West's California Codes

COMMERCIAL CODE

1997 Compact Edition

OFFICIAL CLASSIFICATION
Includes laws through the 1995–1996
Regular and First through Fourth Extraordinary Sessions,
and the November 5, 1996, election

WEST PUBLISHING CO.
ST. PAUL, MINN.

COPYRIGHT © 1990 through 1996 WEST PUBLISHING CO.

COPYRIGHT © 1997
By
WEST PUBLISHING CO.

ISBN 0-314-20504-7

WEST'S and WESTLAW are registered trademarks of West Publishing Co.
Registered in U.S. Patent and Trademark Office.

PRINTED ON 10% POST CONSUMER RECYCLED PAPER

The most complete and current court rules available!

Bay Area Local Court Rules—Superior and Municipal Courts

Bay Area Local Court Rules—Superior and Municipal Courts gives you local court rules and fee schedules for the following counties:

- Alameda
- Contra Costa
- Marin
- Napa
- San Francisco
- San Mateo
- Santa Clara
- Solano
- Sonoma

Clearly organized for faster research! Get complete information today!

Los Angeles County Court Rules—Superior and Municipal Courts

This excellent edition contains the complete text of local rules and fee schedules of the 25 state trial courts in Los Angeles County.

You'll find a consolidated index for the Superior Court materials and an easy-to-use margin index printed on the back cover for fast access.

Southern California Local Court Rules—Superior and Municipal Courts

Southern California Local Court Rules—Superior and Municipal Courts is where you'll find the rules and fee schedules for the superior and municipal courts in the following counties:

- Imperial
- Orange
- Riverside
- San Bernardino
- San Diego
- San Luis Obispo
- Santa Barbara
- Ventura

Central California Local Court Rules Superior and Municipal Courts

Central California Local Court Rules—Superior and Municipal Courts contains local rules and fee schedules for the following counties:

- Fresno
- Inyo
- Kern
- Kings
- Madera
- Mariposa
- Merced
- Monterey
- San Benito
- Santa Cruz
- Stanislaus
- Tulare
- Tuolumne

Northern California Local Court Rules—Superior and Municipal Courts

Northern California Local Court Rules—Superior and Municipal Courts contains local rules and fee schedules for the following 27 counties, and a uniform set of rules:

- Alpine
- Amador
- Butte
- Calaveras
- Colusa
- Del Norte
- El Dorado
- Glenn
- Humboldt
- Lake
- Lassen
- Mendocino
- Modoc
- Mono
- Nevada
- Placer
- Plumas
- Sacramento
- San Joaquin
- Shasta
- Sierra
- Siskiyou
- Sutter
- Tehama
- Trinity
- Yolo
- Yuba
- Uniform Local Rules for Third Appellate District Superior Courts

California Rules of Court, State and Federal

This handy, two-volume edition contains state rules from the California Supreme Court, the Judicial Council of California, and the State Bar of California.

It also includes Federal Rules from the U.S. Court of Appeals for the Ninth Circuit, Bankruptcy Appellate Panel for the Ninth Circuit, and U.S. District and Bankruptcy Courts for the Eastern, Northern, Central and Southern Districts.

Your satisfaction is guaranteed!

For complete information, call toll-free: 1-800-328-9352!

DON'T WAIT! CALL NOW!

WEST

© 1996 West Publishing

Cut research time with the most thoroughly indexed codes yet.

NEW CALIFORNIA RELEASES FOR 1997!

These convenient pamphlets provide fast access to California law wherever and whenever you need it. Each pamphlet pulls together all the relevant and related sections of a given topic of California law into one handy source. There's no need to search through many bound volumes and extra supplements for the complete unannotated text.

- *California Civil Code*
- *California Code of Civil Procedure*
- *California Commercial Code*
- *California Corporations Code*
- *California Education Code*
- *California Environmental Laws*
- *California Evidence Code*
- *California Family Laws and Court Rules*
- *California Insurance Code*
- *California Juvenile Laws & Court Rules*
- *California Penal Code*
- *California Probate Code*
- *California Vehicle Code*

Know the latest local rules.

- *California Rules of Court, State and Federal*
- *Los Angeles County Court Rules Superior and Municipal*
- *Southern California Municipal Court Rules–Superior and Municipal Courts*
- *Bay Area Local Court Rules–Superior and Municipal Courts*

These 1996 Revised Editions are current through August 15, 1996.

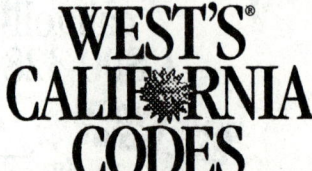

For information about other West Publishing products and services, visit us on the Internet at the URL:
http://www.westpub.com/Practice/CA-home.htm

PREFACE

This edition of the Commercial Code of California, *without court constructions and other annotations*, provides the members of the California Bench and Bar with a compact Code containing the full text of the law, completely indexed, and comments.

It is a companion work to WEST'S ANNOTATED CALIFORNIA CODES in which the user will find exhaustive annotations to the judicial construction and application of the Code, detailed historical notes explaining legislative changes in the provisions, references to law review commentaries, and many other informative features.

All legislative amendments and supplementary provisions through the 1995–1996 Regular and First through Fourth Extraordinary Sessions, and the November 5, 1996, election are integrated in accordance with their official allocations.

As a special feature, this compact edition provides a practical and convenient means of determining the changes which have been made in the text by legislative action. Recent additions or changes effected by amendatory laws are indicated by underlining while deletions are shown by asterisks.

Judicial Council Forms adopted for mandatory use or approved for optional use are set out in a separate two-pamphlet set for convenient reference and use by the bench and bar.

Election Results—November 5, 1996, Election

Proposition		Result
204.	Safe, Clean, Reliable Water Supply Act	Approved
205.	Youthful and Adult Offender Local Facilities Bond Act of 1996	Rejected
206.	Veterans' Bond Act of 1996	Approved
207.	Attorneys. Fees. Right to Negotiate. Frivolous Lawsuits	Rejected
208.	Campaign Contributions and Spending Limits. Restricts Lobbyists	Approved
209.	Prohibition Against Discrimination or Preferential Treatment by State and Other Public Entities	Approved
210.	Minimum Wage Increase	Approved
211.	Attorney-Client Fee Arrangements. Securities Fraud. Lawsuits	Rejected
212.	Campaign Contributions and Spending Limits. Repeals Gift and Honoraria Limits. Restricts Lobbyists	Rejected
213.	Limitation on Recovery to Felons, Uninsured Motorists, Drunk Drivers	Approved
214.	Health Care. Consumer Protection	Rejected
215.	Medical Use of Marijuana	Approved

PREFACE

Proposition		Result
216.	Health Care. Consumer Protection. Taxes on Corporate Restructuring	Rejected
217.	Top Income Tax Brackets. Reinstatement. Revenues to Local Agencies	Rejected
218.	Voter Approval for Local Government Taxes. Limitations on Fees, Assessments, and Charges	Approved

> **Internet Access**
>
> Contact the West Editorial Department directly with your questions and suggestions by e-mail at editor@westpub.com.
>
> Visit West's home page on the World Wide Web at http://www.westpub.com.

THE PUBLISHER

December, 1996

1) Whether there is a contract which is governed under the UCC? a (K) is an intent to be bound by the terms of the (K) in exchange for consideration. In order for the UCC to apply there must be a transaction in goods. A Transaction is Goods means all Things moveable at the time of identification to the contract for Sale. Look TO 2-204
— if Services predominate Purpose Test.
Whether they are merchants? 2-104(1)

2) In order for a (K) to be enforceable the Statute of frauds must be met under 2-201?

3) Whether the goods were accepted by the buyer under UCC 2-606. Whether the buyer may revoke acceptance? 2-608
4) Whether there was a breach of (K)?
5) Whether seller repudiated the (K)? 2-610

IV

COORDINATED RESEARCH IN CALIFORNIA FROM WEST

WEST'S CALIFORNIA LITIGATION FORMS SERIES

West's California Litigation Forms: Civil Procedure Before Trial
Patricia Glaser, Eric Landau, Kirk Pasich, Susan Popik and Laurie Zelon

West's California Litigation Forms: Civil Trials and Evidence
Kathleen V. Fisher, Susan J. Harriman,
Karen Randall and James S. Rummonds

West's California Litigation Forms: Civil Appeals and Writs
Justice J. Anthony Kline and Kent Richland

WEST'S CRIMINAL PRACTICE SERIES

West's California Criminal Law
Douglas Dalton

West's California Criminal Procedure
Laurie L. Levenson

California Criminal Defense Motions Forms Manual
Albert Menaster

JURY SELECTION PRACTICE BOOKS

**Bennett's Guide to Jury Selection and Trial Dynamics:
California Criminal Litigation**

**Bennett's Guide to Jury Selection and Trial Dynamics:
California Civil Litigation**
Cathy E. Bennett, Robert B. Hirschhorn and Dr. Jo-Ellan Dimitrius

WEST'S CALIFORNIA PRACTICE SERIES

Tort Law
Allen Wilkinson and Edward Barker

WEST'S CALIFORNIA CODE FORMS

Business and Professions
Joel S. Primes

Civil
Jeanne P. Robinson

COORDINATED RESEARCH IN CALIFORNIA FROM WEST

Civil Procedure
Gregory L. Ogden and Daryl Fisher-Ogden

Commercial
Stephen N. Hollman and Ray D. Henson

Corporations
Janet E. Kerr

Education
Jay E. Grenig

Elections, Fish & Game, Food & Agricultural, Insurance
Susan J. Orton

Government
Jay E. Grenig and H. Anthony Miller

Labor
W. Robert Morgan and Barbara Spector

Probate
Ann E. Stodden and Timothy A. Whitehouse

Public Utilities
Boris H. Lakusta

Revenue and Taxation
Anthony X. McDermott

CALIFORNIA TRIAL BOOKS

California Civil Trialbook
Richard J. Wharton, Roger S. Haydock and John O. Sonsteng

California Criminal Trialbook
Harry M. Caldwell, Sue Steding and Gary Nichols

JURY INSTRUCTIONS
[Also available in computer disk and looseleaf formats]

California Jury Instructions—Civil (BAJI)

California Jury Instructions—Criminal (CALJIC)

CALIFORNIA HANDBOOK SERIES

California Products Liability
Roy M. Brisbois

California Medical Malpractice
George McDonald

COORDINATED RESEARCH IN CALIFORNIA FROM WEST

California Evidence
Miguel Mendez

California Civil Practice Handbook: The Choice Between State and Federal Courts in California
William Slomanson

WEST'S ANNOTATED CALIFORNIA CODES
[Also available on Westlaw and CD–ROM]

WEST'S CALIFORNIA DIGEST, 2d
[Also available on CD–ROM]

WEST'S CALIFORNIA REPORTER
[Also available on CD–ROM]

PAMPHLETS
West's California Codes—Compact Edition

Civil Code

Code of Civil Procedure

Commercial Code

Corporations Code

Evidence Code

Penal Code

Probate Code

West's California Judicial Council Forms
[Also available in computer disk format]

California Education Code

California Environmental Laws

California Family Laws and Court Rules

California Insurance Code

California Juvenile Laws and Court Rules

COORDINATED RESEARCH IN CALIFORNIA FROM WEST

California Vehicle Code

California Rules of Court, State and Federal

**Bay Area Local Court Rules—
Superior and Municipal Courts**

**Los Angeles County Court Rules—Superior
and Municipal Courts**

**Southern California Local Court Rules—
Superior and Municipal Courts**

THE RUTTER GROUP (TRG) PRACTICE GUIDES
[Also available on CD–ROM]

Alternative Dispute Resolution

Civil Appeals and Writs

Civil Procedure Before Trial

Civil Trials and Evidence

Corporations

Enforcing Judgments and Debts

Family Law

Federal Civil Procedure Before Trial

Federal Civil Procedure Before Trial, 9th Circuit

Insurance Litigation

Landlord-Tenant

Law Office Procedures Manual

Law Practice Management

Legal Secretary's Handbook

Personal Injury

Probate

Real Property Transactions

COORDINATED RESEARCH IN CALIFORNIA FROM WEST

INTERNET
West's California Catalog
The new California print catalog is on the Internet at
http://www.westpub.com/Practice/CA-home.htm

For more information about any of these West California practice tools, please call your West Representative or 1–800–328–9352.

*

WESTLAW ELECTRONIC RESEARCH GUIDE

WESTLAW, Computer Assisted Legal Research

WESTLAW is part of the research system provided by West Publishing Company. With WESTLAW, you find the same quality and integrity that you have come to expect from West books. For the most current and comprehensive legal research, combine the strengths of West books and WESTLAW.

WESTLAW Adds to Your Library

Whether you wish to expand or update your research, WESTLAW can help. For instance, WESTLAW is the most current source for case law, including slip opinions and unreported decisions. In addition to case law, the online availability of statutes, statutory indexes, legislation, court rules and orders, administrative materials, looseleaf publications, texts and periodicals makes WESTLAW an important asset to any library. Check the WESTLAW Directory or the *WESTLAW Database List* for a list of available databases and services. Following is a brief description of some of the capabilities that WESTLAW offers.

You can now search many of the WESTLAW databases using the revolutionary new WIN®, a natural language search method. Instead of formulating a query using terms and connectors, you simply enter a description of your research issue:

> What is the government's obligation to warn military personnel of the danger of past exposure to radiation?

WESTLAW then retrieves the set of documents that has the highest statistical likelihood of matching your description.

Retrieving a Specific Document

When you know the citation to a case, statute, or Constitution section that is not in your library, use FIND to retrieve the document on WESTLAW. The following are sample FIND requests:

> find 639 p2d 939
> find ca elec s 7559
> find ca const art 12 s 1

Updating Your Research

You can use WESTLAW to update your research in many ways:

- Retrieve cases citing a particular statute or Constitution section.
- Update a state statute or Constitution section by typing UPDATE or by using the appropriate jump marker (> or ➤) from the displayed statute or Constitution section.
- Retrieve newly enacted legislation by searching in the appropriate legislative service database.
- Retrieve cases not yet reported by searching in case law databases.
- Read the latest U.S. Supreme Court opinions the same day they are released.
- Update West digests by searching topic and key numbers.

WESTLAW ELECTRONIC RESEARCH GUIDE

Determining Case History

Insta-Cite®, a service of West Publishing, is the most current source for the history of a particular case. Insta-Cite also provides citation verification and parallel citations. Use Insta-Cite when you need to know if the case you are relying on has any subsequent history.

Shepard's® Citations, a service of McGraw-Hill, is also available on WESTLAW. Shepard's on WESTLAW offers several advantages, including the following:

- the consolidation of the books, pocket part and update pamphlet into one result
- the ability to view only those references for a specific jurisdiction, treatment code or headnote
- direct access to citing cases from the West National Reporter System®

Shepard's PreView™ is a WESTLAW exclusive that offers a preview of citing references from the National Reporter System before they are available in print.

Retrieving Citing Cases

You can supplement existing annotations or create your own set of annotations. Simply use the following approach:

1. Determine the format of the statute or case to which you wish to find references.
2. Select a case database in the desired jurisdiction.
3. Run a search containing key portions of the citation, plus any appropriate terms.*

*Because of the great variety of citations and citing styles, you should refer to the *WESTLAW Reference Manual* or consult with the West Reference Attorneys for more specific examples.

Additional Information

For more detailed information or assistance, contact your WESTLAW Account Representative or call 1–800–WESTLAW (1–800–937–8529).

WEST*fax*®

Call 1–800–5622–FAX to order full text cases by fax. Pricing: $7.00 per case plus $1.50 per page and applicable tax. Mail and overnight delivery also available. Cases include current INSTA–CITE® history (reversed, overruled, etc.). Hours: 7:00 a.m.–Midnight, CST. Available only in U.S.A. Order subject to approval of vendor. Price subject to change without notice.

Acknowledgment

Official Comments

Acknowledgment is gratefully made to The American Law Institute and the National Conference of Commissioners on Uniform State Laws for permission to reproduce the Official Comments for the Uniform Commercial Code included in this pamphlet.

THE PUBLISHER

*

TABLE OF CONTENTS

Division		Section
1.	GENERAL PROVISIONS	1101
2.	SALES	2101
3.	NEGOTIABLE INSTRUMENTS	3101
4.	BANK DEPOSITS AND COLLECTIONS	4101
5.	LETTERS OF CREDIT	5101
6.	BULK SALES	6101
7.	WAREHOUSE RECEIPTS, BILLS OF LADING AND OTHER DOCUMENTS OF TITLE	7101
8.	INVESTMENT SECURITIES	8101
9.	SECURED TRANSACTIONS; SALES OF ACCOUNTS, CONTRACT RIGHTS AND CHATTEL PAPER	9101
10.	PERSONAL PROPERTY LEASES	10101
11.	FUNDS TRANSFERS	11101
12.	EFFECTIVE DATE AND TRANSITION PROVISIONS [REPEALED]	12101
13.	EFFECTIVE DATE AND REPEALER	13101
14.	EFFECTIVE DATE AND TRANSITION PROVISIONS	14101
15.	EFFECTIVE DATE AND TRANSITION PROVISIONS	15101
16.	EFFECTIVE DATE AND TRANSITION PROVISIONS	16101

DIVISION 1. GENERAL PROVISIONS

Chapter		
1.	Short Title, Construction, Application and Subject Matter of the Code	1101
2.	General Definitions and Principles of Interpretation	1201

DIVISION 2. SALES

1.	Short Title, General Construction and Subject Matter	2101
2.	Form, Formation and Readjustment of Contract	2201
3.	General Obligation and Construction of Contract	2301
4.	Title, Creditors and Good Faith Purchasers	2401
5.	Performance	2501
6.	Breach, Repudiation and Excuse	2601
7.	Remedies	2701
8.	Retail Sales	2800

TABLE OF CONTENTS

DIVISION 3. NEGOTIABLE INSTRUMENTS

Chapter		Section
1.	General Provisions and Definitions	3101
2.	Negotiation, Transfer, and Indorsement	3201
3.	Enforcement of Instruments	3301
4.	Liability of Parties	3401
5.	Dishonor	3501
6.	Discharge and Payment	3601

DIVISION 4. BANK DEPOSITS AND COLLECTIONS

1.	General Provisions and Definitions	4101
2.	Collection of Items: Depositary and Collecting Banks	4201
3.	Collection of Items: Payor Banks	4301
4.	Relationship Between Payor Bank and Its Customer	4401
5.	Collection of Documentary Drafts	4501

DIVISION 5. LETTERS OF CREDIT
(Sections 5101 to 5117)

APPENDIX TO DIVISION 5—
Letters of Credit

DIVISION 6. BULK SALES
(Sections 6101 to 6111)

DIVISION 7. WAREHOUSE RECEIPTS, BILLS OF LADING AND OTHER DOCUMENTS OF TITLE

1.	General	7101
2.	Warehouse Receipts: Special Provisions	7201
3.	Bills of Lading: Special Provisions	7301
4.	Warehouse Receipts and Bills of Lading: General Obligations	7401
5.	Warehouse Receipts and Bills of Lading: Negotiation and Transfer	7501
6.	Warehouse Receipts and Bills of Lading: Miscellaneous Provisions	7601

DIVISION 8. INVESTMENT SECURITIES

1.	Short Title and General Matters	8101
2.	Issue and Issuer	8201
3.	Transfer of Certificated and Uncertificated Securities	8301
4.	Registration	8401
5.	Security Entitlements	8501
6.	Transition Provisions	8601

TABLE OF CONTENTS

DIVISION 9. SECURED TRANSACTIONS; SALES OF ACCOUNTS, CONTRACT RIGHTS AND CHATTEL PAPER

Chapter		Section
1.	Short Title, Applicability and Definitions	9101
2.	Validity of Security Agreement and Rights of Parties Thereto	9201
3.	Rights of Third Parties; Perfected and Unperfected Security Interests; Rules of Priority	9301
4.	Filing	9401
5.	Default	9501

DIVISION 10. PERSONAL PROPERTY LEASES

1.	General Provisions	10101
2.	Formation and Construction of Lease Contract	10201
3.	Effect of Lease Contract	10301
4.	Performance of Leased Contract: Repudiated, Substituted, and Excused	10401
5.	Default	10501
	Article	
	1. In General	10501
	2. Default by Lessor	10508
	3. Default by Lessee	10523
6.	Transition Provisions	10600

DIVISION 11. FUNDS TRANSFERS

1.	Subject Matter and Definitions	11101
2.	Issue and Acceptance of Payment Order	11201
3.	Execution of Sender's Payment Order by Receiving Bank	11301
4.	Payment	11401
5.	Miscellaneous Provisions	11501

DIVISION 12. EFFECTIVE DATE AND TRANSITION PROVISIONS
[Repealed]
(Sections 12101 to 12104)

DIVISION 13. EFFECTIVE DATE AND REPEALER
(Sections 13101 to 13105)

TABLE OF CONTENTS

DIVISION 14. EFFECTIVE DATE AND TRANSITION PROVISIONS
(Sections 14101 to 14109)

DIVISION 15. EFFECTIVE DATE AND TRANSITION PROVISIONS
(Sections 15101 to 15104)

DIVISION 16. EFFECTIVE DATE AND TRANSITION PROVISIONS
(Sections 16101 to 16104)

INDEX
(Page 623)

COMMERCIAL CODE
SECTIONS AFFECTED BY 1996 LEGISLATION

Sec.	Effect	Chap.	Sec.	Sec.	Effect	Chap.	Sec.
1105	Amended	176	4	prec. 8101 (Div. heading)	Repealed	497	8
		497	4				
1206	Amended	497	5				
2512	Amended	176	5			497	9
3103	Amended	316	1		Added		
3104	Amended	316	2	8101	Repealed	497	8
3416	Amended	316	3		Added	497	9
3417	Amended	316	4	8102	Repealed	497	8
4104	Amended	497	6		Added	497	9
4207	Amended	316	5	8103	Repealed	497	8
4208	Amended	316	6		Added	497	9
5101	Repealed	176	6	8104	Repealed	497	8
	Added	176	7		Added	497	9
5102	Repealed	176	6	8105	Repealed	497	8
	Added	176	7		Added	497	9
5103	Repealed	176	6	8106	Repealed	497	8
	Added	176	7		Added	497	9
5104	Repealed	176	6	8107	Repealed	497	8
	Added	176	7		Added	497	9
5105	Repealed	176	6	8108	Repealed	497	8
	Added	176	7		Added	497	9
5106	Repealed	176	6	8109	Repealed	497	8
	Added	176	7		Added	497	9
5107	Repealed	176	6	8110	Added	497	9
	Added	176	7	8111	Added	497	9
5108	Repealed	176	6	8112	Added	497	9
	Added	176	7	8113	Added	497	9
5109	Repealed	176	6	8114	Added	497	9
	Added	176	7	8115	Added	497	9
5110	Repealed	176	6	8116	Added	497	9
	Added	176	7	prec. 8201 (Ch. heading)	Repealed	497	8
5111	Repealed	176	6				
	Added	176	7				
5112	Repealed	176	6		Added	497	9
	Added	176	7	8201	Repealed	497	8
5113	Repealed	176	6		Added	497	9
	Added	176	7	8202	Repealed	497	8
5114	Repealed	176	6		Added	497	9
	Added	176	7	8203	Repealed	497	8
	Amended	497	7		Added	497	9
5115	Repealed	176	6	8204	Repealed	497	8
	Added	176	7		Added	497	9
5116	Repealed	176	6	8205	Repealed	497	8
	Added	176	7		Added	497	9
5117	Repealed	176	6	8206	Repealed	497	8
	Added	176	7		Added	497	9
prec. 8101 (Ch. heading)	Repealed	497	8	8207	Repealed	497	8
					Added	497	9
	Added	497	9	8208	Repealed	497	8
					Added	497	9

COMMERCIAL CODE TABLE

Sec.	Effect	Chap.	Sec.	Sec.	Effect	Chap.	Sec.
8209	Added	497	9	8406	Repealed	497	8
8210	Added	497	9		Added	497	9
prec. 8301 (Ch. heading)	Repealed	497	8	8407	Repealed	497	8
	Added	497	9		Added	497	9
8301	Repealed	497	8	8408	Repealed	497	8
	Added	497	9	prec. 8501 (Ch. heading)	Added	497	9
8302	Repealed	497	8	8501	Added	497	9
	Added	497	9	8502	Added	497	9
8303	Repealed	497	8	8503	Added	497	9
	Added	497	9	8504	Added	497	9
8304	Repealed	497	8	8505	Added	497	9
	Added	497	9	8506	Added	497	9
8305	Repealed	497	8	8507	Added	497	9
	Added	497	9	8508	Added	497	9
8306	Repealed	497	8	8509	Added	497	9
	Added	497	9	8510	Added	497	9
8307	Repealed	497	8	8511	Added	497	9
8307	Added	497	9	prec. 8601 (Ch. heading)	Added	497	9
8308	Repealed	497	8	8601	Added	497	9
8309	Repealed	497	8	8603	Added	497	9
8310	Repealed	497	8	9103	Amended	176	8
8311	Repealed	497	8		Amended	497	10
8312	Repealed	497	8	9104	Amended	176	9
8313	Repealed	497	8			854	4
8314	Repealed	497	8	9105	Amended	176	10
8315	Repealed	497	8			497	11
8316	Repealed	497	8	9106	Amended	176	11
8317	Repealed	497	8			497	12
8318	Repealed	497	8	9115	Added	497	13
8319	Repealed	497	8	9116	Added	497	14
8320	Repealed	497	8	9203	Amended	497	15
8321	Repealed	497	8	9301	Amended	497	16
prec. 8401 (Ch. heading)	Repealed	497	8	9302	Amended	497	17
	Added	497	9	9304	Amended	176	12
8401	Repealed	497	8			497	18
	Added	497	9	9305	Amended	176	13
8402	Repealed	497	8			497	19
	Added	497	9	9306	Amended	497	20
8403	Repealed	497	8	9309	Amended	497	21
	Added	497	9	9312	Amended	497	22
8404	Repealed	497	8	9501	Amended	124	16
	Added	497	9	15103	Amended	497	23
8405	Repealed	497	8	15104	Amended	497	24
	Added	497	9				

COMMERCIAL CODE

An act to establish a Commercial Code, thereby consolidating and revising the law relating to certain commercial transactions in or regarding personal property and contracts and other documents concerning them, including sales, commercial paper, bank deposits and collections, letters of credit, bulk transfers, warehouse receipts, bills of lading, other documents of title, investment securities, and secured transactions, including certain sales of accounts, chattel paper, and contract rights; providing for public notice to third parties in certain circumstances; regulating procedure, evidence and damages in certain court actions involving such transactions, contracts or documents; to make uniform the law with respect thereto; amending various sections of the Civil Code, Code of Civil Procedure, Corporations Code, Financial Code and Vehicle Code, to make them consistent therewith; adding Chapter 12.5 (commencing with Section 560) to Title 13 of Part 1 of the Penal Code, relating to crimes involving bailments; and repealing legislation inconsistent therewith.

Stats.1963, c. 819

Approved and filed June 8, 1963.

Effective January 1, 1965.

The people of the State of California do enact as follows:

Division	Section
1. General Provisions	1101
2. Sales	2101

Section Numbers

The section numbers of the California Commercial Code correspond to the section numbers of the Uniform Commercial Code but with the dash removed, so that § 1–101 in the Uniform Commercial Code is § 1101 in the California Commercial Code, et cetera.

Effective Date

Section 10101 provides that "this code shall become effective on Jan. 1, 1965. It applies to transactions entered into and events occurring after that date."

Transition—Prior Transactions

Section 10102 provides in part that transactions validly entered into before the effective date specified in Section 10101 and the rights, duties and interests flowing from them remain valid thereafter and may be terminated, completed, consummated or enforced as required or permitted by any statute or other law amended or repealed by this act as though such repeal or amendment had not occurred.

GENERAL COMMENT

By Charles J. Williams

CALIFORNIA LEGISLATIVE CHANGES IN UNIFORM COMMERCIAL CODE SUBSEQUENT TO ADOPTION

The 1967 legislative changes to the California Uniform Commercial Code came principally as a result of recommendations from 2 sources: the Advisory Committee to the California Senate on the Editorial Aspects of the Uniform Commercial Code and the California Law Revision Commission. The following is a brief background of these changes and the reasons for them.

When California adopted the Uniform Commercial Code in 1963 (effective January 1, 1965), it was the 28th state to do so. Since adoption in California, the Code has been adopted by every State except Louisiana and has also been adopted in the District of Columbia and some of the territories of the United States.

The primary purpose of the Code is to provide uniformity of commercial law and when each adopting state began making its own changes, this goal was seriously threatened. Indeed, California made over 120 changes from the Official Text, more than any other state. To discourage local variation and to encourage adoption of the Official Text, the American Law Institute and the National Conference of Commissioners on Uniform State Laws created in 1961 the Permanent Editorial Board for the Uniform Commercial Code.

This board examined and continues to examine every change in the Code which varies from the Official Text. Its first report was published in October 1962. (Report No. 1 of the Permanent Editorial Board for the Uniform Commercial Code, Including the 1962 Official Recommendations for the Amendment of the Code, West Publishing Co., St. Paul, Minn.). Its second report was published in October 1964 and contains the Permanent Editorial Board comments to the California variations. (Report No. 2 of the Permanent Editorial Board for the Uniform Commercial Code, West Publishing Co., St. Paul, Minn.). These comments are quoted in the corresponding California Code Comment.

The Advisory Committee to the California State Senate on the Editorial Aspects of the Uniform Commercial Code was created in 1960. This committee is made up of representatives with diverse interests from the field of business and commerce. It continues to advise the Legislature upon the progress and development of the Uniform Commercial Code and is responsible for recommending most of the changes which California has made since original adoption.

The Advisory Committee reviewed the comments of the Permanent Editorial Board to the California variations. As a result the Advisory Committee concluded that many of the California variations should be eliminated. In so recommending, the committee relied upon Report No. 2 of the Permanent Editorial Board which stated that "the language of the Official Text _____ has the same meaning as the language of the variation _____ adopted in California". Thus, these amendments are not intended to change substantive meaning.

In addition, the Advisory Committee recommended the elimination of other variations in the interests of uniformity and also considered other problems in connection with the Code. Its report to the California Senate Judiciary Committee was printed in the Senate Daily Journal of April 20, 1967, and appears at pages 1235–1240. Excerpts from the report are set forth in the California Code Comments in the supplement whenever the report explains the reason for an amendment or sheds light on the legislative history. The 1967 amendments recommended by the Advisory Committee to the State Senate were embodied in Stats.1967, Chap. 799.

The California Law Revision Commission in its study of the Evidence Code also studied the California Uniform Commercial Code to determine if any changes were needed to conform to the Evidence Code. This study is set forth in its report, California Law Revision Commission, Recommendation Relating to the Evidence Code, No. 3—Commercial Code Revisions (October 1966). With one minor exception, the recommendations of the Commission were accepted and the resulting changes in the California Uniform Commercial Code are contained in Stats.1967, Chap. 703.

In general, the Commission's recommendations stem from the fact that the Evidence Code classifies rebuttable presumptions as being either a presumption affecting the burden of producing evidence or a presumption affecting the burden of proof. The procedural effect of these two kinds of presumptions is set forth in Evidence Code §§ 604, 606 and 607. The Evidence Code does not for the most part tell us whether a particular presumption is of one class or another, but leaves this task to the courts in the light of the standards in Evidence Code §§ 603 and 605. In order to avoid uncertainty as to whether a presumption in the Commercial Code affects the burden of producing evidence or the burden of proof, the Commission recommended that the Commercial Code be amended to designate the effect of the presumptions.

The recommendations of the California Law Revision Commission are intended to be in accordance with the intent of the Uniform Commercial Code. The purpose of defining the presumption as one kind or another is simply to avoid uncertainty and to obviate the need for judicial decisions.

In its recommendations, the California Law Revision Commission says that these suggested revisions to the Uniform Commercial Code "are designed merely to effectuate the intent of the drafters of the Commercial Code and the policies previously approved by the legislature in the light of the subsequent enactment of the Evidence Code". In a footnote to this statement, the Commission states as follows:

> "In most cases, the intent of the drafters of the Commercial Code—*i.e.*, how they would have classified the Commercial Code presumptions had they been aware of and been applying the Evidence Code distinction between presumptions affecting the burden of producing evidence and the presumptions affecting the burden of proof—is relatively clear. In a few cases, the answer is more doubtful, and an educated guess must be made in light of what appears to be the legislative purpose of the part of the Commercial Code in which the particular section appears." (California Law Revision Commission, Recommendation Relating to the Evidence Code, No. 3—Commercial Code Revisions, p. 308.)

Division 1

GENERAL PROVISIONS

Chapter	Section
1. Short Title, Construction, Application and Subject Matter of the Code	1101
2. General Definitions and Principles of Interpretation	1201

CHAPTER 1. SHORT TITLE, CONSTRUCTION, APPLICATION AND SUBJECT MATTER OF THE CODE

Section
1101. Short Title.
1102. Purposes; Rules of Construction; Variation by Agreement.
1103. Supplementary General Principles of Law Applicable.
1104. Construction Against Implicit Repeal.
1105. Multistate or foreign trade transaction; power to choose applicable law; restrictions.
1106. Remedies to be Liberally Administered.
1107. Waiver or Renunciation of Claim or Right After Breach.
1108. Severability.

Introductory Comment

By Charles J. Williams

Division 1 supplies the general principles of construction and definitions which apply throughout the other 8 divisions.

These are significant and should be frequently consulted when a problem in interpretation is encountered.

Of particular significance are the principles set forth in section 1102 concerning variation by agreement and section 1105 relating to the territorial application and choice of law. Course of dealing and usages of the trade (§ 1205) are important factors in determining the meaning of any agreement the parties may have made.

The California version of the Code continues the general rule applicable in all of the other California codes that section captions are not a part of the Code. California Code Comment to section 1–109 of the Official Text explains this omission.

The general definitions contained in section 1201 are very important. Those using the Code should continually consult them in determining the meaning and intent of terms used in the other 8 divisions. The general definitions are subject to the specific definitions which appear in each division. One term may have one meaning for the purpose of one division and a different meaning for the purpose of a different division. For example, "goods" is defined one way in section 2105(1) and another way in section 9105(1)(f).

§ 1101. Short Title

This code shall be known and may be cited as Uniform Commercial Code. *(Stats.1963, c. 819, § 1101.)*

California Code Comment

By John A. Bohn and Charles J. Williams

This is section 1–101 of the Official Text without change.

Uniform Commercial Code Comment

Each Article of the Code (except this Article and Article 10) may also be cited by its own short title. See Sections 2–101, 3–101, 4–101, 5–101, 6–101, 7–101, 8–101 and 9–101.

Cross References

Transactions subject to its application, see Commercial Code § 10102.

§ 1102. Purposes; Rules of Construction; Variation by Agreement

(1) This code shall be liberally construed and applied to promote its underlying purposes and policies.

(2) Underlying purposes and policies of this code are

(a) To simplify, clarify and modernize the law governing commercial transactions;

(b) To permit the continued expansion of commercial practices through custom, usage and agreement of the parties;

(c) To make uniform the law among the various jurisdictions.

(3) The effect of provisions of this code may be varied by agreement, except as otherwise provided in this code and except that the obligations of good faith, diligence, reasonableness and care prescribed by this code may not be disclaimed by agreement but the parties may by agreement determine the standards by which the performance of such obligations is to be measured if such standards are not manifestly unreasonable.

(4) The presence in certain provisions of this code of the words "unless otherwise agreed" or words of similar import does not imply that the effect of other provisions may not be varied by agreement under subdivision (3).

(5) In this code unless the context otherwise requires

(a) Words in the singular number include the plural, and in the plural include the singular;

(b) Words of the masculine or feminine gender include the masculine, the feminine, and the neuter, and when the sense so indicates words of the neuter gender may refer to any gender. *(Stats.1963, c. 819, § 1102. Amended by Stats.1984, c. 927, § 2.5.)*

Legislative Committee Comment—Assembly 1984 Amendment

These changes are intended to make clear that any reference in the Commercial Code to the masculine or the feminine gender includes the masculine, feminine, and neuter. [84 A.J. 18471].

California Code Comment

By John A. Bohn and Charles J. Williams

§ 1102   GENERAL PROVISIONS

Prior California Law

1. The concept of construction to promote the purpose of the Commercial Code in subdivision (1) and to provide uniformity of law among the states who enact it in subdivision (2)(c) have their counterparts in former uniform acts which are superseded by the Commercial Code. See former Civil Code § 1794 (Uniform Sales Act), § 2132a (Uniform Bills of Lading Act), § 1858.03 (Uniform Warehouse Receipts Act).

2. Under subdivision (3) the effect of the Commercial Code may not be varied by agreement in two specific cases: first, if a specific provision itself provides against variation or, second, where the Commercial Code imposes affirmative obligations of "good faith, diligence, reasonableness and care". Existing statutes generally do not prohibit modification of the basic statutory rights and duties by agreement unless modification is contrary to public policy. For example former Civil Code § 1791 (allowing contract under the Uniform Sales Act to be negatived or varied by agreement of parties, course of dealing, or custom), and § 3268 (authorizing waiver of benefit under provisions of the code except when against public policy); and Civil Code § 3513 (authorizing waiver of advantage under law for benefit of that individual, but not under law for public benefit) and cases such as Local 659, I.A.T.S.E. v. Color Corp. of America, 47 Cal.2d 189, 302 P.2d 294 (1956), and Leonard v. Board of Education, 36 Cal.App.2d 595, 97 P.2d 1032 (1940).

Civil Code § 3513 provides for waiver of an advantage under a law conferring a private benefit but not under a law "established for a public reason". The burden is upon the courts in most cases to determine whether a statute is for public or private benefit. In some instances the provisions of the California statutes are expressly made non-waivable. See, for example, former Civil Code § 1801.1 (preventing waiver of the provisions of the "Unruh Act", §§ 1801 to 1812.9), and Civil Code § 1630 (preventing waiver of disclosure requirements in bailment contracts with auto parking lots), and § 2953 (preventing waiver of the statutory protections for borrowers whose loans are secured by liens on real property).

Since no expression of California law appears on the question whether the general obligations of "good faith, diligence, etc." recited in subdivision (3) are for public or private benefit, it is uncertain whether the non-waivability concept of subdivision (3) would or would not change this area of California law.

3. Subdivision (4) is new.

4. The reference to tense and gender in subdivision (5) is similar to Civil Code § 14.

Changes from U.C.C. (1962 Official Text)

5. This is section 1–102 of the Official Text without change.

Uniform Commercial Code Comment
1966 Amendment

Prior Uniform Statutory Provision:

*   *   *

; Section 18, Uniform Trust Receipts Act.

Uniform Commercial Code Comment

Prior Uniform Statutory Provision:

Section 74, Uniform Sales Act; Section 57, Uniform Warehouse Receipts Act; Section 52, Uniform Bills of Lading Act; Section 19, Uniform Stock Transfer Act.

Changes: Rephrased and new material added.

Purposes of Changes:

1. Subsections (1) and (2) are intended to make it clear that:

This Act is drawn to provide flexibility so that, since it is intended to be a semi-permanent piece of legislation, it will provide its own machinery for expansion of commercial practices. It is intended to make it possible for the law embodied in this Act to be developed by the courts in the light of unforeseen and new circumstances and practices. However, the proper construction of the Act requires that its interpretation and application be limited to its reason.

Courts have been careful to keep broad acts from being hampered in their effects by later acts of limited scope. Pacific Wool Growers v. Draper & Co., 158 Or. 1, 73 P.2d 1391 (1937), and compare Section 1–104. They have recognized the policies embodied in an act as applicable in reason to subject-matter which was not expressly included in the language of the act, Commercial Nat. Bank of New Orleans v. Canal-Louisiana Bank & Trust Co., 239 U.S. 520, 36 S.Ct. 194, 60 L.Ed. 417 (1916) (bona fide purchase policy of Uniform Warehouse Receipts Act extended to case not covered but of equivalent nature). They have done the same where reason and policy so required, even where the subject-matter had been intentionally excluded from the act in general. Agar v. Orda, 264 N.Y. 248, 190 N.E. 479 (1934) (Uniform Sales Act change in seller's remedies applied to contract for sale of choses in action even though the general coverage of that Act was intentionally limited to goods "other than things in action.") They have implemented a statutory policy with liberal and useful remedies not provided in the statutory text. They have disregarded a statutory limitation of remedy where the reason of the limitation did not apply. Fiterman v. J. N. Johnson & Co., 156 Minn. 201, 194 N.W. 399 (1923) (requirement of return of the goods as a condition to rescission for breach of warranty; also, partial rescission allowed). Nothing in this Act stands in the way of the continuance of such action by the courts.

The Act should be construed in accordance with its underlying purposes and policies. The text of each section should be read in the light of the purpose and policy of the rule or principle in question, as also of the Act as a whole, and the application of the language should be construed narrowly or broadly, as the case may be, in conformity with the purposes and policies involved.

2. Subsection (3) states affirmatively at the outset that freedom of contract is a principle of the Code: "the effect" of its provisions may be varied by "agreement." The meaning of the statute itself must be found in its text, including its definitions, and in appropriate extrinsic aids; it cannot be varied by agreement. But the Code seeks to avoid the type of interference with evolutionary growth found in Manhattan Co. v. Morgan, 242 N.Y. 38, 150 N.E. 594 (1926). Thus private parties cannot make an instrument negotiable within the meaning of Article 3 except as provided in Section 3–104; nor can they change the meaning of such terms as "bona fide purchaser," "holder in due course," or "due negotiation," as used in this Act. But an agreement can change the legal consequences which would otherwise flow from the provisions of the Act. "Agreement" here includes the effect given to course of dealing, usage of trade and course of performance by Sections 1–201, 1–205 and 2–208; the effect of an agreement on the rights of third parties is left to specific provisions of this Act and to supplementary principles applicable under the next section. The rights of third parties under Section 9–301 when a security interest is unperfected, for example, cannot be destroyed by a clause in the security agreement.

This principle of freedom of contract is subject to specific exceptions found elsewhere in the Act and to the general exceptions stated here. The specific exceptions vary in explicitness: the statute of frauds found in Section 2–201, for example, does not explicitly preclude oral waiver of the requirement of a writing, but a fair reading denies enforcement to such a waiver as part of the "contract" made unenforceable; Section 9–501 (3), on the other hand, is quite explicit. Under the exception for "the obligations of good faith, diligence, reasonableness and care prescribed by this Act," provisions of the Act prescribing such obligations are not to be disclaimed. However, the section also recognizes the prevailing practice of having agreements set forth standards by which due diligence is measured and explicitly provides that, in the absence of a showing that the standards manifestly are unreasonable, the agreement controls. In this connection, Section 1–205 incorporating into the agreement prior course of dealing and usages of trade is of particular importance.

3. Subsection (4) is intended to make it clear that, as a matter of drafting, words such as "unless otherwise agreed" have been used to avoid controversy as to whether the subject matter of a particular section does or does not fall within the exceptions to subsection (3), but absence of such words contains no negative implication since under subsection (3) the general and residual rule is that the effect of all provisions of the Act may be varied by agreement.

4. Subsection (5) is modelled on 1 U.S.C. Section 1 and New York General Construction Law Sections 22 and 35.

Cross References

Construction against implicit repeal, see Commercial Code § 1104.
Construction of uniform acts,
    Fraudulent transfers act, see Civil Code § 3439 et seq.
    Limited partnership act, see Corporations Code § 15528.
    Partnership act, see Corporations Code § 15004.

Liberal administration of remedies, see Commercial Code § 1106.
Maxims of jurisprudence, see Civil Code § 3509 et seq.
Severability, see Commercial Code § 1108.
Statutory construction,
   Amended statutes, see Government Code § 9605.
   Amendment of repealed statutes, see Government Code § 9609.
   Duty of judge, see Code of Civil Procedure § 1858; Evidence Code §§ 310, 400 et seq., 457.
   General rules, see Code of Civil Procedure §§ 1858, 1859; Government Code § 9603 et seq.
   Giving effect to all provisions, see Code of Civil Procedure § 1858.
   Intention of legislature, see Code of Civil Procedure § 1859.
   Particular intent controls general, see Code of Civil Procedure § 1859.
   Question of law for court, see Evidence Code § 310.
   Repeal of repealing statute, see Government Code § 9607.
Uniform operation of laws of a general nature, see Const. Art. 4, § 16.
Waiver of advantage, law established for public reason, see Civil Code § 3513.

§ 1103. Supplementary General Principles of Law Applicable

Unless displaced by the particular provisions of this code, the principles of law and equity, including the law merchant and the law relative to capacity to contract, principal and agent, estoppel, fraud, misrepresentation, duress, coercion, mistake, bankruptcy, or other validating or invalidating cause shall supplement its provisions. (Stats.1963, c. 819, § 1103.)

California Code Comment

By John A. Bohn and Charles J. Williams

Prior California Law

1. This section is similar to former Civil Code § 1793 (Uniform Sales Act), § 2132 (Uniform Bills of Lading Act) § 1858.05 (Uniform Warehouse Receipts Act) and § 3016.13 (Uniform Trust Receipts Law) but restates with greater detail the principle that the general law applies when a case is not covered by statute. The areas of law described in these former sections are enlarged in this section by the addition of the words "estoppel" and "validating".

This section continues the general law relating to capacity and is similar to former Civil Code § 1722 (Uniform Sales Act).

Changes from U.C.C. (1962 Official Text)

2. This is section 1-103 of the Official Text without change.

Uniform Commercial Code Comment
1966 Amendment

Prior Uniform Statutory Provision:

*   *   *

; Section 17, Uniform Trust Receipts Act.

Uniform Commercial Code Comment

Prior Uniform Statutory Provision:

Sections 2 and 73, Uniform Sales Act; Section 196, Uniform Negotiable Instruments Act; Section 56, Uniform Warehouse Receipts Act; Section 51, Uniform Bills of Lading Act; Section 18, Uniform Stock Transfer Act.

Changes: Rephrased, the reference to "estoppel" and "validating" being new.

Purposes of Changes:

1. While this section indicates the continued applicability to commercial contracts of all supplemental bodies of law except insofar as they are explicitly displaced by this Act, the principle has been stated in more detail and the phrasing enlarged to make it clear that the "validating", as well as the "invalidating" causes referred to in the prior uniform statutory provisions, are included here. "Validating" as used here in conjunction with "invalidating" is not intended as a narrow word confined to original validation, but extends to cover any factor which at any time or in any manner renders or helps to render valid any right or transaction.

2. The general law of capacity is continued by express mention to make clear that section 2 of the old Uniform Sales Act (omitted in this Act as stating no matter not contained in the general law) is also consolidated in the present section. Hence, where a statute limits the capacity of a non-complying corporation to sue, this is equally applicable to contracts of sale to which such corporation is a party.

3. The listing given in this section is merely illustrative; no listing could be exhaustive. Nor is the fact that in some sections particular circumstances have led to express reference to other fields of law intended at any time to suggest the negation of the general application of the principles of this section.

Cross References

Agency, see Civil Code §§ 2019 et seq., 2295 et seq.
Contracts by persons without understanding, liability for necessaries, see Civil Code § 38.
Contracts, generally, see Civil Code § 1549 et seq.
Deceit, see Civil Code § 1709 et seq.
Duress, see Civil Code §§ 1569, 1570.
Fraud, see Civil Code §§ 1568, 1571 et seq.
Fraudulent instruments and conveyances, see Civil Code § 3439 et seq.
Husband and wife, contracts with each other and third parties, see Family Code § 721.
Incapacities of minors under age of 18 respecting property interests, see Family Code § 6701.
Married persons over 18 years of age, contractual capacity, see Family Code § 6502.
Menace, see Civil Code § 1570.
Mistake, see Civil Code § 1576 et seq.
Necessities, contracts of minors, see Family Code § 6712.
Noncitizens, rights of, see Const. Art. 1, § 20.
Parties to contract, see Civil Code § 1556 et seq.
Persons authorized to own property, see Civil Code § 671.
Persons capable of contracting, see Civil Code §§ 1556, 1557.
Undue influence, see Civil Code § 1575.

§ 1104. Construction Against Implicit Repeal

This code being a general act intended as a unified coverage of its subject matter, no part of it shall be deemed to be impliedly repealed by subsequent legislation if such construction can reasonably be avoided. (Stats.1963, c. 819, § 1104.)

California Code Comment

By John A. Bohn and Charles J. Williams

Prior California Law

1. This section is consistent with the California law which does not favor repeal by implication (Rexstrew v. City of Huntington Park, 20 Cal.2d 630, 128 P.2d 23 (1942)) and the presumption in California against repeal by implication (Penziner v. West American Finance Co., 10 Cal.2d 160, 74 P.2d 252 (1937)).

Changes from U.C.C. (1962 Official Text)

2. This is section 1-104 of the Official Text without change.

Uniform Commercial Code Comment

Prior Uniform Statutory Provision:
None.

Purposes:

To express the policy that no Act which bears evidence of carefully considered permanent regulative intention should lightly be regarded as impliedly repealed by subsequent legislation. This Act, carefully integrated and intended as a uniform codification of permanent character covering an entire "field" of law, is to be regarded as particular resistant to implied repeal. See Pacific Wool Growers v. Draper & Co., 158 Or. 1, 73 P.2d 1391 (1937).

Cross References

Repeal of statutes, see Government Code § 9606.

§ 1105. Multistate or foreign trade transaction; power to choose applicable law; restrictions

(1) Except as provided hereafter in this section, when a transaction bears a reasonable relation to this state and also to another state or nation the parties may agree that the law either of this state or of such other state or nation shall govern their rights and duties. Failing such agreement this code applies to transactions bearing an appropriate relation to this state.

(2) Where one of the following provisions of this code specifies the applicable law, that provision governs and a contrary agreement is effective only to the extent permitted by the law (including the conflict of laws rules) so specified:

Rights of creditors against sold goods. Section 2402.

Applicability of the division on leases. Sections 10105 and 10106.

Applicability of the division on bank deposits and collections. Section 4102.

Letters of credit. Section 5116.

Bulk sales subject to the division on bulk sales. Section 6103.

Applicability of the division on investment securities. Section 8110.

Perfection provisions of the division on secured transactions. Section 9103. *(Stats. 1963, c. 819, § 1105. Amended by Stats.1974, c. 997, p. 2108, § 1, eff. Jan. 1, 1976; Stats.1988, c. 1359, § 1, operative Jan. 1, 1990; Stats.1990, c. 125 (S.B.1759), § 1; Stats.1990, c. 1191 (A.B.3653), § 1; Stats.1996, c. 176 (S.B.1599), § 4; Stats.1996, c. 497 (S.B.1591), § 4, operative Jan. 1, 1997.)*

California Code Comment

By John A. Bohn and Charles J. Williams

Prior California Law

1. This section adds to and makes more specific the concept expressed in Civil Code § 1646 dealing with contracts in general which provides that a contract is to be interpreted according to the law and usage of the place where it is to be performed, and if a place of performance is not specified then where the contract was made.

This section also sets forth the conflict of laws rules under the Commercial Code. Except for the five areas specified under subdivision (2), the parties may agree on what law governs a commercial transaction if the law of the state selected bears a "reasonable relation" to the transaction. If subdivision (2) does not apply and there is no agreement on what law governs, then the transaction is governed by the law of California, but only if it bears an "appropriate relation" to this state.

The net effect is to make the Commercial Code enforceable in many situations where under previous California law the local law would not have applied.

2. The California cases have recognized the law of other states through the doctrine of comity: Henning's Estate, 128 Cal. 214, 60 Pac. 762 (1900); Commonwealth Acceptance Corp. v. Jordan, 198 Cal. 618, 246 Pac. 796 (1926); Simmons v. Superior Court, 96 Cal.App.2d 119, 214 P.2d 844 (1950), and through the doctrine of full faith and credit: Alaska Packers v. Industrial Accident Commission, 1 Cal.2d 250, 34 P.2d 716 (1934), affd. 294 U.S. 532, 55 S.Ct. 518, 79 L.Ed. 1044.

3. Under subdivision (1) where there is an agreement of the parties as to what law applies the test of "reasonable relation" is used to determine if that law shall apply. The Official Comments state that the test of "reasonable relation" in subdivision (1) is similar to that stated by the Supreme Court in Seeman v. Philadelphia Warehouse Co., 274 U.S. 403, 47 S.Ct. 626, 71 L.Ed. 1123 (1927). As a general rule is California parties may agree on what law shall govern their contract. Boole v. Union Marine Insurance Co., 52 Cal.App. 207, 198 Pac. 416 (1921); Eaton v. Thieme, 15 Cal.App.2d 458, 59 P.2d 638 (1936). However the intention of the parties is not considered on the question of whether a contract has come into existence. (Flittner v. Equitable Life Assurance Society, 30 Cal.App. 209, 159 Pac. 630 (1916). It is suggested in Comment, 12 So.Cal.L.Rev. 335, 346 (1939) that California law limits the parties' range of free choice to states having a "substantial connection" with the transaction. However, in Ehrenzweig, 2 Survey of Calif.Law, 117, 127 (1950) the author states that People v. Globe & Rutgers Fire Insurance Co., 96 Cal.App.2d 571, 216 P.2d 64 (1950) is factually contrary.

If a "reasonable relation" is like a "substantial connection" then apparently this subdivision would not alter California law on the validity of agreements of the parties on the choice of law. On the other hand, to the extent a "substantial relation" is not a "reasonable relation", this subdivision changes the circumstances under which the parties may agree on what law shall govern the transaction. If "reasonable relation" demands more than "substantial connection" the parties' right to agree on choice of law is restricted, and if it demands less, the right is broadened. See Official Comment 1 which states that "ordinarily the law chosen must be that of a jurisdiction where a significant enough portion of the making or performance of the contract is to occur or occurs".

4. Under subdivision (1) in absence of parties' agreement as to what law applies the test of "appropriate relation" is used to determine that law shall apply. The remainder of subdivision (1) provides that in the absence of an agreement by the parties, the Commercial Code applies to transactions bearing an "appropriate relation" to this state. This provision introduces a new term to California law.

In the absence of a valid agreement to the contrary, California courts segregate choice of law rules as follows: (1) matters bearing upon the validity of the contract are determined by the law of the place where the contract is made. See Hutchinson v. Hutchinson, 48 Cal.App.2d 12, 119 P.2d 214 (1941), and 1 Witkin, Summary of California Law, Contracts, § 27 (7th Edition) where cases are collected showing that California courts do not strictly follow this general rule. For an example see Cochran v. Ellsworth, 126 Cal.App.2d 429, 272 P.2d 904 (1954). (2) matters bearing upon the capacity of parties to contract are determined by the law of the place where the contract is made. See Flittner v. Equitable Life Assurance Society, 30 Cal.App. 209, 157 Pac. 630 (1916) and Deason v. Jones, 7 Cal.App.2d 482, 45 P.2d 1025 (1935). (3) matters bearing upon the interpretation or performance of a contract are determined by the law of the place where the contract is to be performed. See Civil Code § 1646 and Sullivan v. Shannon, 25 Cal.App.2d 422, 77 P.2d 498 (1938). Such parcelling out of a commercial transaction would be prevented by subdivision (1) if it is construed to mean that where California has an "appropriate relation" to the transaction, California law governs the *entire* transaction. A State Bar subcommittee stated that:

"It is doubtful that the Uniform Code Commissioners had in mind any such parceling out of a commercial transaction among the laws of several states when they drafted Section 1–105(1). The code says it applies to 'transactions bearing an appropriate relation to this state,' and the implication is that if there is an 'appropriate relation,' the code shall govern the entire transaction. This would create new law in California." Sixth Progress Report to the Legislature by Senate Fact Finding Committee on Judiciary (1959–1961) Part 1, The Uniform Commercial Code, p. 327.

The Official Comments shed no light on the question of the difference between a "reasonable relation" and an "appropriate relation" and do not indicate the source of the term "appropriate relation". However, Official Comment 3 states that where a transaction has significant contacts with another state the question what relation is appropriate is left to judicial decision. This has prompted one writer to say that [the Official Comments] ". . . seem to indicate that having significant contacts is not synonymous with having an appropriate relation—rather that the question is whether the contacts have *enough* significance to justify classifying the relation as appropriate. My guess would be that a relation must be something more than barely reasonable, in order to be considered appropriate. This is on the basis that the Code indicates a policy to give effect to the *parties*' choice of applicable law if at all reasonable, but to condition the *court's* choice of applicable law upon such a relation of the transaction to the state as would of itself suggest appropriateness." (Comment, 48 Kentucky Law Journal, 417, 422 (1960)).

Changes from U.C.C. (1962 Official Text)

5. This is section 1–105 of the Official Text without change.

Uniform Commercial Code Comment
1972 Amendment

Prior Uniform Statutory Provision:
None.

Purposes:

1. Subsection (1) states affirmatively the right of the parties to a multistate transaction or a transaction involving foreign trade to choose their own law. That right is subject to the firm rules stated in the five sections listed in subsection (2), and is limited to jurisdictions to which the transaction bears a "reasonable relation." In general, the test of "reasonable relation" is similar to that laid down by the Supreme Court in Seeman v. Philadelphia Warehouse Co., 274 U.S. 403, 47 S.Ct. 626, 71 L.Ed. 1123 (1927). Ordinarily the law chosen must be that of a jurisdiction where a significant enough portion of the making or performance of the contract is to occur or occurs. But an agreement as to choice of law may sometimes take effect as a shorthand expression of the intent of the parties as to matters governed by their agreement, even though the transaction has no significant contact with the jurisdiction chosen.

2. Where there is no agreement as to the governing law, the Act is applicable to any transaction having an "appropriate" relation to any state which enacts it. Of course, the Act applies to any transaction which takes place in its entirety in a state which has enacted the Act. But the mere fact that suit is brought in a state does not make it appropriate to apply the substantive law of that state. Cases where a relation to the enacting state is not "appropriate" include, for example, those where the parties have clearly contracted on the basis of some other law, as where the law of the place of contracting and the law of the place of contemplated performance are the same and are contrary to the law under the Code.

3. Where a transaction has significant contacts with a state which has enacted the Act and also with other jurisdictions, the question what relation is "appropriate" is left to judicial decision. In deciding that question, the court is not strictly bound by precedents established in other contexts. Thus a conflict-of-laws decision refusing to apply a purely local statute or rule of law to a particular multistate transaction may not be valid precedent for refusal to apply the Code in an analogous situation. Application of the Code in such circumstances may be justified by its comprehensiveness, by the policy of uniformity, and by the fact that it is in large part a reformulation and restatement of the law merchant and of the understanding of a business community which transcends state and even national boundaries. Compare Global Commerce Corp. v. Clark-Babbitt Industries, Inc., 239 F.2d 716, 719 (2d Cir.1956). In particular, where a transaction is governed in large part by the Code, application of another law to some detail of performance because of an accident or geography may violate the commercial understanding of the parties.

4. The Act does not attempt to prescribe choice-of-law rules for states which do not enact it, but this section does not prevent application of the Act in a court of such a state. Common-law choice of law often rests on policies of giving effect to agreements and of uniformity of result regardless of where suit is brought. To the extent that such policies prevail the relevant considerations are similar in such a court to those outlined above.

5. Subsection (2) spells out essential limitations on the parties' right to choose the applicable law. Especially in Article 9 parties taking a security interest or asked to extend credit which may be subject to a security interest must have sure ways to find out whether and where to file and where to look for possible existing filings.

6. Section 9–103 should be consulted as to the rules for perfection of security interests and the effects of perfection and nonperfection.

Uniform Commercial Code Comment

Prior Uniform Statutory Provision:
None.

Purposes:

1. Subsection (1) states affirmatively the right of the parties to a multi-state transaction or a transaction involving foreign trade to choose their own law. That right is subject to the firm rules stated in the six sections listed in subsection (2), and is limited to jurisdictions to which the transaction bears a "reasonable relation." In general, the test of "reasonable relation" is similar to that laid down by the Supreme Court in Seeman v. Philadelphia Warehouse Co., 274 U.S. 403, 47 S.Ct. 626, 71 L.Ed. 1123 (1927). Ordinarily the law chosen must be that of a jurisdiction where a significant enough portion of the making or performance of the contract is to occur or occurs. But an agreement as to choice of law may sometimes take effect as a shorthand expression of the intent of the parties as to matters governed by their agreement, even though the transaction has no significant contact with the jurisdiction chosen.

2. Where there is no agreement as to the governing law, the Act is applicable to any transaction having an "appropriate" relation to any state which enacts it. Of course the Act applies to any transaction which takes place in its entirety in a state which has enacted the Act. But the mere fact that suit is brought in a state does not make it appropriate to apply the substantive law of that state. Cases where a relation to the enacting state is not "appropriate" include, for example, those where the parties have clearly contracted on the basis of some other law, as where the law of the place of contracting and the law of the place of contemplated performance are the same and are contrary to the law under the Code.

3. Where a transaction has significant contacts with a state which has enacted the Act and also with other jurisdictions, the question what relation is "appropriate" is left to judicial decision. In deciding that question, the court is not strictly bound by precedents established in other contexts. Thus a conflict-of-laws decision refusing to apply a purely local statute or rule of law to a particular multi-state transaction may not be valid precedent for refusal to apply the Code in an analogous situation. Application of the Code in such circumstances may be justified by its comprehensiveness, by the policy of uniformity, and by the fact that it is in large part a reformulation and restatement of the law merchant and of the understanding of a business community which transcends state and even national boundaries. Compare Global Commerce Corp. v. Clark-Babbitt Industries, Inc., 239 F.2d 716, 719 (2d Cir.1956). In particular, where a transaction is governed in large part by the Code, application of another law to some detail of performance because of an accident of geography may violate the commercial understanding of the parties.

4. The Act does not attempt to prescribe choice-of-law rules for states which do not enact it, but this section does not prevent application of the Act in a court of such a state. Common-law choice of law often rests on policies of giving effect to agreements and of uniformity of result regardless of where suit is brought. To the extent that such policies prevail, the relevant considerations are similar in such a court to those outlined above.

5. Subsection (2) spells out essential limitations on the parties' right to choose the applicable law. Especially in Article 9 parties taking a security interest or asked to extend credit which may be subject to a security interest must have sure ways to find out whether and where to file and where to look for possible existing filings.

Cross References

Interpretation of contract according to law and usage of place, see Civil Code § 1646.

§ 1106. Remedies to be Liberally Administered

(1) The remedies provided by this code shall be liberally administered to the end that the aggrieved

§ 1106

party may be put in as good a position as if the other party had fully performed but neither consequential or special nor penal damages may be had except as specifically provided in this code or by other rule of law.

(2) Any right or obligation declared by this code is enforceable by action unless the provision declaring it specifies a different and limited effect. *(Stats.1963, c. 819, § 1106.)*

California Code Comment

By John A. Bohn and Charles J. Williams

Prior California Law

1. This section states a general rule for compensatory damages which is similar to the general provision on limitation of damages in Civil Code § 3358. This section disallows "consequential", "special" and "penal" damages except as specifically provided by law. The only other Commercial Code provision for "consequential", "special" or "penal" damages appears in Commercial Code § 2715. Apparently the same results would be obtained under this section and Civil Code § 3300 (providing general damages for breach of contract) and former Civil Code § 1790 (allowing for special damages under the USA. The exception which allows "consequential", "special" and "penal" damages when provided for by "other rule of law" would leave intact any other California rules on the subject.

2. Subdivision (2) is similar to former Civil Code § 1792.

Changes from U.C.C. (1962 Official Text)

3. This is section 1–106 of the Official Text without change.

Uniform Commercial Code Comment

Prior Uniform Statutory Provision: Subsection (1)—none; Subsection (2)—Section 72, Uniform Sales Act.

Changes: Reworded.

Purposes of Changes and New Matter: Subsection (1) is intended to effect three things:

1. First, to negate the unduly narrow or technical interpretation of some remedial provisions of prior legislation by providing that the remedies in this Act are to be liberally administered to the end stated in the section. Second, to make it clear that compensatory damages are limited to compensation. They do not include consequential or special damages, or penal damages; and the Act elsewhere makes it clear that damages must be minimized. Cf. Sections 1–203, 2–706(1), and 2–712(2). The third purpose of subsection (1) is to reject any doctrine that damages must be calculable with mathematical accuracy. Compensatory damages are often at best approximate: they have to be proved with whatever definiteness and accuracy the facts permit, but no more. Cf. Section 2–204(3).

2. Under subsection (2) any right or obligation described in this Act is enforceable by court action, even though no remedy may be expressly provided, unless a particular provision specifies a different and limited effect. Whether specific performance or other equitable relief is available is determined not by this section but by specific provisions and by supplementary principles. Cf. Sections 1–103, 2–716.

3. "Consequential" or "special" damages and "penal" damages are not defined in terms in the Code, but are used in the sense given them by the leading cases on the subject.

Cross References: Sections 1–103, 1–203, 2–204(3), 2–701, 2–706(1), 2–712(2) and 2–716.

Definitional Cross References:

"Action". Section 1–201.
"Aggrieved party". Section 1–201.
"Party". Section 1–201.
"Remedy". Section 1–201.
"Rights". Section 1–201.

Cross References

Action defined, see Code of Civil Procedure § 22.
Actions and proceedings, see Code of Civil Procedure § 307 et seq.
Buyer's remedies, incidental or consequential damages, see Commercial Code § 2712.
Compensatory relief, see Civil Code § 3281 et seq.
Exemplary damages, see Civil Code § 3294.
Liberal construction of code, see Commercial Code § 1102.
Limitation on damages, see Civil Code § 3358.
Liquidated damages, see Civil Code § 1671.
Measure of damages for breach of contract, see Civil Code § 3300.
Obligation of good faith, see Commercial Code § 1203.
Remedies for breach of obligation ancillary to a contract for sale, see Commercial Code § 2701.
Sales,
  Indefiniteness of contract, see Commercial Code § 2204.
  Specific performance, see Commercial Code § 2716.
Seller's remedies, incidental damages, see Commercial Code § 2706.
Supplementation of Code by principles of law and equity, see Commercial Code § 1103.

§ 1107. Waiver or Renunciation of Claim or Right After Breach

Any claim or right arising out of an alleged breach can be discharged in whole or in part without consideration by a written waiver or renunciation signed and delivered by the aggrieved party. *(Stats.1963, c. 819, § 1107.)*

California Code Comment

By John A. Bohn and Charles J. Williams

Prior California Law

1. This section in providing for a waiver or release without consideration if in writing is similar to Civil Code § 1541 which requires a new consideration or a writing to support a release of an obligation. Exception to this general California requirement is found under former Civil Code § 3201 (NIL) providing for the discharge of a person secondarily liable on the instrument and former Civil Code § 3203 providing that the holder may renounce his rights against a party to the instrument.

2. See Civil Code §§ 1605 to 1615 as to what amounts to consideration and Marshall v. Packard-Bell, 106 Cal.App.2d 770, 236 P.2d 201 (1951), for an example of binding written release without consideration.

3. Compare Upper San Joaquin Canal Co. v. Roach, 78 Cal. 552, 21 Pac. 304 (1889) which states that Civil Code § 1541 relates only to formal releases with Sappa v. Crestetto, 78 Cal.App.2d 362, 177 P.2d 950 (1947) which holds a certain document to be a release despite the reason for preparing it.

Changes from U.C.C. (1962 Official Text)

4. This is section 1–107 of the Official Text without change.

Uniform Commercial Code Comment

Prior Uniform Statutory Provision: Compare Section 1, Uniform Written Obligations Act; Sections 119((3), 120(2) and 122, Uniform Negotiable Instruments Law.

Purposes:

This section makes consideration unnecessary to the effective renunciation or waiver of rights or claims arising out of an alleged breach of a commercial contract where such renunciation is in writing and signed and delivered by the aggrieved party. Its provisions, however, must be read in conjunction with the section imposing an obligation of good faith. (Section 1–203). There may, of course, also be an oral renunciation or waiver sustained by consideration but subject to Statute of Frauds provisions and to the section of Article 2 on Sales dealing with the modification of signed writings (Section 2–209). As is made express in the latter section this Act fully recognizes the effectiveness of waiver and estoppel.

Cross References:

Sections 1–203, 2–201 and 2–209. And see Section 2–719.

Definitional Cross References:

"Aggrieved party". Section 1–201.
"Rights". Section 1–201.
"Signed". Section 1–201.
"Written". Section 1–201.

Cross References

Consideration, see Civil Code § 1605 et seq.
Modification, rescission and waiver, see Commercial Code § 2209.
Modification of remedies for breach of sales contract, see Commercial Code § 2719.
Obligation of good faith, see Commercial Code § 1203.
Release, extinction of obligations, see Civil Code § 1541 et seq.
Statute of frauds, see Commercial Code § 2201.
Waiver,
  Advantage of law for own benefit, see Civil Code § 3513.
  Code provisions, see Civil Code § 3268.

§ 1108. Severability

If any provision or clause of this code or application thereof to any person or circumstances is held invalid, such invalidity shall not affect other provisions or applications of the code which can be given effect without the invalid provision or application, and to this end the provisions of this code are declared to be severable. *(Stats.1963, c. 819, § 1108.)*

California Code Comment

By John A. Bohn and Charles J. Williams

Prior California Law

1. This section is the model clause recommended by the National Conference of Commissioners on Uniform State Laws for inclusion in all acts of extensive scope and is identical to former Civil Code § 3016.15. (UTRA).

Changes from U.C.C. (1962 Official Text)

2. This is section 1–108 of the Official Text without change.

Uniform Commercial Code Comment

This is the model severability section recommended by the National Conference of Commissioners on Uniform State Laws for inclusion in all acts of extensive scope.

Definitional Cross Reference:

"Person". Section 1–201.

§ 1109. [Not enacted in California]

California Code Comment

By John A. Bohn and Charles J. Williams

1. This section which appears in the Official Text as section 1–109 is omitted from the California version of the Commercial Code. Section 1–109 of the Official Text reads:

"Section captions are part of this Act".

2. In the California code system section captions do not in any manner affect the scope, meaning or intent of the provisions of a section. This mandate is contained throughout the codes. For example, see Welfare and Institutions Code § 5 and Insurance Code § 6. Similar provisions appear in all existing California codes except the Civil Code and the Code of Civil Procedure.

CHAPTER 2. GENERAL DEFINITIONS AND PRINCIPLES OF INTERPRETATION

Section
1201. General Definitions.
1202. Third Party Documents; Admissibility; Presumption.
1203. Obligation of Good Faith.
1204. Time; Reasonable Time; "Seasonably".
1205. Course of Dealing and Usage of Trade.
1206. Statute of Frauds for Kinds of Personal Property Not Otherwise Covered.
1207. Performance or Acceptance Under Reservation of Rights.
1208. Option to Accelerate at Will.
1209. Subordinated Obligations.
1210. Presumptions; Nature.

§ 1201. General Definitions

Subject to additional definitions contained in the subsequent divisions of this code which are applicable to specific divisions or chapters thereof, and unless the context otherwise requires, in this code:

(1) "Action" in the sense of a judicial proceeding includes recoupment, counterclaim, setoff, suit in equity, and any other proceedings in which rights are determined.

(2) "Aggrieved party" means a party entitled to resort to a remedy.

(3) "Agreement" means the bargain of the parties in fact as found in their language or by implication from other circumstances including course of dealing or usage of trade or course of performance as provided in this code (Sections 1205, 2208, and 10207). Whether an agreement has legal consequences is determined by the provisions of this code, if applicable; otherwise by the law of contracts (Section 1103). (Compare "contract.")

(4) "Bank" means any person engaged in the business of banking.

(5) "Bearer" means the person in possession of an instrument, document of title, or certificated security payable to bearer or indorsed in blank.

(6) "Bill of lading" means a document evidencing the receipt of goods for shipment issued by a person engaged in the business of transporting or forwarding goods, and which, by its terms, evidences the intention of the issuer that the person entitled under the document (Section 7403(4)) has the right to receive, hold and dispose of the document and the goods it covers. Designation of a document by the issuer as a "bill of lading" is conclusive evidence of such intention. "Bill of lading" includes an airbill. "Airbill" means a document serving for air transportation as a bill of lading does for marine or rail transportation, and includes an air consignment note or air waybill.

(7) "Branch" includes a separately incorporated foreign branch of a bank.

(8) "Burden of establishing" a fact means the burden of persuading the triers of fact that the existence of the fact is more probable than its nonexistence.

§ 1201   GENERAL PROVISIONS

(9) "Buyer in ordinary course of business" means a person who in good faith and without knowledge that the sale to him or her is in violation of the ownership rights or security interest of a third party in the goods buys in ordinary course from a person in the business of selling goods of that kind but does not include a pawnbroker. All persons who sell minerals or the like (including oil and gas) at wellhead or mineralhead shall be deemed to be persons in the business of selling goods of that kind. "Buying" may be for cash or by exchange of other property or on secured or unsecured credit and includes receiving goods or documents of title under a preexisting contract for sale but does not include a transfer in bulk or as security for, or in total or partial satisfaction of, a money debt.

(10) "Conspicuous." A term or clause is conspicuous when it is so written that a reasonable person against whom it is to operate ought to have noticed it. A printed heading in capitals (as: <u>Nonnegotiable Bill of Lading</u>) is conspicuous. Language in the body of a form is "conspicuous" if it is in larger or other contrasting type or color. But in a telegram any stated term is "conspicuous." Whether a term or clause is "conspicuous" or not is for decision by the court.

(11) "Contract" means the total legal obligation which results from the parties' agreement as affected by this code and any other applicable rules of law. (Compare "agreement.")

(12) "Creditor" includes a general creditor, a secured creditor, a lien creditor and any representative of creditors, including an assignee for the benefit of creditors, a trustee in bankruptcy, a receiver in equity and an executor or administrator of an insolvent debtor's or assignor's estate.

(13) "Defendant" includes a person in the position of defendant in a cross-action or counterclaim.

(14) "Delivery" with respect to instruments, documents of title, chattel paper or certificated securities means voluntary transfer of possession.

(15) "Document of title" includes bill of lading, dock warrant, dock receipt, warehouse receipt, gin ticket, compress receipt, and also any other document which in the regular course of business or financing is treated as adequately evidencing that the person entitled under the document (Section 7403(4)) has the right to receive, hold and dispose of the document and the goods it covers. To be a document of title, a document shall purport to be issued by a bailee and purport to cover goods in the bailee's possession which are either identified or are fungible portions of an identified mass.

(16) "Fault" means wrongful act, omission or breach.

(17) "Fungible" with respect to goods or securities means goods or securities of which any unit is, by nature or usage of trade, the equivalent of any other like unit. Goods which are not fungible shall be deemed fungible for the purposes of this code to the extent that under a particular agreement or document unlike units are treated as equivalents.

(18) "Genuine" means free of forgery or counterfeiting.

(19) "Good faith" means honesty in fact in the conduct or transaction concerned.

(20) "Holder," with respect to a negotiable instrument, means the person in possession if the instrument is payable to bearer or, in the case of an instrument payable to an identified person, if the identified person is in possession. "Holder," with respect to a document of title, means the person in possession if the goods are deliverable to bearer or to the order of the person in possession.

(21) To "honor" is to pay or to accept and pay, or where a credit so engages to purchase or discount a draft complying with the terms of the credit.

(22) "Insolvency proceedings" includes any assignment for the benefit of creditors or other proceedings intended to liquidate or rehabilitate the estate of the person involved.

(23) A person is "insolvent" who either has ceased to pay his or her debts in the ordinary course of business or cannot pay his or her debts as they become due or is insolvent within the meaning of the federal bankruptcy law.

(24) "Money" means a medium of exchange authorized or adopted by a domestic or foreign government and includes a monetary unit of account established by an intergovernmental organization or by agreement between two or more nations.

(25) A person has "notice" of a fact when any of the following occurs:

(a) He or she has actual knowledge of it.

(b) He or she has received a notice or notification of it.

(c) From all the facts and circumstances known to him or her at the time in question, he or she has reason to know that it exists. A person "knows" or has "knowledge" of a fact when he or she has actual knowledge of it. "Discover" or "learn" or a word or phrase of similar import refers to knowledge rather than to reason to know. The time and circumstances under which a notice or notification may cease to be effective are not determined by this code.

(26) A person "notifies" or "gives" a notice or notification to another by taking such steps as may be reasonably required to inform the other in ordinary course whether or not the other actually comes to know of it. A person "receives" a notice or notification when any of the following occurs:

(a) It comes to his or her attention.

(b) It is duly delivered at the place of business through which the contract was made or at any other place held out by him or her as the place for receipt of such communications.

(27) Notice, knowledge or a notice or notification received by an organization is effective for a particular

transaction from the time when it is brought to the attention of the individual conducting that transaction, and in any event from the time when it would have been brought to his or her attention if the organization had exercised due diligence. An organization exercises due diligence if it maintains reasonable routines for communicating significant information to the person conducting the transaction and there is reasonable compliance with the routines. Due diligence does not require an individual acting for the organization to communicate information unless the communication is part of his or her regular duties or unless he or she has reason to know of the transaction and that the transaction would be materially affected by the information.

(28) "Organization" includes a corporation, government or governmental subdivision or agency, business trust, estate, trust, partnership or association, two or more persons having a joint or common interest, or any other legal or commercial entity.

(29) "Party," as distinct from "third party," means a person who has engaged in a transaction or made an agreement within this division.

(30) "Person" includes an individual or an organization. (See Section 1102.)

(32)[1] "Purchase" includes taking by sale, discount, negotiation, mortgage, pledge, lien, issue or reissue, gift or any other voluntary transaction creating an interest in property.

(33) "Purchaser" means a person who takes by purchase.

(34) "Remedy" means any remedial right to which an aggrieved party is entitled with or without resort to a tribunal.

(35) "Representative" includes an agent, an officer of a corporation or association, and a trustee, executor or administrator of an estate, or any other person empowered to act for another.

(36) "Rights" includes remedies.

(37)(a) "Security interest" means an interest in personal property or fixtures which secures payment or performance of an obligation. The retention or reservation of title by a seller of goods notwithstanding shipment or delivery to the buyer (Section 2401) is limited in effect to a reservation of a "security interest." The term also includes any interest of a buyer of accounts or chattel paper which is subject to Division 9 (commencing with Section 9101). The special property interest of a buyer of goods on identification of those goods to a contract for sale under Section 2401 is not a "security interest," but a buyer may also acquire a "security interest" by complying with Division 9 (commencing with Section 9101). Unless a consignment is intended as security, reservation of title thereunder is not a "security interest," but a consignment in any event is subject to the provisions on consignment sales (Section 2326).

(b) Whether a transaction creates a lease or security interest is determined by the facts of each case; however, a transaction creates a security interest if the consideration the lessee is to pay the lessor for the right to possession and use of the goods is an obligation for the term of the lease not subject to termination by the lessee, and

(i) The original term of the lease is equal to or greater than the remaining economic life of the goods,

(ii) The lessee is bound to renew the lease for the remaining economic life of the goods or is bound to become the owner of the goods,

(iii) The lessee has an option to renew the lease for the remaining economic life of the goods for no additional consideration or nominal additional consideration upon compliance with the lease agreement, or

(iv) The lessee has an option to become the owner of the goods for no additional consideration or nominal additional consideration upon compliance with the lease agreement.

(c) A transaction does not create a security interest merely because it provides that

(i) The present value of the consideration the lessee is obligated to pay the lessor for the right to possession and use of the goods is substantially equal to or is greater than the fair market value of the goods at the time the lease is entered into,

(ii) The lessee assumes risk of loss of the goods, or agrees to pay taxes, insurance, filing, recording, or registration fees, or service or maintenance costs with respect to the goods,

(iii) The lessee has an option to renew the lease or to become the owner of the goods,

(iv) The lessee has an option to renew the lease for a fixed rent that is equal to or greater than the reasonably predictable fair market rent for the use of the goods for the term of the renewal at the time the option is to be performed, * * *

(v) The lessee has an option to become the owner of the goods for a fixed price that is equal to or greater than the reasonably predictable fair market value of the goods at the time the option is to be performed * * *[2] or,

(vi) In the case of a motor vehicle, as defined in Section 415 of the Vehicle Code, or a trailer, as defined in Section 630 of that code, that is not to be used primarily for personal, family, or household purposes, the amount of rental payments may be increased or decreased by reference to the amount realized by the lessor upon sale or disposition of the vehicle or trailer. Nothing in this subparagraph affects the application or administration of the Sales and Use Tax Law (Part 1 (commencing with Section 6001) of Division 2 of the Revenue and Taxation Code).

(d) For purposes of this subdivision (37):

(i) Additional consideration is not nominal if (A) when the option to renew the lease is granted to the lessee, the rent is stated to be the fair market rent for the use of the goods for the term of the renewal determined at the time the option is to be performed, or (B) when the option to become the owner of the goods is granted to the lessee, the price is stated to be the fair market value of the goods determined at the time the option is to be performed. Additional consideration is nominal if it is less than the lessee's reasonably predictable cost of performing under the lease agreement if the option is not exercised;

(ii) "Reasonably predictable" and "remaining economic life of the goods" are to be determined with reference to the facts and circumstances at the time the transaction is entered into; and

(iii) "Present value" means the amount as of a date certain of one or more sums payable in the future, discounted to the date certain. The discount is determined by the interest rate specified by the parties if the rate is not manifestly unreasonable at the time the transaction is entered into; otherwise, the discount is determined by a commercially reasonable rate that takes into account the facts and circumstances of each case at the time the transaction was entered into.

(38) "Send" in connection with any writing or notice means to deposit in the mail or deliver for transmission by any other usual means of communication with postage or cost of transmission provided for and properly addressed and in the case of an instrument to an address specified thereon or otherwise agreed, or if there be none to any address reasonable under the circumstances. The receipt of any writing or notice within the time at which it would have arrived if properly sent has the effect of a proper sending. When a writing or notice is required to be sent by registered or certified mail, proof of mailing is sufficient, and proof of receipt by the addressee is not required unless the words "with return receipt requested" are also used.

(39) "Signed" includes any symbol executed or adopted by a party with present intention to authenticate a writing.

(40) "Surety" includes guarantor.

(41) "Telegram" includes a message transmitted by radio, teletype, cable, any mechanical method of transmission, or the like.

(42) "Term" means that portion of an agreement which relates to a particular matter.

(43) "Unauthorized" signature means one made without actual, implied, or apparent authority and includes a forgery.

(44) "Value". Except as otherwise provided with respect to negotiable instruments and bank collections (Sections 3303, 4210, and 4211), a person gives "value" for rights if he or she acquires them in any of the following ways:

(a) In return for a binding commitment to extend credit or for the extension of immediately available credit whether or not drawn upon and whether or not a chargeback is provided for in the event of difficulties in collection.

(b) As security for, or in total or partial satisfaction of, a preexisting claim.

(c) By accepting delivery pursuant to a preexisting contract for purchase.

(d) Generally, in return for any consideration sufficient to support a simple contract.

(45) "Warehouse receipt" means a document evidencing the receipt of goods for storage issued by a warehouseman (Section 7102), and which, by its terms, evidences the intention of the issuer that the person entitled under the document (Section 7403(4)) has the right to receive, hold and dispose of the document and the goods it covers. Designation of a document by the issuer as a "warehouse receipt" is conclusive evidence of such intention.

(46) "Written" or "writing" includes printing, typewriting or any other intentional reduction to tangible form. *(Stats. 1963, c. 819, § 1201. Amended by Stats.1967, c. 799, p. 2202, § 2; Stats.1974, c. 997, p. 2109, § 2, eff. Jan. 1, 1976; Stats.1984, c. 927, § 3; Stats.1988, c. 1359, § 2, operative Jan. 1, 1990; Stats. 1991, c. 111 (S.B.972), § 1, eff. July 15, 1991; Stats.1992, c. 427 (A.B.3355), § 17; Stats.1992, c. 914 (S.B.833), § 2; Stats.1994, c. 668 (S.B.1405), § 8; Stats.1995, c. 320 (A.B.1159), § 1.)*

1 Chaptered copy contained no subd. (31).

California Comment
Report on the Assembly Committee on Judiciary
August 15, 1988

Uniform Statutory Source: Section 1–201(37), 1978 Official Text of the Act.

Changes: Substantially revised.

Purposes: This amendment to subdivision (37) of Section 1201 is being promulgated at the same time that the Division on Leases (Division 10) is being promulgated as an amendment to this Code.

One of the reasons it was decided to codify the law with respect to leases was to resolve an issue that has created considerable confusion in the courts: what is a lease? The confusion exists, in part, due to the last two sentences of the definition of security interest in the 1978 Official Text of the Code. Subdivision (37), Section 1201. The confusion is compounded by the rather considerable change in the federal, state and local tax laws and accounting rules as they relate to leases of goods. The answer is important because the definition of lease determines not only the rights and remedies of the parties to the lease but also those of third parties. If a transaction creates a lease and not a security interest, the lessee's interest in the goods is limited to its leasehold estate; the residual interest in the goods belongs to the lessor. This has significant implications to the lessee's creditors. "On common law theory, the lessor, since he has not parted with title, is entitled to full protection against the lessee's creditors and trustee in bankruptcy ...." 1 G. Gilmore, *Security Interests in Personal Property* § 3.6, at 76 (1965).

Under pre-Code chattel security law there was generally no requirement that the lessor file the lease, a financing statement, or the like, to enforce the lease agreement against the lessee or any third party; the Division on Secured Transactions (Division 9) did not change the common law in that respect. Coogan, Leasing and the Uniform Commercial Code, in *Equipment Leasing—Leveraged Leasing* 681, 700 n. 25, 729 n. 80 (2d ed.1980). The Division on Leases (Division 10) has not changed the law in that respect, except for leases of fixtures. Section 10309. An examination of the common law will not provide an adequate answer to the question of what is a lease. The definition of security interest in Section 1–201(37) of the 1978 Official Text of the Code provides that the Division on Secured Transactions (Division 9) governs security interests disguised as leases, *i.e.*, leases intended as security; however, the definition is vague and outmoded.

Lease is defined in Division 10 as a transfer of the right to possession and use of goods for a term, in return for consideration. Paragraph (j), subdivision (1), Section 10103. The definition continues by stating that the retention or creation of a security interest is not a lease. Thus, the task of sharpening the line between true leases and security interests disguised as leases continues to be a function of this section.

Paragraph (a) of this definition is a revised version of the first five sentences of the 1978 Official Text of Section 1–201(37). The changes are modest in that they make a style change in the fourth sentence and delete the reference to lease in the fifth sentence. The balance of this definition is new, although it preserves elements of the last two sentences of the prior definition. The focus of the changes was to draw a sharper line between leases and security interests disguised as leases to create greater certainty in commercial transactions.

Prior to this amendment, subdivision (37) of Section 1201 provided that whether a lease was intended as security (*i.e.*, a security interest disguised as a lease) was to be determined from the facts of each case; however, (a) the inclusion of an option to purchase did not itself make the lease one intended for security, and (b) an agreement that upon compliance with the terms of the lease the lessee would become, or had the option to become, the owner of the property for no additional consideration, or for a nominal consideration, did make the lease one intended for security.

Reference to the intent of the parties to create a lease or security interest has led to unfortunate results. In discovering intent, courts have relied upon factors that were thought to be more consistent with sales or loans than leases. Most of these criteria, however, are as applicable to true leases as to security interests. Examples include the typical net lease provisions, a purported lessor's lack of storage facilities or its character as a financing party rather than a dealer in goods. Accordingly, amended subdivision (37) of Section 1201 deletes all reference to the parties' intent.

Paragraph (b) of the new definition is taken from Section 1(2) of the Uniform Conditional Sales Act (act withdrawn 1943), modified to reflect current leasing practice. Thus, reference to the case law prior to this Code will provide a useful source of precedent. Gilmore, *Security Law, Formalism and Article 9*, 47 Neb.L.Rev. 659, 671 (1968). Whether a transaction creates a lease or a security interest continues to be determined by the facts of each case. Paragraph (b) further provides that a transaction creates a security interest if the lessee has an obligation to continue paying consideration for the term of the lease, if the obligation is not terminable by the lessee (thus correcting early statutory gloss, *e.g.*, *In re Royer's Bakery, Inc.*, 1 U.C.C. Rep.Serv. (Callaghan) 342 (Bankr.E.D.Pa.1963)) and if one of four additional tests is met. The first of these four tests, subparagraph (i), is that the original lease term is equal to or greater than the remaining economic life of the goods. The second of these tests, subparagraph (ii), is that the lessee is either bound to renew the lease for the remaining economic life of the goods or to become the owner of the goods. *In re Gehrke Enters.*, 1 Bankr. 647, 651–52 (Bankr.W.D.Wis.1979). The third of these tests, subparagraph (iii), is whether the lessee has an option to renew the lease for the remaining economic life of the goods for no additional consideration or for nominal additional consideration, which is defined later in this section. *In re Celeryvale Transp.*, 44 Bankr. 1007, 1014–15 (Bankr.E.D.Tenn.1984). The fourth of these tests, subparagraph (iv), is whether the lessee has an option to become the owner of the goods for no additional consideration or for nominal additional consideration. All of these tests focus on economics, not the intent of the parties. *In re Berge*, 32 Bankr. 370, 371–73 (Bankr.W.D.Wis.1983).

The focus on economics is reinforced by the next paragraph, which is new. It states that a transaction does not create a security interest merely because the transaction has certain characteristics listed therein. Subparagraph (i) has no statutory derivative; it states that a full payout lease does not *per se* create a security interest. *Rushton v. Shea*, 419 F.Supp. 1349, 1365 (D.Del.1976). Subparagraph (ii) provides the same regarding the provisions of the typical net lease. *Compare All-States Leasing Co. v. Ochs*, 42 Or.App. 319, 600 P.2d 899 (Ct.App.1979) *with In re Tillery*, 571 F.2d 1361 (5th Cir.1978). Subparagraph (iii) restates and expands the provisions of former subdivision (37) of Section 1201 to make clear that the option can be to buy or renew. Subparagraphs (iv) and (v) treat fixed price options and provide that fair market value must be determined at the time the transaction is entered into. *Compare Arnold Mach. Co. v. Balls*, 624 P.2d 678 (Utah 1981) *with Aoki v. Shepherd Mach. Co.*, 665 F.2d 941 (9th Cir.1982).

The relationship of paragraph (b) of this subdivision to paragraph (c) of this subdivision deserves to be explored. The fixed price purchase option provides a useful example. A fixed price purchase option in a lease does not of itself create a security interest. This is particularly true if the fixed price is equal to or greater than the reasonably predictable fair market value of the goods at the time the option is to be performed. A security interest is created only if the option price is nominal and the conditions stated in the introduction to paragraph (b) of this subdivision are met. There is a set of purchase options whose fixed price is less than fair market value but greater than nominal. The fact that the option price is less than the fair market value does not imply that the lease creates a security interest. Whether in these cases the transaction in which the option is included creates a lease or a security interest must be determined on the facts of each case.

It was possible to provide for various other permutations and combinations with respect to options to purchase and renew. For example, this subdivision could have stated a rule to govern the facts of *In re Marhoefer Packing Co.*, 674 F.2d 1139 (7th Cir.1982). This was not done because it would unnecessarily complicate the definition. Further development of this rule is left to the courts.

Paragraph (d) provides definitions and rules of construction.

California Code Comment
By Charles J. Williams

The 1967 amendment amends subdivision (17) to conform to the 1962 Official Text. The addition of this sentence adds some flexibility so that goods which may not be fungible in themselves are deemed fungible if under an agreement or document the parties treated them as fungible.

By John A. Bohn and Charles J. Williams

Prior California Law

1. "Action" defined in subdivision (1) broadens the prior definition of this term in former Civil Code § 1796 (USA); § 1858.04 (UWRA); § 2132(b) (UBLA) and § 3266 (NIL) by adding "recoupment" and "any other proceedings in which rights are determined"; and in the case of former Civil Code § 3266 also adding "suit in equity".

2. "Aggrieved party" defined in subdivision (2) has no statutory counterpart in prior California law.

3. "Agreement" defined in subdivision (3) has no statutory counterpart in prior California law but does include the concepts of a contract contained in Civil Code § 1549 § 1620 and § 1621 (dealing with contracts in general) and is in accord with the rules of interpretation in Civil Code § 13 and § 1644 and Code of Civil Procedure § 16. This definition expands upon the concept of agreement as expressed in the above Civil Code and Code of Civil Procedure sections which formerly stated that a contract was an agreement to do or not to do a certain thing, expressed or implied.

4. "Bank" defined in subdivision (4) appears on its face to be more limited than the definition of this term in former Civil Code § 3266 (NIL) because it does not expressly include an association of persons. However the term "person" is used in subdivision (4) and is broadly defined in subdivision (30) infra to include an "organization" which in turn is defined in subdivision (28) to include incorporated and unincorporated associations. Therefore, by incorporating the broad language of "organization" through the use of "person", the definition of "bank" in subdivision (4) is actually as broad as, if not broader than, the definition of this term in former Civil Code § 3266.

5. "Bearer" defined in subdivision (5) broadens the definition of this term in former Civil Code § 3266 (NIL) by referring to "instrument, document of title, or security" instead of "a bill or note".

6. "Bill of lading" defined in subdivision (6) changes the meaning of this term as expressed in former Civil Code § 2126c and § 2126d (UBLA). These former Civil Code sections used the terms non-negotiable or straight bill and a negotiable or order bill. This definition in the Commercial Code contains language not found in the Official Text. (see note 47 infra)

7. "Branch" defined in subdivision (7) has no statutory counterpart in prior California law.

8. "Burden of establishing" defined in subdivision (8) has not previously been defined in the California statutes but is generally in

§ 1201   GENERAL PROVISIONS   14

accord with the evidentiary provisions of Code of Civil Procedure, §§ 1981, 1826, 1869, and 2061(5) dealing with burden of proof.

9. "Buyer in ordinary course of business" defined in subdivision (9) broadens the terms "buyer" as defined in former Civil Code § 1796 (USA) and "buyer in the ordinary course of trade" as defined in former Civil Code § 3013 (UTRA). The sale of goods under this definition need not be "for new value" as required under former Civil Code § 3013.

10. "Conspicuous" defined in subdivision (7) has no statutory counterpart in prior California law.

11. "Contract" as defined in subdivision (11) is in accord with the definition in Civil Code § 1549 (dealing with contracts in general) and former Civil Code § 1721 (USA). The ordinary concept of a contract in California is not changed by this definition since it specifically recognizes the effect of "any other applicable rules of law".

12. "Creditor" as defined in subdivision (12) broadens the prior definitions of this term in former Civil Code § 3017 (assignment of accounts receivable) and Civil Code §§ 3430 and 3439.01 (special relations of debtor and creditor) by expressly including all classes of creditors and representatives of creditors.

The Report on Proposed Amendments to the Uniform Commercial Code, by Harold Marsh, Jr. and William D. Warren makes the following observations on the effect of subdivision (12) on existing California law.

"The inclusion within the definition of creditor of an assignee, a receiver and a personal representative has the effect under the [Commercial] code principally of permitting such persons to avoid, on behalf of all creditors, certain transfers made by a debtor . . .

"The inclusion of a personal representative within the definition of creditor does not make any change in the California law, since under Probate Code § 579 such a personal representative is already empowered to recover fraudulent conveyances by the decedent or any other 'conveyance that by law is void as against creditors' when the estate is insolvent.

"The inclusion of a receiver in equity within the definition of creditor does not apparently make any change in California law . . . Camerer v. California Savings & Commercial Bank of San Diego, 4 Cal.2d 159, 48 P.2d 39 (1935) . . .

"The inclusion of an assignee for the benefit of creditors in this definition will change the California law. At the present time, such an assignee is held to stand in the shoes of his assignor, and cannot attack any conveyance or security instrument which is valid against the assignor. CC [Civil Code] § 3460; First National Bank of San Jose v. Menke, 128 Cal. 103, 60 P. 675 (1900).

"The inclusion of a trustee in bankruptcy in this definition will neither add to nor subtract from the rights such a trustee has under Section 70(c) of the Bankruptcy Act [11 U.S.C.A. § 110(c)]." Sixth Progress Report to the Legislature by Senate Fact Finding Committee on Judiciary (1959–1961) Part 1, The Uniform Commercial Code, pp. 438, 439.

13. "Defendant" defined in subdivision (13) is similar to the definition of this term in former Civil Code § 1796 (USA) and is in accord with Code of Civil Procedure § 308 and § 1063.

14. "Delivery" defined in subdivision (14) is similar to the definition of this term in former Civil Code § 1796 (USA) § 1858.04 (UWRA) and former Corporations Code § 2453 (USTA) but differs from the definition in former Civil Code § 3266 (NIL) in that section 3266 included constructive transfers and did not include the term "voluntary" in referring to transfers.

15. "Documents of title" defined in subdivision (15) is similar to the definition of "document of title to goods" found in former Civil Code § 1796 (USA), but specifically adds "dock receipt", "gin ticket", and "compress receipt." The Marsh and Warren Report states that the specific mention of "gin ticket" and "compress receipt" not found in the Official Text is an unnecessary addition because they are clearly included in the general definition of this subdivision.

"There can be no doubt that the gin ticket and compress receipt are issued by a bailee (the cotton gin or compress, as the case may be) and purport to cover cotton in the bailee's possession. Therefore, if in the regular course of business or financing they are treated as adequately evidencing that the person in possession of such documents is entitled to receive, hold and dispose of the documents and the goods represented, as the California Bankers Committee states, then they are already included in this definition." Sixth Progress Report to the Legislature by Senate Fact Finding Committee on Judiciary (1959–1961) Part 1, The Uniform Commercial Code, p. 444.

The term "order for the delivery of goods" in the Official Text is deleted to exclude a delivery order from the definition of a document of title. The reason for this deletion is that to include a delivery order in this definition would allow the holder of a warehouse receipt to set up two competing claims of title to the goods. This rationale is explained more fully in reference to Commercial Code § 7502(1) and § 7503(2) in the March and Warren Report, supra, on pp. 526–528. For further explanation of the exclusion of a delivery order see California Code Comments to Commercial Code § 7502(1) and § 7503(2).

16. "Fault" defined in subdivision (16) is defined similarly in former Civil Code § 1796 (USA) except that the term "omission or breach" is substituted for the term "default."

17. "Fungible" defined in subdivision (17) broadens the definitions in former Civil Code § 1796 (USA) and § 1858.04 (UWRA) by including securities in addition to goods.

18. "Genuine" defined in subdivision (18) has no statutory counterpart in prior California law.

19. "Good faith" defined in subdivision (19) is similar to former Civil Code § 1796(2) (USA), § 1858.04(2) (UWRA) and § 2132b(2) (UBLA) and former Corporations Code § 2460 (USTA) but omits the statement contained in these former sections that negligence is not to be considered in determining good faith. This definition fixes a minimum standard. Certain other sections of the Commercial Code such as section 2103(1)(b) and section 7404 impose additional requirements, i.e. the observance of "reasonable commercial standards".

20. "Holder" defined in subdivision (20) broadens the definition of this term in former Civil Code § 2132b (UBLA) and § 3266 (NIL) by specifically including "investment security" and not requiring "a right of property therein" as formerly required in the definition in former Civil Code § 2132b.

21. "Honor" defined in subdivision (21) has no statutory counterpart in prior California law.

22. "Insolvency proceedings" defined in subdivision (22) has no statutory counterpart in prior California law.

23. An "insolvent" person defined in subdivision (23) is similar to former Civil Code § 3077 (NIL), and § 3439.02 and § 3450. Former Civil Code § 1796(3) (USA) also defined insolvency but provided that insolvency under the federal bankruptcy was not to be considered in determining insolvency under the (USA). The definition of "bankrupt" in Corporations Code § 15002 includes insolvency under federal bankruptcy act or any state insolvency act.

24. Although "money" defined in subdivision (24) has no statutory counterpart in prior California law it has been included in the definition of "personal property" in Civil Code § 14(3) and Code of Civil Procedure § 17(3).

25. "Notice" defined in subdivision (25)(a) and (b) is similar to the definitions in Civil Code § 18 and § 19, but the terms "knows", "knowledge", "discovery", and "learn" in subdivision (25)(c) are new to the definition of notice in California law.

26. The definition in subdivision (26) of when a person "gives" notice, "notifies" or "receives" notice has no statutory counterpart in prior California law. Civil Code § 18 and § 19 define actual and constructive notice.

27. Subdivision (27) provides when notice is effective and also explains the concept of due diligence. This subdivision has no statutory counterpart in prior California law. The second and third sentences in this subdivision were included in the 1962 Official Text for the first time and do not appear in the 1958 Official Text. This addition to the previous Official Text is similar to an amendment offered by the California Bankers Committee and an amendment offered by Professors March and Warren. The California Bankers Committee proposed an amendment which would have added to the first sentence of subdivision (27) the following:

"or in the case of an organization maintaining branch offices at the time when it would have been brought to his attention if the personnel of the organization at such branch or office had exercised due diligence."

The March and Warren amendment would have added a sentence to subdivision (27) as follows:

"If notice, knowledge or a notice or notification is brought to the attention of a branch or office of a financial institution other than the branch or office where the individual conducting the transaction is located, due diligence does not require bringing it to the attention of the individual conducting the transaction unless the individual receiving it is aware of the transaction."

The intent of these two amendments was the same and their purpose was

"to preserve the California law that notice to a branch bank other than the branch conducting the transaction is not notice to the bank. See Security-First Nat. Bank v. Taylor, 123 Cal.App.2d 380, 266 P.2d 914 (1954)". Sixth Progress Report to the Legislature by Senate Fact Finding Committee on Judiciary (1959–1961) Part 1, The Uniform Commercial Code, p. 444.

These amendments were unnecessary because the 1962 Official Text additions achieve this same purpose. In addition, in Commercial Code § 4106, amendments were made to the California version to the Official Text to achieve this purpose by the addition of language that notice to one branch is not notice to another branch or separate office of the same bank.

The reason for the addition to the 1962 Official Text stated by the 1962 Official Recommendations on this subdivision in the Permanent Editorial Board for the Uniform Commercial Code, Report No. 1, (1962 Official Text) p. 17, is to remove any basis for the fear that this subdivision "would require any large business organization to make an extensive investigation, before purchasing commercial paper or investment securities, as to whether it had notice of an adverse claim." The Editorial Board also stated that this subdivision with the 1962 addition "retains the same standard for financial institutions as for other organizations, and applies equally to protect an organization located in a single place and an organization operating through two or more branches", and pointed out that "an individual acting for the organization" as used in this subdivision "includes an agent as well as an employee". (See Official Comment 27 for example).

28. "Organization" defined in subdivision (28) is similar to the definition of "person" in former Civil Code § 1796 (USA) § 1858.04 (UWRA), § 2132b (UBLA), § 3013 (UTRA), § 3266 (NIL), § 3369(4) (specific and preventive relief) and present Civil Code § 14 and § 2981(c), but appears to broaden the concept of person by including every type of legal entity. (See Official Comment 28) The term "organization" is included in the definition of "person" in subdivision (30).

29. "Party" defined in subdivision (29) has no statutory counterpart in prior California law.

30. "Person" defined in subdivision (30) broadens the definition of this term contained in former Civil Code § 1796 (USA), § 1858.04 (UWRA), § 2132b (UBLA), § 3013 (UTRA), § 3266 (NIL), § 3369(4) (specific and preventive relief) and present Civil Code § 14 and § 2981, by including "organization" (See California Code Comment 28, supra).

31. The definition of presumption in subdivision (31) of section 1–201 of the Official Text is omitted from the California version because it was thought that the term is ambiguous and possibly contrary to the California law of presumption as expressed in Code of Civil Procedure §§ 1957, 1959 and 1961, and the cases which state that a presumption is evidence, e.g. Scott v. Burke, 39 Cal.2d 388, 247 P.2d 313 (1952). Subdivision (31) of the Official Text reads as follows:

"(31) 'Presumption' or 'presumed' means that the trier of fact must find the existence of the fact presumed unless and until evidence is introduced which would support a finding of its non-existence."

For a discussion on the effect this definition would have had if it had been included, see Sixth Progress Report to the Legislature by Senate Fact Finding Committee on Judiciary (1959–1961) Part 1, The Uniform Commercial Code, pp. 322, 439–441. California State Bar Committee on the Commercial Code, A Special Report, The Uniform Commercial Code, 37 Calif.State Bar J. (March–April, 1962) p. 131.

32. "Purchase" as defined in subdivision (32) broadens the definition of this term in former Civil Code § 3013 (UTRA) by adding "discount", "negotiation", "issue or re-issue", "gift" or "any other voluntary transaction creating an interest in property".

33. "Purchaser" as defined in subdivision (33) broadens the definition of this term in former Civil Code § 3013 (UTRA), § 1858.04 (UWRA), and § 2132b (UBLA) which only provided that a purchaser includes a mortgagee and a pledgee. See California Code Comment 32, supra.

34. "Remedy" defined in subdivision (34) has no statutory counterpart in prior California law although remedies for a buyer on breach of contract are provided in former Civil Code §§ 1786 to 1790 and for the seller in former Civil Code §§ 1783 to 1785 (USA).

35. "Representative" defined in subdivision (35) has no statutory counterpart in prior California law. Although "agent" and "trustee" are specifically included in the definition, neither term is defined in this section. For the definition of "agent" see Civil Code § 2295 and for the definition of "trustee" see Civil Code § 730.03 and § 2219, and former Civil Code § 3013 (UTRA). The State Bar subcommittee has observed that "This subsection broadens the appointive relationship to include 'any other person empowered to act for another,' apparently in any capacity". Sixth Progress Report to the Legislature by Senate Fact Finding Committee on Judiciary (1959–1961) Part 1, The Uniform Commercial Code, p. 331.

36. "Rights" defined in subdivision (36) has no statutory counterpart in prior California law.

37. "Security interest" as defined in subdivision (37) broadens and expands upon the definition of this term in former Civil Code § 3013(12) (UTRA) by including buyers as well as sellers. This definition is broad enough to include the traditional California security devices, (chattel mortgages, conditional sales contracts, pledges, trust receipts, assignments of accounts receivable, and inventory liens) and specifically mentions accounts receivables and leases.

38. "Send" defined in subdivision (38) has no statutory counterpart in prior California law.

39. "Signed" defined in subdivision (39) has no statutory counterpart in prior California law is similar to the definition of "signature or subscription" in Civil Code § 14 and Code of Civil Procedure § 17 to the extent that both recognize signature by mark.

40. "Surety" as defined in subdivision (40) simply states that guarantor is included. Civil Code § 2787 (suretyship) states the same principle but also defines and explains what is a surety or guarantor.

41. "Telegram" defined in subdivision (41) has no statutory counterpart in prior California law.

42. "Term" defined in subdivision (42) has no statutory counterpart in prior California law.

43. "Unauthorized" defined in subdivision (43) has no statutory counterpart in prior California law. In discussing a proposed State Bar amendment to this definition which would have substituted "ostensible" for "implied or apparent", the Marsh and Warren report discussed in detail the various types of authority:

"This subsection [subdivision] provides: ' "Unauthorized" signature or indorsement means one made without actual, implied, or apparent authority and includes a forgery.'

"**Proposed Amendment.** The State Bar Committee proposes that the word 'ostensible' be substituted for the words 'implied or apparent', on the ground that 'ostensible' is defined in CC §§ 2300 and 2317 and is well understood and has been judicially construed in California.

"**Recommendation.** It is recommended that the proposed amendment be rejected.

"**Discussion.** As a preliminary matter, it should be noted that the word 'ostensible' as used in California corresponds *not* to the two words 'implied or apparent' as used elsewhere, but only to the one word 'apparent.' The Restatement of Agency (2d) in §§ 7 and 8, defines actual and apparent authority and treats 'express' and 'implied' authority as subdivisions of *actual* authority. It also states that apparent authority 'is entirely distinct from [actual] authority, either express or implied.' § 8, Comment a. It is equally clear that what the Code intends by 'implied' authority is 'actual authority' as defined in CC § 2316 and not 'ostensible authority' as defined in CC § 2317. Columbia Outfitting Company v. Freeman, 26 C.2d 216, 218, 223 P. 2821, (1950). Therefore, if this amendment is accepted at all, the word 'ostensible' should be substituted only for the word 'apparent' and not for the two words 'implied or apparent.'

"The substitution is recommended on the ground that the courts might interpret the word 'apparent' in this subsection [subdivision] of the Code in a different manner than they have interpreted the word 'ostensible' in CC § 2317, possibly because they would assume that in using a different word, the Legislature intended a different meaning. Ostensible authority is defined in CC § 2317 as authority which a principal, 'intentionally or by want of ordinary care, causes or allows a third person to believe the agent to possess.' The Restatement of Agency (2d, § 8, defines apparent authority as the 'power to affect the legal relations of another person by transactions with third persons, professedly as agent for the other, arising from and in accordance with the other's manifestations to such third persons.'

"The Civil Code section differs from the Restatement definition in that proof of intention or negligence on the part of the principal is required, in addition to objective manifestations by the principal to a third party that the agent has authority. In addition, CC § 2324 provides that a principal is bound by the acts of an agent under ostensible authority 'to those persons only who have in good faith, and without want of ordinary care, incurred a liability or parted with value, upon the faith thereof.' Thus, the California concept of ostensible authority appears to coincide roughly with what the Restatement in § 8B calls 'estoppel.' Hobart v. Hobart Estate Company, 26 C.2d 412, 451, 159 P.2d 958 (1945). However, as the Restatement says, 'In the usual agency case, . . . little turns upon this distinction.' § 8, Comment d.

"If it is assumed that the Civil Code definition of 'ostensible' differs from the meaning of the word 'apparent' in this section in that proof of the elements of an estoppel is required under the first but not under the second, it would appear that the word 'apparent' is preferable despite the fact that its meaning under the Code will not be the same as the meaning of the word 'ostensible' used in other agency cases. The Restatement puts the case this way: 'Apparent authority is based upon the principle which has led to the objective theory of contracts, namely, that in contractual relations one should ordinarily be bound by what he says rather than by what he intends so that the contract which results from the acceptance of an offer is that which the offeree reasonably understands, rather than what the offeror means. It follows, therefore, that when one tells a third person that another is authorized to make a contract of a certain sort, and the other, on behalf of the principal becomes immediately a contracting party, with both rights and liabilities to the third person, irrespective of the fact that he did not intend to contract or that he had directed the "agent" not to contract, and without reference to any change of position by the third party.' In other words, in this area the law of agency is part of the law of contracts, not of torts, and should be so treated." Sixth Progress Report to the Legislature by Senate Fact Finding Committee on Judiciary (1959–1961) Part 1, The Uniform Commercial Code, pp. 441–442.

44. "Value" defined in subdivision (44)(b) and (d) is in the same terms as "value" defined in former Civil Code § 1796 (USA), § 1858.04 (UWRA), § 2132b (UBLA), § 3013 (UTRA) § 3106 (NIL) and § 3266 (NIL). "Value" as defined in subdivision (44)(a) and (c) is within the scope of the phrase "any consideration sufficient to support a simple contract" found in all but the last of the above former Civil Code sections. Therefore, subdivision (44) is not contrary to prior California law but clarifies and expands upon it.

45. "Warehouse Receipt" as defined in subdivision (45) is more detailed and explanatory than the simple definition that " 'receipt' means warehouse receipt" which is found in former Civil Code § 1858.04 (UWRA).

Under prior California law the designation of a document as a "warehouse receipt" did not make it one "if in fact its contents show that it was not such or intended as such" (Harry Hall Company, Inc. v. Consolidated Packing Company, 55 Cal.App.2d 651, 131 P.2d 859 (1942)).

46. "Written" or "writing" defined in subdivision (46) are more broadly defined than each was previously in former Civil Code § 3266 (NIL) which included only printing. These terms are defined similarly in Civil Code § 14, except that the Commercial Code definition is broadened by addition of the catchall phrase "any other intentional reduction to tangible form".

Changes from U.C.C. (1962 Official Text)

47. In subdivision (6) the words "and includes an airbill" were deleted. The language added to the Official Text by the California version is shown in the underlined portion as follows:

" 'Bill of lading' means a document evidencing the receipt of goods for shipment issued by a person engaged in the business of transporting or forwarding goods, and which, by its terms, evidences the intention of the issuer that the person entitled under the document (Section 7403(4)) has the right to receive, hold and dispose of the document and the goods it covers. Designation of a document by the issuer as a 'bill of lading' is conclusive evidence of such intention. 'Bill of lading' includes an airbill. 'Airbill' means a document serving for air transportation as a bill of lading does for marine or rail transportation, and includes an air consignment note or air waybill."

48. The Official Text as amended in California reads as follows:

" 'Document of title' includes bill of lading, dock warrant, dock receipt, warehouse receipt, gin ticket, compress receipt [or order for the delivery of goods] and also any other document which in the regular course of business or financing is treated as adequately evidencing that the person [in possession of it is entitled] entitled under the document (Section 7403(4)) has the right to receive, hold and dispose of the document and the goods it covers. To be a document of title a document must purport to be issued by [or addressed to] a bailee and purport to cover goods in the bailee's possession which are either identified or are fungible portions of an identified mass."

49. In subdivision (17) the second sentence of the Official Text is deleted. The sentence in the Official Text reads:

"Goods which are not fungible shall be deemed fungible for the purposes of this Act to the extent that under a particular agreement or document unlike units are treated as equivalents."

50. Subdivision (31) of section 1–201 of the Official Text is deleted in its entirety. (see note 31, supra)

51. Subdivision (45) is completely rewritten. The Official Text reads:

" 'Warehouse receipt' means a receipt issued by a person engaged in the business of storing goods for hire."

Uniform Commercial Code Comment

Prior Uniform Statutory Provision, Changes and New Matter:

1. "Action". See similar definitions in Section 191, Uniform Negotiable Instruments Law; Section 76, Uniform Sales Act; Section 58, Uniform Warehouse Receipts Act; Section 53, Uniform Bills of Lading Act. The definition has been rephrased and enlarged.

2. "Aggrieved party". New.

3. "Agreement". New. As used in this Act the word is intended to include full recognition of usage of trade, course of dealing, course of performance and the surrounding circumstances as effective parts thereof, and of any agreement permitted under the provisions of this Act to displace a stated rule of law.

4. "Bank". See Section 191, Uniform Negotiable Instruments Law.

5. "Bearer". From Section 191, Uniform Negotiable Instruments Law. The prior definition has been broadened.

6. "Bill of Lading". See similar definitions in Section 1, Uniform Bills of Lading Act. The definition has been enlarged to include freight forwarders' bills and bills issued by contract carriers as well as those issued by common carriers. The definition of airbill is new.

7. "Branch". New.

8. "Burden of establishing a fact". New.

9. "Buyer in ordinary course of business". From Section 1, Uniform Trust Receipts Act. The definition has been expanded to make clear the type of person protected. Its major significance lies in Section 2–403 and in the Article on Secured Transactions (Article 9).

The reference to minerals and the like makes clear that a buyer in ordinary course buying minerals under the circumstances described takes free of a prior mortgage created by the sellers. See Comment to Section 9–103.

A pawnbroker cannot be a buyer in ordinary course of business because the person from whom he buys goods (or acquires ownership after foreclosing an initial pledge) is typically in ordinary user and not a person engaged in selling goods of that kind.

10. "Conspicuous". New. This is intended to indicate some of the methods of making a term attention-calling. But the test is whether attention can reasonably be expected to be called to it.

11. "Contract". New. But see Sections 3 and 71, Uniform Sales Act.

12. "Creditor". New.

13. "Defendant". From Section 76, Uniform Sales Act. Rephrased.

14. "Delivery". Section 76, Uniform Sales Act, Section 191, Uniform Negotiable Instruments Law, Section 58, Uniform Warehouse Receipts Act and Section 53, Uniform Bills of Lading Act.

15. "Document of title". From Section 76, Uniform Sales Act, but rephrased to eliminate certain ambiguities. Thus, by making it explicit that the obligation or designation of a third party as "bailee" is essential

to a document of title, this definition clearly rejects any such result as obtained in Hixson v. Ward, 254 Ill.App. 505 (1929), which treated a conditional sales contract as a document of title. Also the definition is left open so that new types of documents may be included. It is unforeseeable what documents may one day serve the essential purpose now filled by warehouse receipts and bills of lading. Truck transport has already opened up problems which do not fit the patterns of practice resting upon the assumption that a draft can move through banking channels faster than the goods themselves can reach their destination. There lie ahead air transport and such probabilities as teletype transmission of what may some day be regarded commercially as "Documents of Title". The definition is stated in terms of the function of the documents with the intention that any document which gains commercial recognition as accomplishing the desired result shall be included within its scope. Fungible goods are adequately identified within the language of the definition by identification of the mass of which they are a part.

Dock warrants were within the Sales Act definition of document of title apparently for the purpose of recognizing a valid tender by means of such papers. In current commercial practice a dock warrant or receipt is a kind of interim certificate issued by steamship companies upon delivery of the goods at the dock, entitling a designated person to have issued to him at the company's office a bill of lading. The receipt itself is invariably nonnegotiable in form although it may indicate that a negotiable bill is to be forthcoming. Such a document is not within the general compass of the definition, although trade usage may in some cases entitle such paper to be treated as a document of title. If the dock receipt actually represents a storage obligation undertaken by the shipping company, then it is a warehouse receipt within this Section regardless of the name given to the instrument.

The goods must be "described", but the description may be by marks or labels and may be qualified in such a way as to disclaim personal knowledge of the issuer regarding contents or condition. However, baggage and parcel checks and similar "tokens" of storage which identify stored goods only as those received in exchange for the token are not covered by this Article.

The definition is broad enough to include an airway bill.

16. "Fault". From Section 76, Uniform Sales Act.

17. "Fungible". See Sections 5, 6 and 76, Uniform Sales Act; Section 58, Uniform Warehouse Receipts Act. Fungibility of goods "by agreement" has been added for clarity and accuracy. Amendment approved by the Permanent Editorial Board for Uniform Commercial Code November 4, 1995.

[See California Code Comment, note 49.]

18. "Genuine". New.

19. "Good faith". See Section 76(2), Uniform Sales Act; Section 58(2), Uniform Warehouse Receipts Act; Section 53(2), Uniform Bills of Lading Act; Section 22(2), Uniform Stock Transfer Act. "Good faith", whenever it is used in the Code, means at least what is here stated. In certain Articles, by specific provision, additional requirements are made applicable. See, e.g., Secs. 2–103(1)(b), 7–404. To illustrate, in the Article on Sales, Section 2–103, good faith is expressly defined as including in the case of a merchant observance of reasonable commercial standards of fair dealing in the trade, so that throughout that Article wherever a merchant appears in the case an inquiry into his observance of such standards is necessary to determine his good faith.

20. "Holder". See similar definitions in Section 191, Uniform Negotiable Instruments Law; Section 58, Uniform Warehouse Receipts Act; Section 53, Uniform Bills of Lading Act.

21. "Honor". New.

22. "Insolvency proceedings". New.

23. "Insolvent". Section 76(3), Uniform Sales Act. The three tests of insolvency—"ceased to pay his debts in the ordinary course of business," "cannot pay his debts as they become due," and "insolvent within the meaning of the federal bankruptcy law"—are expressly set up as alternative tests and must be approached from a commercial standpoint.

24. "Money". Section 6(5), Uniform Negotiable Instruments Law. The test adopted is that of sanction of government, whether by authorization before issue or adoption afterward, which recognizes the circulating medium as a part of the official currency of that government. The narrow view that money is limited to legal tender is rejected.

25. "Notice". New. Compare N.I.L. Sec. 56. Under the definition a person has notice when he has received a notification of the fact in question. But by the last sentence the act leaves open the time and circumstances under which notice or notification may cease to be effective. Therefore such cases as Graham v. White-Phillips Co., 296 U.S. 27, 56 S.Ct. 21, 80 L.Ed. 20 (1935), are not overruled.

26. "Notifies". New. This is the word used when the essential fact is the proper dispatch of the notice, not its receipt. Compare "Send". When the essential fact is the other party's receipt of the notice, that is stated. The second sentence states when a notification is received.

27. New. This makes clear that reason to know, knowledge, or a notification, although "received" for instance by a clerk in Department A of an organization, is effective for a transaction conducted in Department B only from the time when it was or should have been communicated to the individual conducting that transaction.

28. "Organization". This is the definition of every type of entity or association, excluding an individual, acting as such. Definitions of "person" were included in Section 191, Uniform Negotiable Instruments Law; Section 76, Uniform Sales Act; Section 58, Uniform Warehouse Receipts Act; Section 53, Uniform Bills of Lading Act; Section 22, Uniform Stock Transfer Act; Section 1, Uniform Trust Receipts Act. The definition of "organization" given here includes a number of entities or associations not specifically mentioned in prior definition of "person", namely, government, governmental subdivision or agency, business trust, trust and estate.

29. "Party". New. Mention of a party includes, of course, a person acting through an agent. However, where an agent comes into opposition or contrast to his principal, particular account is taken of that situation.

30. "Person". See Comment to definition of "Organization". The reference to Section 1–102 is to subsection (5) of that section.

31. "Presumption". New.

[Inapplicable in California, see California Code Comment, notes 31, 50.]

32. "Purchase". Section 58, Uniform Warehouse Receipts Act; Section 76, Uniform Sales Act; Section 53, Uniform Bills of Lading Act; Section 22, Uniform Stock Transfer Act; Section 1, Uniform Trust Receipts Act. Rephrased.

33. "Purchaser". Section 58, Uniform Warehouse Receipts Act; Section 76, Uniform Sales Act; Section 53, Uniform Bills of Lading Act; Section 22, Uniform Stock Transfer Act; Section 1, Uniform Trust Receipts Act. Rephrased.

34. "Remedy". New. The purpose is to make it clear that both remedy and rights (as defined) include those remedial rights of "self help" which are among the most important bodies of rights under this Act, remedial rights being those to which an aggrieved party can resort on his own motion.

35. "Representative". New.

36. "Rights". New. See Comment to "Remedy".

37. "Security Interest". See Section 1, Uniform Trust Receipts Act. The present definition is elaborated, in view especially of the complete coverage of the subject in Article 9. Notice that in view of the Article the term includes the interest of certain outright buyers of certain kinds of property. Section 1–201(37) is being amended at the same time that the Article on Leases (Article 2A) is being promulgated as an amendment to this Act.

One of the reasons it was decided to codify the law with respect to leases was to resolve an issue that has created considerable confusion in the courts: what is a lease? The confusion exists, in part, due to the last two sentences of the definition of security interest in the 1978 Official Text of the Act. Section 1–201(37). The confusion is compounded by the rather considerable change in the federal, state and local tax laws and accounting rules as they relate to leases of goods. The answer is important because the definition of lease determines not only the rights and remedies of the parties to the lease but also those of third parties. If a transaction creates a lease and not a security interest, the lessee's interest in the goods is limited to its leasehold estate; the residual interest in the goods belongs to the lessor. This has significant implications to the lessee's creditors. "On common law theory, the lessor, since he has not parted with title, is entitled to full protection against the lessee's creditors and trustee in bankruptcy...." 1 G. Gilmore, *Security Interests in Personal Property* § 3.6, at 76 (1965).

Under pre-Act chattel security law there was generally no requirement that the lessor file the lease, a financing statement, or the like, to enforce the lease agreement against the lessee or any third party; the Article on Secured Transactions (Article 9) did not change the common

§ 1201   GENERAL PROVISIONS

law in that respect. Coogan, Leasing and the Uniform Commercial Code, in *Equipment Leasing—Leveraged Leasing* 681, 700 n. 25, 729 n. 80 (2d ed. 1980). The Article on Leases (Article 2A) has not changed the law in that respect, except for leases of fixtures. Section 2A–309. An examination of the common law will not provide an adequate answer to the question of what is a lease. The definition of security interest in Section 1–201(37) of the 1978 Official Text of the Act provides that the Article on Secured Transactions (Article 9) governs security interests disguised as leases, *i.e.*, leases intended as security; however, the definition is vague and outmoded.

Lease is defined in Article 2A as a transfer of the right to possession and use of goods for a term, in return for consideration. Section 2A–103(1)(j). The definition continues by stating that the retention or creation of a security interest is not a lease. Thus, the task of sharpening the line between true leases and security interests disguised as leases continues to be a function of this section.

The first paragraph of this definition is a revised version of the first five sentences of the 1978 Official Text of Section 1–201(37). The changes are modest in that they make a style change in the fourth sentence and delete the reference to lease in the fifth sentence. The balance of this definition is new, although it preserves elements of the last two sentences of the prior definition. The focus of the changes was to draw a sharper line between leases and security interests disguised as leases to create greater certainty in commercial transactions.

Prior to this amendment, Section 1–201(37) provided that whether a lease was intended as security (*i.e.*, a security interest disguised as a lease) was to be determined from the facts of each case; however, (a) the inclusion of an option to purchase did not itself make the lease one intended for security, and (b) an agreement that upon compliance with the terms of the lease the lessee would become, or had the option to become, the owner of the property for no additional consideration, or for a nominal consideration, did make the lease one intended for security.

Reference to the intent of the parties to create a lease or security interest has led to unfortunate results. In discovering intent, courts have relied upon factors that were thought to be more consistent with sales or loans than leases. Most of these criteria, however, are as applicable to true leases as to security interests. Examples include the typical net lease provisions, a purported lessor's lack of storage facilities or its character as a financing party rather than a dealer in goods. Accordingly, amended Section 1–201(37) deletes all reference to the parties' intent.

The second paragraph of the new definition is taken from Section 1(2) of the Uniform Conditional Sales Act (act withdrawn 1943), modified to reflect current leasing practice. Thus, reference to the case law prior to this Act will provide a useful source of precedent. Gilmore, *Security Law, Formalism and Article 9*, 47 Neb.L.Rev. 659, 671 (1968). Whether a transaction creates a lease or a security interest continues to be determined by the facts of each case. The second paragraph further provides that a transaction creates a security interest if the lessee has an obligation to continue paying consideration for the term of the lease, if the obligation is not terminable by the lessee (thus correcting early statutory gloss, *e.g.*, *In re Royer's Bakery, Inc.*, 1 U.C.C.Rep.Serv. (Callaghan) 342 (Bankr.E.D.Pa.1963)) and if one of four additional tests is met. The first of these four tests, subparagraph (a), is that the original lease term is equal to or greater than the remaining economic life of the goods. The second of these tests, subparagraph (b), is that the lessee is either bound to renew the lease for the remaining economic life of the goods or to become the owner of the goods. *In re Gehrke Enters.*, 1 Bankr. 647, 651–52 (Bankr.W.D.Wis.1979). The third of these tests, subparagraph (c), is whether the lessee has an option to renew the lease for the remaining economic life or the goods for no additional consideration or for nominal additional consideration, which is defined later in this section. *In re Celeryvale Transp.*, 44 Bankr. 1007, 1014–15 (Bankr.E.D.Tenn.1984). The fourth of these tests, subparagraph (d), is whether the lessee has an option to become the owner of the goods for no additional consideration or for nominal additional consideration. All of these tests focus on economics, not the intent of the parties. *In re Berge*, 32 Bankr. 370, 371–73 (Bankr.W.D.Wis.1983).

The focus on economics is reinforced by the next paragraph, which is new. It states that a transaction does not create a security interest merely because the transaction has certain characteristics listed therein. Subparagraph (a) has no statutory derivative; it states that a full payout lease does not *per se* create a security interest. *Rushton v. Shea*, 419 F.Supp. 1349, 1365 (D.Del.1976). Subparagraph (b) provides the same regarding the provisions of the typical net lease. *Compare All–States Leasing Co. v. Ochs*, 42 Or.App. 319, 600 P.2d 899 (Ct.App.1979) *with In re Tillery*, 571 F.2d 1361 (5th Cir.1978). Subparagraph (c) restates and expands the provisions of former Section 1–201(37) to make clear that the option can be to buy or renew. Subparagraphs (d) and (e) treat fixed price options and provide that fair market value must be determined at the time the transaction is entered into. *Compare Arnold Mach. Co. v. Balls*, 624 P.2d 678 (Utah 1981) *with Aoki v. Shepherd Mach. Co.*, 665 F.2d 941 (9th Cir.1982).

The relationship of the second paragraph of this subsection to the third paragraph of this subsection deserves to be explored. The fixed price purchase option provides a useful example. A fixed price purchase option in a lease does not of itself create a security interest. This is particularly true if the fixed price is equal to or greater than the reasonably predictable fair market value of the goods at the time the option is to be performed. A security interest is created only if the option price is nominal and the conditions stated in the introduction to the second paragraph of this subsection are met. There is a set of purchase options whose fixed price is less than fair market value but greater than nominal that must be determined on the facts of each case to ascertain whether the transaction in which the option is included creates a lease or a security interest.

It was possible to provide for various other permutations and combinations with respect to options to purchase and renew. For example, this section could have stated a rule to govern the facts of *In re Marhoefer Packing Co.*, 674 F.2d 1139 (7th Cir.1982). This was not done because it would unnecessarily complicate the definition. Further development of this rule is left to the courts.

The fourth paragraph provides definitions and rules of construction.

38. "Send". New. Compare "notifies".

39. "Signed". New. The inclusion of authentication in the definition of "signed" is to make clear that as the term is used in this Act a complete signature is not necessary. Authentication may be printed, stamped or written; it may be by initials or by thumbprint. It may be on any part of the document and in appropriate cases may be found in a billhead or letterhead. No catalog of possible authentications can be complete and the court must use common sense and commercial experience in passing upon these matters. The question always is whether the symbol was executed or adopted by the party with present intention to authenticate the writing.

40. "Surety". New.

41. "Telegram". New.

42. "Term". New.

43. Under the former version of § 1–201(43), it was not clear whether a reference to an "unauthorized signature" in Articles 3 and 4 applied to indorsements. The words "or indorsement" are deleted so that references to "unauthorized signature" in § 3–406 and elsewhere will unambiguously refer to any signature.

44. "Value". See Sections 25, 26, 27, 191, Uniform Negotiable Instruments Law; Section 76, Uniform Sales Act; Section 53, Uniform Bills of Lading Act; Section 58, Uniform Warehouse Receipts Act; Section 22(1), Uniform Stock Transfer Act; Section 1, Uniform Trust Receipts Act. All the Uniform Acts in the commercial law field (except the Uniform Conditional Sales Act) have carried definitions of "value". All those definitions provided that value was any consideration sufficient to support a simple contract, including the taking of property in satisfaction of or as security for a pre-existing claim. Subsections (a), (b) and (d) in substance continue the definitions of "value" in the earlier acts. Subsection (c) makes explicit that "value" is also given in a third situation: where a buyer by taking delivery under a pre-existing contract converts a contingent into a fixed obligation.

This definition is not applicable to Articles 3 and 4, but the express inclusion of immediately available credit as value follows the separate definitions in those Articles. See Sections 4–208, 4–209, 3–303. A bank or other financing agency which in good faith makes advances against property held as collateral becomes a bona fide purchaser of that property even though provision may be made for charge-back in case of trouble. Checking credit is "immediately available" within the meaning of this section if the bank would be subject to an action for slander of credit in case checks drawn against the credit were dishonored, and when a charge-back is not discretionary with the bank, but may only be made when difficulties in collection arise in connection with the specific transaction involved.

45. "Warehouse receipt". See Section 76(1), Uniform Sales Act; Section 1, Uniform Warehouse Receipts Act. Receipts issued by a field warehouse are included, provided the warehouseman and the depositor of the goods are different persons.
[See California Code Comment, note 51.]
46. "Written" or "writing". This is a broadening of the definition contained in Section 191 of the Uniform Negotiable Instruments Law.

Cross References

Action defined, see Code of Civil Procedure §§ 22, 363.
Actions and proceedings, see Code of Civil Procedure § 307 et seq.
Aggrieved party, motion for new trial, see Code of Civil Procedure § 657.
Banks and Banking,
  Generally, see Financial Code § 99 et seq.
  Branch offices, see Financial Code § 500 et seq.
  Definitions, see Probate Code § 3901; Financial Code §§ 102, 105, 109, 3100, 3360.
  Unauthorized use of term "bank", see Financial Code § 3392.
Burden of proof,
  Generally, see Evidence Code § 500 et seq.
  Instructions on, see Evidence Code § 502.
Civil and criminal remedies, separation, see Code of Civil Procedure § 32.
Civil remedies, preservation, see Penal Code § 9.
Conditional sales contract, automobile sales finance act, see Civil Code § 2981 et seq.
Contracts, see Civil Code § 1549 et seq.
Credit union as bank for purposes of Divisions 3 and 4, see Financial Code § 14867.
Creditor defined, see Civil Code § 3430.
Definitions, priorities and security interests, see Code of Civil Procedure § 697.590.
Disposition of property subject to lien, continuation of lien, and exceptions, see Code of Civil Procedure § 697.610.
Documents of title, see Commercial Code § 7101 et seq.
Implied contract defined, see Civil Code § 1621.
Insolvency defined, see Civil Code § 3439.02.
Judicial remedies defined, see Code of Civil Procedure § 20.
Money, words "personal property" as including, see Code of Civil Procedure § 17.
Notice,
  Actual and constructive, see Civil Code §§ 18, 19.
  Filing and serving, see Code of Civil Procedure § 1010 et seq.
  Principal, notice to agent as notice to principal, see Civil Code § 2332.
  Recorded conveyance as constructive notice, see Civil Code § 1213.
Particular subjects, general definitions,
  Bank deposits and collections, see Commercial Code §§ 4104, 4105.
  Bulk sales, see Commercial Code § 6102.
  Commercial paper, see Commercial Code §§ 3103, 3104.
  Documents of title, see Commercial Code § 7102.
  Investment securities, see Commercial Code § 8102.
  Letters of credit, see Commercial Code § 5103.
  Sales, see Commercial Code § 2103 et seq.
  Secured transactions, see Commercial Code § 9105 et seq.
Payment defined, see Civil Code § 1478.
Person defined, see Code of Civil Procedure § 17; Corporations Code § 18; Financial Code § 18; Government Code § 17; Revenue and Taxation Code § 19.
Personal property not in custody of levying officer transferred or encumbered, exceptions, see Code of Civil Procedure § 697.740.
Proceeds, continuation of lien with same priority, and insolvency, see Code of Civil Procedure § 697.620.
Remedy for wrong, see Civil Code § 3523.
Retail installment contract or contract defined, see Civil Code § 1802.6.
Security interest,
  Retail installment sales, see Civil Code §§ 1802.13, 1802.14, 1810.8.
  Motor vehicles, liens and encumbrances, see Vehicle Code § 6300 et seq.
  Motor vehicles, transfers of title or interest, see Vehicle Code §§ 5905, 5907, 5908.
Subscription of instrument by attorney in fact, see Civil Code § 1095.
Suretyship and guaranty, see Civil Code § 2787 et seq.
Value, issue or transfer of instrument for, see Commercial Code § 3303.
Writing defined, see Code of Civil Procedure § 17; Corporations Code § 8; Financial Code § 8; Government Code § 8.

§ 1202. Third Party Documents; Admissibility; Presumption

(1) * * * A bill of lading, policy or certificate of insurance, official weigher's or inspector's certificate, consular invoice, or any other document authorized or required by the contract to be issued by a third party * * * is admissible as <u>evidence</u> of the facts stated in the document by the third party <u>in any action arising out of the contract which authorized or required the document</u>.

(2) <u>In any action arising out of the contract which authorized or required the document referred to in subdivision (1):</u>

(a) <u>A document in due form purporting to be the document referred to in subdivision (1) is presumed to be authentic and genuine. This presumption is a presumption affecting the burden of producing evidence.</u>

(b) <u>If the document is found to be authentic and genuine, the facts stated in the document by the third party are presumed to be true. This presumption is a presumption affecting the burden of proof.</u> (Stats.1963, c. 819, § 1202. Amended by Stats.1967, c. 703, p. 2077, § 1.)

California Code Comment

By Charles J. Williams

Prior California Law

1. The 1967 amendment incorporates the recommendation of the California Law Revision Commission. The purpose and scope of the Commission's recommendations are described in the General Comment to legislative changes since adoption of the Uniform Commercial Code set forth at pages 7 and 8 of this supplement.

2. This amendment resolves an uncertainty which existed from adoption of the Evidence Code in California as to whether this section as it formerly read established a presumption affecting the burden of producing evidence or a presumption affecting the burden of proof.

3. The procedural effect of the classification in subdivision (2) (a) of the presumption of genuineness is to require the trier of fact to assume the existence of the presumed fact until evidence is introduced which would support a finding of its non-existence. In this case, the trier of fact must determine the existence or non-existence of the presumed fact from the evidence and without regard to the presumption. If contrary evidence is introduced, the presumption is gone from the case and the trier of fact must weigh the inferences arising from the facts that gave rise to the presumption against the contrary evidence and resolve the conflict. (Evidence Code § 604 and Comment.)

4. The effect of the classification in subdivision (2) (b) of the presumption as a presumption affecting the burden of proof is to require the party against whom the presumption operates to prove by a preponderance of the evidence that the facts recited in the document are not true. (Evidence Code § 606 and Comment.)

Changes from U.C.C. (1962 Official Text)

5. This section is a variation from the Official Text. The change was recommended by the California Law Revision Commission in the light of the adoption of the Evidence Code. The classification of the presumptions in the California variation appears to carry out the intent of the drafters of the Uniform Commercial Code. The section is also revised so that it expressly applies only in an action arising out of the contract which authorized or required the document. The California

§ 1202

Law Revision Commission states that this change is consistent with the intent of the drafters of the Uniform Commercial Code.

California Code Comment
By John A. Bohn and Charles J. Williams

Prior California Law

1. The scope of this section is not as broad as Code of Civil Procedure § 1953f (provision of the Uniform Business Records as Evidence Act) which includes "a record of an act, condition or event".

2. Under the Commercial Code a document included in this section is "prima facie evidence of its own authenticity" while under Code of Civil Procedure § 1953f, it is required that a custodian or other qualified witness lay a foundation for admissibility of the document in evidence by testifying as to its identity and preparation.

3. This section reduces the evidentiary requirements for authentication of certain documents under the Commercial Code as compared with the requirements in other cases under the Uniform Business Records as Evidence Act (Code of Civil Procedure §§ 1953e through 1953h).

Changes from U.C.C. (1962 Official Text)

4. This is section 1–202 of the Official Text without change.

Law Revision Commission Comment
1967 Amendment

Section 1202 has been revised to indicate that it applies only in an action arising out of the contract which authorized or required the document referred to in the section. This revision is consistent with the intent of the drafters of the Uniform Commercial Code. Uniform Commercial Code § 1–202 Comment 2 ("This section is concerned only with documents which have been given a preferred status by the parties themselves who have required their procurement in the agreement and for this reason the applicability of the section is limited to actions arising out of the contract which authorized or required the document.").

Paragraph (a) of subdivision (2) classifies the presumption of authenticity and genuineness as a presumption affecting the burden of producing evidence. Under Evidence Code Section 604, a presumption affecting the burden of producing evidence requires the trier of fact to assume the existence of the presumed fact unless and until evidence is introduced which would support a finding of its nonexistence, in which case the trier of fact shall determine the existence or nonexistence of the presumed fact from the evidence and without regard to the presumption. If contrary evidence is introduced, the presumption is gone from the case and the trier of fact must weigh the inferences arising from the facts that gave rise to the presumption against the contrary evidence and resolve the conflict. See Evidence Code Section 604 of the *Comment* to that section.

Paragraph (b) of subdivision (2) classifies the presumption as to the truth of the matters stated in the document by the third party as a presumption affecting the burden of proof. Under Evidence Code Section 606, the effect of this classification is to require the party against whom the presumption operates to prove by a preponderance of the evidence that the facts recited in the authenticated document are not true. See Evidence Code Section 606 and the *Comment* thereto.

Uniform Commercial Code Comment

Prior Uniform Statutory Provision:
None.

Purposes:

1. This section is designed to supply judicial recognition for documents which have traditionally been relied upon as trustworthy by commercial men.

2. This section is concerned only with documents which have been given a preferred status by the parties themselves who have required their procurement in the agreement and for this reason the applicability of the section is limited to actions arising out of the contract which authorized or required the document. The documents listed are intended to be illustrative and not all inclusive.

3. The provisions of this section go no further than establishing the documents in question as prima facie evidence and leave to the court the ultimate determination of the facts where the accuracy or authenticity of the documents is questioned. In this connection the section calls for a commercially reasonable interpretation.

Definitional Cross References:

"Bill of lading". Section 1–201.
"Contract". Section 1–201.
"Genuine". Section 1–201.

Cross References

Prima facie evidence, direct evidence, see Evidence Code §§ 410, 602.
Business records as evidence, see Evidence Code § 1270 et seq.

§ 1203. Obligation of Good Faith

Every contract or duty within this code imposes an obligation of good faith in its performance or enforcement. *(Stats.1963, c. 819, § 1203.)*

California Code Comment
By John A. Bohn and Charles J. Williams

Prior California Law

1. The courts imply in every contract an obligation of "good faith and fair dealing that neither party will do anything which injures the right of the other to receive the benefits of the agreement" (Brown v. Superior Court, 34 Cal.2d 559, 212 P.2d 878 (1949) and Comunale v. Traders and General Insurance Company, 50 Cal.2d 654, 328 P.2d 198 (1958)). This section codifies the implied obligation of good faith and expands the concept of the cases by imposing this obligation on every "duty" as well as every contract within the Commercial Code.

2. For definition of good faith see Commercial Code § 1201(19).

Changes from U.C.C. (1962 Official Text)

3. This is section 1–203 of the Official Text without change.

Uniform Commercial Code Comment

Prior Uniform Statutory Provision:
None.

Purposes:

This section sets forth a basic principle running throughout this Act. The principle involved is that in commercial transactions good faith is required in the performance and enforcement of all agreements or duties. Particular applications of this general principle appear in specific provisions of the Act such as the option to accelerate at will (Section 1–208), the right to cure a defective delivery of goods (Section 2–508), the duty of a merchant buyer who has rejected goods to effect salvage operations (Section 2–603), substituted performance (Section 2–614), and failure of presupposed conditions (Section 2–615). The concept, however, is broader than any of these illustrations and applies generally, as stated in this section, to the performance or enforcement of every contract or duty within this Act. It is further implemented by Section 1–205 on course of dealing and usage of trade. This section does not support an independent cause of action for failure to perform or enforce in good faith. Rather, this section means that a failure to perform or enforce, in good faith, a specific duty or obligation under the contract, constitutes a breach of that contract or makes unavailable, under the particular circumstances, a remedial right or power. This distinction makes it clear that the doctrine of good faith merely directs a court towards interpreting contracts within the commercial context in which they are created, performed, and enforced, and does not create a separate duty of fairness and reasonableness which can be independently breached. See PEB Commentary No. 10, dated February 10, 1994 [Uniform Laws Annotated, UCC, APP II, Comment 10].

Cross References:

Sections 1–201; 1–205; 1–208; 2–103; 2–508; 2–603; 2–614; 2–615.

Definitional Cross References:

"Contract". Section 1–201.
"Good faith". Sections 1–201; 2–103.

Cross References

Acceleration of payment or performance, good faith, see Commercial Code § 1208.
Course of dealing and usage of trade, see Commercial Code § 1205.
Definitions, see Commercial Code §§ 1201, 2103.
Excuse for nondelivery by seller or delay in delivery, see Commercial Code § 2615.
Merchant buyer's duty of good faith after rejection of goods, see Commercial Code § 2603.
Offer of performance to be made in good faith, see Civil Code § 1493.
Rejection of nonconforming tender or delivery, see Commercial Code § 2508.
Substitute performance of sales contract, see Commercial Code § 2614.

§ 1204. Time; Reasonable Time; "Seasonably"

(1) Whenever this code requires any action to be taken within a reasonable time, any time which is not manifestly unreasonable may be fixed by agreement.

(2) What is a reasonable time for taking any action depends on the nature, purpose and circumstances of such action.

(3) An action is taken "seasonably" when it is taken at or within the time agreed or if no time is agreed at or within a reasonable time. *(Stats.1963, c. 819, § 1204.)*

California Code Comment

By John A. Bohn and Charles J. Williams

Prior California Law

1. It has been suggested that the effect of subdivision (1) is to modify former Civil Code § 1791 (USA). In the California Annotations to the Proposed Uniform Commercial Code (1960), the Legislative counsel stated:

"The Pennsylvania annotators, dealing with a statute identical with Civil Code Section 1791 suggest that the effect of this section of U.C.C. permitting modification by agreement if the time specified is not 'manifestly unreasonable' modifies the principle of Civil Code Section 1791 permitting varying of any rights, duties, etc. by express agreement." Sixth Progress Report to the Legislature by Senate Fact Finding Committee on Judiciary (1959–1961) Part 1. The Uniform Commercial Code, p. 33.

2. Subdivision (2) is similar to former Civil Code § 3266b (NIL) in providing what to consider in determining a reasonable time, but the NIL provision also included "usage of trade on business" as a standard to be considered.

3. The term "seasonably" in subdivision (3) has no statutory counterpart in California law.

Changes from U.C.C. (1962 Official Text)

4. This is section 1–204 of the Official Text without change.

Uniform Commercial Code Comment
1966 Amendment

Prior Uniform Statutory Provision:

* * *

Compare Section 193, Negotiable Instruments Law.

Uniform Commercial Code Comment

Prior Uniform Statutory Provision:

None.

Purposes:

1. Subsection (1) recognizes that nothing is stronger evidence of a reasonable time than the fixing of such time by a fair agreement between the parties. However, provision is made for disregarding a clause which whether by inadvertence or overreaching fixes a time so unreasonable that it amounts to eliminating all remedy under the contract. The parties are not required to fix the most reasonable time but may fix any time which is not obviously unfair as judged by the time of contracting.

2. Under the section, the agreement which fixes the time need not be part of the main agreement, but may occur separately. Notice also that under the definition of "agreement" (Section 1–201) the circumstances of the transaction, including course of dealing or usages of trade or course of performance may be material. On the question what is a reasonable time these matters will often be important.

Definitional Cross Reference:

"Agreement". Section 1–201.

Cross References

Obligations, Time of offer of performance, see Civil Code § 1490.
Time of offer of performance not fixed, see Civil Code § 1491.

§ 1205. Course of Dealing and Usage of Trade

(1) A course of dealing is a sequence of previous conduct between the parties to a particular transaction which is fairly to be regarded as establishing a common basis of understanding for interpreting their expressions and other conduct.

(2) A usage of trade is any practice or method of dealing having such regularity of observance in a place, vocation or trade as to justify an expectation that it will be observed with respect to the transaction in question. The existence and scope of such a usage are to be proved as facts. If it is established that such a usage is embodied in a written trade code or similar writing the interpretation of the writing is for the court.

(3) A course of dealing between parties and any usage of trade in the vocation or trade in which they are engaged or of which they are or should be aware give particular meaning to and supplement or qualify terms of an agreement.

(4) The express terms of an agreement and an applicable course of dealing or usage of trade shall be construed wherever reasonable as consistent with each other; but when such construction is unreasonable express terms control both course of dealing and usage of trade and course of dealing controls usage of trade.

(5) An applicable usage of trade in the place where any part of performance is to occur shall be used in interpreting the agreement as to that part of the performance.

(6) Evidence of a relevant usage of trade offered by one party is not admissible unless and until he has given the other party such notice as the court finds sufficient to prevent unfair surprise to the latter. *(Stats.1963, c. 819, § 1205.)*

California Code Comment

By John A. Bohn and Charles J. Williams

§ 1205   GENERAL PROVISIONS   22

Prior California Law

1. "Course of dealing" defined in subdivision (1) has not been previously defined in the California codes. The phrase is used in former Civil Code § 1791 (USA) but has not been interpreted by the courts of this state.

2. "Usage of trade" defined in subdivision (2) has not previously been defined in the California codes. Civil Code § 1644 recognizes special meaning given to words by "usage" in interpreting contracts. In Turner v. Donovan, 3 Cal.App.2d 485, 39 P.2d 858 (1935) the court defines usage as "a uniform practice or course of conduct that is followed in certain lines of business or profession".

3. The "regularity of observance" required in subdivision (2) is similar to the requirement previously imposed by the courts that for custom or usage to be part of the contract it must be either "actually or constructively known" and be "consistent with the contract". Miller v. Germain Seed & Plant Company, 193 Cal. 62, 222 Pac. 817 (1924) and Webster v. Klassen, 109 Cal.App.2d 583, 241 P.2d 302 (1952).

4. The statement in subdivision (2) that the existence and scope of a usage are to be proved as facts is in accordance with California law. Peterson v. Permanente Steamship Corporation, 129 Cal.App.2d 579, 277 P.2d 495 (1954) states: "custom or usage is a matter of fact to be testified to by witnesses qualified by actual knowledge".

5. The last sentence of subdivision (2) which requires the court to interpret usage when reduced to writing is in accord with the general rule that the legal effect and meaning of a contract is a question of law and the meaning of extrinsic evidence (such as usage) is included in this question of law. Citizens Utilities Company v. Wheeler, 156 Cal. App.2d 423, 319 P.2d 763 (1957).

6. Subdivision (3) is similar to the provision in Civil Code § 1644 which allows usage to give a special meaning to the words of a contract. Subdivision (3) also contains terms similar to former Civil Code § 1791 (USA) which provided that "course of dealing" and "custom" may vary obligations under a contract that are implied in law.

7. The provision of subdivision (5) that an applicable usage of trade is to be used in interpreting an agreement is, in general, similar to the reference to local usage in Latta v. Da Roza, 100 Cal.App. 606, 280 Pac. 711, 281 P. 655 (1929), but referring to the usage "in the place where any part of performance is to occur" is a new concept.

8. Subdivision (6) was the source of some criticism and comment before its adoption. Both the State Bar and Professors Marsh and Warren thought the notice required in this subdivision was unnecessary because subdivision (3) provides for the application of a usage of trade that would be known to the parties involved without formal notice. Also, as a procedural requirement subdivision (6) is not clear. The California State Bar subcommittee in a 1960 report said:

"This subsection would appear to create new law in California and the subcommittee recommends that it not be adopted. We feel it is a poor procedural rule and a possible trap that could easily be abused." Sixth Progress Report to the Legislature by Senate Fact Finding Committee on Judiciary (1959–1961) Part 1, The Uniform Commercial Code, p. 333.

Professors Marsh and Warren criticized this subdivision:

"This subsection [subdivision] requires 'notice' by one party in a lawsuit to the other party, if the first intends to rely upon a 'usage of trade' as qualifying the meaning of an express contract. Such evidence is made admissible by subsection [subdivision] (3) of the same section, which provides: 'A course of dealing between parties and any usage of trade in the vocation or trade in which they are engaged or of which they are or should be aware give particular meaning to and supplement or qualify terms of an agreement.'

"This subsection [subdivision] would change the California law. While some of the early cases stated that in order to rely upon a 'custom' which was not so general as to be the subject of judicial notice, it was necessary to plead it, Pray v. Trower Lumber Co., 101 C.A. 482, 489, 281 P. 1036 (1929); the more recent cases have established that a 'custom of the trade' in a contract action between persons who are members of that trade is admissible to show the meaning of their contract without being pleaded on the ground that 'it must be presumed to be known to parties who are specialists in the field.' Iusi v. Chase, 169 C.A.2d 83, 87, 337 P.2d 79 (1959); Associated Lathing and Plastering Company v. Louis C. Dunn, Inc., 135 C.A.2d 40, 286 P.2d 825 (1955) (per Peters, J.); Covely v. C.A.B. Construction Co., 110 C.A.2d 30, 242 P.2d 87 (1952) (per McComb, J.). Although these cases would only specifically cover the first circumstance stated in subsection [subdivision] (3) of this section; i.e., where the usage is 'in the vocation or trade in which [the parties] are engaged', their rationale would also cover the second circumstance; i.e., where the usage is one 'of which [the parties] are or should be aware.'

"The objection to this subsection [subdivision] is that it is either meaningless or undesirable. If it is held that there is 'unfair surprise' only if the other party did not know or have reason to know of the usage, then the evidence is inadmissible in any event and giving the notice will not make it so. If, on the other hand, the subsection [subdivision] means that there may be unfair surprise where the other party is aware or should be aware of the usage, then the subsection [subdivision] seems to create more injustice than it removes. If the party relying on the usage does not give the notice because he knows that the other party is aware or should be aware of the usage, and the judge then excludes his evidence on the ground that the other party has been 'unfairly surprised', this would cause even greater 'unfair surprise' to the proponent of the evidence."

As further pointed out in the above report:

"An additional objection to the subsection [subdivision (6)] is that it is inadequate as a procedural rule, even if a desirable one. It does not say how the notice is to be given, for what length of time, what it is to contan [sic] or what happens if it is not given, except that the evidence is not admissible 'unless and until' it is given. Does this mean that regardless of the circumstances, the proponent of the evidence is entitled to a continuance in the middle of the trial, if he then gives the notice, for such length of time as the judge decides is sufficient to 'prevent unfair surprise' to the other party?" Sixth Progress Report to the Legislature by Senate Fact Finding Committee on Judiciary (1959–1961) Part 1, The Uniform Commercial Code, pp. 442, 443.

9. The requirement of notice in subdivision (6) is not in accord with the statements of the courts to the effect that trade usage is presumed in an action between parties within the trade. ". . . trade usage is admissible, although not pleaded, in an action between parties within the trade, on the theory that it must be presumed to be known to the parties who are specialists in the field" (Iusi v. Chase, 169 Cal.App.2d 83, 337 P.2d 79 (1959) and cases cited therein).

Changes from U.C.C. (1962 Official Text)

10. This is section 1–205 of the Official Text without change.

Uniform Commercial Code Comment

Prior Uniform Statutory Provision:

No such general provision but see Sections 9(1), 15(5), 18(2), and 71, Uniform Sales Act.

Purposes: This section makes it clear that:

1. This Act rejects both the "laydictionary" and the "conveyancer's" reading of a commercial agreement. Instead the meaning of the agreement of the parties is to be determined by the language used by them and by their action, read and interpreted in the light of commercial practices and other surrounding circumstances. The measure and background for interpretation are set by the commercial context, which may explain and supplement even the language of a formal or final writing.

2. Course of dealing under subsection (1) is restricted, literally, to a sequence of conduct between the parties previous to the agreement. However, the provisions of the Act on course of performance make it clear that a sequence of conduct after or under the agreement may have equivalent meaning. (Section 2–208.)

3. "Course of dealing" may enter the agreement either by explicit provisions of the agreement or by tacit recognition.

4. This Act deals with "usage of trade" as a factor in reaching the commercial meaning of the agreement which the parties have made. The language used is to be interpreted as meaning what it may fairly be expected to mean to parties involved in the particular commercial transaction in a given locality or in a given vocation or trade. By adopting in this context the term "usage of trade" this Act expresses its intent to reject those cases which see evidence of "custom" as representing an effort to displace or negate "established rules of law". A distinction is to be drawn between mandatory rules of law such as the Statute of Frauds provisions of Article 2 on Sales whose very office is to control and restrict the actions of the parties, and which cannot be abrogated by agreement, or by a usage of trade, and those rules of law (such as those in Part 3 of Article 2 on Sales) which fill in points which

the parties have not considered and in fact agreed upon. The latter rules hold "unless otherwise agreed" but yield to the contrary agreement of the parties. Part of the agreement of the parties to which such rules yield is to be sought for in the usages of trade which furnish the background and give particular meaning to the language used, and are the framework of common understanding controlling any general rules of law which hold only when there is no such understanding.

5. A usage of trade under subsection (2) must have the "regularity of observance" specified. The ancient English tests for "custom" are abandoned in this connection. Therefore, it is not required that a usage of trade be "ancient or immemorial", "universal" or the like. Under the requirement of subsection (2) full recognition is thus available for new usages and for usages currently observed by the great majority of decent dealers, even though dissidents ready to cut corners do not agree. There is room also for proper recognition of usage agreed upon by merchants in trade codes.

6. The policy of this Act controlling explicit unconscionable contracts and clauses (Sections 1–203, 2–302) applies to implicit clauses which rest on usage of trade and carries forward the policy underlying the ancient requirement that a custom or usage must be "reasonable". However, the emphasis is shifted. The very fact of commercial acceptance makes out a prima facie case that the usage is reasonable, and the burden is no longer on the usage to establish itself as being reasonable. But the anciently established policing of usage by the courts is continued to the extent necessary to cope with the situation arising if an unconscionable or dishonest practice should become standard.

7. Subsection (3), giving the prescribed effect to usages of which the parties "are or should be aware", reinforces the provision of subsection (2) requiring not universality but only the described "regularity of observance" of the practice or method. This subsection also reinforces the point of subsection (2) that such usages may be either general to trade or particular to a special branch of trade.

8. Although the terms in which this Act defines "agreement" include the elements of course of dealing and usage of trade, the fact that express reference is made in some sections to those elements is not to be construed as carrying a contrary intent or implication elsewhere. Compare Section 1–102(4).

9. In cases of a well established line of usage varying from the general rules of this Act where the precise amount of the variation has not been worked out into a single standard, the party relying on the usage is entitled, in any event, to the minimum variation demonstrated. The whole is not to be disregarded because no particular line of detail has been established. In case a dominant pattern has been fairly evidenced, the party relying on the usage is entitled under this section to go to the trier of fact on the question of whether such dominant pattern has been incorporated into the agreement.

10. Subsection (6) is intended to insure that this Act's liberal recognition of the needs of commerce in regard to usage of trade shall not be made into an instrument of abuse.

Cross References:

Point 1: Sections 1–203, 2–104 and 2–202.
Point 2: Section 2–208.
Point 4: Section 2–201 and Part 3 of Article 2.
Point 6: Sections 1–203 and 2–302.
Point 8: Sections 1–102 and 1–201.
Point 9: Section 2–204(3).

Definitional Cross References:

"Agreement". Section 1–201.
"Contract". Section 1–201.
"Party". Section 1–201.
"Term". Section 1–201.

Cross References

Course of performance or practical construction, see Commercial Code § 2208.
Explanation or supplementation of sales agreement by course of dealing or usage of trade, see Commercial Code § 2202.
Final written expression of agreement, effect of this section upon, see Commercial Code § 2202.
Formation of sales contract, see Commercial Code § 2204.

Interpretation of contracts, sense of words, see Civil Code § 1644.
Merchant as one with specialized knowledge or skill, see Commercial Code § 2104.
Obligation and construction of sales contract, see Commercial Code § 2301 et seq.
Obligation of good faith, see Commercial Code § 1203.
Statute of frauds, see Commercial Code § 2201.
Variation by agreement, see Commercial Code § 1102.

§ 1206. Statute of Frauds for Kinds of Personal Property Not Otherwise Covered

(1) Except in the cases described in subdivision (2) of this section a contract for the sale of personal property is not enforceable by way of action or defense beyond five thousand dollars ($5,000) in amount or value of remedy unless there is some writing which indicates that a contract for sale has been made between the parties at a defined or stated price, reasonably identifies the subject matter, and is signed by the party against whom enforcement is sought or by his or her authorized agent.

(2) Subdivision (1) of this section does not apply to contracts for the sale of goods (Section 2201) nor of securities (Section 8113) nor to security agreements (Section 9203). (Stats.1963, c. 819, § 1206. Amended by Stats.1996, c. 497 (S.B.1591), § 5, operative Jan. 1, 1997.)

California Code Comment

By John A. Bohn and Charles J. Williams

Prior California Law

1. This section is the general Commercial Code statute of frauds provision. There are specific provisions requiring a writing in other divisions of the Code, for example, section 2201 (goods), section 8319 (securities) and section 9203 (security interests). Official Comment.

2. Under former Civil Code § 1624a and § 1724(1) and former Code of Civil Procedure § 1973a the writing requirement applied where the value was over $500. Under these former sections part performance could be a substitute for the writing.

Changes from U.C.C. (1962 Official Text)

3. This is section 1–206 of the Official Text without change.

Uniform Commercial Code Comment

Prior Uniform Statutory Provision:

Section 4, Uniform Sales Act (which was based on Section 17 of the Statute of 29 Charles II).

Changes:

Completely rewritten by this and other sections.

Purposes:

To fill the gap left by the Statute of Frauds provisions for goods (Section 2–201) and security interests (Section 9–203). As to securities, see Section 8–113. The Uniform Sales Act covered the sale of "choses in action"; the principal gap relates to sale of the "general intangibles" defined in Article 9 (Section 9–106) and to transactions excluded from Article 9 by Section 9–104. Typical are the sale of bilateral contracts, royalty rights or the like. The informality normal to such transactions is recognized by lifting the limit for oral transactions to $5,000. In such transactions there is often no standard of practice by which to judge, and values can rise or drop without warning; troubling abuses are avoided when the dollar limit is exceeded by requiring that the subject-matter be reasonably identified in a signed writing which indicates that a contract for sale has been made at a defined or stated price. Amendments approved by the Permanent Editorial Board for Uniform Commercial Code November 4, 1995.

§ 1206

Definitional Cross References:

"Action". Section 1–201.
"Agreement". Section 1–201.
"Contract". Section 1–201.
"Contract for sale." Section 2–106.
"Goods". Section 2–105.
"Party". Section 1–201.
"Sale". Section 2–106.
"Signed". Section 1–201.
"Writing". Section 1–201.

Cross References

Authority to enter into contract required to be in writing must be in writing, see Civil Code § 2309.
Contracts required to be in writing generally, see Civil Code § 1624.
Enforceability of security interest, see Commercial Code § 9203.
Formal requirements of sales contract, see Commercial Code § 2201.
Purchase of investment securities, see Commercial Code § 8319.

§ 1207. Performance or Acceptance Under Reservation of Rights

(a) A party who, with explicit reservation of rights, performs or promises performance or assents to performance in a manner demanded or offered by the other party does not thereby prejudice the rights reserved. Such words as "without prejudice," "under protest" or the like are sufficient.

(b) Subdivision (a) does not apply to an accord and satisfaction. *(Stats.1963, c. 819, § 1207. Amended by Stats.1992, c. 914 (S.B.833), § 3.)*

California Code Comment

By John A. Bohn and Charles J. Williams

Prior California Law

1. This section is consistent with former Civil Code § 1769 (USA) which provided that acceptance of the goods by the buyer did not discharge the seller from liability. However the "explicit reservation" required by this section is new.

Changes from U.C.C. (1962 Official Text)

2. This is section 1–207 of the Official Text without change.

Uniform Commercial Code Comment
1992 Amendment

1. This section provides machinery for the continuation of performance along the lines contemplated by the contract despite a pending dispute, by adopting the mercantile device of going ahead with delivery, acceptance, or payment "without prejudice," "under protest," "under reserve," "with reservation of all our rights," and the like. All of these phrases completely reserve all rights within the meaning of this section. The section therefore contemplates that limited as well as general reservations and acceptance by a party may be made "subject to satisfaction of our purchaser," "subject to acceptance by our customers," or the like.

2. This section does not add any new requirement of language of reservation where not already required by law, but merely provides a specific measure on which a party can rely as that party makes or concurs in any interim adjustment in the course of performance. It does not affect or impair the provisions of this Act such as those under which the buyer's remedies for defect survive acceptance without being expressly claimed if notice of the defects is given within a reasonable time. Nor does it disturb the policy of those cases which restrict the effect of a waiver of a defect to reasonable limits under the circumstances, even though no such reservation is expressed.

The section is not addressed to the creation or loss of remedies in the ordinary course of performance but rather to a method of procedure where one party is claiming as of right something which the other believes to be unwarranted.

3. Judicial authority was divided on the issue of whether former Section 1–207 (present subsection (1)) applied to an accord and satisfaction. Typically the cases involved attempted to reach an accord and satisfaction by use of a check tendered in full satisfaction of a claim. Subsection (2) of revised Section 1–207 resolves this conflict by stating that Section 1–207 does not apply to an accord and satisfaction. Section 3–311 of revised Article 3 governs if an accord and satisfaction is attempted by tender of a negotiable instrument as stated in that section. If Section 3–311 does not apply, the issue of whether an accord and satisfaction has been effected is determined by the law of contract. Whether or not Section 3–311 applies, Section 1–207 has no application to an accord and satisfaction.

Uniform Commercial Code Comment

Prior Uniform Statutory Provision:

None.

Purposes:

1. This section provides machinery for the continuation of performance along the lines contemplated by the contract despite a pending dispute, by adopting the mercantile device of going ahead with delivery, acceptance, or payment "without prejudice," "under protest," "under reserve," "with reservation of all our rights," and the like. All of these phrases completely reserve all rights within the meaning of this section. The section therefore contemplates that limited as well as general reservations and acceptance by a party may be made "subject to satisfaction of our purchaser," "subject to acceptance by our customers," or the like.

2. This section does not add any new requirement of language of reservation where not already required by law, but merely provides a specific measure on which a party can rely as he makes or concurs in any interim adjustment in the course of performance. It does not affect or impair the provisions of this Act such as those under which the buyer's remedies for defect survive acceptance without being expressly claimed if notice of the defects is given within a reasonable time. Nor does it disturb the policy of those cases which restrict the effect of a waiver of a defect to reasonable limits under the circumstances, even though no such reservation is expressed.

The section is not addressed to the creation or loss of remedies in the ordinary course of performance but rather to a method of procedure where one party is claiming as of right something which the other feels to be unwarranted.

Cross Reference:

Section 2–607.

Definitional Cross References:

"Party". Section 1–201.
"Rights". Section 1–201.

Cross References

Effect of acceptance of goods, see Commercial Code § 2607.
Notice by buyer to seller, see Commercial Code § 2607.

§ 1208. Option to Accelerate at Will

A term providing that one party or his successor in interest may accelerate payment or performance or require collateral or additional collateral "at will" or "when he deems himself insecure" or in words of similar import shall be construed to mean that he shall have power to do so only if he in good faith believes that the prospect of payment or performance is impaired. The burden of establishing lack of good faith is on the party against whom the power has been exercised. *(Stats.1963, c. 819, § 1208.)*

California Code Comment

By John A. Bohn and Charles J. Williams

Prior California Law

1. This section imposes the obligation of good faith in exercising the right to accelerate payment or require collateral. The provision for this right is sometimes referred to as an "insecurity" clause and is found in such documents as promissory notes, conditional sales contracts, and chattel mortgages.

2. The Legislative Counsel in the California Annotations to the Proposed Uniform Commercial Code states that this section establishes new law:

"Requirement of good faith before exercising acceleration rights is similar to the situation in contract law where there is a promise conditional on the promisor's satisfaction. In this situation California courts have distinguished between two types of cases: (1) That in which the fancy, taste, sensibility or judgment of the party is the issue, in which case the right to terminate cannot be challenged because it was not founded on any practical reason. For example, Kendis v. Cohn, [1928] 90 Cal.App. 41, 265 Pac. 844; Hall v. Webb, [1924] 66 Cal.App. 416, 423, 226 Pac. 403, 406. (2) That in which the question is one of operative or mechanical fitness, in which event the rejection must be reasonable. Allred v. Sheehan, 54 Cal.App. 688, 202 Pac. 681. [1921]" Sixth Progress Report to the Legislature by Senate Fact Finding Committee on Judiciary (1959–1961) Part 1, The Uniform Commercial Code, p. 34.

The good faith that is required by this section of the Commercial Code may be similar to the requirement of good faith where the exercise of the right depends on the promisor's satisfaction.

3. The clause providing for acceleration "when he deems himself insecure" described in this section would prevent an otherwise negotiable instrument from being negotiable under the NIL, former Civil Code §§ 3082 to 3266d. Former Civil Code § 3082(3) states that to be negotiable an instrument "must be payable on demand, or at a fixed or determinable future time" and former Civil Code § 3085 states what constitutes a "determinable future time". However, the cases have held that the typical clause which provides that the holder may accelerate payment so as to make the whole principal and interest due immediately if the interest is not paid when due, does not prevent the instrument from being negotiable. Utah State Nat. Bank v. Smith, 180 Cal. 1, 179 Pac. 160 (1919) and Smith v. Peters, 46 Cal.App. 47, 188 Pac. 811 (1920). A trade acceptance containing an unconditional promise to pay is not made non-negotiable by a provision accelerating maturity upon "suffering a fire loss" or "failure to meet at maturity any prior trade acceptance". People's Finance & Thrift Co. v. Shaw-Leahy Co., 214 Cal. 108, 3 P.2d 1012 (1931). However, cases under the NIL state that if the note is "payable whenever the payee deems himself insecure, the due date is usually held to be uncertain and the note non-negotiable". People's Bank v. Porter, 58 Cal.App. 41, 208 Pac. 200 (1922). See also People's Finance & Thrift Co. v. Shaw-Leahy Co., p. 113, supra.

Under the Commercial Code an acceleration clause does not destroy negotiability since an instrument is payable at a definite time if it is payable "at a definite time subject to *any* acceleration" (emphasis added) as provided in Commercial Code § 3109(1)(c). Therefore, an acceleration clause "when he deems himself insecure" does not make an instrument non-negotiable under the Commercial Code, although California cases decided under the NIL indicate that it would be non-negotiable. However, the acceleration permitted under Commercial Code § 3109(1)(c) must be exercised in "good faith". See Commercial Code § 1201(19) for definition of good faith.

Changes from U.C.C. (1962 Official Text)

4. This is section 1–208 of the Official Text without change.

Uniform Commercial Code Comment

Prior Uniform Statutory Provision:
None.

Purposes:

The increased use of acceleration clauses either in the case of sales on credit or in time paper or in security transactions has led to some confusion in the cases as to the effect to be given to a clause which seemingly grants the power of an acceleration at the whim and caprice of one party. This Section is intended to make clear that despite language which can be so construed and which further might be held to make the agreement void as against public policy or to make the contract illusory or too indefinite for enforcement, the clause means that the option is to be exercised only in the good faith belief that the prospect of payment or performance is impaired.

Obviously this section has no application to demand instruments or obligations whose very nature permits call at any time with or without reason. This section applies only to an agreement or to paper which in the first instance is payable at a future date.

Definitional Cross References:
"Burden of establishing". Section 1–201.
"Good faith". Section 1–201.
"Party". Section 1–201.
"Term". Section 1–201.

Cross References

Acceleration clauses in notes, payment of instrument at definite time, see Commercial Code § 3108.
Obligation of good faith, see Commercial Code § 1203.

§ 1209. Subordinated Obligations

An obligation may be issued as subordinated to payment of another obligation of the person obligated, or a creditor may subordinate his right to payment of an obligation by agreement with either the person obligated or another creditor of the person obligated. Such a subordination does not create a security interest as against either the common debtor or a subordinated creditor. This section shall be construed as declaring the law as it existed prior to the enactment of this section and not as modifying it. *(Added by Stats.1967, c. 799, p. 2206, § 2.5.)*

California Code Comment

By Charles J. Williams

Prior California Law

1. This section is new. It is contained in the 1966 official recommendations for amendments to the Uniform Commercial Code promulgated by the Permanent Editorial Board. It is based upon a section previously adopted in New York.

2. The purpose of this section is to resolve the uncertainty as to whether or not an agreement for the subordination of one debt to another creates a security interest.

Changes from U.C.C. (1962 Official Text)

3. This is section 1–209 of the Official Text without change. This section was added to the Official Text in 1966 as the result of official recommendations for amendment by the Permanent Editorial Board.

Uniform Commercial Code Comment

Prior Uniform Statutory Provision:
None.

Purposes:

1. Billions of dollars of subordinated debt are held by the public and by institutional investors. Commonly, the subordinated debt is subordinated on issue or acquisition and is evidenced by an investment security or by a negotiable or non-negotiable note. Debt is also sometimes subordinated after it arises, either by agreement between the subordinating creditor and the debtor, by agreement between two creditors of the same debtor, or by agreement of all three parties. The subordinated creditor may be a stockholder or other "insider" interested in the common debtor; the subordinated debt may consist of accounts or other rights to payment not evidenced by any instrument. All such

§ 1209

cases are included in the terms "subordinated obligation," "subordination," and "subordinated creditor."

2. Subordination agreements are enforceable between the parties as contracts, and in the bankruptcy of the common debtor dividends otherwise payable to the subordinated creditor are turned over to the superior creditor. This "turn-over" practice has on occasion been explained in terms of "equitable lien," "equitable assignment," or "constructive trust," but whatever the label the practice is essentially an equitable remedy and does not mean that there is a transaction "intended to create a security interest," a "sale of accounts, contract rights or chattel paper," or a "security interest created by contract," within the meaning of Section 9–102. On the other hand, nothing in this section prevents one creditor from assigning his rights to another creditor of the same debtor in such a way as to create a security interest within Article 9, where the parties so intend.

3. The last sentence of this section is intended to negate any implication that the section changes the law. It is intended to be declaratory of pre-existing law. Both the history and the text of Article 9 make it clear that it was not intended to cover subordination agreements. The provisions of Section 9–203 for signature by the "debtor" would be entirely unworkable if read to require signature by public holders of subordinated investment securities. The priorities, filing provisions and remedies on default provided by Article 9 would also be largely inappropriate in many situations. The precautionary language of Section 9–316 preserving subordination of priority by agreement between secured parties points to the conclusion that similar arrangements among unsecured lenders are not covered unless otherwise within the scope of the Article.

4. The enforcement of subordination agreements is largely left to supplementary principles under Section 1–103. If the subordinated debt is evidenced by an investment security, Section 8–202(1) authorizes enforcement against purchasers on terms stated or referred to on the security. If the fact of subordination is noted on a negotiable instrument, a holder under Sections 3–302 and 3–306 is subject to the term because notice precludes him from taking free of the subordination. Sections 3–302(3) (a), 3–306 and 8–317 severely limit the rights of levying creditors of a subordinated creditor in such cases.

Definitional Cross References:

"Agreement". Section 1–201.
"Creditor". Section 1–201.
"Debtor". Section 9–105.
"Person". Section 1–201.
"Rights". Section 1–201.
"Security interest". Section 1–201.

§ 1210. Presumptions; Nature

Except as otherwise provided in Section 1202, the presumptions established by this code are presumptions affecting the burden of producing evidence. *(Added by Stats.1967, c. 703, p. 2077, § 2.)*

California Code Comment

By Charles J. Williams

Prior California Law

1. This section is new and was added upon recommendation of the California Law Revision Commission. Its effect is to classify as presumptions affecting the burden of producing evidence, those presumptions that are established by Commercial Code §§ 3114(3), 3304(3) (c), 3307(1) (b), 3414(2), 3416(4), 3419(2), 3503(2), 3510, and 8105(2) (b).

The procedural effect of classifying these presumptions as presumptions affecting the burden of producing evidence is described in Evidence Code § 604. In general, it means that the trier of fact must assume the existence of the presumed fact unless and until evidence is introduced which would support the finding of its non-existence. If evidence is introduced to support a finding of its non-existence, the trier of the fact must determine the existence or non-existence of the presumed fact from the evidence and without regard to the presumption. When contrary evidence is introduced, the presumption vanishes from the case and the trier of fact must weigh the inferences arising from the facts that gave rise to the presumption and the inferences arising from the contrary evidence and resolve the conflict.

Changes from U.C.C. (1962 Official Text)

2. This section does not appear in the Official Text. The corresponding provision from the Official Text is contained in section 1–201(31). See California Code Comment 31 to section 1201. The California Law Revision Commission states that this section 1210 has the same substantive effect as subdivision (31) of section 1201.

Division 2

SALES

Chapter	Section
1. Short Title, General Construction and Subject Matter	2101
2. Form, Formation and Readjustment of Contract	2201
3. General Obligation and Construction of Contract	2301
4. Title, Creditors and Good Faith Purchasers	2401
5. Performance	2501
6. Breach, Repudiation and Excuse	2601
7. Remedies	2701
8. Retail Sales	2800

WESTLAW Computer Assisted Legal Research

WESTLAW supplements your legal research in many ways. WESTLAW allows you to
- update your research with the most current information
- expand your library with additional resources
- retrieve direct history, precedential history and parallel citations with the Insta-Cite service

For more information on using WESTLAW to supplement your research, see the WESTLAW Electronic Research Guide, which follows the Preface.

CHAPTER 1. SHORT TITLE, GENERAL CONSTRUCTION AND SUBJECT MATTER

Section
2101. Short Title.
2102. Scope; Certain Security and Other Transactions Excluded From This Division.
2103. Definitions and Index of Definitions.
2104. Definitions: "Merchant"; "Between Merchants"; "Financing Agency".
2105. Definitions: Transferability; "Goods"; "Future Goods"; "Lot"; "Commercial Unit".
2106. Definitions; "Contract"; "Agreement"; "Contract for Sale"; "Sale"; "Present Sale"; "Conforming" to Contract; "Termination"; "Cancellation".
2107. Goods to Be Severed From Realty; Recording.

Introductory Comment

By Charles J. Williams

Division 2 replaces the Uniform Sales Act (Civil Code §§ 1721–1800) hereafter referred to as USA which was adopted by California in 1931.

Division 2 is drafted from the standpoint of the businessman. It recognizes that sales contracts are often made without prior approval of the attorneys for the parties. Its basic premise is that a contract which both parties reasonably believe they have made with each other should be enforceable.

Division 2 retains many of the rules of the USA. However, these rules have been modernized and improved to conform more closely with existing commercial practices. For the most part Division 2 represents a change in approach from the Uniform Sales Act.

To a great extent, the passage of title which was so important in determining the rights of the parties under the USA e.g. risk of loss, is abandoned. Division 2 deals directly and separately with each phase of the sales transaction, e.g. time of sale, risk of loss, insurable interest, possessory rights and creditors rights.

Division 2 makes an important distinction between "merchants" and "non-merchants". Merchants are held to a higher standard of knowledge and skill peculiar to the practices or goods involved. For example, an implied warranty of merchantability is imposed upon a seller if he is a merchant (section 2314). Because businessmen rely upon the firm offer which under pre-Commercial Code law was unenforceable for lack of consideration, the firm offer is enforced (section 2205). Special rules also apply to merchants concerning confirmation of a verbal transaction (section 2201(2)) exchange of offer and acceptance forms (section 2207(2)) and oral modification of written contracts (section 2209(2)).

Division 2 revises the statute of frauds by providing more practical rules to deal with partial performance where there is an inadequate writing (section 2201).

Division 2 restates the provisions of the USA involving warranties with important changes in three areas: (1) warranty of fitness for a particular purpose of goods sold under a brand name (section 2315) (2) privity of contract (section 2318) and (3) disclaimer of warranties (section 2316).

In the field of remedies, Division 2 expands those available to both the buyer and the seller. Thus, under section 2705 the seller's right to stop delivery of goods in transit is extended to all cases of breach if the shipment is in carload or similar lots. The buyer need no longer elect his remedy, and under section 2608 he may revoke his acceptance instead of rescinding. He may cancel the contract, return the goods and recover both the purchase price and the damages for the breach (section 2711).

§ 2101. Short Title

This division shall be known and may be cited as Uniform Commercial Code—Sales. *(Stats.1963, c. 819, § 2101.)*

California Code Comment

By John A. Bohn and Charles J. Williams

This is section 2–101 of the Official Text without change.

Uniform Commercial Code Comment

This Article is a complete revision and modernization of the Uniform Sales Act which was promulgated by the National Conference of Commissioners on Uniform State Laws in 1906 and has been adopted in 34 states and Alaska, the District of Columbia and Hawaii.

The coverage of the present Article is much more extensive than that of the old Sales Act and extends to the various bodies of case law which have been developed both outside of and under the latter.

The arrangement of the present Article is in terms of contract for sale and the various steps of its performance. The legal consequences are stated as following directly from the contract and action taken under it without resorting to the idea of when property or title passed or was to pass as being the determining factor. The purpose is to avoid making practical issues between practical men turn upon the location of an intangible something, the passing of which no man can prove by evidence and to substitute for such abstractions proof of words and actions of a tangible character.

§ 2101

Cross References

Construction of instruments, duty of judge, see Code of Civil Procedure § 1858; Evidence Code §§ 310, 400 et seq., 457.
Contracts, interpretation, see Civil Code § 1635 et seq.
Indemnity contracts, interpretation, see Civil Code § 2778.
Obligations, see Civil Code § 1427 et seq.
Personal or movable property, see Civil Code § 946 et seq.
Retail installment sale defined, see Civil Code § 1802.5.
Securities, sale or disposition, see Insurance Code § 822.
Waiver of code provisions, see Civil Code § 3268.

§ 2102. Scope; Certain Security and Other Transactions Excluded From This Division

Unless the context otherwise requires, this division applies to transactions in goods; it does not apply to any transaction which although in the form of an unconditional contract to sell or present sale is intended to operate only as a security transaction nor does this division impair or repeal any statute regulating sales to consumers, farmers or other specified classes of buyers. *(Stats.1963, c. 819, § 2102.)*

California Code Comment

By John A. Bohn and Charles J. Williams

Prior California Law

1. This section rephrases and extends former Civil Code § 1795. It excludes from the operation of Division 2 transactions which, although in the form of a sale or contract to sell, are really only security devices. This section would also exclude certain special statutes pertaining to sales to unique groups of buyers; for example, the provisions of the Vehicle Code relating to sale of and recording of sale of motor vehicles.

Changes from U.C.C. (1962 Official Text)

2. This is section 2–102 of the Official Text without change.

Uniform Commercial Code Comment

Prior Uniform Statutory Provision:

Section 75, Uniform Sales Act.

Changes: Section 75 has been rephrased.

Purposes of Changes and New Matter: To make it clear that:

The Article leaves substantially unaffected the law relating to purchase money security such as conditional sale or chattel mortgage though it regulates the general sales aspects of such transactions. "Security transaction" is used in the same sense as in the Article on Secured Transactions (Article 9).

Cross Reference:

Article 9.

Definitional Cross References:

"Contract". Section 1–201.
"Contract for sale". Section 2–106.
"Present sale". Section 2–106.
"Sale". Section 2–106.

Cross References

Applicability of this division in determining whether a document of title fulfills the obligations of a contract for sale, see Commercial Code § 7509.
Automobile sales finance act, see Civil Code § 2981 et seq.
Motor vehicles, transfer of title or interest, see Vehicle Code § 5600 et seq.
Pawnbrokers, see Financial Code § 21200 et seq.
Retail installment sales, see Civil Code § 1801 et seq.
Secured transactions, see Commercial Code § 9101 et seq.

§ 2103. Definitions and Index of Definitions

(1) In this division unless the context otherwise requires

(a) "Buyer" means a person who buys or contracts to buy goods.

(b) "Good faith" in the case of a merchant means honesty in fact and the observance of reasonable commercial standards of fair dealing in the trade.

(c) "Receipt" of goods means taking physical possession of them.

(d) "Seller" means a person who sells or contracts to sell goods.

(2) Other definitions applying to this division or to specified chapters thereof, and the sections in which they appear are:

"Acceptance."   Section 2606.
"Banker's credit."   Section 2325.
"Between merchants."   Section 2104.
"Cancellation."   Section 2106(4).
"Commercial unit."   Section 2105.
"Confirmed credit."   Section 2325.
"Conforming to contract."   Section 2106.
"Contract for sale."   Section 2106.
"Cover."   Section 2712.
"Entrusting."   Section 2403.
"Financing agency."   Section 2104.
"Future goods."   Section 2105.
"Goods."   Section 2105.
"Identification."   Section 2501.
"Installment contract."   Section 2612.
"Letter of Credit."   Section 2325.
"Lot."   Section 2105.
"Merchant."   Section 2104.
"Overseas."   Section 2323.
"Person in position of seller."   Section 2707.
"Present sale."   Section 2106.
"Sale."   Section 2106.
"Sale on approval."   Section 2326.
"Sale or return."   Section 2326.
"Termination."   Section 2106.

(3) The following definitions in other divisions apply to this division:

"Check."   Section 3104.
"Consignee."   Section 7102.
"Consignor."   Section 7102.
"Consumer goods."   Section 9109.
"Dishonor."   Section 3502.
"Draft."   Section 3104.

(4) In addition Division 1 contains general definitions and principles of construction and interpretation applicable throughout this division. *(Stats.1963, c. 819, § 2103. Amended by Stats.1994, c. 668 (S.B.1405), § 9.)*

California Code Comment

By John A. Bohn and Charles J. Williams

Prior California Law

1. Under the USA (former Civil Code §§ 1721–1800) most relevant definitions were listed in Civil Code § 1796. Under the Commercial Code, most of these definitions are listed in § 1201.

2. As defined in this section:

(a) Subdivision (1)(a): "buyer" is more narrow than the definition contained in former Civil Code § 1796 due to the omission of the words "any legal successor in interest of such person".

(b) Subdivision (1)(b): in the case of merchants defined in section 2104(1), "good faith" broadens the definition contained in former Civil Code § 1796, in that it additionally requires "the observance of reasonable commercial standards of fair dealing in the trade." The general definition of "good faith" contained in section 1201(19) also applies to all transactions under Division 2.

(c) Subdivision (1)(c): "receipt" is a new definition in California statutory law. Its purpose is explained in the Official Comment to section 2–103 of the Official Text.

(d) Subdivision (1)(d): "Seller" is more narrow than the definition contained in former Civil Code § 1796 due to the omission of the words "any legal successor in interest of such person".

Changes from U.C.C. (1962 Official Text)

3. This is section 2–103 of the Official Text without change.

Uniform Commercial Code Comment

Prior Uniform Statutory Provision:

Subsection (1): Section 76, Uniform Sales Act.

Changes:

The definitions of "buyer" and "seller" have been slightly rephrased, the reference in Section 76 of the prior Act to "any legal successor in interest of such person" being omitted. The definition of "receipt" is new.

Purposes of Changes and New Matter:

1. The phrase "any legal successor in interest of such person" has been eliminated since Section 2–210 of this Article, which limits some types of delegation of performance on assignment of a sales contract, makes it clear that not every such successor can be safely included in the definition. In every ordinary case, however, such successors are as of course included.

2. "Receipt" must be distinguished from delivery particularly in regard to the problems arising out of shipment of goods, whether or not the contract calls for making delivery by way of documents of title, since the seller may frequently fulfill his obligations to "deliver" even though the buyer may never "receive" the goods. Delivery with respect to documents of title is defined in Article 1 and requires transfer of physical delivery. Otherwise the many divergent incidents of delivery are handled incident by incident.

Cross References:

Point 1: See Section 2–210 and Comment thereon.
Point 2: Section 1–201.

Definitional Cross Reference:

"Person". Section 1–201.

Cross References

Automobile sales finance act, seller defined, see Civil Code § 2981.
Bulk storage of grain, seller defined, see Civil Code § 1880.1.

Cancellation,
  Contracts, jurisdiction of municipal court, see Code of Civil Procedure § 86.
  Instruments, see Civil Code § 3412 et seq.
Contract,
  Defined, see Civil Code § 1549 et seq.
  Definition, see Civil Code § 1549.
Delegation of performance and assignment of rights, see Commercial Code § 2210.
General definitions, see Commercial Code § 1201.
Obligation of good faith, see Commercial Code § 1203.
Retail installment sale,
  Contract defined, see Civil Code § 1802.6.
  Sale defined, see Civil Code § 1802.5.
Sale defined,
  Alcoholic beverage tax, see Revenue and Taxation Code § 32003.
  Cigarette tax, see Revenue and Taxation Code § 30006.
  Sales and use taxes, see Revenue and Taxation Code § 6006.
Sales and use taxes, seller defined, see Revenue and Taxation Code § 6014.

§ 2104. Definitions: "Merchant"; "Between Merchants"; "Financing Agency"

(1) "Merchant" means a person who deals in goods of the kind or otherwise by his occupation holds himself out as having knowledge or skill peculiar to the practices or goods involved in the transaction or to whom such knowledge or skill may be attributed by his employment of an agent or broker or other intermediary who by his occupation holds himself out as having such knowledge or skill.

(2) "Financing agency" means a bank, finance company or other person who in the ordinary course of business makes advances against goods or documents of title or who by arrangement with either the seller or the buyer intervenes in ordinary course to make or collect payment due or claimed under the contract for sale, as by purchasing or paying the seller's draft or making advances against it or by merely taking it for collection whether or not documents of title accompany the draft. "Financing agency" includes also a bank or other person who similarly intervenes between persons who are in the position of seller and buyer in respect to the goods (Section 2707).

(3) "Between merchants" means in any transaction with respect to which both parties are chargeable with the knowledge or skill of merchants. *(Stats.1963, c. 819, § 2104.)*

California Code Comment

By John A. Bohn and Charles J. Williams

Prior California Law

1. The term "merchant" as defined in subdivision (1) is new to California law. However, the concept of a "merchant" which this section crystallizes is apparent in the USA. Former Civil Code § 1735(2) referred to "a seller who deals in goods of that description" and § 1736(c) made a similar reference, i.e., "if the seller is a dealer in goods of that kind."

2. There is no California precedent, case or statutory, for the treatment given to "merchants" which under this Division have their own special rules regarding behavior between themselves, e.g., §§ 2205, 2207, 2314, 2326 and 2603.

Changes from U.C.C. (1962 Official Text)

3. This is section 2–104 of the Official Text without change.

Uniform Commercial Code Comment

Prior Uniform Statutory Provision:

None. But see Sections 15(2), (5), 16(c), 45(2) and 71, Uniform Sales Act, and Sections 35 and 37, Uniform Bills of Lading Act for examples of the policy expressly provided for in this Article.

Purposes:

1. This Article assumes that transactions between professionals in a given field require special and clear rules which may not apply to a casual or inexperienced seller or buyer. It thus adopts a policy of expressly stating rules applicable "between merchants" and "as against a merchant", wherever they are needed instead of making them depend upon the circumstances of each case as in the statutes cited above. This section lays the foundation of this policy by defining those who are to be regarded as professionals or "merchants" and by stating when a transaction is deemed to be "between merchants".

2. The term "merchant" as defined here roots in the "law merchant" concept of a professional in business. The professional status under the definition may be based upon specialized knowledge as to the goods, specialized knowledge as to business practices, or specialized knowledge as to both and which kind of specialized knowledge may be sufficient to establish the merchant status is indicated by the nature of the provisions.

The special provisions as to merchants appear only in this Article and they are of three kinds. Sections 2–201(2), 2–205, 2–207 and 2–209 dealing with the statute of frauds, firm offers, confirmatory memoranda and modification rest on normal business practices which are or ought to be typical of and familiar to any person in business. For purposes of these sections almost every person in business would, therefore, be deemed to be a "merchant" under the language "who . . . by his occupation holds himself out as having knowledge or skill peculiar to the practices . . . involved in the transaction . . ." since the practices involved in the transaction are non-specialized business practices such as answering mail. In this type of provision, banks or even universities, for example, well may be "merchants." But even these sections only apply to a merchant in his mercantile capacity; a lawyer or bank president buying fishing tackle for his own use is not a merchant.

On the other hand, in Section 2–314 on the warranty of merchantability, such warranty is implied only "if the seller is a merchant with respect to goods of that kind." Obviously this qualification restricts the implied warranty to a much smaller group than everyone who is engaged in business and requires a professional status as to particular kinds of goods. The exception in Section 2–402(2) for retention of possession by a merchant-seller falls in the same class as does Section 2–403(2) on entrusting of possession to a merchant "who deals in goods of that kind".

A third group of sections includes 2–103(1)(b), which provides that in the case of a merchant "good faith" includes observance of reasonable commercial standards of fair dealing in the trade; 2–327(1)(c), 2–603 and 2–605, dealing with responsibilities of merchant buyers to follow seller's instructions, etc.; 2–509 on risk of loss, and 2–609 on adequate assurance of performance. This group of sections applies to persons who are merchants under either the "practices" or the "goods" aspect of the definition of merchant.

3. The "or to whom such knowledge or skill may be attributed by his employment of an agent or broker . . ." clause of the definition of merchant means that even persons such as universities, for example, can come within the definition of merchant if they have regular purchasing departments or business personnel who are familiar with business practices and who are equipped to take any action required.

Cross References:

Point 1: See Sections 1–102 and 1–203.
Point 2: See Sections 2–314, 2–315 and 2–320 to 2–325, of this Article, and Article 9.

Definitional Cross References:

"Bank". Section 1–201.
"Buyer". Section 2–103.
"Contract for sale". Section 2–106.
"Document of title". Section 1–201.
"Draft". Section 3–104.
"Goods". Section 2–105.
"Person". Section 1–201.
"Purchase". Section 1–201.
"Seller". Section 2–103.

Cross References

Agent defined, see Civil Code § 2295.
Definitions, see Commercial Code §§ 2320 to 2325.
Implied warranties, merchantability, see Commercial Code §§ 2314, 2315.
Obligation of good faith, see Commercial Code § 1203.
Produce dealers defined, see Food and Agricultural Code § 56107.
Purposes and construction of code, see Commercial Code § 1102.
Secured transactions, see Commercial Code § 9101 et seq.

§ 2105. Definitions: Transferability; "Goods"; "Future" Goods; "Lot"; "Commercial Unit"

(1) "Goods" means all things (including specially manufactured goods) which are movable at the time of identification to the contract for sale other than the money in which the price is to be paid, investment securities (Division 8) and things in action. "Goods" also includes the unborn young of animals and growing crops and other identified things attached to realty as described in the section on goods to be severed from realty (Section 2107).

(2) Goods must be both existing and identified before any interest in them can pass. Goods which are not both existing and identified are "future" goods. A purported present sale of future goods or of any interest therein operates as a contract to sell.

(3) There may be a sale of a part interest in existing identified goods.

(4) An undivided share in an identified bulk of fungible goods is sufficiently identified to be sold although the quantity of the bulk is not determined. Any agreed proportion of such a bulk or any quantity thereof agreed upon by number, weight or other measure may to the extent of the seller's interest in the bulk be sold to the buyer who then becomes an owner in common.

(5) "Lot" means a parcel or a single article which is the subject matter of a separate sale or delivery, whether or not it is sufficient to perform the contract.

(6) "Commercial unit" means such a unit of goods as by commercial usage is a single whole for purposes of sale and division of which materially impairs its character or value on the market or in use. A commercial unit may be a single article (as a machine) or a set of articles (as a suite of furniture or an assortment of sizes) or a quantity (as a bale, gross, or carload) or any other unit treated in use or in the relevant market as a single whole. (Stats.1963, c. 819, § 2105.)

California Code Comment

By John A. Bohn and Charles J. Williams

Prior California Law

1. The definition of "goods" in subdivision (1) changes the definition in former Civil Code § 1796. The general test now is all things moveable except "the money in which the price is to be paid, investment

securities and things in action." Under former Civil Code § 1796, the test was "chattels personal other than things in action and money."

2. "Investment securities" are excluded under subdivision (1) by definition and are treated separately under Division 8. The California authorities construed the USA (former Civil Code §§ 1721 through 1800) as excluding "securities" from the definition of goods contained therein. Franck v. J. J. Sugarman-Rudolph Co., 40 Cal.2d 81, 251 P.2d 949 (1952); and Porter v. Gibson, 25 Cal.2d 506, 154 P.2d 703 (1944).

3. "Money" is excluded from the definition of "goods" (subdivision (1)) only when it is money "in which the price is to be paid," while under former Civil Code § 1796 all "money" was excluded.

4. The definition of "goods" in subdivision (1) as it relates to realty is consistent with Civil Code § 660 which provides that things attached to the land which are agreed to be severed in accordance with the terms of a sale are treated as goods and are governed by the law regulating the sale of goods. Civil Code § 658 defines "real property".

5. Subdivision (2) is similar to former California law as expressed in former Civil Code §§ 1725(1), 1725(3), 1737 and Schiffman v. Richfield Oil Corp., 8 Cal.2d 211, 64 P.2d 1081 (1937).

6. Subdivisions (3) and (4) are similar to former Civil Code § 1726.

7. Subdivisions (5) and (6) are new and have no counterparts in prior California statutory law.

Changes from U.C.C. (1962 Official Text)

8. This is section 2–105 of the Official Text without change.

Uniform Commercial Code Comment

Prior Uniform Statutory Provision:

Subsections (1), (2), (3) and (4)—Sections 5, 6 and 76, Uniform Sales Act; Subsections (5) and (6)—none.

Changes: Rewritten.

Purposes of Changes and New Matter:

1. Subsection (1) on "goods": The phraseology of the prior uniform statutory provision has been changed so that:

The definition of goods is based on the concept of movability and the term "chattels personal" is not used. It is not intended to deal with things which are not fairly identifiable as movables before the contract is performed.

Growing crops are included within the definition of goods since they are frequently intended for sale. The concept of "industrial" growing crops has been abandoned, for under modern practices fruit, perennial hay, nursery stock and the like must be brought within the scope of this Article. The young of animals are also included expressly in this definition since they, too, are frequently intended for sale and may be contracted for before birth. The period of gestation of domestic animals is such that the provisions of the section on identification can apply as in the case of crops to be planted. The reason of this definition also leads to the inclusion of a wool crop or the like as "goods" subject to identification under this Article.

The exclusion of "money in which the price is to be paid" from the definition of goods does not mean that foreign currency which is included in the definition of money may not be the subject matter of a sales transaction. Goods is intended to cover the sale of money when money is being treated as a commodity but not to include it when money is the medium of payment.

As to contracts to sell timber, minerals, or structures to be removed from the land Section 2–107(1) (Goods to be severed from Realty: recording) controls.

The use of the word "fixtures" is avoided in view of the diversity of definitions of that term. This Article in including within its scope "things attached to realty" adds the further test that they must be capable of severance without material harm thereto. As between the parties any identified things which fall within that definition become "goods" upon the making of the contract for sale.

"Investment securities" are expressly excluded from the coverage of this Article. It is not intended by this exclusion, however, to prevent the application of a particular section of this Article by analogy to securities (as was done with the Original Sales Act in Agar v. Orda, 264 N.Y. 248, 190 N.E. 479, 99 A.L.R. 269 (1934)) when the reason of that section makes such application sensible and the situation involved is not covered by the Article of this Act dealing specifically with such securities (Article 8).

2. References to the fact that a contract for sale can extend to future or contingent goods and that ownership in common follows the sale of a part interest have been omitted here as obvious without need for expression; hence no inference to negate these principles should be drawn from their omission.

3. Subsection (4) does not touch the question of how far an appropriation of a bulk of fungible goods may or may not satisfy the contract for sale.

4. Subsections (5) and (6) on "lot" and "commercial unit" are introduced to aid in the phrasing of later sections.

5. The question of when an identification of goods takes place is determined by the provisions of Section 2–501 and all that this section says is what kinds of goods may be the subject of a sale.

Cross References:

Point 1: Sections 2–107, 2–201, 2–501 and Article 8.
Point 5: Section 2–501.
See also Section 1–201.

Definitional Cross References:

"Buyer". Section 2–103.
"Contract". Section 1–201.
"Contract for sale". Section 2–106.
"Fungible". Section 1–201.
"Money". Section 1–201.
"Present sale". Section 2–106.
"Sale". Section 2–106.
"Seller". Section 2–103.

Cross References

Classification of goods, see Commercial Code § 9109.
Fixtures defined, see Civil Code § 660.
Fraudulent transfers, see Civil Code § 3439 et seq.
General definitions, see Commercial Code § 1201.
Goods to be severed from realty, see Commercial Code § 2107.
Insurable interest, future goods, see Commercial Code § 2501.
Investment securities, see Commercial Code § 8101 et seq.
Personal or movable property, see Civil Code § 946 et seq.
Personal property defined, see Civil Code § 14; Code of Civil Procedure § 17; Penal Code § 7.
Real property defined, see Civil Code § 658.
Sale of timber, etc., as sale of goods, see Commercial Code § 2107.
Statute of frauds, see Commercial Code § 2201.
Things in action, transfer, see Civil Code § 953 et seq.
Transfer defined, see Civil Code § 1039.
Weights and measures generally, see Business and Professions Code § 12001 et seq.

§ 2106. Definitions; "Contract"; "Agreement"; "Contract for Sale"; "Sale"; "Present Sale"; "Conforming" to Contract; "Termination"; "Cancellation"

(1) In this division unless the context otherwise requires "contract" and "agreement" are limited to those relating to the present or future sale of goods. "Contract for sale" includes both a present sale of goods and a contract to sell goods at a future time. A "sale" consists in the passing of title from the seller to the buyer for a price (Section 2401). A "present sale" means a sale which is accomplished by the making of the contract.

(2) Goods or conduct including any part of a performance are "conforming" or conform to the contract when they are in accordance with the obligations under the contract.

§ 2106

(3) "Termination" occurs when either party pursuant to a power created by agreement or law puts an end to the contract otherwise than for its breach. On "termination" all obligations which are still executory on both sides are discharged but any right based on prior breach or performance survives.

(4) "Cancellation" occurs when either party puts an end to the contract for breach by the other and its effect is the same as that of "termination" except that the cancelling party also retains any remedy for breach of the whole contract or any unperformed balance. *(Stats. 1963, c. 819, § 2106.)*

California Code Comment
By John A. Bohn and Charles J. Williams

Prior California Law

1. As defined in this section:
    (a) "Contract for sale" is similar to former Civil Code § 1721.
    (b) "Conforming" is a new definition in California statutory law.
    (c) "Termination" is a new definition in California statutory law. However, see former Civil Code § 1728 (destruction of goods contracted to be sold) and former Civil Code § 1730(1) (sale at a valuation) which speak in terms of a contract being "avoided." Also see former Civil Code § 1793 on avoidance by operation of law and applicable law governing.
    (d) "Cancellation" is a new definition in California statutory law.

Changes from U.C.C. (1962 Official Text)

2. This is section 2–106 of the Official Text without change.

Uniform Commercial Code Comment

Prior Uniform Statutory Provision:

Subsection (1)—Section 1(1) and (2), Uniform Sales Act; Subsection (2)—none, but subsection generally continues policy of Sections 11, 44 and 69, Uniform Sales Act; Subsections (3) and (4)—none.

Changes: Completely rewritten.

Purposes of Changes and New Matter:

1. Subsection (1): "Contract for sale" is used as a general concept throughout this Article, but the rights of the parties do not vary according to whether the transaction is a present sale or a contract to sell unless the Article expressly so provides.

2. Subsection (2): It is in general intended to continue the policy of requiring exact performance by the seller of his obligations as a condition to his right to require acceptance. However, the seller is in part safeguarded against surprise as a result of sudden technicality on the buyer's part by the provisions of Section 2–508 on seller's cure of improper tender or delivery. Moreover usage of trade frequently permits commercial leeways in performance and the language of the agreement itself must be read in the light of such custom or usage and also, prior course of dealing, and in a long term contract, the course of performance.

3. Subsections (3) and (4): These subsections are intended to make clear the distinction carried forward throughout this Article between termination and cancellation.

Cross References:

Point 2: Sections 1–203, 1–205, 2–208 and 2–508.

Definitional Cross References:

"Agreement". Section 1–201.
"Buyer". Section 2–103.

Definitional Cross References:

"Contract". Section 1–201.
"Goods". Section 2–105.

"Party". Section 1–201.
"Remedy". Section 1–201.
"Rights". Section 1–201.
"Seller". Section 2–103.

Cross References

Agreements reduced to writing, exclusion of parol evidence, see Code of Civil Procedure § 1856.
Classification of goods, see Commercial Code § 9109.
Consideration, method of ascertainment, see Civil Code §§ 1612, 1613.
Contract defined, see Civil Code § 1549.
Course of dealing and usage of trade, see Commercial Code § 1205.
Course of performance or practical construction, see Commercial Code § 2208.
Executed and executory contracts, see Civil Code § 1661.
General obligations of parties to sale, see Commercial Code § 2301.
Obligation of good faith, see Commercial Code § 1203.
Passing of title, see Commercial Code § 2401.
Rejection of nonconforming tender or delivery, see Commercial Code § 2508.
Rescission of contracts, see Civil Code § 1688 et seq.
Sale by one having voidable title, see Commercial Code § 2403.
Sale defined, see Revenue and Taxation Code § 6006.

§ 2107. Goods to Be Severed From Realty; Recording

(1) A contract for the sale of minerals or the like <u>(including oil and gas)</u> or a structure or its materials to be removed from realty is a contract for the sale of goods within this division if they are to be severed by the seller but until severance a purported present sale thereof which is not effective as a transfer of an interest in land is effective only as a contract to sell.

(2) A contract for the sale apart from the land of growing crops or other things attached to realty and capable of severance without material harm thereto but not described in subdivision (1) or of timber to be cut is a contract for the sale of goods within this division whether the subject matter is to be severed by the buyer or by the seller even though it forms part of the realty at the time of contracting, and the parties can by identification effect a present sale before severance.

(3) The provisions of this section are subject to any third party rights provided by the law relating to realty records, and the contract for sale may be executed and recorded <u>in the same manner</u> as a document transferring an interest in land and shall then constitute notice to third parties of the buyer's rights under the contract for sale. *(Stats.1963, c. 819, § 2107. Amended by Stats.1974, c. 997, p. 2113, § 3, eff. Jan. 1, 1976.)*

California Code Comment
By John A. Bohn and Charles J. Williams

Prior California Law

1. Under former Civil Code § 1796, "goods" included all things "attached to or forming part of the land" which were to be severed—*by seller or buyer*—"before sale or under the contract of sale." Under section 2107, the things described in subdivision (1) are considered as goods only if severance is to be *by the seller*. Section 2107(1) appears to apply even in situations where severance would or does harm the realty. However, until severance occurs, a transaction involving a sale of things covered by subdivision (1) takes effect only as a contract to sell, subject to the possibility that an effective transfer may be made before severance by virtue of a transfer of an interest in land.

2. Subdivision (2) is consistent with former California law in that it provides that a contract is one for the present sale of goods in the

following cases: the sale of growing crops, things not covered in subdivision (1) which are capable of being severed from realty without causing material harm thereto, and timber to be cut.

The Marsh and Warren report contains this detailed discussion of the California law concerning the nature of a contract for the sale of standing timber:

"Prior to the Uniform Sales Act, a conflict of authority prevailed in the United States on whether the sale of standing timber was a sale of goods or of realty. Williston states that most of the American courts that dealt with the problem held that such a contract was one for the sale of realty. 1 Williston Sales (Rev.Ed.1948) 157. California had no clear judicial expression on the issue before the Uniform Sales Act was passed.

"The English common law rule was that the sale of standing timber, if it was not to be removed immediately, was not a contract for an interest in land. The significance of this to American lawyers is that the English rule was codified in the English Sale of Goods Act and this was, in turn, copied in writing the Uniform Sales Act. Hence, under the Sales Act, the rule came to be that any growing object attached to the soil was to be treated as goods if it was to be severed under the contract, no matter which party was to sever. Williston insists that under the Sales Act definition of goods [§ 76(1); CC § 1796(1)], a contract for the sale of standing timber should be considered the sale of goods only if the timber is to be cut *promptly*. The wording of the statute ('things attached to or forming part of the land which are agreed to be severed before sale or *under the contract of sale*') does not expressly require a prompt severance, but some cases have read in such a requirement. See, e.g., Reid v. Kier, 175 Ore. 192, 152 P.2d 417 (1944).

"However, in Palmer v. Wahler, 133 Cal.App.2d 705, 711, 285 P.2d 8 (1955), the court said:

" 'In California, under the provisions of Civil Code, Sections 658 and 660, standing timber purchased separately from the land under a contract for severance, thereby becomes personalty for all purposes depending upon the contract of purchase. As pointed out by both parties in their briefs, the legal status of standing timber is not uniform throughout the several states, and in California there are no decisions directly upon the point involved here. However, the language of Civil Code, Sections 658 and 660, is in our opinion quite clear and explicit, and regardless of what the rule is elsewhere, we are satisfied that as to those claiming under or by reason of a contract of sale, the California rule is that where standing timber is purchased separately from the land for the purpose of severance, it must thereafter be considered as "goods" or personal property.'

"Devencenzi v. Donkonics, 170 Cal.App.2d 513, 339 P.2d 232 (1959) (sale of Christmas trees to be cut by seller), and Kejr v. Construction Engineers, Inc., 111 Cal.App.2d 817, 245 P.2d 21 (1952) (sale of timber with severance to be done by buyer), lend weight to the statement in the Palmer case.

"Hence, in California under the Sales Act the sale of standing timber to be severed under the contract is a sale of goods without regard to whether the seller or the buyer is to sever. Also, the statements in the Palmer case could be construed to indicate that a sale of timber to be severed by the buyer is a sale of personal property without regard to the time of severance, contrary to the interpretation suggested by Williston.

"This section of the Code clearly categorizes a sale of standing timber to be severed by the *seller* as a sale of goods. Inferentially, sales of standing timber to be severed by the *vendee* are sales of realty. In the latter case, no distinction is made regarding the promptitude required for severance by the agreement. Thus, the Code would modify present law by classifying as a realty contract an agreement for the buyer to go on the land and remove timber without any right to prolonged occupancy of the land. If the California view is, as suggested in the Palmer case, that the time of severance by the vendee is immaterial, the Code provision would clearly change that rule." Sixth Progress Report to the Legislature by Senate Fact Finding Committee on Judiciary (1959–1961) Part 1, The Uniform Commercial Code, pp. 445–446.

3. Subdivision (3) of this section seems entirely consistent with Civil Code § 1220 which allows timber sale contracts to be recorded with like effect as though they were real estate contracts. Civil Code §§ 1213–1215 make recorded transfers in real property constructive notice to subsequent purchasers. Civil Code § 1220 deals with the recordation of contracts for the sale of standing timber.

Changes from U.C.C. (1962 Official Text)

4. Except for the treatment of standing timber, section 2107 is identical with section 2–107 of the 1962 Official Text. In the 1962 Official Text standing timber is considered "goods" only if it is to be severed by the seller. Under section 2107 a contract to sever standing timber is a contract for "goods" regardless of who severs it. Specifically, in subdivision (1) the California Code deleted the word "timber" following the clause "A contract for the sale of" and in subdivision (2) inserted "or of timber to be cut" following the phrase "in subdivision (1)".

Uniform Commercial Code Comment

Prior Uniform Statutory Provision:

See Section 76, Uniform Sales Act on prior policy; Section 7, Uniform Conditional Sales Act.

Purposes:

1. Subsection (1). Notice that this subsection applies only if the minerals or structures "are to be severed by the seller". If the buyer is to sever, such transactions are considered contracts affecting land and all problems of the Statute of Frauds and of the recording of land rights apply to them. Therefore, the Statute of Frauds section of this Article does not apply to such contracts though they must conform to the Statute of Frauds affecting the transfer of interests in land.

2. Subsection (2). "Things attached" to the realty which can be severed without material harm are goods within this Article regardless of who is to effect the severance. The word "fixtures" has been avoided because of the diverse definitions of this term, the test of "severance without material harm" being substituted.

The provision in subsection (3) for recording such contracts is within the purview of this Article since it is a means of preserving the buyer's rights under the contract of sale.

3. The security phases of things attached to or to become attached to realty are dealt with in the Article on Secured Transactions (Article 9) and it is to be noted that the definition of goods in that Article differs from the definition of goods in this Article.

However, both Articles treat as goods growing crops and also timber to be cut under a contract of severance.

Cross References:

Point 1: Section 2–201.
Point 2: Section 2–105.
Point 3: Articles 9 and 9–105.

Definitional Cross References:

"Buyer". Section 2–103.
"Contract". Section 1–201.
"Contract for sale". Section 2–106.
"Goods". Section 2–105.
"Party". Section 1–201.
"Present sale". Section 2–106.
"Rights". Section 1–201.
"Seller". Section 2–103.

Uniform Commercial Code Comment

Prior Uniform Statutory Provision:

See Section 76, Uniform Sales Act on prior policy; Section 7, Uniform Conditional Sales Act.

Purposes:

1. Subsection (1). Notice that this subsection applies only if the timber, minerals or structures "are to be severed by the seller". If the buyer is to sever, such transactions are considered contracts affecting land and all problems of the Statute of Frauds and of the recording of land rights apply to them. Therefore, the Statute of Frauds section of this Article does not apply to such contracts though they must conform to the Statute of Frauds affecting the transfer of interests in land.
[See California Code Comment, note 4.]

2. Subsection (2). "Things attached" to the realty which can be severed without material harm are goods within this Article regardless

§ 2107 SALES

of who is to effect the severance. The word "fixtures" has been avoided because of the diverse definitions of this term, the test of "severance without material harm" being substituted.

The provision in subsection (3) for recording such contracts is within the purview of this Article since it is a means of preserving the buyer's rights under the contract of sale.

3. The security phases of things attached to or to become attached to realty are dealt with in the Article on Secured Transactions (Article 9) and it is to be noted that the definition of goods in that Article differs from the definition of goods in this Article.

Cross References:

Point 1: Section 2–201.
Point 2: Section 2–105.
Point 3: Articles 9 and 9–105.

Definitional Cross References:

"Buyer". Section 2–103.
"Contract". Section 1–201.
"Contract for sale". Section 2–106.
"Goods". Section 2–105.
"Party". Section 1–201.
"Present sale". Section 2–106.
"Rights". Section 1–201.
"Seller". Section 2–103.

Cross References

Conveyance defined, see Civil Code § 1215.
Definitions pertaining to secured transactions, see Commercial Code § 9105.
"Goods" as including growing crops and other identified things attached to realty, see Commercial Code § 2105.
Oil and gas leases, manner of recording and giving constructive notice, see Civil Code § 1219.
Record of conveyances, constructive notice, see Civil Code § 1213.
Recording, effect or the want thereof, see Civil Code § 1213 et seq.
Secured transactions, see Commercial Code § 9101 et seq.
Standing timber or trees, recordation of instruments, see Civil Code § 1220.
Statute of frauds, see Commercial Code § 2201.
Subsequent conveyances, prior recording, see Civil Code § 1214.

CHAPTER 2. FORM, FORMATION AND READJUSTMENT OF CONTRACT

Section

2201. Formal Requirements; Statute of Frauds.
2202. Final Written Expression: Parol or Extrinsic Evidence.
2204. Formation in General.
2205. Firm offers; offers to supply goods to contractors.
2206. Offer and Acceptance in Formation of Contract.
2207. Additional Terms in Acceptance or Confirmation.
2208. Course of Performance or Practical Construction.
2209. Modification, Rescission and Waiver.
2210. Delegation of Performance; Assignment of Rights.

§ 2201. Formal Requirements; Statute of Frauds

(1) Except as otherwise provided in this section a contract for the sale of goods for the price of five hundred dollars ($500) or more is not enforceable by way of action or defense unless there is some writing sufficient to indicate that a contract for sale has been made between the parties and signed by the party against whom enforcement is sought or by his or her authorized agent or broker. A writing is not insufficient because it omits or incorrectly states a term agreed upon but the contract is not enforceable under this paragraph beyond the quantity of goods shown in the writing.

(2) Between merchants if within a reasonable time a writing in confirmation of the contract and sufficient against the sender is received and the party receiving it has reason to know its contents, it satisfies the requirements of subdivision (1) against the party unless written notice of objection to its contents is given within 10 days after it is received.

(3) A contract which does not satisfy the requirements of subdivision (1) but which is valid in other respects is enforceable:

(a) If the goods are to be specially manufactured for the buyer and are not suitable for sale to others in the ordinary course of the seller's business and the seller, before notice of repudiation is received and under circumstances which reasonably indicate that the goods are for the buyer, has made either a substantial beginning of their manufacture or commitments for their procurement; * * *

(b) If the party against whom enforcement is sought admits in his or her pleading, testimony, or otherwise in court that a contract for sale was made, but the contract is not enforceable under this provision beyond the quantity of goods admitted; or

(c) With respect to goods for which payment has been made and accepted or which have been received and accepted (Section 2606). (Stats.1963, c. 819, § 2201. Amended by Stats.1988, c. 1368, § 8, operative Jan. 1, 1990.)

California Code Comment

By John A. Bohn and Charles J. Williams

Prior California Law

1. The California Statute of Frauds, as contained in former Civil Code § 1624a and § 1724, is modified substantially by this section. Under former Civil Code § 1724(1), in order for a memorandum to satisfy the Statute of Frauds, it had to be a "note or memorandum in writing of the contract of sale." The California authorities, however, have been liberal as to the sufficiency of the memorandum. For example, see Skirball v. RKO Radio Pictures, Inc., 134 Cal.App.2d 843, 286 P.2d 954 (1955). Under section 2201 the memorandum is sufficient if it *indicates* "that a contract for sale has been made."

2. Section 2201 apparently liberalizes the prior California Statute of Frauds in all other respects. For example, under this section the memorandum may be indefinite, omit terms, and even incorrectly state a term.

3. With regard to the signature to the memorandum, this section is in accord with prior California cases. See, for example, Murphy v. Munson, 95 Cal.App.2d 306, 212 P.2d 603 (1949).

4. Commercial Code § 1201(39) states that "signed" includes any symbol executed or adopted by a party with present intention to authenticate a writing. This position is similar to the prior California rule as expressed in McNear v. Petroleum Export Corp., 208 Cal. 162, 280 Pac. 684 (1929) and California Canneries Co. v. Scatena, 117 Cal. 447, 49 Pac. 462 (1897).

5. Subdivision (2) of this section changes prior California law by permitting, as between merchants, written confirmation as a substitute for the memorandum in the absence of notice of objection. There was no prior California statutory authorization for such confirmation although, under prior law, the written instrument did not have to be executed at the same time. See Action Rock Co. v. Lone Pine Utilities Co., 44 Cal.App. 597, 186 Pac. 809 (1919).

6. Subdivision (3)(a) is similar to former Civil Code § 1724(2). However, the last clause requiring that the seller have "made either a substantial beginning" or "commitments for their procurement," has no counterpart in prior California law. There are situations where the California courts have recognized an estoppel to assert the statute because of a change of position but the courts required, in addition to the change of position, conduct amounting to a waiver of the statute by the other party. See Wood Lumber Co. v. Moore Lumber Co., 97 F.2d 402 (CCA 9th, 1938).

7. Subdivision (3)(c) is similar to prior California law. Under former Civil Code § 1624a there had to be an acceptance and receipt of or part payment for part of the goods in order to validate the transaction under the Statute of Frauds. However, under former Civil Code § 1624a receipt and acceptance of part of the goods or payment of part of the price validated the entire contract, while under subdivision (3)(c) the transaction is validated "with respect to goods for which payment has been made and accepted or which have been received or accepted." Official Comment 2.

8. Since "goods" as defined in section 2105 does not include "investment securities" and "things in action," section 2201 does not apply to such instruments. The Statute of Frauds provision for investment securities is contained in Commercial Code section 8319.

Changes from U.C.C. (1962 Official Text)

9. Section 2–201(3)(b) of the Official Text is deleted from the California version. That subsection would have removed an oral contract from the Statute of Frauds "if the party against whom enforcement [was] sought admitted in his pleadings, testimony, or otherwise in court that a contract . . ." had been made. A special report of a California State Bar Committee stated the reason for the deletion to be as follows:

". . . Official Text of section 12201 [2201] also provides that the requirement of a writing does not apply 'if the party against whom enforcement is sought admits in his pleading, testimony, or otherwise in court that a contract for sale was made.' . . .

The theory of the Official Text is that the Statute of Frauds intends only to prevent the enforcement of contracts not in fact made. It does not seek to prevent their enforcement just because they were oral. Accordingly, the Code drafters concluded they needed only to prevent the enforcement of oral contracts existing solely in the fraudulent allegations of a plaintiff. When a defendant admits an oral contract was made, the reason for the statute disappears.

However, there are two difficulties with the attempted limitation of the Statute of Frauds to nonexistent oral contracts. First, as drafted, it is not clear what the effect of this attempt would be. For example: Would a demurrer be an 'admission' within the meaning of this provision? Can the plaintiff force the defendant to admit or deny the contract under oath, as, for example, by interrogatories or the testimony of the defendant under section 2055 of the Code of Civil Procedure? What is meant by 'otherwise in court'? Second, even if these questions were resolved, the provisions would reward a defendant's perjured denial. If a defendant denies the existence of the oral contract, no matter how strong the proof he is lying, the contract remains unenforceable. The same contract would be enforceable against a defendant who truthfully admitted an oral contract had been made.

These objections were thought enough to justify leaving the admission innovation out . . ." California State Bar Committee on the Commercial Code, A Special Report, The Uniform Commercial Code, 37 Calif.State Bar J. (March-April, 1962), pp. 141–142.

For a more detailed discussion concerning the deletion of section 2–201(3)(b) see: The Report on Proposed Amendments to the Uniform Commercial Code by Professors Harold Marsh, Jr. and William D. Warren, Sixth Progress Report to the Legislature by Senate Fact Finding Committee on Judiciary (1959–1961), Part 1, The Uniform Commercial Code, pp. 448–450.

Uniform Commercial Code Comment

Prior Uniform Statutory Provision:

Section 4, Uniform Sales Act (which was based on Section 17 of the Statute of 29 Charles II).

Changes: Completely re-phrased; restricted to sale of goods. See also Sections 1–206, 8–319 and 9–203.

Purposes of Changes: The changed phraseology of this section is intended to make it clear that:

1. The required writing need not contain all the material terms of the contract and such material terms as are stated need not be precisely stated. All that is required is that the writing afford a basis for believing that the offered oral evidence rests on a real transaction. It may be written in lead pencil on a scratch pad. It need not indicate which party is the buyer and which the seller. The only term which must appear is the quantity term which need not be accurately stated but recovery is limited to the amount stated. The price, time and place of payment or delivery, the general quality of the goods, or any particular warranties may all be omitted.

Special emphasis must be placed on the permissibility of omitting the price term in view of the insistence of some courts on the express inclusion of this term even where the parties have contracted on the basis of a published price list. In many valid contracts for sale the parties do not mention the price in express terms, the buyer being bound to pay and the seller to accept a reasonable price which the trier of the fact may well be trusted to determine. Again, frequently the price is not mentioned since the parties have based their agreement on a price list or catalogue known to both of them and this list serves as an efficient safeguard against perjury. Finally, "market" prices and valuations that are current in the vicinity constitute a similar check. Thus if the price is not stated in the memorandum it can normally be supplied without danger of fraud. Of course if the "price" consists of goods rather than money the quantity of goods must be stated.

Only three definite and invariable requirements as to the memorandum are made by this subsection. First, it must evidence a contract for the sale of goods; second, it must be "signed", a word which includes any authentication which identifies the party to be charged; and third, it must specify a quantity.

2. "Partial performance" as a substitute for the required memorandum can validate the contract only for the goods which have been accepted or for which payment has been made and accepted.

Receipt and acceptance either of goods or of the price constitutes an unambiguous overt admission by both parties that a contract actually exists. If the court can make a just apportionment, therefore, the agreed price of any goods actually delivered can be recovered without a writing or, if the price has been paid, the seller can be forced to deliver an apportionable part of the goods. The overt actions of the parties make admissible evidence of the other terms of the contract necessary to a just apportionment. This is true even though the actions of the parties are not in themselves inconsistent with a different transaction such as a consignment for resale or a mere loan of money.

Part performance by the buyer requires the delivery of something by him that is accepted by the seller as such performance. Thus, part payment may be made by money or check, accepted by the seller. If the agreed price consists of goods or services, then they must also have been delivered and accepted.

3. Between merchants, failure to answer a written confirmation of a contract within ten days of receipt is tantamount to a writing under subsection (2) and is sufficient against both parties under subsection (1). They only effect, however, is to take away from the party who fails to answer the defense of the Statute of Frauds; the burden of persuading the trier of fact that a contract was in fact made orally prior to the written confirmation is unaffected. Compare the effect of a failure to reply under Section 2–207.

4. Failure to satisfy the requirements of this section does not render the contract void for all purposes, but merely prevents it from being judicially enforced in favor of a party to the contract. For example, a buyer who takes possession of goods as provided in an oral contract which the seller has not meanwhile repudiated, is not a trespasser. Nor would the Statute of Frauds provisions of this section be a defense to a third person who wrongfully induces a party to refuse to perform an oral contract, even though the injured party cannot maintain an action for damages against the party so refusing to perform.

5. The requirement of "signing" is discussed in the comment to Section 1–201.

6. It is not necessary that the writing be delivered to anybody. It need not be signed or authenticated by both parties but it is, of course, not sufficient against one who has not signed it. Prior to a dispute no one can determine which party's signing of the memorandum may be necessary but from the time of contracting each party should be aware that to him it is signing by the other which is important.

§ 2201

7. If the making of a contract is admitted in court, either in a written pleading, by stipulation or by oral statement before the court, no additional writing is necessary for protection against fraud. Under this section it is no longer possible to admit the contract in court and still treat the Statute as a defense. However, the contract is not thus conclusively established. The admission so made by a party is itself evidential against him of the truth of the facts so admitted and of nothing more; as against the other party, it is not evidential at all. [Inapplicable in California, see California Code Comment, note 10.]

Cross References:

See Sections 1–201, 2–202, 2–207, 2–209 and 2–304.

Definitional Cross References:

"Action". Section 1–201.
"Between merchants". Section 2–104.
"Buyer". Section 2–103.
"Contract". Section 1–201.
"Contract for sale". Section 2–106.
"Goods". Section 2–105.
"Notice". Section 1–201.
"Party". Section 1–201.
"Reasonable time". Section 1–204.
"Sale". Section 2–106.
"Seller". Section 2–103.

Cross References

Auctioneers, see Civil Code §§ 2362, 2363.
Authority to enter into contract required to be in writing must be in writing, see Civil Code § 2309.
Enforcement of contract oral by reason of fraud, see Civil Code § 1623.
Execution of instrument defined, see Code of Civil Procedure § 1933.
General definitions, see Commercial Code § 1201.
General provisions of this code relating to statute of frauds not applicable to contracts for sale of goods, see Commercial Code § 1206.
Modification, rescission and waiver, see Commercial Code § 2209.
Price payable in an interest in realty, see Commercial Code § 2304.
Sale or return contracts, see Commercial Code § 2326.
Security interests, formal requirements, see Commercial Code §§ 9203, 9302.
Statute of frauds, see Civil Code § 1624.
Terms in acceptance additional to or different from those agreed upon, see Commercial Code § 2207.
Transfer of personal property, mode, see Commercial Code §§ 2101 et seq., 2401 et seq.
Transfer of real property, mode, see Civil Code § 1091.
Written contracts, effect on negotiations or stipulations, see Civil Code § 1625.

§ 2202. Final Written Expression: Parol or Extrinsic Evidence

Terms with respect to which the confirmatory memoranda of the parties agree or which are otherwise set forth in a writing intended by the parties as a final expression of their agreement with respect to such terms as are included therein may not be contradicted by evidence of any prior agreement or of a contemporaneous oral agreement but may be explained or supplemented

 (a) By course of dealing or usage of trade (Section 1205) or by course of performance (Section 2208); and

 (b) By evidence of consistent additional terms unless the court finds the writing to have been intended also as a complete and exclusive statement of the terms of the agreement. *(Stats.1963, c. 819, § 2202.)*

California Code Comment

By John A. Bohn and Charles J. Williams

Prior California Law

1. Under prior California law, whether the parol evidence rule applied depended upon whether or not there was an "integration" or a complete expression of the agreement of the parties. Pollyanna Homes Inc. v. Berney, 56 Cal.2d 676, 16 Cal.Rptr. 345, 365 P.2d 401 (1961). For an excellent statement of the prior California rule see Spurgeon v. Buchter, 192 Cal.App.2d 198, 13 Cal.Rptr. 354 (1961).

In the absence of ambiguity, the hypothesis of California courts was that the writing of the parties was intended to be a complete "integration" of the agreement and therefore parol evidence was inadmissible. See Mangini v. Wolfschmidt, Ltd., 165 Cal.App.2d 192, 331 P.2d 728 (1958). Certain exceptions to this rule were recognized, for example, in the case of fraud or mistake in the inducement of the contract. See Tillis v. Western Fruit Growers Inc., 44 Cal.App.2d 826, 113 P.2d 267 (1941).

Under this section the theory of the former California parol evidence rule is altered. See Official Comment 1. Rather than assuming that the parties intended a fully integrated document, section 2202(b) assumes that a written contract does not express the full agreement of the parties unless the court expressly so finds.

2. Paragraph (a) enlarges the permissible use of trade usage and custom to explain or supplement a written memorandum or agreement. See Code of Civil Procedure § 1870(12) allowing usage to be put in evidence "as an instrument of interpretation," Wise v. Reeve Electronics, Inc., 183 Cal.App.2d 4, 6 Cal.Rptr. 587 (1960); and Nesbitt Fruit Products, Inc. v. Del Monte Beverages Co., 177 Cal.App.2d 353, 2 Cal.Rptr. 333 (1960).

The premise that "the course of prior dealings between the parties and the usages of trade were taken for granted when the document was phrased" (Official Comment 2), is in accord with prior California law. See California Lettuce Growers Inc. v. Union Sugar Co., 45 Cal.2d 474, 289 P.2d 785 (1955).

3. The California courts under prior law would admit in certain limited situations parol terms that were consistent with the written memorandum or agreement. See Johnson v. Bibb (D.H.) Lbr. Co., 140 Cal. 95, 73 Pac. 730 (1903) and Bouchard v. Cole, 143 Cal.App.2d 93, 299 P.2d 697 (1956).

4. Some of the statutory aids in the interpretation of contracts are contained in Civil Code § 1625 (written agreement supersedes prior negotiations) § 1647 (contract may be explained by circumstances) and Code of Civil Procedure § 1856 (agreement in writing considered as containing the entire agreement) and § 1857 (language of agreement to be interpreted according to its relation to the place of execution).

Changes from U.C.C. (1962 Official Text)

5. This is section 2–202 of the Official Text without change.

Uniform Commercial Code Comment

Prior Uniform Statutory Provision:
None.

Purposes:

1. This section definitely rejects:

 (a) Any assumption that because a writing has been worked out which is final on some matters, it is to be taken as including all the matters agreed upon;

 (b) The premise that the language used has the meaning attributable to such language by rules of construction existing in the law rather than the meaning which arises out of the commercial context in which it was used; and

 (c) The requirement that a condition precedent to the admissibility of the type of evidence specified in paragraph (a) is an original determination by the court that the language used is ambiguous.

2. Paragraph (a) makes admissible evidence of course of dealing, usage of trade and course of performance to explain or supplement the terms of any writing stating the agreement of the parties in order that the true understanding of the parties as to the agreement may be reached. Such writings are to be read on the assumption that the course of prior dealings between the parties and the usages of trade

were taken for granted when the document was phrased. Unless carefully negated they have become an element of the meaning of the words used. Similarly, the course of actual performance by the parties is considered the best indication of what they intended the writing to mean.

3. Under paragraph (b) consistent additional terms, not reduced to writing, may be proved unless the court finds that the writing was intended by both parties as a complete and exclusive statement of all the terms. If the additional terms are such that, if agreed upon, they would certainly have been included in the document in the view of the court, then evidence of their alleged making must be kept from the trier of fact.

Cross References:

Point 3: Sections 1–205, 2–207, 2–302 and 2–316.

Definitional Cross References:

"Agreed" and "agreement". Section 1–201.
"Course of dealing". Section 1–205.
"Parties". Section 1–201.
"Term". Section 1–201.
"Usage of trade". Section 1–205.
"Written" and "writing". Section 1–201.

Cross References

Acceptance stating additional or different terms, see Commercial Code § 2207.
Agreements reduced to writing, exclusion of parol evidence, see Code of Civil Procedure § 1856.
Interpretation of contracts,
  Generally, see Civil Code § 1635 et seq.
  Conclusive effect of recited facts, see Evidence Code § 622.
  Contracts explained by circumstances, see Civil Code § 1647.
  Intent of parties, ascertainment from writing, see Civil Code § 1639.
  Writing disregarded, see Civil Code § 1640.
Sale or return contracts, see Commercial Code § 2326.
Statute of frauds, see Civil Code § 1624.
Usage to explain true character of conduct, facts provable on trial, see Code of Civil Procedure § 1870.
Warranty, words or conduct tending to negate or limit, see Commercial Code § 2316.

§ 2203. [Not enacted in California]

California Code Comment

By John A. Bohn and Charles J. Williams

Prior California Law

1. Section 2–203 of the 1962 Official Text of the Uniform Commercial Code is omitted from the California version of the Commercial Code.

This omitted section is the same in substance as former Civil Code §§ 1629 and 1723 and Code of Civil Procedure § 1932 all of which abolished the distinction between sealed and unsealed writings in California.

Changes from U.C.C. (1962 Official Text)

2. Section 2–203 of the Official Text reads as follows:
"Seals Inoperative.

The affixing of a seal to a writing evidencing a contract for sale or an offer to buy or sell goods does not constitute the writing a sealed instrument and the law with respect to sealed instruments does not apply to such a contract or offer."

§ 2204. Formation in General

(1) A contract for sale of goods may be made in any manner sufficient to show agreement, including conduct by both parties which recognizes the existence of such a contract.

(2) An agreement sufficient to constitute a contract for sale may be found even though the moment of its making is undetermined.

(3) Even though one or more terms are left open a contract for sale does not fail for indefiniteness if the parties have intended to make a contract and there is a reasonably certain basis for giving an appropriate remedy. (Stats.1963, c. 819, § 2204.)

California Code Comment

By John A. Bohn and Charles J. Williams

Prior California Law

1. Subdivisions (1) and (2) are in substantial accord with former Civil Code §§ 1721 and 1723.

2. Although there was no prior California statute comparable to subdivision (3), California courts had formulated a somewhat similar rule. For example, see Ellis v. Klaff, 96 Cal.App.2d 471, 479, 216 P.2d 15, 20 (1950) where the court states, "although the terms of a contract need not be stated in the minutest detail, it is requisite to enforceability that it must evidence a meeting of the minds upon the essential features of the agreement, and that the scope of the duty and limits of acceptable performance be at least sufficiently defined to provide a rational basis for the assessment of damages." Also quoted in Richards v. Oliver, 162 Cal.App.2d 548, 328 P.2d 544 (1958). Subdivision (3) appears to extend this rule in two respects: First, "a meeting of the minds on the essential features of the agreement" is not required but merely an "intent to make a contract" and, second, rather than a "rational basis for the assessment of *damages*" (emphasis added) the section only requires that there be a reasonable basis for giving *an appropriate remedy*. Of course, the actual difference, if any, will depend upon the court's construction of these two new phrases.

Changes from U.C.C. (1962 Official Text)

3. This is section 2–204 of the Official Text without change.

Uniform Commercial Code Comment

Prior Uniform Statutory Provision:

Sections 1 and 3, Uniform Sales Act.

Changes: Completely rewritten by this and other sections of this Article.

Purposes of Changes:

Subsection (1) continues without change the basic policy of recognizing any manner of expression of agreement, oral, written or otherwise. The legal effect of such an agreement is, of course, qualified by other provisions of this Article.

Under subsection (1) appropriate conduct by the parties may be sufficient to establish an agreement. Subsection (2) is directed primarily to the situation where the interchanged correspondence does not disclose the exact point at which the deal was closed, but the actions of the parties indicate that a binding obligation has been undertaken.

Subsection (3) states the principle as to "open terms" underlying later sections of the Article. If the parties intend to enter into a binding agreement, this subsection recognizes that agreement as valid in law, despite missing terms, if there is any reasonably certain basis for granting a remedy. The test is not certainty as to what the parties were to do nor as to the exact amount of damages due the plaintiff. Nor is the fact that one or more terms are left to be agreed upon enough of itself to defeat an otherwise adequate agreement. Rather, commercial standards on the point of "indefiniteness" are intended to be applied, this Act making provision elsewhere for missing terms needed for performance, open price, remedies and the like.

The more terms the parties leave open, the less likely it is that they have intended to conclude a binding agreement, but their actions may be frequently conclusive on the matter despite the omissions.

Cross References:

Subsection (1): Sections 1–103, 2–201 and 2–302.

§ 2204

Subsection (2): Sections 2-205 through 2-209.
Subsection (3): See Part 3.

Definitional Cross References:

"Agreement". Section 1-201.
"Contract". Section 1-201.
"Contract for sale". Section 2-106.
"Goods". Section 2-105.
"Party". Section 1-201.
"Remedy". Section 1-201.
"Term". Section 1-201.

Cross References

Essential elements of contract, see Civil Code § 1550.
Interpretation of contracts, see Civil Code § 1635 et seq.
Manner of creating contracts, see Civil Code § 1619 et seq.
Offer and acceptance, see Commercial Code § 2206.
Open price term, see Commercial Code § 2305.
Requisites of contract, see Commercial Code § 2201.
Statute of frauds, see Commercial Code § 2201.
Supplementation of code by principles of law and equity, see Commercial Code § 1103.
Written contracts, effect on negotiations or stipulations, see Civil Code § 1625.

§ 2205. Firm offers; offers to supply goods to contractors

(a) An offer by a merchant to buy or sell goods in a signed writing which by its terms gives assurance that it will be held open is not revocable, for lack of consideration, during the time stated or if no time is stated for a reasonable time, but in no event may such period of irrevocability exceed three months; but any such term of assurance on a form supplied by the offeree must be separately signed by the offeror.

(b) Notwithstanding subdivision (a), when a merchant renders an offer, oral or written, to supply goods to a contractor licensed pursuant to the provisions of Chapter 9 (commencing with Section 7000) of Division 3 of the Business and Professions Code or a similar contractor's licensing law of another state, and the merchant has actual or imputed knowledge that the contractor is so licensed, and that the offer will be relied upon by the contractor in the submission of its bid for a construction contract with a third party, the offer relied upon shall be irrevocable, notwithstanding lack of consideration, for 10 days after the awarding of the contract to the prime contractor, but in no event for more than 90 days after the date the bid or offer was rendered by the merchant; except that an oral bid or offer, when for a price of two thousand five hundred dollars ($2,500) or more, shall be confirmed in writing by the contractor or his or her agent within 48 hours after it is rendered. Failure by the contractor to confirm such offer in writing shall release the merchant from his or her offer. Nothing in this subdivision shall prevent a merchant from providing that the bid or offer will be held open for less than the time provided for herein. (Stats.1963, c. 819, § 2205. Amended by Stats. 1980, c. 537, p. 1488, § 1.)

California Code Comment

By John A. Bohn and Charles J. Williams

Prior California Law

1. This section replaces former Civil Code §§ 1721 and 1723.

2. In the case of "merchants" (defined in section 2104(1)) this section changes prior California law which required consideration to support an offer that was to remain open. Reese v. House, 162 Cal. 740, 124 Pac. 442 (1912) and Kelley v. Upshaw, 39 Cal.2d 179, 246 P.2d 23 (1952) (See also Civil Code § 1586 for the general rule on revocation of an offer). Apparently an option may still be given for consideration and thereby be made irrevocable for any length of time without any need to rely upon this section.

3. An offer meeting the requirements of this section which states no definite period in which it will be held open is not revocable for a reasonable period of time, but this period may not exceed three calendar months. The three month period is arbitrary. However, a reasonable period may, on the facts, conceivably be a much shorter period of time, especially in a period of a rapidly rising or falling market with respect to the commodity of goods involved in the offer.

4. Note that this section relates only to offers in a signed writing. Apparently the law relating to verbal offers is unaffected by this section.

Changes from U.C.C. (1962 Official Text)

5. This is section 2-205 of the Official Text without change.

Uniform Commercial Code Comment

Prior Uniform Statutory Provision:

Sections 1 and 3, Uniform Sales Act.

Changes: Completely rewritten by this and other sections of this Article.

Purposes of Changes:

1. This section is intended to modify the former rule which required that "firm offers" be sustained by consideration in order to bind, and to require instead that they must merely be characterized as such and expressed in signed writings.

2. The primary purpose of this section is to give effect to the deliberate intention of a merchant to make a current firm offer binding. The deliberation is shown in the case of an individualized document by the merchant's signature to the offer, and in the case of an offer included on a form supplied by the other party to the transaction by the separate signing of the particular clause which contains the offer. "Signed" here also includes authentication but the reasonableness of the authentication herein allowed must be determined in the light of the purpose of the section. The circumstances surrounding the signing may justify something less than a formal signature or initialing but typically the kind of authentication involved here would consist of a minimum of initialing of the clause involved. A handwritten memorandum on the writer's letterhead purporting in its terms to "confirm" a firm offer already made would be enough to satisfy this section, although not subscribed, since under the circumstances it could not be considered a memorandum of mere negotiation and it would adequately show its own authenticity. Similarly, an authorized telegram will suffice, and this is true even though the original draft contained only a type-written signature. However, despite settled courses of dealing or usages of the trade whereby firm offers are made by oral communication and relied upon without more evidence, such offers remain revocable under this Article since authentication by a writing is the essence of this section.

3. This section is intended to apply to current "firm" offers and not to long term options, and an outside time limit of three months during which such offers remain irrevocable has been set. The three month period during which firm offers remain irrevocable under this section need not be stated by days or by date. If the offer states that it is "guaranteed" or "firm" until the happening of a contingency which will occur within the three month period, it will remain irrevocable until that event. A promise made for a longer period will operate under this section to bind the offeror only for the first three months of the period but may of course be renewed. If supported by consideration it may continue for as long as the parties specify. This section deals only with the offer which is not supported by consideration.

4. Protection is afforded against the inadvertent signing of a firm offer when contained in a form prepared by the offeree by requiring that such a clause be separately authenticated. If the offer clause is called to the offeror's attention and he separately authenticates it, he will be bound; Section 2-302 may operate, however, to prevent an unconscio-

nable result which otherwise would flow from other terms appearing in the form.

5. Safeguards are provided to offer relief in the case of material mistake by virtue of the requirement of good faith and the general law of mistake.

Cross References:

Point 1: Section 1–102.
Point 2: Section 1–102.
Point 3: Section 2–201.
Point 5: Section 2–302.

Definitional Cross References:

"Goods". Section 2–105.
"Merchant". Section 2–104.
"Signed". Section 1–201.
"Writing". Section 1–201.

Cross References

Essential elements of contract, see Civil Code § 1550.
Formal requisites of contract, see Commercial Code § 2201.
Purpose of code, see Commercial Code § 1102.
Reasonable time, see Commercial Code § 1204.
Revocation of proposal, time, see Civil Code § 1586.

§ 2206. Offer and Acceptance in Formation of Contract

(1) Unless otherwise unambiguously indicated by the language or circumstances

(a) An offer to make a contract shall be construed as inviting acceptance in any manner and by any medium reasonable in the circumstances;

(b) An order or other offer to buy goods for prompt or current shipment shall be construed as inviting acceptance either by a prompt promise to ship or by the prompt or current shipment of conforming or nonconforming goods, but such a shipment of nonconforming goods does not constitute an acceptance if the seller seasonably notifies the buyer that the shipment is offered only as an accommodation to the buyer.

(2) Where the beginning of a requested performance is a reasonable mode of acceptance an offeror who is not notified of acceptance within a reasonable time may treat the offer as having lapsed before acceptance. (Stats.1963, c. 819, § 2206.)

California Code Comment

By John A. Bohn and Charles J. Williams

Prior California Law

1. Subdivision (1)(a) authorizes acceptance by any reasonable means in the absence of a clear expression by the offeror that acceptance must be by a particular means. This is in accord with prior California law as expressed in Civil Code § 1582; Davis v. Jacoby, 1 Cal.2d 370, 34 P.2d 1026 (1934) and People v. Twedt, 1 Cal.2d 392, 35 P.2d 324 (1934). Also see Civil Code §§ 1565, 1580–1588 for provisions dealing with consent and the acceptance of an offer for contracts in general.

2. The first part of subdivision (1)(b) relating to acceptance by a promise to ship or by a prompt shipment of conforming goods is in accord with prior California law as expressed in Beatty v. Oakland Sheet Metal etc. Co., 111 Cal.App.2d 53, 244 P.2d 25 (1952); Ennis Brown Co. v. W. S. Hurst & Co., 1 Cal.App. 752, 82 Pac. 1056 (1905). The second part of subdivision (1)(b) relating to acceptance by a shipment of non-conforming goods is entirely new law in California.

3. With regard to notice of acceptance of offer and who may accept, see Canney v. S. P. Coast R.R., 63 Cal. 501 (1883). For discussion of reasonable time see Los Angeles Traction Co. v. Wilshire, 135 Cal. 654, 67 Pac. 1086 (1902).

Changes from U.C.C. (1962 Official Text)

4. This is section 2–206 of the Official Text without change.

Uniform Commercial Code Comment

Prior Uniform Statutory Provision:

Sections 1 and 3, Uniform Sales Act.

Changes: Completely rewritten in this and other sections of this Article.

Purposes of Changes: To make it clear that:

1. Any reasonable manner of acceptance is intended to be regarded as available unless the offeror has made quite clear that it will not be acceptable. Former technical rules as to acceptance, such as requiring that telegraphic offers be accepted by telegraphed acceptance, etc., are rejected and a criterion that the acceptance be "in any manner and by any medium reasonable under the circumstances," is substituted. This section is intended to remain flexible and its applicability to be enlarged as new media of communication develop or as the more time-saving present day media come into general use.

2. Either shipment or a prompt promise to ship is made a proper means of acceptance of an offer looking to current shipment. In accordance with ordinary commercial understanding the section interprets an order looking to current shipment as allowing acceptance either by actual shipment or by a prompt promise to ship and rejects the artificial theory that only a single mode of acceptance is normally envisaged by an offer. This is true even though the language of the offer happens to be "ship at once" or the like. "Shipment" is here used in the same sense as in Section 2–504; it does not include the beginning of delivery by the seller's own truck or by messenger. But loading on the seller's own truck might be a beginning of performance under subsection (2).

3. The beginning of performance by an offeree can be effective as acceptance so as to bind the offeror only if followed within a reasonable time by notice to the offeror. Such a beginning of performance must unambiguously express the offeree's intention to engage himself. For the protection of both parties it is essential that notice follow in due course to constitute acceptance. Nothing in this section however bars the possibility that under the common law performance begun may have an intermediate effect of temporarily barring revocation of the offer, or at the offeror's option, final effect in constituting acceptance.

4. Subsection (1)(b) deals with the situation where a shipment made following an order is shown by a notification of shipment to be referable to that order but has a defect. Such a non-conforming shipment is normally to be understood as intended to close the bargain, even though it proves to have been at the same time a breach. However, the seller by stating that the shipment is non-conforming and is offered only as an accommodation to the buyer keeps the shipment or notification from operating as an acceptance.

Definitional Cross References:

"Buyer". Section 2–103.
"Conforming". Section 2–106.
"Contract". Section 1–201.
"Goods". Section 2–105.
"Notifies". Section 1–201.
"Reasonable time". Section 1–204.

Cross References

Acceptance of proposal, see Civil Code §§ 1584, 1585.
Communicating consent and acceptance of proposal, see Civil Code §§ 1581, 1582.
Essentials of consent, nature of contract, see Civil Code § 1565.
Formation of contract, see Commercial Code § 2204.
Mutuality of consent, see Civil Code § 1580.

§ 2206

Revocation of proposal, method, see Civil Code § 1587.

§ 2207. Additional Terms in Acceptance or Confirmation

(1) A definite and seasonable expression of acceptance or a written confirmation which is sent within a reasonable time operates as an acceptance even though it states terms additional to or different from those offered or agreed upon, unless acceptance is expressly made conditional on assent to the additional or different terms.

(2) The additional terms are to be construed as proposals for addition to the contract. Between merchants such terms become part of the contract unless:

(a) The offer expressly limits acceptance to the terms of the offer;

(b) They materially alter it; or

(c) Notification of objection to them has already been given or is given within a reasonable time after notice of them is received.

(3) Conduct by both parties which recognizes the existence of a contract is sufficient to establish a contract for sale although the writings of the parties do not otherwise establish a contract. In such case the terms of the particular contract consist of those terms on which the writings of the parties agree, together with any supplementary terms incorporated under any other provisions of this code. (Stats.1963, c. 819, § 2207.)

California Code Comment

By John A. Bohn and Charles J. Williams

Prior California Law

1. In Apablasa v. Merritt & Co., 176 Cal.App.2d 719, 1 Cal.Rptr. 500 (1959), the court undertook to summarize the California authorities on acceptance in these terms: "It is fundamental that without consent of the parties, which must be mutual, no contract can exist . . . Hence, terms proposed in an offer must be met exactly, precisely and unequivocally for its acceptance to result in the formation of a binding contract (cases cited) and a qualified acceptance amounts to a new proposal or counteroffer putting an end to the original offer. (Cases cited) An offer must be approved in the terms in which it is made. The addition of any condition or limitation is tantamount to a rejection of the original offer and the making of a counteroffer." See, for example, Civil Code § 1585, (acceptance must be absolute); Four Oil Co. v. United Oil Products, 145 Cal. 623, 79 Pac. 366 (1904); Robbins v. Pacific Eastern Corp., 8 Cal.2d 241, 65 P.2d 42 (1937); Born v. Koop, 200 Cal.App.2d 519, 19 Cal.Rptr. 379 (1962). The provisions of this section are probably less of a change in law than might be supposed from the foregoing quoted statement. In a number of cases the California courts were quite liberal in finding that a binding contract had been made even though the offeree added terms to his acceptance. See Kahn v. Lischner, 128 Cal.App.2d 480, 275 P.2d 539 (1954); Turner v. Stock, 79 Cal.App. 662, 251 Pac. 814 (1925); Allen v. Laughlin Fruit Refiners, 57 Cal.App. 46, 206 Pac. 475 (1922); McCowen v. Pew, 18 Cal.App. 302, 123 Pac. 191 (1912); Ennis Brown Co. v. Hurst, 1 Cal.App. 752, 82 Pac. 1056 (1905).

2. The effect of this section is to allow the creation of a valid contract when there is mutual assent between the parties even though the acceptance is not in identical terms with the offer.

3. There are California cases holding that mere silence and inaction constitute consent and assent to an offer such as would be true in the case of merchants under subdivision (2). Taussig v. Bode, et al., 134 Cal. 260, 66 Pac. 259 (1901). Fidelity & Cas. Co. v. Fresno Co., 161 Cal. 466, 119 Pac. 646 (1911). But see, contra, Leslie v. Brown Bros., Inc., 208 Cal. 606, 283 Pac. 936 (1903). There is a necessary implication from subdivision (2) that the parties may still be bound on the agreement though there is a difference arising between them and no agreement on a particular term.

4. It would appear that this section, by virtue of section 10103 of the Commercial Code modifies Civil Code § 1585. See Civil Code §§ 1494, 1497, 1581–1582 for related provisions dealing with obligations and contracts in general.

Changes from U.C.C. (1962 Official Text)

5. This is section 2–207 of the Official Text without change.

Uniform Commercial Code Comment
1966 Amendment

Purposes of Changes:

1. This section is intended to deal with two typical situations. The one is the written confirmation, where an agreement has been reached either orally or by informal correspondence between the parties and is followed by one or both of the parties sending formal memoranda embodying the terms so far as agreed upon and adding terms not discussed. The other situation is offer and acceptance, in which a wire or letter expressed and intended as an acceptance or the closing of an agreement adds further minor suggestions or proposals such as "ship by Tuesday," "rush," "ship draft against bill of lading inspection allowed," or the like. A frequent example of the second situation is the exchange of printed purchase order and acceptance (sometimes called "acknowledgment") forms. Because the forms are oriented to the thinking of the respective drafting parties, the terms contained in them often do not correspond. Often the seller's form contains terms different from or additional to those set forth in the buyer's form. Nevertheless, the parties proceed with the transaction.

2. Under this Article a proposed deal which in commercial understanding has in fact been closed is recognized as a contract. Therefore, any additional matter contained in the confirmation or in the acceptance falls within subsection (2) and must be regarded as a proposal for an added term unless the acceptance is made conditional on the acceptance of the additional or different terms.

* * * * * *

6. If no answer is received within a reasonable time after additional terms are proposed, it is both fair and commercially sound to assume that their inclusion has been assented to. Where clauses on confirming forms sent by both parties conflict each party must be assumed to object to a clause of the other conflicting with one on the confirmation sent by himself. As a result the requirement that there be notice of objection which is found in subsection (2) is satisfied and the conflicting terms do not become a part of the contract. The contract then consists of the terms originally expressly agreed to, terms on which the confirmations agree, and terms supplied by this Act, including subsection (2). The written confirmation is also subject to Section 2–201. Under that section a failure to respond permits enforcement of a prior oral agreement; under this section a failure to respond permits additional terms to become part of the agreement.

7. In many cases, as where goods are shipped, accepted and paid for before any dispute arises, there is no question whether a contract has been made. In such cases, where the writings of the parties do not establish a contract, it is not necessary to determine which act or document constituted the offer and which the acceptance. See Section 2–204. The only question is what terms are included in the contract, and subsection (3) furnishes the governing rule.

Uniform Commercial Code Comment

Prior Uniform Statutory Provision:

Sections 1 and 3, Uniform Sales Act.

Changes: Completely rewritten by this and other sections of this Article.

Purposes of Changes:

1. This section is intended to deal with two typical situations. The one is where an agreement has been reached either orally or by informal correspondence between the parties and is followed by one or both of the parties sending formal acknowledgments or memoranda embodying the terms so far as agreed upon and adding terms not discussed. The

other situation is one in which a wire or letter expressed and intended as the closing or confirmation of an agreement adds further minor suggestions or proposals such as "ship by Tuesday," "rush," "ship draft against bill of lading inspection allowed," or the like.

2. Under this Article a proposed deal which in commercial understanding has in fact been closed is recognized as a contract. Therefore, any additional matter contained either in the writing intended to close the deal or in a later confirmation falls within subsection (2) and must be regarded as a proposal for an added term unless the acceptance is made conditional on the acceptance of the additional terms.

3. Whether or not additional or different terms will become part of the agreement depends upon the provisions of subsection (2). If they are such as materially to alter the original bargain, they will not be included unless expressly agreed to by the other party. If, however, they are terms which would not so change the bargain they will be incorporated unless notice of objection to them has already been given or is given within a reasonable time.

4. Examples of typical clauses which would normally "materially alter" the contract and so result in surprise or hardship if incorporated without express awareness by the other party are: a clause negating such standard warranties as that of merchantability or fitness for a particular purpose in circumstances in which either warranty normally attaches; a clause requiring a guaranty of 90% or 100% deliveries in a case such as a contract by cannery, where the usage of the trade allows greater quantity leeways; a clause reserving to the seller the power to cancel upon the buyer's failure to meet any invoice when due; a clause requiring that complaints be made in a time materially shorter than customary or reasonable.

5. Examples of clauses which involve no element of unreasonable surprise and which therefore are to be incorporated in the contract unless notice of objection is seasonably given are: a clause setting forth and perhaps enlarging slightly upon the seller's exemption due to supervening causes beyond his control, similar to those covered by the provision of this Article on merchant's excuse by failure of presupposed conditions or a clause fixing in advance any reasonable formula of proration under such circumstances; a clause fixing a reasonable time for complaints within customary limits, or in the case of a purchase for subsale, providing for inspection by the sub-purchaser; a clause providing for interest on overdue invoices or fixing the seller's standard credit terms where they are within the range of trade practice and do not limit any credit bargained for; a clause limiting the right of rejection for defects which fall within the customary trade tolerances for acceptance "with adjustment" or otherwise limiting remedy in a reasonable manner (see Sections 2–718 and 2–719).

6. If no answer is received within a reasonable time after additional terms are proposed, it is both fair and commercially sound to assume that their inclusion has been assented to. Where clauses on confirming forms sent by both parties conflict each party must be assumed to object to a clause of the other conflicting with one on the confirmation sent by himself. As a result the requirement that there be notice of objection which is found in subsection (2) is satisfied and the conflicting terms do not become a part of the contract. The contract then consists of the terms originally expressly agreed to, terms on which the confirmations agree, and terms supplied by this Act, including subsection (2).

Cross References:

See generally Section 2–302.
Point 5: Sections 2–513, 2–602, 2–607, 2–609, 2–612, 2–614, 2–615, 2–616, 2–718 and 2–719.
Point 6: Sections 1–102 and 2–104.

Definitional Cross References:

"Between merchants". Section 2–104.
"Contract". Section 1–201.
"Notification". Section 1–201.
"Reasonable time". Section 1–204.
"Seasonably". Section 1–204.
"Send". Section 1–201.
"Term". Section 1–201.
"Written". Section 1–201.

Cross References

Absolute acceptance of proposal, see Civil Code § 1585.
Acceptance of goods by buyer, see Commercial Code § 2607.
Assurance of performance, effect of acceptance of improper delivery or payment, see Commercial Code § 2609.
Communicating acceptance of proposal, see Civil Code § 1582.
Communication of consent, see Civil Code § 1581 et seq.
Conditional offer of performance, see Civil Code § 1494.
Consent to contract, see Civil Code § 1565 et seq.
Construction of code, see Commercial Code § 1102.
Damages for breach, liquidation or limitation, see Commercial Code § 2718.
Delay in delivery or nondelivery, see Commercial Code §§ 2615, 2616.
Extinction of obligation, see Civil Code § 1485 et seq.
Inspection of goods by buyer before payment or acceptance, see Commercial Code § 2513.
Installment contracts, acceptance of goods in separate lots, see Commercial Code § 2612.
Rejection of goods, see Commercial Code § 2602.
Remedies, modification or limitation by terms of contract, see Commercial Code § 2719.
Substituted performance, see Commercial Code § 2614.

§ 2208. Course of Performance or Practical Construction

(1) Where the contract for sale involves repeated occasions for performance by either party with knowledge of the nature of the performance and opportunity for objection to it by the other, any course of performance accepted or acquiesced in without objection shall be relevant to determine the meaning of the agreement.

(2) The express terms of the agreement and any such course of performance, as well as any course of dealing and usage of trade, shall be construed whenever reasonable as consistent with each other; but when such construction is unreasonable, express terms shall control course of performance and course of performance shall control both course of dealing and usage of trade (Section 1205).

(3) Subject to the provisions of the next section on modification and waiver, such course of performance shall be relevant to show a waiver or modification of any term inconsistent with such course of performance. (Stats.1963, c. 819, § 2208.)

California Code Comment

By John A. Bohn and Charles J. Williams

Prior California Law

1. There is no prior California statute comparable to this section. However, California courts did use evidence of "course of performance" or "conduct of the parties" as aids in interpreting the meaning of agreements. This was particularly true when they found ambiguity or uncertainty present. See former Civil Code § 1791 and § 1723. Also see California Code Comment to section 2202, *supra*.

Changes from U.C.C. (1962 Official Text)

2. This is section 2–208 of the Official Text without change.

Uniform Commercial Code Comment

Prior Uniform Statutory Provision:

No such general provision but concept of this section recognized by terms such as "course of dealing", "the circumstances of the case," "the conduct of the parties," etc., in Uniform Sales Act.

Purposes:

1. The parties themselves know best what they have meant by their words of agreement and their action under that agreement is the best indication of what that meaning was. This section thus rounds out the

set of factors which determines the meaning of the "agreement" and therefore also of the "unless otherwise agreed" qualification to various provisions of this Article.

2. Under this section a course of performance is always relevant to determine the meaning of the agreement. Express mention of course of performance elsewhere in this Article carries no contrary implication when there is a failure to refer to it in other sections.

3. Where it is difficult to determine whether a particular act merely sheds light on the meaning of the agreement or represents a waiver of a term of the agreement, the preference is in favor of "waiver" whenever such construction, plus the application of the provisions on the reinstatement of rights waived (see Section 2–209), is needed to preserve the flexible character of commercial contracts and to prevent surprise or other hardship.

4. A single occasion of conduct does not fall within the language of this section but other sections such as the ones on silence after acceptance and failure to specify particular defects can affect the parties' rights on a single occasion (see Sections 2–605 and 2–607).

Cross References:

Point 1: Section 1–201.
Point 2: Section 2–202.
Point 3: Sections 2–209, 2–601 and 2–607.
Point 4: Sections 2–605 and 2–607.

Cross References

Acceptance of goods, see Commercial Code § 2607.
Buyer's options if goods or tender of delivery do not conform to contract, see Commercial Code § 2601.
Definitions, see Commercial Code § 1201.
Explanation or supplementation of terms by course of performance, see Commercial Code § 2202.
Mutual intention to be given effect, see Civil Code § 1636.
Object of contract, see Civil Code § 1595 et seq.
Sense of words, interpretation of contracts, see Civil Code § 1644.
Waiver by buyer of grounds for rejection by failure to particularize, see Commercial Code § 2605.

§ 2209. Modification, Rescission and Waiver

(1) An agreement modifying a contract within this division needs no consideration to be binding.

(2) A * * * <u>signed agreement * * * which excludes modification or rescission</u> except by a signed writing cannot be otherwise modified * * * or <u>rescinded, but except as between merchants such a requirement on a form supplied by the merchant must be separately signed by the other party.</u>

(3) The requirements of the statute of frauds section of this division (Section 2201) must be satisfied if the contract as modified is within its provisions.

(4) Although an attempt at modification or rescission does not satisfy the requirements of subdivision (2) or (3) it can operate as a waiver.

(5) A party who has made a waiver affecting an executory portion of the contract may retract the waiver by reasonable notification received by the other party that strict performance will be required of any term waived, unless the retraction would be unjust in view of a material change of position in reliance on the waiver. (Stats.1963, c. 819, § 2209. Amended by Stats.1967, c. 799, p. 2206, § 3; Stats.1975, c. 7, p. 7, § 1.)

California Code Comment

By Charles J. Williams

The 1967 amendment adds subdivision (3) to this section. Subdivision (4) is amended by adding the reference to subdivision (3). This amendment brings this subdivision of the California version into conformity with the Official Text.

Originally, subdivision (3) was omitted in the California version because of the California variation in subdivision (2), which still exists. See California Code Comments 6 and 7. However, the Permanent Editorial Board comments that the deletion of subdivision (3) "seems to be a mistake based on failure to see that subsection [subdivision] (1) applies to oral modifications of oral contracts". (Permanent Editorial Board for the Uniform Commercial Code, Report No. 2, p. 35.)

California Code Comment

By John A. Bohn and Charles J. Williams

Prior California Law

1. Under prior California law a written contract could be altered "by a contract in writing . . ." Civil Code § 1698. This rule is retained in this section of the code. However, under prior California law a written agreement to modify a pre-existing written contract had to be supported by consideration. See Main Street & Agricultural Park R.R. v. Los Angeles Traction Co., 129 Cal. 301, 61 Pac. 937 (1900). This "pre-existing duty" rule made it difficult for the court to find consideration sufficient to support such an agreement. See Sullivan v. Sullivan, 99 Cal. 187, 33 Pac. 862 (1893) cited in Pacific Finance Corp. v. First Nat. Bank, 4 Cal.2d 47, 47 P.2d 460, (1935). Section 2209(1) eliminates this problem by providing that an oral or written agreement modifying a contract within Division 2 of this code "needs no consideration to be binding."

2. Under prior California law a written contract could be altered by "an executed oral agreement." Civil Code § 1698. The California courts construed the requirement of execution as requiring, in most cases, execution by both parties. Stolenberg v. Harveston, 1 Cal.2d 264, 34 P.2d 472 (1934). However in D. L. Godbey & Sons Const. Co. v. Deane, 39 Cal.2d 429, 246 P.2d 946 (1952) the court held that although an oral modification usually had to be executed by both parties, if the agreement was supported by consideration, then execution by only one of the parties would be sufficient to validate the modification of the prior written contract. Section 2209(2) retains prior California law in requiring execution "by both parties" in the case of oral modification unsupported by consideration and expressly abrogates the rule of D. L. Godbey & Sons v. Deane, 39 Cal.2d 429, 246 P.2d 946 (1952), by providing that the two methods outlined in this section are the "only" means by which a written contract may be modified.

3. While eliminating the requirement of consideration in order to modify a prior written contract, section 2209 does not free one to extort additional consideration by refusing in bad faith to carry out his original commitment. Section 1203 imposes a duty of "good faith" in all transactions. This includes for a merchant (defined in § 2104(1)) the observation of "reasonable commercial standards of fair dealing."

4. Although there was no prior California statute comparable to section 2209(3), the California authorities expressly recognized the doctrine of waiver as an ameliorating factor in cases falling within Civil Code § 1698. See Panno v. Russo, 82 Cal.App.2d 408, 186 P.2d 452 (1947).

5. Under prior California law, a prior oral contract could be modified by a written agreement and no new consideration was required. See Civil Code § 1697. This section is not repealed by the Commercial Code and therefore should be complied with in cases involving modification of an oral contract.

Changes from U.C.C. (1962 Official Text)

6. Subdivision (2) was changed in the California version in order to retain the rule of Civil Code § 1698. Subsection (2) of the Official Text reads as follows: "(2) A signed agreement which excludes modification or rescission except by a signed writing cannot be otherwise modified or rescinded, but except as between merchants such a requirement on a form supplied by the merchant must be separately signed by the other party."

7. Subdivision (3) is omitted from the California version because of the change made in subdivision (2). Sixth Progress Report to the Legislature by Senate Fact Finding Committee on Judiciary (1959–1961) Part 1, The Uniform Commercial Code, p. 454.

Subsection (3) of the Official Text reads as follows: "(3) The requirements of the statute of frauds section of this Article (Section 2-201) must be satisfied if the contract as modified is within its provisions."

8. In subdivision (4) the reference to subdivision (3) is deleted because of the omission of subdivision (3) from the California version.

Law Revision Commission Comment
1975 Amendment

Subdivision (2) of Section 2209 is amended to conform to the language of the Uniform Commercial Code.

Uniform Commercial Code Comment

Prior Uniform Statutory Provision:

Subsection (1)—Compare Section 1, Uniform Written Obligations Act; Subsections (2) to (5)—none.

Purposes of Changes and New Matter:

1. This section seeks to protect and make effective all necessary and desirable modifications of sales contracts without regard to the technicalities which at present hamper such adjustments.

2. Subsection (1) provides that an agreement modifying a sales contract needs no consideration to be binding.

However, modifications made thereunder must meet the test of good faith imposed by this Act. The effective use of bad faith to escape performance on the original contract terms is barred, and the extortion of a "modification" without legitimate commercial reason is ineffective as a violation of the duty of good faith. Nor can a mere technical consideration support a modification made in bad faith.

The test of "good faith" between merchants or as against merchants includes "observance of reasonable commercial standards of fair dealing in the trade" (Section 2-103), and may in some situations require an objectively demonstrable reason for seeking a modification. But such matters as a market shift which makes performance come to involve a loss may provide such a reason even though there is no such unforeseen difficulty as would make out a legal excuse from performance under Sections 2-615 and 2-616.

3. Subsections (2) and (3) [Subsection 3 inapplicable in California, see California Code Comment, notes 7, 8] are intended to protect against false allegations of oral modifications. "Modification or rescission" includes abandonment or other change by mutual consent, contrary to the decision in Green v. Doniger, 300 N.Y. 238, 90 N.E.2d 56 (1949); it does not include unilateral "termination" or "cancellation" as defined in Section 2-106.

The Statute of Frauds provisions of this Article are expressly applied to modifications by subsection (3). Under those provisions the "delivery and acceptance" test is limited to the goods which have been accepted, that is, to the past. "Modification" for the future cannot therefore be conjured up by oral testimony if the price involved is $500.00 or more since such modification must be shown at least by an authenticated memo. And since a memo is limited in its effect to the quantity of goods set forth in it there is safeguard against oral evidence.

Subsection (2) permits the parties in effect to make their own Statute of Frauds as regards any future modification of the contract by giving effect to a clause in a signed agreement which expressly requires any modification to be by signed writing. But note that if a consumer is to be held to such a clause on a form supplied by a merchant it must be separately signed.

4. Subsection (4) is intended, despite the provisions of subsections (2) and (3) [Subsection 3 inapplicable in California, see California Code Comment, notes 7, 8], to prevent contractual provisions excluding modification except by a signed writing from limiting in other respects the legal effect of the parties' actual later conduct. The effect of such conduct as a waiver is further regulated in subsection (5).

Cross References:

Point 1: Section 1-203.
Point 2: Sections 1-201, 1-203, 2-615 and 2-616.
Point 3: Sections 2-106, 2-201 and 2-202.
Point 4: Sections 2-202 and 2-208.

Definitional Cross References:

"Agreement". Section 1-201.
"Between merchants". Section 2-104.
"Contract". Section 1-201.
"Notification". Section 1-201.
"Signed". Section 1-201.
"Term". Section 1-201.
"Writing". Section 1-201.

Cross References

Burden of proof in general, see Evidence Code § 500 et seq.
Consideration defined, see Civil Code § 1605.
Definitions in general, see Commercial Code § 1201.
Definitions of "termination" and "cancellation", see Commercial Code § 2106.
Delay in delivery or nondelivery occasioned by failure of presupposed conditions, see Commercial Code § 2615.
Evidence as to intent of contracting parties, see Code of Civil Procedure § 1856.
Explanation or supplementation of terms, see Commercial Code § 2202.
Failure of consideration as ground for rescission, see Civil Code § 1689.
Final written expression, see Commercial Code § 2202.
Formal requisites of contract, see Commercial Code § 2201.
Modification and cancellation, oral and written contracts, see Civil Code §§ 1697, 1698.
Obligation of good faith, see Commercial Code § 1203.
Rescission of contracts, see Civil Code § 1688 et seq.
Termination and cancellation defined, see Commercial Code § 2106.
Termination or modification by buyer after notification of delay, see Commercial Code § 2616.
Want of consideration, burden of proof, see Civil Code § 1615.
Written instrument presumptive evidence of consideration, see Civil Code § 1614.

§ 2210. Delegation of Performance; Assignment of Rights

(1) A party may perform his duty through a delegate unless otherwise agreed or unless the other party has a substantial interest in having his original promisor perform or control the acts required by the contract. No delegation of performance relieves the party delegating of any duty to perform or any liability for breach.

(2) Unless otherwise agreed all rights of either seller or buyer can be assigned except where the assignment would materially change the duty of the other party, or increase materially the burden or risk imposed on him by his contract, or impair materially his chance of obtaining return performance. A right to damages for breach of the whole contract or a right arising out of the assignor's due performance of his entire obligation can be assigned despite agreement otherwise.

(3) Unless the circumstances indicate the contrary a prohibition of assignment of "the contract" is to be construed as barring only the delegation to the assignee of the assignor's performance.

(4) An assignment of "the contract" or of "all my rights under the contract" or an assignment in similar general terms is an assignment of rights and unless the language or the circumstances (as in an assignment for security) indicate the contrary, it is a delegation of performance of the duties of the assignor and its acceptance by the assignee constitutes a promise by him to perform those duties. This promise is enforceable by

either the assignor or the other party to the original contract.

(5) The other party may treat any assignment which delegates performance as creating reasonable grounds for insecurity and may without prejudice to his rights against the assignor demand assurances from the assignee (Section 2609). *(Stats.1963, c. 819, § 2210.)*

California Code Comment

By John A. Bohn and Charles J. Williams

Prior California Law

1. This section makes no substantive change in prior California law. Subdivision (1) appears to broaden Civil Code § 1457 but is in fact quite similar to section 1457 as it has been interpreted by California authorities. See Farmland Irr. Co. v. Dopplmaier, 48 Cal.2d 208, 308 P.2d 732 (1957).

2. Subdivision (2) appears to be a restatement of Civil Code § 1458 and its construction by California authorities. The court stated in Farmland Irr. Co. v. Dopplmaier, *supra*, at page 22 that "rights . . . cannot be assigned if the assignment would materially impair the non-assigning party's chance of obtaining the performance he expected . . . ." Citing 2 Williston Contracts, 1177–1182 (rev. ed. 1936) and 1 Rest., Contracts, section 151 (1932).

3. Subdivision (3) is a more severe statement of what had, in the past, been expressed by California courts as the "policy" of state statutes in this area, i.e. a policy in favor of free transferability of all types of property including rights under contracts. See Farmland Irr. Co. v. Dopplmaier, 48 Cal.2d 208, 308 P.2d 732 (1957). Subdivision (3) goes further in providing that an express declaration that the contract is non-assignable may be construed to limit only the assignment of duties under the contract.

4. As to subdivision (4) see the cases collected in California Annotations to the Restatement of Contracts, pp. 89–90.

5. The provisions of subdivision (5) are new to California law.

Changes from U.C.C. (1962 Official Text)

6. This is section 2–210 of the Official Text without change.

Uniform Commercial Code Comment

Prior Uniform Statutory Provision:

None.

Purposes:

1. Generally, this section recognizes both delegation of performance and assignability as normal and permissible incidents of a contract for the sale of goods.

2. Delegation of performance, either in conjunction with an assignment or otherwise, is provided for by subsection (1) where no substantial reason can be shown as to why the delegated performance will not be as satisfactory as personal performance.

3. Under subsection (2) rights which are no longer executory such as a right to damages for breach or a right to payment of an "account" as defined in the Article on Secured Transactions (Article 9) may be assigned although the agreement prohibits assignment. In such cases no question of delegation of any performance is involved. The assignment of a "contract right" as defined in the Article on Secured Transactions (Article 9) is not covered by this subsection.

4. The nature of the contract or the circumstances of the case, however, may bar assignment of the contract even where delegation of performance is not involved. This Article and this section are intended to clarify this problem, particularly in cases dealing with output requirement and exclusive dealing contracts. In the first place the section on requirements and exclusive dealing removes from the construction of the original contract most of the "personal discretion" element by substituting the reasonably objective standard of good faith operation of the plant or business to be supplied. Secondly, the section on insecurity and assurances, which is specifically referred to in subsection (5) of this section, frees the other party from the doubts and uncertainty which may afflict him under an assignment of the character in question by permitting him to demand adequate assurance of due performance without which he may suspend his own performance. Subsection (5) is not in any way intended to limit the effect of the section on insecurity and assurances and the word "performance" includes the giving of orders under a requirements contract. Of course, in any case where a material personal discretion is sought to be transferred, effective assignment is barred by subsection (2).

5. Subsection (4) lays down a general rule of construction distinguishing between a normal commercial assignment, which substitutes the assignee for the assignor both as to rights and duties, and a financing assignment in which only the assignor's rights are transferred.

This Article takes no position on the possibility of extending some recognition or power to the original parties to work out normal commercial readjustments of the contract in the case of financing assignments even after the original obligor has been notified of the assignment. This question is dealt with in the Article on Secured Transactions (Article 9).

6. Subsection (5) recognizes that the non-assigning original party has a stake in the reliability of the person with whom he has closed the original contract, and is, therefore, entitled to due assurance that any delegated performance will be properly forthcoming.

7. This section is not intended as a complete statement of the law of delegation and assignment but is limited to clarifying a few points doubtful under the case law. Particularly, neither this section nor this Article touches directly on such questions as the need or effect of notice of the assignment, the rights of successive assignees, or any question of the form of an assignment, either as between the parties or as against any third parties. Some of these questions are dealt with in Article 9.

Cross References:

Point 3: Articles 5 and 9.
Point 4: Sections 2–306 and 2–609.
Point 5: Article 9, Sections 9–317 and 9–318.
Point 7: Article 9.

Definitional Cross References:

"Agreement". Section 1–201.
"Buyer". Section 2–103.
"Contract". Section 1–201.
"Party". Section 1–201.
"Rights". Section 1–201.
"Seller". Section 2–103.
"Term". Section 1–201.

Cross References

Agreement not to assert defenses against assignee, secured transactions, see Commercial Code § 9206.
Assurance of due performance, see Commercial Code § 2609.
Burden of obligation, transfer, see Civil Code § 1457.
Defenses against assignee, see Commercial Code §§ 9206, 9318.
Exclusive dealings, see Commercial Code § 2306.
Identification and proof of assignment of contract, secured transactions, see Commercial Code § 9318.
Letters of credit, see Commercial Code § 5101 et seq.
Non-negotiable instruments, transfer, see Civil Code § 1459.
Retail installment sale contract, assignment, see Civil Code § 1804.2.
Rights arising from obligation transferrable, see Civil Code § 1458.
Secured transactions, see Commercial Code § 9101 et seq.
Security interest or authority giving debtor authority to use or dispose of collateral, see Commercial Code § 9317.
Term of contract prohibiting assignment ineffective, secured transactions, see Commercial Code § 9318.

CHAPTER 3. GENERAL OBLIGATION AND CONSTRUCTION OF CONTRACT

Section
2301. General Obligations of Parties.
2303. Allocation or Division of Risks.
2304. Price Payable in Money, Goods, Realty, or Otherwise.
2305. Open Price Term.

Section
2306. Output, Requirements and Exclusive Dealings.
2307. Delivery in Single Lot or Several Lots.
2308. Absence of Specified Place for Delivery.
2309. Absence of Specific Time Provisions; Notice of Termination.
2310. Open Time for Payment or Running of Credit; Authority to Ship Under Reservation.
2311. Options and Cooperation Respecting Performance.
2312. Warranty of Title and Against Infringement; Buyer's Obligation Against Infringement.
2313. Express Warranties by Affirmation, Promise, Description, Sample.
2314. Implied Warranty; Merchantability; Usage of Trade.
2315. Implied Warranty: Fitness for Particular Purpose.
2316. Exclusion or Modification of Warranties.
2317. Cumulation and Conflict of Warranties Express or Implied.
2319. F.O.B. and F.A.S. Terms.
2320. C.I.F. and C. & F. Terms.
2321. C.I.F. or C. & F.: "Net Landed Weights"; "Payment on Arrival"; Warranty of Condition on Arrival.
2322. Delivery "Ex-Ship".
2323. Form of Bill of Lading Required in Overseas Shipment; "Overseas".
2324. "No Arrival, No Sale" Term.
2325. "Letter of Credit" Term; "Confirmed Credit".
2326. Sale on Approval and Sale or Return; Consignment Sales and Rights of Creditors.
2327. Special Incidents of Sale on Approval and Sale or Return.
2328. Sale by Auction.

§ 2301. General Obligations of Parties

The obligation of the seller is to transfer and deliver and that of the buyer is to accept and pay in accordance with the contract. *(Stats.1963, c. 819, § 2301.)*

California Code Comment

By John A. Bohn and Charles J. Williams

Prior California Law

1. This section is consistent with former Civil Code § 1761 (seller must deliver and buyer accept goods).

Changes from U.C.C. (1962 Official Text)

2. This is section 2–301 of the Official Text without change.

Uniform Commercial Code Comment

Prior Uniform Statutory Provision:

Sections 11 and 41, Uniform Sales Act.

Changes: Rewritten.

Purposes of Changes:

This section uses the term "obligation" in contrast to the term "duty" in order to provide for the "condition" aspects of delivery and payment insofar as they are not modified by other sections of this Article such as those on cure of tender. It thus replaces not only the general provisions of the Uniform Sales Act on the parties' duties, but also the general provisions of that Act on the effect of conditions. In order to determine what is "in accordance with the contract" under this Article usage of trade, course of dealing and performance, and the general background of circumstances must be given due consideration in conjunction with the lay meaning of the words used to define the scope of the conditions and duties.

Cross References:

Section 1–106. See also Sections 1–205, 2–208, 2–209, 2–508 and 2–612.

Definitional Cross References:

"Buyer". Section 2–103.
"Contract". Section 1–201.
"Party". Section 1–201.
"Seller". Section 2–103.

Cross References

Assignment of "account" or "contract right", secured transactions, see Commercial Code § 9318.
Assurance of performance, see Commercial Code § 2609.
Breach, repudiation and excuse, see Commercial Code § 2601 et seq.
Course of dealing and usage of trade, see Commercial Code § 1205.
Course of performance or practical construction, see Commercial Code § 2208.
Installment contracts, see Commercial Code § 2612.
Liberal administration of remedies provided by code, see Commercial Code § 1106.
Modification, rescission and waiver, see Commercial Code § 2209.
Performance of sales contracts, see Commercial Code § 2501 et seq.
Rejection of nonconforming tender or delivery, see Commercial Code § 2508.

§ 2302. [Enacted in California as Civil Code § 1670.5]

California Code Comment

By John A. Bohn and Charles J. Williams

Prior California Law

1. Section 2–302 of the 1962 Official Text of the Uniform Commercial Code is omitted from the California version. The Official Text reads:

Section 2–302. Unconscionable Contract or Clause.

(1) If the court as a matter of law finds the contract or any clause of the contract to have been unconscionable at the time it was made the court may refuse to enforce the contract, or it may enforce the remainder of the contract without the unconscionable clause, or it may so limit the application of any unconscionable clause as to avoid any unconscionable result.

(2) When it is claimed or appears to the court that the contract or any clause thereof may be unconscionable the parties shall be afforded a reasonable opportunity to present evidence as to its commercial setting, purpose and effect to aid the court in making the determination. A California State Bar Committee gives the following reason for the omission in California:

One controversial provision in the Official Text but not in S.B. 1093 [1961 Session 1958 Official Text as amended.] is section 1230 [2302]. If the court finds a contract or a clause "unconscionable," it may refuse to enforce the contract or it may strike out the offending clause. This provision, the subject of much scholarly dispute, was extensively debated in the State Bar Committee and in the Advisory Committee to the Senate Judiciary Committee.

Section 12302 [2302] has been defended on the ground that in an age of "form contracts" not negotiated in any real sense, the courts must have the power to prevent overreaching by one party to a sale, particularly the seller of goods to a retail purchaser who has neither the knowledge nor the bargaining position to influence the contract terms. [Footnote California, like many other states, has placed limitations on the conduct of retail sellers by the enactment of retail installment sales acts. Cal.Civ.Code, secs. 1801–1812.9, 2981–2984.3. For an analysis of this legislation, see note 7, UCLA Law Rev. 618 (1960).] It has also been argued that section 12302 [2302] merely extends to legal actions the ancient rule that "equity will not enforce an unconscionable bargain." Courts often do the same by forced construction. [*Fn:* See, e.g., Burr v. Sherwin Williams Co., 42 C.2d 682, 692, 268 P.2d 1041, 1046 (1954).]

The final recommendation of the Advisory Committee and the decision to delete this section from S.B.1903 [sic] [1093] was based upon the belief that giving courts unqualified power to strike down terms they might consider "unconscionable" could result in the renegotiation of contracts in every case of disagreement with the fairness of provisions the parties had accepted. California State Bar Committee on the Commercial Code, A Special Report, The Uniform Commercial Code, 37 Calif.Bar J. (March–April, 1962) pp. 135–136.

A more detailed discussion of this section of the Official Text and its relation to California law is contained in the Marsh and Warren Report:

"The classic statement of the purpose of this section is to be found in the Official Comment: 'This section is intended to make it possible for the courts to police explicitly against the contracts or clauses which they find to be unconscionable. In the past, such policing has been accomplished by adverse construction of language, by manipulation of the rules of offer and acceptance or by determinations that the clause is contrary to public policy or to the dominant purpose of the contract. This section is intended to allow the court to pass directly on the unconscionability of the contract or particular clause therein and to make a conclusion of law as to its unconscionability. The basic test is whether in the light of the general commercial background and commercial needs of the particular trade or case, the clauses involved are so one-sided as to be unconscionable under the circumstances existing at the time of making of the contract. Subsection [subdivision] (2) makes it clear that it is proper for the court to hear evidence upon these questions.'

"It is difficult to predict how great a change this Section would make in California law. Certainly, the specific legislative grant of power to the courts to refuse to enforce contracts or portions thereof due to the unconscionable nature of these contracts is novel. However, the California Annotations to the Code state that what seems to be new law 'may simply be a restatement of the broad equity powers which the California courts have always assumed they held.' It is well known that judges have by construction and interpretation avoided enforcement of harsh bargains. The cases cited in the Official Comment are only a few of the many instances of this. A recent example is Burr v. Sherwin Williams Co., 42 Cal.2d 682, 268 P.2d 1041 (1954). In that case, the following disclaimer clause was involved: 'Seller makes no warranty of any kind, express or implied, concerning the use of this product. Buyer assumes all risk in use or handling, whether in accordance with directions or not.' Employing the familiar rule that a disclaimer is to be strictly construed against the seller, the court concluded that this disclaimer was insufficient to exclude the implied warranty of merchantable quality.

"Courts may also reach the desired results by finding clauses to be ambiguous or by invoking the doctrine of mutuality. Corbin inventories some of the other weapons in the judicial arsenal in these words: 'There is sufficient flexibility in the concepts of fraud, duress, misrepresentation, and undue influence, not to mention differences in economic bargaining power, to enable the courts to avoid enforcement of a bargain that is shown to be unconscionable by reason of gross inadequacy of consideration accompanied by other relevant factors.' 1 Corbin, Contracts § 128 (1950). In equity, the court's work is simpler for it may resort to the rule that 'equity does not enforce unconscionable bargains.'

"See also Monarco v. Lo Greco, 35 Cal.2d 621, 220 P.2d 737 (1950); State Finance Co. v. Smith, 44 Cal.App.2d 688, 112 P.2d 901 (1941).

". . .

"This is the age of the form contract—sometimes called the contract of adhesion. The buyer of an appliance or an automobile may have excellent bargaining power with regard to price or trade-in allowances, but he usually has no bargaining power at all with regard to the terms of the contract. This section is a strong provision, and strong measures are needed to allow for adequate policing of the great mass of form contracts, the provisions of which are not, in any real sense of the word, negotiated. Although California judges already possess doctrinal tools to achieve the result that this section calls for, it is preferable to allow what has previously been done by indirection, if not subterfuge, to be done openly. It is probable that courts will interpret this section as giving them somewhat greater powers to refuse to enforce harsh contracts or clauses than they now have; this increase in judicial power if it is such, is justified by the proliferation of form contracts in this country within the last few decades.

"The danger which arises under the statute as it appears in the Code is that it seems to give a court the power to cast a clause out of a contract, if it feels that clause is 'nonconscionable', even though the clause or contract had been thoroughly negotiated by the parties. The problem is how to place some sensible limitations on the courts' power. The proposed amendment does this by requiring that the contract be a 'form' contract of the party seeking to enforce it and by excluding the application of the section to contracts 'between merchants', who presumably are of more equal bargaining power." Sixth Progress Report to the Legislature by Senate Fact Finding Committee on Judiciary (1959–1961) Part 1, The Uniform Commercial Code, pp. 455–457.

Uniform Commercial Code Comment

Prior Uniform Statutory Provision:

None.

Purposes:

1. This section is intended to make it possible for the courts to police explicitly against the contracts or clauses which they find to be unconscionable. In the past such policing has been accomplished by adverse construction of language, by manipulation of the rules of offer and acceptance or by determinations that the clause is contrary to public policy or to the dominant purpose of the contract. This section is intended to allow the court to pass directly on the unconscionability of the contract or particular clause therein and to make a conclusion of law as to its unconscionability. The basic test is whether, in the light of the general commercial background and the commercial needs of the particular trade or case, the clauses involved are so one-sided as to be unconscionable under the circumstances existing at the time of the making of the contract. Subsection (2) makes it clear that it is proper for the court to hear evidence upon these questions. The principle is one of the prevention of oppression and unfair surprise (Cf. Campbell Soup Co. v. Wentz, 172 F.2d 80, 3d Cir. 1948) and not of disturbance of allocation of risks because of superior bargaining power. The underlying basis of this section is illustrated by the results in cases such as the following:

Kansas City Wholesale Grocery Co. v. Weber Packing Corporation, 93 Utah 414, 73 P.2d 1272 (1937), where a clause limiting time for complaints was held inapplicable to latent defects in a shipment of catsup which could be discovered only by microscopic analysis; Hardy v. General Motors Acceptance Corporation, 38 Ga.App. 463, 144 S.E. 327 (1928), holding that a disclaimer of warranty clause applied only to express warranties, thus letting in a fair implied warranty; Andrews Bros. v. Singer & Co. (1934 CA) 1 K.B. 17, holding that where a car with substantial mileage was delivered instead of a "new" car, a disclaimer of warranties, including those "implied," left unaffected an "express obligation" on the description, even though the Sale of Goods Act called such an implied warranty; New Prague Flouring Mill Co. v. G. A. Spears, 194 Iowa 417, 189 N.W. 815 (1922), holding that a clause permitting the seller, upon the buyer's failure to supply shipping instructions, to cancel, ship, or allow delivery date to be indefinitely postponed 30 days at a time by the inaction, does not indefinitely postpone the date of measuring damages for the buyer's breach, to the seller's advantage; and Kansas Flour Mills Co. v. Dirks, 100 Kan. 376, 164 P. 273 (1917), where under a similar clause in a rising market the court permitted the buyer to measure his damages for non-delivery at the end of only one 30 day postponement; Green v. Arcos, Ltd. (1931 CA) 47 T.L.R. 336, where a blanket clause prohibiting rejection of shipments by the buyer was restricted to apply to shipments where discrepancies represented merely mercantile variations; Meyer v. Packard Cleveland Motor Co., 106 Ohio St. 328, 140 N.E. 118 (1922), in which the court held that a "waiver" of all agreements not specified did not preclude implied warranty of fitness of a rebuilt dump truck for ordinary use as a dump truck; Austin Co. v. J. H. Tillman Co., 104 Or. 541, 209 P. 131 (1922), where a clause limiting the buyer's remedy to return was held to be applicable only if the seller had delivered a machine needed for a construction job which reasonably met the contract description; Bekkevold v. Potts, 173 Minn. 87, 216 N.W. 790, 59 A.L.R. 1164 (1927), refusing to allow warranty of fitness for purpose imposed by law to be negated by clause excluding all warranties "made" by the seller; Robert A. Munroe & Co. v. Meyer (1930) 2 K.B. 312, holding that the warranty of description overrides a clause reading "with all faults and defects" where adulterated meat not up to the contract description was delivered.

2. Under this section the court, in its discretion, may refuse to enforce the contract as a whole if it is permeated by the unconscionability, or it may strike any single clause or group of clauses which are so

tainted or which are contrary to the essential purpose of the agreement, or it may simply limit unconscionable clauses so as to avoid unconscionable results.

3. The present section is addressed to the court, and the decision is to be made by it. The commercial evidence referred to in subsection (2) is for the court's consideration, not the jury's. Only the agreement which results from the court's action on these matters is to be submitted to the general triers of the facts.

Definitional Cross Reference:

"Contract". Section 1–201.

§ 2303. Allocation or Division of Risks

Where this division allocates a risk or a burden as between the parties "unless otherwise agreed," the agreement may not only shift the allocation but may also divide the risk or burden. *(Stats.1963, c. 819, § 2303.)*

California Code Comment

By John A. Bohn and Charles J. Williams

Prior California Law

1. This section is consistent with former Civil Code § 1742 (Risk of Loss) and § 1791 (Variation of implied obligations). Under section 1742 the rules of regarding risk of loss were not applicable if the parties had agreed otherwise and section 1791 provided, in part, that the parties could vary any right or duty under the contract of sale.

Changes from U.C.C. (1962 Official Text)

This is section 2–303 of the Official Text without change.

Uniform Commercial Code Comment

Prior Uniform Statutory Provision:

None.

Purposes:

1. This section is intended to make it clear that the parties may modify or allocate "unless otherwise agreed" risks or burdens imposed by this Article as they desire, always subject, of course, to the provisions on unconscionability.

Compare Section 1–102(4).

2. The risk or burden may be divided by the express terms of the agreement or by the attending circumstances, since under the definition of "agreement" in this Act the circumstances surrounding the transaction as well as the express language used by the parties enter into the meaning and substance of the agreement.

Cross References:

Point 1: Sections 1–102, 2–302.
Point 2: Section 1–201.

Definitional Cross References:

"Party". Section 1–201.
"Agreement". Section 1–201.

Cross References

Definitions, see Commercial Code § 1201.
Variation of code provisions by agreement, see Commercial Code § 1102.

§ 2304. Price Payable in Money, Goods, Realty, or Otherwise

(1) The price can be made payable in money or otherwise. If it is payable in whole or in part in goods each party is a seller of the goods which he is to transfer.

(2) Even though all or part of the price is payable in an interest in realty the transfer of the goods and the seller's obligations with reference to them are subject to this division, but not the transfer of the interest in realty or the transferor's obligations in connection therewith. *(Stats.1963, c. 819, § 2304.)*

California Code Comment

By John A. Bohn and Charles J. Williams

Prior California Law

1. Subdivision (1) is similar to former Civil Code § 1729(2) which authorized payment "in any personal property." This section uses the broader language authorizing payment "in money or otherwise."

2. Subdivision (2) changes California law. Former Civil Code § 1729(3) provided that the California Uniform Sales Act (former Civil Code §§ 1721 through 1800) did not apply if the transfer of an interest in real estate constituted the whole or any part of the consideration for transfer of goods. See Tozzi v. Lincoln National Life Insurance Co., 103 F.2d 46 (9th Circuit, 1939). Under subdivision (2) the Code applies *to the seller's obligation* with respect to the transfer of the goods.

Changes from U.C.C. (1962 Official Text)

3. This is section 2–304 of the Official Text without change.

Uniform Commercial Code Comment

Prior Uniform Statutory Provision:

Subsections (2) and (3) of Section 9, Uniform Sales Act.

Changes: Rewritten.

Purposes of Changes:

1. This section corrects the phrasing of the Uniform Sales Act so as to avoid misconstruction and produce greater accuracy in commercial result. While it continues the essential intent and purpose of the Uniform Sales Act it rejects any purely verbalistic construction in disregard of the underlying reason of the provisions.

2. Under subsection (1) the provisions of this Article are applicable to transactions where the "price" of goods is payable in something other than money. This does not mean, however, that this whole Article applies automatically and in its entirety simply because an agreed transfer of title to goods is not a gift. The basic purposes and reasons of the Article must always be considered in determining the applicability of any of its provisions.

3. Subsection (2) lays down the general principle that when goods are to be exchanged for realty, the provisions of this Article apply only to those aspects of the transaction which concern the transfer of title to goods but do not affect the transfer of the realty since the detailed regulation of various particular contracts which fall outside the scope of this Article is left to the courts and other legislation. However, the complexities of these situations may be such that each must be analyzed in the light of the underlying reasons in order to determine the applicable principles. Local statutes dealing with realty are not to be lightly disregarded or altered by language of this Article. In contrast, this Article declares definite policies in regard to certain matters legitimately within its scope though concerned with real property situations, and in those instances the provisions of this Article control.

Cross References:

Point 1: Section 1–102.
Point 3: Sections 1–102, 1–103, 1–104 and 2–107.

Definitional Cross References:

"Goods". Section 2–105.
"Money". Section 1–201.
"Party". Section 1–201.
"Seller". Section 2–103.

Cross References

Code as a unified coverage of its subject matter, see Commercial Code § 1104.
Consideration, see Civil Code § 1605 et seq.
Purpose and policy of code, see Commercial Code § 1102.
Seller's action for the price, see Commercial Code § 2709.
Supplementation of code by principles of law and equity, see Commercial Code § 1103.
Waiver or renunciation of claim or right arising out of alleged breach, see Commercial Code § 1107.

§ 2305. Open Price Term

(1) The parties if they so intend can conclude a contract for sale even though the price is not settled. In such a case the price is a reasonable price at the time for delivery if

(a) Nothing is said as to price; or

(b) The price is left to be agreed by the parties and they fail to agree; or

(c) The price is to be fixed in terms of some agreed market or other standard as set or recorded by a third person or agency and it is not so set or recorded.

(2) A price to be fixed by the seller or by the buyer means a price for him to fix in good faith.

(3) When a price left to be fixed otherwise than by agreement of the parties fails to be fixed through fault of one party the other may at his option treat the contract as canceled or himself fix a reasonable price.

(4) Where, however, the parties intend not to be bound unless the price be fixed or agreed and it is not fixed or agreed there is no contract. In such a case the buyer must return any goods already received or if unable so to do must pay their reasonable value at the time of delivery and the seller must return any portion of the price paid on account. *(Stats.1963, c. 819, § 2305.)*

California Code Comment

By John A. Bohn and Charles J. Williams

Prior California Law

1. Subdivision (1)(a) is comparable to former Civil Code § 1729(4) which provided for a reasonable price if the price was not fixed in the contract of sale. See California Lettuce Growers v. Union Sugar Co., 45 Cal.2d 474, 289 P.2d 785 (1955) 289 P.2d 790, where the court said:
"Unexpressed provisions of a contract may be inferred from the writing or external facts. Thus it is well settled that a contract need not specify price if it can be objectively determined. Section 1729 of the Civil Code recognizes three ways of determining price. It can be fixed by the parties, determined from the prior course of dealings of the parties and if these procedures are inapplicable, the contract price may be deemed the reasonable price under the circumstances of the particular case."

2. Under prior California law, leaving the price to be fixed by subsequent agreement of the parties resulted in "an agreement to agree and [is] therefore *nudum pactum* until the price is fixed or agreed upon." California Lettuce Growers Inc. v. Union Sugar Co., 45 Cal.2d 474, 289 P.2d 785 (1955). Under subdivision (1)(b) if the price is to be fixed by subsequent agreement the contract is valid and if the parties do not agree a reasonable price is to be paid.

3. Subdivision (1)(c) is in accord with prior California law as expressed in former Civil Code § 1729 and California Lettuce Growers Inc. v. Union Sugar Co., 45 Cal.2d 474, 289 P.2d 785 (1955).

4. Subdivision (2) is in accord with prior California law as expressed in California Lettuce Growers, Inc. v. Union Sugar Co., 45 Cal.2d 474, 289 P.2d 785 (1955): ". . . where a contract confers on one party a discretionary power affecting the rights of the other, a duty is imposed to exercise that discretion in good faith and in accordance with fair dealing."

5. Under former Civil Code § 1730(2), where there was a contract to sell or a sale of goods at a price to be fixed *by a third person* and that person was prevented from fixing the price through the fault of either the seller or buyer, the party not at fault was entitled to the remedies of the USA (rights of unpaid seller against the goods, former Civil Code §§ 1772–1782, and actions for breach of contract, former Civil Code §§ 1783–1790). Subdivision (3) of section 2305 gives the party not at fault an election between cancellation of the contract or fixing a reasonable price himself. Further, subdivision (3), unlike former Civil Code § 1730, is applicable to all situations where the price is to be fixed "otherwise than by agreement of the parties."

6. Under former Civil Code § 1730(1), if the third person through no fault of the parties would or could not fix the price, then the buyer had to pay a reasonable price for any goods that had been delivered to and appropriated by him. Under section 2305(4) if the buyer has "received" (defined in Commercial Code § 2103(1)(c)) goods under the contract, then he must either return the goods or pay a reasonable price for them. The seller must "return any portion of the price paid on account." Note that subdivision (4) applies only in the case where the parties intend to be bound *only if* the price is fixed or agreed and it is not fixed or agreed.

Changes from U.C.C. (1962 Official Text)

7. This is section 2–305 of the Official Text without change.

Uniform Commercial Code Comment

Prior Uniform Statutory Provision:
Sections 9 and 10, Uniform Sales Act.
Changes: Completely rewritten.

Purposes of Changes:

1. This section applies when the price term is left open on the making of an agreement which is nevertheless intended by the parties to be a binding agreement. This Article rejects in these instances the formula that "an agreement to agree is unenforceable" if the case falls within subsection (1) of this section, and rejects also defeating such agreements on the ground of "indefiniteness". Instead this Article recognizes the dominant intention of the parties to have the deal continue to be binding upon both. As to future performance, since this Article recognizes remedies such as cover (Section 2–712), resale (Section 2–706) and specific performance (Section 2–716) which go beyond any mere arithmetic as between contract price and market price, there is usually a "reasonably certain basis for granting an appropriate remedy for breach" so that the contract need not fail for indefiniteness.

2. Under some circumstances the postponement of agreement on price will mean that no deal has really been concluded, and this is made express in the preamble of subsection (1) ("The parties *if they so intend*") and in subsection (4). Whether or not this is so is, in most cases, a question to be determined by the trier of fact.

3. Subsection (2), dealing with the situation where the price is to be fixed by one party rejects the uncommercial idea that an agreement that the seller may fix the price means that he may fix any price he may wish by the express qualification that the price so fixed must be fixed in good faith. Good faith includes observance of reasonable commercial standards of fair dealing in the trade if the party is a merchant. (Section 2–103). But in the normal case a "posted price" or a future seller's or buyer's "given price," "price in effect," "market price," or the like satisfies the good faith requirement.

4. The section recognizes that there may be cases in which a particular person's judgment is not chosen merely as a barometer or index of a fair price but is an essential condition to the parties' intent to make any contract at all. For example, the case where a known and trusted expert is to "value" a particular painting for which there is no market standard differs sharply from the situation where a named expert is to determine the grade of cotton, and the difference would support a finding that in the one the parties did not intend to make a binding agreement if that expert were unavailable whereas in the other they did so intend. Other circumstances would of course affect the validity of such a finding.

5. Under subsection (3), wrongful interference by one party with any agreed machinery for price fixing in the contract may be treated by the other party as a repudiation justifying cancellation, or merely as a failure to take cooperative action thus shifting to the aggrieved party the reasonable leeway in fixing the price.

6. Throughout the entire section, the purpose is to give effect to the agreement which has been made. That effect, however, is always conditioned by the requirement of good faith action which is made an inherent part of all contracts within this Act. (Section 1–203).

Cross References:

Point 1: Sections 2–204(3), 2–706, 2–712 and 2–716.
Point 3: Section 2–103.
Point 5: Sections 2–311 and 2–610.
Point 6: Section 1–203.

Definitional Cross References:

"Agreement". Section 1–201.
"Burden of establishing". Section 1–201.
"Buyer". Section 2–103.
"Cancellation". Section 2–106.
"Contract". Section 1–201.
"Contract for sale". Section 2–106.
"Fault". Section 1–201.
"Goods". Section 2–105.
"Party". Section 1–201.
"Receipt of goods". Section 2–103.
"Seller". Section 2–103.
"Term". Section 1–201.

Cross References

Action for the price, see Commercial Code § 2709.
Agreement of sale which leaves particulars of performance to be specified by one of the parties, see Commercial Code § 2311.
Buyer's remedies,
 Procurement of substitute goods, see Commercial Code § 2712.
 Specific performance or replevin, see Commercial Code § 2716.
Consideration, see Civil Code § 1605 et seq.
Contract in which one or more terms are left open, see Commercial Code § 2204(3).
Definitions, see Commercial Code § 2103.
Obligation of good faith, see Commercial Code § 1203.
Presumption of consideration, see Civil Code § 1614.
Repudiation of contract with respect to performance not yet due, see Commercial Code § 2610.
Seller's remedies, resale, see Commercial Code § 2706.

§ 2306. Output, Requirements and Exclusive Dealings

(1) A term which measures the quantity by the output of the seller or the requirements of the buyer means such actual output or requirements as may occur in good faith, except that no quantity unreasonably disproportionate to any stated estimate or in the absence of a stated estimate to any normal or otherwise comparable prior output or requirements may be tendered or demanded.

(2) A lawful agreement by either the seller or the buyer for exclusive dealing in the kind of goods concerned imposes unless otherwise agreed an obligation by the seller to use best efforts to supply the goods and by the buyer to use best efforts to promote their sale. *(Stats.1963, c. 819, § 2306.)*

California Code Comment

By John A. Bohn and Charles J. Williams

Prior California Law

1. This section is new. However, the principles of this section are in accord with the rules of interpretation in Civil Code § 1647 (contracts explained by circumstances); § 1655 (reasonable stipulations, when implied); § 1656 (necessary incidents implied); and Code of Civil Procedure § 1860 (The circumstances to be considered in the construction of statutes and instruments). The general policy underlying these Civil Code sections is given in Universal Sales Corp. v. Calif. Press Mfg. Co., 20 Cal.2d 751, 128 P.2d 665 (1942) where the court said: "In every contract there is an implied covenant that neither party shall do anything which will have the effect of destroying or injuring the right of the other party to receive the fruits of the contract, which means that in every contract, there exists an implied covenant of good faith and fair dealing."

2. California courts have previously upheld the validity of output or requirement contracts. See Andersen v. La Rinconada Country Club, 4 Cal.App.2d 197, 40 P.2d 571 (1935) and El Rio Oils v. Pacific Coast Asphalt Co., 95 Cal.App.2d 186, 213 P.2d 1 (1949).

Changes from U.C.C. (1962 Official Text)

3. This is section 2–306 of the Official Text without change.

Uniform Commercial Code Comment

Prior Uniform Statutory Provision:
None.

Purposes:

1. Subsection (1) of this section, in regard to output and requirements, applies to this specific problem the general approach of this Act which requires the reading of commercial background and intent into the language of any agreement and demands good faith in the performance of that agreement. It applies to such contracts of nonproducing establishments such as dealers or distributors as well as to manufacturing concerns.

2. Under this Article, a contract for output or requirements is not too indefinite since it is held to mean the actual good faith output or requirements of the particular party. Nor does such a contract lack mutuality of obligation since, under this section, the party who will determine quantity is required to operate his plant or conduct his business in good faith and according to commercial standards of fair dealing in the trade so that his output or requirements will approximate a reasonably foreseeable figure. Reasonable elasticity in the requirements is expressly envisaged by this section and good faith variations from prior requirements are permitted even when the variation may be such as to result in discontinuance. A shut-down by a requirements buyer for lack of orders might be permissible when a shut-down merely to curtail losses would not. The essential test is whether the party is acting in good faith. Similarly, a sudden expansion of the plant by which requirements are to be measured would not be included within the scope of the contract as made but normal expansion undertaken in good faith would be within the scope of this section. One of the factors in an expansion situation would be whether the market price had risen greatly in a case in which the requirements contract contained a fixed price. Reasonable variation of an extreme sort is exemplified in Southwest Natural Gas Co. v. Oklahoma Portland Cement Co., 102 F.2d 630 (C.C.A.10, 1939). This Article takes no position as to whether a requirements contract is a provable claim in bankruptcy.

3. If an estimate of output or requirements is included in the agreement, no quantity unreasonably disproportionate to it may be tendered or demanded. Any minimum or maximum set by the agreement shows a clear limit on the intended elasticity. In similar fashion, the agreed estimate is to be regarded as a center around which the parties intend the variation to occur.

4. When an enterprise is sold, the question may arise whether the buyer is bound by an existing output or requirements contract. That question is outside the scope of this Article, and is to be determined on other principles of law. Assuming that the contract continues, the output or requirements in the hands of the new owner continue to be measured by the actual good faith output or requirements under the normal operation of the enterprise prior to sale. The sale itself is not grounds for sudden expansion or decrease.

5. Subsection (2), on exclusive dealing, makes explicit the commercial rule embodied in this Act under which the parties to such contracts

§ 2306

are held to have impliedly, even when not expressly, bound themselves to use reasonable diligence as well as good faith in their performance of the contract. Under such contracts the exclusive agent is required, although no express commitment has been made, to use reasonable effort and due diligence in the expansion of the market or the promotion of the product, as the case may be. The principal is expected under such a contract to refrain from supplying any other dealer or agent within the exclusive territory. An exclusive dealing agreement brings into play all of the good faith aspects of the output and requirement problems of subsection (1). It also raises questions of insecurity and right to adequate assurance under this Article.

Cross References:

Point 4: Section 2–210.
Point 5: Sections 1–203 and 2–609.

Definitional Cross References:

"Agreement". Section 1–201.
"Buyer". Section 2–103.
"Contract for sale". Section 2–106.
"Good faith". Section 1–201.
"Goods". Section 2–105.
"Party". Section 1–201.
"Term". Section 1–201.
"Seller". Section 2–103.

Cross References

Adequate assurance of due performance, see Commercial Code § 2609.
Assignment of rights, see Commercial Code § 2210.
Consideration of circumstances in construction of instruments, see Code of Civil Procedure § 1860.
Contracts explained by circumstances, see Civil Code § 1647.
Implied incidents to contract, see Civil Code § 1656.
Obligation of good faith, see Commercial Code § 1203.

§ 2307. Delivery in Single Lot or Several Lots

Unless otherwise agreed all goods called for by a contract for sale must be tendered in a single delivery and payment is due only on such tender but where the circumstances give either party the right to make or demand delivery in lots the price if it can be apportioned may be demanded for each lot. (Stats.1963, c. 819, § 2307.)

California Code Comment

By John A. Bohn and Charles J. Williams

Prior California Law

1. The primary rule of this section is similar to former Civil Code § 1765(1) which provided: "Unless otherwise agreed, the buyer of goods is not bound to accept delivery thereof by installments."

2. The last portion of this section has no prior California statutory counterpart, but is similar in principle to former Civil Code § 1762 which provides that payment should be concurrent with delivery. See Veerkamp v. Hulburd Canning & Drying Co., 58 Cal. 229, 41 Am.Rep. 265 (1881) and L.A. Gas & Elec. v. Amal. Oil Co., 156 Cal. 776, 106 Pac. 55 (1909).

Changes from U.C.C. (1962 Official Text)

3. This is section 2–307 of the Official Text without change.

Uniform Commercial Code Comment

Prior Uniform Statutory Provision:

Section 45(1), Uniform Sales Act.
Changes: Rewritten and expanded.

Purposes of Changes:

1. This section applies where the parties have not specifically agreed whether delivery and payment are to be by lots and generally continues the essential intent of original Act, Section 45(1) by assuming that the parties intended delivery to be in a single lot.

2. Where the actual agreement or the circumstances do not indicate otherwise, delivery in lots is not permitted under this section and the buyer is properly entitled to reject for a deficiency in the tender, subject to any privilege in the seller to cure the tender.

3. The "but" clause of this section goes to the case in which it is not commercially feasible to deliver or to receive the goods in a single lot as for example, where a contract calls for the shipment of ten carloads of coal and only three cars are available at a given time. Similarly, in a contract involving brick necessary to build a building the buyer's storage space may be limited so that it would be impossible to receive the entire amount of brick at once, or it may be necessary to assemble the goods as in the case of cattle on the range, or to mine them.

In such cases, a partial delivery is not subject to rejection for the defect in quantity alone, if the circumstances do not indicate a repudiation or default by the seller as to the expected balance or do not give the buyer ground for suspending his performance because of insecurity under the provisions of Section 2–609. However, in such cases the undelivered balance of goods under the contract must be forthcoming within a reasonable time and in a reasonable manner according to the policy of Section 2–503 on manner of tender of delivery. This is reinforced by the express provisions of Section 2–608 that if a lot has been accepted on the reasonable assumption that its nonconformity will be cured, the acceptance may be revoked if the cure does not seasonably occur. The section rejects the rule of Kelly Construction Co. v. Hackensack Brick Co., 91 N.J.L. 585, 103 A. 417, 2 A.L.R. 685 (1918) and approves the result in Lynn M. Ranger, Inc. v. Gildersleeve, 106 Conn. 372, 138 A. 142 (1927) in which a contract was made for six carloads of coal then rolling from the mines and consigned to the seller but the seller agreed to divert the carloads to the buyer as soon as the car numbers became known to him. He arranged a diversion of two cars and then notified the buyer who then repudiated the contract. The seller was held to be entitled to his full remedy for the two cars diverted because simultaneous delivery of all of the cars was not contemplated by either party.

4. Where the circumstances indicate that a party has a right to delivery in lots, the price may be demanded for each lot if it is apportionable.

Cross References:

Point 1: Section 1–201.
Point 2: Sections 2–508 and 2–601.
Point 3: Sections 2–503, 2–608 and 2–609.

Definitional Cross References:

"Contract for sale". Section 2–106.
"Goods". Section 2–105.
"Lot". Section 2–105.
"Party". Section 1–201.
"Rights". Section 1–201.

Cross References

Assurance of due performance, see Commercial Code § 2609.
Buyer's options in case of nonconforming tender or delivery, see Commercial Code § 2601.
Definitions, see Commercial Code §§ 1201, 2103.
Installment contracts, breach, see Commercial Code § 2612.
Manner, time and place for tender of delivery by seller, see Commercial Code § 2503.
Rejection by buyer of a nonconforming tender or delivery, see Commercial Code § 2508.
Revocation by buyer of acceptance of lot or commercial unit, see Commercial Code § 2608.
Time of performance of contract, see Civil Code § 1657.

§ 2308. Absence of Specified Place for Delivery

Unless otherwise agreed

(a) The place for delivery of goods is the seller's place of business or if he has none his residence; but

(b) In a contract for sale of identified goods which to the knowledge of the parties at the time of contracting are in some other place, that place is the place for their delivery; and

(c) Documents of title may be delivered through customary banking channels. *(Stats.1963, c. 819, § 2308.)*

California Code Comment

By John A. Bohn and Charles J. Williams

Prior California Law

1. Paragraphs (a) and (b) are in accord with prior California law. Under former Civil Code § 1763(1) in the absence of agreement to the contrary, the place of delivery was the seller's place of business or his residence. Where the parties knew that the goods were elsewhere their situs was the place of delivery. Fischer v. Means, 88 Cal.App.2d 137, 198 P.2d 389 (1948) and Robbins v. Pacific Eastern Corp., 8 Cal.2d 241, 65 P.2d 42 (1937).

2. Paragraph (c) permitting delivery of documents of title through customary banking channels has no prior statutory counterpart in California law.

Changes from U.C.C. (1962 Official Text)

3. This is section 2–308 of the Official Text without change.

Uniform Commercial Code Comment

Prior Uniform Statutory Provision:

Paragraphs (a) and (b)—Section 43(1), Uniform Sales Act; Paragraph (c)—none.

Changes: Slight modification in language.

Purposes of Changes and New Matter:

1. Paragraphs (a) and (b) provide for those noncommercial sales and for those occasional commercial sales where no place or means of delivery has been agreed upon by the parties. Where delivery by carrier is "required or authorized by the agreement", the seller's duties as to delivery of the goods are governed not by this section but by Section 2–504.

2. Under paragraph (b) when the identified goods contracted for are known to both parties to be in some location other than the seller's place of business or residence, the parties are presumed to have intended that place to be the place of delivery. This paragraph also applies (unless, as would be normal, the circumstances show that delivery by way of documents is intended) to a bulk of goods in the possession of a bailee. In such a case, however, the seller has the additional obligation to procure the acknowledgment by the bailee of the buyer's right to possession.

3. Where "customary banking channels" call only for due notification by the banker that the documents are on hand, leaving the buyer himself to see to the physical receipt of the goods, tender at the buyer's address is not required under paragraph (c). But that paragraph merely eliminates the possibility of a default by the seller if "customary banking channels" have been properly used in giving notice to the buyer. Where the bank has purchased a draft accompanied by documents or has undertaken its collection on behalf of the seller, Part 5 of Article 4 spells out its duties and relations to its customer. Where the documents move forward under a letter of credit the Article on Letters of Credit spells out the duties and relations between the bank, the seller and the buyer.

4. The rules of this section apply only "unless otherwise agreed." The surrounding circumstances, usage of trade, course of dealing and course of performance, as well as the express language of the parties, may constitute an "otherwise agreement".

Cross References:

Point 1: Sections 2–504 and 2–505.

Point 2: Section 2–503.
Point 3: Section 2–512, Articles 4, Part 5, and 5.

Definitional Cross References:

"Contract for sale". Section 2–106.
"Delivery". Section 1–201.
"Document of title". Section 1–201.
"Goods". Section 2–105.
"Party". Section 1–201.
"Seller". Section 2–103.

Cross References

Collection of documentary drafts, see Commercial Code § 4501 et seq.
Letters of credit, see Commercial Code § 5101 et seq.
Manner, time and place for tender of delivery by seller, see Commercial Code § 2503.
Performance of contracts generally, see Civil Code § 1657.
Shipment of goods by seller, see Commercial Code §§ 2504, 2505.
Tender of required documents, see Commercial Code § 2512.

§ 2309. Absence of Specific Time Provisions; Notice of Termination

(1) The time for shipment or delivery or any other action under a contract if not provided in this division or agreed upon shall be a reasonable time.

(2) Where the contract provides for successive performances but is indefinite in duration it is valid for a reasonable time but unless otherwise agreed may be terminated at any time by either party.

(3) Termination of a contract by one party except on the happening of an agreed event requires that reasonable notification be received by the other party and an agreement dispensing with notification is invalid if its operation would be unconscionable. *(Stats.1963, c. 819, § 2309.)*

California Code Comment

By John A. Bohn and Charles J. Williams

Prior California Law

1. Subdivision (1) is similar to former Civil Code § 1763(2) except that the latter applied only to the *time of delivery* while section 2309(1) applies also to time for "any action under a contract." See Salinas Valley Lumber Co. v. Magne-Silica Co., 159 Cal. 182, 112 Pac. 1089 (1911); and Kuhn v. Valley Meat Co., 23 Cal.App.2d 25, 72 P.2d 164 (1937).

2. Subdivision (2) is in accord with prior California law in making the duration of an indefinite contract a "reasonable" time. The prior California rule was stated in Great Western Distillery Products, Inc., v. John Wathen Distillery Company, 10 Cal.2d 442, 74 P.2d 745 (1937) as follows: "Even where a contract for the sale of goods is silent as to its duration, . . . termination cannot be affected until at least a reasonable time has expired." However, the California courts normally attempt to find the parties' intent regarding duration from various clauses in the contract or the circumstance of the case. Long Beach Drug Co. v. United Drug Co., 13 Cal.2d 158, 88 P.2d 698 (1939); Ravel v. Hubbard, 112 Cal.App.2d 255, 246 P.2d 88 (1952); and Mangini v. Wolfschmidt, Ltd., 165 Cal.App.2d 192, 331 P.2d 728 (1958).

3. The latter part of subdivision (2)—giving either party the right of termination "at any time"—continues prior California law. See Mangini v. Wolfschmidt, Ltd., 165 Cal.App.2d 192, 331 P.2d 728 (1958) and cases cited therein. Subdivision (3) limits the right of termination under subdivision (2) to a right of termination upon reasonable notice and is in accord with prior California law. Great Western Distillery Products, Inc. v. John Wathen Distillery Company, 10 Cal.2d 442, 74 P.2d 745 (1937).

§ 2309

Changes from U.C.C. (1962 Official Text)

4. This is section 2–309 of the Official Text without change.

Uniform Commercial Code Comment

Prior Uniform Statutory Provision:

Subsection (1)—see Sections 43(2), 45(2), 47(1) and 48, Uniform Sales Act, for policy continued under this Article; Subsection (2)—none; Subsection (3)—none.

Changes: Completely different in scope.

Purposes of Changes and New Matter:

1. Subsection (1) requires that all actions taken under a sales contract must be taken within a reasonable time where no time has been agreed upon. The reasonable time under this provision turns on the criteria as to "reasonable time" and on good faith and commercial standards set forth in Sections 1–203, 1–204 and 2–103. It thus depends upon what constitutes acceptable commercial conduct in view of the nature, purpose and circumstances of the action to be taken. Agreement as to a definite time, however, may be found in a term implied from the contractual circumstances, usage of trade or course of dealing or performance as well as in an express term. Such cases fall outside of this subsection since in them the time for action is "agreed" by usage.

2. The time for payment, where not agreed upon, is related to the time for delivery; the particular problems which arise in connection with determining the appropriate time of payment and the time for any inspection before payment which is both allowed by law and demanded by the buyer are covered in Section 2–513.

3. The facts in regard to shipment and delivery differ so widely as to make detailed provision for them in the text of this Article impracticable. The applicable principles, however, make it clear that surprise is to be avoided, good faith judgment is to be protected, and notice or negotiation to reduce the uncertainty to certainty is to be favored.

4. When the time for delivery is left open, unreasonably early offers of or demands for delivery are intended to be read under this Article as expressions of desire or intention, requesting the assent or acquiescence of the other party, not as final positions which may amount without more to breach or to create breach by the other side. See Sections 2–207 and 2–609.

5. The obligation of good faith under this Act requires reasonable notification before a contract may be treated as breached because a reasonable time for delivery or demand has expired. This operates both in the case of a contract originally indefinite as to time and of one subsequently made indefinite by waiver.

When both parties let an originally reasonable time go by in silence, the course of conduct under the contract may be viewed as enlarging the reasonable time for tender or demand of performance. The contract may be terminated by abandonment.

6. Parties to a contract are not required in giving reasonable notification to fix, at peril of breach, a time which is in fact reasonable in the unforeseeable judgment of a later trier of fact. Effective communication of a proposed time limit calls for a response, so that failure to reply will make out acquiescence. Where objection is made, however, or if the demand is merely for information as to when goods will be delivered or will be ordered out, demand for assurances on the ground of insecurity may be made under this Article pending further negotiations. Only when a party insists on undue delay or on rejection of the other party's reasonable proposal is there a question of flat breach under the present section.

7. Subsection (2) applies a commercially reasonable view to resolve the conflict which has arisen in the cases as to contracts of indefinite duration. The "reasonable time" of duration appropriate to a given arrangement is limited by the circumstances. When the arrangement has been carried on by the parties over the years, the "reasonable time" can continue indefinitely and the contract will not terminate until notice.

8. Subsection (3) recognizes that the application of principles of good faith and sound commercial practice normally call for such notification of the termination of a going contract relationship as will give the other party reasonable time to seek a substitute arrangement. An agreement dispensing with notification or limiting the time for the seeking of a substitute arrangement is, of course, valid under this subsection unless the results of putting it into operation would be the creation of an unconscionable state of affairs.

9. Justifiable cancellation for breach is a remedy for breach and is not the kind of termination covered by the present subsection.

10. The requirement of notification is dispensed with where the contract provides for termination on the happening of an "agreed event." "Event" is a term chosen here to contrast with "option" or the like.

Cross References:

Point 1: Sections 1–203, 1–204 and 2–103.
Point 2: Sections 2–320, 2–321, 2–504, and 2–511 through 2–514.
Point 5: Section 1–203.
Point 6: Section 2–609.
Point 7: Section 2–204.
Point 9: Sections 2–106, 2–318, 2–610 and 2–703.

Definitional Cross References:

"Agreement". Section 1–201.
"Contract". Section 1–201.
"Notification". Section 1–201.
"Party". Section 1–201.
"Reasonable time". Section 1–204.
"Termination". Section 2–106.

Cross References

Anticipatory repudiation, see Commercial Code § 2610.
Assurance of due performance, see Commercial Code § 2609.
Cost and freight terms, see Commercial Code §§ 2320, 2321.
Definitions, see Commercial Code §§ 2103, 2106.
Delivery of documents, see Commercial Code § 2514.
Formation of contract, see Commercial Code § 2204.
Inspection of goods by buyer before payment or acceptance, see Commercial Code § 2513.
Obligation of good faith, see Commercial Code § 1203.
Payment by buyer before inspection, see Commercial Code § 2512.
Performance of contracts generally, time for, see Civil Code § 1657.
Reasonable time, see Commercial Code § 1204.
Rescission, grounds, see Civil Code § 1689.
Revocation of proposal, see Civil Code §§ 1586, 1587.
Sellers' remedies in case of breach by buyer, see Commercial Code § 2703.
Shipment of goods by seller, see Commercial Code § 2504.
Tender of payment by buyer, see Commercial Code § 2511.

§ 2310. Open Time for Payment or Running of Credit; Authority to Ship Under Reservation

Unless otherwise agreed

(a) Payment is due at the time and place at which the buyer is to receive the goods even though the place of shipment is the place of delivery; and

(b) If the seller is authorized to send the goods he may ship them under reservation, and may tender the documents of title, but the buyer may inspect the goods after their arrival before payment is due unless such inspection is inconsistent with the terms of the contract (Section 2513); and

(c) If delivery is authorized and made by way of documents of title otherwise than by subdivision (b) then payment is due at the time and place at which the buyer is to receive the documents regardless of where the goods are to be received; and

(d) Where the seller is required or authorized to ship the goods on credit the credit period runs from the time of shipment but postdating the invoice or delaying its dispatch will correspondingly delay the starting of the credit period. *(Stats.1963, c. 819, § 2310.)*

California Code Comment

By John A. Bohn and Charles J. Williams

Prior California Law

1. Paragraph (a) continues the policy of former Civil Code § 1762 which provided that payment and delivery are deemed concurrent conditions. Examples of cases so holding are Wittner Appliances v. Trammell, 193 Cal.App.2d 289, 14 Cal.Rptr. 63 (1961); and S.P. Milling Co. v. Billiwhack Stock Farm, 50 Cal.App.2d 79, 122 P.2d 650 (1942). However, it is important to note that under paragraph (a) receipt of goods rather than "delivery" is a concurrent condition with payment. This provides the buyer with an opportunity to inspect the goods before making payment. Official Comment 1. See also former Civil Code § 1767(1) and (2) (Right to examine goods).

2. The operation and application of paragraph (b) is generally in accord with past California practice. See former Civil Code § 1767(2); Square Deal Machine Co. v. Garrett Corp., 128 Cal.App.2d 286, 275 P.2d 46 (1954); Gladium Co. v. Thatcher, 95 Cal.App. 85, 272 Pac. 340 (1928); Turlock Merchants & Growers, Inc. v. Smith, 80 Cal.App. 263, 251 Pac. 683 (1926).

3. Paragraph (c) continues the rule of former Civil Code § 1767(3) that a buyer of goods shipped under a C.O.D. or similar term is not entitled to examine the goods before payment of the price unless the parties have agreed otherwise.

Changes from U.C.C. (1962 Official Text)

4. This is section 2–310 of the Official Text without change.

Uniform Commercial Code Comment

Prior Uniform Statutory Provision:

Sections 42 and 47(2), Uniform Sales Act.

Changes: Completely rewritten in this and other sections.

Purposes of Changes: This section is drawn to reflect modern business methods of dealing at a distance rather than face to face. Thus:

1. Paragraph (a) provides that payment is due at the time and place "the buyer is to receive the goods" rather than at the point of delivery except in documentary shipment cases (paragraph (c)). This grants an opportunity for the exercise by the buyer of his preliminary right to inspection before paying even though under the delivery term the risk of loss may have previously passed to him or the running of the credit period has already started.

2. Paragraph (b) while providing for inspection by the buyer before he pays, protects the seller. He is not required to give up possession of the goods until he has received payment, where no credit has been contemplated by the parties. The seller may collect through a bank by a sight draft against an order bill of lading "hold until arrival; inspection allowed." The obligations of the bank under such a provision are set forth in Part 5 of Article 4. In the absence of a credit term, the seller is permitted to ship under reservation and if he does payment is then due where and when the buyer is to receive the documents.

3. Unless otherwise agreed, the place for the receipt of the documents and payment is the buyer's city but the time for payment is only after arrival of the goods, since under paragraph (b), and Sections 2–512 and 2–513 the buyer is under no duty to pay prior to inspection.

4. Where the mode of shipment is such that goods must be unloaded immediately upon arrival, too rapidly to permit adequate inspection before receipt, the seller must be guided by the provisions of this Article on inspection which provide that if the seller wishes to demand payment before inspection, he must put an appropriate term into the contract. Even requiring payment against documents will not of itself have this desired result if the documents are to be held until the arrival of the goods. But under (b) and (c) if the terms are C.I.F., C.O.D., or cash against documents payment may be due before inspection.

5. Paragraph (d) states the common commercial understanding that an agreed credit period runs from the time of shipment or from that dating of the invoice which is commonly recognized as a representation of the time of shipment. The provision concerning any delay in sending forth the invoice is included because such conduct results in depriving the buyer of his full notice and warning as to when he must be prepared to pay.

Cross References:

Generally: Part 5.
Point 1: Section 2–509.
Point 2: Sections 2–505, 2–511, 2–512, 2–513 and Article 4.
Point 3: Sections 2–308(b), 2–512 and 2–513.
Point 4: Section 2–513(3)(b).

Definitional Cross References:

"Buyer". Section 2–103.
"Delivery". Section 1–201.
"Document of title". Section 1–201.
"Goods". Section 2–105.
"Receipt of goods". Section 2–103.
"Seller". Section 2–103.
"Send". Section 1–201.
"Term". Section 1–201.

Cross References

Bank deposits and collections, see Commercial Code § 4101 et seq.
Delivery in single lot or several lots, see Commercial Code § 2307.
General obligations of parties, see Commercial Code § 2301.
Inspection by buyer before payment or acceptance, see Commercial Code § 2513.
Payment by buyer before inspection, see Commercial Code § 2512.
Performance, see Commercial Code § 2501 et seq.
Place for delivery in absence of agreements, see Commercial Code § 2308.
Risk of loss, see Commercial Code § 2509.
Shipment by seller with reservation of a security interest, see Commercial Code § 2505.
Tender of payment, see Commercial Code § 2511.
Time of performance of contract, see Civil Code § 1657.

§ 2311. Options and Cooperation Respecting Performance

(1) An agreement for sale which is otherwise sufficiently definite (subdivision (3) of Section 2204) to be a contract is not made invalid by the fact that it leaves particulars of performance to be specified by one of the parties. Any such specification must be made in good faith and within limits set by commercial reasonableness.

(2) Unless otherwise agreed specifications relating to assortment of the goods are at the buyer's opinion and except as otherwise provided in subdivisions (1)(c) and (3) of Section 2319 specifications or arrangements relating to shipment are at the seller's option.

(3) Where such specification would materially affect the other party's performance but is not seasonably made or where one party's co-operation is necessary to the agreed performance of the other but is not seasonably forthcoming, the other party in addition to all other remedies

(a) Is excused for any resulting delay in his own performance; and

(b) May also either proceed to perform in any reasonable manner or after the time for a material part of his own performance treat the failure to specify or to co-operate as a breach by failure to deliver or accept the goods. *(Stats.1963, c. 819, § 2311.)*

California Code Comment

By John A. Bohn and Charles J. Williams

§ 2311 SALES

Prior California Law

1. This section is without direct counterpart in prior California statutory law.

2. Subdivision (1) results basically in a codification of prior California case law. In Mancuso v. Krackov, 110 Cal.App.2d 113, 241 P.2d 1052 (1952) the court stated the California rule in a form which, when taken in conjunction with the related principle given in California Lettuce Growers v. Union Sugar Co., 45 Cal.2d 474, 289 P.2d 785 (1955), could well be taken for the prototype of subdivision (1). In Mancuso v. Krackov, *supra*, at page 115, 241 P.2d 1053, the court said:

"While it is essential that the mutual assent of the parties to the terms of a contract must be sufficiently definite to enable the court to ascertain what they are (case cited), nevertheless it is not necessary that each term be spelled out in minute detail. It is only that the essentials of the contract must have been agreed upon and be ascertainable."

In California Lettuce Growers v. Union Sugar Co., *supra*, at page 484, 289 P.2d 791, the court stated, "where a contract confers on one party a discretionary power affecting the rights of the other, a duty is imposed to exercise that discretion in good faith and in accordance with fair dealing." *Accord*, Automatic Vending Co. v. Wisdom, 182 Cal.App.2d 354, 6 Cal.Rptr. 31 (1960).

In Hylton v. Bowen, 128 Cal.App. 711, 18 P.2d 689 (1933) the court considered the validity of an agreement for the sale of 630 barrels of flour with the buyer having a choice of five different brands or qualities to be selected by him. Held: "The discretion permitted the purchaser . . . did not introduce such an element of uncertainty as would invalidate the contract." *Id.* at 714, 18 P.2d 690, *Contra*, Chipman v. Emeric, 5 Cal. 49, 63 Am.Dec. 80 (1855), (a covenant "to let the lessor have what land he . . . might want for cultivation" held to be void for uncertainty).

3. Whether subdivision (1) changes California law depends upon the construction placed upon Commercial Code § 2204(3) by the California courts.

Under prior California law "only . . . the essentials of the contract" had to "have been agreed upon and be ascertainable." Mancuso v. Krackov, 110 Cal.App.2d 113, 241 P.2d 1052 (1952). Essential terms of the contract under prior California law were stated to be those terms which were necessary to "evidence a meeting of the minds upon the essential features of the agreement" and which sufficiently defined the scope of duties and limits of acceptable performance so as to provide "a rational basis for the assessment of damages." Ellis v. Klaff, 96 Cal.App.2d 471, 216 P.2d 15 (1950).

Subdivision (1) in effect provides that only those terms which are declared by Commercial Code § 2204(3) as essential to the formation of a contract need be ascertainable from the agreement itself. Section 2204(3) states, in effect, that only those terms which are necessary to evidence "an intent to make a contract" and to provide a "reasonable basis for giving an appropriate remedy" are essential to the formation of the contract.

Therefore, both the Commercial Code and prior California law require only that the essential terms be stated in the contract. The actual difference if any between the scope of the language as used in the Commercial Code and prior California law will depend upon the courts construction of the new phrases contained in Commercial Code § 2204(3).

In the California Annotations to the Proposed Uniform Commercial Code, the following position was taken regarding this section:

"[Section 2311] would permit the insertion by either party of terms of a contract after its execution in accordance with established commercial practice. Contracts which under existing California decisions would be treated as too indefinite to enforce are permitted under this section by reference to existing commercial usage. For a collection of these California cases dealing with certainty in terms of a contract see California Annotations to Restatement of Contracts, pp. 21 to 26. Civil Code Section 3538" California Annotations to the Proposed Uniform Commercial Code, printed in Sixth Progress Report to the Legislature by the Senate Fact Finding Committee on Judiciary (1959–1961), Part 1, The Uniform Commercial Code, p. 44.

4. Subdivisions (2) and (3) are without statutory counterpart in prior California law.

Changes from U.C.C. (1962 Official Text)

5. This is section 2–311 of the Official Text without change.

Uniform Commercial Code Comment

Prior Uniform Statutory Provision:

None.

Purposes:

1. Subsection (1) permits the parties to leave certain detailed particulars of performance to be filled in by either of them without running the risk of having the contract invalidated for indefiniteness. The party to whom the agreement gives power to specify the missing details is required to exercise good faith and to act in accordance with commercial standards so that there is no surprise and the range of permissible variation is limited by what is commercially reasonable. The "agreement" which permits one party so to specify may be found as well in a course of dealing, usage of trade, or implication from circumstances as in explicit language used by the parties.

2. Options as to assortment of goods or shipping arrangements are specifically reserved to the buyer and seller respectively under subsection (2) where no other arrangement has been made. This section rejects the test which mechanically and without regard to usage or the purpose of the option gave the option to the party "first under a duty to move" and applies instead a standard commercial interpretation to these circumstances. The "unless otherwise agreed" provision of this subsection covers not only express terms but the background and circumstances which enter into the agreement.

3. Subsection (3) applies when the exercise of an option or cooperation by one party is necessary to or materially affects the other party's performance, but it is not seasonably forthcoming; the subsection relieves the other party from the necessity for performance or excuses his delay in performance as the case may be. The contract-keeping party may at his option under this subsection proceed to perform in any commercially reasonable manner rather than wait. In addition to the special remedies provided, this subsection also reserves "all other remedies". The remedy of particular importance in this connection is that provided for insecurity. Request may also be made pursuant to the obligation of good faith for a reasonable indication of the time and manner of performance for which a party is to hold himself ready.

4. The remedy provided in subsection (3) is one which does not operate in the situation which falls within the scope of Section 2–614 on substituted performance. Where the failure to cooperate results from circumstances set forth in that Section, the other party is under a duty to proffer or demand (as the case may be) substitute performance as a condition to claiming rights against the non-cooperating party.

Cross References:

Point 1: Sections 1–201, 2–204 and 1–203.

Point 3: Sections 1–203 and 2–609.

Point 4: Section 2–614.

Definitional Cross References:

"Agreement". Section 1–201.

"Buyer". Section 2–103.

"Contract for sale". Section 2–106.

"Goods". Section 2–105.

"Party". Section 1–201.

"Remedy". Section 1–201.

"Seasonably". Section 1–204.

"Seller". Section 2–103.

Cross References

Assurance of due performance, see Commercial Code § 2609.

Definitions, see Commercial Code § 1201.

F.O.B. and F.A.S. terms, see Commercial Code § 2319.

Foundation of contract, see Commercial Code § 2204.

Obligation of good faith, see Commercial Code § 1203.

Right to adequate assurance of performance, see Commercial Code § 2609.

Substitute performance, see Commercial Code § 2614.

§ 2312. Warranty of Title and Against Infringement; Buyer's Obligation Against Infringement

(1) Subject to subdivision (2) there is in a contract for sale a warranty by the seller that

(a) The title conveyed shall be good, and its transfer rightful; and

(b) The goods shall be delivered free from any security interest or other lien or encumbrance of which the buyer at the time of contracting has no knowledge.

(2) A warranty under subdivision (1) will be excluded or modified only by specific language or by circumstances which give the buyer reason to know that the person selling does not claim title in himself or that he is purporting to sell only such right or title as he or a third person may have.

(3) Unless otherwise agreed a seller who is a merchant regularly dealing in goods of the kind warrants that the goods shall be delivered free of the rightful claim of any third person by way of infringement or the like but a buyer who furnishes specifications to the seller must hold the seller harmless against any such claim which arises out of compliance with the specifications. *(Stats.1963, c. 819, § 2312.)*

California Code Comment

By John A. Bohn and Charles J. Williams

Prior California Law

1. Subdivision (1)(a) is basically a restatement of the rule of former Civil Code § 1733(1). The few California cases that have considered warranty of title have held that while the seller is not required to give a marketable title, he must give a good and complete title. Loew's Inc. v. Wolfe, 101 F.Supp. 981 (S.D.Cal.1951); Barnum v. Cochrane, 143 Cal. 642, 77 Pac. 656 (1904); Gross v. Kierski, 41 Cal. 111 (1871); Miller v. Van Tassel, 24 Cal. 458 (1864).

2. Subdivision (1)(b) has as its counterpart former Civil Code § 1733(3). Under this subdivision the reference to "knowledge" means actual knowledge (Official Comment 1) whereas former Civil Code § 1733(3) did not specify whether knowledge as used in that section was intended as actual or constructive knowledge. Until the adoption of this section, this was an open question in California.

This section eliminates the warranty of quiet possession contained in former Civil Code § 1733(2) and provides that a "disturbance of quiet possession" is merely one of the ways "in which the breach of warranty of title may be established." Official Comment 1.

3. Subdivision (2) is similar to former Civil Code § 1733(4) which stated that there were no warranties of title in cases where "a sheriff, mortgagee, or other person professing to sell by virtue of authority in fact or law, goods in which a third person has a legal or equitable interest." *Accord,* Routh v. Quinn, 20 Cal.2d 488, 127 P.2d 1 (1942).

4. Subdivision (3) is new statutory law. Its scope is limited to a warranty by a merchant seller that his goods are not subject to a valid third party claim based on patent or trademark infringement. Official Comment 3.

5. For a detailed discussion of this section and prior California law see Ezer, The Impact of The Uniform Commercial Code on The California Law of Sales Warranties, 8 U.C.L.A.L.Rev. 281, 309 (1961).

Changes from U.C.C. (1962 Official Text)

6. This is section 2–312 of the Official Text without change.

Uniform Commercial Code Comment

Prior Uniform Statutory Provision:

Section 13, Uniform Sales Act.

Changes: Completely rewritten, the provisions concerning infringement being new.

Purposes of Changes:

1. Subsection (1) makes provision for a buyer's basic needs in respect to a title which he in good faith expects to acquire by his purchase, namely, that he receive a good, clean title transferred to him also in a rightful manner so that he will not be exposed to a lawsuit in order to protect it.

The warranty extends to a buyer whether or not the seller was in possession of the goods at the time the sale or contract to sell was made.

The warranty of quiet possession is abolished. Disturbance of quiet possession, although not mentioned specifically, is one way, among many, in which the breach of the warranty of title may be established.

The "knowledge" referred to in subsection 1(b) is actual knowledge as distinct from notice.

2. The provisions of this Article requiring notification to the seller within a reasonable time after the buyer's discovery of a breach apply to notice of a breach of the warranty of title, where the seller's breach was innocent. However, if the seller's breach was in bad faith he cannot be permitted to claim that he has been misled or prejudiced by the delay in giving notice. In such case the "reasonable" time for notice should receive a very liberal interpretation. Whether the breach by the seller is in good or bad faith Section 2–725 provides that the cause of action accrues when the breach occurs. Under the provisions of that section the breach of the warranty of good title occurs when tender of delivery is made since the warranty is not one which extends to "future performance of the goods."

3. When the goods are part of the seller's normal stock and are sold in his normal course of business, it is his duty to see that no claim of infringement of a patent or trade-mark by a third party will mar the buyer's title. A sale by a person other than a dealer, however, raises no implication in its circumstances of such a warranty. Nor is there such an implication when the buyer orders goods to be assembled, prepared or manufactured on his own specifications. If, in such a case, the resulting product infringes a patent or trade-mark, the liability will run from buyer to seller. There is, under such circumstances, a tacit representation on the part of the buyer that the seller will be safe in manufacturing according to the specifications, and the buyer is under an obligation in good faith to indemnify him for any loss suffered.

4. This section rejects the cases which recognize the principle that infringements violate the warranty of title but deny the buyer a remedy unless he has been expressly prevented from using the goods. Under this Article "eviction" is not a necessary condition to the buyer's remedy since the buyer's remedy arises immediately upon receipt of notice of infringement; it is merely one way of establishing the fact of breach.

5. Subsection (2) recognizes that sales by sheriffs, executors, foreclosing lienors and persons similarly situated are so out of the ordinary commercial course that their peculiar character is immediately apparent to the buyer and therefore no personal obligation is imposed upon the seller who is purporting to sell only an unknown or limited right. This subsection does not touch upon and leaves open all questions of restitution arising in such cases, when a unique article so sold is reclaimed by a third party as the rightful owner.

6. The warranty of subsection (1) is not designated as an "implied" warranty, and hence is not subject to Section 2–316(3). Disclaimer of the warranty of title is governed instead by subsection (2), which requires either specific language or the described circumstances.

Cross References:

Point 1: Section 2–403.
Point 2: Sections 2–607 and 2–725.
Point 3: Section 1–203.
Point 4: Sections 2–609 and 2–725.
Point 6: Section 2–316.

Definitional Cross References:

"Buyer". Section 2–103.
"Contract for sale". Section 2–106.

Time, reasonable time and seasonably defined, see Commercial Code § 1204.

§ 2312

"Goods". Section 2–105.
"Person". Section 1–201.
"Right". Section 1–201.
"Seller". Section 2–103.

Cross References

Acceptance of goods, see Commercial Code § 2607.
Assurance of due performance, see Commercial Code § 2609.
Buyer's damages for breach in regard to accepted goods, see Commercial Code § 2714.
Damages, measure, see Civil Code § 3300 et seq.
Entrusting of possession of goods, see Commercial Code § 2403.
Exclusion or modification of warranties, see Commercial Code § 2316.
Limitation of action for breach of warranty, see Commercial Code § 2725.
Notice of claim or litigation to person answerable over, see Commercial Code § 2607.
Obligation of good faith, see Commercial Code § 1203.
Sale of personal property, included authority of agents, see Civil Code § 2323.
Warranties on negotiation or transfer of documents of title, see Commercial Code § 7507.
Warranties on presentment and transfer, investment securities, see Commercial Code § 8306.

§ 2313. Express Warranties by Affirmation, Promise, Description, Sample

(1) Express warranties by the seller are created as follows:

(a) Any affirmation of fact or promise made by the seller to the buyer which relates to the goods and becomes part of the basis of the bargain creates an express warranty that the goods shall conform to the affirmation or promise.

(b) Any description of the goods which is made part of the basis of the bargain creates an express warranty that the goods shall conform to the description.

(c) Any sample or model which is made part of the basis of the bargain creates an express warranty that the whole of the goods shall conform to the sample or model.

(2) It is not necessary to the creation of an express warranty that the seller use formal words such as "warrant" or "guarantee" or that he have a specific intention to make a warranty, but an affirmation merely of the value of the goods or a statement purporting to be merely the seller's opinion or commendation of the goods does not create a warranty. (Stats.1963, c. 819, § 2313.)

California Code Comment

By John A. Bohn and Charles J. Williams

Prior California Law

1. Under both the Commercial Code and the prior California law, express warranties arise from the actions or agreement of the parties. Official Comment 1; American Seedless Raisin Co. v. Joshua Hendy Iron Works, 94 Cal.App. 289, 271 Pac. 129 (1928).

2. Subdivision (1)(a) is similar to prior California law as expressed in former Civil Code § 1732 (Definition of expressed warranty). See Burr v. Sherwin Williams Co., 42 Cal.2d 682, 268 P.2d 1041 (1954) ("The principal elements of an express warranty are an affirmation of fact or promise by the seller and reliance thereon by the buyer."). However, the definition contained in subdivision (1)(a) is broader than the definition contained in former Civil Code § 1732. In former Civil Code § 1732 reliance by the buyer was an essential requirement for the creation of an express warranty. Pedroli v. Russell, 157 Cal.App.2d 281, 320 P.2d 873 (1958). Under Subdivision (1) of this section "no particular reliance on [affirmations of fact] need be shown in order to weave them into the fabric of agreement." Official Comment 3.

3. Subdivision (1)(a) changes the prior California rule that in the absence of consideration an express warranty could not be created after the time of sale. See Burdrow v. Wheatcraft, 115 Cal.App.2d 517, 252 P.2d 637 (1953) and Official Comment 7.

4. Subdivision (1)(b) is similar to former Civil Code § 1734, except that this paragraph converts a warranty formerly implied under the USA into an express warranty.

Under Civil Code § 1734, past dealings of the parties did not create implied warranties of description. El Zarape Tortilla Factory, Inc. v. Plant Food Corp., 90 Cal.App.2d 336, 203 P.2d 13 (1949). This position is rejected by the Commercial Code. Official Comment 5 states that "past deliveries may set the description of quality, either expressly or impliedly by course of dealing." Accord, Rosenberg v. Geo. A. Moore Co., 194 Cal. 392, 229 Pac. 34 (1924).

5. Subdivision (1)(c) is similar to former Civil Code § 1736(a) except that this paragraph converts a warranty formerly implied under the USA into an express warranty.

As in the case of warranty by affirmation, prior California law held that a warranty by sample could not be created after the formation of the contract. Alexander v. Stone, 29 Cal.App. 488, 156 Pac. 998 (1916). This rule is altered by subdivision (1)(c) under which the time when the sample is shown is not material. See Official Comment 7.

Former Civil Code § 1763(a) required that the "*bulk* correspond with the sample in quality" (emphasis added). This paragraph requires that the "*whole* . . . conform to the sample or model." (emphasis added). For a discussion of the effect of this change of terms in Pennsylvania, see note, 15 U.Pitt.L.Rev. 331, 336 (1953). Finally, subdivision (1)(c) in addition to using the term sample introduces a new term—"model."

6. The significance of changing an implied warranty into an express warranty lies in the fact that under Commercial Code § 2316 a "disclaimer" is inoperative if it is inconsistent with an express warranty or if it is unreasonable.

7. The provision of subdivision (2) that formal terms such as "warrant" and "guarantee" are not necessary to create an express warranty is in accord with California law. See Steiner v. Jarrett, 130 Cal.App.2d Supp. 869, 280 P.2d 235 (1954).

In providing that the seller's specific intent is not an element in the creation of an express warranty, (Official Comment 3), subdivision (2) is in accord with California law. See Chamberlain Co. v. Allis-Chalmers Co., 51 Cal.App.2d 520, 125 P.2d 113 (1942) ("The Uniform Act [Civil Code, § 1732] does not . . . require any such intent [intent to warrant], and its effect is to dispense with the necessity therefor.") For dictum to the contrary see Sutter v. Associated Seed Growers Inc., 31 Cal.App.2d 543, 88 P.2d 144 (1939). Prior to the adoption of the USA (former Civil Code §§ 1721 through 1800) the California decisions were split on this issue. Compare Hackett v. Lewis, 36 Cal.App. 687, 173 Pac. 111 (1918) and McLennan v. Ohmen, 75 Cal. 558, 17 Pac. 687 (1888) stating that sellers' intent is a requirement for an express warranty with Pepper v. Vedova, 26 Cal.App. 406, 147 Pac. 105 (1915) and Lewin v. Pioneer Hatchery, 99 Cal.App. 473, 278 Pac. 902 (1929) holding that intent is not required.

The second clause of subdivision (2) relating to statements of opinion and value is similar to the last sentence of former Civil Code § 1732. For example see Williams v. Lowenthal, 124 Cal.App. 179, 12 P.2d 75 (1932).

8. The right to inspection implied under former Civil Code § 1736 (b) is preserved in Commercial Code § 2513(1).

9. For a detailed analysis of section 2313 and prior California law see Ezer, The Impact of The Uniform Commercial Code on The California Law of Sales Warranties, 8 U.C.L.A.L.Rev. 281, 284 (1961).

Changes from U.C.C. (1962 Official Text)

10. This is section 2–313 of the Official Text without change.

Uniform Commercial Code Comment

Prior Uniform Statutory Provision:
Sections 12, 14 and 16, Uniform Sales Act.
Changes: Rewritten.

Purposes of Changes: To consolidate and systematize basic principles with the result that:

1. "Express" warranties rest on "dickered" aspects of the individual bargain, and go so clearly to the essence of that bargain that words of disclaimer in a form are repugnant to the basic dickered terms. "Implied" warranties rest so clearly on a common factual situation or set of conditions that no particular language or action is necessary to evidence them and they will arise in such a situation unless unmistakably negated.

This section reverts to the older case law insofar as the warranties of description and sample are designated "express" rather than "implied".

2. Although this section is limited in its scope and direct purpose to warranties made by the seller to the buyer as part of a contract for sale, the warranty sections of this Article are not designed in any way to disturb those lines of case law growth which have recognized that warranties need not be confined either to sales contracts or to the direct parties to such a contract. They may arise in other appropriate circumstances such as in the case of bailments for hire, whether such bailment is itself the main contract or is merely a supplying of containers under a contract for the sale of their contents. The provisions of Section 2–318 on third party beneficiaries expressly recognize this case law development within one particular area. Beyond that, the matter is left to the case law with the intention that the policies of this Act may offer useful guidance in dealing with further cases as they arise.

3. The present section deals with affirmations of fact by the seller, descriptions of the goods or exhibitions of samples, exactly as any other part of a negotiation which ends in a contract is dealt with. No specific intention to make a warranty is necessary if any of these factors is made part of the basis of the bargain. In actual practice affirmations of fact made by the seller about the goods during a bargain are regarded as part of the description of those goods; hence no particular reliance on such statements need be shown in order to weave them into the fabric of the agreement. Rather, any fact which is to take such affirmations, once made, out of the agreement requires clear affirmative proof. The issue normally is one of fact.

4. In view of the principle that the whole purpose of the law of warranty is to determine what it is that the seller has in essence agreed to sell, the policy is adopted of those cases which refuse except in unusual circumstances to recognize a material deletion of the seller's obligation. Thus, a contract is normally a contract for a sale of something describable and described. A clause generally disclaiming "all warranties, express or implied" cannot reduce the seller's obligation with respect to such description and therefore cannot be given literal effect under Section 2–316.

This is not intended to mean that the parties, if they consciously desire, cannot make their own bargain as they wish. But in determining what they have agreed upon good faith is a factor and consideration should be given to the fact that the probability is small that a real price is intended to be exchanged for a pseudo-obligation.

5. Paragraph (1)(b) makes specific some of the principles set forth above when a description of the goods is given by the seller.

A description need not be by words. Technical specifications, blueprints and the like can afford more exact description than mere language and if made part of the basis of the bargain goods must conform with them. Past deliveries may set the description of quality, either expressly or impliedly by course of dealing. Of course, all descriptions by merchants must be read against the applicable trade usages with the general rules as to merchantability resolving any doubts.

6. The basic situation as to statements affecting the true essence of the bargain is no different when a sample or model is involved in the transaction. This section includes both a "sample" actually drawn from the bulk of goods which is the subject matter of the sale, and a "model" which is offered for inspection when the subject matter is not at hand and which has not been drawn from the bulk of the goods.

Although the underlying principles are unchanged, the facts are often ambiguous when something is shown as illustrative, rather than as a straight sample. In general, the presumption is that any sample or model just as any affirmation of fact is intended to become a basis of the bargain. But there is no escape from the question of fact. When the seller exhibits a sample purporting to be drawn from an existing bulk, good faith of course requires that the sample be fairly drawn. But in mercantile experience the mere exhibition of a "sample" does not of itself show whether it is merely intended to "suggest" or to "be" the character of the subject-matter of the contract. The question is whether the seller has so acted with reference to the sample as to make him responsible that the whole shall have at least the values shown by it. The circumstances aid in answering this question. If the sample has been drawn from an existing bulk, it must be regarded as describing values of the goods contracted for unless it is accompanied by an unmistakable denial of such responsibility. If, on the other hand, a model of merchandise not on hand is offered, the mercantile presumption that it has become a literal description of the subject matter is not so strong, and particularly so if modification on the buyer's initiative impairs any feature of the model.

7. The precise time when words of description or affirmation are made or samples are shown is not material. The sole question is whether the language or samples or models are fairly to be regarded as part of the contract. If language is used after the closing of the deal (as when the buyer when taking delivery asks and receives an additional assurance), the warranty becomes a modification, and need not be supported by consideration if it is otherwise reasonable and in order (Section 2–209).

8. Concerning affirmations of value or a seller's opinion or commendation under subsection (2), the basic question remains the same: What statements of the seller have in the circumstances and in objective judgment become part of the basis of the bargain? As indicated above, all of the statements of the seller do so unless good reason is shown to the contrary. The provisions of subsection (2) are included, however, since common experience discloses that some statements or predictions cannot fairly be viewed as entering into the bargain. Even as to false statements of value, however, the possibility is left open that a remedy may be provided by the law relating to fraud or misrepresentation.

Cross References:

Point 1: Section 2–316.
Point 2: Sections 1–102(3) and 2–318.
Point 3: Section 2–316(2)(b).
Point 4: Section 2–316.
Point 5: Sections 1–205(4) and 2–314.
Point 6: Section 2–316.
Point 7: Section 2–209.
Point 8: Section 1–103.

Definitional Cross References:

"Buyer". Section 2–103.
"Conforming". Section 2–106.
"Goods". Section 2–105.
"Seller". Section 2–103.

Cross References

Agent's authority to warrant, see Civil Code § 2323.
Allocation or division of risks, see Commercial Code § 2303.
Consumer warranties, see Civil Code § 1790 et seq.
Course of dealing and usage of trade, see Commercial Code § 1205.
Exclusion or modification of warranties, see Commercial Code § 2316.
Express warranties displacing implied warranties, see Commercial Code § 2317.
Fraud in purchase, sale or exchange of property, see Civil Code § 3343.
Implied warranty,
    Fitness for particular purpose, see Commercial Code § 2315.
Livestock, warranties on sale, see Food and Agricultural Code §§ 18501, 18502.
Modification, rescission and waiver, see Commercial Code § 2209.
Obligation of good faith, see Commercial Code § 1203.
Supplementation of code by principles of law and equity, see Commercial Code § 1103.
Variation from provisions of code by agreement, see Commercial Code § 1102.

§ 2314. Implied Warranty; Merchantability; Usage of Trade

(1) Unless excluded or modified (Section 2316), a warranty that the goods shall be merchantable is implied in a contract for their sale <u>if the seller is a merchant with respect to goods of that kind.</u> Under

§ 2314

this section the serving for value of food or drink to be consumed either on the premises or elsewhere is a sale.

(2) Goods to be merchantable must be at least such as

(a) Pass without objection in the trade under the contract description; and

(b) In the case of fungible goods, are of fair average quality within the description; and

(c) Are fit for the ordinary purposes for which such goods are used; and

(d) Run, within the variations permitted by the agreement, of even kind, quality and quantity within each unit and among all units involved; and

(e) Are adequately contained, packaged, and labeled as the agreement may require; and

(f) Conform to the promises or affirmations of fact made on the container or label if any.

(3) Unless excluded or modified (Section 2316) other implied warranties may arise from course of dealing or usage of trade. *(Stats.1963, c. 819, § 2314.)*

California Code Comment

By John A. Bohn and Charles J. Williams

Prior California Law

1. The first sentence of subdivision (1) continues the basic policy of former Civil Code § 1735(2), but is broader in that it does not limit the implied warranty of merchantability to goods sold by description. Under subdivision (1) the warranty arises under this section if "the seller is a merchant with respect to goods of that kind" while under former Civil Code § 1735(2) the warranty arose when the seller was one who dealt "in goods of that description."

The second sentence of subdivision (1), defining as a sale the serving of food and drink, is in accord with prior California case law. Klein v. Duchess Sandwich Co., 14 Cal.2d 272, 93 P.2d 799 (1939) and Mix v. Ingersoll Candy Co., 6 Cal.2d 674, 59 P.2d 144 (1936).

2. Subdivision (2) gives minimal standards for "merchantable quality." There were no such standards listed in former Civil Code § 1735 (2). However certain minimal requirements were developed by California decisions. For example, see Burr v. Sherwin Williams, 42 Cal.2d 682, 268 P.2d 1041 (1954) and Moore v. Hubbard & Johnson Lbr. Co., 149 Cal.App.2d 236, 308 P.2d 794 (1957).

3. Subdivision (2)(a) is in accord with prior California law as expressed in Burr v. Sherwin Williams, 42 Cal.2d 682, 268 P.2d 1041 (1954) ("goods . . . which are capable of passing in the market under the name or description by which they were sold."). However, paragraph (a) requires that the goods pass "without objection." For a discussion of the possible significance of this phrase, see Ezer, The Impact of The Uniform Commercial Code on The California Law of Sales Warranties, 8 U.C.L.A.L.Rev. 281, 293 (1961).

4. Subdivision (2)(b) changes California law as expressed in a case involving milk, Streff v. Gold Medal Creamery Co., 96 Cal.App. 18, 273 Pac. 831 (1928): "The requirement of merchantability . . . does not require that the goods . . be as good as the average of goods."; and Kenney v. Grogan, 17 Cal.App. 527, 120 Pac. 433 (1911) dealing with olives: "the requirement . . that the goods shall be merchantable, does not require that the goods . . . shall be as good as the average of goods of the sort."

5. Subdivision (2)(c) is in accord with prior California law as expressed in Simmons v. Rhodes & Jamieson, Ltd., 46 Cal.2d 190, 293 P.2d 26 (1956) (" 'Merchantable quality' means that the substance sold is reasonably suitable for the ordinary uses it was manufactured to meet"), and Burr v. Sherwin Williams Co., 42 Cal.2d 682, 268 P.2d 1041 (1954) ("goods which are reasonably suitable for the ordinary uses and purposes of goods of the general type described by the terms of the sale.")

6. Subdivision (2)(e) is in accord with prior California law as expressed in Stella v. Smith, 109 Cal.App. 409, 293 Pac. 656 (1930).

7. Paragraph (2)(f) is in substantial accord with prior California law as expressed in Burr v. Sherwin Williams, 42 Cal.2d 682, 268 P.2d 1041 (1954) and Lane v. C. A. Swanson & Sons, 130 Cal.App.2d 210, 278 P.2d 723 (1954). However, subdivision (2)(f) changes prior California law that such promises or affirmations of fact created *express* warranties. Burr v. Sherwin Williams, *supra,* and Lane v. C. A. Swanson & Sons, *supra.*

8. Subdivision (3) is in accord with but broadens former Civil Code § 1735(5). Under former Civil Code § 1735(5) usage of trade warranties were recognized. Subdivision (3) retains this warranty and adds a "course of dealing" warranty.

9. For a detailed analysis of section 2314 and prior California law, see Ezer, The Impact of The Uniform Commercial Code on The California Law of Sales Warranties, 8 U.C.L.A.L.Rev. 281, 292 (1961).

Changes from U.C.C. (1962 Official Text)

10. This is section 2–314 of the Official Text without change.

Uniform Commercial Code Comment

Prior Uniform Statutory Provision:
Section 15(2), Uniform Sales Act.
Changes: Completely rewritten.
Purposes of Changes: This section, drawn in view of the steadily developing case law on the subject, is intended to make it clear that:

1. The seller's obligation applies to present sales as well as to contracts to sell subject to the effects of any examination of specific goods. (Subsection (2) of Section 2–316). Also, the warranty of merchantability applies to sales for use as well as to sales for resale.

2. The question when the warranty is imposed turns basically on the meaning of the terms of the agreement as recognized in the trade. Goods delivered under an agreement made by a merchant in a given line of trade must be of a quality comparable to that generally acceptable in that line of trade under the description or other designation of the goods used in the agreement. The responsibility imposed rests on any merchant-seller, and the absence of the words "grower or manufacturer or not" which appeared in Section 15(2) of the Uniform Sales Act does not restrict the applicability of this section.

3. A specific designation of goods by the buyer does not exclude the seller's obligation that they be fit for the general purposes appropriate to such goods. A contract for the sale of second-hand goods, however, involves only such obligation as is appropriate to such goods for that is their contract description. A person making an isolated sale of goods is not a "merchant" within the meaning of the full scope of this section and, thus, no warranty of merchantability would apply. His knowledge of any defects not apparent on inspection would, however, without need for express agreement and in keeping with the underlying reason of the present section and the provisions on good faith, impose an obligation that known material but hidden defects be fully disclosed.

4. Although a seller may not be a "merchant" as to the goods in question, if he states generally that they are "guaranteed" the provisions of this section may furnish a guide to the content of the resulting express warranty. This has particular significance in the case of second-hand sales, and has further significance in limiting the effect of fine-print disclaimer clauses where their effect would be inconsistent with large-print assertions of "guarantee."

5. The second sentence of subsection (1) covers the warranty with respect to food and drink. Serving food or drink for value is a sale, whether to be consumed on the premises or elsewhere. Cases to the contrary are rejected. The principal warranty is that stated in subsections (1) and (2)(c) of this section.

6. Subsection (2) does not purport to exhaust the meaning of "merchantable" nor to negate any of its attributes not specifically mentioned in the text of the statute, but arising by usage of trade or through case law. The language used is "must be at least such as . . .," and the intention is to leave open other possible attributes of merchantability.

7. Paragraphs (a) and (b) of subsection (2) are to be read together. Both refer, as indicated above, to the standards of that line of the trade which fits the transaction and the seller's business. "Fair average" is a term directly appropriate to agricultural bulk products and means goods centering around the middle belt of quality, not the least or the worst

that can be understood in the particular trade by the designation, but such as can pass "without objection." Of course a fair percentage of the least is permissible but the goods are not "fair average" if they are all of the least or worst quality possible under the description. In cases of doubt as to what quality is intended, the price at which a merchant closes a contract is an excellent index of the nature and scope of his obligation under the present section.

8. Fitness for the ordinary purposes for which goods of the type are used is a fundamental concept of the present section and is covered in paragraph (c). As stated above, merchantability is also a part of the obligation owing to the purchaser for use. Correspondingly, protection, under this aspect of the warranty, of the person buying for resale to the ultimate consumer is equally necessary, and merchantable goods must therefore be "honestly" resalable in the normal course of business because they are what they purport to be.

9. Paragraph (d) on evenness of kind, quality and quantity follows case law. But precautionary language has been added as a reminder of the frequent usages of trade which permit substantial variations both with and without an allowance or an obligation to replace the varying units.

10. Paragraph (e) applies only where the nature of the goods and of the transaction require a certain type of container, package or label. Paragraph (f) applies, on the other hand, wherever there is a label or container on which representations are made, even though the original contract, either by express terms or usage of trade, may not have required either the labelling or the representation. This follows from the general obligation of good faith which requires that a buyer should not be placed in the position of reselling or using goods delivered under false representations appearing on the package or container. No problem of extra consideration arises in this connection since, under this Article, an obligation is imposed by the original contract not to deliver mislabeled articles, and the obligation is imposed where mercantile good faith so requires and without reference to the doctrine of consideration.

11. Exclusion or modification of the warranty of merchantability, or of any part of it, is dealt with in the section to which the text of the present section makes explicit precautionary references. That section must be read with particular reference to its subsection (4) on limitation of remedies. The warranty of merchantability, wherever it is normal, is so commonly taken for granted that its exclusion from the contract is a matter threatening surprise and therefore requiring special precaution.

12. Subsection (3) is to make explicit that usage of trade and course of dealing can create warranties and that they are implied rather than express warranties and thus subject to exclusion or modification under Section 2-316. A typical instance would be the obligation to provide pedigree papers to evidence conformity of the animal to the contract in the case of a pedigreed dog or blooded bull.

13. In an action based on breach of warranty, it is of course necessary to show not only the existence of the warranty but the fact that the warranty was broken and that the breach of the warranty was the proximate cause of the loss sustained. In such an action an affirmative showing by the seller that the loss resulted from some action or event following his own delivery of the goods can operate as a defense. Equally, evidence indicating that the seller exercised care in the manufacture, processing or selection of the goods is relevant to the issue of whether the warranty was in fact broken. Action by the buyer following an examination of the goods which ought to have indicated the defect complained of can be shown as matter bearing on whether the breach itself was the cause of the injury.

Cross References:

Point 1: Section 2-316.
Point 3: Sections 1-203 and 2-104.
Point 5: Section 2-315.
Point 11: Section 2-316.
Point 12: Sections 1-201, 1-205 and 2-316.

Definitional Cross References:

"Agreement". Section 1-201.
"Contract". Section 1-201.
"Contract for sale". Section 2-106.
"Goods". Section 2-105.
"Merchant". Section 2-104.
"Seller". Section 2-103.

Cross References

Allocation or division of risks, see Commercial Code § 2303.
Consumer warranties, see Civil Code § 1790 et seq.
Course of dealing and usage of trade, see Commercial Code § 1205.
Definitions, see Commercial Code §§ 1201, 2103, 2104.
Exclusion or modification of warranties, see Commercial Code § 2316.
Express warranties displacing implied warranties, see Commercial Code § 2317.
Fraud in purchase, sale or exchange of property, see Civil Code § 3343.
Language sufficient to exclude implied warranties of merchantability and fitness, see Commercial Code § 2316.
Modification, rescission and waiver, see Commercial Code § 2209.
Obligation of good faith, see Commercial Code § 1203.
Retail installment sales, see Civil Code § 1801 et seq.
Sale of animal for slaughter, no implied warranty of merchantable quality, see Food and Agricultural Code § 18502.
Supplementary general principles of law, applicability, see Commercial Code § 1103.
Variation of code by agreement, see Commercial Code § 1102.
Warranties on negotiation or transfer of documents of title, see Commercial Code § 7507.

§ 2315. Implied Warranty: Fitness for Particular Purpose

Where the seller at the time of contracting has reason to know any particular purpose for which the goods are required and that the buyer is relying on the seller's skill or judgment to select or furnish suitable goods, there is unless excluded or modified under the next section an implied warranty that the goods shall be fit for such purpose. (Stats.1963, c. 819, § 2315.)

California Code Comment

By John A. Bohn and Charles J. Williams

Prior California Law

1. Section 2315 is comparable to former Civil Code § 1735(1). One of the requirements for the warranty for a particular purpose under former Civil Code § 1735(1) was that the "buyer, expressly or by implication [make] known to the seller the particular purpose for which the goods are required." Section 2315 removes this limiting language and states that the warranty arises given reliance by the buyer, "when the seller . . . *has reason to know* any particular purpose for which the goods are required." (emphasis added). In interpreting former Civil Code § 1735(1) the California courts stated that the warranty under that section depended upon the buyer informing the seller of the particular purpose for which he was purchasing the goods. In each of these decisions the buyer had expressly informed the seller of the purpose for which they were purchased. There is no case in California in which the court was faced with a situation where an interpretation of knowledge of purpose "by implication" was necessary to the decision. See Lindberg v. Coutches, 167 Cal.App.2d Supp. 828, 334 P.2d 701 (1959); Odell v. Frueh, 146 Cal.App.2d 504, 304 P.2d 45 (1957); Willig v. Brethauer, 127 Cal.App.2d 650, 274 P.2d 202 (1954); Drabkin v. Bigelow, 59 Cal.App.2d 68, 138 P.2d 750 (1943); and Ice Bowl, Inc. v. Spaulding Sales Corp., 56 Cal.App.2d 918, 133 P.2d 846 (1943). However, the phrase "has reason to know" in section 2315 eliminates the problem from the standpoint of the duty upon the buyer to make known his purpose before the implied warranty arises.

2. Former Civil Code § 1735(4) stated that there was no implied warranty for particular purpose in the case of "a specified article under its patent or other trade name . . . ." However, it was held in Drumar Mining Co. v. Morris Ravine Mining Co., 33 Cal.App.2d 492, 92 P.2d 424, (1939) that "the question as to whether the article was described by its trade name or trade mark *is not conclusive* if the other conditions exist which would raise an implied warranty [of fitness for a particular purpose]." (All italicized in original.) This principle was restated in

§ 2315   SALES

Odell v. Frueh, 146 Cal.App.2d 504, 510, 304 P.2d 45, 50 (1956), the court saying:

"If the requisites of an implied warranty for a particular purpose are present—the vendor's knowledge of the special purpose and the vendee's reliance upon his seller's judgment—the fact that the article sold is described by its trade-name does not prevent the imposition of a warranty obligation. (cases cited) . . . [Civil Code § 1735(4)] enacts only the truism that when a consumer purchases a branded item he is more likely to be relying upon his own judgment or the promotional efforts of the manufacturer than upon the skill and judgment of his seller."

Therefore, although section 2315 is drafted in different terms it continues the rule of Civil Code § 1735(4) as construed by the California courts. See Official Comment 5.

3. Section 2315 eliminates the phrase "whether growers or manufacturers" which was contained in former Civil Code § 1735(1).

4. For a detailed analysis of section 2315 and prior California law, see Ezer, The Impact of The Uniform Commercial Code on The California Law of Sales Warranties, 8 U.C.L.A.L.Rev. 281, 296 (1961).

Changes from U.C.C. (1962 Official Text)

5. This is section 2–315 of the Official Text without change.

Uniform Commercial Code Comment

Prior Uniform Statutory Provision:
Section 15(1), (4), (5), Uniform Sales Act.
Changes: Rewritten.

Purposes of Changes:

1. Whether or not this warranty arises in any individual case is basically a question of fact to be determined by the circumstances of the contracting. Under this section the buyer need not bring home to the seller actual knowledge of the particular purpose for which the goods are intended or of his reliance on the seller's skill and judgment, if the circumstances are such that the seller has reason to realize the purpose intended or that the reliance exists. The buyer, of course, must actually be relying on the seller.

2. A "particular purpose" differs from the ordinary purpose for which the goods are used in that it envisages a specific use by the buyer which is peculiar to the nature of his business whereas the ordinary purposes for which goods are used are those envisaged in the concept of merchantability and go to uses which are customarily made of the goods in question. For example, shoes are generally used for the purpose of walking upon ordinary ground, but a seller may know that a particular pair was selected to be used for climbing mountains.

A contract may of course include both a warranty of merchantability and one of fitness for a particular purpose.

The provisions of this Article on the cumulation and conflict of express and implied warranties must be considered on the question of inconsistency between or among warranties. In such a case any question of fact as to which warranty was intended by the parties to apply must be resolved in favor of the warranty of fitness for particular purpose as against all other warranties except where the buyer has taken upon himself the responsibility of furnishing the technical specifications.

3. In connection with the warranty of fitness for a particular purpose the provisions of this Article on the allocation or division of risks are particularly applicable in any transaction in which the purpose for which the goods are to be used combines requirements both as to the quality of the goods themselves and compliance with certain laws or regulations. How the risks are divided is a question of fact to be determined, where not expressly contained in the agreement, from the circumstances of contracting, usage of trade, course of performance and the like, matters which may constitute the "otherwise agreement" of the parties by which they may divide the risk or burden.

4. The absence from this section of the language used in the Uniform Sales Act in referring to the seller, "whether he be the grower or manufacturer or not," is not intended to impose any requirement that the seller be a grower or manufacturer. Although normally the warranty will arise only where the seller is a merchant with the appropriate "skill or judgment," it can arise as to nonmerchants where this is justified by the particular circumstances.

5. The elimination of the "patent or other trade name" exception constitutes the major extension of the warranty of fitness which has been made by the cases and continued in this Article. Under the present section the existence of a patent or other trade name and the designation of the article by that name, or indeed in any other definite manner, is only one of the facts to be considered on the question of whether the buyer actually relied on the seller, but it is not of itself decisive of the issue. If the buyer himself is insisting on a particular brand he is not relying on the seller's skill and judgment and so no warranty results. But the mere fact that the article purchased has a particular patent or trade name is not sufficient to indicate nonreliance if the article has been recommended by the seller as adequate for the buyer's purposes.

6. The specific reference forward in the present section to the following section on exclusion or modification of warranties is to call attention to the possibility of eliminating the warranty in any given case. However it must be noted that under the following section the warranty of fitness for a particular purpose must be excluded or modified by a conspicuous writing.

Cross References:
Point 2: Sections 2–314 and 2–317.
Point 3: Section 2–303.
Point 6: Section 2–316.

Definitional Cross References:
"Buyer". Section 2–103.
"Goods". Section 2–105.
"Seller". Section 2–103.

Cross References

Allocation of risk or burden, see Commercial Code § 2303.
Consumer warranties, see Civil Code § 1790 et seq.
Course of dealing and usage of trade, see Commercial Code § 1205.
Cumulation and conflict of warranties, see Commercial Code § 2317.
Express warranties by affirmation, promise, description or sample, see Commercial Code § 2313.
Language sufficient to exclude warranties of merchantability and fitness, see Commercial Code § 2316.
Modification, rescission and waiver, see Commercial Code § 2209.
Sale of animal for slaughter, no implied warranty of fitness for any particular purpose, see Food and Agricultural Code § 18502.
Sale of livestock, warranties, see Food and Agricultural Code §§ 18501, 18502.
Supplementary general principles of law, applicability, see Commercial Code § 1103.
Variation of code by agreement, see Commercial Code § 1102.

§ 2316. Exclusion or Modification of Warranties

(1) Words or conduct relevant to the creation of an express warranty and words or conduct tending to negate or limit warranty shall be construed wherever reasonable as consistent with each other; but subject to the provisions of this division on parol or extrinsic evidence (Section 2202) negation or limitation is inoperative to the extent that such construction is unreasonable.

(2) Subject to subdivision (3), to exclude or modify the implied warranty of merchantability or any part of it the language must mention merchantability and in case of a writing must be conspicuous, and to exclude or modify any implied warranty of fitness the exclusion must be by a writing and conspicuous. Language to exclude all implied warranties of fitness is sufficient if it states, for example, that "There are no warranties which extend beyond the description on the face hereof."

(3) Notwithstanding subdivision (2)

(a) Unless the circumstances indicate otherwise, all implied warranties are excluded by expressions like "as is," "with all faults" or other language which in common understanding calls the buyer's attention to the exclusion of warranties and makes plain that there is no implied warranty; and

(b) When the buyer before entering into the contract has examined the goods or the sample or model as fully as he desired or has refused to examine the goods there is no implied warranty with regard to defects which an examination ought in the circumstances to have revealed to him; and

(c) An implied warranty can also be excluded or modified by course of dealing or course of performance or usage of trade.

(4) Remedies for breach of warranty can be limited in accordance with the provisions of this division on liquidation or limitation of damages and on contractual modification of remedy (Sections 2718 and 2719). *(Stats.1963, c. 819, § 2316.)*

California Code Comment

In paragraph 2 of the California Code Comment following this section in the main volume, the case of Imperial Gas Engine Co. v. Auteri, 40 Cal.App. 419, 180 Pac. 946 (1919), is cited on the question of the consistency of certain new legislation with existing case law. In so doing the holding of the case was inadvertently misstated. The holding of the case was, in fact, to the effect that there had not been an election to accept certain goods.

By John A. Bohn and Charles J. Williams

Prior California Law

1. Under the USA (former Civil Code §§ 1721 through 1800) the parties could limit warranties or exclude them altogether. See former Civil Code § 1791. However, the California courts limited the effect of clauses disclaiming warranties by: (1) construing them strictly, Burr v. Sherwin Williams Co., 42 Cal.2d 682, 268 P.2d 1041 (1954), and (2) by finding that the buyer had no notice of the disclaimer clause, India Paint & Lacquer Co. v. United Steel Products Corp., 123 Cal.App.2d 597, 267 P.2d 408 (1954). *Contra*, Basin Oil Co. v. Baash-Ross Tool Co., 125 Cal.App.2d 578, 271 P.2d 122 (1954). For a discussion of the approach of courts in California and other states towards disclaimers of warranty under the Uniform Sales Act, see Note, 8 U.C.L.A.L.Rev. 658, 661 (1951) and California State Bar Committee on the Commercial Code, A Special Report, The Uniform Commercial Code, 37 Calif.State Bar J. (March–April, 1962) p. 144.

2. Subdivision (2) both clarifies and broadens the California law as discussed in Burr v. Sherwin Williams Co., 42 Cal.2d 682, 268 P.2d 1041 (1954) by requiring the use of the term "merchantability" in order to exclude or modify the merchantability warranty. In Burr v. Sherwin Williams, *supra*, the label on a drum of insecticide carried the following disclaimer: "Seller makes no warranty of any kind, express or implied, concerning the use of this product. Buyer assumes all risk in use or handling, whether in accordance with directions or not." (on page 693, 268 P.2d 1047, of the opinion). The court held that the language used expressly disclaimed any warranty concerning "use" but went on to say:

"[We] conclude that the Sherwin Williams disclaimer is insufficient to exclude the implied warranty of merchantable quality. The label, after describing the product and listing the ingredients, states merely that there is no warranty as to 'the use of this product' and that the buyer 'assumes all risk in use.' . . . The language does not purport to disclaim the implied warranty that the substance . . . actually meets the description of the product ordered by plaintiffs so as to be generally salable in the same manner as other products of the type described." 42 Cal.2d 682, 694, 695, 268 P.2d 1041, 1048 (1954).

While this section like the Burr case requires the seller to specifically disclaim implied warranties, it does further in establishing a minimum standard, i.e. the seller must mention "merchantability" and in the case of a writing it must be conspicuous.

The requirement of this section that a disclaimer of a warranty of fitness for a particular purpose must be in writing is consistent with prior California law as expressed in Calpetro Producers Syndicate v. Charles M. Woods Co., 206 Cal. 246, 274 Pac. 65 (1929).

The last sentence of subdivision (2) to the effect that the particular purpose warranty can be waived by general language (Official Comment 4) is in accord with prior California law. See, for example, Charles Lomori & Son v. Globe Labs., 35 Cal.App.2d 248, 95 P.2d 173 (1939) and Burr v. Sherwin Williams Co., 42 Cal.2d 682, 268 P.2d 1041 (1954). But see Lindberg v. Coutches, 167 Cal.App.2d Supp. 828, 833, 334 P.2d 701, 704 (1959) ("[O]nly an express disclaimer will eliminate the implied warranty of fitness.").

3. Subdivision (3)(a) is in accord with present California law as expressed in Roberts Distributing Co. v. Kaye-Halbert Corp., 126 Cal.App.2d 664, 272 P.2d 886 (1954) and Budrow v. Wheatcraft, 115 Cal.App.2d 517, 252 P.2d 637 (1957). However, under prior California law terms like "as is" or "with all faults" were construed strictly against the seller. See, for example, Roberts Distrib. Co. v. Kaye-Halbert Corp., 126 Cal.App.2d 664, 669, 272 P.2d 886, 889 (1954) where the court stated:

"A provision that the buyer takes the article in the condition in which it is, or 'as is' prevents representations of the seller, although relied on by the buyer, from constituting express or implied warranties (citing Am.Jur.). But disclaimers of express and implied warranties are construed strictly against the seller."

Accord, Burr v. Sherwin Williams Co., 42 Cal.2d 682, 268 P.2d 1041 (1954).

4. Subdivision (3)(b) is similar to former Civil Code § 1735(3) which provided that where a buyer examined goods there would be no implied warranty "as regards defects which such examinations ought to have revealed." However note that Official Comment 8 points out that in order for there to be a refusal of the buyer to inspect the seller must *demand* that the buyer inspect.

5. Subdivision (3)(c) is in accord with prior California law as expressed in former Civil Code § 1791.

6. For a discussion of subdivision (4) and prior California law see California Code Comments under Commercial Code § 2718 and § 2719.

7. For a detailed analysis of section 2316 and prior California law see Ezer, The Impact of The Uniform Commercial Code on The California Law of Sales Warranties, 8 U.C.L.A.L.Rev. 281, 310 (1961).

Changes from U.C.C. (1962 Official Text)

8. This is section 2–316 of the Official Text without change.

Uniform Commercial Code Comment
1966 Amendment

Prior Uniform Statutory Provision:

* * *

See Sections 15 and 71, Uniform Sales Act.

Uniform Commercial Code Comment

Prior Uniform Statutory Provision:

None.

Purposes:

1. This section is designed principally to deal with those frequent clauses in sales contracts which seek to exclude "all warranties, express or implied." It seeks to protect a buyer from unexpected and unbargained language of disclaimer by denying effect to such language when inconsistent with language of express warranty and permitting the exclusion of implied warranties only by conspicuous language or other circumstances which protect the buyer from surprise.

2. The seller is protected under this Article against false allegations of oral warranties by its provisions on parol and extrinsic evidence and against unauthorized representations by the customary "lack of authority" clauses. This Article treats the limitation or avoidance of consequential damages as a matter of limiting remedies for breach, separate from the matter of creation of liability under a warranty. If no warranty exists, there is of course no problem of limiting remedies for breach of

warranty. Under subsection (4) the question of limitation of remedy is governed by the sections referred to rather than by this section.

3. Disclaimer of the implied warranty of merchantability is permitted under subsection (2), but with the safeguard that such disclaimers must mention merchantability and in case of a writing must be conspicuous.

4. Unlike the implied warranty of merchantability, implied warranties of fitness for a particular purpose may be excluded by general language, but only if it is in writing and conspicuous.

5. Subsection (2) presupposes that the implied warranty in question exists unless excluded or modified. Whether or not language of disclaimer satisfies the requirements of this section, such language may be relevant under other sections to the question whether the warranty was ever in fact created. Thus, unless the provisions of this Article on parol and extrinsic evidence prevent, oral language of disclaimer may raise issues of fact as to whether reliance by the buyer occurred and whether the seller had "reason to know" under the section on implied warranty of fitness for a particular purpose.

6. The exceptions to the general rule set forth in paragraphs (a), (b) and (c) of subsection (3) are common factual situations in which the circumstances surrounding the transaction are in themselves sufficient to call the buyer's attention to the fact that no implied warranties are made or that a certain implied warranty is being excluded.

7. Paragraph (a) of subsection (3) deals with general terms such as "as is," "as they stand," "with all faults," and the like. Such terms in ordinary commercial usage are understood to mean that the buyer takes the entire risk as to the quality of the goods involved. The terms covered by paragraph (a) are in fact merely a particularization of paragraph (c) which provides for exclusion or modification of implied warranties by usage of trade.

8. Under paragraph (b) of subsection (3) warranties may be excluded or modified by the circumstances where the buyer examines the goods or a sample or model of them before entering into the contract. "Examination" as used in this paragraph is not synonymous with inspection before acceptance or at any other time after the contract has been made. It goes rather to the nature of the responsibility assumed by the seller at the time of the making of the contract. Of course if the buyer discovers the defect and uses the goods anyway, or if he unreasonably fails to examine the goods before he uses them, resulting injuries may be found to result from his own action rather than proximately from a breach of warranty. See Sections 2–314 and 2–715 and comments thereto.

In order to bring the transaction within the scope of "refused to examine" in paragraph (b), it is not sufficient that the goods are available for inspection. There must in addition be a demand by the seller that the buyer examine the goods fully. The seller by the demand puts the buyer on notice that he is assuming the risk of defects which the examination ought to reveal. The language "refused to examine" in this paragraph is intended to make clear the necessity for such demand.

Application of the doctrine of "caveat emptor" in all cases where the buyer examines the goods regardless of statements made by the seller is, however, rejected by this Article. Thus, if the offer of examination is accompanied by words as to their merchantability or specific attributes and the buyer indicates clearly that he is relying on those words rather than on his examination, they give rise to an "express" warranty. In such cases the question is one of fact as to whether a warranty of merchantability has been expressly incorporated in the agreement. Disclaimer of such an express warranty is governed by subsection (1) of the present section.

The particular buyer's skill and the normal method of examining goods in the circumstances determine what defects are excluded by the examination. A failure to notice defects which are obvious cannot excuse the buyer. However, an examination under circumstances which do not permit chemical or other testing of the goods would not exclude defects which could be ascertained only by such testing. Nor can latent defects be excluded by a simple examination. A professional buyer examining a product in his field will be held to have assumed the risk as to all defects which a professional in the field ought to observe, while a nonprofessional buyer will be held to have assumed the risk only for such defects as a layman might be expected to observe.

9. The situation in which the buyer gives precise and complete specifications to the seller is not explicitly covered in this section, but this is a frequent circumstance by which the implied warranties may be excluded. The warranty of fitness for a particular purpose would not normally arise since in such a situation there is usually no reliance on the seller by the buyer. The warranty of merchantability in such a transaction, however, must be considered in connection with the next section on the cumulation and conflict of warranties. Under paragraph (c) of that section in case of such an inconsistency the implied warranty of merchantability is displaced by the express warranty that the goods will comply with the specifications. Thus, where the buyer gives detailed specifications as to the goods, neither of the implied warranties as to quality will normally apply to the transaction unless consistent with the specifications.

Cross References:

Point 2: Sections 2–202, 2–718 and 2–719.
Point 7: Sections 1–205 and 2–208.

Definitional Cross References:

"Agreement". Section 1–201.
"Buyer". Section 2–103.
"Contract". Section 1–201.
"Course of dealing". Section 1–205.
"Goods". Section 2–105.
"Remedy". Section 1–201.
"Seller". Section 2–103.
"Usage of trade". Section 1–205.

Cross References

Allocation or division of risks, see Commercial Code § 2303.
Consumer warranties, see Civil Code § 1790 et seq.
Course of dealing and usage of trade, see Commercial Code § 1205.
Course of performance, see Commercial Code § 2208.
Explanation or supplementation of written agreement, see Commercial Code § 2202.
Express warranties by affirmation, promise, description or sample, see Commercial Code § 2313.
Implied warranty,
    Merchantability and usage of trade, see Commercial Code § 2314.
Liquidation of damages, restitution, see Commercial Code § 2718.
Modification of remedies by agreement, see Commercial Code § 2719.
Sale of livestock as not implying warranty for particular purpose, see Food and Agricultural Code §§ 18501, 18502.

§ 2317. Cumulation and Conflict of Warranties Express or Implied

Warranties whether express or implied shall be construed as consistent with each other and as cumulative, but if such construction is unreasonable the intention of the parties shall determine which warranty is dominant. In ascertaining that intention the following rules apply:

(a) Exact or technical specifications displace an inconsistent sample or model or general language of description.

(b) A sample from an existing bulk displaces inconsistent general language of description.

(c) Express warranties displaced [1] inconsistent implied warranties other than an implied warranty of fitness for a particular purpose. *(Stats.1963, c. 819, § 2317.)*

[1] Reads "displace" in official edition.

California Code Comment

By John A. Bohn and Charles J. Williams

Prior California Law

1. This section continues the basic policy of former Civil Code § 1735(6) which provided, "an express warranty or condition does not negative a warranty or condition implied under this act unless inconsistent therewith."

2. Subdivision (1)(a) is in accord with prior California law as expressed in Bancroft v. San Francisco Tool Co., 120 Cal. 228, 52 Pac. 496 (1898), cited as controlling in Remsberg v. Hackney Manufacturing Co., 174 Cal. 799, 164 Pac. 792 (1917). However the rule of this paragraph is controlled by the ultimate determination of the intention of the parties with respect to which warranty should control. One writer has strongly suggested that this was not the case in California prior to the Commercial Code and that this section therefore represents a radical departure from prior California law. See Ezer, The Impact of The Uniform Commercial Code on The California Law of Sales Warranties, 8 U.C.L.A.L.Rev. 281, 320 (1961).

3. Former Civil Code § 1734 provides that in a sale by sample and description, it "is not sufficient that the bulk of the goods corresponds with the sample if the goods do not also correspond with the description." *Accord*, Mayer v. Northwood Textile Mills, 105 Cal. App.2d 406, 233 P.2d 657 (1951). It is not clear whether former Civil Code § 1734 applied to the situation where the warranties—by sample and description—are inconsistent. Under subdivision (1)(b) in the absence of a contrary intent on the part of the parties, conformity with the sample is sufficient without conforming to inconsistent language of description.

4. Subdivision (1)(c) is a rephrasing of former Civil Code § 1735(6) with the modification that an implied particular purpose warranty is not displaced by an inconsistent express warranty. For decisions under former Civil Code § 1735(6) see Gottsdanker v. Cutter Laboratories, 182 Cal.App.2d 602, 6 Cal.Rptr. 320 (1960); North Alaska Salmon Co. v. Hobbs, Wall & Co., 159 Cal. 380, 113 Pac. 870 (1911); and El Zarape Tortilla Factory Inc. v. Plant Food Corp., 90 Cal.App.2d 336, 203 P.2d 13 (1949).

Changes from U.C.C. (1962 Official Text)

5. This is section 2–317 of the Official Text without change.

Uniform Commercial Code Comment

Prior Uniform Statutory Provision:

On cumulation of warranties see Sections 14, 15, and 16, Uniform Sales Act.

Changes: Completely rewritten into one section.

Purposes of Changes:

1. The present section rests on the basic policy of this Article that no warranty is created except by some conduct (either affirmative action or failure to disclose) on the part of the seller. Therefore, all warranties are made cumulative unless this construction of the contract is impossible or unreasonable.

This Article thus follows the general policy of the Uniform Sales Act except that in case of the sale of an article by its patent or trade name the elimination of the warranty of fitness depends solely on whether the buyer has relied on the seller's skill and judgment; the use of the patent or trade name is but one factor in making this determination.

2. The rules of this section are designed to aid in determining the intention of the parties as to which of inconsistent warranties which have arisen from the circumstances of their transaction shall prevail. These rules of intention are to be applied only where factors making for an equitable estoppel of the seller do not exist and where he has in perfect good faith made warranties which later turn out to be inconsistent. To the extent that the seller has led the buyer to believe that all of the warranties can be performed, he is estopped from setting up any essential inconsistency as a defense.

3. The rules in subsections (a), (b) and (c) are designed to ascertain the intention of the parties by reference to the factor which probably claimed the attention of the parties in the first instance. These rules are not absolute but may be changed by evidence showing that the conditions which existed at the time of contracting make the construction called for by the section inconsistent or unreasonable.

Cross Reference:

Point 1: Section 2–315.

Definitional Cross Reference:

"Party". Section 1–201.

Cross References

Express warranties by affirmation, promise, description or sample, see Commercial Code § 2313.
Implied warranty of fitness for particular purpose, see Commercial Code § 2315.
Implied warranty of merchantability, see Commercial Code § 2314.
Livestock, warranties on sale, see Food and Agricultural Code §§ 18501, 18502.
Sale of personal property, included authority of agents, see Civil Code § 2323.

§ 2318. [Not enacted in California]

California Code Comment

By John A. Bohn and Charles J. Williams

Prior California Law

1. Section 2–318 of the 1962 Official Text of the Uniform Commercial Code is omitted from the California version. The Official Text reads:

"A seller's warranty whether express or implied extends to any natural person who is in the family or household of his buyer or who is a guest in his home if it is reasonable to expect that such person may use, consume or be affected by the goods and who is injured in person by breach of the warranty. A seller may not exclude or limit the operation of this section."

Professors Marsh and Warren in their report recommended that section 2–318 be deleted. They submitted the following discussion in support of their recommendation:

"The traditional rule was that a seller was liable in breach of warranty only to his immediate buyer. For clarity, it is convenient to distinguish two situations in which gaps in privity might occur: (1) where *the buyer* sues a manufacturer or other party in the chain of distribution prior to the immediate seller; (2) where *one other than the buyer* sues the immediate seller or prior party in the chain of distribution. This section concerns only the second type of privity gap. The Code takes no stand on first type of privity problem.

"The issuer [sic] in this area of law is the liability of a seller (or his predecessors in interest) to members of the buyer's household, the buyer's employees, his donees, and bystanders for injuries to them caused by defective goods. Due to the somewhat more liberal attitude toward privity taken in cases concerning food, the food cases will be separately treated.

"In Klein v. Duchess Sandwich Company, Ltd., 14 Cal.2d 272, 93 P.2d 799 (1939), the California Supreme Court flatly stated that in food cases the warranty of fitness for human consumption runs to the ultimate consumer; even though that party is not the buyer. Gottsdanker v. Cutter Laboratories [182 Cal.App.2d 602] 6 Cal.Rptr. 320 (1960), extends the rule of the Klein case to drugs.

"Prior to 1960, there was no indication that the California courts were abandoning the privity requirement in nonfood cases involving implied warranties. Burr v. Sherwin Williams, 42 Cal.2d 692 [sic] [682] 269 [sic] [268] P.2d 1041 (1954). However, in Peterson v. Lamb Rubber Co. [54 Cal.2d 339, 5 Cal.Rptr. 863] 353 P.2d 757 [sic] [575] (1960), an employee was found to have a cause of action in breach of implied warranty against the manufacturer of an abrasive wheel purchased by plaintiff's employer which exploded injuring plaintiff.

"This Section of the Code wipes out the distinction between food and drugs and other goods, but it does not go as far in abolishing the privity requirement in terms of the parties eligible to sue as the wording of the California cases does. The wording of the Klein decision would allow any ultimate consumer injured by food to sue whether or not he had any connection with the buyer's family. The Peterson case allows one clearly not connected with the buyer's family—his employee—to recover in a nonfood case. The wording in Peterson suggests that, *a fortiori*, a member of the buyer's household could recover if injured by a nonfood or drug product. Enactment of this Section in its present form threatens to limit the Klein decision and to overturn in its entirety the Peterson holding. Nor is this objection removed by the statement in the Official Comment to the effect that this Section is 'neutral and is not intended to enlarge or restrict the developing case law' on the extent of the warrantor's liability, for Klein and Peterson are present realities and not future developments.

"This Section in its present form is not suitable for enactment in California. Whatever gains accrue from wiping out the distinctions between food and drugs and other goods are more than offset by the restrictions on the designation of parties entitled to sue in warranty— restrictions already rejected by the California courts. Moreover, the 'household' restriction is an awkward and arbitrary one. Is a baby sitter a member of the household? A tenant in a rooming house? A servant?

"This Section, as presently drawn, was apparently intended to extend liability in states having a much more restrictive law of privity of contract than California. In California, it would be a step backward." Sixth Progress Report to The Legislature by Senate Fact Finding Committee on Judiciary (1959–1961), Part 1, The Uniform Commercial Code, pp. 457–458.

The California State Bar Committee made the following comments with regard to the omission of section 2–318 from the California Commercial Code:

"Section 12318 [2318] would contract the scope of a seller's warranty under the California decisions. The California Supreme Court has held that the seller's warranty runs to anyone injured by food and drugs, whether or not he is in the buyer's family, household, or is his guest. [Footnote: Klein v. Dutchess Sandwich Co., Ltd., 14 C.2d 272, 93 P.2d 799 (1939); Gottsdanker v. Cutter Laboratories, 182 C.A.2d 602, 6 Cal.Rptr. 320 (1960).] It has also held that a seller's warranty for other goods extends at least to a buyer's employee, [Footnote: Peterson v. Lamb Rubber Co., 54 C.2d 339, 353 P.2d 575 (1960).] neither a member of the buyer's family or household, nor his guest, and hence under the Code not in privity.

"Since the Official Text of section 12318 [2318] would withdraw protection now given in California to those injured by goods, and its purpose was to extend warranty protection in states where the 'privity' requirement is applied with greater rigor, section 12318 [2318] is not in S.B. 1093 [1961 Session, 1958 official text as amended]." California State Bar Committee on the Commercial Code, A Special Report, The Uniform Commercial Code, 37 Calif. State Bar J. (March–April, 1962) p. 144.

Finally, in The California Annotations to the Proposed Uniform Commercial Code as printed in the Sixth Progress Report to the Legislature by Senate Fact Finding Committee on Judiciary (1959–1961), Part 1, The Uniform Commercial Code, pp. 46–47, the following Comments concerning section 2–318 are made:

"This section spells out new law. The section is obviously designed to extend statutory liability for breach of all the seller's warranties to members of the family household, or guest of buyer. The existing California law is not entirely clear on whether privity is required as basis for warranty action. The older cases held that privity was essential because it was deemed part of the original contract of sale. See Binion v. Sasaki, 5 Cal.App. (2d) 15, 41 Pac. (2d) 585. There is an indication, however, that the California cases are leaving the privity rule and reaching the U.C.C. position by judicial decision, particularly in the food and consumption cases. Dryden v. Continental Baking Co., 11 Cal. (2d) 33, 77 Pac. (2d) 833. (Third party beneficiary theory.) Klein v. Duchess Sandwich Co., 14 Cal. (2d) 272, 93 Pac. (2d) 799; Jensen v. Berris, 31 Cal.App. (2d) 537, 88 Pac. (2d) 220; Free v. Sluss, 87 Cal.App. (2d) Supp. 933, 197 Pac. (2d) 854 (soap case); Odell v. Frueh, 146 Cal.App. (2d) 504, 304 Pac. (2d) 45."

§ 2319. F.O.B. and F.A.S. Terms

(1) Unless otherwise agreed the term F.O.B. (which means "free on board") at a named place, even though used only in connection with the stated price, is a delivery term under which

(a) When the term is F.O.B. the place of shipment, the seller must at that place ship the goods in the manner provided in this division (Section 2504) and bear the expense and risk of putting them into the possession of the carrier; or

(b) When the term is F.O.B. the place of destination, the seller must at his own expense and risk transport the goods to that place and there tender delivery of them in the manner provided in this division (Section 2503);

(c) When under either (a) or (b) the term is also F.O.B. vessel, car or other vehicle, the seller must in addition at his own expense and risk load the goods on board. If the term is F.O.B. vessel the buyer must name the vessel and in an appropriate case the seller must comply with the provisions of this division on the form of bill of lading (Section 2323).

(2) Unless otherwise agreed the term F.A.S. vessel (which means "free alongside") at a named port, even though used only in connection with the stated price, is a delivery term under which the seller must

(a) At his own expense and risk deliver the goods alongside the vessel in the manner usual in that port or on a dock designated and provided by the buyer; and

(b) Obtain and tender a receipt for the goods in exchange for which the carrier is under a duty to issue a bill of lading.

(3) Unless otherwise agreed in any case falling within subdivision (1)(a) or (c) or subdivision (2) the buyer must seasonably give any needed instructions for making delivery, including when the term is F.A.S. or F.O.B. the loading berth of the vessel and in an appropriate case its name and sailing date. The seller may treat the failure of needed instructions as a failure of cooperation under this division (Section 2311). He may also at his option move the goods in any reasonable manner preparatory to delivery or shipment.

(4) Under the term F.O.B. vessel or F.A.S. unless otherwise agreed the buyer must make payment against tender of the required documents and the seller may not tender nor the buyer demand delivery of the goods in substitution for the documents. *(Stats.1963, c. 819, § 2319.)*

California Code Comment

By John A. Bohn and Charles J. Williams

Prior California Law

1. This section has no counterpart in prior California statutory law. The subject of F.O.B. and F.A.S. terms was not specifically covered by the USA (former Civil Code §§ 1721 through 1800).

2. The discussion of the term F.O.B. in notes 3 through 7 of this Comment also applies to the term F.A.S. under subdivision (2). See Meyer v. Sullivan, 40 Cal.App. 723, 730, 181 Pac. 847, 849 (1919) where the court states:

"The only distinction between the two kinds of sales appears to be as to time when the responsibility of the seller ends. In the case of f.a.s. sales, it seems to end with delivery on the dock. In the case of f.o.b. sales, the responsibility of the seller appears to end when the commodity is on board ship."

3. The California cases on this subject matter are quite confusing with regard to exactly what a F.O.B. term signifies.

Subdivision (1) in providing, "unless otherwise agreed the term F.O.B. . . . at a named place . . . is a delivery term" both clarifies and modifies prior California case law. See Meyer v. Sullivan, 40 Cal.App. 723, 730, 181 Pac. 847, 850 (1919):

"The general rule seems to be that 'if the agreement is to sell goods "f.o.b." at a designated place, such place will ordinarily be regarded as the place of delivery; but the effect of the "f.o.b." depends on the connection in which it is used, and if used in connection with the words fixing the price only, it will not be construed as fixing the place of delivery.'"

and Boston Iron & Metal Co. v. Rosenthal, 68 Cal.App.2d 564, 569, 156 P.2d 963, 966 (1945), quoting Pond Creek etc. Co. v. Clark, 270 F.2d 482, 486 (CCA 7th, 1920):

" 'It is quite generally accepted as the law that where in a contract the price of goods is fixed, and in connection with the price is employed the term "f.o.b." at a given point, it means that this refers to and qualifies only the price, and does not indicate that the seller is actually to deliver the goods at the indicated point, and it is construed to have no reference to delivery, but that wheresoever the goods may be shipped the seller will either pay freight to the indicated point, or, if the goods are not shipped there, will deduct or permit the purchaser to deduct from the fixed price an amount equivalent to the freight on such a shipment to the point indicated.' (Identical language is found in 1 Williston on Sales (2d ed.) § 280 h, p. 622)."

and Southern Pac. Co. v. Hyman-Michaels Co., 63 Cal.App.2d 757, 147 P.2d 692 (1944).

Finally, subdivision (1) in placing the risk of loss before delivery under the F.O.B. term upon the seller is in accord with prior California law. See former Civil Code § 1739, (Rules 2, 4 and 5) § 1742, and § 1766 (1) and Lewis v. Farmers Grain and Milling Co., 52 Cal.App. 211, 198 Pac. 426 (1921).

4. Subdivision (1)(a) is in accord with prior California law as expressed in Hackfeld Co. Ltd. v. Castle, 186 Cal. 53, 55, 198 Pac. 1041 (1921) stating that the term f.o.b. "makes it the duty of the seller to load [the goods] at his own expense" and Whitaker v. Dunlap-Morgan Co., 44 Cal.App. 140, 186 Pac. 181 (1919) stating, "The meaning of these words [f.o.b. or free on board] is, that the seller is to put the goods on board at his own expense on account of the person for whom they are shipped." However, see Acton Rock Co. v. Lone Pine Util. Co., 44 Cal.App. 597, 186 Pac. 809 (1919) stating, "the initials f.o.b. . . . imply that the . . . vendor . . . will save the . . . vendee from any expense attending *the bringing of the article* . . . sold *to the point named*, whether it be the initial point of transportation . . . of the final destination of the consignment . . . ." (emphasis added).

5. Subdivision (1)(b) is consistent with prior California law as expressed in Acton Rock Co. v. Lone Pine Util. Co., 44 Cal.App. 597, 186 Pac. 809 (1919) as quoted in California Code Comment 4 above.

6. The first sentence of subdivision (1)(c) probably modifies California law as expressed in Meyer v. Sullivan, 40 Cal.App. 723, 181 Pac. 847 (1919). In Meyer v. Sullivan, 40 Cal.App. 723, 181 Pac. 847 the defendant contracted to sell 250 tons of wheat to plaintiff "f.o.b. Kosmos Steamer at Seattle." At the time of performance under the contract the Kosmos line had cancelled their sailing schedule. Defendant refused to perform on the grounds of impossibility, i.e. that it was impossible to load the wheat upon a Kosmos Steamer. Held: Under contract for the sale of wheat f.o.b. steamer or f.o.b. designated steamer, the seller is obligated to deliver and . . . the buyer to receive and accept the wheat *upon the dock along side of ship's tackle*. (emphasis added). The result in this case was based primarily upon the "general custom, among buyers, sellers, and shippers of wheat in the city of Seattle, and in the city of San Francisco, and, generally, in Pacific Coast Ports." Since trade usage and custom can be taken into consideration in ascertaining the intention of the parties under the Commercial Code (see Commercial Code § 2202(a) and § 2208(2)), the same result might have been obtained under this section.

7. F.O.B., F.A.S. and other mercantile terms are also defined in a set of definitions adopted and recommended by a joint committee representing the Chamber of Commerce of the United States, the National Council of Importers, Inc. and the National Foreign Trade Council. The definitions are entitled "Revised American Foreign Trade Definitions (1941)". These definitions are printed in 2 Williston, Sales §§ 280k–280p (rev. ed. 1948).

Changes from U.C.C. (1962 Official Text)

8. This is section 2–319 of the Official Text without change.

Uniform Commercial Code Comment

Prior Uniform Statutory Provision:

None.

Purposes:

1. This section is intended to negate the uncommercial line of decision which treats an "F.O.B." term as "merely a price term." The distinctions taken in subsection (1) handle most of the issues which have on occasion led to the unfortunate judicial language just referred to. Other matters which have led to sound results being based on unhappy language in regard to F.O.B. clauses are dealt with in this Act by Section 2–311(2) (seller's option re arrangements relating to shipment) and Sections 2–614 and 615 (substituted performance and seller's excuse).

2. Subsection (1)(c) not only specifies the duties of a seller who engages to deliver "F.O.B. vessel," or the like, but ought to make clear that no agreement is soundly drawn when it looks to reshipment from San Francisco or New York, but speaks merely of "F.O.B." the place.

3. The buyer's obligations stated in subsection (1)(c) and subsection (3) are, as shown in the text, obligations of cooperation. The last sentence of subsection (3) expressly, though perhaps unnecessarily, authorizes the seller, pending instructions, to go ahead with such preparatory moves as shipment from the interior to the named point of delivery. The sentence presupposes the usual case in which instructions "fail"; a prior repudiation by the buyer, giving notice that breach was intended, would remove the reason for the sentence, and would normally bring into play, instead, the second sentence of Section 2–704, which duly calls for lessening damages.

4. The treatment of "F.O.B. vessel" in conjunction with F.A.S. fits, in regard to the need for payment against documents, with standard practice and caselaw; but "F.O.B. vessel" is a term which by its very language makes express the need for an "on board" document. In this respect, that term is stricter than the ordinary overseas "shipment" contract (C.I.F., etc., Section 2–320).

Cross References:

Sections 2–311(3), 2–323, 2–503 and 2–504.

Definitional Cross References:

"Agreed". Section 1–201.
"Bill of lading". Section 1–201.
"Buyer". Section 2–103.
"Goods". Section 2–105.
"Seasonably". Section 1–204.
"Seller". Section 2–103.
"Term". Section 1–201.

Cross References

Options and cooperation respecting performance, see Commercial Code § 2311.
Overseas shipment, see Commercial Code § 2323.
Shipment by seller, see Commercial Code § 2504.
Specification by party of particulars of performance, see Commercial Code § 2311.
Tender of delivery by seller, see Commercial Code § 2503.

§ 2320. C.I.F. and C. & F. Terms

(1) The term C.I.F. means that the price includes in a lump sum the cost of the goods and the insurance and freight to the named destination. The term C. & F. or C.F. means that the price so includes cost and freight to the named destination.

(2) Unless otherwise agreed and even though used only in connection with the stated price and destination, the term C.I.F. destination or its equivalent requires the seller at his own expense and risk to

(a) Put the goods into the possession of a carrier at the port for shipment and obtain a negotiable bill or bills of lading covering the entire transportation to the named destination; and

(b) Load the goods and obtain a receipt from the carrier (which may be contained in the bill of lading) showing that the freight has been paid or provided for; and

§ 2320 SALES

(c) Obtain a policy or certificate of insurance, including any war risk insurance, of a kind and on terms then current at the port of shipment in the usual amount, in the currency of the contract, shown to cover the same goods covered by the bill of lading and providing for payment of loss to the order of the buyer or for the account of whom it may concern; but the seller may add to the price the amount of the premium for any such war risk insurance; and

(d) Prepare an invoice of the goods and procure any other documents required to effect shipment or to comply with the contract; and

(e) Forward and tender with commercial promptness all the documents in due form and with any indorsement necessary to perfect the buyer's rights.

(3) Unless otherwise agreed the term C. & F. or its equivalent has the same effect and imposes upon the seller the same obligations and risks as a C.I.F. term except the obligation as to insurance.

(4) Under the term C.I.F. or C. & F. unless otherwise agreed the buyer must make payment against tender of the required documents and the seller may not tender nor the buyer demand delivery of the goods in substitution for the documents. *(Stats.1963, c. 819, § 2320.)*

California Code Comment

By John A. Bohn and Charles J. Williams

Prior California Law

1. This section is without counterpart in prior California law. For a brief discussion of C.I.F. contracts in California, see 1 Witkin, Summary of California Law, Sales § 42 (7th ed. 1960). The following discussion is from California State Bar Committee on the Commercial Code, A Special Report, The Uniform Commercial Code, 37 Calif.State Bar.J. (March–April, 1962) p. 134:

"The Code would define with precision a number of mercantile symbols commonly used in sales transactions, and specify what happens to the delivery obligations of the seller and the risk of loss when these terms are used. Some of these symbols are 'F.O.B.' and 'F.A.S.' (section 12319), [2319] 'C.I.F.' (sections 12320 and 12321), [2320, 2321], 'Ex Ship' (section 12322), [2322] and 'to arrive' and 'no arrival—no sale' (section 12324). [2324]

"Most such symbols are left undefined in the Sales Act, and there has been considerable confusion in the courts as to their meaning. By defining them and specifying the consequences of their use, the Code would clarify and thus improve the law. Businessmen and lawyers would be able to use these symbols with confidence that they have a precise meaning in law as well as in commerce. At the same time, the Code definitions and rules would be variable by express agreement."

Changes from U.C.C. (1962 Official Text)

2. This is section 2–320 of the Official Text without change.

Uniform Commercial Code Comment

Prior Uniform Statutory Provision:
None.

Purposes: To make it clear that:

1. The C.I.F. contract is not a destination but a shipment contract with risk of subsequent loss or damage to the goods passing to the buyer upon shipment if the seller has properly performed all his obligations with respect to the goods. Delivery to the carrier is delivery to the buyer for purposes of risk and "title". Delivery of possession of the goods is accomplished by delivery of the bill of lading, and upon tender of the required documents the buyer must pay the agreed price without awaiting the arrival of the goods and if they have been lost or damaged after proper shipment he must seek his remedy against the carrier or insurer. The buyer has no right of inspection prior to payment or acceptance of the documents.

2. The seller's obligations remain the same even though the C.I.F. term is "used only in connection with the stated price and destination".

3. The insurance stipulated by the C.I.F. term is for the buyer's benefit, to protect him against the risk of loss or damage to the goods in transit. A clause in a C.I.F. contract "insurance—for the account of sellers" should be viewed in its ordinary mercantile meaning that the sellers must pay for the insurance and not that it is intended to run to the seller's benefit.

4. A bill of lading covering the entire transportation from the port of shipment is explicitly required but the provision on this point must be read in the light of its reason to assure the buyer of as full protection as the conditions of shipment reasonably permit, remembering always that this type of contract is designed to move the goods in the channels commercially available. To enable the buyer to deal with the goods while they are afloat the bill of lading must be one that covers only the quantity of goods called for by the contract. The buyer is not required to accept his part of the goods without a bill of lading because the latter covers a larger quantity, nor is he required to accept a bill of lading for the whole quantity under a stipulation to hold the excess for the owner. Although the buyer is not compelled to accept either goods or documents under such circumstances he may of course claim his rights in any goods which have been identified to his contract.

5. The seller is given the option of paying or providing for the payment of freight. He has no option to ship "freight collect" unless the agreement so provides. The rule of the common law that the buyer need not pay the freight if the goods do not arrive is preserved.

Unless the shipment has been sent "freight collect" the buyer is entitled to receive documentary evidence that he is not obligated to pay the freight; the seller is therefore required to obtain a receipt "showing that the freight has been paid or provided for." The usual notation in the appropriate space on the bill of lading that the freight has been prepaid is a sufficient receipt, as at common law. The phrase "provided for" is intended to cover the frequent situation in which the carrier extends credit to a shipper for the freight on successive shipments and receives periodical payments of the accrued freight charges from him.

6. The requirement that unless otherwise agreed the seller must procure insurance "of a kind and on terms then current at the port for shipment in the usual amount, in the currency of the contract, sufficiently shown to cover the same goods covered by the bill of lading", applies to both marine and war risk insurance. As applied to marine insurance, it means such insurance as is usual or customary at the port for shipment with reference to the particular kind of goods involved, the character and equipment of the vessel, the route of the voyage, the port of destination and any other considerations that affect the risk. It is the substantial equivalent of the ordinary insurance in the particular trade and on the particular voyage and is subject to agreed specifications of type or extent of coverage. The language does not mean that the insurance must be adequate to cover all risks to which the goods may be subject in transit. There are some types of loss or damage that are not covered by the usual marine insurance and are excepted in bills of lading or in applicable statutes from the causes of loss or damage for which the carrier or the vessel is liable. Such risks must be borne by the buyer under this Article.

Insurance secured in compliance with a C.I.F. term must cover the entire transportation of the goods to the named destination.

7. An additional obligation is imposed upon the seller in requiring him to procure customary war risk insurance at the buyer's expense. This changes the common law on the point. The seller is not required to assume the risk of including in the C.I.F. price the cost of such insurance, since it often fluctuates rapidly, but is required to treat it simply as a necessary for the buyer's account. What war risk insurance is "current" or usual turns on the standard forms of policy or rider in common use.

8. The C.I.F. contract calls for insurance covering the value of the goods at the time and place of shipment and does not include any increase in market value during transit or any anticipated profit to the buyer on a sale by him.

The contract contemplates that before the goods arrive at their destination they may be sold again and again on C.I.F. terms and that the original policy of insurance and bill of lading will run with the interest in the goods by being transferred to each successive buyer. A buyer who becomes the seller in such an intermediate contract for sale does not thereby, if his sub-buyer knows the circumstances, undertake to insure the goods again at an increased price fixed in the new contract or to cover the increase in price by additional insurance, and his buyer may not reject the documents on the ground that the original policy does not cover such higher price. If such a sub-buyer desires additional insurance he must procure it for himself.

Where the seller exercises an option to ship "freight collect" and to credit the buyer with the freight against the C.I.F. price, the insurance need not cover the freight since the freight is not at the buyer's risk. On the other hand, where the seller prepays the freight upon shipping under a bill of lading requiring prepayment and providing that the freight shall be deemed earned and shall be retained by the carrier "ship and/or cargo lost or not lost," or using words of similar import, he must procure insurance that will cover the freight, because notwithstanding that the goods are lost in transit the buyer is bound to pay the freight as part of the C.I.F. price and will be unable to recover it back from the carrier.

9. Insurance "for the account of whom it may concern" is usual and sufficient. However, for a valid tender the policy of insurance must be one which can be disposed of together with the bill of lading and so must be "sufficiently shown to cover the same goods covered by the bill of lading." It must cover separately the quantity of goods called for by the buyer's contract and not merely insure his goods as part of a larger quantity in which others are interested, a case provided for in American mercantile practice by the use of negotiable certificates of insurance which are expressly authorized by this section. By usage these certificates are treated as the equivalent of separate policies and are good tender under C.I.F. contracts. The term "certificate of insurance", however, does not of itself include certificates or "cover notes" issued by the insurance broker and stating that the goods are covered by a policy. Their sufficiency as substitutes for policies will depend upon proof of an established usage or course of dealing. The present section rejects the English rule that not only brokers' certificates and "cover notes" but also certain forms of American insurance certificates are not the equivalent of policies and are not good tender under a C.I.F. contract.

The seller's failure to tender a proper insurance document is waived if the buyer refuses to make payment on other and untenable grounds at a time when proper insurance could have been obtained and tendered by the seller if timely objection had been made. Even a failure to insure on shipment may be cured by seasonable tender of a policy retroactive in effect; e.g., one insuring the goods "lost or not lost." The provisions of this Article on cure of improper tender and on waiver of buyer's objections by silence are applicable to insurance tenders under a C.I.F. term. Where there is no waiver by the buyer as described above, however, the fact that the goods arrive safely does not cure the seller's breach of his obligations to insure them and tender to the buyer a proper insurance document.

10. The seller's invoice of the goods shipped under a C.I.F. contract is regarded as a usual and necessary document upon which reliance may properly be placed. It is the document which evidences points of description, quality and the like which do not readily appear in other documents. This Article rejects those statements to the effect that the invoice is a usual but not a necessary document under a C.I.F. term.

11. The buyer needs all of the documents required under a C.I.F. contract, in due form and with necessary endorsements, so that before the goods arrive he may deal with them by negotiating the documents or may obtain prompt possession of the goods after their arrival. If the goods are lost or damaged in transit the documents are necessary to enable him promptly to assert his remedy against the carrier or insurer. The seller is therefore obligated to do what is mercantilely reasonable in the circumstances and should make every reasonable exertion to send forward the documents as soon as possible after the shipment. The requirement that the documents be forwarded with "commercial promptness" expresses a more urgent need for action than that suggested by the phrase "reasonable time".

12. Under a C.I.F. contract the buyer, as under the common law, must pay the price upon tender of the required documents without first inspecting the goods, but his payment in these circumstances does not constitute an acceptance of the goods nor does it impair his right of subsequent inspection or his options and remedies in the case of improper delivery. All remedies and rights for the seller's breach are reserved to him. The buyer must pay before inspection and assert his remedy against the seller afterward unless the non-conformity of the goods amounts to a real failure of consideration, since the purpose of choosing this form of contract is to give the seller protection against the buyer's unjustifiable rejection of the goods at a distant port of destination which would necessitate taking possession of the goods and suing the buyer there.

13. A valid C.I.F. contract may be made which requires part of the transportation to be made on land and part on the sea, as where the goods are to be brought by rail from an inland point to a seaport and thence transported by vessel to the named destination under a "through" or combination bill of lading issued by the railroad company. In such a case shipment by rail from the inland point within the contract period is a timely shipment notwithstanding that the loading of the goods on the vessel is delayed by causes beyond the seller's control.

14. Although subsection (2) stating the legal effects of the C.I.F. term is an "unless otherwise agreed" provision, the express language used in an agreement is frequently a precautionary, fuller statement of the normal C.I.F. terms and hence not intended as a departure or variation from them. Moreover, the dominant outlines of the C.I.F. term are so well understood commercially that any variation should, whenever reasonably possible, be read as falling within those dominant outlines rather than as destroying the whole meaning of a term which essentially indicates a contract for proper shipment rather than one for delivery at destination. Particularly careful consideration is necessary before a printed form or clause is construed to mean agreement otherwise and where a C.I.F. contract is prepared on a printed form designed for some other type of contract, the C.I.F. terms must prevail over printed clauses repugnant to them.

15. Under subsection (4) the fact that the seller knows at the time of the tender of the documents that the goods have been lost in transit does not affect his rights if he has performed his contractual obligations. Similarly, the seller cannot perform under a C.I.F. term by purchasing and tendering landed goods.

16. Under the C. & F. term, as under the C.I.F. term, title and risk of loss are intended to pass to the buyer on shipment. A stipulation in a C. & F. contract that the seller shall effect insurance on the goods and charge the buyer with the premium (in effect that he shall act as the buyer's agent for that purpose) is entirely in keeping with the pattern. On the other hand, it often happens that the buyer is in a more advantageous position than the seller to effect insurance on the goods or that he has in force an "open" or "floating" policy covering all shipments made by him or to him, in either of which events the C. & F. term is adequate without mention of insurance.

17. It is to be remembered that in a French contract the term "C.A.F." does not mean "Cost and Freight" but has exactly the same meaning as the term "C.I.F." since it is merely the French equivalent of that term. The "A" does not stand for "and" but for "assurance" which means insurance.

Cross References:

Point 4: Section 2–323.
Point 6: Section 2–509(1)(a).
Point 9: Sections 2–508 and 2–605(1)(a).
Point 12: Sections 2–321(3), 2–512 and 2–513(3) and Article 5.

Definitional Cross References:

"Bill of lading". Section 1–201.
"Buyer". Section 2–103.
"Contract". Section 1–201.
"Goods". Section 2–105.
"Rights". Section 1–201.
"Seller". Section 2–103.
"Term". Section 1–201.

Cross References

Inspection of goods before payment of price, see Commercial Code § 2513.
Letters of credit, see Commercial Code § 5101 et seq.
Marine insurance, see Insurance Code § 103.
Nonconforming tender or delivery, see Commercial Code § 2508.
Overseas shipment, see Commercial Code § 2323.
Particularization of defect relied on by buyer for rejection, see Commercial Code § 2605.
Payment by buyer before inspection, see Commercial Code § 2512.
Shipment of goods by carrier, risk of loss, see Commercial Code § 2509.

§ 2320

Variation of code by agreement, see Commercial Code § 1102.

§ 2321. C.I.F. or C. & F.: "Net Landed Weights"; "Payment on Arrival"; Warranty of Condition on Arrival

Under a contract containing a term C.I.F. or C. & F.

(1) Where the price is based on or is to be adjusted according to "net landed weights," "delivered weights," "out turn" quantity or quality or the like, unless otherwise agreed the seller must reasonably estimate the price. The payment due on tender of the documents called for by the contract is the amount so estimated, but after final adjustment of the price a settlement must be made with commercial promptness.

(2) An agreement described in subdivision (1) or any warranty of quality or condition of the goods on arrival places upon the seller the risk of ordinary deterioration, shrinkage and the like in transportation but has no effect on the place or time of identification to the contract for sale or delivery or on the passing of the risk of loss.

(3) Unless otherwise agreed where the contract provides for payment on or after arrival of the goods the seller must before payment allow such preliminary inspection as is feasible; but if the goods are lost delivery of the documents and payment are due when the goods should have arrived. *(Stats.1963, c. 819, § 2321.)*

California Code Comment

By John A. Bohn and Charles J. Williams

Prior California Law

1. This section is without counterpart in prior California statutory law and the California courts have not discussed any of the specialized terms used in this section.

Changes from U.C.C. (1962 Official Text)

2. This is section 2–321 of the Official Text without change.

Uniform Commercial Code Comment

Prior Uniform Statutory Provision:
None.

Purposes:

This section deals with two variations of the C.I.F. contract which have evolved in mercantile practice but are entirely consistent with the basic C.I.F. pattern. Subsections (1) and (2), which provide for a shift to the seller of the risk of quality and weight deterioration during shipment, are designed to conform the law to the best mercantile practice and usage without changing the legal consequences of the C.I.F. or C. & F. term as to the passing of marine risks to the buyer at the point of shipment. Subsection (3) provides that where under the contract documents are to be presented for payment after arrival of the goods, this amounts merely to a postponement of the payment under the C.I.F. contract and is not to be confused with the "no arrival, no sale" contract. If the goods are lost, delivery of the documents and payment against them are due when the goods should have arrived. The clause for payment on or after arrival is not to be construed as such a condition precedent to payment that if the goods are lost in transit the buyer need never pay and the seller must bear the loss.

Cross Reference:
Section 2–324.

Definitional Cross References:

"Agreement". Section 1–201.
"Contract". Section 1–201.
"Delivery". Section 1–201.
"Goods". Section 2–105.
"Seller". Section 2–103.
"Term". Section 1–201.

Cross References

"No arrival, no sale" terms, see Commercial Code § 2324.
Risk of loss in absence of breach, see Commercial Code § 2509.
Variation of code by agreement, see Commercial Code § 1102.

§ 2322. Delivery "Ex-Ship"

(1) Unless otherwise agreed a term for delivery of goods "ex-ship" (which means from the carrying vessel) or in equivalent language is not restricted to a particular ship and requires delivery from a ship which has reached a place at the named port of destination where goods of the kind are usually discharged.

(2) Under such a term unless otherwise agreed

(a) The seller must discharge all liens arising out of the carriage and furnish the buyer with a direction which puts the carrier under a duty to deliver the goods; and

(b) The risk of loss does not pass to the buyer until the goods leave the ship's tackle or are otherwise properly unloaded. *(Stats.1963, c. 819, § 2322.)*

California Code Comment

By John A. Bohn and Charles J. Williams

Prior California Law

1. This section is without counterpart in prior California statutory law and previous decisions of the California appellate courts do not deal with the subject matter of this section.

Changes from U.C.C. (1962 Official Text)

2. This is section 2–322 of the Official Text without change.

Uniform Commercial Code Comment

Prior Uniform Statutory Provision:
None.

Purposes:

1. The delivery term, "ex ship", as between seller and buyer, is the reverse of the f.a.s. term covered.

2. Delivery need not be made from any particular vessel under a clause calling for delivery "ex ship", even though a vessel on which shipment is to be made originally is named in the contract, unless the agreement by appropriate language, restricts the clause to delivery from a named vessel.

3. The appropriate place and manner of unloading at the port of destination depend upon the nature of the goods and the facilities and usages of the port.

4. A contract fixing a price "ex ship" with payment "cash against documents" calls only for such documents as are appropriate to the contract. Tender of a delivery order and of a receipt for the freight after the arrival of the carrying vessel is adequate. The seller is not required to tender a bill of lading as a document of title nor is he required to insure the goods for the buyer's benefit, as the goods are not at the buyer's risk during the voyage.

Cross Reference:
Point 1: Section 2–319(2).

Definitional Cross References:
"Buyer". Section 2–103.
"Goods". Section 2–105.
"Seller". Section 2–103.
"Term". Section 1–201.

Cross References

F.A.S. terms, see Commercial Code § 2319.
Risk of loss in absence of breach, see Commercial Code § 2509.
Variation of code by agreement, see Commercial Code § 1102.

§ 2323. Form of Bill of Lading Required in Overseas Shipment; "Overseas"

(1) Where the contract contemplates overseas shipment and contains a term C.I.F. or C. & F. or F.O.B. vessel, the seller unless otherwise agreed must obtain a negotiable bill of lading stating that the goods have been loaded on board or, in the case of a term C.I.F. or C. & F., received for shipment.

(2) Where in a case within subdivision (1) a bill of lading has been issued in a set of parts, unless otherwise agreed if the documents are not to be sent from abroad the buyer may demand tender of the full set; otherwise only one part of the bill of lading need be tendered. Even if the agreement expressly requires a full set

(a) Due tender of a single part is acceptable within the provisions of this division on cure of improper delivery (subdivision (1) of Section 2508); and

(b) Even though the full set is demanded, if the documents are sent from abroad the person tendering an incomplete set may nevertheless require payment upon furnishing an indemnity which the buyer in good faith deems adequate.

(3) A shipment by water or by air or a contract contemplating such shipment is "overseas" insofar as by usage of trade or agreement it is subject to the commercial, financing or shipping practices characteristic of international deepwater commerce. *(Stats.1963, c. 819, § 2323.)*

California Code Comment

By John A. Bohn and Charles J. Williams

Prior California Law

1. This section is without counterpart in prior California statutory law and previous decisions of the California appellate courts do not deal with the subject matter of this section.

Changes from U.C.C. (1962 Official Text)

2. This is section 2–323 of the Official Text without change.

Uniform Commercial Code Comment

Prior Uniform Statutory Provision:
None.

Purposes:

1. Subsection (1) follows the "American" rule that a regular bill of lading indicating delivery of the goods at the dock for shipment is sufficient, except under a term "F.O.B. vessel." See Section 2–319 and comment thereto.

2. Subsection (2) deals with the problem of bills of lading covering deep water shipments, issued not as a single bill of lading but in a set of parts, each part referring to the other parts and the entire set constituting in commercial practice and at law a single bill of lading. Commercial practice in international commerce is to accept and pay against presentation of the first part of a set if the part is sent from overseas even though the contract of the buyer requires presentation of a full set of bills of lading provided adequate indemnity for the missing parts is forthcoming.

This subsection codifies that practice as between buyer and seller. Article 5 (Section 5–113) authorizes banks presenting drafts under letters of credit to give indemnities against the missing parts, and this subsection means that the buyer must accept and act on such indemnities if he in good faith deems them adequate. But neither this subsection nor Article 5 decides whether a bank which has issued a letter of credit is similarly bound. The issuing bank's obligation under a letter of credit is independent and depends on its own terms. See Article 5.

Cross References:

Sections 2–508(2), 5–113.

Definitional Cross References:

"Bill of lading". Section 1–201.
"Buyer". Section 2–103.
"Contract". Section 1–201.
"Delivery". Section 1–201.
"Financing agency". Section 2–104.
"Person". Section 1–201.
"Seller". Section 2–103.
"Send". Section 1–201.
"Term". Section 1–201.

Cross References

Bills of lading in a set, see Commercial Code § 7304.
Destroying bills of lading, see Penal Code § 355.
Duplicate receipts or vouchers, see Penal Code § 580.
Erroneous bills of lading issued in good faith, see Penal Code § 579.
F.O.B. and F.A.S. terms, see Commercial Code § 2319.
Fictitious bills of lading, fraudulent issue, see Penal Code §§ 577, 578.
Letters of credit, indemnities, see Commercial Code § 5113.
Manner of seller's tender of delivery, see Commercial Code § 2503.
Substituted performance where agreed berthing, loading or unloading facilities are unavailable, see Commercial Code § 2614.
Substitution for a nonconforming tender, see Commercial Code § 2508.

§ 2324. "No Arrival, No Sale" Term

Under a term "no arrival, no sale" or terms of like meaning, unless otherwise agreed,

(a) The seller must properly ship conforming goods and if they arrive by any means he must tender them on arrival but he assumes no obligation that the goods will arrive unless he has caused the nonarrival; and

(b) Where without fault of the seller the goods are in part lost or have so deteriorated as no longer to conform to the contract or arrive after the contract time, the buyer may proceed as if there had been casualty to identified goods (Section 2613). *(Stats.1963, c. 819, § 2324.)*

California Code Comment

By John A. Bohn and Charles J. Williams

Prior California Law

1. This section is without counterpart in prior California statutory law and prior decisions of the California appellate courts do not discuss the subject matter of this article.

Changes from U.C.C. (1962 Official Text)

2. This is section 2–324 of the Official Text without change.

§ 2324

Uniform Commercial Code Comment

Prior Uniform Statutory Provision:

None.

Purposes:

1. The "no arrival, no sale" term in a "destination" overseas contract leaves risk of loss on the seller but gives him an exemption from liability for nondelivery. Both the nature of the case and the duty of good faith require that the seller must not interfere with the arrival of the goods in any way. If the circumstances impose upon him the responsibility for making or arranging the shipment, he must have a shipment made despite the exemption clause. Further, the shipment made must be a conforming one, for the exemption under a "no arrival, no sale" term applies only to the hazards of transportation and the goods must be proper in all other respects.

The reason of this section is that where the seller is reselling goods bought by him as shipped by another and this fact is known to the buyer, so that the seller is not under any obligation to make the shipment himself, the seller is entitled under the "no arrival, no sale" clause to exemption from payment of damages for non-delivery if the goods do not arrive or if the goods which actually arrive are non-conforming. This does not extend to sellers who arrange shipment by their own agents, in which case the clause is limited to casualty due to marine hazards. But sellers who make known that they are contracting only with respect to what will be delivered to them by parties over whom they assume no control are entitled to the full quantum of the exemption.

2. The provisions of this Article on identification must be read together with the present section in order to bring the exemption into application. Until there is some designation of the goods in a particular shipment or on a particular ship as being those to which the contract refers there can be no application of an exemption for their non-arrival.

3. The seller's duty to tender the agreed or declared goods if they do arrive is not impaired because of their delay in arrival or by their arrival after transshipment.

4. The phrase "to arrive" is often employed in the same sense as "no arrival, no sale" and may then be given the same effect. But a "to arrive" term, added to a C.I.F. or C. & F. contract, does not have the full meaning given by this section to "no arrival, no sale." Such a "to arrive" term is usually intended to operate only to the extent that the risks are not covered by the agreed insurance and the loss or casualty is due to such uncovered hazards. In some instances the "to arrive" term may be regarded as a time of payment term, or, in the case of the reselling seller discussed in point 1 above, as negating responsibility for conformity of the goods, if they arrive, to any description which was based on his good faith belief of the quality. Whether this is the intention of the parties is a question of fact based on all the circumstances surrounding the resale and in case of ambiguity the rules of Sections 2–316 and 2–317 apply to preclude dishonor.

5. Paragraph (b) applies where goods arrive impaired by damage or partial loss during transportation and makes the policy of this Article on casualty to identified goods applicable to such a situation. For the term cannot be regarded as intending to give the seller an unforeseen profit through casualty; it is intended only to protect him from loss due to causes beyond his control.

Cross References:

Point 1: Section 1–203.

Point 2: Section 2–501(a) and (c).

Point 5: Section 2–613.

Definitional Cross References:

"Buyer". Section 2–103.

"Conforming". Section 2–106.

"Contract". Section 1–201.

"Fault". Section 1–201.

"Goods". Section 2–105.

"Sale". Section 2–106.

"Seller". Section 2–103.

"Term". Section 1–201.

Cross References

Casualty to identified goods, see Commercial Code § 2613.

Insurable interest, see Commercial Code § 2501.

Obligation of good faith, see Commercial Code § 1203.

§ 2325. "Letter of Credit" Term; "Confirmed Credit"

(1) Failure of the buyer seasonably to furnish an agreed letter of credit is a breach of the contract for sale.

(2) The delivery to seller of a proper letter of credit suspends the buyer's obligation to pay. If the letter of credit is dishonored, the seller may on seasonable notification to the buyer require payment directly from him.

(3) Unless otherwise agreed the term "letter of credit" or "banker's credit" in a contract for sale means an irrevocable credit issued by a financing agency of good repute and, where the shipment is overseas, of good international repute. The term "confirmed credit" means that the credit must also carry the direct obligation of such an agency which does business in the seller's financial market. *(Stats.1963, c. 819, § 2325.)*

California Code Comment

By John A. Bohn and Charles J. Williams

Prior California Law

1. The subject matter of this section was not covered by the USA (former Civil Code §§ 1721 through 1800) but is related to the former Civil Code sections which deal with "Letter of Credit" (former Civil Code §§ 2858 through 2866).

2. The second sentence of subdivision (2) is consistent with former Civil Code § 2860 which made the writer of a letter of credit, upon default of the debtor, liable to those who had given credit.

3. Subdivision (3) appears to be similar to former Civil Code § 2864 which authorized the use of a letter of credit as a continuing guaranty.

Changes from U.C.C. (1962 Official Text)

4. This is section 2–325 of the Official Text without change. Letters of credit were not covered by the USA (former Civil Code §§ 1721 through 1800). However, its definition, form and legal effect were treated in former Civil Code §§ 2858–2866. Under the Commercial Code letters of credit are treated in Division 5.

Uniform Commercial Code Comment

Prior Uniform Statutory Provision:

None.

Purposes: To express the established commercial and banking understanding as to the meaning and effects of terms calling for "letters of credit" or "confirmed credit":

1. Subsection (2) follows the general policy of this Article and Article 3 (Section 3–802) on conditional payment, under which payment by check or other short-term instrument is not ordinarily final as between the parties if the recipient duly presents the instrument and honor is refused. Thus the furnishing of a letter of credit does not substitute the financing agency's obligation for the buyer's, but the seller must first give the buyer reasonable notice of his intention to demand direct payment from him.

2. Subsection (3) requires that the credit be irrevocable and be a prime credit as determined by the standing of the issuer. It is not necessary, unless otherwise agreed, that the credit be a negotiation credit; the seller can finance himself by an assignment of the proceeds under Section 5–116(2).

3. The definition of "confirmed credit" is drawn on the supposition that the credit is issued by a bank which is not doing direct business in the seller's financial market; there is no intention to require the obligation of two banks both local to the seller.

Cross References:
Sections 2–403, 2–511(3) and 3–802 and Article 5.

Definitional Cross References:
"Buyer". Section 2–103.
"Contract for sale". Section 2–106.
"Draft". Section 3–104.
"Financing agency". Section 2–104.
"Notifies". Section 1–201.
"Overseas". Section 2–323.
"Purchaser". Section 1–201.
"Seasonably". Section 1–204.
"Seller". Section 2–103.
"Term". Section 1–201.

Cross References

Letters of credit, see Commercial Code § 5101 et seq.
Payment by check, see Commercial Code § 2511.
Power of commercial banks to issue letters of credit, see Financial Code § 1224.
Time, reasonable time and seasonably defined, see Commercial Code § 1204.
Title acquired by purchaser, see Commercial Code § 2403.
Transfer and assignment, letters of credit, see Commercial Code § 5116.

§ 2326. Sale on Approval and Sale or Return; Consignment Sales and Rights of Creditors

(1) Unless otherwise agreed, if delivered goods may be returned by the buyer even though they conform to the contract, the transaction is

(a) A "sale on approval" if the goods are delivered primarily for use, and

(b) A "sale or return" if the goods are delivered primarily for resale.

(2) Except as provided in subdivision (3), goods held on approval are not subject to the claims of the buyer's creditors until acceptance; goods held on sale or return are subject to such claims while in the buyer's possession.

(3) Where goods are delivered to a person for sale and the person maintains a place of business at which he or she deals in goods of the kind involved, under a name other than the name of the person making delivery, then with respect to claims of creditors of the person conducting the business the goods are deemed to be on sale or return. The provisions of this subdivision are applicable even though an agreement purports to reserve title to the person making delivery until payment or resale or uses such words as "on consignment" or "on memorandum." However, this subdivision is not applicable if the person making delivery does any of the following:

(b) Establishes that the person conducting the business is generally known by his or her creditors to be substantially engaged in selling the goods of others
* * *

(c) Complies with the filing provisions of the division on secured transactions (Division 9).

(d) Delivers goods which the person making delivery used or bought for use for personal, family, or household purposes.

(4) Any "or return" term of a contract for sale is to be treated as a separate contract for sale within the statute of frauds section of this division (Section 2201) and as contradicting the sale aspect of the contract within the provisions of this division on parol or extrinsic evidence (Section 2202).

(5) If a person delivers or consigns for sale goods which the person used or bought for use for personal, family, or household purposes, these goods do not become the property of the deliveree or consignee unless the deliveree or consignee purchases and fully pays for the goods. Nothing in this subdivision shall prevent the deliveree or consignee from acting as the deliverer's agent to transfer title to these goods to a buyer who pays the full purchase price. Any payment received by the deliveree or consignee from a buyer of these goods, less any amount which the deliverer expressly agreed could be deducted from the payment for commissions, fees, or expenses, is the property of the deliverer and shall not be subject to the claims of the deliveree's or consignee's creditors. *(Stats.1963, c. 819, § 2326. Amended by Stats.1965, c. 1379, p. 3285, § 1; Stats.1984, c. 201, § 1.)*

California Code Comment

By John A. Bohn and Charles J. Williams

Prior California Law

1. Subdivision (1) makes the same fundamental distinction between "sale or return" and "sale on approval" as is made in former Civil Code § 1739, Rule 3(1) (delivery on sale or return) and Rule 3(2) (delivery on approval). People v. Baker, 64 Cal.App. 336, 221 Pac. 654 (1923).

2. Subdivision (2) is consistent with prior California law that in *sale on approval* title remains with the seller and in *sale or return* title vests in the buyer. People v. Baker, 64 Cal.App. 336, 221 Pac. 654 (1923).

3. The Marsh and Warren report discussed the effect of subdivision (3) on California law in extended detail:

"Under the present law there are two methods for allowing a wholesaler to entrust possession of goods to a retailer for purposes of sale on the agreement that they will be paid for when sold. These are by consignment and by sale or return. Each method enables a retailer to finance inventory not suitable for trust receipts financing. By far the most popular method is by consignment wherein the seller retains title to the goods until they are sold. The other method, authorized by CC § 1739(3) (USA § 193), is by 'sale or return.' The sale or return device is explained by the Uniform Sales Act. It states: 'When goods are delivered to the buyer "on sale or return", or on other terms indicating an intention to make a present sale, but to give the buyer an option to return the goods instead of paying the price, the property passes to the buyer on delivery, but he may revest the property in the seller by returning or tendering the goods within the time fixed in the contract, or, if no time has been fixed, within a reasonable time.'

"The advantages to the seller of the consignment device over the sale or return are apparent. Under the sale or return, the goods belong to the buyer and his creditors may reach them; the seller is an unsecured creditor in case of bankruptcy. One advantage to a seller in a sale or return situation is that the buyer bears the risk of loss; while under a consignment, the risk of loss is on the seller. However, risk of loss is subject to the agreement of the parties, and the seller can impose the risk of loss on the buyer by contract in a consignment situation.

"Once one has determined whether a given transaction is a consignment or a sale or return, it is easy to predict what the rights of creditors will be. The difficulty that courts in California and other states have experienced, however, is in deciding when the transaction is one or the other. The agreement drawn by the seller will often attempt to give all the benefits of the contract to him, while imposing the burdens on the buyer. Ambiguous phrases like sale 'on memorandum' may be used to describe the transaction. To determine the rights of creditors and

§ 2326

trustees in bankruptcy, the courts must cut through the verbiage to determine whether the transaction was, in fact, a consignment. Factors examined in this determination are: whether the title was expressly reserved in the wholesaler; whether the retailer had the right to return goods unsold; whether the retailer may be compelled to surrender the goods to the consignor upon demand; whether the retailer has made payments 'on account' to the wholesaler. See Teleking Distributing Company v. Wyle, 218 F.2d 940 (5th Cir. 1955); Chastain v. Belmont, 43 C.2d 45, 271 P.2d 498 (1954); Vermont Marble Co. v. Brow, 109 Cal. 236, 41 Pac. 1031 (1895)."

The general effect of the change made by subdivision (3) is described:

"This subsection [subdivision] greatly simplifies the law in this area by providing that when goods are delivered for purposes of sale to a person maintaining a place of business in which he deals in goods of the kind involved, the goods are deemed to be on sale or return with respect to the creditors of the retailer. This rule applies without regard to the agreement made between the wholesaler and retailer relative to retention of title in the wholesaler. The wholesaler can protect himself only by complying with the filing provisions of Chapter [Division] 9 of the Code or (in States which have 'sign statutes', which California does not) by putting up signs indicating that the goods are on consignment. This subsection [subdivision] relieves the court of the onerous task of determining whether, despite words of 'consignment' in the agreement, the contract was in reality one of sale, thus making the goods available to the retailer's creditors." Sixth Progress Report to The Legislature by Senate Fact Finding Committee on Judiciary (1959–1961), Part 1, The Uniform Commercial Code, pp. 459–460.

4. In The California Annotations to the Proposed Uniform Commercial Code, the Legislative Counsel makes the following comment regarding section 2–326 of the Official Text and prior California law:

"The distinction between sale on approval and sale or return is similar in operative effect to Civil Code Section 1739, Rule 3, (1) and (2), although the California expression is 'delivery on approval.'

"The existing California law under the Sales Act is concerned with the problem—when does title (property) pass. Civil Code Section 1739. The basic emphasis of U.C.C. throughout is away from this concern. The theory of U.C.C. is that the average merchant or businessman knows little and cares less about the concept of 'title' as the lawyer interprets it. Accordingly, from the standpoint of mercantile practice and determining intent, the argument runs, the refinements of 'title' are complete fictions. It will be seen, then, that in this section and in others to follow the emphasis is not 'when' the property passes, but flat rules are laid down regarding rights of creditors, burden of loss, and other incidents of the buyer-seller relationship. Thus the distinction between sale on approval and sale or return depends on whether goods are delivered for use or for resale. For some California cases on the general subject, see Bedell v. Mashburn, 87 Cal.App. (2d) 417, 197 Pac. (2d) 98; People v. Seymour, 54 Cal.App. (2d) 266, 128 Pac. (2d) 726; Metropolitan Finance Corp. v. Morf, 42 Cal.App. (2d) 756, 109 Pac. (2d) 969." Sixth Progress Report to the Legislature by Senate Fact Finding Committee on Judiciary (1959–1961) Part 1, The Uniform Commercial Code, pp. 48, 49.

Changes from U.C.C. (1962 Official Text)

5. Paragraph (a) of subdivision (3) of the Official Text is deleted from the California version. That section reads: "complies with an applicable law providing for a consignor's interest or the like to be evidence by a sign, or"

A special report of a California State Bar Committee states the reason for the deletion to be as follows:

"Section 12326 [2326] in the Official Text . . . treats compliance by a merchant with a 'sign statute' as equivalent to filing under Chapter 9. Since California, unlike some other states, has no 'sign statute,' the State Bar Committee believes this reference might create confusion. Hence the Committee has recommended its deletion . . . ." California State Bar Committee on the Commercial Code, A Special Report, The Uniform Commercial Code, 37 Calif. State Bar J. (March–April, 1962), pp. 136–137.

Uniform Commercial Code Comment
Prior Uniform Statutory Provision:

Section 19(3), Uniform Sales Act.

Changes: Completely rewritten in this and the succeeding section.

Purposes of Changes: To make it clear that:

1. A "sale on approval" or "sale or return" is distinct from other types of transactions with which they have frequently been confused. The type of "sale on approval," "on trial" or "on satisfaction" dealt with involves a contract under which the seller undertakes a particular business risk to satisfy his prospective buyer with the appearance or performance of the goods in question. The goods are delivered to the proposed purchaser but they remain the property of the seller until the buyer accepts them. The price has already been agreed. The buyer's willingness to receive and test the goods is the consideration for the seller's engagement to deliver and sell. The type of "sale or return" involved herein is a sale to a merchant whose unwillingness to buy is overcome only by the seller's engagement to take back the goods (or any commercial unit of goods) in lieu of payment if they fail to be resold. These two transactions are so strongly delineated in practice and in general understanding that every presumption runs against a delivery to a consumer being a "sale or return" and against a delivery to a merchant for resale being a "sale on approval."

The right to return the goods for failure to conform to the contract does not make the transaction a "sale on approval" or "sale or return" and has nothing to do with this and the following section. The present section is not concerned with remedies for breach of contract. It deals instead with a power given by the contract to turn back the goods even though they are wholly as warranted.

This section nevertheless presupposes that a contract for sale is contemplated by the parties although that contract may be of the peculiar character here described.

Where the buyer's obligation as a buyer is conditioned not on his personal approval but on the article's passing a described objective test, the risk of loss by casualty pending the test is properly the seller's and proper return is at his expense. On the point of "satisfaction" as meaning "reasonable satisfaction" where an industrial machine is involved, this Article takes no position.

2. Pursuant to the general policies of this Act which require good faith not only between the parties to the sales contract, but as against interested third parties, subsection (3) resolves all reasonable doubts as to the nature of the transaction in favor of the general creditors of the buyer. As against such creditors words such as "on consignment" or "on memorandum", with or without words of reservation of title in the seller, are disregarded when the buyer has a place of business at which he deals in goods of the kind involved. A necessary exception is made where the buyer is known to be engaged primarily in selling the goods of others or is selling under a relevant sign law [Inapplicable in California, see California Code Comment, note 6.] or the seller complies with the filing provisions of Article 9 as if his interest were a security interest. However, there is no intent in this Section to narrow the protection afforded to third parties in any jurisdiction which has a selling Factors Act. The purpose of the exception is merely to limit the effect of the present subsection itself, in the absence of any such Factors Act, to cases in which creditors of the buyer may reasonably be deemed to have been misled by the secret reservation.

3. Subsection (4) resolves a conflict in the pre-existing case law by recognition that an "or return" provision is so definitely at odds with any ordinary contract for sale of goods that where written agreements are involved it must be contained in a written memorandum. The "or return" aspect of a sales contract must be treated as a separate contract under the Statute of Frauds section and as contradicting the sale insofar as questions of parol or extrinsic evidence are concerned.

Cross References:

Point 2: Article 9.

Point 3: Sections 2–201 and 2–202.

Definitional Cross References:

"Between merchants". Section 2–104.

"Buyer". Section 2–103.

"Conform". Section 2–106.

"Contract for sale". Section 2–106.

"Creditor". Section 1–201.

"Goods". Section 2–105.

"Sale". Section 2–106.

"Seller". Section 2–103.

Cross References

Explanation or supplementation of terms, see Commercial Code § 2202.
Factors, see Civil Code § 2026 et seq.
Secured transactions,
   Generally, see Commercial Code § 9101 et seq.
   Filing, see Commercial Code § 9401 et seq.
Security interest defined, see Commercial Code § 1201.
Statute of frauds, see Commercial Code § 2201.
Variation of code by agreement, see Commercial Code § 1102.

§ 2327. Special Incidents of Sale on Approval and Sale or Return

(1) Under a sale on approval unless otherwise agreed

(a) Although the goods are identified to the contract the risk of loss and the title do not pass to the buyer until acceptance; and

(b) Use of the goods consistent with the purpose of trial is not acceptance but failure seasonably to notify the seller of election to return the goods is acceptance, and if the goods conform to the contract acceptance of any part is acceptance of the whole; and

(c) After due notification of election to return, the return is at the seller's risk and expense but a merchant buyer must follow any reasonable instructions.

(2) Under a sale or return unless otherwise agreed

(a) The option to return extends to the whole or any commercial unit of the goods while in substantially their original condition, but must be exercised seasonably; and

(b) The return is at the buyer's risk and expense. (Stats.1963, c. 819, § 2327.)

California Code Comment

By John A. Bohn and Charles J. Williams

Prior California Law

1. Subdivision (1)(a) has its counterpart in former Civil Code § 1739, Rule 3(2)(a) (delivery on approval) and § 1742 (risk of loss). See 1 Witkin, Summary of California Law, Sales § 36 (7th ed. 1960).

2. Subdivision (1)(b) expands upon certain provisions of Rule 3 contained in former Civil Code § 1739. Rule 3(2)(a) provided that "property" passes when the buyer signifies approval or acceptance to the seller or does "any other act adopting the transaction." An example of such an act includable in this last phrase is an act of conversion of the property. Bedell v. Mashburn, 87 Cal.App.2d 417, 197 P.2d 98 (1948). Rule 3(2)(b) provided that "property" passes if the buyer retains goods without giving notice of rejection for the time fixed for return, or if no fixed time, a reasonable time. Both of these provisions of Rule 3 are in accord with subdivision (1)(b)'s provision that "failure seasonably to notify the seller of election to return the goods is acceptance."

3. Although there is no direct counterpart to subdivision (1)(c) in prior California statutory law, a similar provision was authorized under former Civil Code § 1789(1)(d) in cases involving rescission for breach of warranty and § 1770 (buyer is not bound to return goods wrongfully delivered) and Pacific Western Coml. Co. v. Western Wholesale Drug Co., 41 Cal.App. 696, 183 Pac. 287 (1919).

4. There is no counterpart in prior California statutory law for the provisions relating to a "commercial unit" as used in subdivision (2).

Changes from U.C.C. (1962 Official Text)

5. This is section 2–327 of the Official Text without change.

Uniform Commercial Code Comment

Prior Uniform Statutory Provision:
Section 19(3), Uniform Sales Act.
Changes: Completely rewritten in preceding and this section.
Purposes of Changes: To make it clear that:

1. In the case of a sale on approval:

If all of the goods involved conform to the contract, the buyer's acceptance of part of the goods constitutes acceptance of the whole. Acceptance of part falls outside the normal intent of the parties in the "on approval" situation and the policy of this Article allowing partial acceptance of a defective delivery has no application here. A case where a buyer takes home two dresses to select one commonly involves two distinct contracts; if not, it is covered by the words "unless otherwise agreed".

2. In the case of a sale or return, the return of any unsold unit merely because it is unsold is the normal intent of the "sale or return" provision, and therefore the right to return for this reason alone is independent of any other action under the contract which would turn on wholly different considerations. On the other hand, where the return of goods is for breach, including return of items resold by the buyer and returned by the ultimate purchasers because of defects, the return procedure is governed not by the present section but by the provisions on the effects and revocation of acceptance.

3. In the case of a sale on approval the risk rests on the seller until acceptance of the goods by the buyer, while in a sale or return the risk remains throughout on the buyer.

4. Notice of election to return given by the buyer in a sale on approval is sufficient to relieve him of any further liability. Actual return by the buyer to the seller is required in the case of a sale or return contract. What constitutes due "giving" of notice, as required in "on approval" sales, is governed by the provisions on good faith and notice. "Seasonable" is used here as defined in Section 1–204. Nevertheless, the provisions of both this Article and of the contract on this point must be read with commercial reason and with full attention to good faith.

Cross References:

Point 1: Sections 2–501, 2–601 and 2–603.
Point 2: Sections 2–607 and 2–608.
Point 4: Sections 1–201 and 1–204.

Definitional Cross References:

"Agreed". Section 1–201.
"Buyer". Section 2–103.
"Commercial unit". Section 2–105.
"Conform". Section 2–106.
"Contract". Section 1–201.
"Goods". Section 2–105.
"Merchant". Section 2–104.
"Notifies". Section 1–201.
"Notification". Section 1–201.
"Sale on approval". Section 2–326.
"Sale or return". Section 2–326.
"Seasonably". Section 1–204.
"Seller". Section 2–103.

Cross References

Acceptance of goods, see Commercial Code § 2607.
Consignment sales and rights of creditors, see Commercial Code § 2326.
Definitions, see Commercial Code §§ 1201, 2103, 2104.
Insurable interest, see Commercial Code § 2501.
Options open to buyer in case of nonconforming goods or tender of delivery, see Commercial Code § 2601.
Rejection of goods by merchant buyer, duties, see Commercial Code § 2603.
Revocation of acceptance, see Commercial Code § 2608.
Risk of loss in the absence of breach, see Commercial Code § 2509.
Time, see Commercial Code § 1204.

§ 2327

Variation of code by agreement, see Commercial Code § 1102.

§ 2328. Sale by Auction

(1) In a sale by auction if goods are put up in lots each lot is the subject of a separate sale.

(2) A sale by auction is complete when the auctioneer so announces by the fall of the hammer or in other customary manner. Where a bid is made while the hammer is falling in acceptance of a prior bid the auctioneer may in his discretion reopen the bidding or declare the goods sold under the bid on which the hammer was falling.

(3) Such a sale is with reserve unless the goods are in explicit terms put up without reserve. In an auction with reserve the auctioneer may withdraw the goods at any time until he announces completion of the sale. In an auction without reserve, after the auctioneer calls for bids on an article or lot, that article or lot cannot be withdrawn unless no bid is made within a reasonable time. In either case a bidder may retract his bid until the auctioneer's announcement of completion of the sale, but a bidder's retraction does not revive any previous bid.

(4) If the auctioneer knowingly receives a bid on the seller's behalf or the seller makes or procures such a bid, and notice has not been given that liberty for such bidding is reserved, the buyer may at his option avoid the sale or take the goods at the price of the last good faith bid prior to the completion of the sale. This subdivision shall not apply to any bid at a forced sale. (Stats.1963, c. 819, § 2328.)

California Code Comment

By John A. Bohn and Charles J. Williams

Prior California Law

1. Subdivision (1) is the counterpart of former Civil Code § 1741(1) (sale by auction).

2. The first sentence of subdivision (2) has its counterpart in the first sentence of former Civil Code § 1741(2) (when sale by auction is complete).

The second sentence of subdivision (2) has no counterpart in prior California statutory law.

3. Subdivision (3) retains the basic policy of former Civil Code § 1741(2) but adds to prior statutory law in requiring that "a sale is with reserve unless the goods are in *explicit terms* put up without reserve." (emphasis added).

4. Subdivision (4) is the counterpart of former Civil Code § 1741(4) (failure to give notice in case of sale by auction).

The last sentence of this section permits, for example, an execution creditor to bid at a "forced sale." This avoids a possible problem in construction since an execution creditor is not a seller in the normal sense of the word.

Changes from U.C.C. (1962 Official Text)

5. This is section 2–328 of the Official Text without change.

Uniform Commercial Code Comment

Prior Uniform Statutory Provision:
Section 21, Uniform Sales Act.
Changes: Completely rewritten.
Purposes of Changes: To make it clear that:

1. The auctioneer may in his discretion either reopen the bidding or close the sale on the bid on which the hammer was falling when a bid is made at that moment. The recognition of a bid of this kind by the auctioneer in his discretion does not mean a closing in favor of such a bidder, but only that the bid has been accepted as a continuation of the bidding. If recognized, such a bid discharges the bid on which the hammer was falling when it was made.

2. An auction "with reserve" is the normal procedure. The crucial point, however, for determining the nature of an auction is the "putting up" of the goods. This Article accepts the view that the goods may be withdrawn before they are actually "put up," regardless of whether the auction is advertised as one without reserve, without liability on the part of the auction announcer to persons who are present. This is subject to any peculiar facts which might bring the case within the "firm offer" principle of this Article, but an offer to persons generally would require unmistakable language in order to fall within that section. The prior announcement of the nature of the auction either as with reserve or without reserve will, however, enter as an "explicit term" in the "putting up" of the goods and conduct thereafter must be governed accordingly. The present section continues the prior rule permitting withdrawal of bids in auctions both with and without reserve; and the rule is made explicit that the retraction of a bid does not revive a prior bid.

Cross Reference:
Point 2: Section 2–205.

Definitional Cross References:
"Buyer". Section 2–103.
"Good faith". Section 1–201.
"Goods". Section 2–105.
"Lot". Section 2–105.
"Notice". Section 1–201.
"Sale". Section 2–106.
"Seller". Section 2–103.

Cross References

Auction sales, bulk sales, see Commercial Code § 6108.
Authority of auctioneer, see Civil Code §§ 2362, 2363.
Firm offers, see Commercial Code § 2205.
Punishment for holding mock auction, see Penal Code § 535.
Unlawfully acting as auctioneer, see Penal Code § 436.

CHAPTER 4. TITLE, CREDITORS AND GOOD FAITH PURCHASERS

Section
2401. Passing of Title; Reservation for Security; Limited Application of This Section.
2402. Rights of Seller's Creditors Against Sold Goods.
2403. Power to Transfer; Good Faith Purchase of Goods; "Entrusting".

§ 2401. Passing of Title; Reservation for Security; Limited Application of This Section

Each provision of this division with regard to the rights, obligations and remedies of the seller, the buyer, purchasers or other third parties applies irrespective of title to the goods except where the provision refers to such title. Insofar as situations are not covered by the other provisions of this * * * division and matters concerning title become material the following rules apply:

(1) Title to goods cannot pass under a contract for sale prior to their identification to the contract (Section 2501), and unless otherwise explicitly agreed the buyer acquires by their identification a special property as limited by this code. Any retention or reservation by the seller of the title (property) in goods shipped or delivered to the buyer is limited in effect to a reserva-

tion of a security interest. Subject to these provisions and to the provisions of the division on secured transactions (Division 9), title to goods passes from the seller to the buyer in any manner and on any conditions explicitly agreed on by the parties.

(2) Unless otherwise explicitly agreed title passes to the buyer at the time and place at which the seller completes his performance with reference to the physical delivery of the goods, despite any reservation of a security interest and even though a document of title is to be delivered at a different time or place; and in particular and despite any reservation of a security interest by the bill of lading

(a) If the contract requires or authorizes the seller to send the goods to the buyer but does not require him to deliver them at destination, title passes to the buyer at the time and place of shipment; but

(b) If the contract requires delivery at destination, title passes on tender there.

(3) Unless otherwise explicitly agreed where delivery is to be made without moving the goods,

(a) If the seller is to deliver a document of title, title passes at the time when and the place where he delivers such documents; or

(b) If the goods are at the time of contracting already identified and no documents are to be delivered, title passes at the time and place of contracting.

(4) A rejection or other refusal by the buyer to receive or retain the goods, whether or not justified, or a justified revocation of acceptance revests title to the goods in the seller. Such revesting occurs by operation of law and is not a "sale." (Stats.1963, c. 819, § 2401. Amended by Stats.1965, c. 1379, p. 3286, § 2.)

California Code Comment

By John A. Bohn and Charles J. Williams

Prior California Law

1. Under the USA (former Civil Code §§ 1721 through 1800) many issues revolved around the question of when title passed. Under the Commercial Code the concept of title is subordinated. See Official Comment to Commercial Code § 2101. This section provides rules to determine when "title passes" in those situations under the Commercial Code when passage of title is relevant.

2. Subdivision (1) is comparable to former Civil Code § 1738 and § 1739 which provided rules to determine when title would pass under the Uniform Sales Act (former Civil Code §§ 1721 through 1800).

The provisions of subdivision (1) providing that title passes "in any manner . . . agreed on" is similar to former Civil Code § 1738(1) dealing with ascertained goods, but the qualification "explicitly agreed on" requires a more definite expression of intent than was required under former Civil Code § 1738(1).

3. Subdivision (3) has no statutory counterpart in prior California law; however, subdivision (3)(b) is similar to Rule 1 of former Civil Code § 1739.

4. Subdivision (4) has no statutory counterpart in prior California law.

Changes from U.C.C. (1962 Official Text)

5. This is section 2-401 of the Official Text without change.

Uniform Commercial Code Comment

Prior Uniform Statutory Provision:

See generally, Sections 17, 18, 19 and 20, Uniform Sales Act.

Purposes: To make it clear that:

1. This Article deals with the issues between seller and buyer in terms of step by step performance or non-performance under the contract for sale and not in terms of whether or not "title" to the goods has passed. That the rules of this section in no way alter the rights of either the buyer, seller or third parties declared elsewhere in the Article is made clear by the preamble of this section. This section, however, in no way intends to indicate which line of interpretation should be followed in cases where the applicability of "public" regulation depends upon a "sale" or upon location of "title" without further definition. The basic policy of this Article that known purpose and reason should govern interpretation cannot extend beyond the scope of its own provisions. It is therefore necessary to state what a "sale" is and when title passes under this Article in case the courts deem any public regulation to incorporate the defined term of the "private" law.

2. "Future" goods cannot be the subject of a present sale. Before title can pass the goods must be identified in the manner set forth in Section 2-501. The parties, however, have full liberty to arrange by specific terms for the passing of title to goods which are existing.

3. The "special property" of the buyer in goods identified to the contract is excluded from the definition of "security interest"; its incidents are defined in provisions of this Article such as those on the rights of the seller's creditors, on good faith purchase, on the buyer's right to goods on the seller's insolvency, and on the buyer's right to specific performance or replevin.

4. The factual situations in subsections (2) and (3) upon which passage of title turn actually base the test upon the time when the seller has finally committed himself in regard to specific goods. Thus in a "shipment" contract he commits himself by the act of making the shipment. If shipment is not contemplated subsection (3) turns on the seller's final commitment, i.e. the delivery of documents or the making of the contract.

Cross References:

Point 2: Sections 2-102, 2-501 and 2-502.
Point 3: Sections 1-201, 2-402, 2-403, 2-502 and 2-716.

Definitional Cross References:

"Agreement". Section 1-201.
"Bill of lading". Section 1-201.
"Buyer". Section 2-103.
"Contract". Section 1-201.
"Contract for sale". Section 2-106.
"Delivery". Section 1-201.
"Document of title". Section 1-201.
"Good faith". Section 2-103.
"Goods". Section 2-105.
"Party". Section 1-201.
"Purchaser". Section 1-201.
"Receipt" of goods. Section 2-103.
"Remedy". Section 1-201.
"Rights". Section 1-201.
"Sale". Section 2-106.
"Security interest". Section 1-201.
"Seller". Section 2-103.
"Send". Section 1-201.

Cross References

Buyer protected from seller's security interest, see Commercial Code § 9307.
Buyer's right to goods on seller's insolvency, see Commercial Code § 2502.
Buyer's right to specific performance or replevin, see Commercial Code § 2716.
Definitions, see Commercial Code §§ 1201, 2103, 2104.
Executory and executed contracts defined, see Civil Code § 1661.
Good faith purchase of goods, see Commercial Code § 2403.
Manner of identification of goods, see Commercial Code § 2501.

§ 2401

Motor vehicles, transfer of title by legal owner, see Vehicle Code § 5750.
Offer of performance, see Civil Code § 1485 et seq.
Risk of loss in absence of breach, see Commercial Code § 2509.
Sale defined, see Commercial Code § 2106.
Security interest defined, see Commercial Code § 1201.
Security interests arising under this division as subject to division relating to secured transactions, see Commercial Code § 9113.
Special property acquired by buyer, see Commercial Code §§ 2501, 2502.
Transactions excluded from this division, see Commercial Code § 2102.
Variation of code by agreement, see Commercial Code § 1102.

§ 2402. Rights of Seller's Creditors Against Sold Goods

(1) Except as provided in subdivisions (2) and (3), rights of unsecured creditors of the seller with respect to goods which have been identified to a contract for sale are subject to the buyer's rights to recover the goods under this division (Sections 2502 and 2716).

(2) A creditor of the seller may treat a sale or an identification of goods to a contract for sale as void if as against him or her a retention of possession by the seller is fraudulent or void under any rule of law of the state where the goods are situated, except that retention of possession in good faith and current course of trade by a merchant-seller for a commercially reasonable time after a sale or identification is not fraudulent or void.

(3) Nothing in this division shall be deemed to impair the rights of creditors of the seller:

(a) Under the provisions of the division on secured transactions (Division 9); or

(b) Where identification to the contract or delivery is made not in current course of trade but in satisfaction of or as security for a pre-existing claim for money, security or the like and is made under circumstances which under any rule of law of the state where the goods are situated would apart from this division constitute the transaction a fraudulent transfer or voidable preference. (Stats.1963, c. 819, § 2402. Amended by Stats. 1988, c. 1368, § 9, operative Jan. 1, 1990.)

California Code Comment

By John A. Bohn and Charles J. Williams

Prior California Law

1. Subdivision (1) is without counterpart in prior California statutory law.

2. Subdivision (2) is similar to former Civil Code § 1746 (creditor's rights against sold goods in seller's possession), except that under the Commercial Code there is no fraud if in good faith a merchant seller retains possession for a reasonable time after sale in the course of trade.

3. Subdivision (3) is without counterpart in prior California statutory law.

Changes from U.C.C. (1962 Official Text)

4. This is section 2–402 of the Official Text without change.

Uniform Commercial Code Comment

Prior Uniform Statutory Provision:
Subsection (2)—Section 26, Uniform Sales Act; Subsections (1) and (3)—none.
Changes: Rephrased.

Purposes of Changes and New Matter: To avoid confusion on ordinary issues between current sellers and buyers and issues in the field of preference and hindrance by making it clear that:

1. Local law on questions of hindrance of creditors by the seller's retention of possession of the goods are outside the scope of this Article, but retention of possession in the current course of trade is legitimate. Transactions which fall within the law's policy against improper preferences are reserved from the protection of this Article.

2. The retention of possession of the goods by a merchant seller for a commercially reasonable time after a sale or identification in current course is exempted from attack as fraudulent. Similarly, the provisions of subsection (3) have no application to identification or delivery made in the current course of trade, as measured against general commercial understanding of what a "current" transaction is.

Definitional Cross References:

"Contract for sale". Section 2–106.
"Creditor". Section 1–201.
"Good faith". Section 2–103.
"Goods". Section 2–105.
"Merchant". Section 2–104.
"Money". Section 1–201.
"Reasonable time". Section 1–204.
"Rights". Section 1–201.
"Sale". Section 2–106.
"Seller". Section 2–103.

Cross References

Actual fraud as question of fact, see Civil Code § 1574.
Buyer's right to goods on seller's insolvency, see Commercial Code § 2502.
Buyer's right to specific performance or replevin, see Commercial Code § 2716.
Fraudulent bulk transfers, notice, see Commercial Code § 6105.
Fraudulent instruments and transfers, see Civil Code § 3439 et seq.
Priority of certain liens arising by operation of law, see Commercial Code § 9310.
Rights acquired in the absence of due negotiation, effect of diversion, see Commercial Code § 7504.
Secured transactions, see Commercial Code § 9101 et seq.
Transfers without delivery, see Civil Code § 3440.

§ 2403. Power to Transfer; Good Faith Purchase of Goods; "Entrusting"

(1) A purchaser of goods acquires all title which his transferor had or had power to transfer except that a purchaser of a limited interest acquires rights only to the extent of the interest purchased. A person with voidable title has power to transfer a good title to a good faith purchaser for value. When goods have been delivered under a transaction of purchase the purchaser has such power even though

(a) The transferor was deceived as to the identity of the purchaser, or

(b) The delivery was in exchange for a check which is later dishonored, or

(c) It was agreed that the transaction was to be a "cash sale," or

(d) The delivery was procured through fraud punishable as larcenous under the criminal law.

(2) Any entrusting of possession of goods to a merchant who deals in goods of that kind gives him power to transfer all rights of the entruster to a buyer in ordinary course of business.

(3) "Entrusting" includes any delivery and any acquiescence in retention of possession for the purpose of sale, obtaining offers to purchase, locating a buyer, or the like; regardless of any condition expressed between the parties to the delivery or acquiescence and regardless of whether the procurement of the entrusting or the possessor's disposition of the goods have been such as to be larcenous under the criminal law.

(4) The rights of other purchasers of goods and of lien creditors are governed by the divisions on secured transactions (Division 9), bulk transfers (Division 6) and documents of title (Division 7). *(Stats.1963, c. 819, § 2403. Amended by Stats.1967, c. 799, p. 2207, § 4.)*

California Code Comment

By Charles J. Williams

The 1967 amendment adds the reference to lien creditors of subdivision (4). It is made for the purpose of conforming subdivision (4) to the 1962 Official Text.

The reason for the original variation in the California version is explained in California Code Comment 10, main volume. However, the Permanent Editorial Board comments that the California variation in subdivision (4) "seems to serve no purpose other than to remove an otherwise useful cross-reference. There is no suggestion in the Official Text that the rights of lien creditors are exclusively governed by the Articles [Divisions] referred to". (Permanent Editorial Board for the Uniform Commercial Code, Report No. 2, p. 45.)

California Code Comment

By John A. Bohn and Charles J. Williams

Prior California Law

1. The first sentence of subdivision (1) is consistent with prior California law as expressed in Woodsend v. Chatom, 191 Cal. 72, 214 Pac. 965 (1923) ("a purchaser of personal property acquires only the title or estate of his vendor") and former Civil Code § 1743(1) (sale by a person not the owner). The second sentence in subdivision (1) is a restatement of former Civil Code § 1744 (sale by one having voidable title).

2. Subdivision (1)(a) is probably in accord with prior California law. See Wendling Lumber Co. v. Glenwood Lumber Co., 153 Cal. 411, 95 Pac. 1029 (1908) holding that a purchaser in good faith and for a valuable consideration acquires good title from a fraudulent vendee.

3. Subdivision (1)(b) is in accord with California law as expressed in Keegan v. Kaufman Bros., 68 Cal.App.2d 197, 156 P.2d 261 (1945).

4. Subdivision (1)(c) is contrary to prior California law as expressed in Alonso v. Badger, 58 Cal.App.2d 752, 138 P.2d 24 (1943) (vendee acquires no power to transfer title until cash is in fact paid).

5. Subdivision (1)(d) is contrary to prior California law as expressed in Kelley Kar Co. v. Maryland Cas. Co., 142 Cal.App.2d 263, 298 P.2d 590 (1956); Barthelmess v. Cavalier, 2 Cal.App.2d 477, 38 P.2d 484 (1934) and Crocker Nat. Bank v. Byrne & McDonnell, 178 Cal. 329, 173 Pac. 752 (1918), that one who has stolen a chattel cannot convey good title even to a bona fide purchaser for value.

6. It is important to note that subdivision (1) deals with "a good faith purchaser for value" while subdivisions (2) and (3) deal with "a buyer in ordinary course of business." An example of the importance of this distinction is that a creditor accepting goods in total or partial satisfaction "of a money debt" can be "a good faith purchaser for value" (Commercial Code §§ 1201(32), 1201(33) and 1201(44)), but cannot be "a buyer in ordinary course of business" (Commercial Code § 1201(9)).

7. Under prior California law one entrusted with possession of goods had power to transfer title only if some *indicia* of ownership other than mere possession was present. See former Civil Code § 1743 (sale by a person not the owner); Metropolitan Finance Corporation of California v. Morf, 42 Cal.App.2d 756, 109 P.2d 969 (1941) ("entrusting a third person with mere possession does not constituted holding him out as owner"); and California Jewelry Co. v. Provident Loan Assn., 6 Cal.App.2d 506, 513, 45 P.2d 271, 274 (1935) ("so long as the possession of the goods is not accompanied with some *indicia* of ownership, or of right to sell, the possessor has no more power to divest the owner of his title or to affect it than a mere thief.") But see former Civil Code § 1745 (sale by seller in possession of goods already sold) providing that when a buyer leaves goods in the possession of the seller, a subsequent *bona fide* purchaser will be protected as against the buyer. Also see Civil Code § 3440 (transfer of lien on personal property made without delivery: presumption of fraud) which in effect, with certain exceptions, provides that the making of a transfer of or lien on personal property without a delivery of the property is void as against the transferors, creditors and subsequent purchasers or encumbrancers in good faith.

Under former Civil Code § 1743 the cases usually turned on the question of estoppel or ostensible ownership. For example see General Securities Corp. v. Reo Motor Car Co., 91 Cal.App. 16, 266 Pac. 576 (1928). Therefore, the major problem in this area was the absence of standards whereby one could reasonably predict what *indicia* of ownership would estop the true owner or confer ostensible authority upon the seller. See 2 Williston, Sales, 314–316 (Rev.Ed.1948). Each case was decided on its detailed facts. Sections 2304(2) and 2304(3) of the Commercial Code provide express standards whereby one who entrusts his goods with a merchant can know whether or not he has conferred power upon that merchant to transfer title to the entrusted goods. The seller has power to transfer title when the true owner makes "any delivery" or acquiesces "in retention of possession for the purpose of sale, obtaining offers to purchase, locating a buyer, or the like."

Also note that former Civil Code § 1743 (sale by seller in possession of goods already sold) applied to transfer of title by "a person" while subdivision (2) only applies to "a merchant who deals in goods of that kind."

Changes from U.C.C. (1962 Official Text)

8. Subdivisions (1) and (2) of Section 2403 are subsections (1) and (2) of the Official Text without change.

9. Subdivision (3) of section 2403 is a modified version of subsection 2–403(3) of the Official Text. The subdivision as adopted in California adds "for the purpose of sale, obtaining offers to purchase, locating a buyer, or the like," after "retention of possession." A report of the California State Bar Committee gives the following explanation for the inclusion of additional language in subdivision (3) of this section:

". . . the Official Text of section 12403 [2403] would go further than it needs to. It would also permit the passage of valid title in the ordinary course of business by a merchant entrusted with goods for some purpose other than sale: for example, if one left his watch for repair and the jeweler displayed it in his showcase and sold it, the owner could not replevy it from the purchaser. The State Bar Committee has recommended that section 12403 [2403] be limited to the cases in which the owner entrusts goods to a merchant for the purpose of sale or finding a buyer." California State Bar Committee on the Commercial Code, A Special Report, The Uniform Commercial Code, 37 Calif.State Bar J. p. 148 (March–April, 1962).

Professors Marsh and Warren recommended that subsection 2–403(3) of the Official Text be enacted without modification. See Sixth Progress Report to the Legislature by Senate Fact Finding Committee on Judiciary (1959–1961), Part 1, the Uniform Commercial Code, pp. 461–462 for their discussion of this subdivision.

10. Subdivision (4) of section 2403 is a modified version of subsection 2–403(4) of the Official Text. Subdivision (4) omits the phrase "and lien creditors" after "other purchasers of goods." The rights of lien creditors are governed by Civil Code § 3440.

Professors Marsh and Warren recommended the deletion of the phrase "and of lien creditors" from the California version of subsection 2–403(4). They give the following reasons for their recommendations:

"In view of the recommended deletion of section 19301(3) [9301(3)] containing the definition of 'lien creditor' (see discussion under that Section below) and in view of the fact that the references to 'lien creditor' in these sections have no meaning, it is recommended that the underscored words 'and of lien creditors' in section 12403 [2403] and 'or lien creditor' in section 12702 [2702] be deleted.

"Discussion. Section 12702 [2702] refers the rights of an attaching creditor of the buyer as against a seller attempting to rescind for fraud back to section 12403 [2403]. But Section 12403 [2403] has nothing whatever to do with the rights of lien creditors but only of purchasers.

§ 2403   SALES

It, in turn, says that the rights of lien creditors are governed by Chapter [Division] 9; but there is nothing in Chapter [Division] 9 dealing with the rights of lien creditors of the buyer as against a seller attempting to rescind for fraud. It deals only with the rights of lien creditors as against the holder of an unperfected security interest. Therefore, all of this adds up to zero. That was the conclusion reached in In re Kravitz, 278 F.2d 820 (3d Cir. 1960), which held that the Code 'does not change' prior Pennsylvania law on this subject, since these sections provide nothing and Section 11103 [1103] provides that prior law continues unless displaced by provisions of the Code.

"The Kravitz case held that under Pennsylvania law an attaching creditor of the buyer [and therefore a trustee in bankruptcy under section 70(c) of the Bankruptcy Act] took priority over the defrauded seller in this situation. The California law would appear to be contra. Cf. Blackman v. Pierce, 28 Cal. 508 (1863) (dealing with the analogous right of stoppage in transitu). It is generally true that an attaching creditor in California takes subject to all secret liens and latent equities unless protected by some specific statute, and takes only the interest which his debtor had with all its infirmities. McGee v. Allen, 7 C.2d 468, 60 P.2d 1026 (1936); The Wood Estate Company v. Chanslor, 209 C. 241, 286 P. 1001 (1930); National Bank of The Pacific v. Western Pacific Railway Company, 157 C. 573, 108 P. 676 (1910).

"In any event, whatever the California law may be on this subject, these particular references have no effect on it and they should be deleted in view of the deletion of section 19301(3) [9301(3)], if that recommendation is adopted." Sixth Progress Report to the Legislature by Senate Fact Finding Committee on Judiciary (1959–1961), Part 1, the Uniform Commercial Code, pp. 465, 466.

Uniform Commercial Code Comment

Prior Uniform Statutory Provision:

Sections 20(4), 23, 24, 25, Uniform Sales Act; Section 9, especially 9(2), Uniform Trust Receipts Act; Section 9, Uniform Conditional Sales Act.

Changes: Consolidated and rewritten.

Purposes of Changes: To gather together a series of prior uniform statutory provisions and the case-law thereunder and to state a unified and simplified policy on good faith purchase of goods.

1. The basic policy of our law allowing transfer of such title as the transferor has is generally continued and expanded under subsection (1). In this respect the provisions of the section are applicable to a person taking by any form of "purchase" as defined by this Act. Moreover the policy of this Act expressly providing for the application of supplementary general principles of law to sales transactions wherever appropriate joins with the present section to continue unimpaired all rights acquired under the law of agency or of apparent agency or ownership or other estoppel, whether based on statutory provisions or on case law principles. The section also leaves unimpaired the powers given to selling factors under the earlier Factors Acts. In addition subsection (1) provides specifically for the protection of the good faith purchaser for value in a number of specific situations which have been troublesome under prior law.

On the other hand, the contract of purchase is of course limited by its own terms as in a case of pledge for a limited amount or of sale of a fractional interest in goods.

2. The many particular situations in which a buyer in ordinary course of business from a dealer has been protected against reservation of property or other hidden interest are gathered by subsections (2)–(4) into a single principle protecting persons who buy in ordinary course out of inventory. Consignors have no reason to complain, nor have lenders who hold a security interest in the inventory, since the very purpose of goods in inventory is to be turned into cash by sale.

The principle is extended in subsection (3) to fit with the abolition of the old law of "cash sale" by subsection (1)(c). It is also freed from any technicalities depending on the extended law of larceny; such extension of the concept of theft to include trick, particular types of fraud, and the like is for the purpose of helping conviction of the offender; it has no proper application to the long-standing policy of civil protection of buyers from persons guilty of such trick or fraud. Finally, the policy is extended, in the interest of simplicity and sense, to any entrusting by a bailor; this is in consonance with the explicit provisions of Section 7–205 on the powers of a warehouseman who is also in the business of buying and selling fungible goods of the kind he warehouses. As to entrusting by a secured party, subsection (2) is limited by the more specific provisions of Section 9–307(1), which deny protection to a person buying farm products from a person engaged in farming operations.

3. The definition of "buyer in ordinary course of business" (Section 1–201) is effective here and preserves the essence of the healthy limitations engrafted by the caselaw on the older statutes. The older loose concept of good faith and wide definition of value combined to create apparent good faith purchasers in many situations in which the result outraged common sense; the court's solution was to protect the original title especially by use of "cash sale" or of over-technical construction of the enabling clauses of the statutes. But such rulings then turned into limitations on the proper protection of buyers in the ordinary market. Section 1–201(9) cuts down the category of buyer in ordinary course in such fashion as to take care of the results of the cases, but with no price either in confusion or in injustice to proper dealings in the normal market.

4. Except as provided in subsection (1), the rights of purchasers other than buyers in ordinary course are left to the Articles on Secured Transactions, Documents of Title, and Bulk Sales.

Cross References:

Point 1: Sections 1–103 and 1–201.

Point 2: Sections 1–201, 2–402, 7–205 and 9–307(1).

Points 3 and 4: Sections 1–102, 1–201, 2–104, 2–707 and Articles 6, 7 and 9.

Definitional Cross References:

"Buyer in ordinary course of business". Section 1–201.
"Good faith". Sections 1–201 and 2–103.
"Goods". Section 2–105.
"Person". Section 1–201.
"Purchaser". Section 1–201.
"Signed". Section 1–201.
"Term". Section 1–201.
"Value". Section 1–201.

Cross References

Actual or ostensible agency, see Civil Code §§ 2298, 2299, 3000.
Agents authority, see Civil Code § 2304 et seq.
Bulk sales, see Commercial Code § 6101 et seq.
Buyer in ordinary course of business as taking free of security interest, see Commercial Code § 9307.
Construction of code, see Commercial Code § 1102.
Definitions, see Commercial Code §§ 1201, 2103, 2104.
Documents of title,
   Generally, see Commercial Code § 7101 et seq.
   Where defeated in certain cases, see Commercial Code § 7503.
Payment by buyer before inspection, see Commercial Code § 2512.
Person in the position of a seller, see Commercial Code § 2707.
Secured transactions, see Commercial Code § 9101 et seq.
Seller's remedies on discovery of buyer's insolvency, see Commercial Code § 2702.
Supplementation of code by principles of law and equity, see Commercial Code § 1103.
Theft or larceny, see Penal Code § 484 et seq.
Title under warehouse receipt, see Commercial Code § 7205.
Transfers and liens without delivery, see Civil Code § 3440.
Warranty of title and against infringement, see Commercial Code § 2312.

CHAPTER 5. PERFORMANCE

Section

2501. Insurable Interest in Goods; Manner of Identification of Goods.
2502. Buyer's Right to Goods on Seller's Insolvency.
2503. Manner of Seller's Tender of Delivery.
2504. Shipment by Seller.
2505. Seller's Shipment Under Reservation.
2506. Rights of Financing Agency.
2507. Effect of Seller's Tender; Delivery on Condition.

Section	
2508.	Cure by Seller of Improper Tender or Delivery; Replacement.
2509.	Risk of Loss in the Absence of Breach.
2510.	Effect of Breach on Risk of Loss.
2511.	Tender of Payment by Buyer; Payment by Check.
2512.	Payment by buyer before inspection; nonconformity of goods.
2513.	Buyer's Right to Inspection of Goods.
2514.	When Documents Deliverable on Acceptance; When on Payment.
2515.	Preserving Evidence of Goods in Dispute.

Cross References

Performance of obligations, see Civil Code § 1473 et seq.
Presumption of performance, see Civil Code § 3529.
Time of performance of obligation, contract, see Civil Code §§ 1491, 1657.

§ 2501. Insurable Interest in Goods; Manner of Identification of Goods

(1) The buyer obtains a special property and an insurable interest in goods by identification of existing goods as goods to which the contract refers even though the goods so identified are nonconforming and he has an option to return or reject them. Such identification can be made at any time and in any manner explicitly agreed to by the parties. In the absence of explicit agreement identification occurs

(a) When the contract is made if it is for the sale of goods already existing and identified;

(b) If the contract is for the sale of future goods other than those described in paragraph (c), when goods are shipped, marked or otherwise designated by the seller as goods to which the contract refers;

(c) If the contract is for the sale of unborn young or future crops, when the crops are planted or otherwise become growing crops or the young are conceived.

(2) The seller retains an insurable interest in goods so long as title to or any security interest in the goods remains in him and where the identification is by the seller alone he may until default or insolvency or notification to the buyer that the identification is final substitute other goods for those identified.

(3) Nothing in this section impairs and insurable interest recognized under any other statute or rule of law. (Stats.1963, c. 819, § 2501.)

California Code Comment

By John A. Bohn and Charles J. Williams

Prior California Law

1. Subdivision (1) introduces the concepts of "special property" and "identification" into statutory sales law. The words "identification" or "identified" are now used instead of the words "ascertained" and "appropriated" used in the USA. Former Civil Code § 1737 (no property passes until goods are ascertained) and § 1739, Rule 4 (appropriation of unascertained goods).

2. Under subdivision (1)(a) the buyer unless there is explicit agreement to the contrary obtains a "special property" and an "insurable interest" in existing and identified goods when the contract is made. Under former Civil Code § 1739 subject to a contrary expression of intent the parties were presumed to have intended the property in goods to have passed according to certain rules. In the case of specific goods in a deliverable state the property passed when the contract was made. (Former Civil Code § 1739, Rule 1) where the specific goods were not in a deliverable state, the property passed when the goods were put into a deliverable state. (Former Civil Code § 1739, Rule 2). The rules set forth in former Civil Code § 1739 for ascertaining the intention of the parties applied *unless a different intention appeared*. See Goldberg v. Southwestern Metals Corp., 92 Cal.App.2d 819, 208 P.2d 75 (1949). Subdivision (1) of this section of the Commercial Code requires *explicit agreement* to prevent its provisions as to when identification occurs from applying to the contract.

The Commercial Code makes no distinction between goods in a deliverable state and those upon which the seller is obliged to perform work or labor. "Identification" can occur even though additional labor is to be performed. (See Official Comment 4). Under former Civil Code § 1739, (Rule 2) if the seller was bound to do something to the goods, for the purpose of putting them into a deliverable state, the property in the goods did not pass until such thing was done.

3. Subdivision (1)(a) is comparable to former Civil Code § 1739, Rule 1, pertaining to goods in a deliverable state.

4. Under subdivision (1)(b) the buyer obtains a special property and an insurable interest in future goods, except for unborn young and future crops, when the goods are "designated" by the seller as goods to which the contract refers. Under former Civil Code § 1739, Rule 4, in the absence of a different intention, the property in unascertained or future goods in a deliverable state passed when the goods were "unconditionally appropriated to the contract."

5. Subdivision (1)(c) relating to future goods is similar in effect to former Civil Code § 1725(3) (existing and future goods) which provided,

"Where parties purport to effect a present sale of future goods, the agreement operates as a contract to sell the goods and as soon as the seller acquires the goods the property therein shall pass to the buyer without further act if the parties so intend unless the agreement otherwise provides."

Concerning Civil Code § 1725(3), Professors March and Warren in their report on the Uniform Commercial Code state:

"No authoritative judicial interpretation of . . . [Civil Code § 1725(3)] can be found, and scholars are uncertain about its meaning. Vold, Sales (2d Ed.1959) 240, n. 40. One might speculate that this amendment to the Sales Act was enacted in 1931 in an attempt to codify the result of the Sun-Maid Raisin case [96] Cal.App. 650, 274 Pac. 557 (1929), decided two years before, in which it was held that a contract purporting to make a present sale of raisin grapes to be grown in future years was effective to pass title to the grapes as soon as the grapes came into existence, even though at that time the seller had numerous acts to perform before the grapes would be in a deliverable state." Sixth Progress Report to the Legislature by the Senate Fact Finding Committee on Judiciary (1959–1961), Part 1, The Uniform Commercial Code, p. 464.

Before the USA was adopted in 1931 California followed the common law doctrine of potential possession. Callahan v. Martin, 3 Cal.2d 110, 43 P.2d 788 (1935). Under the doctrine of potential possession, a vendor could enter into a contract for the sale of future crops of the unborn young of animals and title would pass at the time the goods came into existence. Vold, Sales (2d Ed.1959) section 45. This doctrine was abolished in California by the adoption of the USA. Callahan v. Martin, Id.

6. The first part of subdivision (2) probably makes no change in prior California law. While the USA did not deal with the question of insurable interest, the case law under the USA probably gave an insurable interest in both of the situations where the seller has title or an insurable interest described in subdivision (2). For example, see Fageol Truck & Coach Co. v. Pacific Indem. Co., 18 Cal.2d 731, 117 P.2d 661 (1941) holding that "insurable interest" includes the interest which the vendor retained under a conditional sales contract.

7. The second part of subdivision (2) dealing with substitution of goods by the seller is new to California law.

Changes from U.C.C. (1962 Official Text)

8. Except for paragraph (c), this is section 2–501 of the Official Text. Paragraph (c) of the Official Text reads:

"When the crops are planted or otherwise become growing crops or the young are conceived if the contract is for the sale of unborn young to be born within twelve months after contracting or for the sale of crops to be harvested within twelve months or the next normal harvest season after contracting whichever is longer."

9. The California version of paragraph (c) adopts the recommendation of Professors March and Warren:

". . . It is not entirely clear what the draftsmen of the Code intended to accomplish by § 12501(1)(c) [2501(1)(c)]. Under this Section there can be no identification of goods until they are in existence. As soon as goods come into existence, their identification can occur at any time and in any manner explicitly agreed to by the parties. If there is no explicit agreement relative to identification, then identification occurs when crops come into existence or the young of animals are conceived if the contract is for the sale of young to be born in twelve months or crops to be harvested within this period.

"The statute is perfectly clear as far as it goes, but what is its effect on contracts for the sale of crops or animals to be conceived or planted after the twelve month period? The statute does not expressly invalidate such an agreement. The omission to delineate the consequences of contracting for the sale of crops and increase beyond the period of the statute is in contrast to the treatment of future crops in Chapter [Division] 9. In Section 19204(4) [9204(4)], it is expressly provided that no security interest attaches to crops to become such, more than one year after the security agreement is executed.

"With regard to crop and animal contracts not covered by this clause, the following inferences are possible: (1) There is no identification of such goods immediately upon their being conceived or planted unless the contract explicitly so provides; hence, identification must await some further act on the part of the parties. (2) The statute does not apply to such goods; hence, there is a *casus omissus*, and the controlling law must be found outside the Code. Since the Sales Act will be repealed by the Code, presumably the pre-Sales Act doctrine of potential possession, with all of its uncertainties, applies.

"Under the proposed amendment, identification would occur in the sale of future crops or increase of animals when they are conceived or planted, in the absence of an explicit agreement postponing the time of identification. The effect of the amended clause would be similar to that of CC § 1725(3)." Sixth Progress Report to the Legislature by the Senate Fact Finding Committee on Judiciary (1959–1961), Part 1, The Uniform Commercial Code, pp. 463–464.

A special report of a California State Bar Committee gives a similar explanation for the California rewording of subsection (c):

"The Official Text of section 12501 [2501] would leave the identification of crops or animals to the contract unprovided for when the agreement is for the sale of such crops or animals beyond the 12 months' limit. Does the Official Text intend to prohibit contracts for the sale of crops and animals not coming into being until more than 12 months after the agreement? If so, what possible purpose could such a restriction serve? If such a contract should not be prohibited, then identification of the goods to the contract should not simply be left in the air. For these reasons, the 12 months' limitation is not in S.B. 1093 [1961 Session, 1958 official text as amended]. Section 12501 [2501] would now apply to any contract for the sale of future crops or the young of animals." California State Bar Committee on the Commercial Code, A Special Report, The Uniform Commercial Code, 37 Calif.Bar J. 117, 138 (March–April, 1962).

Uniform Commercial Code Comment

Prior Uniform Statutory Provision:

See Sections 17 and 19, Uniform Sales Act.

Purposes:

1. The present section deals with the manner of identifying goods to the contract so that an insurable interest in the buyer and the rights set forth in the next section will accrue. Generally speaking, identification may be made in any manner "explicitly agreed to" by the parties. The rules of paragraphs (a), (b) and (c) apply only in the absence of such "explicit agreement".

2. In the ordinary case identification of particular existing goods as goods to which the contract refers is unambiguous and may occur in one of many ways. It is possible, however, for the identification to be tentative or contingent. In view of the limited effect given to identification by this Article, the general policy is to resolve all doubts in favor of identification.

3. The provision of this section as to "explicit agreement" clarifies the present confusion in the law of sales which has arisen from the fact that under prior uniform legislation all rules of presumption with reference to the passing of title or to appropriation (which in turn depended upon identification) were regarded as subject to the contrary intention of the parties or of the party appropriating. Such uncertainty is reduced to a minimum under this section by requiring "explicit agreement" of the parties before the rules of paragraphs (a), (b) and (c) are displaced—as they would be by a term giving the buyer power to select the goods. An "explicit" agreement, however, need not necessarily be found in the terms used in the particular transaction. Thus, where a usage of the trade has previously been made explicit by reduction to a standard set of "rules and regulations" currently incorporated by reference into the contracts of the parties, a relevant provision of those "rules and regulations" is "explicit" within the meaning of this section.

4. In view of the limited function of identification there is no requirement in this section that the goods be in deliverable state or that all of the seller's duties with respect to the processing of the goods be completed in order that identification occur. For example, despite identification the risk of loss remains on the seller under the risk of loss provisions until completion of his duties as to the goods and all of his remedies remain dependent upon his not defaulting under the contract.

5. Undivided shares in an identified fungible bulk, such as grain in an elevator or oil in a storage tank, can be sold. The mere making of the contract with reference to an undivided share in an identified fungible bulk is enough under subsection (a) to effect an identification if there is no explicit agreement otherwise. The seller's duty, however, to segregate and deliver according to the contract is not affected by such an identification but is controlled by other provisions of this Article.

6. Identification of crops under paragraph (c) [See California Code Comment, notes 8, 9.] is made upon planting only if they are to be harvested within the year or within the next normal harvest season. The phrase "next normal harvest season" fairly includes nursery stock raised for normally quick "harvest," but plainly excludes a "timber" crop to which the concept of a harvest "season" is inapplicable.

Paragraph (c) [See California Code Comment, notes 8, 9.] is also applicable to a crop of wool or the young of animals to be born within twelve months after contracting. The product of a lumbering, mining or fishing operation, though seasonal, is not within the concept of "growing". Identification under a contract for all or part of the output of such an operation can be effected early in the operation.

Cross References:

Point 1: Section 2–502.
Point 4: Sections 2–509, 2–510 and 2–703.
Point 5: Sections 2–105, 2–308, 2–503 and 2–509.
Point 6: Sections 2–105(1), 2–107(1) and 2–402.

Definitional Cross References:

"Agreement". Section 1–201.
"Contract". Section 1–201.
"Contract for sale". Section 2–106.
"Future goods". Section 2–105.
"Goods". Section 2–105.
"Notification". Section 1–201.
"Party". Section 1–201.
"Sale". Section 2–106.
"Security interest". Section 1–201.
"Seller". Section 2–103.

Cross References

Capacity to insure and be insured, see Insurance Code §§ 150, 151.
Contract for sale of growing crops, see Commercial Code § 2107.
Definitions, see Commercial Code §§ 1201, 2103, 2104.
Events subject to insurance, see Insurance Code § 250 et seq.
Insurable interest in general, see Insurance Code § 280 et seq.
Marine insurance, insurable interests, see Insurance Code § 1880 et seq.
Passing of title, see Commercial Code § 2401.
Place for delivery of identified goods, see Commercial Code § 2308.
Remedies of seller for breach by buyer, see Commercial Code § 2703.

Rights of seller's unsecured creditors with respect to goods identified to contract, see Commercial Code § 2402.

Risk of loss,
In absence of breach, see Commercial Code § 2509.
In case of breach, see Commercial Code § 2510.

Tender of delivery, see Commercial Code § 2503.

Transfer of subject insured, effect on insurable interest, see Insurance Code § 300 et seq.

§ 2502. Buyer's Right to Goods on Seller's Insolvency

(1) Subject to subdivision (2) and even though the goods have not been shipped a buyer who has paid a part or all of the price of goods in which he has a special property under the provisions of the immediately preceding section may on making and keeping good a tender of any unpaid portion of their price recover them from the seller if the seller becomes insolvent within 10 days after receipt of the first installment on their price.

(2) If the identification creating his special property has been made by the buyer he acquires the right to recover the goods only if they conform to the contract for sale. *(Stats.1963, c. 819, § 2502.)*

California Code Comment
By John A. Bohn and Charles J. Williams

Prior California Law

1. This section has no counterpart under the USA.

In Latty, Sales and Title and The Proposed Code, 16 Law & Contemp.Prob. 3, 11 (1951) this section is compared with the result in Hopkins v. Bronaugh, 281 Fed. 799 (CCA 9th 1922) where the court held in a case in which certain bonds were set aside by seller for purchaser that title to these bonds had passed.

This section and its effect upon prior California law is discussed by the California State Bar Committee on the Commercial Code.

"At present, if a seller becomes insolvent before delivery of the goods and after the payment of the purchase price, the buyer's right to the goods depends on whether 'title' has passed to him. If it has, he can recover the goods in specie and thus be made whole [*Fn.:* 4 Collier, Bankruptcy 1113–1117 (14th ed. 1942). However, if the seller has retained possession in such a manner as to constitute the sale a "fraud on creditors" (see Cal.Civ.Code, sec. 3440), the trustee in bankruptcy may avoid the sale.] If not, he becomes a general creditor and will likely get only a small portion of the purchase price as a dividend. [*Fn.:* Ibid.] Section 12502 [2502] would establish a new test to determine when the buyer is entitled to the goods: If the buyer has paid all or a part of the purchase price and the goods have been identified to the contract, the buyer could recover the goods by tendering any balance of the purchase price, if the seller becomes insolvent within ten days after receipt of the first installment of the purchase price. Presumably, a buyer could also reclaim goods from an insolvent seller as at present on the basis that title to them had passed to the buyer or that he had a perfected security interest in them, without regard to the ten day limitation." A Special Report, The Uniform Commercial Code, 37 Calif.Bar J. (March–April, 1962) p. 151.

Changes from U.C.C. (1962 Official Text)

2. This is section 2–502 of the Official Text without change.

Uniform Commercial Code Comment

Prior Uniform Statutory Provision:
Compare Sections 17, 18 and 19, Uniform Sales Act.

Purposes:

1. This section gives an additional right to the buyer as a result of identification of the goods to the contract in the manner provided in Section 2–501. The buyer is given a right to the goods on the seller's insolvency occurring within 10 days after he receives the first installment on their price.

2. The question of whether the buyer also acquires a security interest in identified goods and has rights to the goods when insolvency takes place after the ten-day period provided in this section depends upon compliance with the provisions of the Article on Secured Transactions (Article 9).

3. Subsection (2) is included to preclude the possibility of unjust enrichment which exists if the buyer were permitted to recover goods even though they were greatly superior in quality or quantity to that called for by the contract for sale.

Cross References:
Point 1: Sections 1–201 and 2–702.
Point 2: Article 9.

Definitional Cross References:
"Buyer". Section 2–103.
"Conform". Section 2–106.
"Contract for sale". Section 2–106.
"Goods". Section 2–105.
"Insolvent". Section 1–201.
"Right". Section 1–201.
"Seller". Section 2–103.

Cross References

Definitions, see Commercial Code §§ 1201, 2103, 2104.
Fraudulent conveyances, see Civil Code § 3439 et seq.
Insolvency defined, see Civil Code § 3439.02.
Remedies of buyer where seller repudiates or fails to deliver, see Commercial Code § 2711.
Rights of seller's creditors against sold goods, see Commercial Code § 2402.
Secured transactions, see Commercial Code § 9101 et seq.
Seller's remedies on discovery of buyer's insolvency, see Commercial Code § 2702.

§ 2503. Manner of Seller's Tender of Delivery

(1) Tender of delivery requires that the seller put and hold conforming goods at the buyer's disposition and give the buyer any notification reasonably necessary to enable him to take delivery. The manner, time and place for tender are determined by the agreement and this * * * division, and in particular

(a) Tender must be at a reasonable hour, and if it is of goods they must be kept available for the period reasonably necessary to enable the buyer to take possession; but

(b) Unless otherwise agreed the buyer must furnish facilities reasonably suited to the receipt of the goods.

(2) Where the case is within the next section respecting shipment tender requires that the seller comply with its provisions.

(3) Where the seller is required to deliver at a particular destination tender requires that he comply with subdivision (1) and also in any appropriate case tender documents as described in subdivisions (4) and (5) of this section.

(4) Where goods are in the possession of a bailee and are to be delivered without being moved

(a) Tender requires that the seller either tender a negotiable document of title covering such goods or procure acknowledgment by the bailee of the buyer's right to possession of the goods; but

(b) Tender to the buyer of a nonnegotiable document of title or of a written direction to the bailee to

§ 2503   SALES   82

deliver is sufficient tender unless the buyer seasonably objects, and receipt by the bailee of notification of the buyer's rights fixes those rights as against the bailee and all third persons; but risk of loss of the goods and of any failure by the bailee to honor the nonnegotiable document of title or to obey the direction remains on the seller until the buyer has had a reasonable time to present the document or direction, and a refusal by the bailee to honor the document or to obey the direction defeats the tender.

(5) Where the contract requires the seller to deliver documents

(a) He must tender all such documents in correct form, except as provided in this division with respect to bills of lading in a set (subdivision (2) of Section 2323); and

(b) Tender through customary banking channels is sufficient and dishonor of a draft accompanying the documents constitutes nonacceptance or rejection. (Stats.1963, c. 819, § 2503. Amended by Stats.1965, c. 1379, p. 3287, § 3.)

California Code Comment
By John A. Bohn and Charles J. Williams

Prior California Law

1. There is no prior California statute setting forth the general rules governing tender of delivery, although there were isolated statutory sections which were similar.

Subdivision (1) is consistent with the basic policy of former Civil Code § 1771 (buyer's liability for failure to accept delivery). Under § 1771 the buyer was allowed a reasonable time within which to accept or reject a delivery of goods by the seller. This subdivision is consistent to the extent that it requires the seller to give the buyer "notification reasonably necessary to enable him to take delivery." Subdivision (1) differs from former Civil Code § 1771 in that it expressly requires the seller to tender "conforming goods."

2. Subdivision (1)(a) enlarges the rule of former Civil Code § 1763 (4) which required tender of delivery to be made at a reasonable hour.

3. Subdivision (1)(b) is without counterpart in prior California law.

Under former Civil Code § 1771 (buyer's liability for failure to accept delivery) the buyer had an obligation to "take delivery of the goods." Although no cases construing this phrase were found, one could argue that taking delivery would have included doing all acts that would be required of a buyer in order to make delivery possible so that this may not be a change from former law.

4. The California Annotations to the Proposed Uniform Commercial Code make the following observation:

"There is an apparent change made by subdivision (3) in the existing law to the effect that tender by seller is effective when he puts the conforming goods at buyer's disposition and gives notice. Buyer must then furnish facilities to receive them. Under the present statute the property remains the seller's until actually delivered to the buyer or to the place agreed upon for delivery." Sixth Progress Report to the Legislature by the Senate Fact Finding Committee on Judiciary (1959–1961), Part 1, The Uniform Commercial Code, p. 51.

5. Subdivision (4)(a) continues the rule of former Civil Code § 1763(3).

6. Subdivision (4)(b) is basically new to California statutory law. The provisions fixing rights against bailee and third persons upon receipt by the bailee of notification of the buyers rights is apparently a restatement of the provisions of former Civil Code § 1763(3) which states that "as against all others than the seller the buyer shall be regarded as having received delivery from the time when such third person [bailee] first has notice of the sale."

7. Subdivision (5) has no counterpart in prior California statutory law.

Changes from U.C.C. (1962 Official Text)

8. This is section 2–503 of the Official Text without change.

Uniform Commercial Code Comment
Prior Uniform Statutory Provision:

See Sections 11, 19, 20, 43(3) and (4), 46 and 51, Uniform Sales Act.
Changes: The general policy of the above sections is continued and supplemented but subsection (3) changes the rule of prior section 19(5) as to what constitutes a "destination" contract and subsection (4) incorporates a minor correction as to tender of delivery of goods in the possession of a bailee.

Purposes of Changes:

1. The major general rules governing the manner of proper or due tender of delivery are gathered in this section. The term "tender" is used in this Article in two different senses. In one sense it refers to "due tender" which contemplates an offer coupled with a present ability to fulfill all the conditions resting on the tendering party and must be followed by actual performance if the other party shows himself ready to proceed. Unless the context unmistakably indicates otherwise this is the meaning of "tender" in this Article and the occasional addition of the word "due" is only for clarity and emphasis. At other times it is used to refer to an offer of goods or documents under a contract as if in fulfillment of its conditions even though there is a defect when measured against the contract obligation. Used in either sense, however, "tender" connotes such performance by the tendering party as puts the other party in default if he fails to proceed in some manner.

2. The seller's general duty to tender and deliver is laid down in Section 2–301 and more particularly in Section 2–507. The seller's right to a receipt if he demands one and receipts are customary is governed by Section 1–205. Subsection (1) of the present section proceeds to set forth two primary requirements of tender: first, that the seller "put and hold conforming goods at the buyer's disposition" and, second, that he "give the buyer any notice reasonably necessary to enable him to take delivery."

In cases in which payment is due and demanded upon delivery the "buyer's disposition" is qualified by the seller's right to retain control of the goods until payment by the provision of this Article on delivery on condition. However, where the seller is demanding payment on delivery he must first allow the buyer to inspect the goods in order to avoid impairing his tender unless the contract for sale is on C.I.F., C.O.D., cash against documents or similar terms negating the privilege of inspection before payment.

In the case of contracts involving documents the seller can "put and hold conforming goods at the buyer's disposition" under subsection (1) by tendering documents which give the buyer complete control of the goods under the provisions of Article 7 on due negotiation.

3. Under paragraph (a) of subsection (1) usage of the trade and the circumstances of the particular case determine what is a reasonable hour for tender and what constitutes a reasonable period of holding the goods available.

4. The buyer must furnish reasonable facilities for the receipt of the goods tendered by the seller under subsection (1), paragraph (b). This obligation of the buyer is no part of the seller's tender.

5. For the purposes of subsections (2) and (3) there is omitted from this Article the rule under prior uniform legislation that a term requiring the seller to pay the freight or cost of transportation to the buyer is equivalent to an agreement by the seller to deliver to the buyer or at an agreed destination. This omission is with the specific intention of negating the rule, for under this Article the "shipment" contract is regarded as the normal one and the "destination" contract as the variant type. The seller is not obligated to deliver at a named destination and bear the concurrent risk of loss until arrival, unless he has specifically agreed so to deliver or the commercial understanding of the terms used by the parties contemplates such delivery.

6. Paragraph (a) of subsection (4) continues the rule of the prior uniform legislation as to acknowledgment by the bailee. Paragraph (b) of subsection (4) adopts the rule that between the buyer and the seller the risk of loss remains on the seller during a period reasonable for securing acknowledgment of the transfer from the bailee, while as against all other parties the buyer's rights are fixed as of the time the bailee receives notice of the transfer.

7. Under subsection (5) documents are never "required" except where there is an express contract term or it is plainly implicit in the peculiar circumstances of the case or in a usage of trade. Documents may, of course, be "authorized" although not required, but such cases are not within the scope of this subsection. When documents are required, there are three main requirements of this subsection: (1) "All": each required document is essential to a proper tender; (2) "Such": the documents must be the ones actually required by the contract in terms of source and substance; (3) "Correct form": All documents must be in correct form.

When a prescribed document cannot be procured, a question of fact arises under the provision of this Article on substituted performance as to whether the agreed manner of delivery is actually commercially impracticable and whether the substitute is commercially reasonable.

Cross References:

Point 2: Sections 1–205, 2–301, 2–310, 2–507 and 2–513 and Article 7.
Point 5: Sections 2–308, 2–310 and 2–509.
Point 7: Section 2–614(1).

Specific matters involving tender are covered in many additional sections of this Article. See Sections 1–205, 2–301, 2–306 to 2–319, 2–321(3), 2–504, 2–507(2), 2–511(1), 2–513, 2–612 and 2–614.

Definitional Cross References:

"Agreement". Section 1–201.
"Bill of lading". Section 1–201.
"Buyer". Section 2–103.
"Conforming". Section 2–106.
"Contract". Section 1–201.
"Delivery". Section 1–201.
"Dishonor". Section 3–508.
"Document of title". Section 1–201.
"Draft". Section 3–104.
"Goods". Section 2–105.
"Notification". Section 1–201.
"Reasonable time". Section 1–204.
"Receipt" of goods. Section 2–103.
"Rights". Section 1–201.
"Seasonably". Section 1–204.
"Seller". Section 2–103.
"Written". Section 1–201.

Cross References

C.I.F. or C. & F. contracts providing for payment on or after arrival of goods, preliminary inspection, see Commercial Code § 2321.
Course of dealing and usage of trade, see Commercial Code § 1205.
Documents of title,
  Generally, see Commercial Code § 7101 et seq.
  Manner of delivery, see Commercial Code § 2308.
Effect of tender by seller, see Commercial Code § 2507.
F.O.B. and F.A.S. terms, see Commercial Code § 2319.
Inspection of goods by buyer, see Commercial Code § 2513.
Installment contract as requiring or authorizing delivery of goods in separate lots, see Commercial Code § 2612.
Obligations of parties in general, see Commercial Code § 2301.
Overseas shipments, bill of lading issued in set of parts, see Commercial Code § 2323.
Risk of loss, see Commercial Code §§ 2509, 2510.
Shipment of goods, see Commercial Code § 2310.
Single delivery or in several lots, see Commercial Code § 2307.
Substitute performance, tender, see Commercial Code § 2614.
Tender of documents of title, see Commercial Code § 2310.
Tender of payment by buyer, see Commercial Code § 2511.
Time for performance of obligation, contract, see Civil Code §§ 1491, 1657.

§ 2504. Shipment by Seller

Where the seller is required or authorized to send the goods to the buyer and the contract does not require him to deliver them at a particular destination, then unless otherwise agreed he must

(a) Put the goods in the possession of such a carrier and make such a contract for their transportation as may be reasonable having regard to the nature of the goods and other circumstances of the case; and

(b) Obtain and promptly deliver or tender in due form any document necessary to enable the buyer to obtain possession of the goods or otherwise required by the agreement or by usage of trade; and

(c) Promptly notify the buyer of the shipment.

Failure to notify the buyer under paragraph (c) or to make a proper contract under paragraph (a) is a ground for rejection only if material delay or loss ensues. *(Stats.1963, c. 819, § 2504.)*

California Code Comment

By John A. Bohn and Charles J. Williams

Prior California Law

1. Section 2504 is consistent with former Civil Code § 1766 which provided for delivery to a carrier on behalf of the buyer.

2. Paragraph (a) is the counterpart of former Civil Code § 1766(2) which required the seller to make "such contract with the carrier on behalf of the buyer as may be reasonable, having regard to the nature of the goods and the other circumstances of the case."

3. Paragraph (b) has no counterpart in prior California statutory law. However, see Lewis v. Farmers' Grain and Milling Co., 52 Cal.App. 211, 213, 198 Pac. 426 (1921) in which the court stated "Where shipment is made by common carrier it is held that delivery is not completed until the vendor has relinquished his control over the car and given notice to the carrier that it is ready for shipment."

4. Paragraph (c), with the exception of the requirement for prompt notice, is similar to the provisions in former Civil Code § 1766 (2) that if the seller fails to make a reasonable contract with the carrier for delivery of the goods, the buyer may treat the delivery to the carrier not a delivery to himself or hold the seller responsible for any damage.

Changes from U.C.C. (1962 Official Text)

5. This is section 2–504 of the Official Text without change.

Uniform Commercial Code Comment

Prior Uniform Statutory Provision:

Section 46, Uniform Sales Act.

Changes: Rewritten.

Purposes of Changes: To continue the general policy of the prior uniform statutory provision while incorporating certain modifications with respect to the requirement that the contract with the carrier be made expressly on behalf of the buyer and as to the necessity of giving notice of the shipment to the buyer, so that:

1. The section is limited to "shipment" contracts as contrasted with "destination" contracts or contracts for delivery at the place where the goods are located. The general principles embodied in this section cover the special cases of F.O.B. point of shipment contracts and C.I.F. and C. & F. contracts. Under the preceding section on manner of tender of delivery, due tender by the seller requires that he comply with the requirements of this section in appropriate cases.

2. The contract to be made with the carrier under paragraph (a) must conform to all express terms of the agreement, subject to any substitution necessary because of failure of agreed facilities as provided in the later provision on substituted performance. However, under the policies of this Article on good faith and commercial standards and on buyer's rights on improper delivery, the requirements of explicit provisions must be read in terms of their commercial and not their literal meaning. This policy is made express with respect to bills of lading in a set in the provision of this Article on form of bills of lading required in overseas shipment.

3. In the absence of agreement, the provision of this Article on options and cooperation respecting performance gives the seller the choice of any reasonable carrier, routing and other arrangements.

Whether or not the shipment is at the buyer's expense the seller must see to any arrangements, reasonable in the circumstances, such as refrigeration, watering of live stock, protection against cold, the sending along of any necessary help, selection of specialized cars and the like for paragraph (a) is intended to cover all necessary arrangements whether made by contract with the carrier or otherwise. There is, however, a proper relaxation of such requirements if the buyer is himself in a position to make the appropriate arrangements and the seller gives him reasonable notice of the need to do so. It is an improper contract under paragraph (a) for the seller to agree with the carrier to a limited valuation below the true value and thus cut off the buyer's opportunity to recover from the carrier in the event of loss, when the risk of shipment is placed on the buyer by his contract with the seller.

4. Both the language of paragraph (b) and the nature of the situation it concerns indicate that the requirement that the seller must obtain and deliver promptly to the buyer in due form any document necessary to enable him to obtain possession of the goods is intended to cumulate with the other duties of the seller such as those covered in paragraph (a).

In this connection, in the case of pool car shipments a delivery order furnished by the seller on the pool car consignee, or on the carrier for delivery out of a larger quantity, satisfies the requirements of paragraph (b) unless the contract requires some other form of document.

5. This Article, unlike the prior uniform statutory provision, makes it the seller's duty to notify the buyer of shipment in all cases. The consequences of his failure to do so, however, are limited in that the buyer may reject on this ground only where material delay or loss ensues.

A standard and acceptable manner of notification in open credit shipments is the sending of an invoice and in the case of documentary contracts is the prompt forwarding of the documents as under paragraph (b) of this section. It is also usual to send on a straight bill of lading but this is not necessary to the required notification. However, should such a document prove necessary or convenient to the buyer, as in the case of loss and claim against the carrier, good faith would require the seller to send it on request.

Frequently the agreement expressly requires prompt notification as by wire or cable Such a term may be of the essence and the final clause of paragraph (c) does not prevent the parties from making this a particular ground for rejection. To have this vital and irreparable effect upon the seller's duties, such a term should be part of the "dickered" terms written in any "form," or should otherwise be called seasonably and sharply to the seller's attention.

6. Generally, under the final sentence of the section, rejection by the buyer is justified only when the seller's dereliction as to any of the requirements of this section in fact is followed by material delay or damage. It rests on the seller, so far as concerns matters not within the peculiar knowledge of the buyer, to establish that his error has not been followed by events which justify rejection.

Cross References:

Point 1: Sections 2–319, 2–320 and 2–503(2).
Point 2: Sections 1–203, 2–323(2), 2–601 and 2–614(1).
Point 3: Section 2–311(2).
Point 5: Section 1–203.

Definitional Cross References:

"Agreement". Section 1–201.
"Buyer". Section 2–103.
"Contract". Section 1–201.
"Delivery". Section 1–201.
"Goods". Section 2–105.
"Notifies". Section 1–201.
"Seller". Section 2–103.
"Send". Section 1–201.
"Usage of trade". Section 1–205.

Cross References

Bill of lading for overseas shipment, see Commercial Code § 2323.
C.I.F. and C. & F. terms, see Commercial Code § 2320.
F.O.B. and F.A.S. terms, see Commercial Code § 2319.
Obligation of good faith, see Commercial Code § 1203.
Options and cooperation respecting performance, see Commercial Code § 2311.
Remedies of buyer in case of nonconforming tender of delivery, see Commercial Code § 2601.
Right of stoppage in transit, see Commercial Code § 2705.
Risk of loss on shipment by carrier, see Commercial Code § 2509.
Substitute performance, see Commercial Code § 2614.

§ 2505. Seller's Shipment Under Reservation

(1) Where the seller has identified goods to the contract by or before shipment:

(a) His procurement of a negotiable bill of lading to his own order or otherwise reserves in him a security interest in the goods. His procurement of the bill to the order of a financing agency or of the buyer indicates in addition only the seller's expectation of transferring that interest to the person named.

(b) A nonnegotiable bill of lading to himself or his nominee reserves possession of the goods as security but except in a case of conditional delivery (subdivision (2) of Section 2507) a nonnegotiable bill of lading naming the buyer as consignee reserves no security interest even though the seller retains possession of the bill of lading.

(2) When shipment by the seller with reservation of a security interest is in violation of the contract for sale it constitutes an improper contract for transportation within the preceding section but impairs neither the rights given to the buyer by shipment and identification of the goods to the contract nor the seller's powers as a holder of a negotiable document. *(Stats.1963, c. 819, § 2505.)*

California Code Comment
By John A. Bohn and Charles J. Williams

Prior California Law

1. Subdivision (1) continues the provisions of former Civil Code § 1740 which provided for the reservation of right of possession or property when goods are shipped.

2. Subdivision (1)(a) rephrases former Civil Code § 1740(2) and § 1740(3). Under section 1740(2) the seller reserved his property in the goods by shipping them to the order of seller. However section 1740(2) also provided that "if, except for the form of the bill of lading, the property would have passed to the buyer on shipment of the goods," the seller's property was deemed to be only a security interest. Under section 1740(3) the seller reserved his property in goods shipped to order of buyer or buyer's agreement by retaining possession of the bill of lading.

3. Subdivision (2) is without counterpart in prior California statutory law.

Changes from U.C.C. (1962 Official Text)

4. This is section 2–505 of the Official Text without change.

Uniform Commercial Code Comment
Prior Uniform Statutory Provision:

Section 20(2), (3), (4), Uniform Sales Act.

Changes: Completely rephrased, the "powers" of the parties in cases of reservation being emphasized primarily rather than the "rightfulness" of reservation.

Purposes of Changes: To continue in general the policy of the prior uniform statutory provision with certain modifications of emphasis and language, so that:

1. The security interest reserved to the seller under subsection (1) is restricted to securing payment or performance by the buyer and the

seller is strictly limited in his disposition and control of the goods as against the buyer and third parties. Under this Article, the provision as to the passing of interest expressly applies "despite any reservation of security title" and also provides that the "rights, obligations and remedies" of the parties are not altered by the incidence of title generally. The security interest, therefore, must be regarded as a means given to the seller to enforce his rights against the buyer which is unaffected by and in turn does not affect the location of title generally. The rules set forth in subsection (1) are not to be altered by any apparent "contrary intent" of the parties as to passing of title, since the rights and remedies of the parties to the contract of sale, as defined in this Article, rest on the contract and its performance or breach and not on stereotyped presumptions as to the location of title.

This Article does not attempt to regulate local procedure in regard to the effective maintenance of the seller's security interest when the action is in replevin by the buyer against the carrier.

2. Every shipment of identified goods under a negotiable bill of lading reserves a security interest in the seller under subsection (1) paragraph (a).

It is frequently convenient for the seller to make the bill of lading to the order of a nominee such as his agent at destination, the financing agency to which he expects to negotiate the document or the bank issuing a credit to him. In many instances, also, the buyer is made the order party. This Article does not deal directly with the question as to whether a bill of lading made out by the seller to the order of a nominee gives the carrier notice of any rights which the nominee may have so as to limit its freedom or obligation to honor the bill of lading in the hands of the seller as the original shipper if the expected negotiation fails. This is dealt with in the Article on Documents of Title (Article 7).

3. A non-negotiable bill of lading taken to a party other than the buyer under subsection (1) paragraph (b) reserves possession of the goods as security in the seller but if he seeks to withhold the goods improperly the buyer can tender payment and recover them.

4. In the case of a shipment by non-negotiable bill of lading taken to a buyer, the seller, under subsection (1) retains no security interest or possession as against the buyer and by the shipment he *de facto* loses control as against the carrier except where he rightfully and effectively stops delivery in transit. In cases in which the contract gives the seller the right to payment against delivery, the seller, by making an immediate demand for payment, can show that his delivery is conditional, but this does not prevent the buyer's power to transfer full title to a sub-buyer in ordinary course or other purchaser under Section 2–403.

5. Under subsection (2) an improper reservation by the seller which would constitute a breach in no way impairs such of the buyer's rights as result from identification of the goods. The security title reserved by the seller under subsection (1) does not protect his holding of the document or the goods for the purpose of exacting more than is due him under the contract.

Cross References:

Point 1: Section 1–201.
Point 2: Article 7.
Point 3: Sections 2–501(2) and 2–504.
Point 4: Sections 2–403, 2–507(2) and 2–705.
Point 5: Sections 2–310, 2–319(4), 2–320(4), 2–501 and 2–502 and Article 7.

Definitional Cross References:

"Bill of lading". Section 1–201.
"Buyer". Section 2–103.
"Consignee". Section 7–102.
"Contract". Section 1–201.
"Contract for sale". Section 2–106.
"Delivery". Section 1–201.
"Financing agency". Section 2–104.
"Goods". Section 2–105.
"Holder". Section 1–201.
"Person". Section 1–201.
"Security interest". Section 1–201.
"Seller". Section 2–103.

Cross References

Authority to ship under reservation, see Commercial Code § 2310.
Automobile sales finance act, see Civil Code § 2981 et seq.
Buyer's right to replevin for goods identified to contract, see Commercial Code § 2716.
C.I.F. and C. & F. terms, see Commercial Code § 2320.
Definitions, see Commercial Code §§ 1201, 2103, 2104.
Documents of title, see Commercial Code § 7101 et seq.
Entrusting, see Commercial Code § 2403.
Erroneous bills of lading or receipts issued in good faith, see Penal Code § 579.
F.O.B. and F.A.S. terms, see Commercial Code § 2319.
Fraudulent issuance of bills of lading, see Penal Code §§ 577, 578.
Good faith purchase of goods, see Commercial Code § 2403.
Insolvency of seller, recovery of goods by buyer, see Commercial Code § 2502.
Insurable interest in goods, see Commercial Code § 2501.
Payment by buyer as condition to retention or disposition of goods, see Commercial Code § 2507.
Reservation of title for security, see Commercial Code § 2401.
Risk of loss in the absence of breach, see Commercial Code § 2509.
Secured transactions, see Commercial Code § 9101 et seq.
Stoppage of delivery in transit or otherwise, see Commercial Code § 2705.
Unauthorized sale of merchandise for which bill of lading has been issued without consent of holder of bill, see Penal Code § 581.

§ 2506. Rights of Financing Agency

(1) A financing agency by paying or purchasing for value a draft which relates to a shipment of goods acquires to the extent of the payment or purchase and in addition to its own rights under the draft and any document of title securing it any rights of the shipper in the goods including the right to stop delivery and the shipper's right to have the draft honored by the buyer.

(2) The right to reimbursement of a financing agency which has in good faith honored or purchased the draft under commitment to or authority from the buyer is not impaired by subsequent discovery of defects with reference to any relevant document which was apparently regular on its face. (Stats.1963, c. 819, § 2506.)

California Code Comment

By John A. Bohn and Charles J. Williams

Prior California Law

1. This section has no counterpart in prior California statutory law.

Changes from U.C.C. (1962 Official Text)

2. This is section 2–506 of the Official Text without change.

Uniform Commercial Code Comment

Prior Uniform Statutory Provision:
None.

Purposes:

1. "Financing agency" is broadly defined in this Article to cover every normal instance in which a party aids or intervenes in the financing of a sales transaction. The term as used in subsection (1) is not in any sense intended as a limitation and covers any other appropriate situation which may arise outside the scope of the definition.

2. "Paying" as used in subsection (1) is typified by the letter of credit, or "authority to pay" situation in which a banker, by arrangement with the buyer or other consignee, pays on his behalf a draft for the price of the goods. It is immaterial whether the draft is formally drawn on the party paying or his principal, whether it is a sight draft paid in cash or a time draft "paid" in the first instance by acceptance, or

whether the payment is viewed as absolute or conditional. All of these cases constitute "payment" under this subsection. Similarly, "purchasing for value" is used to indicate the whole area of financing by the seller's banker, and the principle of subsection (1) is applicable without any niceties of distinction between "purchase," "discount," "advance against collection" or the like. But it is important to notice that the only right to have the draft honored that is acquired is that *against the buyer*; if any right against any one else is claimed it will have to be under some separate obligation of that other person. A letter of credit does not necessarily protect *purchasers* of drafts. See Article 5. And for the relations of the parties to documentary drafts see Part 5 of Article 4.

3. Subsection (1) is made applicable to payments or advances against a draft which "relates to" a shipment of goods and this has been chosen as a term of maximum breadth. In particular the term is intended to cover the case of a draft against an invoice or against a delivery order. Further, it is unnecessary that there be an explicit assignment of the invoice attached to the draft to bring the transaction within the reason of this subsection.

4. After shipment, "the rights of the shipper in the goods" are merely security rights and are subject to the buyer's right to force delivery upon tender of the price. The rights acquired by the financing agency are similarly limited and, moreover, if the agency fails to procure any outstanding negotiable document of title, it may find its exercise of these rights hampered or even defeated by the seller's disposition of the document to a third party. This section does not attempt to create any new rights in the financing agency against the carrier which would force the latter to honor a stop order from the agency, a stranger to the shipment, or any new rights against a holder to whom a document of title has been duly negotiated under Article 7.

Cross References:

Point 1: Section 2–104(2) and Article 4.
Point 2: Part 5 of Article 4, and Article 5.
Point 4: Sections 2–501 and 2–502(1) and Article 7.

Definitional Cross References:

"Buyer". Section 2–103.
"Document of title". Section 1–201.
"Draft". Section 3–104.
"Financing agency". Section 2–104.
"Good faith". Section 2–103.
"Goods". Section 2–105.
"Honor". Section 1–201.
"Purchase". Section 1–201.
"Rights". Section 1–201.
"Value". Section 1–201.

Cross References

Bank deposits and collections, see Commercial Code § 4101 et seq.
Collection of documentary drafts, see Commercial Code § 4501 et seq.
Definition of "financing agency", see Commercial Code § 2104.
Documents of title, see Commercial Code § 7101 et seq.
Insolvency of seller, buyer's right to goods, see Commercial Code § 2502.
Insurable interest in goods, see Commercial Code § 2501.
Letters of credit, see Commercial Code § 5101 et seq.
Stoppage in transit, see Commercial Code § 2705.

§ 2507. Effect of Seller's Tender; Delivery on Condition

(1) Tender of delivery is a condition to the buyer's duty to accept the goods and, unless otherwise agreed, to his duty to pay for them. Tender entitles the seller to acceptance of the goods and to payment according to the contract.

(2) Where payment is due and demanded on the delivery to the buyer of goods or documents of title, his right as against the seller to retain or dispose of them is conditional upon his making the payment due. *(Stats. 1963, c. 819, § 2507.)*

California Code Comment

By John A. Bohn and Charles J. Williams

Prior California Law

1. Subdivision (1) is in accord with the general principles of former Civil Code § 1731(2) (seller's obligation a condition of the buyer's obligation to perform his promises to accept and pay for the goods); former Civil Code § 1762 (seller must be ready and willing to give possession of the goods to the buyer in exchange for the price) and former Civil Code § 1761 (seller must deliver and buyer accept goods).

2. Subdivision (2) is in accord with the principle expressed in former Civil Code § 1762 that the buyer must be ready and willing to pay the price in exchange for possession of the goods and with former Civil Code § 1761 providing that seller must deliver and buyer accept goods.

Changes from U.C.C. (1962 Official Text)

3. This is section 2–507 of the Official Text without change.

Uniform Commercial Code Comment

1990 Amendment

PEB Commentary No. 1, March 10, 1990

Purposes:

* * * * * *

3. Subsection (2) deals with the effect of a conditional delivery by the seller and in such a situation makes the buyer's "right as against the seller" conditional upon payment. These words are used as words of limitation to conform with the policy set forth in the bona fide purchase sections of this Article. Should the seller after making such a conditional delivery fail to follow up his rights, the condition is waived. This subsection (2) codifies the cash seller's right of reclamation which is in the nature of a lien. There is no specific time limit for a cash seller to exercise the right of reclamation. However, the right will be defeated by delay causing prejudice to the buyer, waiver, estoppel, or ratification of the buyer's right to retain possession. Common law rules and precedents governing such principles are applicable (Section 1–103). If third parties are involved, Section 2–403(1) protects good faith purchasers. See PEB Commentary No. 1, dated March 10, 1990 [Uniform Laws Annotated, UCC, APP II, Comment 1].

* * * * * *

Uniform Commercial Code Comment

Prior Uniform Statutory Provision:

See Sections 11, 41, 42 and 69, Uniform Sales Act.

Purposes:

1. Subsection (1) continues the policies of the prior uniform statutory provisions with respect to tender and delivery by the seller. Under this Article the same rules in these matters are applied to present sales and to contracts for sale. But the provisions of this subsection must be read within the framework of the other sections of this Article which bear upon the question of delivery and payment.

2. The "unless otherwise agreed" provision of subsection (1) is directed primarily to cases in which payment in advance has been promised or a letter of credit term has been included. Payment "according to the contract" contemplates immediate payment, payment at the end of an agreed credit term, payment by a time acceptance or the like. Under this Act, "contract" means the total obligation in law which results from the parties' agreement including the effect of this Article. In this context, therefore, there must be considered the effect in law of such provisions as those on means and manner of payment and on failure of agreed means and manner of payment.

3. Subsection (2) deals with the effect of a conditional delivery by the seller and in such a situation makes the buyer's "right as against the seller" conditional upon payment. These words are used as words of limitation to conform with the policy set forth in the bona fide purchase sections of this Article. Should the seller after making such a

conditional delivery fail to follow up his rights, the condition is waived. The provision of this Article for a ten day limit within which the seller may reclaim goods delivered on credit to an insolvent buyer is also applicable here.

Cross References:

Point 1: Sections 2–310, 2–503, 2–511, 2–601 and 2–711 to 2–713.
Point 2: Sections 1–201, 2–511 and 2–614.
Point 3: Sections 2–401, 2–403, and 2–702(1)(b).

Definitional Cross References:

"Buyer". Section 2–103.
"Contract". Section 1–201.
"Delivery". Section 1–201.
"Document of title". Section 1–201.
"Goods". Section 2–105.
"Rights". Section 1–201.
"Seller". Section 2–103.

Cross References

Definitions, see Commercial Code §§ 1201, 2103, 2104.
Good faith purchasers of goods from buyer, see Commercial Code § 2403.
Implication of term "unless otherwise agreed", see Commercial Code § 1102.
Insolvency of buyer, remedies of seller, see Commercial Code § 2702.
Nonconforming goods or tender of delivery, see Commercial Code § 2601.
Remedies of buyer for breach by seller, see Commercial Code § 2711 et seq.
Seller's shipment under reservation, see Commercial Code § 2505.
Substitute performance, see Commercial Code § 2614.
Tender of delivery by seller, see Commercial Code § 2503.
Tender of payment by buyer, see Commercial Code § 2511.
Time for payment, see Commercial Code § 2310.
Time of performance of contracts, see Civil Code § 1657.
Title to goods, see Commercial Code §§ 2401, 2403.

§ 2508. Cure by Seller of Improper Tender or Delivery; Replacement

(1) Where any tender or delivery by the seller is rejected because nonconforming and the time for performance has not yet expired, the seller may seasonably notify the buyer of his intention to cure and may then within the contract time make a conforming delivery.

(2) Where the buyer rejects a nonconforming tender which the seller had reasonable grounds to believe would be acceptable with or without money allowance the seller may if he seasonably [1] notifies the buyer have a further reasonable time to substitute a conforming tender. (Stats.1963, c. 819, § 2508.)

[1] Reads "seasonably" in official edition.

California Code Comment

By John A. Bohn and Charles J. Williams

Prior California Law

1. This section has no counterpart in prior California statutory law. Under prior California law a seller's tender of nonconforming goods was normally treated as a breach of contract allowing the buyer to reject the goods. 1 Witkin, Summary of California Law 550 (1960). Section 2508 rejects this position and gives the seller an opportunity to cure a breach by substituting a conforming delivery.

2. Under Civil Code § 1490 if an obligation fixes a time for performance an offer of performance had to be made "at that time within reasonable hours, and not before nor afterwards." Subdivision (2) modifies this section in the case of a sales agreement that fixes a time of performance to the extent it permits a non-conforming tender "which the seller had reasonable grounds to believe would be acceptable."

Subdivision (2) is consistent with Civil Code § 1491. Where a time for performance is not fixed Civil Code § 1491 provides that an offer of performance could be made any time before the debtor had refused to perform.

Changes from U.C.C. (1962 Official Text)

3. This is section 2–508 of the Official Text without change.

Uniform Commercial Code Comment

Prior Uniform Statutory Provision:
None.

Purposes:

1. Subsection (1) permits a seller who has made a non-conforming tender in any case to make a conforming delivery within the contract time upon seasonable notification to the buyer. It applies even where the seller has taken back the non-conforming goods and refunded the purchase price. He may still make a good tender within the contract period. The closer, however, it is to the contract date, the greater is the necessity for extreme promptness on the seller's part in notifying of his intention to cure, if such notification is to be "seasonable" under this subsection.

The rule of this subsection, moreover, is qualified by its underlying reasons. Thus if, after contracting for June delivery, a buyer later makes known to the seller his need for shipment early in the month and the seller ships accordingly, the "contract time" has been cut down by the supervening modification and the time for cure of tender must be referred to this modified time term.

2. Subsection (2) seeks to avoid injustice to the seller by reason of a surprise rejection by the buyer. However, the seller is not protected unless he had "reasonable grounds to believe" that the tender would be acceptable. Such reasonable grounds can lie in prior course of dealing, course of performance or usage of trade as well as in the particular circumstances surrounding the making of the contract. The seller is charged with commercial knowledge of any factors in a particular sales situation which require him to comply strictly with his obligations under the contract as, for example, strict conformity of documents in an overseas shipment or the sale of precision parts or chemicals for use in manufacture. Further, if the buyer gives notice either implicitly, as by a prior course of dealing involving rigorous inspections, or expressly, as by the deliberate inclusion of a "no replacement" clause in the contract, the seller is to be held to rigid compliance. If the clause appears in a "form" contract evidence that it is out of line with trade usage or the prior course of dealing and was not called to the seller's attention may be sufficient to show that the seller had reasonable grounds to believe that the tender would be acceptable.

3. The words "a further reasonable time to substitute a conforming tender" are intended as words of limitation to protect the buyer. What is a "reasonable time" depends upon the attending circumstances. Compare Section 2–511 on the comparable case of a seller's surprise demand for legal tender.

4. Existing trade usages permitting variations without rejection but with price allowance enter into the agreement itself as contractual limitations of remedy and are not covered by this section.

Cross References:

Point 2: Section 2–302.
Point 3: Section 2–511.
Point 4: Sections 1–205 and 2–721.

Definitional Cross References:

"Buyer". Section 2–103.
"Conforming". Section 2–106.
"Contract". Section 1–201.
"Money". Section 1–201.
"Notifies". Section 1–201.
"Reasonable time". Section 1–204.
"Seasonably". Section 1–204.
"Seller". Section 2–103.

Cross References

Course of dealing and usage of trade, see Commercial Code § 1205.
Form of bill of lading required in overseas shipment, see Commercial Code § 2323.
Offer of compensation for delay in performance, see Civil Code § 1492.
Remedies for material misrepresentation or fraud, see Commercial Code § 2721.
Tender of payment, see Commercial Code § 2511.
Time of offer of performance, see Civil Code §§ 1490, 1491.

§ 2509. Risk of Loss in the Absence of Breach

(1) Where the contract requires or authorizes the seller to ship the goods by carrier

(a) If it does not require him to deliver them at a particular destination, the risk of loss passes to the buyer when the goods are duly delivered to the carrier even though the shipment is under reservation (Section 2505); but

(b) If it does require him to deliver them at a particular destination and the goods are there duly tendered while in the possession of the carrier, the risk of loss passes to the buyer when the goods are there duly so tendered as to enable the buyer to take delivery.

(2) Where the goods are held by a bailee to be delivered without being moved, the risk of loss passes to the buyer

(a) On his receipt of a negotiable document of title covering the goods; or

(b) On acknowledgment by the bailee of the buyer's right to possession of the goods; or

(c) After his receipt of a nonnegotiable document of title or other written direction to deliver, as provided in subdivision (4)(b) of Section 2503.

(3) In any case not within subdivision (1) or (2), the risk of loss passes to the buyer on his receipt of the goods if the seller is a merchant; otherwise the risk passes to the buyer on tender of delivery.

(4) The provisions of this section are subject to contrary agreement of the parties and to the provisions of this division on sale on approval (Section 2327) and on effect of breach on risk of loss (Section 2510). (Stats.1963, c. 819, § 2509.)

California Code Comment

By John A. Bohn and Charles J. Williams

Prior California Law

1. In accordance with the general policy of the Commercial Code, (See Official Comment to § 2101), this section abolishes the use of "title passage" or "property passage" formerly used in the USA for determining who bears the risk of loss.

2. Subdivision (1)(a) is similar to the rule formed by the conjunction of former Civil Code § 1739, Rules 2 and 4, and § 1742. Under former Civil Code § 1742, unless otherwise agreed, the goods remained at the seller's risk until the property in them was transferred to the buyer. Capitain v. L. A. Wrecking Co., 37 Cal.2d 527, 233 P.2d 544 (1951). Under former Civil Code § 1739, Rule 2, property in goods passed to the buyer when it was unconditionally appropriated to the contract. Under former Civil Code § 1739, Rule 4(2) delivery of the goods by the seller to a carrier for transmission to the buyer resulted in a presumption that the goods had been unconditionally appropriated to the contract.

3. Subdivision (1)(b) is similar to the rule formed by the conjunction of former Civil Code § 1742 and Rule 5 of former Civil Code § 1739. Under former Civil Code § 1742, unless otherwise agreed, the goods remained at the seller's risk until the property in them was transferred to the buyer. Under Rule 5 of former Civil Code § 1739, if the sales contract required the seller to deliver the goods to a particular person or place or pay the transportation costs to a particular place, the property passed when the goods were delivered or reached the place agreed upon.

4. Subdivision (2) is similar to the rule derived from the conjunction of the general rule for risk of loss in former Civil Code § 1742 and § 1753 which provided the rights of a person to whom document was negotiated.

5. Subdivision (3) is a radical departure from prior law. The seller who is a merchant cannot transfer the risk of loss and this risk remains on him until the buyer receives the goods. Official Comment 3.

Changes from U.C.C. (1962 Official Text)

6. This is section 2–509 of the Official Text without change.

Uniform Commercial Code Comment

Prior Uniform Statutory Provision:

Section 22, Uniform Sales Act.

Changes: Rewritten, subsection (3) of this section modifying prior law.

Purposes of Changes: To make it clear that:

1. The underlying theory of these sections on risk of loss is the adoption of the contractual approach rather than an arbitrary shifting of the risk with the "property" in the goods. The scope of the present section, therefore, is limited strictly to those cases where there has been no breach by the seller. Where for any reason his delivery or tender fails to conform to the contract, the present section does not apply and the situation is governed by the provisions on effect of breach on risk of loss.

2. The provisions of subsection (1) apply where the contract "requires or authorizes" shipment of the goods. This language is intended to be construed parallel to comparable language in the section on shipment by seller. In order that the goods be "duly delivered to the carrier" under paragraph (a) a contract must be entered into with the carrier which will satisfy the requirements of the section on shipment by the seller and the delivery must be made under circumstances which will enable the seller to take any further steps necessary to a due tender. The underlying reason of this subsection does not require that the shipment be made after contracting, but where, for example, the seller buys the goods afloat and later diverts the shipment to the buyer, he must identify the goods to the contract before the risk of loss can pass. To transfer the risk it is enough that a proper shipment and a proper identification come to apply to the same goods although, aside from special agreement, the risk will not pass retroactively to the time of shipment in such a case.

3. Whether the contract involves delivery at the seller's place of business or at the situs of the goods, a merchant seller cannot transfer risk of loss and it remains upon him until actual receipt by the buyer, even though full payment has been made and the buyer has been notified that the goods are at his disposal. Protection is afforded him, in the event of breach by the buyer, under the next section.

The underlying theory of this rule is that a merchant who is to make physical delivery at his own place continues meanwhile to control the goods and can be expected to insure his interest in them. The buyer, on the other hand, has no control of the goods and it is extremely unlikely that he will carry insurance on goods not yet in his possession.

4. Where the agreement provides for delivery of the goods as between the buyer and seller without removal from the physical possession of a bailee, the provisions on manner of tender of delivery apply on the point of transfer of risk. Due delivery of a negotiable document of title covering the goods or acknowledgment by the bailee that he holds for the buyer completes the "delivery" and passes the risk.

5. The provisions of this section are made subject by subsection (4) to the "contrary agreement" of the parties. This language is intended as the equivalent of the phrase "unless otherwise agreed" used more frequently throughout this Act. "Contrary" is in no way used as a word of limitation and the buyer and seller are left free to readjust their rights and risks as declared by this section in any manner agreeable to them.

Contrary agreement can also be found in the circumstances of the case, a trade usage or practice, or a course of dealing or performance.

Cross References:

Point 1: Section 2–510(1).
Point 2: Sections 2–503 and 2–504.
Point 3: Sections 2–104, 2–503 and 2–510.
Point 4: Section 2–503(4).
Point 5: Section 1–201.

Definitional Cross References:

"Agreement". Section 1–201.
"Buyer". Section 2–103.
"Contract". Section 1–201.
"Delivery". Section 1–201.
"Document of title". Section 1–201.
"Goods". Section 2–105.
"Merchant". Section 2–104.

Definitional Cross References:

"Party". Section 1–201.
"Receipt" of goods. Section 2–103.
"Sale on approval." Section 2–326.
"Seller". Section 2–103.

Cross References

Capacity to insure and be insured, see Insurance Code §§ 150, 151.
Definitions, see Commercial Code §§ 1201, 2103, 2104.
Events subject to insurance, see Insurance Code § 250 et seq.
Failure of consignee to accept and remove freight, exoneration of carrier, see Civil Code § 2121.
Identified goods, risk of loss, see Commercial Code § 2613.
Insurable interest in general, see Insurance Code § 280 et seq.
Liability of common carrier for loss, see Civil Code §§ 2194, 2195.
Marine insurance, insurable interests, see Insurance Code § 1880 et seq.
Passing of title, see Commercial Code § 2401.
Sale on approval, risk of loss, see Commercial Code § 2327.
Shipment by seller, see Commercial Code § 2504.
Tender of delivery by seller, see Commercial Code § 2503.
Transfer of subject insured, effect on insurable interest, see Insurance Code § 300 et seq.

§ 2510. Effect of Breach on Risk of Loss

(1) Where a tender or delivery of goods so fails to conform to the contract as to give a right of rejection the risk of their loss remains on the seller until cure or acceptance.

(2) Where the buyer rightfully revokes acceptance he may to the extent of any deficiency in his effective insurance coverage treat the risk of loss as having rested on the seller from the beginning.

(3) Where the buyer as to conforming goods already identified to the contract for sale repudiates or is otherwise in breach before risk of their loss has passed to him, the seller may to the extent of any deficiency in his effective insurance coverage treat the risk of loss as resting on the buyer for a commercially reasonable time.
(Stats.1963, c. 819, § 2510.)

California Code Comment

By John A. Bohn and Charles J. Williams

Prior California Law

1. Subdivision (1) is similar to the provision of former Civil Code § 1742(b) so far as that section went in putting the risk of loss on the seller where delivery is delayed through the seller's fault. The cure of defective tender which is a new concept to California law is authorized by section 2508.

2. Subdivision (2) has no counterpart in prior California statutory law. However, the buyer's remedy for breach of warranty was under former Civil Code § 1789(5) which provided that the buyer holds the goods as bailee for the seller where the buyer is entitled to rescind and the seller refuses the offer to rescind.

3. Subdivision (3) has no direct counterpart in prior California statutory law. However, see former Civil Code § 1783(2) (seller has action for the price where title has not passed) and § 1784 (seller has action for damages for nonacceptance of the goods) which would produce a similar result. See Bishop v. Descalzi, 46 Cal.App. 228, 189 Pac. 122 (1920) wrongfully holding that where the buyer refused to accept goods although title did not pass, buyer was still liable for the purchase price upon later damage because such damage was the result of the buyer's refusal.

Changes from U.C.C. (1962 Official Text)

4. This is section 2–510 of the Official Text without change.

Uniform Commercial Code Comment

Prior Uniform Statutory Provision:
None.

Purposes: To make clear that:

1. Under subsection (1) the seller by his individual action cannot shift the risk of loss to the buyer unless his action conforms with all the conditions resting on him under the contract.

2. The "cure" of defective tenders contemplated by subsection (1) applies only to those situations in which the seller makes changes in goods already tendered, such as repair, partial substitution, sorting out from an improper mixture and the like since "cure" by repossession and new tender has no effect on the risk of loss of the goods originally tendered. The seller's privilege of cure does not shift the risk, however, until the cure is completed.

Where defective documents are involved a cure of the defect by the seller or a waiver of the defects by the buyer will operate to shift the risk under this section. However, if the goods have been destroyed prior to the cure or the buyer is unaware of their destruction at the time he waives the defect in the documents, the risk of the loss must still be borne by the seller, for the risk shifts only at the time of cure, waiver of documentary defects or acceptance of the goods.

3. In cases where there has been a breach of the contract, if the one in control of the goods is the aggrieved party, whatever loss or damage may prove to be uncovered by his insurance falls upon the contract breaker under subsections (2) and (3) rather than upon him. The word "effective" as applied to insurance coverage in those subsections is used to meet the case of supervening insolvency of the insurer. The "deficiency" referred to in the text means such deficiency in the insurance coverage as exists without subrogation. This section merely distributes the risk of loss as stated and is not intended to be disturbed by any subrogation of an insurer.

Cross Reference:

Section 2–509.

Definitional Cross References:

"Buyer". Section 2–103.
"Conform". Section 2–106.
"Contract for sale". Section 2–106.
"Goods". Section 2–105.
"Seller". Section 2–103.

Cross References

Buyer's rights on improper delivery, see Commercial Code § 2601.
Capacity to insure and be insured, see Insurance Code §§ 150, 151.
Cure by seller of improper delivery, see Commercial Code § 2508.
Events subject to insurance, see Insurance Code § 250 et seq.
Failure of consignee to accept and remove freight, exoneration of carrier, see Civil Code § 2121.
General obligations of parties, see Commercial Code § 2301.
Insurable interest in general, see Insurance Code § 280 et seq.

Marine insurance, insurable interests, see Insurance Code § 1880 et seq.

Rejection of goods by buyer, see Commercial Code § 2602.

Revocation of acceptance in whole or in part, see Commercial Code § 2608.

Transfer of subject insured, effect on insurable interest, see Insurance Code § 300 et seq.

§ 2511. Tender of Payment by Buyer; Payment by Check

(1) Unless otherwise agreed, tender of payment is a condition to the seller's duty to tender and complete any delivery.

(2) Tender of payment is sufficient when made by any means or in any manner current in the ordinary course of business unless the seller demands payment in legal tender and gives any extension of time reasonably necessary to procure it.

(3) Subject to the provisions of this code on the effect of an instrument on an obligation (Section 3310), payment by check is conditional and is defeated as between the parties by dishonor of the check on due presentment. *(Stats.1963, c. 819, § 2511. Amended by Stats.1992, c. 914 (S.B.833), § 4.)*

California Code Comment
By John A. Bohn and Charles J. Williams

Prior California Law

1. This section is basically a restatement of former Civil Code § 1762 providing that delivery and payment are concurrent conditions.

2. Subdivision (1) is in accord with former Civil Code § 1762 and cases decided before the USA was adopted in California in 1931. For example, Fruit v. Phelps, 4 Cal. 282 (1854) and Pearson v. McKinney, 160 Cal. 649, 117 Pac. 919 (1911).

3. Subdivision (2) adds new language to California statutory law. However the cases state that payment by check is acceptable. The court in O. F. Mefford v. Security Title Insurance Co., 199 Cal.App.2d 578, 584, 18 Cal.Rptr. 877, 880 (1962) states that "Checks are a common means of payment. . . . In California the general rule which prohibits payment to an agent authorized to collect in any form other than money has been relaxed to permit payment by check." Also in Crestline Mobile Homes Mfg. Co. v. Pacific Finance Corp., 54 Cal.2d 773, 779, 8 Cal.Rptr. 448, 452, 356 P.2d 192, 196 (1960) the court states that "Delivery and acceptance of a check in payment of a cash transaction, of course, if it does not amount to payment at least amounts to an agreement to accept the check as a promissory note in payment of the obligation".

4. Subdivision (3) adds new language to California statutory law but is in accord with the law as expressed in Peerless Motor Co. v. Sterling Finance Corp., 139 Cal.App. 621, 624, 34 P.2d 738, 739 (1934): "The mere acceptance of a check in payment for personal property, subject to the payment of the check, does not pass title when the check is subsequently dishonored and is not paid."

5. The provisions of California Vehicle Code § 5600 have been held to supersede the conflicting provisions of former Civil Code § 1762. Coca Cola Bottling Co. v. Feliciano, 32 Cal.App.2d 351, 89 P.2d 686 (1939) and Richter v. Walker, 36 Cal.2d 634, 226 P.2d 593 (1951).

Section 5600 of the Vehicle Code provides that no title or interest in a vehicle passes until the transfer of registration requirements of that section are met. The question should be considered as to whether this or any other section of the Vehicle Code would supersede inconsistent provisions of the Commercial Code. The Commercial Code is intended as a uniform codification of permanent character covering an entire field of law and its repeal or modification by other legislation is not to be lightly indulged in. See section 1104 and the Official Comment to it.

In Division 9 it is provided that in case of conflict certain statutes control over the provisions of that division. See section 9203(2) and the California Code Comments to it.

Changes from U.C.C. (1962 Official Text)

6. This is section 2–511 of the Official Text without change.

Uniform Commercial Code Comment

Prior Uniform Statutory Provision:

Section 42, Uniform Sales Act.

Changes: Rewritten by this section and Section 2–507.

Purposes of Changes:

1. The requirement of payment against delivery in subsection (1) is applicable to noncommercial sales generally and to ordinary sales at retail although it has no application to the great body of commercial contracts which carry credit terms. Subsection (1) applies also to documentary contracts in general and to contracts which look to shipment by the seller but contain no term on time and manner of payment, in which situations the payment may, in proper case, be demanded against delivery of appropriate documents.

In the case of specific transactions such as C.O.D. sales or agreements providing for payment against documents, the provisions of this subsection must be considered in conjunction with the special sections of the Article dealing with such terms. The provision that tender of payment is a condition to the seller's duty to tender and complete "any delivery" integrates this section with the language and policy of the section on delivery in several lots which call for separate payment. Finally, attention should be directed to the provision on right to adequate assurance of performance which recognizes, even before the time for tender, an obligation on the buyer not to impair the seller's expectation of receiving payment in due course.

2. Unless there is agreement otherwise the concurrence of the conditions as to tender of payment and tender of delivery requires their performance at a single place or time. This Article determines that place and time by determining in various other sections the place and time for tender of delivery under various circumstances and in particular types of transactions. The sections dealing with time and place of delivery together with the section on right to inspection of goods answer the subsidiary question as to when payment may be demanded before inspection by the buyer.

3. The essence of the principle involved in subsection (2) is avoidance of commercial surprise at the time of performance. The section on substituted performance covers the peculiar case in which legal tender is not available to the commercial community.

4. Subsection (3) is concerned with the rights and obligations as between the parties to a sales transaction when payment is made by check. This Article recognizes that the taking of a seemingly solvent party's check is commercially normal and proper and, if due diligence is exercised in collection, is not to be penalized in any way. The conditional character of the payment under this section refers only to the effect of the transaction "as between the parties" thereto and does not purport to cut into the law of "absolute" and "conditional" payment as applied to such other problems as the discharge of sureties or the responsibilities of a drawee bank which is at the same time an agent for collection.

The phrase "by check" includes not only the buyer's own but any check which does not effect a discharge under Article 3 (Section 3–802). Similarly the reason of this subsection should apply and the same result should be reached where the buyer "pays" by sight draft on a commercial firm which is financing him.

5. Under subsection (3) payment by check is defeated if it is not honored upon due presentment. This corresponds to the provisions of article on Commercial Paper. (Section 3–802). But if the seller procures certification of the check instead of cashing it, the buyer is discharged. (Section 3–411).

6. Where the instrument offered by the buyer is not a payment but a credit instrument such as a note or a check postdated by even one day, the seller's acceptance of the instrument insofar as third parties are concerned, amounts to a delivery on credit and his remedies are set forth in the section on buyer's insolvency. As between the buyer and the seller, however, the matter turns on the present subsection and the section on conditional delivery and subsequent dishonor of the instrument gives the seller rights on it as well as for breach of the contract for sale.

Cross References:

Point 1: Sections 2–307, 2–310, 2–320, 2–325, 2–503, 2–513 and 2–609.
Point 2: Sections 2–307, 2–310, 2–319, 2–322, 2–503, 2–504 and 2–513.
Point 3: Section 2–614.
Point 5: Article 3, esp. Sections 3–802 and 3–411.
Point 6: Sections 2–507, 2–702, and Article 3.

Definitional Cross References:

"Buyer". Section 2–103.
"Check". Section 3–104.
"Dishonor". Section 3–508.
"Party". Section 1–201.
"Reasonable time". Section 1–204.
"Seller". Section 2–103.

Cross References

Assurance of due performance, see Commercial Code § 2609.
C.I.F. and C. & F. terms, see Commercial Code § 2320.
Certification of check, see Commercial Code § 3409.
Check defined, see Commercial Code § 3104.
Commercial paper, see Commercial Code § 3101 et seq.
Delivery of goods "ex-ship", see Commercial Code § 2322.
Effect of instrument on underlying obligation, see Commercial Code § 3810.
F.O.B. and F.A.S. terms, see Commercial Code § 2319.
Insolvency of buyer, remedies of seller, see Commercial Code § 2702.
Inspection of goods, see Commercial Code § 2513.
Letters of credit, see Commercial Code § 2325.
Shipment of goods by seller, see Commercial Code § 2504.
Single delivery of goods or delivery in several lots, see Commercial Code § 2307.
Substituted performance, see Commercial Code § 2614.
Tender of delivery,
  Cure of improper delivery, see Commercial Code § 2508.
  Effect, see Commercial Code § 2507.
  Manner, see Commercial Code § 2503.
Time for payment, see Commercial Code § 2310.
Transfer of title to good faith purchaser, effect of later dishonor of purchaser's check, see Commercial Code § 2403.

§ 2512. Payment by buyer before inspection; nonconformity of goods

(1) Where the contract requires payment before inspection nonconformity of the goods does not excuse the buyer from so making payment unless (a) the nonconformity appears without inspection or (b) despite tender of the required documents the circumstances would justify injunction against honor under this code (subdivision (b) of Section 5109).

(2) Payment pursuant to subdivision (1) does not constitute an acceptance of goods or impair the buyer's right to inspect or any of his remedies. (Stats.1963, c. 819, § 2512. Amended by Stats.1996, c. 176 (S.B.1599), § 5.)

California Code Comment
By John A. Bohn and Charles J. Williams

Prior California Law

1. Subdivision (1) is without counterpart in prior California statutory law.
2. Subdivision (2) continues the policy expressed in former Civil Code § 1767(1) providing the buyer with the right to examine the goods and § 1769 providing that acceptance does not bar an action for damages.

3. The buyer's right to inspection is set forth in Commercial Code § 2513.

Changes from U.C.C. (1962 Official Text)

4. Paragraph (b) of subsection (1) of the Official Text is omitted. This subsection reads:

"(b) despite tender of the required documents the circumstances would justify injunction against honor under the provisions of this Act (section 5–114)."

This omission coincides with the deletion of the provisions for injunction against honor (part of section 5–114(2)(b) of the Official Text) from Commercial Code § 5114 (see comment to this section). The effect of paragraph (b) is described in Official Comment 4.

Uniform Commercial Code Comment

Prior Uniform Statutory Provision:

None, but see Sections 47 and 49, Uniform Sales Act.

Purposes:

1. Subsection (1) of the present section recognizes that the essence of a contract providing for payment before inspection is the intention of the parties to shift to the buyer the risks which would usually rest upon the seller. The basic nature of the transaction is thus preserved and the buyer is in most cases required to pay first and litigate as to any defects later.

2. "Inspection" under this section is an inspection in a manner reasonable for detecting defects in goods whose surface appearance is satisfactory.

3. Clause (a) of this subsection states an exception to the general rule based on common sense and normal commercial practice. The apparent non-conformity referred to is one which is evident in the mere process of taking delivery.

4. Clause (b) [Inapplicable in California, see California Code Comment, note 4] is concerned with contracts for payment against documents and incorporates the general clarification and modification of the case law contained in the section on excuse of a financing agency. Section 5–114.

5. Subsection (2) makes explicit the general policy of the Uniform Sales Act that the payment required before inspection in no way impairs the buyer's remedies or rights in the event of a default by the seller. The remedies preserved to the buyer are all of his remedies, which include as a matter of reason the remedy for total non-delivery after payment in advance.

The provision on performance or acceptance under reservation of rights does not apply to the situations contemplated here in which payment is made in due course under the contract and the buyer need not pay "under protest" or the like in order to preserve his rights as to defects discovered upon inspection.

6. This section applies to cases in which the contract requires payment before inspection either by the express agreement of the parties or by reason of the effect in law of that contract. The present section must therefore be considered in conjunction with the provision on right to inspection of goods which sets forth the instances in which the buyer is not entitled to inspection before payment.

Cross References:

Point 4: Article 5.
Point 5: Section 1–207.
Point 6: Section 2–513(3).

Definitional Cross References:

"Buyer". Section 2–103.
"Conform". Section 2–106.
"Contract". Section 1–201.
"Financing agency". Section 2–104.
"Goods". Section 2–105.
"Remedy". Section 1–201.
"Rights". Section 1–201.

Cross References

Buyer's right to inspection of goods, see Commercial Code § 2513.

Definitions, see Commercial Code §§ 1201, 2103, 2104.
Goods "conforming" to contract, see Commercial Code § 2106.
Reservation of rights, see Commercial Code § 1207.

§ 2513. Buyer's Right to Inspection of Goods

(1) Unless otherwise agreed and subject to subdivision (3), where goods are tendered or delivered or identified to the contract for sale, the buyer has a right before payment or acceptance to inspect them at any reasonable place and time and in any reasonable manner. When the seller is required or authorized to send the goods to the buyer, the inspection may be after their arrival.

(2) Expenses of inspection must be borne by the buyer but may be recovered from the seller if the goods do not conform and are rejected.

(3) Unless otherwise agreed and subject to the provisions of this division on C.I.F. contracts (subdivision (3) of Section 2321), the buyer is not entitled to inspect the goods before payment of the price when the contract provides

(a) For delivery "C.O.D." or on other like terms; or

(b) For payment against documents of title, except where such payment is due only after the goods are to become available for inspection.

(4) A place or method of inspection fixed by the parties is presumed to be exclusive but unless otherwise expressly agreed it does not postpone identification or shift the place for delivery or for passing the risk of loss. If compliance becomes impossible, inspection shall be as provided in this section unless the place or method fixed was clearly intended as an indispensable condition failure of which avoids the contract. (Stats.1963, c. 819, § 2513.)

California Code Comment

By John A. Bohn and Charles J. Williams

Prior California Law

1. Subdivision (1) is a restatement of the rule of former Civil Code § 1767(2) which provided that the buyer has a reasonable opportunity to examine the goods to see if they conform to the contract.

2. Subdivision (2) is without counterpart in prior California statutory law. In the California Annotations to the proposed Uniform Commercial Code (May, 1960), The Legislative Counsel states: "Subdivision (2) is new language, but is believed to be in accord with general commercial practice". Sixth Progress Report to the Legislature by the Senate Fact Finding Committee on Judiciary (1959–1961) Part 1, The Uniform Commercial Code, p. 53.

3. Subdivision (3) is a restatement of the provisions of former Civil Code § 1767(3) that where goods are not to be delivered to the buyer until he pays the price, the buyer is not entitled to examine the goods before payment.

4. Subdivision (4) is without counterpart in prior California statutory law. However the cases recognize the principle expressed in the second sentence of subdivision (4). In Puritas Coffee & Tea Co. v. De Martini, 56 Cal.App. 628, 206 Pac. 96 (1922) it was held that where the goods are sold by sample, the removal of the goods from the railroad station to the place of business of the buyer for the purpose of inspection does not constitute a waiver of the right of inspection or an acceptance of the goods, where lack of facilities renders inspection at the railroad station impossible. In Bassi v. Walden, 64 Cal.App. 764, 222 Pac. 866 (1923) the court stated: "Ordinarily a purchaser's right of inspection should be exercised at or before the time of delivery and at the place of delivery. (cases cited) There are, of course, well-recognized exceptions to the rule * * *."

Changes from U.C.C. (1962 Official Text)

5. This is section 2–513 of the Official Text without change.

Uniform Commercial Code Comment

Prior Uniform Statutory Provision:

Section 47(2), (3), Uniform Sales Act.

Changes: Rewritten, Subsections (2) and (3) being new.

Purposes of Changes and New Matter: To correspond in substance with the prior uniform statutory provision and to incorporate in addition some of the results of the better case law so that:

1. The buyer is entitled to inspect goods as provided in subsection (1) unless it has been otherwise agreed by the parties. The phrase "unless otherwise agreed" is intended principally to cover such situations as those outlined in subsections (3) and (4) and those in which the agreement of the parties negates inspection before tender of delivery. However, no agreement by the parties can displace the entire right of inspection except where the contract is simply for the sale of "this thing." Even in a sale of boxed goods "as is" inspection is a right of the buyer, since if the boxes prove to contain some other merchandise altogether the price can be recovered back; nor do the limitations of the provision on effect of acceptance apply in such a case.

2. The buyer's right of inspection is available to him upon tender, delivery or appropriation of the goods with notice to him. Since inspection is available to him on tender, where payment is due against delivery he may, unless otherwise agreed, make his inspection before payment of the price. It is also available to him after receipt of the goods and so may be postponed after receipt for a reasonable time. Failure to inspect before payment does not impair the right to inspect after receipt of the goods unless the case falls within subsection (4) on agreed and exclusive inspection provisions. The right to inspect goods which have been appropriated with notice to the buyer holds whether or not the sale was by sample.

3. The buyer may exercise his right of inspection at any reasonable time or place and in any reasonable manner. It is not necessary that he select the most appropriate time, place or manner to inspect or that his selection be the customary one in the trade or locality. Any reasonable time, place or manner is available to him and the reasonableness will be determined by trade usages, past practices between the parties and the other circumstances of the case.

The last sentence of subsection (1) makes it clear that the place of arrival of shipped goods is a reasonable place for their inspection.

4. Expenses of an inspection made to satisfy the buyer of the seller's performance must be assumed by the buyer in the first instance. Since the rule provides merely for an allocation of expense there is no policy to prevent the parties from providing otherwise in the agreement. Where the buyer would normally bear the expenses of the inspection but the goods are rightly rejected because of what the inspection reveals, demonstrable and reasonable costs of the inspection are part of his incidental damage caused by the seller's breach.

5. In the case of payment against documents, subsection (3) requires payment before inspection, since shipping documents against which payment is to be made will commonly arrive and be tendered while the goods are still in transit. This Article recognizes no exception in any peculiar case in which the goods happen to arrive before the documents. However, where by the agreement payment is to await the arrival of the goods, inspection before payment becomes proper since the goods are then "available for inspection."

Where by the agreement the documents are to be held until arrival the buyer is entitled to inspect before payment since the goods are then "available for inspection." Proof of usage is not necessary to establish this right, but if inspection before payment is disputed the contrary must be established by usage or by an explicit contract term to that effect.

For the same reason, that the goods are available for inspection, a term calling for payment against storage documents or a delivery order does not normally bar the buyer's right to inspection before payment under subsection (3)(b). This result is reinforced by the buyer's right under subsection (1) to inspect goods which have been appropriated with notice to him.

6. Under subsection (4) an agreed place or method of inspection is generally held to be intended as exclusive. However, where compliance

with such an agreed inspection term becomes impossible, the question is basically one of intention. If the parties clearly intend that the method of inspection named is to be a necessary condition without which the entire deal is to fail, the contract is at an end if that method becomes impossible. On the other hand, if the parties merely seek to indicate a convenient and reliable method but do not intend to give up the deal in the event of its failure, any reasonable method of inspection may be substituted under this Article.

Since the purpose of an agreed place of inspection is only to make sure at that point whether or not the goods will be thrown back, the "exclusive" feature of the named place is satisfied under this Article if the buyer's failure to inspect there is held to be an acceptance with the knowledge of such defects as inspection would have revealed within the section on waiver of buyer's objections by failure to particularize. Revocation of the acceptance is limited to the situations stated in the section pertaining to that subject. The reasonable time within which to give notice of defects within the section on notice of breach begins to run from the point of the "acceptance."

7. Clauses on time of inspection are commonly clauses which limit the time in which the buyer must inspect and give notice of defects. Such clauses are therefore governed by the section of this Article which requires that such a time limitation must be reasonable.

8. Inspection under this Article is not to be regarded as a "condition precedent to the passing of title" so that risk until inspection remains on the seller. Under subsection (4) such an approach cannot be sustained. Issues between the buyer and seller are settled in this Article almost wholly by special provisions and not by the technical determination of the locus of the title. Thus "inspection as a condition to the passing of title" becomes a concept almost without meaning. However, in peculiar circumstances inspection may still have some of the consequences hitherto sought and obtained under that concept.

9. "Inspection" under this section has to do with the buyer's checkup on whether the seller's performance is in accordance with a contract previously made and is not to be confused with the "examination" of the goods or of a sample or model of them at the time of contracting which may affect the warranties involved in the contract.

Cross References:

Generally: Sections 2–310(b), 2–321(3) and 2–606(1)(b).
Point 1: Section 2–607.
Point 2: Sections 2–501 and 2–502.
Point 4: Section 2–715.
Point 5: Section 2–321(3).
Point 6: Sections 2–606 to 2–608.
Point 7: Section 1–204.
Point 8: Comment to Section 2–401.
Point 9: Section 2–316(3)(b).

Definitional Cross References:

"Buyer". Section 2–103.
"Conform". Section 2–106.
"Contract". Section 1–201.
"Contract for sale". Section 2–106.
"Document of title". Section 1–201.
"Goods". Section 2–105.
"Party". Section 1–201.
"Presumed". Section 1–201.
"Reasonable time". Section 1–204.
"Rights". Section 1–201.
"Seller". Section 2–103.
"Send". Section 1–201.
"Term". Section 1–201.

Cross References

Acceptance of goods,
 Effect, see Commercial Code § 2607.
 Inspection, see Commercial Code § 2606.
 Revocation, see Commercial Code § 2608.
Damages, expenses of inspection, see Commercial Code § 2715.
Implication arising from term "unless otherwise agreed", see Commercial Code § 1102.

Insurable interest, identification of goods, see Commercial Code §§ 2501, 2502.
Payment on or after arrival of goods, preliminary inspection, see Commercial Code § 2321.
Preserving evidence of goods, third party inspection, see Commercial Code § 2515.
Resale of goods, provision for reasonable inspection, see Commercial Code § 2706.
Risk of loss, see Commercial Code §§ 2509, 2510.
Shipment of goods, inspection before payment, see Commercial Code § 2310.
Time, see Commercial Code § 1204.
Title of goods, see Commercial Code § 2401.
Warranties, examination of goods, see Commercial Code § 2316.

§ 2514. When Documents Deliverable on Acceptance; When on Payment

Unless otherwise agreed documents against which a draft is drawn are to be delivered to the drawee on acceptance of the draft if it is payable more than three days after presentment; otherwise, only on payment. *(Stats.1963, c. 819, § 2514.)*

California Code Comment

By John A. Bohn and Charles J. Williams

Prior California Law

1. This section is the counterpart of former Civil Code § 2130e (Uniform Bills of Lading Act) which provided that if a draft is payable (1) before three days after presentment the seller is presumed to have intended that the draft is to be paid before the buyer received the bill; and (2) if beyond three days after presentment, the seller is presumed to have intended that the draft is to be accepted but need not be paid before the buyer received the bill.

2. This section is broader than former Civil Code § 2130e (which only applied to bills of lading) in that it covers all "documents against which a draft is drawn." Where a bill is payable before three days after presentment, this section provides that the document is to be delivered "on payment". Former Civil Code § 2130e(b) required payment "before the buyer should be entitled to receive or retain the bill."

Changes from U.C.C. (1962 Official Text)

3. This is section 2–514 of the Official Text without change.

Uniform Commercial Code Comment

Prior Uniform Statutory Provision:

Section 41, Uniform Bills of Lading Act.

Changes: Rewritten.

Purposes of Changes: To make the provision one of general application so that:

1. It covers any document against which a draft may be drawn, whatever may be the form of the document, and applies to interpret the action of a seller or consignor insofar as it may affect the rights and duties of any buyer, consignee or financing agency concerned with the paper. Supplementary or corresponding provisions are found in Sections 4–503 and 5–112.

2. An "arrival" draft is a sight draft within the purpose of this section.

Cross References:

Point 1: See Sections 2–502, 2–505(2), 2–507(2), 2–512, 2–513, 2–607 concerning protection of rights of buyer and seller, and 4–503 and 5–112 on delivery of documents.

Definitional Cross References:

"Delivery". Section 1–201.
"Draft". Section 3–104.

§ 2514

Cross References

Acceptance, rights of buyer and seller, see Commercial Code § 2607.
Delivery of documents,
    Acceptance or payment of draft, see Commercial Code § 4503.
    Honor or rejection, see Commercial Code § 5112.
Delivery on condition of payment, goods or documents of title, see Commercial Code § 2507.
Draft defined, see Commercial Code § 3104.
Insolvency of seller, buyer's right to goods, see Commercial Code § 2502.
Reservation of security interest by seller, see Commercial Code § 2505.

§ 2515. Preserving Evidence of Goods in Dispute

In furtherance of the adjustment of any claim or dispute

(a) Either party on reasonable notification to the other and for the purpose of ascertaining the facts and preserving evidence has the right to inspect, test and sample the goods including such of them as may be in the possession or control of the other; and

(b) The parties may agree to a third party inspection or survey to determine the conformity or condition of the goods and may agree that the findings shall be binding upon them in any subsequent litigation or adjustment. *(Stats.1963, c. 819, § 2515.)*

California Code Comment

By John A. Bohn and Charles J. Williams

Prior California Law

1. This section is without counterpart in prior California statutory law.

Changes from U.C.C. (1962 Official Text)

2. This is section 2–515 of the Official Text without change.

Uniform Commercial Code Comment

Prior Uniform Statutory Provision:
None.

Purposes:

1. To meet certain serious problems which arise when there is a dispute as to the quality of the goods and thereby perhaps to aid the parties in reaching a settlement, and to further the use of devices which will promote certainty as to the condition of the goods, or at least aid in preserving evidence of their condition.

2. Under paragraph (a), to afford either party an opportunity for preserving evidence, whether or not agreement has been reached, and thereby to reduce uncertainty in any litigation and, in turn perhaps, to promote agreement.

Paragraph (a) does not conflict with the provisions on the seller's right to resell rejected goods or the buyer's similar right. Apparent conflict between these provisions which will be suggested in certain circumstances is to be resolved by requiring prompt action by the parties. Nor does paragraph (a) impair the effect of a term for payment before inspection. Short of such defects as amount to fraud or substantial failure of consideration, non-conformity is neither an excuse nor a defense to an action for non-acceptance of documents. Normally, therefore, until the buyer has made payment, inspected and rejected the goods, there is no occasion or use for the rights under paragraph (a).

3. Under paragraph (b), to provide for third party inspection upon the agreement of the parties, thereby opening the door to amicable adjustments based upon the findings of such third parties.

The use of the phrase "conformity or condition" makes it clear that the parties' agreement may range from a complete settlement of all aspects of the dispute by a third party to the use of a third party merely to determine and record the condition of the goods so that they can be resold or used to reduce the stake in controversy. "Conformity", at one end of the scale of possible issues, includes the whole question of interpretation of the agreement and its legal effect, the state of the goods in regard to quality and condition, whether any defects are due to factors which operate at the risk of the buyer, and the degree of non-conformity where that may be material. "Condition", at the other end of the scale, includes nothing but the degree of damage or deterioration which the goods show. Paragraph (b) is intended to reach any point in the gamut which the parties may agree upon.

The principle of the section on reservation of rights reinforces this paragraph in simplifying such adjustments as the parties wish to make in partial settlement while reserving their rights as to any further points. Paragraph (b) also suggests the use of arbitration, where desired, of any points left open, but nothing in this section is intended to repeal or amend any statute governing arbitration. Where any question arises as to the extent of the parties' agreement under the paragraph, the presumption should be that it was meant to extend only to the relation between the contract description and the goods as delivered, since that is what a craftsman in the trade would normally be expected to report upon. Finally, a written and authenticated report of inspection or tests by a third party, whether or not sampling has been practicable, is entitled to be admitted as evidence under this Act, for it is a third party document.

Cross References:

Point 2: Sections 2–513(3), 2–706 and 2–711(2) and Article 5.
Point 3: Sections 1–202 and 1–207.

Definitional Cross References:

"Conform". Section 2–106.
"Goods". Section 2–105.
"Notification". Section 1–201.
"Party". Section 1–201.

Cross References

Arbitration, see Code of Civil Procedure § 1280 et seq.
Goods as "conforming" to contract, see Commercial Code § 2106.
Inspection,
    Buyer's right before payment or acceptance, see Commercial Code § 2513.
    Prior to public resale by seller, see Commercial Code § 2706.
Letters of credit, see Commercial Code § 5101 et seq.
Prima facie evidence, third party documents, see Commercial Code § 1202.
Remedies of buyer, see Commercial Code § 2711.
Reservation of rights, effect of performance or acceptance, see Commercial Code § 1207.

CHAPTER 6. BREACH, REPUDIATION AND EXCUSE

Section

2601. Buyer's Rights on Improper Delivery.
2602. Manner and Effect of Rightful Rejection.
2603. Merchant Buyer's Duties as to Rightfully Rejected Goods.
2604. Buyer's Options as to Salvage of Rightfully Rejected Goods.
2605. Waiver of Buyer's Objections by Failure to Particularize.
2606. What Constitutes Acceptance of Goods.
2607. Effect of Acceptance; Notice of Breach; Burden of Establishing Breach After Acceptance; Notice of Claim or Litigation to Person Answerable Over.
2608. Revocation of Acceptance in Whole or in Part.
2609. Right to Adequate Assurance of Performance.
2610. Anticipatory Repudiation.
2611. Retraction of Anticipatory Repudiation.
2612. "Installment Contract"; Breach.
2613. Casualty to Identified Goods.
2614. Substituted Performance.

Section
2615. Excuse by Failure of Presupposed Conditions.
2616. Procedure on Notice Claiming Excuse.

§ 2601. Buyer's Rights on Improper Delivery

Subject to the provisions of this division on breach in installment contracts (Section 2612) and unless otherwise agreed under the sections on contractual limitations of remedy (Sections 2718 and 2719), if the goods or the tender of delivery fail in any respect to conform to the contract, the buyer may

(a) Reject the whole; or

(b) Accept the whole; or

(c) Accept any commercial unit or units and reject the rest. *(Stats.1963, c. 819, § 2601.)*

California Code Comment

By John A. Bohn and Charles J. Williams

Prior California Law

1. This section has no direct counterpart in prior California statutory law. However, it is consistent with various provisions of the USA (former Civil Code §§ 1721–1800).

2. This section specifies the three courses of conduct which the buyer has when the seller tenders nonconforming goods. It does not define the buyer's remedies. This section of the Commercial Code is intended to apply to any situation where the tender of delivery fails "in any respect to conform to the contract . . . ." The language of the section and the Official Comments to it indicate that it is broad and is intended to apply to any nonconforming situation.

3. The course of conduct open to the buyer under the USA provided these options when the goods did not conform to the contract:

(a) if the nonconforming tender was a breach of warranty, the buyer could refuse to accept the goods if the property in them had not passed or he could accept the goods and either set up the breach "by way of recoupment in diminution or extinction of the price" or maintain an action against the seller for damages (former Civil Code § 1789(1)).

(b) if the nonconforming tender was the failure of the seller to perform a condition, the buyer could refuse to proceed with the sale (former Civil Code § 1731).

(c) if the goods were less than or more than the contract called for, or were mixed with those not included in the contract, the buyer could reject the whole or the nonconforming part (former Civil Code § 1764).

4. This section broadens the former California law and extends those cases where the buyer has the option to accept, reject or partially accept any situation in which the delivery does not conform to the contract.

Changes from U.C.C. (1962 Official Text)

5. This is section 2–601 of the Official Text without change.

Uniform Commercial Code Comment

Prior Uniform Statutory Provision:

No one general equivalent provision but numerous provisions, dealing with situations of non-conformity where buyer may accept or reject, including Sections 11, 44 and 69(1), Uniform Sales Act.

Changes: Partial acceptance in good faith is recognized and the buyer's remedies on the contract for breach of warranty and the like, where the buyer has returned the goods after transfer of title, are no longer barred.

Purposes of Changes: To make it clear that:

1. A buyer accepting a non-conforming tender is not penalized by the loss of any remedy otherwise open to him. This policy extends to cover and regulate the acceptance of a part of any lot improperly tendered in any case where the price can reasonably be apportioned. Partial acceptance is permitted whether the part of the goods accepted conforms or not. The only limitation on partial acceptance is that good faith and commercial reasonableness must be used to avoid undue impairment of the value of the remaining portion of the goods. This is the reason for the insistence on the "commercial unit" in paragraph (c). In this respect, the test is not only what unit has been the basis of contract, but whether the partial acceptance produces so materially adverse an effect on the remainder as to constitute bad faith.

2. Acceptance made with the knowledge of the other party is final. An original refusal to accept may be withdrawn by a later acceptance if the seller has indicated that he is holding the tender open. However, if the buyer attempts to accept, either in whole or in part, after his original rejection has caused the seller to arrange for other disposition of the goods, the buyer must answer for any ensuing damage since the next section provides that any exercise of ownership after rejection is wrongful as against the seller. Further, he is liable even though the seller may choose to treat his action as acceptance rather than conversion, since the damage flows from the misleading notice. Such arrangements for resale or other disposition of the goods by the seller must be viewed as within the normal contemplation of a buyer who has given notice of rejection. However, the buyer's attempts in good faith to dispose of defective goods where the seller has failed to give instructions within a reasonable time are not to be regarded as an acceptance.

Cross References:

Sections 2–602(2)(a), 2–612, 2–718 and 2–719.

Definitional Cross References:

"Buyer". Section 2–103.
"Commercial unit". Section 2–105.
"Conform". Section 2–106.
"Contract". Section 1–201.
"Goods". Section 2–105.
"Installment contract". Section 2–612.
"Rights". Section 1–201.

Cross References

Acceptance, what constitutes, see Commercial Code § 2606.
Assumption of obligation by acceptance of benefits, see Civil Code § 1589.
Contractual limitations of remedies, see Commercial Code § 2719.
Goods as "conforming" to contract, see Commercial Code § 2106.
Installment contracts, see Commercial Code § 2612.
Rescission of contracts, see Civil Code § 1688 et seq.

§ 2602. Manner and Effect of Rightful Rejection

(1) Rejection of goods must be within a reasonable time after their delivery or tender. It is ineffective unless the buyer seasonably notifies the seller.

(2) Subject to the provisions of the two following sections on rejected goods (Sections 2603 and 2604),

(a) After rejection any exercise of ownership by the buyer with respect to any commercial unit is wrongful as against the seller; and

(b) If the buyer has before rejection taken physical possession of goods in which he does not have a security interest under the provisions of this division (subdivision (3) of Section 2711), he is under a duty after rejection to hold them with reasonable care at the seller's disposition for a time sufficient to permit the seller to remove them; but

(c) The buyer has no further obligations with regard to goods rightfully rejected.

(3) The seller's rights with respect to goods wrongfully rejected are governed by the provisions of this division on seller's remedies in general (Section 2703). *(Stats.1963, c. 819, § 2602.)*

§ 2602

California Code Comment

By John A. Bohn and Charles J. Williams

Prior California Law

1. Subdivision (1) is similar to former Civil Code § 1768 which provided, in part, that a buyer was deemed to have accepted goods if he retained "the goods without intimating to the seller" that he had rejected them and former Civil Code § 1770 which stated that while the buyer did not have to return goods rightfully refused he had to notify seller of the fact that he refused to accept them.

2. Subdivision (2)(a) is consistent with former Civil Code § 1768 in which the buyer was deemed to have accepted goods if he did "any act in relation" to the goods which was "inconsistent with the ownership of the seller."

3. Subdivision (2)(b) is consistent with prior case law as expressed in Gladium Co. v. Thatcher Inc., 95 Cal.App. 85, 90, 272 Pac. 340, 342 (1928). In that case, the consignee attempted to reject the goods, but upon their delivery retained them and conveyed them to a third party. The court held that the consignee could not reject goods after he treated them as his own.

"When goods are shipped . . . [which] are materially defective in quality or quantity . . . they need not be accepted, and under such circumstances the seller becomes a mere volunteer with respect to the shipment, while the consignee then becomes a bailee holding the property for the benefit of the owner, and while he need not necessarily return the property to the shipper, *he must exercise reasonable care to preserve the property against loss or damage.*" (emphasis added)

Regarding the buyer's conduct see also former Civil Code § 1789(3) providing for remedies for breach of warranty.

Changes from U.C.C. (1962 Official Text).

4. This is section 2–602 of the Official Text without change.

Uniform Commercial Code Comment

Purposes of Changes:

To make it clear that:

* * * * * *

2. Subsection (2) lays down the normal duties of the buyer upon rejection, which flow from the relationship of the parties. Beyond his duty to hold the goods with reasonable care for the buyer's [seller's] disposition, this section continues the policy of prior uniform legislation in generally relieving the buyer from any duties with respect to them, except when the circumstances impose the limited obligation of salvage upon him under the next section.

* * * * * *

Uniform Commercial Code Comment

Prior Uniform Statutory Provision:

Section 50, Uniform Sales Act.

Changes: Rewritten.

Purposes of Changes: To make it clear that:

1. A tender or delivery of goods made pursuant to a contract of sale, even though wholly non-conforming, requires affirmative action by the buyer to avoid acceptance. Under subsection (1), therefore, the buyer is given a reasonable time to notify the seller of his rejection, but without such seasonable notification his rejection is ineffective. The sections of this Article dealing with inspection of goods must be read in connection with the buyer's reasonable time for action under this subsection. Contract provisions limiting the time for rejection fall within the rule of the section on "Time" and are effective if the time set gives the buyer a reasonable time for discovery of defects. What constitutes a due "notifying" of rejection by the buyer to the seller is defined in Section 1–201.

2. Subsection (2) lays down the normal duties of the buyer upon rejection, which flow from the relationship of the parties. Beyond his duty to hold the goods with reasonable care for the buyer's [seller's] disposition, this section continues the policy of prior uniform legislation in generally relieving the buyer from any duties with respect to them, except when the circumstances impose the limited obligation of salvage upon him under the next section.

3. The present section applies only to rightful rejection by the buyer. If the seller has made a tender which in all respects conforms to the contract, the buyer has a positive duty to accept and his failure to do so constitutes a "wrongful rejection" which gives the seller immediate remedies for breach. Subsection (3) is included here to emphasize the sharp distinction between the rejection of an improper tender and the non-acceptance which is a breach by the buyer.

4. The provisions of this section are to be appropriately limited or modified when a negotiation is in process.

Cross References:

Point 1: Sections 1–201, 1–204(1) and (3), 2–512(2), 2–513(1) and 2–606(1)(b).
Point 2: Section 2–603(1).
Point 3: Section 2–703.

Definitional Cross References:

"Buyer". Section 2–103.
"Commercial unit". Section 2–105.
"Goods". Section 2–105.
"Merchant". Section 2–104.
"Notifies". Section 1–201.
"Reasonable time". Section 1–204.
"Remedy". Section 1–201.
"Rights". Section 1–201.
"Seasonably". Section 1–204.
"Security interest". Section 1–201.
"Seller". Section 2–103.

Cross References

Acceptance,
  Failure to reject, see Commercial Code § 2606.
  What constitutes, see Commercial Code § 2606.
Buyer's options as to salvage of rightfully rejected goods, see Commercial Code § 2604.
Buyer's security interest in rejected goods, see Commercial Code § 2711.
Definitions, see Commercial Code §§ 1201, 2103, 2104, 2105, 2106.
Payment before inspection, impairment of buyer's remedies, see Commercial Code § 2512.
Reasonable time,
  Agreement as to time, see Commercial Code § 1204.
  Inspection of goods, see Commercial Code § 2513.
Seasonably, see Commercial Code § 1204.
Wrongful rejection, seller's remedies generally, see Commercial Code § 2703.

§ 2603. Merchant Buyer's Duties as to Rightfully Rejected Goods

(1) Subject to any security interest in the buyer (subdivision (3) of Section 2711), when the seller has no agent or place of business at the market of rejection a merchant buyer is under a duty after rejection of goods in his possession or control to follow any reasonable instructions received from the seller with respect to the goods and in the absence of such instructions to make reasonable efforts to sell them for the seller's account if they are perishable or threaten to decline in value speedily. Instructions are not reasonable if on demand indemnity for expenses is not forthcoming.

(2) When the buyer sells goods under subdivision (1), he is entitled to reimbursement from the seller or out of the proceeds for reasonable expenses of caring for and selling them, and if the expenses include no selling commission then to such commission as is usual in the trade or if there is none to a reasonable sum not exceeding 10 percent on the gross proceeds.

(3) In complying with this section the buyer is held only to good faith and good faith conduct hereunder is neither acceptance nor conversion nor the basis of an action for damages. *(Stats.1963, c. 819, § 2603.)*

California Code Comment
By John A. Bohn and Charles J. Williams

Prior California Law

1. Subdivision (1) has no statutory counterpart in prior law. However, in Gladium Co. v. Thatcher, 95 Cal.App. 85, 272 Pac. 340 (1928) the court held that with regard to rejected goods the buyer had an obligation to exercise reasonable care to preserve the property against loss or damage.

2. Subdivisions (2) and (3) have no statutory counterpart in prior law.

Changes from U.C.C. (1962 Official Text).

3. This is section 2–603 of the Official Text without change.

Uniform Commercial Code Comment

Prior Uniform Statutory Provision:

None.

Purposes:

1. This section recognizes the duty imposed upon the merchant buyer by good faith and commercial practice to follow any reasonable instructions of the seller as to reshipping, storing, delivery to a third party, reselling or the like. Subsection (1) goes further and extends the duty to include the making of reasonable efforts to effect a salvage sale where the value of the goods is threatened and the seller's instructions do not arrive in time to prevent serious loss.

2. The limitations on the buyer's duty to resell under subsection (1) are to be liberally construed. The buyer's duty to resell under this section arises from commercial necessity and thus is present only when the seller has "no agent or place of business at the market of rejection". A financing agency which is acting in behalf of the seller in handling the documents rejected by the buyer is sufficiently the seller's agent to lift the burden of salvage resale from the buyer. (See provisions of Sections 4–503 and 5–112 on bank's duties with respect to rejected documents.) The buyer's duty to resell is extended only to goods in his "possession or control", but these are intended as words of wide, rather than narrow, import. In effect, the measure of the buyer's "control" is whether he can practicably effect control without undue commercial burden.

3. The explicit provisions for reimbursement and compensation to the buyer in subsection (2) are applicable and necessary only where he is not acting under instructions from the seller. As provided in subsection (1) the seller's instructions to be "reasonable" must on demand of the buyer include indemnity for expenses.

4. Since this section makes the resale of perishable goods an affirmative duty in contrast to a mere right to sell as under the case law, subsection (3) makes it clear that the buyer is liable only for the exercise of good faith in determining whether the value of the goods is sufficiently threatened to justify a quick resale or whether he has waited a sufficient length of time for instructions, or what a reasonable means and place of resale is.

5. A buyer who fails to make a salvage sale when his duty to do so under this section has arisen is subject to damages pursuant to the section on liberal administration of remedies.

Cross References:

Point 2: Sections 4–503 and 5–112.
Point 5: Section 1–106. Compare generally section 2–706.

Definitional Cross References:

"Buyer". Section 2–103.
"Good faith". Section 1–201.
"Goods". Section 2–105.
"Merchant". Section 2–104.
"Security interest". Section 1–201.
"Seller". Section 2–103.

Cross References

Buyer's resale, damages for failure to sell, see Commercial Code § 1106.
Expenses, reimbursement of bank presenting documentary draft, see Commercial Code § 4503.
Instructions, bank presented with a documentary draft, see Commercial Code §§ 4503, 5112.
Seller's resale, see Commercial Code § 2706.

§ 2604. Buyer's Options as to Salvage of Rightfully Rejected Goods

Subject to the provisions of the immediately preceding section on perishables if the seller gives no instructions within a reasonable time after notification of rejection the buyer may store the rejected goods for the seller's account or reship them to him or resell them for the seller's account with reimbursement as provided in the preceding section. Such action is not acceptance or conversion. *(Stats.1963, c. 819, § 2604.)*

California Code Comment
By John A. Bohn and Charles J. Williams

Prior California Law

1. This section is new.

The California Annotations to the Proposed Uniform Commercial Code states that this section

"probably constitutes a change in the California law in that under [former] Civil Code Section 1768 any act done by buyer 'which is inconsistent with the ownership of seller' constitutes an acceptance of the goods which makes buyer liable for the price." (Sixth Progress Report to the Legislature by the Senate Fact Finding Committee on Judiciary (1959–1961), Part 1, the Uniform Commercial Code, p. 55.) However, this section is in accord with prior California law to the extent it is consistent with the statement of the court in Gladium Co. v. Thatcher, 95 Cal.App. 85, 90, 272 Pac. 340, 342 (1942):

"When goods are shipped . . . when they are materially defective in quality or quantity . . . they need not be accepted, and under such circumstances, the seller becomes a mere volunteer with respect to the shipment, while the consignee then becomes a bailee holding the property for the benefit of the owner, and while he need not necessarily return the property to the shipper, *he must exercise reasonable care to preserve the property against loss or damage.*" (emphasis added).

Changes from U.C.C. (1962 Official Text).

2. This is section 2–604 of the Official Text without change.

Uniform Commercial Code Comment

Prior Uniform Statutory Provision:

None.

Purposes:

The basic purpose of this section is twofold: on the one hand it aims at reducing the stake in dispute and on the other at avoiding the pinning of a technical "acceptance" on a buyer who has taken steps towards realization on or preservation of the goods in good faith. This section is essentially a salvage section and the buyer's right to act under it is conditioned upon (1) non-conformity of the goods, (2) due notification of rejection to the seller under the section on manner of rejection, and (3) the absence of any instructions from the seller which the merchant-buyer has a duty to follow under the preceding section.

This section is designed to accord all reasonable leeway to a rightfully rejecting buyer acting in good faith. The listing of what the buyer may do in the absence of instructions from the seller is intended to be not exhaustive but merely illustrative. This is not a "merchant's" section and the options are pure options given to merchant and non-merchant

§ 2604

buyers alike. The merchant-buyer, however, may in some instances be under a duty rather than an option to resell under the provisions of the preceding section.

Cross References:

Sections 2–602(1), and 2–603(1) and 2–706.

Definitional Cross References:

"Buyer". Section 2–103.
"Notification". Section 1–201.
"Reasonable time". Section 1–204.
"Seller". Section 2–103.

Cross References

Manner of rejection of goods, see Commercial Code § 2602.
Rejection, manner, see Commercial Code § 2602.
Seller's resale, see Commercial Code § 2706.

§ 2605. Waiver of Buyer's Objections by Failure to Particularize

(1) The buyer's failure to state in connection with rejection a particular defect which is ascertainable by reasonable inspection precludes him from relying on the unstated defect to justify rejection or to establish breach

(a) Where the seller could have cured it if stated seasonably; or

(b) Between merchants when the seller has after rejection made a request in writing for a full and final written statement of all defects on which the buyer proposes to rely.

(2) Payment against documents made without reservation of rights precludes recovery of the payment for defects apparent on the face of the documents. *(Stats. 1963, c. 819, § 2605.)*

California Code Comment

By John A. Bohn and Charles J. Williams

Prior California Law

1. While the provisions of this section are basically new to California law, the notice requirement with regard to defects has some precedent under related statutes. Under former Civil Code § 1769, *after acceptance* of the goods the buyer was required to give notice to the seller of "the breach of any promise or warranty within a reasonable time after the buyer knows, or ought to know of such breach . . . ." Under former Civil Code § 1789(3) the buyer could not rescind "if he fails to notify the seller within a reasonable time of the election to rescind . . . ." See Hull v. Ray, 211 Cal. 164, 294 Pac. 700 (1930) for example of the extent to which the grounds for rescission should be stated. The court in that case said that a notice is sufficient if it shows a clear intent to treat the contract at an end, but that if grounds are stated they should not mislead the other party as to what defense he is called upon to make.

2. Whether or not the notice requirement of former Civil Code § 1769 was intended to give the seller an opportunity to correct the defects in the goods sold was an open question under prior California Law. California courts have stated that it is doubtful whether the seller had such a right to correct defects. Reininger v. Eldon Mfg. Co., 114 Cal.App.2d 240, 250 P.2d 4 (1952); Whitfield v. Jessup, 31 Cal.2d 826, 193 P.2d 1 (1948).

Changes from U.C.C. (1962 Official Text).

3. This is section 2–605 of the Official Text without change.

Uniform Commercial Code Comment

Prior Uniform Statutory Provision:

None.

Purposes:

1. The present section rests upon a policy of permitting the buyer to give a quick and informal notice of defects in a tender without penalizing him for omissions in his statement, while at the same time protecting a seller who is reasonably misled by the buyer's failure to state curable defects.

2. Where the defect in a tender is one which could have been cured by the seller, a buyer who merely rejects the delivery without stating his objections to it is probably acting in commercial bad faith and seeking to get out of a deal which has become unprofitable. Subsection (1)(a), following the general policy of this Article which looks to preserving the deal wherever possible, therefore insists that the seller's right to correct his tender in such circumstances be protected.

3. When the time for cure is past, subsection (1)(b) makes it plain that a seller is entitled upon request to a final statement of objections upon which he can rely. What is needed is that he make clear to the buyer exactly what is being sought. A formal demand under paragraph (b) will be sufficient in the case of a merchant-buyer.

4. Subsection (2) applies to the particular case of documents the same principle which the section on effects of acceptance applies to the case of goods. The matter is dealt with in this section in terms of "waiver" of objections rather than of right to revoke acceptance, partly to avoid any confusion with the problems of acceptance of goods and partly because defects in documents which are not taken as grounds for rejection are generally minor ones. The only defects concerned in the present subsection are defects in the documents which are apparent on their face. Where payment is required against the documents they must be inspected before payment, and the payment then constitutes acceptance of the documents. Under the section dealing with this problem, such acceptance of the documents does not constitute an acceptance of the goods or impair any options or remedies of the buyer for their improper delivery. Where the documents are delivered without requiring such contemporary action as payment from the buyer, the reason of the next section on what constitutes acceptance of goods, applies. Their acceptance by non-objection is therefore postponed until after a reasonable time for their inspection. In either situation, however, the buyer "waives" only what is apparent on the face of the documents.

Cross References:

Point 2: Section 2–508.
Point 4: Sections 2–512(2), 2–606(1)(b), 2–607(2).

Definitional Cross References:

"Between merchants". Section 2–104.
"Buyer". Section 2–103.
"Seasonably". Section 1–204.
"Seller". Section 2–103.
"Writing" and "written". Section 1–201.

Cross References

Acceptance,
 Reasonable opportunity to inspect, see Commercial Code § 2606.
 Waiver of objections, see Commercial Code § 2607.
Action taken "seasonably", see Commercial Code § 1204.
Cure by seller of improper tender or delivery, see Commercial Code § 2508.
Manner and effect of rightful rejection, see Commercial Code § 2602.
Payment before inspection, impairment of buyer's remedies, see Commercial Code § 2512.

§ 2606. What Constitutes Acceptance of Goods

(1) Acceptance of goods occurs when the buyer

(a) After a reasonable opportunity to inspect the goods signifies to the seller that the goods are conforming or that he will take or retain them in spite of their nonconformity; or

(b) Fails to make an effective rejection (subdivision (1) of Section 2602), but such acceptance does not occur until the buyer has had a reasonable opportunity to inspect them; or

(c) Does any act inconsistent with the seller's ownership; but if such act is wrongful as against the seller it is an acceptance only if ratified by him.

(2) Acceptance of a part of any commercial unit is acceptance of that entire unit. (Stats.1963, c. 819, § 2606.)

California Code Comment

By John A. Bohn and Charles J. Williams

Prior California Law

1. This section is similar to but expands upon former Civil Code § 1768 which provided what constitutes acceptance under the USA.

2. Subdivision (1)(a) continues the rule formed by the conjunction of former Civil Code § 1767(1) and (2) (right to examine the goods) and § 1768. Former Civil Code § 1767(1) and (2) provided that the buyer should have a reasonable opportunity to examine the goods "for the purpose of ascertaining whether they are in conformity with the contract." Section 1768 provided, in part, that a buyer was "deemed to have accepted the goods when he intimates to the seller that he has accepted them . . . ."

3. Subdivision (1)(b) has its counterpart in former Civil Code § 1767(1) which provided that the buyer is not deemed to have accepted the goods "unless and until he has had a reasonable opportunity of examining them" and former Civil Code § 1768 which provided, in part, that a buyer was deemed to have accepted goods if "after the lapse of a reasonable time, he retains the goods without intimating to the seller that he has rejected them."

4. The first part of subdivision (1)(c) is in accord with former Civil Code § 1768 which provided, in part, that goods were deemed accepted if the buyer "does any act in relation to them which is inconsistent with the ownership of the seller . . . ." However the ratification provision in subdivision (1)(c) has no statutory counterpart in prior California law.

5. Subdivision (2) is new but merely recognizes partial acceptance by making that acceptance apply to the whole of a unit.

Changes from U.C.C. (1962 Official Text).

6. This is section 2–606 of the Official Text without change.

Uniform Commercial Code Comment

Prior Uniform Statutory Provision:

Section 48, Uniform Sales Act.

Changes: Rewritten, the qualification in paragraph (c) and subsection (2) being new; otherwise the general policy of the prior legislation is continued.

Purposes of Changes and New Matter: To make it clear that:

1. Under this Article "acceptance" as applied to goods means that the buyer, pursuant to the contract, takes particular goods which have been appropriated to the contract as his own, whether or not he is obligated to do so, and whether he does so by words, action, or silence when it is time to speak. If the goods conform to the contract, acceptance amounts only to the performance by the buyer of one part of his legal obligation.

2. Under this Article acceptance of goods is always acceptance of identified goods which have been appropriated to the contract or are appropriated by the contract. There is no provision for "acceptance of title" apart from acceptance in general, since acceptance of title is not material under this Article to the detailed rights and duties of the parties. (See Section 2–401). The refinements of the older law between acceptance of goods and of title become unnecessary in view of the provisions of the sections on effect and revocation of acceptance, on effects of identification and on risk of loss, and those sections which free the seller's and buyer's remedies from the complications and confusions caused by the question of whether title has or has not passed to the buyer before breach.

3. Under paragraph (a), payment made after tender is always one circumstance tending to signify acceptance of the goods but in itself it can never be more than one circumstance and is not conclusive. Also, a conditional communication of acceptance always remains subject to its expressed conditions.

4. Under paragraph (c), any action taken by the buyer, which is inconsistent with his claim that he has rejected the goods, constitutes an acceptance. However, the provisions of paragraph (c) are subject to the sections dealing with rejection by the buyer which permit the buyer to take certain actions with respect to the goods pursuant to his options and duties imposed by those sections, without effecting an acceptance of the goods. The second clause of paragraph (c) modifies some of the prior case law and makes it clear that "acceptance" in law based on the wrongful act of the acceptor is acceptance only as against the wrongdoer and then only at the option of the party wronged.

In the same manner in which a buyer can bind himself, despite his insistence that he is rejecting or has rejected the goods, by an act inconsistent with the seller's ownership under paragraph (c), he can obligate himself by a communication of acceptance despite a prior rejection under paragraph (a). However, the sections on buyer's rights on improper delivery and on the effect of rightful rejection, make it clear that after he once rejects a tender, paragraph (a) does not operate in favor of the buyer unless the seller has re-tendered the goods or has taken affirmative action indicating that he is holding the tender open. See also Comment 2 to Section 2–601.

5. Subsection (2) supplements the policy of the section on buyer's rights on improper delivery, recognizing the validity of a partial acceptance but insisting that the buyer exercise this right only as to whole commercial units.

Cross References:

Point 2: Sections 2–401, 2–509, 2–510, 2–607, 2–608 and Part 7.
Point 4: Sections 2–601 through 2–604.
Point 5: Section 2–601.

Definitional Cross References:

"Buyer". Section 2–103.
"Commercial unit". Section 2–105.
"Goods". Section 2–105.
"Seller". Section 2–103.

Cross References

Acceptance of whole or commercial units, see Commercial Code § 2601.
Commercial unit defined, see Commercial Code § 2105.
Documents of title, see Commercial Code § 7101 et seq.
Enforceability of contract not satisfying statute of frauds with respect to goods for which payment has been accepted, see Commercial Code § 2201.
Goods as "conforming to contract", see Commercial Code § 2106.
Rejection,
   Buyer's options as to salvage, see Commercial Code § 2604.
   Manner and effect, see Commercial Code § 2602.
   Merchant buyer's duties, see Commercial Code § 2603.
Remedies, see Commercial Code § 2701 et seq.
Revocation of acceptance,
   Generally, see Commercial Code § 2608.
   Title, see Commercial Code § 2401.
Risk of loss, see Commercial Code §§ 2509, 2510.
Title, effect and revocation of acceptance, see Commercial Code § 2401.

§ 2607. Effect of Acceptance; Notice of Breach; Burden of Establishing Breach After Acceptance; Notice of Claim or Litigation to Person Answerable Over

(1) The buyer must pay at the contract rate for any goods accepted.

(2) Acceptance of goods by the buyer precludes rejection of the goods accepted and, if made with knowledge of a nonconformity, cannot be revoked because of it unless the acceptance was on the reasonable assumption that the nonconformity would be seasonably cured * * *. Acceptance does not of itself impair any other remedy provided by this division for nonconformity.

(3) Where a tender has been accepted:

(A) The buyer must, within a reasonable time after he or she discovers or should have discovered any breach, notify the seller of breach or be barred from any remedy; and

(B) If the claim is one for infringement or the like (subdivision (3) of Section 2312) and the buyer is sued as a result of such a breach * * *, the buyer must so notify the seller within a reasonable time after he or she receives notice of the litigation or be barred from any remedy over for liability established by the litigation.

(4) The burden is on the buyer to establish any breach with respect to the goods accepted.

(5) Where the buyer is sued for breach of a warranty or other obligation for which his or her seller is answerable over:

(A) He or she may give the seller written notice of the litigation. If the notice states that the seller may * * * defend and that if the seller does not do so he or she will be bound in any action against * * * the seller by the buyer by any determination of fact common to the two * * * litigation actions, then unless the seller after seasonable receipt of the notice does * * * defend he or she is so bound.

(B) If the claim is one for infringement or the like (subdivision (3) of Section 2312) the original seller may demand in writing that the buyer turn over to * * * the seller control of the litigation, including settlement, or else be barred from any remedy over and if * * * the seller also agrees to bear all expense and to satisfy any adverse judgment, then unless the buyer after seasonable receipt of the demand does turn over control the buyer is so barred.

(6) The provisions of subdivisions (3), (4) and (5) apply to any obligation of a buyer to hold the seller harmless against infringement or the like (subdivision (3) of Section 2312). *(Stats.1963, c. 819, § 2607. Amended by Stats.1995, c. 91 (S.B.975), § 20.)*

California Code Comment

By John A. Bohn and Charles J. Williams

Prior California Law

1. Subdivision (1) is in accord with the rule of former Civil Code § 1761 requiring the buyer to "accept and pay" for goods "in accordance with the terms of the contract to sell or sale."

2. The first part of subdivision (2) is new to California statutory law but is consistent with the following cases: Stockton Lbr. Co. v. Mulcahy, 86 Cal.App. 505, 260 Pac. 897 (1927) (where buyer's claim that goods were unfit was first asserted a year after delivery in a cross complaint in action by the seller for the price) held that "a buyer to whom delivery of goods is made must inspect the same within a reasonable time after delivery, and if . . . (the) buyer makes use of the goods delivered, he cannot then complain as to their condition." Imperial Gas Engine Co. v. Auteri, 40 Cal.App. 419, 423, 180 Pac. 946, 947 (1919) (where buyer used machinery for two months after delivery knowing of defects and the court held this operated as an election to accept the goods despite the defects):

" 'When personal property is tendered or delivered to a purchaser in fulfillment of a contract for the purchase thereof, the duty devolves upon him to make an examination of the property tendered or delivered for the purpose of determining whether it fills the contract, and if from such examination he finds it does not, *he must promptly reject it* . . . .' (Jackson v. Porter Land & Water Co., 151 Cal. 39 [90 Pac. 125].)" (emphasis added).

Gladium Co. Inc., v. Thatcher, 95 Cal.App. 85, 272 Pac. 340 (1928) (Consignor's duty is to promptly reject goods which are shipped to him, or else he will be deemed to have accepted them.)

3. Subdivision (2) provides that a buyer who accepts with knowledge of nonconformity cannot revoke his acceptance because of the nonconformity unless he reasonably assumes that the non-conformity would be seasonably cured. This provision has no counterpart in prior California statutory law. The cases have recognized that there are situations where the buyer may revoke after acceptance because of misleading behavior of the sellers. In San Francisco Casing Co. v. Mueller, 39 Cal.App. 394, 179 Pac. 211 (1919), there was a contract requirement that rejection of merchandise be made within ten days after it was received. After buyer notified seller of the unsuitability of the goods, the seller repeatedly and persistently requested the buyer to make further trials of the merchandise. The court held that the seller had waived the contract requirement as to time. The court in Advance Rumely Thresher Co. v. McCoy, 213 Cal. 226, 2 P.2d 157 (1931), held that retention by the buyer at the instance of the seller for the purpose of giving the seller an opportunity to remedy defects is not a waiver of the benefits of a specific warranty and the remedy thereunder to rescind the contract.

4. Subdivision (3)(a) continues the rule of former Civil Code § 1769 to the effect that notice by buyer to seller of a breach must be within a reasonable time after he knows or ought to know of the breach. For an example of the application of the notice requirement of former Civil Code § 1769, see Pacific Commercial Co. v. Greer, 129 Cal.App. 751, 19 P.2d 543 (1933) where a notice of rejection of goods 7 months after discovery of a defect was held to be not within a reasonable time.

5. Subdivision (3)(b) adds new language to California statutory law but is consistent with the general provisions of former Civil Code § 1769 requiring the buyer to give notice of a breach within a reasonable time after acceptance.

6. As to standards in determining what is a reasonable time see Commercial Code § 1204 and Official Comment 4. The content of the notice which the buyer must give the seller under subdivision (3) is discussed in Official Comment 4.

7. Subdivision (4) is in accord with the general provisions of Code of Civil Procedure § 1981 that "the party holding the affirmative of the issue must produce the evidence to prove it." Also in accord are: Vogel v. Thrifty Drug Co., 43 Cal.2d 184, 272 P.2d 1 (1954) (the requirement of notice to be given by the buyer charging breach of warranty must be pleaded and proved by the party seeking to recover for such breach) and La Rosa v. Glaze, 18 Cal.App.2d 354, 63 P.2d 1181 (1936) (the burden is on the plaintiff buyer to show the quantity contracted for and the damages sustained by reason of the failure to deliver).

8. Subdivision 5(a) codifies a practice known as "vouching in." Under this provision a dealer (buyer) who is being sued in connection with a product furnished to him by a manufacturer may "vouch in" the manufacturer under subdivision 5(a). If the manufacturer refuses to come in after the notice provided in subdivision 5(a) then he is bound by any judgment rendered in the action in which he was "vouched in."

This vouching in procedure gives collateral estoppel effect against the manufacturer in a case where the dealer and manufacturer may both be liable but the manufacturer is not joined as defendant. Usually, the plaintiff will join the manufacturer and dealer as defendants. However, where the manufacturer is in a different jurisdiction and may not be able to be joined as a defendant, the vouching in procedure becomes particularly valuable.

9. An additional remedy similar to that in subdivision (5) is provided in the 1957 amendment to Code of Civil Procedure § 442 which allows a

defendant to bring a cross-complaint against any person (formerly "party") whether or not a party to the original action. Section 442 as amended enables an intermediate purchaser, who was sued for breach of warranty, to maintain a cross-complaint for declaratory relief against the manufacturer of the product in question. Simon Hardware Co. v. Pacific Tire & Rubber Co., 199 Cal.App.2d 616, 19 Cal.Rptr. 12 (1962) as cited in Dreybus v. Bayless Rents, 213 Cal.App.2d 506, 508, 28 Cal.Rptr. 825, 827 (1963). In the Dreybus case the plaintiff sought damages for breach of warranty for the collapse of crutches sold to him by the defendant dealer. It was held that defendant could bring a cross-complaint against the manufacturer under Code of Civil Procedure § 442. In so holding the court stated:

"It becomes apparent, therefore, that the courts of California have now definitely agreed upon the rule that a defendant may, by cross-complaint for a declaration of the rights of the parties, bring in a party from whom he claims indemnity in case he be held liable in the principal action."

This is also pointed out as the rule under Code of Civil Procedure § 442 in Roylance v. Doelger, 57 Cal.2d 255, 19 Cal.Rptr. 7, 368 P.2d 535 (1962). However, the court in the Roylance case also points out that under Code of Civil Procedure § 1048 the cross-complaint can be severed from the principal action.

Subdivision (5) is an improvement over the cross-complaint as a device of indemnification for the defendant dealer. The "vouching in" procedure of subdivision (5)(a) is not subject to severance as a cross-complaint is. Also a cross-complaint may not aid a defendant in bringing in a manufacturer from a different jurisdiction whereas by voucher such a manufacturer can be held (see Comment 8 immediately preceding).

Changes from U.C.C. (1962 Official Text):

10. This is section 2–607 of the Official Text without change.

Uniform Commercial Code Comment

Prior Uniform Statutory Provision:

Subsection (1)—Section 41, Uniform Sales Act; Subsections (2) and (3)—Sections 49 and 69, Uniform Sales Act.

Changes: Rewritten.

Purposes of Changes: To continue the prior basic policies with respect to acceptance of goods while making a number of minor though material changes in the interest of simplicity and commercial convenience so that:

1. Under subsection (1), once the buyer accepts a tender the seller acquires a right to its price on the contract terms. In cases of partial acceptance, the price of any part accepted is, if possible, to be reasonably apportioned, using the type of apportionment familiar to the courts in quantum valebat cases, to be determined in terms of "the contract rate," which is the rate determined from the bargain in fact (the agreement) after the rules and policies of this Article have been brought to bear.

2. Under subsection (2) acceptance of goods precludes their subsequent rejection. Any return of the goods thereafter must be by way of revocation of acceptance under the next section. Revocation is unavailable for a non-conformity known to the buyer at the time of acceptance, except where the buyer has accepted on the reasonable assumption that the non-conformity would be seasonably cured.

3. All other remedies of the buyer remain unimpaired under subsection (2). This is intended to include the buyer's full rights with respect to future installments despite his acceptance of any earlier non-conforming installment.

4. The time of notification is to be determined by applying commercial standards to a merchant buyer. "A reasonable time" for notification from a retail consumer is to be judged by different standards so that in his case it will be extended, for the rule of requiring notification is designed to defeat commercial bad faith, not to deprive a good faith consumer of his remedy.

The content of the notification need merely be sufficient to let the seller know that the transaction is still troublesome and must be watched. There is no reason to require that the notification which saves the buyer's rights under this section must include a clear statement of all the objections that will be relied on by the buyer, as under the section covering statements of defects upon rejection (Section 2–605). Nor is there reason for requiring the notification to be a claim for damages or of any threatened litigation or other resort to a remedy. The notification which saves the buyer's rights under this Article need only be such as informs the seller that the transaction is claimed to involve a breach, and thus opens the way for normal settlement through negotiation.

5. Under this Article various beneficiaries are given rights for injuries sustained by them because of the seller's breach of warranty. Such a beneficiary does not fall within the reason of the present section in regard to discovery of defects and the giving of notice within a reasonable time after acceptance, since he has nothing to do with acceptance. However, the reason of this section does extend to requiring the beneficiary to notify the seller that an injury has occurred. What is said above, with regard to the extended time for reasonable notification from the lay consumer after the injury is also applicable here; but even a beneficiary can be properly held to the use of good faith in notifying, once he has had time to become aware of the legal situation.

6. Subsection (4) unambiguously places the burden of proof to establish breach on the buyer after acceptance. However, this rule becomes one purely of procedure when the tender accepted was non-conforming and the buyer has given the seller notice of breach under subsection (3). For subsection (2) makes it clear that acceptance leaves unimpaired the buyer's right to be made whole, and that right can be exercised by the buyer not only by way of cross-claim for damages, but also by way of recoupment in diminution or extinction of the price.

7. Subsections (3)(b) and (5)(b) give a warrantor against infringement an opportunity to defend or compromise third-party claims or be relieved of his liability. Subsection (5)(a) codifies for all warranties the practice of voucher to defend. Compare Section 3–803. Subsection (6) makes these provisions applicable to the buyer's liability for infringement under Section 2–312.

8. All of the provisions of the present section are subject to any explicit reservation of rights.

Cross References:

Point 1: Section 1–201.
Point 2: Section 2–608.
Point 4: Sections 1–204 and 2–605.
Point 5: Section 2–318.
Point 6: Section 2–717.
Point 7: Sections 2–312 and 3–803.
Point 8: Section 1–207.

Definitional Cross References:

"Burden of establishing". Section 1–201.
"Buyer". Section 2–103.
"Conform". Section 2–106.
"Contract". Section 1–201.
"Goods". Section 2–105.
"Notifies". Section 1–201.
"Reasonable time". Section 1–204.
"Remedy". Section 1–201.
"Seasonably". Section 1–204.

Cross References

Burden of proof, see Evidence Code § 500 et seq.
Cross-complaint, relief against additional persons, see Code of Civil Procedure § 428.10 et seq.
Damages, recovery after notification of breach, see Commercial Code § 2714.
Definitions, see Commercial Code §§ 1201, 2103, 2104, 2105, 2106.
Goods as "conforming" to contract, see Commercial Code § 2106.
Infringement and like claims of third person, buyer's obligation, see Commercial Code § 2312.
Notice to third parties, see Commercial Code § 3119.
Reasonable time, see Commercial Code § 1204.
Recoupment of damages, see Commercial Code § 2717.
Rescission of contracts, see Civil Code § 1688 et seq.
Reservation of rights, performance or acceptance, see Commercial Code § 1207.
Seasonably, see Commercial Code § 1204.
Seller's remedies, see Commercial Code § 2702 et seq.

§ 2607 SALES 102

Statement of objections, see Commercial Code § 2605.
Warranties, third party beneficiaries, see Commercial Code § 2318.

§ 2608. Revocation of Acceptance in Whole or in Part

(1) The buyer may revoke his acceptance of a lot or commercial unit whose nonconformity substantially impairs its value to him if he has accepted it

(a) On the reasonable assumption that its nonconformity would be cured and it has not been seasonably cured; or

(b) Without discovery of such nonconformity if his acceptance was reasonably induced either by the difficulty of discovery before acceptance or by the seller's assurances.

(2) Revocation of acceptance must occur within a reasonable time after the buyer discovers or should have discovered the ground for it and before any substantial change in condition of the goods which is not caused by their own defects. It is not effective until the buyer notifies the seller of it.

(3) A buyer who so revokes has the same rights and duties with regard to the goods involved as if he had rejected them *(Stats.1963, c. 819, § 2608).*

California Code Comment

By John A. Bohn and Charles J. Williams

Prior California Law

1. This section introduces as a remedy "revocation of acceptance". This replaces the remedy of "rescission" under former Civil Code § 1789(1)(d) as a buyer's remedy for breach of warranty under the USA. Official Comment 1.

2. Subdivision (1) changes prior California law. Although revocation of acceptances by the buyer now requires that there be a substantial impairment of value, substantial impairment of value was not a prerequisite to rescission under former Civil Code § 1789(1)(d). However, see Nye & Nisson v. Weed Lbr. Co., 92 Cal.App. 598, 607, 268 Pac. 659, 663 (1928) ("To permit the cancellation of a contract for 750 cases of processed eggs merely because a minimum number thereof arrived at their destination unfit for use would violate the spirit of the legal maximum de minimis non curat lex.").

3. Subdivision (1)(a) has no counterpart in prior California law.

4. Subdivision (1)(b) modifies prior California law which held that a buyer was deemed to have waived any defects in goods by accepting and using them if he had a reasonable opportunity to inspect them. American Steel Pipe & Tank Company v. Hubbard, 42 Cal.App. 520, 183 Pac. 830 (1919). Subdivision (1)(b) adds that despite acceptance of goods and a reasonable opportunity to inspect them, the buyer may revoke that acceptance if it was induced by difficulty of discovery of the nonconformity on the seller's assurances.

5. Subdivision (2) is similar to former Civil Code § 1789(3) (dealing with the buyer's conduct when he seeks rescission) in that both require the revocation of acceptance or rescission to be done within a reasonable time and before a change in the goods other than that caused by their nonconformity. Subdivision (2) differs in that the buyer need only give notice whereas under former Civil Code § 1789(3) to rescind the buyer was required "to return or to offer to return the goods to the seller."

Changes from U.C.C. (1962 Official Text).

6. This is section 2–608 of the Official Text without change.

Uniform Commercial Code Comment

Prior Uniform Statutory Provision:

Section 69(1)(d), (3), (4) and (5), Uniform Sales Act.
Changes: Rewritten.

Purposes of Changes: To make it clear that:

1. Although the prior basic policy is continued, the buyer is no longer required to elect between revocation of acceptance and recovery of damages for breach. Both are now available to him. The non-alternative character of the two remedies is stressed by the terms used in the present section. The section no longer speaks of "rescission," a term capable of ambiguous application either to transfer of title to the goods or to the contract of sale and susceptible also of confusion with cancellation for cause of an executed or executory portion of the contract. The remedy under this section is instead referred to simply as "revocation of acceptance" of goods tendered under a contract for sale and involves no suggestion of "election" of any sort.

2. Revocation of acceptance is possible only where the nonconformity substantially impairs the value of the goods to the buyer. For this purpose the test is not what the seller had reason to know at the time of contracting; the question is whether the non-conformity is such as will in fact cause a substantial impairment of value to the buyer though the seller had no advance knowledge as to the buyer's particular circumstances.

3. "Assurances" by the seller under paragraph (b) of subsection (1) can rest as well in the circumstances or in the contract as in explicit language used at the time of delivery. The reason for recognizing such assurances is that they induce the buyer to delay discovery. These are the only assurances involved in paragraph (b). Explicit assurances may be made either in good faith or bad faith. In either case any remedy accorded by this Article is available to the buyer under the section on remedies for fraud.

4. Subsection (2) requires notification of revocation of acceptance within a reasonable time after discovery of the grounds for such revocation. Since this remedy will be generally resorted to only after attempts at adjustment have failed, the reasonable time period should extend in most cases beyond the time in which notification of breach must be given, beyond the time for discovery of non-conformity after acceptance and beyond the time for rejection after tender. The parties may by their agreement limit the time for notification under this section, but the same sanctions and considerations apply to such agreements as are discussed in the comment on manner and effect of rightful rejection.

5. The content of the notice under subsection (2) is to be determined in this case as in others by considerations of good faith, prevention of surprise, and reasonable adjustment. More will generally be necessary than the mere notification of breach required under the preceding section. On the other hand the requirements of the section on waiver of buyer's objections do not apply here. The fact that quick notification of trouble is desirable affords good ground for being slow to bind a buyer by his first statement. Following the general policy of this Article, the requirements of the content of notification are less stringent in the case of a non-merchant buyer.

6. Under subsection (2) the prior policy is continued of seeking substantial justice in regard to the condition of goods restored to the seller. Thus the buyer may not revoke his acceptance if the goods have materially deteriorated except by reason of their own defects. Worthless goods, however, need not be offered back and minor defects in the articles reoffered are to be disregarded.

7. The policy of the section allowing partial acceptance is carried over into the present section and the buyer may revoke his acceptance, in appropriate cases, as to the entire lot or any commercial unit thereof.

Cross References:

Point 3: Section 2–721.
Point 4: Sections 1–204, 2–602 and 2–607.
Point 5: Sections 2–605 and 2–607.
Point 7: Section 2–601.

Definitional Cross References:

"Buyer". Section 2–103.
"Commercial unit". Section 2–105.
"Conform". Section 2–106.
"Goods". Section 2–105.
"Lot". Section 2–105.
"Notifies". Section 1–201.
"Reasonable time". Section 1–204.
"Rights". Section 1–201.

"Seasonably". Section 1–204.
"Seller". Section 2–103.

Cross References

Acceptance, whole or any commercial units, see Commercial Code § 2601.
Commercial unit, see Commercial Code § 2105.
Fraud, remedies, see Commercial Code § 2721.
Goods as "conforming" to contract, see Commercial Code § 2106.
Objections of buyer, waiver by failure to particularize, see Commercial Code § 2605.
Reasonable time,
  Generally, see Commercial Code § 1204.
  Rejection of goods, see Commercial Code § 2602.
Remedies of buyer for rightful revocation of acceptance, see Commercial Code § 2711.
Rescission of contracts, see Civil Code § 1688 et seq.

§ 2609. Right to Adequate Assurance of Performance

(1) A contract for sale imposes an obligation on each party that the other's expectation of receiving due performance will not be impaired. When reasonable grounds for insecurity arise with respect to the performance of either party the other may in writing demand adequate assurance of due performance and until he receives such assurance may if commercially reasonable suspend any performance for which he has not already received the agreed return.

(2) Between merchants the reasonableness of grounds for insecurity and the adequacy of any assurance offered shall be determined according to commercial standards.

(3) Acceptance of any improper delivery or payment does not prejudice the aggrieved party's right to demand adequate assurance of future performance.

(4) After receipt of a justified demand failure to provide within a reasonable time not exceeding 30 days such assurance of due performance as is adequate under the circumstances of the particular case is a repudiation of the contract. *(Stats.1963, c. 819, § 2609.)*

California Code Comment

By John A. Bohn and Charles J. Williams

Prior California Law

1. The first sentence of subdivision (1) is consistent with prior California law as expressed in Universal Sales Corp. v. California Press Mfg. Co., 20 Cal.2d 751, 771, 128 P.2d 665, 677 (1942):

"In every contract there is an implied covenant that neither party shall do anything which will have the effect of destroying or injuring the right of the other party to receive the fruits of the contract . . . ."

The remainder of subdivision (1) is without direct statutory counterpart in prior California law, although it is somewhat similar to former Civil Code § 1777 which gave the seller the right to resume possession of goods *in transit* if the buyer was or had been insolvent. Another similar remedy given to the buyer under the USA was former Civil Code § 1783(2) which provided that where the sales price was payable on a day certain the seller was authorized to refuse payment if the seller had "manifested an inability to perform the contract or the sale on his part or an intention not to perform it."

2. Subdivision (2) has no statutory counterpart in prior California law.

3. Subdivision (3) has no direct statutory counterpart in prior California law. However, under former Civil Code § 1765(2) in the case of a material breach of a part of an installment contract by the seller's defective delivery of one or more installments or the buyer's failure to pay or take delivery, the injured party could refuse to proceed further and sue for damages.

4. Subdivision (4) has no statutory counterpart in prior California law and changes the California case law under the USA. Under prior California law a refusal to perform was justification for repudiation of the contract by the party not in default. California Sugar & White Pine Agency v. Penoyar, 167 Cal. 274, 139 Pac. 671 (1914). However, under subdivision (4) failure to give assurance of performance within the time prescribed is a repudiation by the party in default.

5. A California State Bar committee on the Commercial Code had this to say about section 2609:

"Section 12609 [2609] would introduce a new remedy when the conduct or circumstances of one party make the other apprehensive as to whether he will receive the performance contracted for. Now, the conduct of one party which reasonably indicates there may be a default in performance does not give the other any remedy unless it amounts to an 'anticipatory breach' normally requiring a 'repudiation' of the contract, or unless the contract itself expressly covers this situation. [*Fn.:* There is a limited exception to this rule when the buyer is required by the contract to pay for the goods on a given date, regardless of whether title has passed. In such a situation, the buyer can refuse to pay the price if the seller has "manifested an inability to perform." Cal.Civ.Code, sec. 1783(2).] A party must determine at his peril whether a court will subsequently hold the other's conduct to have risen to the level of a 'repudiation,' and if willing to risk this determination, his only recourse is normally a complete termination of the contract.

"Section 12609 [2609] would afford a new remedy. When 'reasonable grounds for insecurity arise with respect to the performance of either party the other may in writing demand adequate assurance of due performance.' He may suspend his own performance until assurance is received. The failure to respond with adequate assurance of future performance within a reasonable time would then be treated as a repudiation. This new remedy should prove beneficial in these situations when one party is not certain whether the other has 'repudiated.' Since conduct by one party which may or may not be a repudiation will normally give the other reasonable grounds for feeling insecure, the other could demand adequate assurance of future performance and either get it or treat the failure to furnish it as a clear repudiation." California State Bar Committee on the Commercial Code, a Special Report. The Uniform Commercial Code, 37 Calif.State Bar J. 117, 148 to 149 (March–April, 1962).

Changes from U.C.C. (1962 Official Text).

6. This is section 2–609 of the Official Text without change.

Uniform Commercial Code Comment

Prior Uniform Statutory Provision:

See Sections 53, 54(1)(b), 55 and 63(2), Uniform Sales Act.

Purposes:

1. The section rests on the recognition of the fact that the essential purpose of a contract between commercial men is actual performance and they do not bargain merely for a promise, or for a promise plus the right to win a lawsuit and that a continuing sense of reliance and security that the promised performance will be forthcoming when due, is an important feature of the bargain. If either the willingness or the ability of a party to perform declines materially between the time of contracting and the time for performance, the other party is threatened with the loss of a substantial part of what he has bargained for. A seller needs protection not merely against having to deliver on credit to a shaky buyer, but also against having to procure and manufacture the goods, perhaps turning down other customers. Once he has been given reason to believe that the buyer's performance has become uncertain, it is an undue hardship to force him to continue his own performance. Similarly, a buyer who believes that the seller's deliveries have become uncertain cannot safely wait for the due date of performance when he has been buying to assure himself of materials for his current manufacturing or to replenish his stock of merchandise.

2. Three measures have been adopted to meet the needs of commercial men in such situations. First, the aggrieved party is permitted to suspend his own performance and any preparation therefor, with excuse for any resulting necessary delay, until the situation has been clarified. "Suspend performance" under this section

means to hold up performance pending the outcome of the demand, and includes also the holding up of any preparatory action. This is the same principle which governs the ancient law of stoppage and seller's lien, and also of excuse of a buyer from prepayment if the seller's actions manifest that he cannot or will not perform. (Original Act, Section 63(2).)

Secondly, the aggrieved party is given the right to require adequate assurance that the other party's performance will be duly forthcoming. This principle is reflected in the familiar clauses permitting the seller to curtail deliveries if the buyer's credit becomes impaired, which when held within the limits of reasonableness and good faith actually express no more than the fair business meaning of any commercial contract.

Third, and finally, this section provides the means by which the aggrieved party may treat the contract as broken if his reasonable grounds for insecurity are not cleared up within a reasonable time. This is the principle underlying the law of anticipatory breach, whether by way of defective part performance or by repudiation. The present section merges these three principles of law and commercial practice into a single theory of general application to all sales agreements looking to future performance.

3. Subsection (2) of the present section requires that "reasonable" grounds and "adequate" assurance as used in subsection (1) be defined by commercial rather than legal standards. The express reference to commercial standards carries no connotation that the obligation of good faith is not equally applicable here.

Under commercial standards and in accord with commercial practice, a ground for insecurity need not arise from or be directly related to the contract in question. The law as to "dependence" or "independence" of promises within a single contract does not control the application of the present section.

Thus a buyer who falls behind in "his account" with the seller, even though the items involved have to do with separate and legally distinct contracts, impairs the seller's expectation of due performance. Again, under the same test, a buyer who requires precision parts which he intends to use immediately upon delivery, may have reasonable grounds for insecurity if he discovers that his seller is making defective deliveries of such parts to other buyers with similar needs. Thus, too, in a situation such as arose in Jay Dreher Corporation v. Delco Appliance Corporation, 93 F.2d 275 (C.C.A.2, 1937), where a manufacturer gave a dealer an exclusive franchise for the sale of his product but on two or three occasions breached the exclusive dealing clause, although there was no default in orders, deliveries or payments under the separate sales contract between the parties, the aggrieved dealer would be entitled to suspend his performance of the contract for sale under the present section and to demand assurance that the exclusive dealing contract would be lived up to. There is no need for an explicit clause tying the exclusive franchise into the contract for the sale of goods since the situation itself ties the agreements together.

The nature of the sales contract enters also into the question of reasonableness. For example, a report from an apparently trustworthy source that the seller had shipped defective goods or was planning to ship them would normally give the buyer reasonable grounds for insecurity. But when the buyer has assumed the risk of payment before inspection of the goods, as in a sales contract on C.I.F. or similar cash against documents terms, that risk is not to be evaded by a demand for assurance. Therefore no ground for insecurity would exist under this section unless the report went to a ground which would excuse payment by the buyer.

4. What constitutes "adequate" assurance of due performance is subject to the same test of factual conditions. For example, where the buyer can make use of a defective delivery, a mere promise by a seller of good repute that he is giving the matter his attention and that the defect will not be repeated, is normally sufficient. Under the same circumstances, however, a similar statement by a known corner-cutter might well be considered insufficient without the posting of a guaranty or, if so demanded by the buyer, a speedy replacement of the delivery involved. By the same token where a delivery has defects, even though easily curable, which interfere with easy use by the buyer, no verbal assurance can be deemed adequate which is not accompanied by replacement, repair, money-allowance, or other commercially reasonable cure.

A fact situation such as arose in Corn Products Refining Co. v. Fasola, 94 N.J.L. 181, 109 A. 505 (1920) offers illustration both of reasonable grounds for insecurity and "adequate" assurance. In that case a contract for the sale of oils on 30 days' credit, 2% off for payment within 10 days, provided that credit was to be extended to the buyer only if his financial responsibility was satisfactory to the seller. The buyer had been in the habit of taking advantage of the discount but at the same time that he failed to make his customary 10 day payment, the seller heard rumors, in fact false, that the buyer's financial condition was shaky. Thereupon, the seller demanded cash before shipment or security satisfactory to him. The buyer sent a good credit report from his banker, expressed willingness to make payments when due on the 30 day terms and insisted on further deliveries under the contract. Under this Article the rumors, although false, were enough to make the buyer's financial condition "unsatisfactory" to the seller under the contract clause. Moreover, the buyer's practice of taking the cash discounts is enough, apart from the contract clause, to lay a commercial foundation for suspicion when the practice is suddenly stopped. These matters, however, go only to the justification of the seller's demand for security, or his "reasonable grounds for insecurity".

The adequacy of the assurance given is not measured as in the type of "satisfaction" situation affected with intangibles, such as in personal service cases, cases involving a third party's judgment as final, or cases in which the whole contract is dependent on one party's satisfaction, as in a sale on approval. Here, the seller must exercise good faith and observe commercial standards. This Article thus approves the statement of the court in James B. Berry's Sons Co. of Illinois v. Monark Gasoline & Oil Co., Inc., 32 F.2d 74 (C.C.A.8, 1929), that the seller's satisfaction under such a clause must be based upon reason and must not be arbitrary or capricious; and rejects the purely personal "good faith" test of the Corn Products Refining Co. case, which held that in the seller's sole judgment, if for *any* reason he was dissatisfied, he was entitled to revoke the credit. In the absence of the buyer's failure to take the 2% discount as was his custom, the banker's report given in that case would have been "adequate" assurance under this Act, regardless of the language of the "satisfaction" clause. However, the seller is reasonably entitled to feel insecure at a sudden expansion of the buyer's use of a credit term, and should be entitled either to security or to a satisfactory explanation.

The entire foregoing discussion as to adequacy of assurance by way of explanation is subject to qualification when repeated occasions for the application of this section arise. This Act recognizes that repeated delinquencies must be viewed as cumulative. On the other hand, commercial sense also requires that if repeated claims for assurance are made under this section, the basis for these claims must be increasingly obvious.

5. A failure to provide adequate assurance of performance and thereby to re-establish the security of expectation, results in a breach only "by repudiation" under subsection (4). Therefore, the possibility is continued of retraction of the repudiation under the section dealing with that problem, unless the aggrieved party has acted on the breach in some manner.

The thirty day limit on the time to provide assurance is laid down to free the question of reasonable time from uncertainty in later litigation.

6. Clauses seeking to give the protected party exceedingly wide powers to cancel or readjust the contract when ground for insecurity arises must be read against the fact that good faith is a part of the obligation of the contract and not subject to modification by agreement and includes, in the case of a merchant, the reasonable observance of commercial standards of fair dealing in the trade. Such clauses can thus be effective to enlarge the protection given by the present section to a certain extent, to fix the reasonable time within which requested assurance must be given, or to define adequacy of the assurance in any commercially reasonable fashion. But any clause seeking to set up arbitrary standards for action is ineffective under this Article. Acceleration clauses are treated similarly in the Articles on Commercial Paper and Secured Transactions.

Cross References:

Point 3: Section 1–203.
Point 5: Section 2–611.
Point 6: Sections 1–203 and 1–208 and Articles 3 and 9.

Definitional Cross References:

"Aggrieved party". Section 1–201.
"Between merchants". Section 2–104.
"Contract". Section 1–201.
"Contract for sale". Section 2–106.
"Party". Section 1–201.

"Reasonable time". Section 1–204.
"Rights". Section 1–201.
"Writing". Section 1–201.

Cross References

Acceleration clauses, see Commercial Code § 1208.
Causes excusing performance of contract, see Civil Code § 1511.
Commercial paper,
  Generally, see Commercial Code § 3101 et seq.
  Acceleration, see Commercial Code §§ 3108, 3304.
Contract requiring payment before inspection, see Commercial Code § 2512.
Delegation of performance and assignment of rights, see Commercial Code § 2210.
Documents of title, see Commercial Code § 7101 et seq.
General obligations of parties, see Commercial Code § 2301.
Good faith as contract obligation, see Commercial Code § 1203.
Good faith in performance of contracts, see Commercial Code § 1203.
Payment against tender of required documents, see Commercial Code §§ 2319, 2320.
Performance of conditional obligations excused, see Civil Code § 1440.
Reasonable time, see Commercial Code § 1204.
Repudiation, retraction of anticipatory repudiation, see Commercial Code § 2611.
Resale by seller, see Commercial Code § 2706.
Secured transactions, see Commercial Code § 9101 et seq.

§ 2610. Anticipatory Repudiation

When either party repudiates the contract with respect to a performance not yet due the loss of which will substantially impair the value of the contract to the other, the aggrieved party may

(a) For a commercially reasonable time await performance by the repudiating party; or

(b) Resort to any remedy for breach (Section 2703 or Section 2711), even though he has notified the repudiating party that he would await the latter's performance and has urged retraction; and

(c) In either case suspend his own performance or proceed in accordance with the provisions of this division on the seller's right to identify goods to the contract notwithstanding breach or to salvage unfinished goods (Section 2704). *(Stats.1963, c. 819, § 2610.)*

California Code Comment

By John A. Bohn and Charles J. Williams

Prior California Law

1. Paragraph (a) modifies prior California law by fixing the time the aggrieved party may wait for performance as "a commercially reasonable time" rather than the date of performance as prescribed by Civil Code § 1440. Under prior California law a declaration by a party of an intention not to be bound by the contract of sale gave the promisee the right to stand on the contract and wait until the time for performance or to act upon the declaration and treat it as a final assertion by the promisor that he was no longer bound by the contract, giving rise to a right to recover for breach of contract. Guerrieri v. Severini, 51 Cal.2d 12, 330 P.2d 635 (1958).

2. Paragraphs (b) and (c) are in accord with prior California law as expressed in Guerrieri v. Severini, 51 Cal.2d 12, 19, 330 P.2d 635, 639 (1958):

"'Manifestation by the injured party of a purpose to allow or to require performance by the promisor in spite of repudiation by him, does not nullify its effect as a breach, or prevent it from excusing performance of conditions and from discharging the duty to render a return performance.'"

Changes from U.C.C. (1962 Official Text).

3. This is section 2–610 of the Official Text without change.

Uniform Commercial Code Comment

Prior Uniform Statutory Provision:

See Sections 63(2) and 65, Uniform Sales Act.

Purposes: To make it clear that:

1. With the problem of insecurity taken care of by the preceding section and with provision being made in this Article as to the effect of a defective delivery under an installment contract, anticipatory repudiation centers upon an overt communication of intention or an action which renders performance impossible or demonstrates a clear determination not to continue with performance.

Under the present section when such a repudiation substantially impairs the value of the contract, the aggrieved party may at any time resort to his remedies for breach, or he may suspend his own performance while he negotiates with, or awaits performance by, the other party. But if he awaits performance beyond a commercially reasonable time he cannot recover resulting damages which he should have avoided.

2. It is not necessary for repudiation that performance be made literally and utterly impossible. Repudiation can result from action which reasonably indicates a rejection of the continuing obligation. And, a repudiation automatically results under the preceding section on insecurity when a party fails to provide adequate assurance of due future performance within thirty days after a justifiable demand therefor has been made. Under the language of this section, a demand by one or both parties for more than the contract calls for in the way of counter-performance is not in itself a repudiation nor does it invalidate a plain expression of desire for future performance. However, when under a fair reading it amounts to a statement of intention not to perform except on conditions which go beyond the contract, it becomes a repudiation.

3. The test chosen to justify an aggrieved party's action under this section is the same as that in the section on breach in installment contracts—namely the substantial value of the contract. The most useful test of substantial value is to determine whether material inconvenience or injustice will result if the aggrieved party is forced to wait and receive an ultimate tender minus the part or aspect repudiated.

4. After repudiation, the aggrieved party may immediately resort to any remedy he chooses provided he moves in good faith (see Section 1–203). Inaction and silence by the aggrieved party may leave the matter open but it cannot be regarded as misleading the repudiating party. Therefore the aggrieved party is left free to proceed at any time with his options under this section, unless he has taken some positive action which in good faith requires notification to the other party before the remedy is pursued.

Cross References:

Point 1: Sections 2–609 and 2–612.
Point 2: Section 2–609.
Point 3: Section 2–612.
Point 4: Section 1–203.

Definitional Cross References:

"Aggrieved party". Section 1–201.
"Contract". Section 1–201.
"Party". Section 1–201.
"Remedy". Section 1–201.

Cross References

Buyer's remedies, see Commercial Code § 2711.
Causes excusing performance of contract, see Civil Code § 1511.
Good faith, enforcement of contracts, see Commercial Code § 1203.
Installment contracts, defective delivery, see Commercial Code §§ 2612, 2616.
Letters of credit,
  Anticipatory repudiation, right of action for wrongful dishonor of, see Commercial Code § 5115.
  Application of remedies under this section for wrongful repudiation, see Commercial Code § 5115.
Performance of conditional obligations excused, see Civil Code § 1440.

§ 2610

Recovery of damages by seller for repudiation, see Commercial Code § 2708.
Rescission of contracts, see Civil Code § 1688 et seq.
Seller's remedies, see Commercial Code § 2703.
Seller's right to identify goods to contract notwithstanding breach, see Commercial Code § 2704.

§ 2611. Retraction of Anticipatory Repudiation

(1) Until the repudiating party's next performance is due he can retract his repudiation unless the aggrieved party has since the repudiation canceled or materially changed his position or otherwise indicated that he considers the repudiation final.

(2) Retraction may be by any method which clearly indicates to the aggrieved party that the repudiating party intends to perform, but must include any assurance justifiably demanded under the provisions of this division (Section 2609).

(3) Retraction reinstates the repudiating party's rights under the contract with due excuse and allowance to the aggrieved party for any delay occasioned by the repudiation. *(Stats.1963, c. 819, § 2611.)*

California Code Comment
By John A. Bohn and Charles J. Williams

Prior California Law

1. This section has no statutory counterpart in prior California law. However, subdivision (1) is in accord with section 320 of the Restatement of Contracts and Salot v. Wershow, 157 Cal.App.2d 352, 357, 320 P.2d 926, 930 (1958), which was quoted with approval in Guerrieri v. Severini, 51 Cal.2d 12, 19, 330 P.2d 635, 639 (1958): " 'among other requirements for application of the doctrine of breach by anticipatory repudiation are that the repudiatee treat the repudiation as a breach, and that there have [sic] been no retraction of the repudiation by the repudiator prior to the time for performance *or prior to a detrimental change in position on the part of the repudiatee in reliance thereon.* (See Rauer's Law & Collection Co. v. Harrell, 32 Cal.App. 45 [162 P. 125.]' (Emphasis added) (And see Abraham Lehr, Inc. v. Cortez, 57 Cal.App.2d 973, 978 [135 P.2d 684]; Big Boy Drilling Corp., Ltd. v. Etheridge, 44 Cal.App.2d 114, 117 [111 P.2d 953].)"

Changes from U.C.C. (1962 Official Text)

2. This is section 2–611 of the Official Text without change.

Uniform Commercial Code Comment

Prior Uniform Statutory Provision:
None.
Purposes: To make it clear that:

1. The repudiating party's right to reinstate the contract is entirely dependent upon the action taken by the aggrieved party. If the latter has cancelled the contract or materially changed his position at any time after the repudiation, there can be no retraction under this section.

2. Under subsection (2) an effective retraction must be accompanied by any assurances demanded under the section dealing with right to adequate assurance. A repudiation is of course sufficient to give reasonable ground for insecurity and to warrant a request for assurance as an essential condition of the retraction. However, after a timely and unambiguous expression of retraction, a reasonable time for the assurance to be worked out should be allowed by the aggrieved party before cancellation.

Cross Reference:
Point 2: Section 2–609.

Definitional Cross References:
"Aggrieved party". Section 1–201.

"Cancellation". Section 2–106.
"Contract". Section 1–201.
"Party". Section 1–201.
"Rights". Section 1–201.

Cross References
Assurance of performance, see Commercial Code § 2609.

§ 2612. "Installment Contract"; Breach

(1) An "installment contract" is one which requires or authorizes the delivery of goods in separate lots to be separately accepted, even though the contract contains a clause "each delivery is a separate contract" or its equivalent.

(2) The buyer may reject any installment which is nonconforming if the nonconformity substantially impairs the value of that installment and cannot be cured or if the nonconformity is a defect in the required documents; but if the nonconformity does not fall within subdivision (3) and the seller gives adequate assurance of its cure the buyer must accept that installment.

(3) Whenever nonconformity or default with respect to one or more installments substantially impairs the value of the whole contract there is a breach of the whole. But the aggrieved party reinstates the contract if he accepts a nonconforming installment without seasonably notifying of cancellation or if he brings an action with respect only to past installments or demands performance as to future installments. *(Stats.1963, c. 819, § 2612.)*

California Code Comment
By John A. Bohn and Charles J. Williams

Prior California Law

1. Subdivision (1) gives a broader definition of an installment contract than was given under the USA in former Civil Code § 1765(2) in which an installment contract was described as "a contract to sell goods to be delivered by stated installments, which are to be separately paid for . . .."

2. Subdivision (2) is without direct statutory counterpart in prior California law. Under former Civil Code § 1765(2) a breach of an installment contract that was severable and did not result in a material breach of the *entire contract* gave rise to "a claim for compensation" but did not authorize a rejection of the non-conforming installment. Although prior California law did not provide for rejection of an installment contract on grounds of a non-conforming installment under former Civil Code § 1789(1)(c) and (d) the buyer was authorized to rescind the contract or reject the goods where there had been a breach of warranty by the seller.

3. The first sentence of subdivision (3) is similar to the provision in former Civil Code § 1765(2) which provided that in cases where a breach of an installment contract was material, the non-defaulting party could refuse to proceed with the contract and sue for damages for breach of the entire contract.

The second sentence of subdivision (3) dealing with "reasonably notifying" of cancellation is similar to the requirement of prior California law regarding notice of breach as expressed in former Civil Code § 1769 which provided that acceptance does not bar action for damages unless the buyer fails to give notice of the breach to the seller "within a reasonable time after the buyer knows, or ought to know of such breach." For a discussion of the notice requirements of former Civil Code § 1769 see Reininger v. Eldon Mfg. Co., 114 Cal.App.2d 240, 250 P.2d 4 (1952). In that case the court quoted Judge Learned Hand to state that the primary purpose of the notice requirement of § 1769 is "to advise the seller that he must meet a claim for damages," and not for the purpose of allowing the seller to revoke the goods.

4. Both Commercial Code § 2612(1) and Civil Code § 1802.6 (Unruh Act) define installment contract. The Unruh Act (Civil Code §§ 1801 to 1812.9) is an important regulatory statute which deals with limited goods and services. It provides special definitions and requirements for retail installment payment contracts (defined in Civil Code § 1802.6). The Unruh Act imposes certain specific requirements in addition to but not in conflict with the Commercial Code. It applies to the sale of certain goods and services whereas the Commercial Code applies only to goods in general. The main regulatory provisions of the Unruh Act cover (1) the terms of the retail installment contract, (2) amount of service charges, (3) payment by buyer, (4) effect of assignment of the contract, (5) collection practice, (6) repossession and resale. (The only changes made by the Commercial Code on the Unruh Act is to substitute the term "security agreement" for the term "chattel mortgage" and "conditional sale contract.")

A subcommittee of the State Bar discussed the relationship between this section of the Commercial Code and Civil Code § 1802.6:

"Article [Chapter] 6 of Chapter [Division] 2 sets forth in detail the remedies of the parties with respect to breach, repudiation and excuse. This is a definite improvement over the Uniform Sales Act. In connection, however, with Section 12612(1) [2612(1)] there is a definition of the term 'installment contract.' The definition of installment contract could give rise to some difficulties in view of Section 1802.6 of the Civil Code (Unruh Act), which also defines an installment contract. The term as used in the Uniform Commercial Code relates to delivery in installments, whereas the term as used in the Unruh Act relates to installment payments. Consideration should therefore be given to the use of a definite term in the Unruh Act so as to preserve the uniformity of the Uniform Commercial Code." Sixth Progress Report to the Legislature by the Senate Fact Finding Committee on Judiciary (1959–1961), Part 1, The Uniform Commercial Code, p. 341.

The concern of the State bar with the possible difficulty between the Unruh Act and section 2612 of the Commercial Code seems unwarranted. Both the provisions of the Unruh Act and the Commercial Code apply to the sale of goods under a retail installment contract, but the applications and purposes of the two are different. The applications are different because an installment contract as defined in the Unruh Act is one which provides for repayment in installments while an installment contract under Commercial Code § 2612 is one which provides for delivery in installments. The purposes are different. The Unruh Act regulates the terms and performances of a retail installment contract. Commercial Code § 2612 describes the circumstances under which the buyer may reject a nonconforming installment delivery or claim breach of the contract. There is no conflict between the definitions of an installment contract under the Unruh Act and Commercial Code § 2612 because each of these definitions serve a different purpose. One would not apply so as to contradict the other.

It should also be noted that section 2612 of the Commercial Code provides for delivery in installments as did former Civil Code § 1765. No difficulty between section 1765 and the Unruh Act has been reported.

A similar possible conflict between the Unruh Act and the Commercial Code exists in connection with Division 9. This conflict is discussed and the Unruh Act is analyzed in the California Code Comments to section 9507.

Changes from U.C.C. (1962 Official Text)

5. This is section 2–612 of the Official Text without change.

Uniform Commercial Code Comment

Prior Uniform Statutory Provision:
Section 45(2), Uniform Sales Act.
Changes: Rewritten.
Purposes of Changes: To continue prior law but to make explicit the more mercantile interpretation of many of the rules involved, so that:

1. The definition of an installment contract is phrased more broadly in this Article so as to cover installment deliveries tacitly authorized by the circumstances or by the option of either party.

2. In regard to the apportionment of the price for separate payment this Article applies the more liberal test of what can be apportioned rather than the test of what is clearly apportioned by the agreement.

This Article also recognizes approximate calculation or apportionment of price subject to subsequent adjustment. A provision for separate payment for each lot delivered ordinarily means that the price is at least roughly calculable by units of quantity, but such a provision is not essential to an "installment contract." If separate acceptance of separate deliveries is contemplated, no generalized contrast between wholly "entire" and wholly "divisible" contracts has any standing under this Article.

3. This Article rejects any approach which gives clauses such as "each delivery is a separate contract" their legalistically literal effect. Such contracts nonetheless call for installment deliveries. Even where a clause speaks of "a separate contract for all purposes", a commercial reading of the language under the section on good faith and commercial standards requires that the singleness of the document and the negotiation, together with the sense of the situation, prevail over any uncommercial and legalistic interpretation.

4. One of the requirements for rejection under subsection (2) is non-conformity substantially impairing the value of the installment in question. However, an installment agreement may require accurate conformity in quality as a condition to the right to acceptance if the need for such conformity is made clear either by express provision or by the circumstances. In such a case the effect of the agreement is to define explicitly what amounts to substantial impairment of value impossible to cure. A clause requiring accurate compliance as a condition to the right to acceptance must, however, have some basis in reason, must avoid imposing hardship by surprise and is subject to waiver or to displacement by practical construction.

Substantial impairment of the value of an installment can turn not only on the quality of the goods but also on such factors as time, quantity, assortment, and the like. It must be judged in terms of the normal or specifically known purposes of the contract. The defect in required documents refers to such matters as the absence of insurance documents under a C.I.F. contract, falsity of a bill of lading, or one failing to show shipment within the contract period or to the contract destination. Even in such cases, however, the provisions on cure of tender apply if appropriate documents are readily procurable.

5. Under subsection (2) an installment delivery must be accepted if the non-conformity is curable and the seller gives adequate assurance of cure. Cure of non-conformity of an installment in the first instance can usually be afforded by an allowance against the price, or in the case of reasonable discrepancies in quantity either by a further delivery or a partial rejection. This Article requires reasonable action by a buyer in regard to discrepant delivery and good faith requires that the buyer make any reasonable minor outlay of time or money necessary to cure an overshipment by severing out an acceptable percentage thereof. The seller must take over a cure which involves any material burden; the buyer's obligation reaches only to cooperation. Adequate assurance for purposes of subsection (2) is measured by the same standards as under the section on right to adequate assurance of performance.

6. Subsection (3) is designed to further the continuance of the contract in the absence of an overt cancellation. The question arising when an action is brought as to a single installment only is resolved by making such action waive the right of cancellation. This involves merely a defect in one or more installments, as contrasted with the situation where there is a true repudiation within the section on anticipatory repudiation. Whether the non-conformity in any given installment justifies cancellation as to the future depends, not on whether such non-conformity indicates an intent or likelihood that the future deliveries will also be defective, but whether the non-conformity substantially impairs the value of the whole contract. If only the seller's security in regard to future installments is impaired, he has the right to demand adequate assurances of proper future performance but has not an immediate right to cancel the entire contract. It is clear under this Article, however, that defects in prior installments are cumulative in effect, so that acceptance does not wash out the defect "waived." Prior policy is continued, putting the rule as to buyer's default on the same footing as that in regard to seller's default.

7. Under the requirement of seasonable notification of cancellation under subsection (3) a buyer who accepts a non-conforming installment which substantially impairs the value of the entire contract should properly be permitted to withhold his decision as to whether or not to cancel pending a response from the seller as to his claim for cure or adjustment. Similarly, a seller may withhold a delivery pending payment for prior ones, at the same time delaying his decision as to cancellation. A reasonable time for notifying of cancellation, judged by

§ 2612

commercial standards under the section on good faith, extends of course to include the time covered by any reasonable negotiation in good faith. However, during this period the defaulting party is entitled, on request, to know whether the contract is still in effect, before he can be required to perform further.

Cross References:

Point 2: Sections 2–307 and 2–607.
Point 3: Section 1–203.
Point 5: Sections 2–208 and 2–609.
Point 6: Section 2–610.

Definitional Cross References:

"Action". Section 1–201.
"Aggrieved party". Section 1–201.
"Buyer". Section 2–103.
"Cancellation". Section 2–106.
"Conform". Section 2–106.
"Contract". Section 1–201.
"Lot". Section 2–105.
"Notifies". Section 1–201.
"Seasonably". Section 1–204.
"Seller". Section 2–103.

Cross References

Anticipatory repudiation, remedies of aggrieved party, see Commercial Code § 2610.
Assurance of performance, see Commercial Code § 2609.
Buyer's remedies, generally, see Commercial Code § 2711.
Course of performance, waiver or modification, see Commercial Code § 2208.
Good faith, performance or enforcement of contract, see Commercial Code § 1203.
Improper delivery, buyer's rights on, see Commercial Code § 2601.
Payment,
   Apportionment upon delivery in lots, see Commercial Code § 2307.
   Contract rate for goods accepted, see Commercial Code § 2607.
Retail installment sales, see Civil Code § 1801 et seq.
Seller's remedies generally, for breach, see Commercial Code § 2703.

§ 2613. Casualty to Identified Goods

Where the contract requires for its performance goods identified when the contract is made, and the goods suffer casualty without fault of either party before the risk of loss passes to the buyer, or in a proper case under a "no arrival, no sale" term (Section 2324) then

(a) If the loss is total the contract is avoided; and

(b) If the loss is partial or the goods have so deteriorated as no longer to conform to the contract the buyer may nevertheless demand inspection and at his option either treat the contract as avoided or accept the goods with due allowance from the contract price for the deterioration or the deficiency in quantity but without further right against the seller. *(Stats.1963, c. 819, § 2613.)*

California Code Comment

By John A. Bohn and Charles J. Williams

Prior California Law

1. Paragraph (a) is the counterpart of former Civil Code § 1727(1) and § 1728(1). Formerly an agreement to sell specific goods was void if the goods had wholly perished either at the time the agreement was made (former Civil Code § 1727(1)) or after the agreement is made but before risk of loss had passed to the buyer (former Civil Code § 1728(1)).

2. Paragraph (b) is the counterpart of former Civil Code § 1727(2) and § 1728(2). Where the goods were sold (1727(2)) or contracted to be sold (1728(2)) "perish[ed] or . . . so deteriorated in quality as to be substantially changed in character" the buyer was given an option to treat the contract as avoided or to accept the goods and pay the full price or the price for the accepted goods depending on whether or not the contract was divisible.

However, each of these former sections were limited in their application. Section 1727(2) applied only when destruction or deterioration occurred "without knowledge of the seller." Section 1728(2) applies only when destruction or deterioration occurred "without any fault of the seller or the buyer."

Under paragraph (b) of section 2613 if the buyer elects to stand on the contract he receives "due allowance from the contract price for the deterioration or deficiency in quality." This puts the emphasis on adjustment in business terms rather than upon the "divisibility" of the contract.

Changes from U.C.C. (1962 Official Text)

3. This is section 2–613 of the Official Text without change.

Uniform Commercial Code Comment

Prior Uniform Statutory Provision:

Sections 7 and 8, Uniform Sales Act.

Changes: Rewritten, the basic policy being continued but the test of a "divisible" or "indivisible" sale or contract being abandoned in favor of adjustment in business terms.

Purposes of Changes:

1. Where goods whose continued existence is presupposed by the agreement are destroyed without fault of either party, the buyer is relieved from his obligation but may at his option take the surviving goods at a fair adjustment. "Fault" is intended to include negligence and not merely wilful wrong. The buyer is expressly given the right to inspect the goods in order to determine whether he wishes to avoid the contract entirely or to take the goods with a price adjustment.

2. The section applies whether the goods were already destroyed at the time of contracting without the knowledge of either party or whether they are destroyed subsequently but before the risk of loss passes to the buyer. Where under the agreement, including of course usage of trade, the risk has passed to the buyer before the casualty, the section has no application. Beyond this, the essential question in determining whether the rules of this section are to be applied is whether the seller has or has not undertaken the responsibility for the continued existence of the goods in proper condition through the time of agreed or expected delivery.

3. The section on the term "no arrival, no sale" makes clear that delay in arrival, quite as much as physical change in the goods, gives the buyer the options set forth in this section.

Cross Reference:

Point 3: Section 2–324.

Definitional Cross References:

"Buyer". Section 2–103.
"Conform". Section 2–106.
"Contract". Section 1–201.
"Fault". Section 1–201.
"Goods". Section 2–105.
"Party". Section 1–201.
"Rights". Section 1–201.
"Seller". Section 2–103.

Cross References

Casualty insurance, see Insurance Code §§ 1850.4, 1853.8.
Goods as "conforming" to contract, see Commercial Code § 2106.
No arrival, no sale, see Commercial Code § 2324.

§ 2614. Substituted Performance

(1) Where without fault of either party the agreed berthing, loading, or unloading facilities fail or an

agreed type of carrier becomes unavailable or the agreed manner of delivery otherwise becomes commercially impracticable but a commercially reasonable substitute is available, such substitute performance must be tendered and accepted.

(2) If the agreed means or manner of payment fails because of domestic or foreign governmental regulation, the seller may withhold or stop delivery unless the buyer provides a means or manner of payment which is commercially a substantial equivalent. If delivery has already been taken, payment by the means or in the manner provided by the regulation discharges the buyer's obligation unless the regulation is discriminatory, oppressive or predatory. *(Stats.1963, c. 819, § 2614.)*

California Code Comment
By John A. Bohn and Charles J. Williams

Prior California Law

1. This section has no statutory counterpart in prior California law. However, subdivision (1) is in accord with prior case law.

In Western Industries Co. v. Mason Malt Whiskey Distilling Co., 56 Cal.App. 355, 205 Pac. 466 (1922) the parties had contemplated delivery by barges in conjunction with railroad tank cars. When it became impossible to use the barges for delivery, the seller sought to avoid the contract. The court, in holding that the seller is not excused because an all rail delivery was a feasible method of delivery, said "mere inconvenience or added expense did not excuse it [the seller] from failing to employ any reasonable method of transportation."

In Meyer v. Sullivan, 40 Cal.App. 723, 181 Pac. 847 (1919) the seller sought to be excused from performance for the reason that the contemplated steamship to be used for delivery was not available because of war conditions. The court held that the seller must still perform since other means of delivery were available. The court stated the rule that parties are not excused from performance of their contract where "conditions rendered the contemplated means of performance unavailable" if the parties were able to perform by other means.

Changes from U.C.C. (1962 Official Text)

2. This is section 2–614 of the Official Text without change.

Uniform Commercial Code Comment

Prior Uniform Statutory Provision:

None.

Purposes:

1. Subsection (1) requires the tender of a commercially reasonable substituted performance where agreed to facilities have failed or become commercially impracticable. Under this Article, in the absence of specific agreement, the normal or usual facilities enter into the agreement either through the circumstances, usage of trade or prior course of dealing.

This section appears between Section 2–613 on casualty to identified goods and the next section on excuse by failure of presupposed conditions, both of which deal with excuse and complete avoidance of the contract where the occurrence or non-occurrence of a contingency which was a basic assumption of the contract makes the expected performance impossible. The distinction between the present section and those sections lies in whether the failure or impossibility of performance arises in connection with an incidental matter or goes to the very heart of the agreement. The differing lines of solution are contrasted in a comparison of International Paper Co. v. Rockefeller, 161 App.Div. 180, 146 N.Y.S. 371 (1914) and Meyer v. Sullivan, 40 Cal.App. 723, 181 P. 847 (1919). In the former case a contract for the sale of spruce to be cut from a particular tract of land was involved. When a fire destroyed the trees growing on that tract the seller was held excused since performance was impossible. In the latter case the contract called for delivery of wheat "f.o.b. Kosmos Steamer at Seattle." The war led to cancellation of that line's sailing schedule after space had been duly engaged and the buyer was held entitled to demand substituted delivery at the warehouse on the line's loading dock. Under this Article, of course, the seller would also be entitled, had the market gone the other way, to make a substituted tender in that manner.

There must, however, be a true commercial impracticability to excuse the agreed to performance and justify a substituted performance. When this is the case a reasonable substituted performance tendered by either party should excuse him from strict compliance with contract terms which do not go to the essence of the agreement.

2. The substitution provided in this section as between buyer and seller does not carry over into the obligation of a financing agency under a letter of credit, since such an agency is entitled to performance which is plainly adequate on its face and without need to look into commercial evidence outside of the documents. See Article 5, especially Sections 5–102, 5–103, 5–109, 5–110, 5–114.

3. Under subsection (2) where the contract is still executory on both sides, the seller is permitted to withdraw unless the buyer can provide him with a commercially equivalent return despite the governmental regulation. Where, however, only the debt for the price remains, a larger leeway is permitted. The buyer may pay in the manner provided by the regulation even though this may not be commercially equivalent provided that the regulation is not "discriminatory, oppressive or predatory."

Cross Reference:

Point 2: Article 5.

Definitional Cross References:

"Buyer". Section 2–103.
"Fault". Section 1–201.
"Party". Section 1–201.
"Seller". Section 2–103.

Cross References

Causes excusing performance of contract, see Civil Code § 1511.
Letters of credit,
   Generally, see Commercial Code § 5101 et seq.
   Availability of credit in portions, see Commercial Code § 5110.
   Definition, see Commercial Code § 5103.
   Issuer's duties, see Commercial Code §§ 5109, 5114.

§ 2615. Excuse by Failure of Presupposed Conditions

Except so far as a seller may have assumed a greater obligation and subject to the preceding section on substituted performance:

(a) Delay in delivery or nondelivery in whole or in part by a seller who complies with paragraphs (b) and (c) is not a breach of his duty under a contract for sale if performance as agreed has been made impracticable by the occurrence of a contingency the nonoccurrence of which was a basic assumption on which the contract was made or by compliance in good faith with any applicable foreign or domestic governmental regulation or order whether or not it later proves to be invalid.

(b) Where the causes mentioned in paragraph (a) affect only a part of the seller's capacity to perform, he must allocate production and deliveries among his customers but may at his option include regular customers not then under contract as well as his own requirements for further manufacture. He may so allocate in any manner which is fair and reasonable.

(c) The seller must notify the buyer seasonably that there will be delay or nondelivery and, when allocation is required under paragraph (b), of the estimated quota

§ 2615

thus made available for the buyer. *(Stats.1963, c. 819, § 2615.)*

California Code Comment
By John A. Bohn and Charles J. Williams

Prior California Law

1. This section is new and has no statutory counterpart in prior California law. However, there are statutes which apply to the impossibility of performance of contracts in general, e.g. Civil Code § 1441 (impossible or unlawful conditions void), § 1598 (when contract wholly void) § 1599 (when contract partially void).

2. The use of the term "impracticable" in paragraph (a) in describing when performance is excused probably does not change the California law. Although the statutes speak in terms of impossibility, the courts have recognized that this logically extends much further. Christin v. Superior Court, 9 Cal.2d 526, 533, 71 P.2d 205, 208 (1937): "Modern cases recognize as a defense (in the enforcement of contract obligations) not only objective impossibility in the true sense, but also impracticability due to excessive and unreasonable difficulty or expense." Lloyd v. Murphy, 25 Cal.2d 48, 153 P.2d 47 (1944) in discussing the meaning of both impossibility of performance and the doctrine of frustration of purpose states that impossibility of performance "includes not only cases of physical impossibility but also cases of extreme impracticability of performance."

3. Paragraph (a) is similar to the rule of 2 Restatement, Contracts § 458 (1932).

4. Paragraph (b) embodies the principle of 2 Restatement, Contracts § 464 (1932).

Changes from U.C.C. (1962 Official Text)

5. This is section 2–615 of the Official Text without change.

Uniform Commercial Code Comment

Prior Uniform Statutory Provision:

None.

Purposes:

1. This section excuses a seller from timely delivery of goods contracted for, where his performance has become commercially impracticable because of unforeseen supervening circumstances not within the contemplation of the parties at the time of contracting. The destruction of specific goods and the problem of the use of substituted performance on points other than delay or quantity, treated elsewhere in this Article, must be distinguished from the matter covered by this section.

2. The present section deliberately refrains from any effort at an exhaustive expression of contingencies and is to be interpreted in all cases sought to be brought within its scope in terms of its underlying reason and purpose.

3. The first test for excuse under this Article in terms of basic assumption is a familiar one. The additional test of commercial impracticability (as contrasted with "impossibility," "frustration of performance" or "frustration of the venture") has been adopted in order to call attention to the commercial character of the criterion chosen by this Article.

4. Increased cost alone does not excuse performance unless the rise in cost is due to some unforeseen contingency which alters the essential nature of the performance. Neither is a rise or a collapse in the market in itself a justification, for that is exactly the type of business risk which business contracts made at fixed prices are intended to cover. But a severe shortage of raw materials or of supplies due to a contingency such as war, embargo, local crop failure, unforeseen shutdown of major sources of supply or the like, which either causes a marked increase in cost or altogether prevents the seller from securing supplies necessary to his performance, is within the contemplation of this section. (See Ford & Sons, Ltd., v. Henry Leetham & Sons, Ltd., 21 Com.Cas. 55 (1915, K.B.D.).)

5. Where a particular source of supply is exclusive under the agreement and fails through casualty, the present section applies rather than the provision on destruction or deterioration of specific goods. The same holds true where a particular source of supply is shown by the circumstances to have been contemplated or assumed by the parties at the time of contracting. (See Davis Co. v. Hoffmann-LaRoche Chemical Works, 178 App.Div. 855, 166 N.Y.S. 179 (1917) and International Paper Co. v. Rockefeller, 161 App.Div. 180, 146 N.Y.S. 371 (1914).) There is no excuse under this section, however, unless the seller has employed all due measures to assure himself that his source will not fail. (See Canadian Industrial Alcohol Co., Ltd., v. Dunbar Molasses Co., 258 N.Y. 194, 179 N.E. 383, 80 A.L.R. 1173 (1932) and Washington Mfg. Co. v. Midland Lumber Co., 113 Wash. 593, 194 P. 777 (1921).)

In the case of failure of production by an agreed source for causes beyond the seller's control, the seller should, if possible, be excused since production by an agreed source is without more a basic assumption of the contract. Such excuse should not result in relieving the defaulting supplier from liability nor in dropping into the seller's lap an unearned bonus of damages over. The flexible adjustment machinery of this Article provides the solution under the provision on the obligation of good faith. A condition to his making good the claim of excuse is the turning over to the buyer of his rights against the defaulting source of supply to the extent of the buyer's contract in relation to which excuse is being claimed.

6. In situations in which neither sense nor justice is served by either answer when the issue is posed in flat terms of "excuse" or "no excuse," adjustment under the various provisions of this Article is necessary, especially the sections on good faith, on insecurity and assurance and on the reading of all provisions in the light of their purposes, and the general policy of this Act to use equitable principles in furtherance of commercial standards and good faith.

7. The failure of conditions which go to convenience or collateral values rather than to the commercial practicability of the main performance does not amount to a complete excuse. However, good faith and the reason of the present section and of the preceding one may properly be held to justify and even to require any needed delay involved in a good faith inquiry seeking a readjustment of the contract terms to meet the new conditions.

8. The provisions of this section are made subject to assumption of greater liability by agreement and such agreement is to be found not only in the expressed terms of the contract but in the circumstances surrounding the contracting, in trade usage and the like. Thus the exemptions of this section do not apply when the contingency in question is sufficiently foreshadowed at the time of contracting to be included among the business risks which are fairly to be regarded as part of the dickered terms, either consciously or as a matter of reasonable, commercial interpretation from the circumstances. (See Madeirense Do Brasil, S.A. v. Stulman-Emrick Lumber Co., 147 F.2d 399 (C.C.A., 2 Cir., 1945).) The exemption otherwise present through usage of trade under the present section may also be expressly negated by the language of the agreement. Generally, express agreements as to exemptions designed to enlarge upon or supplant the provisions of this section are to be read in the light of mercantile sense and reason, for this section itself sets up the commercial standard for normal and reasonable interpretation and provides a minimum beyond which agreement may not go.

Agreement can also be made in regard to the consequences of exemption as laid down in paragraphs (b) and (c) and the next section on procedure on notice claiming excuse.

9. The case of a farmer who has contracted to sell crops to be grown on designated land may be regarded as falling either within the section on casualty to identified goods or this section, and he may be excused, when there is a failure of the specific crop, either on the basis of the destruction of identified goods or because of the failure of a basic assumption of the contract.

Exemption of the buyer in the case of a "requirements" contract is covered by the "Output and Requirements" section both as to assumption and allocation of the relevant risks. But when a contract by a manufacturer to buy fuel or raw material makes no specific reference to a particular venture and no such reference may be drawn from the circumstances, commercial understanding views it as a general deal in the general market and not conditioned on any assumption of the continuing operation of the buyer's plant. Even when notice is given by the buyer that the supplies are needed to fill a specific contract of a normal commercial kind, commercial understanding does not see such a supply contract as conditioned on the continuance of the buyer's further contract for outlet. On the other hand, where the buyer's contract is in reasonable commercial understanding conditioned on a definite and specific venture or assumption as, for instance, a war procurement subcontract known to be based on a prime contract which is subject to termination, or a supply contract for a particular construction venture, the reason of the present section may well apply and entitle the buyer to the exemption.

10. Following its basic policy of using commercial practicability as a test for excuse, this section recognizes as of equal significance either a foreign or domestic regulation and disregards any technical distinctions between "law," "regulation," "order" and the like. Nor does it make the present action of the seller depend upon the eventual judicial determination of the legality of the particular governmental action. The seller's good faith belief in the validity of the regulation is the test under this Article and the best evidence of his good faith is the general commercial acceptance of the regulation. However, governmental interference cannot excuse unless it truly "supervenes" in such a manner as to be beyond the seller's assumption of risk. And any action by the party claiming excuse which causes or colludes in inducing the governmental action preventing his performance would be in breach of good faith and would destroy his exemption.

11. An excused seller must fulfill his contract to the extent which the supervening contingency permits, and if the situation is such that his customers are generally affected he must take account of all in supplying one. Subsections (a) and (b), therefore, explicitly permit in any proration a fair and reasonable attention to the needs of regular customers who are probably relying on spot orders for supplies. Customers at different stages of the manufacturing process may be fairly treated by including the seller's manufacturing requirements. A fortiori, the seller may also take account of contracts later in date than the one in question. The fact that such spot orders may be closed at an advanced price causes no difficulty, since any allocation which exceeds normal past requirements will not be reasonable. However, good faith requires, when prices have advanced, that the seller exercise real care in making his allocations, and in case of doubt his contract customers should be favored and supplies prorated evenly among them regardless of price. Save for the extra care thus required by changes in the market, this section seeks to leave every reasonable business leeway to the seller.

Cross References:

Point 1: Sections 2–613 and 2–614.
Point 2: Section 1–102.
Point 5: Sections 1–203 and 2–613.
Point 6: Sections 1–102, 1–203 and 2–609.
Point 7: Section 2–614.
Point 8: Sections 1–201, 2–302 and 2–616.
Point 9: Sections 1–102, 2–306 and 2–613.

Definitional Cross References:

"Between merchants". Section 2–104.
"Buyer". Section 2–103.
"Contract". Section 1–201.
"Contract for sale". Section 2–106.
"Good faith". Section 1–201.
"Merchant". Section 2–104.
"Notifies". Section 1–201.
"Seasonably". Section 1–204.
"Seller". Section 2–103.

Cross References

Assurance of performance, see Commercial Code § 2609.
Casualty to identified goods, see Commercial Code § 2613.
Causes excusing performance of contract, see Commercial Code § 1511.
Construction of code, see Commercial Code § 1102.
Definitions, see Commercial Code §§ 1201, 2103, 2104, 2105, 2106.
Good faith, performance of contract, see Commercial Code § 1203.
Impossibility defined, see Civil Code § 1597.
Impossible or unlawful conditions, see Civil Code § 1441.
Object of contract, see Civil Code § 1595 et seq.
One of several objects of contract unlawful, see Civil Code § 1599.
Output and requirement provisions, see Commercial Code § 2306.
"Seasonably", time action taken, see Commercial Code § 1204.

Unlawful, impossible or unascertainable object, see Civil Code § 1598.

§ 2616. Procedure on Notice Claiming Excuse

(1) Where the buyer receives notification of a material or indefinite delay or an allocation justified under the preceding section he may by written notification to the seller as to any delivery concerned, and where the prospective deficiency substantially impairs the value of the whole contract under the provisions of this division relating to breach of installment contracts (Section 2612), then also as to the whole,

(a) Terminate and thereby discharge any unexecuted portion of the contract; or

(b) Modify the contract by agreeing to take his available quota in substitution.

(2) If after receipt of such notification from the seller the buyer fails so to modify the contract within a reasonable time not exceeding 30 days the contract lapses with respect to any deliveries affected.

(3) The provisions of this section may not be negated by agreement except insofar as the seller has assumed a greater obligation under the preceding section. *(Stats. 1963, c. 819, § 2616.)*

California Code Comment

By John A. Bohn and Charles J. Williams

Prior California Law

1. This section is without statutory counterpart in prior California Law.

Changes from U.C.C. (1962 Official Text)

2. This is section 2–616 of the Official Text without change.

Uniform Commercial Code Comment

Prior Uniform Statutory Provision:

None.

Purposes:

This section seeks to establish simple and workable machinery for providing certainty as to when a supervening and excusing contingency "excuses" the delay, "discharges" the contract, or may result in a waiver of the delay by the buyer. When the seller notifies, in accordance with the preceding section, claiming excuse, the buyer may acquiesce, in which case the contract is so modified. No consideration is necessary in a case of this kind to support such a modification. If the buyer does not elect so to modify the contract, he may terminate it and under subsection (2) his silence after receiving the seller's claim of excuse operates as such a termination. Subsection (3) denies effect to any contract clause made in advance of trouble which would require the buyer to stand ready to take delivery whenever the seller is excused from delivery by unforeseen circumstances.

Cross References:

Point 1: Sections 2–209 and 2–615.

Definitional Cross References:

"Buyer". Section 2–103.
"Contract". Section 1–201.
"Installment contract". Section 2–612.
"Notification". Section 1–201.
"Reasonable time". Section 1–204.
"Seller". Section 2–103.

§ 2616

"Termination". Section 2–106.
"Written". Section 1–201.

Cross References

Modification of contracts, see Civil Code § 1697 et seq.
Breach of installment contract, see Commercial Code § 2612.
Modification of contract, see Commercial Code § 2209.
Reasonable time, see Commercial Code § 1204.

CHAPTER 7. REMEDIES

Section
2701. Remedies for Breach of Collateral Contracts Not Impaired.
2702. Seller's Remedies on Discovery of Buyer's Insolvency.
2703. Seller's Remedies in General.
2704. Seller's Right to Identify Goods to the Contract Notwithstanding Breach or to Salvage Unfinished Goods.
2705. Seller's Stoppage of Delivery in Transit or Otherwise.
2706. Seller's Resale Including Contract for Resale.
2707. "Person in the Position of a Seller".
2708. Seller's Damages for Non-acceptance or Repudiation.
2709. Action for the Price.
2710. Seller's Incidental Damages.
2711. Buyer's Remedies in General; Buyer's Security Interest in Rejected Goods.
2712. "Cover"; Buyer's Procurement of Substitute Goods.
2713. Buyer's Damages for Non-Delivery or Repudiation.
2714. Buyer's Damages for Breach in Regard to Accepted Goods.
2715. Buyer's Incidental and Consequential Damages.
2716. Buyer's Right to Specific Performance or Replevin.
2717. Deduction of Damages From the Price.
2718. Liquidation or Limitation of Damages; Deposits.
2719. Contractual Modification or Limitation of Remedy.
2720. Effect of "Cancellation" or "Rescission" on Claims for Antecedent Breach.
2721. Remedies for Fraud.
2722. Who Can Sue Third Parties for Injury to Goods.
2723. Proof of Market Price: Time and Place.
2724. Admissibility of Market Quotations.
2725. Statute of Limitations in Contracts for Sale.

§ 2701. Remedies for Breach of Collateral Contracts Not Impaired

Remedies for breach of any obligation or promise collateral or ancillary to a contract for sale are not impaired by the provisions of this division. *(Stats.1963, c. 819, § 2701.)*

California Code Comment

By John A. Bohn and Charles J. Williams

Prior California Law

1. This section has no counterpart in the USA (former Civil Code §§ 1721 through 1800).

Changes from U.C.C. (1962 Official Text)

2. This is section 2–701 of the Official Text without change.

Uniform Commercial Code Comment

Prior Uniform Statutory Provision:

None.

Purposes:

Whether a claim for breach of an obligation collateral to the contract for sale requires separate trial to avoid confusion of issues is beyond the scope of this Article; but contractual arrangements which as a business matter enter vitally into the contract should be considered a part thereof in so far as cross-claims or defenses are concerned.

Definitional Cross References:

"Contract for sale". Section 2–106.
"Remedy". Section 1–201.

§ 2702. Seller's Remedies on Discovery of Buyer's Insolvency

(1) Where the seller discovers the buyer to be insolvent he may refuse delivery except for cash including payment for all goods theretofore delivered under the contract, and stop delivery under this division (Section 2705).

(2) Where the seller discovers that the buyer has received goods on credit while insolvent he may reclaim the goods upon demand made within 10 days after the receipt, but if misrepresentation of solvency has been made to the particular seller in writing within three months before delivery the 10-day limitation does not apply. Except as provided in this subdivision the seller may not base a right to reclaim goods on the buyer's fraudulent or innocent misrepresentation of solvency or of intent to pay.

(3) The seller's right to reclaim under subdivision (2) is subject to the rights of a buyer in ordinary course or other good faith purchaser under this division (Section 2403). Successful reclamation of goods excludes all other remedies with respect to them. *(Stats.1963, c. 819, § 2702.)*

California Code Comment

By John A. Bohn and Charles J. Williams

Prior California Law

1. Subdivision (1) is the counterpart of former Civil Code § 1774(c) which authorized the seller to retain possession of the goods "until payment or tender of the price" in cases where the buyer became insolvent. Former Civil Code § 1777 provided that the seller could stop goods which were in transit if the buyer became insolvent.

2. Subdivisions (2) and (3) relate to the situation where the buyer has received the goods and the seller discovers his insolvency. The USA only covered the situation where the buyer became insolvent while the goods were still in the seller's possession (former Civil Code § 1774(c)) or in transit (former Civil Code § 1777).

3. A California State Bar Committee made the following comments with regard to this section and its effect upon prior California law:

"At present, a seller who has delivered goods on credit to a buyer who thereafter becomes insolvent is a general creditor of the insolvent buyer. [*Fn.:* 4 Collier, op. cit. 1117–1120.] Sellers in this position often try to recover the goods by rescinding the sale contract. [*Fn.:* California Conserving Co. v. D'Avanzo, 62 F.2d 528 (2d Cir.1933); 4 Collier, op. cit. 70.41.] The usual basis for such action is the allegation that the buyer has misrepresented his solvency and his intention to pay. The courts have greatly assisted the seller by presuming that one who buys goods on credit when he manifestly cannot pay for them does not intend to do so. This presumption, along with the rule that a mere purchase of goods on credit is an 'implied representation' of the buyer's intention to pay, has often permitted a seller to reclaim goods from a bankrupt buyer. [*Fn.:* 4 Collier, op. cit. 1322–1323. "Knowledge of inability to pay when the purchase is made is equivalent to a purchase with intent not to pay and such purchase is constructively fraudulent. Good faith which rests only on ignorance due to wilful, reckless, or despairing failure to face the facts is, in proceedings of this nature, the legal equivalent of actual fraud and entitles the seller to reclaim his goods." Matter of Penn Table Co., 26 F.Supp. 887, 889 (S.D.W.Va.1939).] However, a seller's success now depends upon a particular court's assessment of intangible factual issues.

"Section 12702 [2702] would substitute an arbitrary rule of thumb. A seller could recover goods from an insolvent buyer only if the goods are demanded within ten days after the buyer receives them, or if a written misrepresentation of solvency has been made to the particular seller within three months before delivery. The seller's right to recover the goods if the insolvency occurs and demand is made within ten days would not depend upon any proof or 'implication' of fraud. Except for the seller's right to recover the goods within ten days or in the limited case of a written misrepresentation, the seller would have no right to reclaim the goods because of a buyer's misrepresentation of his solvency or his intent to pay, express or implied." California State Bar Committee on the Commercial Code, a Special Report, The Uniform Commercial Code, 37 Calif.State Bar J. 117, 151 to 152 (March–April, 1962).

4. Insolvency has been given two definitions under California law depending upon the nature of the circumstances and the purpose for which the term is used. It can mean an excess of liabilities over assets (Civil Code § 3439.02) or the inability to meet financial obligations as they mature in the ordinary course of business (Civil Code § 3450). Where there is not a controlling statutory definition, the idea of an inability to meet one's financial obligations as they mature in the ordinary course of business has been widely followed. See People v. Biscailuz, 95 Cal.App.2d 635, 213 P.2d 753 (1950).

Changes from U.C.C. (1962 Official Text)

5. The words "or lien creditor" are deleted from subdivision (3) after "good faith purchaser". See California Code Comment 10 to section 2403 in which "lien creditors" is also deleted.

Uniform Commercial Code Comment
1966 Amendment

Purposes of Changes and New Matter:

* * * * * *

3. Because the right of the seller to reclaim goods under this section constitutes preferential treatment as against the buyer's other creditors, subsection (3) provides that such reclamation bars all his other remedies as to the goods involved.

* * * * * *

Uniform Commercial Code Comment

Prior Uniform Statutory Provision:

Subsection (1)—Sections 53(1)(b), 54(1)(c) and 57, Uniform Sales Act; Subsection (2)—none; Subsection (3)—Section 76(3), Uniform Sales Act.

Changes: Rewritten, the protection given to a seller who has sold on credit and has delivered goods to the buyer immediately preceding his insolvency being extended.

Purposes of Changes and New Matter: To make it clear that:

1. The seller's right to withhold the goods or to stop delivery except for cash when he discovers the buyer's insolvency is made explicit in subsection (1) regardless of the passage of title, and the concept of stoppage has been extended to include goods in the possession of any bailee who has not yet attorned to the buyer.

2. Subsection (2) takes as its base line the proposition that any receipt of goods on credit by an insolvent buyer amounts to a tacit business misrepresentation of solvency and therefore is fraudulent as against the particular seller. This Article makes discovery of the buyer's insolvency and demand within a ten day period a condition of the right to reclaim goods on this ground. The ten day limitation period operates from the time of receipt of the goods.

An exception to this time limitation is made when a written misrepresentation of solvency has been made to the particular seller within three months prior to the delivery. To fall within the exception the statement of solvency must be in writing, addressed to the particular seller and dated within three months of the delivery.

3. Subsection (3) subjects the right of reclamation to certain rights of third parties "under this Article (Section 2–403)." The rights so given priority of course include the rights given to purchasers from the buyer by Section 2–403(1) and (2). They also include other rights arising under Article 2, such as the rights of lien creditors of the buyer under Section 2–326(3) on consignment sales. Moreover, since Section 2–403(4) incorporates by reference rights given to other purchasers and to lien creditors by Articles 6, 7 and 9, such rights have the same priority. "Lien creditor" here has the same meaning as in Section 9–301(3). Thus if a seller retains an unperfected security interest, subordinate under Section 9–301(1)(b) to the rights of a levying creditor of the buyer, his right of reclamation under this section is also subject to the creditor's rights. Purchasers or lien creditors may have other rights not arising under this Article; under Section 1–103 such rights may have priority by virtue of supplementary principles not displaced by this Section. See In re Kravitz, 278 F.2d 820 (3d Cir. 1960).

[Deletion of words "or lien creditor" in California, see California Code Comment, note 5.]

Because the right of the seller to reclaim goods under this section constitutes preferential treatment as against the buyer's other creditors, subsection (3) provides that such reclamation bars all his other remedies as to the goods involved.

Cross References:

Point 1: Sections 2–401 and 2–705.
Compare Section 2–502.

Definitional Cross References:

"Buyer". Section 2–103.
"Buyer in ordinary course of business". Section 1–201.
"Contract". Section 1–201.
"Good faith". Section 1–201.
"Goods". Section 2–105.
"Insolvent". Section 1–201.
"Person". Section 1–201.
"Purchaser". Section 1–201.
"Receipt" of goods. Section 2–103.
"Remedy". Section 1–201.
"Rights". Section 1–201.
"Seller". Section 2–103.
"Writing". Section 1–201.

Cross References

Fraudulent conveyances, insolvency, see Civil Code § 3439.02.
Liens in general, see Civil Code § 2872 et seq.; Code of Civil Procedure § 1180 et seq.
Passing of title, see Commercial Code § 2401.
Resale of goods by seller, see Commercial Code § 2706.
Seller's insolvency, buyer's right to goods, see Commercial Code § 2502.
Stoppage in transit, see Commercial Code § 2705.
Title and rights of holder of negotiable document of title notwithstanding stoppage of goods represented by document, see Commercial Code § 7502.

§ 2703. Seller's Remedies in General

Where the buyer wrongfully rejects or revokes acceptance of goods or fails to make a payment due on or before delivery or repudiates with respect to a part or the whole, then with respect to any goods directly affected and, if the breach is of the whole contract (Section 2612), then also with respect to the whole undelivered balance, the aggrieved seller may

(a) Withhold delivery of such goods;

(b) Stop delivery by any bailee as hereinafter provided (Section 2705);

(c) Proceed under the next section respecting goods still unidentified to the contract;

(d) Resell and recover damages as hereafter provided (Section 2706);

(e) Recover damages for nonacceptance (Section 2708) or in a proper case the price (Section 2709);

(f) Cancel. *(Stats.1963, c. 819, § 2703.)*

California Code Comment

By John A. Bohn and Charles J. Williams

Prior California Law

1. This section has no statutory counterpart in prior California law. While there were similar remedies under the USA the basic remedies available to the seller were an action for the contract price (former Civil Code § 1783) an action for damages (former Civil Code § 1784) or rescission (former Civil Code § 1785).

2. The Legislative Counsel in the California Annotations to the Proposed Uniform Commercial Code made the following observation on the difference between the Commercial Code and the Uniform Sales Act (former Civil Code §§ 1721–1800) in regard to the availability of remedies:

"The comments to U.C.C. suggest the section means that an election of remedies is not required (see Official Comment 1). In California, the usual remedies of an aggrieved seller are an action for the price, an action for damages, or rescission, but the seller under the theory of the Civil Code is forced to an election. These remedies under U.C.C. are given irrespective of the situs of title. Under the Civil Code the remedies differ depending on the situs of title. Compare Civil Code section 1783." Sixth Progress Report to the Legislature by the Senate Fact Finding Committee on the Judiciary (1959–1961), Part 1, p. 59.

Changes from U.C.C. (1962 Official Text)

3. This is section 2–703 of the Official Text without change.

Uniform Commercial Code Comment
1966 Amendment

Prior Uniform Statutory Provision:

* * *

See Section 53, Uniform Sales Act.

Uniform Commercial Code Comment

Prior Uniform Statutory Provision:

No comparable index section.

Purposes:

1. This section is an index section which gathers together in one convenient place all of the various remedies open to a seller for any breach by the buyer. This Article rejects any doctrine of election of remedy as a fundamental policy and thus the remedies are essentially cumulative in nature and include all of the available remedies for breach. Whether the pursuit of one remedy bars another depends entirely on the facts of the individual case.

2. The buyer's breach which occasions the use of the remedies under this section may involve only one lot or delivery of goods, or may involve all of the goods which are the subject matter of the particular contract. The right of the seller to pursue a remedy as to all the goods when the breach is as to only one or more lots is covered by the section on breach in installment contracts. The present section deals only with the remedies available after the goods involved in the breach have been determined by that section.

3. In addition to the typical case of refusal to pay or default in payment, the language in the preamble, "fails to make a payment due," is intended to cover the dishonor of a check on due presentment, or the non-acceptance of a draft, and the failure to furnish an agreed letter of credit.

4. It should also be noted that this Act requires its remedies to be liberally administered and provides that any right or obligation which it declares is enforceable by action unless a different effect is specifically prescribed (Section 1–106).

Cross References:

Point 2: Section 2–612.
Point 3: Section 2–325.
Point 4: Section 1–106.

Definitional Cross References:

"Aggrieved party". Section 1–201.
"Buyer". Section 2–103.
"Cancellation". Section 2–106.
"Contract". Section 1–201.
"Goods". Section 2–105.
"Remedy". Section 1–201.
"Seller". Section 2–103.

Cross References

Actions, enforcement of rights or obligations, see Commercial Code § 1106.
Anticipatory repudiation, remedy for breach, see Commercial Code § 2610.
Installment contracts, default as to whole contract, see Commercial Code § 2612.
Letter of credit, failure to furnish, see Commercial Code § 2325.
Person in position of seller, see Commercial Code § 2707.
Remedies, liberal administration, see Commercial Code § 1106.

§ 2704. Seller's Right to Identify Goods to the Contract Notwithstanding Breach or to Salvage Unfinished Goods

(1) An aggrieved seller under the preceding section may

(a) Identify to the contract conforming goods not already identified if at the time he learned of the breach they are in his possession or control;

(b) Treat as the subject of resale goods which have demonstrably been intended for the particular contract even though those goods are unfinished.

(2) Where the goods are unfinished an aggrieved seller may in the exercise of reasonable commercial judgment for the purposes of avoiding loss and of effective realization either complete the manufacture and wholly identify the goods to the contract or cease manufacture and resell for scrap or salvage value or proceed in any other reasonable manner. *(Stats.1963, c. 819, § 2704.)*

California Code Comment

By John A. Bohn and Charles J. Williams

Prior California Law

1. This section considerably broadens remedies previously available to the seller for breach by the buyer under former Civil Code § 1783 (action for the price) and § 1784 (action for damages for nonacceptance of the goods).

2. Subdivision (1)(a) has no statutory counterpart in prior California law. The USA did not provide for "identification" of the goods to the contract and if the goods had not been appropriated to the contract, a seller was limited to an action for the price under former Civil Code § 1783(3) or an action for damages for nonacceptance under former Civil Code § 1784(1). The concept of identification is explained in Commercial Code § 2501 and the California Code Comments to that section.

3. Subdivision (1)(b) has no statutory counterpart in prior California law.

4. Subdivision (2) is a substantial change in California law. Former Civil Code § 1784(4) provided that if the buyer gave notice of a breach while an expenditure for labor or material was still necessary by the

seller to fulfill under the contract, the buyer was liable for no greater damages than the seller would have suffered if he had done nothing more to carry out the contract after receiving notice of the buyer's breach.

Changes from U.C.C. (1962 Official Text)

5. This is section 2–704 of the Official Text without change.

Uniform Commercial Code Comment

Prior Uniform Statutory Provision:

Sections 63(3) and 64(4), Uniform Sales Act.

Changes: Rewritten, the seller's rights being broadened.

Purposes of Changes:

1. This section gives an aggrieved seller the right at the time of breach to identify to the contract any conforming finished goods, regardless of their resalability, and to use reasonable judgment as to completing unfinished goods. It thus makes the goods available for resale under the resale section, the seller's primary remedy, and in the special case in which resale is not practicable, allows the action for the price which would then be necessary to give the seller the value of his contract.

2. Under this Article the seller is given express power to complete manufacture or procurement of goods for the contract unless the exercise of reasonable commercial judgment as to the facts as they appear at the time he learns of the breach makes it clear that such action will result in a material increase in damages. The burden is on the buyer to show the commercially unreasonable nature of the seller's action in completing manufacture.

Cross References:

Sections 2–703 and 2–706.

Definitional Cross References:

"Aggrieved party". Section 1–201.
"Conforming". Section 2–106.
"Contract". Section 1–201.
"Goods". Section 2–105.
"Rights". Section 1–201.
"Seller". Section 2–103.

Cross References

Anticipatory repudiation, see Commercial Code § 2610.
Goods as "conforming" to contract, see Commercial Code § 2106.
Seller's remedies on discovery of buyer's insolvency, see Commercial Code § 2702.
Seller's resale, see Commercial Code § 2706.

§ 2705. Seller's Stoppage of Delivery in Transit or Otherwise

(1) The seller may stop delivery of goods in the possession of a carrier or other bailee when he discovers the buyer to be insolvent (Section 2702) and may stop delivery of carload, truckload, planeload or larger shipments of express or freight when the buyer repudiates or fails to make a payment due before delivery or if for any other reason the seller has a right to withhold or reclaim the goods.

(2) As against such buyer the seller may stop delivery until

(a) Receipt of the goods by the buyer; or

(b) Acknowledgment to the buyer by any bailee of the goods except a carrier that the bailee holds the goods for the buyer; or

(c) Such acknowledgment to the buyer by a carrier by reshipment or as warehouseman; or

(d) Negotiation to the buyer of any negotiable document of title covering the goods.

(3)(a) To stop delivery the seller must so notify as to enable the bailee by reasonable diligence to prevent delivery of the goods.

(b) After such notification the bailee must hold and deliver the goods according to the directions of the seller but the seller is liable to the bailee for any ensuing charges or damages.

(c) If a negotiable document of title has been issued for goods the bailee is not obliged to obey a notification to stop until surrender of the document.

(d) A carrier who has issued a nonnegotiable bill of lading is not obliged to obey a notification to stop received from a person other than the consignor. (Stats.1963, c. 819, § 2705.)

California Code Comment

By John A. Bohn and Charles J. Williams

Prior California Law

1. Subdivision (1) broadens the remedy to stop delivery by including as a cause for it the buyer's repudiation or any other reason giving the seller the right to withhold. Former Civil Code § 1777 authorized the seller to stop delivery only upon the buyer's insolvency.

2. Subdivision (2) is comparable to former Civil Code § 1777 and § 1778. Both provide when the seller's right to stop delivery terminates. Under subdivision (2) the right of the seller to stop delivery continues until one of the acts in paragraphs (a) to (d) occurs.

Former Civil Code § 1778 provided when the seller could stop delivery but spoke in different terms. Section 1777 first stated the general rule that upon the buyer's insolvency the seller could stop delivery of goods "in transit". Section 1778 defined when goods were and were not in transit. In so doing, section 1778 imposed some standards similar to those in subdivision (2) in determining when the right to stop was no longer available to the seller.

Subdivision (2)(a) is a rephrasing of former Civil Code § 1778(1)(a) which provided that goods are in transit "until the buyer, or his agent in that behalf, takes delivery of them".

Subdivision (2)(b) contains a provision on acknowledgment similar to that in former Civil Code § 1778(2)(b) except that in section 1778(2)(b) the carrier as well as any other bailee could effect acknowledgment and the section stated that "it is immaterial that a further destination for the goods may have been indicated by the buyer".

Subdivision (2)(c) and (d) have no similar counterparts in former Civil Code § 1778. However, subdivision (2)(d) is consistent with former Civil Code § 1779(2) which provided that if a negotiable document of title is issued the carrier or other bailee "shall not be obliged to deliver or justified in delivering the goods" until the document is surrendered.

3. The notice requirement of subdivision (3)(a) is similar to former Civil Code § 1779(1). The standard of notice is the same in each case: it must be given so that the bailee can by reasonable diligence prevent delivery.

4. Subdivision (3)(b) makes the seller liable to the bailee for "ensuing charges or damages" when the seller notifies the bailee to stop delivery to the buyer. This liability is broader than that provided under former Civil Code § 1779(2) which made the seller liable to the bailee for the bailee's expenses in redelivering the goods to the seller.

5. Subdivision (3)(c) continues the prior California rule expressed in the last sentence of former Civil Code § 1779(2) (if a negotiable document of title is issued, the carrier or bailee is not required to deliver the goods until the document is surrendered).

6. A California State Bar Committee made the following comments regarding section 2705 and its anticipated effect upon California law:

"A seller's right to stop delivery upon discovery of a buyer's insolvency was recognized at common law and under the Sales Act. [*Fn.:* Cal.Civ.Code, sec. 1777]. This right now extends (under Uniform

§ 2705

Sales Act) only to goods in the possession of a carrier, and it is limited to one circumstance: the buyer's insolvency. A seller cannot now for example stop the delivery of goods upon learning of a buyer's breach or repudiation of the sales contract.

"Section 12705 [2705] would extend a seller's right to stop delivery. A seller could stop delivery of goods in the possession of a warehouseman as well as a carrier upon discovery of the buyer's insolvency. A seller could stop delivery when the buyer repudiates the contract or fails to make payment due before delivery, or if for any other reason the seller has a right to withhold or reclaim the goods. If a seller stops the goods in transit because of the buyer's insolvency, section 12705 [2705] would continue the rule that the right of stoppage in transit extends to less-than-carload lots. However, the new remedy of stoppage in transit based on breach of contract by the buyer is limited to carload shipments. This limitation partially accommodates those carriers who have objected to the present rule on the ground that it is difficult to stop less-than-carload shipments. The Code drafters did not feel the existing right to stop goods in transit upon a buyer's insolvency should be so curtailed. But where the right to stop goods in transit was extended, it was limited to carload shipments.

"Section 12707 [2707] would also give the right of stoppage in transit to a bank or other financing agency with a security interest in the goods shipped. It is now exercisable only by a seller." California State Bar Committee on the Commercial Code, a Special Report. The Uniform Commercial Code, 27 Calif.State Bar J. 117, 152 to 153 (March–April 1962).

7. The rights given to a seller under this section are also given to a "person in the position of a seller" by Civil Code § 2707.

Changes from U.C.C. (1962 Official Text)

8. This is section 2–705 of the Official Text without change.

Uniform Commercial Code Comment

Prior Uniform Statutory Provision:

Sections 57–59, Uniform Sales Act; see also Sections 12, 14 and 42, Uniform Bills of Lading Act and Sections 9, 11 and 49, Uniform Warehouse Receipts Act.

Changes: This section continues and develops the above sections of the Uniform Sales Act in the light of the other uniform statutory provisions noted.

Purposes: To make it clear that:

1. Subsection (1) applies the stoppage principle to other bailees as well as carriers.

It also expands the remedy to cover the situations, in addition to buyer's insolvency, specified in the subsection. But since stoppage is a burden in any case to carriers, and might be a very heavy burden to them if it covered all small shipments in all these situations, the right to stop for reasons other than insolvency is limited to carload, truckload, planeload or larger shipments. The seller shipping to a buyer of doubtful credit can protect himself by shipping C.O.D.

Where stoppage occurs for insecurity it is merely a suspension of performance, and if assurances are duly forthcoming from the buyer the seller is not entitled to resell or divert.

Improper stoppage is a breach by the seller if it effectively interferes with the buyer's right to due tender under the section on manner of tender of delivery. However, if the bailee obeys an unjustified order to stop he may also be liable to the buyer. The measure of his obligation is dependent on the provisions of the Documents of Title Article (Section 7–303). Subsection 3(b) therefore gives him a right of indemnity as against the seller in such a case.

2. "Receipt by the buyer" includes receipt by the buyer's designated representative, the sub-purchaser, when shipment is made direct to him and the buyer himself never receives the goods. It is entirely proper under this Article that the seller, by making such direct shipment to the sub-purchaser, be regarded as acquiescing in the latter's purchase and as thus barred from stoppage of the goods as against him.

As between the buyer and the seller, the latter's right to stop the goods at any time until they reach the place of final delivery is recognized by this section.

Under subsection (3)(c) and (d), the carrier is under no duty to recognize the stop order of a person who is a stranger to the carrier's contract. But the seller's right as against the buyer to stop delivery remains, whether or not the carrier is obligated to recognize the stop order. If the carrier does obey it, the buyer cannot complain merely because of that circumstance; and the seller becomes obligated under subsection (3)(b) to pay the carrier any ensuing damages or charges.

3. A diversion of a shipment is not a "reshipment" under subsection (2)(c) when it is merely an incident to the original contract of transportation. Nor is the procurement of "exchange bills" of lading which change only the name of the consignee to that of the buyer's local agent but do not alter the destination of a reshipment.

Acknowledgment by the carrier as a "warehouseman" within the meaning of this Article requires a contract of a truly different character from the original shipment, a contract not in extension of transit but as a warehouseman.

4. Subsection (3)(c) makes the bailee's obedience of a notification to stop conditional upon the surrender of any outstanding negotiable document.

5. Any charges or losses incurred by the carrier in following the seller's orders, whether or not he was obligated to do so, fall to the seller's charge.

6. After an effective stoppage under this section the seller's rights in the goods are the same as if he had never made a delivery.

Cross References:

Sections 2–702 and 2–703.
Point 1: Sections 2–503 and 2–609, and Article 7.
Point 2: Section 2–103 and Article 7.

Definitional Cross References:

"Buyer". Section 2–103.
"Contract for sale". Section 2–106.
"Document of title". Section 1–201.
"Goods". Section 2–105.
"Insolvent". Section 1–201.
"Notification". Section 1–201.
"Receipt" of goods. Section 2–103.
"Rights". Section 1–201.
"Seller". Section 2–103.

Cross References

Assurance of performance, see Commercial Code § 2609.
Bills of lading,
  Generally, see Commercial Code § 7301 et seq.
  Diversion of shipment, see Commercial Code § 7303.
Definitions, see Commercial Code §§ 1201, 2103, 2104, 2105, 2106.
Duty of carrier to comply with directions, see Civil Code § 2115.
"Person in position of seller", right of stoppage by, see Commercial Code § 2707.
Seller's remedies,
  Generally, see Commercial Code § 2703.
  Insolvency of buyer, see Commercial Code § 2702.
Tender of delivery, see Commercial Code § 2503.
Warehouseman or carrier, obligation to deliver, see Commercial Code § 7403.

§ 2706. Seller's Resale Including Contract for Resale

(1) Under the conditions stated in Section 2703 on seller's remedies, the seller may resell the goods concerned or the undelivered balance thereof. Where the resale is made in good faith and in a commercially reasonable manner the seller may recover the difference between the resale price and the contract price together with any incidental damages allowed under the provisions of this division (Section 2710), but less expenses saved in consequence of the buyer's breach.

(2) Except as otherwise provided in subdivision (3) or unless otherwise agreed resale may be at public or private sale including sale by way of one or more contracts to sell or of identification to an existing contract of the seller. Sale may be as a unit or in

parcels and at any time and place and on any terms but every aspect of the sale including the method, manner, time, place and terms must be commercially reasonable. The resale must be reasonably identified as referring to the broken contract, but it is not necessary that the goods be in existence or that any or all of them have been identified to the contract before the breach.

(3) Where the resale is at private sale the seller must give the buyer reasonable notification of his intention to resell.

(4) Where the resale is at public sale

(a) Only identified goods can be sold except where there is a recognized market for a public sale of futures in goods of the kind; and

(b) It must be made at a usual place or market for public sale if one is reasonably available and except in the case of goods which are perishable or threaten to decline in value speedily the seller must give the buyer reasonable notice of the time and place of the resale; and

(c) If the goods are not to be within the view of those attending the sale the notification of sale must state the place where the goods are located and provide for their reasonable inspection by prospective bidders; and

(d) The seller may buy.

(5) A purchaser who buys in good faith at a resale takes the goods free of any rights of the original buyer even though the seller fails to comply with one or more of the requirements of this section.

(6) The seller is not accountable to the buyer for any profit made on any resale. A person in the position of a seller (Section 2707) or a buyer who has rightfully rejected or justifiably revoked acceptance must account for any excess over the amount of his security interest, as hereinafter defined (subdivision (3) of Section 2711). (Stats.1963, c. 819, § 2706.)

California Code Comment

By John A. Bohn and Charles J. Williams

Prior California Law

1. Subdivision (1) broadens the right of the seller to resell the goods by allowing the exercise of this right upon the conditions stated in section 2703 (buyer's wrongful rejection, revocation of acceptance, failure to pay when due, or repudiation).

Under former Civil Code § 1780(1) the seller could resell the goods only if either (1) the goods were perishable or (2) the seller expressly reserved the right of resale or (3) the buyer was in default an unreasonable length of time.

Subdivision (1) requires the resale to be made "in good faith and in a commercially reasonable manner" while former Civil Code § 1780(5) required the seller to exercise "reasonable care and judgment in making a resale". The differences between these two standards of conduct will necessarily depend upon interpretation of the courts. Official Comment 2 states that the standard in section 2706(1) is intended to be more comprehensive.

2. The right of the seller to sell at public or private sale in former Civil Code § 1780(5) is continued by the first sentence of subdivision (2).

3. Subdivision (3) requires the seller to give the buyer notice of his intention to resell if the resale is at a private sale. However, notice of the time and place of the resale is not necessary. Former Civil Code § 1780(3) provided that notice of an intention to resell was not essential to the validity of a resale, but did provide that, where the resale was based upon the buyer's default in payment of the price for an unreasonable time, the giving of notice in that case would be relevant in determining whether the buyer had been in default for an unreasonable time. The policy behind the notice provision in former Civil Code § 1780(3) was not to require notice in every case but to encourage it. Under this provision the giving of notice by a seller would help a court find that payment had been in default for an unreasonable length of time.

4. Subdivision (4) provides certain requirements when the resale is at a public sale.

The provisions in the main are basically new to California law but are related to some of the provisions in former Civil Code § 1780. Among these requirements is the giving of reasonable notice of the time and place of the sale to the buyer. This changes the rule of former Civil Code § 1780(4) which provided that this notice was not essential to the validity of the sale. However, insofar as the rights of a bona fide purchaser at a resale are concerned, the results are the same because under subdivision (5), failure to give notice would not affect his title. See California Comment 5 below.

Former Civil Code § 1780(5) did not impose specific requirements regarding the manner of resale but only provided that in making a public or private sale the seller must exercise reasonable care and judgment.

5. Subdivision (5) broadens the protection given to the bona fide purchaser at a resale under former Civil Code § 1780(2).

6. The provision of subdivision (6) that a seller is not accountable for a profit upon resale was also in former Civil Code § 1780(1). The remainder of subdivision (6) has no statutory counterpart in prior California law.

7. A California State Bar Committee made the following comments regarding Commercial Code § 2706 and its anticipated effect upon California law:

"Section 12706 [2706] would allow a seller to resell goods when the buyer refuses to accept them, a seller's remedy comparable to the buyer's right to 'cover'. If the seller resells in good faith and in a commercially reasonable manner, he could recover from the buyer the difference between the resale price and the contract price, together with any incidental damages allowed, less expenses saved as a result of the buyer's breach. The seller would not be accountable to the buyer for any profit made on such a resale. Under the Sales Act some courts distinguish between the case where the title had passed and the seller resells to foreclose his vendor's lien, and the case where the title had not passed and the seller resells as the owner. [*Fn.:* Hawkland, Sales and Bulk Sales 150 Cal. 1958.] This distinction would be repudiated by the Code, and the difference between the resale price and the contract price could be recovered by the seller whether or not title to the goods has passed to the buyer." California State Bar Committee on the Commercial Code, A Special Report, The Uniform Commercial Code, 37 Calif.State Bar J. 117, 150 (March–April, 1962).

8. The rights given to a seller under this section are also given to a "person in the position of a seller" by Civil Code § 2707.

Changes from U.C.C. (1962 Official Text)

9. This is section 2–706 of the Official Text without change.

Uniform Commercial Code Comment

Prior Uniform Statutory Provision:

Section 60, Uniform Sales Act.

Changes: Rewritten.

Purposes of Changes: To simplify the prior statutory provision and to make it clear that:

1. The only condition precedent to the seller's right of resale under subsection (1) is a breach by the buyer within the section on the seller's remedies in general or insolvency. Other meticulous conditions and restrictions of the prior uniform statutory provision are disapproved by this Article and are replaced by standards of commercial reasonableness. Under this section the seller may resell the goods after any breach by the buyer. Thus, an anticipatory repudiation by the buyer gives rise to any of the seller's remedies for breach, and to the right of resale. This principle is supplemented by subsection (2) which authorizes a

resale of goods which are not in existence or were not identified to the contract before the breach.

2. In order to recover the damages prescribed in subsection (1) the seller must act "in good faith and in a commercially reasonable manner" in making the resale. This standard is intended to be more comprehensive than that of "reasonable care and judgment" established by the prior uniform statutory provision. Failure to act properly under this section deprives the seller of the measure of damages here provided and relegates him to that provided in Section 2–708.

Under this Article the seller resells by authority of law, in his own behalf, for his own benefit and for the purpose of fixing his damages. The theory of a seller's agency is thus rejected.

3. If the seller complies with the prescribed standard of duty in making the resale, he may recover from the buyer the damages provided for in subsection (1). Evidence of market or current prices at any particular time or place is relevant only on the question of whether the seller acted in a commercially reasonable manner in making the resale.

The distinction drawn by some courts between cases where the title had not passed to the buyer and the seller had resold as owner, and cases where the title had passed and the seller had resold by virtue of his lien on the goods, is rejected.

4. Subsection (2) frees the remedy of resale from legalistic restrictions and enables the seller to resell in accordance with reasonable commercial practices so as to realize as high a price as possible in the circumstances. By "public" sale is meant a sale by auction. A "private" sale may be effected by solicitation and negotiation conducted either directly or through a broker. In choosing between a public and private sale the character of the goods must be considered and relevant trade practices and usages must be observed.

5. Subsection (2) merely clarifies the common law rule that the time for resale is a reasonable time after the buyer's breach, by using the language "commercially reasonable." What is such a reasonable time depends upon the nature of the goods, the condition of the market and the other circumstances of the case; its length cannot be measured by any legal yardstick or divided into degrees. Where a seller contemplating resale receives a demand from the buyer for inspection under the section of preserving evidence of goods in dispute, the time for resale may be appropriately lengthened.

On the question of the place for resale, subsection (2) goes to the ultimate test, the commercial reasonableness of the seller's choice as to the place for an advantageous resale. This Article rejects the theory that the seller is required to resell at the agreed place for delivery and that a resale elsewhere can be permitted only in exceptional cases.

6. The purpose of subsection (2) being to enable the seller to dispose of the goods to the best advantage, he is permitted in making the resale to depart from the terms and conditions of the original contract for sale to any extent "commercially reasonable" in the circumstances.

7. The provision of subsection (2) that the goods need not be in existence to be resold applies when the buyer is guilty of anticipatory repudiation of a contract for future goods, before the goods or some of them have come into existence. In such a case the seller may exercise the right of resale and fix his damages by "one or more contracts to sell" the quantity of conforming future goods affected by the repudiation. The companion provision of subsection (2) that resale may be made although the goods were not identified to the contract prior to the buyer's breach, likewise contemplates an anticipatory repudiation by the buyer but occurring after the goods are in existence. If the goods so identified conform to the contract, their resale will fix the seller's damages quite as satisfactorily as if they had been identified before the breach.

8. Where the resale is to be by private sale, subsection (3) requires that reasonable notification of the seller's intention to resell must be given to the buyer. The length of notification of a private sale depends upon the urgency of the matter. Notification of the time and place of this type of sale is not required.

Subsection (4)(b) requires that the seller give the buyer reasonable notice of the time and place of a public resale so that he may have an opportunity to bid or to secure the attendance of other bidders. An exception is made in the case of goods "which are perishable or threaten to decline speedily in value."

9. Since there would be no reasonable prospect of competitive bidding elsewhere, subsection (4) requires that a public resale "must be made at a usual place or market for public sale if one is reasonably available;" i.e., a place or market which prospective bidders may reasonably be expected to attend. Such a market may still be "reasonably available" under this subsection, though at a considerable distance from the place where the goods are located. In such a case the expense of transporting the goods for resale is recoverable from the buyer as part of the seller's incidental damages under subsection (1). However, the question of availability is one of commercial reasonableness in the circumstances and if such "usual" place or market is not reasonably available, a duly advertised public resale may be held at another place if it is one which prospective bidders may reasonably be expected to attend, as distinguished from a place where there is no demand whatsoever for goods of the kind.

Paragraph (a) of subsection (4) qualifies the last sentence of subsection (2) with respect to resales of unidentified and future goods at public sale. If conforming goods are in existence the seller may identify them to the contract after the buyer's breach and then resell them at public sale. If the goods have not been identified, however, he may resell them at public sale only as "future" goods and only where there is a recognized market for public sale of futures in goods of the kind.

The provisions of paragraph (c) of subsection 4 are intended to permit intelligent bidding.

The provision of paragraph (d) of subsection (4) permitting the seller to bid and, of course, to become the purchaser, benefits the original buyer by tending to increase the resale price and thus decreasing the damages he will have to pay.

10. This Article departs in subsection (5) from the prior uniform statutory provision in permitting a good faith purchaser at resale to take a good title as against the buyer even though the seller fails to comply with the requirements of this section.

11. Under subsection (6), the seller retains profit, if any, without distinction based on whether or not he had a lien since this Article divorces the question of passage of title to the buyer from the seller's right of resale or the consequences of its exercise. On the other hand, where "a person in the position of a seller" or a buyer acting under the section on buyer's remedies, exercises his right of resale under the present section he does so only for the limited purpose of obtaining cash for his "security interest" in the goods. Once that purpose has been accomplished any excess in the resale price belongs to the seller to whom an accounting must be made as provided in the last sentence of subsection (6).

Cross References:

Point 1: Sections 2–610, 2–702 and 2–703.
Point 2: Section 1–201.
Point 3: Sections 2–708 and 2–710.
Point 4: Section 2–328.
Point 8: Section 2–104.
Point 9: Section 2–710.
Point 11: Sections 2–401, 2–707 and 2–711(3).

Definitional Cross References:

"Buyer". Section 2–103.
"Contract". Section 1–201.
"Contract for sale". Section 2–106.
"Good faith". Section 2–103.
"Goods". Section 2–105.
"Merchant". Section 2–104.
"Notification". Section 1–201.
"Person in position of seller". Section 2–707.
"Purchase". Section 1–201.
"Rights". Section 1–201.
"Sale". Section 2–106.
"Security interest". Section 1–201.
"Seller". Section 2–103.

Cross References

Action for price of goods identified to contract on inability of seller to resell, see Commercial Code § 2709.
Anticipatory repudiation, see Commercial Code § 2610.
Auctioneer's authority, see Civil Code §§ 2362, 2363.
Buyer's right of resale, see Commercial Code § 2711.

Damages,
Incidental damages to seller, see Commercial Code § 2710.
Non-acceptance or repudiation by buyer, see Commercial Code § 2708.
Definitions, see Commercial Code §§ 1201, 2103, 2104, 2105, 2106.
Liquidation or limitation of damages, see Commercial Code § 2718.
Passing of title, see Commercial Code § 2401.
"Person in position of seller", resale by, see Commercial Code § 2707.
Preserving evidence of goods in dispute, see Commercial Code § 2515.
Remedies of buyer, see Commercial Code § 2711.
Sale by auction, see Commercial Code § 2328.
Seller's remedies,
Generally, see Commercial Code § 2703.
Insolvency of buyer, see Commercial Code § 2702.

§ 2707. "Person in the Position of a Seller"

(1) A "person in the position of a seller" includes as against a principal an agent who has paid or become responsible for the price of goods on behalf of his principal or anyone who otherwise holds a security interest or other right in goods similar to that of a seller.

(2) A person in the position of a seller may as provided in this division withhold or stop delivery (Section 2705) and resell (Section 2706) and recover incidental damages (Section 2710). *(Stats.1963, c. 819, § 2707.)*

California Code Comment

By John A. Bohn and Charles J. Williams

Prior California Law

1. Subdivision (1) is the counterpart of former Civil Code § 1772(2). It has been rewritten with no significant changes except perhaps to clarify by defining with greater detail to include a person with a security interest or other right in the goods similar to that of a seller.

2. The Legislative Counsel has stated that "This section is similar to but somewhat broader than Civil Code Section 1772." Sixth Progress Report to the Legislature by the Senate Fact Finding Committee on Judiciary (1959–1961), Part 1, The Uniform Commercial Code, p. 60.

Changes from U.C.C. (1962 Official Text)

3. This is section 2–707 of the Official Text without change.

Uniform Commercial Code Comment

Prior Uniform Statutory Provision:

Section 52(2), Uniform Sales Act.

Changes: Rewritten.

Purposes of Changes: To make it clear that:

In addition to following in general the prior uniform statutory provision, the case of a financing agency which has acquired documents by honoring a letter of credit for the buyer or by discounting a draft for the seller has been included in the term "a person in the position of a seller."

Cross Reference:

Article 5, Section 2–506

Definitional Cross References:

"Consignee". Section 7–102.
"Consignor". Section 7–102.
"Goods". Section 2–105.
"Security interest". Section 1–201.
"Seller". Section 2–103.

Cross References

Agency, see Civil Code § 2295 et seq.
Factors, see Civil Code § 2026 et seq.
Financing agencies, rights, see Commercial Code § 2506.
"Financing agency", definition with respect to this section, see Commercial Code § 2104.
Letters of credit,
Generally, see Commercial Code § 5101 et seq.
Remedy for dishonor or repudiation, see Commercial Code § 5115.
Person entitled to honor of draft as person in position of seller, see Commercial Code § 5115.

§ 2708. Seller's Damages for Non-acceptance or Repudiation

(1) Subject to subdivision (2) and to the provisions of this division with respect to proof of market price (Section 2723), the measure of damages for nonacceptance or repudiation by the buyer is the difference between the market price at the time and place for tender and the unpaid contract price together with any incidental damages provided in this division (Section 2710), but less expenses saved in consequence of the buyer's breach. *Lost Volume Seller*

(2) If the measure of damages provided in subdivision (1) is inadequate to put the seller in as good a position as performance would have done then the measure of damages is the profit (including reasonable overhead) which the seller would have made from full performance by the buyer, together with any incidental damages provided in this division (Section 2710), due allowance for costs reasonably incurred and due credit for payments or proceeds of resale. *(Stats.1963, c. 819, § 2708.)*

California Code Comment

By John A. Bohn and Charles J. Williams

Prior California Law

1. Subdivision (1) is the counterpart of former Civil Code § 1784(3). Both use the current market price of the goods as the standard for fixing damages for non-acceptance.

2. Where the goods had a fixed price, the measure of damages (difference between contract price and market price) under former Civil Code § 1784 did not give the seller adequate protection. Although the seller could recover prospective damages, the courts refused to award uncertain and speculative damages. Phillips v. Mathews, 90 Cal.App.2d 161, 202 P.2d 798 (1949); Los Angeles Coin-O-Matic Laundries v. Harow, 195 Cal.App.2d 324, 15 Cal.Rptr. 693 (1961).

Subdivision (2) changes this measure of damages when it is inadequate and substitutes the measure of the seller's expected profit.

3. A measure of damages can be based upon a theory of restitution (putting the parties in the position they were in before the contract was made), reliance (putting the innocent party in a position as if he had not relied on the breaching party's performance), and expectation (putting the innocent party in as good a position as if the breaching party had performed).

The theory behind both measures in this section is to allow the seller to recover an amount equal to the expected performance of the buyer.

Changes from U.C.C. (1962 Official Text)

4. This is section 2–708 of the Official Text without change.

Uniform Commercial Code Comment

Prior Uniform Statutory Provision:

Section 64, Uniform Sales Act.

Changes: Rewritten.

Purposes of Changes: To make it clear that:

1. The prior uniform statutory provision is followed generally in setting the current market price at the time and place for tender as the standard by which damages for nonacceptance are to be determined.

§ 2708

The time and place of tender is determined by reference to the section on manner of tender of delivery, and to the sections on the effect of such terms as FOB, FAS, CIF, C & F, Ex Ship and No Arrival, No Sale.

In the event that there is no evidence available of the current market price at the time and place of tender, proof of a substitute market may be made under the section on determination and proof of market price. Furthermore, the section on the admissibility of market quotations is intended to ease materially the problem of providing competent evidence.

2. The provision of this section permitting recovery of expected profit including reasonable overhead where the standard measure of damages is inadequate, together with the new requirement that price actions may be sustained only where resale is impractical, are designed to eliminate the unfair and economically wasteful results arising under the older law when fixed price articles were involved. This section permits the recovery of lost profits in all appropriate cases, which would include all standard priced goods. The normal measure there would be list price less cost to the dealer or list price less manufacturing cost to the manufacturer. It is not necessary to a recovery of "profit" to show a history of earnings, especially if a new venture is involved.

3. In all cases the seller may recover incidental damages.

Cross References:

Point 1: Sections 2–319 through 2–324, 2–503, 2–723 and 2–724.
Point 2: Section 2–709.
Point 3: Section 2–710.

Definitional Cross References:

"Buyer". Section 2–103.
"Contract". Section 1–201.
"Seller". Section 2–103.

Cross References

Certainty of damages, see Civil Code § 3301.
Determination of damages based on market price, see Commercial Code § 2723.
Estimating damages, value to seller, see Civil Code § 3353.
Limitation of damages, see Civil Code § 3358.
Market price, measure and proof, see Commercial Code §§ 2723, 2724.
Measure of damages for breach of contract, see Civil Code § 3300.
Property of peculiar value, measure of damages, see Civil Code § 3355.
Reasonableness of damages, see Civil Code § 3359.
Tender of delivery,
  Generally, see Commercial Code § 2503.
  C.F., see Commercial Code §§ 2320, 2321, 2323.
  C.I.F., see Commercial Code §§ 2320, 2321, 2323.
  Ex-ship, see Commercial Code § 2322.
  F.A.S., see Commercial Code § 2319.
  F.O.B., see Commercial Code §§ 2319, 2323.
  No arrival, no sale, see Commercial Code § 2324.

§ 2709. Action for the Price

(1) When the buyer fails to pay the price as it becomes due the seller may recover, together with any incidental damages under the next section, the price

(a) Of goods accepted or of conforming goods lost or damaged within a commercially reasonable time after risk of their loss has passed to the buyer; and

(b) Of goods identified to the contract if the seller is unable after reasonable effort to resell them at a reasonable price or the circumstances reasonably indicate that such effort will be unavailing.

(2) Where the seller sues for the price he must hold for the buyer any goods which have been identified to the contract and are still in his control except that if resale becomes possible he may resell them at any time prior to the collection of the judgment. The net proceeds of any such resale must be credited to the buyer and payment of the judgment entitles him to any goods not resold.

(3) After the buyer has wrongfully rejected or revoked acceptance of the goods or has failed to make a payment due or has repudiated (Section 2610), a seller who is held not entitled to the price under this section shall nevertheless be awarded damages for nonacceptance under the preceding section. *(Stats.1963, c. 819, § 2709.)*

California Code Comment

By John A. Bohn and Charles J. Williams

Prior California Law

1. This section lists every case in which the seller has an action for the price. See Official Comment 6.

2. Subdivision (1) liberalizes the remedy formerly given to the seller. Under former Civil Code § 1783(1) the seller could maintain an action for the price *only if title had passed to the buyer* and the buyer had wrongfully refused or neglected to pay for the goods. Under subdivision (1) the passage of title is immaterial to the seller's right to bring an action for the price.

3. Under former Civil Code § 1783(3) the seller had an action for the price though the property in the goods remained in the seller if the goods could not "readily be resold for a reasonable price". For an example of when goods are not readily resalable see Biedebach v. Charles, 96 Cal.App.2d 250, 215 P.2d 114 (1950) in which the court held that there was no duty to resell certain cabinets not accepted by the buyer. The cabinets in this case were of a type which had no sale value on the open market, were made for a highly specialized purpose, and there was no proof that they even had any salvage value.

Subsection (1)(b) is the statutory counterpart of this USA provision but is more definite in that it requires the seller to make a reasonable effort to resell as a condition to maintaining an action for the price.

4. Subdivision (2) has no statutory counterpart in prior California law. It makes clear the seller's right to resell goods at any time before the collection of judgment. This prevents an action for the price being construed as an election of a remedy which would prevent the resale of goods. See also Official Comment 1 to Commercial Code § 2703.

5. Subdivision (3) has no statutory counterpart in prior California law. It makes certain that the seller may recover damages for nonacceptance (under section 2708) if he is not entitled to recover the purchase price. When the seller brings his action he should plead a separate cause of action for the price and for damages. (For propriety of such pleading see Crogan v. Metz, 47 Cal.2d 398, 303 P.2d 1029 (1956).)

Changes from U.C.C. (1962 Official Text)

6. This is section 2–709 of the Official Text without change.

Uniform Commercial Code Comment

Prior Uniform Statutory Provision:

Section 63, Uniform Sales Act

Changes: Rewritten, important commercially needed changes being incorporated.

Purposes of Changes: To make it clear that:

1. Neither the passing of title to the goods nor the appointment of a day certain for payment is now material to a price action.

2. The action for the price is now generally limited to those cases where resale of the goods is impracticable except where the buyer has accepted the goods or where they have been destroyed after risk of loss has passed to the buyer.

3. This section substitutes an objective test by action for the former "not readily resalable" standard. An action for the price under subsection (1)(b) can be sustained only after a "reasonable effort to resell" the goods "at reasonable price" has actually been made or where the circumstances "reasonably indicate" that such an effort will be unavailing.

4. If a buyer is in default not with respect to the price, but on an obligation to make an advance, the seller should recover not under this section for the price as such, but for the default in the collateral (though coincident) obligation to finance the seller. If the agreement between the parties contemplates that the buyer will acquire, on making the advance, a security interest in the goods, the buyer on making the advance has such an interest as soon as the seller has rights in the agreed collateral. See Section 9–204.

5. "Goods accepted" by the buyer under subsection (1)(a) include only goods as to which there has been no justified revocation of acceptance, for such a revocation means that there has been a default by the seller which bars his rights under this section. "Goods lost or damaged" are covered by the section on risk of loss. "Goods identified to the contract" under subsection (1)(b) are covered by the section on identification and the section on identification notwithstanding breach.

6. This section is intended to be exhaustive in its enumeration of cases where an action for the price lies.

7. If the action for the price fails, the seller may nonetheless have proved a case entitling him to damages for non-acceptance. In such a situation, subsection (3) permits recovery of those damages in the same action.

Cross References

Point 4: Section 1–106.
Point 5: Sections 2–501, 2–509, 2–510 and 2–704.
Point 7: Section 2–708.

Definitional Cross References:

"Action". Section 1–201.
"Buyer". Section 2–103.
"Conforming". Section 2–106.
"Contract". Section 1–201.
"Goods". Section 2–105.
"Seller". Section 2–103.

Cross References

Identification of goods, see Commercial Code §§ 2501, 2704.
Measure of damages for breach of contract, see Civil Code § 3300.
Price payable in money, goods, realty, or otherwise, see Commercial Code § 2304.
Remedies,
 Liberal administration, see Commercial Code § 1106.
Risk of loss, goods lost, see Commercial Code §§ 2509, 2510.
Security interest arising from agreement, see Commercial Code § 9203.
Seller's remedies, generally, see Commercial Code § 2703.

§ 2710. Seller's Incidental Damages

Incidental damages to an aggrieved seller include any commercially reasonable charges, expenses or commissions incurred in stopping delivery, in the transportation, care and custody of goods after the buyers' breach, in connection with return or resale of the goods or otherwise resulting from the breach. *(Stats.1963, c. 819, § 2710.)*

California Code Comment

By John A. Bohn and Charles J. Williams

Prior California Law

1. This section is generally in accord with prior California law as expressed in former Civil Code § 1784 (measure of damages in action for nonacceptance of goods) and § 1790 (provision for interest and special damages). However, the term "any commercially reasonable charges" is new.

Changes from U.C.C. (1962 Official Text)

2. This is section 2–710 of the Official Text without change.

Uniform Commercial Code Comment

Prior Uniform Statutory Provision:

See Sections 64 and 70, Uniform Sales Act.

Purposes: To authorize reimbursement of the seller for expenses reasonably incurred by him as a result of the buyer's breach. The section sets forth the principal normal and necessary additional elements of damage flowing from the breach but intends to allow all commercially reasonable expenditures made by the seller.

Definitional Cross References:

"Aggrieved party". Section 1–201.
"Buyer". Section 2–103.
"Goods". Section 2–105.
"Seller". Section 2–103.

Cross References

Incidental damages on wrongful dishonor of draft, see Commercial Code § 5115.
Interest as damages, see Civil Code § 3287 et seq.
Measure of damages for breach of contract, see Civil Code § 3300.
"Person in position of seller", recovery of damages by, see Commercial Code § 2707.
Resale by seller, recovery of incidental damages, see Commercial Code § 2706.
Stoppage of goods in transit, see Commercial Code § 2705.

§ 2711. Buyer's Remedies in General; Buyer's Security Interest in Rejected Goods

(1) Where the seller fails to make delivery or repudiates or the buyer rightfully rejects or justifiably revokes acceptance then with respect to any goods involved, and with respect to the whole if the breach goes to the whole contract (Section 2612), the buyer may cancel and whether or not he has done so may in addition to recovering so much of the price as has been paid

(a) "Cover" and have damages under the next section as to all the goods affected whether or not they have been identified to the contract; or

(b) Recover damages for nondelivery as provided in this division (Section 2713).

(2) Where the seller fails to deliver or repudiates the buyer may also

(a) If the goods have been identified recover them as provided in this division (Section 2502); or

(b) In a proper case obtain specific performance or replevy the goods as provided in this division (Section 2716).

(3) On rightful rejection or justifiable revocation of acceptance a buyer has a security interest in goods in his possession or control for any payments made on their price and any expenses reasonably incurred in their inspection, receipt, transportation, care and custody and may hold such goods and resell them in like manner as an aggrieved seller (Section 2706). *(Stats.1963, c. 819, § 2711.)*

California Code Comment

By John A. Bohn and Charles J. Williams

Prior California Law

1. This index section of buyer's remedies has no counterpart in the Uniform Sales Act (former Civil Code §§ 1721–1800).

§ 2711

Under the Uniform Sales Act the basic remedies available to the buyer for breach of warranty were listed in former Civil Code § 1789 (recoupment, damages or rescission at the buyer's election) and former Civil Code § 1786 (action for converting or detaining), § 1787 (action for failure to deliver goods) and § 1788 (specific performance).

2. Subdivision (1)(b) allows the buyer to cancel and recover whatever was paid *and* to recover damages for non-delivery as provided in Commercial Code § 2713.

3. Subdivision (3) of this section is the counterpart of former Civil Code § 1789(5) which provided that where the buyer rescinds and the seller refuses return of goods, the buyer holds goods as bailee for seller. However, section 1789(5) was limited to breaches of warranty. Subdivision (3) does not have this limitation.

Changes from U.C.C. (1962 Official Text)

4. This is section 2–711 of the Official Text without change.

Uniform Commercial Code Comment

Prior Uniform Statutory Provision:

No comparable index section; Subsection (3)—Section 69(5), Uniform Sales Act.

Changes: The prior uniform statutory provision is generally continued and expanded in Subsection (3).

Purposes of Changes and New Matter:

1. To index in this section the buyer's remedies, subsection (1) covering those remedies permitting the recovery of money damages, and subsection (2) covering those which permit reaching the goods themselves. The remedies listed here are those available to a buyer who has not accepted the goods or who has justifiably revoked his acceptance. The remedies available to a buyer with regard to goods finally accepted appear in the section dealing with breach in regard to accepted goods. The buyer's right to proceed as to all goods when the breach is as to only some of the goods is determined by the section on breach in installment contracts and by the section on partial acceptance.

Despite the seller's breach, proper retender of delivery under the section on cure of improper tender or replacement can effectively preclude the buyer's remedies under this section, except for any delay involved.

2. To make it clear in subsection (3) that the buyer may hold and resell rejected goods if he has paid a part of the price or incurred expenses of the type specified. "Paid" as used here includes acceptance of a draft or other time negotiable instrument or the signing of a negotiable note. His freedom of resale is coextensive with that of a seller under this Article except that the buyer may not keep any profit resulting from the resale and is limited to retaining only the amount of the price paid and the costs involved in the inspection and handling of the goods. The buyer's security interest in the goods is intended to be limited to the items listed in subsection (3), and the buyer is not permitted to retain such funds as he might believe adequate for his damages. The buyer's right to cover, or to have damages for non-delivery, is not impaired by his exercise of his right of resale.

3. It should also be noted that this Act requires its remedies to be liberally administered and provides that any right or obligation which it declares is enforceable by action unless a different effect is specifically prescribed (Section 1–106).

Cross References:

Point 1: Sections 2–508, 2–601(c), 2–608, 2–612 and 2–714.
Point 2: Section 2–706.
Point 3: Section 1–106.

Definitional Cross References:

"Aggrieved party". Section 1–201.
"Buyer". Section 2–103.
"Cancellation". Section 2–106.
"Contract". Section 1–201.
"Cover". Section 2–712.
"Goods". Section 2–105.
"Notifies". Section 1–201.
"Receipt" of goods. Section 2–103.
"Remedy". Section 1–201.
"Security interest". Section 1–201.
"Seller". Section 2–103.

Cross References

Accountability for excess over amount of security interest, see Commercial Code § 2706.
Actions, availability, see Commercial Code § 1106.
Anticipatory repudiation, see Commercial Code § 2610.
Damages, breach as to accepted goods, see Commercial Code § 2714.
Installment contracts, remedies upon breach, see Commercial Code § 2612.
Remedies, liberal administration, see Commercial Code § 1106.
Resale by seller, see Commercial Code § 2706.
Rescission of contracts, see Civil Code § 1688 et seq.
Revocation of acceptance, see Commercial Code § 2608.
Tender of delivery,
  Buyer's rights upon improper tender, see Commercial Code § 2601.
  Cure or replacement, see Commercial Code § 2508.

§ 2712. "Cover"; Buyer's Procurement of Substitute Goods

(1) After a breach within the preceding section the buyer may "cover" by making in good faith and without unreasonable delay any reasonable purchase of or contract to purchase goods in substitution for those due from the seller.

(2) The buyer may recover from the seller as damages the difference between the cost of cover and the contract price together with any incidental or consequential damages as hereinafter defined (Section 2715), but less expenses saved in consequence of the seller's breach.

(3) Failure of the buyer to effect cover within this section does not bar him from any other remedy. *(Stats.1963, c. 819, § 2712.)*

California Code Comment

By John A. Bohn and Charles J. Williams

Prior California Law

1. This section has no statutory counterpart in prior California law.

2. Subdivision (1) introduces the term known as "cover". The concept of cover has been recognized by California courts. Coates v. Lake View Oil and Refining Co., 20 Cal.App.2d 113, 66 P.2d 463 (1937); Olcese v. Davis, 124 Cal.App.2d 58, 268 P.2d 175 (1954).

3. Subdivision (2) changes the measure of damages under the Uniform Sales Act. Former Civil Code § 1787(3) established the measure of damages in the absence of circumstances showing a greater amount as "the difference between the contract price and the market or current price of the goods at the time or times when they ought to have been delivered, or, if no time was fixed, then at the time of the refusal to deliver." However, the court in Coates v. Lake View Oil & Refining Co., 20 Cal.App.2d 113, 117, 66 P.2d 463, 465 (1937) added the concept of cover to this measure by stating:

". . . where a seller agrees to sell a buyer an article which has no established market value and the seller breaches his contract to sell and deliver, the buyer may go into the open market and purchase a similar article of merchandise, or if a similar article is not available and purchasable the buyer may purchase a reasonable substitute. If he does so the difference between the contract price and the reasonable market value of the substitute purchased is of value in furnishing a measure of his damage."

4. A California State Bar Committee makes the following comments regarding Commercial Code § 2712 and its anticipated effect upon California law:

"Under the Sales Act [former Civil Code §§ 1721 to 1800] the normal measure of damages recoverable by a buyer as a result of a seller's failure to deliver is the difference between the contract price and the market price at the time performance was due. [*Fn.*: Cal.Civ.Code, sec. 1787(3). This section does allow recovery of a greater amount if the buyer can establish ". . . special circumstances showing proximate damages of a greater amount. . . ." See Perkins v. Minford, 235 N.Y. 301, 139 N.E. 276 (1923).] If the buyer purchases goods in substitution for those the seller has failed to deliver, the price paid for the other goods does not settle the market price. The buyer's damages may be more or less than any additional amount required to obtain substitute goods. Under section 12712 [2712] the buyer would be able to fix the amount of his damages by purchasing in good faith and without unreasonable delay goods in substitution for those due from the seller. The buyer could then recover the difference between the cost of such 'cover' and the contract price, together with any incidental or consequential damages otherwise allowable, less expenses saved as a result of the seller's breach.

"The buyer's failure to make such substitute purchase would not prevent him from recovering the difference between the contract price and the market price. But under section 12715 [2715] the buyer cannot recover any consequential damages which 'cover' could have reasonably prevented. Section 12713 [2713] would determine the market price for the purpose of computing damages as of the time when the buyer learns of the breach, not at the time when delivery was due under the Sales Act." California State Bar Committee on the Commercial Code, a Special Report, The Uniform Commercial Code, 37 Calif.Bar J. 117, 149 (March–April, 1962).

Changes from U.C.C. (1962 Official Text)

5. This is section 2–712 of the Official Text without change.

Uniform Commercial Code Comment

Prior Uniform Statutory Provision:

None.

Purposes:

1. This section provides the buyer with a remedy aimed at enabling him to obtain the goods he needs thus meeting his essential need. This remedy is the buyer's equivalent of the seller's right to resell.

2. The definition of "cover" under subsection (1) envisages a series of contracts or sales, as well as a single contract or sale; goods not identical with those involved but commercially usable as reasonable substitutes under the circumstances of the particular case; and contracts on credit or delivery terms differing from the contract in breach, but again reasonable under the circumstances. The test of proper cover is whether at the time and place the buyer acted in good faith and in a reasonable manner, and it is immaterial that hindsight may later prove that the method of cover used was not the cheapest or most effective.

The requirement that the buyer must cover "without unreasonable delay" is not intended to limit the time necessary for him to look around and decide as to how he may best effect cover. The test here is similar to that generally used in this Article as to reasonable time and seasonable action.

3. Subsection (3) expresses the policy that cover is not a mandatory remedy for the buyer. The buyer is always free to choose between cover and damages for non-delivery under the next section.

However, this subsection must be read in conjunction with the section which limits the recovery of consequential damages to such as could not have been obviated by cover. Moreover, the operation of the section on specific performance of contracts for "unique" goods must be considered in this connection for availability of the goods to the particular buyer for his particular needs is the test for that remedy and inability to cover is made an express condition to the right of the buyer to replevy the goods.

4. This section does not limit cover to merchants, in the first instance. It is the vital and important remedy for the consumer buyer as well. Both are free to use cover: the domestic or non-merchant consumer is required only to act in normal good faith while the merchant buyer must also observe all reasonable commercial standards of fair dealing in the trade, since this falls within the definition of good faith on his part.

Cross References:

Point 1: Section 2–706.

Point 2: Section 1–204.
Point 3: Sections 2–713, 2–715 and 2–716.
Point 4: Section 1–203.

Definitional Cross References:

"Buyer". Section 2–103.
"Contract". Section 1–201.
"Good faith". Section 2–103.
"Goods". Section 2–105.
"Purchase". Section 1–201.
"Remedy". Section 1–201.
"Seller". Section 2–103.

Cross References

Damages,
  Incidental and consequential, see Commercial Code § 2715.
Good faith, enforcement of contract, see Commercial Code § 1203.
Reasonable time, see Commercial Code § 1204.
Resale by seller as equivalent remedy, see Commercial Code § 2706.
Specific performance or replevin, see Commercial Code § 2716.

§ 2713. Buyer's Damages for Non-Delivery or Repudiation

(1) Subject to the provisions of this division with respect to proof of market price (Section 2723), the measure of damages for nondelivery or repudiation by the seller is the difference between the market price at the time when the buyer learned of the breach and the contract price together with any incidental and consequential damages provided in this division (Section 2715), but less expenses saved in consequence of the seller's breach.

(2) Market price is to be determined as of the place for tender or, in cases of rejection after arrival or revocation of acceptance, as of the place of arrival. (Stats.1963, c. 819, § 2713.)

California Code Comment

By John A. Bohn and Charles J. Williams

Prior California Law

1. This section modifies prior statutory California law. Former Civil Code § 1787(3) provided that the measure of damages would ordinarily be the difference between the contract price and the market price at the time when the goods *ought to have been delivered*, or, if no time was fixed, then at the time of the refusal to deliver. Eskew v. California Fruit Exchange, 203 Cal. 257, 263 Pac. 804 (1928). Subdivision (1) of this section applies the market price at the time when the buyer learns of the breach.

2. The fixing of market price in subdivision (2) adds new language to California statutory law but is in accord with the general damage provision in Civil Code § 3354 that provides, "In estimating damages . . ., the value of property, to a buyer . . ., deprived of its possession, is deemed to be the price at which he might have bought an equivalent thing in the market nearest to the place where the property ought to have been put into his possession . . .."

Changes from U.C.C. (1962 Official Text)

3. This is section 2–713 of the Official Text without change.

Uniform Commercial Code Comment

Prior Uniform Statutory Provision:

Section 67(3), Uniform Sales Act.

Changes: Rewritten.

Purposes of Changes: To clarify the former rule so that:

1. The general baseline adopted in this section uses as a yardstick the market in which the buyer would have obtained cover had he sought

§ 2713

that relief. So the place for measuring damages is the place of tender (or the place of arrival if the goods are rejected or their acceptance is revoked after reaching their destination) and the crucial time is the time at which the buyer learns of the breach.

2. The market or current price to be used in comparison with the contract price under this section is the price for goods of the same kind and in the same branch of trade.

3. When the current market price under this section is difficult to prove the section on determination and proof of market price is available to permit a showing of a comparable market price or, where no market price is available, evidence of spot sale prices is proper. Where the unavailability of a market price is caused by a scarcity of goods of the type involved, a good case is normally made for specific performance under this Article. Such scarcity conditions, moreover, indicate that the price has risen and under the section providing for liberal administration of remedies, opinion evidence as to the value of the goods would be admissible in the absence of a market price and a liberal construction of allowable consequential damages should also result.

4. This section carries forward the standard rule that the buyer must deduct from his damages any expenses saved as a result of the breach.

5. The present section provides a remedy which is completely alternative to cover under the preceding section and applies only when and to the extent that the buyer has not covered.

Cross References:

Point 3: Sections 1–106, 2–716 and 2–723.
Point 5: Section 2–712.

Definitional Cross References:

"Buyer". Section 2–103.
"Contract". Section 1–201.
"Seller". Section 2–103.

Cross References

Buyer's remedies in general, see Commercial Code § 2711.
Damages for breach of contract, see Civil Code § 3300 et seq.
Estimating damages; value to buyer, see Civil Code § 3354.
Market price, measure and proof, see Commercial Code § 2723.
Remedies, liberal administration, see Commercial Code § 1106.
Specific performance, see Commercial Code § 2716.

§ 2714. Buyer's Damages for Breach in Regard to Accepted Goods

(1) Where the buyer has accepted goods and given notification (subdivision (3) of Section 2607) he or she may recover, as damages for any nonconformity of tender, the loss resulting in the ordinary course of events from the seller's breach as determined in any manner that is reasonable.

(2) The measure of damages for breach of warranty is the difference at the time and place of acceptance between the value of the goods accepted and the value they would have had if they had been as warranted, unless special circumstances show proximate damages of a different amount.

(3) In a proper case any incidental and consequential damages under * * * Section 2715 also may be recovered. (Stats.1963, c. 819, § 2714. Amended by Stats. 1995, c. 91 (S.B.975), § 21.)

California Code Comment

By John A. Bohn and Charles J. Williams

Prior California Law

1. Subdivision (1) is in accord with that part of former Civil Code § 1769 which provided that in the absence of express or implied agreement acceptance does not bar an action for damages for breach.

Subdivision (1) is also consistent with former Civil Code § 1789(1)(a) which provided the remedy of recoupment for breach of warranty, and § 1789(6) which provided the measure of damages for breach of warranty.

2. The measure of damages for the seller's breach of warranty in subdivision (2) is similar to former Civil Code § 1789(7) which provided that loss due to breach of warranty of quality was ordinarily the difference between the value of the goods at the time of delivery and the value they would have had if they had met the warranty. However, subdivision (2) is broader because it applies to breach of *any* warranty while section 1789(7) applied only to the warranty of quality.

3. Subdivision (3) providing for "incidental and consequential damages" is consistent with former Civil Code § 1790 which provided for "interest or special damages".

Changes from U.C.C. (1962 Official Text)

4. This is section 2–714 of the Official Text without change.

Uniform Commercial Code Comment

Prior Uniform Statutory Provision:

Section 69(6) and (7), Uniform Sales Act.

Changes: Rewritten.

Purposes of Changes:

1. This section deals with the remedies available to the buyer after the goods have been accepted and the time for revocation of acceptance has gone by. In general this section adopts the rule of the prior uniform statutory provision for measuring damages where there has been a breach of warranty as to goods accepted, but goes further to lay down and explicit provision as to the time and place for determining the loss.

The section on deduction of damages from price provides an additional remedy for a buyer who still owes part of the purchase price, and frequently the two remedies will be available concurrently. The buyer's failure to notify of his claim under the section on effects of acceptance, however, operates to bar his remedies under either that section or the present section.

2. The "non-conformity" referred to in subsection (1) includes not only breaches of warranties but also any failure of the seller to perform according to his obligations under the contract. In the case of such non-conformity, the buyer is permitted to recover for his loss "in any manner which is reasonable."

3. Subsection (2) describes the usual, standard and reasonable method of ascertaining damages in the case of breach of warranty but it is not intended as an exclusive measure. It departs from the measure of damages for non-delivery in utilizing the place of acceptance rather than the place of tender. In some cases the two may coincide, as where the buyer signifies his acceptance upon the tender. If, however, the non-conformity is such as would justify revocation of acceptance, the time and place of acceptance under this section is determined as of the buyer's decision not to revoke.

4. The incidental and consequential damages referred to in subsection (3), which will usually accompany an action brought under this section, are discussed in detail in the comment on the next section.

Cross References:

Point 1: Compare Section 2–711; Sections 2–607 and 2–717.
Point 2: Section 2–106.
Point 3: Sections 2–608 and 2–713.
Point 4: Section 2–715.

Definitional Cross References:

"Buyer". Section 2–103.
"Conform". Section 2–106.
"Goods". Section 1–201.
"Notification". Section 1–201.
"Seller". Section 2–103.

Cross References

Acceptance of goods,
  Effect, see Commercial Code § 2607.
  Revocation, see Commercial Code § 2608.

Consumer warranties, see Civil Code § 1790 et seq.
Definitions, see Commercial Code §§ 1201, 2103, 2104, 2105, 2106.
Measure of damages for breach of contract, see Civil Code § 3300.
Place for determining market price, damages, see Commercial Code § 2713.
Remedies of buyer,
 Generally, see Commercial Code § 2711.
 Deduction of damages from price, see Commercial Code § 2717.
Warranties by seller, see Commercial Code § 2312 et seq.

§ 2715. Buyer's Incidental and Consequential Damages

(1) Incidental damages resulting from the seller's breach include expenses reasonably incurred in inspection, receipt, transportation and care and custody of goods rightfully rejected, any commercially reasonable charges, expenses or commissions in connection with effecting cover and any other reasonable expense incident to the delay or other breach.

(2) Consequential damages resulting from the seller's breach include

(a) Any loss resulting from general or particular requirements and needs of which the seller at the time of contracting had reason to know and which could not reasonably be prevented by cover or otherwise; and

(b) Injury to person or property proximately resulting from any breach of warranty. (Stats.1963, c. 819, § 2715.)

California Code Comment

By John A. Bohn and Charles J. Williams

Prior California Law

1. This section has no counterpart in the USA although it is consistent with rules of damages set forth in former Civil Code § 1787(2) (loss directly and naturally resulting from the breach) and Civil Code § 3300 ("all the detriment proximately caused" by the breach). This section clarifies what damages may be recovered and covers all expenses related to the breach.

2. Subdivision (1) has no statutory counterpart in California law but is in general accord with the cases which allow recovery of incidental damages directly and naturally resulting from the breach. For example see Walpole v. Prefab Mfg. Co., 103 Cal.App.2d 472, 230 P.2d 36 (1951) (damage to good will and expenditures for additional clerical help).

3. The consequential damages provided for in subdivision (2) were recoverable under prior California law. Two examples are the recovery of lost resale profits contemplated at the time of the contract of sale (Tomlinson v. Wander Seed & Bulb Co., 177 Cal.App.2d 462, 2 Cal.Rptr. 310 (1960)) and recovery of damages for time and money spent in efforts to make goods conform to warranty under which they were sold (Roberts Distributing Co. v. Kaye-Halbert Corp., 126 Cal.App. 664, 272 P.2d 886 (1954)).

4. Subdivision (2)(b) is consistent with former Civil Code § 1789(7) and § 1790. See California Code Comments 2 and 3 to section 2714.

Changes from U.C.C. (1962 Official Text)

5. This is section 2–715 of the Official Text without change.

Uniform Commercial Code Comment

Prior Uniform Statutory Provisions: Subsection (2)(b)—Sections 69(7) and 70, Uniform Sales Act.
Changes: Rewritten.

Purposes of Changes and New Matter:

1. Subsection (1) is intended to provide reimbursement for the buyer who incurs reasonable expenses in connection with the handling of rightfully rejected goods or goods whose acceptance may be justifiably revoked, or in connection with effecting cover where the breach of the contract lies in non-conformity or non-delivery of the goods. The incidental damages listed are not intended to be exhaustive but are merely illustrative of the typical kinds of incidental damage.

2. Subsection (2) operates to allow the buyer, in an appropriate case, any consequential damages which are the result of the seller's breach. The "tacit agreement" test for the recovery of consequential damages is rejected. Although the older rule at common law which made the seller liable for all consequential damages of which he had "reason to know" in advance is followed, the liberality of that rule is modified by refusing to permit recovery unless the buyer could not reasonably have prevented the loss by cover or otherwise. Subparagraph (2) carries forward the provisions of the prior uniform statutory provision as to consequential damages resulting from breach of warranty, but modifies the rule by requiring first that the buyer attempt to minimize his damages in good faith, either by cover or otherwise.

3. In the absence of excuse under the section on merchant's excuse by failure of presupposed conditions, the seller is liable for consequential damages in all cases where he had reason to know of the buyer's general or particular requirements at the time of contracting. It is not necessary that there be a conscious acceptance of an insurer's liability on the seller's part, nor is his obligation for consequential damages limited to cases in which he fails to use due effort in good faith.

Particular needs of the buyer must generally be made known to the seller while general needs must rarely be made known to charge the seller with knowledge.

Any seller who does not wish to take the risk of consequential damages has available the section on contractual limitation of remedy.

4. The burden of proving the extent of loss incurred by way of consequential damage is on the buyer, but the section on liberal administration of remedies rejects any doctrine of certainty which requires almost mathematical precision in the proof of loss. Loss may be determined in any manner which is reasonable under the circumstances.

5. Subsection (2)(b) states the usual rule as to breach of warranty, allowing recovery for injuries "proximately" resulting from the breach. Where the injury involved follows the use of goods without discovery of the defect causing the damage, the question of "proximate" cause turns on whether it was reasonable for the buyer to use the goods without such inspection as would have revealed the defects. If it was not reasonable for him to do so, or if he did in fact discover the defect prior to his use, the injury would not proximately result from the breach of warranty.

6. In the case of sale of wares to one in the business of reselling them, resale is one of the requirements of which the seller has reason to know within the meaning of subsection (2)(a).

Cross References:

Point 1: Section 2–608.
Point 3: Sections 1–203, 2–615 and 2–719.
Point 4: Section 1–106.

Definitional Cross References:

"Cover". Section 2–712.
"Goods". Section 1–201.
"Person". Section 1–201.
"Receipt" of goods. Section 2–103.
"Seller". Section 2–103.

Cross References

Consequential damages, limitation by contract, see Commercial Code § 2719
"Cover", damages for, see Commercial Code § 2712.
Excuse by failure of presupposed conditions, see Commercial Code § 2615.
Good faith, enforcement of contract, see Commercial Code § 1203.
Interest as damages, see Commercial Code § 3287 et seq.
Measure of damages for breach of contract, see Civil Code § 3300.
Non-delivery or repudiation, buyer's damages for, see Commercial Code § 2713.
Remedies, liberal administration, see Commercial Code § 1106.

§ 2715

Revocation of acceptance, see Commercial Code §§ 2608, 2703.

§ 2716. Buyer's Right to Specific Performance or Replevin

(1) Specific performance may be decreed where the goods are unique or in other proper circumstances.

(2) The decree for specific performance may include such terms and conditions as to payment of the price, damages, or other relief as the court may deem just.

(3) The buyer has a right of replevin for goods identified to the contract if after reasonable effort he is unable to effect cover for such goods or the circumstances reasonably indicate that such effort will be unavailing or if the goods have been shipped under reservation and satisfaction of the security interest in them has been made or tendered. *(Stats.1963, c. 819, § 2716.)*

California Code Comment
By John A. Bohn and Charles J. Williams

Prior California Law

1. This section continues the same remedy of specific performance available under former Civil Code § 1788. However, section 1788 limited the remedy to cases involving specific or ascertained goods. The availability of the remedy is expanded in this section to include "other proper circumstances". Official Comment 1. The California courts have stated that the adoption of former Civil Code § 1788 was also intended to liberalize the use of the remedy of specific performance in California. Bomberger v. McKelvey, 35 Cal.2d 607, 220 P.2d 729 (1950). This case also indicates the growing tendency to allow specific performance where damages are not the equivalent of the performance.

2. Subdivision (3) giving the buyer the remedy of replevin has no statutory counterpart in prior California law.

Changes from U.C.C. (1962 Official Text)

3. This is section 2–716 of the Official Text without change.

Uniform Commercial Code Comment

Prior Uniform Statutory Provision:
Section 68, Uniform Sales Act.
Changes: Rephrased.
Purposes of Changes: To make it clear that:

1. The present section continues in general prior policy as to specific performance and injunction against breach. However, without intending to impair in any way the exercise of the court's sound discretion in the matter, this Article seeks to further a more liberal attitude than some courts have shown in connection with the specific performance of contracts of sale.

2. In view of this Article's emphasis on the commercial feasibility of replacement, a new concept of what are "unique" goods is introduced under this section. Specific performance is no longer limited to goods which are already specific or ascertained at the time of contracting. The test of uniqueness under this section must be made in terms of the total situation which characterizes the contract. Output and requirements contracts involving a particular or peculiarly available source or market present today the typical commercial specific performance situation, as contrasted with contracts for the sale of heirlooms or priceless works of art which were usually involved in the older cases. However, uniqueness is not the sole basis of the remedy under this section for the relief may also be granted "in other proper circumstances" and inability to cover is strong evidence of "other proper circumstances".

3. The legal remedy of replevin is given the buyer in cases in which cover is reasonably unavailable and goods have been identified to the contract. This is in addition to the buyer's right to recover identified goods on the seller's insolvency (Section 2–502).

4. This section is intended to give the buyer rights to the goods comparable to the seller's rights to the price.

5. If a negotiable document of title is outstanding, the buyer's right of replevin relates of course to the document not directly to the goods. See Article 7, especially Section 7–602.

Cross References:

Point 3: Section 2–502.
Point 4: Section 2–709.
Point 5: Article 7.

Definitional Cross References:

"Buyer". Section 2–103.
"Goods". Section 1–201.
"Rights". Section 1–201.

Cross References

Action for price, comparable right in seller, see Commercial Code § 2709.
Buyer's remedies, generally, see Commercial Code § 2711.
Claim and delivery, see Code of Civil Procedure § 511.010 et seq.
Documents of title,
  Generally, see Commercial Code § 7101 et seq.
  Attachment of covered goods, see Commercial Code § 7602.
Insolvency of seller, buyer's right to goods, see Commercial Code § 2502.
Rights of seller's creditors against sold goods, see Commercial Code § 2402.
Specific performance of obligations, see Civil Code § 3384 et seq.

§ 2717. Deduction of Damages From the Price

The buyer on notifying the seller of his intention to do so may deduct all or any part of the damages resulting from any breach of the contract from any part of the price still due under the same contract. *(Stats. 1963, c. 819, § 2717.)*

California Code Comment
By John A. Bohn and Charles J. Williams

Prior California Law

1. This section liberalizes the USA rule permitting the buyer to deduct his damages from the purchase price. Former Civil Code § 1789(1)(a) provided the remedy of recoupment which permitted the deduction where damage resulted from a breach of warranty by the seller. Under former Civil Code § 1769 where the buyer accepted the goods, notice of the breach was required to be communicated to the seller within a reasonable time.

2. Under this section a deduction is permitted for any breach whereas former Civil Code § 1789(1)(a) applied only to breach of warranty. See Official Comment 1.

3. The requirement that a buyer notify the seller of his intention to make the authorized deduction was not required under prior California law. However, notice *of the fact of the breach of warranty* was required after acceptance of the goods under former Civil Code § 1769.

Changes from U.C.C. (1962 Official Text)

4. This is section 2–717 of the Official Text without change.

Uniform Commercial Code Comment

Prior Uniform Statutory Provision:
See Section 69(1)(a), Uniform Sales Act.

Purposes:

1. This section permits the buyer to deduct from the price damages resulting from any breach by the seller and does not limit the relief to cases of breach of warranty as did the prior uniform statutory provision. To bring this provision into application the breach involved must be of

the same contract under which the price in question is claimed to have been earned.

2. The buyer, however, must give notice of his intention to withhold all or part of the price if he wishes to avoid a default within the meaning of the section on insecurity and right to assurances. In conformity with the general policies of this Article, no formality of notice is required and any language which reasonably indicates the buyer's reason for holding up his payment is sufficient.

Cross Reference:

Point 2: Section 2–609.

Definitional Cross References:

"Buyer". Section 2–103.
"Notifies". Section 1–201.

Cross References

Assurance of performance, see Commercial Code § 2609.

§ 2718. Liquidation or Limitation of Damages; Deposits

(1) Damages for breach by either party may be liquidated in the agreement subject to and in compliance with Section 1671 of the Civil Code. If the agreement provides for liquidation of damages, and such provision does not comply with Section 1671 of the Civil Code, remedy may be had as provided in this division.

(2) Where the seller justifiably withholds delivery of goods because of the buyer's breach, the buyer is entitled to restitution of any amount by which the sum of his or her payments exceeds:

(a) The amount to which the seller is entitled by virtue of terms liquidating the seller's damages in accordance with subdivision (1), or

(b) In the absence of such terms, 20 percent of the value of the total performance for which the buyer is obligated under the contract or five hundred dollars ($500), whichever is smaller.

(3) The buyer's right to restitution under subdivision (2) is subject to offset to the extent that the seller establishes:

(a) A right to recover damages under the provisions of this chapter other than subdivision (1), and

(b) The amount or value of any benefits received by the buyer directly or indirectly by reason of the contract.

(4) Where a seller has received payment in goods their reasonable value or the proceeds of their resale shall be treated as payments for the purposes of subdivision (2); but if the seller has notice of the buyer's breach before reselling goods received in part performance, his or her resale is subject to the conditions laid down in this division on resale by an aggrieved seller (Section 2706). *(Stats.1963, c. 819, § 2718. Amended by Stats.1988, c. 1368, § 10, operative Jan. 1, 1990.)*

California Code Comment

By John A. Bohn and Charles J. Williams

Prior California Law

1. This section has no counterpart in the USA.

2. Subdivision (1) establishes the criterion for determining the validity of a liquidated damage clause.

3. Subdivision (2) limits that portion which the seller can keep from any deposit or payment of the buyer. Paragraph (a) has no counterpart in prior California statutory law. Cases decided before the adoption of this section held that money deposits given as security for performance of a lease were subject to the provisions of Civil Code § 1670 and § 1671 (see Comment 1 above). Redmon v. Graham, 211 Cal. 491, 295 Pac. 1031 (1931); Ricker v. Rombough, 120 Cal.App.2d Supp. 912, 261 P.2d 328 (1953). The percentage or monetary limitations of paragraph (b) is entirely new to California law.

4. Subdivision (3) has no statutory counterpart but is in accord with the holding in Knight v. Marks, 66 Cal.App. 593, 226 Pac. 931 (1924) that although a lease deposit was invalid as a liquidated damage clause under Civil Code § 1670, the deposit could be applied in satisfaction of unpaid rent.

5. Subdivision (4) has no counterpart in prior California law.

Changes from U.C.C. (1962 Official Text)

6. This is section 2–718 of the Official Text without change.

Uniform Commercial Code Comment

Prior Uniform Statutory Provision:

None.

Purposes:

1. [Not applicable].

2. Subsection (2) refuses to recognize a forfeiture unless the amount of the payment so forfeited represents a reasonable liquidation of damages as determined under subsection (1). A special exception is made in the case of small amounts (20% of the price of $500, whichever is smaller) deposited as security. No distinction is made between cases in which the payment is to be applied on the price and those in which it is intended as security for performance. Subsection (2) is applicable to any deposit or down or part payment. In the case of a deposit or turn in of goods resold before the breach, the amount actually received on the resale is to be viewed as the deposit rather than the amount allowed the buyer for the trade in. However, if the seller knows of the breach prior to the resale of the goods turned in, he must make reasonable efforts to realize their true value, and this is assured by requiring him to comply with the conditions laid down in the section on resale by an aggrieved seller.

Cross References:

Point 1: Section 2–302.
Point 2: Section 2–706.

Definitional Cross References:

"Aggrieved party". Section 1–201.
"Agreement". Section 1–201.
"Buyer". Section 2–103.
"Goods". Section 2–105.
"Notice". Section 1–201.
"Party". Section 1–201.
"Remedy". Section 1–201.
"Seller". Section 2–103.
"Term". Section 1–201.

Cross References

Breach of contract to pay liquidated sum, measure of damages, see Civil Code § 3302.
Exclusion or modification of warranties, see Commercial Code § 2316.
Improper delivery, buyer's rights on, see Commercial Code § 2601.
Liquidated damages,
    Circumstances authorizing, see Civil Code § 1671.
    General invalidity, see Civil Code § 1671.
Resale by seller, see Commercial Code § 2706.

§ 2718

Unconscionable clauses, see Civil Code § 1670.5.

§ 2719. Contractual Modification or Limitation of Remedy

(1) Subject to the provisions of subdivisions (2) and (3) of this section and of the preceding section on liquidation and limitation of damages,

(a) The agreement may provide for remedies in addition to or in substitution for those provided in this division and may limit or alter the measure of damages recoverable under this division, as by limiting the buyer's remedies to return of the goods and repayment of the price or to repair and replacement of nonconforming goods or parts; and

(b) Resort to a remedy as provided is optional unless the remedy is expressly agreed to be exclusive, in which case it is the sole remedy.

(2) Where circumstances cause an exclusive or limited remedy to fail of its essential purpose, remedy may be had as provided in this code.

(3) Consequential damages may be limited or excluded unless the limitation or exclusion is unconscionable. Limitation of consequential damages for injury to the person in the case of consumer goods is * * * invalid unless it is proved that the limitation is not unconscionable. Limitation of consequential damages where the loss is commercial is valid unless it is proved that the limitation is unconscionable. *(Stats.1963, c. 819, § 2719. Amended by Stats.1967, c. 703, p. 2077, § 3.)*

California Code Comment
By Charles J. Williams

The 1967 amendment varies subdivision (3) of the California version from the Official Text. No substantive change from the Official Text is intended but the change was made at the recommendation of the California Law Revision Commission to clarify the allocation of the burden of proof.

California Code Comment
By John A. Bohn and Charles J. Williams

Prior California Law

1. Subdivision (1) is in accord with former Civil Code § 1791 which provided that the parties could vary by express agreement any right, duty, or liability imposed by law. Under both former section 1791 and this section the parties may provide their own remedies for breach of contract. However, the Commercial Code in subdivisions (2) and (3) imposes certain limitations on the right of the parties to provide their own remedies by agreement.

2. Subdivision (2) provides that where the remedy provided by agreement "fails in its purpose or operates to deprive either party of the substantial value of the bargain", it will not be enforced. In this case the remedies provided in the Commercial Code govern as if the parties had not agreed to any remedy of their own. Official Comment 1.

3. Subdivision (2) puts a general limitation on the extent that parties may agree on consequential damages (provided for in Commercial Code § 2715). If such an agreement is "unconscionable" it will not be recognized and the statutory remedies of Division 2 apply.

Changes from U.C.C. (1962 Official Text)

4. This is section 2–719 of the Official Text without change.

Law Revision Commission Comment
1967 Amendment

Subdivision (3) of Section 2719 has been revised to make it clear that this subdivision allocates the burden of proof as to the validity of provisions limiting consequential damages.

Uniform Commercial Code Comment

Prior Uniform Statutory Provision:
None.

Purposes:

1. Under this section parties are left free to shape their remedies to their particular requirements and reasonable agreements limiting or modifying remedies are to be given effect.

However, it is of the very essence of a sales contract that at least minimum adequate remedies be available. If the parties intend to conclude a contract for sale within this Article they must accept the legal consequence that there be at least a fair quantum of remedy for breach of the obligations or duties outlined in the contract. Thus any clause purporting to modify or limit the remedial provisions of this Article in an unconscionable manner is subject to deletion and in that event the remedies made available by this Article are applicable as if the stricken clause had never existed. Similarly, under subsection (2), where an apparently fair and reasonable clause because of circumstances fails in its purpose or operates to deprive either party of the substantial value of the bargain, it must give way to the general remedy provisions of this Article.

2. Subsection (1)(b) creates a presumption that clauses prescribing remedies are cumulative rather than exclusive. If the parties intend the term to describe the sole remedy under the contract, this must be clearly expressed.

3. Subsection (3) recognizes the validity of clauses limiting or excluding consequential damages but makes it clear that they may not operate in an unconscionable manner. Actually such terms are merely an allocation of unknown or undeterminable risks. The seller in all cases is free to disclaim warranties in the manner provided in Section 2–316.

Cross References:

Point 1: Section 2–302.
Point 3: Section 2–316.

Definitional Cross References:

"Agreement". Section 1–201.
"Buyer". Section 2–103.
"Conforming". Section 2–106.
"Contract". Section 1–201.
"Goods". Section 2–105.
"Remedy". Section 1–201.
"Seller". Section 2–103.

Cross References

Exclusion or modification of warranties, see Commercial Code § 2316.
Improper delivery, buyer's rights on, see Commercial Code § 2601.
Modification of sales warranties where security agreement exists, see Commercial Code § 9206.
Warranties, see Commercial Code § 2316.

§ 2720. Effect of "Cancellation" or "Rescission" on Claims for Antecedent Breach

Unless the contrary intention clearly appears, expressions of "cancellation" or "rescission" of the contract or the like shall not be construed as a renunciation or discharge of any claim in damages for an antecedent breach. *(Stats.1963, c. 819, § 2720.)*

California Code Comment
By John A. Bohn and Charles J. Williams

Prior California Law

1. This section has no statutory counterpart in prior California law. Civil Code § 3268 and § 3513 allow waiver of a benefit under a provision of a law or a contract unless the waiver is against public policy. Patton v. Patton, 32 Cal.2d 520, 196 P.2d 909 (1948). This section prevents a waiver by the use of certain words unless a contrary intent is clearly shown. The Official Comment explains what language should be used to show the intent to waive rights.

Changes from U.C.C. (1962 Official Text)

2. This is section 2–720 of the Official Text without change.

Uniform Commercial Code Comment

Prior Uniform Statutory Provision:

None.

Purpose:

This section is designed to safeguard a person holding a right of action from any unintentional loss of rights by the ill-advised use of such terms as "cancellation", "rescission", or the like. Once a party's rights have accrued they are not to be lightly impaired by concessions made in business decency and without intention to forego them. Therefore, unless the cancellation of a contract expressly declares that it is "without reservation of rights", or the like, it cannot be considered to be a renunciation under this section.

Cross Reference:

Section 1–107.

Definitional Cross References:

"Cancellation". Section 2–106.
"Contract". Section 1–201.

Cross References

Claims arising from breach, written renunciation, see Commercial Code § 1107.
Waiver of advantage, law established for public reason, see Civil Code § 3513.
Waiver of code provisions, see Civil Code § 3268.

§ 2721. Remedies for Fraud

Remedies for material misrepresentation or fraud include all remedies available under this division for nonfraudulent breach. Neither rescission or a claim for rescission of the contract for sale nor rejection or return of the goods shall bar or be deemed inconsistent with a claim for damages or other remedy. *(Stats.1963, c. 819, § 2721.)*

California Code Comment

By John A. Bohn and Charles J. Williams

Prior California Law

1. This section has no statutory counterpart in the USA. The Legislative Counsel has observed that:

"This section is new, and its purpose, according to the comments, is to make the remedy of buyer or seller where there is fraud as broad as, and coextensive with, the remedies where fraud is absent. This section would perhaps change the rule of Civil Code § 3343 stating the so-called 'out of pocket' rule of damages in fraud cases, and substitute or permit the so-called, 'loss of bargain' rule under which the defrauded party is permitted to get the benefits he would have received if the representation had been true." Sixth Progress Report to the Legislature by the Senate Fact Finding Committee on Judiciary (1959–1961), Part 1, The Uniform Commercial Code, p. 63.

2. The second sentence of this section changes California law. Under former Civil Code § 1789(2), an election of remedies was required between recoupment, damages, or rescission.

Changes from U.C.C. (1962 Official Text)

3. This is section 2–721 of the Official Text without change.

Uniform Commercial Code Comment

Prior Uniform Statutory Provision:

None.

Purposes: To correct the situation by which remedies for fraud have been more circumscribed than the more modern and mercantile remedies for breach of warranty. Thus the remedies for fraud are extended by this section to coincide in scope with those for nonfraudulent breach. This section thus makes it clear that neither rescission of the contract for fraud nor rejection of the goods bars other remedies unless the circumstances of the case make the remedies incompatible.

Definitional Cross References:

"Contract for sale". Section 2–106.
"Goods". Section 1–201.
"Remedy". Section 1–201.

Cross References

Fraud in purchase, sale or exchange of property, see Civil Code § 3343.
Rescission of contract for fraud, see Civil Code §§ 1689, 1690.

§ 2722. Who Can Sue Third Parties for Injury to Goods

Where a third party so deals with goods which have been identified to a contract for sale as to cause actionable injury to a party to that contract

(a) A right of action against the third party is in either party to the contract for sale who has title to or a security interest or a special property or an insurable interest in the goods; and if the goods have been destroyed or converted a right of action is also in the party who either bore the risk of loss under the contract for sale or has since the injury assumed that risk as against the other;

(b) If at the time of the injury the party plaintiff did not bear the risk of loss as against the other party to the contract for sale and there is no arrangement between them for disposition of the recovery, his suit or settlement is, subject to his own interest, as a fiduciary for the other party to the contract;

(c) Either party may with the consent of the other sue for the benefit of whom it may concern. *(Stats. 1963, c. 819, § 2722.)*

California Code Comment

By John A. Bohn and Charles J. Williams

Prior California Law

1. The purpose of this section is to adopt and extend the principle of the statutes providing for suit by the real party in interest. Official Comment. Such statutes are primarily Code of Civil Procedure § 367 (every action is to be brought in the name of the real party in interest) and § 382 (all parties who are "united in interest" must be joined as plaintiffs or defendants).

Changes from U.C.C. (1962 Official Text)

2. This is section 2–722 of the Official Text without change.

Uniform Commercial Code Comment

Prior Uniform Statutory Provision:

None.

§ 2722

Purposes: To adopt and extend somewhat the principle of the statutes which provide for suit by the real party in interest. The provisions of this section apply only after identification of the goods. Prior to that time only the seller has a right of action. During the period between identification and final acceptance (except in the case of revocation of acceptance) it is possible for both parties to have the right of action. Even after final acceptance both parties may have the right of action if the seller retains possession or otherwise retains an interest.

Definitional Cross References:

"Action". Section 1–201.
"Buyer". Section 2–103.
"Contract for sale". Section 2–106.
"Goods". Section 2–105.
"Party". Section 1–201.
"Rights". Section 1–201.
"Security interest". Section 1–201.

Cross References

Enforcement of contract by third party beneficiary, see Civil Code § 1559.
Joinder of persons united in interest, see Code of Civil Procedure § 382.
Real party in interest, necessity in prosecution in name of, see Code of Civil Procedure § 367.

§ 2723. Proof of Market Price: Time and Place

(1) If an action based on anticipatory repudiation comes to trial before the time for performance with respect to some or all of the goods, any damages based on market price (Section 2708 or Section 2713) shall be determined according to the price of such goods prevailing at the time when the aggrieved party learned of the repudiation.

(2) If evidence of a price prevailing at the times or places described in this division is not readily available the price prevailing within any reasonable time before or after the time described or at any other place which in commercial judgment or under usage of trade would serve as a reasonable substitute for the one described may be used, making any proper allowance for the cost of transporting the goods to or from such other place.

(3) Evidence of a relevant price prevailing at a time or place other than the one described in this division offered by one party is not admissible unless and until he has given the other party such notice as the court finds sufficient to prevent unfair surprise. *(Stats.1963, c. 819, § 2723.)*

California Code Comment

By John A. Bohn and Charles J. Williams

Prior California Law

1. This section has no statutory counterpart in prior California law.

2. Under subdivision (1) the market price is determined at the time the aggrieved party learned of the repudiation. This is different from the measure of damages provided in two former USA sections. In former Civil Code § 1784(3) (seller's remedy for nonacceptance of goods) the market price was determined at the time the goods should have been accepted or, if no time for acceptance was fixed, at the time of the refusal to accept the goods. In former Civil Code § 1787(3) (buyer's remedy for nondelivery of goods) the market price was determined at the time the goods should have been delivered or, if no time for delivery was fixed, at the time of the refusal to deliver the goods.

3. In actions for anticipatory breach the courts have applied the general measure of damage formula of Civil Code § 3300 which provides for recovery of an amount which will compensate for all detriment proximately caused by the breach or which would be ordinarily likely to result from the breach. Vitagraph, Inc. v. Liberty Theatres Co., 197 Cal. 694, 242 Pac. 709 (1925).

4. Subdivisions (2) and (3) are new to California statutory law.

Changes from U.C.C. (1962 Official Text)

5. This is section 2–723 of the Official Text without change.

Uniform Commercial Code Comment

Prior Uniform Statutory Provision:

None.

Purposes: To eliminate the most obvious difficulties arising in connection with the determination of market price, when that is stipulated as a measure of damages by some provision of this Article. Where the appropriate market price is not readily available the court is here granted reasonable leeway in receiving evidence of prices current in other comparable markets or at other times comparable to the one in question. In accordance with the general principle of this Article against surprise, however, a party intending to offer evidence of such a substitute price must give suitable notice to the other party.

This section is not intended to exclude the use of any other reasonable method of determining market price or of measuring damages if the circumstances of the case make this necessary.

Definitional Cross References:

"Action". Section 1–201.
"Aggrieved party". Section 1–201.
"Goods". Section 2–105.
"Notifies". Section 1–201.
"Party". Section 1–201.
"Reasonable time". Section 1–204.
"Usage of trade". Section 1–205.

Cross References

Measure of damages for breach of contract, see Civil Code § 3300.
Non-acceptance or repudiation, damages for, see Commercial Code § 2708.
Non-delivery or repudiation by seller, damages for, see Commercial Code § 2713.

§ 2724. Admissibility of Market Quotations

Whenever the prevailing price or value of any goods regularly bought and sold in any established commodity market is in issue, reports in official publications or trade journals or in newspapers or periodicals of general circulation published as the reports of such market shall be admissible in evidence. The circumstances of the preparation of such a report may be shown to affect its weight but not its admissibility. *(Stats.1963, c. 819, § 2724.)*

California Code Comment

By John A. Bohn and Charles J. Williams

Prior California Law

1. This section has no statutory counterpart in the USA.

The section modifies California statutory law by extending the coverage of the Uniform Business Records as Evidence Act (Code of Civil Procedure §§ 1953e to 1953h) by making "reports in official publications or trade journals or in newspapers . . ." admissible as evidence. Under the Uniform Business Records as Evidence Act these reports were admissible only if they were made in the regular course of business. (Code of Civil Procedure § 1953f)

Changes from U.C.C. (1962 Official Text)

2. This is section 2–724 of the Official Text without change.

Uniform Commercial Code Comment

Prior Uniform Statutory Provision:

None.

Purposes: To make market quotations admissible in evidence while providing for a challenge of the material by showing the circumstances of its preparation.

No explicit provision as to the weight to be given to market quotations is contained in this section, but such quotations, in the absence of compelling challenge, offer an adequate basis for a verdict.

Market quotations are made admissible when the price or value of goods traded "in any established market" is in issue. The reason of the section does not require that the market be closely organized in the manner of a produce exchange. It is sufficient if transactions in the commodity are frequent and open enough to make a market established by usage in which one price can be expected to affect another and in which an informed report of the range and trend of prices can be assumed to be reasonably accurate.

This section does not in any way intend to limit or negate the application of similar rules of admissibility to other material, whether by action of the courts or by statute. The purpose of the present section is to assure a minimum of mercantile administration in this important situation and not to limit any liberalizing trend in modern law.

Definitional Cross Reference:

"Goods". Section 2–105.

Cross References

Business records as evidence, see Evidence Code § 1270 et seq.

§ 2725. Statute of Limitations in Contracts for Sale

(1) An action for breach of any contract for sale must be commenced within four years after the cause of action has accrued. By the original agreement the parties may reduce the period of limitation to not less than one year but may not extend it.

(2) A cause of action accrues when the breach occurs, regardless of the aggrieved party's lack of knowledge of the breach. A breach of warranty occurs when tender of delivery is made, except that where a warranty explicitly extends to future performance of the goods and discovery of the breach must await the time of such performance the cause of action accrues when the breach is or should have been discovered.

(3) Where an action commenced within the time limited by subdivision (1) is so terminated as to leave available a remedy by another action for the same breach such other action may be commenced after the expiration of the time limited and within six months after the termination of the first action unless the termination resulted from voluntary discontinuance or from dismissal for failure or neglect to prosecute.

(4) This section does not alter the law on tolling of the statute of limitations nor does it apply to causes of action which have accrued before this code becomes effective. *(Added by Stats.1967, c. 799, p. 2207, § 5.)*

California Code Comment

By Charles J. Williams

Prior California Law

1. This section was not originally included in the California version of the Uniform Commercial Code.

2. The reason for the omission was the view that the statute of limitations was purely a local problem. However, the Permanent Editorial Board comments that uniformity is desirable and the section in the Official Text "was deliberately promulgated to eliminate jurisdictional variations and provide needed relief for concerns doing business on a nationwide scale". (Permanent Editorial Board for the Uniform Commercial Code, Report No. 2, p. 51.)

3. The basic 4-year period for instituting actions is in accord with the present California rule for the time for bringing actions on written contracts.

Changes from U.C.C. (1962 Official Text)

4. This is section 2–725 of the Official Text without change.

California Code Comment

By John A. Bohn and Charles J. Williams

Prior California Law

1. Section 2–725 of the 1962 Official Text of the Uniform Commercial Code is omitted from the California version of the Commercial Code. See California Code Comment 3 for omitted text.

2. A California State Bar Committee gives the following reasons for the omission of this section in California:

"The Official Text of section 12725 [2–725] would establish a uniform four-year period for commencing an action for breach of a sales contract, written or oral. Presently, the periods in California are four years for a written contract [*Fn.*: C.C.P. Sec. 337] and two years for an oral contract [*Fn.*: C.C.P., Sec. 339]. Upon the recommendation of the State Bar Committee and the Advisory Committee, section 12725 [2–725] is not in S.B. 1093 [1961 Session, 1958 Official Text as Amended] [proposed California Commercial Code in 1961 Legislative session]. These Committees believe there is no great need for such uniformity in statutes of limitation, that such statutes may be governed by local policy with little hindrance to commerce among the states, that this section is therefore unnecessary in the Code, and that there is no reason to change existing California law." California State Bar Committee on the Commercial Code, a Special Report, The Uniform Commercial Code, 37 Calif.Bar J. 117, 153 (March–April, 1962).

Professors Marsh and Warren recommended that this section be deleted from the California Commercial Code for the following reasons:

"The purpose of the draftsmen of the Code in writing this section was to introduce a uniform statute of limitations for sales contracts, thereby eliminating variations presently existing among the different states and providing greater certainty for interstate businesses whose contracts have heretofore been governed by different periods of limitation, depending upon the state in which the transaction occurred. This section selects a four-year period of limitations as the most appropriate to modern business practice. The State Bar Committee and the Credit Organizations Committee urge that the statute of limitations, being procedural in nature, is a local problem. This section is also objected to because it increases the period of limitations for an oral contract from two to four years.

"The recommendation that this section be deleted is based on our view that the statute of limitations is a local problem and should not be treated by the Uniform Commercial Code. This recommendation leaves in effect the present periods of limitations of four years for a written contract (CCP § 337) and two years for an oral contract (CCP § 339)." Sixth Progress Report to the Legislature by the Senate Fact Finding Committee on Judiciary (1959–1961), Part 1, The Uniform Commercial Code, p. 465.

Changes from U.C.C. (1962 Official Text)

3. The omitted Official Text of section 2–725 reads as follows:

"(1) An action for breach of any contract for sale must be commenced within four years after the cause of action has accrued. By the original agreement the parties may reduce the period of limitation to not less than one year but may not extend it.

"(2) A cause of action accrues when the breach occurs, regardless of the aggrieved party's lack of knowledge of the breach. A breach of warranty occurs when tender of delivery is made, except that where a warranty explicitly extends to future performance of the goods and discovery of the breach must await the time of such performance the cause of action accrues when the breach is or should have been discovered.

"(3) Where an action commenced within the time limited by subsection (1) is so terminated as to leave available a remedy by another action for the same breach such other action may be commenced after the expiration of the time limited and within six months after the termination of the first action unless the termination resulted from voluntary discontinuance or from dismissal for failure or neglect to prosecute.

"(4) This section does not alter the law on tolling of the statute of limitations nor does it apply to causes of action which have accrued before this Act becomes effective."

Uniform Commercial Code Comment

Prior Uniform Statutory Provision:
None.

Purposes:

To introduce a uniform statute of limitations for sales contracts, thus eliminating the jurisdictional variations and providing needed relief for concerns doing business on a nationwide scale whose contracts have heretofore been governed by several different periods of limitation depending upon the state in which the transaction occurred. This Article takes sales contracts out of the general laws limiting the time for commencing contractual actions and selects a four year period as the most appropriate to modern business practice. This is within the normal commercial record keeping period.

Subsection (1) permits the parties to reduce the period of limitation. The minimum period is set at one year. The parties may not, however, extend the statutory period.

Subsection (2), providing that the cause of action accrues when the breach occurs, states an exception where the warranty extends to future performance.

Subsection (3) states the saving provision included in many state statutes and permits an additional short period for bringing new actions, where suits begun within the four year period have been terminated so as to leave a remedy still available for the same breach.

Subsection (4) makes it clear that this Article does not purport to alter or modify in any respect the law on tolling of the Statute of Limitations as it now prevails in the various jurisdictions.

Definitional Cross References:

"Action". Section 1–201.
"Aggrieved party". Section 1–201.
"Agreement". Section 1–201.
"Contract for sale". Section 2–106.
"Goods". Section 2–105.
"Party". Section 1–201.
"Remedy". Section 1–201.
"Term". Section 1–201.
"Termination". Section 2–106.

CHAPTER 8. RETAIL SALES

Section
2800. Goods Defined.
2801. Warranty; Proof of Purchase Form Completion Requirement; Waiver.

Chapter 8 added by Stats.1970, c. 972, p. 1744, § 1.

§ 2800. Goods Defined

As used in this chapter "goods" means goods used or bought for use primarily for personal, family or household purposes. *(Added by Stats.1970, c. 972, p. 1744, § 1.)*

Cross References

Consumer warranties, see Civil Code § 1790 et seq.

§ 2801. Warranty; Proof of Purchase Form Completion Requirement; Waiver

In any retail sale of goods, if the manufacturer or seller of the goods issues a written warranty or guarantee as to the condition or quality of all or part of the goods which requires the buyer to complete and return any form to the manufacturer or seller as proof of the purchase of the goods, such warranty or guarantee shall not be unenforceable solely because the buyer fails to complete or return the form. This section does not relieve the buyer from proving the fact of purchase and the date thereof in any case in which such a fact is in issue.

The buyer must agree in writing to any waiver of this section for the waiver to be valid. Any waiver by the buyer of the provisions of this section which is not in writing is contrary to public policy and shall be unenforceable and void. *(Added by Stats.1970, c. 972, p. 1744, § 1.)*

Division 3

NEGOTIABLE INSTRUMENTS

Chapter	Section
1. General Provisions and Definitions	3101
2. Negotiation, Transfer, and Indorsement	3201
3. Enforcement of Instruments	3301
4. Liability of Parties	3401
5. Dishonor	3501
6. Discharge and Payment	3601

WESTLAW Computer Assisted Legal Research

WESTLAW supplements your legal research in many ways. WESTLAW allows you to
- update your research with the most current information
- expand your library with additional resources
- retrieve direct history, precedential history and parallel citations with the Insta-Cite service

For more information on using WESTLAW to supplement your research, see the WESTLAW Electronic Research Guide, which follows the Preface.

Cross References

Conflict between Division 3 and Division 4 or Division 9, resolution, see Commercial Code § 3102.

Third-party liability, notice of right to defend action, see Commercial Code § 3119.

CHAPTER 1. GENERAL PROVISIONS AND DEFINITIONS

Section
3101. Short title.
3102. Application of division; conflict with other divisions.
3103. Definitions.
3104. Negotiable instrument; instrument; check; definitions.
3105. Issue; issuer.
3106. Unconditional or conditional promises or orders.
3107. Payable in foreign money.
3108. Payable on demand; payable at a definite time; payable at a fixed date.
3109. Payable to bearer; payable to order.
3110. Person to whom instrument is payable; determination of holder.
3111. Place of payment.
3112. Interest.
3113. Date of instrument.
3114. Contradictory terms in instrument.
3115. Incomplete instruments.
3116. Joint and several liability on instrument; contribution.
3117. Separate agreements affecting instrument.
3118. Limitation of actions.
3119. Third-party liability; notice of right to defend action.
3120 to 3123. Repealed.

Transitional Provisions

Effective date and transitional provisions for repeal and addition of Division 3 by Stats.1992, c. 914, see Commercial Code § 16101 et seq.

Introductory Comment

By Charles J. Williams

Division 3 replaces the Negotiable Instruments Law (former Civil Code §§ 3082–3266(d)) hereafter referred to as the NIL.

The NIL is the oldest of the uniform acts and was adopted in California in 1917. By 1924 every state had adopted it.

The general affect of Division 3 on existing California law was summarized by a subcommittee of the State Bar in its report to the legislature in 1961 which at that time was considering a version of the Uniform Commercial Code based upon the 1958 Official Text:

"Article [Division] 3 of the Uniform Commercial Code is a revision and reorganization of the existing Negotiable Instruments Law now found in our Civil Code. While new language has been used, the changes from the existing NIL are not too great and to all intents and purposes it may be said that the law in this area remains the same. Where in the past there have been conflicts in the interpretation of the NIL, these have been resolved and other sections have been added amplifying the provisions of the NIL or codifying existing case law . . ."

Sixth Progress Report to the Legislature by Senate Fact Finding Committee on Judiciary (1959–1961) Part 1, The Uniform Commercial Code, pp. 342, 343.

Some of the most difficult problems under the NIL involved the rights of parties to a forged check or indorsement. The language of the NIL left many questions unresolved when a forgery occurred. Division 3 resolves many of these problems.

In general, most of the principal rules of the NIL are continued by Division 3 and it makes fewer changes in existing law than any other division of the Commercial Code.

Cross References

Branch or separate office of bank as separate bank for purpose of computation of time, see Commercial Code § 4107.

Forgery of documents of value, see Penal Code § 470.

Items within Division 3, Negotiable Instruments and Division 4, Bank Deposits and Collections, subject to Division 3 except if there is conflict, see Commercial Code § 4102.

Making, possessing or uttering fictitious instruments with intent to defraud, see Penal Code § 476.

Non-negotiable instruments, transfer, see Civil Code § 1459.

Passing worthless checks, see Penal Code § 476a.

Promissory notes serviced by real estate brokers, completion of delivery, transfer and perfection, see Business and Professions Code § 10233.2.

Service of promissory note by real estate broker for lender or purchaser, delivery, transfer and perfection deemed complete for purposes of this division even if possession in broker if recorded, see Business and Professions Code § 10233.2.

§ 3101. Short title

This division may be cited as Uniform Commercial Code—Negotiable Instruments. *(Added by Stats.1992, c. 914 (S.B.833), § 6.)*

California Code Comment

By John A. Bohn and Charles J. Williams

This is section 3–101 of the Official Text without change.

Uniform Commercial Code Comment

This Article represents a complete revision and modernization of the Uniform Negotiable Instruments Law.

The Comments which follow will point out the respects in which this Article changes the Negotiable Instruments Law, which was promulgated by the National Conference of Commissioners on Uniform State Laws in 1896, and was subsequently enacted in every American jurisdiction. Needless to say, in the 50 odd years of the history of that statute, there have been vast changes in commercial practices relating to the handling of negotiable instruments. The need for revision of this important statute was felt for some years before the present project was undertaken.

It should be noted especially that this Article does not apply in any way to the handling of securities. Article 8 deals with that subject. See Sec. 3–103.

§ 3102. Application of division; conflict with other divisions

(a) This division applies to negotiable instruments. It does not apply to money, to payment orders governed by Division 11 (commencing with Section 11101), or to securities governed by Division 8 (commencing with Section 8101).

(b) If there is conflict between this division and Division 4 (commencing with Section 4101) or Division 9 (commencing with Section 9101), Divisions 4 and 9 govern.

(c) Regulations of the Board of Governors of the Federal Reserve System and operating circulars of the Federal Reserve Banks supersede any inconsistent provision of this division to the extent of the inconsistency. *(Added by Stats.1992, c. 914 (S.B.833), § 6.)*

California Code Comment

By John A. Bohn and Charles J. Williams

Prior California Law

1. This section is the statutory counterpart of former Civil Code § 3266. The Commercial Code section is much broader in the scope of the words which it defines and the definitions of words which it incorporates.

2. Subdivision (1)(a) defines "issue" in terms of an instrument which is negotiable and eliminates the requirement in former Civil Code § 3266 that the instrument be "complete in form." This removes the inconsistency which had existed between the general definition in former Civil Code § 3266 which was in terms of completeness and former Civil Code §§ 3095 and 3096 which provided for the completion of instruments not complete in form. The definition is broadened by providing that an instrument is issued when it is delivered to a remitter. Thus, an instrument is issued when a buyer of goods (remitter) obtains from a bank a draft payable to the seller.

3. Subdivision (1)(b) eliminates the restriction of former Civil Code § 3209 that a bill could not be addressed to two or more drawees in the alternative. It retains the restriction in former Civil Code § 3209 that a bill cannot be addressed to two or more drawees in succession. It retains the provision that a bill can be drawn jointly.

4. "Promise" defined in subdivision (c) was not given statutory definition under the NIL.

5. "Secondary party" defined in subdivision (d) was not defined as such under the NIL. However, former Civil Code § 3266a generally defined a party who was secondarily liable as one who was not primarily liable. Section 3266a defined the one primarily liable on the instrument as one "who by the terms of the instrument is absolutely required to pay the same."

6. Subdivision (1)(e) defining "instrument" is the same definition as in former Civil Code § 3266. However, Commercial Code § 3805 makes Division 3 applicable to an instrument not payable to order or bearer (e.g. a check reading "pay John Doe") which is otherwise negotiable. See California Code Comment to section 3805.

Changes from U.C.C. (1962 Official Text)

7. This is section 3–102 of the Official Text without change.

Uniform Commercial Code Comment
1992 Addition

1. Former Article 3 had no provision affirmatively stating its scope. Former Section 3–103 was a limitation on scope. In revised Article 3, Section 3–102 states that Article 3 applies to "negotiable instruments," defined in Section 3–104. Section 3–104(b) also defines the term "instrument" as a synonym for "negotiable instrument." In most places Article 3 uses the shorter term "instrument." This follows the convention used in former Article 3.

2. The reference in former Section 3–103(1) to "documents of title" is omitted as superfluous because these documents contain no promise to pay money. The definition of "payment order" in Section 4A–103(a)(1)(iii) excludes drafts which are governed by Article 3. Section 3–102(a) makes clear that a payment order governed by Article 4A is not governed by Article 3. Thus, Article 3 and Article 4A are mutually exclusive.

Article 8 states in Section 8–103(d) that "A writing that is a security certificate is governed by this Article and not by Article 3, even though it also meets the requirements of that Article." Section 3–102(a) conforms to this provision. With respect to some promises or orders to pay money, there may be a question whether the promise or order is an instrument under Section 3–104(a) or a certificated security under Section 8–102(a)(4) and (15). Whether a writing is covered by Article 3 or Article 8 has important consequences. Among other things, under Section 8–207, the issuer of a certificated security may treat the registered owner as the owner for all purposes until the presentment for registration of a transfer. The issuer of a negotiable instrument, on the other hand, may discharge its obligation to pay the instrument only by paying a person entitled to enforce under Section 3–301. There are also important consequences to an indorser. An indorser of a security does not undertake the issuer's obligation or make any warranty that the issuer will honor the underlying obligation, while an indorser of a negotiable instrument becomes secondarily liable on the underlying obligation. Amendments approved by the Permanent Editorial Board for Uniform Commercial Code November 4, 1995.

Ordinarily the distinction between instruments and certificated securities in non-bearer form should be relatively clear. A certificated security under Article 8 must be in registered form (Section 8–102(a)(13)) so that it can be registered on the issuer's records. By contrast, registration plays no part in Article 3. The distinction between an instrument and a certificated security in bearer form may be somewhat more difficult and will generally lie in the economic functions of the two writings. Ordinarily, negotiable instruments under Article 3 will be separate and distinct instruments, while certificated securities under Article 8 will be either one of a class or series or by their terms divisible into a class or series (Section 8–102(a)(15)(ii)). Thus, a promissory note in bearer form could come under either Article 3 if it were simply an individual note, or under Article 8 if it were one of a series of notes or divisible into a series. An additional distinction is whether the instrument is of the type commonly dealt in on securities exchanges or markets or commonly recognized as a medium for investment (Section 8–102(a)(15)(iii)). Thus, a check written in bearer form (i.e., a check made payable to "cash") would not be a certificated security within Article 8 of the Uniform Commercial Code. Amendments approved by the Permanent Editorial Board for Uniform Commercial Code November 4, 1995.

Occasionally, a particular writing may fit the definition of both a negotiable instrument under Article 3 and of an investment security under Article 8. In such cases, the instrument is subject exclusively to the requirements of Article 8. Section 8–103(d) and Section 3–102(a). Amendments approved by the Permanent Editorial Board for Uniform Commercial Code November 4, 1995.

3. Although the terms of Article 3 apply to transactions by Federal Reserve Banks, federal preemption would make ineffective any Article 3 provision that conflicts with federal law. The activities of the Federal Reserve Banks are governed by regulations of the Federal Reserve Board and by operating circulars issued by the Reserve Banks themselves. In some instances, the operating circulars are issued pursuant to a Federal Reserve Board regulation. In other cases, the Reserve Bank issues the operating circular under its own authority under the Federal Reserve Act, subject to review by the Federal Reserve Board. Section 3–102(c) states that Federal Reserve Board regulations and operating circulars of the Federal Reserve Banks supersede any inconsistent provision of Article 3 to the extent of the inconsistency. Federal Reserve Board regulations, being valid exercises of regulatory authority pursuant to a federal statute, take precedence over state law if there is an inconsistency. Childs v. Federal Reserve Bank of Dallas, 719 F.2d 812 (5th Cir.1983), reh. den. 724 F.2d 127 (5th Cir.1984). Section 3–102(c) treats operating circulars as having the same effect whether issued under the Reserve Bank's own authority or under a Federal Reserve Board regulation. Federal statutes may also preempt Article 3. For example, the Expedited Funds Availability Act, 12 U.S.C. § 4001 et seq., provides that the Act and the regulations issued pursuant to the Act supersede any inconsistent provisions of the UCC. 12 U.S.C. § 4007(b).

4. In Clearfield Trust Co. v. United States, 318 U.S. 363 (1943), the Court held that if the United States is a party to an instrument, its rights and duties are governed by federal common law in the absence of a specific federal statute or regulation. In United States v. Kimbell Foods, Inc., 440 U.S. 715 (1979), the Court stated a three-pronged test to ascertain whether the federal common-law rule should follow the state rule. In most instances courts under the *Kimbell* test have shown a willingness to adopt UCC rules in formulating federal common law on the subject. In *Kimbell* the Court adopted the priorities rules of Article 9.

5. In 1989 the United Nations Commission on International Trade Law completed a Convention on International Bills of Exchange and International Promissory Notes. If the United States becomes a party to this Convention, the Convention will preempt state law with respect to international bills and notes governed by the Convention. Thus, an international bill of exchange or promissory note that meets the definition of instrument in Section 3–104 will not be governed by Article 3 if it is governed by the Convention.

Cross References

Writing that is certificated security and negotiable instrument governed by Division 8, see Commercial Code § 8102.
Presentment, manner of making, see Commercial Code § 3501.

§ 3103. Definitions

(a) In this division:

(1) "Acceptor" means a drawee who has accepted a draft.

(2) "Drawee" means a person ordered in a draft to make payment.

(3) "Drawer" means a person who signs or is identified in a draft as a person ordering payment.

(4) "Good faith" means honesty in fact and the observance of reasonable commercial standards of fair dealing.

(5) "Maker" means a person who signs or is identified in a note as a person undertaking to pay.

(6) "Order" means a written instruction to pay money signed by the person giving the instruction. The instruction may be addressed to any person, including the person giving the instruction, or to one or more persons jointly or in the alternative but not in succession. An authorization to pay is not an order unless the person authorized to pay is also instructed to pay.

(7) "Ordinary care" in the case of a person engaged in business means observance of reasonable commercial standards, prevailing in the area in which the person is located, with respect to the business in which the person is engaged. In the case of a bank that takes an instrument for processing for collection or payment by automated means, reasonable commercial standards do not require the bank to examine the instrument if the failure to examine does not violate the bank's prescribed procedures and the bank's procedures do not vary unreasonably from general banking usage not disapproved by this division or Division 4 (commencing with Section 4101).

(8) "Party" means a party to an instrument.

(9) "Promise" means a written undertaking to pay money signed by the person undertaking to pay. An acknowledgment of an obligation by the obligor is not a promise unless the obligor also undertakes to pay the obligation.

(10) "Prove" with respect to a fact means to meet the burden of establishing the fact (subdivision (8) of Section 1201).

(11) "Remitter" means a person who purchases an instrument from its issuer if the instrument is payable to an identified person other than the purchaser.

(b) Other definitions applying to this division and the sections in which they appear are:

"Acceptance"	Section 3409
"Accommodated party"	Section 3419
"Accommodation party"	Section 3419
"Alteration"	Section 3407
"Anomalous endorsement"	Section 3205
"Blank endorsement"	Section 3205
"Cashier's check"	Section 3104
"Certificate of deposit"	Section 3104
"Certified check"	Section 3409
"Check"	Section 3104
"Consideration"	Section 3303
"Demand Draft"	Section 3104
"Draft"	Section 3104
"Holder in due course"	Section 3302
"Incomplete instrument"	Section 3115
"Indorsement"	Section 3204
"Indorser"	Section 3204
"Instrument"	Section 3104
"Issue"	Section 3105
"Issuer"	Section 3105
"Negotiable instrument"	Section 3104
"Negotiation"	Section 3201
"Note"	Section 3104
"Payable at a definite time"	Section 3108
"Payable on demand"	Section 3108
"Payable to bearer"	Section 3109
"Payable to order"	Section 3109
"Payment"	Section 3602
"Person entitled to enforce"	Section 3301
"Presentment"	Section 3501
"Reacquisition"	Section 3207
"Special indorsement"	Section 3205
"Teller's check"	Section 3104
"Transfer of instrument"	Section 3203

"Traveler's check"	Section 3104
"Value"	Section 3303

(c) The following definitions in other divisions apply to this division:

"Bank"	Section 4105
"Banking day"	Section 4104
"Clearinghouse"	Section 4104
"Collecting bank"	Section 4105
"Depositary bank"	Section 4105
"Documentary draft"	Section 4104
"Intermediary bank"	Section 4105
"Item"	Section 4104
"Payor bank"	Section 4105
"Suspends payments"	Section 4104

(d) In addition, Division 1 (commencing with Section 1101) contains general definitions and principles of construction and interpretation applicable throughout this division. *(Added by Stats.1992, c. 914 (S.B.833), § 6. Amended by Stats.1996, c. 316 (S.B.1742), § 1.)*

California Code Comment

By John A. Bohn and Charles J. Williams

Prior California Law

1. This section is new statutory law. Subdivision (1) excludes the application of Division 3 from documents or instruments which are covered by other divisions of the Commercial Code. (documents of title under Division 7 and investment securities under Division 8). Division 3 has a more restrictive application than the NIL and applies only to commercial paper as it is classified in section 3104(2). Documents of title (such as bills of lading or warehouse receipts) covered under Division 7, or investment securities (such as corporate bonds or debentures) treated under Division 8 may be negotiable under those divisions but Division 3 is not intended to apply to them. Official Comment 1.

2. Subdivision (2) makes Division 3 general in its application and where Division 4 (bank deposits and collections) or Division 9 (secured transactions) applies, Division 3 is subordinate. This means, for example, that an item of commercial paper which is also in the course of bank collection is subject to both Division 3 and Division 4 but where there is a conflict between the provisions of either Division, Division 4 prevails. An item of commercial paper might be held as security thus making it also subject to Division 9.

If an instrument is negotiable under this division and is also a security under Division 8, Division 8 applies. Official Comment 2.

Changes from U.C.C. (1962 Official Text)

3. This is section 3–103 of the Official Text without change.

Uniform Commercial Code Comment
1992 Addition

1. Subsection (a) defines some common terms used throughout the Article that were not defined by former Article 3 and adds the definitions of "order" and "promise" found in former Section 3–102(1)(b) and (c).

2. The definition of "order" includes an instruction given by the signer to another. The most common example of this kind of order is a cashier's check: a draft with respect to which the drawer and drawee are the same bank or branches of the same bank. Former Section 3–118(a) treated a cashier's check as a note. It stated "a draft drawn on the drawer is effective as a note." Although it is technically more correct to treat a cashier's check as a promise by the issuing bank to pay rather than an order to pay, a cashier's check is in the form of a check and it is normally referred to as a check. Thus, revised Article 3 follows banking practice in referring to a cashier's check as both a draft and a check rather than a note. Some insurance companies also follow the practice of issuing drafts in which the drawer draws on itself and makes the draft payable at or through a bank. These instruments are also treated as drafts. The obligation of the drawer of a cashier's check or other draft drawn on the drawer is stated in Section 3–412.

An order may be addressed to more than one person as drawee either jointly or in the alternative. The authorization of alternative drawees follows former Section 3–102(1)(b) and recognizes the practice of drawers, such as corporations issuing dividend checks, who for commercial convenience name a number of drawees, usually in different parts of the country. Section 3–501(b)(1) provides that presentment may be made to any one of multiple drawees. Drawees in succession are not permitted because the holder should not be required to make more than one presentment. Dishonor by any drawee named in the draft entitles the holder to rights of recourse against the drawer or indorsers.

3. The last sentence of subsection (a)(9) is intended to make it clear that an I.O.U. or other written acknowledgment of indebtedness is not a note unless there is also an undertaking to pay the obligation.

4. Subsection (a)(4) introduces a definition of good faith to apply to Articles 3 and 4. Former Articles 3 and 4 used the definition in Section 1–201(19). The definition in subsection (a)(4) is consistent with the definitions of good faith applicable to Articles 2, 2A, 4, and 4A. The definition requires not only honesty in fact but also "observance of reasonable commercial standards of fair dealing." Although fair dealing is a broad term that must be defined in context, it is clear that it is concerned with the fairness of conduct rather than the care with which an act is performed. Failure to exercise ordinary care in conducting a transaction is an entirely different concept than failure to deal fairly in conducting the transaction. Both fair dealing and ordinary care, which is defined in Section 3–103(a)(7), are to be judged in the light of reasonable commercial standards, but those standards in each case are directed to different aspects of commercial conduct.

5. Subsection (a)(7) is a definition of ordinary care which is applicable not only to Article 3 but to Article 4 as well. See Section 4–104(c). The general rule is stated in the first sentence of subsection (a)(7) and it applies both to banks and to persons engaged in businesses other than banking. Ordinary care means observance of reasonable commercial standards of the relevant business prevailing in the area in which the person is located. The second sentence of subsection (a)(7) is a particular rule limited to the duty of a bank to examine an instrument taken by a bank for processing for collection or payment by automated means. This particular rule applies primarily to Section 4–406 and it is discussed in Comment 4 to that section. Nothing in Section 3–103(a)(7) is intended to prevent a customer from proving that the procedures followed by a bank are unreasonable, arbitrary, or unfair.

6. In subsection (c) reference is made to a new definition of "bank" in amended Article 4.

Prior Uniform Statutory Provision:

None.

Purposes:

1. This Article is restricted to commercial paper—that is to say, to drafts, checks, certificates of deposit and notes as defined in Section 3–104(2). Subsection (1) expressly excludes and money, as defined in this Act (Section 1–201), even though the money may be in the form of a bank note which meets all the requirements of Section 3–104(1). Money is of course negotiable at common law or under separate statutes, but no provision of this Article is applicable to it. Subsection (1) also expressly excludes documents of title and investment securities which fall within Articles 7 and 8, respectively. To this extent the section follows decisions which held that interim certificates calling for the delivery of securities were not negotiable instruments under the original statute. Such paper is now covered under Article 8, but is not within any section of this Article. Likewise, bills of lading, warehouse receipts and other documents of title which fall within Article 7 may be negotiable under the provision of that Article, but are not covered by any section of this Article.

2. Instruments which fall within the scope of this Article may also be subject to other Articles of the Code. Many items in course of bank collection will of course be negotiable instruments, and the same may be true of collateral pledged as security for a debt. In such cases this Article, which is general, is, in case of conflicting provisions, subject to the Articles which deal specifically with the type of transaction or

instrument involved: Article 4 (Bank Deposits and Collections) and Article 9 (Secured Transactions). In the case of a negotiable instrument which is subject to Article 4 because it is in course of collection or to Article 9 because it is used as collateral, the provisions of this Article continue to be applicable except insofar as there may be conflicting provisions in the Bank Collection or Secured Transactions Article.

An instrument which qualifies as "negotiable" under this Article may also qualify as a "security" under Article 8. It will be noted that the formal requisites of negotiability (Section 3–104) go to matters of form exclusively; the definition of "security" on the other hand (Section 8–102) looks principally to the manner in which an instrument is used ("commonly dealt in upon securities exchanges . . . or commonly recognized . . . as a medium for investment"). If an instrument negotiable in form under Section 3–104 is, because of the manner of its use, a "security" under Section 8–102, Article 8 and not this Article applies. See subsection (1) of this Section and Section 8–102(1)(b).

Cross References:

Point 1: Articles 7 and 8; Sections 1–201, 3–104(1) and (2), 3–107.
Point 2: Articles 4 and 9; Sections 3–104 and 8–102.

Definitional Cross References:

"Document of title". Section 1–201.
"Money". Section 1–201.

Cross References

Credit union as bank, see Financial Code § 14867.
Money defined, see Commercial Code § 1201.
Bank deposits and collections, see Commercial Code § 4101 et seq.
Definitions, see Commercial Code §§ 1201, 8102.
Demand draft, defined, see Commercial Code § 3104.
Documents of title, see Commercial Code § 7101 et seq.
Investment securities, see Commercial Code § 8101 et seq.
Money, see Commercial Code § 3107.
Secured transactions, see Commercial Code § 9101 et seq.

§ 3104. Negotiable instrument; instrument; check; definitions

(a) Except as provided in subdivisions (c) and (d), "negotiable instrument" means an unconditional promise or order to pay a fixed amount of money, with or without interest or other charges described in the promise or order, if it is all of the following:

(1) Is payable to bearer or to order at the time it is issued or first comes into possession of a holder.

(2) Is payable on demand or at a definite time.

(3) Does not state any other undertaking or instruction by the person promising or ordering payment to do any act in addition to the payment of money, but the promise or order may contain (i) an undertaking or power to give, maintain, or protect collateral to secure payment, (ii) an authorization or power to the holder to confess judgment or realize on or dispose of collateral, or (iii) a waiver of the benefit of any law intended for the advantage or protection of an obligor.

(b) "Instrument" means a negotiable instrument.

(c) An order that meets all of the requirements of subdivision (a), except paragraph (1), and otherwise falls within the definition of "check" in subdivision (f) is a negotiable instrument and a check.

(d) A promise or order other than a check is not an instrument if, at the time it is issued or first comes into possession of a holder, it contains a conspicuous statement, however expressed, to the effect that the promise or order is not negotiable or is not an instrument governed by this division.

(e) An instrument is a "note" if it is a promise and is a "draft" if it is an order. If an instrument falls within the definition of both "note" and "draft," a person entitled to enforce the instrument may treat it as either.

(f) "Check" means (1) a draft, other than a documentary draft, payable on demand and drawn on a bank, (2) a cashier's check or teller's check, or (3) a demand draft. An instrument may be a check even though it is described on its face by another term, such as "money order."

(g) "Cashier's check" means a draft with respect to which the drawer and drawee are the same bank or branches of the same bank.

(h) "Teller's check" means a draft drawn by a bank (1) on another bank, or (2) payable at or through a bank.

(i) "Traveler's check" means an instrument that (1) is payable on demand, (2) is drawn on or payable at or through a bank, (3) is designated by the term "traveler's check" or by a substantially similar term, and (4) requires, as a condition to payment, a countersignature by a person whose specimen signature appears on the instrument.

(j) "Certificate of deposit" means an instrument containing an acknowledgment by a bank that a sum of money has been received by the bank and a promise by the bank to repay the sum of money. A certificate of deposit is a note of the bank.

(k) "Demand draft" means a writing not signed by a customer that is created by a third party under the purported authority of the customer for the purpose of charging the customer's account with a bank. A demand draft shall contain the customer's account number and may contain any or all of the following:

(1) The customer's printed or typewritten name.

(2) A notation that the customer authorized the draft.

(3) The statement "No Signature Required" or words to that effect.

A demand draft shall not include a check purportedly drawn by and bearing the signature of a fiduciary, as defined in paragraph (1) of subdivision (a) of Section 3307. (Added by Stats.1992, c. 914 (S.B.833), § 6. Amended by Stats.1996, c. 316 (S.B.1742), § 2.)

California Code Comment

By John A. Bohn and Charles J. Williams

Prior California Law

1. The requisites of negotiability under subdivision (1) are substantially the same as under former Civil Code § 3082 and the Commercial Code language represents changes in phraseology only.

2. Subdivision (1)(a) through (d) is the counterpart of former Civil Code § 3082. The term "signed" is defined in section 1201(39) and includes any symbol as long as there is an intent to authenticate a writing.

3. Subdivision (2)(a) is similar to former Civil Code § 3207 which defined a bill of exchange as "an unconditional order . . . by one . . . to another . . . requiring the person to whom it is addressed to pay on demand or at a fixed or determinable future time . . . money to order or to bearer."

4. Subdivision (2)(b) is similar to former Civil Code § 3265a which defined a check as a "bill of exchange drawn on a bank payable on demand . . ."

5. Subdivision (2)(c) is a new classification and has not been previously defined by any statute.

6. Subdivision (2)(d) is similar to former Civil Code § 3265 which defined a promissory note as ". . . an unconditional promise . . . by one person to another . . . to pay on demand, or at a fixed or determinable future time . . . money to order or to bearer . . .".

7. Subdivision (3) expresses the policy of section 3805 which makes it possible to attribute aspects of negotiability to non-negotiable instruments except for the doctrine of due course holding. See the California Code Comment and the Official Comment to section 3805.

8. The following is the analysis of the Legislative Counsel to the 1958 Official Text (unchanged in the 1962 Official Text):

"Applicable California Statutes.

Civil Code Sections 3082, 3086, 3091, 3207, and 3265a.

No substantial change in law.

Subdivision (1)(a) is similar to Civil Code Section 3082(1). See Siebenhauer v. Bank of California, 211 Cal. 239, 294 Pac. 1062.

Subdivision (1)(b) is similar to Civil Code Sections 3082(2) and 3086. Adams v. Seaman, 82 Cal. 636, 23 Pac. 53; Westlake Mercantile Fin. Corp. v. Merritt, 204 Cal. 673, 269 Pac. 620.

Subdivision (1)(c) is similar to Civil Code Section 3082(3).

Subdivision (1)(d) is similar to Civil Code Section 3082(4).

Subdivision (2)(a) is similar to but broader than Civil Code Section 3207 defining a bill of exchange.

Subdivision (2)(b) is similar to Civil Code Section 3265a.

Subdivision (2)(c) definition is new. See Civil Code Section 576 as to issue and transferability of certificate of deposit by savings and loan corporations. Defined in People v. California Safe Deposit & Trust Co., 23 Cal.App. 199, 137 Pac. 1111, 1115.

Subdivision (3)—See U.C.C. Section 3–805.

The provisions of Civil Code Section 3086 permitting additional terms have largely been eliminated, but compare U.C.C. Section 3–112. Note the provisions of Civil Code Section 3086(4) permitting an election in holder to require something in lieu of money is omitted.

The provisions of Civil Code Section 3091 permitting looser language is omitted from U.C.C." Sixth Progress Report to the Legislature by Senate Fact Finding Committee on Judiciary (1959–1961) part 1, The Uniform Commercial Code, pp. 65–66.

Changes from U.C.C. (1962 Official Text)

9. This is section 3–104 of the Official Text without change.

Uniform Commercial Code Comment
1992 Addition

1. The definition of "negotiable instrument" defines the scope of Article 3 since Section 3–102 states: "This Article applies to negotiable instruments." The definition in Section 3–104(a) incorporates other definitions in Article 3. An instrument is either a "promise," defined in Section 3–103(a)(9), or "order," defined in Section 3–103(a)(6). A promise is a written undertaking to pay money signed by the person undertaking to pay. An order is a written instruction to pay money signed by the person giving the instruction. Thus, the term "negotiable instrument" is limited to a signed writing that orders or promises payment of money. "Money" is defined in Section 1–201(24) and is not limited to United States dollars. It also includes a medium of exchange established by a foreign government or monetary units of account established by an intergovernmental organization or by agreement between two or more nations. Five other requirements are stated in Section 3–104(a): First, the promise or order must be "unconditional." The quoted term is explained in Section 3–106. Second, the amount of money must be "a fixed amount * * * with or without interest or other charges described in the promise or order." Section 3–112(b) relates to "interest." Third, the promise or order must be "payable to bearer or to order." The quoted phrase is explained in Section 3–109. An exception to this requirement is stated in subsection (c). Fourth, the promise or order must be payable "on demand or at a definite time." The quoted phrase is explained in Section 3–108. Fifth, the promise or order may not state "any other undertaking or instruction by the person promising or ordering payment to do any act in addition to the payment of money" with three exceptions. The quoted phrase is based on the first sentence of N.I.L. Section 5 which is the precursor of "no other promise, order, obligation or power given by the maker or drawer" appearing in former Section 3–104(1)(b). The words "instruction" and "undertaking" are used instead of "order" and "promise" that are used in the N.I.L. formulation because the latter words are defined terms that include only orders or promises to pay money. The three exceptions stated in Section 3–104(a)(3) are based on and are intended to have the same meaning as former Section 3–112(1)(b), (c), (d), and (e), as well as N.I.L. § 5(1), (2), and (3). Subsection (b) states that "instrument" means a "negotiable instrument." This follows former Section 3–102(1)(e) which treated the two terms as synonymous.

2. Unless subsection (c) applies, the effect of subsection (a)(1) and Section 3–102(a) is to exclude from Article 3 any promise or order that is not payable to bearer or to order. There is no provision in revised Article 3 that is comparable to former Section 3–805. The comment to former Section 3–805 states that the typical example of a writing covered by that section is a check reading "Pay John Doe." Such a check was governed by former Article 3 but there could not be a holder in due course of the check. Under Section 3–104(c) such a check is governed by revised Article 3 and there can be a holder in due course of the check. But subsection (c) applies only to checks. The comment to former Section 3–805 does not state any example other than the check to illustrate that section. Subsection (c) is based on the belief that it is good policy to treat checks, which are payment instruments, as negotiable instruments whether or not they contain the words "to the order of". These words are almost always pre-printed on the check form. Occasionally the drawer of a check may strike out these words before issuing the check. In the past some credit unions used check forms that did not contain the quoted words. Such check forms may still be in use but they are no longer common. Absence of the quoted words can easily be overlooked and should not affect the rights of holders who may pay money or give credit for a check without being aware that it is not in the conventional form.

Total exclusion from Article 3 of other promises or orders that are not payable to bearer or to order serves a useful purpose. It provides a simple device to clearly exclude a writing that does not fit the pattern of typical negotiable instruments and which is not intended to be a negotiable instrument. If a writing could be an instrument despite the absence of "to order" or "to bearer" language and a dispute arises with respect to the writing, it might be argued that the writing is a negotiable instrument because the other requirements of subsection (a) are somehow met. Even if the argument is eventually found to be without merit it can be used as a litigation ploy. Words making a promise or order payable to bearer or to order are the most distinguishing feature of a negotiable instrument and such words are frequently referred to as "words of negotiability." Article 3 is not meant to apply to contracts for the sale of goods or services or the sale or lease of real property or similar writings that may contain a promise to pay money. The use of words of negotiability in such contracts would be an aberration. Absence of the words precludes any argument that such contracts might be negotiable instruments.

An order or promise that is excluded from Article 3 because of the requirements of Section 3–104(a) may nevertheless be similar to a negotiable instrument in many respects. Although such a writing cannot be made a negotiable instrument within Article 3 by contract or conduct of its parties, nothing in Section 3–104 or in Section 3–102 is intended to mean that in a particular case involving such a writing a court could not arrive at a result similar to the result that would follow if the writing were a negotiable instrument. For example, a court might find that the obligor with respect to a promise that does not fall within Section 3–104(a) is precluded from asserting a defense against a bona fide purchaser. The preclusion could be based on estoppel or ordinary principles of contract. It does not depend upon the law of negotiable instruments. An example is stated in the paragraph following Case # 2 in Comment 4 to Section 3–302.

Moreover, consistent with the principle stated in Section 1–102(2)(b), the immediate parties to an order or promise that is not an instrument may provide by agreement that one or more of the provisions of Article 3 determine their rights and obligations under the writing. Upholding the parties' choice is not inconsistent with Article 3. Such an agreement may bind a transferee of the writing if the transferee has notice of it or the agreement arises from usage of trade and the agreement does not violate other law or public policy. An example of such an agreement is a provision that a transferee of the writing has the rights of a holder in due course stated in Article 3 if the transferee took rights under the writing in good faith, for value, and without notice of a claim or defense.

Even without an agreement of the parties to an order or promise that is not an instrument, it may be appropriate, consistent with the principles stated in Section 1–102(2), for a court to apply one or more provisions of Article 3 to the writing by analogy, taking into account the expectations of the parties and the differences between the writing and an instrument governed by Article 3. Whether such application is appropriate depends upon the facts of each case.

3. Subsection (d) allows exclusion from Article 3 of a writing that would otherwise be an instrument under subsection (a) by a statement to the effect that the writing is not negotiable or is not governed by Article 3. For example, a promissory note can be stamped with the legend NOT NEGOTIABLE. The effect under subsection (d) is not only to negate the possibility of a holder in due course, but to prevent the writing from being a negotiable instrument for any purpose. Subsection (d) does not, however, apply to a check. If a writing is excluded from Article 3 by subsection (d), a court could, nevertheless, apply Article 3 principles to it by analogy as stated in Comment 2.

4. Instruments are divided into two general categories: drafts and notes. A draft is an instrument that is an order. A note is an instrument that is a promise. Section 3–104(e). The term "bill of exchange" is not used in Article 3. It is generally understood to be a synonym for the term "draft." Subsections (f) through (j) define particular instruments that fall within the categories of draft and note. The term "draft," defined in subsection (e), includes a "check" which is defined in subsection (f). "Check" includes a share draft drawn on a credit union payable through a bank because the definition of bank (Section 4–104) includes credit unions. However, a draft drawn on an insurance payable through a bank is not a check because it is not drawn on a bank. "Money orders" are sold both by banks and non-banks. They vary in form and their form determines how they are treated in Article 3. The most common form of money order sold by banks is that of an ordinary check drawn by the purchaser except that the amount is machine impressed. That kind of money order is a check under Article 3 and is subject to a stop order by the purchaser-drawer as in the case of ordinary checks. The seller bank is the drawee and has no obligation to a holder to pay the money order. If a money order falls within the definition of a teller's check, the rules applicable to teller's checks apply. Postal money orders are subject to federal law. "Teller's check" is separately defined in subsection (h). A teller's check is always drawn by a bank and is usually drawn on another bank. In some cases a teller's check is drawn on a nonbank but is made payable at or through a bank. Article 3 treats both types of teller's check identically, and both are included in the definition of "check." A cashier's check, defined in subsection (g), is also included in the definition of "check." Traveler's checks are issued both by banks and nonbanks and may be in the form of a note or draft. Subsection (i) states the essential characteristics of a traveler's check. The requirement that the instrument be "drawn on or payable at or through a bank" may be satisfied without words on the instrument that identify a bank as drawee or paying agent so long as the instrument bears an appropriate routing number that identifies a bank as paying agent.

The definitions in Regulation CC § 229.2 of the terms "check," "cashier's check," "teller's check," and "traveler's check" are different from the definitions of those terms in Article 3.

Certificates of deposit are treated in former Article 3 as a separate type of instrument. In revised Article 3, Section 3–104(j) treats them as notes.

Prior Uniform Statutory Provision:

Sections 1, 5, 10, 126, 184 and 185, Uniform Negotiable Instruments Law.

Changes: Parts of original sections combined and reworded; new provisions; original Section 10 omitted.

Purposes of Changes and New Matter: The changes are intended to bring together in one section related provisions and definitions formerly widely separated.

1. Under subsection (1)(b) any writing, to be a negotiable instrument within this Article, must be payable in money. In a few states there are special statutes, enacted at an early date when currency was less sound and barter was prevalent, which make promises to pay in commodities negotiable. Even under these statutes commodity notes are now little used and have no general circulation. This Article makes no attempt to provide for such paper, as it is a matter of purely local concern. Even if retention of the old statutes is regarded in any state as important, amendment of this section may not be necessary, since "within this Article" in subsection (1) leaves open the possibility that some writings may be made negotiable by other statutes or by judicial decision. The same is true as to any new type of paper which commercial practice may develop in the future.

2. While a writing cannot be made a negotiable instrument within this Article by contract or by conduct, nothing in this section is intended to mean that in a particular case a court may not arrive at a result similar to that of negotiability by finding that the obligor is estopped by his conduct from asserting a defense against a bona fide purchaser. Such an estoppel rests upon ordinary principles of the law of simple contract; it does not depend upon negotiability, and it does not make the writing negotiable for any other purpose. But a contract to build a house or to employ a workman, or equally a security agreement does not become a negotiable instrument by the mere insertion of a clause agreeing that it shall be one.

3. The words "no other promise, order, obligation or power" in subsection (1)(b) are an expansion of the first sentence of the original Section 5. Section 3–112 permits an instrument to carry certain limited obligations or powers in addition to the simple promise or order to pay money. Subsection (1) of this Section is intended to say that it cannot carry others.

4. Any writing which meets the requirements of subsection (1) and is not excluded under Section 3–103 is a negotiable instrument, and all sections of this Article apply to it, even though it may contain additional language beyond that contemplated by this section. Such an instrument is a draft, a check, a certificate of deposit or a note as defined in subsection (2). Traveler's checks in the usual form, for instance, are negotiable instruments under this Article when they have been completed by the identifying signature.

5. This Article omits the original Section 10, which provided that the instrument need not follow the language of the act if it "clearly indicates an intention to conform" to it. The provision has served no useful purpose, and it has been an encouragement to bad drafting and to liberality in holding questionable paper to be negotiable. The omission is not intended to mean that the instrument must follow the language of this section, or that one term may not be recognized as clearly the equivalent of another, as in the case of "I undertake" instead of "I promise," or "Pay to holder" instead of "Pay to bearer." It does mean that either the language of the section or a clear equivalent must be found, and that in doubtful cases the decision should be against negotiability.

6. Subsection (3) is intended to make clear the same policy expressed in Section 3–805.

Cross References:

Sections 3–105 through 3–112, 3–401, 3–402 and 3–403.
Point 1: Section 3–107.
Point 3: Section 3–112.
Point 4: Sections 3–103 and 3–805.
Point 6: Section 8–805.

Definitional Cross References:

"Bank". Section 1–201.
"Bearer". Section 1–201.
"Definite time". Section 3–109.
"Money". Section 1–201.
"On demand". Section 3–108.
"Order". Section 3–102.
"Promise". Section 3–102.
"Signed". Section 1–201.
"Term". Section 1–201.
"Writing". Section 1–201.

§ 3104

Cross References

Dating, antedating, postdating, see Commercial Code § 3113.
Draft defined, bank deposits and collections, see Commercial Code § 4104.
Holder in due course not subject to execution lien on property transferred or encumbered not in custody of levying officer, see Code of Civil Procedure § 697.740.
Incomplete instruments, see Commercial Code § 3115.
Instrument under seal, negotiability, see Commercial Code § 3113.
Money, see Commercial Code § 3107.
Negotiable documents of title, see Commercial Code § 7104.
Negotiable instrument, payment for goods or services, see Civil Code § 1725.
Payable to bearer, see Commercial Code § 3109.
Payable to order, see Commercial Code § 3109.
Payment of foreign money by dollars, see Commercial Code § 3107.
Personal property not in custody of levying officer transferred or encumbered, exceptions, see Code of Civil Procedure § 697.740.
Restrictive indorsements, effect on negotiability, see Commercial Code § 3206.
Scope of division, see Commercial Code § 3102.
Signature, see Commercial Code § 3401 et seq.
Signature by authorized representative, see Commercial Code § 3403.
Signature in ambiguous capacity, see Commercial Code § 3402.
Signed, see Commercial Code § 1201.
Sum certain, see Commercial Code § 3106.
Terms and omissions not affecting negotiability, see Commercial Code § 3112.
Unconditional promise or order, see Commercial Code § 3106.

§ 3105. Issue; issuer

(a) "Issue" means the first delivery of an instrument by the maker or drawer, whether to a holder or nonholder, for the purpose of giving rights on the instrument to any person.

(b) An unissued instrument, or an unissued incomplete instrument that is completed, is binding on the maker or drawer, but nonissuance is a defense. An instrument that is conditionally issued or is issued for a special purpose is binding on the maker or drawer, but failure of the condition or special purpose to be fulfilled is a defense.

(c) "Issuer" applies to issued and unissued instruments and means a maker or drawer of an instrument. *(Added by Stats.1992, c. 914 (S.B.833), § 6.)*

California Code Comment

By John A. Bohn and Charles J. Williams

Prior California Law

1. This section is a revision and broadening of former Civil Code § 3084 which provided that an unqualified order or promise to pay is unconditional even though coupled with (1) an indication (as distinguished from an order or promise) of a particular fund out of which reimbursement is to be made or (2) a statement of the transaction giving rise to the instrument.

This section resolves conflicts in decisions from the various states under the NIL and is intended to remove any doubt as to the effect of a conditional promise or order upon negotiability. Official Comments 1, 2, 3 and 4.

2. Subdivision (1)(a) is new but is in accord with prior California law. The courts have held that the concurrent execution of a note with a conditional sales contract does not prevent an instrument from being negotiable. Commercial Credit Corp. v. Orange County Machine Works, 34 Cal.2d 766, 214 P.2d 819 (1950); Mann v. Leasko, 179 Cal.App.2d 692, 4 Cal.Rptr. 124 (1960).

3. Subdivision (1)(b) is similar to former Civil Code § 3084(2) and does not change the prior California law. The court in Johnston v. Wolf, 118 Cal.App. 388, 5 P.2d 673 (1932) held a trade acceptance negotiable despite the claim that it was rendered non-negotiable by the language that "the obligation of the acceptor arises out of the purchase of goods from the drawer."

4. Subdivision (1)(c) is new statutory law but is in accord with judicial decisions under former Civil Code § 3084. People's Bank v. Porter, 58 Cal.App. 41, 208 Pac. 200 (1922). However, in Westlake Mercantile Finance Corp. v. Merritt, 204 Cal. 673, 269 Pac. 620, 61 A.L.R. 811, (1928) a draft was held non-negotiable which recited that the obligation arose from a purchase but stated that maturity of the draft was "in conformity with original terms of purchase." Also see California Code Comment 10 and Commercial Code § 3119. Official Comment 2 points out that subdivision (1)(b) is intended to prevent an instrument such as the one in the Westlake case from being held to be non-negotiable.

5. Subdivision (1)(d) is new statutory law. The reasoning of the California cases cited in California Code Comments 3 and 4 preceding as to a statement or reference to a separate agreement or transaction could apply and result in the same rule stated in this subdivision.

6. Subdivision (1)(e) is new statutory law but is in accord with previous judicial decisions. People's Bank v. Porter, Comment 4, supra.

7. Subdivision (1)(f) is similar to former Civil Code § 3084(1).

8. Subdivision (1)(g) is contrary to prior California law as expressed in Kohn v. Sacramento Electric, Gas & Ry. Co., 168 Cal. 1, 141 Pac. 626 (1914). The court in that case held that the bonds issued by the Sacramento Electric, Gas and Railway Company were not negotiable because payable out of a specific fund and not upon the general credit of the maker. The court said that such a provision is "at war with the idea of negotiability." (note: this case was decided before the adoption of the NIL)

9. Subdivision (1)(h) is probably in accord with prior California law. Under the express language of former Civil Code § 3084(1), an instrument issued by a partnership, incorporated association, trust or estate which was limited to payment from its assets could have resulted in non-negotiability. However, in Nelson Co. v. Morton, 106 Cal.App. 144, 288 Pac. 845 (1930), the court held that a note executed by trustees and payable solely out of trust property was negotiable. The court pointed out that when a note is executed by trustees in their trust capacity exclusively it carries the general credit of the trustees as such, and resort is not confined to any particular fund or portion of the trust estate.

10. Subdivision (2)(a) is new statutory law but is in accord with established case law: Pitman v. Walker, 187 Cal. 667, 203 Pac. 739 (1922) holding note not negotiable where a mortgage security was issued concurrently as part of the same transaction; Westlake Mercantile Finance Corp. v. Merritt, 204 Cal. 673, 269 Pac. 620, 61 A.L.R. 811, (1928) holding note not negotiable where the underlying contract was made part of the note for the purpose of determining its maturity date. See also Commercial Code § 3119 as to the effect of other writings upon an instrument.

11. Subdivision (2)(b) is a restatement of the last sentence of former Civil Code § 3084(2). The reference to "except as provided in this section" is to subdivisions (1)(g) and (1)(h).

12. Subdivision (1)(c) of the 1962 Official Text is changed from the 1958 Official Text. It was taken from the language of the New York version of the Uniform Commercial Code. The reason for the change is to remove any doubt that acceleration or pre-payment provisions do not affect negotiability. This is in accord with prior California law that an acceleration clause does not destroy negotiability. Utah State Nat. Bank v. Smith, 180 Cal. 1, 179 Pac. 160 (1919); Smith v. Peters, 46 Cal.App. 47, 188 Pac. 811 (1920). See Comment 3 under section 1208.

Changes from U.C.C. (1962 Official Text)

13. This is section 3–105 of the Official Text without change.

Uniform Commercial Code Comment
1992 Addition

1. Under former Section 3–102(1)(a) "issue" was defined as the first delivery to a "holder or a remitter" but the term "remitter" was neither defined nor otherwise used. In revised Article 3, Section 3–105(a) defines "issue" more broadly to include the first delivery to anyone by the drawer or maker for the purpose of giving rights to anyone on the instrument. "Delivery" with respect to instruments is defined in Section 1–201(14) as meaning "voluntary transfer of possession."

2. Subsection (b) continues the rule that nonissuance, conditional issuance or issuance for a special purpose is a defense of the maker or drawer of an instrument. Thus, the defense can be asserted against a person other than a holder in due course. The same rule applies to nonissuance of an incomplete instrument later completed.

3. Subsection (c) defines "issuer" to include the signer of an unissued instrument for convenience of reference in the statute.

Uniform Commercial Code Comment

Prior Uniform Statutory Provision:

Section 3, Uniform Negotiable Instruments Law.

Changes: Completely revised.

Purposes of Changes: The section is intended to make it clear that, so far as negotiability is affected, the conditional or unconditional character of the promise or order is to be determined by what is expressed in the instrument itself; and to permit certain specific limitations upon the terms of payment.

1. Paragraph (a) of subsection (1) rejects the theory of decisions which have held that a recital in an instrument that it is given in return for an executory promise gives rise to an implied condition that the instrument is not to be paid if the promise is not performed, and that this condition destroys negotiability. Nothing in the section is intended to imply that language may not be fairly construed to mean what it says, but implications, whether of law or fact, are not to be considered in determining negotiability.

2. Paragraph (b) of subsection (1) is an amplification of Section 3(2) of the original act. The final clause is intended to resolve a conflict in the decisions over the effect of such language as "This note is given for payment as per contract for the purchase of goods of even date, maturity being in conformity with the terms of such contract." It adopts the general commercial understanding that such language is intended as a mere recital of the origin of the instrument and a reference to the transaction for information, but is not meant to condition payment according to the terms of any other agreement.

3. Paragraph (c) of subsection (1) likewise is intended to resolve a conflict, and to reject cases in which a reference to a separate agreement was held to mean that payment of the instrument must be limited in accordance with the terms of the agreement, and hence was conditioned by it. Such a reference normally is inserted for the purpose of making a record or giving information to anyone who may be interested, and in the absence of any express statement to that effect is not intended to limit the terms of payment. Inasmuch as rights as to prepayment or acceleration has to do with a "speed-up" in payment and since notes frequently refer to separate agreements for a statement of these rights, such reference does not destroy negotiability even though it has mild aspects of incorporation by reference. The general reasoning with respect to subparagraph (c) also applies to a draft which on its face states that it is drawn under a letter of credit (subparagraph (d)). Paragraphs (c) and (d) therefore adopt the position that negotiability is not affected. If the reference goes further and provides that payment must be made according to the terms of the agreement, it falls under paragraph (a) of subsection (2).

4. Paragraph (e) of subsection (1) is intended to settle another conflict in the decisions, over the effect of "title security notes" and other instruments which recite the security given. It rejects cases which have held that the mere statement that the instrument is secured, by reservation of title or otherwise, carries the implied condition that payment is to be made only if the security agreement is fully performed. Again such a recital normally is included only for the purpose of making a record or giving information, and is not intended to condition payment in any way. The provision adopts the position of the great majority of the courts.

5. Paragraph (f) of subsection (1) is a rewording of Section 3(1) of the original act.

6. Paragraph (g) of subsection (1) is new. It is intended to permit municipal corporations or other governments or governmental agencies to draw checks or to issue other short-term commercial paper in which payment is limited to a particular fund or to the proceeds of particular taxes or other sources of revenue. The provision will permit some municipal warrants to be negotiable if they are in proper form. Normally such warrants lack the words "order" or "bearer," or are marked "Not Negotiable," or are payable only in serial order, which makes them conditional.

7. Paragraph (h) of subsection (1) is new. It adopts the policy of decisions holding that an instrument issued by an unincorporated association is negotiable although its payment is expressly limited to the assets of the association, excluding the liability of individual members; and recognizing as negotiable an instrument issued by a trust estate without personal liability of the trustee. The policy is extended to a partnership and to any estate. The provision affects only the negotiability of the instrument, and is not intended to change the law of any state as to the liability of a partner, trustee, executor, administrator, or any other person on such an instrument.

8. Paragraph (a) of subsection (2) retains the generally accepted rule that where an instrument contains such language as "subject to terms of contract between maker and payee of this date," its payment is conditioned according to the terms of the agreement and the instrument is not negotiable. The distinction is between a mere recital of the existence of the separate agreement or a reference to it for information, which under paragraph (c) of subsection (1) will not affect negotiability, and any language which, fairly construed, requires the holder to look to the other agreement for the terms of payment. The intent of the provision is that an instrument is not negotiable unless the holder can ascertain all of its essential terms from its face. In the specific instance of rights as to prepayment or acceleration, however, there may be a reference to a separate agreement without destroying negotiability.

9. Paragraph (b) of subsection (2) restates the last sentence of Section 3 of the original act. As noted above, exceptions are made by paragraphs (g) and (h) of subsection (1) in favor of instruments issued by governments or governmental agencies, or by a partnership, unincorporated association, trust or estate.

Cross Reference:

Section 3–104.

Definitional Cross References:

"Account". Section 4–104.
"Agreement". Section 1–201.
"Instrument". Section 3–102.
"Issue". Section 3–102.
"Order". Section 3–102.
"Promise". Section 3–102.

Cross References

Acceleration,
  Option to accelerate at will, see Commercial Code § 1208.
Payment of instrument, see Commercial Code § 3108.
Instrument, see Commercial Code § 3103.
Terms and omissions not affecting negotiability, see Commercial Code § 3112.

§ 3106. Unconditional or conditional promises or orders

(a) Except as provided in this section, for the purposes of subdivision (a) of Section 3104, a promise or order is unconditional unless it states (1) an express condition to payment, (2) that the promise or order is subject to or governed by another writing, or (3) that rights or obligations with respect to the promise or order are stated in another writing. A reference to another writing does not of itself make the promise or order conditional.

(b) A promise or order is not made conditional (1) by a reference to another writing for a statement of rights with respect to collateral, prepayment, or acceleration, or (2) because payment is limited to resort to a particular fund or source.

(c) If a promise or order requires, as a condition to payment, a countersignature by a person whose specimen signature appears on the promise or order, the condition does not make the promise or order conditional for the purposes of subdivision (a) of Section 3104. If the person whose specimen signature appears on an instrument fails to countersign the instrument, the failure to countersign is a defense to the obligation of the issuer, but the failure does not prevent a transferee of the instrument from becoming a holder of the instrument.

(d) If a promise or order at the time it is issued or first comes into possession of a holder contains a statement, required by applicable statutory or administrative law, to the effect that the rights of a holder or transferee are subject to claims or defenses that the issuer could assert against the original payee, the promise or order is not thereby made conditional for the purposes of subdivision (a) of Section 3104; but if the promise or order is an instrument, there cannot be a holder in due course of the instrument. *(Added by Stats.1992, c. 914 (S.B.833), § 6.)*

California Code Comment

By John A. Bohn and Charles J. Williams

Prior California Law

1. This section is the statutory counterpart of former Civil Code § 3083. This section clarifies problems which arose under the NIL concerning the effect of interest, discounts or additions, costs and attorneys fees on the requirement that a negotiable instrument be payable in a "sum certain."

2. Subdivision (1)(a) is the same as former Civil Code § 3083(1) and (2).

3. Subdivision (1)(b) is new statutory law but does not change the result under former Civil Code § 3083(1). Under prior California law a different rate of interest before and after maturity did not prevent a note from being for a sum certain. For example, a note bearing interest at 8% until maturity which contained a provision that if the note was not paid at maturity the interest would be 10% on the accrued interest and principal is for a sum certain. Anaheim Nat. Bank v. Dolph, 201 Cal. 17, 255 Pac. 184 (1927).

4. Subdivision (1)(c) is new statutory law but is in accord with prior judicial decisions. Anaheim National Bank v. Dolph, 201 Cal. 17, 255 Pac. 184 (1927).

5. Subdivision (1)(d) is similar to former Civil Code § 3083(4) but clarifies it by providing that an instrument may be payable with exchange deducted as well as added.

6. Subdivision (1)(e) has been reworded but is substantially the same as former Civil Code § 3083(5). California case law is settled to the same effect. Anaheim Nat. Bank v. Dolph, 201 Cal. 17, 255 Pac. 184 (1927).

7. Subdivision (2) is new statutory language but does not change prior California law. The subdivision restricts the applicability of the section to its effect on negotiability only and is not intended to change the law as to the validity of the term itself. Official Comment 5.

Changes from U.C.C. (1962 Official Text)

8. This is section 3–106 of the Official Text without change.

Uniform Commercial Code Comment

1992 Addition

1. This provision replaces former Section 3–105. Its purpose is to define when a promise or order fulfills the requirement in Section 3–104(a) that it be an "unconditional" promise or order to pay. Under Section 3–106(a) a promise or order is deemed to be unconditional unless one of the two tests of the subsection make the promise or order conditional. If the promise or order states an express condition to payment, the promise or order is not an instrument. For example, a promise states, "I promise to pay $100,000 to the order of John Doe if he conveys title to Blackacre to me." The promise is not an instrument because there is an express condition to payment. However, suppose a promise states, "In consideration of John Doe's promise to convey title to Blackacre I promise to pay $100,000 to the order of John Doe." That promise can be an instrument if Section 3–104 is otherwise satisfied. Although the recital of the executory promise of Doe to convey Blackacre might be read as an implied condition that the promise be performed, the condition is not an express condition as required by Section 3–106(a)(i). This result is consistent with former Section 3–105(1)(a) and (b). Former Section 3–105(1)(b) is not repeated in Section 3–106 because it is not necessary. It is an example of an implied condition. Former Section 3–105(1)(d), (e), and (f) and the first clause of former Section 3–105(1)(c) are other examples of implied conditions. They are not repeated in Section 3–106 because they are not necessary. The law is not changed.

Section 3–106(a)(ii) and (iii) carry forward the substance of former Section 3–105(2)(a). The only change is the use of "writing" instead of "agreement" and a broadening of the language that can result in conditionality. For example, a promissory note is not an instrument defined by Section 3–104 if it contains any of the following statements: 1. "This note is subject to a contract of sale dated April 1, 1990 between the payee and maker of this note." 2. "This note is subject to a loan and security agreement dated April 1, 1990 between the payee and maker of this note." 3. "Rights and obligations of the parties with respect to this note are stated in an agreement dated April 1, 1990 between the payee and maker of this note." It is not relevant whether any condition to payment is or is not stated in the writing to which reference is made. The rationale is that the holder of a negotiable instrument should not be required to examine another document to determine rights with respect to payment. But subsection (b)(i) permits reference to a separate writing for information with respect to collateral, prepayment, or acceleration.

Many notes issued in commercial transactions are secured by collateral, are subject to acceleration in the event of default, or are subject to prepayment, or acceleration does not prevent the note from being an instrument if the statement is in the note itself. See Section 3–104(a)(3) and Section 3–108(b). In some cases it may be convenient not to include a statement concerning collateral, prepayment, or acceleration in the note, but rather to refer to an accompanying loan agreement, security agreement or mortgage for that statement. Subsection (b)(i) allows a reference to the appropriate writing for a statement of these rights. For example, a note would not be made conditional by the following statement: "This note is secured by a security interest in collateral described in a security agreement dated April 1, 1990 between the payee and maker of this note. Rights and obligations with respect to the collateral are [stated in] [governed by] the security agreement." The bracketed words are alternatives, either of which complies.

Subsection (b)(ii) addresses the issues covered by former Section 3–105(1)(f), (g), and (h) and Section 3–105(2)(b). Under Section 3–106(a) a promise or order is not made conditional because payment is limited to payment from a particular source or fund. This reverses the result of former Section 3–105(2)(b). There is no cogent reason why the general credit of a legal entity must be pledged to have a negotiable instrument. Market forces determine the marketability of instruments of this kind. If potential buyers don't want promises or orders that are payable only from a particular source or fund, they won't take them, but Article 3 should apply.

2. Subsection (c) applies to traveler's checks or other instruments that may require a countersignature. Although the requirement of a countersignature is a condition to the obligation to pay, traveler's checks are treated in the commercial world as money substitutes and therefore should be governed by Article 3. The first sentence of subsection (c) allows a traveler's check to meet the definition of instrument by stating that the countersignature condition does not make it conditional for the purposes of Section 3–104. The second sentence states the effect of a failure to meet the condition. Suppose a thief steals a traveler's check and cashes it by skillfully imitating the specimen signature so that the countersignature appears to be authentic. The countersignature is for the purpose of identification of the owner of the instrument. It is not an indorsement. Subsection (c) provides that the failure of the owner to countersign does not prevent a transferee from becoming a holder. Thus, the merchant or bank that cashed the traveler's check becomes a holder when the traveler's check is taken. The forged countersignature is a defense to the obligation of the issuer to pay the instrument, and is included in defenses under Section 3–305(a)(2). These defenses may not be asserted against a holder in due course. Whether a holder has

notice of the defense is a factual question. If the countersignature is a very bad forgery, there may be notice. But if the merchant or bank cashed a traveler's check and the countersignature appeared to be similar to the specimen signature, there might not be notice that the countersignature was forged. Thus, the merchant or bank could be a holder in due course.

3. Subsection (d) concerns the effect of a statement to the effect that the rights of a holder or transferee are subject to claims and defenses that the issuer could assert against the original payee. The subsection applies only if the statement is required by Statutory or administrative law. The prime example is the Federal Trade Commission Rule (16 C.F.R. Part 433) preserving consumers' claims and defenses in consumer credit sales. The intent of the FTC rule is to make it impossible for there to be a holder in due course of a note bearing the FTC legend and undoubtedly that is the result. But, under former Article 3, the legend may also have had the unintended effect of making the note conditional, thus excluding the note from former Article 3 altogether. Subsection (d) is designed to make it possible to preclude the possibility of a holder in due course without excluding the instrument from Article 3. Most of the provisions of Article 3 are not affected by the holder-in-due-course doctrine and there is no reason why Article 3 should not apply to a note bearing the FTC legend if holder-in-due-course rights are not involved. Under subsection (d) the statement does not make the note conditional. If the note otherwise meets the requirements of Section 3–104(a) it is a negotiable instrument for all purposes except that there cannot be a holder in due course of the note. No particular form of legend or statement is required by subsection (d). The form of a particular legend or statement may be determined by the other statute or administrative law. For example, the FTC legend required in a note taken by the seller in a consumer sale of goods or services is tailored to that particular transaction and therefore uses language that is somewhat different from that stated in subsection (d), but the difference in expression does not affect the essential similarity of the message conveyed. The effect of the FTC legend is to make the rights of a holder or transferee subject to claims or defenses that the issuer could assert against the original payee of the note.

Prior Uniform Statutory Provision:

Sections 2 and 6(5), Uniform Negotiable Instruments Law.

Changes: Reworded.

Purposes of Changes: The new language is intended to clarify doubts arising under the original section as to interest, discounts or additions, exchange, costs and attorney's fees, and acceleration or extension.

1. The section rejects decisions which have denied negotiability to a note with a term providing for a discount for early payment on the ground that at the time of issue the amount payable was not certain. It is sufficient that at any time of payment the holder is able to determine the amount then payable from the instrument itself with any necessary computation. Thus a demand note bearing interest at six per cent is negotiable. A stated discount or addition for early or late payment does not affect the certainty of the sum so long as the computation can be made, nor do different rates of interest before and after default or a specified date. The computation must be one which can be made from the instrument itself without reference to any outside source, and this section does not make negotiable a note payable with interest "at the current rate."

2. Paragraph (d) recognizes the occasional practice of making the instrument payable with exchange deducted rather than added.

3. In paragraph (e) "upon default" is substituted for the language of the original Section 2(5) in order to include any default in payment of interest or installments.

4. The section contains no specific language relating to the effect of acceleration clauses on the certainty of the sum payable. Section 2(3) of the original act contained a saving clause for provisions accelerating principal on default in payment of an instalment of or interest, which led to doubt as to the effect of other accelerating provisions. This Article (Section 3–109, Definite Time) broadly validates acceleration clauses; it is not necessary to state the matter in this section as well. The disappearance of the language referred to in old Section 2(3) means merely that it was regarded as surplusage.

5. Most states have usury laws prohibiting excessive rates of interest. In some states there are statutes or rules of law invalidating a term providing for increased interest after maturity, or for costs and attorney's fees. Subsection (2) is intended to make it clear that this section is concerned only with the effect of such terms upon negotiability, and is not meant to change the law of any state as to the validity of the term itself.

Cross References:

Section 3–104.
Point 4: Section 3–109.

Definitional Cross Reference:

"Term". Section 1–201.

Cross References

Application of this section to definition of "holder in due course", see Commercial Code § 3302.
Acceleration of time for payment, see Commercial Code § 3108.
Definite time, see Commercial Code § 3109.
Form and contents of negotiable instruments, see Commercial Code § 3104.
Interest,
   Annual rate, see Civil Code § 1916.
   Definition, see Civil Code § 1915.
   Legal rate, see Civil Code § 1916; Const. Art. 15, § 1.
   Presumption, see Civil Code § 1914.
Usury law, see Civil Code § 1916–1 et seq.

§ 3107. Payable in foreign money

Unless the instrument otherwise provides, an instrument that states the amount payable in foreign money may be paid in the foreign money or in an equivalent amount in dollars calculated by using the current bank-offered spot rate at the place of payment for the purchase of dollars on the day on which the instrument is paid. *(Added by Stats.1992, c. 914 (S.B.833), § 6.)*

California Code Comment

By John A. Bohn and Charles J. Williams

Prior California Law

1. This section is an expansion of former Civil Code § 3087(5) into (1) a set of rules for determining when an instrument is payable in money and (2) rules which apply to instruments stated in a foreign currency.

Former Civil Code § 3087(5) merely provided that negotiability was not affected by the fact that an instrument "designates a particular kind of current money in which payment is to be made." This rule is included in the first part of subdivision (2) of this section to the effect that a promise or order to pay a sum in foreign currency is for a sum certain in money. However, the remainder of the section is new.

Changes from U.C.C. (1962 Official Text)

2. Subdivision (1) of section 3107 is the same as subdivision (1) of section 3–107 of the Official Text. However, California has modified subdivision (2) of the Official Text by deleting after the word "money" the phrase "unless a different medium of payment is specified in the instrument" and omitting the second sentence. The Official Text reads as follows:

"(2) A promise or order to pay a sum stated in a foreign currency is for a sum certain in money and, unless a different medium of payment is specified in the instrument, may be satisfied by payment of that number of dollars which the stated foreign currency will purchase at the buying sight rate for that currency on the day on which the instrument is payable or, if payable on demand, on the day of demand. If such an instrument specifies a foreign currency as the medium of payment the instrument is payable in that currency."

3. Subdivision (2) as adopted in California is the same as the New York version. The Permanent Editorial Board for the Uniform Commercial Code rejected this suggested change in subdivision (2) for this reason:

"**Reasons for Rejection:** The New York variation in this subsection and the reasons advanced for it evidence possible misconceptions as to the purpose of the subsection and its potential effect. Part 1 of Article 3, in which Section 3–107 appears, deals with form and interpretation of negotiable instruments. Subsection (2) states affirmatively that a promise or order to pay a sum stated in a foreign currency is for a sum certain in money and, therefore, does not destroy negotiability. The subsection then goes on to state a presumption that such an obligation may be satisfied by payment in dollars in an amount determined by the buying sight rate of the foreign currency on the day the instrument becomes payable. However, New York objects to and has deleted the additional provision that if the instrument specifies a foreign currency as the medium of payment, the instrument is payable in that currency.

"The subsection does not say that every promise or order to pay a sum stated in a foreign currency must be paid in the foreign currency. The general presumption is the other way, namely, that it may be satisfied by payment in dollars at a designated exchange rate. It is only if an instrument specifies a foreign currency as the medium of payment that it then becomes so payable. To come within this special rule, presumably an instrument would have to include a special phrase such as 'This instrument is payable only in French francs' or some equivalent language.

"With the steady increase in international transactions there may be good reason for a drawer of a draft or a maker of a note to specify a particular foreign currency in which payment is to be made. If this is done, there is good reason for a rule of law stating that payment should be made as specifically so prescribed. If such an order is directed to a bank, this will not impose a duty on the bank to pay in the foreign currency unless the drawer has an account with the bank in that currency or has made arrangements with the bank to have such currency available. As specifically provided in subsection (1) of Section 3–409, a check or draft does not of itself operate as an assignment and the drawee is not liable on the instrument until he accepts it. This carries forward the longstanding rule of N.I.L. § 127. Under these rules (absent an acceptance) the drawee's only duty runs to the drawer and if the drawer has not provided the foreign currency to meet the check or draft, the drawee may dishonor in the same way it may dishonor a dollar check or draft where the drawer has no account or there are insufficient funds in the drawer's account to meet the check or draft.

"The fact that Federal and state courts in the United States will grant judgments only in terms of United States dollars is beside the point. American courts will not grant judgments in terms of wheat, aluminum or other property but parties repeatedly obligate themselves to deliver wheat, aluminum and many other kinds of property. American courts render judgments in United States dollars for failure to deliver wheat or aluminum, and, similarly, can render judgments in United States dollars (in appropriate cases against appropriate parties) for failure to pay an instrument in a foreign currency.

"The Editorial Board does not believe the New York criticisms are sound and sees no good reason to amend this subsection." Permanent Editorial Board for the Uniform Commercial Code, Report No. 1 (1962 Official Text), pp. 71–72.

Uniform Commercial Code Comment
1992 Addition

The definition of instrument in Section 3–104 requires that the promise or order be payable in "money." That term is defined in Section 1–201(24) and is not limited to United States dollars. Section 3–107 states that an instrument payable in foreign money may be paid in dollars if the instrument does not prohibit it. It also states a conversion rate which applies in the absence of a different conversion rate stated in the instrument. The reference in former Section 3–107(1) to instruments payable in "currency" or "current funds" has been dropped as superfluous.

Prior Uniform Statutory Provision:

Section 6(5). Uniform Negotiable Instruments Law.

Changes: Completely rewritten.

Purposes of Changes and New Matter: To make clear when an instrument is payable in money and to state rules applicable to instruments drawn payable in a foreign currency.

1. The term "money" is defined in Section 1–201 as "a medium of exchange authorized or adopted by a domestic or foreign government as a part of its currency". That definition rejects the narrow view of some early cases that "money" is limited to legal tender. Legal tender acts do no more than designate a particular kind of money which the obligee will be required to accept in discharge of an obligation. It rejects also the contention sometimes advanced that "money" includes any medium of exchange current and accepted in the particular community, whether it be gold dust, beaver pelts, or cigarettes in occupied Germany. Such unusual "currency" is necessarily of uncertain and fluctuating value, and an instrument intended to pass generally in commerce as negotiable may not be made payable therein.

The test adopted is that of the sanction of government, which recognizes the circulating medium as a part of the official currency of that government. In particular the provision adopts the position that an instrument expressing the amount to be paid in sterling, francs, lire or other recognized currency of a foreign government is negotiable even though payable in the United States.

2. The provision on "currency" or "current funds" accepts the view of the great majority of the decisions, that "currency" or "current funds" means that the instrument is payable in money.

3. Either the amount to be paid or the medium of payment may be expressed in terms of a particular kind of money. A draft passing between Toronto and Buffalo may, according to the desire and convenience of the parties, call for payment of 100 United States dollars or of 100 Canadian dollars; and it may require either sum to be paid in either currency. Under this section an instrument in any of these forms is negotiable, whether payable in Toronto or in Buffalo.

4. As stated in the preceding paragraph the intention of the parties in making an instrument payable in a foreign currency may be that the medium of payment shall be either dollars measured by the foreign currency or the foreign currency in which the instrument is drawn. Under subsection (2) the presumption is, unless the instrument otherwise specifies, that the obligation may be satisfied by payment in dollars in an amount determined by the buying sight rate for the foreign currency on the day the instrument becomes payable. Inasmuch as the buying sight rate will fluctuate from day to day, it might be argued that an instrument expressed in a foreign currency but actually payable in dollars is not for a "sum certain". Subsection (2) makes it clear that for the purposes of negotiability under this Article such an instrument, despite exchange fluctuations, is for a sum certain.

Cross References:

Section 3–104.
Point 1: Section 1–201.
Point 4: Section 4–212(6).

Definitional Cross References:

"Instrument". Section 3–102.
"Money". Section 1–201.
"Order". Section 3–102.
"Promise". Section 3–102.
"Purchase". Section 1–201.

Cross References

Charge-back or refund, see Commercial Code § 4214.
Definitions, see Commercial Code §§ 1201, 3103.
Form and contents of negotiable instruments, see Commercial Code § 3104.
Money of account, see Government Code § 6850 et seq.
Order for payment of money, see Code of Civil Procedure §§ 680.230, 680.270.

§ 3108. Payable on demand; payable at a definite time; payable at a fixed date

(a) A promise or order is "payable on demand" if it (1) states that it is payable on demand or at sight, or otherwise indicates that it is payable at the will of the holder, or (2) does not state any time of payment.

(b) A promise or order is "payable at a definite time" if it is payable on elapse of a definite period of time after sight or acceptance or at a fixed date or dates or at a time or times readily ascertainable at the time the promise or order is issued, subject to rights of (1) prepayment, (2) acceleration, (3) extension at the option of the holder, or (4) extension to a further definite time at the option of the maker or acceptor or automatically upon or after a specified act or event.

(c) If an instrument, payable at a fixed date, is also payable upon demand made before the fixed date, the instrument is payable on demand until the fixed date and, if demand for payment is not made before that date, becomes payable at a definite time on the fixed date. *(Added by Stats.1992, c. 914 (S.B.833), § 6.)*

California Code Comment

By John A. Bohn and Charles J. Williams

Prior California Law

1. This section is substantially the same as former Civil Code § 3088 except that it omits the last sentence of section 3088. The last sentence of former Civil Code § 3088 provided that as to a person issuing, accepting, or indorsing an instrument after maturity, the instrument was payable on demand. This meant that a person taking time paper after maturity could be a holder in due course against an indorser after maturity. The Commercial Code rejects this idea by eliminating this sentence and defining a holder in due course in section 3302 as one who, among other things, takes an instrument without notice that it is overdue.

Changes from U.C.C. (1962 Official Text)

2. This is section 3–108 of the Official Text without change.

Uniform Commercial Code Comment

1992 Addition

This section is a restatement of former Section 3–108 and Section 3–109. Subsection (b) broadens former Section 3–109 somewhat by providing that a definite time includes a time readily ascertainable at the time the promise or order is issued. Subsection (b)(iii) and (iv) restates former Section 3–109(1)(d). It adopts the generally accepted rule that a clause providing for extension at the option of the holder, even without a time limit, does not affect negotiability since the holder is given only a right which the holder would have without the clause. If the extension is to be at the option of the maker or acceptor or is to be automatic, a definite time limit must be stated or the time of payment remains uncertain and the order or promise is not a negotiable instrument. If a definite time limit is stated, the effect upon certainty of time of payment is the same as if the instrument were made payable at the ultimate date with a term providing for acceleration.

Uniform Commercial Code Comment

Prior Uniform Statutory Provision:

Section 7, Uniform Negotiable Instruments Law.

Changes: Reworded, final sentence of original section omitted.

Purposes of Changes: Except for the omission of the final sentence this section restates the substance of original Section 7. The final sentence dealt with the status of a person issuing, accepting or indorsing an instrument after maturity and provided that as to such a person the instrument was payable on demand. That language implied that the ordinary rules relating to demand instruments as to due course, holding, presentment, notice of dishonor and so on were applicable. This Article abandons that concept which served no special purpose except to trap the unwary. Under Section 3–302 (Holder in Due Course) and in view of the deletion from this section of the final sentence of original Section 7 there is no longer the possibility that one taking time paper after maturity may acquire due course rights against a post-maturity indorser. Section 3–501(4), however, provides that the indorser after maturity is not entitled to presentment, notice of dishonor or protest.

Cross References:

Sections 3–104, 3–302 and 3–501(4).

Definitional Cross Reference:

"Instrument". Section 3–102.

Cross References

Form and contents of negotiable instruments, see Commercial Code § 3104.
Holder in due course, see Commercial Code § 3302.
Instrument, see Commercial Code § 3104.
Presentment, notice of dishonor and protest, see Commercial Code § 3505.

§ 3109. Payable to bearer; payable to order

(a) A promise or order is payable to bearer if it is any of the following:

(1) States that it is payable to bearer or to the order of bearer or otherwise indicates that the person in possession of the promise or order is entitled to payment.

(2) Does not state a payee.

(3) States that it is payable to or to the order of cash or otherwise indicates that it is not payable to an identified person.

(b) A promise or order that is not payable to bearer is payable to order if it is payable (1) to the order of an identified person or (2) to an identified person or order. A promise or order that is payable to order is payable to the identified person.

(c) An instrument payable to bearer may become payable to an identified person if it is specially indorsed pursuant to subdivision (a) of Section 3205. An instrument payable to an identified person may become payable to bearer if it is indorsed in blank pursuant to subdivision (b) of Section 3205. *(Added by Stats.1992, c. 914 (S.B.833), § 6.)*

California Code Comment

By John A. Bohn and Charles J. Williams

Prior California Law

1. Subdivision (1)(a) and (1)(b) are similar in effect to former Civil Code § 3085(1).

2. Subdivision (1)(c) has no statutory counterpart in the NIL and resolves a conflict between the judicial decisions in some states as to the effect upon negotiability of acceleration clauses by validating all acceleration clauses. In California, acceleration clauses did not destroy negotiability. People's Finance & Thrift Co. of Vallejo v. Shaw-Leahy Co., 214 Cal. 108, 3 P.2d 1012 (1931). See also the cases cited in California Code Comment 12 under Commercial Code § 3105.

3. Subdivision (1)(d) is new statutory law and probably changes prior California law. This subdivision permits a clause giving the holder an option to extend the due date without destroying negotiability because of indefiniteness as to time of payment. There is a lack of unanimity as to the precise effect of this provision on prior California law. Thus, the Legislative Counsel states that: "Subdivision (1)(d) is new law." Sixth Progress Report to the Legislature by Senate Fact Finding Committee on Judiciary (1959–1961) Part 1, The Uniform Commercial Code, p. 67.

The State Bar Committee says that subdivision (1)(d) ". . . will probably change the present California rule [*Fn.:* see e.g. the discussion in Anaheim National Bank v. Dolph, 201 Cal. 17, 255 Pac. 184 (1927)] but accords with most holdings elsewhere." California State Bar

§ 3109

Committee on the Commercial Code, A Special Report, The Uniform Commercial Code, 37 Calif.State Bar J. (March–April 1962) p. 154. The Final Report of the State Bar sub-committee on Article (Division) 3 states as follows with reference to the effect of subdivision (1)(d) on California law:

"This sub-section expands the existing California rule by providing that an instrument is payable at a definite time, even though it is subject to extension at the option of the holder. This section should be read in conjunction with Sec. 13118(f) [3118(f)] which provides that a holder may not exercise his option to extend an instrument over the objection of a maker or acceptor who tenders full payment upon maturity." Sixth Progress Report to the Legislature by Senate Fact Finding Committee on Judiciary (1959–1961) Part 1, The Uniform Commercial Code, p. 345.

4. Subdivision (2) changes the law of California as to the effect on negotiability of an instrument payable upon an event certain to happen but uncertain as to time. Former Civil Code § 3085(3) provided that an instrument is payable at a determinable future time even though payable "on or at a fixed period after the occurrence of a specified event, which is certain to happen, though the time of happening be uncertain." The reason for the change is the lack of general commercial acceptance of this type of instrument. Official Comment 1.

5. Official Comment 5 describes the background and effect of the rule of subdivision (1)(d). The interpretation of extension clauses is covered in section 3118(f).

Changes from U.C.C. (1962 Official Text)

6. This is section 3–109 of the Official Text without change.

Uniform Commercial Code Comment
1992 Addition

1. Under Section 3–104(a), a promise or order cannot be an instrument unless the instrument is payable to bearer or to order when it is issued or unless Section 3–104(c) applies. The terms "payable to bearer" and "payable to order" are defined in Section 3–109. The quoted terms are also relevant in determining how an instrument is negotiated. If the instrument is payable to bearer it can be negotiated by delivery alone. Section 3–201(b). An instrument that is payable to an identified person cannot be negotiated without the indorsement of the identified person. Section 3–201(b). An instrument payable to order is payable to an identified person. Section 3–109(b). Thus, an instrument payable to order requires the indorsement of the person to whose order the instrument is payable.

2. Subsection (a) states when an instrument is payable to bearer. An instrument is payable to bearer if it states that it is payable to bearer, but some instruments use ambiguous terms. For example, check forms usually have the words "to the order of" printed at the beginning of the line to be filled in for the name of the payee. If the drawer writes in the word "bearer" or "cash," the check reads "to the order of bearer" or "to the order of cash." In each case the check is payable to bearer. Sometimes the drawer will write the name of the payee "John Doe" but will add the words "or bearer." In that case the check is payable to bearer. Subsection (a). Under subsection (b), if an instrument is payable to bearer it can't be payable to order. This is different from former Section 3–110(3). An instrument that purports to be payable both to order and bearer states contradictory terms. A transferee of the instrument should be able to rely on the bearer term and acquire rights as a holder without obtaining the indorsement of the identified payee. An instrument is also payable to bearer if it does not state a payee. Instruments that do not state a payee are in most cases incomplete instruments. In some cases the drawer of a check may deliver or mail it to the person to be paid without filling in the line for the name of the payee. Under subsection (a) the check is payable to bearer when it is sent or delivered. It is also an incomplete instrument. This case is discussed in Comment 2 to Section 3–115. Subsection (a)(3) contains the words "otherwise indicates that it is not payable to an identified person." The quoted words are meant to cover uncommon cases in which an instrument indicates that it is not meant to be payable to a specific person. Such an instrument is treated like a check payable to "cash." The quoted words are not meant to apply to an instrument stating that it is payable to an identified person such as "ABC Corporation" if ABC Corporation is a nonexistent company. Although the holder of the check cannot be the nonexistent company, the instrument is not payable to bearer. Negotiation of such an instrument is governed by Section 3–404(b).

Uniform Commercial Code Comment
Prior Uniform Statutory Provision:
Sections 4 and 17(3), Uniform Negotiable Instruments Law.

Changes: Reworded; new provisions; rule of original Section 4(3) reversed.

Purposes of Changes and New Matter: To remove uncertainties arising under the original section, and to eliminate commercially unacceptable instruments.

1. Subsection (2) reverses the rule of the original Section 4(3) as to instruments payable after events certain to happen but uncertain as to time. Almost the only use of such instruments has been in the anticipation of inheritance or future interests by borrowing on post-obituary notes. These have been much more common in England than in the United States. They are at best questionable paper, not acceptable in general commerce, with no good reason for according them free circulation as negotiable instruments. As in the case of the occasional note payable "one year after the war" or at a similar uncertain date, they are likely to be made under unusual circumstances suggesting good reason for preserving defenses of the maker. They are accordingly eliminated.

2. With this change "definite time" is substituted for "fixed or determinable future time." The time of payment is definite if it can be determined from the face of the instrument.

3. An undated instrument payable "thirty days after date" is not payable at a definite time, since the time of payment cannot be determined on its face. It is, however, an incomplete instrument within the provisions of Section 3–115 dealing with such instruments and may be completed by dating it. It is then payable at a definite time.

4. Paragraph (c) of subsection (1) resolves a conflict in the decisions on the negotiability of instruments containing acceleration clauses as to the meaning and effect of "on or before a fixed or determinable future time" in the original Section 4(2). (Instruments expressly stated to be payable "on or before" a given date are dealt with in subsection (1)(a). So far as certainty of time of payment is concerned a note payable at a definite time but subject to acceleration is no less certain than a note payable on demand, whose negotiability never has been questioned. It is in fact more certain, since it at least states a definite time beyond which the instrument cannot run. Objections to the acceleration clause must be based rather on the possibility of abuse by the holder, which has nothing to do with negotiability and is not limited to negotiable instruments. That problem is now covered by Section 1–208.

Subsection (1)(c) is intended to mean that the certainty of time of payment or the negotiability of the instrument is not affected by any acceleration clause, whether acceleration be at the option of the maker or the holder, or automatic upon the occurrence of some event, and whether it be conditional or unrestricted. If the acceleration term itself is uncertain it may fail on ordinary contract principles, but the instrument then remains negotiable and is payable at the definite time.

The effect of acceleration clauses upon a holder in due course is covered by the new definition of the holder in due course (Section 3–302) and by the section on notice to purchaser (subsection (3) of Section 3–304). If the purchaser is not aware of any acceleration, his delay in making presentment may be excused under the section dealing with excused presentment (subsection (1) of Section 3–511).

5. Paragraph (d) of subsection (1) is new. It adopts the generally accepted rule that a clause providing for extension at the option of the holder, even without a time limit, does not affect negotiability since the holder is given only a right which he would have without the clause. If the extension is to be at the option of the maker or acceptor or is to be automatic, a definite time limit must be stated or the time of payment remains uncertain and the instrument is not negotiable. Where such a limit is stated, the effect upon certainty of time of payment is the same as if the instrument were made payable at the ultimate date with a term providing for acceleration.

The construction and effect of extension clauses is covered by paragraph (f) of Section 3–118 on ambiguous terms and rules of construction, to which reference should be made.

Cross References:
Section 3–104.

Point 3: Section 3–115.
Point 4: Sections 1–208, 3–118(f), 3–304(3), and 3–511(1).
Point 5: Section 3–118(f).

Definitional Cross References:

"Holder". Section 1–201.
"Instrument". Section 3–102.
"Term". Section 1–201.

Cross References

Date, antedating, postdating, see Commercial Code § 3113.
Form and contents of negotiable instruments, see Commercial Code § 3104.
Incomplete instruments, see Commercial Code § 3115.
Instrument, see Commercial Code § 3104.
Payment, acceleration, see Commercial Code §§ 1208, 3118, 3304.
Time of presentment, see Commercial Code § 3501.

§ 3110. Person to whom instrument is payable; determination of holder

(a) The person to whom an instrument is initially payable is determined by the intent of the person, whether or not authorized, signing as, or in the name or behalf of, the issuer of the instrument. The instrument is payable to the person intended by the signer even if that person is identified in the instrument by a name or other identification that is not that of the intended person. If more than one person signs in the name or behalf of the issuer of an instrument and all the signers do not intend the same person as payee, the instrument is payable to any person intended by one or more of the signers.

(b) If the signature of the issuer of an instrument is made by automated means, such as a check-writing machine, the payee of the instrument is determined by the intent of the person who supplied the name or identification of the payee, whether or not authorized to do so.

(c) A person to whom an instrument is payable may be identified in any way, including by name, identifying number, office, or account number. For the purpose of determining the holder of an instrument, the following rules apply:

(1) If an instrument is payable to an account and the account is identified only by number, the instrument is payable to the person to whom the account is payable. If an instrument is payable to an account identified by number and by the name of a person, the instrument is payable to the named person, whether or not that person is the owner of the account identified by number.

(2) If an instrument is payable to:

(A) A trust, an estate, or a person described as trustee or representative of a trust or estate, the instrument is payable to the trustee, the representative, or a successor of either, whether or not the beneficiary or estate is also named.

(B) A person described as agent or similar representative of a named or identified person, the instrument is payable to the represented person, the representative, or a successor of the representative.

(C) A fund or organization that is not a legal entity, the instrument is payable to a representative of the members of the fund or organization.

(D) An office or to a person described as holding an office, the instrument is payable to the named person, the incumbent of the office, or a successor to the incumbent.

(d) If an instrument is payable to two or more persons alternatively, it is payable to any of them and may be negotiated, discharged, or enforced by any or all of them in possession of the instrument. If an instrument is payable to two or more persons not alternatively, it is payable to all of them and may be negotiated, discharged, or enforced only by all of them. If an instrument payable to two or more persons is ambiguous as to whether it is payable to the persons alternatively, the instrument is payable to the persons alternatively. *(Added by Stats.1992, c. 914 (S.B.833), § 6.)*

California Code Comment
By John A. Bohn and Charles J. Williams

1. Subdivision (1) is similar to former Civil Code § 3089 except that this subdivision is expanded by the addition of subdivisions (1)(e) and (1)(g) to include, estates, trusts, funds, partnerships and unincorporated associations.

2. The language in subdivision (1) which provides that an instrument is payable to order when it is payable to "assigns" is new.

3. Subdivision (2) is new statutory law. See Official Comment 5.

4. Subdivision (3) is new statutory law and is intended to clarify a point not previously covered. See Official Comment 6.

Changes from U.C.C. (1962 Official Text)

5. This is section 3–110 of the Official Text without change.

Uniform Commercial Code Comment
1992 Addition

1. Section 3–110 states rules for determining the identity of the person to whom an instrument is initially payable if the instrument is payable to an identified person. This issue usually arises in a dispute over the validity of an indorsement in the name of the payee. Subsection (a) states the general rule that the person to whom an instrument is payable is determined by the intent of "the person, whether or not authorized, signing as, or in the name or behalf of, the issuer of the instrument." "Issuer" means the maker or drawer of the instrument. Section 3–105(c). If X signs a check as drawer of a check on X's account, the intent of X controls. If X, as President of Corporation, signs a check as President in behalf of Corporation as drawer, the intent of X controls. If X forges Y's signature as drawer of a check, the intent of X also controls. Under Section 3–103(a)(3), Y is referred to as the drawer of the check because the signing of Y's name identifies Y as the drawer. But since Y's signature was forged Y has no liability as drawer (Section 3–403(a)) unless some other provision of Article 3 or Article 4 makes Y liable. Since X, even though unauthorized, signed in the name of Y as issuer, the intent of X determines to whom the check is payable.

In the case of a check payable to "John Smith," since there are many people in the world named "John Smith" it is not possible to identify the payee of the check unless there is some further identification or the intention of the drawer is determined. Name alone is sufficient under subsection (a), but the intention of the drawer determines which John Smith is the person to whom the check is payable. The same issue is presented in cases of misdescriptions of the payee. The drawer intends to pay a person known to the drawer as John Smith. In fact that person's name is James Smith or John Jones or some other entirely different name. If the check identifies the payee as John Smith, it is nevertheless payable to the person intended by the drawer. That person may indorse the check in either the name John Smith or the person's correct name or in both names. Section 3–204(d). The intent of the drawer is also controlling in fictitious payee cases. Section 3–404(b). The last sentence of subsection (a) refers to rare cases in which the signature of an organization requires more than one signature and the persons signing on behalf of the organization do not all intend the same person as payee. Any person intended by a signer for the organization is the payee and an indorsement by that person is an effective indorsement.

Subsection (b) recognizes the fact that in a large number of cases there is no human signer of an instrument because the instrument, usually a check, is produced by automated means such as a check-writing machine. In that case, the relevant intent is that of the person who supplied the name of the payee. In most cases that person is an employee of the drawer, but in some cases the person could be an outsider who is committing a fraud by introducing names of payees of checks into the system that produces the checks. A check-writing machine is likely to be operated by means of a computer in which is stored information as to name and address of the payee and the amount of the check. Access to the computer may allow production of fraudulent checks without knowledge of the organization that is the issuer of the check. Section 3–404(b) is also concerned with this issue. See Case #4 in Comment 2 to Section 3–404.

2. Subsection (c) allows the payee to be identified in any way including the various ways stated. Subsection (c)(1) relates to instruments payable to bank accounts. In some cases the account might be identified by name and number, and the name and number might refer to different persons. For example, a check is payable to "X Corporation Account No. 12345 in Bank of Podunk." Under the last sentence of subsection (c)(1), this check is payable to X Corporation and can be negotiated by X Corporation even if Account No. 12345 is some other person's account or the check is not deposited in that account. In other cases the payee is identified by an account number and the name of the owner of the account is not stated. For example, Debtor pays Creditor by issuing a check drawn on Payor Bank. The check is payable to a bank account owned by Creditor but identified only by number. Under the first sentence of subsection (c)(1) the check is payable to Creditor and, under Section 1–201(20), Creditor becomes the holder when the check is delivered. Under Section 3–201(b), further negotiation of the check requires the indorsement of Creditor. But under Section 4–205(a), if the check is taken by a depositary bank for collection, the bank may become a holder without the indorsement. Under Section 3–102(b), provisions of Article 4 prevail over those of Article 3. The depositary bank warrants that the amount of the check was credited to the payee's account.

3. Subsection (c)(2) replaces former Section 3–117 and subsection (1)(e), (f), and (g) of former Section 3–110. This provision merely determines who can deal with an instrument as a holder. It does not determine ownership of the instrument or its proceeds. Subsection (c)(2)(i) covers trusts and estates. If the instrument is payable to the trust or estate or to the trustee or representative of the trust or estate, the instrument is payable to the trustee or representative or any successor. Under subsection (c)(2)(ii), if the instrument states that it is payable to Doe, President of X Corporation, either Doe or X Corporation can be holder of the instrument. Subsection (c)(2)(iii) concerns informal organizations that are not legal entities such as unincorporated clubs and the like. Any representative of the members of the organization can act as holder. Subsection (c)(2)(iv) applies principally to instruments payable to public offices such as a check payable to County Tax Collector.

4. Subsection (d) replaces former Section 3–116. An instrument payable to X or Y is governed by the first sentence of subsection (d). An instrument payable to X and Y is governed by the second sentence of subsection (d). If an instrument is payable to X or Y, either is the payee and if either is in possession that person is the holder and the person entitled to enforce the instrument. Section 3–301. If an instrument is payable to X and Y, neither X nor Y acting alone is the person to whom the instrument is payable. Neither person, acting alone, can be the holder of the instrument. The instrument is "payable to an identified person." The "identified person" is X and Y acting jointly. Section 3–109(b) and Section 1–102(5)(a). Thus, under Section 1–201(20) X or Y, acting alone, cannot be the holder or the person entitled to enforce or negotiate the instrument because neither, acting alone, is the identified person stated in the instrument.

The third sentence of subsection (d) is directed to cases in which it is not clear whether an instrument is payable to multiple payees alternatively. In the case of ambiguity persons dealing with the instrument should be able to rely on the indorsement of a single payee. For example, an instrument payable to X and/or Y is treated like an instrument payable to X or Y.

Prior Uniform Statutory Provision:

Section 8, Uniform Negotiable Instruments Law.

Changes: Reworded, new provisions.

Purposes of Changes and New Matter: The changes are intended to remove uncertainties arising under the original section.

1. Paragraph (d) of subsection (1) replaces the original subsections (4) and (5). It eliminates the word "jointly," which has carried a possible implication of a right of survivorship. Normally an instrument payable to "A and B" is intended to be payable to the two parties as tenants in common, and there is no survivorship in the absence of express language to that effect. The instrument may be payable to "A or B," in which case it is payable to either A or B individually. It may even be made payable to "A and/or B," in which case it is payable either to A or to B singly, or to the two together. The negotiation, enforcement and discharge of the instrument in all such cases are covered by the section on instruments payable to two or more persons (Sec. 3–116).

2. Paragraph (e) of subsection (1) is intended to change the result of decisions which have held that an instrument payable to the order of the estate of a decedent was payable to bearer, on the ground that the name of the payee did not purport to be that of any person. The intent in such cases is obviously not to make the instrument payable to bearer, but to the order of the representative of the estate. The provision extends the same principle to an instrument payable to the order of "Tilden Trust," or "Community Fund". So long as the payee can be identified, it is not necessary that it be a legal entity; and in each case the instrument is treated as payable to the order of the appropriate representative or his successor.

3. Under paragraph (f) of subsection (1) an instrument may be made payable to the office itself ("Swedish Consulate") or to the officer by his title as such ("Treasurer of City Club"). In either case it runs to the incumbent of the office and his successors. The effect of instruments in such a form is covered by the section on instruments payable with words of description (Sec. 3–117).

4. Vestigial theories relating to the lack of "legal entity" of partnerships and various forms of unincorporated associations—such as labor unions and business trusts—make it the part of wisdom to specify that instruments made payable to such groups are order paper payable as designated and not bearer paper (subsection (1)(g)). As in the case of incorporated associations, any person having authority from the partnership or association to whose order the instrument is payable may indorse or otherwise deal with the instrument.

5. Subsection (2) is intended to change the result of cases holding that "payable upon return of this certificate properly indorsed" indicated an intention to make the instrument payable to any indorsee and so must be construed as the equivalent of "Pay to order." Ordinarily the purpose of such language is only to insure return of the instrument with indorsement in lieu of a receipt, and the word "order" is omitted with the intention that the instrument shall not be negotiable.

6. Subsection (3) is directed at occasional instruments reading "Pay to the order of John Doe or bearer." Such language usually is found only where the drawer has filled in the name of the payee on a printed form, without intending the ambiguity or noticing the word "bearer." Under such circumstances the name of the specified payee indicates an intent that the order words shall control. If the word "bearer" is handwritten or typewritten, there is sufficient indication of an intent that the instrument shall be payable to bearer. Instruments payable to "order of bearer" are covered not by this section but by the following Section 3–111.

Cross References:

Sections 3–104 and 3–111.
Point 1: Section 3–116.
Points 2, 3 and 4: Section 3–117.

Definitional Cross References:

"Bearer". Section 1–201.
"Conspicuous". Section 1–201.

"Instrument". Section 3–102.
"Negotiation". Section 3–202.
"Person". Section 1–201.
"Term". Section 1–201.

Cross References

Determination of payee by intent of person, rules applicable, see Commercial Code § 3404.

Special indorsements, application of this section, see Commercial Code § 3206.

§ 3111. Place of payment

Except as otherwise provided for items in Division 4 (commencing with Section 4101), an instrument is payable at the place of payment stated in the instrument. If no place of payment is stated, an instrument is payable at the address of the drawee or maker stated in the instrument. If no address is stated, the place of payment is the place of business of the drawee or maker. If a drawee or maker has more than one place of business, the place of payment is any place of business of the drawee or maker chosen by the person entitled to enforce the instrument. If the drawee or maker has no place of business, the place of payment is the residence of the drawee or maker. *(Added by Stats.1992, c. 914 (S.B.833), § 6.)*

California Code Comment

By John A. Bohn and Charles J. Williams

Prior California Law

1. This section is similar to former Civil Code § 3090(1), (2) and (4). Paragraph (c) is a reworded version of former Civil Code § 3090(4) to make it clear that an instrument which reads "pay to the order of _____" is not payable to bearer. Official Comment 2. This situation did not arise in California under the NIL.

2. The provisions of former Civil Code § 3090(3) which made an instrument payable to bearer when it was payable to a fictitious person and section 3090(5) making an instrument payable to bearer when the last indorsement is an indorsement in blank are omitted from this section but are covered by Commercial Code §§ 3405 and 3204 respectively.

Changes from U.C.C. (1962 Official Text)

3. This is section 3–111 of the Official Text without change.

Uniform Commercial Code Comment
1992 Addition

If an instrument is payable at a bank in the United States, Section 3–501(b)(1) states that presentment must be made at the place of payment, i.e. the bank. The place of presentment of a check is governed by Regulation CC § 229.36.

Uniform Commercial Code Comment

Prior Uniform Statutory Provision:

Section 9, Uniform Negotiable Instruments Law.

Changes: Reworded; original subsections (3) and (5) omitted here but covered by Sections on impostors and signature in name of payee (Section 3–405) and on special and blank indorsements (Section 3–204).

Purposes of Changes: The rewording is intended to remove uncertainties.

1. Language such as "order of bearer" usually results when a printed form is used and the word "bearer" is filled in. Subsection (a) rejects the view that the instrument is payable to order, and adopts the position that "bearer" is the unusual word and should control. Compare Comment 6 to Section 3–110.

2. Paragraph (c) is reworded to remove any possible implication that "Pay to the order of _____" makes the instrument payable to bearer. It is an incomplete order instrument, and falls under Section 3–115. Likewise "Pay Treasurer of X Corporation" does not mean pay bearer, even though there may be no such officer. Instruments payable to the order of an estate, trust, fund, partnership, unincorporated association or office are covered by the preceding section. This subsection applies only to such language as "Pay Cash," "Pay to the order of cash," "Pay bills payable," "Pay to the order of one keg of nails," or other words which do not purport to designate any specific payee.

3. Under Section 40 of the original Act an instrument payable to bearer on its face remained bearer paper negotiable by delivery although subsequently specially indorsed. It should be noted that Section 3–204 on special indorsement reverses this rule and allows the special indorsement to control.

Cross References:

Sections 3–104, 3–405 and 3–204.
Point 2: Sections 3–110(1)(a) and (f) and 3–115.
Point 3: Section 3–204.

Definitional Cross References:

"Bearer". Section 1–201.
"Instrument". Section 3–102.
"Person". Section 1–201.
"Term". Section 1–201.

Cross References

Evidence of debt negotiable by delivery only as subject of embezzlement, see Penal Code § 510.
Form and contents of negotiable instruments, see Commercial Code § 3104.
Impostors, see Commercial Code § 3404.
Incomplete instruments, see Commercial Code § 3115.
Instrument, see Commercial Code § 3104.
Payment to order, see Commercial Code § 3109.
Special or blank indorsements, see Commercial Code § 3205.
Written instruments completed but not delivered as subject of theft, see Penal Code § 494.

§ 3112. Interest

(a) Unless otherwise provided in the instrument, (1) an instrument is not payable with interest, and (2) interest on an interest-bearing instrument is payable from the date of the instrument.

(b) Interest may be stated in an instrument as a fixed or variable amount of money or it may be expressed as a fixed or variable rate or rates. The amount or rate of interest may be stated or described in the instrument in any manner and may require reference to information not contained in the instrument. If an instrument provides for interest, but the amount of interest payable cannot be ascertained from the description, interest is payable at the judgment rate in effect at the place of payment of the instrument and at the time interest first accrues. *(Added by Stats.1992, c. 914 (S.B.833), § 6.)*

California Code Comment

By John A. Bohn and Charles J. Williams

Prior California Law

1. This section is similar to former Civil Code §§ 3086 and 3087 which described provisions or omissions which did not affect the negotiable character of an instrument. There is no substantial change from the law previously specified in those sections of the NIL.

2. Subdivision (1)(a) is similar to former Civil Code § 3087(2) and (3).

3. Subdivision (1)(b) changes former Civil Code § 3086(1) under which the instrument could authorize sale of collateral in the event it was not paid at maturity.

4. Subdivision (1)(c) broadens the scope of terms which do not affect negotiability and which apparently were not within the provisions of the NIL. Official Comment 1. Prior California law is in accord. Kent v. Lampman, 59 Cal.App.2d 407, 139 P.2d 57 (1943) See Commercial Code § 1208 for the interpretation of clauses requiring collateral.

5. Subdivision (1)(d) is similar to former Civil Code § 3086(2). It follows that an instrument which authorizes confession before maturity is not negotiable.

6. Subdivision (1)(e) is the same as former Civil Code § 3086(3). See Official Comment 3.

7. Subdivision (1)(f) is new and clarifies the effect of a clause of acknowledgment of satisfaction upon negotiability which was uncertain under the NIL. Official Comment 4. This subdivision is in accord with the reasoning of Stowel v. Rialto Irrigation District, 155 Cal. 215, 100 Pac. 248 (1909). That case dealt with bonds made payable only upon surrender of its coupons. The issue was whether this provision was a condition not certain of fulfillment and therefore not negotiable under former Civil Code § 3088 (pre NIL version). The court held that the bonds were negotiable and stated the rule that a party paying a negotiable instrument is entitled to demand its surrender as a condition concurrent to its payment by him.

8. Subdivision (1)(g) is new and has no prior statutory counterpart in the NIL.

9. Subdivision (2) is similar to the last paragraph of former Civil Code § 3086. See Official Comment 3.

Changes from U.C.C. (1962 Official Text)

10. Subdivision (1)(b) which is the 1962 Official Text version reflects minor changes made from the 1958 Official Text for the purpose of clarification. The 1958 Official Text read as follows:

"(1)(b) a statement that collateral has been given for the instrument or in case of default on the instrument the collateral may be sold; or"

11. Subdivision (1)(c) was amended in California from the 1962 Official Text to follow the New York version. The 1962 Official Text reads:

"(1)(c) a promise or power to maintain or protect collateral or to give additional collateral; or"

The purpose of the change from the Official Text is to allow additional material to be included in the instrument which would not affect negotiability.

The Permanent Editorial Board for the Uniform Commercial Code rejected the proposed change upon the ground that:

"The additional language introduces a highly elastic standard of negotiability that could well permit an indefinite number of possibly long and complex provisions in negotiable instruments. At the same time, the new standard is sufficiently vague and general to be highly confusing in determining what provisions may or may not be included and what notes are or are not negotiable. It would not only move substantially away from the 'courier without luggage' principle, but, in addition, could produce substantial confusion and litigation." Permanent Editorial Board for the Uniform Commercial Code, Report No. 1 (1962 Official Text), p. 73.

Uniform Commercial Code Comment
1992 Addition

1. Under Section 3–104(a) the requirement of a "fixed amount" applies only to principal. The amount of interest payable is that described in the instrument. If the description of interest in the instrument does not allow for the amount of interest to be ascertained, interest is payable at the judgment rate. Hence, if an instrument calls for interest, the amount of interest will always be determinable. If a variable rate of interest is prescribed, the amount of interest is ascertainable by reference to the formula or index described or referred to in the instrument. The last sentence of subsection (b) replaces subsection (d) of former Section 3–118.

2. The purpose of subsection (b) is to clarify the meaning of "interest" in the introductory clause of Section 3–104(a). It is not intended to validate a provision for interest in an instrument if that provision violates other law.

Uniform Commercial Code Comment
Prior Uniform Statutory Provision:

Sections 5 and 6, Uniform Negotiable Instruments Law.
Changes: Reworded; new provisions; Subsection (4) of original Section 5 omitted. Subsection (4) of the original Section 6 is now covered by Section 3–113, and Subsection (5) by Section 3–107.
Purposes of Changes and New Matter: The changes are intended to remove uncertainties arising under the original sections. Subsection (4) of the original Section 5 is omitted because it has been important only in connection with bonds and other investment securities now covered by Article 8 of this Act. An option to require something to be done in lieu of payment of money is uncommon and not desirable in commercial paper.

This section permits the insertion of certain obligations and powers in addition to the simple promise or order to pay money. Under Section 3–104, dealing with form of negotiable instruments, the instrument may not contain any other promise, order, obligation or power.

1. Paragraph (b) of subsection (1) permits a clause authorizing the sale or disposition of collateral given to secure obligations either on the instrument or otherwise of an obligor on the instrument upon any default in those obligations, including a default in payment of an installment or of interest. It is not limited, as was the original Section 5 (1), to default at maturity. The reference to obligations of an obligor on the instrument is intended to recognize so-called cross collateral provisions that appear in collateral note forms used by banks and others throughout the United States and to permit the use of these provisions without destroying negotiability. Paragraph (c) is new. It permits a clause, apparently not within the original section, containing a promise or power to maintain or protect collateral or to give additional collateral, whether on demand or on some other condition. Such terms frequently are accompanied by a provision for acceleration if the collateral is not given, which is now permitted by the section on what constitutes a definite time. Section 1–208 should be consulted as to the construction to be given such clauses under this Act.

2. As under the original Section 5(2), paragraph (d) is intended to mean that a confession of judgment may be authorized only if the instrument is not paid when due, and that otherwise negotiability is affected. The use of judgment notes in confined to two or three states, and in others the judgment clauses are made illegal or ineffective either by special statutes or by decision. Subsection (2) is intended to say that any such local rule remains unchanged, and that the clause itself may be invalid, although the negotiability of the instrument is not affected.

3. As in the case of the original Section 5(3), paragraph (e) applies not only to any waiver of the benefits of this Article, such as presentment, notice of dishonor or protest, but also to a waiver of the benefits of any other law such as a homestead exemption. Again subsection (2) is intended to mean that any rule which invalidates the waiver itself is not changed, and that while negotiability is not affected, a waiver of the statute of limitations contained in an instrument may be invalid.

This paragraph is to be read together with subsection (1) of Section 3–104 on form of negotiable instruments. A waiver cannot make the instrument negotiable within this Article where it does not comply with the requirements of that section.

4. Paragraph (f) is new. The effect of a clause of acknowledgment of satisfaction upon negotiability has been uncertain under the original section.

5. Paragraph (g) is intended to insure that a condition arising from the statement in question will not adversely affect negotiability.

Cross References:

Sections 3–104 and 3–105.
Point 1: Sections 1–208 and 3–109(1)(c).
Point 3: Section 3–104.

Definitional Cross References:

"Draft". Section 3–104.
"Instrument". Section 3–102.
"On demand". Section 3–108.

"Promise". Section 3–102.
"Term". Section 1–201.

Cross References

Acceleration of payment, see Commercial Code §§ 1208, 3108.
Confession of judgment without action, see Code of Civil Procedure § 1132 et seq.
Instrument, see Commercial Code § 3104.
Instrument payable in money, see Commercial Code § 3107.
Investment securities, see Commercial Code § 8101 et seq.
Statute of limitations, waiver of, see Code of Civil Procedure § 360.5.
Unconditional promise, see Commercial Code §§ 3104, 3106.
Waiver of advantage, law established for public reason, see Civil Code § 3513.
Waiver or renunciation of claim or right after breach, see Commercial Code § 1107.

§ 3113. Date of instrument

(a) An instrument may be antedated or postdated. The date stated determines the time of payment if the instrument is payable at a fixed period after date. Except as provided in subdivision (c) of Section 4401, an instrument payable on demand is not payable before the date of the instrument.

(b) If an instrument is undated, its date is the date of its issue or, in the case of an unissued instrument, the date it first comes into possession of a holder. *(Added by Stats.1992, c. 914 (S.B.833), § 6.)*

California Code Comment

By John A. Bohn and Charles J. Williams

Prior California Law

1. This section is substantially the same as former Civil Code § 3087(4). It is also consistent with Civil Code § 1629 which abolishes seals and provides that they do not affect an instrument.

Changes from U.C.C. (1962 Official Text)

2. This is section 3–113 of the Official Text without change.

Uniform Commercial Code Comment
1992 Addition

This section replaces former Section 3–114. Subsections (1) and (3) of former Section 3–114 are deleted as unnecessary. Section 3–113(a) is based in part on subsection (2) of former Section 3–114. The rule that a demand instrument is not payable before the date of the instrument is subject to Section 4–401(c) which allows the payor bank to pay a postdated check unless the drawer has notified the bank of the postdating pursuant to a procedure prescribed in that subsection. With respect to an undated instrument, the date is the date of issue.

Uniform Commercial Code Comment

Prior Uniform Statutory Provision:

Section 6(4), Uniform Negotiable Instruments Law.

Changes: Reworded.

Purposes of Changes: The revised wording is intended to change the result of decisions holding that while a seal does not affect the negotiability of an instrument it may affect it in other respects falling within the statute, such as the conclusiveness of consideration. The section is intended to place sealed instruments on the same footing as any other instruments so far as all sections of this Article are concerned. It does not affect any other statutes or rules of law relating to sealed instruments except insofar as, in the case of negotiable instruments, they are inconsistent with this Article. Thus a sealed instrument which is within this Article may still be subject to a longer statute of limitations than negotiable instruments not under seal, or to such local rules of procedure as that it may be enforced by an action of special assumpsit.

Cross Reference:

Section 3–104.

Definitional Cross Reference:

"Instrument". Section 3–102.

Cross References

Distinctions between sealed and unsealed instruments abolished, see Civil Code § 1629; Code of Civil Procedure § 1932.
Form and contents of negotiable instruments, see Commercial Code § 3104.
Seal defined, see Code of Civil Procedure §§ 14, 1930, 1931.

§ 3114. Contradictory terms in instrument

If an instrument contains contradictory terms, typewritten terms prevail over printed terms, handwritten terms prevail over both, and words prevail over numbers. *(Added by Stats.1992, c. 914 (S.B.833), § 6.)*

California Code Comment

By John A. Bohn and Charles J. Williams

Prior California Law

1. Subdivision (1) is similar to former Civil Code §§ 3087(1) and 3093 although the NIL spoke in terms of both validity and negotiability. It is also consistent with the pre NIL rule. Collins v. Driscoll, 69 Cal. 550, 11 Pac. 244 (1886). Former Civil Code § 3098(3) provided that an undated instrument would be considered dated as of the date of issuance.

Former Civil Code § 3093 provided that an antedated or postdated instrument is not invalid "provided this is not done for an illegal or fraudulent purpose." This language is omitted. See Official Comment 1.

2. Subdivision (2) is new statutory law. See Official Comment 2. The rule of this subdivision is consistent with American Nat. Bank v. Wheeler, 45 Cal.App. 118, 187 Pac. 128 (1920).

3. Subdivision (3) is similar to former Civil Code § 3092 but extends its application to all signatures on the instrument, not just to an acceptance or indorsement on it.

Changes from U.C.C. (1962 Official Text)

4. This is section 3–114 of the Official Text without change.

Uniform Commercial Code Comment
1992 Addition

Section 3–114 replaces subsections (b) and (c) of former Section 3–118.

Uniform Commercial Code Comment

Prior Uniform Statutory Provision:

Sections 6(1), 11, 12 and 17(3), Uniform Negotiable Instruments Law.

Changes: Reworded; new provision; parts of original section 12 omitted.

Purposes of Changes and New Matter: The rewording is intended to remove uncertainties arising under the original sections.

1. The reference to an "illegal or fraudulent purpose" in the original Section 12 is omitted as inaccurate and misleading. Any fraud or illegality connected with the date of an instrument does not affect its negotiability, but is merely a defense under Sections 3–306 and 3–307 to the same extent as any other fraud or illegality. The provision in the same section as to acquisition of title upon delivery is also omitted, as obvious and unnecessary.

2. Subsection (2) is new. An undated instrument payable "thirty days after date" is uncertain as to time of payment, and does not fall within Section 3–109(1)(a) on definite time. It is, however, an incomplete instrument, and the date may be inserted as provided in the section dealing with such instruments (Section 3–115). When the instrument has been dated, this subsection follows decisions under the original Act in providing that the time of payment is to be determine

from the stated date, even though the instrument is antedated or postdated. An antedated instrument may thus be due before it is issued. As to the liability of indorsers in such a case, see Section 3–501(4), on indorsement after maturity.

3. Subsection (3) extends the original Section 11 to any signature on an instrument. As to the meaning of "presumed," see Section 1–201.

Cross References:

Point 1: Sections 3–306 and 3–307.
Point 2: Sections 3–109(1)(a), 3–115 and 3–501(4).
Point 3: Section 1–201.

Definitional Cross References:

"Instrument". Section 3–102.
"Issue". Section 3–102.
"On demand". Section 3–108.
"Presumed". Section 1–201.
"Signature". Section 3–401.

Cross References

Definitions, see Commercial Code § 1201.
Indorsement after maturity, presentment for payment, see Commercial Code § 3414.
Payment at definite date, see Commercial Code § 3108.
Rights of holder in due course, see Commercial Code § 3305.
Rights of one not holder in due course, see Commercial Code § 3306.
Signatures, burden of establishing validity, see Commercial Code § 3308.

§ 3115. Incomplete instruments

(a) 'Incomplete instrument' means a signed writing, whether or not issued by the signer, the contents of which show at the time of signing that it is incomplete but that the signer intended it to be completed by the addition of words or numbers.

(b) Subject to subdivision (c), if an incomplete instrument is an instrument under Section 3104, it may be enforced according to its terms if it is not completed, or according to its terms as augmented by completion. If an incomplete instrument is not an instrument under Section 3104, but, after completion, the requirements of Section 3104 are met, the instrument may be enforced according to its terms as augmented by completion.

(c) If words or numbers are added to an incomplete instrument without authority of the signer, there is an alteration of the incomplete instrument under Section 3407.

(d) The burden of establishing that words or numbers were added to an incomplete instrument without authority of the signer is on the person asserting the lack of authority. *(Added by Stats.1992, c. 914 (S.B. 833), § 6.)*

California Code Comment

By John A. Bohn and Charles J. Williams

Prior California Law

1. Subdivision (1) is similar to former Civil Code §§ 3094 and 3095 but it has been considerably reduced in length. The rewording of subdivision (1) does not change the prior law. Official Comment 1, 2 and 3.

2. Subdivision (2) by using the words "even though the paper was not delivered" changes the rule of former Civil Code § 3096.

Former Civil Code § 3096 was an inconsistency in an otherwise uniform treatment of the rights and defenses resulting from unauthorized completion of instruments. Under the NIL, the maker did not have a defense against a holder in due course based upon lack of delivery if a completed instrument was stolen from him and then negotiated (former Civil Code § 3097). Likewise, the maker who signed and delivered an incomplete instrument did not have a defense against a holder in due course based upon unauthorized completion by the one in possession (former Civil Code § 3095). However, under former Civil Code § 3096, both the theft of an incomplete instrument and its unauthorized completion did give the maker a good defense against the holder in due course. This anomalous result is changed by subdivision (2) and the loss is put upon the maker in case of non-delivery or unauthorized completion or both. Official Comment 5.

3. In the case of an unauthorized completion, subdivision (2) makes the rules of Commercial Code § 3407 applicable and a holder in due course of a materially altered instrument can enforce it according to its terms as completed. Commercial Code § 3407(3).

4. Under Commercial Code § 4401(2), a similar protection is given to a drawee bank which pays an altered instrument. The Official Comment states that this policy should apply to other drawees as well. Official Comment 5. Although there is no express provision to that effect, this same result could be reached by applying estoppel principles.

5. The "burden of establishing" an unauthorized completion as that phrase is used in subdivision (2) means the burden of persuading the trier of fact that the existence of the fact is more probable than its nonexistence. Commercial Code § 1201(8). This is substituted for the "prima facie authority" which the person in possession had to complete the instrument under former Civil Code § 3095. The California decisions under the former NIL provision reach the same result as this subdivision does. For example, see Schuster v. Bowen, 97 Cal.App.2d 803, 218 P.2d 839 (1950).

Changes from U.C.C. (1962 Official Text)

6. This is section 3–115 of the Official Text without change.

Uniform Commercial Code Comment
1992 Addition

1. This section generally carries forward the rules set out in former Section 3–115. The term "incomplete instrument" applies both to an "instrument," i.e. a writing meeting all the requirements of Section 3–104, and to a writing intended to be an instrument that is signed but lacks some element of an instrument. The test in both cases is whether the contents show that it is incomplete and that the signer intended that additional words or numbers be added.

2. If an incomplete instrument meets the requirements of Section 3–104 and is not completed it may be enforced in accordance with its terms. Suppose, in the following two cases, that a note delivered to the payee is incomplete solely because a space on the pre-printed note form for the due date is not filled in:

Case #1. If the incomplete instrument is never completed, the note is payable on demand. Section 3–108(a)(ii). However, if the payee and the maker agreed to a due date, the maker may have a defense under Section 3–117 if demand for payment is made before the due date agreed to by the parties.

Case #2. If the payee completes the note be filling in the due date agreed to by the parties, the note is payable on the due date stated. However, if the due date filled in was not the date agreed to by the parties there is an alteration of the note. Section 3–407 governs the case.

Suppose Debtor pays Creditor by giving Creditor a check on which the space for the name of the payee is left blank. The check is an instrument but it is incomplete. The check is enforceable in its incomplete form and it is payable to bearer because it does not state a payee. Section 3–109(a)(2). Thus, Creditor is a holder of the check. Normally in this kind of case Creditor would simply fill in the space with Creditor's name. When that occurs the check becomes payable to the Creditor.

3. In some cases the incomplete instrument does not meet the requirements of Section 3–104. An example is a check with the amount not filled in. The check cannot be enforced until the amount is filled in. If the payee fills in an amount authorized by the drawer the check meets the requirements of Section 3–104 and is enforceable as completed. If the payee fills in an unauthorized amount there is an alteration of the check and Section 3–407 applies.

4. Section 3–302(a)(1) also bears on the problem of incomplete instruments. Under that section a person cannot be a holder in due course of the instrument if it is so incomplete as to call into question its validity. Subsection (d) of Section 3–115 is based on the last clause of subsection (2) of former Section 3–115.

Uniform Commercial Code Comment
Prior Uniform Statutory Provision:
Sections 13, 14 and 15, Uniform Negotiable Instruments Law.
Changes: Condensed and reworded; original Section 13 and parts of Section 14 omitted; rule of Section 15 reversed.

Purposes of Changes:

1. The original sections were lengthy and confusing. Section 13 is eliminated because it has suggested some uncertain distinction between undated instruments and those incomplete in other respects, and has carried the inference that only a holder may fill in the date. An instrument lacking in an essential date is merely one kind of incomplete instrument, to be treated like any other. The third sentence of Section 14, providing that the instrument must be filled up strictly in accordance with the authority given and within a reasonable time, is eliminated as entirely superfluous, since any authority must always be exercised in accordance with its limitations, and expires within a reasonable time unless a time limit is fixed.

2. The language "signed while still incomplete in any necessary respect" in subsection (1) is substituted for "wanting in any material particular" in the original Section 14, in order to make it entirely clear that a complete writing which lacks an essential element of an instrument and contains no blanks or spaces or anything else to indicate that what is missing is to be supplied, does not fall within the section. "Necessary" means necessary to a complete instrument. It will always include the promise or order, the designation of the payee, and the amount payable. It may include the time of payment where a blank is left for that time to be filled in; but where it is clear that no time is intended to be stated the instrument is complete, and is payable on demand under Section 3–108. It does not include the date of issue, which under Section 3–114(1) is not essential, unless the instrument is made payable at a fixed period after that date.

3. This section omits the second sentence of the original Section 14, providing that "a signature on a blank paper delivered by the person making the signature in order that the paper may be converted into a negotiable instrument operates as a prima facie authority to fill it up as such for any amount." This had utility only in connection with the ancient practice of signing blank paper to be filled in later as an acceptance, at a time when communications were slow and difficult. The practice has been obsolete for nearly a century. It affords obvious opportunity for fraud, and should not be encouraged by express sanction in the statute. The omission is not intended, however, to mean that any person may not be authorized to write in an instrument over a signature either before or after delivery.

4. Subsection (2) states the rule generally recognized by the courts, that any unauthorized completion is an alteration of the instrument which stands on the same footing as any other alteration. Reference is therefore made to Section 3–407 where the effect of alteration is stated. Subsection (3) of that section provides that a subsequent holder in due course may in all cases enforce the instrument as completed, and replaces the final sentence of the original Section 14.

5. The language "even though the paper was not delivered" reverses the rule of the original Section 15, which provides that where an incomplete instrument has not been delivered it will not, if completed, be a valid contract in the hands of any holder as against any person whose signature was placed thereon before delivery. Since under this Article (Sections 3–305 and 3–407) neither non-delivery nor unauthorized completion is a defense against a holder in due course, it has always been illogical that the two together should invalidate the instrument in his hands. A holder in due course sees and takes the same paper, whether it was complete when stolen or completed afterward by the thief, and in each case he relies in good faith on the maker's signature. The loss should fall upon the party whose conduct in signing blank paper has made the fraud possible, rather than upon the innocent purchaser. The result is consistent with the theory of decisions holding the drawer of a check stolen and afterwards filled in to be estopped from setting up the non-delivery against an innocent party.

A similar provision protecting a depositary bank which pays an item in good faith is contained in Section 4–401. The policy of that Section should apply in favor of drawees other than banks.

6. The language on burden of establishing unauthorized completion is substituted for the "prima facie authority" of the original section 14. It follows the generally accepted rule that the full burden of proof by a preponderance of the evidence is upon the party attacking the completed instrument. "Burden of establishing" is defined in Section 1–201.

Cross References:

Point 2: Sections 3–108 and 3–114(1).
Point 4: Section 3–407.
Point 5: Sections 3–305(2), 3–407(3) and 4–401.
Point 6: Section 1–201.

Definitional Cross References:

"Alteration". Section 3–407.
"Burden of establishing". Section 1–201.
"Delivery". Section 1–201.
"Instrument". Section 3–102.
"Party". Section 1–201.
"Signed". Section 1–201.

Cross References

Acceptor of incomplete instrument, obligation to pay, see Commercial Code § 3413.
Dishonor of item, customer or collecting bank obligation to pay amount due on item according to terms of incomplete item as completed, see Commercial Code § 4207
Drawer of incomplete instrument, obligation to pay, see Commercial Code § 3414.
Indorser of incomplete instrument, obligation to pay, see Commercial Code § 3415.
Issuer of incomplete instrument, obligation to pay, see Commercial Code § 3412.
Alterations, see Commercial Code § 3407.
Altered or completed items, payment by bank, see Commercial Code § 4401.
Definitions, see Commercial Code § 1201.
Essential elements of contracts, see Civil Code § 1550.
Extinction of written contract by material alteration, see Civil Code § 1700.
Instruments payable on demand, see Commercial Code § 3108.
Obligation of issuer, drawer and acceptor as to incomplete instruments, see Commercial Code § 3413 et seq.
Rights of holder in due course, see Commercial Code § 3305.
Undated, antedated or postdated instruments, see Commercial Code § 3113.

§ 3116. Joint and several liability on instrument; contribution

(a) Except as otherwise provided in the instrument, two or more persons who have the same liability on an instrument as makers, drawers, acceptors, indorsers who indorse as joint payees, or anomalous indorsers are jointly and severally liable in the capacity in which they sign.

(b) Except as provided in subdivision (e) of Section 3419 or by agreement of the affected parties, a party having joint and several liability who pays the instrument is entitled to receive from any party having the same joint and several liability contribution in accordance with applicable law.

(c) Discharge of one party having joint and several liability by a person entitled to enforce the instrument does not affect the right under subdivision (b) of a party having the same joint and several liability to receive contribution from the party discharged. *(Added by Stats.1992, c. 914 (S.B.833), § 6.)*

California Code Comment
By John A. Bohn and Charles J. Williams

Prior California Law

1. Paragraph (a) is new statutory law but is in accord with decisions under the NIL. Although there are no California cases on this point, decisions in other states have held under the NIL that an instrument payable in the alternative needed the indorsement of only one payee to indorse. See 5 (Part 1) U.L.A. 484–486.

2. Paragraph (b) requires all payees to join in any negotiation and is consistent with former Civil Code § 3122 (instrument payable to order of 2 or more payees must be indorsed by all).

3. For general contract provisions dealing with the construction of joint and several obligations, see Civil Code §§ 1430–1432.

4. One might infer from the language of paragraph (b) that a payor could be discharged only by performing for all the joint payees. The language is not that explicit. In Cober v. Connolly, 20 Cal.2d 741, 128 P.2d 519, 142 A.L.R. 367 (1942) the court held that a payor of an instrument payable jointly was discharged by performance to one of three joint payees upon the authority of Civil Code § 1475 which reads: "An obligation in favor of several persons is extinguished by performance to any of them . . ." See also Civil Code § 1476; 1 Stanf.L.R. 730–739.

Changes from U.C.C. (1962 Official Text)

5. This is section 3–116 of the Official Text without change.

Uniform Commercial Code Comment
1992 Addition

1. Subsection (a) replaces subsection (e) of former Section 3–118. Subsection (b) states contribution rights of parties with joint and several liability by referring to applicable law. But subsection (b) is subject to Section 3–419(e). If one of the parties with joint and several liability is an accommodation party and the other is the accommodated party, Section 3–419(e) applies. Subsection (c) deals with discharge. The discharge of a jointly and severally liable obligor does not affect the right of other obligors to seek contribution from the discharged obligor.

2. Indorsers normally do not have joint and several liability. Rather, an earlier indorser has liability to a later indorser. But indorsers can have joint and several liability in two cases. If an instrument is payable to two payees jointly, both payees must indorse. The indorsement is a joint indorsement and the indorsers have joint and several liability and subsection (b) applies. The other case is that of two or more anomalous indorsers. The term is defined in Section 3–205(d). An anomalous indorsement normally indicates that the indorser signed as an accommodation party. If more than one accommodation party indorses a note as an accommodation to the maker, the indorsers have joint and several liability and subsection (b) applies.

Uniform Commercial Code Comment

Prior Uniform Statutory Provision:

Section 41, Uniform Negotiable Instruments Law.

Changes: Revised in wording and substance.

Purposes of Changes: The changes are intended to make clear the distinction between an instrument payable to "A or B" and one payable to "A and B." The first names either A or B as payee, so that either of them who is in possession becomes a holder as that term is defined in Section 1–201 and may negotiate, enforce or discharge the instrument. The second is payable only to A and B together, and as provided in the original section both must indorse in order to negotiate the instrument, although one may of course be authorized to sign for the other. Likewise both must join in any action to enforce the instrument, and the rights of one are not discharged without his consent by the act of the other.

If the instrument is payable to "A and/or B," it is payable in the alternative to A, or to B, or to A and B together, and it may be negotiated, enforced or discharged accordingly.

Cross Reference:
Section 1–201.

Definitional Cross References:
"Instrument". Section 3–102.
"Person". Section 1–201.

Cross References
Definitions, see Commercial Code § 1201.

§ 3117. Separate agreements affecting instrument

Subject to applicable law regarding exclusion of proof of contemporaneous or previous agreements, the obligation of a party to an instrument to pay the instrument may be modified, supplemented, or nullified by a separate agreement of the obligor and a person entitled to enforce the instrument, if the instrument is issued or the obligation is incurred in reliance on the agreement or as part of the same transaction giving rise to the agreement. To the extent an obligation is modified, supplemented, or nullified by an agreement under this section, the agreement is a defense to the obligation. *(Added by Stats.1992, c. 914 (S.B.833), § 6.)*

California Code Comment
By John A. Bohn and Charles J. Williams

Prior California Law

1. This section is an expansion of former Civil Code § 3123 to cover instruments payable to a named person with additional words describing him as agent, officer, other fiduciary or which use other words of identification. See Official Comments 1, 2 and 3 for guides to the intent and interpretation of the section.

Changes from U.C.C. (1962 Official Text)

2. This is section 3–117 of the Official Text without change.

Uniform Commercial Code Comment
1992 Addition

1. The separate agreement might be a security agreement or mortgage or it might be an agreement that contradicts the terms of the instrument. For example, a person may be induced to sign an instrument under an agreement that the signer will not be liable on the instrument unless certain conditions are met. Suppose X requested credit from Creditor who is willing to give the credit only if an acceptable accommodation party will sign the note of X as co-maker. Y agrees to sign as co-maker on the condition that Creditor also obtain the signature of Z as co-maker. Creditor agrees and Y signs as co-maker with X. Creditor fails to obtain the signature of Z on the note. Under Sections 3–412 and 3–419(b), Y is obliged to pay the note, but Section 3–117 applies. In this case, the agreement modifies the terms of the note by stating a condition to the obligation of Y to pay the note. This case is essentially similar to a case in which a maker of a note is induced to sign the note by fraud of the holder. Although the agreement that Y not be liable on the note unless Z also signs may not have been fraudulently made, a subsequent attempt by Creditor to require Y to pay the note in violation of the agreement is a bad faith act. Section 3–117, in treating the agreement as a defense, allows Y to assert the agreement against Creditor, but the defense would not be good against a subsequent holder in due course of the note that took it without notice of the agreement. If there cannot be a holder in due course because of Section 3–106(d), a subsequent holder that took the note in good faith, for value and without knowledge of the agreement would not be able to enforce the liability of Y. This result is consistent with the risk that a holder not in due course takes with respect to fraud in inducing issuance of an instrument.

2. The effect of merger or integration clauses to the effect that a writing is intended to be the complete and exclusive statement of the

terms of the agreement or that the agreement is not subject to conditions is left to the supplementary law of the jurisdiction pursuant to Section 1–103. Thus, in the case discussed in Comment 1, whether Y is permitted to prove the condition to Y's obligation to pay the note is determined by that law. Moreover, nothing in this section is intended to validate an agreement which is fraudulent or void as against public policy, as in the case of a note given to deceive a bank examiner.

Uniform Commercial Code Comment

Prior Uniform Statutory Provision:

Section 42, Uniform Negotiable Instruments Law.
Changes: Revised and extended.

Purposes of Changes:

1. Subsection (a) extends the policy of the original Section 42, which covered only cashiers and fiscal officers of banks and corporations, to any case where a payee is named with words describing him as agent or officer of another named person. The intent is to include all such descriptions as "John Doe, Treasurer of Town of Framingham," "John Doe, President Home Telephone Co.," "John Doe, Secretary of City Club," or "John Doe, agent of Richard Roe." In all such cases it is commercial understanding that the description is not added for mere identification but for the purpose of making the instrument payable to the principal, and that the agent or officer is named as payee only for convenience in enabling him to cash the check.

2. Subsection (b) covers such descriptions as "John Doe, Trustee of Smithers Trust," "John Doe, Administrator of the Estate of Richard Roe," or "John Doe, Executor under Will of Richard Roe." In such cases the instrument is payable to the individual named, and he may negotiate it, enforce it or discharge it, but he remains subject to any liability for breach of his obligation as a fiduciary. Any subsequent holder of the instrument is put on notice of the fiduciary position, and under the section on notice to purchaser (Section 3–304) is not a holder in due course if he takes with notice that John Doe has negotiated the instrument in payment of or as security for his own debt or in any transaction for his own benefit, or otherwise in breach of duty.

3. Any other words of description, such as "John Doe, 1121 Main Street," "John Doe, Attorney," or "Jane Doe, unremarried widow," are to be treated as mere identification, and not in any respect as a condition of payment. The same is true of any description of the payee as "Treasurer," "President," "Agent," "Trustee," "Executor," or "Administrator," which does not name the principal or beneficiary. In all such cases the person named may negotiate, enforce or discharge the instrument if he is otherwise identified, even though he does not meet the description. Any subsequent party dealing with the instrument may disregard the description and treat the paper as payable unconditionally to the individual, and is fully protected in the absence of independent notice of other facts sufficient to affect his position.

Cross Reference:

Point 2: Section 3–304(2).

Definitional Cross References:

"Holder". Section 1–201.
"Instrument". Section 3–102.
"Party". Section 1–201.
"Person". Section 1–201.

Cross References

Supplementary general principles of law applicable, see Commercial Code § 1103.
Fiduciary, negotiation in breach of duty, see Commercial Code § 3307.

§ 3118. Limitation of actions

(a) Except as provided in subdivision (e), an action to enforce the obligation of a party to pay a note payable at a definite time shall be commenced within six years after the due date or dates stated in the note or, if a due date is accelerated, within six years after the accelerated due date.

(b) Except as provided in subdivision (d) or (e), if demand for payment is made to the maker of a note payable on demand, an action to enforce the obligation of a party to pay the note shall be commenced within six years after the demand. If no demand for payment is made to the maker, an action to enforce the note is barred if neither principal nor interest on the note has been paid for a continuous period of 10 years.

(c) Except as provided in subdivision (d), an action to enforce the obligation of a party to an unaccepted draft to pay the draft shall be commenced within three years after dishonor of the draft or 10 years after the date of the draft, whichever period expires first.

(d) An action to enforce the obligation of the acceptor of a certified check or the issuer of a teller's check, cashier's check, or traveler's check shall be commenced within three years after demand for payment is made to the acceptor or issuer, as the case may be.

(e) An action to enforce the obligation of a party to a certificate of deposit to pay the instrument shall be commenced within six years after demand for payment is made to the maker, but if the instrument states a due date and the maker is not required to pay before that date, the six-year period begins when a demand for payment is in effect and the due date has passed.

(f) An action to enforce the obligation of a party to pay an accepted draft, other than a certified check, shall be commenced (1) within six years after the due date or dates stated in the draft or acceptance if the obligation of the acceptor is payable at a definite time, or (2) within six years after the date of the acceptance if the obligation of the acceptor is payable on demand.

(g) Unless governed by other law regarding claims for indemnity or contribution, an action (1) for conversion of an instrument, for money had and received, or like action based on conversion, (2) for breach of warranty, or (3) to enforce an obligation, duty, or right arising under this division and not governed by this section shall be commenced within three years after the cause of action accrues. *(Added by Stats.1992, c. 914 (S.B.833), § 6.)*

California Code Comment

By John A. Bohn and Charles J. Williams

Prior California Law

1. Paragraphs (a) through (e) of this section are substantially the same as former Civil Code § 3098 and for the most part constitute a rewording of the NIL.

2. Paragraph (a) is similar to former Civil Code § 3098(5). See Official Comment 2.

3. Paragraph (b) is similar to former Civil Code § 3098(4). See Official Comment 3.

4. Paragraph (c) is similar to former Civil Code § 3098(1). See Official Comment 4.

5. Paragraph (d) clarifies former Civil Code § 3098(2) by adding a provision that the interest rate if none is specified is the judgment rate at the place of payment. The judgment rate in California is 7% a year. California Constitution, Article 20, § 22.

6. Paragraph (e) is similar to former Civil Code § 3098(7) and the last sentence of former Civil Code § 3149. See Official Comment 6.

7. Paragraph (f) is new statutory law. See Official Comment 7.

Changes from U.C.C. (1962 Official Text)

8. This is section 3-118 of the Official Text without change.

Uniform Commercial Code Comment
1992 Addition

1. Section 3-118 differs from former Section 3-122, which states when a cause of action accrues on an instrument. Section 3-118 does not define when a cause of action accrues. Accrual of a cause of action is stated in other sections of Article 3 such as those that state the various obligations of parties to an instrument. The only purpose of Section 3-118 is to define the time within which an action to enforce an obligation, duty, or right arising under Article 3 must be commenced. Section 3-118 does not attempt to state all rules with respect to a statute of limitations. For example, the circumstances under which the running of a limitations period may be tolled is left to other law pursuant to Section 1-103.

2. The first six subsections apply to actions to enforce an obligation of any party to an instrument to pay the instrument. This changes present law in that indorsers who may become liable on an instrument after issue are subject to a period of limitations running from the same date as that of the maker or drawer. Subsections (a) and (b) apply to notes. If the note is payable at a definite time, a six-year limitations period starts at the due date of the note, subject to prior acceleration. If the note is payable on demand, there are two limitations periods. Although a note payable on demand could theoretically be called a day after it was issued, the normal expectation of the parties is that the note will remain outstanding until there is some reason to call it. If the law provides that the limitations period does not start until demand is made, the cause of action to enforce it may never be barred. On the other hand, if the limitations period starts when demand for payment may be made, i.e. at any time after the note was issued, the payee of a note on which interest or portions of principal are being paid could lose the right to enforce the note even though it was treated as a continuing obligation by the parties. Some demand notes are not enforced because the payee has forgiven the debt. This is particularly true in family and other noncommercial transactions. A demand note found after the death of the payee may be presented for payment many years after it was issued. The maker may be a relative and it may be difficult to determine whether the note represents a real or a forgiven debt. Subsection (b) is designed to bar notes that no longer represent a claim to payment and to require reasonably prompt action to enforce notes on which there is default. If a demand for payment is made to the maker, a six-year limitations period starts to run when demand is made. The second sentence of subsection (b) bars an action to enforce a demand note if no demand has been made on the note and no payment of interest or principal has been made for a continuous period of 10 years. This covers the case of a note that does not bear interest or a case in which interest due on the note has not been paid. This kind of case is likely to be a family transaction in which a failure to demand payment may indicate that the holder did not intend to enforce the obligation but neglected to destroy the note. A limitations period that bars stale claims in this kind of case is appropriate if the period is relatively long.

3. Subsection (c) applies primarily to personal uncertified checks. Checks are payment instruments rather than credit instruments. The limitations period expires three years after the date of dishonor or 10 years after the date of the check, whichever is earlier. Teller's checks, cashier's checks, certified checks, and traveler's checks are treated differently under subsection (d) because they are commonly treated as cash equivalents. A great delay in presenting a cashier's check for payment in most cases will occur because the check was mislaid during that period. The person to whom traveler's checks are issued may hold them indefinitely as a safe form of cash for use in an emergency. There is no compelling reason for barring the claim of the owner of the cashier's check or traveler's check. Under subsection (d) the claim is never barred because the three-year limitations period does not start to run until demand for payment is made. The limitations period in subsection (d) in effect applies only to cases in which there is a dispute about the legitimacy of the claim of the person demanding payment.

4. Subsection (e) covers certificates of deposit. The limitations period of six years doesn't start to run until the depositor demands payment. Most certificates of deposit are payable on demand even if they state a due date. The effect of a demand for payment before maturity is usually that the bank will pay, but that a penalty will be assessed against the depositor in the form of a reduction in the amount of interest that is paid. Subsection (e) also provides for cases in which the bank has no obligation to pay until the due date. In that case the limitations period doesn't start to run until there is a demand for payment in effect and the due date has passed.

5. Subsection (f) applies to accepted drafts other than certified checks. When a draft is accepted it is in effect turned into a note of the acceptor. In almost all cases the acceptor will agree to pay at a definite time. Subsection (f) states that in that case the six-year limitations period starts to run on the due date. In the rare case in which the obligation of the acceptor is payable on demand, the six-year limitations period starts to run at the date of the acceptance.

6. Subsection (g) covers warranty and conversion cases and other actions to enforce obligations or rights arising under Article 3. A three-year period is stated and subsection (g) follows general law in stating that the period runs from the time the cause of action accrues. Since the traditional term "cause of action" may have been replaced in some states by "claim for relief" or some equivalent term, the words "cause of action" have been bracketed to indicate that the words may be replaced by an appropriate substitute to conform to local practice.

Uniform Commercial Code Comment

Prior Uniform Statutory Provision:

Sections 17 and 68, Uniform Negotiable Instruments Law.

Changes: Reworded; new provisions; original subsections (3) and (6) of Section 17 omitted. The original Section 17(3) is covered, so far as the question can arise, by Sections 3-109(1)(a) and 3-114 of this Article. The original Section 17(6) is now covered by Section 3-402.

Purposes of Changes and New Matter:

1. The purpose of this section is to protect holders and to encourage the free circulation of negotiable paper by stating rules of law which will preclude a resort to parol evidence for any purpose except reformation of the instrument. Except as to such reformation, these rules cannot be varied by any proof that any party intended the contrary.

2. Subsection (a): The language of the original Section 17(5) is changed to make it clear that the provision is not limited to ambiguities of phrasing, but extends to any case where the form of the instrument leaves its character as a draft or a note in doubt.

3. Subsection (b): The original Section 17(4) is revised to cover typewriting because of its frequent use in instruments, particularly in promissory notes.

4. Subsection (c): The rewording of the original Section 17(1) is intended to make it clear that figures control only where the words are ambiguous and the figures are not.

5. Subsection (d): The revision of the original Section 17(2) is intended to make it clear that where the instrument provides for payment "with interest" without specifying the rate, the judgment rate of interest of the place of payment is to be taken as intended.

6. Subsection (e): This subsection combines and revises the original Section 17(7) and the last sentence of the original Section 68. The rule applies to any two or more persons who sign in the same capacity, whether as makers, drawers, acceptors or indorsers. It applies only where such parties sign as a part of the same transaction; successive indorsers are, of course, liable severally but not jointly.

7. Subsection (f): This provision is new. It has reference to such clauses as "The makers and indorsers of this note consent that it may be extended without notice to them." Such terms usually are inserted to obtain the consent of the indorsers and any accommodation maker to extension which might otherwise discharge them under Section 3-606 dealing with impairment of recourse or collateral. An extension in accord with these terms binds secondary parties. The holder may not force an extension on a maker or acceptor who makes due tender; the holder is not free to refuse payment and keep interest running on a good note or other instrument by extending it over the objection of a maker or acceptor or other party who in accordance with Section 3-604 tenders full payment when the instrument is due. Where consent to extension has been given, the subsection provides that unless otherwise specified the consent is to be construed as authorizing only one extension for not longer than the original period of the note.

Cross References:

Sections 3–109, 3–114, 3–402 and 3–606.
Point 7: Sections 3–604 and 3–606.

Definitional Cross References:

"Draft". Section 3–104.
"Holder". Section 1–201.
"Instrument". Section 3–102.
"Issue". Section 3–102.
"Note". Section 3–104.
"Person". Section 1–201.
"Promise". Section 3–102.
"Signed". Section 1–201.
"Term". Section 1–201.

Cross References

Actions commenced prior to Jan. 1, 1993, application of this section, see Commercial Code § 16103.
Impairment of recourse or of collateral, see Commercial Code § 3605.
Interpretation of contracts, see Civil Code § 1635 et seq.
Interest,
   Annual rate, see Civil Code § 1916.
   Definition, see Civil Code § 1915.
   Legal rate of interest, see Const. Art. 15, § 1.
   Presumption, see Civil Code § 1914.
Joint authority construed, see Civil Code § 12; Code of Civil Procedure § 15.
Joint or several obligations, see Civil Code § 1430 et seq.
Payment at definite time, see Commercial Code § 3108.
Signature in ambiguous capacity, see Commercial Code § 3402.
Tender of payment, see Commercial Code § 3603.
Undated, antedated or postdated instruments, time of payment, see Commercial Code § 3113.
Usury law, see Civil Code § 1916–1 et seq.
Writing as including printing and typewriting, see Civil Code § 14; Code of Civil Procedure § 17.
Written parts of contract as controlling printed parts, see Civil Code § 1651.

§ 3119. Third-party liability; notice of right to defend action

In an action for breach of an obligation for which a third person is answerable over pursuant to this division or Division 4 (commencing with Section 4101), the defendant may give the third person written notice of the litigation, and the person notified may then give similar notice to any other person who is answerable over. If the notice states (1) that the person notified may come in and defend and (2) that failure to do so will bind the person notified in an action later brought by the person giving the notice as to any determination of fact common to the two litigations, the person notified is so bound unless after seasonable receipt of the notice the person notified does come in and defend.
(Added by Stats.1992, c. 914 (S.B.833), § 6.)

California Code Comment

By John A. Bohn and Charles J. Williams

Prior California Law

1. This section has no statutory counterpart in prior California law. However, it is in accord with and consistent with prior California decisions. Williams v. Silverstein, 213 Cal. 269, 2 P.2d 165 (1931); Kent v. Lampman, 59 Cal.App.2d 407, 139 P.2d 57 (1943).

Changes from U.C.C. (1962 Official Text)

2. This is section 3–119 of the Official Text without change.

Uniform Commercial Code Comment
1992 Addition

This section is a restatement of former Section 3–803.

Uniform Commercial Code Comment

Prior Uniform Statutory Provision:

None.

Purposes: This section is new. It is intended to resolve conflicts as to the effect of a separate writing upon a negotiable instrument.

1. This Article does not attempt to state general rules as to when an instrument may be varied or affected by parol evidence, except to the extent indicated by the comment to the preceding section. This section is limited to the effect of a separate written agreement executed as a part of the same transaction. The separate writing is most commonly an agreement creating or providing for a security interest such as a mortgage, chattel mortgage, conditional sale or pledge. It may, however, be any type of contract, including an agreement that upon certain conditions the instrument shall be discharged or is not to be paid, or even an agreement that it is a sham and not to be enforced at all. Nothing in this section is intended to validate any such agreement which is fraudulent or void as against public policy, as in the case of a note given to deceive a bank examiner.

2. Other parties, such as an accommodation indorser, are not affected by the separate writing unless they were also parties to it as a part of the transaction by which they became bound on the instrument.

3. The section applies to negotiable instruments the ordinary rule that writings executed as a part of the same transaction are to be read together as a single agreement. As between the immediate parties a negotiable instrument is merely a contract, and is no exception to the principle that the courts will look to the entire contract in writing. Accordingly a note may be affected by an acceleration clause, a clause providing for discharge under certain conditions, or any other relevant term in the separate writing. "May be modified or affected" does not mean that the separate agreement must necessarily be given effect. There is still room for construction of the writing as not intended to affect the instrument at all, or as intended to affect it only for a limited purpose such as foreclosure or other realization of collateral. If there is outright contradiction between the two, as where the note is for $1,000 but the accompanying mortgage recites that it is for $2,000, the note may be held to stand on its own feet and not to be affected by the contradiction.

4. Under this Article a purchaser of the instrument may become a holder in due course although he takes it with knowledge that it was accompanied by a separate agreement, if he has no notice of any defense or claim arising from the terms of the agreement. If any limitation in the separate writing in itself amounts to a defense or claim, as in the case of an agreement that the note is a sham and cannot be enforced, a purchaser with notice of it cannot be a holder in due course. The section also covers limitations which do not in themselves give notice of any present defense or claim, such as conditions providing that under certain conditions the note shall be extended for one year. A purchaser with notice of such limitations may be a holder in due course, but he takes the instrument subject to the limitation. If he is without such notice, he is not affected by such a limiting clause in the separate writing.

5. Subsection (2) rejects decisions which have carried the rule that contemporaneous writings must be read together to the length of holding that a clause in a mortgage affecting a note destroyed the negotiability of the note. The negotiability of an instrument is always to be determined by what appears on the face of the instrument alone, and if it is negotiable in itself a purchaser without notice of a separate writing is in no way affected by it. If the instrument itself states that it is subject to or governed by any other agreement, it is not negotiable under this Article; but if it merely refers to a separate agreement or states that it arises out of such an agreement, it is negotiable.

Cross References:

Point 1: Section 3–119.
Point 4: Section 3–304(4)(b).
Point 5: Section 3–105(2)(a) and (1)(c).

§ 3119

Definitional Cross References:

"Agreement". Section 1–201.
"Holder in due course". Section 3–302.
"Instrument". Section 3–102.
"Notice". Section 1–201.
"Rights". Section 1–201.
"Term". Section 1–201.
"Written" and "writing". Section 1–201.

Cross References

Instrument, see Commercial Code § 3104.
Several contracts as parts of one transaction, see Civil Code § 1642.
Taker, notice of defense or claim, see Commercial Code § 3307.
Unconditional promise or order, see Commercial Code § 3106.

§§ 3120 to 3123. Repealed by Stats.1992, c. 914 (S.B. 833), § 5

CHAPTER 2. NEGOTIATION, TRANSFER, AND INDORSEMENT

Section
3201. Negotiation.
3202. Effective negotiation; rescission and other remedies.
3203. Transfer of instrument; rights acquired by transfer.
3204. Indorsement; indorser.
3205. Special indorsement; blank indorsement; anomalous indorsement.
3206. Restrictive indorsements.
3207. Reacquisition of instrument; cancellation of indorsements.
3208. Repealed.

Transitional Provisions

Effective date and transitional provisions for repeal and addition of Division 3 by Stats.1992, c. 914, see Commercial Code § 16101 et seq.

§ 3201. Negotiation

(a) "Negotiation" means a transfer of possession, whether voluntary or involuntary, of an instrument by a person other than the issuer to a person who thereby becomes its holder.

(b) Except for negotiation by a remitter, if an instrument is payable to an identified person, negotiation requires transfer of possession of the instrument and its indorsement by the holder. If an instrument is payable to bearer, it may be negotiated by transfer of possession alone. *(Added by Stats.1992, c. 914 (S.B.833), § 6.)*

California Code Comment

By John A. Bohn and Charles J. Williams

Prior California Law

1. Subdivision (1) is similar to former Civil Code § 3139. Subdivision (2) is similar to former Civil Code § 3108. Each of these subdivisions embodies the rule that a holder may transfer whatever he has and continue the shelter principle to provide the holder a free market. These provisions apply to any transfer whether or not for value. Official Comments 1, 2 and 3. Examples of the operation of these principles appear in Official Comment 3.

2. Subdivision (3) is in part new and in part a restatement of former Civil Code § 3130. The transferee is now given a specifically enforceable right to the transferor's indorsement while formerly he had "the right to have the indorsement of the transferor" and could sue on the note without the indorsement. Cassetta v. Baima, 106 Cal.App. 196, 288 Pac. 830 (1930). The last phrase providing that until indorsement there is no presumption that the transferee is the owner is new.

3. If this section does not change prior California law, it at least strengthens the shelter principle and the rights which a transferee without an indorsement obtains in contrast to the view of the court in Cassetta v. Baima, supra, that the transferee is not protected against equities which exist against the transferor. Also see Britton, Bills & Notes (1961) 173–177.

Changes from U.C.C. (1962 Official Text)

4. This is section 3–201 of the Official Text without change.

Uniform Commercial Code Comment
1992 Addition

1. Subsections (a) and (b) are based in part on subsection (1) of former Section 3–202. A person can become holder of an instrument when the instrument is issued to that person, or the status of holder can arise as the result of an event that occurs after issuance. "Negotiation" is the term used in Article 3 to describe this post-issuance event. Normally, negotiation occurs as the result of a voluntary transfer of possession of an instrument by a holder to another person who becomes the holder as a result of the transfer. Negotiation always requires a change in possession of the instrument because nobody can be a holder without possessing the instrument, either directly or through an agent. But in some cases the transfer of possession is involuntary and in some cases the person transferring possession is not a holder. In defining "negotiation" former Section 3–202(1) used the word "transfer," an undefined term, and "delivery," defined in Section 1–201(14) to mean voluntary change of possession. Instead, subsections (a) and (b) use the term "transfer of possession" and, subsection (a) states that negotiation can occur by an involuntary transfer of possession. For example, if an instrument is payable to bearer and it is stolen by Thief or is found by Finder, Thief or Finder becomes the holder of the instrument when possession is obtained. In this case there is an involuntary transfer of possession that results in negotiation to Thief or Finder.

2. In most cases negotiation occurs by a transfer of possession by a holder or remitter. Remitter transactions usually involve a cashier's or teller's check. For example, Buyer buys goods from Seller and pays for them with a cashier's check of Bank that Buyer buys from Bank. The check is issued by Bank when it is delivered to Buyer, regardless of whether the check is payable to Buyer or to Seller. Section 3–105(a). If the check is payable to Buyer, negotiation to Seller is done by delivery of the check to Seller after it is indorsed by Buyer. It is more common, however, that the check when issued will be payable to Seller. In that case Buyer is referred to as the "remitter." Section 3–103(a)(11). The remitter, although not a party to the check, is the owner of the check until ownership is transferred to Seller by delivery. This transfer is a negotiation because Seller becomes the holder of the check when Seller obtains possession. In some cases Seller may have acted fraudulently in obtaining possession of the check. In those cases Buyer may be entitled to rescind the transfer to Seller because of the fraud and assert a claim of ownership to the check under Section 3–306 against Seller or a subsequent transferee of the check. Section 3–202(b) provides for rescission of negotiation, and that provision applies to rescission by a remitter as well as by a holder.

3. Other sections of Article 3 may modify the rule stated in the first sentence of subsection (b). See for example, Sections 3–404, 3–405 and 3–406.

Prior Uniform Statutory Provision:

Sections 27, 49 and 58, Uniform Negotiable Instruments Law.

Changes: Combined and reworded; new provisions.

Purposes of Changes and New Matter: To make it clear that:

1. The section applies to any transfer, whether by a holder or not. Any person who transfers an instrument transfers whatever rights he has in it. The transferee acquires those rights even though they do not amount to "title."

2. The transfer of rights is not limited to transfers for value. An instrument may be transferred as a gift, and the donee acquires whatever rights the donor had.

3. A holder in due course may transfer his rights as such. The "shelter" provision of the last sentence of the original Section 58 is

merely one illustration of the rule that anyone may transfer what he has. Its policy is to assure the holder in due course a free market for the paper, and that policy is continued in this section. The provision is not intended and should not be used to permit any holder who has himself been a party to any fraud or illegality affecting the instrument, or who has received notice of any defense or claim against it, to wash the paper clean by passing it into the hands of a holder in due course and then repurchasing it. The operation of the provision is illustrated by the following examples:

(a) A induces M by fraud to make an instrument payable to A, A negotiates it to B, who takes as a holder in due course. After the instrument is overdue B gives it to C, who has notice of the fraud. C succeeds to B's rights as a holder in due course, cutting off the defense.

(b) A induces M by fraud to make an instrument payable to A, A negotiates it to B, who takes as a holder in due course. A then repurchases the instrument from B. A does not succeed to B's rights as a holder in due course, and remains subject to the defense of fraud.

(c) A induces M by fraud to make an instrument payable to A, A negotiates it to B, who takes with notice of the fraud. B negotiates it to C, a holder in due course, and then repurchases the instrument from C. B does not succeed to C's rights as a holder in due course, and remains subject to the defense of fraud.

(d) The same facts as (c), except that B had no notice of the fraud when he first acquired the instrument, but learned of it while he was a holder and with such knowledge negotiated to C. B does not succeed to C's rights as a holder in due course, and his position is not improved by the negotiation and repurchase.

4. The rights of a transferee with respect to collateral for the instrument are determined by Article 9 (Secured Transactions).

5. Subsection (2) restates original Section 27 and is intended to make it clear that a transfer of a limited interest in the instrument passes the rights of the transferor to the extent of the interest given. Thus a transferee for security acquires all such rights subject of course to the provisions of Article 9 (Secured Transactions).

6. Subsection (3) applies only to the transfer for value of an instrument payable to order or specially indorsed. It has no application to a gift, or to an instrument payable or indorsed to bearer or indorsed in blank. The transferee acquires, in the absence of any agreement to the contrary, the right to have the indorsement of the transferor. This right is now made enforceable by an action for specific performance. Unless otherwise agreed, it is a right to the general indorsement of the transferor with full liability as indorser, rather than to an indorsement without recourse. The question commonly arises where the purchaser has paid in advance and the indorsement is omitted fraudulently or through oversight; a transferor who is willing to indorse only without recourse or unwilling to indorse at all should make his intentions clear. The agreement for the transferee to take less than an unqualified indorsement need not be an express one, and the understanding may be implied from conduct, from past practice, or from the circumstances of the transaction.

7. Subsection (3) follows the second sentence of the original Section 49 in providing that there is no effective negotiation until the indorsement is made. Until that time the purchaser does not become a holder, and if he receives earlier notice of defense against or claim to the instrument he does not qualify as a holder in due course under Section 3–302(1)(c).

8. The final clause of subsection (3), which is new, is intended to make it clear that the transferee without indorsement of an order instrument is not a holder and so is not aided by the presumption that he is entitled to recover on the instrument provided in Section 3–307(2). The terms of the obligation do not run to him, and he must account for his possession of the unindorsed paper by proving the transaction through which he acquired it. Proof of a transfer to him by a holder is proof that he has acquired the rights of a holder and that he is entitled to the presumption.

Cross References:

Sections 3–202 and 3–416.
Point 5: Article 9.
Point 7: Section 3–302(1)(c).
Point 8: Section 3–307(2).

Definitional Cross References:

"Bearer". Section 1–201.
"Holder". Section 1–201.
"Holder in due course". Section 3–302.
"Instrument". Section 3–102.
"Negotiation". Section 3–202.
"Notice". Section 1–201.
"Party". Section 1–201.
"Presumption". Section 1–201.
"Rights". Section 1–201.
"Security interest". Section 1–201.

Cross References

Holder in due course, see Commercial Code § 3302.
Negligence contributing to alteration or forged signature, see Commercial Code § 3406.
Rights of one not holder in due course, see Commercial Code § 3306.
Secured transactions, see Commercial Code § 9101 et seq.
Signatures, burden of establishing validity, see Commercial Code § 3308.
Transfer of non-negotiable instruments, see Civil Code §§ 955, 1459.
Transfer of obligations, see Civil Code § 1457 et seq.
Transfer of things in action, see Civil Code § 953 et seq.

§ 3202. Effective negotiation; rescission and other remedies

(a) Negotiation is effective even if obtained (1) from an infant, a corporation exceeding its powers, or a person without capacity, (2) by fraud, duress, or mistake, or (3) in breach of duty or as part of an illegal transaction.

(b) To the extent permitted by other law, negotiation may be rescinded or may be subject to other remedies, but those remedies may not be asserted against a subsequent holder in due course or a person paying the instrument in good faith and without knowledge of facts that are a basis for rescission or other remedy. *(Added by Stats.1992, c. 914 (S.B.833), § 6.)*

California Code Comment

By John A. Bohn and Charles J. Williams

Prior California Law

1. Subdivision (1) is substantially the same as former Civil Code § 3111.

2. Subdivision (2) follows former Civil Code § 3112 but adds language to require the separate paper containing the indorsement to be so firmly fixed as to become a part of it.

3. Subdivision (3) continues the rule of the first sentence of former Civil Code § 3113 on transfer of the amount due.

However, the last sentence in subdivision (3) is new and changes the rule in California. Former Civil Code § 3113 provided in part that "an indorsement which purports to transfer to the indorsee a part only of the amount payable . . . does not operate as a negotiation of the instrument." In Wright v. Shoenhair, 100 Cal.App. 163, 280 Pac. 174 (1929) the court held that an indorsement of a $6,000 interest in a $14,000 note was invalid and conveyed no interest to the indorsee and that the assignment of a part of the interest was invalid under Civil Code § 3113. The last sentence of subdivision (3) changes the California law to the extent that the indorsement of a partial interest is a partial assignment. The Uniform Commercial Code makes no attempt to state the legal effect of a partial assignment. This is left to local law. See Official Comment 4.

4. Subdivision (4) is new statutory law. See Official Comments 5 and 6 for an explanation of the intent. There is a difference of opinion as to its effect upon prior California law, due more likely to the factual variety of the cases and the courts view of the parties' intent than to a difference in principle.

§ 3202

The Legislative Counsel states that:

"Subdivision (4) is new statutory law, although perhaps the California case law is in accord. See Adolph Ramish Inc. v. Woodruff, 2 Cal.2d 190, 40 Pac.2d, 509." Sixth Progress Report to the Legislature by Senate Fact Finding Committee on Judiciary (1959–1961) Part 1, The Uniform Commercial Code, p. 70.

The sub-committee of the State Bar on Article [Division] 3 comments to the effect that:

"This section makes it clear that words of assignment or guaranty do not affect an endorsement as such. This probably changes California law as found in such cases as Kern v. Henry, 138 Cal.App. 46 (1934), holding that words of assignment make the endorsement a qualified endorsement." Sixth Progress Report to the Legislature by Senate Fact Finding Committee on Judiciary (1959–1961) Part 1, The Uniform Commercial Code p. 345.

The State Bar Committee on the Commercial Code in its special report states:

"Section 13202 [3202] provides that words of 'assignment, condition, waiver, guaranty, limitation or disclaimer of liability and the like' accompanying an indorsement do not affect its character as an indorsement. This would reject decisions such as those in California holding that the addition of words of assignment prevent a signature from operating as an indorsement. [*Fn.:* Title Insurance & Trust Co. v. Bandini Estate Co., 26 C.A.2d 157, 79 P.2d 141 (1938); see also, Kern v. Henry, 138 Cal.App. 46, 31 P.2d 454 (1934)]." California State Bar Committee on the Commercial Code, A Special Report, The Uniform Commercial Code, 37 Calif.State Bar J. 161 (March–April 1962).

An extended discussion of the problem and analysis of American decisions is presented in Ramish (Adolph) Inc., v. Woodruff, 2 C.2d 190, 40 P.2d 509, 96 A.L.R. 1146 (1934).

Changes from U.C.C. (1962 Official Text)

5. This is section 3–202 of the Official Text without change.

Uniform Commercial Code Comment
1992 Addition

1. This section is based on former Section 3–207. Subsection (2) of former Section 3–207 prohibited rescission of a negotiation against holders in due course. Subsection (b) of Section 3–202 extends this protection to payor banks.

2. Subsection (a) applies even though the lack of capacity or the illegality, is of a character which goes to the essence of the transaction and makes it entirely void. It is inherent in the character of negotiable instruments that any person in possession of an instrument which by its terms is payable to that person or to bearer is a holder and may be dealt with by anyone as a holder. The principle finds its most extreme application in the well settled rule that a holder in due course may take the instrument even from a thief and be protected against the claim of the rightful owner. The policy of subsection (a) is that any person to whom an instrument is negotiated is a holder until the instrument has been recovered from that person's possession. The remedy of a person with a claim to an instrument is to recover the instrument by replevin or otherwise; to impound it or to enjoin its enforcement, collection or negotiation; to recover its proceeds from the holder; or to intervene in any action brought by the holder against the obligor. As provided in Section 3–305(c), the claim of the claimant is not a defense to the obligor unless the claimant defends the action.

3. There can be no rescission or other remedy against a holder in due course or a person who pays in good faith and without notice, even though the prior negotiation may have been fraudulent or illegal in its essence and entirely void. As against any other party the claimant may have any remedy permitted by law. This section is not intended to specify what that remedy may be, or to prevent any court from imposing conditions or limitations such as prompt action or return of the consideration received. All such questions are left to the law of the particular jurisdiction. Section 3–202 gives no right that would not otherwise exist. The section is intended to mean that any remedies afforded by other law are cut off only by a holder in due course.

Uniform Commercial Code Comment
Prior Uniform Statutory Provision:

Sections 30, 31 and 32, Uniform Negotiable Instruments Law.

Changes: Combined and reworded; new provisions.

Purposes of Changes and New Matter: To make it clear that:

1. Negotiation is merely a special form of transfer, the importance of which lies entirely in the fact that it makes the transferee a holder as defined in Section 1–201. Any negotiation carries a transfer of rights as provided in the section on transfer (subsections (1) and (2) of Section 3–201).

2. Any instrument which has been specially indorsed can be negotiated only with the indorsement of the special indorsee as provided in Section 3–204 on special indorsement. An instrument indorsed in blank may be negotiated by delivery alone, provided that it bears the indorsement of all prior special indorsees.

3. Subsection (2) follows decisions holding that a purported indorsement on a mortgage or other separate paper pinned or clipped to an instrument is not sufficient for negotiation. The indorsement must be on the instrument itself or on a paper intended for the purpose which is so firmly affixed to the instrument as to become an extension or part of it. Such a paper is called an allonge.

4. The cause of action on an instrument cannot be split. Any indorsement which purports to convey to any party less than the entire amount of the instrument is not effective for negotiation. This is true of either "Pay A one-half," or "Pay A two-thirds and B one-third," and neither A nor B becomes a holder. On the other hand an indorsement reading merely "Pay A and B" is effective, since it transfers the entire cause of action to A and B as tenants in common.

The partial indorsement does, however, operate as a partial assignment of the cause of action. The provision makes no attempt to state the legal effect of such an assignment, which is left to the local law. In a jurisdiction in which a partial assignee has any rights, either at law or in equity, the partial indorsee has such rights; and in any jurisdiction where a partial assignee has no rights the partial indorsee has none.

5. Subsection (4) is intended to reject decisions holding that the addition of such words as "I hereby assign all my right, title and interest in the within note" prevents the signature from operating as an indorsement. Such words usually are added by laymen out of an excess of caution and a desire to indicate formally that the instrument is conveyed, rather than with any intent to limit the effect of the signature.

6. Subsection (4) is also intended to reject decisions which have held that the addition of "I guarantee payment" indicates an intention not to indorse but merely to guarantee. Any signature with such added words is an indorsement, and if it is made by a holder is effective for negotiation; but the liability of the indorser may be affected by the words of guarantee as provided in the section on the contract of a guarantor. (Section 3–416.)

Cross References:

Section 3–417.
Point 1: Sections 1–201 and 3–201(1) and (2).
Point 2: Section 3–204.
Point 6: Section 3–416.

Definitional Cross References:

"Bearer". Section 1–201.
"Delivery". Section 1–201.
"Holder". Section 1–201.
"Instrument". Section 3–102.
"Written". Section 1–201.

Cross References

Definitions, see Commercial Code § 1201.
Documents of title, negotiation, see Commercial Code § 7501 et seq.
Negotiation by indorsement, see Commercial Code § 3204 et seq.
Obligation of guarantor, see Commercial Code § 3419.
Transfer of non-negotiable instruments, see Civil Code § 1459.
Transfer of things in action, see Civil Code § 953 et seq.
Warranties on presentment and transfer, see Commercial Code §§ 3416, 3417.

§ 3203. Transfer of instrument; rights acquired by transfer

(a) An instrument is transferred when it is delivered by a person other than its issuer for the purpose of giving to the person receiving delivery the right to enforce the instrument.

(b) Transfer of an instrument, whether or not the transfer is a negotiation, vests in the transferee any right of the transferor to enforce the instrument, including any right as a holder in due course, but the transferee cannot acquire rights of a holder in due course by a transfer, directly or indirectly, from a holder in due course if the transferee engaged in fraud or illegality affecting the instrument.

(c) Unless otherwise agreed, if an instrument is transferred for value and the transferee does not become a holder because of lack of indorsement by the transferor, the transferee has a specifically enforceable right to the unqualified indorsement of the transferor, but negotiation of the instrument does not occur until the indorsement is made.

(d) If a transferor purports to transfer less than the entire instrument, negotiation of the instrument does not occur. The transferee obtains no rights under this division and has only the rights of a partial assignee. *(Added by Stats.1992, c. 914 (S.B.833), § 6.)*

California Code Comment

By John A. Bohn and Charles J. Williams

Prior California Law

1. This section expands former Civil Code § 3124 to permit the payor to compel signature in both names.

Changes from U.C.C. (1962 Official Text)

2. This is section 3–203 of the Official Text without change.

Uniform Commercial Code Comment

1992 Addition

1. Section 3–203 is based on former Section 3–201 which stated that a transferee received such rights as the transferor had. The former section was confusing because some rights of the transferor are not vested in the transferee unless the transfer is a negotiation. For example, a transferee that did not become the holder could not negotiate the instrument, a right that the transferor had. Former Section 3–201 did not define "transfer." Subsection (a) defines transfer by limiting it to cases in which possession of the instrument is delivered for the purpose of giving to the person receiving delivery the right to enforce the instrument.

Although transfer of an instrument might mean in a particular case that title to the instrument passes to the transferee, that result does not follow in all cases. The right to enforce an instrument and ownership of the instrument are two different concepts. A thief who steals a check payable to bearer becomes the holder of the check and a person entitled to enforce it, but does not become the owner of the check. If the thief transfers the check to a purchaser the transferee obtains the right to enforce the check. If the purchaser is not a holder in due course, the owner's claim to the check may be asserted against the purchaser. Ownership rights in instruments may be determined by principles of the law of property, independent of Article 3, which do not depend upon whether the instrument was transferred under Section 3–203. Moreover, a person who has an ownership right in an instrument might not be a person entitled to enforce the instrument. For example, suppose X is the owner and holder of an instrument payable to X. X sells the instrument to Y but is unable to deliver immediate possession to Y. Instead, X signs a document conveying all of X's right, title, and interest in the instrument to Y. Although the document may be effective to give Y a claim to ownership of the instrument, Y is not a person entitled to enforce the instrument until Y obtains possession of the instrument.

No transfer of the instrument occurs under Section 3–203(a) until it is delivered to Y.

An instrument is a reified right to payment. The right is represented by the instrument itself. The right to payment is transferred by delivery of possession of the instrument "by a person other than its issuer for the purpose of giving to the person receiving delivery the right to enforce the instrument." The quoted phrase excludes issue of an instrument, defined in Section 3–105, and cases in which a delivery of possession is for some purpose other than transfer of the right to enforce. For example, if a check is presented for payment by delivering the check to the drawee, no transfer of the check to the drawee occurs because there is no intent to give the drawee the right to enforce the check.

2. Subsection (b) states that transfer vests in the transferee any right of the transferor to enforce the instrument "including any right as a holder in due course." If the transferee is not a holder because the transferor did not indorse, the transferee is nevertheless a person entitled to enforce the instrument under Section 3–301 if the transferor was a holder at the time of transfer. Although the transferee is not a holder, under subsection (b) the transferee obtained the rights of the transferor as holder. Because the transferee's rights are derivative of the transferor's rights, those rights must be proved. Because the transferee is not a holder, there is no presumption under Section 3–308 that the transferee, by producing the instrument, is entitled to payment. The instrument, by its terms, is not payable to the transferee and the transferee must account for possession of the unindorsed instrument by proving the transaction through which the transferee acquired. it. Proof of a transfer to the transferee by a holder is proof that the transferee has acquired the rights of a holder. At that point the transferee is entitled to the presumption under Section 3–308.

Under subsection (b) a holder in due course that transfers an instrument transfers those rights as a holder in due course to the purchaser. The policy is to assure the holder in due course a free market for the instrument. There is one exception to this rule stated in the concluding clause of subsection (b). A person who is party to fraud or illegality affecting the instrument is not permitted to wash the instrument clean by passing it into the hands of a holder in due course and then repurchasing it.

3. Subsection (c) applies only to a transfer for value. It applies only if the instrument is payable to order or specially indorsed to the transferor. The transferee acquires, in the absence of a contrary agreement, the specifically enforceable right to the indorsement of the transferor. Unless otherwise agreed, it is a right to the general indorsement of the transferor with full liability as indorser, rather than to an indorsement without recourse. The question may arise if the transferee has paid in advance and the indorsement is omitted fraudulently or through oversight. A transferor who is willing to indorse only without recourse or unwilling to indorse at all should make those intentions clear before transfer. The agreement of the transferee to take less than an unqualified indorsement need not be an express one, and the understanding may be implied from conduct, from past practice, or from the circumstances of the transaction. Subsection (c) provides that there is no negotiation of the instrument until the indorsement by the transferor is made. Until that time the transferee does not become a holder, and if earlier notice of a defense or claim is received, the transferee does not qualify as a holder in due course under Section 3–302.

4. The operation of Section 3–203 is illustrated by the following cases. In each case Payee, by fraud, induced Maker to issue a note to Payee. The fraud is a defense to the obligation of Maker to pay the note under Section 3–305(a)(2).

Case #1. Payee negotiated the note to X who took as a holder in due course. After the instrument became overdue X negotiated the note to Y who had notice of the fraud. Y succeeds to X's rights as a holder in due course and takes free of Maker's defense of fraud.

Case #2. Payee negotiated the note to X who took as a holder in due course. Payee then repurchased the note from X. Payee does not succeed to X's rights as a holder in due course and is subject to Maker's defense of fraud.

Case #3. Payee negotiated the note to X who took as a holder in due course. X sold the note to Purchaser who received possession. The note, however, was indorsed to X and X failed to indorse it. Purchaser is a person entitled to enforce the instrument under Section 3–301 and succeeds to the rights of X as holder in due course. Purchaser is not a holder, however, and under Section 3–308 Purchaser will have to prove the transaction with X under which the rights of X as holder in due course were acquired.

Case #4. Payee sold the note to Purchaser who took for value, in good faith and without notice of the defense of Maker. Purchaser received possession of the note but Payee neglected to indorse it. Purchaser became a person entitled to enforce the instrument but did not become the holder because of the missing indorsement. If Purchaser received notice of the defense of Maker before obtaining the indorsement of Payee, Purchaser cannot become a holder in due course because at the time notice was received the note had not been negotiated to Purchaser. If indorsement by Payee was made after Purchaser received notice, Purchaser had notice of the defense when it became the holder.

5. Subsection (d) restates former Section 3–202(3). The cause of action on an instrument cannot be split. Any indorsement which purports to convey to any party less than the entire amount of the instrument is not effective for negotiation. This is true of either "Pay A one-half," or "Pay A two-thirds and B one-third." Neither A nor B becomes a holder. On the other hand an indorsement reading merely "Pay A and B" is effective, since it transfers the entire cause of action to A and B as tenants in common. An indorsement purporting to convey less than the entire instrument does, however, operate as a partial assignment of the cause of action. Subsection (d) makes no attempt to state the legal effect of such an assignment, which is left to other law. A partial assignee of an instrument has rights only to the extent the applicable law gives rights, either at law or in equity, to a partial assignee.

Uniform Commercial Code Comment

Prior Uniform Statutory Provision:

Section 43, Uniform Negotiable Instruments Law.

Changes: Reworded.

Purposes of Changes: To make it clear that:

1. The party whose name is wrongly designated or misspelled may make an indorsement effective for negotiation by signing in his true name only. This is not commercially satisfactory, since any subsequent purchaser may be left in doubt as to the state of the title; but whether it is done intentionally or through oversight, the party transfers his rights and is liable on his indorsement, and there is a negotiation if identity exists.

2. He may make an effective indorsement in the wrongly designated or misspelled name only. This again is not commercially satisfactory, since his liability as an indorser may require proof of identity.

3. He may indorse in both names. This is the proper and desirable form of indorsement, and any person called upon to pay an instrument or under contract to purchase it may protect his interest by demanding indorsement in both names, and is not in default if such demand is refused.

Cross Reference:

Section 3–401(2).

Definitional Cross References:

"Instrument". Section 3–102.
"Person". Section 1–201.
"Signature". Section 3–401.

Cross References

Signatures, see Commercial Code § 3401.

§ 3204. Indorsement; indorser

(a) "Indorsement" means a signature, other than that of a signer as maker, drawer, or acceptor, that alone or accompanied by other words is made on an instrument for the purpose of (1) negotiating the instrument, (2) restricting payment of the instrument, or (3) incurring indorser's liability on the instrument, but regardless of the intent of the signer, a signature and its accompanying words is an indorsement unless the accompanying words, terms of the instrument, place of the signature, or other circumstances unambiguously indicate that the signature was made for a purpose other than indorsement. For the purpose of determining whether a signature is made on an instrument, a paper affixed to the instrument is a part of the instrument.

(b) "Indorser" means a person who makes an indorsement.

(c) For the purpose of determining whether the transferee of an instrument is a holder, an indorsement that transfers a security interest in the instrument is effective as an unqualified indorsement of the instrument.

(d) If an instrument is payable to a holder under a name that is not the name of the holder, indorsement may be made by the holder in the name stated in the instrument or in the holder's name or both, but signature in both names may be required by a person paying or taking the instrument for value or collection. (Added by Stats.1992, c. 914 (S.B.833), § 6.)

California Code Comment

By John A. Bohn and Charles J. Williams

Prior California Law

1. This section generally follows former Civil Code §§ 3090(5), 3114, 3115, 3116, 3117, and changes the rule of former Civil Code § 3121.

2. The first sentence of subdivision (1) is similar to former Civil Code § 3115.

The second sentence of subdivision (1) reverses the rule of former Civil Code § 3121. Formerly an instrument drawn payable to bearer which was specifically indorsed could still be negotiated by delivery alone. Under the Commercial Code the last indorsement controls the manner of negotiation.

3. The first sentence of subdivision (2) expands the definition of a blank indorsement in the last sentence of former Civil Code § 3115 by adding that it may consist of a signature. The second sentence of subdivision (2) adopts the principle of subdivision (1) that a special indorser as the owner has the right to direct payment and require the indorsement of his indorsee as evidence of the satisfaction of the special indorser's obligation. Official Comment.

4. Subdivision (3) is identical to former Civil Code § 3116.

Changes from U.C.C. (1962 Official Text)

5. This is section 3–204 of the Official Text without change.

Uniform Commercial Code Comment
1992 Addition

1. Subsection (a) is a definition of "indorsement," a term which was not defined in former Article 3. Indorsement is defined in terms of the purpose of the signature. If a blank or special indorsement is made to give rights as a holder to a transferee the indorsement is made for the purpose of negotiating the instrument. Subsection (a)(i). If the holder of a check has an account in the drawee bank and wants to be sure that payment of the check will be made by credit to the holder's account, the holder can indorse the check by signing the holder's name with the accompanying words "for deposit only" before presenting the check for payment to the drawee bank. In that case the purpose of the quoted words is to restrict payment of the instrument. Subsection (a)(ii). If X wants to guarantee payment of a note signed by Y as maker, X can do so by signing X's name to the back of the note as an indorsement. This indorsement is known as an anomalous indorsement (Section 3–205(d)) and is made for the purpose of incurring indorser's liability on the note. Subsection (a)(iii). In some cases an indorsement may serve more than one purpose. For example, if the holder of a check deposits it to the

holder's account in a depositary bank for collection and indorses the check by signing the holder's name with the accompanying words "for deposit only" the purpose of the indorsement is both to negotiate the check to the depositary bank and to restrict payment of the check.

The "but" clause of the first sentence of subsection (a) elaborates on former Section 3–402. In some cases it may not be clear whether a signature was meant to be that of an indorser, a party to the instrument in some other capacity such as drawer, maker or acceptor, or a person who was not signing as a party. The general rule is that a signature is an indorsement if the instrument does not indicate an unambiguous intent of the signer not to sign as an indorser. Intent may be determined by words accompanying the signature, the place of signature, or other circumstances. For example, suppose a depositary bank gives cash for a check properly indorsed by the payee. The bank requires the payee's employee to sign the back of the check as evidence that the employee received the cash. If the signature consists only of the initials of the employee it is not reasonable to assume that it was meant to be an indorsement. If there was a full signature but accompanying words indicated that it was meant as a receipt for the cash given for the check, it is not an indorsement. If the signature is not qualified in any way and appears in the place normally used for indorsements, it may be an indorsement even though the signer intended the signature to be a receipt. To take another example, suppose the drawee of a draft signs the draft on the back in the space usually used for indorsements. No words accompany the signature. Since the drawee has no reason to sign a draft unless the intent is to accept the draft, the signature is effective as an acceptance. Custom and usage may be used to determine intent. For example, by long-established custom and usage, a signature in the lower right hand corner of an instrument indicates an intent to sign as the maker of a note or the drawer of a draft. Any similar clear indication of an intent to sign in some other capacity or for some other purpose may establish that a signature is not an indorsement. For example, if the owner of a traveler's check countersigns the check in the process of negotiating it, the countersignature is not an indorsement. The countersignature is a condition to the issuer's obligation to pay and its purpose is to provide a means of verifying the identity of the person negotiating the traveler's check by allowing comparison of the specimen signature and the countersignature. The countersignature is not necessary for negotiation and the signer does not incur indorser's liability. See Comment 2 to Section 3–106.

The last sentence of subsection (a) is based on subsection (2) of former Section 3–202. An indorsement on an allonge is valid even though there is sufficient space on the instrument for an indorsement.

2. Assume that Payee indorses a note to Creditor as security for a debt. Under subsection (b) of Section 3–203 Creditor takes Payee's rights to enforce or transfer the instrument subject to the limitations imposed by Article 9. Subsection (c) of Section 3–204 makes clear that Payee's indorsement to Creditor, even though it mentions creation of a security interest, is an unqualified indorsement that gives to Creditor the right to enforce the note as its holder.

3. Subsection (d) is a restatement of former Section 3–203. Section 3–110(a) states that an instrument is payable to the person intended by the person signing as or in the name or behalf of the issuer even if that person is identified by a name that is not the true name of the person. In some cases the name used in the instrument is a misspelling of the correct name and in some cases the two names may be entirely different. The payee may indorse in the name used in the instrument, in the payee's correct name, or in both. In each case the indorsement is effective. But because an indorsement in a name different from that used in the instrument may raise a question about its validity and an indorsement in a name that is not the correct name of the payee may raise a problem of identifying the indorser, the accepted commercial practice is to indorse in both names. Subsection (d) allows a person paying or taking the instrument for value or collection to require indorsement in both names.

Uniform Commercial Code Comment

Prior Uniform Statutory Provision:

Sections 9(5), 33, 34, 35, 36, and 40, Uniform Negotiable Instruments Law.

Changes: Combined and reworded; rule of Section 40 reversed.

Purposes of Changes:

The last sentence of subsection (1) reverses the rule of the original Section 40, under which an instrument drawn payable to bearer and specially indorsed could be further negotiated by delivery alone. The principle here adopted is that the special indorser, as the owner even of a bearer instrument, has the right to direct the payment and to require the indorsement of his indorsee as evidence of the satisfaction of his own obligation. The special indorsee may of course make it payable to bearer again by himself indorsing in blank.

Cross Reference:

Section 3–202.

Definitional Cross References:

"Bearer". Section 1–201.
"Delivery". Section 1–201.
"Instrument". Section 3–102.
"Person". Section 1–201.
"Signature". Section 3–401.

Cross References

Evidence of debt as subject of embezzlement, see Penal Code § 510.
Negotiation, see Commercial Code § 3202.
Signature, see Commercial Code § 3401.

§ 3205. Special indorsement; blank indorsement; anomalous indorsement

(a) If an indorsement is made by the holder of an instrument, whether payable to an identified person or payable to bearer, and the indorsement identifies a person to whom it makes the instrument payable, it is a "special indorsement." When specially indorsed, an instrument becomes payable to the identified person and may be negotiated only by the indorsement of that person. The principles stated in Section 3110 apply to special indorsements.

(b) If an indorsement is made by the holder of an instrument and it is not a special indorsement, it is a "blank indorsement." When indorsed in blank, an instrument becomes payable to bearer and may be negotiated by transfer of possession alone until specially indorsed.

(c) The holder may convert a blank indorsement that consists only of a signature into a special indorsement by writing, above the signature of the indorser, words identifying the person to whom the instrument is made payable.

(d) "Anomalous indorsement" means an indorsement made by a person who is not the holder of the instrument. An anomalous indorsement does not affect the manner in which the instrument may be negotiated. (Added by Stats.1992, c. 914 (S.B.833), § 6.)

California Code Comment

By John A. Bohn and Charles J. Williams

Prior California Law

1. This section is a regrouping of the classes of restrictive indorsements and conditional indorsements which were treated separately under the NIL, the former under former Civil Code § 3117 and the latter under former Civil Code § 3120.

2. Paragraph (a) includes within the classification of restrictive indorsements the conditional indorsement described and treated separately in former Civil Code § 3120.

3. Paragraph (b) is similar to former Civil Code § 3117(1) to the extent that the type of indorsement described is classified the same way. However, this subdivision together with section 3206(1) change the rule as to whether a restrictive indorsement prevents further negotiation. Under the express language of former Civil Code § 3117(1), a restrictive indorsement could prohibit further negotiation. By the provisions of section 3206(1) a restrictive indorsement cannot prevent further negotiation. See California Code Comment to section 3206.

4. Paragraph (c) covers the types of indorsements included in former Civil Code § 3117(2).

5. Paragraph (d) covers the types of indorsements included within former Civil Code § 3117(2) and (3).

Changes from U.C.C. (1962 Official Text)

6. This is section 3–205 of the Official Text without change.

Uniform Commercial Code Comment
1992 Addition

1. Subsection (a) is based on subsection (1) of former Section 3–204. It states the test of a special indorsement to be whether the indorsement identifies a person to whom the instrument is payable. Section 3–110 states rules for identifying the payee of an instrument. Section 3–205(a) incorporates the principles stated in Section 3–110 in identifying an indorsee. The language of Section 3–110 refers to language used by the issuer of the instrument. When that section is used with respect to an indorsement, Section 3–110 must be read as referring to the language used by the indorser.

2. Subsection (b) is based on subsection (2) of former Section 3–204. An indorsement made by the holder is either a special or blank indorsement. If the indorsement is made by a holder and is not a special indorsement, it is a blank indorsement. For example, the holder of an instrument, intending to make a special indorsement, writes the words "Pay to the order of" without completing the indorsement by writing the name of the indorsee. The holder's signature appears under the quoted words. The indorsement is not a special indorsement because it does not identify a person to whom it makes the instrument payable. Since it is not a special indorsement it is a blank indorsement and the instrument is payable to bearer. The result is analogous to that of a check in which the name of the payee is left blank by the drawer. In that case the check is payable to bearer. See the last paragraphs of Comment 2 to Section 3–115.

A blank indorsement is usually the signature of the indorser on the back of the instrument without other words. Subsection (c) is based on subsection (3) of former Section 3–204. A "restrictive indorsement" described in Section 3–206 can be either a blank indorsement or a special indorsement. "Pay to T, in trust for B" is a restrictive indorsement. It is also a special indorsement because it identifies T as the person to whom the instrument is payable. "For deposit only" followed by the signature of the payee of a check is a restrictive indorsement. It is also a blank indorsement because it does not identify the person to whom the instrument is payable.

3. The only effect of an "anomalous indorsement," defined in subsection (d), is to make the signer liable on the instrument as an indorser. Such an indorsement is normally made by an accommodation party. Section 3–419.

Uniform Commercial Code Comment
Prior Uniform Statutory Provision:
Sections 36 and 39, Uniform Negotiable Instruments Law.
Changes: Combined and reworded; new provisions.
Purposes of Changes and New Matter:

1. This section is intended to provide a definition of restrictive indorsements which will include the varieties of indorsement described in original Sections 36 and 39. The separate mention of conditional indorsements, those prohibiting transfer, indorsements in the bank deposit or collection process, and other indorsements to a fiduciary, permits separate treatment in subsequent sections where policy so requires.

2. This is part of a series of changes of the prior uniform statutory provisions effected by Sections 3–102, 3–205, 3–206, 3–304, 3–419, 3–603, and in Article 4, Sections 4–203 and 4–205. The purpose of the changes is generally to require a taker or payor under restrictive indorsement to apply or pay value given consistently with the indorsement, but to provide certain exceptions applying to banks in the collection process (other than depositary banks), and to some other takers and payors.

Cross References:

Sections 3–102, 3–202(2), 3–205, 3–206, 3–304, 3–419, 3–603, 4–203 and 4–205.

Definitional Cross References:

"Instrument". Section 3–102.
"Person". Section 1–201.

Cross References

Bank deposits and collections, effect of instructions, see Commercial Code § 4203.
Conversion of instrument, see Commercial Code § 3420.
Definitions, see Commercial Code § 3103.
Missing indorsement, see Commercial Code § 4205.
Negotiation, see Commercial Code § 3202.
Payable to bearer or to order, application of principles stated in this section, see Commercial Code § 3109.
Payment, discharge of obligation, see Commercial Code § 3602.
Taker, notice of claim or defense, see Commercial Code § 3307.

§ 3206. Restrictive indorsements

(a) An indorsement limiting payment to a particular person or otherwise prohibiting further transfer or negotiation of the instrument is not effective to prevent further transfer or negotiation of the instrument.

(b) An indorsement stating a condition to the right of the indorsee to receive payment does not affect the right of the indorsee to enforce the instrument. A person paying the instrument or taking it for value or collection may disregard the condition, and the rights and liabilities of that person are not affected by whether the condition has been fulfilled.

(c) If an instrument bears an indorsement (i) described in subdivision (b) of Section 4201, or (ii) in blank or to a particular bank using the words "for deposit," "for collection," or other words indicating a purpose of having the instrument collected by a bank for the indorser or for a particular account, the following rules apply:

(1) A person, other than a bank, who purchases the instrument when so indorsed converts the instrument unless the amount paid for the instrument is received by the indorser or applied consistently with the indorsement.

(2) A depositary bank that purchases the instrument or takes it for collection when so indorsed converts the instrument unless the amount paid by the bank with respect to the instrument is received by the indorser or applied consistently with the indorsement.

(3) A payor bank that is also the depositary bank or that takes the instrument for immediate payment over the counter from a person other than a collecting bank converts the instrument unless the proceeds of the instrument are received by the indorser or applied consistently with the indorsement.

(4) Except as otherwise provided in paragraph (3), a payor bank or intermediary bank may disregard the indorsement and is not liable if the proceeds of the

instrument are not received by the indorser or applied consistently with the indorsement.

(d) Except for an indorsement covered by subdivision (c), if an instrument bears an indorsement using words to the effect that payment is to be made to the indorsee as agent, trustee, or other fiduciary for the benefit of the indorser or another person, the following rules apply:

(1) Unless there is notice of breach of fiduciary duty as provided in Section 3307, a person who purchases the instrument from the indorsee or takes the instrument from the indorsee for collection or payment may pay the proceeds of payment or the value given for the instrument to the indorsee without regard to whether the indorsee violates a fiduciary duty to the indorser.

(2) A subsequent transferee of the instrument or person who pays the instrument is neither given notice nor otherwise affected by the restriction in the indorsement unless the transferee or payor knows that the fiduciary dealt with the instrument or its proceeds in breach of fiduciary duty.

(e) The presence on an instrument of an indorsement to which this section applies does not prevent a purchaser of the instrument from becoming a holder in due course of the instrument unless the purchaser is a converter under subdivision (c) or has notice or knowledge of breach of fiduciary duty as stated in subdivision (d).

(f) In an action to enforce the obligation of a party to pay the instrument, the obligor has a defense if payment would violate an indorsement to which this section applies and the payment is not permitted by this section. (Added by Stats.1992, c. 914 (S.B.833), § 6.)

California Code Comment

By John A. Bohn and Charles J. Williams

Prior California Law

1. This section is a complete revision of former Civil Code §§ 3117, 3118, 3120 and 3128. It represents a change in the California law expressed in those sections.

2. This section makes it clear that a transferee under a restrictive indorsement can be a holder in due course, a conclusion which was in doubt because of the language of former Civil Code §§ 3118 and 3128. Official Comment 1.

3. Subdivision (1) changes the rule of former Civil Code § 3117(1) that a restrictive indorsement could prevent further negotiation of the instrument. Official Comment 2.

4. Subdivision (2) may change California law. Its effect is to permit a bank other than a depository bank to disregard any restrictive indorsement except the bank's immediate transferor. The purpose is to simplify the collection process for banks because they handle the instrument in bulk and have no practicable opportunity to consider the effect of restrictive indorsements. Official Comment 3. Under former Civil Code § 3118, a subsequent indorsee acquired only the title of the first indorsee under a restrictive indorsement. In Nordin v. Eagle Rock State Bank, 139 Cal.App. 584, 34 P.2d 490 (1934) the court cited with approval the statement that a restrictive indorsement is notice to all persons that the indorser has not parted with his title.

5. Subdivision (3) reverses the rule of former Civil Code § 3120 and permits a transferee under a conditional indorsement to become a holder in due course free of the conditional indorser's claim. Official Comments 4 and 5.

6. Subdivision (4) applies the principle of subdivision (3) to trust indorsements other than those for deposit or collection. See Official Comment 6.

7. The subcommittee on Article [Division] 3 of the State Bar classified the change made by this section as minor and described its effect thusly:

"This section probably changes the existing California law. It is made clear that there may be a holder in due course after a restrictive endorsement. The first taker under certain types of restrictive endorsement must however pay or apply any value given in a manner consistent with the restrictive endorsement." Sixth Progress Report to the Legislature by Senate Fact Finding Committee on Judiciary (1959–1961) Part 1, The Uniform Commercial Code, p. 345.

Changes from U.C.C. (1962 Official Text)

8. This is section 3–206 of the Official Text without change.

Uniform Commercial Code Comment
1992 Addition

1. This section replaces former Sections 3–205 and 3–206 and clarifies the law of restrictive indorsements.

2. Subsection (a) provides that an indorsement that purports to limit further transfer or negotiation is ineffective to prevent further transfer or negotiation. If a payee indorses "Pay A only," A may negotiate the instrument to subsequent holders who may ignore the restriction on the indorsement. Subsection (b) provides that an indorsement that states a condition to the right of a holder to receive payment is ineffective to condition payment. Thus if a payee indorses "Pay A if A ships goods complying with our contract," the right of A to enforce the instrument is not affected by the condition. In the case of a note, the obligation of the maker to pay A is not affected by the indorsement. In the case of a check, the drawee can pay A without regard to the condition, and if the check is dishonored the drawer is liable to pay A. If the check was negotiated by the payee to A in return for a promise to perform a contract and the promise was not kept, the payee would have a defense or counterclaim against A if the check were dishonored and A sued the payee as indorser, but the payee would have that defense or counterclaim whether or not the condition to the right of A was expressed in the indorsement. Former Section 3–206 treated a conditional indorsement like indorsements for deposit or collection. In revised Article 3, Section 3–206(b) rejects that approach and makes the conditional indorsement ineffective with respect to parties other than the indorser and indorsee. Since the indorsements referred to in subsections (a) and (b) are not effective as restrictive indorsements, they are no longer described as restrictive indorsements.

3. The great majority of restrictive indorsements are those that fall within subsection (c) which continues previous law. The depositary bank or the payor bank, if it takes the check for immediate payment over the counter, must act consistently with the indorsement, but an intermediary bank or payor bank that takes the check from a collecting bank is not affected by the indorsement. Any other person is also bound by the indorsement. For example, suppose a check is payable to X, who indorses in blank but writes above the signature the words "For deposit only." The check is stolen and is cashed at a grocery store by the thief. The grocery store indorses the check and deposits it in Depositary Bank. The account of the grocery store is credited and the check is forwarded to Payor Bank which pays the check. Under subsection (c), the grocery store and Depositary Bank are converters of the check because X did not receive the amount paid for the check. Payor Bank and any intermediary bank in the collection process are not liable to X. This Article does not displace the law of waiver as it may apply to restrictive indorsements. The circumstances under which a restrictive indorsement may be waived by the person who made it is not determined by this Article.

4. Subsection (d) replaces subsection (4) of former Section 3–206. Suppose Payee indorses a check "Pay to T in trust for B." T indorses in blank and delivers it to (a) Holder for value; (b) Depositary Bank for collection; or (c) Payor Bank for payment. In each case these takers can safely pay T so long as they have no notice under Section 3–307 of any breach of fiduciary duty that T may be committing. For example, under subsection (a) of Section 3–307 these takers have notice of a breach of trust if the check was taken in any transaction known by the taker to be for T's personal benefit. Subsequent transferees of the

check from Holder or Depositary Bank are not affected by the restriction unless they have knowledge that T dealt with the check in breach of trust.

5. Subsection (f) allows a restrictive indorsement to be used as a defense by a person obliged to pay the instrument if that person would be liable for paying in violation of the indorsement.

Prior Uniform Statutory Provision:
Sections 36, 37, 39 and 47, Uniform Negotiable Instruments Law.
Changes: Completely revised.
Purposes of Changes:

1. Subsections (1) and (2) apply to all four classes of restrictive indorsements defined in Section 3–205. Conditional indorsements and indorsements for deposit or collection, defined in paragraphs (a) and (c) of Section 3–205, are also subject to subsection (3); and trust indorsements as defined in paragraph (d) of Section 3–205 are subject to subsection (4). This section negates the implication which has sometimes been found in the original Sections 37 and 47, that under a restrictive indorsement neither the indorsee nor any subsequent taker from him could become a holder in due course. By omitting the original Section 47, this Article also avoids any implication that a discharge is effective against a holder in due course. See Section 3–602.

2. Under subsection (1) an indorsement reading "Pay A only," or any other indorsement purporting to prohibit further transfer, is without effect for that purpose. Such indorsements have rarely appeared in reported American cases. Ordinarily further negotiation will be contemplated by the indorser, if only for bank collection. The indorsee becomes a holder, and the indorsement does not of itself give notice to subsequent parties of any defense or claim of the indorser. Hence this section gives such an indorsement the same effect as an unrestricted indorsement.

3. Subsection (2) permits an intermediary bank (Sections 3–102 (3) and 4–105) or a payor bank which is not a depositary bank (Sections 3–102(3) and 4–105) to disregard any restrictive indorsement except that of the bank's immediate transferor. Such banks ordinarily handle instruments, especially checks, in bulk and have no practicable opportunity to consider the effect of restrictive indorsements. Subsection (2) does not affect the rights of the restrictive indorser against parties outside the bank collection process or against the first bank in the collection process; such rights are governed by subsections (3) and (4) and Section 3–603.

4. Conditional indorsements are treated by this section like indorsements for deposit or collection. Under subsection (3) any transferee under such an indorsement except an intermediary bank becomes a holder for value to the extent that he acts consistently with the indorsement in paying or applying any value given by him for or on the security of the instrument. Contrary to the original Section 39, subsection (3) permits a transferee under a conditional indorsement to become a holder in due course free of the conditional indorser's claim.

5. Of the indorsements covered by this section those "for collection", "for deposit" and "pay any bank" are overwhelmingly the most frequent. Indorsements "for collection" or "for deposit" may be either special or blank; indorsements "pay any bank" are governed by Section 4–201(2). Instruments so indorsed are almost invariably destined to be lodged in a bank for collection. Subsection (3) requires any transferee other than an intermediary bank to act consistently with the purpose of collection, and Section 3–603 lays down a similar rule for payors not covered by subsection (2).

6. Subsection (4), applying to trust indorsements other than those for deposit or collection (paragraph (d) of Section 3–205) is similar to subsection (3); but in subsection (4) the duty to act consistently with the indorsement is limited to the first taker under it. If an instrument is indorsed "Pay T in trust for B" or "Pay T for B" or "Pay T for account of B" or "Pay T as agent for B," whether B is the indorser or a third person, T is of course subject to liability for any breach of his obligation as fiduciary. But trustees commonly and legitimately sell trust assets in transactions entirely outside the bank collection process; the trustee therefore had power to negotiate the instrument and make his transferee a holder in due course. Whether transferees from T have notice of a breach of trust such as to deny them the status of holders in due course is governed by the section on notice to purchasers (Section 3–304); the trust indorsement does not of itself give such notice. Payors are immunized either by subsection (2) of this section or by Section 3–603: payment to the trustee or to a purchaser from the trustee is "consistent with the terms" of the trust indorsement under Section 3–603(1)(b).

7. Several sections of Article 3 and Article 4 are explicitly made subject to the rules stated in this section. See Sections 3–306, 3–419, 4–203 and 4–205.

Cross References:

Point 1: Sections 3–205 and 3–602.
Point 2: Section 3–205(b).
Point 3: Sections 3–102(3), 3–419(4), 3–603, 4–105, 4–205(2).
Point 4: Section 3–205(a).
Point 5: Sections 3–205, 3–603 and 4–201.
Point 6: Sections 3–205, 3–304 and 3–603.
Point 7: Sections 3–306, 3–419, 4–203 and 4–205.

Definitional Cross References:

"Bank". Section 1–201.
"Depositary bank". Sections 3–102(3) and 4–105.
"Holder in due course". Section 3–302.
"Intermediary bank". Sections 3–102(3) and 4–105.
"Negotiation". Sections 3–102(2) and 3–202.
"Payor bank". Sections 3–102(3) and 4–105.
"Restrictive indorsement". Section 3–205.
"Transfer". Section 3–201.

Cross References

Bank deposits and collections, effect of instructions, see Commercial Code § 4203.
Conversion of instrument, see Commercial Code § 3420.
Definitions, see Commercial Code §§ 3103, 4105.
Holder in due course, effect of discharge, see Commercial Code § 3601.
Items indorsed "pay any bank", see Commercial Code § 4201.
Missing indorsements, see Commercial Code § 4205.
Negotiation by fiduciary in payment of his own debt, notice to taker of, see Commercial Code § 3307.
Nonliability of collecting bank to prior parties for action taken pursuant to instructions from transferor subject to restrictive endorsements, see Commercial Code § 4203.
Payment, discharge of obligation, see Commercial Code § 3602.
Rights of one not holder in due course, see Commercial Code § 3306.
Taker, notice of claim or defense, see Commercial Code § 3307.

§ 3207. Reacquisition of instrument; cancellation of indorsements

Reacquisition of an instrument occurs if it is transferred to a former holder, by negotiation or otherwise. A former holder who reacquires the instrument may cancel indorsements made after the reacquirer first became a holder of the instrument. If the cancellation causes the instrument to be payable to the reacquirer or to bearer, the reacquirer may negotiate the instrument. An indorser whose indorsement is canceled is discharged, and the discharge is effective against any subsequent holder. *(Added by Stats.1992, c. 914 (S.B. 833), § 6.)*

California Code Comment
By John A. Bohn and Charles J. Williams

Prior California Law

1. Subdivision (1)(a) extends former Civil Code § 3103 which was limited to infants or corporations to include negotiation by any person without capacity. The term negotiation as used in this section is defined in section 3202. It is delivery or delivery with an indorsement depending on the type of instrument. Acquisition of possession by a thief is not negotiation under this section. However, delivery by the thief to another person may be. Official Comment 3.

2. Subdivision (1)(b), (c) and (d) is a broadening of the principle of former Civil Code § 3103. The language of this section now makes it clear that any negotiation of a character which would make the transaction entirely void is subject to the provision that negotiation is effective to transfer the instrument. See Official Comment 2 for the reasoning and policy behind this rule.

The decisions in California have approached the position set forth in subdivisions (1)(b) and (c) without the detailed statutory language.

Subdivision (1)(b) is in accord with Allenberg v. Rapken & Co., 108 Cal.App. 99, 291 Pac. 281 (1930). In that case the defendant alleged collusion in the negotiation of the instrument and facts were present to show fraud or mistake. The court held that under the facts negotiation to a holder in due course was not prevented.

Subdivision (1)(c) is in accord with Drukker v. Howe & Haun Inv. Co., 136 Cal.App. 437, 29 P.2d 289 (1934) in which the court held that negotiation to a holder in due course is not prevented by a prior breach of an agreement of which he had no notice.

Both of the above cited cases also point out the extent of the notice of any infirmity which is required to prevent one from being a holder in due course. The notice must be actual. Facts sufficient to put one on notice are not adequate unless the circumstances are of a very obvious nature or there is something on the face of the instrument to arouse suspicion. See also Sasner v. Ornsten, 93 Cal.App.2d 467, 209 P.2d 44 (1949) and California Code Comment 2 to Commercial Code § 3302 for the amount of notice required.

3. Subdivision (2) continues that part of former Civil Code § 3138 to the effect that a holder in due course took the instrument free of defects in title. As against a holder in due course no remedy is available even though a prior negotiation is fraudulent and void, but against any other party the claimant may have any other remedy which is permitted by local law. Subdivision (2) does preserve the remedies available under the law of California but does not give a right where it would not otherwise exist. Official Comment 5.

Changes from U.C.C. (1962 Official Text)

4. This is section 3–207 of the Official Text without change.

Uniform Commercial Code Comment
1992 Addition

Section 3–207 restates former Section 3–208. Reacquisition refers to cases in which a former holder reacquires the instrument either by negotiation from the present holder or by a transfer other than negotiation. If the reacquisition is by negotiation, the former holder reacquires the status of holder. Although Section 3–207 allows the holder to cancel all indorsements made after the holder first acquired holder status, cancellation is not necessary. Status of holder is not affected whether or not cancellation is made. But if the reacquisition is not the result of negotiation the former holder can obtain holder status only by striking the former holder's indorsement and any subsequent indorsements. The latter case is an exception to the general rule that if an instrument is payable to an identified person, the indorsement of that person is necessary to allow a subsequent transferee to obtain the status of holder. Reacquisition without indorsement by the person to whom the instrument is payable is illustrated by two examples:

Case #1. X, a former holder, buys the instrument from Y, the present holder. Y delivers the instrument to X but fails to indorse it. Negotiation does not occur because the transfer of possession did not result in X's becoming holder. Section 3–201(a). The instrument by its terms is payable to Y, not to X. But X can obtain the status of holder by striking X's indorsement and all subsequent indorsements. When these indorsements are struck, the instrument by its terms is payable either to X or to bearer, depending upon how X originally became holder. In either case X becomes holder. Section 1–201(20).

Case #2. X, the holder of an instrument payable to X, negotiates it to Y by special indorsement. The negotiation is part of an underlying transaction between X and Y. The underlying transaction is rescinded by agreement of X and Y, and Y returns the instrument without Y's indorsement. The analysis is the same as that in Case #1. X can obtain holder status by canceling X's indorsement to Y.

In Case #1 and Case #2, X acquired ownership of the instrument after reacquisition, but X's title was clouded because the instrument by its terms was not payable to X. Normally, X can remedy the problem by obtaining Y's indorsement, but in some cases X may not be able to conveniently obtain that indorsement. Section 3–207 is a rule of convenience which relieves X of the burden of obtaining an indorsement that serves no substantive purpose. The effect of cancellation of any indorsement under Section 3–207 is to nullify it. Thus, the person whose indorsement is canceled is relieved of indorser's liability. Since cancellation is notice of discharge, discharge is effective even with respect to the rights of a holder in due course. Sections 3–601 and 3–604.

Uniform Commercial Code Comment
Prior Uniform Statutory Provision:

Sections 22, 58 and 59, Uniform Negotiable Instruments Law.

Changes: Completely revised.

Purposes of Changes: To make it clear that:

1. The original Section 22, which covered only negotiation by an infant or a corporation, is extended by this section to include other negotiations which may be rescinded. The provision applies even though the party's lack of capacity, or the illegality, is of a character which goes to the essence of the transaction and makes it entirely void, and even though the party negotiating has incurred no liability and is entitled to recover the instrument and have his indorsement cancelled.

2. It is inherent in the character of negotiable paper that any person in possession of an instrument which by its terms runs to him is a holder, and that anyone may deal with him as a holder. The principle finds its most extreme application in the well settled rule that a holder in due course may take the paper even from a thief and be protected against the claim of the rightful owner. Where there is actual negotiation, even in an entirely void transaction, it is no less effective. The policy of this provision, as well as of the last sentence of the original Section 59, is that any person to whom an instrument is negotiated is a holder until the instrument has been recovered from his possession; and that any person who negotiates an instrument thereby parts with all his rights in it until such recovery. The remedy of any such claimant is to recover the paper by replevin or otherwise; to impound it or to enjoin its enforcement, collection or negotiation; to recover its proceeds from the holder; or to intervene in any action brought by the holder against the obligor. As provided in the section on the rights of one not a holder in due course (Section 3–306) his claim is not a defense to the obligor unless he himself defends the action.

3. Negotiation under this Article always includes delivery. (Section 3–202, and see Section 1–201(14)). Acquisition of possession by a thief can therefore never be negotiation under this section. But delivery by the thief to another person may be.

4. Nothing in this section is intended to impose any liability on the party negotiating. He may assert any defense available to him under Sections 3–305, 3–306 and 3–307.

5. A holder in due course takes the instrument free from all claims to it on the part of any person (Section 3–305(1)). Against him there can be no rescission or other remedy, even though the prior negotiation may have been fraudulent or illegal in its essence and entirely void. As against any other party the claimant may have any remedy permitted by law. This section is not intended to specify what that remedy may be, or to prevent any court from imposing conditions or limitations such as prompt action or return of the consideration received. All such questions are left to the law of the particular jurisdiction. Subsection (2) of Section 3–207 gives no right where it would not otherwise exist. The section is intended to mean that any remedies afforded by the local law are cut off only by a holder in due course, and that other parties, such as a bona fide purchaser with notice that the instrument is overdue, take it subject to the claim as provided in paragraph (a) of the section of the rights of one not a holder in due course (Section 3–306).

Cross References:

Point 2: Sections 1–201 and 3–306(d).
Point 3: Sections 1–201 and 3–202.
Point 4: Sections 3–305, 3–306 and 3–307.
Point 5: Sections 3–305(1) and 3–306(a).

Definitional Cross References:

"Holder in due course". Section 3–302.
"Instrument". Section 3–102.
"Negotiation". Section 3–202.

"Person". Section 1–201.
"Remedy". Section 1–201.

Cross References

Definitions, see Commercial Code § 1201.
Duress, absence of consent to contract, see Civil Code § 1569.
Fraud, absence of consent to contract, see Civil Code § 1571 et seq.
Holder in due course, see Commercial Code § 3302.
Menace, absence of consent to contract, see Civil Code § 1570.
Minors' power to contract, see Family Code § 6700.
Mistake, absence of consent to contract, see Civil Code § 1576 et seq.
Parol evidence to establish fraud or to correct mistake in written agreement, see Code of Civil Procedure § 1856.
Partially void contracts, one of several objects unlawful, see Civil Code § 1599.
Persons capable of contracting, generally, see Civil Code § 1556.
Persons with unsound mind, contracts by, see Civil Code §§ 38, 39, 1556, 1557.
Powers of corporations, in general, see Corporations Code § 207.
Ratification of voidable contract, see Civil Code § 1588.
Rescission of contracts, see Civil Code §§ 1566, 1688 et seq.
Revision of contracts for fraud or mutual mistake, see Civil Code § 3399.
Rights of holder in due course, see Commercial Code § 3305.
Rights of one not holder in due course, see Commercial Code § 3306.
Signatures, burden of establishing validity, see Commercial Code § 3308.
Undue influence, absence of consent to contract, see Civil Code § 1575.
Unlawful contracts, see Civil Code § 1667 et seq.
Void contracts, unlawful object, see Civil Code § 1598.
Want of consideration as defense, see Commercial Code § 3303.

§ 3208. Repealed by Stats.1992, c. 914 (S.B.833), § 5

California Code Comment

By John A. Bohn and Charles J. Williams

Prior California Law

1. This section is a combination and rewording of former Civil Code §§ 3129, 3131 and 3202. No change in the law is intended. See Official Comment.

Changes from U.C.C. (1962 Official Text)

2. This is section 3–208 of the Official Text without change.

Uniform Commercial Code Comment
1992 Addition

Prior Uniform Statutory Provision:

Sections 48, 50 and 121, Uniform Negotiable Instruments Law.

Changes: Parts of original sections combined and rephrased.

Purposes of Changes: No change in the substance of the law is intended. "Returned to or reacquired by" is substituted for "negotiated back to" in the original Section 50 in order to make it clear that the section applies to a return by an indorsee who does not himself indorse. "Discharged" is substituted for the original language to make it clear that the discharge of the intervening party is included within the rule of the section on effect of discharge against a holder in due course (Section 3–602) and is not effective against a subsequent holder in due course who takes without notice of it.

The reacquirer may keep the instrument himself or he may further negotiate it. On further negotiation he may or may not cancel intervening indorsements. In any case intervening indorsers are discharged as to the reacquirer, since if he attempted to enforce it against them they would have an action back against him. Where the reacquirer negotiates without cancelling the intervening indorsements, the section provides that such indorsers are discharged except against subsequent holders in due course. The intervening indorser whose indorsement is stricken is, in conformity with Section 3–605, discharged even as against subsequent holders in due course.

Cross References:

Sections 3–602, 3–603(2) and 3–605.

Definitional Cross References:

"Holder in due course". Section 3–302.
"Instrument". Section 3–102.
"Party". Section 1–201.

Cross References

Cancellation and renunciation, see Commercial Code § 3604.
Holder in due course,
   Generally, see Commercial Code § 3302.
   Effect of discharge, see Commercial Code § 3601.
Payment, discharge of obligation, see Commercial Code § 3602.

CHAPTER 3. ENFORCEMENT OF INSTRUMENTS

Section
3301. Person entitled to enforce instrument.
3302. Holder in due course.
3303. Value and consideration.
3304. Overdue instruments.
3305. Enforcement of obligations; defenses; claims in recoupment.
3306. Claims to instruments.
3307. Breach of fiduciary duty; notice.
3308. Signatures; validity; presumptions and proof.
3309. Enforcement of instrument by person without possession.
3310. Effect of instrument on obligation for which it was taken.
3311. Satisfaction of claim by use of instrument.
3312. Enforcement of claim to amount of a check.

Transitional Provisions

Effective date and transitional provisions for repeal and addition of Division 3 by Stats.1992, c. 914, see Commercial Code § 16101 et seq.

§ 3301. Person entitled to enforce instrument

"Person entitled to enforce" an instrument means (a) the holder of the instrument, (b) a nonholder in possession of the instrument who has the rights of a holder, or (c) a person not in possession of the instrument who is entitled to enforce the instrument pursuant to Section 3309 or subdivision (d) of Section 3418. A person may be a person entitled to enforce the instrument even though the person is not the owner of the instrument or is in wrongful possession of the instrument. *(Added by Stats.1992, c. 914 (S.B.833), § 6.)*

California Code Comment

By John A. Bohn and Charles J. Williams

Prior California Law

1. This section is substantially in accord with former Civil Code § 3132. It is a rewording of that section with the addition to it of the right of the holder to transfer and negotiate the instrument. Former Civil Code § 3132 also provided that payment to the holder in due course discharged the instrument. This provision is now covered in Commercial Code § 3603(1).

Changes from U.C.C. (1962 Official Text)

2. This is section 3–301 of the Official Text without change.

Uniform Commercial Code Comment
1992 Addition

This section replaces former Section 3–301 that stated the rights of a holder. The rights stated in former Section 3–301 to transfer, negotiate, enforce, or discharge an instrument are stated in other sections of Article 3. In revised Article 3, Section 3–301 defines "person entitled to enforce" an instrument. The definition recognizes that enforcement is not limited to holders. The quoted phrase includes a person enforcing a lost or stolen instrument. Section 3–309. It also includes a person in possession of an instrument who is not a holder. A nonholder in possession of an instrument includes a person that acquired rights of a holder by subrogation or under Section 3–203(a). It also includes any other person who under applicable law is a successor to the holder or otherwise acquires the holder's rights.

Prior Uniform Statutory Provision:
Section 51, Uniform Negotiable Instruments Law.
Changes: Reworded. The provision in the original Section 51 as to discharge by payment is now covered by Section 3–603(1).
Purposes of Changes: The section is revised to state in one provision all the rights of a holder, and to make it clear that every holder has such rights. The only limitations are those found in Section 3–603 on payment or satisfaction. That section provides (with stated exceptions) that payment to a holder discharges the liability of the party paying even though made with knowledge of a claim of another person to the instrument, unless the adverse claimant posts indemnity or procures the issuance of appropriate legal process restraining the payment. Thus payment to a holder in an adverse claim situation would not give discharge if the adverse claimant had followed either of the procedures provided for in the "unless" clause of Section 3–603; nor would a discharge result from payment in two other specific situations described in Section 3–603.

Cross References:
Sections 1–201, 3–307 and 3–603(1).

Definitional Cross References:
"Holder". Section 1–201.
"Instrument". Section 3–102.
"Rights". Section 1–201.

Cross References
Attachment of commercial paper, see Code of Civil Procedure § 487.010.
Definitions, see Commercial Code § 1201.
Discharge, see Commercial Code § 3601 et seq.
General limitations, special cases, see Code of Civil Procedure § 312.
Joinder of persons severally liable upon same obligation, see Code of Civil Procedure § 383.
Obligation of accommodation party, see Commercial Code § 3419.
Payment, discharge of obligation, see Commercial Code § 3602.
Presumption of consideration, see Civil Code § 1614.
Property subject to transfer, see Civil Code § 1044.
Real party in interest, necessity of prosecution in name of, see Code of Civil Procedure § 367.
Restrictive indorsement, see Commercial Code § 3206.
Right of reacquirer to negotiate instrument, see Commercial Code § 3207.
Right to payment on proof of entitlement to enforce instrument under this section, see Commercial Code § 3308.
Signatures, burden of establishing validity, see Commercial Code § 3308.
Transfer of nonnegotiable instrument, see Civil Code § 955.
Transfer of obligations, see Civil Code § 1457 et seq.
Transfer of things in action, see Civil Code § 953 et seq.
Want of consideration, effect, see Commercial Code § 3303.

§ 3302. Holder in due course

(a) Subject to subdivision (c) and subdivision (d) of Section 3106, "holder in due course" means the holder of an instrument if both of the following apply:

(1) The instrument when issued or negotiated to the holder does not bear such apparent evidence of forgery or alteration or is not otherwise so irregular or incomplete as to call into question its authenticity.

(2) The holder took the instrument (A) for value, (B) in good faith, (C) without notice that the instrument is overdue or has been dishonored or that there is an uncured default with respect to payment of another instrument issued as part of the same series, (D) without notice that the instrument contains an unauthorized signature or has been altered, (E) without notice of any claim to the instrument described in Section 3306, and (F) without notice that any party has a defense or claim in recoupment described in subdivision (a) of Section 3305.

(b) Notice of discharge of a party, other than discharge in an insolvency proceeding, is not notice of a defense under subdivision (a), but discharge is effective against a person who became a holder in due course with notice of the discharge. Public filing or recording of a document does not of itself constitute notice of a defense, claim in recoupment, or claim to the instrument.

(c) Except to the extent a transferor or predecessor in interest has rights as a holder in due course, a person does not acquire rights of a holder in due course of an instrument taken (1) by legal process or by purchase in an execution, bankruptcy, or creditor's sale or similar proceeding, (2) by purchase as part of a bulk transaction not in ordinary course of business of the transferor, or (3) as the successor in interest to an estate or other organization.

(d) If, under paragraph (1) of subdivision (a) of Section 3303, the promise of performance that is the consideration for an instrument has been partially performed, the holder may assert rights as a holder in due course of the instrument only to the fraction of the amount payable under the instrument equal to the value of the partial performance divided by the value of the promised performance.

(e) If (1) the person entitled to enforce an instrument has only a security interest in the instrument and (2) the person obliged to pay the instrument has a defense, claim in recoupment, or claim to the instrument that may be asserted against the person who granted the security interest, the person entitled to enforce the instrument may assert rights as a holder in due course only to an amount payable under the instrument which, at the time of enforcement of the instrument, does not exceed the amount of the unpaid obligation secured.

(f) To be effective, notice shall be received at a time and in a manner that gives a reasonable opportunity to act on it.

(g) This section is subject to any law limiting status as a holder in due course in particular classes of transactions. *(Added by Stats.1992, c. 914 (S.B.833), § 6.)*

California Code Comment

By John A. Bohn and Charles J. Williams

Prior California Law

1. This section is in part similar to former Civil Code § 3133 but is a rewording of it and also adds new provisions. The changes are intended not as a substantive revision but to remove uncertainties under former Civil Code § 3133.

2. Subdivision (1)(a) and (b) are similar to former Civil Code § 3133(3). The term "good faith" is defined in Commercial Code § 1201 (19) as "honesty in fact in the conduct or transaction concerned." The presence of suspicious circumstances sufficient to put a reasonably prudent person on inquiry does not negative existence of good faith. Mann v. Leasko, 179 Cal.App.2d 692, 4 Cal.Rptr. 124 (1960).

3. Subdivision (1)(c) changes the rule under former Civil Code § 3133(2) by requiring only that the holder take the instrument "without notice that it is overdue." Former Civil Code § 3133(2) required that a holder to be a holder in due course, take the instrument "before it was overdue." Bliss v. California Co-op. Producers, 30 Cal.2d 240, 181 P.2d 369, 170 ALR 1009 (1947). For a critical analysis, see Britton, Holder in Due Course, A Comparison of the Provisions of the Negotiable Instruments Law with those of Article 3 of the proposed Uniform Commercial Code, 49 Northwestern U.L.R. 417, 421–430 (1954).

4. Subdivision (2) resolves the conflict under the NIL as to whether a payee could be a holder in due course. Official Comment 2. Britton, Bills & Notes (1961) 308. This is in accord with prior California law. Johnson v. Ulrey, 201 Cal. 456, 257 Pac. 505 (1927) and Pasadena Nat. Bank v. Shorten, 96 Cal.App. 451, 274 Pac. 358 (1929). There is dictum that a payee could not be a holder in due course in Hockett v. Pacific States Auxiliary Corp., 15 P.2d 547 (1932), on review by Supreme Court, 218 Cal. 382, 23 P.2d 512 (1933).

5. Subdivision (3) is new law to the extent that it supplies authority where none had existed before that a person acquiring an instrument (a) under legal process or (b) by taking over an estate or (c) purchasing it as part of a bulk transaction not in the regular course of business can be a holder in due course. However, there is no intent to change case law under the NIL. It clarifies the few situations in which the purchaser takes an instrument under unusual circumstances. Official Comment 3.

6. Subdivision (4) is similar to former Civil Code § 3108.

Changes from U.C.C. (1962 Official Text)

7. This is section 3–302 of the Official Text without change.

Uniform Commercial Code Comment
1992 Addition

1. Subsection (a)(1) is a return to the N.I.L. rule that the taker of an irregular or incomplete instrument is not a person the law should protect against defenses of the obligor or claims of prior owners. This reflects a policy choice against extending the holder in due course doctrine to an instrument that is so incomplete or irregular "as to call into question its authenticity." The term "authenticity" is used to make it clear that the irregularity or incompleteness must indicate that the instrument may not be what it purports to be. Persons who purchase or pay such instruments should do so at their own risk. Under subsection (1) of former Section 3–304, irregularity or incompleteness gave a purchaser notice of a claim or defense. But it was not clear from that provision whether the claim or defense had to be related to the irregularity or incomplete aspect of the instrument. This ambiguity is not present in subsection (a)(1).

2. Subsection (a)(2) restates subsection (1) of former Section 3–302. Section 3–305(a) makes a distinction between defenses to the obligation to pay an instrument and claims in recoupment by the maker or drawer that may be asserted to reduce the amount payable on the instrument. Because of this distinction, which was not made in former Article 3, the reference in subsection (a)(2)(vi) is to both a defense and a claim in recoupment. Notice of forgery or alteration is stated separately because forgery and alteration are not technically defenses under subsection (a) of Section 3–305.

3. Discharge is also separately treated in the first sentence of subsection (b). Except for discharge in an insolvency proceeding, which is specifically stated to be a real defense in Section 3–305(a)(1), discharge is not expressed in Article 3 as a defense and is not included in Section 3–305(a)(2). Discharge is effective against anybody except a person having rights of a holder in due course who took the instrument without notice of the discharge. Notice of discharge does not disqualify a person from becoming a holder in due course. For example, a check certified after it is negotiated by the payee may subsequently be negotiated to a holder. If the holder had notice that the certification occurred after negotiation by the payee, the holder necessarily had notice of the discharge of the payee as indorser. Section 3–415(d). Notice of that discharge does not prevent the holder from becoming a holder in due course, but the discharge is effective against the holder. Section 3–601(b). Notice of a defense under Section 3–305(a)(1) of a maker, drawer or acceptor based on a bankruptcy discharge is different. There is no reason to give holder in due course status to a person with notice of that defense. The second sentence of subsection (b) is from former Section 3–304(5).

4. Professor Britton in his treatise Bills and Notes 309 (1961) stated: "A substantial number of decisions before the [N.I.L.] indicates that at common law there was nothing in the position of the payee as such which made it impossible for him to be a holder in due course." The courts were divided, however, about whether the payee of an instrument could be a holder in due course under the N.I.L. Some courts read N.I.L. § 52(4) to mean that a person could be a holder in due course only if the instrument was "negotiated" to that person. N.I.L. § 30 stated that "an instrument is negotiated when it is transferred from one person to another in such manner as to constitute the transferee the holder thereof." Normally, an instrument is "issued" to the payee; it is not transferred to the payee. N.I.L. § 191 defined "issue" as the "first delivery of the instrument * * * to a person who takes it as a holder." Thus, some courts concluded that the payee never could be a holder in due course. Other courts concluded that there was no evidence that the N.I.L. was intended to change the common law rule that the payee could be a holder in due course. Professor Britton states on p. 318: "The typical situations which raise the [issue] are those where the defense of a maker is interposed because of fraud by a [maker who is] principal debtor * * * against a surety co-maker, or where the defense of fraud by a purchasing remitter is interposed by the drawer of the instrument against the good faith purchasing payee."

Former Section 3–302(2) stated: "A payee may be a holder in due course." This provision was intended to resolve the split of authority under the N.I.L. It made clear that there was no intent to change the common-law rule that allowed a payee to become a holder in due course. See Comment 2 to former Section 3–302. But there was no need to put subsection (2) in former Section 3–302 because the split in authority under the N.I.L. was caused by the particular wording of N.I.L. § 52(4). The troublesome language in that section was not repeated in former Article 3 nor is it repeated in revised Article 3. Former Section 3–302(2) has been omitted in revised Article 3 because it is surplusage and may be misleading. The payee of an instrument can be a holder in due course, but use of the holder-in-due-course doctrine by the payee of an instrument is not the normal situation.

The primary importance of the concept of holder in due course is with respect to assertion of defenses or claims in recoupment (Section 3–305) and of claims to the instrument (Section 3–306). The holder-in-due-course doctrine assumes the following case as typical. Obligor issues a note or check to Obligee. Obligor is the maker of the note or drawer of the check. Obligee is the payee. Obligor has some defense to Obligor's obligation to pay the instrument. For example, Obligor issued the instrument for goods that Obligee promised to deliver. Obligee never delivered the goods. The failure of Obligee to deliver the goods is a defense. Section 3–303(b). Although Obligor has a defense against Obligee, if the instrument is negotiated to Holder and the requirements of subsection (a) are met, Holder may enforce the instrument against Obligor free of the defense. Section 3–305(b). In the typical case the holder in due course is not the payee of the instrument. Rather, the holder in due course is an immediate or remote transferee of the payee. If Obligor in our example is the only obligor on the check or note, the holder-in-due-course doctrine is irrelevant in determining rights between Obligor and Obligee with respect to the instrument.

But in a small percentage of cases it is appropriate to allow the payee of an instrument to assert rights as a holder in due course. The cases are like those referred to in the quotation from Professor Britton referred to above, or other cases in which conduct of some third party is the basis of the defense of the issuer of the instrument. The following are examples:

Case #1. Buyer pays for goods bought from Seller by giving to Seller a cashier's check bought from Bank. Bank has a defense to its obligation to pay the check because Buyer bought the check from Bank with a check known to be drawn on an account with insufficient funds to cover the check. If Bank issued the check to Buyer as payee and Buyer indorsed it over to Seller, it is clear that Seller can be a holder in due course taking free of the defense if Seller had no notice of the defense. Seller is a transferee of the check. There is no good reason why Seller's position should be any different if Bank drew the check to the order of Seller as payee. in that case, when Buyer took delivery of the check from Bank, Buyer became the owner of the check even though Buyer was not the holder. Buyer was a remitter. Section 3–103(a)(11). At that point nobody was the holder. When Buyer delivered the check to Seller, ownership of the check was transferred to Seller who also became the holder. This is a negotiation. Section 3–201. The rights of Seller should not be affected by the fact that in one case the negotiation to Seller was by a holder and in the other case the negotiation was by a remitter. Morever [sic], it should be irrelevant whether Bank delivered the check to Buyer and Buyer delivered it to Seller or whether Bank delivered it directly to Seller. In either case Seller can be a holder in due course that takes free of Bank's defense.

Case #2. X fraudulently induces Y to join X in a spurious venture to purchase a business. The purchase is to be financed by a bank loan for part of the price. Bank lends money to X and Y by deposit in a joint account of X and Y who sign a note payable to Bank for the amount of the loan. X then withdraws the money from the joint account and absconds. Bank acted in good faith and without notice of the fraud of X against Y. Bank is payee of the note executed by Y, but its right to enforce the note against Y should not be affected by the fact that Y was induced to execute the note by the fraud of X. Bank can be a holder in due course that takes free of the defense of Y. Case #2 is similar to Case #1. In each case the payee of the instrument has given value to the person committing the fraud in exchange for the obligation of the person against whom the fraud was committed. In each case the payee was not party to the fraud and had no notice of it.

Suppose in Case #2 that the note does not meet the requirements of Section 3–104(a) and thus is not a negotiable instrument covered by Article 3. In that case, Bank cannot be a holder in due course but the result should be the same. Bank's rights are determined by general principles of contract law. Restatement Second, Contracts § 164(2) governs the case. If Y is induced to enter into a contract with Bank by a fraudulent misrepresentation by X, the contract is voidable by Y unless Bank "in good faith and without reason to know of the misrepresentation either gives value or relies materially on the transaction." Comment e to § 164(2) states:

"This is the same principle that protects an innocent person who purchases goods or commercial paper in good faith, without notice and for value from one who obtained them from the original owner by a misrepresentation. See Uniform Commercial Code §§ 2–403(1), 3–305. In the cases that fall within [§ 164(2)], however, the innocent person deals directly with the recipient of the misrepresentation, which is made by one not a party to the contract."

The same result follows in Case #2 if Y had been induced to sign the note as an accommodation party (Section 3–419). If Y signs as co-maker of a note for the benefit of X, Y is a surety with respect to the obligation of X to pay the note but is liable as maker of the note to pay Bank. Section 3–419(b). If Bank is a holder in due course, the fraud of X cannot be asserted against Bank under Section 3–305(b). But the result is the same without resort to holder-in-due-course doctrine. If the note is not a negotiable instrument governed by Article 3, general rules of suretyship apply. Restatement, Security § 119 states that the surety (Y) cannot assert a defense against the creditor (Bank) based on the fraud of the principal (X) if the creditor "without knowledge of the fraud * * * extended credit to the principal on the security of the surety's promise * * *." The underlying principle of § 119 is the same as that of § 164(2) of Restatement Second, Contracts.

Case #3. Corporation draws a check payable to Bank. The check is given to an officer of Corporation who is instructed to deliver it to Bank in payment of a debt owed by Corporation to Bank. Instead, the officer, intending to defraud Corporation, delivers the check to Bank in payment of the officer's personal debt, or the check is delivered to Bank for deposit to the officer's personal account. If Bank obtains payment of the check, Bank has received funds of Corporation which have been used for the personal benefit of the officer. Corporation in this case will assert a claim to the proceeds of the check against Bank. If Bank was a holder in due course of the check it took the check free of Corporation's claim. Section 3–306. The issue in this case is whether Bank had notice of the claim when it took the check. If Bank knew that the officer was a fiduciary with respect to the check, the issue is governed by Section 3–307.

Case #4. Employer, who owed money to X, signed a blank check and delivered it to Secretary with instructions to complete the check by typing in X's name and the amount owed to X. Secretary fraudulently completed the check by typing in the name of Y, a creditor to whom Secretary owed money. Secretary then delivered the check to Y in payment of Secretary's debt. Y obtained payment of the check. This case is similar to Case #3. Since Secretary was authorized to complete the check, Employer is bound by Secretary's act in making the check payable to Y. The drawee bank properly paid the check. Y received funds of Employer which were used for the personal benefit of Secretary. Employer asserts a claim to these funds against Y. If Y is a holder in due course, Y takes free of the claim. Whether Y is a holder in due course depends upon whether Y had notice of Employer's claim.

5. Subsection (c) is based on former Section 3–302(3). Like former Section 3–302(3), subsection (c) is intended to state existing case law. It covers a few situations in which the purchaser takes an instrument under unusual circumstances. The purchaser is treated as a successor in interest to the prior holder and can acquire no better rights. But if the prior holder was a holder in due course, the purchaser obtains rights of a holder in due course.

Subsection (c) applies to a purchaser in an execution sale or sale in bankruptcy. It applies equally to an attaching creditor or any other person who acquires the instrument by legal process or to a representative, such as an executor, administrator, receiver or assignee for the benefit of creditors, who takes the instrument as part of an estate. Subsection (c) applies to bulk purchases lying outside of the ordinary course of business of the seller. For example, it applies to the purchase by one bank of a substantial part of the paper held by another bank which is threatened with insolvency and seeking to liquidate its assets. Subsection (c) would also apply when a new partnership takes over for value all of the assets of an old one after a new member has entered the firm, or to a reorganized or consolidated corporation taking over the assets of a predecessor.

In the absence of controlling state law to the contrary, subsection (c) applies to a sale by a state bank commissioner of the assets of an insolvent bank. However, subsection (c) may be preempted by federal law if the Federal Deposit Insurance Corporation takes over an insolvent bank. Under the governing federal law, the FDIC and similar financial institution insurers are given holder in due course status and that status is also acquired by their assignees under the shelter doctrine.

6. Subsections (d) and (e) clarify two matters not specifically addressed by former Article 3:

Case #5. Payee negotiates a $1,000 note to Holder who agrees to pay $900 for it. After paying $500, Holder learns that Payee defrauded Maker in the transaction giving rise to the note. Under subsection (d) Holder may assert rights as a holder in due course to the extent of $555.55 ($500 ÷ $900 = .555 × $1,000 = $555.55). This formula rewards Holder with a ratable portion of the bargained for profit.

Case #6. Payee negotiates a note of Maker for $1,000 to Holder as security for payment of Payee's debt to Holder of $600. Maker has a defense which is good against Payee but of which Holder has no notice. Subsection (e) applies. Holder may assert rights as a holder in due course only to the extent of $600. Payee does not get the benefit of the holder-in-due-course status of Holder. With respect to $400 of the note, Maker may assert any rights that Maker has against Payee. A different result follows if the payee of a note negotiated it to a person who took it as a holder in due course and that person pledged the note as security for a debt. Because the defense cannot be asserted against the pledgor, the pledgee can assert rights as a holder in due course for the full amount of the note for the benefit of both the pledgor and the pledgee.

7. There is a large body of state statutory and case law restricting the use of the holder in due course doctrine in consumer transactions as well as some business transactions that raise similar issues. Subsection (g) subordinates Article 3 to that law and any other similar law that may evolve in the future. Section 3–106(d) also relates to statutory or administrative law intended to restrict use of the holder-in-due-course doctrine. See Comment 3 to Section 3–106.

Uniform Commercial Code Comment

Prior Uniform Statutory Provision:
Section 52, Uniform Negotiable Instruments Law.
Changes: Reworded; new provisions.
Purposes of Changes and New Matter: The changes are intended to remove uncertainties arising under the original section.

1. The language "without notice that it is overdue" is substituted for that of the original subsection (2) in order to make it clear that the purchaser of an instrument which is in fact overdue may be a holder in due course if he takes it without notice that it is overdue. Such notice is covered by the section on notice to purchaser (Section 3–304).

2. Subsection (2) is intended to settle the long continued conflict over the status of the payee as a holder in due course. This conflict has turned very largely upon the word "negotiated" in the original Section 52(4), which is now eliminated. The position here taken is that the payee may become a holder in due course to the same extent and under the same circumstances as any other holder. This is true whether he takes the instrument by purchase from a third person or directly from the obligor. All that is necessary is that the payee meet the requirements of this section. In the following cases, among others, the payee is a holder in due course:

   a. A remitter, purchasing goods from P, obtains a bank draft payable to P and forwards it to P, who takes it for value, in good faith and without notice as required by this section.

   b. The remitter buys the bank draft payable to P, but it is forwarded by the bank directly to P, who takes it in good faith and without notice in payment of the remitter's obligation to him.

   c. A and B sign a note as co-makers. A induces B to sign by fraud, and without authority from B delivers the note to P, who takes it for value, in good faith and without notice.

   d. A defrauds the maker into signing an instrument payable to P. P pays A for it in good faith and without notice, and the maker delivers the instrument directly to P.

   e. D draws a check payable to P and gives it to his agent to be delivered to P in payment of D's debt. The agent delivers it to P, who takes it in good faith and without notice in payment of the agent's debt to P. But as to this case see Section 3–304(2), which may apply.

   f. D draws a check payable to P but blank as to the amount, and gives it to his agent to be delivered to P. The agent fills in the check with an excessive amount, and P takes it for value, in good faith and without notice.

   g. D draws a check blank as to the name of the payee, and gives it to his agent to be filled in with the name of A and delivered to A. The agent fills in the name of P, and P takes the check in good faith, for value and without notice.

3. Subsection (3) is intended to state existing case law. It covers a few situations in which the purchaser takes the instrument under unusual circumstances which indicate that he is merely a successor in interest to the prior holder and can acquire no better rights. (If such prior holder was himself a holder in due course, the purchaser succeeds to that status under Section 3–201 on Transfer.) The provision applies to a purchaser at an execution sale, a sale in bankruptcy or a sale by a state bank commissioner of the assets of an insolvent bank. It applies equally to an attaching creditor or any other person who acquires the instrument by legal process, even under an antecedent claim; and equally to a representative, such as an executor, administrator, receiver or assignee for the benefit of creditors, who takes over the instrument as part of an estate, even though he is representing antecedent creditors.

   Subsection (3)(c) applies to bulk purchases lying outside of the ordinary course of business of the seller. It applies, for example, when a new partnership takes over for value all of the assets of an old one after a new member has entered the firm, or to a reorganized or consolidated corporation taking over in bulk the assets of a predecessor. It has particular application to the purchase by one bank of a substantial part of the paper held by another bank which is threatened with insolvency and seeking to liquidate its assets.

4. A purchaser of a limited interest—as a pledgee in a security transaction—may become a holder in due course, but he may enforce the instrument over defenses only to the extent of his interest, and defenses good against the pledgor remain available insofar as the pledgor retains an equity in the instrument. This is merely a special application of the general rule (Section 1–201) that a purchaser of a limited interest acquires rights only to the extent of the interest purchased. Section 27 of the original Act contained a similar provision.

Cross References:

Sections 1–201, 3–303, 3–305 and 3–306.
Point 1: Section 3–304(5).
Point 3: Section 3–201.
Point 4: Section 1–201.

Definitional Cross References:

"Good faith". Section 1–201.
"Holder". Section 1–201.
"Instrument". Section 3–102.
"Notice". Section 1–201.
"Notice of dishonor". Section 3–508.
"Person". Section 1–201.
"Purchase". Section 1–201.
"Purchaser". Section 1–201.
"Value". Section 3–303.

Cross References

Definitions, see Commercial Code § 1201.
Depositary bank as holder in due course, see Commercial Code § 4205.
Determination of bank as holder in due course, value given to extent of security interest in item, see Commercial Code § 4211.
Letters of credit, issuer's duty to honor a draft or demand for payment, see Commercial Code § 5114.
Negotiable instrument issued by corporation for purchase or redemption of shares, enforcement by holder in due course, see Corporations Code § 511.
Personal property not in custody of levying officer transferred or encumbered, exceptions, see Code of Civil Procedure § 697.740.
Restrictive indorsement, effect of, see Commercial Code § 3206.
Rights of holder in due course, see Commercial Code § 3305.
Rights of one not holder in due course, see Commercial Code § 3306.
Secured transactions, protection of purchasers of instruments and documents, see Commercial Code § 9309.
Taker, notice of claim or defense, see Commercial Code § 3307.
Transfer, see Commercial Code § 3203.
When bank gives value for purposes of holder in due course, see Commercial Code § 4211.

§ 3303. Value and consideration

(a) An instrument is issued or transferred for value if any of the following apply:

(1) The instrument is issued or transferred for a promise of performance, to the extent the promise has been performed.

(2) The transferee acquires a security interest or other lien in the instrument other than a lien obtained by judicial proceeding.

(3) The instrument is issued or transferred as payment of, or as security for, an antecedent claim against any person, whether or not the claim is due.

(4) The instrument is issued or transferred in exchange for a negotiable instrument.

(5) The instrument is issued or transferred in exchange for the incurring of an irrevocable obligation to a third party by the person taking the instrument.

(b) "Consideration" means any consideration sufficient to support a simple contract. The drawer or maker of an instrument has a defense if the instrument is issued without consideration. If an instrument is issued for a promise of performance, the issuer has a defense to the extent performance of the promise is due and the promise has not been performed. If an instrument is issued for value as stated in subdivision (a), the instrument is also issued for consideration. *(Added by Stats.1992, c. 914 (S.B.833), § 6.)*

California Code Comment

By John A. Bohn and Charles J. Williams

Prior California Law

1. This section restates former Civil Code §§ 3106, 3108 and 3135 for the purpose of removing uncertainties. Former Civil Code § 3107 provided "where value has at any time been given for the instrument, the holder is deemed a holder for value in respect to all parties who become such prior to that time." This had reference to the liability of an accommodation party.

Division 3 separates value from consideration. Consideration (section 3408) is important only on the issue of whether the obligation of a party can be enforced against him. Value is important only on the issue of whether the holder acquiring the obligation qualifies as a particular kind of holder. Official Comment 2.

2. Paragraph (a) resolves the conflict between the first sentence of former Civil Code §§ 3106 ("value is any consideration sufficient to support a simple contract") and 3135 ("where the transferee receives notice of any infirmity in the instrument or defect in the title of the person negotiating the same before he has paid the full amount agreed to be paid therefor, he will be deemed a holder in due course only to the extent of the amount theretofore paid by him"). See Official Comment 3. The holder in due course receives protection only to the extent that executory consideration is paid. This is in accord with prior California law. People's Finance & Thrift Co. v. Matthews Fruit Co., 104 Cal.App. 630, 286 Pac. 710 (1930).

Paragraph (a) expressly eliminates as a holder any person who acquires a lien by legal process. This is in accord with decisions under the NIL. Official Comment 4.

3. Paragraph (b) is a restatement of the last sentence of former Civil Code § 3106 which provided: ". . . An antecedent or preexisting debt constitutes value; and is deemed such whether the instrument is payable on demand or at a future time." Official Comment 5.

4. Paragraph (c) is new statutory law and an exception to the rule that an executory promise is not value. Official Comment 6. Prior California case law is in accord that a note for a note is valuable consideration, Tumansky v. Woodruff, 14 Cal.App.2d 279, 57 P.2d 1372 (1936).

Changes from U.C.C. (1962 Official Text)

5. This is section 3–303 of the Official Text without change.

Uniform Commercial Code Comment
1992 Addition

1. Subsection (a) is a restatement of former Section 3–303 and subsection (b) replaces former Section 3–408. The distinction between value and consideration in Article 3 is a very fine one. Whether an instrument is taken for value is relevant to the issue of whether a holder is a holder in due course. If an instrument is not issued for consideration the issuer has a defense to the obligation to pay the instrument. Consideration is defined in subsection (b) as "any consideration sufficient to support a simple contract." The definition of value in Section 1–201(44), which doesn't apply to Article 3, includes "any consideration sufficient to support a simple contract." Thus, outside Article 3, anything that is consideration is also value. A different rule applies in Article 3. Subsection (b) of Section 3–303 states that if an instrument is issued for value it is also issued for consideration.

Case # 1. X owes Y $1,000. The debt is not represented by a note. Later X issues a note to Y for the debt. Under subsection (a)(3) X's note is issued for value. Under subsection (b) the note is also issued for consideration whether or not, under contract law, Y is deemed to have given consideration for the note.

Case # 2. X issues a check to Y in consideration of Y's promise to perform services in the future. Although the executory promise is consideration for issuance of the check it is value only to the extent the promise is performed. Subsection (a)(1).

Case # 3. X issues a note to Y in consideration of Y's promise to perform services. If at the due date of the note Y's performance is not yet due, Y may enforce the note because it was issued for consideration. But if at the due date of the note, Y's performance is due and has not been performed, X has a defense. Subsection (b).

2. Subsection (a), which defines value, has primary importance in cases in which the issue is whether the holder of an instrument is a holder in due course and particularly to cases in which the issuer of the instrument has a defense to the instrument. Suppose Buyer and Seller signed a contract on April 1 for the sale of goods to be delivered on May 1. Payment of 50% of the price of the goods was due upon signing of the contract. On April 1 Buyer delivered to Seller a check in the amount due under the contract. The check was drawn by X to Buyer as payee and was indorsed to Seller. When the check was presented for payment to the drawee on April 2, it was dishonored because X had stopped payment. At that time Seller had not taken any action to perform the contract with Buyer. If X has a defense on the check, the defense can be asserted against Seller who is not a holder in due course because Seller did not give value for the check. Subsection (a)(1). The policy basis for subsection (a)(1) is that the holder who gives an executory promise of performance will not suffer an out-of-pocket loss to the extent the executory promise is unperformed at the time the holder learns of dishonor of the instrument. When Seller took delivery of the check on April 1, Buyer's obligation to pay 50% of the price on that date was suspended, but when the check was dishonored on April 2 the obligation revived. Section 3–310(b). If payment for goods is due at or before delivery and the Buyer fails to make the payment, the Seller is excused from performing the promise to deliver the goods. Section 2–703. Thus, Seller is protected from an out-of-pocket loss even if the check is not enforceable. Holder-in-due-course status is not necessary to protect Seller.

3. Subsection (a)(2) equates value with the obtaining of a security interest or a nonjudicial lien in the instrument. The term "security interest" covers Article 9 cases in which an instrument is taken as collateral as well as bank collection cases in which a bank acquires a security interest under Section 4–210. The acquisition of a common-law or statutory banker's lien is also value under subsection (a)(2). An attaching creditor or other person who acquires a lien by judicial proceedings does not give value for the purposes of subsection (a)(2).

4. Subsection (a)(3) follows former Section 3–303(b) in providing that the holder takes for value if the instrument is taken in payment of or as security for an antecedent claim, even though there is no extension of time or other concession, and whether or not the claim is due. Subsection (a)(3) applies to any claim against any person; there is no requirement that the claim arise out of contract. In particular the provision is intended to apply to an instrument given in payment of or as security for the debt of a third person, even though no concession is made in return.

5. Subsection (a)(4) and (5) restate former Section 3–303(c). They state generally recognized exceptions to the rule that an executory promise is not value. A negotiable instrument is value because it carries the possibility of negotiation to a holder in due course, after which the party who gives it is obliged to pay. The same reasoning applies to any irrevocable commitment to a third person, such as a letter of credit issued when an instrument is taken.

Prior Uniform Statutory Provision:
Sections 25, 26, 27 and 54, Uniform Negotiable Instruments Law.
Changes: Combined and reworded; original Section 26 omitted.
Purposes of Changes: The changes are intended to remove uncertainties arising under the original Act.

1. The original Section 26 which had reference to the liability of accommodation parties is omitted as erroneous and misleading, since a holder who does not himself give value cannot qualify as a holder in due course in his own right merely because value has previously been given for the instrument.

2. In this Article value is divorced from consideration (Section 3–408). The latter is important only on the question of whether the obligation of a party can be enforced against him; while value is important only on the question of whether the holder who has acquired that obligation qualifies as a particular kind of holder.

3. Paragraph (a) resolves an apparent conflict between the original Section 54 and the first sentence of the original Section 25, by requiring that the agreed consideration shall actually have been given. An

executory promise to give value is not itself value, except as provided in paragraph (c). The underlying reason of policy is that when the purchaser learns of a defense against the instrument or of a defect in the title he is not required to enforce the instrument, but is free to rescind the transaction for breach of the transferor's warranty (Section 3–417). There is thus not the same necessity for giving him the status of a holder in due course, cutting off claims and defenses, as where he has actually paid value. A common illustration is the bank credit not drawn upon, which can be and is revoked when a claim or defense appears.

4. Paragraph (a) limits the language of the original Section 27, eliminating the attaching creditor or any other person who acquires a lien by legal process. Any such lienor has been uniformly held not to be a holder in due course.

5. Paragraph (b) restates the last sentence of the original Section 25. It adopts the generally accepted rule that the holder takes for value when he takes the instrument as security for an antecedent debt, even though there is no extension of time or other concession, and whether or not the debt is due. The provision extends the same rule to any claim against any person; there is no requirement that the claim arise out of contract. In particular the provision is intended to apply to an instrument given in payment of or as security for the debt of a third person, even though no concession is made in return.

6. Paragraph (c) is new, but states generally recognized exceptions to the rule that an executory promise is not value. A negotiable instrument is value because it carries the possibility of negotiation to a holder in due course, after which the party who gives it cannot refuse to pay. The same reasoning applies to any irrevocable commitment to a third person, such as a letter of credit issued when an instrument is taken.

Cross References:

Sections 3–302 and 3–415.
Point 1: Section 3–415.
Point 2: Section 3–408.
Point 3: Section 3–417.

Definitional Cross References:

"Holder". Section 1–201.
"Instrument". Section 3–102.
"Person". Section 1–201.
"Security interest". Section 1–201.

Cross References

Definition of new value,
 Generally, see Commercial Code § 1201.
 Secured transactions, see Commercial Code § 9105.
Obligation of accommodation party, see Commercial Code § 3419.
Warranties on presentment and transfer, see Commercial Code §§ 3426, 3417.

§ 3304. Overdue instruments

(a) An instrument payable on demand becomes overdue at the earliest of the following times:

(1) On the day after the day demand for payment is duly made.

(2) If the instrument is a check, 90 days after its date.

(3) If the instrument is not a check, when the instrument has been outstanding for a period of time after its date which is unreasonably long under the circumstances of the particular case in light of the nature of the instrument and usage of the trade.

(b) With respect to an instrument payable at a definite time the following rules apply:

(1) If the principal is payable in installments and a due date has not been accelerated, the instrument becomes overdue upon default under the instrument for nonpayment of an installment, and the instrument remains overdue until the default is cured.

(2) If the principal is not payable in installments and the due date has not been accelerated, the instrument becomes overdue on the day after the due date.

(3) If a due date with respect to principal has been accelerated, the instrument becomes overdue on the day after the accelerated due date.

(c) Unless the due date of principal has been accelerated, an instrument does not become overdue if there is default in payment of interest but no default in payment of principal. *(Added by Stats.1992, c. 914 (S.B.833), § 6.)*

California Code Comment

By John A. Bohn and Charles J. Williams

Prior California Law

1. This section which provides the circumstances in which notice of a defense or claim exists treats the subject in more detail than under the NIL.

2. The term "notice" as used in this section is defined in Commercial Code § 1201(25) as actual knowledge or notice of the existence of facts and circumstances known at the time which gives reason to know that the fact exists. This replaces former Civil Code § 3137 which provided that notice of an infirmity in the instrument or defect in title was "actual knowledge . . . or knowledge of such facts that . . . taking the instrument amounted to bad faith."

3. Subdivision (1)(a) replaces former Civil Code § 3133(1) which used the phrase "complete and regular upon its face." The Legislative Counsel has stated that:

"Subdivision (1)(a) is narrower in its restriction on negotiability than Civil Code Section 3133. See In Re Home Furniture Co., 7 Fed. (2d) 299; and Goodale v. Thorn, 199 Cal. 307, 249 Pac. 11." Sixth Progress Report to the Legislature by Senate Fact Finding Committee on Judiciary (1959–1961) Part 1, The Uniform Commercial code, p. 73. In the special report of the State Bar Committee on the Uniform Commercial Code the effect of section 3304 and in particular subdivision (1)(a) on existing California law is discussed:

"**d. Incomplete or Irregular Instruments.** Under the N.I.L. one cannot be a holder in due course if he takes an instrument incomplete and irregular on its face. [*Fn.:* Cal.Civ.Code, sec. 3133(1).] One not a holder in due course is subject to all defenses and adverse claims, whether or not they relate to the instrument's completeness or regularity. Code section 13304 [3304] would continue this N.I.L. rule, but may relax the standards of completeness and regularity. Under the Code, a purchaser would have notice of a defense or adverse claim if the instrument 'is so incomplete, bears such visible evidence of forgery or alteration, or is otherwise so irregular as to call into question its validity, terms or ownership, or to create an ambiguity as to the party to pay.' It is hard to say whether or how much this language would change present standards of completeness and regularity, but it seems on its face to impose less of a duty than the N.I.L. upon the holder. But since the Code treats the matter of incompleteness or irregularity as giving notice of a claim or defense, rather than disqualifying a holder from being a holder in due course, it may also be possible to interpret incompleteness or irregularity as giving notice only of a claim or defense associated with the defect. This is not clear and the Code has also been interpreted as continuing the N.I.L. rule unchanged. [*Fn.:* See Hawkland, Commercial Paper 81–82 (A.L.I.1959).]" California State Bar Committee on the Commercial Code, A Special Report, The Uniform Commercial Code, 37 Calif.State Bar J. 159 (March–April 1962).

4. Subdivision (1)(b) rewords former Civil Code § 3133(4) which referred to "notice of any infirmity in the instrument or defect in the title of the person negotiating it" and replaces former Civil Code § 3136 which defined defect in title as title obtained by ". . . fraud, duress, or force and fear, or other unlawful means, or for an illegal consideration . . . or" when an instrument is negotiated ". . . in breach of faith, or under such circumstances as amount to a fraud." This subdivision

expands the former provisions to include the case where a purchaser has notice of the discharge. Official Comment 4. Subdivision (1)(b) is intended to apply to notice of defenses which would permit a party to avoid his original obligation. Official Comment 3.

Subdivision (1)(b) appears more restrictive on negotiability than former Civil Code §§ 3133(4), 3136 and 3137 as interpreted by the courts because the latter were limited to "actual knowledge of defects" (Mann v. Leasko, 179 Cal.App.2d 692, 4 Cal.Rptr. 124 (1960)) while "notice" in subdivision (1)(b) includes knowledge of facts and circumstances which might put a person on his guard.

5. Subdivision (2) is based upon the policy of the Uniform Fiduciaries Act. See Official Comment 5. This uniform act was never adopted in California. This subdivision is consistent with case law under the NIL even in the absence of the Uniform Fiduciaries Act. Britton, Bills & Notes (1961) 289.

6. Subdivision (3)(a) continues the rule of former Civil Code § 3133(2). For an example of its application, see Bliss v. California Co-op. Producers, 30 Cal.2d 240, 181 P.2d 369, 170 ALR 1009 (1947).

This subdivision distinguishes an instrument in which an installment is overdue from one in which interest is overdue. Under subdivision (4)(f) the fact that interest is overdue does not prevent the holder from taking in due course.

7. Under subdivision (3)(b) a purchaser may be a holder in due course if he does not have reason to know that an instrument has been accelerated. This clarifies a problem under former Civil Code § 3133(2) under which an acceleration would make the instrument actually overdue and yet a purchaser could take it without notice of the exercise of the acceleration clause. See Britton, Bills & Notes (1961) 305–308.

Query: should an acceleration clause which makes an instrument due for failure to pay interest plus knowledge that interest is overdue constitute knowledge that instrument is overdue? Although the Commercial Code doesn't answer this, it would seem to depend on how the acceleration clause works: is it automatic or optional, is notice necessary, etc. See Britton, Bills & Notes (1961) 305.

This subdivision also eliminates former Civil Code § 3126 (negotiation deemed made prima facie before instrument overdue) since the presumption that the negotiation of instrument is deemed prima facie to have been effected before the instrument was overdue was only of importance in determining whether a person was a holder in due course. Official Comment 7.

8. Under subdivision (3)(c) as well as under former Civil Code § 3134 the taking of an instrument for more than a reasonable length of time after its issue would prevent the holder from being a holder in due course. See Commercial Code § 1204 for meaning of reasonable time. The last sentence in subdivision (3) adding the presumption that a domestic check is stale after 30 days is new.

9. Subdivision (4)(a) is new statutory law. There are no California decisions on this point but the authority under the NIL from other jurisdictions was generally that the antedating or postdating of an instrument did not prevent the holder from being a holder in due course. Britton, Bills and Notes (1961) 287.

10. Subdivision (4)(b) is new statutory law but is in accord with the California decisions. One taking a note with knowledge of an underlying executory contract is not prevented by that fact from being a holder in due course, unless he also has notice of a breach of that agreement. See Flood v. Petry, 165 Cal. 309, 132 Pac. 256, 46 LRA, N.S. 579 (1913); Mann v. Andrus, 169 Cal.App.2d 455, 337 P.2d 473 (1959). (see also Bliss v. California Co-op. Producers cited in Comment 6 above)

11. Subdivision (4)(c) is new statutory law but probably is in accord with the existing judicial decisions. In Commercial Security v. Modesto Drug Co., 43 Cal.App. 162, 184 Pac. 964 (1919) the court stated that a guaranty in lieu of the customary indorsement on a note is not a fact which would cause suspicion that the note was improper.

12. Subdivision (4)(d) continues the policy of Civil Code § 3115 permitting the completion of incomplete instruments. Official Comment 10. This subdivision is consistent with California decisions under the NIL. Transcontinental & Western Air, Inc. v. Bank of America, N.T. & S.A., 46 Cal.App.2d 708, 116 P.2d 791 (1941) dealt with the negotiation of travelers checks. The court held that although the checks were wrongfully completed, the holder had no notice of improper completion and therefore took as a holder in due course.

13. Subdivision (4)(e) is new statutory law. It is in accord with the Uniform Fiduciaries Act.

14. Subdivision (4)(f) is new statutory law.

15. Subdivision (5) is new statutory law. Its purpose is to remove an uncertainty under the NIL. Official Comment 11.

16. Subdivision (6) is new statutory law but is in accord with Goodale v. Thorn, 199 Cal. 307, 249 Pac. 11 (1926) in which the court stated that notice of infirmities in an instrument subsequent to the time it was acquired would not prevent one from recovering on the instrument. See Official Comment 12. A similar provision appeared in the USA (former Civil Code § 1779(1)). See also section 2705(3)(a).

Changes from U.C.C. (1962 Official Text)

17. This is section 3–304 of the Official Text without change.

Uniform Commercial Code Comment
1992 Addition

1. To be a holder in due course, one must take without notice that an instrument is overdue. Section 3–302(a)(2)(iii). Section 3–304 replaces subsection (3) of former Section 3–304. For the sake of clarity it treats demand and time instruments separately. Subsection (a) applies to demand instruments. A check becomes stale after 90 days.

Under former Section 3–304(3)(c), a holder that took a demand note had notice that it was overdue if it was taken "more than a reasonable length time after its issue." In substitution for this test, subsection (a)(3) requires the trier of fact to look at both the circumstances of the particular case and the nature of the instrument and trade usage. Whether a demand note is stale may vary a great deal depending on the facts of the particular case.

2. Subsections (b) and (c) cover time instruments. They follow the distinction made under former Article 3 between defaults in payment of principal and interest. In subsection (b) installment instruments and single payment instruments are treated separately. If an installment is late, the instrument is overdue until the default is cured.

Uniform Commercial Code Comment

Prior Uniform Statutory Provision:

Sections 45, 52, 53, 55 and 56, Uniform Negotiable Instruments Law.

Changes: Combined and reworded; new provisions.

Purposes of Changes and New Matter: The original sections are expanded, with the addition of specific provisions intended to remove uncertainties in the existing law.

1. "Notice" is defined in Section 1–201.

2. Paragraph (a) of subsection (1) replaces the provision in the original Section 52(1) requiring that the instrument be "complete and regular on its face." An instrument may be blank as to some unnecessary particular, may contain minor erasures, or even have an obvious change in the date, as where "January 2, 1948" is changed to "January 2, 1949", without even exciting suspicion. Irregularity is properly a question of notice to the purchaser of something wrong, and is so treated here.

3. "Voidable" obligation in paragraph (b) of subsection (1) is intended to limit the provision to notice of defense which will permit any party to avoid his original obligation on the instrument, as distinguished from a set-off or counterclaim.

4. Notice that one party has been discharged is not notice to the purchaser of an infirmity in the obligation of other parties who remain liable on the instrument. A purchaser with notice that an indorser is discharged takes subject to that discharge as provided in the section on effect of discharge against a holder in due course (Section 3–602) but is not prevented from taking the obligation of the maker in due course. If he has notice that all parties are discharged he cannot be a holder in due course.

5. Subsection (2) follows the policy of Section 6 of the Uniform Fiduciaries Act, and specifies the same elements as notice of improper conduct of a fiduciary. Under paragraph (e) of subsection (4) mere notice of the existence of the fiduciary relation is not enough in itself to prevent the holder from taking in due course, and he is free to take the instrument on the assumption that the fiduciary is acting properly. The purchaser may pay cash into the hands of the fiduciary without notice of any breach of the obligation. Section 3–206 should be consulted for the effect of a restrictive indorsement.

6. Subsection (3) removes an uncertainty in the original Act by providing that reason to know of an overdue installment or other part of the principal amount is notice that the instrument is overdue and thus prevents the purchaser from taking in due course. On the other hand subsection (4)(f) makes notice that interest is overdue insufficient, on the basis of banking and commercial practice, the decisions under the original Act, and the frequency with which interest payments are in fact delayed. Notice of default in payment of any other instrument, except an uncured default in another instrument of the same series, is likewise insufficient.

7. Subsection (3) departs from the original Section 52(2) by providing that the purchaser may take accelerated paper, or a demand instrument on which demand has in fact been made, as a holder in due course if he takes without notice of the acceleration or demand. With this change the original Section 45 is eliminated, as the presumption that any negotiation has taken place before the instrument was in fact overdue is of importance only in aid of a holder in due course. Under this section it is not conclusive that the instrument was in fact overdue when it was negotiated, if the holder takes without notice of that fact.

The "reasonable time after issue" is retained from the original Section 53, but paragraph (c) adds a presumption, as that term is defined in this Act (Section 1–201), that a domestic check is stale after thirty days.

8. Paragraph (a) of subsection (4) rejects decisions holding that an instrument known to be antedated or postdated is not "regular." Such knowledge does not prevent a holder from taking in due course.

9. Paragraph (b) of subsection (4) is to be read together with the provisions of this Article as to when a promise or order is unconditional and as to other writings affecting the instrument (Sections 3–105 and 3–119). Mere notice of the existence of an executory promise or a separate agreement does not prevent the holder from taking in due course, and such notice may even appear in the instrument itself. If the purchaser has notice of any default in the promise or agreement which gives rise to a defense or claim against the instrument, he is on notice to the same extent as in the case of any other information as to the existence of a defense or claim.

10. Paragraph (d) of subsection (4) follows the policy of the original Section 14, under which any person in possession of an instrument has prima facie authority to fill blanks. It is intended to mean that the holder may take in due course even though a blank is filled in his presence, if he is without notice that the filling is improper. Section 3–407 on alteration should be consulted as to the rights of subsequent holders following such an alteration.

11. Subsection (5) is new. It removes an uncertainty arising under the original Act as to the effect of "constructive notice" through public filing or recording.

12. Subsection (6) is new. It means that notice must be received with a sufficient margin of time to afford a reasonable opportunity to act on it, and that a notice received by the president of a bank one minute before the bank's teller cashes a check is not effective to prevent the bank from becoming a holder in due course. See in this connection the provision on notice to an organization, Sec. 1–201(27).

Cross References:

Sections 3–201 and 3–302.
Point 1: Section 1–201.
Point 4: Section 3–602.
Point 5: Section 3–206.
Point 7: Section 1–201.
Point 9: Sections 3–105(1)(b) and (c) and 3–119.
Point 10: Section 3–407.
Point 12: Section 1–201.

Definitional Cross References:

"Accommodation party". Section 3–415.
"Agreement". Section 1–201.
"Alteration". Section 3–407.
"Bank". Section 1–201.
"Check". Section 3–104.
"Holder in due course". Section 3–302.
"Instrument". Section 3–102.
"Issue". Section 3–102.
"Negotiation". Section 3–202.
"Notice". Section 1–201.
"Party". Section 1–201.
"Person". Section 1–201.
"Presumed". Section 1–201.
"Promise". Section 3–102.
"Purchaser". Section 1–201.
"Reasonable time". Section 1–204.
"Signed". Section 1–201.
"Term". Section 1–201.

Cross References

Accommodation party, see Commercial Code § 3419.
Alteration, see Commercial Code § 3407.
Conditional delivery as defense, see Commercial Code § 3306.
Conveyances, effect of recording, see Civil Code § 1213 et seq.
Definitions, see Commercial Code § 1201.
Forged signature, see Commercial Code § 3406.
Holder in due course,
    Generally, see Commercial Code § 3302.
    Effect of discharge, see Commercial Code § 3601.
Negotiation, see Commercial Code § 3202.
Promise,
    Generally, see Commercial Code § 3103.
    When conditional, see Commercial Code § 3106.
Reasonable time, see Commercial Code § 1204.
Restrictive indorsement, effect, see Commercial Code § 3206.
Separate writings affecting instrument, see Commercial Code § 3117.
Transfer, see Commercial Code § 3203.
Unconditional promise or order, see Commercial Code § 3106.
Value, see Commercial Code § 1201.

§ 3305. Enforcement of obligations; defenses; claims in recoupment

(a) Except as stated in subdivision (b), the right to enforce the obligation of a party to pay an instrument is subject to all of the following:

(1) A defense of the obligor based on (A) infancy of the obligor to the extent it is a defense to a simple contract, (B) duress, lack of legal capacity, or illegality of the transaction which, under other law, nullifies the obligation of the obligor, (C) fraud that induced the obligor to sign the instrument with neither knowledge nor reasonable opportunity to learn of its character or its essential terms, or (D) discharge of the obligor in insolvency proceedings.

(2) A defense of the obligor stated in another section of this division or a defense of the obligor that would be available if the person entitled to enforce the instrument were enforcing a right to payment under a simple contract.

(3) A claim in recoupment of the obligor against the original payee of the instrument if the claim arose from the transaction that gave rise to the instrument; but the claim of the obligor may be asserted against a transferee of the instrument only to reduce the amount owing on the instrument at the time the action is brought.

(b) The right of a holder in due course to enforce the obligation of a party to pay the instrument is subject to defenses of the obligor stated in paragraph (1) of subdivision (a), but is not subject to defenses of the obligor stated in paragraph (2) of subdivision (a) or claims in recoupment stated in paragraph (3) of subdivision (a) against a person other than the holder.

(c) Except as stated in subdivision (d), in an action to enforce the obligation of a party to pay the instrument, the obligor may not assert against the person entitled to enforce the instrument a defense, claim in recoupment, or claim to the instrument (Section 3306) of another person, but the other person's claim to the instrument may be asserted by the obligor if the other person is joined in the action and personally asserts the claim against the person entitled to enforce the instrument. An obligor is not obliged to pay the instrument if the person seeking enforcement of the instrument does not have rights of a holder in due course and the obligor proves that the instrument is a lost or stolen instrument.

(d) In an action to enforce the obligation of an accommodation party to pay an instrument, the accommodation party may assert against the person entitled to enforce the instrument any defense or claim in recoupment under subdivision (a) that the accommodated party could assert against the person entitled to enforce the instrument, except the defenses of discharge in insolvency proceedings, infancy, and lack of legal capacity. *(Added by Stats.1992, c. 914 (S.B.833), § 6.)*

California Code Comment

By John A. Bohn and Charles J. Williams

Prior California Law

1. Former Civil Code § 3138 merely provided that a holder in due course held the instrument free from "any defect of title of prior parties" and "free from defenses available to prior parties among themselves".

Subdivision (1) in describing freedom from defenses substitutes the phrase "claims to it [the instrument] on the part of any person" for the language "any defect of title of prior parties" in former Civil Code § 3138. It is language of clarification rather than change. Official Comment 2.

2. In subdivision (2) the reference to "all defenses" includes nondelivery and when read together with Commercial Code §§ 3115 (incomplete instruments) and 3407 (alteration) cuts off the defense of nondelivery of an incomplete instrument against a holder in due course. This changes the rule under former Civil Code § 3096.

3. Subdivision (2)(a) is new statutory law. The NIL did not characterize the defense of infancy as real or personal but both before the NIL and after it the defense was held to be real and assertable against a holder in due course. Official Comment 4; Britton, Bills and Notes (1961) 334–335. However, the question of when the defense of infancy is available is left to local law. See Civil Code §§ 1557 and 2542 for provisions dealing with capacity in general.

4. Subdivision (2)(b) is new statutory law. However, it leaves the effect of whether or not the defense is cut off to local law. The defense of insanity has been held a real defense. Hellman Commercial Trust & Savings Bank v. Alden, 206 Cal. 592, 275 Pac. 794 (1929). See also Civil Code § 1557. Fraud has been held a real defense. C.I.T. Corp. v. Panac, 25 Cal.2d 547, 154 P.2d 710, 160 ALR 1285 (1944).

5. Paragraph (2)(c) is new statutory law but is in accord with prior California decisions which recognized that fraud in the essence or fraud in the factum is a real defense and is effective against a holder in due course. C.I.T. Corp. v. Panac, cited in Comment 4; United States v. Klatt, (D.C.Cal.1955) 135 F.Supp. 648. See Official Comment 7.

6. Subdivision (2)(d) is new statutory law. Commercial Code § 1201(22) defines an insolvency proceeding as a proceeding intended to liquidate or rehabilitate the estate of the person involved.

7. Subdivision (2)(e) is new statutory law. Official Comment 9.

Changes from U.C.C. (1962 Official Text)

8. This is section 3–305 of the Official Text without change.

Uniform Commercial Code Comment
1992 Addition

1. Subsection (a) states the defenses to the obligation of a party to pay the instrument. Subsection (a)(1) states the "real defenses" that may be asserted against any person entitled to enforce the instrument.

Subsection (a)(1)(i) allows assertion of the defense of infancy against a holder in due course, even though the effect of the defense is to render the instrument voidable but not void. The policy is one of protection of the infant even at the expense of occasional loss to an innocent purchaser. No attempt is made to state when infancy is available as a defense or the conditions under which it may be asserted. In some jurisdictions it is held that an infant cannot rescind the transaction or set up the defense unless the holder is restored to the position held before the instrument was taken which, in the case of a holder in due course, is normally impossible. In other states an infant who has misrepresented age may be estopped to assert infancy. Such questions are left to other law, as an integral part of the policy of each state as to the protection of infants.

Subsection (a)(1)(ii) covers mental incompetence, guardianship, ultra vires acts or lack of corporate capacity to do business, or any other incapacity apart from infancy. Such incapacity is largely statutory. Its existence and effect is left to the law of each state. If under the state law the effect is to render the obligation of the instrument entirely null and void, the defense may be asserted against a holder in due course. If the effect is merely to render the obligation voidable at the election of the obligor, the defense is cut off.

Duress, which is also covered by subsection (a)(ii), is a matter of degree. An instrument signed at the point of a gun is void, even in the hands of a holder in due course. One signed under threat to prosecute the son of the maker for theft may be merely voidable, so that the defense is cut off. Illegality is most frequently a matter of gambling or usury, but may arise in other forms under a variety of statutes. The statutes differ in their provisions and the interpretations given them. They are primarily a matter of local concern and local policy. All such matters are therefore left to the local law. If under that law the effect of the duress or the illegality is to make the obligation entirely null and void, the defense may be asserted against a holder in due course. Otherwise it is cut off.

Subsection (a)(1)(iii) refers to "real" or "essential" fraud, sometimes called fraud in the essence or fraud in the factum, as effective against a holder in due course. The common illustration is that of the maker who is tricked into signing a note in the belief that it is merely a receipt or some other document. The theory of the defense is that the signature on the instrument is ineffective because the signer did not intend to sign such an instrument at all. Under this provision the defense extends to an instrument signed with knowledge that it is a negotiable instrument, but without knowledge of its essential terms. The test of the defense is that of excusable ignorance of the contents of the writing signed. The party must not only have been in ignorance, but must also have had no reasonable opportunity to obtain knowledge. In determining what is a reasonable opportunity all relevant factors are to be taken into account, including the intelligence, education, business experience, and ability to read or understand English of the signer. Also relevant is the nature of the representations that were made, whether the signer had good reason to rely on the representations or to have confidence in the person making them, the presence or absence of any third person who might read or explain the instrument to the signer, or any other possibility of obtaining independent information, and the apparent necessity, or lack of it, for acting without delay. Unless the misrepresentation meets this test, the defense is cut off by a holder in due course.

Subsection (a)(1)(iv) states specifically that the defense of discharge in insolvency proceedings is not cut off when the instrument is purchased by a holder in due course. "Insolvency proceedings" is defined in Section 1–201(22) and it includes bankruptcy whether or not the debtor is insolvent. Subsection (2)(e) of former Section 3–305 is omitted. The substance of that provision is stated in Section 3–601(b).

2. Subsection (a)(2) states other defenses that, pursuant to subsection (b), are cut off by a holder in due course. These defenses comprise those specifically stated in Article 3 and those based on common law contract principles. Article 3 defenses are nonissuance of the instrument, conditional issuance, and issuance for a special purpose (Section 3–105(b)); failure to countersign a traveler's check (Section 3–106(c)); modification of the obligation by a separate agreement (Section 3–117); payment that violates a restrictive indorsement (Section 3–206(f));

instruments issued without consideration or for which promised performance has not been given (Section 3–303(b)), and breach of warranty when a draft is accepted (Section 3–417(b)). The most prevalent common law defenses are fraud, misrepresentation or mistake in the issuance of the instrument. In most cases the holder in due course will be an immediate or remote transferee of the payee of the instrument. In most cases the holder-in-due-course doctrine is irrelevant if defenses are being asserted against the payee of the instrument, but in a small number of cases the payee of the instrument may be a holder in due course. Those cases are discussed in Comment 4 to Section 3–302.

Assume Buyer issues a note to Seller in payment of the price of goods that Seller fraudulently promises to deliver but which are never delivered. Seller negotiates the note to Holder who has no notice of the fraud. If Holder is a holder in due course, Holder is not subject to Buyer's defense of fraud. But in some cases an original party to the instrument is a holder in due course. For example, Buyer fraudulently induces Bank to issue a cashier's check to the order of Seller. The check is delivered by Bank to Seller, who has no notice of the fraud. Seller can be a holder in due course and can take the check free of Bank's defense of fraud. This case is discussed as Case # 1 in Comment 4 to Section 3–302. Former Section 3–305 stated that a holder in due course takes free of defenses of "any party to the instrument with whom the holder has not dealt." The meaning of this language was not at all clear and if read literally could have produced the wrong result. In the hypothetical case, it could be argued that Seller "dealt" with Bank because Bank delivered the check to Seller. But it is clear that Seller should take free of Bank's defense against Buyer regardless of whether Seller took delivery of the check from Buyer or from Bank. The quoted language is not included in Section 3–305. It is not necessary. If Buyer issues an instrument to Seller and Buyer has a defense against Seller, that defense can obviously be asserted. Buyer and Seller are the only people involved. The holder-in-due-course doctrine has no relevance. The doctrine applies only to cases in which more than two parties are involved. Its essence is that the holder in due course does not have to suffer the consequences of a defense of the obligor on the instrument that arose from an occurrence with a third party.

3. Subsection (a)(3) is concerned with claims in recoupment which can be illustrated by the following example. Buyer issues a note to the order of Seller in exchange for a promise of Seller to deliver specified equipment. If Seller fails to deliver the equipment or delivers equipment that is rightfully rejected, Buyer has a defense to the note because the performance that was the consideration for the note was not rendered. Section 3–303(b). This defense is included in Section 3–305(a)(2). That defense can always be asserted against Seller. This result is the same as that reached under former Section 3–408.

But suppose Seller delivered the promised equipment and it was accepted by Buyer. The equipment, however, was defective. Buyer retained the equipment and incurred expenses with respect to its repair. In this case, Buyer does not have a defense under Section 3–303(b). Seller delivered the equipment and the equipment was accepted. Under Article 2, Buyer is obliged to pay the price of the equipment which is represented by the note. But Buyer may have a claim against Seller for breach of warranty. If Buyer has a warranty claim, the claim may be asserted against Seller as a counterclaim or as a claim in recoupment to reduce the amount owing on the note. It is not relevant whether Seller is or is not a holder in due course of the note or whether Seller knew or had notice that Buyer had the warranty claim. It is obvious that holder-in-due-course doctrine cannot be used to allow Seller to cut off a warranty claim that Buyer has against Seller. Subsection (b) specifically covers this point by stating that a holder in due course is not subject to a "claim in recoupment * * * against a person other than the holder."

Suppose Seller negotiates the note to Holder. If Holder had notice of Buyer's warranty claim at the time the note was negotiated to Holder, Holder is not a holder in due course (Section 3–302(a)(2)(iv)) and Buyer may assert the claim against Holder (Section 3–305(a)(3)) but only as a claim in recoupment, i.e. to reduce the amount owed on the note. If the warranty claim is $1,000 and the unpaid note is $10,000, Buyer owes $9,000 to Holder. If the warranty claim is more than the unpaid amount of the note, Buyer owes nothing to Holder, but Buyer cannot recover the unpaid amount of the warranty claim from Holder. If Buyer had already partially paid the note, Buyer is not entitled to recover the amounts paid. The claim can be used only as an offset to amounts owing on the note. If Holder had no notice of Buyer's claim and otherwise qualifies as a holder in due course, Buyer may not assert the claim against Holder. Section 3–305(b).

The result under Section 3–305 is consistent with the result reached under former Article 3, but the rules for reaching the result are stated differently. Under former Article 3 Buyer could assert rights against Holder only if Holder was not a holder in due course, and Holder's status depended upon whether Holder had notice of a defense by Buyer. Courts have held that Holder had that notice if Holder had notice of Buyer's warranty claim. The rationale under former Article 3 was "failure of consideration." This rationale does not distinguish between cases in which the seller fails to perform and those in which the buyer accepts the performance of seller but makes a claim against the seller because the performance is faulty. The term "failure of consideration" is subject to varying interpretations and is not used in Article 3. The use of the term "claim in recoupment" in Section 3–305(a)(3) is a more precise statement of the nature of Buyer's right against Holder. The use of the term does not change the law because the treatment of a defense under subsection (a)(2) and a claim in recoupment under subsection (a)(3) is essentially the same.

Under former Article 3, case law was divided on the issue of the extent to which an obligor on a note could assert against a transferee who is not a holder in due course a debt or other claim that the obligor had against the original payee of the instrument. Some courts limited claims to those that arose in the transaction that gave rise to the note. This is the approach taken in Section 3–305(a)(3). Other courts allowed the obligor on the note to use any debt or other claim, no matter how unrelated to the note, to offset the amount owed on the note. Under current judicial authority and non-UCC statutory law, there will be many cases in which a transferee of a note arising from a sale transaction will not qualify as a holder in due course. For example, applicable law may require the use of a note to which there cannot be a holder in due course. See Section 3–106(d) and Comment 3 to Section 3–106. It is reasonable to provide that the buyer should not be denied the right to assert claims arising out of the sale transaction. Subsection (a)(3) is based on the belief that it is not reasonable to require the transferee to bear the risk that wholly unrelated claims may also be asserted. The determination of whether a claim arose from the transaction that gave rise to the instrument is determined by law other than this Article and thus may vary as local law varies.

4. Subsection (c) concerns claims and defenses of a person other than the obligor on the instrument. It applies principally to cases in which an obligation is paid with the instrument of a third person. For example, Buyer buys goods from Seller and negotiates to Seller a cashier's check issued by Bank in payment of the price. Shortly after delivering the check to Seller, Buyer learns that Seller had defrauded Buyer in the sale transaction. Seller may enforce the check against Bank even though Seller is not a holder in due course. Bank has no defense to its obligation to pay the check and it may not assert defenses, claims in recoupment, or claims to the instrument of Buyer, except to the extent permitted by the "but" clause of the first sentence of subsection (c). Buyer may have a claim to the instrument under Section 3–306 based on a right to rescind the negotiation to Seller because of Seller's fraud. Section 3–202(b) and Comment 2 to Section 3–201. Bank cannot assert that claim unless Buyer is joined in the action in which Seller is trying to enforce payment of the check. In that case Bank may pay the amount of the check into court and the court will decide whether that amount belongs to Buyer or Seller. The last sentence of subsection (c) allows the issuer of an instrument such as a cashier's check to refuse payment in the rare case in which the issuer can prove that the instrument is a lost or stolen instrument and the person seeking enforcement does not have rights of a holder in due course.

5. Subsection (d) applies to instruments signed for accommodation (Section 3–419) and this subsection equates the obligation of the accommodation party to that of the accommodated party. The accommodation party can assert whatever defense or claim the accommodated party had against the person enforcing the instrument. The only exceptions are discharge in bankruptcy, infancy and lack of capacity. The same rule does not apply to an indorsement by a holder of the instrument in negotiating the instrument. The indorser, as transferor, makes a warranty to the indorsee, as transferee, that no defense or claim in recoupment is good against the indorser. Section 3–416(a)(4). Thus, if the indorsee sues the indorser because of dishonor of the instrument, the indorser may not assert the defense or claim in recoupment of the maker or drawer against the indorsee.

Section 3–305(d) must be read in conjunction with Section 3–605, which provides rules (usually referred to as suretyship defenses) for determining when the obligation of an accommodation party is discharged, in whole or in part, because of some act or omission of a person entitled to enforce the instrument. To the extent a rule stated in Section 3–605 is inconsistent with Section 3–305(d), the Section 3–605 rule governs. For example, under Section 3–605(b), discharge under Section 3–604 of the accommodated party does not discharge the accommodation party. As explained in Comment 3 to Section 3–605, discharge of the accommodated party is normally part of a settlement under which the holder of a note accepts partial payment from an accommodated party who is financially unable to pay the entire amount of the note. If the holder then brings an action against the accommodation party to recover the remaining unpaid amount of the note, the accommodation party cannot use Section 3–305(d) to nullify Section 3–605(b) by asserting the discharge of the accommodated party as a defense. On the other hand, suppose the accommodated party is a buyer of goods who issued the note to the seller who took the note for the buyer's obligation to pay for the goods. Suppose the buyer has a claim for breach of warranty with respect to the goods against the seller and the warranty claim may be asserted against the holder of the note. The warranty claim is a claim in recoupment. If the holder and the accommodated party reach a settlement under which the holder accepts payment less than the amount of the note in full satisfaction of the note and the warranty claim, the accommodation party could defend an action on the note by the holder by asserting the accord and satisfaction under Section 3–305(d). There is no conflict with Section 3–605(b) because that provision is not intended to apply to settlement of disputed claims. Another example of the use of Section 3–305(d) in cases in which Section 3–605 applies is stated in Comment 4 to Section 3–605. See PEB Commentary No. 11, dated February 10, 1994 [Uniform Laws Annotated, UCC, APP II, Comment 11].

Uniform Commercial Code Comment

Prior Uniform Statutory Provision:

Sections 15, 16 and 57, Uniform Negotiable Instruments Law.

Changes: Combined and reworded; new provisions; rule of original Section 15 reversed.

Purposes of Changes and New Matter:

1. The section applies to any person who is himself a holder in due course, and equally to any transferee who acquires the rights of one (Section 3–201). "Takes" is substituted for "holds" in the original Section 57 because a holder in due course may still be subject to any claims or defenses which arise against him after he has taken the instrument.

2. The language "all claims to it on the part of any person" is substituted for "any defect of title of prior parties" in the original Section 57 in order to make it clear that the holder in due course takes the instrument free not only from any claim of legal title but also from all liens, equities or claims of any other kind. This includes any claim for rescission of a prior negotiation, in accordance with the provisions of the section on reacquisition (Section 3–208).

3. "All defenses" includes nondelivery, conditional delivery or delivery for a special purpose. Under this Article such nondelivery or qualified delivery is a defense (Sections 3–306 and 3–307) and the defendant has the full burden of establishing it. Accordingly the "conclusive presumption" of the third sentence of the original Section 16 is abrogated in favor of a rule of law cutting off the defense.

The effect of this section, together with the sections dealing with incomplete instruments (Section 3–115) and alteration (Section 3–407) is to cut off the defense of nondelivery of an incomplete instrument against a holder in due course, and to change the rule of the original Section 15.

4. Paragraph (a) of subsection (2) is new. It follows the decisions under the original Act in providing that the defense of infancy may be asserted against a holder in due course, even though its effect is to render the instrument voidable but not void. The policy is one of protection of the infant against those who take advantage of him, even at the expense of occasional loss to an innocent purchaser. No attempt is made to state when infancy is available as a defense or the conditions under which it may be asserted. In some jurisdictions it is held that an infant cannot rescind the transaction or set up the defense unless he restores the holder to his former position, which in the case of a holder in due course is normally impossible. In other states an infant who has misrepresented his age may be estopped to assert his infancy. Such questions are left to the local law, as an integral part of the policy of each state as to the protection of infants.

5. Paragraph (b) of subsection (2) is new. It covers mental incompetence, guardianship, ultra vires acts or lack of corporate capacity to do business, any remaining incapacity of married women, or any other incapacity apart from infancy. Such incapacity is largely statutory. Its existence and effect is left to the law of each state. If under the local law the effect is to render the obligation of the instrument entirely null and void, the defense may be asserted against a holder in due course. If the effect is merely to render the obligation voidable at the election of the obligor, the defense is cut off.

6. Duress is a matter of degree. An instrument signed at the point of a gun is void, even in the hands of a holder in due course. One signed under threat to prosecute the son of the maker for theft may be merely voidable, so that the defense is cut off. Illegality is most frequently a matter of gaming or usury, but may arise in many other forms under a great variety of statutes. The statutes differ greatly in their provisions and the interpretations given them. They are primarily a matter of local concern and local policy. All such matters are therefore left to the local law. If under that law the effect of the duress or the illegality is to make the obligation entirely null and void, the defense may be asserted against a holder in due course. Otherwise it is cut off.

7. Paragraph (c) of subsection (2) is new. It follows the great majority of the decisions under the original Act in recognizing the defense of "real" or "essential" fraud, sometimes called fraud in the essence or fraud in the factum, as effective against a holder in due course. The common illustration is that of the maker who is tricked into signing a note in the belief that it is merely a receipt or some other document. The theory of the defense is that his signature on the instrument is ineffective because he did not intend to sign such an instrument at all. Under this provision the defense extends to an instrument signed with knowledge that it is a negotiable instrument, but without knowledge of its essential terms.

The test of the defense here stated is that of excusable ignorance of the contents of the writing signed. The party must not only have been in ignorance, but must also have had no reasonable opportunity to obtain knowledge. In determining what is a reasonable opportunity all relevant factors are to be taken into account, including the age and sex of the party, his intelligence, education and business experience; his ability to read or to understand English, the representations made to him and his reason to rely on them or to have confidence in the person making them; the presence or absence of any third person who might read or explain the instrument to him, or any other possibility of obtaining independent information; and the apparent necessity, or lack of it, for acting without delay.

Unless the misrepresentation meets this test, the defense is cut off by a holder in due course.

8. Paragraph (d) is also new. It is inserted to make it clear that any discharge in bankruptcy or other insolvency proceedings, as defined in this Article, is not cut off when the instrument is purchased by a holder in due course.

9. Paragraph (e) of subsection (2) is also new. Under the notice to purchaser section of this Article (Section 3–304), notice of any discharge which leaves other parties liable on the instrument does not prevent the purchaser from becoming a holder in due course. The obvious case is that of the cancellation of an indorsement, which leaves the maker and prior indorsers liable. As to such parties the purchaser may be a holder in due course, but he takes the instrument subject to the discharge of which he has notice. If he is without such notice, the discharge is not effective against him (Section 3–602).

Cross References:

Point 1: Section 3–201(1).
Point 2: Section 3–208.
Point 3: Sections 3–115(2), 3–306(c), 3–307(2) and 3–407(3).
Point 9: Sections 3–304(1)(b) and 3–602.

Definitional Cross References:

"Contract". Section 1–201.
"Holder in due course". Section 3–302.

"Insolvency proceedings". Section 1–201.
"Instrument". Section 3–102.
"Notice". Section 1–201.
"Party". Section 1–201.
"Person". Section 1–201.
"Term". Section 1–201.

Cross References

Transfer warranty, item not subject to defense or claim in recoupment, see Commercial Code § 4207.
Alteration, see Commercial Code § 3407.
Capacity to contract, see Civil Code §§ 1556, 1557.
Definitions,
    Delivery, see Commercial Code § 1201.
    Holder in due course, see Commercial Code § 3302.
Effect of discharge, see Commercial Code § 3601.
Illegality,
    Consideration, see Civil Code §§ 1607, 1608, 1667 et seq.
    Object of contract, see Civil Code § 1598.
Incomplete instruments, see Commercial Code § 3115.
Acquisition of lien for value, see Commercial Code § 3303.
Minors,
    Capacity to contract, see Civil Code §§ 1556, 1557; Family Code §6700 et seq.
    Disaffirmance of contracts, see Family Code § 6710.
Negotiation of bearer paper by transfer of possession, see Commercial Code § 3202.
Object of contract, see Civil Code § 1595 et seq.
Persons of unsound mind, rescission of contracts, see Civil Code § 39.
Reacquisition, see Commercial Code § 3207.
Rescission, grounds, see Civil Code § 1689.
Signatures, see Commercial Code § 3307.
Taker, notice of claim or defense, see Commercial Code § 3307.
Transfer, see Commercial Code § 3203.
Usury law, see Civil Code § 1916–1 et seq.
Want or failure of consideration as defense, see Commercial Code § 3303.

§ 3306. Claims to instruments

A person taking an instrument, other than a person having rights of a holder in due course, is subject to a claim of a property or possessory right in the instrument or its proceeds, including a claim to rescind a negotiation and to recover the instrument or its proceeds. A person having rights of a holder in due course takes free of the claim to the instrument. *(Added by Stats.1992, c. 914 (S.B.833), § 6.)*

California Code Comment

By John A. Bohn and Charles J. Williams

Prior California Law

1. This section specifies the rights of a person who is neither a holder in due course nor a person who has acquired the rights of a holder in due course by transfer under Commercial Code § 3201. Official Comment 1.

2. Subdivision (a) is new statutory language and expands former Civil Code § 3139 which provided that one not a holder in due course was subject to the same defenses as if the instrument were non-negotiable. Official Comment 2.

3. Subdivision (b) is a restatement of the first sentence of former Civil Code § 3139.

4. The part of subdivision (c) which deals with want or failure of consideration adopts the rule of former Civil Code § 3109. The remainder of subdivision (c) is similar to former Civil Code § 3097. See Official Comment 4.

The last sentence of former Civil Code § 3097 provided that "And where the instrument is no longer in the possession of a party whose signature appears thereon, a valid and intentional delivery by him is presumed until the contrary is proved." This is deleted and is covered by the rule in Commercial Code § 3307. Official Comment 4.

5. Subdivision (d) replaces the last sentence of former Civil Code § 3140. Former Civil Code § 3140 established a presumption that every holder was a holder in due course but if the defendant showed that the title of anyone who negotiated it was defective, the holder had to prove he was a holder in due course or a successor to one. The last sentence removed the burden of proof from a holder when the defendant became liable before the defect. This means that the defendant in this instance would be one who had no defense of his own but was asserting that plaintiff had a defective title and that the equity of ownership was in another not a party to the action (jus tertii). The defendant has the burden of proving that the plaintiff is not a holder in due course.

Subdivision (d) removes the right of a defendant to assert the ownership of a third party not a party to the action except for theft or inconsistency with a restrictive indorsement. The burden of establishing it is on the defendant (Commercial Code § 3307(2)) and when it is established, the holder must prove that he is a holder in due course in order to recover (Commercial Code § 3307(3)).

Changes from U.C.C. (1962 Official Text)

6. This is section 3–306 of the Official Text without change.

Uniform Commercial Code Comment

1992 Addition

This section expands on the reference to "claims to" the instrument mentioned in former Sections 3–305 and 3–306. Claims covered by the section include not only claims to ownership but also any other claim of a property or possessory right. It includes the claim to a lien or the claim of a person in rightful possession of an instrument who was wrongfully deprived of possession. Also included is a claim based on Section 3–202(b) for rescission of a negotiation of the instrument by the claimant. Claims to an instrument under Section 3–306 are different from claims in recoupment referred to in Section 3–305(a)(3).

Uniform Commercial Code Comment

Prior Uniform Statutory Provision:

Sections 16, 28, 58 and 59, Uniform Negotiable Instruments Law.

Changes: Combined, condensed and reworded.

Purposes of Changes: The changes are intended to remove the following uncertainties arising under the original sections:

1. Any transferee who acquires the rights of a holder in due course under the transfer section of this Article (Section 3–201) is included within the provisions of the preceding Section 305. This section covers any person who neither qualifies in his own right as a holder in due course nor has acquired the rights of one by transfer. In particular the section applies to a bona fide purchaser with notice that the instrument is overdue.

2. "All valid claims to it on the part of any person" includes not only claims of legal title, but all liens, equities, or other claims of right against the instrument or its proceeds. It includes claims to rescind a prior negotiation and to recover the instrument or its proceeds.

3. Paragraph (b) restates the first sentence of the original Section 58.

4. Paragraph (c) condenses the original Sections 16 and 28. Want or failure of consideration is specifically mentioned, as in the original Section 28, in order to make it clear that either is a defense which the defendant has the burden of establishing under the following section of this Article. The language as to an "ascertained or liquidated amount or otherwise" in the original Section 28 is omitted because it is believed to be superfluous. The third sentence of Section 16 is now covered by the preceding section. The fourth sentence is omitted in favor of the rule stated in the following section, which places the full burden of establishing the defense of non-delivery, conditional delivery or delivery for a special purpose upon the defendant, and makes any presumption unnecessary.

5. Paragraph (d) is substituted for the last sentence of the original Section 59, as a more detailed and explicit statement of the same policy, which is also found in the original Section 22. The contract of the obligor is to pay the holder of the instrument, and the claims of other persons against the holder are generally not his concern. He is not

required to set up such a claim as a defense, since he usually will have no satisfactory evidence of his own on the issue; and the provision that he may not do so is intended as much for his protection as for that of the holder. The claimant who has lost possession of an instrument so payable or indorsed that another may become a holder has lost his rights on the instrument, which by its terms no longer runs to him. The provision includes all claims for rescission of a negotiation, whether based in incapacity, fraud, duress, mistake, illegality, breach of trust or duty or any other reason. It includes claims based on conditional delivery or delivery for a special purpose. It includes claims of legal title, lien, constructive trust or other equity against the instrument or its proceeds. The exception made in the case of theft is based on the policy which refuses to aid a proved thief to recover, and refuses to aid him indirectly by permitting his transferee to recover unless the transferee is a holder in due course. The exception concerning restrictive indorsements is intended to achieve consistency with Section 3–603 and related sections.

Nothing in this section is intended to prevent the claimant from intervening in the holder's action against the obligor or defending the action for the latter, and asserting his claim in the course of such intervention or defense. Nothing here stated is intended to prevent any interpleader, deposit in court or other available procedure under which the defendant may bring the claimant into court or be discharged without himself litigating the claim as a defense. Compare Section 3–803 on vouching in other parties alleged to be liable.

Cross References:

Section 3–302.
Point 1: Sections 3–201(1) and 3–305.
Point 2: Section 3–207.
Point 3: Section 3–307(2).
Point 4: Sections 3–305 and 3–307(2).
Point 5: Section 3–803.

Definitional Cross References:

"Action". Section 1–201.
"Contract". Section 1–201.
"Delivery". Section 1–201.
"Holder in due course". Section 3–302.
"Instrument". Section 3–102.
"Party". Section 1–201.
"Person". Section 1–201.
"Rights". Section 1–201.

Cross References

Payment made with knowledge of claim to instrument under this section by another person as discharge of party obliged to pay, see Commercial Code § 3602.

§ 3307. Breach of fiduciary duty; notice

(a) In this section:

(1) "Fiduciary" means an agent, trustee, partner, corporate officer or director, <u>limited liability company manager,</u> or other representative owing a fiduciary duty with respect to an instrument.

(2) "Represented person" means the principal, beneficiary, partnership, corporation, <u>limited liability company,</u> or other person to whom the duty stated in paragraph (1) is owed.

(b) If (i) an instrument is taken from a fiduciary for payment or collection or for value, (ii) the taker has knowledge of the fiduciary status of the fiduciary, and (iii) the represented person makes a claim to the instrument or its proceeds on the basis that the transaction of the fiduciary is a breach of fiduciary duty, the following rules apply:

(1) Notice of breach of fiduciary duty by the fiduciary is notice of the claim of the represented person.

(2) In the case of an instrument payable to the represented person or the fiduciary as such, the taker has notice of the breach of fiduciary duty if the instrument is (A) taken in payment of or as security for a debt known by the taker to be the personal debt of the fiduciary, (B) taken in a transaction known by the taker to be for the personal benefit of the fiduciary, or (C) deposited to an account other than an account of the fiduciary, as such, or an account of the represented person.

(3) If an instrument is issued by the represented person or the fiduciary as such, and made payable to the fiduciary personally, the taker does not have notice of the breach of fiduciary duty unless the taker knows of the breach of fiduciary duty.

(4) If an instrument is issued by the represented person or the fiduciary as such, to the taker as payee, the taker has notice of the breach of fiduciary duty if the instrument is (A) taken in payment of or as security for a debt known by the taker to be the personal debt of the fiduciary, (B) taken in a transaction known by the taker to be for the personal benefit of the fiduciary, or (C) deposited to an account other than an account of the fiduciary, as such, or an account of the represented person. *(Added by Stats.1992, c. 914 (S.B.833), § 6. Amended by Stats.1994, c. 1200 (S.B.469), § 8, eff. Sept. 30, 1994.)*

California Code Comment

By John A. Bohn and Charles J. Williams

Prior California Law

1. The first sentence of subdivision (1) is in accord with Code of Civil Procedure § 437. A signature upon an instrument may be denied upon information and belief.

2. Subdivision (1)(a) is in accord with existing California law. Code of Civil Procedure § 1981. The burden of establishing is defined in Commercial Code § 1201(8) as the burden of persuading the trier of fact that the existence of the fact is more probable than its nonexistence. See Official Comment 1 for an explanation of the effect of subdivision (1).

3. Subdivision (1)(b) puts the burden of going forward with the evidence on the party attacking the signature except where the purported signer is dead or incompetent.

4. Subdivision (2) replaces the first clause of former Civil Code § 3140 which read: "every holder is deemed prima facie to be a holder in due course . . ." and which entitled a holder to recover unless a defense is established. See Official Comment 2.

5. Subdivision (3) replaces the last clause of the first sentence of former Civil Code § 3140 which read as follows: "but when it is shown that the title of any person who has negotiated the instrument was defective, the burden is on the holder to prove that he or some person under whom he claims acquired the title as holder in due course."

For a critical examination of this section see Britton, Holder in Due Course, A Comparison of the Provisions of the Negotiable Instruments Law with those of Article 3 of the proposed Uniform Commercial Code, 49 Northwestern U.L.R. 417, 447–450, 452–455 (1954).

Changes from U.C.C. (1962 Official Text)

6. This is section 3–307 of the Official Text without change.

Uniform Commercial Code Comment
1992 Addition

1. This section states rules for determining when a person who has taken an instrument from a fiduciary has notice of a breach of fiduciary duty that occurs as a result of the transaction with the fiduciary. Former Section 3–304(2) and (4)(e) related to this issue, but those provisions were unclear in their meaning. Section 3–307 is intended to clarify the law by stating rules that comprehensively cover the issue of when the taker of an instrument has notice of a breach of a fiduciary duty and thus notice of a claim to the instrument or its proceeds.

2. Subsection (a) defines the terms "fiduciary" and "represented person" and the introductory paragraph of subsection (b) describes the transaction to which the section applies. The basic scenario is one in which the fiduciary in effect embezzles money of the represented person by applying the proceeds of an instrument that belongs to the represented person to the personal use of the fiduciary. The person dealing with the fiduciary may be a depositary bank that takes the instrument for collection or a bank or other person that pays value for the instrument. The section also covers a transaction in which an instrument is presented for payment to a payor bank that pays the instrument by giving value to the fiduciary. Subsections (b)(2), (3), and (4) state rules for determining when the person dealing with the fiduciary has notice of breach of fiduciary duty. Subsection (b)(1) states that notice of breach of fiduciary duty is notice of the represented person's claim to the instrument or its proceeds.

Under Section 3–306, a person taking an instrument is subject to a claim to the instrument or its proceeds, unless the taker has rights of a holder in due course. Under Section 3–302(a)(2)(v), the taker cannot be a holder in due course if the instrument was taken with notice of a claim under Section 3–306. Section 3–307 applies to cases in which a represented person is asserting a claim because a breach of fiduciary duty resulted in a misapplication of the proceeds of an instrument. The claim of the represented person is a claim described in Section 3–306. Section 3–307 states rules for determining when a person taking an instrument has notice of the claim which will prevent assertion of rights as a holder in due course. It also states rules for determining when a payor bank pays an instrument with notice of breach of fiduciary duty.

Section 3–307(b) applies only if the person dealing with the fiduciary "has knowledge of the fiduciary status of the fiduciary." Notice which does not amount to knowledge is not enough to cause Section 3–307 to apply. "Knowledge" is defined in Section 1–201(25). In most cases, the "taker" referred to in Section 3–307 will be a bank or other organization. Knowledge of an organization is determined by the rules stated in Section 1–201(27). In many cases, the individual who receives and processes an instrument on behalf of the organization that is the taker of the instrument "for payment or collection or for value" is a clerk who has no knowledge of any fiduciary status of the person from whom the instrument is received. In such cases, Section 3–307 doesn't apply because, under Section 1–201(27), knowledge of the organization is determined by the knowledge of the "individual conducting that transaction," i.e. the clerk who receives and processes the instrument. Furthermore, paragraphs (2) and (4) each require that the person acting for the organization have knowledge of facts that indicate a breach of fiduciary duty. In the case of an instrument taken for deposit to an account, the knowledge is found in the fact that the deposit is made to an account other than that of the represented person or a fiduciary account for benefit of that person. In other cases the person acting for the organization must know that the instrument is taken in payment or as security for a personal debt of the fiduciary or for the personal benefit of the fiduciary. For example, if the instrument is being used to buy goods or services, the person acting for the organization must know that the goods or services are for the personal benefit of the fiduciary. The requirement that the taker have knowledge rather than notice is meant to limit Section 3–307 to relatively uncommon cases in which the person who deals with the fiduciary knows all the relevant facts: the fiduciary status and that the proceeds of the instrument are being used for the personal debt or benefit of the fiduciary or are being paid to an account that is not an account of the represented person or of the fiduciary, as such. Mere notice of these facts is not enough to put the taker on notice of the breach of fiduciary duty and does not give rise to any duty of investigation by the taker.

3. Subsection (b)(2) applies to instruments payable to the represented person or the fiduciary as such. For example, a check payable to Corporation is indorsed in the name of Corporation by Doe as its President. Doe gives the check to Bank as partial repayment of a personal loan that Bank had made to Doe. The check was indorsed either in blank or to Bank. Bank collects the check and applies the proceeds to reduce the amount owed on Doe's loan. If the person acting for Bank in the transaction knows that Doe is a fiduciary and that the check is being used to pay a personal obligation of Doe, subsection (b)(2) applies. If Corporation has a claim to the proceeds of the check because the use of the check by Doe was a breach of fiduciary duty, Bank has notice of the claim and did not take the check as a holder in due course. The same result follows if Doe had indorsed the check to himself before giving it to Bank. Subsection (b)(2) follows Uniform Fiduciaries Act § 4 in providing that if the instrument is payable to the fiduciary, as such, or to the represented person, the taker has notice of a claim if the instrument is negotiated for the fiduciary's personal debt. If fiduciary funds are deposited to a personal account of the fiduciary or to an account that is not an account of the represented person or of the fiduciary, as such, there is a split of authority concerning whether the bank is on notice of a breach of fiduciary duty. Subsection (b)(2)(iii) states that the bank is given notice of breach of fiduciary duty because of the deposit. The Uniform Fiduciaries Act § 9 states that the bank is not on notice unless it has knowledge of facts that makes its receipt of the deposit an act of bad faith.

The rationale of subsection (b)(2) is that it is not normal for an instrument payable to the represented person or the fiduciary, as such, to be used for the personal benefit of the fiduciary. It is likely that such use reflects an unlawful use of the proceeds of the instrument. If the fiduciary is entitled to compensation from the represented person for services rendered or for expenses incurred by the fiduciary the normal mode of payment is by a check drawn on the fiduciary account to the order of the fiduciary.

4. Subsection (b)(3) is based on Uniform Fiduciaries Act § 6 and applies when the instrument is drawn by the represented person or the fiduciary as such to the fiduciary personally. The term "personally" is used as it is used in the Uniform Fiduciaries Act to mean that the instrument is payable to the payee as an individual and not as a fiduciary. For example, Doe as President of Corporation writes a check on Corporation's account to the order of Doe personally. The check is then indorsed over to Bank as in Comment 3. In this case there is no notice of breach of fiduciary duty because there is nothing unusual about the transaction. Corporation may have owed Doe money for salary, reimbursement for expenses incurred for the benefit of Corporation, or for any other reason. If Doe is authorized to write checks on behalf of Corporation to pay debts of Corporation, the check is a normal way of paying a debt owed to Doe. Bank may assume that Doe may use the instrument for his personal benefit.

5. Subsection (b)(4) can be illustrated by a hypothetical case. Corporation draws a check payable to an organization. X, an officer or employee of Corporation, delivers the check to a person acting for the organization. The person signing the check on behalf of Corporation is X or another person. If the person acting for the organization in the transaction knows that X is a fiduciary, the organization is on notice of a claim by Corporation if it takes the instrument under the same circumstances stated in subsection (b)(2). If the organization is a bank and the check is taken in repayment of a personal loan of the bank to X, the case is like the case discussed in Comment 3. It is unusual for Corporation, the represented person, to pay a personal debt of Doe by issuing a check to the bank. It is more likely that the use of the check by Doe reflects an unlawful use of the proceeds of the check. The same analysis applies if the check is made payable to an organization in payment of goods or services. If the person acting for the organization knew of the fiduciary status of X and that the goods or services were for X's personal benefit, the organization is on notice of a claim by Corporation to the proceeds of the check. See the discussion in the last paragraph of Comment 2.

Uniform Commercial Code Comment
Prior Uniform Statutory Provision:
Section 59, Uniform Negotiable Instruments Law.
Changes: Reworded; new provisions.

Purposes of Changes and New Matter:

1. Subsection (1) is new, although similar provisions are found in a number of states. The purpose of the requirement of a specific denial in the pleadings is to give the plaintiff notice that he must meet a claim

of forgery or lack of authority as to the particular signature, and to afford him an opportunity to investigate and obtain evidence. Where local rules of pleading permit, the denial may be on information and belief, or it may be a denial of knowledge or information sufficient to form a belief. It need not be under oath unless the local statutes or rules require verification. In the absence of such specific denial the signature stands admitted, and is not in issue. Nothing in this section is intended, however, to prevent amendment of the pleading in a proper case.

The question of the burden of establishing the signature arises only when it has been put in issue by specific denial. "Burden of establishing" is defined in the definitions section of this Act (Section 1–201). The burden is on the party claiming under the signature, but he is aided by the presumption that it is genuine or authorized [as] stated in paragraph (b). "Presumption" is also defined in this Act (Section 1–201). It means that until some evidence is introduced which would support a finding that the signature is forged or unauthorized the plaintiff is not required to prove that it is authentic. The presumption rests upon the fact that in ordinary experience forged or unauthorized signatures are very uncommon, and normally any evidence is within the control of the defendant or more accessible to him. He is therefore required to make some sufficient showing of the grounds for his denial before the plaintiff is put to his proof. His evidence need not be sufficient to require a directed verdict in his favor, but it must be enough to support his denial by permitting a finding in his favor. Until he introduces such evidence the presumption requires a finding for the plaintiff. Once such evidence is introduced the burden of establishing the signature by a preponderance of the total evidence is on the plaintiff.

Under paragraph (b) this presumption does not arise where the action is to enforce the obligation of a purported signer who has died or become incompetent before the evidence is required, and so is disabled from obtaining or introducing it. "Action" of course includes a claim asserted against the estate of a deceased or an incompetent.

2. Subsection (2) is substituted for the first clause of the original Section 59. Once signatures are proved or admitted, a holder makes out his case by mere production of the instrument, and is entitled to recover in the absence of any further evidence. The defendant has the burden of establishing any and all defenses, not only in the first instance but by a preponderance of the total evidence. The provision applies only to a holder, as defined in this Act (Section 1–201). Any other person in possession of an instrument must prove his right to it and account for the absence of any necessary indorsement. If he establishes a transfer which gives him the rights of a holder (Section 3–201), this provision becomes applicable, and he is then entitled to recover unless the defendant establishes a defense.

3. Subsection (3) rephrases the last clause of the first sentence of the original Section 59. Until it is shown that a defense exists the issue as to whether the holder is a holder in due course does not arise. In the absence of a defense any holder is entitled to recover and there is no occasion to say that he is deemed prima facie to be a holder in due course. When it is shown that a defense exists the plaintiff may, if he so elects, seek to cut off the defense by establishing that he is himself a holder in due course, or that he has acquired the rights of a prior holder in due course (Section 3–201). On this issue he has the full burden of proof by a preponderance of the total evidence. "In all respects" means that he must sustain this burden by affirmative proof that the instrument was taken for value, that it was taken in good faith, and that it was taken without notice (Section 3–302).

Nothing in this section is intended to say that the plaintiff must necessarily prove that he is a holder in due course. He may elect to introduce no further evidence, in which case a verdict may be directed for the plaintiff or the defendant, or the issue of the defense may be left to the jury, according to the weight and sufficiency of the defendant's evidence. He may elect to rebut the defense itself by proof to the contrary, in which case again a verdict may be directed for either party or the issue may be for the jury. This subsection means only that if the plaintiff claims the rights of a holder in due course against the defense he has the burden of proof upon that issue.

Cross References

Sections 3–305, 3–306, 3–401, 3–403, and 3–404.
Point 1: Section 1–201.
Point 2: Sections 1–201 and 3–201(1).
Point 3: Sections 3–201(1) and 3–302.

Definitional Cross References:

"Action". Section 1–201.
"Burden of establishing". Section 1–201.
"Defendant". Section 1–201.
"Genuine". Section 1–201.
"Holder". Section 1–201.
"Holder in due course". Section 3–302.
"Instrument". Section 3–102.
"Party". Section 1–201.
"Person". Section 1–201.
"Presumed". Section 1–201.
"Rights". Section 1–201.
"Signature". Section 3–401.

Cross References

Indorsement for payment to indorsee, notice of breach of fiduciary duty as provided in this section, see Commercial Code § 3206.
Complaint, uncontroverted allegations deemed true, see Code of Civil Procedure § 431.20.
Definitions, see Commercial Code § 1201.
Holder in due course, see Commercial Code § 3302.
Instrument, see Commercial Code § 3104.
Liability of parties, signature, see Commercial Code § 3401 et seq.
Rights,
    Generally, see Commercial Code § 1201.
    Holder in due course, see Commercial Code § 3305.
Signature,
    Generally, see Commercial Code § 3401.
    Ambiguous capacity, see Commercial Code § 3402.
    Authorized representative, see Commercial Code § 3403.
    Including mark, see Civil Code § 14; Code of Civil Procedure § 17.
    Unauthorized, see Commercial Code § 3403.
Transfer, see Commercial Code § 3203.

§ 3308. Signatures; validity; presumptions and proof

(a) In an action with respect to an instrument, the authenticity of, and authority to make, each signature on the instrument is admitted unless specifically denied in the pleadings. If the validity of a signature is denied in the pleadings, the burden of establishing validity is on the person claiming validity, but the signature is presumed to be authentic and authorized unless the action is to enforce the liability of the purported signer and the signer is dead or incompetent at the time of trial of the issue of validity of the signature. If an action to enforce the instrument is brought against a person as the undisclosed principal of a person who signed the instrument as a party to the instrument, the plaintiff has the burden of establishing that the defendant is liable on the instrument as a represented person under subdivision (a) of Section 3402.

(b) If the validity of signatures is admitted or proved and there is compliance with subdivision (a), a plaintiff producing the instrument is entitled to payment if the plaintiff proves entitlement to enforce the instrument under Section 3301, unless the defendant proves a defense or claim in recoupment. If a defense or claim in recoupment is proved, the right to payment of the plaintiff is subject to the defense or claim, except to the extent the plaintiff proves that the plaintiff has rights of a holder in due course which are not subject to the defense or claim. *(Added by Stats.1992, c. 914 (S.B. 833), § 6.)*

Uniform Commercial Code Comment
1992 Addition

1. Section 3–308 is a modification of former Section 3–307. The first two sentences of subsection (a) are a restatement of former Section 3–307(1). The purpose of the requirement of a specific denial in the pleadings is to give the plaintiff notice of the defendant's claim of forgery or lack of authority as to the particular signature, and to afford the plaintiff an opportunity to investigate and obtain evidence. If local rules of pleading permit, the denial may be on information and belief, or it may be a denial of knowledge or information sufficient to form a belief. It need not be under oath unless the local statutes or rules require verification. In the absence of such specific denial the signature stands admitted, and is not in issue. Nothing in this section is intended, however, to prevent amendment of the pleading in a proper case.

The question of the burden of establishing the signature arises only when it has been put in issue by specific denial. "Burden of establishing" is defined in Section 1–201. The burden is on the party claiming under the signature, but the signature is presumed to be authentic and authorized except as stated in the second sentence of subsection (a). "Presumed" is defined in Section 1–201 and means that until some evidence is introduced which would support a finding that the signature is forged or unauthorized, the plaintiff is not required to prove that it is valid. The presumption rests upon the fact that in ordinary experience forged or unauthorized signatures are very uncommon, and normally any evidence is within the control of, or more accessible to, the defendant. The defendant is therefore required to make some sufficient showing of the grounds for the denial before the plaintiff is required to introduce evidence. The defendant's evidence need not be sufficient to require a directed verdict, but it must be enough to support the denial by permitting a finding in the defendant's favor. Until introduction of such evidence the presumption requires a finding for the plaintiff. Once such evidence is introduced the burden of establishing the signature by a preponderance of the total evidence is on the plaintiff. The presumption does not arise if the action is to enforce the obligation of a purported signer who has died or become incompetent before the evidence is required, and so is disabled from obtaining or introducing it. "Action" is defined in Section 1–201 and includes a claim asserted against the estate of a deceased or an incompetent.

The last sentence of subsection (a) is a new provision that is necessary to take into account Section 3–402(a) that allows an undisclosed principal to be liable on an instrument signed by an authorized representative. In that case the person enforcing the instrument must prove that the undisclosed principal is liable.

2. Subsection (b) restates former Section 3–307(2) and (3). Once signatures are proved or admitted a holder, by mere production of the instrument, proves "entitlement to enforce the instrument" because under Section 3–301 a holder is a person entitled to enforce the instrument. Any other person in possession of an instrument may recover only if that person has the rights of a holder. Section 3–301. That person must prove a transfer giving that person such rights under Section 3–203(b) or that such rights were obtained by subrogation or succession.

If a plaintiff producing the instrument proves entitlement to enforce the instrument, either as a holder or a person with rights of a holder, the plaintiff is entitled to recovery unless the defendant proves a defense or claim in recoupment. Until proof of a defense or claim in recoupment is made, the issue as to whether the plaintiff has rights of a holder in due course does not arise. In the absence of a defense or claim in recoupment, any person entitled to enforce the instrument is entitled to recover. If a defense or claim in recoupment is proved, the plaintiff may seek to cut off the defense or claim in recoupment by proving that the plaintiff is a holder in due course or that the plaintiff has rights of a holder in due course under Section 3–203(b) or by subrogation or succession. All elements of Section 3–302(a) must be proved.

Nothing in this section is intended to say that the plaintiff must necessarily prove rights as a holder in due course. The plaintiff may elect to introduce no further evidence, in which case a verdict may be directed for the plaintiff or the defendant, or the issue of the defense or claim in recoupment may be left to the trier of fact, according to the weight and sufficiency of the defendant's evidence. The plaintiff may elect to rebut the defense or claim in recoupment by proof to the contrary, in which case a verdict may be directed for either party or the issue may be for the trier of fact. Subsection (b) means only that if the plaintiff claims the rights of a holder in due course against the defense or claim in recoupment, the plaintiff has the burden of proof on that issue.

§ 3309. Enforcement of instrument by person without possession

(a) A person not in possession of an instrument is entitled to enforce the instrument if (1) the person was in possession of the instrument and entitled to enforce it when loss of possession occurred, (2) the loss of possession was not the result of a transfer by the person or a lawful seizure, and (3) the person cannot reasonably obtain possession of the instrument because the instrument was destroyed, its whereabouts cannot be determined, or it is in the wrongful possession of an unknown person or a person that cannot be found or is not amenable to service of process.

(b) A person seeking enforcement of an instrument under subdivision (a) shall prove the terms of the instrument and the person's right to enforce the instrument. If that proof is made, Section 3308 applies to the case as if the person seeking enforcement had produced the instrument. The court may not enter judgment in favor of the person seeking enforcement unless it finds that the person required to pay the instrument is adequately protected against loss that might occur by reason of a claim by another person to enforce the instrument. Adequate protection may be provided by any reasonable means. *(Added by Stats.1992, c. 914 (S.B.833), § 6.)*

Uniform Commercial Code Comment
1992 Addition

Section 3–309 is a modification of former Section 3–804. The rights stated are those of "a person entitled to enforce the instrument" at the time of loss rather than those of an "owner" as in former Section 3–804. Under subsection (b), judgment to enforce the instrument cannot be given unless the court finds that the defendant will be adequately protected against a claim to the instrument by a holder that may appear at some later time. The court is given discretion in determining how adequate protection is to be assured. Former Section 3–804 allowed the court to "require security indemnifying the defendant against loss." Under Section 3–309 adequate protection is a flexible concept. For example, there is substantial risk that a holder in due course may make a demand for payment if the instrument was payable to bearer when it was lost or stolen. On the other hand if the instrument was payable to the person who lost the instrument and that person did not indorse the instrument, no other person could be a holder of the instrument. In some cases there is risk of loss only if there is doubt about whether the facts alleged by the person who lost the instrument are true. Thus, the type of adequate protection that is reasonable in the circumstances may depend on the degree of certainty about the facts in the case.

Cross References

Enforcement of lost, destroyed, or wrongfully possessed cashier's check, teller's check or certified check, see Commercial Code § 3312.
Person entitled to enforce instrument, definition, see Commercial Code § 3301.

§ 3310. Effect of instrument on obligation for which it was taken

(a) Unless otherwise agreed, if a certified check, cashier's check, or teller's check is taken for an obligation, the obligation is discharged to the same extent discharge would result if an amount of money equal to the amount of the instrument were taken in payment of the obligation. Discharge of the obligation does not affect any liability that the obligor may have as an indorser of the instrument.

(b) Unless otherwise agreed and except as provided in subdivision (a), if a note or an uncertified check is taken for an obligation, the obligation is suspended to the same extent the obligation would be discharged if an amount of money equal to the amount of the instrument were taken, and the following rules apply:

(1) In the case of an uncertified check, suspension of the obligation continues until dishonor of the check or until it is paid or certified. Payment or certification of the check results in discharge of the obligation to the extent of the amount of the check.

(2) In the case of a note, suspension of the obligation continues until dishonor of the note or until it is paid. Payment of the note results in discharge of the obligation to the extent of the payment.

(3) Except as provided in paragraph (4), if the check or note is dishonored and the obligee of the obligation for which the instrument was taken is the person entitled to enforce the instrument, the obligee may enforce either the instrument or the obligation. In the case of an instrument of a third person which is negotiated to the obligee by the obligor, discharge of the obligor on the instrument also discharges the obligation.

(4) If the person entitled to enforce the instrument taken for an obligation is a person other than the obligee, the obligee may not enforce the obligation to the extent the obligation is suspended. If the obligee is the person entitled to enforce the instrument but no longer has possession of it because it was lost, stolen, or destroyed, the obligation may not be enforced to the extent of the amount payable on the instrument, and to that extent the obligee's rights against the obligor are limited to enforcement of the instrument.

(c) If an instrument other than one described in subdivision (a) or (b) is taken for an obligation, the effect is (1) that stated in subdivision (a) if the instrument is one on which a bank is liable as maker or acceptor, or (2) that stated in subdivision (b) in any other case. *(Added by Stats.1992, c. 914 (S.B.833), § 6.)*

Uniform Commercial Code Comment
1992 Addition

1. Section 3–310 is a modification of former Section 3–802. As a practical matter, application of former Section 3–802 was limited to cases in which a check or a note was given for an obligation. Subsections (a) and (b) of Section 3–310 are therefore stated in terms of checks and notes in the interests of clarity. Subsection (c) covers the rare cases in which some other instrument is given to pay an obligation.

2. Subsection (a) deals with the case in which a certified check, cashier's check or teller's check is given in payment of an obligation. In that case the obligation is discharged unless there is an agreement to the contrary. Subsection (a) drops the exception in former Section 3–802 for cases in which there is a right of recourse on the instrument against the obligor. Under former Section 3–802(1)(a) the obligation was not discharged if there was a right of recourse on the instrument against the obligor. Subsection (a) changes this result. The underlying obligation is discharged, but any right of recourse on the instrument is preserved.

3. Subsection (b) concerns cases in which an uncertified check or a note is taken for an obligation. The typical case is that in which a buyer pays for goods or services by giving the seller the buyer's personal check, or in which the buyer signs a note for the purchase price. Subsection (b) also applies to the uncommon cases in which a check or note of a third person is given in payment of the obligation. Subsection (b) preserves the rule under former Section 3–802(1)(b) that the buyer's obligation to pay the price is suspended, but subsection (b) spells out the effect more precisely. If the check or note is dishonored, the seller may sue on either the dishonored instrument or the contract of sale if the seller has possession of the instrument and is the person entitled to enforce it. If the right to enforce the instrument is held by somebody other than the seller, the seller can't enforce the right to payment of the price under the sales contract because that right is represented by the instrument which is enforceable by somebody else. Thus, if the seller sold the note or the check to a holder and has not reacquired it after dishonor, the only right that survives is the right to enforce the instrument.

The last sentence of subsection (b)(3) applies to cases in which an instrument of another person is indorsed over to the obligee in payment of the obligation. For example, Buyer delivers an uncertified personal check of X payable to the order of Buyer to Seller in payment of the price of goods. Buyer indorses the check over to Seller. Buyer is liable on the check as indorser. If Seller neglects to present the check for payment or to deposit it for collection within 30 days of the indorsement, Buyer's liability as indorser is discharged. Section 3–415(e). Under the last sentence of Section 3–310(b)(3) Buyer is also discharged on the obligation to pay for the goods.

4. There was uncertainty concerning the applicability of former Section 3–802 to the case in which the check given for the obligation was stolen from the payee, the payee's signature was forged, and the forger obtained payment. The last sentence of subsection (b)(4) addresses this issue. If the payor bank pays a holder, the drawer is discharged on the underlying obligation because the check was paid. Subsection (b)(1). If the payor bank pays a person not entitled to enforce the instrument, as in the hypothetical case, the suspension of the underlying obligation continues because the check has not been paid. Section 3–602(a). The payee's cause of action is against the depositary bank or payor bank in conversion under Section 3–420 or against the drawer under Section 3–309. In the latter case, the drawer's obligation under Section 3–414(b) is triggered by dishonor which occurs because the check is unpaid. Presentment for payment to the drawee is excused under Section 3–504(a)(i) and, under Section 3–502(e), dishonor occurs without presentment if the check is not paid. The payee cannot merely ignore the instrument and sue the drawer on the underlying contract. This would impose on the drawer the risk that the check when stolen was indorsed in blank or to bearer.

A similar analysis applies with respect to lost instruments that have not been paid. If a creditor takes a check of the debtor in payment of an obligation, the obligation is suspended under the introductory paragraph of subsection (b). If the creditor then loses the check, what are the creditor's rights? The creditor can request the debtor to issue a new check and in many cases, the debtor will issue a replacement check after stopping payment on the lost check. In that case both the debtor and creditor are protected. But the debtor is not obliged to issue a new check. If the debtor refuses to issue a replacement check, the last sentence of subsection (b)(4) applies. The creditor may not enforce the obligation of debtor for which the check was taken. The creditor may assert only rights on the check. The creditor can proceed under Section 3–309 to enforce the obligation of the debtor, as drawer, to pay the check.

5. Subsection (c) deals with rare cases in which other instruments are taken for obligations. If a bank is the obligor on the instrument, subsection (a) applies and the obligation is discharged. In any other case subsection (b) applies.

§ 3311. Satisfaction of claim by use of instrument

(a) If a person against whom a claim is asserted proves that (1) that person in good faith tendered an instrument to the claimant as full satisfaction of the claim, (2) the amount of the claim was unliquidated or subject to a bona fide dispute, and (3) the claimant obtained payment of the instrument, the following subdivisions apply.

(b) Unless subdivision (c) applies, the claim is discharged if the person against whom the claim is asserted proves that the instrument or an accompanying written communication contained a conspicuous statement to the effect that the instrument was tendered as full satisfaction of the claim.

(c) Subject to subdivision (d), a claim is not discharged under subdivision (b) if either of the following applies:

(1) The claimant, if an organization, proves that (A) within a reasonable time before the tender, the claimant sent a conspicuous statement to the person against whom the claim is asserted that communications concerning disputed debts, including an instrument tendered as full satisfaction of a debt, are to be sent to a designated person, office, or place, and (B) the instrument or accompanying communication was not received by that designated person, office, or place.

(2) The claimant, whether or not an organization, proves that within 90 days after payment of the instrument, the claimant tendered repayment of the amount of the instrument to the person against whom the claim is asserted. This paragraph does not apply if the claimant is an organization that sent a statement complying with subparagraph (A) of paragraph (1).

(d) A claim is discharged if the person against whom the claim is asserted proves that within a reasonable time before collection of the instrument was initiated, the claimant, or an agent of the claimant having direct responsibility with respect to the disputed obligation, knew that the instrument was tendered in full satisfaction of the claim. *(Added by Stats.1992, c. 914 (S.B. 833), § 6.)*

Uniform Commercial Code Comment
1992 Addition

1. This section deals with an informal method of dispute resolution carried out by use of a negotiable instrument. In the typical case there is a dispute concerning the amount that is owed on a claim.

Case #1. The claim is for the price of goods or services sold to a consumer who asserts that he or she is not obliged to pay the full price for which the consumer was billed because of a defect or breach of warranty with respect to the goods or services.

Case #2. A claim is made on an insurance policy. The insurance company alleges that it is not liable under the policy for the amount of the claim.

In either case the person against whom the claim is asserted may attempt an accord and satisfaction of the disputed claim by tendering a check to the claimant for some amount less than the full amount claimed by the claimant. A statement will be included on the check or in a communication accompanying the check to the effect that the check is offered as full payment or full satisfaction of the claim. Frequently, there is also a statement to the effect that obtaining payment of the check is an agreement by the claimant to a settlement of the dispute for the amount tendered. Before enactment of revised Article 3, the case law was in conflict over the question of whether obtaining payment of the check had the effect of an agreement to the settlement proposed by the debtor. This issue was governed by a common law rule, but some courts hold that the common law was modified by former Section 1–207 which they interpreted as applying to full settlement checks.

2. Comment d. to Restatement of Contracts, Section 281 discusses the full satisfaction check and the applicable common law rule. In a case like Case #1, the buyer can propose a settlement of the disputed bill by a clear notation on the check indicating that the check is tendered as full satisfaction of the bill. Under the common law rule the seller, by obtaining payment of the check accepts the offer of compromise by the buyer. The result is the same if the seller adds a notation to the check indicating that the check is accepted under protest or in only partial satisfaction of the claim. Under the common law rule the seller can refuse the check or can accept it subject to the condition stated by the buyer, but the seller can't accept the check and refuse to be bound by the condition. The rule applies only to an unliquidated claim or a claim disputed in good faith by the buyer. The dispute in the courts was whether Section 1–207 changed the common law rule. The Restatement states that section "need not be read as changing this well-established rule."

3. As part of the revision of Article 3, Section 1–207 has been amended to add subsection (2) stating that Section 1–207 "does not apply to an accord and satisfaction." Because of that amendment and revised Article 3, Section 3–311 governs full satisfaction checks. Section 3–311 follows the common law rule with some minor variations to reflect modern business conditions. In cases covered by Section 3–311 there will often be an individual on one side of the dispute and a business organization on the other. This section is not designed to favor either the individual or the business organization. In Case #1 the person seeking the accord and satisfaction is an individual. In Case #2 the person seeking the accord and satisfaction is an insurance company. Section 3–311 is based on a belief that the common law rule produces a fair result and that informal dispute resolution by full satisfaction checks should be encouraged.

4. Subsection (a) states three requirements for application of Section 3–311. "Good faith" in subsection (a)(i) is defined in Section 3–103(a)(4) as not only honesty in fact, but the observance of reasonable commercial standards of fair dealing. The meaning of "fair dealing" will depend upon the facts in the particular case. For example, suppose an insurer tenders a check in settlement of a claim for personal injury in an accident clearly covered by the insurance policy. The claimant is necessitous and the amount of the check is very small in relationship to the extent of the injury and the amount recoverable under the policy. If the trier of fact determines that the insurer was taking unfair advantage of the claimant, an accord and satisfaction would not result from payment of the check because of the absence of good faith by the insurer in making the tender. Another example of lack of good faith is found in the practice of some business debtors in routinely printing full satisfaction language on their check stocks so that all or a large part of the debts of the debtor are paid by checks bearing the full satisfaction language, whether or not there is any dispute with the creditor. Under such a practice the claimant cannot be sure whether a tender in full satisfaction is or is not being made. Use of a check on which full satisfaction language was affixed routinely pursuant to such a business practice may prevent an accord and satisfaction on the ground that the check was not tendered in good faith under subsection (a)(i).

Section 3–311 does not apply to cases in which the debt is a liquidated amount and not subject to a bona fide dispute. Subsection (a)(ii). Other law applies to cases in which a debtor is seeking discharge of such a debt by paying less than the amount owed. For the purpose of subsection (a)(iii) obtaining acceptance of a check is considered to be obtaining payment of the check.

The person seeking the accord and satisfaction must prove that the requirements of subsection (a) are met. If that person also proves that the statement required by subsection (b) was given, the claim is discharged unless subsection (c) applies. Normally the statement required by subsection (b) is written on the check. Thus, the canceled check can be used to prove the statement as well as the fact that the claimant obtained payment of the check. Subsection (b) requires a "conspicuous" statement that the instrument was tendered in full satisfaction of the claim. "Conspicuous" is defined in Section 1–201(10). The statement is conspicuous if "it is so written that a reasonable person against whom it is to operate ought to have noticed it." If the claimant can reasonably be expected to examine the check, almost any statement on the check should be noticed and is therefore conspicuous. In cases in which the claimant is an individual the claimant will receive the check and will normally indorse it. Since the statement concerning tender in full satisfaction normally will appear above the space provided for the claimant's indorsement of the check, the claimant "ought to have noticed" the statement.

5. Subsection (c)(1) is a limitation on subsection (b) in cases in which the claimant is an organization. It is designed to protect the claimant against inadvertent accord and satisfaction. If the claimant is an organization payment of the check might be obtained without notice to the personnel of the organization concerned with the disputed claim. Some business organizations have claims against very large numbers of customers. Examples are department stores, public utilities and the like. These claims are normally paid by checks sent by customers to a designated office at which clerks employed by the claimant or a bank acting for the claimant process the checks and record the amounts paid. If the processing office is not designed to deal with communications extraneous to recording the amount of the check and the account number of the customer, payment of a full satisfaction check can easily be obtained without knowledge by the claimant of the existence of the full satisfaction statement. This is particularly true if the statement is written on the reverse side of the check in the area in which indorsements are usually written. Normally, the clerks of the claimant have no reason to look at the reverse side of checks. Indorsement by the claimant normally is done by mechanical means or there may be no indorsement at all. Section 4–205(a). Subsection (c)(1) allows the claimant to protect itself by advising customers by a conspicuous statement that communications regarding disputed debts must be sent to a particular person, office, or place. The statement must be given to the customer within a reasonable time before the tender is made. This requirement is designed to assure that the customer has reasonable notice that the full satisfaction check must be sent to a particular place. The reasonable time requirement could be satisfied by a notice on the billing statement sent to the customer. If the full satisfaction check is sent to the designated destination and the check is paid, the claim is discharged. If the claimant proves that the check was not received at the designated destination the claim is not discharged unless subsection (d) applies.

6. Subsection (c)(2) is also designed to prevent inadvertent accord and satisfaction. It can be used by a claimant other than an organization or by a claimant as an alternative to subsection (c)(1). Some organizations may be reluctant to use subsection (c)(1) because it may result in confusion of customers that causes checks to be routinely sent to the special designated person, office, or place. Thus, much of the benefit of rapid processing of checks may be lost. An organization that chooses not to send a notice complying with subsection (c)(1)(i) may prevent an inadvertent accord and satisfaction by complying with subsection (c)(2). If the claimant discovers that it has obtained payment of a full satisfaction check, it may prevent an accord and satisfaction if, within 90 days of the payment of the check, the claimant tenders repayment of the amount of the check to the person against whom the claim is asserted.

7. Subsection (c) is subject to subsection (d). If a person against whom a claim is asserted proves that the claimant obtained payment of a check known to have been tendered in full satisfaction of the claim by "the claimant or an agent of the claimant having direct responsibility with respect to the disputed obligation," the claim is discharged even if (i) the check was not sent to the person, office, or place required by a notice complying with subsection (c)(1), or (ii) the claimant tendered repayment of the amount of the check in compliance with subsection (c)(2).

A claimant knows that a check was tendered in full satisfaction of a claim when the claimant "has actual knowledge" of that fact. Section 1–201(25). Under Section 1–201(27), if the claimant is an organization, it has knowledge that a check was tendered in full satisfaction of the claim when that fact is

"brought to the attention of the individual conducting that transaction, and in any event when it would have been brought to his attention if the organization had exercised due diligence. An organization exercises due diligence if it maintains reasonable routines for communicating significant information to the person conducting the transaction and there is reasonable compliance with the routines. Due diligence does not require an individual acting for the organization to communicate information unless such communication is part of his regular duties or unless he has reason to know of the transaction and that the transaction would be materially affected by the information."

With respect to an attempted accord and satisfaction the "individual conducting that transaction" is an employee or other agent of the organization having direct responsibility with respect to the dispute.

For example, if the check and communication are received by a collection agency acting for the claimant to collect the disputed claim, obtaining payment of the check will result in an accord and satisfaction even if the claimant gave notice, pursuant to subsection (c)(1), that full satisfaction checks be sent to some other office. Similarly, if a customer asserting a claim for breach of warranty with respect to defective goods purchased in a retail outlet of a large chain store delivers the full satisfaction check to the manager of the retail outlet at which the goods were purchased, obtaining payment of the check will also result in an accord and satisfaction. On the other hand, if the check is mailed to the chief executive officer of the chain store subsection (d) would probably not be satisfied. The chief executive officer of a large corporation may have general responsibility for operations of the company, but does not normally have direct responsibility for resolving a small disputed bill to a customer. A check for a relatively small amount mailed to a high executive officer of a large organization is not likely to receive the executive's personal attention. Rather, the check would normally be routinely sent to the appropriate office for deposit and credit to the customer's account. If the check does receive the personal attention of the high executive officer and the officer is aware of the full-satisfaction language, collection of the check will result in an accord and satisfaction because subsection (d) applies. In this case the officer has assumed direct responsibility with respect to the disputed transaction.

If a full satisfaction check is sent to a lock box or other office processing checks sent to the claimant, it is irrelevant whether the clerk processing the check did or did not see the statement that the check was tendered as full satisfaction of the claim. Knowledge of the clerk is not imputed to the organization because the clerk has no responsibility with respect to an accord and satisfaction. Moreover, there is no failure of "due diligence" under Section 1–201(27) if the claimant does not require its clerks to look for full satisfaction statements on checks or accompanying communications. Nor is there any duty of the claimant to assign that duty to its clerks. Section 3–311(c) is intended to allow a claimant to avoid an inadvertent accord and satisfaction by complying with either subsection (c)(1) or (2) without burdening the check-processing operation with extraneous and wasteful additional duties.

8. In some cases the disputed claim may have been assigned to a finance company or bank as part of a financing arrangement with respect to accounts receivable. If the account debtor was notified of the assignment, the claimant is the assignee of the account receivable and the "agent of the claimant" in subsection (d) refers to an agent of the assignee.

Cross References

Check or draft tendered in full discharge of disputed claim, effect of acceptance, see Civil Code § 1526.

§ 3312. Enforcement of claim to amount of a check

(a) In this section:

(1) "Check" means a cashier's check, teller's check, or certified check.

(2) "Claimant" means a person who claims the right to receive the amount of a cashier's check, teller's check, or certified check that was lost, destroyed, or stolen.

(3) "Declaration of loss" means a written statement, made under penalty of perjury, to the effect that (i) the declarer lost possession of a check, (ii) the declarer is the drawer or payee of the check, in the case of a certified check, or the remitter or payee of the check, in the case of a cashier's check or teller's check, (iii) the loss of possession was not the result of a transfer by the declarer or a lawful seizure, and (iv) the declarer cannot reasonably obtain possession of the check because the check was destroyed, its whereabouts cannot be determined, or it is in the wrongful possession of an unknown person or a person that cannot be found or is not amenable to service of process.

§ 3312

(4) "Obligated bank" means the issuer of a cashier's check or teller's check or the acceptor of a certified check.

(b) A claimant may assert a claim to the amount of a check by a communication to the obligated bank describing the check with reasonable certainty and requesting payment of the amount of the check, if (i) the claimant is the drawer or payee of a certified check or the remitter or payee of a cashier's check or teller's check, (ii) the communication contains or is accompanied by a declaration of loss of the claimant with respect to the check, (iii) the communication is received at a time and in a manner affording the bank a reasonable time to act on it before the check is paid, and (iv) the claimant provides reasonable identification if requested by the obligated bank. Delivery of a declaration of loss is a warranty of the truth of the statements made in the declaration. The warranty is made to the obligated bank and any person entitled to enforce the check. If a claim is asserted in compliance with this subdivision, the following rules apply:

(1) The claim becomes enforceable at the later of (i) the time the claim is asserted, or (ii) the 90th day following the date of the check, in the case of a cashier's check or teller's check, or the 90th day following the date of the acceptance, in the case of a certified check.

(2) Until the claim becomes enforceable, it has no legal effect and the obligated bank may pay the check or, in the case of a teller's check, may permit the drawee to pay the check. Payment to a person entitled to enforce the check discharges all liability of the obligated bank with respect to the check.

(3) If the claim becomes enforceable before the check is presented for payment, the obligated bank is not obliged to pay the check.

(4) When the claim becomes enforceable, the obligated bank becomes obliged to pay the amount of the check to the claimant if payment of the check has not been made to a person entitled to enforce the check. Subject to paragraph (1) of subdivision (a) of Section 4302, payment to the claimant discharges all liability of the obligated bank with respect to the check.

(c) If the obligated bank pays the amount of a check to a claimant under paragraph (4) of subdivision (b) and, after the claim became enforceable, the check is presented for payment by a person having rights of a holder in due course, the claimant is obliged to (i) refund the payment to the obligated bank if the check is paid, or (ii) pay the amount of the check to the person having rights of a holder in due course if the check is dishonored.

(d) If a claimant has the right to assert a claim under subdivision (b) and is also a person entitled to enforce a cashier's check, teller's check, or certified check which is lost, destroyed, or stolen, the claimant may assert rights with respect to the check either under this section or Section 3309. *(Added by Stats.1992, c. 914 (S.B.833), § 6.)*

Uniform Commercial Code Comment
1992 Addition

1. This section applies to cases in which a cashier's check, teller's check, or certified check is lost, destroyed, or stolen. In one typical case a customer of a bank closes his or her account and takes a cashier's check or teller's check of the bank as payment of the amount of the account. The customer may be moving to a new area and the check is to be used to open a bank account in that area. In such a case the check will normally be payable to the customer. In another typical case a cashier's check or teller's check is bought from a bank for the purpose of paying some obligation of the buyer of the check. In such a case the check may be made payable to the customer and then negotiated to the creditor by indorsement. But often, the payee of the check is the creditor. In the latter case the customer is a remitter. The section covers loss of the check by either the remitter or the payee. The section also covers loss of a certified check by either the drawer or payee.

Under Section 3–309 a person seeking to enforce a lost, destroyed, or stolen cashier's check or teller's check may be required by the court to give adequate protection to the issuing bank against loss that might occur by reason of the claim by another person to enforce the check. This might require the posting of an expensive bond for the amount of the check. Moreover, Section 3–309 applies only to a person entitled to enforce the check. It does not apply to a remitter of a cashier's check or teller's check or to the drawer of a certified check. Section 3–312 applies to both. The purpose of Section 3–312 is to offer a person who loses such a check a means of getting refund of the amount of the check within a reasonable period of time without the expense of posting a bond and with full protection of the obligated bank.

2. A claim to the amount of a lost, destroyed, or stolen cashier's check, teller's check, or certified check may be made under subsection (b) if the following requirements of that subsection are met. First, a claim may be asserted only by the drawer or payee of a certified check or the remitter or payee of a cashier's check or teller's check. An indorsee of a check is not covered because the indorsee is not an original party to the check or a remitter. Limitation to an original party or remitter gives the obligated bank the ability to determine, at the time it becomes obligated on the check, the identity of the person or persons who can assert a claim with respect to the check. The bank is not faced with having to determine the rights of some person who was not a party to the check at that time or with whom the bank had not dealt. If a cashier's check is issued to the order of the person who purchased it from the bank and that person indorses it over to a third person who loses the check, the third person may assert rights to enforce the check under Section 3–309 but has no rights under Section 3–312.

Second, the claim must be asserted by a communication to the obligated bank describing the check with reasonable certainty and requesting payment of the amount of the check. "Obligated bank" is defined in subsection (a)(4). Third, the communication must be received in time to allow the obligated bank to act on the claim before the check is paid, and the claimant must provide reasonable identification if requested. Subsections (b)(iii) and (iv). Fourth, the communication must contain or be accompanied by a declaration of loss described in subsection (b). This declaration is an affidavit or other writing made under penalty of perjury alleging the loss, destruction, or theft of the check and stating that the declarer is a person entitled to assert a claim, i.e. the drawer or payee of a certified check or the remitter or payee of a cashier's check or teller's check.

A claimant who delivers a declaration of loss makes a warranty of the truth of the statements made in the declaration. The warranty is made to the obligated bank and anybody who has a right to enforce the check. If the declaration of loss falsely alleges loss of a cashier's check that did not in fact occur, a holder of the check who was unable to obtain payment because subsection (b)(3) and (4) caused the obligated bank to dishonor the check would have a cause of action against the declarer for breach of warranty.

The obligated bank may not impose additional requirements on the claimant to assert a claim under subsection (b). For example, the obligated bank may not require the posting of a bond or other form of security. Section 3–312(b) states the procedure for asserting claims covered by the section. Thus, procedures that may be stated in other law for stating claims to property do not apply and are displaced within the meaning of Section 1–103.

3. A claim asserted under subsection (b) does not have any legal effect, however, until the date it becomes enforceable, which cannot be

earlier than 90 days after the date of a cashier's check or teller's check or 90 days after the date of acceptance of a certified check. Thus, if a lost check is presented for payment within the 90-day period, the bank may pay a person entitled to enforce the check without regard to the claim and is discharged of all liability with respect to the check. This ensures the continued utility of cashier's checks, teller's checks, and certified checks as cash equivalents. Virtually all such checks are presented for payment within 90 days.

If the claim becomes enforceable and payment has not been made to a person entitled to enforce the check, the bank becomes obligated to pay the amount of the check to the claimant. Subsection (b)(4). When the bank becomes obligated to pay the amount of the check to the claimant, the bank is relieved of its obligation to pay the check. Subsection (b)(3). Thus, any person entitled to enforce the check, including even a holder in due course, loses the right to enforce the check after a claim under subsection (b) becomes enforceable.

If the obligated bank pays the claimant under subsection (b)(4), the bank is discharged of all liability with respect to the check. The only exception is the unlikely case in which the obligated bank subsequently incurs liability under Section 4-302(a)(1) with respect to the check. For example, Obligated Bank is the issuer of a cashier's check and, after a claim becomes enforceable, it pays the claimant under subsection (b)(4). Later the check is presented to Obligated Bank for payment over the counter. Under subsection (b)(3), Obligated Bank is not obliged to pay the check and may dishonor the check by returning it to the person who presented it for payment. But the normal rules of check collection are not affected by Section 3-312. If Obligated Bank retains the check beyond midnight of the day of presentment without settling for it, it becomes accountable for the amount of the check under Section 4-302(a)(1) even though it had no obligation to pay the check.

An obligated bank that pays the amount of a check to a claimant under subsection (b)(4) is discharged of all liability on the check so long as the assertion of the claim meets the requirements of subsection (b) discussed in Comment 2. This is important in cases of fraudulent declarations of loss. For example, if the claimant falsely alleges a loss that in fact did not occur, the bank, subject to Section 1-203, may rely on the declaration of loss. On the other hand, a claim may be asserted only by a person described in subsection (b)(i). Thus, the bank is discharged under subsection (a)(4) only if it pays such a person. Although it is highly unlikely, it is possible that more than one person could assert a claim under subsection (b) to the amount of a check. Such a case could occur if one of the claimants makes a false declaration of loss. The obligated bank is not required to determine whether a claimant who complies with subsection (b) is acting wrongfully. The bank may utilize procedures outside this Article, such as interpleader, under which the conflicting claims may be adjudicated.

Although it is unlikely that a lost check would be presented for payment after the claimant was paid by the bank under subsection (b)(4), it is possible for it to happen. Suppose the declaration of loss by the claimant fraudulently alleged a loss that in fact did not occur. If the claimant negotiated the check, presentment for payment would occur shortly after negotiation in almost all cases. Thus, a fraudulent declaration of loss is not likely to occur unless the check is negotiated after the 90-day period has already expired or shortly before expiration. In such a case the holder of the check, who may not have noticed the date of the check, is not entitled to payment from the obligated bank if the check is presented for payment after the claim becomes enforceable. Subsection (b)(3). The remedy of the holder who is denied payment in that case is an action against the claimant under subsection (c) if the holder is a holder in due course, or for breach of warranty under subsection (b). The holder would also have common law remedies against the claimant under the law of restitution or fraud.

4. The following cases illustrate the operation of Section 3-312:

Case # 1. Obligated Bank (OB) certified a check drawn by its customer, Drawer (D), payable to Payee (P). Two days after the check was certified, D lost the check and then asserted a claim pursuant to subsection (b). The check had not been presented for payment when D's claim became enforceable 90 days after the check was certified. Under subsection (b)(4), at the time D's claim became enforceable OB became obliged to pay D the amount of the check. If the check is later presented for payment, OB may refuse to pay the check and has no obligation to anyone to pay the check. Any obligation owed by D to P, for which the check was intended as payment, is unaffected because the check was never delivered to P.

Case # 2. Obligated Bank (OB) issued a teller's check to Remitter (R) payable to Payee (P). R delivered the check to P in payment of an obligation. P lost the check and then asserted a claim pursuant to subsection (b). To carry out P's order, OB issued an order pursuant to Section 4-403(a) to the drawee of the teller's check to stop payment of the check effective on the 90th day after the date of the teller's check. The check was not presented for payment. On the 90th day after the date of the teller's check P's claim becomes enforceable and OB becomes obliged to pay P the amount of the check. As in Case # 1, OB has no further liability with respect to the check to anyone. When R delivered the check to P, R's underlying obligation to P was discharged under Section 3-310. Thus, R suffered no loss. Since P received the amount of the check, P also suffered no loss except with respect to the delay in receiving the amount of the check.

Case # 3. Obligated Bank (OB) issued a cashier's check to its customer, Payee (P). Two days after issue, the check was stolen from P who then asserted a claim pursuant to subsection (b). Ten days after issue, the check was deposited by X in an account in Depositary Bank (DB). X had found the check and forged the indorsement of P. DB promptly presented the check to OB and obtained payment on behalf of X. On the 90th day after the date of the check P's claim becomes enforceable and P is entitled to receive the amount of the check from OB. Subsection (b)(4). Although the check was presented for payment before P's claim became enforceable, OB is not discharged. Because of the forged indorsement X was not a holder and neither was OB. Thus, neither is a person entitled to enforce the check (Section 3-301) and OB is not discharged under Section 3-602(a). Thus, under subsection (b)(4), because OB did not pay a person entitled to enforce the check, OB must pay P. OB's remedy is against DB for breach of warranty under Section 4-208(a)(1). As an alternative to the remedy under Section 3-312, P could recover from DB for conversion under Section 3-420(a).

Case # 4. Obligated Bank (OB) issued a cashier's check to its customer, Payee (P). P made an unrestricted blank indorsement of the check and mailed the check to P's bank for deposit to P's account. The check was never received by P's bank. When P discovered the loss, P asserted a claim pursuant to subsection (b). X found the check and deposited it in X's account in Depositary Bank (DB) after indorsing the check. DB presented the check for payment before the end of the 90-day period after its date. OB paid the check. Because of the unrestricted blank indorsement by P, X became a holder of the check. DB also became a holder. Since the check was paid before P's claim became enforceable and payment was made to a person entitled to enforce the check, OB is discharged of all liability with respect to the check. Subsection (b)(2). Thus, P is not entitled to payment from OB. Subsection (b)(4) doesn't apply.

Case # 5. Obligated Bank (OB) issued a cashier's check to its customer, Payee (P). P made an unrestricted blank indorsement of the check and mailed the check to P's bank for deposit to P's account. The check was never received by P's bank. When P discovered the loss, P asserted a claim pursuant to subsection (b). At the end of the 90-day period after the date of the check, OB paid the amount of the check to P under subsection (b)(4). X then found the check and deposited it to X's account in Depositary Bank (DB). DB presented the check to OB for payment. OB is not obliged to pay the check. Subsection (b)(4). If OB dishonors the check, DB's remedy is to charge back X's account. Section 4-214(a). Although P, as an indorser, would normally have liability to DB under Section 3-415(a) because the check was dishonored, P is released from that liability under Section 3-415(e) because collection of the check was initiated more than 30 days after the indorsement. DB has a remedy only against X. A depositary bank that takes a cashier's check that cannot be presented for payment before expiration of the 90-day period after its date is on notice that the check might not be paid because of the possibility of a claim asserted under subsection (b) which would excuse the issuer of the check from paying the check. Thus, the depositary bank cannot safely release funds with respect to the check until it has assurance that the check has been paid. DB cannot be a holder in due course of the check because it took the check when the check was overdue. Section 3-304(a)(2). Thus, DB has no action against P under subsection (c).

Case # 6. Obligated Bank (OB) issued a cashier's check payable to bearer and delivered it to its customer, Remitter (R). R held the check for 90 days and then wrongfully asserted a claim to the amount of the check under subsection (b). The declaration of loss fraudulently stated that the check was lost. R received payment from OB under subsection (b)(4). R then negotiated the check to X for value. X presented the check to OB for payment. Although OB, under subsection (b)(2), was not obliged to pay the check, OB paid X by mistake. OB's teller did not notice that the check was more than 90 days old and was not aware that OB was not obliged to pay the check. If X took the check in good faith, OB may not recover from X. Section 3–418(c). OB's remedy is to recover from R for fraud or for breach of warranty in making a false declaration of loss. Subsection (b).

CHAPTER 4. LIABILITY OF PARTIES

Section
3401. Signature.
3402. Representative's signature.
3403. Unauthorized signatures.
3404. Imposters; fictitious payees.
3405. Fraudulent indorsement by employee; responsibility of employer.
3406. Altered instruments; forged signatures; contributory negligence.
3407. Alteration; effect on obligation.
3408. Liability of drawee.
3409. Acceptance of draft; certified check.
3410. Acceptance varying from terms of draft.
3411. Cashier's checks; teller's checks; certified checks; refusal to pay; liability.
3412. Issuer's obligation.
3413. Acceptor's obligation.
3414. Drawer's obligation.
3415. Indorser's obligation.
3416. Transfer warranties.
3417. Presentment warranties.
3418. Payment or acceptance by mistake.
3419. Instruments signed for accommodation.
3420. Conversion of instrument.

Transitional Provisions

Effective date and transitional provisions for repeal and addition of Division 3 by Stats.1992, c. 914, see Commercial Code § 16101 et seq.

§ 3401. Signature

(a) A person is not liable on an instrument unless (1) the person signed the instrument, or (2) the person is represented by an agent or representative who signed the instrument and the signature is binding on the represented person under Section 3402.

(b) A signature may be made (1) manually or by means of a device or machine, and (2) by the use of any name, including a trade or assumed name, or by a word, mark, or symbol executed or adopted by a person with present intention to authenticate a writing. *(Added by Stats.1992, c. 914 (S.B.833), § 6.)*

California Code Comment

By John A. Bohn and Charles J. Williams

Prior California Law

1. Subdivision (1) continues the rule of the first sentence of former Civil Code § 3099. An undisclosed principal on an instrument signed by an authorized agent may not be sued on the instrument. Although one whose signature does not appear on the instrument is not liable on the instrument, he may be held liable for money had and received based on an implied agreement. Schwaegler Co. v. Marchesotti, 88 Cal. App.2d 738, 199 P.2d 331 (1948).

This rule also applies in the case where an agent signs for an undisclosed principal. See also Commercial Code § 3403(2).

2. Subdivision (2) expands the last sentence of former Civil Code § 3099. As to what may serve as a signature see Official Comment 2.

Subdivision (2) by recognizing other than a written signature is in accord with California law prior to the adoption of the NIL in 1917. The court in Pennington v. Baehr, 48 Cal. 565 (1874) recognized a printed facsimile of the maker's signature as being sufficient to bind him on the instrument. The effect of this decision was continued by former Civil Code § 3099 which provided that the signature "appear" on the instrument. Subdivision (2) now further liberalizes the requirement for a signature by providing that it may be "any word or mark used in lieu of a written signature."

Changes from U.C.C. (1962 Official Text)

3. This is section 3–401 of the Official Text without change.

Uniform Commercial Code Comment
1992 Addition

1. Obligation on an instrument depends on a signature that is binding on the obligor. The signature may be made by the obligor personally or by an agent authorized to act for the obligor. Signature by agents is covered by Section 3–402. It is not necessary that the name of the obligor appear on the instrument, so long as there is a signature that binds the obligor. Signature includes an indorsement.

2. A signature may be handwritten, typed, printed or made in any other manner. It need not be subscribed, and may appear in the body of the instrument, as in the case of "I, John Doe, promise to pay * * *" without any other signature. It may be made by mark, or even by thumb-print. It may be made in any name, including any trade name or assumed name, however false and fictitious, which is adopted for the purpose. Parol evidence is admissible to identify the signer, and when the signer is identified the signature is effective. Indorsement in a name other than that of the indorser is governed by Section 3–204(d).

This section is not intended to affect any other law requiring a signature by mark to be witnessed, or any signature to be otherwise authenticated, or requiring any form of proof.

Uniform Commercial Code Comment

Prior Uniform Statutory Provision:

Section 18, Uniform Negotiable Instruments Law.

Changes: Reworded.

Purposes of Changes: To make it clear that:

1. No one is liable on an instrument unless and until he has signed it. The chief application of the rule has been in cases holding that a principal whose name does not appear on an instrument signed by his agent is not liable on the instrument even though the payee knew when it was issued that it was intended to be the obligation of one who did not sign. The exceptions made as to collateral and virtual acceptances by the original Sections 134 and 135 are now abrogated by the definition of an acceptance and the rules governing its operation. An allonge is part of the instrument to which it is affixed. Section 3–202(2).

Nothing in this section is intended to prevent any liability arising apart from the instrument itself. The party who does not sign may still be liable on the original obligation for which the instrument was given, or for breach of any agreement to sign, or in tort for misrepresentation, or even on an oral guaranty of payment where the statute of frauds is satisfied. He may of course be liable under any separate writing. The provision is not intended to prevent an estoppel to deny that the party has signed, as where the instrument is purchased in good faith reliance upon his assurance that a forged signature is genuine.

2. A signature may be handwritten, typed, printed or made in any other manner. It need not be subscribed, and may appear in the body of the instrument, as in the case of "I, John Doe, promise to pay—" without any other signature. It may be made by mark, or even by thumbprint. It may be made in any name, including any trade name or assumed name, however false and fictitious, which is adopted for the purpose. Parol evidence is admissible to identify the signer, and when he is identified the signature is effective.

This section is not intended to affect any local statute or rule of law requiring a signature by mark to be witnessed, or any signature to be otherwise authenticated, or requiring any form of proof. It is to be read together with the provision under which a person paying or giving value for the instrument may require indorsement in both the right name and the wrong one; and with the provision that the absence of an indorsement in the right name may make an instrument so irregular as to call its ownership into question and put a purchaser upon notice which will prevent his taking as a holder in due course.

Cross References:

Sections 3–202(2), 3–402 through 3–406.
Point 1: Section 3–410.
Point 2: Section 3–203.

Definitional Cross References:

"Person". Section 1–201.
"Instrument". Section 3–102.
"Signed". Section 1–201.
"Written". Section 1–201.

Cross References

Acceptance, definition and operation, see Commercial Code § 3409.
Agent, personal liability of, see Commercial Code § 3101.
Authorized representative, signature, see Commercial Code § 3403.
Impostors, see Commercial Code § 3404.
Instrument, see Commercial Code § 3104.
Negligence contributing to alteration or forged signature, see Commercial Code § 3406.
Negotiation, see Commercial Code § 3202.
Signature as including mark, see Civil Code § 14; Code of Civil Procedure § 17.
Signed, see Commercial Code § 1201.
Unauthorized signature, see Commercial Code § 3403.
Wrong name, see Commercial Code § 3204.

§ 3402. Representative's signature

(a) If a person acting, or purporting to act, as a representative signs an instrument by signing either the name of the represented person or the name of the signer, the represented person is bound by the signature to the same extent the represented person would be bound if the signature were on a simple contract. If the represented person is bound, the signature of the representative is the "authorized signature of the represented person" and the represented person is liable on the instrument, whether or not identified in the instrument.

(b) If a representative signs the name of the representative to an instrument and the signature is an authorized signature of the represented person, the following rules apply:

(1) If the form of the signature shows unambiguously that the signature is made on behalf of the represented person who is identified in the instrument, the representative is not liable on the instrument.

(2) Subject to subdivision (c), if (A) the form of the signature does not show unambiguously that the signature is made in a representative capacity or (B) the represented person is not identified in the instrument, the representative is liable on the instrument to a holder in due course that took the instrument without notice that the representative was not intended to be liable on the instrument. With respect to any other person, the representative is liable on the instrument unless the representative proves that the original parties did not intend the representative to be liable on the instrument.

(c) If a representative signs the name of the representative as drawer of a check without indication of the representative status and the check is payable from an account of the represented person who is identified on the check, the signer is not liable on the check if the signature is an authorized signature of the represented person. *(Added by Stats.1992, c. 914 (S.B.833), § 6.)*

California Code Comment

By John A. Bohn and Charles J. Williams

Prior California Law

1. This section combines and rewords former Civil Code §§ 3098(6) (signature so placed upon instrument that it is not clear in what capacity the person intended to sign is deemed indorser) and 3144 (person signing instrument other than as maker, drawer, or accepter, is deemed an indorser, unless other intent is clearly indicated by appropriate words). Under the NIL parol evidence was not admissible to change the character of the indorsement. Schaeffle v. Nolan, 115 Cal.App.2d 651, 252 P.2d 732, 35 ALR2d 1027 (1953). This result is intended under the Commercial Code. See Official Comment.

Changes from U.C.C. (1962 Official Text)

2. This is section 3–402 of the Official Text without change.

Uniform Commercial Code Comment

1992 Addition

1. Subsection (a) states when the represented person is bound on an instrument if the instrument is signed by a representative. If under the law of agency the represented person would be bound by the act of the representative in signing either the name of the represented person or that of the representative, the signature is the authorized signature of the represented person. Former Section 3–401(1) stated that "no person is liable on an instrument unless his signature appears thereon." This was interpreted as meaning that an undisclosed principal is not liable on an instrument. This interpretation provided an exception to ordinary agency law that binds an undisclosed principal on a simple contract.

It is questionable whether this exception was justified by the language of former Article 3 and there is no apparent policy justification for it. The exception is rejected by subsection (a) which returns to ordinary rules of agency. If P, the principal, authorized A, the agent, to borrow money on P's behalf and A signed A's name to a note without disclosing that the signature was on behalf of P, A is liable on the instrument. But if the person entitled to enforce the note can also prove that P authorized A to sign on P's behalf, why shouldn't P also be liable on the instrument? To recognize the liability of P takes nothing away from the utility of negotiable instruments. Furthermore, imposing liability on P has the merit of making it impossible to have an instrument on which nobody is liable even though it was authorized by P. That result could occur under former Section 3–401(1) if an authorized agent signed "as agent" but the note did not identify the principal. If the dispute was between the agent and the payee of the note, the agent could escape liability on the note by proving that the agent and the payee did not intend that the agent be liable on the note when the note was issued. Former Section 3–403(2)(b). Under the prevailing interpretation of former Section 3–401(1), the principal was not liable on the note under former Section 3–401(1) because the principal's name did not appear on the note. Thus, nobody was liable on the note even though all parties knew that the note was signed by the agent on behalf of the principal. Under Section 3–402(a) the principal would be liable on the note.

2. Subsection (b) concerns the question of when an agent who signs an instrument on behalf of a principal is bound on the instrument. The approach followed by former Section 3–403 was to specify the form of signature that imposed or avoided liability. This approach was unsatisfactory. There are many ways in which there can be ambiguity about a signature. It is better to state a general rule. Subsection (b)(1) states that if the form of the signature unambiguously shows that it is made on behalf of an identified represented person (for example, "P, by A, Treasurer") the agent is not liable. This is a workable standard for a court to apply. Subsection (b)(2) partly changes former Section 3–

§ 3402

403(2). Subsection (b)(2) relates to cases in which the agent signs on behalf of a principal but the form of the signature does not fall within subsection (b)(1). The following cases are illustrative. In each case John Doe is the authorized agent of Richard Roe and John Doe signs a note on behalf of Richard Roe. In each case the intention of the original parties to the instrument is that Roe is to be liable on the instrument but Doe is not to be liable.

Case #1. Doe signs "John Doe" without indicating in the note that Doe is signing as agent. The note does not identify Richard Roe as the represented person.

Case #2. Doe signs "John Doe, Agent" but the note does not identify Richard Roe as the represented person.

Case #3. The name "Richard Roe" is written on the note and immediately below that name Doe signs "John Doe" without indicating that Doe signed as agent.

In each case Doe is liable on the instrument to a holder in due course without notice that Doe was not intended to be liable. In none of the cases does Doe's signature unambiguously show that Doe was signing as agent for an identified principal. A holder in due course should be able to resolve any ambiguity against Doe.

But the situation is different if a holder in due course is not involved. In each case Roe is liable on the note. Subsection (a). If the original parties to the note did not intend that Doe also be liable, imposing liability on Doe is a windfall to the person enforcing the note. Under subsection (b)(2) Doe is prima facie liable because his signature appears on the note and the form of the signature does not unambiguously refute personal liability. But Doe can escape liability by proving that the original parties did not intend that he be liable on the note. This is a change from former Section 3–403(2)(a).

A number of cases under former Article 3 involved situations in which an agent signed the agent's name to a note, without qualification and without naming the person represented, intending to bind the principal but not the agent. The agent attempted to prove that the other party had the same intention. Some of these cases involved mistake, and in some there was evidence that the agent may have been deceived into signing in that manner. In some of the cases the court refused to allow proof of the intention of the parties and imposed liability on the agent based on former Section 3–403(2)(a) even though both parties to the instrument may have intended that the agent not be liable. Subsection (b)(2) changes the result of those cases, and is consistent with Section 3–117 which allows oral or written agreements to modify or nullify apparent obligations on the instrument.

Former Section 3–403 spoke of the represented person being "named" in the instrument. Section 3–402 speaks of the represented person being "identified" in the instrument. This change in terminology is intended to reject decisions under former Section 3–403(2) requiring that the instrument state the legal name of the represented person.

3. Subsection (c) is directed at the check cases. It states that if the check identifies the represented person the agent who signs on the signature line does not have to indicate agency status. Virtually all checks used today are in personalized form which identify the person on whose account the check is drawn. In this case, nobody is deceived into thinking that the person signing the check is meant to be liable. This subsection is meant to overrule cases decided under former Article 3 such as Griffin v. Ellinger, 538 S.W.2d 97 (Texas 1976).

Uniform Commercial Code Comment

Prior Uniform Statutory Provision:

Sections 17(6) and 63, Uniform Negotiable Instruments Law.

Changes: Combined and reworded.

Purposes of Changes: The revised language is intended to say that any ambiguity as to the capacity in which a signature is made must be resolved by a rule of law that it is an indorsement. Parol evidence is not admissible to show any other capacity, except for the purpose of reformation of the instrument as it may be permitted under the rules of the particular jurisdiction. The question is to be determined from the face of the instrument alone, and unless the instrument itself makes it clear that he has signed in some other capacity the signer must be treated as an indorser.

The indication that the signature is made in another capacity must be clear without reference to anything but the instrument. It may be found in the language used. Thus if John Doe signs after "I, John Doe, promise to pay," he is clearly a maker; and "John Doe, witness" is not liable at all. The capacity may be found in any clearly evidenced purpose of the signature, as where a drawee signing in an unusual place on the paper has no visible reason to sign at all unless he is an acceptor. It may be found in usage or custom. Thus by long established practice judicially noticed or otherwise established a signature in the lower right hand corner of an instrument indicates an intent to sign as the maker of a note or the drawer of a draft. Any similar clear indication of an intent to sign in some other capacity may be enough to remove the signature from the application of this section.

Cross Reference:

Section 3–401.

Definitional Cross References:

"Instrument". Section 3–102.
"Signature". Section 3–401.

Cross References

Burden of establishment of liability of defendant as represented party, see Commercial Code § 3308.
Obligation of issuer, drawer and acceptor, see Commercial Code § 3413 et seq.
Instrument, see Commercial Code § 3104.
Liability of indorser, see Commercial Code § 3415.
Manner of signing, see Commercial Code § 3401.

§ 3403. Unauthorized signatures

(a) Unless otherwise provided in this division or Division 4 (commencing with Section 4101), an unauthorized signature is ineffective except as the signature of the unauthorized signer in favor of a person who in good faith pays the instrument or takes it for value. An unauthorized signature may be ratified for all purposes of this division.

(b) If the signature of more than one person is required to constitute the authorized signature of an organization, the signature of the organization is unauthorized if one of the required signatures is lacking.

(c) The civil or criminal liability of a person who makes an unauthorized signature is not affected by any provision of this division which makes the unauthorized signature effective for the purposes of this division. *(Added by Stats.1992, c. 914 (S.B.833), § 6.)*

California Code Comment

By John A. Bohn and Charles J. Williams

Prior California Law

1. Subdivision (1) is substantially the same as former Civil Code § 3100. Cignetti v. American Trust Co., 139 Cal.App.2d 744, 294 P.2d 490 (1956). Former Civil Code § 3100 also applied to ratification of the signature. Volandri v. Hlobil, 170 Cal.App.2d 656, 339 P.2d 218 (1959).

2. Subdivision (2) is substantially the same as former Civil Code § 3101. Unless it is indicated upon the face of the instrument who is the principal, the agent who executed the instrument is personally liable even though authorized by the principal to so execute the instrument. Pratt v. Hopper, 12 Cal.App.2d 291, 55 P.2d 517 (1936). This subdivision assumes that the representative who signs is authorized. If he is not authorized Commercial Code § 3404 applies. See Official Comment 3.

3. Subdivision (3) is new statutory law but is consistent with prior California case law. Charles Nelson Co. v. Morton, 106 Cal.App. 144, 288 Pac. 845 (1930). Earlier California case law was to the contrary, however. Chamberlain v. Pacific Wool-Growing Co., 54 Cal. 103, 5 PCLJ 2 (1880); Hobson v. Hassett, 76 Cal. 203, 18 Pac. 320, 9 Am.St.Rep. 193 (1888).

4. This section also replaces former Civil Code § 3102 which provided that a signature by "procuration" is notice that the agent has only limited authority to sign, and the principal is bound only if the agent in signing acted within the limits of his authority. This provision is not found in the Commercial Code because the English practice of adding "per procuration" to a signature is unknown in the United States. It does not mean that a signature can not have the same effect as set forth in former Civil Code § 3102. Official Comment 4.

Changes from U.C.C. (1962 Official Text)

5. This is section 3–403 of the Official Text without change.

Uniform Commercial Code Comment
1992 Addition

1. "Unauthorized" signature is defined in Section 1–201(43) as one that includes a forgery as well as a signature made by one exceeding actual or apparent authority. Former Section 3–404(1) stated that an unauthorized signature was inoperative as the signature of the person whose name was signed unless that person "is precluded from denying it." Under former Section 3–406 if negligence by the person whose name was signed contributed to an unauthorized signature, that person "is precluded from asserting the * * * lack of authority." Both of these sections were applied to cases in which a forged signature appeared on an instrument and the person asserting rights on the instrument alleged that the negligence of the purported signer contributed to the forgery. Since the standards for liability between the two sections differ, the overlap between the sections caused confusion. Section 3–403(a) deals with the problem by removing the preclusion language that appeared in former Section 3–404.

2. The except clause of the first sentence of subsection (a) states the generally accepted rule that the unauthorized signature, while it is wholly inoperative as that of the person whose name is signed, is effective to impose liability upon the signer or to transfer any rights that the signer may have in the instrument. The signer's liability is not in damages for breach of warranty of authority, but is full liability on the instrument in the capacity in which the signer signed. It is, however, limited to parties who take or pay the instrument in good faith; and one who knows that the signature is unauthorized cannot recover from the signer on the instrument.

3. The last sentence of subsection (a) allows an unauthorized signature to be ratified. Ratification is a retroactive adoption of the unauthorized signature by the person whose name is signed and may be found from conduct as well as from express statements. For example, it may be found from the retention of benefits received in the transaction with knowledge of the unauthorized signature. Although the forger is not an agent, ratification is governed by the rules and principles applicable to ratification of unauthorized acts of an agent.

Ratification is effective for all purposes of this Article. The unauthorized signature becomes valid so far as its effect as a signature is concerned. Although the ratification may relieve the signer of liability on the instrument, it does not of itself relieve the signer of liability to the person whose name is signed. It does not in any way affect the criminal law. No policy of the criminal law prevents a person whose name is forged to assume liability to others on the instrument by ratifying the forgery, but the ratification cannot affect the rights of the state. While the ratification may be taken into account with other relevant facts in determining punishment, it does not relieve the signer of criminal liability.

4. Subsection (b) clarifies the meaning of "unauthorized" in cases in which an instrument contains less than all of the signatures that are required as authority to pay a check. Judicial authority was split on the issue whether the one-year notice period under former Section 4–406(4) (now Section 4–406(f)) barred a customer's suit against a payor bank that paid a check containing less than all of the signatures required by the customer to authorize payment of the check. Some cases took the view that if a customer required that a check contain the signatures of both A and B to authorize payment and only A signed, there was no unauthorized signature within the meaning of that term in former Section 4–406(4) because A's signature was neither unauthorized nor forged. The other cases correctly pointed out that it was the customer's signature at issue and not that of A; hence, the customer's signature was unauthorized if all signatures required to authorize payment of the check were not on the check. Subsection (b) follows the latter line of cases. The same analysis applies if A forged the signature of B.

Because the forgery is not effective as a signature of B, the required signature of B is lacking.

Subsection (b) refers to "the authorized signature of an organization." The definition of "organization" in Section 1–201(28) is very broad. It covers not only commercial entities but also "two or more persons having a joint or common interest." Hence subsection (b) would apply when a husband and wife are both required to sign an instrument.

Uniform Commercial Code Comment

Prior Uniform Statutory Provision:

Sections 19, 20 and 21, Uniform Negotiable Instruments Law.

Changes: Combined and reworded; original Section 21 omitted.

Purposes of Changes:

1. The definition of "representative" in this Act (Section 1–201) includes an officer of a corporation or association, a trustee, an executor or administrator of an estate, or any person empowered to act for another. It is not intended to mean that a trust or an estate is necessarily a legal entity with the capacity to issue negotiable instruments, but merely that if it can issue them they may be signed by the representative.

The power to sign for another may be an express authority, or it may be implied in law or in fact, or it may rest merely upon apparent authority. It may be established as in other cases of representation, and when relevant parol evidence is admissible to prove or to deny it.

2. Subsection (2) applies only to the signature of a representative whose authority to sign for another is established. If he is not authorized his signature has the effect of an unauthorized signature (Section 3–404). Even though he is authorized the principal is not liable on the instrument, under the provisions (Section 3–401) relating to signatures, unless the instrument names him and clearly shows that the signature is made on his behalf.

3. Assuming that Peter Pringle is a principal and Arthur Adams is his agent, an instrument might, for example, bear the following signatures affixed by the agent—

(a) "Peter Pringle", or

(b) "Arthur Adams", or

(c) "Peter Pringle by Arthur Adams, Agent", or

(d) "Arthur Adams, Agent", or

(e) "Peter Pringle Arthur Adams", or

(f) "Peter Pringle Corporation Arthur Adams".

A signature in form (a) does not bind Adams if authorized (Sections 3–401 and 3–404).

A signature as in (b) personally obligates the agent and parol evidence is inadmissible under subsection (2)(a) to disestablish his obligation.

The unambiguous way to make the representation clear is to sign as in (c). Any other definite indication is sufficient, as where the instrument reads "Peter Pringle promises to pay" and it is signed "Arthur Adams, Agent." Adams is not bound if he is authorized (Section 3–404).

Subsection 2(b) adopts the New York (minority) rule of Megowan v. Peterson, 173 N.Y. 1 (1902), in such a case as (d); and adopts the majority rule in such a case as (e). In both cases the section admits parol evidence in litigation between the immediate parties to prove signature by the agent in his representative capacity. Case (f) is subject to the same rule.

4. The original Section 21, covering signatures by "procuration," is omitted. It was based on English practice under which the words "per procuration" added to any signature are understood to mean that the signer is acting under a power of attorney which the holder is free to examine. The holder is thus put on notice of the limited authority, and there can be no apparent authority extending beyond the power of attorney. This meaning of "per procuration" is almost unknown in the United States, and the words are understood by the ordinary banker or attorney to be merely the equivalent of "by." The omission is not intended to suggest that a signature "by procuration" can no longer have the effect which it had under the original Section 21, in any case where a party chooses to use the expression.

Cross References:
   Point 1: Section 1–201.
   Point 2: Sections 3–401(1), 3–404 and 3–405.

Definitional Cross References:
   "Instrument". Section 3–102.
   "Person". Section 1–201.
   "Representative". Section 1–201.
   "Signature". Section 3–401.

Cross References

Agent or broker, warranties by, see Commercial Code § 3417.
Agents in general, see Civil Code § 2019 et seq.
Authority of agents, see Civil Code § 2304 et seq.
Definitions, see Commercial Code § 1201.
Duties of collecting agent, see Civil Code § 2021.
Indorsement in representative capacity, see Commercial Code § 3414.
Instrument, see Commercial Code § 3104.
Liability on instrument, necessity of signature, see Commercial Code § 3401.
Signature, see Commercial Code § 3401.

§ 3404. Imposters; fictitious payees

(a) If an impostor, by use of the mails or otherwise, induces the issuer of an instrument to issue the instrument to the impostor, or to a person acting in concert with the impostor, by impersonating the payee of the instrument or a person authorized to act for the payee, an indorsement of the instrument by any person in the name of the payee is effective as the indorsement of the payee in favor of a person who, in good faith, pays the instrument or takes it for value or for collection.

(b) If (i) a person whose intent determines to whom an instrument is payable (subdivision (a) or (b) of Section 3110) does not intend the person identified as payee to have any interest in the instrument, or (ii) the person identified as payee of an instrument is a fictitious person, the following rules apply until the instrument is negotiated by special indorsement:

(1) Any person in possession of the instrument is its holder.

(2) An indorsement by any person in the name of the payee stated in the instrument is effective as the indorsement of the payee in favor of a person who, in good faith, pays the instrument or takes it for value or for collection.

(c) Under subdivision (a) or (b), an indorsement is made in the name of a payee if (1) it is made in a name substantially similar to that of the payee or (2) the instrument, whether or not indorsed, is deposited in a depositary bank to an account in a name substantially similar to that of the payee.

(d) With respect to an instrument to which subdivision (a) or (b) applies, if a person paying the instrument or taking it for value or for collection fails to exercise ordinary care in paying or taking the instrument and that failure contributes to loss resulting from payment of the instrument, the person bearing the loss may recover from the person failing to exercise ordinary care to the extent the failure to exercise ordinary care contributed to the loss. *(Added by Stats.1992, c. 914 (S.B.833), § 6.)*

California Code Comment
By John A. Bohn and Charles J. Williams

Prior California Law

1. The first portion of subdivision (1) is a rewording of former Civil Code § 3104 which provided that a forged or unauthorized signature was "wholly inoperative, and no right to retain the instrument, . . . to give a discharge . . ., or to enforce payment . . . against any party . . . can be acquired through or under such signature, unless the party, against whom it is sought to enforce such right is precluded from setting up the forgery or want of authority." An estoppel to deny authority may exist where apparent authority exists by virtue of negligence. Walsh v. American Trust Co., 7 Cal.App.2d 654, 47 P.2d 323 (1935). Britton, Bills & Notes (1961) 343.

The language of subdivision (1) providing that an unauthorized signature can be ratified is new statutory law.

An unauthorized signature is defined in Commercial Code § 1201(43) and includes a forgery.

The last clause of subdivision (1) providing that an unauthorized signature is operative in favor of a person who pays the instrument in good faith or takes the instrument for value is new statutory law. Although the unauthorized signature does not operate against the person whose name is signed it is effective to impose liability upon the person who actually signed it and to transfer any rights that the actual signer may have had. Official Comment 2.

2. Subdivision (2) is new statutory law. There is no California decision upon the question of whether a forgery may be ratified although there is conflict in the decisions of other states under the NIL. Britton, Bills & Notes (1961) 342. This subdivision is probably in accord with prior California Law.

The court in The California Bank v. Sayre, 85 Cal. 102, 24 Pac. 713 (1890) held that mere silence in that case did not amount to ratification, but recognized that under certain circumstances failure to repudiate the signature might be ratification of an unauthorized signature. See also Gates v. Bank of America Nat. Trust & Sav. Ass'n, 120 Cal.App.2d 571, 261 P.2d 545 (1953) for a discussion of ratification of unauthorized transactions.

Changes from U.C.C. (1962 Official Text)

3. This is section 3–404 of the Official Text without change.

Uniform Commercial Code Comment
1992 Addition

1. Under former Article 3, the impostor cases were governed by former Section 3–405(1)(a) and the fictitious payee cases were governed by Section 3–405(1)(b). Section 3–404 replaces former Section 3–405(1)(a) and (b) and modifies the previous law in some respects. Former Section 3–405 was read by some courts to require that the indorsement be in the exact name of the named payee. Revised Article 3 rejects this result. Section 3–404(c) requires only that the indorsement be made in a name "substantially similar" to that of the payee. Subsection (c) also recognizes the fact that checks may be deposited without indorsement. Section 4–205(a).

Subsection (a) changes the former law in a case in which the impostor is impersonating an agent. Under former Section 3–405(1)(a), if Impostor impersonated Smith and induced the drawer to draw a check to the order of Smith, Impostor could negotiate the check. If Impostor impersonated Smith, the president of Smith Corporation, and the check was payable to the order of Smith Corporation, the section did not apply. See the last paragraph of Comment 2 to former Section 3–405. In revised Article 3, Section 3–404(a) gives Impostor the power to negotiate the check in both cases.

2. Subsection (b) is based in part on former Section 3–405(1)(b) and in part on N.I.L. § 9(3). It covers cases in which an instrument is payable to a fictitious or nonexisting person and to cases in which the payee is a real person but the drawer or maker does not intend the payee to have any interest in the instrument. Subsection (b) applies to any instrument, but its primary importance is with respect to checks of corporations and other organizations. It also applies to forged check cases. The following cases illustrate subsection (b):

Case #1. Treasurer is authorized to draw checks in behalf of Corporation. Treasurer fraudulently draws a check of Corporation payable to Supplier Co., a non-existent company. Subsection (b) applies because Supplier Co. is a fictitious person and because Treasurer did not intend Supplier Co. to have any interest in the check. Under subsection (b)(1) Treasurer, as the person in possession of the check, becomes the holder of the check. Treasurer indorses the check in the name "Supplier Co." and deposits it in Depositary Bank. Under subsection (b)(2) and (c)(i), the indorsement is effective to make Depositary Bank the holder and therefore a person entitled to enforce the instrument. Section 3–301.

Case #2. Same facts as Case #1 except that Supplier Co. is an actual company that does business with Corporation. If Treasurer intended to steal the check when the check was drawn, the result in Case #2 is the same as the result in Case #1. Subsection (b) applies because Treasurer did not intend Supplier Co. to have any interest in the check. It does not make any difference whether Supplier Co. was or was not a creditor of Corporation when the check was drawn. If Treasurer did not decide to steal the check until after the check was drawn, the case is covered by Section 3–405 rather than Section 3–404(b), but the result is the same. See Case #6 in Comment 3 to Section 3–405.

Case #3. Checks of Corporation must be signed by two officers. President and Treasurer both sign a check of Corporation payable to Supplier Co., a company that does business with Corporation from time to time but to which Corporation does not owe any money. Treasurer knows that no money is owed to Supplier Co. and does not intend that Supplier Co. have any interest in the check. President believes that money is owed to Supplier Co. Treasurer obtains possession of the check after it is signed. Subsection (b) applies because Treasurer is "a person whose intent determines to whom an instrument is payable" and Treasurer does not intend Supplier Co. to have any interest in the check. Treasurer becomes the holder of the check and may negotiate it by indorsing it in the name "Supplier Co."

Case #4. Checks of Corporation are signed by a check-writing machine. Names of payees of checks produced by the machine are determined by information entered into the computer that operates the machine. Thief, a person who is not an employee or other agent of Corporation, obtains access to the computer and causes the check-writing machine to produce a check payable to Supplier Co., a non-existent company. Subsection (b)(ii) applies. Thief then obtains possession of the check. At that point Thief becomes the holder of the check because Thief is the person in possession of the instrument. Subsection (b)(1). Under Section 3–301 Thief, as holder, is the "person entitled to enforce the instrument" even though Thief does not have title to the check and is in wrongful possession of it. Thief indorses the check in the name "Supplier Co." and deposits it in an account in Depositary Bank which Thief opened in the name "Supplier Co." Depositary Bank takes the check in good faith and credits the "Supplier Co." account. Under subsection (b)(2) and (c)(i), the indorsement is effective. Depositary Bank becomes the holder and the person entitled to enforce the check. The check is presented to the drawee bank for payment and payment is made. Thief then withdraws the credit to the account. Although the check was issued without authority given by Corporation, the drawee bank is entitled to pay the check and charge Corporation's account if there was an agreement with Corporation allowing the bank to debit Corporation's account for payment of checks produced by the check-writing machine whether or not authorized. The indorsement is also effective if Supplier Co. is a real person. In that case subsection (b)(i) applies. Under Section 3–110(b) Thief is the person whose intent determines to whom the check is payable, and Thief did not intend Supplier Co. to have any interest in the check. When the drawee bank pays the check, there is no breach of warranty under Section 3–417(a)(1) or 4–208(a)(1) because Depositary Bank was a person entitled to enforce the check when it was forwarded for payment.

Case #5. Thief, who is not an employee or agent of Corporation, steals check forms of Corporation. John Doe is president of Corporation and is authorized to sign checks on behalf of Corporation as drawer. Thief draws a check in the name of Corporation as drawer by forging the signature of Doe. Thief makes the check payable to the order of Supplier Co. with the intention of stealing it. Whether Supplier Co. is a fictitious person or a real person, Thief becomes the holder of the check and the person entitled to enforce it. The analysis is the same as that in Case #4. Thief deposits the check in an account in Depositary Bank which Thief opened in the name "Supplier Co." Thief either indorses the check in a name other than "Supplier Co." or does not indorse the check at all. Under Section 4–205(a) a depositary bank may become holder of a check deposited to the account of a customer if the customer was a holder, whether or not the customer indorses. Subsection (c)(ii) treats deposit to an account in a name substantially similar to that of the payee as the equivalent of indorsement in the name of the payee. Thus, the deposit is an effective indorsement of the check. Depositary Bank becomes the holder of the check and the person entitled to enforce the check. If the check is paid by the drawee bank, there is no breach of warranty under Section 3–417(a)(1) or 4–208(a)(1) because Depositary Bank was a person entitled to enforce the check when it was forwarded for payment and, unless Depositary Bank knew about the forgery of Doe's signature, there is no breach of warranty under Section 3–417(a)(3) or 4–208(a)(3). Because the check was a forged check the drawee bank is not entitled to charge Corporation's account unless Section 3–406 or Section 4–406 applies.

3. In cases governed by subsection (a) the dispute will normally be between the drawer of the check that was obtained by the impostor and the drawee bank that paid it. The drawer is precluded from obtaining recredit of the drawer's account by arguing that the check was paid on a forged indorsement so long as the drawee bank acted in good faith in paying the check. Cases governed by subsection (b) are illustrated by Cases #1 through #5 in Comment 2. In Cases #1, #2, and #3 there is no forgery of the check, thus the drawer of the check takes the loss if there is no lack of good faith by the banks involved. Cases #4 and #5 are forged check cases. Depositary Bank is entitled to retain the proceeds of the check if it didn't know about the forgery. Under Section 3–418 the drawee bank is not entitled to recover from Depositary Bank on the basis of payment by mistake because Depositary Bank took the check in good faith and gave value for the check when the credit given for the check was withdrawn. And there is no breach of warranty under Section 3–417(a)(1) or (3) or 4–208(a)(1) or (3). Unless Section 3–406 applies the loss is taken by the drawee bank if a forged check is paid, and that is the result in Case #5. In Case #4 the loss is taken by Corporation, the drawer, because an agreement between Corporation and the drawee bank allowed the bank to debit Corporation's account despite the unauthorized use of the check-writing machine.

If a check payable to an impostor, fictitious payee, or payee not intended to have an interest in the check is paid, the effect of subsections (a) and (b) is to place the loss on the drawer of the check rather than on the drawee or the Depositary Bank that took the check for collection. Cases governed by subsection (a) always involve fraud, and fraud is almost always involved in cases governed by subsection (b). The drawer is in the best position to avoid the fraud and thus should take the loss. This is true in Case #1, Case #2, and Case #3. But in some cases the person taking the check might have detected the fraud and thus have prevented the loss by the exercise of ordinary care. In those cases, if that person failed to exercise ordinary care, it is reasonable that that person bear loss to the extent the failure contributed to the loss. Subsection (d) is intended to reach that result. It allows the person who suffers loss as a result of payment of the check to recover from the person who failed to exercise ordinary care. In Case #1, Case #2, and Case #3, the person suffering the loss is Corporation, the drawer of the check. In each case the most likely defendant is the depositary bank that took the check and failed to exercise ordinary care. In those cases, the drawer has a cause of action against the offending bank to recover a portion of the loss. The amount of loss to be allocated to each party is left to the trier of fact. Ordinary care is defined in Section 3–103(a)(7). An example of the type of conduct by a depositary bank that could give rise to recovery under subsection (d) is discussed in Comment 4 to Section 3–405. That comment addresses the last sentence of Section 3–405(b) which is similar to Section 3–404(d).

In Case #1, Case #2, and Case #3, there was no forgery of the drawer's signature. But cases involving checks payable to a fictitious payee or a payee not intended to have an interest in the check are often forged check cases as well. Examples are Case #4 and Case #5. Normally, the loss in forged check cases is on the drawee bank that paid the check. Case #5 is an example. In Case #4 the risk with respect to the forgery is shifted to the drawer because of the agreement between the drawer and the drawee bank. The doctrine that prevents a drawee bank from recovering payment with respect to a forged check if the payment was made to a person who took the check for value and in good faith is incorporated into Section 3–418 and Sections 3–417(a)(3) and 4–208(a)(3). This doctrine is based on the assumption that the depositary bank normally has no way of detecting the forgery becau

§ 3404

the drawer is not that bank's customer. On the other hand, the drawee bank, at least in some cases, may be able to detect the forgery by comparing the signature on the check with the specimen signature that the drawee has on file. But in some forged check cases the depositary bank is in a position to detect the fraud. Those cases typically involve a check payable to a fictitious payee or a payee not intended to have an interest in the check. Subsection (d) applies to those cases. If the depositary bank failed to exercise ordinary care and the failure substantially contributed to the loss, the drawer in Case #4 or the drawee bank in Case #5 has a cause of action against the depositary bank under subsection (d). Comment 4 to Section 3–405 can be used as a guide to the type of conduct that could give rise to recovery under Section 3–404(d).

Uniform Commercial Code Comment

Prior Uniform Statutory Provision:

Section 23, Uniform Negotiable Instruments Law.

Changes: Reworded; new provisions.

Purpose of Changes and New Matter: The changes are intended to remove uncertainties arising under the original section:

1. "Unauthorized signature" is a defined term (Section 1–201). It includes both a forgery and a signature made by an agent exceeding his actual or apparent authority.

2. The final clause of subsection (1) is new. It states the generally accepted rule that the unauthorized signature, while it is wholly inoperative as that of the person whose name is signed, is effective to impose liability upon the actual signer or to transfer any rights that he may have in the instrument. His liability is not in damages for breach of a warranty of his authority, but is full liability on the instrument in the capacity in which he has signed. It is, however, limited to parties who take or pay the instrument in good faith; and one who knows that the signature is unauthorized cannot recover from the signer on the instrument.

3. Subsection (2) is new. It settles the conflict which has existed in the decisions as to whether a forgery may be ratified. A forged signature may at least be adopted; and the word "ratified" is used in order to make it clear that the adoption is retroactive, and that it may be found from conduct as well as from express statements. Thus it may be found from the retention of benefits received in the transaction with knowledge of the unauthorized signature; and although the forger is not an agent, the ratification is governed by the same rules and principles as if he were.

This provision makes ratification effective only for the purposes of this Article. The unauthorized signature becomes valid so far as its effect as a signature is concerned. The ratification relieves the actual signer from liability on the signature. It does not of itself relieve him from liability to the person whose name is signed. It does not in any way affect the criminal law. No policy of the criminal law requires that the person whose name is forged shall not assume liability to others on the instrument; but he cannot affect the rights of the state. While the ratification may be taken into account with other relevant facts in determining punishment, it does not relieve the signer of criminal liability.

4. The words "or is precluded from denying it" are retained in subsection (1) to recognize the possibility of an estoppel against the person whose name is signed, as where he expressly or tacitly represents to an innocent purchaser that the signature is genuine; and to recognize the negligence which precludes a denial of the signature.

Cross References:

Sections 3–307, 3–401, 3–403 and 3–405.
Point 1: Section 1–201.
Point 4: Section 3–406.

Definitional Cross References:

"Good faith". Section 1–201.
"Instrument". Section 3–102.
"Person". Section 1–201.
"Rights". Section 1–201.
"Signature". Section 3–401.
"Signed". Section 1–201.

"Unauthorized signature". Section 1–201.
"Value". Section 3–303.

Cross References

Altered instrument, see Commercial Code § 3407.
Burden of establishing signatures validity, see Commercial Code § 3308.
Defective title, see Commercial Code § 3304.
Defense against drawee on claim for breach of warranty by proof of effectiveness of indorsement, see Commercial Code §§ 3417, 4208.
Definitions, see Commercial Code § 1201.
Instrument, see Commercial Code § 3104.
Limitation of action against bank for paying forged check, see Code of Civil Procedure § 340.
Manner of signing, see Commercial Code § 3401.
Negligence, contributing to alteration or forged signature, see Commercial Code § 3406.
Offenses and punishment, see Penal Code § 470 et seq.
Signature, generally, see Commercial Code § 3401.
Unauthorized signature, see Commercial Code § 1201.
Value, see Commercial Code § 3303.

§ 3405. Fraudulent indorsement by employee; responsibility of employer

(a) In this section:

(1) "Employee" includes an independent contractor and employee of an independent contractor retained by the employer.

(2) "Fraudulent indorsement" means (A) in the case of an instrument payable to the employer, a forged indorsement purporting to be that of the employer, or (B) in the case of an instrument with respect to which the employer is the issuer, a forged indorsement purporting to be that of the person identified as payee.

(3) "Responsibility" with respect to instruments means authority (A) to sign or indorse instruments on behalf of the employer, (B) to process instruments received by the employer for bookkeeping purposes, for deposit to an account, or for other disposition, (C) to prepare or process instruments for issue in the name of the employer, (D) to supply information determining the names or addresses of payees of instruments to be issued in the name of the employer, (E) to control the disposition of instruments to be issued in the name of the employer, or (F) to act otherwise with respect to instruments in a responsible capacity. "Responsibility" does not include authority that merely allows an employee to have access to instruments or blank or incomplete instrument forms that are being stored or transported or are part of incoming or outgoing mail, or similar access.

(b) For the purpose of determining the rights and liabilities of a person who, in good faith, pays an instrument or takes it for value or for collection, if an employer entrusted an employee with responsibility with respect to the instrument and the employee or a person acting in concert with the employee makes a fraudulent indorsement of the instrument, the indorsement is effective as the indorsement of the person to whom the instrument is payable if it is made in the name of that person. If the person paying the instrument or taking it for value or for collection fails to exercise ordinary care in paying or taking the instrument and that failure contributes to loss resulting from the fraud, the person bearing the loss may recover from the person failing to exercise ordinary care to the extent the failure to exercise ordinary care contributed to the loss.

(c) Under subdivision (b), an indorsement is made in the name of the person to whom an instrument is payable if (1) it is made in a name substantially similar to the name of that person or (2) the instrument, whether or not indorsed, is deposited in a depositary bank to an account in a name substantially similar to the name of that person. *(Added by Stats.1992, c. 914 (S.B.833), § 6.)*

California Code Comment

By John A. Bohn and Charles J. Williams

Prior California Law

1. This section is consistent with former Civil Code § 3090(3) but extends the rule of that section to additional situations which were not originally covered by it.

2. Former Civil Code § 3090(3) provided that an instrument was payable to bearer "when it is payable to the order of a fictitious or nonexisting or living person not intended to have any interest in it and such fact was known to the person making it so payable or known to his employee or the other agent who supplies the name of such payee . . .". By its express terms former Civil Code § 3090 prior to amendment in 1945 did not apply when the payee was a real person or when the fraudulent employee did not himself sign the check. In Edgington v. Security-First National Bank of Los Angeles, 78 Cal. App.2d 849, 179 P.2d 640 (1947), the court held that an instrument signed by someone other than the dishonest employee was not payable to bearer and the employee could recover against the bank. Section 3090(3) was amended in 1945 to protect the bank in this situation and to put the loss on the corporation which hired the dishonest employee.

This section continues this rule but instead of using the device that an instrument is payable to bearer when it is made out to a fictitious or other person not intended to have any interest in it, the Commercial Code provides that such an indorsement is not a forgery. Under section 3405 an indorsement by anyone using the payee's name will be effective if the person signing it for the maker or drawer intends that the payee have no interest in the instrument or if an agent or employee of the maker or drawer supplied the signer with the name of the payee intending the payee to have no interest in the instrument. This applies whether or not the named payee exists. The instrument does not become bearer paper.

In the typical case, a dishonest corporate employee may arrange for the issuance of checks. These checks might be payable to a nonexistent person or to a real person who is owed nothing by the employer. The employee then indorses the name of the fictitious payee and cashes it. Can the drawee bank which makes payments on these checks charge the drawers account? Under former Civil Code § 3090(3) such a check became a bearer instrument and could be passed by delivery without the necessity for indorsement. Under Commercial Code § 3405 an indorsement is still necessary to negotiation. However, a chain of indorsements which purports to be regular is necessary although any person can effectively indorse in the name of the payee. See California State Bar Committee on the Commercial Code, A Special Report, The Uniform Commercial Code, 37 California State Bar J. 157–159 (March–April 1962).

3. Subdivision (1)(a) is new statutory law and covers a situation not specifically covered by former Civil Code § 3090(3).

There appears to be no case in California which distinguishes between an impostor who worked face to face and one who worked by mail. Official Comment 2 states that this subdivision is intended to reject those decisions under the NIL which made this distinction.

4. Subdivision (1)(b) is a restatement of former Civil Code § 3090(3).

5. Subdivision (1)(c) is new statutory law. It extends the rule of former Civil Code § 3090(3) to include padded payroll cases where the dishonest agent or employee furnishes the officer signing the check with the name of a payee. This is consistent with prior judicial decisions. The cases have held that the question of whether the maker was bound on the instrument turned on the intent of the agent or employee when indorsing. If he intended to make the instrument payable to a fictitious payee it was payable to the bearer under former Civil Code § 3090(3). Union Bank & Trust Co. of Los Angeles v. Security First Nat. Bank of Los Angeles, 8 Cal.2d 303, 65 P.2d 355 (1937); Edgington v. Security First National Bank of Los Angeles, 78 Cal.App.2d 849, 179 P.2d 640.

Subdivision (1)(c) continues this emphasis on intent by providing that the indorsement is effective if the agent or employee intends the payee to have no interest.

6. Subdivision (2) is new. Even though a signature transfers the instrument, this subdivision makes it clear that the signature can be a forgery or subject the signer to civil liability. Official Comment 5.

Changes from U.C.C. (1962 Official Text)

7. This is section 3–405 of the Official Text without change.

Uniform Commercial Code Comment

1992 Addition

1. Section 3–405 is addressed to fraudulent indorsements made by an employee with respect to instruments with respect to which the employer has given responsibility to the employee. It covers two categories of fraudulent indorsements: indorsements made in the name of the employer to instruments payable to the employer and indorsements made in the name of payees of instruments issued by the employer. This section applies to instruments generally but normally the instrument will be a check. Section 3–405 adopts the principle that the risk of loss for fraudulent indorsements by employees who are entrusted with responsibility with respect to checks should fall on the employer rather than the bank that takes the check or pays it, if the bank was not negligent in the transaction. Section 3–405 is based on the belief that the employer is in a far better position to avoid the loss by care in choosing employees, in supervising them, and in adopting other measures to prevent forged indorsements on instruments payable to the employer or fraud in the issuance of instruments in the name of the employer. If the bank failed to exercise ordinary care, subsection (b) allows the employer to shift loss to the bank to the extent the bank's failure to exercise ordinary care contributed to the loss. "Ordinary care" is defined in Section 3–103(a)(7). The provision applies regardless of whether the employer is negligent.

The first category of cases governed by Section 3–405 are those involving indorsements made in the name of payees of instruments issued by the employer. In this category, Section 3–405 includes cases that were covered by former Section 3–405(1)(c). The scope of Section 3–405 in revised Article 3 is, however, somewhat wider. It covers some cases not covered by former Section 3–405(1)(c) in which the entrusted employee makes a forged indorsement to a check drawn by the employer. An example is Case #6 in Comment 3. Moreover, a larger group of employees is included in revised Section 3–405. The key provision is the definition of "responsibility" in subsection (a)(1) which identifies the kind of responsibility delegated to an employee which will cause the employer to take responsibility for the fraudulent acts of that employee. An employer can insure this risk by employee fidelity bonds.

The second category of cases governed by Section 3–405—fraudulent indorsements of the name of the employer to instruments payable to the employer—were covered in former Article 3 by Section 3–406. Under former Section 3–406, the employer took the loss only if negligence of the employer could be proved. Under revised Article 3, Section 3–406 need not be used with respect to forgeries of the employer's indorsement. Section 3–405 imposes the loss on the employer without proof of negligence.

2. With respect to cases governed by former Section 3–405(1)(c), Section 3–405 is more favorable to employers in one respect. The bank was entitled to the preclusion provided by former Section 3–405(1)(c) if it took the check in good faith. The fact that the bank acted negligently did not shift the loss to the bank so long as the bank acted in good faith. Under revised Section 3–405 the loss may be recovered from the bank to the extent the failure of the bank to exercise ordinary care contributed to the loss.

3. Section 3–404(b) and Section 3–405 both apply to cases of employee fraud. Section 3–404(b) is not limited to cases of employee

fraud, but most of the cases to which it applies will be cases of employee fraud. The following cases illustrate the application of Section 3–405. In each case it is assumed that the bank that took the check acted in good faith and was not negligent.

Case #1. Janitor, an employee of Employer, steals a check for a very large amount payable to Employer after finding it on a desk in one of Employer's offices. Janitor forges Employer's indorsement on the check and obtains payment. Since Janitor was not entrusted with "responsibility" with respect to the check, Section 3–405 does not apply. Section 3–406 might apply to this case. The issue would be whether Employer was negligent in safeguarding the check. If not, Employer could assert that the indorsement was forged and bring an action for conversion against the depositary or payor bank under Section 3–420.

Case #2. X is Treasurer of Corporation and is authorized to write checks on behalf of Corporation by signing X's name as Treasurer. X draws a check in the name of Corporation and signs X's name as Treasurer. The check is made payable to X. X then indorses the check and obtains payment. Assume that Corporation did not owe any money to X and did not authorize X to write the check. Although the writing of the check was not authorized, Corporation is bound as drawer of the check because X had authority to sign checks on behalf of Corporation. This result follows from agency law and Section 3–402(a). Section 3–405 does not apply in this case because there is no forged indorsement. X was payee of the check so the indorsement is valid. Section 3–110(a).

Case #3. The duties of Employee, a bookkeeper, include posting the amounts of checks payable to Employer to the accounts of the drawers of the checks. Employee steals a check payable to Employer which was entrusted to Employee and forges Employer's indorsement. The check is deposited by Employee to an account in Depositary Bank which Employee opened in the same name as Employer, and the check is honored by the drawee bank. The indorsement is effective as Employer's indorsement because Employee's duties include processing checks for bookkeeping purposes. Thus, Employee is entrusted with "responsibility" with respect to the check. Neither Depositary Bank nor the drawee bank is liable to Employer for conversion of the check. The same result follows if Employee deposited the check in the account in Depositary Bank without indorsement. Section 4–205(a). Under subsection (c) deposit in a depositary bank in an account in a name substantially similar to that of Employer is the equivalent of an indorsement in the name of Employer.

Case #4. Employee's duties include stamping Employer's unrestricted blank indorsement on checks received by Employer and depositing them in Employer's bank account. After stamping Employer's unrestricted blank indorsement on a check, Employee steals the check and deposits it in Employee's personal bank account. Section 3–405 doesn't apply because there is no forged indorsement. Employee is authorized by Employer to indorse Employer's checks. The fraud by Employee is not the indorsement but rather the theft of the indorsed check. Whether Employer has a cause of action against the bank in which the check was deposited is determined by whether the bank had notice of the breach of fiduciary duty by Employee. The issue is determined under Section 3–307.

Case #5. The computer that controls Employer's check-writing machine was programmed to cause a check to be issued to Supplier Co. to which money was owed by Employer. The address of Supplier Co. was included in the information in the computer. Employee is an accounts payable clerk whose duties include entering information into the computer. Employee fraudulently changed the address of Supplier Co. in the computer data bank to an address of Employee. The check was subsequently produced by the check-writing machine and mailed to the address that Employee had entered into the computer. Employee obtained possession of the check, indorsed it in the name of Supplier Co, and deposited it to an account in Depositary Bank which Employee opened in the name "Supplier Co." The check was honored by the drawee bank. The indorsement is effective under Section 3–405(b) because Employee's duties allowed Employee to supply information determining the address of the payee of the check. An employee that is entrusted with duties that enable the employee to determine the address to which a check is to be sent controls the disposition of the check and facilitates forgery of the indorsement. The employer is held responsible. The drawee may debit the account of Employer for the amount of the check. There is no breach of warranty by Depositary Bank under Section 3–417(a)(1) or 4–208(a)(1).

Case #6. Treasurer is authorized to draw checks in behalf of Corporation. Treasurer draws a check of Corporation payable to Supplier Co., a company that sold goods to Corporation. The check was issued to pay the price of these goods. At the time the check was signed Treasurer had no intention of stealing the check. Later, Treasurer stole the check, indorsed it in the name "Supplier Co." and obtained payment by depositing it to an account in Depositary Bank which Treasurer opened in the name "Supplier Co.". The indorsement is effective under Section 3–405(b). Section 3–404(b) does not apply to this case.

Case #7. Checks of Corporation are signed by Treasurer in behalf of Corporation as drawer. Clerk's duties include the preparation of checks for issue by Corporation. Clerk prepares a check payable to the order of Supplier Co. for Treasurer's signature. Clerk fraudulently informs Treasurer that the check is needed to pay a debt owed to Supplier Co, a company that does business with Corporation. No money is owed to Supplier Co. and Clerk intends to steal the check. Treasurer signs it and returns it to Clerk for mailing. Clerk does not indorse the check but deposits it to an account in Depositary Bank which Clerk opened in the name "Supplier Co.". The check is honored by the drawee bank. Section 3–404(b)(i) does not apply to this case because Clerk, under Section 3–110(a), is not the person whose intent determines to whom the check is payable. But Section 3–405 does apply and it treats the deposit by Clerk as an effective indorsement by Clerk because Clerk was entrusted with responsibility with respect to the check. If Supplier Co. is a fictitious person Section 3–404(b)(ii) applies. But the result is the same. Clerk's deposit is treated as an effective indorsement of the check whether Supplier Co. is a fictitious or a real person or whether money was or was not owing to Supplier Co. The drawee bank may debit the account of Corporation for the amount of the check and there is no breach of warranty by Depositary Bank under Section 3–417(1)(a).

4. The last sentence of subsection (b) is similar to subsection (d) of Section 3–404 which is discussed in Comment 3 to Section 3–404. In Case #5, Case #6, or Case #7 the depositary bank may have failed to exercise ordinary care when it allowed the employee to open an account in the name "Supplier Co.," to deposit checks payable to "Supplier Co." in that account, or to withdraw funds from that account that were proceeds of checks payable to Supplier Co. Failure to exercise ordinary care is to be determined in the context of all the facts relating to the bank's conduct with respect to the bank's collection of the check. If the trier of fact finds that there was such a failure and that the failure substantially contributed to loss, it could find the depositary bank liable to the extent the failure contributed to the loss. The last sentence of subsection (b) can be illustrated by an example. Suppose in Case #5 that the check is not payable to an obscure "Supplier Co." but rather to a well-known national corporation. In addition, the check is for a very large amount of money. Before depositing the check, Employee opens an account in Depositary Bank in the name of the corporation and states to the person conducting the transaction for the bank that Employee is manager of a new office being opened by the corporation. Depositary Bank opens the account without requiring Employee to produce any resolutions of the corporation's board of directors or other evidence of authorization of Employee to act for the corporation. A few days later, the check is deposited, the account is credited, and the check is presented for payment. After Depositary Bank receives payment, it allows Employee to withdraw the credit by a wire transfer to an account in a bank in a foreign country. The trier of fact could find that Depositary Bank did not exercise ordinary care and that the failure to exercise ordinary care contributed to the loss suffered by Employer. The trier of fact could allow recovery by Employer from Depositary Bank for all or part of the loss suffered by Employer.

Uniform Commercial Code Comment

Prior Uniform Statutory Provision:

Section 9(3), Uniform Negotiable Instruments Law.
Changes: Reworded; new provisions.

Purposes of Changes and New Matter:

1. This section enlarges the original subsection to include additional situations which it has not been held to cover. The words "fictitious or nonexisting person" have been eliminated as misleading, since the existence or nonexistence of the named payee is not decisive and is important only as it may bear on the intent that he shall have no interest in the instrument. The instrument is not made payable to bearer and indorsements are still necessary to negotiation. The section however

recognizes as effective indorsement of the types of paper covered no matter by whom made. This solution is thought preferable to making such instruments bearer paper; on the face of things they are payable to order and a subsequent taker should require what purports to be a regular chain of indorsements. On the other hand it is thought to be unduly restrictive to require that the actual indorsement be made by the impostor or other fraudulent actor. In most cases the person whose fraud procured the instrument to be issued will himself indorse; when some other third person indorses it will most probably be a case of theft or a second independent fraud superimposed upon the original fraud. In neither case does there seem to be sufficient reason to reverse the rule of the section. To recapitulate: the instrument does not become bearer paper, a purportedly regular chain in indorsements is required, but any person—first thief, second impostor or third murderer—can effectively indorse in the name of the payee.

2. Subsection (1)(a) is new. It rejects decisions which distinguish between face-to-face imposture and imposture by mail and hold that where the parties deal by mail the dominant intent of the drawer is to deal with the name rather than with the person so that the resulting instrument may be negotiated only by indorsement of the payee whose name has been taken in vain. The result of the distinction has been under some prior law, to throw the loss in the mail imposture forward to a subsequent holder or to the drawee. Since the maker or drawer believes the two to be one and the same, the two intentions cannot be separated, and the "dominant intent" is a fiction. The position here taken is that the loss, regardless of the type of fraud which the particular impostor has committed, should fall upon the maker or drawer.

"Impostor" refers to impersonation, and does not extend to a false representation that the party is the authorized agent of the payee. The maker or drawer who takes the precaution of making the instrument payable to the principal is entitled to have his indorsement.

3. Subsection (1)(b) restates the substance of the original subsection 9(3). The test stated is not whether the named payee is "fictitious," but whether the signer intends that he shall have no interest in the instrument. The following situations illustrate the application of the subsection.

    a. The drawer of a check, for his own reasons, makes it payable to P knowing that P does not exist.

    b. The drawer makes the check payable in the name of P. A person named P exists, but the drawer does not know it.

    c. The drawer makes the check payable to P, an existing person whom he knows, intending to receive the money himself and that P shall have no interest in the check.

    d. The treasurer of a corporation draws its check payable to P, who to the knowledge of the treasurer does not exist.

    e. The treasurer of a corporation draws its check payable to P. P exists but the treasurer has fraudulently added his name to the payroll intending that he shall not receive the check.

    f. The president and the treasurer of a corporation both sign its check payable to P. P does not exist. The treasurer knows it but the president does not.

    g. The same facts as f, except that P exists and the treasurer knows it, but intends that P shall have no interest in the check.

In all the cases stated an indorsement by any person in the name of P is effective.

4. Paragraph (c) is new. It extends the rule of the original Subsection 9(3) to include the padded payroll cases, where the drawer's agent or employee prepares the check for signature or otherwise furnishes the signing officer with the name of the payee. The principle followed is that the loss should fall upon the employer as a risk of his business enterprise rather than upon the subsequent holder or drawee. The reasons are that the employer is normally in a better position to prevent such forgeries by reasonable care in the selection or supervision of his employees, or, if he is not, is at least in a better position to cover the loss by fidelity insurance; and that the cost of such insurance is properly an expense of his business rather than of the business of the holder or drawee.

The provision applies only to the agent or employee of the drawer, and only to the agent or employee who supplies him with the name of the payee. The following situations illustrate its application.

    a. An employee of a corporation prepares a padded payroll for its treasurer, which includes the name of P. P does not exist, and the employee knows it, but the treasurer does not. The treasurer draws the corporation's check payable to P.

    b. The same facts as a, except that P exists and the employee knows it but intends him to have no interest in the check. In both cases an indorsement by any person in the name of P is effective and the loss falls on the corporation.

5. The section is not intended to affect criminal liability for forgery or any other crime, or civil liability to the drawer or to any other person. It is to be read together with the section under which an unauthorized signer is personally liable on the signature to any person who takes the instrument in good faith (3–404(1)).

Cross References:

Sections 3–401, 3–403, 3–404 and 3–406.
Point 5: Section 3–404(1).

Definitional Cross References:

"Instrument". Section 3–102.
"Issue". Section 3–102.
"Person". Section 1–201.
"Signature". Section 3–401.

Cross References

Defense against drawee on claim for breach of warranty by proof of
    effectiveness of indorsement, see Commercial Code §§ 3417, 4208.
Embezzlement, see Penal Code § 510.
False personation, see Penal Code §§ 529, 530.
Forgery, see Penal Code § 470 et seq.
Indorsement, see Commercial Code § 3204 et seq.
Instrument, see Commercial Code § 3104.
Issue, see Commercial Code § 3105.
Manner of signing, see Commercial Code § 3401.
Signature,
    Generally, see Commercial Code § 3401.
    Authorized representative, see Commercial Code § 3403.
Unauthorized signatures, see Commercial Code § 3403.

§ 3406. Altered instruments; forged signatures; contributory negligence

(a) A person whose failure to exercise ordinary care contributes to an alteration of an instrument or to the making of a forged signature on an instrument is precluded from asserting the alteration or the forgery against a person who, in good faith, pays the instrument or takes it for value or for collection.

(b) Under subdivision (a), if the person asserting the preclusion fails to exercise ordinary care in paying or taking the instrument and that failure contributes to loss, the loss is allocated between the person precluded and the person asserting the preclusion according to the extent to which the failure of each to exercise ordinary care contributed to the loss.

(c) Under subdivision (a), the burden of proving failure to exercise ordinary care is on the person asserting the preclusion. Under subdivision (b), the burden of proving failure to exercise ordinary care is on the person precluded. *(Added by Stats.1992, c. 914 (S.B.833), § 6.)*

California Code Comment

By John A. Bohn and Charles J. Williams

Prior California Law

1. This section is new statutory law. However, it is probably a restatement of existing California case law. While Commercial Code § 3406 is stated in terms of estoppel, the effect is that the negligent drawer is liable to a drawee who pays an altered instrument. The report of the sub-committee of the State Bar on article [Division] 3 of t¹

Uniform Commercial Code summarizes the effect of section 3406 upon existing law:

"This section codifies and broadens the case law rule on negligence of a maker or drawer which contributes to forgery or alteration. Negligence must contribute 'substantially' to the alteration or forgery, but such negligence will preclude the maker or drawer from asserting a defense based on the alteration or lack of authority against a holder, as well as a drawee. The drawee or other payor must, however, pay the instrument in good faith and in accordance with the 'reasonable commercial standards' of the drawee's business. Presumably this is a question of fact and is substantially equivalent to the present case law requirement that a drawee bank must first show itself free of negligence. See Basch v. Bank of America, 22 Cal.2d 316 (1943)." Sixth Progress Report to the Legislature by Senate Fact Finding Committee on Judiciary (1959–1961) Part 1, The Uniform Commercial Code, p. 346.

2. In the absence of this kind of statutory provision, the decisions in the various jurisdictions have permitted the drawee bank to charge the drawer's account for payment on an instrument with a forged indorsement. The basis for charging the drawer was placed upon (1) an implied term in the contract between the drawer and drawee, (2) an implied duty in law, or (3) estoppel as a result of the drawer's acts by which he is estopped to assert against the drawee that he did not sign the instrument. California has followed the estoppel theory. In Basch v. Bank of America Nat. Trust & Sav. Ass'n, 22 Cal.2d 316, 139 P.2d 1 (1943), the court stated:

"It is settled law that a bank in receiving ordinary deposits becomes the debtor of the depositor, that its implied contract with him is to discharge this indebtedness by honoring such checks as he may draw upon it, and that in so doing it is charged with knowledge of its depositor's signature. . . . Consequently, a bank pays a forged check at its peril; and in such event, payment in legal contemplation will be considered to have been made from the bank's own funds so that it has no right to charge the depositor's account with the amount disbursed contrary to his genuine order, and it will be liable to him for so doing. Its responsibility in such case is, and should be, rigid. . . . While no degree of care on the part of the bank will excuse it from liability, it may justify the payment of a forged check on principles of estoppel, or on the basis of negligent or misleading conduct of the depositor which directly or proximately caused the bank to pay. However, the bank must show due diligence before it can assert such defenses . . .". Page 321 of 22 Cal.2d.

In that case the court enumerates, among other duties which exist upon the drawer, the duty to (1) examine the periodic bank statements which are forwarded to him without delay and to report discrepancies revealed upon the comparison of his own records, (2) to properly supervise the conduct of his trusted employees, and (3) to take the steps that the careful and prudent businessman would take after knowledge that his funds seem to be disappearing or that there may be a leak in his business.

3. The Official Comments contain a detailed analysis of how this section is intended to operate and should be interpreted.

See also Commercial Code § 4406 for the duty of customers to examine bank statements and report irregularities.

Changes from U.C.C. (1962 Official Text)

4. This is section 3–406 of the Official Text without change.

Uniform Commercial Code Comment
1992 Addition

1. Section 3–406(a) is based on former Section 3–406. With respect to alteration, Section 3–406 adopts the doctrine of Young v. Grote, 4 Bing. 253 (1827), which held that a drawer who so negligently draws an instrument as to facilitate its material alteration is liable to a drawee who pays the altered instrument in good faith. Under Section 3–406 the doctrine is expanded to apply not only to drafts but to all instruments. It includes in the protected class any "person who, in good faith, pays the instrument or takes it for value or for collection." Section 3–406 rejects decisions holding that the maker of a note owes no duty of care to the holder because at the time the instrument is issued there is no contract between them. By issuing the instrument and "setting it afloat upon a sea of strangers" the maker or drawer voluntarily enters into a relation with later holders which justifies imposition of a duty of care. In this respect an instrument so negligently drawn as to facilitate alteration does not differ in principle from an instrument containing blanks which may be filled. Under Section 3–407 a person paying an altered instrument or taking it for value, in good faith and without notice of the alteration may enforce rights with respect to the instrument according to its original terms. If negligence of the obligor substantially contributes to an alteration, this section gives the holder or the payor the alternative right to treat the altered instrument as though it had been issued in the altered form.

No attempt is made to define particular conduct that will constitute "failure to exercise ordinary care [that] substantially contributes to an alteration." Rather, "ordinary care" is defined in Section 3–103(a)(7) in general terms. The question is left to the court or the jury for decision in the light of the circumstances in the particular case including reasonable commercial standards that may apply.

Section 3–406 does not make the negligent party liable in tort for damages resulting from the alteration. If the negligent party is estopped from asserting the alteration the person taking the instrument is fully protected because the taker can treat the instrument as having been issued in the altered form.

2. Section 3–406 applies equally to a failure to exercise ordinary care that substantially contributes to the making of a forged signature on an instrument. Section 3–406 refers to "forged signature" rather than "unauthorized signature" that appeared in former Section 3–406 because it more accurately describes the scope of the provision. Unauthorized signature is a broader concept that includes not only forgery but also the signature of an agent which does not bind the principal under the law of agency. The agency cases are resolved independently under agency law. Section 3–406 is not necessary in those cases.

The "substantially contributes" test of former Section 3–406 is continued in this section in preference to a "direct and proximate cause" test. The "substantially contributes" test is meant to be less stringent than a "direct and proximate cause" test. Under the less stringent test the preclusion should be easier to establish. Conduct "substantially contributes" to a material alteration or forged signature if it is a contributing cause of the alteration or signature and a substantial factor in bringing it about. The analysis of "substantially contributes" in former Section 3–406 by the court in Thompson Maple Products v. Citizens National Bank of Corry, 234 A.2d 32 (Pa.Super.Ct.1967), states what is intended by the use of the same words in revised Section 3–406(b). Since Section 3–404(d) and Section 3–405(b) also use the words "substantially contributes" the analysis of these words also applies to those provisions.

3. The following cases illustrate the kind of conduct that can be the basis of a preclusion under Section 3–406(a):

Case #1. Employer signs checks drawn on Employer's account by use of a rubber stamp of Employer's signature. Employer keeps the rubber stamp along with Employer's personalized blank check forms in an unlocked desk drawer. An unauthorized person fraudulently uses the check forms to write checks on Employer's account. The checks are signed by use of the rubber stamp. If Employer demands that Employer's account in the drawee bank be recredited because the forged check was not properly payable, the drawee bank may defend by asserting that Employer is precluded from asserting the forgery. The trier of fact could find that Employer failed to exercise ordinary care to safeguard the rubber stamp and the check forms and that the failure substantially contributed to the forgery of Employer's signature by the unauthorized use of the rubber stamp.

Case #2. An insurance company draws a check to the order of Sarah Smith in payment of a claim of a policyholder, Sarah Smith, who lives in Alabama. The insurance company also has a policyholder with the same name who lives in Illinois. By mistake, the insurance company mails the check to the Illinois Sarah Smith who indorses the check and obtains payment. Because the payee of the check is the Alabama Sarah Smith, the indorsement by the Illinois Sarah Smith is a forged indorsement. Section 3–110(a). The trier of fact could find that the insurance company failed to exercise ordinary care when it mailed the check to the wrong person and that the failure substantially contributed to the making of the forged indorsement. In that event the insurance company could be precluded from asserting the forged indorsement against the drawee bank that honored the check.

Case #3. A company writes a check for $10. The figure "10" and the word "ten" are typewritten in the appropriate spaces on the check form. A large blank space is left after the figure and the word. The payee of the check, using a typewriter with a typeface similar to that used on the check, writes the word "thousand" after the word "ten" and a comma and three zeros after the figure "10". The drawee bank in good faith pays $10,000 when the check is presented for payment and debits the account of the drawer in that amount. The trier of fact could find that the drawer failed to exercise ordinary care in writing the check and that the failure substantially contributed to the alteration. In that case the drawer is precluded from asserting the alteration against the drawee if the check was paid in good faith.

4. Subsection (b) differs from former Section 3–406 in that it adopts a concept of comparative negligence. If the person precluded under subsection (a) proves that the person asserting the preclusion failed to exercise ordinary care and that failure substantially contributed to the loss, the loss may be allocated between the two parties on a comparative negligence basis. In the case of a forged indorsement the litigation is usually between the payee of the check and the depositary bank that took the check for collection. An example is a case like Case #1 of Comment 3 to Section 3–405. If the trier of fact finds that Employer failed to exercise ordinary care in safeguarding the check and that the failure substantially contributed to the making of the forged indorsement, subsection (a) of Section 3–406 applies. If Employer brings an action for conversion against the depositary bank that took the checks from the forger, the depositary bank could assert the preclusion under subsection (a). But suppose the forger opened an account in the depositary bank in a name identical to that of Employer, the payee of the check, and then deposited the check in the account. Subsection (b) may apply. There may be an issue whether the depositary bank should have been alerted to possible fraud when a new account was opened for a corporation shortly before a very large check payable to a payee with the same name is deposited. Circumstances surrounding the opening of the account may have suggested that the corporation to which the check was payable may not be the same as the corporation for which the account was opened. If the trier of fact finds that collecting the check under these circumstances was a failure to exercise ordinary care, it could allocate the loss between the depositary bank and Employer, the payee.

Uniform Commercial Code Comment

Prior Uniform Statutory Provision:
None.

Purposes:

1. This section is new. It adopts the doctrine of Young v. Grote, 4 Bing. 253 (1827), which held that a drawer who so negligently draws an instrument as to facilitate its material alteration is liable to a drawee who pays the altered instrument in good faith. It should be noted that the rule as stated in the section requires that the negligence "substantially" contribute to the alteration.

2. The section extends the above principle to the protection of a holder in due course and of payors who may not technically be drawees. It rejects decisions which have held that the maker of a note owes no duty of care to the holder because at the time the instrument is drawn there is no contract between them. By drawing the instrument and "setting it afloat upon a sea of strangers" the maker or drawer voluntarily enters into a relation with later holders which justifies his responsibility. In this respect an instrument so negligently drawn as to facilitate alteration does not differ in principle from an instrument containing blanks which may be filled.

The holder in due course under the rules governing alteration (Section 3–407) may enforce the altered instrument according to its original tenor. Where negligence of the obligor has substantially contributed to the alteration, this section gives the holder the alternative right to enforce the instrument as altered.

3. No attempt is made to define negligence which will contribute to an alteration. The question is left to the court or the jury upon the circumstances of the particular cases. Negligence usually has been found where spaces are left in the body of the instrument in which words or figures may be inserted. No unusual precautions are required, and the section is not intended to change decisions holding that the drawer of a bill is under no duty to use sensitized paper, indelible ink or a protectograph; or that it is not negligence to leave spaces between the lines or at the end of the instrument in which a provision for interest or the like can be written.

4. The section applies only where the negligence contributes to the alteration. It must afford an opportunity of which advantage is in fact taken. The section approves decisions which have refused to hold the drawer responsible where he has left spaces in a check but the payee erased all the writing with chemicals and wrote in an entirely new check.

5. This section does not make the negligent party liable in tort for damages resulting from the alteration. Instead it estops him from asserting it against the holder in due course or drawee. The reason is that in the usual case the extent of the loss, which involves the possibility of ultimate recovery from the wrongdoer, cannot be determined at the time of litigation, and the decision would have to be made on the unsatisfactory basis of burden of proof. The holder or drawee is protected by an estoppel, and the task of pursuing the wrongdoer is left to the negligent party. Any amount in fact recovered from the wrongdoer must be held for the benefit of the negligent party under ordinary principles of equity.

6. The section protects parties who act not only in good faith, (Section 1–201) but also in observance of the reasonable standards of their business. Thus any bank which takes or pays an altered check which ordinary banking standards would require it to refuse cannot take advantage of the estoppel.

7. The section applies the same rule to negligence which contributes to a forgery or other unauthorized signature, as defined in this Act (Section 1–201). The most obvious case is that of the drawer who makes use of a signature stamp or other automatic signing device and is negligent in looking after it. The section extends, however, to cases where the party has notice that forgeries of his signature have occurred and is negligent in failing to prevent further forgeries by the same person. It extends to negligence which contributes to a forgery of the signature of another, as in the case where a check is negligently mailed to the wrong person having the same name as the payee. As in the case of alteration, no attempt is made to specify what is negligence, and the question is one for the court or the jury on the facts of the particular case.

Cross References:

Section 3–401 and 3–404.
Point 2: Section 3–407(3).
Point 6: Section 1–201.
Point 7: Section 1–201.

Definitional Cross References:

"Alteration". Section 3–407.
"Good faith". Section 1–201.
"Holder in due course". Section 3–302.
"Instrument". Section 3–102.
"Person". Section 1–201.
"Unauthorized signature". Section 1–201.

Cross References

Defense against drawee on claim for breach of warranty based on unauthorized indorsement or alteration, see Commercial Code §§ 3417, 4208.
Definitions, see Commercial Code § 1201.
Holder in due course, see Commercial Code § 3302.
Innocent persons, which of two must suffer, see Civil Code § 3543.
Liability on instrument, necessity of signature, see Commercial Code § 3401.
Responsibility for negligence, see Civil Code § 1714.
Unauthorized signatures, see Commercial Code §§ 1201, 3404.

§ 3407. Alteration; effect on obligation

(a) "Alteration" means (1) an unauthorized change in an instrument that purports to modify in any respect the obligation of a party, or (2) an unauthorized addition of words or numbers or other change to an incomplete instrument relating to the obligation of a party.

(b) Except as provided in subdivision (c), an alteration fraudulently made discharges a party whose obligation is affected by the alteration unless that party assents or is precluded from asserting the alteration.

§ 3407

No other alteration discharges a party, and the instrument may be enforced according to its original terms.

(c) A payor bank or drawee paying a fraudulently altered instrument or a person taking it for value, in good faith and without notice of the alteration, may enforce rights with respect to the instrument (1) according to its original terms, or (2) in the case of an incomplete instrument altered by unauthorized completion, according to its terms as completed. *(Added by Stats.1992, c. 914 (S.B.833), § 6.)*

California Code Comment
By John A. Bohn and Charles J. Williams

Prior California Law

1. Subdivision (1) is similar to former Civil Code § 3206.

2. Subdivision (2) is a revision of former Civil Code § 3205 which provided that where a negotiable instrument was materially altered without the assent of all parties liable on it, the instrument was voided except as against a party who had made or agreed to the alteration and except as to subsequent indorsers. Under former Civil Code § 3205, a material alteration discharged a party unless he were in some way involved in the alteration or was a subsequent indorser. Subdivision (2) modifies this rule to the extent that a material alteration does not discharge any party unless it is made by a holder, is made for fraudulent purpose, and is material.

3. The discharge which is provided by subdivision (2) is a personal defense. This means it cannot be asserted by one whose contract is not affected. Official Comment 3 c.

4. Subdivision (3) is a combination of the last sentences of both former Civil Code §§ 3205 and 3095. The effect of this subdivision is to reverse the rule of former Civil Code § 3096 which gave a real defense where an incomplete instrument had not been delivered. Official Comment 4.

Changes from U.C.C. (1962 Official Text)

5. This is section 3-407 of the Official Text without change.

Uniform Commercial Code Comment
1992 Addition

1. This provision restates former Section 3-407. Former Section 3-407 defined a "material" alteration as any alteration that changes the contract of the parties in any respect. Revised Section 3-407 refers to such a change as an alteration. As under subsection (2) of former Section 3-407, discharged because of alteration occurs only in the case of an alteration fraudulently made. There is no discharge if a blank is filled in the honest belief that it is authorized or if a change is made with a benevolent motive such as a desire to give the obligor the benefit of a lower interest rate. Changes favorable to the obligor are unlikely to be made with any fraudulent intent, but if such an intent is found the alteration may operate as a discharge.

Discharge is a personal defense of the party whose obligation is modified and anyone whose obligation is not affected is not discharged. But if an alteration discharges a party there is also discharge of any party having a right of recourse against the discharged party because the obligation of the party with the right of recourse is affected by the alteration. Assent to the alteration given before or after it is made will prevent the party from asserting the discharge. The phrase "or is precluded from asserting the alteration" in subsection (b) recognizes the possibility of an estoppel or other ground barring the defense which does not rest on assent.

2. Under subsection (c) a person paying a fraudulently altered instrument or taking it for value, in good faith and without notice of the alteration, is not affected by a discharge under subsection (b). The person paying or taking the instrument may assert rights with respect to the instrument according to its original terms or, in the case of an incomplete instrument that is altered by unauthorized completion, according to its terms as completed. If blanks are filled or an incomplete instrument is otherwise completed, subsection (c) places the loss upon the party who left the instrument incomplete by permitting enforcement in its completed form. This result is intended even though the instrument was stolen from the issuer and completed after the theft.

Uniform Commercial Code Comment

Prior Uniform Statutory Provision:

Sections 14, 15, 124 and 125, Uniform Negotiable Instruments Law.
Changes: Combined and reworded; new provisions; rule of original Section 15 reversed.

Purposes of Changes and New Matter: The changes are intended to remove uncertainties arising under the original sections, and to modify the rules as to discharge:

1. Subsection (1) substitutes a general definition for the list of illustrations in the original Section 125. Any alteration is material only as it may change the contract of a party to the instrument; and the addition or deletion of words which do not in any way affect the contract of any previous signer is not material. But any change in the contract of a party, however slight, is a material alteration; and the addition of one cent to the amount payable, or an advance of one day in the date of payment, will operate as a discharge if it is fraudulent.

Specific mention is made of a change in the number or relations of the parties in order to make it clear that any such change is material only if it changes the contract of one who has signed. The addition of a co-maker or a surety does not change in most jurisdictions the contract of one who has already signed as maker and should not be held material as to him. The addition of the name of an alternative payee is material, since it changes his obligation. Paragraph (c) makes special mention of a change in the writing signed in order to cover occasional cases of addition of sticker clauses, scissoring or perforating instruments where the separation is not authorized.

2. Paragraph (b) of subsection (1) is to be read together with Section 3-115 on incomplete instruments. Where an instrument contains blanks or is otherwise incomplete, it may be completed in accordance with the authority given and is then valid and effective as completed. If the completion is unauthorized and has the effect of changing the contract of any previous signer, this provision follows the generally accepted rule in treating it as a material alteration which may operate as a discharge.

3. Subsection (2) modifies the very rigorous rule of the original Section 124. The changes made are as follows:

a. A material alteration does not discharge any party unless it is made by the holder. Spoliation by any meddling stranger does not affect the rights of the holder. It is of course intended that the acts of the holder's authorized agent or employee, or of his confederates are to be attributed to him.

b. A material alteration does not discharge any party unless it is made for a fraudulent purpose. There is no discharge where a blank is filled in the honest belief that it is as authorized; or where a change is made with a benevolent motive such as a desire to give the obligor the benefit of a lower interest rate. Changes favorable to the obligor are unlikely to be made with any fraudulent intent; but if such an intent is found the alteration may operate as a discharge.

c. The discharge is a personal defense of the party whose contract is changed by the alteration and anyone whose contract is not affected cannot assert it. The contract of any party is necessarily affected, however, by the discharge of any party against whom he has a right of recourse on the instrument. Assent to the alteration given before or after it is made will prevent the party from asserting the discharge. "Or is precluded from asserting the defense" is added in paragraph (a) to recognize the possibility of an estoppel or other ground barring the defense which does not rest on assent.

d. If the alteration is not material or if it is not made for a fraudulent purpose there is no discharge, and the instrument may be enforced according to its original tenor. Where blanks are filled or an incomplete instrument is otherwise completed there is no original tenor, but the instrument may be enforced according to the authority in fact given.

4. Subsection (3) combines the final sentences of the original Sections 14 and 124, and provides that a subsequent holder in due course takes free of the discharge in all cases. The provision is merely one form of the general rule governing the effect of discharge against a holder in due course (Section 3-602). The holder in due course may enforce the instrument according to its original tenor. In this connec-

tion reference should be made to the section giving the holder in due course the right, where the maker's or drawer's negligence has substantially contributed to the alteration, to enforce the instrument in its altered form (Section 3–406). Reference should also be made to Section 4–401 covering a bank's right to charge its customer's account in the case of altered instruments.

Where blanks are filled or an incomplete instrument is otherwise completed, this subsection follows the original Section 14 in placing the loss upon the party who left the instrument incomplete and permitting the holder to enforce it in its completed form. As indicated in the comment to Section 3–115 on incomplete instruments, this result is intended even though the instrument was stolen from the maker or drawer and completed after the theft; and the effect of this subsection, together with the section on incomplete instruments is to reverse the rule of the original Section 15.

There is no inconsistency between subsection (3) and paragraph (b) of subsection (2). The holder in due course may elect to enforce the instrument either as provided in that paragraph or as provided in subsection (3).

It should be noted that a purchaser who takes the instrument with notice of any material alteration, including the unauthorized completion of an incomplete instrument, takes with notice of a claim or defense and cannot be a holder in due course (Section 3–304).

Cross References:

Sections 3–305, 3–306 and 3–307.

Point 2: Section 3–115.

Point 4: Sections 3–115, 3–304(2), 4–401 and 3–602.

Definitional Cross References:

"Contract". Section 1–201.

"Holder". Section 1–201.

"Holder in due course". Section 3–302.

"Instrument". Section 3–102.

"Party". Section 1–201.

"Person". Section 1–201.

"Signed". Section 1–201.

"Writing". Section 1–201.

Cross References

Acceptor of incomplete instrument, obligation to pay, see Commercial Code § 3413 et seq.
Altered or completed items, payment by bank, see Commercial Code § 4401.
Burden of establishing signatures validity, see Commercial Code § 3308.
Discharge of parties, see Commercial Code § 3601.
Dishonor of item customer or collecting bank obligation to pay amount due on item according to terms of incomplete item as collected, see Commercial Code § 4207.
Drawer of incomplete instrument, obligation to pay, see Commercial Code § 3414.
Extinction of written contract by material alteration, see Civil Code § 1700.
Holder in due course,
 Generally, see Commercial Code § 3302.
 Effect of discharge, see Commercial Code § 3601.
Incomplete instruments, see Commercial Code § 3115.
Indorser of incomplete instrument, obligation to pay, see Commercial Code § 3415.
Instrument, see Commercial Code § 3104.
Issuer of incomplete instrument, obligation to pay, see Commercial Code § 3412.
Party producing altered writing to account for it, see Evidence Code § 1402.
Taker, notice of claims or defense, see Commercial Code § 3307.
Rights of holder in due course, see Commercial Code § 3305.
Rights of one not holder in due course, see Commercial Code § 3306.

Taker, notice of claims or defense, see Commercial Code § 3307.

§ 3408. Liability of drawee

A check or other draft does not of itself operate as an assignment of funds in the hands of the drawee available for its payment, and the drawee is not liable on the instrument until the drawee accepts it. *(Added by Stats.1992, c. 914 (S.B.833), § 6.)*

California Code Comment

By John A. Bohn and Charles J. Williams

Prior California Law

1. This section is similar to former Civil Code § 3109. This section also supersedes former Civil Code §§ 3105 and 3106. Although under the NIL consideration and value were synonymous, Division 3 distinguishes between them. Official Comment 1. Also see California Code Comment to section 3303 and Official Comment 2 to section 3303.

2. The language within the exception clause in the first sentence to the effect that no consideration is necessary for an instrument or an obligation on an instrument given in payment or security for an antecedent obligation is new statutory language but it is in accord with prior California decisions holding that a pre-existing debt is sufficient consideration for the execution or transfer of a negotiable instrument. The cases decided under former Civil Code § 3106 (which provided that an antecedent or pre-existing debt constitutes value) hold that a pre-existing debt is a valuable consideration. Fowles v. National Bank of Calif., 167 Cal. 653, 140 Pac. 271 (1914); Silberschmidt v. Moran, 79 Cal.App. 533, 250 Pac. 205 (1926). Britton Bills & Notes (1961) 221–233.

Changes from U.C.C. (1962 Official Text)

3. This is section 3–408 of the Official Text without change.

Uniform Commercial Code Comment
1992 Addition

1. This section is a restatement of former Section 3–409(1). Subsection (2) of former Section 3–409 is deleted as misleading and superfluous. Comment 3 says of subsection (2): "It is intended to make it clear that this section does not in any way affect any liability which may arise apart from the instrument." In reality subsection (2) did not make anything clear and was a source of confusion. If all it meant was that a bank that has not certified a check may engage in other conduct that might make it liable to a holder, it stated the obvious and was superfluous. Section 1–103 is adequate to cover those cases.

2. Liability with respect to drafts may arise under other law. For example, Section 4–302 imposes liability on a payor bank for late return of an item.

Uniform Commercial Code Comment

Prior Uniform Statutory Provision:

Sections 24, 25 and 28, Uniform Negotiable Instruments Law.
Changes: Combined and reworded.

Purposes of Changes:

1. "Consideration" is distinguished from "value" throughout this Article. "Consideration" refers to what the obligor has received for his obligation, and is important only on the question of whether his obligation can be enforced against him.

2. The "except" clause is intended to remove the difficulties which have arisen where a note or a draft, or an indorsement of either, is given as payment or as security for a debt already owed by the party giving it, or by a third person. The provision is intended to change the result of decisions holding that where no extension of time or other concession is given by the creditor the new obligation fails for lack of legal consideration. It is intended also to mean that an instrument given for more or less than the amount of a liquidated obligation does not fail by reason of the common law rule that an obligation for a lesser liquidated amount cannot be consideration for the surrender of a greater.

§ 3408

3. With respect to the necessity or sufficiency of consideration other obligations on an instrument are subject to the ordinary rules of contract law relating to contracts not under seal. Promissory estoppel or any other equivalent or substitute for consideration is to be recognized as in other contract cases. The provision of the original Section 28 as to absence or failure of consideration is now covered by the section dealing with the rights of one not a holder in due course; and the "presumption" of consideration in the original Section 24 is replaced by the provision relating to the burden of establishing defenses.

Cross References:

Point 1: Section 3–303.

Point 3: Sections 3–306(c) and 3–307(2).

Definitional Cross References:

"Holder in due course". Section 3–302.

"Instrument". Section 3–102.

"Person". Section 1–201.

"Rights". Section 1–201.

Cross References

Burden of establishing signatures validity, see Commercial Code § 3308.
Consideration, see Civil Code § 1605 et seq.
Cause or consideration as essential element of contract, see Civil Code § 1550.
Contracts in general, consideration, see Civil Code § 1605.
Holder in due course, see Commercial Code § 3302.
Instrument, see Commercial Code § 3104.
Issue or transfer for value, see Commercial Code § 3303.
Presumption from written instrument, see Civil Code § 1614.
Rescission of contract for failure of consideration, see Civil Code § 1689.
Rights of one not holder in due course, see Commercial Code § 3306.
Signatures, presumptions and proof, see Commercial Code § 3308.

§ 3409. Acceptance of draft; certified check

(a) "Acceptance" means the drawee's signed agreement to pay a draft as presented. It shall be written on the draft and may consist of the drawee's signature alone. Acceptance may be made at any time and becomes effective when notification pursuant to instructions is given or the accepted draft is delivered for the purpose of giving rights on the acceptance to any person.

(b) A draft may be accepted although it has not been signed by the drawer, is otherwise incomplete, is overdue, or has been dishonored.

(c) If a draft is payable at a fixed period after sight and the acceptor fails to date the acceptance, the holder may complete the acceptance by supplying a date in good faith.

(d) "Certified check" means a check accepted by the bank on which it is drawn. Acceptance may be made as stated in subdivision (a) or by a writing on the check which indicates that the check is certified. The drawee of a check has no obligation to certify the check, and refusal to certify is not dishonor of the check. *(Added by Stats.1992, c. 914 (S.B.833), § 6.)*

California Code Comment

By John A. Bohn and Charles J. Williams

Prior California Law

1. Subdivision (1) combines the provisions of former Civil Code §§ 3208 and 3265 e. The rule of this subdivision was also the pre NIL rule. Guggenhime & Co. v. Lamantia, 207 Cal. 96, 276 Pac. 995 (1929).

2. Subdivision (2) is new statutory law. This subdivision means that liability of any kind apart from the instrument is unaffected by subdivision 1. It is intended only as a clarification. Official Comment 3.

Changes from U.C.C. (1962 Official Text)

3. This is section 3–409 of the Official Text without change.

Uniform Commercial Code Comment
1992 Addition

1. The first three subsections of Section 3–409 are a restatement of former Section 3–410. Subsection (d) adds a definition of certified check which is a type of accepted draft.

2. Subsection (a) states the generally recognized rule that the mere signature of the drawee on the instrument is a sufficient acceptance. Customarily the signature is written vertically across the face of the instrument, but since the drawee has no reason to sign for any other purpose a signature in any other place, even on the back of the instrument, is sufficient. It need not be accompanied by such words as "Accepted," "Certified," or "Good." It must not, however, bear any words indicating an intent to refuse to honor the draft. The last sentence of subsection (a) states the generally recognized rule that an acceptance written on the draft takes effect when the drawee notifies the holder or gives notice according to instructions.

3. The purpose of subsection (c) is to provide a definite date of payment if none appears on the instrument. An undated acceptance of a draft payable "thirty days after sight" is incomplete. Unless the acceptor writes in a different date the holder is authorized to complete the acceptance according to the terms of the draft by supplying a date of acceptance. Any date supplied by the holder is effective if made in good faith.

4. The last sentence of subsection (d) states the generally recognized rule that in the absence of agreement a bank is under no obligation to certify a check. A check is a demand instrument calling for payment rather than acceptance. The bank may be liable for breach of any agreement with the drawer, the holder, or any other person by which it undertakes to certify. Its liability is not on the instrument, since the drawee is not so liable until acceptance. Section 3–408. Any liability is for breach of the separate agreement.

Uniform Commercial Code Comment

Prior Uniform Statutory Provision:

Sections 127 and 189, Uniform Negotiable Instruments Law.
Changes: Combined and reworded; new provisions.

Purposes of Changes and New Matter:

The two original sections are combined, brought forward to appear in connection with acceptance, and reworded to remove uncertainties.

1. As under the original sections, a check or other draft does not of itself operate as an assignment in law or equity. The assignment may, however, appear from other facts, and particularly from other agreements, express or implied; and when the intent to assign is clear the check may be the means by which the assignment is effected.

2. The language of the original Section 189, that the drawee is not liable "to the holder", is changed as inaccurate and not intended. The drawee is not liable on the instrument until he accepts; but he remains subject to any other liability to the holder. In this connection reference should be made to Section 4–302 on the payor bank's liability for late return. Such a bank if it does not either make prompt settlement or return on an item received by it will become liable to a holder of the item.

3. Subsection (2) is new. It is intended to make it clear that this section does not in any way affect any liability which may arise apart from the instrument itself. The drawee who fails to accept may be liable to the drawer or to the holder for breach of the terms of a letter of credit or any other agreement by which he is obligated to accept. He may be liable in tort or upon any other basis because of his

representation that he has accepted, or that he intends to accept. The section leaves unaffected any liability of any kind apart from the instrument.

Cross References:

Sections 3–410, 3–411, 3–412 and 3–415.
Point 2: Section 4–302.

Definitional Cross References:

"Acceptance". Section 3–410.
"Check". Section 3–104.
"Contract". Section 1–201.
"Draft". Section 3–104.
"Instrument". Section 3–102.
"Letter of credit". Section 5–104.

Cross References

Certificate of deposit, see Commercial Code § 3104.
Check, see Commercial Code § 3104.
Obligation of accommodation party, see Commercial Code § 3419.
Obligation of issuer, drawer, or acceptor, see Commercial Code § 3413 et seq.
Draft, see Commercial Code § 3104.
Instrument, see Commercial Code § 3104.
Letter of credit, see Commercial Code § 5104.
Liability of bank to customer for nonpayment of check, see Commercial Code § 4402.
Note, see Commercial Code § 3104.
Payor bank's responsibility for late return of item, see Commercial Code § 4302.

§ 3410. Acceptance varying from terms of draft

(a) If the terms of a drawee's acceptance vary from the terms of the draft as presented, the holder may refuse the acceptance and treat the draft as dishonored. In that case, the drawee may cancel the acceptance.

(b) The terms of a draft are not varied by an acceptance to pay at a particular bank or place in the United States, unless the acceptance states that the draft is to be paid only at that bank or place.

(c) If the holder assents to an acceptance varying the terms of a draft, the obligation of each drawer and indorser that does not expressly assent to the acceptance is discharged. *(Added by Stats.1992, c. 914 (S.B.833), § 6.)*

California Code Comment

By John A. Bohn and Charles J. Williams

Prior California Law

1. Subdivision (1) continues the rule of former Civil Code § 3213 that acceptance must be in writing and signed by the drawee.

Subdivision (1) by requiring acceptance on the draft eliminates former Civil Code §§ 3215 (collateral acceptance) and 3216 (virtual acceptance) both of which are practices which no longer exist and are not in accordance with good banking practice. Official Comment 3.

Subdivision (1) also eliminates former Civil Code § 3218 which provided that delay or refusal to return the instrument amounted to acceptance.

2. Subdivision (2) continues the rule of the first sentence of former Civil Code § 3219.

3. Subdivision (3) changes the rule of the last sentence of former Civil Code § 3219 which provided:

". . . But when a bill payable after sight is dishonored by non-acceptance and the drawee subsequently accepts it, the holder in the absence of any different agreement is entitled to have the bill accepted as of the date of the first presentment."

The effect of subdivision (3) is to permit the holder to write in an effective date to provide a definite date of payment where none appears on the instrument. Official Comment 6.

4. Former Civil Code §§ 3242–3251 providing for acceptance for honor are eliminated entirely as obsolete. Official Comment 1.

Changes from U.C.C. (1962 Official Text)

5. This is section 3–410 of the Official Text without change.

Uniform Commercial Code Comment

1992 Addition

1. This section is a restatement of former Section 3–412. It applies to conditional acceptances, acceptances for part of the amount, acceptances to pay at a different time from that required by the draft, or to the acceptance of less than all of the drawees. It applies to any other engagement changing the essential terms of the draft. If the drawee makes a varied acceptance the holder may either reject it or assent to it. The holder may reject by insisting on acceptance of the draft as presented. Refusal by the drawee to accept the draft as presented is dishonor. In that event the drawee is not bound by the varied acceptance and is entitled to have it canceled.

If the holder assents to the varied acceptance, the drawee's obligation as acceptor is according to the terms of the varied acceptance. Under subsection (c) the effect of the holder's assent is to discharge any drawer or indorser who does not also assent. The assent of the drawer or indorser must be affirmatively expressed. Mere failure to object within a reasonable time is not assent which will prevent the discharge.

2. Under subsection (b) an acceptance does not vary from the terms of the draft if it provides for payment at any particular bank or place in the United States unless the acceptance states that the draft is to be paid only at such bank or place. Section 3–501(b)(1) states that if an instrument is payable at a bank in the United States presentment must be made at the place of payment (Section 3–111) which in this case is at the designated bank.

Uniform Commercial Code Comment

Prior Uniform Statutory Provision:

Sections 132, 133, 134, 135, 136, 137, 138, 161–170, and 191, Uniform Negotiable Instruments Law.

Changes: Combined, reworded; original Sections 134, 135, 137 and 161–170 eliminated.

Purposes of Changes:

1. The original Sections 161–170 providing for acceptance for honor are omitted from this Article. This ancient practice developed at a time when communications were slow, and particularly in overseas transactions there might be a delay of several months before the drawer could be notified of dishonor by non-acceptance and take steps to protect his credit. The need for intervention by a third party has passed with the development of the cable transfer, the letter of credit, and numerous other devices by which a substitute arrangement is promptly made. The practice has been obsolete for many years, and the sections are therefore eliminated.

2. Under Section 3–417 a person obtaining acceptance gives a warranty against alteration of the instrument before acceptance.

3. Subsection (1) adopts the rule of Section 17 of the English Bills of Exchange Act that the acceptance must be written on the draft. It eliminates the original Sections 134 and 135, providing for "virtual" acceptance by a written promise to accept drafts to be drawn, and "collateral" acceptance by a separate writing. Both have been anomalous exceptions to the policy that no person is liable on an instrument unless his signature appears on it. Both are derived from a line of early American cases decided at a time when difficulties of communication, particularly overseas, might leave the holder in doubt for a long period whether the draft was accepted. Such conditions have long since ceased to exist, and the "virtual" or "collateral" acceptance is now almost entirely obsolete. Good commercial and banking practice does not sanction acceptance by any separate writing because of the dangers and uncertainties arising when it becomes separated from the draft. The instrument is now forwarded to the drawee for his acceptance upon it, or reliance is placed upon the obligation of the separate writing itself, as in the case of a letter of credit.

Nothing in this section is intended to eliminate any liability of the drawee in contract, tort or otherwise arising from the separate writing or any other obligation or representation, as provided in Section 3–409.

Subsection (1) likewise eliminates the original section 137, providing for acceptance by delay or refusal to return the instrument but the drawee may be liable for a conversion of the instrument under Section 3–419.

4. Subsection (1) states the generally recognized rule that the mere signature of the drawee on the instrument is a sufficient acceptance. Customarily the signature is written vertically across the face of the instrument; but since the drawee has no reason to sign for any other purpose his signature in any other place, even on the back of the instrument, is sufficient. It need not be accompanied by such words as "Accepted," "Certified," or "Good." It must not, however, bear any words indicating an intent to refuse to honor the bill; and nothing in this provision is intended to change such decisions as Norton v. Knapp, 64 Iowa 112, 19 N.W. 867 (1884), holding that the drawee's signature accompanied by the words "Kiss my foot" is not an acceptance.

5. The final sentence of subsection (1) expressly states the generally recognized rule, implied in the definition of acceptance in the original Section 191, that an acceptance written on the draft takes effect when the drawee notifies the holder or gives notice according to his instructions. Acceptance is thus an exception to the usual rule that no obligation on an instrument is effective until delivery.

6. Subsection (3) changes the last sentence of the original Section 138. The purpose of the provision is to provide a definite date of payment where none appears on the instrument. An undated acceptance of a draft payable "thirty days after sight" is incomplete; and unless the acceptor himself writes in a different date the holder is authorized to complete the acceptance according to the terms of the draft by supplying a date of presentment. Any date which the holder chooses to write in is effective providing his choice of date is made in good faith. Any different agreement not written on the draft is not effective, and parol evidence is not admissible to show it.

Cross References:

Sections 3–411, 3–412 and 3–418.
Point 2: Section 3–417.
Point 3: Sections 3–401(1), 3–409(2) and 3–419.
Point 6: Section 3–412.

Definitional Cross References:

"Delivery". Section 1–201.
"Dishonor". Section 3–507.
"Draft". Section 3–104.
"Good faith". Section 1–201.
"Holder". Section 1–201.
"Honor". Section 1–201.
"Notification". Section 1–201.
"Presentment". Section 3–504.
"Signature". Section 3–401.
"Signed". Section 1–201.
"Written". Section 1–201.

Cross References

Certified checks, see Financial Code §§ 970, 971.
Commercial banks, acceptance of drafts and bills, see Financial Code § 1224 et seq.
Conversion of instrument, see Commercial Code § 3420.
Dishonor, see Commercial Code § 3502.
Draft, see Commercial Code § 3104.
International banks, dealing with acceptances, see Financial Code § 3504.
Liability on instrument, necessity of signature, see Commercial Code § 3401.
Notice of dishonor, see Commercial Code § 3503.
Payment or acceptance, finality, see Commercial Code § 3418.
Presentment, how made, see Commercial Code § 3501.
Protest, see Commercial Code § 3505.
Rights of party to whom presentment made, see Commercial Code § 3501.
Savings associations, investment in bankers' acceptances, see Financial Code § 7250.
Signature, see Commercial Code § 3401.
Time allowed for acceptance, see Commercial Code § 3501.
Warranties on presentment and transfer, see Commercial Code §§ 3416, 3417.

§ 3411. Cashier's checks; teller's checks; certified checks; refusal to pay; liability

(a) In this section, "obligated bank" means the acceptor of a certified check or the issuer of a cashier's check or teller's check bought from the issuer.

(b) If the obligated bank wrongfully (1) refuses to pay a cashier's check or certified check, (2) stops payment of a teller's check, or (3) refuses to pay a dishonored teller's check, the person asserting the right to enforce the check is entitled to compensation for expenses and loss of interest resulting from the nonpayment and may recover consequential damages if the obligated bank refuses to pay after receiving notice of particular circumstances giving rise to the damages.

(c) Expenses or consequential damages under subdivision (b) are not recoverable if the refusal of the obligated bank to pay occurs because (1) the bank suspends payments, (2) the obligated bank asserts a claim or defense of the bank that it has reasonable grounds to believe is available against the person entitled to enforce the instrument, (3) the obligated bank has a reasonable doubt whether the person demanding payment is the person entitled to enforce the instrument, or (4) payment is prohibited by law. (Added by Stats.1992, c. 914 (S.B.833), § 6.)

California Code Comment

By John A. Bohn and Charles J. Williams

Prior California Law

1. The first sentence of subdivision (1) is similar to former Civil Code § 3265 c.

The second sentence of subdivision (1) is similar to former Civil Code § 3265 d. Official Comment 1. Under prior California law certification was an acceptance by the bank and its effect was "to impose a primary liability on the acceptor to pay the amount of the check on demand to the payee or holder". Umbsen v. Crocker First National Bank of San Francisco, 33 Cal.2d 599, 203 P.2d 752 (1949).

2. Subdivision (2) is new statutory law. It is in accord with the little authority under the NIL which exists on this point. Wachtel v. Rosen, 249 N.Y. 386, 164 N.E. 326, 62 ALR 374 (1928); Britton, Bills & Notes (1961) 517.

3. Subdivision (3) is new statutory law. It is statutory recognition of banking practice. Official Comment 3.

Changes from U.C.C. (1962 Official Text)

4. This is section 3–411 of the Official Text without change.

Uniform Commercial Code Comment
1992 Addition

1. In some cases a creditor may require that the debt be paid by an obligation of a bank. The debtor may comply by obtaining certification of the debtor's check, but more frequently the debtor buys from a bank a cashier's check or teller's check payable to the creditor. The check is taken by the creditor as a cash equivalent on the assumption that the bank will pay the check. Sometimes, the debtor wants to retract payment by inducing the obligated bank not to pay. The typical case involves a dispute between the parties to the transaction in which the

check is given in payment. In the case of a certified check or cashier's check, the bank can safely pay the holder of the check despite notice that there may be an adverse claim to the check (Section 3–602). It is also clear that the bank that sells a teller's check has no duty to order the bank on which it is drawn not to pay it. A debtor using any of these types of checks has no right to stop payment. Nevertheless, some banks will refuse payment as an accommodation to a customer. Section 3–411 is designed to discourage this practice.

2. The term "obligated bank" refers to the issuer of the cashier's check or teller's check and the acceptor of the certified check. If the obligated bank wrongfully refuses to pay, it is liable to pay for expenses and loss of interest resulting from the refusal to pay. There is no express provision for attorney's fees, but attorney's fees are not meant to be necessarily excluded. They could be granted because they fit within the language "expenses * * * resulting from the nonpayment." In addition the bank may be liable to pay consequential damages if it has notice of the particular circumstances giving rise to the damages.

3. Subsection (c) provides that expenses or consequential damages are not recoverable if the refusal to pay is because of the reasons stated. The purpose is to limit that recovery to cases in which the bank refuses to pay even though its obligation to pay is clear and it is able to pay. Subsection (b) applies only if the refusal to honor the check is wrongful. If the bank is not obliged to pay there is no recovery. The bank may assert any claim or defense that it has, but normally the bank would not have a claim or defense. In the usual case it is a remitter that is asserting a claim to the check on the basis of a rescission of negotiation to the payee under Section 3–202. See Comment 2 to Section 3–201. The bank can assert that claim if there is compliance with Section 3–305(c), but the bank is not protected from damages under subsection (b) if the claim of the remitter is not upheld. In that case, the bank is insulated from damages only if payment is enjoined under Section 3–602(b)(1). Subsection (c)(iii) refers to cases in which the bank may have a reasonable doubt about the identity of the person demanding payment. For example, a cashier's check is payable to "Supplier Co." The person in possession of the check presents it for payment over the counter and claims to be an officer of Supplier Co. The bank may refuse payment until it has been given adequate proof that the presentment in fact is being made for Supplier Co., the person entitled to enforce the check.

Uniform Commercial Code Comment
Prior Uniform Statutory Provision:
Sections 187 and 188, Uniform Negotiable Instruments Law.
Changes: Combined and reworded; new provisions.

Purposes of Changes and New Matter:

1. The second sentence of subsection (1) continues the rule of original Section 188 that, while certification procured by a holder discharges the drawer and other prior parties, certification procured by the drawer leaves him liable. Under this provision any certification procured by a holder discharges the drawer and prior indorsers. Any indorsement made after a certification so procured remains effective; and where it is intended that any indorser shall remain liable notwithstanding certification, he may indorse with the words "after certification" to make his liability clear.

2. Subsection (2) is new. It states the generally recognized rule that in the absence of agreement a bank is under no obligation to certify a check, because it is a demand instrument calling for payment rather than acceptance. The bank may be liable for breach of any agreement with the drawer, the holder, or any other person by which it undertakes to certify. Its liability is not on the instrument, since the drawee is not so liable until acceptance (Section 3–409(1)). Any liability is for breach of the separate agreement.

3. Subsection (3) is new. It recognizes the banking practice of certifying a check which is returned for proper indorsement in order to protect the drawer against a longer contingent liability. It is consistent with the provision of Section 3–410(2) permitting certification although the check has not been signed or is otherwise incomplete.

Cross References:
Sections 3–412, 3–413, 3–417 and 3–418.
Point 2: Section 3–409(1).
Point 3: Section 3–410(2).

Definitional Cross References:
"Acceptance". Section 3–410.
"Bank". Section 1–201.
"Check". Section 3–104.
"Holder". Section 1–201.

Cross References
Bank,
Generally, see Commercial Code § 1201.
Return of items, see Commercial Code § 4301.
Right of charge back or refund, see Commercial Code § 4214.
Check, see Commercial Code § 3104.
Definition and operation of acceptance, see Commercial Code § 3409.
Discharge of parties, see Commercial Code § 3601.
Draft as assignment, see Commercial Code § 3409.
Obligation of issuer, drawer and acceptor, see Commercial Code § 3413 et seq.
Payment or acceptance, finality, see Commercial Code § 3418.
Warranties on presentment and transfer, see Commercial Code §§ 3416, 3417.

§ 3412. Issuer's obligation

The issuer of a note or cashier's check or other draft drawn on the drawer is obliged to pay the instrument (a) according to its terms at the time it was issued or, if not issued, at the time it first came into possession of a holder, or (b) if the issuer signed an incomplete instrument, according to its terms when completed, to the extent stated in Sections 3115 and 3407. The obligation is owed to a person entitled to enforce the instrument or to an indorser who paid the instrument under Section 3415. *(Added by Stats.1992, c. 914 (S.B.833), § 6.)*

California Code Comment
By John A. Bohn and Charles J. Williams

Prior California Law

1. This section applies to any acceptance which changes the essential terms of the instrument. It speaks in terms of an acceptance which varies the draft rather than the terminology of general, qualified, conditional, partial or local acceptance under the NIL.

2. Subdivision (1) substitutes as the standard an acceptance which "varies the draft" for the term "qualified acceptance" used in former Civil Code §§ 3220, 3222 and 3223.

This subdivision continues the rule of former Civil Code § 3223 which permits the holder to refuse an acceptance which varies the draft and to treat the draft as dishonored.

3. Subdivision (2) combines former Civil Code §§ 3221 and 3222(3) and continues the rule that an acceptance to pay at a particular place does not vary the terms unless it restricts payment to the place specified.

Commercial Code § 3504(4) provides that a draft accepted as payable at a bank in the United States must be presented at the bank designated.

4. Under subdivision (3) the effect of failing to assent to the acceptance which varies the terms of the instrument is the same as under former Civil Code §§ 3223. If the holder takes the acceptance, indorsers who do not agree to the acceptance are discharged.

However, subdivision (3) changes the manner by which the assent to the acceptance is given. Under former Civil Code § 3223, the drawer or indorser were deemed to have agreed if each did not specifically object to the holder within a reasonable time after receiving notice of the holder's qualified acceptance.

This rule is changed and under subdivision (3) the drawer and indorsers are discharged unless they "affirmatively assent" to the acceptance which varies the draft.

Changes from U.C.C. (1962 Official Text)

5. This is section 3–412 of the Official Text without change.

Uniform Commercial Code Comment
1992 Addition

1. The obligations of the maker, acceptor, drawer, and indorser are stated in four separate sections. Section 3–412 states the obligation of the maker of a note and is consistent with former Section 3–413(1). Section 3–412 also applies to the issuer of a cashier's check or other draft drawn on the drawer. Under former Section 3–118(a), since a cashier's check or other draft drawn on the drawer was "effective as a note," the drawer was liable under former Section 3–413(1) as a maker. Under Sections 3–103(a)(6) and 3–104(f) a cashier's check or other draft drawn on the drawer is treated as a draft to reflect common commercial usage, but the liability of the drawer is stated by Section 3–412 as being the same as that of the maker of a note rather than that of the drawer of a draft. Thus, Section 3–412 does not in substance change former law.

2. Under Section 3–105(b) nonissuance of either a complete or incomplete instrument is a defense by a maker or drawer against a person that is not a holder in due course.

3. The obligation of the maker may be modified in the case of alteration if, under Section 3–406, the maker is precluded from asserting the alteration.

Uniform Commercial Code Comment

Prior Uniform Statutory Provision:

Sections 139, 140, 141 and 142, Uniform Negotiable Instruments Law.
Changes: Combined and reworded; law changed as to qualified acceptances.

Purposes of Changes:

1. The section applies to conditional acceptances, acceptances for part of the amount, acceptances to pay at a different time from that required by the draft, or to the acceptance of less than all of the drawees, all of which are covered by the original Section 141. It applies to any other engagement changing the essential terms of the draft.

2. Where the drawee offers such a varied engagement the holder has an election. He may reject the offer, insist on acceptance of the draft as presented, and treat the refusal to give it as a dishonor. In that event the drawee is not bound by his engagement, and is entitled to have it cancelled. After any necessary notice of dishonor and protest the holder may have his recourse against the drawer and indorsers.

If the holder elects to accept the offer, this section does not invalidate the drawee's varied engagement. It remains his effective obligation, which the holder may enforce against him. By his assent, however, the holder discharges any drawer or indorser who does not also assent. The rule of the original Section 142 is changed to require that the assent of the drawer or indorser be affirmatively expressed. Mere failure to object within a reasonable time is not assent which will prevent the discharge.

3. The rule of original Section 140 that an acceptance to pay at a particular place is an unqualified acceptance is modified by the provision of subsection (2) that the terms of the draft are not varied by an acceptance to pay at any particular bank or place in the United States unless the acceptance states that the draft is to be paid only at such bank or place. Section 3–504(4) provides that a draft accepted payable at a bank in the United States must be presented at the bank designated.

Cross References:

Sections 3–410 and 3–413.
Point 3: Section 3–504(4).

Definitional Cross References:

"Acceptance". Section 3–410.
"Bank". Section 1–201.
"Dishonor". Section 3–507.
"Draft". Section 3–104.
"Holder". Section 1–201.
"Term". Section 1–201.
"Written". Section 1–201.

Cross References

Acceptance, see Commercial Code § 3409.
Definition and operation of acceptance, see Commercial Code § 3409.
Discharge of parties, see Commercial Code § 3601.
Dishonor, see Commercial Code § 3502.
Draft, see Commercial Code § 3104.
Presentment of draft for acceptance, manner of making, see Commercial Code § 3501.

§ 3413. Acceptor's obligation

(a) The acceptor of a draft is obliged to pay the draft (1) according to its terms at the time it was accepted, even though the acceptance states that the draft is payable "as originally drawn" or equivalent terms, (2) if the acceptance varies the terms of the draft, according to the terms of the draft as varied, or (3) if the acceptance is of a draft that is an incomplete instrument, according to its terms when completed, to the extent stated in Sections 3115 and 3407. The obligation is owed to a person entitled to enforce the draft or to the drawer or an indorser who paid the draft under Section 3414 or 3415.

(b) If the certification of a check or other acceptance of a draft states the amount certified or accepted, the obligation of the acceptor is that amount. If (1) the certification or acceptance does not state an amount, (2) the amount of the instrument is subsequently raised, and (3) the instrument is then negotiated to a holder in due course, the obligation of the acceptor is the amount of the instrument at the time it was taken by the holder in due course. *(Added by Stats.1992, c. 914 (S.B.833), § 6.)*

California Code Comment
By John A. Bohn and Charles J. Williams

Prior California Law

1. This section generally adopts the rules of former Civil Code §§ 3141–3143 inclusive.

2. Subdivision (1) is similar to the first part of former Civil Code § 3141. The remainder of former Civil Code § 3141 to the effect that the maker admits the existence of the payee and his capacity to indorse is covered by subdivision (3). An agreement outside the terms of the note cannot be used to defeat the maker's liability on the instrument. The court in Kent v. Lampman, 59 Cal.App.2d 407, 139 P.2d 57 (1943) held that a certain bonus agreement executed contemporaneously with a promissory note could not modify the obligation to pay the note.

Subdivision (1) also replaces former Civil Code § 3143 which provided that an acceptor engaged to pay according to the tenor of his acceptance. This was interpreted to mean the tenor at the time of acceptance. Wells Fargo Bank & Union Trust Co. v. Bank of Italy, 214 Cal. 156, 4 P.2d 781 (1931). This subdivision continues the rule of former Civil Code § 3143 as interpreted in California. See Official Comment.

3. Subdivision (2) is similar to former Civil Code § 3142.

4. Subdivision (3) combines parts of former Civil Code §§ 3141, 3142 and 3143 relating to admissions made by a maker, drawer or acceptor of the payee's existence and his capacity to exist.

Changes from U.C.C. (1962 Official Text)

5. This is section 3–413 of the Official Text without change.

Uniform Commercial Code Comment
1992 Addition

Subsection (a) is consistent with former Section 3–413(1). Subsection (b) has primary importance with respect to certified checks. It protects the holder in due course of a certified check that was altered after certification and before negotiation to the holder in due course. A bank can avoid liability for the altered amount by stating on the check the amount the bank agrees to pay. The subsection applies to other accepted drafts as well.

Uniform Commercial Code Comment

Prior Uniform Statutory Provision:

Sections 60, 61 and 62, Uniform Negotiable Instruments Law.
Changes: Combined and reworded.

Purposes of Changes:

The original sections are combined for convenience and condensed to avoid duplication of language. This section should be read in connection with the sections on incomplete instruments (3–115), negligence contributing to alteration or unauthorized signature (3–406), alteration (3–407), acceptances varying a draft (3–412) and finality of payment or acceptance (3–418). Thus a maker who signs an incomplete note engages under this section to pay it according to its tenor at the time he signs it, but by virtue of Sections 3–115 and 3–407 the note may thereafter be completed and enforced against him. In the same way, if the maker's negligence substantially contributes to alteration of the instrument, he will become liable on his note as altered under Section 3–406. When a holder assents to an acceptance varying a draft (Section 3–412) he can of course hold the acceptor only according to the form of acceptance to which the holder agreed. Section 3–418 applies the rule of Price v. Neal both to acceptance and payment; thus an acceptor may not, after acceptance, assert that the drawer's signature is unauthorized.

Subsection (1) applies to all drafts (including checks) the rule that the acceptance relates to the instrument as it was at the time of its acceptance and not (in case of alteration before acceptance) to its original tenor. The cases on this point under the original act (all of which involved checks) have been in conflict. It should be noted that under Section 3–417 a person who obtains acceptance warrants to the acceptor that the instrument has not been materially altered.

Except as indicated in the foregoing comment the section makes no change in substance from the provision of the original act.

Cross References:

Sections 3–115, 3–406, 3–407, 3–412, 3–417 and 3–418.

Definitional Cross References:

"Contract". Section 1–201.
"Dishonor". Section 3–507.
"Draft". Section 3–104.
"Holder". Section 1–201.
"Instrument". Section 3–102.
"Notice of dishonor". Section 3–508.
"Party". Section 1–201.
"Protest". Section 3–509.

Cross References

Acceptance, see Commercial Code § 3409.
Acceptance varying draft, see Commercial Code § 3410.
Alteration, see Commercial Code § 3407.
Contract, see Commercial Code § 1201; Civil Code § 1549.
Dishonor, see Commercial Code § 3502.
Draft, see Commercial Code § 3104.
Incomplete instruments, see Commercial Code § 3115.
Instrument, see Commercial Code § 3104.
Liability of acceptor on bills drawn in sets, see Commercial Code § 3801.
Liability of maker where signature forged, see Commercial Code § 3406.
Negligence contributing to alteration or forged signature, see Commercial Code § 3406.
Notice of dishonor, see Commercial Code § 3503.
Payment or acceptance, finality, see Commercial Code § 3418.
Persons capable of contracting,
  Generally, see Civil Code § 1556,
  Minors' contracts, see Family Code § 6701.
Protest, see Commercial Code § 3505.

Time of payment, see Commercial Code § 3108.
Transfer without recourse, see Commercial Code § 3417.
Variation by agreement, see Commercial Code § 1102.
Warranties on presentment and transfer, see Commercial Code §§ 3426, 3417.

§ 3414. Drawer's obligation

(a) This section does not apply to cashier's checks or other drafts drawn on the drawer.

(b) If an unaccepted draft is dishonored, the drawer is obliged to pay the draft (1) according to its terms at the time it was issued or, if not issued, at the time it first came into possession of a holder, or (2) if the drawer signed an incomplete instrument, according to its terms when completed, to the extent stated in Sections 3115 and 3407. The obligation is owed to a person entitled to enforce the draft or to an indorser who paid the draft under Section 3415.

(c) If a draft is accepted by a bank, the drawer is discharged, regardless of when or by whom acceptance was obtained.

(d) If a draft is accepted and the acceptor is not a bank, the obligation of the drawer to pay the draft if the draft is dishonored by the acceptor is the same as the obligation of an indorser under subdivisions (a) and (c) of Section 3415.

(e) If a draft states that it is drawn "without recourse" or otherwise disclaims liability of the drawer to pay the draft, the drawer is not liable under subdivision (b) to pay the draft if the draft is not a check. A disclaimer of the liability stated in subdivision (b) is not effective if the draft is a check.

(f) If (1) a check is not presented for payment or given to a depositary bank for collection within 30 days after its date, (2) the drawee suspends payments after expiration of the 30-day period without paying the check, and (3) because of the suspension of payments, the drawer is deprived of funds maintained with the drawee to cover payment of the check, the drawer to the extent deprived of funds may discharge its obligation to pay the check by assigning to the person entitled to enforce the check the rights of the drawer against the drawee with respect to the funds. *(Added by Stats.1992, c. 914 (S.B.833), § 6.)*

California Code Comment

By John A. Bohn and Charles J. Williams

Prior California Law

1. Subdivision (1) replaces the last paragraph of former Civil Code § 3147 which provided that the indorser engaged to pay the instrument according to its tenor. This subdivision adds "at the time of his indorsement" and makes it consistent with the liability of an acceptor under Commercial Code § 3413.

Subdivision (1) continues the right of an indorser under former Civil Code § 3119 to limit his liability by using such words as "without recourse."

Former Civil Code § 3125 which permitted one signing in a representative capacity to limit his liability is deleted. It is necessarily included under the broader right to disclaim any liability. Official Comment 1.

The general statement of an indorser's liability in this subdivision includes the substance of former Civil Code § 3148 which imposed similar liabilities on the indorser of bearer paper.

2. If the indorser is also a transferor, he warrants to his transferee as provided in Commercial Code § 3417.

3. Subdivision (2) is a restatement of former Civil Code § 3149 and is intended to clarify it. See Official Comment 4.

Changes from U.C.C. (1962 Official Text)

4. This is section 3–414 of the Official Text without change.

Uniform Commercial Code Comment
1992 Addition

1. Subsection (a) excludes cashier's checks because the obligation of the issuer of a cashier's check is stated in Section 3–412.

2. Subsection (b) states the obligation of the drawer on an unaccepted draft. It replaces former Section 3–413(2). The requirement under former Article 3 of notice of dishonor or protest has been eliminated. Under revised Article 3, notice of dishonor is necessary only with respect to indorser's liability. The liability of the drawer of an unaccepted draft is treated as a primary liability. Under former Section 3–102(1)(d) the term "secondary party" was used to refer to a drawer or indorser. The quoted term is not used in revised Article 3. The effect of a draft drawn without recourse is stated in subsection (e).

3. Under subsection (c) the drawer is discharged of liability on a draft accepted by a bank regardless of when acceptance was obtained. This changes former Section 3–411(1) which provided that the drawer is discharged only if the holder obtains acceptance. Holders that have a bank obligation do not normally rely on the drawer to guarantee the bank's solvency. A holder can obtain protection against the insolvency of a bank acceptor by a specific guaranty of payment by the drawer or by obtaining an indorsement by the drawer. Section 3–205(d).

4. Subsection (d) states the liability of the drawer if a draft is accepted by a drawee other than a bank and the acceptor dishonors. The drawer of an unaccepted draft is the only party liable on the instrument. The drawee has no liability on the draft. Section 3–408. When the draft is accepted, the obligations change. The drawee, as acceptor, becomes primarily liable and the drawer's liability is that of a person secondarily liable as a guarantor of payment. The drawer's liability is identical to that of an indorser, and subsection (d) states the drawer's liability that way. The drawer is liable to pay the person entitled to enforce the draft or any indorser that pays pursuant to Section 3–415. The drawer in this case is discharged if notice of dishonor is required by Section 3–503 and is not given in compliance with that section. A drawer that pays has a right of recourse against the acceptor. Section 3–413(a).

5. Subsection (e) does not permit the drawer of a check to avoid liability under subsection (b) by drawing the check without recourse. There is no legitimate purpose served by issuing a check on which nobody is liable. Drawing without recourse is effective to disclaim liability of the drawer if the draft is not a check. Suppose, in a documentary sale, Seller draws a draft on Buyer for the price of goods shipped to Buyer. The draft is payable upon delivery to the drawee of an order bill of lading covering the goods. Seller delivers the draft with the bill of lading to Finance Company that is named as payee of the draft. If Seller draws without recourse Finance Company takes the risk that Buyer will dishonor. If Buyer dishonors, Finance Company has no recourse against Seller but it can obtain reimbursement by selling the goods which it controls through the bill of lading.

6. Subsection (f) is derived from former Section 3–502(1)(b). It is designed to protect the drawer of a check against loss resulting from suspension of payments by the drawee bank when the holder of the check delays collection of the check. For example, X writes a check payable to Y for $1,000. The check is covered by funds in X's account in the drawee bank. Y delays initiation of collection of the check for more than 30 days after the date of the check. The drawee bank suspends payments after the 30-day period and before the check is presented for payment. If the $1,000 of funds in X's account have not been withdrawn, X has a claim for those funds against the drawee bank and, if subsection (e) were not in effect, X would be liable to Y on the check because the check was dishonored. Section 3–502(e). If the suspension of payments by the drawee bank will result in payment to X of less than the full amount of the $1,000 in the account or if there is a significant delay in payment to X, X will suffer a loss which would not have been suffered if Y had promptly initiated collection of the check. In most cases, X will not suffer any loss because of the existence of federal bank deposit insurance that covers accounts up to $100,000. Thus, subsection (e) has relatively little importance. There might be some cases, however, in which the account is not fully insured because it exceeds $100,000 or because the account doesn't qualify for deposit insurance. Subsection (f) retains the phrase "deprived of funds maintained with the drawee" appearing in former Section 3–502(1)(b). The quoted phrase applies if the suspension of payments by the drawee prevents the drawer from receiving the benefit of funds which would have paid the check if the holder had been timely in initiating collection. Thus, any significant delay in obtaining full payment of the funds is a deprivation of funds. The drawer can discharge drawer's liability by assigning rights against the drawee with respect to the funds to the holder.

Uniform Commercial Code Comment

Prior Uniform Statutory Provision:

Sections 38, 44, 66, 67 and 68, Uniform Negotiable Instruments Law.
Changes: Combined and reworded.

Purposes of Changes:

1. Subsection (1) states the contract of indorsement—that if the instrument is dishonored and any protest or notice of dishonor which may be necessary under Section 3–501 is given, the indorser will pay the instrument. The indorser's engagement runs to any holder (whether or not for value) and to any indorser subsequent to him who has taken the instrument up. An indorser may disclaim his liability on the contract of indorsement, but only if the indorsement itself so specifies. Since the disclaimer varies the written contract of indorsement, the disclaimer itself must be written on the instrument and cannot be proved by parol. The customary manner of disclaiming the indorser's liability under this section is to indorse "without recourse". Apart from such a disclaimer all indorsers incur this liability, without regard to whether or not the indorser transferred the instrument for value or received consideration for his indorsement.

Original Section 44, permitting a representative to indorse in such terms as to exclude personal liability, is omitted as unnecessary and included in the broader right to disclaim any liability. No change in the law is intended by this omission.

2. In addition to his liability on the contract of indorsement, an indorser, if a transferor, gives the warranties stated in Section 3–417.

3. As in the case of acceptor's liability (Section 3–413), this section conditions the indorser's liability on the tenor of the instrument at the time of his indorsement. Thus if a person indorses an altered instrument he assumes liability as indorser on the instrument as altered.

4. Subsection (2) is intended to clarify existing law under original Section 68.

The section states two presumptions: One is that the indorsers are liable to one another in the order in which they have in fact indorsed. The other is that they have in fact indorsed in the order in which their names appear. Parol evidence is admissible to show that they have indorsed in another order, or that they have otherwise agreed as to their liability to one another.

The last sentence of the original Section 68 is now covered by Section 3–118(e) (Ambiguous Terms and Rules of Construction).

Cross References:

Point 1: Section 3–501.
Point 2: Section 3–417.
Point 3: Section 3–413.
Point 4: Section 3–118(e).

Definitional Cross References:

"Contract". Section 1–201.
"Dishonor". Section 3–507.
"Holder". Section 1–201.
"Instrument". Section 3–102.
"Notice of dishonor". Section 3–508.
"Presumed". Section 1–201.

"Protest". Section 3–509.
"Signature". Section 3–401.

Cross References

Cancellation of indorsement, see Commercial Code §§ 3207, 3605.
Contract, see Commercial Code § 1201; Civil Code § 1549.
Dishonor, see Commercial Code § 3502.
Enforcement of obligation of drawer, conditions, see Commercial Code § 3503.
Instrument, see Commercial Code § 3104.
Liability of multiple signatories, see Commercial Code § 3118.
Liability of person signing as representative, see Commercial Code § 3402.
Notice of dishonor, see Commercial Code § 3503.
Presentment, notice of dishonor and protest, see Commercial Code § 3505.
Presumptions, see Civil Code § 1614.
Protest, see Commercial Code § 3505.
Rules of construction, see Commercial Code § 3118.
Signature, see Commercial Code § 3401.
Striking out indorsement, see Commercial Code §§ 3208, 3604.
Transfer of right arising from obligation, see Civil Code § 1458.
Transfer of things in action, see Civil Code § 954.
Variation by agreement, see Commercial Code § 1102.
Warranties on presentment and transfer, see Commercial Code §§ 3416, 3417.

§ 3415. Indorser's obligation

(a) Subject to subdivisions (b), (c), and (d) and to subdivision (d) of Section 3419, if an instrument is dishonored, an indorser is obliged to pay the amount due on the instrument (1) according to the terms of the instrument at the time it was indorsed, or (2) if the indorser indorsed an incomplete instrument, according to its terms when completed, to the extent stated in Sections 3115 and 3407. The obligation of the indorser is owed to a person entitled to enforce the instrument or to a subsequent indorser who paid the instrument under this section.

(b) If an indorsement states that it is made "without recourse" or otherwise disclaims liability of the indorser, the indorser is not liable under subdivision (a) to pay the instrument.

(c) If notice of dishonor of an instrument is required by Section 3503 and notice of dishonor complying with that section is not given to an indorser, the liability of the indorser under subdivision (a) is discharged.

(d) If a draft is accepted by a bank after an indorsement is made, the liability of the indorser under subdivision (a) is discharged.

(e) If an indorser of a check is liable under subdivision (a) and the check is not presented for payment, or given to a depositary bank for collection, within 30 days after the day the indorsement was made, the liability of the indorser under subdivision (a) is discharged. (Added by Stats.1992, c. 914 (S.B.833), § 6.)

California Code Comment

By John A. Bohn and Charles J. Williams

Prior California Law

1. Subdivision (1) is similar to the first sentence of former Civil Code § 3110 except that the requirement that the accommodation party sign the instrument "without receiving value" is eliminated upon the basis that the essential characteristic in an accommodation party transaction is the suretyship liability and not the fact that the accommodation party receives no consideration. Official Comments 1 and 2.

Under former Civil Code § 3110 a person who signed an instrument and received value for it could not be an accommodation maker. Holtman v. Ledford, 170 Cal.App.2d 481, 339 P.2d 150 (1959).

2. Subdivision (2) is similar to the second sentence of former Civil Code § 3110. A holder for value may enforce the instrument against the accommodation party even though he knows of the accommodation. In First National Bank of Santa Ana v. Kinslow, 2 Cal.App.2d 456, 38 Pac.2d 163 (1934) the court pointed out that an accommodation party will be held as a principal as between himself and the payee, even though the payee knows that he was only a surety between himself and the other makers.

3. Subdivision (3) is new statutory law but is consistent with prior case law. Seth v. Lew Hing, 125 Cal.App. 729, 14 P.2d 537 (1932); Brown v. Volz, 90 Cal.App.2d 793, 204 P.2d 110 (1949). These cases point out that as between parties parol evidence is admissible to show the capacity of one as an accommodation maker, but this is limited to situations where no value was received as required under former Civil Code § 3110.

4. Subdivision (4) is new statutory law. The courts have not stated their opinions in terms of notice or chain of title as does subdivision (4). The courts have dealt with the situation where one indorses a note as a guaranty after its execution. This would be an indorsement out of the chain of title. In such cases liability turned on whether there was consideration for the indorsement (Leverone v. Hildreth, 80 Cal. 139, 22 Pac. 72 (1889); Rusk v. Johnston, 18 Cal.App.2d 408, 63 P.2d 1167 (1937); Pierce v. Wright, 117 Cal.App.2d 718, 256 P.2d 1049 (1953)) or whether the indorsement was pursuant to an agreement at the time the note was given. (Pauly v. Murray, 110 Cal. 13, 42 Pac. 313 (1895); Stroud v. Thomas, 139 Cal. 274, 72 Pac. 1008, 96 Am.St.R. 111 (1903)).

5. Subdivision (5) is new statutory law but is in accord with prior California decisions. Western Hardwood Lumber Co. v. Superior Furniture Mfrs. Ltd., 18 Cal.App.2d 287, 63 P.2d 828 (1937). Official Comments 4 and 5.

6. This section also replaces former Civil Code § 3109 (absence or failure of consideration is a defense against one other than a holder in due course) and former Civil Code § 3145 (liability of an irregular indorser).

7. The effect of this section on prior California law is described in these terms:

"Under the Code as under the N.I.L., a surety who signs a negotiable instrument as an accommodation maker for the party primarily liable on the transaction, would appear as a principal party. Therefore, he would have no suretyship defenses (such as extension of time, etc.) against a holder in due course. But under the N.I.L., most courts, including those in California, hold that even as against one not a holder in due course an accommodation maker cannot rely upon a suretyship defense. [Fn.: 1 Witkin, Summary of California Law 616–617 (1960); Hawkland, Commercial Paper 92–93 (A.L.I. 1959).] Code sections 13415 [3415] and 13306 [3306] reject this view. They would permit parol proof of the accommodation character of a maker's signature, except as against a holder in due course, and give the accommodation party the benefit of discharges dependent on his character as such." California State Bar Committee, A Special Report, The Uniform Commercial Code, 37 California State Bar J. 162 (March–April 1962).

8. General provisions dealing with suretyship are covered in Civil Code §§ 2787–2854.

Changes from U.C.C. (1962 Official Text)

9. This is section 3–415 of the Official Text without change.

Uniform Commercial Code Comment

1992 Addition

1. Subsections (a) and (b) restate the substance of former Section 3–414(1). Subsection (2) of former Section 3–414 has been dropped because it is superfluous. Although notice of dishonor is not mentioned in subsection (a), it must be given in some cases to charge an indorser. It is covered in subsection (c). Regulation CC § 229.35(b) provides that a bank handling a check for collection or return is liable to a bank that subsequently handles the check to the extent the latter bank does not receive payment for the check. This liability applies whether or not the bank incurring the liability indorsed the check.

§ 3415

2. Section 3–503 states when notice of dishonor is required and how it must be given. If required notice of dishonor is not given in compliance with Section 3–503, subsection (c) of Section 3–415 states that the effect is to discharge the indorser's obligation.

3. Subsection (d) is similar in effect to Section 3–414(c) if the draft is accepted by a bank after the indorsement is made. See Comment 3 to Section 3–414. If a draft is accepted by a bank before the indorsement is made, the indorser incurs the obligation stated in subsection (a).

4. Subsection (e) modified former Sections 3–503(2)(b) and 3–502(1)(a) by stating a 30-day rather than a seven-day period, and stating it as an absolute rather than a presumptive period.

5. As stated in subsection (a), the obligation of an indorser to pay the amount due on the instrument is generally owed not only to a person entitled to enforce the instrument but also to a subsequent indorser who paid the instrument. But if the prior indorser and the subsequent indorser are both anomalous indorsers, this rule does not apply. In that case, Section 3–116 applies. Under Section 3–116(a), the anomalous indorsers are jointly and severally liable and if either pays the instrument the indorser who pays has a right of contribution against the other. Section 3–116(b). The right to contribution in Section 3–116(b) is subject to "agreement of the affected parties." Suppose the subsequent indorser can prove an agreement with the prior indorser under which the prior indorser agreed to treat the subsequent indorser as a guarantor of the obligation of the prior indorser. Rights of the two indorsers between themselves would be governed by the agreement. Under suretyship law, the subsequent indorser under such an agreement is referred to as a sub-surety. Under the agreement, if the subsequent indorser pays the instrument there is a right to reimbursement from the prior indorser; if the prior indorser pays the instrument, there is no right of recourse against the subsequent indorser. See PEB Commentary No. 11, dated February 10, 1994 [Uniform Laws Annotated, UCC, APP II, Comment 11].

Uniform Commercial Code Comment

Prior Uniform Statutory Provision:

Sections 28, 29 and 64, Uniform Negotiable Instruments Law.

Changes: Combined and reworded; new provisions.

Purposes of Changes and New Matter: To make it clear that:

1. Subsection (1) recognizes that an accommodation party is always a surety (which includes a guarantor), and it is his only distinguishing feature. He differs from other sureties only in that his liability is on the instrument and he is a surety for another party to it. His obligation is therefore determined by the capacity in which he signs. An accommodation maker or acceptor is bound on the instrument without any resort to his principal, while an accommodation indorser may be liable only after presentment, notice of dishonor and protest. The subsection recognizes the defenses of a surety in accordance with the provisions subjecting one not a holder in due course to all simple contract defenses, as well as his rights against his principal after payment. Under subsection (3) except as against a holder in due course without notice of the accommodation, parol evidence is admissible to prove that the party has signed for accommodation. In any case, however, under subsection (4) an indorsement which is not in the chain of title (the irregular or anomalous indorsement) is notice to all subsequent takers of the instrument of the accommodation character of the indorsement.

2. Subsection (1) eliminates the language of the old Section 29 requiring that the accommodation party sign the instrument "without receiving value therefor." The essential characteristic is that the accommodation party is a surety, and not that he has signed gratuitously. He may be a paid surety, or receive other compensation from the party accommodated. He may even receive it from the payee, as where A and B buy goods and it is understood that A is to pay for all of them and that B is to sign a note only as a surety for A.

3. The obligation of the accommodation party is supported by any consideration for which the instrument is taken before it is due. Subsection (2) is intended to change occasional decisions holding that there is no sufficient consideration where an accommodation party signs a note after it is in the hands of a holder who has given value. The party is liable to the holder in such a case even though there is no extension of time or other concession. This is consistent with the provision as to antecedent obligations as consideration (Section 3–408). The limitation to "before it is due" is one of suretyship law, by which the obligation of the surety is terminated at the time limit unless in the meantime the obligation of the principal has become effective.

4. As a surety the accommodation party is not liable to the party accommodated; but he is otherwise liable on the instrument in the capacity in which he has signed. This general statement of the rule makes unnecessary the detailed provisions of the original Section 64, which is therefore eliminated, without any change in substance.

5. Subsection (5) is intended to change the result of such decisions as Quimby v. Varnum, 190 Mass. 211, 76 N.E. 671 (1906), which held that an accommodation indorser who paid the instrument could not maintain an action on it against the accommodated party since he had no "former rights" to which he was remitted. Under ordinary principles of suretyship the accommodation party who pays is subrogated to the rights of the holder paid, and should have his recourse on the instrument.

Cross References:

Sections 3–305, 3–408, 3–603, 3–604 and 3–606.
Point 1: Section 3–306(b).
Point 3: Section 3–408.

Definitional Cross References:

"Holder in due course". Section 3–302.
"Instrument". Section 3–102.
"Notice". Section 1–201.
"Party". Section 1–201.
"Presentment". Section 3–504.
"Signed". Section 1–201.
"Writing". Section 1–201.

Cross References

Enforcement of obligation of indorser, conditions, see Commercial Code § 3503.
Defined, see Evidence Code § 140.

§ 3416. Transfer warranties

(a) A person who transfers an instrument for consideration warrants all of the following to the transferee and, if the transfer is by indorsement, to any subsequent transferee:

(1) The warrantor is a person entitled to enforce the instrument.

(2) All signatures on the instrument are authentic and authorized.

(3) The instrument has not been altered.

(4) The instrument is not subject to a defense or claim in recoupment of any party which can be asserted against the warrantor.

(5) The warrantor has no knowledge of any insolvency proceeding commenced with respect to the maker or acceptor or, in the case of an unaccepted draft, the drawer.

(6) If the instrument is a demand draft, creation of the instrument according to the terms on its face was authorized by the person identified as drawer.

(b) A person to whom the warranties under subdivision (a) are made and who took the instrument in good faith may recover from the warrantor as damages for breach of warranty an amount equal to the loss suffered as a result of the breach, but not more than the amount of the instrument plus expenses and loss of interest incurred as a result of the breach.

(c) The warranties stated in subdivision (a) cannot be disclaimed with respect to checks. Unless notice of a claim for breach of warranty is given to the warrantor within 30 days after the claimant has reason to know of the breach and the identity of the warrantor, the liability of the warrantor under subdivision (b) is discharged to the extent of any loss caused by the delay in giving notice of the claim.

(d) A cause of action for breach of warranty under this section accrues when the claimant has reason to know of the breach.

(e) If the warranty in paragraph (6) of subdivision (a) is not given by a transferor under applicable conflict of law rules, then the warranty is not given to that transferor when that transferor is a transferee. *(Added by Stats.1992, c. 914 (S.B.833), § 6. Amended by Stats.1996, c. 316 (S.B.1742), § 3.)*

California Code Comment

By John A. Bohn and Charles J. Williams

Prior California Law

1. This section is new statutory law. Its purpose is to state the commercial understanding of the meaning and effect of words of guaranty added to a signature on an instrument. See Official Comment.

2. Suretyship obligations are treated generally in Civil Code §§ 2787–2854. Civil Code § 2787 abolishes the distinction between sureties and guarantors and provides that the terms as used in any statute in effect or which may be enacted shall have the same meaning as defined in that section. Section 2787 defines surety or guarantor as:

". . . one who promises to answer for the debt, default, or miscarriage of another, or hypothecates property as security therefor. Guaranties of collection and continuing guaranties are forms of suretyship obligations, and except insofar as necessary in order to give effect to provisions specially relating thereto, shall be subject to all provisions of law relating to suretyships in general."

3. In connection with subdivision (2) relating to the guaranty of collection, see Civil Code § 2800 which provides that a guaranty that an obligation is collectible "imports that the debtor is solvent, and that the demand is collectible by the usual legal proceedings, if taken with reasonable diligence."

4. In connection with subdivision (6) see Civil Code §§ 2793 and 2794 for the rule and exceptions to it that the ordinary suretyship obligation must be in writing.

Changes from U.C.C. (1962 Official Text)

5. This is section 3–416 of the Official Text without change.

Uniform Commercial Code Comment

1992 Addition

1. Subsection (a) is taken from subsection (2) of former Section 3–417. Subsections (3) and (4) of former Section 3–417 are deleted. Warranties under subsection (a) in favor of the immediate transferee apply to all persons who transfer an instrument for consideration whether or not the transfer is accompanied by indorsement. Any consideration sufficient to support a simple contract will support those warranties. If there is an indorsement the warranty runs with the instrument and the remote holder may sue the indorser-warrantor directly and thus avoid a multiplicity of suits.

2. Since the purpose of transfer (Section 3–203(a)) is to give the transferee the right to enforce the instrument, subsection (a)(1) is a warranty that the transferor is a person entitled to enforce the instrument (Section 3–301). Under Section 3–203(b) transfer gives the transferee any right of the transferor to enforce the instrument. Subsection (a)(1) is in effect a warranty that there are no unauthorized or missing indorsements that prevent the transferor from making the transferee a person entitled to enforce the instrument.

3. The rationale of subsection (a)(4) is that the transferee does not undertake to buy an instrument that is not enforceable in whole or in part, unless there is a contrary agreement. Even if the transferee takes as a holder in due course who takes free of the defense or claim in recoupment, the warranty gives the transferee the option of proceeding against the transferor rather than litigating with the obligor on the instrument the issue of the holder-in-due-course status of the transferee. Subsection (3) of former Section 3–417 which limits this warranty is deleted. The rationale is that while the purpose of a "no recourse" indorsement is to avoid a guaranty of payment, the indorsement does not clearly indicate an intent to disclaim warranties.

4. Under subsection (a)(5) the transferor does not warrant against difficulties of collection, impairment of the credit of the obligor or even insolvency. The transferee is expected to determine such questions before taking the obligation. If insolvency proceedings as defined in Section 1–201(22) have been instituted against the party who is expected to pay and the transferor knows it, the concealment of that fact amounts to a fraud upon the transferee, and the warranty against knowledge of such proceedings is provided accordingly.

5. Transfer warranties may be disclaimed with respect to any instrument except a check. Between the immediate parties disclaimer may be made by agreement. In the case of an indorser, disclaimer of transferor's liability, to be effective, must appear in the indorsement with words such as "without warranties" or some other specific reference to warranties. But in the case of a check, subsection (c) of Section 3–416 provides that transfer warranties cannot be disclaimed at all. In the check collection process the banking system relies on these warranties.

6. Subsection (b) states the measure of damages for breach of warranty. There is no express provision for attorney's fees, but attorney's fees are not meant to be necessarily excluded. They could be granted because they fit within the phrase "expenses * * * incurred as a result of the breach." The intention is to leave to other state law the issue as to when attorney's fees are recoverable.

7. Since the traditional term "cause of action" may have been replaced in some states by "claim for relief" or some equivalent term, the words "cause of action" in subsection (d) have been bracketed to indicate that the words may be replaced by an appropriate substitute to conform to local practice.

Uniform Commercial Code Comment

Prior Uniform Statutory Provision:
None.

Purposes: The section is new. It states the commercial understanding as to the meaning and effect of words of guaranty added to a signature.

An indorser who guarantees payment waives not only presentment, notice of dishonor and protest, but also all demand upon the maker or drawee. Words of guaranty do not affect the character of the indorsement as an indorsement (Section 3–202(4)); but the liability of the indorser becomes indistinguishable from that of a co-maker. A guaranty of collection likewise waives formal presentment, notice of dishonor and protest, but requires that the holder first proceed against the maker or acceptor by suit and execution, or show that such proceeding would be useless.

Subsection (6) is concerned chiefly with the type of statute of frauds which provides that no promise to answer for the debt, default or miscarriage of another is enforceable unless it is evidenced by a writing which states the consideration for the promise. It is unusual to state any consideration when a guaranty is added to a signature on a negotiable instrument, which in itself sufficiently shows the nature of the transaction; and such statutes have commonly been held not to apply to such guaranties.

Cross References:
Sections 3–202(4) and 3–415.

Definitional Cross References:
"Holder". Section 1–201.
"Insolvent". Section 1–201.
"Instrument". Section 3–102.
"Notice of dishonor". Section 3–508.

"Party". Section 1–201.
"Presumption". Section 1–201.
"Protest". Section 3–509.
"Signature". Section 3–401.
"Written". Section 1–201.

Cross References

Demand draft, defined, see Commercial Code § 3104.
Holder's promise on transfer for precedent debt or new consideration as original obligation which need not be in writing, see Civil Code § 2794.
Instrument, see Commercial Code § 3104.
Negotiation, effect of words of guaranty, see Commercial Code § 3202.
Notice of dishonor, see Commercial Code § 3503.
Obligation, accommodation party, see Commercial Code § 3419.
Presumption, see Commercial Code § 1201; Evidence Code § 600.
Protest, see Commercial Code § 3505.
Signature, see Commercial Code § 3401.
Statute of frauds, special promise to answer for the debt, default or miscarriage of another, see Civil Code § 1624.
Suretyship, see Civil Code § 2787 et seq.
Variation by agreement, see Commercial Code § 1102.
Words of guaranty accompanying indorsement, effect, see Commercial Code § 3202.

§ 3417. Presentment warranties

(a) If an unaccepted draft is presented to the drawee for payment or acceptance and the drawee pays or accepts the draft, (i) the person obtaining payment or acceptance, at the time of presentment, and (ii) a previous transferor of the draft, at the time of transfer, warrant all of the following to the drawee making payment or accepting the draft in good faith:

(1) The warrantor is, or was, at the time the warrantor transferred the draft, a person entitled to enforce the draft or authorized to obtain payment or acceptance of the draft on behalf of a person entitled to enforce the draft.

(2) The draft has not been altered.

(3) The warrantor has no knowledge that the signature of the drawer of the draft is unauthorized.

(4) If the draft is a demand draft, creation of the demand draft according to the terms on its face was authorized by the person identified as drawer.

(b) A drawee making payment may recover from any warrantor damages for breach of warranty equal to the amount paid by the drawee less the amount the drawee received or is entitled to receive from the drawer because of the payment. In addition, the drawee is entitled to compensation for expenses and loss of interest resulting from the breach. The right of the drawee to recover damages under this subdivision is not affected by any failure of the drawee to exercise ordinary care in making payment. If the drawee accepts the draft, breach of warranty is a defense to the obligation of the acceptor. If the acceptor makes payment with respect to the draft, the acceptor is entitled to recover from any warrantor for breach of warranty the amounts stated in this subdivision.

(c) If a drawee asserts a claim for breach of warranty under subdivision (a) based on an unauthorized indorsement of the draft or an alteration of the draft, the warrantor may defend by proving that the indorsement is effective under Section 3404 or 3405 or the drawer is precluded under Section 3406 or 4406 from asserting against the drawee the unauthorized indorsement or alteration.

(d) If (i) a dishonored draft is presented for payment to the drawer or an indorser or (ii) any other instrument is presented for payment to a party obliged to pay the instrument, and (iii) payment is received, the following rules apply:

(1) The person obtaining payment and a prior transferor of the instrument warrant to the person making payment in good faith that the warrantor is, or was, at the time the warrantor transferred the instrument, a person entitled to enforce the instrument or authorized to obtain payment on behalf of a person entitled to enforce the instrument.

(2) The person making payment may recover from any warrantor for breach of warranty an amount equal to the amount paid plus expenses and loss of interest resulting from the breach.

(e) The warranties stated in subdivisions (a) and (d) cannot be disclaimed with respect to checks. Unless notice of a claim for breach of warranty is given to the warrantor within 30 days after the claimant has reason to know of the breach and the identity of the warrantor, the liability of the warrantor under subdivision (b) or (d) is discharged to the extent of any loss caused by the delay in giving notice of the claim.

(f) A cause of action for breach of warranty under this section accrues when the claimant has reason to know of the breach.

(g) A demand draft is a check, as provided in subdivision (f) of Section 3104.

(h) If the warranty in paragraph (4) of subdivision (a) is not given by a transferor under applicable conflict of law rules, then the warranty is not given to that transferor when that transferor is a transferee. (Added by Stats.1992, c. 914 (S.B.833), § 6. Amended by Stats.1996, c. 316 (S.B.1742), § 4.)

California Code Comment

By John A. Bohn and Charles J. Williams

Prior California Law

1. The rights of the various parties where there was a mistake in the payment process by the party making payment was not satisfactorily covered by the NIL. It was left to the courts to resolve the rights of the parties and they were not always consistent or uniform in the way they resolved the disputes between the parties.

The Commercial Code treats the solution to the problems of the rights of the various parties upon the basis of warranties. Under the NIL the justification used by the courts was payment under a mistake of fact and the application of quasi contract principles. As in the case of other warranties, the warranties set forth in this section are intended to carry with them all of the usual rules of law applicable to warranties. As in the case of other warranties these warranties may be disclaimed by agreement between the immediate parties. Official Comment 1.

2. In general, subdivision (1) of this section is new statutory law but continues the principles of prior judicial decisions. It also clarifies some situations upon which there is no specific California authority. The effect of subdivision (1) upon the rights of the parties follows closely the principles of Price v. Neal, 3 Burr. 1354 (1762). Official Comment 4.

§ 3417 · LIABILITY OF PARTIES · 215

3. Subdivision (1)(a) continues the rule of former Civil Code § 3146(2). The effect of this subdivision is to permit the drawee to recover payment from a holder in due course when that payment is made upon a forged indorsement. Where the maker's or drawer's signature is forged (subdivision (1)(b)), the drawee who pays to a holder in due course cannot recover the amount paid. The supposed justification for distinguishing the right of recovery between the forgery of the drawer's signature and the forgery of an indorser's signature is that the drawee is in a better position to detect the drawer's forgery while in the case of the indorser's signature the drawee ordinarily does not have the opportunity to verify an indorsement. Official Comment 3. In this age of expert forgery, this distinction is more probably justifiable upon the basis of commercial convenience.

4. Subdivision (1)(b) deals with the situation where the maker's or drawer's signature is forged.

The basic warranty established by subdivision (1)(b) is the state of mind concerning knowledge of the authenticity of the maker's signature. One who presents an instrument knowing that the maker's signature is forged breaches the warranty. Under the NIL a person presenting an instrument knowing the maker's signature is forged committed a fraud and recovery was permitted.

Different fact situations can produce parties with equities of differing strengths. The exceptions in subparagraphs (i), (ii) and (iii) are designed to provide flexibility. They apply where one or more innocent parties have taken the instrument in good faith. In this case there is no warranty as to the state of knowledge of the person presenting the instrument. Thus in subparagraph (i) a holder in due course does not warrant to the maker as to the maker's own signature and if the maker pays an instrument containing his forged signature to the holder in due course he may not recover. This was also the rule under Price v. Neal, supra. In subparagraph (ii) the result under subparagraph (i) is applied to the drawer. Under subparagraph (iii) the drawee (in accepting or paying an instrument) is given the benefit of a warranty by a holder except where the holder takes the instrument after the drawee accepted it or where the holder obtained acceptance without knowledge of the forgery. See the last paragraph of Official Comment 4.

5. Subdivision (1)(c) is new statutory law but is in accord with the common law rule that a party who pays or accepts an altered instrument can recover or void the acceptance upon the basis of mutual mistake of fact. Official Comment 5.

The exceptions to the rule in subparagraphs (i) and (ii) are based upon the same reasoning as subparagraphs (i) and (ii) in subdivision (1)(b) that no warranty is made to the issuer because he should know his own signature and the instrument which he signed. The basis for the exception in subparagraph (iv) has a similar rationale. Wells Fargo Bank and Union Trust Co. v. Bank of Italy, 214 Cal. 156, 4 P.2d 781 (1931), (drawee certifies a check after the alteration, check is presented and paid by the drawee, held that the drawee may not recover).

6. Subdivision (2) extends the warranties of an indorser to all indorsers beyond the immediate transferee. Former Civil Code § 3146 limited the warranties to the immediate transferee of the person negotiating the instrument. Under subdivision (2) the warranties accompanying the indorsement run with the instrument and remote holders may sue upon them. Official Comments 8 and 9.

7. Subdivision (2)(a) is similar to former Civil Code §§ 3146(2) and 3147(1).

8. Subdivision (2)(b) is similar to former Civil Code §§ 3146(1), (2) and 3147(1).

9. Subdivision (2)(c) rewords former Civil Code § 3146(1) which provided that an indorser warranted that the instrument was "genuine and . . . what it purports to be."

10. Subdivision (2)(d) clarifies the warranty intended to be included under former Civil Code § 3147(2). That section provided that an indorser warranted that the instrument at the time of indorsement was "valid and subsisting." The language was changed so that it is now clear that the indorser warrants the absence of defenses. Official Comment 9.

11. Subdivision (2)(e) replaces former Civil Code § 3146(4) which provided that a person negotiating an instrument warranted that he had no knowledge of any fact which would "impair . . . [its] validity . . . or render it valueless." Official Comment 10.

12. Subdivision (3) is new statutory law but is in accord with prior California law. Under prior California law "without recourse" or similar language was a qualified indorsement (former Civil Code § 3119) and the party so signing would not be held as a regular indorser. Hammond Lumber Co. v. Kearsley, 36 Cal.App. 431, 172 Pac. 404 (1918). However, a party so signing was still liable as a transferor of the instrument and held to the warranties under former Civil Code § 3146. Quatman v. Superior Court of Glenn County, 64 Cal.App. 203, 221 Pac. 666 (1923). An indorsement "without recourse" carries the same warranties as any other transfer except that the (2)(d) warranty is limited to no knowledge. Official Comment 9.

13. Subdivision (4) is similar to former Civil Code § 3150 but is limited to "selling agents," while former Civil Code § 3150 applied to an "agent for collection". Official Comment 11.

Changes from U.C.C. (1962 Official Text)

14. This is section 3–417 of the Official Text without change.

Uniform Commercial Code Comment

1992 Addition

1. This section replaces subsection (1) of former Section 3–417. The former provision was difficult to understand because it purported to state in one subsection all warranties given to any person paying any instrument. The result was a provision replete with exceptions that could not be readily understood except after close scrutiny of the language. In revised Section 3–417, presentment warranties made to drawees of uncertified checks and other unaccepted drafts are stated in subsection (a). All other presentment warranties are stated in subsection (d).

2. Subsection (a) states three warranties. Subsection (a)(1) in effect is a warranty that there are no unauthorized or missing indorsements. "Person entitled to enforce" is defined in Section 3–301. Subsection (a)(2) is a warranty that there is no alteration. Subsection (a)(3) is a warranty of no knowledge that there is a forged drawer's signature. Subsection (a) states that the warranties are made to the drawee and subsections (b) and (c) identify the drawee as the person entitled to recover for breach of warranty. There is no warranty made to the drawer under subsection (a) when presentment is made to the drawee. Warranty to the drawer is governed by subsection (d) and that applies only when presentment for payment is made to the drawer with respect to a dishonored draft. In Sun 'N Sand, Inc. v. United California Bank, 582 P.2d 920 (Cal.1978), the court held that under former Section 3–417(1) a warranty was made to the drawer of a check when the check was presented to the drawee for payment. The result in that case is rejected.

3. Subsection (a)(1) retains the rule that the drawee does not admit the authenticity of indorsements and subsection (a)(3) retains the rule of Price v. Neal, 3 Burr. 1354 (1762), that the drawee takes the risk that the drawer's signature is unauthorized unless the person presenting the draft has knowledge that the drawer's signature is unauthorized. Under subsection (a)(3) the warranty of no knowledge that the drawer's signature is unauthorized is also given by prior transferors of the draft.

4. Subsection (d) applies to presentment for payment in all cases not covered by subsection (a). It applies to presentment of notes and accepted drafts to any party obliged to pay the instrument, including an indorser, and to presentment of dishonored drafts if made to the drawer or an indorser. In cases covered by subsection (d), there is only one warranty and it is the same as that stated in subsection (a)(1). There are no warranties comparable to subsections (a)(2) and (a)(3) because they are appropriate only in the case of presentment to the drawee of an unaccepted draft. With respect to presentment of an accepted draft to the acceptor, there is no warranty with respect to alteration or knowledge that the signature of the drawer is unauthorized. Those warranties were made to the drawee when the draft was presented for acceptance (Section 3–417(a)(2) and (3)) and breach of that warranty is a defense to the obligation of the drawee as acceptor to pay the draft. If the drawee pays the accepted draft the drawee may recover the payment from any warrantor who was in breach of warranty when the draft was accepted. Section 3–417(b). Thus, there is no necessity for these warranties to be repeated when the accepted draft is presented for payment. Former Section 3–417(1)(b)(iii) and (c)(iii) are not included in revised Section 3–417 because they are unnecessary. Former Section 3–417(1)(c)(iv) is not included because it is also unnecessary. The acceptor should know what the terms of the draft were at the time acceptance was made.

§ 3417   NEGOTIABLE INSTRUMENTS   216

If presentment is made to the drawer or maker, there is no necessity for a warranty concerning the signature of that person or with respect to alteration. If presentment is made to an indorser, the indorser had itself warranted authenticity of signatures and that the instrument was not altered. Section 3–416(a)(2) and (3).

5. The measure of damages for breach of warranty under subsection (a) is stated in subsection (b). There is no express provision for attorney's fees, but attorney's fees are not meant to be necessarily excluded. They could be granted because they fit within the language "expenses * * * resulting from the breach." Subsection (b) provides that the right of the drawee to recover for breach of warranty is not affected by a failure of the drawee to exercise ordinary care in paying the draft. This provision follows the result reached under former Article 3 in Hartford Accident & Indemnity Co. v. First Pennsylvania Bank, 859 F.2d 295 (3d Cir.1988).

6. Subsection (c) applies to checks and other unaccepted drafts. It gives to the warrantor the benefit of rights that the drawee has against the drawer under Section 3–404, 3–405, 3–406, or 4–406. If the drawer's conduct contributed to a loss from forgery or alteration, the drawee should not be allowed to shift the loss from the drawer to the warrantor.

7. The first sentence of subsection (e) recognizes that checks are normally paid by automated means and that payor banks rely on warranties in making payment. Thus, it is not appropriate to allow disclaimer of warranties appearing on checks that normally will not be examined by the payor bank. The second sentence requires a breach of warranty claim to be asserted within 30 days after the drawee learns of the breach and the identity of the warrantor.

8. Since the traditional term "cause of action" may have been replaced in some states by "claim for relief" or some equivalent term, the words "cause of action" in subsection (f) have been bracketed to indicate that the words may be replaced by an appropriate substitute to conform to local practice.

Uniform Commercial Code Comment

Prior Uniform Statutory Provision:

Sections 65 and 69, Uniform Negotiable Instruments Law.
Changes: Combined and reworded; new provisions added.

Purposes of Changes and New Matter:

1. The obligations imposed by this section are stated in terms of warranty. Warranty terms, which are not limited to sale transactions, are used with the intention of bringing in all the usual rules of law applicable to warranties, and in particular the necessity of reliance in good faith and the availability of all remedies for breach of warranty, such as rescission of the transaction or an action for damages. Like other warranties, those stated in this section may be disclaimed by agreement between the immediate parties. In the case of an indorser, disclaimer of his liability as a transferor, to be effective, must appear in the form of the indorsement, and no parol proof of "agreement otherwise" is admissible. For corresponding warranties in the case of items in the bank collection process, Section 4–207 should be consulted.

2. Subsection (1) is new. It is intended to state the undertaking to a party who accepts or pays of one who obtains payment or acceptance or of any prior transferor. It is closely connected with the following section on the finality of acceptance or payment (Section 3–418), and should be read together with it.

3. Subsection (1)(a) retains the generally accepted rule that the party who accepts or pays does not "admit" the genuineness of indorsements, and may recover from the person presenting the instrument when they turn out to be forged. The justification for the distinction between forgery of the signature of the drawer and forgery of an indorsement is that the drawee is in a position to verify the drawer's signature by comparison with one in his hands, but has ordinarily no opportunity to verify an indorsement.

4. Subsection (1)(b) recognizes and deals with competing equities of parties accepting or paying instruments bearing unauthorized maker's or drawer's signatures and those obtaining acceptances or receiving payment. The warranties prescribed and exceptions thereto follow closely principles established at common law, particularly, those under Price v. Neal, 3 Burr. 1354 (1762).

The basic warranty that the person obtaining payment or acceptance and any prior transferor warrants that he has no knowledge that the signature of the maker or drawer is unauthorized stems from the general principle that one who presents an instrument knowing that the signature of the maker or drawer is forged or unauthorized commits an obvious fraud upon the party to whom presentment is made. However, few cases present this simple fact situation. If the signature of a maker or drawer has been forged, the parties include the dishonest forger himself and usually one or more innocent holders taking from him. Frequently, the state of knowledge of a holder is difficult to determine and sometimes a holder takes such a forged instrument in perfect good faith but subsequently learns of the forgery. Since in different fact situations holders have equities of varying strength, it is necessary to have some exceptions to the basic warranty.

The exceptions apply only in favor of a holder in due course and, within the provisions of Section 3–201, to all subsequent transferees from a holder in due course. Since a condition of the status of a holder in due course under Section 3–302(1)(a) is that the holder takes the instrument without notice of any defense against it, this condition presupposes that at the time of taking such a holder had no knowledge of the unauthorized signature. Consequently, the warranty of subsection (1)(b) is pertinent in the case of a holder in due course only in the relatively few cases where he acquires knowledge of the forgery after the taking but before the presentment. In this situation the holder in due course must continue to act in good faith to be exempted from the basic warranty.

The first exemption from the warranty by such a holder, made by subparagraph (i), is that the warranty does not run to a maker of a note with respect to the maker's own signature. This codifies the rule of Price v. Neal, and related cases. Since a maker of a note is presumed to know his own signature, if he fails to detect a forgery of his own signature and pays the note, under the Price v. Neal principle he should not be permitted to recover such payment from a holder in due course acting in good faith. Similarly, under subparagraph (ii) a drawer of a draft is presumed to know his own signature and if he fails to detect a forgery of his signature and pays a draft he may not recover that payment from a holder in due course acting in good faith. This rule applies if the drawer pays the instrument as drawer and also if he pays the instrument as drawee in a case where he is both drawer and drawee.

Under the principle of Price v. Neal a drawee of a draft is presumed to know the signature of his customer, the drawer. However, under subsection (1)(b) and subparagraph (iii) of this subsection this presumption is not strong enough to deprive such a drawee (either in accepting or paying an instrument) of the warranty of no knowledge of the unauthorized drawer's signature, unless the holder in due course took the instrument and became such a holder after the drawee's acceptance; or obtained the acceptance without knowledge that the drawer's signature was unauthorized. In the former case, the holder taking after and thereby presumably in reliance on the acceptance should be protected as against the drawee who accepted without detecting the unauthorized signature. In the latter case the holder, having no knowledge of the unauthorized signature at the time of the drawee's acceptance, would not be charged with this warranty and would be entitled to enforce such acceptance under Section 3–418, even if thereafter he acquired knowledge of the unauthorized signature prior to enforcement of the acceptance. Such right of the holder to enforce the acceptance would be valueless if immediately upon enforcing it and obtaining payment the holder became obligated to return the payment by reason of breach of the warranty of no knowledge at the time of payment.

5. Subsection (1)(c) retains the common law rule, followed by several decisions under the original Act, which has permitted a party paying a materially altered instrument in good faith to recover, and a party who accepts such an instrument to avoid such acceptance. As in the case of subsection (1)(b) this warranty is not imposed against a holder in due course acting in good faith in favor of a maker of a note or a drawer of a draft on the ground that such maker or drawer should know the form and amount of the note or draft which he has signed. The exception made by subparagraph (iii) in the case of a holder in due course of a draft accepted after the alteration follows the decisions in National City Bank of Chicago v. National Bank of Republic of Chicago, 300 Ill. 103, 132 N.E. 832, 22 A.L.R. 1153 (1921), and Wells Fargo Bank & Union Trust Company v. Bank of Italy, 214 Cal. 156, 4 P.2d 781 (1931), and is based on the principle that an acceptance is an undertaking relied upon in good faith by an innocent party. The attempt to avoid this result by certifying checks "payable as originally drawn" leaves the subsequent purchaser in uncertainty as to the amount

for which the instrument is certified, and so defeats the entire purpose of certification, which is to obtain the definite obligation of the bank to honor a definite instrument. Subparagraph (iii) accordingly provides that such language is not sufficient to impose on the holder in due course the warranty of no material alteration where the holder took the draft after the acceptance and presumably in reliance on it.

Subparagraph (iv) of subsection (1)(c) exempts a holder in due course from the warranty of no material alteration to the acceptor of a draft with respect to an alteration made after the acceptance. A drawee accepting a draft has an opportunity of ascertaining the form and particularly the amount of the draft accepted. If, thereafter, the draft is materially altered and is thereupon presented for payment to the acceptor, the acceptor has the necessary information in its records to verify the form and particularly the amount of the draft. If in spite of this available information it pays the draft, there is as much reason to leave the responsibility for such payment upon the acceptor (as against a holder in due course acting in good faith) as there is in the case of a maker or drawer paying a materially altered note or draft.

6. Under Section 3–201 parties taking from or holding under a holder in due course, within the limits of that section, will have the same rights under Section 4–317(1) as a holder in due course. Of course such parties claiming under a holder in due course must act in good faith and be free from fraud, illegality and notice as provided in Section 3–201.

7. The liabilities imposed by subsection (2) in favor of the immediate transferee apply to all persons who transfer an instrument for consideration whether or not the transfer is accompanied by indorsement. Any consideration sufficient to support a simple contract will support those warranties.

8. Subsection (2) changes the original Section 65 to extend the warranties of any *indorser* beyond the immediate transferee in all cases. Where there is an indorsement the warranty runs with the instrument and the remote holder may sue the indorser-warrantor directly and thus avoid a multiplicity of suits which might be interrupted by the insolvency of an intermediate transferor. The language of subsections (2)(b) and (2)(c) is substituted for "genuine and what it purports to be" in the original Section 65(1). The language of subsection (2)(a) is substituted for that of Section 65(2) in order to cover the case of the agent who transfers for another.

9. Subsection (2)(d) resolves a conflict in the decisions as to whether the transferor warrants that there are no defenses to the instrument good against him. The position taken is that the buyer does not undertake to buy an instrument incapable of enforcement, and that in the absence of contrary understanding the warranty is implied. Even where the buyer takes as a holder in due course who will cut off the defense, he still does not undertake to buy a lawsuit with the necessity of proving his status. Subsection (3) however provides that an indorsement "without recourse" limits the (2)(d) warranty to one that the indorser has no knowledge of such defenses. With this exception the liabilities of a "without recourse" indorser under this section are the same as those of any other transferor. Under Section 3–414 "without recourse" in an indorsement is effective to disclaim the general contract of the indorser stated in that section.

10. Subsection (2)(e) is substituted for Section 65(4). The transferor does not warrant against difficulties of collection, apart from defenses, or against impairment of the credit of the obligor or even his insolvency in the commercial sense. The buyer is expected to determine such questions for himself before he takes the obligation. If insolvency proceedings as defined in this Act (Section 1–201) have been instituted against the party who is expected to pay and the transferor knows it, the concealment of that fact amounts to a fraud upon the buyer, and the warranty against knowledge of such proceedings is provided accordingly.

11. Subsection (4) is substituted for Section 69 of the original Act. It applies only to a selling agent, as distinguished from an agent for collection. It follows the rule generally accepted that an agent who makes the disclosure warrants his good faith and authority and may not by contract assume a lesser warranty.

Cross References:

Sections 3–404, 3–405, 3–406, 3–414 and 4–207.
Point 1: Section 4–207.
Point 2: Section 3–418.
Point 4: Sections 3–201, 3–302 and 3–418.
Point 9: Section 3–414.
Point 10: Section 1–201.

Definitional Cross References:

"Acceptance". Section 3–410.
"Alteration". Section 3–407.
"Bank". Section 1–201.
"Draft". Section 3–104.
"Genuine". Section 1–201.
"Good faith". Section 1–201.
"Holder in due course". Section 3–302.
"Instrument". Section 3–102.
"Note". Section 3–104.
"Party". Section 1–201.
"Person". Section 1–201.
"Signature". Section 3–401.
"Term". Section 1–201.

Cross References

Acceptance, see Commercial Code § 3409.
Alteration, see Commercial Code § 3407.
Definitions, see Commercial Code § 1201.
Demand draft, defined, see Commercial Code § 3104.
Draft, see Commercial Code § 3104.
Holder in due course, see Commercial Code § 3302.
Impostors, see Commercial Code § 3404.
Indorsement in name of fictitious payee, see Commercial Code § 3404.
Instrument, see Commercial Code § 3104.
Negligence contributing to alteration or forged signature, see Commercial Code § 3406.
Note, see Commercial Code § 3104.
Obligation of indorser, see Commercial Code § 3414.
Rights of transferee, see Commercial Code § 3203.
Signature, see Commercial Code § 3401.
Signature by representative, see Commercial Code § 3402.
Transfer, see Commercial Code § 3203.
Unauthorized signature, see Commercial Code § 3403.
Variation by agreement, see Commercial Code § 1102.
Warranties,
    Collecting bank as to documents, see Commercial Code § 7508.
    Customer and collecting bank, see Commercial Code § 4207.
    Letters of credit, transfer and presentment, see Commercial Code § 5111.
    Negotiation or transfer of document of title, see Commercial Code § 7507.
Sales, see Commercial Code § 2312 et seq.
Without recourse, indorsement, see Commercial Code § 3414.

§ 3418. Payment or acceptance by mistake

(a) Except as provided in subdivision (c), if the drawee of a draft pays or accepts the draft and the drawee acted on the mistaken belief that (1) payment of the draft had not been stopped pursuant to Section 4403 or (2) the signature of the drawer of the draft was authorized, the drawee may recover the amount of the draft from the person to whom or for whose benefit payment was made or, in the case of acceptance, may revoke the acceptance. Rights of the drawee under this subdivision are not affected by failure of the drawee to exercise ordinary care in paying or accepting the draft.

(b) Except as provided in subdivision (c), if an instrument has been paid or accepted by mistake and the case is not covered by subdivision (a), the person paying or accepting may, to the extent permitted by the law governing mistake and restitution, (1) recover the payment from the person to whom or for whose benefit payment was made or (2) in the case of acceptance, may revoke the acceptance.

(c) The remedies provided by subdivision (a) or (b) may not be asserted against a person who took the instrument in good faith and for value or who in good faith changed position in reliance on the payment or acceptance. This subdivision does not limit remedies provided by Section 3417 or 4407.

(d) Notwithstanding Section 4215, if an instrument is paid or accepted by mistake and the payor or acceptor recovers payment or revokes acceptance under subdivision (a) or (b), the instrument is deemed not to have been paid or accepted and is treated as dishonored, and the person from whom payment is recovered has rights as a person entitled to enforce the dishonored instrument. *(Added by Stats.1992, c. 914 (S.B.833), § 6.)*

California Code Comment
By John A. Bohn and Charles J. Williams

Prior California Law

1. This section restates the rule of former Civil Code § 3143.

Any payment or acceptance becomes final in favor of a holder in due course or his transferee. This is true whether it is made on a forged instrument or by mistake for any reason. This prevents an opening up of a previous transaction or series of transactions upon an instrument which is later discovered to have been forged or paid in error for any reason. Official Comments 1, 2, 3 and 4.

2. This principle of finality is in accord with prior judicial decisions. The court in Crocker-Woolworth Nat. Bank v. Nevada Bank, 139 Cal. 564, 73 Pac. 456, 63 ALR 245, 96 AmStR 169 (1903), pointed out that when a holder moves in reliance upon acceptance or payment the party paying is precluded by ordinary rules of estoppel from denying payment. This section is also in accord with the rule that a holder in due course can enforce an instrument against the acceptor according to its tenor at the time of acceptance. Wells Fargo Bank & Union Trust Co. v. Bank of Italy, 214 Cal. 156, 4 P.2d 781 (1931)

Changes from U.C.C. (1962 Official Text)

4. This is section 3–418 of the Official Text without change.

Uniform Commercial Code Comment
1992 Addition

1. This section covers payment or acceptance by mistake and replaces former Section 3–418. Under former Article 3, the remedy of a drawee that paid or accepted a draft by mistake was based on the law of mistake and restitution, but that remedy was not specifically stated. It was provided by Section 1–103. Former Section 3–418 was simply a limitation on the unstated remedy under the law of mistake and restitution. Under revised Article 3, Section 3–418 specifically states the right of restitution in subsections (a) and (b). Subsection (a) allows restitution in the two most common cases in which the problem is presented: payment or acceptance of forged checks and checks on which the drawer has stopped payment. If the drawee acted under a mistaken belief that the check was not forged or had not been stopped, the drawee is entitled to recover the funds paid or to revoke the acceptance whether or not the drawee acted negligently. But in each case, by virtue of subsection (c), the drawee loses the remedy if the person receiving payment or acceptance was a person who took the check in good faith and for value or who in good faith changed position in reliance on the payment or acceptance. Subsections (a) and (c) are consistent with former Section 3–418 and the rule of Price v. Neal. The result in the two cases covered by subsection (a) is that the drawee in most cases will not have a remedy against the person paid because there is usually a person who took the check in good faith and for value or who in good faith changed position in reliance on the payment or acceptance.

2. If a check has been paid by mistake and the payee receiving payment did not give value for the check or did not change position in reliance on the payment, the drawee bank is entitled to recover the amount of the check under subsection (a) regardless of how the check was paid. The drawee bank normally pays a check by a credit to an account of the collecting bank that presents the check for payment. The payee of the check normally receives the payment by a credit to the payee's account in the depositary bank. But in some cases the payee of the check may have received payment directly from the drawee bank by presenting the check for payment over the counter. In those cases the payee is entitled to receive cash, but the payee may prefer another form of payment such as a cashier's check or teller's check issued by the drawee bank. Suppose Seller contracted to sell goods to Buyer. The contract provided for immediate payment by Buyer and delivery of the goods 20 days after payment. Buyer paid by mailing a check for $10,000 drawn on Bank payable to Seller. The next day Buyer gave a stop payment order to Bank with respect to the check Buyer had mailed to Seller. A few days later Seller presented Buyer's check to Bank for payment over the counter and requested a cashier's check as payment. Bank issued and delivered a cashier's check for $10,000 payable to Seller. The teller failed to discover Buyer's stop order. The next day Bank discovered the mistake and immediately advised Seller of the facts. Seller refused to return the cashier's check and did not deliver any goods to Buyer.

Under Section 4–215, Buyer's check was paid by Bank at the time it delivered its cashier's check to Seller. See Comment 3 to Section 4–215. Bank is obliged to pay the cashier's check and has no defense to that obligation. The cashier's check was issued for consideration because it was issued in payment of Buyer's check. Although Bank has no defense on its cashier's check, it may have a right to recover $10,000, the amount of Buyer's check, from Seller under Section 3–418(a). Bank paid Buyer's check by mistake. Seller did not give value for Buyer's check because the promise to deliver goods to Buyer was never performed. Section 3–303(a)(1). And, on these facts, Seller did not change position in reliance on the payment of Buyer's check. Thus, the first sentence of Section 3–418(c) does not apply and Seller is obliged to return $10,000 to Bank. Bank is obliged to pay the cashier's check but it has a counterclaim against Seller based on its rights under Section 3–418(a). This claim can be asserted against Seller, but it cannot be asserted against some other person with rights of a holder in due course of the cashier's check. A person without rights of a holder in due course of the cashier's check would take subject to Bank's claim against Seller because it is a claim in recoupment. Section 3–305(a)(3).

If Bank recovers from Seller under Section 3–418(a), the payment of Buyer's check is treated as unpaid and dishonored. Section 3–418(d). One consequence is that Seller may enforce Buyer's obligation as drawer to pay the check. Section 3–414. Another consequence is that Seller's rights against Buyer on the contract of sale are also preserved. Under Section 3–310(b) Buyer's obligation to pay for the goods was suspended when Seller took Buyer's check and remains suspended until the check is either dishonored or paid. Under Section 3–310(b)(2) the obligation is discharged when the check is paid. Since Section 3–418(d) treats Buyer's check as unpaid and dishonored, Buyer's obligation is not discharged and suspension of the obligation terminates. Under Section 3–310(b)(3), Seller may enforce either the contract of sale or the check subject to defenses and claims of Buyer.

If Seller had released the goods to Buyer before learning about the stop order, Bank would have no recovery against Seller under Section 3–418(a) because Seller in that case gave value for Buyer's check. Section 3–418(c). In this case Bank's sole remedy is under Section 4–407 by subrogation.

3. Subsection (b) covers cases of payment or acceptance by mistake that are not covered by subsection (a). It directs courts to deal with those cases under the law governing mistake and restitution. Perhaps the most important class of cases that falls under subsection (b), because it is not covered by subsection (a), is that of payment by the drawee bank of a check with respect to which the bank has no duty to the drawer to pay either because the drawer has no account with the bank or because available funds in the drawer's account are not sufficient to cover the amount of the check. With respect to such a case, under Restatement of Restitution § 29, if the bank paid because of a mistaken belief that there were available funds in the drawer's account sufficient to cover the amount of the check, the bank is entitled to restitution. But § 29 is subject to Restatement of Restitution § 33 which denies restitution if the holder of the check receiving payment paid value in good faith for the check and had no reason to know that the check was paid by mistake when payment was received.

The result in some cases is clear. For example, suppose Father gives Daughter a check for $10,000 as a birthday gift. The check is drawn on

Bank in which both Father and Daughter have accounts. Daughter deposits the check in her account in Bank. An employee of Bank, acting under the belief that there were available funds in Father's account to cover the check, caused Daughter's account to be credited for $10,000. In fact, Father's account was overdrawn and Father did not have overdraft privileges. Since Daughter received the check gratuitously there is clear unjust enrichment if she is allowed to keep the $10,000 and Bank is unable to obtain reimbursement from Father. Thus, Bank should be permitted to reverse the credit to Daughter's account. But this case is not typical. In most cases the remedy of restitution will not be available because the person receiving payment of the check will have given value for it in good faith.

In some cases, however, it may not be clear whether a drawee bank should have a right of restitution. For example, a check-kiting scheme may involve a large number of checks drawn on a number of different banks in which the drawer's credit balances are based on uncollected funds represented by fraudulently drawn checks. No attempt is made in Section 3–418 to state rules for determining the conflicting claims of the various banks that may be victimized by such a scheme. Rather, such cases are better resolved on the basis of general principles of law and the particular facts presented in the litigation.

4. The right of the drawee to recover a payment or to revoke an acceptance under Section 3–418 is not affected by the rules under Article 4 that determine when an item is paid. Even though a payor bank may have paid an item under Section 4–215, it may have a right to recover the payment under Section 3–418. National Savings & Trust Co. v. Park Corp., 722 F.2d 1303 (6th Cir.1983), cert. denied, 466 U.S. 939 (1984), correctly states the law on the issue under former Article 3. Revised Article 3 does not change the previous law.

Uniform Commercial Code Comment

Prior Uniform Statutory Provision:

Section 62, Uniform Negotiable Instruments Law.

Changes: Completely restated.

Purposes of Changes:

The rewording is intended to remove a number of uncertainties arising under the original section.

1. The section follows the rule of Price v. Neal, 3 Burr. 1354 (1762), under which a drawee who accepts or pays an instrument on which the signature of the drawer is forged is bound on his acceptance and cannot recover back his payment. Although the original Act is silent as to payment, the common law rule has been applied to it by all but a very few jurisdictions. The traditional justification for the result is that the drawee is in a superior position to detect a forgery because he has the maker's signature and is expected to know and compare it; a less fictional rationalization is that it is highly desirable to end the transaction on an instrument when it is paid rather than reopen and upset a series of commercial transactions at a later date when the forgery is discovered.

The rule as stated in the section is not limited to drawees, but applies equally to the maker of a note or to any other party who pays an instrument.

2. The section follows the decisions under the original Act applying the rule of Price v. Neal to the payment of overdrafts, or any other payment made in error as to the state of the drawer's account. The same argument for finality applies, with the additional reason that the drawee is responsible for knowing the state of the account before he accepts or pays.

3. The section follows decisions under the original Act, in making payment or acceptance final only in favor of a holder in due course, or a transferee who has the rights of a holder in due course under the shelter principle. If no value has been given for the instrument the holder loses nothing by the recovery of the payment or the avoidance of the acceptance, and is not entitled to profit at the expense of the drawee; and if he has given only an executory promise or credit he is not compelled to perform it after the forgery or other reason for recovery is discovered. If he has taken the instrument in bad faith or with notice he has no equities as against the drawee.

4. The section rejects decisions under the original Act permitting recovery on the basis of mere negligence of the holder in taking the instrument. If such negligence amounts to a lack of good faith as defined in this Act (Section 1–201) or to notice under the rules (Section 3–304) relating to notice to a purchaser of an instrument, the holder is not a holder in due course and is not protected; but otherwise the holder's negligence does not affect the finality of the payment or acceptance.

5. This section is to be read together with the preceding section, which states the warranties given by the person obtaining acceptance or payment. It is also limited by the bank collection provision (Section 4–301) permitting a payor bank to recover a payment improperly paid if it returns the item or sends notice of dishonor within the limited time provided in that section. But notice that the latter right is sharply limited in time, and terminates in any case when the bank has made final payment, as defined in Section 4–213.

Cross References:

Sections 3–302, 3–303 and 3–417.
Point 2: Section 3–201(1).
Point 4: Sections 1–201, 3–302 and 3–304.
Point 5: Sections 3–417, 4–213 and 4–301.

Definitional Cross References:

"Acceptance". Section 3–410.
"Account". Section 4–104.
"Bank". Section 1–201.
"Holder in due course". Section 3–302.
"Instrument". Section 3–102.
"Presentment". Section 3–504.

Cross References

Acceptance, see Commercial Code § 3409.
Account, see Commercial Code § 4104.
Bank deposits and collections, see Commercial Code § 4101 et seq.
Definitions, see Commercial Code § 1201.
Final payment of item by payor bank, see Commercial Code § 4215.
Holder in due course, see Commercial Code § 3302.
Improperly made payments, recovery by bank, see Commercial Code § 4301.
Instrument, see Commercial Code § 3104.
Issue or transfer for value, see Commercial Code § 3303.
Liability of acceptor of single part of draft drawn in a set, see Commercial Code § 3801.
Person entitled to enforce instrument, definition, see Commercial Code § 3301.
Presentment, see Commercial Code § 3501.
Provisional bank debits and credits, finality, see Commercial Code § 4215.
Taker, notice of claims or defenses, see Commercial Code § 3307.
Recovery of payment by return of item, see Commercial Code § 4301.
Rights of transferee, see Commercial Code § 3203.
Warranties on presentment and transfer, see Commercial Code §§ 3416, 3417.

§ 3419. Instruments signed for accommodation

(a) If an instrument is issued for value given for the benefit of a party to the instrument ("accommodated party") and another party to the instrument ("accommodation party") signs the instrument for the purpose of incurring liability on the instrument without being a direct beneficiary of the value given for the instrument, the instrument is signed by the accommodation party "for accommodation."

(b) An accommodation party may sign the instrument as maker, drawer, acceptor, or indorser and, subject to subdivision (d), is obliged to pay the instrument in the capacity in which the accommodation party signs. The obligation of an accommodation party may be enforced notwithstanding any statute of frauds and whether or not the accommodation party receives consideration for the accommodation.

(c) A person signing an instrument is presumed to be an accommodation party and there is notice that the instrument is signed for accommodation if the signature is an anomalous indorsement or is accompanied by words indicating that the signer is acting as surety or guarantor with respect to the obligation of another party to the instrument. Except as provided in Section 3605, the obligation of an accommodation party to pay the instrument is not affected by the fact that the person enforcing the obligation had notice when the instrument was taken by that person that the accommodation party signed the instrument for accommodation.

(d) If the signature of a party to an instrument is accompanied by words indicating unambiguously that the party is guaranteeing collection rather than payment of the obligation of another party to the instrument, the signer is obliged to pay the amount due on the instrument to a person entitled to enforce the instrument only if (1) execution of judgment against the other party has been returned unsatisfied, (2) the other party is insolvent or in an insolvency proceeding, (3) the other party cannot be served with process, or (4) it is otherwise apparent that payment cannot be obtained from the other party.

(e) An accommodation party who pays the instrument is entitled to reimbursement from the accommodated party and is entitled to enforce the instrument against the accommodated party. An accommodated party who pays the instrument has no right of recourse against, and is not entitled to contribution from, an accommodation party. *(Added by Stats.1992, c. 914 (S.B.833), § 6.)*

California Code Comment

By John v. Bohn and Charles J. Williams

Prior California Law

1. This section changes the rule of former Civil Code § 3218 and adds new provisions.

2. Under former Civil Code § 3218, the failure of a drawee to accept within 24 hours or such other period as the holder allowed was treated as an acceptance. Under subdivision (1)(a) and (b) this same conduct is treated as a conversion. The reason for the change is explained in Official Comment 1.

3. Subdivision (1)(c) is new statutory law and reverses the rule in California. Under the NIL, there was a split of authority on whether the drawee bank paying on a forged indorsement is liable to the holder whose indorsement was forged. In those jurisdictions which gave the payee a right of action against the drawee bank, the theory was upon constructive acceptance or conversion. Britton, Bills & Notes (1961) 418. California adopted the rule that the drawee in this situation was not liable upon the ground that there was no privity. United States Rubber Co. v. Union Bank & Trust Co., 194 Cal.App.2d 703, 15 Cal.Rptr. 385 (1961). In denying the payee a right of action for conversion against a drawee bank which has paid a check upon the payee's forged signature the court reasoned:

"The payee never had any contract right against the bank as the bank never received any money from the payee, it had no money belonging to the payee and never promised to pay it anything. (see Jones v. Bank of America, supra, [49 Cal.App.2d 115, 124, 121 P.2d 94, (1942).] If the payee had no right against the bank it is difficult indeed to see how the bank could convert anything of the payee's. The right which the payee had was a claim against the maker of the check and it still has that right.

"To say that the piece of paper upon which the lettering was printed and the wording written was the instrument which was converted, is without merit. The check was never rightfully endorsed and was not a bearer instrument; it was merely an order to pay (§ 3207) and is of no value unless accepted. The forged instrument was in effect a nullity (§ 3104) and worthless and could not be the subject of conversion as contemplated in this proceeding." (194 Cal.App.2d) at pp. 708–709).

The effect of subdivision (1)(c) is described in the California State Bar Committee on the Commercial Code, A Special Report, The Uniform Commercial Code, 37 Calif.State Bar J. pp. 155–156 (March–April, 1962):

"Under the N.I.L. a drawee bank which pays a check upon a forged payee's signature has been forged cannot charge the drawer's account.

[*Fn:* Britton, Bills and Notes, sec. 142 (1961).]

But a conflict of authority exists as to the right of the payee to recover against the drawee bank when the bank has paid another upon the payee's forged indorsement. Some courts have given the payee a right of action against the drawee bank, either on the theory that such payment is a constructive acceptance or on the theory that it is a conversion by the drawee.

[*Fn:* Blacker & Shepard Co. v. Granite Trust Co., 284 Mass. 9, 187 N.E. 53 (1933); Henderson v. Lincoln Rochester Trust Co., 303 N.Y. 27, 100 N.E.2d 117 (1951); Atlanta & St. A.B. Ry. v. Barnes, 96 F.2d 18 (5th Cir. 1938).]

In California, the payee has no right of action, because there is no privity between the payee and the drawee bank and payment on a forged indorsement does not discharge either the bank's liability to the drawer or the drawer's liability to the payee.

[*Fn:* Jones v. Bank of America, 49 C.A.2d 115, 121 P.2d 94 (1942); United States Rubber Co. v. Union Bank and Trust Co., 194 A.C.A. 740 (1961).]

Section 13419 [3419] would resolve this conflict among states and would change California law. Section 13419 [3419] would make payment of an instrument on a forged indorsement a conversion of the instrument, and give the payee a right of action against the drawee bank. The payee's action against the bank for conversion would be a ratification of the payment on the forged indorsement, and the bank could then charge the item against the drawer's account. Section 13419 [3419] would not increase the bank's liability; it would substitute a direct action by the payee, if the payee wanted it, for actions first by the payee against the drawer and then by the drawer against the bank. The bank, of course, would still be out of pocket the duplicate payment made on the forged indorsement. Under section 13417 [3417] (discussed next) the bank could recover this from the one receiving the payment, if it can find him."

4. Subdivision (2) is new statutory law and is a variation from subdivision (2) of section 3–419 of the 1962 Official Text. See California Code Comment 7.

5. Subdivision (3) is new statutory law. Its basic premise that a person dealing in good faith with the property of another is not liable for conversion is consistent with prior California law on the tort of conversion.

6. Subdivision (4) is new statutory law. It makes the provisions of subdivision (3) applicable to restrictive indorsements. This is probably consistent with existing California law.

Changes from U.C.C. (1962 Official Text)

7. Except for subdivision (2) this is section 3–419 of the Official Text without change. Subdivision (2) of the Official Text reads as follows:

"In an action against a drawee under subsection (1) the measure of the drawee's liability is the face amount of the instrument. In any other action under subsection (1) the measure of liability is presumed to be the face amount of the instrument."

The California version of subdivision (2) was adopted as a result of criticism of the 1962 Official Text. The California Bankers Association commented that:

"Section 3–419 codifies in part the existing rules concerning conversion of an instrument by a bank which refuses to return it to the rightful owner, or pays it on a forged endorsement. Subsection (2) sets forth the measure of damages in various fact situations. As presently worded, the plaintiff in an action against a drawee bank would be entitled to recover the face amount of the instrument notwithstanding conclusive proof that he had been damaged in a lesser amount. It is suggested, therefore, that this subsection be amended as follows:

(2) ~~In an action against a drawee under subsection (1) the measure of the drawee's liability is the face amount of the instrument.~~ In any other action under subsection (1) the measure of liability is presumed to be the face amount of the instrument." Sixth Progress Report to the Legislature by Senate Fact Finding Committee on Judiciary (1959–1961), Part 1, The Uniform Commercial Code, pp. 403–404.

Professors Marsh and Warren recommended the adoption of this proposed amendment and made the following statement in its support:

"The New York Law Commission Report states that the present law on the subject is that the drawee would not be liable for the face value of the instrument, if it could be shown that the actual value of the instrument is less. 2 N.Y.Law Rev.Comm., Study of the Uniform Commercial Code (1955) 1079. The California authorities recognize the liability to the payee of a drawee bank which pays out on a forged indorsement, but they are obscure on the measure of damages. In Hensley-Johnson v. Citizens National Bank, 122 Cal.App.2d, 22, 25, 264 P.2d 973 (1953) the court states: 'The general rule is that a bank which has paid out money on a forged endorsement is liable to the payee of the check for the amount which he should have received thereon.' There is no indication in the California cases that the drawee's liability must in all cases be the face amount of the instrument.

"No reason is given by the draftsmen of the Code for imposing liability on the drawee to the extent of the face amount of the instrument in the cases set out in § 13419(1) [3419(1)] while measuring the liability of other parties by a different standard. The proposed amendment seems sound in that it allows for the possibility that under some circumstances it would be unjust to hold the drawee for the face amount of the instrument." Sixth Progress Report to the Legislature by the Senate Fact Finding Committee on Judiciary (1959–1961) Part 1, The Uniform Commercial Code, p. 468.

Uniform Commercial Code Comment
1992 Addition

1. Section 3–419 replaces former Sections 3–415 and 3–416. An accommodation party is a person who signs an instrument to benefit the accommodated party either by signing at the time value is obtained by the accommodated party or later, and who is not a direct beneficiary of the value obtained. An accommodation party will usually be a co-maker or anomalous indorser. Subsection (a) distinguishes between direct and indirect benefit. For example, if X cosigns a note of Corporation that is given for a loan to Corporation, X is an accommodation party if no part of the loan was paid to X or for X's direct benefit. This is true even though X may receive indirect benefit from the loan because X is employed by Corporation or is a stockholder of Corporation, or even if X is the sole stockholder so long as Corporation and X are recognized as separate entities.

2. It does not matter whether an accommodation party signs gratuitously either at the time the instrument is issued or after the instrument is in the possession of a holder. Subsection (b) of Section 3–419 takes the view stated in Comment 3 to former Section 3–415 that there need be no consideration running to the accommodation party: "The obligation of the accommodation party is supported by any consideration for which the instrument is taken before it is due. Subsection (2) is intended to change occasional decisions holding that there is no sufficient consideration where an accommodation party signs a note after it is in the hands of a holder who has given value. The [accommodation] party is liable to the holder in such a case even though there is no extension of time or other concession."

3. As stated in Comment 1, whether a person is an accommodation party is a question of fact. But it is almost always the case that a co-maker who signs with words of guaranty after the signature is an accommodation party. The same is true of an anomalous indorser. In either case a person taking the instrument is put on notice of the accommodation status of the co-maker or indorser. This is relevant to Section 3–605(h). But, under subsection (c), signing with words of guaranty or as an anomalous indorser also creates a presumption that the signer is an accommodation party. A party challenging accommodation party status would have to rebut this presumption by producing evidence that the signer was in fact a direct beneficiary of the value given for the instrument.

An accommodation party is always a surety. A surety who is not a party to the instrument, however, is not an accommodation party. For example, if M issues a note payable to the order of P, and S signs a separate contract in which S agrees to pay P the amount of the instrument if it is dishonored, S is a surety but is not an accommodation party. In such a case, S's rights and duties are determined under the general law of suretyship. In unusual cases two parties to an instrument may have a surety relationship that is not governed by Article 3 because the requirements of Section 3–419(a) are not met. In those cases the general law of suretyship applies to the relationship. See PEB Commentary No. 11, dated February 10, 1994 [Uniform Laws Annotated, UCC, APP II, Comment 11].

4. Subsection (b) states that an accommodation party is liable on the instrument in the capacity in which the party signed the instrument. In most cases that capacity will be either that of a maker or indorser of a note. But subsection (d) provides a limitation on subsection (b). If the signature of the accommodation party is accompanied by words indicating unambiguously that the party is guaranteeing collection rather than payment of the instrument, liability is limited to that stated in subsection (d), which is based on former Section 3–416(2).

Former Article 3 was confusing because the obligation of a guarantor was covered both in Section 3–415 and in Section 3–416. The latter section suggested that a signature accompanied by words of guaranty created an obligation distinct from that of an accommodation party. Revised Article 3 eliminates that confusion by stating in Section 3–419 the obligation of a person who uses words of guaranty. Portions of former Section 3–416 are preserved. Former Section 3–416(2) is reflected in Section 3–416(d) and former Section 3–416(4) is reflected in Section 3–419(c). Words added to an anomalous indorsement indicating that payment of the instrument is guaranteed by the indorser do not change the liability of the indorser as stated in Section 3–415. This is a change from former Section 3–416(5). See PEB Commentary No. 11, supra.

5. Subsection (e) like former 3–415(5), provides that an accommodation party that pays the instrument is entitled to enforce the instrument against the accommodated party. Since the accommodation party that pays the instrument is entitled to enforce the instrument against the accommodated party, the accommodation party also obtains rights to any security interest or other collateral that secures payment of the instrument. Subsection (e) also provides that an accommodation party that pays the instrument is entitled to reimbursement from the accommodated party. See PEB Commentary No. 11, supra.

6. In occasional cases, the accommodation party might pay the instrument even though the accommodated party had a defense to its obligation that was available to the accommodation party under Section 3–305(d). In such cases, the accommodation party's right to reimbursement may conflict with the accommodated party's right to raise its defense. For example, suppose the accommodation party pays the instrument without being aware of the defense. In that case the accommodation party should be entitled to reimbursement. Suppose the accommodation party paid the instrument with knowledge of the defense. In that case, to the extent of the defense, reimbursement ordinarily would not be justified, but under some circumstances reimbursement may be justified depending upon the facts of the case. The resolution of this conflict is left to the general law of suretyship. Section 1–103. See PEB Commentary No. 11, supra.

7. Section 3–419, along with Section 3–116(a) and (b), Section 3–305(d) and Section 3–605, provides rules governing the rights of accommodation parties. In addition, except to the extent that it is displaced by provisions of this Article, the general law of suretyship also applies to the rights of accommodation parties. Section 1–103. See PEB Commentary No. 11, supra.

Uniform Commercial Code Comment
Prior Uniform Statutory Provision:
Section 137, Uniform Negotiable Instruments Law.
Changes: Rule changed; new provisions.
Purposes of Changes and New Matter: To remove difficulties arising under the original section, and to cover additional situations:

1. The provision of the original Section 137 that refusal to return a bill presented for acceptance is deemed to be acceptance has led to difficulties. If the bill is accepted it is not dishonored, and the holder is left without recourse against the drawer and indorsers when he has most need for immediate recourse. The drawee does not in fact accept and does everything he can to display an intention not to accept; and the "acceptance" is useless to the holder for any purpose other than an action against the drawee, since he has nothing that he can negotiate. The original rule has therefore been changed (see Section 3–410).

2. A negotiable instrument is the property of the holder. It is a mercantile specialty which embodies rights against other parties, and a thing of value. This section adopts the generally recognized rule that a refusal to return it on demand is a conversion. The provision is not limited to drafts presented for acceptance, but extends to any instrument presented for payment, including a note presented to the maker. The action is not on the instrument, but in tort for its conversion.

The detention of an instrument voluntarily delivered is not wrongful unless and until there is demand for its return. Demand for a return at a particular time may, however, be made at the time of delivery; or it may be implied under the circumstances or understood as a matter of custom. If the holder is to call for the instrument and fails to do so, he is to be regarded as extending the time. "Refuses" is meant to cover any intentional failure to return the instrument, including its intentional destruction. It does not cover a negligent loss or destruction, or any other unintentional failure to return. In such a case the party may be liable in tort for any damage sustained as a result of his negligence, but he is not liable as a converter under this section.

3. Subsection (1)(c) is new. It adopts the prevailing view of decisions holding that payment on a forged indorsement is not an acceptance, but that even though made in good faith it is an exercise of dominion and control over the instrument inconsistent with the rights of the owner, and results in liability for conversion.

4. Subsection (2) is new. [Changes in California from U.C.C. (1962 Official Text), see California Code Comment, note 7.] It adopts the rule generally applied to the conversion of negotiable instruments, that the obligation of any party on the instrument is presumed, in the sense that the term is defined in this Act (Section 1–201), to be worth its face value. Evidence is admissible to show that for any reason such as insolvency or the existence of a defense the obligation is in fact worth less, or even that it is without value. In the case of the drawee, however, the presumption is replaced by a rule of absolute liability.

5. Subsection (3), which is new, is intended to adopt the rule of decisions which has held that a representative, such as a broker or depositary bank, who deals with a negotiable instrument for his principal in good faith is not liable to the true owner for conversion of the instrument or otherwise, except that he may be compelled to turn over to the true owner the instrument itself or any proceeds of the instrument remaining in his hands. The provisions of subsection (3) are, however, subject to the provisions of this Act concerning restrictive indorsements (Sections 3–205, 3–206 and related sections).

6. The provisions of this section are not intended to eliminate any liability on warranties of presentment and transfer (Section 3–417). Thus a collecting bank might be liable to a drawee bank which had been subject to liability under this section, even though the collecting bank might not be liable directly to the owner of the instrument.

Cross References:

Sections 3–409, 3–410, 3–411 and 3–603.
Point 4: Section 1–201.
Point 5: Sections 1–201, 3–205 and 3–206.
Point 6: Section 3–417.

Definitional Cross References:

"Acceptance". Section 3–410.
"Action". Section 1–201.
"Bank". Section 1–201.
"Collecting bank". Sections 3–102 and 4–105.
"Depositary bank". Sections 3–102 and 4–105.
"Good faith". Section 1–201.
"Instrument". Section 3–102.
"Intermediary bank". Sections 3–102 and 4–105.
"On demand". Section 3–108.
"Person". Section 1–201.
"Presumed". Section 1–201.
"Representative". Section 1–201.

Cross References

Discharge of accommodation party unless knowledge of signature for accommodation known by person entitled to enforce instrument, see Commercial Code § 3605.

Joint and several liability on instrument, exception to contribution, see Commercial Code § 3116.
Acceptance, definition and operation, see Commercial Code § 3409.
Certification of check, see Commercial Code § 3409.
Check or draft, operation and effect, see Commercial Code § 3409.
Collecting bank, see Commercial Code § 4105.
Definitions, see Commercial Code § 1201.
Depositary bank, see Commercial Code § 4105.
Instructions from, or agreement with, transferor, as relieving collecting bank from liability for conversion, see Commercial Code § 4203.
Instrument, see Commercial Code § 3104.
Intermediary bank, see Commercial Code § 4105.
On demand, see Commercial Code § 3108.
Payment with knowledge of claim, non-discharge, see Commercial Code § 3602.
Restrictive indorsements,
  Generally, see Commercial Code § 3206.
  Effect, see Commercial Code § 3206.
Warranties on presentment and transfer, see Commercial Code §§ 3416, 3417.

§ 3420. Conversion of instrument

(a) The law applicable to conversion of personal property applies to instruments. An instrument is also converted if it is taken by transfer, other than a negotiation, from a person not entitled to enforce the instrument or a bank makes or obtains payment with respect to the instrument for a person not entitled to enforce the instrument or receive payment. An action for conversion of an instrument may not be brought by (1) the issuer or acceptor of the instrument or (2) a payee or indorsee who did not receive delivery of the instrument either directly or through delivery to an agent or a copayee.

(b) In an action under subdivision (a), the measure of liability is presumed to be the amount payable on the instrument, but recovery may not exceed the amount of the plaintiff's interest in the instrument.

(c) A representative, other than a depositary bank, who has in good faith dealt with an instrument or its proceeds on behalf of one who was not the person entitled to enforce the instrument is not liable in conversion to that person beyond the amount of any proceeds that it has not paid out. *(Added by Stats.1992, c. 914 (S.B.833), § 6.)*

Uniform Commercial Code Comment
1992 Addition

1. Section 3–420 is a modification of former Section 3–419. The first sentence of Section 3–420(a) states a general rule that the law of conversion applicable to personal property also applies to instruments. Paragraphs (a) and (b) of former Section 3–419(1) are deleted as inappropriate in cases of noncash items that may be delivered for acceptance or payment in collection letters that contain varying instructions as to what to do in the event of nonpayment on the day of delivery. It is better to allow such cases to be governed by the general law of conversion that would address the issue of when, under the circumstances prevailing, the presenter's right to possession has been denied. The second sentence of Section 3–420(a) states that an instrument is converted if it is taken by transfer other than a negotiation from a person not entitled to enforce the instrument or taken for collection or payment from a person not entitled to enforce the instrument or receive payment. This covers cases in which a depositary or payor bank takes an instrument bearing a forged indorsement. It also covers cases in which an instrument is payable to two persons and the two persons are not alternative payees, e.g., a check payable to John and Jane Doe. Under Section 3–110(d) the check can be negotiated or

enforced only by both persons acting jointly. Thus, neither payee acting without the consent of the other, is a person entitled to enforce the instrument. If John indorses the check and Jane does not, the indorsement is not effective to allow negotiation of the check. If Depositary Bank takes the check for deposit to John's account, Depositary Bank is liable to Jane for conversion of the check if she did not consent to the transaction. John, acting alone, is not the person entitled to enforce the check because John is not the holder of the check. Section 3–110(d) and Comment 4 to Section 3–110. Depositary Bank does not get any greater rights under Section 4–205(1). If it acted for John as its customer, it did not become holder of the check under that provision because John, its customer, was not a holder.

Under former Article 3, the cases were divided on the issue of whether the drawer of a check with a forged indorsement can assert rights against a depositary bank that took the check. The last sentence of Section 3–420(a) resolves the conflict by following the rule stated in Stone & Webster Engineering Corp. v. First National Bank & Trust Co., 184 N.E.2d 358 (Mass.1962). There is no reason why a drawer should have an action in conversion. The check represents an obligation of the drawer rather than property of the drawer. The drawer has an adequate remedy against the payor bank for recredit of the drawer's account for unauthorized payment of the check.

There was also a split of authority under former Article 3 on the issue of whether a payee who never received the instrument is a proper plaintiff in a conversion action. The typical case was one in which a check was stolen from the drawer or in which the check was mailed to an address different from that of the payee and was stolen after it arrived at that address. The thief forged the indorsement of the payee and obtained payment by depositing the check to an account in a depositary bank. The issue was whether the payee could bring an action in conversion against the depositary bank or the drawee bank. In revised Article 3, under the last sentence of Section 3–420(a), the payee has no conversion action because the check was never delivered to the payee. Until delivery, the payee does not have any interest in the check. The payee never became the holder of the check nor a person entitled to enforce the check. Section 3–301. Nor is the payee injured by the fraud. Normally the drawer of a check intends to pay an obligation owed to the payee. But if the check is never delivered to the payee, the obligation owed to the payee is not affected. If the check falls into the hands of a thief who obtains payment after forging the signature of the payee as an indorsement, the obligation owed to the payee continues to exist after the thief receives payment. Since the payee's right to enforce the underlying obligation is unaffected by the fraud of the thief, there is no reason to give any additional remedy to the payee. The drawer of the check has no conversion remedy, but the drawee is not entitled to charge the drawer's account when the drawee wrongfully honored the check. The remedy of the drawee is against the depositary bank for breach of warranty under Section 3–417(a)(1) or 4–208(a)(1). The loss will fall on the person who gave value to the thief for the check.

The situation is different if the check is delivered to the payee. If the check is taken for an obligation owed to the payee, the last sentence of Section 3–310(b)(4) provides that the obligation may not be enforced to the extent of the amount of the check. The payee's rights are restricted to enforcement of the payee's rights in the instrument. In this event the payee is injured by the theft and has a cause of action for conversion.

The payee receives delivery when the check comes into the payee's possession, as for example when it is put into the payee's mailbox. Delivery to an agent is delivery to the payee. If a check is payable to more than one payee, delivery to one of the payees is deemed to be delivery to all of the payees. Occasionally, the person asserting a conversion cause of action is an indorsee rather that the original payee. If the check is stolen before the check can be delivered to the indorsee and the indorsee's indorsement is forged, the analysis is similar. For example, a check is payable to the order of A. A indorses it to B and puts it into an envelope addressed to B. The envelope is never delivered to B. Rather, Thief steals the envelope, forges B's indorsement to the check and obtains payment. Because the check was never delivered to B, the indorsee, B has no cause of action for conversion, but A does have such an action. A is the owner of the check. B never obtained rights in the check. If A intended to negotiate the check to B in payment of an obligation, that obligation was not affected by the conduct of Thief. B can enforce that obligation. Thief stole A's property not B's.

2. Subsection (2) of former Section 3–419 is amended because it is not clear why the former law distinguished between the liability of the drawee and that of other converters. Why should there be a conclusive presumption that the liability is face amount if a drawee refuses to pay or return an instrument or makes payment on a forged indorsement, while the liability of a maker who does the same thing is only presumed to be the face amount? Moreover, it was not clear under former Section 3–419(2) what face amount meant. If a note for $10,000 is payable in a year at 10% interest, it is common to refer to $10,000 as the face amount, but if the note is converted the loss to the owner also includes the loss of interest. In revised Article 3, Section 3–420(b), by referring to "amount payable on the instrument," allows the full amount due under the instrument to be recovered.

The "but" clause in subsection (b) addresses the problem of conversion actions in multiple payee checks. Section 3–110(d) states that an instrument cannot be enforced unless all payees join in the action. But an action for conversion might be brought by a payee having no interest or a limited interest in the proceeds of the check. This clause prevents such a plaintiff from receiving a windfall. An example is a check payable to a building contractor and a supplier of building material. The check is not payable to the payees alternatively. Section 3–110(d). The check is delivered to the contractor by the owner of the building. Suppose the contractor forges supplier's signature as an indorsement of the check and receives the entire proceeds of the check. The supplier should not, without qualification, be able to recover the entire amount of the check from the bank that converted the check. Depending upon the contract between the contractor and the supplier, the amount of the check may be due entirely to the contractor, in which case there should be no recovery, entirely to the supplier, in which case recovery should be for the entire amount, or part may be due to one and the rest to the other, in which case recovery should be limited to the amount due to the supplier.

3. Subsection (3) of former Section 3–419 drew criticism from the courts, that saw no reason why a depositary bank should have the defense stated in the subsection. See Knesz v. Central Jersey Bank & Trust Co., 477 A.2d 806 (N.J.1984). The depositary bank is ultimately liable in the case of a forged indorsement check because of its warranty to the payor bank under Section 4–208(a)(1) and it is usually the most convenient defendant in cases involving multiple checks drawn on different banks. There is no basis for requiring the owner of the check to bring multiple actions against the various payor banks and to require those banks to assert warranty rights against the depositary bank. In revised Article 3, the defense provided by Section 3–420(c) is limited to collecting banks other than the depositary bank. If suit is brought against both the payor bank and the depositary bank, the owner, of course, is entitled to but one recovery.

Cross References

Nonliability of collecting bank to prior parties for action taken pursuant to instructions from transferor subject to conversion of instrument, see Commercial Code § 4203.

CHAPTER 5. DISHONOR

Section
3501. Presentment.
3502. Dishonor.
3503. Notice of dishonor.
3504. Excused presentment and notice of dishonor.
3505. Dishonor and notice of dishonor; evidence and presumptions.
3506 to 3511. Repealed.

Transitional Provisions

Effective date and transitional provisions for repeal and addition of Division 3 by Stats.1992, c. 914, see Commercial Code § 16101 et seq.

§ 3501. Presentment

(a) "Presentment" means a demand made by or on behalf of a person entitled to enforce an instrument (1) to pay the instrument made to the drawee or a party

§ 3501

obliged to pay the instrument or, in the case of a note or accepted draft payable at a bank, to the bank, or (2) to accept a draft made to the drawee.

(b) The following rules are subject to Division 4 (commencing with Section 4101), agreement of the parties, and clearinghouse rules and the like:

(1) Presentment may be made at the place of payment of the instrument and shall be made at the place of payment if the instrument is payable at a bank in the United States; may be made by any commercially reasonable means, including an oral, written, or electronic communication; is effective when the demand for payment or acceptance is received by the person to whom presentment is made; and is effective if made to any one of two or more makers, acceptors, drawees, or other payors.

(2) Upon demand of the person to whom presentment is made, the person making presentment shall (A) exhibit the instrument, (B) give reasonable identification and, if presentment is made on behalf of another person, reasonable evidence of authority to do so, and (C) sign a receipt on the instrument for any payment made or surrender the instrument if full payment is made.

(3) Without dishonoring the instrument, the party to whom presentment is made may (A) return the instrument for lack of a necessary indorsement, or (B) refuse payment or acceptance for failure of the presentment to comply with the terms of the instrument, an agreement of the parties, or other applicable law or rule.

(4) The party to whom presentment is made may treat presentment as occurring on the next business day after the day of presentment if the party to whom presentment is made has established a cutoff hour not earlier than 2 p.m. for the receipt and processing of instruments presented for payment or acceptance and presentment is made after the cutoff hour. *(Added by Stats.1992, c. 914 (S.B.833), § 6.)*

California Code Comment

By John A. Bohn and Charles J. Williams

Prior California Law

1. This section is a combination and rewording of a series of sections dealing with the subject of presentment, notice of dishonor and protest under the NIL. There is no important substantive change. Official Comment 1.

2. The effect of failure to present or to give notice or to protest is set forth in the following sections of this chapter.

3. Subdivision (1)(a) continues the rules of presentment for acceptance contained in former Civil Code §§ 3224, 3225 and 3231. The last sentence of subdivision (1)(a) states the rule that a time draft may be presented for acceptance at any time. Official Comment 3.

4. Subdivision (1)(b) is similar to the last sentence of former Civil Code § 3151. Failure to present discharges an indorser whether or not the failure causes a loss. Commercial Code § 3502(1)(a). This was also the rule under the NIL. Kern v. Henry, 138 Cal.App. 46, 31 P.2d 454 (1934) (where the court used the failure to present along with the fact that the indorsement was qualified to support its holding that the indorser was not liable on the note.)

5. Subdivision (1)(c) is similar to former Civil Code §§ 3151 and 3265(b) except that the rule of former Civil Code § 3265(b) is extended and made applicable to all drafts.

Under both the NIL and the Commercial Code, presentment for payment is necessary in order to charge a drawer, unless there is an excuse under Commercial Code § 3511. The failure to present resulted in a discharge of the drawer except that in the case of a check, the drawer was only discharged "to the extent of the loss caused by the delay". Former Civil Code § 3265(b). Subdivision (1)(c) extends this rule to all drafts. Thus, the rule is now that presentment is necessary to charge an indorser but in the case of failure to present for payment there is a discharge only to the extent of the loss caused by the delay. This measure of discharge is set forth in Commercial Code § 3502(1)(b).

6. Subdivision (2)(a) adopts the rule of former Civil Code § 3170 for an indorser. Failure to give notice discharges an indorser. Commercial Code § 3502(1).

7. Subdivision (2)(b) is similar to former Civil Code § 3170 except that the failure to give notice of dishonor was a complete discharge under former Civil Code § 3170. Under subdivision (2)(b) it is a discharge only to the extent of the loss caused by the failure to give notice. Commercial Code § 3502(1)(b). The rules as to the necessity of notice of dishonor are parallel to the rules as to the necessity of presentment in subdivision (1). Official Comment 5.

8. Subdivision (3) continues the rules of former Civil Code §§ 3210, 3199 and 3233. This subdivision eliminates the requirement of protest of dishonor (necessary to charge the drawer or indorser of a draft) except upon a draft which is either drawn or payable outside of the United States. The only change is that subdivision (3) substitutes the phrase "states and territories of the United States and the District of Columbia" for the term "the continental limits of the United States" previously used in former Civil Code § 3210 in fixing the geographical area where a draft may be drawn or payable which need not be protested for dishonor.

One of the reasons for protest is to authenticate the failure to pay. In short, it is an evidentiary aid. Britton, Bills & Notes (1961) 583.

The part of subdivision (3) which permits a protest for better security in the case of a foreign draft is the same as former Civil Code § 3239.

9. Subdivision (4) is new statutory law and changes the rule adopted in Janssen v. Gordon, 35 Cal.App.2d 410, 96 P.2d 152 (1939) that an instrument indorsed after maturity was deemed payable on demand as to an indorser indorsing after maturity. Subdivision (4) eliminates the requirement of presentment or notice of dishonor or protest in order to charge an indorser who indorses after maturity. The rule is changed to meet normal commercial expectation.

10. Before the adoption of the NIL, the rule was that mere delay in presenting a bill was not a discharge or an exoneration of the liability of any party but that notice of dishonor to the indorser was necessary in order to fix the indorser's liability. Merchants Nat. Bank v. Bentel, 15 Cal.App. 170, 113 Pac. 708 (1911). It was necessary to make a demand or have shown reasonable excuse for not so doing although mere delay was not a release from liability. Wills v. Booth, 6 Cal.App. 197, 91 Pac. 759 (1907).

11. Under the NIL, when an action was brought against an indorser it was necessary to allege presentment to the principal debtor within the requisite time. Harris v. Hilland, 2 Cal.App.2d 404, 38 P.2d 164 (1934).

Changes from U.C.C. (1962 Official Text)

12. This is section 3–501 of the Official Text without change.

Uniform Commercial Code Comment

1992 Addition

Subsection (a) defines presentment. Subsection (b)(1) states the place and manner of presentment. Electronic presentment is authorized. The communication of the demand for payment or acceptance is effective when received. Subsection (b)(2) restates former Section 3–505. Subsection (b)(2)(i) allows the person to whom presentment is made to require exhibition of the instrument, unless the parties have agreed otherwise as in an electronic presentment agreement. Former Section 3–507(3) is the antecedent of subsection (b)(3)(i). Since a payor must decide whether to pay or accept on the day of presentment, subsection (b)(4) allows the payor to set a cut-off hour for receipt of instruments presented.

Uniform Commercial Code Comment

Prior Uniform Statutory Provision:

Sections 70, 89, 118, 129, 143, 144, 150, 151, 152, 157, 158 and 186, Uniform Negotiable Instruments Law.

Changes: Combined and simplified.

Purposes of Changes:

1. Part 5 simplifies the requirements of the original Act as to presentment for acceptance or payment, notice of dishonor and protest. This section assembles in one place all provisions as to when any such proceeding is necessary. It eliminates some of the requirements and simplifies others. The effect of unexcused delay in any such proceeding as a discharge is covered by the next section, and the sections following prescribe the details of the proceedings.

2. The words "Necessary to charge" are retained from the original Act. They mean that the necessary proceeding is a condition precedent to any right of action against the drawer or indorser. He is not liable and cannot be sued without the proceedings however long delayed. Under some circumstances delay is excused. If it is not excused it may operate as a discharge under the next section. Under some circumstances the proceeding may be entirely excused and the drawer or indorser is then liable as if the proceeding had been duly taken. Section 3–511 states the circumstances under which delay may be excused or the proceeding entirely excused.

3. Subsection (1)(a) retains the substance of the original Sections 143, 144 and 150. The last sentence of the subsection states the rule of the decisions both at common law and under the original Act, that the holder may at his option present any time draft for acceptance, and is not required to wait until the due date to know whether the drawee will accept it; but that if he does make presentment and acceptance is refused he must give notice of dishonor. There is no similar right to present for acceptance a draft payable on demand, since a demand draft entitles the holder to immediate payment but not to acceptance.

4. Subdivisions (1)(b) and (1)(c) on presentment for payment follow Section 70 of the original Act with one important change. Under the original Act and under this section, ((1)(b)), presentment for payment is necessary (unless excused) to charge any drawer. Under the original Act drawers of drafts other than checks were wholly discharged by a failure to make due presentment but drawers of checks (Section 70 in conjunction with Section 186) were discharged only "to the extent of the loss caused by the delay"—that is to say, when insolvency of the drawee bank occurred after the time when presentment was due. The check rule of the original Act (somewhat modified—see Section 3–502(1)(b) and Comment thereto) is by subsection (1)(c) extended to all drawers, and also to the acceptors and makers of domiciled—"payable at a bank"—drafts and notes. Thus drawers of drafts other than checks are not, as they were under Section 70, wholly discharged by failure to make due presentment but, like drawers of checks, are discharged only as they may have suffered loss as provided in Section 3–502(1)(b). As to domiciled paper original Section 70 provided that ability and willingness to pay at the place named at maturity were "equivalent to a tender of payment"—that is to say would stop the running of interest, but had no other effect. Accordingly cases have held that makers and acceptors of domiciled paper were not discharged to any extent by the holder's failure to make presentment even when the obligor had funds available in the paying bank on the date for presentment and the bank subsequently failed. Subsection (1)(c) applies the check rule to such makers and acceptors; the "tender" language of Section 70 is eliminated; and the result in the cases referred to in the preceding sentence is reversed. Under this section as under the original act presentment for payment is not necessary to charge primary parties (makers and acceptors of undomiciled paper).

5. Under subsection (2) the rules as to necessity of notice of dishonor run parallel with the rules as to necessity of presentment stated in subsection (1).

6. Under the original Sections 129 and 152 protest is required in the case of every "foreign draft", defined as a draft which on its face is not both drawn and payable "within this state." The result has been that upon dishonor in New York a check which appears on its face to be drawn in Jersey City must be protested in order to sue the drawer or any indorser. This has led to great inconvenience and expense of protest fees. The only function of protest is that of proof of dishonor, and it adds nothing to notice of dishonor as such.

Subsection (3) eliminates the requirement of protest except upon dishonor of a draft which on its face appears to be either drawn or payable outside of the United States. The requirement is left as to such international drafts because it is generally required by foreign law, which this Article cannot affect. The formalities of protest are covered by Section 3–509 on protest, and substitutes for protest as proof of dishonor are provided for in Section 3–510 on evidence of dishonor and of notice.

This provision retains from the original Section 118 the rule permitting the holder at his option to make protest of any dishonor of any other instrument. Even where not required protest may have definite convenience where process does not run to another state and the taking of depositions is a slow and expensive matter. Even where the instrument is drawn and payable entirely within a state there may be convenience in saving the trip of a witness from Buffalo to New York to testify to dishonor, where the substitute evidence of dishonor and notice of dishonor cannot be relied on. Either required or optional protest is presumptive evidence of dishonor. (Section 3–510.)

7. The permissible "protest for better security" of original Section 158 is retained in the case of a foreign draft, as the practice is common in certain foreign countries.

8. Under the final sentence of Section 7 of the original Act an instrument indorsed when overdue became payable on demand as to the indorser. That language has been deleted from this Article—see Section 3–108 and Comment. It meant, among other things and in view of the provisions of the original Act as to demand paper, that such an indorser was discharged unless the instrument was presented for payment within a reasonable time after his indorsement. Presentment of overdue paper for the purpose of charging an indorser is unusual and not an expected commercial practice; the rule has been little more than a trap for those not familiar with the Act. Subsection (4), reversing the original Act, provides that as to indorsers after maturity neither presentment nor notice of dishonor nor protest is necessary; like primary parties therefore they will remain liable on the instrument for the period of the applicable statute of limitations.

Cross References:

Point 1: Sections 3–502 through 3–508.
Point 2: Sections 3–413, 3–414 and 3–511.
Point 3: Sections 3–413, 3–414 and 3–511.
Point 4: Section 3–502.
Point 6: Sections 3–413, 3–414, 3–509, 3–510 and 3–511.
Point 8: Section 3–108.

Definitional Cross References:

"Acceptance". Section 3–410.
"Bank". Section 1–201.
"Certificate of deposit". Section 3–104.
"Dishonor". Section 3–507.
"Draft". Section 3–104.
"Holder". Section 1–201.
"Instrument". Section 3–102.
"Note". Section 3–104.
"Notice of dishonor". Section 3–508.
"Party". Section 1–201.
"Presentment". Section 3–504.
"Protest". Section 3–509.
"Secondary party". Section 3–102.
"Signature". Section 3–401.

Cross References

Acceptance, see Commercial Code § 3409.
Certificate of deposit, see Commercial Code § 3104.
Dishonor and notice of dishonor, evidence, see Commercial Code § 3505.
Draft, see Commercial Code § 3104.
Effect of discharge against holder in due course, see Commercial Code § 3601.
Excused delay, see Commercial Code § 3503.
Instrument, see Commercial Code § 3104.
Instrument dishonored by nonpayment, see Commercial Code § 3507.
Instruments payable on demand, see Commercial Code § 3108.

§ 3501

Note, see Commercial Code § 3104.
Notice of dishonor, see Commercial Code § 3503.
Obligation of drawer, see Commercial Code § 3414.
Obligation of indorser, see Commercial Code § 3415.
Payable at a bank, see Commercial Code § 4106.
Presentment of notice for items, not payable by, through or at a bank, see Commercial Code § 4212.
Protest, see Commercial Code § 3505.
Reasonable time; computation, see Commercial Code §§ 1204, 3503.
Secondary party, see Commercial Code § 3102.
Signature, see Commercial Code § 3401.
Time for presenting check to bank, see Commercial Code § 4404.
Time for presentment, see Commercial Code § 3503.
Excused delay, see Commercial Code § 3503.
Waiver or excuse, see Commercial Code § 3504.
Warranties on presentment, see Commercial Code § 3417.

§ 3502. Dishonor

(a) Dishonor of a note is governed by the following rules:

(1) If the note is payable on demand, the note is dishonored if presentment is duly made to the maker and the note is not paid on the day of presentment.

(2) If the note is not payable on demand and is payable at or through a bank or the terms of the note require presentment, the note is dishonored if presentment is duly made and the note is not paid on the day it becomes payable or the day of presentment, whichever is later.

(3) If the note is not payable on demand and paragraph (2) does not apply, the note is dishonored if it is not paid on the day it becomes payable.

(b) Dishonor of an unaccepted draft other than a documentary draft is governed by the following rules:

(1) If a check is duly presented for payment to the payor bank otherwise than for immediate payment over the counter, the check is dishonored if the payor bank makes timely return of the check or sends timely notice of dishonor or nonpayment under Section 4301 or 4302, or becomes accountable for the amount of the check under Section 4302.

(2) If a draft is payable on demand and paragraph (1) does not apply, the draft is dishonored if presentment for payment is duly made to the drawee and the draft is not paid on the day of presentment.

(3) If a draft is payable on a date stated in the draft, the draft is dishonored if (A) presentment for payment is duly made to the drawee and payment is not made on the day the draft becomes payable or the day of presentment, whichever is later, or (B) presentment for acceptance is duly made before the day the draft becomes payable and the draft is not accepted on the day of presentment.

(4) If a draft is payable on elapse of a period of time after sight or acceptance, the draft is dishonored if presentment for acceptance is duly made and the draft is not accepted on the day of presentment.

(c) Dishonor of an unaccepted documentary draft occurs according to the rules stated in paragraphs (2), (3), and (4) of subdivision (b), except that payment or acceptance may be delayed without dishonor until no later than the close of the third business day of the drawee following the day on which payment or acceptance is required by those paragraphs.

(d) Dishonor of an accepted draft is governed by the following rules:

(1) If the draft is payable on demand, the draft is dishonored if presentment for payment is duly made to the acceptor and the draft is not paid on the day of presentment.

(2) If the draft is not payable on demand, the draft is dishonored if presentment for payment is duly made to the acceptor and payment is not made on the day it becomes payable or the day of presentment, whichever is later.

(e) In any case in which presentment is otherwise required for dishonor under this section and presentment is excused under Section 3504, dishonor occurs without presentment if the instrument is not duly accepted or paid.

(f) If a draft is dishonored because timely acceptance of the draft was not made and the person entitled to demand acceptance consents to a late acceptance, from the time of acceptance the draft is treated as never having been dishonored. *(Added by Stats.1992, c. 914 (S.B.833), § 6.)*

California Code Comment

By John A. Bohn and Charles J. Williams

Prior California Law

1. This section supplements the preceding section 3501 which specifies when presentment, notice or protest is necessary, and states the effect of failing to present, give notice or protest. This section rewords and combines several NIL provisions.

In general and except as provided in this section a delay operates as a discharge unless it is excused under Commercial Code § 3511.

2. Subdivision (1)(a) combines former Civil Code §§ 3151, 3170, 3225 and 3231. The indorser is discharged whether or not the delay causes actual loss. See California Code Comment 4 to this section.

3. Subdivision (1)(b) extends the rule of former Civil Code § 3265(b) which discharged liability for failure to present a check only "to the extent of the loss caused by the delay." This measure of damages formerly applicable to checks is now extended to the drawer or the maker or accepter of a draft or note payable at a bank.

Under prior California law the drawer of a draft was absolutely discharged by failure to make presentment and the rule of partial discharge in the event of delay in presentment applied only to the drawer of a check. This rule of partial discharge is now broadened in its application.

The phrase "to the extent of the loss caused by the delay" in former Civil Code § 3265(b) meant the loss resulting from the insolvency of the drawee or payor. This was the only type of loss to which the partial discharge rule of former Civil Code § 3265(b) was ever applied. Official Comment 2.

4. Subdivision (2) is similar to the rule of former Civil Code § 3233 that an unexcused delay in protesting is a discharge of the drawer and indorsers.

Changes from U.C.C. (1962 Official Text)

5. This is section 3–502 of the Official Text without change.

Uniform Commercial Code Comment
1992 Addition

1. Section 3–415 provides that an indorser is obliged to pay an instrument if the instrument is dishonored and is discharged if the indorser is entitled to notice of dishonor and notice is not given. Under Section 3–414, the drawer is obliged to pay an unaccepted draft if it is dishonored. The drawer, however, is not entitled to notice of dishonor except to the extent required in a case governed by Section 3–414(d). Part 5 tells when an instrument is dishonored (Section 3–502) and what it means to give notice of dishonor (Section 3–503). Often dishonor does not occur until presentment (Section 3–501), and frequently presentment and notice of dishonor are excused (Section 3–504).

2. In the great majority of cases presentment and notice of dishonor are waived with respect to notes. In most cases a formal demand for payment to the maker of the note is not contemplated. Rather, the maker is expected to send payment to the holder of the note on the date or dates on which payment is due. If payment is not made when due, the holder usually makes a demand for payment, but in the normal case in which presentment is waived, demand is irrelevant and the holder can proceed against indorsers when payment is not received. Under former Article 3, in the small minority of cases in which presentment and dishonor were not waived with respect to notes, the indorser was discharged from liability (former Section 3–502(1)(a)) unless the holder made presentment to the maker on the exact day the note was due (former Section 3–503(1)(c)) and gave notice of dishonor to the indorser before midnight of the third business day after dishonor (former Section 3–508(2)). These provisions are omitted from Revised Article 3 as inconsistent with practice which seldom involves face-to-face dealings.

3. Subsection (a) applies to notes. Subsection (a)(1) applies to notes payable on demand. Dishonor requires presentment, and dishonor occurs if payment is not made on the day of presentment. There is no change from previous Article 3. Subsection (a)(2) applies to notes payable at a definite time if the note is payable at or through a bank or, by its terms, presentment is required. Dishonor requires presentment, and dishonor occurs if payment is not made on the due date or the day of presentment if presentment is made after the due date. Subsection (a)(3) applies to all other notes. If the note is not paid on its due date it is dishonored. This allows holders to collect notes in ways that make sense commercially without having to be concerned about a formal presentment on a given day.

4. Subsection (b) applies to unaccepted drafts other than documentary drafts. Subsection (b)(1) applies to checks. Except for checks presented for immediate payment over the counter, which are covered by subsection (b)(2), dishonor occurs according to rules stated in Article 4. When a check is presented for payment through the check-collection system, the drawee bank normally makes settlement for the amount of the check to the presenting bank. Under Section 4–301 the drawee bank may recover this settlement if it returns the check within its midnight deadline (Section 4–104). In that case the check is not paid and dishonor occurs under Section 3–502(b)(1). If the drawee bank does not return the check or give notice of dishonor or nonpayment within the midnight deadline, the settlement becomes final payment of the check. Section 4–215. Thus, no dishonor occurs regardless of whether the check is retained or is returned after the midnight deadline. In some cases the drawee bank might not settle for the check when it is received. Under Section 4–302 if the drawee bank is not also the depositary bank and retains the check without settling for it beyond midnight of the day it is presented for payment, the bank becomes "accountable" for the amount of the check, i.e. it is obliged to pay the amount of the check. If the drawee bank is also the depositary bank, the bank is accountable for the amount of the check if the bank does not pay the check or return it or send notice of dishonor within the midnight deadline. In all cases in which the drawee bank becomes accountable, the check has not been paid and, under Section 3–502(b)(1), the check is dishonored. The fact that the bank is obliged to pay the check does not mean that the check has been paid. When a check is presented for payment, the person presenting the check is entitled to payment not just the obligation of the drawee to pay. Until that payment is made, the check is dishonored. To say that the drawee bank is obliged to pay the check necessarily means that the check has not been paid. If the check is eventually paid, the drawee bank no longer is accountable.

Subsection (b)(2) applies to demand drafts other than those governed by subsection (b)(1). It covers checks presented for immediate payment over the counter and demand drafts other than checks. Dishonor occurs if presentment for payment is made and payment is not made on the day of presentment.

Subsection (b)(3) and (4) applies to time drafts. An unaccepted time draft differs from a time note. The maker of a note knows that the note has been issued, but the drawee of a draft may not know that a draft has been drawn on it. Thus, with respect to drafts, presentment for payment or acceptance is required. Subsection (b)(3) applies to drafts payable on a date stated in the draft. Dishonor occurs if presentment for payment is made and payment is not made on the day the draft becomes payable or the day of presentment if presentment is made after the due date. The holder of an unaccepted draft payable on a stated date has the option of presenting the draft for acceptance before the day the draft becomes payable to establish whether the drawee is willing to assume liability by accepting. Under subsection (b)(3)(ii) dishonor occurs when the draft is presented and not accepted. Subsection (b)(4) applies to unaccepted drafts payable on elapse of a period of time after sight or acceptance. If the draft is payable 30 days after sight, the draft must be presented for acceptance to start the running of the 30-day period. Dishonor occurs if it is not accepted. The rules in subsection (b)(3) and (4) follow former Section 3–501(1)(a).

5. Subsection (c) gives drawees an extended period to pay documentary drafts because of the time that may be needed to examine the documents. The period prescribed is that given by Section 5–112 in cases in which a letter of credit is involved.

6. Subsection (d) governs accepted drafts. If the acceptor's obligation is to pay on demand the rule, stated in subsection (d)(1), is the same as for that of a demand note stated in subsection (a)(1). If the acceptor's obligation is to pay at a definite time the rule, stated in subsection (d)(2), is the same as that of a time note payable at a bank stated in subsection (b)(2).

7. Subsection (e) is a limitation on subsection (a)(1) and (2), subsection (b), subsection (c), and subsection (d). Each of those provisions states dishonor as occurring after presentment. If presentment is excused under Section 3–504, dishonor occurs under those provisions without presentment if the instrument is not duly accepted or paid.

8. Under subsection (b)(3)(ii) and (4) if a draft is presented for acceptance and the draft is not accepted on the day of presentment, there is dishonor. But after dishonor, the holder may consent to late acceptance. In that case, under subsection (f), the late acceptance cures the dishonor. The draft is treated as never having been dishonored. If the draft is subsequently presented for payment and payment is refused dishonor occurs at that time.

Uniform Commercial Code Comment

Prior Uniform Statutory Provision:

Sections 7, 70, 89, 144, 150, 152 and 186, Uniform Negotiable Instruments Law.

Changes: Combined and simplified.

Purposes of Changes:

This section is the complement of the preceding section. It covers in one section widely scattered provisions of the original Act:

1. The circumstances under which presentment or notice of dishonor or protest or delay therein are excused are stated in Section 3–511. When not excused delay operates as a discharge as provided in this section.

2. Subsection (1)(b) applies to any drawer, as well as to the makers and acceptors of drafts and notes payable at a bank, the rule of the original Section 186 providing for discharge only where the drawer of a check has sustained loss through the delay. This section expressly limits the rule to loss sustained through insolvency of the drawee or payor which was the only type of loss to which the Section 186 rule has ever been applied in the cases arising under it.

The purpose of the rule is to avoid hardship upon the holder through complete discharge, and unjust enrichment of the drawer or other party who normally has received goods or other consideration for the issue of the instrument. He is "deprived of funds" in any case where bank failure or other insolvency of the drawee or payor has prevented him from receiving the benefit of funds which would have paid the instrument if it had been duly presented.

The original language discharging the drawer "to the extent of the loss caused by the delay" has not worked out satisfactorily in the decided cases, since the amount of the loss caused by the failure of a bank is almost never ascertainable at the time of suit and may not be ascertained until some years later. The decisions have turned upon burden of proof, and the drawer has seldom succeeded in proving his discharge. Subsection (1)(b) therefore substitutes a right to discharge liability by written assignment to the holder of rights against the drawee or payor as to the funds which cover the particular instrument. The assignment is intended to give the holder an effective right to claim against the drawee or payor.

3. Subsection (2) retains the rule of the original Section 152, that any unexcused delay of a required protest is a complete discharge of all drawers and indorsers.

Cross References:

Point 1: Section 3–511(1).
Point 2: Section 3–501.
Point 3: Section 3–509.

Definitional Cross References:

"Bank". Section 1–201.
"Draft". Section 3–104.
"Holder". Section 1–201.

Definitional Cross References:

"Insolvent". Section 1–201.
"Instrument". Section 3–102.
"Note". Section 3–104.
"Notice of dishonor". Section 3–508.
"Payor bank". Section 4–105.
"Presentment". Section 3–504.
"Protest". Section 3–509.
"Rights". Section 1–201.
"Signature". Section 3–401.
"Written". Section 1–201.

Cross References

Discharge in general, see Commercial Code § 3601 et seq.
Draft, see Commercial Code § 3104.
Effect of discharge against holder in due course, see Commercial Code § 3601.
Excused delay, see Commercial Code § 3504.
Instrument, see Commercial Code § 3104.
Notary public, protest by, see Government Code § 8208.
Note, see Commercial Code § 3104.
Notice of dishonor, see Commercial Code § 3503.
Payable at a bank, see Commercial Code § 4106.
Payor bank, see Commercial Code § 4105.
Presentment, time of, see Commercial Code § 3503.
Protest, see Commercial Code § 3505.
Reasonable time, see Commercial Code §§ 1204, 3503.
Signature, see Commercial Code § 3401.
Time for presenting check to bank, see Commercial Code § 4404.
Waiver of notice, see Commercial Code § 3504.

§ 3503. Notice of dishonor

(a) The obligation of an indorser stated in subdivision (a) of Section 3415 and the obligation of a drawer stated in subdivision (d) of Section 3414 may not be enforced unless (1) the indorser or drawer is given notice of dishonor of the instrument complying with this section or (2) notice of dishonor is excused under subdivision (b) of Section 3504.

(b) Notice of dishonor may be given by any person; may be given by any commercially reasonable means, including an oral, written, or electronic communication; and is sufficient if it reasonably identifies the instrument and indicates that the instrument has been dishonored or has not been paid or accepted. Return of an instrument given to a bank for collection is sufficient notice of dishonor.

(c) Subject to subdivision (c) of Section 3504, with respect to an instrument taken for collection by a collecting bank, notice of dishonor shall be given (1) by the bank before midnight of the next banking day following the banking day on which the bank receives notice of dishonor of the instrument, or (2) by any other person within 30 days following the day on which the person receives notice of dishonor. With respect to any other instrument, notice of dishonor shall be given within 30 days following the day on which dishonor occurs. *(Added by Stats.1992, c. 914 (S.B.833), § 6.)*

California Code Comment

By John A. Bohn and Charles J. Williams

Prior California Law

1. This section consolidates several widely scattered NIL provisions and adds some new provisions to meet either commercial understanding or convenience.

2. Subdivision (1)(a) is similar to the first part of former Civil Code § 3226.

3. Subdivision (1)(b) combines the rule of former Civil Code §§ 3224(1) and 3225.

4. Subdivision (1)(c) is similar to former Civil Code § 3152.

5. Subdivision (1)(d) is new statutory law. Although there were few cases on point, it is believed the rule under the NIL was or should have been the same. See Britton, Bills & Notes (1961) 540.

6. Subdivision (1)(e) is similar to former Civil Code § 3225.

7. Former Civil Code § 3167, which provided that the time of payment for an instrument payable at a fixed or ascertainable date was determined by excluding the first day from which the time is to begin to run and including the date of payment, is omitted as unnecessary in view of the fact that it states the universal rule applied to all time calculations. There are comparable provisions in other California Codes. For example, Government Code § 6800, Code of Civil Procedure § 12.

8. Subdivision (2) retains the general standard for determining what is a reasonable time which was set forth in former Civil Code § 3266b.

The remainder of subdivision (2) including the presumptions of reasonable periods set forth in (2)(a) and (2)(b) is new statutory law. Under former Civil Code § 3265b it was necessary to present a check for payment within a reasonable time after its issue. A reasonable time under former Civil Code § 3265b depended upon the facts and circumstances in each case. However, the indication from the pre NIL cases and the decisions from other states under the NIL point to a much shorter period of time in general than that which is permitted by the presumptions under subdivisions (2)(a) and (b) of this section. For a general discussion of presentment of checks for payment at common law, see R. H. Herron Co. v. Mawby, 5 Cal.App. 39, 89 Pac. 872 (1907).

Official Comment 3 suggests that the presumptions in subdivisions (2)(a) and (b) apply to uncertified checks drawn and payable within the "continental" United States only, although the qualifying term "continental" is not used. (Compare e.g. Commercial Code §§ 3412 and 3504 which were changed in the 1962 Official Text from the 1958 version by the deletion of "continental" to take account of the admission of Alaska and Hawaii). The term presumption is defined in subdivision (31) of section 1–201 of the Official Text but this definition has been omitted in California. See California Code Comment 31 to Commercial Code § 1201. The use of the word "presumed" and its effect in subdivision (2) is therefore to be determined by the general Code of Civil Procedure provisions as to presumptions. Code of Civil Procedure §§ 1959–1963.

9. Subdivision (3) modifies the rule under the NIL. Under former Civil Code § 3227 the day on which an instrument could be presented was the same as the day upon which an instrument could be paid under former Civil Code § 3166. Subdivision (3) changes this rule. Instead

of specifying in detail as former Civil Code § 3166 did, subdivision (3) merely takes into account the widespread practice of businesses closing on Saturday or other days of the week. See Official Comment 4.

10. Subdivision (4) combines former Civil Code § 3153(2) and part of § 3156. The part of former Civil Code § 3156 which permitted presentment "at any hour before the bank is closed" when the drawer has insufficient funds has been eliminated in order to avoid inconvenience to the bank. Official Comment 5.

Changes from U.C.C. (1962 Official Text)

11. This is section 3–503 of the Official Text without change.

Uniform Commercial Code Comment
1992 Addition

1. Subsection (a) is consistent with former Section 3–501(2)(a), but notice of dishonor is no longer relevant to the liability of a drawer except for the case of a draft accepted by an acceptor other than a bank. Comments 2 and 4 to Section 3–414. There is no reason why drawers should be discharged on instruments they draw until payment or acceptance. They are entitled to have the instrument presented to the drawee and dishonored (Section 3–414(b)) before they are liable to pay, but no notice of dishonor need be made to them as a condition of liability. Subsection (b), which states how notice of dishonor is given, is based on former Section 3–508(3).

2. Subsection (c) replaces former Section 3–508(2). It differs from that section in that it provides a 30-day period for a person other than a collecting bank to give notice of dishonor rather than the three-day period allowed in former Article 3. Delay in giving notice of dishonor may be excused under Section 3–504(c).

Uniform Commercial Code Comment
Prior Uniform Statutory Provision:

Sections 71, 72, 75, 85, 86, 144, 145, 146, 186 and 193, Uniform Negotiable Instruments Law.
Changes: Combined and simplified; new provisions.

Purposes of Changes and New Matter:

1. This section states in one place all of the rules applicable to the time of presentment. Excused delay is covered by Section 3–511 on waiver and excuse, and the effect of unexcused delay by Section 3–502 on discharge.

The original Section 86, as to the determination of the time of payment by calculation from the day the time is to run, is omitted as superfluous. It states a rule universally applied to all time calculations in the law of contracts, and has no special application to negotiable instruments. No change in the law is intended.

2. Subsection (1) contains new provisions stating the commercial understanding as to the presentment of instruments payable after sight, and of accelerated paper.

3. Subsection (2) retains the substance of the original Section 193 as to the determination of a reasonable time. It provides specific time limits which are presumed, as that term is defined in this Act (Section 1–201), to be reasonable for uncertified checks drawn and payable within the continental limits of the United States. The court-made time limit of the day after the receipt of the instrument found in decisions under the original Act has proved to be too short a time for some holders, such as the department store or other large business clearing many checks through its books shortly after the first of the month, as well as the farmer or other individual at a distance from a bank.

The time limit provided differs as to drawer and indorser. The drawer, who has himself issued the check and normally expects to have it paid and charged to his account is reasonably required to stand behind it for a longer period, especially in view of the protection now provided by Federal Deposit Insurance. The thirty days specified coincides with the time after which a purchaser has notice that a check has become stale (Section 3–304(3)(c)). The indorser, who has normally merely received the check and passed it on, and does not expect to have to pay it, is entitled to know more promptly whether it is to be dishonored, in order that he may have recourse against the person with whom he has dealt.

4. Subsection (3) replaces the original Sections 85 and 146. It is intended to make allowance for the increasing practice of closing banks or businesses on Saturday or other days of the week. It is not intended to mean that any drawee or obligor can avoid dishonor of instruments by extended closing.

5. Subsection (4) eliminates the provision of the original Section 75 permitting presentment "at any hour before the bank is closed" if the drawer has no funds in the bank. The change is made to avoid inconvenience to the bank.

"Banking day" is defined in Section 4–104.

Cross References:

Point 1: Sections 3–501, 3–502, 3–505, 3–506 and 3–511.
Point 3: Section 1–201 and 3–304(3)(c).
Point 5: Section 4–104.

Definitional Cross References:

"Acceptance". Section 3–410.
"Bank". Section 1–201.
"Banking day". Section 4–104.
"Check". Section 3–104.
"Draft". Section 3–104.
"Instrument". Section 3–102.
"Issue". Section 3–102.
"Party". Section 1–201.
"Person". Section 1–201.
"Presentment". Section 3–504.
"Presumed". Section 1–201.
"Reasonable time". Section 1–204.
"Secondary party". Section 3–102.
"Usage of trade". Section 1–205.

Cross References

Failure to notify indorser of dishonor, discharge of liability, see Commercial Code § 3415.
Acceptance, see Commercial Code § 3409.
Acceptance or payment, time, see Commercial Code § 3501.
Banking day, see Commercial Code § 4104.
Business days, see Civil Code § 9.
Check, see Commercial Code § 3104.
Computation of time, see Civil Code § 10; Code of Civil Procedure § 12; Government Code § 6800 et seq.
Definitions, see Commercial Code §§ 1201, 4104.
Document or instrument, last day for filing falling on holiday, see Government Code § 6707.
Draft, see Commercial Code § 3104.
Duties of collecting agent, see Civil Code § 2021.
Excuse in making presentment, see Commercial Code § 3504.
Holidays, acts performable on next business day, see Civil Code § 11; Code of Civil Procedure § 13; Government Code § 6706.
Holidays falling on Sunday, see Government Code § 6701.
Instrument, see Commercial Code § 3104.
Issue, see Commercial Code § 3105.
Overdue demand instrument, see Commercial Code § 3304.
Party to whom presentment is made, rights, see Commercial Code § 3501.
Payable at a bank, see Commercial Code § 4106.
Payable on demand, see Commercial Code § 3108.
Presentment, see Commercial Code § 3501.
Qualified acceptance, time for drawer or indorser to express assent, see Commercial Code § 3410.
Reasonable time, see Commercial Code § 1204.
Saturday half-holiday, see Government Code § 6702.
Secondary party, see Commercial Code § 3102.
Special or limited holidays, see Code of Civil Procedure § 13a; Government Code § 6705.
State holidays, see Civil Code § 7; Code of Civil Procedure § 10; Government Code § 6700.
Taker, notice that check became stale, see Commercial Code § 3307.
Time for presenting check to bank, see Commercial Code § 4404.
Time of maturity, optional bank holidays, see Commercial Code § 3123.

Time of performance of contract, see Civil Code § 1657.

§ 3504. Excused presentment and notice of dishonor

(a) Presentment for payment or acceptance of an instrument is excused if (1) the person entitled to present the instrument cannot with reasonable diligence make presentment, (2) the maker or acceptor has repudiated an obligation to pay the instrument or is dead or in insolvency proceedings, (3) by the terms of the instrument presentment is not necessary to enforce the obligation of indorsers or the drawer, (4) the drawer or indorser whose obligation is being enforced has waived presentment or otherwise has no reason to expect or right to require that the instrument be paid or accepted, or (5) the drawer instructed the drawee not to pay or accept the draft or the drawee was not obligated to the drawer to pay the draft.

(b) Notice of dishonor is excused if (1) by the terms of the instrument notice of dishonor is not necessary to enforce the obligation of a party to pay the instrument, or (2) the party whose obligation is being enforced waived notice of dishonor. A waiver of presentment is also a waiver of notice of dishonor.

(c) Delay in giving notice of dishonor is excused if the delay was caused by circumstances beyond the control of the person giving the notice and the person giving the notice exercised reasonable diligence after the cause of the delay ceased to operate. *(Added by Stats.1992, c. 914 (S.B.833), § 6.)*

California Code Comment

By John A. Bohn and Charles J. Williams

Prior California Law

1. Subdivision (1) is similar to former Civil Code § 3153(1) and part of former Civil Code § 3226 which required presentment to be made by the holder or some person authorized to receive payment on his behalf. However, the NIL did not separately define presentment. The reason for defining presentment is to make it clear that any demand to pay is a presentment. This then separates the problem of what is presentment from how presentment may be made. Official Comment 1. Under the NIL presentment was indirectly defined in terms of the requirements as to how presentment was made.

2. Subdivision (2)(a) is new statutory law but is in accord with prior judicial decisions. For example, Thompson v. Dubois, 215 Cal. 577, 11 P.2d 862 (1932), held that mailing a copy to the maker's last place of residence and leaving a copy at the place where the notes were payable was sufficient where the maker had left the place of residence or was hiding and personal demand could not be made upon him.

This subdivision at least liberalizes the requirement of presentment by permitting it to be made by mail, while under the NIL it appears that some excuse for not presenting it in person had to be shown before presentment by mail was permitted.

3. Subdivision (2)(b) is new statutory language but in substance is within former Civil Code § 3154. The method which a collecting bank may use in presenting an item is set forth in Commercial Code § 4210.

4. Subdivision (2)(c) follows the rules of former Civil Code § 3154 as to the proper place for presentment. However, this subdivision excuses presentment where neither the payor nor his representative is present or accessible at the place for presentment. The same result was reached under the NIL because under former Civil Code § 3163(1) presentment for payment was excused where presentment as required could not be made with the exercise of reasonable diligence.

5. Subdivision (3)(a) changes California law. It provides that presentment may be made to any one of two or more makers, acceptors, drawees or other payors. Under former Civil Code §§ 3226(1), 3158 and 3159, presentment for payment had to be made to all persons primarily liable on the instrument unless they were partners. Official Comment 3.

6. Subdivision (3)(b) is new statutory law but is in accord with commercial understanding.

7. Subdivision (4) is new statutory language but is in substance included within the provisions of former Civil Code § 3154.

8. Subdivision (5) is new statutory law. It modifies former California law to the extent that it makes presentment under Commercial Code § 4210 proper presentment under this section. See the California Code Comment and the Official Comment to section 4210.

Changes from U.C.C. (1962 Official Text)

9. Subdivision (2)(b) was changed from the 1962 Official Text by the addition of the phrase "or a place designated by the party to accept or pay." This amendment was made at the suggestion of the State Bar Committee in its Supplemental Report After the Enactment of the Uniform Commercial Code With Changes by New York. The added language is intended to handle the problem of presentment at electric computer centers.

Uniform Commercial Code Comment

1992 Addition

Section 3–504 is largely a restatement of former Section 3–511. Subsection (4) of former Section 3–511 is replaced by Section 3–502(f).

Uniform Commercial Code Comment

Prior Uniform Statutory Provision:

Sections 72, 73, 77, 78 and 145, Uniform Negotiable Instruments Law.

Changes: Combined and simplified.

Purposes of Changes:

1. This section is intended to simplify the rules as to how presentment is made and to make it clear that any demand upon the party to pay is a presentment no matter where or how. Former technical requirements of exhibition of the instrument and the like are not required unless insisted upon by the party to pay (Section 3–505).

2. Paragraph (a) of subsection (2) authorizes presentment by mail directly to the obligor. The presentment is sufficient and the instrument is dishonored by non-acceptance or non-payment even though the party making presentment may be liable for improper collection methods. "Through a clearing-house" means that presentment is not made when the demand reaches the clearing-house, but when it reaches the obligor. Section 4–210 should also be consulted for the methods of presenting which may properly be employed by a collecting bank. Subsection (5) of this section makes it clear that presentment made under Section 4–210 is proper presentment.

3. Paragraph (a) of subsection (3) eliminates the requirement of the original Sections 78 and 145(1) that presentment be made to each of two or more makers, acceptors or drawees unless they are partners or one has authority to act for the others. The holder is entitled to expect that any one of the named parties will pay or accept, and should not be required to go to the trouble and expense of making separate presentment to a number of them.

4. Section 3–412 provides that an acceptance made payable at a bank in the United States does not vary the draft. Subsection (4) of this section makes it clear that a draft so accepted must be presented at the bank so designated. The same rule is applied to notes made payable at a bank. The rule of the subsection is in conformity with the provisions of Section 3–501 on presentment and Section 3–502 on the effect of failure to make presentment with reference to domiciled paper.

Cross References:

Point 1: Sections 3–501, 3–502, 3–505 and 3–511.
Point 2: Section 4–210.
Point 5: Sections 3–412, 3–501 and 3–502.

Definitional Cross References:

"Acceptance". Section 3–410.
"Bank". Section 1–201.
"Clearing house". Section 4–104.

"Draft". Section 3–104.
"Holder". Section 1–201.
"Instrument". Section 3–102.
"Note". Section 3–104.
"Party". Section 1–201.
"Person". Section 1–201.

Cross References

Acceptance, see Commercial Code § 3409.
Acceptance varying terms of draft, see Commercial Code § 3410.
Clearing house, see Commercial Code § 4104.
Collecting bank, method of presentment, see Commercial Code § 4212.
Delay in presentment, see Commercial Code § 3415.
Draft, see Commercial Code § 3104.
Duties of collecting agent as to negotiable instrument, see Civil Code § 2021.
Instrument, see Commercial Code § 3104.
Note, see Commercial Code § 3104.
Party to whom presentment is made, rights, see Commercial Code § 3501.
Presentment, see Commercial Code § 3501.

§ 3505. Dishonor and notice of dishonor; evidence and presumptions

(a) The following are admissible as evidence and create a presumption of dishonor and of any notice of dishonor stated:

(1) A document regular in form as provided in subdivision (b) which purports to be a protest.

(2) A purported stamp or writing of the drawee, payor bank, or presenting bank on or accompanying the instrument stating that acceptance or payment has been refused unless reasons for the refusal are stated and the reasons are not consistent with dishonor.

(3) A book or record of the drawee, payor bank, or collecting bank, kept in the usual course of business which shows dishonor, even if there is no evidence of who made the entry.

(b) A protest is a certificate of dishonor made by a United States consul or vice consul, or a notary public or other person authorized to administer oaths by the law of the place where dishonor occurs. It may be made upon information satisfactory to that person. The protest shall identify the instrument and certify either that presentment has been made or, if not made, the reason why it was not made, and that the instrument has been dishonored by nonacceptance or nonpayment. The protest may also certify that notice of dishonor has been given to some or all parties. *(Added by Stats.1992, c. 914 (S.B.833), § 6.)*

California Code Comment

By John A. Bohn and Charles J. Williams

Prior California Law

1. Subdivision (1)(a) changes the rule under former Civil Code § 3155. Former Civil Code § 3155 made it mandatory that the instrument be exhibited upon presentment. This requirement is now optional at the request of the party to whom presentment is made.

Commercial Code § 3804 prescribes the course of action where an instrument has been lost, destroyed or stolen. Prior to the NIL a California court had held that loss of an instrument excused presentment. California Nat. Bank v. Weldon, 14 Cal.App. 765, 113 Pac. 334 (1911). There are no California cases under the NIL. Former Civil Code § 3241 provided that ". . . protest could be made on a copy or a writing containing its terms." New York courts had held under this section that loss did not excuse notice of dishonor or protest. Heinrich v. First Nat. Bank of Middletown, 219 N.Y. 1, 113 N.E. 531, LRA1917A, 655 (1916)

2. Subdivision (1)(b) is new statutory law. However, the right under certain circumstances to require identification would appear to be in accordance with general commercial practice and seems reasonable whether or not specific statutory language authorizes it.

3. Subdivision (1)(c) supplements Commercial Code § 3504(2)(c) which provides that presentment may be made at the place specified. This is also in accord with former Civil Code § 3154. The language permitting the party to whom presentment is made to require presentment in any reasonable place where none is specified is new statutory law. Former Civil Code § 3154(3) and (4) specified that where no place of payment was designated, the place of payment was the last known business or residence address.

4. The requirement of subdivision (1)(d) that the instrument be surrendered is in accord with former Civil Code § 3155. The right to a receipt is new statutory law.

5. Subdivision (2) is new. It protects the presenting party where the party to whom presentment is made requires any of the items set forth in subdivision (1).

Changes from U.C.C. (1962 Official Text)

6. This is section 3–505 of the Official Text without change.

Uniform Commercial Code Comment

1992 Addition

Protest is no longer mandatory and must be requested by the holder. Even if requested, protest is not a condition to the liability of indorsers or drawers. Protest is a service provided by the banking system to establish that dishonor has occurred. Like other services provided by the banking system, it will be available if market incentives, interbank agreements, or governmental regulations require it, but liabilities of parties no longer rest on it. Protest may be a requirement for liability on international drafts governed by foreign law which this Article cannot affect.

Uniform Commercial Code Comment

Prior Uniform Statutory Provision:

Section 74, Uniform Negotiable Instruments Law.

Changes: Expanded and modified.

Purposes of Changes: To supplement the provision as to how presentment is made, by permitting the party to whom it is made to insist on additional requirements:

1. In the first instance a mere demand for acceptance or payment is sufficient presentment, and if the payment is unqualifiedly refused nothing more is required. The party to whom presentment is made may, however, require exhibition of the instrument, its production at the proper place, identification of the party making presentment, and a signed receipt on the instrument, or its surrender on full payment. Failure to comply with any such requirement invalidates the presentment and means that the instrument is not dishonored. The time for presentment is, however, extended to give the person presenting a reasonable opportunity to comply with the requirements.

2. "Reasonable identification" means identification reasonable under all the circumstances. If the party on whom demand is made knows the person making presentment, no requirement of identification is reasonable, while if the circumstances are suspicious a great deal may be required. The requirement applies whether the instrument presented is payable to order or to bearer.

Cross References:

Point 1: Sections 3–504 and 3–506.

Definitional Cross References:

"Acceptance". Section 3–410.
"Dishonor". Section 3–507.
"Instrument". Section 3–102.
"Party". Section 1–201.
"Person". Section 1–201.

"Presentment". Section 3–504.
"Reasonable time." Section 1–204.
"Signed". Section 1–201.

Cross References

Acceptance, see Commercial Code § 3409.
Dishonor, see Commercial Code § 3502.
Instrument, see Commercial Code § 3104.
Lost, destroyed or stolen instruments, see Commercial Code § 3309.
Manner of presentment, see Commercial Code § 3501.
Time for acceptance or payment, see Commercial Code § 3501.

§§ 3506 to 3511. Repealed by Stats.1992, c. 914 (S.B. 833), § 5

CHAPTER 6. DISCHARGE AND PAYMENT

Section
3601. Discharge; effect of discharge.
3602. Payment; discharge of obligation.
3603. Tender of payment.
3604. Discharge by cancellation or renunciation.
3605. Indorsers and accommodation parties; discharge.
3606 to 3805. Repealed.

Chapter 6, added as Part 6 by Stats.1992, c. 914 (S.B.833), § 6, was editorially classified as Chapter 6 due to its subject matter and placement following Chapters 1 to 5 of Division 3.

Transitional Provisions

Effective date and transitional provisions for repeal and addition of Division 3 by Stats.1992, c. 914, see Commercial Code § 16101 et seq.

§ 3601. Discharge; effect of discharge

(a) The obligation of a party to pay the instrument is discharged as stated in this division or by an act or agreement with the party which would discharge an obligation to pay money under a simple contract.

(b) Discharge of the obligation of a party is not effective against a person acquiring rights of a holder in due course of the instrument without notice of the discharge. *(Added by Stats.1992, c. 914 (S.B.833), § 6.)*

California Code Comment

By John A. Bohn and Charles J. Williams

Prior California Law

1. Subdivision (1) is an index of all sections in Division 3 which provide when a party is discharged. This list is exclusive within the limits of Division 3 but a discharge created by other statute does apply and may result in a discharge, for example a discharge in bankruptcy or because of illegality. Official Comment 1.

The NIL counterpart to this section was former Civil Code § 3200 which spoke in terms of the discharge of the instrument, while this section is in terms of the discharge of the parties.

2. Subdivision (2) is similar to former Civil Code § 3200(4) which provided a discharge by "any other act which will discharge a simple contract for the payment of money". See Official Comment 2.

3. Subdivision (3) specifies those situations in which all parties are discharged from liability.

Subdivision (3)(a) is similar to former Civil Code § 3200(5) except that changes have been made in wording to clarify certain difficulties under the former language. See Official Comment 4.

Subdivision (3)(b) picks up and applies the other grounds stated for discharge and provides that when a party who has no right of action or recourse on the instrument is discharged under any such provision, all of the parties are discharged. To this extent is it similar in effect to former Civil Code §§ 3200(1), (2) and (5), 3201(1) and (3), and 3202. It is an expression of the general principle that when no party is left with rights against any other party on the paper, all parties to the instrument are discharged. Official Comment 3.

Changes from U.C.C. (1962 Official Text)

4. This is section 3–601 of the Official Text without change.

Uniform Commercial Code Comment
1992 Addition

Subsection (a) replaces subsections (1) and (2) of former Section 3–601. Subsection (b) restates former Section 3–602. Notice of discharge is not treated as notice of a defense that prevents holder in due course status. Section 3–302(b). Discharge is effective against a holder in due course only if the holder had notice of the discharge when holder in due course status was acquired. For example, if an instrument bearing a canceled indorsement is taken by a holder, the holder has notice that the indorser has been discharged. Thus, the discharge is effective against the holder even if the holder is a holder in due course.

Uniform Commercial Code Comment

Prior Uniform Statutory Provision:

Sections 119, 120 and 121, Uniform Negotiable Instruments Law.

Changes: Portions of original sections combined and reworded; new provisions.

Purposes of Changes:

1. Subsection (1) contains an index referring to all of the sections of this Article which provide for the discharge of any party. The list is exclusive so far as the provisions of this Article are concerned, but it is not intended to prevent or affect any discharge arising apart from this statute, as for example a discharge in bankruptcy or a statutory provision for discharge if the instrument is negotiated in a gaming transaction.

2. A negotiable instrument is in itself merely a piece of paper bearing a writing, and strictly speaking is incapable of being discharged. The parties are rather discharged from liability on their contracts on the instrument. The language of the original Section 119 as to discharge of the instrument itself has left uncertainties as to the effect of the discharge upon the rights of a subsequent holder in due course. It is therefore eliminated, and this section now distinguishes instead between the discharge of a single party and the discharge of all parties.

So far as the discharge of any one party is concerned a negotiable instrument differs from any other contract only in the special rules arising out of its character to which paragraphs (a) to (i) of subsection (1) are an index, and in the effect of the discharge against a subsequent holder in due course (Section 3–602). Subsection (2) therefore retains from the original Section 119(4) the provision for discharge by "any other act which will discharge a simple contract for the payment of money," and specifically recognizes the possibility of a discharge by agreement.

The discharge of any party is a defense available to that party as provided in sections on rights of those who are and are not holders in due course (Sections 3–305 and 3–306). He has the burden of establishing the defense (Section 3–307).

3. Subsection (3) substitutes for the "discharge of the instrument" the discharge of all parties from liability on their contracts on the instrument. It covers a part of the substance of the original Section 119(1), (2) and (5), the original Section 120(1) and (3), and the original Section 121(1) and (2). It states a general principle in lieu of the original detailed provisions. The principle is that all parties to an instrument are discharged when no party is left with rights against any other party on the paper.

When any party reacquires the instrument in his own right his own liability is discharged; and any intervening party to whom he was liable is also discharged as provided in Section 3–208 on reacquisition. When he is left with no right of action against an intervening party and no right of recourse against any prior party, all parties are obviously discharged. The instrument itself is not necessarily extinct, since it may be reissued or renegotiated with a new and further liability; and if it subsequently reaches the hands of a holder in due course without notice of the discharge he may still enforce it as provided in Section 3–602 on effect of discharge against a holder in due course.

Under Section 3–606 on impairment of recourse or collateral, the discharge of any party discharges those who have a right of recourse against him, except in the case of a release with reservation of rights or a failure to give notice of dishonor. A discharge of one who has himself no right of action or recourse on the instrument may thus discharge all parties. Again the instrument itself is not necessarily extinct, and if it is negotiated to a subsequent holder in due course without notice of the discharge he may enforce it as provided in Section 3–602 on effect of discharge against a holder in due course.

4. The language "any party who has himself no right of action or recourse on the instrument" is substituted for "principal debtor," which is not defined by the original Act and has been misleading. This Article also omits the original Section 192, defining the "person primarily liable." Under Section 3–415 on accommodation parties an accommodation maker or acceptor, although he is primarily liable on the instrument in the sense that he is obligated to pay it without recourse upon another, has himself a right of recourse against the accommodated payee; and his reacquisition or discharge leaves the accommodated party liable to him. The accommodated payee, although he is not primarily liable to others, has no right of action or recourse against the accommodation maker, and his reacquisition or discharge may discharge all parties.

Cross References:

Sections 3–406, 3–411, 3–412, 3–509, 3–603, 3–604 and 3–605.
Point 2: Sections 3–305, 3–306, 3–307 and 3–602.
Point 3: Sections 3–208, 3–602 and 3–606.
Point 4: Section 3–415.

Definitional Cross References:

"Action". Section 1–201.
"Agreement". Section 1–201.
"Alteration". Section 3–407.
"Certification". Section 3–411.
"Check". Section 3–104.
"Contract". Section 1–201.
"Draft". Section 3–104.
"Instrument". Section 3–102.
"Money". Section 1–201.
"Notice of dishonor". Section 3–508.
"Party". Section 1–201.
"Presentment". Section 3–504.
"Rights". Section 1–201.

Cross References

Accommodation party, recourse against accommodated payee, see Commercial Code § 3419.
Accord and satisfaction, extinction of obligation, see Civil Code § 1521 et seq.
Action, see Commercial Code § 1201; Code of Civil Procedure §§ 22, 30, 363.
Agreement,
    Generally, see Commercial Code § 1201.
    Reduced to writing, exclusion of parol evidence, exceptions, see Code of Civil Procedure § 1856.
Alteration or forged signature, negligence constituting, see Commercial Code § 3406.
Cancellation of written contract, see Civil Code §§ 1699, 1700.
Certification, see Commercial Code § 3409.
Discharge by failure to give notice of dishonor, see Commercial Code § 3415.
Extinction of,
    Contracts, see Civil Code § 1682 et seq.
    Obligations, see Civil Code § 1473 et seq.
Holder in due course,
    Rights, see Commercial Code § 3305.
Holder's right to enforce instrument, see Commercial Code § 3301.
Modification,
    Generally, see Commercial Code § 3407.
    Contracts, see Civil Code § 1697 et seq.
    Writings, burden of explanation, see Evidence Code § 1402.
Notice of dishonor, see Commercial Code § 3503.
Novation, substitution of obligation, see Civil Code § 1530 et seq.
Obligation defined, see Civil Code § 1427; Code of Civil Procedure § 26.
Offer of performance, extinction of obligation, see Civil Code § 1485 et seq.
One not holder in due course, rights, see Commercial Code § 3306.
Performance, extinction of obligation by, see Civil Code § 1473 et seq.
Presentment, see Commercial Code § 3501.
Presumption of payment of obligation delivered up to debtor, see Evidence Code § 633.
Prevention of performance or offer, extinction of obligation, see Civil Code § 1511 et seq.
Release, extinction of obligations, see Civil Code § 1541 et seq.
Rescission, see Civil Code § 1688 et seq.
Signatures, burden of establishing validity, see Commercial Code § 3307.
Waiver or renunciation of claim or right arising out of breach, see Commercial Code § 1107.

§ 3602. Payment; discharge of obligation

(a) Subject to subdivision (b), an instrument is paid to the extent payment is made (1) by or on behalf of a party obliged to pay the instrument, and (2) to a person entitled to enforce the instrument. To the extent of the payment, the obligation of the party obliged to pay the instrument is discharged even though payment is made with knowledge of a claim to the instrument under Section 3306 by another person.

(b) The obligation of a party to pay the instrument is not discharged under subdivision (a) if either of the following applies:

(1) A claim to the instrument under Section 3306 is enforceable against the party receiving payment and (A) payment is made with knowledge by the payor that payment is prohibited by injunction or similar process of a court of competent jurisdiction, or (B) in the case of an instrument other than a cashier's check, teller's check, or certified check, the party making payment accepted, from the person having a claim to the instrument, indemnity against loss resulting from refusal to pay the person entitled to enforce the instrument.

(2) The person making payment knows that the instrument is a stolen instrument and pays a person it knows is in wrongful possession of the instrument. *(Added by Stats.1992, c. 914 (S.B.833), § 6.)*

California Code Comment

By John A. Bohn and Charles J. Williams

Prior California Law

1. This section is new statutory law. The preliminary review of Article [Division] 3 by a section of the State Bar subcommittee described the effect of this section of California law: "Although . . . there is no corresponding section in the present Civil Code, the rule stated is probably the law in California." Sixth Progress Report to the Legislature by Senate Fact Finding Committee on Judiciary (1959–1961), Part 1, The Uniform Commercial Code, pp. 355–356.

2. A holder in due course takes an instrument free of all personal defenses. The effect of this section is to make the defense of discharge a personal defense which is cut off by a holder in due course. The NIL did not specifically settle the question whether or not a discharge in

every case was a real or personal defense and the issue was rarely raised because most acts of discharge by their nature prevent a transferee from being a holder in due course. See Britton, Bills and Notes (1961) 647–653.

This section is probably in accord with prior California decisions. For example, in Schoen v. Houghton, 50 Cal. 528 (1875), a purchaser prior to maturity who purchased after the payee executed a release of the note was held to be bona fide holder even though the note was purchased for less than the face value and by the exercise of slight diligence the purchaser might have ascertained that the release had been given. In Allenberg v. Rapken & Co., 108 Cal.App. 99, 291 Pac. 281 (1930), payment by a maker without requiring surrender of the instrument was insufficient as against a subsequent transferee and the maker was held to be liable to him.

Changes from U.C.C. (1962 Official Text)

3. This is section 3–602 of the Official Text without change.

Uniform Commercial Code Comment
1992 Addition

This section replaces former Section 3–603(1). The phrase "claim to the instrument" in subsection (a) means, by reference to Section 3–306, a claim of ownership or possession and not a claim in recoupment. Subsection (b)(1)(ii) is added to conform to Section 3–411. Section 3–411 is intended to discourage an obligated bank from refusing payment of a cashier's check, certified check or dishonored teller's check at the request of a claimant to the check who provided the bank with indemnity against loss. See Comment 1 to Section 3–411. An obligated bank that refuses payment under those circumstances not only remains liable on the check but may also be liable to the holder of the check for consequential damages. Section 3–602(b)(1)(ii) and Section 3–411, read together, change the rule of former Section 3–603(1) with respect to the obligation of the obligated bank on the check. Payment to the holder of a cashier's check, teller's check, or certified check discharges the obligation of the obligated bank on the check to both the holder and the claimant even though indemnity has been given by the person asserting the claim. If the obligated bank pays the check in violation of an agreement with the claimant in connection with the indemnity agreement, any liability that the bank may have for violation of the agreement is not governed by Article 3, but is left to other law. This section continues the rule that the obligor is not discharged on the instrument if payment is made in violation of an injunction against payment. See Section 3–411(c)(iv).

Uniform Commercial Code Comment
Prior Uniform Statutory Provision:
None.

Purposes:

The section is intended to remove an uncertainty as to which the original Act is silent. It rests on the principle that any discharge of a party provided under any section of this Article is a personal defense of the party, which is cut off when a subsequent holder in due course takes the instrument without notice of the defense. Thus where an instrument is paid without surrender such a subsequent purchase cuts off the defense. This section applies only to discharges arising under the provisions of this Article, and it has no application to any discharge arising apart from it, such as a discharge in bankruptcy.

Under Section 3–304(1)(b) on notice to purchaser it is possible for a holder to take the instrument in due course even though he has notice that one or more parties have been discharged, so long as any party remains undischarged. Thus he may take with notice that an indorser of a note has been released, and still be a holder in due course as to the liability of the maker. In that event, the holder in due course is subject to the defense of the discharge of which he had notice when he took the instrument.

Cross References:

Sections 3–302, 3–304, 3–305 and 3–601.

Definitional Cross References:

"Holder in due course". Section 3–302.

"Instrument". Section 3–102.
"Notice". Section 1–201.
"Party". Section 1–201.

Cross References

Extinction of obligations, see Civil Code § 1473 et seq.
Holder in due course, definition and rights, see Commercial Code §§ 3302, 3305.
Taker, notice of claim or defense, see Commercial Code § 3307.

§ 3603. Tender of payment

(a) If tender of payment of an obligation to pay an instrument is made to a person entitled to enforce the instrument, the effect of tender is governed by principles of law applicable to tender of payment under a simple contract.

(b) If tender of payment of an obligation to pay an instrument is made to a person entitled to enforce the instrument and the tender is refused, there is discharge, to the extent of the amount of the tender, of the obligation of an indorser or accommodation party having a right of recourse with respect to the obligation to which the tender relates.

(c) If tender of payment of an amount due on an instrument is made to a person entitled to enforce the instrument, the obligation of the obligor to pay interest after the due date on the amount tendered is discharged. If presentment is required with respect to an instrument and the obligor is able and ready to pay on the due date at every place of payment stated in the instrument, the obligor is deemed to have made tender of payment on the due date to the person entitled to enforce the instrument. *(Added by Stats.1992, c. 914 (S.B.833), § 6.)*

California Code Comment
By John A. Bohn and Charles J. Williams

Prior California Law

1. Under former Civil Code §§ 3132, 3169 and 3200 an instrument was discharged by "payment in due course." Subdivision (1) eliminates this concept and, by providing for a discharge to the extent of payment or satisfaction with knowledge of a claim, removes from the payor the burden of determining which of two adverse claimants is entitled to payment. Official Comment 1.

2. Subdivision (1) eliminates the requirement of former Civil Code § 3169 that payment be made in good faith and without notice that the title of the holder is defective. Payment to the holder under this subdivision discharges the party who makes it. This rule is qualified by paragraphs (a) and (b) of subdivision (1) regarding persons who acquire an instrument by theft or through a restrictive indorsement.

Is payment made and discharge obtained where a new negotiable instrument is issued in exchange for one previously executed? The California courts have held generally that there is a presumption that the renewal or new note is not taken by the payee in payment and therefore the issuance of a new or renewal note is not payment. Selig Cahn Inc. v. California Wrecking Co., 9 Cal.2d 617, 71 P.2d 113 (1937).

3. Code of Civil Procedure § 1962 (9) establishes a presumption that an obligation "delivered up to the debtor has been paid". Although Commercial Code § 3307(2) puts the burden of establishing a defense, of which payment is one, upon the person asserting it, the effect of the presumption is to show the existence of a defense under Commercial Code § 3307(3) and the holder then has the burden of going forward with the evidence to establish that he is a holder in due course and that the defense does not apply to him.

4. Subdivision (2) supersedes former Civil Code §§ 3252–3258 which dealt with the payment of a draft "for honor" after protest and permits payment to be made by any person including a stranger to the instrument as long as the holder consents. Official Comment 2.

This subdivision omits the provision of former Civil Code § 3202 under the terms of which a party secondarily liable who paid the instrument was "remitted to his former rights."

The person who pays and to whom an instrument is surrendered receives the rights of a transferee under Commercial Code § 3201.

The Legislative Counsel states that:

"Subdivision (2) is in accord with the spirit of California cases such as Foster v. Beau De Zart, 13 Cal.App. 52, 108 Pac. 875, and Wright v. Shoenhair, 100 Cal.App. 163, 280 Pac. 174." Sixth Progress Report to the Legislature by Senate Fact Finding Committee on Judiciary, (1959–1961) Part 1, The Uniform Commercial Code, p. 84.

5. Preliminary review by a section of the State Bar subcommittee makes this comment with regard to the effect of this section on California law:

"Basically this section appears to be in the main a combination and rewording of the Civil Code Sections noted; however, a new provision has been added to provide that payment made in due course may permit the discharge of a party even though payment is made with the knowledge of third party claims unless the third party claimant file a bond or obtain an injunction." Sixth Progress Report to the Legislature by Senate Fact Finding Committee on Judiciary, (1959–1961) Part 1, The Uniform Commercial Code, p. 356.

6. A person who makes payment is discharged from liability. See Official Comment 5 for the effect of payment upon the liability of other parties to the instrument.

Changes from U.C.C. (1962 Official Text)

7. This is section 3–603 of the Official Text without change.

Uniform Commercial Code Comment
1992 Addition

Section 3–603 replaces former Section 3–604. Subsection (a) generally incorporates the law of tender of payment applicable to simple contracts. Subsections (b) and (c) state particular rules. Subsection (b) replaces former Section 3–604(2). Under subsection (b) refusal of a tender of payment discharges any indorser or accommodation party having a right of recourse against the party making the tender. Subsection (c) replaces former Section 3–604(1) and (3).

Uniform Commercial Code Comment
Prior Uniform Statutory Provision:

Sections 51, 88, 119, 121 and 171–177, Uniform Negotiable Instruments Law.

Changes: Parts of original sections combined and reworded; law changed.

Purposes of Changes: This section changes the law as follows:

1. It eliminates the "payment in due course" found in the original Sections 51, 88 and 119. "Payment in due course" discharged all parties where it was made by one who has no right of recourse on the instrument; but this is true of any other discharge of such a party, and is now covered by Section 3–601(3) on discharge of parties. Such payment was effective as a discharge against a subsequent purchaser; but since it is made at or after maturity of the instrument a purchaser with notice of that fact cannot be a holder in due course, and one who takes without notice of the payment and the maturity should be protected against failure to take up the instrument. The matter is now covered by Section 3–602.

2. The original Sections 171–177 provide for payment of a draft "for honor" after protest. The practice originated at a time when communications were slow and difficult, and in overseas transactions there might be a delay of several months before the drawer could act upon any dishonor. It provided a method by which a third party might intervene to protect the credit of the drawer and at the same time preserve his own rights. Cable, telegraph and telephone have made the practice obsolete for nearly a century, and it is today almost entirely unknown. It has been replaced by the cable transfer, the letter of credit and numerous other devices by which a substitute arrangement is promptly made. "Payment for honor" is therefore eliminated; and subsection (2) now provides that any person may pay with the consent of the holder.

3. Payment to the holder discharges the party who makes it from his own liability on the instrument, and a part payment discharges him pro tanto. The same is true of any other satisfaction. Subsection (1) changes the law by eliminating the requirement of the original Section 88 that the payment be made in good faith and without notice that the title of the holder is defective. It adopts as a general principle the position that a payor is not required to obey an order to stop payment received from an indorser. However, this general principle is qualified by the provisions of subsection (1)(a) and (b) respecting persons who acquire an instrument by theft, or through a restrictive indorsement (Section 3–205). These provisions are thus consistent with Section 3–306 covering the rights of one not a holder in due course.

When the party to pay is notified of an adverse claim to the instrument he has normally no means of knowing whether the assertion is true. The "unless" clause of subsection (1) follows statutes which have been passed in many states on adverse claims to bank deposits. The paying party may pay despite notification of the adverse claim unless the adverse claimant supplies indemnity deemed adequate by the paying party or procures the issuance of process restraining payment in an action in which the adverse claimant and the holder of the instrument are both parties. If the paying party chooses to refuse payment and stand suit, even though not indemnified or enjoined, he is free to do so, although, under Section 3–306(d) on the rights of one not a holder in due course, except where theft or taking through a restrictive indorsement is alleged the payor must rely on the third party claimant to litigate the issue and may not himself defend on such a ground. His contract is to pay the holder of the instrument, and he performs it by making such payment. Except in cases of theft or restrictive indorsement there is no good reason to put him to inconvenience because of a dispute between two other parties unless he is indemnified or served with appropriate process.

4. With the elimination of "payment for honor", subsection (2) provides that with the consent of the holder payment may be made by anyone, including a stranger. The subsection omits the provision of the original Section 121 by which the payor is "remitted to his former rights". It rejects such decisions as Quimby v. Varnum, 190 Mass. 211, 76 N.E. 671 (1906), holding that an irregular indorser who makes payment cannot recover on the instrument. The same result is reached under Section 3–415(5) on accommodation parties. Upon payment and surrender of the paper the payor succeeds to the rights of the holder, subject to the limitation found in Section 3–201 on transfer that one who has himself been a party to any fraud or illegality affecting the instrument or who as a prior holder had notice of a defense or claim against it cannot improve his position by taking from a later holder in due course.

5. Payment discharges the liability of the person making it. It discharges the liability of other parties only as

a. The discharge of the payor discharges others who have a right of recourse against him under Section 3–606; or

b. Reacquisition of the instrument discharges intervening parties under Section 3–208 on reacquisition; or

c. The discharge of one who has himself no right of recourse on the instrument discharges all parties under Section 3–601 on discharge of parties.

Cross References:

Sections 3–604 and 3–606.
Point 1: Section 3–601(3).
Point 3: Sections 3–205 and 3–306(d).
Point 4: Sections 3–201 and 3–415(5).
Point 5: Sections 3–606, 3–208, 3–601.

Definitional Cross References:

"Action". Section 1–201.
"Holder". Section 1–201.
"Instrument". Section 3–102.
"Order". Section 3–102.
"Party". Section 1–201.
"Person". Section 1–201.
"Rights". Section 1–201.

Cross References

Accommodation party, recourse against accommodated payee, see Commercial Code § 3419.
Accord and satisfaction, extinction of obligation, see Civil Code § 1521 et seq.
Action, see Commercial Code § 1201; Code of Civil Procedure §§ 22, 30, 363.
Discharge of parties in general, see Commercial Code § 3601.
Extinction of obligations, see Civil Code § 1473 et seq.
Holder's right to enforce instrument, see Commercial Code § 3301.
Impairment of recourse or of collateral, see Commercial Code § 3605.
Obligation of payment extinguished by offer and deposit, see Civil Code § 1500.
Party defined, see Commercial Code § 1201.
Party not holder in due course, rights, see Commercial Code § 3306.
Party to fraud, subsequent taking from holder in due course, see Commercial Code § 3203.
Payment, see Civil Code § 1478.
Presumption of payment of obligation delivered up to debtor, see Evidence Code § 633.
Reacquisition of instrument, see Commercial Code § 3207.
Rejected offer of payment equivalent to tender, see Code of Civil Procedure § 2074.
Restrictive indorsement defined, see Commercial Code § 3206.
Right to receipt for payment, see Code of Civil Procedure § 2075.
Tender of payment, see Commercial Code § 3603.

§ 3604. Discharge by cancellation or renunciation

(a) A person entitled to enforce an instrument, with or without consideration, may discharge the obligation of a party to pay the instrument (1) by an intentional voluntary act, such as surrender of the instrument to the party, destruction, mutilation, or cancellation of the instrument, cancellation or striking out of the party's signature, or the addition of words to the instrument indicating discharge, or (2) by agreeing not to sue or otherwise renouncing rights against the party by a signed writing.

(b) Cancellation or striking out of an indorsement pursuant to subdivision (a) does not affect the status and rights of a party derived from the indorsement. *(Added by Stats.1992, c. 914 (S.B.833), § 6.)*

California Code Comment

By John A. Bohn and Charles J. Williams

Prior California Law

1. Subdivision (1) is new statutory law. However it is in accord with prior California decisions. Rottman v. Hevener, 54 Cal.App. 474, 202 Pac. 329 (1921); Walsh v. Walsh, 42 Cal.App.2d 293, 108 P.2d 768 (1940).

2. Subdivision (2) is similar to former Civil Code § 3201(4) which provided that a person secondarily liable is discharged by a valid tender of payment made by a prior party. This was also the pre NIL rule. Daneri v. Gazzola, 139 Cal. 416, 73 Pac. 179 (1903) (surety released from obligation by the principal's offer of payment).

Subdivision (2) is not limited to a prior party so that any party may make tender and the party having recourse against him is discharged.

3. Subdivision (3) is similar to the second clause in the first sentence of former Civil Code § 3151. This makes it clear that when an instrument is payable at more than one place the maker or acceptor must be ready to pay at each of them. Official Comment 3.

At common law in the United States and under the NIL the prevailing view is that where a note is payable at a particular time and place, neither demand nor presentment is necessary in order to permit the holder to maintain an action against the maker. The failure to make presentment at the place named was not a discharge of the debt. First sentence of former Civil Code § 3151; Rottman v. Hevener, cited in California Code Comment 1 above. The Commercial Code changes this rule. See Official Comment 3.

4. Civil Code § 1500 provides that "an obligation for the payment of money is extinguished by a due offer of payment, if the amount is immediately deposited in the name of the creditor, with some bank of deposit within this State, of good repute, and notice thereof is given to the creditor."

Changes from U.C.C. (1962 Official Text)

5. This is section 3–604 of the Official Text without change.

Uniform Commercial Code Comment
1992 Addition

Section 3–604 replaces former Section 3–605.

Uniform Commercial Code Comment

Prior Uniform Statutory Provision:

Sections 70 and 120, Uniform Negotiable Instruments Law.
Changes: Parts of original sections combined and reworded; new provisions.

Purposes of Changes and New Matter:

1. Subsection (1) is new. It states the generally accepted rule as to the effect of tender.

2. Subsection (2) rewords the original subsection 120(4). The party discharged is one who has a right of recourse against the party making tender, whether the latter be a prior party or a subsequent one who has been accommodated.

3. Subsection (3) rewords the final clause of the first sentence of the original Section 70. Where the instrument is payable at any one of two or more specified places, the maker or acceptor must be able and ready to pay at each of them. The language in original Section 70 was taken to mean that makers and acceptors of notes and drafts payable at a bank were not discharged by failure of a holder to make due presentment of such paper at the designated bank. This Article reverses that rule. See Section 3–501 on necessity of presentment, 3–504 on how presentment is made, and 3–502 on effect of delay in presentment.

Cross References:

Section 3–601.
Point 3: Sections 3–501, 3–502 and 3–504.

Definitional Cross References:

"Holder". Section 1–201.
"Instrument". Section 3–102.
"On demand". Section 3–108.
"Party". Section 1–201.
"Right". Section 1–201.

Cross References

Obligation of indorser or accommodation party, effect of discharge, see Commercial Code § 3605.

§ 3605. Indorsers and accommodation parties; discharge

(a) In this section, the term "indorser" includes a drawer having the obligation described in subdivision (d) of Section 3414.

(b) Discharge, under Section 3604, of the obligation of a party to pay an instrument does not discharge the obligation of an indorser or accommodation party having a right of recourse against the discharged party.

(c) If a person entitled to enforce an instrument agrees, with or without consideration, to an extension of the due date of the obligation of a party to pay the instrument, the extension discharges an indorser or accommodation party having a right of recourse against the party whose obligation is extended to the extent the indorser or accommodation party proves that the extension caused loss to the indorser or accommodation party with respect to the right of recourse.

(d) If a person entitled to enforce an instrument agrees, with or without consideration, to a material modification of the obligation of a party other than an extension of the due date, the modification discharges the obligation of an indorser or accommodation party having a right of recourse against the person whose obligation is modified to the extent the modification causes loss to the indorser or accommodation party with respect to the right of recourse. The loss suffered by the indorser or accommodation party as a result of the modification is equal to the amount of the right of recourse unless the person enforcing the instrument proves that no loss was caused by the modification or that the loss caused by the modification was an amount less than the amount of the right of recourse.

(e) If the obligation of a party to pay an instrument is secured by an interest in collateral and a person entitled to enforce the instrument impairs the value of the interest in collateral, the obligation of an indorser or accommodation party having a right of recourse against the obligor is discharged to the extent of the impairment. The value of an interest in collateral is impaired to the extent (1) the value of the interest is reduced to an amount less than the amount of the right of recourse of the party asserting discharge, or (2) the reduction in value of the interest causes an increase in the amount by which the amount of the right of recourse exceeds the value of the interest. The burden of proving impairment is on the party asserting discharge.

(f) If the obligation of a party is secured by an interest in collateral not provided by an accommodation party and a person entitled to enforce the instrument impairs the value of the interest in collateral, the obligation of any party who is jointly and severally liable with respect to the secured obligation is discharged to the extent the impairment causes the party asserting discharge to pay more than that party would have been obliged to pay, taking into account rights of contribution, if impairment had not occurred. If the party asserting discharge is an accommodation party not entitled to discharge under subdivision (e), the party is deemed to have a right to contribution based on joint and several liability rather than a right to reimbursement. The burden of proving impairment is on the party asserting discharge.

(g) Under subdivision (e) or (f), impairing value of an interest in collateral includes (1) failure to obtain or maintain perfection or recordation of the interest in collateral, (2) release of collateral without substitution of collateral of equal value, (3) failure to perform a duty to preserve the value of collateral owed, under Division 9 (commencing with Section 9101) or other law, to a debtor or surety or other person secondarily liable, or

(4) failure to comply with applicable law in disposing of collateral.

(h) An accommodation party is not discharged under subdivision (c), (d), or (e) unless the person entitled to enforce the instrument knows of the accommodation or has notice under subdivision (c) of Section 3419 that the instrument was signed for accommodation.

(i) A party is not discharged under this section if (1) the party asserting discharge consents to the event or conduct that is the basis of the discharge, or (2) the instrument or a separate agreement of the party provides for waiver of discharge under this section either specifically or by general language indicating that parties waive defenses based on suretyship or impairment of collateral. *(Added by Stats.1992, c. 914 (S.B.833), § 6.)*

California Code Comment
By John A. Bohn and Charles J. Williams

Prior California Law

1. Subdivision (1) recognizes cancellation and renunciation as two methods of discharge which operate as a discharge even without consideration.

2. Subdivision (1)(a) combines the rules of former Civil Code §§ 3200(3), 3201(2), 3129 and 3204.

While former Civil Code § 3129 provided that cancellation is effected by the striking of indorsements, subdivision (1) specifies in detail how cancellation is effected. The methods described are exclusive. Official Comment 1.

In general contract law an obligation can be extinguished by destruction or cancellation of the written instrument. Civil Code §§ 1699–1700.

3. Subdivision (1)(b) is similar to former Civil Code § 3203.

4. Subdivision (2) is new statutory law. See Official Comment 3.

Changes from U.C.C. (1962 Official Text)

5. This is section 3–605 of the Official Text without change.

Uniform Commercial Code Comment
1992 Addition

1. Section 3–605, which replaces former Section 3–606, can be illustrated by an example. Bank lends $10,000 to Borrower who signs a note under which Borrower is obliged to pay $10,000 to Bank on a due date stated in the note. Bank insists, however, that Accommodation Party also become liable to pay the note. Accommodation Party can incur this liability by signing the note as a co-maker or by indorsing the note. In either case the note is signed for accommodation and Borrower is the accommodated party. Rights and obligations of Accommodation Party in this case are stated in Section 3–419. Suppose that after the note is signed, Bank agrees to a modification of the rights and obligations between Bank and Borrower. For example, Bank agrees that Borrower may pay the note at some date after the due date, or that Borrower may discharge Borrower's $10,000 obligation to pay the note by paying Bank $3,000, or that Bank releases collateral given by Borrower to secure the note. Under the law of suretyship Borrower is usually referred to as the principal debtor and Accommodation Party is referred to as the surety. Under that law, the surety can be discharged under certain circumstances if changes of this kind are made by Bank, the creditor, without the consent of Accommodation Party, the surety. Rights of the surety to discharge in such cases are commonly referred to as suretyship defenses. Section 3–605 is concerned with this kind of problem in the context of a negotiable instrument to which the principal debtor and the surety are parties. But Section 3–605 has a wider scope. It also applies to indorsers who are not accommodation parties. Unless an indorser signs without recourse, the indorser's liability under Section 3–415(a) is that of a guarantor of payment. If Bank in our hypothetical case indorsed the note and transferred it to Second Bank, Bank has

rights given to an indorser under Section 3–605 if it is Second Bank that modifies rights and obligations of Borrower. Both accommodation parties and indorsers will be referred to in these Comments as sureties. The scope of Section 3–605 is also widened by subsection (e) which deals with rights of a non-accommodation party co-maker when collateral is impaired.

2. The importance of suretyship defenses is greatly diminished by the fact that they can be waived. The waiver is usually made by a provision in the note or other writing that represents the obligation of the principal debtor. It is standard practice to include a waiver of suretyship defenses in notes given to financial institutions or other commercial creditors. Section 3–605(i) allows waiver. Thus, Section 3–605 applies to the occasional case in which the creditor did not include a waiver clause in the instrument or in which the creditor did not obtain the permission of the surety to take the action that triggers the suretyship defense.

3. Subsection (b) addresses the effect of discharge under Section 3–604 of the principal debtor. In the hypothetical case stated in Comment 1, release of Borrower by Bank does not release Accommodation Party. As a practical matter, Bank will not gratuitously release Borrower. Discharge of Borrower normally would be part of a settlement with Borrower if Borrower is insolvent or in financial difficulty. If Borrower is unable to pay all creditors, it may be prudent for Bank to take partial payment, but Borrower will normally insist on a release of the obligation. If Bank takes $3,000 and releases Borrower from the $10,000 debt, Accommodation Party is not injured. To the extent of the payment Accommodation Party's obligation to Bank is reduced. The release of Borrower by Bank does not affect the right of Accommodation party to obtain reimbursement from Borrower or to enforce the note against Borrower if Accommodation Party pays Bank. Section 3–419(e). Subsection (b) is designed to allow a creditor to settle with the principal debtor without risk of losing rights against sureties. Settlement is in the interest of sureties as well as the creditor. Subsection (b), however, is not intended to apply to a settlement of a disputed claim which discharges the obligation.

Subsection (b) changes the law stated in former Section 3–606 but the changes relates largely to formalities rather than substance. Under former Section 3–606, Bank in the hypothetical case stated in Comment 1 could settle with and release Borrower without releasing Accommodation Party, but to accomplish that result Bank had to either obtain the consent of Accommodation Party or make an express reservation of rights against Accommodation Party at the time it released Borrower. The reservation of rights was made in the agreement between Bank and Borrower by which the release of Borrower was made. There was no requirement in former Section 3–606 that any notice be given to Accommodation Party. Section 3–605 eliminates the necessity that Bank formally reserve rights against Accommodation Party in order to retain rights of recourse against Accommodation Party. See PEB Commentary No. 11, dated February 10, 1994 [Uniform Laws Annotated, UCC, APP. II, Comment 11].

4. Subsection (c) relates to extensions of the due date of the instrument. In most cases an extension of time to pay a note is a benefit to both the principal debtor and sureties having recourse against the principal debtor. In relatively few cases the extension may cause loss if deterioration of the financial condition of the principal debtor reduces the amount that the surety will be able to recover on its right of recourse when default occurs. Former Section 3–606(1)(a) did not take into account the presence or absence of loss to the surety. For example, suppose the instrument is an installment note and the principal debtor is temporarily short of funds to pay a monthly installment. The payee agrees to extend the due date of the installment for a month or two to allow the debtor to pay when funds are available. Under former Section 3–606 surety was discharged if consent was not given unless the payee expressly reserved rights against the surety. It did not matter that the extension of time was a trivial change in the guaranteed obligation and that there was no evidence that the surety suffered any loss because of the extension. Wilmington Trust Co. v. Gesullo, 29 U.C.C. Rep. 144 (Del.Super.Ct. 1980). Under subsection (c) an extension of time results in discharge only to the extent the surety proves that the extension caused loss. For example, if the extension is for a long period the surety might be able to prove that during the period of extension the principal debtor became insolvent, thus reducing the value of the right of recourse of the surety. By putting the burden on the surety to prove loss, subsection (c) more accurately reflects what the parties would have done by agreement, and it facilitates workouts.

Under other provisions of Article 3, what is the effect of an extension agreement between the holder of a note and the maker who is an accommodated party? The question is illustrated by the following case:

Case #1. A borrows money from Lender and issues a note payable on April 1, 1992. B signs the note for accommodation at the request of Lender. B signed the note either as co-maker or as an anomalous indorser. In either case Lender subsequently makes an agreement with A extending the due date of A's obligation to pay the note to July 1, 1992. In either case B did not agree to the extension.

What is the effect of the extension agreement on B? Could Lender enforce the note against B if the note is not paid on April 1, 1992? A's obligation to Lender to pay the note on April 1, 1992 may be modified by the agreement of Lender. If B is an anomalous indorser Lender cannot enforce the note against B unless the note has been dishonored. Section 3–415(a). Under Section 3–502(a)(3) dishonor occurs if it is not paid on the day it becomes payable. Since the agreement between A and the Lender extended the due date of A's obligation to July 1, 1992 there is no dishonor because A was not obligated to pay Lender on April 1, 1992. If B is a co-maker the analysis is somewhat different. Lender has no power to amend the terms of the note without the consent of both A and B. By an agreement with A, Lender can extend the due date of A's obligation to Lender to pay the note but B's obligation is to pay the note according to the terms of the note at the time of issue. Section 3–412. However, B's obligation to pay the note is subject to a defense because B is an accommodation party. B is not obliged to pay Lender if A is not obliged to pay Lender. Under Section 3–305(d), B as an accommodation party can assert against Lender any defense of A. A has a defense based on the extension agreement. Thus, the result is that Lender could not enforce the note against B until July 1, 1992. This result is consistent with the right of B if B is an anomalous indorser.

As a practical matter an extension of the due date will normally occur when the accommodated party is unable to pay on the due date. The interest of the accommodation party normally is to defer payment to the holder rather than to pay right away and rely on an action against the accommodated party that may have little or no value. But in unusual cases the accommodation party may prefer to pay the holder on the original due date. In such cases, the accommodation party may do so. This is because the extension agreement between the accommodated party and the holder cannot bind the accommodation party to a change in its obligation without the accommodation party's consent. The effect on the recourse of the accommodation party against the accommodated party of performance by the accommodation party on the original due date is not addressed in § 3–419 and is left to the general law of suretyship.

Even though an accommodation party has the option of paying the instrument on the original due date, the accommodation party is not precluded from asserting its rights to discharge under Section 3–605(c) if it does not exercise that option. The critical issue is whether the extension caused the accommodation party a loss by increasing the difference between its cost of performing its obligation on the instrument and the amount recoverable from the accommodated party pursuant to Section 3–419(e). The decision by the accommodation party not to exercise its option to pay on the original due date may, under the circumstances, be a factor to be considered in the determination of that issue. See PEB Commentary No. 11, supra.

5. Former Section 3–606 applied to extensions of the due date of a note but not to other modifications of the obligation of the principal debtor. There was no apparent reason why former Section 3–606 did not follow general suretyship law in covering both. Under Section 3–605(d) a material modification of the obligation of the principal debtor, other than an extension of the due date, will result in discharge of the surety to the extent the modification caused loss to the surety with respect to the right of recourse. The loss caused by the modification is deemed to be the entire amount of the right of recourse unless the person seeking enforcement of the instrument proves that no loss occurred or that the loss was less than the full amount of the right of recourse. In the absence of that proof, the surety is completely discharged. The rationale for having different rules with respect to loss for extensions of the due date and other modifications is that extensions are likely to be beneficial to the surety and they are often made. Other modifications are less common and they may very well be detrimental to the surety. Modification of the obligation of the principal debtor without permission of the surety is unreasonable unless the modification is benign. Subsection (d) puts the burden on the person seeking

enforcement of the instrument to prove the extent to which loss was not caused by the modification.

The following is an illustration of the kind of case to which Section 3–605(d) would apply:

Case #2. Corporation borrows money from Lender and issues a note payable to Lender. X signs the note as accommodation party for Corporation. The loan agreement under which the note was issued states various events of default which allow Lender to accelerate the due date of the note. Among the events of default are breach of covenants not to incur debt beyond specified limits and not to engage in any line of business substantially different from that currently carried on by Corporation. Without consent of X, Lender agrees to modify the covenants to allow Corporation to enter into a new line of business that X considers to be risky, and to incur debt beyond the limits specified in the loan agreement to finance the new venture. This modification releases X unless Lender proves that the modification did not cause loss to X or that the loss caused by the modification was less than X's right of recourse.

Sometimes there is both an extension of the due date and some other modification. In that case both subsections (c) and (d) apply. The following is an example:

Case #3. Corporation was indebted to Lender on a note payable on April 1, 1992 and X signed the note as an accommodation party for Corporation. The interest rate on the note was 12 percent. Lender and Corporation agreed to a six-month extension of the due date of the note to October 1, 1992 and an increase in the interest rate to 14 percent after April 1, 1992. Corporation defaulted on October 1, 1992. Corporation paid no interest during the six-month extension period. Corporation is insolvent and has no assets from which unsecured creditors can be paid. Lender demanded payment from X.

Assume X is an anomalous indorser. First consider Section 3–605(c) alone. If there had been no change in the interest rate, the fact that Lender gave an extension of six months to Corporation would not result in discharge unless X could prove loss with respect to the right of recourse because of the extension. If the financial condition of Corporation on April 1, 1992 would not have allowed any recovery on the right of recourse, X can't show any loss as a result of the extension with respect to the amount due on the note on April 1, 1992. Since the note accrued interest during the six-month extension, is there a loss equal to the accrued interest? Since the interest rate was not raised, only Section 3–605(c) would apply and X could not prove any loss. The obligation of X includes interest on the note until the note is paid. To the extent payment was delayed X had the use of the money that X otherwise would have had to pay to Lender. X could have prevented the running of interest by paying the debt. Since X did not do so, X suffered no loss as the result of the extension.

If the interest rate was raised, Section 3–605(d) also must be considered. If X is an anomalous indorser, X's liability is to pay the note according to its terms at the time of indorsement. Section 3–415(a). Thus, X's obligation to pay interest is measured by the terms of the note (12%) rather than by the increased amount of 14 percent. The same analysis applies if X had been a co-maker. Under Section 3–412 the liability of the issuer of a note is to pay the note according to its terms at the time it was issued. Either obligation could be changed by contract and that occurred with respect to Corporation when it agreed to the increase in the interest rate, but X did not join in that agreement and is not bound by it. Thus, the most that X can be required to pay is the amount due on the note plus interest at the rate of 12 percent.

Does the modification discharge X under Section 3–605(d)? Any modification that increases the monetary obligation of X is material. An increase of the interest rate from 12 percent to 14 percent is certainly a material modification. There is a presumption that X is discharged because Section 3–605(d) creates a presumption that the modification caused a loss to X equal to the amount of the right of recourse. Thus, Lender has the burden of proving absence of loss or a loss less than the amount of the right of recourse. Since Corporation paid no interest during the six-month period, the issue is like the issue presented under Section 3–605(c) which we have just discussed. The increase in the interest rate could not have affected the right of recourse because no interest was paid by Corporation. X is in the same position as X would have been in if there had been an extension without an increase in the interest rate.

The analysis with respect to Section 3–605(c) and (d) would have been different if we change the assumptions. Suppose Corporation was not insolvent on April 1, 1992, that Corporation paid interest at the higher rate during the six-month period, and that Corporation was insolvent at the end of the six-month period. In this case it is possible that the extension and the additional burden placed on Corporation by the increased interest rate may have been detrimental to X.

There are difficulties in properly allocating burden of proof when the agreement between Lender and Corporation involves both an extension under Section 3–605(c) and a modification under Section 3–605(d). The agreement may have caused loss to X but it may be difficult to identify the extent to which the loss was caused by the extension or the other modification. If neither Lender nor X introduces evidence on the issue, the result is full discharge because Section 3–605(d) applies. Thus, Lender has the burden of overcoming the presumption in Section 3–605(d). In doing so, Lender should be entitled to a presumption that the extension of time by itself caused no loss. Section 3–605(c) is based on such a presumption and X should be required to introduce evidence on the effect of the extension on the right of recourse. Lender would have to introduce evidence on the effect of the increased interest rate. Thus both sides will have to introduce evidence. On the basis of this evidence the court will have to make a determination of the overall effect of the agreement on X's right of recourse. See PEB Commentary No. 11, supra.

6. Subsection (e) deals with discharge of sureties by impairment of collateral. It generally conforms to former Section 3–606(1)(b). Subsection (g) states common examples of what is meant by impairment. By using the term "includes," it allows a court to find impairment in other cases as well. There is extensive case law on impairment of collateral. The surety is discharged to the extent the surety proves that impairment was caused by a person entitled to enforce the instrument. For example, suppose the payee of a secured note fails to perfect the security interest. The collateral is owned by the principal debtor who subsequently files in bankruptcy. As a result of the failure to perfect, the security interest is not enforceable in bankruptcy. If the payee obtains payment from the surety, the surety is subrogated to the payee's security interest in the collateral. In this case the value of the security interest is impaired completely because the security interest is unenforceable. If the value of the collateral is as much or more than the amount of the note there is a complete discharge.

In some states a real property grantee who assumes the obligation of the grantor as maker of a note secured by the real property becomes by operation of law a principal debtor and the grantor becomes a surety. The meager case authority was split on whether former Section 3–606 applied to release the grantor if the holder released or extended the obligation of the grantee. Revised Article 3 takes no position on the effect of the release of the grantee in this case. Section 3–605(b) does not apply because the holder has not discharged the obligation of a "party," a term defined in Section 3–103(a)(8) as "party to an instrument." The assuming grantee is not a party to the instrument. The resolution of this question is governed by general principles of law, including the law of suretyship. See PEB Commentary No. 11, supra.

7. Subsection (f) is illustrated by the following case. X and Y sign a note for $1,000 as co-makers. Neither is an accommodation party. X grants a security interest in X's property to secure the note. The collateral is worth more than $1,000. Payee fails to perfect the security interest in X's property before X files in bankruptcy. As a result the security interest is not enforceable in bankruptcy. Had Payee perfected the security interest, Y could have paid the note and gained rights to X's collateral by subrogation. If the security interest had been perfected, Y could have realized on the collateral to the extent of $500 to satisfy its right of contribution against X. Payee's failure to perfect deprived Y of the benefit of the collateral. Subsection (f) discharges Y to the extent of its loss. If there are no assets in the bankruptcy for unsecured claims, the loss is $500, the amount of Y's contribution claim against X which now has a zero value. If some amount is payable on unsecured claims, the loss is reduced by the amount receivable by Y. The same result follows if Y is an accommodation party but Payee has no knowledge of the accommodation or notice under Section 3–419(c). In that event Y is not discharged under subsection (e), but subsection (f) applies because X and Y are jointly and severally liable on the note. Under subsection (f), Y is treated as a co-maker with a right of contribution rather than an accommodation party with a right of reimbursement. Y is discharged to the extent of $500. If Y is the principal debtor and X is the accommodation party subsection (f) doesn't apply. Y, as principal debtor, is not injured by the impairment of collateral because Y wou¹

have been obliged to reimburse X for the entire $1,000 even if Payee had obtained payment from sale of the collateral.

8. Subsection (i) is a continuation of former law which allowed suretyship defenses to be waived. As the subsection provides, a party is not discharged under this section if the instrument or a separate agreement of the party waives discharge either specifically or by general language indicating that defenses based on suretyship and impairment of collateral are waived. No particular language or form of agreement is required, and the standards for enforcing such a term are the same as the standards for enforcing any other term in an instrument or agreement.

Subsection (i), however, applies only to a "discharge under this section." The right of an accommodation party to be discharged under Section 3–605(e) because of an impairment of collateral can be waived. But with respect to a note secured by personal property collateral, Article 9 also applies. If an accommodation party is a "debtor" under Section 9–105(1)(d), the accommodation party has rights under Article 9. Under Section 9–501(3)(b) rights of an Article 9 debtor under Section 9–504(3) and 9–505(1), which deal with disposition of collateral, cannot be waived except as provided in Article 9. These Article 9 rights are independent of rights under Section 3–605. Since Section 3–605(i) is specifically limited to discharge under Section 3–605, a waiver of rights with respect to Section 3–605 has no effect on rights under Article 9. With respect to Article 9 rights, Section 9–501(3)(b) controls. See PEB Commentary No. 11, supra.

Uniform Commercial Code Comment

Prior Uniform Statutory Provision:

Sections 48, 119(3), 120(2), 122 and 123, Uniform Negotiable Instruments Law.

Changes: Combined and reworded.

Purposes of Changes:

1. The original Act does not state how cancellation is to be effected, except as to striking indorsements under the original Section 48. It must be done in such a manner as to be apparent on the face of the instrument, and the methods stated, which are supported by the decisions, are exclusive.

2. Subsection (1)(b) restates the original Section 122. The provision as to "discharge of the instrument" is not covered by discharge, Section 3–601(3); that as to subsequent holders in due course by Section 3–602 on effect of discharge against a holder in due course.

3. Subsection (2) is new. It is intended to make it clear that the striking of an indorsement, or any other cancellation or renunciation, does not affect the title.

Cross References:

Point 2: Sections 3–601 and 3–602.

Definitional Cross References:

"Holder". Section 1–201.
"Instrument". Section 3–102.
"Party". Section 1–201.
"Rights". Section 1–201.
"Signature". Section 3–401.
"Signed". Section 1–201.
"Writing". Section 1–201.

Cross References

Accommodation party, obligation to pay instrument not affected by notice to person enforcing obligation of signature as accommodation, see Commercial Code § 3419.
Cancellation of written contract,
  Extinction, see Civil Code §§ 1699, 1700.
  Instruments, see Civil Code § 3412 et seq.
Discharge,
  Failure to give notice of dishonor, see Commercial Code § 3415.
  Parties in general, see Commercial Code § 3601.
Extinction of obligations, see Civil Code § 1473 et seq.
Holder in due course, effect of discharge of parties, see Commercial Code § 3601.
Release, extinction of obligations, see Civil Code § 1541 et seq.
Rescission, see Civil Code § 1688 et seq.
Waiver or renunciation of claim or right after breach, see Commercial Code § 1107.

§§ 3606 to 3805. Repealed by Stats.1992, c. 914 (S.B. 833), § 5

Division 4

BANK DEPOSITS AND COLLECTIONS

Chapter	Section
1. General Provisions and Definitions	4101
2. Collection of Items: Depositary and Collecting Banks	4201
3. Collection of Items: Payor Banks	4301
4. Relationship Between Payor Bank and Its Customer	4401
5. Collection of Documentary Drafts	4501

Introductory Comment

By Charles J. Williams

Division 4 provides uniform rules governing the (1) collection by banks of checks and other instruments for the payment of money and (2) relationship of banks with their depositors in connection with the collection and payment of items.

Division 4 went through several successive drafts and much of Division 4 reflects criticism made by New York studies.[1]

The bank collection process is a complex one in view of the millions of checks and bank items which are processed each day. California is one of the few states which had its own comprehensive bank collection statute. Former Financial Code §§ 1010–1019.

Division 4 was discussed and disputed in California to great extent. Nevertheless, the California version of Division 4 generally follows the Official Text with some amendments to accommodate California banking practices. These changes from the Official Text are explained in the California Code comments to the sections affected.

Division 4 adopts a flexible approach which permits parties to vary the rules by agreement. Flexibility in this field is particularly important:

". . . Because of the complexity of the subject matter . . . and the certainty that whatever may be the practice today, there is certain to be a change tomorrow. In fact, the complex nature of the subject matter and the difficulty of drafting rules that today appear to be satisfactory suggest the extreme naivete of thinking that these rules will remain immutable and continually wise throughout the years that the Code may be law." [2]

Prior to the adoption of the Code the regulations of the Federal Reserve system also applied to bank collections and deposits. These regulations will continue to apply under the Code and the relationship between Division 4 and these regulations is set forth in Section 4103. The principal regulations are Regulations G and J, 12 CFR, §§ 207.1–207.4, 210.1–210.6 (1959).

[1] Clarke, Bailey and Young, Bank Deposits and Collections, 12 to 15 (A.L.I.1963).

[2] Malcolm, Article 4—A Battle with Complexity, 1952 Wisc.L.Rev. 265, 276.

WESTLAW Computer Assisted Legal Research

WESTLAW supplements your legal research in many ways. WESTLAW allows you to
- update your research with the most current information
- expand your library with additional resources
- retrieve direct history, precedential history and parallel citations with the Insta-Cite service

For more information on using WESTLAW to supplement your research, see the WESTLAW Electronic Research Guide, which follows the Preface.

Cross References

Conflict between Division 3 and Division 4, resolution, see Commercial Code § 3102.

Third-party liability, notice of right to defend action, see Commercial Code § 3119.

CHAPTER 1. GENERAL PROVISIONS AND DEFINITIONS

Section
4101. Short Title.
4102. Construction with Divisions 3 and 8; choice of law.
4103. Variation by Agreement; Measure of Damages; Certain Action Constituting Ordinary Care.
4104. Definitions and Index of Definitions.
4105. Bank; definitions.
4106. Payable through; payable at.
4107. Separate office of bank.
4108. Cutoff hours.
4109. Waiver of time limits; delays.
4110. Agreement for electronic presentment.
4111. Limitation of actions.

Transitional Provisions

Effective date and transitional provisions for sections in Division 4 affected by Stats.1992, c. 914, see Commercial Code § 16101 et seq.

Cross References

Action for breach of obligation, notice to third person answerable over pursuant to this division, see Commercial Code § 3119.

Place of payment, exceptions for items in this division, see Commercial Code § 3111.

Presentment, rules subject to this division, see Commercial Code § 3501.

§ 4101. Short Title

This division may * * * be cited as Uniform Commercial Code—Bank Deposits and Collections. *(Stats. 1963, c. 819, § 4101. Amended by Stats.1992, c. 914 (S.B.833), § 7.)*

California Code Comment

By John A. Bohn and Charles J. Williams

This is section 4–101 of the Official Text without change.

Uniform Commercial Code Comment

Official Reasons for 1990 Change

Modified to conform with current drafting practices; no intent to change substance.

1990 Change

1. The great number of checks handled by banks and the country-wide nature of the bank collection process require uniformity in the law of bank collections. There is needed a uniform statement of the principal rules of the bank collection process with ample provision for flexibility to meet the needs of the large volume handled and the

changing needs and conditions that are bound to come with the years. This Article meets that need.

2. In 1950 at the time Article 4 was drafted, 6.7 billion checks were written annually. By the time of the 1990 revision of Article 4 annual volume was estimated by the American Bankers Association to be about 50 billion checks. The banking system could not have coped with this increase in check volume had it not developed in the late 1950s and early 1960s an automated system for check collection based on encoding checks with machine-readable information by Magnetic Ink Character Recognition (MICR). An important goal of the 1990 revision of Article 4 is to promote the efficiency of the check collection process by making the provisions of Article 4 more compatible with the needs of an automated system and, by doing so, increase the speed and lower the cost of check collection for those who write and receive checks. An additional goal of the 1990 revision of Article 4 is to remove any statutory barriers in the Article to the ultimate adoption of programs allowing the presentment of checks to payor banks by electronic transmission of information captured from the MICR line on the checks. The potential of these programs for saving the time and expense of transporting the huge volume of checks from depositary to payor banks is evident.

3. Article 4 defines rights between parties with respect to bank deposits and collections. It is not a regulatory statute. It does not regulate the terms of the bank-customer agreement, nor does it prescribe what constraints different jurisdictions may wish to impose on that relationship in the interest of consumer protection. The revisions in Article 4 are intended to create a legal frame-work that accommodates automation and truncation for the benefit of all bank customers. This may raise consumer problems which enacting jurisdictions may wish to address in individual legislation. For example, with respect to Section 4–401(c), jurisdictions may wish to examine their unfair and deceptive practices laws to determine whether they are adequate to protect drawers who postdate checks from unscrupulous practices that may arise on the part of persons who induce drawers to issue postdated checks in erroneous belief that the checks will not be immediately payable. Another example arises from the fact that under various truncation plans customers will no longer receive their cancelled checks and will no longer have the cancelled check to prove payment. Individual legislation might provide that a copy of a bank statement along with a copy of the check is prima facie evidence of payment.

Uniform Commercial Code Comment

The tremendous number of checks handled by banks and the countrywide nature of the bank collection process require uniformity in the law of bank collections. Individual Federal Reserve banks process as many as 1,000,000 items a day; large metropolitan banks average 300,000 a day; banks with less than $5,000,000 on deposit handle from 1,000 to 2,000 daily. There is needed a uniform statement of the principal rules of the bank collection process with ample provision for flexibility to meet the needs of the large volume handled and the changing needs and conditions that are bound to come with the years.

The American Bankers Association Bank Collection Code, enacted in eighteen states, has stated many of the bank collection rules that have developed, and more recently Deferred Posting statutes have developed and varied further rules. With items flowing in great volume not only in and around metropolitan and smaller centers but also continuously across state lines and back and forth across the entire country, a proper situation exists for uniform rules that will state in modern concepts at least some of the rights of the parties and in addition aid this flow and not interfere with its progress.

This Article adopts many of the rules of the American Bankers Association Code that are still in current operation, the principles and rules of the Deferred Posting and other statutes, codifies some rules established by court decisions and in addition states certain patterns and procedures that exist even though not heretofore covered by statute.

§ 4102. Construction with Divisions 3 and 8; choice of law

(a) To the extent that items within this division are also within * * * Divisions 3 (commencing with Section 3101) and 8 (commencing with Section 8101), they are subject to * * * those divisions. * * * If there is conflict * * *, this division * * * governs Division 3 (commencing with Section 3101), but * * * Division 8 * * * (commencing with Section 8101) governs this division.

(b) The liability of a bank for action or nonaction with respect to an item handled by it for purposes of presentment, payment, or collection is governed by the law of the place where the bank is located. In the case of action or nonaction by or at a branch or separate office of a bank, its liability is governed by the law of the place where the branch or separate office is located. (Stats.1963, c. 819, § 4102. Amended by Stats.1992, c. 914 (S.B.833), § 8.)

California Code Comment

By John A. Bohn and Charles J. Williams

Prior California Law

1. This section is new statutory law.
2. Subdivision (1) clarifies applicability where Divisions 3, 4 and 8 overlap. See California Code Comment 2 to Commercial Code § 3103.
3. Subdivision (2) states the conflicts of law rule in determining the liability of a bank for items handled by it. There is no prior statutory law or case precedent precisely on point. However, this subdivision is similar to Restatement, Conflict of Laws, §§ 349 and 336. See Official Comment 2. The parties may select the law to apply to a transaction as long as the transaction bears a reasonable relation to the place whose law is selected. Official Comment 2d. See Commercial Code § 1105.

Changes from U.C.C. (1962 Official Text)

4. This is section 4–102 of the Official Text without change.

Uniform Commercial Code Comment

Official Reasons for 1990 Change

Modified to conform with current drafting practices; no intent to change substance.

1990 Change

1. The rules of Article 3 governing negotiable instruments, their transfer, and the contracts of the parties thereto apply to the items collected through banking channels wherever no specific provision is found in this Article. In the case of conflict, this Article governs. See Section 3–102(b).

Bonds and like instruments constituting investment securities under Article 8 may also be handled by banks for collection purposes. Various sections of Article 8 prescribe rules of transfer some of which (see Sections 8–304 and 8–306) may conflict with provisions of this Article (Sections 4–205, 4–207, and 4–208). In the case of conflict, Article 8 governs.

Section 4–210 deals specifically with overlapping problems and possible conflicts between this Article and Article 9. However, similar reconciling provisions are not necessary in the case of Articles 5 and 7. Sections 4–301 and 4–302 are consistent with Section 5–112. In the case of Article 7 documents of title frequently accompany items but they are not themselves items. See Section 4–104(a)(9).

In Clearfield Trust Co. v. United States, 318 U.S. 363 (1943), the Court held that if the United States is a party to an instrument, its rights and duties are governed by federal common law in the absence of a specific federal statute or regulation. In United States v. Kimbell Foods, Inc., 440 U.S. 715 (1979), the Court stated a three-pronged test to ascertain whether the federal common-law rule should follow the state rule. In most instances courts under the *Kimbell* test have shown a willingness to adopt UCC rules in formulating federal common law on the subject. In *Kimbell* the Court adopted the priorities rules of Article 9.

In addition, applicable federal law may supersede provisions of this Article. One federal law that does so is the Expedited Funds Availability Act, 12 U.S.C. § 4001 et seq., and its implementing Regulation CC, 12 CFR Pt. 229. In some instances this law is alluded to in the statute, e.g., Section 4–215(e) and (f). In other instances, although not referred to in this Article, the provisions of the EFAA and Regulation CC control with respect to checks. For example, except between the depositary bank and its customer, all settlements are final and not provisional (Regulation CC, Section 229.36(d)), and the midnight deadline may be extended (Regulation CC, Section 229.30(c)). The comments to this Article suggest in most instances the relevant Regulation CC provisions.

2. Subsection (b) is designed to state a workable rule for the solution of otherwise vexatious problems of the conflicts of laws:

a. The routine and mechanical nature of bank collections makes it imperative that one law govern the activities of one office of a bank. The requirement found in some cases that to hold an indorser notice must be given in accordance with the law of the place of indorsement, since that method of notice became an implied term of the indorser's contract, is more theoretical than practical.

b. Adoption of what is in essence a tort theory of the conflict of laws is consistent with the general theory of this Article that the basic duty of a collecting bank is one of good faith and the exercise of ordinary care. Justification lies in the fact that, in using an ambulatory instrument, the drawer, payee, and indorsers must know that action will be taken with respect to it in other jurisdictions. This is especially pertinent with respect to the law of the place of payment.

c. The phrase "action or non-action with respect to any item handled by it for purposes of presentment, payment, or collection" is intended to make the conflicts rule of subsection (b) apply from the inception of the collection process of an item through all phases of deposit, forwarding, presentment, payment and remittance or credit of proceeds. Specifically the subsection applies to the initial act of a depositary bank in receiving an item and to the incidents of such receipt. The conflicts rule of Weissman v. Banque de Bruxelles, 254 N.Y. 488, 173 N.E. 835 (1930), is rejected. The subsection applies to questions of possible vicarious liability of a bank for action or non-action of sub-agents (see Section 4–202(c)), and tests these questions by the law of the state of the location of the bank which uses the sub-agent. The conflicts rule of St. Nicholas Bank of New York v. State Nat. Bank, 128 N.Y. 26, 27 N.E. 849, 13 L.R.A. 241 (1891), is rejected. The subsection applied to action or non-action of a payor bank in connection with handling an item (see Sections 4–215(a), 4–301, 4–302, 4–303) as well as action or non-action of a collecting bank (Sections 4–201 through 4–216); to action or non-action of a bank which suspends payment or is affected by another bank suspending payment (Section 4–216); to action or non-action of a bank with respect to an item under the rule of Part 4 of Article 4.

d. In a case in which subsection (b) makes this Article applicable, Section 4–103(a) leaves open the possibility of an agreement with respect to applicable law. This freedom of agreement follows the general policy of Section 1–105.

Uniform Commercial Code Comment

Prior Uniform Statutory Provision:

None.

Purposes:

1. The rules governing negotiable instruments, their transfer, and the contracts of the parties thereto apply to the items collected through banking channels wherever no specific provision is found in this Article. In the case of conflict, this Article governs. See Section 3–103(2).

Bonds and like instruments constituting investment securities under Article 8 may also be handled by banks for collection purposes. Various sections of Article 8 prescribe rules of transfer some of which (see Sections 8–304 and 8–306) may conflict with provisions of this Article (Sections 4–205 and 4–207). In the case of conflict, Article 8 governs.

Section 4–208 deals specifically with overlapping problems and possible conflicts between this Article and Article 9. However, similar reconciling provisions are not necessary in the case of Articles 5 and 7. Sections 4–301 and 4–302 are consistent with Section 5–112. In the case of Article 7 documents of title frequently accompany items but they are not themselves items. See Section 4–104(g).

2. Subsection (2) is designed to state a workable rule for the solution of otherwise vexatious problems of the conflicts of laws:

a. The routine and mechanical nature of bank collections makes it imperative that one law govern the activities of one office of a bank. The requirement found in some cases that to hold an indorser notice must be given in accordance with the law of the place of indorsement, since that method of notice became an implied term of the indorser's contract, is more theoretical than practical.

b. Adoption of what is in essence a tort theory of the conflict of laws is consistent with the general theory of this Article that the basic duty of a collecting bank is one of good faith and the exercise of ordinary care. Justification lies in the fact that, in using an ambulatory instrument, the drawer, payee, and indorsers must know that action will be taken with respect to it in other jurisdictions. This is especially pertinent with respect to the law of the place of payment.

c. The phrase "action or non-action with respect to any item handled by it for purposes of presentment, payment or collection" is intended to make the conflicts rule of subsection (2) apply from the inception of the collection process of an item through all phases of deposit, forwarding, presentment, payment and remittance or credit of proceeds. Specifically the subsection applies to the initial act of a depositary bank in receiving an item and to the incidents of such receipt. The conflicts rule of Weissman v. Banque de Bruxelles, 254 N.Y. 488, 173 N.E. 835 (1930), is rejected. The subsection applies to questions of possible vicarious liability of a bank for action or non-action of sub-agents (see Section 4–202(3)) and tests these questions by the law of the state of the location of the bank which uses the sub-agent. The conflicts rule of St. Nicholas Bank of New York v. State Nat. Bank, 128 N.Y. 26, 27 N.E. 849, 13 L.R.A. 241 (1891), is rejected. The subsection applies to action or non-action of a payor bank in connection with handling an item (see Sections 4–213(1), 4–301, 4–302, 4–303) as well as action or non-action of a collecting bank (Sections 4–201 through 4–214); to action or non-action of a bank which suspends payment or is affected by another bank suspending payment (Section 4–214); to action or non-action of a bank with respect to an item under the rules of Part 4 of Article 4.

d. Where subsection (2) makes this Article applicable, Section 4–103(1) leaves open the possibility of an agreement with respect to applicable law. Such freedom of agreement follows the general policy of Section 1–105.

Cross References:

Sections 1–105; 3–103(2) and Article 3; all sections of Article 4; 5–112; Article 7; 8–304 and 8–306; Article 9.

Definitional Cross References:

"Bank". Section 1–201.
"Branch". Section 1–201.
"Item". Section 4–104.

Cross References

Accountability of payor bank upon final payment, see Commercial Code § 4215.
Adverse claims, notice to purchaser of investment securities, see Commercial Code § 8304.
Applicable law, variations by agreement, see Commercial Code § 4103.
Branch offices, within state, see Financial Code § 500 et seq.
Collection of items,
　Depositary and collecting banks, see Commercial Code § 4201 et seq.
　Payor banks, see Commercial Code § 4301 et seq.
Commercial paper,
　Generally, see Commercial Code § 3101 et seq.
　Effect of this division, see Commercial Code § 3102.
Deferred posting, see Commercial Code § 4301.
Documents of title, see Commercial Code § 7101 et seq.
Instructions, effect of, see Commercial Code § 4203.
Investment securities,
　Generally, see Commercial Code § 8101 et seq.
　Warranties on presentment and transfer, see Commercial Code § 8306.
Letters of credit, honor or rejection, see Commercial Code § 5112.
Methods of sending and presenting items, see Commercial Code § 4204.
Missing indorsement, see Commercial Code § 4205.
Payor bank's responsibility for late return of item, see Commercial Code § 4302.

§ 4102

Payor or collecting bank, suspension of payments, see Commercial Code § 4216.
Purchaser of securities, notice of adverse claims, see Commercial Code § 8304.
Relationship between payor bank and customer, see Commercial Code § 4401 et seq.
Secured transactions, see Commercial Code § 9101 et seq.
Security interest of collecting bank, see Commercial Code § 4210.
Standard of care for collection, see Commercial Code § 4202.
Territorial applicability, see Commercial Code § 1105.
Warranties, see Commercial Code § 4207.

§ 4103. Variation by Agreement; Measure of Damages; Certain Action Constituting Ordinary Care

(a) The effect of the provisions of this division may be varied by agreement * * *, but the parties to the agreement cannot disclaim a bank's responsibility for its * * * lack of good faith or failure to exercise ordinary care or * * * limit the measure of damages for the lack or failure * * *. However, the parties may determine by agreement * * * the standards by which * * * the bank's responsibility is to be measured if those standards are not manifestly unreasonable.

(b) Federal Reserve regulations and operating * * * circulars, clearing house rules, and the like * * * have the effect of agreements under subdivision (a), whether or not specifically assented to by all parties interested in items handled.

(c) Action or nonaction approved by this division or pursuant to Federal Reserve regulations or operating * * * circulars is the exercise of ordinary care and, in the absence of special instructions, action or nonaction consistent with * * * clearing house rules and the like or with a general banking usage not disapproved by this division, is prima facie * * * the exercise of ordinary care.

(d) The specification or approval of certain procedures by this division is not * * * disapproval of other procedures that may be reasonable under the circumstances.

(e) The measure of damages for failure to exercise ordinary care in handling an item is the amount of the item reduced by an amount that could not have been realized by the exercise of ordinary care * * *. If there is also bad faith it includes any other damages * * * the party suffered as a proximate consequence. (Stats.1963, c. 819, § 4103. Amended by Stats.1992, c. 914 (S.B.833), § 9.)

California Code Comment

By John A. Bohn and Charles J. Williams

Prior California Law

1. Subdivision (1) is the statutory counterpart of former Financial Code § 1019. Subdivision (1) continues the rule that the parties may vary the statute by agreement but omits the requirement that the agreement must be in writing.

The part of subdivision (1) prohibiting disclaimer of a bank's responsibility or limiting the measure of damages is in accord with prior California law. In Luckehe v. First Nat. Bank of Marysville, 81 Cal.App. 254, 253 Pac. 337 (1927) the court held that a bank's certificate of deposit could not be used to avoid liability of the bank for failure to use due care.

Subdivision (1) and subdivision (2) read together are both more explicit and much broader in the scope of matters which may be included in an agreement and in the effect of an agreement upon parties interested in an item but who have not specifically entered into the agreement. This wide latitude in varying this Division reflects the freedom of contract philosophy which it is hoped will permit flexibility to meet changing conditions. Official Comments 1, 2 and 3.

2. Subdivision (2) lists official and semi official rules of collection which may vary the application of Division 4 and which affect parties concerned with the collection of an item even though they have not specifically agreed with all the other persons similarly concerned. Official Comment 3 describes the kinds of matters included under this subdivision.

Under prior California law, although clearing house rules were considered binding agreements among the member banks (Merchants' Nat. Bank v. Continental Nat. Bank, 98 Cal.App. 523, 277 Pac. 354 (1929)) these rules did not govern the rights of a drawer and payee who were not members of the clearing house and who did not contract with express reference to those rules. Sneider v. Bank of Italy, 184 Cal. 595, 194 Pac. 1021, 12 A.L.R. 993 (1920).

3. An amendment to subdivision (2) was suggested by the subcommittee of the State Bar on Article [Division] 4 by including the term "circulars" after "operating letters." The purpose of this recommendation was to make sure that federal reserve circulars were included in this provision. In recommending against adopting this amendment, the Marsh and Warren Report describes the breadth and intent of the subdivision:

"This section permits parties to banking transactions to agree to vary the rules established by the Code; furthermore, this Section gives to certain official and quasi-official regulations the same force as agreements of the parties. The reason for the proposed amendment [The State Bar subcommittee's proposal to amend subdivision (2)] is to make clear that Federal Reserve 'circulars' are included. The recommendation for rejection of the amendment is made because the Official Comments make clear that circulars are included under the term 'operating letters.' This term is used to describe the instructions issued pursuant to Federal Reserve regulations and concerned with operating details. There is no need to specify the exact designation currently used by the Federal Reserve Board and Federal Reserve Banks to describe such instructions. Furthermore, if the philosophy of this proposed amendment is adopted, Chapter [Division] 4 might have to be amended any time the designation of these instructions is changed." Sixth Progress Report to the Legislature by Senate Fact Finding Committee on Judiciary (1959–1961) Part 1, The Uniform Commercial Code, p. 471.

4. Subdivision (3) has no counterpart in prior statutory law. However, prior California decisions are in accord with the provision of subdivision (3) that banking usage may be set up as the standard of ordinary care. Luckehe v. First Nat. Bank of Marysville, 81 Cal.App. 254, 253 Pac. 337 (1927).

The standard of "ordinary care" is the one used in tort law. Official Comment 4.

The same recommendation for the addition of "circulars" was made in subdivision (3) as it was in subdivision (2). This recommendation was rejected for the same reasons. See California Code Comment 3 to this section.

5. Subdivision (4) is new. It reflects the principle of flexibility in the bank collection process designed to meet changing conditions. Official Comment 5. If a different procedure is questioned as being unreasonable, the court must make a determination in each case whether the action taken was reasonable rather than determining whether the action was authorized by a statute.

6. Subdivision (5) has no statutory counterpart in prior California law. The maximum recovery is the amount of the item unless bad faith is established. Official Comment 6.

The prior California rule was that the measure of damages was "prima facie" the face amount of the instrument. Kriste v. International Savings & Exchange Bank, 17 Cal.App. 301, 119 Pac. 666 (1911) quoting Bolles' Modern Law of Banking.

Subdivision (5) is in accord with the statement in this case but adds flexibility to the measure of damages by stating the plus and minus factors in the basic liability for the face amount of the instrument.

The measure of damages in subdivision (5) cannot be limited by agreement by virtue of subdivision (1).

Changes from U.C.C. (1962 Official Text)

7. This is section 4–103 of the Official Text without change.

Uniform Commercial Code Comment

Official Reasons for 1990 Change

Modified to conform with current drafting practices; no intent to change substance.

1990 Change

1. Section 1–102 states the general principles and rules for variation of the effect of this Act by agreement and the limitations to this power. Section 4–103 states the specific rules for variation of Article 4 by agreement and also certain standards of ordinary care. In view of the technical complexity of the field of bank collections, the enormous number of items handled by banks, the certainty that there will be variations from the normal in each day's work in each bank, the certainty of changing conditions and the possibility of developing improved methods of collection to speed the process, it would be unwise to freeze present methods of operation by mandatory statutory rules. This section, therefore, permits within wide limits variation of the effect of provisions of the Article by agreement.

2. Subsection (a) confers blanket power to vary all provisions of the Article by agreements of the ordinary kind. The agreements may not disclaim a bank's responsibility for its own lack of good faith or failure to exercise ordinary care and may not limit the measure of damages for the lack or failure, but this subsection like Section 1–102(3) approves the practice of parties determining by agreement the standards by which the responsibility is to be measured. In the absence of a showing that the standards manifestly are unreasonable, the agreement controls. Owners of items and other interested parties are not affected by agreements under this subsection unless they are parties to the agreement or are bound by adoption, ratification, estoppel or the like.

As here used "agreement" has the meaning given to it by Section 1–201(3). The agreement may be direct, as between the owner and the depositary bank; or indirect, as in the case in which the owner authorizes a particular type of procedure and any bank in the collection chain acts pursuant to such authorization. It may be with respect to a single item; or to all items handled for a particular customer, e.g., a general agreement between the depositary bank and the customer at the time a deposit account is opened. Legends on deposit tickets, collection letters and acknowledgments of items, coupled with action by the affected party constituting acceptance, adoption, ratification, estoppel or the like, are agreements if they meet the tests of the definition of "agreement." See Section 1–201(3). First Nat. Bank of Denver v. Federal Reserve Bank, 6 F.2d 339 (8th Cir.1925) (deposit slip); Jefferson County Bldg. Ass'n v. Southern Bank & Trust Co., 225 Ala. 25, 142 So. 66 (1932) (signature card and deposit slip); Semingson v. Stock Yards Nat. Bank, 162 Minn. 424, 203 N.W. 412 (1925) (passbook); Farmers State Bank v. Union Nat. Bank, 42 N.D. 449, 454, 173 N.W. 789, 790 (1919) (acknowledgment of receipt of item).

3. Subsection (a) (subject to its limitations with respect to good faith and ordinary care) goes far to meet the requirements of flexibility. However, it does not by itself confer fully effective flexibility. Since it is recognized that banks handle a great number of items every business day and that the parties interested in each item include the owner of the item, the drawer (if it is a check), all nonbank indorsers, the payor bank and from one to five or more collecting banks, it is obvious that it is impossible, practically, to obtain direct agreements from all of these parties on all items. In total, the interested parties constitute virtually every adult person and business organization in the United States. On the other hand they may become bound to agreements on the principle that collecting banks acting as agents have authority to make binding agreements with respect to items being handled. This conclusion was assumed but was not flatly decided in Federal Reserve Bank of Richmond v. Malloy, 264 U.S. 160, at 167, 44 S.Ct. 296, at 298, 68 L.Ed. 617, 31 A.L.R. 1261 (1924).

To meet this problem subsection (b) provides that official or quasi-official rules of collection, that is Federal Reserve regulations and operating circulars, clearing-house rules, and the like, have the effect of agreements under subsection (a), whether or not specifically assented to by all parties interested in items handled. Consequently, such official or quasi-official rules may, standing by themselves but subject to the good faith and ordinary care limitations, vary the effect of the provisions of Article 4.

Federal Reserve regulations. Various sections of the Federal Reserve Act (12 U.S.C. § 221 et seq.) authorize the Board of Governors of the Federal Reserve System to direct the Federal Reserve banks to exercise bank collection functions. For example, Section 16 (12 U.S.C. § 248(*o*)) authorizes the Board to require each Federal Reserve bank to exercise the functions of a clearing house for its members and Section 13 (12 U.S.C. § 342) authorizes each Federal Reserve bank to receive deposits from nonmember banks solely for the purposes of exchange or of collection. Under this statutory authorization the Board has issued Regulation J (Subpart A—Collection of Checks and Other Items). Under the supremacy clause of the Constitution, federal regulations prevail over state statutes. Moreover, the Expedited Funds Availability Act, 12 U.S.C. Section 4007(b) provides that the Act and Regulation CC, 12 CFR 229, supersede "any provision of the law of any State, including the Uniform Commercial Code as in effect in such State, which is inconsistent with this chapter or such regulations." See Comment 1 to Section 4–102.

Federal Reserve operating circulars. The regulations of the Federal Reserve Board authorize the Federal Reserve banks to promulgate operating circulars covering operating details. Regulation J, for example, provides that "Each Reserve Bank shall receive and handle items in accordance with this subpart, and shall issue operating circulars governing the details of its handling of items and other matters deemed appropriate by the Reserve Bank." This Article recognizes that "operating circulars" issued pursuant to the regulations and concerned with operating details as appropriate may, within their proper sphere, vary the effect of the Article.

Clearing-House Rules. Local clearing houses have long issued rules governing the details of clearing; hours of clearing, media of remittance, time for return of mis-sent items and the like. The case law has recognized these rules, within their proper sphere, as binding on affected parties and as appropriate sources for the courts to look to in filling out details of bank collection law. Subsection (b) in recognizing clearing-house rules as a means of preserving flexibility continues the sensible approach indicated in the cases. Included in the terms "clearing houses" are county and regional clearing houses as well as those within a single city or town. There is, of course, no intention of authorizing a local clearing house or a group of clearing houses to rewrite the basic law generally. The term "clearing-house rules" should be understood in the light of functions the clearing houses have exercised in the past.

And the like. This phrase is to be construed in the light of the foregoing. "Federal Reserve regulations and operating circulars" cover rules and regulations issued by public or quasi-public agencies under statutory authority. "Clearing-house rules" cover rules issued by a group of banks which have associated themselves to perform through a clearing house some of their collection, payment and clearing functions. Other agencies or associations of this kind may be established in the future whose rules and regulations could be appropriately looked on as constituting means of avoiding absolute statutory rigidity. The phrase "and the like" leaves open possibilities for future development. An agreement between a number of banks or even all the banks in an area simply because they are banks, would not of itself, by virtue of the phrase "and the like," meet the purposes and objectives of subsection (b).

4. Under this Article banks come under the general obligations of the use of good faith and the exercise of ordinary care. "Good faith" is defined in Section 3–103(a)(4). The term "ordinary care" is defined in Section 3–103(a)(7). These definitions are made to apply to Article 4 by Section 4–104(c). Section 4–202 states respects in which collecting banks must use ordinary care. Subsection (c) of Section 4–103 provides that action or non-action approved by the Article or pursuant to Federal Reserve regulations or operating circulars constitutes the exercise of ordinary care. Federal Reserve regulations and operating circulars constitute an affirmative standard of ordinary care equally with the provisions of Article 4 itself.

Subsection (c) further provides that, absent special instructions, action or non-action consistent with clearing-house rules and the like or with a general banking usage not disapproved by the Article, prima facie constitutes the exercise of ordinary care. Clearing-house rules and the phrase "and the like" have the significance set forth above in these Comments. The term "general banking usage" is not defined but should be taken to mean a general usage common to banks in the area concerned. See Section 1–205(2). In a case in which the adjective "general" is used, the intention is to require a usage broader than a mere practice between two or three banks but it is not intended to require anything as broad as a country-wide usage. A usage followed generally throughout a state, a substantial portion of a state, a metropolitan area or the like would certainly be sufficient. Consistently with the principle of Section 1–205(3), action or non-action consistent with clearing-house rules or the like or with banking usages prima facie constitutes the exercise of ordinary care. However, the phrase "in the absence of special instructions" affords owners of items an opportunity to prescribe other standards and although there may be no direct supervision or control of clearing houses or banking usages by official supervisory authorities, the confirmation of ordinary care by compliance with these standards is prima facie only, thus conferring on the courts the ultimate power to determine ordinary care in any case in which it should appear desirable to do so. The prima facie rule does, however, impose on the party contesting the standards to establish that they are unreasonable, arbitrary or unfair as used by the particular bank.

5. Subsection (d), in line with the flexible approach required for the bank collection process is designed to make clear that a novel procedure adopted by a bank is not to be considered unreasonable merely because that procedure is not specifically contemplated by this Article or by agreement, or because it has not yet been generally accepted as a bank usage. Changing conditions constantly call for new procedures and someone has to use the new procedure first. If this procedure is found to be reasonable under the circumstances, provided, of course, that it is not inconsistent with any provision of the Article or other law or agreement, the bank which has followed the new procedure should not be found to have failed in the exercise of ordinary care.

6. Subsection (e) sets forth a rule for determining the measure of damages for failure to exercise ordinary care which, under subsection (a), cannot be limited by agreement. In the absence of bad faith the maximum recovery is the amount of the item concerned. The term "bad faith" is not defined; the connotation is the absence of good faith (Section 3–103). When it is established that some part or all of the item could not have been collected even by the use of ordinary care the recovery is reduced by the amount that would have been in any event uncollectible. This limitation on recovery follows the case law. Finally, if bad faith is established the rule opens to allow the recovery of other damages, whose "proximateness" is to be tested by the ordinary rules applied in comparable cases. Of course, it continues to be as necessary under subsection (e) as it has been under ordinary common law principles that, before the damage rule of the subsection becomes operative, liability of the bank and some loss to the customer or owner must be established.

Uniform Commercial Code Comment

Prior Uniform Statutory Provision:

None; but see Sections 5 and 6 of the American Bankers Association Bank Collection Code.

Purposes:

1. Section 1–102 states the general principles and rules for variation of the effect of this Act by agreement and the limitations to this power. Section 4–103 states the specific rules for variation of Article 4 by agreement and also certain standards of ordinary care. In view of the technical complexity of the field of bank collections, the enormous number of items handled by banks, the certainty that there will be variations from the normal in each day's work in each bank, the certainty of changing conditions and the possibility of developing improved methods of collection to speed the process, it would be unwise to freeze present methods of operation by mandatory statutory rules. This section, therefore, permits within wide limits variation of provisions of the Article by agreement.

2. Subsection (1) confers blanket power to vary all provisions of the Article by agreements of the ordinary kind. The agreements may not disclaim a bank's responsibility for its own lack of good faith or failure to exercise ordinary care and may not limit the measure of damages for such lack or failure, but this subsection like Section 1–102(3) approves the practice of parties determining by agreement the standards by which such responsibility is to be measured. In the absence of a showing that the standards manifestly are unreasonable, the agreement controls. Owners of items and other interested parties are not affected by agreements under this subsection unless they are parties to the agreement or are bound by adoption, ratification, estoppel or the like.

As here used "agreement" has the meaning given to it by Section 1–201(3). The agreement may be direct, as between the owner and the depositary bank; or indirect, as where the owner authorizes a particular type of procedure and any bank in the collection chain acts pursuant to such authorization. It may be with respect to a single item; or to all items handled for a particular customer, e.g., a general agreement between the depositary bank and the customer at the time a deposit account is opened. Legends on deposit tickets, collection letters and acknowledgments of items, coupled with action by the affected party constituting acceptance, adoption, ratification, estoppel or the like, are agreements if they meet the tests of the definition of "agreement". See Section 1–201(3). First Nat. Bank of Denver v. Federal Reserve Bank, 6 F.2d 339 (8th Cir. 1925) (deposit slip); Jefferson County Bldg. Ass'n v. Southern Bank & Trust Co., 225 Ala. 25, 142 So. 66 (1932) (signature card and deposit slip); Semingson v. Stock Yards Nat. Bank, 162 Minn. 424, 203 N.W. 412 (1925) (passbook); Farmers State Bank v. Union Nat. Bank, 42 N.D. 449, 454, 173 N.W. 789, 790 (1919) (acknowledgment of receipt of item).

3. Subsection (1) (subject to its limitations with respect to good faith and ordinary care) goes far to meet the requirements of flexibility. However, it does not by itself confer fully effective flexibility. When it is recognized that banks handle probably 25,000,000 items every business day and that the parties interested in each item include the owner of the item, the drawer (if it is a check), all non-bank indorsers, the payor bank and from one to five or more collecting banks, it is obvious that it is impossible, practically, to obtain direct agreements from all of these parties on all items. *En masse*, the interested parties constitute virtually every adult person and business organization in the United States. On the other hand they may become bound to agreements on the principle that collecting banks acting as agents have authority to make binding agreements with respect to items being handled. This conclusion was assumed but was not flatly decided in Federal Reserve Bank of Richmond v. Malloy, 264 U.S. 160, at 167, 44 S.Ct. 296, at 298, 68 L.Ed. 617, 31 A.L.R. 1261 (1924).

To meet this problem subsection (2) provides that official or quasi-official rules of collection, that is Federal Reserve regulations and operating letters, clearing house rules, and the like, have the effect of agreements under subsection (1), whether or not specifically assented to by all parties interested in items handled. Consequently, such official or quasi-official rules may, standing by themselves but subject to the good faith and ordinary care limitations, vary the effect of the provisions of Article 4.

Federal Reserve regulations. Various sections of the Federal Reserve Act (12 U.S.C.A. § 221 et seq.) authorize the Board of Governors of the Federal Reserve System to direct the Federal Reserve banks to exercise bank collection functions. For example, Section 16 (12 U.S.C.A. § 248(*o*)) authorizes the Board to require each Federal Reserve bank to exercise the functions of a clearing house for its members and Section 13 (12 U.S.C.A. § 342) authorizes each Federal Reserve bank to receive deposits from non-member banks solely for the purposes of exchange or of collection. Under this statutory authorization the Board has issued Regulation J (Check Clearing and Collection), which has been infrequently amended over the many years during which it has been in force. (Regulation G, issued under comparable statutory authority, covers the handling of "non-cash items"). Where regulations issued by the Board in pursuance of its statutory mandate may be said to have some force of law and constitute an effective means of maintaining flexibility, it is appropriate to provide that such regulations may vary this Article even though not specifically assented to by all parties interested in items handled.

Federal Reserve operating letters. The regulations of the Federal Reserve Board authorize the Federal Reserve banks to promulgate rules covering operating details. Regulation J, for example, provides that each bank may promulgate rules "not inconsistent with the terms of the law or of this regulation governing the sorting, listing, packaging and transmission of items and other details of its check clearing and collection operation. Such rules . . . shall be set forth . . . in . . . letters of instructions to . . . member and non-member clearing banks." The term "operating letters" means these "letters of instructions", sometimes called "operating circulars", issued by the Federal Reserve banks under appropriate regulation of the Board. This Article recognizes such "operating letters" issued pursuant to the regulations and concerned with operating details as appropriate means, within their proper sphere, to vary the effect of the Article.

Clearing House Rules. Local clearing houses have long issued rules governing the details of clearing; hours of clearing, media of remittance, time for return of mis-sent items and the like. The case law has recognized such rules, within their proper sphere, as binding on affected parties and as appropriate sources for the courts to look to in filling out details of bank collection law. Subsection (2) in recognizing clearing house rules as a means of preserving flexibility continues the sensible approach indicated in the cases. Included in the term "clearing houses" are county and regional clearing houses as well as those within a single city or town. There is, of course, no intention of authorizing a local clearing house or a group of clearing houses to rewrite the basic law generally. The term "clearing house rules" should be understood in the light of functions the clearing houses have exercised in the past.

And the like. This phrase is to be construed in the light of the foregoing. "Federal Reserve regulations and operating letters" cover rules and regulations issued by public or quasi-public agencies under statutory authority. "Clearing house rules" cover rules issued by a group of banks which have associated themselves to perform through a clearing house some of their collection, payment and clearing functions. Other such agencies or associations may be established in the future whose rules and regulations could be appropriately looked on as constituting means of avoiding absolute statutory rigidity. The phrase "and the like" leaves open such possibilities of future development. An agreement between a number of banks or even all the banks in an area simply because they are banks, would not of itself, by virtue of the phrase "and the like," meet the purposes and objectives of subsection (2).

4. Under this Article banks come under the general obligations of the use of good faith and the exercise of ordinary care. "Good faith" is defined in this Act (Section 1–201(19)) as "honesty in fact in the conduct or transaction concerned." The term "ordinary care" is not defined and is here used with its normal tort meaning and not in any special sense relating to bank collections. No attempt is made in the Article to define *in toto* what constitutes ordinary care or lack of it. Section 4–202 states respects in which collecting banks must use ordinary care. Subsection (3) of 4–103 provides that action or non-action approved by the Article or pursuant to Federal Reserve regulations or operating letters constitutes the exercise of ordinary care. Where Federal Reserve regulations and operating letters are issued pursuant to statutory mandate as indicated above, they constitute an affirmative standard of ordinary care equally with the provisions of Article 4 itself.

Subsection (3) further provides that, absent special instructions, action or non-action consistent with clearing house rules and the like or with a general banking usage not disapproved by the Article, prima facie constitutes the exercise of ordinary care. Clearing house rules and the phrase "and the like" have the significance set forth above in these Comments. The term "general banking usage" is not defined but should be taken to mean a general usage common to banks in the area concerned. See Section 1–205(2). Where the adjective "general" is used, the intention is to require a usage broader than a mere practice between two or three banks but it is not intended to require anything as broad as a country-wide usage. A usage followed generally throughout a state, a substantial portion of a state, a metropolitan area or the like would certainly be sufficient. Consistently with the principle of Section 1–205(3), action or non-action consistent with clearing house rules or the like or with such banking usages prima facie constitutes the exercise of ordinary care. However, the phrase "in the absence of special instructions" affords owners of items an opportunity to prescribe other standards and where there may be no direct supervision or control of clearing houses or banking usages by official supervisory authorities, the confirmation of ordinary care by compliance with these standards is *prima facie* only, thus conferring on the courts the ultimate power to determine ordinary care in any case where it should appear desirable to do so. The *prima facie* rule does, however, impose on the party contesting the standards to establish that they are unreasonable, arbitrary or unfair.

5. Subsection (4), in line with the flexible approach required for the bank collection process is designed to make clear that a novel procedure adopted by a bank is not to be considered unreasonable merely because that procedure is not specifically contemplated by this Article or by agreement, or because it has not yet been generally accepted as a bank usage. Changing conditions constantly call for new procedures and someone has to use the new procedure first. If such a procedure when called in question is found to be reasonable under the circumstances, provided, of course, that it is not inconsistent with any provision of the Article or other law or agreement, the bank which has followed the new procedure should not be found to have failed in the exercise of ordinary care.

6. Subsection (5) sets forth a rule for determining the measure of damages which, under subsection (1), cannot be limited by agreement. In the absence of bad faith the maximum recovery is the amount of the item concerned. When it is established that some part or all of the item could not have been collected even by the use of ordinary care the recovery is reduced by the amount which would have been in any event uncollectible. This limitation on recovery follows the case law. Finally, when bad faith is established the rule opens to allow the recovery of other damages, whose "proximateness" is to be tested by the ordinary rules applied in comparable cases. Of course, it continues to be as necessary under subsection (5) as it has been under ordinary common law principles that, before the damage rule of the subsection becomes operative, liability of the bank and some loss to the customer or owner must be established.

Cross References:

Sections 1–102(3), 1–203, 1–205 and 4–202.

Definitional Cross References:

"Bank". Section 1–201.
"Good faith". Section 1–201.
"Item". Section 4–104.
"Usage". Section 1–205.

Cross References

Agreement, see Commercial Code § 1201.
Clearinghouse, see Commercial Code § 4104.
Course of dealing and usage of trade, see Commercial Code § 1205.
Deposits in general, see Financial Code § 850 et seq.
Good faith, see Commercial Code § 1201.
Measure of damages,
   Breach of contract, see Civil Code § 3300 et seq.
   General provision, see Civil Code § 3353 et seq.
   Wrongs, see Civil Code § 3333 et seq.
Obligation of good faith, see Commercial Code § 1203.
Ordinary care,
   Standard of care of collecting bank, see Commercial Code § 4202.
   Want of, responsibility for injury, see Civil Code § 1714.
Variation by agreement of effect of provisions, see Commercial Code § 1102.

§ 4104. Definitions and Index of Definitions

(a) In this division unless the context otherwise requires:

(1) "Account" means any deposit or credit account with a bank, including a demand, time, savings, passbook, share draft, or like account, other than an account evidenced by a certificate of deposit.

(2) "Afternoon" means the period of a day between noon and midnight.

(3) "Banking day" means the part of a day on which a bank is open to the public for carrying on substantially all of its banking functions.

(4) "Clearing house" means an association of banks or other payors regularly clearing items.

(5) "Customer" means a person having an account with a bank or for whom a bank has agreed to collect items, including a bank that maintains an account at another bank.

(6) "Documentary draft" means a draft to be presented for acceptance or payment if specified docu-

ments, certificated securities (Section 8102) or instructions for uncertificated securities (Section 8102), or other certificates, statements, or the like are to be received by the drawee or other payor before acceptance or payment of the draft.

(7) "Draft" means a draft as defined in Section 3104 or an item, other than an instrument, that is an order.

(8) "Drawee" means a person ordered in a draft to make payment.

(9) "Item" means an instrument or a promise or order to pay money handled by a bank for collection or payment. The term does not include a payment order governed by Division 11 (commencing with Section 11101) or a credit or debit card slip.

(10) "Midnight deadline" with respect to a bank is midnight on its next banking day following the banking day on which it receives the relevant item or notice or from which the time for taking action commences to run, whichever is later.

(11) "Settle" means to pay in cash, by clearinghouse settlement, in a charge or credit or by remittance, or otherwise as agreed. A settlement may be either provisional or final.

(12) "Suspends payments" with respect to a bank means that it has been closed by order of the supervisory authorities, that a public officer has been appointed to take it over or that it ceases or refuses to make payments in the ordinary course of business.

(b) Other definitions applying to this division and the sections in which they appear are:

"Agreement for electronic presentment"	Section 4110
"Bank"	Section 4105
"Collecting bank"	Section 4105
"Depositary bank"	Section 4105
"Intermediary bank"	Section 4105
"Payor bank"	Section 4105
"Presenting bank"	Section 4105
"Presentment notice"	Section 4110

(c) The following definitions in other divisions apply to this division:

"Acceptance"	Section 3409
"Alteration"	Section 3407
"Cashier's check"	Section 3104
"Certificate of deposit"	Section 3104
"Certified check"	Section 3409
"Check"	Section 3104
"Good faith"	Section 3103
"Holder in due course"	Section 3302
"Instrument"	Section 3104
"Notice of dishonor"	Section 3503
"Order"	Section 3103
"Ordinary care"	Section 3103
"Person entitled to enforce"	Section 3301
"Presentment"	Section 3501
"Promise"	Section 3103
"Prove"	Section 3103
"Teller's check"	Section 3104
"Unauthorized signature"	Section 3403

(d) In addition, Division 1 (commencing with Section 1101) contains general definitions and principles of construction and interpretation applicable throughout this division. *(Stats.1963, c. 819, § 4104. Amended by Stats.1992, c. 914 (S.B.833), § 10; Stats.1996, c. 497 (S.B.1591), § 6, operative Jan. 1, 1997.)*

California Code Comment

By John A. Bohn and Charles J. Williams

Prior California Law

1. The definitions in this section are new to California law and for the most part have no statutory counterpart in prior California law. See the Official Comments for further explanation of some of the terms.

2. The definition of the term "item" in subdivision (1)(g) is substantially the same definition contained in former Financial Code § 1010.

Changes from U.C.C. (1962 Official Text)

3. This is section 4–104 of the Official Text without change.

Uniform Commercial Code Comment

Official Reasons for 1990 Change

The definition of "account" is amended to make clear that it includes both asset accounts in which a customer has deposited money and accounts from which a customer may draw on a line of credit. The remainder of the definition is amended to bring it more into conformity with the definition of "deposit account" in Section 9–105(1)(e).

The definition of "documentary draft" is amended to recognize the existence of uncertificated securities. The reference to "accompanying documents" is deleted as obsolete. It is enough that the documents are to be received by the drawee or other payor before acceptance or payment of the draft.

The definition of "draft" is new and is explained in the Official Comment.

The definition of "drawee" is new and is explained in the Official Comment.

The definition of "item" is amended because the term "instrument" as defined in Section 3–104 and as used in Article 4 is narrower than the term "item." See the Official Comment.

The definition of "properly payable" is deleted. In former Article 4 there is no affirmative definition of the term "properly payable." Former Section 4–104(1)(i) merely implies that if the customer's account is insufficient to pay the item the item is not properly payable. The phrase is defined in proposed Section 4–401(1) in terms of the items authorized by the customer and in accordance with the bank-customer agreement. This is done to give meaning to "properly payable" in Sections 4–401(1) and 4–402(1). The latter provision makes clear that a bank that fails to pay an overdraft has not wrongfully dishonored unless it had agreed to pay the overdraft.

The definition of "settle" is amended in changing "instructed" to "agreed" to conform to Section 4–213.

The terms "remitting bank," "protest," and "second party" are deleted because they are not used in Article 4.

The other modifications are made to conform with current legislative drafting practices, with no intent to change substance.

1990 Change

1. Paragraph (a)(1): "Account" is defined to include both asset accounts in which a customer has deposited money and accounts from which a customer may draw on a line of credit. The limiting factor is that the account must be in a bank.

2. Paragraph (a)(3): "Banking day." Under this definition that part of a business day when a bank is open only for limited functions, e.g., to receive deposits and cash checks, but with loan, bookkeeping and other departments closed, is not part of a banking day.

3. Paragraph (a)(4): "Clearing house." Occasionally express companies, governmental agencies and other nonbanks deal directly with a clearing house; hence the definition does not limit the term to an association of banks.

4. Paragraph (a)(5): "Customer." It is to be noted that this term includes a bank carrying an account with another bank as well as the more typical nonbank customer or depositor.

5. Paragraph (a)(6): "Documentary draft" applies even though the documents do not accompany the draft but are to be received by the drawee or other payor before acceptance or payment of the draft.

6. Paragraph (a)(7): "Draft" is defined in Section 3–104 as a form of instrument. Since Article 4 applies to items that may not fall within the definition of instrument, the term is defined here to include an item that is a written order to pay money, even though the item may not qualify as an instrument. The term "order" is defined in Section 3–103.

7. Paragraph (a)(8): "Drawee" is defined in Section 3–103 in terms of an Article 3 draft which is a form of instrument. Here "drawee" is defined in terms of an Article 4 draft which includes items that may not be instruments.

8. Paragraph (a)(9): "Item" is defined broadly to include an instrument, as defined in Section 3–104, as well as promises or orders that may not be within the definition of "instrument." The terms "promise" and "order" are defined in Section 3–103. A promise is a written undertaking to pay money. An order is a written instruction to pay money. But see Section 4–110(c). Since bonds and other investment securities under Article 8 may be within the term "instrument" or "promise," they are items and when handled by banks for collection are subject to this Article. See Comment 1 to Section 4–102. The functional limitation on the meaning of this term is the willingness of the banking system to handle the instrument, undertaking or instruction for collection or payment.

9. Paragraph (a)(10): "Midnight deadline." The use of this phrase is an example of the more mechanical approach used in this Article. Midnight is selected as a termination point or time limit to obtain greater uniformity and definiteness than would be possible from other possible terminating points, such as the close of the banking day or business day.

10. Paragraph (a)(11): The term "settle" has substantial importance throughout Article 4. In the American Bankers Association Bank Collection Code, in deferred posting statutes, in Federal Reserve regulations and operating circulars, in clearing-house rules, in agreements between banks and customers and in legends on deposit tickets and collection letters, there is repeated reference to "conditional" or "provisional" credits or payments. Tied in with this concept of credits or payments being in some way tentative, has been a related but somewhat different problem as to when an item is "paid" or "finally paid" either to determine the relative priority of the item as against attachments, stop-payment orders and the like or in insolvency situations. There has been extensive litigation in the various states on these problems. To a substantial extent the confusion, the litigation and even the resulting court decisions fail to take into account that in the collection process some debits or credits are provisional or tentative and others are final and that very many debits or credits are provisional or tentative for awhile but later become final. Similarly, some cases fail to recognize that within a single bank, particularly a payor bank, each item goes through a series of processes and that in a payor bank most of these processes are preliminary to the basic act of payment or "final payment."

The term "settle" is used as a convenient term to characterize a broad variety of conditional, provisional, tentative and also final payments of items. Such a comprehensive term is needed because it is frequently difficult or unnecessary to determine whether a particular action is tentative or final or when a particular credit shifts from the tentative class to the final class. Therefore, its use throughout the Article indicates that in that particular context it is unnecessary or unwise to determine whether the debit or the credit or the payment is tentative or final. However, if qualified by the adjective "provisional" its tentative nature is intended, and if qualified by the adjective "final" its permanent nature is intended.

Examples of the various types of settlement contemplated by the term include payments in cash; the efficient but somewhat complicated process of payment through the adjustment and offsetting of balances through clearing houses; debit or credit entries in accounts between banks; the forwarding of various types of remittance instruments, sometimes to cover a particular item but more frequently to cover an entire group of items received on a particular day.

11. Paragraph (a)(12): "Suspends payments." This term is designed to afford an objective test to determine when a bank is no longer operating as a part of the banking system.

Uniform Commercial Code Comment

Prior Uniform Statutory Provision:

None.

Purposes:

1. Subsection (1)(c): "Banking Day". Under this definition that part of a business day when a bank is open only for limited functions, e.g., on Saturday evenings to receive deposits and cash checks, but with loan, bookkeeping and other departments closed, is not part of a banking day.

2. Subsection (1)(d): "Clearing House". Occasionally express companies, governmental agencies and other non-banks deal directly with a clearing house; hence the definition does not limit the term to an association of banks.

3. Subsection (1)(e): "Customer". It is to be noted that this term includes a bank carrying an account with another bank as well as the more typical non-bank customer or depositor.

4. Subsection (1)(g): The word "item" is chosen because it is "banking language" and includes non-negotiable as well as negotiable paper calling for money and also similar paper governed by the Article on Investment Securities (Article 8) as well as that governed by the Article on Commercial Paper (Article 3).

5. Subsection (1)(h): "Midnight Deadline". The use of this phrase is an example of the more mechanical approach used in this Article. Midnight is selected as a termination point or time limit to obtain greater uniformity and definiteness than would be possible from other possible termination points, such as the close of the banking day or business day.

6. Subsection (1)(j): The term "settle" is a new term in bank collection language that has substantial importance throughout Article 4. In the American Bankers Association Bank Collection Code, in deferred posting statutes, in Federal Reserve regulations and operating letters, in clearing house rules, in agreements between banks and customers and in legends on deposit tickets and collection letters, there is repeated reference to "conditional" or "provisional" credits or payments. Tied in with this concept of credits or payments being in some way tentative, has been a related but somewhat different problem as to when an item is "paid" or "finally paid" either to determine the relative priority of the item as against attachments, stop payment orders and the like or in insolvency situations. There has been extensive litigation in the various states on these problems. To a substantial extent the confusion, the litigation and even the resulting court decisions fail to take into account that in the collection process some debits or credits are provisional or tentative and others are final and that very many debits or credits are provisional or tentative for awhile but later become final. Similarly, some cases fail to recognize that within a single bank, particularly a payor bank, each item goes through a series of processes and that in a payor bank most of these processes are preliminary to the basic act of payment or "final payment".

The term "settle" is used as a convenient term to characterize a broad variety of conditional, provisional, tentative and also final payments of items. Such a comprehensive term is needed because it is frequently difficult or unnecessary to determine whether a particular action is tentative or final or when a particular credit shifts from the tentative class to the final class. Therefore, its use throughout the Article indicates that in that particular context it is unnecessary or unwise to determine whether the debit or the credit or the payment is tentative or final. However, when qualified by the adjective "provisional" its tentative nature is intended, and when qualified by the adjective "final" its permanent nature is intended.

Examples of the various types of settlement contemplated by the term include payments in cash; the efficient but somewhat complicated process of payment through the adjustment and offsetting of balances through clearing houses; debit or credit entries in accounts between banks; the forwarding of various types of remittance instruments, sometimes to cover a particular item but more frequently to cover an entire group of items received on a particular day.

7. Subsection (1)(k): "Suspends payments". This term is designed to afford an objective test to determine when a bank is no longer operating as a part of the banking system.

Definitional Cross References:

"Bank". Section 1–201.
"Documents". Section 1–201.
"Money". Section 1–201.
"Negotiable". Section 3–104.
"Notice". Section 1–201.
"Person". Section 1–201.
"Securities". Section 8–102.

Cross References

Bank business days, see Civil Code § 9.
Branch offices, see Financial Code § 500 et seq.
Check or draft, see Commercial Code § 3104.
Deposits in general, see Financial Code § 850 et seq.
Duties of collecting agent, see Civil Code § 2021.
Form of negotiable instruments, see Commercial Code § 3104.
Holidays, see Civil Code §§ 7, 9; Code of Civil Procedure § 10; Government Code § 6700 et seq.
Negotiable instruments in general, see Commercial Code § 3101 et seq.
Optional bank holidays, see Commercial Code § 3123.

§ 4105. Bank; definitions

In this division * * *:

(1) "Bank" means a person engaged in the business of banking, including a savings bank, savings and loan association, credit union, or trust company.

(2) "Depositary bank" means the first bank to take an item * * * even though it is also the payor bank * * *, unless the item is presented for immediate payment over the counter.

(3) "Payor bank" means a bank * * * that is the drawee of a draft.

(4) "Intermediary bank" means a bank to which an item is transferred in course of collection except the depositary or payor bank.

(5) "Collecting bank" means a bank handling an item for collection except the payor bank.

(6) "Presenting bank" means a bank presenting an item except a payor bank.

* * * (Stats.1963, c. 819, § 4105). Amended by Stats.1992, c. 914 (S.B.833), § 11.)

California Code Comment

By John A. Bohn and Charles J. Williams

Prior California Law

1. This section defines banks in terms of the transfer of the item in process of collection. This manner of defining banks is new statutory law and these definitions apply only within this division of the Commercial Code.

In the Financial Code, banks are defined in terms of their functions. Financial Code § 102 defines "bank" generally and §§ 103 to 109 describe the three classes of banks, commercial, savings, and trust and defines a fourth type known as "departmental" which is a bank that performs the functions of more than one of the classes of banks. These definitions in the Financial Code apply for purposes other than Division 4.

Changes from U.C.C. (1962 Official Text)

2. Paragraphs (a) through (f) are the same as their counterparts in Section 4–105 of the Official Text.

Paragraph (g) is not in the Official Text. It was added as a result of the recommendation of Professors Marsh and Warren. An amendment similar in effect by including branch banks in paragraphs (b) and (d) was offered by the State Bar subcommittee.

The reason for the addition of paragraph (g) is explained in the Marsh and Warren Report:

"The amendments are proposed to make sure that the branch on which an item is drawn is considered to be the payor bank and a different branch of the same bank handling the item for collection is considered to be the collecting bank. No reason is given by the State Bar Committee or is apparent from the section under study why the words 'or the branch or separate office of a bank' should be inserted in subsections [subparagraphs] (b) and (d) and not in the other four subsections [subdivisions] of this Section. It seems to us that a separate branch should be considered a separate bank in all six subsections [subdivisions] of this Section. This is accomplished by the new subsection [subdivision] proposed. The wording of the recommended amendment is based on FC § 1012(c)." Sixth Progress Report to the Legislature by Senate Fact Finding Committee on Judiciary (1959–1961) Part 1, The Uniform Commercial Code, p. 472.

Uniform Commercial Code Comment

Official Reasons for 1990 Change

The definition of "bank" is added and is in conformity with that found in Section 4A–105(a)(2). See the Official Comment.

The definition of "depositary bank" is amended. The term "transferred for collection" is too limiting as the purpose for which the item is taken. The amendment makes clear that a payor bank is not also a depositary bank with respect to an item presented for immediate payment over the counter.

The definition of "payor bank" is amended to require that in order for a bank to be a payor bank it must be instructed rather than authorized to pay and that the instruction must be contained in the item. As explained in the Official Comment, this result follows from the use of the defined terms "drawee" and "draft."

The definition of "remitting bank" is deleted because the term is not used in Article 4.

The other modifications are made to conform with current legislative drafting practices, with no intent to change substance.

1990 Change

1. The definitions in general exclude a bank to which an item is issued, as this bank does not take by transfer except in the particular case covered in which the item is issued to payee for collection, as in the case in which a corporation is transferring balances from one account to another. Thus, the definition of "depositary bank" does not include the bank to which a check is made payable if a check is given in payment of a mortgage. This bank has the status of a payee under Article 3 on Negotiable Instruments and not that of a collecting bank.

2. Paragraph (1): "Bank" is defined in Section 1–201(4) as meaning "any person engaged in the business of banking." The definition in paragraph (1) makes clear that "bank" includes savings banks, savings and loan associations, credit unions and trust companies, in addition to the commercial banks commonly denoted by use of the term "bank."

3. Paragraph (2): A bank that takes an "on us" item for collection, for application to a customer's loan, or first handles the item for other reasons is a depositary bank even though it is also the payor bank. However, if the holder presents the item for immediate payment over the counter, the payor bank is not a depositary bank.

4. Paragraph (3): The definition of "payor bank" is clarified by use of the term "drawee." That term is defined in Section 4–104 as meaning "a person ordered in a draft to make payment." An "order" is defined in Section 3–103 as meaning "a written instruction to pay money . . . An authorization to pay is not an order unless the person authorized to pay is also instructed to pay." The definition of order is incorporated into Article 4 by Section 4–104(c). Thus a payor bank is one instructed to pay in the item. A bank does not become a payor bank by being merely authorized to pay or by being given an instruction to pay not contained in the item.

5. Paragraph (4): The term "intermediary bank" includes the last bank in the collection process if the drawee is not a bank. Usually the last bank is also a presenting bank.

Uniform Commercial Code Comment

Prior Uniform Statutory Provision:

None.

Purposes:

1. The definitions in general exclude a bank to which an item is issued, as such bank does not take by transfer except in the particular case covered where the item is issued to a payee for collection, as where a corporation is transferring balances from one account to another. Thus, the definition of "depositary bank" does not include the bank to which a check is made payable where a check is given in payment of a mortgage. Such a bank has the status of a payee under Article 3 on Commercial Paper and not that of a collecting bank.

2. The term payor bank includes a drawee bank and also a bank at which an item is payable if the item constitutes an order on the bank to pay, for it is then "payable by" the bank. If the "at" item is not an order in the particular state, (See Section 3–121) then the bank is not a payor, but will be a presenting or collecting bank.

3. Items are sometimes drawn or accepted "payable through" a particular bank. Under this Section and Section 3–120 the "payable through" bank (if it in fact handles the item) will be a collecting (and often a presenting) bank; it is not a "payor bank."

4. The term intermediary bank includes the last bank in the collection process where the payor is not a bank. Usually the last bank is also a presenting bank.

Cross References:

Article 3, especially Sections 3–120 and 3–121.

Definitional Cross References:

"Bank". Section 1–201.
"Customer". Section 4–104.
"Item". Section 4–104.

Cross References

Branch offices, within state, see Financial Code § 500 et seq.
Commercial paper, see Commercial Code § 3101 et seq.
Credit union as bank, see Financial Code § 14867
Items "payable through" bank or at bank, see Commercial Code § 4106.
Separate offices, see Commercial Code § 4107.

§ 4106. Payable through; payable at

(a) If an item states that it is "payable through" a bank identified in the item, (1) the item designates the bank as a collecting bank and does not by itself authorize the bank to pay the item, and (2) the item may be presented for payment only by or through the bank.

(b) If an item states that it is "payable at" a bank identified in the item, (1) the item designates the bank as a collecting bank and does not by itself authorize the bank to pay the item, and (2) the item may be presented for payment only by or through the bank.

(c) If a draft names a nonbank drawee and it is unclear whether a bank named in the draft is a co-drawee or a collecting bank, the bank is a collecting bank. *(Added by Stats.1992, c. 914 (S.B.833), § 12.)*

California Code Comment

By John A. Bohn and Charles J. Williams

Prior California Law

1. This section is of special importance in California because of the prevalence of branch banking. In many other states branch banking is prohibited.

2. This section replaces former Financial Code §§ 1012(c) ("each branch or office of a bank shall be deemed a separate bank") and 1018 (an item payable at one bank office and received at another office of the same bank is deemed payable at another bank).

Changes from U.C.C. (1962 Official Text)

3. The first part of the section as it reads down to and including the words "under Division 3" is the 1962 Official Text with the optional phrase "maintaining its own deposit ledgers" deleted. The 1962 Official Text with the optional language reads as follows:

"A branch or separate office of a bank [maintaining its own deposit ledgers] is a separate bank for the purpose of computing the time within which and determining the place at or to which action may be taken or notices or orders shall be given under this Article and under Article 3."

4. The language following the phrase "under Division 3" in the California version is the same as the New York version and does not appear in the Official Text. It was added to make it clear that notice to one branch of a bank would not impair the status of another branch as a holder in due course. California State Bar Committee on the Commercial Code, A Special Report, The Uniform Commercial Code, 37 Calif.State Bar J. (March–April, 1962) p. 165.

This addition was made at the recommendation of the State Bar subcommittee which stated that its purpose is "to make certain that the knowledge of one branch or office is not imputed to another branch or office, and that such other branch or office may be a holder in due course." Sixth Progress Report of the Legislature by the Senate Fact Finding Committee on Judiciary (1959–1961), Part 1, The Uniform Commercial Code, p. 359.

The California Bankers Association commented on the addition of this language by stating:

"The suggested change amplifies the section to bring in the provisions of Sections 991, 1012(c) and 1018 of the California Financial Code, concerning notice to one branch as not being notice to another branch, also the right of one branch to be a holder in due course of an item drawn on or payable at another branch." Sixth Progress Report of the Legislature by the Senate Fact Finding Committee on Judiciary (1959–1961), Part 1, The Uniform Commercial Code, p. 406.

The added language also conforms to the change in Commercial Code § 1201(27). See the California Code Comment 27 under section 1201.

5. This additional language was considered by the Permanent Editorial Board for the Uniform Commercial Code and rejected for the following reason: "The added words merely elaborate or restate other provisions of the Code." Permanent Editorial Board for the Uniform Commercial Code, Report No. 1 (1962 Official Text), p. 78.

Uniform Commercial Code Comment

Official Reasons for 1990 Change

New section. See the Official Comment.

1990 Change

1. This section replaces former Sections 3–120 and 3–121. Some items are made "payable through" a particular bank. Subsection (a) states that such language makes the bank a collecting bank and not a payor bank. An item identifying a "payable through" bank can be presented for payment to the drawee only by the "payable through" bank. The item cannot be presented to the drawee over the counter for immediate payment or by a collecting bank other than the "payable through" bank.

2. Subsection (b) retains the alternative approach of the present law. Under Alternative A a note payable at a bank is the equivalent of a draft drawn on the bank and the midnight deadline provisions of Sections 4–301 and 4–302 apply. Under Alternative B a "payable at" bank is in the same position as a "payable through" bank under subsection (a).

3. Subsection (c) rejects the view of some cases that a bank named below the name of a drawee is itself a drawee. The commercial understanding is that this bank is a collecting bank and is not accountable under Section 4–302 for holding an item beyond its deadline. The liability of the bank is governed by Sections 4–202(a) and 4–103(e).

Uniform Commercial Code Comment

Prior Uniform Statutory Provision:

None; but see Section 1, American Bankers Association Bank Collection Code.

Purposes:

1. A rule with respect to the status of a branch or separate office of a bank as a part of any statute on bank collections is highly desirable if not absolutely necessary. However, practices in the operations of branches and separate offices vary substantially in the different states and it has not been possible to find any single rule that is logically correct, fair in all situations and workable under all different types of practices.

2. In many states and for many purposes a branch or separate office of the bank needs to be treated as a separate bank. Many branches function as separate banks in the handling and payment of items and require time for doing so similar to that of a separate bank. This is particularly true where branch banking is permitted throughout a state or in different towns and cities. Similarly, where there is this separate functioning a particular branch or separate office is the only proper place for various types of action to be taken or orders or notices to be given. Examples include the drawing of a check on a particular branch by a customer whose account is carried at that branch; the presentment of that same check at that branch; the issuance of an order to the branch to stop payment on the check.

3. Section 1 of the American Bankers Association Bank Collection Code provides simply: "A branch or office of any such bank shall be deemed a bank." Although this rule appears to be brief and simple, as applied to particular sections of the ABA Code it produces illogical and, in some cases, unreasonable results. For example, under Section 11 of the ABA Code it seems anomalous for one branch of a bank to have charged an item to the account of the drawer and another branch to have the power to elect to treat the item as dishonored. Similar logical problems would flow from applying the same rule to Article 4. Warranties by one branch to another branch under Section 4–207 (each considered a separate bank) do not make sense.

4. Assuming that it is not desirable to make each branch a separate bank for all purposes, this Section provides that a branch or separate office is a separate bank for certain purposes. In so doing the single legal entity of the bank as a whole is preserved, thereby carrying with it the liability of the institution as a whole on such obligations as it may be under. On the other hand, where the Article provides a number of time limits for different types of action by banks, if a branch functions as a separate bank, it should have the time limits available to a separate bank. Similarly if in its relations to customers a branch functions as a separate bank, notices and orders with respect to accounts of customers of the branch should be given at the branch. For example, whether a branch has notice sufficient to affect its status as a holder in due course of an item taken by it should depend upon what notice that branch has received with respect to the item. Similarly the receipt of a stop payment order at one branch should not be notice to another branch so as to impair the right of the second branch to be a holder in due course of the item, although in circumstances in which ordinary care requires the communication of a notice or order to the proper branch of a bank, such notice or order would be effective at such proper branch from the time it was or should have been received. See Section 1–201(27).

5. Whether a branch functions as a separate bank may vary depending upon the type of activity taking place and upon practices in the different states. If the activity is that of a payor bank paying items, a branch will usually function as a separate bank if it maintains its own deposit ledgers. Similarly whether a branch functions as a separate bank in the collection of items usually depends also on whether it maintains its own deposit ledgers. Conversely, if a particular bank having branches does all of its bookkeeping at its head office, the branches of that bank do not usually function as separate banks either in the payment or collection of items.

On the other hand, in its relations to customers a branch may function as a separate bank regardless of whether it maintains its own deposit ledgers. Checks may be drawn on a particular branch and notices and stop orders delivered to that branch even though all the bookkeeping is done at the head office or another branch.

Where the words "maintaining its own deposit ledgers" are bracketed, the option is given to each state enacting the Code to include these words as a test of separateness. In those states where the maintenance by a branch of its own deposit ledgers will serve as a satisfactory standard, the bracketed words should be retained. In those states where these words will cause more problems than benefits, they may be deleted. Insofar as this latter rule allows extra time to banks maintaining branches where such extra time is not needed, it is not ideal. However, it has not been found possible to find a rule that will meet this problem and will work in all cases. Further, it is highly unlikely that large banks maintaining branches will needlessly take advantage of extra time under this rule.

Cross References:

Sections 3–504, 4–102(2).

Definitional Cross References:

"Bank". Section 1–201.
"Branch". Section 1–201.

Cross References

Branch offices, generally, see Financial Code § 500 et seq.
Commercial paper, see Commercial Code § 3101 et seq.
Deposits in general, see Financial Code § 850 et seq.
Forwarding for collection, see Commercial Code § 4204.
Holder in due course,
   Generally, see Commercial Code § 3302.
   Security interest of bank as value given, see Commercial Code § 4211.
Liability for action or non-action, law governing, see Commercial Code § 4102(b).
Midnight deadline, see Commercial Code § 4104.
Notice,
   Generally, see Commercial Code § 1201.
   Adverse claims to deposits, see Financial Code § 952.
   Alteration or unauthorized signature, see Commercial Code § 4406.
Statement of account, see Financial Code § 861.
Stop payment orders, see Commercial Code § 4403.
Trust deposit, effect of failure to give, see Probate Code § 5404 et seq.
Order, see Commercial Code § 3103.
Presentment, manner of making, see Commercial Code §§ 3501, 4212.
Time of receipt of items, see Commercial Code § 4108.

§ 4107. Separate office of bank

A branch or separate office of a bank is a separate bank for the purpose of computing the time within which and determining the place at or to which action may be taken or <u>notice</u> or orders shall be given under this division and under Division 3 * * * (commencing with Section 3101). *(Formerly § 4106, added by Stats. 1963, c. 819, § 4106. Renumbered § 4107 and amended by Stats.1992, c. 914 (S.B.833), § 13.)*

California Code Comment

By John A. Bohn and Charles J. Williams

Prior California Law

1. Subdivision (1) in fixing the cutoff hour has no counterpart in prior California law. See Official Comment 1 for an explanation of the operating convenience which a cutoff hour affords.

Some questions have been raised under this subdivision. For example, may a bank select a cutoff hour without giving notice to its customers and others with whom it does business? What is the cutoff hour on Saturday for banks open that day? Clarke, Bailey and Young, Bank Deposits and Collections (A.L.I.1963) 24–26.

2. Subdivision (2) is similar to former Financial Code § 1012(a). However, subdivision (2) provides that the item *may* be treated as received on the next banking day, while section 1012(a) made it mandatory.

Changes from U.C.C. (1962 Official Text)

3. This is section 4–107 of the Official Text without change.

Uniform Commercial Code Comment
Official Reasons for 1990 Change

The bracketed language in former Section 4–106 is deleted. Today banks keep records on customer accounts by electronic data storage. This has led most banks with branches to centralize to some degree their record keeping. The place where records are kept has little meaning if the information is electronically stored and is instantly retrievable at all branches of the bank. Hence, the inference to be drawn from the deletion of the bracketed language is that where record keeping is done is no longer an important factor in determining whether a branch is a separate bank.

1990 Change

1. A rule with respect to the status of a branch or separate office of a bank as a part of any statute on bank collections is highly desirable if not absolutely necessary. However, practices in the operations of branches and separate offices vary substantially in the different states and it has not been possible to find any single rule that is logically correct, fair in all situations and workable under all different types of practices. The decision not to draft the section with greater specificity leaves to the courts the resolution of the issues arising under this section on the basis of the facts of each case.

2. In many states and for many purposes a branch or separate office of the bank should be treated as a separate bank. Many branches function as separate banks in the handling and payment of items and require time for doing so similar to that of a separate bank. This is particularly true if branch banking is permitted throughout a state or in different towns and cities. Similarly, if there is this separate functioning a particular branch or separate office is the only proper place for various types of action to be taken or orders or notices to be given. Examples include the drawing of a check on a particular branch by a customer whose account is carried at that branch; the presentment of that same check at that branch; the issuance of an order to the branch to stop payment on the check.

3. Section 1 of the American Bankers Association Bank Collection Code provided simply: "A branch or office of any such bank shall be deemed a bank." Although this rule appears to be brief and simple, as applied to particular sections of the ABA Code it produces illogical and, in some cases, unreasonable results. For example, under Section 11 of the ABA Code it seems anomalous for one branch of a bank to have charged an item to the account of the drawer and another branch to have the power to elect to treat the item as dishonored. Similar logical problems would flow from applying the same rule to Article 4. Warranties by one branch to another branch under Sections 4–207 and 4–208 (each considered a separate bank) do not make sense.

4. Assuming that it is not desirable to make each branch a separate bank for all purposes, this section provides that a branch or separate office is a separate bank for certain purposes. In so doing the single legal entity of the bank as a whole is preserved, thereby carrying with it the liability of the institution as a whole on such obligations as it may be under. On the other hand, in cases in which the Article provides a number of time limits for different types of action by banks, if a branch functions as a separate bank, it should have the time limits available to a separate bank. Similarly if in its relations to customers a branch functions as a separate bank, notices and orders with respect to accounts of customers of the branch should be given at the branch. For example, whether a branch has notice sufficient to affect its status as a holder in due course of an item taken by it should depend upon what notice that branch has received with respect to the item. Similarly the receipt of a stop-payment order at one branch should not be notice to another branch so as to impair the right of the second branch to be a holder in due course of the item, although in circumstances in which ordinary care requires the communication of a notice or order to the proper branch of a bank, the notice or order would be effective at the proper branch from the time it was or should have been received. See Section 1–201(27).

5. The bracketed language ("maintaining its own deposit ledger") in former Section 4–106 is deleted. Today banks keep records on customer accounts by electronic data storage. This has led most banks with branches to centralize to some degree their record keeping. The place where records are kept has little meaning if the information is electronically stored and is instantly retrievable at all branches of the bank. Hence, the inference to be drawn from the deletion of the bracketed language is that where record keeping is done is no longer an important factor in determining whether a branch is a separate bank.

Uniform Commercial Code Comment

Prior Uniform Statutory Provision:
None.

Purposes:

1. After an item has been received by a bank it goes through a series of processes varying with the type of item that it is. It moves from the teller's window, branch office, or mail desk at which it is received through settlement and proving departments until it is forwarded or presented to a clearing house or another bank, if it is a transit item, or until it reaches the bookkeeping department, if the bank receiving it is the payor bank. In addition, in order that the books of the bank always remain in balance while items are moving through it, the amount of each item is included in lists or proofs of debits or credits several times as it progresses through the bank. The running of proofs, the making of debit and credit entries in subsidiary and general ledgers and the striking of a general balance for each day requires a considerable amount of time. If these processes are to be completed on any particular day during normal working hours without the employment of night forces, a number of banks have found it necessary to establish a "cut-off hour" to allow time to obtain final figures to be incorporated into the bank's position for the day. Subsection (1) approves a cut-off hour of this type provided it is not earlier than 2 P.M. Subsection (2) provides that if such a cut-off hour is fixed, items received after the cut-off hour may be treated as being received at the opening of the next banking day. Where the number of items received either through the mail or over the counter tends to taper off radically as the afternoon hours progress, a 2 P.M. cut-off hour does not involve a large portion of the items received but at the same time permits a bank using such a cut-off hour to leave its doors open later in the afternoon without forcing into the evening the completion of its settling and proving process.

2. The alternative provision in Subsection (2) that items or deposits received after the close of the banking day may be treated as received at the opening of the next banking day is important in cases where a bank closes at twelve or one o'clock, e.g., on a Saturday, but continues to receive some items by mail or over the counter if, for example, it opens Saturday evening for the limited purpose of receiving deposits and cashing checks.

Definitional Cross References:

"Afternoon". Section 4–104.
"Bank". Section 1–201.
"Banking day". Section 4–404.
"Item". Section 4–104.
"Money." Section 1–201.

Cross References

Business days, banks, see Civil Code § 9.
Deposits in general, see Financial Code § 850 et seq.

§ 4108. Cutoff hours

* * * (a) For the purpose of allowing time to process items, prove balances, and make the necessary entries on its books to determine its position for the day, a bank may fix an afternoon hour of 2 p.m. or later as a cutoff hour for the handling of money and items and the making of entries on its books.

* * * (b) An item or deposit of money received on any day after a cutoff hour so fixed or after the close of the banking day may be treated as being received at the opening of the next banking day. *(Formerly § 4107, added by Stats.1963, c. 819, § 4107. Renumbered § 4108 and amended by Stats.1992, c. 914 (S.B.833), § 14.)*

California Code Comment

By John A. Bohn and Charles J. Williams

Prior California Law

1. Subdivision (1) is new. Other sections in this division fix time limits in the handling of items by banks which banks must follow if they are to follow the standard of ordinary care. See Commercial Code §§ 4202(2), 4212, 4301 and 4302. This subdivision permits a 1 day extension in the collection process in connection with a good faith effort to secure payment. Official Comments 1, 2 and 3.

The courts have imposed only general standards of care upon banks in their activities. The court in Davis v. First Nat. Bank, 118 Cal. 600, 50 Pac. 666 (1897) stated that the basis of a bank's liability for failure to collect was negligence and that "if in making the collection it followed the course usually taken by banks under similar circumstances it cannot be held to be negligent." In First Nat. Bank of Ely v. Hamaker, 83 Cal.App. 670, 257 Pac. 454 (1927) there was a 6 weeks delay between the drawee's repudiation of a draft and the bank's notice of dishonor, but the court held that there was no evidence of negligence on the part of the banks involved. Subdivision (1) now adds a statutory provision for liability in addition to the general doctrine of negligence and custom imposed by the courts.

2. The extra days' extension under subdivision (1) also extends the time for payment or presentment under Division 3. Official Comment 3. Under former Civil Code §§ 3169, 3183, 3184, giving an additional day risked the discharge of secondary parties.

3. Subdivision (2) excuses delays caused by suspension of another bank or by force majeure and imposes a standard of diligence in facing the delay. This is in accord with prior California law that a collecting bank is liable only for negligence and is not an insurer. Banking custom and usage could be used to determine whether diligence or reasonable care was exercised by the bank. Luckehe v. First Nat. Bank of Marysville, 193 Cal. 184, 223 Pac. 547 (1924); Davis v. First Nat. Bank, 118 Cal. 600, 50 Pac. 666 (1897).

4. Under subdivision (2) the bank asserting the excuse has the burden of establishing the excuse. Official Comment 4.

Changes from U.C.C. (1962 Official Text)

5. This is section 4–108 of the Official Text without change.

Uniform Commercial Code Comment

Official Reasons for 1990 Change

Modified to conform with current drafting practices; no intent to change substance.

1990 Change

1. Each of the huge volume of checks processed each day must go through a series of accounting procedures that consume time. Many banks have found it necessary to establish a cutoff hour to allow time for these procedures to be completed within the time limits imposed by Article 4. Subsection (a) approves a cutoff hour of this type provided it is not earlier than 2 P.M. Subsection (b) provides that if such a cutoff hour is fixed, items received after the cutoff hour may be treated as being received at the opening of the next banking day. If the number of items received either through the mail or over the counter tends to taper off radically as the afternoon hours progress, a 2 P.M. cutoff hour does not involve a large portion of the items received but at the same time permits a bank using such a cutoff hour to leave its doors open later in the afternoon without forcing into the evening the completion of its settling and proving process.

2. The provision in subsection (b) that items or deposits received after the close of the banking day may be treated as received at the opening of the next banking day is important in cases in which a bank closes at twelve or one o'clock, e.g., on a Saturday, but continues to receive some items by mail or over the counter if, for example, it opens Saturday evening for the limited purpose of receiving deposits and cashing checks.

Uniform Commercial Code Comment

Prior Uniform Statutory Provision:

None.

Purposes:

1. Sections 4–202(2), 4–212, 4–301 and 4–302 prescribe various time limits for the handling of items. These are the limits of time within which a bank, in fulfilment of its obligation to exercise ordinary care, must handle items entrusted to it for collection or payment. Under Section 4–103 they may be varied by agreement or by Federal Reserve regulations or operating letters, clearing house rules, or the like.

2. Subsection (1) of this section permits a limited extension of these time limits in special cases. It permits collecting banks to grant, within a rather narrow field, an additional banking day and to do so with or without the approval of any interested party. Such one-day extension can only be granted in a good faith effort to secure payment and only with respect to specific items. It cannot be exercised if the customer instructs otherwise. Thus limited the escape provision should afford a limited degree of flexibility in special cases but should not interfere with the overall requirement and objective of speedy collections.

3. Notice that an extension granted under Subsection (1) is "without discharge of secondary parties". It therefore extends also the times for presentment or payment, as the case may be, specified in Article 3. See Sections 3–503 and 3–506. Where this Article and Article 3 conflict, this Article controls. See Sections 3–103(2) and 4–102(1).

4. Subsection (2) is another escape clause from time limits. This clause operates not only with respect to time limits imposed by the article itself but also time limits imposed by special instructions, by agreement or by Federal Reserve regulations or operating letters, clearing house rules or the like. The latter time limits are "permitted" by the Code. This clause operates, however, only in the types of situation specified. Examples of these situations include blizzards, floods, or hurricanes, and other "Act of God" events or conditions, and wrecks or disasters, interfering with mails; suspension of payments by another bank; abnormal operating conditions such as substantial increased volume or substantial shortage of personnel during war or emergency situations. When delay is sought to be excused under this subsection the bank must "exercise such diligence as the circumstances require" and it has the burden of proof. See Section 4–202(2).

Cross References:

Sections 3–103(2), 3–503, 3–506, 4–102(1), 4–103, 4–104, 4–202(2), 4–212, 4–213, 4–301, 4–302.

Definitional Cross References:

"Bank". Section 1–201.
"Banking day". Section 4–104.
"Collecting bank". Section 4–105.
"Good faith". Section 1–201.
"Item". Section 4–104.
"Party". Section 1–201.

Cross References

Banking day, see Commercial Code § 4104.
Business day for banks, see Civil Code § 9.
Charge-back or refund upon provisional settlement, see Commercial Code § 4214.
Collecting bank, see Commercial Code § 4105.
Commercial paper, effect of this division, see Commercial Code § 3102.
Conflicting provisions, operation and effect of this division, see Commercial Code § 4102(a).
Deferred acceptance or payment, see Commercial Code § 3501.
Deferred posting of items, see Commercial Code § 4301.
Definitions, see Commercial Code § 4104.
Good faith, see Commercial Code § 1201.
Handling of items, variation, see Commercial Code § 4103.
Improperly paid items, recovery by payor bank, see Commercial Code § 4301.
Item, see Commercial Code § 4104.
Late return of items, payor bank's responsibility, see Commercial Code § 4302.
Ordinary care, standard of care of collecting bank, see Commercial Code § 4202.
Payment of items by payor bank, finality, see Commercial Code § 4215.
Payor bank, see Commercial Code § 4105.
Propriety of action of collecting bank, burden of proof, see Commercial Code § 4202(b).

Time of presentment, see Commercial Code § 3501.

§ 4109. Waiver of time limits; delays

* * * (a) Unless otherwise instructed, a collecting bank in a good faith effort to secure payment * * * of a specific * * * item drawn on a payor other than a bank, and with or without the approval of any person involved, may waive, modify, or extend time limits imposed or permitted by this code for a period not * * * exceeding two additional banking days without discharge of * * * drawers or indorsers or liability to its transferor or a prior party.

(b) Delay by a collecting bank or payor bank beyond time limits prescribed or permitted by this code or by instructions is excused if (1) the delay is caused by interruption of communication or computer facilities, suspension of payments by another bank, war, emergency conditions, failure of equipment, or other circumstances beyond the control of the bank * * *, and (2) the bank exercises such diligence as the circumstances require. *(Formerly § 4108, added by Stats.1963, c. 819, § 4108. Renumbered § 4109 and amended by Stats. 1992, c. 914 (S.B.833), § 15.)*

California Code Comment

By John A. Bohn and Charles J. Williams

Section 4–109 of the 1962 Official Text is deleted from the California version of the Uniform Commercial Code. The section defines the process of posting referred to in section 4–213(1)(c) and 4–303(1)(d) of the Official Text.

Sections 4213 and 4303 of the California version delete references to the process of posting and therefore the definitions of the terms in section 4–109 become meaningless. See California Code Comment 5 to Commercial Code § 4213.

The 1962 Official Text and the Official Comment follow:

Section 4–109. Process of Posting.

The "process of posting" means the usual procedure followed by a payor bank in determining to pay an item and in recording the payment including one or more of the following or other steps as determined by the bank:

(a) verification of any signature;
(b) ascertaining that sufficient funds are available;
(c) affixing a "paid" or other stamp;
(d) entering a charge or entry to a customer's account;
(e) correcting or reversing an entry or erroneous action with respect to the item.

Prior Uniform Statutory Provisions:

None.

Purposes:

Completion of the "process of posting" is one of the measuring points for determining when an item is finally paid (subsection (1)(c) of Section 4–213) and when knowledge, notice, stop order, legal process and set-off come too late to affect a payor bank's right or duty to pay an item (subsection (1)(d) of Section 4–303). This Section defines what is meant by the "process of posting". It is the "usual procedure followed by a payor bank in determining to pay an item and in recording the payment . . .". It involves the two basic elements of some decision to pay and some recording of the payment with a listing of some of the typical steps that might be involved. Procedures followed by banks in determining to pay an item and in recording the payment vary. Examples of some of these procedures will illustrate what is meant by completion of the "process of posting".

Example 1. A payor bank receives an item through the clearing on Monday morning. It is sorted under the name of the customer on Monday and under deferred posting routines (Section 4–301) reaches the bookkeeper for that customer on Tuesday morning. The bookkeeper examines the signature, verifies there are sufficient funds and decides at 11 a.m. on Tuesday to pay the item. A debit entry for or including the amount of the item is entered in the customer's account at 12 noon on Tuesday. The process of posting is completed at 12 noon on Tuesday.

Example 2. A payor bank with branches receives an item through the clearing on Monday morning. One branch does all the bookkeeping for itself and nine other branches. The item is sent to that branch and a provisional debit is entered to the customer's account for the amount of the item on Monday. After this entry is made the item is sent to the branch where the customer transacts business and at this branch a clerk verifies the signature on Tuesday, e.g. at 12 noon. If the clerk determines the signature is valid and makes a decision to pay, the process of posting is completed at 12 noon on Tuesday because there has been both a charge to the customer's account and a determination to pay. If, however, the clerk determines the signature is not valid or that the item should not be paid for some other reason, the item is then returned to the presenting bank through the clearing house and an offsetting credit entry is made in the customer's account by the bookkeeping branch. In this case there has been no determination to pay the item, no completion of the process of posting and no payment of the item.

Example 3. A payor bank receives in the mail on Monday an item drawn upon it. The item is sorted and otherwise processed on Monday and during Monday night is provisionally recorded on tape by an electronic computer as charged to the customer's account. On Tuesday a clerk examines the signature on the item and makes other checks to determine finally whether the item should be paid. If the clerk determines the signature is valid and makes a decision to pay and all processing of this item is complete, e.g., at 12 noon on Tuesday, the "process of posting" is completed at that time. If, however, the clerk determines the signature is not valid or that the item should not be paid for some other reason, the item is returned to the presenting bank and in the regular Tuesday night run of the computer the debit to the customer's account for the item is reversed or an offsetting credit entry is made. In this case, as in Example 2, there has been no determination to pay the item, no completion of the process of posting and no payment of the item.

Uniform Commercial Code Comment

Official Reasons for 1990 Change

Subsection (a) is amended to exclude checks and other items drawn on banks from its application so that the provision will not impede the speedy collection of these items. The amended subsection authorizes a collecting bank to take additional time, not in excess of two days, in a good faith effort to collect drafts drawn on nonbank payors with or without the approval of any interested party. The term "secondary parties" is deleted because it is no longer used in Articles 3 and 4. Subsection (b) is amended to make clear that the delay is excused for one of the reasons stated only if the bank exercises such diligence as the circumstances require. With the addition of references to the interruption of computer facilities and the failure of equipment, the permissible reasons for delay enumerated are made to conform to those stated in Regulation CC Section 229.38(e). The other modifications are made to conform with current legislative drafting practices, with no intent to change substance.

1990 Change

1. Sections 4–202(b), 4–214, 4–301, and 4–302 prescribe various time limits for the handling of items. These are the limits of time within which a bank, in fulfillment of its obligation to exercise ordinary care, must handle items entrusted to it for collection or payment. Under Section 4–103 they may be varied by agreement or by Federal Reserve regulations or operating circular, clearing-house rules, or the like. Subsection (a) permits a very limited extension of these time limits. It authorizes a collecting bank to take additional time in attempting to collect drafts drawn on nonbank payors with or without the approval of any interested party. The right of a collecting bank to waive time limits under subsection (a) does not apply to checks. The two-day extension can only be granted in a good faith effort to secure payment and only with respect to specific items. It cannot be exercised if the customer instructs otherwise. Thus limited the escape provision should afford

§ 4109

limited degree of flexibility in special cases but should not interfere with the overall requirement and objective of speedy collections.

2. An extension granted under subsection (a) is without discharge of drawers or indorsers. It therefore extends the times for presentment or payment as specified in Article 3.

3. Subsection (b) is another escape clause from time limits. This clause operates not only with respect to time limits imposed by the Article itself but also time limits imposed by special instructions, by agreement or by Federal regulations or operating circulars, clearing-house rules or the like. The latter time limits are "permitted" by the Code. For example, a payor bank that fails to make timely return of a dishonored item may be accountable for the amount of the item. Subsection (b) excuses a bank from this liability when its failure to meet its midnight deadline resulted from, for example, a computer breakdown that was beyond the control of the bank, so long as the bank exercised the degree of diligence that the circumstances required. In Port City State Bank v. American National Bank, 486 F.2d 196 (10th Cir.1973), the court held that a bank exercised sufficient diligence to be excused under this subsection. If delay is sought to be excused under this subsection, the bank has the burden of proof on the issue of whether it exercised "such diligence as the circumstances require." The subsection is consistent with Regulation CC, Section 229.38(e).

Cross References:

Sections 4–213(1)(c), 4–303(1)(d).

Definitional Cross References:

"Account". Section 4–104(1)(a).
"Customer". Section 4–104(1)(e).
"Item". Section 4–104(1)(g).
"Payor bank". Section 4–105(b).

§ 4110. Agreement for electronic presentment

(a) "Agreement for electronic presentment" means an agreement, clearing house rule, or Federal Reserve regulation or operating circular, providing that presentment of an item may be made by transmission of an image of an item or information describing the item ("presentment notice") rather than delivery of the item itself. The agreement may provide for procedures governing retention, presentment, payment, dishonor, and other matters concerning items subject to the agreement.

(b) Presentment of an item pursuant to an agreement for presentment is made when the presentment notice is received.

(c) If presentment is made by presentment notice, a reference to "item" or "check" in this division means the presentment notice unless the context otherwise indicates. *(Added by Stats.1992, c. 914 (S.B.833), § 16.)*

Uniform Commercial Code Comment

Official Reasons for 1990 Change

New section. See Official Comment.

1990 Change

1. "An agreement for electronic presentment" refers to an agreement under which presentment may be made to a payor bank by a presentment notice rather than by presentment of the item. Under imaging technology now under development, the presentment notice might be an image of the item. The electronic presentment agreement may provide that the item may be retained by a depositary bank, other collecting bank, or even a customer of the depositary bank, or it may provide that the item will follow the presentment notice. The identifying characteristic of an electronic presentment agreement is that presentment occurs when the presentment notice is received. "An agreement for electronic presentment" does not refer to the common case of retention of items by payor banks because the item itself is presented to the payor bank in these cases. Payor bank check retention is a matter of agreement between payor banks and their customers. Provisions on payor bank check retention are found in Section 4–406(b).

2. The assumptions under which the electronic presentment amendments are based are as follows: No bank will participate in an electronic presentment program without an agreement. These agreements may be either bilateral (Section 4–103(a)), under which two banks that frequently do business with each other may agree to depositary bank check retention, or multilateral (Section 4–103(b)), in which large segments of the banking industry may participate in such a program. In the latter case, federal or other uniform regulatory standards would likely supply the substance of the electronic presentment agreement, the application of which could be triggered by the use of some form of identifier on the item. Regulation CC, Section 229.36(c) authorizes truncation agreements but forbids them from extending return times or otherwise varying requirements of the part of Regulation CC governing check collection without the agreement of all parties interested in the check. For instance, an extension of return time could damage a depositary bank which must make funds available to its customers under mandatory availability schedules. The Expedited Funds Availability Act, 12 U.S.C. Section 4008(b)(2), directs the Federal Reserve Board to consider requiring that banks provide for check truncation.

3. The parties affected by an agreement for electronic presentment, with the exception of the customer, can be expected to protect themselves. For example, the payor bank can probably be expected to limit its risk of loss from drawer forgery by limiting the dollar amount of eligible items (Federal Reserve program), by reconcilement agreements (ABA Safekeeping program), by insurance (credit union share draft program), or by other means. Because agreements will exist, only minimal amendments are needed to make clear that the UCC does not prohibit electronic presentment.

§ 4111. Limitation of actions

An action to enforce an obligation, duty, or right arising under this division shall be commenced within three years after the cause of action accrues. *(Added by Stats.1992, c. 914 (S.B.833), § 17.)*

Uniform Commercial Code Comment

Official Reasons for 1990 Change

New section. See Official Comment.

1990 Change

This section conforms to the period of limitations set by Section 3–118(g) for actions for breach of warranty and to enforce other obligations, duties or rights arising under Article 3. Bracketing "cause of action" recognizes that some states use a different term, such as "claim for relief."

Cross References

Actions commenced prior to Jan. 1, 1993, application of this section, see Commercial Code § 16103.

CHAPTER 2. COLLECTION OF ITEMS: DEPOSITARY AND COLLECTING BANKS

Section
4201. Agency status of collecting bank; application of division; item indorsed "pay any bank".
4202. Standard of care; scope of liability.
4203. Instructions; liability.
4204. Methods of sending and presenting.
4205. Delivery of item to depositary bank; effect.
4206. Transfer Between Banks.
4207. Transfer of item by customer or collecting bank; warranties; damages for breach.

Section
4208. Drawee payment or acceptance of unaccepted draft; warranties; damages for breach; payment of dishonored draft.
4209. Encoded information; agreements for electronic presentment; warranties.
4210. Security interest of collecting bank.
4211. Holder in due course; status of bank.
4212. Items not payable by, through or at bank; presentment of notice.
4213. Settlement by bank.
4214. Revocation of settlement; return of item; right to charge back.
4215. Final payment by payor bank; credits available for withdrawal.
4216. Insolvency and preference.

Transitional Provisions

Effective date and transitional provisions for sections in Division 4 affected by Stats.1992, c. 914, see Commercial Code § 16101 et seq.

§ 4201. Agency status of collecting bank; application of division; item indorsed "pay any bank"

(a) Unless a contrary intent clearly appears and * * * <u>before</u> the time that a settlement given by a collecting bank for an item is or becomes final * * * the bank, <u>with respect to the item,</u> is an agent or subagent of the owner of the item and any settlement given for the item is provisional. This provision applies regardless of the form of indorsement or lack of indorsement and even though credit given for the item is subject to immediate withdrawal as of right or is in fact withdrawn; but the continuance of ownership of an item by its owner and any rights of the owner to proceeds of the item are subject to rights of a collecting bank, such as those resulting from outstanding advances on the item and * * * rights of <u>recoupment or</u> setoff. If an item is handled by banks for purposes of presentment, payment, collection, <u>or return,</u> the relevant provisions of this division apply even though action of <u>the</u> parties clearly establishes that a particular bank <u>has</u> purchased the item and is the owner of it.

(b) After an item has been indorsed with the words "pay any bank" or the like, only a bank may acquire the rights of a holder * * * <u>until</u> the item has been * * * <u>either of the following:</u>

<u>(1) Returned</u> to the customer initiating collection * * *<u>;</u>

* * * <u>(2)</u> Specially <u>indorsed</u> by a bank to a person who is not a bank. *(Stats.1963, c. 819, § 4201. Amended by Stats.1992, c. 914 (S.B.833), § 18.)*

California Code Comment

By John A. Bohn and Charles J. Williams

Prior California Law

1. Subdivision (1) is new.

The last sentence of subdivision (1) expresses the principle also present in other Divisions that the rules and answers to major problems should exist without reference to status or ownership (e.g. title and risk of loss in Division 2) to the extent possible. Official Comment 1.

At the same time, subdivision (1) attempts to resolve the problem of whether the bank which receives an item takes it as a collecting agent or as an owner. The answer is important in solving residual problems such as fixing the risk of loss, e.g. availability of the item to creditors, loss in case of insolvency. Prior case law from the various jurisdictions on status of a bank taking an item was irreconcilable. See Official Comment 1. The rule under subdivision (1) is that a bank taking an item is presumably an agent and settlement given is presumptively provisional. The agency status terminates when settlement is final. At this point the bank becomes the customer's debtor. See Duggan v. Hopkins, 147 Cal.App.2d 67, 304 P.2d 823 (1956).

The determination of this status is not dependent upon the type of indorsement or whether the bank gives credit for the item to the transferor which is subject to immediate withdrawal. However, if the owner draws upon or uses this credit, the collecting bank has a security interest in the item under Commercial Code § 4208.

2. Subdivision (2) is new statutory law but is in accord with prior California law on the nature of indorsements such as "pay any bank." This was a restrictive indorsement under former Civil Code § 3117 and under the case law. In Nordin v. Eagle Rock State Bank, 139 Cal.App. 584, 34 P.2d 490 (1934), "pay to the order of any bank or banker" was held to be a restrictive indorsement. Similar indorsements were held to be restrictive in Crocker-Woolworth Nat. Bank v. Nevada Bank, 139 Cal. 564, 73 P. 456 (1903) ("pay only through clearing house") and Christian v. California Bank, 30 Cal.2d 421, 182 P.2d 554 (1947) (where indorsement named particular bank). This indorsement is also restrictive under Commercial Code § 3205.

An indorsement to a bank is the designation of that bank as an agent for collection and any subsequent indorsee holds as trustee of the owner. Nordin v. Eagle Rock State Bank, supra. Under prior California law the bank was regarded as a holder in due course of a deposit for collection when it "allows the depositor to draw against the deposit", the bank thereby paying value. Anglo-Calif. Trust Co. v. French American Bank, 108 Cal.App. 354, 291 Pac. 621 (1930).

3. The purpose of subdivision (2) is to protect the rights of ownership of the item. In effect it makes an indorsement "pay any bank" or the like restrictive. See Commercial Code §§ 3205 and 3206 concerning nature and effect of restrictive indorsements. Since only a bank may be a holder under this subdivision, a transfer is ineffectual if by anyone other than the bank who might improperly obtain the instrument. If the item is returned to the customer under subdivision (2)(a), he assumes his original rights as owner and may cancel the indorsement. If the item is indorsed specially under subdivision (2)(b), the special indorsee then takes as a holder. However, if a bank so indorses to one not a bank, that bank is liable for loss resulting if the transfer was in bad faith or with lack of ordinary care. Official Comment 7.

4. The effect of subdivision (2) in simplifying the bank collection process is commented upon by a California State Bar Committee as follows:

"Under section 14021 [sic] [4201] only a bank could acquire a holder's rights after an item had been indorsed 'pay any bank,' until the item is indorsed specially to a person other than a bank or returned to the customer. This would permit a bank to lock an item into the collection process by one such indorsement at the outset." California State Bar Committee on the Commercial Code, A Special Report, The Uniform Commercial Code, 37 Calif. State Bar J. (March–April, 1962) 166.

Changes from U.C.C. (1962 Official Text)

5. This is section 4–201 of the Official Text without change.

Uniform Commercial Code Comment

Official Reasons for 1990 Change

Subsection (a) is amended to delete the cross references to former Sections 4–211, 4–212 and 4–213. The reason for the deletion is to remove any implication that final settlement is determined only by these provisions. Sections 4–213(c) and (d) and 4–215(c) provide when final settlement occurs with respect to certain kinds of settlements, but these provisions are not intended to be exclusive. Since it is impossible to contemplate all the kinds of settlements that will be utilized, no attempt is made in Article 4 to provide when settlement is final in all cases. "Recoupment" is added to the second sentence to clarify the collecting bank's rights against the item or its proceeds. Terms like "valid" or "binding" have been deleted entirely from Article 4 as superfluous. "Or return" is added to the third sentence to make clear that the effect of the provision is not restricted to the forward collection activities of banks but also extends to their acts in returning items. The other modifications are made to conform with current legislative drafting practices, with no intent to change substance.

1990 Change

1. This section states certain basic rules of the bank collection process. One basic rule, appearing in the last sentence of subsection (a), is that, to the extent applicable, the provisions of the Article govern without regard to whether a bank handling an item owns the item or is an agent for collection. Historically, much time has been spent and effort expended in determining or attempting to determine whether a bank was a purchaser of an item or merely an agent for collection. See discussion of this subject and cases cited in 11 A.L.R. 1043, 16 A.L.R. 1084, 42 A.L.R. 492, 68 A.L.R. 725, 99 A.L.R. 486. See also Section 4 of the American Bankers Association Bank Collection Code. The general approach of Article 4, similar to that of other articles, is to provide, within reasonable limits, rules or answers to major problems known to exist in the bank collection process without regard to questions of status and ownership but to keep general principles such as status and ownership available to cover residual areas not covered by specific rules. In line with this approach, the last sentence of subsection (a) says in effect that Article 4 applies to practically every item moving through banks for the purpose of presentment, payment or collection.

2. Within this general rule of broad coverage, the first two sentences of subsection (a) state a rule of agency status. "Unless a contrary intent clearly appears" the status of a collecting bank is that of an agent or subagent for the owner of the item. Although as indicated in Comment 1 it is much less important under Article 4 to determine status than has been the case heretofore, status may have importance in some residual areas not covered by specific rules. Further, since status has been considered so important in the past, to omit all reference to it might cause confusion. The status of agency "applies regardless of the form of indorsement or lack of indorsement and even though credit given for the item is subject to immediate withdrawal as of right or is in fact withdrawn." Thus questions heretofore litigated as to whether ordinary indorsements "for deposit," "for collection" or in blank have the effect of creating an agency status or a purchase, no longer have significance in varying the prima facie rule of agency. Similarly, the nature of the credit given for an item or whether it is subject to immediate withdrawal as of right or is in fact withdrawn, does not alter the agency status. See A.L.R. references supra in Comment 1.

A contrary intent can change agency status but this must be clear. An example of a clear contrary intent would be if collateral papers established or the item bore a legend stating that the item was sold absolutely to the depositary bank.

3. The prima facie agency status of collecting banks is consistent with prevailing law and practice today. Section 2 of the American Bankers Association Bank Collection Code so provided. Legends on deposit tickets, collection letters and acknowledgments of items and Federal Reserve operating circulars consistently so provide. The status is consistent with rights of charge-back (Section 4–214 and Section 11 of the ABA Code) and risk of loss in the event of insolvency (Section 4–216 and Section 13 of the ABA Code). The right of charge-back with respect to checks is limited by Regulation CC, Section 226.36(d).

4. Affirmative statement of a prima facie agency status for collecting banks requires certain limitations and qualifications. Under current practices substantially all bank collections sooner or later merge into bank credits, at least if collection is effected. Usually, this takes place within a few days of the initiation of collection. An intermediary bank receives final collection and evidences the result of its collection by a "credit" on its books to the depositary bank. The depositary bank evidences the results of its collection by a "credit" in the account of its customer. As used in these instances the term "credit" clearly indicates a debtor-credit relationship. At some stage in the bank collection process the agency status of a collecting bank changes to that of debtor, a debtor of its customer. Usually at about the same time it also becomes a creditor for the amount of the item, a creditor of some intermediary payor or other bank. Thus the collection is completed, all agency aspects are terminated and the identity of the item has become completely merged in bank accounts, that of the customer with the depositary bank and that of one bank with another.

Although Section 4–215(a) provides that an item is finally paid when the payor bank takes or fails to take certain action with respect to the item, the final payment of the item may or may not result in the simultaneous final settlement for the item in the case of all prior parties. If a series of provisional debits and credits for the item have been entered in accounts between banks, the final payment of the item by the payor bank may result in the automatic firming up of all these provisional debits and credits under Section 4–215(c), and the consequent receipt of final settlement for the item by each collecting bank and the customer of the depositary bank simultaneously with such action of the payor bank. However, if the payor bank or some intermediary bank accounts for the item with a remittance draft, the next prior bank usually does not receive final settlement for the item until the remittance draft finally clears. See Section 4–213(c). The first sentence of subsection (a) provides that the agency status of a collecting bank (whether intermediary or depositary) continues until the settlement given by it for the item is or becomes final. In the case of the series of provisional credits covered by Section 4–215(c), this could be simultaneously with the final payment of the item by the payor bank. In cases in which remittance drafts are used or in straight noncash collections, this would not be until the times specified in Sections 4–213(c) and 4–215(d). With respect to checks Regulation CC Sections 229.31(c), 229.32(b) and 229.36(d) provide that all settlements between banks are final in both the forward collection and return of checks.

Under Section 4–213(a) settlements for items may be made by any means agreed to by the parties. Since it is impossible to contemplate all the kinds of settlements that will be utilized, no attempt is made in Article 4 to provide when settlement is final in all cases. The guiding principle is that settlements should be final when the presenting person has received usable funds. Section 4–213(c) and (d) and Section 4–215(c) provide when final settlement occurs with respect to certain kinds of settlement, but these provisions are not intended to be exclusive.

A number of practical results flow from the rule continuing the agency status of a collecting bank until its settlement for the item is or becomes final, some of which are specifically set forth in this Article. One is that risk of loss continues in the owner of the item rather than the agent bank. See Section 4–214. Offsetting rights favorable to the owner are that pending such final settlement, the owner has the preference rights of Section 4–216 and the direct rights of Section 4–302 against the payor bank. It also follows from this rule that the dollar limitations of Federal Deposit Insurance are measured by the claim of the owner of the item rather than that of the collecting bank. With respect to checks, rights of the parties in insolvency are determined by Regulation CC Section 229.39 and the liability of a bank handling a check to a subsequent bank that does not receive payment because of suspension of payments by another bank is stated in Regulation CC Section 229.35(b).

5. In those cases in which some period of time elapses between the final payment of the item by the payor bank and the time that the settlement of the collecting bank is or becomes final, e.g., if the payor bank or an intermediary bank accounts for the item with a remittance draft or in straight noncash collections, the continuance of the agency status of the collecting bank necessarily carries with it the continuance of the owner's status as principal. The second sentence of subsection (a) provides that whatever rights the owner has to proceeds of the item are subject to the rights of collecting banks for outstanding advances on the item and other valid rights, if any. The rule provides a sound rule to govern cases of attempted attachment of proceeds of a noncash item in the hands of the payor bank as property of the absent owner. If a collecting bank has made an advance on an item which is still outstanding, its right to obtain reimbursement for this advance should be superior to the rights of the owner to the proceeds or to the rights of a creditor of the owner. An intentional crediting of proceeds of an item to the account of a prior bank known to be insolvent, for the purpose of acquiring a right of setoff, would not produce a valid setoff. See 8 Zollman, Banks and Banking (1936) Sec. 5443.

6. This Section and Article 4 as a whole represent an intentional abandonment of the approach to bank collection problems appearing in Section 4 of the American Bankers Association Bank Collection Code. Because the tremendous volume of items handled makes impossible the examination by all banks of all indorsements on all items and thus in fact this examination is not made, except perhaps by depositary banks, it is unrealistic to base the rights and duties of all banks in the collection chain on variations in the form of indorsements. It is anomalous to provide throughout the ABA Code that the prima facie status of

collecting banks is that of agent or sub-agent but in Section 4 to provide that subsequent holders (sub-agents) shall have the right to rely on the presumption that the bank of deposit (the primary agent) is the owner of the item. It is unrealistic, particularly in this background, to base rights and duties on status of agent or owner. Thus Section 4–201 makes the pertinent provisions of Article 4 applicable to substantially all items handled by banks for presentment, payment or collection, recognizes the prima facie status of most banks as agents, and then seeks to state appropriate limits and some attributes to the general rules so expressed.

7. Subsection (b) protects the ownership rights with respect to an item indorsed "pay any bank or banker" or in similar terms of a customer initiating collection or of any bank acquiring a security interest under Section 4–210, in the event the item is subsequently acquired under improper circumstances by a person who is not a bank and transferred by that person to another person, whether or not a bank. Upon return to the customer initiating collection of an item so indorsed, the indorsement may be cancelled (Section 3–207). A bank holding an item so indorsed may transfer the item out of banking channels by special indorsement; however, under Section 4–103(e), the bank would be liable to the owner of the item for any loss resulting therefrom if the transfer had been made in bad faith or with lack of ordinary care. If briefer and more simple forms of bank indorsements are developed under Section 4–206 (e.g., the use of bank transit numbers in lieu of present lengthy forms of bank indorsements), a depositary bank having the transit number "X100" could make subsection (b) operative by indorsements such as "Pay any bank—X100." Regulation CC Section 229.35(c) states the effect of an indorsement on a check by a bank.

Uniform Commercial Code Comment

Prior Uniform Statutory Provision:

None; but see Sections 2 and 4 of the American Bankers Association Bank Collection Code.

Purposes:

1. This section states certain basic rules and presumptions of the bank collection process. One basic rule, appearing in the last sentence of subsection (1), is that, to the extent applicable, the provisions of the Article govern without regard to whether a bank handling an item owns the item or is an agent for collection. Historically, much time has been spent and effort expended in determining or attempting to determine whether a bank was a purchaser of an item or merely an agent for collection. See discussion of this subject and cases cited in 11 A.L.R. 1043, 16 A.L.R. 1084, 42 A.L.R. 492, 68 A.L.R. 725, 99 A.L.R. 486. See also Section 4 of the American Bankers Association Bank Collection Code. The general approach of Article 4, similar to that of other articles, is to provide, within reasonable limits, rules or answers to major problems known to exist in the bank collection process without regard to questions of status and ownership but to keep general principles such as status and ownership available to cover residual areas not covered by specific rules. In line with this approach, the last sentence of subsection (1) says in effect that Article 4 applies to practically every item moving through banks for the purpose of presentment, payment or collection.

2. Within this general rule of broad coverage, the first two sentences of subsection (1) state a rule of status in terms of a strong presumption. "Unless a contrary intent clearly appears" the status of a collecting bank is that of an agent or sub-agent for the owner of the item. Although as indicated in Comment 1 it is much less important under Article 4 to determine status than has been the case heretofore, such status may have importance in some residual areas not covered by specific rules. Further, where status has been considered so important in the past, to omit all reference to it might cause confusion. The presumption of agency "applies regardless of the form of indorsement or lack of indorsement and even though credit given for the item is subject to immediate withdrawal as of right or is in fact withdrawn". Thus questions heretofore litigated as to whether ordinary indorsements "for deposit", "for collection" or in blank have the effect of creating an agency status or a purchase, no longer have significance in varying the prima facie rule of agency. Similarly, the nature of the credit given for an item or whether it is subject to immediate withdrawal as of right or is in fact withdrawn, do not rebut the general presumption. See A.L.R. references supra in Comment 1.

A contrary intent can rebut the presumption but this must be clear. An example of a clear contrary intent would be if collateral papers established or the item bore a legend stating that the item was sold absolutely to the depositary bank.

3. The prima facie agency status of collecting banks is consistent with prevailing law and practice today. Section 2 of the American Bankers Association Bank Collection Code so provides. Legends on deposit tickets, collection letters and acknowledgments of items and Federal Reserve operating letters consistently so provide. The status is consistent with charge-back (Section 4–212 and Section 11 of the ABA Code) and risk of loss in the event of insolvency (Section 4–214 and Section 13 of the ABA Code).

4. Affirmative statement of a prima facie agency status for collecting banks requires certain limitations and qualifications. Under current practices substantially all bank collections sooner or later merge into bank credits, at least if collection is effected. Usually, this takes place within a few days of the initiation of collection. An intermediary bank receives final collection and evidences the result of its collection by a "credit" on its books to the depositary bank. The depositary bank evidences the results of its collection by a "credit" in the account of its customer. As used in these instances the term "credit" clearly indicates a debtor-creditor relationship. At some stage in the bank collection process the agency status of a collecting bank changes to that of debtor, a debtor of its customer. Usually at about the same time it also becomes a creditor for the amount of the item, a creditor of some intermediary, payor or other bank. Thus the collection is completed, all agency aspects are terminated and the identity of the item has become completely merged in bank accounts, that of the customer with the depositary bank and that of one bank with another.

Although Section 4–213(1) provides that an item is finally paid when the payor bank takes certain action with respect to the item such final payment of the item may or may not result in the simultaneous *final settlement* for the item in the case of all prior parties. If a series of provisional debits and credits for the item have been entered in accounts between banks, the final payment of the item by the payor bank may result in the automatic firming up of all these provisional debits and credits under Section 4–213(2), and the consequent receipt of final settlement for the item by each collecting bank and the customer of the depositary bank simultaneously with such action of the payor bank. However, if the payor bank or some intermediary bank accounts for the item with a remittance draft, the next prior bank usually does not receive final settlement for the item until such remittance draft finally clears. See Section 4–211(3)(a). The first sentence of subsection (1) provides that the agency status of a collecting bank (whether intermediary or depositary) continues until the settlement *given by it for the item* is or becomes final, referring to Sections 4–211(3), 4–212, and 4–213. In the case of the series of provisional credits covered by Section 4–213(2), this could be simultaneously with the final payment of the item by the payor bank. In cases where remittance drafts are used or in straight non-cash collections, this would not be until the times specified in Sections 4–211(3) and 4–213(3).

A number of practical results flow from this rule continuing the agency status of a collecting bank until its settlement for the item is or becomes final, some of which are specifically set forth in this Article. One is that risk of loss continues in the owner of the item rather than the agent bank. See Section 4–212. Off-setting rights favorable to the owner are that pending such final settlement, the owner has the preference rights of Section 4–214 and the direct rights of Section 4–302 against the payor bank. It also follows from this rule that the dollar limitations of Federal Deposit Insurance are measured by the claim of the owner of the item rather than that of the collecting bank.

5. In those cases where some period of time elapses between the final payment of the item by the payor bank and the time that the settlement of the collecting bank is or becomes final, e.g., where the payor bank or an intermediary bank accounts for the item with a remittance draft or in straight non-cash collections, the continuance of the agency status of the collecting bank necessarily carries with it the continuance of the owner's status as principal. The second sentence of subsection (1) provides that whatever rights the owner has to proceeds of the item are subject to the rights of collecting banks for outstanding advances on the item and other valid rights, if any. The rule provides a sound rule to govern cases of attempted attachment of proceeds of a non-cash item in the hands of the payor bank as property of the absent owner. If a collecting bank has made an advance on an item which is still outstanding, its right to obtain reimbursement for this advance should be superior to the rights of the owner to the proceeds or to the rights of a creditor of the owner. The phrase "other valid rights, if any"

is broad enough to cover legitimate rights of set-off of accounts between banks without attempting to provide that all set-offs may be valid. An intentional crediting of proceeds of an item to the account of a prior bank known to be insolvent, for the purpose of acquiring a right of set-off, would not produce a valid set-off. See 8 Zollman, Banks and Banking (1936) Sec. 5443.

6. This section and Article 4 as a whole represent an intentional abandonment of the approach to bank collection problems appearing in Section 4 of the American Bankers Association Bank Collection Code. Where the tremendous volume of items handled makes impossible the examination by all banks of all indorsements on all items and where in fact this examination is not made, except perhaps by depositary banks, it is unrealistic to base the rights and duties of all banks in the collection chain on variations in the form of indorsements. It is anomalous to provide throughout the ABA Code that the prima facie status of collecting banks is that of agent or sub-agent but in Section 4 to provide that subsequent holders (sub-agents) shall have the right to rely on the presumption that the bank of deposit (the primary agent) is the owner of the item. It is unrealistic, particularly in this background, to base rights and duties on status of agent or owner. This Section 4–201 makes the pertinent provisions of Article 4 applicable to substantially all items handled by banks for presentment, payment or collection, recognizes the prima facie status of most banks as agents, and then seeks to state appropriate limits and some attributes to the general rules and presumptions so expressed.

7. Subsection (2) protects the ownership rights with respect to an item indorsed "pay any bank or banker" or in similar terms of a customer initiating collection or of any bank acquiring a security interest under Section 4–208, in the event the item is subsequently acquired under improper circumstances by a person who is not a bank and transferred by that person to another person, whether or not a bank. Upon return to the customer initiating collection of an item so indorsed, the indorsement may be cancelled (Section 3–208). A bank holding an item so indorsed may transfer the item out of banking channels by special indorsement; however, under Section 4–103(5), such bank would be liable to the owner of the item for any loss resulting therefrom if the transfer had been made in bad faith or with lack of ordinary care. If briefer and more simple forms of bank indorsements are developed under Section 4–206 (e.g., the use of bank transit numbers in lieu of present lengthy forms of bank indorsements), a depositary bank having the transit number "X100" could make subsection (2) operative by indorsements such as "Pay any bank—X100".

Cross References:

Sections 3–206, 3–208, 4–103, 4–206, 4–208, 4–212, 4–213, 4–214, 4–302.

Definitional Cross References:

"Bank". Section 1–201.
"Collecting bank". Section 4–105.
"Customer". Section 4–104.
"Depositary bank". Section 4–105.
"Holder". Section 1–201.
"Item". Section 4–104.
"Indorsements". Sections 3–202, 3–204, 3–205 and 3–206.
"Person". Section 1–201.
"Settle". Section 4–104.

Cross References

Application of rules on restrictive indorsements on indorsements described in this section, see Commercial Code § 3206.
Bad faith or lack of ordinary care, liability of bank, see Commercial Code § 4103.
Charge-back or refund upon provisional settlement, see Commercial Code § 4214.
Discharge of parties by reacquisition, see Commercial Code § 3207.
Insolvency and preference, see Commercial Code § 4216.
Late return of item, responsibility of payor bank, see Commercial Code § 4302.
Media of remittance, see Commercial Code § 4211.
Negotiation, see Commercial Code § 3202.
Payment, discharge of obligation, see Commercial Code § 3602.
Payment of items by payor bank, finality, see Commercial Code § 4215.

Restrictive indorsements,
  Generally, see Commercial Code § 3206.
  Effect, see Commercial Code § 3206.
  Rules applicable, item indorsed "pay any bank", see Commercial Code § 3206.
Security interest of collecting bank, see Commercial Code § 4210.
Special indorsement, see Commercial Code § 3205.
Transfer between banks, see Commercial Code § 4206.

§ 4202. Standard of care; scope of liability

(a) A collecting bank * * * <u>shall exercise</u> ordinary care in <u>all of the following:</u>

(1) Presenting an item or sending it for presentment * * *<u>.</u>

(2) Sending notice of dishonor or nonpayment or returning an item other than a documentary draft to the bank's transferor after learning that the item has not been paid or accepted, as the case may be * * *<u>.</u>

(3) Settling for an item when the bank receives final settlement * * *<u>.</u>

* * *

(4) Notifying its transferor of any loss or delay in transit within a reasonable time after discovery thereof.

(b) A collecting bank <u>exercises ordinary care under subdivision (a) by</u> taking proper action before its midnight deadline following receipt of an item, notice * * *, or settlement. Taking proper action within a reasonably longer time may * * * <u>constitute the exercise of ordinary care,</u> but the bank has the burden of * * * establishing <u>timeliness.</u>

(c) Subject to <u>paragraph (1)</u> of subdivision <u>(a)</u>, a bank is not liable for the insolvency, neglect, misconduct, mistake<u>,</u> or default of another bank or person or for loss or destruction of * * * an item in * * * the possession of others <u>or in transit</u>. (Stats.1963, c. 819, § 4202. Amended by Stats.1992, c. 914 (S.B.833), § 19.)

California Code Comment

By John A. Bohn and Charles J. Williams

Prior California Law

1. Subdivision (1) states the basic responsibilities of the collecting bank. Official Comment 1. Ordinary care is not defined but the standard of care it commands is the same as that used in tort law. Official Comment 4 to Commercial Code § 4103.

This subdivision is new statutory law but is in accord with pre Commercial Code cases holding a bank liable for negligence in performing the acts listed in subdivision (1). For example see Kriste v. International Sav. and Exchange Bank, 17 Cal.App. 301, 119 Pac. 666 (1911) holding a bank negligent in delaying to give notice of dishonor. Davis v. First Nat. Bank, 118 Cal. 600, 50 Pac. 666 (1897); First Nat. Bank of Ely v. Hamaker, 83 Cal.App. 670, 257 Pac. 454 (1927).

2. Subdivision (2) is similar to former Financial Code § 1014 which provided that an item received and allowed provisional credit and drawn on shall be forwarded for collection before midnight of the bank's next business day following the day of receipt. See Official Comment 3.

3. Subdivision (3) is similar to former Financial Code § 1016 which limited the liability of a bank for loss in forwarding an item in the usual course of business. This incorporates the so-called "Massachusetts rule" that a bank is not responsible for the action of subsequent banks in the collection chain. Official Comment 4.

DEPOSITARY AND COLLECTING BANKS § 4202

Changes from U.C.C. (1962 Official Text)

4. In subdivision (1)(b) the optional language contained in the 1962 Official Text "or directly to the depository bank under subsection (2) of Section 4–212." which follows the phrase "bank's transferor" is omitted. This corresponds with the deletion of subdivision (2) of Section 4–212 of the 1962 Official Text from the California version of the Commercial Code. Both of these provisions refer to direct returns and are optional provisions in the Official Text because direct returns are not an established bank practice in every state. Both of these provisions of the Official Text are omitted to conform to California banking practice. The supplemental report of the Uniform Commercial Code committee of the State Bar as a result of further consideration since enactment by New York recommended that the optional language be retained.

5. In subdivision (3) "inability to obtain repossession of" was added to the California version of the Commercial Code. The provision in former Financial Code § 1016(c) that a bank is not liable for the "inability to obtain repossession of the item" is specifically carried over into subdivision (3). The purpose is "to make clear that a bank is not liable if unable to obtain repossession of an item, as set forth in [former] section 1016(c) of the Financial Code". Recommendations and Comments of the California Bankers Association, Sixth Progress Report to the Legislature by Senate Fact Finding Committee on Judiciary (1959–1961) Part 1, The Uniform Commercial Code, p. 406.

Uniform Commercial Code Comment
Official Reasons for 1990 Change

The term "timely" is substituted for "seasonable" throughout the section. The bracketed material in paragraph (2) of subsection (a) is deleted because the provision to which it refers in former Section 4–212 is deleted. Paragraph (d) of former subsection (1) is deleted because Article 4 has no requirement of protest. Subsection (b) is a restatement of former subsection (2). The other modifications are made to conform with current legislative drafting practices, with no intent to change substance.

1990 Change

1. Subsection (a) states the basic responsibilities of a collecting bank. Of course, under Section 1–203 a collecting bank is subject to the standard requirement of good faith. By subsection (a) it must also use ordinary care in the exercise of its basic collection tasks. By Section 4–103(a) neither requirement may be disclaimed.

2. If the bank makes presentment itself, subsection (a)(1) requires ordinary care with respect both to the time and manner of presentment. (Sections 3–501 and 4–212.) If it forwards the item to be presented the subsection requires ordinary care with respect to routing (Section 4–204), and also in the selection of intermediary banks or other agents.

3. Subsection (a) describes types of basic action with respect to which a collecting bank must use ordinary care. Subsection (b) deals with the time for taking action. It first prescribes the general standard for timely action, namely, for items received on Monday, proper action (such as forwarding or presenting) on Monday or Tuesday is timely. Although under current "production line" operations banks customarily move items along on regular schedules substantially briefer than two days, the subsection states an outside time within which a bank may know it has taken timely action. To provide flexibility from this standard norm, the subsection further states that action within a reasonably longer time may be timely but the bank has the burden of proof. In the case of time items, action after the midnight deadline, but sufficiently in advance of maturity for proper presentation, is a clear example of a "reasonably longer time" that is timely. The standard of requiring action not later than Tuesday in the case of Monday items is also subject to possibilities of variation under the general provisions of Section 4–103, or under the special provisions regarding time of receipt of items (Section 4–108), and regarding delays (Section 4–109). This subsection (b) deals only with collecting banks. The time limits applicable to payor banks appear in Sections 4–301 and 4–302.

4. At common law the so-called New York collection rule subjected the initial collecting bank to liability for the actions of subsequent banks in the collection chain; the so-called Massachusetts rule was that each bank, subject to the duty of selecting proper intermediaries, was liable only for its own negligence. Subsection (c) adopts the Massachusetts rule. But since this is stated to be subject to subsection (a)(1) a collecting bank remains responsible for using ordinary care in selecting properly qualified intermediary banks and agents and in giving proper instructions to them. Regulation CC, Section 229.36(d) states the liability of a bank during the forward collection of checks.

Uniform Commercial Code Comment
Prior Uniform Statutory Provision:

None; but see Sections 5 and 6, American Bankers Association Bank Collection Code.

Purposes:

1. Subsection (1) states the basic responsibilities of a collecting bank. Of course, under Section 1–203 a collecting bank is subject to the standard requirement of good faith. By subsection (1) it must also use ordinary care in the exercise of its basic collection tasks. By Section 4–103(1) neither requirement may be disclaimed.

2. If the bank makes presentment itself, subsection 1(a) requires ordinary care with respect both to the time and manner of presentment. (Sections 3–503, 3–504, 4–210.) If it forwards the item to be presented the subsection requires ordinary care with respect to routing (Section 4–204), and also in the selection of intermediary banks or other agents.

3. Subsection (1) describes *types* of basic action with respect to which a collecting bank must use ordinary care. Subsection (2) deals with the *time* for taking action. It first prescribes the general standard for seasonable action, namely, for items received on Monday, proper action (such as forwarding or presenting) on Monday or Tuesday is seasonable. Although under current "production line" operations banks customarily move items along on regular schedules substantially briefer than two days, the subsection states an outside time within which a bank may know it has acted seasonably. To provide flexibility from this standard norm, the subsection further states that action within a reasonably longer time may be seasonable but the bank has the burden of proof. In the case of time items, action after the midnight deadline, but sufficiently in advance of maturity for proper presentation, is a clear example of a "reasonably longer time" that is seasonable. The standard of requiring action not later than Tuesday in the case of Monday items is also subject to possibilities of variation under the general provisions of Section 4–103, or under the special provisions regarding time of receipt of items (Section 4–107), and regarding delays (Section 4–108). This subsection (2) deals only with collecting banks. The time limits applicable to payor banks appear in Sections 4–301 and 4–302.

4. At common law the so-called New York collection rule subjected the initial collecting bank to liability for the actions of subsequent banks in the collection chain; the so-called Massachusetts rule was that each bank, subject to the duty of selecting proper intermediaries, was liable only for its own negligence. Subsection (3) adopts the Massachusetts rule. But since this is stated to be subject to subsection (1)(a) a collecting bank remains responsible for using ordinary care in selecting properly qualified intermediary banks and agents and in giving proper instructions to them.

Cross References:

Sections 1–203, 4–103, 4–107, 4–108, 4–301, and 4–302.

Definitional Cross References:

"Collecting bank". Section 4–105.
"Depositary bank". Section 4–105.
"Documentary draft". Section 4–104.
"Item". Section 4–104.
"Midnight deadline". Section 4–104.
"Presentment". Article 3, Part 5.
"Protest". Section 3–505.

Cross References

Business days, banks, see Civil Code § 9.
Deferred posting of items, see Commercial Code § 4301.
Delays, see Commercial Code § 4109.
Duties of collecting agent, see Civil Code § 2021.
Forwarding of item, see Commercial Code § 4204.
Improperly made payments, recovery by payor bank, see Commercial Code § 4301.
Late return of item, responsibility of payor bank, see Commercial Code § 4302.

Liability of acceptor of negotiable instruments, see Commercial Code § 3413.
Obligation of good faith, see Commercial Code § 1203.
Ordinary care,
    Acts constituting, see Commercial Code § 4103.
    Responsibility for want of, see Civil Code § 1714.
Payment, what may be accepted in, see Commercial Code § 4211.
Presentment,
    By notice, see Commercial Code § 4212.
    Manner, see Commercial Code § 3501.
    Necessity, see Commercial Code § 3501.
    Time, see Commercial Code § 3501.
Protest, see Commercial Code § 3505.
Provisional credit for item, see Commercial Code § 4201.
Receipt of items, time, see Commercial Code § 4108.
Right of charge-back or refund, see Commercial Code § 4214.
Settlement, recovery of payment by return, see Commercial Code § 4301.

§ 4203. Instructions; liability

Subject to * * * Division 3 (commencing with Section 3101) concerning conversion of instruments (Section 3420) and * * * restrictive indorsements (Section 3206), only a collecting bank's transferor can give instructions that affect the bank or constitute notice to it, and a collecting bank is not liable to prior parties for any action taken pursuant to the instructions or in accordance with any agreement with its transferor. *(Stats.1963, c. 819, § 4203. Amended by Stats.1992, c. 914 (S.B.833), § 20.)*

California Code Comment

By John A. Bohn and Charles J. Williams

Prior California Law

1. This section is new. By its terms, a collecting bank need not determine the authority of its transferor. See the Official Comment. The rule that the collecting bank need follow only its transferor's instructions is subject to two exceptions: its liability for conversion under Commercial Code § 3419; and the effect of remote restrictive indorsement if it is also the depository bank.

2. The provision limiting the liability of the collecting bank is in accord with the general rule in California that a forwarding bank is not liable for the negligence of its correspondent bank as a sub-agent for collection. First Nat. Bank of Ely v. Hamaker, 83 Cal.App. 670, 257 Pac. 454 (1927) and Luckehe v. First Nat. Bank of Marysville, 193 Cal. 184, 223 Pac. 547 (1924). Earlier cases applied the principle that a bank receiving an item for collection is an independent contractor and as such is liable for the negligence of the correspondent bank. San Francisco Nat. Bank v. American Nat. Bank, 5 Cal.App. 408, 90 Pac. 558 (1907); Smith v. Nat. Bank of D. O. Mills & Co., 191 Fed. 226 (1911).

Changes from U.C.C. (1962 Official Text)

3. This is section 4–203 of the Official Text without change.

Uniform Commercial Code Comment
Official Reasons for 1990 Change

Article 4 no longer has provisions on restrictive indorsements; hence, the reference to "this Article" is deleted. The other modifications are made to conform with current legislative drafting practices, with no intent to change substance.

1990 Change

This section adopts a "chain of command" theory which renders it unnecessary for an intermediary or collecting bank to determine whether its transferor is "authorized" to give the instructions. Equally the bank is not put on notice of any "revocation of authority" or "lack of authority" by notice received from any other person. The desirability of speed in the collection process and the fact that, by reason of advances made, the transferor may have the paramount interest in the item requires the rule.

The section is made subject to the provisions of Article 3 concerning conversion of instruments (Section 3–420) and restrictive indorsements (Section 3–206). Of course instructions from or an agreement with its transferor does not relieve a collecting bank of its general obligation to exercise good faith and ordinary care. See Section 4–103(a). If in any particular case a bank has exercised good faith and ordinary care and is relieved of responsibility by reason of instructions of or an agreement with its transferor, the owner of the item may still have a remedy for loss against the transferor (another bank) if such transferor has given wrongful instructions.

The rules of the section are applied only to collecting banks. Payor banks always have the problem of making proper payment of an item; whether such payment is proper should be based upon all of the rules of Articles 3 and 4 and all of the facts of any particular case, and should not be dependent exclusively upon instructions from or an agreement with a person presenting the item.

Uniform Commercial Code Comment

Prior Uniform Statutory Provision:

None; but see Section 2 of the American Bankers Association Bank Collection Code.

Purposes:

This Section adopts a "chain of command" theory which renders it unnecessary for an intermediary or collecting bank to determine whether its transferor is "authorized" to give the instructions. Equally the bank is not put on notice of any "revocation of authority" or "lack of authority" by notice received from any other person. The desirability of speed in the collection process and the fact that, by reason of advances made, the transferor may have the paramount interest in the item requires the rule.

The Section is made subject to the provisions of Article 3 concerning conversion of instruments (Section 3–419) and other provisions of Article 3 and this Article concerning restrictive indorsements (Sections 3–205, 3–206, 3–419, 3–603, 4–205). Of course instructions from or an agreement with its transferor does not relieve a collecting bank of its general obligation to exercise good faith and ordinary care. See Section 4–103(1). If in any particular case a bank has exercised good faith and ordinary care and is relieved of responsibility by reason of instructions of or an agreement with its transferor, the owner of the item may still have a remedy for loss against the transferor (another bank) if such transferor has given wrongful instructions.

The rules of the Section are applied only to collecting banks. Payor banks always have the problem of making proper payment of an item; whether such payment is proper should be based upon all of the rules of Articles 3 and 4 and all of the facts of any particular case, and should not be dependent exclusively upon instructions from or an agreement with a person presenting the item.

Cross References:

Sections 3–205, 3–206, 3–419, 3–603, 4–103(1) and 4–205.

Definitional Cross References:

"Collecting bank". Section 4–105.
"Restrictive indorsement". Section 3–205.

Cross References

Conversion of instruments, see Commercial Code § 3420.
Good faith or ordinary care, bank's responsibility, see Commercial Code § 4103.
Missing indorsements, see Commercial Code § 4205.
Restrictive indorsement,
    Defined, see Commercial Code § 3206.
    Operation and effect, see Commercial Code § 3206.
Restrictively indorsed instruments, liability for payment, see Commercial Code § 3206.

Variation of provisions of this division, scope of agreement, see Commercial Code § 4103(a).

§ 4204. Methods of sending and presenting

(a) A collecting bank shall send items by reasonably prompt method, taking into consideration * * * relevant instructions, the nature of the item, the number of those items on hand, * * * the cost of collection involved, and the method generally used by it or others to present those items.

(b) A collecting bank may send:

* * * (1) An item directly to the payor bank.

* * * (2) An item to a nonbank payor if authorized by its transferor.

* * * (3) An item other than documentary drafts to a nonbank payor, if authorized by Federal Reserve regulation or operating * * * circular, clearing house rule, or the like.

* * *

(c) Presentment may be made by a presenting bank at a place where the payor bank or other payor has requested that presentment be made. (Stats.1963, c. 819, § 4204. Amended by Stats.1992, c. 914 (S.B.833), § 21.)

California Code Comment
By John A. Bohn and Charles J. Williams

Prior California Law

1. Subdivision (1) substitutes the standard for a collecting bank of a "reasonably prompt method" in sending items for the more specific requirements of former Financial Code §§ 1013 and 1014.

Each former section fixed a specific time limit within which the bank had to act on an item after extending credit on it. Former Financial Code § 1013 provided that the bank had until midnight of the next business day after receipt of an item to dishonor or refuse payment of that item. Former Financial Code § 1014 required the bank to forward an item for collection before midnight of the next business day after receipt of the item.

Subdivision (1) provides flexibility in the time requirements for such action by requiring a "reasonably prompt method" rather than a specific time limit. Official Comment 1.

2. The provision of subdivision (1) requiring a collecting bank to send items by a "method generally used by it or others" is in accord with those cases which state that a bank exercises reasonable care if it follows banking custom and usage. Davis v. First Nat. Bank, 118 Cal. 600, 50 Pac. 666 (1897) and Luckehe v. First Nat. Bank of Marysville, 193 Cal. 184, 223 Pac. 547 (1924).

3. Subdivision (2) in paragraphs (a), (d) and (e) continues the rule of former Financial Code § 1014 that a bank may send an item for collection directly to the payor bank, any Federal Reserve Bank, or any other bank or agency.

Paragraphs (b) and (c) of subdivision (2) are new statutory provisions. See Official Comment 3 for explanation of these paragraphs.

Changes from U.C.C. (1962 Official Text)

4. Paragraphs (d) and (e) of subdivision (2) are peculiar to this California version and do not appear in the Official Text. These paragraphs were added at the recommendation of the State Bar committee on Chapter [Division] 4, to insure the inclusion of Federal Reserve Banks and other banks which were specifically included in former Financial Code § 1014. The recommendation to add these paragraphs was criticized by Professors Marsh and Warren in their report to the legislature on the Commercial Code:

"It is obvious that a bank should be able to send items to a Federal Reserve bank or any other bank. This subsection [subdivision] would have been better drafted if it had included these two additional clauses. However, it is also clear that the enumeration in this subsection [subdivision] is not intended to be exclusive, both from the use of the word 'may' and from the express statement to that effect in Section 14103(4) [4103(4)]. If California should insert these additional clauses, then the courts in some other state which adopted the Code without them might be inclined to hold that these procedures were excluded (although it is difficult to see how a court could hold this under any circumstances). Solely in the interests of uniformity, and because we think that there is no possibility that the Code would be interpreted to exclude these procedures, we recommend rejection of the proposed additional clauses." Sixth Progress Report to the Legislature by the Senate Fact Finding Committee on Judiciary (1959–1961), Part 1, The Uniform Commercial Code p. 473.

The State Bar also recommended the insertion of the term "circular" after "Federal Reserve regulation" in paragraph (e) of subdivision (2) but this was rejected. See California Code Comment 3 to Commercial Code § 4103 for the reason for rejection.

5. The last paragraph in subdivision (2) is language peculiar to the California version and does not appear in the Official Text. It was substituted in the California version for subdivision (3) of the Official Text which is omitted. Subdivision (3) in the 1962 Official Text provides:

"(3) Presentment may be made by a presenting bank at a place where the payor bank has requested that presentment be made."

Subdivision (3) was added to the Official Text in 1962 for the following reason:

"The new subsection (3) is intended to make it clear that a presenting bank may make presentment of any item at any place requested by the payor bank, even though that place may not be one of those mentioned in Section 3–504. This subsection will thus remove any doubt as to the validity of presentment by a presenting bank at a centralized bookkeeping center or electronic processing center maintained or used by the payor bank." Permanent Editorial Board for the Uniform Commercial Code, Report No. 1, (1962), p. 27.

Subdivision (3) is limited to places requested by the payor bank. The California language in the last paragraph of subdivision (2) which is substituted for subdivision (3) is broader in that it includes any place requested by any of those listed in paragraphs (a) through (e), not just the payor bank (paragraph (a)).

Uniform Commercial Code Comment
Official Reasons for 1990 Change

Subsection (c) is amended to allow nonbank payors to request a place of payment. The other modifications are made to conform with current legislative drafting practices, with no intent to change substance.

1990 Change

1. Subsection (a) prescribes the general standards applicable to proper sending or forwarding of items. Because of the many types of methods available and the desirability of preserving flexibility any attempt to prescribe limited or precise methods is avoided.

2. Subsection (b)(1) codifies the practice of direct mail, express, messenger or like presentment to payor banks. The practice is now country-wide and is justified by the need for speed, the general responsibility of banks, Federal Deposit Insurance protection and other reasons.

3. Full approval of the practice of direct sending is limited to cases in which a bank is a payor. Since nonbank drawees or payors may be of unknown responsibility, substantial risks may be attached to placing in their hands the instruments calling for payments from them. This is obviously so in the case of documentary drafts. However, in some cities practices have long existed under clearing-house procedures to forward certain types of items to certain nonbank payors. Examples include insurance loss drafts drawn by field agents on home offices. For the purpose of leaving the door open to legitimate practices of this kind, subsection (b)(3) affirmatively approves direct sending of any item other than documentary drafts to any nonbank payor, if authorized by Federal Reserve regulation or operating circular, clearing-house rule or the like.

On the other hand subsection (b)(2) approves sending any item directly to a nonbank payor if authorized by a collecting bank's transferor. This permits special instructions or agreements out of the norm and is consistent with the "chain of command" theory of Section

4-203. However, if a transferor other than the owner of the item, e.g., a prior collecting bank, authorizes a direct sending to a nonbank payor, such transferor assumes responsibility for the propriety or impropriety of such authorization.

4. Section 3–501(b) provides where presentment may be made. This provision is expressly subject to Article 4. Section 4–204(c) specifically approves presentment by a presenting bank at any place requested by the payor bank or other payor. The time when a check is received by a payor bank for presentment is governed by Regulation CC Section 229.36(b).

Uniform Commercial Code Comment

Prior Uniform Statutory Provision:

None; but see Section 6, American Bankers Association Bank Collection Code.

Purposes:

1. Subsection (1) prescribes the general standards applicable to proper sending or forwarding of items. Because of the many types of methods available and the desirability of preserving flexibility any attempt to prescribe limited or precise methods is avoided.

2. Subsection (2)(a) codifies the practice of direct mail, express, messenger or like presentment to payor banks. The practice is now countrywide and is justified by the need for speed, the general responsibility of banks, Federal Deposit Insurance protection and other reasons.

3. Full approval of the practice of direct sending is limited to cases where a bank is a payor. Where non-bank drawees or payors may be of unknown responsibility, substantial risks may be attached to placing in their hands the instruments calling for payments from them. This is obviously so in the case of documentary drafts. However, in some cities practices have long existed under clearing house procedures to forward certain types of items to certain non-bank payors. Examples include insurance loss drafts drawn by field agents on home offices. For the purpose of leaving the door open to legitimate practices of this kind, subsection (2)(c) affirmatively approves direct sending of any item other than documentary drafts to any non-bank payor, if authorized by Federal Reserve regulation or operating letter, clearing house rule or the like.

On the other hand subsection (2)(b) approves sending any item direct to a non-bank payor if authorized by a collecting bank's transferor. This permits special instructions or agreements out of the norm and is consistent with the "chain of command" theory of Section 4–203. However, if a transferor other than the owner of the item, e.g., a prior collecting bank, authorizes a direct sending to a non-bank payor, such transferor assumes responsibility for the propriety or impropriety of such authorization.

4. Section 3–504 states how presentment is made and subsection (2) of that Section affirmatively approves three specific methods by which presentment may be made. The methods so specified are permissive and do not foreclose other possible methods. However, in view of the substantial increase in recent years of presentment at centralized bookkeeping centers and electronic processing centers maintained or used by payor banks, many of which are at locations other than the banks themselves, subsection (3) specifically approves presentment by a presenting bank at any place requested by the payor bank. [Changes in California from U.C.C. (1962 Official Text, see California Code Comment, note 5.]

Cross References:

Sections 3–504, 4–501 and 4–502.

Definitional Cross References:

"Collecting bank". Section 4–105.
"Documentary draft". Section 4–104.
"Item". Section 4–104.
"Payor bank". Section 4–105.
"Presenting bank". Section 4–105.

Cross References

Business days, banks, see Civil Code § 9.

Charging back of item to party from whom received, see Commercial Code § 4214.
Credit for item to be provisional, see Commercial Code § 4201.
Deferred posting, recovery of payment by return, see Commercial Code § 4301.
Documentary drafts, manner of handling, see Commercial Code § 4501.
Notice of dishonor, see Commercial Code § 3503.
"On arrival" drafts, manner of presentment, see Commercial Code § 4502.
Presentment, manner of making, see Commercial Code § 3501.

§ 4205. Delivery of item to depositary bank; effect

If a customer delivers an item to a depositary bank for collection both of the following apply:

(a) The depositary bank becomes a holder of the item at the time it receives the item for collection if the customer at the time of delivery was a holder of the item, whether or not the customer indorses the item, and, if the bank satisfies the other requirements of Section 3302, it is a holder in due course.

(b) The depositary bank warrants to collecting banks, the payor bank or other payor, and the drawer that the amount of the item was paid to the customer or deposited to the customer's account. *(Added by Stats. 1992, c. 914 (S.B.833), § 23.)*

California Code Comment

By John A. Bohn and Charles J. Williams

Prior California Law

1. Subdivision (1) has no statutory counterpart in prior California law. It is consistent with accepted banking practice. It also is in accord with the rule that where an intended payee actually receives the proceeds, the drawer cannot recover from the payor. 9 C.J.S. 737. In the California Annotations to the proposed Uniform Commercial Code (1960), the Legislative Council made the following observation:

"There is no California statutory precedent for the power given a collecting bank in subdivision (1) to insert a missing indorsement, but it is believed to be common commercial practice." Sixth Progress Report to the Legislature by the Senate Fact Finding Committee on Judiciary (1959–1961) Part 1, The Uniform Commercial Code, p. 90.

2. Subdivision (2) provides that an intermediary bank or a payor bank not a depositary may ignore a restrictive indorsement. This is an exception to the general rule under prior California law that a restrictive indorsement is notice to a bank that further negotiation is prohibited. Nordin v. Eagle Rock State Bank, 139 Cal.App. 584, 594, 34 P.2d 490 (1934) and Christian v. California Bank, 30 Cal.2d 421, 182 P.2d 554 (1947).

3. Subdivision (2) is the same as section 3206(2) except that section 3206(2) adds at the end "or the person presenting for payment."

Changes from U.C.C. (1962 Official Text)

4. This is section 4–205 of the Official Text without change.

Uniform Commercial Code Comment
Official Reasons for 1990 Change

New section. See Official Comment.

1990 Change

Section 3–201(b) provides that negotiation of an instrument payable to order requires indorsement by the holder. The rule of former Section 4–205(1) was that the depositary bank may supply a missing indorsement of its customer unless the item contains the words "payee's indorsement required" or the like. The cases have differed on the status of the depositary bank as a holder if it fails to supply its customer's indorsement. Marine Midland Bank, N.A. v. Price, Miller, Evans & Flowers, 446 N.Y.S.2d 797 (N.Y.App.Div. 4th Dept.1981), rev'd, 455 N.Y.S.2d 565 (N.Y.1982). It is common practice for depositary banks to receive unindorsed checks under so-called "lockbox" agreements from customers who receive a high volume of checks. No function would be served by requiring a depositary bank to run these items through a machine that would supply the customer's indorsement except to afford the drawer and the subsequent banks evidence that the proceeds of the item reached the customer's account. Paragraph (1) provides that the depositary bank becomes a holder when it takes the item for deposit if the depositor is a holder. Whether it supplies the customer's indorsement is immaterial. Paragraph (2) satisfies the need for a receipt of funds by the depositary bank by imposing on that bank a warranty that it paid the customer or deposited the item to the customer's account. This warranty runs not only to collecting banks and to the payor bank or nonbank drawee but also to the drawer, affording protection to these parties that the depositary bank received the item and applied it to the benefit of the holder.

Uniform Commercial Code Comment

Prior Uniform Statutory Provision:
None.

Purposes:

1. Subsection (1) is designed to speed up collections by eliminating any necessity to return to a non-bank depositor any items he may have failed to indorse.

2. For the purpose of permitting items to move rapidly through banking channels, intermediary banks and payor banks which are not also depositary banks are permitted to ignore restrictive indorsements of any person except the bank's immediate transferor. However, depositary banks may not so ignore restrictive indorsements. If an owner of an item indorses it "for deposit" or "for collection" he usually does so in the belief such indorsement will guard against further negotiation of the item to a holder in due course by a finder or a thief. This belief is reasonably justified if at least one bank in any chain of banks collecting the item has a responsibility to act consistently with the indorsement.

Cross References:

Sections 3–205, 3–206, 3–419, 3–603, 4–203.

Definitional Cross References:

"Collecting bank." Section 4–105.
"Customer." Section 4–104.
"Depositary bank." Section 4–105.
"Intermediary bank." Section 4–105.
"Item." Section 4–104.
"Payor bank." Section 4–105.
"Restrictive indorsement." Section 3–205.

Cross References

Burden of establishing signatures validity, see Commercial Code § 3308.
Conversion of instruments, see Commercial Code § 3420.
Effect of instructions, see Commercial Code § 4203.
Incomplete instruments, see Commercial Code § 3115.
Negotiation, see Commercial Code § 3202.
Restrictive indorsement,
    Defined, see Commercial Code § 3206.
    Operation and effect, see Commercial Code § 3206.
Restrictively indorsed instruments, liability for payment, see Commercial Code § 3206.
Right to indorsement on transfer, see Commercial Code § 3203.

§ 4206. Transfer Between Banks

Any agreed method that identifies the transferor bank is sufficient for the item's further transfer to another bank. *(Stats.1963, c. 819, § 4206. Amended by Stats.1992, c. 914 (S.B.833), § 24.)*

California Code Comment

By John A. Bohn and Charles J. Williams

Prior California Law

1. This section is new statutory law. The requirements of indorsement and negotiation are covered by Commercial Code §§ 3201–3208. However, when the transfer is between banks this section takes the place of the more formal requirements of section 3202. Official Comment.

2. A California State Bar committee made the following comment on the effect of this section:

"Section 14206 [4206] provides that any agreed method which identifies the transferor bank is sufficient to transfer an item to another bank. A bank could transfer an item merely by stamping on it an identifying number or symbol, such as its transit number." [Fn.: Clarke, Bailey and Young, Bank Deposits and Collections 60 (A.L.I. 1963)]. California State Bar Committee on the Commercial Code, A Special Report, The Uniform Commercial Code, 37 Calif.State Bar J. (March–April, 1962) 166.

Changes from U.C.C. (1962 Official Text)

3. This is section 4–206 of the Official Text without change.

Uniform Commercial Code Comment

Official Reasons for 1990 Change

Modified to conform with current drafting practices; no intent to change substance.

1990 Change

This section is designed to permit the simplest possible form of transfer from one bank to another, once an item gets in the bank collection chain, provided only identity of the transferor bank is preserved. This is important for tracing purposes and if recourse is necessary. However, since the responsibilities of the various banks appear in the Article it becomes unnecessary to have liability or responsibility depend on more formal indorsements. Simplicity in the form of transfer is conducive to speed. If the transfer is between banks, this section takes the place of the more formal requirements of Section 3–201.

Uniform Commercial Code Comment

Prior Uniform Statutory Provision:
None.

Purposes:

This section is designed to permit the simplest possible form of transfer from one bank to another, once an item gets in the bank collection chain, provided only identity of the transferor bank is preserved. This is important for tracing purposes and if recourse is necessary. However, since the responsibilities of the various banks appear in the Article it becomes unnecessary to have liability or responsibility depend on more formal indorsements. Simplicity in the form of transfer is conducive to speed. Where the transfer is between banks this section takes the place of the more formal requirements of Section 3–202.

Cross References:

Sections 3–201, 3–202.

Definitional Cross References:

"Bank". Section 1–201.
"Item". Section 4–104.

Cross References

Transfer and negotiation, see Commercial Code § 3201 et seq.

§ 4207. Transfer of item by customer or collecting bank; warranties; damages for breach

(a) A customer or collecting bank that transfers an item and receives a settlement or other consideration warrants to the transferee and to any subsequent collecting bank that all of the following are applicable:

(1) The warrantor is a person entitled to enforce the item.

(2) All signatures on the item are authentic and authorized.

(3) The item has not been altered.

(4) The item is not subject to a defense or claim in recoupment (subdivision (a) of Section 3305) of any party that can be asserted against the warrantor.

(5) The warrantor has no knowledge of any insolvency proceeding commenced with respect to the maker or acceptor or, in the case of an unaccepted draft, the drawer.

(6) If the item is a demand draft, creation of the item according to the terms on its face was authorized by the person identified as drawer.

(b) If an item is dishonored, a customer or collecting bank transferring the item and receiving settlement or other consideration is obliged to pay the amount due on the item (1) according to the terms of the item at the time it was transferred, or (2) if the transfer was of an incomplete item, according to its terms when completed as stated in Sections 3115 and 3407. The obligation of a transferor is owed to the transferee and to any subsequent collecting bank that takes the item in good faith. A transferor cannot disclaim its obligation under this subdivision by an indorsement stating that it is made "without recourse" or otherwise disclaiming liability.

(c) A person to whom the warranties under subdivision (a) are made and who took the item in good faith may recover from the warrantor as damages for breach of warranty an amount equal to the loss suffered as a result of the breach, but not more than the amount of the item plus expenses and loss of interest incurred as a result of the breach.

(d) The warranties stated in subdivision (a) cannot be disclaimed with respect to checks. Unless notice of a claim for breach of warranty is given to the warrantor within 30 days after the claimant has reason to know of the breach and the identity of the warrantor, the warrantor is discharged to the extent of any loss caused by the delay in giving notice of the claim.

(e) A cause of action for breach of warranty under this section accrues when the claimant has reason to know of the breach.

(f) If the warranty in paragraph (6) of subdivision (a) is not given by a transferor or collecting bank under applicable conflict of law rules, then the warranty is not given by that transferor when that transferor is a transferee nor to any prior collecting bank of that transferee. *(Added by Stats.1992, c. 914 (S.B.833), § 26. Amended by Stats.1996, c. 316 (S.B.1742), § 5.)*

California Code Comment

By John A. Bohn and Charles J. Williams

Prior California Law

1. This section provides that a person transferring an item for collection gives certain warranties to certain parties. The general result of this subsection is for the most part in accord with the general result under prior law. This section changes prior law only in that it changes the basis of a recovery to a warranty theory. Section 4207 fixes the same warranties for the collection of items through the banking system that Commercial Code § 3417 establishes for the transfer of commercial paper not collected through the banking system.

Under prior California law the liability of a bank in connection with the transfer of an item was based on negligence rather than upon breach of warranty. Kirby v. Bank of America, 4 Cal.App.2d 370, 40 P.2d 943 (1935).

2. The result under subdivision (1)(b) is the same as under prior law. This continues a Price v. Neal, 3 Burr. 1354 (1762) exception. Under prior California law the cases imposed liability by holding that a bank was charged with knowledge of the depositor's signature as a result of the implied contractual relationship between the bank and the depositor. Basch v. Bank of America, 22 Cal.2d 316, 139 P.2d 1 (1943). Part of the implied agreement is that the bank would pay the check only upon a genuine indorsement and the bank must determine the genuineness at its own peril. This duty was imposed upon the bank because it had the opportunity of ascertaining genuineness when the check is presented, either by requiring identification or a responsible guaranty. Los Angeles Inv. Co. v. Home Sav. Bank of Los Angeles, 180 Cal. 601, 182 Pac. 293, 5 A.L.R. 1193 (1919). A bank which paid out money on an altered or forged indorsement was liable to the payee unless it could show it was free from negligence and the depositor was negligent or estopped to deny that payment was correct. Hensley-Johnson Motors v. Citizens Nat. Bank, 122 Cal.App.2d 22, 264 P.2d 973 (1953); Pac. Coast Cheese Inc. v. Security-First Nat. Bank, 45 Cal.2d 75, 286 P.2d 353 (1955).

An exception to a bank's liability for the genuineness of an indorsement is where the check is made payable to a fictitious and non-existing person. The court in Metropolitan Life Ins. Co. v. San Francisco Bank, 58 Cal.App.2d 528, 136 P.2d 853 (1943) stated that in such a case

"no contractual obligation arises in favor of the drawer upon the guarantee of the collecting bank of the validity of the forged indorsement of the signature of the fictitious payee for the reason that the very act of the drawer, in signing a check made payable to a fictitious payee under the circumstances alleged, makes impossible any valid indorsement of such check." (58 Cal.App.2d at p. 533, 136 P.2d at p. 533)

3. A California State Bar Committee observed one of the important effects of this section in its comment on this section:

Section 14207 [4207] would make an indorsement unnecessary to transfer an item from one bank to another. The warranties provided for in that section arise upon transfer despite lack of indorsement. These provisions should eliminate many of the overlapping indorsements on the back of an item which now often make earlier indorsements unreadable, and should reduce the chance of items being misdirected. California State Bar Committee on the Commercial Code, A Special Report, The Uniform Commercial Code, 37 Calif.State Bar J. (March–April, 1962) 166.

Changes from U.C.C. (1962 Official Text)

4. This is section 4–207 of the Official Text without change.

Uniform Commercial Code Comment

Official Reasons for 1990 Change

New section. See Official Comment.

1990 Change

Except for subsection (b), this section conforms to Section 3–416 and extends its coverage to items. The substance of this section is discussed in the Comment to Section 3–416. Subsection (b) provides that customers or collecting banks that transfer items, whether by indorsement or not, undertake to pay the item if the item is dishonored. This obligation cannot be disclaimed by a "without recourse" indorsement or otherwise. With respect to checks, Regulation CC Section 229.34 states the warranties made by paying and returning banks.

Uniform Commercial Code Comment

Prior Uniform Statutory Provision:

None; but see American Bankers Association Bank Collection Code, Section 4.

Purposes:

1. Subject to certain exceptions peculiar to the bank collection process and except that they apply only to customers and collecting banks, the warranties and engagements to honor in this section are identical in substance with those provided in the Article on Commercial Paper (Article 3). See Sections 3–414, 3–417. For a more complete explanation of the purposes of these warranties and engagements see the Comments to Sections 3–414 and 3–417.

2. In addition to imposing upon customers and collecting banks the warranties and engagements imposed by the original Sections 65 and 66 of the Uniform Negotiable Instruments Law and those of Sections 3–414 and 3–417 of Article 3, with some variations, this Section 4–207 is intended to give the effect presently obtained in bank collections by the words "prior indorsements guaranteed" in collection transfers and presentments between banks. The warranties and engagements arise automatically as a part of the bank collection process. Receipt of a settlement or other consideration by a customer or collecting bank is a requirement but any settlement is sufficient regardless of whether the settlement is concurrent with the transfer, as in the case of a cash item, or delayed, as in the case of a non-cash straight collection item. Further, the warranties and engagements run with the item with the result that a collecting bank may sue a remote prior collecting bank or a remote customer and thus avoid multiplicity of suits. This section is also intended to make it clear that the so-called equitable defense of "payment over" does not apply to a collecting bank and that no statute of frauds provision will defeat recovery. Subsections (2) and (3) indicate that these results are intended notwithstanding the absence of indorsement or words of guarantee or warranty in a transfer or presentment. Consequently, if for purposes of simplification or the speeding up of the bank collection process, banks desire to cut down the length or size of indorsements (Section 4–206), they may do so and the standard warranties and engagements to honor still apply.

3. With respect to the exceptions to the warranties in favor of a holder in due course specified in sub-paragraphs (b) and (c) of subsection (1), collecting banks usually have holder in due course status (Sections 4–208, 4–209). However, if in any case there is a holder in due course but a subsequent collecting bank does not have holder in due course status (e.g., in a straight non-cash collection where no settlement of any kind is made until the bank itself receives final settlement) the bank still has the benefit of the exceptions (if it acts in good faith) under the shelter provisions of Section 3–201. It is to be noted that these shelter provisions, by virtue of successive transfers, benefit not only the immediate transferee from a holder in due course but also subsequent transferees.

4. In this section as in Section 3–417, the (a), (b) and (c) warranties to transferees and collecting banks under subsection (2) are in general similar to the (a), (b) and (c) warranties to payors under subsection (1); but the warranties to payors are less inclusive because of exceptions reflecting the rule of Price v. Neal, 3 Burr. 1354 (1762), and related principles. See Comment to Section 3–417. Thus collecting banks are given not only all the warranties given to payors by subsection (1), without those exceptions, but also the (d) and (e) warranties of subsection (2).

5. The last sentence of subsection (3) provides that damages for breach of warranties or the engagement to honor shall not exceed the consideration received by the customer or collecting bank responsible "plus finance charges and expenses related to the item, if any". The "expenses" referred to in this phrase may be ordinary collecting expenses and in appropriate cases could also include such expenses as attorneys fees. "Finance charges" are also referred to because in some cases interest or a finance charge is charged by the collecting bank for the time that the bank's advance on the item is outstanding prior to receipt of proceeds of collection. An example of this type of case would be where a bank undertakes a foreign collection in South America or Europe and makes an advance on the item at the time of receipt but may not receive proceeds of the foreign collection for three months or more.

Cross References:

Sections 3–201, 3–414, 3–417, 3–418, 4–206, 4–208, 4–209 and 4–406.

Definitional Cross References:

"Collecting bank". Section 4–105.
"Customer". Section 4–104.
"Draft". Section 3–104.
"Genuine". Section 1–201.
"Good faith". Section 1–201.
"Holder". Section 1–201.
"Holder in due course". Section 3–302.
"Insolvency proceedings". Section 1–201.
"Item". Section 4–104.
"Party". Section 1–201.
"Payor bank". Section 4–105.
"Person". Section 1–201.
"Presentment". Section 3–504.
"Protest". Section 3–509.
"Unauthorized signature". Section 1–201.

Cross References

Demand draft, defined, see Commercial Code § 3104.
Finality of payment or collection of commercial paper, see Commercial Code § 3418.
Indorsement, investment securities, see Commercial Code § 8308.
Obligation of indorser, see Commercial Code § 3415.
Presentment, how made, see Commercial Code § 3501.
Status of collecting bank, see Commercial Code § 4210.
Transfer and negotiation of commercial paper, see Commercial Code § 3201 et seq.
Transfer between banks, method, see Commercial Code § 4206.
Unauthorized signature or alteration, discovery and report by bank's customer, see Commercial Code § 4406.
Warranties on presentment or transfer,
  Investment securities, see Commercial Code § 8306.
  Letters of credit, see Commercial Code § 5111.
  Negotiable instruments, see Commercial Code §§ 3416, 3417.

§ 4208. Drawee payment or acceptance of unaccepted draft; warranties; damages for breach; payment of dishonored draft

(a) If an unaccepted draft is presented to the drawee for payment or acceptance and the drawee pays or accepts the draft, (i) the person obtaining payment or acceptance, at the time of presentment, and (ii) a previous transferor of the draft, at the time of transfer, warrant to the drawee that pays or accepts the draft in good faith that all of the following apply:

(1) The warrantor is, or was, at the time the warrantor transferred the draft, a person entitled to enforce the draft or authorized to obtain payment or acceptance of the draft on behalf of a person entitled to enforce the draft.

(2) The draft has not been altered.

(3) The warrantor has no knowledge that the signature of the purported drawer of the draft is unauthorized.

(4) If the draft is a demand draft, creation of the demand draft according to the terms on its face was authorized by the person identified as drawer.

(b) A drawee making payment may recover from a warrantor damages for breach of warranty equal to the amount paid by the drawee less the amount the drawee received or is entitled to receive from the draw-

because of the payment. In addition, the drawee is entitled to compensation for expenses and loss of interest resulting from the breach. The right of the drawee to recover damages under this subdivision is not affected by any failure of the drawee to exercise ordinary care in making payment. If the drawee accepts the draft (1) breach of warranty is a defense to the obligation of the acceptor, and (2) if the acceptor makes payment with respect to the draft, the acceptor is entitled to recover from a warrantor for breach of warranty the amounts stated in this subdivision.

(c) If a drawee asserts a claim for breach of warranty under subdivision (a) based on an unauthorized indorsement of the draft or an alteration of the draft, the warrantor may defend by proving that the indorsement is effective under Section 3404 or 3405 or the drawer is precluded under Section 3406 or 4406 from asserting against the drawee the unauthorized indorsement or alteration.

(d) If (1) a dishonored draft is presented for payment to the drawer or an indorser or (2) any other item is presented for payment to a party obliged to pay the item, and the item is paid, the person obtaining payment and a prior transferor of the item warrant to the person making payment in good faith that the warrantor is, or was, at the time the warrantor transferred the item, a person entitled to enforce the item or authorized to obtain payment on behalf of a person entitled to enforce the item. The person making payment may recover from any warrantor for breach of warranty an amount equal to the amount paid plus expenses and loss of interest resulting from the breach.

(e) The warranties stated in subdivisions (a) and (d) cannot be disclaimed with respect to checks. Unless notice of a claim for breach of warranty is given to the warrantor within 30 days after the claimant has reason to know of the breach and the identity of the warrantor, the warrantor is discharged to the extent of any loss caused by the delay in giving notice of the claim.

(f) A cause of action for breach of warranty under this section accrues when the claimant has reason to know of the breach.

(g) A demand draft is a check, as provided in subdivision (f) of Section 3104.

(h) If the warranty in paragraph (4) of subdivision (a) is not given by a transferor under applicable conflict of law rules, then the warranty is not given to that transferor when that transferor is a transferee. *(Added by Stats.1992, c. 914 (S.B.833), § 27. Amended by Stats.1996, c. 316 (S.B.1742), § 6.)*

California Code Comment

By John A. Bohn and Charles J. Williams

Prior California Law

1. Subdivision (1) is new statutory law. The security interest provided by subdivision (1) is in addition to the banker's lien given by Civil Code § 3054 on the customer's property in the bank's possession for the balance owed by the customer and is not intended to replace it. The unanimous view of the commentators in California, including the State Bar, the California Banker's Association and Professors Marsh and Warren was that this subdivision would not and should not replace or derogate from the banker's common law lien or right of set-off against indebtedness owing in deposit accounts. Sixth Progress Report to the Legislature by the Senate Fact Finding Committee on Judiciary (1959–1961), Part 1, The Uniform Commercial Code pp. 359, 406, 473 to 474.

2. Section 3054 of the Civil Code gives a banker a general lien "dependent on possession, upon all property in his hands belonging to a customer, for the balance due to him from such customer in the course of the business." The "lien" on the depositor's funds on deposit is not technically a lien because the bank is the owner of the funds and the debtor of the depositor and the bank cannot have a lien on its own property. The banker's right to charge the depositors fund is more correctly termed a right of set-off based upon general equitable principles. Although this right of the bank may not technically be a lien, it is in the nature of a lien or security interest and is enforceable by the bank's own account without the aid of the court. Gonsalves v. Bank of America, 16 C.2d 169, 105 P.2d 118 (1940).

3. To the extent the bank has a security interest pursuant to subdivision (1) it is a holder for value under sections 4209 and 3303, and is a holder in due course if it satisfies the other requirements of section 3302. Official Comment 1.

4. Subdivision (2) is new statutory law. See Official Comment 2.

5. The first sentence of subdivision (3) reflects the self-liquidating nature of the bank's security interest. Official Comment 3. The remainder of subdivision (3) explains the relationship between the bank's security interest provided in subdivision (1) and Division 9. Division 9 applies to the security interest created by subdivision (1) except as stated in paragraphs (a), (b) and (c).

Changes from U.C.C. (1962 Official Text)

6. This is section 4–208 of the Official Text without change.

Uniform Commercial Code Comment

Official Reasons for 1990 Change

New section. See Official Comment.

1990 Change

This section conforms to Section 3–417 and extends its coverage to items. The substance of this section is discussed in the comment to Section 3–417. "Draft" is defined in Section 4–104 as including an item that is an order to pay so as to make clear that the term "draft" in Article 4 may include items that are not instruments within Section 3–104.

Uniform Commercial Code Comment

Prior Uniform Statutory Provision:

None; but see American Bankers Association Bank Collection Code, Section 2.

Purposes:

1. Subsection (1) states a rational rule for the interest of a bank in an item. The customer of the depositary bank is normally the owner of the item and the several collecting banks are his agents (Section 4–201). A collecting agent may properly make advances on the security of paper held by him for collection, and when he does acquires at common law a possessory lien for his advances. Subsection (1) applies an analogous principle to a bank in the collection chain which extends credit on items in the course of collection. The bank has a security interest to the extent stated in this section. To the extent of its security interest it is a holder for value (Sections 3–303, 4–209) and a holder in due course if it satisfies the other requirements for that status (Section 3–302). Subsection (1) does not derogate from the banker's general common-law lien or right of set-off against indebtedness owing in deposit accounts. See Section 1–103. Rather subsection (1) specifically implements and extends the principle as a part of the bank collection process.

2. Subsection (2) spreads the security interest of the bank over all items in a single deposit or received under a single agreement and a single giving of credit. It also adopts the "first-in, first-out" rule.

3. Collection statistics establish that in excess of ninety-nine per cent of items handled for collection are in fact collected. The first sentence of subsection (3) reflects the fact that in such normal case the bank's security interest is self-liquidating. The remainder of the subsection correlates the security interest with the provisions of Article 9, particularly for use in the cases of non-collection where the security interest may be important.

Cross References:

Sections 3–302, 3–303, 4–201, 4–209, 9–203(1)(b) and 9–302.

Definitional Cross References:

"Account". Section 4–104.
"Agreement". Section 1–201.
"Bank". Section 1–201.
"Item". Section 4–104.
"Security interest". Section 1–201.
"Settlement". Section 4–104.

Cross References

Agency status of collecting bank, see Commercial Code § 4201.
Collecting bank, see Commercial Code § 4105.
Definitions, see Commercial Code § 1201.
Demand draft, defined, see Commercial Code § 3104.
Depository bank, see Commercial Code § 4105.
Enforceability of security interest, see Commercial Code § 9203.
Holder in due course,
  Bank's status, see Commercial Code § 4211.
  Defined, see Commercial Code § 3302.
Issue or transfer of instrument for value, see Commercial Code § 3303.
Items being collected by collecting bank holding security interest not subject to execution lien, see Code of Civil Procedure § 697.740.
Payment, discharge of obligation, see Commercial Code § 3602.
Payor bank's responsibility for late return of item, liability subject to defenses on breach of presentment warranty, see Commercial Code § 4302.
Perfection of security interest, see Commercial Code § 9302.
Preferences, see Commercial Code § 4216.
Priorities among conflicting security interests in the same collateral, see Commercial Code § 9312.
Recovery for breach of warranty under this section by payor bank with respect to unauthorized signature or alteration, see Commercial Code § 4406.
Secured transactions,
  Generally, see Commercial Code § 9101 et seq.
  Prerequisites of security interest, see Commercial Code § 9203.
Security agreement, see Commercial Code § 9105.

§ 4209. Encoded information; agreements for electronic presentment; warranties

(a) A person who encodes information on or with respect to an item after issue warrants to any subsequent collecting bank and to the payor bank or other payor that the information is correctly encoded. If the customer of a depositary bank encodes, that bank also makes the warranty.

(b) A person who undertakes to retain an item pursuant to an agreement for electronic presentment warrants to any subsequent collecting bank and to the payor bank or other payor that retention and presentment of the item comply with the agreement. If a customer of a depositary bank undertakes to retain an item, that bank also makes this warranty.

(c) A person to whom warranties are made under this section and who took the item in good faith may recover from the warrantor as damages for breach of warranty an amount equal to the loss suffered as a result of the breach, plus expenses and loss of interest incurred as a result of the breach. *(Added by Stats.1992, c. 914 (S.B.833), § 29.)*

California Code Comment

By John A. Bohn and Charles J. Williams

Prior California Law

1. This section implements Commercial Code § 4208. It is similar to former Civil Code § 3108 which provided that one with a lien on an instrument is deemed a holder for value to the extent of that lien. Both sections provide that the security interest given is value for the purpose of determining whether one is a holder in due course.

Changes from U.C.C. (1962 Official Text)

2. This is section 4–209 of the Official Text without change.

Uniform Commercial Code Comment
Official Reasons for 1990 Change

New section. See Official Comment.

1990 Change

1. Encoding and retention warranties are included in Article 4 because they are unique to the bank collection process. These warranties are breached only by the person doing the encoding or retaining the item and not by subsequent banks handling the item. Encoding and check retention may be done by customers who are payees of a large volume of checks; hence, this section imposes warranties on customers as well as banks. If a customer encodes or retains, the depositary bank is also liable for any breach of this warranty.

2. A miscoding of the amount on the MICR line is not an alteration under Section 3–407(a) which defines alteration as changing the contract of the parties. If a drawer wrote a check for $2,500 and the depository bank encoded $25,000 on the MICR line, the payor bank could debit the drawer's account for only $2,500. This subsection would allow the payor bank to hold the depositary bank liable for the amount paid out over $2,500 without first pursuing the person who received payment. Intervening collecting banks would not be liable to the payor bank for the depositary bank's error. If a drawer wrote a check for $25,000 and the depositary bank encoded $2,500, the payor bank becomes liable for the full amount of the check. The payor bank's rights against the depositary bank depend on whether the payor bank has suffered a loss. Since the payor bank can debit the drawer's account for $25,000, the payor bank has a loss only to the extent that the drawer's account is less than the full amount of the check. There is no requirement that the payor bank pursue collection against the drawer beyond the amount in the drawer's account as a condition to the payor bank's action against the depositary bank for breach of warranty. See Georgia Railroad Bank & Trust Co. v. First National Bank & Trust, 229 S.E.2d 482 (Ga.App.1976), aff'd, 235 S.E.2d 1 (Ga.1977), and First National Bank of Boston v. Fidelity Bank, National Association, 724 F.Supp. 1168 (E.D.Pa.1989).

3. A person retaining items under an electronic presentment agreement (Section 4–110) warrants that it has complied with the terms of the agreement regarding its possession of the item and its sending a proper presentment notice. If the keeper is a customer, its depositary bank also makes this warranty.

Uniform Commercial Code Comment

Prior Uniform Statutory Provision:

Negotiable Instruments Law, Section 27.

Purpose:

The section completes the thought of the previous section and makes clear that a security interest in an item is "value" for the purpose of determining the holder's status as a holder in due course. The provision is in accord with the prior law (N.I.L. Section 27) and with Article 3 (Section 3–303). The section does not prescribe a security interest under Section 4–208 as a test of "value" generally because the meaning of "value" under other Articles is adequately defined in Section 1–201.

§ 4209

Cross References:

Sections 1–201, 3–302, 3–303 and 4–208.

Definitional Cross References:

"Bank". Section 1–201.
"Holder in due course". Section 3–302.
"Item". Section 4–104.
"Security interest". Section 1–201.

Cross References

Collecting bank, see Commercial Code § 4105.
Collecting bank's security interest, see Commercial Code § 4210.
Definitions, see Commercial Code § 1201.
Holder in due course, see Commercial Code § 3302.
Security interest of collecting bank, see Commercial Code § 4210.
Issue or transfer for value, see Commercial Code § 3303.

§ 4210. Security interest of collecting bank

* * * (a) A collecting bank has a security interest in an item and any accompanying documents or the proceeds of either:

(1) In case of an item deposited in an account to the extent to which credit given for the item has been withdrawn or applied.

(2) In case of an item for which it has given credit available for withdrawal as of right, to the extent of the credit given, whether or not the credit is drawn upon or there is a right of * * * charge-back.

(3) If it makes an advance on or against the item.

* * * (b) If credit * * * given for several items received at one time or pursuant to a single agreement is withdrawn or applied in part, the security interest remains upon all the items, any accompanying documents or the proceeds of either. For the purpose of this section, credits first given are first withdrawn.

(c) Receipt by a collecting bank of a final settlement for an item is a realization on its security interest in the item, accompanying documents, and proceeds. * * * So long as the bank does not receive final settlement for the item or give up possession of the item or accompanying documents for purposes other than collection, the security interest continues to that extent and is subject to * * * Division 9 * * * (commencing with Section 9101), but all of the following are applicable:

(1) No security agreement is necessary to make the security interest enforceable (paragraph (1) of subdivision (a) of Section 9203) * * *.

(2) No filing is required to perfect the security interest * * *.

(3) The security interest has priority over conflicting perfected security interests in the item, accompanying documents, or proceeds. *(Formerly § 4208, added by Stats.1963, c. 819, § 4208. Renumbered § 4210 and amended by Stats.1992, c. 914 (S.B.833), § 28.)*

California Code Comment

By John A. Bohn and Charles J. Williams

Prior California Law

1. This section permits a bank to make presentment of an item on a non-bank payor by sending written notice. This method of presentment was not authorized under the NIL (former Civil Code §§ 3082 to 3266d) and although it is recognized by custom, is said to be a legislative novelty at least in this country. Clarke, Bailey and Young, Bank Deposits and Collections (A.L.I.1963) 71, 76.

2. Former Civil Code § 3155 required that the instrument be exhibited upon presentment. Commercial Code § 3505(1)(a) permits the party to whom presentment is made to require exhibition of the instrument and subdivision (1) of this section provides that the bank must meet the requirements of the party under Commercial Code § 3505. As a practical matter the bank presenting the item must be close enough to the drawee to exhibit the instrument before the close of the next business day after it is requested. Official Comment 3.

3. Presentment under this section is good presentment under Commercial Code § 3504(5).

Changes from U.C.C. (1962 Official Text)

4. This is section 4–210 of the Official Text without change.

Uniform Commercial Code Comment
Official Reasons for 1990 Change

The addition of "collecting" in subsection (a) is a clarification. The other modifications are made to conform with current legislative drafting practices, with no intent to change substance.

1990 Change

1. Subsection (a) states a rational rule for the interest of a bank in an item. The customer of the depositary bank is normally the owner of the item and the several collecting banks are agents of the customer (Section 4–201). A collecting agent may properly make advances on the security of paper held for collection, and acquires at common law a possessory lien for these advances. Subsection (a) applies an analogous principle to a bank in the collection chain which extends credit on items in the course of collection. The bank has a security interest to the extent stated in this section. To the extent of its security interest it is a holder for value (Sections 3–303, 4–211) and a holder in due course if it satisfies the other requirements for that status (Section 3–302). Subsection (a) does not derogate from the banker's general common law lien or right of setoff against indebtedness owing in deposit accounts. See Section 1–103. Rather subsection (a) specifically implements and extends the principle as a part of the bank collection process.

2. Subsection (b) spreads the security interest of the bank over all items in a single deposit or received under a single agreement and a single giving of credit. It also adopts the "first-in, first-out" rule.

3. Collection statistics establish that the vast majority of items handled for collection are in fact collected. The first sentence of subsection (c) reflects the fact that in the normal case the bank's security interest is self-liquidating. The remainder of the subsection correlates the security interest with the provisions of Article 9, particularly for use in the cases of noncollection in which the security interest may be important.

Uniform Commercial Code Comment

Prior Uniform Statutory Provision:

None.

Purposes:

1. This section codifies a practice extensively followed in presentation of trade acceptances and documentary and other drafts drawn on non-bank payors. It imposes a duty on the payor to respond to the notice of the item if the item is not to be considered dishonored. Notice of such a dishonor charges parties secondarily liable. Presentment under this Section is good presentment under Article 3. Section 3–504(5).

2. A drawee not receiving notice is not, of course, liable to the drawer for wrongful dishonor.

3. A bank so presenting an instrument must be sufficiently close to the drawee to be able to exhibit the instrument on the day it is requested to do so or the next business day at the latest.

Cross References:

Sections 3–501 through 3–508, 4–501 and 4–502.

Definitional Cross References:

"Acceptance". Section 3–410.
"Banking day". Section 4–104.
"Collecting bank". Section 105.
"Item". Section 4–104.
"Party". Section 1–201.
"Presentment". Section 3–504.
"Secondary party". Section 3–102.
"Send". Section 1–201.

Cross References

Business days, banks, see Civil Code § 9.
Documentary drafts, manner of handling, see Commercial Code § 4501.
Negotiable instruments, presentment and notice of dishonor, see Commercial Code § 3501 et seq.
"On arrival" drafts, presentment, see Commercial Code § 4502.
Party to whom presentment is made, rights, see Commercial Code § 3501.
Personal property not in custody of levying officer transferred or encumbered, exceptions, see Code of Civil Procedure § 697.740.
State tax lien, invalidity against collecting bank holding security interest in items being collected, accompanying documents and proceeds, see Government Code § 7170.

§ 4211. Holder in due course; status of bank

For purposes of determining its status as a holder in due course, a bank has given value to the extent * * * it has a security interest in an item * * *, if the bank otherwise complies with the requirements of Section 3302 on what constitutes a holder in due course. (Formerly § 4209, added by Stats.1963, c. 819, § 4209. Renumbered § 4211 and amended by Stats.1992, c. 914 (S.B.833), § 30.)

California Code Comment

By John A. Bohn and Charles J. Williams

Prior California Law

1. Subdivision (1) lists the approved forms of remittance. However, this list is not exclusive. Official Comment 5, second paragraph.

Subdivision (1) is similar to Financial Code § 1015 except that the items in subdivision (1)(b) and (1)(c) are new. See Official Comments 1–5.

2. Subdivision (2) relieves the collecting bank of liability if an approved form of remittance is later unpaid. Official Comment 6.

The midnight deadline for dishonor is similar to former Financial Code § 1013.

3. Subdivision (3) has no statutory counterpart in prior California law. It states the general rules as to when a settlement by remittance instrument becomes final. Official Comment 7.

Paragraph (a) of subdivision (3) states the general rule that settlement by an approved remittance instrument becomes final when it is paid. See Commercial Code § 4213 for what constitutes final payment.

The provision of subdivision (3) regarding an unauthorized remittance is in accord with prior California law. In Midway Five Oil Co. v. Citizens Nat. Bank, 25 Cal.App. 366, 143 Pac. 800 (1914) the bank accepted a means of payment not authorized (certified check instead of cash) and the court held that it assumed the risk that the other means of payment is good for the amount stated until it is paid by the payor (bank issuing the certified check).

Changes from U.C.C. (1962 Official Text)

4. Paragraphs (e) and (f) in subdivision (1) are peculiar to the California version and do not appear in Section 4–211 of the Official Text.

Each is taken from former Financial Code § 1015 and included for the following reasons:

". . . the Official Text of section 14211 [4211] lists that which a bank may accept in settlement of an item in the collection process, but does not mention 'money.' The Code drafters did not intend to forbid acceptance of money. [Official Comment 5] [Footnote: Comments to Code, Sec. 4–211, Note 5] Section 14211 [4211] sought only to eliminate the common law rule that a bank could accept nothing but money. But a bank should not have to decide at its own risk that taking money is reasonable. Hence this section has been amended in S.B. 1093 [1961 Session, 1958 Official Text as Amended] to include money, as well as credit on the books of a Federal Reserve Bank or other bank designated by the collecting bank, also left out of the Official Text." California State Bar Committee on the Commercial Code, A Special Report, The Uniform Commercial Code, 37 Calif.State Bar J. (March–April 1962) 164.

Professors Marsh and Warren disagreed with the inclusion of these paragraphs:

". . . Obviously, this subsection [subdivision (1)] was not intended to prevent a bank from taking 'money' in settlement of an item, although it would certainly have been better to mention money in the subsection [subdivision] as originally drafted. The same considerations apply here as under Section 14204(2) [4202(2)] above. See the discussion under that section. In the interests of uniformity, we recommend the rejection of the amendment." Sixth Progress Report to the Legislature by the Senate Fact Finding Committee on Judiciary (1959–1961) Part 1, The Uniform Commercial Code, p. 474.

Uniform Commercial Code Comment

Official Reasons for 1990 Change

Modified to conform with current drafting practices; no intent to change substance.

1990 Change

The section completes the thought of the previous section and makes clear that a security interest in an item is "value" for the purpose of determining the holder's status as a holder in due course. The provision is in accord with the prior law (N.I.L. Section 27) and with Article 3 (Section 3–303). The section does not prescribe a security interest under Section 4–210 as a test of "value" generally because the meaning of "value" under other Articles is adequately defined in Section 1–201.

Uniform Commercial Code Comment

Prior Uniform Statutory Provision:

None; but see Sections 9 and 10 American Bankers Association Bank Collection Code.

Purposes:

1. Subsection (1) states various types of remittance instruments and authorities to charge which may be received by a collecting bank in a settlement for an item, without the collecting bank being responsible if such form of remittance is not itself paid. The action of the collecting bank in receiving these provisional forms of remittance is approved and the risk that they are not paid is placed on the owner of the item, and not on the collecting bank. Justification for these results lies in the fact that with the tremendous volume of items collected it is simply not mechanically feasible to remit or pay in money or other forms of technical "legal tender". Since it is not feasible for banks to perform their collection functions except with the use of these provisional remittances, they should not be penalized for acting in the only way they can act.

2. The first approved form of provisional remittance having these results is a check of the remitting bank or of another bank on any bank except the remitting bank (subsection (1)(a)). A check on the remitting bank itself is not approved because this would merely be substituting for the original item another item on the same payor.

3. A cashier's check or similar primary obligation of the remitting bank which is a member of or clears through a member of the same clearing house or group as the collecting bank is approved by subsection (1)(b) because this is just as speedy and effective a means of settlement through a clearing house as any other type of instrument or a check on

§ 4211 BANK DEPOSITS AND COLLECTIONS 272

another bank. On the other hand such cashier's checks or primary obligations are not approved for use at the owner's risk, outside a single clearing house or clearing area because when so used they do not constitute a means of final settlement but merely substitute one item on the remitting bank for another one on the same bank. To the remitting bank they may have benefit in maintaining "float" or having the use of money even though drawn against, but this is not looked upon as sound practice.

4. Subsection (1)(d) recognizes and approves the general and consistent practice of collecting banks to accept cashier's checks, certified checks or other bank checks or obligations as a proper means of remittance from non-bank payors, with the owner of the original item carrying the risk of non-payment of these bank instruments rather than the collecting bank, to the extent there is any risk. Here again this rule and practice is justified by the fact that payment in money for all practical purposes is no longer feasible and consequently is not used except in rare instances. Subsection (1)(d) recognizes the standard medium that is used.

5. This section does not purport to deal with all kinds of settlements for items. It does not purport to deal with settlements for "cash items" (described in Comments to Section 4–212), settlements merely by debits and credits in accounts between banks (Section 4–213) or settlements through clearing houses. The section is limited to those situations where a collecting or payor bank or a non-bank payor receives an item and accounts for it by "remitting" or "sending back" something for the item, usually some form of a remittance instrument, order or authorization. Some specific rules are needed for remittance cases because of time required to process the remittance instrument.

Failure to mention in subsection (1) entries in accounts between banks and clearing house settlements carries no implication of impropriety of these types of provisional or final settlement. Approval of these means of settlement is evidenced by the definition of "settle" in Section 4–104(j), provision for charge-back and refund in Section 4–212, and provisions regarding settlements becoming final (Section 4–213). Further, the specific listing in subsection (1) of certain usual types of remittances does not imply that all other types of remittances are improper (Section 4–103(4)).

6. Subsection (2) provides that if a remittance is one of the kinds approved by subsection (1) and the collecting bank receiving the item acts seasonably in handling it before the bank's midnight deadline, the bank is not liable to prior parties in the event of dishonor. The subsection also provides for an additional situation. If without any authorization whatsoever the payor or remitting bank or person remits with an improper remittance instrument, the collecting bank should not be penalized where it is without fault. Nevertheless, the owner of the item may not be served if the collecting bank rejects the improper instrument. In many cases the best course would be to collect the instrument as rapidly as possible. Subsection (2) provides that if this is done the collecting bank is not responsible in the event of dishonor.

7. Subsection (3) complements subsections (1) and (2) by providing when a settlement by means of a remittance instrument or authorization to charge becomes final. Subparagraph (a) provides that in situations specified in subsection (2) the settlement becomes final at the time the remittance instrument or authorization is finally paid by the payor by which it is payable. The standards determining this final payment are those prescribed in Section 4–213. Conversely, under subparagraph (b) if the person receiving the settlement has authorized remittance by certain specified media not approved by subsection (1) the settlement becomes final at the time of receipt of such check or obligation. In this event the person receiving the settlement assumes the risk that the remittance instrument is not itself paid. A prior course of dealing of receiving unapproved forms of remittances from the payor or remitting person in question would be the equivalent of an authorization and effective as such. Subparagraph (c) provides for most, if not all, remaining remittance situations. Here settlement becomes final at the midnight deadline of the person receiving the remittance.

Subsection (3) provides that the times of final settlement prescribed apply both to the person making and the person receiving the settlement. Further, by use of the term "person", these rules also apply to non-bank payors of items and non-bank customers for whom items are being collected, as well as to collecting and payor banks.

8. When settlement is by credit in an account with another bank Section 4–213 controls.

Cross Reference:

Section 4–213.

Definitional Cross References:

"Account". Section 4–104.
"Bank". Section 1–201.
"Clearing house". Section 4–104.
"Collecting bank". Section 4–105.
"Item". Section 4–104.
"Midnight deadline". Section 4–104.
"Money". Section 1–201.
"Payor bank". Section 4–105.
"Person". Section 1–201.
"Remitting bank". Section 4–105.
"Settle". Section 4–104.

Cross References

Business days, banks, see Civil Code § 9.
Certification, see Commercial Code § 3409.
Charging back item, see Commercial Code § 4214.
Check, see Commercial Code § 3104.
Deferred posting, recovery of payment by return, see Commercial Code § 4301.
Finality of payment, see Commercial Code § 4215.
Forwarding item for collection, see Commercial Code § 4204.
Notice of dishonor, see Commercial Code § 3503.
Provisional status of credits, see Commercial Code § 4201.

§ 4212. Items not payable by, through or at bank; presentment of notice

* * * (a) Unless otherwise instructed, a collecting bank may present an item not payable by, through, or at a bank by sending to the party to accept or pay a written notice that the bank holds the item for acceptance or payment. The notice shall be sent in time to be received on or before the day when presentment is due and the bank shall meet any requirement of the party to accept or pay under Section 3501 by the close of the bank's next banking day after it knows of the requirement.

* * * (b) If presentment is made by notice and * * * payment, acceptance, or request for compliance with a requirement under Section 3501 is not received by the close of business on the day after maturity or, in the case of demand items, by the close of business on the third banking day after notice was sent, the presenting bank may treat the item as dishonored and charge any * * * drawer or indorser by sending it notice of the facts. (Formerly § 4210, added by Stats.1963, c. 819, § 4210. Renumbered § 4212 and amended by Stats. 1992, c. 914 (S.B.833), § 31.)

California Code Comment

By John A. Bohn and Charles J. Williams

Prior California Law

1. Subdivision (1) is similar to former Financial Code § 1017 which provided both a right of charge back and also gave a right "to collect the amount of the item". The main difference appears to be that under subdivision (1) something more is required by the bank than just charging the customer's account. The bank must return the item or send notification either by its midnight deadline or such longer reasonable time when it cannot act by the midnight deadline. The court in Anthony v. Crocker First Nat. Bank, 95 Cal.App. 347, 272 Pac. 767 (1928) recognized the right of charge back when it held that the bank

could charge the account of one who deposited worthless paper for collection.

2. Subdivision (2) of the Official Text is omitted in California. See California Code Comment 4 to section 4202 for an explanation of the omission. Official Comment 4 explains the purpose of the subdivision.

3. Subdivision (3) is in accord with prior California law. It refers to the methods for charging back or obtaining a refund.

Former Financial Code § 1017 did not specify the precise method by which the bank could collect but the substance of subdivision (3) appears to fall within its general intent and purpose. For example, see Anthony v. Crocker First Nat. Bank, 95 Cal.App. 347, 272 Pac. 767 (1928).

4. Subdivision (4)(a) is in accord with prior California law. Subdivision (4)(b) is new. See Official Comments 5 and 6.

5. Subdivision (5) is new to California law but is consistent with the cases allowing the bank to charge back without limiting the bank's rights. Anthony v. Crocker First Nat. Bank, 95 Cal.App. 347, 272 Pac. 767 (1928); Faulkner v. Bank of Italy, 69 Cal.App. 370, 231 Pac. 380 (1924).

6. Subdivision (6) provides the rule for determining the rate of exchange in collections involving foreign currency. The time fixed for determining the rate of exchange can be changed by agreement. Official Comment 7.

7. Subdivision (7) preserves the right to obtain refund. It complements subdivision (4) which preserves the right to charge back. Its purpose is explained as follows:

". . . the right to obtain a refund should no more be affected by the prior use of the credit than the right to charge back. Further, the bank's liability for negligence might be less than the credit used, and the bank should not be barred from recovering the difference. Therefore, in S.B. 1093 [1961 Session, 1958 Official Text as amended] a new subdivision added to section 14212 [4212] would provide that the bank's right to obtain a refund is not affected by the prior use of the credit or by the bank's negligence 'except to the extent of the bank's liability therefor.'" California State Bar Committee on the Commercial Code, A Special Report, The Uniform Commercial Code, 37 Calif.State Bar J. (March–April, 1962) 167.

Changes from U.C.C. (1962 Official Text)

8. Subdivision (2) of section 4–212 of the Official Text is omitted in the California version. Subdivision (2) reads as follows:

"(2) Within the time and manner prescribed by this section and Section 4–301, an intermediary or payor bank, as the case may be, may return an unpaid item directly to the depositary bank and may send for collection a draft on the depositary bank and obtain reimbursement. In such case, if the depositary bank has received provisional settlement for the item, it must reimburse the bank drawing the draft and any provisional credits for the item between banks shall become and remain final."

9. Subdivision (7) does not appear in section 4–212 of the 1962 Official Text. See California Code Comment 7, supra, for the reason why it was added in California. The inclusion of a similar provision in an earlier version of the code was criticized in the Marsh and Warren Report:

The State Bar Committee report gives no reason for the proposed amendment [which would add the right to obtain a refund], and the California Bankers Committee did not consider the amendment necessary. We wonder if the State Bar Committee did not believe that the right to a refund had been inadvertently left out of subsection [subdivision] (3) since every other time this section mentions the right to charge back it is coupled with the right of refund. The Official Comments, however, show that the omission of the right of refund in this subsection [subdivision] (3) was deliberate. [Comment 5]

This Section gives a collecting bank that has made a provisional settlement with its customer the right to revoke the settlement if it fails to obtain a settlement for an item and to charge back the amount credited to the customer's account or to obtain a refund from its customer. We assume that the right to obtain a refund will be used in cases when the credit has been drawn on, or the provisional settlement was made in cash or in some other manner that does not produce a book credit subject to a chargeback. See 2 N.Y.Law Rev. Comm., Study of the Uniform Commercial Code (1955) 1362. The Official Comments indicate that subsection [subdivision] (3) allows a chargeback even in cases where the nonpayment results from the depositary bank's own negligence. The Comments state: "Any other rule would result in litigation based upon a claim for wrongful dishonor of other checks of the customer, with potential damages far in excess of the amount of the item. Any other rule would require a bank to determine difficult questions of fact." [Official Comment 5] If we assume that the right of refund will be used when there is no book credit in the customer's account, the policy reason given for allowing a negligent depositary bank a right of chargeback does not support granting it a right of refund. In our opinion, there is no justification for giving a negligent depositary bank a right of refund against a customer. Sixth Progress Report to the Legislature by Senate Fact Finding Committee on Judiciary (1959–1961) Part 1, The Uniform Commercial Code, p. 475.

Uniform Commercial Code Comment

Official Reasons for 1990 Change

The term "secondary party" is no longer used in Articles 3 and 4. The other modifications are made to conform with current legislative drafting practices, with no intent to change substance.

1990 Change

1. This section codifies a practice extensively followed in presentation of trade acceptances and documentary and other drafts drawn on nonbank payors. It imposes a duty on the payor to respond to the notice of the item if the item is not to be considered dishonored. Notice of such a dishonor charges drawers and indorsers. Presentment under this section is good presentment under Article 3. See Section 3–501.

2. A drawee not receiving notice is not, of course, liable to the drawer for wrongful dishonor.

3. A bank so presenting an instrument must be sufficiently close to the drawee to be able to exhibit the instrument on the day it is requested to do so or the next business day at the latest.

Uniform Commercial Code Comment

Prior Uniform Statutory Provision:

None; but see Sections 2 and 11, American Bankers Association Bank Collection Code.

Purposes:

1. Under current bank practice, in a major portion of cases banks make provisional settlement for items when they are first received and then await subsequent determination of whether the item will be finally paid. This is the principal characteristic of what are referred to in banking parlance as "cash items". Statistically, this practice of settling provisionally first and then awaiting final payment is justified because more than ninety-nine per cent of such cash items are finally paid, with the result that in this great preponderance of cases it becomes unnecessary for the banks making the provisional settlements to make any further entries. In due course the provisional settlements become final simply with the lapse of time. However, in those cases where the item being collected is not finally paid or where for various reasons the bank making the provisional settlement does not itself receive final payment, under the American Bankers Association Bank Collection Code, under Federal Reserve Regulations and operating letters and under various types of agreements between banks and between customers and banks, provision is made for the reversal of the provisional settlements, charge-back of provisional credits and the right to obtain refund. Subsection (1) codifies and simplifies the statement of these rights.

2. Various causes of a bank not receiving final payment, with the resulting right of charge-back or refund, are stated or suggested in subsection (1). These include dishonor of the original item; dishonor of a remittance instrument given for it; reversal of a provisional credit for the item; suspension of payments by another bank. The causes stated are illustrative; the right of charge-back or refund is stated to exist whether the failure to receive final payment in ordinary course arises through one of them "or otherwise".

3. The right of charge-back or refund exists if a collecting bank has made a provisional settlement for an item with its customer but terminates if and when a settlement received by the bank for the item is or becomes final. If the bank fails to receive such a final settlement the right of charge-back or refund must be exercised promptly after the

bank learns the facts. The right exists (if so promptly exercised) whether or not the bank is able to return the item.

4. Subsection (2) [Inapplicable in California, see California Code Comment, note 8] is an affirmative provision for so-called "direct returns". This is a new practice that is currently in the process of developing in a few sections of the country. Its purpose is to speed up the return of unpaid items by avoiding handling by one or more intermediate banks. The subsection is bracketed because the practice is not yet well established and some bankers and bank lawyers would prefer to let the practice develop by agreement. The contention is made that substantive rights between banks may be affected, e.g. available set-offs, but proponents contend advantages of direct returns outweigh possible detriments. However, if the subsection were omitted, the election to use direct returns would be on the depositary bank and it would probably be necessary for that bank to specifically authorize direct returns with each outgoing letter. This is a cumbersome way of meeting the problem. If the subsection is retained the payor bank, unless it has been specifically directed otherwise, will have the right to make the decision whether it will return an unpaid item directly. Since the subsection is permissive and its inclusion tends toward greater flexibility, its retention is recommended.

5. The rule of subsection (4) relating to charge-back (as distinguished from claim for refund) applies irrespective of the cause of the nonpayment, and of the person ultimately liable for nonpayment. Thus charge-back is permitted even where nonpayment results from the depositary bank's own negligence. Any other rule would result in litigation based upon a claim for wrongful dishonor of other checks of the customer, with potential damages far in excess of the amount of the item. Any other rule would require a bank to determine difficult questions of fact. The customer's protection is found in the general obligation of good faith (Sections 1–203 and 4–103). If bad faith is established the customer's recovery "includes other damages, if any, suffered by the party as a proximate consequence" (Section 4–103(5); see also Section 4–402).

6. It is clear that the charge-back does not relieve the bank from any liability for failure to exercise ordinary care in handling the item. The measure of damages for such failure is stated in Section 4–103(5).

7. Subsection (6) states a rule fixing the time for determining the rate of exchange if there is a charge-back or refund of a credit given in dollars for an item payable in a foreign currency. Compare Section 3–107(2). Fixing such a rule is desirable to avoid disputes. If in any case the parties wish to fix a different time for determining the rate of exchange, they may do so by agreement.

Cross References:

Sections 1–203, 3–107, 4–103, 4–211(3), 4–213(2) and (3), 4–402.

Definitional Cross References:

"Account". Section 4–104.
"Collecting bank". Section 4–105.
"Customer". Section 4–104.
"Depositary bank". Section 4–105.
"Intermediary bank". Section 4–105.
"Item". Section 4–104.
"Midnight deadline". Section 4–104.
"Payor bank". Section 4–105.
"Send". Section 1–201.
"Settlement". Section 4–104.
"Suspension of payment". Section 4–104.

Cross References

Agency status of collecting banks, see Commercial Code § 4201.
Damages for failure to exercise ordinary care, see Commercial Code § 4103(e).
Discharge of negotiable instruments, methods of, see Commercial Code § 3601 et seq.
Forwarding for collection, see Commercial Code § 4204.
Holder's right of recourse, see Commercial Code § 3507.
Medium of exchange, see Commercial Code § 3107.
Obligation,
  Indorser, see Commercial Code § 3415.
  Issuer, drawer and acceptor, see Commercial Code § 3413 et seq.
Obligation of good faith, see Commercial Code §§ 1203, 4103.
Payment,
  Generally, see Civil Code § 1478.
  Charging against accounts, see Commercial Code § 4401.
  Discharge, see Commercial Code § 3602.
  Final, see Commercial Code § 4215.
  Finality of, see Commercial Code § 3418.
  Suspended, see Commercial Code § 4216.
  Time, see Commercial Code §§ 3108, 3501.
Provisional credit, see Commercial Code § 4201.
Provisional debits and credits, finality, see Commercial Code § 4215.
Recovery of payment by return of item, see Commercial Code § 4301.
Standard of care for collection, see Commercial Code § 4202.
Settlement in remittance cases, finality, see Commercial Code § 4211(3).
Warranties on presentment and transfer, see Commercial Code §§ 3416, 3417.
Wrongful dishonor, bank's liability, see Commercial Code § 4402.

§ 4213. Settlement by bank

(a) With respect to settlement by a bank, the medium and time of settlement may be prescribed by Federal Reserve regulations or circulars, clearing house rules, and the like, or agreement. In the absence of that prescription, the following are applicable:

(1) The medium of settlement is cash or credit to an account in a federal reserve bank of or specified by the person to receive settlement.

(2) The time of settlement is any of the following:

(A) With respect to tender of settlement by cash, a cashier's check, or teller's check, when the cash or check is sent or delivered.

(B) With respect to tender of settlement by credit in an account in a federal reserve bank, when the credit is made.

(C) With respect to tender of settlement by a credit or debit to an account in a bank, when the credit or debit is made or, in the case of tender of settlement by authority to charge an account, when the authority is sent or delivered.

(D) With respect to tender of settlement by a funds transfer, when payment is made pursuant to subdivision (a) of Section 11406 to the person receiving settlement.

(b) If the tender of settlement is not by a medium authorized by subdivision (a) or the time of settlement is not fixed by subdivision (a), no settlement occurs until the tender of settlement is accepted by the person receiving settlement.

(c) If settlement for an item is made by cashier's check or teller's check and the person receiving settlement, before its midnight deadline either:

(1) Presents or forwards the check for collection, settlement is final when the check is finally paid.

(2) Fails to present or forward the check for collection, settlement is final at the midnight deadline of the person receiving settlement.

(d) If settlement for an item is made by giving authority to charge the account of the bank giving settlement in the bank receiving settlement, settlement is final when the charge is made by the bank receiving settlement if there are funds available in the account for the amount of the item. *(Added by Stats.1992, c. 914 (S.B.833), § 33.)*

California Code Comment

By John A. Bohn and Charles J. Williams

Prior California Law

1. Subdivision (1) provides a uniform standard determining the time when final payment of an item occurs. The standard for determining final payment is based solely upon action of the payor bank and is not affected by whether payment is made by a remittance draft or whether such draft is itself paid. Official Comment 2.

When an item is finally paid is important in (1) determining priority as between the owner of the item and the drawer or creditors of the drawer (Commercial Code § 4303) and (2) fixing preferential rights if the payor bank becomes insolvent (Commercial Code § 4214(1), (2)). Official Comment 1, second paragraph.

2. Subdivision (1) is new statutory law.

There is no prior statutory case law rule as to what act of the payor bank constituted final payment and there was uncertainty as to when an item was finally paid.

Subdivision (1)(a) restates what is generally agreed to be a universal rule that payment in cash is final payment. Official Comment 3, second paragraph; Clarke, Bailey and Young, Bank Deposits and Collections, 76 (A.L.I.1963). This same rule was assumed although not stated in Larrus v. First Nat. Bank, 122 Cal.App.2d 884, 266 P.2d 143 (1954). In Utah Construction Co. v. Western Pacific Ry., 174 Cal. 156, 162 Pac. 631 (1916) the court held that credit given by a payor bank on its books to the account of the presenting bank was final payment.

Subdivisions (1)(b) and (1)(d) are new. Rather than modify prior law, they fill a gap in it.

3. Subdivision (2) codifies the practice of "firming up." See Official Comment 8. This subdivision is new statutory law but is consistent with Utah Construction Co. v. Western Pacific Ry. cited in California Code Comment 2 above.

4. Subdivision (3) is new. See Official Comment 9.
5. Subdivision (4) is new. See Official Comments 10 and 11.
6. Subdivision (5) is new. See Official Comment 12.

Changes from U.C.C. (1962 Official Text)

7. Subdivisions (2), (3), (4) and (5) are the same as the corresponding subdivisions of section 4–213 of the 1962 Official Text.

Subdivision (1) of section 4–213 of the 1962 Official Text has been changed in California. The Official Text with the California changes read:

"4213. (1) An item is finally paid by a payor bank when the bank has done any of the following, whichever happens first:

"(a) Paid the item in cash; or

"(b) Settled for the item without [reserving] having a right to revoke the settlement [and without having such right] under any of the following: statute, clearinghouse rule, [or] agreement, or reservation thereof; or

"[(c) Completed the process of posting the item to the indicated account of the drawer, maker, or other person to be charged therewith; or]

"(d) [Made a provisional settlement] Settled for the item having a right to revoke the settlement under any one or more of the following: statute, clearinghouse rule, agreement or reservation thereof, and failed to revoke the settlement in the time and manner permitted [by statute, clearinghouse rule or agreement] under such right.

Upon final payment under [subparagraphs] paragraphs (b), [, (c)] or (d) the payor bank shall be accountable for the amount of the item."

8. Paragraph (c) of subdivision (1) is omitted because California banks have centralized bookkeeping systems:

"The proposed deletion of clause (c) of the original subsection [subdivision] is suggested in the light of the practice of California banks of having centralized bookkeeping systems where items are posted first and thereafter sent to the proper branch for checking of signatures, stop payments, and the like. If clause (c) were retained in its present form the unfortunate consequences would be that an item would be considered to be finally paid by a bank before the signature had been verified. This raises the question whether to amend clause (c) to provide that an item is not finally paid until verified and posted or whether it is best to delete it. California bankers and bank lawyers believe it should be deleted because of the uncertainty and indefiniteness of relating 'payment' to the procedures of bookkeeping systems, whether mechanical or manual. They prefer to relate 'payment' to failure to revoke within the time allotted by statute, clearinghouse rule or agreement." Marsh and Warren Report, Sixth Progress Report to the Legislature by Senate Fact Finding Committee on Judiciary (1959–1961) Part 1, The Uniform Commercial Code, p. 476.

Also see California State Bar Committee on the Commercial Code, A Special Report, The Uniform Commercial Code, 37 Calif.State Bar J. 117, 165.

9. The reason for the change in subdivision (1)(b) is explained in the Marsh and Warren Report:

"The proposed change of 'and' to 'or' in clause (b) is suggested because of the belief of the State Bar Committee and the California Bankers Committee that the clause in its present form might be interpreted as requiring that a bank have a right to revoke under *both* a clearinghouse rule and a reservation of such right before the settlement was considered provisional. If this were correct, it would require the reintroduction of lengthy 'collection legends' on deposit slips and the like, which were abandoned by California banks many years ago. On the other hand, Walter Malcolm, the distinguished attorney and one of the authors of Chapter [Division] 4, in a letter to the Chairman of the Commissioners on Uniform State Laws commenting on this proposal, states that in his opinion the change to 'or' will have exactly the effect which these California committees think the 'and' will have.

"When such distinguished counsel disagree, it is obvious that a court might be confused by the use of either word and it seems the part of prudence to avoid the 'and/or' problem altogether. This we have attempted to do in the proposed revision of clauses (b) and (c) [formerly (d)]. In this recommended revision we have attempted to state explicitly, without the use of 'and' or 'or,' that the right to revoke need not exist under *only one* of these sources in order for the settlement to be provisional." Sixth Progress Report to the Legislature by Senate Fact Finding Committee on Judiciary (1959–1961) Part 1, The Uniform Commercial Code, pp. 476–477.

Uniform Commercial Code Comment

Official Reasons for 1990 Change

New section. See the Official Comment. Former Section 4–211 applied only to settlements by remittance instruments and authorities to charge which could be received in settlement by a collecting bank without the collecting bank's being responsible if the remittance wasn't paid. The new section is much broader in stating general rules for all types of settlements with respect to the time settlement is made and the medium which the person receiving settlement must accept. Subsections (c) and (d) apply to the issues treated in former Section 4–211.

1990 Change

1. Subsection (a) sets forth the medium of settlement that the person receiving settlement must accept. In nearly all cases the medium of settlement will be determined by agreement or by Federal Reserve regulations and circulars, clearing-house rules, and the like. In the absence of regulations, rules or agreement, the person receiving settlement may demand cash or credit in a Federal Reserve bank. If the person receiving settlement does not have an account in a Federal Reserve bank, it may specify the account of another bank in a Federal Reserve bank. In the unusual case in which there is no agreement on the medium of settlement and the bank making settlement tenders settlement other than cash or Federal Reserve bank credit, no settlement has occurred under subsection (b) unless the person receiving settlement accepts the settlement tendered. For example, if a payor bank, without agreement, tenders a teller's check, the bank receiving the settlement may reject the check and return it to the payor bank or it may accept the check as settlement.

2. In several provisions of Article 4 the time that a settlement occurs is relevant. Subsection (a) sets out a general rule that the time of settlement, like the means of settlement, may be prescribed by agreement. In the absence of agreement, the time of settlement for tender of the common agreed media of settlement is that set out in subsection (a)(2). The time of settlement by cash, cashier's or teller's

check or authority to charge an account is the time the cash, check or authority is sent, unless presentment is over the counter in which case settlement occurs upon delivery to the presenter. If there is no agreement on the time of settlement and the tender of settlement is not made by one of the media set out in subsection (a), under subsection (b) the time of settlement is the time the settlement is accepted by the person receiving settlement.

3. Subsections (c) and (d) are special provisions for settlement by remittance drafts and authority to charge an account in the bank receiving settlement. The relationship between final settlement and final payment under Section 4-215 is addressed in subsection (b) of Section 4-215. With respect to settlement by cashier's checks or teller's checks, other than in response to over-the-counter presentment, the bank receiving settlement can keep the risk that the check will not be paid on the bank tendering the check in settlement by acting to initiate collection of the check within the midnight deadline of the bank receiving settlement. If the bank fails to initiate settlement before its midnight deadline, final settlement occurs at the midnight deadline, and the bank receiving settlement assumes the risk that the check will not be paid. If there is no agreement that permits the bank tendering settlement to tender a cashier's or teller's check, subsection (b) allows the bank receiving the check to reject it, and, if it does, no settlement occurs. However, if the bank accepts the check, settlement occurs and the time of final settlement is governed by subsection (c).

With respect to settlement by tender of authority to charge the account of the bank making settlement in the bank receiving settlement, subsection (d) provides that final settlement does not take place until the account charged has available funds to cover the amount of the item. If there is no agreement that permits the bank tendering settlement to tender an authority to charge an account as settlement, subsection (b) allows the bank receiving the tender to reject it. However, if the bank accepts the authority, settlement occurs and the time of final settlement is governed by subsection (d).

Uniform Commercial Code Comment

Prior Uniform Statutory Provisions: None; but see Section 11, American Bankers Association Bank Collection Code.

Purposes:

1. By the definition and use of the term "settle" (Section 4-104(j)) this Article recognizes that various debits or credits, remittances, settlements or payments given for an item may be either provisional or final, that settlements sometimes are provisional and sometimes are final and sometimes are provisional for awhile but later become final. Subsection (1) of Section 4-213 defines when settlement for an item or other action with respect to it constitutes final payment.

Final payment of an item is important for a number of reasons. It is one of several factors determining the relative priorities between items and notices, stop-orders, legal process and set-offs (Section 4-303). It is the "end of the line" in the collection process and the "turn around" point commencing the return flow of proceeds. It is the point at which many provisional settlements become final. See Section 4-213(2). Final payment of an item by the payor bank fixes preferential rights under Section 4-214(1) and (2).

2. If an item being collected moves through several states, e.g., is deposited for collection in California, moves through two or three California banks to the Federal Reserve Bank of San Francisco, to the Federal Reserve Bank of Boston, to a payor bank in Maine, the collection process involves the eastward journey of the item from California to Maine and the westward journey of the proceeds from Maine to California. Subsection (1) adopts the basic policy that final payment occurs at some point in the processing of the item by the payor bank. This policy recognizes that final payment does not take place, in such hypothetical case, on the journey of the item eastward. It also adopts the view that neither does final payment occur on the journey westward because what in fact is journeying westward are *proceeds* of the item. Because the true tests of final payment are the same in all cases and to avoid the confusion resulting from variable standards, the rule basing final payment exclusively on action of the payor bank is not affected by whether payment is made by a remittance draft or whether such draft is itself paid. Consequently, subsection (1) rejects those cases which base time of payment of the item in remittance cases on whether the remittance draft was *accepted* by the presenting bank; Page v. Holmes-Darst Coal Co., 269 Mich. 159, 256 N.W. 840 (1934);

Tobiason v. First State Bank of Ashby, 173 Minn. 533, 217 N.W. 934 (1928); Bohlig v. First Nat. Bank in Wadena, 233 Minn. 523, 48 N.W.2d 445 (1951); Dewey v. Margolis & Brooks, 195 N.C. 307, 142 S.E. 22 (1928); Texas Electric Service Co. v. Clark, 47 S.W.2d 483 (Tex.Civ. App.1932); cf. Ellis Way Drug Co. v. McLean, 176 Miss. 830, 170 So. 288 (1936); 2 Paton's Digest 1332; or whether the remittance draft was itself *paid;* Cleve v. Craven Chemical Co., 18 F.2d 711 (4th Cir. 1927); Holdingford Milling Co. v. Hillman Farmers' Cooperative Creamery, 181 Minn. 212, 231 N.W. 928 (1930); or upon an election of a collecting bank under Section 11 of the American Bankers Association Bank Collection Code; United States Pipe & Foundry Co. v. City of Hornell, 146 Misc. 812, 263 N.Y.S. 89 (1933); Jones v. Board of Education, 242 App.Div. 17, 272 N.Y.S. 5 (1934); Matter of State Bank of Binghamton, 156 Misc. 353, 281 N.Y.S. 706 (1935); cf. Malcolm, Inc. v. Burlington City Loan & Trust Co., 115 N.J.Eq. 227, 170 A. 32 (1934). Of course, the time of payment of the remittance draft will be governed by subsection (1) but payment or nonpayment of the remittance draft will not change the time of payment of the original item.

3. In fixing the point of time within the payor bank when an item is finally paid, subsection (1) recognizes and is framed on the basis that in a payor bank an item goes through a series of processes before its handling is completed. The item is received first from the clearing house or over the counter or through the mail. When received over the counter, the bank may receipt for it in some way by making a notation in the customer's passbook or by receipting a duplicate deposit slip. After the initial receipt the item moves to the sorting and proving departments. When sorted and proved it may be photographed. Still later it moves to the bookkeeping department where it is examined for form and signature and compared against the ledger account of the customer to whom it is to be charged. If it is in good form and there are funds to cover it, it is posted to the drawer's account, either immediately or at a later time. If paid, it is so marked and filed with other items of the same customer. This process may take either a few hours or substantially all of the day of receipt and of the next banking day.

Within this period of processing by the payor bank subsection (1) first recognizes two types of overt external acts constituting final payment. Traditionally and under various decisions payment in cash of an item by a payor bank has been considered final payment. Chambers v. Miller, 13 C.B.N.S. 125 (Eng.1862); Fidelity & Casualty Co. of New York v. Planenscheck, 200 Wis. 304, 309, 227 N.W. 387, 389, 71 A.L.R. 331 (1929); see Bellevue Bank of Allen Kimberly & Co. v. Security Nat. Bank of Sioux City, 168 Iowa 707, 712, 150 N.W. 1076, 1077 (1915); 1 Paton's Digest 1066. Subsection (1)(a) first recognizes and provides that payment of an item in cash by a payor bank is final payment.

4. Section 4-104(j) defines "settle" as meaning "to pay in cash, by clearing house settlement, in a charge or credit or by remittance, or otherwise as instructed. A settlement may be either provisional or final;" Subsection (1)(b) of Section 4-213 provides that an item is finally paid by a payor bank when the bank has "settled for the item without reserving a right to revoke the settlement and without having such right under statute, clearing house rule or agreement". Subsection (1)(b) provides in effect that if the payor bank finally settles for an item this constitutes final payment of the item. The subsection operates if nothing has occurred and no situation exists making the settlement provisional. If at the time of settlement the payor bank reserves a right to revoke the settlement, the settlement is provisional. In the alternative, if under statute, clearing house rule or agreement, a right of revocation of the settlement exists the settlement is provisional. Conversely, if there is an absence of a reservation of the right to revoke and also an absence of a right to revoke under statute, clearing house rule or agreement, the settlement is final and such final settlement constitutes final payment of the item.

A primary example of a statutory right on the part of the payor bank to revoke a settlement is the right to revoke conferred by Section 4-301. The underlying theory and reason for deferred posting statutes (Section 4-301) is to require a settlement on the date of receipt of an item but to keep that settlement provisional with the right to revoke prior to the midnight deadline. In any case where Section 4-301 is applicable, any settlement by the payor bank is provisional solely by virtue of the statute, subsection (1)(b) of Section 4-213 does not operate and such provisional settlement does not constitute final payment of the item.

A second important example of a right to revoke a settlement is that arising under clearing house rules. It is very common for clearing house rules to provide that items exchanged and settled for in a clearing (e.g., before 10:00 a.m. on Monday) may be returned and the settlements revoked up to but not later than 2:00 p.m. on the same day (Monday) or under deferred posting at some hour on the next business day (e.g., 2:00 p.m. Tuesday). Under this type of rule the Monday morning settlement is provisional and being provisional does not constitute a final payment of the item.

An example of a reservation of a right to revoke a settlement is where the payor bank is also the depositary bank and has signed a receipt or duplicate deposit ticket or has made an entry in a passbook acknowledging receipt, for credit to the account of A, of a check drawn on it by B. If the receipt, deposit ticket, passbook or other agreement with A is to the effect that any credit so entered is provisional and may be revoked pending the time required by the payor bank to process the item to determine if it is in good form and there are funds to cover it, such reservation or agreement keeps the receipt or credit provisional and avoids it being either final settlement or final payment.

In other ways the payor bank may keep settlements provisional: by general or special agreement with the presenting party or bank; by simple reservation at the time the settlement is made; or otherwise. Thus a payor bank (except in the case of statutory provisions) has control whether a settlement made by it is provisional or final, by participating in general agreements or clearing house rules or by special agreement or reservation. If it fails to keep a settlement provisional and if no applicable statute keeps the settlement provisional, its settlement is final and, unless the item had previously been paid by one of the other methods prescribed in subsection (1), such final settlement constitutes final payment. In this manner payor banks may without difficulty avoid the effect of such cases as: Cohen v. First Nat. Bank of Nogales, 22 Ariz. 394, 400, 198 P. 122, 124, 15 A.L.R. 701 (1921); Briviesca v. Coronado, 19 Cal.2d 244, 120 P.2d 649 (1941); White Brokerage Co. v. Cooperman, 207 Minn. 239, 290 N.W. 790 (1940); Scotts Bluff County v. First Nat. Bank of Gering, 115 Neb. 273, 212 N.W. 617 (1927); Provident Savings Bank & Trust Co. v. Hildebrand, 49 Ohio App. 207, 196 N.E. 790, 791 (1934); Schaer v. First Nat. Bank of Brenham, 132 Tex. 499, 124 S.W.2d 108 (1939) (bill of exchange); Union State Bank of Lancaster v. Peoples State Bank of Lancaster, 192 Wis. 28, 33, 211 N.W. 931, 933 (1927); 1 Paton's Digest 1067.

5. If a payor bank has not previously paid an item in cash or finally settled for it, certain internal acts or procedures will produce final payment of the item. Exclusive of the external acts of payment in cash or final settlement, the key point at which the decision of the bank to pay or dishonor is made is when the bookkeeper for the drawer's account determines or verifies that the check is in good form and that there are sufficient funds in the drawer's account to cover it. Previous steps in the processing of an item are preliminary to this vital step and in no way indicate a decision to pay. However, a more tangible measuring point is desirable than a mere examination of the account of the person to be charged. The mechanical step that usually indicates that the examination has been completed and the decision to pay has been made is the posting of the item to the account to be charged. Therefore, subsection (1)(c) [Inapplicable in California, see California Code Comment, note 8] adopts as the third measuring point the completion of the process of posting. The phrase "completed the process of posting" is used rather than simple "posting" because under current machine operations posting is a process and something more than simply making entries on the customer's ledger. Subsection (1) follows fairly closely the New York statute, 37 McKinney's Consolidated Laws of New York, Negotiable Instruments, Art. 19–A, Sec. 350–b as amended by L.1950, C. 153, Sec. 1. However, subsections (1)(a) and (b) furnish more precise rules for determining "final settlement" by the payor bank than does the New York statute in using the term "irrevocable credit", the definition of which is not helpful.

6. Subsection (1)(d) covers the situation where the payor bank makes a provisional settlement for an item, which settlement becomes final at a later time by reason of the failure of the payor bank to revoke it in the time and manner permitted by statute, clearing house rule or agreement. An example of this type of situation is the clearing house settlement referred to in Comment 4. In the illustration there given if the time limit for the return of items received in the Monday morning clearing is 2:00 p.m. on Tuesday and the provisional settlement has not been revoked at that time in a manner permitted by the clearing house rules, the provisional settlement made on Monday morning becomes final at 2:00 p.m. on Tuesday. Subsection (1)(d) provides specifically that in this situation the item is finally paid at 2:00 p.m. Tuesday. If on the other hand a payor bank receives an item in the mail on Monday and makes some provisional settlement for the item on Monday, it has until midnight on Tuesday to return the item or give notice and revoke any settlement under Section 4–301. In this situation subsection (1)(d) of Section 4–213 provides that if the provisional settlement made on Monday is not revoked before midnight on Tuesday as permitted by Section 4–301, the item is finally paid at midnight on Tuesday even if the process of posting the item to the account of the drawer has not been completed at that time.

7. Subsection (1) provides that an item is finally paid by the payor bank when any one of the four events set forth in subparagraphs (a), (b), (c) and (d) have occurred, whichever happens first, and then provides that upon a final payment under subparagraphs (b), (c) or (d) the payor bank shall be accountable for the amount of the item. It is not made accountable if it has paid the item in cash because such payment is itself a sufficient accounting. The term "accountable" is used as imposing a duty to account, which duty is met if and when a settlement for the item satisfactorily clears. The fact that determination of the time of final payment is based exclusively upon action of the payor bank is not detrimental to the interests of owners of items or collecting banks because of the general obligations of payors to honor or dishonor and the time limits for action imposed by Sections 4–301 and 4–302.

8. Subsection (2) states the country-wide usage that when the item is finally paid by the payor bank under subsection (1) this final payment automatically without further action "firms up" other provisional settlements made for it. However, the subsection makes clear that this "firming up" occurs only where the settlement between the presenting and payor banks was made either through a clearing house or by debits and credits in accounts between them. It does not take place where the payor bank remits for the item with some form of remittance instrument. Further, the "firming up" continues only to the extent that provisional debits and credits are entered seriatim in accounts between banks which are successive to the presenting bank. The automatic "firming up" is broken at any time that any collecting bank remits for the item with a remittance draft, because final payment to the remittee then usually depends upon final payment of the remittance draft.

9. Subsection (3) states the general rule that if a collecting bank receives settlement for an item which is or becomes final, the bank is accountable to its customer for the amount of the item. One means of accounting is to remit to its customer the amount it has received on the item. If previously it gave to its customer a provisional credit for the item in an account its receipt of final settlement for the item "firms up" this provisional credit and makes it final. When this credit given by it so becomes final, in the usual case its agency status terminates and it becomes a debtor to its customer for the amount of the item. See Section 4–201(1). If the accounting is by a remittance instrument or authorization to charge further time will usually be required to complete its accounting (Section 4–211).

10. Subsection (4) states when certain credits given by a bank to its customer become available for withdrawal as of right. Subsection (4)(a) deals with the situation where a bank has given a credit (usually provisional) for an item to its customer and in turn has received a provisional settlement for the item from an intermediary or payor bank to which it has forwarded the item. In this situation before the provisional credit entered by the collecting bank in the account of its customer becomes available for withdrawal as of right, it is not only necessary that the provisional settlement received by the bank for the item becomes final but also that the collecting bank has a reasonable time to learn that this is so. Hence, subsection (4)(a) imposes both of these conditions. If the provisional settlement received is a provisional debit or credit in an account with the intermediary or payor bank or a remittance instrument on some bank other than the collecting bank itself, the collecting bank will usually learn that this debit or credit is final or that the remittance instrument has been paid merely by not learning the opposite within a reasonable time. How much time is "reasonable" for these purposes will of course depend on the distance the item has to travel and the number of banks through which it must pass (having in mind not only travel time by regular lines of transmission but also the successive midnight deadlines of the several banks) and other pertinent facts. Also, if the provisional settlement received is some form of a remittance instrument or authorization to charge, the "reasonable" time depends on the identity and location of the payor of the remittance instrument, the means for clearing such instrument and other pertinent facts.

11. Subsection (4)(6) deals with the situation of a bank which is both a depositary bank and a payor bank. The subsection recognizes that where A and B are both customers of a depositary-payor bank and A

deposits B's check on the depositary-payor in A's account on Monday, time must be allowed to permit the check under the deferred posting rules of Section 4–301 to reach the bookkeeper for B's account at some time on Tuesday, and if there are insufficient funds in B's account to reverse or charge back the provisional credit in A's account. Consequently this provisional credit in A's account does not become available for withdrawal as of right until the opening of business on Wednesday. If it is determined on Tuesday that there are insufficient funds in B's account to pay the check the credit to A's account can be reversed on Tuesday. On the other hand if the item is in fact paid on Tuesday, the rule of subsection (4)(b) is desirable to avoid uncertainty and possible disputes between the bank and its customer as to exactly what hour within the day the credit is available.

12. Subsection (5) recognizes that even when A makes a deposit of cash in his account on Monday it takes some period of time to record that cash deposit and communicate it to A's bookkeeper (the bookkeeper handling A's account) so that A's bookkeeper has a record of it when she considers whether there are available funds to pay A's check. Where as indicated in Comment 5 A's bookkeeper is the particular employee in the bank to determine, in most cases and subject to supervisory control, whether the item may be paid, the effectiveness of a deposit of cash as a basis for paying a check must of necessity rest upon when the record of that deposit reaches such bookkeeper rather than when it passes through the teller's window. Consequently, although the bank is charged with responsibility for cash deposited from the moment it is received on Monday the cash is not effective as a basis for paying checks until the opening of business on Tuesday.

Cross References:

Sections 3–418, 4–107, 4–201, 4–211, 4–212, 4–214, 4–301, 4–302, 4–303.

Definitional Cross References:

"Account". Section 4–104.
"Agreement". Section 1–201.
"Banking day". Section 4–104.
"Clearing house". Section 4–104.
"Collecting bank". Section 4–105.
"Customer". Section 4–104.
"Depositary bank". Section 4–105.
"Item". Section 4–104.
"Money". Section 1–201.
"Notice". Section 1–201.
"Payor bank". Section 4–105.
"Presenting bank". Section 4–105.
"Settlement". Section 4–104.

Cross References

Agency status of bank, see Commercial Code § 4201.
Charge-back or refund, see Commercial Code § 4214.
Commercial paper, finality of payment or acceptance, see Commercial Code § 3418.
Deferred posting of items, see Commercial Code § 4301.
Insolvency and preference, see Commercial Code § 4216.
Items subject to notice, stop-order, legal process or set-offs, see Commercial Code § 4303.
Late return of items, payor bank's responsibility, see Commercial Code § 4302.
Provisional and final settlement in remittance cases, see Commercial Code § 4211.
Receipt of items, time, see Commercial Code § 4108.
Recovery of payment by return of items, see Commercial Code § 4301.

§ 4214. Revocation of settlement; return of item; right to charge back

(a) If a collecting bank has made provisional settlement with its customer for an item and * * * fails by reason of dishonor, suspension of payments by a bank, or otherwise to receive * * * settlement for the item which is or becomes final, the bank may revoke the settlement given by it, charge back the amount of any credit given for the item to its customer's account, or obtain refund from its customer, whether or not it is able to return the * * * item, if by its midnight deadline or within a longer reasonable time after it learns the facts it returns the item or sends notification of the facts. If the return or notice is delayed beyond the bank's midnight deadline or a longer reasonable time after it learns the facts, the bank may revoke the settlement, charge back the credit, or obtain refund from its customer, but it is liable for any loss resulting from the delay. These rights to revoke, charge back and obtain refund terminate if and when a settlement for the item received by the bank is or becomes final * * *.

* * *

(b) A collecting bank returns an item when it is sent or delivered to the bank's customer or transferor or pursuant to its instructions.

(c) A depositary bank that is also the payor may charge back the amount of an item to its customer's account or obtain refund in accordance with the section governing return of an item received by a payor bank for credit on its books (Section 4301).

(d) The right to charge back is not affected by either of the following:

* * * (1) Previous use of a credit given for the item * * * :

(2) Failure by any bank to exercise ordinary care with respect to the item, but a bank so failing remains liable.

(e) A failure to charge back or claim refund does not affect other rights of the bank against the customer or any other party.

(f) If credit is given in dollars as the equivalent of the value of an item payable in * * * foreign * * * money, the dollar amount of any charge-back or refund shall be calculated on the basis of the * * * bank-offered spot rate for the foreign money prevailing on the day when the person entitled to the charge-back or refund learns that it will not receive payment in ordinary course.

* * * (Formerly § 4212, added by Stats.1963, c. 819, § 4212. Amended by Stats.1983, c. 1011, § 1. Renumbered § 4214 and amended by Stats.1992, c. 914 (S.B. 833), § 34.)

California Code Comment

By John A. Bohn and Charles J. Williams

Prior California Law

1. This section fixes a cut-off point which determines when items in the process of collection must be sent back (subdivision (1)) and when they may be continued through the collection process (subdivisions (2), (3) and (4)). Official Comments 1 and 2.

This section does not apply to national banks in the absence of federal legislation. Official Comment 3.

2. This section is new. There was no prior systematic treatment of preferences in the event of insolvency. Former Financial Code § 1016 provided that a bank forwarding an item for collection in the usual course of business was not liable for the loss of that item resulting from the insolvency of any other bank.

Changes from U.C.C. (1962 Official Text)

3. This is section 4–214 of the Official Text without change.

Uniform Commercial Code Comment
Official Reasons for 1990 Change

Subsection (a) is amended by the addition of the second sentence which adopts the view of Appliance Buyers Credit Corp. v. Prospect National Bank, 708 F.2d 290 (7th Cir.1983), that if the midnight deadline for returning an item or giving notice is not met, a collecting bank loses its rights only to the extent of damages for any loss resulting from the delay. The cross references to former Sections 4–211 and 4–213 are deleted. The reason for the deletion is to remove any implication that final settlement is determined by only these provisions. See Reasons for 1990 Change for Section 4–201.

Former subsection (2) is replaced by subsection (b). Former subsection (2) broadly allowed for direct return of all types of unpaid items. The purpose of the amendment is to limit the right of direct return with respect to noncheck items. This purpose is accomplished by subsection (b) when read against the background of Regulation CC Section 229.31 which allows for the direct return of checks but does not apply to noncheck items. Since Regulation CC preempts subsection (b) with respect to checks, the result is that the limitation on direct return found in subsection (b) applies only to noncheck items.

Subsection (f) is amended to conform to the terminology ("bank-offered spot rate") used in Section 3–107.

The other modifications are made to conform with current legislative drafting practices, with no intent to change substance.

1990 Change

1. Under current bank practice, in a major portion of cases banks make provisional settlement for items when they are first received and then await subsequent determination of whether the item will be finally paid. This is the principal characteristic of what are referred to in banking parlance as "cash items." Statistically, this practice of settling provisionally first and then awaiting final payment is justified because the vast majority of such cash items are finally paid, with the result that in this great preponderance of cases it becomes unnecessary for the banks making the provisional settlements to make any further entries. In due course the provisional settlements become final simply with the lapse of time. However, in those cases in which the item being collected is not finally paid or if for various reasons the bank making the provisional settlement does not itself receive final payment, provision is made in subsection (a) for the reversal of the provisional settlements, charge-back of provisional credits and the right to obtain refund.

2. Various causes of a bank's not receiving final payment, with the resulting right of charge-back or refund, are stated or suggested in subsection (a). These include dishonor of the original item; dishonor of a remittance instrument given for it; reversal of a provisional credit for the item; suspension of payments by another bank. The causes stated are illustrative; the right of charge-back or refund is stated to exist whether the failure to receive final payment in ordinary course arises through one of them "or otherwise."

3. The right of charge-back or refund exists if a collecting bank has made a provisional settlement for an item with its customer but terminates if and when a settlement received by the bank for the item is or becomes final. If the bank fails to receive such a final settlement the right of charge-back or refund must be exercised promptly after the bank learns the facts. The right exists (if so promptly exercised) whether or not the bank is able to return the item. The second sentence of subsection (a) adopts the view of Appliance Buyers Credit Corp. v. Prospect National Bank, 708 F.2d 290 (7th Cir.1983), that if the midnight deadline for returning an item or giving notice is not met, a collecting bank loses its rights only to the extent of damages for any loss resulting from the delay.

4. Subsection (b) states when an item is returned by a collecting bank, Regulation CC, Section 229.31 preempts this subsection with respect to checks by allowing direct return to the depositary bank. Because a returned check may follow a different path than in forward collection, settlement given for the check is final and not provisional except as between the depositary bank and its customer. Regulation CC, Section 229.36(d). See also Regulations CC, Sections 229.31(c) and 229.32(b). Thus owing to the federal preemption, this subsection applies only to noncheck items.

5. The rule of subsection (d) relating to charge-back (as distinguished from claim for refund) applies irrespective of the cause of the nonpayment, and of the person ultimately liable for nonpayment. Thus charge-back is permitted even if nonpayment results from the depositary bank's own negligence. Any other rule would result in litigation based upon a claim for wrongful dishonor of other checks of the customer, with potential damages far in excess of the amount of the item. Any other rule would require a bank to determine difficult questions of fact. The customer's protection is found in the general obligation of good faith (Sections 1–203 and 4–103). If bad faith is established the customer's recovery "includes other damages, if any, suffered by the party as a proximate consequence" (Section 4–103(e); see also Section 4–402).

6. It is clear that the charge-back does not relieve the bank from any liability for failure to exercise ordinary care in handling the item. The measure of damages for such failure is stated in Section 4–103(e).

7. Subsection (f) states a rule fixing the time for determining the rate of exchange if there is a charge-back or refund of a credit given in dollars for an item payable in a foreign currency. Compare Section 3–107. Fixing such a rule is desirable to avoid disputes. If in any case the parties wish to fix a different time for determining the rate of exchange, they may do so by agreement.

Uniform Commercial Code Comment

Prior Uniform Statutory Provision:

None; but see Section 13, American Bankers Association Bank Collection Code.

Purposes:

1. The underlying purpose of the provisions of this section is not to confer upon banks, holders of items or anyone else preferential positions in the event of bank failures over general depositors or any other creditors of the failed banks. The purpose is to fix as definitely as possible the cut-off point of time for the completion or cessation of the collection process in the case of items that happen to be in such process at the time a particular bank suspends payments. It must be remembered that in bank collections as a whole and in the handling of items by an individual bank, items go through a whole series of processes. It must also be remembered that at any particular point of time a particular bank (at least one of any size) is functioning as a depositary bank for some items, as an intermediary bank for others, as a presenting bank for still others and as a payor bank for still others, and that when it suspends payments it will have close to its normal load of items working through its various processes. For the convenience of receivers, owners of items, banks, and in fact substantially everyone concerned, it is recognized that at the particular moment of time that a bank suspends payment, a certain portion of the items being handled by it have progressed far enough in the bank collection process that it is preferable to permit them to continue the remaining distance, rather than to send them back and reverse the many entries that have been made or the steps that have been taken with respect to them. Therefore, having this background and these purposes in mind, the section states what items must be turned backward at the moment suspension intervenes and what items have progressed far enough that the collection process with respect to them continues, with the resulting necessary statement of rights of various parties flowing from this prescription of the cut-off time.

2. The rules stated are similar to those stated in the American Bankers Association Bank Collection Code, but with the abandonment of any theory of trust. Although for practical purposes Federal Deposit Insurance affects materially the result of bank failures on holders of items and banks, no attempt is made to vary the rules of the section by reason of such insurance.

3. It is recognized that in view of Jennings v. United States Fidelity & Guaranty Co., 294 U.S. 216, 55 S.Ct. 394, 79 L.Ed. 869, 99 A.L.R. 1248 (1935), amendment of the National Bank Act would be necessary to have this section apply to national banks. But there is no reason why it should not apply to others. See Section 1–108.

Cross References:

Sections 1–108, 4–211(3) and 4–213.

§ 4214

Definitional Cross References:
"Collecting bank". Section 4–105.
"Customer". Section 4–104.
"Item". Section 4–104.
"Payor bank". Section 4–105.
"Presenting bank". Section 4–105.
"Settlement". Section 4–104.
"Suspends payment". Section 4–104.

Cross References

Acceptance of deposits when bank insolvent, see Financial Code § 3367.
Fraudulent insolvency, see Financial Code § 3362.
Liquidation, see Financial Code §§ 3100 et seq., 3220 et seq.
Payment of item by payor bank, finality, see Commercial Code § 4215.
Priorities, negotiable instruments forwarded for collection and remittance, see Financial Code § 3240.
Provisional debits and credits, finality, see Commercial Code § 4215.
Settlement by means of remittance instrument or authorization, finality, see Commercial Code § 4211(3).
Severability provisions, see Commercial Code § 1108.

§ 4215. Final payment by payor bank; credits available for withdrawal

(a) An item is finally paid by a payor bank when the bank has <u>first</u> done any of the following * * *:

(1) Paid the item in cash * * *<u>.</u>

(2) Settled for the item without having a right to revoke the settlement under * * * statute, * * * <u>clearing house</u> rule, <u>or</u> agreement * * *<u>.</u>

* * * (3) Made a provisional settlement * * * <u>for the item and failed to revoke the settlement in the time and manner permitted by</u> statute, * * * <u>clearing house</u> rule, <u>or</u> agreement * * *.

* * *

(b) <u>If provisional settlement for an item does not become final, the item is not finally paid.</u>

(c) If provisional settlement for an item between the presenting and payor banks is made through a * * * <u>clearing house</u> or by debits or credits in an account between them, then to the extent that provisional debits or credits for the item are entered in accounts between the presenting and payor banks or between the presenting and successive prior collecting banks seriatim, they become final upon final payment of the <u>items</u> by the payor bank.

(d) If a collecting bank receives a settlement for an item which is or becomes final * * *<u>,</u> the bank is accountable to its customer for the amount of the item and any provisional credit given for the item in an account with its customer becomes final.

(e) Subject to <u>(i) applicable law stating a time for availability of funds and (ii)</u> any right of <u>the</u> bank * * * to apply the credit to an obligation of the customer, credit <u>given</u> by a bank * * * for an item in * * * <u>a customer's</u> account * * * becomes available for withdrawal as of right:

* * * (1) If the bank * * * has received a provisional settlement for the item, * * * when the settlement * * * <u>becomes</u> final and the bank * * * has had a reasonable time to receive * * * return of the item * * * and the item has not been received within that time.

* * * (2) If the bank * * * is both the depositary bank and the payor bank, and the item is finally paid * * *, the opening of the <u>bank's</u> second <u>banking</u> day following receipt of the item.

* * * (f) Subject to <u>applicable law stating a time for availability of funds and</u> any right of <u>a</u> bank to apply <u>a</u> deposit to an obligation of the * * * <u>depositor, a</u> deposit <u>of money</u> becomes available for withdrawal as of right at the opening of the bank's next banking day <u>after receipt of the deposit.</u> (Formerly § 4213, added by Stats.1963, c. 819, § 4213. Amended by Stats.1983, c. 1011, § 1.5. Renumbered § 4215 and amended by Stats.1992, c. 914 (S.B.833), § 35.)

Uniform Commercial Code Comment
Official Reasons for 1990 Change

Subsection (a)(2) is amended to provide that a payor bank cannot make settlement provisional by unilaterally reserving a right to revoke the settlement. The right to revoke must come from a statute (e.g., Section 4–301), clearing-house rule or other agreement. Former subsection (1)(c) is deleted for the reason stated in the Reason for 1990 Change for former Section 4–109. Subsection (a)(3) is amended to remove the final sentence as an unnecessary source of confusion. Initially the view that payor bank may be accountable for, that is, liable for the amount of, an item that it has already paid seems incongruous. This is particularly true in the light of the language formerly found in former Section 4–302 stating that the payor bank can defend against liability for accountability by showing that it has already settled for the item. But, at least with respect to former Section 4–213(1)(c), such a provision was needed because under the process-of-posting test a payor bank may have paid an item without settling for it. Now that Article 4 has abandoned the process-of-posting test, the sentence is no longer needed. If the payor bank has neither paid the item nor returned it within its midnight deadline, the payor bank is accountable under Section 4–302.

Subsection (b) was added to clarify the relationship of final settlement to final payment under Section 4–215. For example, if a payor bank makes provisional settlement for an item by sending a cashier's or teller's check and that settlement fails to become final under Section 4–213(c), subsection (b) provides that final payment has not occurred. Under Section 4–302(a) the payor bank is accountable unless it has returned the item before its midnight deadline. In this regard, subsection (b) is an exception to subsection (a)(3). Even if the payor bank has not returned an item by its midnight deadline there is still no final payment if provisional settlement had been made and settlement failed to become final. However, if presentment of the item was over the counter for immediate payment, final payment has occurred under Section 4–215(a)(2). Subsection (b) does not apply because the settlement was not provisional. Section 4–301(a). In this case the presenting person, often the payee of the item, has the right to demand cash or the cash equivalent of federal reserve credit. If the presenting person accepts another medium of settlement such as a cashier's or teller's check, the presenting person takes the risk that the payor bank may fail to pay a cashier's check because of insolvency or that the drawee of a teller's check may dishonor it.

Subsection (d) is amended to delete the cross references to former Sections 4–211 and 4–213. The reason for the deletion is to remove any implication that final settlement is determined by only those provisions. See Reasons for 1990 Change for Section 4–201.

The preamble to subsection (e), as well as subsection (f), is amended to recognize that Regulation CC Sections 229.10–229.13 and the laws of several states (Regulation CC Section 229.20) prescribe times for availability of a depositor's funds. Subsections (e) and (f) are expressly made subject to these funds availability laws. Paragraph (1) of subsection (e) is amended to delete the test that a customer may withdraw funds after the bank has had a reasonable time to "learn that the settlement is final." The depositary bank may never affirmatively learn that a settlement is final. The substituted test is that the bank may delay making funds available to a customer until it has had a reasonable time to receive return of the item and the item has not been returned. The other modifications are made to conform with current legislative drafting practices, with no intent to change substance.

1990 Change

1. By the definition and use of the term "settle" (Section 4–104(a)(11)) this Article recognizes that various debits or credits, remittances, settlements or payments given for an item may be either provisional or final, that settlements sometimes are provisional and sometimes are final and sometimes are provisional for awhile but later become final. Subsection (a) defines when settlement for an item constitutes final payment.

Final payment of an item is important for a number of reasons. It is one of several factors determining the relative priorities between items and notices, stop-payment orders, legal process and setoffs (Section 4–303). It is the "end of the line" in the collection process and the "turn around" point commencing the return flow of proceeds. It is the point at which many provisional settlements become final. See Section 4–215(c). Final payment of an item by the payor bank fixes preferential rights under Section 4–216.

2. If an item being collected moves through several states, e.g., is deposited for collection in California, moves through two or three California banks to the Federal Reserve Bank of San Francisco, to the Federal Reserve Bank of Boston, to a payor bank in Maine, the collection process involves the eastward journey of the item from California to Maine and the westward journey of the proceeds from Maine to California. Subsection (a) recognizes that final payment does not take place, in this hypothetical case, on the journey of the item eastward. It also adopts the view that neither does final payment occur on the journey westward because what in fact is journeying westward are *proceeds* of the item.

3. Traditionally and under various decisions payment in cash of an item by a payor bank has been considered final payment. Subsection (a)(1) recognizes and provides that payment of an item in cash by a payor bank is final payment.

4. Section 4–104(a)(11) defines "settle" as meaning "to pay in cash, by clearing-house settlement, in a charge or credit or by remittance, or otherwise as agreed. A settlement may be either provisional or final." Subsection (a)(2) of Section 4–215 provides that an item is finally paid by a payor bank when the bank has "settled for the item without having a right to revoke the settlement under statute, clearing-house rule or agreement." Former subsection (1)(b) is modified by subsection (a)(2) to make clear that a payor bank cannot make settlement provisional by unilaterally reserving a right to revoke the settlement. The right must come from a statute (e.g., Section 4–301), clearing-house rule or other agreement. Subsection (a)(2) provides in effect that if the payor bank finally settles for an item this constitutes final payment of the item. The subsection operates if nothing has occurred and no situation exists making the settlement provisional. If under statute, clearing-house rule or agreement, a right of revocation of the settlement exists, the settlement is provisional. Conversely, if there is an absence of a right to revoke under statute, clearing-house rule or agreement, the settlement is final and such final settlement constitutes final payment of the item.

A primary example of a statutory right on the part of the payor bank to revoke a settlement is the right to revoke conferred by Section 4–301. The underlying theory and reason for deferred posting statutes (Section 4–301) is to require a settlement on the date of receipt of an item but to keep that settlement provisional with the right to revoke prior to the midnight deadline. In any case in which Section 4–301 is applicable, any settlement by the payor bank is provisional solely by virtue of the statute, subsection (a)(2) of Section 4–215 does not operate, and such provisional settlement does not constitute final payment of the item. With respect to checks, Regulation CC Section 229.36(d) provides that settlement between banks for the forward collection of checks is final. The relationship of this provision to Article 4 is discussed in the Commentary to that section.

A second important example of a right to revoke a settlement is that arising under clearing-house rules. It is very common for clearing-house rules to provide that items exchanged and settled for in a clearing (e.g., before 10:00 a.m. on Monday) may be returned and the settlements revoked up to but not later than 2:00 p.m. on the same day (Monday) or under deferred posting at some hour on the next business day (e.g., 2:00 p.m. Tuesday). Under this type of rule the Monday morning settlement is provisional and being provisional does not constitute a final payment of the item.

An example of an agreement allowing the payor bank to revoke a settlement is a case in which the payor bank is also the depositary bank and has signed a receipt or duplicate deposit ticket or has made an entry in a passbook acknowledging receipt, for credit to the account of A, of a check drawn on it by B. If the receipt, deposit ticket, passbook or other agreement with A is to the effect that any credit so entered is provisional and may be revoked pending the time required by the payor bank to process the item to determine if it is in good form and there are funds to cover it, the agreement keeps the receipt or credit provisional and avoids its being either final settlement or final payment.

The most important application of subsection (a)(2) is that in which presentment of an item has been made over the counter for immediate payment. In this case Section 4–301(a) does not apply to make the settlement provisional, and final payment has occurred unless a rule or agreement provides otherwise.

5. Former Section 4–213(1)(c) provided that final payment occurred when the payor bank completed the "process of posting." The term was defined in former Section 4–109. In the present Article, Section 4–109 has been deleted and the process-of-posting test has been abandoned in Section 4–215(a) for determining when final payment is made. Difficulties in determining when the events described in former Section 4–109 take place make the process-of-posting test unsuitable for a system of automated check collection or electronic presentment.

6. The last sentence of former Section 4–213(1) is deleted as an unnecessary source of confusion. Initially the view that payor bank may be accountable for, that is, liable for the amount of, an item that it has already paid seems incongruous. This is particularly true in the light of the language formerly found in Section 4–302 stating that the payor bank can defend against liability for accountability by showing that it has already settled for the item. But, at least with respect to former Section 4–213(1)(c), such a provision was needed because under the process-of-posting test a payor bank may have paid an item without settling for it. Now that Article 4 has abandoned the process-of-posting test, the sentence is no longer needed. If the payor bank has neither paid the item nor returned it within its midnight deadline, the payor bank is accountable under Section 4–302.

7. Subsection (a)(3) covers the situation in which the payor bank makes a provisional settlement for an item, and this settlement becomes final at a later time by reason of the failure of the payor bank to revoke it in the time and manner permitted by statute, clearing-house rule or agreement. An example of this type of situation is the clearing-house settlement referred to in Comment 4. In the illustration there given if the time limit for the return of items received in the Monday morning clearing is 2:00 p.m. on Tuesday and the provisional settlement has not been revoked at that time in a manner permitted by the clearing-house rules, the provisional settlement made on Monday morning becomes final at 2:00 p.m. on Tuesday. Subsection (a)(3) provides specifically that in this situation the item is finally paid at 2:00 p.m. Tuesday. If on the other hand a payor bank receives an item in the mail on Monday and makes some provisional settlement for the item on Monday, it has until midnight on Tuesday to return the item or give notice and revoke any settlement under Section 4–301. In this situation subsection (a)(3) of Section 4–215 provides that if the provisional settlement made on Monday is not revoked before midnight on Tuesday as permitted by Section 4–301, the item is finally paid at midnight on Tuesday. With respect to checks, Regulation CC Section 229.30(c) allows an extension of the midnight deadline under certain circumstances. If a bank does not expeditiously return a check, liability may accrue under Regulation CC, Section 229.38. For the relationship of that liability to responsibility under this Article, see Regulation CC, Sections 229.30 and 229.38.

8. Subsection (b) relates final settlement to final payment under Section 4–215. For example, if a payor bank makes provisional settlement for an item by sending a cashier's or teller's check and that settlement fails to become final under Section 4–213(c), subsection (b) provides that final payment has not occurred. If the item is not paid, the drawer remains liable, and under Section 4–302(a) the payor bank is accountable unless it has returned the item before its midnight deadline. In this regard, subsection (b) is an exception to subsection (a)(3). Even if the payor bank has not returned an item by its midnight deadline there is still no final payment if provisional settlement had been made and settlement failed to become final. However, if presentment of the item was over the counter for immediate payment, final payment has occurred under Section 4–215(a)(2). Subsection (b) does not apply

because the settlement was not provisional. Section 4–301(a). In this case the presenting person, often the payee of the item, has the right to demand cash or the cash equivalent of federal reserve credit. If the presenting person accepts another medium of settlement such as a cashier's or teller's check, the presenting person takes the risk that the payor bank may fail to pay a cashier's check because of insolvency or that the drawee of a teller's check may dishonor it.

9. Subsection (c) states the country-wide usage that when the item is finally paid by the payor bank under subsection (a) this final payment automatically without further action "firms up" other provisional settlements made for it. However, the subsection makes clear that this "firming up" occurs only if the settlement between the presenting and payor banks was made either through a clearing-house or by debits and credits in accounts between them. It does not take place if the payor bank remits for the item by sending some form of remittance instrument. Further, the "firming up" continues only to the extent that provisional debits and credits are entered seriatim in accounts between banks which are successive to the presenting bank. The automatic "firming up" is broken at any time that any collecting bank remits for the item by sending a remittance draft, because final payment to the remittee then usually depends upon final payment of the remittance draft.

10. Subsection (d) states the general rule that if a collecting bank receives settlement for an item which is or becomes final, the bank is accountable to its customer for the amount of the item. One means of accounting is to remit to its customer the amount it has received on the item. If previously it gave to its customer a provisional credit for the item in an account its receipt of final settlement for the item "firms up" this provisional credit and makes it final. When this credit given by it so becomes final, in the usual case its agency status terminates and it becomes a debtor to its customer for the amount of the item. See Section 4–201(a). If the accounting is by a remittance instrument or authorization to charge, further time will usually be required to complete its accounting (Section 4–213).

11. Subsection (e) states when certain credits given by a bank to its customer become available for withdrawal as of right. Subsection (e)(1) deals with the situation in which a bank has given a credit (usually provisional) for an item to its customer and in turn has received a provisional settlement for the item from an intermediary or payor bank to which it has forwarded the item. In this situation before the provisional credit entered by the collecting bank in the account of its customer becomes available for withdrawal as of right, it is not only necessary that the provisional settlement received by the bank for the item becomes final but also that the collecting bank has a reasonable time to receive return of the item and the item has not been received within that time. How much time is "reasonable" for these purposes will of course depend on the distance the item has to travel and the number of banks through which it must pass (having in mind not only travel time by regular lines of transmission but also the successive midnight deadlines of the several banks) and other pertinent facts. Also, if the provisional settlement received is some form of a remittance instrument or authorization to charge, the "reasonable" time depends on the identity and location of the payor of the remittance instrument, the means for clearing such instrument, and other pertinent facts. With respect to checks Regulation CC Sections 229.10–229.13 or similar applicable state law (Section 229.20) control. This is also time for the situation described in Comment 12.

12. Subsection (e)(2) deals with the situation of a bank that is both a depositary bank and a payor bank. The subsection recognizes that if A and B are both customers of a depositary-payor bank and A deposits B's check on the depositary-payor in A's account on Monday, time must be allowed to permit the check under the deferred posting rules of Section 4–301 to reach the bookkeeper for B's account at some time on Tuesday, and, if there are insufficient funds in B's account, to reverse or charge back the provisional credit in A's account. Consequently this provisional credit in A's account does not become available for withdrawal as of right until the opening of business on Wednesday. If it is determined on Tuesday that there are insufficient funds in B's account to pay the check, the credit to A's account can be reversed on Tuesday. On the other hand, if the item is in fact paid on Tuesday, the rule of subsection (e)(2) is desirable to avoid uncertainty and possible disputes between the bank and its customer as to exactly what hour within the day the credit is available.

Cross References

Person from whom payment is recovered or acceptance is revoked, rights to enforce as dishonored instrument, see Commercial Code § 3418.

§ 4216. Insolvency and preference

* * * (a) If an item is in or comes into the possession of a payor or collecting bank that suspends payment and the item has not been finally paid, the item shall be returned by the receiver, trustee, or agent in charge of the closed bank to the presenting bank or the closed bank's customer.

(b) If a payor bank finally pays an item and suspends payments without making a settlement for the item with its customer or the presenting bank which settlement is or becomes final, the owner of the item has a preferred claim against the payor bank.

(c) If a payor bank gives or a collecting bank gives or receives a provisional settlement for an item and thereafter suspends payments, the suspension does not prevent or interfere with the settlement's becoming final if the finality occurs automatically upon the lapse of certain time or the happening of certain events * * *.

(d) If a collecting bank receives from subsequent parties settlement for an item, which settlement is or becomes final and the bank suspends payments without making a settlement for the item with its customer which settlement is or becomes final, the owner of the item has a preferred claim against the collecting bank. (Formerly § 4214, added by Stats.1963, c. 819, § 4214. Renumbered § 4216 and amended by Stats.1992, c. 914 (S.B.833), § 36.)

Uniform Commercial Code Comment
Official Reasons for 1990 Change

Subsection (c) is amended to delete the cross references to former Sections 4–211 and 4–213. The reason for the deletion is to remove any implication that final settlement is determined by only those provisions. See Reasons for 1990 Change for Section 4–201. The other modifications are made to conform with current legislative drafting practices, with no intent to change substance.

1990 Change

1. The underlying purpose of the provisions of this section is not to confer upon banks, holders of items or anyone else preferential positions in the event of bank failures over general depositors or any other creditors of the failed banks. The purpose is to fix as definitely as possible the cut-off point of time for the completion or cessation of the collection process in the case of items that happen to be in the process at the time a particular bank suspends payments. It must be remembered that in bank collections as a whole and in the handling of items by an individual bank, items go through a whole series of processes. It must also be remembered that at any particular point of time a particular bank (at least one of any size) is functioning as a depositary bank for some items, as an intermediary bank for others, as a presenting bank for still others and as a payor bank for still others, and that when it suspends payments it will have close to its normal load of items working through its various processes. For the convenience of receivers, owners of items, banks, and in fact substantially everyone concerned, it is recognized that at the particular moment of time that a bank suspends payment, a certain portion of the items being handled by it have progressed far enough in the bank collection process that it is preferable to permit them to continue the remaining distance, rather than to send them back and reverse the many entries that have been made or the steps that have been taken with respect to them. Therefore, having this

background and these purposes in mind, the section states what items must be turned backward at the moment suspension intervenes and what items have progressed far enough that the collection process with respect to them continues, with the resulting necessary statement of rights of various parties flowing from this prescription of the cut-off time.

2. The rules stated are similar to those stated in the American Bankers Association Bank Collection Code, but with the abandonment of any theory of trust. On the other hand, some law previous to this Act may be relevant. See Note, Uniform Commercial Code: Stopping Payment of an Item Deposited with an Insolvent Depositary Bank, 40 Okla.L.Rev. 689 (1987). Although for practical purposes Federal Deposit Insurance affects materially the result of bank failures on holders of items and banks, no attempt is made to vary the rules of the section by reason of such insurance.

3. It is recognized that in view of Jennings v. United States Fidelity & Guaranty Co., 294 U.S. 216, 55 S.Ct. 394, 79 L.Ed. 869, 99 A.L.R. 1248 (1935), amendment of the National Bank Act would be necessary to have this section apply to national banks. But there is no reason why it should not apply to others. See Section 1–108.

CHAPTER 3. COLLECTION OF ITEMS: PAYOR BANKS

Section
4301. Deferred posting; recovery of payment by return of items; time of dishonor; return of items by payor bank.
4302. Payor Bank's Responsibility for Late Return of Item.
4303. When Items Subject to Notice, Stop-Order, Legal Process or Setoff; Order in Which Items May Be Charged or Certified.

Transitional Provisions

Effective date and transitional provisions for sections in Division 4 affected by Stats.1992, c. 914, see Commercial Code § 16101 et seq.

§ 4301. Deferred posting; recovery of payment by return of items; time of dishonor; return of items by payor bank

* * * (a) If a payor bank settles for a demand item * * * other than a documentary draft * * * presented otherwise than for immediate payment over the counter before midnight of the banking day of receipt, the payor bank may revoke the settlement and recover * * * the settlement if, before it has made final payment * * * and before its midnight deadline, it either:

(1) Returns the item * * *.

(2) Sends written notice of dishonor or nonpayment if the item is * * * unavailable for return.

(b) If a demand item is received by a payor bank for credit on its books, it may return the item or send notice of dishonor and may revoke any credit given or recover the amount thereof withdrawn by its customer, if it acts within the time limit and in the manner specified in * * * subdivision (a).

(c) Unless previous notice of dishonor has been sent an item is dishonored at the time when for purposes of dishonor it is returned or notice sent in accordance with this section.

(d) An item is returned either:

(1) As to an item presented through a * * * clearing house, when it is delivered to the presenting or last collecting bank or to the * * * clearing house or is sent or delivered in accordance with * * * clearing house rules * * *.

(2) In all other cases, when it is sent or delivered to the bank's customer or transferor or pursuant to his instructions. *(Stats.1963, c. 819, § 4301. Amended by Stats.1992, c. 914 (S.B.833), § 37.)*

California Code Comment

By John A. Bohn and Charles J. Williams

Prior California Law

1. Subdivision (1) is similar to former Financial Code § 1013, the California deferred posting statute. It applies normally to the case of an item drawn on one bank and deposited at another. Official Comment 1 explains deferred posting.

2. Subdivision (2) applies the deferred posting rules of subdivision (1) to the case where the payor bank is also the depositary bank. Official Comment 2.

3. Subdivision (3) is in accord with former Financial Code § 1013.

4. Subdivision (4) is new statutory law.

Changes from U.C.C. (1962 Official Text)

5. This is section 4–301 of the Official Text without change.

Uniform Commercial Code Comment

Official Reasons for 1990 Change

The term "authorized settlement" is deleted in subsection (a) because Section 4–213 makes the term superfluous. That section prescribes the medium of settlement that a bank must accept. References to settlement throughout Article 4 assume that settlement was made by tender of the proper medium; hence, the word "settles" in subsection (a) means an authorized settlement. Substitution of "settlement" for "payment" in subsection (a) is consistent with the usage throughout Article 4 in distinguishing the act of settlement from the issue of whether the settlement constitutes final payment. The cross reference to former Section 4–213 is deleted. The reason for the deletion is to remove any implication that final settlement is determined only by that provision. See Reason for 1990 Change for Section 4–201. The reference to protest is deleted in paragraph (2) of subsection (a) because Article 4 no longer deals with protest. The other modifications are made to conform with current legislative drafting practices, with no intent to change substance.

1990 Change

1. The term "deferred posting" appears in the caption of Section 4–301. This refers to the practice permitted by statute in most of the states before the UCC under which a payor bank receives items on one day but does not post the items to the customer's account until the next day. Items dishonored were then returned after the posting on the day after receipt. Under Section 4–301 the concept of "deferred posting" merely allows a payor bank that has settled for an item on the day of receipt to return a dishonored item on the next day before its midnight deadline, without regard to when the item was actually posted. With respect to checks Regulation CC Section 229.30(c) extends the midnight deadline under the UCC under certain circumstances. See the Commentary to Regulation CC Section 229.38(d) on the relationship between the UCC and Regulation CC on settlement.

2. The function of this section is to provide the circumstances under which a payor bank that has made timely settlement for an item may return the item and revoke the settlement so that it may recover any settlement made. These circumstances are: (1) the item must be a demand item other than a documentary draft; (2) the item must be presented otherwise than for immediate payment over the counter; and (3) the payor bank must return the item (or give notice if the item is unavailable for return) before its midnight deadline and before it has paid the item. With respect to checks, see Regulation CC Section

229.31(f) on notice in lieu of return and Regulation CC Section 229.33 as to the different requirement of notice of nonpayment. An instance of when an item may be unavailable for return arises under a collecting bank check retention plan under which presentment is made by a presentment notice and the item is retained by the collecting bank. Section 4–215(a)(2) provides that final payment occurs if the payor bank has settled for an item without a right to revoke the settlement under statute, clearing-house rule or agreement. In any case in which Section 4–301(a) is applicable, the payor bank has a right to revoke the settlement by statute; therefore, Section 4–215(a)(2) is inoperable, and the settlement is provisional. Hence, if the settlement is not over the counter and the payor bank settles in a manner that does not constitute final payment, the payor bank can revoke the settlement by returning the item before its midnight deadline.

3. The relationship of Section 4–301(a) to final settlement and final payment under Section 4–215 is illustrated by the following case. Depositary Bank sends by mail an item to Payor Bank with instructions to settle by remitting a teller's check drawn on a bank in the city where Depositary Bank is located. Payor Bank sends the teller's check on the day the item was presented. Having made timely settlement, under the deferred posting provisions of Section 4–301(a), Payor Bank may revoke that settlement by returning the item before its midnight deadline. If it fails to return the item before its midnight deadline, it has finally paid the item if the bank on which the teller's check was drawn honors the check. But if the teller's check is dishonored there has been no final settlement under Section 4–213(c) and no final payment under Section 4–215(b). Since the Payor Bank has neither paid the item nor made timely return, it is accountable for the item under Section 4–302(a).

4. The time limits for action imposed by subsection (a) are adopted by subsection (b) for cases in which the payor bank is also the depositary bank, but in this case the requirement of a settlement on the day of receipt is omitted.

5. Subsection (c) fixes a base point from which to measure the time within which notice of dishonor must be given. See Section 3–503.

6. Subsection (d) leaves banks free to agree upon the manner of returning items but establishes a precise time when an item is "returned." For definition of "sent" as used in paragraphs (1) and (2) see Section 1–201(38). Obviously the subsection assumes that the item has not been "finally paid" under Section 4–215(a). If it has been, this provision has no operation.

7. The fact that an item has been paid under proposed Section 4–215 does not preclude the payor bank from asserting rights of restitution or revocation under Section 3–418. National Savings and Trust Co. v. Park Corp., 722 F.2d 1303 (6th Cir.1983), cert. denied, 466 U.S. 939 (1984), is the correct interpretation of the present law on this issue.

Uniform Commercial Code Comment

Prior Uniform Statutory Provision:

None; but see American Bankers Association Model Deferred Posting Statute.

Purposes:

1. Deferred posting and delayed returns is that practice whereby a payor bank sorts and proves items received by it on the day they are received, e.g. Monday, but does not post the items to the customer's account or return "not good" items until the next day, e.g. Tuesday. The practice typifies "production line" methods currently used in bank collection and is based upon the necessity of an even flow of items through payor banks on a day by day basis in a manner which can be handled evenly by employee personnel without abnormal peak load periods, night work, and other practices objectionable to personnel. Since World War II statutes authorizing deferred posting and delayed returns have been passed in almost all of the forty-eight states. This section codifies the content of these statutes and approves the practice.

2. The time limits for action imposed by Subsection (1) are adopted by Subsection (2) for cases where the payor bank is also the depositary bank, but in this case the requirement of a settlement on the day of receipt is omitted.

3. Subsection (3) fixes a base point from which to measure the time within which notice of dishonor must be given. See Section 3–508.

4. Subsection (4) leaves banks free to agree upon the manner of returning items but establishes a precise time when an item is "returned". For definition of "sent" as used in subsections (a) and (b) see Section 1–201(38).

5. Obviously the section assumes that the item has not been "finally paid" under Section 4–213(1). If it has been, this section has no operation.

Cross References:

Sections 3–508, 4–213, 4–302.

Definitional Cross References:

"Banking day". Section 4–104.
"Clearing house". Section 4–104.
"Collecting bank". Section 4–105.
"Customer". Section 4–104.
"Documentary draft". Section 4–104.
"Item". Section 4–104.
"Midnight deadline". Section 4–104.
"Notice of dishonor". Section 3–508.
"Payor bank". Section 4–105.
"Presenting bank". Section 4–105.
"Sent". Section 1–201(38).
"Settlement". Section 4–104.

Cross References

Banking day, see Commercial Code § 4104.
Business days, banks, see Civil Code § 9.
Charging back item, see Commercial Code § 4214.
Demand instrument, see Commercial Code § 3108.
Dishonor of check if payor bank timely returns check or sends timely notice of dishonor or nonpayment under this section, see Commercial Code § 3502.
Dishonor of instrument, see Commercial Code § 3502.
Finality of payment, see Commercial Code § 4215.
Late return of item, bank's responsibility, see Commercial Code § 4302.
Notice of dishonor, see Commercial Code § 3503.
Revocation of settlement by payor depositary bank, charge back amount of item to customer's account or obtain refund in accordance with this section, see Commercial Code § 4214.
Right of charge-back or refund, see Commercial Code § 4214.

§ 4302. Payor Bank's Responsibility for Late Return of Item

* * * <u>(a)</u> If an item is presented <u>to</u> and received by a payor bank<u>,</u> the bank is accountable for the amount of either:

<u>(1)</u> A demand item<u>,</u> other than a documentary draft<u>,</u> whether properly payable or not<u>,</u> if the bank, in any case * * * <u>in which</u> it is not also the depositary bank, retains the item beyond midnight of the banking day of receipt without settling for it or, * * * whether <u>or not</u> it is also the depositary bank, does not pay or return the item or send notice of dishonor until after its midnight deadline * * *<u>;</u>

<u>(2)</u> Any other properly payable item unless<u>,</u> within the time allowed for acceptance or payment of that item<u>,</u> the bank either accepts or pays the item or returns it and accompanying documents.

<u>(b) The liability of a payor bank to pay an item pursuant to subdivision (a) is subject to defenses based on breach of a presentment warranty (Section 4208) or proof that the person seeking enforcement of the liability presented or transferred the item for the purpose of defrauding the payor bank.</u> (Stats.1963, c. 819, § 4302. Amended by Stats.1992, c. 914 (S.B.833), § 38.)

California Code Comment

By John A. Bohn and Charles J. Williams

Prior California Law

1. This section states the results if a payor bank fails to take action within the time limit provided in section 4301.

If the bank fails to act by its midnight deadline, the bank is accountable for the amount of the item. This is in accord with prior California law. Kriste v. International Savings and Exchange Bank, 17 Cal.App. 301, 119 Pac. 666 (1911) (failure to give notice of dishonor within prescribed time limits resulted in the bank being held liable for the amount of the item).

Changes from U.C.C. (1962 Official Text)

2. This is section 4–302 of the Official Text without change.

Uniform Commercial Code Comment
Official Reasons for 1990 Change

Subsection (b) is added to clarify the deleted introductory language of former Section 4–302: "In the absence of a valid defense such as breach of a presentment warranty (subsection (1) of Section 4–207), settlement effected or the like...." A payor bank can defend an action against it based on accountability by showing that the item contained a forged indorsement or a fraudulent alteration. Section 4–208. Proposed subsection (b) drops the ambiguous "or the like" language and provides that the payor bank may also raise the defense of fraud. Decisions that hold an accountable bank's liability to be "absolute" are rejected. A payor bank that makes a late return of an item should not be liable to a defrauder operating a check kiting scheme. In Bank Leumi Trust Co. v. Balley's Park Place Inc., 528 F.Supp. 349 (S.D.N.Y.1981), and American National Bank v. Foodbasket, 497 P.2d 546 (Wyo.1972) banks that were accountable under Section 4–302 for missing their midnight deadline were successful in defending against parties who initiated collection knowing that the check would not be paid. The "settlement effected" language is deleted as unnecessary. If a payor bank is accountable for an item it is liable to pay it. If it has made final payment for an item, it is no longer accountable for the item. The other modifications are made to conform with current legislative drafting practices, with no intent to change substance.

1990 Change

1. Subsection (a)(1) continues the former law distinguishing between cases in which the payor bank is not also the depositary bank and those in which the payor bank is also the depositary bank ("on us" items). For "on us" items the payor bank is accountable if it retains the item beyond its midnight deadline without settling for it. If the payor bank is not the depositary bank it is accountable if it retains the item beyond midnight of the banking day of receipt without settling for it. It may avoid accountability either by settling for the item on the day of receipt and returning the item before its midnight deadline under Section 4–301 or by returning the item on the day of receipt. This rule is consistent with the deferred posting practice authorized by Section 4–301 which allows the payor bank to make provisional settlement for an item on the day of receipt and to revoke that settlement by returning the item on the next day. With respect to checks, Regulation CC Section 229.36(d) provides that settlements between banks for forward collection of checks are final when made. See the Commentary on that provision for its effect on the UCC.

2. If the settlement given by the payor bank does not become final, there has been no payment under Section 4–215(b), and the payor bank giving the failed settlement is accountable under subsection (a)(1) of Section 4–302. For instance, the payor bank makes provisional settlement by sending a teller's check that is dishonored. In such a case settlement is not final under Section 4–213(c) and no payment occurs under Section 4–215(b). Payor bank is accountable on the item. The general principle is that unless settlement provides the presenting bank with usable funds, settlement has failed and the payor bank is accountable for the amount of the item.

3. Subsection (b) is an elaboration of the deleted introductory language of former Section 4–302: "In the absence of a valid defense such as breach of a presentment warranty (subsection (1) of Section 4–207), settlement effected or the like...." A payor bank can defend an action against it based on accountability by showing that the item contained a forged indorsement or a fraudulent alteration. Subsection (b) drops the ambiguous "or the like" language and provides that the payor bank may also raise the defense of fraud. Decisions that hold an accountable bank's liability to be "absolute" are rejected. A payor bank that makes a late return of an item should not be liable to a defrauder operating a check kiting scheme. In Bank of Leumi Trust Co. v. Bally's Park Place Inc., 528 F.Supp. 349 (S.D.N.Y.1981), and American National Bank v. Foodbasket, 497 P.2d 546 (Wyo.1972), banks that were accountable under Section 4–302 for missing their midnight deadline were successful in defending against parties who initiated collection knowing that the check would not be paid. The "settlement effected" language is deleted as unnecessary. If a payor bank is accountable for an item it is liable to pay it. If it has made final payment for an item, it is no longer accountable for the item.

Uniform Commercial Code Comment

Prior Uniform Statutory Provision:

None; but see American Bankers Association Model Deferred Posting Statute.

Purposes:

Under Section 4–301, time limits are prescribed within which a payor bank must take action if it receives an item payable by it. Section 4–302 states the rights of the customer if the payor bank fails to take the action required within the time limits prescribed.

Cross Reference:

Section 4–301.

Definitional Cross References:

"Acceptance". Section 3–410.
"Banking day". Section 4–104.
"Customer". Section 4–104.
"Depositary bank". Section 4–105.
"Documentary draft". Section 4–104.
"Item". Section 4–104.
"Midnight deadline". Section 4–104.
"Notice of dishonor". Section 3–508.
"Payor bank". Section 4–105.
"Properly payable". Section 4–104.
"Settle". Section 4–104.

Cross References

Bank's action upon receipt of item, time, see Commercial Code § 4301.
Business days, banks, see Civil Code § 9.
Charging back item, see Commercial Code § 4214.
Deferred posting, recovery of payment by return, see Commercial Code § 4301.
Discharge of liability of obligated bank with respect to check on payment to claimant, exception, see Commercial Code § 3312.
Dishonor of check if payor bank timely returns check or sends timely notice of dishonor or nonpayment or becomes accountable for amount of check under this section, see Commercial Code § 3502.
Warranties of customer and collecting bank on transfer or presentment of items, see Commercial Code § 4207.

§ 4303. When Items Subject to Notice, Stop-Order, Legal Process or Setoff; Order in Which Items May Be Charged or Certified

(a) Any knowledge, notice, or <u>stop-payment</u> order received by, legal process served upon, or setoff exercised by a payor bank * * * <u>comes too late</u> to terminate, suspend, or modify the bank's right or duty to pay an item or to charge its customer's account for the item * * * if the knowledge, notice, <u>stop-payment</u> order, or legal process is received or served and <u>a reasonable time for the bank</u> * * * <u>to act thereon</u> * * * <u>expires</u> or the

§ 4303

setoff is exercised after * * * the earliest of the following:

(1) The bank * * * accepts or certifies the item.

(2) The bank * * * pays the item in cash.

(3) The bank * * * settles for the item without having a right to revoke the settlement under * * * statute, * * * clearing house rule, or agreement * * *.
* * *

(4) The bank * * * becomes accountable for the amount of the item under * * * Section 4302 dealing with the payor bank's responsibility for late return of items * * *.
* * *

(5) With respect to checks, a cutoff hour no earlier than one hour after the opening of the next banking day after the banking day on which the bank received the check and no later than the close of that next banking day or, if no cutoff hour is fixed, the close of the next banking day after the banking day on which the bank received the check.

(b) Subject to * * * subdivision * * * (a), items may be accepted, paid, certified, or charged to the indicated account of its customer in any order * * *. *(Stats.1963, c. 819, § 4303. Amended by Stats.1992, c. 914 (S.B.833), § 39.)*

California Code Comment
1992 Amendment

1. While a payor bank is processing an item presented for payment, it may receive knowledge or a legal notice affecting the item, such as knowledge or a notice that the drawer has filed a petition in bankruptcy or made an assignment for the benefit of creditors; may receive an order of the drawer stopping payment on the item; may have served on it an attachment of the account of the drawer; or the bank itself may exercise a right of setoff against the drawer's account. Each of these events affects the account of the drawer and may eliminate or freeze all or part of whatever balance is available to pay the item. Subsection (a) states the rule for determining the relative priorities between these various legal events and the item.

2. The rule is that if any one of several things has been done to the item or if it has reached any one of several stages in its processing at the time the knowledge, notice, stop-payment order or legal process is received or served and a reasonable time for the bank to act thereon expires or the setoff is exercised, the knowledge, notice, stop-payment order, legal process or setoff comes too late, the item has priority and a charge to the customer's account may be made and is effective. With respect to the effect of the customer's bankruptcy, the bank's rights are governed by Bankruptcy Code Section 542(c) which codifies the result of Bank of Marin v. England, 385 U.S. 99 (1966). Section 4–405 applies to the death or incompetence of the customer.

3. Once a payor bank has accepted or certified an item or has paid the item in cash, the event has occurred that determines priorities between the item and the various legal events usually described as the "four legals." Paragraphs (1) and (2) of subsection (a) so provide. If a payor bank settles for an item presented over the counter for immediate payment by a cashier's check or teller's check which the presenting person agrees to accept, paragraph (3) of subsection (a) would control and the event determining priority has occurred. Because presentment was over the counter, Section 4–301(a) does not apply to give the payor bank the statutory right to revoke the settlement. Thus the requirements of paragraph (3) have been met unless a clearinghouse rule or agreement of the parties provides otherwise.

4. In the usual case settlement for checks is by entries in bank accounts. Since the process-of-posting test has been abandoned as inappropriate for automated check collection, the determining event for priorities is a given hour on the day after the item is received. (Paragraph (5) of subsection (a).) The hour may be fixed by the bank no earlier than one hour after the opening on the next banking day after the bank received the check and no later than the close of that banking day. If an item is received after the payor bank's regular Section 4–108 cutoff hour, it is treated as received the next banking day. If a bank receives an item after its regular cutoff hour on Monday and an attachment is levied at noon on Tuesday, the attachment is prior to the item if the bank had not before that hour taken the action described in paragraphs (1), (2), and (3) of subsection (a). The Commentary to Regulation CC Section 229.36(d) explains that even though settlement by a paying bank for a check is final for Regulation CC purposes, the paying bank's right to return the check before its midnight deadline under the UCC is not affected.

5. Another event conferring priority for an item and a charge to the customer's account based upon the item is stated by the language "become accountable for the amount of the item under Section 4–302 dealing with the payor bank's responsibility for late return of items." Expiration of the deadline under Section 4–302 with resulting accountability by the payor bank for the amount of the item, establishes priority of the item over notices, stop-payment orders, legal process or setoff.

6. In the case of knowledge, notice, stop-payment orders and legal process the effective time for determining whether they were received too late to affect the payment of an item and a charge to the customer's account by reason of such payment, is receipt plus a reasonable time for the bank to act on any of these communications. Usually a relatively short time is required to communicate to the accounting department advice of one of these events but certainly some time is necessary. Compare Sections 1–201(27) and 4–403. In the case of setoff the effective time is when the setoff is actually made.

7. Subsection (b) provides that a payor bank may accept or pay items in any order. For example, three checks drawn on a customer's account are presented for payment to the payor bank as follows: an $850 check to the Internal Revenue Service, a $300 check to a department store and a $200 check to John Doe. The balance of available funds in the customer's account is $900. Since the three checks overdraw the customer's account by $450 the payor bank has no duty to the customer to pay all three checks. Under subsection (b) if the bank chooses not to pay all of the checks, it may either pay the $850 check to the IRS and return the other two smaller checks or pay the two smaller checks and return the $850 check. In this example, it may well be that the customer would prefer that the check to the IRS be paid because nonpayment may have more serious consequences than nonpayment of the other two checks, but that is not necessarily true. Payment of one of the smaller checks may be more vital or the customer may prefer to minimize the number of checks returned because the payor bank normally charges a fee with respect to each returned check. The bank has no way of knowing the wishes of the customer, but it may be able to identify a check that appears to be particularly important. It is necessary to give discretion to the payor bank because it is impossible to state a rule that will be fair to the customer in all cases, having in mind the almost infinite number of combinations of large and small checks in relation to the available balance on hand in the drawer's account; the possible methods of receipt; and other variables. Further, the drawer has drawn all the checks, the drawer should have funds available to meet all of them and has no basis for urging one should be paid before another; and the holders have no direct right against the payor bank in any event, unless of course, the bank has accepted, certified or finally paid a particular item, or has become liable for it under Section 4–302.

The only restraint on the discretion given to the payor bank under subsection (b) is that the bank act in good faith. For example, the bank could not properly follow an established practice of maximizing the number of returned checks for the sole purpose of increasing the amount of returned check fees charged to the customer. On the other hand, the bank has the right to pay items for which it is itself liable ahead of those for which it is not. (1992 Senate Daily Journal 7350)

California Code Comment
By John A. Bohn and Charles J. Williams

Prior California Law

1. Subdivision (1) provides when the bank's knowledge or notice, a stop payment order, legal process or set off comes too late to nullify a

prior act so that the bank may nevertheless charge the customer's account. It states the rules for determining the winner between the owner of the item and the creditors of the drawer or the drawer himself. Official Comments 1 through 5.

2. Subdivision (1) is new statutory law but the principle is adopted in Rosen v. Rosen, 17 Cal.App.2d 601, 62 P.2d 384 (1936). In that case execution was levied on a customer's account the day after a check on the account was received and posted. The issue was whether the bank had accepted the check before the levy. The court held that the bank could pay the item and charge the drawer's account.

3. Subdivision (2) in its first sentence allows the bank to pay items in any order it chooses. See Official Comment 6. This latitude is subject to the requirement of good faith and ordinary care. This subdivision is new statutory law. There does not appear to be case authority in California on the question of what order the bank may pay or charge items. Other jurisdictions have been divided, e.g. Castaline v. National City Bank, 244 Mass. 416, 138 N.E. 398, 26 A.L.R. 1484 (1923); Louisville & Nashville R.R. Co. v. Federal Reserve Bank, 157 Tenn. 297, 10 S.W.2d 683, 61 A.L.R. 954 (1928).

Changes from U.C.C. (1962 Official Text)

4. The California version of section 4–303 of the 1962 Official Text contains several variations. The 1962 Official Text as amended in California reads:

"4303. (1) Any knowledge, notice or stop order received by, legal process served upon or setoff exercised by a payor bank, whether or not effective under other rules of law to terminate, suspend or modify the bank's right or duty to pay an item or to charge its customer's account for the item, comes too late to so terminate, suspend or modify such right or duty if the knowledge, notice, stop order or legal process is received or served and [a reasonable time for the bank to act thereon expires] the bank does not have a reasonable time to act thereon before, or the setoff is exercised after [the bank has done], the happening of any of the following:

"(a) The bank has accepted or certified the item;

"(b) The bank has paid the item in cash;

"(c) The bank has settled for the item without [reserving] having a right to revoke the settlement [and without having such right.] under any of the following: statute, clearinghouse rule, [or] agreement, or reservation thereof;

"(d) The cutoff hour (Section 4107) or the close of the banking day if no cutoff hour is fixed of the day on which the bank received the item; [completed the process of posting the item to the indicated account of the drawer, maker or other person to be charged therewith or otherwise has evidenced by examination of such indicated account and by action its decision to pay the item; or]

"(e) The bank has become accountable for the amount of the item under [subsection] subdivision (1)(d) of Section 4213 and Section 4302 dealing with the payor bank's responsibility for late return of items; or

"(f) The item has been deposited or received for deposit for credit in an account of a customer with the payor bank.

"(2). Subject to the provisions of [subsection] subdivision (1) items may be accepted, paid, certified or charged to the indicated account of its customer in any order convenient to the bank [.] and before or after its regular banking hours. A bank is under no obligation to determine the time of day an item is received and without liability may withhold the amount thereof pending a determination of the effect, consequence or priority of any knowledge, notice, stop order or legal process concerning the same, or interplead such amount and the claimants thereto."

5. Subdivision (1)(d) of section 4–303 of the Official Text is deleted. The new paragraph (d) is substituted to eliminate uncertainty of "completed the process of posting." Sixth Progress Report to the Legislature by Senate Fact Finding Committee on Judiciary (1959–1961) Part 1, The Uniform Commercial Code, pp. 360, 407 and 477.

6. Paragraph (f) of subdivision (1) is an addition to the Official Text. It was added as a result of recommendations of the State Bar and California Bankers Association. Its purpose is to retain the rule that final payment occurs when a customer deposits an item in his account with the payor bank and receives credit in his account. Briviesca v. Coronado, 19 Cal.2d 244, 120 P.2d 649 (1941).

The Marsh and Warren report recommended against including paragraph (f) in subdivision (1):

"Where the holder of a check deposits the check in the drawee bank in his own name (in which case the item is known as an 'on us' item), the California rule is that he receives immediate payment. In Briviesca v. Coronado, 19 C.2d 244, 120 P.2d 661 (1941), the court stated that when a holder of a check deposits it in the drawee bank 'In effect he receives the money from the bank and immediately deposits it therein. . . . The liability of the bank to the depositor-payee is not based upon the check or any promise by the bank to pay the check, but arises from the relationship of debtor and creditor that exists between a bank and a depositor. In the instant case, this relationship came into existence at the time the deposit was made, not at the time the check was stamped and the account posted in the ledger.' As stated in the Official Comments, the draftsmen of the Code clearly intended to apply the same rule to 'on us' items as to all other items and to abrogate the Briviesca rule. There is no convincing reason, in our opinion, why the right of third parties to assert priority over an item being processed should be abolished because of the happenstance that the bank in which the item is deposited is also the drawee bank. It is worth pointing out that the proposed amendments of the State Bar Committee would reduce to the vanishing point the time during which third parties may claim priority over 'on us' items being processed; but they would increase to an indeterminate period the time during which the payor bank may exercise its right of setoff in priority over these same items. It is recommended that proposed new clause (f) be rejected." Sixth Progress Report to the Legislature by Senate Fact Finding Committee on Judiciary (1959–1961) Part 1, The Uniform Commercial Code, p. 478.

The State Bar gives the following reason for adding paragraph (f):

"When a payee deposits a check in his own account in the bank on which it is drawn, it is known as an 'on us' item. The Official Text would treat such 'on us' checks no differently from items deposited in a bank other than the drawee bank. There would be a certain period after deposit of the 'on us' item during which stop-payment orders, garnishments or setoffs might take priority over the item. The rule in California is that such a check is considered paid at the moment deposited. [Footnote: Briviesca v. Coronado, 19 C.2d 244, 120 P.2d 649 (1941).] Since the payee could have cashed the check and immediately deposited the cash in his own account in the same bank, his rights should not be curtailed just because he did not go through this process. The State Bar Committee and the Advisory Committee believe the California rule preferable because the Code rule would be unfair to the depositor. Section 14303 [4303] has therefore been amended in S.B. 1093 [1961 Session, 1958 Official Text as amended] to retain the California law." California State Bar Committee on the Commercial Code, A Special Report, The Uniform Commercial Code, 37 Calif.State Bar J. (March–April, 1962) p. 166.

7. In subdivision (2) the reference to payment before or after banking hours at the end of the first sentence and the second sentence were added to eliminate any question of the propriety of action outside regular banking hours. Payment or certification before or after regular banking hours was recognized under former Financial Code § 993. The reason for this change and its effect on California law is described in the Marsh and Warren report:

". . . [It] would bring into this [subdivision 2] subsection the provisions of FC [former Financial Code section] § 993 and eliminate any possible objection to action outside of banking hours. The amendment seems desirable.

"The State Bar Committee proposes the addition of a second sentence in this [subdivision 2] subsection stating that a bank is under no obligation to ascertain the time when an item is received and allowing a bank to withhold the amount of an item pending a determination of the priority of any knowledge, notice, stop order or legal process or the bank may interplead the claimants. If proposed Section 14303(1)(f) [4303(1)(f)] . . . were adopted, [it was] it would create a problem of ascertaining the exact time the item was received. We are informed that banks make no attempt to record the time of day an item is received. Even if Section 14303(1)(f) [4303(1)(f)] is not adopted, . . . Section 14303(1)(b) [4303(1)(b)] states that the time a bank pays an item in cash cuts off the rights of third parties, and it seems this time might also be hard to determine. Since a bank does not know the time of day when it receives items, the State Bar proposal gives to banks a means of protecting themselves when caught between competing claimants. In shaping the law to conform to the legitimate practices of the banking community, this proposal is in keeping with the spirit of the Code and should be adopted. However, we have added the words 'of day' after 'time' in order to make clear that this provision does not relieve a bank of responsibility for determining what day it received an item." Sixth Progress Report to the Legislature by Senate Fact Finding Committee on Judiciary (1959–1961) Part 1, The Uniform Commercial Code, p. 480.

Uniform Commercial Code Comment
Official Reasons for 1990 Change

The preamble of subsection (a) is restated in order to improve comprehension. Paragraphs (1)–(4) of subsection (a) are restated to accommodate the addition of paragraph (5) which is stated in terms of the reaching of a cutoff hour rather than the doing of an act. Subsection (a)(3) is amended to conform to Section 4–215(a)(2) which provides that a payor bank cannot make settlement provisional by unilaterally reserving a right to revoke the settlement. The right to revoke must come from a statute (e.g. Section 4–301), a clearing-house rule or other agreement. Former subsection (1)(d) is deleted for the reason stated in the Reason for 1990 Change for former Section 4–109. The reference to former Section 4–213 is deleted from subsection (a)(4) because the reference to accountability in former Section 4–213 is deleted from what is now Section 4–215.

Subsection (a)(5) is added to allow payor banks, under time pressure to return checks to meet Regulation CC deadlines, to fix a cutoff hour earlier than the close of the next banking day after the banking day on which the checks are received. Banks must have time after receiving an attachment or effecting a setoff to return a check if the attachment or setoff renders the customer's account insufficient to pay the check. Since banks are now returning checks earlier during the next banking day after the banking day of receipt owing to Regulation CC, they need a cutoff hour earlier than the close of the banking day after that of receipt because they may be returning their checks before the close of that banking day.

Subsection (b) is amended to delete "convenient to the bank" as being superfluous. The other modifications are made to conform with current legislative drafting practices with no intent to change substance.

1990 Change

1. While a payor bank is processing an item presented for payment, it may receive knowledge or a legal notice affecting the item, such as knowledge or a notice that the drawer has filed a petition in bankruptcy or made an assignment for the benefit of creditors; may receive an order of the drawer stopping payment on the item; may have served on it an attachment of the account of the drawer; or the bank itself may exercise a right of setoff against the drawer's account. Each of these events affects the account of the drawer and may eliminate or freeze all or part of whatever balance is available to pay the item. Subsection (a) states the rule for determining the relative priorities between these various legal events and the item.

2. The rule is that if any one of several things has been done to the item or if it has reached any one of several stages in its processing at the time the knowledge, notice, stop-payment order or legal process is received or served and a reasonable time for the bank to act thereon expires or the setoff is exercised, the knowledge, notice, stop-payment order, legal process or setoff comes too late, the item has priority and a charge to the customer's account may be made and is effective. With respect to the effect of the customer's bankruptcy, the bank's rights are governed by Bankruptcy Code Section 542(c) which codifies the result of Bank of Marin v. England, 385 U.S. 99 (1966). Section 4–405 applies to the death or incompetence of the customer.

3. Once a payor bank has accepted or certified an item or has paid the item in cash, the event has occurred that determines priorities between the item and the various legal events usually described as the "four legals." Paragraphs (1) and (2) of subsection (a) so provide. If a payor bank settles for an item presented over the counter for immediate payment by a cashier's check or teller's check which the presenting person agrees to accept, paragraph (3) of subsection (a) would control and the event determining priority has occurred. Because presentment was over the counter, Section 4–301(a) does not apply to give the payor bank the statutory right to revoke the settlement. Thus the requirements of paragraph (3) have been met unless a clearing-house rule or agreement of the parties provides otherwise.

4. In the usual case settlement for checks is by entries in bank accounts. Since the process-of-posting test has been abandoned as inappropriate for automated check collection, the determining event for priorities is a given hour on the day after the item is received. (Paragraph (5) of subsection (a).) The hour may be fixed by the bank no earlier than one hour after the opening on the next banking day after the bank received the check and no later than the close of that banking day. If an item is received after the payor bank's regular Section 4–108 cutoff hour, it is treated as received the next banking day. If a bank receives an item after its regular cutoff hour on Monday and an attachment is levied at noon on Tuesday, the attachment is prior to the item if the bank had not before that hour taken the action described in paragraphs (1), (2), and (3) of subsection (a). The Commentary to Regulation CC Section 229.36(d) explains that even though settlement by a paying bank for a check is final for Regulation CC purposes, the paying bank's right to return the check before its midnight deadline under the UCC is not affected.

5. Another event conferring priority for an item and a charge to the customer's account based upon the item is stated by the language "become accountable for the amount of the item under Section 4–302 dealing with the payor bank's responsibility for late return of items." Expiration of the deadline under Section 4–302 with resulting accountability by the payor bank for the amount of the item, establishes priority of the item over notices, stop-payment orders, legal process or setoff.

6. In the case of knowledge, notice, stop-payment orders and legal process the effective time for determining whether they were received too late to affect the payment of an item and a charge to the customer's account by reason of such payment, is receipt plus a reasonable time for the bank to act on any of these communications. Usually a relatively short time is required to communicate to the accounting department advice of one of these events but certainly some time is necessary. Compare Sections 1–201(27) and 4–403. In the case of setoff the effective time is when the setoff is actually made.

7. As between one item and another no priority rule is stated. This is justified because of the impossibility of stating a rule that would be fair in all cases, having in mind the almost infinite number of combinations of large and small checks in relation to the available balance on hand in the drawer's account; the possible methods of receipt; and other variables. Further, the drawer has drawn all the checks, the drawer should have funds available to meet all of them and has no basis for urging one should be paid before another; and the holders have no direct right against the payor or bank in any event, unless of course, the bank has accepted, certified or finally paid a particular item, or has become liable for it under Section 4–302. Under subsection (b) the bank has the right to pay items for which it is itself liable ahead of those for which it is not.

Uniform Commercial Code Comment
Prior Uniform Statutory Provision:
None.

Purposes:

1. The comments to Section 4–213 describe the process through which an item passes in the payor bank. Prior to this process or at any time while it is going on, the payor bank may receive knowledge or a legal notice affecting the item, such as knowledge or a notice that the drawer has filed a petition in bankruptcy or made an assignment for the benefit of creditors; may receive an order of the drawer stopping payment on the item; may have served on it an attachment of the account of the drawer; or the bank itself may exercise a right of setoff against the drawer's account. Each of these events affects the account of the drawer and may eliminate or freeze all or part of whatever balance is available to pay the item. Subsection (1) states the rule for determining the relative priorities between these various legal events and the item.

2. The rule is that if any one of several things has been done to the item or if it has reached any one of several stages in its processing at the time the knowledge, notice, stop-order or legal process is received or served and a reasonable time for the bank to act thereon expires or the setoff is exercised, the knowledge, notice, stop-order, legal process or setoff comes too late, the item has priority and a charge to the customer's account may be made and is effective. Certain of the tests determining the priority status of the item are the same as for final payment under Section 4–213(1), but additional tests apply in the context of the present section. The first event mentioned, namely, acceptance, means formal acceptance as that term is used and defined in

Section 3–410. Certification is the type of certification defined in Section 3–411. Payment of the item in cash under Section 4–213(1)(a), final settlement for the item under Section 4–213(1)(b) and completion of the process of posting under Section 4–213(1)(c) all constitute final payment of the item and confer priority. After a cash payment, final settlement or the completion of the process of posting any knowledge, notice, stop-order, legal process or setoff comes too late and cannot interfere with either the payment of the item or a charge to the customer's account based upon such payment.

3. The sixth event conferring priority is stated by the language "or otherwise has evidenced by examination of such indicated account and by action its decision to pay the item." This general "omnibus" language is necessary to pick up other possible types of action impossible to specify particularly but where the bank has examined the account to see if there are sufficient funds and has taken some action indicating an intention to pay. An example is what has sometimes been called "sight posting" where the bookkeeper examines the account and makes a decision to pay but postpones posting. The clause should be interpreted in the light of Nineteenth Ward Bank v. First Nat. Bank of South Weymouth, 184 Mass. 49, 67 N.E. 670 (1903). It is not intended to refer to various preliminary acts in no way close to a true decision of the bank to pay the item, such as receipt of the item over the counter for deposit, entry of a provisional credit in a passbook, or the making of a provisional settlement for the item through the clearing house, by entries in accounts, remittance or otherwise. All actions of this type are provisional and none of them evidences the bank's decision to pay the item. In this Section as in Section 4–213 reasoning such as appears in Cohen v. First Nat. Bank of Nogales, 22 Ariz. 394, 400, 198 P. 122, 124 (1921); Briviesca v. Coronado, 19 Cal.2d 244, 120 P.2d 649 (1941); White Brokerage Co. v. Cooperman, 207 Minn. 239, 290 N.W. 790 (1940); Scotts Bluff County v. First Nat. Bank of Gering, 115 Neb. 273, 212 N.W. 617, 618 (1927); Provident Savings Bank & Trust Co. v. Hildebrand, 49 Ohio App. 207, 196 N.E. 790, 791 (1934); Schaer v. First Nat. Bank of Brenham, 132 Tex. 499, 124 S.W.2d 108 (1939) (bill of exchange); Union State Bank of Lancaster v. People's State Bank of Lancaster, 192 Wis. 28, 33, 211 N.W. 931, 933 (1927); 1 Paton's Digest 1067, is rejected.

4. The seventh and last event conferring priority for an item and a charge to the customer's account based upon the item is stated by the language "become accountable for the amount of the item under subsection (1)(d) of Section 4–213 and Section 4–302 dealing with the payor bank's responsibility for late return of items". Under Section 4–213(1)(d) if a payor bank makes a provisional settlement for an item and fails to revoke the settlement in the time and manner permitted by statute, clearing house rule or agreement, such combination of events constitutes final payment of the item. Under Section 4–302 a payor bank may also become accountable for the amount of an item in certain other situations even though there has been no provisional settlement for the item or such action as constitutes final payment under Section 4–213(1). Expiration of the deadlines under Sections 4–213(1)(d) or 4–302 with resulting accountability by the payor bank for the amount of the item, establish priority of the item over notices, stop-orders, legal process or setoff.

5. In the case of knowledge, notice, stop-orders and legal process the effective time for determining whether they were received too late to affect the payment of an item and a charge to the customer's account by reason of such payment, is receipt plus a reasonable time for the bank to act on any of these communications. Usually a relatively short time is required to communicate to the bookkeeping department advice of one of these events but certainly some time is necessary. Compare Sections 1–201(27) and 4–403. In the case of setoff the effective time is when the setoff is actually made.

6. As between one item and another no priority rule is stated, other than the convenience of the bank. This rule is justified because of the impossibility of stating a rule that would be fair in all cases, having in mind the almost infinite number of combinations of large and small checks in relation to the available balance on hand in the drawer's account; the possible methods of receipt; and other difficulties. Further, where the drawer has drawn all the checks, he should have funds available to meet all of them and has no basis for urging one should be paid before another; and the holders have no direct right against the payor bank in any event, unless of course, the bank has accepted, certified or finally paid a particular item, or has become liable for it under Section 4–302. Under subsection (2) the bank obviously has the right to pay items for which it is itself liable ahead of those for which it is not.

Cross References:

Sections 3–410, 3–411, 4–213(1), 4–301, 4–302.

Definitional Cross References:

"Accepted". Section 3–410.
"Account". Section 4–104.
"Agreement". Section 1–201.
"Certified". Section 3–411.
"Clearing house". Section 4–104.
"Customer". Section 4–104.
"Item". Section 4–104.
"Notice". Section 1–201.
"Payor bank". Section 4–105.
"Settle". Section 4–104.

Cross References

Acceptance, definition and operation, see Commercial Code § 3409.
Business days of banks, see Civil Code § 9.
Certification defined, see Commercial Code § 3409.
Check subject to stop-payment order, charges against customer's account, see Commercial Code § 4401.
Customer's right to stop payment, see Commercial Code § 4403.
Deferred posting, see Commercial Code § 4301.
Final payment, act constituting, see Commercial Code § 4215.
Late return items, accountability, see Commercial Code § 4302.

CHAPTER 4. RELATIONSHIP BETWEEN PAYOR BANK AND ITS CUSTOMER

Section
4401. Charges against customer's account; liability of customer.
4402. Wrongful dishonor; liability to customer.
4403. Stop-payment orders.
4404. Checks presented over six months past date.
4405. Death or Incompetence of Customer.
4406. Statement of account; customer's duty to examine statement; remedies.
4406. Statement of account; customer's duty to examine statement; remedies.
4407. Improper payment; subrogation rights of payor bank.

Transitional Provisions

Effective date and transitional provisions for sections in Division 4 affected by Stats.1992, c. 914, see Commercial Code § 16101 et seq.

§ 4401. Charges against customer's account; liability of customer

* * * (a) A bank may charge against the account * * * of a customer an item that is * * * properly payable from that account even though the charge creates an overdraft * * *. An item is properly payable if it is authorized by the customer and is in accordance with any agreement between the customer and bank.

(b) A customer is not liable for the amount of an overdraft if the customer neither signed the item nor benefited from the proceeds of the item.

(c) A bank may charge against the account of a customer a check that is otherwise properly payable from the account, even though payment was made before the date of the check, unless the customer has given notice to the bank of the postdating describing the check with reasonable certainty. The notice is effective for the period stated in subdivision (b) of Section 4403 for stop-payment orders, and shall be received at such time and in such manner as to afford the bank a reasonable opportunity to act on it before the bank takes any action with respect to the check described in Section 4303. If a bank charges against the account of a customer a check before the date stated in the notice of postdating, the bank is liable for damages for the loss resulting from its act. The loss may include damages for dishonor of subsequent items under Section 4402.

(d) A bank that in good faith makes payment to a holder may charge the indicated account of its customer according to either:

(1) The original * * * terms of the altered item * * *;

* * * (2) The terms of the completed item, even though the bank knows the item has been completed unless the bank has notice that the completion was improper. *(Stats.1963, c. 819, § 4401. Amended by Stats.1992, c. 914 (S.B.833), § 40.)*

California Code Comment

By John A. Bohn and Charles J. Williams

Prior California Law

1. Subdivision (1) is new statutory law but is in accord with prior judicial decisions to the effect that a bank may charge against a customer's account even if this would create an overdraft. Bank of America v. Universal Finance Co., 131 Cal.App. 116, 125, 21 P.2d 147 (1933).

2. Subdivision (2) is new statutory law. Its provisions parallel Commercial Code §§ 3115 and 3407. Redington v. Woods, 45 Cal. 406, 13 Am.Rep. 190, 75 A.L.R.2d 614 (1873) recognized the rule that the drawee could recover the excess paid on an altered instrument even if paid to an innocent holder.

However, the courts have held that a bank could not charge its depositor's account on an altered check unless the bank could show negligence or acts raising estoppel on the part of the customer and in addition show that the bank itself was free from negligence. Pacific Coast Cheese, Inc. v. Security First National Bank, 45 Cal.2d 75, 286 P.2d 353 (1955).

Changes from U.C.C. (1962 Official Text)

3. Subdivision (1) of the California version adds the following language:

"and in such event recover or obtain refund of the amount of the overdraft."

This addition was recommended to make it clear that the amount of the overdraft can be recovered:

"Under section 14401 [4401] a bank could charge an item against a customer's account even though it creates an overdraft, if it is otherwise properly payable. This Code section as it stands in the Official Text was probably intended to change California law. Torrance National Bank v. Enesco Federal Credit Union [Footnote: 134 C.A.2d 316, 285 P.2d 737 (1955)] held that an agent (e.g., an officer of a corporation) lacks the power to write a check creating an overdraft on the principal's account without authority from the principal to borrow money. S.B. 1093 [1961 Session, 1958 Official Text as amended] amends section 14401 [4401] to make it clear that the bank may not only charge the account but may recover the amount of the overdraft from the customer." California State Bar Committee on the Commercial Code, A Special Report, The Uniform Commercial Code, 37 Calif.State Bar J. (March–April, 1962) pp. 167 to 168.

Professors Marsh and Warren felt that this addition was not necessary:

"This subsection [subdivision (1)] deals with the situation where the bank pays a draft even though there are insufficient funds in the customer's account. Because of a doubt raised in some cases, it was thought advisable by the draftsmen of the Code expressly to give a bank the right to pay the overdraft rather than dishonoring it. If the bank does so pursuant to this express right, and charges its customer's account, it obviously follows that it can recover the amount from the customer. No court would hold that it was limited to charging the account, but could take no action to collect the amount charged—that the bookkeeping entry could be made only for its own amusement. Even though it might have been better to include the proposed additional language in the original draft of the subsection, the same considerations apply here as under Section 14204(2) [4204(2)] above." Sixth Progress Report to the Legislature by Senate Fact Finding Committee on Judiciary (1959–1961) Part 1, The Uniform Commercial Code, pp. 480–481.

Uniform Commercial Code Comment
Official Reasons for 1990 Change

Subsection (a) is amended by the addition of the second sentence which provides a more general definition of "properly payable" than the narrow definition that was contained in former Section 4–104(1)(i). An item is properly payable from a customer's account if the customer has authorized the payment and the payment does not violate the customer-bank agreement concerning the account. An item drawn for more than the balance of the customer's account may be properly payable.

Subsection (b) is added to adopt the view of case authority holding that if there is more than one customer who can draw on an account, the nonsigning customer is not liable for an overdraft unless that person benefits from the proceeds of the item.

Subsection (c) is added because the automated check collection system cannot accommodate postdated checks. A check is usually paid upon presentment without respect to the date of the check. Under the former law, if a payor bank paid a postdated check before its stated date, it could not charge the customer's account because the check was not "properly payable." Hence, the bank might have been liable for wrongfully dishonoring subsequent checks of the drawer that would have been paid had the postdated check not been prematurely paid. Under subsection (c) a customer wishing to postdate a check must notify the payor bank of its postdating in time to allow the bank to act on the customer's notice before the bank has to commit itself to pay the check. If the bank fails to act on the customer's timely notice, it may be liable for damages for the resulting loss which may include damages for dishonor of subsequent items.

The other modifications are made to conform with current legislative drafting practices, with no intent to change substance.

1990 Change

1. An item is properly payable from a customer's account if the customer has authorized the payment and the payment does not violate any agreement that may exist between the bank and its customer. For an example of a payment held to violate an agreement with a customer, see Torrance National Bank v. Enesco Federal Credit Union, 285 P.2d 737 (Cal.App.1955). An item drawn for more than the amount of a customer's account may be properly payable. Thus under subsection (a) a bank may charge the customer's account for an item even though payment results in an overdraft. An item containing a forged drawer's signature or forged indorsement is not properly payable. Concern has arisen whether a bank may require a customer to execute a stop-payment order when the customer notifies the bank of the loss of an unindorsed or specially indorsed check. Since such a check cannot be properly payable from the customer's account, it is inappropriate for a bank to require a stop-payment order in such a case.

2. Subsection (b) adopts the view of case authority holding that if there is more than one customer who can draw on an account, the nonsigning customer is not liable for an overdraft unless that person benefits from the proceeds of the item.

3. Subsection (c) is added because the automated check collection system cannot accommodate postdated checks. A check is usually paid upon presentment without respect to the date of the check. Under the former law, if a payor bank paid a postdated check before its stated

date, it could not charge the customer's account because the check was not "properly payable." Hence, the bank might have been liable for wrongfully dishonoring subsequent checks of the drawer that would have been paid had the postdated check not been prematurely paid. Under subsection (c) a customer wishing to postdate a check must notify the payor bank of its postdating in time to allow the bank to act on the customer's notice before the bank has to commit itself to pay the check. If the bank fails to act on the customer's timely notice, it may be liable for damages for the resulting loss which may include damages for dishonor of subsequent items. This Act does not regulate fees that banks charge their customers for a notice of postdating or other services covered by the Act, but under principles of law such as unconscionability or good faith and fair dealing, courts have reviewed fees and the bank's exercise of a discretion to set fees. Perdue v. Crocker National Bank, 38 Cal.3d 913 (1985) (unconscionability); Best v. United Bank of Oregon, 739 P.2d 554, 562–566 (1987) (good faith and fair dealing). In addition, Section 1–203 provides that every contract or duty within this Act imposes an obligation of good faith in its performance or enforcement.

4. Section 3–407(c) states that a payor bank or drawee which pays a fraudulently altered instrument in good faith and without notice of the alteration may enforce rights with respect to the instrument according to its original terms or, in the case of an incomplete instrument altered by unauthorized completion, according to its terms as completed. Section 4–401(d) follows the rules stated in Section 3–407(c) by applying it to an altered item and allows the bank to enforce rights with respect to the altered item by charging the customer's account.

Uniform Commercial Code Comment

Prior Uniform Statutory Provision:

None.

Purposes:

1. It is fundamental that upon proper payment of a draft the drawee may charge the account of the drawer. This is true even though the draft is an overdraft since the draft itself authorizes the payment for the drawer's account and carries an implied promise to reimburse the drawee.

2. Subsection (2) parallels the provision which protects a holder in due course against discharge by reason of alteration and permits him to enforce the instrument according to its original tenor. Section 3–407(3). It adopts the rule of cases extending the same protection to a drawee who pays in good faith. The subsection also follows the policy of Sections 3–115 and 3–407(3) by protecting the drawee who pays a completed instrument in good faith according to the instrument as completed.

Cross References:

Sections 3–115 and 3–407.

Definitional Cross References:

"Account". Section 4–104.
"Bank". Section 1–201.
"Customer". Section 4–104.
"Good faith". Section 1–201.
"Holder". Section 1–201.
"Item". Section 4–104.
"Properly payable". Section 4–104.

Cross References

Alteration of instruments, definition and effect, see Commercial Code § 3407.
Conditions for person to require or request consumer to issue postdated check, see Business and Professions Code § 17538.6.
Enforcement of altered instruments, see Commercial Code § 3407.
Finality of items or payments, see Commercial Code § 4215.
Incomplete instruments, see Commercial Code § 3115.
Instrument payable on demand, date of payment, see Commercial Code § 3113.
Right of charge back or refund, see Commercial Code § 4214.
Security interest of collecting bank, see Commercial Code § 4210.
Statement, correctness conclusively presumed after four years, see Financial Code § 861.
Warranties on transfer or presentment, see Commercial Code § 4207.

§ 4402. Wrongful dishonor; liability to customer

(a) Except as otherwise provided in this division, a payor bank wrongfully dishonors an item if it dishonors an item that is properly payable, but a bank may dishonor an item that would create an overdraft unless it has agreed to pay the overdraft.

(b) A payor bank is liable to its customer for damages proximately caused by the wrongful dishonor of an item. * * * Liability is limited to actual damages proved and may include damages for an arrest or prosecution of the customer or other consequential damages. Whether any consequential damages are proximately caused by the wrongful dishonor is a question of fact to be determined in each case.

(c) A payor bank's determination of the customer's account balance on which a decision to dishonor for insufficiency of available funds is based may be made at any time between the time the item is received by the payor bank and the time that the payor bank returns the item or gives notice in lieu of return, and no more than one determination need be made. If, at the election of the payor bank, a subsequent balance determination is made for the purpose of reevaluating the bank's decision to dishonor the item, the account balance at that time is determinative of whether a dishonor for insufficiency of available funds is wrongful. (Stats.1963, c. 819, § 4402. Amended by Stats.1992, c. 914 (S.B.833), § 41.)

California Code Comment
1992 Amendment

1. Subsection (a) states positively what has been assumed under the original article: that if a bank fails to honor a properly payable item it may be liable to its customer for wrongful dishonor. Under subsection (b) the payor bank's wrongful dishonor of an item gives rise to a statutory cause of action. Damages may include consequential damages. Confusion has resulted from the attempts of courts to reconcile the first and second sentences of former Section 4–402. The second sentence implied that the bank was liable for some form of damages other than those proximately caused by the dishonor if the dishonor was other than by mistake. But nothing in the section described what these noncompensatory damages might be. Some courts have held that in distinguishing between mistaken dishonors and nonmistaken dishonors, the so-called "trader" rule has been retained that allowed a "merchant or trader" to recover substantial damages for wrongful dishonor without proof of damages actually suffered. Comment 3 to former Section 4–402 indicated that this was not the intent of the drafters. White & Summers, Uniform Commercial Code, Section 18–4 (1988), states: "The negative implication is that when wrongful dishonors occur not 'through mistake' but willfully, the court may impose damages greater than 'actual damages'.... Certainly the reference to 'mistake' in the second sentence of 4–402 invites a court to adopt the relevant pre-code distinction." Subsection (b) by deleting the reference to mistake in the second sentence precludes any inference that Section 4–402 retains the "trader" rule. Whether a bank is liable for noncompensatory damages, such as punitive damages, must be decided by Section 1–103 and Section 1–106 ("by other rule of law").

2. Wrongful dishonor is different from "failure to exercise ordinary care in handling an item," and the measure of damages is that stated in this section, not that stated in Section 4–103(e). By the same token, if a dishonor comes within this section, the measure of damages of this section applies and not another measure of damages. If the wrongful

refusal of the beneficiary's bank to make funds available from a funds transfer causes the beneficiary's check to be dishonored, no specific guidance is given as to whether recovery is under this section or Article 4A. In each case this issue must be viewed in its factual context, and it was thought unwise to seek to establish certainty at the cost of fairness.

3. The second and third sentences of the subsection (b) reject decisions holding that as a matter of law the dishonor of a check is not the "proximate cause" of the arrest and prosecution of the customer and leave to determination in each case as a question of fact whether the dishonor is or may be the "proximate cause."

4. Banks commonly determine whether there are sufficient funds in an account to pay an item after the close of banking hours on the day of presentment when they post debit and credit items to the account. The determination is made on the basis of credits available for withdrawal as of right or made available for withdrawal by the bank as an accommodation to its customer. In determining whether a check presented for payment will create an overdraft, the prevailing banking practice is to first credit the customer's account for deposits made on the day of presentment. If that credit represents funds available for withdrawal as of right, it is taken into account in determining whether the check presented for payment will or will not create an overdraft. A bank failing to follow that practice would not be acting in good faith if the failure caused the customer's account to be considered withdrawn.

When it is determined that payment of a check would overdraw the customer's account, the check may be returned at any time before the bank's midnight deadline the following day. In the case of large banks, the determination of the customer's account balance is made in a central operations center. The check may be returned immediately after it is determined that there is an overdraft, but the bank may want to hold the check until the following day to ask the manager of the branch that maintains the customer's account whether the check should be returned or paid. In many cases, after branch review, checks of a trustworthy customer are paid in spite of an overdraft. But suppose the check is returned after the branch review and, before the return, the customer made a deposit to the account that represented funds withdrawable as of right. Must the deposit be taken into account in determining whether the dishonor of the check was wrongful? Under former Section 4–402 it was unclear whether a dishonor of the check on the day following presentment was wrongful if the bank failed to make another determination of the account balance before the check was returned. The first sentence of subsection (c) makes clear in a case of this kind that the bank is not required to make another determination of the account balance on the day the check is returned. Obtaining an accurate reading of the customer's account balance during the course of a banking day is difficult for most banks because, while the bank is open, there may be withdrawals or deposits to the account at any time. Moreover, a substantial cost in money and time may be incurred by a second review of the customer's account balance. Requirement of a "second look" is a disincentive to the practice of some banks of obtaining branch review before dishonoring a check. Faced with the expense and difficulty of making a second review of the account balance many banks undoubtedly would abandon branch review and would return checks on the day of presentment following the late night processing. The first sentence of revised Section 4–402(c) was drafted to encourage banks not to automatically dishonor insufficient funds checks. There is a strong public policy in minimizing dishonor of checks.

The last sentence of Section 4–402(c) covers the case in which the payor bank elects to make a second determination of the customer's account balance. If the bank makes such a determination before dishonoring the check, the account balance at that time governs the question of whether the dishonored check did or did not create an overdraft.

5. Section 4–402 has been construed to preclude an action for wrongful dishonor by a plaintiff other than the bank's customer. *Loucks v. Albuquerque National Bank,* 418 P.2d 191 (N.Mex.1966). Some courts have allowed a plaintiff other than the customer to sue when the customer is a business entity that is one and the same with the individual or individuals operating it. *Murdaugh Volkswagen, Inc. v. First National Bank,* 801 F.2d 719 (4th Cir.1986) and *Karsh v. American City Bank,* 113 Cal.App.3d 419, 169 Cal.Rptr. 851 (1980). However, where the wrongful dishonor impugns the reputation of an operator of the business, the issue is not merely, as the court in *Koger v. East First National Bank* 433 So.2d 141 (Fla.App.1983), put it, one of the literal versus a liberal interpretation of Section 4–402. Rather the issue is whether the statutory cause of action in Section 4–402 displaces, in accordance with Section 1–103, any cause of action that existed at common law in a person who is not the customer whose reputation was damaged. *See Marcum v. Security Trust and Savings Co.,* 221 Ala. 419, 129 So. 74 (1930). While Section 4–402 should not be interpreted to displace the latter cause of action, the section itself gives no cause of action to other than a "customer," however that definition is construed, and thus confers no cause of action of the holder of a dishonored item. *First American National Bank v. Commerce Union Bank,* 692 S.W.2d 642 (Tenn.App.1985). (1992 Senate Daily Journal 7350).

California Code Comment

By John A. Bohn and Charles J. Williams

Prior California Law

1. This section is consistent with former Civil Code § 3320 which provided that a bank is not liable for nonpayment through mistake or error unless the depositor shows actual damage. Former Civil Code § 3320 also limited the bank's liability to damages actually proved. See Weaver v. Bank of America, 59 Cal.2d 428, 30 Cal.Rptr. 4, 380 P.2d 644 (1963) for an excellent statement of the background and purpose of Civil Code § 3320.

Commercial Code § 4402 and former Civil Code § 3320 both prevent the award of punitive damages for dishonor caused by mistake.

Changes from U.C.C. (1962 Official Text)

2. The last two sentences of section 4–402 of the Official Text are omitted from the California version. These provided:

"If so proximately caused and proved damages may include damages for an arrest or prosecution of the customer or other consequential damages. Whether any consequential damages are proximately caused by the wrongful dishonor is a question of fact to be determined in each case."

The language was omitted upon recommendation of the State Bar:

"Section 14402 [4402] would govern a bank's liability for damages proximately caused by the wrongful dishonor of a check. As in Civil Code section 3320, section 14402 [4402] rejects the common-law rule that a 'trader' is entitled to substantial damages for the wrongful dishonor of his check without proof of any actual damage.

"The Code section, however, goes on to provide that damages recoverable may include damages for a customer's arrest or prosecution if proximately caused by wrongful dishonor. Either this is contrary to the California rule of Hartford v. All Night and Day Bank [Footnote: 170 Cal. 538, 150 P. 356 (1915) Cf. Abramowitz v. Bank of America, 131 C.A.2d Supp. 892, 281 P.2d 380 (1955).] or it adds nothing to the rest of the section. This case held as a matter of law that a person's arrest and prosecution for writing a bad check could not be the proximate result of the wrongful dishonor of the check since there was an intervening agency. This part of section 14402 [4402] is not in S.B. 1093 [1961 Session, 1958 Official Text as amended] because one particular item of damage should not be singled out for special treatment. As now in S.B. 1093 [1961 Session, 1958 Official Text as amended] section 14402 [4402] takes no position on the rule of the Hartford case." California State Bar Committee on the Commercial Code, A Special Report, The Uniform Commercial Code, 37 Calif. State Bar J. (March–April 1962) p. 169.

The Marsh and Warren report discussed this recommendation thoroughly and concluded that the 1962 Official Text should be retained:

"Before 1917 the common-law rule prevailed in this State to the effect that substantial damages were recoverable against a bank for wrongfully dishonoring a check of its depositor. However, a distinction was made between traders and nontraders; in the case of the former it was presumed, without further proof, that substantial damages had been sustained. In 1917 California enacted CC § 3320, sponsored by the American Bankers Association, which states: 'No bank shall be liable to a depositor because of the nonpayment through mistake or error, and without malice, of a check which should have been paid unless the depositor shall allege and prove actual damage by reason of such nonpayment and in such event the liability shall not exceed the amount of damage so proved.' Section 3320 abolished the distinction recognized at common law between traders and nontraders; under this statute all parties must prove actual damage and can recover only the amount proved. Abramowitz v. Bank of America, 131 C.A.2d (Supp.) 892, 281 P.2d 380 (1955), states that 'the actual damage' under CC § 3320 is to be determined under CC § 3333 covering tort damages; hence, the test is injury proximately caused, rather than the contract measure of what was reasonably contemplated by the parties.

"This Section [4402] also rejects the distinction between traders and nontraders. Like present California law, it speaks in terms of computing damages on the basis of proximate cause. The State Bar Committee proposes deletion of the last two sentences of this Section on the ground that what damages are proximately caused should be determined by each state and not by a uniform act.

"The objection of the State Bar Committee apparently goes to the statement that the damages recoverable may include damages for arrest or prosecution of the customer if these damages are proximately caused by the wrongful dishonor. In Hartford v. All Night and Day Bank, 170 Cal. 538, 150 P. 356 (1915), the court held, apparently as a matter of law, that the wrongful dishonor of a check is not the proximate cause of the maker's arrest for the crime of drawing a check with intent to defraud. The court stated: 'There was an interruption and the intervention of an entirely separate cause, which cause was an independent human agency acting with an independent mind.' 170 Cal. at 541. Beardon v. Bank of Italy, 57 Cal.App. 337, 207 P. 270 (1922), is a similar holding, although the Abramowitz case, supra, recently questioned this rule.

"The Official Comments [Comment 3] indicate that the intent of the draftsmen of the Code was to overrule decisions holding as a matter of law that dishonor is not the proximate cause of arrest and prosecution. This Section leaves to determination in each case as a question of fact whether dishonor is or may be the proximate cause.

"However sympathetic one might be to the proposition that a determination of what damages are proximately caused is a local problem, the effect of this Section is to abolish the highly arbitrary rule which has been followed in this State to the effect that dishonor as a matter of law cannot be the proximate cause of arrest and prosecution. When a bank bounces a check of a customer even though he has sufficient funds, and the payee has the arm of the law put on him, to say that the bank's action had nothing to do with his incarceration is fantastic. It is recommended that California seize the opportunity afforded by the Code to abrogate this unrealistic rule." Sixth Progress Report to the Legislature by Senate Fact Finding Committee on Judiciary, (1959–1961) Part 1, The Uniform Commercial Code, pp. 481–482.

Uniform Commercial Code Comment
Official Reasons for 1990 Change

Subsection (a) is added for the purpose of stating positively what has been assumed under the original Article: that if a bank fails to honor a properly payable item it may be liable to its customer for wrongful dishonor. Subsection (b) is amended for clarification. Under this subsection the payor bank's wrongful dishonor of an item gives rise to a statutory cause of action. Damages may include consequential damages. Confusion has resulted from the attempts of courts to reconcile the first and second sentences of former Section 4–402. The second sentence implied that the bank was liable for some form of damages other than those proximately caused by the dishonor if the dishonor was other than by mistake. But nothing in the section described what these noncompensatory damages might be. Some courts have held that in distinguishing between mistaken dishonors and nonmistaken dishonors, the so-called "trader" rule has been retained that allowed a "merchant or trader" to recover substantial damages for wrongful dishonor without proof of damages actually suffered. Comment 3 to former Section 4–402 indicated that this was not the intent of the drafters. White & Summers, Uniform Commercial Code, Section 18–4 (1988), states: "The negative implication is that when wrongful dishonors occur not 'through mistake' but willfully, the court may impose damages greater than 'actual damages'.... Certainly the reference to 'mistake' in the second sentence of 4–402 invites a court to adopt the relevant pre-Code distinction." Subsection (b) by deleting the reference to mistake in the second sentence precludes any inference that Section 4–402 retains the "trader" rule. Whether a bank is liable for noncompensatory damages, such as punitive damages, must be decided by Section 1–103 and Section 1–106 ("by other rule of law").

Subsection (c) is added for clarification. Banks commonly determine whether there are sufficient funds in an account to pay an item after the close of banking hours on the day of presentment when they post debit and credit items to the account. The determination is made on the basis of credits available for withdrawal as of right or made available for withdrawal by the bank as an accommodation to its customer. When it is determined that payment of the item would overdraw the account, the item may be returned at any time before the bank's midnight deadline the following day. Before the item is returned new credits that are withdrawable as of right may have been added to the account. Subsection (c) eliminates uncertainty under Article 4 as to whether the failure to make a second determination before the item is returned on the day following presentment is a wrongful dishonor if new credits were added to the account on that day that would have covered the amount of the check.

1990 Change

1. Subsection (a) states positively what has been assumed under the original Article: that if a bank fails to honor a properly payable item it may be liable to its customer for wrongful dishonor. Under subsection (b) the payor bank's wrongful dishonor of an item gives rise to a statutory cause of action. Damages may include consequential damages. Confusion has resulted from the attempts of courts to reconcile the first and second sentences of former Section 4–402. The second sentence implied that the bank was liable for some form of damages other than those proximately caused by the dishonor if the dishonor was other than by mistake. But nothing in the section described what these noncompensatory damages might be. Some courts have held that in distinguishing between mistaken dishonors and nonmistaken dishonors, the so-called "trader" rule has been retained that allowed a "merchant or trader" to recover substantial damages for wrongful dishonor without proof of damages actually suffered. Comment 3 to former Section 4–402 indicated that this was not the intent of the drafters. White & Summers, Uniform Commercial Code, Section 18–4 (1988), states: "The negative implication is that when wrongful dishonors occur not 'through mistake' but willfully, the court may impose damages greater than 'actual damages'.... Certainly the reference to 'mistake' in the second sentence of 4–402 invites a court to adopt the relevant pre-Code distinction." Subsection (b) by deleting the reference to mistake in the second sentence precludes any inference that Section 4–402 retains the "trader" rule. Whether a bank is liable for noncompensatory damages, such as punitive damages, must be decided by Section 1–103 and Section 1–106 ("by other rule of law").

2. Wrongful dishonor is different from "failure to exercise ordinary care in handling an item," and the measure of damages is that stated in this section not that stated in Section 4–103(e). By the same token, if a dishonor comes within this section, the measure of damages of this section applies and not another measure of damages. If the wrongful refusal of the beneficiary's bank to make funds available from a funds transfer causes the beneficiary's check to be dishonored, no specific guidance is given as to whether recovery is under this section or Article 4A. In each case this issue must be viewed in its factual context, and it was thought unwise to seek to establish certainty at the cost of fairness.

3. The second and third sentences of the subsection (b) reject decisions holding that as a matter of law the dishonor of a check is not the "proximate cause" of the arrest and prosecution of the customer and leave to determination in each case as a question of fact whether the dishonor is or may be the "proximate cause."

4. Banks commonly determine whether there are sufficient funds in an account to pay an item after the close of banking hours on the day of presentment when they post debit and credit items to the account. The determination is made on the basis of credits available for withdrawal as of right or made available for withdrawal by the bank as an accommodation to its customer. When it is determined that payment of the item would overdraw the account, the item may be returned at any time before the bank's midnight deadline the following day. Before the item is returned new credits that are withdrawable as of right may have been added to the account. Subsection (c) eliminates uncertainty under Article 4 as to whether the failure to make a second determination before the item is returned on the day following presentment is a wrongful dishonor if new credits were added to the account on that day that would have covered the amount of the check.

5. Section 4–402 has been construed to preclude an action for wrongful dishonor by a plaintiff other than the bank's customer. Loucks v. Albuquerque National Bank, 418 P.2d 191 (N.Mex.1966). Some courts have allowed a plaintiff other than the customer to sue when the customer is a business entity that is one and the same with the

individual or individuals operating it. Murdaugh Volkswagen, Inc. v. First National Bank, 801 F.2d 719 (4th Cir.1986) and Karsh v. American City Bank, 113 Cal.App.3d 419, 169 Cal.Rptr. 851 (1980). However, where the wrongful dishonor impugns the reputation of an operator of the business, the issue is not merely, as the court in Koger v. East First National Bank, 443 So.2d 141 (Fla.App.1983), put it, one of a literal versus a liberal interpretation of Section 4–402. Rather the issue is whether the statutory cause of action in Section 4–402 displaces, in accordance with Section 1–103, any cause of action that existed at common law in a person who is not the customer whose reputation was damaged. See Marcum v. Security Trust and Savings Co., 221 Ala. 419, 129 So. 74 (1930). While Section 4–402 should not be interpreted to displace the latter cause of action, the section itself gives no cause of action to other than a "customer," however that definition is construed, and thus confers no cause of action on the holder of a dishonored item. First American National Bank v. Commerce Union Bank, 692 S.W.2d 642 (Tenn.App.1985).

Uniform Commercial Code Comment

Prior Uniform Statutory Provision:
None.

Purposes:

1. This section is new to the Uniform Laws, although similar statutory provisions are in existence in twenty-three jurisdictions.

2. The liability of the drawee for dishonor has sometimes been stated as one for breach of contract, sometimes as for negligence or other breach of a tort duty, and sometimes as for defamation. This section does not attempt to specify a theory. "Wrongful dishonor" excludes any permitted or justified dishonor, as where the drawer has no credit extended by the drawee, or where the draft lacks a necessary indorsement or is not properly presented.

3. This section rejects decisions which have held that where the dishonored item has been drawn by a merchant, trader or fiduciary he is defamed in his business, trade or profession by a reflection on his credit and hence that substantial damages may be awarded on the basis of defamation "per se" without proof that damage has occurred. The merchant, trader and fiduciary are placed on the same footing as any other drawer and in all cases of dishonor by mistake damages recoverable are limited to those actually proved.

4. Wrongful dishonor is different from "failure to exercise ordinary care in handling an item" and the measure of damages is that stated in this section, not that stated in Section 4–103(5).

5. The fourth sentence of the section [Inapplicable in California, see California Code Comment, note 2] rejects decisions holding that as a matter of law the dishonor of a check is not the "proximate cause" of the arrest and prosecution of the customer, and leaves to determination in each case as a question of fact whether the dishonor is or may be the "proximate cause".

Definitional Cross References:

"Bank". Section 1–201.
"Customer". Section 4–104.
"Item". Section 4–104.

Cross References

Allowance of damages exclusive of exemplary damages and interest, exceptions, see Civil Code § 3357.
Breach of obligation to pay money only, damages, see Civil Code § 3302.
Certainty of damages, see Civil Code § 3301.
Check defined, see Commercial Code § 3104.
Customer loss from payment of item contrary to stop-payment order, inclusion of damages for dishonor of subsequent items under this section, see Commercial Code § 4403.
Damages as species of relief, see Civil Code § 3274.
Detriment suffered, damages, see Civil Code § 3281 et seq.
Dishonor, see Commercial Code § 3502.
Exemplary damages, see Civil Code § 3294.
Limitation of damages, see Civil Code § 3358.
Measure of damages,
 Breach of contract, see Civil Code § 3300 et seq.
 Failure to exercise ordinary care in handling an item, see Commercial Code § 4103.
 Torts, see Civil Code § 3333.
Nominal damages, see Civil Code § 3360.
Ordinary care, duty to exercise, see Commercial Code § 4103.
Reasonableness of damages, see Civil Code § 3359.
Stop payment order, see Commercial Code §§ 4303, 4403.

§ 4403. Stop-payment orders

(a) A customer * * * or any * * * person authorized to draw on the account if there is more than one * * * person may stop payment of any item * * * drawn * * * on the customer's * * * account * * * or close the account by an order to the bank * * * describing the item or account with reasonable certainty * * * received at a time and in a manner that affords the bank a reasonable opportunity to act on it * * * before any * * * action by the bank with respect to the item described in Section 4303. If the signature of more than one person is required to draw on an account, any of these persons may stop payment or close the account.

* * *

(b) A stop-payment order is effective for six months, but it lapses after 14 calendar days if the original order was oral and was not confirmed in writing within that period. A stop-payment order may be renewed for additional six-month periods by a writing given to the bank within a period during which the stop-payment order is effective.

* * * (c) The burden of establishing the fact and amount of loss resulting from the payment of an item contrary to a * * * stop-payment order or order to close an account is on the customer. The loss from payment of an item contrary to a stop-payment order may include damages for dishonor of subsequent items under Section 4402. (Stats.1963, c. 819, § 4403. Amended by Stats.1992, c. 914 (S.B.833), § 42.)

California Code Comment
By John A. Bohn and Charles J. Williams

Prior California Law

1. This section replaces former Financial Code §§ 990 to 995. Before treatment of these sections regulating stop-payment orders the attempt by banks to limit liability by use of printed stop-payment forms with exculpatory clauses was repudiated by the courts on the ground of public policy. Hiroshima v. Bank of Italy, 78 Cal.App. 362, 248 Pac. 947 (1926).

2. Subdivision (1) provides that the bank may disregard to stop order unless it has a "reasonable opportunity" to act upon the stop order. Former Financial Code § 990 required only that the stop order be delivered before the check is certified or paid.

3. Subdivision (2) makes a minor change in the rule under former Financial Code § 994. Under former Financial Code § 994 a written stop payment order was effective indefinitely except that 6 months after the order was first given, the bank could notify the drawer that the order must be renewed in writing to remain in effect.

4. The first sentence of subdivision (3) continues the rule of former Financial Code §§ 992 and 993. The second sentence states merely the usual rule that the burden of proof is upon the party seeking damages.

Changes from U.C.C. (1962 Official Text)

5. California has extensively rewritten section 4–403 of the Official Text. The changes are shown as follows:

4403. (1) A customer, or any customer if there is more than one, or any person authorized to sign checks or make withdrawals thereon may [by order to his bank] stop payment of any item payable for or drawn against such customer's or customers' [his] account but [the order must be] the bank may disregard the same unless the order is in writing, is signed by such customer or authorized person, describes with certainty the item on which payment is to be stopped, and is received [at] by the bank in such time and in such manner as to afford the bank a reasonable opportunity to act on it prior to [any action by the bank with respect to the item] the happening of any of the events described in Section 4303.

(2) [An oral order is binding upon the bank only for fourteen calendar days unless confirmed in writing within that period. A written order is effective for only six months unless renewed in writing.] An order may be disregarded by the bank six months after receipt unless renewed in writing.

(3) The bank is liable to its customer for the actual loss incurred by him resulting from the payment of an item contrary to a binding stop payment order, not exceeding the amount of the item unless the bank is guilty of negligence. The burden of establishing the fact and amount of loss resulting from the payment of an item contrary to a binding stop payment order is on the customer.

The purpose of changing subdivisions (1) and (2) of the Official Text is to eliminate oral stop orders and to preserve the requirement of former Financial Code § 990 that stop orders must be in writing.

Extensive comment has been made on the desirability of retaining California law on stop orders. The following statement by the Special Committee of the California Bankers Association appointed to study Division 4 of the Commercial Code gives some interesting background information on the subject:

"One of the more important differences between California law and Article [Division] 4 has to do with stop payments. The Code provides for oral stop payment orders, whereas California law, since 1935, has provided for orders in writing, with the right on the part of the bank to waive such requirement. Through the years since 1951, until the current year, opposition to this change in the California law has been unanimous. During this past year there have been some who have ventured the opinion that, since several states have already adopted Article [Division] 4, with an oral stop payment provision, and bankers in those states have reported the law is working well and they are satisfied with it, banks in California should have no objection to the adoption of the Code with this provision included.

"This Committee checked the stop payment laws of the various states, and found that all of the states which have thus far adopted the Code had theretofore had a law providing for oral stop payment orders. The Code therefore did not change their law in this respect, and there was no reason for them to object. We then checked with bankers in the various states which have laws similar to ours, providing for written stop payment orders. Each of those who answered made in clear they would be against the oral stop payment provision in Article [Division] 4 of the Code. From this it is evident this same problem will have to be faced when an attempt is made to introduce the Code in each of these other states." Sixth Progress Report to the Legislature by Senate Fact Finding Committee on Judiciary (1959–1961) Part 1, The Uniform Commercial Code, p. 405.

The State Bar Committee on the Commercial Code expresses its position on this section as follows:

"The Official Text of section 14403 [4403] would make an oral as well as a written stop payment order binding on a bank. California [former] Financial Code section 990 requires a stop payment order to be in writing before a bank must observe it. The Advisory Committee believes that only a written order should require a bank to dishonor its customer's check. A bank is liable to its customer, who has himself created the situation by issuing the check, [Footnote: See Report of the New York Clearing House Association on the Uniform Commercial Code 25 (1961): 'Although no statistics are available, it is probable that in most cases of stop payment orders, the drawer of the check imprudently or carelessly issued it in the first place. Indeed, there are many cases where a drawer issues the check intending to stop payment on it.'] for the wrongful payment of the check in disregard of a stop payment order. In these circumstances, it was felt a bank's liability should rest upon better evidence than an alleged oral instruction. S.B. 1093 [1961 Session, 1958 Official Text as amended] therefore amends section 14403 [4403] to continue the present California requirement of a written stop payment order." California State Bar Committee on the Commercial Code, A Special Report, The Uniform Commercial Code, 37 Calif.State Bar J. (March–April, 1962) p. 168.

The most thorough commentary is made by Professors Marsh and Warren in their report to the legislature. The changes to each subdivision are discussed.

Regarding subdivision (1):

"The question of desirability of requiring written stop payment orders has been much debated; little can be accomplished by rearguing the question. California has required written stop orders by [former] FC § 990 for many years. Banks and bank lawyers are strongly in favor of retaining this rule. The danger of the rule is that customers are probably unaware of it. The usual way in which a customer would learn that only a written stop order will bind the bank is to be told by the bank; but it is against the interest of the bank to make this disclosure. Therefore, unless the bank tells the customer who desires to stop payment on an item that he must sign a form, the customer is led to believe that his phone call or oral order is sufficient. Nonetheless, the evidential aspects of the rule requiring written stop orders is desirable. It is recommended that the present California rule be retained and that only written stop orders be made binding on a bank.

"The State Bar Committee also proposes adding to this subsection an amendment giving anyone authorized to sign checks on an account the right to stop payment of any items drawn on that account. This apparently is contrary to present law; there are no cases on the matter, but [former] FC § 990 states that a bank may disregard an order unless the order is 'in writing, is signed by the *drawer*.' At first it may seem like a radical proposal to allow one other than the drawer to stop payment on a check, but when it is realized that the other customer could draw all the money out of the account and stop payment on the check in that way, the amendment seems less radical. The State Bar Committee amendment would prove a great convenience to customers in allowing either depositor to stop payment on items drawn on their joint account. This is particularly true in situations where the customers live a long distance from the bank and where it would be a hardship on the wife to travel downtown to a bank which her husband may pass each day on his way to work. Therefore, it is recommended that this amendment also be adopted." Sixth Progress Report to the Legislature by Senate Fact Finding Committee on Judiciary (1959–1961) Part 1, The Uniform Commercial Code, p. 483.

Regarding subdivision (2):

"Some amendment is necessary in view of the change recommended in subsection (1) of this same section. Under [former] FC § 994, to terminate its duty to observe a stop payment order the bank must give the drawer notice that the order must be renewed to remain effective. This notice can be given at any time after six months have elapsed from the date of receipt of the stop order, and if the drawer fails to renew the order within 30 days after receiving the notice, the stop order ceases to be effective. The effect of this subsection, both as originally drafted and as amended by the State Bar Committee and the California Bankers Committee proposals would be to relieve the bank of any duty to remind the drawer that he must be renew to keep his stop order effective, as now required by FC § 994. There is something to be said for the policy adopted in FC § 994, but since neither the Code draftsmen nor the local groups favor retaining it, it is recommended that this subsection be amended . . . ." Sixth Progress Report to the Legislature by Senate Fact Finding Committee on Judiciary (1959–1961) Part 1, The Uniform Commercial Code, p. 484.

Regarding subdivision (3):

"The amendment proposed by the State Bar Committee differs from that proposed by the California Bankers Committee, but their purpose is similar: to make clear that a bank improperly paying an item on which there was a valid stop payment order is liable only for actual damages. The proposed amendments are based on [former] FC § 992. The proposed amendments also limit the liability of the bank to the amount of the item unless the bank is 'guilty of negligence' (as provided by the California Bankers Committee amendment) or is 'guilty of gross negligence or bad faith' (as provided by the State Bar Committee amendment). FC § 992 limits liability to the amount of the check 'unless the bank is guilty of negligence.' It is recommended that the California Bankers Committee amendment, which substantially incorporates FC § 992, be adopted. [This was done] The State Bar Committee version of the amendment places on the customer the burden of proving gross negligence or bad faith before he can recover for *actual loss* sustained by him exceeding the amount of the item; in our opinion this is an unjustifiable burden to impose on the customer."

Sixth Progress Report to the Legislature by Senate Fact Finding Committee on Judiciary (1959–1961) Part 1, The Uniform Commercial Code, pp. 484–485.

Uniform Commercial Code Comment
Official Reasons for 1990 Change

Subsection (a) removes any ambiguity that may have been present under former subsection (1) by making clear that if there is more than one person authorized to draw on a customer's account any one of them can stop payment of any check drawn on the account or can order the account closed. Moreover, if there is a customer, such as a corporation, that requires its checks to bear the signatures of more than one person, any of these persons may stop payment on a check. In describing the item, the customer, in the absence of a contrary agreement, must meet the standard of what information allows the bank under the technology then existing to identify the item with reasonable certainty. An order to close an account is assimilated to an order to stop payment in this section and in Section 4–407.

Subsection (b) restates and clarifies former subsection (2). Subsection (c) is amended by the addition of the last sentence to provide expressly for what was only assumed under the former section: that a customer's damages for payment contrary to a stop-payment order may include damages for wrongful dishonor of subsequent items. The word "binding" is deleted as superfluous.

The other modifications are made to conform with current legislative drafting practices, with no intent to change substance.

1990 Change

1. The position taken by this section is that stopping payment or closing an account is a service which depositors expect and are entitled to receive from banks notwithstanding its difficulty, inconvenience and expense. The inevitable occasional losses through failure to stop or close should be borne by the banks as a cost of the business of banking.

2. Subsection (a) follows the decisions holding that a payee or indorsee has no right to stop payment. This is consistent with the provision governing payment or satisfaction. See Section 3–602. The sole exception to this rule is found in Section 4–405 on payment after notice of death, by which any person claiming an interest in the account can stop payment.

3. Payment is commonly stopped only on checks; but the right to stop payment is not limited to checks, and extends to any item payable by any bank. If the maker of a note payable at a bank is in a position analogous to that of a drawer (Section 4–106) the maker may stop payment of the note. By analogy the rule extends to drawees other than banks.

4. A cashier's check or teller's check purchased by a customer whose account is debited in payment for the check is not a check drawn on the customer's account within the meaning of subsection (a); hence, a customer purchasing a cashier's check or teller's check has no right to stop payment of such a check under subsection (a). If a bank issuing a cashier's check or teller's check refuses to pay the check as an accommodation to its customer or for other reasons, its liability on the check is governed by Section 3–411. There is no right to stop payment after certification of a check or other acceptance of a draft, and this is true no matter who procures the certification. See Sections 3–411 and 4–303. The acceptance is the drawee's own engagement to pay, and it is not required to impair its credit by refusing payment for the convenience of the drawer.

5. Subsection (a) makes clear that if there is more than one person authorized to draw on a customer's account any one of them can stop payment of any check drawn on the account or can order the account closed. Moreover, if there is a customer, such as a corporation, that requires its checks to bear the signatures of more than one person, any of these persons may stop payment on a check. In describing the item, the customer, in the absence of a contrary agreement, must meet the standard of what information allows the bank under the technology then existing to identify the item with reasonable certainty.

6. Under subsection (b), a stop-payment order is effective after the order, whether written or oral, is received by the bank and the bank has a reasonable opportunity to act on it. If the order is written it remains in effect for six months from that time. If the order is oral it lapses after 14 days unless there is written confirmation. If there is written confirmation within the 14-day period, the six-month period dates from the giving of the oral order. A stop-payment order may be renewed any number of times by written notice given during a six-month period while a stop order is in effect. A new stop-payment order may be given after a six-month period expires, but such a notice takes effect from the date given. When a stop-payment order expires it is as though the order had never been given, and the payor bank may pay the item in good faith under Section 4–404 even though a stop-payment order had once been given.

7. A payment in violation of an effective direction to stop payment is an improper payment, even though it is made by mistake or inadvertence. Any agreement to the contrary is invalid under Section 4–103(a) if in paying the item over the stop-payment order the bank has failed to exercise ordinary care. An agreement to the contrary which is imposed upon a customer as part of a standard form contract would have to be evaluated in the light of the general obligation of good faith. Sections 1–203 and 4–104(c). The drawee is, however, entitled to subrogation to prevent unjust enrichment (Section 4–407); retains common law defenses, e.g., that by conduct in recognizing the payment the customer has ratified the bank's action in paying over a stop-payment order (Section 1–103); and retains common law rights, e.g., to recover money paid under a mistake under Section 3–418. It has sometimes been said that payment cannot be stopped against a holder in due course, but the statement is inaccurate. The payment can be stopped but the drawer remains liable on the instrument to the holder in due course (Sections 3–305, 3–414) and the drawee, if it pays, becomes subrogated to the rights of the holder in due course against the drawer. Section 4–407. The relationship between Sections 4–403 and 4–407 is discussed in the comments to Section 4–407. Any defenses available against a holder in due course remain available to the drawer, but other defenses are cut off to the same extent as if the holder were bringing the action.

Uniform Commercial Code Comment

Prior Uniform Statutory Provision:

None.

Purposes:

1. This section is new. It is intended to replace separate statutes in twenty-nine states which regulate stop-payment orders.

2. The position taken by this section is that stopping payment is a service which depositors expect and are entitled to receive from banks notwithstanding its difficulty, inconvenience and expense. The inevitable occasional losses through failure to stop should be borne by the banks as a cost of the business of banking.

3. Subsection (1) follows the decisions holding that a payee or indorsee has no right to stop payment. This is consistent with the provision governing payment or satisfaction. See Section 3–603. The sole exception to this rule is found in Section 4–405 on payment after notice of death, by which any person claiming an interest in the account can stop payment.

4. Payment is commonly stopped only on checks; but the right to stop payment is not limited to checks, and extends to any item payable by any bank. Where the maker of a note payable at a bank is in a position analogous to that of a drawer (Section 3–121) he may stop payment of the note. By analogy the rule extends to drawees other than banks.

5. There is no right to stop payment after certification of a check or other acceptance of a draft, and this is true no matter who procures the certification. See Sections 3–411 and 4–303. The acceptance is the drawee's own engagement to pay, and he is not required to impair his credit by refusing payment for the convenience of the drawer.

6. Normally a direction to stop payment is first given by telephone. Notwithstanding statutes which require a written order, banks customarily accept such directions, and have been held to waive the writing. Subsection (2) is intended to protect both parties by making the oral direction effective for only a short time during which the drawer must confirm it in writing, and by eliminating thereafter any claim of waiver by acceptance of the oral direction. [Changes in California from U.C.C. (1962 Official Text), see California Code Comment, note 5.]

7. The existing statutes all specify a time limit after which any direction to stop payment becomes ineffective unless it is renewed in writing; and the majority of them have specified six months. The purpose of the provision is, of course, to facilitate stopping payment by clearing the records of the drawee of accumulated unrevoked stop

orders, as where the drawer has found a lost instrument or has settled his controversy with the payee, but has failed to notify the drawee. The last sentence of subsection (2), together with the second clause in Section 4–404, rejects the reasoning of such cases as Goldberg v. Manufacturers Trust Company, 199 Misc. 167, 102 N.Y.S.2d 144 (1951).

8. A payment in violation of an effective direction to stop payment is an improper payment, even though it is made by mistake or inadvertence. Any agreement to the contrary is invalid under Section 4–103(1) if in paying the item over the stop payment order the bank has failed to exercise ordinary care. The drawee is, however, entitled to subrogation to prevent unjust enrichment (Section 4–407); retains common-law defenses, e.g., that by conduct in recognizing the payment the customer has ratified the bank's action in paying over a stop payment order (Section 1–103); and retains common-law rights, e.g., to recover money paid under a mistake (Section 1–103) in cases where the payment is not made final by Section 3–418. It has sometimes been said that payment cannot be stopped against a holder in due course, but the statement is inaccurate. The payment can be stopped but the drawer remains liable on the instrument to the holder in due course (Sections 3–305, 3–413) and the drawee, if he pays, becomes subrogated to the rights of the holder in due course against the drawer. Section 4–407. Any defenses available against a holder in due course remain available to the drawer, but other defenses are cut off to the same extent as if the holder himself were bringing the action.

Cross References:

Point 3: Sections 3–603(1), 4–405.
Point 4: Section 3–121.
Point 5: Sections 3–411 and 4–303.
Point 8: Sections 3–305, 3–413, 3–418, 4–103 and 4–407.

Definitional Cross References:

"Account". Section 4–104.
"Bank". Section 1–201.
"Burden of establishing". Section 1–201.
"Customer". Section 4–104.
"Item". Section 4–104.
"Send". Section 1–201.

Cross References

Bank may disregard stop payment order, when, see Commercial Code § 4303.
Certification, definition, see Commercial Code §§ 3409, 4303.
Certified checks, see Financial Code §§ 970, 971.
Finality of payment or acceptance, see Commercial Code § 3418.
Items payable at bank, see Commercial Code § 4106.
Liability of drawer, see Commercial Code § 3414.
Ordinary care, liability for failure to exercise, see Commercial Code § 4103.
Payment of draft by drawee on mistaken belief stop payment order not in effect, see Commercial Code § 3418.
Payment, discharge of obligation, see Commercial Code § 3602.
Payment over stop payment, subrogation, see Commercial Code § 4407.
Payment upon notice of death, exception, see Commercial Code § 4405.

§ 4404. Checks presented over six months past date

A bank is under no obligation to a customer having a checking account to pay a check, other than a certified check, which is presented more than six months after its date, but it may charge its customer's account for a payment made thereafter in good faith. *(Stats.1963, c. 819, § 4404. Amended by Stats.1992, c. 914 (S.B.833), § 43.)*

California Code Comment

By John A. Bohn and Charles J. Williams

Prior California Law

1. This section replaces former Financial Code § 950. Although the two provisions are similar, former Financial Code § 950 provided that the bank could refuse payment "unless expressly instructed by the drawer or maker to pay it." This section instead leaves it entirely to the bank's discretion.

Changes from U.C.C. (1962 Official Text)

2. The California version omits the words "in good faith" which appear in section 4–404 of the Official Text at the end of the section after the word "thereafter." This amendment was made to eliminate uncertainty:

"Under section 14404 [4404] a bank would not have to pay an uncertified check presented more than six months after its date, but it could do so if it acts 'in good faith.' This section appears to offer a choice of paying or dishonoring a check more than six months old. Without a clear definition of what might constitute 'bad faith,' a careful bank might not be willing to pay any check more than six months old without consulting its customer. For practical purposes the apparent alternative given to the bank is thus taken away. This result would be disruptive following the end of a year when many people continue to write the old year on checks out of habit. If a bank receives a check dated January 10, 1961, on January 15, 1962, it may not be able to tell whether the check is five days or a year old. It would be impossible for a large metropolitan bank to ask its customer every time such an item is received during the first few weeks of the new year. [Footnote: The foregoing paragraph is based upon Marsh and Warren, Report on Proposed Amendments to the Uniform Commercial Code, pp. 4–25–4–26 (April 1, 1961). Compare Report of the New York Clearing House Association on the Uniform Commercial Code at 26 (Dec. 1, 1961).] Therefore, the words 'in good faith' in this section are not in S.B. 1093 [1961 Session, 1958 Official Text as Amended] and a bank can pay or not pay checks more than six months old, as it sees fit. [Footnote: Since section 11203 [1203] would impose an obligation of 'good faith' in the performance of every contract and duty under the Code, it might be that nothing has been accomplished by deleting this phrase from section 14404 [4404]. If the legislature accepts the State Bar Committee view, some further amendment might be necessary. [Eds.]]." California State Bar Committee on the Commercial Code, A Special Report, the Uniform Commercial Code, 37 Calif.State Bar J. (March–April, 1962) p. 168.

Professors Marsh and Warren agreed with this position:

"About half the states have statutes similar to [former] FC § 951 allowing a bank to refuse payment of a check presented for payment more than six months from the date of the instrument. This Section adopts this view and in addition gives the bank the privilege of paying the check after the six-month period if its payment is in good faith. The State Bar Committee recommends deleting the good faith requirement on the ground that it is uncertain what is meant by good faith in this context. The definition of good faith in Section 11201(19) [1201(19)] is: ' "Good faith" means honesty in fact in the conduct or transaction concerned.'

"The Official Comments do not disclose what situations the Code draftsmen had in mind in adding the good faith requirement. The following situation might raise the good faith issue: Suppose a stop order has been entered against a certain check but has expired by elapse of time at the date the stale check is presented for payment. Is the bank protected in paying this stale item? In Goldberg v. Manufacturers Trust Co., 199 Misc. 167, 102 N.Y.S.2d 144 (1951), the court held on facts similar to these that a stale check raises a duty of inquiry, and had the bank inquired, it would have found the expired stop order. The existence of the expired stop order, said the court, was sufficient to put the bank under a duty to inquire of the drawer before making payment.

"The existence of the good faith requirement would cause the prudent banker to inquire of his depositor before paying a stale check. This is true because he can never be sure whether payment of such a check is in good faith. This Section seems to give the bank the privilege of paying stale items, but this privilege is immediately taken away, for all practical purposes, by the addition of the words 'in good faith' in the same sentence.

"This matter is of considerable importance because, in many cases, the bank cannot be sure whether the item is stale or not. For example, if a bank receives an item on January 15, 1961, dated January 5, 1960, it frequently cannot tell whether the item is a year old or only 10 days old, since thousands of persons continue writing the old year through habit for some time after New Year's Day. It would be impossible for large banks to inquire of their customers with respect to all such items received each January." Sixth Progress Report to the Legislature by Senate Fact Finding Committee on Judiciary (1959–1961) Part 1, The Uniform Commercial Code, pp. 485–486.

Uniform Commercial Code Comment
1990 Change

This section incorporates a type of statute that had been adopted in 26 jurisdictions before the Code. The time limit is set at six months because banking and commercial practice regards a check outstanding for longer than that period as stale, and a bank will normally not pay such a check without consulting the depositor. It is therefore not required to do so, but is given the option to pay because it may be in a position to know, as in the case of dividend checks, that the drawer wants payment made.

Certified checks are excluded from the section because they are the primary obligation of the certifying bank (Sections 3–409 and 3–413). The obligation runs directly to the holder of the check. The customer's account was presumably charged when the check was certified.

Uniform Commercial Code Comment

Prior Uniform Statutory Provision:

None.

Purposes:

This section incorporates a type of statute adopted in twenty-six jurisdictions. The time limit is set at six months because banking and commercial practice regards a check outstanding for longer than that period as stale, and a bank will normally not pay such a check without consulting the depositor. It is therefore not required to do so, but is given the option to pay because it may be in a position to know, as in the case of dividend checks, that the drawer wants payment made.

Certified checks are excluded from the section because they are the primary obligation of the certifying bank (Sections 3–411 and 3–413), which obligation runs direct to the holder of the check. The customer's account was charged when the check was certified.

Cross References:

Sections 3–411 and 3–413.

Definitional Cross References:

"Account". Section 4–104.
"Bank". Section 1–201.
"Check". Section 3–104.
"Customer". Section 4–104.
"Good faith". Section 1–201.
"Present". Section 3–504.

Cross References

Certification of check, see Commercial Code § 3409.
Check defined, see Commercial Code § 3104.
Commercial bank defined, see Financial Code §§ 105, 109.
Liability of bank for wrongful dishonor, see Commercial Code § 4402.
Obligation of issuer, drawer and acceptor, see Commercial Code § 3413 et seq.
Time for presenting check, see Commercial Code § 3503.

§ 4405. Death or Incompetence of Customer

(a) A payor or collecting bank's authority to accept, pay$_2$ or collect an item or to account for proceeds of its collection$_2$ if otherwise effective$_2$ is not rendered ineffective by incompetence of a customer of either bank existing at the time the item is issued or its collection is undertaken if the bank does not know of an adjudication of incompetence. Neither death nor incompetence of a customer revokes the authority to accept, pay, collect$_2$ or account until the bank knows of the fact of death or of an adjudication of incompetence and has reasonable opportunity to act on it.

(b) Even with knowledge * * *$_2$ a bank may, for 10 days after the date of death, pay or certify checks drawn * * * on or * * * before that date unless * * * ordered to stop payment by a person claiming an interest in the account.

* * * (Stats.1963, c. 819, § 4405. Amended by Stats.1992, c. 914 (S.B.833), § 44.)

California Code Comment
By Charles J. Williams
1992 Amendment

In addition to the change which California made in subdivision (2) of the 1962 Official Text, subdivision (3) and (4) of this section as enacted in California do not appear in the Official Text. These two subdivisions were added at the suggestion of the State Bar. Sixth Progress Report to the Legislature by Senate Fact Finding Committee on Judiciary (1959–1961) Part 1, the Uniform Commercial Code, pp. 367, 487–488.

California Code Comment
By John A. Bohn and Charles J. Williams

Prior California Law

1. Subdivision (1) is new statutory law but is in accord with prior California case law. Paddock v. Anglo-California Trust Co., 107 Cal.App. 430, 290 Pac. 550 (1930) (bank not liable to depositor's estate for payment of check after his death when done in good faith, in the regular course of business, and without knowledge of the depositor's death). The rule is based upon considerations stemming from the impracticability of having to determine the state of the drawer's health before paying a check. Official Comment 2.

2. Subdivision (2) is new statutory law but is in accord with prior case law which is based upon the principle that the death of the drawer does not affect the rights of a checkholder who has given value for it. Nassano v. Tuolumne County Bank, 20 Cal.App. 603, 130 Pac. 29 (1912).

3. Subdivision (3) is new statutory law. Its purpose is described by the State Bar Committee:

"Section 14405 [4405] has also been amended in S.B. 1093 [1961 session, 1958 official text as amended] by adding a new subdivision [subdivision (3)] to deal with a customer's incompetence when another is also authorized to draw on the account. At present, a bank would be reluctant to permit one joint account depositor to withdraw money if it had knowledge of the incompetency of the other, or might be on notice of facts indicating such incompetence. Under section 14405(3) [4405(3)] in S.B. 1093 [1961 session, 1958 official text as amended], a bank could honor an item drawn by one customer, despite the incompetence of another, if the item would have been effective prior to such incompetence. The limitation would for example prevent a bank from honoring an item with only one signature if the terms of the deposit required two. But this new subsection would often permit a depositor to use funds for the benefit of the incompetent when the small amount of money involved would not justify a guardianship proceeding. It does not, of course, affect any liability between the customers." California State Bar Committee on the Commercial Code, A Special Report, The Uniform Commercial Code, 37 Calif.State Bar J. (March–April 1962) p. 170.

This language has been criticized:

"The . . . proposal seems . . . too broad. It would allow a bank to cash a check drawn by an agent at any time after the death of the principal, even though the bank knew of the death at the time it cashed the check. This rule would allow an agent to deplete the assets of the decedent's estate, in violation of the familiar rule that death revokes the agent's authority. Admittedly, exceptions must be made to this rule of agency, but an entirely unlimited one should not be created. In addition, . . . the bank may, even with the knowledge of the death of 'a customer,' pay any item drawn 'by any other customer.' This would include joint accounts which are *not* payable to the survivor. . . . the subsection [subdivision 3] should specify what kind of customers are contemplated. . . .

"In view of the California law to the effect that an account in form a joint tenancy can be shown by parol evidence to be community property, Paterson v. Comastri, 39 C.2d 66, 244 P.2d 902 (1952); Solon v. Lichtenstein, 39 C.2d 75, 244 P.2d 907 (1952); Hotle v. Miller, 51 C.2d 541, 334 P.2d 849 (1959); FC § 852 as amended in 1951 (removing former 'conclusive' presumption upon death of one depositor), we have added the provision allowing an interested party or court to stop payment. A bank should not be allowed to pay the money in a joint account to a surviving spouse after it has been notified by a legatee of the decedent that the account was in fact community property." Marsh and Warren Report, Sixth Progress Report to the Legislature by Senate Fact Finding Committee on Judiciary, (1959–1961) Part 1, The Uniform Commercial Code, pp. 487–488.

4. Subdivision (4) is in substance the same as former Financial Code § 951. This subdivision differs from former § 951 only in that it adds the reference to an affidavit stating a disability under this subdivision.

Changes from U.C.C. (1962 Official Text)

5. Subdivision (2) is changed in the California version by the following changes from the Official Text:

"(2) Even with knowledge <u>of the death of a customer or of any person authorized to sign checks or make withdrawals</u> a bank may, for 10 days after the date of death, pay or certify checks drawn <u>by the decedent</u> on or prior to that date unless [ordered to stop payment by a person claiming an interest in the account.] <u>the bank has received notice pursuant to Section 852 or Section 952 of the Financial Code.</u>"

This change was made to make it clear that certain checks may be stopped without having to stop payment on all checks. The State Bar makes the following observation on this change:

"Presently, a bank may not pay a customer's check after it learns of his death. Death 'revokes the agency.' [Footnote: Sneider v. Bank of Italy, 184 Cal. 595, 194 P. 1021 (1921).] Section 14405 [4405] would modify this rule. It would allow a bank with knowledge of a customer's death to pay checks presented within ten days after death unless notified to stop payment by someone claiming an interest in the account. This would enable holders of outstanding checks drawn by a decedent to cash them without having to file a claim in probate. An amendment to this section [subdivision 2] in S.B. 1093 [1901 session, 1958 official text as amended] extends it clearly to cover checks written by a customer's agent and presented for payment after the agent's death." California State Bar Committee on the Commercial Code, A Special Report, The Uniform Commercial Code, 37 Calif.State Bar J. (March–April, 1962) p. 170.

Professors Marsh and Warren agreed with this change:

"The purpose of the proposed amendments is to make clear that checks drawn by an authorized person other than the customer may be paid in the same way as the customer's check and to make clear that payment may be stopped under the last clause on one check without stopping payment on all outstanding checks.

"This subsection [subdivision 2] is a desirable change in the rule prevailing in California and elsewhere to the effect that a bank's authorization to pay a check ceases when it learns of the death of the customer drawing the check. Sneider v. Bank of Italy, 184 Cal. 595, 194 Pac. 1021 (1921). The Official Comments [Comment 3] explain that the purpose of the provision is to permit holders of checks drawn and issued shortly before death to cash them without the necessity of filing claims in probate.

"The major substantive change embodied in the State Bar Committee proposal is the addition of the words 'or of any person authorized to sign checks or make withdrawals.' Such a party is probably not encompassed by the definition of customer as 'any person having an account with a bank.' As amended by the State Bar Committee proposal, this subsection covers items drawn by customers or their agents presented for payment at the drawer's death. We have revised the language somewhat to take care of the case where the item is drawn by one authorized to draw checks and the *customer* (rather than the agent) dies before the check is presented. If such a check is drawn or issued before the death of the customer, it should be paid if presented within the 10-day period. It is not certain whether this case (i.e., where the decedent is not the drawer of the check but the principal who authorized the drawing of the check) is covered by the original version of this subsection, but the State Bar Committee's language would clearly exclude it.

"We have omitted the proposed additional and, we think, superfluous reference to 'any check' etc. We do not think the original language requires stopping payment on all checks or none, but would permit stopping a particular check.

"We have also added a reference to an order of a court stopping payment, since the probate court may be involved in some cases." Sixth Progress Report to the Legislature by Senate Fact Finding Committee on Judiciary (1959–1961) Part 1, The Uniform Commercial Code, p. 486–487.

The language changes recommended by the Marsh and Warren report appears in this action as finally adopted.

Uniform Commercial Code Comment

Official Reasons for 1990 Change

Modified to conform with current drafting practices; no intent to change substance.

1990 Change

1. Subsection (a) follows existing decisions holding that a drawee (payor) bank is not liable for the payment of a check before it has notice of the death or incompetence of the drawer. The justice and necessity of the rule are obvious. A check is an order to pay which the bank must obey under penalty of possible liability for dishonor. Further, with the tremendous volume of items handled any rule that required banks to verify the continued life and competency of drawers would be completely unworkable.

One or both of these same reasons apply to other phases of the bank collection and payment process and the rule is made wide enough to apply to these other phases. It applies to all kinds of "items"; to "customers" who own items as well as "customers" who draw or make them; to the function of collecting items as well as the function of accepting or paying them; to the carrying out of instructions to account for proceeds even though these may involve transfers to third parties; to depositary and intermediary banks as well as payor banks; and to incompetency existing at the time of the issuance of an item or the commencement of the collection or payment process as well as to incompetency occurring thereafter. Further, the requirement of actual knowledge makes inapplicable the rule of some cases that an adjudication of incompetency is constructive notice to all the world because obviously it is as impossible for banks to keep posted on such adjudications (in the absence of actual knowledge) as it is to keep posted as to death of immediate or remote customers.

2. Subsection (b) provides a limited period after death during which a bank may continue to pay checks (as distinguished from other items) even though it has notice. The purpose of the provision, as of the existing statutes, is to permit holders of checks drawn and issued shortly before death to cash them without the necessity of filing a claim in probate. The justification is that these checks normally are given in immediate payment of an obligation, that there is almost never any reason why they should not be paid, and that filing in probate is a useless formality, burdensome to the holder, the executor, the court and the bank.

This section does not prevent an executor or administrator from recovering the payment from the holder of the check. It is not intended to affect the validity of any gift causa mortis or other transfer in contemplation of death, but merely to relieve the bank of liability for the payment.

3. Any surviving relative, creditor or other person who claims an interest in the account may give a direction to the bank not to pay checks, or not to pay a particular check. Such notice has the same effect as a direction to stop payment. The bank has no responsibility to determine the validity of the claim or even whether it is "colorable." But obviously anyone who has an interest in the estate, including the person named as executor in a will, even if the will has not yet been admitted to probate, is entitled to claim an interest in the account.

Uniform Commercial Code Comment

Prior Uniform Statutory Provision:

None.

Purposes:

1. This section is new, although similar statutory provisions are in existence in seven states.

2. Subsection (1) follows existing decisions which hold that a drawee (payor) bank is not liable for the payment of a check before it has notice of the death or incompetence of the drawer. The justice and necessity of the rule are obvious. A check is an order to pay which the bank must obey under penalty of possible liability for dishonor. Further, with the tremendous volume of items handled any rule which required banks to verify the continued life and competency of drawers would be completely unworkable.

One or both of these same reasons apply to other phases of the bank collection and payment process and the rule is made wide enough to apply to these other phases. It applies to all kinds of "items"; to "customers" who own items as well as "customers" who draw or make them; to the function of collecting items as well as the function of accepting or paying them; to the carrying out of instructions to account for proceeds even though these may involve transfers to third parties; to depositary and intermediary banks as well as payor banks; and to incompetency existing at the time of the issuance of an item or the commencement of the collection or payment process as well as to incompetency occurring thereafter. Further, the requirement of actual knowledge makes inapplicable the rule of some cases that an adjudication of incompetency is constructive notice to all the world because obviously it is as impossible for banks to keep posted on such adjudications (in the absence of actual knowledge) as it is to keep posted as to death of immediate or remote customers.

3. Subsection (2) provides a limited period after death during which a bank may continue to pay checks (as distinguished from other items) even though it has notice. The purpose of the provision, as of the existing statutes, is to permit holders of checks drawn and issued shortly before death to cash them without the necessity of filing a claim in probate. The justification is that such checks normally are given in immediate payment of an obligation, that there is almost never any reason why they should not be paid, and that filing in probate is a useless formality, burdensome to the holder, the executor, the court and the bank.

This section does not prevent an executor or administrator from recovering the payment from the holder of the check. It is not intended to affect the validity of any gift causa mortis or other transfer in contemplation of death, but merely to relieve the bank of liability for the payment.

4. Any surviving relative, creditor or other person who claims an interest in the account may give a direction to the bank not to pay checks, or not to pay a particular check. Such notice has the same effect as a direction to stop payment. The bank has no responsibility to determine the validity of the claim or even whether it is "colorable". But obviously anyone who has an interest in the estate, including the person named as executor in a will, even if the will has not yet been admitted to probate, is entitled to claim an interest in the account. [See California Code Comment, note 5.]

Definitional Cross References:

"Accept". Section 3–410.
"Bank". Section 1–201.
"Certify". Section 3–411.
"Check". Section 3–104.
"Customer". Section 4–104.
"Depositary bank". Section 4–105.
"Item". Section 4–104.
"Payor bank". Section 4–105.

Cross References

Contracts by persons of unsound mind, see Civil Code § 39.
Contracts by persons without understanding, see Civil Code § 38.
Deposits by minors, see Financial Code § 850.
Fiduciary deposits, danger of misappropriation, see Financial Code § 952.
Multiple party accounts, see Financial Code § 852.
Notice of adverse claims, see Financial Code § 952.

Trust accounts, see Probate Code § 5404 et seq.

§ 4406. Statement of account; customer's duty to examine statement; remedies

Text of section operative until Jan. 1, 1998.

(a) A bank that sends or makes available to a customer a statement of account showing payment of items for the account shall either return or make available to the customer the items paid or provide information in the statement of account sufficient to allow the customer reasonably to identify the items paid. The statement of account provides sufficient information if the item is described by item number, amount, and date of payment. If the bank does not return the items, it shall provide in the statement of account the telephone number that the customer may call to request an item or a legible copy thereof pursuant to subdivision (b).

(b) If the items are not returned to the customer, the person retaining the items shall either retain the items or, if the items are destroyed, maintain the capacity to furnish legible copies of the items until the expiration of seven years after receipt of the items. A customer may request an item from the bank that paid the item, and that bank shall provide in a reasonable time either the item or, if the item has been destroyed or is not otherwise obtainable, a legible copy of the item. A bank shall provide, upon request and without charge to the customer, at least two items or a legible copy thereof with respect to each statement of account sent to the customer.

(c) If a bank sends or makes available a statement of account or items pursuant to subdivision (a), the customer shall exercise reasonable promptness in examining the statement or the items to determine whether any payment was not authorized because of an alteration of an item or because a purported signature by or on behalf of the customer was not authorized. If, based on the statement or items provided, the customer should reasonably have discovered the unauthorized payment, the customer shall promptly notify the bank of the relevant facts.

(d) If the bank proves that the customer failed, with respect to an item, to comply with the duties imposed on the customer by subdivision (c), the customer is precluded from asserting any of the following against the bank:

(1) The customer's unauthorized signature or any alteration on the item if the bank also proves that it suffered a loss by reason of the failure.

(2) The customer's unauthorized signature or alteration by the same wrongdoer on any other item paid in good faith by the bank if the payment was made before the bank received notice from the customer of the unauthorized signature or alteration and after the customer had been afforded a reasonable period of time, not exceeding 30 days, in which to examine the item or statement of account and notify the bank.

(e) If subdivision (d) applies and the customer proves that the bank failed to exercise ordinary care in paying the item and that the failure contributed to loss, the loss is allocated between the customer precluded and the bank asserting the preclusion according to the extent to which the failure of the customer to comply with subdivision (c) and the failure of the bank to exercise ordinary care contributed to the loss. If the customer proves that the bank did not pay the item in good faith, the preclusion under subdivision (d) does not apply.

(f) Without regard to care or lack of care of either the customer or the bank, a customer who does not within one year after the statement or items are made available to the customer (subdivision (a)) discover and report the customer's unauthorized signature on or any alteration on the item is precluded from asserting against the bank the unauthorized signature or alteration. If there is a preclusion under this subdivision, the payor bank may not recover for breach of warranty under Section 4208 with respect to the unauthorized signature or alteration to which the preclusion applies.

(g) This section shall remain in effect only until January 1, 1998, and as of that date is repealed, unless a later enacted statute, which is enacted before January 1, 1998, deletes or extends that date. *(Stats.1963, c. 819, § 4406. Amended by Stats.1992, c. 914 (S.B.833), § 45; Stats.1993, c. 589 (A.B.2211), § 29.)*

For text of section operative Jan. 1, 1998, see § 4406, post.

California Code Comment

By John A. Bohn and Charles J. Williams

Prior California Law

1. Subdivision (1) sets the standard of reasonable care for the customer in examining his statements. Official Comment 2.

This subdivision is new statutory law but is in accord with the standard of care prescribed in prior judicial decisions. Janin v. London & San Francisco Banks, 92 Cal. 14, 27 Pac. 1100, 14 L.R.A. 320 (1891); Union Tool Co. v. Farmers & Merchants Nat. Bank, 192 Cal. 40, 218 Pac. 424 (1923); Basch v. Bank of America, 22 Cal.2d 316, 139 P.2d 1 (1943). See also California Code Comment to Commercial Code § 3406.

2. Subdivision (2) is new statutory law but follows generally the result under prior California decisions.

Subdivision (2) states the effect of the customer's failure to comply with subdivision (1). Official Comment 3.

3. Subdivision (2)(a) requires that the bank must suffer an actual loss resulting from the customer's conduct and the bank has the burden of so showing. This is in accord with Hensley-Johnson Motors v. Citizens Nat. Bank, 122 Cal.App.2d 22, 264 P.2d 973 (1953) and Edgington v. Security-First Nat. Bank, 78 Cal.App.2d 849, 179 P.2d 640 (1947).

4. Subdivision (2)(b) extends the effect of the customer's failure to other items forged or altered by the same wrongdoer. It is new statutory law but is consistent with the rule of the prior cases cited in California Code Comment 1.

5. Under subdivision (3), even if the bank shows negligence of the customer, the bank is liable if the customer shows that the bank itself was also negligent. Official Comment 4. This is in accord with the prior cases holding that a bank cannot assert the depositor's negligence unless the bank itself was free from negligence. Basch v. Bank of America, 22 Cal.2d 316, 139 P.2d 1 (1943); Pacific Coast Cheese, Inc. v. Security First Nat. Bank, 45 Cal.2d 75, 286 P.2d 353 (1955).

6. The first sentence of subdivision (4) is consistent with the 1 year statute of limitation on a drawer's right of action against a bank which paid on a forged or altered item or indorsement. Code of Civil Procedure § 340(3).

The last sentence which imposes the burden upon the customer is new statutory law.

7. Subdivision (5) is new law in California. Its effect is to extend the protection of subdivision (4) to collecting banks. See Official Comment 7.

Changes from U.C.C. (1962 Official Text)

8. California modified subdivision (4) of section 4–406 of the Official Text. The changes are indicated as follows:

"(4) Without regard to care or lack of care of either the customer or the bank a customer who does not within one year from the time the statement and items are made available to the customer ([subsection] subdivision (1)) discover and report his unauthorized signature or any alteration on the face or back of the item or [does not within three years from that time discover and report any unauthorized indorsement] any unauthorized indorsement, and if the bank so requests exhibit the item to the bank for inspection, is precluded from asserting against the bank such unauthorized signature or indorsement or such alteration. The burden of establishing the fact of such unauthorized signature or indorsement or such alteration is on the customer."

This reason for these changes is explained in this statement by the State Bar:

"The Official Text of section 14406 [4406] provides that a customer may not assert a claim against a bank for the payment of a forged or raised check, or a check bearing a forged endorsement unless he reports such irregularity to the bank within a specified period after his statement is sent to him. The customer would have to report a forged signature or a raised check in one year, a forged endorsement in three years. The distinction rests on the questionable theory that the customer is more likely promptly to discover a forgery of his own signature or an alteration than a forged endorsement. Under California Code of Civil Procedure section 340(3), a one-year statute of limitations at present applies to both. In S.B. 1093, [1961 Session, 1958 Official text as amended] section 14406 [4406] has been amended to a one-year period for the reporting of a forged endorsement as well as a forged signature or an alteration. Since S.B. 1093 [1961 Session, 1958 Official Text as amended] does not repeal section 340(3) of the Code of Civil Procedure, the customer would be required not only to report within the one-year period under Code section 14406 [4406] but also to commence an action within such one-year period, as at present." California State Bar Committee on the Commercial Code, A Special Report, The Uniform Commercial Code, 37 Calif. State Bar J. (March–April, 1962) pp. 169 to 170.

The Marsh and Warren report agreed:

"The purpose of this subsection [subdivision (4)] is to set an absolute time limit on the right of a customer to make a claim against the payor bank, without regard to the care or lack of care of either the customer or the bank. In California this matter is covered at present by CCP § 340(3) which sets a one-year limitation on actions by a depositor against a bank for the payment of a forged or raised check or a check bearing forged or unauthorized indorsements.

"The one-year limitation in CCP § 340(3) applies both to forged indorsements and cases where the drawer's signature is forged. This subsection [the Official Text] provides a longer period of limitation for the discovery of a forged indorsement (three years) than for a forged signature of a drawer (one year), on the ground that the drawer is less likely to discover a forged indorsement. The State Bar Committee proposes retaining the present one-year limitation for both cases. There is no indication that this rule has been unsatisfactory in the past, and it is recommended that the State Bar Committee proposal on this point be adopted. . . .". Sixth Progress Report to the Legislature by Senate Fact Finding Committee on Judiciary, (1959–1961) Part 1, The Uniform Commercial Code, p. 489.

9. Subdivision (5) does not expressly bar a possible right of action by the drawer of a check bearing a forged indorsement against a collection bank. However, such an action was not permitted in California under prior law. California Mill Supply Co. v. Bank of America N.T. & S.A., 36 Cal.2d 334, 223 P.2d 849 (1950); Clarke, Bailey and Young, Bank Deposits and Collections 60 (A.L.I.1963) pp. 166–167.

Uniform Commercial Code Comment
Official Reasons for 1990 Change

Subsection (a), (b) and (c) restate and enlarge on former subsection (1). Subsection (a) recognizes that the parties may agree that the payor, a collecting bank or other person may retain the items drawn on the customer's account. In these cases the payor bank must provide sufficient information in a statement of account to allow the customer to reasonably identify the items paid. A safe harbor rule is stated that provides that the payor bank has satisfied its obligation if the item is described by item number, amount and the date of payment. This information is selected because it can be captured by the payor bank by automation without manual processing of the item.

Subsection (b) allows the bank retaining the item to destroy the item so long as it maintains the capacity to furnish legible copies for seven years. During this period the customer is entitled to demand from its payor bank the item or a copy of it. If the item is being retained by a collecting bank or other person, the payor bank must obtain the item or copy from that bank for its customer.

Subsection (c) continues the rule of former subsection (1) of requiring the customer to exercise reasonable promptness in examining the statement or items for an unauthorized signature of the customer or an alteration and to notify the bank promptly.

Subsection (d)(2) restates the conditions of the customer's preclusion and extends the 14-day period under former subsection (2) to a 30-day period. Although the 14-day period may have been sufficient when the original version of Article 4 was drafted, given the huge increase in the volume of checks, a longer period is viewed as more appropriate today.

Subsection (e) replaces former subsection (3) and poses a modified comparative negligence test for determining liability. See the discussion on this point in the Official Comments to Sections 3–404, 3–405 and 3–406. The term "good faith" is defined in Section 3–103(a)(4) as including "observance of reasonable commercial standards of fair dealing." The connotation of this standard is fairness and not absence of negligence. The term "ordinary care" used in subsection (e) is defined in Section 3–103(a)(7) to provide that sight examination by a payor bank is not required if its procedure is reasonable and is commonly followed by other comparable banks in the area. The case law is divided on this issue. The definition of "ordinary care" in Section 3–103 rejects those authorities that hold in effect, that failure to use sight examination is negligence as a matter of law.

Subsection (f) amends former subsection (4) to delete the reference to a three-year period to discover an unauthorized indorsement. Section 4–406 imposes no duty on a customer to discover a forged indorsement. Section 4–111 sets out a statute of limitations allowing a customer a three-year period to seek a credit to an account improperly charged by payment of an item bearing an unauthorized indorsement. The final sentence added to subsection (f) incorporates the substance of former subsection (5).

The other modifications are made to conform with current legislative drafting practices, with no intent to change substance.

1990 Change

1. In order to impose on its customer the duty stated in subsection (c) to examine a statement or the returned items and report unauthorized signatures of the customer or alterations, the bank must comply with subsection (a) in sending or making available to the customer a statement of account. Whether the bank returns to the customer the items paid is a matter for bank-customer agreement. If the agreement is that the bank does not return the items paid, a general standard is stated that the customer must be given information "sufficient to allow the customer reasonably to identify the items paid." If the bank supplies its customer with an image of an item, it complies with this standard. But a safe harbor rule is provided. The bank complies with the standard of providing "sufficient information" if "the item is described by item number, amount, and date of payment." This means that the customer's duties under subsection (c) are triggered if the bank sends the statement of account without returning the paid items. However, a customer is bound to consider only "the statement or items provided" and to make reasonable discovery on that basis. If a bank elects to provide the minimum information that is "sufficient" under subsection (a), the customer has only a limited basis for the customer's duty of discovery and notification. For example, if a check is fraudulently altered by changing the name of the payee, the customer could not normally detect the fraud unless the customer were given the paid check, or otherwise informed of the name of the payee of the altered check. In such circumstances, the customer might not be able to "reasonably have discovered the unauthorized payment" under subsection (c) and, therefore, would not be precluded under subsection (d) from asserting the alteration.

The provision in subsection (a) that a statement of account contains "sufficient information if the item is described by item number, amount, and date of payment" is based upon the existing state of technology. This information was chosen because it can be obtained by the bank's computer from the check's MICR line without examination of the items involved. The other two items of information that the customer would normally want to know—the name of the payee and the date of the item—cannot currently be obtained from the MICR line. The safe harbor rule is important in determining the feasibility of payor or collecting bank check retention plans. A customer who keeps a record of items written will have sufficient information to identify the item on the basis of item number, amount and date of payment. But customers who don't keep records may not. The policy decision is that accommodating these customers is not as desirable as accommodating others who keep more careful records at less cost to the check collection system, and thus, to all customers of the system. It is expected that technological advances may make it possible for banks to give customers more information in the future in a manner that is fully compatible with automation or truncation systems. At that time the Permanent Editorial Board may wish to make recommendations for an amendment revising the safe harbor requirements in the light of those advances.

2. Subsection (b) applies if the items are not returned to the customer. Check retention plans may include a simple payor bank check retention plan or the kind of check retention plan that would be authorized by a truncation agreement in which a collecting bank or the payee may retain the items. Even after agreeing to a check retention plan, a customer may need to see one or more checks for litigation or other purposes. The customer's request for the check may always be made to the payor bank. Under subsection (b) retaining banks may destroy items but must maintain the capacity to furnish legible copies for seven years. A legible copy may include an image of an item. This act does not define the length of the reasonable period of time for a bank to provide the check or copy of the check. What is reasonable depends on the capacity of the bank and the needs of the customer. This act requires a bank to provide a customer with a minimum of two items or a legible copy thereof with respect to each statement of account that is sent to a customer. A statement customarily is sent for each 30-day period. This act does not specify sanctions for failure to retain or furnish the items or legible copies; this is left to other laws regulating banks. See Comment 3 to Section 4–101. Moreover, this act does not regulate fees that banks charge their customers for furnishing items or copies or other services covered by the act, but under principles of law such as unconscionability or good faith and fair dealing, courts have reviewed fees and the bank's exercise of a discretion to set fees. *Perdue v. Crocker National Bank,* 38 Cal.3d 913 (1985) (unconscionability); *Best v. United Bank of Oregon,* 739 P.2d 554, 562–566 (1987) (good faith and fair dealing). In addition, Section 1–203 provides that every contract or duty within this act imposes an obligation of good faith in its performance or enforcement.

3. Subsection (c) imposes on the customer the duty to examine for and report unauthorized payments. Subsection (d)(2) changes former subsection (2)(b) by adopting a 30-day period in place of a 14-day period. Although the 14-day period may have been sufficient when the original version of Article 4 was drafted in the 1950s, given the much greater volume of checks at the time of the revision, a longer period was viewed as more appropriate. The rule of subsection (d)(2) follows pre-code case law that payment of an additional item or items bearing an authorized signature or alteration by the same wrongdoer is a loss suffered by the bank traceable to the customer's failure to exercise reasonable care in examining the statement and notifying the bank of objections to it. One of the most serious consequences of failure of the customer to comply with the requirements of subsection (c) is the opportunity presented to the wrongdoer to repeat the misdeeds. Conversely, one of the best ways to keep down losses in this type of situation is for the customer to promptly examine the statement and notify the bank of an unauthorized signature or alteration so that the bank will be alerted to stop paying further items. Hence, the rule of subsection (d)(2) is prescribed, and to avoid dispute a specific time limit, 30 days, is designated for cases to which the subsection applies. These

considerations are not present if there are no losses resulting from the payment of additional items. In these circumstances, a reasonable period for the customer to comply with its duties under subsection (c) would depend on the circumstances (Section 1–204(2)) and the subsection (d)(2) time limit should not be imported by analogy into subsection (c).

4. Subsection (e) replaces former subsection (3) and poses a modified comparative negligence test for determining liability. See the discussion on this point in the Comments to Sections 3–404, 3–405, and 3–406. The term "good faith" is defined in Section 3–103(a)(4) as including "observance of reasonable commercial standards of fair dealing." The connotation of this standard is fairness and not absence of negligence.

The term "ordinary care" used in subsection (e) is defined in Section 3–103(a)(7), made applicable to Article 4 by Section 4–104(c), to provide that sight examination by a payor bank is not required if its procedure is reasonable and is commonly followed by other comparable banks in the area. The case law is divided on this issue. The definition of "ordinary care" in Section 3–103 rejects those authorities that hold, in effect, that failure to use sight examination is negligence as a matter of law. The effect of the definition of "ordinary care" on Section 4–406 is only to provide that in the small percentage of cases in which a customer's failure to examine its statement or returned items has led to loss under subsection (d) a bank should not have to share that loss solely because it has adopted an automated collection or payment procedure in order to deal with the great volume of items at a lower cost to all customers.

5. Several changes are made in former Section 4–406(5). First, former subsection (5) is deleted and its substance is made applicable only to the one-year notice preclusion in former subsection (4) (subsection (f)). Thus if a drawer has not notified the payor bank of an unauthorized check or material alteration within the one-year period, the payor bank may not choose to recredit the drawer's account and pass the loss to the collecting banks on the theory of breach of warranty. Second, the reference in former subsection (4) to unauthorized indorsements is deleted. Section 4–406 imposes no duties on the drawer to look for unauthorized indorsements. Section 4–111 sets out a statute of limitations allowing a customer a three-year period to seek a credit to an account improperly charged by payment of an item bearing an unauthorized indorsement. Third, subsection (c) is added to Section 4–208 to assure that if a depositary bank is sued for breach of a presentment warranty, it can defend by showing that the drawer is precluded by Section 3–406 or Section 4–406(c) and (d). (1992 Senate Daily Journal 7350)

Uniform Commercial Code Comment

Prior Uniform Statutory Provision:
None.

Purposes:

1. This section is new to Uniform Laws. It is to replace statutes in forty jurisdictions dealing with the general subject of a depositor's duty to discover and report forgeries and alterations. In these statutes there is substantial variation in rules prescribed as to the following matters: application of the statute to unauthorized signatures, raised checks or altered checks; inclusion of special provisions with respect to fictitious payees; periods of time prescribed for termination of right of customer to assert claims against bank; time when limitation period begins to run; restriction of rights of customer stated in terms of liability for loss, preclusion of rights or limitations on time in which suits may be brought.

2. Subsection (1) states the general duty of a customer to exercise reasonable care and promptness to examine his bank statements and items to discover his unauthorized signature or any alteration and to promptly notify the bank if he discovers an unauthorized signature or alteration. This duty becomes operative when the bank does any one of three things with respect to the statement of account and supporting items paid in good faith. The first action is the sending of the statement and items to the customer. The sending may be either by mailing or any other action within the definition of "send" (Section 1–201). The second action is the holding of such statement and items available for the customer pursuant to a request for instructions of the customer. The third action is stated as "or otherwise in a reasonable manner makes the statement and items available to the customer." Such wider residual language is desirable to cover unusual situations. An example might be where the bank knows a customer has left a former address but does not know any new address to which to send the statement or item or to obtain instructions from the customer. The third residual type of action, however, must be "reasonable" and any court has the power to determine that a particular action or practice of a bank, other than sending statements and items or holding them pursuant to instructions, is not reasonable.

3. Subsection (2) states the effect of a failure of a customer to comply with subsection (1). The first effect stated in subparagraph (a) is that he is precluded from asserting against the bank his unauthorized signature and alteration if the bank establishes that it suffered a loss by reason of the customer's failure. The bank has the burden of establishing that it suffered some loss.

Under subparagraph (b) if, after the first item and statement becomes available plus a reasonable period not exceeding fourteen calendar days, the bank pays in good faith any other item on which there is an unauthorized signature or alteration by the same wrongdoer, which payment is prior to receipt by the bank of notification of such unauthorized signature or alteration on the first item, the customer is precluded from asserting the additional unauthorized signature or alteration. This rule follows substantial case law that payment of an additional item or items bearing an unauthorized signature or alteration by the same wrongdoer is a loss suffered by the bank traceable to the customer's failure to exercise reasonable care in examining his statement and notifying the bank of objections to it. One of the most serious consequences of failure of the customer to comply with the requirements of subsection (1) is the opportunity presented to the wrongdoer to repeat his misdeeds. Conversely, one of the best ways to keep down losses in this type of situation is for the customer to promptly examine his statement and notify the bank of an unauthorized signature or alteration so that the bank will be alerted to stop paying further items. Hence, the rule of subparagraph (b) is prescribed and to avoid dispute a specific time limit for action by the customer is designated, namely fourteen calendar days.

4. The two effects on the customer of his failure to comply with subsection (1) (subparagraphs (a) and (b) of subsection (2)) are stated in terms of preclusion from asserting a claim against the bank. However, these two effects occur only if the customer has failed to exercise reasonable care and promptness in examining his statement and items and notifying the bank and as to this question of fact the burden is upon the bank to establish such failure. Further, even if the bank succeeds in establishing that the customer has failed to exercise ordinary care, if in turn the customer succeeds in establishing that the bank failed to exercise ordinary care in paying the item(s) the preclusion rule does not apply. This distribution of the burden of establishing between the customer and the bank provides reasonable equality of treatment and requires each person asserting the negligence to establish such negligence rather than requiring either person to establish that his entire course of conduct constituted ordinary care.

5. Whether the preclusion rule of subsection (2) operates or does not operate depends upon determinations as to ordinary care of the customer and possibly of the bank. However, subsection (4) places an absolute time limit on the right of a customer to make claim for payment of altered or forged paper without regard to care or lack of care of either the customer or the bank. In the case of alteration or the unauthorized signature of the customer himself the absolute time limit is one year. In the case of unauthorized indorsements it is three years [Changes in California from U.C.C. (1962 Official Text), see California Code Comment, note 8.] This recognizes that there is little excuse for a customer not detecting an alteration of his own check or a forgery of his own signature. However, he does not know the signatures of indorsers and may be delayed in learning that indorsements are forged. The three year absolute time limit on the discovery of forged indorsements should be ample, because in the great preponderance of cases the customer will learn of the forged indorsements within this time and if in any exceptional case he does not, the balance in favor of a mechanical termination of the liability of the bank outweighs what few residuary risks the customer may still have. In thirteen of the existing statutes there are limitations on the liability of a bank for payment of items bearing forged indorsements which limitation periods range from thirty days to two years. In the remaining twenty-seven no provision is made for forged indorsements.

6. Nothing in this section is intended to affect any decision holding that a customer who has notice of something wrong with an indorsement must exercise reasonable care to investigate and to notify the bank.

§ 4406

should be noted that under the rules relating to impostors and signatures in the name of the payee (Section 3–405) certain forged indorsements on which the bank has paid the item in good faith may be treated as effective notwithstanding such discovery and notice. If the alteration or forgery results from the drawer's negligence the drawee who pays in good faith is also protected. Section 3–406.

7. The forty existing statutes on the subject as well as Section 4–406 evidence a public policy in favor of imposing on customers the duty of prompt examination of their bank statements and the notification of banks of forgeries and alterations and in favor of reasonable time limitations on the responsibility of banks for payment of forged or altered items. In two New York cases, however, it has been held that a payor bank may waive defenses of the kind prescribed by the section and ignore the public policy indicated by these defenses and recover the full amount of a forged or altered item from a collecting bank. Fallick v. Amalgamated Bank of New York, 232 App.Div. 127, 249 N.Y.S. 238 (1st Dep't. 1931); National Surety Corp. v. Federal Reserve Bank of New York, 188 Misc. 207, 70 N.Y.S.2d 636 (1946), affirmed without opinion 188 Misc. 213, 70 N.Y.S.2d 642 (1946). Subsection (5) is intended to reject the holding of these and like cases. Although the principle of subsection (5) might well be applied to other types of claims of customers against banks and defenses to these claims, the rule of the subsection is limited to defenses of a payor bank under this section. No present need is known to give the rule wider effect.

Cross References:

Sections 3–404, 3–405, 3–406, 3–407, 3–417 and 4–207.

Definitional Cross References:

"Alteration". Section 3–407.
"Bank". Section 1–201.
"Collecting bank". Section 4–105.
"Customer". Section 4–104.
"Good faith". Section 1–201.
"Indorsement". Section 3–204.
"Item". Section 4–104.
"Payor bank". Section 4–105.
"Send". Section 1–201.
"Unauthorized signature". Section 1–201.

Cross References

Alteration, definition and effect, see Commercial Code § 3407.
Alteration or forged signature, negligence contributing, see Commercial Code § 3406.
Defense against drawee on claim for breach of warranty based on unauthorized indorsement or alteration, see Commercial Code §§ 3417, 4208.
Impostors, see Commercial Code § 3404.
Limitation of actions, forged or raised check, see Code of Civil Procedure § 340.
Statement, correctness conclusively presumed after four years, see Financial Code § 861.
Unauthorized signatures, see Commercial Code §§ 1201, 3403.
Warranties on presentment and transfer, see Commercial Code §§ 3416, 3417.

§ 4406. Statement of account; customer's duty to examine statement; remedies

Text of section operative Jan. 1, 1998.

(a) A bank that sends or makes available to a customer a statement of account showing payment of items for the account shall either return or make available to the customer the items paid or provide information in the statement of account sufficient to allow the customer to identify the items paid. If the bank does not return the items, it shall provide in the statement of account the telephone number that the customer may call to request an item or a legible copy thereof pursuant to subdivision (b).

(b) If the items are not returned to the customer, the person retaining the items shall either retain the items or, if the items are destroyed, maintain the capacity to furnish legible copies of the items until the expiration of seven years after receipt of the items. A customer may request an item from the bank that paid the item, and that bank shall provide in a reasonable time either the item or, if the item has been destroyed or is not otherwise obtainable, a legible copy of the item. A bank shall provide, upon request and without charge to the customer, at least two items or a legible copy thereof with respect to each statement of account sent to the customer.

(c) If a bank sends or makes available a statement of account or items pursuant to subdivision (a), the customer shall exercise reasonable promptness in examining the statement or the items to determine whether any payment was not authorized because of an alteration of an item or because a purported signature by or on behalf of the customer was not authorized. If, based on the statement or items provided, the customer should reasonably have discovered the unauthorized payment, the customer shall promptly notify the bank of the relevant facts.

(d) If the bank proves that the customer failed, with respect to an item, to comply with the duties imposed on the customer by subdivision (c), the customer is precluded from asserting any of the following against the bank:

(1) The customer's unauthorized signature or any alteration on the item if the bank also proves that it suffered a loss by reason of the failure.

(2) The customer's unauthorized signature or alteration by the same wrongdoer on any other item paid in good faith by the bank if the payment was made before the bank received notice from the customer of the unauthorized signature or alteration and after the customer had been afforded a reasonable period of time, not exceeding 30 days, in which to examine the item or statement of account and notify the bank.

(e) If subdivision (d) applies and the customer proves that the bank failed to exercise ordinary care in paying the item and that the failure contributed to loss, the loss is allocated between the customer precluded and the bank asserting the preclusion according to the extent to which the failure of the customer to comply with subdivision (c) and the failure of the bank to exercise ordinary care contributed to the loss. If the customer proves that the bank did not pay the item in good faith, the preclusion under subdivision (d) does not apply.

(f) Without regard to care or lack of care of either the customer or the bank, a customer who does not within one year after the statement or items are made available to the customer (subdivision (a)) discover and report the customer's unauthorized signature on or any alteration on the item is precluded from asserting against the bank the unauthorized signature or alteration. If there is a preclusion under this subdivision, the payor bank may not recover for breach of warranty under Section 4208 with respect to the unauthorized signature or alteration to which the preclusion applies.

(g) This section shall become operative on January 1, 1998. *(Added by Stats.1992, c. 914 (S.B.833), § 45.5, operative Jan. 1, 1998. Amended by Stats.1993, c. 589 (A.B.2211), § 30, operative Jan. 1, 1998.)*

For text of section operative until Jan. 1, 1998, see § 4406, ante.

§ 4407. Improper payment; subrogation rights of payor bank

If a payor bank has paid an item over the * * * order of the drawer or maker to stop payment, or after an account has been closed, or otherwise under circumstances giving a basis for objection by the drawer or maker, to prevent unjust enrichment and only to the extent necessary to prevent loss to the bank by reason of its payment of the item, the payor bank * * * is subrogated to the rights of all of the following:

(a) Of any holder in due course on the item against the drawer or maker * * *.

(b) Of the payee or any other holder of the item against the drawer or maker either on the item or under the transaction out of which the item arose * * *.

(c) Of the drawer or maker against the payee or any other holder of the item with respect to the transaction out of which the item arose. *(Stats.1963, c. 819, § 4407. Amended by Stats.1992, c. 914 (S.B.833), § 46.)*

California Code Comment

By John A. Bohn and Charles J. Williams

Prior California Law

1. This section is new statutory law. Its purpose is to give a bank remedies to get its money back when it has improperly paid an item.

The principles underlying this section are familiar but there are no parallels in prior California case law.

Changes from U.C.C. (1962 Official Text)

2. This is section 4–407 of the Official Text without change.

Uniform Commercial Code Comment

Official Reasons for 1990 Change

An order to close an account is assimilated to an order to stop payment in this section and in Section 4–403. The other modifications are made to conform with current legislative drafting practices, with no intent to change substance.

1990 Change

1. Section 4–403 states that a stop-payment order or an order to close an account is binding on a bank. If a bank pays an item over such an order it is prima facie liable, but under subsection (c) of Section 4–403 the burden of establishing the fact and amount of loss from such payment is on the customer. A defense frequently interposed by a bank in an action against it for wrongful payment over a stop-payment order is that the drawer or maker suffered no loss because it would have been liable to a holder in due course in any event. On this argument some cases have held that payment cannot be stopped against a holder in due course. Payment can be stopped but if it is, the drawer or maker is liable and the sound rule is that the bank is subrogated to the rights of the holder in due course. The preamble and paragraph (1) of this section state this rule.

2. Paragraph (2) also subrogates the bank to the rights of the payee or other holder against the drawer or maker either on the item or under the transaction out of which it arose. It may well be that the payee is not a holder in due course but still has good rights against the drawer. These may be on the check but also may not be as, for example, where the drawer buys goods from the payee and the goods are partially defective so that the payee is not entitled to the full price, but the goods are still worth a portion of the contract price. If the drawer retains the goods it is obligated to pay a part of the agreed price. If the bank has paid the check it should be subrogated to this claim of the payee against the drawer.

3. Paragraph (3) subrogates the bank to the rights of the drawer or maker against the payee or other holder with respect to the transaction out of which the item arose. If, for example, the payee was a fraudulent salesman inducing the drawer to issue a check for defective securities, and the bank pays the check over a stop-payment order but reimburses the drawer for such payment, the bank should have a basis for getting the money back from the fraudulent salesman.

4. The limitations of the preamble prevent the bank itself from getting any double recovery or benefits out of its subrogation rights conferred by the section.

5. The spelling out of the affirmative rights of the bank in this section does not destroy other existing rights (Section 1–103). Among others these may include the defense of a payor bank that by conduct in recognizing the payment a customer has ratified the bank's action in paying in disregard of a stop-payment order or right to recover money paid under a mistake.

Uniform Commercial Code Comment

Prior Uniform Statutory Provision:

None.

Purposes:

1. Section 4–403 states that a stop payment order is binding on a bank. If a bank pays an item over such a stop order it is prima facie liable, but under subsection (3) of 4–403 the burden of establishing the fact and amount of loss from such payment is on the customer. A defense frequently interposed by a bank in an action against it for wrongful payment over a stop-order is that the drawer or maker suffered no loss because he would have been liable to a holder in due course in any event. On this argument some cases have held that payment cannot be stopped against a holder in due course. Payment can be stopped, but if it is, the drawer or maker is liable and the sound rule is that the bank is subrogated to the rights of the holder in due course. The preamble and subsection (a) of this section state this rule.

2. Subsection (b) also subrogates the bank to the rights of the payee or other holder against the drawer or maker either on the item or under the transaction out of which it arose. It may well be that the payee is not a holder in due course but still has good rights against the drawer. These may be on the check but also may not be as, for example, where the drawer buys goods from the payee and the goods are partially defective so that the payee is not entitled to the full price, but the goods are still worth a portion of the contract price. If the drawer retains the goods he is obligated to pay a part of the agreed price. If the bank has paid the check it should be subrogated to this claim of the payee against the drawer.

3. Subsection (c) subrogates the bank to the rights of the drawer or maker against the payee or other holder with respect to the transaction out of which the item arose. If, for example, the payee was a fraudulent salesman inducing the drawer to issue his check for defective securities, and the bank pays the check over a stop order but reimburses the drawer for such payment, the bank should have a basis for getting the money back from the fraudulent salesman.

4. The limitations of the preamble prevent the bank itself from getting any double recovery or benefits out of its subrogation rights conferred by the section.

5. The spelling out of the affirmative rights of the bank in this section does not destroy other existing rights (Section 1–103). Among others these may include the defense of a payor bank that by conduct in recognizing the payment a customer has ratified the bank's action in paying in disregard of a stop payment order or rights to recover money paid under a mistake.

§ 4407

Cross Reference:

Section 4-403.

Definitional Cross References:

"Holder". Section 1-201.
"Holder in due course". Section 3-302.
"Item". Section 4-104.
"Payor bank". Section 4-105.

Cross References

Stop payment, see Commercial Code § 4403.
Subrogation on redemption from lien, see Civil Code §§ 2903, 2904.

CHAPTER 5. COLLECTION OF DOCUMENTARY DRAFTS

Section
4501. Handling of Documentary Drafts; Duty to Send for Presentment and to Notify Customer of Dishonor.
4502. Presentment of "On Arrival" Drafts.
4503. Responsibility of Presenting Bank for Documents and Goods; Report of Reasons for Dishonor; Referee in Case of Need.
4504. Privilege of Presenting Bank to Deal With Goods; Security Interest for Expenses.

Transitional Provisions

Effective date and transitional provisions for sections in Division 4 affected by Stats.1992, c. 914, see Commercial Code § 16101 et seq.

§ 4501. Handling of Documentary Drafts; Duty to Send for Presentment and to Notify Customer of Dishonor

A bank that takes a documentary draft for collection shall present or send the draft and accompanying documents for presentment and, upon learning that the draft has not been paid or accepted in due course * * *, shall seasonably notify its customer of the fact even though it may have discounted or bought the draft or extended credit available for withdrawal as of right. (Stats.1963, c. 819, § 4501. Amended by Stats.1992, c. 914 (S.B.833), § 47.)

California Code Comment

By John A. Bohn and Charles J. Williams

Prior California Law

1. This section is new. It is a codification of California banking practice. It is consistent with the duty of a collecting bank to present an item or forward it for presentment. Under pre Commercial Code practice a bank was liable for an unreasonable delay in notifying the customer of non payment or non acceptance. Kriste v. International Savings and Exchange Bank, 17 Cal.App. 301, 119 Pac. 666 (1911).

2. It should be noted that Commercial Code §§ 4501-4504 make no provision for warranties in connection with a documentary draft given by a collecting bank. Commercial Code § 7508 deals with warranties of a collecting bank with respect to documents of title accompanying a documentary draft. Clarke, Bailey and Young, Bank Deposits and Collections 60 (A.L.I.1963) pp. 124-129.

Changes from U.C.C. (1962 Official Text)

3. This is section 4-501 of the Official Text without change.

Uniform Commercial Code Comment

Official Reasons for 1990 Change

Modified to conform with current drafting practices; no intent to change substance.

1990 Change

This section states the duty of a bank handling a documentary draft for a customer. "Documentary draft" is defined in Section 4-104. The duty stated exists even if the bank has bought the draft. This is because to the customer the draft normally represents an underlying commercial transaction, and if that is not going through as planned the customer should know it promptly.

Uniform Commercial Code Comment

Prior Uniform Statutory Provision:

None.

Purposes:

To state the duty of a bank handling a documentary draft for a customer. "Documentary draft" is defined in Section 4-104. Notice that the duty stated exists even when the bank has bought the draft. This is because to the customer the draft normally represents an underlying commercial transaction, and if that is not going through as planned he should know it promptly.

Cross References:

In Article 4: Sections 4-201, 4-202, 4-203, 4-204 and 4-210.
In Article 5: Sections 5-110, 5-111, 5-112 and 5-113.

Definitional Cross References:

"Documentary draft". Sections 4-104, 5-103.

Cross References

Collection of items, see Commercial Code §§ 4201 et seq., 4301 et seq.
Effect of instructions, see Commercial Code § 4203.
Honor or rejection of letters of credit, see Commercial Code § 5112.
Indemnity agreement inducing honor, negotiation or reimbursement, see Commercial Code § 5113.
Letters of credit, presenter's reservation of lien or claim, see Commercial Code § 5110.
Ordinary care, standard of care of collecting bank, see Commercial Code § 4202.
Presentment, notice of dishonor, negotiable instruments, see Commercial Code § 3501 et seq.
Presentment by notice of item not payable by, through, or at bank, see Commercial Code § 4212.
Provisional status of credits, see Commercial Code § 4201.
Relinquishment of claim to documents when draft honored, see Commercial Code § 5110.
Sending and collecting items, method, see Commercial Code § 4204.
Time allowed for honor or rejection of draft under a credit, see Commercial Code § 5112.
Warranties of collecting bank as to documents, see Commercial Code § 7508.
Warranties of customer and collecting bank on transfer or presentment of items, see Commercial Code § 4207.
Warranties on transfer and presentment of letters of credit, see Commercial Code § 5111.

§ 4502. Presentment of "On Arrival" Drafts

If a draft or the relevant instructions require presentment "on arrival," "when goods arrive" or the like, the collecting bank need not present until in its judgment a reasonable time for arrival of the goods has expired. Refusal to pay or accept because the goods have not arrived is not dishonor; the bank shall notify its transferor of the refusal but need not present the draft again until it is instructed to do so or learns of the arrival of the goods. *(Stats.1963, c. 819, § 4502. Amended by Stats.1992, c. 914 (S.B.833), § 48.)*

California Code Comment

By John A. Bohn and Charles J. Williams

Prior California Law

1. This section is new.

There is no California precedent on this point. However, this section changes the earlier rule because it is said that under pre-Commercial Code practice, a presenting bank might risk violating the rule requiring prompt presentment if it delayed presentment until the goods arrived. Bank Deposits and Collections, Clarke, Bailey and Young 60 (A.L.I. 1963) p. 114.

Changes from U.C.C. (1962 Official Text)

2. This is section 4–502 of the Official Text without change.

Uniform Commercial Code Comment
Official Reasons for 1990 Change

Modified to conform with current drafting practices; no intent to change substance.

1990 Change

The section is designed to establish a definite rule for "on arrival" drafts. The term includes not only drafts drawn payable "on arrival" but also drafts forwarded with instructions to present "on arrival." The term refers to the arrival of the relevant goods. Unless a bank has actual knowledge of the arrival of the goods, as for example, when it is the "notify" party on the bill of lading, the section only requires the exercise of such judgment in estimating time as a bank may be expected to have. Commonly the buyer-drawee will want the goods and will therefore call for the documents and take up the draft when they do arrive.

Uniform Commercial Code Comment

Prior Uniform Statutory Provision:

None.

Purposes:

The section is designed to establish a definite rule for "on arrival" drafts. The term includes not only drafts drawn payable "on arrival" but also drafts forwarded with instructions to present "on arrival". The term refers to the arrival of the relevant goods. Unless a bank has actual knowledge of the arrival of the goods, as for example, when it is the "notify" party on the bill of lading, the section only requires the exercise of such judgment in estimating time as a bank may be expected to have. Commonly the buyer-drawee will want the goods and will therefore call for the documents and take up the draft when they do arrive.

Cross References:

In Article 4: Sections 4–202 and 4–203.
In Article 5: Section 5–112.

Definitional Cross References:

"Collecting bank". Section 4–105.

Cross References

Collecting bank, see Commercial Code § 4105.
Effect of instructions, see Commercial Code § 4203.
Honor or rejection of letters of credit, see Commercial Code § 5112.
Indemnity agreement inducing honor, negotiation or reimbursement, see Commercial Code § 5113.
Ordinary care, standard of care of collecting bank, see Commercial Code § 4202.

§ 4503. Responsibility of Presenting Bank for Documents and Goods; Report of Reasons for Dishonor; Referee in Case of Need

Unless otherwise instructed and except as provided in Division 5 (commencing with Section 5101), a bank presenting a documentary draft:

(a) Shall deliver the documents to the drawee on acceptance of the draft if it is payable more than three days after presentment; otherwise, only on payment * * *;

(b) Upon dishonor, either in the case of presentment for acceptance or presentment for payment, may seek and follow instructions from any referee in case of need designated in the draft or, if the presenting bank does not choose to utilize * * * the referee's services, it shall use diligence and good faith to ascertain the reason for dishonor, shall notify its transferor of the dishonor and of the results of its effort to ascertain the reasons therefor, and shall request instructions. * * *

However, the presenting bank is under no obligation with respect to goods represented by the documents except to follow any reasonable instructions seasonably received; it has a right to reimbursement for any expense incurred in following instructions and to prepayment of or indemnity for those expenses. *(Stats. 1963, c. 819, § 4503. Amended by Stats.1992, c. 914 (S.B.833), § 49.)*

California Code Comment

By John A. Bohn and Charles J. Williams

Prior California Law

1. Paragraph (a) is similar to former Civil Code § 2130e which was a part of the former Uniform Bills of Lading Act. However, this section extends the rule to all documentary drafts.

2. Paragraph (b) is new. Former Civil Code § 3212 (NIL) authorized the drawer or indorser to place on the item the name of a person to whom the holder may resort in case of need. That person was known as the "referee in case of need." Resort would normally have been made to a referee under this provision to obtain acceptance or payment for honor after a draft had been protested for dishonor by non acceptance or non payment. Britton, Bills & Notes (1961) 607–613 Former Civil Code § 3212 has not been carried over into the Commercial Code and there is no other specific provision for a referee in case of need. His function under this paragraph is as an alternate source of instructions for the presenting bank upon dishonor.

Changes from U.C.C. (1962 Official Text)

3. This is section 4–503 of the Official Text without change.

Uniform Commercial Code Comment
Official Reasons for 1990 Change

Modified to conform with current drafting practices; no intent to change substance.

1990 Change

1. This section states the rules governing, in the absence of instructions, the duty of the presenting bank in case either of honor or of dishonor of a documentary draft. The section should be read in connection with Section 2–514 or when documents are deliverable c acceptance, when on payment.

2. If the draft is drawn under a letter of credit, Article 5 controls. See Sections 5–109 through 5–114.

Uniform Commercial Code Comment

Prior Uniform Statutory Provision:

Section 131(3), Uniform Negotiable Instruments Law.

Changes: Completely rewritten and enlarged.

Purposes:

1. To state the rules governing, in the absence of instructions, the duty of the presenting bank in case either of honor or of dishonor of a documentary draft. The section should be read in connection with Section 2–514 on when documents are deliverable on acceptance, when on payment.

2. If the draft is drawn under a letter of credit, Article 5 controls. See Sections 5–109 through 5–114.

Cross References:

Point 1. Section 2–514; see also Section 4–504.
Point 2. Article 5, especially Sections 5–109 through 5–114.

Definitional Cross References:

"Documentary draft". Sections 4–104, 5–103.
"Presenting bank". Section 4–105.

Cross References

Disposition of goods upon dishonor, see Commercial Code § 4504.
Letters of credit, see Commercial Code § 5101 et seq.
Sales, documents deliverable on acceptance or payment, see Commercial Code § 2514.

§ 4504. Privilege of Presenting Bank to Deal With Goods; Security Interest for Expenses

(a) A presenting bank that, following the dishonor of a documentary draft, has seasonably requested instructions but does not receive them within a reasonable time may store, sell, or otherwise deal with the goods in any reasonable manner.

(b) For its reasonable expenses incurred by action under subdivision * * * (a), the presenting bank has a lien upon the goods or their proceeds, which may be foreclosed in the same manner as an unpaid seller's lien. (Stats.1963, c. 819, § 4504. Amended by Stats.1992, c. 914 (S.B.833), § 50.)

California Code Comment

By John A. Bohn and Charles J. Williams

Prior California Law

1. This section establishes new California law.
2. Subdivision (2) gives the presenting bank an unpaid seller's lien intended to be enforced under Commercial Code § 2706.

Changes from U.C.C. (1962 Official Text)

3. This is section 4–504 of the Official Text without change.

Uniform Commercial Code Comment
Official Reasons for 1990 Change

Modified to conform with current drafting practices; no intent to change substance.

1990 Change

The section gives the presenting bank, after dishonor, a privilege to deal with the goods in any commercially reasonable manner pending instructions from its transferor and, if still unable to communicate with its principal after a reasonable time, a right to realize its expenditures as if foreclosing on an unpaid seller's lien (Section 2–706). The provision includes situations in which storage of goods or other action becomes commercially necessary pending receipt of any requested instructions, even if the requested instructions are later received.

The "reasonable manner" referred to means one reasonable in the light of business factors and the judgment of a business man.

Uniform Commercial Code Comment

Prior Uniform Statutory Provision:

None.

Purposes:

To give the presenting bank, after dishonor, a privilege to deal with the goods in any commercially reasonable manner pending instructions from its transferor and, if still unable to communicate with its principal after a reasonable time, a right to realize its expenditures as if foreclosing on an unpaid seller's lien (Section 2–706). The provision includes situations in which storage of goods or other action becomes commercially necessary pending receipt of any requested instructions, even if the requested instructions are later received.

The "reasonable manner" referred to means one reasonable in the light of business factors and the judgment of a business man.

Cross References:

Sections 4–503 and 2–706.

Definitional Cross References:

"Presenting bank". Section 4–105.
"Documentary draft". Sections 4–104, 5–103.

Cross References

Responsibility of presenting bank with respect to goods, see Commercial Code § 4503.
Seller's resale, and contract for resale, see Commercial Code § 2706.

Division 5
LETTERS OF CREDIT

Section
5101. Short title.
5102. Definitions.
5103. Scope; changes to effect of division; rights and obligations of issuer.
5104. Form requirements.
5105. Consideration.
5106. Time of issuance; amendment, cancellation, or revocation; duration.
5107. Confirmer; rights and obligations; nominated person; adviser; notification of terms.
5108. Issuer's obligations and rights.
5109. Forgery or material fraud; honor of presentation.
5110. Warranties.
5111. Remedies; improper dishonor or repudiation.
5112. Transfers.
5113. Successor of beneficiary; rights and obligations.
5114. Issuer's duty and privilege to honor; right of reimbursement.
5114. Assignment of proceeds.
5115. Limitation of actions.
5116. Governing law and forum.
5117. Subrogation.

Former Division 5 was repealed by Stats.1996, c. 176 (S.B.1599), § 6. For text and continuing application of former Division 5, see Appendix to Division 5—Letters of Credit, post.

WESTLAW Computer Assisted Legal Research

WESTLAW supplements your legal research in many ways. WESTLAW allows you to
• update your research with the most current information
• expand your library with additional resources
• retrieve direct history, precedential history and parallel citations with the Insta-Cite service
For more information on using WESTLAW to supplement your research, see the WESTLAW Electronic Research Guide, which follows the Preface.

---

§ 5101. Short title

This division may be cited as Uniform Commercial Code—Letters of Credit. *(Added by Stats.1996, c. 176 (S.B.1599), § 7.)*

Uniform Commercial Code Comment

The Official Comment to the original Section 5-101 was a remarkably brief inaugural address. Noting that letters of credit had not been the subject of statutory enactment and that the law concerning them had been developed in the cases, the Comment stated that Article 5 was intended "within its limited scope" to set an independent theoretical frame for the further development of letters of credit. That statement addressed accurately conditions as they existed when the statement was made, nearly half a century ago. Since Article 5 was originally drafted, the use of letters of credit has expanded and developed, and the case law concerning these developments is, in some respects, discordant.

Revision of Article 5 therefore has required reappraisal both of the statutory goals and of the extent to which particular statutory provisions further or adversely affect achievement of those goals.

The statutory goal of Article 5 was originally stated to be: (1) to set a substantive theoretical frame that describes the function and legal nature of letters of credit; and (2) to preserve procedural flexibility in order to accommodate further development of the efficient use of letters of credit. A letter of credit is an idiosyncratic form of undertaking that supports performance of an obligation incurred in a separate financial, mercantile, or other transaction or arrangement. The objectives of the original and revised Article 5 are best achieved (1) by defining the peculiar characteristics of a letter of credit that distinguish it and the legal consequences of its use from other forms of assurance such as secondary guarantees, performance bonds, and insurance policies, and from ordinary contracts, fiduciary engagements, and escrow arrangements; and (2) by preserving flexibility through variation by agreement in order to respond to and accommodate developments in custom and usage that are not inconsistent with the essential definitions and substantive mandates of the statute. No statute can, however, prescribe the manner in which such substantive rights and duties are to be enforced or imposed without risking stultification of wholesome developments in the letter of credit mechanism. Letter of credit law should remain responsive to commercial reality and in particular to the customs and expectations of the international banking and mercantile community. Courts should read the terms of this article in a manner consistent with these customs and expectations.

The subject matter in Article 5, letters of credit, may also be governed by an international convention that is now being drafted by UNCITRAL, the draft Convention on Independent Guarantees and Standby Letters of Credit. The Uniform Customs and Practice is an international body of trade practice that is commonly adopted by international and domestic letters of credit and as such is the "law of the transaction" by agreement of the parties. Article 5 is consistent with and was influenced by the rules in the existing version of the UCP. In addition to the UCP and the international convention, other bodies of law apply to letters of credit. For example, the federal bankruptcy law applies to letters of credit with respect to applicants and beneficiaries that are in bankruptcy; regulations of the Federal Reserve Board and the Comptroller of the Currency lay out requirements for banks that issue letters of credit and describe how letters of credit are to be treated for calculating asset risk and for the purpose of loan limitations. In addition there is an array of anti-boycott and other similar laws that may affect the issuance and performance of letters of credit. All of these laws are beyond the scope of Article 5, but in certain circumstances they will override Article 5.

Cross References

Definition of acceptance, see Commercial Code §§ 3409, 5103.
Scope of division, see Commercial Code § 5102.

§ 5102. Definitions

(a) In this division:

(1) "Adviser" means a person who, at the request of the issuer, a confirmer, or another adviser, notifies or requests another adviser to notify the beneficiary that a letter of credit has been issued, confirmed, or amended.

(2) "Applicant" means a person at whose request or for whose account a letter of credit is issued. The term includes a person who requests an issuer to issue a letter of credit on behalf of another if the person making the

§ 5102   LETTERS OF CREDIT

request undertakes an obligation to reimburse the issuer.

(3) "Beneficiary" means a person who under the terms of a letter of credit is entitled to have its complying presentation honored. The term includes a person to whom drawing rights have been transferred under a transferable letter of credit.

(4) "Confirmer" means a nominated person who undertakes, at the request or with the consent of the issuer, to honor a presentation under a letter of credit issued by another.

(5) "Dishonor" of a letter of credit means failure timely to honor or to take an interim action, such as acceptance of a draft, that may be required by the letter of credit.

(6) "Document" means a draft or other demand, document of title, investment security, certificate, invoice, or other record, statement, or representation of fact, law, right, or opinion (i) which is presented in a written or other medium permitted by the letter of credit or, unless prohibited by the letter of credit, by the standard practice referred to in subdivision (e) of Section 5108 and (ii) which is capable of being examined for compliance with the terms and conditions of the letter of credit. A document may not be oral.

(7) "Good faith" means honesty in fact in the conduct or transaction concerned.

(8) "Honor" of a letter of credit means performance of the issuer's undertaking in the letter of credit to pay or deliver an item of value. Unless the letter of credit otherwise provides, "honor" occurs

(i) upon payment,

(ii) if the letter of credit provides for acceptance, upon acceptance of a draft and, at maturity, its payment, or

(iii) if the letter of credit provides for incurring a deferred obligation, upon incurring the obligation and, at maturity, its performance.

(9) "Issuer" means a bank or other person that issues a letter of credit, but does not include an individual who makes an engagement for personal, family, or household purposes.

(10) "Letter of credit" means a definite undertaking that satisfies the requirements of Section 5104 by an issuer to a beneficiary at the request or for the account of an applicant or, in the case of a financial institution, to itself or for its own account, to honor a documentary presentation by payment or delivery of an item of value.

(11) "Nominated person" means a person whom the issuer (i) designates or authorizes to pay, accept, negotiate, or otherwise give value under a letter of credit and (ii) undertakes by agreement or custom and practice to reimburse.

(12) "Presentation" means delivery of a document to an issuer or nominated person for honor or giving of value under a letter of credit.

(13) "Presenter" means a person making a presentation as or on behalf of a beneficiary or nominated person.

(14) "Record" means information that is inscribed on a tangible medium, or that is stored in an electronic or other medium and is retrievable in perceivable form.

(15) "Successor of a beneficiary" means a person who succeeds to substantially all of the rights of a beneficiary by operation of law, including a corporation with or into which the beneficiary has been merged or consolidated, an administrator, executor, personal representative, trustee in bankruptcy, debtor in possession, liquidator, and receiver.

(b) Definitions in other divisions applying to this division and the sections in which they appear are:

"Accept" or "Acceptance" Section 3409

"Value" Sections 3303, 4211

(c) Division 1 contains certain additional general definitions and principles of construction and interpretation applicable throughout this division. *(Added by Stats.1996, c. 176 (S.B.1599), § 7.)*

Uniform Commercial Code Comment

1. Since no one can be a confirmer unless that person is a nominated person as defined in Section 5–102(a)(11), those who agree to "confirm" without the designation or authorization of the issuer are not confirmers under Article 5. Nonetheless, the undertakings to the beneficiary of such persons may be enforceable by the beneficiary as letters of credit issued by the "confirmer" for its own account or as guarantees or contracts outside of Article 5.

2. The definition of "document" contemplates and facilitates the growing recognition of electronic and other nonpaper media as "documents," however, for the time being, data in those media constitute documents only in certain circumstances. For example, a facsimile received by an issuer would be a document only if the letter of credit explicitly permitted it, if the standard practice authorized it and the letter did not prohibit it, or the agreement of the issuer and beneficiary permitted it. The fact that data transmitted in a nonpaper (unwritten) medium can be recorded on paper by a recipient's computer printer, facsimile machine, or the like does not under current practice render the data so transmitted a "document." A facsimile or S.W.I.F.T. message received directly by the issuer is in an electronic medium when it crosses the boundary of the issuer's place of business. One wishing to make a presentation by facsimile (an electronic medium) will have to procure the explicit agreement of the issuer (assuming that the standard practice does not authorize it). Where electronic transmissions are authorized neither by the letter of credit nor by the practice, the beneficiary may transmit the data electronically to its agent who may be able to put it in written form and make a conforming presentation.

3. "Good faith" continues in revised Article 5 to be defined as "honesty in fact." "Observance of reasonable standards of fair dealing" has not been added to the definition. The narrower definition of "honesty in fact" reinforces the "independence principle" in the treatment of "fraud," "strict compliance," "preclusion," and other tests affecting the performance of obligations that are unique to letters of credit. This narrower definition—which does not include "fair dealing"—is appropriate to the decision to honor or dishonor a presentation of documents specified in a letter of credit. The narrower definition is also appropriate for other parts of revised Article 5 where greater certainty of obligations is necessary and is consistent with the goals of speed and low cost. It is important that U.S. letters of credit have continuing vitality and competitiveness in international transactions.

For example, it would be inconsistent with the "independence" principle if any of the following occurred: (i) the beneficiary's failure to adhere to the standard of "fair dealing" in the underlying transaction or otherwise in presenting documents were to provide applicants and issuers with an "unfairness" defense to dishonor even when the documents complied with the terms of the letter of credit; (ii) the issuer's obligation to honor in "strict compliance in accordance with standard practice" were changed to "reasonable compliance" by use of the "fair dealing" standard, or (iii) the preclusion against the issuer (Section 5–108(d)) were modified under the "fair dealing" standard to enable the issuer later to raise additional deficiencies in the presentation. The rights and obligations arising from presentation, honor, dishonor and reimbursement, are independent and strict, and thus "honesty in fact" is an appropriate standard.

The contract between the applicant and beneficiary is not governed by Article 5, but by applicable contract law, such as Article 2 or the general law of contracts. "Good faith" in that contract is defined by other law, such as Section 2–103(1)(b) or Restatement of Contracts 2d, § 205, which incorporate the principle of "fair dealing" in most cases, or a State's common law or other statutory provisions that may apply to that contract.

The contract between the applicant and the issuer (sometimes called the "reimbursement" agreement) is governed in part by this article (e.g., Sections 5–108(i), 5–111(b), and 5–103(c)) and partly by other law (e.g., the general law of contracts. The definition of good faith in Section 5–102(a)(7) applies only to the extent that the reimbursement contract is governed by provisions in this article; for other purposes good faith is defined by other law.

4. Payment and acceptance are familiar modes of honor. A third mode of honor, incurring an unconditional obligation, has legal effects similar to an acceptance of a time draft but does not technically constitute an acceptance. The practice of making letters of credit available by "deferred payment undertaking" as now provided in UCP 500 has grown up in other countries and spread to the United States. The definition of "honor" will accommodate that practice.

5. The exclusion of consumers from the definition of "issuer" is to keep creditors from using a letter of credit in consumer transactions in which the consumer might be made the issuer and the creditor would be the beneficiary. If that transaction were recognized under Article 5, the effect would be to leave the consumer without defenses against the creditor. That outcome would violate the policy behind the Federal Trade Commission Rule in 16 CFR Part 433. In a consumer transaction, an individual cannot be an issuer where that person would otherwise be either the principal debtor or a guarantor.

6. The label on a document is not conclusive; certain documents labelled "guarantees" in accordance with European (and occasionally, American) practice are letters of credit. On the other hand, even documents that are labelled "letter of credit" may not constitute letters of credit under the definition in Section 5–102(a). When a document labelled a letter of credit requires the issuer to pay not upon the presentation of documents, but upon the determination of an extrinsic fact such as applicant's failure to perform a construction contract, and where that condition appears on its face to be fundamental and would, if ignored, leave no obligation to the issuer under the document labelled letter of credit, the issuer's undertaking is not a letter of credit. It is probably some form of suretyship or other contractual arrangement and may be enforceable as such. See Sections 5–102(a)(10) and 5–103(d). Therefore, undertakings whose fundamental term requires an issuer to look beyond documents and beyond conventional reference to the clock, calendar, and practices concerning the form of various documents are not governed by Article 5. Although Section 5–108(g) recognizes that certain nondocumentary conditions can be included in a letter of credit without denying the undertaking the status of letter of credit, that section does not apply to cases where the nondocumentary condition is fundamental to the issuer's obligation. The rules in Sections 5–102(a)(10), 5–103(d), and 5–108(g) approve the conclusion in *Wichita Eagle & Beacon Publishing Co. v. Pacific Nat. Bank*, 493 F.2d 1285 (9th Cir.1974).

The adjective "definite" is taken from the UCP. It approves cases that deny letter of credit status to documents that are unduly vague or incomplete. See, e.g., *Transparent Products Corp. v. Paysaver Credit Union*, 864 F.2d 60 (7th Cir.1988). Note, however, that no particular phrase or label is necessary to establish a letter of credit. It is sufficient if the undertaking of the issuer shows that it is intended to be a letter of credit. In most cases the parties' intention will be indicated by a label on the undertaking itself indicating that it is a "letter of credit," but no such language is necessary.

A financial institution may be both the issuer and the applicant or the issuer and the beneficiary. Such letters are sometimes issued by a bank in support of the bank's own lease obligations or on behalf of one of its divisions as an applicant or to one of its divisions as beneficiary, such as an overseas branch. Because wide use of letters of credit in which the issuer and the applicant or the issuer and the beneficiary are the same would endanger the unique status of letters of credit, only financial institutions are authorized to issue them.

In almost all cases the ultimate performance of the issuer under a letter of credit is the payment of money. In rare cases the issuer's obligation is to deliver stock certificates or the like. The definition of letter of credit in Section 5–102(a)(10) contemplates those cases.

7. Under the UCP any bank is a nominated bank where the letter of credit is "freely negotiable." A letter of credit might also nominate by the following: "We hereby engage with the drawer, indorsers, and bona fide holders of drafts drawn under and in compliance with the terms of this credit that the same will be duly honored on due presentation" or "available with any bank by negotiation." A restricted negotiation credit might be "available with x bank by negotiation" or the like.

Several legal consequences may attach to the status of nominated person. First, when the issuer nominates a person, it is authorizing that person to pay or give value and is authorizing the beneficiary to make presentation to that person. Unless the letter of credit provides otherwise, the beneficiary need not present the documents to the issuer before the letter of credit expires; it need only present those documents to the nominated person. Secondly, a nominated person that gives value in good faith has a right to payment from the issuer despite fraud. Section 5–109(a)(1).

8. A "record" must be in or capable of being converted to a perceivable form. For example, an electronic message recorded in a computer memory that could be printed from that memory could constitute a record. Similarly, a tape recording of an oral conversation could be a record.

9. Absent a specific agreement to the contrary, documents of a beneficiary delivered to an issuer or nominated person are considered to be presented under the letter of credit to which they refer, and any payment or value given for them is considered to be made under that letter of credit. As the court held in *Alaska Textile Co. v. Chase Manhattan Bank, N.A.*, 982 F.2d 813, 820 (2d Cir.1992), it takes a "significant showing" to make the presentation of a beneficiary's documents for "collection only" or otherwise outside letter of credit law and practice.

10. Although a successor of a beneficiary is one who succeeds "by operation of law," some of the successions contemplated by Section 5–102(a)(15) will have resulted from voluntary action of the beneficiary such as merger of a corporation. Any merger makes the successor corporation the "successor of a beneficiary" even though the transfer occurs partly by operation of law and partly by the voluntary action of the parties. The definition excludes certain transfers, where no part of the transfer is "by operation of law"—such as the sale of assets by one company to another.

11. "Draft" in Article 5 does not have the same meaning it has in Article 3. For example, a document may be a draft under Article 5 even though it would not be a negotiable instrument, and therefore would not qualify as a draft under Section 3–104(e).

§ 5103. Scope; changes to effect of division; rights and obligations of issuer

(a) This division applies to letters of credit and to certain rights and obligations arising out of transactions involving letters of credit.

(b) The statement of a rule in this division does not by itself require, imply, or negate application of the same or a different rule to a situation not provided for, or to a person not specified, in this division.

(c) With the exception of this subdivision, subdivisions (a) and (d), paragraphs 9 and 10 of subdivision (a) of Section 5102, subdivision (d) of Section 5106, and subdivision (d) of Section 5114, and except to the extent prohibited in subdivision (3) of Section 1102 and subdivision (d) of Section 5117, the effect of this division may be varied by agreement or by a provision stated or incorporated by reference in an undertaking.

A term in an agreement or undertaking generally excusing liability or generally limiting remedies for failure to perform obligations is not sufficient to vary obligations prescribed by this division.

(d) Rights and obligations of an issuer to a beneficiary or a nominated person under a letter of credit are independent of the existence, performance, or nonperformance of a contract or arrangement out of which the letter of credit arises or which underlies it, including contracts or arrangements between the issuer and the applicant and between the applicant and the beneficiary. *(Added by Stats.1996, c. 176 (S.B.1599), § 7.)*

Uniform Commercial Code Comment

1. Sections 5–102(a)(10) and 5–103 are the principal limits on the scope of Article 5. Many undertakings in commerce and contract are similar, but not identical to the letter of credit. Principal among those are "secondary," "accessory," or "suretyship" guarantees. Although the word "guarantee" is sometimes used to describe an independent obligation like that of the issuer of a letter of credit (most often in the case of European bank undertakings but occasionally in the case of undertakings of American banks), in the United States the word "guarantee" is more typically used to describe a suretyship transaction in which the "guarantor" is only secondarily liable and has the right to assert the underlying debtor's defenses. This article does not apply to secondary or accessory guarantees and it is important to recognize the distinction between letters of credit and those guarantees. It is often a defense to a secondary or accessory guarantor's liability that the underlying debt has been discharged or that the debtor has other defenses to the underlying liability. In letter of credit law, on the other hand, the independence principle recognized throughout Article 5 states that the issuer's liability is independent of the underlying obligation. That the beneficiary may have breached the underlying contract and thus have given a good defense on that contract to the applicant against the beneficiary is no defense for the issuer's refusal to honor. Only staunch recognition of this principle by the issuers and the courts will give letters of credit the continuing vitality that arises from the certainty and speed of payment under letters of credit. To that end, it is important that the law not carry into letter of credit transactions rules that properly apply only to secondary guarantees or to other forms of engagement.

2. Like all of the provisions of the Uniform Commercial Code, Article 5 is supplemented by Section 1–103 and, through it, by many rules of statutory and common law. Because this article is quite short and has no rules on many issues that will affect liability with respect to a letter of credit transaction, law beyond Article 5 will often determine rights and liabilities in letter of credit transactions. Even within letter of credit law, the article is far from comprehensive; it deals only with "certain" rights of the parties. Particularly with respect to the standards of performance that are set out in Section 5–108, it is appropriate for the parties and the courts to turn to customs and practice such as the Uniform Customs and Practice for Documentary Credits, currently published by the International Chamber of Commerce as I.C.C. Pub. No. 500 (hereafter UCP). Many letters of credit specifically adopt the UCP as applicable to the particular transaction. Where the UCP are adopted but conflict with Article 5 and except where variation is prohibited, the UCP terms are permissible contractual modifications under Sections 1–102(3) and 5–103(c). See Section 5–116(c). Normally Article 5 should not be considered to conflict with practice except when a rule explicitly stated in the UCP or other practice is different from a rule explicitly stated in Article 5.

Except by choosing the law of a jurisdiction that has not adopted the Uniform Commercial Code, it is not possible entirely to escape the Uniform Commercial Code. Since incorporation of the UCP avoids only "conflicting" Article 5 rules, parties who do not wish to be governed by the nonconflicting provisions of Article 5 must normally either adopt the law of a jurisdiction other than a State of the United States or state explicitly the rule that is to govern. When rules of custom and practice are incorporated by reference, they are considered to be explicit terms of the agreement or undertaking.

Neither the obligation of an issuer under Section 5–108 nor that of an adviser under Section 5–107 is an obligation of the kind that is invariable under Section 1–102(3). Section 5–103(c) and Comment 1 to Section 5–108 make it clear that the applicant and the issuer may agree to almost any provision establishing the obligations of the issuer to the applicant. The last sentence of subsection (c) limits the power of the issuer to achieve that result by a nonnegotiated disclaimer or limitation of remedy.

What the issuer could achieve by an explicit agreement with its applicant or by a term that explicitly defines its duty, it cannot accomplish by a general disclaimer. The restriction on disclaimers in the last sentence of subsection (c) is based more on procedural than on substantive unfairness. Where, for example, the reimbursement agreement provides explicitly that the issuer need not examine any documents, the applicant understands the risk it has undertaken. A term in a reimbursement agreement which states generally that an issuer will not be liable unless it has acted in "bad faith" or committed "gross negligence" is ineffective under Section 5–103(c). On the other hand, less general terms such as terms that permit issuer reliance on an oral or electronic message believed in good faith to have been received from the applicant or terms that entitle an issuer to reimbursement when it honors a "substantially" though not "strictly" complying presentation, are effective. In each case the question is whether the disclaimer or limitation is sufficiently clear and explicit in reallocating a liability or risk that is allocated differently under a variable Article 5 provision.

Of course, no term in a letter of credit, whether incorporated by reference to practice rules or stated specifically, can free an issuer from a conflicting contractual obligation to its applicant. If, for example, an issuer promised its applicant that it would pay only against an inspection certificate of a particular company but failed to require such a certificate in its letter of credit or made the requirement only a nondocumentary condition that had to be disregarded, the issuer might be obliged to pay the beneficiary even though its payment might violate its contract with its applicant.

3. Parties should generally avoid modifying the definitions in Section 5–102. The effect of such an agreement is almost inevitably unclear. To say that something is a "guarantee" in the typical domestic transaction is to say that the parties intend that particular legal rules apply to it. By acknowledging that something is a guarantee, but asserting that it is to be treated as a "letter of credit," the parties leave a court uncertain about where the rules on guarantees stop and those concerning letters of credit begin.

4. Section 5–102(2) and (3) of Article 5 are omitted as unneeded; the omission does not change the law.

§ 5104. Form requirements

A letter of credit, confirmation, advice, transfer, amendment, or cancellation may be issued in any form that is a record and is authenticated (i) by a signature or (ii) in accordance with the agreement of the parties or the standard practice referred to in subdivision (e) of Section 5108. *(Added by Stats.1996, c. 176 (S.B.1599), § 7.)*

Uniform Commercial Code Comment

1. Neither Section 5–104 nor the definition of letter of credit in Section 5–102(a)(10) requires inclusion of all the terms that are normally contained in a letter of credit in order for an undertaking to be recognized as a letter of credit under Article 5. For example, a letter of credit will typically specify the amount available, the expiration date, the place where presentation should be made, and the documents that must be presented to entitle a person to honor. Undertakings that have the formalities required by Section 5–104 and meet the conditions specified in Section 5–102(a)(10) will be recognized as letters of credit even though they omit one or more of the items usually contained in a letter of credit.

2. The authentication specified in this section is authentication only of the identity of the issuer, confirmer, or adviser.

An authentication agreement may be by system rule, by standard practice, or by direct agreement between the parties. The reference to practice is intended to incorporate future developments in the UCP and other practice rules as well as those that may arise spontaneously in commercial practice.

3. Many banking transactions, including the issuance of many letters of credit, are now conducted mostly by electronic means. For example, S.W.I.F.T. is currently used to transmit letters of credit from issuing to advising banks. The letter of credit text so transmitted may be printed at the advising bank, stamped "original" and provided to the beneficiary in that form. The printed document may then be used as a way of controlling and recording payments and of recording and authorizing assignments of proceeds or transfers of rights under the letter of credit. Nothing in this section should be construed to conflict with that practice.

To be a record sufficient to serve as a letter of credit or other undertaking under this section, data must have a durability consistent with that function. Because consideration is not required for a binding letter of credit or similar undertaking (Section 5–105) yet those undertakings are to be strictly construed (Section 5–108), parties to a letter of credit transaction are especially dependent on the continued availability of the terms and conditions of the letter of credit or other undertaking. By declining to specify any particular medium in which the letter of credit must be established or communicated, Section 5–104 leaves room for future developments.

Prior Uniform Statutory Provision:

None.

Purposes:

1. Subsection (1) is to make clear that, except for the statement or title required by Section 5–102(1)(c) to bring certain transactions within the scope of this Article, no particular form need be followed; it is sufficient that the credit is in writing and signed by the issuer. The subsection also states that any modification is subject to the same requirements of signing and writing. Compare Section 2–209(3) on sale of goods. Questions of mistake, waiver or estoppel are left to supplementary principles of law. See Section 1–103.

2. Subsection (2), although perhaps unnecessary in view of the definition of "signed" in Section 1–201, is inserted here to make certain that code and authorized naming of an issuer is a sufficient signing. These forms of signing are so customary that their explicit inclusion is useful to eliminate all controversy on the point.

Cross References:

Point 1: Sections 5–102, 2–209, 1–103.
Point 2: Section 1–201.

Definitional Cross References:

"Confirming bank". Section 5–103.
"Credit". Section 5–103.
"Issuer". Section 5–103.
"Signed". Section 1–201.
"Telegram". Section 1–201.
"Term". Section 1–201.
"Writing". Section 1–201.

Cross References

Breach of carrier's obligation to receive messages, see Civil Code § 3315.
Consideration, see Commercial Code § 5105.
Definitions, see Commercial Code § 1201.
Effect of written contract on negotiations or stipulations, see Civil Code § 1625.
Enforcement of contract oral by reason of fraud, see Civil Code § 1623.
Representation as to credit of third person; necessity of writing, see Code of Civil Procedure § 1974.
Sales, modification, rescission and waiver of terms of agreement, see Commercial Code § 2209.
Scope of division, see Commercial Code § 5102.
Statute of frauds, promise to answer for debt, default or miscarriage of another, see Civil Code § 1624.
Supplementary principles of law, application, see Commercial Code § 1103.

Telegraphic messages, order of transmission, see Civil Code § 2207.

§ 5105. Consideration

Consideration is not required to issue, amend, transfer, or cancel a letter of credit, advice, or confirmation. *(Added by Stats.1996, c. 176 (S.B.1599), § 7.)*

Uniform Commercial Code Comment

It is not to be expected that any issuer will issue its letter of credit without some form of remuneration. But it is not expected that the beneficiary will know what the issuer's remuneration was or whether in fact there was any identifiable remuneration in a given case. And it might be difficult for the beneficiary to prove the issuer's remuneration. This section dispenses with this proof and is consistent with the position of Lord Mansfield in *Pillans v. Van Mierop*, 97 Eng.Rep. 1035 (K.B. 1765) in making consideration irrelevant.

Prior Uniform Statutory Provision:

None.

Purposes:

It is not to be expected that a financial institution will engage its credit without some form of expected remuneration. But it is not expected that the beneficiary will know what the issuer's remuneration was, or whether in fact there was any identifiable remuneration in a given case. And it would be extraordinarily difficult for the beneficiary to *prove* the issuer's remuneration. This section dispenses with such proof.

Definitional Cross References:

"Credit". Section 5–103.
"Terms". Section 1–201.

Cross References

Cause or consideration,
  Generally, see Civil Code § 1605 et seq.
  Essential element of contract, see Civil Code § 1550.
Firm offers, lack of consideration, see Commercial Code § 2205.
Modification of sales contract without consideration, see Commercial Code § 2209.
Negotiable instruments, see Commercial Code § 3303.
Term "letter of credit" in contract of sale, see Commercial Code § 2325.
Value, see Commercial Code § 1201.
Waiver or renunciation of claim or right after breach without consideration, see Commercial Code § 1107.

§ 5106. Time of issuance; amendment, cancellation, or revocation; duration

(a) A letter of credit is issued and becomes enforceable according to its terms against the issuer when the issuer sends or otherwise transmits it to the person requested to advise or to the beneficiary. A letter of credit is revocable only if it so provides.

(b) After a letter of credit is issued, rights and obligations of a beneficiary, applicant, confirmer, and issuer are not affected by an amendment or cancellation to which that person has not consented except to the extent the letter of credit provides that it is revocable or that the issuer may amend or cancel the letter of credit without that consent.

(c) If there is no stated expiration date or other provision that determines its duration, a letter of credit expires one year after its stated date of issuance or, if none is stated, after the date on which it is issued.

(d) A letter of credit that states that it is perpetual expires five years after its stated date of issuance, or if

§ 5106

none is stated, after the date on which it is issued. *(Added by Stats.1996, c. 176 (S.B.1599), § 7.)*

Uniform Commercial Code Comment

1. This section adopts the position taken by several courts, namely that letters of credit that are silent as to revocability are irrevocable. See, e.g., *Weyerhaeuser Co. v. First Nat. Bank*, 27 UCC Rep.Serv. 777 (S.D. Iowa 1979); *West Va. Hous. Dev. Fund v. Sroka*, 415 F.Supp. 1107 (W.D.Pa.1976). This is the position of the current UCP (500). Given the usual commercial understanding and purpose of letters of credit, revocable letters of credit offer unhappy possibilities for misleading the parties who deal with them.

2. A person can consent to an amendment by implication. For example, a beneficiary that tenders documents for honor that conform to an amended letter of credit but not to the original letter of credit has probably consented to the amendment. By the same token an applicant that has procured the issuance of a transferable letter of credit has consented to its transfer and to performance under the letter of credit by a person to whom the beneficiary's rights are duly transferred. If some, but not all of the persons involved in a letter of credit transaction consent to performance that does not strictly conform to the original letter of credit, those persons assume the risk that other nonconsenting persons may insist on strict compliance with the original letter of credit. Under subsection (b) those not consenting are not bound. For example, an issuer might agree to amend its letter of credit or honor documents presented after the expiration date in the belief that the applicant has consented or will consent to the amendment or will waive presentation after the original expiration date. If that belief is mistaken, the issuer is bound to the beneficiary by the terms of the letter of credit as amended or waived, even though it may be unable to recover from the applicant.

In general, the rights of a recognized transferee beneficiary cannot be altered without the transferee's consent, but the same is not true of the rights of assignees of proceeds from the beneficiary. When the beneficiary makes a complete transfer of its interest that is effective under the terms for transfer established by the issuer, adviser, or other party controlling transfers, the beneficiary no longer has an interest in the letter of credit, and the transferee steps into the shoes of the beneficiary as the one with rights under the letter of credit. Section 5–102(a)(3). When there is a partial transfer, both the original beneficiary and the transferee beneficiary have an interest in performance of the letter of credit and each expects that its rights will not be altered by amendment unless it consents.

The assignee of proceeds under a letter of credit from the beneficiary enjoys no such expectation. Notwithstanding an assignee's notice to the issuer of the assignment of proceeds, the assignee is not a person protected by subsection (b). An assignee of proceeds should understand that its rights can be changed or completely extinguished by amendment or cancellation of the letter of credit. An assignee's claim is precarious, for it depends entirely upon the continued existence of the letter of credit and upon the beneficiary's preparation and presentation of documents that would entitle the beneficiary to honor under Section 5–108.

3. The issuer's right to cancel a revocable letter of credit does not free it from a duty to reimburse a nominated person who has honored, accepted, or undertaken a deferred obligation prior to receiving notice of the amendment or cancellation. Compare UCP Article 8.

4. Although all letters of credit should specify the date on which the issuer's engagement expires, the failure to specify an expiration date does not invalidate the letter of credit, or diminish or relieve the obligation of any party with respect to the letter of credit. A letter of credit that may be revoked or terminated at the discretion of the issuer by notice to the beneficiary is not "perpetual."

Cross References

Advice or confirmation of credit, see Commercial Code § 5107.
Alteration of instruments,
  Bank items, see Commercial Code § 4406.
  Bills of lading, see Commercial Code § 7306.
  Investment securities, see Commercial Code §§ 8206, 8306.
  Negotiable instruments, see Commercial Code §§ 3406, 3407, 3415.
  Warehouse receipts, see Commercial Code § 7208.
Cancellation, negotiable instruments, see Commercial Code §§ 3207, 3604.

Consideration unnecessary, see Commercial Code § 5105.
"Letter of credit" and "confirmed credit" defined, see Commercial Code § 2325.
Modification and cancellation of contracts, see Civil Code § 1697 et seq.
Modification of obligation in negotiable instrument, see Commercial Code § 3117.
Reimbursement, see Commercial Code § 5114.
Rescission, negotiable instruments, see Commercial Code § 3202.

§ 5107. Confirmer; rights and obligations; nominated person; adviser; notification of terms

(a) A confirmer is directly obligated on a letter of credit and has the rights and obligations of an issuer to the extent of its confirmation. The confirmer also has rights against and obligations to the issuer as if the issuer were an applicant and the confirmer had issued the letter of credit at the request and for the account of the issuer.

(b) A nominated person who is not a confirmer is not obligated to honor or otherwise give value for a presentation.

(c) A person requested to advise may decline to act as an adviser. An adviser that is not a confirmer is not obligated to honor or give value for a presentation. An adviser undertakes to the issuer and to the beneficiary accurately to advise the terms of the letter of credit, confirmation, amendment, or advice received by that person and undertakes to the beneficiary to check the apparent authenticity of the request to advise. Even if the advice is inaccurate, the letter of credit, confirmation, or amendment is enforceable as issued.

(d) A person who notifies a transferee beneficiary of the terms of a letter of credit, confirmation, amendment, or advice has the rights and obligations of an adviser under subdivision (c). The terms in the notice to the transferee beneficiary may differ from the terms in any notice to the transferor beneficiary to the extent permitted by the letter of credit, confirmation, amendment, or advice received by the person who so notifies. *(Added by Stats.1996, c. 176 (S.B.1599), § 7.)*

Uniform Commercial Code Comment

1. A confirmer has the rights and obligations identified in Section 5–108. Accordingly, unless the context otherwise requires, the terms "confirmer" and "confirmation" should be read into this article wherever the terms "issuer" and "letter of credit" appear.

A confirmer that has paid in accordance with the terms and conditions of the letter of credit is entitled to reimbursement by the issuer even if the beneficiary committed fraud (see Section 5–109(a)(1)(ii)) and, in that sense, has greater rights against the issuer than the beneficiary has. To be entitled to reimbursement from the issuer under the typical confirmed letter of credit, the confirmer must submit conforming documents, but the confirmer's presentation to the issuer need not be made before the expiration date of the letter of credit.

A letter of credit confirmation has been analogized to a guarantee of issuer performance, to a parallel letter of credit issued by the confirmer for the account of the issuer or the letter of credit applicant or both, and to a back-to-back letter of credit in which the confirmer is a kind of beneficiary of the original issuer's letter of credit. Like letter of credit undertakings, confirmations are both unique and flexible, so that no one of these analogies is perfect, but unless otherwise indicated in the letter of credit or confirmation, a confirmer should be viewed by the letter of credit issuer and the beneficiary as an issuer of a parallel letter of credit for the account of the original letter of credit issuer. Absent a direct agreement between the applicant and a confirmer, normally the obligations of a confirmer are to the issuer not the applicant, but the applicant might have a right to injunction against a confirmer under Section 5–109 or warranty claim under Section 5–110, and either might have claims against the other under Section 5–117.

2. No one has a duty to advise until that person agrees to be an adviser or undertakes to act in accordance with the instructions of the issuer. Except where there is a prior agreement to serve or where the silence of the adviser would be an acceptance of an offer to contract, a person's failure to respond to a request to advise a letter of credit does not in and of itself create any liability, nor does it establish a relationship of issuer and adviser between the two. Since there is no duty to advise a letter of credit in the absence of a prior agreement, there can be no duty to advise it timely or at any particular time. When the adviser manifests its agreement to advise by actually doing so (as is normally the case), the adviser cannot have violated any duty to advise in a timely way. This analysis is consistent with the result of *Sound of Market Street v. Continental Bank International*, 819 F.2d 384 (3d Cir.1987) which held that there is no such duty. This section takes no position on the reasoning of that case, but does not overrule the result. By advising or agreeing to advise a letter of credit, the adviser assumes a duty to the issuer and to the beneficiary accurately to report what it has received from the issuer, but, beyond determining the apparent authenticity of the letter, an adviser has no duty to investigate the accuracy of the message it has received from the issuer. "Checking" the apparent authenticity of the request to advise means only that the prospective adviser must attempt to authenticate the message (e.g., by "testing" the telex that comes from the purported issuer), and if it is unable to authenticate the message must report that fact to the issuer and, if it chooses to advise the message, to the beneficiary. By proper agreement, an adviser may disclaim its obligation under this section.

3. An issuer may issue a letter of credit which the adviser may advise with different terms. The issuer may then believe that it has undertaken a certain engagement, yet the text in the hands of the beneficiary will contain different terms, and the beneficiary would not be entitled to honor if the documents it submitted did not comply with the terms of the letter of credit as originally issued. On the other hand, if the adviser also confirmed the letter of credit, then as a confirmer it will be independently liable on the letter of credit as advised and confirmed. If in that situation the beneficiary's ultimate presentation entitled it to honor under the terms of the confirmation but not under those in the original letter of credit, the confirmer would have to honor but might not be entitled to reimbursement from the issuer.

4. When the issuer nominates another person to "pay," "negotiate," or otherwise to take up the documents and give value, there can be confusion about the legal status of the nominated person. In rare cases the person might actually be an agent of the issuer and its act might be the act of the issuer itself. In most cases the nominated person is not an agent of the issuer and has no authority to act on the issuer's behalf. Its "nomination" allows the beneficiary to present to it and earns it certain rights to payment under Section 5–109 that others do not enjoy. For example, when an issuer issues a "freely negotiable credit," it contemplates that banks or others might take up documents under that credit and advance value against them, and it is agreeing to pay those persons but only if the presentation to the issuer made by the nominated person complies with the credit. Usually there will be no agreement to pay, negotiate, or to serve in any other capacity by the nominated person, therefore the nominated person will have the right to decline to take the documents. It may return them or agree merely to act as a forwarding agent for the documents but without giving value against them or taking any responsibility for their conformity to the letter of credit.

Cross References

Definitions, see Commercial Code § 5103.
Issuer's obligation to its customer, see Commercial Code § 5109.
Letter of advice of international sight draft, see Commercial Code § 3701.

§ 5108. Issuer's obligations and rights

(a) Except as otherwise provided in Section 5109, an issuer shall honor a presentation that, as determined by the standard practice referred to in subdivision (e), appears on its face strictly to comply with the terms and conditions of the letter of credit. Except as otherwise provided in Section 5113 and unless otherwise agreed with the applicant, an issuer shall dishonor a presentation that does not appear so to comply.

(b) An issuer has a reasonable time after presentation, but not beyond the end of the seventh business day of the issuer after the day of its receipt of documents:

(1) to honor,

(2) if the letter of credit provides for honor to be completed more than seven business days after presentation, to accept a draft or incur a deferred obligation, or

(3) to give notice to the presenter of discrepancies in the presentation.

(c) Except as otherwise provided in subdivision (d), an issuer is precluded from asserting as a basis for dishonor any discrepancy if timely notice is not given, or any discrepancy not stated in the notice if timely notice is given.

(d) Failure to give the notice specified in subdivision (b) or to mention fraud, forgery, or expiration in the notice does not preclude the issuer from asserting as a basis for dishonor fraud or forgery as described in subdivision (a) of Section 5109 or expiration of the letter of credit before presentation.

(e) An issuer shall observe standard practice of financial institutions that regularly issue letters of credit. Determination of the issuer's observance of the standard practice is a matter of interpretation for the court. The court shall offer the parties a reasonable opportunity to present evidence of the standard practice.

(f) An issuer is not responsible for:

(1) the performance or nonperformance of the underlying contract, arrangement, or transaction,

(2) an act or omission of others, or

(3) observance or knowledge of the usage of a particular trade other than the standard practice referred to in subdivision (e).

(g) If an undertaking constituting a letter of credit under paragraph (10) of subdivision (a) of Section 5102 contains nondocumentary conditions, an issuer shall disregard the nondocumentary conditions and treat them as if they were not stated.

(h) An issuer that has dishonored a presentation shall return the documents or hold them at the disposal of, and send advice to that effect to, the presenter.

(i) An issuer that has honored a presentation as permitted or required by this division:

(1) is entitled to be reimbursed by the applicant in immediately available funds not later than the date of its payment of funds;

(2) takes the documents free of claims of the beneficiary or presenter;

(3) is precluded from asserting a right of recourse on a draft under Sections 3414 and 3415;

(4) except as otherwise provided in Sections 5110 and 5117, is precluded from restitution of money paid or other value given by mistake to the extent the mistake concerns discrepancies in the documents or tender which are apparent on the face of the presentation; and

(5) is discharged to the extent of its performance under the letter of credit unless the issuer honored a presentation in which a required signature of a beneficiary was forged. *(Added by Stats.1996, c. 176 (S.B. 1599), § 7.)*

Uniform Commercial Code Comment

1. This section combines some of the duties previously included in Sections 5–114 and 5–109. Because a confirmer has the rights and duties of an issuer, this section applies equally to a confirmer and an issuer. See Section 5–107(a).

The standard of strict compliance governs the issuer's obligation to the beneficiary and to the applicant. By requiring that a "presentation" appear strictly to comply, the section requires not only that the documents themselves appear on their face strictly to comply, but also that the other terms of the letter of credit such as those dealing with the time and place of presentation are strictly complied with. Typically, a letter of credit will provide that presentation is timely if made to the issuer, confirmer, or any other nominated person prior to expiration of the letter of credit. Accordingly, a nominated person that has honored a demand or otherwise given value before expiration will have a right to reimbursement from the issuer even though presentation to the issuer is made after the expiration of the letter of credit. Conversely, where the beneficiary negotiates documents to one who is not a nominated person, the beneficiary or that person acting on behalf of the beneficiary must make presentation to a nominated person, confirmer, or issuer prior to the expiration date.

This section does not impose a bifurcated standard under which an issuer's right to reimbursement might be broader than a beneficiary's right to honor. However, the explicit deference to standard practice in Section 5–108(a) and (e) and elsewhere expands issuers' rights of reimbursement where that practice so provides. Also, issuers can and often do contract with their applicants for expanded rights of reimbursement. Where that is done, the beneficiary will have to meet a more stringent standard of compliance as to the issuer than the issuer will have to meet as to the applicant. Similarly, a nominated person may have reimbursement and other rights against the issuer based on this article, the UCP, bank-to-bank reimbursement rules, or other agreement or undertaking of the issuer. These rights may allow the nominated person to recover from the issuer even when the nominated person would have no right to obtain honor under the letter of credit.

The section adopts strict compliance, rather than the standard that commentators have called "substantial compliance," the standard arguably applied in *Banco Español de Credito v. State Street Bank and Trust Company*, 385 F.2d 230 (1st Cir.1967) and *Flagship Cruises Ltd. v. New England Merchants Nat. Bank*, 569 F.2d 699 (1st Cir.1978). Strict compliance does not mean slavish conformity to the terms of the letter of credit. For example, standard practice (what issuers do) may recognize certain presentations as complying that an unschooled layman would regard as discrepant. By adopting standard practice as a way of measuring strict compliance, this article indorses the conclusion of the court in *New Braunfels Nat. Bank v. Odiorne*, 780 S.W.2d 313 (Tex.Ct. App. 1989) (beneficiary could collect when draft requested payment on "Letter of Credit No. 86–122–5" and letter of credit specified "Letter of Credit No. 86–122–S" holding strict compliance does not demand oppressive perfectionism). The section also indorses the result in *Tosco Corp. v. Federal Deposit Insurance Corp.*, 723 F.2d 1242 (6th Cir.1983). The letter of credit in that case called for "drafts Drawn under Bank of Clarksville Letter of Credit Number 105." The draft presented stated "drawn under Bank of Clarksville, Clarksville, Tennessee letter of Credit No. 105." The court correctly found that despite the change of upper case "L" to a lower case "l" and the use of the word "No." instead of "Number," and despite the addition of the words "Clarksville, Tennessee," the presentation conformed. Similarly a document addressed by a foreign person to General Motors as "Jeneral Motors" would strictly conform in the absence of other defects.

Identifying and determining compliance with standard practice are matters of interpretation for the court, not for the jury. As with similar rules in Sections 4A–202(c) and 2–302, it is hoped that there will be more consistency in the outcomes and speedier resolution of disputes if the responsibility for determining the nature and scope of standard practice is granted to the court, not to a jury. Granting the court authority to make these decisions will also encourage the salutary practice of courts' granting summary judgment in circumstances where there are no significant factual disputes. The statute encourages outcomes such as *American Coleman Co. v. Intrawest Bank*, 887 F.2d 1382 (10th Cir.1989), where summary judgment was granted.

In some circumstances standards may be established between the issuer and the applicant by agreement or by custom that would free the issuer from liability that it might otherwise have. For example, an applicant might agree that the issuer would have no duty whatsoever to examine documents on certain presentations (e.g., those below a certain dollar amount). Where the transaction depended upon the issuer's payment in a very short time period (e.g., on the same day or within a few hours of presentation), the issuer and the applicant might agree to reduce the issuer's responsibility for failure to discover discrepancies. By the same token, an agreement between the applicant and the issuer might permit the issuer to examine documents exclusively by electronic or electro-optical means. Neither those agreements nor others like them explicitly made by issuers and applicants violate the terms of Section 5–108(a) or (b) or Section 5–103(c).

2. Section 5–108(a) balances the need of the issuer for time to examine the documents against the possibility that the examiner (at the urging of the applicant or for fear that it will not be reimbursed) will take excessive time to search for defects. What is a "reasonable time" is not extended to accommodate an issuer's procuring a waiver from the applicant. See Article 14c of the UCP.

Under both the UCC and the UCP the issuer has a reasonable time to honor or give notice. The outside limit of that time is measured in business days under the UCC and in banking days under the UCP, a difference that will rarely be significant. Neither business nor banking days are defined in Article 5, but a court may find useful analogies in Regulation CC, 12 CFR 229.2, in state law outside of the Uniform Commercial Code, and in Article 4.

Examiners must note that the seven-day period is not a safe harbor. The time within which the issuer must give notice is the lesser of a reasonable time or seven business days. Where there are few documents (as, for example, with the mine run standby letter of credit), the reasonable time would be less than seven days. If more than a reasonable time is consumed in examination, no timely notice is possible. What is a "reasonable time" is to be determined by examining the behavior of those in the business of examining documents, mostly banks. Absent prior agreement of the issuer, one could not expect a bank issuer to examine documents while the beneficiary waited in the lobby if the normal practice was to give the documents to a person who had the opportunity to examine those together with many others in an orderly process. That the applicant has not yet paid the issuer or that the applicant's account with the issuer is insufficient to cover the amount of the draft is not a basis for extension of the time period.

This section does not preclude the issuer from contacting the applicant during its examination; however, the decision to honor rests with the issuer, and it has no duty to seek a waiver from the applicant or to notify the applicant of receipt of the documents. If the issuer dishonors a conforming presentation, the beneficiary will be entitled to the remedies under Section 5–111, irrespective of the applicant's views.

Even though the person to whom presentation is made cannot conduct a reasonable examination of documents within the time after presentation and before the expiration date, presentation establishes the parties' rights. The beneficiary's right to honor or the issuer's right to dishonor arises upon presentation at the place provided in the letter of credit even though it might take the person to whom presentation has been made several days to determine whether honor or dishonor is the proper course. The issuer's time for honor or giving notice of dishonor may be extended or shortened by a term in the letter of credit. The time for the issuer's performance may be otherwise modified or waived in accordance with Section 5–106.

The issuer's time to inspect runs from the time of its "receipt of documents." Documents are considered to be received only when they are received at the place specified for presentation by the issuer or other party to whom presentation is made.

Failure of the issuer to act within the time permitted by subsection (b) constitutes dishonor. Because of the preclusion in subsection (c) and the liability that the issuer may incur under Section 5–111 for wrongful dishonor, the effect of such a silent dishonor may ultimately be the same as though the issuer had honored, i.e., it may owe damages in the amount drawn but unpaid under the letter of credit.

3. The requirement that the issuer send notice of the discrepancies or be precluded from asserting discrepancies is new to Article 5. It is taken from the similar provision in the UCP and is intended to promote certainty and finality.

The section thus substitutes a strict preclusion principle for the doctrines of waiver and estoppel that might otherwise apply under Section 1–103. It rejects the reasoning in *Flagship Cruises Ltd. v. New England Merchants' Nat. Bank*, 569 F.2d 699 (1st Cir.1978) and *Wing On Bank Ltd. v. American Nat. Bank & Trust Co.*, 457 F.2d 328 (5th Cir.1972) where the issuer was held to be estopped only if the beneficiary relied on the issuer's failure to give notice.

Assume, for example, that the beneficiary presented documents to the issuer shortly before the letter of credit expired, in circumstances in which the beneficiary could not have cured any discrepancy before expiration. Under the reasoning of *Flagship* and *Wing On*, the beneficiary's inability to cure, even if it had received notice, would absolve the issuer of its failure to give notice. The virtue of the preclusion obligation adopted in this section is that it forecloses litigation about reliance and detriment.

Even though issuers typically give notice of the discrepancy of tardy presentation when presentation is made after the expiration of a credit, they are not required to give that notice and the section permits them to raise late presentation as a defect despite their failure to give that notice.

4. To act within a reasonable time, the issuer must normally give notice without delay after the examining party makes its decision. If the examiner decides to dishonor on the first day, it would be obliged to notify the beneficiary shortly thereafter, perhaps on the same business day. This rule accepts the reasoning in cases such as *Datapoint Corp. v. M & I Bank*, 665 F.Supp. 722 (W.D.Wis.1987) and *Esso Petroleum Canada, Div. of Imperial Oil, Ltd. v. Security Pacific Bank*, 710 F.Supp. 275 (D.Or.1989).

The section deprives the examining party of the right simply to sit on a presentation that is made within seven days of expiration. The section requires the examiner to examine the documents and make a decision and, having made a decision to dishonor, to communicate promptly with the presenter. Nevertheless, a beneficiary who presents documents shortly before the expiration of a letter of credit runs the risk that it will never have the opportunity to cure any discrepancies.

5. Confirmers, other nominated persons, and collecting banks acting for beneficiaries can be presenters and, when so, are entitled to the notice provided in subsection (b). Even nominated persons who have honored or given value against an earlier presentation of the beneficiary and are themselves seeking reimbursement or honor need notice of discrepancies in the hope that they may be able to procure complying documents. The issuer has the obligations imposed by this section whether the issuer's performance is characterized as "reimbursement" of a nominated person or as "honor."

6. In many cases a letter of credit authorizes presentation by the beneficiary to someone other than the issuer. Sometimes that person is identified as a "payor" or "paying bank," or as an "acceptor" or "accepting bank," in other cases as a "negotiating bank," and in other cases there will be no specific designation. The section does not impose any duties on a person other than the issuer or confirmer, however a nominated person or other person may have liability under this article or at common law if it fails to perform an express or implied agreement with the beneficiary.

7. The issuer's obligation to honor runs not only to the beneficiary but also to the applicant. It is possible that an applicant who has made a favorable contract with the beneficiary will be injured by the issuer's wrongful dishonor. Except to the extent that the contract between the issuer and the applicant limits that liability, the issuer will have liability to the applicant for wrongful dishonor under Section 5–111 as a matter of contract law. A good faith extension of the time in Section 5–108(b) by agreement between the issuer and beneficiary binds the applicant even if the applicant is not consulted or does not consent to the extension.

The issuer's obligation to dishonor when there is no apparent compliance with the letter of credit runs only to the applicant. No other party to the transaction can complain if the applicant waives compliance with terms or conditions of the letter of credit or agrees to a less stringent standard for compliance than that supplied by this article. Except as otherwise agreed with the applicant, an issuer may dishonor a noncomplying presentation despite an applicant's waiver.

Waiver of discrepancies by an issuer or an applicant in one or more presentations does not waive similar discrepancies in a future presentation. Neither the issuer nor the beneficiary can reasonably rely upon honor over past waivers as a basis for concluding that a future defective presentation will justify honor. The reasoning of *Courtaulds of North America Inc. v. North Carolina Nat. Bank*, 528 F.2d 802 (4th Cir.1975) is accepted and that expressed in *Schweibish v. Pontchartrain State Bank*, 389 So.2d 731 (La.App.1980) and *Titanium Metals Corp. v. Space Metals, Inc.*, 529 P.2d 431 (Utah 1974) is rejected.

8. The standard practice referred to in subsection (e) includes (i) international practice set forth in or referenced by the Uniform Customs and Practice, (ii) other practice rules published by associations of financial institutions, and (iii) local and regional practice. It is possible that standard practice will vary from one place to another. Where there are conflicting practices, the parties should indicate which practice governs their rights. A practice may be overridden by agreement or course of dealing. See Section 1–205(4).

9. The responsibility of the issuer under a letter of credit is to examine documents and to make a prompt decision to honor or dishonor based upon that examination. Nondocumentary conditions have no place in this regime and are better accommodated under contract or suretyship law and practice. In requiring that nondocumentary conditions in letters of credit be ignored as surplusage, Article 5 remains aligned with the UCP (see UCP 500 Article 13c), approves cases like *Pringle-Associated Mortgage Corp. v. Southern National Bank*, 571 F.2d 871, 874 (5th Cir.1978), and rejects the reasoning in cases such as *Sherwood & Roberts, Inc. v. First Security Bank*, 682 P.2d 149 (Mont. 1984).

Subsection (g) recognizes that letters of credit sometimes contain nondocumentary terms or conditions. Conditions such as a term prohibiting "shipment on vessels more than 15 years old," are to be disregarded and treated as surplusage. Similarly, a requirement that there be an award by a "duly appointed arbitrator" would not require the issuer to determine whether the arbitrator had been "duly appointed." Likewise a term in a standby letter of credit that provided for differing forms of certification depending upon the particular type of default does not oblige the issuer independently to determine which kind of default has occurred. These conditions must be disregarded by the issuer. Where the nondocumentary conditions are central and fundamental to the issuer's obligation (as for example a condition that would require the issuer to determine in fact whether the beneficiary had performed the underlying contract or whether the applicant had defaulted) their inclusion may remove the undertaking from the scope of Article 5 entirely. See Section 5–102(a)(10) and Comment 6 to Section 5–102.

Subsection (g) would not permit the beneficiary or the issuer to disregard terms in the letter of credit such as place, time, and mode of presentation. The rule in subsection (g) is intended to prevent an issuer from deciding or even investigating extrinsic facts, but not from consulting the clock, the calendar, the relevant law and practice, or its own general knowledge of documentation or transactions of the type underlying a particular letter of credit.

Even though nondocumentary conditions must be disregarded in determining compliance of a presentation (and thus in determining the issuer's duty to the beneficiary), an issuer that has promised its applicant that it will honor only on the occurrence of those nondocumentary conditions may have liability to its applicant for disregarding the conditions.

10. Subsection (f) condones an issuer's ignorance of "any usage of a particular trade"; that trade is the trade of the applicant, beneficiary, or others who may be involved in the underlying transaction. The issuer is expected to know usage that is commonly encountered in the course of document examination. For example, an issuer should know the common usage with respect to documents in the maritime shipping trade but would not be expected to understand synonyms used in a particular trade for product descriptions appearing in a letter of credit or an invoice.

§ 5108

11. Where the issuer's performance is the delivery of an item of value other than money, the applicant's reimbursement obligation would be to make the "item of value" available to the issuer.

12. An issuer is entitled to reimbursement from the applicant after honor of a forged or fraudulent drawing if honor was permitted under Section 5–109(a).

13. The last clause of Section 5–108(i)(5) deals with a special case in which the fraud is not committed by the beneficiary, but is committed by a stranger to the transaction who forges the beneficiary's signature. If the issuer pays against documents on which a required signature of the beneficiary is forged, it remains liable to the true beneficiary.

§ 5109. Forgery or material fraud; honor of presentation

(a) If a presentation is made that appears on its face strictly to comply with the terms and conditions of the letter of credit, but a required document is forged or materially fraudulent, or honor of the presentation would facilitate a material fraud by the beneficiary on the issuer or applicant:

(1) the issuer shall honor the presentation, if honor is demanded by (i) a nominated person who has given value in good faith and without notice of forgery or material fraud, (ii) a confirmer who has honored its confirmation in good faith, (iii) a holder in due course of a draft drawn under the letter of credit which was taken after acceptance by the issuer or nominated person, or (iv) an assignee of the issuer's or nominated person's deferred obligation that was taken for value and without notice of forgery or material fraud after the obligation was incurred by the issuer or nominated person; and

(2) the issuer, acting in good faith, may honor or dishonor the presentation in any other case.

(b) If an applicant claims that a required document is forged or materially fraudulent or that honor of the presentation would facilitate a material fraud by the beneficiary on the issuer or applicant, a court of competent jurisdiction may temporarily or permanently enjoin the issuer from honoring a presentation or grant similar relief against the issuer or other persons only if the court finds that:

(1) the relief is not prohibited under the law applicable to an accepted draft or deferred obligation incurred by the issuer;

(2) a beneficiary, issuer, or nominated person who may be adversely affected is adequately protected against loss that it may suffer because the relief is granted;

(3) all of the conditions to entitle a person to the relief under the law of this state have been met; and

(4) on the basis of the information submitted to the court, the applicant is more likely than not to succeed under its claim of forgery or material fraud and the person demanding honor does not qualify for protection under paragraph (1) of subdivision (a). *(Added by Stats.1996, c. 176 (S.B.1599), § 7.)*

Uniform Commercial Code Comment

1. This recodification makes clear that fraud must be found either in the documents or must have been committed by the beneficiary on the issuer or applicant. See *Cromwell v. Commerce & Energy Bank*, 464 So.2d 721 (La.1985).

Secondly, it makes clear that fraud must be "material." Necessarily courts must decide the breadth and width of "materiality." The use of the word requires that the fraudulent aspect of a document be material to a purchaser of that document or that the fraudulent act be significant to the participants in the underlying transaction. Assume, for example, that the beneficiary has a contract to deliver 1,000 barrels of salad oil. Knowing that it has delivered only 998, the beneficiary nevertheless submits an invoice showing 1,000 barrels. If two barrels in a 1,000 barrel shipment would be an insubstantial and immaterial breach of the underlying contract, the beneficiary's act, though possibly fraudulent, is not materially so and would not justify an injunction. Conversely, the knowing submission of those invoices upon delivery of only five barrels would be materially fraudulent. The courts must examine the underlying transaction when there is an allegation of material fraud, for only by examining that transaction can one determine whether a document is fraudulent or the beneficiary has committed fraud and, if so, whether the fraud was material.

Material fraud by the beneficiary occurs only when the beneficiary has no colorable right to expect honor and where there is no basis in fact to support such a right to honor. The section indorses articulations such as those stated in *Intraworld Indus. v. Girard Trust Bank*, 336 A.2d 316 (Pa.1975), *Roman Ceramics Corp. v. People's Nat. Bank*, 714 F.2d 1207 (3d Cir.1983), and similar decisions and embraces certain decisions under Section 5–114 that relied upon the phrase "fraud in the transaction." Some of these decisions have been summarized as follows in *Ground Air Transfer, Inc. v. Westate's Airlines, Inc.*, 899 F.2d 1269, 1272–73 (1st Cir.1990):

We have said throughout that courts may not *"normally"* issue an injunction because of an important exception to the general "no injunction" rule. The exception, as we also explained in Itek, 730 F.2d at 24–25, concerns "fraud" so serious as to make it obviously pointless and unjust to permit the beneficiary to obtain the money. Where the circumstances *"plainly"* show that the underlying contract forbids the beneficiary to call a letter of credit, Itek, 730 F.2d at 24; where they show that the contract deprives the beneficiary of even a *"colorable"* right to do so, id., at 25; where the contract and circumstances reveal that the beneficiary's demand for payment has "absolutely no basis in fact," id.; see Dynamics Corp. of America, 356 F.Supp. at 999; where the beneficiary's conduct has "so vitiated the entire transaction that the legitimate purposes of the independence of the issuer's obligation would no longer be served," Itek, 730 F.2d at 25 (quoting *Roman Ceramics Corp. v. Peoples National Bank*, 714 F.2d 1207, 1212 n.12, 1215 (3d Cir.1983) (quoting Intraworld Indus., 336 A.2d at 324–25)); *then* a court may enjoin payment.

2. Subsection (a)(2) makes clear that the issuer may honor in the face of the applicant's claim of fraud. The subsection also makes clear what was not stated in former Section 5–114, that the issuer may dishonor and defend that dishonor by showing fraud or forgery of the kind stated in subsection (a). Because issuers may be liable for wrongful dishonor if they are unable to prove forgery or material fraud, presumably most issuers will choose to honor despite applicant's claims of fraud or forgery unless the applicant procures an injunction. Merely because the issuer has a right to dishonor and to defend that dishonor by showing forgery or material fraud does not mean it has a duty to the applicant to dishonor. The applicant's normal recourse is to procure an injunction, if the applicant is unable to procure an injunction, it will have a claim against the issuer only in the rare case in which it can show that the issuer did not honor in good faith.

3. Whether a beneficiary can commit fraud by presenting a draft under a clean letter of credit (one calling only for a draft and no other documents) has been much debated. Under the current formulation it would be possible but difficult for there to be fraud in such a presentation. If the applicant were able to show that the beneficiary were committing material fraud on the applicant in the underlying transaction, then payment would facilitate a material fraud by the beneficiary on the applicant and honor could be enjoined. The courts should be skeptical of claims of fraud by one who has signed a "suicide" or clean credit and thus granted a beneficiary the right to draw by mere presentation of a draft.

4. The standard for injunctive relief is high, and the burden remains on the applicant to show, by evidence and not by mere allegation, that such relief is warranted. Some courts have enjoined payments on letters of credit on insufficient showing by the applicant. For example,

in *Griffin Cos. v. First Nat. Bank*, 374 N.W.2d 768 (Minn.App.1985), the court enjoined payment under a standby letter of credit, basing its decision on plaintiff's allegation, rather than competent evidence, of fraud.

There are at least two ways to prohibit injunctions against honor under this section after acceptance of a draft by the issuer. First is to define honor (see Section 5–102(a)(8)) in the particular letter of credit to occur upon acceptance and without regard to later payment of the acceptance. Second is explicitly to agree that the applicant has no right to an injunction after acceptance—whether or not the acceptance constitutes honor.

5. Although the statute deals principally with injunctions against honor, it also cautions against granting "similar relief" and the same principles apply when the applicant or issuer attempts to achieve the same legal outcome by injunction against presentation (see *Ground Air Transfer, Inc. v. Westates Airlines, Inc.*, 899 F.2d 1269 (1st Cir.1990)), interpleader, declaratory judgment, or attachment. These attempts should face the same obstacles that face efforts to enjoin the issuer from paying. Expanded use of any of these devices could threaten the independence principle just as much as injunctions against honor. For that reason courts should have the same hostility to them and place the same restrictions on their use as would be applied to injunctions against honor. Courts should not allow the "sacred cow of equity to trample the tender vines of letter of credit law."

6. Section 5–109(a)(1) also protects specified third parties against the risk of fraud. By issuing a letter of credit that nominates a person to negotiate or pay, the issuer (ultimately the applicant) induces that nominated person to give value and thereby assumes the risk that a draft drawn under the letter of credit will be transferred to one with a status like that of a holder in due course who deserves to be protected against a fraud defense.

7. The "loss" to be protected against—by bond or otherwise under subsection (b)(2)—includes incidental damages. Among those are legal fees that might be incurred by the beneficiary or issuer in defending against an injunction action.

§ 5110. Warranties

(a) If its presentation is honored, the beneficiary warrants:

(1) to the issuer, any other person to whom presentation is made, and the applicant that there is no fraud or forgery of the kind described in subdivision (a) of Section 5109; and

(2) to the applicant that the drawing does not violate any agreement between the applicant and beneficiary or any other agreement intended by them to be augmented by the letter of credit.

(b) The warranties in subdivision (a) are in addition to warranties arising under Division 3 (commencing with Section 3101), Division 4 (commencing with Section 4101), Division 7 (commencing with Section 7101), and Division 8 (commencing with Section 8101) because of the presentation or transfer of documents covered by any of those divisions. *(Added by Stats.1996, c. 176 (S.B.1599), § 7.)*

Uniform Commercial Code Comment

1. Since the warranties in subsection (a) are not given unless a letter of credit has been honored, no breach of warranty under this subsection can be a defense to dishonor by the issuer. Any defense must be based on Section 5–108 or 5–109 and not on this section. Also, breach of the warranties by the beneficiary in subsection (a) cannot excuse the applicant's duty to reimburse.

2. The warranty in Section 5–110(a)(2) assumes that payment under the letter of credit is final. It does not run to the issuer, only to the applicant. In most cases the applicant will have a direct cause of action for breach of the underlying contract. This warranty has primary application in standby letters of credit or other circumstances where the applicant is not a party to an underlying contract with the beneficiary. It is not a warranty that the statements made on the presentation of the documents presented are truthful nor is it a warranty that the documents strictly comply under Section 5–108(a). It is a warranty that the beneficiary has performed all the acts expressly and implicitly necessary under any underlying agreement to entitle the beneficiary to honor. If, for example, an underlying sales contract authorized the beneficiary to draw only upon "due performance" and the beneficiary drew even though it had breached the underlying contract by delivering defective goods, honor of its draw would break the warranty. By the same token, if the underlying contract authorized the beneficiary to draw only upon actual default or upon its or a third party's determination of default by the applicant and if the beneficiary drew in violation of its authorization, then upon honor of its draw the warranty would be breached. In many cases, therefore, the documents presented to the issuer will contain inaccurate statements (concerning the goods delivered or concerning default or other matters), but the breach of warranty arises not because the statements are untrue but because the beneficiary's drawing violated its express or implied obligations in the underlying transaction.

3. The damages for breach of warranty are not specified in Section 5–111. Courts may find damage analogies in Section 2–714 in Article 2 and in warranty decisions under Articles 3 and 4.

Unlike wrongful dishonor cases—where the damages usually equal the amount of the draw—the damages for breach of warranty will often be much less than the amount of the draw, sometimes zero. Assume a seller entitled to draw only on proper performance of its sales contract. Assume it breaches the sales contract in a way that gives the buyer a right to damages but no right to reject. The applicant's damages for breach of the warranty in subsection (a)(2) are limited to the damages it could recover for breach of the contract of sale. Alternatively assume an underlying agreement that authorizes a beneficiary to draw only the "amount in default." Assume a default of $200,000 and a draw of $500,000. The damages for breach of warranty would be no more than $300,000.

§ 5111. Remedies; improper dishonor or repudiation

(a) If an issuer wrongfully dishonors or repudiates its obligation to pay money under a letter of credit before presentation, the beneficiary, successor, or nominated person presenting on its own behalf may recover from the issuer the amount that is the subject of the dishonor or repudiation. If the issuer's obligation under the letter of credit is not for the payment of money, the claimant may obtain specific performance or, at the claimant's election, recover an amount equal to the value of performance from the issuer. In either case, the claimant may also recover incidental but not consequential damages. The claimant is not obligated to take action to avoid damages that might be due from the issuer under this subdivision. If, although not obligated to do so, the claimant avoids damages, the claimant's recovery from the issuer must be reduced by the amount of damages avoided. The issuer has the burden of proving the amount of damages avoided. In the case of repudiation the claimant need not present any document.

(b) If an issuer wrongfully dishonors a draft or demand presented under a letter of credit or honors a draft or demand in breach of its obligation to the applicant, the applicant may recover damages resulting from the breach, including incidental but not consequential damages, less any amount saved as a result of the breach.

(c) If an adviser or nominated person other than a confirmer breaches an obligation under this article or a issuer breaches an obligation not covered in subdivi

§ 5111

(a) or (b), a person to whom the obligation is owed may recover damages resulting from the breach, including incidental but not consequential damages, less any amount saved as a result of the breach. To the extent of the confirmation, a confirmer has the liability of an issuer specified in this subdivision and subdivisions (a) and (b).

(d) An issuer, nominated person, or adviser who is found liable under subdivision (a), (b), or (c) shall pay interest on the amount owed thereunder from the date of wrongful dishonor or other appropriate date.

(e) Reasonable attorney's fees and other expenses of litigation must be awarded to the prevailing party in an action in which a remedy is sought under this article.

(f) Damages that would otherwise be payable by a party for breach of an obligation under this article may be liquidated by agreement or undertaking, but only in an amount or by a formula that is reasonable in light of the harm anticipated. *(Added by Stats.1996, c. 176 (S.B.1599), § 7.)*

Uniform Commercial Code Comment

1. The right to specific performance is new. The express limitation on the duty of the beneficiary to mitigate damages adopts the position of certain courts and commentators. Because the letter of credit depends upon speed and certainty of payment, it is important that the issuer not be given an incentive to dishonor. The issuer might have an incentive to dishonor if it could rely on the burden of mitigation falling on the beneficiary, (to sell goods and sue only for the difference between the price of the goods sold and the amount due under the letter of credit). Under the scheme contemplated by Section 5–111(a), the beneficiary would present the documents to the issuer. If the issuer wrongfully dishonored, the beneficiary would have no further duty to the issuer with respect to the goods covered by documents that the issuer dishonored and returned. The issuer thus takes the risk that the beneficiary will let the goods rot or be destroyed. Of course the beneficiary may have a duty of mitigation to the applicant arising from the underlying agreement, but the issuer would not have the right to assert that duty by way of defense or setoff. See Section 5–117(d). If the beneficiary sells the goods covered by dishonored documents or if the beneficiary sells a draft after acceptance but before dishonor by the issuer, the net amount so gained should be subtracted from the amount of the beneficiary's damages—at least where the damage claim against the issuer equals or exceeds the damage suffered by the beneficiary. If, on the other hand, the beneficiary suffers damages in an underlying transaction in an amount that exceeds the amount of the wrongfully dishonored demand (e.g., where the letter of credit does not cover 100 percent of the underlying obligation), the damages avoided should not necessarily be deducted from the beneficiary's claim against the issuer. In such a case, the damages would be the lesser of (i) the amount recoverable in the absence of mitigation (that is, the amount that is subject to the dishonor or repudiation plus any incidental damages) and (ii) the damages remaining after deduction for the amount of damages actually avoided.

A beneficiary need not present documents as a condition of suit for anticipatory repudiation, but if a beneficiary could never have obtained documents necessary for a presentation conforming to the letter of credit, the beneficiary cannot recover for anticipatory repudiation of the letter of credit. *Doelger v. Battery Park Bank*, 201 A.D. 515, 194 N.Y.S. 582 (1922) and *Decor by Nikkei Int'l, Inc. v. Federal Republic of Nigeria*, 497 F.Supp. 893 (S.D.N.Y.1980), aff'd, 647 F.2d 300 (2d Cir.1981), cert. denied, 454 U.S. 1148 (1982). The last sentence of subsection (c) does not expand the liability of a confirmer to persons to whom the confirmer would not otherwise be liable under Section 5–107.

Almost all letters of credit, including those that call for an acceptance, are "obligations to pay money" as that term is used in Section 5–111(a).

2. What damages "result" from improper honor is for the courts to decide. Even though an issuer pays a beneficiary in violation of Section 5–108(a) or of its contract with the applicant, it may have no liability to an applicant. If the underlying contract has been fully performed, the applicant may not have been damaged by the issuer's breach. Such a case would occur when *A* contracts for goods at $100 per ton, but, upon delivery, the market value of conforming goods has decreased to $25 per ton. If the issuer pays over discrepancies, there should be no recovery by *A* for the price differential if the issuer's breach did not alter the applicant's obligation under the underlying contract, i.e., to pay $100 per ton for goods now worth $25 per ton. On the other hand, if the applicant intends to resell the goods and must itself satisfy the strict compliance requirements under a second letter of credit in connection with its sale, the applicant may be damaged by the issuer's payment despite discrepancies because the applicant itself may then be unable to procure honor on the letter of credit where it is the beneficiary, and may be unable to mitigate its damages by enforcing its rights against others in the underlying transaction. Note that an issuer found liable to its applicant may have recourse under Section 5–117 by subrogation to the applicant's claim against the beneficiary or other persons.

One who inaccurately advises a letter of credit breaches its obligation to the beneficiary, but may cause no damage. If the beneficiary knows the terms of the letter of credit and understands the advice to be inaccurate, the beneficiary will have suffered no damage as a result of the adviser's breach.

3. Since the confirmer has the rights and duties of an issuer, in general it has an issuer's liability, see subsection (c). The confirmer is usually a confirming bank. A confirming bank often also plays the role of an adviser. If it breaks its obligation to the beneficiary, the confirming bank may have liability as an issuer or, depending upon the obligation that was broken, as an adviser. For example, a wrongful dishonor would give it liability as an issuer under Section 5–111(a). On the other hand a confirming bank that broke its obligation to advise the credit but did not commit wrongful dishonor would be treated under Section 5–111(c).

4. Consequential damages for breach of obligations under this article are excluded in the belief that these damages can best be avoided by the beneficiary or the applicant and out of the fear that imposing consequential damages on issuers would raise the cost of the letter of credit to a level that might render it uneconomic. *A fortiori* punitive and exemplary damages are excluded, however, this section does not bar recovery of consequential or even punitive damages for breach of statutory or common law duties arising outside of this article.

5. The section does not specify a rate of interest. It leaves the setting of the rate to the court. It would be appropriate for a court to use the rate that would normally apply in that court in other situations where interest is imposed by law.

6. The court must award attorney's fees to the prevailing party, whether that party is an applicant, a beneficiary, an issuer, a nominated person, or adviser. Since the issuer may be entitled to recover its legal fees and costs from the applicant under the reimbursement agreement, allowing the issuer to recover those fees from a losing beneficiary may also protect the applicant against undeserved losses. The party entitled to attorneys' fees has been described as the "prevailing party." Sometimes it will be unclear which party "prevailed," for example, where there are multiple issues and one party wins on some and the other party wins on others. Determining which is the prevailing party is in the discretion of the court. Subsection (e) authorizes attorney's fees in all actions where a remedy is sought "under this article." It applies even when the remedy might be an injunction under Section 5–109 or when the claimed remedy is otherwise outside of Section 5–111. Neither an issuer nor a confirmer should be treated as a "losing" party when an injunction is granted to the applicant over the objection of the issuer or confirmer; accordingly neither should be liable for fees and expenses in that case.

"Expenses of litigation" is intended to be broader than "costs." For example, expense of litigation would include travel expenses of witnesses, fees for expert witnesses, and expenses associated with taking depositions.

7. For the purposes of Section 5–111(f) "harm anticipated" must be anticipated at the time when the agreement that includes the liquidated damage clause is executed or at the time when the undertaking that includes the clause is issued. See Section 2A–504.

§ 5112. Transfers

(a) Except as otherwise provided in Section 5113, unless a letter of credit provides that it is transferable, the right of a beneficiary to draw or otherwise demand performance under a letter of credit may not be transferred.

(b) Even if a letter of credit provides that it is transferable, the issuer may refuse to recognize or carry out a transfer if:

(1) the transfer would violate applicable law; or

(2) the transferor or transferee has failed to comply with any requirement stated in the letter of credit or any other requirement relating to transfer imposed by the issuer which is within the standard practice referred to in subdivision (e) of Section 5108 or is otherwise reasonable under the circumstances. *(Added by Stats. 1996, c. 176 (S.B.1599), § 7.)*

Uniform Commercial Code Comment

1. In order to protect the applicant's reliance on the designated beneficiary, letter of credit law traditionally has forbidden the beneficiary to convey to third parties its right to draw or demand payment under the letter of credit. Subsection (a) codifies that rule. The term "transfer" refers to the beneficiary's conveyance of that right. Absent incorporation of the UCP (which make elaborate provision for partial transfer of a commercial letter of credit) or similar trade practice and absent other express indication in the letter of credit that the term is used to mean something else, a term in the letter of credit indicating that the beneficiary has the right to transfer should be taken to mean that the beneficiary may convey to a third party its right to draw or demand payment. Even in that case, the issuer or other person controlling the transfer may make the beneficiary's right to transfer subject to conditions, such as timely notification, payment of a fee, delivery of the letter of credit to the issuer or other person controlling the transfer, or execution of appropriate forms to document the transfer. A nominated person who is not a confirmer has no obligation to recognize a transfer.

The power to establish "requirements" does not include the right absolutely to refuse to recognize transfers under a transferable letter of credit. An issuer who wishes to retain the right to deny all transfers should not issue transferable letters of credit or should incorporate the UCP. By stating its requirements in the letter of credit an issuer may impose any requirement without regard to its conformity to practice or reasonableness. Transfer requirements of issuers and nominated persons must be made known to potential transferors and transferees to enable those parties to comply with the requirements. A common method of making such requirements known is to use a form that indicates the information that must be provided and the instructions that must be given to enable the issuer or nominated person to comply with a request to transfer.

2. The issuance of a transferable letter of credit with the concurrence of the applicant is *ipso facto* an agreement by the issuer and applicant to permit a beneficiary to transfer its drawing right and permit a nominated person to recognize and carry out that transfer without further notice to them. In international commerce, transferable letters of credit are often issued under circumstances in which a nominated person or adviser is expected to facilitate the transfer from the original beneficiary to a transferee and to deal with that transferee. In those circumstances it is the responsibility of the nominated person or adviser to establish procedures satisfactory to protect itself against double presentation or dispute about the right to draw under the letter of credit. Commonly such a person will control the transfer by requiring that the original letter of credit be given to it or by causing a paper copy marked as an original to be issued where the original letter of credit was electronic. By keeping possession of the original letter of credit the nominated person or adviser can minimize or entirely exclude the possibility that the original beneficiary could properly procure payment from another bank. If the letter of credit requires presentation of the original letter of credit itself, no other payment could be procured. In addition to imposing whatever requirements it considers appropriate to protect itself against double payment the person that is facilitating the transfer has a right to charge an appropriate fee for its activity.

"Transfer" of a letter of credit should be distinguished from "assignment of proceeds." The former is analogous to a novation or a substitution of beneficiaries. It contemplates not merely payment to but also performance by the transferee. For example, under the typical terms of transfer for a commercial letter of credit, a transferee could comply with a letter of credit transferred to it by signing and presenting its own draft and invoice. An assignee of proceeds, on the other hand, is wholly dependent on the presentation of a draft and invoice signed by the beneficiary.

By agreeing to the issuance of a transferable letter of credit, which is not qualified or limited, the applicant may lose control over the identity of the person whose performance will earn payment under the letter of credit.

§ 5113. Successor of beneficiary; rights and obligations

(a) A successor of a beneficiary may consent to amendments, sign and present documents, and receive payment or other items of value in the name of the beneficiary without disclosing its status as a successor.

(b) A successor of a beneficiary may consent to amendments, sign and present documents, and receive payment or other items of value in its own name as the disclosed successor of the beneficiary. Except as otherwise provided in subdivision (e), an issuer shall recognize a disclosed successor of a beneficiary as beneficiary in full substitution for its predecessor upon compliance with the requirements for recognition by the issuer of a transfer of drawing rights by operation of law under the standard practice referred to in subdivision (e) of Section 5108 or, in the absence of such a practice, compliance with other reasonable procedures sufficient to protect the issuer.

(c) An issuer is not obliged to determine whether a purported successor is a successor of a beneficiary or whether the signature of a purported successor is genuine or authorized.

(d) Honor of a purported successor's apparently complying presentation under subdivision (a) or (b) has the consequences specified in subdivision (i) of Section 5108 even if the purported successor is not the successor of a beneficiary. Documents signed in the name of the beneficiary or of a disclosed successor by a person who is neither the beneficiary nor the successor of the beneficiary are forged documents for the purposes of Section 5109.

(e) An issuer whose rights of reimbursement are not covered by subdivision (d) or substantially similar law and any confirmer or nominated person may decline to recognize a presentation under subdivision (b).

(f) A beneficiary whose name is changed after the issuance of a letter of credit has the same rights and obligations as a successor of a beneficiary under this section. *(Added by Stats.1996, c. 176 (S.B.1599), § 7.)*

Uniform Commercial Code Comment

This section affirms the result in *Pastor v. Nat. Republic Bank of Chicago*, 76 Ill.2d 139, 390 N.E.2d 894 (Ill.1979) and *Federal Deposit Insurance Co. v. Bank of Boulder*, 911 F.2d 1466 (10th Cir.1990).

An issuer's requirements for recognition of a successor's status might include presentation of a certificate of merger, a court order appointing a bankruptcy trustee or receiver, a certificate of appointment as bankruptcy trustee, or the like. The issuer is entitled to rely upon such documents which on their face demonstrate that presentation is made by a successor of a beneficiary. It is not obliged to make an independent investigation to determine the fact of succession.

§ 5114. Issuer's duty and privilege to honor; right of reimbursement

(1) An issuer must honor a draft or demand for payment that complies with the terms of the relevant credit regardless of whether the goods or documents conform to the underlying contract for sale or other contract between the customer and the beneficiary. The issuer is not excused from honor of the draft or demand by reason of an additional general term that all documents must be satisfactory to the issuer, but an issuer may require that specified documents must be satisfactory to it.

(2) Unless otherwise agreed, when documents appear on their face to comply with the terms of a credit but a required document does not in fact conform to the warranties made on the negotiation or transfer of a document of title (Section 7507) or of a certificated security (Section 8108) or is forged or fraudulent or there is fraud in the transaction:

(a) The issuer must honor the draft or demand for payment if honor is demanded by a negotiating bank or other holder of the draft or demand which has taken the draft or demand under the credit and under circumstances which would make it a holder in due course (Section 3302) and in an appropriate case would make it a person to whom a document of title has been duly negotiated (Section 7501) or a bona fide purchaser of a certificated security (Section 8302).

(b) In all other cases as against its customer, an issuer acting in good faith may honor the draft or demand for payment despite notification from the customer of fraud, forgery or other defect not apparent on the face of the documents.

(3) Unless otherwise agreed, an issuer which has duly honored a draft or demand for payment is entitled to immediate reimbursement of any payment made under the credit and to be put in effectively available funds not later than the day before maturity of any acceptance made under the credit. (Stats.1963, c. 819, § 5114. Amended by Stats.1984, c. 927, § 4; Stats.1994, c. 611 (S.B.1612), § 4, eff. Sept. 16, 1994; Stats.1996, c. 497 (S.B.1591), § 7, operative Jan. 1, 1997.)

For another section of the same number, added by Stats.1996, c. 176 (S.B.1599), § 7, see Commercial Code § 5114, post.

California Code Comment

By John A. Bohn and Charles J. Williams

Prior California Law

1. This section is new. The problem with which this section deals is described in this statement:

"Section 15114 [5114] deals with the difficult problem which arises when a buyer asserts that the seller has breached the underlying sales contract, but the issuing bank has received documents fully complying with the requirements of the letter of credit along with a draft for payment. Without a court order, the bank may pay the draft despite the buyer's allegations, since, as this section provides, the letter of credit requires only documents. In addition, a holder in due course of the draft would be entitled to payment regardless of any breach of the underlying transaction." California State Bar Committee on the Commercial Code, A Special Report, The Uniform Commercial Code, 37 Calif.State Bar J. (March–April, 1962) pp. 172–173.

2. Subdivision (1) reflects the concept that the letter of credit is independent from the underlying sales contract. This is in accord with prior California law:

"On the question of the interaction of the letter of credit and the underlying commercial transaction, the California decisions accord with Section 11514(1) [sic] [5114(1)] of the bill and hold the issuer liable on the letter of credit even though there has been a breach of the underlying commercial transaction. Continental National Bank, et al v. National City Bank of New York, 69 F.2d 312 (9th Cir. 1934), Cert. denied, 293 U.S. 557, 55 S.Ct. 69, 97 L.Ed. 659; Crocker First National Bank of San Francisco v. De Sousa, supra; Banco National De Credito Ejidal, S.A. v. Bank of America et al, supra." Preliminary Report of the [State Bar] UCC Subcommittee on Articles [Divisions] 1 and 5. Sixth Progress Report to the Legislature by Senate Fact Finding Committee on Judiciary, (1959–1961) Part 1, The Uniform Commercial Code, p. 335.

3. Subdivision (2)(a) requires the issuer to honor a draft even if the documents are faulty in one of the ways listed but are proper on their face. This supplements the general statement of the issuer's obligation in Commercial Code § 5109(2) that the issuer is not responsible for the genuineness of the document but only that, on its face, it comply with the terms of the credit. The requirement to honor is limited to the case where an intermediary bank is the presenter and qualifies under the section listed in this provision. See Official Comment 2 for explanation of purpose and application of subdivision (2)(a).

4. While honor in subdivision (2)(a) is mandatory on the issuer, honor in subdivision (2)(b) is permissive. This permits the bank to honor or dishonor the draft or demand in good faith without incurring liability in cases other than stated in subdivision (2)(a).

5. Subdivision (3) states the standard form of reimbursement. Official Comment 3. This is also in accord with Article 8, Uniform Customs and Practice for Documentary Credits (1962 Revision).

Changes from U.C.C. (1962 Official Text)

6. The phrase "but a court of appropriate jurisdiction may enjoin such honor," which appears at the end of subdivision 2(b) of the 1962 Official Text is omitted.

This provision for a protective injunction was omitted because:

"By giving the courts power to enjoin the honor of drafts drawn upon documents which appear to be regular on their face, the Commissioners on Uniform State Laws do violence to one of the basic concepts of the letter of credit, to wit, that the letter of credit agreement is independent of the underlying commercial transaction. However, the injunction would give the customer protection he probably would not have under California law and it probably would not create legal problems for banks although it might strain business relations between corresponding banks." Preliminary Report of the [State Bar] UCC Subcommittee on Articles [Divisions] 1 and 5. Sixth Progress Report to the Legislature by Senate Fact Finding Committee on Judiciary, (1959–1961), Part 1, The Uniform Commercial Code, p. 337.

The reasons for this change in the California version are stated even more strongly by the State Bar Committee:

"The decisions are not clear as to whether a buyer can now obtain an injunction against the bank to prevent it from honoring a draft presented by one other than a holder in due course, if the buyer establishes fraud by the seller. [Footnote: See 3 N.Y.Law Rev.Comm., Study of the Uniform Commercial Code, 1667–1670 (1955).] In such a case, except as against a holder in due course, the Official Text of section 15114 [5114] would provide that 'a court of appropriate jurisdiction may enjoin such honor.'

"The State Bar Committee and the Advisory Committee believe this part of section 15114 [5114] would undermine the parties' basic understanding of a letter of credit transaction, namely that the seller is assured of payment upon tender of the called for documents, and that the buyer must sue the seller in his own country for any claimed breach of contract. To permit a court to enjoin the honor of the draft would throw the burden on the seller of litigating in the buyer's country whenever the buyer raised a claim of 'fraud.' For this reason, this provision is contrary to one of the basic concepts of the letter of credit: its independence of the underlying commercial transaction. This part of section 15114 [5114] is therefore not in S.B. 1093 [1961 Session, 1958 Official text as amended]" California State Bar Committee on the Commercial Code, A Special Report, The Uniform Commercial Code, 37 Calif.State Bar J. (March–April, 1962) p. 173.

Professors Marsh and Warren explore the policy problem raised by the State Bar Committee recommendations:

"The last portion of clause (b) under consideration involves the following type of situation: A, a buyer, procures a letter of credit from his bank, the X Bank, in California, and sends it to B, a seller, in a foreign country, to induce B to sell goods to him. The drafts under the letter of credit are to be paid if accompanied by bills of lading showing the shipment of the goods ordered, which are pineapples. The X Bank receives from B or his agent a draft drawn under the letter of credit with bills of lading attached which are perfectly in order. A, however, notifies the X Bank that he has information that B has actually shipped barrels of bones rather than pineapples. The X Bank may tell A, as provided in the first part of this clause, 'We deal only with documents, and therefore we must honor the draft.' A then to court to enjoin such honor.

"There can be no doubt that if A, the X Bank and B were all before the court, the court could issue such injunction. The crucial question is, can it do so in the absence of B, whom it will almost always be impossible to serve? See 3 N.Y.Law Rev.Comm., Study of the Uniform Commercial Code (1955) 1667–1670. This question the Code provision wholly fails to answer, but conceals in the ambiguous phrase 'court of appropriate jurisdiction.' It may be that the answer is suggested by the use of this phrase, since there would normally be *no* court with jurisdiction over both the issuing bank and the seller-beneficiary, and the provision implies that there must be some court with 'jurisdiction.' Surely, however, it is better to answer this question frankly, and not leave the result to any such tenuous argument. Despite the criticism of the 1952 Text of the Code for failure to answer this question, no improvement was made in the 1956 Text in this regard.

"We have found no case which supports the assertion of the State Bar Committee that under 'present California law' an injunction would not issue in the circumstances. There are cases in New York in which such an injunction has been issued, by Professor Schlesinger concludes that a permanent injunction in the absence of the beneficiary is probably improper in New York. 3 N.Y.Law Rev.Comm., Study of the Uniform Commercial Code (1955) 1669.

"In order to resolve this policy question, it is important to keep in mind the reason for the issuance of the letter of credit in the first place. It is because the seller wants assurance of being paid without equivocation, and the essence of the transaction is that it throws the risk on the buyer of pursuing the seller in his own country with any claim of breach of contract. It seems improper to destroy this basic understanding of the parties whenever the buyer raises a claim of 'fraud.' If the injunction is issued, then the seller must pursue the buyer in his own country in a breach of contract action. Certainly the issuing bank will not adequately represent the seller in the injunction action, since it is merely in the position of a stake holder and, if it is protected by an injunction, it doesn't care who wins. If anything, the bank is on the side of the buyer, since, if the claims of fraud is true, its security in the goods is impaired.

"It is suggested that no permanent injunction should be issued in the absence of the seller-beneficiary, but that the buyer does need the protection of a temporary injunction until such time as he can institute an action in the seller's country. The goods may be on the high seas, and if he has no means of preventing payment of the draft until an investigation can be made, he has to reimburse the bank, and he may never be able to recover the money from the seller even though the documents submitted were entirely fraudulent." Sixth Progress Report to the Legislature by Senate Fact Finding Committee on Judiciary (1959–1961) Part 1, The Uniform Commercial Code, pp. 494–495.

7. Subdivisions (4) and (5) of section 5–114 of the 1962 Official Text are optional provisions which are omitted in the California version. They provide as follows:

"[(4) When a credit provides for payment by the issuer on receipt of notice that the required documents are in the possession of a correspondent or other agent of the issuer

"(a) any payment made on receipt of such notice is conditional; and

"(b) the issuer may reject documents which do not comply with the credit if it does so within three banking days following its receipt of the documents; and

(c) in the event of such rejection, the issuer is entitled by charge back of otherwise to return of the payment made.]

"[(5) In the case covered by subsection (4) failure to reject documents within the time specified in sub-paragraph (b) constitutes acceptance of the documents and makes the payment final in favor of the beneficiary.]"

Subdivisions (4) and (5) were deleted from the California version for the following reason:

". . . The issuing bank, in selecting an agent to receive the documents in its behalf, ought to accept the risk of proper performance by that agent and, in the case of improper performance, assert its claim against the agent—in any event, not against the beneficiary." California Banker's Association Committee on Uniform Commercial Code, Sixth Progress Report to the Legislature by the Senate Fact Finding Committee on Judiciary, (1959–1961) Part 1, The Uniform Commercial Code p. 409.

Uniform Commercial Code Comment
1977 Amendment

Subsec. (2) (a) was amended in 1977 to conform to Revised Article 8 of the Code. The 1977 amendment added the word "certificated" preceding "security" in two instances to conform to the new definitions in revised section 8–102.

Uniform Commercial Code Comment

Prior Uniform Statutory Provision:
None.

Purposes:

To define the areas in which the issuer must honor drafts or demands for payment under a credit and those in which he has an option to do so and to make explicit the customer's duty of reimbursement.

1. The letter of credit is essentially a contract between the issuer and the beneficiary and is recognized by this Article as independent of the underlying contract between the customer and the beneficiary (See Section 5–109 and Comment thereto). In view of this independent nature of the letter of credit engagement, the issuer is under a duty to honor the drafts or demands for payment which in fact comply with the terms of the credit without reference to their compliance with the terms of the underlying contract. This is stated in subsection (1). Attempts by the issuer to reserve a right to dishonor by including a clause that all documents must be satisfactory to itself are declared invalid as essentially repugnant to an irrevocable letter of credit. Such a reservation can be made by issuing a revocable credit. See Section 5–106. Particular documents, such as bills of lading or inspection or weight certificates can, of course, be required to be satisfactory to the issuer. The duty of the issuer to honor where there is factual compliance with the terms of the credit is also independent of any instructions from its customer once the credit has been issued and received by the beneficiary. See Section 5–106.

2. Documents, however, may appear regular on their face and apparently conforming to the credit whereas in fact they are forged or fraudulent or in other respects non-conforming to the warranties which arise under other Articles of the Code on their transfer or negotiation. Since the issuer's duties to its customer are limited to examination of the documents with care (Section 5–109) and since it is important to preserve both the independent character of the issuer's engagement and the reasonable reliance on that engagement of persons dealing with papers regular on their face and in apparent compliance with the terms of the credit, subsection (2)(a) includes as an area in which the issuer's duty to honor exists cases in which persons have acted in a manner which would make them the equivalent of holders in due course under Article 3 or, where relevant, persons to whom documents have been duly negotiated under Article 7 or bona fide purchasers of securities under Article 8. The risk of the original bad-faith action of the beneficiary is thus thrown upon the customer who selected him rather than upon innocent third parties or the issuer. So, too, is the risk of fraud in the transaction placed upon the customer.

When, however, no innocent third parties as defined in subsection (a) are involved the issuer is no longer under a duty to honor; but since

§ 5114　　　　　　　LETTERS OF CREDIT　　　　　　324

these matters frequently involve situations in which the determination of the fact of the non-conformance may be difficult or time-consuming, the issuer if he acts in good faith is given the privilege of honoring the draft as against its customer, that is to say, with a right of reimbursement against him. The issuer may, however, refuse honor. In the event of honor, an action by the customer against the beneficiary will lie by virtue of either the underlying contract or Section 5–111(1) of this Article. In the event of dishonor, if the presenter is a person who has parted with value, he also may recover against the beneficiary under Section 5–111(1).

3. Subsection (3) represents the standard form for reimbursement. The words "duly honored" include not only situations where the issuer has honored because it was his duty to do so but also where he was privileged to do so as in subsection (2)(b) or has done so as under Section 5–106(4).

4. Optional subsections (4) and (5) [inapplicable in California, see California Code Comment, note 7] are for the purpose of clarifying a situation which has arisen under the currency restrictions of a few nations and in which payment is required to be made under the credit before opportunity exists to examine the documents. The Article resolves this situation by making clear that the payment is conditional in nature and may be reversed by subsequent timely discovery of defects in the documents.

Cross References:

Point 1: Sections 5–106 and 5–109.
Point 2: Sections 5–106, 5–109, 5–111 and Articles 3, 7 and 8.
Point 3: Section 5–106.

Definitional Cross References:

"Bank". Section 1–201.
"Beneficiary". Section 5–103.
"Contract". Section 1–201.
"Contract for sale". Section 2–106.
"Credit". Section 5–103.
"Customer". Section 5–103.
"Document". Section 5–103.
"Document of title". Section 1–201.
"Draft". Section 3–104.
"Good faith". Section 1–201.
"Holder". Section 1–201.
"Honor". Section 1–201.
"Issuer". Section 5–103.
"Notification". Section 1–201.
"Receives notice". Section 1–201.
"Security". Section 8–102.
"Term". Section 1–201.

Cross References

Commercial paper, see Commercial Code § 3101 et seq.
Documents of title,
　Generally, see Commercial Code § 7101 et seq.
　Warranties, see Commercial Code §§ 7507, 7508.
Establishment of credit, time and effect, see Commercial Code § 5106.
Investment securities,
　Generally, see Commercial Code § 8101 et seq.
　Warranties, see Commercial Code § 8306.
Issuer's obligation to its customer, see Commercial Code § 5109.
Reimbursement, see Commercial Code § 5106(4).
Warranties on presentment and transfer, see Commercial Code § 5111.

§ 5114. Assignment of proceeds

(a) In this section, "proceeds of a letter of credit" means the cash, check, accepted draft, or other item of value paid or delivered upon honor or giving of value by the issuer or any nominated person under the letter of credit. The term does not include a beneficiary's drawing rights or documents presented by the beneficiary.

(b) A beneficiary may assign its right to part or all of the proceeds of a letter of credit. The beneficiary may do so before presentation as a present assignment of its right to receive proceeds contingent upon its compliance with the terms and conditions of the letter of credit.

(c) An issuer or nominated person need not recognize an assignment of proceeds of a letter of credit until it consents to the assignment.

(d) An issuer or nominated person has no obligation to give or withhold its consent to an assignment of proceeds of a letter of credit, but consent may not be unreasonably withheld if the assignee possesses and exhibits the letter of credit and presentation of the letter of credit is a condition to honor.

(e) Rights of a transferee beneficiary or nominated person are independent of the beneficiary's assignment of the proceeds of a letter of credit and are superior to the assignee's right to the proceeds.

(f) Neither the rights recognized by this section between an assignee and an issuer, transferee beneficiary, or nominated person nor the issuer's or nominated person's payment of proceeds to an assignee or third person affect the rights between the assignee and any person other than the issuer, transferee beneficiary, or nominated person. The mode of creating and perfecting a security interest in or granting an assignment of a beneficiary's rights to proceeds is governed by Division 9 (commencing with Section 9101) or other law. Against persons other than the issuer, transferee beneficiary, or nominated person, the rights and obligations arising upon the creation of a security interest or other assignment of a beneficiary's right to proceeds and its perfection are governed by Division 9 (commencing with Section 9101) or other law. *(Added by Stats.1996, c. 176 (S.B.1599), § 7.)*

For another section of the same number, amended by Stats.1996, c. 497 (S.B.1591), § 7, see Commercial Code § 5114, ante.

Uniform Commercial Code Comment

1. Subsection (b) expressly validates the beneficiary's present assignment of letter of credit proceeds if made after the credit is established but before the proceeds are realized. This section adopts the prevailing usage—"assignment of proceeds"—to an assignee. That terminology carries with it no implication, however, that an assignee acquires no interest until the proceeds are paid by the issuer. For example, an "assignment of the right to proceeds" of a letter of credit for purposes of security that meets the requirements of Section 9–203(1) would constitute the present creation of a security interest in that right. This security interest can be perfected by possession (Section 9–305) if the letter of credit is in written form. Although subsection (a) explains the meaning of "'proceeds' of a letter of credit," it should be emphasized that those proceeds also may be Article 9 proceeds of other collateral. For example, if a seller of inventory receives a letter of credit to support the account that arises upon the sale, payments made under the letter of credit are Article 9 proceeds of the inventory, account, and any document of title covering the inventory. Thus, the secured party who had a perfected security interest in that inventory, account, or document has a perfected security interest in the proceeds collected under the letter of credit, so long as they are identifiable cash proceeds (Section 9–306(2), (3)). This perfection is continuous, regardless of whether the secured party perfected a security interest in the right to letter of credit proceeds.

2. An assignee's rights to enforce an assignment of proceeds against an issuer and the priority of the assignee's rights against a nominated person or transferee beneficiary are governed by Article 5. Those rights and that priority are stated in subsections (c), (d), and (e). Note also that Section 4–210 gives first priority to a collecting bank that has given value for a documentary draft.

3. By requiring that an issuer or nominated person consent to the assignment of proceeds of a letter of credit, subsections (c) and (d) follow more closely recognized national and international letter of credit practices than did prior law. In most circumstances, it has always been advisable for the assignee to obtain the consent of the issuer in order better to safeguard its right to the proceeds. When notice of an assignment has received, issuers normally have required signatures on a consent form. This practice is reflected in the revision. By unconditionally consenting to such an assignment, the issuer or nominated person becomes bound, subject to the rights of the superior parties specified in subsection (e), to pay to the assignee the assigned letter of credit proceeds that the issuer or nominated person would otherwise pay to the beneficiary or another assignee.

Where the letter of credit must be presented as a condition to honor and the assignee holds and exhibits the letter of credit to the issuer or nominated person, the risk to the issuer or nominated person of having to pay twice is minimized. In such a situation, subsection (d) provides that the issuer or nominated person may not unreasonably withhold its consent to the assignment.

§ 5115. Limitation of actions

An action to enforce a right or obligation arising under this article must be commenced within one year after the expiration date of the relevant letter of credit or one year after the cause of action accrues, whichever occurs later. A cause of action accrues when the breach occurs, regardless of the aggrieved party's lack of knowledge of the breach. *(Added by Stats.1996, c. 176 (S.B.1599), § 7.)*

Uniform Commercial Code Comment

1. This section is based upon Sections 4–111 and 2–725(2).

2. This section applies to all claims for which there are remedies under Section 5–111 and to other claims made under this article, such as claims for breach of warranty under Section 5–110. Because it covers all claims under Section 5–111, the statute of limitations applies not only to wrongful dishonor claims against the issuer but also to claims between the issuer and the applicant arising from the reimbursement agreement. These might be for reimbursement (issuer v. applicant) or for breach of the reimbursement contract by wrongful honor (applicant v. issuer).

3. The statute of limitations, like the rest of the statute, applies only to a letter of credit issued on or after the effective date and only to transactions, events, obligations, or duties arising out of or associated with such a letter. If a letter of credit was issued before the effective date and an obligation on that letter of credit was breached after the effective date, the complaining party could bring its suit within the time that would have been permitted prior to the adoption of Section 5–115 and would not be limited by the terms of Section 5–115.

§ 5116. Governing law and forum

(a) The liability of an issuer, nominated person, or adviser for action or omission is governed by the law of the jurisdiction chosen by an agreement in the form of a record signed or otherwise authenticated by the affected parties in the manner provided in Section 5104 or by a provision in the person's letter of credit, confirmation, or other undertaking. The jurisdiction whose law is chosen need not bear any relation to the transaction.

(b) Unless subdivision (a) applies, the liability of an issuer, nominated person, or adviser for action or omission is governed by the law of the jurisdiction in which the person is located. The person is considered to be located at the address indicated in the person's undertaking. If more than one address is indicated, the person is considered to be located at the address from which the person's undertaking was issued. For the purpose of jurisdiction, choice of law, and recognition of interbranch letters of credit, but not enforcement of a judgment, all branches of a bank are considered separate juridical entities and a bank is considered to be located at the place where its relevant branch is considered to be located under this subdivision.

(c) Except as otherwise provided in this subdivision, the liability of an issuer, nominated person, or adviser is governed by any rules of custom or practice, such as the Uniform Customs and Practice for Documentary Credits, to which the letter of credit, confirmation, or other undertaking is expressly made subject. If (i) this article would govern the liability of an issuer, nominated person, or adviser under subdivision (a) or (b), (ii) the relevant undertaking incorporates rules of custom or practice, and (iii) there is conflict between this article and those rules applied to that undertaking, those rules govern except to the extent of any conflict with the nonvariable provisions specified in subdivision (c) of Section 5103.

(d) If there is conflict between this division and Division 3 (commencing with Section 3101), Division 4 (commencing with Section 4101), or Division 9 (commencing with Section 9101), this division governs.

(e) The forum for settling disputes arising out of an undertaking within this article may be chosen in the manner and with the binding effect that governing law may be chosen in accordance with subdivision (a). *(Added by Stats.1996, c. 176 (S.B.1599), § 7.)*

Uniform Commercial Code Comment

1. Although it would be possible for the parties to agree otherwise, the law normally chosen by agreement under subsection (a) and that provided in the absence of agreement under subsection (b) is the substantive law of a particular jurisdiction not including the choice of law principles of that jurisdiction. Thus, two parties, an issuer and an applicant, both located in Oklahoma might choose the law of New York. Unless they agree otherwise, the section anticipates that they wish the substantive law of New York to apply to their transaction and they do not intend that a New York choice of law principle might direct a court to Oklahoma law. By the same token, the liability of an issuer located in New York is governed by New York substantive law—in the absence of agreement—even in circumstances in which choice of law principles found in the common law of New York might direct one to the law of another State. Subsection (b) states the relevant choice of law principles and it should not be subordinated to some other choice of law rule. Within the States of the United States *renvoi* will not be a problem once every jurisdiction has enacted Section 5–116 because every jurisdiction will then have the same choice of law rule and in a particular case all choice of law rules will point to the same substantive law.

Subsection (b) does not state a choice of law rule for the "liability of an applicant." However, subsection (b) does state a choice of law rule for the liability of an issuer, nominated person, or adviser, and since some of the issues in suits by applicants against those persons involve the "liability of an issuer, nominated person, or adviser," subsection (b) states the choice of law rule for those issues. Because an issuer may have liability to a confirmer both as an issuer (Section 5–108(a), Comment 5 to Section 5–108) and as an applicant (Section 5–107(a), Comment 1 to Section 5–107, Section 5–108(i)), subsection (b) may

§ 5116

state the choice of law rule for some but not all of the issuer's liability in a suit by a confirmer.

2. Because the confirmer or other nominated person may choose different law from that chosen by the issuer or may be located in a different jurisdiction and fail to choose law, it is possible that a confirmer or nominated person may be obligated to pay (under their law) but will not be entitled to payment from the issuer (under its law). Similarly, the rights of an unreimbursed issuer, confirmer, or nominated person against a beneficiary under Section 5–109, 5–110, or 5–117, will not necessarily be governed by the same law that applies to the issuer's or confirmer's obligation upon presentation. Because the UCP and other practice are incorporated in most international letters of credit, disputes arising from different legal obligations to honor have not been frequent. Since Section 5–108 incorporates standard practice, these problems should be further minimized—at least to the extent that the same practice is and continues to be widely followed.

3. This section does not permit what is now authorized by the nonuniform Section 5–102(4) in New York. Under the current law in New York a letter of credit that incorporates the UCP is not governed in any respect by Article 5. Under revised Section 5–116 letters of credit that incorporate the UCP or similar practice will still be subject to Article 5 in certain respects. First, incorporation of the UCP or other practice does not override the nonvariable terms of Article 5. Second, where there is no conflict between Article 5 and the relevant provision of the UCP or other practice, both apply. Third, practice provisions incorporated in a letter of credit will not be effective if they fail to comply with Section 5–103(c). Assume, for example, that a practice provision purported to free a party from any liability unless it were "grossly negligent" or that the practice generally limited the remedies that one party might have against another. Depending upon the circumstances, that disclaimer or limitation of liability might be ineffective because of Section 5–103(c).

Even though Article 5 is generally consistent with UCP 500, it is not necessarily consistent with other rules or with versions of the UCP that may be adopted after Article 5's revision, or with other practices that may develop. Rules of practice incorporated in the letter of credit or other undertaking are those in effect when the letter of credit or other undertaking is issued. Except in the unusual cases discussed in the immediately preceding paragraph, practice adopted in a letter of credit will override the rules of Article 5 and the parties to letter of credit transactions must be familiar with practice (such as future versions of the UCP) that is explicitly adopted in letters of credit.

4. In several ways Article 5 conflicts with and overrides similar matters governed by Articles 3 and 4. For example, "draft" is more broadly defined in letter of credit practice than under Section 3–104. The time allowed for honor and the required notification of reasons for dishonor are different in letter of credit practice than in the handling of documentary and other drafts under Articles 3 and 4.

5. Subsection (e) must be read in conjunction with existing law governing subject matter jurisdiction. If the local law restricts a court to certain subject matter jurisdiction not including letter of credit disputes, subsection (e) does not authorize parties to choose that forum. For example, the parties' agreement under Section 5–116(e) would not confer jurisdiction on a probate court to decide a letter of credit case.

If the parties choose a forum under subsection (e) and if—because of other law—that forum will not take jurisdiction, the parties' agreement or undertaking should then be construed (for the purpose of forum selection) as though it did not contain a clause choosing a particular forum. That result is necessary to avoid sentencing the parties to eternal purgatory where neither the chosen State nor the State which would have jurisdiction but for the clause will take jurisdiction—the former in disregard of the clause and the latter in honor of the clause.

§ 5117. Subrogation

(a) An issuer that honors a beneficiary's presentation is subrogated to the rights of the beneficiary to the same extent as if the issuer were a secondary obligor of the underlying obligation owed to the beneficiary and of the applicant to the same extent as if the issuer were the secondary obligor of the underlying obligation owed to the applicant.

(b) An applicant that reimburses an issuer is subrogated to the rights of the issuer against any beneficiary, presenter, or nominated person to the same extent as if the applicant were the secondary obligor of the obligations owed to the issuer and has the rights of subrogation of the issuer to the rights of the beneficiary stated in subdivision (a).

(c) A nominated person who pays or gives value against a draft or demand presented under a letter of credit is subrogated to the rights of:

(1) the issuer against the applicant to the same extent as if the nominated person were a secondary obligor of the obligation owed to the issuer by the applicant;

(2) the beneficiary to the same extent as if the nominated person were a secondary obligor of the underlying obligation owed to the beneficiary; and

(3) the applicant to the same extent as if the nominated person were a secondary obligor of the underlying obligation owed to the applicant.

(d) Notwithstanding any agreement or term to the contrary, the rights of subrogation stated in subdivisions (a) and (b) do not arise until the issuer honors the letter of credit or otherwise pays and the rights in subdivision (c) do not arise until the nominated person pays or otherwise gives value. Until then, the issuer, nominated person, and the applicant do not derive under this section present or prospective rights forming the basis of a claim, defense, or excuse. *(Added by Stats.1996, c. 176 (S.B.1599), § 7.)*

Uniform Commercial Code Comment

1. By itself this section does not grant any right of subrogation. It grants only the right that would exist if the person seeking subrogation "were a secondary obligor." (The term "secondary obligor" refers to a surety, guarantor, or other person against whom or whose property an obligee has recourse with respect to the obligation of a third party. See Restatement of the Law Third, Suretyship and Guaranty § 1 (1996).) If the secondary obligor would not have a right to subrogation in the circumstances in which one is claimed under this section, none is granted by this section. In effect, the section does no more than to remove an impediment that some courts have found to subrogation because they conclude that the issuer's or other claimant's rights are "independent" of the underlying obligation. If, for example, a secondary obligor would not have a subrogation right because its payment did not fully satisfy the underlying obligation, none would be available under this section. The section indorses the position of Judge Becker in *Tudor Development Group, Inc. v. United States Fidelity and Guaranty*, 968 F.2d 357 (3rd Cir.1991).

2. To preserve the independence of the letter of credit obligation and to insure that subrogation not be used as an offensive weapon by an issuer or others, the admonition in subsection (d) must be carefully observed. Only one who has completed its performance in a letter of credit transaction can have a right to subrogation. For example, an issuer may not dishonor and then defend its dishonor or assert a setoff on the ground that it is subrogated to another person's rights. Nor may the issuer complain after honor that its subrogation rights have been impaired by any good faith dealings between the beneficiary and the applicant or any other person. Assume, for example, that the beneficiary under a standby letter of credit is a mortgagee. If the mortgagee were obliged to issue a release of the mortgage upon payment of the underlying debt (by the issuer under the letter of credit), that release might impair the issuer's rights of subrogation, but the beneficiary would have no liability to the issuer for having granted that release.

APPENDIX TO DIVISION 5—LETTERS OF CREDIT

Section
5101. Short Title.
5102. Scope.
5103. Definitions.
5104. Formal Requirements; Signing.
5105. Consideration,.
5106. Time and Effect of Establishment of Credit.
5107. Advice of Credit; Confirmation; Error in Statement of Terms.
5108. "Notation Credit"; Exhaustion of Credit.
5109. Issuer's Obligation to Its Customer.
5110. Availability of Credit in Portions; Presenter's Reservation of Lien or Claim.
5111. Warranties on Transfer and Presentment.
5112. Time Allowed for Honor or Rejection; Withholding Honor or Rejection by Consent; "Presenter".
5113. Indemnities.
5114. Issuer's duty and privilege to honor; right of reimbursement.
5115. Remedy for Improper Dishonor or Anticipatory Repudiation.
5116. Transfer and assignment.
5117. Insolvency of Bank Holding Funds for Documentary Credit.

This Appendix contains former Division 5 of the Commercial Code, Letters of Credit, repealed by Stats.1996, c. 176 (S.B.1599). Application of former Division 5 to letters of credit issued before the effective date of act, see §§ 14 and 15 of that act.

§ 5101. Short Title

This division shall be known and may be cited as Uniform Commercial Code—Letters of Credit. *(Stats. 1963, c. 819, § 5101.)*

§ 5102. Scope

(1) This division applies

(a) To a credit issued by a bank if the credit requires a documentary draft or a documentary demand for payment; and

(b) To a credit issued by a person other than a bank if the credit requires that the draft or demand for payment be accompanied by a document of title; and

(c) To a credit issued by a bank or other person if the credit is not within paragraph (a) or (b) but conspicuously states that it is a letter of credit or is conspicuously so entitled.

(2) Unless the engagement meets the requirements of subdivision (1), this division does not apply to engagements to make advances or to honor drafts or demands for payment, to authorities to pay or purchase, to guarantees or to general agreements.

(3) This division deals with some but not all of the rules and concepts of letters of credit as such rules or concepts have developed prior to this act or may hereafter develop. The fact that this division states a rule does not by itself require, imply or negate application of the same or a converse rule to a situation not provided for or to a person not specified by this division. *(Stats.1963, c. 819, § 5102.)*

§ 5103. Definitions

(1) In this division unless the context otherwise requires

(a) "Credit" or "letter of credit" means an engagement by a bank or other person made at the request of a customer and of a kind within the scope of this division (Section 5102) that the issuer will honor drafts or other demands for payment upon compliance with the conditions specified in the credit. A credit may be either revocable or irrevocable. The engagement may be either an agreement to honor or a statement that a bank or other person is authorized to honor.

(b) A "documentary draft" or a "documentary demand for payment" is one honor of which is conditioned upon the presentation of a document or documents. "Document" means any paper including document of title, security, invoice, certificate, notice of default and the like.

(c) An "issuer" is a bank or other person issuing a credit.

(d) A "beneficiary" of a credit is a person who is entitled under its terms to draw or demand payment.

(e) An "advising bank" is a bank which gives notification of the issuance of a credit by another bank.

(f) A "confirming bank" is a bank which engages either that it will itself honor a credit already issued by another bank or that such a credit will be honored by the issuer or a third bank.

(g) A "customer" is a buyer or other person who causes an issuer to issue a credit. The term also includes a bank which procures issuance or confirmation on behalf of that bank's customer.

(2) Other definitions applying to this division and the sections in which they appear are:

"Notation of credit." Section 5108.

"Presenter." Section 5112(3).

(3) Definitions in other divisions applying to this division and the sections in which they appear are:

"Accept" or "acceptance." Section 3409.

"Contract for sale." Section 2106.

"Draft." Section 3104.

"Holder in due course." Section 3302.

"Midnight deadline." Section 4104.

"Security." Section 8102.

(4) In addition, Division 1 contains general definitions and principles of construction and interpretation applicable throughout this division. *(Stats.1963, c. 819,*

§ 5103. Amended by Stats.1994, c. 668 (S.B.1405), § 10.)

§ 5104. Formal Requirements; Signing

(1) Except as otherwise required in subdivision (1)(c) of Section 5102 on scope, no particular form of phrasing is required for a credit. A credit must be in writing and signed by the issuer and a confirmation must be in writing and signed by the confirming bank. A modification of the terms of a credit or confirmation must be signed by the issuer or confirming bank.

(2) A telegram may be a sufficient signed writing if it identifies its sender by an authorized authentication. The authentication may be in code and the authorized naming of the issuer in an advice of credit is a sufficient signing. *(Stats.1963, c. 819, § 5104.)*

§ 5105. Consideration,

No consideration is necessary to establish a credit or to enlarge or otherwise modify its terms. *(Stats.1963, c. 819, § 5105.)*

§ 5106. Time and Effect of Establishment of Credit

(1) Unless otherwise agreed a credit is established

(a) As regards the customer as soon as a letter of credit is sent to him or the letter of credit or an authorized written advice of its issuance is sent to the beneficiary; and

(b) As regards the beneficiary when he receives a letter of credit or an authorized written advice of its issuance.

(2) Unless otherwise agreed once an irrevocable credit is established as regards the customer it can be modified or revoked only with the consent of the customer and once it is established as regards the beneficiary it can be modified or revoked only with his consent.

(3) Unless otherwise agreed after a revocable credit is established it may be modified or revoked by the issuer without notice to or consent from the customer or beneficiary.

(4) Notwithstanding any modification or revocation of a revocable credit any person authorized to honor or negotiate under the terms of the original credit is entitled to reimbursement for or honor of any draft or demand for payment duly honored or negotiated before receipt of notice of the modification or revocation and the issuer in turn is entitled to reimbursement from its customer. *(Stats.1963, c. 819, § 5106.)*

§ 5107. Advice of Credit; Confirmation; Error in Statement of Terms

(1) Unless otherwise specified an advising bank by advising a credit issued by another bank does not assume any obligation to honor drafts drawn or demands for payment made under the credit but it does assume obligation for the accuracy of its own statement.

(2) A confirming bank by confirming a credit becomes directly obligated on the credit to the extent of its confirmation as though it were its issuer and acquires the rights of an issuer.

(3) Even though an advising bank incorrectly advises the terms of a credit it has been authorized to advise the credit is established as against the issuer to the extent of its original terms.

(4) Unless otherwise specified the customer bears as against the issuer all risks of transmission and reasonable translation or interpretation of any message relating to a credit. *(Stats.1963, c. 819, § 5107.)*

§ 5108. "Notation Credit"; Exhaustion of Credit

(1) A credit which specifies that any person purchasing or paying drafts drawn or demands for payment made under it must note the amount of the draft or demand on the letter or advice of credit is a "notation credit."

(2) Under a notation credit

(a) A person paying the beneficiary or purchasing a draft or demand for payment from him acquires a right to honor only if the appropriate notation is made and by transferring or forwarding for honor the documents under the credit such a person warrants to the issuer that the notation has been made; and

(b) Unless the credit or a signed statement that an appropriate notation has been made accompanies the draft or demand for payment the issuer may delay honor until evidence of notation has been procured which is satisfactory to it but its obligation and that of its customer continue for a reasonable time not exceeding 30 days to obtain such evidence.

(3) If the credit is not a notation credit

(a) The issuer may honor complying drafts or demands for payment presented to it in the order in which they are presented and is discharged pro tanto by honor of any such draft or demand;

(b) As between competing good faith purchasers of complying drafts or demands the person first purchasing has priority over a subsequent purchaser even though the later purchased draft or demand has been first honored. *(Stats.1963, c. 819, § 5108.)*

§ 5109. Issuer's Obligation to Its Customer

(1) An issuer's obligation to its customer includes good faith and observance of any general banking usage but unless otherwise agreed does not include liability or responsibility

(a) For performance of the underlying contract for sale or other transaction between the customer and the beneficiary; or

(b) For any act or omission of any person other than itself or its own branch or for loss or destruction of a draft, demand or document in transit or in the possession of others; or

(c) Based on knowledge or lack of knowledge of any usage of any particular trade.

(2) An issuer must examine documents with care so as to ascertain that on their face they appear to comply with the terms of the credit but unless otherwise agreed assumes no liability or responsibility for the genuineness, falsification or effect of any document which appears on such examination to be regular on its face.

(3) A nonbank issuer is not bound by any banking usage of which it has no knowledge. *(Stats.1963, c. 819, § 5109.)*

§ 5110. Availability of Credit in Portions; Presenter's Reservation of Lien or Claim

(1) Unless otherwise specified a credit may be used in portions in the discretion of the beneficiary.

(2) Unless otherwise specified a person by presenting a documentary draft or demand for payment under a credit relinquishes upon its honor all claims to the documents and a person by transferring such draft or demand or causing such presentment authorizes such relinquishment. An explicit reservation of claim makes the draft or demand noncomplying. *(Stats.1963, c. 819, § 5110).)*

§ 5111. Warranties on Transfer and Presentment

(1) Unless otherwise agreed the beneficiary by transferring or presenting a documentary draft or demand for payment warrants to all interested parties that the necessary conditions of the credit have been complied with. This is in addition to any warranties arising under Divisions 3, 4, 7, and 8.

(2) Unless otherwise agreed a negotiating, advising, confirming, collecting or issuing bank presenting or transferring a draft or demand for payment under a credit warrants only the matters warranted by a collecting bank under Division 4 and any such bank transferring a document warrants only the matters warranted by an intermediary under Divisions 7 and 8. *(Stats.1963, c. 819, § 5111.)*

§ 5112. Time Allowed for Honor or Rejection; Withholding Honor or Rejection by Consent; "Presenter"

(1) A bank to which a documentary draft or demand for payment is presented under a credit may without dishonor of the draft, demand or credit

(a) Defer honor until the close of the third banking day following receipt of the documents; and

(b) Further defer honor if the presenter has expressly or impliedly consented thereto.

Failure to honor within the time here specified constitutes dishonor of the draft or demand and of the credit.

(2) Upon dishonor the bank may unless otherwise instructed fulfill its duty to return the draft or demand and the documents by holding them at the disposal of the presenter and sending him an advice to that effect.

(3) "Presenter" means any person presenting a draft or demand for payment for honor under a credit even though that person is a confirming bank or other correspondent which is acting under an issuer's authorization. *(Stats.1963, c. 819, § 5112.)*

§ 5113. Indemnities

(1) A bank seeking to obtain (whether for itself or another) honor, negotiation or reimbursement under a credit may give an indemnity to induce such honor, negotiation or reimbursement.

(2) An indemnity agreement inducing honor, negotiation or reimbursement unless otherwise explicitly agreed applies to defects in the documents but not in the goods. *(Stats.1963, c. 819, § 5113.)*

§ 5114. Issuer's duty and privilege to honor; right of reimbursement

(1) An issuer must honor a draft or demand for payment that complies with the terms of the relevant credit regardless of whether the goods or documents conform to the underlying contract for sale or other contract between the customer and the beneficiary. The issuer is not excused from honor of the draft or demand by reason of an additional general term that all documents must be satisfactory to the issuer, but an issuer may require that specified documents must be satisfactory to it.

(2) Unless otherwise agreed, when documents appear on their face to comply with the terms of a credit but a required document does not in fact conform to the warranties made on the negotiation or transfer of a document of title (Section 7507) or of a certificated security (Section 8108) or is forged or fraudulent or there is fraud in the transaction:

(a) The issuer must honor the draft or demand for payment if honor is demanded by a negotiating bank or other holder of the draft or demand which has taken the draft or demand under the credit and under circumstances which would make it a holder in due course (Section 3302) and in an appropriate case would make it a person to whom a document of title has been duly negotiated (Section 7501) or a bona fide purchaser of a certificated security (Section 8302).

(b) In all other cases as against its customer, an issuer acting in good faith may honor the draft or demand for payment despite notification from the customer of fraud, forgery or other defect not apparent on the face of the documents.

(3) Unless otherwise agreed, an issuer which has duly honored a draft or demand for payment is entitled to immediate reimbursement of any payment made under the credit and to be put in effectively available funds not later than the day before maturity of any acceptance made under the credit. *(Stats.1963, c. 819, § 5114. Amended by Stats.1984, c. 927, § 4; Stats.1994, c. 611*

(S.B.1612), § 4, eff. Sept. 16, 1994; Stats.1996, c. 497 (S.B.1591), § 7, operative Jan. 1, 1997.)

§ 5115. Remedy for Improper Dishonor or Anticipatory Repudiation

(1) When an issuer wrongfully dishonors a draft or demand for payment presented under a credit the person entitled to honor has with respect to any documents the rights of a person in the position of a seller (Section 2707) and may recover from the issuer the face amount of the draft or demand together with incidental damages under Section 2710 on seller's incidental damages and interest but less any amount realized by resale or other use or disposition of the subject matter of the transaction. In the event no resale or other utilization is made the documents, goods or other subject matter involved in the transaction must be turned over to the issuer on payment of judgment.

(2) When an issuer wrongfully cancels or otherwise repudiates a credit before presentment of a draft or demand for payment drawn under it the beneficiary has the rights of a seller after anticipatory repudiation by the buyer under Section 2610 if he learns of the repudiation in time reasonably to avoid procurement of the required documents. Otherwise the beneficiary has an immediate right of action for wrongful dishonor. *(Stats.1963, c. 819, § 5115.)*

§ 5116. Transfer and assignment

(1) The right to draw under a credit can be transferred or assigned only when the credit is expressly designated as transferable or assignable.

(2) Even though the credit specifically states that it is nontransferable or nonassignable the beneficiary may before performance of the conditions of the credit assign his right to proceeds. Such an assignment is an assignment of an account under Division 9 on secured transactions and is governed by that division except that

(a) The assignment is ineffective until the letter of credit or advice of credit is delivered to the assignee which delivery constitutes perfection of the security interest under Division 9; and

(b) The issuer may honor drafts or demands for payment drawn under the credit until it receives a notification of the assignment signed by the beneficiary which reasonably identifies the credit involved in the assignment and contains a request to pay the assignee; and

(c) After what reasonably appears to be such a notification has been received the issuer may without dishonor refuse to accept or pay even to a person otherwise entitled to honor until the letter of credit or advice of credit is exhibited to the issuer.

(3) Except where the beneficiary has effectively assigned his right to draw or his right to proceeds, nothing in this section limits his right to transfer or negotiate drafts or demands drawn under the credit. *(Stats.1963, c. 819, § 5116. Amended by Stats.1967, c. 799, p. 2209, § 9; Stats.1974, c. 997, p. 2114, § 4, eff. Jan. 1, 1976.)*

§ 5117. Insolvency of Bank Holding Funds for Documentary Credit

(1) Where an issuer or an advising or confirming bank or a bank which has for a customer procured issuance of a credit by another bank becomes insolvent before final payment under the credit and the credit is one to which this division is made applicable by paragraph (a) or (b) of Section 5102(1) on scope, the receipt or allocation of funds or collateral to secure or meet obligations under the credit shall have the following results:

(a) To the extent of any funds or collateral turned over after or before the insolvency as indemnity against or specifically for the purpose of payment of drafts or demands for payment drawn under the designated credit, the drafts or demands are entitled to payment in preference over depositors or other general creditors of the issuer or bank; and

(b) On expiration of the credit or surrender of the beneficiary's rights under it unused any person who has given such funds or collateral is similarly entitled to return thereof; and

(c) A charge to a general or current account with a bank if specifically consented to for the purpose of indemnity against or payment of drafts or demands for payment drawn under the designated credit falls under the same rules as if the funds had been drawn out in cash and then turned over with specific instructions.

(2) After honor or reimbursement under this section the customer or other person for whose account the insolvent bank has acted is entitled to receive the documents involved. *(Stats.1963, c. 819, § 5117.)*

Division 6

BULK SALES

Section
6101. Short title.
6102. Definitions and Index of Definitions.
6103. Bulk sales governed by this division; exceptions.
6104. Buyers; seller's list; notice; compliance with § 6106.2.
6105. Notice; requirements for compliance.
6106. Repealed.
6106.1. Repealed.
6106.2. Payment of consideration to satisfy claims of seller's creditors; disputed claims; attachment; interpleader; notice; security interest.
6106.4. Escrow; filing claims; distribution; notice.
6107. Liability for Noncompliance.
6108. Auction sales.
6109. Repealed.
6110. Limitation of actions.
6111. Application of division.

Application

Bulk sales on or after and before Jan. 1, 1991, application of division and former division, see § 6111.

Cross References

Alcoholic beverages, temporary retail permits, extension of credit or receipt of payment in unauthorized manner with knowledge established by evidence of recording and publishing notice pursuant to this division, see Business and Professions Code § 24045.5.

Attachment, ex parte hearing procedure, see Code of Civil Procedure § 485.010.

Taxes due on property advertised for bulk transfer, seizure prior to delinquency, exemption from declaration, see Revenue and Taxation Code § 2953.1.

§ 6101. Short title

This division shall be known and may be cited as Uniform Commercial Code—Bulk Sales. *(Added by Stats.1990, c. 1191 (A.B.3653), § 3.)*

Application

Bulk sales on or after and before Jan. 1, 1991, application of division and former division, see § 6111.

Uniform Commercial Code Comment
1990 Addition

Prior Uniform Statutory Provision: Section 6–101 (1987 Official Text).

Change: This Article applies only to sales, as defined in Section 2–103(1), and not to other transfers.

Purpose of Change: Transfers other than sales, *e.g.*, grants of security interests, do not present risks to creditors necessitating advance notice in accordance with the provisions of this Article. The Uniform Fraudulent Transfer Act affords a remedy to creditors who are injured by donative transfers.

Rationale for Revision of the Article:

Article 6 (1987 Official Text) imposes upon transferees in bulk several duties toward creditors of the transferor. These duties include the duty to notify the creditors of the impending bulk transfer and, in those jurisdictions that have adopted optional Section 6–106, the duty to assure that the new consideration for the transfer is applied to pay debts of the transferor.

Compliance with the provisions of Article 6 can be burdensome, particularly when the transferor has a large number of creditors. When the transferor is actively engaged in business at a number of locations, assembling a current list of creditors may not be possible. Mailing a notice to each creditor may prove costly. When the goods that are the subject of the transfer are located in several jurisdictions, the transferor may be obligated to comply with Article 6 as enacted in each jurisdiction. The widespread enactment of nonuniform amendments makes compliance with Article 6 in multiple-state transactions problematic. Moreover, the Article requires compliance even when there is no reason to believe that the transferor is conducting a fraudulent transfer, *e.g.*, when the transferor is scaling down the business but remaining available to creditors.

Article 6 imposes strict liability for noncompliance. Failure to comply with the provisions of the Article renders the transfer ineffective, even when the transferor has attempted compliance in good faith, and even when no creditor has been injured by the noncompliance. The potential liability for minor noncompliance may be high. If the transferor should enter bankruptcy before the expiration of the limitation period, Bankruptcy Code §§ 544(b), 550(a), 11 U.S.C. §§ 544(b), 550(a), may enable the transferor's bankruptcy trustee to set aside the entire transaction and recover from the noncomplying transferee all the goods transferred or their value. The trustee has this power even though the noncompliance was with respect to only a single creditor holding a small claim.

The benefits that compliance affords to creditors do not justify the substantial burdens and risks that the Article imposes upon good faith purchasers of business assets. The Article requires that notice be sent only ten days before the transferee takes possession of the goods or pays for them, whichever happens first. Given the delay between sending the notice and its receipt, creditors have scant opportunity to avail themselves of a judicial or nonjudicial remedy before the transfer has been consummated.

In some cases Article 6 may have the unintended effect of injuring, rather than aiding, creditors of the transferor. Those transferees who recognize the burdens and risks that Article 6 imposes upon them sometimes agree to purchase only at a reduced price. Others refuse to purchase at all, leaving the creditors to realize only the liquidation value, rather than the going concern value, of the business goods.

As a response to these inadequacies and others, the National Conference of Commissioners on Uniform State Laws has completely revised Article 6. This revision is designed to reduce the burdens and risks imposed upon good-faith buyers of business assets while increasing the protection afforded to creditors. Among the major changes it makes are the following:

—this Article applies only when the buyer has notice, or after reasonable inquiry would have had notice, that the seller will not continue to operate the same or a similar kind of business after the sale (Section 6–102(1)(c)).

—this Article does not apply to sales in which the value of the property otherwise available to creditors is less than $10,000 or those in which the value of the property is greater than $25,000,000 (Section 6–103(3)(*l*)).

—the choice-of-law provision (Sections 6–103(1)(b) and 6–103(2)) limits the applicable law to that of one jurisdiction.

—when the seller if indebted to a large number of persons, the buyer need neither obtain a list of those persons nor send individual notices to each person but instead may give notice by filing (Sections 6–105(2) and 6–104(2)).

—the notice period is increased from 10 days to 45 days (Section 6–105(5)), and the statute of limitations is extended from six months to one year (Section 6–110).

—the notice must include a copy of a "schedule of distribution," which sets forth how the net contract price is to be distributed (Sections 6–105(3) and 6–106(1)).

—a buyer who makes a good faith effort to comply with the requirements of this Article or to exclude the sale from the application of this Article, or who acts on the good faith belief that this Article does not apply to the sale, is not liable for noncompliance (Section 6–107(3)).

—a buyer's noncompliance does not render the sale ineffective or otherwise affect the buyer's title to the goods; rather, the liability of a noncomplying buyer is for damages caused by the noncompliance (Sections 6–107(1) and 6–107(8)).

In addition to making these and other major substantive changes, revised Article 6 resolves the ambiguities that three decades of law practice, judicial construction, and scholarly inquiry have disclosed.

Cross References

Auction sales, see Commercial Code § 6108.
Notice,
   Generally, see Commercial Code § 6105.
   Contents, see Commercial Code § 6105 et seq.
Requisites of effective transfers, see Commercial Code § 6105 et seq.
Tax liability of successors, see Revenue and Taxation Code §§ 6811, 6812; Unemployment Insurance Code § 1731 et seq.
Transfers and enterprises subject to this division, see Commercial Code § 6102.
Transfers excepted from this division, see Commercial Code § 6103.
Uniform Fraudulent Conveyance Act, see Civil Code § 3439 et seq.

§ 6102. Definitions and Index of Definitions

(a) In this division, unless the context otherwise requires:

(1) "Assets" means the inventory and equipment that is the subject of a bulk sale and any tangible and intangible personal property used or held for use primarily in, or arising from, the seller's business and sold in connection with that inventory and equipment, but the term does not include any of the following:

(i) Fixtures (paragraph (a) of subdivision (1) of Section 9313) other than readily removable factory and office machines.

(ii) The lessee's interest in a lease of real property.

(iii) Property to the extent it is generally exempt from creditor process under nonbankruptcy law.

(2) "Auctioneer" means a person whom the seller engages to direct, conduct, control, or be responsible for a sale by auction.

(3) "Bulk sale" means either of the following:

(i) In the case of a sale by auction or a sale or series of sales conducted by a liquidator on the seller's behalf, a sale or series of sales not in the ordinary course of the seller's business of more than half of the seller's inventory and equipment, as measured by a value on the date of the bulk-sale agreement.

(ii) In all other cases, a sale not in the ordinary course of the seller's business of more than half the seller's inventory and equipment, as measured by value on the date of the bulk-sale agreement.

(4) "Claim" means a right to payment from the seller, whether or not the right is reduced to judgment, liquidated, fixed, matured, disputed, secured, legal, or equitable. The term includes costs of collection and attorney's fees only to the extent that the laws of this state permit the holder of the claim to recover them in an action against the obligor.

(5) "Claimant" means a person holding a claim incurred in the seller's business other than any of the following:

(i) An unsecured and unmatured claim for employment compensation and benefits, including commissions and vacation, severance, and sick-leave pay.

(ii) A claim for injury to an individual or to property, or for breach of warranty, unless all of the following are satisfied:

(A) A right of action for the claim has accrued.

(B) The claim has been asserted against the seller.

(C) The seller knows the identity of the person asserting the claim and the basis upon which the person has asserted it.

(iii) A claim for taxes owing to a governmental unit, if both of the following are satisfied:

(A) A statute governing the enforcement of the claim permits or requires notice of the bulk sale to be given to the governmental unit in a manner other than by compliance with the requirements of this division.

(B) Notice is given in accordance with the statute.

(6) "Creditor" means a claimant or other person holding a claim.

(7) (i) "Date of the bulk sale" means either of the following:

(A) If the sale is by auction or is conducted by a liquidator on the seller's behalf, the date on which more than 10 percent of the net proceeds is paid to or for the benefit of the seller.

(B) In all other cases, the later of the date on which either of the following occurs:

(I) More than 10 percent of the net contract price is paid to or for the benefit of the seller.

(II) More than 10 percent of the assets, as measured by value, are transferred to the buyer.

(ii) For purposes of this subdivision the following shall apply:

(A) Delivery of a negotiable instrument (subdivision (1) of Section 3104) to or for the benefit of the seller in exchange for assets constitutes payment of the contract price pro tanto.

(B) To the extent that the contract price is deposited in an escrow, the contract price is paid to or for the benefit of the seller when the seller acquires the unconditional right to receive the deposit or when the deposit is delivered to the seller or for the benefit of the seller, whichever is earlier.

(C) An asset is transferred when a person holding an unsecured claim can no longer obtain through judicial proceedings rights to the asset that are superior to those of the buyer arising as a result of the bulk sale. A person holding an unsecured claim can obtain those superior rights to a tangible asset at least until the buyer has an unconditional right, under the bulk-sale agreement, to possess the asset, and a person holding an unsecured claim can obtain those superior rights to an intangible asset at least until the buyer has an unconditional right, under the bulk-sale agreement, to use the asset.

(8) "Date of the bulk-sale agreement" means either of the following:

(i) In the case of a sale by auction or conducted by a liquidator (subparagraph (i) of paragraph (3)), the date on which the seller engages the auctioneer or liquidator.

(ii) In all other cases, the date on which a bulk-sale agreement becomes enforceable between the buyer and the seller.

(9) "Debt" means liability on a claim.

(10) "Liquidator" means a person who is regularly engaged in the business of disposing of assets for businesses contemplating liquidation or dissolution.

(11) "Net contract price" means the new consideration the buyer is obligated to pay for the assets less each of the following:

(i) The amount of any proceeds of the sale of an asset, to the extent the proceeds are applied in partial or total satisfaction of a debt secured by the asset.

(ii) The amount of any debt to the extent it is secured by a security interest or lien that is enforceable against the asset before and after it has been sold to a buyer. If a debt is secured by an asset and other property of the seller, the amount of the debt secured by a security interest or lien that is enforceable against the asset is determined by multiplying the debt by a fraction, the numerator of which is the value of the new consideration for the asset on the date of the bulk sale and the denominator of which is the value of all property securing the debt on the date of the bulk sale.

(12) "Net proceeds" means the new consideration received for assets sold at a sale by auction or a sale conducted by a liquidator on the seller's behalf less each of the following:

(i) Commissions and reasonable expenses of the sale.

(ii) The amount of any proceeds of the sale of an asset, to the extent the proceeds are applied in partial or total satisfaction of a debt secured by the asset.

(iii) The amount of any debt to the extent it is secured by a security interest or lien that is enforceable against the asset before and after it has been sold to a buyer. If a debt is secured by an asset and other property of the seller, the amount of the debt secured by a security interest or lien that is enforceable against the asset is determined by multiplying the debt by a fraction, the numerator of which is the value of the new consideration for the asset on the date of the bulk sale and the denominator of which is the value of all property securing the debt on the date of the bulk sale.

(13) A sale is "in the ordinary course of the seller's business" if the sale comports with usual or customary practices in the kind of business in which the seller is engaged or with the seller's own usual or customary practices.

(14) "United States" includes its territories and possessions and the Commonwealth of Puerto Rico.

(15) "Value" means fair market value.

(16) "Verified" means signed and sworn to or affirmed.

(b) The following definitions in other divisions apply to this division:

(1) "Buyer." Paragraph (a) of subdivision (1) of Section 2103.

(2) "Equipment." Subdivision (2) of Section 9109.

(3) "Inventory." Subdivision (4) of Section 9109.

(4) "Sale." Subdivision (1) of Section 2106.

(5) "Seller." Paragraph (d) of subdivision (1) of Section 2103.

(c) In addition, Division 1 (commencing with Section 1101) contains general definitions and principles of construction and interpretation applicable throughout this division. *(Added by Stats.1990, c. 1191 (A.B.3653), § 3.)*

Application

Bulk sales on or after and before Jan. 1, 1991, application of division and former division, see § 6111.

Uniform Commercial Code Comment
1990 Addition

1. (a) "Assets". New. The term generally includes only "personal property." Whether particular property is "personal property" is to be determined by law outside this Article; however, for purposes of this Article, (i) the term includes "readily removable factory and office machines" (compare Section 9–313(4)(c)), even if they are covered by applicable real estate law and thus are "fixtures" as defined in Section 9–313(1)(a); (ii) the term does not include the lessee's interest in a lease of real property, even if that interest is considered to be personal property under other applicable law; and (iii) the term does not include property to the extent that it is "generally exempt from creditor process under nonbankruptcy law."

(b) "Auctioneer". Compare Section 6–108(3) (1987 Official Text).

(c) "Bulk Sale". Bulk sales are of two kinds. Subsection (1)(c)(i) describes bulk sales conducted by a professional intermediary (*i.e.*, an auctioneer or liquidator), as to which sales Section 6–108 applies. If these indirect sales occur as a series of related sales, then the entire series is treated as a single "bulk sale" and the term applies to the sales in the aggregate. Sales made directly by the seller to the buyer, described in subsection (1)(c)(ii), include sales conducted by an auctioneer or liquidator for its own account.

The elements of both direct and indirect sales are the same. Some of these elements have been borrowed from the 1987 Official Text of Article 6 and restated. For example, the term includes only sales that are not "in the ordinary course of the seller's business" (subsection (1)(m)). The sale must be of "more than half of the seller's inventory, as measured by value [subsection (1)(*o*)] on the date of the bulk-sale agreement [subsection (1)(h)]." All inventory owned by the seller should be included in the calculation, regardless of where it is located. Inventory that is encumbered by a security interest or lien should be counted at its gross value, although the fact that it is encumbered may affect the applicability of this Article to the sale.

§ 6102

The determination whether a sale is a "bulk sale" and thus subject to this Article is not affected by whether other types of property are sold in connection with inventory. However, other provisions of this Article take account of the fact that other property may be sold in connection with inventory. For example, the availability of the exclusion in Section 6–103(3)(*l*) turns on the value of all the "assets," not just the inventory. Similarly, the notice required by Section 6–105 must describe the "assets," not just the inventory. And Section 6–107(4) measures the buyer's maximum cumulative liability for noncompliance by the value of the inventory and equipment sold in the bulk sale.

In an effort to limit its coverage to sales posing the greatest risks to creditors, this Article adds an additional element to the definition of "bulk sale." A sale is not a "bulk sale" unless the buyer, auctioneer, or liquidator has notice, or after a reasonable inquiry would have had notice, that the seller will not continue to operate the same or a similar kind of business after the sale. Whether a person has "notice" depends upon what the person knows and what the person would have known had the person conducted a reasonable inquiry. The issue of whether a transaction was a bulk sale is likely to be litigated only when the seller has absconded with the sale proceeds. This Article requires that the matters as to which the buyer, auctioneer, or liquidator had notice be determined only by reference to facts that the person knew or would have known at the date of the bulk-sale agreement. Reference to what actually occurred is inappropriate.

Whether an inquiry is "reasonable" depends on the facts and circumstances of each case. These facts and circumstances may include the identities of the buyer and seller and the type of assets being sold. In some cases, a reasonable inquiry may consist of no inquiry at all concerning the seller's future.

Not every change in business operations poses a substantial enough risk to creditors to justify the costs of compliance with this Article. Thus, in determining whether post-sale business is of a kind that is "the same" or "similar" to the business conducted before the sale, a court should consider whether, viewed from the perspective of the creditors of the seller, the change poses extraordinary risks or whether the change is a normal risk that creditors can be assumed to take. In particular, when the post-bulk sale business differs from the pre-bulk sale business only in the size of the business conducted, the seller should be considered to be continuing in the same or a similar kind of business and the sale should not be considered a bulk sale.

The seller must "continue to operate" the same or a similar kind of business as owner. If the owner sells the business assets to a buyer and continues to manage the business as an employee of the buyer, the seller is not continuing to operate the business within the meaning of this Article.

(d) "Claim". New. The first sentence derives from Bankruptcy Code § 101(4), 11 U.S.C. § 101(4). Changes, including the deletion of Section 101(4)(B), were made for stylistic purposes only.

(e) "Claimant". New. This term defines the category of claim holders who are the primary beneficiaries of the duties that this Article imposes. Compare "Creditor" (subsection (1)(f)).

States that choose not to afford taxing authorities the benefits of this Article should adopt Alternative A. Adoption of Alternative B would afford the benefits of this Article to taxing authorities except with respect to those taxes as to which there has been compliance with another statute requiring that notice of the bulk sale be given to the taxing authority.

(f) "Creditor". New. The term includes all holders of claims against the seller, even holders of claims arising from consumer transactions. Compare "Claimant" (subsection (1)(e)).

(g) "Date of the bulk sale". New. The parties are able to control the date of the bulk sale in several ways. They can keep the proceeds of the sale in escrow, thereby delaying the date of payment, or they can specifically agree that the assets remain subject to the reach of the seller's creditors, thereby delaying the date that the assets are transferred. By adjusting the time that the buyer acquires an unconditional right to possess tangible assets and the time the buyer acquires an unconditional right to use intangible assets, the parties may affect the substantive rights of creditors and thereby control the date the assets are transferred.

The connection between the time of transfer and the buyer's rights under the bulk-sale agreement appears only for purposes of sales to which this Article applies. Subsection (1)(g) does not purport to affect the rights of creditors of a seller of property for other purposes or under other circumstances.

(h) "Date of the bulk-sale agreement". New. Law outside this Article, including the provisions of Article 2, determines when an agreement for a bulk sale becomes enforceable between the buyer and the seller and when an auctioneer or liquidator is engaged.

(i) "Debt". New. This subsection is borrowed from Bankruptcy Code Section 101(11).

(j) "Liquidator". New. Although the definition of "liquidator" is quite broad, the term is used with respect to sales that are "conducted" by a liquidator on behalf of the seller. See subsection (1)(c)(i). Thus only those liquidators that "conduct" sales will be affected by this Article.

(k) "Net contract price". New. Consideration is not "new consideration" to the extent that it consists of the partial or total satisfaction of an antecedent debt owed to the buyer by the seller. When the buyer buys assets along with property other than assets, the "net contract price" is that portion of the new consideration allocable to the assets.

(*l*) "Net proceeds". New. The term appears, without definition, in Section 6–108 (1987 Official Text).

(m) "In the ordinary course of the seller's business". New.

(n) "United States". New. This subsection derives from Section 9–103(3)(c).

(o) "Value". New. The definition in Section 1–201(44) is not appropriate in the context of this Article.

(p) "Verified". New.

2. "Good faith". This Article adopts the definition of "good faith" in Article 1 in all cases, even when the buyer is a merchant.

Cross-References:

Point 1(a): Section 9–313.
Point 1(c): Sections 1–201 and 6–103.
Point 1(g): Article 2 generally.
Point 1(h): Section 2–201 and Article 2 generally.

Cross References

Bank deposits and collections, see Commercial Code § 4101 et seq.
Classification of goods, see Commercial Code § 9109.
Commercial paper, see Commercial Code § 3101 et seq.
Investment securities, see Commercial Code § 8101 et seq.
Parties' power to choose applicable law, see Commercial Code § 1105.
Personal property, law of domicile, see Civil Code § 946.
Secured transactions,
  Generally, see Commercial Code § 9101 et seq.
  Assignment of interest, see Commercial Code §§ 9102, 9206, 9302, 9318, 9406.
  Nonapplicability of bulk transfer laws, see Commercial Code § 9111.
Transfer in general, see Civil Code § 1039 et seq.
Transfer of personal property, see Commercial Code §§ 2101 et seq., 2401 et seq.
Transfers excepted from this division, see Commercial Code § 6103.
Uniform Fraudulent Conveyance Act, see Civil Code § 3439 et seq.

§ 6103. Bulk sales governed by this division; exceptions

(a) Except as otherwise provided in subdivision (c), this division applies to a bulk sale if both of the following are satisfied:

(1) The seller's principal business is the sale of inventory from stock, including those who manufacture what they sell, or that of a restaurant owner.

(2) On the date of the bulk-sale agreement the seller is located in this state or, if the seller is located in a jurisdiction that is not a part of the United States, the seller's major executive office in the United States is in this state.

(b) A seller is deemed to be located at its place of business. If a seller has more than one place of business, the seller is deemed located at its chief executive office.

(c) This division does not apply to any of the following:

(1) A transfer made to secure payment or performance of an obligation.

(2) A transfer of collateral to a secured party pursuant to Section 9503.

(3) A sale of collateral pursuant to Section 9504.

(4) Retention of collateral pursuant to Section 9505.

(5) A sale of an asset encumbered by a security interest or lien if (i) all the proceeds of the sale are applied in partial or total satisfaction of the debt secured by the security interest or lien or (ii) the security interest or lien is enforceable against the asset after it has been sold to the buyer and the net contract price is zero.

(6) A general assignment for the benefit of creditors or to a subsequent transfer by the assignee.

(7) A sale by an executor, administrator, receiver, trustee in bankruptcy, debtor in possession, or any public officer under judicial process.

(8) A sale made in the course of judicial or administrative proceedings for the dissolution or reorganization of an organization.

(9) A sale to a buyer whose principal place of business is in the United States and who satisfies each of the following:

(i) Not earlier than 21 days before the date of the bulk sale, (A) obtains from the seller a verified and dated list of claimants of whom the seller has notice three days before the seller sends or delivers the list to the buyer or (B) conducts a reasonable inquiry to discover the claimants.

(ii) Assumes in full the debts owed to claimants of whom the buyer has knowledge on the date the buyer receives the list of claimants from the seller or on the date the buyer completes the reasonable inquiry, as the case may be.

(iii) Is not insolvent after the assumption.

(iv) Records and publishes notice of the assumption not later than 30 days after the date of the bulk sale in the manner provided in Section 6105.

(10) A sale to a buyer whose principal place of business is in the United States and who satisfies each of the following:

(i) Assumes in full the debts that were incurred in the seller's business before the date of the bulk sale.

(ii) Is not insolvent after the assumption.

(iii) Records and publishes notice of the assumption not later than 30 days after the date of the bulk sale in the manner provided by Section 6105.

(11) A sale to a new organization that is organized to take over and continue the business of the seller and that has its principal place of business in the United States if each of the following conditions are satisfied:

(i) The buyer assumes in full the debts that were incurred in the seller's business before the date of the bulk sale.

(ii) The seller receives nothing from the sale except an interest in the new organization that is subordinate to the claims against the organization arising from the assumption.

(iii) The buyer records and publishes notice of the assumption not later than 30 days after the date of the bulk sale in the manner provided in Section 6105.

(12) A sale of assets having either of the following:

(i) A value, net of liens and security interests, of less than ten thousand dollars ($10,000). If a debt is secured by assets and other property of the seller, the net value of the assets is determined by subtracting from their value an amount equal to the product of the debt multiplied by a fraction, the numerator of which is the value of the assets on the date of the bulk sale and the denominator of which is the value of all property securing the debt on the date of the bulk sale.

(ii) A value of more than five million dollars ($5,000,000) on the date of the bulk-sale agreement.

(13) A sale required by, and made pursuant to, statute.

(14) A transfer of personal property, if the personal property is leased back to the transferor immediately following the transfer and either there has been compliance with subdivision (h) of Section 3440.1 of the Civil Code or the transfer is exempt under subdivision (k) of Section 3440.1 of the Civil Code.

(15) A transfer which is subject to and complies with Article 5 (commencing with Section 24070) of Chapter 6 of Division 9 of the Business and Professions Code, if the transferee records and publishes notice of the transfer at least 12 business days before the transfer is to be consummated in the manner provided in Section 6105 and the notice contains the information set forth in paragraphs (1) to (4) inclusive, of subdivision (a) of Section 6105.

(16) A transfer of goods in a warehouse where a warehouse receipt has been issued therefor by a warehouseman (Section 7102) and a copy of the receipt is kept at the principal place of business of the warehouseman and at the warehouse in which the goods are stored.

(d) The notice under subparagraph (iv) of paragraph (9) of subdivision (c) shall state each of the following:

(1) That a sale that may constitute a bulk sale has been or will be made.

(2) The date or prospective date of the bulk sale.

(3) The individual, partnership, or corporate names and the addresses of the seller and buyer.

(4) The address to which inquiries about the sale may be made, if different from the seller's address.

(5) That the buyer has assumed or will assume in full the debts owed to claimants of whom the buyer has knowledge on the date the buyer receives the list of claimants from the seller or completes a reasonable inquiry to discover the claimants.

(e) The notice under subparagraph (iii) of paragraph (10) of subdivision (c) and subparagraph (iii) of paragraph (11) of subdivision (c) shall state each of the following:

(1) That a sale that may constitute a bulk sale has been or will be made.

(2) The date or prospective date of the bulk sale.

(3) The individual, partnership, or corporate names and the addresses of the seller and buyer.

(4) The address to which inquiries about the sale may be made, if different from the seller's address.

(5) That the buyer has assumed or will assume the debts that were incurred in the seller's business before the date of the bulk sale.

(f) For purposes of paragraph (12) of subdivision (c), the value of assets is presumed to be equal to the price the buyer agrees to pay for the assets. However, in a sale by auction or a sale conducted by a liquidator on the seller's behalf, the value of assets is presumed to be the amount the auctioneer or liquidator reasonably estimates the assets will bring at auction or upon liquidation. *(Added by Stats.1990, c. 1191 (A.B.3653), § 3.)*

Application

Bulk sales on or after and before Jan. 1, 1991, application of division and former division, see § 6111.

Uniform Commercial Code Comment
1990 Addition

Prior Uniform Statutory Provision: Sections 6–102 and 6–103 (1987 Official Text).

Changes: New choice-of-law provision; exclusions from the Article clarified, revised, and expanded.

Purposes of Changes and New Matter:

1. Subsection (1)(a) follows Section 6–102(3) of the 1987 Official Text and makes Article 6 applicable only when the seller's principal business is the sale of inventory from stock. This Article does not apply to a sale by a seller whose principal business is the sale of goods other than inventory, *e.g.,* a farmer, is the sale of inventory not from stock, *e.g.,* a manufacturer who produces goods to order, or is the sale of services, *e.g.,* a dry cleaner, barber, or operator of a hotel, tavern, or restaurant.

2. The choice-of-law rule in subsections (1)(b) and (2) derives from Section 9–103(3) and should be interpreted consistently with the Official Comment and case law construing that Section. Any agreement between the buyer and the seller with regard to the law governing a bulk sale does not affect the choice-of-law rule in this Article.

3. Some of the transactions excluded by subsection (3), *e.g.,* those excluded by subsection (3)(a), may not be bulk sales. This Article nevertheless specifically excludes them in order to allay any doubts about the Article's applicability. Certain transactions, *e.g.,* the sale of fully encumbered inventory that remains subject to a security interest, may be excluded by more than one subsection.

4. Subsections (3)(a), (b), (c), (d), and (e) derive from subsections (1) and (3) of Section 6–103 (1987 Official Text).

5. Subsections (3)(f), (g), and (h) restate subsections (2), (4), and (5) of Section 6–103 with minor changes.

6. Subsections (3)(i), (j), and (k) relate to sales in which the buyer assumes specified debts of the seller. A bulk sale does not fall within any of these subsections unless the buyer's assumption of debts is binding and irrevocable.

Subsection (3)(j) derives from subsection (6) of Section 6–103 (1987 Official Text) and is available to buyers who are not insolvent (as defined in Section 1–201(23)), assume all the seller's business debts in full, and give notice of the assumption. Subsection (3)(k) derives from subsection (7) of Section 6–103 (1987 Official Text) and excludes transactions in which the risks to creditors are minimal. Like subsection (3)(j), this subsection applies only if the buyer assumes all the seller's business debts in full and gives notice of the assumption. In addition, the buyer must be a new organization that is organized to take over and continue the seller's business, the seller must receive nothing from the sale other than an interest in the new organization, and the seller's interest must be subordinate to the claims arising from the assumption. Sales that may qualify for the exclusion include the incorporation of a partnership or sole proprietorship.

Buyers often are reluctant to assume debts of which they have no knowledge. Subsection (3)(i), which is new, permits a qualifying buyer to exclude a sale from this Article by assuming only those debts owed to claimants of whom the buyer has knowledge after the buyer either conducts a reasonable inquiry to discover claimants or obtains a list of claimants from the seller. A buyer who takes a verified list from the seller is held to have knowledge of the claimants on the list and is entitled to rely in good faith on the list without making further inquiry. The protection afforded by the assumption of these debts, while not perfect, is sufficiently great to eliminate the need for compliance with Article 6.

7. Subsection (3)(*l*) is new. Although the bulk sale of even a very small business may be of concern to some creditors, losses to creditors from sales of assets in which the seller's equity is less than $10,000 are not likely to justify the costs of complying with this Article. Sales of assets having a value of more than $25,000,000 have not presented serious risks to creditors. Publicity normally attends sales of that magnitude, and the sellers are unlikely to be able successfully to remove the proceeds from the reach of creditors. As used in this subsection, "price" includes all consideration for the assets, not only new consideration. Compare "Net contract price" (Section 6–102(1)(k)). If the auctioneer or liquidator does not make an estimation, then no presumption arises.

8. Subsection (3)(m) is new. This Article assumes that creditors are aware of statutes that may require their debtors to conduct bulk sales under specified circumstances, *e.g.,* upon the termination of a franchise or of a contract between a dealer and supplier, and are able to take account of any risk that those sales may impose.

Cross-References:
Point 1: Section 9–109.
Point 2: Sections 1–105 and 9–103.
Point 3: Section 6–102.
Point 4: Sections 9–111, 9–503, 9–504, and 9–505.
Point 6: Sections 1–201 and 1–203.
Point 7: Section 6–102.

Definitional Cross-References:
"Asset". Section 6–102.
"Auctioneer". Section 6–102.
"Bulk sale". Section 6–102.
"Buyer". Section 2–103.
"Claimant". Section 6–102.
"Collateral". Section 9–105.
"Date of the bulk sale". Section 6–102.
"Date of the bulk-sale agreement". Section 6–102.
"Debt". Section 6–102.
"Insolvent". Section 1–201.
"Inventory". Section 9–109.
"Knowledge". Section 1–201.
"Liquidator". Section 6–102.
"Net contract price". Section 6–102.
"Notice". Section 1–201.
"Organization". Section 1–201.
"Presumed". Section 1–201.
"Proceeds". Section 9–306.

"Sale". Section 2-106.
"Secured party". Section 9-105.
"Security interest". Section 1-201.
"Seller". Section 2-103.
"Send". Section 1-201.
"United States". Section 6-102.
"Value". Section 6-102.
"Verified". Section 6-102.

Cross References

Creation of security interest, operation, see Commercial Code § 9111.
Creditor, see Commercial Code § 1201.
Requisites of effective transfers, see Commercial Code § 6105 et seq.
Sales by personal representative, see Probate Code § 10000 et seq.
Sales under execution, see Code of Civil Procedure § 701.170 et seq.
Secured transactions, see Commercial Code § 9101 et seq.
Transfers and enterprises subject to this division, see Commercial Code § 6111.

§ 6104. Buyers; seller's list; notice; compliance with § 6106.2

In a bulk sale as defined in subparagraph (ii) of paragraph (3) of subdivision (a) of Section 6102 the buyer shall do each of the following:

(a) Obtain from the seller a list of all business names and addresses used by the seller within three years before the date the list is sent or delivered to the buyer.

(b) Give notice of the bulk sale in accordance with Section 6105.

(c) Comply with Section 6106.2 if the bulk sale is within the scope of that section. *(Added by Stats.1990, c. 1191 (A.B.3653), § 3.)*

Application

Bulk sales on or after and before Jan. 1, 1991, application of division and former division, see § 6111.

§ 6105. Notice; requirements for compliance

In order to comply with subdivision (b) of Section 6104 each of the following shall be satisfied:

(a) The notice shall comply with each of the following:

(1) State that a bulk sale is about to be made.

(2) State the name and business address of the seller together with any other business name and address listed by the seller (subdivision (a) of Section 6104) and the name and business address of the buyer.

(3) State the location and general description of the assets.

(4) State the place and the anticipated date of the bulk sale.

(5) State whether or not the bulk sale is subject to Section 6106.2 and, if so subject, the matters required by subdivision (f) of Section 6106.2.

(b) At least 12 business days before the date of the bulk sale, the notice shall be:

(1) Recorded in the office of the county recorder in the county or counties in this state in which the tangible assets are located and, if different, in the county in which the seller is located (paragraph (2) of subdivision (a) of Section 6103).

(2) Published at least once in a newspaper of general circulation published in the judicial district in this state in which the tangible assets are located and in the judicial district, if different, in which the seller is located (paragraph (2) of subdivision (a) of Section 6103), if in either case there is one, and if there is none, then in a newspaper of general circulation in the county in which the judicial district is located.

(3) Delivered or sent by registered or certified mail to the county tax collector in the county or counties in this state in which the tangible assets are located. <u>If delivered during the period from March 1 to the last Friday in May, inclusive, the notice shall be accompanied by a completed business property statement with respect to property involved in the bulk sale pursuant to Section 441 of the Revenue and Taxation Code.</u>

If the tangible assets are located in more than one judicial district in this state, the publication required in paragraph (2) shall be in a newspaper of general circulation published in the judicial district in this state in which a greater portion of the tangible assets are located, on the date the notice is published, than in any other judicial district in this state and, if different, in the judicial district in which the seller is located (paragraph (2) of subdivision (a) of Section 6103). As used in this subdivision, "business day" means any day other than a Saturday, Sunday, or day observed as a holiday by the state government. *(Added by Stats.1990, c. 1191 (A.B. 3653), § 3. Amended by Stats.1991, c. 532 (S.B.1064), § 1.)*

Application

Bulk sales on or after and before Jan. 1, 1991, application of division and former division, see § 6111.

Cross References

Auction sales, see Commercial Code § 6108.
Contents and requisites of notice, see Commercial Code § 6105 et seq.
Protected creditors, see Commercial Code § 6109.
Uniform Fraudulent Conveyance Act, see Civil Code § 3439 et seq.

§ 6106. Repealed by Stats.1990, c. 1191 (A.B.3653), § 2

§ 6106.1. Repealed by Stats.1990, c. 1191 (A.B.3653), § 2

§ 6106.2. Payment of consideration to satisfy claims of seller's creditors; disputed claims; attachment; interpleader; notice; security interest

(a) This section applies only to a bulk sale where the consideration is two million dollars ($2,000,000) or less and is substantially all cash or an obligation of the buyer to pay cash in the future to the seller or a combination thereof.

(b) Upon every bulk sale subject to this section except one made by sale at auction or a sale or series of sales conducted by a liquidator on the seller's behalf, it

§ 6106.2

is the duty of the buyer or, if the transaction is handled through an escrow, the escrow agent to apply the cash consideration in accordance with this section so far as necessary to pay those debts of the seller for which claims are due and payable on or before the date of the bulk sale and are received in writing on or prior to the date specified as the last date to file claims with the person designated in the notice to receive claims. This duty of the buyer or escrow agent runs to each claimant timely filing the claim.

(c) If the seller disputes whether a claim is due and payable on the date of the bulk sale or the amount of any claim, the buyer or escrow agent shall withhold from distribution an amount equal to (1) 125 percent of the first seven thousand five hundred dollars ($7,500) of the claim, and (2) an amount equal to that portion of the claim in excess of the first seven thousand five hundred dollars ($7,500), or the pro rata amount under subdivision (b) of Section 6106.4, if applicable, and shall send a written notice to the claimant filing the claim on or before two business days after the distribution that the amount will be paid to the seller, or to the other claimants in accordance with subdivision (b) of Section 6106.4, as the case may be, unless attached within 25 days from the mailing of the notice. Any portion of the amount withheld which is not attached by the claimant within that time shall be paid by the buyer or escrow agent to the seller, or to the other claimants in accordance with subdivision (b) of Section 6106.4 if they have not been paid in full. An attachment of any amount so withheld shall be limited in its effect to the amount withheld for the attaching claimant and shall give the attaching claimant no greater priority or rights with respect to its claim than the claimant would have had if the claim had not been disputed. For purposes of this subdivision, a claimant may obtain the issuance of an attachment for a claim which is less than five hundred dollars ($500) and which otherwise meets the requirements of Section 483.010 of the Code of Civil Procedure or which is a secured claim or lien of the type described in Section 483.010 of the Code of Civil Procedure. The remedy in this subdivision shall be in addition to any other remedies the claimant may have, including any right to attach the property intended to be transferred or any other property.

(d) If the cash consideration payable is not sufficient to pay all of the claims received in full, where no escrow has been established pursuant to Section 6106.4, the buyer shall follow the procedures specified in subdivisions (a) to (c), inclusive, of Section 6106.4, and the immunity established by paragraph (3) of subdivision (a) of that section shall apply to the buyer.

(e) The buyer or escrow agent shall, within 45 days after the buyer takes legal title to any of the goods, either pay to the extent of the cash consideration the claims filed and not disputed, or the applicable portion thereof to the extent of the cash consideration under subdivision (b) of Section 6106.4, or institute an action in interpleader pursuant to subdivision (b) of Section 386 of the Code of Civil Procedure and deposit the consideration with the clerk of the court pursuant to subdivision (c) of that section. The action shall be brought in the appropriate court in the county where the seller had its principal place of business in this state. Sections 386.1 and 386.6 of the Code of Civil Procedure shall apply in the action.

(f) The notice shall state, in addition to the matters required by Section 6105, the name and address of the person with whom claims may be filed and the last date for filing claims, which shall be the business day before the date stated in the notice pursuant to paragraph (4) of subdivision (a) of Section 6105. Claims shall be deemed timely filed only if actually received by the person designated in the notice to receive claims before the close of business on the day specified in the notice as the last date for filing claims.

(g) This section shall not be construed to release any security interest or other lien on the property which is the subject of the bulk sale except upon a voluntary release by the secured party or lienholder. *(Added by Stats.1990, c. 1191 (A.B.3653), § 4.)*

Application

Bulk sales on or after and before Jan. 1, 1991, application of division and former division, see § 6111.

§ 6106.4. Escrow; filing claims; distribution; notice

In any case where the notice of a bulk sale subject to Section 6106.2 states that claims may be filed with an escrow agent, the intended buyer shall deposit with the escrow agent the full amount of the purchase price or consideration. If, at the time the bulk sale is otherwise ready to be consummated, the amount of cash deposited or agreed to be deposited at or prior to consummation in the escrow is insufficient to pay in full all of the claims filed with the escrow agent, the escrow agent shall do each of the following:

(a) (1) Delay the distribution of the consideration and the passing of legal title for a period of not less than 25 days nor more than 30 days from the date the notice required in paragraph (2) is mailed.

(2) Within five business days after the time the bulk sale would otherwise have been consummated, send a written notice to each claimant who has filed a claim stating the total consideration deposited or agreed to be deposited in the escrow, the name of each claimant who filed a claim against the escrow and the amount of each claim, the amount proposed to be paid to each claimant, the new date scheduled for the passing of legal title pursuant to paragraph (1) and the date on or before which distribution will be made to claimants which shall not be more than five days after the new date specified for the passing of legal title.

(3) If no written objection to the distribution described in the notice required by paragraph (2) is received by the escrow agent prior to the new date specified in the notice for the passing of legal title, the escrow agent shall not be liable to any person to whom

the notice required by paragraph (2) was sent for any good faith error that may have been committed in allocating and distributing the consideration as stated in the notice.

(b) Distribute the consideration in the following order of priorities:

(1) All obligations owing to the United States, to the extent given priority by federal law.

(2) Secured claims, including statutory and judicial liens, to the extent of the consideration fairly attributable to the value of the properties securing the claims and in accordance with the priorities provided by law. A secured creditor shall participate in the distribution pursuant to this subdivision only if a release of lien is deposited by the secured creditor conditioned only upon receiving an amount equal to the distribution.

(3) Escrow and professional charges and brokers' fees attributable directly to the sale.

(4) Wage claims given priority by Section 1205 of the Code of Civil Procedure.

(5) All other tax claims.

(6) All other unsecured claims pro rata, including any deficiency claims of partially secured creditors.

(c) To the extent that an obligation of the buyer to pay cash in the future is a part of the consideration and the cash consideration is not sufficient to pay all claims filed in full, apply all principal and interest received on the obligation to the payment of claims in accordance with subdivision (b) until they are paid in full before making any payment to the seller. In that case, the notice sent pursuant to subdivision (a) shall state the amount, terms, and due dates of the obligation and the portion of the claims expected to be paid thereby.

No funds may be drawn from the escrow, prior to the actual closing and completion of the escrow, for the payment, in whole or in part, of any commission, fee, or other consideration as compensation for a service that is contingent upon the performance of any act, condition, or instruction set forth in the escrow. (Added by Stats.1990, c. 1191 (A.B.3653), § 3. Amended by Stats. 1991, c. 111 (S.B.972), § 1.5, eff. July 15, 1991.)

Application

Bulk sales on or after and before Jan. 1, 1991, application of division and former division, see § 6111.

§ 6107. Liability for Noncompliance

(a) Except as provided in subdivision (c), and subject to the limitation in subdivision (d), a buyer who fails to comply with the requirements of Section 6104 with respect to a claimant is liable to the claimant for damages in the amount of the claim, reduced by any amount that the claimant would not have realized if the buyer had complied.

(b) In an action under subdivision (a), the claimant has the burden of establishing the validity and amount of the claim, and the buyer has the burden of establishing the amount that the claimant would not have realized if the buyer had complied.

(c) A buyer who made a good faith and commercially reasonable effort to comply with the requirements of Section 6104 or to exclude the sale from the application of this division under subdivision (c) of Section 6103 is not liable to creditors for failure to comply with the requirements of Section 6104. The buyer has the burden of establishing the good faith and commercial reasonableness of the effort.

(d) In a single bulk sale the cumulative liability of the buyer for failure to comply with the requirements of Section 6104 may not exceed an amount equal to any of the following:

(1) If the assets consist only of inventory and equipment, twice the net contract price, less the amount of any part of the net contract price paid to or applied for the benefit of the seller or a creditor except to the extent that the payment or application is applied to a debt which is secured by the assets and which has been taken into consideration in determining the net contract price.

(2) If the assets include property other than inventory and equipment, twice the net value of the inventory and equipment less the amount of the portion of any part of the net contract price paid to or applied for the benefit of the seller or a creditor which is allocable to the inventory and equipment except to the extent that the payment or application is applied to a debt which is secured by the assets and which has been taken into consideration in determining the net contract price.

(e) For the purposes of paragraph (2) of subdivision (d), the "net value" of an asset is the value of the asset less each of the following:

(1) The amount of any proceeds of the sale of an asset, to the extent the proceeds are applied in partial or total satisfaction of a debt secured by the asset.

(2) The amount of any debt to the extent it is secured by a security interest or lien that is enforceable against the asset before and after it has been sold to a buyer. If a debt is secured by an asset and other property of the seller, the amount of the debt secured by a security interest or lien that is enforceable against the asset is determined by multiplying the debt by a fraction, the numerator of which is the value of the asset on the date of the bulk sale and the denominator of which is the value of all property securing the debt on the date of the bulk sale. The portion of a part of the net contract price paid to or applied for the benefit of the seller or a creditor that is "allocable to the inventory and equipment" is the portion that bears the same ratio to that part of the net contract price as the net value of the inventory and equipment bears to the net value of all of the assets.

(f) A payment made by the buyer to a person to whom the buyer is, or believes it is, liable under

§ 6107

subdivision (a) reduces pro tanto the buyer's cumulative liability under subdivision (d).

(g) No action may be brought under subdivision (a) by or on behalf of a claimant whose claim is unliquidated or contingent.

(h) A buyer's failure to comply with the requirements of Section 6104 does not do any of the following:

(1) Impair the buyer's rights in or title to the assets.

(2) Render the sale ineffective, void, or voidable.

(3) Entitle a creditor to more than a single satisfaction of its claim.

(4) Create liability other than as provided in this division.

(i) Payment of the buyer's liability under subdivision (a) discharges pro tanto the seller's debt to the creditor.

(j) Unless otherwise agreed, a buyer has an immediate right of reimbursement from the seller for any amount paid to a creditor in partial or total satisfaction of the buyer's liability under subdivision (a). *(Added by Stats.1990, c. 1191 (A.B.3653), § 3.)*

Application

Bulk sales on or after and before Jan. 1, 1991, application of division and former division, see § 6111.

Uniform Commercial Code Comment
1990 Addition

Prior Uniform Statutory Provision: None.

Purposes:

1. This section sets forth the consequences of noncompliance with the requirements of Section 6–104. Although other legal consequences may result from a bulk sale—*e.g.,* the buyer may be liable to the seller under Article 2 or to the seller's creditors under the Uniform Fraudulent Transfer Act—no other consequences may be imposed by reason of the buyer's failure to comply with the requirements of this Article.

The two subsections of Section 6–107(1) reflect the duties set forth in Section 6–104. The duties generally run only to claimants, but the duty to distribute the net contract price in accordance with the schedule of distribution (Section 6–104(1)(e)) may run also to certain creditors.

2. Article 6 (1987 Official Text), like many of its nonuniform predecessors, makes a noncomplying transfer ineffective against aggrieved creditors. In contrast, noncompliance with this Article neither renders the sale ineffective nor otherwise affects the buyer's rights in or title to the assets.

Liability under this Article is for breach of a statutory duty. The buyer's only liability is personal (*in personam*) liability. Aggrieved creditors may only recover money damages. *In rem* remedies, which are available upon noncompliance with Article 6 (1987 Official Text), are not available under this Article. Thus, aggrieved creditors no longer may treat the sale as if it had not occurred and use the judicial process to apply assets purchased by the buyer toward the satisfaction of their claims against the seller.

The change in the theory of liability and in the available remedy should be of particular significance if the seller enters bankruptcy after the sale is consummated. When an aggrieved creditor of the transferor has a nonbankruptcy right to avoid a transfer in whole or in part, as may be the case under Article 6 (1987 Official Text), the transferor's bankruptcy trustee may avoid the entire transfer. See Bankruptcy Code § 544(b), 11 U.S.C. § 544(b). Under this Article, a person who is aggrieved by the buyer's noncompliance may not avoid the sale. Rather, the person is entitled only to recover damages as provided in this section. Because no creditor has the right to avoid the transaction or to assert a remedy that is the functional equivalent of avoidance, the seller's bankruptcy trustee likewise should be unable to do so.

3. This Article makes explicit what is implicit in Article 6 (1987 Official Text): only those persons as to whom there has been noncompliance are entitled to a remedy. For example, if notices are sent to each claimant other than claimant A, claimant B cannot recover. Similarly, a creditor who acquires a claim after notice is given has no remedy unless the buyer undertakes in the schedule of distribution to pay that creditor and the buyer fails to meet the obligation.

4. Unlike Article 6 (1987 Official Text), which imposes strict liability upon a noncomplying transferee, this Article imposes liability for noncompliance only when the failure to comply actually has injured a creditor and only to the extent of the injury. Each creditor's damages are measured by the injury that the particular creditor sustained as a consequence of the buyer's failure to comply. This measure is stated as the amount of the debt reduced by any amount that the person would not have realized if the buyer had complied. Compare Section 4–103(5).

5. A buyer is liable only for the buyer's own noncompliance with the requirements of Section 6–104. Under that section, the only step the buyer must take to discover the identity of the seller's claimants is to obtain a list of claimants from the seller. If the seller's list is incomplete and the buyer lacks knowledge of claimant C, then claimant C has no remedy under subsection (1)(b) of this section.

6. The creditor has the burden of establishing the validity and amount of the debt owed by the seller as well as the fact of the buyer's noncompliance. In contesting the allegation of noncompliance, the buyer may introduce evidence tending to show either that the sale was not a bulk sale or that the sale was a bulk sale to which this Article does not apply. In contesting the validity and amount of the debt, the buyer may introduce evidence tending to show that the seller had a defense to the debt. The buyer has the burden of establishing the amount that the creditor would not have realized even if the buyer had complied. Implicit in subsection (2) is that certain failures to comply with the requirements of this Article will cause no injury and thus result in no liability.

The following examples illustrate the operation of subsection (2):

Example 1: The buyer fails to give notice of the bulk sale. Claimant D, who appears on seller's list of claimants, admits to having had actual knowledge of the impending sale two months before it occurred. The buyer is likely to be able to meet the burden of establishing that even had the buyer given notice of the sale, claimant D would not have recovered any more than the claimant actually recovered.

Example 2: The buyer failed to obtain a list of seller's business names (Section 6–104(1)(a)) or to make available the list of claimants. (Section 6–104(1)(f)). In many cases, the buyer may be able to meet the burden of establishing that compliance with those subsections would not have enabled claimants to recover any more than they actually recovered.

7. Subsection (3) may afford a complete defense to a noncomplying buyer. This defense is available to buyers who establish that they made a good faith effort to comply with the requirements of this Article or made a good faith effort to exclude the sale from the application of this Article (*e.g.,* by assuming debts and attempting to comply with the notice requirements of Section 6–103(3)(i), (j), or (k)). When a buyer makes a good faith effort to comply with this Article or to exclude the transaction from its coverage, the injury caused by noncompliance is likely to be *de minimis*. In any event, the primary responsibility for satisfying claims rests with the creditors, and this Article imposes no greater duty upon buyers who attempt to comply with this Article or to exclude a sale from its application than to make a good faith effort to do so.

The defense of subsection (3) also is available to buyers who act on the good faith belief that this Article does not apply to the sale (*e.g.,* because the sale is not a bulk sale or is excluded under Section 6–103). The good-faith-belief defense is an acknowledgement that reasonable people may disagree over whether a given transaction is or is not a bulk sale and over whether Section 6–103 excludes a particular transaction. A buyer acting in good faith should be protected from the liability that this Article otherwise would impose on buyers who may be completely innocent of wrongdoing. A buyer who is unaware of the requirements of this Article holds no belief concerning the applicability of the Article and so may not use the defense.

8. Even a buyer who completely fails to comply with this Article may not be liable in an amount equal to sum of the seller's debts. Subsection (4) limits the aggregate recovery for "any one bulk sale," which term includes a series of sales by a liquidator. The maximum cumulative liability for noncompliance with this Article parallels the maximum recovery generally available to creditors under the 1987 Official Text of Article 6. Under that Article, the noncomplying transferee may have to "pay twice" for the goods. First, the transferee may pay the purchase price to the transferor; then, the transferee may lose the goods to aggrieved creditors.

Under this Article, the maximum cumulative liability is an amount equal to twice the net contract price of the inventory and equipment (*i.e.*, twice the amount that would be available to unsecured creditors from the inventory and equipment), less the amount of any portion of that net contract price paid to or applied for the benefit of the seller or a creditor of the seller. Unless the buyer receives credit for amounts paid to the seller (which amounts the creditors have a right to apply to payment of their claims), the buyer might wind up paying an amount equal to the net contract price three times (once to the seller and twice to aggrieved creditors). The grant of credit for amounts paid to the seller's creditors recognizes that ordinarily the seller has no obligation to pay creditors pro rata.

When the assets sold consist of only inventory and equipment, calculation of the maximum cumulative liability is relatively simple. But when the assets sold include property in addition to inventory and equipment, the calculation becomes more difficult. When inventory or equipment secures a debt that also is secured by other collateral and the aggregate value of the collateral exceeds the secured debt, a determination of the amount in clause (ii) of subsection (5) may require an allocation of the collateral to the debt in accordance with the statutory formula. In addition, one may need to determine which portion of payments of the net contract price is allocable to inventory and equipment. Subsection (5) directs that this allocation be made by multiplying the part of the net contract price paid to or applied for the benefit of the seller or a creditor by a fraction whose nominator is the net value of the inventory and equipment and whose denominator is the net value of all the assets.

Sometimes the seller may receive the net contract price and pay some or all of it to one or more creditors. In determining whether a payment to a creditor was made from the net contract price or from another source, courts are free to employ tracing rules. Amounts paid to secured parties usually are taken into account in determining the net contract price; if so, the buyer should not receive credit for them.

9. The buyer need not wait for judgment to be entered before paying a person believed to be a creditor of the seller. Indeed, the buyer is entitled to credit for amounts paid to persons who in fact may not be creditors of the seller, as long as the buyer acts with the belief that the seller is so indebted. As is the case with respect to all obligations under the Code, the buyer's belief must be held in good faith.

10. Any amounts paid by the buyer in satisfaction of the liability created by Section 6–107(1) reduce the seller's liability to the recipient pro tanto. Consequently, the buyer is entitled to immediate reimbursement of those amounts from the seller. The right of reimbursement is available only for amounts paid to actual creditors. Amounts paid to those whom the buyer incorrectly believes to be creditors ordinarily are not recoverable from the seller, although the buyer is entitled to credit for those amounts against the aggregate liability in subsection (4). Of course, the buyer and seller may vary the seller's reimbursement obligation by agreement.

11. Because of the difficulty in valuing claims that are unliquidated or contingent, persons holding claims of that kind may not bring an action under subsection (1)(b). If the claim remains unliquidated or contingent throughout the limitation period in Section 6–110, then these creditors have no remedy for noncompliance under that subsection. They may, however, be entitled to a remedy under subsection (1)(a) or (11) for failure to distribute the net contract price in accordance with the schedule of distribution.

12. In certain circumstances, subsection (11) imposes liability on a person in direct or indirect control of a seller that is an organization. Excuse under Section 6–106(6) is a "legal justification" that prevents liability from attaching under subsection (11). No special provision applies to the seller who fails to comply with the schedule. The seller already owes the debt to the creditor, and other law governs the consequences of a debtor who fails to pay a debt when promised.

Cross-References:
Point 1: Section 6–104.
Point 4: Section 4–103.
Point 5: Sections 6–104 and 6–105.
Point 6: Sections 1–201, 6–102, 6–103, and 6–104.
Point 7: Sections 1–102, 1–201, 6–102, and 6–103.
Point 8: Section 6–102.
Point 9: Section 1–203.
Point 10: Section 1–102.
Point 11: Sections 6–102 and 6–110.
Point 12: Section 6–106.

Definitional Cross-References:
"Assets". Section 6–102.
"Bulk sale". Section 6–102.
"Burden of establishing". Section 1–201.
"Buyer". Section 2–103.
"Claim". Section 6–102.
"Claimant". Section 6–102.
"Creditor". Section 6–102.
"Date of the bulk sale". Section 6–102.
"Equipment". Section 6–102.
"Good faith". Section 6–102.
"Inventory". Section 9–109.
"Net contract price". Section 6–102.
"Organization". Section 1–201.
"Person". Section 1–201.
"Proceeds". Section 9–306.
"Security interest". Section 1–201.
"Seller". Section 2–103.
"Written". Section 1–201.

Cross References

Auction sales, notice, see Commercial Code § 6108.
Necessity of notice, see Commercial Code § 6105.
Recording in office of county recorder, see Government Code § 27320.

§ 6108. Auction sales

(a) Sections 6104, 6105, and 6107 apply to a bulk sale by auction and a bulk sale conducted by a liquidator on the seller's behalf with the following modifications:

(1) "Buyer" refers to auctioneer or liquidator, as the case may be.

(2) "Net contract price" refers to net proceeds of the auction or net proceeds of the sale, as the case may be.

(3) The written notice required under subdivision (a) of Section 6105 shall be accompanied by a statement that the sale is to be by auction or by liquidation, the name of the auctioneer or liquidator, and the time and place of the auction or the time and place on or after which the liquidator will begin to sell assets on the seller's behalf.

(4) In a single bulk sale the cumulative liability of the auctioneer or liquidator for failure to comply with the requirements of this section may not exceed the amount of the net proceeds of the sale allocable to inventory and equipment sold less the amount of the portion of any part of the net proceeds paid to or applied for the benefit of a creditor which is allocable to the inventory and equipment.

(b) A payment made by the auctioneer or liquidator to a person to whom the auctioneer or liquidator is, or believes it is, liable under this section reduces pro tanto

§ 6108

the auctioneer's or liquidator's cumulative liability under paragraph (4) of subdivision (a).

(c) A person who buys at a bulk sale by auction or conducted by a liquidator need not comply with the requirements of Section 6104 and is not liable for the failure of an auctioneer or liquidator to comply with the requirements of this section. *(Added by Stats.1990, c. 1191 (A.B.3653), § 3.)*

Application

Bulk sales on or after and before Jan. 1, 1991, application of division and former division, see § 6111.

Uniform Commercial Code Comment
1990 Addition

Prior Uniform Statutory Provision: Section 6–108.

Changes: Revised, expanded to include sales conducted by a liquidator on the seller's behalf, and form of notice added.

Purposes of Changes and New Matter:

1. This section applies only to bulk sales by auction or conducted by a liquidator on the seller's behalf, as defined in Section 6–102(1)(c). Bulk sales conducted by an auctioneer or liquidator on its own behalf are treated as ordinary bulk sales and are not subject to this section.

2. Regardless of whether the assets are sold directly from the seller to the buyer, are sold to a variety of buyers at auction, or are sold on the seller's behalf by a liquidator to one or more buyers, a going-out-of-business sale of inventory presents similar risks to claimants. Auctioneers and liquidators are likely to be in a better position to ascertain whether the sale they are conducting is, or is part of, a bulk sale than are their customers. Accordingly, buyers at auctions and from liquidators selling assets of others need not be concerned with complying with this Article. Instead, this Section imposes upon auctioneers and liquidators duties and liabilities that are similar, but not always identical, to those of a buyer under Sections 6–104(1) and 6–107. Except to the extent that this section treats bulk sales by auctioneers and liquidators differently from those conducted by the seller on its own behalf, the Official Comments to Sections 6–105(1) and 6–107, as well as the Comments to Sections 6–105 and 6–106, which those sections incorporate by reference, are applicable to sales to which this section applies.

3. Subsection (1)(d) sets forth the maximum cumulative liability for auctioneers and liquidators "in any one bulk sale," which term includes a series of sales by a liquidator. This liability is to be calculated in a manner similar to that set forth in Sections 6–107(4) and 6–107(5). The term "net proceeds of the auction or sale allocable to inventory and equipment" is analogous to the term "net value of the inventory and equipment"; however, the former takes into account the reasonable expenses of the auction or sale whereas the latter does not. Also, the latter is doubled whereas the former is not. The "amount of the portion of any part of the net proceeds paid to or applied for the benefit of a creditor which is allocable to inventory and equipment" is determined by multiplying the part of the net proceeds paid to or applied for the benefit of a creditor by a fraction whose numerator is the net proceeds of the sale allocable to inventory and equipment and whose denominator is the total net proceeds of the auction or sale. Because the amount of the net proceeds allocable to inventory and equipment is not doubled, the auctioneer or liquidator is not entitled to credit for payments made to the seller.

4. Section 6–107(3) applies to all bulk sales. Accordingly, an auctioneer or liquidator who makes a good faith effort to comply with the requirements of this Article or to exclude the sale from this Article or who acts under a good faith belief that this Article does not apply to the sale faces no liability whatsoever.

Cross–References:
Point 1: Section 6–102.
Point 2: Sections 6–102, 6–104, 6–105, 6–106, and 6–107.
Point 3: Sections 6–102 and 6–107.
Point 4: Section 6–107.

Definitional Cross–References:
"Assets". Section 6–102.
"Auctioneer". Section 6–102.
"Bulk sale". Section 6–102.
"Claimants". Section 6–102.
"Creditor". Section 6–102.
"Debt". Section 6–102.
"Equipment". Section 9–109.
"Inventory". Section 9–109.
"Liquidator". Section 6–102.
"Net proceeds". Section 6–102.
"Person". Section 1–201.
"Seller". Section 2–103.
"Written". Section 1–201.

Cross References

Additional requisites for effective transfers, see Commercial Code § 6105 et seq.
Authority of auctioneers, see Civil Code §§ 2362, 2363.
Creditor, see Commercial Code § 1201.
Notice to creditors, see Commercial Code § 6105 et seq.
Sale by auction, see Commercial Code § 2328.

§ 6109. Repealed by Stats.1990, c. 1191 (A.B.3653), § 2

§ 6110. Limitation of actions

(a) Except as provided in subdivision (b), an action under this division against a buyer, auctioneer, or liquidator shall be commenced within one year after the date of the bulk sale.

(b) If the buyer, auctioneer, or liquidator conceals the fact that the sale has occurred, the limitation is tolled and an action under this division may be commenced within the earlier of the following:

(1) One year after the person bringing the action discovers that the sale has occurred.

(2) One year after the person bringing the action should have discovered that the sale has occurred, but no later than two years after the date of the bulk sale. Complete noncompliance with the requirements of this division does not of itself constitute concealment. *(Added by Stats.1990, c. 1191 (A.B.3653), § 3.)*

Application

Bulk sales on or after and before Jan. 1, 1991, application of division and former division, see § 6111.

Uniform Commercial Code Comment
1990 Addition

Prior Uniform Statutory Provision: Section 6–111 (1987 Official Text).

Changes: Statute of limitations extended and clarified.

Purposes of Changes and New Matter:

1. This Article imposes liability upon only those who do not make a good faith and commercially reasonable effort to comply with the requirements of the Article or to exclude the sale from the application of the Article and who do not hold a good faith and commercially reasonable belief that the Article is inapplicable to the sale. Consequently, it extends the six-month limitation period of the 1987 Official Text, which applies to good faith transferees as well as those not in good faith, to one year. The period commences with the date of the bulk sale.

2. Cases decided under the 1987 Official Text of Article 6 disagree over whether the complete failure to comply with the requirements of that Article constitutes a concealment that tolls the limitation. This

Article adopts the view that noncompliance does not of itself constitute concealment.

3. This Article does not contemplate tolling the limitation for actions against a person in control of the seller who fails to distribute the net contract price in accordance with the schedule of distribution. Those actions must be commenced within one year after the alleged violation occurs.

Cross–References:

Point 1: Sections 1–201, 6–102, 6–107 and 6–108.

Point 3: Section 6–107.

Definitional Cross–References:

"Action". Section 1–201.

"Auctioneer". Section 6–102.

"Buyer". Section 2–103.

"Date of the bulk sale". Section 6–102.

"Liquidator". Section 6–102.

Cross References

Actual and constructive notice, see Civil Code §§ 18, 19.
Excepted transfers, see Commercial Code § 6103.
Transfers and enterprises subject to this division, see Commercial Code § 6102.

§ 6111. Application of division

(a) Except to the extent provided in subdivision (b), this division shall apply to a bulk sale if the date of the bulk sale is on or after January 1, 1991.

(b) If the date of a bulk sale is on or after January 1, 1991, and the date of the bulk-sale agreement is before January 1, 1991, all of the following shall apply:

(1) Paragraph (2) of subdivision (a) of Section 6103 and subdivision (b) of Section 6103 shall not apply and this division shall apply only if the goods are located in this state.

(2) Subdivision (a) of Section 6104 shall not apply.

(3) The buyer is required under subdivision (b) of Section 6104 to give notice in accordance with Section 6107, as in effect on December 31, 1990, rather than Section 6105.

(4) The buyer is required under subdivision (c) of Section 6104 to comply with Section 6106, as in effect on December 31, 1990, if the bulk sale is within the scope of that section, rather than Section 6106.2.

(5) Section 6105 shall not apply, and Section 6107, as in effect on December 31, 1990, shall apply.

(6) Sections 6106.2 and 6106.4 shall not apply, and Sections 6106 and 6106.1, as in effect on December 31, 1990, shall apply.

(7) No action may be brought under this division, as in effect either before or on or after January 1, 1991, if the provisions of this division, as in effect on December 31, 1990, have been complied with. *(Added by Stats. 1990, c. 1191 (A.B.3653), § 3.)*

Cross References

Action for relief on ground of fraud or mistake, limitation of actions, see Code of Civil Procedure § 338.
One year statute of limitations generally, see Code of Civil Procedure § 340.
Time of commencing civil actions, see Code of Civil Procedure §§ 312 et seq., 350 et seq.

Division 7

WAREHOUSE RECEIPTS, BILLS OF LADING AND OTHER DOCUMENTS OF TITLE

Chapter	Section
1. General	7101
2. Warehouse Receipts: Special Provisions	7201
3. Bills of Lading: Special Provisions	7301
4. Warehouse Receipts and Bills of Lading: General Obligations	7401
5. Warehouse Receipts and Bills of Lading: Negotiation and Transfer	7501
6. Warehouse Receipts and Bills of Lading: Miscellaneous Provisions	7601

Introductory Comment
By Charles J. Williams

Documents of title are made up principally of two types: bills of lading and warehouse receipts. These can be negotiable but more often are nonnegotiable. A document of title is used by a carrier or a warehouseman when goods are stored or shipped as a receipt for the goods. Since most railroad transportation is interstate, it is conducted under the nonnegotiable bill of lading.[1] While documents of title have a part in the mechanics of the storage and shipment of merchandise, they are also purchased and sold as symbols of the goods. These documents are used as a basis of credit to finance their storage and shipment.

Before the adoption of Division 7, documents of title were regulated by three uniform acts. The Uniform Sales Act (USA)[2] dealt with the negotiation and transfer of documents of title. Bills of lading were regulated by the Uniform Bills of Lading Act (UBLA).[3] Warehouse receipts were covered by the Uniform Warehouse Receipts Act (UWRA).[4] Interstate shipments and exports were covered by the Federal Bills of Lading Act (FBLA).[5] The FBLA was for the most part identical with the UBLA.

Federal law and state regulatory laws are left unrepealed by the adoption of Division 7. These laws will regulate many document of title transactions and will supersede Division 7. This is especially true with bills of lading. Division 7 is superseded in interstate shipments by the FBLA and the Carmack Amendment to the Interstate Commerce Act (49 USCA Section 20(11). Overseas shipments are governed by the Harter Act (46 U.S.C.A. sections 190–196) and the Carriage of Goods by Sea Act (46 USCA Sections 1300–1315). The United States Warehouse Act (7 USCA Sections 241–273) regulates agricultural warehouses in which products are stored under federal programs and it also supersedes Division 7.

State regulatory statutes also prevail over this division (Commercial Code § 7103).

Division 7 combines and integrates the USA, UBLA and UWRA to the extent that it covers problems common to all documents. Chapters 1, 4, 5 and 6 apply to all documents of title. Chapter 2 contains special rules applicable to warehouse receipts and Chapter 3 states special rules applicable to bills of lading. One of the differences between Chapter 2 and Chapter 3 is the existence of detailed formal requirements for a warehouse receipt while no such requirements exist for a bill of lading. The reason for this is that federal law supersedes in the case of bills of lading. See California Code Comment 1 to Commercial Code Section 7301.

[1] Braucher, Documents of Title, 2 (A.L.I.1958).
[2] Former Civil Code §§ 1721 to 1800.
[3] Former Civil Code §§ 2126 to 2132c.
[4] Former Civil Code §§ 1858.01 to 1858.85.
[5] 49 USCA §§ 81 to 124 (1952).

Cross References
Form or contents of documents of title or business of bailees, effect of this division, see Commercial Code § 13104.

CHAPTER 1. GENERAL

Section
7101. Short Title.
7102. Definitions and Index of Definitions.
7103. Relation of Division to Treaty, Statute, Tariff, Classification or Regulation.
7104. Negotiable and Non-Negotiable Warehouse Receipt, Bill of Lading, or Other Document of Title.
7105. Construction Against Negative Implication.

Cross References
Fish marketing associations, receipts from warehouses owned by, see Corporations Code § 13334.
Self-service storage facilities, application of this division, see Business and Professions Code § 21701.

§ 7101. Short Title

This division shall be known and may be cited as Uniform Commercial Code—Documents of Title. *(Stats.1963, c. 819, § 7101.)*

California Code Comment
By John A. Bohn and Charles J. Williams

This is section 7–101 of the Official Text without change.

Uniform Commercial Code Comment

This Article is a consolidation and revision of the Uniform Warehouse Receipts Act and the Uniform Bills of Lading Act, and embraces also the provisions of the Uniform Sales Act relating to negotiation of documents of title.

The only substantial omissions of material covered in the previous uniform acts are the criminal provisions found in the Warehouse Receipts and Bills of Lading acts. These criminal provisions are inappropriate to a Commercial Code, and for the most part duplicate portions of the ordinary criminal law relating to frauds.

The Article does not attempt to define the tort liability of bailees, except to hold certain classes of bailees to a minimum standard of reasonable care. For important classes of bailees, liabilities in case of loss, damage or destruction, as well as other legal questions associated with particular documents of title, are governed by federal statutes, international treaties, and in some cases regulatory state laws, which supersede the provisions of this Article in case of inconsistency. See Section 7–103.

Cross References
Collection of documentary drafts, see Commercial Code § 4501 et seq.
Preference of producer's lien, exception, see Food and Agricultural Code § 55633.

§ 7102. Definitions and Index of Definitions

(1) In this division, unless the context otherwise requires:

(a) "Bailee" means the person who by a warehouse receipt, bill of lading or other document of title acknowledges possession of goods and contracts to deliver them.

(b) "Consignee" means the person named in a bill to whom or to whose order the bill promises delivery.

(c) "Consignor" means the person named in a bill as the person from whom the goods have been received for shipment.

(e) "Document" means document of title as defined in the general definitions in Division 1 (Section 1201).

(f) "Goods" means all things which are treated as movable for the purposes of a contract of storage or transportation.

(g) "Issuer" means a bailee who issues a document. Issuer includes any person for whom an agent or employee purports to act in issuing a document if the agent or employee has real or apparent authority to issue documents, notwithstanding that the issuer received no goods or that the goods were misdescribed or that in any other respect the agent or employee violated his instructions.

(h) "Warehouseman" is a person engaged in the business of storing goods for hire.

(2) Other definitions applying to this division or to specified chapters thereof, and the sections in which they appear are:

"Duly negotiate." Section 7501.

"Person entitled under the document." Section 7403(4).

(3) Definitions in other divisions applying to this division and the sections in which they appear are:

"Contract for sale." Section 2106.

"Overseas." Section 2323.

"Receipt" of goods. Section 2103.

(4) In addition Division 1 contains general definitions and principles of construction and interpretation applicable throughout this division. (Stats.1963, c. 819, § 7102.)

California Code Comment

By Charles J. Williams

The California version changed the 1962 Official Text by deleting all references to delivery orders. The Permanent Editorial Board for the Uniform Commercial Code made these comments to this California change:

"California has eliminated all references to delivery orders, amending Sections 1–201(15), 7–502 and 7–503. These changes appear to be based on a misunderstanding of criticisms made by the New York Law Revision Commission and upon an erroneous belief that the draftsmen of the Code invented delivery orders.

"The Uniform Sales Act included any "order for the delivery of goods" in its definition of "document of title to goods." According to the draftsman, that provision followed the English Factors' Act of 1889 and Sale of Goods Act of 1894. See 2 Williston, Sales § 405a (Rev.ed.1948). Negotiable delivery orders in both order form and bearer form have frequently been involved in reported cases. See, e.g., Ant. Jurgens Margarinefabriken v. Louis Dreyfus & Co., [1914] 3 K.B. 40; Laurie v. Dudin, [1925] 1 K.B. 383, affirmed [1926] 1 K.B. 223;

Comptoir d'Achat v. Luis de Ridder, Ltd., [1949] A.C. 293, 297 (H.L.); Anderson v. Read, 106 N.Y. 333, 13 N.E. 292 (1887); Maurice O'Meara Co. v. National Park Bank, 239 N.Y. 386, 146 N.E. 636 (1925); Kirsch v. Roulston, 178 N.Y.Supp. 246 (1919); Robinson v. All-Lite Sales Co., 202 N.Y.Supp. 260 (1923); Transmares Corp. v. George F. Smith, Inc., 76 N.Y.S.2d 737, affirmed 81 N.Y.S.2d 670 (1947). For a delivery order in non-negotiable form, see Cundill v. Lewis, 245 N.Y. 383, 157 N.E. 502 (1927). Several of those cases deal with rights between buyer and seller, governed by Section 2–503(4) of the Code.

"The 1952 version of the Code contained provisions as to delivery orders which were criticized and were revised in Supplement No. 1, January 1955. The revised provisions were subjected to further criticism. See 3 Report N.Y. Law Rev.Comm. 1840–1843 (1955); id. 448–449 (1956). Further revision in 1956 substantially complied with those criticisms. See Committee on Uniform State Laws of the Ass'n of the Bar of the City of New York, Report on the Uniform Commercial Code 69 (1962).

"The revised provisions simply spell out the consequences of the common practice of issuing a delivery order, as explained in Braucher, Documents of Title 67–70 (2d ed.1958). The California consultants criticized that explanation for complexity, but the possible complexities are much the same whether there is a statute on the subject or not. Indeed, it is fairly arguable that the same results will follow under the common law or the Uniform Sales Act as under the Code." Permanent Editorial Board for the Uniform Commercial Code, Report No. 2 (1962 Official Text), pp. 121–122.

Uniform Commercial Code Comment

Prior Uniform Statutory Provision:

Section 76, Uniform Sales Act; Section 58, Uniform Warehouse Receipts Act; Sections 1 and 53, Uniform Bills of Lading Act.

Changes: Applicable definitions from the uniform acts have been consolidated and revised; definition of delivery order is new.

Purposes of Changes and New Matter:

1. "Bailee" was not defined in the old uniform acts. It is used in this Article as a blanket term to designate carriers, warehousemen and others who normally issue documents of title on the basis of goods which they have received. The definition does not, however, require actual possession of the goods. If a bailee acknowledges possession when he does not have it he is bound by sections of this Article which declare the "bailee's" obligations. (See definition of "Issuer" in this section and Sections 7–203 and 7–301 on liability in case of non-receipt.)

2. The definition of warehouse receipt contained in the general definitions section of this Act (Section 1–201) eliminates the requirement of the Uniform Warehouse Receipts Act that the issuing warehouseman be "lawfully engaged" in business. The warehouseman's compliance with applicable state regulations such as the filing of a bond has no bearing on the substantive issues dealt with in this Article. Certainly the issuer's violations of law should not diminish his responsibility on documents he has put in commercial circulation. The Uniform Warehouse Receipts Act requirement that the warehouseman be engaged "for profit" has also been eliminated in view of the existence of state operated and co-operative warehouses. But it is still essential that the business be storing goods "for hire" (Section 1–201 and this section). A person does not become a warehouseman by storing his own goods.

3. [Not applicable in California].

Cross References:

Point 1: Sections 7–203 and 7–301.

Point 2: Sections 1–201 and 7–203.

See general comment to document of title in Section 1–201.

Definitional Cross References:

"Bill of lading". Section 1–201.

"Contract". Section 1–201.

"Contract for sale". Section 2–106.

"Delivery". Section 1–201.

"Document of title". Section 1–201.

"Person". Section 1–201.

"Purchase". Section 1–201.

"Receipt of goods". Section 2–103.

"Right". Section 1–201.

"Warehouse receipt". Section 1–201.
"Written" Section 1–201.

Cross References

Crimes involving bailments, see Penal Code § 560 et seq.
Non-receipt or misdescription, liability, see Commercial Code §§ 7203, 7301.

§ 7103. Relation of Division to Treaty, Statute, Tariff, Classification or Regulation

To the extent that any treaty or statute of the United States, regulatory statute of this State, or tariff, classification or regulation filed or issued pursuant thereto is applicable, the provisions of this division are subject thereto. *(Stats.1963, c. 819, § 7103.)*

California Code Comment

By John A. Bohn and Charles J. Williams

Prior California Law

1. This section is new statutory law. It is a restatement of the rule that federal legislation and regulations pursuant to federal legislation are paramount, Art. VI, U.S.Constitution; Seaboard Air Line Ry. Co. v. Daniel, 333 U.S. 118, 68 S.Ct. 426, 92 L.Ed. 580 (S.C.1948), but adds state regulatory statutes and regulations to this supremacy rule.

Interstate shipments and foreign exports were and continue to be governed by the Federal Bills of Lading Act (FBLA), 49 USC §§ 81–124. Chesapeake & Ohio Ry. v. Martin, 283 U.S. 209, 51 S.Ct. 453, 75 L.Ed. 983 (Va.1931). The FBLA is for the most part identical with The Uniform Bills of Lading Act (UBLA).

Ocean bills of lading for exports and imports must comply with the Carriage of Goods by Sea Act, 46 USC §§ 1300–1315.

Statutes regulating the business of carriers and warehousemen also affect documents of title. On the federal level, e.g. the Interstate Commerce Act, 49 USC § 20. On the state level, e.g. warehousemen are public utilities and subject to regulation as such. Pub.U.C. §§ 216, 2501–2574.

Related to this principle of subordination are the provisions of Commercial Code § 10104 which preserves all regulatory statutes dealing with bailees. See also Commercial Code § 7201(2) which covers the situation of receipts issued by a bonded warehouse under regulatory statutes, e.g. whiskey (26 USC Chapter 26).

Changes from U.C.C. (1962 Official Text)

2. This is section 7–103 of the Official Text without change.

Uniform Commercial Code Comment

Prior Uniform Statutory Provision:
None.

Purposes:

1. To make clear what would of course be true without the Section, that applicable Federal law is paramount.

2. To make clear also that *regulatory* state statutes (such as those fixing or authorizing a commission to fix rates and prescribe services, authorizing different charges for goods of different values, and limiting liability for loss to the declared value on which the charge was based) are not affected by the Article and are controlling on the matters which they cover. Notice that the reference is not only to such statutes, but to tariffs, classifications and regulations filed or issued pursuant to them.

Cross References:
Sections 7–201, 7–202, 7–204, 7–206, 7–309, 7–401, 7–403.

Definitional Cross Reference:
"Bill of lading". Section 1–201.

Cross References

Duty of care, limitation of liability, see Commercial Code §§ 7204, 7309.
Form and terms of warehouse receipt, see Commercial Code § 7202.
Interpretation of contract, law governing, see Civil Code § 1646.
Irregularities in issue of receipt or bill, effect, see Commercial Code § 7401.
Law of domicile, personal property, see Civil Code § 946.
Obligation to deliver, see Commercial Code § 7403.
Storage under government bond, see Commercial Code § 7201.
Termination of storage, see Commercial Code § 7206.

§ 7104. Negotiable and Non-Negotiable Warehouse Receipt, Bill of Lading, or Other Document of Title

(1) A warehouse receipt, bill of lading or other document of title is negotiable

(a) If by its terms the goods are to be delivered to bearer or to the order of a named person; or

(b) Where recognized in overseas trade, if it runs to a named person or assigns.

(2) Any other document is nonnegotiable. A bill of lading in which it is stated that the goods are consigned to a named person is not made negotiable by a provision that the goods are to be delivered only against a written order signed by the same or another named person.

(3) A nonnegotiable warehouse receipt and a nonnegotiable bill of lading must be conspicuously (Section 1201) marked "nonnegotiable." In case of the bailee's failure to do so, a holder of the document who purchased it for value supposing it to be negotiable may, at his option, treat such document as imposing upon the bailee the same liabilities he would have incurred had the document been negotiable. *(Stats.1963, c. 819, § 7104.)*

California Code Comment

By John A. Bohn and Charles J. Williams

Prior California Law

1. The classification of negotiability or non-negotiability established in this section is important because the negotiable document more nearly represents the goods and the bailee may not deliver the goods without receiving the document. Commercial Code § 7403(3). The holder of a negotiable document can acquire greater rights than his transferor. Official Comment.

2. Subdivision (1) replaces former Civil Code §§ 1858.14 (UWRA), 2126d (UBLA), and 1747 (USA).

Subdivision (1)(a) is similar to former Civil Code §§ 1858.14 (UWRA) and 1747 (USA), both of which also conditioned negotiability upon the obligation to deliver the goods to the bearer of the document or to the order of a specified person. The definition in former Civil Code § 2126d (UBLA) which this subdivision replaces defined a negotiable bill as one "in which it is stated that the goods are consigned or destined to the order of any person named in such bill. . . ."

Former Civil Code §§ 1747 (USA), 1858.14 (UWRA) and 2126d (UBLA) all provided that a statement in a document to the effect that the document was non-negotiable would have no effect upon its negotiability. The Commercial Code does not contain a similar provision but it would appear that a statement of non-negotiability in a document which meets all requirements of negotiability should be treated as surplusage.

Former Civil Code §§ 1858–1858f which was a 1901 law dealing with warehouse receipts was found to be inconsistent with and superseded at least in part by the UWRA in Sampsell v. Lawrence Warehouse Co. (CCA 9 1948) 167 F.2d 885, certiorari denied 69 S.Ct. 42, 335 U.S. 820, 93 L.Ed. 375, and Sampsell v. Security-First Nat. Bank, 92 C.A.2d 648, 207 P.2d 1088 (1949).

3. Subdivision (1)(b) is new.

4. This first sentence of subdivision (2) defines all documents which do not meet the conditions of negotiability under subdivision (1) as non-negotiable. This replaces former Civil Code § 1858.13 (UWRA) defining a non-negotiable receipt as a "receipt in which it is stated that the goods received will be delivered to the depositor or to any other specified person . . ." and former Civil Code § 2126c (UBLA)

defining a non-negotiable bill as a "bill in which it is stated that the goods are consigned or destined to a specified person."

The second sentence of subdivision (2) is new.

5. Subdivision (3) of this section continues the rule of former Civil Code §§ 1858.16 (UWRA) and 2126g (UBLA) which required a non-negotiable receipt or bill to be plainly marked "non-negotiable" or "not negotiable" upon its face. Former Civil Code § 1858.16 (UWRA) provided that failure to mark the receipt in this manner permitted a holder for value to enforce it against the warehouseman as if it were negotiable. Former Civil Code § 2126g (UBLA) did not expressly state the consequences for failure to mark the bill.

Changes from U.C.C. (1962 Official Text)

6. Subdivision (3) of this section does not appear in section 7-104 of the Official Text.

Subdivision (3) was included in the California version because the requirement to plainly mark was felt to be desirable. The State Bar stated:

"Under the Uniform Warehouse Receipts Act and the Uniform Bills of Lading Act, the issuer must mark 'nonnegotiable' on a nonnegotiable warehouse receipt or bill of lading. An issuer who fails to so mark a nonnegotiable document is liable as if it had been negotiable [Footnote: (Cal.Civ.Code, §§ 1858b, 1858.16, 2126g.)] to a purchaser who supposes it to be negotiable. This marking requirement has been a great convenience to financing institutions which handle these documents in bulk. The Official Text of section 17104 [7104] would eliminate it. The Comments offer no explanation why. The State Bar Committee believes that clear labeling of nonnegotiable bills of lading is desirable and should be continued." California State Bar Committee on the Commercial Code, A Special Report, The Uniform Commercial Code, 37 Calif.State Bar J. (March–April, 1962), p. 181.

The interested groups which studied this section were in unanimous agreement that the requirement be included. As expressed by Professors Marsh and Warren:

"The abandonment by this section of the present requirements of the Uniform Warehouse Receipts Act and the Uniform Bills of Lading Act that a non-negotiable document be earmarked clearly changes California law as well as that of all other states. No reason is given for this abandonment by the draftsmen of the Code and studies of the Code merely note it without suggesting any reason for it. Braucher, Documents of Title under the Uniform Commercial Code (ALI 1958) 18; 3 N.Y.Law Rev.Comm., Study of the Uniform Commercial Code (1955) 1783.

"It is difficult to imagine why it was felt necessary to abandon the universal and, in our opinion, salutary, requirement for the earmarking of non-negotiable documents of title for the convenience of persons dealing with them. The only reason which we can think of is that it might have been considered unwise to impose this requirement upon the miscellaneous documents which are brought under Chapter [Division] 7 but which are not covered by the Warehouse Receipts Act and the Bill of Lading Act, and with respect to which the custom of earmarking non-negotiable documents may not be as widespread. Therefore, we have suggested that this requirement be retained only with respect to warehouse receipts and bills of lading." Sixth Progress Report to the Legislature by Senate Fact Finding Committee on Judiciary (1959-1961), Part 1, the Uniform (Commercial Code, p. 517.

For additional comments to the same effect by the public utility warehouse and field warehouse industries, see, Sixth Progress Report to the Legislature by Senate Fact Finding Committee on Judiciary (1959–1961), Part 1, The Uniform Commercial Code, 370 (Bankers Committee), 616 and 622.

Interestingly but by apparent coincidence only, the definition of "conspicuous" in Commercial Code § 1201(10) uses the phrase "Non-Negotiable Bill of Lading" as an example to illustrate what is intended by the word "conspicuous".

Uniform Commercial Code Comment

Prior Uniform Statutory Provision:

Sections 27 and 76, Uniform Sales Act; Sections 2, 3, 4 and 5, Uniform Warehouse Receipts Act; Sections 2, 3, 4, 5 and 53, Uniform Bills of Lading Act.

Changes: Consolidated and rewritten.

Purposes of Changes:

This Article deals with a class of commercial paper representing commodities in storage or transportation. This "commodity paper" is to be distinguished from what might be called "money paper" dealt with in the Article of this Act on Commercial Paper (Article 3) and "investment paper" dealt with in the Article of this Act on Investment Securities (Article 8). The class of "commodity paper" is designated "document of title" following the terminology of the Uniform Sales Act Section 76. Section 1–201. The distinctions between negotiable and nonnegotiable documents in this section makes the most important subclassification employed in the Article, in that the holder of negotiable documents may acquire more rights than his transferor had (See Section 7–502).

A document of title is negotiable only if it satisfies this section. "Deliverable on proper indorsement and surrender of this receipt" will not render a document negotiable. Bailees often include such provisions as a means of insuring return of non-negotiable receipts for record purposes. Such language may be regarded as insistence by the bailee upon a particular kind of receipt in connection with delivery of the goods. Subsections (1)(a) and (2) make it clear that a document is not negotiable which provides for delivery to order or bearer only if written instructions to that effect are given by a named person.

Cross Reference:

Section 7–502.

Definitional Cross References:

"Bearer". Section 1–201.
"Bill of lading". Section 1–201.
"Delivery". Section 1–201.
"Document of title". Section 1–201.
"Overseas". Section 2–323.
"Person". Section 1–201.
"Warehouse receipt". Section 1–201.

Cross References

Document of title, definition, see Commercial Code § 1201.
Due negotiation, rights acquired, see Commercial Code § 7502.
Form and contents of warehouse receipts, see Commercial Code § 7202.
Issuing fictitious bill of lading, see Penal Code §§ 577, 578.

§ 7105. Construction Against Negative Implication

The omission from either Chapter 2 or Chapter 3 of this division of a provision corresponding to a provision made in the other chapter does not imply that a corresponding rule of law is not applicable. *(Stats.1963, c. 819, § 7105.)*

California Code Comment

By John A. Bohn and Charles J. Williams

Prior California Law

1. This section is new statutory law. It was added to the Official Text as a result of suggestions from the Report of The New York Law Revision Commission, dated February 29, 1956. Its purpose is described in the Official Comment.

Changes from U.C.C. (1962 Official Text)

2. This is section 7–105 of the Official Text without change.

Uniform Commercial Code Comment

Prior Uniform Statutory Provision:
None.

Purposes:

To avoid any impairment, for example, of any common-law right of indemnity a warehouseman may have corresponding to Section 7–301(5), or of any contractual security interest a carrier might have corresponding to Section 7–209(2).

Cross References:
Parts 2 and 3 of Article 7.

Cross References

Bills of lading, special provisions, see Commercial Code § 7301 et seq.

Warehouse receipts, special provisions, see Commercial Code § 7201 et seq.

CHAPTER 2. WAREHOUSE RECEIPTS: SPECIAL PROVISIONS

Section
7201. Who May Issue a Warehouse Receipt; Storage Under Government Bond.
7202. Form of Warehouse Receipt; Essential Terms; Optional Terms.
7203. Liability for Non-Receipt or Misdescription.
7204. Duty of Care; Contractual Limitation of Warehouseman's Liability.
7205. Title Under Warehouse Receipt Defeated in Certain Cases.
7206. Termination of Storage at Warehouseman's Option.
7207. Goods Must Be Kept Separate; Fungible Goods.
7208. Altered Warehouse Receipts.
7209. Lien of Warehouseman.
7210. Enforcement of Warehouseman's Lien.

§ 7201. Who May Issue a Warehouse Receipt; Storage Under Government Bond

(1) A warehouse receipt may be issued by any warehouseman.

(2) Where goods including distilled spirits and agricultural commodities are stored under a statute requiring a bond against withdrawal or a license for the issuance of receipts in the nature of warehouse receipts, a receipt issued for the goods has like effect as a warehouse receipt even though issued by a person who is the owner of the goods and is not a warehouseman. *(Stats.1963, c. 819, § 7201.)*

California Code Comment

By John A. Bohn and Charles J. Williams

Prior California Law
1. Subdivision (1) is the same as former Civil Code § 1858.10 (UWRA).
2. Subdivision (2) is new statutory law. See Official Comment.

Changes from U.C.C. (1962 Official Text)
3. This is section 7–201 of the Official Text without change.

Uniform Commercial Code Comment

Prior Uniform Statutory Provision:
Section 1, Uniform Warehouse Receipts Act.

Changes: Provision added to cover storage under government bond or under licensing statute.

Purposes:
It is not intended by reenactment of subsection (1) to repeal any provisions of special licensing or other statutes regulating who may become a warehouseman. See Section 10–103. Subsection (2) covers receipts issued by the owner for whiskey or other goods stored in bonded warehouses under such statutes as 26 U.S.C. Chapter 26. Limitations on the transfer of the receipts and criminal sanctions for violation of such limitations are not impaired. Section 7–103. Compare Section 7–401(d) on the liability of the issuer in such cases.

Cross References:
Sections 7–103, 7–401, 10–103.

Definitional Cross References:
"Warehouse receipt". Section 1–201.
"Warehouseman". Section 7–102.

Cross References
Crimes involving bailments, see Penal Code § 560 et seq.
Definition of warehouseman, see Commercial Code § 7102.
Fictitious warehouse receipts, penal provision, see Penal Code § 578.
Obligations imposed by this division, application, see Commercial Code § 7401.
Treaty, statute, etc., effect, see Commercial Code § 7103.

§ 7202. Form of Warehouse Receipt; Essential Terms; Optional Terms

(1) A warehouse receipt need not be in any particular form.

(2) Unless a warehouse receipt embodies within its written or printed terms each of the following, the warehouseman is liable for damages caused by the omission to a person injured thereby:

(a) The location of the warehouse where the goods are stored;

(b) The date of issue of the receipt;

(c) The consecutive number of the receipt;

(d) A statement whether the goods received will be delivered to the bearer, to a specified person, or to a specified person or his order;

(e) The rate of storage and handling charges, except that where goods are stored under a field warehousing arrangement a statement of that fact is sufficient on a nonnegotiable receipt and except that where goods are stored in a public utility warehouse having a lawful tariff on file with the Public Utilities Commission, a statement that the rate of storage and handling charges are as provided in such tariff is sufficient;

(f) A description of the goods or of the packages containing them;

(g) The signature of the warehouseman, which may be made by his authorized agent;

(h) If the receipt is issued for goods of which the warehouseman is owner, either solely or jointly or in common with others, the fact of such ownership; and

(i) A statement of the amount of advances made and of liabilities incurred for which the warehouseman claims a lien or security interest (Section 7209). If the precise amount of such advances made or of such liabilities incurred is, at the time of the issue of the receipt, unknown to the warehouseman or to his agent who issues it, a statement of the fact that advances have been made or liabilities incurred and the purpose thereof is sufficient.

(3) A warehouseman may insert in his receipt any other terms which are not contrary to the provisions of this code and do not impair his obligation of delivery (Section 7403) or his duty of care (Section 7204). Any contrary provisions shall be ineffective. *(Stats.1963, c. 819, § 7202.)*

California Code Comment

By John A. Bohn and Charles J. Williams

§ 7202

Prior California Law

1. Subdivision (1) continues the rule stated in the first sentence of former Civil Code § 1858.11 (UWRA).

2. Subdivision (2) prescribing the contents of the warehouse receipt is substantially the same as former Civil Code § 1858.11 (UWRA) with the following exception:

The paragraph (e) requirement is expanded from the paragraph (e) requirement of former Civil Code § 1858.11 which only included the rate of storage charges.

3. If a document does not comply with the form prescribed the issuer is nevertheless subject to the same obligations as if it were in correct form. Commercial Code § 7401(a).

4. A warehouseman's liability for damages for failure to include the required terms is broadened in subdivision (2) to cover "any" (i.e. negotiable or non-negotiable) warehouse receipt. Former Civil Code § 1858.11 limited liability for the omission of required terms to negotiable warehouse receipts only.

5. Subdivision (3) is similar to former Civil Code § 1858.12(a) and part of (b) (UWRA). Former Civil Code § 1858.12(b) also fixed the standard of care of a warehouseman. This is now covered by Commercial Code § 7204.

Changes from U.C.C. (1962 Official Text)

6. Subdivision (2)(e) of the 1962 Official Text was modified in California by the addition of the following language:

"and except that where goods are stored in a public utility warehouse having a lawful tariff on file with the Public Utilities Commission, a statement that the rate of storage and handling charges are as provided in such tariff is sufficient."

Subsection (2)(e) of the Official Text reads:

"(e) The rate of storage and handling charges, except that where goods are stored under a field warehousing arrangement a statement of that fact is sufficient on a nonnegotiable receipt;"

The California change was made because the industry is regulated in California as a public utility:

"One item required by section 17202 [7202] would be statement of 'the rate of storage and handling charges.' The State Bar Committee recommends that this clause be amended to permit the incorporation of rates and charges on file with the Public Utilities Commission by a reference in the warehouse receipt to such established charges. Unlike most states California regulates the business of warehousing as a public utility when the warehouse holds itself out as serving the public. The rates and charges must be on file with the Public Utilities Commission. Any departure from them is prohibited. There is no need to require specification of public utility warehouse charges on the receipt." California State Bar Committee on the Commercial Code, A Special Report, The Uniform Commercial Code, 37 Calif. State Bar J. (March–April, 1962) p. 182.

Uniform Commercial Code Comment

Prior Uniform Statutory Provision:
Section 2, Uniform Warehouse Receipts Act.

Changes: Exemption for field warehouse receipts added in subsection (2)(e).

Purposes:
To make clear that the formal requirements of the Uniform Warehouse Receipts Act are continued but not to displace particular legislation requiring other or different specifications of form, see Sections 7–103 and 10–103. This section does not require that a receipt be issued but states formal requirements for those which are issued.

Cross References:
Sections 7–103 and 10–103.

Definitional Cross References:
"Bearer". Section 1–201.
"Delivery". Section 1–201.
"Goods". Section 7–102.
"Person". Section 1–201.
"Security interest". Section 1–201.
"Term". Section 1–201.
"Warehouse receipt". Section 1–201.
"Warehouseman". Section 7–102.
"Written". Section 1–201.

Cross References

Treaty, statute, etc., effect, see Commercial Code § 7103.

§ 7203. Liability for Non-Receipt or Misdescription

A party to or purchaser for value in good faith of a document of title other than a bill of lading relying in either case upon the description therein of the goods may recover from the issuer damages caused by the nonreceipt or misdescription of the goods, except to the extent that the document conspicuously indicates that the issuer does not know whether any part or all of the goods in fact were received or conform to the description, as where the description is in terms of marks or labels or kind, quantity or condition, or the receipt or description is qualified by "contents, condition and quality unknown," "said to contain" or the like, if such indication be true, or the party or purchaser otherwise has notice. (Stats.1963, c. 819, § 7203.)

California Code Comment

By John A. Bohn and Charles J. Williams

Prior California Law

1. This section is a rewording of former Civil Code § 1858.29 (UWRA) which provided for the liability of a warehouseman in the case of nonexistence of the goods or failure of the goods to correspond with the description on the warehouse receipt.

This section is confined to liability for non-receipt or misdescription of the goods. Although liability for non-existence is not expressly stated, the Official Comment characterizes the change made by this section as a "simplified restatement of existing law." Other authorities are in accord. Further Comments of The State Bar, Sixth Progress Report to the Legislature by Senate Fact Finding Committee on Judiciary (1959–1961), Part 1, The Uniform Commercial Code, pp. 619, 624; 3 New York Law Revision Commission, Study of the Uniform Commercial Code (1955) 1788–1790.

Changes from U.C.C. (1962 Official Text)

2. This is section 7–203 of the Official Text without change.

Uniform Commercial Code Comment

Prior Uniform Statutory Provision:
Section 20, Uniform Warehouse Receipts Act.

Changes: New section confined to problem of non-receipt and misdescription.

Purposes of Changes and New Matter:
This section is a simplified restatement of existing law as to the method by which a bailee may avoid responsibility for the accuracy of descriptions which are made by or in reliance upon information furnished by the depositor. The issuer is liable on documents issued by an agent, contrary to instructions of his principal, without receiving goods. No disclaimer of the latter liability is permitted.

Cross References:
Sections 7–301 and 7–203.

Definitional Cross References:
"Conspicuous". Section 1–201.
"Document". Section 7–102.
"Document of title". Section 1–201.
"Goods". Section 7–102.
"Issuer". Section 7–102.
"Notice". Section 1–201.
"Party". Section 1–201.
"Purchaser". Section 1–201.
"Receipt of goods". Section 2–103.
"Value". Section 1–201.

Cross References

Document, see Commercial Code § 7102.

Document of title, see Commercial Code § 1201.
Liability for non-receipt or misdescription under bill of lading, see Commercial Code § 7301.
Liability for overissue or failure to identify duplicate documents, see Commercial Code § 7402.
Obligation of warehouseman or carrier to deliver, see Commercial Code § 7403.

§ 7204. Duty of Care; Contractual Limitation of Warehouseman's Liability

(1) A warehouseman is liable for damages for loss of or injury to the goods caused by his failure to exercise such care in regard to them as a reasonably careful man would exercise under like circumstances but unless otherwise agreed he is not liable for damages which could not have been avoided by the exercise of such care.

(2) Damages may be limited by a term in the warehouse receipt or storage agreement limiting the amount of liability in case of loss or damage, and setting forth a specific liability per article or item, or value per unit of weight, beyond which the warehouseman shall not be liable; provided, however, that such liability may on written request of the bailor at the time of signing such storage agreement or within a reasonable time after receipt of the warehouse receipt be increased on part or all of the goods thereunder, in which event increased rates may be charged based on such increased valuation, but that no such increase shall be permitted contrary to a lawful limitation of liability contained in the warehouseman's tariff, if any, nor permit recovery in excess of the actual value of the goods. No such limitation is effective with respect to the warehouseman's liability for conversion to his own use.

(3) Reasonable provisions as to the time and manner of presenting claims and instituting actions based on the bailment may be included in the warehouse receipt or tariff.

(4) This section does not impair or repeal Section 1630 of the Civil Code nor any of the provisions of the Public Utilities Code or the Agricultural Code or any lawful regulations issued thereunder. *(Stats.1963, c. 819, § 7204.)*

California Code Comment

By John A. Bohn and Charles J. Williams

Prior California Law

1. Subdivision (1) establishes the standard of care provided by former Civil Code § 1858.30 (UWRA) which required the warehouseman to exercise such care ". . . as a reasonably careful owner of similar goods would exercise."

Subdivision (1) is in accord with the provision of former Civil Code § 1858.30 that the liability of a warehouseman may be increased by contract.

2. Subdivision (2) which permits the warehouseman to limit the amount of his liability by agreement is new statutory law. However, it is in accord with prior case law. George v. Bekins Van and Storage Co., 33 Cal.2d 834, 205 P.2d 1037, (1949) (terms limiting the warehouseman's liability for damages to the declared value of the goods held valid and not prohibited by former Civil Code § 1858.12).

Subdivision (2) of this section avoids any problem with regard to damage of goods whose declared value may exceed their actual value by providing that recovery may not exceed actual value. See discussion under California Code Comment 5.

3. Subdivision (3) is new statutory law but is in accord with prior California case law. In Home Ins. Co. of New York v. Los Angeles Warehouse Co., 16 Cal.App.2d 737, 61 P.2d 510 (1936), a warehouse receipt issued by defendant required all claims for loss to be filed within 30 days after damage to or loss of the goods. The receipt was held valid and not in violation of former Civil Code § 1858.12.

4. Subdivision (4) is new. It permits the imposition of a higher standard of care by statute. Official Comment.

Changes from U.C.C. (1962 Official Text)

5. California modified subdivision (2) by adding to the first sentence the following phrase: "nor permit recovery in excess of the actual value of the goods" at the end of the first sentence of that subsection.

This was done out of an excess of caution for fear of a technical court interpretation. The Marsh and Warren Report criticized this change:

"It seems highly improbable that any court would construe the wording of § 17204(1) [7204(1)] and (2) to subject a warehouseman to liability for loss or injury to goods exceeding the value of the goods. The warehousemen apparently base their concern in this matter on the proviso in § 17204(2) [7204(2)] which allows the bailor and bailee to agree on an increase in the liability of the bailee. Their contention is that this proviso might be construed to increase the liability of a warehouseman set forth in § 17204(1) [7204(1)] which provides that a warehouseman is liable 'for damages for loss of or injury to the goods.' The suggested amendment should clear up the matter.

"We do not understand the basis of the criticism of the warehousemen regarding the ability of the parties to agree to an increased liability with regard to part of the goods in a lot. We see nothing in existing statute or case law which would prohibit the parties from agreeing to increased liability for only part of the goods in the lot. The problem in determining the bailee's liability for loss would simply be one of identifying those goods upon which there is increased liability. Obviously, if the depositor wanted to declare an increased valuation on only one-half of 100 boxes or crates stored, the ones on which the increased valuation was declared would have to be earmarked. He could not say: 'I will wait to see which ones are lost before saying which ones have the increased value.'" Sixth Progress Report to the Legislature by Senate Fact Finding Committee on Judiciary (1959–1961) Part 1, The Uniform Commercial Code, pp. 625–626.

6. Subdivision (4) is an optional subdivision in section 7–204 of the 1962 Official Text which imposes higher statutory standards of care than are set forth in subdivision (1). The reason for the specific statutes included in the California version is described in the Marsh and Warren Report:

"A note to the Official Text of the Code suggests that in subsection (4) there should be inserted a reference 'to any statute which imposes a higher responsibility upon the warehouseman or invalidates contractual limitations which would be permissible under this section. The only such statute of which we are aware is Section 1630 of the Civil Code enacted in 1957, which requires that a limitation of liability must be conspicuously printed on a contract of bailment 'for the parking or storage of a motor vehicle.' There may perhaps be others which we have not found. In addition, we consider that it would be wise to insert a general reference to the regulatory provisions of the Public Utilities Code and the Agricultural Code covering warehouses and agricultural warehouses, since this Section is clearly not intended to supersede any present or future regulation of the business of warehousing under those laws." Sixth Progress Report to the Legislature by Senate Fact Finding Committee on Judiciary (1959–1961), Part 1, The Uniform Commercial Code, p. 518.

7. California added the phrase "Section 1630 of the Civil Code nor any of the provisions of the Public Utilities Code or the Agricultural Code or any lawful regulations issued thereunder" to subdivision (4) of section 7–204 of the Official Text. This is in accord with the recommendation of Professors Marsh and Warren quoted in California Code Comment 6.

Uniform Commercial Code Comment

Prior Uniform Statutory Provision:
Sections 3 and 21, Uniform Warehouse Receipts Act.

Changes: Consolidated and rewritten; material on limitation of remedy is new.

Purposes of Changes:

The old uniform acts provided that receipts could not contain terms impairing the obligation of reasonable care. Whether this is violated by a stipulation that in case of loss the bailee's liability is limited to stated amounts has been much controverted. The section is intended to eliminate that controversy by setting forth the conditions under which liability is so limited. However, as subsection (4) makes clear, the states as well as the federal government may supplement this section with more rigid standards of responsibility for some or all bailees.

Cross References:

Sections 7–103 and 10–103.

Definitional Cross References:

"Action". Section 1–201.
"Agreed". Section 1–201.
"Goods". Section 7–102.
"Reasonable time". Section 1–204.
"Sign". Section 1–201.
"Term". Section 1–201.
"Value". Section 1–201.
"Warehouse receipt". Section 1–201.
"Warehouseman". Section 7–102.
"Written". Section 1–201.

Cross References

Crimes involving bailments, see Penal Code § 560 et seq.
Degree of care required of depositary for hire, see Civil Code § 1852.
Duty of care; contractual limitation of carrier's liability, see Commercial Code § 7309.
Negligence, limitation of liability of depositary, see Civil Code § 1840.
Obligations of depositary, see Civil Code § 1822 et seq.
Treaty, statute, etc., effect, see Commercial Code § 7103.

§ 7205. Title Under Warehouse Receipt Defeated in Certain Cases

A buyer in the ordinary course of business of fungible goods sold and delivered by a warehouseman who is also in the business of buying and selling such goods takes free of any claim under a warehouse receipt even though it has been duly negotiated. *(Stats.1963, c. 819, § 7205.)*

California Code Comment

By John A. Bohn and Charles J. Williams

Prior California Law

1. This section is new.

In response to a criticism that this section would seem to permit a buyer with knowledge of the outstanding negotiable receipt to take good title, the State Bar Committee commented on the purpose and effect of this section:

". . . Under § 17205 [7205] a buyer of fungible goods does not take free of the rights of the holder of the warehouse receipt covering those goods unless he is a 'buyer in the ordinary course of business'. Under § 11201(9) [1201(9)] such a buyer is one 'who in good faith and without knowledge that the sale to him is in violation of the ownership rights or *security interest* of a third party in the goods buys. . . .' (Emphasis added.) Thus, a buyer with knowledge of outstanding warehouse receipts would not qualify as a 'buyer in the ordinary course of business'.

"The reference in the report [criticizing this section] . . . to 'knowledge of *the* outstanding negotiable receipt' seems to be meaningless in the case of fungible goods, which is all that this section deals with. There is no 'the' outstanding receipt in such case. As explained in the comments, in a case where there has been an issuance of receipts for more fungible goods than there are in storage, a purchaser from the warehouseman who is also in the business of buying and selling such goods nevertheless takes free of the claims of the receipt holders. Even though this reverses the present law, it is a risk which should properly be placed on the depositors where they store fungible goods with a warehouseman who is in the business of selling goods of that kind."

Further Comments of The State Bar, Sixth Progress Report to the Legislature by Senate Fact Finding Committee on Judiciary (1959–1961), Part 1, The Uniform Commercial Code, p. 626.

Changes from U.C.C. (1962 Official Text)

2. This is section 7–205 of the Official Text without change.

Uniform Commercial Code Comment

Prior Uniform Statutory Provision:

None.

Purposes:

The typical case covered by this section is that of the warehouseman-dealer in grain, and the substantive question at issue is whether in case the warehouseman becomes insolvent the receipt holders shall be able to trace and recover grain shipped to farmers and other purchasers from the elevator. This was possible under the old acts, although courts were eager to find estoppels to prevent it. The practical difficulty of tracing fungible grain means that the preservation of this theoretical right adds little to the commercial acceptability of negotiable grain receipts, which really circulate on the credit of the warehouseman. Moreover, on default of the warehouseman, the receipt holders at least share in what grain remains, whereas retaking the grain from a good faith cash purchaser reduces him completely to the status of general creditor in a situation where there was very little he could do to guard against the loss. Compare 15 U.S.C. Section 714p, enacted in 1955.

Cross References:

Sections 2–403 and 9–307.

Definitional Cross References:

"Buyer in ordinary course of business". Section 1–201.
"Delivery". Section 1–201.
"Duly negotiate". Section 7–501.
"Fungible" goods. Section 1–201.
"Goods". Section 7–102.
"Value". Section 1–201.
"Warehouse receipt". Section 1–201.
"Warehouseman". Section 7–102.

Cross References

Buyer in ordinary course of business, protection, see Commercial Code § 9307.
Fungible goods, see Commercial Code § 1201.
Good faith purchase of goods, see Commercial Code § 2403.
Rights acquired by due negotiation, see Commercial Code § 7502.

§ 7206. Termination of Storage at Warehouseman's Option

(1) A warehouseman may on notifying the person on whose account the goods are held and any other person known to claim an interest in the goods require payment of any charges and removal of the goods from the warehouse at the termination of the period of storage fixed by the document, or, if no period is fixed, within a stated period not less than 30 days after the notification. If the goods are not removed before the date specified in the notification, the warehouseman may sell them in accordance with the provisions of the section on enforcement of a warehouseman's lien (Section 7210).

(2) If a warehouseman in good faith believes that the goods are about to deteriorate or decline in value to less than the amount of his lien within the time prescribed in subdivision (1) for notification, advertisement and sale, the warehouseman may specify in the notification any reasonable shorter time for removal of the goods and in case the goods are not removed, may sell them at public sale held not less than one week after a single advertisement or posting.

(3) If as a result of a quality or condition of the goods of which the warehouseman had no notice at the time of

deposit the goods are a hazard to other property or to the warehouse or to persons, the warehouseman may sell the goods at public or private sale without advertisement on reasonable notification to all persons known to claim an interest in the goods. If the warehouseman after a reasonable effort is unable to sell the goods he may dispose of them in any lawful manner and shall incur no liability by reason of such disposition.

(4) The warehouseman must deliver the goods to any person entitled to them under this division upon due demand made at any time prior to sale or other disposition under this section and payment of any amount necessary to satisfy the warehouseman's lien and reasonable expenses incurred under this section.

(5) The warehouseman may satisfy his lien from the proceeds of any sale or disposition under this section but must hold the balance for delivery on the demand of any person to whom he would have been bound to deliver the goods.   *(Stats.1963, c. 819, § 7206.)*

California Code Comment

By John A. Bohn and Charles J. Williams

Prior California Law

1. Subdivision (1) may modify prior California law regulating the storage of personal property for hire. Civil Code § 1854 provided that in the absence of an agreement with regard to how long a deposit is to continue, the depositary may terminate the deposit upon reasonable notice. Subdivision (1), in effect, provides that in no circumstances will a notice period of less than 30 days constitute "reasonable notice". While Civil Code § 1854 was not specifically repealed by Stats.1963, Chapter 819, Commercial Code § 10103 provides that "all . . . parts of acts inconsistent with this act are hereby repealed."

The Uniform Warehouse Receipts Act (former Civil Code §§ 1858.01–1858.85) did not contain provisions regulating the warehouseman's right to terminate storage in cases other than non-payment of storage charges and perishable or hazardous goods. See California Code Comment 2 to this section.

2. Subdivision (2) modifies the rule of former Civil Code § 1858.57 (UWRA) by allowing the sale of perishable, deteriorating or hazardous goods only at a public sale and not earlier than one week after a single advertisement or posting. Under former Civil Code § 1858.57, a warehouseman could sell perishable or hazardous goods at a public or private sale without advertising after giving notice.

Both subdivision (2) and subdivision (3) make a distinction between the situation where the warehouseman knew of the hazardous or perishable nature of the goods and the situation where he had no such knowledge. See Official Comment 2. This distinction was not made in former Civil Code § 1858.57 (UWRA).

3. Subdivision (3) applies to goods of whose condition or character the warehouseman had no notice at the time of deposit that they are a "hazard". Former Civil Code § 1858.57 was not limited to the case where the warehouseman had no knowledge.

On the other hand former Civil Code § 1858.57 limited the right to terminate storage to goods which by their odor, leakage, inflammability or explosive nature would be liable to injure other property. The term hazard in subdivision (3) is more general.

4. With regard to subdivisions (2) and (3) of this section also see Civil Code § 1837 which provides, in part, that "if a thing deposited is in actual danger of perishing before instructions can be obtained from the depositor, the depositary may sell it . . . .".

5. Subdivision (4) is a restatement without substantive change of the last paragraph of former Civil Code § 1858.56 (UWRA) which dealt with the satisfaction of a warehouseman's lien.

6. Subdivision (5) of this section is a restatement without substantive change of the next to last paragraph of former Civil Code § 1858.56 (UWRA).

Changes from U.C.C. (1962 Official Text)

7. In the California version, the following clause was added to subdivision (4): "and payment of any amount necessary to satisfy the warehouseman's lien and reasonable expenses incurred under this section."

This language was added because of an objection that this section in the 1962 Official Text would require warehousemen to deliver the goods upon demand without payment of the charges, etc. then due:

"The draftsmen of the UCC doubtless intended this section to be read in the light of the extensive provisions of § 17209 [7209] giving the warehouseman a lien for such charges, and § 17403(2) [7403(2)] which states: 'A person claiming goods covered by a document of title must satisfy the bailee's lien where the bailee so requests. . . .' The suggested amendment should clear up the point . . ." Further Comments of The State Bar, Sixth Progress Report to the Legislature by Senate Fact Finding Committee on Judiciary (1959–1961) Part 1, The Uniform Commercial Code, p. 627.

Uniform Commercial Code Comment

Prior Uniform Statutory Provision:

Section 34, Uniform Warehouse Receipts Act.

Changes: Rewritten and expanded to define the warehouseman's right to terminate the storage not only where the goods are perishable or hazardous as in Uniform Warehouse Receipts Act, Section 34, but also for any other reason including decline in value of the goods imperilling the warehouseman's security for charges.

Purposes of Changes:

1. Most warehousing is for an indefinite term, the bailor being entitled to delivery on reasonable demand. It is necessary to define the warehouseman's power to terminate the bailment, since it would be commercially intolerable to allow warehousemen to order removal of the goods on short notice. The thirty day period provided where the document does not carry its own period of termination corresponds to commercial practice of computing rates on a monthly basis. The right to terminate under subsection (1) includes a right to require payment of "any charges", but does not depend on the existence of unpaid charges.

2. In permitting expeditious disposition of perishable and hazardous goods Uniform Warehouse Receipts Act, Section 34, made no distinction between cases where the warehouseman knowingly undertook to store such goods and cases where the goods were discovered to be of that character subsequent to storage. The former situation presents no such emergency as justifies the summary power of removal and sale. Subsections (2) and (3) distinguish between the two situations.

3. Protection of his lien is the only interest which the warehouseman has to justify summary sale of perishable goods which are not hazardous. This same interest must be recognized when the stored goods, although not perishable, decline in market value to a point which threatens the warehouseman's security.

4. The right to order removal of stored goods is subject to provisions of the public warehousing laws of some states forbidding warehousemen from discriminating among customers. Nor does the section relieve the warehouseman of any obligation under the state laws to secure the approval of a public official before disposing of deteriorating goods. Such *regulatory* statutes and the regulations under them remain in force and operative. Sections 7–103, 10–103.

Cross References:

Sections 7–103, 7–403, 10–103.

Definitional Cross References:

"Delivery". Section 1–201.
"Document". Section 7–102.
"Good faith". Section 1–201.
"Goods". Section 7–102.
"Notice". Section 1–201.
"Notification". Section 1–201.
"Person". Section 1–201.
"Reasonable time". Section 1–204.
"Value". Section 1–201.
"Warehouseman". Section 7–102.

Cross References

Depositary's lien, see Civil Code §§ 1856, 1857.
Liens in general, see Civil Code § 2872 et seq.
Obligation to deliver goods, see Commercial Code § 7403.

Sale of thing deposited in danger of perishing, see Civil Code § 1837.
Termination of deposit, see Civil Code §§ 1854, 1855.
Treaty, statute, etc., effect, see Commercial Code § 7103.

§ 7207. Goods Must Be Kept Separate; Fungible Goods

(1) Unless the warehouse receipt otherwise provides, a warehouseman must keep separate the goods covered by each receipt so as to permit at all times identification and delivery of those goods except that different lots of fungible goods may be commingled.

(2) Fungible goods so commingled are owned in common by the persons entitled thereto and the warehouseman is severally liable to each owner for that owner's share. Where because of overissue a mass of fungible goods is insufficient to meet all the receipts which the warehouseman has issued against it, the persons entitled include all holders to whom overissued receipts have been duly negotiated. *(Stats.1963, c. 819, § 7207.)*

California Code Comment

By John A. Bohn and Charles J. Williams

Prior California Law

1. Subdivision (1) restates the provisions of former Civil Code § 1858.31 (UWRA), duty to keep goods separate, and replaces the first sentence of § 1858.32 (UWRA) which permitted the mingling of fungible goods where it was authorized by custom or agreement.

2. Subdivision (2) changes prior California law by permitting all holders of overissued receipts to share in a mass of fungible goods. Former Civil Code § 1858 expressly prohibited the issuance of overissued receipts and former Civil Code § 1858f made the issuance of overissued receipts a felony.

The first sentence of subdivision (2) is a consolidation and restatement of the second sentence of former Civil Code §§ 1858.32, 1858.33 (UWRA).

The second sentence of subdivision (2) is new. The reason for this provision is stated in the Official Comment.

Changes from U.C.C. (1962 Official Text)

3. This is section 7–207 of the Official Text without change.

Uniform Commercial Code Comment

Prior Uniform Statutory Provision:

Sections 22, 23 and 24, Uniform Warehouse Receipts Act.

Changes: Consolidated and revised; holders of overissued receipts permitted to share in mass of fungible goods.

Purposes of Changes:

No change of substance is made other than the explicit statement that holders to whom overissued receipts have been duly negotiated shall share in a mass of fungible goods. Where individual ownership interests are merged into claims on a common fund, as is necessarily the case with fungible goods, there is no policy reason for discriminating between successive purchasers of similar claims.

Definitional Cross References:

"Delivery". Section 1–201.
"Duly negotiate". Section 7–501.
"Fungible" goods. Section 1–201.
"Goods". Section 7–102.
"Holder". Section 1–201.
"Person". Section 1–201.
"Warehouse receipt". Section 1–201.
"Warehouseman". Section 7–102.

Cross References

Fungible goods, see Commercial Code § 1201.

§ 7208. Altered Warehouse Receipts

Where a blank in a negotiable warehouse receipt has been filled in without authority, a purchaser for value and without notice of the want of authority may treat the insertion as authorized. Any other unauthorized alteration leaves any receipt enforceable against the issuer according to its original tenor. *(Stats.1963, c. 819, § 7208.)*

California Code Comment

By John A. Bohn and Charles J. Williams

Prior California Law

1. Section 7208 condenses and simplifies former Civil Code § 1858.22 (UWRA).

Former Civil Code § 1858.22 did not excuse a warehouseman from liability in case of an altered receipt if the alteration was "(a) immaterial, (b) authorized, or (c) made without fraudulent intent." If the alteration was authorized the warehouseman was liable according to the terms of the altered receipt. If the alteration was immaterial or unauthorized but made without fraudulent intent, the warehouseman was liable according to the original terms of the receipt. A material or fraudulent alteration under section 1858.22 excused the warehouseman from all liability to the person who made the alteration or to one who took with notice except for the obligation to "deliver, according to the terms of the receipt as originally issued, the goods for which it was issued."

Commercial Code § 7208 simplifies this detail by stating that an alteration except one involving the filling of a blank is "enforceable against the issuer according to its original tenor."

The first sentence of this section is new. It is in accord with the principle of the Commercial Code which treats unauthorized completion as an alteration. For example, Commercial Code §§ 3407(1)(b), 8206(1)(b).

Changes from U.C.C. (1962 Official Text)

2. This is section 7–208 of the Official Text without change.

Uniform Commercial Code Comment

Prior Uniform Statutory Provision:

Section 13, Uniform Warehouse Receipts Act.

Changes: Generally revised and simplified; explicit treatment of the situation where a blank in an executed document is filled without authority.

Purposes of Changes:

1. The execution of warehouse receipts in blank is a dangerous practice. As between the issuer and an innocent purchaser the risks should clearly fall on the former.

2. An unauthorized alteration whether made with or without fraudulent intent does not relieve the issuer of his liability on the warehouse receipt as originally executed. The unauthorized alteration itself is of course ineffective against the warehouseman.

Definitional Cross References:

"Issuer". Section 7–102.
"Notice". Section 1–201.
"Purchaser". Section 1–201.
"Value". Section 1–201.
"Warehouse receipt". Section 1–201.

Cross References

Alteration of writing, explanation by party producing, see Evidence Code § 1402.
Extinction of written contract by material alteration, see Civil Code § 1700.

Fictitious warehouse receipts, penal provision, see Penal Code § 578.

§ 7209. Lien of Warehouseman

(1) A warehouseman has a lien against the bailor on the goods deposited or on the proceeds thereof in his possession for charges for storage, processing incidental to storage, or transportation, including demurrage and terminal charges, insurance, labor, or charges present or future in relation to the goods, and for expenses necessary for preservation of the goods or reasonably incurred in their sale pursuant to law. If the person on whose account the goods are held is liable for like charges or expenses in relation to other goods whenever deposited, the warehouseman also has a lien against him for such charges and expenses whether or not the other goods have been delivered by the warehouseman. But against a person to whom a negotiable warehouse receipt is duly negotiated a warehouseman's lien is limited to charges specified on the receipt or if no charges are so specified then to a reasonable charge for storage of the goods covered by the receipt subsequent to the date of the receipt.

(2) The warehouseman may also reserve a security interest against the bailor for charges other than those specified in subdivision (1), such as for money advanced and interest, but if a receipt is issued for the goods such a security interest is not valid as against third persons without notice unless the maximum amount thereof is conspicuously specified (Section 1201) on the receipt. Such a security interest is governed by the division on secured transactions (Division 9).

(3) (a) A warehouseman's lien for charges and expenses under subdivision (1) or a security interest under subdivision (2) is also effective against any person who so entrusted the bailor with possession of the goods that a pledge of them by him to a good faith purchaser for value would have been valid but is not effective against a person as to whom the document confers no right in the goods covered by it under Section 7503.

(b) A warehouseman's lien on household goods for charges and expenses in relation to the goods under subdivision (1) is also effective against all persons if the depositor was the legal possessor of the goods at the time of deposit. "Household goods" means furniture, furnishings and personal effects used by the depositor in a dwelling.

(4) A warehouseman loses his lien on any goods which he voluntarily delivers or which he unjustifiably refuses to deliver. *(Stats.1963, c. 819, § 7209. Amended by Stats.1965, c. 1379, p. 3288, § 5.5.)*

California Code Comment

By John A. Bohn and Charles J. Williams

Prior California Law

1. The first sentence of subdivision (1) of this section is essentially a restatement of former Civil Code § 1858.50 (UWRA) which authorized the warehouseman's lien under prior California law.

The second sentence of subdivision (1) restates the principle of former Civil Code § 1858.51(a) (UWRA) which authorized a warehouseman's lien against all goods owned by a depositor regardless of the time of deposit if the depositor was liable "as debtor for the claims in regard to which the lien is asserted". In San Angelo Wine & Spirits Corp. v. South End Warehouse Co., 19 Cal.App.2d Supp. 749, 61 P.2d 1235 (1936) the court held that former Civil Code §§ 1858.51(a) and 1858.50 authorized a warehouseman to assert his lien against personal property deposited by plaintiff liquor company in satisfaction of charges arising from the advance of money by the warehouseman for the payment of taxes on liquor stored by plaintiff prior to the deposit in question.

The final sentence in subdivision (1) restates the rule of former Civil Code § 1858.53 (UWRA) but limits it to the case where a negotiable receipt is negotiated rather than, as under the UWRA, applying it to all negotiable receipts.

2. Subdivision (2) changes California law by treating the warehouseman's interest resulting from advances as a security interest. Under former Civil Code § 1858.50, (UWRA), this interest was a lien. The importance is that the security interest is enforced under Division 9 rather than under Division 7. See Official Comment 2.

3. Subdivision (3) is the counterpart of former Civil Code § 1858.51(b) (UWRA) which provided for a warehouseman's lien against goods deposited by a non-owner so long as "such person was in legal possession of the goods when they were deposited." See Official Comment 3.

4. Subsection (4) of this section restates the rule of former Civil Code § 1858.52 (UWRA) without substantive change.

Changes from U.C.C. (1962 Official Text)

5. Subdivision (1) of the Official Text as modified in California reads as follows:

"A warehouseman has a lien against the bailor on the goods deposited [covered by a warehouse receipt] or on the proceeds thereof in his possession for charges for storage processing incidental to storage, or transportation, [(]including demurrage and terminal charges[)], insurance, labor, or charges present or future in relation to the goods, and for expenses necessary for preservation of the goods or reasonably incurred in their sale pursuant to law. If the person on whose account the goods are held is liable for like charges or expenses in relation to other goods whenever deposited [and it is stated in the receipt that a lien is claimed for charges and expenses in relation to other goods], the warehouseman also has a lien against him for such charges and expenses whether or not the other goods have been delivered by the warehouseman. But against a person to whom a negotiable warehouse receipt is duly negotiated a warehouseman's lien is limited to charges [in an amount or at a rate] specified on the receipt or if no charges are so specified then to a reasonable charge for storage of the goods covered by the receipt subsequent to the date of the receipt."

The changes made in subdivision (1) are in accord with the recommendations of the California State Bar and the comments of the California Warehouse Industry:

" 'Section 17209 [7209] states "a warehouseman has a lien against the bailor on goods covered by a warehouse receipt ...", whereas Section 1858.50 of the Warehouse Receipts Act provides "... (a) a warehouseman shall have a lien on goods deposited by the owner ...". The difference in the wording of these two sections is obvious. If a warehouseman does not issue a receipt under wording proposed in Section 17209, [7209] then he does not have a lien against the bailor, whereas at the present time the lien runs against the goods deposited. This section indicates a difference in the amount of lien which a warehouseman has "against the bailor" or against the person to whom a negotiable receipt has been negotiated even though the person to whom it has been negotiated may at the time of the negotiations, have been fully aware of the charges claimed. It would seem to prevent a warehouseman from recovering against a person to whom a receipt has been negotiated, perfectly proper advances such as Federal floor tax on liquor stocks, etc., which could be very difficult to set forth at the time of the issuance of receipt. This section also only gives to the warehouseman a security interest for moneys advanced and interest, in lieu of a lien on the goods deposited as now permitted in the Warehouse Receipts Act. This type of limitation would work a hardship on many of the warehouseman's depositors who look for their financing in this manner and who cannot obtain financing through banking institutions at the present time.'

"**Recommendation.** The section should be amended to read: '(1) A warehouseman has a lien against the bailor on the goods deposited or on the proceeds thereof in his possession for charges for storage or transportation (including demurrage and terminal charges), insurance, labor, or charges present or future in relation to the goods, and for expenses necessary for preservation of the goods or reasonably incurred in their sale pursuant to law. If the person on whose account the goods are held is liable for like charges or expenses in relation to other goods whenever deposited, the warehouseman also has a lien against him for such charges and expenses whether or not the other goods have been delivered by the warehouseman. But against a person to whom a negotiable warehouse receipt is duly negotiated a warehouseman's lien is limited to charges specified on the receipt or if no charges are so specified then to a reasonable charge for storage of the goods covered by the receipt subsequent to the date of the receipt.'

"Discussion. These are valid criticisms. The amendment to the first sentence retains the rule in effect under CC 1858.50 which grants the warehouseman a lien on goods deposited whether a warehouse receipt was issued on the goods or not.

"The second sentence or § 17209(1) [7209(1)] gives a general lien only where it is stated in the receipt that such a lien is claimed. The deletion we suggest restores the rule prevailing under CC § 1858.51.

"In the case of a negotiable receipt, CC § 1858.53 provides that the warehouseman has a lien for charges other than for storage of the goods covered by the receipt only if such other charges are 'expressly enumerated' on the receipt, but the amount of the other charges need not be stated. In response to the objections of the warehousemen in this respect, we have suggested that deletions be made in the third sentence of § 17209(1) [7209(1)] which will restore the present rule in this respect.

"The warehousemen object to § 17209(2) [7209(2)] which gives a warehouseman a security interest for money advanced in lieu of a lien on the goods deposited, as they contend the Warehouse Receipts Act now allows. (See the discussion on pages 7–6 and 7–7 of the Preliminary Draft for a discussion of the rights of a warehouseman under present law to a lien for money advanced.) Their objection is based on the belief that this change will 'work a hardship on many of the warehouseman's depositors who look for their financing in this manner and who cannot obtain financing through banking institutions at the present time.' The warehousemen do not explain why this change in law will inhibit this kind of financing. Giving the warehouseman a security interest for such advances would seem to be ample protection for him. Such a security interest is subject to Chapter [Division] 9 of the UCC. Section 19305 [9305] provides that possession without filing perfects a security interest; hence, the warehouseman would not have to file to obtain a security interest in goods in his possession. Then, too, subsequent advances by the warehouseman would have priority over conflicting security interests from the time the security interest was perfected, ordinarily the time he took possession. We fail to see how the provisions of subsection (2) are going to work a hardship on warehousemen or their customers, since all that the warehouseman has to do to advance money against the goods and reserve a security interest for such advance is to set forth the maximum amount of the advances conspicuously on the receipt." Further Comments of The State Bar, Sixth Progress Report to the Legislature by Senate Fact Finding Committee on Judiciary (1959–1961), Part 1, The Uniform Commercial Code, pp. 627–628.

9. Subdivision (2) in the California version has been substantially reworded from the Official Text. Subdivision (2) of 7–209 of the Official Text with the California changes reads as follows:

"(2) The warehouseman may also reserve a security interest against the bailor for [a maximum amount specified on the receipt for] charges other than those specified in subdivision [subsection] (1), such as for money advanced and interest, but if a receipt is issued for the goods such a security interest is not valid as against third persons without notice unless the maximum amount thereof is conspicuously specified (Section 1201) on the receipt. Such a security interest is governed by the division [article] on secured transactions (Division [Article] 9)." This change is in accord with although not identical to the recommendation of Professors Marsh and Warren:

"Subsection (2), which permits a warehouseman to reserve a consensual lien for other money loaned to a depositor by specifying it in the receipt, is a provision not contained in the Warehouse Receipts Act. [Although Section 27 (CC § 1858.50) refers to 'all lawful claims for money advanced,' it is doubtful whether this refers to *any* loan by the warehouseman to the depositor.] However, as pointed out by Professor Ernest N. Warren, there is nothing in present law to prevent a warehouseman from contracting for a pledge of the property in his possession to secure any debt owed by the depositor to him, and in the case of a non-negotiable receipt without any notation at all in the receipt. 3 N.Y.Law Rev.Comm., Study of the Uniform Commercial Code (1955) 1800. See San Angelo Wine & Spirits Corp. v. South End Warehouse Co., 19 C.A.2d (Supp.) 749, 61 P.2d 1235 (1936). And presumably, even in the case of a *negotiable* receipt, a statement in the receipt that the warehouseman claims a right as pledgee would be sufficient to put a subsequent taker on notice and prevent him from being a holder in due course. Subsection (2) increases the protection to the subsequent taker in the case of a non-negotiable receipt by requiring that there be notice of the lien on the receipt.

"The statement . . . that subsection (2) creates a 'statutory lien' appears to be wholly without foundation. The subsection states that the lien is governed by Chapter 9, which covers only consensual liens, and the Official Comments expressly state that it is not a statutory lien.

"Nevertheless, and despite the fact that it would probably change the present law, we think that it would better promote the free flow of commerce not to permit a warehouseman to reserve a lien for other advances by some fine print in a *negotiable* warehouse receipt. And even in the case of a non-negotiable receipt, it would seem that the subsequent taker is entitled to unmistakable notice of the claim of the warehouseman of a lien for other advances. Therefore, we have suggested the above amendment which would require that the notice of the claim be 'conspicuously' placed on the receipt [see Section 11201(10)] [1201(10)]." Sixth Progress Report to the Legislature by Senate Fact Finding Committee on Judiciary (1959–1961) Part 1, The Uniform Commercial Code, pp. 519–520.

10. The following general comment concerning this section was made by the California State Bar Committee on the Commercial Code:

"The Uniform Warehouse Receipts Act gives the warehouseman a general lien for charges upon all goods deposited by the same owner. [Footnote: Cal.Civ.Code, Secs. 1858.50, 1858.51] The lien applies whether or not the warehouseman issues a receipt. If a receipt is issued, it extends to all enumerated charges (e.g., insurance, transportation, expenses of preservation, and so on).

"Though the Official Text of section 17209 [7209] would establish a warehouseman's lien, it would make several important changes. It would give a general lien only if a receipt is issued and then only if a general lien is claimed in the receipt. It would extend the lien only to those charges other than for storage the *amount* of which are specified, even though many of such other charges would be incurred after the issuance of the receipt and their exact amount could not be known when the receipt is issued.

"The State Bar Committee saw no reason for these changes and some of them would be detrimental to the California warehousing industry. Accordingly, Code section 17209 [7209] . . . has restored in substance the lien provisions of section 28 of the Uniform Warehouse Receipts Act." California State Bar Committee on the Commercial Code, A Special Report, The Uniform Commercial Code, 37 Calif.State Bar J. (March–April, 1962) p. 183.

California Code Comment—1965 Amendment

By Charles J. Williams

The 1965 amendment added subparagraph (b) to subdivision (3). This is a variation from the 1962 Official Text.

Subdivision (1) gives the warehouseman a lien on specific goods and a general lien as to other goods. This lien differs in amount against a third person who holds the warehouse receipt depending upon whether the receipt is negotiable or non-negotiable.

Subdivision (3) makes this warehouseman's lien good against certain strangers to the storage transaction.

Subdivision (3) (a) makes the lien effective against those persons who permitted the bailor to have possession or control of the goods, i.e. gave the bailor the power to pledge them.

Subdivision (3) (b) added by California in 1965 makes a different test in the case of "household goods": the lien is good against "all persons if the depositor was the legal possessor of the goods . . . ." The reason for the addition of subparagraph (b) is not readily apparent. The brief legislative history indicates that it restates the same rule giving the warehouseman a lien on household goods which existed under former Civil Code Sections 1858.50 and 1858.51 (UWRA). However, if the Uniform Commercial Code eliminated the warehouseman's lien on household goods, it was not discussed during consideration of the Code in California.

Uniform Commercial Code Comment [amended 1966]
Prior Uniform Statutory Provision:
Sections 27 through 32, Uniform Warehouse Receipts Act.
Changes: Rewritten.
Purposes of Changes:

1. Subsection (1) defines the warehouseman's statutory lien. A specific lien attaches automatically, without express notation on the receipt, to goods stored under a non-negotiable receipt. That lien is limited to the usual charges arising out of a storage transaction; by notation on the receipt it can be made a general lien extending to like charges in relation to other goods. The same rules apply where the receipt is negotiable, except that as against a holder by due negotiation the lien is limited to the amount or rate specified on the receipt, or, if none is specified, to a reasonable charge for storage of the specific goods after the date of the receipt.

2. Subsection (2) provides for a security interest based upon agreement. Such a security interest arises out of relations between the parties other than bailment for storage or transportation, as where the bailee assumes the role of financer or performs a manufacturing operation, extending credit in reliance upon the goods covered by the receipt. Such a security interest is not a statutory lien. Compare Sections 9–102(2) and 9–310. It is governed in all respects by Article 9, except that subsection (2) requires that the receipt specify a maximum amount and limits the security interest to the amount specified.

3. Subsections (1) and (2) validate the lien and security interest "against the bailor." As against third parties, subsection (3) (a) continues the rule under the prior uniform statutory provision that to validate the lien the owner must have entrusted the goods to the depositor, and that the circumstances must be such that a pledge by the depositor to a good faith purchaser for value would have been valid. Thus the owner's interest will not be subjected to a lien or security interest arising out of a deposit of his goods by a thief. The warehouseman may be protected because of the actual, implied or apparent authority of the depositor, because of a Factor's Act, or because of other circumstances which would protect a bona fide pledgee, unless those circumstances are denied effect under Section 7–503. Where the third party is the holder of a security interest, the rights of the warehouseman depend on the priority given to a hypothetical bona fide pledgee by Article 9, particularly Section 9–312. Thus the special priority granted to statutory liens by Section 9–310 does not apply to liens under subsection (1) of this section, since subsection (3) "expressly provides otherwise" within the meaning of Section 9–310. As to household goods, however, subsection (3) (b) makes the warehouseman's lien "for charges and expenses in relation to the goods" effective against all persons if the depositor was the legal possessor. The purpose of the exception is to permit the warehouseman to accept household goods for storage in sole reliance on the value of the goods themselves, especially in situations of family emergency. (As amended in 1966).

4. It is unnecessary to state here, as in Uniform Warehouse Receipts Act 31, that a bailee with a valid lien need not deliver until the lien is satisfied. Section 7–403 provides that a person demanding delivery under a document must be prepared to satisfy the bailee's lien.

5. Where goods have been stored under a non-negotiable warehouse receipt and are sold by the person to whom the receipt has been issued, frequently the goods are not withdrawn by the new owner. The obligations of the seller of the goods in this situation are set forth in Section 2–503(4) on tender of delivery and include procurement of an acknowledgment by the bailee of the buyer's right to possession of the goods. If a new receipt is requested, such an acknowledgment can be withheld until storage charges have been paid or provided for. The statutory lien for charges on the goods sold, granted by the first sentence of subsection (1), continues valid unless the bailee gives it up. But once a new receipt is issued to the buyer, the buyer becomes "the person on whose account the goods are held" under the second sentence of subsection (1); unless he undertakes liability for charges in relation to other goods stored by the seller, there is no general lien against the buyer for such charges. Of course, the bailee may preserve the general lien in such a case either by an arrangement by which the buyer "is liable for" such charges, or by reserving a security interest under subsection (2).

Cross References:
Point 2: Sections 9–102(2) and 9–310.
Point 3: Sections 7–503, 9–310 and 9–312.
Point 4: Section 7–403.
Point 5: Section 2–503.
Definitional Cross References:
"Deliver". Section 1–201.
"Document". Section 7–102.
"Goods". Section 7–102.
"Money". Section 1–201.
"Person". Section 1–201.
"Purchaser". Section 1–201.
"Right". Section 1–201.
"Security interest". Section 1–201.
"Value". Section 1–201.
"Warehouse receipt". Section 1–201.
"Warehouseman". Section 7–102.

Cross References
Conflicting security interests in same collateral, priorities, see Commercial Code § 9312.
Depositary's lien, see Civil Code § 1856.
Lien of carrier, see Commercial Code § 7307.
Liens arising by operation of law, priority, see Commercial Code § 9310.
Liens in general, see Civil Code § 2872 et seq.
Obligation to deliver goods, see Commercial Code §§ 7403, 7503.
Possessory liens for services, repairs, etc., see Civil Code § 3051 et seq.
Security interest, law governing, see Commercial Code § 9102.
Seller's tender of delivery, manner, see Commercial Code § 2503.

§ 7210. Enforcement of Warehouseman's Lien

(1) Except as provided in subdivision (2), a warehouseman's lien may be enforced by public or private sale of the goods in bloc or in parcels, at any time or place and on any terms which are commercially reasonable, after notifying all persons known to claim an interest in the goods. Such notification must include a statement of the amount due, the nature of the proposed sale and the time and place of any public sale. The fact that a better price could have been obtained by a sale at a different time or in a different method from that selected by the warehouseman is not of itself sufficient to establish that the sale was not made in a commercially reasonable manner. If the warehouseman either sells the goods in the usual manner in any recognized market therefor, or if he sells at the price current in such market at the time of his sale, or if he has otherwise sold in conformity with commercially reasonable practices among dealers in the type of goods sold, he has sold in a commercially reasonable manner. A sale of more goods than apparently necessary to be offered to insure satisfaction of the obligation is not commercially reasonable except in cases covered by the preceding sentence.

(2) A warehouseman's lien on goods other than goods stored by a merchant in the course of his business may be enforced only as follows:

(a) All persons known to claim an interest in the goods must be notified.

(b) The notification must be delivered in person or sent by registered or certified letter to the last known address of any person to be notified.

§ 7210

(c) The notification must include an itemized statement of the claim, a description of the goods subject to the lien, a demand for payment within a specified time not less than 10 days after receipt of the notification, and a conspicuous statement that unless the claim is paid within that time the goods will be advertised for sale and sold by auction at a specified time and place.

(d) The sale must conform to the terms of the notification.

(e) The sale must be held at the nearest suitable place to that where the goods are held or stored.

(f) After the expiration of the time given in the notification, an advertisement of the sale must be published once a week for two weeks consecutively in a newspaper of general circulation published in the judicial district where the sale is to be held. The advertisement must include a description of the goods, the name of the person on whose account they are being held, and the time and place of the sale. The sale must take place at least 15 days after the first publication. If there is no newspaper of general circulation published in the judicial district where the sale is to be held, the advertisement must be posted at least 10 days before the sale in not less than six conspicuous places in the neighborhood of the proposed sale.

(3) Before any sale pursuant to this section any person claiming a right in the goods may pay the amount necessary to satisfy the lien and the reasonable expenses incurred under this section. In that event the goods must not be sold, but must be retained by the warehouseman subject to the terms of the receipt and this division.

(4) The warehouseman may buy at any public sale pursuant to this section.

(5) A purchaser in good faith of goods sold to enforce a warehouseman's lien takes the goods free of any rights of persons against whom the lien was valid, despite noncompliance by the warehouseman with the requirements of this section.

(6) The warehouseman may satisfy his lien from the proceeds of any sale pursuant to this section but must hold the balance, if any, for delivery on demand to any person to whom he would have been bound to deliver the goods.

(7) The rights provided by this section shall be in addition to all other rights allowed by law to a creditor against his debtor.

(8) Where a lien is on goods stored by a merchant in the course of his business the lien may be enforced in accordance with either subdivision (1) or (2).

(9) The warehouseman is liable for damages caused by failure to comply with the requirements for sale under this section and in case of willful violation is liable for conversion. *(Stats.1963, c. 819, § 7210.)*

California Code Comment

By John A. Bohn and Charles J. Williams

Prior California Law

1. This section is a reorganization and a simplification of former Civil Code § 1858.56 (UWRA) dealing with foreclosure of warehousemen's liens.

2. Subdivision (1) is new statutory law. It substitutes the standard of commercial reasonableness for satisfaction of warehouseman's lien in lieu of former Civil Code § 1858.56 which went into extensive detail with regard to the notice of sale and its contents, advertisement of sale, place of sale, and time of sale. Official Comment 1.

Subdivision (1) applies to commercial storage, i.e. goods stored by a merchant. Official Comment 1. No such distinction was made in the UWRA. However, at his option the warehouseman may enforce his lien at a public sale under subdivision (2). Subdivision 8. For a criticism of this distinction see Marsh and Warren Report, Sixth Progress Report to the Legislature by Senate Fact Finding Committee on Judiciary (1959–1961) Part 1, The Uniform Commercial Code, p. 523. One objection was that "merchant" for the purpose of this distinction is not defined. California Commercial Code § 2104(1).

3. Subdivision (2) applies to the manner of enforcing the lien of a warehouseman who has stored noncommercial goods.

Paragraph (a) continues the rule stated in the second sentence of the first paragraph of former Civil Code § 1858.56.

Paragraph (b) is similar to the third sentence of the first paragraph of former Civil Code § 1858.56.

Paragraph (c) restates with slight variation the provisions of paragraphs (a), (b), (c) and (d) of former Civil Code § 1858.56. Paragraph (c) of former Civil Code § 1858.56 authorized a demand that accrued charges be paid within ten days after the date "when the notice (of sale) should reach its destination, according to the due course of post, if the notice is sent by mail." Subdivision (2)(c) provides that the demand for payment may not specify a time for payment which is less than 10 days after actual receipt of notification. Further, unlike subdivision (2)(c), there was no requirement under section 1858.56 that the demand for payment be "conspicuous."

Subdivision (2)(d) is in accord with former Civil Code § 1858.56.

Subdivision (2)(e) restates in simpler form that part of former Civil Code § 1858.56 which required the sale to be held "in the place where the lien was acquired, or, if such place is manifestly unsuitable at the nearest suitable place."

Subdivision (2)(f) restates the provisions contained in the latter part of the second paragraph of former Civil Code § 1858.56. A minor change is made in the advertising requirement. Former Civil Code § 1858.56 required advertising "pursuant to section 6066 of the Government Code" (once a week for two successive weeks) in the place where the sale is to be held. Subdivision (2)(f) requires advertising twice, once a week for two weeks, "in the judicial district where the sale is to be held."

4. Subdivision (3) is a restatement and simplification without substantive change of the last paragraph of former Civil Code § 1858.56.

5. Subdivision (4) is new law in California. The point has not previously been covered by statute or case law in California. However, the Marsh and Warren Report states that this subdivision changes the prior law:

". . . With respect to the provision that a warehouseman or carrier may buy at a public sale held to satisfy its own lien, this would change the present law. See 3 N.Y.Law Rev.Comm., Study of the Uniform Commercial Code (1955) 1802. However, we can see no reason to prohibit the warehouseman or carrier from buying even at a public sale, when other secured parties under the Code may buy at public sale and also at some private sales. Section 19504(3) [9504(3)]." Sixth Progress Report to the Legislature by Senate Fact Finding Committee on Judiciary (1959–1961) Part 1, The Uniform Commercial Code, p. 523.

6. Subdivision (5) is new statutory law.

7. Subdivision (6) is a restatement without substantive change of the next to last paragraph of former Civil Code § 1858.56.

8. Subdivision (7) integrates and continues the principles of former Civil Code §§ 1858.55 and 1858.58 (UWRA).

Former Civil Code § 1858.55 provided that the warehouseman was "entitled to all remedies allowed by law to a creditor against his debtor" regardless of whether or not the warehouseman had a lien. Former Civil Code § 1858.58 stated that the warehousemen's lien provided in former Civil Code § 1858.56 did not "preclude any other remedies allowed by law for the enforcement of a lien against personal property nor bar the right to recover so much of the warehouseman's claim as shall not be paid by the proceeds of the sale of the property."

Also see Civil Code §§ 3051–3052 regulating liens for services. Although the Commercial Code does not specifically repeal these sections of the Civil Code, Jewett v. City Transfer & Storage Co., 128 Cal.App. 556, 18 P.2d 351 (1933) held that the remedy of Civil Code §§ 3051–3052 insofar as it applied to warehousemen was repealed by the adoption of former Civil Code § 1858.56.

9. Subdivision (8) is new. See California Code Comment 2.

10. The distinction made between "a willful violation" and "a failure to comply" in subdivision (9) is new statutory law but is consistent with prior California case law. In George v. Bekins Van & Storage Co., 33 Cal.2d 834, 205 P.2d 1037–1040 (1949) the court stated that "negligence in caring for the goods is not an act of dominion over them such as is necessary to make the bailee liable as a converter."

Changes from U.C.C. (1962 Official Text)

11. The California version contains 2 minor variations from section 7–210 of the 1962 Official Text:

The words "or certified" were added after the word "registered" in subdivision (2)(b).

The phrase "published in the judicial district" was added after the phrase "newspaper of general circulation" in the first and fourth sentences of subdivision (2)(f).

Uniform Commercial Code Comment
Prior Uniform Statutory Provision:
Section 33, Uniform Warehouse Receipts Act.
Changes: Rewritten; simplified foreclosure proceeding provided for all liens other than warehousemen's lien in non-commercial storage.
Purposes of Changes:

1. Subsection (1) makes "commercial reasonableness" the standard for foreclosure proceedings in all cases except noncommercial storage with a warehouseman. The latter category embraces principally storage of household goods by private owners; and for such cases the detailed provisions as to notification, publication and public sale, found in Section 33 of the Uniform Warehouse Receipts Act, are retained in subsection (2). The swifter, more flexible procedure of subsection (1) is appropriate to commercial storage. Compare seller's power of resale on breach by buyer under the provisions of the Article on Sales (Section 2–706).

2. The provisions of subsections (4) and (5) permitting the bailee to bid at public sales and confirming the title of purchasers at foreclosure sales are designed to secure more bidding and better prices.

Cross Reference:
Section 7–403.
Definitional Cross References:
"Bill of lading". Section 1–201.
"Conspicuous". Section 1–201.
"Creditor". Section 1–201.
"Delivery". Section 1–201.
"Document". Section 7–102.
"Good faith". Section 1–201.
"Goods". Section 7–102.
"Notification". Section 1–201.
"Notifies". Section 1–201.
"Person". Section 1–201.
"Purchaser". Section 1–201.
"Rights". Section 1–201.
"Term". Section 1–201.
"Warehouseman". Section 7–102.

Cross References
Damages for conversion of personal property, see Civil Code § 3336 et seq.
Depositary's lien, sale, see Civil Code § 1857.
Enforcement of carrier's lien, see Commercial Code § 7308.
Obligation to deliver goods, excuse, see Commercial Code § 7403.
Possessory liens for services, repairs, etc., see Civil Code § 3051 et seq.

Sale by lien holder at auction, see Civil Code § 3052.

CHAPTER 3. BILLS OF LADING: SPECIAL PROVISIONS

Section
7301. Liability for Non-Receipt or Misdescription; "Said to Contain"; "Shipper's Load and Count"; Improper Handling.
7302. Through Bills of Lading and Similar Documents.
7303. Diversion; Reconsignment; Change of Instructions.
7304. Bills of Lading in a Set.
7305. Destination Bills.
7306. Altered Bills of Lading.
7307. Lien of Carrier.
7308. Enforcement of Carrier's Lien.
7309. Duty of Care; Contractual Limitation of Carrier's Liability.

Cross References
Crimes involving bailments, see Penal Code § 560 et seq.
Fraudulent issue of documents of title to merchandise, see Penal Code § 577 et seq.

§ 7301. Liability for Non-Receipt or Misdescription; "Said to Contain"; "Shipper's Load and Count"; Improper Handling

(1) A consignee of a nonnegotiable bill who has given value in good faith or a holder to whom a negotiable bill has been duly negotiated relying in either case upon the description therein of the goods, or upon the date therein shown, may recover from the issuer damages caused by the misdating of the bill or the nonreceipt or misdescription of the goods, except to the extent that the document indicates that the issuer does not know whether any part or all of the goods in fact were received or conform to the description, as where the description is in terms of marks or labels or kind, quantity, or condition or the receipt or description is qualified by "contents or condition of contents of packages unknown," "said to contain," "shipper's weight, load and count" or the like, if such indication be true.

(2) When goods are loaded by an issuer who is a common carrier, the issuer must count the packages of goods if package freight and ascertain the kind and quantity if bulk freight. In such cases "shipper's weight, load and count" or other words indicating that the description was made by the shipper are ineffective except as to freight concealed by packages.

(3) When bulk freight is loaded by a shipper who makes available to the issuer adequate facilities for weighing such freight, an issuer who is a common carrier must ascertain the kind and quantity within a reasonable time after receiving the written request of the shipper to do so. In such cases "shipper's weight" or other words of like purport are ineffective.

(4) The issuer may by inserting in the bill the words "shipper's weight, load and count" or other words of like purport indicate that the goods were loaded by the shipper; and if such statement be true the issuer shall not be liable for damages caused by the improper

§ 7301

loading. But their omission does not imply liability for such damages.

(5) The shipper shall be deemed to have guaranteed to the issuer the accuracy at the time of shipment of the description, marks, labels, number, kind, quantity, condition and weight, as furnished by him; and the shipper shall indemnify the issuer against damage caused by inaccuracies in such particulars. The right of the issuer to such indemnity shall in no way limit his responsibility and liability under the contract of carriage to any person other than the shipper. *(Stats.1963, c. 819, § 7301.)*

California Code Comment

By John A. Bohn and Charles J. Williams

Prior California Law

1. Under the Interstate Commerce Act, 49 USCA section 1–27 the Interstate Commerce Commission has prescribed uniform bills of lading which interstate rail carriers must use. Since these forms must be used in interstate shipments, carriers also generally use them in intrastate shipments as a matter of convenience. Therefore for practical purposes the uniform bills of lading forms prescribed by the Interstate Commerce Commission may be treated as the standard forms.

It has been stated that a bill of lading performs 3 functions, serving as (1) a receipt for the goods, (2) a contract for carriage of goods and (3) evidence of title to the goods. In the matter of Bills of Lading 52, I.C.C. 671 (1919). The functions of a bill of lading as documentary evidence of title is true only with respect to a negotiable bill. Braucher, Documents of Title, 18–71 (A.L.I.1963).

A bill of lading in its role as a receipt may be explained or contradicted by parol evidence, but as a contract it may not.

2. Subdivision (1) simplifies and restates former Civil Code § 2128g (UBLA). Subdivision (1) broadens liability for damages by including damages resulting from misdating of a bill of lading. See Official Comment 1. Former Civil Code § 2128g authorized damages only in cases of non-receipt or misdescription of goods.

3. Subdivision (2) is new. It is in accord with the FBLA. Official Comment 1.

4. Subdivision (3) is new. It is in accord with the FBLA. Official Comment 1.

5. Subdivision (4) restates the last sentence of former Civil Code § 2128g which required the carrier to check the loading upon request by the shipper but at the shipper's expense and to issue a clean bill. The absolute obligation to check the loading at the shipper's request is eliminated under this subdivision. The carrier is no longer protected by being compelled to check but he may now insert in the bill of lading words indicating that the goods were loaded by the shipper. See Official Comment 4.

6. Subdivision (5) is new. See Official Comment 5.

Changes from U.C.C. (1962 Official Text)

7. This is section 7–301 of the Official Text without change.

Uniform Commercial Code Comment

Prior Uniform Statutory Provision:
Section 23, Uniform Bills of Lading Act.

Changes: Rewritten in part.

Purposes of Changes:

1. The provision as to misdating in subsection (1) conforms to the policy of the amendment to the Federal Bills of Lading Act by 44 Stat. 1450 (1927), as amended 49 U.S.C. Section 102, after the holding in Browne v. Union Pac. R. Co., 113 Kan. 726, 216 P. 299 (1923), affirmed on other grounds 267 U.S. 255, 45 S.Ct. 315, 69 L.Ed. 601 (1925). Subsections (2) and (3) conform to the policy of the Federal Bills of Lading Act, 49 U.S.C. Sections 100, 101, and the laws of several states. See, e.g., N.Y.Pers.Prop.Law Section 209; Report of N.Y. Law Revision Commission, N.Y.Leg.Doc. (1941) No. 65(F).

2. The language of the old Uniform Act suggested that a carrier is ordinarily liable for damage caused by improper loading, but may relieve himself of liability by disclosing on the bill that shipper actually loaded. A more accurate statement of the law is that the carrier is not liable for losses caused by act or default of the shipper, which would include improper loading. There is some question whether under present law a carrier is liable even to a good faith purchaser of a negotiable bill for such losses, if the shipper's faulty loading in fact caused the loss. It is this doubtful liability which subsection (4) permits the carrier to bar by disclosure of shipper's loading. There is no implication that decisions such as Modern Tool Corp. v. Pennsylvania R. Co., 100 F.Supp. 595 (D.N.J.1951), are disapproved.

3. This section is a simplified restatement of existing law as to the method by which a bailee may avoid responsibility for the accuracy of descriptions which are made by or in reliance upon information furnished by the depositor or shipper. The issuer is liable on documents issued by an agent, contrary to instructions of his principal, without receiving goods. No disclaimer of this liability is permitted since it is not a matter either of the care of the goods or their description.

4. The shipper's erroneous report to the carrier concerning the goods may cause damage to the carrier. Subsection (5) therefore provides appropriate indemnity.

Cross References:
Sections 7–203 and 7–309.

Definitional Cross References:
"Bill of lading". Section 1–201.
"Consignee". Section 7–102.
"Document". Section 7–102.
"Duly negotiate". Section 7–501.
"Good faith". Section 1–201.
"Goods". Section 7–102.
"Holder". Section 1–201.
"Issuer". Section 7–102.
"Notice". Section 1–201.
"Party". Section 1–201.
"Purchaser". Section 1–201.
"Receipt of goods". Section 2–103.
"Value". Section 1–201.

Cross References

Carrier's liability, contractual limitation, see Commercial Code § 7309.
Common carriers of property, see Civil Code § 2194 et seq.
Construction against negative implication, see Commercial Code § 7105.
Liability for non-receipt or misdescription under warehouse receipt, see Commercial Code § 7203.
Liability of issuer for overissue or failure to identify duplicate document, see Commercial Code § 7402.
Obligation of carrier to deliver, see Commercial Code § 7403.
Obligations of carrier, in general, see Civil Code §§ 2114, 2115, 2118 et seq.
Obligations of depositary, see Civil Code § 1822 et seq.

§ 7302. Through Bills of Lading and Similar Documents

(1) The issuer of a through bill of lading or other document embodying an undertaking to be performed in part by persons acting as its agents or by connecting carriers is liable to anyone entitled to recover on the document for any breach by such other persons or by a connecting carrier of its obligation under the document but to the extent that the bill covers an undertaking to be performed overseas or in territory not contiguous to the continental United States or an undertaking including matters other than transportation this liability may be varied by agreement of the parties.

(2) Where goods covered by a through bill of lading or other document embodying an undertaking to be performed in part by persons other than the issuer are received by any such person, he is subject with respect to his own performance while the goods are in his

possession to the obligation of the issuer. His obligation is discharged by delivery of the goods to another such person pursuant to the document, and does not include liability for breach by any other such persons or by the issuer.

(3) The issuer of such through bill of lading or other document shall be entitled to recover from the connecting carrier or such other person in possession of the goods when the breach of the obligation under the document occurred, the amount it may be required to pay to anyone entitled to recover on the document therefor, as may be evidenced by any receipt, judgment, or transcript thereof, and the amount of any expense reasonably incurred by it in defending any action brought by anyone entitled to recover on the document therefor. *(Stats.1963, c. 819, § 7302.)*

California Code Comment

By John A. Bohn and Charles J. Williams

Prior California Law

1. This section changes California law. Former Civil Code § 2201 provided that, in the absence of agreement to the contrary, a common carrier's responsibility for freight shipped over his lines to an address beyond his usual route ended with his delivery of the freight to another competent carrier carrying to the place of address. McCaslin v. Southern Pac. Co., 187 Cal. 716, 203 Pac. 742 (1922).

This section imposes a responsibility for breach of contract upon the issuer of a through bill as a matter of law until the freight has reached the place of address and this responsibility cannot be modified by contract except in cases of overseas shipments. See Official Comments 1 and 3. The issuer who is liable for the fault of another under this subdivision has a right of recourse under subdivision (3). Official Comment 4.

Subdivision (1) is based upon section 20(11) of the Interstate Commerce Act (49 U.S.C.A. § 20(11) (1952)).

2. Subdivision (2) is new statutory law but is in accord with prior case law holding that each connecting carrier of a given freight shipment was responsible for the freight while it was in his possession. Cavallaro v. Texas & P. Ry. Co., 110 Cal. 348, 42 Pac. 918, 52 Am.St.R. 94 (1895). McCaslin v. Southern Pac. Co., *supra.*

3. Subdivision (3) is new statutory law. It is substantially the same as section 20(12) of the Interstate Commerce Act (49 U.S.C.A. § 20(12) (1952)). See Kansas City & M. Ry. Co. v. New York Cent. & H.R.R. Co., 110 Ark. 612, 163 S.W. 171 (1914).

Changes from U.C.C. (1962 Official Text)

4. This is section 7–302 of the Official Text without change.

Uniform Commercial Code Comment

Prior Uniform Statutory Provision:
None.

Purposes:

1. The purpose of this section is to subject the initial carrier under a through bill to suit for breach of the contract of carriage by any connecting carrier and to make it clear that any such connecting carrier holds the goods on terms which are defined by the document of title even though such connecting carrier did not issue the document. Since the connecting carrier does hold on the terms of the document, it must honor a proper demand for delivery or a diversion order just as the original bailee would have to. Similarly it has the benefits of the excuses for nondelivery and limitations of liability provided for the original bailee. Unlike the original bailee-issuer, the connecting carrier's responsibility is limited to the period while the goods are in its possession. The section is patterned generally after the Interstate Commerce Act, but does not impose any obligation to issue through bills.

2. The reference to documents other than through bills looks to the possibility that multi-purpose documents may come into use, e.g., combination warehouse receipts and bills of lading.

3. Where the obligations or standards applicable to different parties bound by a document of title are different, the initial carrier's responsibility for portions of the journey not on its own lines will be determined by the standards appropriate to the connecting carrier. Thus a land carrier issuing a through bill of lading involving water carriage at a later stage will have the benefit of the water carrier's immunity from liability for negligence of its servants in navigating the vessel, where the law provides such an immunity for water carriers and the loss occurred while the goods were in the water carrier's possession.

4. Under Subsection (1) the issuer of a through bill of lading may become liable for the fault of another person. Subsection (3) gives it appropriate rights of recourse.

Definitional Cross References:
"Agreement". Section 1–201.
"Bailee". Section 7–102.
"Bill of lading". Section 1–201.
"Delivery". Section 1–201.
"Document". Section 7–102.
"Goods". Section 7–102.
"Issuer". Section 7–102.
"Overseas". Section 2–323.
"Party". Section 1–201.
"Person". Section 1–201.

Cross References
Damages for breach of carrier's obligation to deliver, see Civil Code § 3316.
Delivery, in general, see Civil Code § 2118 et seq.
Obligation of carrier to deliver, see Commercial Code § 7403.
Variation by agreement, see Commercial Code § 1102.

§ 7303. Diversion; Reconsignment; Change of Instructions

(1) Unless the bill of lading otherwise provides, the carrier may deliver the goods to a person or destination other than that stated in the bill or may otherwise dispose of the goods on instructions from

(a) The holder of a negotiable bill; or

(b) The consignor on a nonnegotiable bill notwithstanding contrary instructions from the consignee; or

(c) The consignee on a nonnegotiable bill in the absence of contrary instructions from the consignor, if the goods have arrived at the billed destination or if the consignee is in possession of the bill; or

(d) The consignee on a nonnegotiable bill if he is entitled as against the consignor to dispose of them.

(2) Unless such instructions are noted on a negotiable bill of lading, a person to whom the bill is duly negotiated can hold the bailee according to the original terms. *(Stats.1963, c. 819, § 7303.)*

California Code Comment

By John A. Bohn and Charles J. Williams

Prior California Law

1. Subdivision (1) has no statutory counterpart in the UBLA. See Official Comment 1.

Subdivision (1) limits Civil Code § 2115 which provides that subject to this section of the Commercial Code, a "carrier must comply with the directions of the consignor or consignee . . ." and modifies former Civil Code § 2116 which did not specifically recognize the right to divert or reconsign.

Former Civil Code § 2127a (UBLA) dealing with justification for delivery is superseded by this section.

Former Civil Code § 2116 provided that where the directions of the consignor and consignee conflicted, the consignor's prevailed "in respect to all matters except the delivery of the freight." With regard to delivery the carrier had to comply with the directions of the consignee unless the consignor had "specially forbidden the carrier to receive orders inconsistent with his own."

Subdivision (1) distinguishes between a negotiable bill in which case the carrier must obey the holder and a nonnegotiable bill in which case the carrier must obey the consignor and may obey the consignee only in the absence of contrary instructions from the consignor and then only if the goods have arrived at the billed destination *or* if the consignee is in possession of the goods *or* if the consignee is entitled to dispose of the goods.

2. Subdivision (1)(a) protects the carrier who follows the instructions of a holder of a negotiable bill of lading. Under former Civil Code § 2127a (UBLA) a carrier was protected if he delivered to "(c) A person in possession of a negotiable bill for the goods by the terms of which the goods are deliverable to his order, or which has been indorsed to him or in blank by the consignee or by the mediate or immediate indorsee of the consignee." However under former Civil Code § 2127b (UBLA) a carrier was not protected if he had been requested prior to delivery by a person having a right in the property, not to deliver or if the carrier had information that the delivery was to a person not entitled to possession.

Subdivision (1)(b) and (1)(c) increase the consignor's control beyond that provided in former Civil Code §§ 2127a(b) and 2127b.

Subdivision (1)(b) is similar to paragraph (a) of former Civil Code § 2127a.

3. Subdivision (2) is new statutory law.

Changes from U.C.C. (1962 Official Text)

4. This is section 7-303 of the Official Text without change.

Uniform Commercial Code Comment

Prior Uniform Statutory Provision:
None.

Purposes:

1. The old Acts contained no reference to diversion, a very common commercial practice which defeats delivery to the consignee originally named in a bill of lading. The carrier was protected under the heading of "justified delivery" if the substituted consignee who received delivery was "a person lawfully entitled to possession of the goods." Cf. subsection (1)(d). This in turn depended on whether the person ordering the diversion was the owner of the goods or empowered to dispose of them, which again might depend upon whether under sales law title had passed from the consignor-seller to the consignee-buyer. The carrier is plainly not in a position to decide such questions when directed by the person with whom it has contracted for transportation to change the destination of the goods in transit. Carriers may as a business matter be willing to accept instructions from consignees in which case, as under the old uniform acts, the carrier will be liable for misdelivery if the consignee was not the owner or otherwise empowered to dispose of the goods. The section imposes no duty on carriers to undertake diversion; it is of course subject to the provisions of filed tariffs. Section 7-103.

2. It should be noted that the section provides only an immunity for carriers against liability for "misdelivery." It does not, for example, defeat the title to the goods which the consignee-buyer may have acquired from the consigner-seller upon delivery of the goods to the carrier under a non-negotiable bill of lading. Thus if the carrier, upon instructions from the consignor, returns the goods to him, the consignee may recover the goods from the consignor or his insolvent estate. However, under certain circumstances, the consignee's title may be defeated by diversion of the goods in transit to a different consignee.

Cross References:
Point 2: Sections 7-403 and 7-504(3).

Definitional Cross References:
"Bailee". Section 7-102.
"Bill of lading". Section 1-201.
"Consignee". Section 7-102.
"Consignor". Section 7-102.
"Delivery". Section 1-201.
"Goods". Section 7-102.
"Holder". Section 1-201.
"Notice". Section 1-201.
"Person". Section 1-201.
"Purchaser". Section 1-201.
"Term". Section 1-201.

Cross References

Damages for breach of carrier's obligation to deliver goods, see Civil Code § 3316.
Delivery, in general, see Civil Code § 2118 et seq.
Duty of carrier to comply with directions, see Civil Code § 2115.
Effect of diversion, see Commercial Code § 7504.
Obligation to deliver goods, excuse, see Commercial Code § 7403.

§ 7304. Bills of Lading in a Set

(1) Except where customary in overseas transportation, a bill of lading must not be issued in a set of parts. The issuer is liable for damages caused by violation of this subdivision.

(2) Where a bill of lading is lawfully drawn in a set of parts, each of which is numbered and expressed to be valid only if the goods have not been delivered against any other part, the whole of the parts constitute one bill.

(3) Where a bill of lading is lawfully issued in a set of parts and different parts are negotiated to different persons, the title of the holder to whom the first due negotiation is made prevails as to both the document and the goods even though any later holder may have received the goods from the carrier in good faith and discharged the carrier's obligation by surrender of his part.

(4) Any person who negotiates or transfers a single part of a bill of lading drawn in a set is liable to holders of that part as if it were the whole set.

(5) The bailee is obliged to deliver in accordance with Chapter 4 of this division against the first presented part of a bill of lading lawfully drawn in a set. Such delivery discharges the bailee's obligation on the whole bill. *(Stats.1963, c. 819, § 7304.)*

California Code Comment

Prior California Law

1. Subdivision (1) replaces former Civil Code § 2126e (UBLA). See Official Comment.

The prohibition of bills in a set was limited to the south 48 states under former Civil Code § 2126e while subdivision (1) prohibits them "except where customary in overseas transportation."

Former Civil Code § 2126e was limited to negotiable bills but Commercial Code § 7304 applies to all bills of lading.

2. Subdivisions (2)-(5) are new. See Commercial Code § 3801(1), (2) for parallel provisions to subdivision (2), (3) and (4) of this section.

Changes from U.C.C. (1962 Official Text)

3. This is Section 7-304 of the Official Text without change.

Uniform Commercial Code Comment

Prior Uniform Statutory Provision:
Section 6, Uniform Bills of Lading Act.

Changes: This section adds to existing legislation, which merely prohibits bills in a set in ordinary domestic trade, a statement of the legal effect of a lawfully issued set.

Purposes of Changes:

The statement of the legal effect of a lawfully issued set is in accord with existing commercial law relating to maritime and other overseas bills. This law has been codified in the Hague and Warsaw Conventions and in the Carriage of Goods by Sea Act, the provisions of which would ordinarily govern in situations where bills in a set are recognized by this Article.

Cross Reference:
Section 10–103.

Definitional Cross References:
"Bailee". Section 7–102.
"Bill of lading". Section 7–102.
"Delivery". Section 1–201.
"Document". Section 7–102.
"Duly negotiate". Section 7–501.
"Good faith". Section 1–201.
"Goods". Section 7–102.
"Holder". Section 1–201.
"Issuer". Section 7–102.
"Overseas". Section 2–323.
"Person". Section 1–201.
"Receipt of goods". Section 2–103.

Cross References

Irregularities in issue of bill, see Commercial Code § 7401.
Liability for failure to identify duplicate document, see Commercial Code § 7402.
Negotiation and transfer of documents of title, see Commercial Code § 7501 et seq.
Obligation of carrier to deliver, see Commercial Code § 7403.

§ 7305. Destination Bills

(1) Instead of issuing a bill of lading to the consignor at the place of shipment a carrier may at the request of the consignor procure the bill to be issued at destination or at any other place designated in the request.

(2) Upon request of anyone entitled as against the carrier to control the goods while in transit and on surrender of any outstanding bill of lading or other receipt covering such goods, the issuer may procure a substitute bill to be issued at any place designated in the request. *(Stats.1963, c. 819, § 7305.)*

California Code Comment

By John A. Bohn and Charles J. Williams

Prior California Law
1. This section is new. It is intended to meet the problem caused by arrival of the goods before the bill of lading covering them due to modern high speed methods of transportation. See Official Comment.

Changes from U.C.C. (1962 Official Text)
2. This is section 7–305 of the Official Text without change.

Uniform Commercial Code Comment

Prior Uniform Statutory Provision:
None.

Purposes:
This proposal is designed to facilitate the use of order bills in connection with fast shipments. Use of order bills on high speed shipments is impeded by the fact that the goods may arrive at destination before the documents, so that no one is ready to take delivery from the carrier. This is especially inconvenient for carriers by truck and air, who do not have terminal facilities where shipments can be held to await consignee's appearance. Order bills would be useful to take advantage of bank collection. This may be preferable to C.O.D. shipment in which the carrier, e.g. a truck driver, is the collecting and remitting agent. Financing of shipments under this plan would be handled as follows: seller at San Francisco delivers the goods to an airline with instructions to issue a bill in New York to a named bank. Seller receives a receipt embodying this undertaking to issue a destination bill. Airline wires its New York freight agent to issue the bill as instructed by the seller. Seller wires the New York bank a draft on buyer. New York bank indorses the bill to buyer when he honors the draft. Normally seller would act through his own bank in San Francisco, which would extend him credit in reliance on the airline's contract to deliver a bill to the order of its New York correspondent. This section is entirely permissive; it imposes no duty to issue such bills. Whether a connecting carrier will act as issuing agent is left to agreement between carriers.

Definitional Cross References:
"Bill of lading". Section 1–201.
"Consignor". Section 7–102.
"Goods". Section 7–102.
"Issuer". Section 7–102.
"Receipt of goods". Section 2–103.

§ 7306. Altered Bills of Lading

An unauthorized alteration or filling in of a blank in a bill of lading leaves the bill enforceable according to its original tenor. *(Stats.1963, c. 819, § 7306.)*

California Code Comment

By John A. Bohn and Charles J. Williams

Prior California Law
1. This section restates and simplifies without substantive change former Civil Code § 2128 (UBLA). See the Official Comment.

Changes from U.C.C. (1962 Official Text)
2. This is section 7–306 of the Official Text without change.

Uniform Commercial Code Comment

Prior Uniform Statutory Provision:
Section 16, Uniform Bills of Lading Act.

Changes: Generally revised and simplified; explicit treatment of the situation where a blank in an executed document is filled without authority.

Purposes of Changes:
An unauthorized alteration whether made with or without fraudulent intent does not relieve the issuer of his liability on the document as originally executed. Uniform Warehouse Receipts Act 13 excused the issuer from any liability to a fraudulent alterer, other than the liability to deliver the goods according to the terms of the original document. It is difficult to conceive what liability the draftsman intended to excuse. Uniform Bills of Lading Act 16 contains no such excuse provision, and is followed in this respect in the present section. Uniform Bills of Lading Act 16 characterizes an unauthorized alteration as "void" but apparently nothing more was intended than that the alteration did not change the obligation of the issuer. This is sufficiently covered by the terms of this Section. Moreover cases are conceivable in which an alteration would not be "void"; for example, an alteration made by common consent of a transferor and transferee of a document might evidence an enforceable contract between them. The same rule is made applicable to the filling in of blanks, a matter on which the prior Acts were silent.

Definitional Cross References:
"Bill of lading". Section 1–201.
"Issuer". Section 7–102.

Cross References

Alteration of writing, explanation by party producing, see Evidence Code § 1402.
Fictitious bills of lading, penal provision, see Penal Code § 578.
Modification of contracts, see Civil Code § 1697 et seq.

§ 7307. Lien of Carrier

(1) A carrier has a lien on the goods covered by a bill of lading for charges subsequent to the date of its receipt of the goods for storage or transportation (including demurrage and terminal charges) and for expenses necessary for preservation of the goods incident to their transportation or reasonably incurred in their sale pursuant to law. But against a purchaser for

value of a negotiable bill of lading a carrier's lien is limited to charges stated in the bill or the applicable tariffs, or if no charges are stated then to a reasonable charge.

(2) A lien for charges and expenses under subdivision (1) on goods which the carrier was required by law to receive for transportation is effective against the consignor or any person entitled to the goods unless the carrier had notice that the consignor lacked authority to subject the goods to such charges and expenses. Any other lien under subdivision (1) is effective against the consignor and any person who permitted the bailor to have control or possession of the goods unless the carrier had notice that the bailor lacked such authority.

(3) A carrier loses his lien on any goods which he voluntarily delivers or which he unjustifiably refuses to deliver. *(Stats.1963, c. 819, § 7307.)*

California Code Comment
By John A. Bohn and Charles J. Williams

Prior California Law

1. Subdivision (1) is similar to former Civil Code § 2128j (UBLA) with the following differences noted: former Civil Code § 2128j recognized a carrier's lien for "freight, storage, demurrage and terminal charges, and expenses necessary for the preservation of the goods or incident to their transportation subsequent to the date of the bill." Any other charges claimed as a part of the lien had to be expressly enumerated in the bill. Former Civil Code § 2128j was limited to negotiable bills. This subdivision recognizes the lien on goods shipped under a negotiable or non-negotiable bill.

Subdivision (1) modifies prior law as expressed in former Civil Code § 2128j by limiting the lien, as against a purchaser for value, to charges (i) stated in the bill, (ii) stated in an applicable tariff, or (iii) if not stated, then to reasonable charges.

Prior to the adoption of the UBLA in 1919, California recognized a lien for the carrier for freightage and services. Civil Code § 2144 recognizes a carrier's lien for freightage or services rendered at the shipper's or consignee's request "in and about the transportation, care and preservation of the property" and for money advanced at the request of the shipper or consignee to discharge a prior lien. This section was not repealed as a result of adoption of the Commercial Code. It would be subordinate to the specific provisions of the Commercial Code. See Commercial Code §§ 1102 and 10104. Civil Code § 2144 provides that the lien given by that section is regulated by the title on liens. Civil Code §§ 2872–3075.

2. Subdivision (2) is new statutory law. It extends the lien to any person who permits the bailor to have possession of the goods. Official Comment.

3. Subdivision (3) is a restatement of former Civil Code § 1858.52 (UWRA) without substantive change.

Changes from U.C.C. (1962 Official Text)

4. This is section 7–307 of the Official Text without change.

Uniform Commercial Code Comment

Prior Uniform Statutory Provision:
Sections 27 through 32, Uniform Warehouse Receipts Act.

Changes: Rewritten; lien extended to carrier. Lien of common carrier validated unless carrier had notice that consignor lacked authority to subject the goods to charges and expenses. Where the carrier is not required by law to receive the goods for transportation, lien validated against anyone who permitted the bailor to have possession even if he had no real or apparent authority.

Purposes of Changes:

The section is intended to give carriers a specific statutory lien for charges and expenses similar to that given to warehousemen by the first sentence of Section 7–209. But since carriers do not commonly claim a lien for charges in relation to other goods or lend money on the security of goods in their hands, provisions for a general lien or a security interest similar to those in Section 7–209(1) and (2) are omitted. See Comment to Section 7–105. Since the lien given by this section is specific, and the storage or transportation often preserves or increases the value of the goods, subsection (2) validates the lien against anyone who permitted the bailor to have possession of the goods. Where the carrier is required to receive the goods for transportation, the owner's interest may be subjected to charges and expenses arising out of deposit of his goods by a thief. Cf. Section 9–310. The crucial mental element is the carrier's knowledge or reason to know of the bailor's lack of authority.

Cross References:
Sections 7–209, 9–102(2) and 9–310.

Definitional Cross References:
"Bill of lading". Section 1–201.
"Consignor". Section 7–102.
"Delivery". Section 1–201.
"Goods". Section 7–102.
"Person". Section 1–201.
"Purchaser". Section 1–201.
"Value". Section 1–201.

Cross References

Carrier's lien, in general, see Civil Code § 2144.
Liens,
  Generally, see Civil Code § 2872 et seq.
  Arising by operation of law, priority, see Commercial Code § 9310.
  Law governing, see Commercial Code § 9102.
  Priorities among conflicting security interests, see Commercial Code § 9312.
  Warehouseman, see Commercial Code § 7209.
Possessory liens for services, repairs, etc., see Civil Code § 3051 et seq.
Storage by bailee until freight and charges paid, see Civil Code § 2081.

§ 7308. Enforcement of Carrier's Lien

(1) A carrier's lien may be enforced by public or private sale of the goods, in bloc or in parcels, at any time or place and on any terms which are commercially reasonable, after notifying all persons known to claim an interest in the goods. Such notification must include a statement of the amount due, the nature of the proposed sale and the time and place of any public sale. The fact that a better price could have been obtained by a sale at a different time or in a different method from that selected by the carrier is not of itself sufficient to establish that the sale was not made in a commercially reasonable manner. If the carrier either sells the goods in the usual manner in any recognized market therefor or if he sells at the price current in such market at the time of his sale or if he has otherwise sold in conformity with commercially reasonable practices among dealers in the type of goods sold he has sold in a commercially reasonable manner. A sale of more goods than apparently necessary to be offered to ensure satisfaction of the obligation is not commercially reasonable except in cases covered by the preceding sentence.

(2) Before any sale pursuant to this section any person claiming a right in the goods may pay the amount necessary to satisfy the lien and the reasonable expenses incurred under this section. In that event the goods must not be sold, but must be retained by the carrier subject to the terms of the bill and this division.

(3) The carrier may buy at any public sale pursuant to this section.

(4) A purchaser in good faith of goods sold to enforce a carrier's lien takes the goods free of any rights of persons against whom the lien was valid, despite noncompliance by the carrier with the requirements of this section.

(5) The carrier may satisfy his lien from the proceeds of any sale pursuant to this section but must hold the balance, if any, for delivery on demand to any person to whom he would have been bound to deliver the goods.

(6) The rights provided by this section shall be in addition to all other rights allowed by law to a creditor against his debtor.

(7) A carrier's lien may be enforced in accordance with either subdivision (1) or the procedure set forth in subdivision (2) of Section 7210.

(8) The carrier is liable for damages caused by failure to comply with the requirements for sale under this section and in case of willful violation is liable for conversion. *(Stats.1963, c. 819, § 7308.)*

California Code Comment

By John A. Bohn and Charles J. Williams

Prior California Law

1. This section is substantially the same as Commercial Code § 7210 which deals with enforcement of warehouseman's lien. Subdivision (2) of Commercial Code § 7210 is not repeated in this section. See California Code Comments to Commercial Code § 7210 for the parallel provisions of this section.

2. Subdivision (1) of this section is essentially the same as subdivision (1) of section 7210.

3. Subdivision (2) of this section is essentially the same as subdivision (3) of section 7210.

4. Subdivision (3) of this section is essentially the same as subdivision (4) of section 7210.

5. Subdivision (4) of this section is essentially the same as subdivision (5) of section 7210.

6. Subdivision (5) of this section is essentially the same as subdivision (6) of section 7210.

7. Subdivision (6) of this section is essentially the same as subdivision (7) of section 7210.

8. Subdivision (8) of this section is essentially the same as subdivision (9) of section 7210.

Changes from U.C.C. (1962 Official Text)

9. This is section 7-308 of the Official Text without change.

Uniform Commercial Code Comment

Prior Uniform Statutory Provision:
Section 33, Uniform Warehouse Receipts Act.

Changes: Rewritten; provisions extended to carriers' liens; simplified foreclosure proceeding provided.

Purposes of Changes:
This section is intended to give the carrier an enforcement procedure of his lien coextensive with that given the warehousemen in cases other than those covering noncommercial storage by him. See Comment to Section 7-210.

Cross Reference:
Section 7-210.

Definitional Cross References:
"Bill of lading". Section 1-201.
"Creditor". Section 1-201.
"Delivery". Section 1-201.
"Good faith". Section 1-201.
"Goods". Section 7-102.
"Notification." Section 1-201.
"Notifies". Section 1-201.
"Person". Section 1-201.
"Purchaser". Section 1-201.
"Rights". Section 1-201.
"Term". Section 1-201.

Cross References

Carrier's lien, in general, see Civil Code § 2144.
Crimes involving bailments, see Penal Code § 560 et seq.
Damages for conversion of personal property, see Civil Code § 3336 et seq.
Enforcement of warehouseman's lien, see Commercial Code § 7210.
Extinction of liens, see Civil Code § 2909 et seq.
Perishable property, sale for freightage, see Civil Code § 2204.
Redemption from lien, see Civil Code § 2903 et seq.
Sale by lien holder at auction, see Civil Code § 3052.
Unclaimed property, storage by bailee until freight and charges paid, see Civil Code § 2081.

§ 7309. Duty of Care; Contractual Limitation of Carrier's Liability

(1) A carrier who issues a bill of lading whether negotiable or nonnegotiable must exercise the degree of care in relation to the goods which a reasonably careful man would exercise under like circumstances. This subdivision does not repeal or change any law or rule of law which imposes liability upon a common carrier for damages not caused by its negligence.

(2) Damages may be limited by a provision that the carrier's liability shall not exceed a value stated in the document if the carrier's rates are dependent upon value and the consignor by the carrier's tariff is afforded an opportunity to declare a higher value or a value as lawfully provided in the tariff, or where no tariff is filed he is otherwise advised of such opportunity; but no such limitation is effective with respect to the carrier's liability for conversion to its own use.

(3) Reasonable provisions as to the time and manner of presenting claims and instituting actions based on the shipment may be included in a bill of lading or tariff. *(Stats.1963, c. 819, § 7309.)*

California Code Comment

By John A. Bohn and Charles J. Williams

Prior California Law

1. This section is patterned after 49 USCA § 20(11), a provision of the Interstate Commerce Act known as the Carmack Amendment. Official Comment.

2. The first sentence of subdivision (1) imposes the same standard as under former Civil Code § 2126b (UBLA) which imposed an obligation upon a carrier "to exercise at least that degree of care in the transportation and safekeeping of the goods entrusted to him which a reasonably careful man would exercise in regard to similar goods *of his own*." (emphasis added).

Subdivision (1) of this section does not require the carrier to care for the goods as a reasonable man would care for "his own" but rather as a reasonable man would "under like circumstances."

The second sentence of subdivision (1) leaves certain prior statutes unaffected by the adoption of this section. Civil Code §§ 2174 (obligations of carrier can be limited only by special agreement), 2175 (agreement to exonerate carrier from liability for gross negligence or willful act is void), and 2176 (effect of written contract).

Subdivision (2) is new statutory law but is in accord with prior case law. In Franklin v. Southern Pacific Co., 203 Cal. 680, 265 Pac. 936, (1928), cert. den. 278 U.S. 621, the court stated:

"... What amounts to a limitation of liability may be made by special contract with the shipper where the charges are graduated according to the value of the property as fixed by the shipper, he having at all times the privilege of securing full coverage by paying the stipulated charge for such protection."

Also see Civil Code § 2176 dealing with limitation of liability in case of loss or injury to property "carried in packages, trunks, or boxes" and "live animals carried"; Civil Code § 2177 dealing with limitation of carriers liability in cases involving "loss or miscarriage of a letter or package in the form of a letter" containing money or papers of value; Civil Code § 2178 dealing with the limitation of liability for loss of or damage to baggage by railroad companies; and Civil Code § 2200 dealing with limitation of liability for valuables.

Changes from U.C.C. (1962 Official Text)

3. This is section 7–309 of the Official Text without change.

Uniform Commercial Code Comment

Prior Uniform Statutory Provision:
Section 3, Uniform Bills of Lading Act.

Changes: Consolidated and rewritten.

Purposes of Changes:

The old uniform act provided that bills of lading could not contain terms impairing the obligation of reasonable care. Whether this is violated by a stipulation that in case of loss the bailee's liability is limited to stated amounts has been much controverted. For interstate rail transportation the matter is settled by the Carmack Amendment to the Interstate Commerce Act (See 49 U.S.C.A. § 20(11)). The present section is a generalized version of the Interstate Commerce Act provisions. The obligation of due care is radically qualified, in the case of maritime bills and international airbills, by federal legislation and treaty. All this special legislation would remain in effect even if Congress enacts this Code, including the present Article. See Section 7–103.

Subsection (1) does not impair any rule of law imposing the liability of an insurer on a common carrier in intrastate commerce. Subsection (2), however, applies to such liability as well as to liability based on negligence. The entire section is subject under Section 7–103 to applicable provisions in filed tariffs, such as the common disclaimer of responsibility for undeclared articles of extraordinary value, hidden from view. Tariffs which lawfully provide a maximum unit value beyond which goods are not taken fall within the same principle, and are expressly covered by the words "value as lawfully provided in the tariff."

Cross Reference:
Section 7–103.

Definitional Cross References:
"Action". Section 1–201.
"Bill of lading". Section 1–201.
"Consignor". Section 7–102.
"Document". Section 7–102.
"Goods". Section 7–102.
"Value". Section 1–201.

Cross References

Common carriers of property, see Civil Code § 2194 et seq.
Damages for conversion of personal property, see Civil Code § 3336 et seq.
Duty of care; contractual limitation of warehouseman's liability, see Commercial Code § 7204.
Invalid agreements of exoneration by common carrier, see Civil Code § 2175.
Liability of issuer for non-receipt or misdescription, see Commercial Code § 7301.
Limitation of carrier's liability by contract, see Civil Code § 2176.
Limitation of carrier's obligations, see Civil Code § 2174.
No liability for good faith delivery pursuant to bill of lading, see Commercial Code § 7404.
Obligation of carrier to deliver, see Commercial Code § 7403.
Obligations of depositary, see Civil Code § 1822 et seq.
Treaty, statute, etc., effect, see Commercial Code § 7103.

Valuables, limitation of liability by carrier, see Civil Code § 2200.

CHAPTER 4. WAREHOUSE RECEIPTS AND BILLS OF LADING: GENERAL OBLIGATIONS

Section
7401. Irregularities in Issue of Receipt or Bill or Conduct of Issuer.
7402. Duplicate Receipt or Bill; Overissue.
7403. Obligation of Warehouseman or Carrier to Deliver; Excuse.
7404. No Liability for Good Faith Delivery Pursuant to Receipt or Bill.

§ 7401. Irregularities in Issue of Receipt or Bill or Conduct of Issuer

The obligations imposed by this division on an issuer apply to a document of title regardless of the fact that

(a) The document may not comply with the requirements of this division or of any other law or regulation regarding its issue, form or content; or

(b) The issuer may have violated laws regulating the conduct of his business; or

(c) The goods covered by the document were owned by the bailee at the time the document was issued; or

(d) The person issuing the document does not come within the definition of warehouseman if it purports to be a warehouse receipt. *(Stats.1963, c. 819, § 7401.)*

California Code Comment
By John A. Bohn and Charles J. Williams

Prior California Law

1. This section is largely new. It is intended to make the issuer subject to the obligations of Division 7 even though neither the document nor the issuer of it may have complied with Division 7. Official Comment. It effectively prevents an issuer from pleading his own violation of Division 7 as a defense in an action against him.

2. Paragraph (a) is new.

3. Paragraph (b) is new. It is consistent with former Civil Code §§ 1858.29 (UWRA) and 2128g (UBLA) which covered only non-receipt and misdescription. Official Comment.

4. Paragraph (c) is new. However, it is similar in principle to former Civil Code §§ 1858.25 (UWRA) and 2128c (UBLA) which stated that a warehouseman (carrier) was not excused from liability for refusing to deliver the goods because he had title to the goods unless such title was derived from the depositor (consignor or consignee) or warehouseman's (carrier's) lien.

5. Paragraph (d) is new.

Changes from U.C.C. (1962 Official Text)

6. This is section 7–401 of the Official Text without change.

Uniform Commercial Code Comment

Prior Uniform Statutory Provision:
Section 20, Uniform Warehouse Receipts Act; Section 23, Uniform Bills of Lading Act.

Changes: Most of the material is new; the uniform act sections cited deal only with non-receipt and misdescription.

Purposes of Changes and New Matter:

The bailee's liability on his document despite non-receipt or misdescription of the goods is affirmed in Sections 7–203 and 7–301. The purpose of this section is to make it clear that regardless of irregularities a document which falls within the definition of document of title imposes on the issuer the obligations stated in this Article. For example, a bailee will not be permitted to avoid his obligation to deliver the goods (Section 7–403) or his obligation of due care with respect to them (Sections 7–204 and 7–309) by taking the position that no valid "document" was issued because he failed to file a statutory bond or did not pay stamp taxes or did not disclose the place of storage in the document. Sanctions against violations of statutory or administrative duties with respect to documents should be limited to revocation of license or other measures prescribed by the regulation imposing the duty. As to the continuing vitality of regulations, in addition to those found in this Article, of documents of title, see Sections 7–103 and 10–103.

Cross References:
Sections 7–103, 7–203, 7–204, 7–301, 7–309 and 10–103.

Definitional Cross References:
"Bailee". Section 7–102.
"Document". Section 7–102.
"Document of title". Section 1–201.
"Goods". Section 7–102.
"Issuer". Section 7–102.
"Person". Section 1–201.
"Warehouse receipt". Section 1–201.
"Warehouseman". Section 7–102.

Cross References

Crimes involving bailments, see Penal Code § 560 et seq.
Duty of care in relation to goods, see Commercial Code §§ 7204, 7309.
Fraudulent issue of documents of title to merchandise, see Penal Code § 577 et seq.
Non-delivery or misdescription of goods, liability, see Commercial Code §§ 7203, 7301.
Obligation of warehouseman or carrier to deliver, see Commercial Code § 7403.
Obligations of carrier, see Civil Code §§ 2114, 2115, 2118 et seq.
Obligations of depositary, see Civil Code § 1822 et seq.
Treaty, statute, etc., effect, see Commercial Code § 7103.

§ 7402. Duplicate Receipt or Bill; Overissue

Neither a duplicate nor any other document of title purporting to cover goods already represented by an outstanding document of the same issuer confers any right in the goods, except as provided in the case of bills in a set, overissue of documents for fungible goods and substitutes for lost, stolen or destroyed documents. But the issuer is liable for damages caused by his overissue or failure to identify a duplicate document as such by conspicuous notation on its face. *(Stats.1963, c. 819, § 7402.)*

California Code Comment

By John A. Bohn and Charles J. Williams

Prior California Law

1. This section combines and restates the rule of former Civil Code §§ 1858.15 (UWRA) and 2126f (UBLA) requiring duplicate documents to be plainly marked as such.

The basic changes effected by this section are that its provisions are extended to (1) non-negotiable documents and (2) deliberate overissue. Former Civil Code §§ 1858.15 and 2126f did not apply to non-negotiable documents or overissue.

This section is an exception to the general rule that the transferee of a non-negotiable document takes only the rights of his transferee. Official Comment 2.

2. In response to the suggestion that this section might conflict with Commercial Code § 7502 (rights acquired by due negotiation), the Marsh and Warren Report commented:

"There is no conflict between this Section and Section 17502 [7502]. As expressly pointed out in the comments to this Section, it deals only with the situation where two documents for the same goods have been issued *by the same issuer*. Where there is an outstanding warehouse receipt and an outstanding delivery order issued by the holder of the warehouse receipt, there are not two outstanding documents '*of the same issue*' and this Section has no application. Therefore, there is no need for an exception to this Section.

"The California Bankers Committee does not say in what other respect they think this Section 'unclear.' They state that Comment 3 indicates that there may be more than one outstanding document against the same goods. That is precisely the situation with which this Section deals. However, Comment 3 points out situations where the two outstanding documents may be *of different issuers* and therefore not within the scope of this Section." Sixth Progress Report to the Legislature by Senate Fact Finding Committee on Judiciary (1959–1961), Part 1, The Uniform Commercial Code, p. 524.

3. The following analysis of the State Bar Committee which recommended adoption of this section was in response to a proposal limiting this section to negotiable receipts.

"Under CC § 1858.15 when more than one negotiable receipt is issued for the same goods, the word 'duplicate' shall be plainly placed upon the face of every such receipt, except the first one issued, and a warehouseman will be liable for all damage caused by his failure to do this to anyone who purchased the subsequent receipt for value supposing it to be an original. Section 17402 [7402] applies to non-negotiable receipts as well as negotiable ones; hence, the purchaser of a non-negotiable receipt is given a cause of action against the issuer of an unmarked duplicate. It is this extension of protection to purchasers of non-negotiable receipts that is objected to by the warehousemen.

"In view of the widespread use of non-negotiable receipts in financing, we believe the greater protection afforded purchasers of non-negotiable receipts under § 17402 [7402] is desirable. The warehouseman is the only party in the position to exercise control over the issuance of duplicate warehouse receipts. A purchaser of a non-negotiable warehouse receipt must realize that he is not taking as complete rights as he would were he purchasing a negotiable receipt, but, with regard to an action against the warehouseman, he should not be bound to determine at his peril whether the warehouse has issued duplicate receipts on the same goods." Further Comments of State Bar, Sixth Progress Report to the Legislature by Senate Fact Finding Committee on Judiciary (1959–1961), Part 1, The Uniform Commercial Code, p. 630.

Changes from U.C.C. (1962 Official Text)

4. This is section 7–402 of the Official Text without change.

Uniform Commercial Code Comment

Prior Uniform Statutory Provision:
Section 6, Uniform Warehouse Receipts Act; Section 7, Uniform Bills of Lading Act.

Changes: Consolidated and rewritten.

Purposes of Changes:

1. This section treats a duplicate which is not properly identified as such like any other overissue of documents: a purchaser of such a document acquires no title but only a cause of action for damages against the person who made his deception possible, except in the cases noted in the section. But parts of a bill lawfully issued in a set of parts are not "overissue" (Section 7–304). Of course, if the issuer has clearly indicated that a document is a duplicate so that no one can be deceived by it, and in fact the duplicate is a correct copy of the original, the warehouseman is not liable for preparing and delivering such a duplicate copy.

2. The section applies to non-negotiable documents to the extent of providing an action for damages for one who acquires an unmarked duplicate from a transferor who knew the facts and would therefore himself have had no cause of action against the issuer of the duplicate. Ordinarily the transferee of a non-negotiable document acquires only the rights of his transferor.

3. Overissue is defined so as to exclude the common situation where two valid documents of different issuers are outstanding for the same goods at the same time. Thus freight forwarders commonly issue bills of lading to their customers for small shipments to be combined into carload shipments for which the railroad will issue a bill of lading to the forwarder. So also a warehouse receipt may be outstanding against goods, and the holder of the receipt may issue delivery orders against the same goods. In these cases dealings with the subsequently issued documents may be effective to transfer title; e.g. negotiation of a delivery order will effectively transfer title in the ordinary case where no

dishonesty has occurred and the goods are available to satisfy the orders. Section 7–503 provides for cases of conflict between documents of different issuers.

Cross References:
Point 1: Sections 7–207, 7–304, and 7–601.
Point 3: Section 7–503.

Definitional Cross References:
"Bill of lading". Section 1–201.
"Conspicuous". Section 1–201.
"Document". Section 7–102.
"Document of title". Section 1–201.
"Fungible" goods. Section 1–201.
"Goods". Section 7–102.
"Issuer". Section 7–102.
"Right". Section 1–201.

Cross References

Bills of lading in a set, see Commercial Code § 7304.
Commingled fungible goods, persons entitled in case of overissue of receipts, see Commercial Code § 7207.
Document of title to goods, operation and effect, see Commercial Code § 7503.
Duplicate receipts, penalty for failure to mark as duplicate, see Penal Code § 580.
Lost and missing documents, delivery of goods, see Commercial Code § 7601.
Unlawful issuance of duplicate or additional negotiable document of title, see Penal Code § 560.4.

§ 7403. Obligation of Warehouseman or Carrier to Deliver; Excuse

(1) The bailee must deliver the goods to a person entitled under the document who complies with subdivisions (2) and (3), unless and to the extent that the bailee establishes any of the following:

(a) Delivery of the goods to a person whose receipt was rightful as against the claimant;

(b) Damage to or delay, loss or destruction of the goods for which the bailee is not liable, but the burden of establishing negligence in case of damage or destruction by fire is on the person entitled under the document;

(c) Previous sale or other disposition of the goods in lawful enforcement of a lien or on warehouseman's lawful termination of storage;

(d) The exercise by a seller of his right to stop delivery pursuant to the provisions of the division on sales (Section 2705);

(e) A diversion, reconsignment or other disposition pursuant to the provisions of this division (Section 7303) or tariff regulating such right;

(f) Release, satisfaction or any other fact affording a personal defense against the claimant;

(g) Any other lawful excuse.

(2) A person claiming goods covered by a document of title must satisfy the bailee's lien where the bailee so requests or where the bailee is prohibited by law from delivering the goods until the charges are paid.

(3) * * * Unless the person claiming is one against whom the document confers no right under subdivision (1) of Section 7503, he must surrender for cancellation or notation of partial deliveries any outstanding negotiable document covering the goods, and the bailee must cancel the document or conspicuously note the partial delivery thereon or be liable to any person to whom the document is duly negotiated.

(4) "Person entitled under the document" means holder in the case of a negotiable document, or the person to whom delivery is to be made by the terms of or pursuant to written instructions under a nonnegotiable document. *(Stats.1963, c. 819, § 7403. Amended by Stats.1967, c. 799, p. 2210, § 11.)*

California Code Comment

By Charles J. Williams

Prior California Law

1. The 1967 amendment brings subdivision (3) into conformity with the Official Text. Subdivision (1)(b) still contains a California variation. See California Code Comments 6 and 7, main volume, for an explanation of these variations from the Official Text.

2. The California variation in subdivision (2) was not apparently intended to change substance. (Permanent Editorial Board for the Uniform Commercial Code, Report No. 2, p. 135.)

Changes from U.C.C. (1962 Official Text)

3. The California variation from the Official Text in subdivision (1)(b) still exists. The reason for this California variation is to retain prior California law. (California Code Comments 2 and 6, ante.)

Uniform Commercial Code Comment

Prior Uniform Statutory Provision:
Sections 8 through 12, 16 and 19, Uniform Warehouse Receipts Act; Sections 11 through 15, 19 and 22, Uniform Bills of Lading Act.

Changes: Consolidated and rewritten.

Purposes of Changes:

1. The general and primary purpose of this revision is to simplify the statement of the bailee's obligation on the document. The interrelations of the separate sections of the old uniform acts dealing with "obligation to deliver," "justification in delivering," and "liability for misdelivery" are obscure. The present section is constructed on the basis of stating what previous deliveries or other circumstances operate to excuse the bailee's normal obligation on the document. Accordingly, "justified" deliveries under the old uniform acts now find their place as "excuse" under subsection (1). Unjustified deliveries, i.e., "misdeliveries" under the old acts, are simply omitted from the list of excuses, thus permitting the normal obligation on the document to be asserted.

2. The principal case covered by subsection (1)(a) is delivery to a person whose title is paramount to the rights represented by the document. For example, if a thief deposits stolen goods in a warehouse and takes a negotiable receipt, the warehouseman is not liable on the receipt if he has surrendered the goods to the true owner, even though the receipt is held by a good faith purchaser. See Section 7–503(1). However, if the owner entrusted the goods to a person with power of disposition, and that person deposited the goods and took a negotiable document, the owner's receipt would not be rightful as against a holder to whom the negotiable document was duly negotiated, and delivery to the owner would not give the bailee a defense against such a holder. See Sections 7–502(1)(b), 7–503(1)(a).

3. Subsection (1)(b) amounts to a cross reference to all the tort law that determines the varying responsibilities and standards of care applicable to commercial bailees. A restatement of this tort law would be beyond the scope of this Act. Much of the applicable law as to responsibility of bailees for the preservation of the goods and limitation of liability in case of loss has been codified for particular classes of bailees in interstate and foreign commerce by federal legislation and treaty and for intrastate carriers and other bailees by the regulatory state laws preserved by Section 7–103. In the absence of governing legislation the common law will prevail subject to the minimum standard of reasonable care prescribed by Sections 7–204 and 7–309 of this Article. The optional language in subsection (1)(b) states the rule laid down for interstate carriers in many federal cases. State decisions are

in conflict as to both carriers and warehousemen. Particular states may prefer to adopt the federal rule.

4. Subsection (2) eliminates the implication of the old uniform acts that a request for delivery must be accompanied by a formal tender of the amount of the charges due. Rather, the bailee must request payment of the amount of his lien when asked to deliver, and only in case this request is refused is he justified in declining to deliver because of nonpayment of charges. Where delivery without payment is forbidden by law, the request is treated as implicit. Such a prohibition reflects a policy of uniformity to prevent discrimination by failure to request payment in particular cases.

5. Subsection (3) states the obvious duty of a bailee to take up a negotiable document or note partial deliveries conspicuously thereon, and the result of failure in that duty. It is subject to only one exception, that stated in subsection 1(a) of this section and in Section 7–503(1). It is limited to cases of delivery to a claimant; it has no application, for example, where goods held under a negotiable document are lawfully sold to enforce the bailee's lien.

Cross References:

Point 2: Sections 7–502 and 7–503.
Point 3: Sections 7–103, 7–204, 7–309 and 10–103.
Point 5: Section 7–503(1).

Definitional Cross References:

"Bailee". Section 7–102.
"Conspicuous". Section 1–201.
"Delivery". Section 1–201.
"Document". Section 7–102.
"Document of title". Section 1–201.
"Duly negotiate". Section 7–501.
"Goods". Section 7–102.
"Person". Section 1–201.
"Receipt of goods". Section 2–103.
"Right". Section 1–201.
"Terms". Section 1–201.
"Warehouseman". Section 7–102.
"Written". Section 1–201.

Cross References

Common carriers of property, see Civil Code § 2194 et seq.
Damages,
　Breach of carrier's obligation to deliver, see Civil Code § 3316.
　Carrier's delay in delivery, see Civil Code § 3317.
Degree of care, see Commercial Code §§ 7204, 7309.
Delivery, in general, see Civil Code § 2118 et seq.
Delivery on demand, see Civil Code § 1822.
Document of title, effect, see Commercial Code § 7503.
Due negotiation, rights acquired, see Commercial Code § 7502.
Extinction of obligation by performance, see Civil Code § 1473.
Unlawful delivery of goods, punishment, see Penal Code § 560.2.

§ 7404. No Liability for Good Faith Delivery Pursuant to Receipt or Bill

A bailee who in good faith including observance of reasonable commercial standards has received goods and delivered or otherwise disposed of them according to the terms of the document of title or pursuant to this division is not liable therefor. This rule applies even though the person from whom he received the goods had no authority to procure the document or to dispose of the goods and even though the person to whom he delivered the goods had no authority to receive them. *(Stats.1963, c. 819, § 7404.)*

California Code Comment

By John A. Bohn and Charles J. Williams

Prior California Law

1. This section combines and rewrites former Civil Code §§ 1858.19 (UWRA) and 2127b (UBLA) which enumerated the conditions under which the bailee was obligated to deliver goods. This section states explicitly what was a necessary implication under the former uniform sections. See Official Comment.

2. In answer to objections to the use of the standard "reasonable commercial standard," the Marsh and Warren Report discussed the effect of this section: "The Warehouse Receipts Acts, § 10, [former CC § 1858.19] and the Bills of Lading Act, § 13, [former CC § 2175b] provided for two situations where the warehouseman or carrier might be liable for misdelivery even though he delivered in accordance with the terms of the receipt or bill of lading: (a) Where he had been requested by the true owner not to make delivery; and (b) Where he had information that the delivery was to one not lawfully entitled to the goods. CC §§ 1858.19, 2127b. This Section eliminates this specification and provides instead that the warehouseman or carrier may be liable for misdelivery even though in accordance with the terms of the receipt or bill of lading if he does not observe 'reasonable commercial standards.' It thus substitutes a general standard for a particularization of two circumstances which will make the warehouseman or carrier liable regardless of all other circumstances existing at the time.

"This change may work in favor of the warehouseman or carrier in some cases and against him in others, but we think that the generalized standard of good faith including observance of reasonable commercial standards will permit the courts to reach juster results in the cases." Sixth Progress Report to the Legislature by Senate Fact Finding Committee on Judiciary (1959–1961), Part 1, The Uniform Commercial Code, p. 525.

Changes from U.C.C. (1962 Official Text)

3. This is section 7–404 of the Official Text without change.

Uniform Commercial Code Comment

Prior Uniform Statutory Provision:

Section 10, Uniform Warehouse Receipts Act; Section 13, Uniform Bills of Lading Act.

Changes: Consolidated and rewritten.

Purposes of Changes:

The generalized test of good faith and observance of reasonable commercial standards is substituted for the attempts to particularize what constitutes good faith in the cited sections of the old uniform acts. The section states explicitly what is perhaps an implication from the old acts that the common law rule of "innocent conversion" by unauthorized "intermeddling" with another's property is inapplicable to the operations of commercial carriers and warehousemen, who in good faith and with reasonable observance of commercial standards perform obligations which they have assumed and which generally they are under a legal compulsion to assume. The section applies to delivery to a fraudulent holder of a valid document as well as to delivery to the holder of an invalid document.

Definitional Cross References:

"Bailee". Section 7–102.
"Delivery". Section 1–201.
"Document of title". Section 1–201.
"Good faith". Section 1–201.
"Goods". Section 7–102.
"Person". Section 1–201.
"Receipt of goods". Section 2–103.
"Term". Section 1–201.

Cross References

Authority of agents, see Civil Code § 2304 et seq.
Damages for breach of carrier's obligation to deliver, see Civil Code § 3316.
Damages for conversion, see Civil Code § 3336 et seq.
Investment securities, no conversion by good faith delivery, see Commercial Code § 8318.
Notice to beneficiary of deposit of adverse claims, see Civil Code § 1825.

Restoration of thing wrongfully acquired, see Civil Code §§ 1712, 1713.

CHAPTER 5. WAREHOUSE RECEIPTS AND BILLS OF LADING: NEGOTIATION AND TRANSFER

Section
7501. Form of Negotiation and Requirements of "Due Negotiation".
7502. Rights Acquired by Due Negotiation.
7503. Document of Title to Goods Defeated in Certain Cases.
7504. Rights Acquired in the Absence of Due Negotiation; Effect of Diversion; Seller's Stoppage of Delivery.
7505. Indorser Not a Guarantor for Other Parties.
7506. Delivery Without Indorsement; Right to Compel Indorsement.
7507. Warranties on Negotiation or Transfer of Receipt or Bill.
7508. Warranties of Collecting Bank as to Documents.
7509. Receipt or Bill: When Adequate Compliance With Commercial Contract.

§ 7501. Form of Negotiation and Requirements of "Due Negotiation"

(1) A negotiable document of title running to the order of a named person is negotiated by his indorsement and delivery. After his indorsement in blank or to bearer any person can negotiate it by delivery alone.

(2)(a) A negotiable document of title is also negotiated by delivery alone when by its original terms it runs to bearer.

(b) When a document running to the order of a named person is delivered to him the effect is the same as if the document had been negotiated.

(3) Negotiation of a negotiable document of title after it has been indorsed to a specified person requires indorsement by the special indorsee as well as delivery.

(4) A negotiable document of title is "duly negotiated" when it is negotiated in the manner stated in this section to a holder who purchases it in good faith without notice of any defense against or claim to it on the part of any person and for value.

(5) Indorsement of a nonnegotiable document neither makes it negotiable nor adds to the transferee's rights.

(6) The naming in a negotiable bill of a person to be notified of the arrival of the goods does not limit the negotiability of the bill nor constitute notice to a purchaser thereof of any interest of such person in the goods. *(Stats.1963, c. 819, § 7501.)*

California Code Comment

By John A. Bohn and Charles J. Williams

Prior California Law

1. Under prior California law, separate sections of the Civil Code regulated negotiation of documents of title by delivery and indorsement under the USA, UWRA and the UBLA.

Subdivision (1) of this section integrates and rephrases these former Civil Code sections without substantive change: former Civil Code §§ 1748 (negotiation of negotiable documents of title by delivery) and 1749 (negotiation of negotiable documents by delivery); former Civil Code § 1858b (classification and effect of warehouse receipts); former Civil Code § 1858.65 (negotiation of negotiable receipts by delivery); former Civil Code § 2129 (negotiation of negotiable bills by delivery), and § 2129a (negotiation of negotiable bills by delivery).

2. Subdivision (2)(a) integrates and restates provisions of former Civil Code §§ 1748 (USA) and 1858.65 (UWRA) both of which dealt with negotiation of a negotiable document by delivery. Former Civil Code § 2129 (UBLA) did not make provision for "bearer bills."

Subdivision (2)(b) is new statutory language. However, the rule of this paragraph is implicit in former Civil Code §§ 1748 and 1749 (USA), 1858.65 and 1858.66 (UWRA) and 2129 and 2129a (UBLA). See Official Comment 3.

The rule of subdivision (2)(b) complements the rule of Commercial Code § 3302(2) that a payee of a negotiable instrument may be a holder in due course.

3. Subdivision (3) integrates and restates without substantive change a provision of former Civil Code §§ 1749 (USA), 1858.66 (UWRA), and 2129a (UBLA).

4. Subdivision (4) integrates and restates the provisions of former Civil Code §§ 1752 and 1758 (USA), 1858.68 and 1858.75 (UWRA), and 2129c and 2130b (UBLA) all of which provided that negotiation of the negotiable document of title was valid if the person to whom the document was negotiated paid value in good faith without notice of breach of duty, or loss, theft, fraud, accident, mistake, duress or conversion. This subdivision is a variation from the 1962 Official Text and does not change prior California law because of the change in the California version of subdivision (4) eliminating the requirement that a due negotiation must be in the regular course of trade. See California Code Comment 1.

5. Subdivision (5) of this section integrates are restates the last sentence of former Civil Code §§ 1751 (USA), 1858.67 (UWRA), and 2129b (UBLA) all of which, in effect, stated: "a non-negotiable document [of title] cannot be negotiated, and the indorsement of such a document [of title] gives the transferee no additional right." See Ward-Lewis Lumber Co. v. Mahony, 70 Cal.App. 708, 234 Pac. 417 (1925).

6. Subdivision (6) restates the rule of former Civil Code § 2126h (UBLA) without substantive change.

Changes from U.C.C. (1962 Official Text)

7. The last clause of subdivision (4) of Section 7–501 of the 1962 Official Text is deleted from the California version of that section. That clause reads: "unless it is established that the negotiation is not in the regular course of business or financing or involves receiving the document in settlement or payment of a money obligation".

The effect is to eliminate the requirement that due negotiation be in the regular course of business.

This variation was discussed and approved by Professors Marsh and Warren in their Report:

"This subsection states the requirements for a person to be a holder in due course of a negotiable document of title. The requirement in the last clause underscored above is entirely new to the law. [Referring to the requirement that due negotiation be in the regular course of business or financing]

"The purpose . . ., as stated in the [Official] Comments, is to eliminate the possibility of anyone being a holder in due course of a document except in the 'great run of commercial transactions which are patently usual and normal.' Therefore, a person taking such a document for value must determine at his peril whether the transaction is 'patently usual and normal.' This seems to us to put an impossible burden upon institutions dealing with such documents.

"The Comments go on to say: 'In regard to documents of title the only holder whose possession appears, commercially, to be in order is almost invariably a person in the trade. No commercial purpose is served by allowing a tramp or a professor . . . to "duly negotiate" an order bill of lading for hides or cotton not his own, and since such a transfer is obviously not in the regular course of business, it is excluded from the scope of the protection of subsection (4).' Furthermore, 'the snapping up of goods for quick resale at a price suspiciously below the market deserves no protection as a matter of policy: it is also clearly outside the range of regular course.'

"The Comments go on to say that the transfer of a document of title as additional security for a debt usually is in the regular course of business or financing (the comments to the 1952 Text interpreted substantially the same language in exactly the opposite manner—an indication of how clear this language is: even its authors are undecided as to what it means). Nevertheless, 'the matter has moved out of the regular courses of financing if the debtor is thought to be insolvent, the credit previously extended is in effect canceled, and the creditor snatches a plank in the shipwreck under the guise of a demand for additional collateral.' So the court must decide whether there is a demand for additional collateral or only the 'guise' of a demand for additional collateral.

"All of this in our opinion would seriously impair the negotiability of documents of title and their value for use as collateral and in other aspects of trade and commerce. So far as we know, the proponents of the Code have offered no proof that this radical new concept is necessary to correct any particular evil which has arisen under the Uniform Acts. . . .

"Nor can we see any reason to deny the status of a holder in due course to a person who receives a document in 'settlement or payment' of an obligation, whereas a person who takes a document as *security* for an obligation, even a pre-existing obligation, is granted that status. Furthermore, under this provision, if a person holding documents as security and who was a holder in due course agreed to accept them in settlement of the same obligation, he would thereupon lose that status. This result is irrational. But that, of course, would be the most common case where a document would be received in settlement or payment of an obligation." Sixth Progress Report to the Legislature by Senate Fact Finding Committee on Judiciary (1959–1961), Part 1, The Uniform Commercial Code, pp. 525, 526.

8. The following comments were made by a committee of the California State Bar regarding subdivision (4) of Section 7–501:

"Section 17501 [7501] would govern the negotiability of documents of title. As at present [Footnote: Cal.Civ.Code, Secs. 1858.75, 2130b.] a good faith purchaser of a negotiable document without notice of a defense or adverse claim would take free of such defense or claim. However, the Official Text of section 17501 [7501] would deny the status of a good faith purchaser to one who acquires the document if 'the negotiation is not in the regular course of business or financing or involves receiving the document in settlement or payment of a money obligation.'

"The Comments justify this qualification on the ground that no one should be regarded as a good faith purchaser except in 'the great run of commercial transactions which are patently usual and normal.' Financing institutions would have to determine at their peril whether each transaction was 'patently usual and normal.' To the State Bar Committee this would be an unreasonable burden upon those dealing with such documents in bulk.

"Further, the State Bar Committee cannot see why one who takes such a document in payment of an obligation should not be a good faith purchaser when the same section grants that status to one who takes such a document as security for a debt, even a pre-existing debt. One who held such a document as security and was a good faith purchaser would lose that status by accepting the document in settlement.

"Accordingly, the Official Text qualification upon negotiability is not in S.B. 1249 [1961 Session 1958 Official Text as amended]." California State Bar Committee on The Commercial Code, A Special Report, The Uniform Commercial Code, 37 Calif.State Bar J. (March–April, 1962) p. 184.

Uniform Commercial Code Comment
Prior Uniform Statutory Provision:
Sections 28, 29, 31, 32 and 38, Uniform Sales Act; Sections 37, 38, 39, 40 and 47, Uniform Warehouse Receipts Act; Sections 9, 28, 29, 30, 31 and 38, Uniform Bills of Lading Act.

Changes: Consolidated and rewritten.

Purposes of Changes:

1. In general this section is intended to clarify the language of the old acts and to restate the effect of the better decisions thereunder. An important new concept is added, however, in the requirement of "regular course of business or financing" to effect the "due negotiation" which will transfer greater rights than those held by the person negotiating. The foundation of the mercantile doctrine of good faith purchase for value has always been, as shown by the case situations, the furtherance and protection of the regular course of trade. The reason for allowing a person, in bad faith or in error, to convey away rights which are not his own has from the beginning been to make possible the speedy handling of that great run of commercial transactions which are patently usual and normal.

There are two aspects to the usual and normal course of mercantile dealings, namely, the person making the transfer and the nature of the transaction itself. The first question which arises is: Is the transferor a person with whom it is reasonable to deal as having full powers? In regard to documents of title the only holder whose possession appears, commercially, to be in order is almost invariably a person in the trade. No commercial purpose is served by allowing a tramp or a professor to "duly negotiate" an order bill of lading for hides or cotton not his own, and since such a transfer is obviously not in the regular course of business, it is excluded from the scope of the protection of subsection (4) [Changes in California from U.C.C. (1962 Official Text), see California Code Comment, note 7].

The second question posed by the "regular course" qualification is: Is the transaction one which is normally proper to pass full rights without inquiry, even though the transferor himself may not have such rights to pass, and even though he may be acting in breach of duty? In raising this question the "regular course" criterion has the further advantage of limiting the effective wrongful disposition to transactions whose protection will really further trade. Obviously, the snapping up of goods for quick resale at a price suspiciously below the market deserves no protection as a matter of policy: it is also clearly outside the range of regular course.

Any notice from the face of the document sufficient to put a merchant on inquiry as to the "regular course" quality of the transaction will frustrate a "due negotiation". Thus irregularity of the document on its face or unexplained staleness of a bill of lading may appropriately be recognized as negating a negotiation in "regular" course.

A pre-existing claim constitutes value, and "due negotiation" does not require "new value." A usual and ordinary transaction in which documents are received as security for credit previously extended may be in "regular" course, even though there is a demand for additional collateral because the creditor "deems himself insecure." But the matter has moved out of the regular course of financing if the debtor is thought to be insolvent, the credit previously extended is in effect cancelled, and the creditor snatches a plank in the shipwreck under the guise of a demand for additional collateral. Where a money debt is "paid" in commodity paper, any question of "regular" course disappears, as the case is explicitly excepted from "due negotiation".

2. Negotiation under this section may be made by any holder no matter how he acquired possession of the document. The present section follows in this respect the Uniform Bills of Lading Act and amendments of the original Uniform Sales Act and Uniform Warehouse Receipts Act proposed by the Commissioners on Uniform State Laws in 1922.

3. Subsection (2)(b) makes explicit a matter upon which the intent of the old acts was clear but the language somewhat obscure: a negotiation results from a delivery to a banker or buyer to whose order the document has been taken by the person making the bailment. There is no presumption of irregularity in such a negotiation; it may very well be in "regular course".

4. This Article does not contain any provision creating a presumption of due negotiation to, and full rights in, a holder of a document of title akin to that created by Sections 16, 24 and 59 of the Negotiable Instruments Law. But the reason of the provisions of this Act (Section 1–202) on the prima facie authenticity and accuracy of third party documents, joins with the reason of the present section to work such a presumption in favor of any person who has power to make a due negotiation. It would not make sense for this Act to authorize a purchaser to indulge the presumption of regularity if the courts were not also called upon to do so.

Cross References:
Point 1: Sections 7–502 and 7–503.
Point 2: Section 7–502.

Definitional Cross References:
"Bearer". Section 1–201.
"Delivery". Section 1–201.
"Document". Section 7–102.
"Document of title". Section 1–201.
"Good faith". Section 1–201.
"Holder". Section 1–201.
"Notice". Section 1–201.

"Person". Section 1-201.
"Purchase". Section 1-201.
"Rights". Section 1-201.
"Term". Section 1-201.
"Value". Section 1-201.

Cross References

Buyer of fungible goods not deprived of title by due negotiation of document, see Commercial Code § 7205.
Disposition of property subject to lien, continuation of lien, and exceptions, see Code of Civil Procedure § 697.610.
Document of title,
Operation and effect, see Commercial Code § 7503.
Unlawful negotiation by depositor not having title to goods, see Penal Code § 560.3.
Unlawful negotiation in general, punishment, see Penal Code § 560.
Due negotiation, rights acquired, see Commercial Code § 7502.
Goods, wares or merchandise stored or deposited in warehouse, unlawful issuance or transfer of receipt, see Penal Code § 560.6.
Indorser not a guarantor for other parties, see Commercial Code § 7505.
Mode of transfer, see Civil Code § 1052 et seq.
Personal property not in custody of levying officer transferred or encumbered, exceptions, see Code of Civil Procedure § 697.740.
Right to compel indorsement, see Commercial Code § 7506.
Secured transactions, protection of purchasers of instruments and documents, see Commercial Code § 9309.
Warranties on negotiation or transfer of receipt or bill, see Commercial Code § 7507.

§ 7502. Rights Acquired by Due Negotiation

(1) Subject to the following section and to the provisions of Section 7205 on fungible goods, a holder to whom a negotiable document of title has been duly negotiated acquires thereby:

(a) Title to the document;

(b) Title to the goods;

(c) All rights accruing under the law of agency or estoppel, including rights to goods delivered to the bailee after the document was issued; and

(d) The direct obligation of the issuer to hold or deliver the goods according to the terms of the document free of any defense or claim by him except those arising under the terms of the document or under this division.

(2) Subject to the following section, title and rights so acquired are not defeated by any stoppage of the goods represented by the document or by surrender of such goods by the bailee, and are not impaired even though the negotiation or any prior negotiation constituted a breach of duty or even though any person has been deprived of possession of the document by misrepresentation, fraud, accident, mistake, duress, loss, theft or conversion, or even though a previous sale or other transfer of the goods or document has been made to a third person. *(Stats.1963, c. 819, § 7502.)*

California Code Comment

By John A. Bohn and Charles J. Williams

Prior California Law

1. Subdivision (1)(a) is new statutory law. It makes explicit that which was implicit in former Civil Code §§ 1753 (USA), 1858.69 (UWRA) and 2129d (UBLA) which enumerated the rights of a person to whom a document had been negotiated.

Subdivision (1)(b) integrates and restates the provisions of former Civil Code §§ 1753(a) (USA), 1858.69(a) (UWRA), and 2129d(a) (UBLA) all of which in effect stated that the person to whom a negotiable document had been negotiated acquired such title to the goods as the person negotiating the document to him had or had ability to convey and also such title to the goods as the person to whose order the goods were to be delivered had or had ability to convey.

Subdivision (1)(c) is new and has no counterpart in the prior uniform acts. See Official Comment 2.

Subdivision (1)(d) integrates and restates the provisions of former Civil Code §§ 1753(b) (USA), 1858.69(b) (UWRA), and 2129d(b) (UBLA) all of which stated in effect that the person to whom the document was negotiated acquired the direct obligation of the carrier to hold possession of the goods for him according to the terms of the document as fully as if the carrier had contracted directly with him.

2. Subdivision (2) in part adds new statutory language and also integrates the following sections of prior uniform acts: former Civil Code §§ 1740(4) (USA) and 2130d(d) (UBLA) dealing with the rights of a good faith purchaser for value to whom a negotiable bill of lading or bill of exchange is negotiated by a buyer who has refused payment of acceptance of a draft accompanying the bill; former Civil Code § 1745 (USA) dealing with the rights of a good faith purchaser for value of goods already sold but still in the possession of the seller; former Civil Code §§ 1758 (USA), 1858.75 (UWRA) and 2130b (UWRA) all of which stated that negotiation was not impaired by a breach of duty by the person negotiating the document or by the fact that the true owner of the document was wrongfully deprived of its possession so long as the person to whom the document was negotiated was a good faith purchaser for value; former Civil Code §§ 1858.76 (UWRA) and 2130c (UBLA) dealing with a negotiable bill or receipt covering goods already sold and the right of a good faith purchaser for value to whom the receipt or bill is subsequently negotiated; and former Civil Code §§ 1782 (USA), 1858.77 (UWRA), and 2130f (UBLA) dealing with the effect of negotiation of a document which covers goods subject to a seller's lien stoppage in transit.

The phrase "or by surrender of such goods by the bailee" has no counterpart in the prior uniform acts.

Changes from U.C.C. (1962 Official Text)

3. The last sentence of subdivision (1)(d) in section 7-502 of The 1962 Official Text is omitted in California. It provides:

"In the case of a delivery order the bailee's obligation accrues only upon acceptance and the obligation acquired by the holder is that the issuer and any indorser will procure the acceptance of the bailee."

This reference to delivery order was deleted because of the elimination of the concept from the California version of the Commercial Code. See California Code Comment 8 to Commercial Code § 7102.

Professor Braucher describes the operation of the provision which was deleted in the California version:

"As to negotiable delivery orders, the bailee's position is somewhat similar to that of a bank on which a check is drawn: such a bank is, of course, not liable on the check until it accepts or certifies. The application of a similar rule to negotiable delivery orders frees the bailee of any obligation to cancel such documents outstanding at the time it delivers the goods. On the other hand, a delivery order issued by the holder of a negotiable document could not safely be honored without surrender of, or conspicuous notation of partial deliveries on, the negotiable document. The limitation in Section 7–502(1)(d), however, may not protect the bailee in ignoring a delivery order entirely; a cautious bailee may well be concerned as to the scope of his obligation of good faith in cases of doubt.

"Title to goods based on a negotiable delivery order is not limited by Section 7-502, but that Section is expressly made subject to Section 7-503. If O, the owner of goods subject to a non-negotiable warehouse receipt, transfers the document to X, X becomes the owner. If O then issues and duly negotiates a delivery order to Y covering the same goods, Section 7-503(1) denies effect to the delivery order unless X 'delivered or entrusted' to O or to Y with the authority or power described in that Section or 'acquiesced' in the procurement of a document by O or by Y. Until the bailee receives notification of the transfer to X, he is protected in good faith dealings with O, and O has power of disposition to a buyer in ordinary course. Under Section 7-503(2), Y's rights as the holder of an unaccepted delivery order can be defeated to the same extent as the rights of X. The result seems to be that priority of notification to the bailee will ordinarily determine the rights between X and Y.

"If a similar fraud were accomplished by the issue of two delivery orders for the same goods, the same reasoning might apply. In such a case, Section 7–402 on 'overissue' would also be applicable, providing that the second document of the same issuer confers no right in the goods. Even so, however, the holder of the invalid second document might be a buyer in ordinary course and might be protected if the bailee received notification of his rights first. Section 7–207(2) on fungible goods does not apply unless the overissue is that of a warehouseman.

"Section 2–503(2) also provides that title based on an unaccepted delivery order may be defeated by due negotiation of a negotiable warehouse receipt or bill of lading covering the same goods. If the delivery order is negotiable, this rule is a corollary of the rule that the bailee is not obligated before acceptance. Its reason is also clear as applied to a delivery order issued by the holder of a negotiable document. After acceptance of the delivery order, the rule does not apply; an accepted delivery order 'is for practical purposes indistinguishable from a warehouse receipt' and the accepting bailee seems to fall within the definition of issuer.

"But there may be difficulty in one situation. Suppose that O, the owner of goods under a non-negotiable warehouse receipt, issues a non-negotiable delivery order to X, and that X promptly notifies the warehouseman. If O then procured a negotiable document in substitution for his non-negotiable document, and negotiates the new document to Y, Section 7–503(2) can be read as subjecting X's rights to those of Y. It would be more consistent with the other provisions on delivery orders, however, to hold that notification to the bailee fixed X's rights, and that the subsequent issue of a negotiable document for the same goods was a void 'overissue' under Section 7–402." Braucher, Documents of Title, 68–70. "Copyright (ALI 1958). Reprinted with the permission of the American Law Institute."

A committee of the California State Bar made the following comments regarding Section 7–502(1)(d):

"The Official Text of sections 11201(15) [1201(15)], 17102 [7102], 17502 [7502] and 17503 [7503] would make a 'delivery order' issued by a holder of an outstanding document of title itself a document of title representing the same goods as the bill of lading or warehouse receipt. If B held a negotiable warehouse receipt covering certain goods, he could execute an order directing them to be delivered 'to the order of C' and deliver this document to C, retaining the negotiable warehouse receipt himself. The delivery order in C's hands would become another negotiable document of title representing the same goods as the negotiable warehouse receipt still in B's hands. B could then negotiate the warehouse receipt to X, and C could negotiate the delivery order to Y. The Official Text would try to define the rights of X and Y to the goods as between them.

"The Official Text thus contemplates two documents outstanding at the same time, covering the same goods and being transferred in different chains of title. The Official Text then attempts to unravel the confusion it has created. [Footnote: See Braucher, Documents of Title, 68–70 (A.L.I.1958).]

"The Comments suggest that a 'delivery order' is like a check drawn on a bank account: it should therefore be recognized as a document of title in the same way that a check is recognized as a negotiable instrument. The analogy is not apt since a check is not an assignment of any particular funds in the bank's hands. A closer analogy would be to allow the holder of a cashier's check to write a check against the outstanding cashier's check, which could then be transferred independently of the cashier's check.

"The State Bar Committee concluded that these delivery order provisions are undesirable, and no documents now used in the warehouse and carrier industries in California suggest the need for them. They are therefore not in S.B. 1249 [1961 Session, 1958 Official Text as amended] except as to a delivery order 'accepted' by the bailee, which the Official Text recognizes as indistinguishable, for practical purposes, from a warehouse receipt or bill of lading. Since no such documents are now used in California the State Bar Committee also recommends the elimination from S.B. 1249 [1961 Session, 1958 Official Text as amended] of the provisions for the negotiability of an 'accepted delivery order.' If goods under a non-negotiable warehouse receipt have been ordered delivered to one who wants to leave them with the warehouseman under a document of title, the warehouseman could issue a new warehouse receipt as easily as he could 'accept' the delivery order." California State Bar Committee on The Commercial Code, A Special Report, the Uniform Commercial Code, 37 Calif.State Bar J. (March–April, 1962) pp. 180, 181.

Uniform Commercial Code Comment

Prior Uniform Statutory Provision:
Sections 20(4), 25, 33, 38 and 62, Uniform Sales Act; Sections 41, 47, 48 and 49, Uniform Warehouse Receipts Act; Sections 32, 38, 39, 40 and 42, Uniform Bills of Lading Act.

Changes: Rewritten.

Purposes of Changes:

1. The several necessary qualifications of the broad principle that the holder of a document acquired in a due negotiation is the owner of the document and the goods have been brought together in the next section.

2. Subsection (1)(c) covers the case of "feeding" of a duly negotiated document by subsequent delivery to the bailee of such goods as the document falsely purported to cover; the bailee in such case is estopped as against the holder of the document.

3. The explicit statement in subsection (1)(d) of the bailee's direct obligation to the holder precludes the defense, sometimes successfully asserted under the old acts, that the document in question was "spent" after the carrier had delivered the goods to a previous holder. But the holder is subject to such defenses as non-negligent destruction even though not apparent on the face of the document, and the bailee's obligation is of course subject to lawful provisions in filed classifications and tariffs. See Sections 7–103, 7–403. The sentence on delivery orders [Omitted in California] applies only to delivery orders in negotiable form which have been duly negotiated. On delivery orders, see also Section 7–503(2) and Comment.

4. Subsection (2) condenses and continues the law of a number of sections of the prior acts which gave full effect to the issuance or due negotiation of a negotiable document. The subsection adds nothing to the effect of the rules stated in subsection (1), but it has been included since such explicit references were relied upon under the prior acts to preserve the rights of a purchaser by due negotiation unimpaired. The listing is not exhaustive. Only those matters have been repeated in this subsection which were explicitly reserved in the prior acts except in the case of stoppage in transit. Here, the language has been broadened to include "any stoppage" lest an inference be drawn that a stoppage of the goods before or after transit might cut off or otherwise impair the purchaser's rights.

Cross References:
Sections 7–103, 7–205, 7–403 and 7–503.

Definitional Cross References:
"Bailee". Section 7–102.
"Delivery". Section 1–201.
"Delivery order". Section 7–102.
"Document". Section 7–102.
"Document of title". Section 1–201.
"Duly negotiate". Section 7–501.
"Fungible". Section 1–201.
"Goods". Section 7–102.
"Holder". Section 1–201.
"Issuer". Section 7–102.
"Person". Section 1–201.
"Rights". Section 1–201.
"Term". Section 1–201.
"Warehouse receipt". Section 1–201.

Cross References

Agency, see Civil Code § 2295 et seq.
Document of title to goods, operation and effect, see Commercial Code § 7503.
Financing agency, right to stop delivery of goods, see Commercial Code § 2506.
Letters of credit, issuer's duty to honor a draft or demand for payment, see Commercial Code § 5114.
Lost and missing documents, order of delivery by court, see Commercial Code § 7601.
Obligation to deliver goods, excuse, see Commercial Code § 7403.
Purchases in ordinary course of business, effect, see Commercial Code § 7205.

Sale of undivided share in identified bulk of fungible goods, see Commercial Code § 2105.

Stoppage of delivery in transit by seller, see Commercial Code § 2705.

Title acquired by purchaser of goods, see Commercial Code § 2403.

Treaty, statute, etc., effect, see Commercial Code § 7103.

§ 7503. Document of Title to Goods Defeated in Certain Cases

(1) A document of title confers no right in goods against a person who before issuance of the document had a legal interest or a perfected security interest in them and who neither

(a) Delivered nor entrusted them nor any document of title covering them to the bailor or his nominee with actual or apparent authority to ship, store or sell or with power to obtain delivery under this division (Section 7403) or with power of disposition under this Code (Sections 2403 and 9307) or other statute or rule of law * * *, nor

(b) Acquiesced in the procurement by the bailor or his nominee of any document of title.

* * * (2) Title to goods based upon a bill of lading issued to a freight forwarder is subject to the rights of anyone to whom a bill issued by the freight forwarder is duly negotiated; but delivery by the carrier in accordance with Chapter 4 of this division pursuant to its own bill of lading discharges the carrier's obligation to deliver. *(Stats.1963, c. 819, § 7503. Amended by Stats. 1967, c. 799, p. 2211, § 12.)*

California Code Comment

By John A. Bohn and Charles J. Williams

Prior California Law

1. Subdivision (1) modifies the prior California rules for determining when a document holder's title may be defeated.

Under former Civil Code §§ 1753 (USA), 1858.69 (UWRA) and 2129d (UBLA) the good faith purchaser for value acquired such title as the person negotiating the document or the depositor or person to whose order the goods were to be delivered "had or had ability to convey." One "had ability to convey" if (i) he had voidable title to the goods or (ii) if the facts surrounding the transaction were such that the owner was "estopped to deny either that the party in possession [was] the owner, or that the party in possession [had] authority to dispose of the goods", or (iii) where the party in possession of the goods was "a former owner and . . . remained in possession after the first sale and resold to a second purchaser who obtained possession." William E. Britton, *Negotiable Documents of Title*, 5 Hastings L.J. 103, 113–115 (1954).

Under subdivision (1) the good faith purchaser for value acquires only such title as the true owner, by *entrusting* the goods or the document of title covering the goods, has actually or apparently given the transferor authority, power or disposition to convey. Official Comment 1, 2.

2. Subdivision (3) is new. See Official Comment 3.

Changes from U.C.C. (1962 Official Text)

3. Subdivision (1)(b) of section 7–503 the 1962 Official Text is omitted in California. It reads:

"(b) acquiesced in the procurement by the bailor or his nominee of any document of title".

The objection to subdivision (1)(b) is explained in the Marsh and Warren Report:

"The Official Comments to this Section state that 'acquiescence' under clause (b) does not require 'active consent', but that 'knowledge of the likelihood of storage or shipment with no objection or effort to control it is sufficient to defeat [the owner's] rights as against one who takes by "due" negotiation of a negotiable document.' This provision is clearly intended to make a change in existing law. See Braucher (Documents of Title under the Uniform Commercial Code (ALI 1958) 64–65; 3 N.Y.Law Rev.Comm., Study of the Uniform Commercial Code (1955) 1847; Ruud, Analyses of Article 7 of the Uniform Commercial Code (Tex.Legis.Council 1952) 108–115.

"Williston states the existing law as follows: 'As a general proposition it needs no argument to show that a bailor having no title to goods cannot, by depositing them with a warehouseman, or carrier, and receiving a document of title in return, whatever its form, give a good title to them to a purchaser of the document, however innocent he may be. The only qualification to this principle is that if the depositor of the goods, though he had no title, had ability or capacity to transfer a title to a purchaser for value, either by virtue of actual authority or because the owner had allowed a situation to arise which would estop him from asserting his title to the goods, the same reason should protect a purchaser of the document of title that would protect a purchaser of the goods.' 2 Williston, Sales (Rev.Ed.1948) § 421. See, also, Britton, *Negotiable Documents of Title*, 5 Hastings L.J. 103, 113–115 (1954). This exception stated by Williston, where the person in possession has power to pass title *to the goods*, and therefore can pass title to a negotiable document substituted for the goods, is covered by clause (a) of this subsection (enlarged somewhat by other provisions of the Code.) It would seem that there is another exception, even if the possessor had no power to pass title to the goods, in a case where the owner *authorized* him to 'ship or warehouse goods and to take documents therefor.' 3 N.Y.Law Rev.Comm., Study of the Uniform Commercial Code (1955) 1847, citing Dows v. Kidder, 84 N.Y. 121 (1881); Pollard v. Reardon, 65 F. 848 (1st Cir. 1895). This exception is also covered by clause (a) in its reference to 'actual or apparent authority to ship [or] store.'

"Clause (b) of this subsection enlarges this second exception, however, to include any case where the owner parted with possession of goods with a 'knowledge of the likelihood of storage or shipment', if the courts accept the comments as an authoritative gloss on the text. In the ordinary meaning of the word, of course, this goes far beyond 'acquiescence.' One does not 'acquiesce' in everything of which he has a 'knowledge of the likelihood.'

"It seems to us that if an owner has actually consented to the procurement of a document of title to his goods by another or if he has permitted such procurement under circumstances showing that he was negligent in so doing, his equities are certainly less than those of a bona fide purchaser of a negotiable document of title so procured. These situations, we think are sufficiently covered by the language of clause (a). However, the rule stated in clause (b) of this Section as interpreted by the comments seems to us to go far beyond anything that is necessary to protect the negotiability of documents of title, and would subject an owner of goods to a risk of their loss any time he entrusted their possession to another. Furthermore, what is the meaning of 'likelihood?' A 20 percent chance? A 95 percent chance? We believe that clause (b) would be uncertain and unjust in operation, and therefore recommend its deletion." Sixth Progress Report to the Legislature by Senate Fact Finding Committee on Judiciary (1959–1961), Part 1, The Uniform Commercial Code, pp. 529, 530.

4. Subdivision (2) section 7–503 of the 1962 Official Text is omitted in California. The deletion in the California version is based upon the elimination of the concept of "delivery orders" from the California Commercial Code. See California Code Comment 9 to section 7102.

Subdivision (2) of section 7503 of the 1962 Official Text provides:

"(2) Title to goods based upon an unaccepted delivery order is subject to the rights of anyone to whom a negotiable warehouse receipt or bill of lading covering the goods has been duly negotiated. Such a title may be defeated under the next section to the same extent as the rights of the issuer or a transferee from the issuer."

California Code Comment—1967 Amendment

By Charles J. Williams

1. The 1967 amendment adds subparagraph (b) to subdivision (1) and brings subdivision (1) into conformity with the Official Text. For discussion of the reason for this variation from the Official Text, see California Code Comment 3, ante.

2. In recommending that the Official Text be followed, the Advisory Committee states that:

"Subsection (b) of the official text of this section was deleted in California in adopting the Code primarily because of a comment which seemed to indicate that any "knowledge of the likelihood" of shipment or storage of the goods on the part of the true owner would result in the title of the true owner being cut off by negotiation of the document. In its Report No. 2 the permanent Editorial Board has stated "an expansive reading of that comment would seem to be precluded by the statutory text." The Advisory Committee is relying upon that statement of the Permanent Editorial Board limiting the effect of the official comment to this section in recommending that subsection (b) of the official text of this section be adopted so as to make the law of California uniform with that of the other jurisdictions adopting the Code." (Report of the Advisory Committee, Senate Journal, April 20, 1967, 1967 Regular Session, p. 1238.)

3. The amendment also renumbers as subdivision (2) what is designated in the Official Text as subdivision (3). The Official Text still contains a suggested subdivision (2) relating to delivery orders. All references to delivery orders have been deleted from the California version. (California Code Comment 4, ante.)

Uniform Commercial Code Comment
Prior Uniform Statutory Provision:
Section 33, Uniform Sales Act; Section 41, Uniform Warehouse Receipts Act; Section 32, Uniform Bills of Lading Act.
Changes: Subsection (1) narrows, as compared to the cited sections, the occasions for defeating the document holder's title.
Purposes of Changes:

1. In general it may be said that the title of a purchaser by due negotiation prevails over almost any interest in the goods which existed prior to the procurement of the document of title if the possession of the goods by the person obtaining the document derived from any action by the prior claimant which introduced the goods into the stream of commerce or carried them along that stream. A thief of the goods cannot indeed by shipping or storing them to his own order acquire power to transfer them to a good faith purchaser. Nor can a tenant or mortgagor defeat any rights of a landlord or mortgagee which have been perfected under the local law merely by wrongfully shipping or storing a portion of the crop or other goods. However, "acquiescence" by the landlord or tenant does not require active consent under subsection (1)(b) [Changes in California from U.C.C. (1962 Official Text), see California Code Comment, note 3] and knowledge of the likelihood of storage or shipment with no objection or effort to control it is sufficient to defeat his rights as against one who takes by "due" negotiation of a negotiable document.

On the other hand, where goods are delivered to a factor for sale, even though the factor has made no advances and is limited in his duty to sell for cash, the goods are "entrusted" to him "with actual . . . authority . . . to sell" under subsection (1)(a), and if he procures a negotiable document of title he can transfer the owner's interest to a purchaser by due negotiation. Further, where the factor is in the business of selling, goods entrusted to him simply for safekeeping or storage may be entrusted under circumstances which give him "apparent authority to ship, store or sell" under subsection (1)(a), or power of disposition under 2–403, 7–205 or 9–307, or under a statute such as the earlier Factors Acts, or under a rule of law giving effect to apparent ownership. See Section 1–103.

Persons having an interest in goods also frequently deliver or entrust them to agents or servants other than factors for the purpose of shipping or warehousing or under circumstances reasonably contemplating such action. Rounding out the case law development under the prior Acts, this Act is clear that such persons assume full risk that the agent to whom the goods are so delivered may ship or store in breach of duty, take a document to his own order and then proceed to misappropriate it. This Act makes no distinction between possession or mere custody in such situations and finds no exception in the case of larceny by a bailee or the like. The safeguard in such situations lies in the requirement that a due negotiation can occur only "in the regular course of business or financing" and that the purchase be in good faith and without notice. See Section 7–501. Documents of title have no market among the commercially inexperienced and the commercially experienced do not take them without inquiry from persons known to be truck drivers or petty clerks even though such persons purport to be operating in their own names.

Again, where the seller allows a buyer to receive goods under a contract for sale, though as a "conditional delivery" or under "cash sale" terms and on explicit agreement for immediate payment, the buyer thereby acquires power to defeat the seller's interest by transfer of the goods to certain good faith purchasers. See Section 2–403. Both in policy and under the language of subsection (1)(a) that same power must be extended to accomplish the same result if the buyer procures a negotiable document of title to the goods and duly negotiates it.

2. Under subsection (1) a delivery order issued by a person having no right in or power over the goods is ineffective unless the owner acts as provided in subsection (1)(a) or (b). Thus the rights of a transferee of a non-negotiable warehouse receipt can be defeated by a delivery order subsequently issued by the transferor only if the transferee "delivers or entrusts" to the "person procuring" the delivery order or "acquiesces" in his procurement. Similarly, a second delivery order issued by the same issuer for the same goods will ordinarily be subject to the first, both under this section and under Section 7–402. After a delivery order is validly issued but before it is accepted, it may nevertheless be defeated under subsection (2) [Changes in California from U.C.C. (1962 Official Text), see California Code Comment, note 4] in much the same way that the rights of a transferee may be defeated under Section 7–504. For example, a buyer in ordinary course from the issuer may defeat the rights of the holder of a prior delivery order if the bailee receives notification of the buyer's rights before notification of the holder's rights. Section 7–504(2)(b). But an accepted delivery order has the same effect as a document issued by the bailee.

3. Under subsection (3) a bill of lading issued to a freight forwarder is subordinated to the freight forwarder's certificate, since the bill on its face gives notice of the fact that a freight forwarder is in the picture and has in all probability issued a certificate. But the carrier is protected in following the terms of its own bill of lading.

Cross References:
Point 1: Sections 2–403, 7–205, 7–501, 9–307, and 9–309.
Point 2: Sections 7–402 and 7–504.
Point 3: Sections 7–402, 7–403 and 7–404.
Definitional Cross References:
"Bill of lading". Section 1–201.
"Contract for sale". Section 2–106.
"Delivery". Section 1–201.
"Delivery order". Section 7–102.
"Document". Section 7–102.
"Document of title". Section 1–201.
"Duly negotiate". Section 7–501.
"Goods". Section 7–102.
"Person". Section 1–201.
"Right". Section 1–201.
"Warehouse receipt". Section 1–201.

Cross References
Actual agency, defined, see Civil Code § 2299.
Attachment of goods covered by a negotiable document, see Commercial Code § 7602.
Buyer in ordinary course of business, see Commercial Code §§ 7205, 7504, 9307.
Conflicting claims, see Commercial Code § 7603.
Due negotiation, requisites, see Commercial Code § 7501.
Duly negotiated documents of title, rights of holders, see Commercial Code § 9309.
Duplicate receipt or bill, operation, see Commercial Code § 7402.
Good faith delivery, effect, see Commercial Code § 7404.
Obligation to deliver goods, see Commercial Code § 7403.
Ostensible authority of agent, see Civil Code §§ 2300, 2317, 2334.
Protection of buyers of goods, see Commercial Code § 9307.
Purchaser, power to transfer, see Commercial Code § 2403.

§ 7504. Rights Acquired in the Absence of Due Negotiation; Effect of Diversion; Seller's Stoppage of Delivery

(1) A transferee of a document, whether negotiable or nonnegotiable, to whom the document has been delivered but not duly negotiated, acquires the title and rights which his transferor had or had actual authority to convey.

(2) In the case of a nonnegotiable document, until but not after the bailee receives notification of the transfer, the rights of the transferee may be defeated

(a) By those creditors of the transferor who could treat the sale as void under Section 2402; or

(b) By a buyer from the transferor in ordinary course of business if the bailee has delivered the goods to the buyer or received notification of his rights; or

(c) As against the bailee by good faith dealings of the bailee with the transferor.

(3) A diversion or other change of shipping instructions by the consignor in a nonnegotiable bill of lading which causes the bailee not to deliver to the consignee defeats the consignee's title to the goods if they have been delivered to a buyer in ordinary course of business and in any event defeats the consignee's rights against the bailee.

(4) Delivery pursuant to a nonnegotiable document may be stopped by a seller under Section 2705, and subject to the requirement of due notification there provided. A bailee honoring the seller's instructions is entitled to be indemnified by the seller against any resulting loss or expense. *(Stats.1963, c. 819, § 7504.)*

California Code Comment

By John A. Bohn and Charles J. Williams

Prior California Law

1. Subdivision (1) has its counterpart in the first sentence of former Civil Code §§ 1754 (USA), 1858.70 (UWRA) and 2129e (UBLA) all of which provided that where a document had been transferred but not negotiated the transferee, as against the transferor, received title to the goods. Subdivision (1) of this section states that the transferee "acquires the title and rights which his transferor had or had actual authority to convey." Prior California law is therefore modified to the extent that the transferee no longer gets title automatically as against the transferor. See Official Comment 2.

2. Subdivision (2) continues the rule of the last paragraph of former Civil Code §§ 1754 (USA), 1858.70 (UWRA), and the second paragraph of former Civil Code § 2129e (UBLA) all of which enumerated certain classes of person or events that could defeat the rights of a transferee of a non-negotiable document.

Subdivision (2)(a) by incorporating Commercial Code § 2402 continues the basic rule under former Civil Code §§ 1754, 1858.70 and 2129e that a creditor of the transferor could defeat the rights of the transferee if the garnishment or attachment was initiated before notification of the bailee.

Subdivision (2)(b) continues the rule under former Civil Code §§ 1754, 1858.70 and 2129e without substantive change.

Subdivision (2)(c) is new but its rule is implicitly stated in former Civil Code §§ 1754 (USA), 1858.70 (UWRA), and 2129e (UBLA).

3. Subdivision (3) is new. See Official Comment 3.

In the California annotations to the proposed Uniform Commercial Code, the Legislative Counsel states that subdivision (3) changes California law:

"subdivision (3) would change the present law which now recognizes a transfer of title to the consignee when there has been delivery to the carrier under subdivision (3). This title could be defeated by diversion of the shipment made under a non-negotiable bill at the order of consignor and a sale to a 'buyer in the ordinary course of business.'" Sixth Progress Report to the Legislature by Senate Fact Finding Committee on Judiciary (1959–1961) Part 1, The Uniform Commercial Code, p. 110.

Former Civil Code § 1858d provided that when a non-negotiable warehouse receipt was issued, neither the issuer or the bailee could deliver the property except upon the order of the person to whom the receipt was issued.

The Official Comment 3 states that subdivision (3) is in accordance with common commercial practice.

Subdivision (3) deals with the carrier's immunity if it honors the consignor's instructions to divert and also protects the title of the new consignee. However the diversion or change of instructions by the consignor in violation of his agreement with the consignee may be a conversion of the consignee's property. Braucher, Documents of Title, 77 (A.L.I.1958).

Changes from U.C.C. (1962 Official Text)

4. This is section 7–504 of the Official Text without change.

Uniform Commercial Code Comment

Prior Uniform Statutory Provision:

Section 34, Uniform Sales Act; Sections 41(b) and 42, Uniform Warehouse Receipts Act; Sections 32(b) and 33, Uniform Bills of Lading Act.

Changes: Generally rewritten; Subsection (3) is new.

Purposes of Changes and New Matter:

1. Under the general principles controlling negotiable documents, it is clear that in the absence of due negotiation a transferor cannot convey greater rights than he himself has, even when the negotiation is formally perfect. This section recognizes the transferor's power to transfer rights which he himself has or has "actual authority to convey." Thus, where a negotiable document of title is being transferred the operation of the principle of estoppel is not recognized, as contrasted with situations involving the transfer of the goods themselves. (Compare Section 2–403 on good faith purchase of goods.)

A necessary part of the price for the protection of regular dealings with negotiable documents of title is an insistence that no dealing which is in any way irregular shall be recognized as a good faith purchase of the document or of any rights pertaining to it. So, where the transfer of a negotiable document fails as a negotiation because a requisite indorsement is forged or otherwise missing, the purchaser in good faith and for value may be in the anomalous position of having less rights, in part, than if he had purchased the goods themselves. True, his rights are not subject to defeat by attachment of the goods or surrender of them to his transferor [Contrast subsection (2)]; but on the other hand, he cannot acquire enforceable rights to control or receive the goods over the bailee's objection merely by giving notice to the bailee. Similarly, a consignee who makes payment to his consignor against a straight bill of lading can thereby acquire the position of a good faith purchaser of goods under provisions of the Article of this Act on Sales (Section 2–403), whereas the same payment made in good faith against an unindorsed order bill would not have such effect. The appropriate remedy of a purchaser in such a situation is to regularize his status by compelling indorsement of the document (see Section 7–506).

2. As in the case of transfer—as opposed to "due negotiation"—of negotiable documents, subsection (1) empowers the transferor of a nonnegotiable document to transfer only such rights as he himself has or has "actual authority" to convey. In contrast to situations involving the goods themselves the operation of estoppel or agency principles is not here recognized to enable the transferor to convey greater rights than he actually has. Subsection (2) makes it clear, however, that the transferee of a nonnegotiable document may acquire rights greater in some respects than those of his transferor by giving notice of the transfer to the bailee.

3. Subsection (3) is in part a reiteration of the carrier's immunity from liability if it honors instructions of the consignor to divert, but there is added a provision protecting the title of the substituted consignee if the latter is a buyer in ordinary course of business. A typical situation would be where a manufacturer, having shipped a lot of standardized goods to A on nonnegotiable bill of lading, diverts the goods to customer B who pays for them. Under orthodox passage-of-title-by-appropriation doctrine A might reclaim the goods from B. However, no consideration of commercial policy supports this involvement of an innocent third party in the default of the manufacturer on his contract to A; and the common commercial practice of diverting goods in transit suggests a trade understanding in accordance with this subsection.

4. Subsection (4) gives the carrier an express right to indemnity where he honors a seller's request to stop delivery.

5. Section 1–201(27) gives the bailee protection, if due diligence is exercised, similar to that found in the third paragraph of Section 33, Uniform Bills of Lading Act, where the bailee's organization has not had time to act on a notification.

Cross References:
Point 1: Sections 2–403 and 7–506.
Point 2: Section 2–403.
Point 3: Sections 7–303 and 7–403(1)(e).
Point 4: Sections 2–705 and 7–403(1)(d).

Definitional Cross References:
"Bailee". Section 7–102.
"Bill of lading". Section 1–201.
"Buyer in ordinary course of business". Section 1–201.
"Consignee". Section 7–102.
"Consignor". Section 7–102.
"Creditor". Section 1–201.
"Delivery". Section 1–201.
"Document". Section 7–102.
"Duly negotiate". Section 7–501.
"Good faith". Section 1–201.
"Goods". Section 7–102.
"Honor". Section 1–201.
"Notification". Section 1–201.
"Purchaser". Section 1–201.
"Rights". Section 1–201.

Cross References

Authority of agents, see Civil Code § 2304 et seq.
Diversion of goods upon change of instructions, see Commercial Code § 7303.
Good faith purchase of goods, see Commercial Code § 2403.
Obligation to deliver, excuse, see Commercial Code § 7403.
Seller's stoppage of delivery, see Commercial Code § 2705.
Transferee of negotiable document of title, compelling indorsement, see Commercial Code § 7506.

§ 7505. Indorser Not a Guarantor for Other Parties

The indorsement of a document of title issued by a bailee does not make the indorser liable for any default by the bailee or by previous indorsers. *(Stats.1963, c. 819, § 7505.)*

California Code Comment

By John A. Bohn and Charles J. Williams

Prior California Law

1. Section 7505 consolidates and restates without substantive change former Civil Code §§ 1757 (USA), 1858.73 (UWRA) and 2130 (UBLA). See Official Comment.

Changes from U.C.C. (1962 Official Text)

2. This is section 7–505 of the Official Text without change.

Uniform Commercial Code Comment

Prior Uniform Statutory Provision:
Section 37, Uniform Sales Act; Section 45, Uniform Warehouse Receipts Act; Section 36, Uniform Bills of Lading Act.

Changes: No substantial change.

Purposes of Changes:
The indorsement of a document of title is generally understood to be directed towards perfecting the transferee's rights rather than towards assuming additional obligations. The language of the present section, however, does not preclude the one case in which an indorsement given for value guarantees future action, namely, that in which the bailee has not yet become liable upon the document at the time of the indorsement. Under such circumstances the indorser, of course, engages that appropriate honor of the document by the bailee will occur. See Section 7–502(1)(d) as to negotiable delivery orders. However, even in such a case, once the bailee attorns to the transferee, the indorser's obligation has been fulfilled and the policy of this section excludes any continuing obligation on the part of the indorser for the bailee's ultimate actual performance.

Cross Reference:
Section 7–502.

Definitional Cross References:
"Bailee". Section 7–102.
"Document of title". Section 1–201.
"Party". Section 1–201.

Cross References

Due negotiation, rights acquired, see Commercial Code § 7502.

§ 7506. Delivery Without Indorsement; Right to Compel Indorsement

The transferee of a negotiable document of title has a specifically enforceable right to have his transferor supply any necessary indorsement but the transfer becomes a negotiation only as of the time the indorsement is supplied. *(Stats.1963, c. 819, § 7506.)*

California Code Comment

By John A. Bohn and Charles J. Williams

Prior California Law

1. This section consolidates and restates the rule of former Civil Code §§ 1755 (USA) 1858.71 (UWRA) and 2129f (UBLA). However, Commercial Code § 7506 modifies these prior uniform provisions by eliminating the requirement that the transfer be for value.

Changes from U.C.C. (1962 Official Text)

2. This is section 7–506 of the Official Text without change.

Uniform Commercial Code Comment

Prior Uniform Statutory Provision:
Section 35, Uniform Sales Act; Section 43, Uniform Warehouse Receipts Act; Section 34, Uniform Bills of Lading Act.

Changes: Consolidated and rewritten; former requirement that transfer be "for value" eliminated.

Purposes of Changes:

1. From a commercial point of view the intention to transfer a negotiable document of title which requires an indorsement for its transfer, is incompatible with an intention to withhold such indorsement and so defeat the effective use of the document. This position is sustained by the absence of any reported case applying the prior provisions in almost forty years of decisions. Further, the preceding section and the Comment thereto make it clear that an indorsement generally imposes no responsibility on the indorser.

2. Although this section provides that delivery of a document of title without the necessary indorsement is effective as a transfer, the transferee, of course, has not regularized his position until such indorsement is supplied. Until this is done he cannot claim rights under due negotiation within the requirements of this Article (subsection (4) of Section 7–501) on "due negotiation." Similarly, despite the transfer to him of his transferor's title, he cannot demand the goods from the bailee until the negotiation has been completed and the document is in proper form for surrender. See Section 7–403(3).

Cross References:
Point 1: Section 7–505.
Point 2: Sections 7–501(4) and 7–403(2).

Definitional Cross References:
"Document of title". Section 1–201.
"Rights". Section 1–201.

Cross References

Indorser, liability for other parties, see Commercial Code § 7505.
Obligation to deliver goods, see Commercial Code § 7403.

§ 7506

Requisites of due negotiation, see Commercial Code § 7501.

§ 7507. Warranties on Negotiation or Transfer of Receipt or Bill

Where a person negotiates or transfers a document of title for value otherwise than as a mere intermediary * * * under the next following section, then unless otherwise agreed he warrants to his immediate purchaser only in addition to any warranty made in selling the goods

(a) That the document is genuine; and

(b) That he has no knowledge of any fact which would impair its validity or worth; and

(c) That his negotiation or transfer is rightful and fully effective with respect to the title to the document and the goods it represents. *(Stats.1963, c. 819, § 7507. Amended by Stats.1967, c. 799, p. 2211, § 13.)*

California Code Comment

By John A. Bohn and Charles J. Williams

Prior California Law

1. This section consolidates and restates former Civil Code §§ 1756 (USA), 1758.72 (UWRA), and 2129g (UWRA) without substantive change. Each of these uniform sections specifically referred to warranty of title, merchantability and warranty for particular purpose. This is omitted as unnecessary and incomplete. Official Comment 1.

2. Paragraph (a) restates the rule of former Civil Code §§ 1757(a) (USA), 1858.72(a) (UWRA) and 2129g(a) (UBLA) without substantive change.

3. Paragraph (b) restates former Civil Code §§ 1756(c) (USA), 1858.72(c) (UWRA) and 2129g(c) (UBLA) without substantive change.

4. Paragraph (c) restates former Civil Code §§ 1756(b) (USA), 1858.72(b) (UWRA), and 2129g(b) (UBLA) without substantive change.

Changes from U.C.C. (1962 Official Text)

5. In the preamble of the California version the phrase "or secured party" was added after the words "as a mere intermediary". This was included in order to conform this section to the amendment in Commercial Code § 7508. See Comment 3 of the California Code Comment to Commercial Code § 7508.

California Code Comment—1967 Amendment

By Charles J. Williams

Prior California Law

1. The 1967 amendment simply eliminates the words "or secured party" after the word "intermediary". The 1967 amendment brings this section into conformity with the Official Text. The reason for this original variation is explained in California Code Comment 5, ante, and California Code Comment 3 to § 7508, post.

2. In spite of the intended reason for the California variation, the Permanent Editorial Board comments that the California change was apparently intended for clarification, but it seemed unnecessary for that purpose. (Permanent Editorial Board for the Uniform Commercial Code, Report No. 2, p. 140.)

Changes from U.C.C. (1962 Official Text)

3. This is section 7-507 of the Official Text without change.

Uniform Commercial Code Comment

Prior Uniform Statutory Provision:

Section 36, Uniform Sales Act; Section 44, Uniform Warehouse Receipts Act; Section 35, Uniform Bills of Lading Act.

Changes: Consolidated and rewritten without change in policy.

Purposes of Changes:

1. This section omits provisions of the prior acts on warranties as to the goods as unnecessary and incomplete. It is unnecessary because such warranties derive from the contract of sale and not from the transfer of the documents. The fact that transfer of control occurs by way of a document of title does not limit or displace the ordinary obligations of a seller. The former provision, moreover, was incomplete because it did not expressly include all of the warranties which might rest upon a seller under such circumstances. This Act handles the problem by means of the precautionary reference to "any warranty made in selling the goods." If the transfer of documents attends or follows the making of a contract for the sale of goods, the general obligations on warranties as to the goods (Sections 2–312 through 2–318) are brought to bear as well as the special warranties under this section.

2. The limited warranties of a delivering or collecting intermediary are stated in Section 7–508.

Cross References:

Point 1: Sections 2–312 through 2–318.
Point 2: Section 7–508.

Definitional Cross References:

"Document". Section 7–102.
"Document of title". Section 1–201.
"Genuine". Section 1–201.
"Goods". Section 7–102.
"Person". Section 1–201.
"Purchaser". Section 1–201.
"Value". Section 1–201.

Cross References

Agents, warranty of authority, see Civil Code § 2342.
Breach of warranty of agents' authority, see Civil Code § 3318.
Letters of credit,
   Issuer's duty to honor a draft or demand for payment, see Commercial Code § 5114.
   Warranties of transfer and presentment, see Commercial Code § 5111.
Sale of goods, warranties, see Commercial Code § 2312 et seq.
Warranties of collecting bank as to documents, see Commercial Code § 7508.

§ 7508. Warranties of Collecting Bank as to Documents

A collecting bank or other intermediary known to be entrusted with documents on behalf of another or with collection of a draft or other claim against delivery of documents * * * warrants by such delivery of the documents * * * only * * * its own good faith and authority. This rule applies even though the intermediary has purchased or made advances against the claim or draft to be collected. *(Stats.1963, c. 819, § 7508. Amended by Stats.1967, c. 799, p. 2212, § 14.)*

California Code Comment

By John A. Bohn and Charles J. Williams

Prior California Law

1. This section is an extension of the provisions of former Civil Code §§ 1858.74 (UWRA) and 2130a (UBLA) to expressly include banks and other intermediaries. Former Civil Code §§ 1858.74 and 2130a were phrased negatively and provided that a holder of a document for security did not warrant either the genuineness of the document or the goods covered by the document.

2. The warranties made by an intermediary under the prior uniform acts were not defined by California case law. In other jurisdictions (including decisions under the FBLA, 49 USCA 116) there was a split of authority. One view held that an intermediary warranted only its good faith and authority. American State Bank v. Mueller Grain Co. (CCA 7th 1926) 15 F.2d 899, reversed on other grounds, 275 U.S. 493, 48 S.Ct. 34, 72 L.Ed. 390 (Ill.1927). The other view extended the warranties to the document. Fort Worth Elevator Co. v. State Guaranty Bank, 93 Okla. 191, 220 Pac. 340 (1923).

Changes from U.C.C. (1962 Official Text)

3. This section was changed in California from section 7–508 of the 1962 Official Text for the purpose of continuing the rule under the prior uniform acts. The Official Text with the California changes reads as follows:

"A collecting bank or other intermediary known to be entrusted with documents on behalf of another or with collection of a draft or other claim against delivery of document [warrants by such delivery of the documents], and a holder of documents for security, warrant by delivery of documents against payment only their [its] own good faith and authority. This rule applies even though the intermediary has purchased or made advances against the claim or draft to be collected."

Because the Official Text did not expressly include a security holder as one whose warranties were limited, it was feared that a bank which held a document as security would upon releasing it be warranting such things as genuineness of the document. Since this would change the prior law, the Official Text was modified.

The Marsh and Warren Report made the recommendations for this change:

"Section 46 of the U.W.R.A. [Former CC § 1858.74] and Section 37 of the U.B.L.A. [Former CC § 2130a] are not cited as sources for this provision of the Code. Nevertheless, it has been argued that this Section would cover a secured party who delivered the documents against payment. 3 N.Y. Law Rev.Comm., Study of the Uniform Commercial Code (1955) 1862–1864. It seems to us that it would be very difficult to describe such a party as an 'intermediary.' The suggestion that a bank holding documents as security would be acting as an 'intermediary' of its own customer in making collection and delivering the documents seems to us a little far fetched.

"There certainly seems to be no reason why these provisions of the Uniform Acts should be repealed. It is impossible to determine whether the draftsmen of the Code intended to repeal them or not. We have suggested the foregoing amendment in order explicitly to continue this rule of the Uniform Acts in effect." Sixth Progress Report to the Legislature by Senate Fact Finding Committee on Judiciary (1959–1961), Part 1, The Uniform Commercial Code p. 531.

California Code Comment—1967 Amendment

By Charles J. Williams

Prior California Law

1. This section originally contained a California variation from the Official Text. California Code Comment 3, ante. The 1967 amendment brings this section into conformity with the Official Text.

2. The original California change was apparently intended for clarification, but seems unnecessary for that purpose. "Under the last sentence of this section, a secured party may be an 'intermediary'. Moreover, the limitation of warranties should apply to a delivery of documents whether or not the delivery is 'against payment.'" (Permanent Editorial Board for the Uniform Commercial Code, Report No. 2, p. 140.)

Changes from U.C.C. (1962 Official Text)

3. This is section 7–508 of the Official Text without change.

Uniform Commercial Code Comment

Prior Uniform Statutory Provision:
None.

Purposes:

1. To state the limited warranties given with respect to the documents accompanying a documentary draft.

2. In warranting its authority a bank only warrants its authority from its transferor. See Section 4–203. It does not warrant the genuineness or effectiveness of the document. Compare Section 7–507.

3. Other duties and rights of banks handling documentary drafts for collection are stated in Article 4, Part 5.

Cross References:

Sections 4–203 and 7–507, 4–501 through 4–504.

Definitional Cross References:

"Collecting bank". Section 4–105.
"Delivery". Section 1–201.
"Document". Section 7–102.
"Draft". Section 5–103.
"Good faith". Section 1–201.

Cross References

Agents, warranty of authority, see Civil Code § 2342.
Breach of warranty of agents' authority, see Civil Code § 3318.
Collection of documentary drafts, see Commercial Code § 4501 et seq.
Effect of instructions, see Commercial Code § 4203.
Negotiation or transfer of receipt or bill, warranties, see Commercial Code § 7507.

§ 7509. Receipt or Bill: When Adequate Compliance With Commercial Contract

The question whether a document is adequate to fulfill the obligations of a contract for sale or the conditions of a credit is governed by the divisions on sales (Division 2) and on letters of credit (Division 5). (Stats.1963, c. 819, § 7509.)

California Code Comment

By John A. Bohn and Charles J. Williams

Prior California Law

1. This section is new. See Official Comment.

Changes from U.C.C. (1962 Official Text)

2. This is section 7–509 of the Official Text without change.

Uniform Commercial Code Comment

Prior Uniform Statutory Provision:
None.

Purposes:

To cross-refer to the Articles of this Act which deal with the substantive issues of the type of document of title required under the contract entered into by the parties.

Cross References:

Articles 2 and 5.

Definitional Cross References:

"Contract for sale". Section 2–106.
"Document". Section 7–102.

Cross References

Consideration for letters of credit, see Commercial Code § 5105.
Document, see Commercial Code § 7102.
Form, formation and readjustment of sales contract, see Commercial Code § 2201 et seq.
Formal requirements of letters of credit, see Commercial Code § 5104.
Letters of credit, see Commercial Code § 5101 et seq.
Sales, see Commercial Code § 2101 et seq.

CHAPTER 6. WAREHOUSE RECEIPTS AND BILLS OF LADING: MISCELLANEOUS PROVISIONS

Section
7601. Lost and Missing Documents.
7602. Attachment of Goods Covered by a Negotiable Document.
7603. Conflicting Claims; Interpleader.

§ 7601. Lost and Missing Documents

(1) If a document has been lost, stolen or destroyed, a court may order delivery of the goods or issuance of a substitute document and the bailee may without liability to any person comply with such order. If the document was negotiable the claimant must post * * * an undertaking approved by the court to indemnify any person who may suffer loss as a result of nonsurrender of the document. If the document was not negotiable, * * * an undertaking may be required at the discretion of the

§ 7601

court. The court may also in its discretion order payment of the bailee's reasonable costs and counsel fees.

(2) A bailee who without court order delivers goods to a person claiming under a missing negotiable document is liable to any person injured thereby, and if the delivery is not in good faith becomes liable for conversion. Delivery in good faith is not conversion if made in accordance with a filed classification or tariff or, where no classification or tariff is filed, if the claimant posts * * * an undertaking with the bailee in an amount at least double the value of the goods at the time of posting to indemnify any person injured by the delivery who files a notice of claim within one year after the delivery. (Stats.1963, c. 819, § 7601. Amended by Stats.1982, c. 517, p. 2364, § 185.)

California Code Comment

By John A. Bohn and Charles J. Williams

Prior California Law

1. This section consolidates and revises the prior California statutory law expressed in former Civil Code §§ 1858.23 (UWRA) and 2128a (UBLA).

2. Subdivision (1) makes several modifications in prior California Law.

Under subdivision (1) the court is authorized to order either delivery of the goods or issuance of a substitute document where a document is lost, stolen, or destroyed. Under former Civil Code §§ 1858.23 and 2128a the court was authorized only to compel the delivery of the goods, there being no provision for the issuance of a substitute document and this authority only applied to negotiable documents which were lost or destroyed. Official Comments 2 and 3.

Subdivision (1) authorizes the bailee to comply with a court order for delivery without incurring personal liability. This changes the rule under former Civil Code §§ 1858.23 and 2128a which provided that the delivery of the goods under an order of the court as provided in this section shall not relieve the warehouseman from liability to a purchaser for value without notice.

Former Civil Code §§ 1858.23 and 2128a expressly conditioned the authority of the court to order delivery of the goods upon "satisfactory proof of such loss or destruction (see Civil Code § 3415) and upon the giving of a bond with sufficient sureties to be approved by the court to protect the warehouseman from any liability or expense. . . ." Subdivision (1) eliminates the phrase "upon satisfactory proof . . ." as unnecessary. Official Comment 4.

Subdivision (1) continues the requirement of posting security in the case of a negotiable document. The third sentence in subdivision (1) making the security requirement in the case of a non-negotiable document is new since former Civil Code §§ 1858.23 and 2128a did not apply to non-negotiable bills and receipts. This subdivision is extended to non-negotiable documents to protect the bailee in case the document would be held to be negotiable. Official Comment 2, second paragraph. For comments of The State Bar Committee recommending against extension of subdivision (1) to non-negotiable documents see, Further Comments of State Bar, Sixth Progress Report to the Legislature by Senate Fact Finding Committee on Judiciary (1959–1961) Part 1, The Uniform Commercial Code, pp. 619, 634.

The last sentence of subdivision (1) continues the rule of the last sentence of former Civil Code §§ 1858.23 and 2128a without substantive change.

3. Subdivision (2) applies only to negotiable documents.

Subdivision (2) is consistent with the prior California law expressed in former Civil Code §§ 1858.20 (UWRA) and 2127c (UBLA) which imposed liability upon a bailee to a good faith purchaser for delivery of goods to a claimant without taking up the negotiable bill or receipt.

Under the prior uniform acts there was some doubt as to whether or not there was an absolute liability for delivery without taking up the bill or receipt. See former Civil Code § 1858.84 and Official Comment 1.

Further, former Civil Code §§ 1858.19 (UWRA) and 2127b (UBLA) probably imposed liability for conversion in the case of delivery to a person not entitled to the goods whether there was good faith or not. See McMullin v. Lyon Fireproof Storage Co., 74 Cal.App. 87, 239 Pac. 422, (1925). Subdivision (2) by spelling out the liability of the bailee for delivery to one other than the person legally entitled to the goods thereby clarifies the prior law.

4. Division 7 treats carriers and warehousemen uniformly as to their liability for delivery without taking up the document of title. Former Civil Code § 1858.84 (UWRA) made it a crime to issue goods without taking up a receipt but there was not a similar provision applicable in the case of bills of lading. Official Comment 1.

5. Division 7 omits entirely the penal provisions contained in former Civil Code §§ 1858.80–1858.93 (UWRA) and 2131–2131f (UBLA).

It was proposed by the California Bankers Committee to retain the penal provisions of the Uniform Warehouse Receipts Act and the Uniform Bills of Lading Act upon the basis that they contributed materially to the high degree of confidence which banks have been able to place in documents of title. Recommendations and Comments of the California Bankers Association, Sixth Progress Report to the Legislature by Senate Fact Finding Committee on Judiciary (1959–1961) Part 1, The Uniform Commercial Code, p. 416.

The Marsh and Warren Report suggested that if these provisions were retained, they should be placed in the penal code. Sixth Progress Report to the Legislature by Senate Fact Finding Committee on Judiciary (1959–1961) Part 1, The Uniform Commercial Code, p. 531. In accordance with this suggestion these criminal provisions appear as sections 560–560.6, Penal Code.

Changes from U.C.C. (1962 Official Text)

6. This is section 7–601 of the Official Text without change.

Law Revision Commission Comment
1982 Amendment

Section 7601 is amended for consistency with the Bond and Undertaking Law. See Code Civ.Proc. § 995.020 (application of provisions). (16 Cal.L.Rev.Comm. Reports 501).

Uniform Commercial Code Comment

Prior Uniform Statutory Provision:

Section 14, Uniform Warehouse Receipts Act; Section 17, Uniform Bills of Lading Act.

Changes: General Revision. Principal innovations include: affirmation of bailee's privilege to deliver to claimant without resort to judicial proceedings if the bailee acts in good faith and is willing to take the full risk of loss in case the lost document turns up in the hands of an innocent purchaser; explicit authorization to the court to order bailee to issue a substitute document rather than make physical delivery of the goods; inclusion of "stolen" as well as lost documents; extension of section to non-negotiable documents.

Purposes of Changes: The purposes of the changes insofar as they are not self-evident are as follows:

1. As to bailee's privilege to deliver without court order, doubt had arisen as to the propriety of such action under Section 54 of the Uniform Warehouse Receipts Act, which made it a crime to deliver goods covered by negotiable receipts without taking up the receipts "except in the cases provided for in Section 14" (the lost receipts section). This has been interpreted by one court as exempting from criminal liability only if the judicial procedure of Section 14 was followed. Dahl v. Winter-Truesdell-Diercks Co., 61 N.D. 84, 237 N.W. 202 (1931). Although the criminal provisions are not being reenacted in this Act (and the Uniform Bills of Lading Act never did include such a criminal provision), it seems advisable to clarify the legality of the well established commercial practice of bailees to make delivery where they are satisfied that the claimant is the person entitled under a lost document. Since the bailee remains liable on the document in such cases, he will usually insist that the claimant provide an indemnity bond.

2. The old acts provide only for compulsory delivery of goods; this Section provides also for compulsory issuance of a substitute document. If continuance of the bailment is desirable there is no reason to require the goods to be withdrawn and redeposited in order to secure a negotiable document. The present acts would probably be so interpreted. Section 20 of the Federal Warehouse Act and some state laws

expressly require issuance of a new receipt on proof of loss and posting of bond.

3. Claimants on non-negotiable instruments are permitted to avail themselves of this procedure because straight bills of lading sometimes contain provisions that the goods shall not be delivered except upon production of the bill. If the carrier should choose to insist upon production of the bill, the consignee should have some means of compelling delivery on satisfactory proof of entitlement.

Ordinarily no security would be necessary to indemnify a bailee in delivering to the person named in a non-negotiable document. But disputes as to negotiability may arise, in which case if there is a reasonable doubt on the point the bailee should be protected against the possibility that the missing document would, in the hands of an innocent purchaser for value, be held negotiable.

4. It seems unnecessary to state, as do the present acts, that the court shall act "on satisfactory proof of such loss or destruction." The right of action created by the section is conditioned on a document being lost, stolen or destroyed. Plaintiff must of course bring himself within the section. There is nothing in the language of the old acts to suggest that they intended to impose anything but the normal burden of proof on the plaintiff in such proceedings.

5. Subsection (2) makes it clear that after delivery without court order the bailee remains liable for actual damages. Liability for conversion is provided where the delivery is dishonest, but excluded where a filed classification or tariff is followed in good faith, or where the described bond is posted in good faith and no classification or tariff is filed. Liability for conversion in other cases is left to judicial decision.

Definitional Cross References:
"Bailee". Section 7–102.
"Bill of lading". Section 1–201.
"Delivery". Section 1–201.
"Document". Section 7–102.
"Good faith". Section 1–201.
"Goods". Section 7–102.
"Person". Section 1–201.
"Warehouse receipt". Section 1–201.
"Warehouseman". Section 7–102.

Cross References

Lost, destroyed and stolen certificated securities, see Commercial Code § 8405.
Lost or destroyed documents, establishment, issuance of duplicate, see Civil Code § 3415.
Lost or destroyed writing, see Evidence Code § 1500 et seq.
Private records destroyed in disaster or calamity, procedure to establish, see Code of Civil Procedure § 1953.10 et seq.
Rights acquired by due negotiation notwithstanding loss, theft or conversion of document, see Commercial Code § 7502.
Treaty, statute, etc., effect, see Commercial Code § 7103.
Unlawful delivery of goods, exception of cases provided for in this section, see Penal Code § 560.2.

§ 7602. Attachment of Goods Covered by a Negotiable Document

Except where the document was originally issued upon delivery of the goods by a person who had no power to dispose of them, no lien attaches by virtue of any judicial process to goods in the possession of a bailee for which a negotiable document of title is outstanding unless the document be first surrendered to the bailee or its negotiation enjoined, and the bailee shall not be compelled to deliver the goods pursuant to process until the document is surrendered to him or impounded by the court. One who purchases the document for value without notice of the process or injunction takes free of the lien imposed by judicial process. *(Stats.1963, c. 819, § 7602.)*

California Code Comment
By John A. Bohn and Charles J. Williams

Prior California Law

1. This section consolidates and restates former Civil Code §§ 1759 (USA), 1858.34 (UWRA) and 2128h (UBLA). The section protects the bailee from the conflicting claims by the document holder and the judgment creditor of the person who deposited the goods. Official Comment 1.

The last sentence is new statutory law. See Official Comment 2. See former Civil Code §§ 1858.35 (UWRA) and 2128i (UBLA) which authorized aids to the creditor of the document holder by injunction or otherwise.

Changes from U.C.C. (1962 Official Text)

2. This is section 7–602 of the Official Text without change.

Uniform Commercial Code Comment

Prior Uniform Statutory Provisions: Section 25, Uniform Warehouse Receipts Act; Section 24, Uniform Bills of Lading Act.
Changes: Consolidated and rewritten.
Purposes of Changes:

1. The purpose of the section is to protect the bailee from conflicting claims of the document holder and the judgment creditors of the person who deposited the goods. The rights of the former prevail unless, in effect, the judgment creditors immobilize the negotiable document. However, if the document was issued upon deposit of the goods by a person who had no power to dispose of the goods so that the document is ineffective to pass title, judgment liens are valid to the extent of the debtor's interest in the goods.

2. The last sentence covers the possibility that the holder of a document who has been enjoined from negotiating it will violate the injunction by negotiating to an innocent purchaser for value. In such case the lien will be defeated.

Cross Reference:
Point 1: Section 7–503.

Definitional Cross References:
"Bailee". Section 7–102.
"Delivery". Section 1–201.
"Document". Section 7–102.
"Goods". Section 7–102.
"Notice". Section 1–201.
"Person". Section 1–201.
"Purchase". Section 1–201.
"Value". Section 1–201.

Cross References

Document of title, operation and effect, see Commercial Code § 7503.
Unlawful delivery of goods, exception of cases provided for in this section, see Penal Code § 560.2.

§ 7603. Conflicting Claims; Interpleader

If more than one person claims title or possession of the goods, the bailee or warehouseman is excused from delivery until he has had a reasonable time to ascertain the validity of the adverse claims or to bring an action to compel all claimants to interplead and may compel such interpleader, either in defending an action for nondelivery of the goods, or by original action, whichever is appropriate. *(Stats.1963, c. 819, § 7603.)*

California Code Comment
By John A. Bohn and Charles J. Williams

Prior California Law

1. This section consolidates and restates former Civil Code §§ 1858.26 and 1858.27 (UWRA) and 2128d and 2128e (UBLA).

Former Civil Code § 1858.27 provided that the warehouseman had a reasonable time to ascertain the validity of the adverse claim or to bring

§ 7603

an interpleader action, but imposed this stringent limitation on an adverse claimant: "If such adverse claimant shall not bring suit and serve summons on the warehouseman within 48 hours after the service of notice of his adverse claim, such failure shall act as a complete abandonment of such adverse claim." This provision is omitted from Commercial Code § 7603.

3. Also see Code of Civil Procedure § 386 dealing with interpleader.

Changes from U.C.C. (1962 Official Text)

4. In the California version, the words "or warehouseman" were inserted after the word "bailee".

Uniform Commercial Code Comment

Prior Uniform Statutory Provision:
Sections 16 and 17, Uniform Warehouse Receipts Act; Sections 20 and 21, Uniform Bills of Lading Act.

Changes: Consolidation without substantial change.

Purposes of Changes:
The section enables a bailee faced with conflicting claims to the goods to compel the claimants to litigate their claims with each other rather than with him.

Definitional Cross References:

"Action". Section 1–201.

"Bailee". Section 7–102.

"Delivery". Section 1–201.

"Goods". Section 7–102.

"Person". Section 1–201.

"Reasonable time". Section 1–204.

Cross References

Interpleader proceedings, see Code of Civil Procedure § 386.

Division 8

INVESTMENT SECURITIES

Chapter	Section
1. Short Title And General Matters	8101
2. Issue and Issuer	8201
3. Transfer of Certificated and Uncertificated Securities	8301
4. Registration	8401
5. Security Entitlements	8501
6. Transition Provisions	8601

CHAPTER 1. SHORT TITLE AND GENERAL MATTERS

Section
8101. Short title.
8102. Definitions; index of definitions.
8103. Specified obligations and interests; characterization as security or financial asset.
8104. Acquisition of security, interest therein, or financial asset; satisfaction of transfer requirement.
8105. Adverse claims; notice.
8106. Control of security or security entitlement agreement.
8107. Appropriate person; effective endorsement, instruction or entitlement.
8108. Transfer of certificated security or endorsement; warranties.
8109. Entitlement orders; security account credits; warranties.
8110. Choice of law.
8111. Clearing corporation rules.
8112. Creditors; legal process.
8113. Enforcement of contracts; writing requirements.
8114. Evidence; burden of proof.
8115. Liability to persons with adverse claims.
8116. Security intermediary; purchaser for value.

Cross References

Corporate securities law, see Corporations Code § 25000 et seq.
Investment securities included within definition of goods, see Commercial Code § 2105.
Items within Division 4, Bank Deposits and Collections, and this division subject to and governed by this division, see Commercial Code § 4102.

§ 8101. Short title

This division may be cited as Uniform Commercial Code—Investment Securities. *(Added by Stats.1996, c. 497 (S.B.1591), § 9, operative Jan. 1, 1997.)*

Cross References

Inapplicability of Division 3 to investment securities, see Commercial Code § 3102.

§ 8102. Definitions; index of definitions

(a) In this division:

(1) "Adverse claim" means a claim that a claimant has a property interest in a financial asset and that it is a violation of the rights of the claimant for another person to hold, transfer, or deal with the financial asset.

(2) "Bearer form," as applied to a certificated security, means a form in which the security is payable to the bearer of the security certificate according to its terms but not by reason of an indorsement.

(3) "Broker" means a person defined as a broker or dealer under the federal securities laws, but without excluding a bank acting in that capacity.

(4) "Certificated security" means a security that is represented by a certificate.

(5) "Clearing corporation" means any of the following:

(A) A person that is registered as a "clearing agency" under the federal securities laws.

(B) A federal reserve bank.

(C) Any other person that provides clearance or settlement services with respect to financial assets that would require it to register as a clearing agency under the federal securities laws but for an exclusion or exemption from the registration requirement, if its activities as a clearing corporation, including promulgation of rules, are subject to regulation by a federal or state governmental authority.

(6) "Communicate" means to either:

(A) Send a signed writing.

(B) Transmit information by any mechanism agreed upon by the persons transmitting and receiving the information.

(7) "Entitlement holder" means a person identified in the records of a securities intermediary as the person having a security entitlement against the securities intermediary. If a person acquires a security entitlement by virtue of paragraph (2) or (3) of subdivision (b) of Section 8501, that person is the entitlement holder.

(8) "Entitlement order" means a notification communicated to a securities intermediary directing transfer or redemption of a financial asset to which the entitlement holder has a security entitlement.

(9) "Financial asset," except as otherwise provided in Section 8103, means any of the following:

(A) A security.

(B) An obligation of a person or a share, participation, or other interest in a person or in property or an enterprise of a person, that is, or is of a type, dealt in or traded on financial markets, or that is recognized in any area in which it is issued or dealt in as a medium for investment.

(C) Any property that is held by a securities intermediary for another person in a securities account if the securities intermediary has expressly agreed with the

§ 8102

other person that the property is to be treated as a financial asset under this division. As context requires, the term means either the interest itself or the means by which a person's claim to it is evidenced, including a certificated or uncertificated security, a security certificate, or a security entitlement.

(10) "Good faith," for purposes of the obligation of good faith in the performance or enforcement of contracts or duties within this division, means honesty in fact and the observance of reasonable commercial standards of fair dealing.

(11) "Endorsement" means a signature that alone or accompanied by other words is made on a security certificate in registered form or on a separate document for the purpose of assigning, transferring, or redeeming the security or granting a power to assign, transfer, or redeem it.

(12) "Instruction" means a notification communicated to the issuer of an uncertificated security that directs that the transfer of the security be registered or that the security be redeemed.

(13) "Registered form," as applied to a certificated security, means a form in which both of the following apply:

(A) The security certificate specifies a person entitled to the security.

(B) A transfer of the security may be registered upon books maintained for that purpose by or on behalf of the issuer, or the security certificate so states.

(14) "Securities intermediary" means either:

(A) A clearing corporation.

(B) A person, including a bank or broker, that in the ordinary course of its business maintains securities accounts for others and is acting in that capacity.

(15) "Security," except as otherwise provided in Section 8103, means an obligation of an issuer or a share, participation, or other interest in an issuer or in property or an enterprise of an issuer that is all of the following:

(A) It is represented by a security certificate in bearer or registered form, or the transfer of it may be registered upon books maintained for that purpose by or on behalf of the issuer.

(B) It is one of a class or series or by its terms is divisible into a class or series of shares, participations, interests, or obligations.

(C) It is either of the following:

(i) It is, or is of a type, dealt in or traded on securities exchanges or securities markets.

(ii) It is a medium for investment and by its terms expressly provides that it is a security governed by this division.

(16) "Security certificate" means a certificate representing a security.

(17) "Security entitlement" means the rights and property interest of an entitlement holder with respect to a financial asset specified in Chapter 5 (commencing with Section 8501).

(18) "Uncertificated security" means a security that is not represented by a certificate.

(b) Other definitions applying to this division and the sections in which they appear are:

Appropriate person. Section 8107.

Control. Section 8106.

Delivery. Section 8301.

Investment company security. Section 8103.

Issuer. Section 8201.

Overissue. Section 8210.

Protected purchaser. Section 8303.

Securities account. Section 8501.

(c) In addition, Division 1 (commencing with Section 1101) contains general definitions and principles of construction and interpretation applicable throughout this division.

(d) The characterization of a person, business, or transaction for purposes of this division does not determine the characterization of the person, business, or transaction for purposes of any other law, regulation, or rule. *(Added by Stats.1996, c. 497 (S.B.1591), § 9, operative Jan. 1, 1997.)*

Uniform Commercial Code Comment

1. "Adverse claim." The definition of the term "adverse claim" has two components. First, the term refers only to property interests. Second, the term means not merely that a person has a property interest in a financial asset but that it is a violation of the claimant's property interest for the other person to hold or transfer the security or other financial asset.

The term adverse claim is not, of course, limited to ownership rights, but extends to other property interests established by other law. A security interest, for example, would be an adverse claim with respect to a transferee from the debtor since any effort by the secured party to enforce the security interest against the property would be an interference with the transferee's interest.

The definition of adverse claim in the prior version of Article 8 might have been read to suggest that any wrongful action concerning a security, even a simple breach of contract, gave rise to an adverse claim. Insofar as such cases as *Fallon v. Wall Street Clearing Corp.*, 586 N.Y.S.2d 953, 182 A.D.2d 245, (1992) and *Pentech Intl. v. Wall St. Clearing Co.*, 983 F.2d 441 (2d Cir. 1993), were based on that view, they are rejected by the new definition which explicitly limits the term adverse claim to property interests. Suppose, for example, that A contracts to sell or deliver securities to B, but fails to do so and instead sells or pledges the securities to C. B, the promisee, has an action against A for breach of contract, but absent unusual circumstances the action for breach would not give rise to a property interest in the securities. Accordingly, B does not have an adverse claim. An adverse claim might, however, be based upon principles of equitable remedies that give rise to property claims. It would, for example, cover a right established by other law to rescind a transaction in which securities were transferred. Suppose, for example, that A holds securities and is induced by B's fraud to transfer them to B. Under the law of contract or restitution, A may have a right to rescind the transfer, which gives A a property claim to the securities. If so, A has an adverse claim to the securities in B's hands. By contrast, if B had committed no fraud, but had merely committed a breach of contract in connection with the transfer from A to B, A may have only a right to damages for breach, not a right to rescind. In that case, A would not have an adverse claim to the securities in B's hands.

2. "Bearer form." The definition of "bearer form" has remained substantially unchanged since the early drafts of the original version of Article 8. The requirement that the certificate be payable to bearer by its terms rather than by an indorsement has the effect of preventing instruments governed by other law, such as chattel paper or Article 3 negotiable instruments, from being inadvertently swept into the Article 8 definition of security merely by virtue of blank indorsements. Although the other elements of the definition of security in Section 8–102(a)(14) probably suffice for that purpose in any event, the language used in the prior version of Article 8 has been retained.

3. "Broker." Broker is defined by reference to the definitions of broker and dealer in the federal securities laws. The only difference is that banks, which are excluded from the federal securities law definition, are included in the Article 8 definition when they perform functions that would bring them within the federal securities law definition if it did not have the clause excluding banks. The definition covers both those who act as agents ("brokers" in securities parlance) and those who act as principals ("dealers" in securities parlance). Since the definition refers to persons "defined" as brokers or dealers under the federal securities law, rather than to persons required to "register" as brokers or dealers under the federal securities law, it covers not only registered brokers and dealers but also those exempt from the registration requirement, such as purely intrastate brokers. The only substantive rules that turn on the defined term broker are one provision of the section on warranties, Section 8–108(i), and the special perfection rule in Article 9 for security interests granted by brokers, Section 9–115(4)(c).

4. "Certificated security." The term "certificated security" means a security that is represented by a security certificate.

5. "Clearing corporation." The definition of clearing corporation limits its application to entities that are subject to a rigorous regulatory framework. Accordingly, the definition includes only federal reserve banks, persons who are registered as "clearing agencies" under the federal securities laws (which impose a comprehensive system of regulation of the activities and rules of clearing agencies), and other entities subject to a comparable system of regulatory oversight.

6. "Communicate." The term "communicate" assures that the Article 8 rules will be sufficiently flexible to adapt to changes in information technology. Sending a signed writing always suffices as a communication, but the parties can agree that a different means of transmitting information is to be used. Agreement is defined in Section 1–201(3) as "the bargain of the parties in fact as found in their language or by implication from other circumstances including course of dealing or usage of trade or course of performance." Thus, use of an information transmission method might be found to be authorized by agreement, even though the parties have not explicitly so specified in a formal agreement. The term communicate is used in Sections 8–102(a)(7) (definition of entitlement order), 8–102(a)(11) (definition of instruction), and 8–403 (demand that issuer not register transfer).

7. "Entitlement holder." This term designates those who hold financial assets through intermediaries in the indirect holding system. Because many of the rules of Part 5 impose duties on securities intermediaries in favor of entitlement holders, the definition of entitlement holder is, in most cases, limited to the person specifically designated as such on the records of the intermediary. The last sentence of the definition covers the relatively unusual cases where a person may acquire a security entitlement under Section 8–501 even though the person may not be specifically designated as an entitlement holder on the records of the securities intermediary.

A person may have an interest in a security entitlement, and may even have the right to give entitlement orders to the securities intermediary with respect to it, even though the person is not the entitlement holder. For example, a person who holds securities through a securities account in its own name may have given discretionary trading authority to another person, such as an investment adviser. Similarly, the control provisions in Section 8–106 and the related provisions in Article 9 are designed to facilitate transactions in which a person who holds securities through a securities account uses them as collateral in an arrangement where the securities intermediary has agreed that if the secured party so directs the intermediary will dispose of the positions. In such arrangements, the debtor remains the entitlement holder but has agreed that the secured party can initiate entitlement orders.

8. "Entitlement order." This term is defined as a notification communicated to a securities intermediary directing transfer or redemption of the financial asset to which an entitlement holder has a security entitlement. The term is used in the rules for the indirect holding system in a fashion analogous to the use of the terms "indorsement" and "instruction" in the rules for the direct holding system. If a person directly holds a certificated security in registered form and wishes to transfer it, the means of transfer is an indorsement. If a person directly holds an uncertificated security and wishes to transfer it, the means of transfer is an instruction. If a person holds a security entitlement, the means of disposition is an entitlement order. As noted in Comment 7, an entitlement order need not be initiated by the entitlement holder in order to be effective, so long as the entitlement holder has authorized the other party to initiate entitlement orders. See Section 8–107(b).

9. "Financial asset." The definition of "financial asset," in conjunction with the definition of "securities account" in Section 8–501, sets the scope of the indirect holding system rules of Part 5 of Revised Article 8. The Part 5 rules apply not only to securities held through intermediaries, but also to other financial assets held through intermediaries. The term financial asset is defined to include not only securities but also a broader category of obligations, shares, participations, and interests.

Having separate definitions of security and financial asset makes it possible to separate the question of the proper scope of the traditional Article 8 rules from the question of the proper scope of the new indirect holding system rules. Some forms of financial assets should be covered by the indirect holding system rules of Part 5, but not by the rules of Parts 2, 3, and 4. The term financial asset is used to cover such property. Because the term security entitlement is defined in terms of financial assets rather than securities, the rules concerning security entitlements set out in Part 5 of Article 8 and in Revised Article 9 apply to the broader class of financial assets.

The fact that something does or could fall within the definition of financial asset does not, without more, trigger Article 8 coverage. The indirect holding system rules of Revised Article 8 apply only if the financial asset is in fact held in a securities account, so that the interest of the person who holds the financial asset through the securities account is a security entitlement. Thus, questions of the scope of the indirect holding system rules cannot be framed as "Is such-and-such a 'financial asset' under Article 8?" Rather, one must analyze whether the relationship between an institution and a person on whose behalf the institution holds an asset falls within the scope of the term securities account as defined in Section 8–501. That question turns in large measure on whether it makes sense to apply the Part 5 rules to the relationship.

The term financial asset is used to refer both to the underlying asset and the particular means by which ownership of that asset is evidenced. Thus, with respect to a certificated security, the term financial asset may, as context requires, refer either to the interest or obligation of the issuer or to the security certificate representing that interest or obligation. Similarly, if a person holds a security or other financial asset through a securities account, the term financial asset may, as context requires, refer either to the underlying asset or to the person's security entitlement.

10. "Good faith." Good faith is defined in Article 8 for purposes of the application to Article 8 of Section 1–203, which provides that "Every contract or duty within this Act imposes an obligation of good faith in its performance or enforcement." The sole function of the good faith definition in Revised Article 8 is to give content to the Section 1–203 obligation as it applies to contracts and duties that are governed by Article 8. The standard is one of "reasonable commercial standards of fair dealing." The reference to commercial standards makes clear that assessments of conduct are to be made in light of the commercial setting. The substantive rules of Article 8 have been drafted to take account of the commercial circumstances of the securities holding and processing system. For example, Section 8–115 provides that a securities intermediary acting on an effective entitlement order, or a broker or other agent acting as a conduit in a securities transaction, is not liable to an adverse claimant, unless the claimant obtained legal process or the intermediary acted in collusion with the wrongdoer. This, and other similar provisions, see Sections 8–404 and 8–503(e), do not depend on notice of adverse claims, because it would impair rather than advance the interest of investors in having a sound and efficient securities clearance and settlement system to require intermediaries to investigate the propriety of the transactions they are processing. The good faith obligation does not supplant the standards of conduct established in provisions of this kind.

In Revised Article 8, the definition of good faith is not germane to the question whether a purchaser takes free from adverse claims. The rules on such questions as whether a purchaser who takes in suspicious circumstances is disqualified from protected purchaser status are treated not as an aspect of good faith but directly in the rules of Section 8–105 on notice of adverse claims.

11. "Indorsement" is defined as a signature made on a security certificate or separate document for purposes of transferring or redeeming the security. The definition is adapted from the language of Section 8–308(1) of the prior version and from the definition of indorsement in the Negotiable Instruments Article, see Section 3–204(a). The definition of indorsement does not include the requirement that the signature be made by an appropriate person or be authorized. Those questions are treated in the separate substantive provision on whether the indorsement is effective, rather than in the definition of indorsement. See Section 8–107.

12. "Instruction" is defined as a notification communicated to the issuer of an uncertificated security directing that transfer be registered or that the security be redeemed. Instructions are the analog for uncertificated securities of indorsements of certificated securities.

13. "Registered form." The definition of "registered form" is substantially the same as in the prior version of Article 8. Like the definition of bearer form, it serves primarily to distinguish Article 8 securities from instruments governed by other law, such as Article 3.

14. "Securities intermediary." A "securities intermediary" is a person that in the ordinary course of its business maintains securities accounts for others and is acting in that capacity. The most common examples of securities intermediaries would be clearing corporations holding securities for their participants, banks acting as securities custodians, and brokers holding securities on behalf of their customers. Clearing corporations are listed separately as a category of securities intermediary in subparagraph (i) even though in most circumstances they would fall within the general definition in subparagraph (ii). The reason is to simplify the analysis of arrangements such as the NSCC–DTC system in which NSCC performs the comparison, clearance, and netting function, while DTC acts as the depository. Because NSCC is a registered clearing agency under the federal securities laws, it is a clearing corporation and hence a securities intermediary under Article 8, regardless of whether it is at any particular time or in any particular aspect of its operations holding securities on behalf of its participants.

The terms securities intermediary and broker have different meanings. Broker means a person engaged in the business of buying and selling securities, as agent for others or as principal. Securities intermediary means a person maintaining securities accounts for others. A stockbroker, in the colloquial sense, may or may not be acting as a securities intermediary.

The definition of securities intermediary includes the requirement that the person in question is "acting in the capacity" of maintaining securities accounts for others. This is to take account of the fact that a particular entity, such as a bank, may act in many different capacities in securities transactions. A bank may act as a transfer agent for issuers, as a securities custodian for institutional investors and private investors, as a dealer in government securities, as a lender taking securities as collateral, and as a provider of general payment and collection services that might be used in connection with securities transactions. A bank that maintains securities accounts for its customers would be a securities intermediary with respect to those accounts; but if it takes a pledge of securities from a borrower to secure a loan, it is not thereby acting as a securities intermediary with respect to the pledged securities, since it holds them for its own account rather than for a customer. In other circumstances, those two functions might be combined. For example, if the bank is a government securities dealer it may maintain securities accounts for customers and also provide the customers with margin credit to purchase or carry the securities, in much the same way that brokers provide margin loans to their customers.

15. "Security." The definition of "security" has three components. First, there is the subparagraph (i) test that the interest or obligation be fully transferable, in the sense that the issuer either maintains transfer books or the obligation or interest is represented by a certificate in bearer or registered form. Second, there is the subparagraph (ii) test that the interest or obligation be divisible, that is, one of a class or series, as distinguished from individual obligations of the sort governed by ordinary contract law or by Article 3. Third, there is the subparagraph (iii) functional test, which generally turns on whether the interest or obligation is, or is of a type, dealt in or traded on securities markets or securities exchanges. There is, however, an "opt-in" provision in subparagraph (iii) which permits the issuer of any interest or obligation that is "a medium of investment" to specify that it is a security governed by Article 8.

The divisibility test of subparagraph (ii) applies to the security—that is, the underlying intangible interest—not the means by which that interest is evidenced. Thus, securities issued in book-entry only form meet the divisibility test because the underlying intangible interest is divisible via the mechanism of the indirect holding system. This is so even though the clearing corporation is the only eligible direct holder of the security.

The third component, the functional test in subparagraph (iii), provides flexibility while ensuring that the Article 8 rules do not apply to interests or obligations in circumstances so unconnected with the securities markets that parties are unlikely to have thought of the possibility that Article 8 might apply. Subparagraph (iii)(A) covers interests or obligations that either are dealt in or traded on securities exchanges or securities markets, or are of a type dealt in or traded on securities exchanges or securities markets. The "is dealt in or traded on" phrase eliminates problems in the characterization of new forms of securities which are to be traded in the markets, even though no similar type has previously been dealt in or traded in the markets. Subparagraph (iii)(B) covers the broader category of media for investment, but it applies only if the terms of the interest or obligation specify that it is an Article 8 security. This opt-in provision allows for deliberate expansion of the scope of Article 8.

Section 8–103 contains additional rules on the treatment of particular interests as securities or financial assets.

16. "Security certificate." The term "security" refers to the underlying asset, e.g., 1000 shares of common stock of Acme, Inc. The term "security certificate" refers to the paper certificates that have traditionally been used to embody the underlying intangible interest.

17. "Security entitlement" means the rights and property interest of a person who holds securities or other financial assets through a securities intermediary. A security entitlement is both a package of personal rights against the securities intermediary and an interest in the property held by the securities intermediary. A security entitlement is not, however, a specific property interest in any financial asset held by the securities intermediary or by the clearing corporation through which the securities intermediary holds the financial asset. See Sections 8–104(c) and 8–503. The formal definition of security entitlement set out in subsection (a)(17) of this section is a cross-reference to the rules of Part 5. In a sense, then, the entirety of Part 5 is the definition of security entitlement. The Part 5 rules specify the rights and property interest that comprise a security entitlement.

18. "Uncertificated security." The term "uncertificated security" means a security that is not represented by a security certificate. For uncertificated securities, there is no need to draw any distinction between the underlying asset and the means by which a direct holder's interest in that asset is evidenced. Compare "certificated security" and "security certificate."

Definitional Cross References

"Agreement" Section 1–201(3)

"Bank" Section 1–201(4)

"Person" Section 1–201(30)

"Send" Section 1–201(38)

"Signed" Section 1–201(39)

"Writing" Section 1–201(46)

Cross References

Certificated securities as documentary draft, see Commercial Code § 4104.

Commercial paper, inapplicability to investment securities, see Commercial Code § 3102.

Effect of issuer's restrictions on transfer, see Commercial Code § 8204.

"Instrument" defined, see Commercial Code § 9105.

§ 8103. Specified obligations and interests; characterization as security or financial asset

(a) A share or similar equity interest issued by a corporation, business trust, joint stock company, or similar entity is a security.

(b) An "investment company security" is a security. "Investment company security" means a share or similar equity interest issued by an entity that is registered as an investment company under the federal investment company laws, an interest in a unit investment trust that is so registered, or a face-amount certificate issued by a face-amount certificate company that is so registered. Investment company security does not include an insurance policy or endowment policy or annuity contract issued by an insurance company.

(c) An interest in a partnership or limited liability company is not a security unless it is dealt in or traded on securities exchanges or in securities markets, its terms expressly provide that it is a security governed by this division, or it is an investment company security. However, an interest in a partnership or limited liability company is a financial asset if it is held in a securities account.

(d) A writing that is a security certificate is governed by this division and not by Division 3 (commencing with Section 3101), even though it also meets the requirements of that division. However, a negotiable instrument governed by Division 3 (commencing with Section 3101) is a financial asset if it is held in a securities account.

(e) An option or similar obligation issued by a clearing corporation to its participants is not a security, but is a financial asset.

(f) A commodity contract, as defined in Section 9115, is not a security or a financial asset. *(Added by Stats.1996, c. 497 (S.B.1591), § 9, operative Jan. 1, 1997.)*

Uniform Commercial Code Comment

1. This section contains rules that supplement the definitions of "financial asset" and "security" in Section 8–102. The Section 8–102 definitions are worded in general terms, because they must be sufficiently comprehensive and flexible to cover the wide variety of investment products that now exist or may develop. The rules in this section are intended to foreclose interpretive issues concerning the application of the general definitions to several specific investment products. No implication is made about the application of the Section 8–102 definitions to investment products not covered by this section.

2. Subsection (a) establishes an unconditional rule that ordinary corporate stock is a security. That is so whether or not the particular issue is dealt in or traded on securities exchanges or in securities markets. Thus, shares of closely held corporations are Article 8 securities.

3. Subsection (b) establishes that the Article 8 term "security" includes the various forms of the investment vehicles offered to the public by investment companies registered as such under the federal Investment Company Act of 1940, as amended. This clarification is prompted principally by the fact that the typical transaction in shares of open-end investment companies is an issuance or redemption, rather than a transfer of shares from one person to another as is the case with ordinary corporate stock. For similar reasons, the definitions of indorsement, instruction, and entitlement order in Section 8–102 refer to "redemptions" as well as "transfers," to ensure that the Article 8 rules on such matters as signature guaranties, Section 8–306, assurances, Sections 8–402 and 8–507, and effectiveness, Section 8–107, apply to directions to redeem mutual fund shares. The exclusion of insurance products is needed because some insurance company separate accounts are registered under the Investment Company Act of 1940, but these are not traded under the usual Article 8 mechanics.

4. Subsection (c) is designed to foreclose interpretive questions that might otherwise be raised by the application of the "of a type" language of Section 8–102(a)(15)(iii) to partnership interests. Subsection (c) establishes the general rule that partnership interests or shares of limited liability companies are not Article 8 securities unless they are in fact dealt in or traded on securities exchanges or in securities markets. The issuer, however, may explicitly "opt-in" by specifying that the interests or shares are securities governed by Article 8. Partnership interests or shares of limited liability companies are included in the broader term "financial asset." Thus, if they are held through a securities account, the indirect holding system rules of Part 5 apply, and the interest of a person who holds them through such an account is a security entitlement.

5. Subsection (d) deals with the line between Article 3 negotiable instruments and Article 8 investment securities. It continues the rule of the prior version of Article 8 that a writing that meets the Article 8 definition is covered by Article 8 rather than Article 3, even though it also meets the definition of negotiable instrument. However, subsection (d) provides that an Article 3 negotiable instrument is a "financial asset" so that the indirect holding system rules apply if the instrument is held through a securities intermediary. This facilitates making items such as money market instruments eligible for deposit in clearing corporations.

6. Subsection (e) is included to clarify the treatment of investment products such as traded stock options, which are treated as financial assets but not securities. Thus, the indirect holding system rules of Part 5 apply, but the direct holding system rules of Parts 2, 3, and 4 do not.

7. Subsection (f) excludes commodity contracts from all of Article 8. However, the Article 9 rules on security interests in investment property do apply to security interests in commodity positions. See Section 9–115 and Comment 8 thereto. "Commodity contract" is defined in Section 9–115.

Definitional Cross References

"Clearing corporation" Section 8–102(a)(5)
"Commodity contract" Section 9–115
"Financial asset" Section 8–102(a)(9)
"Security" Section 8–102(a)(15)
"Security certificate" Section 8–102(a)(16)

§ 8104. Acquisition of security, interest therein, or financial asset; satisfaction of transfer requirement

(a) A person acquires a security or an interest therein, under this division, if either of the following applies:

(1) The person is a purchaser to whom a security is delivered pursuant to Section 8301; or

(2) The person acquires a security entitlement to the security pursuant to Section 8501.

(b) A person acquires a financial asset, other than a security, or an interest therein, under this division, if the person acquires a security entitlement to the financial asset.

(c) A person who acquires a security entitlement to a security or other financial asset has the rights specified in Chapter 5 (commencing with Section 8501), but is a purchaser of any security, security entitlement, or other financial asset held by the securities intermediary only to the extent provided in Section 8503.

(d) Unless the context shows that a different meaning is intended, a person who is required by other law, regulation, rule, or agreement to transfer, deliver, present, surrender, exchange, or otherwise put in the possession of another person a security or financial asset satisfies that requirement by causing the other person to acquire an interest in the security or financial asset pursuant to subdivision (a) or (b). *(Added by Stats.1996, c. 497 (S.B.1591), § 9, operative Jan. 1, 1997.)*

Uniform Commercial Code Comment

1. This section lists the ways in which interests in securities and other financial assets are acquired under Article 8. In that sense, it describes the scope of Article 8. Subsection (a) describes the two ways that a person may acquire a security or interest therein under this Article: (1) by delivery (Section 8–301), and (2) by acquiring a security entitlement. Each of these methods is described in detail in the relevant substantive provisions of this Article. Part 3, beginning with the definition of "delivery" in Section 8–301, describes how interests in securities are acquired in the direct holding system. Part 5, beginning with the rules of Section 8–501 on how security entitlements are acquired, describes how interests in securities are acquired in the indirect holding system.

Subsection (b) specifies how a person may acquire an interest under Article 8 in a financial asset other than a security. This Article deals with financial assets other than securities only insofar as they are held in the indirect holding system. For example, a bankers' acceptance falls within the definition of "financial asset," so if it is held through a securities account the entitlement holder's right to it is a security entitlement governed by Part 5. The bankers' acceptance itself, however, is a negotiable instrument governed by Article 3, not by Article 8. Thus, the provisions of Parts 2, 3, and 4 of this Article that deal with the rights of direct holders of securities are not applicable. Article 3, not Article 8, specifies how one acquires a direct interest in a bankers' acceptance. If a bankers' acceptance is delivered to a clearing corporation to be held for the account of the clearing corporation's participants, the clearing corporation becomes the holder of the bankers' acceptance under the Article 3 rules specifying how negotiable instruments are transferred. The rights of the clearing corporation's participants, however, are governed by Part 5 of this Article.

2. The distinction in usage in Article 8 between the term "security" (and its correlatives "security certificate" and "uncertificated security") on the one hand, and "security entitlement" on the other, corresponds to the distinction between the direct and indirect holding systems. For example, with respect to certificated securities that can be held either directly or through intermediaries, obtaining possession of a security certificate and acquiring a security entitlement are both means of holding the underlying security. For many other purposes, there is no need to draw a distinction between the means of holding. For purposes of commercial law analysis, however, the form of holding may make a difference. Where an item of property can be held in different ways, the rules on how one deals with it, including how one transfers it or how one grants a security interest in it, differ depending on the form of holding.

Although a security entitlement is means of holding the underlying security or other financial asset, a person who has a security entitlement does not have any direct claim to a specific asset in the possession of the securities intermediary. Subsection (c) provides explicitly that a person who acquires a security entitlement is a "purchaser" of any security, security entitlement, or other financial asset held by the securities intermediary only in the sense that under Section 8–503 a security entitlement is treated as a *sui generis* form of property interest.

3. Subsection (d) is designed to ensure that parties will retain their expected legal rights and duties under Revised Article 8. One of the major changes made by the revision is that the rules for the indirect holding system are stated in terms of the "security entitlements" held by investors, rather than speaking of them as holding direct interests in securities. Subsection (d) is designed as a translation rule to eliminate problems of co-ordination of terminology, and facilitate the continued use of systems for the efficient handling of securities and financial assets through securities intermediaries and clearing corporations. The efficiencies of a securities intermediary or clearing corporation are, in part, dependent on the ability to transfer securities credited to securities accounts in the intermediary or clearing corporation to the account of an issuer, its agent, or other person by book entry in a manner that permits exchanges, redemptions, conversions, and other transactions (which may be governed by pre-existing or new agreements, constitutional documents, or other instruments) to occur and to avoid the need to withdraw from immobilization in an intermediary or clearing corporation physical securities in order to deliver them for such purposes. Existing corporate charters, indentures and like documents may require the "presentation," "surrender," "delivery," or "transfer" of securities or security certificates for purposes of exchange, redemption, conversion or other reason. Likewise, documents may use a wide variety of terminology to describe, in the context for example of a tender or exchange offer, the means of putting the offeror or the issuer or its agent in possession of the security. Subsection (d) takes the place of provisions of prior law which could be used to reach the legal conclusion that book-entry transfers are equivalent to physical delivery to the person to whose account the book entry is credited.

Definitional Cross References

"Delivery"   Section 8–301
"Financial asset"   Section 8–102(a)(9)
"Person"   Section 1–201(30)
"Purchaser"   Sections 1–201(33) & 8–116
"Security"   Section 8–102(a)(15)
"Security entitlement"   Section 8–102(a)(17)

§ 8105. Adverse claims; notice

(a) A person has notice of an adverse claim if any of the following applies:

(1) The person knows of the adverse claim.

(2) The person is aware of facts sufficient to indicate that there is a significant probability that the adverse claim exists and deliberately avoids information that would establish the existence of the adverse claim.

(3) The person has a duty, imposed by statute or regulation, to investigate whether an adverse claim exists, and the investigation so required would establish the existence of the adverse claim.

(b) Having knowledge that a financial asset or interest therein is or has been transferred by a representative imposes no duty of inquiry into the rightfulness of a transaction and is not notice of an adverse claim. However, a person who knows that a representative has transferred a financial asset or interest therein in a transaction that is, or whose proceeds are being used, for the individual benefit of the representative or otherwise in breach of duty has notice of an adverse claim.

(c) An act or event that creates a right to immediate performance of the principal obligation represented by a security certificate or sets a date on or after which the certificate is to be presented or surrendered for redemption or exchange does not itself constitute notice of an adverse claim except in the case of a transfer more than either of the following:

(1) One year after a date set for presentment or surrender for redemption or exchange.

(2) Six months after a date set for payment of money against presentation or surrender of the certificate, if money was available for payment on that date.

(d) A purchaser of a certificated security has notice of an adverse claim if the security certificate is any of the following:

(1) Whether in bearer or registered form, has been endorsed "for collection" or "for surrender" or for some other purpose not involving transfer.

(2) Is in bearer form and has on it an unambiguous statement that it is the property of a person other than the transferor, but the mere writing of a name on the certificate is not such a statement.

(e) Filing of a financing statement under Division 9 (commencing with Section 9101) is not notice of an adverse claim to a financial asset. *(Added by Stats.1996, c. 497 (S.B.1591), § 9, operative Jan. 1, 1997.)*

Uniform Commercial Code Comment

1. The rules specifying whether adverse claims can be asserted against persons who acquire securities or security entitlements, Sections 8–303, 8–502, and 8–510, provide that one is protected against an adverse claim only if one takes without notice of the claim. This section defines notice of an adverse claim.

The general Article 1 definition of "notice" in Section 1–201(25)—which provides that a person has notice of a fact if "from all the facts and circumstances known to him at the time in question he has reason to know that it exists"—does not apply to the interpretation of "notice of adverse claims." The Section 1–201(25) definition of "notice" does, however, apply to usages of that term and its cognates in Article 8 in contexts other than notice of adverse claims.

2. This section must be interpreted in light of the definition of "adverse claim" in Section 8–102(a)(1). "Adverse claim" does not include all circumstances in which a third party has a property interest in securities, but only those situations where a security is transferred in violation of the claimant's property interest. Therefore, awareness that someone other than the transferor has a property interest is not notice of an adverse claim. The transferee must be aware that the transfer violates the other party's property interest. If A holds securities in which B has some form of property interest, and A transfers the securities to C, C may know that B has an interest, but infer that A is acting in accordance with A's obligations to B. The mere fact that C knew that B had a property interest does not mean that C had notice of an adverse claim. Whether C had notice of an adverse claim depends on whether C had sufficient awareness that A was acting in violation of B's property rights. The rule in subsection (b) is a particularization of this general principle.

3. Paragraph (a)(1) provides that a person has notice of an adverse claim if the person has knowledge of the adverse claim. Knowledge is defined in Section 1–201(25) as actual knowledge.

4. Paragraph (a)(2) provides that a person has notice of an adverse claim if the person is aware of a significant probability that an adverse claim exists and deliberately avoids information that might establish the existence of the adverse claim. This is intended to codify the "willful blindness" test that has been applied in such cases. See *May v. Chapman*, 16 M. & W. 355, 153 Eng. Rep. 1225 (1847); *Goodman v. Simonds*, 61 U.S. 343 (1857).

The first prong of the willful blindness test of paragraph (a)(2) turns on whether the person is aware facts sufficient to indicate that there is a significant probability that an adverse claim exists. The "awareness" aspect necessarily turns on the actor's state of mind. Whether facts known to a person make the person aware of a "significant probability" that an adverse claim exists turns on facts about the world and the conclusions that would be drawn from those facts, taking account of the experience and position of the person in question. A particular set of facts might indicate a significant probability of an adverse claim to a professional with considerable experience in the usual methods and procedures by which securities transactions are conducted, even though the same facts would not indicate a significant probability of an adverse claim to a non-professional.

The second prong of the willful blindness test of paragraph (a)(2) turns on whether the person "deliberately avoids information" that would establish the existence of the adverse claim. The test is the character of the person's response to the information the person has. The question is whether the person deliberately failed to seek further information because of concern that suspicions would be confirmed.

Application of the "deliberate avoidance" test to a transaction by an organization focuses on the knowledge and the actions of the individual or individuals conducting the transaction on behalf of the organization. Thus, an organization that purchases a security is not willfully blind to an adverse claim unless the officers or agents who conducted that purchase transaction are willfully blind to the adverse claim. Under the two prongs of the willful blindness test, the individual or individuals conducting a transaction must know of facts indicating a substantial probability that the adverse claim exists and deliberately fail to seek further information that might confirm or refute the indication. For this purpose, information known to individuals within an organization who are not conducting or aware of a transaction, but not forwarded to the individuals conducting the transaction, is not pertinent in determining whether the individuals conducting the transaction had knowledge of a substantial probability of the existence of the adverse claim. Cf. Section 1–201(27). An organization may also "deliberately avoid information" if it acts to preclude or inhibit transmission of pertinent information to those individuals responsible for the conduct of purchase transactions.

5. Paragraph (a)(3) provides that a person has notice of an adverse claim if the person would have learned of the adverse claim by conducting an investigation that is required by other statute or regulation. This rule applies only if there is some other statute or regulation that explicitly requires persons dealing with securities to conduct some investigation. The federal securities laws require that brokers and banks, in certain specified circumstances, check with a stolen securities registry to determine whether securities offered for sale or pledge have been reported as stolen. If securities that were listed as stolen in the registry are taken by an institution that failed to comply with requirement to check the registry, the institution would be held to have notice of the fact that they were stolen under paragraph (a)(3). Accordingly, the institution could not qualify as a protected purchaser under Section 8–303. The same result has been reached under the prior version of Article 8. See *First Nat'l Bank of Cicero v. Lewco Securities*, 860 F.2d 1407 (7th Cir. 1988).

6. Subsection (b) provides explicitly for some situations involving purchase from one described or identifiable as a representative. Knowledge of the existence of the representative relation is not enough in itself to constitute "notice of an adverse claim" that would disqualify the purchaser from protected purchaser status. A purchaser may take a security on the inference that the representative is acting properly. Knowledge that a security is being transferred to an individual account of the representative or that the proceeds of the transaction will be paid into that account is not sufficient to constitute "notice of an adverse claim," but knowledge that the proceeds will be applied to the personal indebtedness of the representative is. See *State Bank of Binghamton v. Bache*, 162 Misc. 128, 293 N.Y.S. 667 (1937).

7. Subsection (c) specifies whether a purchaser of a "stale" security is charged with notice of adverse claims, and therefore disqualified from protected purchaser status under Section 8–303. The fact of "staleness" is viewed as notice of certain defects after the lapse of stated periods, but the maturity of the security does not operate automatically to affect holders' rights. The periods of time here stated are shorter than those appearing in the provisions of this Article on staleness as notice of defects or defenses of an issuer (Section 8–203) since a purchaser who takes a security after funds or other securities are available for its redemption has more reason to suspect claims of ownership than issuer's defenses. An owner will normally turn in a security rather than transfer it at such a time. Of itself, a default never constitutes notice of a possible adverse claim. To provide otherwise would not tend to drive defaulted securities home and would serve only to disrupt current financial markets where many defaulted securities are actively traded. Unpaid or overdue coupons attached to a bond do not bring it within the operation of this subsection, though they may be relevant under the general test of notice of adverse claims in subsection (a).

8. Subsection (d) provides the owner of a certificated security with a means of protection while a security certificate is being sent in for redemption or exchange. The owner may endorse it "for collection" or "for surrender," and this constitutes notice of the owner's claims, under subsection (d).

Definitional Cross References

"Adverse claim"   Section 8–102(a)(1)
"Bearer form"   Section 8–102(a)(2)
"Certificated security"   Section 8–102(a)(4)
"Financial asset"   Section 8–102(a)(9)
"Knowledge"   Section 1–201(25)
"Person"   Section 1–201(30)
"Purchaser"   Sections 1–201(33) & 8–116
"Registered form"   Section 8–102(a)(13)
"Representative"   Section 1–201(35)
"Security certificate"   Section 8–102(a)(16)

§ 8106. Control of security or security entitlement agreement

(a) A purchaser has "control" of a certificated security in bearer form if the certificated security is delivered to the purchaser.

(b) A purchaser has "control" of a certificated security in registered form if the certificated security is delivered to the purchaser, and either of the following applies:

(1) The certificate is endorsed to the purchaser or in blank by an effective endorsement.

(2) The certificate is registered in the name of the purchaser, upon original issue or registration of transfer by the issuer.

(c) A purchaser has "control" of an uncertificated security if either of the following applies:

(1) The uncertificated security is delivered to the purchaser; or

(2) The issuer has agreed that it will comply with instructions originated by the purchaser without further consent by the registered owner.

(d) A purchaser has "control" of a security entitlement if either of the following applies:

(1) The purchaser becomes the entitlement holder.

(2) The securities intermediary has agreed that it will comply with entitlement orders originated by the purchaser without further consent by the entitlement holder.

(e) If an interest in a security entitlement is granted by the entitlement holder to the entitlement holder's own securities intermediary, the securities intermediary has control.

(f) A purchaser who has satisfied the requirements of paragraph (2) of subdivision (c) or paragraph (2) of subdivision (d) has control even if the registered owner in the case of paragraph (2) of subdivision (c) or the entitlement holder in the case of paragraph (2) of subdivision (d) retains the right to make substitutions for the uncertificated security or security entitlement, to originate instructions or entitlement orders to the issuer or securities intermediary, or otherwise to deal with the uncertificated security or security entitlement.

(g) An issuer or a securities intermediary may not enter into an agreement of the kind described in paragraph (2) of subdivision (c) or paragraph (2) of subdivision (d) without the consent of the registered owner or entitlement holder, but an issuer or a securities intermediary is not required to enter into such an agreement even though the registered owner or entitlement holder so directs. An issuer or securities intermediary that has entered into such an agreement is not required to confirm the existence of the agreement to another party unless requested to do so by the registered owner or entitlement holder. *(Added by Stats. 1996, c. 497 (S.B.1591), § 9, operative Jan. 1, 1997.)*

Uniform Commercial Code Comment

1. The concept of "control" plays a key role in various provisions dealing with the rights of purchasers, including secured parties. See Sections 8–303 (protected purchasers); 8–503(e) (purchasers from securities intermediaries); 8–510 (purchasers of security entitlements from entitlement holders); 9–115(4) (perfection of security interests); 9–115(5) (priorities among conflicting security interests).

Obtaining "control" means that the purchaser has taken whatever steps are necessary, given the manner in which the securities are held, to place itself in a position where it can have the securities sold, without further action by the owner.

2. Subsection (a) provides that a purchaser obtains "control" with respect to a certificated security in bearer form by taking "delivery," as defined in Section 8–301. Subsection (b) provides that a purchaser obtains "control" with respect to a certificated security in registered form by taking "delivery," as defined in Section 8–301, provided that the security certificate has been indorsed to the purchaser or in blank. Section 8–301 provides that delivery of a certificated security occurs when the purchaser obtains possession of the security certificate, or when an agent for the purchaser (other than a securities intermediary) either acquires possession or acknowledges that the agent holds for the purchaser.

3. Subsection (c) specifies the means by which a purchaser can obtain control over uncertificated securities which the transferor holds directly. Two mechanisms are possible.

Under subsection (c)(1), securities can be "delivered" to a purchaser. Section 8–301(b) provides that "delivery" of an uncertificated security occurs when the purchaser becomes the registered holder. So far as the issuer is concerned, the purchaser would then be entitled to exercise all rights of ownership. See Section 8–207. As between the parties to a purchase transaction, however, the rights of the purchaser are determined by their contract. Cf. Section 9–202. Arrangements covered by this paragraph are analogous to arrangements in which bearer certificates are delivered to a secured party—so far as the issuer or any other parties are concerned, the secured party appears to be the outright owner, although it is in fact holding as collateral property that belongs to the debtor.

Under subsection (c)(2), a purchaser has control if the issuer has agreed to act on the instructions of the purchaser, even though the owner remains listed as the registered owner. The issuer, of course, would be acting wrongfully against the registered owner if it entered into such an agreement without the consent of the registered owner. Subsection (g) makes this point explicit. The subsection (c)(2) provision makes it possible for issuers to offer a service akin to the registered pledge device of the 1978 version of Article 8, without mandating that all issuers offer that service.

4. Subsection (d) specifies the means by which a purchaser can obtain control over a security entitlement. Two mechanisms are possible, analogous to those provided in subsection (c) for uncertificated securities. Under subsection (d)(1), a purchaser has control if it is the entitlement holder. This subsection would apply whether the purchaser holds through the same intermediary that the debtor used, or has the securities position transferred to its own intermediary.

Subsection (d)(2) provides that a purchaser has control if the securities intermediary has agreed to act on entitlement orders originated by the purchaser, even though the transferor remains listed as the entitlement holder. This section specifies only the minimum requirements that such an arrangement must meet to confer "control"; the details of the arrangement can be specified by agreement. The arrangement might cover all of the positions in a particular account or subaccount, or only specified positions. There is no requirement that the control party's right to give entitlement orders be exclusive. The arrangement might provide that only the control party can give entitlement orders, or that either the entitlement holder or the control party can give entitlement orders. See subsection (f).

The following examples illustrate the rules of subsection (d):

Example 1. Debtor grants Alpha Bank a security interest in 1000 shares of XYZ Co. stock that Debtor holds through an account with Able & Co. Alpha Bank also has an account with Able. Debtor instructs Able to transfer the shares to Alpha Bank, and Able does so. Alpha Bank has control of the 1000 shares under subsection (d)(1), because Alpha Bank is the entitlement holder.

Example 2. Debtor grants Alpha Bank a security interest in 1000 shares of XYZ Co. stock that Debtor holds through an account with Able & Co. Alpha Bank does not have an account with Able. Alpha Bank uses Beta Bank as its securities custodian. Debtor instructs Able to transfer the shares to Beta Bank, for the account of Alpha Bank, and Able does so. Alpha Bank has control of the 1000 shares under subsection (d)(1), because Alpha Bank is the entitlement holder.

Example 3. Debtor grants Alpha Bank a security interest in 1000 shares of XYZ Co. stock that Debtor holds through an account with Able & Co. Debtor, Able, and Alpha Bank enter into an agreement under which Debtor will continue to receive dividends and distributions, and will continue to have the right to direct dispositions, but Alpha Bank also has the right to direct dispositions. Alpha Bank has control of the 1000 shares under subsection (d)(2).

Example 4. Able & Co., a securities dealer, grants Alpha Bank a security interest in 1000 shares of XYZ Co. stock that Able holds through an account with Clearing Corporation. Able causes Clearing Corporation to transfer the shares into Alpha Bank's account at Clearing Corporation. Alpha Bank has control of the 1000 shares under subsection (d)(1).

Example 5. Able & Co., a securities dealer, grants Alpha Bank a security interest in 1000 shares of XYZ Co. stock that Able holds through an account with Clearing Corporation. Alpha Bank does not have an account with Clearing Corporation. It holds its securities through Beta Bank, which does have an account with Clearing Corporation. Able causes Clearing Corporation to transfer the shares into Beta Bank's account at Clearing Corporation. Beta Bank credits the position to Alpha Bank's account with Beta Bank. Alpha Bank has control of the 1000 shares under subsection (d)(1).

Example 6. Able & Co. a securities dealer, grants Alpha Bank a security interest in 1000 shares of XYZ Co. stock that Able holds through an account with Clearing Corporation. Able causes Clearing Corporation to transfer the shares into a pledge account, pursuant to an agreement under which Able will continue to receive dividends, distributions, and the like, but Alpha Bank has the right to direct dispositions. Alpha Bank has control of the 1000 shares under subsection (d)(2).

Example 7. Able & Co. a securities dealer, grants Alpha Bank a security interest in 1000 shares of XYZ Co. stock that Able holds through an account with Clearing Corporation. Able, Alpha, and Clearing Corporation enter into an agreement under which Clearing Corporation will act on instructions from Alpha with respect to the XYZ Co. stock carried in Able's account, but Able will continue to receive dividends, distributions, and the like, and will also have the right to direct dispositions. Alpha Bank has control of the 1000 shares under subsection (d)(2).

Example 8. Able & Co. a securities dealer, holds a wide range of securities through its account at Clearing Corporation. Able enters into an arrangement with Alpha Bank pursuant to which Alpha provides financing to Able secured by securities identified as the collateral on lists provided by Able to Alpha on a daily or other periodic basis. Able, Alpha, and Clearing Corporation enter into an agreement under which Clearing Corporation agrees that if at any time Alpha directs Clearing Corporation to do so, Clearing Corporation will transfer any securities from Able's account at Alpha's instructions. Because Clearing Corporation has agreed to act on Alpha's instructions with respect to any securities carried in Able's account, at the moment that Alpha's security interest attaches to securities listed by Able, Alpha obtains control of those securities under subsection (d)(2). There is no requirement that Clearing Corporation be informed of which securities Able has pledged to Alpha.

5. For a purchaser to have "control" under subsection (c)(2) or (d)(2), it is essential that the issuer or securities intermediary, as the case may be, actually be a party to the agreement. If a debtor gives a secured party a power of attorney authorizing the secured party to act in the name of the debtor, but the issuer or securities intermediary does not specifically agree to this arrangement, the secured party does not have "control" within the meaning of subsection (c)(2) or (d)(2) because the issuer or securities intermediary is not a party to the agreement. The secured party does not have control under subsection (c)(1) or (d)(1) because, although the power of attorney might give the secured party authority to act on the debtor's behalf as an agent, the secured party has not actually become the registered owner or entitlement holder.

6. Subsection (e) provides that if an interest in a security entitlement is granted by an entitlement holder to the securities intermediary through which the security entitlement is maintained, the securities intermediary has control. A common transaction covered by this provision is a margin loan from a broker to its customer.

7. The term "control" is used in a particular defined sense. The requirements for obtaining control are set out in this section. The concept is not to be interpreted by reference to similar concepts in other bodies of law. In particular, the requirements for "possession" derived from the common law of pledge are not to be used as a basis for interpreting subsection (c)(2) or (d)(2). Those provisions are designed to supplant the concepts of "constructive possession" and the like. A principal purpose of the "control" concept is to eliminate the uncertainty and confusion that results from attempting to apply common law possession concepts to modern securities holding practices.

The key to the control concept is that the purchaser has the present ability to have the securities sold or transferred without further action by the transferor. There is no requirement that the powers held by the purchaser be exclusive. For example, in a secured lending arrangement, if the secured party wishes, it can allow the debtor to retain the right to make substitutions, or to direct the disposition of the uncertificated security or security entitlement. Subsection (f) is included to make clear the general point stated in subsection (c) that the test of control is whether the purchaser has obtained the requisite power, not whether the debtor has retained other powers. There is no implication that retention by the debtor of powers other than those mentioned in subsection (f) is inconsistent with the purchaser having control.

Definitional Cross References

"Bearer form" Section 8–102(a)(2)
"Certificated security" Section 8–102(a)(4)
"Delivery" Section 8–301
"Effective" Section 8–107
"Entitlement holder" Section 8–102(a)(7)
"Entitlement order" Section 8–102(a)(8)
"Indorsement" Section 8–102(a)(11)
"Instruction" Section 8–102(a)(12)
"Purchaser" Sections 1–201(33) & 8–116
"Registered form" Section 8–102(a)(13)
"Securities intermediary" Section 8–102(a)(14)
"Security entitlement" Section 8–102(a)(17)
"Uncertificated security" Section 8–102(a)(18)

§ 8107. Appropriate person; effective endorsement, instruction or entitlement

(a) "Appropriate person" means any of the following:

(1) With respect to an endorsement, the person specified by a security certificate or by an effective special endorsement to be entitled to the security.

(2) With respect to an instruction, the registered owner of an uncertificated security.

(3) With respect to an entitlement order, the entitlement holder.

(4) If the person designated in paragraph (1), (2), or (3) is deceased, the designated person's successor taking under other law or the designated person's personal representative acting for the estate of the decedent.

(5) If the person designated in paragraph (1), (2), or (3) lacks capacity, the designated person's guardian, conservator, or other similar representative who has power under other law to transfer the security or financial asset.

(b) An endorsement, instruction, or entitlement order is effective if it is made by any of the following:

(1) It is made by the appropriate person.

(2) It is made by a person who has power under the law of agency to transfer the security or financial asset on behalf of the appropriate person, including, in the case of an instruction or entitlement order, a person who has control under paragraph (2) of subdivision (c) or paragraph (2) of subdivision (d) of Section 8106.

(3) The appropriate person has ratified it or is otherwise precluded from asserting its ineffectiveness.

(c) An endorsement, instruction, or entitlement order made by a representative is effective even if:

(1) The representative has failed to comply with a controlling instrument or with the law of the state having jurisdiction of the representative relationship, including any law requiring the representative to obtain court approval of the transaction.

(2) The representative's action in making the endorsement, instruction, or entitlement order or using the proceeds of the transaction is otherwise a breach of duty.

(d) If a security is registered in the name of or specially endorsed to a person described as a representative, or if a securities account is maintained in the name of a person described as a representative, an endorsement, instruction, or entitlement order made by the person is effective even though the person is no longer serving in the described capacity.

(e) Effectiveness of an endorsement, instruction, or entitlement order is determined as of the date the endorsement, instruction, or entitlement order is made, and an endorsement, instruction, or entitlement order does not become ineffective by reason of any later change of circumstances. *(Added by Stats.1996, c. 497 (S.B.1591), § 9, operative Jan. 1, 1997.)*

Uniform Commercial Code Comment

1. This section defines two concepts, "appropriate person" and "effective." Effectiveness is a broader concept than appropriate person. For example, if a security or securities account is registered in the name of Mary Roe, Mary Roe is the "appropriate person," but an indorsement, instruction, or entitlement order made by John Doe is "effective" if, under agency or other law, Mary Roe is precluded from denying Doe's authority. Treating these two concepts separately facilitates statement of the rules of Article 8 that state the legal effect of an indorsement, instruction, or entitlement order. For example, a securities intermediary is protected against liability if it acts on an effective entitlement order, but has a duty to comply with an entitlement order only if it is originated by an appropriate person. See Sections 8–115 and 8–507.

One important application of the "effectiveness" concept is in the direct holding system rules on the rights of purchasers. A purchaser of a certificated security in registered form can qualify as a protected purchaser who takes free from adverse claims under Section 8–303 only if the purchaser obtains "control." Section 8–106 provides that a purchaser of a certificated security in registered form obtains control if there has been an "effective" indorsement.

2. Subsection (a) provides that the term "appropriate person" covers two categories: (1) the person who is actually designated as the person entitled to the security or security entitlement, and (2) the successor or legal representative of that person if that person has died or otherwise lacks capacity. Other law determines who has power to transfer a security on behalf of a person who lacks capacity. For example, if securities are registered in the name of more than one person and one of the designated persons dies, whether the survivor is the appropriate person depends on the form of tenancy. If the two were registered joint tenants with right of survivorship, the survivor would have that power under other law and thus would be the "appropriate person." If securities are registered in the name of an individual and the individual dies, the law of decedents' estates determines who has power to transfer the decedent's securities. That would ordinarily be the executor or administrator, but if a "small estate statute" permits a widow to transfer a decedent's securities without administration proceedings, she would be the appropriate person. If the registration of a security or a securities account contains a designation of a death beneficiary under the Uniform Transfer on Death Security Registration Act or comparable legislation, the designated beneficiary would, under that law, have power to transfer upon the person's death and so would be the appropriate person. Article 8 does not contain a list of such representatives, because any list is likely to become outdated by developments in other law.

3. Subsection (b) sets out the general rule that an indorsement, instruction, or entitlement order is effective if it is made by the appropriate person or by a person who has power to transfer under agency law or if the appropriate person is precluded from denying its effectiveness. The control rules in Section 8–106 provide for arrangements where a person who holds securities through a securities intermediary, or holds uncertificated securities directly, enters into a control agreement giving the secured party the right to initiate entitlement orders of instructions. Paragraph 2 of subsection (b) states explicitly that an entitlement order or instruction initiated by a person who has obtained such a control agreement is "effective."

Subsections (c), (d), and (e) supplement the general rule of subsection (b) on effectiveness. The term "representative," used in subsections (c) and (d), is defined in Section 1–201(35).

4. Subsection (c) provides that an indorsement, instruction, or entitlement order made by a representative is effective even though the representative's action is a violation of duties. The following example illustrates this subsection:

Example 1. Certificated securities are registered in the name of John Doe. Doe dies and Mary Roe is appointed executor. Roe indorses the security certificate and transfers it to a purchaser in a transaction that is a violation of her duties as executor.

Roe's indorsement is effective, because Roe is the appropriate person under subsection (a)(4). This is so even though Roe's transfer violated her obligations as executor. The policies of free transferability of securities that underlie Article 8 dictate that neither a purchaser to whom Roe transfers the securities nor the issuer who registers transfer should be required to investigate the terms of the will to determine whether Roe is acting properly. Although Roe's indorsement is effective under this section, her breach of duty may be such that her beneficiary has an adverse claim to the securities that Roe transferred. The question whether that adverse claim can be asserted against purchasers is governed not by this section but by Section 8–303. Under Section 8–404, the issuer has no duties to an adverse claimant unless the claimant obtains legal process enjoining the issuer from registering transfer.

5. Subsection (d) deals with cases where a security or a securities account is registered in the name of a person specifically designated as a representative. The following example illustrates this subsection:

Example 2. Certificated securities are registered in the name of "John Jones, trustee of the Smith Family Trust." John Jones is removed as trustee and Martha Moe is appointed successor trustee. The securities, however, are not reregistered, but remain registered in the name of "John Jones, trustee of the Smith Family Trust." Jones indorses the security certificate and transfers it to a purchaser.

Subsection (d) provides that an indorsement by John Jones as trustee is effective even though Jones is no longer serving in that capacity. Since the securities were registered in the name of "John Jones, trustee of the Smith Family Trust," a purchaser, or the issuer when called upon to register transfer, should be entitled to assume without further inquiry that Jones has the power to act as trustee for the Smith Family Trust.

Note that subsection (d) does not apply to a case where the security or securities account is registered in the name of principal rather than the representative as such. The following example illustrates this point:

Example 3. Certificated securities are registered in the name of John Doe. John Doe dies and Mary Roe is appointed executor. The securities are not reregistered in the name of Mary Roe as executor. Later, Mary Roe is removed as executor and Martha Moe is appointed as her successor. After being removed, Mary Roe indorses the security certificate that is registered in the name of John Doe and transfers it to a purchaser.

Mary Roe's indorsement is not made effective by subsection (d), because the securities were not registered in the name of Mary Roe as representative. A purchaser or the issuer registering transfer should be required to determine whether Roe has power to act for John Doe. Purchasers and issuers can protect themselves in such cases by requiring signature guarantees. See Section 8–306.

6. Subsection (e) provides that the effectiveness of an indorsement, instruction, or entitlement order is determined as of the date it is made. The following example illustrates this subsection:

Example 4. Certificated securities are registered in the name of John Doe. John Doe dies and Mary Roe is appointed executor. Mary Roe indorses the security certificate that is registered in the name of John Doe and transfers it to a purchaser. After the indorsement and transfer, but before the security certificate is presented to the issuer for registration of transfer, Mary Roe is removed as executor and Martha Moe is appointed as her successor.

Mary Roe's indorsement is effective, because at the time Roe indorsed she was the appropriate person under subsection (a)(4). Her later removal as executor does not render the indorsement ineffective. Accordingly, the issuer would not be liable for registering the transfer. See Section 8–404.

Definitional Cross References

"Entitlement order"   Section 8–102(a)(8)
"Financial asset"   Section 8–102(a)(9)
"Indorsement"   Section 8–102(a)(11)
"Instruction"   Section 8–102(a)(12)
"Representative"   Section 1–201(35)
"Securities account"   Section 8–501
"Security"   Section 8–102(a)(15)
"Security certificate"   Section 8–102(a)(16)
"Security entitlement"   Section 8–102(a)(17)
"Uncertificated security"   Section 8–102(a)(18)

§ 8108. Transfer of certificated security or endorsement; warranties

(a) A person who transfers a certificated security to a purchaser for value warrants to the purchaser, and an endorser, if the transfer is by endorsement, warrants to any subsequent purchaser, all of the following:

(1) The certificate is genuine and has not been materially altered.

(2) The transferor or endorser does not know of any fact that might impair the validity of the security.

(3) There is no adverse claim to the security.

(4) The transfer does not violate any restriction on transfer.

(5) If the transfer is by endorsement, the endorsement is made by an appropriate person, or if the endorsement is by an agent, the agent has actual authority to act on behalf of the appropriate person.

(6) The transfer is otherwise effective and rightful.

(b) A person who originates an instruction for registration of transfer of an uncertificated security to a purchaser for value warrants to the purchaser all of the following:

(1) The instruction is made by an appropriate person, or if the instruction is by an agent, the agent has actual authority to act on behalf of the appropriate person.

(2) The security is valid.

(3) There is no adverse claim to the security.

(4) At the time the instruction is presented to the issuer, all of the following will be applicable:

(A) The purchaser will be entitled to the registration of transfer.

(B) The transfer will be registered by the issuer free from all liens, security interests, restrictions, and claims other than those specified in the instruction.

(C) The transfer will not violate any restriction on transfer.

(D) The requested transfer will otherwise be effective and rightful.

(c) A person who transfers an uncertificated security to a purchaser for value and does not originate an instruction in connection with the transfer warrants all of the following:

(1) The uncertificated security is valid.

(2) There is no adverse claim to the security.

(3) The transfer does not violate any restriction on transfer.

(4) The transfer is otherwise effective and rightful.

(d) A person who endorses a security certificate warrants all of the following to the issuer:

(1) There is no adverse claim to the security.

(2) The endorsement is effective.

(e) A person who originates an instruction for registration of transfer of an uncertificated security warrants all of the following to the issuer:

(1) The instruction is effective.

(2) At the time the instruction is presented to the issuer the purchaser will be entitled to the registration of transfer.

(f) A person who presents a certificated security for registration of transfer or for payment or exchange warrants to the issuer that the person is entitled to the registration, payment, or exchange, but a purchaser for value and without notice of adverse claims to whom transfer is registered warrants only that the person has no knowledge of any unauthorized signature in a necessary endorsement.

(g) If a person acts as agent of another in delivering a certificated security to a purchaser, the identity of the principal was known to the person to whom the certificate was delivered, and the certificate delivered by the agent was received by the agent from the principal or received by the agent from another person at the direction of the principal, the person delivering the security certificate warrants only that the delivering person has authority to act for the principal and does not know of any adverse claim to the certificated security.

(h) A secured party who redelivers a security certificate received, or after payment and on order of the debtor delivers the security certificate to another person, makes only the warranties of an agent under subdivision (g).

(i) Except as otherwise provided in subdivision (g), a broker acting for a customer makes to the issuer and a purchaser the warranties provided in subdivisions (a) to (f), inclusive. A broker that delivers a security certificate to its customer, or causes its customer to be registered as the owner of an uncertificated security, makes to the customer the warranties provided in subdivision (a) or (b), and has the rights and privileges of a purchaser under this section. The warranties of and in favor of the broker acting as an agent are in addition to applicable warranties given by and in favor of the customer. *(Added by Stats.1996, c. 497 (S.B. 1591), § 9, operative Jan. 1, 1997.)*

Uniform Commercial Code Comment

1. Subsections (a), (b), and (c) deal with warranties by security transferors to purchasers. Subsections (d) and (e) deal with warranties by security transferors to issuers. Subsection (f) deals with presentment warranties.

2. Subsection (a) specifies the warranties made by a person who transfers a certificated security to a purchaser for value. Paragraphs (3), (4), and (5) make explicit several key points that are implicit in the general warranty of paragraph (6) that the transfer is effective and rightful. Subsection (b) sets forth the warranties made to a purchaser for value by one who originates an instruction. These warranties are quite similar to those made by one transferring a certificated security, subsection (a), the principal difference being the absolute warranty of validity. If upon receipt of the instruction the issuer should dispute the validity of the security, the burden of proving validity is upon the transferor. Subsection (c) provides for the limited circumstances in which an uncertificated security could be transferred without an instruction, see Section 8–301(b)(2). Subsections (d) and (e) give the issuer the benefit of the warranties of an indorser or originator on those matters not within the issuer's knowledge.

3. Subsection (f) limits the warranties made by a purchaser for value without notice whose presentation of a security certificate is defective in some way but to whom the issuer does register transfer. The effect is to deny the issuer a remedy against such a person unless at the time of presentment the person had knowledge of an unauthorized signature in a necessary indorsement. The issuer can protect itself by refusing to make the transfer or, if it registers the transfer before it discovers the defect, by pursuing its remedy against a signature guarantor.

4. Subsection (g) eliminates all substantive warranties in the relatively unusual case of a delivery of certificated security by an agent of a disclosed principal where the agent delivers the exact certificate that it received from or for the principal. Subsection (h) limits the warranties given by a secured party who redelivers a certificate. Subsection (i) specifies the warranties of brokers in the more common scenarios.

5. Under Section 1–102(3) the warranty provisions apply "unless otherwise agreed" and the parties may enter into express agreements to allocate the risks of possible defects. Usual estoppel principles apply with respect to transfers of both certificated and uncertificated securities whenever the purchaser has knowledge of the defect, and these warranties will not be breached in such a case.

Definitional Cross References

"Adverse claim" Section 8–102(a)(1)
"Appropriate person" Section 8–107
"Broker" Section 8–102(a)(3)
"Certificated security" Section 8–102(a)(4)
"Indorsement" Section 8–102(a)(11)
"Instruction" Section 8–102(a)(12)
"Issuer" Section 8–201
"Person" Section 1–201(30)
"Purchaser" Sections 1–201(33) & 8–116
"Secured party" Section 9–105(1)(m)
"Security"Section 8–102(a)(15)
"Security certificate" Section 8–102(a)(16)
"Uncertificated security" Section 8–102(a)(18)
"Value" Sections 1–201(44) & 8–116

§ 8109. Entitlement orders; security account credits; warranties

(a) A person who originates an entitlement order to a securities intermediary warrants all of the following to the securities intermediary:

(1) The entitlement order is made by an appropriate person, or if the entitlement order is by an agent, the agent has actual authority to act on behalf of the appropriate person.

(2) There is no adverse claim to the security entitlement.

(b) A person who delivers a security certificate to a securities intermediary for credit to a securities account or originates an instruction with respect to an uncertificated security directing that the uncertificated security be credited to a securities account makes to the securities intermediary the warranties specified in subdivision (a) or (b) of Section 8108.

(c) If a securities intermediary delivers a security certificate to its entitlement holder or causes its entitlement holder to be registered as the owner of an uncertificated security, the securities intermediary makes to the entitlement holder the warranties specified in subdivision (a) or (b) of Section 8108. *(Added by Stats.1996, c. 497 (S.B.1591), § 9, operative Jan. 1, 1997.)*

Uniform Commercial Code Comment

1. Subsection (a) provides that a person who originates an entitlement order warrants to the securities intermediary that the order is authorized, and warrants the absence of adverse claims. Subsection (b) specifies the warranties that are given when a person who holds securities directly has the holding converted into indirect form. A person who delivers a certificate to a securities intermediary or originates an instruction for an uncertificated security gives to the securities intermediary the transfer warranties under Section 8–108. If the securities intermediary in turn delivers the certificate to a higher level securities intermediary, it gives the same warranties.

2. Subsection (c) states the warranties that a securities intermediary gives when a customer who has been holding securities in an account with the securities intermediary requests that certificates be delivered or that uncertificated securities be registered in the customer's name. The warranties are the same as those that brokers make with respect to securities that the brokers sell to or buy on behalf of the customers. See Section 8–108(i).

3. As with the Section 8–108 warranties, the warranties specified in this section may be modified by agreement under Section 1–102(3).

Definitional Cross References

"Adverse claim" Section 8–102(a)(1)
"Appropriate person" Section 8–107
"Entitlement holder" Section 8–102(a)(7)
"Entitlement order" Section 8–102(a)(8)

"Instruction" Section 8–102(a)(12)
"Person" Section 1–201(30)
"Securities account" Section 8–501
"Securities intermediary" Section 8–102(a)(14)
"Security certificate" Section 8–102(a)(16)
"Uncertificated security" Section 8–102(a)(18)

§ 8110. Choice of law

(a) The local law of the issuer's jurisdiction, as specified in subdivision (d), governs the following:

(1) The validity of a security.

(2) The rights and duties of the issuer with respect to registration of transfer.

(3) The effectiveness of registration of transfer by the issuer.

(4) Whether the issuer owes any duties to an adverse claimant to a security.

(5) Whether an adverse claim can be asserted against a person to whom transfer of a certificated or uncertificated security is registered or a person who obtains control of an uncertificated security.

(b) The local law of the securities intermediary's jurisdiction, as specified in subdivision (e), governs the following:

(1) Acquisition of a security entitlement from the securities intermediary.

(2) The rights and duties of the securities intermediary and entitlement holder arising out of a security entitlement.

(3) Whether the securities intermediary owes any duties to an adverse claimant to a security entitlement.

(4) Whether an adverse claim can be asserted against a person who acquires a security entitlement from the securities intermediary or a person who purchases a security entitlement or interest therein from an entitlement holder.

(c) The local law of the jurisdiction in which a security certificate is located at the time of delivery governs whether an adverse claim can be asserted against a person to whom the security certificate is delivered.

(d) "Issuer's jurisdiction" means the jurisdiction under which the issuer of the security is organized or, if permitted by the law of that jurisdiction, the law of another jurisdiction specified by the issuer. An issuer organized under the law of this state may specify the law of another jurisdiction as the law governing the matters specified in paragraphs (2) to (5), inclusive, of subdivision (a).

(e) The following rules determine a "securities intermediary's jurisdiction" for purposes of this section:

(1) If an agreement between the securities intermediary and its entitlement holder specifies that it is governed by the law of a particular jurisdiction, that jurisdiction is the securities intermediary's jurisdiction.

(2) If an agreement between the securities intermediary and its entitlement holder does not specify the governing law as provided in paragraph (1), but expressly specifies that the securities account is maintained at an office in a particular jurisdiction, that jurisdiction is the securities intermediary's jurisdiction.

(3) If an agreement between the securities intermediary and its entitlement holder does not specify a jurisdiction as provided in paragraph (1) or (2), the securities intermediary's jurisdiction is the jurisdiction in which is located the office identified in an account statement as the office serving the entitlement holder's account.

(4) If an agreement between the securities intermediary and its entitlement holder does not specify a jurisdiction as provided in paragraph (1) or (2) and an account statement does not identify an office serving the entitlement holder's account as provided in paragraph (3), the securities intermediary's jurisdiction is the jurisdiction in which is located the chief executive office of the securities intermediary.

(f) A securities intermediary's jurisdiction is not determined by the physical location of certificates representing financial assets, or by the jurisdiction in which is organized the issuer of the financial asset with respect to which an entitlement holder has a security entitlement, or by the location of facilities for data processing or other record keeping concerning the account. *(Added by Stats.1996, c. 497 (S.B.1591), § 9, operative Jan. 1, 1997.)*

Uniform Commercial Code Comment

1. This section deals with applicability and choice of law issues concerning Article 8. The distinction between the direct and indirect holding systems plays a significant role in determining the governing law. An investor in the direct holding system is registered on the books of the issuer and/or has possession of a security certificate. Accordingly, the jurisdiction of incorporation of the issuer or location of the certificate determine the applicable law. By contrast, an investor in the indirect holding system has a security entitlement, which is a bundle of rights against the securities intermediary with respect to a security, rather than a direct interest in the underlying security. Accordingly, in the rules for the indirect holding system, the jurisdiction of incorporation of the issuer of the underlying security or the location of any certificates that might be held by the intermediary or a higher tier intermediary, do not determine the applicable law.

The phrase "local law" refers to the law of a jurisdiction other than its conflict of laws rules. See Restatement (Second) of Conflict of Laws § 4.

2. Subsection (a) provides that the law of an issuer's jurisdiction governs certain issues where the substantive rules of Article 8 determine the issuer's rights and duties. Paragraph (1) of subsection (a) provides that the law of the issuer's jurisdiction governs the validity of the security. This ensures that a single body of law will govern the questions addressed in Part 2 of Article 8, concerning the circumstances in which an issuer can and cannot assert invalidity as a defense against purchasers. Similarly, paragraphs (2), (3), and (4) of subsection (a) ensure that the issuer will be able to look to a single body of law on the questions addressed in Part 4 of Article 8, concerning the issuer's duties and liabilities with respect to registration of transfer.

Paragraph (5) of subsection (a) applies the law of an issuer's jurisdiction to the question whether an adverse claim can be asserted against a purchaser to whom transfer has been registered, or who has obtained control over an uncertificated security. Although this issue deals with the rights of persons other than the issuer, the law of the issuer's jurisdiction applies because the purchasers to whom the provision applies are those whose protection against adverse claims depends on the fact that their interests have been recorded on the books of the issuer.

The principal policy reflected in the choice of law rules in subsection (a) is that an issuer and others should be able to look to a single body of law on the matters specified in subsection (a), rather than having to look to the law of all of the different jurisdictions in which security holders may reside. The choice of law policies reflected in this subsection do not require that the body of law governing all of the matters specified in subsection (a) be that of the jurisdiction in which the issuer is incorporated. Thus, subsection (d) provides that the term "issuer's jurisdiction" means the jurisdiction in which the issuer is organized, or, if permitted by that law, the law of another jurisdiction selected by the issuer. Subsection (d) also provides that issuers organized under the law of a State which adopts this Article may make such a selection, except as to the validity issue specified in paragraph (1). The question whether an issuer can assert the defense of invalidity may implicate significant policies of the issuer's jurisdiction of incorporation. See, e.g., Section 8–202 and Comments thereto.

Although subsection (a) provides that the issuer's rights and duties concerning registration of transfer are governed by the law of the issuer's jurisdiction, other matters related to registration of transfer, such as appointment of a guardian for a registered owner or the existence of agency relationships, might be governed by another jurisdiction's law. Neither this section nor Section 1–105 deals with what law governs the appointment of the administrator or executor; that question is determined under generally applicable choice of law rules.

3. Subsection (b) provides that the law of the securities intermediary's jurisdiction governs the issues concerning the indirect holding system that are dealt with in Article 8. Paragraphs (1) and (2) cover the matters dealt with in the Article 8 rules defining the concept of security entitlement and specifying the duties of securities intermediaries. Paragraph (3) provides that the law of the security intermediary's jurisdiction determines whether the intermediary owes any duties to an adverse claimant. Paragraph (4) provides that the law of the security intermediary's jurisdiction determines whether adverse claims can be asserted against entitlement holders and others.

Subsection (e) determines what is a "securities intermediary's jurisdiction." The policy of subsection (b) is to ensure that a securities intermediary and all of its entitlement holders can look to a single, readily-identifiable body of law to determine their rights and duties. Accordingly, subsection (e) sets out a sequential series of tests to facilitate identification of that body of law. Paragraph (1) of subsection (e) permits specification of the governing law by agreement. Because the policy of this section is to enable parties to determine, in advance and with certainty, what law will apply to transactions governed by this Article, the validation of selection of governing law by agreement is not conditioned upon a determination that the jurisdiction whose law is chosen bear a "reasonable relation" to the transaction. See Section 4A–507; compare Section 1–105(1). That is also true with respect to the similar provisions in subsection (d) of this section and in Section 9–103(6).

Subsection (f) makes explicit a point that is implicit in the Article 8 description of a security entitlement as a bundle of rights against the intermediary with respect to a security or other financial asset, rather than as a direct interest in the underlying security or other financial asset. The governing law for relationships in the indirect holding system is not determined by such matters as the jurisdiction of incorporation of the issuer of the securities held through the intermediary, or the location of any physical certificates held by the intermediary or a higher tier intermediary.

4. Subsection (c) provides a choice of law rule for adverse claim issues that may arise in connection with delivery of security certificates in the direct holding system. It applies the law of the place of delivery. If a certificated security issued by an Idaho corporation is sold, and the sale is settled by physical delivery of the certificate from Seller to Buyer in New York, under subsection (c), New York law determines whether Buyer takes free from adverse claims. The domicile of Seller, Buyer, and any adverse claimant is irrelevant.

5. The following examples illustrate how a court in a jurisdiction which has enacted this section would determine the governing law:

Example 1. John Doe, a resident of Kansas, maintains a securities account with Able & Co. Able is incorporated in Delaware. Its chief executive offices are located in Illinois. The office where Doe transacts business with Able is located in Missouri. The agreement between Doe and Able specifies that it is governed by Illinois law. Through the account, Doe holds securities of a Colorado corporation, which Able holds through Clearing Corporation. The rules of Clearing Corporation provide that the rights and duties of Clearing Corporation and its participants are governed by New York law. Subsection (a) specifies that a controversy concerning the rights and duties as between the issuer and Clearing Corporation is governed by Colorado law. Subsections (b) and (e) specify that a controversy concerning the rights and duties as between the Clearing Corporation and Able is governed by New York law, and that a controversy concerning the rights and duties as between Able and Doe is governed by Illinois law.

Example 2. Same facts as to Doe and Able as in Example 1. Through the account, Doe holds securities of a Senegalese corporation, which Able holds through Clearing Corporation. Clearing Corporation's operations are located in Belgium, and its rules and agreements with its participants provide that they are governed by Belgian law. Clearing Corporation holds the securities through a custodial account at the Paris branch office of Global Bank, which is organized under English law. The agreement between Clearing Corporation and Global Bank provides that it is governed by French law. Subsection (a) specifies that a controversy concerning the rights and duties as between the issuer and Global Bank is governed by Senegalese law. Subsections (b) and (e) specify that a controversy concerning the rights and duties as between Global Bank and Clearing Corporation is governed by French law, that a controversy concerning the rights and duties as between Clearing Corporation and Able is governed by Belgian law, and that a controversy concerning the rights and duties as between Able and Doe is governed by Illinois law.

6. To the extent that this section does not specify the governing law, general choice of law rules apply. For example, suppose that in either of the examples in the preceding Comment, Doe enters into an agreement with Roe, also a resident of Kansas, in which Doe agrees to transfer all of his interests in the securities held through Able to Roe. Article 8 does not deal with whether such an agreement is enforceable or whether it gives Roe some interest in Doe's security entitlement. This section specifies what jurisdiction's law governs the issues that are dealt with in Article 8. Article 8, however, does specify that securities intermediaries have only limited duties with respect to adverse claims. See Section 8–115. Subsection (b)(3) of this section provides that Illinois law governs whether Able owes any duties to an adverse claimant. Thus, if Illinois has adopted Revised Article 8, Section 8–115 as enacted in Illinois determines whether Roe has any rights against Able.

7. The choice of law provisions concerning security interests in securities and security entitlements are set out in Section 9–103(6).

Definitional Cross References

"Adverse claim"   Section 8–102(a)(1)
"Agreement"   Section 1–201(3)
"Certificated security"   Section 8–102(a)(4)
"Entitlement holder"   Section 8–102(a)(7)
"Financial asset"   Section 8–102(a)(9)
"Issuer"   Section 8–201
"Person"   Section 1–201(30)
"Purchase"   Section 1–201(32)
"Securities intermediary"   Section 8–102(a)(14)
"Security"   Section 8–102(a)(15)
"Security certificate"   Section 8–102(a)(16)
"Security entitlement"   Section 8–102(a)(17)
"Uncertificated security"   Section 8–102(a)(18)

§ 8111. Clearing corporation rules

A rule adopted by a clearing corporation governing rights and obligations among the clearing corporation and its participants in the clearing corporation is effective even if the rule conflicts with this division and affects another party who does not consent to the rule. *(Added by Stats.1996, c. 497 (S.B.1591), § 9, operative Jan. 1, 1997.)*

Uniform Commercial Code Comment

1. The experience of the past few decades shows that securities holding and settlement practices may develop rapidly, and in unforesee-

able directions. Accordingly, it is desirable that the rules of Article 8 be adaptable both to ensure that commercial law can conform to changing practices and to ensure that commercial law does not operate as an obstacle to developments in securities practice. Even if practices were unchanging, it would not be possible in a general statute to specify in detail the rules needed to provide certainty in the operations of the clearance and settlement system.

The provisions of this Article and Article 1 on the effect of agreements provide considerable flexibility in the specification of the details of the rights and obligations of participants in the securities holding system by agreement. See Sections 8–504 through 8–509, and Section 1–102(3) and (4). Given the magnitude of the exposures involved in securities transactions, however, it may not be possible for the parties in developing practices to rely solely on private agreements, particularly with respect to matters that might affect others, such as creditors. For example, in order to be fully effective, rules of clearing corporations on the finality or reversibility of securities settlements must not only bind the participants in the clearing corporation but also be effective against their creditors. Section 8–111 provides that clearing corporation rules are effective even if they indirectly affect third parties, such as creditors of a participant. This provision does not, however, permit rules to be adopted that would govern the rights and obligations of third parties other than as a consequence of rules that specify the rights and obligations of the clearing corporation and its participants.

2. The definition of clearing corporation in Section 8–102 covers only federal reserve banks, entities registered as clearing agencies under the federal securities laws, and others subject to comparable regulation. The rules of registered clearing agencies are subject to regulatory oversight under the federal securities laws.

Definitional Cross References

"Clearing corporation"   Section 8–102(a)(5)

§ 8112. Creditors; legal process

(a) The interest of a debtor in a certificated security may be reached by a creditor only by actual seizure of the security certificate by the officer making the attachment or levy, except as otherwise provided in subdivision (d). However, a certificated security for which the certificate has been surrendered to the issuer may be reached by a creditor by legal process upon the issuer.

(b) The interest of a debtor in an uncertificated security may be reached by a creditor only by legal process upon the issuer at its chief executive office in the United States, except as otherwise provided in subdivision (d).

(c) The interest of a debtor in a security entitlement may be reached by a creditor only by legal process upon the securities intermediary with whom the debtor's securities account is maintained, except as otherwise provided in subdivision (d).

(d) The interest of a debtor in a certificated security for which the certificate is in the possession of a secured party, or in an uncertificated security registered in the name of a secured party, or a security entitlement maintained in the name of a secured party, may be reached by a creditor by legal process upon the secured party.

(e) A creditor whose debtor is the owner of a certificated security, uncertificated security, or security entitlement is entitled to aid from a court of competent jurisdiction, by injunction or otherwise, in reaching the certificated security, uncertificated security, or security entitlement or in satisfying the claim by means allowed at law or in equity in regard to property that cannot readily be reached by other legal process. *(Added by Stats.1996, c. 497 (S.B.1591), § 9, operative Jan. 1, 1997.)*

Uniform Commercial Code Comment

1. In dealing with certificated securities the instrument itself is the vital thing, and therefore a valid levy cannot be made unless all possibility of the certificate's wrongfully finding its way into a transferee's hands has been removed. This can be accomplished only when the certificate is in the possession of a public officer, the issuer, or an independent third party. A debtor who has been enjoined can still transfer the security in contempt of court. See *Overlock v. Jerome-Portland Copper Mining Co.*, 29 Ariz. 560, 243 P. 400 (1926). Therefore, although injunctive relief is provided in subsection (e) so that creditors may use this method to gain control of the certificated security, the security certificate itself must be reached to constitute a proper levy whenever the debtor has possession.

2. Subsection (b) provides that when the security is uncertificated and registered in the debtor's name, the debtor's interest can be reached only by legal process upon the issuer. The most logical place to serve the issuer would be the place where the transfer records are maintained, but that location might be difficult to identify, especially when the separate elements of a computer network might be situated in different places. The chief executive office is selected as the appropriate place by analogy to Section 9–103(3)(d). See Comment 5(c) to that section. This section indicates only how attachment is to be made, not when it is legally justified. For that reason there is no conflict between this section and *Shaffer v. Heitner*, 433 U.S. 186 (1977).

3. Subsection (c) provides that a security entitlement can be reached only by legal process upon the debtor's security intermediary. Process is effective only if directed to the debtor's own security intermediary. If Debtor holds securities through Broker, and Broker in turn holds through Clearing Corporation, Debtor's property interest is a security entitlement against Broker. Accordingly, Debtor's creditor cannot reach Debtor's interest by legal process directed to the Clearing Corporation. See also Section 8–115.

4. Subsection (d) provides that when a certificated security, an uncertificated security, or a security entitlement is controlled by a secured party, the debtor's interest can be reached by legal process upon the secured party. This section does not attempt to provide for rights as between the creditor and the secured party, as, for example, whether or when the secured party must liquidate the security.

Definitional Cross References

"Certificated security"   Section 8–102(a)(4)
"Issuer"   Section 8–201
"Secured party"   Section 9–105(1)(m)
"Securities intermediary"   Section 8–102(a)(14)
"Security certificate"   Section 8–102(a)(16)
"Security entitlement"   Section 8–102(a)(17)
"Uncertificated security"   Section 8–102(a)(18)

§ 8113. Enforcement of contracts; writing requirements

A contract or modification of a contract for the sale or purchase of a security is enforceable whether or not there is a writing signed or record authenticated by a party against whom enforcement is sought, even if the contract or modification is not capable of performance within one year of its making. *(Added by Stats.1996, c. 497 (S.B.1591), § 9, operative Jan. 1, 1997.)*

Uniform Commercial Code Comment

This section provides that the statute of frauds does not apply to contracts for the sale of securities, reversing prior law which had a special statute of frauds in Section 8–319 (1978). With the increasing use of electronic means of communication, the statute of frauds is unsuited to the realities of the securities business. For securities transactions, whatever benefits a statute of frauds may play in filtering out fraudulent claims are outweighed by the obstacles it places in the development of modern commercial practices in the securities business.

§ 8113

Definitional Cross References

"Action" Section 1–201(1)
"Contract" Section 1–201(11)
"Writing" Section 1–201(46)

§ 8114. Evidence; burden of proof

The following rules apply in an action on a certificated security against the issuer:

(a) Unless specifically denied in the pleadings, each signature on a security certificate or in a necessary endorsement is admitted.

(b) If the effectiveness of a signature is put in issue, the burden of establishing effectiveness is on the party claiming under the signature, but the signature is presumed to be genuine or authorized.

(c) If signatures on a security certificate are admitted or established, production of the certificate entitles a holder to recover on it unless the defendant establishes a defense or a defect going to the validity of the security.

(d) If it is shown that a defense or defect exists, the plaintiff has the burden of establishing that the plaintiff or some person under whom the plaintiff claims is a person against whom the defense or defect cannot be asserted. *(Added by Stats.1996, c. 497 (S.B.1591), § 9, operative Jan. 1, 1997.)*

Uniform Commercial Code Comment

This section adapts the rules of negotiable instruments law concerning procedure in actions on instruments, see Section 3–308, to actions on certificated securities governed by this Article. An "action on a security" includes any action or proceeding brought against the issuer to enforce a right or interest that is part of the security, such as an action to collect principal or interest or a dividend, or to establish a right to vote or to receive a new security under an exchange offer or plan of reorganization. This section applies only to certificated securities; actions on uncertificated securities are governed by general evidentiary principles.

Definitional Cross References

"Action" Section 1–201(1)
"Burden of establishing" Section 1–201(8)
"Certificated security" Section 8–102(a)(4)
"Indorsement" Section 8–102(a)(11)
"Issuer" Section 8–201
"Presumed" Section 1–201(31)
"Security" Section 8–102(a)(15)
"Security certificate" Section 8–102(a)(16)

§ 8115. Liability to persons with adverse claims

A securities intermediary that has transferred a financial asset pursuant to an effective entitlement order, or a broker or other agent or bailee that has dealt with a financial asset at the direction of its customer or principal, is not liable to a person having an adverse claim to the financial asset, unless the securities intermediary, or broker or other agent or bailee did one or more of the following:

(1) Took the action after it had been served with an injunction, restraining order, or other legal process enjoining it from doing so, issued by a court of competent jurisdiction, and had a reasonable opportunity to act on the injunction, restraining order, or other legal process.

(2) Acted in collusion with the wrongdoer in violating the rights of the adverse claimant.

(3) In the case of a security certificate that has been stolen, acted with notice of the adverse claim. *(Added by Stats.1996, c. 497 (S.B.1591), § 9, operative Jan. 1, 1997.)*

Uniform Commercial Code Comment

1. Other provisions of Article 8 protect certain purchasers against adverse claims, both for the direct holding system and the indirect holding system. See Sections 8–303 and 8–502. This section deals with the related question of the possible liability of a person who acted as the "conduit" for a securities transaction. It covers both securities intermediaries—the "conduits" in the indirect holding system—and brokers or other agents or bailees—the "conduits" in the direct holding system. The following examples illustrate its operation:

Example 1. John Doe is a customer of the brokerage firm of Able & Co. Doe delivers to Able a certificate for 100 shares of XYZ Co. common stock, registered in Doe's name and properly indorsed, and asks the firm to sell it for him. Able does so. Later, John Doe's spouse Mary Doe brings an action against Able asserting that Able's action was wrongful against her because the XYZ Co. stock was marital property in which she had an interest, and John Doe was acting wrongfully against her in transferring the securities.

Example 2. Mary Roe is a customer of the brokerage firm of Baker & Co. and holds her securities through a securities account with Baker. Roe instructs Baker to sell 100 shares of XYZ Co. common stock that she carried in her account. Baker does so. Later, Mary Roe's spouse John Roe brings an action against Baker asserting that Baker's action was wrongful against him because the XYZ Co. stock was marital property in which he had an interest, and Mary Roe was acting wrongfully against him in transferring the securities.

Under common law conversion principles, Mary Doe might be able to assert that Able & Co. is liable to her in Example 1 for exercising dominion over property inconsistent with her rights in it. On that or some similar theory John Roe might assert that Baker is liable to him in Example 2. Section 8–115 protects both Able and Baker from liability.

2. The policy of this section is similar to that of many other rules of law that protect agents and bailees from liability as innocent converters. If a thief steals property and ships it by mail, express service, or carrier, to another person, the recipient of the property does not obtain good title, even though the recipient may have given value to the thief and had no notice or knowledge that the property was stolen. Accordingly, the true owner can recover the property from the recipient or obtain damages in a conversion or similar action. An action against the postal service, express company, or carrier presents entirely different policy considerations. Accordingly, general tort law protects agents or bailees who act on the instructions of their principals or bailors. See Restatement (Second) of Torts § 235. See also UCC Section 7–404.

3. Except as provided in paragraph 3, this section applies even though the securities intermediary, or the broker or other agent or bailee, had notice or knowledge that another person asserts a claim to the securities. Consider the following examples:

Example 3. Same facts as in Example 1, except that before John Doe brought the XYZ Co. security certificate to Able for sale, Mary Doe telephoned or wrote to the firm asserting that she had an interest in all of John Doe's securities and demanding that they not trade for him.

Example 4. Same facts as in Example 2, except that before Mary Roe gave an entitlement order to Baker to sell the XYZ Co. securities from her account, John Roe telephoned or wrote to the firm asserting that he had an interest in all of Mary Roe's securities and demanding that they not trade for her.

Section 8–115 protects Able and Baker from liability. The protections of Section 8–115 do not depend on the presence or absence of notice of adverse claims. It is essential to the securities settlement system that brokers and securities intermediaries be able to act promptly on the directions of their customers. Even though a firm has notice that someone asserts a claim to a customer's securities or security entitlements, the firm should not be placed in the position of having to make a legal judgment about the validity of the claim at the risk of liability either to its customer or to the third party for guessing wrong. Under this section, the broker or securities intermediary is privileged to act on the instructions of its customer or entitlement holder, unless it has been served with a restraining order or other legal process enjoining it from doing so. This is already the law in many jurisdictions. For example a section of the New York Banking Law provides that banks need not recognize any adverse claim to funds or securities on deposit with them unless they have been served with legal process. N.Y. Banking Law § 134. Other sections of the UCC embody a similar policy. See Sections 3–602, 5–114(2)(b).

Paragraph (1) of this section refers only to a court order enjoining the securities intermediary or the broker or other agent or bailee from acting at the instructions of the customer. It does not apply to cases where the adverse claimant tells the intermediary or broker that the customer has been enjoined, or shows the intermediary or broker a copy of a court order binding the customer.

Paragraph (3) takes a different approach in one limited class of cases, those where a customer sells stolen certificated securities through a securities firm. Here the policies that lead to protection of securities firms against assertions of other sorts of claims must be weighed against the desirability of having securities firms guard against the disposition of stolen securities. Accordingly, paragraph (3) denies protection to a broker, custodian, or other agent or bailee who receives a stolen security certificate from its customer, if the broker, custodian, or other agent or bailee had notice of adverse claims. The circumstances that give notice of adverse claims are specified in Section 8–105. The result is that brokers, custodians, and other agents and bailees face the same liability for selling stolen certificated securities that purchasers face for buying them.

4. As applied to securities intermediaries, this section embodies one of the fundamental principles of the Article 8 indirect holding system rules—that a securities intermediary owes duties only to its own entitlement holders. The following examples illustrate the operation of this section in the multi-tiered indirect holding system:

Example 5. Able & Co., a broker-dealer, holds 50,000 shares of XYZ Co. stock in its account at Clearing Corporation. Able acquired the XYZ shares from another firm, Baker & Co., in a transaction that Baker contends was tainted by fraud, giving Baker a right to rescind the transaction and recover the XYZ shares from Able. Baker sends notice to Clearing Corporation stating that Baker has a claim to the 50,000 shares of XYZ Co. in Able's account. Able then initiates an entitlement order directing Clearing Corporation to transfer the 50,000 shares of XYZ Co. to another firm in settlement of a trade. Under Section 8–115, Clearing Corporation is privileged to comply with Able's entitlement order, without fear of liability to Baker. This is so even though Clearing Corporation has notice of Baker's claim, unless Baker obtains a court order enjoining Clearing Corporation from acting on Able's entitlement order.

Example 6. Able & Co., a broker-dealer, holds 50,000 shares of XYZ Co. stock in its account at Clearing Corporation. Able initiates an entitlement order directing Clearing Corporation to transfer the 50,000 shares of XYZ Co. to another firm in settlement of a trade. That trade was made by Able for its own account, and the proceeds were devoted to its own use. Able becomes insolvent, and it is discovered that Able has a shortfall in the shares of XYZ Co. stock that it should have been carrying for its customers. Able's customers bring an action against Clearing Corporation asserting that Clearing Corporation acted wrongfully in transferring the XYZ shares on Able's order because those were shares that should have been held by Able for its customers. Under Section 8–115, Clearing Corporation is not liable to Able's customers, because Clearing Corporation acted on an effective entitlement order of its own entitlement holder, Able. Clearing Corporation's protection against liability does not depend on the presence or absence of notice or knowledge of the claim by Clearing Corporation.

5. If the conduct of a securities intermediary or a broker or other agent or bailee rises to a level of complicity in the wrongdoing of its customer or principal, the policies that favor protection against liability do not apply. Accordingly, paragraph (2) provides that the protections of this section do not apply if the securities intermediary or broker or other agent or bailee acted in collusion with the customer or principal in violating the rights of another person. The collusion test is intended to adopt a standard akin to the tort rules that determine whether a person is liable as an aider or abettor for the tortious conduct of a third party. See Restatement (Second) of Torts § 876.

Knowledge that the action of the customer is wrongful is a necessary but not sufficient condition of the collusion test. The aspect of the role of securities intermediaries and brokers that Article 8 deals with is the clerical or ministerial role of implementing and recording the securities transactions that their customers conduct. Faithful performance of this role consists of following the instructions of the customer. It is not the role of the record-keeper to police whether the transactions recorded are appropriate, so mere awareness that the customer may be acting wrongfully does not itself constitute collusion. That, of course, does not insulate an intermediary or broker from responsibility in egregious cases where its action goes beyond the ordinary standards of the business of implementing and recording transactions, and reaches a level of affirmative misconduct in assisting the customer in the commission of a wrong.

Definitional Cross References

"Broker" Section 8–102(a)(3)
"Effective" Section 8–107
"Entitlement order" Section 8–102(a)(8)
"Financial asset" Section 8–102(a)(9)
"Securities intermediary" Section 8–102(a)(14)
"Security certificate" Section 8–102(a)(16)

§ 8116. Security intermediary; purchaser for value

A securities intermediary that receives a financial asset and establishes a security entitlement to the financial asset in favor of an entitlement holder is a purchaser for value of the financial asset. A securities intermediary that acquires a security entitlement to a financial asset from another securities intermediary acquires the security entitlement for value if the securities intermediary acquiring the security entitlement establishes a security entitlement to the financial asset in favor of an entitlement holder. *(Added by Stats.1996, c. 497 (S.B.1591), § 9, operative Jan. 1, 1997.)*

Uniform Commercial Code Comment

1. This section is intended to make explicit two points that, while implicit in other provisions, are of sufficient importance to the operation of the indirect holding system that they warrant explicit statement. First, it makes clear that a securities intermediary that receives a financial asset and establishes a security entitlement in respect thereof in favor of an entitlement holder is a "purchaser" of the financial asset that the securities intermediary received. Second, it makes clear that by establishing a security entitlement in favor of an entitlement holder a securities intermediary gives value for any corresponding financial asset that the securities intermediary receives or acquires from another party, whether the intermediary holds directly or indirectly.

In many cases a securities intermediary that receives a financial asset will also be transferring value to the person from whom the financial asset was received. That, however, is not always the case. Payment may occur through a different system than settlement of the securities side of the transaction, or the securities might be transferred without a corresponding payment, as when a person moves an account from one securities intermediary to another. Even though the securities intermediary does not give value to the transferor, it does give value by incurring obligations to its own entitlement holder. Although the general definition of value in Section 1–201(44)(d) should be interpreted to cover the point, this section is included to make this point explicit.

2. The following examples illustrate the effect of this section:

Example 1. Buyer buys 1000 shares of XYZ Co. common stock through Buyer's broker Able & Co. to be held in Buyer's securities account. In settlement of the trade, the selling broker delivers to Able a security certificate in street name, indorsed in blank, for 1000 shares XYZ Co. stock, which Able holds in its vault. Able credits Buyer's account for securities in that amount. Section 8–116 specifies that Able is a purchaser of the XYZ Co. stock certificate, and gave value for it. Thus, Able can obtain the benefit of Section 8–303, which protects purchasers for value, if it satisfies the other requirements of that section.

§ 8116

Example 2. Buyer buys 1000 shares XYZ Co. common stock through Buyer's broker Able & Co. to be held in Buyer's securities account. The trade is settled by crediting 1000 shares XYZ Co. stock to Able's account at Clearing Corporation. Able credits Buyer's account for securities in that amount. When Clearing Corporation credits Able's account, Able acquires a security entitlement under Section 8–501. Section 8–116 specifies that Able acquired this security entitlement for value. Thus, Able can obtain the benefit of Section 8–502, which protects persons who acquire security entitlements for value, if it satisfies the other requirements of that section.

Example 3. Thief steals a certificated bearer bond from Owner. Thief sends the certificate to his broker Able & Co. to be held in his securities account, and Able credits Thief's account for the bond. Section 8–116 specifies that Able is a purchaser of the bond and gave value for it. Thus, Able can obtain the benefit of Section 8–303, which protects purchasers for value, if it satisfies the other requirements of that section.

Definitional Cross References

"Financial asset"   Section 8–102(a)(9)
"Securities intermediary"   Section 8–102(a)(14)
"Security entitlement"   Section 8–102(a)(17)
"Entitlement holder"   Section 8–102(a)(7)

CHAPTER 2. ISSUE AND ISSUER

Section
8201. Issuer.
8202. Terms included in certificated security; notice of defect; defenses.
8203. Notice of defect or defense.
8204. Security transfers; restrictions.
8205. Unauthorized signatures.
8206. Signed but incomplete certificates; improper alterations.
8207. Registered owner; treatment by issuer or indenture trustee prior to transfer.
8208. Authenticating signers; warranties.
8209. Liens.
8210. Overissue of securities.

§ 8201. Issuer

(a) With respect to an obligation on or a defense to a security, an "issuer" includes a person that does any of the following:

(1) Places or authorizes the placing of its name on a security certificate, other than as authenticating trustee, registrar, transfer agent, or the like, to evidence a share, participation, or other interest in its property or in an enterprise, or to evidence its duty to perform an obligation represented by the certificate.

(2) Creates a share, participation, or other interest in its property or in an enterprise, or undertakes an obligation, that is an uncertificated security.

(3) Directly or indirectly creates a fractional interest in its rights or property, if the fractional interest is represented by a security certificate.

(4) Becomes responsible for, or in place of, another person described as an issuer in this section.

(b) With respect to an obligation on or defense to a security, a guarantor is an issuer to the extent of its guaranty, whether or not its obligation is noted on a security certificate.

(c) With respect to a registration of a transfer, issuer means a person on whose behalf transfer books are maintained. *(Added by Stats.1996, c. 497 (S.B.1591), § 9, operative Jan. 1, 1997.)*

Uniform Commercial Code Comment

1. The definition of "issuer" in this section functions primarily to describe the persons whose defenses may be cut off under the rules in Part 2. In large measure it simply tracks the language of the definition of security in Section 8–102(a)(15).

2. Subsection (b) distinguishes the obligations of a guarantor as issuer from those of the principal obligor. However, it does not exempt the guarantor from the impact of subsection (d) of Section 8–202. Whether or not the obligation of the guarantor is noted on the security is immaterial. Typically, guarantors are parent corporations, or stand in some similar relationship to the principal obligor. If that relationship existed at the time the security was originally issued the guaranty would probably have been noted on the security. However, if the relationship arose afterward, e.g., through a purchase of stock or properties, or through merger or consolidation, probably the notation would not have been made. Nonetheless, the holder of the security is entitled to the benefit of the obligation of the guarantor.

3. Subsection (c) narrows the definition of "issuer" for purposes of Part 4 of this Article (registration of transfer). It is supplemented by Section 8–407.

Definitional Cross References

"Person"   Section 1–201(30)
"Security"   Section 8–102(a)(15)
"Security certificate"   Section 8–102(a)(16)
"Uncertificated security"   Section 8–102(a)(18)

Cross References

Definitions, see Commercial Code § 8102.
Registration of transfer, see Commercial Code § 8401 et seq.
Uncertificated securities, interests in, governing law, effective date and transition provisions, see Commercial Code §§ 15103, 15104.

§ 8202. Terms included in certificated security; notice of defect; defenses

(a) Even against a purchaser for value and without notice, the terms of a certificated security include terms stated on the certificate and terms made part of the security by reference on the certificate to another instrument, indenture, or document or to a constitution, statute, ordinance, rule, regulation, order, or the like, to the extent the terms referred to do not conflict with terms stated on the certificate. A reference under this subdivision does not of itself charge a purchaser for value with notice of a defect going to the validity of the security, even if the certificate expressly states that a person accepting it admits notice. The terms of an uncertificated security include those stated in any instrument, indenture, or document or in a constitution, statute, ordinance, rule, regulation, order, or the like, pursuant to which the security is issued.

(b) The following rules apply if an issuer asserts that a security is not valid:

(1) A security other than one issued by a government or governmental subdivision, agency, or instrumentality, even though issued with a defect going to its validity, is valid in the hands of a purchaser for value and without notice of the particular defect unless the defect involves a violation of a constitutional provision. In that case, the security is valid in the hands of a purchaser for value

and without notice of the defect, other than one who takes by original issue.

(2) Paragraph (1) applies to an issuer that is a government or governmental subdivision, agency, or instrumentality only if there has been substantial compliance with the legal requirements governing the issue or the issuer has received a substantial consideration for the issue as a whole or for the particular security and a stated purpose of the issue is one for which the issuer has power to borrow money or issue the security.

(c) Except as otherwise provided in Section 8205, lack of genuineness of a certificated security is a complete defense, even against a purchaser for value and without notice.

(d) All other defenses of the issuer of a security, including nondelivery and conditional delivery of a certificated security, are ineffective against a purchaser for value who has taken the certificated security without notice of the particular defense.

(e) This section does not affect the right of a party to cancel a contract for a security "when, as and if issued" or "when distributed" in the event of a material change in the character of the security that is the subject of the contract or in the plan or arrangement pursuant to which the security is to be issued or distributed.

(f) If a security is held by a securities intermediary against whom an entitlement holder has a security entitlement with respect to the security, the issuer may not assert any defense that the issuer could not assert if the entitlement holder held the security directly. (Added by Stats.1996, c. 497 (S.B.1591), § 9, operative Jan. 1, 1997.)

Uniform Commercial Code Comment

1. In this Article the rights of the purchaser for value without notice are divided into two aspects, those against the issuer, and those against other claimants to the security. Part 2 of this Article, and especially this section, deal with rights against the issuer.

Subsection (a) states, in accordance with the prevailing case law, the right of the issuer (who prepares the text of the security) to include terms incorporated by adequate reference to an extrinsic source, so long as the terms so incorporated do not conflict with the stated terms. Thus, the standard practice of referring in a bond or debenture to the trust indenture under which it is issued without spelling out its necessarily complex and lengthy provisions is approved. Every stock certificate refers in some manner to the charter or articles of incorporation of the issuer. At least where there is more than one class of stock authorized applicable corporation codes specifically require a statement or summary as to preferences, voting powers and the like. References to constitutions, statutes, ordinances, rules, regulations or orders are not so common, except in the obligations of governments or governmental agencies or units; but where appropriate they fit into the rule here stated.

Courts have generally held that an issuer is estopped from denying representations made in the text of a security. *Delaware–New Jersey Ferry Co. v. Leeds*, 21 Del.Ch. 279, 186 A. 913 (1936). Nor is a defect in form or the invalidity of a security normally available to the issuer as a defense. *Bonini v. Family Theatre Corporation*, 327 Pa. 273, 194 A. 498 (1937); *First National Bank of Fairbanks v. Alaska Airmotive*, 119 F.2d 267 (C.C.A.Alaska 1941).

2. The rule in subsection (a) requiring that the terms of a security be noted or referred to on the certificate is based on practices and expectations in the direct holding system for certificated securities. This rule does not express a general rule or policy that the terms of a security are effective only if they are communicated to beneficial owners in some particular fashion. Rather, subsection (a) is based on the principle that a purchaser who does obtain a certificate is entitled to assume that the terms of the security have been noted or referred to on the certificate. That policy does not come into play in a securities holding system in which purchasers do not take delivery of certificates.

The provisions of subsection (a) concerning notation of terms on security certificates are necessary only because paper certificates play such an important role for certificated securities that a purchaser should be protected against assertion of any defenses or rights that are not noted on the certificate. No similar problem exists with respect to uncertificated securities. The last sentence of subsection (a) is, strictly speaking, unnecessary, since it only recognizes the fact that the terms of an uncertificated security are determined by whatever other law or agreement governs the security. It is included only to preclude any inference that uncertificated securities are subject to any requirement analogous to the requirement of notation of terms on security certificates.

The rule of subsection (a) applies to the indirect holding system only in the sense that if a certificated security has been delivered to the clearing corporation or other securities intermediary, the terms of the security should be noted or referred to on the certificate. If the security is uncertificated, that principle does not apply even at the issuer-clearing corporation level. The beneficial owners who hold securities through the clearing corporation are bound by the terms of the security, even though they do not actually see the certificate. Since entitlement holders in an indirect holding system have not taken delivery of certificates, the policy of subsection (a) does not apply.

3. The penultimate sentence of subsection (a) and all of subsection (b) embody the concept that it is the duty of the issuer, not of the purchaser, to make sure that the security complies with the law governing its issue. The penultimate sentence of subsection (a) makes clear that the issuer cannot, by incorporating a reference to a statute or other document, charge the purchaser with notice of the security's invalidity. Subsection (b) gives to a purchaser for value without notice of the defect the right to enforce the security against the issuer despite the presence of a defect that otherwise would render the security invalid. There are three circumstances in which a purchaser does not gain such rights: first, if the defect involves a violation of constitutional provisions, these rights accrue only to a subsequent purchaser, that is, one who takes other than by original issue. This Article leaves to the law of each particular State the rights of a purchaser on original issue of a security with a constitutional defect. No negative implication is intended by the explicit grant of rights to a subsequent purchaser.

Second, governmental issuers are distinguished in subsection (b) from other issuers as a matter of public policy, and additional safeguards are imposed before governmental issues are validated. Governmental issuers are estopped from asserting defenses only if there has been substantial compliance with the legal requirements governing the issue or if substantial consideration has been received and a stated purpose of the issue is one for which the issuer has power to borrow money or issue the security. The purpose of the substantial compliance requirement is to make certain that a mere technicality as, e.g., in the manner of publishing election notices, shall not be a ground for depriving an innocent purchaser of rights in the security. The policy is here adopted of such cases as *Tommie v. City of Gadsden*, 229 Ala. 521, 158 So. 763 (1935), in which minor discrepancies in the form of the election ballot used were overlooked and the bonds were declared valid since there had been substantial compliance with the statute.

A long and well established line of federal cases recognizes the principle of estoppel in favor of purchasers for value without notices where municipalities issue bonds containing recitals of compliance with governing constitutional and statutory provisions, made by the municipal authorities entrusted with determining such compliance. *Chaffee County v. Potter*, 142 U.S. 355 (1892); *Oregon v. Jennings*, 119 U.S. 74 (1886); *Gunnison County Commissioners v. Rollins*, 173 U.S. 255 (1898). This rule has been qualified, however, by requiring that the municipality have power to issue the security. *Anthony v. County of Jasper*, 101 U.S. 693 (1879); *Town of South Ottawa v. Perkins*, 94 U.S. 260 (1876). This section follows the case law trend, simplifying the rule by setting up two conditions for an estoppel against a governmental issuer: (1) substantial consideration given, and (2) power in the issuer to borrow money or issue the security for the stated purpose. As a practical matter the problem of policing governmental issuers has been alleviated by the present practice of requiring legal opinions as to the validity of the issue.

§ 8202

The bulk of the case law on this point is nearly 100 years old and it may be assumed that the question now seldom arises.

Section 8–210, regarding overissue, provides the third exception to the rule that an innocent purchase for value takes a valid security despite the presence of a defect that would otherwise give rise to invalidity. See that section and its Comment for further explanation.

4. Subsection (e) is included to make clear that this section does not affect the presently recognized right of either party to a "when, as and if" or "when distributed" contract to cancel the contract on substantial change.

5. Subsection (f) has been added because the introduction of the security entitlement concept requires some adaptation of the Part 2 rules, particularly those that distinguish between purchasers who take by original issue and subsequent purchasers. The basic concept of Part 2 is to apply to investment securities the principle of negotiable instruments law that an obligor is precluded from asserting most defenses against purchasers for value without notice. Section 8–202 describes in some detail which defenses issuers can raise against purchasers for value and subsequent purchasers for value. Because these rules were drafted with the direct holding system in mind, some interpretive problems might be presented in applying them to the indirect holding. For example, if a municipality issues a bond in book-entry only form, the only direct "purchaser" of that bond would be the clearing corporation. The policy of precluding the issuer from asserting defenses is, however, equally applicable. Subsection (f) is designed to ensure that the defense preclusion rules developed for the direct holding system will also apply to the indirect holding system.

Definitional Cross References

"Certificated security"   Section 8–102(a)(4)
"Notice"   Section 1–201(25)
"Purchaser"   Sections 1–201(33) & 8–116
"Security"   Section 8–102(a)(15)
"Uncertificated security"   Section 8–102(a)(18)
"Value"   Sections 1–201(44) & 8–116

Cross References

Completion or alteration, see Commercial Code § 8206.
Defects or defenses, staleness as notice, see Commercial Code § 8203.
Definitions, see Commercial Code §§ 1201, 8102, 8104.
Effect of overissue, see Commercial Code § 8104.
Issuer's lien, see Commercial Code § 8103.
Notice, actual and constructive, see Civil Code §§ 18, 19.
Staleness as notice of adverse claims, see Commercial Code § 8305.
Unauthorized signature, effect on issue, see Commercial Code § 8205.
Uncertificated securities, interests in, governing law, effective date and transition provisions, see Commercial Code §§ 15103, 15104.

§ 8203. Notice of defect or defense

After an act or event, other than a call that has been revoked, creating a right to immediate performance of the principal obligation represented by a certificated security or setting a date on or after which the security is to be presented or surrendered for redemption or exchange, a purchaser is charged with notice of any defect in its issue or defense of the issuer, if the act or event either:

(1) Requires the payment of money, the delivery of a certificated security, the registration of transfer of an uncertificated security, or any of them on presentation or surrender of the security certificate, the money or security is available on the date set for payment or exchange, and the purchaser takes the security more than one year after that date.

(2) Is not covered by paragraph (1) and the purchaser takes the security more than two years after the date set for surrender or presentation or the date on which performance became due. *(Added by Stats.1996, c. 497 (S.B.1591), § 9, operative Jan. 1, 1997.)*

Uniform Commercial Code Comment

1. The problem of matured or called securities is here dealt with in terms of the effect of such events in giving notice of the issuer's defenses and not in terms of "negotiability". The substance of this section applies only to certificated securities because certificates may be transferred to a purchaser by delivery after the security has matured, been called, or become redeemable or exchangeable. It is contemplated that uncertificated securities which have matured or been called will merely be canceled on the books of the issuer and the proceeds sent to the registered owner. Uncertificated securities which have become redeemable or exchangeable, at the option of the owner, may be transferred to a purchaser, but the transfer is effectuated only by registration of transfer, thus necessitating communication with the issuer. If defects or defenses in such securities exist, the issuer will necessarily have the opportunity to bring them to the attention of the purchaser.

2. The fact that a security certificate is in circulation long after it has been called for redemption or exchange must give rise to the question in a purchaser's mind as to why it has not been surrendered. After the lapse of a reasonable period of time a purchaser can no longer claim "no reason to know" of any defects or irregularities in its issue. Where funds are available for the redemption the security certificate is normally turned in more promptly and a shorter time is set as the "reasonable period" than is set where funds are not available.

Defaulted certificated securities may be traded on financial markets in the same manner as unmatured and undefaulted instruments and a purchaser might not be placed upon notice of irregularity by the mere fact of default. An issuer, however, should at some point be placed in a position to determine definitely its liability on an invalid or improper issue, and for this purpose a security under this section becomes "stale" two years after the default. A different rule applies when the question is notice not of issuer's defenses but of claims of ownership. Section 8–105 and Comment.

3. Nothing in this section is designed to extend the life of preferred stocks called for redemption as "shares of stock" beyond the redemption date. After such a call, the security represents only a right to the funds set aside for redemption.

Definitional Cross References

"Certificated security"   Section 8–102(a)(4)
"Notice"   Section 1–201(25)
"Purchaser"   Sections 1–201(33) & 8–116
"Security"   Section 8–102(a)(15)
"Security certificate"   Section 8–102(a)(16)
"Uncertificated security"   Section 8–102(a)(18)

Cross References

Adverse claims, staleness as notice, see Commercial Code § 8305.
Liability of transferee of corporate shares, see Corporations Code §§ 411, 412.
Notice, actual and constructive, see Civil Code §§ 18, 19.
Notice of defects or defense, see Commercial Code § 8202.
Overissue, effect, see Commercial Code § 8104.
Redemption of corporate shares, see Corporations Code §§ 402, 509, 510.
Rights of issuer with respect to registered owners, see Commercial Code § 8207.
Uncertificated securities, interests in, governing law, effective date and transition provisions, see Commercial Code §§ 15103, 15104.

§ 8204. Security transfers; restrictions

A restriction on transfer of a security imposed by the issuer, even if otherwise lawful, is ineffective against a person without knowledge of the restriction unless either of the following applies:

(1) The security is certificated and the restriction is noted conspicuously on the security certificate.

(2) The security is uncertificated and the registered owner has been notified of the restriction. *(Added by Stats.1996, c. 497 (S.B.1591), § 9, operative Jan. 1, 1997.)*

Uniform Commercial Code Comment

1. Restrictions on transfer of securities are imposed by issuers in a variety of circumstances and for a variety of purposes, such as to retain control of a close corporation or to ensure compliance with federal securities laws. Other law determines whether such restrictions are permissible. This section deals only with the consequences of failure to note the restriction on a security certificate.

This section imposes no bar to enforcement of a restriction on transfer against a person who has actual knowledge of it.

2. A restriction on transfer of a certificated security is ineffective against a person without knowledge of the restriction unless the restriction is noted conspicuously on the certificate. The word "noted" is used to make clear that the restriction need not be set forth in full text. Refusal by an issuer to register a transfer on the basis of an unnoted restriction would be a violation of the issuer's duty to register under Section 8–401.

3. The policy of this section is the same as in Section 8–202. A purchaser who takes delivery of a certificated security is entitled to rely on the terms stated on the certificate. That policy obviously does not apply to uncertificated securities. For uncertificated securities, this section requires only that the registered owner has been notified of the restriction. Suppose, for example, that A is the registered owner of an uncertificated security, and that the issuer has notified A of a restriction on transfer. A agrees to sell the security to B, in violation of the restriction. A completes a written instruction directing the issuer to register transfer to B, and B pays A for the security at the time A delivers the instruction to B. A does not inform B of the restriction, and B does not otherwise have notice or knowledge of it at the time B pays and receives the instruction. B presents the instruction to the issuer, but the issuer refuses to register the transfer on the grounds that it would violate the restriction. The issuer has complied with this section, because it did notify the registered owner A of the restriction. The issuer's refusal to register transfer is not wrongful. B has an action against A for breach of transfer warranty, see Section 8–108(b)(4)(iii). B's mistake was treating an uncertificated security transaction in the fashion appropriate only for a certificated security. The mechanism for transfer of uncertificated securities is registration of transfer on the books of the issuer; handing over an instruction only initiates the process. The purchaser should make arrangements to ensure that the price is not paid until it knows that the issuer has or will register transfer.

4. In the indirect holding system, investors neither take physical delivery of security certificates nor have uncertificated securities registered in their names. So long as the requirements of this section have been satisfied at the level of the relationship between the issuer and the securities intermediary that is a direct holder, this section does not preclude the issuer from enforcing a restriction on transfer. See Section 8–202(a) and Comment 2 thereto.

5. This section deals only with restrictions imposed by the issuer. Restrictions imposed by statute are not affected. See *Quiner v. Marblehead Social Co.*, 10 Mass. 476 (1813); *Madison Bank v. Price*, 79 Kan. 289, 100 P. 280 (1909); *Healey v. Steele Center Creamery Ass'n*, 115 Minn. 451, 133 N.W. 69 (1911). Nor does it deal with private agreements between stockholders containing restrictive covenants as to the sale of the security.

Definitional Cross References

"Certificated security"   Section 8–102(a)(4)
"Conspicuous"   Section 1–201(10)
"Issuer"   Section 8–201
"Knowledge"   Section 1–201(25)
"Notify"   Section 1–201(25)
"Purchaser"   Sections 1–201(33) & 8–116
"Security"   Section 8–102(a)(15)
"Security certificate"   Section 8–102(a)(16)
"Uncertificated security"   Section 8–102(a)(18)

Cross References

By-laws, restrictions on right to transfer or hypothecate shares, see Corporations Code § 204.
Issuer, see Commercial Code § 8201.
Issuer's lien, see Commercial Code § 8103.
Registration of transfer, see Commercial Code § 8401 et seq.
Shares, contents of certificate, see Corporations Code § 416 et seq.
Statements required to be included in certificates to bind transferees, see Corporations Code § 416 et seq.
Unauthorized endorsement, assertion of ineffectiveness against issuer, see Commercial Code § 8311.
Uncertificated securities, interests in, governing law, effective date and transition provisions, see Commercial Code §§ 15103, 15104.

§ 8205. Unauthorized signatures

An unauthorized signature placed on a security certificate before or in the course of issue is ineffective, but the signature is effective in favor of a purchaser for value of the certificated security if the purchaser is without notice of the lack of authority and the signing has been done by one of the following:

(1) An authenticating trustee, registrar, transfer agent, or other person entrusted by the issuer with the signing of the security certificate or of similar security certificates, or the immediate preparation for signing of any of them.

(2) An employee of the issuer, or of any of the persons listed in paragraph (1), entrusted with responsible handling of the security certificate. *(Added by Stats.1996, c. 497 (S.B.1591), § 9, operative Jan. 1, 1997.)*

Uniform Commercial Code Comment

1. The problem of forged or unauthorized signatures may arise where an employee of the issuer, transfer agent, or registrar has access to securities which the employee is required to prepare for issue by affixing the corporate seal or by adding a signature necessary for issue. This section is based upon the issuer's duty to avoid the negligent entrusting of securities to such persons. Issuers have long been held responsible for signatures placed upon securities by parties whom they have held out to the public as authorized to prepare such securities. See *Fifth Avenue Bank of New York v. The Forty–Second & Grand Street Ferry Railroad Co.*, 137 N.Y. 231, 33 N.E. 378, 19 L.R.A. 331, 33 Am.St.Rep. 712 (1893); *Jarvis v. Manhattan Beach Co.*, 148 N.Y. 652, 43 N.E. 68, 31 L.R.A. 776, 51 Am.St.Rep. 727 (1896). The "apparent authority" concept of some of the case-law, however, is here extended and this section expressly rejects the technical distinction, made by courts reluctant to recognize forged signatures, between cases where forgers sign signatures they are authorized to sign under proper circumstances and those in which they sign signatures they are never authorized to sign. *Citizens' & Southern National Bank v. Trust Co. of Georgia*, 50 Ga.App. 681, 179 S.E. 278 (1935). Normally the purchaser is not in a position to determine which signature a forger, entrusted with the preparation of securities, has "apparent authority" to sign. The issuer, on the other hand, can protect itself against such fraud by the careful selection and bonding of agents and employees, or by action over against transfer agents and registrars who in turn may bond their personnel.

2. The issuer cannot be held liable for the honesty of employees not entrusted, directly or indirectly, with the signing, preparation, or responsible handling of similar securities and whose possible commission of forgery it has no reason to anticipate. The result in such cases as *Hudson Trust Co. v. American Linseed Co.*, 232 N.Y. 350, 134 N.E. 178 (1922), and *Dollar Savings Fund & Trust Co. v. Pittsburgh Plate Glass Co.*, 213 Pa. 307, 62 A. 916, 5 Ann.Cas. 248 (1906) is here adopted.

3. This section is not concerned with forged or unauthorized indorsements, but only with unauthorized signatures of issuers, transfer agents, etc., placed upon security certificates during the course of their issue. The protection here stated is available to all purchasers for value without notice and not merely to subsequent purchasers.

§ 8205

Definitional Cross References

"Certificated security" Section 8–102(a)(4)
"Issuer" Section 8–201
"Notice" Section 1–201(25)
"Purchaser" Sections 1–201(33) & 8–116
"Security certificate" Section 8–102(a)(14)
"Unauthorized signature" Section 1–201(43)

Cross References

Extinction of written contract by material alteration, see Civil Code § 1700.
Forgery, see Penal Code § 470 et seq.
Genuineness, lack as defense, see Commercial Code § 8202.
Notice of defect or defense, see Commercial Code § 8202.
Signature, presumptions, see Commercial Code § 8105.
Unauthorized indorsement, effect, see Commercial Code § 8311.
Uncertificated securities, interests in, governing law, effective date and transition provisions, see Commercial Code §§ 15103, 15104.

§ 8206. Signed but incomplete certificates; improper alterations

(a) If a security certificate contains the signatures necessary to its issue or transfer but is incomplete in any other respect, the following apply:

(1) Any person may complete it by filling in the blanks as authorized.

(2) Even if the blanks are incorrectly filled in, the security certificate as completed is enforceable by a purchaser who took it for value and without notice of the incorrectness.

(b) A complete security certificate that has been improperly altered, even if fraudulently, remains enforceable, but only according to its original terms. *(Added by Stats.1996, c. 497 (S.B.1591), § 9, operative Jan. 1, 1997.)*

Uniform Commercial Code Comment

1. The problem of forged or unauthorized signatures necessary for the issue or transfer of a security is not, involved here, and a person in possession of a blank certificate is not, by this section, given authority to fill in blanks with such signatures. Completion of blanks left in a transfer instruction is dealt with elsewhere (Section 8–305(a)).

2. Blanks left upon issue of a security certificate are the only ones dealt with here, and a purchaser for value without notice is protected. A purchaser is not in a good position to determine whether blanks were completed by the issuer or by some person not authorized to complete them. On the other hand the issuer can protect itself by not placing its signature on the writing until the blanks are completed or, if it does sign before all blanks are completed, by carefully selecting the agents and employees to whom it entrusts the writing after authentication. With respect to a security certificate that is completed by the issuer but later is altered, the issuer has done everything it can to protect the purchaser and thus is not charged with the terms as altered. However, it is charged according to the original terms, since it is not thereby prejudiced. If the completion or alteration is obviously irregular, the purchaser may not qualify as a purchaser who took without notice under this section.

3. Only the purchaser who physically takes the certificate is directly protected. However, a transferee may receive protection indirectly through Section 8–302(a).

4. The protection granted a purchaser for value without notice under this section is modified to the extent that an overissue may result where an incorrect amount is inserted into a blank (Section 8–210).

Definitional Cross References

"Notice" Section 1–201(25)
"Purchaser" Sections 1–201(33) & 8–116

INVESTMENT SECURITIES 404

"Security certificate" Section 8–102(a)(16)
"Unauthorized signature" Section 1–201(43)
"Value" Sections 1–201(44) & 8–116

Cross References

Effect of delivery without indorsement, see Commercial Code § 8307.
Effect of overissue, see Commercial Code § 8104.
Forgery, see Penal Code § 470 et seq.
Indorsements, manner of making, see Commercial Code § 8308.
Negotiable instruments,
  Alteration of instruments, see Commercial Code § 3407.
  Incomplete instruments, see Commercial Code § 3115.
Non-delivery as defense, see Commercial Code § 8202.
Rights acquired by purchaser, see Commercial Code § 8301.
Material alteration of contract, see Civil Code § 1700.
Unauthorized indorsement, effect, see Commercial Code § 8311.
Unauthorized signature, effect, see Commercial Code § 8205.
Uncertificated securities, interests in, governing law, effective date and transition provisions, see Commercial Code §§ 15103, 15104.

§ 8207. Registered owner; treatment by issuer or indenture trustee prior to transfer

(a) Before due presentment for registration of transfer of a certificated security in registered form or of an instruction requesting registration of transfer of an uncertificated security, the issuer or indenture trustee may treat the registered owner as the person exclusively entitled to vote, receive notifications, and otherwise exercise all the rights and powers of an owner.

(b) This division does not affect the liability of the registered owner of a security for a call, assessment, or the like. *(Added by Stats.1996, c. 497 (S.B.1591), § 9, operative Jan. 1, 1997.)*

Uniform Commercial Code Comment

1. Subsection (a) states the issuer's right to treat the registered owner of a security as the person entitled to exercise all the rights of an owner. This right of the issuer is limited by the provisions of Part 4 of this article. Once there has been due presentation for registration of transfer, the issuer has a duty to register ownership in the name of the transferee. Section 8–401. Thus its right to treat the old registered owner as exclusively entitled to the rights of ownership must cease.

The issuer may under this section make distributions of money or securities to the registered owners of securities without requiring further proof of ownership, provided that such distributions are distributable to the owners of all securities of the same issue and the terms of the security do not require surrender of a security certificate as a condition of payment or exchange. Any such distribution shall constitute a defense against a claim for the same distribution by a person, even if that person is in possession of the security certificate and is a protected purchaser of the security. See PEB Commentary No. 4, dated March 10, 1990.

2. Subsection (a) is permissive and does not require that the issuer deal exclusively with the registered owner. It is free to require proof of ownership before paying out dividends or the like if it chooses to. *Barbato v. Breeze Corporation*, 128 N.J.L. 309, 26 A.2d 53 (1942).

3. This section does not operate to determine who is finally entitled to exercise voting and other rights or to receive payments and distributions. The parties are still free to incorporate their own arrangements as to these matters in seller-purchaser agreements which may be definitive as between them.

4. No change in existing state laws as to the liability of registered owners for calls and assessments is here intended; nor is anything in this section designed to estop record holders from denying ownership when assessments are levied if they are otherwise entitled to do so under state law. See *State ex rel. Squire v. Murfey, Blosson & Co.*, 131 Ohio St. 289, 2 N.E.2d 866 (1936); *Willing v. Delaplaine*, 23 F.Supp. 579 (1937).

5. No interference is intended with the common practice of closing the transfer books or taking a record date for dividend, voting, and other purposes, as provided for in by-laws, charters, and statutes.

Definitional Cross References

"Certificated security" Section 8–102(a)(4)
"Instruction" Section 8–102(a)(12)
"Issuer" Section 8–201
"Registered form" Section 8–102(a)(13)
"Security" Section 8–102(a)(15)
"Uncertificated security" Section 8–102(a)(18)

Cross References

Assessments, see Corporations Code § 423.
Duty of authenticating trustee, transfer agent or registrar, see Commercial Code § 8406.
Liability of transferees, see Corporations Code § 411.
Notice of redemption, see Corporations Code § 509.
Persons entitled to vote, see Corporations Code § 701.
Record date for determining shareholders, closing books to transfers, see Corporations Code § 701.
Registered form, see Commercial Code § 8102.
Registration of transfers, see Commercial Code § 8401 et seq.
Statements required to be included in certificates to bind transferees, see Corporations Code § 418.
Uncertificated securities, interests in, governing law, effective date and transition provisions, see Commercial Code §§ 15103, 15104.
Voting rights, see Corporations Code §§ 400, 603, 604, 701 et seq.

§ 8208. Authenticating signers; warranties

(a) A person signing a security certificate as authenticating trustee, registrar, transfer agent, or the like, warrants all of the following to a purchaser for value of the certificated security, if the purchaser is without notice of a particular defect:

(1) The certificate is genuine.

(2) The person's own participation in the issue of the security is within the person's capacity and within the scope of the authority received by the person from the issuer.

(3) The person has reasonable grounds to believe that the certificated security is in the form and within the amount the issuer is authorized to issue.

(b) Unless otherwise agreed, a person signing under subdivision (a) does not assume responsibility for the validity of the security in other respects. *(Added by Stats.1996, c. 497 (S.B.1591), § 9, operative Jan. 1, 1997.)*

Uniform Commercial Code Comment

1. The warranties here stated express the current understanding and prevailing case law as to the effect of the signatures of authenticating trustees, transfer agents, and registrars. See *Jarvis v. Manhattan Beach Co.*, 148 N.Y. 652, 43 N.E. 68, 31 L.R.A. 776, 51 Am.St.Rep. 727 (1896). Although it has generally been regarded as the particular obligation of the transfer agent to determine whether securities are in proper form as provided by the by-laws and Articles of Incorporation, neither a registrar nor an authenticating trustee should properly place a signature upon a certificate without determining whether it is at least regular on its face. The obligations of these parties in this respect have therefore been made explicit in terms of due care. See *Feldmeier v. Mortgage Securities, Inc.*, 34 Cal.App.2d 201, 93 P.2d 593 (1939).

2. Those cases which hold that an authenticating trustee is not liable for any defect in the mortgage or property which secures the bond or for any fraudulent misrepresentations made by the issuer are not here affected since these matters do not involve the genuineness or proper form of the security. *Ainsa v. Mercantile Trust Co.*, 174 Cal. 504, 163 P. 898 (1917); *Tschetinian v. City Trust Co.*, 186 N.Y. 432, 79 N.E. 401 (1906); *Davidge v. Guardian Trust Co. of New York*, 203 N.Y. 331, 96 N.E. 751 (1911).

3. The charter or an applicable statute may affect the capacity of a bank or other corporation undertaking to act as an authenticating trustee, registrar, or transfer agent. See, for example, the Federal Reserve Act (U.S.C.A., Title 12, Banks and Banking, Section 248) under which the Board of Governors of the Federal Reserve Bank is authorized to grant special permits to National Banks permitting them to act as trustees. Such corporations are therefore held to certify as to their legal capacity to act as well as to their authority.

4. Authenticating trustees, registrars, and transfer agents have normally been held liable for an issue in excess of the authorized amount. *Jarvis v. Manhattan Beach Co.*, supra; *Mullen v. Eastern Trust & Banking Co.*, 108 Me. 498, 81 A. 948 (1911). In imposing upon these parties a duty of due care with respect to the amount they are authorized to help issue, this section does not necessarily validate the security, but merely holds persons responsible for the excess issue liable in damages for any loss suffered by the purchaser.

5. Aside from questions of genuineness and excess issue, these parties are not held to certify as to the validity of the security unless they specifically undertake to do so. The case law which has recognized a unique responsibility on the transfer agent's part to testify as to the validity of any security which it countersigns is rejected.

6. This provision does not prevent a transfer agent or issuer from agreeing with a registrar of stock to protect the registrar in respect of the genuineness and proper form of a security certificate signed by the issuer or the transfer agent or both. Nor does it interfere with proper indemnity arrangements between the issuer and trustees, transfer agents, registrars, and the like.

7. An unauthorized signature is a signature for purposes of this section if and only if it is made effective by Section 8–205.

Definitional Cross References

"Certificated security" Section 8–102(a)(4)
"Genuine" Section 1–201(18)
"Issuer" Section 8–201
"Notice" Section 1–201(25)
"Purchaser" Sections 1–201(33) & 8–116
"Security" Section 8–102(a)(15)
"Security certificate" Section 8–102(a)(16)
"Uncertificated security" Section 8–102(a)(18)
"Value" Sections 1–201(44) & 8–116

Cross References

Definitions, see Commercial Code § 8102.
Duty and obligation of authenticating trustee, transfer agent or registrar, see Commercial Code § 8406.
Effect of unauthorized signature on issue, see Commercial Code § 8205.
Signature, presumptions, see Commercial Code § 8105.
Uncertificated securities, interests in, governing law, effective date and transition provisions, see Commercial Code §§ 15103, 15104.

§ 8209. Liens

A lien in favor of an issuer upon a certificated security is valid against a purchaser only if the right of the issuer to the lien is noted conspicuously on the security certificate. *(Added by Stats.1996, c. 497 (S.B. 1591), § 9, operative Jan. 1, 1997.)*

Uniform Commercial Code Comment

This section is similar to Sections 8–202 and 8–204 which require that the terms of a certificated security and any restriction on transfer imposed by the issuer be noted on the security certificate. This section differs from those two sections in that the purchaser's knowledge of the issuer's claim is irrelevant. "Noted" makes clear that the text of the lien provisions need not be set forth in full. However, this would not override a provision of an applicable corporation code requiring statement in haec verba. This section does not apply to uncertificated securities. It applies to the indirect holding system in the same fashion as Sections 8–202 and 8–204, see Comment 2 to Section 8–202.

Definitional Cross References

"Certificated security" Section 8–102(a)(4)
"Issuer" Section 8–201

"Purchaser"   Sections 1–201(33) & 8–116
"Security"   Section 8–102(a)(15)
"Security certificate"   Section 8–102(a)(16)

§ 8210.   Overissue of securities

(a) In this section, "overissue" means the issue of securities in excess of the amount the issuer has corporate power to issue, but an overissue does not occur if appropriate action has cured the overissue.

(b) Except as otherwise provided in subdivisions (c) and (d), the provisions of this division that validate a security or compel its issue or reissue do not apply to the extent that validation, issue, or reissue would result in overissue.

(c) If an identical security not constituting an overissue is reasonably available for purchase, a person entitled to issue or validation may compel the issuer to purchase the security and deliver it if certificated or register its transfer if uncertificated, against surrender of any security certificate the person holds.

(d) If a security is not reasonably available for purchase, a person entitled to issue or validation may recover from the issuer the price the person or the last purchaser for value paid for it with interest from the date of the person's demand. *(Added by Stats.1996, c. 497 (S.B.1591), § 9, operative Jan. 1, 1997.)*

Uniform Commercial Code Comment

1. Deeply embedded in corporation law is the conception that "corporate power" to issue securities stems from the statute, either general or special, under which the corporation is organized. Corporation codes universally require that the charter or articles of incorporation state, at least as to capital shares, maximum limits in terms of number of shares or total dollar capital. Historically, special incorporation statutes are similarly drawn and sometimes similarly limit the face amount of authorized debt securities. The theory is that issue of securities in excess of the authorized amounts is prohibited. See, for example, *McWilliams v. Geddes & Moss Undertaking Co.*, 169 So. 894 (1936, La.); *Crawford v. Twin City Oil Co.*, 216 Ala. 216, 113 So. 61 (1927); *New York and New Haven R.R. Co. v. Schuyler*, 34 N.Y. 30 (1865). This conception persists despite modern corporation codes under which, by action of directors and stockholders, additional shares can be authorized by charter amendment and thereafter issued. This section does not give a person entitled to validation, issue, or reissue of a security, the right to compel amendment of the charter to authorize additional shares. Therefore, in a case where issue of an additional security would require charter amendment, the plaintiff is limited to the two alternate remedies set forth in subsections (c) and (d). The last clause of subsection (a), which is added in Revised Article 8, does, however, recognize that under modern conditions, overissue may be a relatively minor technical problem that can be cured by appropriate action under governing corporate law.

2. Where an identical security is reasonably available for purchase, whether because traded on an organized market, or because one or more security owners may be willing to sell at a not unreasonable price, the issuer, although unable to issue additional shares, will be able to purchase them and may be compelled to follow that procedure. *West v. Tintic Standard Mining Co.*, 71 Utah 158, 263 P. 490 (1928).

3. The right to recover damages from an issuer who has permitted an overissue to occur is well settled. *New York and New Haven R.R. Co. v. Schuyler*, 34 N.Y. 30 (1865). The measure of such damages, however, has been open to question, some courts basing them upon the value of stock at the time registration is refused; some upon the value at the time of trial; and some upon the highest value between the time of refusal and the time of trial. *Allen v. South Boston Railroad*, 150 Mass. 200, 22 N.E. 917, 5 L.R.A. 716, 15 Am.St.Rep. 185 (1889); *Commercial Bank v. Kortright*, 22 Wend. (N.Y.) 348 (1839). The purchase price of the security to the last purchaser who gave value for it is here adopted as being the fairest means of reducing the possibility of speculation by the purchaser. Interest may be recovered as the best available measure of compensation for delay.

Definitional Cross References

"Issuer"   Section 8–201
"Security"   Section 8–102(a)(15)
"Security certificate"   Section 8–102(a)(16)
"Uncertificated security"   Section 8–102(a)(18)

CHAPTER 3.   TRANSFER OF CERTIFICATED AND UNCERTIFICATED SECURITIES

Section
8301.   Delivery of security.
8302.   Rights acquired on delivery.
8303.   Protected purchaser.
8304.   Endorsements.
8305.   Instructions.
8306.   Signature guarantee; warranties.
8307.   Transferor's proof of authority.
8308 to 8321.   Repealed.

§ 8301.   Delivery of security

(a) Delivery of a certificated security to a purchaser occurs when any of the following occur:

(1) The purchaser acquires possession of the security certificate.

(2) Another person, other than a securities intermediary, either acquires possession of the security certificate on behalf of the purchaser or, having previously acquired possession of the certificate, acknowledges that it holds for the purchaser.

(3) A securities intermediary acting on behalf of the purchaser acquires possession of the security certificate, only if the certificate is in registered form and has been specially endorsed to the purchaser by an effective endorsement.

(b) Delivery of an uncertificated security to a purchaser occurs when any of the following occur:

(1) The issuer registers the purchaser as the registered owner, upon original issue or registration of transfer.

(2) Another person, other than a securities intermediary, either becomes the registered owner of the uncertificated security on behalf of the purchaser or, having previously become the registered owner, acknowledges that it holds for the purchaser. *(Added by Stats.1996, c. 497 (S.B.1591), § 9, operative Jan. 1, 1997.)*

Uniform Commercial Code Comment

1. This section specifies the requirements for "delivery" of securities. Delivery is used in Article 8 to describe the formal steps necessary for a purchaser to acquire a direct interest in a security under this Article. The concept of delivery refers to the implementation of a transaction, not the legal categorization of the transaction which is consummated by delivery. Issuance and transfer are different kinds of transaction, though both may be implemented by delivery. Sale and pledge are different kinds of transfers, but both may be implemented by delivery.

2. Subsection (a) defines delivery with respect to certificated securities. Paragraph (1) deals with simple cases where purchasers themselves acquire physical possession of certificates. Paragraphs (2)

and (3) of subsection (a) specify the circumstances in which delivery to a purchaser can occur although the certificate is in the possession of a person other than the purchaser. Paragraph (2) contains the general rule that a purchaser can take delivery through another person, so long as the other person is actually acting on behalf of the purchaser or acknowledges that it is holding on behalf of the purchaser. Paragraph (2) does not apply to acquisition of possession by a securities intermediary, because a person who holds securities through a securities account acquires a security entitlement, rather than having a direct interest. See Section 8–501. Subsection (a)(3) specifies the limited circumstances in which delivery of security certificates to a securities intermediary is treated as a delivery to the customer.

3. Subsection (b) defines delivery with respect to uncertificated securities. Use of the term "delivery" with respect to uncertificated securities, does, at least on first hearing, seem a bit solecistic. The word "delivery" is, however, routinely used in the securities business in a broader sense than manual tradition. For example, settlement by entries on the books of a clearing corporation is commonly called "delivery," as in the expression "delivery versus payment." The diction of this section has the advantage of using the same term for uncertificated securities as for certificated securities, for which delivery is conventional usage. Paragraph (1) of subsection (b) provides that delivery occurs when the purchaser becomes the registered owner of an uncertificated security, either upon original issue or registration of transfer. Paragraph (2) provides for delivery of an uncertificated security through a third person, in a fashion analogous to subsection (a)(2).

Definitional Cross References

"Certificated security"   Section 8–102(a)(4)
"Effective"   Section 8–107
"Issuer"   Section 8–201
"Purchaser"   Sections 1–201(33) & 8–116
"Registered form"   Section 8–102(a)(13)
"Securities intermediary"   Section 8–102(a)(14)
"Security certificate"   Section 8–102(a)(16)
"Special indorsement"   Section 8–304(a)
"Uncertificated security"   Section 8–102(a)(18)

§ 8302. Rights acquired on delivery

(a) Except as otherwise provided in subdivisions (b) and (c), upon delivery of a certificated or uncertificated security to a purchaser, the purchaser acquires all rights in the security that the transferor had or had power to transfer.

(b) A purchaser of a limited interest acquires rights only to the extent of the interest purchased.

(c) A purchaser of a certificated security who as a previous holder had notice of an adverse claim does not improve his position by taking from a protected purchaser. *(Added by Stats.1996, c. 497 (S.B.1591), § 9, operative Jan. 1, 1997.)*

Uniform Commercial Code Comment

1. Subsection (a) provides that if a certificated or uncertificated security is delivered (Section 8–301) to a purchaser in a transfer, the purchaser acquires all rights that the transferor had or had power to transfer. This statement of the familiar "shelter" principle is qualified by the exceptions that a purchaser of a limited interest acquires only that interest, subsection (b), and that a person who does not qualify as a protected purchaser cannot improve its position by taking from a subsequent protected purchaser, subsection (c).

2. Although this section provides that a purchaser acquires a property interest in a certificated or uncertificated security upon "delivery," it does not state that a person can acquire an interest in a security only by delivery. Article 8 is not a comprehensive codification of all of the law governing the creation or transfer of interests in securities. For example, the grant of a security interest is a transfer of a property interest, but the formal steps necessary to effectuate such a transfer are governed by Article 9 not by Article 8. Under the Article 9 rules, a security interest in a certificated or uncertificated security can be created by execution of a security agreement under Section 9–203 and can be perfected by filing. A transfer of an Article 9 security interest can be implemented by an Article 8 delivery, but need not be.

Similarly, Article 8 does not determine whether a property interest in certificated or uncertificated security is acquired under other law, such as the law of gifts, trusts, or equitable remedies. Nor does Article 8 deal with transfers by operation of law. For example, transfers from decedent to administrator, from ward to guardian, and from bankrupt to trustee in bankruptcy are governed by other law as to both the time they occur and the substance of the transfer. The Article 8 rules do, however, determine whether the issuer is obligated to recognize the rights that a third party, such as a transferee, may acquire under other law. See Sections 8–207, 8–401, and 8–404.

Definitional Cross References

"Certificated security"   Section 8–102(a)(4)
"Notice of adverse claim"   Section 8–105
"Protected purchaser"   Section 8–303
"Purchaser"   Sections 1–201(33) & 8–116
"Uncertificated security"   Section 8–102(a)(18)
"Delivery"   Section 8–301

Cross References

Action for possession, see Commercial Code § 8315.
Effect of delivery without indorsement, see Commercial Code § 8307.
Lost, destroyed or stolen securities, see Commercial Code § 8405.
Notice, actual and constructive, see Civil Code §§ 18, 19.
Notice to purchaser of adverse claims, see Commercial Code § 8304.
Personal property not in custody of levying officer transferred or encumbered, exceptions, see Code of Civil Procedure § 697.740.
Staleness as notice of adverse claims, see Commercial Code § 8305.
Staleness as notice of defects or defenses, see Commercial Code § 8203.
Uncertificated securities, interests in, governing law, effective date and transition provisions, see Commercial Code §§ 15103, 15104.

§ 8303. Protected purchaser

(a) "Protected purchaser" means a purchaser of a certificated or uncertificated security, or of an interest therein, who does all of the following:

(1) Gives value.

(2) Does not have notice of any adverse claim to the security.

(3) Obtains control of the certificated or uncertificated security.

(b) In addition to acquiring the rights of a purchaser, a protected purchaser also acquires its interest in the security free of any adverse claim. *(Added by Stats. 1996, c. 497 (S.B.1591), § 9, operative Jan. 1, 1997.)*

Uniform Commercial Code Comment

1. Subsection (a) lists the requirements that a purchaser must meet to qualify as a "protected purchaser." Subsection (b) provides that a protected purchaser takes its interest free from adverse claims. "Purchaser" is defined broadly in Section 1–201. A secured party as well as an outright buyer can qualify as a protected purchaser. Also, "purchase" includes taking by issue, so a person to whom a security is originally issued can qualify as a protected purchaser.

2. To qualify as a protected purchaser, a purchaser must give value, take without notice of any adverse claim, and obtain control. Value is used in the broad sense defined in Section 1–201(44). See also Section 8–116 (securities intermediary as purchaser for value). Adverse claim is defined in Section 8–102(a)(1). Section 8–105 specifies whether a purchaser has notice of an adverse claim. Control is defined in Section 8–106. To qualify as a protected purchaser there must be a time at which all of the requirements are satisfied. Thus if a purchaser obtains notice of an adverse claim before giving value or satisfying the

requirements for control, the purchaser cannot be a protected purchaser. See also Section 8–304(d).

The requirement that a protected purchaser obtain control expresses the point that to qualify for the adverse claim cut-off rule a purchaser must take through a transaction that is implemented by the appropriate mechanism. By contrast, the rules in Part 2 provide that any purchaser for value of a security without notice of a defense may take free of the issuer's defense based on that defense. See Section 8–202.

3. The requirements for control differ depending on the form of the security. For securities represented by bearer certificates, a purchaser obtains control by delivery. See Sections 8–106(a) and 8–301(a). For securities represented by certificates in registered form, the requirements for control are: (1) delivery as defined in Section 8–301(b), plus (2) either an effective indorsement or registration of transfer by the issuer. See Section 8–106(b). Thus, a person who takes through a forged indorsement does not qualify as a protected purchaser by virtue of the delivery alone. If, however, the purchaser presents the certificate to the issuer for registration of transfer, and the issuer registers transfer over the forged indorsement, the purchaser can qualify as a protected purchaser of the new certificate. If the issuer registers transfer on a forged indorsement, the true owner will be able to recover from the issuer for wrongful registration, see Section 8–404, unless the owner's delay in notifying the issuer of a loss or theft of the certificate results in preclusion under Section 8–406.

For uncertificated securities, a purchaser can obtain control either by delivery, see Sections 8–106(c)(1) and 8–301(b), or by obtaining an agreement pursuant to which the issuer agrees to act on instructions from the purchaser without further consent from the registered owner, see Section 8–106(c)(2). The control agreement device of Section 8–106(c)(2) takes the place of the "registered pledge" concept of the 1978 version of Article 8. A secured lender who obtains a control agreement under Section 8–106(c)(2) can qualify as a protected purchaser of an uncertificated security.

4. This section states directly the rules determining whether one takes free from adverse claims without using the phrase "good faith." Whether a person who takes under suspicious circumstances is disqualified is determined by the rules of Section 8–105 on notice of adverse claims. The term "protected purchaser," which replaces the term "bona fide purchaser" used in the prior version of Article 8, is derived from the term "protected holder" used in the Convention on International Bills and Notes prepared by the United Nations Commission on International Trade Law ("UNCITRAL").

Definitional Cross References

"Adverse claim"   Section 8–102(a)(1)
"Certificated security"   Section 8–102(a)(4)
"Control"   Section 8–106
"Notice of adverse claim"   Section 8–105
"Purchaser"   Sections 1–201(33) & 8–116
"Uncertificated security"   Section 8–102(a)(18)
"Value"   Sections 1–201(44) & 8–116

§ 8304. Endorsements

(a) An endorsement may be in blank or special. An endorsement in blank includes an endorsement to bearer. A special endorsement specifies to whom a security is to be transferred or who has power to transfer it. A holder may convert a blank endorsement to a special endorsement.

(b) An endorsement purporting to be only of part of a security certificate representing units intended by the issuer to be separately transferable is effective to the extent of the endorsement.

(c) An endorsement, whether special or in blank, does not constitute a transfer until delivery of the certificate on which it appears or, if the endorsement is on a separate document, until delivery of both the document and the certificate.

(d) If a security certificate in registered form has been delivered to a purchaser without a necessary endorsement, the purchaser may become a protected purchaser only when the endorsement is supplied. However, against a transferor, a transfer is complete upon delivery and the purchaser has a specifically enforceable right to have any necessary endorsement supplied.

(e) An endorsement of a security certificate in bearer form may give notice of an adverse claim to the certificate, but it does not otherwise affect a right to registration that the holder possesses.

(f) Unless otherwise agreed, a person making an endorsement assumes only the obligations provided in Section 8108 and not an obligation that the security will be honored by the issuer. *(Added by Stats.1996, c. 497 (S.B.1591), § 9, operative Jan. 1, 1997.)*

Uniform Commercial Code Comment

1. By virtue of the definition of indorsement in Section 8–102 and the rules of this section, the simplified method of indorsing certificated securities previously set forth in the Uniform Stock Transfer Act is continued. Although more than one special indorsement on a given security certificate is possible, the desire for dividends or interest, as the case may be, should operate to bring the certificate home for registration of transfer within a reasonable period of time. The usual form of assignment which appears on the back of a stock certificate or in a separate "power" may be filled up either in the form of an assignment, a power of attorney to transfer, or both. If it is not filled up at all but merely signed, the indorsement is in blank. If filled up either as an assignment or as a power of attorney to transfer, the indorsement is special.

2. Subsection (b) recognizes the validity of a "partial" indorsement, e.g., as to fifty shares of the one hundred represented by a single certificate. The rights of a transferee under a partial indorsement to the status of a protected purchaser are left to the case law.

3. Subsection (c) deals with the effect of an indorsement without delivery. There must be a voluntary parting with control in order to effect a valid transfer of a certificated security as between the parties. *Levey v. Nason,* 279 Mass. 268, 181 N.E. 193 (1932), and *National Surety Co. v. Indemnity Insurance Co. of North America,* 237 App.Div. 485, 261 N.Y.S. 605 (1933). The provision in Section 10 of the Uniform Stock Transfer Act that an attempted transfer without delivery amounts to a promise to transfer is omitted. Even under that Act the effect of such a promise was left to the applicable law of contracts, and this Article by making no reference to such situations intends to achieve a similar result. With respect to delivery there is no counterpart to subsection (d) on right to compel indorsement, such as is envisaged in *Johnson v. Johnson,* 300 Mass. 24, 13 N.E.2d 788 (1938), where the transferee under a written assignment was given the right to compel a transfer of the certificate.

4. Subsection (d) deals with the effect of delivery without indorsement. As between the parties the transfer is made complete upon delivery, but the transferee cannot become a protected purchaser until indorsement is made. The indorsement does not operate retroactively, and notice may intervene between delivery and indorsement so as to prevent the transferee from becoming a protected purchaser. Although a purchaser taking without a necessary indorsement may be subject to claims of ownership, any issuer's defense of which the purchaser had no notice at the time of delivery will be cut off, since the provisions of this Article protect all purchasers for value without notice (Section 8–202).

The transferee's right to compel an indorsement where a security certificate has been delivered with intent to transfer is recognized in the case law. See *Coats v. Guaranty Bank & Trust Co.,* 170 La. 871, 129 So. 513 (1930). A proper indorsement is one of the requisites of transfer which a purchaser of a certificated security has a right to obtain (Section 8–307). A purchaser may not only compel an indorsement under that section but may also recover for any reasonable expense incurred by the transferor's failure to respond to the demand for an indorsement.

5. Subsection (e) deals with the significance of an indorsement on a security certificate in bearer form. The concept of indorsement applies only to registered securities. A purported indorsement of bearer paper is normally of no effect. An indorsement "for collection," "for surrender" or the like, charges a purchaser with notice of adverse claims (Section 8–105(d)) but does not operate beyond this to interfere with any right the holder may otherwise possess to have the security registered.

6. Subsection (f) makes clear that the indorser of a security certificate does not warrant that the issuer will honor the underlying obligation. In view of the nature of investment securities and the circumstances under which they are normally transferred, a transferor cannot be held to warrant as to the issuer's actions. As a transferor the indorser, of course, remains liable for breach of the warranties set forth in this Article (Section 8–108).

Definitional Cross References

"Bearer form"   Section 8–102(a)(2)
"Certificated security"   Section 8–102(a)(4)
"Indorsement"   Section 8–102(a)(11)
"Purchaser"   Sections 1–201(33) & 8–116
"Registered form"   Section 8–102(a)(13)
"Security certificate"   Section 8–102(a)(16)

§ 8305. Instructions

(a) If an instruction has been originated by an appropriate person but is incomplete in any other respect, any person may complete it as authorized and the issuer may rely on it as completed, even though it has been completed incorrectly.

(b) Unless otherwise agreed, a person initiating an instruction assumes only the obligations imposed by Section 8108 and not an obligation that the security will be honored by the issuer. *(Added by Stats.1996, c. 497 (S.B.1591), § 9, operative Jan. 1, 1997.)*

Uniform Commercial Code Comment

1. The term instruction is defined in Section 8–102(a)(12) as a notification communicated to the issuer of an uncertificated security directing that transfer be registered. Section 8–107 specifies who may initiate an effective instruction.

Functionally, presentation of an instruction is quite similar to the presentation of an indorsed certificate for reregistration. Note that instruction is defined in terms of "communicate," see Section 8–102(a)(6). Thus, the instruction may be in the form of a writing signed by the registered owner or in any other form agreed upon by the issuer and the registered owner. Allowing nonwritten forms of instructions will permit the development and employment of means of transmitting instructions electronically.

When a person who originates an instruction leaves a blank and the blank later is completed, subsection (a) gives the issuer the same rights it would have had against the originating person had that person completed the blank. This is true regardless of whether the person completing the instruction had authority to complete it. Compare Section 8–206 and its Comment, dealing with blanks left upon issue.

2. Subsection (b) makes clear that the originator of an instruction, like the indorser of a security certificate, does not warrant that the issuer will honor the underlying obligation, but does make warranties as a transferor under Section 8–108.

Definitional Cross References

"Appropriate person"   Section 8–107
"Instruction"   Section 8–102(a)(12)
"Issuer"   Section 8–201

§ 8306. Signature guarantee; warranties

(a) A person who guarantees a signature of an endorser of a security certificate warrants that at the time of signing all of the following were true:

(1) The signature was genuine.

(2) The signer was an appropriate person to endorse, or if the signature is by an agent, the agent had actual authority to act on behalf of the appropriate person.

(3) The signer had legal capacity to sign.

(b) A person who guarantees a signature of the originator of an instruction warrants that at the time of signing all of the following were true:

(1) The signature was genuine.

(2) The signer was an appropriate person to originate the instruction, or if the signature is by an agent, the agent had actual authority to act on behalf of the appropriate person, if the person specified in the instruction as the registered owner was, in fact, the registered owner, as to which fact the signature guarantor does not make a warranty.

(3) The signer had legal capacity to sign.

(c) A person who specially guarantees the signature of an originator of an instruction makes the warranties of a signature guarantor under subdivision (b) and also warrants that at the time the instruction is presented to the issuer all of the following are true:

(1) The person specified in the instruction as the registered owner of the uncertificated security will be the registered owner.

(2) The transfer of the uncertificated security requested in the instruction will be registered by the issuer free from all liens, security interests, restrictions, and claims other than those specified in the instruction.

(d) A guarantor under subdivisions (a) and (b) or a special guarantor under subdivision (c) does not otherwise warrant the rightfulness of the transfer.

(e) A person who guarantees an endorsement of a security certificate makes the warranties of a signature guarantor under subdivision (a) and also warrants the rightfulness of the transfer in all respects.

(f) A person who guarantees an instruction requesting the transfer of an uncertificated security makes the warranties of a special signature guarantor under subdivision (c) and also warrants the rightfulness of the transfer in all respects.

(g) An issuer may not require a special guaranty of signature, a guaranty of endorsement, or a guaranty of instruction as a condition to registration of transfer.

(h) The warranties under this section are made to a person taking or dealing with the security in reliance on the guaranty, and the guarantor is liable to the person for loss resulting from their breach. An endorser or originator of an instruction whose signature, endorsement, or instruction has been guaranteed is liable to a guarantor for any loss suffered by the guarantor as a result of breach of the warranties of the guarantor. *(Added by Stats.1996, c. 497 (S.B.1591), § 9, operative Jan. 1, 1997.)*

Uniform Commercial Code Comment

1. Subsection (a) provides that a guarantor of the signature of the indorser of a security certificate warrants that the signature is genuine, that the signer is an appropriate person or has actual authority to indorse on behalf of the appropriate person, and that the signer has legal capacity. Subsection (b) provides similar, though not identical, warranties for the guarantor of a signature of the originator of an instruction for transfer of an uncertificated security.

Appropriate person is defined in Section 8–107(a) to include a successor or person who has power under other law to act for a person who is deceased or lacks capacity. Thus if a certificate registered in the name of Mary Roe is indorsed by Jane Doe as executor of Mary Roe, a guarantor of the signature of Jane Doe warrants that she has power to act as executor.

Although the definition of appropriate person in Section 8–107(a) does not itself include an agent, an indorsement by an agent is effective under Section 8–107(b) if the agent has authority to act for the appropriate person. Accordingly, this section provides an explicit warranty of authority for agents.

2. The rationale of the principle that a signature guarantor warrants the authority of the signer, rather than simply the genuineness of the signature, was explained in the leading case of *Jennie Clarkson Home for Children v. Missouri, K. & T. R. Co.*, 182 N.Y. 47, 74 N.E. 571, 70 A.L.R. 787 (1905), which dealt with a guaranty of the signature of a person indorsing on behalf of a corporation. "If stock is held by an individual who is executing a power of attorney for its transfer, the member of the exchange who signs as a witness thereto guarantees not only the genuineness of the signature affixed to the power of attorney, but that the person signing is the individual in whose name the stock stands. With reference to stock standing in the name of a corporation, which can only sign a power of attorney through its authorized officers or agents, a different situation is presented. If the witnessing of the signature of the corporation is only that of the signature of a person who signs for the corporation, then the guaranty is of no value, and there is nothing to protect purchasers or the companies who are called upon to issue new stock in the place of that transferred from the frauds of persons who have signed the names of corporations without authority. If such is the only effect of the guaranty, purchasers and transfer agents must first go to the corporation in whose name the stock stands and ascertain whether the individual who signed the power of attorney had authority to so do. This will require time, and in many cases will necessitate the postponement of the completion of the purchase by the payment of the money until the facts can be ascertained. The broker who is acting for the owner has an opportunity to become acquainted with his customer, and may readily before sale ascertain, in case of a corporation, the name of the officer who is authorized to execute the power of attorney. It was therefore, we think, the purpose of the rule to cast upon the broker who witnesses the signature the duty of ascertaining whether the person signing the name of the corporation had authority to so do, and making the witness a guarantor that it is the signature of the corporation in whose name the stock stands."

3. Subsection (b) sets forth the warranties that can reasonably be expected from the guarantor of the signature of the originator of an instruction, who, though familiar with the signer, does not have any evidence that the purported owner is in fact the owner of the subject uncertificated security. This is in contrast to the position of the person guaranteeing a signature on a certificate who can see a certificate in the signer's possession in the name of or indorsed to the signer or in blank. Thus, the warranty in paragraph (2) of subsection (b) is expressly conditioned on the actual registration's conforming to that represented by the originator. If the signer purports to be the owner, the guarantor under paragraph (2), warrants only the identity of the signer. If, however, the signer is acting in a representative capacity, the guarantor warrants both the signer's identity and authority to act for the purported owner. The issuer needs no warranty as to the facts of registration because those facts can be ascertained from the issuer's own records.

4. Subsection (c) sets forth a "special guaranty of signature" under which the guarantor additionally warrants both registered ownership and freedom from undisclosed defects of record. The guarantor of the signature of an indorser of a security certificate effectively makes these warranties to a purchaser for value on the evidence of a clean certificate issued in the name of the indorser, indorsed to the indorser or indorsed in blank. By specially guaranteeing under subsection (c), the guarantor warrants that the instruction will, when presented to the issuer, result in the requested registration free from defects not specified.

5. Subsection (d) makes clear that the warranties of a signature guarantor are limited to those specified in this section and do not include a general warranty of rightfulness. On the other hand subsections (e) and (f) provide that a person guaranteeing an indorsement or an instruction does warrant that the transfer is rightful in all respects.

6. Subsection (g) makes clear what can be inferred from the combination of Sections 8–401 and 8–402, that the issuer may not require as a condition to transfer a guaranty of the indorsement or instruction nor may it require a special signature guaranty.

7. Subsection (h) specifies to whom the warranties in this section run, and also provides that a person who gives a guaranty under this section has an action against the indorser or originator for any loss suffered by the guarantor.

Definitional Cross References

"Appropriate person"   Section 8–107
"Genuine"   Section 1–201(18)
"Indorsement"   Section 8–102(a)(11)
"Instruction"   Section 8–102(a)(12)
"Issuer"   Section 8–201
"Security certificate"   Section 8–102(a)(16)
"Uncertificated security"   Section 8–102(a)(18)

Cross References

Agency, warranty of authority, see Civil Code § 2342.
Bona fide purchaser, rights and title, see Commercial Code § 8302.
Damages for breach of warranty of agent's authority, see Civil Code § 3318.
Issuer's lien, see Commercial Code § 8103.
Letters of credit,
   Issuer's duty to honor a draft or demand for payment, see Commercial Code § 5114.
   Warranties of transfer and presentment, see Commercial Code § 5111.
Lost, destroyed and stolen certificated securities, see Commercial Code § 8405.
Unauthorized indorsement, effect, see Commercial Code § 8311.
Uncertificated securities, interests in, governing law, effective date and transition provisions, see Commercial Code §§ 15103, 15104.
Variation agreements, see Commercial Code § 1102.
Warranties on sales of goods, see Commercial Code § 2312 et seq.

§ 8307. Transferor's proof of authority

Unless otherwise agreed, the transferor of a security on due demand shall supply the purchaser with proof of authority to transfer or with any other requisite necessary to obtain registration of the transfer of the security, but if the transfer is not for value, a transferor need not comply unless the purchaser pays the necessary expenses. If the transferor fails within a reasonable time to comply with the demand, the purchaser may reject or rescind the transfer. *(Added by Stats.1996, c. 497 (S.B.1591), § 9, operative Jan. 1, 1997.)*

Uniform Commercial Code Comment

1. Because registration of the transfer of a security is a matter of vital importance, a purchaser is here provided with the means of obtaining such formal requirements for registration as signature guaranties, proof of authority, transfer tax stamps and the like. The transferor is the one in a position to supply most conveniently whatever documentation may be requisite for registration of transfer, and the duty to do so upon demand within a reasonable time is here stated affirmatively. If an essential item is peculiarly within the province of the transferor so that the transferor is the only one who can obtain it, the purchaser may specifically enforce the right to obtain it. Compare Section 8–304(d). If a transfer is not for value the transferor need not pay expenses.

2. If the transferor's duty is not performed the transferee may reject or rescind the contract to transfer. The transferee is not bound to do so. An action for damages for breach of contract may be preferred.

Definitional Cross References

"Purchaser" Sections 1–201(33) & 8–116
"Security" Section 8–102(a)(15)
"Value" Sections 1–201(44) & 8–116

§§ 8308 to 8321. Repealed by Stats.1996, c. 497 (S.B. 1591), § 8, operative Jan. 1, 1997

CHAPTER 4. REGISTRATION

Section
8401. Transfer registration; conditions required; liability.
8402. Assurances required by issuer.
8403. Demand to not register transfer of security; notice by issuer following demand; liability of issuer.
8404. Wrongful registration of transfer; issuer's liability.
8405. Lost, destroyed, or wrongfully taken certificates; duty and liability of issuer.
8406. Lost, destroyed or wrongfully taken certificate; failure to notify issuer.
8407. Agent of issuer; obligations.
8408. Repealed.

§ 8401. Transfer registration; conditions required; liability

(a) If a certificated security in registered form is presented to an issuer with a request to register transfer or an instruction is presented to an issuer with a request to register transfer of an uncertificated security, the issuer shall register the transfer as requested if the following conditions are met:

(1) Under the terms of the security the person seeking registration of transfer is eligible to have the security registered in its name.

(2) The endorsement or instruction is made by the appropriate person or by an agent who has actual authority to act on behalf of the appropriate person.

(3) Reasonable assurance is given that the endorsement or instruction is genuine and authorized (Section 8402).

(4) Any applicable law relating to the collection of taxes has been complied with.

(5) The transfer does not violate any restriction on transfer imposed by the issuer in accordance with Section 8204.

(6) A demand that the issuer not register transfer has not become effective under Section 8403, or the issuer has complied with subdivision (b) of Section 8403 but no legal process or indemnity bond is obtained as provided in subdivision (d) of Section 8403.

(7) The transfer is in fact rightful or is to a protected purchaser.

(b) If an issuer is under a duty to register a transfer of a security, the issuer is liable to a person presenting a certificated security or an instruction for registration or to the person's principal for loss resulting from unreasonable delay in registration or failure or refusal to register the transfer. *(Added by Stats.1996, c. 497 (S.B.1591), § 9, operative Jan. 1, 1997.)*

Uniform Commercial Code Comment

1. This section states the duty of the issuer to register transfers. A duty exists only if certain preconditions exist. If any of the preconditions do not exist, there is no duty to register transfer. If an indorsement on a security certificate is a forgery, there is no duty. If an instruction to transfer an uncertificated security is not originated by an appropriate person, there is no duty. If there has not been compliance with applicable tax laws, there is no duty. If a security certificate is properly indorsed but nevertheless the transfer is in fact wrongful, there is no duty unless the transfer is to a protected purchaser (and the other preconditions exist).

This section does not constitute a mandate that the issuer must establish that all preconditions are met before the issuer registers a transfer. The issuer may waive the reasonable assurances specified in paragraph (a)(3). If it has confidence in the responsibility of the persons requesting transfer, it may ignore questions of compliance with tax laws. Although an issuer has no duty if the transfer is wrongful, the issuer has no duty to inquire into adverse claims, see Section 8–404.

2. By subsection (b) the person entitled to registration may not only compel it but may hold the issuer liable in damages for unreasonable delay.

3. Section 8–201(c) provides that with respect to registration of transfer, "issuer" means the person on whose behalf transfer books are maintained. Transfer agents, registrars or the like within the scope of their respective functions have rights and duties under this Part similar to those of the issuer. See Section 8–407.

Definitional Cross References

"Appropriate person" Section 8–107
"Certificated security" Section 8–102(a)(4)
"Genuine" Section 1–201(18)
"Indorsement" Section 8–102(a)(11)
"Instruction" Section 8–102(a)(12)
"Issuer" Section 8–201
"Protected purchaser" Section 8–303
"Registered form" Section 8–102(a)(13)
"Uncertificated security" Section 8–102(a)(18)

Cross References

Authenticating trustee, transfer agent or registrar, duties, see Commercial Code § 8406.
Bona fide purchaser, rights and title acquired, see Commercial Code § 8302.
By-law provisions restricting right to transfer or hypothecate shares, see Corporations Code § 204.
Delivery without indorsement, effect, see Commercial Code § 8307.
Execution of certificate for shares, see Corporations Code § 416.
Failure to transfer shares on books or issue certificate, penalty, see Corporations Code § 2201.
Indorsement by appropriate person, see Commercial Code § 8308.
Indorsement without delivery, effect, see Commercial Code § 8309.
Issuance of certificate to purchaser at sale for delinquent assessments, see Corporations Code § 423.
"Issuer", defined, see Commercial Code § 8201.
Issuer's restrictions on transfer, effect, see Commercial Code § 8204.
Law governing registration, see Commercial Code § 8106.
Liability for registration, see Commercial Code § 8404.
Married persons, transfer of shares, see Corporations Code § 420.
Unauthorized indorsement, effect, see Commercial Code § 8311.
Uncertificated securities, interests in, governing law, effective date and transition provisions, see Commercial Code §§ 15103, 15104.

§ 8402. Assurances required by issuer

(a) An issuer may require the following assurance that each necessary endorsement or each instruction is genuine and authorized:

(1) In all cases, a guaranty of the signature of the person making an endorsement or originating an

struction including, in the case of an instruction, reasonable assurance of identity.

(2) If the endorsement is made or the instruction is originated by an agent, appropriate assurance of actual authority to sign.

(3) If the endorsement is made or the instruction is originated by a fiduciary pursuant to paragraph (4) or (5) of Section 8107, appropriate evidence of appointment or incumbency.

(4) If there is more than one fiduciary, reasonable assurance that all who are required to sign have done so.

(5) If the endorsement is made or the instruction is originated by a person not covered by another provision of this subdivision, assurance appropriate to the case corresponding as nearly as may be to the provisions of this subdivision.

(b) An issuer may elect to require reasonable assurance beyond that specified in this section.

(c) In this section:

(1) "Guaranty of the signature" means a guaranty signed by or on behalf of a person reasonably believed by the issuer to be responsible. An issuer may adopt standards with respect to responsibility if they are not manifestly unreasonable.

(2) "Appropriate evidence of appointment or incumbency" means:

(A) In the case of a fiduciary appointed or qualified by a court, a certificate issued by or under the direction or supervision of the court or an officer thereof and dated within 60 days before the date of presentation for transfer.

(B) In any other case, a copy of a document showing the appointment or a certificate issued by or on behalf of a person reasonably believed by an issuer to be responsible or, in the absence of that document or certificate, other evidence the issuer reasonably considers appropriate. *(Added by Stats.1996, c. 497 (S.B. 1591), § 9, operative Jan. 1, 1997.)*

Uniform Commercial Code Comment

1. An issuer is absolutely liable for wrongful registration of transfer if the indorsement or instruction is ineffective. See Section 8–404. Accordingly, an issuer is entitled to require such assurance as is reasonable under the circumstances that all necessary indorsements are effective, and thus to minimize its risk. This section establishes the requirements the issuer may make in terms of documentation which, except in the rarest of instances, should be easily furnished. Subsection (b) provides that an issuer may require additional assurances if that requirement is reasonable under the circumstances, but if the issuer demands more than reasonable assurance that the instruction or the necessary indorsements are genuine and authorized, the presenter may refuse the demand and sue for improper refusal to register. Section 8–401(b).

2. Under subsection (a)(1), the issuer may require in all cases a guaranty of signature. See Section 8–306. When an instruction is presented the issuer always may require reasonable assurance as to the identity of the originator. Subsection (c) allows the issuer to require that the person making these guaranties be one reasonably believed to be responsible, and the issuer may adopt standards of responsibility which are not manifestly unreasonable. Regulations under the federal securities laws, however, place limits on the requirements transfer agents may impose concerning the responsibility of eligible signature guarantors. See 17 CFR 240.17Ad–15.

3. This section, by paragraphs (2) through (5) of subsection (a), permits the issuer to seek confirmation that the indorsement or instruction is genuine and authorized. The permitted methods act as a double check on matters which are within the warranties of the signature guarantor. See Section 8–306. Thus, an agent may be required to submit a power of attorney, a corporation to submit a certified resolution evidencing the authority of its signing officer to sign, an executor or administrator to submit the usual "short-form certificate," etc. But failure of a fiduciary to obtain court approval of the transfer or to comply with other requirements does not make the fiduciary's signature ineffective. Section 8–107(c). Hence court orders and other controlling instruments are omitted from subsection (a).

Subsection (a)(3) authorizes the issuer to require "appropriate evidence" of appointment or incumbency, and subsection (c) indicates what evidence will be "appropriate". In the case of a fiduciary appointed or qualified by a court that evidence will be a court certificate dated within sixty days before the date of presentation, subsection (c)(2)(i). Where the fiduciary is not appointed or qualified by a court, as in the case of a successor trustee, subsection (c)(2)(ii) applies. In that case, the issuer may require a copy of a trust instrument or other document showing the appointment, or it may require the certificate of a responsible person. In the absence of such a document or certificate, it may require other appropriate evidence. If the security is registered in the name of the fiduciary as such, the person's signature is effective even though the person is no longer serving in that capacity, see Section 8–107(d), hence no evidence of incumbency is needed.

4. Circumstances may indicate that a necessary signature was unauthorized or was not that of an appropriate person. Such circumstances would be ignored at risk of absolute liability. To minimize that risk the issuer may properly exercise the option given by subsection (b) to require assurance beyond that specified in subsection (a). On the other hand, the facts at hand may reflect only on the rightfulness of the transfer. Such facts do not create a duty of inquiry, because the issuer is not liable to an adverse claimant unless the claimant obtains legal process. See Section 8–404.

Definitional Cross References

"Appropriate person" Section 8–107
"Genuine" Section 1–201(18)
"Indorsement" Section 8–102(a)(11)
"Instruction" Section 8–102(a)(12)
"Issuer" Section 8–201

Cross References

Appropriate person, indorsement, see Commercial Code § 8308.
Breach of warranties in respect of signature or indorsement, see Commercial Code § 8312.
Computation of time, see Government Code § 6800 et seq.
Duty of inquiry, see Commercial Code § 8403.
Guarantee of signature, see Commercial Code § 8312.
Improper refusal to register, liability, see Commercial Code § 8401.
Indorsement, manner of making, see Commercial Code § 8308.
Liability arising from registration, see Commercial Code § 8404.
Notice, actual and constructive, see Civil Code §§ 18, 19.
Obligation of good faith, see Commercial Code § 1203.
Sale of securities upon order of probate court, see Probate Code § 10200.
Unauthorized indorsement, see Commercial Code § 8311.
Uncertificated securities, interests in, governing law, effective date and transition provisions, see Commercial Code §§ 15103, 15104.

§ 8403. Demand to not register transfer of security; notice by issuer following demand; liability of issuer

(a) A person who is an appropriate person to make an endorsement or originate an instruction may demand that the issuer not register transfer of a security by communicating to the issuer a notification that identifies the registered owner and the issue of which the security is a part and provides an address for communications directed to the person making the demand. The demand is effective only if it is received by the issuer at a time and in a manner affording the issuer reasonable opportunity to act on it.

(b) If a certificated security in registered form is presented to an issuer with a request to register transfer or an instruction is presented to an issuer with a request to register transfer of an uncertificated security after a demand that the issuer not register transfer has become effective, the issuer shall promptly communicate to (A) the person who initiated the demand at the address provided in the demand and (B) the person who presented the security for registration of transfer or initiated the instruction requesting registration of transfer a notification stating all of the following:

(1) The certificated security has been presented for registration of transfer or the instruction for registration of transfer of the uncertificated security has been received.

(2) A demand that the issuer not register transfer had previously been received.

(3) The issuer will withhold registration of transfer for a period of time stated in the notification in order to provide the person who initiated the demand an opportunity to obtain legal process or an indemnity bond.

(c) The period described in paragraph (3) of subdivision (b) may not exceed 30 days after the date of communication of the notification. A shorter period may be specified by the issuer if it is not manifestly unreasonable.

(d) An issuer is not liable to a person who initiated a demand that the issuer not register transfer for any loss the person suffers as a result of registration of a transfer pursuant to an effective endorsement or instruction if the person who initiated the demand does not, within the time stated in the issuer's communication, either:

(1) Obtain an appropriate restraining order, injunction, or other process from a court of competent jurisdiction enjoining the issuer from registering the transfer.

(2) File with the issuer an indemnity bond, sufficient in the issuer's judgment to protect the issuer and any transfer agent, registrar, or other agent of the issuer involved from any loss it or they may suffer by refusing to register the transfer.

(e) This section does not relieve an issuer from liability for registering transfer pursuant to an endorsement or instruction that was not effective. *(Added by Stats.1996, c. 497 (S.B.1591), § 9, operative Jan. 1, 1997.)*

Uniform Commercial Code Comment

1. The general rule under this Article is that if there has been an effective indorsement or instruction, a person who contends that registration of the transfer would be wrongful should not be able to interfere with the registration process merely by sending notice of the assertion to the issuer. Rather, the claimant must obtain legal process. See Section 8–404. Section 8–403 is an exception to this general rule. It permits the registered owner—but not third parties—to demand that the issuer not register a transfer.

2. This section is intended to alleviate the problems faced by registered owners of certificated securities who lose or misplace their certificates. A registered owner who realizes that a certificate may have been lost or stolen should promptly report that fact to the issuer, lest the owner be precluded from asserting a claim for wrongful registration. See Section 8–406. The usual practice of issuers and transfer agents is that when a certificate is reported as lost, the owner is notified that a replacement can be obtained if the owner provides an indemnity bond. See Section 8–405. If the registered owner does not plan to transfer the securities, the owner might choose not to obtain a replacement, particularly if the owner suspects that the certificate has merely been misplaced.

Under this section, the owner's notification that the certificate has been lost would constitute a demand that the issuer not register transfer. No indemnity bond or legal process is necessary. If the original certificate is presented for registration of transfer, the issuer is required to notify the registered owner of that fact, and defer registration of transfer for a stated period. In order to prevent undue delay in the process of registration, the stated period may not exceed thirty days. This gives the registered owner an opportunity to either obtain legal process or post an indemnity bond and thereby prevent the issuer from registering transfer.

3. Subsection (e) makes clear that this section does not relieve an issuer from liability for registering a transfer pursuant to an ineffective indorsement. An issuer's liability for wrongful registration in such cases does not depend on the presence or absence of notice that the indorsement was ineffective. Registered owners who are confident that they neither indorsed the certificates, nor did anything that would preclude them from denying the effectiveness of another's indorsement, see Sections 8–107(b) and 8–406, might prefer to pursue their rights against the issuer for wrongful registration rather than take advantage of the opportunity to post a bond or seek a restraining order when notified by the issuer under this section that their lost certificates have been presented for registration in apparently good order.

Definitional Cross References

"Appropriate person"   Section 8–107
"Certificated security"   Section 8–102(a)(4)
"Communicate"   Section 8–102(a)(6)
"Effective"   Section 8–107
"Indorsement"   Section 8–102(a)(11)
"Instruction"   Section 8–102(a)(12)
"Issuer"   Section 8–201
"Registered form"   Section 8–102(a)(13)
"Uncertificated security"   Section 8–102(a)(18)

Cross References

Adverse claims, notice to purchaser, see Commercial Code § 8304.
Duty of authenticating trustee, transfer agent or registrar, see Commercial Code § 8406.
Effectiveness of indorsements, assurance, see Commercial Code § 8402.
Good faith, defined, see Commercial Code § 1201.
Injunction, see Civil Code § 3420 et seq.; Code of Civil Procedure § 525 et seq.
Liability arising from registration, see Commercial Code § 8404.
Lost, destroyed and stolen certificated securities, see Commercial Code § 8405.
Notice, actual and constructive, see Civil Code §§ 18, 19.
Obligation of good faith, see Commercial Code § 1203.
Sale of securities upon order of probate court, see Probate Code § 10200.
Uncertificated securities, interests in, governing law, effective date and transition provisions, see Commercial Code §§ 15103, 15104.
Unreasonable delay in registration, liability, see Commercial Code § 8401.

§ 8404. Wrongful registration of transfer; issuer's liability

(a) Except as otherwise provided in Section 8406, an issuer is liable for wrongful registration of transfer if the issuer has registered a transfer of a security to a person not entitled to it, and the transfer was registered in any of the following circumstances:

(1) Pursuant to an ineffective endorsement or instruction.

(2) After a demand that the issuer not register transfer became effective under subdivision (a) of Section 8403(a) and the issuer did not comply with subdivision (b) of Section 8403.

(3) After the issuer had been served with an injunction, restraining order, or other legal process enjoining it from registering the transfer, issued by a court of competent jurisdiction, and the issuer had a reasonable opportunity to act on the injunction, restraining order, or other legal process.

(4) By an issuer acting in collusion with the wrongdoer.

(b) An issuer that is liable for wrongful registration of transfer under subdivision (a) on demand shall provide the person entitled to the security with a like certificated or uncertificated security, and any payments or distributions that the person did not receive as a result of the wrongful registration. If an overissue would result, the issuer's liability to provide the person with a like security is governed by Section 8210.

(c) Except as otherwise provided in subdivision (a) or in a law relating to the collection of taxes, an issuer is not liable to an owner or other person suffering loss as a result of the registration of a transfer of a security if registration was made pursuant to an effective endorsement or instruction. (Added by Stats.1996, c. 497 (S.B.1591), § 9, operative Jan. 1, 1997.)

Uniform Commercial Code Comment

1. Subsection (a)(1) provides that an issuer is liable if it registers transfer pursuant to an indorsement or instruction that was not effective. For example, an issuer that registers transfer on a forged indorsement is liable to the registered owner. The fact that the issuer had no reason to suspect that the indorsement was forged or that the issuer obtained the ordinary assurances under Section 8–402 does not relieve the issuer from liability. The reason that issuers obtain signature guaranties and other assurances is that they are liable for wrongful registration.

Subsection (b) specifies the remedy for wrongful registration. Pre-Code cases established the registered owner's right to receive a new security where the issuer had wrongfully registered a transfer, but some cases also allowed the registered owner to elect between an equitable action to compel issue of a new security and an action for damages. Cf. *Casper v. Kalt–Zimmers Mfg. Co.*, 159 Wis. 517, 149 N.W. 754 (1914). Article 8 does not allow such election. The true owner of a certificated security is required to take a new security except where an overissue would result and a similar security is not reasonably available for purchase. See Section 8–210. The true owner of an uncertificated security is entitled and required to take restoration of the records to their proper state, with a similar exception for overissue.

2. Read together, subsections (c) and (a) have the effect of providing that an issuer has no duties to an adverse claimant unless the claimant serves legal process on the issuer to enjoin registration. Issuers, or their transfer agents, perform a record-keeping function for the direct holding system that is analogous to the functions performed by clearing corporations and securities intermediaries in the indirect holding system. This section applies to the record-keepers for the direct holding system the same standard that Section 8–115 applies to the record-keepers for the indirect holding system. Thus, issuers are not liable to adverse claimants merely on the basis of notice. As in the case of the analogous rules for the indirect holding system, the policy of this section is to protect the right of investors to have their securities transfers processed without the disruption or delay that might result if the record-keepers risked liability to third parties. It would be undesirable to apply different standards to the direct and indirect holding systems, since doing so might operate as a disincentive to the development of a book-entry direct holding system.

3. This section changes prior law under which an issuer could be held liable, even though it registered transfer on an effective indorsement or instruction, if the issuer had in some fashion been notified that the transfer might be wrongful against a third party, and the issuer did not appropriately discharge its duty to inquire into the adverse claim. See Section 8–403 (1978).

The rule of former Section 8–403 was anomalous inasmuch as Section 8–207 provides that the issuer is entitled to "treat the registered owner as the person exclusively entitled to vote, receive notifications, and otherwise exercise all the rights and powers of an owner." Under Section 8–207, the fact that a third person notifies the issuer of a claim does not preclude the issuer from treating the registered owner as the person entitled to the security. See *Kerrigan v. American Orthodontics Corp.*, 960 F.2d 43 (7th Cir. 1992). The change made in the present version of Section 8–404 ensures that the rights of registered owners and the duties of issuers with respect to registration of transfer will be protected against third-party interference in the same fashion as other rights of registered ownership.

Definitional Cross References

"Certificated security" Section 8–102(a)(4)
"Effective" Section 8–107
"Indorsement" Section 8–102(a)(11)
"Instruction" Section 8–102(a)(12)
"Issuer" Section 8–201
"Security" Section 8–102(a)(15)
"Uncertificated security" Section 8–102(a)(18)

Cross References

Certificate held in joint tenancy, immunity of corporation for transfer of, see Corporations Code § 420.
Duty of authenticating trustee, transfer agent or registrar, see Commercial Code § 8406.
Duty of inquiry, see Commercial Code § 8403.
Effectiveness of indorsements, assurance, see Commercial Code § 8402.
Indorsements, manner of making, see Commercial Code § 8308.
Lost, destroyed and stolen certificated securities, see Commercial Code § 8405.
Minor or incompetent, immunity of corporation for transfer by, see Corporations Code § 420.
Notice, actual or constructive, see Civil Code §§ 18, 19.
Overissue, definition and effect, see Commercial Code § 8104.
Uncertificated securities, interests in, governing law, effective date and transition provisions, see Commercial Code §§ 15103, 15104.

§ 8405. Lost, destroyed, or wrongfully taken certificates; duty and liability of issuer

(a) If an owner of a certificated security, whether in registered or bearer form, claims that the certificate has been lost, destroyed, or wrongfully taken, the issuer shall issue a new certificate if the owner does all of the following:

(1) So requests before the issuer has notice that the certificate has been acquired by a protected purchaser.

(2) Files with the issuer a sufficient indemnity bond.

(3) Satisfies other reasonable requirements imposed by the issuer.

(b) If, after the issue of a new security certificate, a protected purchaser of the original certificate presents it for registration of transfer, the issuer shall register the transfer unless an overissue would result. In that case, the issuer's liability is governed by Section 8210. In addition to any rights on the indemnity bond, an issuer may recover the new certificate from a person to whom it was issued or any person taking under that person, except a protected purchaser. *(Added by Stats.1996, c. 497 (S.B.1591), § 9, operative Jan. 1, 1997.)*

Uniform Commercial Code Comment

1. This section enables the owner to obtain a replacement of a lost, destroyed or stolen certificate, provided that reasonable requirements are satisfied and a sufficient indemnity bond supplied.

2. Where an "original" security certificate has reached the hands of a protected purchaser, the registered owner—who was in the best position to prevent the loss, destruction or theft of the security certificate—is now deprived of the new security certificate issued as a replacement. This changes the pre-UCC law under which the original certificate was ineffective after the issue of a replacement except insofar as it might represent an action for damages in the hands of a purchaser for value without notice. *Keller v. Eureka Brick Mach. Mfg. Co.*, 43 Mo.App. 84, 11 L.R.A. 472 (1890). Where both the original and the new certificate have reached protected purchasers the issuer is required to honor both certificates unless an overissue would result and the security is not reasonably available for purchase. See Section 8–210. In the latter case alone, the protected purchaser of the original certificate is relegated to an action for damages. In either case, the issuer itself may recover on the indemnity bond.

Definitional Cross References

"Bearer form"   Section 8–102(a)(2)
"Certificated security"   Section 8–102(a)(4)
"Issuer"   Section 8–201
"Notice"   Section 1–201(25)
"Overissue"   Section 8–210
"Protected purchaser"   Section 8–303
"Registered form"   Section 8–102(a)(13)
"Security certificate"   Section 8–102(a)(16)

Cross References

Duty of inquiry, see Commercial Code § 8403.
Effectiveness of indorsements, assurance, see Commercial Code § 8402.
Liability arising from registration, see Commercial Code § 8404.
Lost and missing documents of title, see Commercial Code § 7601.
Lost, stolen or destroyed bonds, etc., action for new certificate, see Corporations Code § 419.
Lost or destroyed documents, issuance of duplicate, see Civil Code § 3415.
Notice, actual or constructive, see Civil Code §§ 18, 19.
Overissue, effect, see Commercial Code § 8104.
Signature or indorsement, effect of guaranteeing, see Commercial Code § 8312.
Unauthorized indorsement, see Commercial Code § 8311.
Uncertificated securities, interests in, governing law, effective date and transition provisions, see Commercial Code §§ 15103, 15104.

§ 8406. Lost, destroyed or wrongfully taken certificate; failure to notify issuer

If a security certificate has been lost, apparently destroyed, or wrongfully taken, and the owner fails to notify the issuer of that fact within a reasonable time after the owner has notice of it and the issuer registers a transfer of the security before receiving notification, the owner may not assert against the issuer a claim for registering the transfer under Section 8404 or a claim to a new security certificate under Section 8405. *(Added by Stats.1996, c. 497 (S.B.1591), § 9, operative Jan. 1, 1997.)*

Uniform Commercial Code Comment

An owner who fails to notify the issuer within a reasonable time after the owner knows or has reason to know of the loss or theft of a security certificate is estopped from asserting the ineffectiveness of a forged or unauthorized indorsement and the wrongfulness of the registration of the transfer. If the lost certificate was indorsed by the owner, then the registration of the transfer was not wrongful under Section 8–404, unless the owner made an effective demand that the issuer not register transfer under Section 8–403.

Definitional Cross References

"Issuer"   Section 8–201
"Notify"   Section 1–201(25)
"Security certificate"   Section 8–102(a)(16)

§ 8407. Agent of issuer; obligations

A person acting as authenticating trustee, transfer agent, registrar, or other agent for an issuer in the registration of a transfer of its securities, in the issue of new security certificates or uncertificated securities, or in the cancellation of surrendered security certificates has the same obligation to the holder or owner of a certificated or uncertificated security with regard to the particular functions performed as the issuer has in regard to those functions. *(Added by Stats.1996, c. 497 (S.B.1591), § 9, operative Jan. 1, 1997.)*

Uniform Commercial Code Comment

1. Transfer agents, registrars, and the like are here expressly held liable both to the issuer and to the owner for wrongful refusal to register a transfer as well as for wrongful registration of a transfer in any case within the scope of their respective functions where the issuer would itself be liable. Those cases which have regarded these parties solely as agents of the issuer and have therefore refused to recognize their liability to the owner for mere non-feasance, i.e., refusal to register a transfer, are rejected. *Hulse v. Consolidated Quicksilver Mining Corp.*, 65 Idaho 768, 154 P.2d 149 (1944); *Nicholson v. Morgan*, 119 Misc. 309, 196 N.Y.Supp. 147 (1922); *Lewis v. Hargadine–McKittrick Dry Goods Co.*, 305 Mo. 396, 274 S.W. 1041 (1924).

2. The practice frequently followed by authenticating trustees of issuing certificates of indebtedness rather than authenticating duplicate certificates where securities have been lost or stolen became obsolete in view of the provisions of Section 8–405, which makes express provision for the issue of substitute securities. It is not a breach of trust or lack of due diligence for trustees to authenticate new securities. Cf. *Switzerland General Ins. Co. v. N.Y.C. & H.R.R. Co.*, 152 App.Div. 70, 136 N.Y.S. 726 (1912).

Definitional Cross References

"Certificated security"   Section 8–102(a)(4)
"Issuer"   Section 8–201
"Security"   Section 8–102(a)(15)
"Security certificate"   Section 8–102(a)(16)
"Uncertificated security"   Section 8–102(a)(18)

§ 8408. Repealed by Stats.1996, c. 497 (S.B.1591), § 8, operative Jan. 1, 1997

CHAPTER 5. SECURITY ENTITLEMENTS

Section
8501. Security account; acquisition of entitlement.
8502. Adverse claims.
8503. Interest or security entitlement held by securities intermediary; property interest of entitlement holder; actions.
8504. Aggregate of security entitlements; maintenance of quantity by securities intermediary.

Section
8505. Payment or distribution by issuer of financial asset; duty of securities intermediary.
8506. Entitlement holder rights in asset; exercise by securities intermediary.
8507. Entitlement orders; duty of securities intermediary to comply.
8508. Change of entitlement to another form of holding; duty of securities intermediary.
8509. Duty of securities intermediary; compliance with federal law; standard of care.
8510. Adverse claims; priorities.
8511. Priority of claims.

§ 8501. Security account; acquisition of entitlement

(a) "Securities account" means an account to which a financial asset is or may be credited in accordance with an agreement under which the person maintaining the account undertakes to treat the person for whom the account is maintained as entitled to exercise the rights that comprise the financial asset.

(b) Except as otherwise provided in subdivisions (d) and (e), a person acquires a security entitlement if a securities intermediary does any of the following:

(1) Indicates by book entry that a financial asset has been credited to the person's securities account.

(2) Receives a financial asset from the person or acquires a financial asset for the person and, in either case, accepts it for credit to the person's securities account.

(3) Becomes obligated under other law, regulation, or rule to credit a financial asset to the person's securities account.

(c) If a condition of subdivision (b) has been met, a person has a security entitlement even though the securities intermediary does not itself hold the financial asset.

(d) If a securities intermediary holds a financial asset for another person, and the financial asset is registered in the name of, payable to the order of, or specially endorsed to the other person, and has not been endorsed to the securities intermediary or in blank, the other person is treated as holding the financial asset directly rather than as having a security entitlement with respect to the financial asset.

(e) Issuance of a security is not establishment of a security entitlement. *(Added by Stats.1996, c. 497 (S.B.1591), § 9, operative Jan. 1, 1997.)*

Uniform Commercial Code Comment

1. Part 5 rules apply to security entitlements, and Section 8–501(b) provides that a person has a security entitlement when a financial asset has been credited to a "securities account." Thus, the term "securities account" specifies the type of arrangements between institutions and their customers that are covered by Part 5. A securities account is a consensual arrangement in which the intermediary undertakes to treat the customer as entitled to exercise the rights that comprise the financial asset. The consensual aspect is covered by the requirement that the account be established pursuant to agreement. The term agreement is used in the broad sense defined in Section 1–201(3). There is no requirement that a formal or written agreement be signed.

As the securities business is presently conducted, several significant relationships clearly fall within the definition of a securities account, including the relationship between a clearing corporation and its participants, a broker and customers who leave securities with the broker, and a bank acting as securities custodian and its custodial customers. Given the enormous variety of arrangements concerning securities that exist today, and the certainty that new arrangements will evolve in the future, it is not possible to specify all of the arrangements to which the term does and does not apply.

Whether an arrangement between a firm and another person concerning a security or other financial asset is a "securities account" under this Article depends on whether the firm has undertaken to treat the other person as entitled to exercise the rights that comprise the security or other financial asset. Section 1–102, however, states the fundamental principle of interpretation that the Code provisions should be construed and applied to promote their underlying purposes and policies. Thus, the question whether a given arrangement is a securities account should be decided not by dictionary analysis of the words of the definition taken out of context, but by considering whether it promotes the objectives of Article 8 to include the arrangement within the term securities account.

The effect of concluding that an arrangement is a securities account is that the rules of Part 5 apply. Accordingly, the definition of "securities account" must be interpreted in light of the substantive provisions in Part 5, which describe the core features of the type of relationship for which the commercial law rules of Revised Article 8 concerning security entitlements were designed. There are many arrangements between institutions and other persons concerning securities or other financial assets which do not fall within the definition of "securities account" because the institutions have not undertaken to treat the other persons as entitled to exercise the ordinary rights of an entitlement holder specified in the Part 5 rules. For example, the term securities account does not cover the relationship between a bank and its depositors or the relationship between a trustee and the beneficiary of an ordinary trust, because those are not relationships in which the holder of a financial asset has undertaken to treat the other as entitled to exercise the rights that comprise the financial asset in the fashion contemplated by the Part 5 rules.

In short, the primary factor in deciding whether an arrangement is a securities account is whether application of the Part 5 rules is consistent with the expectations of the parties to the relationship. Relationships not governed by Part 5 may be governed by other parts of Article 8 if the relationship gives rise to a new security, or may be governed by other law entirely.

2. Subsection (b) of this section specifies what circumstances give rise to security entitlements. Paragraph (1) of subsection (b) sets out the most important rule. It turns on the intermediary's conduct, reflecting a basic operating assumption of the indirect holding system that once a securities intermediary has acknowledged that it is carrying a position in a financial asset for its customer or participant, the intermediary is obligated to treat the customer or participant as entitled to the financial asset. Paragraph (1) does not attempt to specify exactly what accounting, record-keeping, or information transmission steps suffice to indicate that the intermediary has credited the account. That is left to agreement, trade practice, or rule in order to provide the flexibility necessary to accommodate varying or changing accounting and information processing systems. The point of paragraph (1) is that once an intermediary has acknowledged that it is carrying a position for the customer or participant, the customer or participant has a security entitlement. The precise form in which the intermediary manifests that acknowledgment is left to private ordering.

Paragraph (2) of subsection (b) sets out a different operational test, turning not on the intermediary's accounting system but on the facts that accounting systems are supposed to represent. Under paragraph (b)(2) a person has a security entitlement if the intermediary has received and accepted a financial asset for credit to the account of its customer or participant. For example, if a customer of a broker or bank custodian delivers a security certificate in proper form to the broker or bank to be held in the customer's account, the customer acquires a security entitlement. Paragraph (b)(2) also covers circumstances in which the intermediary receives a financial asset from a third person for credit to the account of the customer or participant. Paragraph (b)(2) is not limited to circumstances in which the intermediary receives security certificates or other financial assets in physical form. Paragraph (b)(2) also covers circumstances in which the intermediary acquires a security entitlement with respect to a financial asset which is to be credited to the account of the intermediary's own customer. For example, if a customer transfers her account from Broker A to Broker B, she acquires security entitlements against Broker B once the clearing corporation has credited the positions to Broker B's account. It should be noted, however, that paragraph (b)(2) provides that a person acquires a security entitlement when the intermediary not only receives but also accepts the financial asset for credit to the account. This limitation is included to take account of the fact that there may be circumstances in which an intermediary has received a financial asset but is not willing to undertake the obligations that flow from establishing a security entitlement. For example, a security certificate which is sent to an intermediary may not be in proper form, or may represent a type of financial asset which the intermediary is not willing to carry for others. It should be noted that in all but extremely unusual cases, the circumstances covered by paragraph (2) will also be covered by paragraph (1), because the intermediary will have credited the positions to the customer's account.

Paragraph (3) of subsection (b) sets out a residual test, to avoid any implication that the failure of an intermediary to make the appropriate entries to credit a position to a customer's securities account would prevent the customer from acquiring the rights of an entitlement holder under Part 5. As is the case with the paragraph (2) test, the paragraph (3) test would not be needed for the ordinary cases, since they are covered by paragraph (1).

3. In a sense, Section 8–501(b) is analogous to the rules set out in the provisions of Sections 8–313(1)(d) and 8–320 of the prior version of Article 8 that specified what acts by a securities intermediary or clearing corporation sufficed as a transfer of securities held in fungible bulk. Unlike the prior version of Article 8, however, this section is not based on the idea that an entitlement holder acquires rights only by virtue of a "transfer" from the securities intermediary to the entitlement holder. In the indirect holding system, the significant fact is that the securities intermediary has undertaken to treat the customer as entitled to the financial asset. It is up to the securities intermediary to take the necessary steps to ensure that it will be able to perform its undertaking. It is, for example, entirely possible that a securities intermediary might make entries in a customer's account reflecting that customer's acquisition of a certain security at a time when the securities intermediary did not itself happen to hold any units of that security. The person from whom the securities intermediary bought the security might have failed to deliver and it might have taken some time to clear up the problem, or there may have been an operational gap in time between the crediting of a customer's account and the receipt of securities from another securities intermediary. The entitlement holder's rights against the securities intermediary do not depend on whether or when the securities intermediary acquired its interests. Subsection (c) is intended to make this point clear. Subsection (c) does not mean that the intermediary is free to create security entitlements without itself holding sufficient financial assets to satisfy its entitlement holders. The duty of a securities intermediary to maintain sufficient assets is governed by Section 8–504 and regulatory law. Subsection (c) is included only to make it clear the question whether a person has acquired a security entitlement does not depend on whether the intermediary has complied with that duty.

4. Part 5 of Article 8 sets out a carefully designed system of rules for the indirect holding system. Persons who hold securities through brokers or custodians have security entitlements that are governed by Part 5, rather than being treated as the direct holders of securities. Subsection (d) specifies the limited circumstance in which a customer who leaves a financial asset with a broker or other securities intermediary has a direct interest in the financial asset, rather than a security entitlement.

The customer can be a direct holder only if the security certificate, or other financial asset, is registered in the name of, payable to the order of, or specially indorsed to the customer, and has not been indorsed by the customer to the securities intermediary or in blank. The distinction between those circumstances where the customer can be treated as direct owner and those where the customer has a security entitlement is essentially the same as the distinction drawn under the federal bankruptcy code between customer name securities and customer property. The distinction does not turn on any form of physical identification or segregation. A customer who delivers certificates to a broker with blank indorsements or stock powers is not a direct holder but has a security entitlement, even though the broker holds those certificates in some form of separate safe-keeping arrangement for that particular customer. The customer remains the direct holder only if there is no indorsement or stock power so that further action by the customer is required to place the certificates in a form where they can be transferred by the broker.

The rule of subsection (d) corresponds to the rule set out in Section 8–301(a)(3) specifying when acquisition of possession of a certificate by a securities intermediary counts as "delivery" to the customer.

5. Subsection (e) is intended to make clear that Part 5 does not apply to an arrangement in which a security is issued representing an interest in underlying assets, as distinguished from arrangements in which the underlying assets are carried in a securities account. A common mechanism by which new financial instruments are devised is that a financial institution that holds some security, financial instrument, or pool thereof, creates interests in that asset or pool which are sold to others. In many such cases, the interests so created will fall within the definition of "security" in Section 8–102(a)(15). If so, then by virtue of subsection (e) of Section 8–501, the relationship between the institution that creates the interests and the persons who hold them is not a security entitlement to which the Part 5 rules apply. Accordingly, an arrangement such as an American depositary receipt facility which creates freely transferable interests in underlying securities will be issuance of a security under Article 8 rather than establishment of a security entitlement to the underlying securities.

The subsection (e) rule can be regarded as an aspect of the definitional rules specifying the meaning of securities account and security entitlement. Among the key components of the definition of security in Section 8–102(a)(15) are the "transferability" and "divisibility" tests. Securities, in the Article 8 sense, are fungible interests or obligations that are intended to be tradable. The concept of security entitlement under Part 5 is quite different. A security entitlement is the package of rights that a person has against the person's own intermediary with respect to the positions carried in the person's securities account. That package of rights is not, as such, something that is traded. When a customer sells a security that she had held through a securities account, her security entitlement is terminated; when she buys a security that she will hold through her securities account, she acquires a security entitlement. In most cases, settlement of a securities trade will involve termination of one person's security entitlement and acquisition of a security entitlement by another person. That transaction, however, is not a "transfer" of the same entitlement from one person to another. That is not to say that an entitlement holder cannot transfer an interest in her security entitlement as such; granting a security interest in a security entitlement is such a transfer. On the other hand, the nature of a security entitlement is that the intermediary is undertaking duties only to the person identified as the entitlement holder.

Definitional Cross References

"Financial asset" Section 8–102(a)(9)
"Indorsement" Section 8–102(a)(11)
"Securities intermediary" Section 8–102(a)(14)
"Security" Section 8–102(a)(15)
"Security entitlement" Section 8–102(a)(17)

§ 8502. Adverse claims

An action based on an adverse claim to a financial asset, whether framed in conversion, replevin, constructive trust, equitable lien, or other theory, may not be asserted against a person who acquires a security entitlement under Section 8501 for value and without notice of the adverse claim. *(Added by Stats.1996, c. 497 (S.B.1591), § 9, operative Jan. 1, 1997.)*

Uniform Commercial Code Comment

1. The section provides investors in the indirect holding system with protection against adverse claims by specifying that no adverse claim can be asserted against a person who acquires a security entitlement under Section 8–501 for value and without notice of the adverse claim. It plays a role in the indirect holding system analogous to the rule of the direct holding system that protected purchasers take free from adverse claims (Section 8–303).

This section does not use the locution "takes free from adverse claims" because that could be confusing as applied to the indirect holding system. The nature of indirect holding system is that an entitlement holder has an interest in common with others who hold positions in the same financial asset through the same intermediary. Thus, a particular entitlement holder's interest in the financial assets held by its intermediary is necessarily "subject to" the interests of others. See Section 8–503. The rule stated in this section might have been expressed by saying that a person who acquires a security entitlement under Section 8–501 for value and without notice of adverse claims takes "that security entitlement" free from adverse claims. That formulation has not been used, however, for fear that it would be misinterpreted as suggesting that the person acquires a right to the underlying financial assets that could not be affected by the competing rights of others claiming through common or higher tier intermediaries. A security entitlement is a complex bundle of rights. This section does not deal with the question of what rights are in the bundle. Rather, this section provides that once a person has acquired the bundle, someone else cannot take it away on the basis of assertion that the transaction in which the security entitlement was created involved a violation of the claimant's rights.

2. Because securities trades are typically settled on a net basis by book-entry movements, it would ordinarily be impossible for anyone to trace the path of any particular security, no matter how the interest of parties who hold through intermediaries is described. Suppose, for example, that S has a 1000 share position in XYZ common stock through an account with a broker, Able & Co. S's identical twin impersonates S and directs Able to sell the securities. That same day, B places an order with Baker & Co., to buy 1000 shares of XYZ common stock. Later, S discovers the wrongful act and seeks to recover "her shares." Even if S can show that, at the stage of the trade, her sell order was matched with B's buy order, that would not suffice to show that "her shares" went to B. Settlement between Able and Baker occurs on a net basis for all trades in XYZ that day; indeed Able's net position may have been such that it received rather than delivered shares in XYZ through the settlement system.

In the unlikely event that this was the only trade in XYZ common stock executed in the market that day, one could follow the shares from S's account to B's account. The plaintiff in an action in conversion or similar legal action to enforce a property interest must show that the defendant has an item of property that belongs to the plaintiff. In this example, B's security entitlement is not the same item of property that formerly was held by S, it is a new package of rights that B acquired against Baker under Section 8–501. Principles of equitable remedies might, however, provide S with a basis for contending that if the position B received was the traceable product of the wrongful taking of S's property by S's twin, a constructive trust should be imposed on B's property in favor of S. See G. Palmer, The Law of Restitution § 2.14. Section 8–502 ensures that no such claims can be asserted against a person, such as B in this example, who acquires a security entitlement under Section 8–501 for value and without notice, regardless of what theory of law or equity is used to describe the basis of the assertion of the adverse claim.

In the above example, S would ordinarily have no reason to pursue B unless Able is insolvent and S's claim will not be satisfied in the insolvency proceedings. Because S did not give an entitlement order for the disposition of her security entitlement, Able must recredit her account for the 1000 shares of XYZ common stock. See Section 8–507(b).

3. The following examples illustrate the operation of Section 8–502.

Example 1. Thief steals bearer bonds from Owner. Thief delivers the bonds to Broker for credit to Thief's securities account, thereby acquiring a security entitlement under Section 8–501(b). Under other law, Owner may have a claim to have a constructive trust imposed on the security entitlement as the traceable product of the bonds that Thief misappropriated. Because Thief was himself the wrongdoer, Thief obviously had notice of Owner's adverse claim. Accordingly, Section 8–502 does not preclude Owner from asserting an adverse claim against Thief.

Example 2. Thief steals bearer bonds from Owner. Thief owes a personal debt to Creditor. Creditor has a securities account with Broker. Thief agrees to transfer the bonds to Creditor as security for or in satisfaction of his debt to Creditor. Thief does so by sending the bonds to Broker for credit to Creditor's securities account. Creditor thereby acquires a security entitlement under Section 8–501(b). Under other law, Owner may have a claim to have a constructive trust imposed on the security entitlement as the traceable product of the bonds that Thief misappropriated. Creditor acquired the security entitlement for value, since Creditor acquired it as security for or in satisfaction of Thief's debt to Creditor. See Section 1–201(44). If Creditor did not have notice of Owner's claim, Section 8–502 precludes any action by Owner against Creditor, whether framed in constructive trust or other theory. Section 8–105 specifies what counts as notice of an adverse claim.

Example 3. Father, as trustee for Son, holds XYZ Co. shares in a securities account with Able & Co. In violation of his fiduciary duties, Father sells the XYZ Co. shares and uses the proceeds for personal purposes. Father dies, and his estate is insolvent. Assume—implausibly—that Son is able to trace the XYZ Co. shares and show that the "same shares" ended up in Buyer's securities account with Baker & Co. Section 8–502 precludes any action by Son against Buyer, whether framed in constructive trust or other theory, provided that Buyer acquired the security entitlement for value and without notice of adverse claims.

Example 4. Debtor holds XYZ Co. shares in a securities account with Able & Co. As collateral for a loan from Bank, Debtor grants Bank a security interest in the security entitlement to the XYZ Co. shares. Bank perfects by a method which leaves Debtor with the ability to dispose of the shares. See Section 9–115. In violation of the security agreement, Debtor sells the XYZ Co. shares and absconds with the proceeds. Assume—implausibly—that Bank is able to trace the XYZ Co. shares and show that the "same shares" ended up in Buyer's securities account with Baker & Co. Section 8–502 precludes any action by Bank against Buyer, whether framed in constructive trust or other theory, provided that Buyer acquired the security entitlement for value and without notice of adverse claims.

Example 5. Debtor owns controlling interests in various public companies, including Acme and Ajax. Acme owns 60% of the stock of another public company, Beta. Debtor causes the Beta stock to be pledged to Lending Bank as collateral for Ajax's debt. Acme holds the Beta stock through an account with a securities custodian, C Bank, which in turn holds through Clearing Corporation. Lending Bank is also a Clearing Corporation participant. The pledge of the Beta stock is implemented by Acme instructing C Bank to instruct Clearing Corporation to debit C Bank's account and credit Lending Bank's account. Acme and Ajax both become insolvent. The Beta stock is still valuable. Acme's liquidator asserts that the pledge of the Beta stock for Ajax's debt was wrongful as against Acme and seeks to recover the Beta stock from Lending Bank. Because the pledge was implemented by an outright transfer into Lending Bank's account at Clearing Corporation, Lending Bank acquired a security entitlement to the Beta stock under Section 8–501. Lending Bank acquired the security entitlement for value, since it acquired it as security for a debt. See Section 1–201(44). If Lending Bank did not have notice of Acme's claim, Section 8–502 will preclude any action by Acme against Lending Bank, whether framed in constructive trust or other theory.

4. Although this section protects entitlement holders against adverse claims, it does not protect them against the risk that their securities intermediary will not itself have sufficient financial assets to satisfy the claims of all of its entitlement holders. Suppose that Customer A holds 1000 shares of XYZ Co. stock in an account with her broker, Able & Co. Able in turn holds 1000 shares of XYZ Co. through its account with Clearing Corporation, but has no other positions in XYZ Co. shares, either for other customers or for its own proprietary account. Customer B places an order with Able for the purchase of 1000 shares of XYZ Co. stock, and pays the purchase price. Able credits B's account with a 1000 share position in XYZ Co. stock, but Able does not itself buy any additional XYZ Co. shares. Able fails, having only 1000 shares to satisfy the claims of A and B. Unless other insolvency law establishes a different distributional rule, A and B would share the 1000 shares held by Able pro rata, without regard to the time that their respective entitlements were established. See Section 8–503(b). Section 8–502 protects entitlement holders, such as A and B, against adverse claimants. In this case, however, the problem that A and B face is not that someone is trying to take away their entitlements, but that the entitlements are not worth what they thought. The only role that Section 8–502 plays in this case is to preclude any assertion that A has some form of claim against B by virtue of the fact that Able's establishment of an entitlement in favor of B diluted A's rights to the limited assets held by Able.

Definitional Cross References
"Adverse claim" Section 8–102(a)(1)
"Financial asset" Section 8–102(a)(9)
"Notice of adverse claim" Section 8–105
"Security entitlement" Section 8–102(a)(17)
"Value" Sections 1–201(44) & 8–116

§ 8503. Interest or security entitlement held by securities intermediary; property interest of entitlement holder; actions

(a) To the extent necessary for a securities intermediary to satisfy all security entitlements with respect to a particular financial asset, all interests in that financial asset held by the securities intermediary are held by the securities intermediary for the entitlement holders, are not property of the securities intermediary, and are not subject to claims of creditors of the securities intermediary, except as otherwise provided in Section 8511.

(b) An entitlement holder's property interest with respect to a particular financial asset under subdivision (a) is a pro rata property interest in all interests in that financial asset held by the securities intermediary, without regard to the time the entitlement holder acquired the security entitlement or the time the securities intermediary acquired the interest in that financial asset.

(c) An entitlement holder's property interest with respect to a particular financial asset under subdivision (a) may be enforced against the securities intermediary only by exercise of the entitlement holder's rights under Sections 8505 to 8508, inclusive.

(d) An entitlement holder's property interest with respect to a particular financial asset under subdivision (a) may be enforced against a purchaser of the financial asset or interest therein only if all of the following conditions are met:

(1) Insolvency proceedings have been initiated by or against the securities intermediary.

(2) The securities intermediary does not have sufficient interests in the financial asset to satisfy the security entitlements of all of its entitlement holders to that financial asset.

(3) The securities intermediary violated its obligations under Section 8504 by transferring the financial asset or interest therein to the purchaser.

(4) The purchaser is not protected under subdivision (e). The trustee or other liquidator, acting on behalf of all entitlement holders having security entitlements with respect to a particular financial asset, may recover the financial asset, or interest therein, from the purchaser. If the trustee or other liquidator elects not to pursue that right, an entitlement holder whose security entitlement remains unsatisfied has the right to recover its interest in the financial asset from the purchaser.

(e) An action based on the entitlement holder's property interest with respect to a particular financial asset under subdivision (a), whether framed in conversion, replevin, constructive trust, equitable lien, or other theory, may not be asserted against any purchaser of a financial asset or interest therein who gives value, obtains control, and does not act in collusion with the securities intermediary in violating the securities intermediary's obligations under Section 8504. *(Added by Stats.1996, c. 497 (S.B.1591), § 9, operative Jan. 1, 1997.)*

Uniform Commercial Code Comment

1. This section specifies the sense in which a security entitlement is an interest in the property held by the securities intermediary. It expresses the ordinary understanding that securities that a firm holds for its customers are not general assets of the firm subject to the claims of creditors. Since securities intermediaries generally do not segregate securities in such fashion that one could identify particular securities as the ones held for customers, it would not be realistic for this section to state that "customers' securities" are not subject to creditors' claims. Rather subsection (a) provides that to the extent necessary to satisfy all customer claims, all units of that security held by the firm are held for the entitlement holders, are not property of the securities intermediary, and are not subject to creditors' claims, except as otherwise provided in Section 8–511.

An entitlement holder's property interest under this section is an interest with respect to a specific issue of securities or financial assets. For example, customers of a firm who have positions in XYZ common stock have security entitlements with respect to the XYZ common stock held by the intermediary, while other customers who have positions in ABC common stock have security entitlements with respect to the ABC common stock held by the intermediary.

Subsection (b) makes clear that the property interest described in subsection (a) is an interest held in common by all entitlement holders who have entitlements to a particular security or other financial asset. Temporal factors are irrelevant. One entitlement holder cannot claim that its rights to the assets held by the intermediary are superior to the rights of another entitlement holder by virtue of having acquired those rights before, or after, the other entitlement holder. Nor does it matter whether the intermediary had sufficient assets to satisfy all entitlement holders' claims at one point, but no longer does. Rather, all entitlement holders have a pro rata interest in whatever positions in that financial asset the intermediary holds.

Although this section describes the property interest of entitlement holders in the assets held by the intermediary, it does not necessarily determine how property held by a failed intermediary will be distributed in insolvency proceedings. If the intermediary fails and its affairs are being administered in an insolvency proceeding, the applicable insolvency law governs how the various parties having claims against the firm are treated. For example, the distributional rules for stockbroker liquidation proceedings under the Bankruptcy Code and Securities Investor Protection Act ("SIPA") provide that all customer property is distributed pro rata among all customers in proportion to the dollar value of their total positions, rather than dividing the property on an issue by issue basis. For intermediaries that are not subject to the Bankruptcy Code and SIPA, other insolvency law would determine what distributional rule is applied.

2. Although this section recognizes that the entitlement holders of a securities intermediary have a property interest in the financial assets held by the intermediary, the incidents of this property interest are established by the rules of Article 8, not by common law property concepts. The traditional Article 8 rules on certificated securities were based on the idea that a paper certificate could be regarded as a nearly complete reification of the underlying right. The rules on transfer and the consequences of wrongful transfer could then be written using the same basic concepts as the rules for physical chattels. A person's claim of ownership of a certificated security is a right to a specific identifiable physical object, and that right can be asserted against any person who ends up in possession of that physical certificate, unless cut off by the rules protecting purchasers for value without notice. Those concepts do not work for the indirect holding system. A security entitlement is not a claim to a specific identifiable thing; it is a package of rights and interests that a person has against the person's securities intermediary and the property held by the intermediary. The idea that discrete objects might be traced through the hands of different persons has no place in the Revised Article 8 rules for the indirect holding system. The fundamental principles of the indirect holding system rules are that an entitlement holder's own intermediary has the obligation to see to it that

the entitlement holder receives all of the economic and corporate rights that comprise the financial asset, and that the entitlement holder can look only to that intermediary for performance of the obligations. The entitlement holder cannot assert rights directly against other persons, such as other intermediaries through whom the intermediary holds the positions, or third parties to whom the intermediary may have wrongfully transferred interests, except in extremely unusual circumstances where the third party was itself a participant in the wrongdoing. Subsections (c) through (e) reflect these fundamental principles.

Subsection (c) provides that an entitlement holder's property interest can be enforced against the intermediary only by exercise of the entitlement holder's rights under Sections 8–505 through 8–508. These are the provisions that set out the duty of an intermediary to see to it that the entitlement holder receives all of the economic and corporate rights that comprise the security. If the intermediary is in insolvency proceedings and can no longer perform in accordance with the ordinary Part 5 rules, the applicable insolvency law will determine how the intermediary's assets are to be distributed.

Subsections (d) and (e) specify the limited circumstances in which an entitlement holder's property interest can be asserted against a third person to whom the intermediary transferred a financial asset that was subject to the entitlement holder's claim when held by the intermediary. Subsection (d) provides that the property interest of entitlement holders cannot be asserted against any transferee except in the circumstances therein specified. So long as the intermediary is solvent, the entitlement holders must look to the intermediary to satisfy their claims. If the intermediary does not hold financial assets corresponding to the entitlement holders' claims, the intermediary has the duty to acquire them. See Section 8–504. Thus, paragraphs (1), (2), and (3) of subsection (d) specify that the only occasion in which the entitlement holders can pursue transferees is when the intermediary is unable to perform its obligation, and the transfer to the transferee was a violation of those obligations. Even in that case, a transferee who gave value and obtained control is protected by virtue of the rule in subsection (e), unless the transferee acted in collusion with the intermediary.

Subsections (d) and (e) have the effect of protecting transferees from an intermediary against adverse claims arising out of assertions by the intermediary's entitlement holders that the intermediary acted wrongfully in transferring the financial assets. These rules, however, operate in a slightly different fashion than traditional adverse claim cut-off rules. Rather than specifying that a certain class of transferee takes free from all claims, subsections (d) and (e) specify the circumstances in which this particular form of claim can be asserted against a transferee. Revised Article 8 also contains general adverse claim cut-off rules for the indirect holding system. See Sections 8–502 and 8–510. The rule of subsections (d) and (e) takes precedence over the general cut-off rules of those sections, because Section 8–503 itself defines and sets limits on the assertion of the property interest of entitlement holders. Thus, the question whether entitlement holders' property interest can be asserted as an adverse claim against a transferee from the intermediary is governed by the collusion test of Section 8–503(e), rather than by the "without notice" test of Sections 8–502 and 8–510.

3. The limitations that subsections (c) through (e) place on the ability of customers of a failed intermediary to recover securities or other financial assets from transferees are consistent with the fundamental policies of investor protection that underlie this Article and other bodies of law governing the securities business. The commercial law rules for the securities holding and transfer system must be assessed from the forward-looking perspective of their impact on the vast number of transactions in which no wrongful conduct occurred or will occur, rather than from the *post hoc* perspective of what rule might be most advantageous to a particular class of persons in litigation that might arise out of the occasional case in which someone has acted wrongfully. Although one can devise hypothetical scenarios where particular customers might find it advantageous to be able to assert rights against someone other than the customers' own intermediary, commercial law rules that permitted customers to do so would impair rather than promote the interest of investors and the safe and efficient operation of the clearance and settlement system. Suppose, for example, that Intermediary A transfers securities to B, that Intermediary A acted wrongfully as against its customers in so doing, and that after the transaction Intermediary A did not have sufficient securities to satisfy its obligations to its entitlement holders. Viewed solely from the standpoint of the customers of Intermediary A, it would seem that permitting the property to be recovered from B, would be good for investors. That, however, is not the case. B may itself be an intermediary with its own customers, or may be some other institution through which individuals invest, such as a pension fund or investment company. There is no reason to think that rules permitting customers of an intermediary to trace and recover securities that their intermediary wrongfully transferred work to the advantage of investors in general. To the contrary, application of such rules would often merely shift losses from one set of investors to another. The uncertainties that would result from rules permitting such recoveries would work to the disadvantage of all participants in the securities markets.

The use of the collusion test in Section 8–503(e) furthers the interests of investors generally in the sound and efficient operation of the securities holding and settlement system. The effect of the choice of this standard is that customers of a failed intermediary must show that the transferee from whom they seek to recover was affirmatively engaged in wrongful conduct, rather than casting on the transferee any burden of showing that the transferee had no awareness of wrongful conduct by the failed intermediary. The rule of Section 8–503(e) is based on the long-standing policy that it is undesirable to impose upon purchasers of securities any duty to investigate whether their sellers may be acting wrongfully.

Rather than imposing duties to investigate, the general policy of the commercial law of the securities holding and transfer system has been to eliminate legal rules that might induce participants to conduct investigations of the authority of persons transferring securities on behalf of others for fear that they might be held liable for participating in a wrongful transfer. The rules in Part 4 of Article 8 concerning transfers by fiduciaries provide a good example. Under *Lowry v. Commercial & Farmers' Bank*, 15 F. Cas. 1040 (C.C.D. Md. 1848) (No. 8551), an issuer could be held liable for wrongful transfer if it registered transfer of securities by a fiduciary under circumstances where it had any reason to believe that the fiduciary may have been acting improperly. In one sense that seems to be advantageous for beneficiaries who might be harmed by wrongful conduct by fiduciaries. The consequence of the *Lowry* rule, however, was that in order to protect against risk of such liability, issuers developed the practice of requiring extensive documentation for fiduciary stock transfers, making such transfers cumbersome and time consuming. Accordingly, the rules in Part 4 of Article 8, and in the prior fiduciary transfer statutes, were designed to discourage transfer agents from conducting investigations into the rightfulness of transfers by fiduciaries.

The rules of Revised Article 8 implement for the indirect holding system the same policies that the rules on protected purchasers and registration of transfer adopt for the direct holding system. A securities intermediary is, by definition, a person who is holding securities on behalf of other persons. There is nothing unusual or suspicious about a transaction in which a securities intermediary sells securities that it was holding for its customers. That is exactly what securities intermediaries are in business to do. The interests of customers of securities intermediaries would not be served by a rule that required counterparties to transfers from securities intermediaries to investigate whether the intermediary was acting wrongfully against its customers. Quite the contrary, such a rule would impair the ability of securities intermediaries to perform the function that customers want.

The rules of Section 8–503(c) through (e) apply to transferees generally, including pledgees. The reasons for treating pledgees in the same fashion as other transferees are discussed in the Comments to Section 8–511. The statement in subsection (a) that an intermediary holds financial assets for customers and not as its own property does not, of course, mean that the intermediary lacks power to transfer the financial assets to others. For example, although Article 9 provides that for a security interest to attach the debtor must have "rights" in the collateral, see Section 9–203, the fact that an intermediary is holding a financial asset in a form that permits ready transfer means that it has such rights, even if the intermediary is acting wrongfully against its entitlement holders in granting the security interest. The question whether the secured party takes subject to the entitlement holder's claim in such a case is governed by Section 8–511, which is an application to secured transactions of the general principles expressed in subsections (d) and (e) of this section.

Definitional Cross References

"Control" Section 8–106

"Entitlement holder" Section 8–102(a)(7)

"Financial asset" Section 8–102(a)(9)
"Insolvency proceedings" Section 1–201(22)
"Purchaser" Sections 1–201(33) & 8–116
"Securities intermediary" Section 8–102(a)(14)
"Security entitlement" Section 8–102(a)(17)
"Value" Sections 1–201(44) & 8–116

§ 8504. Aggregate of security entitlements; maintenance of quantity by securities intermediary

(a) A securities intermediary shall promptly obtain and thereafter maintain a financial asset in a quantity corresponding to the aggregate of all security entitlements it has established in favor of its entitlement holders with respect to that financial asset. The securities intermediary may maintain those financial assets directly or through one or more other securities intermediaries.

(b) Except to the extent otherwise agreed by its entitlement holder, a securities intermediary may not grant any security interests in a financial asset it is obligated to maintain pursuant to subdivision (a).

(c) A securities intermediary satisfies the duty in subdivision (a) if it does either of the following:

(1) The securities intermediary acts with respect to the duty as agreed upon by the entitlement holder and the securities intermediary.

(2) In the absence of agreement, the securities intermediary exercises due care in accordance with reasonable commercial standards to obtain and maintain the financial asset.

(d) This section does not apply to a clearing corporation that is itself the obligor of an option or similar obligation to which its entitlement holders have security entitlements. *(Added by Stats.1996, c. 497 (S.B.1591), § 9, operative Jan. 1, 1997.)*

Uniform Commercial Code Comment

1. This section expresses one of the core elements of the relationships for which the Part 5 rules were designed, to wit, that a securities intermediary undertakes to hold financial assets corresponding to the security entitlements of its entitlement holders. The locution "shall promptly obtain and shall thereafter maintain" is taken from the corresponding regulation under federal securities law, 17 C.F.R. § 240.15c3–3. This section recognizes the reality that as the securities business is conducted today, it is not possible to identify particular securities as belonging to customers as distinguished from other particular securities that are the firm's own property. Securities firms typically keep all securities in fungible form, and may maintain their inventory of a particular security in various locations and forms, including physical securities held in vaults or in transit to transfer agents, and book entry positions at one or more clearing corporations. Accordingly, this section states that a securities intermediary shall maintain a quantity of financial assets corresponding to the aggregate of all security entitlements it has established. The last sentence of subsection (a) provides explicitly that the securities intermediary may hold directly or indirectly. That point is implicit in the use of the term "financial asset," inasmuch as Section 8–102(a)(9) provides that the term "financial asset" may refer either to the underlying asset or the means by which it is held, including both security certificates and security entitlements.

2. Subsection (b) states explicitly a point that is implicit in the notion that a securities intermediary must maintain financial assets corresponding to the security entitlements of its entitlement holders, to wit, that it is wrongful for a securities intermediary to grant security interests in positions that it needs to satisfy customers' claims, except as authorized by the customers. This statement does not determine the rights of a secured party to whom a securities intermediary wrongfully grants a security interest; that issue is governed by Sections 8–503 and 8–511.

Margin accounts are common examples of arrangements in which an entitlement holder authorizes the securities intermediary to grant security interests in the positions held for the entitlement holder. Securities firms commonly obtain the funds needed to provide margin loans to their customers by "rehypothecating" the customers' securities. In order to facilitate rehypothecation, agreements between margin customers and their brokers commonly authorize the broker to commingle securities of all margin customers for rehypothecation to the lender who provides the financing. Brokers commonly rehypothecate customer securities having a value somewhat greater than the amount of the loan made to the customer, since the lenders who provide the necessary financing to the broker need some cushion of protection against the risk of decline in the value of the rehypothecated securities. The extent and manner in which a firm may rehypothecate customers' securities are determined by the agreement between the intermediary and the entitlement holder and by applicable regulatory law. Current regulations under the federal securities laws require that brokers obtain the explicit consent of customers before pledging customer securities or commingling different customers' securities for pledge. Federal regulations also limit the extent to which a broker may rehypothecate customer securities to 110% of the aggregate amount of the borrowings of all customers.

3. The statement in this section that an intermediary must obtain and maintain financial assets corresponding to the aggregate of all security entitlements it has established is intended only to capture the general point that one of the key elements that distinguishes securities accounts from other relationships, such as deposit accounts, is that the intermediary undertakes to maintain a direct correspondence between the positions it holds and the claims of its customers. This section is not intended as a detailed specification of precisely how the intermediary is to perform this duty, nor whether there may be special circumstances in which an intermediary's general duty is excused. Accordingly, the general statement of the duties of a securities intermediary in this and the following sections is supplemented by two other provisions. First, each of Sections 8–504 through 8–508 contains an "agreement/due care" provision. Second, Section 8–509 sets out general qualifications on the duties stated in these sections, including the important point that compliance with corresponding regulatory provisions constitutes compliance with the Article 8 duties.

4. The "agreement/due care" provision in subsection (c) of this section is necessary to provide sufficient flexibility to accommodate the general duty stated in subsection (a) to the wide variety of circumstances that may be encountered in the modern securities holding system. For the most common forms of publicly traded securities, the modern depository-based indirect holding system has made the likelihood of an actual loss of securities remote, though correctable errors in accounting or temporary interruptions of data processing facilities may occur. Indeed, one of the reasons for the evolution of book-entry systems is to eliminate the risk of loss or destruction of physical certificates. There are, however, some forms of securities and other financial assets which must still be held in physical certificated form, with the attendant risk of loss or destruction. Risk of loss or delay may be a more significant consideration in connection with foreign securities. An American securities intermediary may well be willing to hold a foreign security in a securities account for its customer, but the intermediary may have relatively little choice of or control over foreign intermediaries through which the security must in turn be held. Accordingly, it is common for American securities intermediaries to disclaim responsibility for custodial risk of holding through foreign intermediaries.

Subsection (c)(1) provides that a securities intermediary satisfies the duty stated in subsection (a) if the intermediary acts with respect to that duty in accordance with the agreement between the intermediary and the entitlement holder. Subsection (c)(2) provides that if there is no agreement on the matter, the intermediary satisfies the subsection (a) duty if the intermediary exercises due care in accordance with reasonable commercial standards to obtain and maintain the financial asset in question. This formulation does not state that the intermediary has a universally applicable statutory duty of due care. Section 1–102(3) provides that statutory duties of due care cannot be disclaimed by agreement, but the "agreement/due care" formula contemplates that there may be particular circumstances where the parties do not wish to create a specific duty of due care, for example, with respect to foreign securities. Under subsection (c)(1), compliance with the agreement constitutes satisfaction of the subsection (a) duty, whether or not the agreement provides that the intermediary will exercise due care.

In each of the sections where the "agreement/due care" formula is used, it provides that entering into an agreement and performing in accordance with that agreement is a method by which the securities intermediary may satisfy the statutory duty stated in that section. Accordingly, the general obligation of good faith performance of statutory and contract duties, see Sections 1–203 and 8–102(a)(10), would apply to such an agreement. It would not be consistent with the obligation of good faith performance for an agreement to purport to establish the usual sort of arrangement between an intermediary and entitlement holder, yet disclaim altogether one of the basic elements that define that relationship. For example, an agreement stating that an intermediary assumes no responsibilities whatsoever for the safekeeping any of the entitlement holder's securities positions would not be consistent with good faith performance of the intermediary's duty to obtain and maintain financial assets corresponding to the entitlement holder's security entitlements.

To the extent that no agreement under subsection (c)(1) has specified the details of the intermediary's performance of the subsection (a) duty, subsection (c)(2) provides that the intermediary satisfies that duty if it exercises due care in accordance with reasonable commercial standards. The duty of care includes both care in the intermediary's own operations and care in the selection of other intermediaries through whom the intermediary holds the assets in question. The statement of the obligation of due care is meant to incorporate the principles of the common law under which the specific actions or precautions necessary to meet the obligation of care are determined by such factors as the nature and value of the property, the customs and practices of the business, and the like.

5. This section necessarily states the duty of a securities intermediary to obtain and maintain financial assets only at the very general and abstract level. For the most part, these matters are specified in great detail by regulatory law. Broker-dealers registered under the federal securities laws are subject to detailed regulation concerning the safeguarding of customer securities. See 17 C.F.R. § 240.15c3–3. Section 8–509(a) provides explicitly that if a securities intermediary complies with such regulatory law, that constitutes compliance with Section 8–504. In certain circumstances, these rules permit a firm to be in a position where it temporarily lacks a sufficient quantity of financial assets to satisfy all customer claims. For example, if another firm has failed to make a delivery to the firm in settlement of a trade, the firm is permitted a certain period of time to clear up the problem before it is obligated to obtain the necessary securities from some other source.

6. Subsection (d) is intended to recognize that there are some circumstances, where the duty to maintain a sufficient quantity of financial assets does not apply because the intermediary is not holding anything on behalf of others. For example, the Options Clearing Corporation is treated as a "securities intermediary" under this Article, although it does not itself hold options on behalf of its participants. Rather, it becomes the issuer of the options, by virtue of guaranteeing the obligations of participants in the clearing corporation who have written or purchased the options cleared through it. See Section 8–103(e). Accordingly, the general duty of an intermediary under subsection (a) does not apply, nor would other provisions of Part 5 that depend upon the existence of a requirement that the securities intermediary hold financial assets, such as Sections 8–503 and 8–508.

Definitional Cross References

"Agreement"   Section 1–201(3)
"Clearing corporation"   Section 8–102(a)(5)
"Entitlement holder"   Section 8–102(a)(7)
"Financial asset"   Section 8–102(a)(9)
"Securities intermediary"   Section 8–102(a)(14)
"Security entitlement"   Section 8–102(a)(17)

§ 8505. Payment or distribution by issuer of financial asset; duty of securities intermediary

(a) A securities intermediary shall take action to obtain a payment or distribution made by the issuer of a financial asset. A securities intermediary satisfies the duty if it does either of the following:

(1) The securities intermediary acts with respect to the duty as agreed upon by the entitlement holder and the securities intermediary.

(2) In the absence of agreement, the securities intermediary exercises due care in accordance with reasonable commercial standards to attempt to obtain the payment or distribution.

(b) A securities intermediary is obligated to its entitlement holder for a payment or distribution made by the issuer of a financial asset if the payment or distribution is received by the securities intermediary. *(Added by Stats.1996, c. 497 (S.B.1591), § 9, operative Jan. 1, 1997.)*

Uniform Commercial Code Comment

1. One of the core elements of the securities account relationships for which the Part 5 rules were designed is that the securities intermediary passes through to the entitlement holders the economic benefit of ownership of the financial asset, such as payments and distributions made by the issuer. Subsection (a) expresses the ordinary understanding that a securities intermediary will take appropriate action to see to it that any payments or distributions made by the issuer are received. One of the main reasons that investors make use of securities intermediaries is to obtain the services of a professional in performing the record-keeping and other functions necessary to ensure that payments and other distributions are received.

2. Subsection (a) incorporates the same "agreement/due care" formula as the other provisions of Part 5 dealing with the duties of a securities intermediary. See Comment 4 to Section 8–504. This formulation permits the parties to specify by agreement what action, if any, the intermediary is to take with respect to the duty to obtain payments and distributions. In the absence of specification by agreement, the intermediary satisfies the duty if the intermediary exercises due care in accordance with reasonable commercial standards. The provisions of Section 8–509 also apply to the Section 8–505 duty, so that compliance with applicable regulatory requirements constitutes compliance with the Section 8–505 duty.

3. Subsection (b) provides that a securities intermediary is obligated to its entitlement holder for those payments or distributions made by the issuer that are in fact received by the intermediary. It does not deal with the details of the time and manner of payment. Moreover, as with any other monetary obligation, the obligation to pay may be subject to other rights of the obligor, by way of set-off counterclaim or the like. Section 8–509(c) makes this point explicit.

Definitional Cross References

"Agreement"   Section 1–201(3)
"Entitlement holder"   Section 8–102(a)(7)
"Financial asset"   Section 8–102(a)(9)
"Securities intermediary"   Section 8–102(a)(14)
"Security entitlement"   Section 8–102(a)(17)

§ 8506. Entitlement holder rights in asset; exercise by securities intermediary

A securities intermediary shall exercise rights with respect to a financial asset if directed to do so by an entitlement holder. A securities intermediary satisfies the duty if it does either of the following:

(1) The securities intermediary acts with respect to the duty as agreed upon by the entitlement holder and the securities intermediary.

(2) In the absence of agreement, the securities intermediary either places the entitlement holder in a

position to exercise the rights directly or exercises due care in accordance with reasonable commercial standards to follow the direction of the entitlement holder. *(Added by Stats.1996, c. 497 (S.B.1591), § 9, operative Jan. 1, 1997.)*

Uniform Commercial Code Comment

1. Another of the core elements of the securities account relationships for which the Part 5 rules were designed is that although the intermediary may, by virtue of the structure of the indirect holding system, be the party who has the power to exercise the corporate and other rights that come from holding the security, the intermediary exercises these powers as representative of the entitlement holder rather than at its own discretion. This characteristic is one of the things that distinguishes a securities account from other arrangements where one person holds securities "on behalf of" another, such as the relationship between a mutual fund and its shareholders or a trustee and its beneficiary.

2. The fact that the intermediary exercises the rights of security holding as representative of the entitlement holder does not, of course, preclude the entitlement holder from conferring discretionary authority upon the intermediary. Arrangements are not uncommon in which investors do not wish to have their intermediaries forward proxy materials or other information. Thus, this section provides that the intermediary shall exercise corporate and other rights "if directed to do so" by the entitlement holder. Moreover, as with the other Part 5 duties, the "agreement/due care" formulation is used in stating how the intermediary is to perform this duty. This section also provides that the intermediary satisfies the duty if it places the entitlement holder in a position to exercise the rights directly. This is to take account of the fact that some of the rights attendant upon ownership of the security, such as rights to bring derivative and other litigation, are far removed from the matters that intermediaries are expected to perform.

3. This section, and the two that follow, deal with the aspects of securities holding that are related to investment decisions. For example, one of the rights of holding a particular security that would fall within the purview of this section would be the right to exercise a conversion right for a convertible security. It is quite common for investors to confer discretionary authority upon another person, such as an investment adviser, with respect to these rights and other investment decisions. Because this section, and the other sections of Part 5, all specify that a securities intermediary satisfies the Part 5 duties if it acts in accordance with the entitlement holder's agreement, there is no inconsistency between the statement of duties of a securities intermediary and these common arrangements.

4. Section 8–509 also applies to the Section 8–506 duty, so that compliance with applicable regulatory requirements constitutes compliance with this duty. This is quite important in this context, since the federal securities laws establish a comprehensive system of regulation of the distribution of proxy materials and exercise of voting rights with respect to securities held through brokers and other intermediaries. By virtue of Section 8–509(a), compliance with such regulatory requirement constitutes compliance with the Section 8–506 duty.

Definitional Cross References

"Agreement" Section 1–201(3)
"Entitlement holder" Section 8–102(a)(7)
"Financial asset" Section 8–102(a)(9)
"Securities intermediary" Section 8–102(a)(14)
"Security entitlement" Section 8–102(a)(17)

§ 8507. Entitlement orders; duty of securities intermediary to comply

(a) A securities intermediary shall comply with an entitlement order if the entitlement order is originated by the appropriate person, the securities intermediary has had reasonable opportunity to assure itself that the entitlement order is genuine and authorized, and the securities intermediary has had reasonable opportunity to comply with the entitlement order. A securities intermediary satisfies the duty if it does either of the following:

(1) The securities intermediary acts with respect to the duty as agreed upon by the entitlement holder and the securities intermediary.

(2) In the absence of agreement, the securities intermediary exercises due care in accordance with reasonable commercial standards to comply with the entitlement order.

(b) If a securities intermediary transfers a financial asset pursuant to an ineffective entitlement order, the securities intermediary shall reestablish a security entitlement in favor of the person entitled to it, and pay or credit any payments or distributions that the person did not receive as a result of the wrongful transfer. If the securities intermediary does not reestablish a security entitlement, the securities intermediary is liable to the entitlement holder for damages. *(Added by Stats.1996, c. 497 (S.B.1591), § 9, operative Jan. 1, 1997.)*

Uniform Commercial Code Comment

1. Subsection (a) of this section states another aspect of duties of securities intermediaries that make up security entitlements—the securities intermediary's duty to comply with entitlement orders. One of the main reasons for holding securities through securities intermediaries is to enable rapid transfer in settlement of trades. Thus the right to have one's orders for disposition of the security entitlement honored is an inherent part of the relationship. Subsection (b) states the correlative liability of a securities intermediary for transferring a financial asset from an entitlement holder's account pursuant to an entitlement order that was not effective.

2. The duty to comply with entitlement orders is subject to several qualifications. The intermediary has a duty only with respect to an entitlement order that is in fact originated by the appropriate person. Moreover, the intermediary has a duty only if it has had reasonable opportunity to assure itself that the order is genuine and authorized, and reasonable opportunity to comply with the order. The same "agreement/due care" formula is used in this section as in the other Part 5 sections on the duties of intermediaries, and the rules of Section 8–509 apply to the Section 8–507 duty.

3. Appropriate person is defined in Section 8–107. In the usual case, the appropriate person is the entitlement holder, see Section 8–107(a)(3). Entitlement holder is defined in Section 8–102(a)(7) as the person "identified in the records of a securities intermediary as the person having a security entitlement." Thus, the general rule is that an intermediary's duty with respect to entitlement orders runs only to the person with whom the intermediary has established a relationship. One of the basic principles of the indirect holding system is that securities intermediaries owe duties only to their own customers. See also Section 8–115. The only situation in which a securities intermediary has a duty to comply with entitlement orders originated by a person other than the person with whom the intermediary established a relationship is covered by Section 8–107(a)(4) and (a)(5), which provide that the term "appropriate person" includes the successor or personal representative of a decedent, or the custodian or guardian of a person who lacks capacity. If the entitlement holder is competent, another person does not fall within the defined term "appropriate person" merely by virtue of having power to act as an agent for the entitlement holder. Thus, an intermediary is not required to determine at its peril whether a person who purports to be authorized to act for an entitlement holder is in fact authorized to do so. If an entitlement holder wishes to be able to act through agents, the entitlement holder can establish appropriate arrangements in advance with the securities intermediary.

One important application of this principle is that if an entitlement holder grants a security interest in its security entitlements to a third-party lender, the intermediary owes no duties to the secured party, unless the intermediary has entered into a "control" agreement in which it agrees to act on entitlement orders originated by the secured party. See Section 8–106. Even though the security agreement or some other document may give the secured party authority to act as agent for the debtor, that would not make the secured party an "appropriate person" to whom the security intermediary owes duties. If the entitlement holder and securities intermediary have agreed to such a control arrangement, then the intermediary's action in following instructions from the secured party would satisfy the subsection (a) duty. Although an agent, such as the secured party in this example, is not an "appropriate person," an entitlement order is "effective" if originated by an authorized person. See Section 8–107(a) and (b). Moreover, Section 8–507(a) provides that the intermediary satisfies its duty if it acts in accordance with the entitlement holder's agreement.

4. Subsection (b) provides that an intermediary is liable for a wrongful transfer if the entitlement order was "ineffective." Section 8–107 specifies whether an entitlement order is effective. An "effective entitlement order" is different from an "entitlement order originated by an appropriate person." An entitlement order is effective under Section 8–107(b) if it is made by the appropriate person, or by a person who has power to act for the appropriate person under the law of agency, or if the appropriate person has ratified the entitlement order or is precluded from denying its effectiveness. Thus, although a securities intermediary does not have a duty to act on an entitlement order originated by the entitlement holder's agent, the intermediary is not liable for wrongful transfer if it does so.

Subsection (b), together with Section 8–107, has the effect of leaving to other law most of the questions of the sort dealt with by Article 4A for wire transfers of funds, such as allocation between the securities intermediary and the entitlement holder of the risk of fraudulent entitlement orders.

5. The term entitlement order does not cover all directions that a customer might give a broker concerning securities held through the broker. Article 8 is not a codification of all of the law of customers and stockbrokers. Article 8 deals with the settlement of securities trades, not the trades. The term entitlement order does not refer to instructions to a broker to make trades, that is, enter into contracts for the purchase or sale of securities. Rather, the entitlement order is the mechanism of transfer for securities held through intermediaries, just as indorsements and instructions are the mechanism for securities held directly. In the ordinary case the customer's direction to the broker to deliver the securities at settlement is implicit in the customer's instruction to the broker to sell. The distinction is, however, significant in that this section has no application to the relationship between the customer and broker with respect to the trade itself. For example, assertions by a customer that it was damaged by a broker's failure to execute a trading order sufficiently rapidly or in the proper manner are not governed by this Article.

Definitional Cross References

"Agreement" Section 1–201(3)
"Appropriate person" Section 8–107
"Effective" Section 8–107
"Entitlement holder" Section 8–102(a)(7)
"Entitlement order" Section 8–102(a)(8)
"Financial asset" Section 8–102(a)(9)
"Securities intermediary" Section 8–102(a)(14)
"Security entitlement" Section 8–102(a)(17)

§ 8508. Change of entitlement to another form of holding; duty of securities intermediary

A securities intermediary shall act at the direction of an entitlement holder to change a security entitlement into another available form of holding for which the entitlement holder is eligible, or to cause the financial asset to be transferred to a securities account of the entitlement holder with another securities intermediary. A securities intermediary satisfies the duty if it does either of the following:

(1) The securities intermediary acts as agreed upon by the entitlement holder and the securities intermediary.

(2) In the absence of agreement, the securities intermediary exercises due care in accordance with reasonable commercial standards to follow the direction of the entitlement holder. *(Added by Stats.1996, c. 497 (S.B. 1591), § 9, operative Jan. 1, 1997.)*

Uniform Commercial Code Comment

1. This section states another aspect of the duties of securities intermediaries that make up security entitlements—the obligation of the securities intermediary to change an entitlement holder's position into any other form of holding for which the entitlement holder is eligible or to transfer the entitlement holder's position to an account at another intermediary. This section does not state unconditionally that the securities intermediary is obligated to turn over a certificate to the customer or to cause the customer to be registered on the books of the issuer, because the customer may not be eligible to hold the security directly. For example, municipal bonds are now commonly issued in "book-entry only" form, in which the only entity that the issuer will register on its own books is a depository.

If security certificates in registered form are issued for the security, and individuals are eligible to have the security registered in their own name, the entitlement holder can request that the intermediary deliver or cause to be delivered to the entitlement holder a certificate registered in the name of the entitlement holder or a certificate indorsed in blank or specially indorsed to the entitlement holder. If security certificates in bearer form are issued for the security, the entitlement holder can request that the intermediary deliver or cause to be delivered a certificate in bearer form. If the security can be held by individuals directly in uncertificated form, the entitlement holder can request that the security be registered in its name. The specification of this duty does not determine the pricing terms of the agreement in which the duty arises.

2. The same "agreement/due care" formula is used in this section as in the other Part 5 sections on the duties of intermediaries. So too, the rules of Section 8–509 apply to the Section 8–508 duty.

Definitional Cross References

"Agreement" Section 1–201(3)
"Entitlement holder" Section 8–102(a)(7)
"Financial asset" Section 8–102(a)(9)
"Securities intermediary" Section 8–102(a)(14)
"Security entitlement" Section 8–102(a)(17)

§ 8509. Duty of securities intermediary; compliance with federal law; standard of care

(a) If the substance of a duty imposed upon a securities intermediary by Sections 8504 to 8508, inclusive, is the subject of a federal statute, regulation, or rule, compliance with that statute, regulation, or rule satisfies the duty.

(b) To the extent that specific standards for the performance of the duties of a securities intermediary or the exercise of the rights of an entitlement holder are not specified by other statute, regulation, or rule or by agreement between the securities intermediary and entitlement holder, the securities intermediary shall perform its duties and the entitlement holder shall exercise its rights in a commercially reasonable manner.

(c) The obligation of a securities intermediary to perform the duties imposed by Sections 8504 to 8508, inclusive, is subject to the following:

(1) Rights of the securities intermediary arising out of a security interest under a security agreement with the entitlement holder or otherwise.

(2) Rights of the securities intermediary under other law, regulation, rule, or agreement to withhold performance of its duties as a result of unfulfilled obligations of the entitlement holder to the securities intermediary.

(d) Sections 8504 to 8508, inclusive, do not require a securities intermediary to take any action that is prohibited by other statute, regulation, or rule. *(Added by Stats.1996, c. 497 (S.B.1591), § 9, operative Jan. 1, 1997.)*

Uniform Commercial Code Comment

This Article is not a comprehensive statement of the law governing the relationship between broker-dealers or other securities intermediaries and their customers. Most of the law governing that relationship is the common law of contract and agency, supplemented or supplanted by regulatory law. This Article deals only with the most basic commercial/property law principles governing the relationship. Although Sections 8–504 through 8–508 specify certain duties of securities intermediaries to entitlement holders, the point of these sections is to identify what it means to have a security entitlement, not to specify the details of performance of these duties.

For many intermediaries, regulatory law specifies in great detail the intermediary's obligations on such matters as safekeeping of customer property, distribution of proxy materials, and the like. To avoid any conflict between the general statement of duties in this Article and the specific statement of intermediaries' obligations in such regulatory schemes, subsection (a) provides that compliance with applicable regulation constitutes compliance with the duties specified in Sections 8–504 through 8–508.

Definitional Cross References

"Agreement"   Section 1–201(3)

"Entitlement holder"   Section 8–102(a)(7)

"Securities intermediary"   Section 8–102(a)(14)

"Security agreement"   Section 9–105(1)(*l*)

"Security interest"   Section 1–201(37)

§ 8510. Adverse claims; priorities

(a) An action based on an adverse claim to a financial asset or security entitlement, whether framed in conversion, replevin, constructive trust, equitable lien, or other theory, may not be asserted against a person who purchases a security entitlement, or an interest therein, from an entitlement holder if the purchaser gives value, does not have notice of the adverse claim, and obtains control.

(b) If an adverse claim could not have been asserted against an entitlement holder under Section 8502, the adverse claim cannot be asserted against a person who purchases a security entitlement, or an interest therein, from the entitlement holder.

(c) In a case not covered by the priority rules in Division 9 (commencing with Section 9101), a purchaser for value of a security entitlement, or an interest therein, who obtains control has priority over a purchaser of a security entitlement, or an interest therein, who does not obtain control. Purchasers who have control rank equally, except that a securities intermediary as purchaser has priority over a conflicting purchaser who has control unless otherwise agreed by the securities intermediary. *(Added by Stats.1996, c. 497 (S.B.1591), § 9, operative Jan. 1, 1997.)*

Uniform Commercial Code Comment

1. This section specifies certain rules concerning the rights of persons who purchase interests in security entitlements from entitlement holders. The rules of this section are provided to take account of cases where the purchaser's rights are derivative from the rights of another person who is and continues to be the entitlement holder.

2. Subsection (a) provides that no adverse claim can be asserted against a purchaser of an interest in a security entitlement if the purchaser gives value, obtains control, and does not have notice of the adverse claim. The primary purpose of this rule is to give adverse claim protection to persons who take security interests in security entitlements and obtain control, but do not themselves become entitlement holders.

The following examples illustrate subsection (a):

Example 1. X steals a certificated bearer bond from Owner. X delivers the certificate to Able & Co. for credit to X's securities account. Later, X borrows from Bank and grants bank a security interest in the security entitlement. Bank obtains control under Section 8–106(d)(2) by virtue of an agreement in which Able agrees to comply with entitlement orders originated by Bank. X absconds.

Example 2. Same facts as in Example 1, except that Bank does not obtain a control agreement. Instead, Bank perfects by filing a financing statement.

In both of these examples, when X deposited the bonds X acquired a security entitlement under Section 8–501. Under other law, Owner may be able to have a constructive trust imposed on the security entitlement as the traceable product of the bonds that X misappropriated. X granted a security interest in that entitlement to Bank. Bank was a purchaser of an interest in the security entitlement from X. In Example 1, although Bank was not a person who acquired a security entitlement from the intermediary, Bank did obtain control. If Bank did not have notice of Owner's claim, Section 8–510(a) precludes Owner from asserting an adverse claim against Bank. In Example 2, Bank had a perfected security interest, but did not obtain control. Accordingly, Section 8–510(a) does not preclude Owner from asserting its adverse claim against Bank.

3. Subsection (b) applies to the indirect holding system a limited version of the "shelter principle." The following example illustrates the relatively limited class of cases for which it may be needed:

Example 3. Thief steals a certificated bearer bond from Owner. Thief delivers the certificate to Able & Co. for credit to Thief's securities account. Able forwards the certificate to a clearing corporation for credit to Able's account. Later Thief instructs Able to sell the positions in the bonds. Able sells to Baker & Co., acting as broker for Buyer. The trade is settled by book-entries in the accounts of Able and Baker at the clearing corporation, and in the accounts of Thief and Buyer at Able and Baker respectively. Owner may be able to reconstruct the trade records to show that settlement occurred in such fashion that the "same bonds" that were carried in Thief's account at Able are traceable into Buyer's account at Baker. Buyer later decides to donate the bonds to Alma Mater University and executes an assignment of its rights as entitlement holder to Alma Mater.

Buyer had a position in the bonds, which Buyer held in the form of a security entitlement against Baker. Buyer then made a gift of the position to Alma Mater. Although Alma Mater is a purchaser, Section 1–201(33), it did not give value. Thus, Alma Mater is a person who purchased a security entitlement, or an interest therein, from an entitlement holder (Buyer). Buyer was protected against Owner's adverse claim by the Section 8–502 rule. Thus, by virtue of Section 8–510(b), Owner is also precluded from asserting an adverse claim against Alma Mater.

4. Subsection (c) specifies a priority rule for cases where an entitlement holder transfers conflicting interests in the same security entitlement to different purchasers. It follows the same principle as the Article 9 priority rule for investment property, that is, control trumps non-control. Indeed, the most significant category of conflicting "purchasers" may be secured parties. Priority questions for security interests, however, are governed by the rules in Article 9. Subsection (c) applies only to cases not covered by the Article 9 rules. It is intended primarily for disputes over conflicting claims arising out of repurchase agreement transactions that are not covered by the other rules set out in Articles 8 and 9.

The following example illustrates subsection (c):

Example 4. Dealer holds securities through an account at Alph Bank. Alpha Bank in turns holds through a clearing corporatio account. Dealer transfers securities to RP1 in a "hold in custody" repo transaction. Dealer then transfers the same securities to RP2 in another repo transaction. The repo to RP2 is implemented by transferring the securities from Dealer's regular account at Alpha Bank to a special account maintained by Alpha Bank for Dealer and RP2. The agreement among Dealer, RP2, and Alpha Bank provides that Dealer can make substitutions for the securities but RP2 can direct Alpha Bank to sell any securities held in the special account. Dealer becomes insolvent. RP1 claims a prior interest in the securities transferred to RP2.

In this example Dealer remained the entitlement holder but agreed that RP2 could initiate entitlement orders to Dealer's security intermediary, Alpha Bank. If RP2 had become the entitlement holder, the adverse claim rule of Section 8–502 would apply. Even if RP2 does not become the entitlement holder, the arrangement among Dealer, Alpha Bank, and RP2 does suffice to give RP2 control. Thus, under Section 8–510(c), RP2 has priority over RP1, because RP2 is a purchaser who obtained control, and RP1 is a purchaser who did not obtain control. The same result could be reached under Section 8–510(a) which provides that RP1's earlier in time interest cannot be asserted as an adverse claim against RP2. The same result would follow under the Article 9 priority rules if the interests of RP1 and RP2 are characterized as "security interests," see Section 9–115(5)(a). The main point of the rules of Section 8–510(c) is to ensure that there will be clear rules to cover the conflicting claims of RP1 and RP2 without characterizing their interests as Article 9 security interests.

The priority rules in Article 9 for conflicting security interests also include a default rule of pro rata treatment for cases where multiple secured parties have obtained control but omitted to specify their respective rights by agreement. See Section 9–115(5)(b) and Comment 6 to Section 9–115. Because the purchaser priority rule in Section 8–510(c) is intended to track the Article 9 priority rules, it too has a pro rata rule for cases where multiple non-secured party purchasers have obtained control but omitted to specify their respective rights by agreement.

Definitional Cross References

"Adverse claim" Section 8–102(a)(1)
"Control" Section 8–106
"Entitlement holder" Section 8–102(a)(7)
"Notice of adverse claim" Section 8–105
"Purchase" Section 1–201(32)
"Purchaser" Sections 1–201(33) & 8–116
"Securities intermediary" Section 8–102(a)(14)
"Security entitlement" Section 8–102(a)(17)
"Value" Sections 1–201(44) & 8–116

§ 8511. Priority of claims

(a) Except as otherwise provided in subdivisions (b) and (c), if a securities intermediary does not have sufficient interests in a particular financial asset to satisfy both its obligations to entitlement holders who have security entitlements to that financial asset and its obligation to a creditor of the securities intermediary who has a security interest in that financial asset, the claims of entitlement holders, other than the creditor, have priority over the claim of the creditor.

(b) A claim of a creditor of a securities intermediary who has a security interest in a financial asset held by a securities intermediary has priority over claims of the securities intermediary's entitlement holders who have security entitlements with respect to that financial asset if the creditor has control over the financial asset.

(c) If a clearing corporation does not have sufficient financial assets to satisfy both its obligations to entitlement holders who have security entitlements with respect to a financial asset and its obligation to a creditor of the clearing corporation who has a security interest in that financial asset, the claim of the creditor has priority over the claims of entitlement holders. *(Added by Stats.1996, c. 497 (S.B.1591), § 9, operative Jan. 1, 1997.)*

Uniform Commercial Code Comment

1. This section sets out priority rules for circumstances in which a securities intermediary fails leaving an insufficient quantity of securities or other financial assets to satisfy the claims of its entitlement holders and the claims of creditors to whom it has granted security interests in financial assets held by it. Subsection (a) provides that entitlement holders' claims have priority except as otherwise provided in subsection (b), and subsection (b) provides that the secured creditor's claim has priority if the secured creditor obtains control, as defined in Section 8–106. The following examples illustrate the operation of these rules.

Example 1. Able & Co., a broker, borrows from Alpha Bank and grants Alpha Bank a security interest pursuant to a written agreement which identifies certain securities that are to be collateral for the loan, either specifically or by category. Able holds these securities in a clearing corporation account. Able becomes insolvent and it is discovered that Able holds insufficient securities to satisfy the claims of customers who have paid for securities that they held in accounts with Able and the collateral claims of Alpha Bank. Alpha Bank's security interest in the security entitlements that Able holds through the clearing corporation account may be perfected under the automatic perfection rule of Section 9–115(4)(c), but Alpha Bank did not obtain control under Section 8–106. Thus, under Section 8–511(a) the entitlement holders' claims have priority over Alpha Bank's claim.

Example 2. Able & Co., a broker, borrows from Beta Bank and grants Beta Bank a security interest in securities that Able holds in a clearing corporation account. Pursuant to the security agreement, the securities are debited from Alpha's account and credited to Beta's account in the clearing corporation account. Able becomes insolvent and it is discovered that Able holds insufficient securities to satisfy the claims of customers who have paid for securities that they held in accounts with Able and the collateral claims of Alpha Bank. Although the transaction between Able and Beta took the form of an outright transfer on the clearing corporation's books, as between Able and Beta, Able remains the owner and Beta has a security interest. In that respect the situation is no different than if Able had delivered bearer bonds to Beta in pledge to secure a loan. Beta's security interest is perfected, and Beta obtained control. See Sections 8–106 and 9–115. Under Section 8–511(b), Beta Bank's security interest has priority over claims of Able's customers.

The result in Example 2 is an application to this particular setting of the general principle expressed in Section 8–503, and explained in the Comments thereto, that the entitlement holders of a securities intermediary cannot assert rights against third parties to whom the intermediary has wrongfully transferred interests, except in extremely unusual circumstances where the third party was itself a participant in the transferor's wrongdoing. Under subsection (b) the claim of a secured creditor of a securities intermediary has priority over the claims of entitlement holders if the secured creditor has obtained control. If, however, the secured creditor acted in collusion with the intermediary in violating the intermediary's obligation to its entitlement holders, then under Section 8–503(e), the entitlement holders, through their representative in insolvency proceedings, could recover the interest from the secured creditor, that is, set aside the security interest.

2. The risk that investors who hold through an intermediary will suffer a loss as a result of a wrongful pledge by the intermediary is no different than the risk that the intermediary might fail and not have the securities that it was supposed to be holding on behalf of its customers, either because the securities were never acquired by the intermediary or because the intermediary wrongfully sold securities that should have been kept to satisfy customers' claims. Investors are protected against that risk by the regulatory regimes under which securities intermediaries operate. Intermediaries are required to maintain custody, through clearing corporation accounts or in other approved locations, of their customers' securities and are prohibited from using customers' securities in their own business activities. Securities firms who are carrying both customer and proprietary positions are not permitted to grant blanket liens to lenders covering all securities which they hold, for their own account or for their customers. Rather, securities firms designate specifically which positions they are pledging. Under SEC Rules 8c–1

and 15c2–1, customers' securities can be pledged only to fund loans to customers, and only with the consent of the customers. Customers' securities cannot be pledged for loans for the firm's proprietary business; only proprietary positions can be pledged for proprietary loans. SEC Rule 15c3–3 implements these prohibitions in a fashion tailored to modern securities firm accounting systems by requiring brokers to maintain a sufficient inventory of securities, free from any liens, to satisfy the claims of all of their customers for fully paid and excess margin securities. Revised Article 8 mirrors that requirement, specifying in Section 8–504 that a securities intermediary must maintain a sufficient quantity of investment property to satisfy all security entitlements, and may not grant security interests in the positions it is required to hold for customers, except as authorized by the customers.

If a failed brokerage has violated the customer protection regulations and does not have sufficient securities to satisfy customers' claims, its customers are protected against loss from a shortfall by the Securities Investor Protection Act ("SIPA"). Securities firms required to register as brokers or dealers are also required to become members of the Securities Investor Protection Corporation ("SIPC"), which provides their customers with protection somewhat similar to that provided by FDIC and other deposit insurance programs for bank depositors. When a member firm fails, SIPC is authorized to initiate a liquidation proceeding under the provisions of SIPA. If the assets of the securities firm are insufficient to satisfy all customer claims, SIPA makes contributions to the estate from a fund financed by assessments on its members to protect customers against losses up to $500,000 for cash and securities held at member firms.

Article 8 is premised on the view that the important policy of protecting investors against the risk of wrongful conduct by their intermediaries is sufficiently treated by other law.

3. Subsection (c) sets out a special rule for secured financing provided to enable clearing corporations to complete settlement. The reasons that secured financing arrangements are needed in such circumstances are explained in Comment 7 to Section 9–115. In order to permit clearing corporations to establish liquidity facilities where necessary to ensure completion of settlement, subsection (c) provides a priority for secured lenders to such clearing corporations. Subsection (c) does not turn on control because the clearing corporation may be the top tier securities intermediary for the securities pledged, so that there may be no practicable method for conferring control on the lender.

Definitional Cross References

"Clearing corporation" Section 8–102(a)(5)

"Control" Section 8–106

"Entitlement holder" Section 8–102(a)(7)

"Financial asset" Section 8–102(a)(9)

"Securities intermediary" Section 8–102(a)(14)

"Security entitlement" Section 8–102(a)(17)

"Security interest" Section 1–201(37)

"Value" Sections 1–201(44) & 8–116

CHAPTER 6. TRANSITION PROVISIONS

Section
8601. Operative date.
8603. Actions or proceedings pending before operative date of division; perfection of security interest at division operative date.

§ 8601. Operative date

This division becomes operative January 1, 1997. *(Added by Stats.1996, c. 497 (S.B.1591), § 9, operative Jan. 1, 1997.)*

§ 8603. Actions or proceedings pending before operative date of division; perfection of security interest at division operative date

(a) This division does not affect an action or proceeding commenced before this division becomes operative.

(b) If a security interest in a security is perfected at the date this division becomes operative, and the action by which the security interest was perfected would suffice to perfect a security interest under this division, no further action is required to continue perfection. If a security interest in a security is perfected at the date this division takes effect but the action by which the security interest was perfected would not suffice to perfect a security interest under this division, the security interest remains perfected for a period of four months after the operative date and continues perfected thereafter if appropriate action to perfect under this division is taken within that period. If a security interest is perfected at the date this division becomes operative and the security interest can be perfected by filing under this division, a financing statement signed by the secured party instead of the debtor may be filed within that period to continue perfection or thereafter to perfect and that financing statement shall contain a statement that it is being filed pursuant to this section. *(Added by Stats.1996, c. 497 (S.B.1591), § 9, operative Jan. 1, 1997.)*

Uniform Commercial Code Comment

The revision of Article 8 should present few significant transition problems. Although the revision involves significant changes in terminology and analysis, the substantive rules are, in large measure, based upon the current practices and are consistent with results that could be reached, albeit at times with some struggle, by proper interpretation of the rules of present law. Thus, the new rules can be applied, without significant dislocations, to transactions and events that occurred prior to enactment.

The enacting provisions should not, whether by applicability, transition, or savings clause language, attempt to provide that old Article 8 continues to apply to "transactions," "events," "rights," "duties," "liabilities," or the like that occurred or accrued before the effective date and that new Article 8 applies to those that occur or accrue after the effective date. The reason for revising Article 8 and corresponding provisions of Article 9 is the concern that the provisions of old Article 8 could be interpreted or misinterpreted to yield results that impede the safe and efficient operation of the national system for the clearance and settlement of securities transactions. Accordingly, it is not the case that any effort should be made to preserve the applicability of old Article 8 to transactions and events that occurred before the effective date.

Only two circumstances seem to warrant continued application of rules of old Article 8. First, to avoid disruption in the conduct of litigation, it may make sense to provide for continued application of the old Article 8 rules to lawsuits pending before the effective date. Second, there are some limited circumstances in which prior law permitted perfection of security interests by methods that are not provided for in the revised version. Section 8–313(1)(h) (1978) permitted perfection of security interests in securities held through intermediaries by notice to the intermediary. Under Revised Articles 8 and 9, security interests can be perfected in such cases by control, which requires the agreement of the intermediary, or by filing. It is likely that secured parties who relied strongly on such collateral under prior law did not simply send notices but obtained agreements from the intermediaries that would suffice for control under the new rules. However, it seems appropriate to include a provision that gives a secured creditor some opportunity after the effective date to perfect in this or any other case in which there is doubt whether the method of perfection used under prior law would be sufficient under the new version.

① Whether the UCC applies?
   a) applies if goods, Transaction - 2-103

② Whether the parties were merchants?
   2-104

③ Whether there are any warranties?
   Expressed
   Implied

④ Whether there are any expressed warranties?
   In all K's for goods, absent a specific waiver the seller/warrants that the goods are merchantable.
   To find an expressed warranty there must be an affirmation of fact that induces reliance.

⑤ Whether there is an implied warranty - 2-314
   a) Warranties of Merchantability?
      Implied - The warranty of merch. Protect the buyer by assuring that the goods will pass w/o objection in the trade and are fit for the ordinary purpose which such goods are used.
   b) Implied warranty for fit for a Particular Purpose? 2-315
      When goods are specially made + the buyer describes to the seller the purpose for which the goods are intended & relies on the seller expertise + seller has reason to know of the reliance then an implied w/ of F.f.P.

⑥ Whether the warranties were Excluded? 2-316   "Puffing" or "opinion"
   a) Expressed warranty 2-316(1) are difficult to limit or exclude.
   b) Implied warranty of merchantability 2-316(2)
   c) Implied warranty for fitness for a particular - writing 10 pt or larger.

⑦ Whether there was acceptance? 2-606
(7.5) SOL?
⑧ Whether there was a breach? 2-607

⑩ Whether there are any remedies? 2-714 etc
                    Modification of warranties
UCC-2-316 allows both express + implied warranties to be disclaimed. So long
as the words or conduct relevant to the creation of an express warranty
and the words or conduct, limitation may be construed as reasonably consistent
with each other. If they are inconsistent the limitation will fail.

To exclude im war of Mech - the words used to exclude the warranty must
include the words of merchantability, "as is" or "with all faults."

Modification or exclusion must be written & conspicuous.

Mod or limitation of Remedies?
- Parties may agree to a specific penalty or a specific nature of dmgs -
provisions are enforceable unless circum. cause the limitation or exclusion to "fail of its
essential purpose." 2-719(2) (unconscionable) if limitation deprives either party of the
Substantial value of the bargain.   2-718(3) - exclusion of conseq. dmgs - OK unless
                                                                    unconscionable.

Division 9

SECURED TRANSACTIONS; SALES OF ACCOUNTS, CONTRACT RIGHTS AND CHATTEL PAPER

Chapter	Section
1. Short Title, Applicability and Definitions	9101
2. Validity of Security Agreement and Rights of Parties Thereto	9201
3. Rights of Third Parties; Perfected and Unperfected Security Interests; Rules of Priority	9301
4. Filing	9401
5. Default	9501

Introductory Comment

By Charles J. Williams

Division 9 is the greatest advancement which the Code presents in the field of commercial law. It is the first comprehensive treatment of the entire system of personal property security law and replaces the patchwork and hodgepodge of various personal property security devices.

Under prior California law, personal property security devices consisted of the (1) pledge, a concept developed by the common law; (2) chattel mortgage, former Civil Code §§ 2955–2978; (3) trust receipt, former Civil Code §§ 3012–3016.16; (4) conditional sale, former Civil Code §§ 2980–2980.5; (5) inventory lien, former Civil Code §§ 3030–3043 and (6) assignment of accounts receivable, former Civil Code §§ 3017–3029. The applicable rules depended upon the nature of the security device employed and there were as many sets of rules as there were devices. The differences were based not upon any logical basis but because the statutes were drafted by different persons at different times.[1]

Division 9 eliminates this diversity of treatment, abolishes the formal distinctions between each of these security devices and provides a uniform set of rules for the unitary concept described as the "security interest". All of the statutes dealing with the six various security devices are superseded. Such regulatory laws for consumer retail installment sales such as the Unruh Act (Civil Code §§ 1802–1812.9) or the Rees-Levering Motor Vehicle and Finance Act (Civil Code §§ 2981–2984.3) are not affected.

Division 9 is not based upon any prior uniform act. However, it does follow in those instances noted parts of the Uniform Trust Receipts Act (UTRA) and the Uniform Conditional Sales Act.

The broad approach of Division 9 is to cover (1) the creation of a security interest with priorities and (2) the giving of notice of a security interest to third parties.

In adopting Division 9, as in the case of Division 6, California departed from its policy of adopting the Code in its Official Text form. Each change is shown and the reason for it explained in the California Code Comment. Although the changes do affect in part the uniformity sought to be obtained, this division adopts in principle the approach of the Official Text.

There should be little question that Division 9 will be far superior to the laws which it supersedes.

[1] California State Bar Committee on the Commercial Code, A Special Report, The Uniform Commercial Code, 37 Calif.State Bar J. 199.

Cross References

Conflict between Division 3 and Division 9, resolution, see Commercial Code § 3102.

CHAPTER 1. SHORT TITLE, APPLICABILITY AND DEFINITIONS

Section
9101. Short Title.

Section
9102. Policy and Scope of Division.
9103. Perfection of security interests in multiple transactions.
9104. Transactions excluded from division.
9105. Definitions; index of definitions.
9106. Account; general intangibles.
9107. Definitions: "Purchase Money Security Interest".
9108. When After-Acquired Collateral Not Security for Antecedent Debt.
9109. Classification of Goods; "Consumer Goods"; "Equipment"; "Farm Products"; "Inventory".
9110. Sufficiency of Description.
9111. Repealed.
9112. Where Collateral Is Not Owned by Debtor.
9113. Security Interests Arising Under Divisions on Sales or Leases.
9114. Consignment.
9115. Security interest in securities account; attachment or perfection; investment property; priorities.
9116. Financial assets bought through securities intermediary; delivery of certificated security or other financial asset; security interest.

Cross References

Assignment of lottery prizes, collateral as loan pursuant to this Division, see Government Code § 8880.32.
Attachment, effect of security interest, see Code of Civil Procedure § 483.010.
Collecting bank, security interest in item subject to this division, see Commercial Code § 4210.
Promissory notes serviced by real estate brokers, completion of delivery, transfer and perfection, see Business and Professions Code § 10233.2.
Sales,
　Passing of title, see Commercial Code § 2401.
　Rights of seller's creditors against sold goods, see Commercial Code § 2402.
Security interest, definition of, see Commercial Code § 1201.

§ 9101. Short Title

This division shall be known and may be cited as Uniform Commercial Code—Secured Transactions. *(Stats.1963, c. 819, § 9101.)*

California Code Comment

By John A. Bohn and Charles J. Williams

This is section 9–101 of the 1962 Official Text without change.

Uniform Commercial Code Comment

This Article sets out a comprehensive scheme for the regulation of security interests in personal property and fixtures. It supersedes prior legislation dealing with such security devices as chattel mortgages, conditional sales, trust receipts, factor's liens and assignments of accounts receivable (see Note to Section 9–102).

Consumer installment sales and consumer loans present special problems of a nature which makes special regulation of them inappropriate in a general commercial codification. Many states now regulate such loans and sales under small loan acts, retail installment selling acts and the like. The National Conference of Commissioners on Uniform State Laws has proposed a Uniform Consumer Credit Code dealing with this subject. While this Article applies generally to security interests in consumer goods, it is not designed to supersede such regulatory legislation (see Notes to Sections 9–102 and 9–203). Nor is this Article designed as a substitute for small loan acts or retail installment selling acts in any state which does not presently have such legislation.

Pre-Code law recognized a wide variety of security devices, which came into use at various times to make possible different types of secured financing. Differences between one device and another persisted, in formal requisites, in the secured party's rights against the debtor and third parties, in the debtor's rights against the secured party, and in filing requirements, although many of those differences no longer served any useful function. Thus an unfiled chattel mortgage was by the law of many states "void" against creditors generally; a conditional sale, often available as a substitute for the chattel mortgage, was in some states valid against all creditors without filing, and in states where filing is required was, if unfiled, void only against lien creditors. The recognition of so many separate security devices had the result that half a dozen filing systems covering chattel security devices might be maintained within a state, some on a county basis, others on a state-wide basis, each of which had to be separately checked to determine a debtor's status.

Nevertheless, despite the great number of security devices there remained gaps in the structure. In many states, for example, a security interest could not be taken in inventory or a stock in trade although there was a real need for such financing. It was often baffling to try to maintain a technically valid security interest when financing a manufacturing process, where the collateral starts out as raw materials, becomes work in process and ends as finished goods. Furthermore, it was by no means clear, even to specialists, how under pre-Code law a security interest might be taken in many kinds of intangible property—such as television or motion picture rights—which have come to be an important source of commercial collateral.

While the chattel mortgage was adaptable for use in almost any situation where goods are collateral, there were limitations, sometimes highly technical, on the use of other devices, such as the conditional sale and particularly the trust receipt. The cases are many in which a security transaction described by the parties as a conditional sale or a trust receipt was later determined by a court to be something else, usually a chattel mortgage. The consequence of such a determination was typically to void the security interest against creditors because the security agreement was not filed *as a chattel mortgage* (even though it may have been filed as a conditional sale or a trust receipt). The already mentioned difficulty of financing on the security of inventory has been got around to some extent by the device known as "field warehousing" as well as by the use of the trust receipt. After 1940 a number of states generally authorized inventory financing by enacting statutes, similar although not uniform, known as "factor's lien" acts. Also after 1940 the increasingly important business of lending against accounts receivable inspired new statutes in that field in more than thirty states.

The growing complexity of financing transactions forced legislatures to keep piling new statutory provisions on top of our inadequate and already sufficiently complicated nineteenth-century structure of security law. The results of this continuing development were increasing costs to both parties and increasing uncertainty as to their rights and the rights of third parties dealing with them.

The aim of this Article is to provide a simple and unified structure within which the immense variety of present-day secured financing transactions can go forward with less cost and with greater certainty.

Under this Article the traditional distinctions among security devices, based largely on form, are not retained; the Article applies to all transactions intended to create security interests in personal property and fixtures, and the single term "security interest" substitutes for the variety of descriptive terms which had grown up at common law and under a hundred-year accretion of statutes. This does not mean that the old forms may not be used, and Section 9–102(2) makes it clear that they may be.

This Article does not determine whether "title" to collateral is in the secured party or in the debtor and adopts neither a "title theory" nor a "lien theory" of security interests. Rights, obligations and remedies under the Article do not depend on the location of title (Section 9–202). The location of title may become important for other purposes—as, for example, in determining the incidence of taxation—and in such a case the parties are left free to contract as they will. In this connection the use of a form which has traditionally been regarded as determinative of title (e.g., the conditional sale) could reasonably be regarded as evidencing the parties' intention with respect to title to the collateral.

Under the Article distinctions based on form (except as between pledge and non-possessory interests) are no longer controlling. For some purposes there are distinctions based on the type of property which constitutes the collateral—industrial and commercial equipment, business inventory, farm products, consumer goods, accounts receivable, documents of title and other intangibles—and, where appropriate, the Article states special rules applicable to financing transactions involving a particular type of property. Despite the statutory simplification a greater degree of flexibility in the financing transaction is allowed than is possible under existing law.

The scheme of the Article is to make distinctions, where distinctions are necessary, along functional rather than formal lines.

This has made possible a radical simplification in the formal requisites for creation of a security interest.

A more rational filing system replaces the present system of different files for each security device which is subject to filing requirements. Thus not only is the information contained in the files made more accessible but the cost of procuring credit information, and, incidentally, of maintaining the files, is greatly reduced.

The Article's flexibility and simplified formalities should make it possible for new forms of secured financing, as they develop, to fit comfortably under its provisions, thus avoiding the necessity, so apparent in recent years, of year by year passing new statutes and tinkering with the old ones to allow legitimate business transactions to go forward.

The rules set out in this Article are principally concerned with the limits of the secured party's protection against purchasers from and creditors of the debtor. Except for procedure on default, freedom of contract prevails between the immediate parties to the security transaction.

Cross References

Aircraft repair, special liens, see Business and Professions Code § 9798.1.

Displaced homemaker emergency loans, default, remedies, see Government Code § 8258.1.

§ 9102. Policy and Scope of Division

(1) Except as otherwise provided in Section 9104 on excluded transactions, this division applies

(a) To any transaction (regardless of its form) which is intended to create a security interest in personal property or fixtures including goods, documents, instruments, general intangibles, chattel paper or accounts; and also

(b) To any sale of accounts or chattel paper.

(2) This division applies to security interests created by contract including pledge, assignment, chattel mortgage, chattel trust, trust deed, inventory lien, equipment trust, conditional sale, trust receipt, other lien or title retention contract and lease or consignment intended as security. This division does not apply to statutory liens except as provided in Section 9310.

(3) The application of this division to a security interest in a secured obligation is not affected by the fact that the obligation is itself secured by a transaction or interest to which this division does not apply.

(4) Notwithstanding anything to the contrary contained in this division, but subject to subdivisions (5), (6), and (7), no nonpossessory security interest, other than a purchase money security interest, may be given

or taken in or to the inventory of a retail merchant held for sale consisting of beer, wine, or liquor. The phrase "purchase money security interest" as used in this subdivision does not extend to any after-acquired property other than the initial property sold by a secured party or taken by a lender as security as provided in Section 9107.

(5) Except as provided in this subdivision, any nonpossessory security interest in the inventory, other than beer, wine, or liquor, of a retail merchant shall be effective with respect to goods in which the debtor acquires rights before, on, or after July 1, 1985, provided the requirements of subdivision (1) of Section 9203 are met before, on, or after July 1, 1985. Any nonpossessory security interest in the inventory, other than beer, wine, or liquor, of a retail merchant whose sales of goods for personal, family, or household purposes exceeded 75 percent in dollar volume of his or her total sales of all goods during the 12 months preceding the filing of the financing statement perfecting the security interest shall not be valid unless:

(a) The security interest is a purchase money security interest as defined in Section 9107; or

(b) The security interest secures a debt as to which the secured party has made no restrictions as to use of funds, other than those which are commercially reasonable and made in good faith.

(6) Subdivisions (4) and (5) do not apply to the following:

(a) Inventory consisting of durable goods having a unit retail value of at least five hundred dollars ($500) or motor vehicles, housetrailers, trailers, semitrailers, farm machinery, construction machinery, or aircraft, or repair parts of any of the foregoing.

(b) Inventory of a debtor which is a cooperative association organized pursuant to Chapter 1 (commencing with Section 54001) of Division 20 of the Food and Agricultural Code (agricultural cooperative associations) or Part 3 (commencing with Section 13200) of Division 3 of Title 1 of the Corporations Code (Fish Marketing Act) * * *.

(7) For purposes of this section, a "retail merchant" is a merchant whose sales for resale did not exceed 75 percent in dollar volume of his or her total sales of all goods during the 12 months preceding the filing of the financing statement perfecting the security interest; and for the purpose of this subdivision, a sale of goods to a contractor, who is required to be licensed, for the purpose of incorporating such goods at any time into improvements or repairs to real property, is a sale for resale.

(8) A financing statement or a continuation statement filed on or before July 1, 1985, if otherwise sufficient in accordance with this division (other than Section 9102), shall be effective with respect to a security interest which first becomes permissible under Section 9102 on or after July 1, 1985.

(9) This section shall become effective on July 1, 1985. *(Stats.1963, c. 819, § 9102. Amended by Stats. 1965, c. 1379, p. 3293, § 16; Stats.1974, c. 997, p. 2115, § 6, eff. Jan. 1, 1976; Stats.1978, c. 38, p. 121, § 1, eff. March 13, 1978; Stats.1980, c. 1156, p. 3857, § 2; Stats.1984, c. 1197, § 1, operative July 1, 1985.)*

California Code Comment

By John A. Bohn and Charles J. Williams

Prior California Law

1. The preamble to subdivision (1) stating the rule concerning personal property within the jurisdiction of this state is in accord with the rule of the Restatement of Conflicts, §§ 265 and 272 (1932) fixing the situs of the chattel as the law which governs the validity of a security agreement concerning that chattel.

2. The test of the applicability of Division 9 in subdivision (1)(a) is whether the parties intended the transaction to have effect as security. Official Comment 1. This approach is similar to the approach of judicial decisions under prior California law which determined the question of whether a transaction was an absolute sale or intended as security is determined by the intention of the parties, not the language or form. Teater v. Good Hope Development Corp., 14 Cal.2d 196, 93 P.2d 112 (1939); Project, California Chattel Security and Article Nine of the Uniform Commercial Code, 8 UCLA L.Rev. 806, 826, 1961, hereafter cited merely as 8 UCLA L.Rev.

3. Subdivision (1)(b) makes a transaction involving the sale of an account, contract right or chattel paper subject to Division 9 regardless of the parties' intent. This means that the assignor's creditors get notice whether the transaction is a sale or a loan. This is consistent with prior Civil Code § 3017(2) which included "sale" within the meaning of "assignment" which made it subject to the assignment of accounts receivable statute.

4. Subdivision (1)(c) is consistent with prior judicial decisions that goods may remain personal as between the secured party and the debtor and still become fixtures governed by the law relating to real property as between the secured party and third persons. R. Barcroft & Sons Co., v. Cullen, 217 Cal. 708, 20 P.2d 665 (1933).

5. Subdivision (2) is new. Commercial Code § 1201(37) defining "security interest" sets forth tests for determining intent.

For a discussion of the inclusion of leases and consignments, see 8 UCLA L.Rev. 806, 826–827. Under prior California law a lease or a consignment could be the subject of a security interest in a chattel if the parties intended to create a security interest.

In California law the term "factors lien" has a limited meaning. By using the term "inventory lien", this subdivision replaces former Civil Code §§ 3030–3043 relating to inventory liens. This change was made to make it clear that these former Civil Code sections were replaced. Sixth Progress Report to the Legislature by Senate Fact Finding Committee on Judiciary (1959–1961) Part 1, The Uniform Commercial Code, p. 418.

6. Subdivision (3) is new. See Official Comment 4 for an illustration of its application.

7. Subdivision (4) has the effect of prohibiting certain forms of retail inventory financing except as there set forth.

Under prior California law the only non-possessory security interest which could be created on existing retail inventory was pursuant to former Civil Code § 3014.5 (Uniform Trust Receipts Act).

Subdivision (4) was amended in the California version to continue the law under former Civil Code § 3014.5 and uses language similar to that former section. This approach was criticized by the State Bar Committee on the Commercial Code:

"Present California statutes forbid a chattel mortgage on 'stock in trade.' [Fn.: Cal.Civ.Code, sec. 2955.] This prohibition is limited to the inventory of a retail or wholesale merchant. According to the California Supreme Court, a manufacturer's inventory is not a 'stock in trade.' [Fn.: Phillips v. Byers, 189 Cal. 665, 209 P. 557 (1922).] Yet based upon this limited statutory prohibition, the statement has been made, apparently in earnest, that a 'lien upon inventory' is impossible in California. [Fn.: This statement was made at the hearing on S.B. 1093 before the Senate Judiciary Committee on May 11, 1961.] This statement is not true. Aside from the possibility of a chattel mortgage on a manufacturer's inventory, other security devices are not limited in the same way as a chattel mortgage. Under the Inventory Lien Law [Fn.: Cal.Civ.Code, secs. 3030–3043] enacted in 1957, a lien may be created on the inventory of any manufacturer or wholesale merchant, though not upon the inventory of a retail merchant. [Fn.: Cal.Civ. Code, sec. 3030(3).] Under the Uniform Trust Receipts Act, [Fn.: Cal.Civ.Code, secs. 3012–3016.16] a purchase-money lien may be created on the inventory of a retail merchant, [Fn.: Cal.Civ.Code, sec. 3014(3).] as well as upon that of a wholesale merchant or manufacturer, if the business is of a type suitable for the mechanics of trust receipts financing. Under a California addition to the Uniform Trust Receipts Act (Civ.Code section 3014.5), a non-purchase-money lien (i.e., one given on existing stock previously owned) may be given on a retail merchant's inventory if he is a dealer in automobiles, aircraft, trailers, house trailers, or other durable goods having a per unit retail value of at least $500. [Fn.: See Crestline Mobile Homes Manufacturing Co., v. Pacific Finance Corp., 54 C.2d 773, 8 Cal.Rptr. 448, 356 P.2d 192 (1960).] A pledge, or a field warehouse which is a species of pledge, may be made of any merchant's inventory if his business can adapt to the required change of possession. [Fn.: McCaffey Canning Co. v. Bank of America, 109 C.A. 415, 294 P. 45 (1930); Heffron v. Bank of America, 113 F.2d 239, 133 A.L.R. 203 (9th Cir.1940).]

"Chapter [Division] 9 would permit a security interest to be given upon the inventory of any business, without the present irrational distinctions. Fifty years ago this would have been a radical departure from California law, but not today. However, because of objections to thus consummating the logical development of the California law as it has changed over the past half century, the Advisory Committee recommended an amendment to preserve substantially the present California law. That amendment, section 19102 [9102] of S.B. 1093 [1961 Session 1958 Official Text as amended], would forbid a non-possessory security interest, other than a purchase-money security interest, upon the inventory of a retail merchant, except upon those types of inventory upon which a non-purchase-money security interest can presently be given under Civil Code section 3014.5. Yet after S.B. 1093 was drafted, the limitation in Civil Code section 3014.5 on non-purchase money trust receipts was reduced from $1,000 to $500 by the 1961 Legislature. [Fn.: Cal.Stats.1961, Ch. 549.]

"The State Bar Committee has recommended that the Advisory Committee amendment be eliminated from S.B. 1093 [1961 Session 1958 Official Text as amended], restoring the original Code provisions to permit a security interest upon the inventory of any business. The State Bar Committee believes that the age of inventory financing has long since arrived. Even if it were desirable, which the members do not believe, it is impossible to turn back the clock. Simply to continue California law, the amendment to section 19102 [9102] in S.B. 1093 [1961 Session 1958 Official Text as amended] preserves nothing but accidental distinctions." California State Bar Committee on the Commercial Code, A Special Report, The Uniform Commercial Code, 37 Calif. State Bar J. (March-April, 1962) pp. 203–204.

Although subdivision (4) is intended to maintain prior California law concerning types of retail financing arrangements, a question is raised as to whether or not subdivision (4) successfully accomplishes this purpose:

"The retailer is now expressly excluded from the benefits of the Inventory Lien statute. [Fn.: Cal.Civ.Code § 3030(3).] Even under the California version of the Code, however, the retailer may be able to create the equivalent of an inventory lien so long as the funds advanced by the financier are initially utilized in the acquisition of new inventory, thereby enabling the newly created security interest to be denominated a purchase money security interest as defined in the Code. The retailer involved in such a security transaction could thereby in effect tie up all his inventory assets with a single secured lender to the possible derogation of his unsecured creditors. The California amendment would appear to have been clearly directed at avoiding such a result." 8 U.C.L.A.L.Rev. 806, 829.

Changes from U.C.C. (1962 Official Text)

8. Section 9–102 of the Official Text with the California changes reads as follows:

(1) Except as otherwise provided in Section 9103 [9–103] on multiple state transactions and in Section 9104 [9–104] on excluded transactions, this [Article] division applies so far as concerns any personal property and fixtures within the jurisdiction of this State

(a) To any transaction (regardless of its form) which is intended to create a security interest in personal property [or fixtures] including goods, documents, instruments, general intangibles, chattel paper, accounts or contract rights; and also

(b) To any sale of accounts, contract rights or chattel paper; and also

(c) To any transaction (regardless of its form) which is intended to create a security interest in goods which are or later become "fixtures" under the law of this State, but as against third parties having or acquiring an interest in or a lien on the real property, the rights and duties of the parties to the secured transaction are governed by the law of this State relating to real property and fixtures.

(2) This [Article] division applies to security interests created by contract including pledge, assignment, chattel mortgage, chattel trust, trust deed, [factor's], inventory lien, equipment trust, conditional sale, trust receipt, other lien or title retention contract and lease or consignment intended as security. This [Article] division does not apply to statutory liens except as provided in Section 9310 [9–310].

(3) The application of this [Article] division to a security interest in a secured obligation is not affected by the fact that the obligation is itself secured by a transaction or interest to which this [Article] division does not apply.

(4) Notwithstanding anything to the contrary in this division, no non-possessory security interest, other than a purchase money security interest, may be given or taken in or to the inventory of a retail merchant held for sale, except in or to inventory consisting of durable goods having a unit retail value of at least five hundred dollars ($500) or motor vehicles, house trailers, semitrailers, farm and construction machinery and repair parts thereof, or aircraft.

9. In subdivision (1)(a) the word "fixtures" was deleted in order to maintain the existing California law of fixtures. Sixth Progress Report to the Legislature by Senate Fact Finding Committee on Judiciary (1959–1961) Part 1, The Uniform Commercial Code, pp. 417–418. Also see California Code Comment to section 9313.

10. In subdivision (2) the change from "factor's lien" to "inventory lien" was made to conform to California terminology.

11. Subdivision (4) does not appear in the Official Text. The purpose of subdivision (4) is to continue the prior California law concerning retail inventory financing. See California Code Comment 7 above. This subdivision was also in the S.B. 1093 (1961 Session, 1958 Official Text as amended) with the exception that the dollar limit was $1,000.

California Code Comment

By Charles J. Williams

In 1965, the word "trailers" was added to subdivision (4) to correct an oversight made when the section was originally enacted in 1963.

Uniform Commercial Code Comment

Neither Section 9-102 nor any other provision of Article 9 is intended to prevent the transfer of ownership of accounts or chattel paper. The determination of whether a particular transfer of accounts or chattel paper constitutes a sale or a transfer for security purposes (such as in connection with a loan) is not governed by Article 9. Article 9 applies both to sales of accounts or chattel paper and loans secured by accounts or chattel paper primarily to incorporate Article 9's perfection rules. The use of terminology such as 'security interest' to include the interest of a buyer of accounts or chattel paper, 'secured party' to include a buyer of accounts or chattel paper, 'debtor' to include a seller of accounts or chattel paper, and 'collateral' to include accounts or chattel paper that have been sold is intended solely as a drafting technique to achieve this end and is not relevant to the sale or secured transaction determination. See PEB Commentary No. 14, dated June 10, 1994.

Prior Uniform Statutory Provision:
None.

Purposes:

The main purpose of this Section is to bring all consensual security interests in personal property and fixtures under this Article, except for certain types of transactions excluded by Section 9–104. In addition certain sales of accounts and chattel paper are brought within this Article to avoid difficult problems of distinguishing between transactions intended for security and those not so intended. As to security interests in fixtures created under the law applicable to real estate, see Section 9–313(1).

§ 9102 APPLICATION AND DEFINITIONS

1. Except for sales of accounts and chattel paper, the principal test whether a transaction comes under this Article is: is the transaction intended to have effect as security? For example, Section 9–104 excludes certain transactions where the security interest (such as an artisan's lien) arises under statute or common law by reason of status and not by consent of the parties. Transactions in the form of consignments or leases are subject to this Article if the understanding of the parties or the effect of the arrangement shows that a security interest was intended. (As to consignments the provisions of Sections 2–326, 9–114 and 9–408 should be consulted.) When it is found that a security interest as defined in Section 1–201(37) was intended, this Article applies regardless of the form of the transaction or the name by which the parties may have christened it. The list of traditional security devices in subsection (2) is illustrative only; other old devices, as well as any new ones which the ingenuity of lawyers may invent, are included, so long as the requisite intent is found. The controlling definition is that contained in subsection (1).

The Article does not in terms abolish existing security devices. The conditional sale or bailment-lease, for example, is not prohibited; but even though it is used, the rules of this Article govern.

2. If an obligation is to repay money lent and is not part of chattel paper, it is either an instrument or a general intangible. A sale of an instrument or general intangible is not within this Article, but a transfer intended to have effect as security for an obligation of the transferor is covered by subsection (1)(a). In either case the nature of the transaction is not affected by the fact that collateral is transferred with the instrument or general intangible. Such a transfer is treated as a transfer by operation of law, whether or not it is articulated in the agreement.

An assignment of accounts or chattel paper as security for an obligation is covered by subsection (1)(a). Commercial financing on the basis of accounts and chattel paper is often so conducted that the distinction between a security transfer and a sale is blurred, and a sale of such property is therefore covered by subsection (1)(b) whether intended for security or not, unless excluded by Section 9–104. The buyer then is treated as a secured party, and his interest as a security interest. See Sections 9–105(1)(m), 1–201(37). Certain sales which have nothing to do with commercial financing transactions are excluded by Section 9–104(f); compare Spurlin v. Sloan, 368 S.W.2d 314 (Ky.1963). See also Section 9–302(1)(e), exempting from filing casual or isolated assignments, and Section 9–302(2), preserving the perfected status of a security interest against the original debtor when a secured party assigns his interest.

3. In general, problems of choice of law in this Article as to the validity of security agreements are governed by Section 1–105. Problems of choice of law as to perfection of security interests and the effect of perfection or non-perfection thereof, including rules requiring reperfection, are governed by Section 9–103.

4. An illustration of subsection (3) is as follows:

The owner of Blackacre borrows $10,000 from his neighbor, and secures his note by a mortgage on Blackacre. This Article is not applicable to the creation of the real estate mortgage. Nor is it applicable to a sale of the note by the mortgagee, even though the mortgage continues to secure the note. However, when the mortgagee pledges the note to secure his own obligation to X, this Article applies to the security interest thus created, which is a security interest in an instrument even though the instrument is secured by a real estate mortgage. This Article leaves to other law the question of the effect on rights under the mortgage of delivery or non-delivery of the mortgage or of recording or nonrecording of an assignment of the mortgage's interest. See Section 9–104(j). But under Section 3–304(5) recording of the assignment does not of itself prevent X from holding the note in due course.

5. While most sections of this Article apply to a security interest without regard to the nature of the collateral or its use, some sections state special rules with reference to particular types of collateral. An index of sections where such special rules are stated follows:

ACCOUNTS

Section	
9–102(1)(b)	Sale of accounts subject to Article
9–103(1)	When Article applies; conflict of laws rules
9–104(f)	Certain sales of accounts excluded from Article
9–106	Definitions
9–205	Permissible for debtor to make collections
9–206(1)	Agreement not to assert defenses against assignee
9–301(1)(d)	Unperfected security interest subordinate to certain transferees
9–302(1)(e)	What assignments need not be filed
9–306(5)	Rule when goods whose sale gave rise to an account return to seller's possession
9–318(1)	Rights of assignee subject to defenses
9–318(2)	Modification of contract after assignment of contract right
9–318(3)	When account debtor may pay assignor
9–318(4)	Term prohibiting assignment ineffective
9–401	Place of filing
9–502	Collection rights of secured party
9–504(2)	Rights on default where underlying transaction was sale of accounts or contract rights

CHATTEL PAPER

9–102(1)(b)	Sale subject to Article
9–104(f)	Certain sales excluded from Article
9–105(1)(b)	Definition
9–205	Permissible for debtor to make collections
9–206(1)	Agreement not to assert defenses against assignee
9–207(1)	Duty of secured party in possession to preserve rights against prior parties
9–301(1)(c)	Unperfected security interest subordinate to certain transferees
9–304(1)	Perfection by filing
9–305	When possession by secured party perfects security interest
9–306(5)	Rule when goods whose sale results in chattel paper return to seller's possession
9–308	When purchasers of chattel paper have priority over security interest
9–318(1)	Rights of assignee subject to defenses
9–318(3)	When account debtor may pay assignor
9–502	Collection rights of secured party
9–504(2)	Rights on default where underlying transaction was sale

DOCUMENTS AND INSTRUMENTS

9–105(1)(e)	Definition of document (and see 1–201)
9–105(1)(g)	Definition of instrument
9–206(1)	Rule where buyer of goods signs both negotiable instrument and security agreement
9–207(1)	Duty of secured party in possession of instrument to preserve rights against prior parties
9–301(1)(c)	Unperfected security interest subordinate to certain transferees
9–302(1)(b) and (f)	What interests need not be filed
9–304(1)	How security interest can be perfected
9–304(2, 3)	Perfection of security interest in goods in possession of issuer of negotiable document or of other bailee
9–304(4, 5)	Perfection of security interest in instruments or negotiable documents without filing or transfer of possession
9–305	When possession by secured party perfects security interest
9–308	When purchasers of instruments have priority over security interest
9–309	When purchasers of negotiable instruments or negotiable documents have priority over security interest
9–501(1)	Rights on default when collateral is documents
9–502	Collection rights of secured party

GENERAL INTANGIBLES

9–103(2)	When Article applies; conflict of laws rules
9–105	Obligor is "account debtor"
9–106	Definition
9–301(1)(d)	Unperfected security interest subordinate to certain transferees

§ 9102

Section	
9–318(1)	Rights of assignee subject to defenses
9–318(3)	When account debtor may pay assignor
9–502	Collection rights of secured party

GOODS
(See also Consumer Goods, Equipment, Farm Products, Inventory)

9–103	When Article applies with regard to goods of a type normally used in more than one jurisdiction; goods covered by certificate of title; conflict of laws rules
9–105(1)(h)	Definition
9–109	Classification of goods as consumer goods, equipment, farm products and inventory
9–203	Formal requisites of security agreement covering certain types of goods (crops or timber)
9–204	Validity of after-acquired property clause covering certain types of goods (crops, consumer goods)
9–205	Permissible for debtor to accept returned goods
9–206(2)	When security agreement can limit or modify warranties on sale
9–301(1)(c)	Unperfected security interest subordinate to certain transferees
9–304(2, 3)	Perfection of security interest in goods in possession of issuer of negotiable document or of other bailee
9–304(5)	Perfection of security interest without filing or transfer of possession where goods in possession of certain bailees
9–305	When possession by secured party perfects security interest
9–306(5)	Rule when goods whose sale gave rise to account or chattel paper return to seller's possession
9–307	When buyers of goods from debtor take free of security interest
9–313	Goods which are or become fixtures
9–314	Goods affixed to other goods
9–315	Goods commingled in a product
9–401(1)	Place of filing for fixtures
9–402	Form of financing statement covering fixtures
9–504(1)	Sale of goods by secured party after default subject to Article 2 (Sales)

CONSUMER GOODS

9–109(1)	Definition
9–203(2)	Transaction, although subject to this Article, may also be subject to certain regulatory statutes
9–204(2)	Validity of after-acquired property clause
9–206(1)	Buyer's agreement not to assert defenses against an assignee subject to statute or decision which establishes rule for buyers of consumer goods
9–302(1)(d)	When filing not required
9–307(2)	When buyers from debtor take free of security interest
9–401(1)(a)	Place of filing
9–505(1)	Secured party's duty to dispose of repossessed consumer goods
9–507(1)	Secured party's liability for improper disposition of consumer goods after default

EQUIPMENT

9–103(2)	When Article applies with regard to certain types of equipment normally used in more than one jurisdiction; conflict of laws rules
9–109(2)	Definition
9–302(1)(c)	When filing not required to perfect security interest in certain farm equipment
9–307(2)	When buyers of certain farm equipment from debtor take free of security interest

Section	
9–401(1)	Place of filing for equipment used in farming operation
9–503	Secured party's right after default to remove or to render equipment unusable

FARM PRODUCTS

9–109(3)	Definition
9–203(1)(b)	Formal requisites of security agreement covering crops
9–307	When a buyer of farm products takes free of security interest
9–312(2)	Priority of secured party who gives new value to enable debtor to produce crops
9–401(1)	Place of filing
9–402(1) and (3)	Form of financing statement covering crops

INVENTORY

9–103(3)	When Article applies with regard to certain types of inventory normally used in more than one jurisdiction; conflict of laws rules
9–109(4)	Definition
9–114	Consigned goods
9–306(5)	Rule where goods whose sale gave rise to account or chattel paper return to seller's possession
9–307(1)	When buyers from debtor take free of security interest
9–312(3), 9–304(5)	When purchase money security interest takes priority over conflicting security interest
9–408	Financing statements covering consigned or leased goods

Cross References:

Sections 9–103 and 9–104.

Point 1: Section 2–326.

Point 2: Section 1–105.

Definitional Cross References:

"Account". Section 9–106.

"Chattel paper". Section 9–105.

"Contract". Section 1–201.

"Document". Section 9–105.

"General intangibles". Section 9–106.

"Goods". Section 9–105.

"Instrument". Section 9–105.

"Security interest". Section 1–201.

Cross References

Application of 1979–1980 legislation relating to fixtures, see Commercial Code § 14109.
Consignment sales, see Commercial Code § 2326.
Contracts, generally, see Civil Code § 1549 et seq.
Effective date and transition provisions of Stats.1974, c. 997, see Commercial Code § 14101 et seq.
Excluded transactions, see Commercial Code § 9104.
Personal representatives, mortgaging property, see Probate Code § 9800 et seq.
Factor, no authority to mortgage or pledge, see Civil Code § 2368.
Fixtures,
   Affixing without agreement to remove, see Civil Code § 1013.
   Defined, see Civil Code § 660.
   Removal, see Civil Code §§ 1013.5, 1019.
General definitions and principles of interpretation, see Commercial Code § 1201 et seq.
Liens, in general, see Civil Code § 2872 et seq.
Multiple state transactions, see Commercial Code § 9103.
Personal property, generally, see Civil Code § 946 et seq.
Property, in general, see Civil Code § 654 et seq.

Territorial application of act, see Commercial Code § 1105.

§ 9103. Perfection of security interests in multiple transactions

(1)(a) This subdivision applies to documents, instruments, <u>rights to proceeds of written letters of credit,</u> and * * * goods other than those covered by a certificate of title described in subdivision (2), mobile goods described in subdivision (3), and minerals described in subdivision (5).

(b) Except as otherwise provided in this subdivision, perfection and the effect of perfection or nonperfection of a security interest in collateral are governed by the law of the jurisdiction where the collateral is when the last event occurs on which is based the assertion that the security interest is perfected or unperfected.

(c) If the parties to a transaction creating a purchase money security interest in goods in one jurisdiction understand at the time that the security interest attaches that the goods will be kept in another jurisdiction, then the law of the other jurisdiction governs the perfection and the effect of perfection or nonperfection of the security interest from the time it attaches until 30 days after the debtor receives possession of the goods and thereafter if the goods are taken to the other jurisdiction before the end of the 30–day period.

(d) When collateral is brought into and kept in this state while subject to a security interest perfected under the law of the jurisdiction from which the collateral was removed, the security interest remains perfected, but if action is required by Chapter 3 (commencing with Section 9301) to perfect the security interest:

(i) If the action is not taken before the expiration of the period of perfection in the other jurisdiction or the end of four months after the collateral is brought into this state, whichever period first expires, the security interest becomes unperfected at the end of that period and is thereafter deemed to have been unperfected as against a person who became a purchaser after removal.

(ii) If the action is taken before the expiration of the period specified in subparagraph (i), the security interest continues perfected thereafter.

(iii) For the purpose of priority over a buyer of consumer goods (subdivision (2) of Section 9307), the period of the effectiveness of a filing in the jurisdiction from which the collateral is removed is governed by the rules with respect to perfection in subparagraphs (i) and (ii).

(e) If goods are or become fixtures (Section 9313(1)(a)) in relation to real estate located in this state, the conflicting interest of an encumbrancer or owner of the real estate is governed by Section 9313.

(2)(a) This subdivision applies to goods covered by a certificate of title issued under a statute of this state or of another jurisdiction under the law of which indication of a security interest on the certificate is required as a condition of perfection whether such certificate is designated a "certificate of title," "certificate of ownership," or otherwise.

(b) Except as otherwise provided in this subdivision, perfection and the effect of perfection or nonperfection of the security interest are governed by the law (including the conflict of laws rules) of the jurisdiction issuing the certificate until four months after the goods are removed from that jurisdiction and thereafter until the goods are registered in another jurisdiction, but in any event not beyond surrender of the certificate. After the expiration of that period, the goods are not covered by the certificate of title within the meaning of this section.

(c) Except with respect to the rights of a buyer described in the next paragraph, a security interest, perfected in another jurisdiction otherwise than by notation on a certificate of title, in goods brought into this state and thereafter covered by a certificate of title issued by this state is subject to the rules stated in paragraph (d) of subdivision (1).

(d) If goods are brought into this state while a security interest therein is perfected in any manner under the law of the jurisdiction from which the goods are removed and a certificate of title is issued by this state and the certificate does not show that the goods are subject to the security interest or that they may be subject to a security interest not shown on the certificate, the security interest is subordinate to the rights of a buyer of the goods who is not in the business of selling goods of that kind to the extent that he or she gives value and receives delivery of the goods after issuance of the certificate and without knowledge of the security interest.

(3)(a) This subdivision applies to accounts (other than an account described in subdivision (5) on minerals) and general intangibles (other than uncertificated securities) and to goods which are mobile and which are of a type normally used in more than one jurisdiction, such as motor vehicles, trailers, rolling stock, airplanes, shipping containers, roadbuilding and construction machinery and commercial harvesting machinery and the like, if the goods are equipment or are inventory leased or held for lease by the debtor to others, and are not covered by a certificate of title described in subdivision (2).

(b) The law (including the conflict of laws rules) of the jurisdiction in which the debtor is located governs the perfection and the effect of perfection or nonperfection of the security interest.

(c) If, however, the debtor is located in a jurisdiction which is not a part of the United States, and which does not provide for perfection of the security interest by filing or recording in that jurisdiction, the law of the jurisdiction in the United States in which the debtor has its major executive office in the United States governs the perfection and the effect of perfection or nonperfection of the security interest through filing. In the alternative, if the debtor is located in a jurisdiction which is not a part of the United States or Canada and the collateral is accounts or general intangibles for

§ 9103

money due or to become due, the security interest may be perfected by notification to the account debtor. As used in this paragraph, "United States" includes its territories and possessions and the Commonwealth of Puerto Rico.

(d) A debtor shall be deemed located at the debtor's place of business if he or she has one, at the debtor's chief executive office if he or she has more than one place of business, or otherwise at the debtor's residence. If, however, the debtor is a foreign air carrier under the Federal Aviation Act of 1958, as amended, it shall be deemed located at the designated office of the agent upon whom service of process may be made on behalf of the foreign air carrier.

(e) A security interest perfected under the law of the jurisdiction of the location of the debtor is perfected until the expiration of four months after a change of the debtor's location to another jurisdiction, or until perfection would have ceased by the law of the first jurisdiction, whichever period first expires. Unless perfected in the new jurisdiction before the end of that period, it becomes unperfected thereafter and is deemed to have been unperfected as against a person who became a purchaser after the change.

(4) The rules stated for goods in subdivision (1) apply to a possessory security interest in chattel paper. The rules stated for accounts in subdivision (3) apply to a nonpossessory security interest in chattel paper, but the security interest may not be perfected by notification to the account debtor.

(5) Perfection and the effect of perfection or nonperfection of a security interest which is created by a debtor who has an interest in minerals or the like (including oil and gas) before extraction and which attaches thereto as extracted, or which attaches to an account resulting from the sale thereof at the wellhead or minehead are governed by the law (including the conflict of laws rules) of the jurisdiction wherein the wellhead or minehead is located.

* * *

(6)(a) This subdivision applies to investment property.

(b) Except as otherwise provided in paragraph (f), during the time that a security certificate is located in a jurisdiction, perfection of a security interest, the effect of perfection or nonperfection, and the priority of a security interest in the certificated security represented thereby are governed by the local law of that jurisdiction.

(c) Except as otherwise provided in paragraph (f), perfection of a security interest, the effect of perfection or nonperfection, and the priority of a security interest in an uncertificated security are governed by the local law of the issuer's jurisdiction as specified in subdivision (d) of Section 8110.

(d) Except as otherwise provided in paragraph (f), perfection of a security interest, the effect of perfection or nonperfection, and the priority of a security interest in a security entitlement or securities account are governed by the local law of the securities intermediary's jurisdiction as specified in subdivision (e) of Section 8110.

(e) Except as otherwise provided in paragraph (f), perfection of a security interest, the effect of perfection or nonperfection, and the priority of a security interest in a commodity contract or commodity account are governed by the local law of the commodity intermediary's jurisdiction. The following rules determine a "commodity intermediary's jurisdiction" for purposes of this paragraph:

(i) If an agreement between the commodity intermediary and commodity customer specifies that it is governed by the law of a particular jurisdiction, that jurisdiction is the commodity intermediary's jurisdiction.

(ii) If an agreement between the commodity intermediary and commodity customer does not specify the governing law as provided in subparagraph (i), but expressly specifies that the commodity account is maintained at an office in a particular jurisdiction, that jurisdiction is the commodity intermediary's jurisdiction.

(iii) If an agreement between the commodity intermediary and commodity customer does not specify a jurisdiction as provided in subparagraphs (i) or (ii), the commodity intermediary's jurisdiction is the jurisdiction in which is located the office identified in an account statement as the office serving the commodity customer's account.

(iv) If an agreement between the commodity intermediary and commodity customer does not specify a jurisdiction as provided in subparagraphs (i) or (ii) and an account statement does not identify an office serving the commodity customer's account as provided in subparagraph (iii), the commodity intermediary's jurisdiction is the jurisdiction in which is located the chief executive office of the commodity intermediary.

(f) Perfection of a security interest by filing, automatic perfection of a security interest in investment property granted by a broker or securities intermediary, and automatic perfection of a security interest in a commodity contract or commodity account granted by a commodity intermediary are governed by the local law of the jurisdiction in which the debtor is located. The rules in paragraphs (c), (d), and (e) of subdivision (3) apply to security interests to which this paragraph applies. *(Added by Stats.1974, c. 997, p. 2116, § 8, eff. Jan. 1, 1976. Amended by Stats.1980, c. 1156, p. 3858, § 3; Stats.1984, c. 927, § 7; Stats.1996, c. 176 (S.B. 1599), § 8; Stats.1996, c. 497 (S.B.1591), § 10, operative Jan. 1, 1997.)*

**Legislative Committee Comment—Assembly
1984 Addition**

These changes conform to the Official Text, except that the phrase "(including the conflict of laws rules)" has been deleted from Section 9103(6) in order to retain an existing California nonuniform variation. [84 A.J. 18471].

Uniform Commercial Code Comment

Official Reasons for 1977 Change

Uncertificated securities are included in the definition of "General intangibles" under Section 9–106. Since the perfection of a security interest in an uncertificated security is normally accomplished by registration of pledge or transfer under Article 8, uncertificated securities are excluded from the coverage of subsection (3) under which the location of the debtor would govern. New subsection (6) prescribes the law of the issuer's jurisdiction of organization as the governing law, consistent with Section 8–106.

Prior Uniform Statutory Provisions:

Paragraph 1(d): Section 14, Uniform Conditional Sales Act.

Purposes:

1. The general rules on choice of law between the original parties in Section 1–105 apply to this Article. However, when conflicting claims to collateral arise, the question depends on *perfection* of security interests, and thus on the effect of perfection or non-perfection. These problems are dealt with in this section. The general rule (paragraph (1) (b)) is that these questions are governed by the law of the jurisdiction where the collateral is when the last event occurs on which is based the assertion that the security interest is perfected or unperfected. This event will frequently be the filing. If the last event is not filing and perfection is through filing, the filing required is in the jurisdiction where the collateral is when the last event occurs; prior filing in another jurisdiction is not effective and is not saved by the four-month rule discussed below, which applies only when the security interest was *perfected* in the jurisdiction from which the collateral was removed. If the security interest was perfected in one jurisdiction and then removed to another jurisdiction, maintenance of perfection in the latter jurisdiction or failure to do so is the "last event" to which the basic rule refers.

There are, however, exceptions to this basic rule:

2. If the parties to a transaction creating a purchase money security interest in goods understand when the security interest attaches that the collateral will be kept in another jurisdiction, the law of that jurisdiction governs perfection and the effect of perfection or non-perfection until 30 days after the debtor receives possession of the goods (paragraph (1) (c)). A filing in that jurisdiction perfects the security interest even before the goods are removed. The 30-day period is not a period of grace during which filing is unnecessary or has retroactive effect, but merely states the period during which the other jurisdiction is the place of filing. The effect of late filing is governed by other provisions, such as Sections 9–301 and 9–312.

3. If the goods reach that jurisdiction within the 30 days, the effectiveness of the filing in that jurisdiction continues without interruption. If the collateral is not kept in that jurisdiction before the end of the 30-day period, paragraph (1) (c) ceases to be applicable and thereafter the law of the jurisdiction where the collateral is controls perfection. A failure of the collateral to reach the intended destination jurisdiction before the expiration of the 30-day period because of a conflicting claim or otherwise may cause disappointment of expectations that the law of the destination jurisdiction will govern continuously, and caution may dictate filing both in that jurisdiction and in the jurisdiction where the security interest attaches.

This section uses the concepts that goods are "kept" in a state or "brought" into a state, and related terms. These concepts imply a stopping place of a permanent nature in the state, not merely transit or storage intended to be transitory.

4. (a) Where the collateral is an automobile or other goods covered by a certificate of title issued by any state and the security interest is perfected by notation on the certificate of title, perfection is controlled by the certificate of title rather than by the law of the state wherein the security interest attached (subsection (2)).

(b) It has long been hoped that "exclusive certificate of title laws" would provide a sure means of controlling property interests in goods like automobiles, which because of their nature cannot readily be controlled by local or statewide filing alone. In theory the certificate of title should control the property interests in the vehicle wherever the vehicle may be. However, two circumstances operate to prevent the perfect operation of the certificate of title device:

First, some states have never adopted certificate of title laws. This results in a problem in the issuance of a certificate of title when the vehicle moves from a non-certificate to a certificate state, because the certificate-issuing officer is in no position to conduct a complete search to ascertain the condition of the title in a state of origin which requires no filing or in which filing could be in any one or more of several localities. Also, it seems that when a vehicle moves from a certificate to a non-certificate state, the officers issuing a new registration for the vehicle are not always meticulous to notify secured parties shown on the certificate to give them a chance to perfect their security interests in the non-certificate state when a new registration is issued. Moreover, some vehicles like mobile homes are not always registered and title certificates are not always issued even in a state which may have certificate laws applicable thereto, because the certificate laws may apply only if the mobile homes use the highways. Registration plates of a mobile home having a certificate could be removed and there would be nothing visible to show that a certificate had ever been issued for it.

Second, various fraudulent devices based on allegations of loss of the certificate of title enable a dishonest person to obtain both an original and a duplicate of title; to have a security interest shown on only one thereof; and then to effect a transfer into a new state on the basis of the clean certificate, no matter how diligent the officers in the second state may be.

Given these practical problems, the choice of applicable rules of law after interstate removals of vehicles subject to certificate of title laws is most difficult. This Article provides the rules set forth below.

(c) The security interest perfected by notation on a certificate of title will be recognized without limit as to time; but, of course, perfection by this method ceases if the certificate of title is surrendered (paragraph (2) (b)). Since the secured party ordinarily holds the certificate, surrender thereof could not occur without his action in the matter in some respect. If the vehicle is reregistered in another jurisdiction while the secured party still holds the certificate, a danger of deception to third parties arises. The section provides that the certificate ceases to control after 4 months following removal if reregistration has occurred, but during the 4 months the secured party has the same protection for cases of interstate removal as is set forth in paragraph (1) (d) of the section and Comment 7, subject to additional limitation if the reregistration also involves a new "clean" certificate of title in the removal jurisdiction and a non-professional buyer buys while that new certificate is outstanding. See paragraph (2) (d) and Comment 4(e).

(d) If a vehicle not described in the preceding paragraph (*i.e.*, not covered by a certificate of title) is removed to a certificate state and a certificate is issued therefor, the holder of a security interest has the same 4-month protection, subject to the provision discussed in the next paragraph of Comment.

(e) Where "this state" issues a certificate of title on collateral that has come from another state subject to a security interest perfected in any manner, problems will arise if this state, from whatever cause, fails to show on its certificate the security interest perfected in the other jurisdiction. This state will have every reason, nevertheless, to make its certificate of title reliable to the type of person who most needs to rely on it. Paragraph (2) (d) of the section therefore provides that the security interest perfected in the other jurisdiction is subordinate to the rights of a limited class of persons buying the goods while there is a clean certificate of title issued by this state, without knowledge of the security interest perfected in the other jurisdiction. The limited class are buyers who are non-professionals, i.e., not dealers and not secured parties, because these are ordinarily professionals. The protective rule mentioned does not apply if this state adopts a device used under some certificate of title laws, namely, stating on the certificate of title that the vehicle may be subject to security interests not shown on the certificate, where the collateral came from a non-certificate state.

In any event the security interest perfected out of state becomes unperfected unless reperfected in this state under the usual 4-month rule (paragraph (2) (d) of the section). States which place a cautionary statement on a certificate of title coming from a non-certificate state make provision to reissue the certificate without the caution after 4 months.

One difficulty is that no state's certificate of title law makes any provision by which a foreign security interest may be reperfected in that state, without the cooperation of the owner or other person holding the certificate in temporarily surrendering the certificate. But that cooperation is not likely to be forthcoming from an owner who wrongfully procured the issuance of a new certificate not showing the out-of-state security interest, or from a local secured party finding himself in a priority contest with the out-of-state secured party. The only solution for the out-of-state secured party under present certificate of title laws seems to be to reperfect by possession, i.e., by repossessing the goods.

5. The general rules of the section based on location of the collateral could not be applied to certain types of intangible collateral which have no location in any realistic sense, or to certain movable chattels which have no permanent location.

(a) For accounts and general intangibles there is no indispensable or symbolic document which represents the underlying claim, whose endorsement or delivery is the one effectual means of transfer. There is a considerable body of case law dealing with the situs of choses in action such as these. This case law is in the highest degree confused, contradictory and uncertain: it affords no base on which to build a statutory rule.

An account arises typically out of a sale; the contract of sale may be executed in State A, the goods shipped from a warehouse in State B to buyer (account debtor) in State C. The account may then be assigned to an assignee in State D. The seller-assignor may keep his principal records in State E. Under the non-notification system of accounts financing, the seller-assignor, despite the assignment, bills and collects from the account debtor; under notification financing the account debtor makes payment to the assignee, but the bills may be prepared and sent out by either assignor or assignee. The contacts of the transaction are with many jurisdictions: to which one is it appropriate to look for the governing law? Even more complicated situations may be anticipated when the collateral consists of novel or uncommon types of personal property, which fall within the definition of general intangibles.

If we bear in mind that our principal question is where certain financing statements shall be filed, two things become clear. *First:* since the purpose of filing is to allow subsequent creditors of the *debtor-assignor* to determine the true status of his affairs, the place chosen must be one which such creditors would normally associate with the assignor; thus the place of business of the assignee and the places of business or residences of the various account debtors must be rejected in ordinary situations. *Second:* the place chosen must be one which can be determined with the least possible risk of error. The place chosen by subsection (3) is the debtor's location, which is ordinarily the location of its chief executive office. This concept is discussed below.

(b) Another class of collateral for which a special rule is stated in subsection (3) is mobile goods of types which are normally moved for use from one jurisdiction to another. Such goods are generally classified as equipment; sometimes they may be classified as inventory, for example, goods leased by a professional lessor. Subsection (3) provides that a security interest in such equipment or inventory is subject to this Article when the debtor's location, i.e., ordinarily its chief executive office, is in this state.

While automobiles are obviously mobile goods, they will in most cases be covered by subsection (2) of this section and therefore excluded from subsection (3) by paragraph (a) thereof. If an automobile is not covered by a certificate of title and is classified as equipment or as inventory under lease, it will be subject to subsection (3). Automobiles and other mobile goods which are classified as consumer goods are not subject to subsection (3).

The rule of subsection (3) applies to goods of a type "normally used" in more than one jurisdiction; there is no requirement that particular goods be in fact used out of state. Thus, if an enterprise whose chief executive office is in State X keeps in State Y goods of the type covered by subsection (3), the rule of subsection (3) requires filing in State X even though the goods never leave State Y.

(c) "Chief executive office" does not mean the place of incorporation; it means the place from which in fact the debtor manages the main part of his business operations. This is the place where persons dealing with the debtor would normally look for credit information, and is the appropriate place for filing. The term "chief executive office" is not defined in this Section or elsewhere in this Act. Doubt may arise as to which is the "chief executive office" of a multi-state enterprise, but it would be rare that there could be more than two possibilities. A secured party in such a case may easily protect himself at no great additional burden by filing in each possible place. The subsection states a rule which will be simple to apply in most cases, and which makes it possible to dispense with much burdensome and useless filing.

(d) If the location of the debtor is moved after a security interest has been perfected in another jurisdiction, the secured party has four months within which to refile, unless the perfection in the original jurisdiction would have expired earlier (paragraph (3) (e)).

(e) Under subsection (3) each state other than that of the debtor's location in effect disclaims jurisdiction over certain accounts and general intangibles which, by common law rules, might be held to be within its jurisdiction; in the same way there is a disclaimer of jurisdiction over mobile chattels, even though they may be physically located within the state much of the time. If the jurisdiction whose law controls under this rule is a United States jurisdiction or has enacted legislation permitting perfection of the security interest by filing or recording in that jurisdiction, the law of that jurisdiction will be recognized in the disclaiming jurisdiction as perfecting the security interest. The jurisdiction of the debtor's location may not, however, have such legislation. For example, mobile equipment is used in New York; the debtor's chief place of business is in a Canadian jurisdiction which will not permit or recognize filing as to property not physically located therein. Paragraph (3) (c) solves this difficulty by permitting perfection through filing in the jurisdiction in the United States in which the debtor has his major executive office in the United States. Where the debtor is not located in the United States or Canada and the collateral is accounts or general intangibles for money due or to become due, the secured party may alternatively perfect by notification to account debtors.

(f) A sentence in paragraph (3) (d) provides a special rule for security interests in airplanes owned by a foreign air carrier. Without that sentence subsection (3) might refer such a case to the law of a foreign nation whose law is difficult or impossible to ascertain. The sentence clears up such doubts by treating as the location of the carrier the office designated for service of process in the United States under the Federal Aviation Act of 1958. To the extent that it is applicable, the Convention on the International Recognition of Rights in Aircraft (Geneva Convention) supersedes state legislation on this subject, as set forth in Section 9–302(3), but some nations are not parties to that Convention.

6. Subsection (4) deals with chattel paper, a semi-intangible security interest which may be perfected either by possession or by filing (Sections 9–304(1), 9–305). As to possessory security, subsection (4) provides that chattel paper shall be subject to the same rule as goods in subsection (1). As to non-possessory security, subsection (4) provides that it shall be subject to the same rule as the intangibles under subsection (3), except that notification to the account debtor is ruled out as an optional means of perfection under paragraph (3) (c). The reason for this is that a different alternative, possession, is available for chattel paper.

7. In addition to the foregoing rules defining which jurisdiction governs perfection of a security interest in the first instance, "this state" (i.e., a destination state after removal) adds its own rules requiring reperfection following removal of collateral other than that described in subsections (2), (3), and (5). "This state" will for four months recognize perfection under the law of the jurisdiction from which the collateral came, unless the remaining period of effectiveness of the perfection in that jurisdiction was less than four months (paragraph (1) (d)). After the four month period or the remaining period of effectiveness, whichever is shorter, the secured party must comply with perfection requirements in this state. This rule differs from the former rule of Section 14 of the Uniform Conditional Sales Act. Under that section a conditional seller was required to file within 10 days after he "received notice" that the goods had been removed into this state. Apparently, under the Uniform Conditional Sales Act, if the seller never "received notice" his interest continued or became perfected in this state without filing. Paragraph (1) (d) proceeds on the theory that not only the secured party whose collateral has been removed but also creditors of and purchasers from the debtor "in this state" should be considered.

The four-month period is long enough for a secured party to discover in most cases that the collateral has been removed and refile in this state; thereafter, if he has not done so, his interest, although originally perfected in the jurisdiction from which the collateral was removed, is subject to defeat here by purchasers of the collateral. Compare the situation arising under Section 9–403(2) when a filing lapses.

It should be noted that a "purchaser" includes a secured party. Section 1–201(32) and (33). The rights of a purchaser with a security interest against an unperfected security interest are governed by Section 9–312.

In case of delay beyond the four-month period, there is no "relation back"; and this is also true where the security interest is perfected for the first time in this state.

If the removal occurs within a short period, like two weeks, before the lapse of the filing in the original state, the secured party has only that period, not the full four months, to reperfect in "this state". But ordinarily he would have filed a continuation statement in the original jurisdiction; and he may do so to avoid lapse and allow himself the full four months if he is searching for the collateral and needs more time.

Paragraph (1) (d) does not apply to the case of goods removed from one filing district to another within this state (see subsection (3) of Section 9–401), but only to property brought into this state from another jurisdiction.

8. Subsection (5) deals with problems relating to the financing of minerals (including oil and gas) as these products come from the ground. In some cases rights in oil and gas in the ground have been split into a large variety of interests. As the oil or gas issues from the ground, it may be encumbered by the group of persons having interests therein. Or the product may be sold at minehead or wellhead and the resulting accounts assigned. The question arises as to the place of filing. The usual rule of this section in subsection (3) would make the place to search for encumbrances on the accounts the locations of the respective assignors; but the assignors might be a number of individuals located throughout the country. To avoid the difficult problems of search thus created, subsection (5) provides that the place for filing with respect to security interests in the minerals as they issue from the ground at minehead or wellhead or in the accounts arising out of the sale of the minerals at minehead or wellhead shall be in the state where the minehead or wellhead is located. Section 9–401 similarly provides that the place to file within the state is in the real property records in the county where the minehead or wellhead is located. These rules conform to pre-Code practice and to practice which seems to have continued in the early Code period before express provision was made for these situations.

The term "at wellhead" is intended to encompass arrangements based on sale of the product as soon as it issues from the ground and is measured, without technical distinctions as to whether title passes at the "Christmas tree" or the far side of a gathering tank or at some other point. The term "at minehead" is a comparable concept.

9. Subsection (6) of Section 9–103 specifies choice of law rules for perfection of security interests in investment property. Paragraph (b) covers security interests in certificated securities. Paragraph (c) covers security interests in uncertificated securities. Paragraph (d) covers security interests in security entitlements and securities accounts. Paragraph (e) covers security interests in commodity contracts and commodity accounts. The approach of each of these paragraphs is essentially the same. They identify the jurisdiction's law that governs questions of perfection and priority on the basis of the same principles that are used in Article 8 to determine other questions concerning that form of investment property. Thus, for certificated securities, the law of the jurisdiction where the certificate is located governs. Cf. Section 8–110(c). For uncertificated securities, the law of the issuer's jurisdiction governs. Cf. Section 8–110(a). For security entitlements and securities accounts, the law of the securities intermediary's jurisdiction governs. Cf. Section 8–110(b). For commodity contracts and commodity accounts, the law of the commodity intermediary's jurisdiction governs. Since commodity contracts and commodity accounts are not governed by Article 8, paragraph (e) contains rules that specify the commodity intermediary's jurisdiction. These are analogous to the rules in Section 8–110(e) specifying a securities intermediary's jurisdiction.

Under this subsection, if litigation about perfection or priority arises in this state, the relevant choice of law rule of paragraphs (b) through (e) may point to the law of this State of to the law of another State. If the litigation were in a tribunal of a jurisdiction that has not enacted this section, it would follow its own choice of law rules. The choice of law rules prescribed here by statute conform to generally accepted principles of choice of law. The simplicity and clarity in the choice of law rules, couples with the explicit recognition that the parties to some securities transactions may agree on a governing law, are intended to assure that there will be one clear choice of law regardless of forum.

Paragraph (f) adapts the general choice of law principles of this subsection to cases where a secured party claims perfection on the basis of filing, or by virtue of the automatic perfection rules in Section 9–115(4)(c) and (d). In such a case, the law of the debtor's jurisdiction determines whether the requirements for that form of perfection have been satisfied. The rules in Section 9–103(3) on the debtor's location and effect of change of location apply to cases governed by paragraph (f)*. The main reason for the paragraph (f) rule is to specify the proper filing office. Under the substantive rules of this Act, a security interest in investment property perfected only by filing is enforceable against the debtor or lien creditors, but not against most other claimants. See Sections 9–115(5) and (6), 8–105(e), 8–303, and 8–502. Because the choice of law rules in this section may, in some circumstances, have the effect of directing a court in a jurisdiction that has adopted this Act to look to the law of another jurisdiction, it is possible that the jurisdiction so specified will be one that has not adopted rules concerning the effect of filing as a method of perfection for investment property. In such cases, or other circumstances where the governing substantive law is not this Act, the effect of filing on the rights of other parties should be interpreted in light of the role of that form of perfection under this Act; that is, the rights of a secured party in investment property as determined under this Act perfected only by filing against another secured party or any other person who purchases or otherwise deals with the investment property should be interpreted to be no greater than the rights of that secured party under this Act. *Amendments approved by the Permanent Editorial Board for Uniform Commercial Code November 4, 1995.

The following examples illustrate these rules:

Example 1. A customer residing in New Jersey maintains a securities account with Able & Co. The agreement between the customer and Able specifies that it is governed by Pennsylvania law. Through the account the customer holds securities of a Massachusetts corporation, which Able holds through a clearing corporation located in New York. The customer obtains a margin loan from Able. Subsection (6)(d) provides that Pennsylvania law—the law of the securities intermediary's jurisdiction—governs perfection and priority of the security interest.

Example 2. A customer residing in New Jersey maintains a securities account with Able & Co. The agreement between the customer and Able specifies that it is governed by Pennsylvania law. Through the account the customer holds securities of a Massachusetts corporation, which Able holds through a clearing corporation located in New York. The customer obtains a loan from a lender located in Illinois. The lender takes a security interest and perfects by obtaining an agreement among the debtor, itself, and Able, which satisfies the requirement of Section 8–106(d)(2) to give the lender control. Subsection (6)(d) provides that Pennsylvania law—the law of the securities intermediary's jurisdiction—governs perfection and priority of the security interest.

Example 3. A customer residing in New Jersey maintains a securities account with Able & Co. The agreement between the customer and Able specifies that it is governed by Pennsylvania law. Through the account, the customer holds securities of a Massachusetts corporation, which Able holds through a clearing corporation located in New York. The customer borrows from SP1, and SP1 files a financing statement in New Jersey. Later, the customer obtains a loan from SP2. SP2 takes a security interest and perfects by obtaining an agreement among the debtor, itself, and Able, which satisfies the requirement of Section 8–106(d)(2) to give the SP2 control. Subsection (6)(f) provides that perfection of SP1's security interest by filing is governed by the location of the debtor, so the filing in New Jersey was appropriate—assuming New Jersey has adopted the revisions of Article 9 permitting perfection of security interests in investment property by filing. Subsection (6)(d), however, provides that Pennsylvania law—the law of the securities intermediary's jurisdiction—governs all other questions of perfection and priority. Thus, Pennsylvania law governs perfection of SP2's security interest, and Pennsylvania law also governs the priority of the security interests of SP1 and SP2.

Cross References:

Sections 1–105, 9–302, and 9–401.

Definitional Cross References:

"Accounts". Section 9–106.
"Attaches". Section 9–203.
"Chattel paper". Section 9–105.
"Collateral". Section 9–105.
"Consumer goods". Section 9–109.
"Debtor". Section 9–105.
"Document". Section 9–105.
"Equipment". Section 9–109.
"General intangibles". Section 9–106.

"Goods". Section 9–105.
"Instrument". Section 9–109.
"Purchase money security interest". Section 9–107.
"Purchaser". Section 1–201(33).
"Security interest". Section 1–201(37).

Cross References

Application of 1979–1980 legislation relating to fixtures, see Commercial Code § 14109.
California housing and infrastructure finance agency, perfection of security interest in collateral on loans to qualified mortgage lenders, see Health and Safety Code § 51153.
Conflicting security interests, priorities, see Commercial Code § 9312.
Contracts, law governing interpretation, see Civil Code § 1646.
Effective date and transition provisions of Stats.1974, c. 997, see Commercial Code § 14101 et seq.
Filing provision, inapplicability to certain security interests, see Commercial Code § 9302.
Financing statement, formal requisites, see Commercial Code § 9402.
Law of domicile, personal property, see Civil Code § 946.
Mortgage or sale of corporate assets, see Corporations Code § 1000 et seq.
Motor vehicles, effect of foreign certificates of title, see Vehicle Code § 4304.
Place of filing, see Commercial Code § 9401.
Policy and scope of division, see Commercial Code § 9102.
Territorial application of act, see Commercial Code § 1105.
Unperfected security interests, subordination, see Commercial Code § 9301.

§ 9104. Transactions excluded from division

This division does not apply:

(a) To a security interest subject to any statute of the United States to the extent that such statute governs the rights of parties to and third parties affected by transactions in particular types of property; or

(c)[1] To a lien given by statute or other rule of law for services or materials except as provided in Section 9310 on priority of such liens; or

(d) To a transfer of a claim for wages, salary or other compensation of an employee; or

(e) To a transfer, including creation of a security interest, by a government or governmental subdivision or agency; or

(f) To a sale of accounts or chattel paper as part of a sale of the business out of which they arose, or an assignment of accounts or chattel paper which is for the purpose of collection only, or a transfer of a right to payment under a contract to an assignee who is also to do the performance under the contract or a transfer of a single account to an assignee in whole or partial satisfaction of a preexisting indebtedness; or

(g) To any loan made by an insurance company pursuant to the provisions of a policy or contract issued by it and upon the sole security of the policy or contract; or

(h) To a right represented by a judgment (other than a judgment taken in a right to payment which was collateral); or

(i) To any right of setoff; or

(j) Except to the extent that provision is made for fixtures in Section 9313, to the creation or transfer of an interest in or lien on real estate, including a lease or rents thereunder and to any interest of a lessor and lessee in any such lease or rents; or

(k) To a transfer in whole or in part of any claim arising out of tort.

(*l*) To any security interest created by the assignment of the benefits of any public construction contract under the Improvement Act of 1911 (Division 7 (commencing with Section 5000), Streets and Highways Code).

(m) To transition property, as defined in Section 840 of the Public Utilities Code, except to the extent that the provisions of this division are referenced in Article 5.5 (commencing with Section 840) of Chapter 4 of Part 1 of Division 1 of the Public Utilities Code. *(Stats.1963, c. 819, § 9104. Amended by Stats.1967, c. 799, p. 2214, § 20; Stats.1969, c. 871, p. 1713, § 1; Stats.1974, c. 997, p. 2118, § 9, eff. Jan. 1976; Stats.1980, c. 1156, p. 3860, § 4; Stats.1996, c. 176 (S.B.1599), § 9; Stats.1996, c. 854 (A.B.1890), § 4, eff. Sept. 24, 1996.)*

[1] Enrolled bill contains no subd. (b).

California Code Comment

By John A. Bohn and Charles J. Williams

Prior California Law

1. This section is new statutory law.

2. With reference to security interests subject to federal statute, see Official Comment 1. Other security interests which are to some extent covered by federal statutes include those created in aircraft (49 USCA § 1403), railroads (49 USCA § 20), patents (35 USCA § 261), and copyrights (17 USCA §§ 18, 20). It is not clear whether they would require an exclusion of security interests from coverage by the Commercial Code. The language of Official Comment 1 by analogy would not appear to require an exclusion. 8 UCLA L.Rev. 806, 831.

3. Paragraph (c) is consistent with the approach of the Commercial Code to cover consensual security interests, not statutory or common law liens which arise by reason of the status of the parties. See Official Comment 4 to section 9102.

4. With reference to paragraphs (c) to (k), see Official Comments 3 to 8.

5. The effect of paragraph (g) is to narrow the exclusion to cover only loans made by an insurance company against its own policy. A loan made by one insurance company against a policy issued by another insurance company is treated the same as any other transaction involving a general intangible. In commenting upon the proposal to limit paragraph (g) the Marsh and Warren Report describes the effect upon prior California law:

"... At the present time such an assignment would be subject to the requirements of Section 955.1 of the Civil Code, requiring notice to the obligor (the insurance company) in order to perfect the assignment against any subsequent bona fide assignee, but would be perfected against creditors of assignor without any notice or other action. McIntyre v. Hauser, 131 C. 11, 63 P. 69 (1900); Smith v. Harris, 127 C.A.2d 311, 273 P.2d 835 (1954)." Sixth Progress Report to the Legislature by Senate Fact Finding Committee on Judiciary (1959–1961) Part 1, The Uniform Commercial Code, p. 552.

6. Paragraph (k) as it applies to a tort claim continues the rule under prior law which held that a tort claim before final judgment is not assignable. Pacific Gas & Electric Co. v. Nakano, 12 Cal.2d 711, 87 P.2d 700, 121 A.L.R. 417 (1939).

Changes from U.C.C. (1962 Official Text)

7. Section 9–104 of the Official Text as changed in the California version reads as follows:

[Section 9–104. Transactions Excluded From Article.]

9104. This [Article] division does not apply

(a) To a security interest subject to any statute of the United States such as the Ship Mortgage Act, 1920, to the extent that such statute governs the rights of parties to and third parties affected by transactions in particular types of property; or

[(b) to a landlord's lien; or]

(c) To a lien given by statute or other rule of law for services or materials except as provided in Section 9310 on priority of such liens; or

(d) To a transfer of a claim for wages, salary or other compensation of an employee; or

(e) To an equipment trust covering railway rolling stock; or

(f) To a sale of accounts, contract rights or chattel paper as part of a sale of the business out of which they arose, or an assignment of accounts, contract rights or chattel paper which is for the purpose of collection only, or a transfer of a contract right to an assignee who is also to do the performance under the contract; or

(g) [To a transfer of an interest or claim in or under any policy of insurance; or] To any loan made by an insurance company pursuant to the provisions of a policy or contract issued by it and upon the sole security of such policy or contract; or

(h) To a right represented by a judgment; or

(i) To any right of setoff; or to a security interest of a bank, savings and loan association, credit union or like organization in any deposit, savings, passbook or like account maintained with such organization; or

(j) [except to the extent that provision is made for fixtures in Section 9–313], To the creation or transfer of an interest in or lien on real estate, including a lease or rents thereunder; or

(k) To a transfer in whole or in part of any [of the following:] any claim arising out of tort; [any deposit, savings, passbook or like account maintained with a bank, savings and loan association, credit union or like organization].

8. The change made in subdivision (g) is in accord with suggestions by the California Bankers Association Committee:

"This exclusion should be narrowed to cover only advances made by insurance companies against their own policies. Loans made by others against insurance policies should be treated the same as other transactions involving general intangibles. (See Appendix 2.)" Sixth Progress Report to the Legislature by Senate Fact Finding Committee on Judiciary (1959–1961) Part 1, The Uniform Commercial Code, p. 418.

9. The change in paragraph (j) is made to conform to the deletion of fixtures from coverage of Division 9. See California Code Comment to Commercial Code § 9102.

10. In subdivision (k) this language was deleted in order to avoid narrowing the definition of general intangibles in section 9106 and in order to make Division 9 cover substantially all of the field of secured transactions and personal property. Sixth Progress Report to the Legislature by Senate Fact Finding Committee on Judiciary (1959–1961) Part 1, The Uniform Commercial Code, pp. 418, 553 and 641.

California Code Comment—1967 Amendment
By Charles J. Williams

The 1967 amendment to this section adds a new subdivision (*l*) for the purpose of making it clear that public securities are not included in the transactions referred to in Division 9. (Report of the Advisory Committee Senate Journal, April 20, 1967, pp. 1238–9.)

This subdivision does not appear in the Official Text. The exemption of public securities is not a substantive change from the Official Text.

Uniform Commercial Code Comment
Prior Uniform Statutory Provisions:
None.
Purposes:
To exclude certain security transactions from this Article.

1. Where a federal statute regulates the incidents of security interests in particular types of property, those security interests are of course governed by the federal statute and excluded from this Article. The Ship Mortgage Act, 1920, is an example of such a federal act. The present provisions of the Federal Aviation Act of 1958 (49 U.S.C. § 1403 et seq.) call for registration of title to and liens upon aircraft with the Civil Aeronautics Administrator and such registration is recognized as equivalent to filing under this Article (Section 9–302(3)); but to the extent that the Federal Aviation Act does not regulate the rights of parties to and third parties affected by such transactions, security interests in aircraft remain subject to this Article.

Although the Federal Copyright Act contains provisions permitting the mortgage of a copyright and for the recording of an assignment of a copyright (17 U.S.C. §§ 28, 30) such a statute would not seem to contain sufficient provisions regulating the rights of the parties and third parties to exclude security interests in copyrights from the provisions of this Article. Compare Republic Pictures Corp. v. Security-First National Bank of Los Angeles, 197 F.2d 767 (9th Cir. 1952). Compare also with respect to patents, 35 U.S.C. § 47. The filing provisions under these Acts, like the filing provisions of the Federal Aviation Act, are recognized as the equivalent to filing under this Article. Section 9–302(3) and (4).

Even such a statute as the Ship Mortgage Act is far from a comprehensive regulation of all aspects of ship mortgage financing. That Act contains provisions on formal requisites, on recordation and on foreclosure but not much more. If problems arise under a ship mortgage which are not covered by the Act, the federal admiralty court must decide whether to improvise an answer under "federal law" or to follow the law of some state with which the mortgage transaction has appropriate contacts. The exclusionary language in paragraph (a) is that this Article does not apply to such security interest "to the extent" that the federal statute governs the rights of the parties. Thus if the federal statute contained no relevant provision, this Article could be looked to for an answer.

2. Except for fixtures (Section 9–313) [Changes in California from U.C.C. (1962 official Text) see California Code Comment, Note 7], the Article applies only to security interests in personal property. The exclusion of landlord's liens by paragraph (b) and of leases and other interests in or liens on real estate by paragraph (j) [Paragraphs (b) and (j) not applicable in California, see California Code Comment, Note 7] merely reiterates the limitations on coverage already made explicit in Section 9–102(3). See Comment 4 to that section.

3. In all jurisdictions liens are given suppliers of many types of services and materials either by statute or by common law. It was thought to be both inappropriate and unnecessary for this Article to attempt a general codification of that lien structure which is in considerable part determined by local conditions and which is far removed from ordinary commercial financing. Moreover, federal law may displace state law in situations such as admiralty liens. Paragraph (c) therefore excludes statutory liens from the Article. Section 9–310 states a rule for determining priorities between such liens and the consensual security interests covered by this Article.

4. In many states assignments of wage claims and the like are regulated by statute. Such assignments present important social problems whose solution should be a matter of local regulation. Paragraph (d) therefore excludes them from this Article.

5. Certain governmental borrowings include collateral in the form of assignments of water, electricity or sewer charges, rents on dormitories or industrial buildings, tools, etc. Since these assignments are usually governed by special provisions of law, these governmental transfers are excluded from this Article.

6. In general sales as well as security transfers of accounts and chattel paper are within the Article (see Section 9–102). Paragraph (f) excludes from the Article certain transfers of such intangibles which, by their nature, have nothing to do with commercial financing transactions.

Similarly, this paragraph excludes from the Article such transactions as that involved in Lyon v. Ty-Wood Corporation, 212 Pa.Super. 69, 239 A.2d 819 (1968) and Spurlin v. Sloan, 368 S.W.2d 314 (Ky.1963).

7. Rights under life insurance and other policies, and deposit accounts, are often put up as collateral. Such transactions are often quite special, do not fit easily under a general commercial statute and are adequately covered by existing law. Paragraphs (g) and (*l*) make appropriate exclusions, but provision is made for coverage of deposit accounts and certain insurance money as proceeds. [California adopted different pars. (g) and (*l*), see California Code Comment, note 8, under this section, and note 3 under section 9106].

8. The remaining exclusions go to other types of claims which do not customarily serve as commercial collateral: judgments under paragraph (h), set-offs under paragraph (i) and tort claims under paragraph (k).

Cross References:
Point 1: Section 9–302(3).
Point 2: Sections 9–102(3) and 9–313.
Point 3: Sections 9–102(2) and 9–310.
Point 6: Section 9–102.

Definitional Cross References:

"Account". Section 9-106.
"Chattel paper". Section 9-105.
"Contract". Section 1-201.
"Deposit account". Section 9-105.
"Party." Section 1-201.
"Rights". Section 1-201.
"Security interest". Section 1-201.

Cross References

Filing provisions, inapplicability to certain circumstances, see Commercial Code § 9302.

Liens arising by operation of law, priority, see Commercial Code § 9310.

Perfection of sale or transfer of accounts, sale of accounts or chattel paper as part of sale of business out of which they arose, see Civil Code § 955.

Policy and scope of division, see Commercial Code § 9102.

Vessels numbered under Vehicle Code, exclusive method of perfecting security interest, see Vehicle Code § 9922.

§ 9105. Definitions; index of definitions

(1) In this division unless the context otherwise requires:

(a) "Account debtor" means the person who is obligated on an account, chattel paper or general intangible.

(b) "Chattel paper" means a writing or writings which evidence both a monetary obligation and a security interest in or a lease of specific goods, but a charter or other contract involving the use or hire of a vessel is not chattel paper. When a transaction is evidenced both by a security agreement or a lease and by an instrument or a series of instruments, the group of writings taken together constitutes chattel paper.

(c) "Collateral" means the property subject to a security interest, and includes accounts and chattel paper which have been sold.

(d) "Debtor" means the person who owes payment or other performance of the obligation secured, whether or not he or she owns or has rights in the collateral, and includes the seller of accounts or chattel paper. Where the debtor and the owner of the collateral are not the same person, "debtor" means the owner of the collateral in any provision of the division dealing with the collateral, the obligor in any provision dealing with the obligation, and may include both where the context so requires.

(e) "Deposit account" means a demand, time, savings, passbook or like account maintained with a bank, savings and loan association, credit union or like organization, other than an account evidenced by a negotiable certificate of deposit.

(f) "Document" means document of title as defined in the general definitions of Division 1 (Section 1201), and a receipt of the kind described in subdivision (2) of Section 7201.

(g) "Encumbrance" includes real estate mortgages and other liens on real estate and all other rights in real estate that are not ownership interests.

(h) "Goods" includes all things which are movable at the time the security interest attaches or which are fixtures (Section 9313), but does not include money, documents, instruments, investment property, accounts, chattel paper, general intangibles or minerals or the like (including oil and gas) before extraction. "Goods" also includes standing timber which is to be cut and removed under a conveyance or contract for sale, the unborn young of animals, and growing crops.

(i) "Instrument" means a negotiable instrument (defined in Section 3104) * * * or any other writing which evidences a right to the payment of money and is not itself a security agreement or lease and is of a type which is in ordinary course of business transferred by delivery with any necessary endorsement or assignment. The term does not include investment property.

(j) "Mortgage" means a consensual interest created by a real estate mortgage, a trust deed on real estate, or the like.

(k) An advance is made "pursuant to commitment" if the secured party has bound himself or herself to make it, whether or not a subsequent event of default or other event not within his or her control has relieved or may relieve him or her from his or her obligation.

(*l*) "Security agreement" means an agreement which creates or provides for a security interest.

(m) "Secured party" means a lender, seller or other person in whose favor there is a security interest, including a person to whom accounts or chattel paper have been sold. * * * If a security interest is in favor of a trustee, indenture trustee, agent, collateral agent, or other representative, the representative is the secured party.

(n) "Transmitting utility" means any person primarily engaged in the railroad, street railway or trolley bus business, the electric or electronics communications transmission business, the transmission of goods by pipeline, or the transmission or the production and transmission of electricity, steam, gas or water, or the provision of sewer service.

(o) "New value" includes new advances or loans made, or new obligations incurred, or the release of a valid and existing security interest, or the release of a claim to proceeds; but "new value" shall not be construed to include extension or renewals of existing obligations of the debtor, nor obligations substituted for such existing obligations.

(2) Other definitions applying to this division and the sections in which they appear are:

"Account." Section 9106.

"Attach." Section 9203.

"Commodity contract." Section 9115.

"Commodity customer." Section 9115.

"Commodity intermediary." Section 9115.

"Consumer goods." Section 9109(1).

"Construction mortgage." Section 9313(1).

"Control." Section 9115.

"Equipment." Section 9109(2).

"Farm products." Section 9109(3).

"Fixture." Section 9313(1).

"Fixture filing." Section 9313(1).

"General intangibles." Section 9106.

"Inventory." Section 9109(4).

"Investment property." Section 9115.

"Lien creditor." Section 9301(3).

"Proceeds." Section 9306(1).

"Purchase money security interest." Section 9107.

"United States." Section 9103.

(3) The following definitions in other divisions apply to this division:

"Broker." Section 8102.

"Certificated security." Section 8102.

"Check." Section 3104.

"Clearing corporation." Section 8102.

"Contract for sale." Section 2106.

"Control." Section 8106.

"Delivery." Section 8301.

"Entitlement holder." Section 8102.

"Financial asset." Section 8102.

"Holder in due course." Section 3302.

"Letter of credit." Section 5102.

"Note." Section 3104.

"Proceeds of a letter of credit." Subdivision (a) of Section 5114.

"Sale." Section 2106.

"Securities intermediary." Section 8102.

"Security." Section 8102.

"Security certificate." Section 8102.

"Security entitlement." Section 8102.

"Uncertificated security." Section 8102.

(4) In addition, Division 1 (commencing with Section 1101) contains general definitions and principles of construction and interpretation applicable throughout this division. *(Stats.1963, c. 819, § 9105. Amended by Stats.1974, c. 997, p. 2119, § 10, eff. Jan. 1, 1976; Stats.1980, c. 1156, p. 3861, § 5; Stats.1984, c. 927, § 8; Stats.1996, c. 176 (S.B.1599), § 10; Stats.1996, c. 497 (S.B.1591), § 11, operative Jan. 1, 1997.)*

California Code Comment

By John A. Bohn and Charles J. Williams

Prior California Law

1. The Commercial Code does not use the terms associated with the former security devices. It uses the concept of "security interest" rather than "pledge", "chattel mortgage", "conditional sale", "trust receipt", "inventory lien" or "assignment of account receivable". The legal terminology formerly associated with these security devices is abandoned to avoid any implication that prior law referrable to a specific form was to be used in construing or interpreting the Commercial Code. Official Comment 1.

2. The term "security agreement" includes all of the security devices formerly used in California. Such terms as conditional vendor and vendee, chattel mortgagor and mortgagee, entruster and trustee, lender and borrower, are no longer used.

3. Because of the approach of the Commercial Code, the definitions of the same terms in this section which appeared in prior statutory law have no applicability and are of no value. However, for purposes of comparison the prior definitional counterparts where they existed are set forth: "Debtor" was defined in former Civil Code § 3017(5) as a person "by whom an account is owing to the assignor"; also see Civil Code § 3429 defining a debtor as one who "is or may become liable to pay". "Goods" was variously defined in Civil Code §§ 1796 (USA), 2132(b) and 3013(4) (NIL). "Document" was previously defined in Civil Code § 1796 (USA) and Civil Code § 3013(2) (UTRA). "Instrument" was formerly defined in Civil Code § 3013(5) (NIL). "New value" is defined substantially in the same terms in former Civil Code § 3013(7) (UTRA).

Changes from U.C.C. (1962 Official Text)

4. Section 9–105 of the Official Text is changed in subdivisions (1)(f) and (1)(j) of the California version:

(f) "Goods" includes all things which are movable at the time the security interest attaches or which are fixtures [(Section 9–313)] (other than goods incorporated into a structure in the manner of lumber, bricks, tile, cement, glass, metalwork and the like unless the structure remains personal property under applicable law), but does not include money, documents, instruments, accounts, chattel paper, general intangibles, contract rights and other things in action. "Goods" also include the unborn young of animals, [and] growing crops, and standing timber which is to be cut and removed under a conveyance or contract for sale;

(j) "New value" includes new advances or loans made, or new obligations incurred, or the release of a valid and existing security interest, or the release of a claim to proceeds; but "new value" shall not be construed to include extension or renewals of existing obligations of the debtor, nor obligations substituted for such existing obligations.

5. In subdivision (1)(f), the addition of the language in parenthesis is added for clarification. The "standing timber" provision is added to continue the rule of Civil Code §§ 658 and 660 to permit continued financing of contracts covering standing timber in accordance with prior California practice. Sixth Progress Report to the Legislature by Senate Fact Finding Committee on Judiciary (1959–1961) Part 1, The Uniform Commercial Code, pp. 419, 641–642.

6. Subdivision (1)(j) defining new value is based upon the definition in former Civil Code § 3013. In former Civil Code § 3013 (UTRA) this definition was added because it is an important term used throughout Division 9 but is not defined. The comments under section 9108 of the Official Text could invite the definition by the courts in any way they wish. Sixth Progress Report to the Legislature by Senate Fact Finding Committee on Judiciary (1959–1961) Part 1, The Uniform Commercial Code, p. 419.

Uniform Commercial Code Comment

Official Reasons for 1977 Change

Because Section 8–102 now defines "security" as either a certificated or an uncertificated security, the word "certificated" is inserted to limit the definition only to those securities which are represented by instruments.

Prior Uniform Statutory Provisions:

Various.

Purposes:

1. **General.** It is necessary to have a set of terms to describe the parties to a secured transaction, the agreement itself, and the property involved therein; but the selection of the set of terms applicable to any one of the existing forms (e.g., mortgagor and mortgagee) might carry to some extent the implication that the existing law referable to that form was to be used for the construction and interpretation of this Article. Since it is desired to avoid any such implication, a set of terms has been chosen which have no common law or statutory roots tying them to a particular form.

In place of such terms as "chattel mortgage," "conditional sale," "assignment of accounts receivable," "trust receipt," etc., this Article substitutes the general term "security agreement" defined in paragraph (1) (*l*). In place of "mortgagor," "mortgagee," "conditional vendee," "conditional vendor," etc., this Article substitutes "debtor", defined in paragraph (1) (d), and "secured party", defined in paragraph (1) (m). The property subject to the security agreement is "collateral", defined in paragraph (1) (c). The interest in the collateral which is conveyed by the debtor to the secured party is a "security interest", defined in Section 1–201(37).

2. **Parties.** The parties to the security agreement are the "debtor" and the "secured party."

"Debtor": In all but a few cases the person who owes the debt and the person whose property secures the debt will be the same. Occasionally, one person furnishes security for another's debt, and sometimes property is transferred subject to a secured debt of the transferor which the transferee does not assume; in such cases, under the second sentence of the definition, the term "debtor" may, depending upon the context, include either or both such persons. Section 9–112 sets out special rules which are applicable where collateral is owned by a person who does not owe a debt.

"Secured party": The term includes any person in whose favor there is a security interest (defined in Section 1–201). The term is used equally to refer to a person who as a seller retains a lien on or title to goods sold, to a person whose interest arises initially from a loan transaction, and to an assignee of either. Note that a seller is a "secured party" in relation to his customer; the seller becomes a "debtor" if he assigns the chattel paper as collateral. This is also true of a lender who assigns the debt as collateral. With the exceptions stated in Section 9–104(f) the Article applies to any sale of accounts or chattel paper: the term "secured party" includes an assignee of such intangibles whether by sale or for security, to distinguish him from the payee of the account, for example, who becomes a "debtor" by pledging the account as security for a loan.

On the applicability of the terms "debtor" and "secured party" to consignments and leases see Section 9–408 and Comment thereto.

"Account debtor": Where the collateral is an account, chattel paper or general intangible the original obligor is called the "account debtor", defined in paragraph (1) (a).

3. **Property subject to the security agreement.** "Collateral", defined in paragraph (1) (c), is a general term for the tangible and intangible property subject to a security interest. For some purposes the Code makes distinctions between different types of collateral and therefore further classification of collateral is necessary. Collateral which consists of tangible property is "goods", defined in paragraph (1) (h); and "goods" are again subdivided in Section 9–109. For purposes of this Article all intangible collateral fits one of five categories, two of which, "accounts", and "general intangibles" are defined in the following Section 9–106; the other three, "documents", "instruments" and "chattel paper", are defined in paragraphs (1) (f), (1) (i) and (1) (b) of this section.

"Goods": the definition in paragraph (1) (h) is similar to that contained in Section 2–105 except that the Sales Article definition refers to "time of identification to the contract for sale", while this definition refers to "the time the security interest attaches."

For the treatment of fixtures, Section 9–313 should be consulted. It will be noted that the treatment of fixtures under Section 9–313 does not at all points conform to their treatment under Section 2–107 (goods to be severed from realty). Section 2–107 relates to sale of such goods; Section 9–313 to security interests in them. The discrepancies between the two sections arise from the differences in the types of interest covered. A comparable discrepancy exists as to minerals. In the case of timber, both sections treat it as goods if it is to be severed under a contract of sale, but not otherwise.

If in any state minerals before severance are deemed to be personal property, they fall outside the Article's definition of "goods" and would therefore fall in the catch-all definition, "general intangibles", in Section 9–106. The special provisions of Section 9–103(5) would not apply and those of Section 9–103(3) would apply. The resulting problems should be considered locally.

For the purpose of this Article, goods are classified as "consumer goods", "equipment", "farm products", and "inventory"; those terms are defined in Section 9–109. When the general term "goods" is used in this Article, it includes, as may be appropriate in the context, the subclasses of goods defined in Section 9–109.

"Instrument": the term as defined in paragraph (1)(i) includes not only negotiable instruments but also any other intangibles evidenced by writings which are in ordinary course of business transferred by delivery. As in the case of chattel paper "delivery" is only the minimum stated and may be accompanied by other steps. Amendment approved by the Permanent Editorial Board for Uniform Commercial Code November 4, 1995.

If a writing is itself a security agreement or lease with respect to specific goods it is not an instrument although it otherwise meets the term of the definition. See Comment below on "chattel paper".

The fact that an instrument is secured by collateral, whether the collateral be other instruments, documents, goods, accounts or general intangibles, does not change the character of the principal obligation as an instrument or convert the combination of instrument and collateral into a separate Code classification of personal property. The single qualification to this principle is that an instrument which is secured by chattel paper is itself part of the chattel paper, while also retaining its identity as an instrument.

"Document": See the Comments under Sections 1–201(15) and 7–201.

"Chattel paper": To secure his own financing a secured party may wish to borrow against or sell the security agreement itself along with his interest in the collateral which he has received from his debtor. Since the refinancing of paper secured by specific goods presents some problems of its own, the term "chattel paper" is used to describe this kind of collateral. The Comments under Section 9–308 further describe this concept.

Charters of vessels are excluded from the definition of chattel paper because they fit under the definition of accounts. See Comment to Section 9–106. The term "charter" as used herein and in Section 9–106 includes bareboat charters, time charters, successive voyage charters, contracts of affreightment, contracts of carriage, and all other arrangements for use of vessels.

4. The following transactions illustrate the use of the term "chattel paper" and some of the other terms defined in this section.

A dealer sells a tractor to a farmer on conditional sales contract or purchase money security interest. The conditional sales contract is a "security agreement", the farmer is the "debtor", the dealer is the "secured party" and the tractor is the type of "collateral" defined in Section 9–109 as "equipment". But now the dealer transfers the contract to his bank, either by outright sale or to secure a loan. Since the conditional sales contract is a security agreement relating to specific equipment, the conditional sales contract is now the type of collateral called "chattel paper". In this transaction between the dealer and his bank, the bank is the "secured party", the dealer is the "debtor", and the farmer is the "account debtor".

Under the definition of "security interest" in Section 1–201(37) a lease does not create a security interest unless intended as security. Whether or not the lease itself is a security agreement, it is chattel paper when transferred if it relates to specific goods. Thus, if the dealer enters into a straight lease of the tractor to the farmer (not intended as security), and then arranges to borrow money on the security of the lease, the lease is chattel paper.

Security agreements of the type formerly known as chattel mortgages and conditional sales contracts are frequently executed in connection with a negotiable note or a series of such notes. Under the definitions in paragraphs (1) (b) and (1) (i) the rules applicable to chattel paper, rather than those relating to instruments, are applicable to the group of writings (contract plus note) taken together.

5. **Miscellaneous definitions.** "Deposit account" is a type of collateral excluded from this Article under Section 9–104(*l*), except when it constitutes proceeds of other collateral under Section 9–306.

The terms "encumbrance" and "mortgage" are defined for use in the section on fixtures, Section 9–113.

The term "transmitting utility" is defined to designate a special class of debtors for whom separate filing rules are provided in Part 4, thus obviating all local filing and particularly the several local filings that would be necessary under the usual rules of Section 9–401 for the fixture collateral of a far-flung public utility debtor. See Comments under Sections 9–401 and 9–403.

The term "pursuant to commitment" is defined for use in the rules relating to priority of future advances in Sections 9–301(4), 9–307(3), and 9–312(7).

6. Comments to the definitions indexed in subsections (2) and (3) follow the sections in which the definitions are contained.

Cross References:

Point 2: Sections 9–104(f) and 9–112.
Point 3: Sections 2–105, 2–107, 9–106, 9–109, 9–308 and 9–313.

Definitional Cross References:

"Account". Section 9–106.
"Agreement". Section 1–201.
"Document of title". Sections 1–201, 7–201.
"General intangibles". Section 9–106.
"Holder". Section 1–201.
"Money". Section 1–201.
"Negotiable instrument". Section 3–104.
"Person". Section 1–201.
"Representative". Section 1–201.
"Rights". Section 1–201.
"Security". Section 8–102.
"Security interest". Section 1–201.
"Writing". Section 1–201.

Cross References

Chattel paper and instruments, priorities, see Commercial Code § 9308.
Collateral, ownership by other than debtor, see Commercial Code § 9112.
Debtor, defined, see Civil Code § 3429.
Definitions, see Commercial Code §§ 2105, 9106, 9109.
Driving cattle from their range, damages, secured parties excepted, see Food and Agricultural Code § 21855.
Excluded transactions, see Commercial Code § 9104.
Sale of property covered by security agreement and willful failure to pay secured party and appropriations to own use as embezzlement, see Penal Code § 504b.
Transfer of general intangibles, see Civil Code § 955.1.
Unemployment compensation delinquent contributions, penalties, or interest, levy on bank or savings and loan, application to credits and personal property in deposit account, see Unemployment Insurance Code § 1755.

§ 9106. Account; general intangibles

"Account" means any right to payment for goods sold or leased or for services rendered which is not evidenced by an instrument or chattel paper, whether or not it has been earned by performance. "General intangibles" means any personal property (including things in action) other than goods, accounts, chattel paper, documents, instruments, <u>investment property, rights to proceeds of written letters of credit</u>, and money. All rights to payment earned or unearned under a charter or other contract involving the use or hire of a vessel and all rights incident to the charter or contract are accounts. *(Stats.1963, c. 819, § 9106. Amended by Stats.1974, c. 997, p. 2121, § 11, eff. Jan. 1, 1976; Stats.1996, c. 176 (S.B.1599), § 11; Stats.1996, c. 497 (S.B.1591), § 12, operative Jan. 1, 1997.)*

California Code Comment

By John A. Bohn and Charles J. Williams

Prior California Law

1. The definition of "account" is broader than the term as defined in former Civil Code § 3017(1), the former Assignment of Accounts Receivable statute. Former Civil Code § 3017(1) specifically excluded debts arising under a lease of personal property.

Under prior California practice there could be an assignment of an account due to arise out of a contract not yet in existence. H.S. Mann Corporation v. Moody, 144 Cal.App.2d 310, 301 P.2d 28 (1956). The language of this section does not necessarily preclude this but the Official Comment states that a contract right is a right to be earned by future performance under an *existing* contract. Official Comment, 2nd paragraph.

2. The definition of general intangible brings within the Commercial Code the miscellaneous types of rights which are personal property and which could become used as a commercial security. Official Comment, 1st paragraph.

Changes from U.C.C. (1962 Official Text)

3. The last sentence in this section does not appear in section 9–106 of the Official Text. This was added in California to conform with the deletion of this same language from paragraph (g) of Commercial Code § 9104. California specifically includes an interest or claim under an insurance policy within the coverage of Division 9. The Official Text specifically excludes it.

Uniform Commercial Code Comment

Prior Uniform Statutory Provision:
None.

Purposes:
The terms defined in this section round out the classification of intangibles: see the definitions of "document", "chattel paper" and "instrument" in Section 9–105. Those three terms cover the various categories of commercial paper which are either negotiable or to a greater or less extent dealt with as if negotiable. The term "account" covers most choses in action which may be the subject of commercial financing transactions but which are not evidenced by an indispensable writing. The term "general intangibles" brings under this Article miscellaneous types of contractual rights and other personal property which are used or may become customarily used as commercial security. Examples are goodwill, literary rights and rights to performance. Other examples are copyrights, trademarks and patents, except to the extent that they may be excluded by Section 9–104(a). This Article solves the problems of filing of security interests in these types of intangibles (Sections 9–103(3) and 9–401). Note that this catch-all definition does not apply to money or to types of intangibles which are specifically excluded from the coverage of the Article (Section 9–104) and note also that under Section 9–302 filing under a federal statute may satisfy the filing requirements of this Article.

A right to the payment of money is frequently buttressed by ancillary covenants to insure the preservation of collateral, such as covenants in a purchase agreement, note or mortgage requiring insurance on the collateral or forbidding removal of the collateral; or covenants to preserve credit-worthiness of the promisor, such as covenants restricting dividends, etc. While these miscellaneous ancillary rights might conceivably be thought to fall within the definition of "general intangibles", it is not the intention of the Code to treat them separately and require the perfection of assignment thereof by filing in the manner required for perfection of an assignment of general intangibles. Whatever perfection is required for the perfection of an assignment of the right to the payment of money will also carry these ancillary rights.

Similarly, when the right to the payment of money is not yet earned by performance, there are frequently ancillary rights designed to assure that an assignee may complete the performance and crystallize the right to payment of money. Such rights are frequently present in a "maintenance" lease where the lessor has continuing duties to perform, or in a ship charter. These ancillary rights, if considered in the abstract, might be thought to be "general intangibles", since they do not themselves involve the payment of money; but it is not the intent of the Code to split up the rights to the payment of money and its ancillary supports, and thereby multiply the problem of perfection of assignments. Therefore, all rights of the lessor in a lease are to be perfected as "chattel paper", and all rights of the owner in a ship charter are to be perfected as "accounts".

"Account" is defined as a right to payment for goods sold or leased or services rendered; the ordinary commercial account receivable. In some special cases a right to receive money not yet earned by performance crystallizes not into an account but into a general intangible, for it is a right to payment of money that is not "for goods sold or leased or for services rendered." Examples of such rights are the right to receive payment of a loan not evidenced by an instrument or chattel paper; a right to receive partial refund of purchase prices paid by reason of retroactive volume discounts; rights to receive payment under licenses of patents and copyrights, exhibition contracts, etc.

This Article rejects any lingering common law notion that only rights already earned can be assigned. In the triangular arrangement following assignment, there is reason to allow the original parties—assignor and account debtor—more flexibility in modifying the underlying contract before performance than after performance (see Section 9–318). It will, however, be found that in most situations the same rules apply to accounts both before and after performance.

Cross References:
Sections 9–103(2), 9–104, 9–302(3), 9–318 and 9–401.

Definitional Cross References:
"Chattel paper". Section 9–105.
"Contract". Section 1–201.
"Document". Section 9–105.
"Goods". Section 9–105.
"Instrument". Section 9–105.

Cross References

Assignment of general intangibles, see Civil Code § 955.1.
Contracts, generally, see Civil Code § 1549 et seq.
Excluded transactions, see Commercial Code § 9104.
Filing under federal regulations, see Commercial Code § 9302.
Modification of contract after notification of assignment, see Commercial Code § 9318.
Perfection of security interest, law governing, see Commercial Code § 9103.
Place of filing, see Commercial Code § 9401.

§ 9107. Definitions: "Purchase Money Security Interest"

A security interest is a "purchase money security interest" to the extent that it is

(a) Taken or retained by the seller of the collateral to secure all or part of its price; or

(b) Taken by a person who by making advances or incurring an obligation gives value to enable the debtor to acquire rights in or the use of collateral if such value is in fact so used. *(Stats.1963, c. 819, § 9107.)*

California Code Comment

By John A. Bohn and Charles J. Williams

Prior California Law

1. The term "purchase money security interest" conforms with the unitary concept and approach in the Code. Its counterpart under prior California law was the "purchase money mortgage" or security interest purchase money "deed of trust". In scope, the "purchase money security interest" overlaps the former devices of the conditional sale, chattel mortgage, trust receipt and inventory lien.

2. This is section 9–107 of the Official Text without change.

Uniform Commercial Code Comment

Prior Uniform Statutory Provision:
None.

Purposes:

1. Under existing rules of law and under this Article purchase money obligations often have priority over other obligations. Thus a purchase money obligation has priority over an interest acquired under an after-acquired property clause (Section 9–312(3) and (4)); where filing is required a grace period of ten days is allowed against creditors and transferees in bulk (Section 9–301(2)); and in some instances filing may not be necessary (Section 9–302(1) (d)).

Under this section a seller has a purchase money security interest if he retains a security interest in the goods; a financing agency has a purchase money security interest when it advances money to the seller, taking back an assignment of chattel paper, and also when it makes advances to the buyer (e.g., on chattel mortgage) to enable him to buy, and he uses the money for that purpose.

2. When a purchase money interest is claimed by a secured party who is not a seller, he must of course have given present consideration. This section therefore provides that the purchase money party must be one who gives value "by making advances or incurring an obligation": the quoted language excludes from the purchase money category any security interest taken as security for or in satisfaction of a pre-existing claim or antecedent debt.

Cross References:
Point 1: Sections 9–301, 9–302 and 9–312.
Point 2: Section 9–108.

Definitional Cross References:
"Collateral". Section 9–105.
"Debtor". Section 9–105.
"Person". Section 1–201.
"Rights". Section 1–201.
"Security interest". Section 1–201.
"Value". Section 1–201.

Cross References

Antecedent debt, effect of after-acquired collateral, see Commercial Code § 9108.
Collateral, defined, see Commercial Code § 9105.
Conflicting security interests, priorities, see Commercial Code § 9312.
Perfection of security interest, necessity of filing, see Commercial Code § 9302.
Personal property not in custody of levying officer transferred or encumbered, exceptions, see Code of Civil Procedure § 697.740.
Priorities of party's filing with respect to purchase money security interest, see Commercial Code § 9301.
Security interest, defined, see Commercial Code § 1201.

§ 9108. When After-Acquired Collateral Not Security for Antecedent Debt

Where a secured party makes an advance, incurs an obligation, releases a perfected security interest, or otherwise gives new value which is to be secured in whole or in part by afteracquired property his security interest in the afteracquired collateral shall be deemed to be taken for new value and not as security for an antecedent debt if the debtor acquires his rights in such collateral either in the ordinary course of his business or under a contract of purchase made pursuant to the security agreement within a reasonable time after new value is given. *(Stats.1963, c. 819, § 9108.)*

California Code Comment

By John A. Bohn and Charles J. Williams

Prior California Law

1. The operation and effect of this section are described in the Marsh and Warren Report:

"This Section is intended to operate only in bankruptcy and to provide that property acquired by a debtor and becoming security for an antecedent debt pursuant to an after-acquired property clause in the original loan agreement shall be 'deemed' *not* to be for an antecedent debt and, therefore, not a recoverable preference in bankruptcy, even though it is acquired within four months of bankruptcy and while the debtor is insolvent to the knowledge of the secured party. In our opinion, this is an attempt to amend Section 60 of the Bankruptcy Act, which is clearly beyond the power of California or any other state. The Official Comments state that what is an 'antecedent debt' under Section 60 of the Bankruptcy Act is a matter of State law. No authority is cited for this proposition and, in our opinion, it is erroneous. So far from leaving the definition of this term to State law, Congress has provided 8 subdivisions to Section 60a, containing pages of practically incomprehensible verbiage, explaining what is meant by antecedent debt (or, what amounts to the same thing, when a transfer shall be considered to have occurred) and when some transfers shall be 'deemed' not to be for an antecedent debt by virtue of a limited relation back. The situation covered by Section 19108 is not among the latter. It is obvious as a matter of fact, rather than fiction, that in this situation the debt is incurred first, the security interest is transferred at a later time (since the property *cannot* have been transferred before it was acquired by the debtor), and therefore it is a transfer for an antecedent debt. See Comment, *The Commercial Code and Bankruptcy Act: Potential Conflicts*, 53 NW.U.L.Rev. (1958) 411, 412–418.

"Without going into the merits of the proposed rule of this Section, it is a matter which, in our opinion, should properly be left to Congress where it belongs. The retention of this Section will only lead to extensive and probably useless litigation." Sixth Progress Report to the Legislature by Senate Fact Finding Committee on Judiciary (1959–1961) Part 1, The Uniform Commercial Code, p. 556.

In response to this comment the State Bar Committee disagreed: "We believe it is desirable to retain Section 19108 [9108] in the California Draft for the following reasons:

"(a) The position of a secured party should be as strong under the Code in California as in other States which have adopted the Official Draft with this section.

"(b) The Supreme Court is tending toward the rule that State rules creating or regulating interests in property are entitled to greater weight in the Federal courts than had been previously believed (see for example the recent cases involving asserted priority of Federal tax liens) and several Federal cases have relied upon State law to sustain the validity of liens on after acquired property in bankruptcy: Pearson v. Rapstine, 203 F.2d 313 (5th Cir. 1953); Mason v. Citizens Nat. Trust & Savings Bank, 71 F.2d 246 (9th Cir. 1934).

"(c) The rule of the Official Draft is carefully drafted to effect a proper limitation on the scope of a floating lien on after acquired property. It may be granted that no well advised lender will rely upon the effectiveness of this section until it has been tested in the courts, but it is undesirable that California should be the only State adopting the Uniform Commercial Code in which such a test case could not be litigated." Sixth Progress Report to the Legislature by Senate Fact Finding Committee on Judiciary (1959–1961) Part 1, The Uniform Commercial Code, p. 647.

In response to these State Bar comments Professor Marsh maintained the earlier position of the Marsh and Warren Report:

"It seems to me that the discussions of this section proceed under a misapprehension. No one questions the fact that the 'validity' of a chattel mortgage and an after-acquired property clause in a chattel mortgage (or other security device) is governed in bankruptcy by State law. The question is whether the time when an otherwise valid transfer is 'deemed' to have occurred, for the purpose of testing whether it is a voidable preference, is determined by state law. Therefore, the cases cited are beside the point. Section 60 of the Bankruptcy Act is an explicit refutation of any affirmative answer to the real question (except to the extent expressly provided therein). See Curtis v. Knox, 254 F.2d 433 (7th Cir. 1958).

"A chattel mortgage given one month prior to bankruptcy while the mortgagor is insolvent to secure a debt incurred six months prior to bankruptcy is 'valid' under State law, but is nevertheless a recoverable preference in bankruptcy if the other requirements of Section 60 are met. Could a State enact a law saying in this situation that the chattel mortgage shall be 'deemed' to have been given at the time the debt was incurred, thereby making it not for an antecedent debt and not a recoverable preference? It is inconceivable to me, and I think it would be to any bankruptcy lawyer, that the Supreme Court would uphold such a statute. Yet there is no difference in theory between such a statute and Section 19108 [9108]. If 'state law' determines when a transfer is 'deemed' to have been made, then a state could destroy the effectiveness of Section 60. And of course Section 19108 would apply to no independent state question—it does not have 'particular significance' in bankruptcy; it has significance only in bankruptcy. No state law question turns upon whether a transfer is for an 'antecedent debt' or not. Therefore, such cases as *Aquilino* and *Bess*, aside from the fact that they deal with entirely different subjects, have no relevance here." Sixth Progress Report to the Legislature by Senate Fact Finding Committee on Judiciary (1959–1961) Part 1, The Uniform Commercial Code, p. 642.

Changes from U.C.C. (1962 Official Text)

2. This is section 9–108 without change.

Uniform Commercial Code Comment

Prior Uniform Statutory Provision:
None.

Purposes:

1. Many financing transactions contemplate that the collateral will include both the debtor's existing assets and also assets thereafter acquired by him in the operation of his business. This Article generally validates such after-acquired property interests (see Section 9–204 and Comment) although they may be subordinated to later purchase money interests under Section 9–312(3) and (4).

Interests in after-acquired property have never been considered as involving transfers of property for antecedent debt merely because of the after-acquired feature, nor should they be so considered. The section makes explicit what has been true under the case law: an after-acquired property interest is not, by virtue of that fact alone, security for a pre-existing claim. This rule is of importance principally in insolvency proceedings under the federal Bankruptcy Act or state statutes which make certain transfers for antecedent debt voidable as preferences. The determination of when a transfer is for antecedent debt is largely left by the Bankruptcy Act to state law.

Two tests must be met under this section for an interest in after-acquired property to be one not taken for an antecedent debt. *First*: the secured party must, at the inception of the transaction, have given new value in some form. *Second*: the after-acquired property must come in either in the ordinary course of the debtor's business or as an acquisition which is made under a contract of purchase entered into within a reasonable time after the giving of new value and pursuant to the security agreement. The reason for the first test needs no comment. The second is in line with limitations which judicial construction has placed on the operation of after-acquired property clauses. Their coverage has been in many cases restricted to subsequent ordinary course acquisitions: this Article does not go so far (see Section 9–204 and Comment), but it does deny present value status to out of ordinary course acquisitions not made pursuant to the original loan agreement. This solution gives the secured party full protection as to the collateral which he may be reasonably thought to have contracted for; it gives other creditors the possibility, under the law of preferences, of subjecting to their claims windfall or uncontemplated acquisitions shortly before bankruptcy.

2. The term "value" is defined in Section 1–201(44) and discussed in the accompanying Comment. In this section and in other sections of this Article the term "new value" is used but is left without statutory definition. The several illustrations of "new value" given in the text of this section (making an advance, incurring an obligation, releasing a perfected security interest) as well as the "purchase money security interest" definition in Section 9–107 indicate the nature of the concept. In other situations it is left to the courts to distinguish between "new" and "old" value, between present considerations and antecedent debt.

Cross References:

Point 1: Sections 9–204 and 9–312.
Point 2: Section 9–107.

Definitional Cross References:

"Collateral". Section 9–105.
"Contract". Section 1–201.
"Debtor". Section 9–105.
"Purchase". Section 1–201.
"Rights". Section 1–201.
"Secured party". Section 9–105.
"Security agreement". Section 9–105.
"Security interest". Section 1–201.
"Value". Section 1–201.

Cross References

Conflicting security interests, priorities, see Commercial Code § 9312.
Purchase money security interest defined, see Commercial Code § 9107.
Security agreement, after-acquired property, see Commercial Code § 9204.

§ 9109. Classification of Goods; "Consumer Goods"; "Equipment"; "Farm Products"; "Inventory"

Goods are

§ 9109

(1) "Consumer goods" if they are used or bought for use primarily for personal, family or household purposes;

(2) "Equipment" if they are used or bought for use primarily in business (including farming or a profession) or by a debtor who is a nonprofit organization or a governmental subdivision or agency or if the goods are not included in the definitions of inventory, farm products or consumer goods;

(3) "Farm products" if they are crops or livestock or supplies used or produced in farming operations or if they are products of crops or livestock in their unmanufactured states (such as ginned cotton, wool clip, maple syrup, * * * milk and eggs), and if they are in the possession of a debtor engaged in raising, fattening, grazing or other farming operations. If goods are farm products they are neither equipment nor inventory;

(4) "Inventory" if they are held by a person who holds them for sale or lease or to be furnished under contracts of service or if he has so leased or furnished them, or if they are raw materials, work in process or materials used or consumed in a business. Inventory of a person is not to be classified as his equipment. (Stats.1963, c. 819, § 9109. Amended by Stats.1974, c. 997, p. 2121, § 12, eff. Jan. 1, 1976.)

California Code Comment

By John A. Bohn and Charles J. Williams

Prior California Law

1. The classification of goods in this section is new statutory law. The significance of this classification is described in Official Comment 1.

Although goods cannot belong to more than one category at any time, they may change their classification depending upon who holds them and for what reason. Each classification is mutually exclusive but the four classifications described are intended to include all goods. Official Comment 2.

Changes from U.C.C. (1962 Official Text)

2. In subdivision (3) the word "honey" has been added to the enumeration.

3. In subdivision (4) the words "leased or" have been added before the phrase "so furnished them". This language was added to clarify the subdivision.

Uniform Commercial Code Comment

Prior Uniform Statutory Provision:
None.

Purposes:

1. This section classifies goods as consumer goods, equipment, farm products and inventory. The classification is important in many situations: it is relevant, for example, in determining the rights of persons who buy from a debtor goods subject to a security interest (Section 9–307), in certain questions of priority (Section 9–312), in determining the place of filing (Section 9–401) and in working out rights after default (Part 5). Comment 5 to Section 9–102 contains an index of the special rules applicable to different classes of collateral.

2. The classes of goods are mutually exclusive; the same property cannot at the same time and as to the same person be both equipment and inventory, for example. In borderline cases—a physician's car or a farmer's jeep which might be either consumer goods or equipment—the principal use to which the property is put should be considered as determinative. Goods can fall into different classes at different times; a radio is inventory in the hands of a dealer and consumer goods in the hands of a householder.

3. The principal test to determine whether goods are inventory is that they are held for immediate or ultimate sale. Implicit in the definition is the criterion that the prospective sale is in the ordinary course of business. Machinery used in manufacturing, for example, is equipment and not inventory even though it is the continuing policy of the enterprise to sell machinery when it becomes obsolete. Goods to be furnished under a contract of service are inventory even though the arrangement under which they are furnished is not technically a sale. When an enterprise is engaged in the business of leasing a stock of products to users (for example, the fleet of cars owned by a car rental agency), that stock is also included within the definition of "inventory". It should be noted that one class of goods which is not held for disposition to a purchaser or user is included in inventory: "Materials used or consumed in a business". Examples of this class of inventory are fuel to be used in operations, scrap metal produced in the course of manufacture, and containers to be used to package the goods. In general it may be said that goods used in a business are equipment when they are fixed assets or have, as identifiable units, a relatively long period of use; but are inventory, even though not held for sale, if they are used up or consumed in a short period of time in the production of some end product.

4. Goods are "farm products" only if they are in the possession of a debtor engaged in farming operations. Animals in a herd of livestock are covered whether they are acquired by purchase or result from natural increase. Products of crops or livestock remain farm products so long as they are in the possession of a debtor engaged in farming operations and have not been subjected to a manufacturing process. The terms "crops", "livestock" and "farming operations" are not defined; however, it is obvious from the text that "farming operations" includes raising livestock as well as crops; similarly, since eggs are products of livestock, livestock includes fowl.

When crops or livestock or their products come into the possession of a person not engaged in farming operations they cease to be "farm products". If they come into the possession of a marketing agency for sale or distribution or of a manufacturer or processor as raw materials, they become inventory.

Products of crops or livestock, even though they remain in the possession of a person engaged in farming operations, lose their status as farm products if they are subjected to a manufacturing process. What is and what is not a manufacturing operation is not determined by this Article. At one end of the scale some processes are so closely connected with farming—such as pasteurizing milk or boiling sap to produce maple syrup or maple sugar—that they would not rank as manufacturing. On the other hand an extensive canning operation would be manufacturing. The line is one for the courts to draw. After farm products have been subjected to a manufacturing operation, they become inventory if held for sale.

Note that the buyer in ordinary course who under Section 9–307 takes free of a security interest in goods held for sale does not include one who buys farm products from a person engaged in farming operations.

5. The principal definition of equipment is a negative one: goods used in a business (including farming or a profession) which are not inventory and not farm products. Trucks, rolling stock, tools, machinery are typical. It will be noted furthermore that any goods which are not covered by one of the other definitions in this section are to be treated as equipment.

Cross References:

Point 1: Sections 9–102, 9–307, 9–312, 9–401 and Part 5.
Point 3: Section 9–307.
Point 4: Section 9–307.

Definitional Cross References:

"Contract". Section 1–201.
"Debtor". Section 9–105.
"Goods". Section 9–105.
"Organization". Section 1–201.
"Person". Section 1–201.
"Sale". Sections 2–106 and 9–105.

Cross References

Conflicting security interests, priorities, see Commercial Code § 9312.
Default, see Commercial Code § 9501 et seq.
Place of filing, see Commercial Code § 9401.
Policy and scope of division, see Commercial Code § 9102.

Protection of buyers of goods, see Commercial Code § 9307.

§ 9110. Sufficiency of Description

For the purposes of this division any description of personal property or real estate is sufficient whether or not it is specific if it reasonably identifies what is described. Personal property may be referred to by general kind or class if the property can be reasonably identified as falling within such kind or class or if it can be so identified when it is acquired by the debtor. * * * (Stats.1963, c. 819, § 9110. Amended by Stats. 1974, c. 997, p. 2122, § 13, eff. Jan. 1, 1976.)

California Code Comment

By John A. Bohn and Charles J. Williams

Prior California Law

1. This section is consistent with prior California law.

There was no prior statute generally setting forth the test of the sufficiency of a description. However the description of collateral required in a chattel mortgage under former Civil Code § 2956 is similar to the requirement of this section. The second sentence of this section continues the rule under former Civil Code § 3031, the Inventory Lien statute which permitted the property to be referred to by its general kind or class when it could be reasonably so identified.

Changes from U.C.C. (1962 Official Text)

2. The second and third sentences of this section do not appear in section 9–110 of the Official Text. This additional language was added as a result of the suggestion proposed by the California Bankers Committee. The Marsh and Warren Report recommended against the amendment upon the basis that it was not necessary. Sixth Progress Report to the Legislature by Senate Fact Finding Committee on Judiciary (1959–1961) Part 1, The Uniform Commercial Code, pp. 419, 595.

Uniform Commercial Code Comment

Prior Uniform Statutory Provision:

None.

Purposes:

The requirement of description of collateral (see Section 9–203 and Comment thereto) is evidentiary. The test of sufficiency of a description laid down by this section is that the description do the job assigned to it—that it make possible the identification of the thing described. Under this rule courts should refuse to follow the holdings, often found in the older chattel mortgage cases, that descriptions are insufficient unless they are of the most exact and detailed nature, the so-called "serial number" test. The same test of reasonable identification applies where a description of real estate is required in a financing statement. See Section 9–402.

Cross References:

Sections 9–203 and 9–402.

Cross References

Financing statement, formal requisites, see Commercial Code § 9402.
Requisites of description, see Commercial Code § 9203.
Sale of property, contents of notice of sale, description of personal property or fixtures under this section, see Civil Code § 2924f.

§ 9111. Repealed by Stats.1979, c. 294, p. 1099, § 8, eff. July 24, 1979

§ 9112. Where Collateral Is Not Owned by Debtor

Unless otherwise agreed, when a secured party knows that collateral is owned by a person who is not the debtor, the owner of the collateral is entitled to receive from the secured party any surplus under Section 9502(2) or under Section 9504(1), and is not liable for the debt or for any deficiency after resale, and he has the same right as the debtor

(a) To receive statements under Section 9208;

(b) To receive notice of and to object to a secured party's proposal to retain the collateral in satisfaction of the indebtedness under Section 9505;

(c) To redeem the collateral under Section 9506;

(d) To obtain injunctive or other relief under Section 9507(1); and

(e) To recover losses caused to him under Section 9208(2). (Stats.1963, c. 819, § 9112. Amended by Stats. 1974, c. 997, p. 2122, § 14, eff. Jan. 1, 1976.)

California Code Comment

By John A. Bohn and Charles J. Williams

Prior California Law

1. This section establishes the rights of a third party who furnished collateral for the obligation of the debtor. In effect the third party has the rights of the debtor without personal obligation on the underlying debt. See the Official Comment.

Changes from U.C.C. (1962 Official Text)

2. This is section 9–112 of the Official Text without change.

Uniform Commercial Code Comment

Prior Uniform Statutory Provision:

None.

Purposes:

Under the definition of Section 9–105, in any provisions of the Article dealing with the collateral the term "debtor" means the owner of the collateral even though he is not the person who owes payment or performance of the obligation secured. The section covers several situations in which the implications of this definition are specifically set out.

The duties which this section imposes on a secured party toward such an owner of collateral are conditioned on the secured party's knowledge of the true state of facts. Short of such knowledge he may continue to deal exclusively with the person who owes the obligation. Nor does the section suggest that the secured party is under any duty of inquiry. It does not purport to cut across the law of conversion or of ultra vires. Whether a person who does not own property has authority to encumber it for his own debts and whether a person is free to encumber his property as collateral for the debts of another, are matters to be decided under other rules of law and are not covered by this section.

The section does not purport to be an exhaustive treatment of the subject. It isolates certain problems which may be expected to arise and states rules as to them. Others will no doubt arise: their solution is left to the courts.

Cross References:

Sections 9–105, 9–208 and Part 5.

Definitional Cross References:

"Collateral". Section 9–105.
"Debtor". Section 9–105.
"Notice". Section 1–201.
"Person". Section 1–201.
"Receive notice". Section 1–201.
"Right". Section 1–201.
"Secured party". Section 9–105.

Cross References

Account or list of collateral, request for statement, see Commercial Code § 9208.
Default, see Commercial Code § 9501 et seq.

§ 9113. Security Interests Arising Under Divisions on Sales or Leases

A security interest arising solely under the division on sales (Division 2) or the division on leases (Division 10) is subject to the provisions of this division except that to the extent that and so long as the debtor does not have or does not lawfully obtain possession of the goods

(a) No security agreement is necessary to make the security interest enforceable; and

(b) No filing is required to perfect the security interest; and

(c) The rights of the secured party on default by the debtor are governed (i) by the division on sales (Division 2) in the case of a security interest arising solely under that division or (ii) by the division on leases (Division 10) in the case of a security interest arising solely under that division. *(Stats.1963, c. 819, § 9113. Amended by Stats.1988, c. 1359, § 3, operative Jan. 1, 1990.)*

Uniform Commercial Code Comment

Prior Uniform Statutory Provision:
None.

Purposes:

1. Under the provisions of Article 2 on Sales, a seller of goods may reserve a security interest (see, e.g., Sections 2–401 and 2–505); and in certain circumstances, whether or not a security interest is reserved, the seller has rights of resale and stoppage under Sections 2–703, 2–705, and 2–706 which are similar to the rights of a secured party. Similarly, under such sections as Sections 2–506, 2–707 and 2–711, a financing agency, an agent, a buyer or another person may have a security interest or other right in goods similar to that of a seller. The use of the term "security interest" in the Sales Article is meant to bring the interests so designated within this Article. This section makes it clear, however, that such security interests are exempted from certain provisions of this Article. Compare Section 4–208(3), making similar special provisions for security interests arising in the bank collection process.

2. The security interests to which this section applies commonly arise by operation of law in the course of a sales transaction. Since the circumstances under which they arise are defined in the Sales Article, there is no need for the "security agreement" defined in Section 9–105(1) (*l*) and required by Section 9–203(1) and paragraph (a) dispenses with such requirements. The requirement of filing may be inapplicable under Sections 9–302(1) (a) and (b), 9–304 and 9–305, where the goods are in the possession of the secured party or of a bailee other than the debtor. To avoid difficulty in the residual cases, as for example where a bailee does not receive notification of the secured party's interest until after the security interest arises, paragraph (b) dispenses with any filing requirement. Finally, paragraph (c) makes inapplicable the default provisions of Part 5 of this Article, since the Sales Article contains detailed provisions governing stoppage of delivery and resale after breach. See Sections 2–705, 2–706, 2–707(2) and 2–711(3).

3. These limitations on the applicability of this Article to security interests arising under the Sales Article are appropriate only so long as the debtor does not have or lawfully obtain possession of the goods. Compare Section 56(b) of the Uniform Sales Act. A secured party who wishes to retain a security interest after the debtor lawfully obtains possession must comply fully with all the provisions of this Article and ordinarily must file a financing statement to perfect his interest. This is the effect of the "except" clause in the preamble to this section. Note that in the case of a buyer who has a security interest in rejected goods under Section 2–711(3), the buyer is the "secured party" and the seller is the "debtor".

4. This section applies only to a "security interest". The definition of "security interest" in Section 1–201(37) expressly excludes the special property interest of a buyer of goods on identification under Section 2–401(1). The seller's interest after identification and before delivery may be more than a security interest by virtue of explicit agreement under Section 2–401(1) or 2–501(1), by virtue of the provisions of Section 2–401(2), (3) or (4), or by virtue of substitution pursuant to Section 2–501(2). In such cases, Article 9 is inapplicable by the terms of Section 9–102(1) (a).

5. Where there is a "security interest", this section applies only if the security interest arises "solely" under the Sales Article. Thus Section 1–201(37) permits a buyer to acquire by agreement a security interest in goods not in his possession or control; such a security interest does not impair his rights under the Sales Article, but any rights based on the security agreement are fully subject to this Article without regard to the limitations of this section. Similarly, a seller who reserves a security interest by agreement does not lose his rights under the Sales Article, but rights other than those conferred by the Sales Article depend on full compliance with this Article.

6. This section is amended to include security interests arising under the Article on Leases (Article 2A), which is being promulgated at the same time as this amendment. Section 2A–508(5). After the effective date of the amendment to this section all references in the Act to Section 9–113 will be deemed to refer to this section, as amended. *E.g.,* Sections 9–203(1) and 9–302(1)(f).

Cross References:

Point 1: Sections 2–401, 2–505, 2–506, 2–705, 2–706, 2–707, 2–711(3), 4–208(3).

Point 2: Sections 2–705, 2–706, 2–707(2), 2–711(3), 9–203(1), 9–302(1) (a) and (b), 9–304, 9–305 and Part 5.

Point 3: Section 2–711(3).

Point 4: Sections 2–401, 2–501 and 9–102(1) (a).

Point 6: Article 2A, esp. Section 2A–508(5).

Definitional Cross References:

"Agreement". Section 1–201(3).
"Debtor". Section 9–105.
"Goods". Sections 2A–103(1)(h), 9–105.
"Lease". Section 2A–103(1)(j).
"Party". Section 1–201(29).
"Rights". Section 1–201(36).
"Sale". Section 2–106(1).
"Secured party". Section 9–105.
"Security agreement". Section 9–105.
"Security interest". Section 1–201(37).

Cross References

Buyer's insurable interest in goods, see Commercial Code § 2501.
Buyer's security interest in rejected goods, see Commercial Code § 2711.
Default, see Commercial Code § 9501 et seq.
Enforceability of security interest, see Commercial Code § 9203.
Financing agency, rights, see Commercial Code § 2506.
Goods in possession of secured party or bailee other than debtor, filing requirement, see Commercial Code §§ 9302, 9304, 9305.
Perfection of security interest, necessity of filing, see Commercial Code § 9302.
Perfection of security interest in instruments, documents and goods covered by documents, see Commercial Code § 9304.
Policy and scope of division, see Commercial Code § 9102.
Remedies of seller, in general, see Commercial Code § 2702 et seq.
Reservation of security, see Commercial Code § 2401.
Security agreement, defined, see Commercial Code § 9105.
Security interest, defined, see Commercial Code § 1201.
Security interest of collecting bank, see Commercial Code § 4210.
Seller's rights of resale and stoppage, see Commercial Code § 2703 et seq.
Seller's shipment under reservation, see Commercial Code § 2505.

§ 9114. Consignment

(1) A person who delivers goods under a consignment which is not a security interest and who would be required to file under this division by paragraph (3) (c) of Section 2326 has priority over a secured party who is or becomes a creditor of the consignee and who would

have a perfected security interest in the goods if they were the property of the consignee, and also has priority with respect to identifiable cash proceeds received on or before delivery of the goods to a buyer, if

(a) The consignor complies with the filing provision of the division on sales with respect to consignments (paragraph (3) (c) of Section 2326) before the consignee receives possession of the goods; and

(b) The consignor gives notification in writing to the holder of the security interest if the holder has filed a financing statement covering the same types of goods before the date of the filing made by the consignor; and

(c) The holder of the security interest receives the notification within five years before the consignee receives possession of the goods; and

(d) The notification states that the consignor expects to deliver goods on consignment to the consignee describing the goods by item or type.

(2) In the case of a consignment which is not a security interest and in which the requirements of the preceding subdivision have not been met, a person who delivers goods to another is subordinate to a person who would have a perfected security interest in the goods if they were the property of the debtor. *(Added by Stats.1974, c. 997, p. 2122, § 15, eff. Jan. 1, 1976.)*

Uniform Commercial Code Comment
Prior Uniform Statutory Provisions:
None.
Purposes:
1. This section requires that where goods are furnished to a merchant under the arrangement known as consignment rather than in a security transaction, the consignor must, in order to protect his position as against an inventory secured party of the consignee, give to that party the same notice and at the same time that he would give to that party if that party had filed first with respect to inventory and if the consignor were furnishing the goods under an inventory security agreement instead of under a consignment.

For the distinction between true consignment and security arrangements, see Section 1–201(37). For the assimilation of consignments under certain circumstances to goods on sale or return and the requirement of filing in the case of consignments, see Section 2–326.

The requirements of notice in this section conform closely to the concepts and the language of Section 9–312(3), which should be consulted together with the relevant Comments.

Except in the limited cases of identifiable cash proceeds received on or before delivery of the goods to a buyer, no attempt has been made to provide rules as to perfection of a claim to proceeds of consignments (compare Section 9–306) or the priority thereof (compare Section 9–312). It is believed that under many true consignments the consignor acquires a claim for an agreed amount against the consignee at the moment of sale, and does not look to the proceeds of sale. In contrast to the assumption of this Article that rights to proceeds of security interests under Section 9–306 represent the presumed intent of the parties (compare Section 9–203(3)), the Article goes on the assumption that if consignors intend to claim the proceeds of sale, they will do so by expressly contracting for them and will perfect their security interests therein.

Cross References:
Sections 2–326 and 9–312(3).
Definitional Cross References:
"Consignment". Section 1–201(37).
"Debtor". Section 9–105.
"Goods". Section 9–105.
"Notification". Section 1–201(26).
"Proceeds". Section 9–306.
"Security interest". Section 1–201(37).

§ 9115. Security interest in securities account; attachment or perfection; investment property; priorities

(1) In this division:

(a) "Commodity account" means an account maintained by a commodity intermediary in which a commodity contract is carried for a commodity customer.

(b) "Commodity contract" means a commodity futures contract, an option on a commodity futures contract, a commodity option, or other contract that, in each case, is either of the following:

(i) Traded on or subject to the rules of a board of trade that has been designated as a contract market for such a contract pursuant to the federal commodities laws.

(ii) Traded on a foreign commodity board of trade, exchange, or market, and is carried on the books of a commodity intermediary for a commodity customer.

(c) "Commodity customer" means a person for whom a commodity intermediary carries a commodity contract on its books.

(d) "Commodity intermediary" means either of the following:

(i) A person who is registered as a futures commission merchant under the federal commodities laws.

(ii) A person who in the ordinary course of its business provides clearance or settlement services for a board of trade that has been designated as a contract market pursuant to the federal commodities laws.

(e) "Control" with respect to a certificated security, uncertificated security, or security entitlement has the meaning specified in Section 8106. A secured party has control over a commodity contract if by agreement among the commodity customer, the commodity intermediary, and the secured party, the commodity intermediary has agreed that it will apply any value distributed on account of the commodity contract as directed by the secured party without further consent by the commodity customer. If a commodity customer grants a security interest in a commodity contract to its own commodity intermediary, the commodity intermediary as secured party has control. A secured party has control over a securities account or commodity account if the secured party has control over all security entitlements or commodity contracts carried in the securities account or commodity account.

(f) "Investment property" means any of the following:

(i) A security, whether certificated or uncertificated.

(ii) A security entitlement.

(iii) A securities account.

(iv) A commodity contract.

(v) A commodity account.

(2) Attachment or perfection of a security interest in a securities account is also attachment or perfection of a security interest in all security entitlements carried in the securities account. Attachment or perfection of a security interest in a commodity account is also attachment or perfection of a security interest in all commodity contracts carried in the commodity account.

(3) A description of collateral in a security agreement or financing statement is sufficient to create or perfect a security interest in a certificated security, uncertificated security, security entitlement, securities account, commodity contract, or commodity account whether it describes the collateral by those terms, or as investment property, or by description of the underlying security, financial asset, or commodity contract. A description of investment property collateral in a security agreement or financing statement is sufficient if it identifies the collateral by specific listing, by category, by quantity, by a computational or allocational formula or procedure, or by any other method, if the identity of the collateral is objectively determinable.

(4) Perfection of a security interest in investment property is governed by the following rules:

(a) A security interest in investment property may be perfected by control.

(b) Except as otherwise provided in paragraphs (c) and (d), a security interest in investment property may be perfected by filing.

(c) If the debtor is a broker or securities intermediary, a security interest in investment property is perfected when it attaches. The filing of a financing statement with respect to a security interest in investment property granted by a broker or securities intermediary has no effect for purposes of perfection or priority with respect to that security interest.

(d) If a debtor is a commodity intermediary, a security interest in a commodity contract or a commodity account is perfected when it attaches. The filing of a financing statement with respect to a security interest in a commodity contract or a commodity account granted by a commodity intermediary has no effect for purposes of perfection or priority with respect to that security interest.

(5) Priority between conflicting security interests in the same investment property is governed by the following rules:

(a) A security interest of a secured party who has control over investment property has priority over a security interest of a secured party who does not have control over the investment property.

(b) Except as otherwise provided in paragraphs (c) and (d), conflicting security interests of secured parties each of whom has control rank equally.

(c) Except as otherwise agreed by the securities intermediary, a security interest in a security entitlement or a securities account granted to the debtor's own securities intermediary has priority over any security interest granted by the debtor to another secured party.

(d) Except as otherwise agreed by the commodity intermediary, a security interest in a commodity contract or a commodity account granted to the debtor's own commodity intermediary has priority over any security interest granted by the debtor to another secured party.

(e) Conflicting security interests granted by a broker, a securities intermediary, or a commodity intermediary that are perfected without control rank equally.

(f) In all other cases, priority between conflicting security interests in investment property is governed by subdivisions (5), (6), and (7) of Section 9312. Subdivision (4) of Section 9312 does not apply to investment property.

(6) If a security certificate in registered form is delivered to a secured party pursuant to agreement, a written security agreement is not required for attachment or enforceability of the security interest, delivery suffices for perfection of the security interest, and the security interest has priority over a conflicting security interest perfected by means other than control, even if a necessary endorsement is lacking. *(Added by Stats. 1996, c. 497 (S.B.1591), § 13, operative Jan. 1, 1997.)*

Uniform Commercial Code Comment

1. Overview. This section sets out the principal rules on security interests in investment property. Investment property, defined in subsection (1)(f) is a new term for a category of collateral that includes securities, whether held directly or through intermediaries, and commodity futures. The term investment property is used in Article 9 as one of the general categories of collateral, such as goods or instruments. Investment property is excluded from the definitions of goods, instruments, and general intangibles. See Sections 9–105(1)(h), 9–105(1)(i), and 9–106.

This section is added as part of the revision of Article 8 on investment securities. It relies in part on terms and concepts defined in Revised Article 8. For an overview of Revised Article 8, see the Prefatory Note to that Article. Prior to the 1978 amendments to Article 8, the rules on security interests in securities were included in Article 9. The 1978 amendments moved the key rules to Article 8. The revision of Article 8 returns these matters to Article 9. In order to avoid disruption of section numbering, the new rules on security interests in investment property are collected in this section, rather than being distributed among the various sections of Article 9 dealing with corresponding issues for other categories of collateral. On matters not covered by rules set out in this section, security interests in investment property are governed by the general rules in other sections of this Article.

The distinction between the direct and indirect holding systems plays an important role in the rules on security interests in securities. Consider two investors, X and Y, each of whom owns 1000 shares of XYZ Co. common stock. X has a certificate representing 1000 shares and is registered on the books maintained by XYZ Co.'s transfer agent as the holder of record of those 1000 shares. X has a direct relationship with the issuer, and receives dividends, distributions, and proxies directly from the issuer. In Revised Article 8 terminology, X has a direct claim to a "certificated security." If X wishes to use the investment position as collateral for a loan, X would grant the lender a security interest in the "certificated security." The Article 9 rules for such transactions are explained in Comment 2. XYZ Co. might not issue certificates, but register investors such as X directly on its stockholder books. In that case, X's interest would be an "uncertificated security." The Article 9 rules for uncertificated securities are explained in Comment 3. By contrast to these direct relationships, Y holds the securities through an account with Y's broker. Y does not have a certificate and is not registered on XYZ Co.'s stock books as a holder of record. Rather, Y holds the securities through a chain of securities intermediaries. Under Revised Article 8, Y's interest in XYZ common stock is described as a "securities entitlement." If Y wishes to use the investment position as collateral for a loan, Y would grant the lender a security interest in the "securities entitlement." The Article 9 rules for security entitlements are explained in Comment 4.

A commercial setting in which security interests in investment property play a most economically significant role is the "wholesale" level, that is, finance of securities firms and security interests that support the extension of credit in the settlement system. Comments 6 and 7 deal with these transactions. The rules on security interests in investment property also apply to commodity futures. Comment 8 deals with these transactions.

The rules on security interests in investment property are based on the concept of "control," defined in Sections 8–106 and 9–115(1)(e). If the secured party has control the security interest can attach even without a written security agreement. See Section 9–203. A security interest in investment property can also be created by a written security agreement pursuant to Section 9–203. Security interests in investment property can be perfected by control. See subsection (4)(a). Although other methods of perfection are also permitted, the basic priority rule, set out in subsection (5)(a), is that a secured party who obtains control has priority over a secured party who relies on some other method of perfection. The control priority rule is explained in Comment 5.

2. Security interests in certificated securities. A security interest in a certificated security can be created by conferring control on the secured party. Section 8–106 provides that a secured party has control of a certificated security if the certificate has been delivered, see Section 8–301, and any necessary indorsement has been supplied. Section 9–203 provides that a security interest can attach, even without a written security agreement, if the secured party has control. Section 9–115(4)(a) provides that control is a permissible method of perfection.

A security interest in a certificated security can also be created by a written security agreement pursuant to Section 9–203, and can be perfected by filing, see subsection (4)(b). (The perfection by filing rule does not apply if the debtor is a broker or securities intermediary.) However, a security interest perfected only by filing is subordinate to a conflicting security interest perfected by control. See subsection (5)(a) and Comment 5. Also, perfection by filing would not give the secured party protection against other types of adverse claims, since the Article 8 adverse claim cut-off rules require control. See Section 8–510.

Section 9–115(6) deals with cases where a secured party has taken possession of an unindorsed security certificate in registered form. It provides that even though the indorsement is lacking, delivery of the certificate to the secured party suffices for attachment and perfection of the security interest in the certificated security. It also provides that such a possessory security interest has priority over a conflicting non-control security interest, such as a security interest perfected by filing. However, without the indorsement the secured party would not get the other protections against adverse claims that flow from obtaining control. See Section 8–510.

3. Security interests in uncertificated securities. The rules on security interests in uncertificated securities apply only where the debtor is the direct holder of an uncertificated security. For example, mutual funds typically do not issue certificates, but the beneficial owners of mutual funds shares commonly are the direct holders of the shares, whose interests are recorded on the books of the issuer. If such an investor grants a security interest in the mutual funds shares, the rules in this section on security interests in uncertificated securities apply. These rules are not germane to situations where a debtor holds securities through a securities intermediary. Security interests in positions held through securities intermediaries are governed by the rules on security entitlements and securities accounts, not the rules on uncertificated securities.

A security interest in an uncertificated security can be perfected either by control or by filing. See subsection (4)(a) and (b). (The filing rule does not apply if the debtor is itself a broker or securities intermediary.) Priority disputes among conflicting security interests in an uncertificated security are governed by subsection (5). Under subsection (5)(a), a secured party who obtains control has priority over a secured party who does not have control. Thus, although filing is a permissible method of perfection, a secured party who perfects by filing takes the risk that the debtor has granted or will grant a security interest in the same property to another party who obtains control. See Comment 5.

The requirements for control with respect to uncertificated securities are set out in Section 8–106(c). There are two possibilities. First, a secured party has control if the uncertificated security is transferred from debtor to secured party on the books of the issuer. See Sections 8–106(c)(1) (control by "delivery") and 8–301(b) (defining "delivery" of uncertificated security). So far as the issuer is concerned, the secured party is the registered owner entitled to all rights of ownership, though as between the debtor and secured party the debtor remains the owner and the secured party holds its interest as secured party. Second, a secured party has control over an uncertificated security if the issuer agrees that it will comply with "instructions" originated by the secured party without further consent by the registered owner. See Section 8–106(c)(2). If the debtor, secured party, and issuer agree that the secured party has the right to direct the issuer to dispose of the security without further action by the debtor, the secured party has control even though the debtor remains listed as the registered owner and continues to receive dividends and distributions. Note, though, that there is no statutory requirement that issuers of uncertificated securities offer such arrangements.

4. Security interests in security entitlements and securities accounts. This section establishes a structure for creating security interests in securities and other financial assets that a debtor holds through an account with a securities intermediary. Under Revised Article 8, the interest of a person who holds securities through a securities account with a broker or other securities intermediary is described as a security entitlement. Thus, the Article 9 rules governing the use of that person's investment position as collateral are the rules for security entitlements and securities accounts, not the rules for certificated securities or uncertificated securities.

Attachment of security interests in security entitlements and securities accounts is governed by Section 9–203 and subsections (2) and (3) of this section. Unless the secured party has control, a written security agreement is necessary for attachment. For purposes of description of the collateral in a security agreement, it is not essential that the precise Article 8 terminology be used. See subsection (3). For example, if a debtor who holds 1000 shares of XYZ Co. common stock through a securities account signs a security agreement which describes the collateral as "1000 shares of XYZ Co. common stock," that description is sufficient, even though the debtor's interest would be described under Revised Article 8 as a "security entitlement" to 1000 shares of XYZ Co. common stock.

The Article 8 term security entitlement also covers the interest of a person in a "financial asset," if the person holds that financial asset through a securities account. "Financial asset" is a broader term than "security." See Section 8–102(a)(9). For example, a bankers' acceptance is an Article 3 negotiable instrument and hence an instrument under Section 9–105(1)(i). If a person who holds a bankers' acceptance directly wishes to grant a security interest in it, the Article 9 rules for instruments apply. However, if a person holds a bankers' acceptance through a securities account, the person has a security entitlement to the bankers' acceptance. If the person wishes to grant a security interest in the security entitlement to the bankers' acceptance, the Article 9 rules for investment property apply.

Subsection (1)(f)(iii) provides that the term investment property also includes "securities account." This is intended to facilitate transactions in which a debtor wishes to grant a security interest in all of the investment positions held through a particular account rather than in particular positions carried in the account. Just as a debtor may grant a security interest either in specifically listed items of equipment or in all of the debtor's equipment, so too a debtor who holds securities or other financial assets through a securities account may grant a security interest either in specifically listed security entitlements or in all of the security entitlements held through that account. Referring to the collateral as the securities account is a simple way of describing all of the security entitlements carried in the account. Section 9–115(2) provides that attachment or perfection of a security interest in a securities account is also attachment or perfection of a security interest in all security entitlements carried in the securities account. A security interest in a securities account would also include all other rights of the debtor against the securities intermediary arising out of the securities account. For example, a security interest in a securities account would include credit balances due to the debtor from the securities intermediary, whether or not they are proceeds of a security entitlement.

A security interest in a security entitlement or securities account can be perfected either by control or by filing. See subsections (4)(a) and (4)(b), (The filing rule does not apply if the debtor is itself a broker or securities intermediary.) Priority disputes among conflicting security interests in a security entitlement or securities account are governed by subsection (5). The basic rule of subsection (5)(a) is that a secured party who obtains control has priority over a secured party who does not have control. Thus, although filing is a permissible method of perfection, a secured party who perfects by filing takes the risk that the debtor has granted or will grant a security interest in the same property to another party who obtains control. See Comment 5.

The requirements for control with respect to security entitlements and securities accounts are set out in Sections 8–106(d) and 9–115(1)(e). There are two possibilities. First, Section 8–106(d)(1) provides that a secured party has control over a security entitlement if the secured party becomes the entitlement holder, that is, the position is transferred from debtor to secured party on the books of a securities intermediary. See Examples 1 and 2 in Comment 4 to Section 8–106. Second, Section 8–106(d)(2) provides that a secured party has control over a security entitlement if the securities intermediary agrees that it will comply with entitlement orders originated by the secured party without further consent by the debtor. See Example 3 in Comment 4 to Section 8–106. If the debtor, secured party, and issuer agree that the secured party has the right to direct the securities intermediary to dispose of the collateral without further action by the debtor, the secured party has control even though the debtor remains listed as the entitlement holder and continues to receive dividends and distributions. The secured party can obtain control even though the debtor is also allowed to continue to trade. See Section 8–106(f) and Comment 7 thereto. The three-party control agreement device is based on arrangements that have already developed in the securities business. Even under prior law, some securities brokers developed standard forms of such agreements. Note though that, as is the case with respect to issuers of uncertificated securities, there is no statutory requirement that securities intermediaries offer such control agreement arrangements.

Subsection (1)(e) provides that a secured party has control over a securities account if it has control over all security entitlements carried in the account. Thus, the rules in Section 8–106(d) on control with respect to security entitlements determine whether a secured party has control over a securities account. Control with respect to a securities account is defined in terms of obtaining control over the security entitlements simply for drafting convenience. Of course, an agreement that provides that the securities intermediary will honor instructions from the secured party concerning a securities account described as such is sufficient since such an agreement necessarily implies that the secured party has control over all security entitlements carried in the account.

If a customer borrows from its own securities intermediary, e.g., to purchase securities "on margin" or for other purposes, and grants a security interest to its intermediary, the intermediary has control. See Section 8–106(e). A securities firm could also provide control financing arrangements to its customers through a different legal entity than the securities intermediary itself, e.g., the securities trading, custody, and credit services might be provided by different corporate entities within the financial services firm's "family." So long as the agreement with the customer provides that the entity providing the custodial function (the "securities intermediary") will act on instructions received from entity providing the credit, the credit entity has control.

5. Priority Rules. Subsection (5) specifies the priority rules for conflicting security interests in the same investment property. Subsection (5)(a) states the most important general rule—that a secured party who obtains control has priority over a secured party who does not obtain control. The other priority rules, in subsections (5)(b) through (5)(e), deal with relatively unusual circumstances not covered by the control priority rule. Subsection (5)(f) provides that the general priority rules of Section 9–312 apply to cases not covered by the specific rules in subsection (5). The principal application of this residual rule is that the usual first in time of filing rule applies to conflicting security interests that are perfected only by filing. Because the control priority rule of subsection (5)(a) provides for the ordinary cases in which persons purchase securities on margin credit from their brokers, there is no need for special rules for purchase money security interests. Accordingly, subsection (5)(f) provides that the purchase money priority rule of Section 9–312(4) does not apply to investment property.

The following examples illustrate the basic priority rules of this section:

Example 1. Debtor borrows from Alpha and grants Alpha a security interest in a variety of collateral, including all of Debtor's investment property. At that time Debtor owns 1000 shares of XYZ Co. stock for which Debtor has a certificate. Alpha perfects by filing. Later, Debtor borrows from Beta and grants Beta a security interest in the 1000 shares of XYZ Co. stock. Debtor delivers the certificate, properly indorsed, to Beta. Alpha and Beta both have perfected security interests in the XYZ Co. stock. Beta has control, see Section 8–106(b)(1), and hence has priority over Alpha.

Example 2. Debtor borrows from Alpha and grants Alpha a security interest in a variety of collateral, including all of Debtor's investment property. At that time Debtor owns 1000 shares of XYZ Co. stock, held through a securities account with Able & Co. Alpha perfects by filing. Later, Debtor borrows from Beta and grants Beta a security interest in the 1000 shares of XYZ Co. stock. Debtor instructs Able to have the 1000 shares transferred through the clearing corporation to Custodian Bank, to be credited to Beta's account with Custodian Bank. Alpha and Beta both have perfected security interests in the XYZ Co. stock. Beta has control, see Section 8–106(d)(1), and hence has priority over Alpha.

Example 3. Debtor borrows from Alpha and grants Alpha a security interest in a variety of collateral, including all of Debtor's investment property. At that time Debtor owns 1000 shares of XYZ Co. stock, which is held through a securities account with Able & Co. Alpha perfects by filing. Later, Debtor borrows from Beta and grants Beta a security interest in the 1000 shares of XYZ Co. stock. Debtor, Able, and Beta enter into an agreement under which Debtor will continue to receive dividends and distributions, and will continue to have the right to direct dispositions, but Beta will also have the right to direct dispositions and receive the proceeds. Alpha and Beta both have perfected security interests in the XYZ Co. stock. Beta has control, see Section 8–106(d)(2), and hence has priority over Alpha.

Example 4. Debtor borrows from Alpha and grants Alpha a security interest in a variety of collateral, including all of Debtor's investment property. At that time Debtor owns 1000 shares of XYZ Co. stock, held through a securities account with Able & Co. Alpha perfects by filing. Debtor's agreement with Able & Co. provides that Able has a security interest in all securities carried in the account as security for any obligations of Debtor to Able. Debtor incurs obligations to Able and later defaults on the obligations to Alpha and Able. Able has control by virtue of the rule of Section 8–106(e) that if a customer grants a security interest to its own intermediary, the intermediary has control. Since Alpha does not have control, Able has priority over Alpha under the general control priority rule of subsection (5)(a).

Example 5. Debtor holds securities through a securities account with Able & Co. Debtor's agreement with Able & Co. provides that Able has a security interest in all securities carried in the account as security for any obligations of Debtor to Able. Debtor borrows from Beta and grants Beta a security interest in 1000 shares of XYZ Co. stock carried in the account. Debtor, Able, and Beta enter into an agreement under which Debtor will continue to receive dividends and distributions and will continue to have the right to direct dispositions, but Beta will also have the right to direct dispositions and receive the proceeds. Debtor incurs obligations to Able and later defaults on the obligations to Beta and Able. Both Beta and Able have control, so the general control priority rule of subsection (5)(a) does not apply. Compare Example 4. Subsection (5)(c) provides that a security interest held by a securities intermediary in positions of its own customer has priority over a conflicting security interest of an external lender, so Able has priority over Beta. (Subsection (5)(d) has a parallel rule for commodities intermediaries.) The agreement among Able, Beta, and Debtor could, of course, determine the relative priority of the security interests of Able and Beta, see Section 9–316, but the fact that the intermediary has agreed to act on the instructions of a secured party such as Beta does not itself imply any agreement by the intermediary to subordinate.

The control priority rule does not turn on either temporal sequence or awareness of conflicting security interests. Rather, it is a structural rule, based on the principle that a lender should be able to rely on the collateral without question if the lender has taken the necessary steps to assure itself that it is in a position where it can foreclose on the collateral without further action by the debtor. The control priority rule is necessary because the perfection rules provide considerable flexibility in structuring secured financing arrangements. For example, at the "retail" level, a secured lender to an investor who wants the full measure of protection can obtain control, but the creditor may be willing to accept the greater measure of risk that follows from perfection by filing. Similarly, at the "wholesale" level, a lender to securities firms can leave the collateral with the debtor and obtain a perfected security interest under the automatic perfection rule of subsection (4)(c), but a lender who wants to be entirely sure of its position will want to obtain control. The control priority rule of subsection (5)(a) is an essential part of this system of flexibility. It is feasible to provide more than one method of perfecting secured transactions only if the rules ensure that those who take the necessary steps to obtain the full measure of protection do not run the risk of subordination to those who have not taken such steps. A secured party who is unwilling to run the risk that the debtor has granted or will grant a conflicting control security interest should not make a loan without obtaining control of the collateral.

As applied to the retail level, the control priority rule means that a secured party who obtains control has priority over a conflicting security interest perfected by filing without regard to inquiry into whether the control secured party was aware of the filed security interest. Prior to enactment of this section, Article 9 did not permit perfection of security interests in securities by filing. Accordingly, parties who deal in securities have never developed a practice of searching the UCC files before conducting securities transactions. Although filing is now a permissible method of perfection, in order to avoid disruption of existing practices in this business it is necessary to give perfection by filing a different and more limited effect for securities than for some other forms of collateral. The priority rules are not based on the assumption that parties who perfect by the usual method of obtaining control will search the files. Quite the contrary, the control priority rule is intended to ensure that secured parties who do obtain control are entirely unaffected by filings. To state the point another way, perfection by filing is intended to affect only general creditors or other secured creditors who rely on filing. The rule that a security interest perfected by filing can be primed by a control security interest, without regard to awareness, is a consequence of the system of perfection and priority rules for investment property. These rules are designed to take account of the circumstances of the securities markets, where filing is not given the same effect as for some other forms of property. No implication is made about the effect of filing with respect to security interests in other forms of property, nor about other Article 9 rules, e.g., Section 9–308, which govern the circumstances in which security interests in other forms of property perfected by filing can be primed by subsequent perfected security interests.

6. Secured finance of securities firms. Modernization of the commercial law rules governing secured finance of securities dealers and security interest arrangements in the clearance and settlement system is essential to the safe and efficient functioning of the securities markets.

Secured financing arrangements for securities firms are currently implemented in various ways. In some circumstances lenders may require that the transactions be structured as "hard pledges," where the securities are transferred on the books of a clearing corporation from the debtor's account to the lender's account or to a special pledge account for the lender where they cannot be disposed of without the specific consent of the lender. In other circumstances, lenders are content with so-called "agreement to pledge" or "agreement to deliver" arrangements, where the debtor retains the positions in its own account, but reflects on its books that the positions have been hypothecated and promises that the securities will be transferred to the secured party's account on demand.

The perfection and priority rules of this section are designed to facilitate current secured financing arrangements for securities firms as well as to provide sufficient flexibility to accommodate new arrangements that develop in the future. Hard pledge arrangements are covered by the concept of control. If the lender obtains control, the security interest is perfected and has priority over a conflicting non-control security interest. For examples of control arrangements in this setting see Examples 4 through 8 in Comment 4 to Section 8–106. The secured party can obtain control even though the debtor retains the right to trade or otherwise dispose of the collateral. See Section 8–106(f) and Examples 7 and 8 in Comment 4 to Section 8–106.

Non-control secured financing arrangements for securities firms are covered by the automatic perfection rule of subsection (4)(c). Under prior law, agreement to pledge arrangements could be implemented under a provision that a security interest in securities given for new value under a written security agreement was perfected without filing or possession for a period of 21 days. Although the security interests were temporary in legal theory, the financing arrangements could, in practice, be continued indefinitely by rolling over the loans at least every 21 days. Accordingly, a knowledgeable creditor of a securities firm realizes that the firm's securities may be subject to security interests that are not discoverable from any public records. The perfection rule of subsection (4)(c) makes it unnecessary to engage in the purely formal practice of rolling over these arrangements every 21 days.

Priority questions concerning security interests granted by brokers and securities intermediaries are governed by the general control priority rule of subsection (5)(a), as supplemented by the special rules set out in subsections (b), (c), and (e). In cases not covered by the control priority rule, conflicting security interests rank equally. The following examples illustrate the priority rules as applied to this setting. (In all cases it is assumed that the debtor retains sufficient other securities to satisfy all customers' claims. This section deals with the relative rights of secured lenders to a securities firm. Disputes between a secured lender and the firm's own customers are governed by Section 8–511.)

Example 6. Able & Co., a securities dealer, enters into financing arrangements with two lenders, Alpha Bank and Beta Bank. In each case the agreements provide that the lender will have a security interest in the securities identified on lists provided to the lender on a daily basis, that the debtor will deliver the securities to the lender on demand, and that the debtor will not list as collateral any securities which the debtor has pledged to any other lender. Upon Able's insolvency it is discovered that Able has listed the same securities on the collateral lists provided to both Alpha and Beta. Alpha and Beta both have perfected security interests under the automatic perfection rule of subsection (4)(c). Neither Alpha nor Beta has control. Subsection (5)(e) provides that the security interests of Alpha and Beta rank equally, because each of them has a non-control security interest granted by a securities firm. They share pro-rata.

Example 7. Able enters into financing arrangements, with Alpha Bank and Beta Bank as in Example 6. At some point, however, Beta decides that it is unwilling to continue to provide financing on a non-control basis. Able directs the clearing corporation where it holds its principal inventory of securities to move specified securities into Beta's account. Upon Able's insolvency it is discovered that a list of collateral provided to Alpha includes securities that had been moved to Beta's account. Both Alpha and Beta have perfected security interests; Alpha under the automatic perfection rule of subsection (4)(c), and Beta under that rule and also the subsection (4)(a) control perfection rule. Beta has control but Alpha does not. Beta has priority over Alpha under subsection (5)(a).

Example 8. Able & Co. carries its principal inventory of securities through Clearing Corporation, which offers a "shared control" facility whereby a participant securities firm can enter into an arrangement with a lender under which the securities firm will retain the power to trade and otherwise direct dispositions of securities carried in its account, but Clearing Corporation agrees that, at any time the lender so directs, Clearing Corporation will transfer any securities from the firm's account to the lender's account or otherwise dispose of them as directed by the lender. Able enters into financing arrangements with two lenders, Alpha and Beta, each of which obtains such a control agreement from Clearing Corporation. The agreement with each lender provides that Able will designate specific securities as collateral on lists provided to the lender on a daily or other periodic basis, and that it will not pledge the same securities to different lenders. Upon Able's insolvency, it is discovered that Able has listed the same securities on the collateral lists provided to both Alpha and Beta. Both Alpha and Beta have control over the disputed securities. They share pro rata under subsection (5)(b).

7. Secured financing arrangement in the settlement system. Under the rules or agreements governing the relationship between a clearing corporation and its participants, the clearing corporation may have a security interest in securities that the participants have deposited with the clearing corporation pursuant to guaranty fund arrangements or in securities that are in the process of delivery to or from a participant's account in the settlement process. The control rules protect the clearing corporation's rights as secured party in such arrangements, since the clearing corporation would have control over the collateral under the Section 8–106 rules. The control rules also protect the rights of "upper-tier" intermediaries that are not themselves clearing corporations. For example, if a securities dealer carries its inventory through a clearing bank that provides both custodial and credit services, the clearing bank as secured party would have control and hence be assured of perfection and priority over any potential conflicting security interests granted by the securities dealer.

In some circumstances, a clearing corporation may be the debtor in a secured financing arrangement. For example, a clearing corporation that settles delivery-versus-payment transactions among its participants on a net, same-day basis relies on timely payments from all participants with net obligations due to the system. If a participant that is a net debtor were to default on its payment obligation, the clearing corporation would not receive some of the funds needed to settle with participants that are net creditors to the system. To complete end-of-day settlement after a payment default by a participant, a clearing corporation that settles on a net, same-day basis may need to draw on credit lines and pledge securities of the defaulting participant or other securities pledged by participants in the clearing corporation to secure such drawings. The clearing corporation may be the top tier securities intermediary for the securities pledged, so that it would not be practical for the lender to obtain control. Even where the clearing corporation holds some types of securities through other intermediaries, however, the clearing corporation is unlikely to be able to complete the arrangements necessary to convey "control" over the securities to be pledged in time to complete settlement in a timely manner. However, the term "securities intermediary" is defined in Section 8–102(a)(14) to include clearing corporations. Thus, the perfection rule of subsection (4)(c) applies to security interests in investment property granted by clearing corporations.

In secured financing arrangements for clearing corporations and other securities intermediaries, it is sometimes necessary to specify that a secured lender will have a security interest in a certain bundle of securities that, after all the calculations necessary to complete a processing cycle are completed, turn out to be appropriate and available for pledge. At the time the security interest attaches, the necessary computations may not have been completed, though the information that ultimately will determine what positions are to be pledged has been entered. Accordingly, subsection (3) provides that the description of collateral in a security agreement may identify the collateral by means of a computational or allocational formula.

8. Security interests in commodity futures. Section 9–115 establishes rules on security interests in commodity contracts and commodity accounts that are, in general, parallel to the rules on security interests in security entitlements and securities accounts. Note, though, that commodity contracts are not "securities" or "financial assets" under Article 8. See Section 8–103(f). Thus, the relationship between commodity intermediaries and commodity customers is not governed by the indirect holding system rules Part 5 of Article 8. For securities, the UCC establishes rules in Article 9 rules on security interests, and rules in Article 8 on the rights of transferees, including secured parties, on such matters as the rights of a transferee if the transfer was itself wrongful so that another party has an adverse claim. For commodity contracts, Article 9 establishes rules on security interests, but questions of the sort dealt with in Article 8 for securities are left to other law.

Subsection (1) contains the definitions of the terms used in substantive rules on security interests in commodity contracts and commodity accounts. The key term "commodity contract" is defined in subsection (1)(b). Section 8–103(f) provides that a commodity contract, as defined in Section 9–115, is not a security or a financial asset. The result is that the indirect holding system rules in Revised Article 8 Part 5 do not apply to anything that falls within the definition of commodity contract in this section. The indirect holding system rules of Article 8, however, are intended to be sufficiently flexible that they can be applied to new developments in the securities and financial markets, where that is appropriate. Accordingly, the "commodity contract" definition in this section is narrowly drafted to ensure that it does not operate as an obstacle to the application of the new Article 8 indirect holding system rules to new products. The term commodity contract covers those contracts that are traded on or subject to the rules of a designated contract market, and foreign commodity contracts that are carried on the books of American commodity intermediaries. The effect of this definition is that the category of commodity contracts that are excluded from Article 8 but governed by Article 9 is essentially the same as the category of contracts that fall within the exclusive regulatory jurisdiction of the federal Commodities Futures Trading Commission.

Commodity contracts are rather different from securities or other financial assets. A person who enters into a commodity futures contract is not buying an asset having a certain value and holding it in anticipation of increase in value. Rather the person is entering into a contract to buy or sell a commodity at set price for delivery at a future time. That contract may become advantageous or disadvantageous as the price of the commodity fluctuates during the term of the contract. The rules of the commodity exchanges require that the contracts be marked to market on a daily basis, that is the customer pays or receives any increment attributable to that day's price change. Because commodity customers may incur obligations on their contracts, they are required to provide collateral at the outset, known as "original margin," and may be required to provide additional amounts, known as "variation margin," during the term of the contract.

The most likely setting in which a person would want to take a security interest in a commodity contract is where a lender who is advancing funds to finance an inventory of a physical commodity requires the borrower to enter into a commodity contract as a hedge against the risk of decline in the value of the commodity. The lender will want to take a security interest in both the commodity itself and the hedging commodity contract. Typically, such arrangements are structured as security interests in the entire commodity account in which the borrower carries the hedging contracts, rather than in individual contracts. Section 9–115 provides a simple mechanism for implementation of such arrangements, either by granting a security interest in the commodity account, or in particular commodity contracts carried in the account. The security interest can be perfected by filing or by control. Under subsection (1)(e) the secured party can obtain control over a commodity contract or commodity account by obtaining an agreement among the commodity customer, the secured party, and the commodity intermediary in which the commodity intermediary agrees to apply any value distributed as directed by the secured party. This provides a clear and certain legal framework for practices that have already developed in the industry.

One important effect of including commodity contracts and commodity accounts in the new Article 9 rules is to provide a clearer legal structure for the analysis of the rights of commodity clearing organizations against their participants and futures commission merchants against their customers. The rules and agreements of commodity clearing organizations generally provide that the clearing organization has the right to liquidate any participant's positions in order to satisfy obligations of the participant to the clearing corporation. Similarly, agreements between futures commission merchants and their customers generally provide that the futures commission merchant has the right to liquidate a customer's positions in order to satisfy obligations of the customer to the futures commission merchant. Section 9–115 treats these rights as security interests and applies to them the same priority rules that apply to the somewhat analogous relationships between securities clearing corporations or securities intermediaries and their participants or customers. Subsection (1)(e) provides that the commodity intermediary has control, and therefore the security interest is perfected under subsection (4)(a). Subsection (5)(d) provides that the security interest of a commodity clearing organization in its participant's commodity contracts has priority over any security interest granted by the participant to a third-party lender. Similarly, an FCM's security interest would have priority over any security interest granted by its customer to a third-party lender.

The main property that a commodity intermediary holds as collateral for the obligations that the commodity customer may incur under its commodity contracts is not other commodity contracts carried by the customer but the other property that the customer has posted as margin. Typically, this property will be securities. The commodity intermediary's security interest in such securities is governed by the rules of this section on security interests in securities, not the rules on security interests in commodity contracts or commodity accounts.

Although there are significant analytic and regulatory differences between commodities and securities, the development of commodity contracts on financial products in the past few decades has resulted in a system in which the commodity markets and security markets are closely linked. The Section 9–115 rules on security interests in commodity contracts and commodity accounts provide a structure that may be essential in times of stress in the financial markets. Suppose, for example that a firm has a position in a securities market that is hedged by a position in a commodity market, so that payments that the firm is obligated to make with respect to the securities position will be covered by the receipt of funds from the commodity position. Depending upon the settlement cycles of the different markets, it is possible that the firm could find itself in a position where it is obligated to make the payment with respect to the securities position before it receives the matching funds from the commodity position. If cross-margining arrangements have not been developed between the two markets, the firm may need to borrow funds temporarily to make the earlier payment. The Section

9–115 rules would facilitate the use of positions in one market as collateral for loans needed to cover obligations in the other market.

9. Relation to other law. Section 1–103 provides that "unless displaced by particular provisions of this Act, the principles of law and equity ... shall supplement its provisions." There may be circumstances in which a secured party's action in acquiring a security interest that has priority under this section constitutes conduct that is wrongful under other law. Though the possibility of such resort to other law may provide an appropriate "escape valve" for cases of egregious conduct, care must be taken to ensure that this does not impair the certainty and predictability of the priority rules. Whether a court may appropriately look to other law to impose liability upon or estop a party from asserting its Article 9 priority depends on an assessment of the party's conduct under the standards established by such other law as well as a determination of whether the particular application of such other law is displaced by the UCC.

Some circumstances in which other law is clearly displaced by the UCC rules are readily identifiable. Common law "first in time, first in right" principles, or correlative tort liability rules such as common law conversion principles under which a purchaser may incur liability to a party with a prior property interest without regard to awareness of that claim, are necessarily displaced by the priority rules set out in this section since these rules determine the relative ranking of security interests in investment property. So too, Article 8 provides protections against adverse claims to certain purchasers of interests in investment property. In circumstances where a secured party not only has priority under Section 9–115, but also qualifies for protection against adverse claims under Section 8–303, 8–502, or 8–510, resort to other law would be precluded.

In determining whether it is appropriate in a particular case to look to other law, account must also be taken of the policies that underlie the commercial law rules on securities markets and security interests in securities. A principal objective of the revision of Article 8 and corresponding provisions of Article 9 is to ensure that secured financing transactions can be implemented on a simple, timely, and certain basis. One of the circumstances that led to the revision was the concern that uncertainty in the application of the rules on secured transactions involving securities and other financial assets could contribute to systemic risk by impairing the ability of financial institutions to provide liquidity to the markets in times of stress. The control priority rule is designed to provide a clear and certain rule to ensure that lenders who have taken the necessary steps to establish control do not face a risk of subordination to other lenders who have not done so.

The control priority rule does not turn on an inquiry into the state of a party's awareness of potential conflicting claims because a rule under which a party's rights depended on that sort of after the fact inquiry could introduce an unacceptable measure of uncertainty. If an inquiry into awareness could provide a complete and satisfactory resolution of the problem in all cases, the priority rule of this section would have incorporated that test. The fact that it does not necessarily means that resort to other law based solely on that factor is precluded, though the question whether a control secured party induced or encouraged its financing arrangement with actual knowledge that the debtor would be violating the rights of another secured party may, in some circumstances, appropriately be treated as a factor in determining whether the control party's action is the kind of egregious conduct for which resort to other law is appropriate.

Definitional Cross References

"Broker" Section 8–102(a)(3)
"Certificated security" Section 8–102(a)(4)
"Collateral" Section 9–105(1)(c)
"Control" Section 8–106
"Debtor" Section 9–105(1)(d)
"Delivery" Section 8–301
"Entitlement holder" Section 8–102(a)(7)
"Secured party" Section 9–105(1)(m)
"Securities account" Section 8–501
"Securities intermediary" Section 8–102(a)(14)
"Security" Section 8–102(a)(15)
"Security agreement" Section 9–105(1)(*l*)
"Security certificate" Section 8–102(a)(16)
"Security entitlement" Section 8–102(a)(17)
"Security interest" Section 1–201(37)
"Uncertificated security" Section 8–102(a)(18)

§ 9116. Financial assets bought through securities intermediary; delivery of certificated security or other financial asset; security interest

(1) If a person buys a financial asset through a securities intermediary in a transaction in which the buyer is obligated to pay the purchase price to the securities intermediary at the time of the purchase, and the securities intermediary credits the financial asset to the buyer's securities account before the buyer pays the securities intermediary, the securities intermediary has a security interest in the buyer's security entitlement securing the buyer's obligation to pay. A security agreement is not required for attachment or enforceability of the security interest, and the security interest is automatically perfected.

(2) If a certificated security, or other financial asset represented by a writing that in the ordinary course of business is transferred by delivery with any necessary endorsement or assignment is delivered pursuant to an agreement between persons in the business of dealing with those securities or financial assets and the agreement calls for delivery versus payment, the person delivering the certificate or other financial asset has a security interest in the certificated security or other financial asset securing the seller's right to receive payment. A security agreement is not required for attachment or enforceability of the security interest, and the security interest is automatically perfected. *(Added by Stats.1996, c. 497 (S.B.1591), § 14, operative Jan. 1, 1997.)*

Uniform Commercial Code Comment

1. This section establishes two special rules concerning security interests in investment property in order to provide certainty in the securities settlement system.

2. Depending upon a securities intermediary's arrangements with its entitlement holders, the securities intermediary may treat the entitlement holder as entitled to the securities in question before the entitlement holder has actually made payment for them. For example, many brokers permit retail customers to pay for securities by check. The broker may not receive final payment of the check until several days after the broker has credited the customer's securities account for the securities. Thus, the customer will have acquired a security entitlement prior to payment. Subsection (1) provides that in such circumstances the securities intermediary has a security interest in the entitlement holder's security entitlement as security for the payment obligation. This is a codification and adaptation to the indirect holding system of the so-called "broker's lien," which has long been recognized in existing law. See Restatement of Security § 12. An intermediary who has a security interest under this section will have control by virtue of Section 8–106(e). The security interest has priority over conflicting security interests granted by the entitlement holder, under Section 9–115(5)(a) and (c).

3. Subsection (2) specifies the rights of persons who deliver certificated securities or other financial assets in physical form, such as money market instruments, if the agreed payment is not received. In the typical arrangement for settlement of physical securities, the seller's securities custodian will deliver the physical certificates to the buyer's securities custodian and receive a time-stamped delivery receipt. The buyer's securities custodian will examine the certificate to ensure that it is in good order, and that the delivery matches a trade in which the buyer has instructed the seller to deliver to that custodian. If all is in order, the receiving custodian will settle with the delivering custodian through whatever funds settlement system has been agreed upon or is

used by custom and usage in that market. The understanding of the trade, however, is that the delivery is conditioned upon payment, so that if payment is not made for any reason, the security will be returned to the deliverer. Subsection (2) is intended to clarify the rights of persons making deliveries in such circumstances. It specifies that the person making delivery has a security interest in the securities or other financial assets, securing the right to receive payment. No security agreement is required for attachment, and no filing or other action is required for perfection.

Definitional Cross References

"Certificated security" Section 8–102(a)(4)
"Financial asset" Section 8–102(a)(9)
"Securities account" Section 8–501
"Securities intermediary" Section 8–102(a)(14)
"Security agreement" Section 9–105(1)(*l*)
"Security entitlement" Section 8–102(a)(17)
"Security interest" Section 1–201(37)

CHAPTER 2. VALIDITY OF SECURITY AGREEMENT AND RIGHTS OF PARTIES THERETO

Section
9201. General Validity of Security Agreement.
9202. Title to Collateral Immaterial.
9203. Attachment and Enforceability of Security Interest; Proceeds; Formal Requisites.
9204. After-Acquired Property; Future Advances.
9205. Use or Disposition of Collateral Without Accounting Permissible.
9206. Agreement Not to Assert Defenses Against Assignee; Modification of Sales Warranties Where Security Agreement Exists.
9207. Rights and Duties When Collateral Is in Secured Party's Possession.
9208. Request for Statement of Account or List of Collateral.

§ 9201. General Validity of Security Agreement

Except as otherwise provided by this code a security agreement is effective according to its terms between the parties, against purchasers of the collateral and against creditors. Nothing in this division validates any charge or practice illegal under any statute or regulation thereunder governing usury, small loans, retail installment sales, or the like or extends the application of any such statute or regulation to any transaction not otherwise subject thereto. *(Stats.1963, c. 819, § 9201.)*

California Code Comment

By John A. Bohn and Charles J. Williams

Prior California Law

1. The first sentence of this section combines parts of former Civil Code § 3016.1 and 3015 (UTRA). The language of the section is patterned after section 4 of the Uniform Conditional Sales Act, a uniform act which was not adopted in California. The second sentence which states that the division does not take the place of regulatory legislation refers to such laws as:

The Retail Installment Sales Act Civil Code §§ 1801 to 1812.95.
The Automobile Sales Finance Act Civil Code §§ 2981 to 2985.4.
The Industrial Loan Law Financial Code §§ 18000 to 18858.
The Pawnbroker Law Financial Code §§ 21000 to 21209.
The Personal Property Brokers Law Financial Code §§ 22000 to 22653.
The California Small Loan Law Financial Code §§ 24000 to 24651.

The California Usury Statute, West's Annotated California Civil Code §§ 1916–1 to 1916–5.
See Official Comment. Also see Commercial Code § 9203(2).

Changes from U.C.C. (1962 Official Text)

2. This section 9–201 of the Official Text without change.

Uniform Commercial Code Comment

Prior Uniform Statutory Provisions: Section 4, Uniform Conditional Sales Act; Section 3, Uniform Trust Receipts Act.

Purposes:

This section states the general validity of a security agreement. In general the security agreement is effective between the parties; it is likewise effective against third parties. Exceptions to this general rule arise where there is a specific provision in any Article of this Act, for example, where Article 1 invalidates a disclaimer of the obligations of good faith, etc. (Section 1–102(3)), or this Article subordinates the security interest because it has not been perfected (Section 9–301) or for other reasons (see Section 9–312 on priorities) or defeats the security interest where certain types of claimants are involved (for example Section 9–307 on buyers of goods). As pointed out in the Note to Section 9–102, there is no intention that the enactment of this Article should repeal retail installment selling acts or small loan acts. Nor of course are the usury laws of any state repealed. These are mentioned in the text of Section 9–201 as examples of applicable laws, outside this Code entirely, which might invalidate the terms of a security agreement.

Cross References:

Sections 1–102(3), 9–301, 9–307 and 9–312.

Definitional Cross References:

"Collateral". Section 9–105.
"Creditor". Section 1–201.
"Party". Section 1–201.
"Purchaser". Section 1–201.
"Security agreement". Section 9–105.

Cross References

Automobile sales finance act, see Civil Code § 2981 et seq.
Buyer in ordinary course of business, see Commercial Code § 9307.
California housing and infrastructure finance agency, perfection of security interest in collateral on loans to qualified mortgage lenders, see Health and Safety Code § 51153.
Conflicting security interests, priorities, see Commercial Code § 9312.
Finance lenders law, see Financial Code § 22000 et seq.
Industrial loan law, see Financial Code § 18000 et seq.
Installment contracts, in general, see Commercial Code § 2612.
Pawnbroker law, see Financial Code § 21000 et seq.
Retail installment sales, see Civil Code § 1801 et seq.
Unperfected security interests, subordination, see Commercial Code § 9301.
Legal rate of interest, see Const. Art. 15, § 1; Civil Code § 1916–1 et seq.
Variation agreements, see Commercial Code § 1102.

§ 9202. Title to Collateral Immaterial

Each provision of this division with regard to rights, obligations and remedies applies whether title to collateral is in the secured party or in the debtor. *(Stats. 1963, c. 819, § 9202.)*

California Code Comment

By John A. Bohn and Charles J. Williams

Prior California Law

1. This section emphasizes the abandonment of the concept of title in the Code. However, the location of title can be important for purposes outside this Division. See the Official Comment.

This approach is a departure from prior California law. However, there is a difference of opinion as to the degree this approach affects prior California law.

In the California Annotations to the Uniform Commercial Code (1960), the Legislative Counsel states:

"This section would change rather drastically the law of California, since the existing law makes the location of title all-important in both defining the various devices and in determining substantive rights and priorities. Thus, in the pledge situation the pledgor retains title, as does the conditional vendor. This is so in some instances by definition. See, for example, Civil Code Section 2981(a) 1 regarding motor vehicles. Title has been equally important in determining risk of loss, and priority among creditors, etc. Under the traditional California view creation of a lien vests no legal title in the creditor (Civil Code Section 2888). In most instances, however, irrespective of the situs of title the secured creditor is protected by recording. For example, chattel mortgages (Civil Code Section 2963), conditional sales contract on certain types of personalty (Civil Code Section 2980), etc." Sixth Progress Report to the Legislature by Senate Fact Finding Committee on Judiciary (1959–1961) Part 1, The Uniform Commercial Code, p. 125.

In Project, 8 U.C.L.A.L.Rev. 806, 821 (1961) it is said that "the Code's position has more theoretical than practical significance, since the Code gives effect to many existing rules which were developed under theories of title."

Changes from U.C.C. (1962 Official Text)

2. This is section 9–202 of the Official Text without change.

Uniform Commercial Code Comment
Prior Uniform Statutory Provision:
None.
Purposes:
The rights and duties of the parties to a security transaction and of third parties are stated in this Article without reference to the location of "title" to the collateral. Thus the incidents of a security interest which secures the purchase price of goods are the same under this Article whether the secured party appears to have retained title or the debtor appears to have obtained title and then conveyed it or a lien to the secured party. This Article in no way determines which line of interpretation (title theory v. lien theory or retained title v. conveyed title) should be followed in cases where the applicability of some other rule of law depends upon who has title. Thus if a revenue law imposes a tax on the "legal" owner of goods or if a corporation law makes a vote of the stockholders prerequisite to a corporation "giving" a security interest but not if it acquires property "subject" to a security interest, this Article does not attempt to define whether the secured party is a "legal" owner or whether the transaction "gives" a security interest for the purpose of such laws. Other rules of law or the agreement of the parties determine the location of "title" for such purposes.

Petitions for reclamation brought by a secured party in his debtor's insolvency proceedings have often been granted or denied on a title theory: where the secured party has title, reclamation will be granted; where he has "merely a lien", reclamation may be denied. For the treatment of such petitions under this Article, see Point 1 of Comment to Section 9–507.

Cross References:
Sections 2–401 and 2–507.
Definitional Cross References:
"Collateral". Section 9–105.
"Debtor". Section 9–105.
"Remedy". Section 1–201.
"Rights". Section 1–201.
"Secured party". Section 9–105.

Cross References

Conditional delivery by seller, see Commercial Code § 2507.
Passing of title, reservation of security interest, see Commercial Code § 2401.
Reclamation of goods, see Commercial Code § 9507.

§ 9203. Attachment and Enforceability of Security Interest; Proceeds; Formal Requisites

(1) Subject to the provisions of Section 4210 on the security interest of a collecting bank, * * * Sections 9115 and 9116 on security interests in * * * investment property, and Section 9113 on a security interest arising under the divisions on sales and leases, a security interest is not enforceable against the debtor or third parties with respect to the collateral and does not attach unless all of the following are applicable:

(a) The collateral is in the possession of the secured party pursuant to agreement, the collateral is investment property and the secured party has control pursuant to agreement, or the debtor has signed a security agreement which contains a description of the collateral and in addition, when the security interest covers crops growing or to be grown or timber to be cut, a description of the land concerned.

(b) Value has been given.

(c) The debtor has rights in the collateral.

(2) A security interest attaches when it becomes enforceable against the debtor with respect to the collateral. Attachment occurs as soon as all of the events specified in subdivision (1) have taken place unless explicit agreement postpones the time of attaching.

(3) Unless otherwise agreed, a security agreement gives the secured party the rights to proceeds provided by Section 9306.

(4) A transaction, although subject to this division, is also subject to the Retail Installment Sales Act, Chapter 1 (commencing with Section 1801) of Title 2 of Part 4 of Division 3 of the Civil Code; the Automobile Sales Finance Act, Chapter 2b (commencing with Section 2981) of Title 14 of Part 4 of Division 3 of the Civil Code; the Industrial Loan Law, Division 7 (commencing with Section 18000) of the Financial Code; the Pawnbroker Law, Division 8 (commencing with Section 21000) of the Financial Code; the Personal Property Brokers Law, Division 9 (commencing with Section 22000) of the Financial Code; the Consumer Finance Lenders Law, Division 10 (commencing with Section 24000) of the Financial Code; the Commercial Finance Lenders Law, Division 11 (commencing with Section 26000) of the Financial Code; and the Mobilehomes–Manufactured Housing Act of 1980, Part 2 (commencing with Section 18000) of Division 13 of the Health and Safety Code, and in the case of conflict between the provisions of this division and that statute, the provisions of that statute control. Failure to comply with any applicable statute has only the effect which is specified in that statute. *(Stats.1963, c. 819, § 9203. Amended by Stats.1974, c. 977, p. 2123, § 16, eff. Jan. 1, 1976; Stats.1981, c. 724, p. 2838, § 5; Stats.1982, c. 1082, p. 3922, § 4; Stats.1983, c. 1124, § 13, operative July 1, 1984; Stats.1984, c. 927, § 9; Stats.1994, c. 668 (S.B. 1405), § 11; Stats.1996, c. 497 (S.B.1591), § 15, operative Jan. 1, 1997.)*

Uniform Commercial Code Comment

Official Reasons for 1977 Change

The added language in subsection (1) expressly makes this section subject to Section 8–321. Section 8–321(1) provides that an enforceable security interest in a security can be created only by a transfer which complies with Section 8–313(1).

It should be noted that both subsection (1) of this section and Section 8–321(2) contain the requirements that value be given and that the debtor have rights in the collateral. Subparagraph (1)(a) of this section, however, requires either possession by the secured party or a security agreement signed by the debtor. Of the various provisions of Section 8–313(1), some require possession by the secured party, some require a signed security agreement and the rest require procedures which are functionally equivalent to possession.

It is intended that compliance with some provision of Section 8–313(1) is essential to the creation of an enforceable security interest in a security and, conversely, that compliance with the requirements of subsection (1) of this section will not, of itself, suffice.

Uniform Commercial Code Comment

Prior Uniform Statutory Provision:
Section 2, Uniform Trust Receipts Act.

Purposes:

1. Subsection (1) states three basic prerequisites to the existence of a security interest: agreement, value, and collateral. In addition, the agreement must be in writing unless the collateral is in the possession of the secured party (including an agent on his behalf—see Comment 2 to Section 9–305). When all of these elements exist, the security agreement becomes enforceable between the parties and is said to "attach". Perfection of a security interest (see Section 9–303) will in many cases depend on the additional step of filing a financing statement (see Section 9–302) or possession of the collateral (Sections 9–304(1) and 9–305). Section 9–301 states who will take priority over a security interest which has attached but which was not been perfected. Subsection (2) states a rule of construction under which the security interest, unless postponed by explicit agreement, attaches automatically when the stated events have occurred.

2. As to the type of description of collateral in a written security agreement which will satisfy the requirements of this section, see Section 9–110 and Comment thereto.

In the case of crops growing or to be grown or timber to be cut the best identification is by describing the land, and subsection (1)(a) requires such a description.

3. One purpose of the formal requisites stated in subsection (1)(a) is evidentiary. The requirement of written record minimizes the possibility of future dispute as to the terms of a security agreement and as to what property stands as collateral for the obligation secured. Where the collateral is in the possession of the secured party, the evidentiary need for a written record is much less than where the collateral is in the debtor's possession; customarily, of course, as a matter of business practice the written record will be kept, but, in this Article as at common law, the writing is not a formal requisite. Subsection (1)(a), therefore, dispenses with the written agreement—and thus with signature and description—if the collateral is in the secured party's possession.

4. The definition of "security agreement" (Section 9–105) is "an agreement which creates or provides for a security interest". Under that definition the requirement of this section that the debtor sign a security agreement is not intended to reject, and does not reject, the deeply rooted doctrine that a bill of sale although absolute in form may be shown to have been in fact given as security. Under this Article as under prior law a debtor may show by parol evidence that a transfer purporting to be absolute was in fact for security and may then, on payment of the debt, assert his fundamental right to return of the collateral and execution of an acknowledgment of satisfaction.

5. The formal requisite of a writing stated in this section is not only a condition to the enforceability of a security interest against third parties, it is in the nature of a Statute of Frauds. Unless the secured party is in possession of the collateral, his security interest, absent a writing which satisfies paragraph (1)(a), is not enforceable even against the debtor, and cannot be made so on any theory of equitable mortgage or the like. If he has advanced money, he is of course a creditor and, like any creditor, is entitled after judgment to appropriate process to enforce his claim against his debtor's assets; he will not, however, have against his debtor the rights given a secured party by Part 5 of this Article on Default. The theory of equitable mortgage, insofar as it has operated to allow creditors to enforce informal security agreements against debtors, may well have developed as a necessary escape from the elaborate requirements of execution, acknowledgment and the like which the nineteenth century chattel mortgage acts vainly relied on as a deterrent to fraud. Since this Article reduces formal requisites to a minimum, the doctrine is no longer necessary or useful. More harm than good would result from allowing creditors to establish a secured status by parol evidence after they have neglected the simple formality of obtaining a signed writing.

6. Subsection (4) states that the provisions of regulatory statutes covering the field of consumer finance prevail over the provisions of this Article in case of conflict. The second sentence of the subsection is added to make clear that no doctrine of total voidness for illegality is intended: failure to comply with the applicable regulatory statute has whatever effect may be specified in that statute, but no more.

Cross References:
Sections 4–208 and 9–113.
Point 1: Section 9–110.
Point 5: Part 5.

Definitional Cross References:
"Collateral". Section 9–105.
"Debtor". Section 9–105.
"Party". Section 1–201.
"Proceeds". Section 9–306.
"Secured party". Section 9–105.
"Security agreement". Section 9–105.
"Security interest". Section 1–201.
"Signed". Section 1–201.

Cross References

Collecting banks, security interest, see Commercial Code § 4210.
Default, see Commercial Code § 9501 et seq.
Enforcement of security interest of collecting bank, see Commercial Code § 4210.
Form of mortgage of real property, see Civil Code § 2948.
Formalities of mortgage, necessity of writing, see Civil Code § 2922.
General provisions of statute of frauds not applicable to security agreements, see Commercial Code § 1206.
Security interests arising under division on sales, see Commercial Code § 9113.
Sufficiency of description, see Commercial Code § 9110.

§ 9204. After-Acquired Property; Future Advances

(1) * * * Except as provided in subdivision * * * (2) a security agreement may provide that * * * any or all obligations covered by the security agreement are to be secured by afteracquired collateral.

(2) No security interest attaches under an afteracquired property clause * * * to consumer goods other than accessions (Section 9314) * * * when given as additional security unless the debtor acquires rights in them within 10 days after the secured party gives value.

(3) Obligations covered by a security agreement may include future advances or other value whether or not the advances or value are given pursuant to commitment (subdivision (1) of Section 9105). *(Stats.1963, c. 819, § 9204. Amended by Stats.1974, c. 997, p. 2123, § 17, eff. Jan. 1, 1976.)*

California Code Comment

By John A. Bohn and Charles J. Williams

Prior California Law

1. This section is in accord with prior California law. In discussing this section The California State Bar Committee describes its effect on California law:

"Section 19204 [9204] would not change California law. After-acquired property clauses in a chattel mortgage are valid here and create a legal lien upon the property when it is acquired by the mortgagor. [*Fn.:* Bank of California v. McCoy, 23 C.A.2d 192, 72 P.2d 923 (1937).] Similarly, the assignment of accounts to be created in the future creates a legal lien upon the accounts when they come into existence. [*Fn.:* H.S. Mann Corporation v. Moody, 144 C.A.2d 310, 301 P.2d 28 (1956).] And under the Inventory Lien Law, a manufacturer or wholesale merchant may give a 'continuing lien upon all merchandise .... then owned or thereafter acquired by the borrower. ....' [*Fn.:* Cal.Sec. 3031.]" California State Bar Committee on the Commercial Code, A Special Report, The Uniform Commercial Code, 37 Calif.State Bar.J. (March–April, 1962) pp. 205, 206.

2. Subdivision (1) provides that a security interest attaches when there is an agreement, value has passed and the debtor has rights in a collateral. Official Comment 1.

3. Subdivision (2) fixes the rule in the case of certain specified classes of personal property. Official Comment 4.

4. Subdivision (3) makes both after-acquired property clauses and "cross security" clauses valid. Official Comments 2–5.

In discussing an amendment which would have deleted subdivision (3) from this section, Professors Marsh and Warren describe the effect of the deletion of this subdivision as well as the existing California law on the subject of after-acquired property clauses:

"This amendment would change the California law relating to almost every type of personal property security device. An after-acquired property clause in a chattel mortgage is valid in California. CC § 2883; Bank of California v. McCoy, 23 C.A.2d 192, 72 P.2d 923 (1937); cf. CC § 2977. An after-acquired property clause in an assignment of accounts receivable is valid in California. H.S. Mann Corporation v. Moody, 144 C.A.2d 310, 301 P.2d 28 (1956). An after-acquired property clause in an inventory lien agreement is valid in California, provided that the merchandise 'is from time to time .... designated in one or more separate written statements dated and signed by the borrower and delivered to the lender.' CC § 3031.

"We see no reason for thus changing the California law or for invalidating all after-acquired property clauses in connection with personal property security agreements." Sixth Progress Report to the Legislature by Senate Fact Finding Committee on Judiciary (1959–1961) Part 1, The Uniform Commercial Code, p. 558.

5. Under former Civil Code § 2883, an agreement could be made which would create a lien upon property not yet acquired or not yet in existence. The lien would attach when the mortgagor acquired an interest in the property actually in existence. There were special provisions relating to livestock and other animate chattels which provided for the equivalent of a purchase money mortgage. Former Civil Code §§ 2976–2977.

This subdivision is in accord with prior judicial decisions which recognized after-acquired property clauses. Phillips v. Byers, 189 Cal. 665, 209 Pac. 557 (1922); In Re Los Angeles Mfg. Co., 7 F.Supp. 567 (S.D.Cal.1933); 8 UCLA L.Rev. 806, 861–862.

6. Subdivision (4) sets forth one exception to the after-acquired property rule stated in subdivisions (1) and (3). The exception as to crops in subdivision (4)(a) of the Official Text is deleted in the California version. See California Code Comment 9.

7. Subdivision (5) covers what is known as "future advances". See Official Comment 8.

Under California law future advances were recognized as a part of the pledge transaction. Citizens' Sav. Bank of San Diego v. Mack, 180 Cal. 246, 180 Pac. 618 (1919); 8 UCLA L.Rev. 806, 854. Subdivision (5) continues the prior California rule.

The point is made that in order for the secured party to be protected in all cases, there must be a prior agreement to the maximum amount of future advances. Otherwise an intervening right will prevail over a secured party who makes advances with knowledge of the intervening right. 8 UCLA L.Rev. 806, 854.

Prior California chattel mortgage law also recognized the validity of future advances in the idea of "cross-security" under which collateral acquired anytime could secure advances whenever made. Official Comment 5.

Changes from U.C.C. (1962 Official Text)

8. In subdivision (2) California has deleted from the end of that subdivision the phrase "in timber until it is cut".

This change was made to continue the prior California law regarding financing timber contracts.

9. Paragraph (a) of subdivision (4) of the Official Text was deleted in California. It provides:

"To crops which become such more than one year after the security agreement is executed except that a security interest in crops which is given in conjunction with a lease or a land purchase or improvement transaction evidenced by a contract, mortgage or deed of trust may if so agreed attach to crops to be grown on the land concerned during the period of such real estate transaction."

Paragraph (a) was deleted in order to avoid any changes in California law. The following excerpt from the Marsh and Warren Report explains prior California law and questions the reason for the provision in the original text:

"This clause is contrary to the present California law. Although Section 2977 of the Civil Code specifically permits a chattel mortgage of afteracquired property only in the case of 'live stock, or other animate chattels', Section 2883 of the Civil Code provides that 'An agreement may be made to create a lien upon property not yet acquired by the party agreeing to give the lien, or not yet in existence. In such case, the lien agreed for attaches from the time when the party agreeing to give it acquires an interest in the thing, to the extent of such interest.' This Section was construed in Bank of California v. McCoy, 23 C.A.2d 192, 72 P.2d 923 (1937), generally to validate afteracquired property clauses in chattel mortgages, in a transaction occurring before the enactment of Section 2977.

"No reason is assigned by the drafters of the Code for the invalidation of mortgages of future crops which are to be grown more than one year after the execution of the agreement. .... It is believed that the retention of this clause would seriously disrupt the established method of financing a number of crops in this State." Sixth Progress Report to the Legislature by Senate Fact Finding Committee on Judiciary (1959–1961) Part 1, The Uniform Commercial Code, p. 559.

In subdivision (4)(b) the words "or replacements" was added after the word "accessions".

No reason appears for this California change from the Official Text.

Uniform Commercial Code Comment
Prior Uniform Statutory Provision:
None.
Purposes:
1. Subsection (1) makes clear that a security interest arising by virtue of an after-acquired property clause has equal status with a security interest in collateral in which the debtor has rights at the time value is given under the security agreement. That is to say: the security interest in after-acquired property is not merely an "equitable" interest; no further action by the secured party—such as the taking of a supplemental agreement covering the new collateral—is required. This does not however mean that the interest is proof against subordination or defeat: Section 9–108 should be consulted on when a security interest in after-acquired collateral is not security for antecedent debt, and section 9–312(3) and (4) on when such a security interest may be subordinated to a conflicting purchase money security interest in the same collateral.

2. This Article accepts the principle of a "continuing general lien". It rejects the doctrine—of which the judicial attitude toward after-acquired property interests was one expression—that there is reason to invalidate as a matter of law what has been variously called the floating charge, the free-handed mortgage and the lien on a shifting stock. This Article validates a security interest in the debtor's existing and future assets, even though (see Section 9–205) the debtor has liberty to use or dispose of collateral without being required to account for proceeds or substitute new collateral. (See further, however, Section 9–306 on Proceeds and Comment thereto.)

The widespread nineteenth century prejudice against the floating charge was based on a feeling, often inarticulate in the opinions, that a commercial borrower should not be allowed to encumber all his assets present and future, and that for the protection not only of the borrower but of his other creditors a cushion of free assets should be preserved. That inarticulate premise has much to recommend it. This Article decisively rejects it not on the ground that it was wrong in policy but on the ground that it was not effective. In pre-Code law there was a multiplication of security devices designed to avoid the policy: field warehousing, trust receipts, factor's lien acts and so on. The cushion of free assets was not preserved. In almost every state is was possible before the Code for the borrower to give a lien on everything he held or would have. There have no doubt been sufficient economic reasons for the change. This Article, in expressly validating the floating charge,

§ 9204

merely recognizes an existing state of things. The substantive rules of law set forth in the balance of the Article are designed to achieve the protection of the debtor and the equitable resolution of the conflicting claims of creditors which the old rules no longer give.

Notice that the question of assignment of future accounts is treated like any other case of after-acquired property: no periodic list of accounts is required by this Act. Where less than all accounts are assigned such a list may of course be necessary to permit identification of the particular accounts assigned.

3. Subsection (1) has been already referred to in connection with after-acquired property. It also serves to validate the so-called "cross-security" clause under which collateral acquired at any time may secure advances whenever made.

4. Subsection (2) limits the operation of the after-acquired property clause against consumers. No such interest can be claimed as additional security in consumer goods (defined in Section 9–109), except accessions (see Section 9–314), acquired more than ten days after the giving of value.

5. Under subsection (3) collateral may secure future as well as present advances when the security agreement so provides. At common law and under chattel mortgage statutes there seems to have been a vaguely articulated prejudice against future advance agreements comparable to the prejudice against after-acquired property interests. Although only a very few jurisdictions went to the length of invalidating interests claimed by virtue of future advances, judicial limitations severely restricted the usefulness of such arrangements. A common limitation was that an interest claimed in collateral existing at the time the security transaction was entered into for advances made thereafter was good only to the extent that the original security agreement specified the amount of such later advances and even the times at which they should be made. In line with the policy of this Article toward after-acquired property interests this subsection validates the future advance interest, provided only that the obligation be covered by the security agreement.

The effect of after-acquired property and future advance clauses in the security agreement should not be confused with the use of financing statements in notice filing. The references to after-acquired property clauses and future advance clauses in Section 9–204 are limited to security agreements. This section follows Section 9–203, the section requiring a written security agreement, and its purpose is to make clear that confirmatory agreements are not necessary where the basic agreement has the clauses mentioned. This section has no reference to the operation of financing statements. The filing of a financing statement is effective to perfect security interests as to which the other required elements for perfection exist, whether the security agreement involved is one existing at the date of filing with an after-acquired property clause or a future advance clause, or whether the applicable security agreement is executed later. Indeed, Section 9–402(1) expressly contemplates that a financing statement may be filed when there is no security agreement. There is no need to refer to after-acquired property or future advances in the financing statement.

As in the case of interests in after-acquired collateral, a security interest based on future advances may be subordinated to conflicting interests in the same collateral. See Sections 9–301(4); 9–307(3); 9–312(3), (4), and (7).

Cross References:
  Point 1: Sections 9–108 and 9–312.
  Point 2: Sections 9–205 and 9–306.
  Point 4: Sections 9–109 and 9–314.
  Point 5: Sections 9–301(4); 9–307(3); 9–312(3), (4), and (7).
Definitional Cross References:
  "Account". Section 9–106.
  "Agreement". Section 1–201.
  "Collateral". Section 9–105.
  "Consumer goods". Section 9–109.
  "Contract". Section 1–201.
  "Debtor". Section 9–105.
  "Purchase". Section 1–201.
  "Pursuant to commitment". Section 9–105.
  "Rights". Section 1–201.
  "Secured party". Section 9–105.
  "Security agreement". Section 9–105.
  "Security interest". Section 1–201.
  "Value". Section 1–201.

Cross References

Accessions, see Commercial Code § 9314.
Antecedent debt, after-acquired property as security, see Commercial Code § 9108.
Contract to create a lien for obligations not in existence, see Civil Code § 2884.
Crop production loan, priority, see Commercial Code § 9312.
Definitions, see Commercial Code § 9109.
Disposition of collateral, secured party's rights, see Commercial Code § 9306.
Enforceability of security interest, requisites, see Commercial Code § 9203.
Lien on property not yet acquired, see Civil Code § 2883.
Perfection of security interest, necessity of filing, see Commercial Code § 9302.
Priorities among conflicting security interests in the same collateral, see Commercial Code § 9312.
Purchase money security interest, priority, see Commercial Code § 9312.
Sufficiency of description, see Commercial Code § 9110.
Title subsequently acquired by mortgagor, see Civil Code § 2930.
Unperfected security interests, subordination, see Commercial Code § 9301.
Use or disposition of collateral without accounting, see Commercial Code § 9205.

§ 9205. Use or Disposition of Collateral Without Accounting Permissible

A security interest is not invalid or fraudulent against creditors by reason of liberty in the debtor to use, commingle or dispose of all or part of the collateral (including returned or repossessed goods) or to collect or compromise accounts * * * or chattel paper, or to accept the return of goods or make repossessions, or to use, commingle or dispose of proceeds, or by reason of the failure of the secured party to require the debtor to account for proceeds or replace collateral. This section does not relax the requirements of possession where perfection of a security interest depends upon possession of the collateral by the secured party or by a bailee. (Stats.1963, c. 819, § 9205. Amended by Stats.1974, c. 997, p. 2124, § 18, eff. Jan. 1, 1976.)

California Code Comment

By John A. Bohn and Charles J. Williams

Prior California Law

1. This section validates the "floating lien" recognized in English and Canadian law but rejected by the case of Benedict v. Ratner, 268 U.S. 353, 45 S.Ct. 566, 69 L.Ed. 991 (D.C.N.Y.1925). Official Comment 1.

The floating lien permits the debtor to commingle or dispose of all or part of the collateral without having to account for proceeds or to substitute new collateral.

2. The effect of this section and its impact on prior California law is described by the California State Bar Committee:

"The second much discussed topic is the so-called 'floating lien,' a term borrowed from the so-called 'floating charge' of English and Canadian law. [Fn.: See Gower, Modern Company Law 389 et seq. (2d Ed. 1957)] It denotes a lien on a changeable mass of items, such as accounts receivable or inventory. Such a lien is not conceived of as attaching to any particular item, but as hovering or 'floating' over the mass as it exists from time to time. The owner is free to exercise complete dominion over the mass until insolvency or foreclosure. The lien becomes fully effective on whatever items are present at the moment of insolvency or foreclosure.

"Two rules have retarded or prevented a similar development in American law. One is the rule in some states that an after-acquired property clause in a chattel mortgage creates only an 'equitable' lien, not perfected against the mortgagor's unsecured creditors until the mortgagee takes possession of the property. [*Fn.*: 1 Jones, Chattel Mortgages and Conditional Sales sec. 138 (6th ed. 1933)] This rule almost always makes a lien on the after-acquired property invalid in bankruptcy as a preference. [*Fn.*: Curtis v. Knox, 254 F.2d 433 (C.A.Ill.1958)]

"The second is the famous rule of Benedict v. Ratner, [*Fn.*: 268 U.S. 353, 45 S.Ct. 566, 69 L.Ed. 991 (D.C.N.Y.1925)] followed in many states. The case itself held that under New York law a clause in an assignment of accounts receivable giving the assignor power to dispose of the property subject to the lien, without using the proceeds to pay the debt or replace the collateral, rendered the assignment wholly void. Subsequent cases held that under this rule, even if the chattel mortgage or account assignment required accounting by the mortgagor or assignor for the proceeds, a failure by the mortgagee or assignee adequately to 'police' the carrying out of this agreement also rendered the entire transaction void. [*Fn.*: Lee v. State Bank & Trust Co., 38 F.2d 45 (2d Cir. 1930)] The rule of Benedict v. Ratner does not prevent the same result as a 'floating lien' but it requires elaborate measures for partial repayment of the loan upon each sale of an inventory item or collection of an account, and the relending of the same money upon the acquisition of new inventory or the creation of new accounts. [*Fn.*: See, for a discussion of such measures, the opinion of Judge Medina in In Re New Haven Clock & Watch Co., 253 F.2d 577 (2d Cir. 1958)]

"The Code would sweep away these obstacles to a 'floating lien' by generally validating after-acquired property clauses (section 19204) [9204], and by abrogating the doctrine of Benedict v. Ratner (section 19205) [9205]. Section 19204 [9204] would not change California law. After-acquired property clauses in a chattel mortgage are valid here and create a legal lien upon the property when it is acquired by the mortgagor. [*Fn.*: (Bank of California v. McCoy, 23 C.A.2d 192, 72 P.2d 923 (1937))] Similarly, the assignment of accounts to be created in the future creates a legal lien upon the accounts when they come into existence. [*Fn.*: H. S. Mann Corporation v. Moody, 144 C.A.2d 310, 301 P.2d 28 (1956)] And under the Inventory Lien Law, a manufacturer or wholesale merchant may give a 'continuing lien upon all merchandise . . . then owned or thereafter acquired by the borrower. . . .' [*Fn.*: Cal.Civ.Code, sec. 3031] The California Supreme Court has never ruled on whether the rule of Benedict v. Ratner is law in this state. [*Fn.*: Cf. Matter of Oest Fruit Company, 12 Am.Bkr.Rpts. (n.s.) 678 (N.D.Cal.1928)] Hence, it is not clear that section 19205 would change California law. Only as to the inventory of a retail merchant, and then only as to inventory not now covered by Civil Code section 3014.5, would the Code clearly change California law." California State Bar Committee on the Commercial Code, A Special Report, The Uniform Commercial Code, 37 Calif.State Bar J. (March–April 1962) pp. 204–206.

Changes from U.C.C. (1962 Official Text)
2. This is the Official Text without change.

Uniform Commercial Code Comment
Prior Uniform Statutory Provision:
None.

Purposes:
1. This Article expressly validates the floating charge or lien on a shifting stock. (See Sections 9–201, 9–204, and Comment to Section 9–204.) This section provides that a security interest is not invalid or fraudulent by reason of liberty in the debtor to dispose of the collateral without being required to account for proceeds or substitute new collateral. It repeals the rule of Benedict v. Ratner, 268 U.S. 353, 45 S.Ct. 566, 69 L.Ed. 991 (1925), and other cases which held such arrangements void as a matter of law because the debtor was given unfettered dominion or control over the collateral. The principal effect of the Benedict rule has been, not to discourage or eliminate security transactions in inventory and accounts receivable—on the contrary such transactions have vastly increased in volume—but rather to force financing arrangements in this field toward a self-liquidating basis. Furthermore, several lower court cases drew implications from Justice Brandeis' opinion in Benedict v. Ratner which required lenders operating in this field to observe a number of needless and costly formalities: for example it was thought necessary for the debtor to make daily remittances to the lender of all collections received, even though the amount remitted is immediately returned to the debtor in order to keep the loan at an agreed level.

2. The Benedict rule was, in the accounts receivable field, repealed in many of the state accounts receivable statutes enacted after 1943, and, in the inventory field, by some of the factor's lien statutes. (Benedict v. Ratner purported to state the law of New York and not a rule of federal bankruptcy law. Since its acceptance is a matter of state law, it can of course be rejected by state statute.)

3. The requirement of "policing" is the substance of the Benedict rule. While this section repeals Benedict in matters of form, the filing requirements (Section 9–302) give other creditors the opportunity to ascertain from public sources whether property of their debtor or prospective debtor is subject to secured claims, and the provisions about proceeds (Section 9–306(4)) enable creditors to claim collections which were made by the debtor more than 10 days before insolvency proceedings and commingled or deposited in a bank account before institution of the insolvency proceedings. The repeal of the Benedict rule under this section must be read in the light of these provisions.

4. Other decisions reaching results like that in the Benedict case, but relating to other aspects of dominion (of which Lee v. State Bank & Trust Co., 54 F.2d 518 (2d Cir.1931), is an example) are likewise rejected.

5. Nothing in Section 9–205 prevents such "policing" or dominion as the secured party and the debtor may agree upon; business and not legal reasons will determine the extent to which strict accountability, segregation of collections, daily reports and the like will be employed.

6. The last sentence is added to make clear that the section does not mean that the holder of an unfiled security interest, whose perfection depends on possession of the collateral by the secured party or by a bailee (such as a field warehouseman), can allow the debtor access to and control over the goods without thereby losing his perfected interest. The common law rules on the degree and extent of possession which are necessary to perfect a pledge interest or to constitute a valid field warehouse are not relaxed by this or any other section of this Article.

Cross References:
Point 1: Sections 9–201 and 9–204.
Point 3: Sections 9–302 and 9–306(4).
Point 6: Sections 9–304 and 9–305.

Definitional Cross References:
"Account". Section 9–106.
"Chattel paper". Section 9–105.
"Collateral". Section 9–105.
"Creditor". Section 1–201.
"Debtor". Section 9–105.
"Goods". Section 9–105.
"Proceeds". Section 9–306.
"Secured party". Section 9–105.
"Security interest". Section 1–201.

Cross References
Disposition of collateral, secured party's rights, see Commercial Code § 9306.
Fraudulent conveyances, see Civil Code § 3439 et seq.
Insolvency of debtor, secured party's interest in proceeds, see Commercial Code § 9306.
Instruments, documents and goods covered by documents, perfection of security interests, see Commercial Code § 9304.
Perfection of security interest, necessity of filing, see Commercial Code § 9302.
Possession by secured party, perfection of security interest, see Commercial Code § 9305.
Sale of property covered by security agreement and willful failure to pay secured party and appropriations to own use as embezzlement, see Penal Code § 504b.
Security agreements, see Commercial Code §§ 9201, 9204.

§ 9206. Agreement Not to Assert Defenses Against Assignee; Modification of Sales Warranties Where Security Agreement Exists

(1) Subject to any statute or decision which establishes a different rule for buyers or lessees of consumer

§ 9206

goods, an agreement by a buyer or lessee that he will not assert against an assignee any claim or defense which he may have against the seller or lessor is enforceable by an assignee who takes his assignment for value, in good faith and without notice of a claim or defense, except as to defenses of a type which may be asserted against a holder in due course of a negotiable instrument under the division on * * * negotiable instruments (Division 3). A buyer who as part of one transaction signs both a negotiable instrument and a security agreement makes such an agreement.

(2) When a seller retains a purchase money security interest in goods the division on sales (Division 2) governs the sale and any disclaimer, limitation or modification of the seller's warranties. *(Stats.1963, c. 819, § 9206. Amended by Stats.1974, c. 997, p. 2124, § 19, eff. Jan. 1, 1976; Stats.1994, c. 668 (S.B.1405), § 12.)*

California Code Comment
By John A. Bohn and Charles J. Williams

Prior California Law

1. This section is based on section 2 of the Uniform Conditional Sales Act. This uniform act was not adopted in California.

2. Subdivision (1) changes prior California law.

Before the adoption of the Commercial Code in California, the waiver of a defense clause was invalid upon the ground that it created a new form of negotiable instrument by contract. American National Bank of San Francisco v. A. G. Sommerville, Inc., 191 Cal. 364, 216 Pac. 376 (1923); Banco Mercantil S.A. v. Sauls Inc., 140 Cal.App.2d 316, 295 P.2d 55 (1956); 8 UCLA L.Rev. 806, 970–972; Official Comment 1.

In effect subdivision (1) makes the contract negotiable to the extent that personal defenses are cut off.

Because the section by its express terms is subject to a statute which establishes a different rule for the buyer-consumer, this change in prior California law is not as drastic as would first appear. In non-consumer transactions the rule is as stated in this section. In the case of consumer transactions the Unruh Act raises a question of interpretation:

"However, the Unruh Act raises a question as to the continued efficacy of this rule in California. CC § 1804.1 prohibits in any retail installment sale contract subject to that act a provision by which 'The buyer agrees not to assert against a seller a claim or defense arising out of the sale or agrees not to assert against an assignee such a claim or defense *other than as provided in Section 1804.2.*' (Emphasis supplied.) CC § 1804.2 provides that 'No right or defense arising out of a retail installment sale which the buyer has against the seller, *and which would be cut off by assignment*, shall be cut off by assignment of the contract to any third party whether or not he acquires the contract in good faith and for value unless the assignee gives notice of the assignment to the buyer as provided in this Section and within 15 days of the mailing of such notice receives no written notice of the facts giving rise to the claim or defense of the buyer.' (Emphasis supplied.)

"There are two possible interpretations of these provisions of the Unruh Act: (1) They are intended to deal only with defenses which could be cut off by assignment under the *Sommerville* case, i.e., defenses arising *subsequent* to notice of the assignment (CC § 1459), and merely regulate the type of notice necessary to cut off such subsequent defenses. (2) They are intended to validate generally waiver of defenses clauses, and thus overrule the *Sommerville* case, subject only to the notice provisions of the Act. See 7 UCLA Law Rev. 618, at 744–758 (1960). It would seem that the first interpretation is the more reasonable one, in view of the underscored language in CC § 1804.2, above, and in view of the fact that this legislation was designed to protect installment buyers, not to destroy the protection which they already had under the California decisions." Marsh and Warren Report, Sixth Progress Report to the Legislature by Senate Fact Finding Committee on Judiciary (1959–1961) Part 1, The Uniform Commercial Code, pp. 560, 561.

3. Subdivision (2) is based upon section 2 of the Uniform Conditional Sales Act. It clarifies the relationship between Divisions 2 and 9.

Changes from U.C.C. (1962 Official Text)

4. In subdivision (1) wherever the word "buyer" appears the California version adds the words "or lessee". This was done to assure that the same rules would apply to the rental as to the sale of property. Marsh and Warren Report, Sixth Progress Report to the Legislature by Senate Fact Finding Committee on Judiciary (1959–1961), Part 1, The Uniform Commercial Code, pp. 596–597.

5. In subdivision (1) of the Official Text the phrase "or decision" which appears after the word "statute" has been deleted from the California version. This change was the subject of intensive consideration by the Bar, the Bankers and Professors Marsh and Warren. The Report of the Subcommittee of the State Bar stated that:

"The Unruh Act is an existing statute which establishes to some extent a different rule for buyers of consumer goods. The retention of the words 'or decision' is an invitation to judicial legislation and they should not be retained, especially in view of the fact that a statute on the subject already exists." Sixth Progress Report to the Legislature by Senate Fact Finding Committee on Judiciary (1959–1961) Part 1, The Uniform Commercial Code, p. 398.

Although the Bankers Committee agreed in substance with this, Professors Marsh and Warren stated:

"The effect of the deletion of the words 'or decision' in this subsection would be a clear legislative reversal of the *Sommerville* decision and a general validation of waiver of defenses clauses, subject only to the notice requirements of the Unruh Act in transactions subject to that Act. The subsection as it now stands, of course, constitutes a reversal of that decision with respect to all buyers except consumers. To this extent the clause would seem to be justified, since consumers are the ones who are most in need of protection in connection with provisions of this nature.

"We do not believe that a reversal of the *Sommerville* case in toto is justified. The financing agency which regularly purchases the paper of a retail merchant is the one which ought to bear the risk of his fraud or failure to deliver the consideration, and not the casual purchaser who buys from him in a single transaction and undoubtedly does not understand the legal effect of a waiver of defenses clause in the form contract which he signs. It is perfectly obvious that the invalidation of such clauses for many years in this State has imposed no obstacle to installment selling. . . . ." Sixth Progress Report to the Legislature by Senate Fact Finding Committee on Judiciary (1959–1961) Part 1, The Uniform Commercial Code, p. 561.

After further consideration and in light of suggestions made by the State Bar Committee and the Bankers Committee, Professor Marsh reaffirmed his earlier position. Sixth Progress Report to the Legislature by Senate Fact Finding Committee on Judiciary (1959–1961) Part 1, The Uniform Commercial Code, p. 643.

The further comments by the State Bar Committee following Professor Marsh's comments stated the basis for its earlier opinion that this change should be made:

"In drafting the Official Draft, the words 'any statute *or decision*' were included for the purpose of recognizing, in a Uniform Act, that some States might establish a special rule, by statute, regulating the waiver of defenses by buyers or consumer goods, whereas other States might establish such a rule by decision.

"California is a State which has established a special rule by statute and the words 'or decision' are not appropriate to the California Draft.

"The retention of such language in the California Draft creates uncertainty whether a decision inconsistent with the statute is valid, which is an unfortunate result.

"For these reasons, we feel that the words 'or decision' should be deleted." Sixth Progress Report to the Legislature by Senate Fact Finding Committee on Judiciary (1959–1961) Part 1, The Uniform Commercial Code, p. 648.

Uniform Commercial Code Comment

Prior Uniform Statutory Provision:

Section 2, Uniform Conditional Sales Act.

Purposes:

1. Clauses are frequently inserted in installment purchase contracts under which the conditional vendee agrees not to assert defenses against an assignee of the contract. These clauses have led to litigation and

their present status under the case law is in confusion. In some jurisdictions they have been held void as attempts to create negotiable instruments outside the framework of Article 3 or on grounds of public policy; in others they have been allowed to operate to cut off at least defenses based on breach of warranty. Under subsection (1) such clauses in a security agreement are validated outside the consumer field, but only as to defenses which could be cut off if a negotiable instrument were used. This limitation is important since if the clauses were allowed to have full effect as typically drafted, they would operate to cut off real as well as personal defenses. The execution of a negotiable note in connection with a security agreement is given like effect as the execution of an agreement containing a waiver of defense clause. The same rules are made applicable to leases as to security agreements, whether or not the lease is intended as security.

2. This Article takes no position on the controversial question whether a buyer of consumer goods may effectively waive defenses by contractual clause or by execution of a negotiable note. In some states such waivers have been invalidated by statute. In other states the course of judicial decision has rendered them ineffective or unreliable—courts have found that the assignee is not protected against the buyer's defense by a clause in the contract or that the holder of a note, by reason of his too close connection with the underlying transaction, does not have the rights of a holder in due course. This Article neither adopts nor rejects the approach taken in such statutes and decisions, except that the validation of waivers in subsection (1) is expressly made "subject to any statute or decision" which may restrict the waiver's effectiveness in the case of a buyer of consumer goods.

3. Subsection (2) makes clear, as did Section 2 of the Uniform Conditional Sales Act, that purchase money security transactions are sales, and warranty rules for sales are applicable. It also prevents a buyer from inadvertently abandoning his warranties by a "no warranties" term in the security agreement when warranties have already been created under the sales arrangement. Where the sales arrangement and the purchase money security transaction are evidenced by only one writing, that writing may disclaim, limit or modify warranties to the extent permitted by Article 2.

Cross References:
  Point 1: Section 3–305.
  Point 2: Section 9–203(2).
  Point 3: Sections 2–102 and 2–316.

Definitional Cross References:
  "Agreement". Section 1–201.
  "Consumer goods". Section 9–109.
  "Good faith". Section 1–201.
  "Goods". Section 9–105.
  "Holder". Section 1–201.
  "Holder in due course". Sections 3–302 and 9–105.
  "Negotiable instrument". Section 3–104.
  "Notice". Section 1–201.
  "Purchase money security interest". Section 9–107.
  "Sale". Sections 2–106 and 9–105.
  "Security agreement". Section 9–105.
  "Security interest". Section 1–201.
  "Value". Section 1–201.

Cross References

Defenses against assignee, see Commercial Code § 9318.
Enforceability of security interest, see Commercial Code § 9203.
Exclusion or modification of warranties, see Commercial Code § 2316.
Holder in due course, rights, see Commercial Code § 3305.
Sales intended to operate only as security transactions, see Commercial Code § 2102.

§ 9207. Rights and Duties When Collateral Is in Secured Party's Possession

(1) A secured party must use reasonable care in the custody and preservation of collateral in his possession. In the case of an instrument or chattel paper reasonable care includes taking necessary steps to preserve rights against prior parties unless otherwise agreed.

(2) Unless otherwise agreed, when collateral is in the secured party's possession

(a) Reasonable expenses (including the cost of any insurance and payment of taxes or other charges) incurred in the custody, preservation, use or operation of the collateral are chargeable to the debtor and are secured by the collateral;

(b) The risk of accidental loss or damage is on the debtor to the extent of any deficiency in any effective insurance coverage;

(c) The secured party may hold as additional security any increase or profits (except money) received from the collateral, but money so received, unless remitted to the debtor, shall be applied in reduction of the secured obligation;

(d) The secured party must keep the collateral identifiable but fungible collateral may be commingled;

(e) The secured party may repledge the collateral upon terms which do not impair the debtor's right to redeem it.

(3) A secured party is liable for any loss caused by his failure to meet any obligation imposed by the preceding subdivisions but does not lose his security interest.

(4) A secured party may use or operate the collateral for the purpose of preserving the collateral or its value or pursuant to the order of a court of appropriate jurisdiction or, except in the case of consumer goods, in the manner and to the extent provided in the security agreement. *(Stats.1963, c. 819, § 9207.)*

California Code Comment

By John A. Bohn and Charles J. Williams

Prior California Law

1. This section imposes upon a secured party in possession of the security the duty to use reasonable care to preserve it.

This restates common law rules. The section also corresponds to principles contained in the Restatement of Security. Official Comments 1–4. In the California Annotations To The Proposed Uniform Commercial Code (1960), the Legislative Counsel correlates the rules of this section with the Restatement of Security:

"There is a general correlation between this section and the American Law Institute Restatement of Security, as follows: Subdivision (1), Sections 17 and 18 of the Restatement; subdivision (2), Section 14; subdivision (2)(a), Sections 25 and 26; subdivision (2)(b), Sections 17 and 18 of the Restatement.

"As to subdivision (2)(c), any increase of property is likewise subject to the pledge. (See Civil Code Section 2989.) The rule is the same as to chattel mortgages of livestock (Civil Code Section 2976), and see Sections 3, 27, and 46 of the Restatement.

"As to subdivision (2)(e) see Restatement of Security, Section 22.

"As to subdivision (3) see Restatement of Security, Section 20.

"Subdivision (4) is new." Sixth Progress Report to the Legislature by Senate Fact Finding Committee on Judiciary (1959–1961) Part 1, The Uniform Commercial Code, p. 126.

The effect of this section upon prior California law is described in 8 UCLA L.Rev. 806, 968:

"While this section does not depart from the present California law, [*Fn.*: See Ferro v. Citizens Nat. Trust & Sav. Bank, 44 Cal.2d 401, 282 P.2d 849 (1955); Hudgens v. Chamberlain, 161 Cal. 710, 120 Pac. 422 (1911).] it is more explicit in stating the rights and duties of the secured party. Heretofore the statutory provisions provided that ordinary care must be used in preservation of the property, [*Fn.*: Cal.Civ.Code §§ 1714, 1852, 2997] and the courts held that the secured party in possession kept the collateral as trustee for the benefit of the debtor. [*Fn.*: Cases cited note 1009 supra.] Any special rights and duties were left to the terms of the security agreement."

2. Subdivision (2) describes standards which control the conduct of the parties in the absence of agreement. Official Comment 2.

Changes from U.C.C. (1962 Official Text)

3. This is section 9–207 of the Official Text without change.

Uniform Commercial Code Comment

Prior Uniform Statutory Provision:

None.

Purposes:

1. Subsection (1) states the duty to preserve collateral imposed on a pledge at common law. See Restatement of Security, §§ 17, 18. In many cases a secured party having collateral in his possession may satisfy this duty by notifying the debtor of any act which must be taken and allowing the debtor to perform such act himself. If the secured party himself takes action, his reasonable expenses may be added to the secured obligation.

Under Section 1–102(3) the duty to exercise reasonable care may not be disclaimed by agreement, although under that section the parties remain free to determine by agreement, in any manner not manifestly unreasonable, what shall constitute reasonable care in a particular case.

2. Subsection (2) states rules, which follow common law precedents, and which apply, unless there is agreement otherwise, in typical situations during the period while the secured party is in possession of the collateral.

3. The right of a secured party holding instruments or documents to have them indorsed or transferred to him or his order is dealt with in the relevant sections of Articles 3 (Commercial Paper), 7 (Warehouse Receipts, Bills of Lading and Other Documents) and 8 (Investment Securities). (Sections 3–201, 7–506, 8–304(d).) Amendments approved by the Permanent Editorial Board for Uniform Commercial Code November 4, 1995.

4. This section applies when the secured party has possession of the collateral before default, as a pledgee, and also when he has taken possession of the collateral after default. See Section 9–501(1) and (2). Subsection (4) permits operation of the collateral in the circumstances stated, and subsection (2)(a) authorizes payment of or provision for expenses of such operation. Agreements providing for such operation are common in trust indentures securing corporate bonds and are particularly important when the collateral is a going business. Such an agreement cannot of course disclaim the duty of care established by subsection (1), nor can it waive or modify the rights of the debtor contrary to Section 9–501(3).

Cross References:

Point 1: Section 1–102(3).

Point 3: Sections 3–201, 7–506 and 8–304(d). Amendments approved by the Permanent Editorial Board for Uniform Commercial Code November 4, 1995.

Point 4: Section 9–501(2) and Part 5.

Definitional Cross References:

"Chattel paper". Section 9–105.
"Collateral". Section 9–105.
"Debtor". Section 9–105.
"Instrument". Section 9–105.
"Money". Section 1–201.
"Party". Section 1–201.
"Secured party". Section 9–105.
"Security interest". Section 1–201.

Cross References

Debtor's remedies after default, see Commercial Code § 9501.
Default, in general, see Commercial Code § 9501 et seq.
Documents of title, compelling indorsement, see Commercial Code § 7506.
Investment securities, compelling indorsement, see Commercial Code § 8307.
Obligations of depositary, see Civil Code § 1822 et seq.
Owner as entitled to accessions of property, see Civil Code § 732.
Responsibility for willful acts and negligence, see Civil Code § 1714.
Right to increase of thing lent, see Civil Code § 1885.
Title to products of thing hired, see Civil Code § 1926.
Transfer of security interest in commercial paper, see Commercial Code § 3201.
Unauthorized pledge by warehouseman or carrier, see Penal Code § 581.
Variation agreements, see Commercial Code § 1102.

§ 9208. Request for Statement of Account or List of Collateral

(1) A debtor may sign a statement indicating what he believes to be the aggregate amount of unpaid indebtedness as of a specified date and may send it to the secured party with a request that the statement be approved or corrected and returned to the debtor. When the security agreement or any other record kept by the secured party identifies the collateral a debtor may similarly request the secured party to approve or correct a list of the collateral.

(2) The secured party must comply with such a request within two weeks after receipt by sending a written correction or approval. If the secured party claims a security interest in all of a particular type of collateral owned by the debtor he may indicate that fact in his reply and need not approve or correct an itemized list of such collateral. If the secured party without reasonable excuse fails to comply he is liable for any loss caused to the debtor thereby; and if the debtor has properly included in his request a good faith statement of the obligation or a list of the collateral or both the secured party may claim a security interest only as shown in the statement against persons misled by his failure to comply. If he no longer has an interest in the obligation or collateral at the time the request is received he must disclose the name and address of any successor in interest known to him and he is liable for any loss caused to the debtor as a result of failure to disclose. A successor in interest is not subject to this section until a request is received by him.

(3) A debtor is entitled to such a statement once every six months without charge. The secured party may require payment of a charge not exceeding ten dollars ($10) for each additional statement furnished.

(4) If the secured party is an organization maintaining branches or branch offices the requests herein provided for shall be sent to the branch or branch office at which the security transaction was entered into or at which the debtor is to make payment of his obligation, and the secured party's statement, unless otherwise specified, shall be deemed to apply only to indebtedness entered into at or payable to such branch or branch office and to any collateral taken by such branch or branch office. (Stats.1963, c. 819, § 9208.)

California Code Comment

By John A. Bohn and Charles J. Williams

Prior California Law

1. This section is new. The rationale for it is explained in Official Comments 1–2.

2. Similar duties to provide information upon the debtor's request were imposed by statutes upon the assignee of an account (former Civil Code § 3026) and the lender under an inventory lien (former Civil Code § 3041). Under each of these former provisions, the secured party rather than the debtor was required to prepare the information and there was no limit on the frequency of requests. However, there was also no liability on the secured party for his refusal to supply the information.

3. Subdivision (3) imposes liability upon the secured party for his refusal to comply with the debtor's request. An interesting question is raised in the case of a mistake by the secured party in supplying the information requested:

"The sanctions discussed previously are provided in cases of the secured party's refusal to return the statement of the debtor's current position. But what if the secured party in good faith returns an understatement of his interest? The subsequent creditor who relied on the returned statement would appear to have an excellent defense of estoppel to any such excuse by the secured party. In contrast, what if a good faith *overstatement* were returned? Such statement may prevent successful negotiations by the debtor, and yet the Code imposes sanctions only on the *failure* to reply. Perhaps future cases may imply the word 'properly' after reply to cover this eventuality". 8 UCLA L.Rev. 806, 891.

Changes from U.C.C. (1962 Official Text)

2. Subdivision (4) does not appear in the Official Text. It is part of a series of "branch office" amendments which California has made to the Official Text to meet the branch banking practice prevalent in California. Sixth Progress Report to the Legislature by Senate Fact Finding Committee on Judiciary (1959–1961) Part 1, The Uniform Commercial Code, p. 654.

Uniform Commercial Code Comment

Prior Uniform Statutory Provision:
None.

Purposes:

1. To provide a procedure whereby a debtor may obtain from the secured party a statement of the amount due on the obligation and in some cases a statement of the collateral.

2. The financing statement required to be filed under this Article (see Section 9–402) may disclose only that a secured party may have a security interest in specified types of collateral owned by the debtor. Unless a copy of the security agreement itself is filed as the financing statement third parties are told neither the amount of the obligation secured nor which particular assets are covered. Since subsequent creditors and purchasers may legitimately need more detailed information, it is necessary to provide a procedure under which the secured party will be required to make disclosure. On the other hand, the secured party should not be under a duty to disclose details of business operations to any casual inquirer or competitor who asks for them. This section gives the right to demand disclosure only to the debtor, who will typically request a statement in connection with negotiations with subsequent creditors and purchasers, or for the purpose of establishing his credit standing and proving which of his assets are free of the security interest. The secured party is further protected against onerous requests by the provisions that he need furnish a statement of collateral only when his own records identify the collateral and that if he claims all of a particular type of collateral owned by the debtor he is not required to approve an itemized list.

Cross Reference:
Point 2: Section 9–402.

Definitional Cross References:
"Collateral". Section 9–105.
"Debtor". Section 9–105.
"Good faith". Section 1–201.
"Know". Section 1–201.
"Person". Section 1–201.
"Receive". Section 1–201.
"Secured party". Section 9–105.
"Security agreement". Section 9–105.
"Security interest". Section 1–201.

"Send". Section 1–201.
"Written". Section 1–201.

Cross References

Financing statement, formal requisites, see Commercial Code § 9402. Where collateral is not owned by debtor, right of owner to receive statements under this section, see Commercial Code § 9112.

CHAPTER 3. RIGHTS OF THIRD PARTIES; PERFECTED AND UNPERFECTED SECURITY INTERESTS; RULES OF PRIORITY

Section

9301. Persons Who Take Priority Over Unperfected Security Interests; Rights of "Lien Creditor"; Service of Judgment Lien on Personal Property.

9302. When Filing Is Required to Perfect Security Interest; Security Interests to Which Filing Provisions of This Division Do Not Apply.

9303. When Security Interest is Perfected; Continuity of Perfection.

9304. Perfection of security interests; instruments, documents, proceeds of a written letter of credit, and goods covered by documents.

9305. Security interest perfected by possession of collateral.

9306. "Proceeds"; Secured Party's Rights on Disposition of Collateral.

9307. Protection of Buyers of Goods.

9308. Purchase of Chattel Paper and Instruments.

9309. Protection of Purchasers of Instruments and Documents.

9310. Priority of Certain Liens Arising by Operation of Law.

9311. Alienability of Debtor's Rights: Judicial Process.

9312. Priorities Among Conflicting Security Interests in the Same Collateral.

9313. Fixtures; fixture filing; construction mortgage; priorities.

9314. Accessions.

9315. Priority When Goods Are Commingled or Processed.

9316. Priority Subject to Subordination.

9317. Secured Party Not Obligated on Contract of Debtor.

9318. Defenses against Assignee; Modification of Contract After Notification of Assignment; Term Prohibiting Assignment Ineffective; Identification and Proof of Assignment.

§ 9301. Persons Who Take Priority Over Unperfected Security Interests; Rights of "Lien Creditor"; Service of Judgment Lien on Personal Property

(1) Except as otherwise provided in subdivision (2), an unperfected security interest is subordinate to the rights of all of the following:

(a) Persons entitled to priority under Section 9312.

(b) A person who becomes a lien creditor before the security interest is perfected.

(c) In the case of goods, instruments, documents, and chattel paper, a person who is not a secured party and who is a transferee in bulk or other buyer not in ordinary course of business to the extent that he or she gives value and receives delivery of the collateral without knowledge of the security interest and before it is perfected.

(d) In the case of accounts, general intangibles, and investment property, a person who is not a secured party and who is a transferee to the extent that he or she gives value without knowledge of the security interest and before it is perfected.

(2) If the secured party files with respect to a purchase money security interest before or within 20 days after the debtor receives possession of the collateral, he or she takes priority over the rights of a transferee in bulk or of a lien creditor which arise between the time the security interest attaches and the time of filing.

(3) A "lien creditor" means a creditor who has acquired a lien on the property involved by attachment, levy or the like and includes an assignee for benefit of creditors from the time of assignment, and a trustee in bankruptcy from the date of the filing of the petition or a receiver in equity from the time of appointment. "Lien creditor" does not include a creditor who by filing a notice with the Secretary of State has acquired only an attachment or judgment lien on personal property, or both.

(4) A person who becomes a lien creditor while a security interest is perfected takes subject to the security interest only to the extent that it secures advances made before he or she becomes a lien creditor or within 45 days thereafter or made without knowledge of the lien or pursuant to a commitment entered into without knowledge of the lien. (Stats.1963, c. 819, § 9301. Amended by Stats.1967, c. 799, p. 2215, § 21; Stats.1974, c. 997, p. 2124, § 20, eff. Jan. 1, 1976; Stats.1982, c. 497, p. 2180, § 82.5, operative July 1, 1983; Stats.1984, c. 538, § 33.5; Stats.1993, c. 91 (A.B.707), § 1; Stats.1996, c. 497 (S.B.1591), § 16, operative Jan. 1, 1997.)

California Code Comment

By John A. Bohn and Charles J. Williams

Prior California Law

1. This section lists those classes of persons who take priority over an unperfected security interest. The term "perfected" is used in the sense that a security interest cannot be defeated by insolvency or by general creditors. Official Comment 1.

2. Subdivision (1)(a) gives the security interests listed in Commercial Code § 9312 priority over an unperfected security interest. Section 9312 contains general rules for determining priorities among conflicting security interests and is also an index section for other sections which state special rules for priority in various situations. The interests which are given priority under section 9312 take priority over perfected and unperfected security interests. Official Comment 2.

3. Subdivision (1)(b) is the subject of this extensive discussion in the Marsh and Warren Report:

"This clause deals with the most fundamental problem with respect to a recording or filing system in connection with secured transactions, i.e., what effect does nonrecordation or failure to file have on the rights of other persons who are creditors of the debtor.

"Under present California law, at one extreme, a failure to record a real estate mortgage or deed of trust gives no rights whatever to other creditors of the mortgagor, and the holder of the unrecorded mortgage can come in and gain priority even after levy of attachment or execution by another creditor. First National Bank v. Maxwell, 123 C. 360, 55 P. 980 (1899); Bank of Ukiah v. Petaluma Savings Bank, 100 C. 590, 35 P. 170 (1893). Only by becoming a bona fide purchaser at his own execution sale can the other creditor gain priority over the unrecorded mortgage. Foorman v. Wallace, 75 C. 552, 17 P. 680 (1888).

"On the other hand, a failure to record a chattel mortgage 'immediately or as soon thereafter as practicable' gives priority to any creditor of the mortgagor who was such before the mortgage was executed or became such after its execution and before its recordation, Wolpert v. Gripton, 213 C. 474, 2 P.2d 767 (1931); Cardenas v. Miller, 108 C. 250, 39 P. 783 (1895); CC § 2973; even though attachment or execution is not levied by such other creditor until after recordation or even until after foreclosure and taking of possession by the mortgagee. Chelhar v. Acme Garage, 18 C.A.2d (Supp.) 775, 61 P.2d 1232 (1936) (reviewing the cases).

"With respect to other security devices in California, the Assignment of Accounts Receivable Act follows generally the chattel mortgage rules, CC § 3018, with a five-day period for filing. (See Costello v. Bank of America, 246 F.2d 807 (9th Circ.1957), holding that collection of the account terminates any right of the other creditors to gain priority.) The Inventory Lien Law provides that the rights of other creditors who have not levied attachment or execution is cut off 10 days after filing, regardless of when the filing is done, CC § 3031, thus attempting to combine the functions of a bulk sales notice and a recordation. The Trust Receipts Act provides that the rights of the holder of a trust receipt is superior to that of any other creditor if filing is made before levy of attachment or execution by the other creditor, no matter how belated such filing may be, in accord with this clause of the Code, CC § 3016.4, but contrary to the Code the Trust Receipts Act gives a 30–day grace period for filing. *Ibid.*

"There are several questions involved in this problem:

"(a) Should a failure to file within some required period give any rights to creditors of the debtor who extended credit *before* the execution of the security instrument? When such persons become unsecured creditors, they do so with knowledge that his assets may subsequently be encumbered by him. When such a transaction occurs, a filing or recordation cannot help them and a failure to file or record cannot prejudice them. The only situation in which it might be argued that such a prior creditor should have a right to insist upon prompt filing or recording is one where he has a 'negative pledge clause' in his loan agreement and an acceleration provision for breach of this clause. To put him upon notice of the breach by making a public record of it would enable him to take action to protect his rights. However, this presupposes that he will be constantly searching the records to determine whether any secured transaction has been placed of record, which is unlikely in most cases, and that the secured lender had no knowledge of the negative pledge clause. If he had knowledge of it, it is probable that he would be subordinated in equity regardless of recordation or lack thereof.

"(b) Should there be some specified period after the execution which the secured lender is given to file, and during which he will not be subject even to attachment or execution liens of other creditors? All of the existing statutes, other than the Inventory Lien Law, give some period of time for the secured lender to file, in acknowledgment of the fact that it is impractical to carry out chattel security transactions through an escrow as one would a real estate transaction, with a search of the records up to the last second before the new instrument is placed of record. (Even under the Inventory Lien Law, the filing can be made 10 days before the money is paid over, and thus the secured lender can protect himself.) Unless such a period is given, with relation back of the filing if made during that period, the secured lender may find that an attachment or execution has been levied between the time of the execution of the security instrument and the time when he can get to the proper office to place it of record. The Bankruptcy Act, in § 60a, recognizes and permits such relation back under State law up to a maximum period of 21 days.

"(c) If the filing or recordation is unreasonably delayed, should a person who advances credit to the debtor while it is off record take priority over the security interest even though he does not levy attachment or execution until after it is recorded? An affirmative answer is the long standing policy of this State as evidenced by our chattel mortgage statutes and the Assignment of Accounts Receivable Act. It is true that this policy was discarded in the Trust Receipts Act, but that merely shows that the Commissioners on Uniform State Laws adopted this provision of the Code once before, not that it is right. It would seem that unless the unsecured lender can rely upon the records at the time he advances his money, the filing or recordation is no protection to him at all. That is the point at which he is committed, and a filing or recordation three or fourth months later does him not good at all, even if he learns of it. This clause as written would permit a secured lender to take a secret lien, to keep it in his pocket six months, while other persons extend credit to the debtor relying upon the apparently unencumbered status of his assets, to keep it secret another period while their debts mature, and then to gain priority over them by rushing down and filing the day before they levy attachment or execution. This makes a mockery out of any pretense that other creditors are protected against secret liens by this provision of the Code.

"(d) If the filing or recordation is unreasonably delayed, should a person who advances credit to the debtor after it is recorded take priority over the security interest? Clearly, the answer to this question should be no, in accord with CC § 2973 and our other present statutes. If the interest is on record at the time he advances his money, he cannot have been prejudiced by the delay.

"It is in the light of these considerations that the revision of this clause (b) suggested above has been drafted.

"One other point should be mentioned. This clause in its original form has the virtue that it eliminates the effect of the decision in Constance v. Harvey, 215 F.2d 571 (2d Cir.1954), cert. denied. That case held that, in the case of a belated recording of a chattel mortgage under a statute such as California's, even though no creditor in fact extended credit while the mortgage was off record a trustee in bankruptcy could 'pretend' to be such a creditor under the provisions of Section 70c of the Bankruptcy Act and invalidate the mortgage. This makes every chattel mortgage where there is a failure to record seasonably forever voidable in bankruptcy. This decision does not apply if the state statute requires a creditor to acquire a *lien* while the mortgage is off record in order to prevail. In the Matter of P.T.G. Grain Service, 185 F.Supp. 332 (D.Minn.1960).

"However, the Sixth Circuit held *contra* to the Constance case in In re Alikasovich, 275 F.2d 454 (6th Cir.1960), and this case is now before the Supreme Court on certiorari (*sub nom.* Lewis v. Manufacturers National Bank). Also, Congress at its last session enacted a bill sponsored by the National Bankruptcy Conference to over turn the Constance case (H.R. 7242), but this bill was pocket-vetoed by the President in September, 1960, because of entirely unrelated provisions dealing with the Federal tax lien. Therefore, it appears highly probable that the Constance case will be overruled either by Supreme Court or Congressional action.

"In any event, it appears to us unwise to attempt to solve Bankruptcy Act problems by state enactments and at the cost of imposing unjust results in non-bankruptcy cases. Certainly the experience of all the states rushing to enact accounts receivable statutes after Corn Exchange Bank v. Klauder, 318 U.S. 434 (1943), and then having these statutes rendered meaningless, or worse, after the amendment of Section 60a in 1950 should demonstrate this." Sixth Progress Report to the Legislature by Senate Fact Finding Committee on Judiciary (1959–1961) Part 1, The Uniform Commercial Code, pp. 562 to 564.

The prior California law differed depending upon the old security device used:

"Generally, an unperfected security interest is subordinate under the present law and under the Code to the claims of unsecured creditors who subsequently attach or levy upon the property. However, this general statement has many qualifications. For example, are prior creditors protected as well as subsequent creditors? Does the creditor have to levy before perfection, or merely extend credit before perfection? Is any grace period to be provided during which perfection will relate back to the creation of the security interest? Does the unsecured creditor have to levy prior to foreclosure of the security interest?

"At present, there is a bewildering variety of answers to these questions, depending upon the type of secured transaction. Under the Uniform Trust Receipts Act, the secured party has 30 days in which to file, and a filing at any time before a levy by the unsecured creditor will give the holder of the trust receipt priority. [*Fn.*: Cal.Civ.Code, sec. 3016.4.] Under the chattel mortgage statutes, recording must be done at once 'or as soon thereafter as practicable.' [*Fn.*: Wolpert v. Gripton, 213 Cal. 474, 2 P.2d 767 (1931).] If recording is not prompt, the secured party will be subordinate to a prior or subsequent unsecured creditor who levies after recording or even after foreclosure. [*Fn.*: Chelhar v. Acme Garage, 18 Cal.App.2d Supp. 775, 61 P.2d 1232 (1936).] Still different rules apply to assignments of accounts receivable [*Fn.*: Cal.Civ.Code, sec. 3018] and to inventory liens. [*Fn.*: Cal.Civ. Code, sec. 3031.]" California State Bar Committee on the Commercial Code, A Special Report, The Uniform Commercial Code, 37 Calif.State Bar J. (March–April, 1962) p. 214.

An analysis of the prior California law dealing with priority over unperfected security interest is contained in 8 UCLA L.Rev. 806, 901–914.

4. Subdivisions (1)(c) and (1)(d) concern the purchaser of property subject to a perfected security interest who is given priority over an unperfected security interest. Subdivision (1)(c) applies to property which is transferred by physical delivery and subdivision (1)(d) applies to intangible personal property. To receive priority the purchaser must give value and, in the case of tangible personal property must also receive delivery. Official Comment 4.

5. The idea of the grace period allowed in subdivision (2) for the perfection of a purchase money security interest is similar in principle to the grace period permitted under the California Trust Receipts Act. Subdivision (2) protects the secured party for 10 days against a creditor if he perfects his security interest within that period. Prior California law gave the entruster a 30 day grace period during which he was protected automatically and without filing against creditors, bulk transferees and bona fide purchasers and encumbrances unless they gave new value and took possession (former Civil Code §§ 3016.4(1), 3016.5(1), (2)).

Changes from U.C.C. (1962 Official Text)

6. Section 9–301 of the Official Text as changed in the California version reads as follows:

9301. (1) Except as otherwise provided in [subsection] subdivision (2), an unperfected security interest is subordinate to the rights of

(a) Persons entitled to priority under Section [9–312] 9312;

(b) A person who becomes a lien creditor without knowledge of the security interest and before it is perfected; after the security interest attaches and before it is perfected unless the security interest is perfected within 10 days after it attaches and a person who becomes a lien creditor before the security interest attaches;

(c) in the case of goods, instruments, documents, and chattel paper, a person who is not a secured party and who is a transferee in bulk or other buyer not in ordinary course of business to the extent that he gives value and receives delivery of the collateral [without knowledge of the security interest and before it is perfected;]

(d) in the case of accounts, contract rights, and general intangibles, a person who is not a secured party and who is a transferee to the extent that he gives value without knowledge of the security interest and before it is perfected.

(2) If the secured party files with respect to a purchase money security interest before or within ten days after the collateral comes into possession of the debtor, he takes priority over the rights of a transferee in bulk or [of a lien creditor] other buyer not in the ordinary course of business which arise between the time the security interest attaches and the time of filing.

(3) A "lien creditor" means a creditor who has acquired a lien on the property involved by attachment, levy or the like. [and includes an assignee for benefit of creditors from the time of assignment, and a trustee in bankruptcy from the date of the filing of the petition or a receiver in equity from the time of appointment. Unless all the creditors represented had knowledge of the security interest such a representative of creditors is a lien creditor without knowledge even though he personally has knowledge of the security interest.]

7. For the discussion of the change in subdivision (1)(b) see California Code Comment 3 above.

8. The deletion of the phrase in subdivision (1)(c) conforms with the change made in subdivision (1)(b).

9. Subdivision (2) was changed to make it consistent with Commercial Code § 9301(1)(b). 8 UCLA L.Rev. 806, 851–852.

10. Subdivision (3) was changed to keep the assignee for the benefit of creditors in the same position as he was under prior California law and to take advantage of any favorable change in the Bankruptcy Act. Report of California Bankers Association Committee, Sixth Progress Report to the Legislature by Senate Fact Finding Committee on Judiciary (1959–1961) Part 1, The Uniform Commercial Code, p. 421.

Subdivision (3) was also changed to avoid the rule of "void against one, void against all":

"The last sentence of this subsection incorporates the 'void against one, void against all' principle of Moore v. Bay, 284 U.S. 4 (1931), so that if one creditor with a $100 claim had no knowledge of the security interest, it is totally void in insolvency proceedings for the benefit of other creditors holding $500,000 of claims even though they all had knowledge and could not have gained priority outside of insolvency. There is nothing the State of California can do about this doctrine in bankruptcy, despite the apparent belief of the drafters of the Code to the contrary, but it can avoid adopting it for all insolvency proceedings outside of bankruptcy and avoid incorporating it into State law so that it would persist in bankruptcy in this State even if Moore v. Bay were overturned." Sixth Progress Report to the Legislature by Senate Fact Finding Committee on Judiciary (1959–1961) Part 1, The Uniform Commercial Code, p. 566.

See also 8 UCLA L.Rev. 806, 900–901.

California Code Comment
By Charles J. Williams

Subdivision (1) (b), as changed in California from the 1962 Official Text, reads as follows:

"(b) a person who becomes a lien creditor [without knowledge of the security interest] after the security interest attaches and before it is perfected unless the security interest is perfected within 10 days after it attaches and a person who becomes a lien creditor before the security interest attaches;"

In rejecting this proposed change in the Official Text, the Permanent Editorial Board stated:

"The Code in the Official Text permits a ten-day retroactive effect against lien creditors only for purchase money interests, which typically are handled by non-professionals, and in any event bring in new assets to the extent of the security interest. Other security interests typically secure loans where they represent new value. Filing in advance by the professionals who make most loans is always possible and usually feasible. Where old obligations are secured, equity is served by the Code's usual provisions. The California variation substitutes for the Code's race-of-diligence standard with respect to competing lien creditors, a rule which protects any person extending credit before a competing security interest is perfected by filing, unless the filing occurs within a ten-day grace period.

Subdivision (3) in the original California version changed the Official Text. (California Code Comment 10, [ante].)

"In Section 9–301(1) (b) California also, probably unintentionally, reversed a change made earlier in the Official Text, one which in 9–302(2) dates the ten days not from the time of attachment but from the earliest time another creditor could be misled—the time the debtor gets possession of the collateral. In this respect, the California texts of 9–301(1) (a) and 9–301(2) are inconsistent." Permanent Editorial Board for the Uniform Commercial Code, Report No. 2 (1962 Official Text), p. 189.

The 1967 amendment amends subdivision (3) so that the first sentence of subdivision (3) now conforms with the Official Text. The California version originally omitted as assignee for the benefit of creditors and the trustee in bankruptcy from the definition of "lien creditor". Because the trustee in bankruptcy has the power of a lien creditor under the Bankruptcy Act and because credit organizations requested that the assignee for the benefit of creditors be included in the definition, the 1967 amendment to subdivision (3) was adopted. (Report of the Advisory Committee, Senate Journal April 20, 1967, p. 1238.)

However, subdivision (3) does not in its entirety conform with the Official Text. The last sentence of subdivision (3) in the Official Text is still omitted in the California version.

Legislative Committee Comment—Assembly
1982 Amendment

Subdivision (3) of Section 9301 is amended to make clear that a judgment creditor who acquires a judgment lien on personal property pursuant to Code of Civil Procedure Sections 697.510–697.670 is a "lien creditor." See Code Civ.Proc. § 697.590 (priority of judgment lien on personal property against security interest).

Subdivision (5) requires a judgment creditor who seeks to establish the priority of a judgment lien on personal property to serve a copy of the notice of judgment lien on the secured party as a prerequisite to a determination that the secured party had knowledge of the judgment lien. (15 Cal.L.Rev.Comm. Reports 2001; 82 A.J. 9356).

Uniform Commercial Code Comment
P.E.B. Commentary No. 2, March 10, 1990

Purposes:

* * * * * *

8. The word "only" in subsection (4) is limited in its effect to the lien creditor's subjection to the specified advances. It does not limit the lien creditor's subjection to whatever other rights the secured party may have by contract or law, e.g., the right to interest before or after the attachment of the judgment lien to the collateral or the right to foreclosure expenses or other collection expenses. See PEB Commentary No. 2, dated March 10, 1990 [Uniform Laws Annotated, UCC, APP II, Comment 2].

P.E.B. Commentary No. 6, March 10, 1990

9. There is no conflict between the principle of § 9–301(1) and the "shelter principle," which is applied at several points in the statute, but is most explicitly stated in § 2–403(1): "A purchaser of goods acquires all title which his transferor had...."

Although § 9–301(1) fails to state the shelter principle expressly, that principle is applicable where a person who had met the conditions for prevailing over an unperfected security interest transfers his right to another person after the security interest is perfected. See PEB Commentary No. 6, dated March 10, 1990 [Uniform Laws Annotated, UCC, APP II, Comment 6].

The rules for subordination of unperfected security interests have a purpose—in common with similar rules in all filing and recording systems—to impose sanctions for not adhering to filing or recording requirements. Such rules are necessary to make the system effective and enforce the policy against secret liens. The shelter principle recognizes that when a person in a protected class transfers his right after the security interest has been perfected, the right will be diminished in value unless the sanction is continued. The sanction imposed by § 9–301(1) is that members of protected classes take free of an unperfected security interest. That sanction should be continued to protect transferees from those members in order to fulfill the purpose of the section.

* * * * * *

Uniform Commercial Code Comment
Prior Uniform Statutory Provision:

Sections 8(2) and 9(2) (b), Uniform Trust Receipts Act; Section 5, Uniform Conditional Sales Act.

Purposes:

1. This section lists the classes of persons who take priority over an unperfected security interest. As in Section 60 of the Federal Bankruptcy Act, the term "perfected" is used to describe a security interest in personal property which cannot be defeated in insolvency proceedings or in general by creditors. A security interest is "perfected" when the secured party has taken whatever steps are necessary to give him such an interest. These steps are explained in the five following sections (9–302 through 9–306).

2. Section 9–312 states general rules for the determination of priorities among conflicting security interests and in addition refers to other sections which state special rules of priority in a variety of situations. The interests given priority under Section 9–312 and the other sections therein cited take such priority in general even over a perfected security interest. A fortiori they take priority over an unperfected security interest, and paragraph (1) (a) of this section so states.

3. Paragraph (1) (b) provides that an unperfected security interest is subordinate to the rights of lien creditors. The section rejects the rule applied in many jurisdictions in pre-Code law that an unperfected security interest is subordinated to all creditors, but requires the lien obtained by legal proceedings to attach to the collateral before the security interest is perfected. The section subordinates the unperfected security interest but does not subordinate the secured debt to the lien.

4. Paragraphs (1) (c) and (1) (d) deal with purchasers (other than secured parties) of collateral who would take subject to a perfected security interest but who are by these subsections given priority over an unperfected security interest. In the cases of goods and of intangibles of the type whose transfer is effected by physical delivery of the

representative piece of paper (instruments, documents and chattel paper) the purchaser who takes priority must both give value and receive delivery of the collateral without knowledge of the existing security interest and before perfection (paragraph (1) (c)). Thus even if the purchaser gave value without knowledge and before perfection, he would take subject to the security interest if perfection occurred before physical delivery of the collateral to him. The paragraph (1) (c) rule is obviously not appropriate where the collateral consists of intangibles and there is no representative piece of paper whose physical delivery is the only or the customary method of transfer. Therefore with respect to such intangibles (accounts and general intangibles), paragraph (1) (d) gives priority to any transferee who has given value without knowledge and before perfection of the security interest.

The term "buyer in ordinary course of business" referred to in paragraph (1) (c) is defined in Section 1–201(9).

Other secured parties are excluded from paragraphs (1) (c) and (1) (d) because their priorities are covered in Section 9–312 (see point 2 of this Comment).

5. Except to the extent provided in subsection (2), this Article does not permit a secured party to file or take possession after another interest has received priority under subsection (1) and thereby protect himself against the intervening interest.

A few chattel mortgage statutes did have grace periods, i.e., a filing within x days after the mortgage was given related back to the day the mortgage was given. The Uniform Conditional Sales Act had a ten-day period which cut off all intervening interests. The Uniform Trust Receipts Act had a thirty-day period but did not cut off the interest of a purchaser who took delivery before the filing.

Subsection (2) gives a grace period for perfection by filing as to purchase money security interests only (that term is defined in Section 9–107). The grace period runs for ten days after the debtor receives possession of the collateral but operates to cut off only the interests of intervening lien creditors or bulk purchasers.

6. Subsection (3) defines "lien creditor", following in substance the provisions of the Uniform Trust Receipts Act.

7. Subsection (4) deals with the question whether advances under an existing security interest in collateral, made after rights of lien creditors have attached to that collateral, will take precedence over rights of lien creditors. See related problems in Sections 9–307(3) and 9–312(7). In this section, because of the impact of the rule chosen on the question whether the security interest for future advances is "protected" under Sections 6323(c) (2) and (d) of the Internal Revenue Code as amended by the Federal Tax Lien Act of 1966, the priority of the security interest for future advances over a judgment lien is made absolute for 45 days regardless of knowledge of the secured party concerning the judgment lien. If, however, the advance is made after the 45 days, the advance will not have priority unless it was made or committed without knowledge of the lien obtained by legal proceedings. The importance of the rule chosen for actual conflicts between secured parties making subsequent advances and judgment lien creditors may not be great; but the rule chosen for the first 45 days is important in effectuating the intent of the Federal Tax Lien Act of 1966.

Cross References:
Section 9–312.
Point 1: Sections 9–302 through 9–306.
Point 7: Sections 9–204, 9–307(3) and 9–312(7).

Definitional Cross References:
"Account". Section 9–106.
"Buyer in ordinary course of business". Section 1–201.
"Chattel paper". Section 9–105.
"Collateral". Section 9–105.
"Creditor". Section 1–201.
"Delivery". Section 1–201.
"Document". Section 9–105.
"General intangibles". Section 9–106.
"Goods". Section 9–105.
"Instrument". Section 9–105.
"Knowledge". Section 1–201.
"Person". Section 1–201.
"Purchase money security interest". Section 9–107.
"Pursuant to commitment". Section 9–105.
"Representative". Section 1–201.
"Rights". Section 1–201.
"Secured party". Section 9–105.
"Security interest". Section 1–201.
"Value". Section 1–201.

Cross References

Conditional sale of railroad equipment, see Public Utilities Code § 7576 et seq.
Conflicting security interests, priorities, see Commercial Code § 9312.
Fraudulent conveyances, see Civil Code § 3439.
Motor vehicles,
  Legal owner, see Vehicle Code § 370.
  Recording of security interest, see Vehicle Code § 6300.
  Transfer requirements, see Vehicle Code § 5600.
Perfection of security interest, see Commercial Code § 9302 et seq.

§ 9302. When Filing Is Required to Perfect Security Interest; Security Interests to Which Filing Provisions of This Division Do Not Apply

(1) A financing statement must be filed to perfect all security interests except the following:

(a) A security interest in collateral in possession of the secured party under Section 9305.

(b) A security interest temporarily perfected in instruments, certificated securities, or documents without delivery under Section 9304 or in proceeds for a 10-day period under Section 9306.

(c) A security interest created by an assignment of a beneficial interest in a trust or a decedent's estate.

(d) A purchase money security interest in consumer goods; but filing is required for a motor vehicle or boat required to be registered; and fixture filing is required for priority over conflicting interests in fixtures to the extent provided in Section 9313.

(e) A security interest of a collecting bank (Section 4210) * * * or arising under the divisions on sales and leases (see Section 9113) or covered in subdivision (3) of this section.

(f) An assignment for the benefit of all the creditors of the transferor, and subsequent transfers by the assignee thereunder.

(g) A security interest in a deposit account. Such a security interest is perfected:

(i) As to a deposit account maintained with the secured party, when the security agreement is executed.

(ii) As to a deposit account not described in subparagraph (i), when notice thereof is given in writing to the organization with whom the deposit account is maintained.

(h) A security interest in investment property that is perfected without filing under Section 9115 or 9116.

(i) A security interest in or claim in or under any policy of insurance including unearned premiums. Such interest shall be perfected when notice thereof is given in writing to the insurer.

(2) If a secured party assigns a perfected security interest, no filing under this division is required in ord' to continue the perfected status of the security int'

against creditors of and transferees from the original debtor.

(3) The filing of a financing statement otherwise required by this division is not necessary or effective to perfect a security interest in property subject to any of the following:

(a) A statute or treaty of the United States which provides for a national or international registration or a national or international certificate of title or which specifies a place of filing different from that specified in this division for filing of the security interest.

(b) The provisions of the Vehicle Code which require registration of a vehicle or boat, or provisions of the Health and Safety Code which require registration of a mobilehome or commercial coach; but during any period in which collateral is inventory, the filing provisions of this division (Chapter 4 (commencing with Section 9401)) apply to a security interest in that collateral.

(c) A certificate of title statute of another jurisdiction under the law of which indication of a security interest on the certificate is required as a condition of perfection (subdivision (2) of Section 9103).

(d) The provisions of the Health and Safety Code which require registration of all interests in approved air contaminant emission reductions (Sections 40709 to 40713, inclusive, of the Health and Safety Code).

(4) Compliance with a statute or treaty described in subdivision (3) is equivalent to the filing of a financing statement under this division and a security interest in property subject to the statute or treaty can be perfected only by compliance therewith except as provided in Section 9103 on multiple state transactions. Duration and renewal of perfection of a security interest perfected by compliance with the statute or treaty are governed by the provisions of the statute or treaty; in other respects the security interest is subject to this division. (Stats.1963, c. 819, § 9302. Amended by Stats.1967, c. 799, p. 2215, § 22; Stats.1970, c. 1428, p. 2731, § 2; Stats.1974, c. 997, p. 2126, § 21, eff. Jan. 1, 1976; Stats.1975, c. 650, p. 1407, § 1; Stats.1980, c. 692, p. 2086, § 1, eff. July 24, 1980; Stats.1980, c. 1149, p. 3739, § 13; Stats.1980, c. 1156, p. 3863, § 6; Stats.1981, c. 134, p. 912, § 7, eff. July 1, 1981, operative July 1, 1981; Stats.1984, c. 927, § 10; Stats.1994, c. 668 (S.B.1405), § 13; Stats.1996, c. 497 (S.B.1591), § 17, operative Jan. 1, 1997.)

California Code Comment

By John A. Bohn and Charles J. Williams

Prior California Law

1. In general the Commercial Code provides that a financing statement must be filed to perfect a security interest except where specifically exempted. In the case of those situations where the filing of a financial statement is specifically excused, the Commercial Code provides that the security interest is perfected in another manner. Official Comments 1–6 explain the background and reasons for the provisions.

2. The prior California law is described in the California Annotations to the Proposed Uniform Commercial Code (1960) prepared by the Legislative Counsel:

"Subdivision (1)(a) is to be compared with Civil Code Sections 2988 and 3015 wherein possession is necessary to perfect a pledge without the necessity of a filing. In none of the other security devices is possession a controlling element.

"With reference to the filing (or recording) provisions of the remainder of the section, comparison should be made with the various California security instruments.

"Recording is required to perfect all chattel mortgages (Civil Code Section 2957), except on motor vehicles, where the mortgagee must be designated as the legal owner on the certificate of ownership (Vehicle Code Section 6300). This is similar to Alternative A. No special treatment is given to purchase money chattel mortgages. Possession by a chattel mortgagee is the equivalent of record. See Chelhar v. Acme Garage, 18 Cal.App.2d 775, 61 Pac.2d 1232.

"Recording or filing is not required in order to perfect a security interest under a conditional sales contract except as to livestock and animate chattels (Civil Code Section 2980.5); mining machinery and equipment (Civil Code Section 2980) and railroad equipment (Public Utilities Code Section 7579). Under Civil Code Section 955 a recording is not required to perfect the transfer of a conditional sales contract but it must be endorsed, or assigned in writing and delivered to the transferee.

"No filing is necessary to perfect a pledge.

"Filing or possession is necessary to perfect a trust receipt under Civil Code Sections 3016.3, 3016.4, and 3016.5.

"Filing is necessary to perfect accounts receivable under Civil Code Sections 3019 and 3020.

"Filing is necessary to perfect an inventory lien under Civil Code Section 3031.

"Ship mortgages must be recorded with the Collector of Customs under Civil Code Section 2958. Aircraft mortgages must be recorded in accordance with the laws of the United States. (Civil Code Section 2958a.)" Sixth Progress Report to the Legislature by Senate Fact Finding Committee on Judiciary, (1959–1961) Part 1, The Uniform Commercial Code, pp. 127–128.

3. Subdivision (1)(g) incorporates substantially the provisions of former Civil Code § 955.1. This allows the first bona fide assignee of a general intangible consisting of a right to payment who gives notice to the account debtor to prevail regardless of which assignee was first in time. 8 UCLA L.Rev. 806, 847.

4. The effect of subdivision (1)(h) is described in the Marsh and Warren report:

"The Assignment of Claims statutes (31 U.S.C. § 203 and 41 U.S.C. § 15) require as a condition of an assignment of a claim against the United States as security that the consent of the department head involved be secured and that notice be given to the Government.

"If an assignment of a claim is made *without compliance* with the Assignment of Claims statutes, it is void against the United States, but it is nevertheless generally valid as between the assignor and assignee and as against third parties. Mayo v. Pioneer Bank & Trust Company, 270 F.2d 823, 834 (5th Cir.1959); California Bank v. United States Fidelity & Guaranty Co., 129 F.2d 751, 753 (9th Cir.1942). However, such an assignment is only valid against third persons *'if it is perfected according to local law.'* M.M. Landy, Inc. v. Nicholas, 221 F.2d 923, 927 (5th Cir.1955) (holding that compliance with the Florida Assignment of Accounts Receivable Act was necessary in that case to perfect the interest of the assignee). We see no reason why, if there is an assignment of a claim against the United States in violation of the Assignment of Claims statutes, it should be perfected without any filing under the Code (which would be the effect of the language suggested by the California Bankers Committee).

"On the other hand, if the Assignment of Claims statute is complied with, it is probable that a State *cannot* require any additional filing to perfect the assignment. By amendment in 1951 (65 Stat. 41) those statutes declare: 'Notwithstanding any law to the contrary governing the validity of assignments, any assignment pursuant to this section shall constitute a valid assignment *for all purposes.*' While the immediate purpose of this amendment was to prevent the Government from recovering from the assignee, see American Fidelity Company v. National City Bank of Evansville, 266 F.2d 910, at 915 (D.C.Cir.1959), it appears to be a sweeping pre-emption of the field by the Federal

Government, and such a pre-emption is consonant with the main purpose of the statutes to 'encourage the private financing of government contracts.' Central Bank v. United States, 345 U.S. 639, at 646 (1953). Therefore, although we have found no case so holding and despite the contrary suggestion in the Official Comment to Section 9-302 of the Code, we believe that filing under the Code probably cannot be required if there has been compliance with the Assignment of Claims statutes. [See Baruch Investment Co. v. California Equities, Inc., 3 Cal.Rptr. 763 (Cal.App.1960), where there was a filing under the California Assignment of Accounts Receivable Act with respect to a claim against the United States, but the court did not discuss this point nor indicate whether there had been any compliance with the Assignment of Claims statutes.]

"We believe that it is preferable not to leave this question up in the air subject to future litigation, but expressly to exempt from filing under the Code where there has been compliance with the Federal Assignment of Claims statutes, since the Federal Government has probably already pre-empted this field." Sixth Progress Report to the Legislature by Senate Fact Finding Committee on Judiciary (1959–1961) Part 1, The Uniform Commercial Code, p. 569.

Changes from U.C.C. (1962 Official Text)

5. Section 9–302 as changed in the California version reads as follows:

9302. (1) A financing statement must be filed to perfect all security interests except the following:

(a) A security interest in collateral in possession of the secured party under Section [9–305] 9305;

(b) A security interest temporarily perfected in instruments or documents without delivery under Section [9–304] 9304 or in proceeds for a 10–day period under Section [9–306] 9306;

(c) A purchase money security interest in farm equipment having a purchase price not in excess of two thousand five hundred dollars ($2,500); but [filing is required for a fixture under Section 9–313 or for a motor vehicle required to be licensed;] compliance with subdivision (4) is required for a motor vehicle required to be registered;

(d) A purchase money security interest in consumer goods; but [filing is required for a fixture under Section 9–313 or for a motor vehicle required to be licensed] compliance with subdivision (4) is required for a motor vehicle or boat required to be registered;

[(e) an assignment of accounts or contract rights which does not alone or in conjunction with other assignments to the same assignee transfer a significant part of the outstanding accounts or contract rights of the assignor;]

(f) A security interest of a collecting bank (Section [4–208] 4208) or arising under the division on sales (see Section [9–113] 9113) or covered in subdivision (3) of this section;

(g) A security interest in general intangibles; provided, however, that as between bona fide assignees for value without notice of the same general intangible consisting of any right to payment, the assignee first giving notice thereof to the account debtor in writing shall have priority, but the assignment of such general intangible shall not be of itself notice to the account debtor so as to invalidate any payments made by him to the transferor;

(h) An assignment of any claim against the United States made pursuant to and in conformity with 31 U.S.C. Section 203 or 41 U.S.C. Section 15 (the Assignment of Claims statutes) or any statutes amendatory thereof or in substitution therefor.

(2) If a secured party assigns a perfected security interest, no filing under this [Article] division is required in order to continue the perfected status of the security interest against creditors of and transferees from the original debtor.

(3) The filing provisions of this [Article] division do not apply to a security interest

(a) In property subject to a statute of the United States which provides for a national registration or filing of all security interests in such property; or [Alternative A—]

[(b) of this state which provides for central filing of, or which requires indication on a certificate of title of, such security interests in such property.

Alternative B—]

[(b) of this state which provides for central filing of security interests in such property, or in a motor vehicle which is not inventory held for sale for which a certificate of title is required under the statutes of this state if a notation of such a security interest can be indicated by a public official on a certificate or a duplicate thereof.]

(b) In a vehicle required to be registered under the Vehicle Code, unless such vehicle is inventory, or in a boat required to be registered under the Harbors and Navigation Code, unless such boat is inventory.

(4) A security interest in property [covered by a statute described in subsection (3) can be perfected only by registration or filing under that statute or by indication of the security interest on a certificate of title or a duplicate thereof by a public official.] subject to a statute of the United States which provides for national registration or filing of all security interests in such property may be perfected only by filing or registration under such statute. A security interest in a vehicle required to be registered under the Vehicle Code which is not inventory may be perfected only as provided in the Vehicle Code. A security interest in a boat required to be registered under the Harbors and Navigation Code which is not inventory may be perfected only as provided in the Harbors and Navigation Code.

6. Subdivision (1)(d) was changed to harmonize with the system of licensing motor vehicles in California. Sixth Progress Report to the Legislature by Senate Fact Finding Committee on Judiciary (1959–1961) Part 1, The Uniform Commercial Code, p. 421.

7. The reason for the deletion of subdivision (1)(e) is described in the Marsh and Warren report:

"The Official Comments to the Code state that the purpose of this clause is to exempt from the filing requirement 'casual or isolated assignments.' We approve of this purpose and would approve of this clause if it had any tendency to accomplish it. However, under this clause if A assigns to B an account receivable, which is the only account that A owns, and this transaction has nothing to do with any business which either one of them is engaged in, filing is required because certainly an assignment of 100 percent of the accounts of A is an assignment of a 'significant part' of his accounts. On the other hand, if a manufacturing corporation assigns to a finance company 5 percent of its outstanding accounts receivable, then filing is not required if 5 percent is determined not to be a 'significant part.' Thus the clause has no tendency to accomplish its stated purpose. Furthermore, the meaning of 'significant part' is wholly ambiguous and would take extensive litigation to determine." Sixth Progress Report to the Legislature by Senate Fact Finding Committee on Judiciary (1959–1961) Part 1, The Uniform Commercial Code, p. 567.

8. Subdivision (1)(g) was added to continue the rule under former Civil Code § 955.1. California Code Comment 3 above.

9. Subdivision (1)(h) was added for the reason described in the Marsh and Warren report quoted in California Code Comment 4 above.

10. Subdivision (3)(b) was changed to harmonize with the existing system of licensing motor vehicles and boats.

California Code Comment

By Charles J. Williams

The 1967 amendment revises subdivision (1)(h). This change has no counterpart in the Official Text. In its report to the legislature, the Advisory Committee explains the reason for the amendment: . . .

". . . this subsection, has the effect of exempting assignments of claims against the United States made in conformity with the Federal Assignment of Claims Act from the requirement of filing a financing statement in order to perfect them. The Assignment of Claims Act is not designed to give notice to third persons of the Assignment and the Advisory Committee believes it would be preferable to require the filing of a financing statement to perfect the assignment of accounts or contract rights on which the United States is the account debtor as is required in the official text adopted in other states. At the same time, the Advisory Committee believes that the filing of a financing statement of perfect the assignment of the accounts and contract rights to an assignee for the benefit of all the creditors of the assignor serves no useful purpose and therefore recommends the adoption of a new Section 9302(1)(h) . . .". (Report of the Advisory Committee, Senate Journal, April 20, 1967, 1967 Regular Session, p. 1238.)

Uniform Commercial Code Comment
Official Reasons for 1977 Change

Section 8-321(2) provides that security interests in securities created in accordance with its provisions are perfected. Since none of its provisions, including the provisions of Section 8-313(1) incorporated therein, require filing, security interests in securities are excepted from the normal filing requirements of Article 9 by the language added to subparagraph (1)(f) of this section. Note that most of the requirements of Section 8-313(1) involve either possession or its functional equivalent.

Uniform Commercial Code Comment

9. Perfection of a security interest under a state or federal statute of the type referred to in subsection (3) has all the consequences of perfection under the provisions of this Article. Subsection (4).

10. If a security interest has been perfected under the applicable certificate of title statute and is thereafter assigned, and that statute does not expressly require the assignee to take some further action with respect to the certificate of title to reflect that it has become the secured party in order to continue such perfection, § 9-302(2) is applicable and the assignee is not required to note its name on the certificate of title "in order to continue the perfected status of the security interest against creditors of and transferees from the original debtor." See PEB Commentary No. 12, dated February 10, 1994 [Uniform Laws Annotated, UCC, APP II, Comment 12].

Prior Uniform Statutory Provision:

Section 5, Uniform Conditional Sales Act; Section 8, Uniform Trust Receipts Act.

Purposes:

1. Subsection (1) states the general rule that to perfect a security interest under this Article a financing statement must be filed. Paragraphs (1) (a) through (1) (g) exempt from the filing requirement the transactions described. Subsection (3) further sets out certain transactions to which the filing provisions of this Article do not apply, but it does not defer to another state statute on the filing of inventory security interests. The cases recognized are those where suitable alternative systems for giving public notice of a security interest are available. Subsection (4) states the consequences of such other form of notice.

Section 9-303 states the time when a security interest is perfected by filing or otherwise. Part 4 of the Article deals with the mechanics of filing: place of filing, form of financing statement and so on.

2. As at common law, there is no requirement of filing when the secured party has possession of the collateral in a pledge transaction (paragraph (1) (a)). Section 9-305 should be consulted on what collateral may be pledged and on the requirements of possession.

3. Under this Article, as under the Uniform Trust Receipts Act, filing is not effective to perfect a security interest in instruments. See Section 9-304(1).

4. Where goods subject to a security interest are left in the debtor's possession, the only permanent exception from the general filing requirement is that stated in paragraph (1) (d): purchase money security interests in consumer goods. For temporary exceptions, see Sections 9-304(5) (a) and 9-306.

In many jurisdictions under prior law security interests in consumer goods under conditional sale or bailment leases were not subject to filing requirements. Paragraph (1) (d) follows the policy of those jurisdictions. The paragraph changes prior law in jurisdictions where all conditional sales and bailment leases were subject to a filing requirement, except that filing is required for purchase money security interests in consumer fixtures to attain priority under Section 9-313 against real estate interests.

Although the security interests described in paragraph (1) (d) are perfected without filing, Section 9-307(2) provides that unless a financing statement is filed certain buyers may take free of the security interest even though perfected. See that section and the Comment thereto.

On filing for security interests in motor vehicles under certificate of title laws see subsection (3) of this section.

5. A financing statement must be filed to perfect a security interest in accounts except for the transactions described in paragraphs (1) (e) [changes in California from U.C.C. (1962 Official Text), see California Code Comment, notes 5, 7] and (g). It should be noted that this Article applies to sales of accounts and chattel paper as well as to transfers thereof for security (Section 9-102(1) (b)); the filing requirement of this section applies both to sales and to transfers thereof for security. In this respect this Article follows many of the pre-Code statutes regulating assignments of accounts receivable.

Over forty jurisdictions had enacted accounts receivable statutes. About half of these statutes required filing to protect or perfect assignments; of the remainder, one was a so-called "bookmarking" statute and the others validated assignments without filing. This Article adopts the filing requirement, on the theory that there is no valid reason why public notice is less appropriate for assignments of accounts than for any other type of nonpossessory interest. Section 9-305, furthermore, excludes accounts from the types of collateral which may be the subject of a possessory security interest: filing is thus the only means of perfection contemplated by this Article. See Section 9-306 on accounts as proceeds.

The purpose of the subsection (1) (e) [changes in California from U.C.C. (1962 Official Text), see California Code Comment, notes 5, 7] exemption is to save from *ex post facto* invalidation casual or isolated assignments: some accounts receivable statutes were so broadly drafted that all assignments, whatever their character or purpose, fell within their filing provisions. Under such statutes many assignments which no one would think of filing might have been subject to invalidation. The paragraph (1) (e) exemption goes to that type of assignment. Any person who regularly takes assignments of any debtor's accounts should file. In this connection Section 9-104(f) which excludes certain transfers of accounts from the Article should be consulted.

Assignments of interests in trusts and estates are not required to be filed because they are often not thought of as collateral comparable to the types dealt with by this Article. Assignments for the benefit of creditors are not required to be filed because they are not financing transactions and the debtor will not ordinarily be engaging in further credit transactions.

6. With respect to the paragraph (1) (f) exemptions, see the sections cited therein and Comments thereto.

7. The following example will explain the operation of subsection (2): Buyer buys goods from seller who retains a security interest in them which he perfects. Seller assigns the perfected security interest to X. The security interest, in X's hands and without further steps on his part, continues perfected against *Buyer's* transferees and creditors. If, however, the assignment from Seller to X was itself intended for security (or was a sale of accounts or chattel paper), X must take whatever steps may be required for perfection in order to be protected against *Seller's* transferees and creditors.

8. Subsection (3) exempts from the filing provisions of this Article transactions as to which an adequate system of filing, state or federal, has been set up outside this Article and subsection (4) makes clear that when such a system exists perfection of a relevant security interest can be had only through compliance with that system (i.e., filing under this Article is not a permissible alternative).

Examples of the type of federal statute referred to in paragraph (3) (a) are the provisions of 17 U.S.C. §§ 28, 30 (copyrights), 49 U.S.C. § 1403 (aircraft), 49 U.S.C. § 20(c) (railroads). The Assignment of Claims Act of 1940, as amended, provides for notice to contracting and disbursing officers and to sureties on bonds but does not establish a national filing system and therefore is not within the scope of paragraph (3) (a). An assignee of a claim against the United States, who must of course comply with the Assignment of Claims Act, must also file under this Article in order to perfect his security interest against creditors and transferees of his assignor.

Some states have enacted central filing statutes with respect to security transactions in kinds of property which are of special importance in the local economy. Subsection (3) adopts such statutes as the appropriate filing system for such property.

In addition to such central filing statutes many states have enacted certificate of title laws covering motor vehicles and the like. Subsection (3) exempts transactions covered by such laws from the filing requirements of this Article.

For a discussion of the operation of state motor vehicle certificate of title laws in interstate contexts, see Comment 4 to Section 9-103.

Cross References:

Point 1: Section 9-303 and Part 4.
Point 2: Section 9-305.

Point 3: Section 9–304(1).
Point 4: Section 9–307(2).
Point 5: Sections 9–102(1) (b), 9–104(f) and 9–305.
Point 6: Sections 4–208 and 9–113.

Definitional Cross References:
"Account". Section 9–106.
"Collateral". Section 9–105.
"Consumer goods". Section 9–109.
"Creditor". Section 1–201.
"Debtor". Section 9–105.
"Delivery". Section 1–201.
"Document". Section 9–105.
"Equipment". Section 9–109.
"Fixture". Section 9–313.
"Fixture filing". Section 9–313.
"Instrument". Section 9–105.
"Inventory". Section 9–109.
"Proceeds". Section 9–306.
"Purchase". Section 1–201.
"Purchase money security interest". Section 9–107.
"Sale". Sections 2–106 and 9–105.
"Secured party". Section 9–105.
"Security interest". Section 1–201.

Cross References

Automobile sales finance act, see Civil Code § 2981 et seq.
Collecting bank, security interest, see Commercial Code § 4210.
Consumer goods and farm equipment, purchase without knowledge of security interest, see Commercial Code § 9307.
Continuity of perfection, see Commercial Code § 9303.
Excluded transactions, see Commercial Code § 9104.
Filing, see Commercial Code § 9401 et seq.
Motor vehicles,
  Perfection of security interest, see Vehicle Code § 6301.
  Recording of security instrument, see Vehicle Code § 6300.
  Transfers of title to, or interest in, see Vehicle Code § 5600 et seq.
Perfection of security interest, time, see Commercial Code § 9303.
Policy and scope of division, see Commercial Code § 9102.
Possession of collateral by secured party, see Commercial Code § 9305.
Security interest in instruments, perfection, see Commercial Code § 9304.
Security interests arising under division on sales, see Commercial Code § 9113.
Transfer of interest in undocumented vessels, see Vehicle Code § 9900 et seq.
Transfer of nonnegotiable instruments, general intangibles, see Civil Code §§ 955, 955.1.

§ 9303. When Security Interest is Perfected; Continuity of Perfection

(1) A security interest is perfected when it has attached and when all of the applicable steps required for perfection have been taken. Such steps are specified in Sections 9302, 9304, 9305 and 9306. If such steps are taken before the security interest attaches, it is perfected at the time when it attaches.

(2) If a security interest is originally perfected in any way permitted under this division and is subsequently perfected in some other way under this division, without an intermediate period when it was unperfected, the security interest shall be deemed to be perfected continuously for the purposes of this division. * * *
(Stats.1963, c. 819, § 9303. Amended by Stats.1974, c. 997, p. 2126, § 22, effective Jan. 1, 1976.)

California Code Comment

By John A. Bohn and Charles J. Williams

Prior California Law

1. Prior California law relating to the time of perfection of security interest was as follows:

(a) For a chattel mortgage, the date of execution if the mortgage is recorded within a reasonable time. Former Civil Code § 2957.

(b) For a trust receipt, the date of delivery of the goods if notice is filed within 30 days. Former Civil Code § 3016.4.

(c) For an assignment of an account, generally upon the date of filing; but as to a creditor it was the date of execution of the assignment if notice was filed within 5 days. Former Civil Code § 3018.

(d) For an inventory lien, the date of execution if notice was filed within 10 days. Former Civil Code § 3031.

(e) For a conditional sales contract, the date of execution, subject to recordation if the contract was for mining or oil drilling machinery or livestock. Former Civil Code §§ 2980 and 2980.5.

(f) For a pledge, the date of delivery except that under certain circumstances delivery within 10 days could relate back to the date of the agreement. Former Civil Code §§ 2988 and 3015.

(g) For an inventory lien, 10 days after the filing of a proper notice of inventory lien. Former Civil Code §§ 3031, 3036, 3042.

Uniform Commercial Code Comment

Prior Uniform Statutory Provision:
None.

Purposes:

1. The term "attach" is used in this Article to describe the point at which property becomes subject to a security interest. The requisites for attachment are stated in Section 9–203. When it attaches a security interest may be either perfected or unperfected: "Perfected" means that the secured party has taken all the steps required by this Article as specified in the several sections listed in subsection (1). A perfected security interest may still be or become subordinate to other interests (see Section 9–312) but in general after perfection the secured party is protected against creditors and transferees of the debtor and in particular against any representative of creditors in insolvency proceedings instituted by or against the debtor. Subsection (1) states the truism that the time of perfection is when the security interest has attached and any necessary steps for perfection (such as taking possession or filing) have been taken. If the steps for perfection have been taken in advance (as when the secured party files a financing statement before giving value or before the debtor acquires rights in the collateral), then the interest is perfected automatically when it attaches.

2. The following example will illustrate the operation of subsection (2): A bank which has issued a letter of credit honors drafts drawn under the credit and receives possession of the negotiable bill of lading covering the goods shipped. Under Sections 9–304(2) and 9–305 the bank now has a perfected security interest in the document and the goods. The bank releases the bill of lading to the debtor for the purpose of procuring the goods from the carrier and selling them. Under Section 9–304(5) the bank continues to have a perfected security interest in the document and goods for 21 days. The bank files before the expiration of the 21 day period. Its security interest now continues perfected for as long as the filing is good. The goods are sold by the debtor. The bank continues to have a security interest in the proceeds of the sale to the extent stated in Section 9–306.

If the successive stages of the bank's security interest succeed each other without an intervening gap, the security interest is "continuously perfected" and the date of perfection is when the interest first became perfected (i.e., in the example given, when the bank received possession of the bill of lading against honor of the drafts). If, however, there is a gap between stages—for example, if the bank does not file until after the expiration of the 21 day period specified in Section 9–304(5), the collateral still being in the debtor's possession—then, the chain being broken, the perfection is no longer continuous. The date of perfection would now be the date of filing (after expiration of the 21 day period); the bank's interest might now become subject to attack under Section 60 of the Federal Bankruptcy Act and would be subject to any interests arising during the gap period which under Section 9–301 take priority over an unperfected security interest.

The rule of subsection (2) would also apply to the case of collateral brought into this state subject to a security interest which became perfected in another state or jurisdiction. See Section 9–103(1) (d).

Cross References:

§ 9303

Sections 9–302, 9–304, 9–305 and 9–306.
Point 1: Sections 9–204 and 9–312.
Point 2: Sections 9–103(1)(d) and 9–301.

Definitional Cross References:
"Attach". Section 9–203.
"Security interest". Section 1–201.

Cross References

Acquisition of title subsequent to execution of mortgage, see Civil Code § 2930.
California housing and infrastructure finance agency, perfection of security interest in collateral on loans to qualified mortgage lenders, see Health and Safety Code § 51153.
Classification of goods, see Commercial Code § 9109.
Conflicting interests, priorities, see Commercial Code § 9312.
Disposition of collateral, secured party's rights, see Commercial Code § 9306.
Incoming goods already subject to security interest, see Commercial Code § 9103.
Motor vehicles, recording of security interest, see Vehicle Code § 6300.
Necessity of filing, see Commercial Code § 9302.
Property not yet acquired, creation of lien, see Civil Code § 2883.
Requisites for attachment of security interests, see Commercial Code § 9203.
Security interest in goods and documents, see Commercial Code §§ 9304, 9305.
Transfer of nonnegotiable instruments, see Civil Code § 955.
Unperfected security interests, subordination, see Commercial Code § 9301.

§ 9304. Perfection of security interests; instruments, documents, proceeds of a written letter of credit, and goods covered by documents

(1) A security interest in chattel paper or negotiable documents may be perfected by filing. <u>A security interest in the rights to proceeds of a written letter of credit can be perfected only by the secured party's taking possession of the letter of credit.</u> A security interest in money or instruments (other than * * * instruments which constitute part of chattel paper) can be perfected only by the secured party's taking possession, except as provided in subdivisions (4), (5), and (7) of this section and subdivisions (2) and (3) of Section 9306 on proceeds.

(2) During the period that goods are in the possession of the issuer of a negotiable document therefor, a security interest in the goods is perfected by perfecting a security interest in the document, and any security interest in the goods otherwise perfected during the period is subject thereto.

(3) A security interest in goods in the possession of a bailee other than one who has issued a negotiable document therefor is perfected by issuance of a document in the name of the secured party or by the bailee's receipt of notification of the secured party's interest or by filing as to the goods.

(4) A security interest in instruments * * *$_2$ certificated securities,$_2$ or negotiable documents is perfected without filing or the taking of possession for a period of 21 days from the time it attaches to the extent that it arises for new value given under a written security agreement.

(5) A security interest remains perfected for a period of 21 days without filing where a secured party having a perfected security interest in an instrument * * *$_2$ a certificated security * * *, a negotiable document, or goods in possession of a bailee other than one who has issued a negotiable document therefor does either of the following:

(a) Makes available to the debtor the goods or documents representing the goods for the purpose of ultimate sale or exchange or for the purpose of loading, unloading, storing, shipping, transshipping, manufacturing, processing or otherwise dealing with them in a manner preliminary to their sale or exchange, but priority between conflicting security interests in the goods is subject to subdivision (3) of Section 9312.

(b) Delivers the instrument <u>or certificated security</u> to the debtor for the purpose of ultimate sale or exchange or of presentation, collection, renewal or registration of transfer.

(6) After the 21–day period in subdivisions (4) and (5), perfection depends upon compliance with applicable provisions of this division.

(7) If an instrument claimed as proceeds (other than cash proceeds) under Section 9306 is in the custody of a levying officer, a secured party may perfect a security interest in such instrument by filing a third-party claim with the levying officer pursuant to Chapter 3 (commencing with Section 720.210) of Division 4 of Title 9 of Part 2 of the Code of Civil Procedure within the 10–day period allowed under Section 9306. *(Stats.1963, c. 819, § 9304. Amended by Stats.1974, c. 997, p. 2126, § 23, eff. Jan. 1, 1976; Stats.1982, c. 497, p. 2181, § 82.7, operative July 1, 1983; Stats.1984, c. 927 § 11; Stats. 1996, c. 176 (S.B.1599), § 12; Stats.1996, c. 497 (S.B. 1591), § 18, operative Jan. 1, 1997.)*

California Code Comment

By John A. Bohn and Charles J. Williams

Prior California Law

1. This section follows in general the Uniform Trust Receipts Act. The comparable provisions in California law were contained in former Civil Code §§ 3015, 3016.3, 3016.4 and 3016.5. See Official Comments 1–4.

Changes from U.C.C. (1962 Official Text)

2. This is section 9–304 of the Official Text without change.

Legislative Committee Comment—Senate
1982 Amendment

Subdivision (7) is added to Section 9304 to provide a method of perfecting a security interest in an instrument constituting proceeds (other than cash proceeds) of collateral when the instrument is in the custody of a levying officer. (15 Cal.L.Rev.Comm. Reports 2001; 82 S.J. 11394).

Uniform Commercial Code Comment
Official Reasons for 1977 Change

The definition of "instrument" in Section 9–105(1)(i) includes a certificated security and the perfection of security interests in all securities is governed by Section 8–321. Hence, certificated securities are expressly excluded from this section.

Note that a perfected security interest under Section 8–321 must be created by a transfer under Section 8–313(1) which, when certificated securities are involved, requires possession or a functional equivalent thereof. The 21 day initial grace period of subsection (4) is reflected in

Section 8–313(1)(i) and the reference thereto in Section 8–321(2). The 21 day grace period of subsection (5) is reflected in Section 8–321(4).

Uniform Commercial Code Comment
Prior Uniform Statutory Provision:
Sections 3 and 8(1), Uniform Trust Receipts Act.
Purposes:
1. For most types of property, filing and taking possession are alternative methods of perfection. For some types of intangibles (i.e., accounts and general intangibles) filing is the only available method (see Section 9–305 and point 1 of Comment thereto). With respect to instruments subsection (1) provides that, except for the cases of "temporary perfection" covered in subsections (4) and (5), taking possession is the only available method; this provision follows the Uniform Trust Receipts Act. The rule is based on the thought that where the collateral consists of instruments, it is universal practice for the secured party to take possession of them in pledge; any surrender of possession to the debtor is for a short time; therefore it would be unwise to provide the alternative of perfection for a long period by filing which, since it in no way corresponds with commercial practice, would serve no useful purpose.

For similar reasons, filing is not permitted as to money. Perfection of security interests in certificated securities, which are covered by the definition of instruments, is governed by Section 8–321 and, therefore, excluded from this section.

Subsection (1) further provides that filing is available as a method of perfection for security interests in chattel paper and negotiable documents, which also come within Section 9–305 on perfection by possession. Chattel paper is sometimes delivered to the assignee, sometimes left in the hands of the assignor for collection; subsection (1) allows the assignee to perfect his interest by filing in the latter case. Negotiable documents may be, and usually are, delivered to the secured party; subsection (1) follows the Uniform Trust Receipts Act in allowing filing as an alternative method of perfection. Perfection of an interest in goods through a non-negotiable document is covered in subsection (3).

2. Subsection (2), following prior law and consistently with the provisions of Article 7, takes the position that, so long as a negotiable document covering goods is outstanding, title to the goods is, so to say, locked up in the document and the proper way of dealing with such goods is through the document. Perfection therefore is to be made with respect to the document and, when made, automatically carries over to the goods. Any interest perfected directly in the goods while the document is outstanding (for example, a chattel mortgage type of security interest on goods in a warehouse) is subordinated to an outstanding negotiable document.

3. Subsection (3) takes a different approach to the problem of goods covered by a non-negotiable document or otherwise in the possession of a bailee who has not issued a negotiable document. Here title to the goods is not looked on as being locked up in the document and the secured party may perfect his interest directly in the goods by filing as to them. The subsection states two other methods of perfection: issuance of the document in the secured party's name (as consignee of a straight bill of lading or the person to whom delivery would be made under a non-negotiable warehouse receipt) and receipt of notification of the secured party's interest by the bailee which, under Section 9–305, is looked on as equivalent to taking possession by the secured party.

4. Subsections (4) and (5) follow the Uniform Trust Receipts Act in giving perfected status to security interests in instruments (other than certificated securities, which are governed by Section 8–321) and documents for a short period although there has been no filing and the collateral is in the debtor's possession. The period of 21 days is chosen to conform to the provisions of Section 60 of the Federal Bankruptcy Act. There are a variety of legitimate reasons—some of them are described in subsections (5) (a) and (5) (b)—why such collateral has to be temporarily released to a debtor and no useful purpose would be served by cluttering the files with records of such exceedingly short term transactions. Under subsection (4) the 21 day perfection runs from the date of attachment; there is no limitation on the purpose for which the debtor is in possession but the secured party must have given new value under a written security agreement. Under subsection (5) the 21 day perfection runs from the date a secured party who already has a perfected security interest turns over the collateral to the debtor (an example is a bank which has acquired a bill of lading by honoring drafts drawn under a letter of credit and subsequently turns over the bill of lading to its customer); there is no new value requirement but the turn-over must be for one or more of the purposes stated in subsections (5) (a) and (5) (b). Note that while subsection (4) is restricted to instruments and *negotiable* documents, subsection (5) extends to goods covered by non-negotiable documents as well. Thus the letter of credit bank referred to in the example could make a subsection (5) turn-over without regard to the form of the bill of lading, provided that, in the case of a non-negotiable document, it had previously perfected its interest under one of the methods stated in subsection (3). But note that the discussion of subsection (5) in this Comment deals only with perfection. Priority of a security interest in inventory after surrender of the document depends on compliance with the requirements of Section 9–312(3) on notice to prior inventory financer.

Finally, it should be noted that the 21 days applies only to the documents and to the goods obtained by surrender thereof. If the goods are sold, the security interest will continue in proceeds for only 10 days under Section 9–306, unless a further perfection occurs as to the security interest in proceeds.

Cross References:
Article 7 and Sections 9–303, 9–305 and 9–312(3).
Definitional Cross References:
"Chattel paper". Section 9–105.
"Debtor". Section 9–105.
"Document". Section 9–105.
"Goods". Section 9–105.
"Instrument". Section 9–105.
"Receives" notification. Section 1–201.
"Sale". Sections 2–106 and 9–105.
"Secured party". Section 9–105.
"Security agreement". Section 9–105.
"Security interest". Section 1–201.
"Value". Section 1–201.
"Written". Section 1–201.

Cross References
Commercial paper, see Commercial Code § 3101 et seq.
Computation of time,
  Generally, see Government Code § 6800 et seq.
  Last day a holiday, see Code of Civil Procedure § 12a; Government Code § 6800.
Continuity of perfection, see Commercial Code § 9303.
Documents of title, see Commercial Code § 7101 et seq.
Investment securities, see Commercial Code § 8101 et seq.
Possession of collateral by secured party, see Commercial Code § 9305.
Priorities among conflicting security interests in the same collateral, see Commercial Code § 9312.
Priority of chattel paper and instruments over security interests perfected under this section, see Commercial Code § 9308.
Time for perfection, see Commercial Code § 9303.
Transfer or pledge of investment securities by bookkeeping entry, see Commercial Code § 8320.

§ 9305. Security interest perfected by possession of collateral

A security interest in * * * goods, instruments * * *, money, negotiable documents or chattel paper may be perfected by the secured party's taking possession of the collateral. <u>A security interest in the right to proceeds of a written letter of credit may be perfected by the secured party's taking possession of the letter of credit.</u> If such collateral other than goods covered by a negotiable document is held by a bailee, the secured party is deemed to have possession from the time the bailee receives notification of the secured party's interest. A security interest is perfected by possession from the time possession is taken without relation back and continues only so long as possession is retained, unless otherwise specified in this division. The security interest may be otherwise perfected as provided in this division before or after the period of possession by the secured party. *(Stats.1963, c. 819, § 9305. Amended by Stats.1974, c. 997, p. 2127, § 24, eff. Jan. 1, 1976; Stats.1984, c. 927, § 12; Stats.1996, c. 176 (S.B.1599), § 13; Stats.1996, c. 497 (S.B.1591), § 19, operative Jan. 1, 1997.)*

California Code Comment

By John A. Bohn and Charles J. Williams

Prior California Law

1. The Commercial Code retains the common law idea of perfecting a security interest by possession.

Under this section a security interest can be perfected by transfer of possession when the collateral is goods, instruments, documents or chattel paper. If the collateral is an account, contract right or general intangible, the security interest can be perfected only by filing. Official Comment 1.

2. The Commercial Code does not define "possession". However the language of Official Comment 2 and the analogy which is made to the common law pledge indicates that the common law determinations of "possession" under the pledge would probably apply. 8 UCLA L.Rev. 806, 850.

3. Prior California law recognized that a security interest could be perfected in certain situations by a transfer of possession:

(a) For a trust receipt. Former Civil Code §§ 3016.3, 3016.4.

(b) For a chattel mortgage. Chelhar v. Acme Garage, 18 Cal.App.2d Supp. 775, 61 P.2d 1232 (1937).

(c) For a pledge. Former Civil Code § 2988. No filing was required in the case of field warehousing situations where the arrangements constituted a valid pledge. Heffron v. Bank of America Nat. Trust & Savings Ass'n, 113 Fed.2d 239, 133 ALR 203 (C.C.A.9th 1940).

Possession did not perfect the security interest in an assignment of an account, in an inventory lien, or in a conditional sale.

4. Official Comment 2 indicates that neither the debtor nor any person in the debtor's control can qualify as an agent for the secured party. If this section is so interpreted, it would change the rule under prior California law that a pledge holder can be the pledger's agent or that a pledgee can temporarily allow goods to remain in the hands of the pledgor for some purposes. Stephan v. Lagerqvest, 52 Cal.App. 519, 199 Pac. 52 (1921); Sequeira v. Collins, 153 Cal. 426, 95 Pac. 876 (1908).

Changes from U.C.C. (1962 Official Text)

5. This is section 9–305 of the Official Text without change.

Uniform Commercial Code Comment

Official Reasons for 1977 Change

The definition of "instrument" in Section 9–105(1)(i) includes a certificated security and the perfection of security interests in all securities is governed by Section 8–321. Hence, certificated securities are expressly excluded from this section.

The typical pledge of a certificated security is unaffected by this change since Section 8–313(1)(a) provides for transfer by delivery and Section 8–321(2) provides that a security interest thus transferred is perfected. Section 9–305 has been relied on to perfect security interests in securities in the hands of third parties (first pledgees, brokers, custodian banks, etc.) by notifying such third parties and assuming that they are bailees of certificated securities. When certificated securities have been repledged, held in nominee name or deposited in a securities depository, there is some doubt as to the identity of the bailee or, indeed, whether there is even an instrument that can be identified as the subject matter of the security interest.

The transfer rules of Section 8–313(1), which are incorporated in Section 8–321, are intended to settle such questions with respect to both certificated securities and uncertificated securities, which, by definition, cannot be "possessed." Note that Section 8–313(1)(h) deals explicitly with the problem of perfection by notice, provides that the notice be signed by the debtor-transferor and identifies the proper party to be notified.

Uniform Commercial Code Comment

Prior Uniform Statutory Provision:

None.

Purposes:

1. As under the common law of pledge, no filing is required by this Article to perfect a security interest where the secured party has possession of the collateral. Compare Section 9–302(1)(a). This section permits a security interest to be perfected by transfer of possession only when the collateral is goods, rights to proceeds of letters or credit (if written), *instruments, documents or chattel paper: that is to say, accounts and general intangibles are excluded. As to perfection of security interests in certificated securities by possession, see the general rules on perfection of security interests in investment property in Section 9–115(4) and the special rule in Section 9–115(6) dealing with cases where a secured party takes possession of a security certificate in registered form without obtaining an indorsement. A security interest in accounts and general intangibles—property not ordinarily represented by any writing whose delivery operates to transfer the claim—may under this Article be perfected only by filing, and this rule would not be affected by the fact that a security agreement or other writing described the assignment of such collateral as a "pledge". Section 9–302(1)(e) exempts from filing certain assignments of accounts which are out of the ordinary course of financing: such exempted assignments are perfected when they attach under Section 9–303(1); they do not fall within this section. *Amendments approved by the Permanent Editorial Board for Uniform Commercial Code November 4, 1995.

2. Possession may be by the secured party himself or by an agent on his behalf: it is of course clear, however, that the debtor or a person controlled by him cannot qualify as such an agent for the secured party. See also the last sentence of Section 9–205. Where the collateral (except for goods covered by a negotiable document) is held by a bailee, the time of perfection of the security interest, under the second sentence of the section, is when the bailee receives notification of the secured party's interest: this rule rejects the common law doctrine that it is necessary for the bailee to attorn to the secured party or acknowledge that he now holds on his behalf.

3. The third sentence of the section rejects the "equitable pledge" theory of relation back, under which the taking possession was deemed to relate back to the date of the original security agreement. The relation back theory has had little vitality since the 1938 revision of the Federal Bankruptcy Act, which introduced in Section 60(a) provisions designed to make such interests voidable as preferences in bankruptcy proceedings. This section now brings state law into conformity with the overriding federal policy: where a pledge transaction is contemplated, perfection dates only from the time possession is taken, although a security interest may attach, unperfected, before that under the rules stated in Section 9–204. The only exception to this rule is the short twenty-one day period of perfection provided in Section 9–304(4) and (5), during which a debtor may have possession of specified collateral in which there is a perfected security interest.

Cross References:

Sections 5–116, 9–204, 9–302, 9–303 and 9–304.

Definitional Cross References:

"Chattel paper". Section 9–105.
"Collateral". Section 9–105.
"Documents". Section 9–105.
"Goods". Section 9–105.
"Instruments". Section 9–105.
"Receives" notification. Section 1–201.
"Secured party". Section 9–105.
"Security interest". Section 1–201.

Cross References

Attachment of security interests, see Commercial Code § 9203.
Commercial paper, see Commercial Code § 3101 et seq.
Continuity of perfection, see Commercial Code § 9303.
Documents of title, see Commercial Code § 7101.
Instruments or negotiable documents, perfection of security interest, see Commercial Code § 9304.

Letter of advice of international sight draft, see Commercial Code § 3701.
Letters of credit, see Commercial Code § 5101 et seq.
Manufactured homes, mobilehomes or commercial coaches, priority of security interests perfected pursuant to this section, see Health and Safety Code § 18105.
Necessity of filing, exceptions, see Commercial Code § 9302.
Suspension, revocation, or cancellation of certificate of title of manufactured homes, mobilehomes and commercial coaches, affect on perfected security interest, see Health and Safety Code § 18122.
Time for perfection, see Commercial Code § 9303.
Transfer of personal property, actual change of possession indicating pledge, see Civil Code § 2924.
Transfer or assignment of letters of credit, see Commercial Code § 5116.
Transfer or pledge of investment securities by bookkeeping entry, see Commercial Code § 8320.
Transfers and liens without delivery, see Civil Code § 3440.

§ 9306. "Proceeds"; Secured Party's Rights on Disposition of Collateral

(1) "Proceeds" includes whatever is received upon the sale, exchange, collection or other disposition of collateral or proceeds. Insurance payable by reason of loss or damage to the collateral is proceeds, except to the extent that it is payable to a person other than a party to the security agreement. <u>Any payments or distributions made with respect to investment property collateral are proceeds.</u> Money, checks, deposit accounts, and the like are "cash proceeds." All other proceeds are "noncash proceeds."

(2) Except where this division or subdivision (4) of Section 8321 otherwise provides, a security interest continues in collateral notwithstanding sale, exchange or other disposition thereof unless the disposition was authorized by the secured party in the security agreement or otherwise, and also continues in any identifiable proceeds including collections received by the debtor.

(3) The security interest in proceeds is a continuously perfected security interest if the interest in the original collateral was perfected but it ceases to be a perfected security interest and becomes unperfected 10 days after receipt of the proceeds by the debtor unless any of the following apply:

(a) A filed financing statement covers the original collateral and the proceeds are collateral in which a security interest may be perfected by filing in the office or offices where the financing statement has been filed and, if the proceeds are acquired with cash proceeds, the description of collateral in the financing statement indicates the types of property constituting the proceeds.

(b) A filed financing statement covers the original collateral and the proceeds are identifiable cash proceeds.

<u>(c) The original collateral was investment property and the proceeds are identifiable cash proceeds.</u>

(d) The security interest in the proceeds is perfected before the expiration of the 10-day period.

Except as provided in this section, a security interest in proceeds can be perfected only by the methods or under the circumstances permitted in this division or Division 8 (commencing with Section 8101) for original collateral of the same type.

(4) In the event of insolvency proceedings instituted by or against a debtor, a secured party with a perfected security interest in proceeds has a perfected security interest only in all of the following proceeds:

(a) In identifiable noncash proceeds and in a separate deposit account containing only proceeds.

(b) In identifiable cash proceeds in the form of money which is neither commingled with other money nor deposited in a deposit account prior to the insolvency proceedings.

(c) In identifiable cash proceeds in the form of checks and the like which are not deposited in a deposit account prior to the insolvency proceedings.

(d) In all cash and deposit accounts of the debtor in which proceeds have been commingled with other funds, but the perfected security interest under this paragraph (d) is both:

(i) Subject to any right of setoff.

(ii) Limited to an amount not greater than the amount of any cash proceeds received by the debtor within 10 days before the institution of the insolvency proceedings less the sum of (I) the payments to the secured party on account of cash proceeds received by the debtor during such period and (II) the cash proceeds received by the debtor during such period to which the secured party is entitled under paragraphs (a), (b), and (c).

(5) If a sale of goods results in an account or chattel paper which is transferred by the seller to a secured party, and if the goods are returned to or are repossessed by the seller or the secured party, the following rules determine priorities:

(a) If the goods were collateral at the time of sale, for an indebtedness of the seller which is still unpaid, the original security interest attaches again to the goods and continues as a perfected security interest if it was perfected at the time when the goods were sold. If the security interest was originally perfected by a filing which is still effective, nothing further is required to continue the perfected status; in any other case, the secured party must take possession of the returned or repossessed goods or must file.

(b) An unpaid transferee of the chattel paper has a security interest in the goods against the transferor. Such security interest is prior to a security interest asserted under paragraph (a) to the extent that the transferee of the chattel paper was entitled to priority under Section 9308.

(c) An unpaid transferee of the account has a security interest in the goods against the transferor. Such security interest is subordinate to a security interest asserted under paragraph (a).

(d) A security interest of an unpaid transferee asserted under paragraph (b) or (c) must be perfected for protection against creditors of the transferor and purchasers of the returned or repossessed goods.

(6) Cash proceeds retain their character as cash proceeds while in the possession of a levying officer pursuant to Title 6.5 (commencing with Section 481.010) or Title 9 (commencing with Section 680.010) of Part 2 of the Code of Civil Procedure. *(Stats.1963, c. 819, § 9306. Amended by Stats.1974, c. 997, p. 2127, § 25, eff. Jan. 1, 1976; Stats.1982, c. 497, p. 2182, § 82.8, operative July 1, 1983; Stats.1984, c. 927, § 13; Stats. 1996, c. 497 (S.B.1591), § 20, operative Jan. 1, 1997.)*

California Code Comment

By John A. Bohn and Charles J. Williams

Prior California Law

1. This section, except for subdivision (4) relating to insolvency proceedings, provides the right to perfect a security interest only in proceeds which are identifiable. This perfection can take place in two ways: first, automatically when the debtor receives proceeds and the financing statement also covers proceeds; second, upon filing within 10 days of the date when the debtor receives the proceeds.

2. Changes from prior California law:

(a) For a chattel mortgage, conditional sale, and pledge, there were no special provisions on the right of a secured party to proceeds. The right to proceeds under these transactions depended upon the ability to trace the funds in accordance with common law rules. This section eliminates the problem of tracing.

(b) For trust receipt, former Civil Code § 3016.6 attempted to give the entruster a right to identifiable proceeds and to proceeds received within 10 days of insolvency proceedings. See Peoples Finance & Thrift Co. of Visalia v. Bowman, 58 Cal.App.2d 729, 137 P.2d 729 (1943). In re Crosstown Motors Inc., 272 F.2d 244, (CCA 7th 1959) held that former Civil Code § 3016.6 created a priority under state law but not in bankruptcy.

(c) For an assignment of an account, former Civil Code § 3025 made the assignor trustee of the proceeds for the assignee.

(d) For an inventory lien, former Civil Code § 3037 provided that the lien attached to the proceeds of merchandise sold.

3. The effect of subdivision (4) is described in the Marsh and Warren Report:

"This subsection [subdivision] deals with the situation where the debtor has sold the collateral pursuant to permission to do so in the loan agreement, but has not accounted to the secured party for the proceeds of sale at the time when insolvency supervenes. Under present law, the right of the secured party generally depends upon whether he can 'trace' the proceeds, and, this in turn, depends upon difficult and confusing doctrines regarding 'tracing' (e.g., first-in, first-out; non-trust-funds used first; etc.). The drafters of the Uniform Trust Receipts Act apparently attempted to give the secured party a lien upon 'all assets' of the debtor to the extent of proceeds received within 10 days prior to insolvency, but In re Crosstown Motors, Inc., 272 F.2d 224 (7th Cir.1959), held that that Act only created a State 'priority' which is invalid in bankruptcy. Contra: In re Harpeth Motors, 135 F.Supp. 863 (M.D.Tenn.1955).

"This subsection [subdivision] solves the problem by eliminating the requirement of 'tracing' and clearly giving to the secured party a lien upon 'all cash and bank accounts' of the debtor to the extent of proceeds received within 10 days of insolvency. The secured party also has a right to any 'identifiable' proceeds which have not been commingled with other funds. Presumably, where the proceeds have been commingled, the right of the secured party to 'trace' into a bank account beyond the 10-day period is lost, although the subsection does not expressly say so.

"It is not clear whether the term 'identifiable noncash proceeds' would include a separate bank account in which the debtor is required to deposit proceeds and in which he deposits only proceeds. If not, then the right of the secured party to such a bank account would be limited under clause (d) to proceeds deposited in it within the 10-day period. Since such a bank account includes only 'his' money, certainly the secured party should have a right to it regardless of when the proceeds were received and this interpretation should not be left to inference.

"With respect to 'commingled' cash and bank accounts, the original clause (d) would give the secured party a lien to the amount of proceeds received within the 10-day period upon *all* cash and bank accounts of the debtor, even though as to some or most of them it could be demonstrated that *no* proceeds had gone into them. In other words, suppose the debtor had four bank accounts, and he commingled proceeds in only one of them, which had a zero balance on the date of insolvency; the secured party would have a lien on the other three bank accounts in which no proceeds had been commingled. This seems to go too far in favoring the secured party over unsecured creditors. Therefore, the amendment proposed by the California Bankers Committee is recommended, which would limit this lien to those bank accounts in which commingling has occurred.

"The proposed amendment of the Credit Organizations Committee would leave in effect the present law regarding 'tracing' with all of its uncertainties. We believe that the substitution of a simple and arbitrary rule such as that of the Code is preferable from the point of view of both the secured creditor and the unsecured creditors." Sixth Progress Report to the Legislature by Senate Fact Finding Committee on Judiciary (1959–1961) Part 1, The Uniform Commercial Code, pp. 571, 572.

Changes from U.C.C. (1962 Official Text)

4. Subdivision (4) of the Official Text as changed in California reads as follows:

(4) In the event of insolvency proceedings instituted by or against a debtor, a secured party with a perfected security interest in proceeds has a perfected security interest

(a) In identifiable noncash proceeds and in a separate bank account containing only proceeds:

(b) In identifiable cash proceeds in the form of money which is not commingled with other money or deposited in a bank account prior to the insolvency proceedings;

(c) In identifiable cash proceeds in the form of checks and the like which are not deposited in a bank account prior to the insolvency proceedings; and

(d) In all cash and bank accounts of the debtor [if other] in which [cash] proceeds have been commingled [or deposited in] a [bank account] with other funds, but the perfected security interest under this paragraph (d) is

(i) Subject to any right of set-off; and

(ii) Limited to an amount not greater than the amount of any cash proceeds received by the debtor within 10 days before the institution of the insolvency proceedings [and commingled or deposited in a bank account prior to the insolvency proceedings less the amount of cash proceeds received by the debtor and paid over to the secured party during the ten day period] less the sum of (I) the payments to the secured party on account of cash proceeds received by the debtor during such period and (II) the cash proceeds received by the debtor during such period to which the secured party is entitled under paragraphs (a) through (c) of this subdivision (4).

5. The changes made in subdivision (4) of the California version follow suggestions of the California State Bar Committee and the California Bankers Committee. See the Marsh and Warren report quoted in California Code Comment 3 above.

Legislative Committee Comment—Assembly
1982 Amendment

Subdivision (6) is added to Section 9306 to make clear that custody of cash proceeds by a levying officer does not affect the status of the cash proceeds provided by this section. (15 Cal.L.Rev.Comm. Reports 2001; 82 A.J. 9356).

Uniform Commercial Code Comment
P.E.B. Commentary No. 3, March 10, 1990

Purposes:

* * * * *

3. In most cases when a debtor makes an unauthorized disposition of collateral, the security interest, under prior law and under this

Article, continues in the original collateral in the hands of the purchaser or other transferee. That is to say, since the transferee takes subject to the security interest, the secured party may repossess the collateral from him or in an appropriate case maintain an action for conversion. Subsection (2) codifies this rule. The secured party may claim both proceeds and collateral, but may of course have only one satisfaction.

In many cases a purchaser or other transferee of collateral will take free of a security interest: in such cases the secured party's only right will be to proceeds. A transferee will acquire the collateral free and clear of a pre-existing security interest only if the disposition of the collateral by the debtor was authorized by the secured party free and clear of the secured party's security interest. If the disposition was not authorized by the secured party, or was authorized by the secured party subject to the secured party's security interest, the transferee will not acquire the collateral free and clear of the security interest. The authorization may be contained in the security agreement or otherwise given. The right to proceeds, either under the rules of this section or under specific mention thereof in a security agreement or financing statement does not in itself constitute an authorization of sale. PEB Commentary No. 3, dated March 10, 1990, analyzes the interplay between this Section and Section 9–402(7) [Uniform Laws Annotated, UCC, APP II, comment 3].

* * * * * *

P.E.B. Commentary No. 5, March 10, 1990

5. "Creditors" and "purchasers" as used in paragraph (5)(d) do not include the original secured inventory financer of the seller of goods under subsection (a). If a purchaser of chattel paper generated by a sale of the goods attains priority over the seller's inventory financer under Section 9–308, the purchaser retains that priority in the event the goods covered by the chattel paper are returned to the seller, without having to further perfect against the inventory financer. This priority issue will usually arise in the context of the original inventory financer and the chattel paper purchaser both claiming the goods or the proceeds of any sale or disposition thereof by the seller See PEB Commentary No. 5, dated March 10, 1990 [Uniform Laws Annotated, UCC, APP II, Comment 5].

6. Where a debtor has granted to a secured party a security interest in goods and the debtor later leases those goods as lessor, the lease rentals constitute proceeds of the secured party's collateral consisting of the goods. See PEB Commentary No. 9, dated June 25, 1992 [Uniform Laws Annotated, UCC, APP II, Comment 9].

* * * * * *

Uniform Commercial Code Comment

Prior Uniform Statutory Provision:
Section 10, Uniform Trust Receipts Act.
Purposes:

1. This section states a secured party's right to the proceeds received by a debtor on disposition of collateral and states when his interest in such proceeds is perfected.

It makes clear that insurance proceeds from casualty loss of collateral are proceeds within the meaning of this section.

As to the proceeds of consigned goods, see Section 9–114 and the Comment thereto.

2. (a) Whether a debtor's sale of collateral was authorized or unauthorized, prior law generally gave the secured party a claim to the proceeds. Sometimes it was said that the security interest attached to the "property" received in substitution; sometimes it was said the debtor held the proceeds as "trustee" or "agent" for the secured party. Whatever the formulation of the rule, the secured party, if he could identify the proceeds, could reclaim them or their equivalent from the debtor or his trustee in bankruptcy. This section provides new rules for insolvency proceedings. Paragraphs 4(a) through (c) substitute specific rules of identification for general principles of tracing. Paragraph 4(d) limits the security interest in proceeds not within these rules to an amount of the debtor's cash and deposit accounts not greater than cash proceeds received within ten days of insolvency proceedings less the cash proceeds during this period already paid over and less the amounts for which the security interest is recognized under paragraphs 4(a) through (c).

(b) Subsections (2) and (3) make clear that the four-month period for calculating a voidable preference in bankruptcy begins with the date of the secured party's obtaining the security interest in the original collateral and not with the date of his obtaining control of the proceeds. The interest in the proceeds "continues" as a perfected interest if the original interest was perfected; but the interest ceases to be perfected after the expiration of ten days unless a filed financing statement covered the original collateral and the proceeds are collateral of a type as to which a security interest could be perfected by a filing in the same office or unless the secured party perfects his interest in the proceeds themselves—*i.e.*, by filing a financing statement covering them or by taking possession. See Section 9–312(6) and Comment thereto for priority of rights in proceeds perfected by a filing as to original collateral.

(c) Where cash proceeds are covered into the debtor's checking account and paid out in the operation of the debtor's business, recipients of the funds of course take free of any claim which the secured party may have in them as proceeds. What has been said relates to payments and transfers in ordinary course. The law of fraudulent conveyances would no doubt in appropriate cases support recovery of proceeds by a secured party from a transferee out of ordinary course or otherwise in collusion with the debtor to defraud the secured party.

3. In most cases when a debtor makes an unauthorized disposition of collateral, the security interest, under prior law and under this Article, continues in the original collateral in the hands of the purchaser or other transferee. That is to say, since the transferee takes subject to the security interest, the secured party may repossess the collateral from him or in an appropriate case maintain an action for conversion. Subsection (2) codifies this rule. The secured party may claim both proceeds and collateral, but may of course have only one satisfaction.

In many cases a purchaser or other transferee of collateral will take free of a security interest: in such cases the secured party's only right will be to proceeds. The transferee will take free whenever the disposition was authorized; the authorization may be contained in the security agreement or otherwise given. The right to proceeds, either under the rules of this section or under specific mention thereof in a security agreement or financing statement does not in itself constitute an authorization of sale.

Section 9–301 states when transferees take free of unperfected security interests. Sections 9–307 on goods, 9–308 on chattel paper and instruments and 9–309 on negotiable instruments, negotiable documents and securities state when purchasers of such collateral take free of a security interest even though perfected and even though the disposition was not authorized.

4. Subsection (5) states rules to determine priorities when collateral which has been sold is returned to the debtor: for example goods returned to a department store by a dissatisfied customer. The most typical problems involve sale and return of inventory, but the subsection can also apply to equipment. Under the rule of Benedict v. Ratner, failure to segregate such returned goods sometimes led to invalidation of the entire security arrangement. This Article rejects the Benedict v. Ratner line of cases (see Section 9–205 and Comment). Subsection (5) (a) of this section reinforces the rule of Section 9–205: as between secured party and debtor (and debtor's trustee in bankruptcy) the original security interest continues on the returned goods. Whether or not the security interest in the returned goods is perfected depends upon factors stated in the text.

Paragraphs (5)(b), (c) and (d) deal with a different aspect of the returned goods situation. Assume that a dealer has sold an automobile and transferred the chattel paper or the account arising on the sale to Bank X (which had not previously financed the car as inventory). Thereafter the buyer of the automobile rightfully rescinds the sale, say for breach of warranty, and the car is returned to the dealer. Paragraph (5)(b) gives the bank as transferee of the chattel paper or the account a security interest in the car against the dealer. For protection against dealer's creditors or purchasers from him (other than buyers in the ordinary course of business, see Section 9–307), Bank X as the transferee, under paragraph (5)(d), must perfect its interest by taking possession of the car or by filing as to it. Perfection of his original interest in the chattel paper or the account does not automatically carry over to the returned car, as it does under paragraph (5)(a) where the secured party originally financed the dealer's inventory.

In the situation covered by (5)(b) and (5)(c) a secured party who financed the inventory and a secured party to whom the chattel paper or the account was transferred may both claim the returned goods—the inventory financer under paragraph (5)(a), the transferee under paragraphs (5) (b) and (5) (c). With respect to chattel paper, Section 9–308 regulates the priorities. With respect to an account, paragraph (5) (c) subordinates the security interest of the transferee of the account to that of the inventory financer. However, if the inventory security interest was unperfected, the transferee's interest could become entitled to priority under the rules stated in Section 9–312(5).

In cases of repossession by the dealer and also in cases where the chattel was returned to the dealer by the voluntary act of the account debtor, the dealer's position may be that of a mere custodian; he may be an agent for resale, but without any other obligation to the holder of the chattel paper; he may be obligated to repurchase the chattel, the chattel paper or the account from the secured party or to hold it as collateral for a loan secured by a transfer of the chattel paper or the account.

If the dealer thereafter sells the chattel to a buyer in ordinary course of business in any of the foregoing cases, the buyer is fully protected under Section 2–403(2) as well as under Section 9–307(1), whichever is technically applicable.

Cross References:
Sections 9–307, 9–308 and 9–309.
Point 3: Sections 1–205 and 9–301.
Point 4: Sections 2–403(2), 9–205 and 9–312.

Definitional Cross References:
"Account". Section 9–106.
"Bank". Section 1–201.
"Chattel paper". Section 9–105.
"Check". Sections 3–104 and 9–105.
"Collateral". Section 9–105.
"Creditors". Section 1–201.
"Debtor". Section 9–105.
"Deposit account". Section 9–105.
"Goods". Section 9–105.
"Insolvency proceedings". Section 1–201.
"Money" Section 1–201.
"Purchaser". Section 1–201.
"Sale". Sections 2–106 and 9–105.
"Secured party". Section 9–105.
"Security agreement". Section 9–105.
"Security interest". Section 1–201.

Cross References

Collection rights of secured party, see Commercial Code § 9502.
Computation of time,
  Generally, see Government Code § 6800 et seq.
  Last day a holiday, see Code of Civil Procedure § 12a; Government Code § 6800.
Conflicting security interests, priorities, see Commercial Code § 9312.
Course of dealing and usage of trade, see Commercial Code § 1205.
Formal requisites of financing statements, see Commercial Code § 9402.
Good faith purchaser for value, see Commercial Code § 2403.
Purchasers, taking free from security interest, see Commercial Code § 9307 et seq.
Rights of seller's creditors against sold goods, see Commercial Code § 2402.
Unperfected security interests, subordination, see Commercial Code § 9301.
Use or disposition of security without accounting, see Commercial Code § 9205.

§ 9307. Protection of Buyers of Goods

(1) A buyer in ordinary course of business (subdivision (9) of Section 1201) * * * takes free of a security interest created by his seller even though the security interest is perfected and even though the buyer knows of its existence.

(3) [1] A buyer other than a buyer in ordinary course of business (subdivision (1) of this section) takes free of a security interest to the extent that it secures future advances made after the secured party acquires knowledge of the purchase, unless made pursuant to a commitment entered into without knowledge of the purchase. *(Stats.1963, c. 819, § 9307. Amended by Stats.1974, c. 997, p. 2129, § 26, eff. Jan. 1, 1976.)*

[1] Section 26 of Stats.1974, c. 997, p. 2129, contains no subd. (2).

California Code Comment

By John A. Bohn and Charles J. Williams

Prior California Law

1. Subdivision (1) continues the rule under prior California law to the effect that a person who buys goods in the ordinary course of business in good faith and without knowledge of a security interest takes the goods free of the security interest.

The rule of this subdivision is consistent with the Uniform Trust Receipts Act and the Uniform Conditional Sales Act. Official Comments 1 and 2.

2. Under prior California law the rule as to each security device was as follows:

(a) For a chattel mortgage, the question was academic because a mortgage could not be taken on the stock in trade of a merchant. Former Civil Code § 2955.

(b) For a conditional sales contract, the rule was substantially the same as this section but it was based upon principles of estoppel against the seller to assert his title. Asp v. Lowry, 117 Cal.App.2d 81, 254 P.2d 967 (1953).

(c) For a pledge, the security interest was perfected by possession and no purchaser could acquire a right prior to the pledgee under former Civil Code § 2988. However, under former Civil Code § 3015, a pledge was valid for 10 days even though possession was not taken. In this case a purchaser without notice would acquire a prior right.

(d) For a trust receipt, the rule was in accord with subdivision (1). Former Civil Code § 3016.5.

(e) For an inventory lien, the rule was in accord with subdivision (1) because the lien terminated when the goods it covers were sold in the ordinary course of business. Former Civil Code § 3037.

(f) For an assignment of account, a perfected assignment was valid as against a subsequent purchaser. Former Civil Code §§ 3018 and 3019.

Changes from U.C.C. (1962 Official Text)

3. Subdivision (2) of section 9–307 of the Official Text is omitted in the California version. This section reads as follows:

[(2) In the case of consumer goods and in the case of farm equipment having an original purchase price not in excess of $2500 (other than fixtures, see Section 9–313), a buyer takes free of a security interest even though perfected if he buys without knowledge of the security interest, for value and for his own personal, family or household purposes or his own farming operations unless prior to the purchase the secured party has filed a financing statement covering such goods.]

4. The reason for deleting subdivision (2) was that it would have required the installment seller of consumer goods and farm equipment to file:

"The Code does not require filing to perfect a purchase money security interest in consumer goods or in farm equipment costing less than $2500 as against a creditor of the buyer or a purchaser from the buyer. Section 19302 [9302]. This is to eliminate from the filing requirement the thousands of retail sales per day which are now handled under conditional sale contract and not required to be filed or recorded. However, by this subsection unless there is a filing with respect to these transactions, the security interest is not perfected as against purchaser who buys 'for his own personal, family or household purposes or for his own farming operations.' Thus, a filing requirement is reintroduced through the back door, and in order to be completely protected, the installment seller must file. We think such a requirement is impractical, and that the secured party should not be subjected to this risk because he does not file. Even if he did file, and therefore retained his priority over the purchaser from his buyer, the chances are a 1,000 to 1 that a purchaser of the type described in this subsection would not check the records anyway. To say that the installment seller must file in order to give such a purchaser notice ignores realities." Marsh and Warren Report, Sixth Progress Report to the Legislature by Senate Fact Finding

Committee on Judiciary, (1959–1961) Part 1, The Uniform Commercial Code, pp. 572–573.

Uniform Commercial Code Comment

Prior Uniform Statutory Provision:

Section 9, Uniform Conditional Sales Act; Section 9(2), Uniform Trust Receipts Act.

Purposes:

1. This section states when buyers of goods take free of a security interest even though perfected. A buyer who takes free of a perfected security interest of course takes free of an unperfected one. Section 9–301 should be consulted to determine what purchasers, in addition to the buyers covered in this section, take free of an unperfected security interest.

Article 2 (Sales) states general rules on purchase of goods from a seller with defective or voidable title (Section 2–403).

2. The definition of "buyer in ordinary course of business" in Section 1–201(9) restricts the application of subsection (1) to buyers (except pawnbrokers) "from a person in the business of selling goods of that kind": thus the subsection applies, in the terminology of this Article, primarily to inventory. Subsection (1) further excludes from its operation buyers of "farm products", defined in Section 9–109(3), from a person engaged in farming operations. The buyer in ordinary course of business is defined as one who buys "in good faith and without knowledge that the sale to him is in violation of the ownership rights or security interest of a third party." This section provides that such a buyer takes free of a security interest, even though perfected, and although he knows the security interest exists. Reading the two provisions together, it results that the buyer takes free if he merely knows that there is a security interest which covers the goods but takes subject if he knows, in addition, that the sale is in violation of some term in the security agreement not waived by the words or conduct of the secured party.

The limitations which this section imposes on the persons who may take free of a security interest apply of course only to unauthorized sales by the debtor. If the secured party has authorized the sale in the security agreement or otherwise, the buyer takes free without regard to the limitations of this section. Section 9–306 states the right of a secured party to the proceeds of a sale, authorized or unauthorized.

3. [Subsection 2 not enacted in California, see California Code Comment, note 3].

4. Although a buyer is of course subject to the Code's system of notice from filing or possession, subsection (3) makes clear that he will not be subject to future advances under a security interest after the secured party has knowledge that the buyer has purchased the collateral and in any event after 45 days after the purchase unless the advances were made pursuant to a commitment entered into before the expiration of the 45 days and without knowledge of the purchase. Of course, a buyer in ordinary course who takes free of the security interest under subsection (1) is not subject to any future advances. Compare Sections 9–301(4) and 9–312(7).

Cross References:

Point 1: Sections 2–403 and 9–301.
Point 2: Section 9–306.
Point 3: Sections 9–301 and 9–302.
Point 4: Sections 9–301(4) and 9–312(7).

Definitional Cross References:

"Buyer in ordinary course of business". Section 1–201.
"Consumer goods". Section 9–109.
"Goods". Section 9–105.
"Knows" and "Knowledge". Section 1–201.
"Person". Section 1–201.
"Purchase". Section 1–201.
"Pursuant to commitment". Section 9–105.
"Secured party". Section 9–105.
"Security interest". Section 1–201.
"Value". Section 1–201.

Cross References

Disposition of collateral, secured party's rights, see Commercial Code § 9306.

Disposition of property subject to lien, continuation of lien, and exceptions, see Code of Civil Procedure § 697.610.
Document of title to goods defeated in certain cases, see Commercial Code § 7503.
Good faith purchase of goods, see Commercial Code § 2403.
Necessity of filing, exceptions, see Commercial Code § 9302.
Personal property not in custody of levying officer transferred or encumbered, exceptions, see Code of Civil Procedure § 697.740.
Priorities among conflicting security interests in the same collateral, see Commercial Code § 9312.
Unperfected security interests, subordination, see Commercial Code § 9301.

§ 9308. Purchase of Chattel Paper and Instruments

A purchaser of chattel paper or * * * an instrument who gives new value and takes possession of it in the ordinary course of his business * * * has priority over a security interest in the chattel paper or instrument

(a) Which is perfected under Section 9304 (permissive filing and temporary perfection) or under Section 9306 (perfection as to proceeds) if he acts without knowledge that the specific paper or instrument is subject to a security interest; or

(b) Which is claimed merely as proceeds of inventory subject to a security interest (Section 9306) even though he knows that the specific paper or instrument is subject to the security interest. (Stats.1963, c. 819, § 9308. Amended by Stats.1974, c. 997, p. 2129, § 27, eff. Jan. 1, 1976.)

California Code Comment

By John A. Bohn and Charles J. Williams

Prior California Law

1. The effect of this section is to make the purchaser of a nonnegotiable instrument of chattel paper who gives new value in the ordinary course of business prevail over all prior security interests except the security interest of a collecting bank. Commercial Code § 4208 provides for the security interest of a collecting bank.

2. There were no prior comparable statutory provisions. This section alters former Civil Code §§ 3016.5 and 3016.5(a) and 3016.6 to fit the concept of chattel paper. See the Official Comments.

3. The effect of this section on prior California law is described by the Legislative Counsel in the California Annotations to the Proposed Uniform Commercial Code (1960):

"As to chattel mortgages, an assignment of chattel mortgage may be recorded and from the time it is recorded it is constructive notice to all persons except the debtor. See Civil Code Sections 2934 and 2935. A mortgage cannot be assigned independently of the debts secured by the mortgage. See Polhemus v. Trainer, 30 Cal. 686.

"An assignment of a conditional sales contract is not perfected against third persons until the contract is indorsed or assigned in writing and delivered to the buyer under Civil Code Section 955. There are no provisions for filing or recording the instrument.

"As to pledges, trust receipts, assignments of accounts receivable, and inventory liens, the section is new." Sixth Progress Report to the Legislature by Senate Fact Finding Committee on Judiciary (1959–1961) Part 1, The Uniform Commercial Code, p. 131.

Changes from U.C.C. (1962 Official Text)

4. This is section 9–308 of the Official Text without change.

Uniform Commercial Code Comment

3. Clause (a) deals with the case where the non-possessory security interest in the chattel paper is more than a mere claim to proceeds—i.e., exists in favor of a secured party who has given value against the paper, whether or not he financed the inventory whose sale gave rise to it. I this case the purchaser, to take priority, must not only give new v and take possession in the ordinary course of his business; he m

§ 9308

take without knowledge of the existing security interest. Thus a secured party, who has a specific interest in the chattel paper and not merely a claim to proceeds, and who wishes to leave the paper in the debtor's possession can, because of the knowledge requirement, protect himself against purchasers by stamping or noting on the paper the fact that it has been assigned to him. A chattel paper financer who gives new value and takes possession of chattel paper in the ordinary course of his business and is without knowledge of prior security interests in the chattel paper has no duty to search for Article 9 filings against the chattel paper or to make other inquiries which might reveal perfected prior interests in the paper, even though the chattel paper financer is aware of the possibility that a prior security interest exists. Mere knowledge of an Article 9 filing against chattel paper does not give knowledge of the existence of a security interest in the chattel paper itself. See PEB Commentary No. 8, dated December 10, 1991 [Uniform Laws Annotated, UCC, APP II, comment 8].

Prior Uniform Statutory Provision:
Sections 9(a) and 10 of Uniform Trust Receipts Act.

Purposes:

1. Chattel paper is defined (Section 9–105) as "a writing or writings which evidence both a monetary obligation and a security interest in or a lease of specific goods". Such paper has become an important class of collateral in financing arrangements, which may—as in the automobile and some other fields—follow an earlier financing arrangement covering inventory or which may begin with the chattel paper itself.

Arrangements where the chattel paper is delivered to the secured party who then makes collections, as well as arrangements where the debtor, whether or not he is left in possession of the paper, makes the collections, are both widely used, and are known respectively as notification (or "direct collection") and non-notification (or "indirect collection") arrangements. In the automobile field, for example, when a car is sold to a consumer buyer under an installment purchase agreement and the resulting chattel paper is assigned, the assignee usually takes possession, the obligor is notified of the assignment and is directed to make payments to the assignee. In the furniture field, for an example on the other hand, the chattel paper may be left in the dealer's hands or delivered to the assignee; in either case the obligor may not be notified, and payments are made to the dealer-assignor who receives them under a duty to remit to his assignee. The widespread use of both methods of dealing with chattel paper is recognized by the provisions of this Article, which permit perfection of a chattel paper security interest either by filing or by taking possession.

2. Although perfection by filing is permitted as to chattel paper, certain purchasers of chattel paper allowed to remain in the debtor's possession take free of the security interest despite the filing.

Clause (b) of the section deals with the case where the security interest in the chattel paper is claimed merely as proceeds—i.e., on behalf of an inventory financer who has not by some new transaction with the debtor acquired a specific interest in the chattel paper. In that case a purchaser, even though he knows of the inventory financer's proceeds interest, takes priority provided he gives new value and takes possession of the paper in the ordinary course of his business.

The same basic rule applies in favor of a purchaser of other instruments who claims priority against a proceeds interest therein of which he has knowledge. Thus a purchaser of a negotiable instrument might prevail under clause (b) even though his knowledge of the conflicting proceeds claim precluded his having holder in due course status under Section 9–309.

4. It should be noted that under Section 9–304(1) a security interest in an instrument, negotiable or non-negotiable, cannot be perfected by filing (except where the instrument constitutes part of chattel paper). Thus the only types of perfected non-possessory security interest that can arise in an instrument are the temporary 21 day perfection provided for in Section 9–304(4) and (5) or the 10 day perfection in proceeds of Section 9–306. Where such a perfected interest exists in a non-negotiable instrument, purchasers will take free if they qualify under clause (a) of the section.

Cross References:
Point 1: Sections 9–304(1) and 9–305.
Point 2: Section 9–306.
Point 4: Sections 9–304 and 9–306.

Definitional Cross References:
"Chattel paper". Section 9–105.
"Instrument". Section 9–105.
"Inventory". Section 9–109.
"Knowledge". Section 1–201.
"Proceeds". Section 9–306.
"Purchaser". Section 1–201.
"Security interest". Section 1–201.
"Value". Section 1–201.

Cross References

Assignment of mortgage or beneficial interest under trust deed, see Civil Code § 2934.
Disposition of collateral, secured party's rights, see Commercial Code § 9306.
Documents of title, rights acquired, see Commercial Code § 7502 et seq.
Perfection of security interest in instruments, documents and goods covered by documents, see Commercial Code § 9304.
Possession by secured party, see Commercial Code § 9305.
Priorities among conflicting security interests in the same collateral, see Commercial Code § 9312.
Record of assignment of mortgage or beneficial interest under trust deed not notice to debtor, see Civil Code § 2935.
Rights of holder of negotiable instrument, see Commercial Code § 3301.
Transfer of nonnegotiable instruments, see Civil Code § 955.

§ 9309. Protection of Purchasers of Instruments and Documents

Nothing in this division limits the rights of a holder in due course of a negotiable instrument (Section 3302) or a holder to whom a negotiable document of title has been duly negotiated (Section 7501) or a * * * protected purchaser of a security (Section 8303) and the holders or purchasers take priority over an earlier security interest even though perfected. Filing under this division does not constitute notice of the security interest to the holders or purchasers. (Stats.1963, c. 819, § 9309. Amended by Stats.1974, c. 997, p. 2129, § 28, eff. Jan. 1, 1976; Stats.1984, c. 927, § 14; Stats. 1996, c. 497 (S.B.1591), § 21, operative Jan. 1, 1997.)

California Code Comment

By John A. Bohn and Charles J. Williams

Prior California Law

1. This section is consistent with the policy under prior California law which gave the holder in due course priority over an earlier security interest.

Under prior California law, a prior security interest was subordinate to the right of a holder in due course of a negotiable instrument or a negotiable document of title. Former Civil Code §§ 3138, 1858.69, 2129d. The Uniform Trust Receipts Act did not limit the right of a holder in due course of a negotiable instrument or a document of title. Former Civil Code § 3016.5(1). In the case of an inventory lien, a holder in due course prevailed over merchandise subject to an inventory lien which has been sold and reduced to proceeds. Former Civil Code § 3037(b).

Changes from U.C.C. (1962 Official Text)

2. This is section 9–309 of the Official Text without change.

Uniform Commercial Code Comment

P.E.B. Commentary No. 7, March 10, 1990

Purposes:

* * * * * *

3. The operation of this section can be seen when two secured parties have a perfected security interest in an account, chattel paper, or general intangible and the secured party that does not have priority receives a payment by check directly or indirectly from the account

debtor. If the recipient takes the check under circumstances that give the recipient the rights of a holder in due course (Section 3–302), then the recipient's security interest and the recipient will be entitled to keep the payment. See PEB Commentary No. 7, dated March 10, 1990 [Uniform Laws Annotated, UCC, App II, Comment 7].

*   *   *   *   *   *

Uniform Commercial Code Comment
Official Reasons for 1977 Change

This section presently resolves the conflict which may result when a financial intermediary or secured party wrongfully transfers a certificated security he controls. Since the term "security" now includes, under revised Section 8–102, uncertificated securities, this section will also cover the situation where a financial intermediary or secured party who is the registered owner or registered pledgee of an uncertificated security wrongfully causes the registration of transfer or pledge. In either case, a bona fide purchaser (including a pledgee) from the financial intermediary or secured party will prevail over a secured creditor of the beneficial owner who has created and perfected his security interest by notice to or acknowledgment from the wrongful transferor under Section 8–321.

Uniform Commercial Code Comment
Prior Uniform Statutory Provision:
Section 9(a), Uniform Trust Receipts Act.

Purposes:

1. Under this Article as at common law and under prior statutes the rights of purchasers of negotiable paper, including negotiable documents of title and investment securities, are determined by the rules of holding in due course and the like which are applicable to the type of paper concerned. (Articles 3, 7, and 8.) This section, as did Section 9(a) of the Uniform Trust Receipts Act, makes explicit the rule which was implicitly but universally recognized under the earlier statutes.

2. Under Section 9–304(1) filing is ineffective to perfect a security interest in instruments (including securities) except those instruments which are part of chattel paper, and of course is ineffective to constitute notice to subsequent purchasers. Although filing is permissible as a method of perfection for a security interest in documents, this section follows the policy of the Uniform Trust Receipts Act in providing that the filing does not constitute notice to purchasers.

Cross References:
Articles 3, 7, and 8 and Sections 9–304(1) and 9–308.

Definitional Cross References:
"Bona fide purchaser". Section 8–302.
"Document of title". Section 1–201.
"Duly negotiated". Section 7–501.
"Holder". Section 1–201.
"Holder in due course". Sections 3–302 and 9–105.
"Negotiable instrument". Sections 3–104 and 9–105.
"Notice". Section 1–201.
"Purchaser". Section 1–201.
"Security". Sections 8–102 and 9–105.
"Security interest". Section 1–201.

Cross References

Commercial paper, see Commercial Code § 3101 et seq.
Documents of title, see Commercial Code § 7101 et seq.
Investment securities, see Commercial Code § 8101 et seq.
Possession, perfection of security interest in instruments, see Commercial Code § 9304.
Priority among conflicting security interests in the same collateral, see Commercial Code § 9312.

§ 9310. Priority of Certain Liens Arising by Operation of Law

When a person in the ordinary course of his business furnishes services or materials with respect to goods subject to a security interest, a lien upon goods in the possession of such person given by statute or rule of law for such materials or services takes priority over a perfected security interest unless the lien is statutory and the statute expressly provides otherwise. *(Stats. 1963, c. 819, § 9310.)*

California Code Comment
By John A. Bohn and Charles J. Williams

Prior California Law

1. This section leaves to state law the priority between statutory and common law liens as opposed to consensual liens, i.e. security interests created with the consent of the parties.

This leaves the law concerning priority as it was prior to the adoption of the Commercial Code. This is summarized in 8 UCLA L.Rev. 806, 930–931 as follows:

"The Code, in effect, leaves to state law the priority of possessory liens on goods arising from the furnishing of services or materials. [*Fn.:* UCC § 9–310, Cal.Civ.Code § 19310 (proposed)] This leaves unaltered the present position of persons who perform services on goods at the request of the person in possession. The persons rendering the services are granted a lien on the goods, dependent on possession, for the amount of the debt. [*Fn.:* Cal.Civ.Code § 3051] It is settled that a possessory lien for the value of services takes priority over a security interest in the goods [*Fn.:* See, e.g., Mortgage Securities Co. v. Pfaffmann, 177 Cal. 109, 169 Pac. 1033 (1917); Woodruff v. Benbow, 118 Cal.App. 318, 5 P.2d 73 (1931) (chattel mortgages); Davenport v. Grundy Motor Sales Co., 28 Cal.App. 409, 152 Pac. 932 (1915) (conditional sale). The Uniform Trust Receipts Act provides that 'specific liens arising out of contractual acts of the trustee with reference to the processing, warehousing, shipping or otherwise dealing with specific goods in the usual course of the trustee's business preparatory to the sale shall attach against the interest of the entruster. . . .' Cal.Civ.Code § 3016.7] with the partial exception that the legal owner, if known and if not the person requesting the services, must be given notice before work is begun to validate as much of the lien as exceeds $200 against his interest. [*Fn.:* Cal.Civ.Code § 3051(a)] Among secured parties the notice provisions apply clearly to conditional sellers. When the lien is on a vehicle the holder of legal title for the purpose of determining whether notice is required is the person named as legal owner in the registration certificate. [*Fn.:* Cal.Civ.Code § 3068(b).] Since a mortgagee as well as a conditional vendor is listed in vehicle registration certificates as legal owner, [*Fn.:* Cal.Veh.Code § 6300] the mortgagee must be given notice in order to enforce a lien over $200 for the full amount. Whether or not an entruster be regarded as legal title holder the terms of the Uniform Trust Receipts Act would seem to subject his interest to a lien for services regardless of notice. [*Fn.:* Cal.Civ.Code § 3016.7] The scope of possessory liens for materials furnished is not so broad as that of liens for services performed. The Uniform Trust Receipts Act, while not explicit on the point may be read to include liens for materials furnished a trustee in the usual course of business among the liens good against an entruster. [*Fn.:* See quotation from Cal.Civ.Code § 3016.7] Persons engaged in performing work on watches, clocks, or jewelry are given a lien for the value of materials supplied for the work. [*Fn.:* Cal.Civ.Code § 3052a] And persons who furnish materials or supplies for vehicles also have liens enforceable against the vehicle while in their possession [*Fn.:* Cal.Civ. Code § 3068(a)] subject to the same requisite of notice to the legal owner as provided for in the case of liens for services. [*Fn.:* Cal.Civ.Code § 3068(b)]".

Changes from U.C.C. (1962 Official Text)

3. This is section 9–310 of the Official Text without change.

Uniform Commercial Code Comment
Prior Uniform Statutory Provision:
Section 11, Uniform Trust Receipts Act.

Purposes:

1. To provide that liens securing claims arising from work intended to enhance or preserve the value of the collateral take priority over an earlier security interest even though perfected.

2. Apart from the Uniform Trust Receipts Act which had a section similar to this one, there was generally no specific statutory rule as to priority between security devices and liens for services or materials.

Under chattel mortgage or conditional sales law many decisions made the priority of such liens turn on whether the secured party did or did not have "title". This section changes such rules and makes the lien for services or materials prior in all cases where they are furnished in the ordinary course of the lienor's business and the goods involved are in the lienor's possession. Some of the statutes creating such liens expressly make the lien subordinate to a prior security interest. This section does not repeal such statutory provisions. If the statute creating the lien is silent, even though it has been construed by decision to make the lien subordinate to the security interest, this section provides a rule of interpretation that the lien should take priority over the security interest.

Cross References:
Sections 9–102(2), 9–104(c) and 9–312(1).

Definitional Cross References:
"Goods". Section 9–105.
"Person". Section 1–201.
"Security interest". Section 1–201.

Cross References

Aircraft liens, see Code of Civil Procedure § 1208.61 et seq.
Animals, liens upon, see Code of Civil Procedure § 1208.5.
Artisan and service lien, see Civil Code § 3051.
Banker's lien, see Civil Code § 3054.
Cleaner's and renovator's liens, see Civil Code § 3066.
Conflicting security interests, priority, see Commercial Code § 9312.
Enforcement of liens in general, see Code of Civil Procedure § 1180 et seq.
Excluded transactions, see Commercial Code § 9104.
Factor's lien, see Civil Code § 3053.
Jeweler's lien, see Civil Code § 3052a.
Liens in general, see Civil Code § 2872 et seq.
Logging and sawmill liens, see Civil Code § 3065 et seq.
Mechanics liens, see Civil Code §§ 3059, 3110.
Mining liens, see Civil Code § 3060.
Officer's lien, see Code of Civil Procedure § 488.100.
Oil and gas liens, see Code of Civil Procedure § 1203.50 et seq.
Policy and scope of division, see Commercial Code § 9102.
Priority of liens in general, see Civil Code § 2897 et seq.
Salary and wages, lien for, see Code of Civil Procedure § 1204 et seq.
Statutory liens, applicability of division to, see Commercial Code § 9102.
Storage lien, see Civil Code § 1856.
Thresher's lien, see Civil Code § 3061.
Vehicles, liens on, see Civil Code §§ 3051, 3067 et seq.
Vessels, liens on, see Harbors and Navigation Code § 450 et seq.

§ 9311. Alienability of Debtor's Rights: Judicial Process

The debtor's rights in collateral may be voluntarily or involuntarily transferred (by way of sale, creation of a security interest, attachment, levy, garnishment or other judicial process) notwithstanding a provision in the security agreement prohibiting any transfer but a provision in the security agreement making the transfer constitute a default is valid. *(Stats.1963, c. 819, § 9311. Amended by Stats.1982, c. 454, p. 1834, § 15.)*

California Code Comment

By John A. Bohn and Charles J. Williams

Prior California Law

1. This section is consistent with prior California law. The prior California law in the light of the possible impact of this section on it is described in the Marsh and Warren Report:

"This Section is clearly in accord with the California law in permitting a levy upon the owner's equity in encumbered property despite any provision in the mortgage or conditional sale 'for default or forfeiture in case of levy or change of possession.' CCP § 689a.

"This section would also appear to be in accord with the present California law in permitting a voluntary conveyance of the owner's equity in encumbered property. Section 538 of the Penal Code makes it a crime for the mortgagor to sell his equity without notifying the purchaser of the mortgage and notifying the mortgagee of the sale. However, it is said that even a violation of this Section does 'not prevent title passing to the purchaser, subject to the mortgage lien . . .'. Schwartzler v. Lemas, 11 C.A.2d 442, 450, 53 P.2d 1039 (1936). With respect to property held under a conditional sale contract, in Bowden v. Bank of America, 36 C.2d 406, 413, 224 P.2d 713 (1950) the court said that 'The interest of [the] purchaser . . ., though it does not amount to a legal title, may be made the subject of a chattel mortgage which will be good otherwise than as against the vendor . . . Likewise, the buyer's interest may be conveyed subject to the rights of the conditional seller.' See, also, Luke v. Mercantile Acceptance Corp., 111 C.A.2d 431, 244 P.2d 764 (1952). While these cases do not expressly deal with a situation where the vendee of the owner's equity had knowledge of a provision prohibiting its transfer, there would seem to be no reason to sanction such a restraint on alienation. This Section is said to be in accord with the law of New York. 3 N.Y. Law Rev.Comm., Study of the Uniform Commercial Code (1955) 2060.

"This Section does not, of course, invalidate a provision making such a transfer of the owner's equity an event of default or take away any other remedies which the secured party may have reserved to himself. However, as stated in the Luke case, supra, 'The sole interest of the [conditional] seller is in the receipt of the price, and his reserved title cannot be used for any other purpose.' Therefore, if the buyer should tender payment in full, it would seem that the secured party would have no right to complain." Sixth Progress Report to the Legislature by Senate Fact Finding Committee on Judiciary (1959–1961) Part 1, The Uniform Commercial Code, pp. 573–574.

Changes from U.C.C. (1962 Official Text)

2. Section 9–311 of the Official Text as changed in California reads as follows:

9311. The debtor's rights in collateral may be voluntarily or involuntarily transferred (by way of sale, creation of a security interest, attachment, levy, garnishment or other judicial process) notwithstanding a provision in the security agreement prohibiting any transfer [or making the transfer constitute a default] but a provision in the security agreement making the transfer constitute a default is valid.

The purpose of the California change is to clarify the Official Text:

"This will at least clarify something which is obscure under the Official Draft, namely, that a debtor whose rights in collateral are transferred in violation of an express provision in the security agreement is in default under the agreement with whatever consequences may follow from such a default. This was the intention of the draftsmen of the Official Draft, but fears have been expressed by many good lawyers to the effect that the language of the Official Draft makes such a contractual provision invalid for the purpose of determining a default as well as for the purpose of preventing the transfer of the debtor's rights." Further Comments from the State Bar, Sixth Progress Report to the Legislature by Senate Fact Finding Committee on Judiciary, (1959–1961) Part 1, The Uniform Commercial Code, p. 650.

Uniform Commercial Code Comment

Prior Uniform Statutory Provision:
None.

Purposes:

1. To make clear that in all security transactions under this Article, the debtor has an interest (whether legal title or an equity) which he can dispose of and which his creditors can reach.

2. Some jurisdictions have held that when a mortgagee or conditional seller has "title" to the collateral, creditors may not proceed against the mortgagor's or vendee's interest by levy, attachment or other judicial process. This section changes those rules by providing that in all security interests the debtor's interest in the collateral remains subject to claims of creditors who take appropriate action. It is left to the law of each state to determine the form of "appropriate process".

3. Where the security interest is in inventory, difficult problems arise with reference to attachment and levy. Assume that a debt of $100,000 is secured by inventory worth twice that amount. If by attachment or levy certain units of the inventory are seized, the determination of the debtor's equity in the units seized is not a simple matter. The section leaves the solution of this problem to the courts. Procedures such as marshalling may be appropriate.

Cross References:

Sections 9–301(4), 9–307(3) and 9–312(7).
Definitional Cross References:
"Collateral". Section 9–105.
"Debtor". Section 9–105.
"Rights". Section 1–201.
"Sale". Sections 2–106 and 9–105.
"Security agreement". Section 9–105.
"Security interest". Section 1–201.

Cross References

Attachment, see Code of Civil Procedure § 484.010 et seq.
Conditions in restraint of alienation, see Civil Code § 711.
Execution of judgment,
  Generally, see Code of Civil Procedure §§ 683.010, 683.020, 699.510, 712.010.
  Personal property under writ, see Code of Civil Procedure § 720.210 et seq.
Sale of property covered by security agreement and willful failure to pay secured party and appropriations to own use as embezzlement, see Penal Code § 504b.

§ 9312. Priorities Among Conflicting Security Interests in the Same Collateral

(1) The rules of priority stated in other sections of this chapter and in the following sections shall govern where applicable: Section 4210 with respect to the security interest of collecting banks in items being collected, accompanying documents and proceeds; Section 9103 on security interests related to other jurisdictions; Section 9114 on consignments; Section 9115 on security interests in investment property.

(3)¹ A perfected purchase money security interest in inventory has priority over a conflicting security interest in the same inventory and also has priority in identifiable cash proceeds received on or before the delivery of the inventory to a buyer if all of the following occur:

(a) The purchase money security interest is perfected at the time the debtor receives possession of the inventory.

(b) The purchase money secured party gives notification in writing to the holder of the conflicting security interest if the holder had filed a financing statement covering the same types of inventory (i) before the date of the filing made by the purchase money secured party, or (ii) before the beginning of the 21–day period where the purchase money security interest is temporarily perfected without filing or possession (subdivision (5) of Section 9304).

(c) The holder of the conflicting security interest receives the notification within five years before the debtor receives possession of the inventory.

(d) The notification states that the person giving the notice has or expects to acquire a purchase money security interest in inventory of the debtor, describing such inventory by item or type.

(4) A purchase money security interest in collateral other than inventory has priority over a conflicting security interest in the same collateral or its proceeds if the purchase money security interest is perfected at the time the debtor receives possession of the collateral or within 20 days thereafter.

(5) In all cases not governed by other rules stated in this section (including cases of purchase money security interests which do not qualify for the special priorities set forth in subdivisions (3) and (4)), priority between conflicting security interests in the same collateral shall be determined according to the following rules:

(a) Conflicting security interests rank according to priority in time of filing or perfection. Priority dates from the time a filing is first made covering the collateral or the time the security interest is first perfected, whichever is earlier, provided that there is no period thereafter when there is neither filing nor perfection.

(b) So long as conflicting security interests are unperfected, the first to attach has priority.

(6) For the purposes of subdivision (5) a date of filing or perfection as to collateral is also a date of filing or perfection as to proceeds.

(7) If future advances are made while a security interest is perfected by filing, the taking of possession, or under Section * * * 9115 or 9116 on investment property, the security interest has the same priority for the purposes of subdivision (5) with respect to the future advances as it does with respect to the first advance. If a commitment is made before or while the security interest is so perfected, the security interest has the same priority with respect to advances made pursuant thereto. In other cases a perfected security interest has priority from the date the advance is made. (Stats. 1963, c. 819, § 9312. Amended by Stats.1965, c. 1379, p. 3293, § 17; Stats.1974, c. 997, p. 2130, § 30, eff. Jan. 1, 1976; Stats.1984, c. 927, § 15; Stats.1985, c. 606, § 1; Stats.1994, c. 668 (S.B.1405), § 14; Stats.1996, c. 497 (S.B.1591), § 22, operative Jan. 1, 1997.)

1 Enrolled bill contains no subd. (2).

California Code Comment

By John A. Bohn and Charles J. Williams

Prior California Law

1. Official Comments 1, 3 and 4 explain the general operation and effect of this section.

2. Prior California law did not contain comprehensive detailed rules to cover the various situations described in this section.

In the California Annotations to the Proposed Uniform Commercial Code by the Legislative Counsel, this section is described as stating the basic rule that security interests rank in the order of the time of perfection. Upon this basis it has been said that the section has the following effect upon California law:

(a) For a chattel mortgage, there was no requirement under former Civil Code § 2957 or Vehicle Code § 6300 that a subsequent encumbrancer must first perfect his interest to be protected;

(b) For a conditional sales contract, the interest was generally perfected without filing or recording against all persons and would take precedence over any subsequent security interest, except as to livestock, mine machinery, equipment and railroad equipment;

(c) For a pledge, the interest was perfected merely by a change of possession;

(d) For a trust receipt, priority was not upon the basis of time of perfection since the priority of a trust receipt did not depend upon who perfected first. Former Civil Code § 3016.5; C.I.T. Corp. v. Commercial Bank, 64 Cal.App.2d 722, 149 P.2d 439 (1944);

(e) For an assignment of an account receivable and an inventory lien, the basic rule that security interests rank in order of perfection was followed in former Civil Code §§ 3018 and 3036.

California Annotations to the Proposed Uniform Commercial Code, Sixth Progress Report to the Legislature by Senate Fact Finding Committee on Judiciary (1959–1961) Part 1, The Uniform Commercial Code pp. 132–133.

Changes from U.C.C. (1962 Official Text)

3. Subdivision (1) of the California version omits the reference to section 9–313 from the enumeration.

This phrase was omitted to conform to the deletion of the entire section 9–313 from the California version of the Commercial Code.

4. Subdivision (2) of the Official Text is omitted in the California version. It provides as follows:

"(2) A perfected security interest in crops for new value given to enable the debtor to produce the crops during the production season and given not more than three months before the crops become growing crops by planting or otherwise takes priority over an earlier perfected security interest to the extent that such earlier interest secures obligations due more than six months before the crops become growing crops by planting or otherwise, even though the person giving new value had knowledge of the earlier security interest."

It was omitted because of the novel effect it would have had on California law. Marsh and Warren Report, Sixth Progress Report to the Legislature by Senate Fact Finding Committee on Judiciary (1959–1961) Part 1, The Uniform Commercial Code p. 574.

5. Subdivision (3) is peculiar to the California version of the Commercial Code and does not appear in the Official Text. Its purpose is to continue the rule under former Civil Code § 2975. Substantially the same subdivision was proposed as an amendment to the Uniform Commercial Code when it was introduced in the California legislature at the 1961 session except that it was set forth as subdivision (2). California has a long history involving the distinction between optional and obligatory future advances and because the Commercial Code does not treat this subject in detail, this subdivision was added. The legislative and decisional history of optional and obligatory future advances is contained in 8 UCLA L.Rev. 806, 862–865.

California Code Comment

By Charles J. Williams

The 1965 amendment to this section deletes subdivision (7).

Subdivision (7) stated a rule of priority as to future advances which conformed to the former California rule. This subdivision was not a part of the 1962 Official Text so that its deletion in California brings California in line with the Official Text in this regard.

Uniform Commercial Code Comment

P.E.B. Commentary No. 7, March 10, 1990

Purposes:

* * * * * *

9. Under some circumstances, a secured party who does not have priority in an account, chattel paper, or general intangible may be entitled to keep a cash payment received directly or indirectly from the account debtor. See PEB Commentary No. 7, dated March 10, 1990 [Uniform Laws Annotated, UCC, APP II, Comment 7].

* * * * * *

Uniform Commercial Code Comment

Official Reasons for 1977 Change

The insertion in subsection (7) protects the future advances of a secured party who has perfected his security interest in securities under Section 8–321 even if the method did not involve his taking possession of the collateral.

Uniform Commercial Code Comment

Prior Uniform Statutory Provision:
None.
Purposes:

1. In a variety of situations two or more people may claim an interest in the same property. The several sections specified in subsection (1) contain rules for determining priorities between security interests and such other claims in the situations covered in those sections. For cases not covered in those sections this section states general rules of priority between conflicting security interests.

2. Subsection (2) [Subsection 2 not enacted in California, see California Code Comment, note 4] gives priority to a new value security interest in crops based on a current crop production loan over an earlier security interest in the crop which secured obligations (such as rent, interest or mortgage principal amortization) due more than six months before the crops become growing crops. This priority is not affected by the fact that the person making the crop loan knew of the earlier security interest.

3. Subsections (3) and (4) give priority to a purchase money security interest (defined in Section 9–107) under certain conditions over non-purchase money interests, which in this context will usually be interests asserted under after-acquired property clauses. See Section 9–204 on the extent to which after-acquired property interests are validated and Section 9–108 on when a security interest in after-acquired property is deemed taken for new value.

Prior law, under one or another theory, usually contrived to protect purchase money interests over after-acquired property interests (to the extent to which the after-acquired property interest was recognized at all). For example, in the field of industrial equipment financing it was possible, by manipulation of title theory, for the purchase money financer of new equipment (under conditional sale or equipment trust) to protect himself against the claims of prior mortgagees or bondholders under an after-acquired clause in the mortgage or trust indenture: the result was arrived at on the theory that since "title" to the equipment was never in the vendee or lessee there was nothing for the lien of the mortgage to attach to. While this Article broadly validates the after-acquired property interest, it also recognizes as sound the preference which prior law gave to the purchase money interest. That policy is carried out in subsections (3) and (4).

Subsection (4) states a general rule applicable to all types of collateral except inventory: the purchase money interest takes priority if it is perfected when the debtor receives possession of the collateral or within ten days thereafter. As to the ten day grace period, compare Section 9–301(2). The perfection requirement means that the purchase money secured party either has filed a financing statement before that time or has a temporarily perfected interest in goods covered by documents under Section 9–304(4) and (5) (which is continued in a perfected status by filing before the expiration of the 21 day period specified in that section). There is no requirement that the purchase money secured party be without notice or knowledge of the other interest; he takes priority although he knows of it or it has been filed.

Under subsection (3) the same rule of priority, but without the ten day grace period for filing, applies to a purchase money security interest in inventory, with the additional requirement that the purchase money secured party give notification, as stated in subsection (3), to any other secured party who filed earlier for the same item or type of inventory. The reason for the additional requirement of notification is that typically the arrangement between an inventory secured party and his debtor will require the secured party to make periodic advances against incoming inventory or periodic releases of old inventory as new inventory is received. A fraudulent debtor may apply to the secured party for advances even though he has already given a security interest in the inventory to another secured party. The notification requirement protects the inventory financer in such a situation: if he has received notification, he will presumably not make an advance; if he has not received notification (or if the other interest does not qualify as a purchase money interest), any advance he may make will have priority. Since an arrangement for periodic advances against incoming property is unusual outside the inventory field, no notification requirement is included in subsection (4).

Where the purchase money inventory financing began by possession of a negotiable document of title by the secured party, he must in order to retain priority give the notice required by subsection (3) at or before the usual time, i.e., when the debtor gets possession of the inventory, even though his security interest remains perfected for 21 days under Section 9–304(5).

When under these rules the purchase money secured party has priority over another secured party, the question arises whether this priority extends to the proceeds of the original collateral. Under subsection (4) which deals with non-inventory collateral and where there was no ordinary expectation that the goods would be sold, the section gives an affirmative answer. In the case of inventory collateral under subsection (3), where it was expected that the goods would be sold and where financing frequently is based on the resulting accounts, chattel paper, or other proceeds, the subsection gives an answer limited to the preservation of the purchase money priority only in so far as the proceeds are cash received on or before the delivery of the inventory to a buyer, that is, without the creation of an intervening account to which conflicting rights might attach. The conflicting rights to proceeds consisting of accounts are governed by subsection (5). See Comment 8.

The foregoing rules applicable to purchase money security interests in inventory apply also to the rights in consigned merchandise. See Section 9–114.

4. Subsection (5) states a rule for determining priority between conflicting security interests in cases not covered in the sections referred to in subsection (1) or in subsections (2), (3) and (4) of this section. Note that subsection (5) applies to cases of purchase money security interests which do not qualify for the special priorities set forth in subsections (3) and (4).

There is a single priority rule based on precedence in the time as of which the competing parties either filed their security interests or perfected their security interests. The form of the claim to priority, i.e., filing or perfection, may shift from time to time, and the rank will be based on the first filing or perfection so long as there is no intervening period without filing or perfection. Filing may occur as to particular collateral before the collateral comes into existence. Under the standards of Section 9–203 perfection cannot occur as to particular collateral until the collateral itself (and not prior collateral) comes into existence and the debtor has rights therein; but under subsection (6) of this section the secured party's priority may date from his time of perfection as to the prior collateral, if perfection or filing has been continuously maintained. Subsection (6) provides that a date of filing or perfection as to original collateral is also a date of filing or perfection as to proceeds. This rule should also be read with Section 9–306, which makes it unnecessary to claim proceeds expressly in a financing statement and provides in effect that a filing as to original collateral is also a filing as to proceeds (with exceptions therein stated). Thus, if a financing statement is filed covering inventory, then (subject to the exception involving multistate problems) this filing is also a filing as to the resulting accounts and constitutes the date of filing as to the accounts.

The party who may have had a prior security interest in inventory or may have had the only such security interest does not automatically for that reason have priority as to the accounts. His claim to accounts may or may not have priority over competing filed claims to accounts. The priority is based on precedence as to the accounts under the rules stated in the preceding paragraph.

5. The operation of this section is illustrated by the examples set forth under this and the succeeding Points.

Example 1. A files against X (debtor) on February 1. B files against X on March 1. B makes a non-purchase money advance against certain collateral on April 1. A makes an advance against the same collateral on May 1. A has priority even though B's advance was made earlier and was perfected when made. It makes no difference whether or not A knew of B's interest when he made his advance.

The problem stated in the example is peculiar to a notice filing system under which filing may be made before the security interest attaches (see Section 9–402). The Uniform Trust Receipts Act, which first introduced such a filing system, contained no hint of a solution and case law under it was unpredictable. This Article follows several of the accounts receivable statutes in determining priority by order of filing. The justification for the rule lies in the necessity of protecting the filing system—that is, of allowing the secured party who has first filed to make subsequent advances without each time having, as a condition of protection, to check for filings later than his. Note, however, that his protection is not absolute: if, in the example, B's advance creates a purchase money security interest, he has priority under subsection (4), or, in the case of inventory, under subsection (3) provided he has properly notified A. (See further Example 3 below.)

Example 2. A and B make nonpurchase money advances against the same collateral. The collateral is in the debtor's possession and neither interest is perfected when the second advance is made. Whichever secured party first perfects his interest (by taking possession of the collateral or by filing) takes priority and it makes no difference whether or not he knows of the other interest at the time he perfects his own.

This result may be regarded as an adoption, in this type of situation, of the idea, deeply rooted at common law, of a race of diligence among creditors. Subsection (5) (b) adds the thought that so long as neither of the interests is perfected, the one which first attached (i.e., under the advance first made) has priority. The last mentioned rule may be thought to be of merely theoretical interest, since it is hard to imagine a situation where the case would come into litigation without either A or B having perfected his interest. If neither interest had been perfected at the time of the filing of a petition in bankruptcy, of course neither would be good against the trustee in bankruptcy.

Example 3. A has a temporarily perfected (21 day) security interest, unfiled, in a negotiable document in the debtor's possession under Section 9–304(4) or (5). On the fifth day B files and thus perfects a security interest in the same document. On the tenth day A files. A has priority, whether or not he knows of B's interest when he files, because he perfected first and has maintained continuous perfection or filing.

6. The application of the priority rules to after-acquired property must be considered separately for each item of collateral. Priority does not depend only on time of perfection, but may also be based on priority in filing before perfection.

Example 4. On February 1 A makes advances to X under a security agreement which covers "all the machinery in X's plant" and contains an after-acquired property clause. A promptly files his financing statement. On March 1 X acquires a new machine, B makes an advance against it and files his financing statement. On April 1 A, under the original security agreement, makes an advance against the machine acquired March 1. If B's advance creates a purchase money security interest, he has priority under subsection (4) (provided he filed before X received possession of the machine or within ten days thereafter). If B's advance, although he gave new value, did not create a purchase money interest, A has priority as to both of his advances by virtue of his priority in filing, although the parties perfected simultaneously on March 1 as to the new machine.

The application of the priority rules to proceeds presents special features discussed in Comment 8.

7. The application of the priority rules to future advances is complicated. In general, since any secured party must operate in reference to the Code's system of notice, he takes subject to future advances under a prior security interest while it is perfected through filing or possession, whether the advances are committed or non-committed, and to any advances subsequently made "pursuant to commitment" (Section 9–105) during that period. In the rare case when a future advance is made without commitment while the security interest is perfected temporarily without either filing or possession, the future advance has priority from the date it is made. These rules are more liberal toward the priority of future advances than the corresponding rules applicable to an intervening buyer (Section 9–307(3)) because of the different characteristics of the intervening party. Compare the corresponding rule applicable to an intervening judgment creditor. (Section 9–301(4)).

Example 5. On February 1 A makes an advance against machinery in the debtor's possession and files his financing statement. On March 1 B makes an advance against the same machinery and files his financing statement. On April 1 A makes a further advance, under the original security agreement, against the same machinery (which is covered by the original financing statement and thus perfected when made). A has priority over B both as to the February 1 and as to the April 1 advance and it makes no difference whether or not A knows of B's intervening advance when he makes his second advance.

A wins, as to the April 1 advance, because he first filed even though B's interest attached, and indeed was perfected, before the April 1 advance. The same rule would apply if either A or B had perfected through possession. Section 9–204(3) and the Comment thereto should be consulted for the validation of future advances.

The same result would be reached even though A's April 1 advance was not under the original security agreement, but was under a new security agreement under A's same financing statement or during the continuation of A's possession.

8. The application of the priority rules of subsections (5) and (6) to proceeds is shown by the following examples:

§ 9312

Example 6. A files a financing statement covering a described type of inventory then owned or thereafter acquired. B subsequently takes a purchase money security interest in certain inventory described in A's financing statement and achieves priority over A under subsection (3) as to this inventory. This inventory is then sold, producing proceeds.

If the proceeds of the inventory are instruments or chattel paper, the rights of A and B on the one hand and any adverse claimant to these proceeds on the other are governed by Sections 9–308 and 9–309. If the proceeds are cash, subsection (3) indicates that B's priority as to the inventory carries over to the cash. Proceeds which are accounts constitute different collateral and the priorities as to the original collateral do not control the priority as to the accounts. Under Sections 9–306 and 9–312(6), A's first filing as to the inventory constitutes a first filing as to the accounts, provided that the same filing office would be appropriate for filing as to accounts under the rules of Section 9–306(3). Therefore, A has priority as to the accounts.

Many parties financing inventory are quite content to protect their first security interest in the inventory itself, realizing that when inventory is sold, someone else will be financing the accounts and the priority for inventory will not run forward to the accounts. Indeed, the cash supplied by the accounts financer will be used to pay the inventory financing. In some situations, the party financing the inventory on a purchase money basis makes contractual arrangements that the proceeds of accounts financing by another be devoted to paying off the first inventory security interest.

Example 7. In the foregoing case, if B had filed directly as to accounts, the date of that filing as to accounts would be compared with the date of A's first filing as to the inventory, and the first-to-file rule would prevail.

Subsection (6) provides that a filing as to original collateral determines the date of a filing as to the proceeds thereof. This rule implies, of course, that the filing as to the original collateral is effective as to proceeds under the rule of Section 9–306(3).

Example 8. If C had filed as to accounts in Example 6 above before either A or B had filed as to inventory, C's first filing as to accounts would have priority over the filings of A and B, which would also constitute filings as to accounts under the rule just mentioned. A's and B's position as to the inventory gives them no automatic claim to the proceeds of the inventory consisting of accounts against someone who has filed earlier as to accounts. If, on the other hand, either A's or B's filings as to the inventory constituted good filings as to accounts and these filings preceded C's direct filings as to accounts, A or B would outrank C as to the accounts.

If the filings as to inventory were not effective under subsection (6) for filing as to accounts because a filing for accounts would have to be in a different filing office under Section 9–103(3), these inventory filings would nevertheless be effective for 10 days as to accounts. If the perfection of the security interest in accounts was continued within the 10 days by appropriate filings, then A and B's interests in the accounts would date from the date of filing as to inventory.

Cross References:

Sections 9–204(1) and 9–303.

Point 1: Sections 4–208, 9–114, 9–301, 9–304, 9–306, 9–307, 9–308, 9–309, 9–310, 9–313, 9–314, 9–315 and 9–316.
Point 3: Sections 9–108, 9–204, 9–304(4) and (5).
Points 4 to 7: Sections 9–204, 9–301(4), 9–304(4) and (5), 9–306, 9–307(3) and 9–402(1).
Point 8: Sections 9–103(6), 9–306(3).

Definitional Cross References:
 "Chattel paper". Section 9–105.
 "Collateral". Section 9–105.
 "Collecting bank". Section 4–105.
 "Debtor". Section 9–105.
 "Documents". Section 9–105.
 "Give notice". Section 1–201.
 "Goods". Section 9–105.
 "Instruments". Section 9–105.
 "Inventory". Section 9–109.
 "Knowledge". Section 1–201.
 "Person". Section 1–201.
 "Proceeds". Section 9–306.
 "Purchase money security interest". Section 9–107.
 "Pursuant to commitment". Section 9–105.
 "Receives" notification. Section 1–201.
 "Secured party". Section 9–105.
 "Security". Sections 8–102 and 9–105.
 "Security interest". Section 1–201.
 "Value". Section 1–201.

Cross References

Accessions, see Commercial Code § 9314.
Account or list of collateral, statement, see Commercial Code § 9208.
After-acquired collateral as security for antecedent debt, see Commercial Code § 9108.
Attachment of security interest, see Commercial Code § 9203.
Commingled or processed goods, see Commercial Code § 9315.
Definitions, priorities and security interests, see Code of Civil Procedure § 697.590.
Financial statement, formal requisites, see Commercial Code § 9402.
Goods covered by documents, see Commercial Code § 9304.
Liens arising by operation of law, see Commercial Code § 9310.
Manufactured homes, mobilehomes or commercial coaches, priority regarding conflicting security interests, see Health and Safety Code § 18105.
Motor vehicles, filing instruments evidencing liens or encumbrances, see Vehicle Code § 6300 et seq.
Proceeds and repossessions, see Commercial Code § 9306.
Protection of buyers of goods, see Commercial Code § 9307.
Purchaser of chattel paper or instruments, see Commercial Code § 9308.
Security agreements, see Commercial Code § 9204.
Security interest in negotiable instruments, documents or securities, see Commercial Code § 9309.
Security interest of collecting bank in items, accompanying documents and proceeds, see Commercial Code § 4210.
Subordination agreement, see Commercial Code § 9316.
Unperfected security interests, subordination, see Commercial Code § 9301.
When security interest perfected, see Commercial Code § 9303.

§ 9313. Fixtures; fixture filing; construction mortgage; priorities

(1) In this section and in the provisions of Chapter 4 (commencing with Section 9401) referring to fixture filing, unless the context otherwise requires

(a) Goods are "fixtures" when they become so related to particular real estate that an interest in them arises under real estate law.

(b) A "fixture filing" is the filing in the office where a mortgage on the real estate would be recorded of a financing statement covering goods which are or are to become fixtures and conforming to the requirements of subdivision (5) of Section 9402.

(c) A mortgage is a "construction mortgage" to the extent that it secures an obligation incurred for the construction of an improvement on land including the acquisition cost of the land, if the recorded writing so indicates.

(2) A security interest under this division may be created in goods which are fixtures or may continue in goods which become fixtures, but no security interest exists under this division in ordinary building materials incorporated into an improvement on land.

(3) This division does not prevent creation of an encumbrance upon fixtures pursuant to real estate law.

(4) A perfected security interest in fixtures has priority over the conflicting interest of an encumbrancer or owner of the real estate where

(a) The security interest is a purchase money security interest, the interest of the encumbrancer or owner arises before the goods become fixtures, a fixture filing covering the fixtures is filed before the goods become fixtures or within 10 days thereafter, and the debtor has an interest of record in the real estate or is in possession of the real estate; or

(b) A fixture filing covering the fixtures is filed before the interest of the encumbrancer or owner is of record, the security interest has priority over any conflicting interest of a predecessor in title of the encumbrancer or owner, and the debtor has an interest of record in the real estate or is in possession of the real estate; or

(c) The fixtures are readily removable factory or office machines or readily removable replacements of domestic appliances which are consumer goods; or

(d) The conflicting interest is a lien on the real estate obtained by legal or equitable proceedings after the security interest was perfected by any method permitted by this division.

(5) A security interest in fixtures, whether or not perfected, has priority over the conflicting interest of an encumbrancer or owner of the real estate where

(a) The encumbrancer or owner has consented in writing to the security interest or has disclaimed an interest in the goods as fixtures; or

(b) The debtor has a right to remove the goods as against the encumbrancer or owner. If the debtor's right terminates, the priority of the security interest continues for a reasonable time.

(6) Notwithstanding paragraph (a) of subdivision (4) but otherwise subject to subdivisions (4) and (5), a security interest in fixtures is subordinate to a construction mortgage recorded before the goods become fixtures if the goods become fixtures before the completion of the construction. To the extent that it is given to refinance a construction mortgage, a mortgage has this priority to the same extent as the construction mortgage.

(7) In the cases not within the preceding subdivisions, a security interest in fixtures is subordinate to the conflicting interest of an encumbrancer or owner of the related real estate who is not the debtor.

(8) When the secured party has priority over all owners and encumbrancers of the real estate, he may, on default, subject to the provisions of Chapter 5 (commencing with Section 9501), remove his collateral from the real estate but he must reimburse any encumbrancer or owner of the real estate who is not the debtor and who has not otherwise agreed for the cost of repair of any physical injury, but not for any diminution in value of the real estate caused by the absence of the goods removed or by any necessity of replacing them. A person entitled to reimbursement may refuse permission to remove until the secured party gives adequate security for the performance of this obligation. *(Added by Stats.1980, c. 1156, p. 3864, § 7.)*

Uniform Commercial Code Comment
Prior Uniform Statutory Provision:
Section 7, Uniform Conditional Sales Act.
Purposes:

1. Section 9–313 deals with the problem that certain goods which are the subject of chattel financing become so affixed or otherwise so related to real estate that they become part of the real estate, and that chattel interests would be subordinate to real estate interests except as protected by the priorities regulated by the section. These goods are called "fixtures". Some fixtures also retain their chattel nature in that a chattel financing with respect to them may exist and may continue to be recognized, if notice thereof is given to real estate interests in accordance with this section. But this concept does not apply if the goods are integrally incorporated into the real estate.

The term "fixture filing" has been introduced and defined. It emphasizes that when a filing is intended to give the priority advantages herein discussed against real estate interests, the filing must (except as stated below) be for record in the real estate records an indexed therein, so that it will be found in a real estate search.

Since the determination in advance of judicial decision of the question whether goods have become fixtures is a difficult one, no inference may be drawn from a fixture filing that the secured party concedes that the goods are or will become fixtures. The fixture filing may be merely precautionary.

2. "Fixture" is defined to include any goods which become so related to particular real estate that an interest in them arises under real estate law and therefore, goods integrally incorporated into the real estate are clearly fixtures. But under subsection (2) no security interest exists under Article 9 in ordinary building materials incorporated into an improvement on land.

Goods may be technically "ordinary building materials," e.g., window glass, but if they are incorporated into a structure which as a whole has not become an integral part of the real estate, the rules applicable to the ordinary building materials follow the rules applicable to the structure itself. The outstanding examples presenting this kind of problem are the modern "mobile homes" and the modern pre-fabricated steel buildings usable as warehouses, garages, factories, etc. In the case of the mobile homes, most of them are erected on leased land and the right of the debtor under a mobile home purchase contract to remove the goods as lessee will make clear that his secured party ordinarily has a similar right. See paragraph (5)(b).

In cases where mobile homes or pre-fabricated steel buildings are erected by a person having an ownership interest in the land, the question into which category the buildings fall is one determined by local law. In general, the governing local law will not be that applicable in determining whether goods have become real property between landlord and tenant, or between mortgagor and mortgagee, or between grantor and grantee, but rather that applicable in a three-party situation, determining whether chattel financing can survive as against parties who acquire rights through the affixation of the goods to the real estate.

The assertion that no security interest exists in ordinary building materials is only for the operation of the priority provisions of this section. It is without prejudice to any rights which the secured party may have against the debtor himself if he incorporated the goods into real estate or against any party guilty of wrongful incorporation thereof in violation of the secured party's rights.

3. Under these concepts the section recognizes three categories of goods: (1) those which retain their chattel character entirely and are not part of the real estate; (2) ordinary building materials which have become an integral part of the real estate and cannot retain their chattel character for purposes of finance; and (3) an intermediate class which has become real estate for certain purposes, but as to which chattel financing may be preserved. This third and intermediate class is the primary subject of this section. The demarcation between these classifications is not delineated by this section.

4. In considering fixture priority problems, there will always first be a preliminary question whether real estate interests per se have an interest in the goods as part of real estate. If not, it is immaterial, so far as concerns real estate parties as such, whether a chattel security interest

is perfected or unperfected. In no event does a real estate party acquire an interest in a "pure" chattel just because a security interest therein is unperfected. If on the other hand real estate law gives real estate parties an interest in the goods, a conflict arises and this section states the priorities.

(a) The principal exception to the general rule of priority stated in Comment 4(b) based on time of filing or recording is a priority given in paragraph (4)(a) to purchase money security interest in fixtures as against *prior* recorded real estate interest, provided that the purchase money security interest is filed as a fixture filing in the real estate records before the goods become fixtures or within 10 days thereafter. This priority corresponds to one given in Section 9–312(4), and the 10 days of grace represents a reduction of the purchase money priority as against prior interests in the real estate under the present Section 9–313, where the purchase money priority exists even though the security interest is *never* filed.

It should be emphasized that this purchase money priority with the 10-day grace period for filing is limited to rights against *prior* real estate interests. There is no such priority with the 10-day grace period as against subsequent real estate interests. The fixture security interest can defeat subsequent real estate interests only if it is filed first and prevails under the usual conveyancing rule recognized in paragraph (4)(b).

(b) The general principle of priority announced in this section is set forth in paragraph (4)(b). It is basically that a fixture filing gives to the fixture security interest priority as against other real estate interests according to the usual priority rule of conveyancing, that is, the first to file or record prevails. An apparent limitation to this principle set forth in paragraph (4)(b), namely that the secured party must have had priority over any interest of a predecessor in title of the conflicting encumbrancer or owner, is not really a limitation, but is an expression of the usual rule that a person must be entitled to transfer what he has. Thus, if the fixture security interest is subordinate to a mortgage, it is subordinate to an interest of an assignee of the mortgage even though the assignment is a later recorded instrument. Similarly if the fixture security interest is subordinate to the rights of an owner, it is subordinate to a subsequent grantee of the owner and likewise subordinate to a subsequent mortgagee of the owner.

(c) A qualification to the rule based on priority of filing or recording is paragraph (4)(d), where priority based on precedence in filing or recording is preserved, but there is no requirement that as against a judgment lienor of the real estate, the prior filing of the fixture security interest must be in the real estate records. The fixture security interest if perfected first should prevail even though not filed or recorded in real estate records, because generally a judgment creditor is not a reliance creditor who would have searched records. Thus, even a prior filing in the chattel records protects the priority of a fixture security interest against a subsequent judgment lien.

It is hoped that this rule will have the effect of preserving a fixture security interest so filed against invalidation by a trustee in bankruptcy. That would, of course, be the result under Section 60a of the Bankruptcy Act if the time of perfection of the fixture security interest were measured by the judgment creditor test applicable to personal property. It would not be the result if the time of perfection were measured by the purchaser test applicable to real estate. Since the fixture security interest arises against the goods in their capacity as chattels, the bankruptcy courts should apply the judgment creditor test. The effectiveness of the drafting to achieve its purpose cannot be known certainly until the courts adjudicate the question or until it is settled by amendment to Section 60a of the Bankruptcy Act.

The phrase "lien by legal or equitable proceedings" is suggested by Section 70c of the Bankruptcy Act, and is intended to encompass all liens on real estate obtained by any of the creditor action therein described.

(d) A special exception to the usual rule of priority based on precedence in time is the one of paragraph (4)(c) in favor of holders of security interests in factory and office machines, and in certain replacement domestic appliances, as discussed below. This is not as broad an exception as it might seem. To repeat, a fixture conflict is not reached if the goods are held as a matter of local law not to have become part of the real estate, which will frequently be the holding for goods of these types. If the opposite is held, the rule of paragraph (4)(c) operates only if the fixture security interest is perfected before the goods become fixtures. Having been perfected, it would of course have priority over subsequent real estate interests under the rule of paragraph (4)(b). Since it would in almost all cases be a purchase money security interest, it would also have priority over other real estate interests under the purchase-money priority of paragraph (4)(a), discussed in paragraph (a) above. The rule is stated separately because the permitted perfection is by any method permitted by the Article, and not exclusively by fixture filing in the real estate records. This rule is made necessary by the confusions of the law as to whether certain machinery and appliances become fixtures.

As an additional point, in the case of machinery, the separate statement of this rule makes clear that it is not overridden by the construction mortgage priority of subsection (6) discussed in Comment 4(e) below, as would have been true if reliance had been solely on the purchase money priority. Factory and office machines are not always financed as part of a construction mortgage, and the mortgagee should be alert to conflicting chattel financing of these machines.

As to appliances, the rule stated is limited to readily removable replacements, not original installations, of appliances which are consumer goods in the hands of the debtor (Section 9–109). To facilitate financing of original appliances in new dwellings as part of the real estate financing of the dwellings, no special priority is given to chattel financing of original appliances. The section leaves to other law of the state the question whether original installations are fixtures to which the protection accorded by this section to construction mortgages would be applicable. Likewise, it is recognized that (when not supplied by tenants) appliances in commercial apartment buildings are intended as permanent improvements, and no special rule is stated for appliances in that case. The special priority rule here stated in favor of chattel financing is limited to situations where the installation of appliances may not be intended to be permanent, i.e., replacement appliances used by the debtor or his family (consumer goods). The principal effect of the rule is to make clear that a secured party financing occasional replacements of domestic appliances in noncommercial owner-occupied contexts need not concern himself with real estate descriptions or records; indeed, for a purchase-money replacement of consumer goods, perfection without any filing will be possible. (The priority of the construction mortgage has no application to replacement appliances.)

(e) The purchase money priority presents a difficult problem in relation to construction mortgages. The latter will ordinarily have been recorded even before the commencement of delivery of materials to the job, and therefore would be prior in rank to the fixture security interests were it not for the problem of the purchase money priority. Subsection (6) expressly gives priority to the construction mortgage recorded before the filing of the fixture security interest, but this priority of a construction mortgage applies only during the construction period leading to the completion of the improvement. As to additions to the building made long after completion of the improvement, the construction priority will not apply simply because the additions are financed by the real estate mortgagee under an open end clause of his construction mortgage. In such case, the applicable principles will be those of paragraphs (4)(a) and (4)(b). A refinancing of a construction mortgage has the same priority as the mortgage itself.

The phrase "an obligation incurred for the construction of an improvement" covers both optional advances and advances pursuant to commitment, and both types of advances have the same priority under the section.

5. The section makes it impossible for a fixture supplier to retain a security interest against a contractor, to the possible surprise and deception of real estate interests, unless the debtor has an interest of record in the real estate. See paragraphs (4)(a) and (b).

On the other hand, these paragraphs do recognize that fixture filing may be necessary when the debtor is in possession of the real estate (e.g., a lessee) even without an interest of record. This possibility of a filing against a debtor who is not in the real estate chain of title makes it necessary to require the furnishing of the name of a record owner in such cases. See Sections 9–402(3), item 3; 9–402(5); 9–403(7).

6. The status of fixtures installed by tenants (as well as such persons as licensees and holders of easements) is defined by paragraph (5)(b) to the effect that if the debtor (tenant or other interest mentioned) has the right to remove the fixture as against a real estate interest, the secured party has priority over that real estate interest.

7. Real estate lenders and title companies will have little difficulty in locating relevant fixture security interests applicable to particular parcels of real estate because of the provisions as to real estate description in fixture filings, the indexing thereof, and other related provisions in Part 4 of Article 9.

8. Real estate lending is typically long-term, and is usually done by institutional investors who can afford to take a long view of the matter rather than concentrating on the results of any particular case. It is apparent that the rule which permits and encourages purchase money fixture financing, which in contrast is typically short-term, will result in the modernization and improvement of real estate rather than in its deterioration and will on balance benefit long-term real estate lenders. Because of the short-term character of the chattel financing, it will rarely produce any conflict in fact with the real estate lender. The contrary rule would chill the availability of short-term credit for modernization of real estate by installation of new fixtures and in the long run could not help real estate lenders.

9. Subsection (8) is an important departure from Section 7 of the Uniform Conditional Sales Act and from much other conditional sales legislation. Under the Uniform Conditional Sales Act a conditional vendor could not sever and remove the affixed chattel if a "material injury to the freehold" would result. The courts of various jurisdictions were in sharp disagreement on the meaning of "material injury"; some held that only physical injury was meant; others adopted the so-called "institutional theory" and denied removal whenever the "going value" of the structure would be materially diminished by the removal. Under these rules the conditional vendor either could not remove at all, or, if he could, could damage the structure on removal without becoming accountable to the real estate claimant. The situation was complicated by the fact that it became increasingly difficult to predict what types of goods the courts in a given jurisdiction would hold not subject to removal.

Subsection (8) abandons the "material injury to the freehold" rule. Instead a secured party entitled to priority may in all cases sever and remove his collateral, subject, however, to a duty to reimburse any real estate claimant (other than the debtor himself) for any physical injury caused by the removal. The right to reimbursement is implemented by the last sentence of subsection (8) which gives the real estate claimant a statutory right to security or indemnity failing which he may refuse permission to remove. The subsection (8) rule thus accomplishes two things: it puts an end to the uncertainty which has grown up under the "material injury" rule, while at the same time it protects the real estate claimant under the reimbursement provisions.

Cross References:
Sections 2–107, 9–102(1), 9–104(j) and 9–312(1), and Parts 4 and 5.

Definitional Cross References:
"Collateral". Section 9–105.
"Contract". Section 1–201.
"Creditor". Section 1–201.
"Debtor". Section 9–105.
"Encumbrance". Section 9–105.
"Goods". Section 9–105.
"Knowledge". Section 1–201.
"Mortgage". Section 9–105.
"Person". Section 1–201.
"Purchase". Section 1–201.
"Purchaser". Section 1–201.
"Secured party". Section 9–105.
"Security interest". Section 1–201.
"Value". Section 1–201.
"Writing". Section 1–201.

Cross References

Application of 1979–1980 legislation relating to fixtures, see Commercial Code § 14109.

Recording fixture filing without acknowledgment, see Government Code § 27282.

§ 9314. Accessions

(1) A security interest in goods which attaches before they are installed in or affixed to other goods takes priority as to the goods installed or affixed (called in this section "accessions") over the claims of all persons to the whole except as stated in subdivision (3) and subject to Section 9315(1).

(2) A security interest which attaches to goods after they become part of a whole is valid against all persons subsequently acquiring interests in the whole except as stated in subdivision (3) but is invalid against any person with an interest in the whole at the time the security interest attaches to the goods who has not in writing consented to the security interest or disclaimed an interest in the goods as part of the whole.

(3) The security interests described in subdivisions (1) and (2) do not take priority over

(a) A subsequent purchaser for value of any interest in the whole; or

(b) A creditor with a lien on the whole subsequently obtained by judicial proceedings; or

(c) A creditor with a prior perfected security interest in the whole to the extent that he makes subsequent advances

if the subsequent purchase is made, the lien by judicial proceedings obtained or the subsequent advance under the prior perfected security interest is made or contracted for without knowledge of the security interest and before it is perfected. A purchaser of the whole at a foreclosure sale other than the holder of a perfected security interest purchasing at his own foreclosure sale is a subsequent purchaser within this section.

(4) When under subdivisions (1) or (2) and (3) a secured party has an interest in accessions which has priority over the claims of all persons who have interests in the whole, he may on default subject to the provisions of Chapter 5 remove his collateral from the whole but he must reimburse any encumbrancer or owner of the whole who is not the debtor and who has not otherwise agreed for the cost of repair of any physical injury but not for any diminution in value of the whole caused by the absence of the goods removed or by any necessity for replacing them. A person entitled to reimbursement may refuse permission to remove until the secured party gives adequate security for the performance of this obligation. *(Stats.1963, c. 819, § 9314.)*

California Code Comment

By John A. Bohn and Charles J. Williams

Prior California Law

1. The prior California law relating to ownership in the case of accession is contained in Civil Code §§ 1025–1030. The general rule of Civil Code § 1025 states that when things belonging to different owners have been united to form a single thing and cannot be separated without injury an accession occurs. The California accession statute contains several ambiguities which have not yet been resolved by judicial decision. For a detailed treatment of the California accession statute, see 8 UCLA L.Rev. 806, 943–948.

This comment concerning the impact of this section on prior California law is made:

"The Code would make some significant changes in the effects of a determination that there has been an accession. Furthermore, rather than leaving the factual determination to prior state law, as is done in fixtures questions, the Code itself determines what is an accession. An accession occurs whenever goods are attached or installed in other goods, so long as the goods affixed are still identifiable. [Fn.: UCC § 9–314, Cal.Civ.Code 19314 (proposed). If the goods are no longer separately identifiable but their identity is lost in a product or mass, the secured party's interest is determined by UCC § 9–315, Cal.Civ.Code § 19315 (proposed), discussed infra.] Thus, the rights and remedies of the California accession statute, which presently would apply only when the accessory is not removable without physical injury to the principal part, are superseded by the Code." 8 UCLA L.Rev. 806, 946.

Changes from U.C.C. (1962 Official Text)

2. This is section 9–314 of the Official Text without change.

Uniform Commercial Code Comment

Prior Uniform Statutory Provision:
None.

Purposes:

1. To state when a secured party claiming an interest in goods installed in or affixed to other goods is entitled to priority over a party with a security interest in the whole.

2. This section changes prior law in that the secured party claiming an interest in a part (e.g., a new motor in an old car) is entitled to priority and has a right to remove even though under other rules of law the part now belongs to the whole.

3. This section does not apply to goods which, for example, are so commingled in a manufacturing process that their original identity is lost. That type of situation is covered in Section 9–315. Section 9–315 should also be consulted for the effect of a financing statement which claims both component parts and the resulting product.

Cross References:

Sections 9–203(1), 9–303 and 9–312(1) and Part 5.
Point 3: Section 9–315.

Definitional Cross References:

"Collateral". Section 9–105.
"Creditor". Section 1–201.
"Debtor". Section 9–105.
"Goods". Section 9–105.
"Knowledge". Section 1–201.
"Person". Section 1–201.
"Purchaser". Section 1–201.
"Secured party". Section 9–105.
"Security interest". Section 1–201.
"Value". Section 1–201.
"Writing". Section 1–201.

Cross References

Acquisition of property by accession, see Civil Code §§ 1000, 1013 et seq.
Default, see Commercial Code § 9501 et seq.
Letters of credit, see Commercial Code § 5101 et seq.
Products and accessions of property, see Civil Code § 732.
Property not yet acquired, creation of lien, see Civil Code § 2883.
Security interests,
    Attachment, see Commercial Code § 9203.
    Perfection, in general, see Commercial Code § 9303.
    Perfection in instruments, documents, and goods covered by documents, see Commercial Code § 9304.
    Priorities, in general, see Commercial Code § 9312.

§ 9315. Priority When Goods Are Commingled or Processed

(1) If a security interest in goods was perfected and subsequently the goods or a part thereof have become part of a product or mass, the security interest continues in the product or mass if

(a) The goods are so manufactured, processed, assembled or commingled that their identity is lost in the product or mass; or

(b) A financing statement covering the original goods also covers the product into which the goods have been manufactured, processed or assembled.

In a case to which paragraph (b) applies, no separate security interest in that part of the original goods which has been manufactured, processed or assembled into the product may be claimed under Section 9314.

(2) When under subdivision (1) more than one security interest attaches to the product or mass, they rank equally according to the ratio that the cost of the goods to which each interest originally attached bears to the cost of the total product or mass. *(Stats.1963, c. 819, § 9315.)*

California Code Comment

By John A. Bohn and Charles J. Williams

Prior California Law

1. There was no proper comparable statutory provision. In some cases it was possible for the secured party to shift his interest in raw materials to the finished product by using the inventory lien. This however was much more restrictive than Commercial Code § 9315. See in general 8 UCLA L.Rev. 806, 950–951.

2. Section 9315 does not answer the question as to when goods have in fact lost their identity. This will have to be resolved by judicial decision. Some suggestions for interpretation are contained in 8 UCLA L.Rev. 806, 948 (footnote 863):

"An analogous concept emphasizing physical identity is applied in the area of Specification—i.e., cases in which a converter takes a party's goods and through his labor shapes them into a new product. The question of whether the new product's title is in the innocent converter or the original owner of the materials is frequently settled by considering whether the materials have lost their identity. However, loss of identity, at least in this context, does not merely mean change of form. What exactly is meant is quite uncertain. See Evans, Some Applications of Title by Accession, 16 U.Cinc.L.Rev. 267, 294 (1942). California would give the product to the materials owner unless the workmanship is more valuable than the materials. The party who gets the product must reimburse the other for his contribution in materials or workmanship. See Cal.Civ.Code § 1029. However, if both have contributed materials and there is integration, a common interest is created in proportion to the value of materials of one party compared with the materials-workmanship contribution of the other. See Cal.Civ. Code § 1030."

Changes from U.C.C. (1962 Official Text)

3. This is section 9–315 of the Official Text without change.

Uniform Commercial Code Comment

Prior Uniform Statutory Provision:
None.

Purposes:

1. To state when a secured party whose collateral contributes to a product has priority over others who have conflicting claims in the same product.

2. This section changes the law in some jurisdictions where a security interest in goods (e.g., raw materials) was lost when the goods lost their identity by being commingled or processed. Under this section the security interest continues in the resulting mass or product in the cases stated in subsection (1).

3. This section applies not only to cases where flour, sugar and eggs are commingled into cake mix or cake, but also to cases where components are assembled into a machine. In the latter case a secured party is put to an election at the time of filing, by the last sentence of subsection (1), whether to claim under this section or to claim a security interest in one component under Section 9–314.

4. Subsection (2) is new and is needed because under subsection (1) it is possible to have more than one secured party claiming an interest in a product. The rule stated treats all such interests as being of equal priority entitled to share ratably in the product.

Cross References:

Sections 9–203(1), 9–303, 9–312(1) and 9–314.

Definitional Cross References:

"Goods". Section 9–105.
"Security interest". Section 1–201.

Cross References

Accessions, see Commercial Code § 9314.
Attachment of security interests, requisites, see Commercial Code § 9203.
Ownership of thing made from materials of several owners, see Civil Code § 1030.
Perfection of security interests, requisites, see Commercial Code § 9303.
Priorities among security interests, see Commercial Code §§ 9312, 9314.

§ 9316. Priority Subject to Subordination

Nothing in this division prevents subordination by agreement by any person entitled to priority. *(Stats. 1963, c. 819, § 9316.)*

California Code Comment

By John A. Bohn and Charles J. Williams

Prior California Law
1. This section is consistent with prior California law which did recognize subordination agreements. For example, Civil Code § 2934.

Changes from U.C.C. (1962 Official Text)
2. This is section 9–316 of the Official Text without change.

Uniform Commercial Code Comment

Prior Uniform Statutory Provision:
None.

Purposes:
The several preceding sections deal elaborately with questions of priority. This section is inserted to make it entirely clear that a person entitled to priority may effectively agree to subordinate his claim. Only the person entitled to priority may make such an agreement: his rights cannot be adversely affected by an agreement to which he is not a party.

Cross References:
Sections 1–102 and 9–312(1).

Definitional Cross References:
"Agreement". Section 1–201.
"Person". Section 1–201.

Cross References

Assignments, instruments subordinating or waiving priority, see Civil Code § 2934.
Conflicting security interests, priorities, see Commercial Code § 9312.
Variation by agreement, see Commercial Code § 1102.

§ 9317. Secured Party Not Obligated on Contract of Debtor

The mere existence of a security interest or authority given to the debtor to dispose of or use collateral does not impose contract or tort liability upon the secured party for the debtor's acts or omissions. *(Stats.1963, c. 819, § 9317.)*

California Code Comment

By John A. Bohn and Charles J. Williams

Prior California Law
1. This section is a generalized version of former Civil Code § 3016.8 (UTRA). See the Official Comment.

Changes from U.C.C. (1962 Official Text)
2. This is section 9–317 of the Official Text without change.

Uniform Commercial Code Comment

Prior Uniform Statutory Provision:
Section 12, Uniform Trust Receipts Act.

Purposes:
There were a few common law decisions, mostly in cases involving trust receipts, which suggested, if they did not hold, that a secured party who gave his debtor liberty of sale might be liable (for example, for breach of warranty) on the debtor's contracts of sale. The theory was grounded on the law of agency; the debtor being regarded as selling agent for the secured party as principal. This section rejects that theory. Section 12 of the Uniform Trust Receipts Act provided that the entruster was not subject to liability, merely because of his status as entruster, on sale of the goods subject to trust receipt. This section adopts the policy of the prior act and states it in general terms.

Cross Reference:
Section 2–210(4).

Definitional Cross References:
"Collateral". Section 9–105.
"Contract". Section 1–201.
"Debtor". Section 9–105.
"Secured party". Section 9–105.
"Security interest". Section 1–201.

Cross References

Burden of obligation not transferable, see Civil Code § 1457.
Sales, assignments of rights and duties, see Commercial Code § 2210.

§ 9318. Defenses against Assignee; Modification of Contract After Notification of Assignment; Term Prohibiting Assignment Ineffective; Identification and Proof of Assignment

(1) Unless an account debtor has made an enforceable agreement not to assert defenses or claims arising out of a sale as provided in Section 9206 the rights of an assignee are subject to:

(a) All the terms of the contract between the account debtor and assignor and any defense or claim arising therefrom; and

(b) Any other defense or claim of the account debtor against the assignor which accrues before the account debtor receives notification of the assignment.

(2) So far as the right to payment or a part thereof under an assigned contract has not been fully earned by performance, and notwithstanding notification of the assignment, any modification of or substitution for the contract made in good faith and in accordance with reasonable commercial standards is effective against an assignee unless the account debtor has otherwise agreed but the assignee acquires corresponding rights under the modified or substituted contract. The assignment may provide that the modification or substitution is a breach by the assignor.

(3) The account debtor is authorized to pay the assignor until the account debtor receives notification that the amount due or to become due has been assigned and that payment is to be made to the assignee. A notification which does not reasonably identify the rights assigned is ineffective. If requested by the account debtor, the assignee must seasonably furnish reasonable proof that the assignment has been made and unless he or she does so the account debtor may pay the assignor.

(4) A term in any contract between an account debtor and an assignor is ineffective if it prohibits assignment of an account or prohibits creation of a security interest in chattel paper or a security interest in

a general intangible for money due or to become due or requires the account debtor's consent to the assignment or security interest. *(Stats.1963, c. 819, § 9318. Amended by Stats.1974, c. 997, p. 2131, § 32, eff. Jan. 1, 1976; Stats.1988, c. 1368, § 11, operative Jan. 1, 1990.)*

California Code Comment

By John A. Bohn and Charles J. Williams

Prior California Law

1. Subdivision (1) is a generalized version of former Civil Code § 3016.5(3) (UTRA). See Official Comment 1.

2. Subdivision (3) is in accord with prior California law and business practice. Former Civil Code § 3018; Nanny v. Pogue (H.E.) Distillery Co., 56 Cal.App.2d 817, 133 P.2d 686 (1943), 8 UCLA L.Rev. 806, 974.

3. Subdivision (4) makes ineffective any clause which prohibits assignment of contract rights. Although there is no specific decision upon this point, it has been held that a trustee in bankruptcy could not reach the bankrupt's accounts receivable which had been assigned contrary to an express prohibition in the contract and it has been argued that California probably under prior law would have upheld the clause if the obligor had defended upon it. Bass v. Aetna Factors Co., 272 F.2d 707 (CCA 9, 1959); 8 UCLA L.Rev. 806, 973.

Changes from U.C.C. (1962 Official Text)

4. In subdivision (4) a California amendment adds the following phrase between the words "parties" and the phrase "is ineffective": "or which requires the account debtor's consent to such assignment"

This language was added for the purpose of clarifying the meaning of the section. It follows the suggestions of the California Bankers Committee and the Marsh and Warren Report. Sixth Progress Report to the Legislature by Senate Fact Finding Committee on Judiciary (1959–1961) Part 1, The Uniform Commercial Code, pp. 424, 599.

Uniform Commercial Code Comment

Prior Uniform Statutory Provision:

Section 9(3), Uniform Trust Receipts Act.

Purposes:

1. Subsection (1) makes no substantial change in prior law. An assignee has traditionally been subject to defenses or set-offs existing before an account debtor is notified of the assignment. When the account debtor's defenses on an assigned claim arise from the contract between him and the assignor, it makes no difference whether the breach giving rise to the defense occurs before or after the account debtor is notified of the assignment (paragraph (1) (a)). The account debtor may also have claims against the assignor which arise independently of that contract: an assignee is subject to all such claims which accrue before, and free of all those which accrue after, the account debtor is notified (paragraph (1) (b)). The account debtor may waive his right to assert claims or defenses against an assignee to the extent provided in Section 9–206.

2. Prior law was in confusion as to whether modification of an executory contract by account debtor and assignor without the assignee's consent was possible after notification of an assignment. Subsection (2) makes good faith modifications by assignor and account debtor without the assignee's consent effective against the assignee even after notification. This rule may do some violence to accepted doctrines of contract law. Nevertheless it is a sound and indeed a necessary rule in view of the realities of large scale procurement. When for example it becomes necessary for a government agency to cut back or modify existing contracts, comparable arrangements must be made promptly in hundreds and even thousands of subcontracts lying in many tiers below the prime contract. Typically the right to payments under these subcontracts will have been assigned. The government, as sovereign, might have the right to amend or terminate existing contracts apart from statute. This subsection gives the prime contractor (the account debtor) the right to make the required arrangements directly with his subcontractors without undertaking the task of procuring assents from the many banks to whom rights under the contracts may have been assigned. Assignees are protected by the provision which gives them automatically corresponding rights under the modified or substituted contract. Notice that subsection (2) applies only so far as the right to payment has not been earned by performance, and therefore its application ends entirely when the work is done or the goods furnished.

3. Subsection (3) clarifies the right of an account debtor to make payment to his seller-assignor in an "indirect collection" situation (see Comment to Section 9–308). So long as the assignee permits the assignor to collect claims or leaves him in possession of chattel paper which does not indicate that payment is to be made at some place other than the assignor's place of business, the account debtor may pay the assignor even though he may know of the assignment. In such a situation an assignee who wants to take over collections must notify the account debtor to make further payments to him.

4. Subsection (4) breaks sharply with the older contract doctrines by denying effectiveness to contractual terms prohibiting assignment of sums due and to become due under contracts of sale, construction contracts and the like. Under the rule as stated, an assignment would be effective even if made to an assignee who took with full knowledge that the account debtor had sought to prohibit or restrict assignment of the claims.

It is only for the past hundred years that our law has recognized the possibility of assigning choses in action. The history of this development, at law and equity, is in broad outline well known. Lingering traces of the absolute common law prohibition have survived almost to our own day.

There can be no doubt that a term prohibiting assignment of proceeds was effective against an assignee with notice through the nineteenth century and well into the twentieth. Section 151 of the Restatement of Contracts (1932) so states the law without qualification, but the changing character of the law is shown in the proposed Section 154 of the Restatement, Second, Contracts.

The original rule of law has been progressively undermined by a process of erosion which began much earlier than the cited section of the Restatement of Contracts would suggest. The cases are legion in which courts have construed the heart out of prohibitory or restrictive terms and held the assignment good. The cases are not lacking where courts have flatly held assignments valid without bothering to construe away the prohibition. See 4 Corbin on Contracts (1951) §§ 872, 873. Such cases as Allhusen v. Caristo Const. Corp., 303 N.Y. 446, 103 N.E.2d 891 (1952), are rejected by this subsection.

This gradual and largely unacknowledged shift in legal doctrine has taken place in response to economic need: as accounts and other rights under contracts have become the collateral which secures an ever increasing number of financing transactions, it has been necessary to reshape the law so that these intangibles, like negotiable instruments and negotiable documents of title, can be freely assigned.

Subsection (4) thus states a rule of law which is widely recognized in the cases and which corresponds to current business practices. It can be regarded as a revolutionary departure only by those who still cherish the hope that we may yet return to the views entertained some two hundred years ago by the Court of King's Bench.

5. The Federal Assignment of Claims Act of 1940—to which of course this section is subject—requires that assignments of claims against the United States be filed as provided in that Act. Many large business enterprises, situated like the United States in that claims against them are held by hundreds or thousands of subcontractors or suppliers, often require in their contract or purchase order forms that assignments against them be filed in a prescribed way. Subsection (3) requires reasonable identification of the account assigned and recognizes the right of an account debtor to require reasonable proof of the making of the assignment and to that extent validates such requirements in contracts or purchase order forms. If the notification does not contain such reasonable identification or if such reasonable proof is not furnished on request, the account debtor may disregard the assignment and make payment to the assignor. What is "reasonable" is not left to the arbitrary decision of the account debtor; if there is doubt as to the adequacy either of a notification or of proof submitted after request, the account debtor may not be safe in disregarding it unless he has notified the assignee with commercial promptness as to the respects in which identification or proof is considered defective.

6. If the thing to be assigned is the beneficiary's right under a letter of credit, Section 5–116 should be consulted.

Cross References:

Point 1: Section 9–206.
Point 3: Sections 9–205 and 9–308.
Point 4: Section 2–210(2) and (3).

Point 6: Section 5–116.
Definitional Cross References:
"Account". Section 9–106.
"Account debtor". Section 9–105.
"Agreement". Section 1–201.
"Contract". Section 1–201.
"Good faith". Section 1–201.
"Party". Section 1–201.
"Receives" notification. Section 1–201.
"Rights". Section 1–201.
"Sale". Sections 2–106 and 9–105.
"Seasonably". Section 1–204.
"Term". Section 1–201.

Cross References

Agreement not to assert claims or defenses, see Commercial Code § 9206.
Collateral, use or disposition by debtor, see Commercial Code § 9205.
Letters of credit, assignments, see Commercial Code § 5116.
Purchase of chattel paper and instruments, see Commercial Code § 9308.
Sales, limitations on assignments, see Commercial Code § 2210.
Transfer of non-negotiable instruments, see Civil Code § 1459.

CHAPTER 4. FILING

Section
9401. Place of Filing; Erroneous Filing; Removal of Collateral.
9401.5. Renumbered.
9402. Formal Requisites of Financing Statement; Amendments; Mortgage as Financing Statement.
9403. Filing requirements; duration of filing; effect of lapsed filing; continuation statement; duties of filing officer; fees; recordation and indexing; standard form wording.
9403. Filing requirements; duration of filing; effect of lapsed filing; continuation statement; duties of filing officer; fees; recordation and indexing; standard form wording.
9403.1. Destruction of Financing Statement Index.
9403.5. Financing or continuation statements; effective dates.
9404. Termination Statement.
9404. Termination Statement.
9405. Release of Security Interest; Duties of Filing Officer; Fees.
9405. Release of Security Interest; Duties of Filing Officer; Fees.
9406. Assignment or Transfer of Security Interest; Duties of Filing Officer; Fees; Statement of Assignment.
9406. Assignment or Transfer of Security Interest; Duties of Filing Officer; Fees; Statement of Assignment.
9407. Information From Filing Officer.
9407.1. Recordation in Lieu of Filing; Microphotography, Optical Disk, or Other Reproduction Techniques; Safekeeping.
9407.2. Recordation; File Numbers; Index.
9407.3. Return of Originals to Parties After Recordation.
9408. Financing Statements Covering Consigned or Leased Goods.
9409. Combined Certificate.

§ 9401. Place of Filing; Erroneous Filing; Removal of Collateral

(1) The proper place to file in order to perfect a security interest is as follows:

(a) When the collateral is consumer goods, then in the office of the county recorder in the county of the debtor's residence or if the debtor is not a resident of this state, then in the office of county recorder of the county in which the goods are kept;

(b) When the collateral is crops growing or to be grown, timber to be cut or is minerals or the like (including oil and gas) or accounts subject to subdivision (5) of Section 9103, then in the office where a mortgage on the real estate would be recorded.

(c) In all other cases, in the office of the Secretary of State.

(2) A filing which is made in good faith in an improper place or not in all of the places required by this section is nevertheless effective with regard to any collateral as to which the filing complied with the requirements of this division and is also effective with regard to collateral covered by the financing statement against any person who has knowledge of the contents of such financing statement.

(3) A filing which is made in the proper place in this state continues effective even though the debtor's residence or place of business or the location of the collateral or its use, whichever controlled the original filing, is thereafter changed.

(4) The rules stated in Section 9103 determine whether filing is necessary in this state.

(5) Notwithstanding subdivision (1), and subject to subdivision (3) of Section 9302, the proper place to file in order to perfect a security interest in collateral, including fixtures, of a transmitting utility is the office of the Secretary of State. This filing also constitutes a fixture filing (Section 9313) as to the collateral described therein which is or is to become fixtures.

(6) For the purposes of this section, the residence of an organization is its place of business if it has one or its chief executive office if it has more than one place of business.

(7) The proper place to file a financing statement filed as a fixture filing is in the office where a mortgage on the real estate would be recorded. (Stats.1963, c. 819, § 9401. Amended by Stats.1970, c. 310, p. 702, § 1, operative Jan. 1, 1971; Stats.1974, c. 997, p. 2131, § 33, eff. Jan. 1, 1976; Stats.1980, c. 1156, p. 3865, § 8.)

California Code Comment

By John A. Bohn and Charles J. Williams

Prior California Law

1. In order to perfect almost all security interests under Division 9 it is necessary to file a financing statement. Prior California law also required recordation as a means of protecting the interest of the secured party:

(a) for a chattel mortgage. Former Civil Code § 2957.
(b) for a trust receipt. Former Civil Code § 3016.4.
(c) for an assignment of an account. Former Civil Code § 3018.
(d) for an inventory lien. Former Civil Code §§ 3031–3033.
(e) for a conditional sale there was no extensive recordation requirement. However, recordation was required in the case of a conditional sale of mining and oil drilling equipment and machinery (former Civil

Code § 2980), animate chattels (former Civil Code § 2980.5), railroad equipment (Public Utilities Code § 7578). In the case of the conditional sale of chattel which is found to be a fixture, the California courts imposed the requirement of recordation. Oakland Bank of Savings v. California Pressed Brick Co., 183 Cal. 295, 191 Pac. 524 (1920).

2. Under prior California law the filing provisions were local except in the case of trust receipts:

"Cal.Civ.Code §§ 2957 (chattel mortgage) ((a) animate property—county of the mortgagor's residence; (b) crops—county in which crops are grown; (c) all other personalty—county where the mortgaged property is located and county where mortgagor resides if he is state resident), 2980 (conditional sales of mining and oil drilling equipment) (county of property's location and county of buyer's residence if he is a state resident), 2980.5 (conditional sales of animate property) (same as requirements for chattel mortgages of animate property *supra* this footnote), 3017 (assignment of accounts receivable) (county of assignor's chief place of business, or if he has no place of business, county of his residence), 3033 (inventory lien) (county in which borrower has his chief place of business, if within the state, and county of location of merchandise).

"Trust receipt financing is the major exception to local filing requirements. Perfection with the Secretary of State is permitted, although the entruster may elect to file locally. Local filing will not protect the entruster as against subsequent lienors or buyers in the ordinary course of trade, however. Cal.Civ.Code §§ 3016.9, 3016.12. Conditional sales of railroad equipment are also required to be centrally recorded. Pub.Util.Code § 7578." 8 UCLA L.Rev. 806, 883.

3. Subdivision (2) is similar in effect to former Civil Code § 2962 which provided that a chattel mortgage required to be recorded in different places was valid to the extent that it was recorded in the correct place. However, the Commercial Code is more liberal in disregarding errors which would not mislead third parties. A more strict view was taken under prior law. Rolando v. Everett, 72 Cal.App.2d 629, 165 P.2d 33 (1946) (chattel mortgage); In re San Clemente Elec. Supply, 101 F.Supp. 252 (S.D.Cal.1951) (trust receipt).

Changes from U.C.C. (1962 Official Text)

4. Subdivisions (2) and (4) are the same as subdivisions (2) and (4) of section 9–401 of the Official Text.

5. Subdivision (1) uses as a basic framework the second alternative subsection (1) of the 1962 Official Text with changes carried over as a result of interim study from the 1961 session. Sixth Progress Report to the Legislature by Senate Fact Finding Committee on Judiciary (1959–1961) Part 1, The Uniform Commercial Code, pp. 644, 651.

6. In subdivision (3) the phrase "or place of business" after the word "residence" is omitted in the California version.

7. Subdivision (5) does not appear in the Official Text.

Uniform Commercial Code Comment

Prior Uniform Statutory Provision:

Section 4, Uniform Trust Receipts Act; Sections 6 and 7, Uniform Conditional Sales Act.

Purposes:

1. Under chattel mortgage acts, the Uniform Conditional Sales Act and other conditional sales legislation the geographical unit for filing or recording was local: the county or township in which the mortgagor or vendee resided or in which the goods sold or mortgaged were kept. The Uniform Trust Receipts Act used the state as the geographical filing unit: under that Act statements of trust receipt financing were filed with an official in the state capital and were not filed locally. The state-wide filing system of the Trust Receipts Act has been followed in many accounts receivable and factor's lien acts.

Both systems have their advocates and both their own advantages and drawbacks. The principal advantage of state-wide filing is ease of access to the credit information which the files exist to provide. Consider for example the national distributor who wishes to have current information about the credit standing of the thousands of persons he sells to on credit. The more completely the files are centralized on a state-wide basis, the easier and cheaper it becomes to procure credit information; the more the files are scattered in local filing units, the more burdensome and costly. On the other hand, it can be said that most credit inquiries about local businesses, farmers and consumers come from local sources; convenience is served by having the files locally available and there is not great advantage in centralized filing.

This section does not attempt to resolve the controversy between the advocates of a completely centralized state-wide filing system and those of a large degree of local autonomy. Instead the section is drafted in a series of alternatives; local considerations of policy will determine the choice to be made.

2. Fortunately there is general agreement that the proper filing place for security interests in fixtures is in the office where a mortgage on the real estate concerned would be filed or recorded, and paragraph (1)(a) in the First Alternative and paragraph (1)(b) in the Second and Third Alternatives so provide. This provision follows the Uniform Conditional Sales Act. Note that there is no requirement for an additional filing with the chattel records.

3. In states where it is felt wise to preserve local filing for transactions of essentially local interest, either the Second or Third Alternative of subsection (1) should be adopted. Paragraph (1)(a) in both alternatives provides county (township, etc.) filing for consumer goods transactions and for agricultural transactions (farm equipment, farm products, farm accounts and crops). Note that the subsection departs from Section 6 of the Uniform Conditional Sales Act and adopts instead the policy of many chattel mortgage acts in selecting the county of the debtor's residence, rather than the county where the goods are located, as the normal filing place. Where, however, the debtor is an out-of-state resident, the filing must of necessity be in the county where the goods are, and the subsection so provides. Though not expressly stated, it is evident that filing for an assignment of accounts arising from the sale of farm products by a farmer who is not a resident must be in the county where the debtor keeps his farm products. In the case of crops growing or to be grown, where the land is in one county and the debtor's residence in another, filing must be made in both counties. Neither this filing for crops in the county where the land is nor the requirements that the security agreement (Section 9–203(1)(a)) and the financing statement (Section 9–402(1) and (3)) contain a description of the real estate point to the conclusion that a financing statement for a security interest in crops must be filed in the real estate records. This Article follows pre-Code law which recognized such a financing as a chattel mortgage. The policy of the subsection is to require filing in the place or places where a creditor would normally look for information concerning interests created by the debtor.

For some incorporated farmers, reference to residence is an anomaly. Therefore subsection (6) provides that the residence of an organization is its place of business, or its chief executive office if it has more than one place of business. Compare Section 9–103(3), which reaches essentially the same concept as a definition of the "location" of a debtor.

4. It is thought that sound policy requires a state-wide filing system for all transactions except the essentially local ones covered in paragraph (1)(a) of the Second and Third Alternatives and land-related transactions covered in paragraph (1)(b) of the Second and Third Alternatives. Paragraph (1)(c) so provides in both alternatives, as does paragraph (1)(b) in the First Alternative. In a state which has adopted either the Second or Third Alternative, central filing would be required when the collateral was goods except consumer goods, farm equipment or farm products (including crops), or was documents or chattel paper or was accounts or general intangibles, unless related to a farm. Note that the filing provisions of this Article do not apply to instruments (see Section 9–304).

If the Third Alternative subsection (1) is adopted, then local filing, in addition to the central filing, is required in all the cases stated in the preceding paragraph, with respect to any debtor whose places of business within the state are all within a single county (township, etc.) or a debtor who is not engaged in business. The last event test stated in Section 9–103(1)(b) and Comment thereto applies to determine whether local filing is required under the present section, as well as to determine in which state filing is required.

In states where the arguments for a completely centralized set of files (except for fixtures) prevail, the First Alternative subsection (1) should be adopted. That alternative provides for exclusive central filing of all security interests except those in fixtures.

5. When a secured party has in good faith attempted to comply with the filing requirements but has not done so correctly, subsection (2) makes his filing effective in so far as it was proper, and also makes it good for all collateral covered by the financing statement against any person who actually knows the contents of the improperly filed statement. The subsection rejects the occasional decisions that an improperly filed record is ineffective to give notice even to a person who

knows of it. But if the Third Alternative subsection (1) is adopted, the requirements of paragraph (1) (c) are not complied with unless there is filing in both offices specified; filing in only one of two required places is not effective except as against one with actual knowledge of the contents of the defective financing statement.

6. Subsection (3) deals with change of residence or place of business or the location or use of the goods *after* a proper filing has been made. The subsection is important only when local filing is required, and covers only changes between local filing units in the state. For changes of location between states see Section 9–103(1) (d).

Subsection (3) is presented in alternative forms. Under the first, no new filing is required in the county to which the collateral has been removed. Under alternative subsection (3) the original filing lapses four months after the change in location; this is basically the same rule that is applied by Section 9–103(1) (d) to the case of collateral brought into the state subject to a security interest which attached elsewhere.

7. The usual filing rules do not apply well for a transmitting utility (defined in Section 9–105). Many pre-Code statutes provided special filing rules for railroads and in some cases for other public utilities to avoid the requirements for filing with legal descriptions in every county in which such debtors had property. The Code recreates and broadens these provisions by subsection (5) of this section, which provides that for transmitting utilities the filing need only be in the office of the Secretary of State. The nature of the debtor will inform persons searching the record as to where to make a search.

Cross References:
Sections 9–302, 9–304 and 9–307(2).
Point 2: Section 9–313.
Point 6: Section 9–103(3).
Point 7: Sections 9–402(5) and 9–403(6).

Definitional Cross References:
"Account". Section 9–106.
"Collateral". Section 9–105.
"Consumer goods". Section 9–109.
"Debtor". Section 9–105.
"Equipment". Section 9–109.
"Farm products". Section 9–109.
"Financing statement". Section 9–402.
"Fixture filing". Section 9–313.
"Good faith". Section 1–201.
"Goods". Section 9–105.
"Knowledge". Section 1–201.
"Person". Section 1–201.
"Secured party". Section 9–105.
"Security interest". Section 1–201.
"Signed". Section 1–201.
"Transmitting utility". Section 9–105.

Cross References

Changes of location between states, see Commercial Code § 9103.
County recorder, see Government Code § 27201 et seq.
Effect of recording or the want thereof, see Civil Code § 1213 et seq.
Filing prior to Jan. 1, 1971, of financing statement or continuation with county recorder, validity and future filings, see Commercial Code § 13105.
Mode of recording, see Civil Code § 1169 et seq.
Perfection of security interests, filing, see Commercial Code §§ 9302, 9304.
Recording and indexing fees, see Government Code § 27361.
Recording of instruments, see Government Code § 27320 et seq.
Secretary of state, custodian of records, see Government Code § 12160.

§ 9401.5. Renumbered § 10105 and amended by Stats.1974, c. 997, p. 2132, § 34, eff. Jan. 1, 1976

§ 9402. Formal Requisites of Financing Statement; Amendments; Mortgage as Financing Statement

(1) A financing statement is sufficient if it gives the names of the debtor and the secured party, is signed by the debtor, gives an address of the secured party from which information concerning the security interest may be obtained, gives a mailing address of the debtor, and contains a statement indicating the types, or describing the items, of collateral. A financing statement should include the debtor's trade name or style, if any, if known to the secured party, * * * but a failure to include the trade name or style * * * shall not under any circumstances affect the validity of the financing statement. A financing statement may be filed before a security agreement is made or a security interest otherwise attaches. When the financing statement covers crops growing or to be grown, the statement must also contain a description of the real estate concerned. When the financing statement covers timber to be cut or covers minerals or the like (including oil and gas) or accounts subject to subdivision (5) of Section 9103, or when the financing statement is filed as a fixture filing (Section 9313) and the collateral is goods which are or are to become fixtures, the statement must also comply with subdivision (5). A copy of the security agreement is sufficient as a financing statement if it contains the above information and is signed by the debtor. A certified copy of a financing statement or security agreement is sufficient as a financing statement if the original thereof was filed in this state.

(2) A financing statement which otherwise complies with subdivision (1) is sufficient when it is signed by the secured party instead of the debtor if it is filed to perfect a security interest in or as a fixture filing covering any of the following:

(a) Collateral already subject to a security interest in another jurisdiction when it is brought into this state or when the debtor's location is changed to this state. The financing statement must state that the collateral was brought into this state or that the debtor's location was changed to this state under such circumstances.

(b) Proceeds under Section 9306, if the security interest in the original collateral was perfected. The financing statement must describe the original collateral and give the date of filing and the file number of the prior financing statement.

(c) Collateral as to which the filing has lapsed. The financing statement must include a statement to the effect that the prior financing statement has lapsed and give the date of filing and the file number of the prior financing statement* * *.

(d) Collateral acquired after a change of name, identity or corporate structure of the debtor (subdivision (7)). The financing statement must include a statement that the name, identity or corporate structure of the debtor has been changed and give the date of filing and the file number of the prior financing statement and the name of the debtor as shown in the prior financing statement.

(3) A form substantially as follows is sufficient to comply with subdivision (1):

Name of debtor (or assigner) _____

Address _____

§ 9402   SECURED TRANSACTIONS

Name of secured party (or assignee) _____

Address _____

Debtor's trade name or style, if any _____

1. This financing statement covers the following types (or items) of property: (Describe) _____

2. (If collateral is crops) The above-described crops are growing or are to be grown on: (Describe real estate) _____

3. (If applicable) The above goods are or are to become fixtures on* (Describe real estate) _____ and this financing statement is to be recorded in the real estate records. (If the debtor does not have an interest of record) The name of a record owner is _____

4. (If products of collateral are claimed) Products of the collateral are also covered.

(Use whichever is applicable)   Signature of debtor (or assignor)

                   Signature of secured party (or assignee)

*Where appropriate substitute either "The above timber is standing on ......" or "The above mineral or the like (including oil and gas) or accounts will be financed at the wellhead or minehead of the well or mine located on ......"

(4) A financing statement may be amended by filing a writing signed by both the debtor and the secured party, or by the secured party alone in the case of an amendment pursuant to subdivision (7). An amendment does not extend the period of effectiveness of a financing statement. If any amendment adds collateral, it is effective as to the added collateral only from the filing date of the amendment. In this division, unless the context otherwise requires, the term "financing statement" means the original financing statement and any amendments.

(5) A financing statement covering timber to be cut or covering minerals or the like (including oil and gas) or accounts subject to subdivision (5) of Section 9103, or a financing statement filed as a fixture filing (Section 9313) where the debtor is not a transmitting utility, must show that it covers this type of collateral, must recite that it is to be recorded in the real estate records, and the financing statement must contain a description of the real estate sufficient if it were contained in a mortgage of the real estate to give constructive notice of the mortgage under the law of this state. If the debtor does not have an interest of record in the real estate, the financing statement must show the name of a record owner. A financing statement filed as a fixture filing (Section 9313) where the debtor is not a transmitting utility must also recite either that it is filed as a fixture filing or that it covers goods which are or are to become fixtures.

(6) A mortgage is effective as a financing statement filed as a fixture filing from the date of its recording if all of the following conditions are met:

(a) The goods are described in the mortgage by item or type.

(b) The goods are or are to become fixtures related to the real estate described in the mortgage.

(c) The mortgage complies with the requirements for a financing statement in this section other than a recital that it is to be filed in the real estate records* * *.

(d) The mortgage is duly recorded.

No fee with reference to the financing statement is required other than the regular recording and satisfaction fees with respect to the mortgage.

(7) A financing statement sufficiently shows the name of the debtor if it gives the individual, partnership or corporate name of the debtor, whether or not it adds other trade names or names of partners. Where the debtor so changes his or her name or in the case of an organization its name, identity or corporate structure that a filed financing statement becomes seriously misleading, the filing is not effective to perfect a security interest in collateral acquired by the debtor more than four months after the change, unless a new appropriate financing statement or an appropriate amendment to the filed financing statement is filed before the acquisition of the collateral by the debtor. A filed financing statement remains effective with respect to collateral transferred by the debtor even though the secured party knows of or consents to the transfer.

(8) A financing statement substantially complying with the requirements of this section is effective even though it contains minor errors which are not seriously misleading. A financing statement filed as a fixture filing (Section 9313) where the debtor is not a transmitting utility is not effective if it does not recite that it is to be recorded in the real estate records and either that it is filed as a fixture filing or that it covers goods which are or are to become fixtures.

(9) A financing statement substantially complying with the requirements of this section creates a security interest only to the extent of the interest of the debtor.

(10) No person or entity acting for or on behalf of the parties to a financing statement shall incur any liability for the consequences of recording a financing statement in the real estate records, and no action may be brought or maintained against that person or entity as a result of the recordation. (Stats.1963, c. 819, § 9402. Amended by Stats.1965, c. 1379, p. 3294, § 18; Stats.1974, c. 997, p. 2133, § 35, eff. Jan. 1, 1976; Stats.1980, c. 1156, p. 3866, § 9; Stats.1981, c. 148, p. 946, § 1, eff. July 8, 1981; Stats.1982, c. 1174, p. 4191, § 2, eff. Sept. 20, 1982; Stats.1988, c. 1368, § 12, operative Jan. 1, 1990; Stats.1989, c. 464, § 1.)

California Code Comment

By John A. Bohn and Charles J. Williams

Prior California Law

1. The form of the financing statement required by this section is similar to former Civil Code § 3016.9 which prescribed the trust receipt financing statement.

This form does not require as much detail as the form of statement formerly prescribed in the case of an assignment of account receivable (former Civil Code § 3019) or inventory lien (former Civil Code § 3032). The chattel mortgage statute required that the mortgage itself be recorded Former Civil Code § 2957. In addition the description of the mortgage property in a chattel mortgage required more detail and also a statement of the amount of the secured debt. Former Civil Code § 2956.

2. In general under prior California law certain statements had to be acknowledged:

(a) chattel mortgage. Former Civil Code § 2957.

(b) conditional sale of mining & oil drilling equipment, or livestock, (former Civil Code §§ 2980, 2980.5) or railroad equipment (Public Utilities Code § 7578).

Changes from U.C.C. (1962 Official Text)

3. Subdivisions (2) and (5) are the same as subdivisions (2) and (5) of section 9–402 of the Official Text.

However, subdivisions (1) and (4) of the Official Text as changed in California reads as follows:

9402. (1) A financing statement is sufficient if it is signed by the debtor and by the secured party, gives [an] the name and mailing address of the secured party, [from which information concerning the security interest may be obtained,] the name and mailing address of the debtor and contains a statement indicating the types of collateral or describing the items of collateral. [A financing statement may be filed before a security agreement is made or before a security interest otherwise attaches. When the financing statement covers crops growing or to be grown or goods which are or are to become fixtures, the statement must also contain a description of the real estate concerned. A copy of the security agreement is sufficient as a financing statement if it contains the above information and is signed by both parties.] The financing statement shall also set forth: if the debtor is an individual, the address of his residence and the address of his chief place of business, if any; if the debtor is an organization, the address of its chief place of business; if the debtor is doing business under a trade name or style, such trade name or style. A financing statement may be filed before a security agreement is made or before a security interest otherwise attaches. When the financing statement covers crops growing or to be grown or timber to be cut, the statement must also contain a description of the real property concerned. A copy of the security agreement is sufficient as a financing statement if it contains the above information and is signed by both parties.

(4) The term "financing statement" as used in this [Article] code means the original financing statement and any amendments signed by the debtor and the secured party or a financing statement signed only by the secured party under Section 9402(2) and any amendments thereto, but if any amendment adds collateral, it is effective as to the added collateral only from the filing date of the amendment.

The form as set forth in subdivision (3) of the California version is changed from the form prescribed in subdivision (3) of the Official Text to conform to the changes made in subdivision (1) which describes the form.

California Code Comment

By Charles J. Williams

The form of financing statement originally included an optional provision stating the maximum amount of the indebtedness to be secured at any one time. This optional provision was deleted in 1965 because it is no longer necessary in view of the deletion of subdivision (7) from Section 9312.

Legislative Committee Comment—Senate
1974 Amendment

The second sentence of Section 9402(1) expresses the sense of the Legislature that it is desirable that a financing statement contain any trade names or styles of the debtor known to the secured party since this enhances the usefulness of the records to all parties. However, the use of the word "should" in that sentence is intended to be entirely precatory as indicated by the last part of the sentence. Even if the omission of a trade name should be found to be willful on the part of the secured party or to have seriously misled another party searching the records, the "but clause" of this sentence clearly states that the financing statement is nevertheless valid if otherwise in proper form. The validity of a filing should not be made to depend on difficult factual inquiries regarding subjective intent or reliance.

Uniform Commercial Code Comment
P.E.B. Commentary No. 3, March 10, 1990

Purposes:

1.

* * * * * *

Nothing in Article 9 mandates a particular mode of transmission to the filing office of the data required to be supplied for a financing statement or other filing, mandates that a filing be on paper or any particular medium, or limits the filing officer's use of any particular technology for the receipt, storage, or retrieval of filings. Accordingly, data transmitted electronically to the filing office and reduces to tangible form constitute a financing statement or other filing under Article 9 if they provide all the information required under the applicable provision of Article 9. See PEB Commentary No. 15, dated July 16, 1996. [Uniform Laws Annotated, UCC, APP II, Comment 15].

* * * * * *

8. Subsection (7) also deals with a different problem, namely whether a new filing is necessary where the collateral has been transferred from one debtor to another. This question has been much debated both in pre-Code law and under the Code. This Article now answers the question in the negative. Thus, any person searching the condition of the ownership of a debtor must make inquiry as to the debtor's source of title, and must search in the name of a former owner if circumstances seem to require it.

PEB Commentary No. 3, dated March 10, 1990 [Uniform Laws Annotated, UCC, APP II, Comment 3], explains the interplay between this Section and Section 9–306(2). As explained in this Commentary, this Section is consistent with Section 9–306(2) since Section 9–306(2) deals with the continuation or termination of a security interest in collateral following a disposition of the collateral. The last sentence of Section 9–402(7), on the other hand, deals with the continued effectiveness of a filed financing statement to perfect any security interest that continues in the collateral following its disposition.

* * * * * *

Uniform Commercial Code Comment

Prior Uniform Statutory Provision:

Sections 13(3), 13(4), Uniform Trust Receipts Act.

Purposes:

1. Subsection (1) sets out the simple formal requisites of a financing statement under this Article. These requirements are: (1) signature of the debtor; (2) addresses of both parties; (3) a description of the collateral by type or item.

Where the collateral is crops growing or to be grown or when the financing statement is filed as a fixture filing (Section 9–313) or when the collateral is timber to be cut or minerals or the like (including oil and gas) financed at wellhead or minehead or accounts resulting from the sale thereof, the financing statement must also contain a description of the lands concerned. On description generally, see Section 9–110 and Comment 5 to the present section. An important distinction must be drawn, however, between the function of the description of land in reference to crops and its function in the other cases mentioned. For crops it is merely part of the description of the crops concerned, and the security interest in crops is a Code security interest, like the pre-Code "crop mortgage" which was a *chattel* mortgage. In contrast, in the other cases mentioned the function of the description of land is to have the financing statement filed in the county where the land is situated and in the realty records, as distinguished from the chattel records. Subsection (3) suggests a form which complies with the statutory requirements and makes clear that for the types of collateral mentioned other than crops, the financing statement containing a description of the land concerned is to go in the realty records. Note also subsection (5) on the adequacy of the description of land where the filing is to be in the real estate records. See also Section 9–403(7) on the indexing of these filings in the real estate records.

A copy of the security agreement may be filed in place of a separate financing statement, if it contains the required information and signature.

2. This section adopts the system of "notice filing" which proved successful under the Uniform Trust Receipts Act. What is required to be filed is not, as under chattel mortgage and conditional sales acts, the security agreement itself, but only a simple notice which may be filed before the security interest attaches or thereafter. The notice itself indicates merely that the secured party who has filed may have a security interest in the collateral described. Further inquiry from the parties concerned will be necessary to disclose the complete state of affairs. Section 9–208 provides a statutory procedure under which the secured party, at the debtor's request, may be required to make disclosure. Notice filing has proved to be of great use in financing transactions involving inventory, accounts and chattel paper, since it obviates the necessity of refiling on each of a series of transactions in a continuing arrangement where the collateral changes from day to day. Where other types of collateral are involved, the alternative procedure of filing a signed copy of the security agreement may prove to be the simplest solution. Sometimes more than one copy of a financing statement or of a security agreement used as a financing statement is needed for filing. In such a case the section permits use of a carbon copy or photographic copy of the paper, including signatures.

However, even in the case of filings that do not necessarily involve a series of transactions the financing statement is effective to encompass transactions under a security agreement not in existence and not contemplated at the time the notice was filed, if the description of collateral in the financing statement is broad enough to encompass them. Similarly, the financing statement is valid to cover after-acquired property and future advances under security agreements whether or not mentioned in the financing statement.

3. This section departs from the requirements of many pre-Code chattel mortgage statutes that the instrument filed be acknowledged or witnessed or accompanied by affidavits of good faith. Those requirements did not seem to have been successful as a deterrent to fraud; their principal effect was to penalize good faith mortgagees who had inadvertently failed to comply with the statutory niceties. They are here abandoned in the interest of a simplified and workable filing system.

4. Subsection (2) allows the secured party to file a financing statement signed only by himself where the filing is required by any of the events listed, each of which occurs after the commencement of the financing, and therefore under circumstances where the cooperation of the debtor is not certain. Section 9–401(3), alternative provision, contains similar permission on removal between counties in this state. The secured party should not be penalized for failure to make a timely filing by reason of difficulty in procuring the signature of a possibly reluctant or hostile debtor. Financing statements filed under this subsection must explain the circumstances under which they are filed with the signature of the secured party rather than that of the debtor.

In contrast to the signatures on original financing statements, an amendment to a financing statement must be signed by both parties, to preclude either from adversely affecting the interests of the other.

The reference in subsection (4) to an amendment which "adds collateral" refers to additional types of collateral. A security interest on additional units of a type of collateral already described can be created under an after acquired property clause or a new security agreement. See Comment 5 to Section 9–204. On priorities in such cases see Section 9–312 and Comments thereto.

5. [California did not adopt provisions on fixture financing statements]. A description of real estate must be sufficient to identify it. See Section 9–110. This formulation rejects the view that the real estate description must be by metes and bounds, or otherwise conforming to traditional real estate practice in conveyancing, but of course the incorporation of such a description by reference to the recording data of a deed, mortgage or other instrument containing the description should suffice under the most stringent standards. The proper test is that a description of real estate must be sufficient so that the fixture financing statement will fit into the real estate search system and the financing statement be found by a real estate searcher. Optional language has been added by which the test of adequacy of the description is whether it would be adequate in a mortgage of the real estate. As suggested in the Note, more detail may be required if there is a tract indexing system or a land registration system.

Where the debtor does not have an interest of record in the real estate, a fixture financing statement must show the name of a record owner, and Section 9–403(7) requires the financing statement to be indexed in the name of that owner. Thus the fixture financing statement will fit into the real estate search system.

6. [California did not adopt subsection 6 from U.C.C. (1972 official text)]. A real estate mortgage may provide that it constitutes a security agreement with respect to fixtures (or other goods) in conformity with this Article. Combined mortgages on real estate and chattels are common and useful for certain purposes. This section goes further and makes provision that the recording of the real estate mortgage (if it complies with the requirements of a financing statement) shall constitute the filing of a financing statement as to the fixtures (but not, of course, as to the other goods). Section 9–403(6) makes the usual five-year maximum life for financing statements inapplicable to real estate mortgages which operate as financing statements under Section 9–402(6), and they are effective for the duration of the real estate recording.

Of course, if a combined mortgage covers chattels which are not fixtures, a regular chattel filing is necessary, and subsection (6) is inapplicable to such chattels. Likewise, filing as a "fixture filing" provided in Section 9–401 does not apply to true chattels.

7. Subsection (7) undertakes to deal with some of the problems as to who is the debtor. In the case of individuals, it contemplates filing only in the individual name, not in a trade name. In the case of partnerships it contemplates filing in the partnership name, not in the names of any of the partners, and not in any other trade names. Trade names are deemed to be too uncertain and too likely not to be known to the secured party or person searching the record, to form the basis for a filing system. However, provision is made in Section 9–403(5) for indexing in a trade name if the secured party so desires.

Subsection (7) also deals with the case of a change of name of a debtor and provides some guidelines when mergers or other changes of corporate structure of the debtor occur with the result that a filed financing statement might become seriously misleading. Not all cases can be imagined and covered by statutes in advance; however, the principle sought to be achieved by the subsection is that after a change which would be seriously misleading, the old financing statement is not effective as to new collateral acquired more than four months after the change, unless a new appropriate financing statement is filed before the expiration of the four months. The old financing statement, if legally still valid under the circumstances, would continue to protect collateral acquired before the change and, if still operative under the particular circumstances, would also protect collateral acquired within the four months. Obviously, the subsection does not undertake to state whether the old security agreement continues to operate between the secured party and the party surviving the corporate change of the debtor.

8. Subsection (7) also deals with a different problem, namely whether a new filing is necessary where the collateral has been transferred from one debtor to another. This question has been much debated both in pre-Code law and under the Code. This Article now answers the question in the negative. Thus, any person searching the condition of the ownership of a debtor must make inquiry as to the debtor's source of title, and must search in the name of a former owner if circumstances seem to require it.

9. Subsection (8) is in line with the policy of this Article to simplify formal requisites and filing requirements and is designed to discourage the fanatical and impossibly refined reading of such statutory requirements in which courts have occasionally indulged themselves. As an example of the sort of reasoning which this subsection rejects, see General Motors Acceptance Corporation v. Haley, 329 Mass. 559, 109 N.E.2d 143 (1952).

Cross References:
Point 1: Section 9–110.
Point 2: Section 9–208.
Point 4: Sections 9–103, 9–306 and 9–401(3).
Point 5: Section 9–110.
Point 6: Section 9–403(6).
Point 7: Section 9–403(8).
Point 8: Section 9–311.

Definitional Cross References:
"Collateral". Section 9–105.
"Debtor". Section 9–105.

"Fixture". Section 9–313.
"Fixture filing". Section 9–313.
"Goods". Section 9–105.
"Party". Section 1–201.
"Proceeds". Section 9–306.
"Secured party". Section 9–105.
"Security agreement". Section 9–105.
"Security interest". Section 1–201.
"Signed". Section 1–201.
"Transmitting utility". Section 9–105.

Cross References

Description of property, see Commercial Code § 9110.

Disclosure by secured party, indebtedness and collateral, see Commercial Code § 9208.

Filing,
Collateral brought into state, see Commercial Code § 9103.
Refiling, see Commercial Code § 9306.

§ 9403. Filing requirements; duration of filing; effect of lapsed filing; continuation statement; duties of filing officer; fees; recordation and indexing; standard form wording

Text of section operative until January 1, 2000.

(1) Presentation for filing of a financing statement, tender of the filing fee and acceptance of the statement by the filing officer constitutes filing under this division.

(2) Except as provided in subdivision (6), a filed financing statement is effective for a period of five years from the date of filing. The effectiveness of a filed financing statement lapses on the expiration of such five-year period unless a continuation statement is filed prior to the lapse. If a security interest perfected by filing exists at the time insolvency proceedings are commenced by or against the debtor, the security interest remains perfected until termination of the insolvency proceedings and thereafter for a period of 60 days or until expiration of the five-year period, whichever occurs later. Upon such lapse the security interest becomes unperfected unless it is perfected without filing. If the security interest becomes unperfected upon lapse, it is deemed to have been unperfected as against a person who became a purchaser or lien creditor before lapse. If a fixture filing is effective at the time insolvency proceedings are commenced by or against the debtor, the fixture filing remains effective until termination of the insolvency proceedings and thereafter for a period of 60 days or until expiration of the five-year period or termination pursuant to subdivision (6), whichever occurs later. Upon lapse of a fixture filing, it is deemed to have been ineffective as against a person who became a purchaser or lien creditor before lapse.

(3) A continuation statement may be filed by the secured party of record within six months prior to the expiration of the five-year period specified in subdivision (2). Any such continuation statement must be signed by the secured party of record, identify the original statement by giving the date and the names of the parties thereto and the file number thereof and state that the original statement is continued. A continuation statement filed to continue the effectiveness of a financing statement filed as a fixture filing (Section 9313) is not effective unless the following requirements are met:

(a) If the debtor did not have an interest of record in the real estate as of the date of the filing of the original statement, the continuation statement shall contain the name of a record owner of the real estate as of the date of the filing of the original statement.

(b) The continuation statement shall contain substantially the following statement: "This continuation statement is filed to continue the effectiveness of a financing statement filed as a fixture filing"; provided, that such statement shall clearly indicate the intent to continue the effectiveness of a financing statement as a fixture filing.

Upon timely filing of the continuation statement, the effectiveness of the original statement is continued for five years after the last date to which the filing was effective whereupon it lapses in the same manner as provided in subdivision (2) unless another continuation statement is filed prior to such lapse. Succeeding continuation statements may be filed in the same manner to continue the effectiveness of the original statement. The filing officer may remove a lapsed financing statement and related filings from the files and destroy them immediately if he or she has retained a microfilm or other photographic record, or in other cases after one year after the lapse. The filing officer shall so arrange matters by physical annexation of financing statements to continuation statements or other related filings, or by other means, that if he or she physically destroys the financing statements of a period more than five years past, those which have been continued by a continuation statement or which are still effective under subdivision (6) shall be retained. The filing officer shall not destroy a financing statement and related filings as to which he or she has received written notice that there is an action pending relative thereto or that insolvency proceedings have been commenced by or against the debtor.

(4) Except as provided in subdivision (7) a filing officer shall mark each financing statement with a consecutive file number and with the date and time of filing and shall hold the statement or a microfilm or other photographic copy thereof for public inspection. In addition the filing officer shall index the statement according to the name of the debtor and shall note in the index the file number and the address of the debtor given in this statement. The filing officer shall mark each continuation statement with the date and time of filing and shall index the same under the file number of the original financing statement.

(5) The uniform fee for filing, indexing and furnishing filing data (subdivision (1) of Section 9407) for an original financing statement, an amendment or a continuation statement shall be <u>twenty</u> dollars ($20) if the statement is in the standard form prescribed by the Secretary of State and otherwise shall be <u>thirty</u> dollars ($<u>30</u>).

(6) If the debtor is a transmitting utility (subdivision (5) of Section 9401) and a filed financing statement so states, it is effective until a termination statement is filed. A real estate mortgage which is effective as a fixture filing under subdivision (6) of Section 9402 remains effective as a fixture filing until the mortgage is released or satisfied of record or its effectiveness otherwise terminates as to the real estate.

(7) A financing or continuation statement covering collateral described in paragraph (b) of subdivision (1) of Section 9401 or filed as a fixture filing shall be recorded and indexed by the filing officer in the real property index of grantors under the name of the debtor and any owner of record shown on the financing statement. A financing or continuation statement so recorded and indexed and containing a description of real property affected thereby shall constitute constructive notice from the time of its acceptance for recording to any purchaser or encumbrancer of the real property of the security interest in such collateral.

(8) The standard form of original financing statement prescribed by the Secretary of State pursuant to subdivision (5) shall include the wording "Financing statements are effective, with certain exceptions, only for five years from the date of filing, pursuant to Section 9403 of the California Commercial Code" or substantially equivalent warning language as prescribed by the Secretary of State.

(9) This section shall remain in effect only until January 1, 2000, and as of that date is repealed, unless a later enacted statute, that is enacted before January 1, 2000, deletes or extends that date. *(Stats.1963, c. 819, § 9403. Amended by Stats.1971, c. 1307, p. 2593, § 1; Stats.1974, c. 997, p. 4194, § 36, eff. Jan. 1, 1976; Stats.1980, c. 1156, p. 3869, § 10; Stats.1981, c. 148, p. 948, § 2, eff. July 8, 1981; Stats.1982, c. 1174, p. 4194, § 3, eff. Sept. 20, 1982; Stats.1987, c. 1348, § 9; Stats.1989, c. 464, § 2; Stats.1992, c. 1333 (S.B.1434), § 3; Stats.1995, c. 656 (S.B.888), § 5.)*

Repeal

This section is repealed by its own terms on January 1, 2000.

For text of section operative January 1, 2000, see § 9403, post.

California Code Comment

By John A. Bohn and Charles J. Williams

Prior California Law

1. Subdivision (1) is consistent with Civil Code § 1170 which applies to recordation of instruments by a county recorder. Subdivision (1) is also in accord with prior California law:

(a) for a chattel mortgage. Watkins v. Wilhoit, 104 Cal. 395, 38 Pac. 53 (1894). However, when the question involved a subsequent third party relying upon the record, in giving value the mortgage was not considered as recorded as against that subsequent party. Cady v. Purser, 131 Cal. 552, 63 Pac. 844 (1901). The rationale for the rule was that the recording officer is like the agent of the mortgagee and the mortgagee cannot avoid the consequences of errors in recordation by shifting the blame to the recorder. 8 UCLA L.Rev. 806, 895.

(b) for a trust receipt. Former Civil Code § 3016.9(4).

(c) for an assignment of account receivable. Former Civil Code § 3021.

(d) for an inventory lien. Former Civil Code § 3035.

2. Subdivision (2) provides for the lapse of the financing statement. Prior California law differed depending upon the kind of security transaction:

(a) for a chattel mortgage, four years. Former Civil Code § 2957.

(b) for a trust receipt, one year. Former Civil Code § 3016.9(4).

(c) for an assignment of account receivable, three years. Former Civil Code § 3022.

(d) for an inventory lien, three years. Former Civil Code § 3038.

(e) For a conditional sale contract for livestock, four years. Former Civil Code § 2980.5(d) incorporating the same period applicable to chattel mortgages. There was no refiling requisite for the conditional sale of mining or oil drilling or railroad equipment.

Similarly the recordation statements differed depending upon the type of security transaction:

(a) For a chattel mortgage the certificate of recordation had to be signed by the mortgagee, contain the names of the parties and refer to the index of the original file mortgage.

(b) For a trust receipt, assignment of account and inventory lien, both parties had to sign or had to submit an affidavit by the secured party and it must have been in the same form as the original statement. 8 UCLA L.Rev. 806, 896.

3. The Commercial Code makes changes in the priorities under conflicting claims when the first claim has lapsed.

Under subdivision (2) the effect of the failure to refile is a loss of perfection of the security interest. This means that if a later creditor had perfected his interest, his knowledge is immaterial and the second perfected interest takes priority if the first interest lapses. Official Comment 3.

In general, the statutes dealing with the various security interests provided that a lapsed mortgage or security interest was void against a creditor or subsequent purchaser and encumbrancer who took without actual knowledge of the outstanding but lapsed interest: chattel mortgage (former Civil Code § 2957), trust receipt (former Civil Code § 3016.4(2)), assignment of account (former Civil Code § 3018), and inventory lien (former Civil Code § 3042).

Changes from U.C.C. (1962 Official Text)

4. Section 9–403 of the Official Text as changed in the California version reads as follows:

(1) Presentation for filing of a financing statement, [and] tender of the filing fee [or] and acceptance of the statement by the filing officer constitutes filing under this [Article] code.

(2) A filed financing statement [which states a maturity date of the obligation secured of five years or less] is effective [until such maturity date and thereafter] for a period of [sixty days]. Any other filed financing statement is effective for a period of] five years from the date of filing. The effectiveness of a filed financing statement lapses on the expiration of such [sixty day period after a stated maturity date or on the expiration of such] five-year period [, as the case may be,] unless a continuation statement is filed prior to such [the] lapse. Upon such lapse the security interest becomes unperfected. [A filed financing statement which states that the obligation secured is payable on demand is effective for five years from the date of filing.]

(3) A continuation statement may be filed by the secured party of record [(i)] within six months [before and sixty days after a stated maturity date of five years or less, and (ii) otherwise within six months] prior to the end [expiration] of the five-year period [specified in subsection (2)]. Any such continuation statement must be signed by the secured party of record, identify the original statement by giving the date and the names of the parties thereto and the [by] file number thereof and state that the original statement is [still effective] continued. Upon timely filing of the continuation statement, the effectiveness of the original statement is continued for five years from the time when it would otherwise have lapsed, [after the last date to which the filing was effective] whereupon it lapses in the same manner as provided in [subsection] subdivision (2) unless another continuation statement is filed prior to such lapse. Succeeding continuation statements may be filed in the same manner to continue the effectiveness of the original *financing* statement.

[Unless a statute on disposition of public records provides otherwise, the filing officer may remove a lapsed statement from the files and destroy it].

(4)(a)[A] The filing officer shall mark each financing statement with a consecutive file number and with the date and [hour] time of filing. [and shall hold the statement for public inspection. In addition to the filing officer] He shall index the statements according to the name of the debtor (or assignor or seller) and shall note in the index the file number and the mailing address of the debtor (or assignor or seller) given in the statement. (b) The filing officer shall mark each such continuation statement with the date and time of filing and shall index the same under the name of the debtor (or assignor or seller) and under the file number of the original financing statement. (c) A financing or continuation statement relating to crops or timber shall also be indexed by the filing officer in the real property index of grantors under the name of the debtor. A financing or continuation statement relating to crops or timber so indexed and containing a description of real property affected thereby shall constitute constructive notice from the time of its acceptance for filing to any purchaser or encumbrancer of said real property of the security interest in the crops or timber.

(5) The uniform fee for filing, indexing and furnishing filing data (subdivision (1) of section 9407) for an original or a continuation statement on a form conforming to standards prescribed by the Secretary of State shall be [$......] two dollars ($2) or, if the statement otherwise conforms to the requirements of this division, three dollars ($3).

5. The legislative history of changes made in the Official Text is scant. The last sentence in subdivision (3) of the Official Text is covered in the California version by Commercial Code § 9408.

Uniform Commercial Code Comment
Prior Uniform Statutory Provision:
Sections 13(3), 13(4), Uniform Trust Receipts Act; Section 10, Uniform Conditional Sales Act.

Purposes:

1. Prior law was not always clear whether a mortgage filed for record gave constructive notice from the time of presentation to the filing officer or only from the time of indexing. Subsection (1) adopts the former position.

2. Prior statutes have usually limited the effectiveness of a filing to a specified period of time after which refiling is necessary. Subsection (2) follows the same policy, establishing five years as the filing period, with an exception for the cases mentioned in subsection (6). Subsection (3) provides for the filing of one or more continuation statements (which need be signed only by the secured party) if it is desired to continue the effectiveness of the original filing.

The theory of this Article is that the public files of financing statements are self-clearing, because the filing officer may automatically discard each financing statement after a period of five years plus the year after lapse required by subsection (3), unless a continuation statement is filed, or the financing statement is still effective under subsection (6). This theory materially lessens the tension that would otherwise exist to have the files cleared by termination statements under Section 9–404. Similarly, a person searching the files need not go back past this five years plus one year; and if the indices are arranged by years, he has a limited and defined search problem. The section asks the filing officer to attach financing statements whose life has been continued by continuation statements to the latter statements, so that anything contained in the files of old years can be discarded.

Subsection (6) provides certain special filing rules, namely, filings against transmitting utilities (Section 9–105), for which financing statements are filed in the office of the [Secretary of State]; and real estate mortgages [California did not adopt provisions on real estate mortgages which serve as fixture financing statements] which serve as fixture financing statements and which are filed in the real estate records. In both of these cases the financing statement is valid for the life of the obligations secured. No confusion as to the required scope of search should result, because of the special nature of the filings involved.

3. Under subsection (2) the security interest becomes unperfected when filing lapses. Thereafter, the interest of the secured party is subject to defeat by purchasers and lienors even though before lapse the conflicting interest may have been junior. Compare the situation arising under Section 9–103(1)(d) when a perfected security interest under the law of another jurisdiction is not perfected in this state within four months after the property is brought into this state.

Thus if A and B both make nonpurchase money advances against the same collateral, and both perfect security interests by filing, A who files first is entitled to priority under Section 9–312(5). But if no continuation statement is filed, A's filing may lapse first. So long as B's interest remains perfected thereafter, he is entitled to priority over A's unperfected interest. This rule avoids the circular priority which arose under some prior statutes, under which A was subordinate to the debtor's trustee in bankruptcy. A retained priority over B, and B's interest was valid against the trustee in bankruptcy. In re Andrews, 172 F.2d 996 (7th Cir.1949).

4. Subsection (7) makes clear that the filings in real estate records (Sections 9–401 and 9–402(3) and (5)) shall be indexed in the real estate records, where they will be found by a real estate searcher. Where the debtor is not an owner of record, the financing statement must show the name of an owner of record, and the statement is to be indexed in his name. See Sections 9–313(4)(b) and (c); 9–402(3); 9–402(5).

Cross References:

Point 3: Sections 9–103(3), 9–301 and 9–312(5).

Point 4: Sections 9–313(4)(b) and (c), 9–401(1), 9–402(3) and (5), 9–405(2).

Definitional Cross References:

"Debtor". Section 9–105.
"Financing statement". Section 9–402.
"Fixture". Section 9–313.
"Fixture filing". Section 9–313.
"Secured party". Section 9–105.
"Security interest". Section 1–201.
"Transmitting utility". Section 9–105.

Cross References

Filing prior to Jan. 1, 1971, with county recorder, filing of continuation in accordance with this section, see Commercial Code § 13105.
Recording, in general, see Government Code § 27320 et seq.
Refiling on removal, see Commercial Code § 9401.
Security interests,
    Perfection as to goods entering state, see Commercial Code § 9103.
    Priority over unperfected interests, see Commercial Code §§ 9301, 9312.

§ 9403. Filing requirements; duration of filing; effect of lapsed filing; continuation statement; duties of filing officer; fees; recordation and indexing; standard form wording

Text of section operative January 1, 2000.

(1) Presentation for filing of a financing statement, tender of the filing fee and acceptance of the statement by the filing officer constitutes filing under this division.

(2) Except as provided in subdivision (6), a filed financing statement is effective for a period of five years from the date of filing. The effectiveness of a filed financing statement lapses on the expiration of such five-year period unless a continuation statement is filed prior to the lapse. If a security interest perfected by filing exists at the time insolvency proceedings are commenced by or against the debtor, the security interest remains perfected until termination of the insolvency proceedings and thereafter for a period of 60 days or until expiration of the five-year period, whichever occurs later. Upon such lapse the security interest becomes unperfected unless it is perfected without filing. If the security interest becomes unperfected upon lapse, it is deemed to have been unperfected as against a person who became a purchaser or lien

creditor before lapse. If a fixture filing is effective at the time insolvency proceedings are commenced by or against the debtor, the fixture filing remains effective until termination of the insolvency proceedings and thereafter for a period of 60 days or until expiration of the five-year period or termination pursuant to subdivision (6), whichever occurs later. Upon lapse of a fixture filing, it is deemed to have been ineffective as against a person who became a purchaser or lien creditor before lapse.

(3) A continuation statement may be filed by the secured party of record within six months prior to the expiration of the five-year period specified in subdivision (2). Any such continuation statement must be signed by the secured party of record, identify the original statement by giving the date and the names of the parties thereto and the file number thereof and state that the original statement is continued. A continuation statement filed to continue the effectiveness of a financing statement filed as a fixture filing (Section 9313) is not effective unless the following requirements are met:

(a) If the debtor did not have an interest of record in the real estate as of the date of the filing of the original statement, the continuation statement shall contain the name of a record owner of the real estate as of the date of the filing of the original statement.

(b) The continuation statement shall contain substantially the following statement: "This continuation statement is filed to continue the effectiveness of a financing statement filed as a fixture filing"; provided, that such statement shall clearly indicate the intent to continue the effectiveness of a financing statement as a fixture filing.

Upon timely filing of the continuation statement, the effectiveness of the original statement is continued for five years after the last date to which the filing was effective whereupon it lapses in the same manner as provided in subdivision (2) unless another continuation statement is filed prior to such lapse. Succeeding continuation statements may be filed in the same manner to continue the effectiveness of the original statement. The filing officer may remove a lapsed financing statement and related filings from the files and destroy them immediately if he or she has retained a microfilm or other photographic record, or in other cases after one year after the lapse. The filing officer shall so arrange matters by physical annexation of financing statements to continuation statements or other related filings, or by other means, that if he or she physically destroys the financing statements of a period more than five years past, those which have been continued by a continuation statement or which are still effective under subdivision (6) shall be retained. The filing officer shall not destroy a financing statement and related filings as to which he or she has received written notice that there is an action pending relative thereto or that insolvency proceedings have been commenced by or against the debtor.

(4) Except as provided in subdivision (7) a filing officer shall mark each financing statement with a consecutive file number and with the date and time of filing and shall hold the statement or a microfilm or other photographic copy thereof for public inspection. In addition the filing officer shall index the statement according to the name of the debtor and shall note in the index the file number and the address of the debtor given in this statement. The filing officer shall mark each continuation statement with the date and time of filing and shall index the same under the file number of the original financing statement.

(5) The uniform fee for filing, indexing and furnishing filing data (subdivision (1) of Section 9407) for an original financing statement, an amendment or a continuation statement shall be five dollars ($5) if the statement is in the standard form prescribed by the Secretary of State and otherwise shall be ten dollars ($10).

(6) If the debtor is a transmitting utility (subdivision (5) of Section 9401) and a filed financing statement so states, it is effective until a termination statement is filed. A real estate mortgage which is effective as a fixture filing under subdivision (6) of Section 9402 remains effective as a fixture filing until the mortgage is released or satisfied of record or its effectiveness otherwise terminates as to the real estate.

(7) A financing or continuation statement covering collateral described in paragraph (b) of subdivision (1) of Section 9401 or filed as a fixture filing shall be recorded and indexed by the filing officer in the real property index of grantors under the name of the debtor and any owner of record shown on the financing statement. A financing or continuation statement so recorded and indexed and containing a description of real property affected thereby shall constitute constructive notice from the time of its acceptance for recording to any purchaser or encumbrancer of the real property of the security interest in such collateral.

(8) The standard form of original financing statement prescribed by the Secretary of State pursuant to subdivision (5) shall include the wording 'Financing statements are effective, with certain exceptions, only for five years from the date of filing, pursuant to Section 9403 of the California Commercial Code' or substantially equivalent warning language as prescribed by the Secretary of State.

(9) This section shall become operative on January 1, 2000. *(Added by Stats.1995, c. 656 (S.B.888), § 5.5, operative Jan. 1, 2000.)*

For text of section operative until January 1, 2000, see § 9403, ante.

§ 9403.1. Destruction of Financing Statement Index

The county recorder may destroy any index of financing statements, including any amendments, releases, continuations, terminations, assignments, any other document relating to an original financing statement, if the last entry in the index is six or more years old. *(Added by Stats.1982, c. 843, p. 3176, § 4.)*

§ 9403.5. Financing or continuation statements; effective dates

For purposes of Section 9403:

(1) A financing statement becomes effective on the date when filed, other than that portion of the day preceding the time of filing.

(2) The final day of effectiveness of a financing statement or continuation statement is, except as provided in subdivision (3), the same day of the year as the filing of the financing statement, in five-year increments specified in Section 9403. The financing statement or continuation statement is in effect for the entirety of its final day of effectiveness.

(3) If, under subdivision (2), the final day of effectiveness of a financing statement or continuation statement would occur on a Saturday, Sunday, or legal holiday, the effectiveness thereof is extended until the next day that is not a Saturday, Sunday, or legal holiday. If, under subdivision (2), the last day of effectiveness would occur on February 29 in any calendar year that does not include February 29, the final day of effectiveness is February 28.

(4) A continuation statement may be filed at any time on the final day of effectiveness of the financing statement or prior continuation statement.

(5) This section clarifies the meaning of Section 9403. As this section affects lapse and continuation, it shall be applied to all financing and continuation statements, whether filed before or on or after January 1, 1986, so long as the effectiveness of the financing statement has not lapsed prior to that date. *(Added by Stats.1985, c. 89, § 1.)*

§ 9404. Termination Statement

Text of section operative until January 1, 2000.

(1) Whenever there is no outstanding secured obligation and no commitment to make advances, incur obligations or otherwise give value, the secured party of record must on written demand by the debtor send the debtor a statement that he or she no longer claims a security interest under the financing statement, which shall be identified by date, names of parties thereto and file number. If the affected secured party of record fails to send such a termination statement within 10 days after proper demand therefor he or she shall be liable to the debtor for all actual damages suffered by the debtor by reason of such failure, and if the failure is in bad faith for a penalty of one hundred dollars ($100).

(2) The filing officer shall mark each such termination statement with the date and time of filing and shall index the same under the name of the debtor and under the file number of the original financing statement. If the filing officer has a microfilm or other photographic record of the financing statement and related filings, the filing officer may remove the originals from the files at any time after receipt of the termination statement and destroy them, or if he or she has no such record, he or she may remove them from his or her files at any time after one year after receipt of the termination statement and destroy them.

(3) The uniform fee for filing, indexing and furnishing filing data (subdivision (1) of Section 9407) for a termination statement shall be twenty dollars ($20) if the statement is in the standard form prescribed by the Secretary of State and otherwise shall be thirty dollars ($30).

(4) This section shall remain in effect only until January 1, 2000, and as of that date is repealed, unless a later enacted statute, that is enacted before January 1, 2000, deletes or extends that date. *(Stats.1963, c. 819, § 9404. Amended by Stats.1971, c. 1307, p. 2594, § 2; Stats.1974, c. 997, p. 2136, § 37, eff. Jan. 1, 1976; Stats.1987, c. 1348, § 10.); Stats.1992, c. 1333 (S.B. 1434), § 4; Stats.1995, c. 656 (S.B.888), § 6.)*

Repeal

This section is repealed by its own terms on January 1, 2000.

For text of section operative January 1, 2000, see § 9404, post.

California Code Comment

By John A. Bohn and Charles J. Williams

Prior California Law

1. Provisions for termination statements existed under prior law:

(a) for a chattel mortgage. The penalty for failure to respond was automatic forfeiture of $300 and liability for loss. In addition the mortgagee who refused to respond was also guilty of a misdemeanor. Former Civil Code §§ 2941, 2941.5.

(b) for an inventory lien. The penalty for failure to respond was $100 penalty if there was bad faith. In addition there was liability for damages limited to "actual direct damages." Former Civil Code § 3040.

(c) for an assignment of account. The penalty for failure to respond was the same as for an inventory lien. Former Civil Code § 3024.

Subdivision (1) provides for liability for all "actual damages" for failure to respond.

Changes from U.C.C. (1962 Official Text)

2. Section 9–404 of the Official Text as changed in California reads as follows:

[Section 9–404. Termination Statement.]

9404. (1) Whenever there is no outstanding secured obligation and no commitment to make advances, incur obligations or otherwise give value, the secured party of record must on written demand by the debtor send the debtor a statement that he no longer claims a security interest under the financing statement, which shall be identified by file number. [A termination statement signed by a person other than the secured party of record must include or be accompanied by the assignment or a statement by the secured party of record that he has assigned the security interest to the signer of the termination statement. The uniform fee for filing and indexing such an assignment or statement thereof shall be $......] If the affected secured party of record fails to send such a termination statement within 10 days after proper demand therefor he shall be liable to the debtor for [one hundred dollars, and in addition for any loss caused to the debtor by such failure]. All actual damages suffered by the debtor by reason of such failure, and if the failure is in bad faith for a penalty of one hundred dollars ($100).

[(2) On presentation to the filing officer of such a termination statement he must note it in the index. The filing officer shall remove from the files, mark "terminated" and send or deliver to the secured party the financing statement and any continuation statement, statement of assignment or statement of release pertaining thereto].

(2) The filing officer shall mark each such termination statement with the date and time of filing and shall index the same under the name of the debtor and under the file number of the original financing statement.

(3) The uniform fee for filing [and indexing a termination statement including sending or delivering the financing statement shall be $......]., indexing and furnishing filing data (subdivision (1) of Section 9407) for a termination statement on a form conforming to standards prescribed by the Secretary of State shall be two dollars ($2) or, if such a statement otherwise conforms to the requirements of this section, three dollars ($3).

3. The deletion of the language of the Official Text providing for a flat penalty regardless of good faith follows the suggestions of the California Bankers Association Committee to the effect that the penalties should be assessed only in the case of bad faith. See also 8 UCLA L.Rev. 806, 889.

Uniform Commercial Code Comment
Prior Uniform Statutory Provision:
Section 12, Uniform Conditional Sales Act.
Purposes:

1. To provide a procedure for noting discharge of the secured obligation on the records and for noting that a financing arrangement has been terminated.

Since most financing statements expire in five years unless a continuation statement is filed (Section 9–403), no compulsion is placed on the secured party to file a termination statement unless demanded by the debtor, except in the case of consumer goods. Because many consumers will not realize the importance of clearing the situation as it appears on file, an affirmative duty is put on the secured party in that case. But many purchase money security interests in consumer goods will not be filed, except for motor vehicles (Section 9–302(1) (d)); and in the case of motor vehicles a certificate of title law may control instead of the provisions of Article 9.

2. This section adds to the usual provisions one covering the problem which arises because a secured party under a notice filing system may file notice of an intention to make advances which may never be made. Under this section a debtor may require a secured party to send a termination statement when there is no outstanding obligation and no commitment to make future advances.

Cross References:
Point 2: Section 9–402(1).

Definitional Cross References:
"Consumer goods". Section 9–109.
"Debtor". Section 9–105.
"Financing statement". Section 9–402.
"Person". Section 1–201.
"Secured party". Section 9–105.
"Security interest". Section 1–201.
"Send". Section 1–201.
"Value". Section 1–201.
"Written". Section 1–201.

Cross References
Financing statements, filing before security interest attaches, see Commercial Code § 9402.
Notation by filing officer upon copy of statement, see Commercial Code § 9407.
Recording, in general, see Government Code § 27320 et seq.
Satisfaction of judgment, see Code of Civil Procedure § 697.640.

§ 9404. Termination Statement

Text of section operative January 1, 2000.

(1) Whenever there is no outstanding secured obligation and no commitment to make advances, incur obligations or otherwise give value, the secured party of record must on written demand by the debtor send the debtor a statement that he or she no longer claims a security interest under the financing statement, which shall be identified by date, names of parties thereto and file number. If the affected secured party of record fails to send such a termination statement within 10 days after proper demand therefor he or she shall be liable to the debtor for all actual damages suffered by the debtor by reason of such failure, and if the failure is in bad faith for a penalty of one hundred dollars ($100).

(2) The filing officer shall mark each such termination statement with the date and time of filing and shall index the same under the name of the debtor and under the file number of the original financing statement. If the filing officer has a microfilm or other photographic record of the financing statement and related filings, the filing officer may remove the originals from the files at any time after receipt of the termination statement and destroy them, or if he or she has no such record, he or she may remove them from his or her files at any time after one year after receipt of the termination statement and destroy them.

(3) The uniform fee for filing, indexing and furnishing filing data (subdivision (1) of Section 9407) for a termination statement shall be five dollars ($5) if the statement is in the standard form prescribed by the Secretary of State and otherwise shall be ten dollars ($10).

(4) This section shall become operative on January 1, 2000. *(Added by Stats.1995, c. 656 (S.B.888), § 6.5, operative Jan. 1, 2000.)*

For text of section operative until January 1, 2000, see § 9404, ante.

§ 9405. Release of Security Interest; Duties of Filing Officer; Fees

Text of section operative until January 1, 2000.

(1) A secured party of record may by a writing release his or her security interest in all or a part of the collateral covered by a filed financing statement. A statement of release is sufficient if it is signed by the secured party of record, contains a statement describing the collateral being released, the name and address of the debtor, and the file number of the original financing statement.

(2) The filing officer shall mark each such statement with the date and time of filing and index the same under the name of the debtor and under the file number of the original financing statement.

(3) The uniform fee for filing, indexing and furnishing filing data (subdivision (1) of Section 9407) for a statement of release on a form conforming to standards prescribed by the Secretary of State shall be twenty dollars ($20) or, if such a statement otherwise conforms to the requirements of this section, thirty dollars ($30).

(4) This section shall remain in effect only until January 1, 2000, and as of that date is repealed, unless a later enacted statute, that is enacted before January 1, 2000, deletes or extends that date. *(Stats.1963, c. 819, § 9405. Amended by Stats.1971, c. 1307, p. 2595, § 3;*

Stats.1987, c. 1348, § 11; Stats.1992, c. 1333 (S.B.1434), § 5; Stats.1995, c. 656 (S.B.888), § 7.)

Repeal

This section is repealed by its own terms on January 1, 2000.

For text of section operative January 1, 2000, see § 9405, post.

California Code Comment

By John A. Bohn and Charles J. Williams

Prior California Law

1. The principle of cancellation statements is consistent with prior California law relating to a chattel mortgage (former Civil Code § 2939), the assignment of an account (former Civil Code § 3023) and an inventory lien (former Civil Code § 3039).

Changes from U.C.C. (1962 Official Text)

2. The California version of the Commercial Code reverses the numbering of sections 9–405 and 9–406 of the Official Text. Commercial Code § 9405 is comparable to section 9–406 of the Official Text. Because the change is merely in the numbering the text of California section 9405 is compared with the text of section 9–406 of the Official Text for the purposes of this Comment. Section 9–406 of the Official Text as it is changed by section 9–405 of the California version reads as follows:

(1) A secured party of record may by a writing [his signed statement] release his security interest in all or a part of the [any] collateral covered by [described in] a filed financing statement. A [The] statement of release is sufficient if it is signed by the secured party of record, contains a statement describing [description of] the collateral being released, the name and address of the debtor, [the name and address of the secured party,] and the file number of the original financing statement.

(2) [Upon presentation of such a statement to] The filing officer [he] shall mark [the] each such statement with the [hour and] date and time of filing and [shall note] index the same [upon the margin of the index of the filing] under the name of the debtor and under the file number of the original financing statement.

(3) The uniform fee for filing, indexing and furnishing filing data (subdivision (1) of Section 9407) [and noting] for [such] a statement of release on a form conforming to standards prescribed by the Secretary of State shall be [$. . . . .] two dollars ($2) or, if such a statement otherwise conforms to the requirements of this section, three dollars ($3).

3. The change in numbering was made because it seemed more logical to reverse the order of these two sections. Sixth Progress Report to the Legislature by Senate Fact Finding Committee on Judiciary (1959–1961) Part 1, The Uniform Commercial Code, p. 425.

Uniform Commercial Code Comment [Section 9–406]

Prior Uniform Statutory Provision:
None.

Purposes:

Like the preceding section [Section 9406 of California version of Commercial Code, see California Code Comment, note 2], this section provides a permissive device for noting of record any release of collateral. There is no requirement that such a statement be filed when collateral is released (cf. Section 9–404 on Termination Statements). It is merely a method of making the record reflect the true state of affairs so that fewer inquiries will have to be made by persons who consult the files.

[Change in numbering in California version of Commercial Code, see California Code Comment, note 2.]

[Change in Uniform Commercial Code Comment necessitated by the 1972 Amendment of the official text not applicable in California].

Cross Reference:
Section 9–404.

Definitional Cross References:
"Collateral". Section 9–105.
"Debtor". Section 9–105.
"Financing statement". Section 9–402.
"Secured party". Section 9–105.
"Signed". Section 1–201.

Cross References

Erroneously identified property owner, lien, release, and attorney fees, see Code of Civil Procedure § 697.660.
Formal requisites of financing statement, see Commercial Code § 9402.
Recording, in general, see Government Code § 27320 et seq.
Release, extinction of obligations, see Civil Code § 1541 et seq.
Secured party, see Commercial Code § 9105.
Termination statements, see Commercial Code § 9404.
When filing required to perfect security interest, see Commercial Code § 9302.

§ 9405. Release of Security Interest; Duties of Filing Officer; Fees

Text of section operative January 1, 2000.

(1) A secured party of record may by a writing release his or her security interest in all or a part of the collateral covered by a filed financing statement. A statement of release is sufficient if it is signed by the secured party of record, contains a statement describing the collateral being released, the name and address of the debtor, and the file number of the original financing statement.

(2) The filing officer shall mark each such statement with the date and time of filing and index the same under the name of the debtor and under the file number of the original financing statement.

(3) The uniform fee for filing, indexing and furnishing filing data (subdivision (1) of Section 9407) for a statement of release on a form conforming to standards prescribed by the Secretary of State shall be five dollars ($5) or, if such a statement otherwise conforms to the requirements of this section, ten dollars ($10).

(4) This section shall become operative on January 1, 2000. (Added by Stats.1995, c. 656 (S.B.888), § 7.5, operative Jan. 1, 2000.)

For text of section operative until January 1, 2000, see § 9405, ante.

§ 9406. Assignment or Transfer of Security Interest; Duties of Filing Officer; Fees; Statement of Assignment

Text of section operative until January 1, 2000.

(1) If a secured party assigns or transfers his or her security interest in any collateral as to which a financing statement has been filed, a statement of such assignment may be filed. Such statement shall be signed by the secured party, describe the collateral as to which the security interest has been assigned, give the name and mailing address of the assignee or transferee, the name and address of the debtor and the file number of the original financing statement.

(2) The filing officer shall mark each such statement of assignment or transfer with the date and time of filing and shall index the same under the name of the debtor and under the file number of the original financing statement.

(3) A statement of assignment may be filed at the time of the filing of the financing statement, in which event the filing officer shall first file the financing statement and index the assignment under the name of the debtor and under the file number given the financing statement. An assignment endorsed on the financing statement before it is filed with the filing officer need not be indexed by the filing officer.

(4) The uniform fee for filing, indexing and furnishing filing data (subdivision (1) of Section 9407) for a separate statement of assignment on a form conforming to standards prescribed by the Secretary of State shall be <u>twenty</u> dollars ($<u>20</u>) or, if such a statement otherwise conforms to the requirements of this section, <u>thirty</u> dollars ($<u>30</u>).

(5) Whenever a continuation statement, an amendment to a financing statement, a termination statement, a statement of release or a statement of assignment signed by one other than the secured party of record is presented for filing it must be accompanied by a statement of assignment signed by the secured party of record covering the collateral to which such continuation statement, amendment, termination statement, release, or assignment applies.

(6) Wherever in this code reference is made to the secured party of record it means the secured party named in the original financing statement or, if a statement of assignment has been filed, or an assignee has been named in the financing statement before it is filed, the assignee or transferee of the security interest in the collateral affected. Any continuation statement, amendment to a financing statement, termination statement, statement of release or statement of assignment signed by one other than the secured party of record as to the collateral affected thereby shall be ineffective for any purpose except as between the parties thereto.

<u>(7) This section shall remain in effect only until January 1, 2000, and as of that date is repealed, unless a later enacted statute, that is enacted before January 1, 2000, deletes or extends that date.</u> (Stats.1963, c. 819, § 9406. Amended by Stats.1965, c. 1379, p. 3296, § 19; Stats.1971, c. 1307, p. 2595, § 4; Stats.1987, c. 1348, § 12; Stats.1992, c. 1333 (S.B.1434), § 6; Stats.1995, c. 656 (S.B.888), § 8.)

Repeal

This section is repealed by its own terms on January 1, 2000.

For text of section operative January 1, 2000, see § 9406, post.

California Code Comment

By John A. Bohn and Charles J. Williams

Prior California Law

1. This section permits a former creditor who has assigned his interest to personally correct the record thereby avoiding further inquiry. See Official Comment.

There is no similar prior California statute.

2. Commercial Code § 9406 is comparable to section 9–405 of the Official Text. See California Code Comment 2 to Commercial Code § 9405.

Changes from U.C.C. (1962 Official Text)

3. Section 9–405 of the Official Text as changed by Commercial Code § 9406 in the California version reads as follows:

(1) If a secured party assigns or transfers his [A financing statement may disclose an assignment of a] security interest in [the] any collateral as to which a financing [described in the] statement has been filed, a statement of such assignment may be filed. [by indication in the statement of the name and address of the assignee or by an assignment itself or a copy thereof on the face or back of the statement.] Such statement shall be signed by the [Either the original] secured party, [or the assignee may sign this statement as the secured party. On presentation to the filing officer of such a financing statement the filing officer shall mark the same as provided in Section 9–403(4). The uniform fee for filing, indexing and furnishing filing data for a financing statement so indicating an assignment shall be $......] describe the collateral as to which the security interest has been assigned, give the name and mailing address of the assignee or transferee, the name and address of the debtor and the file number of the original financing statement.

(2) [A secured party may assign of record all or a part of his rights under a financing statement by the filing of a separate written statement of assignment signed by the secured party of record and setting forth the name of the secured party of record and the debtor, the file number and the date of filing of the financing statement and the name and address of the assignee and containing a description of the collateral assigned. A copy of the assignment is sufficient as a separate statement if it complies with the preceding sentence. On presentation to the filing officer of such a separate statement,] The filing officer shall mark each such [separate] statement of assignment or transfer with the date and time [hour] of [the] filing and shall index the same under the name of the debtor and under the file number of the original financing statement.

(3) [He shall note the assignment on the index of the financing statement.] A statement of assignment may be filed at the time of the filing of the financing statement, in which event the filing officer shall first file the financing statement and index the assignment under the name of the debtor and under the file number given the financing statement. An assignment endorsed on the financing statement before it is filed with the filing officer need not be indexed by him.

(4) The uniform fee for filing, indexing and furnishing filing data (subdivision (1) of section 9407) for [about such] a separate statement of assignment on a form conforming to standards prescribed by the Secretary of State shall be [$......] two dollars ($2), or, if such a statement otherwise conforms to the requirements of this section, three dollars ($3).

[(3) After the disclosure or filing of an assignment under this section, the assignee is the secured party of record.]

(5) Whenever a continuation statement, an amendment to a financing statement, a termination statement, a statement of release or a statement of assignment signed by one other than the secured party of record is presented for filing it must be accompanied by a statement of assignment signed by the secured party of record covering the collateral to which such continuation statement, amendment, termination statement, release, or assignment applies.

(6) Wherever in this code reference is made to the secured party of record it means the secured party named in the original financing statement or, if a statement of assignment has been filed, the assignee or transferee of the security interest in the collateral affected. Any continuation statement, amendment to a financing statement, termination statement, statement of release or statement or assignment signed by one other than the secured party of record as to the collateral affected thereby shall be ineffective for any purpose except as between the parties thereto.

California Code Comment

By Charles J. Williams

Subdivision (6) was amended in 1965 to include an assignee named in a financing statement within the definition of "the secured party of record". The purpose of the amendment is to make certain that a financing agency which purchases dealer paper and is listed in the financing statement as an assignee is a secured party of record within the meaning of the Commercial Code.

Uniform Commercial Code Comment [Section 9–405]
Prior Uniform Statutory Provision:
None.
Purposes:
This section provides a permissive device whereby a secured party who has assigned all or part of his interest may have the assignment noted of record. Note that under Section 9–302(2) no filing of such an assignment is required as a condition of continuing the perfected status of the security interest against creditors and transferees of the original debtor. A secured party who has assigned his interest might wish to have the fact noted of record, so that inquiries concerning the transaction would be addressed not to him but to the assignee (see Point 2 of Comment to Section 9–402). After a secured party has assigned his rights of record, the assignee becomes the "secured party of record" and may file a continuation statement under Section 9–403, a termination statement under Section 9–404, or a statement of release under Section 9–406.

[Change in numbering in California version of Commercial Code, see California Code Comment, note 3.]

[Change in Uniform Commercial Code Comment necessitated by the 1972 Amendment of the Official Text not applicable in California].
Cross References:
Sections 9–302(2) and 9–402 through 9–406.
Definitional Cross References:
"Collateral". Section 9–105.
"Debtor". Section 9–105.
"Financing statement". Section 9–402.
"Rights". Section 1–201.
"Secured party". Section 9–105.
"Signed". Section 1–201.
"Written". Section 1–201.

Cross References
Financing statements,
  Filing, see Commercial Code § 9403.
  Formal requisites, see Commercial Code § 9402.
  Release of security interest in collateral, see Commercial Code § 9405.
  Termination statements, see Commercial Code § 9404.
Recording, in general, see Government Code § 27320 et seq.
Security interests, filing of assignment, see Commercial Code § 9302.

§ 9406. Assignment or Transfer of Security Interest; Duties of Filing Officer; Fees; Statement of Assignment

Text of section operative January 1, 2000.

(1) If a secured party assigns or transfers his or her security interest in any collateral as to which a financing statement has been filed, a statement of such assignment may be filed. Such statement shall be signed by the secured party, describe the collateral as to which the security interest has been assigned, give the name and mailing address of the assignee or transferee, the name and address of the debtor and the file number of the original financing statement.

(2) The filing officer shall mark each such statement of assignment or transfer with the date and time of filing and shall index the same under the name of the debtor and under the file number of the original financing statement.

(3) A statement of assignment may be filed at the time of the filing of the financing statement, in which event the filing officer shall first file the financing statement and index the assignment under the name of the debtor and under the file number given the financing statement. An assignment endorsed on the financing statement before it is filed with the filing officer need not be indexed by the filing officer.

(4) The uniform fee for filing, indexing and furnishing filing data (subdivision (1) of Section 9407) for a separate statement of assignment on a form conforming to standards prescribed by the Secretary of State shall be five dollars ($5) or, if such a statement otherwise conforms to the requirements of this section, ten dollars ($10).

(5) Whenever a continuation statement, an amendment to a financing statement, a termination statement, a statement of release or a statement of assignment signed by one other than the secured party of record is presented for filing it must be accompanied by a statement of assignment signed by the secured party of record covering the collateral to which such continuation statement, amendment, termination statement, release, or assignment applies.

(6) Wherever in this code reference is made to the secured party of record it means the secured party named in the original financing statement or, if a statement of assignment has been filed, or an assignee has been named in the financing statement before it is filed, the assignee or transferee of the security interest in the collateral affected. Any continuation statement, amendment to a financing statement, termination statement, statement of release or statement of assignment signed by one other than the secured party of record as to the collateral affected thereby shall be ineffective for any purpose except as between the parties thereto.

(7) This section shall become operative on January 1, 2000. *(Added by Stats.1995, c. 656 (S.B.888), § 8.5, operative Jan. 1, 2000.)*

For text of section operative until January 1, 2000, see § 9406, ante.

§ 9407. Information From Filing Officer

(1) If the person filing any financing statement, amendment, termination statement, statement of assignment, continuation statement, or statement of release, furnishes the filing officer a copy thereof, the filing officer shall upon request note upon the copy of a financing statement the file number and upon the copy of any of such statements the date and time of the filing of the original and deliver or send the copy to such person.

(2) Upon request of any person, the filing officer shall issue his or her certificate showing whether there is on file on the date and time stated therein, any presently effective financing statement naming a particular debtor and any statement of assignment thereof and if there is, giving the date and time of filing of each such statement and the names and addresses of each secured party therein. The certificate shall not include any statement as to the possibility of insolvency proceedings which might have the effect of preventing the

§ 9407

lapse of effectiveness of a filed financing statement pursuant to Section 9403 whether actual insolvency proceedings are known or unknown to the filing officer. Upon request, the filing officer shall furnish a copy of any filed financing statement or related filings. If the filing officer is a county recorder, the * * * fee for * * * a certificate for each name searched shall be set by the filing officer in an amount that covers actual costs, but that, in no event, exceeds fifteen dollars ($15), and the fee for copies shall be in accordance with Section 27366 of the Government Code. If the filing officer is the Secretary of State, the certificate shall be issued as part of a combined certificate pursuant to Section 9409 of the Commercial Code, and the fee for the certificate and copies shall be in accordance with that section.

(3) Fees to be charged by the Secretary of State for daily or less frequent summaries or compilations of filings, which he or she may furnish, shall be sufficient to pay at least the actual cost of such service. Fees shall be determined by the Secretary of State with the approval of the Department of Finance. Such summaries or compilations may be in the form of microfilm copies or such other form as may be provided for the required information. (Stats.1963, c. 819, § 9407. Amended by Stats.1964, c. 1, § 1; Stats.1967, c. 93, p. 1008, § 1; Stats.1974, c. 997, p. 2137, § 39, eff. Jan. 1, 1976; Stats.1982, c. 1327, p. 4898, § 1; Stats.1988, c. 393, § 11.)

California Code Comment
By John A. Bohn and Charles J. Williams

Prior California Law

1. Subdivisions (1) and (2) are in accord with prior statutory law regarding the assignment of an account (former Civil Code § 3020) and an inventory lien (former Civil Code § 3034).

2. In the Official Text subdivisions (1) and (2) are optional provisions. The advisability of adopting them depends upon local law and practices. See note to Official Text.

Changes from U.C.C. (1962 Official Text)

3. Section 9–407 of the Official Text does not include a specific recommended fee for the certificate. This is left to local option.

Subdivision (3) does not appear in the Official Text. It was added at the 1964 Special Session of the Legislature.

After the adoption of the Code it became apparent that financing agencies and other interested persons would be interested in summaries or compilations of filings. Under the section as it formerly read, the Secretary of State would have to charge $1 for the information furnished concerning each filing. The cost to a person interested in frequent summaries would be prohibitive. Subdivision (3) permits the Secretary of State to furnish frequent summaries to those who may be interested at a reasonable cost.

Uniform Commercial Code Comment
Prior Uniform Statutory Provision:
None.
Purposes:

1. Subsection (1) requires the filing officer upon request to return to the secured party a copy of the financing statement on which the material data concerning the filing are noted. Receipt of such a copy will assure the secured party that the mechanics of filing have been complied with. Note, however, that under Section 9–403(1) the secured party does not bear the risk that the filing officer will not properly perform his duties: under that Section the secured party has complied with the filing requirements when he presents his financing statement for filing and the filing fee has been tendered or the statement accepted by the filing officer.

2. Subsection (2) requires the filing officer on request to issue to any person who has tendered the proper fee his certificate as to what filings have been made against any particular debtor and to furnish copies of such filed financing statements. In view of the centralized filing system adopted by this Article (see Section 9–401 and Comment thereto), this provision is of obvious convenience to a person who wishes to know what the files contain but who cannot conveniently consult files located in the state capital.

Cross References:
Point 1: Section 9–403(1).
Point 2: Section 9–401.

Definitional Cross References:
"Debtor". Section 9–105.
"Financing statement". Section 9–402.
"Person". Section 1–201.
"Secured party". Section 9–105.
"Send". Section 1–201.

Cross References
Accessions, see Commercial Code § 9314.
Certified copies from secretary of state, see Government Code § 12168.
County recorder, fees for copies of records, see Government Code § 27366.
Filing,
  Acts constituting, see Commercial Code § 9403.
  Place of filing, see Commercial Code § 9401.
Authentication, inspection, and copying of public records, see Evidence Code §§ 1400 et seq., 1506 et seq.; Government Code § 6250 et seq.

§ 9407.1. Recordation in Lieu of Filing; Microphotography, Optical Disk, or Other Reproduction Techniques; Safekeeping

In lieu of filing all financing statements, termination statements, partial releases, assignments, or other related papers falling under this code, the filing officer may record those papers. The filing officer may employ a system of microphotography, optical disk, or reproduction by other techniques which do not permit additions, deletions, or changes to the original document.

All film used in the microphotography process shall comply with minimum standards of quality approved by the United States Bureau of Standards and the American National Standards Institute. A true copy of the microfilm, optical disk, or other storage medium shall be kept in a safe and separate place for security purposes. * * * A reproduction of any document filed, recorded, stored, or retained on microfilm * * * , optical disk, or by other technology pursuant to this section shall be as admissible in any court * * * as the original itself. (Added by Stats.1973, c. 591, p. 1114, § 1. Amended by Stats.1987, c. 1348, § 13; Stats.1991, c. 1059 (S.B.563), § 1.)

§ 9407.2. Recordation; File Numbers; Index

Should the filing officer choose to record rather than file all financing statements and related papers, he shall mark each financing statement with a consecutive file number. All other related papers affecting such financing statement shall thereafter bear the same file number. He shall index the same under the name of the debtor (or assignor or seller) in a separate index or in his general index, and under the file number of the original statement. *(Added by Stats.1973, c. 591, p. 1114, § 2.)*

§ 9407.3. Return of Originals to Parties After Recordation

Upon recording the financing statement or other related papers, the originals or copy of the same shall be returned to the parties entitled thereto. *(Added by Stats.1973, c. 591, p. 1114, § 3.)*

§ 9408. Financing Statements Covering Consigned or Leased Goods

A consignor or lessor of goods may file a financing statement using the terms "consignor," "consignee," "lessor," "lessee" or the like instead of the terms specified in Section 9402. The provisions of this part shall apply as appropriate to such a financing statement but its filing shall not of itself be a factor in determining whether or not the consignment or lease is intended as security (Section 1201(37)). However, if it is determined for other reasons that the consignment or lease is so intended, a security interest of the consignor or lessor which attaches to the consigned or leased goods is perfected by such filing. *(Added by Stats.1974, c. 997, p. 2137, § 41, eff. Jan. 1, 1976.)*

Uniform Commercial Code Comment

Prior Uniform Statutory Provision:

None.

Purposes:

1. Where filing is required under Sections 2–326(3) and 9–114 for a consignment which is not a security interest (Section 1–201(37)), this section authorizes the appropriate adaptations of terminology.

Apart from the rules in Part 4, the rules of this article using the terms "debtor" and "secured party" will not apply to consignments if they are not security interests. Section 9–114 on consignments essentially parallels Section 9–312(3) on inventory priorities, and the latter rule therefore does not apply to consignments. Section 2–326 states the rights of creditors of a consignee who has not filed or otherwise complied with subsection (3), and Section 9–301 on unperfected security interests is therefore not applicable. Section 2–326 and the law of consignments supply rules which are provided by Section 9–311 for security interests and that section is therefore not applicable to consignments. For reasons indicated in the Comment to Section 9–114, Section 9–306 on proceeds is inapplicable to consignments. An equivalent to the protection of a buyer in ordinary course of business against a security interest under Section 9–307(1) is provided against consignments by Section 2–403(2) and (3).

2. If a lease is actually intended as security (Section 1–201(37)), this Article applies in full. But this question of intention is a doubtful one, and the lessor may choose to file for safety even while contending that the lease is a true lease for which no filing is required. This section authorizes filing with appropriate changes of terminology, and without affecting the substantive question of classification of the lease. If the lease is a true lease, none of the provisions of the Article is applicable to the lease as an interest in the chattel. Note, however, that the Article may be applicable to the lease in its aspect as chattel paper. See Section 9–105(b).

Cross References

Financing statement, see Commercial Code § 9402.
Statement of assignment or transfer of security interest, see Commercial Code § 9406.
Statement of release of security interest, see Commercial Code § 9405.
Termination statement, see Commercial Code § 9404.

§ 9409. Combined Certificate

(a) Upon request of any person, the Secretary of State shall issue a combined certificate showing the information as to financing statements as specified in Section 9407, the information as to state tax liens as specified in Section 7226 of the Government Code, the information as to attachment liens as specified in Sections 488.375 and 488.405 of the Code of Civil Procedure, the information as to judgment liens as specified in Section 697.580 of the Code of Civil Procedure, and the information as to federal liens as specified in Section 2103 of the Code of Civil Procedure.

(b) The fee for the certificate shall be ten dollars ($10). * * * The fee for copies shall be one dollar ($1) for the first page and fifty cents ($0.50) for each page thereafter. *(Added by Stats.1979, c. 330, p. 1187, § 3. Amended by Stats.1982, c. 497, p. 2184, § 83, operative July 1, 1983; Stats.1982, c. 1198, p. 4326, § 65, operative July 1, 1983; Stats.1987, c. 1348, § 14; Stats.1988, c. 393, § 12; Stats.1995, c. 656 (S.B.888), § 9.)*

Legislative Committee Comment—Senate
1982 Amendment

Section 9409 is amended to add a provision requiring that judgment liens on personal property be included in the combined certificate and to correct the cross-references to provisions relating to attachment liens. (15 Cal.L.Rev.Comm. Reports 2001; 82 S.J. 11394).

CHAPTER 5. DEFAULT

Section
9501. Default; Procedure When Security Agreement Covers Both Real and Personal Property.
9501. Default; Procedure When Security Agreement Covers Both Real and Personal Property.
9502. Collection Rights of Secured Party.
9502. Collection Rights of Secured Party.
9503. Secured Party's Rights to Take Possession After Default.
9504. Secured Party's Right to Dispose of Collateral After Default; Notification of Sale; Publication; Effect of Disposition.
9504. Secured Party's Right to Dispose of Collateral After Default; Notification of Sale; Publication; Effect of Disposition.
9505. Compulsory Disposition of Collateral; Acceptance of the Collateral as Discharge of Obligation.
9506. Debtor's Right to Redeem Collateral.
9507. Secured Party's Liability for Failure to Comply With This Chapter.
9508. Validity of Renunciation or Modification of Rights by Debtor.

§ 9501. Default; Procedure When Security Agreement Covers Both Real and Personal Property

Text of section operative until Jan. 1, 1999.

(1) When a debtor is in default under a security agreement, a secured party has the rights and remedies provided in this chapter and, except as limited by subdivision (3), those provided in the security agree-

ment. The secured party may reduce his or her claim to judgment, foreclose, or otherwise enforce the security interest by any available judicial procedure. If the collateral is documents the secured party may proceed either as to the documents or as to the goods covered thereby. A secured party in possession has the rights, remedies, and duties provided in Section 9207. The rights and remedies referred to in this subdivision are cumulative.

(2) After default, the debtor has the rights and remedies provided in this chapter, those provided in the security agreement, and those provided in Section 9207.

(3) To the extent that they give rights to the debtor and impose duties on the secured party, the rules stated in the subdivisions referred to below may not be waived or varied except as provided with respect to compulsory disposition of collateral (subdivision (3) of Section 9504 and Section 9505) and with respect to redemption of collateral (Section 9506), but the parties may by agreement determine the standards by which the fulfillment of these rights and duties is to be measured if those standards are not manifestly unreasonable:

(a) Subdivision (2) of Section 9502 and subdivision (2) of Section 9504, insofar as they require accounting for surplus proceeds of collateral and deal with the debtor's liability for any deficiency;

(b) Subdivision (3) of Section 9504 and subdivision (1) of Section 9505 that deal with disposition of collateral;

(c) Subdivision (2) of Section 9505 that deals with acceptance of collateral as discharge of obligation;

(d) Section 9506 that deals with redemption of collateral; and

(e) Subdivision (1) of Section 9507 that deals with the secured party's liability for failure to comply with this chapter.

(4) If an obligation secured by a security interest in personal property or fixtures (Section 9313(1)(a)) is also secured by an interest in real property or an estate therein:

(a) The secured party may do any of the following:

(i) Proceed, in any sequence, (1) in accordance with the secured party's rights and remedies in respect of real property as to the real property security, and (2) in accordance with this chapter as to the personal property or fixtures.

(ii) Proceed in any sequence, as to both some or all of the real property and some or all of the personal property or fixtures in accordance with the secured party's rights and remedies in respect of the real property, by including the portion of the personal property or fixtures selected by the secured party in the judicial or nonjudicial foreclosure of the real property in accordance with the procedures applicable to real property. In proceeding under this subparagraph, (A) no provision of this chapter other than this subparagraph, subparagraph (iii) of paragraph (d), and paragraphs (g) and (h) shall apply to any aspect of the foreclosure; (B) a power of sale under the deed of trust or mortgage shall be exercisable with respect to both the real property and the personal property or fixtures being sold; and (C) the sale may be conducted by the mortgagee under the mortgage or by the trustee under the deed of trust. The secured party shall not be deemed to have elected irrevocably to proceed as to both real property and personal property or fixtures as provided in this subparagraph with respect to any particular property, unless and until that particular property actually has been * * * disposed of pursuant to a unified sale (judicial or nonjudicial) conducted in accordance with the procedures applicable to real property, and then only as to the property so sold.

(iii) Proceed, in any sequence, as to part of the personal property or fixtures as provided in subparagraph (i), and as to other of the personal property or fixtures as provided in subparagraph (ii).

(b)(i) Except as otherwise provided in paragraph (c), provisions and limitations of any law respecting real property and obligations secured by an interest in real property or an estate therein, including, but not limited to, Section 726 of the Code of Civil Procedure, provisions regarding acceleration or reinstatement of obligations secured by an interest in real property or an estate therein, prohibitions against deficiency judgments, limitations on deficiency judgments based on the value of the collateral, limitations on the right to proceed as to collateral, and requirements that a creditor resort either first or at all to its security, do not in any way apply to either (1) any personal property or fixtures other than personal property or fixtures as to which the secured party has proceeded or is proceeding under subparagraph (ii) of paragraph (a), or (2) the obligation.

(ii) Pursuant to, but without limiting subparagraph (i), in the event that an obligation secured by personal property or fixtures would otherwise become unenforceable by reason of Section 726 of the Code of Civil Procedure or any requirement that a creditor resort first to its security, then, notwithstanding that section or any similar requirement, the obligation shall nevertheless remain enforceable to the full extent necessary to permit a secured party to proceed against personal property or fixtures securing the obligation in accordance with the secured party's rights and remedies as permitted under this chapter.

(c)(i) Paragraph (b) does not limit the application of Section 580b of the Code of Civil Procedure.

(ii) If the secured party commences an action, as defined in Section 22 of the Code of Civil Procedure, and the action seeks a monetary judgment on the debt, paragraph (b) does not prevent the debtor's assertion of any right to require the inclusion in the action of any interest in real property or an estate therein securing the debt. If a monetary judgment on the debt is entered in the action, paragraph (b) does not prevent the debtor's assertion of the subsequent unenforceability of the encumbrance on any interest in real property or an estate therein securing the debt and not included in the action.

(iii) Nothing in paragraph (b) shall be construed to excuse compliance with Section 2924c of the Civil Code as a prerequisite to the sale of real property, but that section has no application to the right of a secured party to proceed as to personal property or fixtures except, and then only to the extent that, the secured party is proceeding as to personal property or fixtures in a unified sale as provided in subparagraph (ii) of paragraph (a).

(iv) Paragraph (b) does not deprive the debtor of the protection of Section 580d of the Code of Civil Procedure against a deficiency judgment following a sale of the real property collateral pursuant to a power of sale in a deed of trust or mortgage.

(v) Paragraph (b) shall not affect, nor shall it determine the applicability or inapplicability of, any law respecting real property or obligations secured in whole or in part by real property with respect to a loan or a credit sale made to any individual primarily for personal, family, or household purposes.

(vi) Paragraph (b) does not deprive the debtor of the protection of Section 580a of the Code of Civil Procedure following a sale of real property collateral.

(vii) If the secured party violates any statute or rule of law that requires a creditor who holds an obligation secured by an interest in real property or an estate therein to resort first to its security before resorting to any property of the debtor that does not secure the obligation, paragraph (b) does not prevent the debtor's assertion of any right to require correction of the violation, any right of the secured party to correct the violation, or the debtor's assertion of the subsequent unenforceability of the encumbrance on any interest in real property or an estate therein securing the obligation, or the debtor's assertion of the subsequent unenforceability of the obligation except to the extent that the obligation is preserved by subparagraph (ii) of paragraph (b).

(d) If the secured party realizes proceeds from the disposition of collateral that is personal property or fixtures, the following provisions shall apply:

(i) The disposition of the collateral, the realization of the proceeds, the application of the proceeds, or any one or more of the foregoing shall not operate to cure any nonmonetary default.

(ii) The disposition of the collateral, the realization of the proceeds, the application of the proceeds, or any one or more of the foregoing shall not operate to cure any monetary default (although the application of the proceeds shall, to the extent of those proceeds, satisfy the secured obligation) so as to affect in any way the secured party's rights and remedies under this chapter with respect to any remaining personal property or fixtures collateral.

(iii) All proceeds so realized shall be applied by the secured party to the secured obligation in accordance with the agreement of the parties and applicable law.

(e) An action by the secured party utilizing any available judicial procedure, as provided in subdivision (1), shall in no way be affected by omission of a prayer for a monetary judgment on the debt. Notwithstanding Section 726 of the Code of Civil Procedure, any prohibition against splitting causes of action or any other statute or rule of law, a judicial action that neither seeks nor results in a monetary judgment on the debt shall not preclude a subsequent action seeking a monetary judgment on the debt or any other relief.

(f) As used in this subdivision, "monetary judgment on the debt" means a judgment for the recovery from the debtor of all or part of the principal amount of the secured obligation, including, for purposes of this subdivision, contractual interest thereon. "Monetary judgment on the debt" does not include a judgment that provides only for other relief (whether or not that other relief is secured by the collateral), such as one or more forms of nonmonetary relief, and monetary relief ancillary to any of the foregoing, such as attorneys' fees and costs incurred in seeking the relief.

(g) If a secured party fails to comply with the procedures applicable to real property in proceeding as to both real and personal property under subparagraph (ii) of paragraph (a), a purchaser for value of any interest in the real property at judicial or nonjudicial foreclosure proceedings conducted pursuant to subparagraph (ii) of paragraph (a) takes that interest free from any claim or interest of another person, or any defect in title, based upon that noncompliance, unless:

(i) The purchaser is the secured party and the failure to comply with this chapter occurred other than in good faith; or

(ii) The purchaser is other than the secured party and at the time of sale of the real property at that foreclosure the purchaser had knowledge of the failure to comply with this chapter and that the noncompliance occurred other than in good faith.

Even if the purchaser at the foreclosure sale does not take his or her interest free of claims, interests, or title defects based upon that noncompliance with this chapter, a subsequent purchaser for value who acquires an interest in that real property from the purchaser at that foreclosure takes that interest free from any claim or interest of another person, or any defect in title, based upon that noncompliance, unless at the time of acquiring the interest the subsequent purchaser has knowledge of the failure to comply with this chapter and that the noncompliance occurred other than in good faith.

(h) If a secured party proceeds by way of a unified sale under subparagraph (ii) of paragraph (a), then, for purposes of applying Section 580a or subdivision (b) of Section 726 of the Code of Civil Procedure to any such unified sale, the personal property or fixtures included in the unified sale shall be deemed to be included in the

§ 9501

"real property or other interest sold," as that term is used in Section 580a or subdivision (b) of Section 726 of the Code of Civil Procedure.

(5) When a secured party has reduced his or her claim to judgment, the lien of any levy that may be made upon his or her collateral by virtue of any execution based upon the judgment shall relate back to the date of the perfection of the security interest in the collateral. A judicial sale, pursuant to that execution, is a foreclosure of the security interest by judicial procedure within the meaning of this section, and the secured party may purchase at the sale and thereafter hold the collateral free of any other requirements of this division.

(6) This section shall be repealed on January 1, 1999. (Stats.1963, c. 819, § 9501. Amended by Stats.1974, c. 997, p. 2138, § 42, eff. Jan. 1, 1976; Stats.1980, c. 1156, p. 3871, § 11; Stats.1985, c. 974, § 1; Stats.1985, c. 1368, § 12; Stats.1990, c. 1125 (A.B.3881), § 2; Stats. 1992, c. 1095 (A.B.2734), § 6; Stats.1995, c. 591 (A.B. 1689), § 6; Stats.1996, c. 124 (A.B.3470), § 16.)

Repeal

This section is repealed by its own terms on Jan. 1, 1999.

For text of section operative Jan. 1, 1999, see Commercial Code § 9501, post.

California Code Comment

By John A. Bohn and Charles J. Williams

Prior California Law

1. Commercial Code §§ 9501–9506 which relate to default in general are limited to stating the secured party's rights and remedies without specifying what acts constitute default.

Under prior California law, the remedies of the secured creditor depended upon the nature of the security device and there were as many sets of rules as there were devices. As with the other chapters in this division, this chapter provides a uniform set of rules based upon business practice and experience. The object of the remedies in this chapter is to permit disposal of the collateral without unnecessary restrictions.

In general the secured party's debt may be satisfied after default by:

(1) reduction of the claim to judgment and execution (Commercial Code § 9501(5));

(2) foreclosure or enforcement under any available judicial procedure (Commercial Code § 9501(1));

(3) retention of the collateral (Commercial Code § 9505); or

(4) disposition of the collateral in a commercially reasonable manner (Commercial Code § 9504).

2. Prior California law contained a set of rules which differed depending upon the nature of the security device used. A more extended and detailed discussion of the remedies available under each of the prior security devices is contained in 8 UCLA L.Rev. 806, 957–968.

Prior California law in general followed these principles:

(a) pledge: upon default, the pledgee could (1) sue on the debt and obtain and enforce judgment, (2) sell the pledged property at public auction after notice and demand for performance, or (3) bring a foreclosure proceeding and have a judicial sale. Former Civil Code §§ 3000–3011.

Prior decisional law upheld a pledge agreement which limited the manner of sale and waived statutory requirements of demand, notice of sale and presence of collateral at the sale. Retention of the collateral was void and an actual sale was necessary. Faivret v. First Nat. Bank, 160 F.2d 827, (CCA 9, 1947); Lowe v. Ozmun, 3 Cal.App. 387, 86 Pac. 729 (1906).

(b) chattel mortgage: upon default the mortgagee could (1) conduct a summary sale as in the case of a pledge (2) foreclose by judicial procedure under Code of Civil Procedure § 726 or (3) proceed in accordance with the power of sale incorporated in the mortgage. Former Civil Code § 2932. Podrat v. Oberndorff, 207 Cal. 457, 278 Pac. 1035 (1929); Dohrman v. Durston, 90 Cal.App.2d 236, 202 P.2d 607 (1949). In addition the mortgage could give the mortgagee the right to take possession in order to conduct a sale. Wixom v. Davis, 57 Cal.App. 620, 207 Pac. 694 (1922).

(c) trust receipt: the entruster could take peaceful possession of the property, sell at public or private sale with the right to purchase at the public sale. The entruster could also recover a deficiency. Former Civil Code § 3016.2.

(d) inventory lien: the lender could take possession of the inventory and dispose of it in the manner and upon the notice prescribed for a pledge agreement or in any other manner agreed upon by the parties. Former Civil Code § 3031.

(e) account receivable financing: there were no statutes regulating the default procedure in the case of an assignment of an account and there are no decisions indicating what the procedure would be in this type of financing. 8 UCLA L.Rev. 806, 964.

(f) conditional sale: the doctrine of election of remedies applied to the conditional vendor's rights upon default and the cases permitted the vendor to (1) sue upon the debt and obtain judgment or (2) repossess the goods. However, the vendor could not do both. Johnson v. Kaeser, 196 Cal. 686, 239 Pac. 324 (1925); James v. Allen, 23 Cal.App.2d 205, 72 P.2d 570 (1937); Holt Mfg. Co. v. Ewing, 109 Cal. 353, 42 Pac. 435 (1895). The rationale for the doctrine of election of remedies is that by bringing an action for the price, the seller forfeits his security interest and becomes a general creditor and confirms title in the purchaser. By repossessing the goods the seller is considered as sacrificing his deficiency claim since repossession constitutes a rescission of the contract and is inconsistent with the claim based upon a price. However, courts have permitted the parties to control their rights and liabilities by the conditional sales agreement and have therefore avoided applying the doctrine. Ravizza v. Budd & Quinn Inc., 19 Cal.2d 289, 120 P.2d 865 (1942); 8 UCLA L.Rev. 806, 965.

Remedies under a retail installment sales contract for consumer goods are covered by the Unruh Act and are excluded from the scope of Division 9. For a discussion of remedies under the Unruh Act see 7 UCLA L.Rev. 618, 706–744 (1960); 8 UCLA L.Rev. 806, 965–968.

3. Subdivisions (1) and (2) of this section permit the parties to state their rights and remedies in addition to those specifically provided by statute. Official Comment 1.

To the extent that the rights and duties are specified in subdivision (3) they may not be waived or varied except as stated. Official Comment 4.

Changes from U.C.C. (1962 Official Text)

4. Subdivision (3) in the California version has been modified to conform to the deletion of subdivision (1) from Commercial Code § 9505.

Uniform Commercial Code Comment

Prior Uniform Statutory Provision:

Section 6, Uniform Trust Receipts Act; Sections 16 through 26, Uniform Conditional Sales Act.

Purposes:

1. The rights of the secured party in the collateral after the debtor's default are of the essence of a security transaction. These are the rights which distinguish the secured from the unsecured lender. This section and the following six sections state those rights as well as the limitations on their free exercise which legislative policy requires for the protection not only of the defaulting debtor but of other creditors. But subsections (1) and (2) make it clear that the statement of rights and remedies in this Part does not exclude other remedies provided by agreement.

2. Following default and the taking possession of the collateral by the secured party, there is no longer any distinction between the security interest which before default was non-possessory and that which was possessory under a pledge. Therefore no general distinction is taken in this Part between the rights of a non-possessory secured party and those of a pledgee; the latter, being in possession of the collateral at default, will of course not have to avail himself of the right to take possession under Section 9–503.

3. Section 9–207 states rights, remedies and duties with respect to collateral in the secured party's possession. That section applies not only to the situation where he is in possession before default, as a pledgee, but also, by subsections (1) and (2) of this section, to the secured party in possession after default. Nevertheless the relations of the parties have been changed by default, and Section 9–207 as it applies after default must be read together with this Part. In particular, agreements permitted under Section 9–207 cannot waive or modify the rights of the debtor contrary to subsection (3) of this section.

4. Section 1–102(3) states rules to determine which provisions of this Act are mandatory and which may be varied by agreement. In general, provisions which relate to matters which come up between immediate parties may be varied by agreement. In the area of rights after default our legal system has traditionally looked with suspicion on agreements designed to cut down the debtor's rights and free the secured party of his duties: no mortgage clause has even been allowed to clog the equity of redemption. The default situation offers great scope for overreaching; the suspicious attitude of the courts has been grounded in common sense.

Subsection (3) of this section contains a codification of this long-standing and deeply rooted attitude: the specified rights of the debtor and duties of the secured party may not be waived or varied except as stated. Provisions not specified in subsection (3) are subject to the general rules stated in Section 1–102(3).

5. The collateral for many corporate security issues consists of both real and personal property. In the interest of simplicity and speed subsection (4) permits, although it does not require, the secured party to proceed as to both real and personal property in accordance with his rights and remedies in respect of the real property. Except for the permission so granted, this Act leaves to other state law all questions of procedure with respect to real property. For example, this Act does not determine whether the secured party can proceed against the real estate alone and later proceed in a separate action against the personal property in accordance with his rights and remedies against the real estate. By such separate actions the secured party "proceeds as to both," and this Part does not apply in either action. But subsection (4) does give him an option to proceed under this Part as to the personal property.

6. Under subsection (1) a secured party is entitled to reduce his claim to judgment or to foreclose his interest by any available procedure, outside this Article, which state law may provide. The first sentence of subsection (5) makes clear that any judgment lien which the secured party may acquire against the collateral is, so to say, a continuation of his original interest (if perfected) and not the acquisition of a new interest or a transfer of property to satisfy an antecedent debt. The judgment lien is therefore stated to relate back to the date of perfection of the security interest. The second sentence of the subsection makes clear that a judicial sale following judgment, execution and levy is one of the methods of foreclosure contemplated by subsection (1); such a sale is governed by other law and not by this Article and the restrictions which this Article imposes on the right of a secured party to buy in the collateral at a sale under Section 9–504 do not apply.

Cross References:
Point 2: Section 9–503.
Point 3: Section 9–207.
Point 4: Section 1–102(3).
Point 5: Sections 9–102(1) and 9–104(j).
Point 6: Section 9–504.

Definitional Cross References:
"Agreement". Section 1–201.
"Collateral". Section 9–105.
"Debtor". Section 9–105.
"Documents". Section 9–105.
"Goods". Section 9–105.
"Remedy". Section 1–201.
"Rights". Section 1–201.
"Secured party". Section 9–105.
"Security agreement". Section 9–105.
"Security interest". Section 1–201.

§ 9501. Default; Procedure When Security Agreement Covers Both Real and Personal Property

Text of section operative Jan. 1, 1999.

(1) When a debtor is in default under a security agreement, a secured party has the rights and remedies provided in this chapter and except as limited by subdivision (3) those provided in the security agreement. The secured party may reduce his or her claim to judgment, foreclose or otherwise enforce the security interest by any available judicial procedure. If the collateral is documents the secured party may proceed either as to the documents or as to the goods covered thereby. A secured party in possession has the rights, remedies and duties provided in Section 9207. The rights and remedies referred to in this subdivision are cumulative.

(2) After default, the debtor has the rights and remedies provided in this chapter, those provided in the security agreement and those provided in Section 9207.

(3) To the extent that they give rights to the debtor and impose duties on the secured party, the rules stated in the subdivisions referred to below may not be waived or varied except as provided with respect to compulsory disposition of collateral (subdivision (3) of Section 9504 and Section 9505) and with respect to redemption of collateral (Section 9506) but the parties may by agreement determine the standards by which the fulfillment of these rights and duties is to be measured if such standards are not manifestly unreasonable:

(a) Subdivision (2) of Section 9502 and subdivision (2) of Section 9504 insofar as they require accounting for surplus proceeds of collateral;

(b) Subdivision (3) of Section 9504 and subdivision (1) of Section 9505 which deal with disposition of collateral;

(c) Subdivision (2) of Section 9505 which deals with acceptance of collateral as discharge of obligation;

(d) Section 9506 which deals with redemption of collateral; and

(e) Subdivision (1) of Section 9507 which deals with the secured party's liability for failure to comply with this chapter.

(4) If an obligation secured by <u>a security interest in</u> personal property or fixtures (Section 9313(1)(a)) is also secured by <u>an interest in</u> real property <u>or an estate therein</u>:

(a) The secured party may do any of the following:

(i) Proceed, in any sequence, (1) in accordance with the secured party's rights and remedies in respect of real property as to the real property security, and (2) in accordance with this chapter as to the personal property or fixtures.

(ii) Proceed in any sequence, as to both some or all of the real property and some or all of the personal property or fixtures in accordance with the secured party's rights and remedies in respect of the real property, by including the portion of the personal property or fixtures selected by the secured party in the judicial or nonjudicial foreclosure of the real property in accordance with the procedures applicable to real property. In proceeding under this subparagraph, (A) no provision of this chapter other than this subparagraph, subparagraph (iii) of paragraph (d), and paragraphs (g) and (h) shall apply to any aspect of the foreclosure; (B) a power of sale under the deed of trust or mortgage shall be exercisable with respect to both the real property and the personal property or fixtures being sold; and (C) the sale may be conducted by the mortgagee under the mortgage or by the trustee under the deed of trust. The secured party shall not be deemed to have elected irrevocably to proceed as to both real property and personal property or fixtures as provided in this subparagraph with respect to any particular property, unless and until that particular property has been actually disposed of pursuant to a unified sale (judicial or nonjudicial) conducted in accordance with the procedures applicable to real property, and then only as to the property so sold.

(iii) Proceed, in any sequence, as to part of the personal property or fixtures as provided in subparagraph (i), and as to other of the personal property or fixtures as provided in subparagraph (ii).

(b) (i) Except as otherwise provided in paragraph (c), provisions and limitations of any law respecting real property and obligations secured by an interest in real property or an estate therein, including, but not limited to, Section 726 of the Code of Civil Procedure, provisions regarding acceleration or reinstatement of obligations secured by an interest in real property or an estate therein, prohibitions against deficiency judgments, * * * limitations on deficiency judgments based on the value of the collateral, limitations on the right to proceed as to collateral, and requirements that a creditor resort either first or at all to its security, do not in any way apply to either (1) any personal property or fixtures other than personal property or fixtures as to which the secured party has proceeded or is proceeding * * * under subparagraph (ii) of paragraph (a), or (2) the obligation * * *.

(ii) Pursuant to, but without limiting subparagraph (i), in the event that an obligation secured by personal property or fixtures would otherwise become unenforceable by reason of Section 726 of the Code of Civil Procedure or any requirement that a creditor resort first to its security, then, notwithstanding that section or any similar requirement, the obligation shall nevertheless remain enforceable to the full extent necessary to permit a secured party to proceed against personal property or fixtures securing the obligation in accordance with the secured party's rights and remedies as permitted under this chapter.

(c) (i) Paragraph (b) does not limit the application of Section 580b of the Code of Civil Procedure.

(ii) If * * * the secured party commences * * * an action * * *, as defined in Section 22 of the Code of Civil Procedure * * *, and the action seeks a monetary judgment on the debt * * *, paragraph (b) does not prevent the debtor's assertion of any right to require the inclusion in the action of any interest in real property or an estate therein securing the debt. If a monetary judgment on the debt is entered in the action, paragraph (b) does not prevent the debtor's assertion of the subsequent unenforceability of the encumbrance on any interest in real property or an estate therein securing the debt and not included in the action * * *.

(iii) Nothing in paragraph (b) shall be construed to excuse compliance with Section 2924c of the Civil Code as a prerequisite to the * * * sale of real property, but that section has no application to the right of a secured party to proceed as to personal property or fixtures except, and then only to the extent that the secured party is proceeding as to personal property or fixtures in a unified sale as provided in subparagraph (ii) of paragraph (a).

(iv) Paragraph (b) does not deprive the debtor of the protection of Section 580d of the Code of Civil Procedure against a deficiency judgment following a sale of the real property collateral pursuant to a power of sale in a deed of trust or mortgage.

(v) Paragraph (b) * * * shall not affect, nor shall it determine the applicability or inapplicability of, any law respecting real property or obligations secured in whole or in part by real property with respect to a loan or a credit sale made to any individual primarily for personal, family, or household purposes.

(vi) Paragraph (b) does not deprive the debtor of the protection of Section 580a of the Code of Civil Procedure following a sale of real property collateral.

(vii) If the secured party violates any statute or rule of law that requires a creditor who holds an obligation secured by an interest in real property or an estate therein to resort first to its security before resorting to any property of the debtor that does not secure the obligation, paragraph (b) does not prevent the debtor's assertion of any right to require correction of the violation, any right of the secured party to correct the violation, or the debtor's assertion of the subsequent unenforceability of the encumbrance on any interest in real property or an estate therein securing the obligation, or the debtor's assertion of the subsequent unenforceability of the obligation except to the extent that the obligation is preserved by subparagraph (ii) of paragraph (b).

(d) If the secured party realizes proceeds from the disposition of collateral that is personal property or fixtures, the following provisions shall apply:

(i) The disposition of the collateral, the realization of the proceeds, the application of the proceeds, or any one or more of the foregoing shall not operate to cure any nonmonetary default.

(ii) The disposition of the collateral, the realization of the proceeds, the application of the proceeds, or any one or more of the foregoing shall not operate to cure any monetary default (although the application of the proceeds shall, to the extent of those proceeds, satisfy the secured obligation) so as to affect in any way the secured party's rights and remedies under this chapter with respect to any remaining personal property or fixtures collateral.

(iii) All proceeds so realized shall be applied by the secured party to the secured obligation in accordance with the agreement of the parties and applicable law.

(e) An action by the secured party utilizing any available judicial procedure, as provided in subdivision (1), shall in no way be affected by omission of a prayer for a monetary judgment on the debt. * * * Notwithstanding Section 726 of the Code of Civil Procedure, any prohibition against splitting causes of action or any other statute or rule of law, a judicial action which neither * * * seeks nor results in a monetary judgment on the debt shall not preclude a subsequent action seeking a monetary judgment on the debt or any other relief.

(f) As used in this subdivision, "monetary judgment on the debt" means a judgment for the recovery from the debtor of all or part of the principal amount of the secured obligation, including, for purposes of this subdivision, contractual interest thereon. "Monetary judgment on the debt" does not include a judgment which provides only for other relief (whether or not that other relief is secured by the collateral), such as one or more forms of nonmonetary relief, and monetary relief ancillary to any of the foregoing, such as attorneys' fees and costs incurred in seeking the relief.

(g) If a secured party fails to comply with * * * the procedures applicable to real property in proceeding as to both real and personal property under subparagraph (ii) of paragraph (a) * * *, a purchaser for value of any interest in the real property at judicial or nonjudicial foreclosure proceedings conducted pursuant to subparagraph (ii) of paragraph (a) takes that interest free from any claim or interest of another person, or any defect in title, based upon that noncompliance, unless:

(i) The purchaser is the secured party and the failure to comply with this chapter occurred other than in good faith; or

(ii) The purchaser is other than the secured party and at the time of sale of the real property at that foreclosure the purchaser had * * * knowledge of the failure to comply with this chapter and that the noncompliance occurred other than in good faith.

Even if the purchaser at the foreclosure sale does not take his or her interest free of claims, interests, or title defects based upon that noncompliance with this chapter, a subsequent purchaser for value who acquires an interest in that real property from the purchaser at that foreclosure takes that interest free from any claim or interest of another person, or any defect in title, based upon that noncompliance, unless at the time of acquiring the interest the subsequent purchaser has knowledge of the failure to comply with this chapter and that the noncompliance occurred other than in good faith.

* * * (h) If a secured party proceeds by way of a unified sale under subparagraph (ii) of paragraph (a) * * *, then, for purposes of applying Section 580a or subdivision (b) of Section 726 of the Code of Civil Procedure to any such unified sale, the personal property or fixtures included in the unified sale shall be deemed to be included in the "real property or other interest sold," as that term is used in Section 580a or subdivision (b) of Section 726 of the Code of Civil Procedure.

(5) When a secured party has reduced his or her claim to judgment the lien of any levy which may be made upon his or her collateral by virtue of any execution based upon the judgment shall relate back to the date of the perfection of the security interest in the collateral. A judicial sale, pursuant to that execution, is a foreclosure of the security interest by judicial procedure within the meaning of this section, and the secured party may purchase at the sale and thereafter hold the collateral free of any other requirements of this division. (Added by Stats.1990, c. 1125 (A.B.3881), § 2.5, operative Jan. 1, 1999. Amended by Stats.1992, c. 1095 (A.B. 2734), § 7, operative Jan. 1, 1999.)

For text of section operative until Jan. 1, 1999, see Commercial Code § 9501, ante.

Cross References

Applicability as to personalty, fixtures, or realty, see Commercial Code §§ 9102, 9104.
Attachment, see Code of Civil Procedure § 484.010 et seq.
Collateral,
   Disposal after default, see Commercial Code § 9504.
   Rights and duties when in secured party's possession, see Commercial Code § 9207.
Secured party's right to possession, see Commercial Code § 9503.
Displaced homemaker emergency loans, default, remedies, see Government Code § 8258.1.
Execution of judgment, see Code of Civil Procedure §§ 683.010, 683.020, 699.510, 712.010.
Foreclosure of mortgages, see Code of Civil Procedure § 725a et seq.
Mortgages, transactions or security interests governed by the Commercial Code, exception by reason of election under this section, see Civil Code § 2944.
Possession of mortgaged property, see Civil Code § 2927.
Power of sale, see Civil Code § 2932.
Retail installment sales, repossession and resale, see Civil Code § 1812.2 et seq.
Sale of property, unified sale as provided by this section, contents of notice, see Civil Code § 2924f.
Variation by agreement, see Commercial Code § 1102.

§ 9502. Collection Rights of Secured Party

Text of section operative until Jan. 1, 1999.

(1) When so agreed and in any event on default the secured party is entitled to notify an account debtor or the obligor on an instrument to make payment to him or her whether or not the assignor was theretofore making collections on the collateral, and also to take control of any proceeds to which he or she is entitled under Section 9306.

(2)(a) A secured party who by agreement is entitled to charge back uncollected collateral or otherwise to f˙ or limited recourse against the debtor and who u˙ takes to collect from the account debtors or must proceed in a commercially reasonable manner and may deduct his or her reasonable expenses of realization from the collections.

(b) If the security agreement secures an indebtedness, the secured party must account to the debtor for any surplus.

(c) If the security agreement secures an indebtedness, the debtor is liable for any deficiency unless otherwise agreed, but only (i) if the secured party in collection pursuant to this section has proceeded in a commercially reasonable manner, or (ii) as provided in paragraph (d).

(d) If the secured party in collecting pursuant to this section has not proceeded in a commercially reasonable manner, the debtor is liable, subject to paragraph (e), for any deficiency only if the balance of the indebtedness immediately before the collection exceeds the amount that the secured party establishes would have been realized had the secured party in collecting pursuant to this section proceeded in a commercially reasonable manner, and the liability is limited to the excess.

(e) Notwithstanding paragraph (d), if the secured party in collecting pursuant to this section has not proceeded in a commercially reasonable manner, and if the transaction was entered into by the debtor primarily for personal, family, or household purposes or if the amount of the indebtedness immediately before the collection was one hundred thousand dollars ($100,000) or less, then the debtor is not liable for any deficiency.

(f) Upon entry of a final judgment that the debtor is not liable for a deficiency by reason of either paragraph (d) or paragraph (e), the secured party may neither obtain a deficiency judgment nor retain a security interest in any other collateral of the debtor that secured the indebtedness for which the debtor is no longer liable.

(g) To the extent, subsequent to a collection that does not satisfy the conditions set forth in clause (i) of paragraph (c), or subsequent to a disposition that does not satisfy any one or more of the conditions set forth in clause (i) of paragraph (b) of subdivision (2) of Section 9504, the secured party collects pursuant to this section on other collateral securing the same indebtedness, the debtor may, to the extent he or she is no longer liable for a deficiency judgment by reason of paragraph (d) or paragraph (e), or by reason of paragraph (c) or paragraph (d) of subdivision (2) of Section 9504, recover the proceeds realized from those subsequent collections, as well as any damages to which the debtor may be entitled if the subsequent collection is itself noncomplying or otherwise wrongful. Except for secured transactions entered by the debtor primarily for personal, family, or household purposes, neither the subsequent collections nor the exercise of any other remedy by the secured party subsequent to a noncomplying collection or disposition shall be deemed tortious or otherwise wrongful based, in whole or in part, on the fact that it occurred subsequent to a noncomplying collection or disposition.

(h) If the underlying transaction was a sale of accounts or chattel paper, the debtor is entitled to any surplus or is liable for any deficiency only if the security agreement so provides. The provisions of subdivision (b) of Section 701.040 of the Code of Civil Procedure relating to the payment of proceeds apply only if the security agreement provides that the debtor is entitled to any surplus.

(i) Nothing herein shall deprive the debtor of any right to recover damages from the secured party under subdivision (1) of Section 9507 or to offset any such damages against any claim by the secured party for a deficiency, or of any right or remedy to which the debtor may be entitled under any other law. However, except in the case of any secured party that has willfully failed to proceed in a commercially reasonable manner in collection pursuant to this section, or in the case of a debtor who entered the secured transaction primarily for personal, family, or household purposes, any damages recoverable by the debtor shall be reduced by the amount of any deficiency that would have resulted had the secured party in collecting pursuant to this section proceeded in conformity with the condition set forth in clause (i) of paragraph (c) regardless whether or not the debtor is liable for the deficiency under paragraph (c) or (d).

(3) This section shall be repealed on January 1, 1999. (Stats.1963, c. 819, § 9502. Amended by Stats.1974, c. 997, p. 2139, § 43, eff. Jan. 1, 1976; Stats.1990, c. 1125 (A.B.3881), § 3; Stats.1992, c. 1095 (A.B.2734), § 8; Stats.1995, c. 591 (A.B.1689), § 7.)

Repeal

This section is repealed by its own terms on Jan. 1, 1999.

For text of section operative Jan. 1, 1999, see Commercial Code § 9502, post.

California Code Comment

By John A. Bohn and Charles J. Williams

Prior California Law

1. This section deals with the collection rights of a secured party after default when the collateral consists of intangibles rather that tangible personal property. Official Comments 1 and 2 explain the reasons for treating tangibles and intangibles differently.

There was no prior statutory law dealing with this subject. For a discussion of prior California law dealing with the general rights of the secured creditor in the case of default, see California Code Comment 2 to Commercial Code § 9501.

Changes from U.C.C. (1962 Official Text)

2. This is section 9–502 of the Official Text without change.

Uniform Commercial Code Comment

Prior Uniform Statutory Provision:
None.

Purposes:

1. The assignee of accounts, chattel paper, or instruments holds as collateral property which is not only the most liquid asset of the debtor's business but also property which may be collected without any

interruption of the business, assuming it to continue after default. The situation is far different from that where the collateral is inventory or equipment, whose removal may bring the business to a halt. Furthermore the problems of valuation and identification, present where the collateral is tangible chattels, do not arise so sharply on the assignment of intangibles. Considerations, similar although not identical, apply to assignments of general intangibles, which are also covered by the rule of the section. Consequently, this section recognizes the fact that financing by assignment of intangibles lacks many of the complexities which arise after default in other types of financing, and allows the assignee to liquidate in the regular course of business by collecting whatever may become due on the collateral, whether or not the method of collection contemplated by the security arrangement before default was direct (i.e., payment by the account debtor to the assignee, "notification" (financing) or indirect (i.e., payment by the account debtor to the assignor, "non-notification" financing). By agreement, of course, the secured party may have the right to give notice and to make collections before default.

2. In one form of accounts receivable financing, which is found in the "factoring" arrangements which are common in the textile industry, the assignee assumes the credit risk—that is, he buys the account under an agreement which does not provide for recourse or charge-back against the assignor in the event the account proves uncollectible. Under such an arrangement, neither the debtor nor his creditors have any legitimate concern with the disposition which the assignee makes of the accounts. Under another form of accounts receivable financing, however, the assignee does not assume the credit risk and retains a right of full or limited recourse or charge-back for uncollectible accounts. In such a case both debtor and creditors have a right that the assignee not dump the accounts, if the result will be to increase a possible deficiency claim or to reduce a possible surplus.

3. Where an assignee has a right of charge-back or a right of recourse, subsection (2) provides that liquidation must be made with due regard to the interest of the assignor and of his other creditors—"in a commercially reasonable manner" (compare Section 9–504 and see Section 9–507(2))—and the proceeds allocated to the expenses of realization and to the indebtedness. If the "charge-back" provisions of the assignment arrangement provide only for "charge-back" of bad accounts against a reserve, the debtor's claim to surplus and his liability for a deficiency are limited to the amount of the reserve.

4. Financing arrangements of the type dealt with by this section are between business men. The last sentence of subsection (2) therefore preserves freedom of contract, and the subsection recognizes that there may be a true sale of accounts or chattel paper although recourse exists. The determination whether a particular assignment constitutes a sale or a transfer for security is left to the courts. Note that, under Section 9–102, this Article applies both to sales and to security transfers of such intangibles.

Cross References:

Sections 9–205 and 9–306.

Point 3: Sections 9–504 and 9–507(2).

Point 4: Sections 9–102(1)(b) and 9–104(f).

Definitional Cross References:

"Account". Section 9–106.

"Account debtor". Section 9–105.

"Agreement". Section 1–201.

"Chattel paper". Section 9–105.

"Collateral". Section 9–105.

"Debtor". Section 9–105.

"Instrument". Section 9–105.

"Notify". Section 1–201.

"Proceeds". Section 9–306.

"Secured party". Section 9–105.

"Security agreement". Section 9–105.

Cross References

Applicability to personalty, fixtures, intangibles, and realty, see Commercial Code §§ 9102, 9104.

Collateral, use or disposition, see Commercial Code §§ 9205, 9306, 9504, 9507.

§ 9502. Collection Rights of Secured Party

Text of section operative Jan. 1, 1999.

(1) When so agreed and in any event on default the secured party is entitled to notify an account debtor or the obligor on an instrument to make payment to him or her whether or not the assignor was theretofore making collections on the collateral, and also to take control of any proceeds to which he or she is entitled under Section 9306.

(2) A secured party who by agreement is entitled to charge back uncollected collateral or otherwise to full or limited recourse against the debtor and who undertakes to collect from the account debtors or obligors must proceed in a commercially reasonable manner and may deduct his or her reasonable expenses of realization from the collections. If the security agreement secures an indebtedness, the secured party must account to the debtor for any surplus, and unless otherwise agreed, the debtor is liable for any deficiency. But, if the underlying transaction was a sale of accounts or chattel paper, the debtor is entitled to any surplus or is liable for any deficiency only if the security agreement so provides. (Added by Stats.1990, c. 1125 (A.B.3881), § 3.5, operative Jan. 1, 1999.)

For text of section operative until Jan. 1, 1999, see Commercial Code § 9502, ante.

§ 9503. Secured Party's Rights to Take Possession After Default

Unless otherwise agreed a secured party has on default the right to take possession of the collateral. In taking possession a secured party may proceed without judicial process if this can be done without breach of the peace or may proceed by action. If the security agreement so provides the secured party may require the debtor to assemble the collateral and make it available to the secured party at a place to be designated by the secured party which is reasonably convenient to both parties. Without removal a secured party may render equipment unusable, and may dispose of collateral on the debtor's premises under Section 9504. (Stats.1963, c. 819, § 9503.)

California Code Comment

By John A. Bohn and Charles J. Williams

Prior California Law

1. This section gives the secured party the remedy of taking possession of the collateral without the issuance of judicial process. Commercial Code § 9505 governs the situation where the secured party retains the collateral in discharge of the obligation.

This section also recognizes the situation where the collateral is such that physical removal is impractical. See Official Comment.

The right granted under this section is similar to the right granted under former Civil Code § 3016.2 (UTRA).

See California Code Comment 2 to section 9501 for a discussion of the prior California law relating to remedies upon default.

Changes from U.C.C. (1962 Official Text)

2. This is section 9–503 of the Official Text without change.

Uniform Commercial Code Comment

Prior Uniform Statutory Provision:

Section 6, Uniform Trust Receipts Act; Sections 16 and 17, Uniform Conditional Sales Act.

Purposes:

Under this Article the secured party's right to possession of the collateral (if he is not already in possession as pledgee) accrues on default unless otherwise agreed in the security agreement. This Article follows the provisions of the earlier uniform legislation in allowing the secured party in most cases to take possession without the issuance of judicial process. In the case of collateral such as heavy equipment, the physical removal from the debtor's plant and the storage of the equipment pending resale may be exceedingly expensive and in some cases impractical. The section therefore provides that in lieu of removal the lender may render equipment unusable or dispose of collateral on the debtor's premises. The authorization to render equipment unusable or to dispose of collateral without removal would not justify unreasonable action by the secured party, since, under Section 9–504(3), all his actions in connection with disposition must be taken in a "commercially reasonable manner".

Cross Reference:

Section 9–504.

Definitional Cross References:

"Action". Section 1–201.
"Collateral". Section 9–105.
"Debtor". Section 9–105.
"Equipment". Section 9–109.
"Rights". Section 1–201.
"Secured party". Section 9–105.
"Security agreement". Section 9–105.

Cross References

Collateral, disposal after default, see Commercial Code § 9504.

Fighting, noise, offensive words, see Penal Code § 415.

Retail installment sales, repossession and resale on default by buyer, see Civil Code § 1812.2 et seq.

Right of owner to surplus where collateral not owned by debtor, see Commercial Code § 9112.

§ 9504. Secured Party's Right to Dispose of Collateral After Default; Notification of Sale; Publication; Effect of Disposition

Text of section operative until Jan. 1, 1999.

(1) A secured party after default may sell, lease or otherwise dispose of any or all of the collateral in its then condition or following any commercially reasonable preparation or processing. Any sale of goods is subject to the division on sales (Division 2). The proceeds of disposition shall be applied in the order following to:

(a) The reasonable expenses of retaking, holding, preparing for sale or lease, selling, leasing and the like and, to the extent provided for in the agreement and not prohibited by law, the reasonable attorneys' fees and legal expenses incurred by the secured party;

(b) The satisfaction of indebtedness secured by the security interest under which the disposition is made;

(c) The satisfaction of indebtedness secured by any subordinate security interest in the collateral if written notification of demand therefor is received before distribution of the proceeds is completed and to the satisfaction of any subordinate attachment lien or execution lien pursuant to subdivision (b) of Section 701.040 of the Code of Civil Procedure if notice of the levy of attachment or execution is received before distribution of the proceeds is completed. If requested by the secured party, the holder of a subordinate security interest must seasonably furnish reasonable proof of his or her interest, and unless he or she does so, the secured party need not comply with his or her demand.

(2)(a) If the security interest secures an indebtedness, the secured party must account to the debtor for any surplus except as provided in Section 701.040 of the Code of Civil Procedure.

(b) If the security interest secures an indebtedness, the debtor is liable for any deficiency unless otherwise agreed or otherwise provided in the Retail Installment Sales Act, and in particular Section 1812.5 of the Civil Code or any other statute, but only (i) if the debtor was given notice, if and as required by subdivision (3), of the disposition of the collateral in accordance with subdivision (3), and the disposition of the collateral by the secured party pursuant to this section was conducted in good faith and in a commercially reasonable manner, or (ii) except for secured transactions entered by a debtor primarily for personal, family, or household purposes, as provided in paragraph (c).

(c) If the secured party has provided notice to the debtor pursuant to subdivision (3), if so required, but has not proceeded in a commercially reasonable manner in the disposition of the collateral, the debtor is liable, subject to paragraphs (b) and (d), for any deficiency only if the balance of the indebtedness immediately before the disposition exceeds the amount that the secured party establishes would have been realized had the disposition of the collateral by the secured party pursuant to this section been conducted in conformity with the conditions set forth in clause (i) of paragraph (b), and the liability is limited to the excess. This paragraph does not apply to secured transactions entered by a debtor primarily for personal, family, or household purposes.

(d) Notwithstanding paragraph (c), if any one or more of the conditions set forth in clause (i) of paragraph (b) are not proved by the secured party to be satisfied with respect to the disposition, then the debtor is not liable for any deficiency if either:

(i) All of the collateral immediately before the disposition was consumer goods and the amount of the indebtedness immediately before the disposition was one hundred thousand dollars ($100,000) or less.

(ii) The amount of the indebtedness immediately before the disposition was fifty thousand dollars ($50,000) or less.

(e) Upon entry of a final judgment that the debtor is not liable for a deficiency by reason of either paragraph (c) or paragraph (d), the secured party may neither obtain a deficiency judgment nor retain a security interest in any other collateral of the debtor that secured the indebtedness for which the debtor is no longer liable.

(f) To the extent, subsequent to a disposition that does not satisfy any one or more of the conditions set forth in clause (i) of paragraph (b), or subsequent to a collection that does not satisfy the condition set forth in clause (i) of paragraph (c) of subdivision (2) of Section 9502, the secured party disposes pursuant to this section of other collateral securing the same indebtedness, the debtor may, to the extent he or she is no longer liable for a deficiency judgment by reason of paragraph (c) or paragraph (d), or by reason of paragraph (d) or paragraph (e) of subdivision (2) of Section 9502, recover the proceeds realized from the subsequent dispositions, as well as any damages to which the debtor may be entitled if the subsequent disposition is itself noncomplying or otherwise wrongful. Except for secured transactions entered by a debtor primarily for personal, family, or household purposes, neither the subsequent dispositions nor the exercise of any other remedy by the secured party subsequent to a noncomplying disposition or collection shall be deemed tortious or otherwise wrongful based, in whole or in part, on the fact that it occurred subsequent to a noncomplying disposition or collection.

(g) If the underlying transaction was a sale of accounts or chattel paper, the debtor is entitled to any surplus or is liable for any deficiency only if the security agreement so provides. The provisions of subdivision (b) of Section 701.040 of the Code of Civil Procedure relating to the payment of proceeds and the liability of the secured party apply only if the security agreement provides that the debtor is entitled to any surplus.

(h) Nothing herein shall deprive the debtor of any right to recover damages from the secured party under subdivision (1) of Section 9507 or to offset any such damages against any claim by the secured party for a deficiency, or of any right or remedy to which the debtor may be entitled under any other law; provided, however, that, except in the case of any secured party that has willfully failed to conduct the disposition of collateral in good faith and in a commercially reasonable manner or in the case of a debtor who entered the secured transaction primarily for personal, family, or household purposes, any damages recoverable by the debtor shall be reduced by the amount of any deficiency that would have resulted had the disposition of the collateral by the secured party been conducted in conformity with the conditions set forth in clause (i) of paragraph (b) regardless whether or not the debtor is liable for the deficiency under paragraph (b) or (c).

(3) A sale or lease of collateral may be as a unit or in parcels, at wholesale or retail and at any time and place and on any terms, provided the secured party acts in good faith and in a commercially reasonable manner. Unless collateral is perishable or threatens to decline speedily in value or is of a type customarily sold on a recognized market, the secured party must give to the debtor, if he or she has not signed after default a statement renouncing or modifying his or her right to notification of sale, and to any other person who has a security interest in the collateral and who has filed with the secured party a written request for notice giving his or her address (before that secured party sends his or her notification to the debtor or before debtor's renunciation of his or her rights), a notice in writing of the time and place of any public sale or of the time on or after which any private sale or other intended disposition is to be made. Such notice must be delivered personally or be deposited in the United States mail postage prepaid addressed to the debtor at his or her address as set forth in the financing statement or as set forth in the security agreement or at such other address as may have been furnished to the secured party in writing for this purpose, or, if no address has been so set forth or furnished, at his or her last known address, and to any other secured party at the address set forth in his or her request for notice, at least five days before the date fixed for any public sale or before the day on or after which any private sale or other disposition is to be made. Notice of the time and place of a public sale shall also be given at least five days before the date of sale by publication once in a newspaper of general circulation published in the county in which the sale is to be held or in case no newspaper of general circulation is published in the county in which the sale is to be held, in a newspaper of general circulation published in the county in this state that (1) is contiguous to the county in which the sale is to be held and (2) has, by comparison with all similarly contiguous counties, the highest population based upon total county population as determined by the most recent federal decennial census published by the Bureau of the Census. Any public sale shall be held in the county or place specified in the security agreement, or if no county or place is specified in the security agreement, in the county in which the collateral or any part thereof is located or in the county in which the debtor has his or her residence or chief place of business, or in the county in which the secured party has his or her residence or a place of business if the debtor does not have a residence or chief place of business within this state. If the collateral is located outside of this state or has been removed from this state, a public sale may be held in the locality in which the collateral is located. Any public sale may be postponed from time to time by public announcement at the time and place last scheduled for the sale. The secured party may buy at any public sale and if the collateral is customarily sold in a recognized market or is the subject of widely or regularly distributed standard price quotations he or she may buy at private sale. Any sale of which notice is delivered or mailed and published as herein provided and that is held as herein provided is a public sale.

(4) When collateral is disposed of by a secured party after default, the disposition transfers to a purchaser for value all of the debtor's rights therein, discharges the security interest under which it is made and any security interest or lien subordinate thereto. The purchaser takes free of all such rights and interest even though the secured party fails to comply with the requirements of this chapter or of any judicial proceedings.

(a) In the case of a public sale, if the purchaser has no knowledge of any defects in the sale and if he or she does not buy in collusion with the secured party, other bidders or the person conducting the sale; or

(b) In any other case, if the purchaser acts in good faith.

(5) A person who is liable to a secured party under a guaranty, indorsement, repurchase agreement or the like and who receives a transfer of collateral from the secured party or is subrogated to his or she [1] rights has thereafter the rights and duties of the secured party. Such a transfer of collateral is not a sale or disposition of the collateral under this division.

(6) This section shall be repealed on January 1, 1999. (Stats.1963, c. 819, § 9504. Amended by Stats.1974, c. 997, p. 2139, § 44, eff. Jan. 1, 1976; Stats.1982, c. 497, p. 2184, § 83.5, operative July 1, 1983; Stats.1985, c. 102, § 2, eff. June 26, 1985. Amended by Stats.1990, c. 1125 (A.B.3881), § 4; Stats.1995, c. 591 (A.B.1689), § 8.)

[1] So in chaptered copy.

Repeal

This section is repealed by its own terms on Jan. 1, 1999.

For text of section operative Jan. 1, 1999, see Commercial Code § 9504, post.

California Code Comment

By Charles J. Williams

In considering the extensive deviation which California made in subdivision (3) from the 1962 Official Text, the Permanent Editorial Board gives these reasons for rejecting the California changes:

". . . The provisions of Part 5 of Article 9 with respect to the rights of parties in the event of default were carefully considered and long debated with the objective of meeting the reasonable needs of the secured party, the debtor and other parties having possible interests in the collateral. Recognizing that Article 9 would apply to all types of collateral ranging anywhere from a diesel locomotive or a jet airplane to a box of apples or from a trademark or a copyright to a household refrigerator, one major objective of these provisions was to preserve maximum flexibility for this extremely wide range of collateral. Another motivating factor was the belief that if reasonable private sales of collateral were encouraged, this could well result in higher realization on collateral for the benefit of all parties than if standardized or stereotyped public sales were predominantly used. Thus, the general standards of good faith and commercial reasonableness were adopted in preference to rigid mandatory formulae for either public or private sales. However, substantial protection was provided for secured parties in the provision of subsection (3) of Section 9–501 that the parties may by agreement determine the standards by which the fulfillment of rights and duties is to be measured if such standards are not manifestly unreasonable; by the provisions of subsection (3) of Section 9–504 and subsection (2) of Section 9–507 prescribing various types of disposition that are commercially reasonable; and by the specification of numerous things the secured party can do, many of which were at least doubtful under pre-Code law.

"The Editorial Board considers that the California variations constitute unsound policy. It believes that the elaborate rules relating to notice tend to destroy desirable flexibility now appearing in the Official Code Text and, by providing for stereotyped forms of notice in public sales, could well decrease realization on collateral to the detriment of all parties.

"The requirement that any other secured party is entitled to notice of a sale only if he has previously filed a request for such notice makes a second lien imprudent unless the holder of the subordinate security interest immediately files such a notice with the holder of the priority security interest. Where notice to the subordinate party is not required in the case of consumer goods and in the case of other goods only if the subordinate party has duly filed a financing statement indexed in the name of the debtor in the enacting state or who is known to the primary secured party, notice to a subordinate party imposes no unreasonable burden on the primary secured party. Conversely, the California variation gives the primary party an undesirable advantage.

"The Editorial Board further believes that changes made for clarification do not have sufficient merit to justify modification of the Official Code Text." Permanent Editorial Board for the Uniform Commercial Code, Report No. 2 (1962 Official Text), pp. 294–295.

Legislative Committee Comment—Assembly
1982 Amendment

Section 9504 is amended to clarify the manner of disposition of proceeds of collateral remaining after satisfaction of the indebtedness to a secured party who has a priority over a lien creditor. (15 Cal.L.Rev. Comm. Reports 2001; 82 A.J. 9356).

Uniform Commercial Code Comment

Prior Uniform Statutory Provision:

Section 6, Uniform Trust Receipts Act; Sections 19, 20, 21, and 22, Uniform Conditional Sales Act.

Purposes:

1. The Uniform Trust Receipts Act provides that an entruster in possession after default holds the collateral with the rights and duties of a pledgee, and, in particular, that he may sell such collateral at public or private sale with a right to claim deficiency and a duty to account for any surplus. The Uniform Conditional Sales Act insisted on a sale at public auction with elaborate provisions for the giving of notice of sale. This section follows the more liberal provisions of the Trust Receipts Act. Although public sale is recognized, it is hoped that private sale will be encouraged where, as is frequently the case, private sale through commercial channels will result in higher realization on collateral for the benefit of all parties. The only restriction placed on the secured party's method of disposition is that it must be commercially reasonable. In this respect this section follows the provisions of the section on resale by a seller following a buyer's rejection of goods (Section 2–706). Subsection (1) does not restrict disposition to sale: the collateral may be sold, leased, or otherwise disposed of—subject of course to the general requirement of subsection (2) that all aspects of the disposition be "commercially reasonable". Section 9–507(2) states some tests as to what is "commercially reasonable".

2. Subsection (1) in general follows prior law in its provisions for the application of proceeds and for the debtor's right to surplus and liability for deficiency. Under paragraph (1) (c) the secured party, after paying expenses of retaking and disposition and his own debt, is required to pay over remaining proceeds to the extent necessary to satisfy the holder of any junior security interest in the same collateral if the holder of the junior interest has made a written demand and furnished on request reasonable proof of his interest: this provision is necessary in view of the fact that under subsection (4) the junior interest is discharged by the disposition. Since the requirement is conditioned on written demand, it should not result in undue burden on the secured party making the disposition. It should be noted also that under Section 9–112 where the secured party knows that the collateral is owned by a person who is not the debtor, the owner of the collateral and not the debtor is entitled to any surplus.

3. In any security transaction the debtor (or the owner of the collateral if other than the debtor: see Section 9–112) is entitled to any surplus which results from realization on the collateral; the debtor will also, unless otherwise agreed, be liable for any deficiency. Subsection (2) so provides. Since this Article covers sales of certain intangibles as well as transfers for security, the subsection also provides that apart from agreement the right to surplus or liability for deficiency does not accrue where the transaction between debtor and secured party was a sale and not a security transaction.

4. Subsection (4) provides that a purchaser for value from a secured party after default takes free of any rights of the debtor and of the holders of junior security interests and liens, even though the secured party has not complied with the requirements of this Part or of any judicial proceedings. This subsection follows a similar provision in the Uniform Trust Receipts Act and in the section of this Act on resale by a

seller (Section 2–706). Where the purchaser for value has bought at a public sale he is protected under paragraph (a) if he has no knowledge of any defects in the sale and was not guilty of collusive practices. Where the purchaser for value has bought at a private sale he must, to receive the protection of paragraph (b), qualify in all respects as a purchaser in good faith. Thus while the purchaser at a private sale is required to proceed in the exercise of good faith, the purchaser at public sale is protected so long as he is not acting in bad faith, and is put under no duty to inquire into the circumstances of the sale.

5. Both the Uniform Trust Receipts Act and the Uniform Conditional Sales Act required a waiting period after repossession and before sale (five days in the Trust Receipts Act, ten days in the Conditional Sales Act). Under subsection (3), the secured party in most cases is required to give reasonable notification of disposition to the debtor unless the debtor has after default signed a statement renouncing or modifying his right to notification of sale.

The secured party must also (except for consumer goods) give notice to any other secured parties who have in writing given notice of a claim of an interest in the collateral. This latter notice must be given before the debtor renounces his rights or before the secured party gives his notification to the debtor. Compare Section 9–505(2). Except for the requirement of notification there is no statutory period during which the collateral must be held before disposition. "Reasonable notification" is not defined in this Article; at a minimum it must be sent in such time that persons entitled to receive it will have sufficient time to take appropriate steps to protect their interests by taking part in the sale or other disposition if they so desire.

6. Section 19 of the Uniform Conditional Sales Act required that sale be made not more than thirty days after possession taken by the conditional vendor. The Uniform Trust Receipts Act contained no comparable provision. Here again this Article follows the Trust Receipts Act, and no period is set within which the disposition must be made, except in the case of consumer goods which under Section 9–505(1) must in certain instances be sold within ninety days after the secured party has taken possession. The failure to prescribe a statutory period during which disposition must be made is in line with the policy adopted in this Article to encourage disposition by private sale through regular commercial channels. It may, for example, be wise not to dispose of goods when the market has collapsed, or to sell a large inventory in parcels over a period of time instead of in bulk. Note, however, that under subsection (3) every aspect of the sale or other disposition of the collateral must be commercially reasonable; this specifically includes method, manner, time, place and terms. See Section 9–507(2). Under that provision a secured party who without proceeding under Section 9–505(2) held collateral a long time without disposing of it, thus running up large storage charges against the debtor, where no reason existed for not making a prompt sale, might well be found not to have acted in a "commercially reasonable" manner. See also Section 1–203 on the general obligation of good faith.

Cross References:
Point 1: Sections 2–706 and 9–507(2).
Point 2: Section 9–112.
Point 3: Sections 9–102(1) (b) and 9–112.
Point 4: Section 2–706.
Point 6: Sections 9–505 and 9–507(2).

Definitional Cross References:
"Account". Section 9–106.
"Agreement". Section 1–201.
"Chattel paper". Section 9–105.
"Collateral". Section 9–105.
"Consumer goods". Section 9–109.
"Contract". Section 1–201.
"Debtor". Section 9–105.
"Financing statement". Section 9–402.
"Gives" notification. Section 1–201.
"Good faith". Section 1–201.
"Goods". Section 9–105.
"Knowledge". Section 1–201.
"Person". Section 1–201.
"Proceeds". Section 9–306.
"Purchaser". Section 1–201.
"Receives" notification. Section 1–201.
"Rights". Section 1–201.
"Sale". Sections 2–106 and 9–105.
"Secured party". Section 9–105.
"Security agreement". Section 9–105.
"Security interest". Section 1–201.
"Send". Section 1–201.
"Term". Section 1–201.
"Value". Section 1–201.
"Written". Section 1–201.

Cross References

Applicability to intangibles, see Commercial Code § 9102.
Commercially reasonable dispositions, see Commercial Code § 9507.
Continuation of lien, and transfer or encumbrance of property subject to lien, see Code of Civil Procedure § 697.920.
Costs, see Code of Civil Procedure § 1021 et seq.
Debtor's right to redeem collateral, see Commercial Code § 9506.
Disposition of property subject to lien, continuation of lien, and exceptions, see Code of Civil Procedure § 697.610.
Execution, in general, see Code of Civil Procedure § 699.510.
Good faith, see Commercial Code §§ 1201, 1203.
Growing crops, timber to be cut, and minerals transferred or encumbered, see Code of Civil Procedure § 697.750.
Obligation of good faith, see Commercial Code § 1203.
Personal property not in custody of levying officer transferred or encumbered, exceptions, see Code of Civil Procedure § 697.740.
Publication in newspapers, see Government Code § 6000 et seq.
Resale by seller, see Commercial Code § 2706.
Retail installment sales, repossession and resale on default by buyer, see Civil Code § 1812.2 et seq.
Sale on execution, see Code of Civil Procedure §§ 701.510, 701.520.
Surplus, collateral not owned by debtor, see Commercial Code § 9112.

§ 9504. Secured Party's Right to Dispose of Collateral After Default; Notification of Sale; Publication; Effect of Disposition

Text of section operative Jan. 1, 1999.

(1) A secured party after default may sell, lease or otherwise dispose of any or all of the collateral in its then condition or following any commercially reasonable preparation or processing. Any sale of goods is subject to the division on sales (Division 2). The proceeds of disposition shall be applied in the order following to:

(a) The reasonable expenses of retaking, holding, preparing for sale or lease, selling, leasing and the like and, to the extent provided for in the agreement and not prohibited by law, the reasonable attorneys' fees and legal expenses incurred by the secured party;

(b) The satisfaction of indebtedness secured by the security interest under which the disposition is made;

(c) The satisfaction of indebtedness secured by any subordinate security interest in the collateral if written notification of demand therefor is received before distribution of the proceeds is completed and to the satisfaction of any subordinate attachment lien or execution lien pursuant to subdivision (b) of Section 701.040 of the Code of Civil Procedure if notice of the levy of attachment or execution is received before distribution of the proceeds is completed. If requested by the secured party, the holder of a subordinate security interest must seasonably furnish reasonable proof of his or her interest, and unless he or she does so, the secured party need not comply with his or her demand.

§ 9504

(2) If the security interest secures an indebtedness, the secured party must account to the debtor for any surplus except as provided in Section 701.040 of the Code of Civil Procedure, and, unless otherwise agreed, the debtor is liable for any deficiency. But if the underlying transaction was a sale of accounts or chattel paper, the debtor is entitled to any surplus or is liable for any deficiency only if the security agreement so provides and the provisions of Section 701.040 of the Code of Civil Procedure relating to payment of proceeds and the liability of the secured party apply only if the security agreement provides that the debtor is entitled to any surplus.

(3) A sale or lease of collateral may be as a unit or in parcels, at wholesale or retail and at any time and place and on any terms, provided the secured party acts in good faith and in a commercially reasonable manner. Unless collateral is perishable or threatens to decline speedily in value or is of a type customarily sold on a recognized market, the secured party must give to the debtor, if he or she has not signed after default a statement renouncing or modifying his or her right to notification of sale, and to any other person who has a security interest in the collateral and who has filed with the secured party a written request for notice giving his or her address (before that secured party sends his or her notification to the debtor or before debtor's renunciation of his or her rights), a notice in writing of the time and place of any public sale or of the time on or after which any private sale or other intended disposition is to be made. Such notice must be delivered personally or be deposited in the United States mail postage prepaid addressed to the debtor at his or her address as set forth in the financing statement or as set forth in the security agreement or at such other address as may have been furnished to the secured party in writing for this purpose, or, if no address has been so set forth or furnished, at his or her last known address, and to any other secured party at the address set forth in his or her request for notice, at least five days before the date fixed for any public sale or before the day on or after which any private sale or other disposition is to be made. Notice of the time and place of a public sale shall also be given at least five days before the date of sale by publication once in a newspaper of general circulation published in the county in which the sale is to be held or in case no newspaper of general circulation is published in the county in which the sale is to be held, in a newspaper of general circulation published in the county in this state that (1) is contiguous to the county in which the sale is to be held and (2) has, by comparison with all similarly contiguous counties, the highest population based upon total county population as determined by the most recent federal decennial census published by the Bureau of the Census. Any public sale shall be held in the county or place specified in the security agreement, or if no county or place is specified in the security agreement, in the county in which the collateral or any part thereof is located or in the county in which the debtor has his or her residence

SECURED TRANSACTIONS 526

or chief place of business, or in the county in which the secured party has his or her residence or a place of business if the debtor does not have a residence or chief place of business within this state. If the collateral is located outside of this state or has been removed from this state, a public sale may be held in the locality in which the collateral is located. Any public sale may be postponed from time to time by public announcement at the time and place last scheduled for the sale. The secured party may buy at any public sale and if the collateral is customarily sold in a recognized market or is the subject of widely or regularly distributed standard price quotations he or she may buy at private sale. Any sale of which notice is delivered or mailed and published as herein provided and which is held as herein provided is a public sale.

(4) When collateral is disposed of by a secured party after default, the disposition transfers to a purchaser for value all of the debtor's rights therein, discharges the security interest under which it is made and any security interest or lien subordinate thereto. The purchaser takes free of all such rights and interest even though the secured party fails to comply with the requirements of this chapter or of any judicial proceedings.

(a) In the case of a public sale, if the purchaser has no knowledge of any defects in the sale and if he or she does not buy in collusion with the secured party, other bidders or the person conducting the sale; or

(b) In any other case, if the purchaser acts in good faith.

(5) A person who is liable to a secured party under a guaranty, indorsement, repurchase agreement or the like and who receives a transfer of collateral from the secured party or is subrogated to his or her rights has thereafter the rights and duties of the secured party. Such a transfer of collateral is not a sale or disposition of the collateral under this division. *(Added by Stats. 1990, c. 1125 (A.B.3881), § 4.5, operative Jan. 1, 1999.)*

For text of section operative until Jan. 1, 1999, see Commercial Code § 9504, ante.

§ 9505. **Compulsory Disposition of Collateral; Acceptance of the Collateral as Discharge of Obligation**

(1) If the debtor has paid 60 percent of the cash price in the case of a purchase money security interest in consumer goods or 60 percent of the loan in the case of another security interest in consumer goods, and has not signed after default a statement renouncing or modifying his rights under this chapter a secured party who has taken possession of collateral must dispose of it under Section 9504 and if he fails to do so within 90 days after he takes possession or within a reasonable time after such 90-day period, the debtor at his option may recover in conversion or under Section 9507(1) on secured party's liability.

(2) In any other case involving consumer goods or any other collateral a secured party in possession may, after default, propose to retain the collateral in satisfaction of the obligation. Written notice of such proposal

shall be sent to the debtor if he has not signed after default a statement renouncing or modifying his rights under this subdivision. In the case of consumer goods no other notice need be given. In other cases notice shall be sent to any other secured party from whom the secured party has received (before sending his notice to the debtor or before the debtor's renunciation of his rights) written notice of a claim of an interest in the collateral. If the secured party receives objection in writing from a person entitled to receive notification within 21 days after the notice was sent, the secured party must dispose of the collateral under Section 9504. In the absence of such written objection the secured party may retain the collateral in satisfaction of the debtor's obligation. *(Added by Stats.1974, c. 997, p. 2141, § 46, eff. Jan. 1, 1976.)*

Uniform Commercial Code Comment
Prior Uniform Statutory Provision:
Section 23, Uniform Conditional Sales Act.
Purposes:
1. Experience has shown that the parties are frequently better off without a resale of the collateral; hence this section sanctions an alternative arrangement. In lieu of resale or other disposition, the secured party may propose under subsection (2) that he keep the collateral as his own, thus discharging the obligation and abandoning any claim for a deficiency. This right may not be exercised in the case of consumer goods where the debtor has paid 60% of the price or obligation and thus has a substantial equity, and may be exercised in other cases only on notification to the debtor, unless the debtor has signed after default a statement renouncing or modifying his rights under this section, and (except in the case of consumer goods) to any other secured party who has given written notice of a claim of an interest in the collateral. In the latter case, notice must be given before the secured party receives the debtor's renunciation or before he sends his notice to the debtor. The secured party may keep the goods in lieu of sale on failure of anyone receiving notification to object within twenty-one days.

2. When an objection is received by the secured party he must then proceed to dispose of the collateral in accordance with Section 9–504, and on failure to do so would incur the liabilities set out in Section 9–507. In the case of consumer goods where 60% of the price or obligation has been paid the disposition must be made within 90 days after possession taken. For failure to make the sale within the 90-day period the secured party is liable in conversion or alternatively may incur the liabilities set out in Section 9–507.

In the absence of objection the secured party is bound by his notice.

3. After default (but not before) a consumer-debtor who has paid 60% of the cash price may sign a written renunciation of his rights to require resale of the collateral.

Cross References:
Sections 9–504 and 9–507(1).
Definitional Cross References:
"Collateral". Section 9–105.
"Consumer goods". Section 9–109.
"Debtor". Section 9–105.
"Knows" Section 1–201.
"Notice". Section 1–201.
"Person". Section 1–201.
"Purchase money security interest". Section 9–107.
"Receives" notification. Section 1–201.
"Rights". Section 1–201.
"Secured party". Section 9–105.
"Security interest". Section 1–201.
"Send". Section 1–201.
"Signed". Section 1–201.
"Written". Section 1–201.

Cross References
Collateral, disposition by secured party, see Commercial Code §§ 9504, 9507.
Computation of time,
   Generally, see Government Code § 6800 et seq.
   Extension of time when last day a holiday, see Code of Civil Procedure § 12a; Government Code § 6800.
Debtor's right to redeem collateral, see Commercial Code § 9506.
Where collateral not owned by debtor, right of owner to object to proposal to retain collateral in satisfaction of indebtedness, see Commercial Code § 9112.

§ 9506. Debtor's Right to Redeem Collateral

At any time before the secured party has disposed of collateral or entered into a contract for its disposition under Section 9504 or before the obligation has been discharged under Section 9505(2) the debtor or any other secured party may unless otherwise agreed in writing after default redeem the collateral by tendering fulfillment of all obligations secured by the collateral as well as the expenses reasonably incurred by the secured party in retaking, holding and preparing the collateral for disposition, in arranging for the sale, and to the extent provided in the agreement and not prohibited by law, his reasonable attorneys' fees and legal expenses. *(Stats.1963, c. 819, § 9506. Amended by Stats.1974, c. 997, p. 2141, § 47, eff. Jan. 1, 1976; Stats.1975, c. 678, p. 1475, § 8.)*

California Code Comment
By John A. Bohn and Charles J. Williams

Prior California Law

1. This section preserves the equity of redemption which existed under prior California law. Under this section the debtor has an equity of redemption before the collateral is disposed of. This equity of redemption cannot be terminated before the debtor's default. See Official Comment.

2. Prior California statutory law upon the debtor's right of redemption was as follows:

(a) pledge: the right of redemption existed at any time before the sale by the pledgor. Bell v. Bank of California, 153 Cal. 234, 94 Pac. 889 (1908).

(b) chattel mortgage: there was no statutory right of redemption but the mortgaged property could be redeemed at any time before its disposition. A provision in the mortgage which gave the mortgagee absolute title was void as an attempt to cut off the mortgagor's equity of redemption before default. Ely v. Williams, 6 Cal.App. 455, 92 Pac. 393 (1907); A. Paladini, Inc. v. Durchman, 216 Cal. 212, 13 P.2d 731 (1932).

(c) trust receipt: there was no specific provision in the UTRA relating to a trustee's equity of redemption. However, because the entruster in possession held the property as a pledgee, the trustee should be able to redeem as a pledgor. Former Civil Code § 3016.2(3)(a); 8 UCLA L.Rev. 806, 961.

(d) inventory lien: the remedies under default were controlled more by practice under the inventory lien agreement. The lender was entitled to possession and he could dispose of the inventory in the manner provided in the agreement. However, the language of the statute was broad enough to permit strict foreclosure of the borrower's interest. It has been pointed out that under this type of financing the parties were in an unequal bargaining position and that in an effort to obtain a loan, the borrower would allow a forfeiture clause to be inserted. This would violate the principle of default remedies to the effect that the debtor's equity of redemption could not be cut off before default. A. Paladini, Inc. v. Durchman, 216 Cal. 212, 13 P.2d 731 (1932); Wakabashi v. Stafford Packing Co., 186 Cal. 632, 200 Pac. 392 (1921); Bonestell v. Western Automotive Finance Corp., 69 Cal.App. 719, 725, 232 Pac. 734 (1924); 8 UCLA L.Rev. 806, 963–964.

§ 9506

(e) assignment of account: there were no prior statutes regulating default procedure.

(f) conditional sale: the right of redemption did exist but a contract term making time of the essence could deprive the buyer of this right within a reasonable time. Silverthorne v. Simon, 59 Cal.App. 494, 211 Pac. 26 (1922); 8 UCLA L.Rev. 806, 965.

Changes from U.C.C. (1962 Official Text)
3. This is section 9–506 of the Official Text without change.

Uniform Commercial Code Comment
Prior Uniform Statutory Provision:
Section 18, Uniform Conditional Sales Act.

Purposes:
Except in the case stated in Section 9–505(1) (consumer goods) the secured party is not required to dispose of collateral within any stated period of time. Under this section so long as the secured party has not disposed of collateral in his possession or contracted for its disposition, and so long as his right to retain it has not become fixed under Section 9–505(2), the debtor or another secured party may redeem. The debtor must tender fulfillment of all obligations secured, plus certain expenses: if the agreement contains a clause accelerating the entire balance due on default in one installment, the entire balance would have to be tendered. "Tendering fulfillment" obviously means more than a new promise to perform the existing promise; it requires payment in full of all monetary obligations then due and performance in full of all other obligations then matured. If unmatured obligations remain, the security interest continues to secure them as if there had been no default.

Under Section 9–504 the secured party may make successive sales of parts of the collateral in his possession. The fact that he may have sold or contracted to sell part of the collateral would not affect the debtor's right under this section to redeem what was left. In such a case, of course, in calculating the amount required to be tendered the debtor would receive credit for net proceeds of the collateral sold.

Cross References:
Sections 9–504 and 9–505.

Definitional Cross References:
"Agreement". Section 1–201.
"Collateral". Section 9–105.
"Contract". Section 1–201.
"Debtor". Section 9–105.
"Secured party". Section 9–105.
"Writing". Section 1–201.

Cross References

Costs, see Code of Civil Procedure § 1021 et seq.
Permissive disposition of collateral by secured party, see Commercial Code § 9504.
Where collateral not owned by debtor, right of owner to redeem collateral, see Commercial Code § 9112.

§ 9507. Secured Party's Liability for Failure to Comply With This Chapter

(1) If it is established that the secured party is not proceeding in accordance with the provisions of this chapter disposition may be ordered or restrained on appropriate terms and conditions. If the disposition has occurred the debtor or any person entitled to notification or whose security interest has been made known to the secured party prior to the disposition has a right to recover from the secured party any loss caused by a failure to comply with the provisions of this chapter.

(2) The fact that a better price could have been obtained by a sale at a different time or in a different method from that selected by the secured party is not of itself sufficient to establish that the sale was not made in a commercially reasonable manner. If the secured party either sells the collateral in the usual manner in any recognized market therefor or if he sells at the price current in such market at the time of his sale or if he has otherwise sold in conformity with reasonable commercial practices among dealers in the type of property sold he has sold in a commercially reasonable manner. The principles stated in the two preceding sentences with respect to sales also apply as may be appropriate to other types of disposition. A disposition which has been approved in any judicial proceeding or by any bona fide creditors' committee or representative of creditors shall conclusively be deemed to be commercially reasonable, but this sentence does not indicate that any such approval must be obtained in any case nor does it indicate that any disposition not so approved is not commercially reasonable. *(Stats.1963, c. 819, § 9507.)*

California Code Comment
By John A. Bohn and Charles J. Williams

Prior California Law

1. This section is new statutory law. Under prior California law, the mortgagee's failure to follow the statutory procedure in dealing with collateral could be a conversion. Metheny v. Davis, 107 Cal.App. 137, 290 Pac. 91 (1930). This may also have been true in the case of a trust receipt. Former Civil Code § 3016.2(3)(c).

2. Under prior California law in the case of a pledge, the pledgee was under a duty to act in good faith and to make reasonable efforts to obtain the best price. Hudgens v. Chamberlain, 161 Cal. 710, 120 Pac. 422 (1911).

3. In connection with a proposal to delete this section, the Marsh and Warren Report explains the background and effect of the section:

"Subsection [subdivision] (1) of this Section sets forth the remedies available to the debtor and other creditors in cases where the secured party violates the provisions of Chapter [Division] 9 in disposing of collateral. It grants to debtors a remedy that can be applied prospectively before the secured party has completed the unreasonable disposition. It also provides for damages in cases where the unreasonable disposition has already occurred, and provides for a minimum recovery when consumer goods are involved.

"The minimum recovery provided in consumer goods cases is the amount of the finance charge plus 10 per cent of the principal amount of the debt. This compares with the provision in the Uniform Conditional Sales Act allowing the buyer to recover from a seller who has violated the act "one-fourth of the sum of all payments which have been made under the contract, with interest." (U.C.S.A. § 25). The penalty set out in the Unruh Act in CC § 1812.7 bars the person violating the act from recovering any finance charge and grants the buyer the right to recover the amount of such charges already paid by the buyer. CC § 1812.9 allows the buyer to recover treble the finance charges contracted for in cases where there is a willful violation of certain provisions of the Unruh Act. CC § 1812.6 imposes criminal penalties on willful violators of the Unruh Act.

"Another statute to be compared with the Code is the Motor Vehicle Conditional Sales Act. CC § 2982(e) and (f) provide that for the violation of certain parts of that act, the buyer may recover from the seller or holder the total amount he has paid on the contract balance. The California courts have held that under these provisions the buyer gets his money back and can keep the vehicle without offset or allowance for its use. This is probably the harshest penalty for violation of such a statute in the nation.

"These comparisons have been drawn to show (1) that statutes dealing with the disposition of collateral by secured parties ordinarily provide for penalties for violations, and (2) that the Code penalty is a moderate sanction. Since the California Bankers Commission proposal would leave the debtor with no statutory remedy at all for violations of the provisions of Chapter [Division], its rejection is recommended.

. . . .

"Subdivision (2) of this Section is an explanation of what types of disposition of collateral are to be considered commercially reasonable.

This subdivision is an important elaboration of the theory of the draftsmen of the Code that the law should 'encourage disposition [of collateral] by private sale through regular commercial channels.'" Sixth Progress Report to the Legislature by Senate Fact Finding Committee on Judiciary (1959–1961) Part 1, The Uniform Commercial Code, pp. 590–591.

4. The relation between consumer protection statutes such as the Unruh Act and the Commercial Code was considered but, as finally adopted, the Code does not apply in this area of retail installment sales. Professors Marsh and Warren recommended the adoption of one set of rules:

"It is recommended that the following sections of the Unruh Act and the Motor Vehicle Conditional Sales Act be repealed by this Section: CC §§ 1812.2, 1812.3, 1812.4, 1812.5, and CC § 2982(g). . . .

"The repeal of these provisions of the Unruh Act and the Motor Vehicle Act is suggested on three grounds:

"(1) Much confusion would result in having three statutes with different provisions covering the same problem. Businessmen and lawyers would have to familiarize themselves with three sets of rules for the disposition of collateral upon default by a debtor. This, in itself, is undesirable, but perhaps even more difficult is the task of determining which transactions are covered by each of the statutes. In every case of default by a debtor who has given a security interest in a chattel, the secured party would have to decide first whether the transaction fell within the Unruh Act (if non-vehicular chattels were involved) or Motor Vehicle Act; if not, then Chapter 9 of the Code would govern.

"(2) There is no cogent reason for having different sets of rules covering what is essentially the same problem, i.e., how to protect the rights of both the secured party and the debtor when the former forecloses. If the provisions covering this matter are left in the Unruh Act and Motor Vehicle Act, there will be entirely different rules governing the debtor's default depending, for example, on whether the security interest he gave in his furniture was a purchase money security interest (covered by the Unruh Act) or whether the security interest was given on furniture already owned by the debtor (not covered by the Unruh Act, thus governed by Chapter 9). The secured party's rights upon default by the debtor should not vary depending on whether the security interest was a purchase money interest or not.

"(3) Chapter 9 (amended as suggested above) is better legislation on the question of disposition of collateral than is the Unruh Act. The Motor Vehicle Act at present has only fragmentary coverage of the problem, but it is expected that a new motor vehicle retail installment sales act is to be presented to the Legislature in 1961 which will cover this matter in detail. It is, of course, impossible to predict what this statute will provide." Sixth Progress Report to the Legislature by Senate Fact Finding Committee on Judiciary (1959–1961) Part 1, The Uniform Commercial Code, pp. 611–612.

A discussion and analysis of the effect of the Commercial Code on the Unruh Act is contained in 8 UCLA L.Rev. 806, 965–968:

"California has changed significantly Part [Chapter] 5 of Article [Division] 9 by excluding from its scope security agreements in regard to sale of consumer goods. Section 9–203 [9203] specifies that in the case of a conflict between Article [Division] 9 and any statute regulating retail installment sales, the local statute is to control. A note appended to the section in the official version states that any provisions in such act covering filing or default should be repealed. Despite this suggestion, Part [Chapter] 5 has been modified so that the Unruh Act will govern default remedies in regard to consumer goods.

"Retail installment sales acts are designed to protect the buyer from the unequal bargaining power which normally exists between retailer and consumer. On the other hand, the policy of Part [Chapter] 5 is to provide simple, efficient remedies producing the maximum realization upon the collateral so that credit will not only be easier but cheaper to procure. While not necessarily inconsistent, these policies have different goals for which the legislature requires different sets of rules. Although it is the Unruh Act which is designed to protect consumers, surprisingly enough it does not afford as much protection as the Code which, while not so directed, also recognizes the need of the consumer.

"a. *Modified Election Doctrine Preserved.* Although consistently attacked by writers in the field, the legislature, in the Unruh Act, preserved the election of remedies doctrine in a modified form. The secured party must elect either to sue for the price or to repossess the goods. However, the old rule was changed to the extent that if the goods are repossessed and sold, the secured party may then maintain an action for any resulting deficiency.

"Since an action for the price means that the secured party will not be able to repossess the property in order to satisfy the judgment, repossession is the remedy favored by creditors. By repossession, the secured party need not worry about satisfying a judgment against an insolvent debtor. Moreover, he will be able to claim a deficiency if the property sold does not satisfy the obligation.

"b. *Forfeiture.* Under the Unruh Act the secured party may also notify the debtor that he intends to retain the collateral in satisfaction of the obligation. The debtor then has 10 days in which to redeem the property. Since the debtor has just defaulted, his financial condition is likely to be such that it will be difficult to redeem the collateral and to prevent title to it from vesting in the secured party. This result obtains regardless of the size of the debtor's equity in the property; thus it is not difficult to conjure up a situation in which the procedure would work a severe forfeiture.

"Section 9–501 [9501] of the Code specifies that the rights and remedies under Part [Chapter] 5 are cumulative. Hence the secured party does not run the risk of losing his security interest by suing for the price. Consequently, if the secured party pursues this course of action the debtor might have time to raise the price with which to redeem the security during the pendency of the litigation. Moreover, the harshness of the forfeiture possibility is abrogated by section 9–505 [9505] (1) which, unfortunately, the legislature rejected in its entirety. Section 9–505(1) [9505(1)] provides that if the debtor has paid 60% of the price or obligation then, unless he had signed a statement after default renouncing or modifying his rights, disposition of the collateral must be made under section 19504 [9504] within 90 days.

"c. *Repossession and Resale.* If the collateral is repossessed and sold under the Unruh Act, Civil Code section 1812.2 specifies that the sale must be a public one. Since public sales are perfunctory in nature and often take place with no one but the creditor bidding, there is no reason why the goods may not be sold at a private sale through normal commercial channels. The Unruh Act simply does not recognize the economic reality that private sales through normal business channels may result in larger realization upon the collateral.

"The secured party also wants the maximum return upon the collateral rather than run the risk of a deficiency against an insolvent debtor. Part [Chapter] 5 provides for private as well as public sales and since the obligations of good faith and diligence are imposed upon the secured party, the consumer-debtor is not only adequately protected but may benefit by the private sale.

"The only significant protection to the consumer under the Unruh Act which is missing from the Code is that if repossession is taken by the secured party when 80% or more has been paid upon the price or the obligation, the debtor can not be held for a deficiency. However, this does not protect the debtor's equity nor prevent the possibility of forfeiture.

"Retail installment sales legislation is designed to protect the unwary buyer. But under the Unruh Act the consumer is given less protection than his wary businessman counterpart is given by the UCC. Such a result is not rationally justifiable and warrants legislative re-examination." 8 UCLA L.Rev. 806, 965–968.

Changes from U.C.C. (1962 Official Text)

5. The last sentence in subdivision (1) of section 9–507 of the Official Text is omitted in the California Version. This sentence reads:

"If the collateral is consumer goods, the debtor has a right to recover in any event an amount not less than the credit service charge plus ten per cent of the principal amount of the debt or the time price differential plus ten per cent of the cash price."

This change was made to conform to the deletion from the scope and coverage of Division 9 of consumer goods.

Uniform Commercial Code Comment
Prior Uniform Statutory Provision:
None.
Purposes:
1. The principal limitation on the secured party's right to dispose of collateral is the requirement that he proceed in good faith (Section 1–203) and in a commercially reasonable manner see Section 9–504. In the case where he proceeds, or is about to proceed, in a contrary manner, it is vital both to the debtor and other creditors to provide a remedy for the failure to comply with the statutory duty. This remedy

will be of particular importance when it is applied prospectively before the unreasonable disposition has been concluded. This section therefore provides that a secured party proposing to dispose of collateral in an unreasonable manner, may, by court order, be restrained from doing so, and such an order might appropriately provide either that he proceed with the sale or other disposition under specified terms and conditions, or that the sale be made by a representative of creditors where insolvency proceedings have been instituted. The section further provides for damages where the unreasonable disposition has been concluded, and, in the case of consumer goods, states a minimum recovery.

A case may be put in which the liquidation value of an insolvent estate would be enhanced by disposing of all the debtor's property (including that subject to a security interest) in the liquidation proceeding and in which, if a secured party repossesses and sells that part of the property which he holds as collateral, the remainder will have little or no resale value. In such a case the question may arise whether a particular court has the power to control the manner of disposition, although reasonable in other respects, in order to preserve the estate for the benefit of creditors. Such a power is no doubt inherent in a Federal bankruptcy court, and perhaps also in other courts of equity administering insolvent estates. Traditionally it was not exercised where the secured party claimed under a title retention device, such as conditional sale or trust receipt. See In re Lake's Laundry, Inc., 79 F.2d 326 (2d Cir. 1935) and the remarks of Clark, J., concurring, in In re White Plains Ice Service, Inc., 109 F.2d 913 (2d Cir. 1940). It has been held that distinctions in results based on these distinctions in form have been made obsolete by this Article. In re Yale Express System, Inc., 370 F.2d 433 (2d Cir. 1966), 384 F.2d 990 (2d Cir. 1967).

2. In view of the remedies provided the debtor and other creditors in subsection (1) when a secured party does not dispose of collateral in a commercially reasonable manner, it is of great importance to make clear what types of disposition are to be considered commercially reasonable, and in an appropriate case to give the secured party means of getting, by court order or negotiation with a creditors' committee or a representative of creditors, approval of a proposed method of disposition as a commercially reasonable one. Subsection (2) states rules to assist in the determination, and provides for such advance approval in appropriate situations. One recognized method of disposing of repossessed collateral is for the secured party to sell the collateral to or through a dealer—a method which in the long run may realize better average returns since the secured party does not usually maintain his own facilities for making such sales. Such a method of sale, fairly conducted, is recognized as commercially reasonable under the second sentence of subsection (2). However, none of the specific methods of disposition set forth in subsection (2) is to be regarded as either required or exclusive, provided only that the disposition made or about to be made by the secured party is commercially reasonable.

Cross References:
Point 1: Sections 1–203, 9–202 and 9–504.

Definitional Cross References:
"Collateral". Section 9–105.
"Consumer goods". Section 9–109.
"Creditor". Section 1–201.
"Debtor". Section 9–105.
"Knows". Section 1–201.
"Notification". Section 1–201.
"Person". Section 1–201.
"Representative". Section 1–201.
"Rights". Section 1–201.
"Secured party". Section 9–105.
"Security interest". Section 1–201.

Cross References

Collateral,
Disposition in commercially reasonable manner, see Commercial Code § 9504.
Title immaterial, see Commercial Code § 9202.
Good faith, enforcement of contract, see Commercial Code § 1203.
Injunction, see Civil Code § 3420 et seq.; Code of Civil Procedure § 525 et seq.
Where collateral not owned by debtor owner's right to injunctive relief, see Commercial Code § 9112.

§ 9508. Validity of Renunciation or Modification of Rights by Debtor

No renunciation or modification by the debtor of any of his rights under this chapter as to consumer goods shall be valid or enforceable unless the renunciation or modification is in consideration of a waiver by the secured party of any right to a deficiency on the debt. *(Added by Stats.1974, c. 997, p. 2141, § 47.5, eff. Jan. 1, 1976.)*

Division 10

PERSONAL PROPERTY LEASES

Chapter	Section
1. General Provisions	10101
2. Formation and Construction of Lease Contract	10201
3. Effect of Lease Contract	10301
4. Performance of Leased Contract: Repudiated, Substituted, and Excused	10401
5. Default	10501
6. Transition Provisions	10600

Application

Application of Division 10, see § 10600.

CHAPTER 1. GENERAL PROVISIONS

Section
10101. Short Title.
10102. Scope.
10103. Definitions and Index of Definitions.
10104. Leases Subject to Other Statutes.
10105. Territorial Application of Article to Goods Covered by Certificate of Title.
10106. Limitation on Power of Parties to Consumer Lease to Choose Applicable Law and Judicial Forum.
10107. Waiver or Renunciation of Claim or Right After Default.

Cross References

Consumers Legal Remedies Act, see Civil Code § 1750 et seq.
Hiring of personal property, see Civil Code § 1955 et seq.
Personal property, law of domicile, see Civil Code § 946.
Vehicle Leasing Act, see Civil Code § 2985.7 et seq.

§ 10101. Short Title

This division shall be known and may be cited as the Uniform Commercial Code—Leases. *(Added by Stats. 1988, c. 1359, § 5, operative Jan. 1, 1990.)*

California Comment
Report of the Assembly Committee on Judiciary
August 15, 1989

There are several reasons for codifying the law with respect to leases of goods. An analysis of the case law as it applies to leases of goods suggests at least three significant issues to be resolved by codification. First, what is a lease? It is necessary to define lease to determine whether a transaction creates a lease or a security interest disguised as a lease. If the transaction creates a security interest disguised as a lease, the lessor will be required to file a financing statement or take other action to perfect its interest in the goods against third parties. There is no such requirement with respect to leases. Yet the distinction between a lease and a security interest disguised as a lease is not clear. Second, will the lessor be deemed to have made warranties to the lessee? If the transaction is a sale the express and implied warranties of Division 2 of the Uniform Commercial Code apply. However, the warranty law with respect to leases is uncertain. Third, what remedies are available to the lessor upon the lessee's default? If the transaction is a security interest disguised as a lease, the answer is stated in Chapter 5 of the Division on Secured Transactions (Division 9). There is no clear answer with respect to leases.

There are reasons to codify the law with respect to leases of goods in addition to those suggested by a review of the reported cases. The answer to this important question should not be limited to the issues raised in these cases. Is it not also proper to determine the remedies available to the lessee upon the lessor's default? It is, but that issue is not reached through a review of the reported cases. This is only one of the many issues presented in structuring, negotiating and documenting a lease of goods.

After it was decided to proceed with the codification project, the drafting committee of the National Conference of Commissioners on Uniform State Laws looked for a statutory analogue, gradually narrowing the focus to the Division on Sales (Division 2) and the Division on Secured Transactions (Division 9). A review of the literature with respect to the sale of goods reveals that Division 2 is predicated upon certain assumptions: Parties to the sales transaction frequently are without counsel; the agreement of the parties often is oral or evidenced by scant writings; obligations between the parties are bilateral; and applicable law is influenced by the need to preserve freedom of contract. A review of the literature with respect to personal property security law reveals that Division 9 is predicated upon very different assumptions: Parties to a secured transaction regularly are represented by counsel; the agreement of the parties frequently is reduced to a writing, extensive in scope; the obligations between the parties are essentially unilateral; and applicable law seriously limits freedom of contract.

The lease is closer in spirit and form to the sale of goods than to the creation of a security interest. While parties to a lease are sometimes represented by counsel and their agreement is often reduced to a writing, the obligations of the parties are bilateral and the common law of leasing is dominated by the need to preserve freedom of contract. Thus the drafting committee concluded that Division 2 was the appropriate statutory analogue.

The drafting committee then identified and resolved several issues critical to codification:

Scope: The scope of the Division was limited to leases (Section 10102). There was no need to include leases intended as security, *i.e.*, security interests disguised as leases, as they are adequately treated in Division 9. Further, even if leases intended as security were included, the need to preserve the distinction would remain, as policy suggests treatment significantly different from that accorded leases.

Definition of Lease: Lease was defined to exclude leases intended as security (paragraph (j), subdivision (1), Section 10101). Given the litigation to date a revised definition of security interest was suggested for inclusion in the Code. (subdivision (37), Section 1201). This revision sharpens the distinction between leases and security interests disguised as leases.

Filing: The lessor was not required to file a financing statement against the lessee or take any other action to protect the lessor's interest in the goods (Section 10301). The refined definition of security interest will more clearly signal the need to file to potential lessors of goods. Those lessors who are concerned will file a protective financing statement (Section 9408).

Warranties: All of the express and implied warranties of the Division on Sales (Division 2) were included (Sections 10210 through 10216), revised to reflect differences in lease transactions. The lease of goods is sufficiently similar to the sale of goods to justify this decision. Further, many courts have reached the same decision.

Certificate of Title Laws: Many leasing transactions involve goods subject to certificate of title statutes. To avoid conflict with those statutes, this Division is subject to them (paragraph (b), subdivision (1), Section 10104).

Consumer Leases: Many leasing transactions involve parties subject to consumer protection laws and statutes. To avoid conflict with those laws and statutes this Division is subject to them (paragraphs (a) and (d), subdivision (1), Section 10104). Further, certain consumer protections have been incorporated in the Division.

Finance Leases: Certain leasing transactions substitute the seller of the goods for the lessor as the party responsible to the lessee with respect to warranties and the like. The definition of finance lease (paragraph (g), subdivision (1), Section 10103) was developed to describe these transactions. Various sections of the Division implement the substitution of the seller for the lessor, including Sections 10209 and 10407.

Sale and Leaseback: Sale and leaseback transactions are becoming increasingly common. A number of state statutes (e.g., Section 3440, Civil Code) treat transactions where possession is retained by the seller as fraudulent *per se* or *prima facie* fraudulent. That position is not balanced and thus is changed by the Division "if the buyer bought for value and in good faith" (subdivision (3), Section 10308).

Remedies: The Division has not only provided for lessor's remedies upon default by the lessee (Sections 10523 through 10531), but also for lessee's remedies upon default by the lessor (Sections 10508 through 10522). This is a significant departure from Division 9, which provides remedies only for the secured party upon default by the debtor. This difference is compelled by the bilateral nature of the obligations between the parties to a lease.

Damages: Many leasing transactions are predicated on the parties' ability to stipulate an appropriate measure of damages in the event of default. The rule with respect to sales of goods (Section 2718) is not sufficiently flexible to accommodate this practice. Consistent with the common law emphasis upon freedom to contract, the Division has created a revised rule that allows greater flexibility with respect to leases of goods (subdivision (1), Section 10504).

This Division is a revision of the Uniform Personal Property Leasing Act, which was approved by the National Conference of Commissioners on Uniform State Laws in August, 1985. However, it was believed that the subject matter of the Uniform Personal Property Leasing Act would be better treated as an article of this Code. Thus, although the Conference promulgated the Uniform Personal Property Leasing Act as a Uniform Law, activity was modest to allow time to restate the Uniform Personal Property Leasing Act as Division 10.

In August, 1986 the Conference approved and recommended this Division (including conforming amendments to Division 1 and Division 9) for promulgation as an amendment to this Code. In December, 1986 the Council of the American Law Institute approved and recommended this Division (including conforming amendments to Division 1 and Division 9), with comments, for promulgation as an amendment to this Code. In March, 1987 the Permanent Editorial Board for the Uniform Commercial Code approved and recommended this Division (including conforming amendments to Division 1 and Division 9), with comments, for promulgation as an amendment to this Code. In May, 1987 the American Law Institute approved and recommended this Division (including conforming amendments to Division 1 and Division 9), with comments, for promulgation as an amendment to this Code. In August, 1987 the Conference confirmed its approval of the final text of this Division.

The Division on Sales provided a useful point of reference for codifying the law of leases. Many of the provisions of that Division were carried over, changed to reflect differences in style, leasing terminology or leasing practices. Thus, the comments to those sections of Division 2 whose provisions were carried over are incorporated by reference in Division 10, as well; further, any case law interpreting those provisions should be viewed as persuasive but not binding on a court when deciding a similar issue with respect to leases. Any change in the sequence that has been made when carrying over a provision from Division 2 should be viewed as a matter of style, not substance. This is not to suggest that in other instances Division 10 did not also incorporate substantially revised provisions of Division 2, Division 9 or otherwise where the revision was driven by a concern over the substance; but for the lack of a mandate, the drafting committee would have made the same or a similar change in the statutory analogue. Those sections in Division 10 include Section 10104; Section 10105; Section 10106; subdivisions (2) and (4) of Section 10108; subdivision (2) of Section 10109; Section 10108; subdivision (2) and paragraph (a) of subdivision (3) of Section 10214; Section 10216; Section 10303; Section 10306; Section 10503; paragraph (b) of subdivision (3) of Section 10504; subdivision (2) of Section 10506; and Section 10515. For lack of relevance or significance not all of the provisions of Division 2 were incorporated in Division 10.

This codification was greatly influenced by the fundamental tenet of the common law as it has developed with respect to leases of goods: freedom of the parties to contract. Note that, like all other Divisions of this Code, the principles of construction and interpretation contained in Division 1 are applicable throughout Division 10 (subdivision (4), Section 10103). These principles include the ability of the parties to vary the effect of the provisions of Division 10, subject to certain limitations including those that relate to the obligations of good faith, diligence, reasonableness and care (subdivision (3), Section 1102). Consistent with those principles no negative inference is to be drawn by the episodic use of the phrase "unless otherwise agreed" in certain provisions of Division 10. Subdivision (4), Section 1102. Indeed, the contrary is true, as the general rule in the Code, including this Division, is that the effect of the Code's provisions may be varied by agreement. Subdivision (3), Section 1102. This conclusion follows even where the statutory analogue contains the phrase and the correlative provision in Division 10 does not.

§ 10102. Scope

This division applies to any transaction, regardless of form, that creates a lease. *(Added by Stats.1988, c. 1359, § 5, operative Jan. 1, 1990.)*

California Comment
Report of the Assembly Committee on Judiciary
August 15, 1989

Uniform Statutory Source: Section 9–102(1). Throughout this Division, unless otherwise stated, references to "Section" are to other sections of this Code.

Changes: Substantially revised.

Purposes: This Division governs transactions as diverse as the lease of a hand tool to an individual for a few hours and the leveraged lease of a complex line of industrial equipment to a multi-national organization for a number of years.

To achieve that end it was necessary to provide that this Division applies to any transaction, regardless of form, that creates a lease. Since lease is defined as a transfer of an interest in goods (paragraph (j), subdivision (1), Section 10103) and goods is defined to include fixtures (paragraph (h), subdivision (1), Section 10103), application is limited to the extent the transaction relates to goods, including fixtures. Further, since the definition of lease does not include a sale (subdivision (1), Section 2106) or retention or creation of a security interest (subdivision (37), Section 1201), application is further limited; sales and security interests are governed by other Divisions of this Code.

Finally, in recognition of the diversity of the transactions to be governed, the sophistication of many of the parties to these transactions, and the common law tradition as it applies to the bailment for hire or lease, freedom of contract has been preserved. DeKoven, Proceedings After Default by the Lessee Under a True Lease of Equipment, in 1C P. Coogan, W. Hogan, D. Vagts, *Secured Transactions Under the Uniform Commercial Code*, § 29B.02[2] (1986). Thus, despite the extensive regulatory scheme established by this Division, the parties to a lease will be able to create private rules to govern their transaction. Subdivision (4), Section 10103 and subdivision (3), Section 1102. However, there are special rules in this Division governing consumer leases, as well as other state and federal statutes, that may further limit freedom of contract with respect to consumer leases.

A court may apply this Division by analogy to any transaction, regardless of form, that creates a lease of personal property other than goods, taking into account the expressed intentions of the parties to the transaction and any differences between a lease of goods and a lease of other property. Such application has precedent as the provisions of the Division on Sales (Division 2) have been applied by analogy to leases of goods. *E.g.,* Hawkland, *The Impact of the Uniform Commercial Code on Equipment Leasing*, 1972 Ill. L.F. 446; Murray, *Under the Spreading Analogy of Article 2 of the Uniform Commercial Code*, 39 Fordham L.Rev. 447 (1971). Whether such application would be appropriate for other bailments of personal property, gratuitous or for hire, should be determined by the facts of each case. See *Mieske v. Bartell Drug Co.*, 92 Wash.2d 40, 46–48, 593 P.2d 1308, 1312 (1979).

Further, parties to a transaction creating a lease of personal property other than goods, or a bailment of personal property may provide by agreement that this Division applies. Upholding the parties' choice is consistent with the spirit of this Division.

Cross References:

Subdivision (3), Section 10102; subdivision (37), Section 1201; Division 2, esp. subdivision (1), Section 2106; paragraph (h), subdivision (1), Section 10103; paragraph (j), subdivision (1), Section 10103; and subdivision (4), Section 10103.

Definitional Cross Reference:

"Lease". Paragraph (j), subdivision (1), Section 10103.

Cross References

Security interest, general definitions, see Commercial Code § 1201.

§ 10103. Definitions and Index of Definitions

(a) In this division, unless the context otherwise requires:

(1) "Buyer in ordinary course of business" means a person who, in good faith and without knowledge that the sale to him or her is in violation of the ownership rights or security interest or leasehold interest of a third party in the goods, buys in ordinary course from a person in the business of selling goods of that kind, but does not include a pawnbroker. "Buying" may be for cash or by exchange of other property or on secured or unsecured credit and includes receiving goods or documents of title under a preexisting contract for sale but does not include a transfer in bulk or as security for or in total or partial satisfaction of a money debt.

(2) "Cancellation" occurs when either party puts an end to the lease contract for default by the other party.

(3) "Commercial unit" means such a unit of goods as by commercial usage is a single whole for purposes of lease and division of which materially impairs its character or value on the market or in use. A commercial unit may be a single article, as a machine, or a set of articles, as a suite of furniture or a line of machinery, or a quantity, as a gross or carload, or any other unit treated in use or in the relevant market as a single whole.

(4) "Conforming" goods or performance under a lease contract means goods or performance that are in accordance with the obligations under the lease contract.

(5) "Consumer lease" means a lease that a lessor regularly engaged in the business of leasing or selling makes to a lessee who is * * * an individual and who takes under the lease primarily for a personal, family, or household purpose.

(6) "Fault" means wrongful act, omission, breach, or default.

(7) "Finance lease" means a lease * * * with respect to which (A) the lessor does not select, manufacture, or supply the goods, (B) the lessor acquires the goods or the right to possession and use of the goods in connection with the lease, and * * * (C) one of the following occurs:

(i) The lessee receives a copy of the contract * * * by which the lessor acquired the goods or the right to possession and use of the goods * * * before signing the lease contract * * *.

(ii) The lessee's approval of the contract * * * by which the lessor acquired the goods or the right to possession and use of the goods is a condition to effectiveness of the lease contract.

(iii) The lessee, before signing the lease contract, receives an accurate and complete statement designating the promises and warranties, and any disclaimers of warranties, limitations or modifications of remedies, or liquidated damages, including those of a third party, such as the manufacturer of the goods, provided to the lessor by the person supplying the goods in connection with or as part of the contract by which the lessor acquired the goods or the right to possession and use of the goods.

(iv) The lessor * * *, before the lessee signs the lease contract, informs the lessee in writing (aa) of the identity of the * * * person supplying the goods to the lessor, unless the lessee has selected * * * that person and directed the lessor to acquire the goods * * * or the right to possession and use of the goods from that person, (bb) * * * that the lessee is entitled under this division to the promises and warranties, including those of any third party, provided to the lessor by the person supplying the goods in connection with or as part of the contract by which the lessor acquired the goods or the right to possession and use of the goods, and (cc) that the lessee may communicate with the person supplying the goods to the lessor and receive an accurate and complete statement of those promises and warranties, including any disclaimers and limitations of them or of remedies.

(8) "Goods" means all things that are movable at the time of identification to the lease contract, or are fixtures (Section 10309), but the term does not include money, documents, instruments, accounts, chattel paper, general intangibles, or minerals or the like, including oil and gas, before extraction. The term also includes the unborn young of animals.

(9) "Installment lease contract" means a lease contract that authorizes or requires the delivery of goods in separate lots to be separately accepted, even though the lease contract contains a clause "each delivery is a separate lease" or its equivalent.

(10) "Lease" means a transfer of the right to possession and use of goods for a term in return for consideration, but a sale, including a sale on approval or a sale or return, or retention or creation of a security interest is not a lease. Unless the context clearly indicates otherwise, the term includes a sublease.

(11) "Lease agreement" means the bargain, with respect to the lease, of the lessor and the lessee in fact as found in their language or by implication from other circumstances including course of dealing or usage of trade or course of performance as provided in this division. Unless the context clearly indicates otherwise, the term includes a sublease agreement.

(12) "Lease contract" means the total legal obligation that results from the lease agreement as affected

by this division and any other applicable rules of law. Unless the context clearly indicates otherwise, the term includes a sublease contract.

(13) "Leasehold interest" means the interest of the lessor or the lessee under a lease contract.

(14) "Lessee" means a person who acquires the right to possession and use of goods under a lease. Unless the context clearly indicates otherwise, the term includes a sublessee.

(15) "Lessee in ordinary course of business" means a person who, in good faith and without knowledge that the lease to him or her is in violation of the ownership rights or security interest or leasehold interest of a third party in the goods, leases in ordinary course from a person in the business of selling or leasing goods of that kind, but does not include a pawnbroker. "Leasing" may be for cash or by exchange of other property or on secured or unsecured credit and includes receiving goods or documents of title under a preexisting lease contract but does not include a transfer in bulk or as security for or in total or partial satisfaction of a money debt.

(16) "Lessor" means a person who transfers the right to possession and use of goods under a lease. Unless the context clearly indicates otherwise, the term includes a sublessor.

(17) "Lessor's residual interest" means the lessor's interest in the goods after expiration, termination, or cancellation of the lease contract.

(18) "Lien" means a charge against or interest in goods to secure payment of a debt or performance of an obligation, but the term does not include a security interest.

(19) "Lot" means a parcel or a single article that is the subject matter of a separate lease or delivery, whether or not it is sufficient to perform the lease contract.

(20) "Merchant lessee" means a lessee that is a merchant with respect to goods of the kind subject to the lease.

(21) "Present value" means the amount as of a date certain of one or more sums payable in the future, discounted to the date certain. The discount is determined by the interest rate specified by the parties if the rate was not manifestly unreasonable at the time the transaction was entered into; otherwise, the discount is determined by a commercially reasonable rate that takes into account the facts and circumstances of each case at the time the transaction was entered into.

(22) "Purchase" includes taking by sale, lease, mortgage, security interest, pledge, gift, or any other voluntary transaction creating an interest in goods.

(23) "Sublease" means a lease of goods the right to possession and use of which was acquired by the lessor as a lessee under an existing lease.

(24) "Supplier" means a person from whom a lessor buys or leases goods to be leased under a finance lease.

(25) "Supply contract" means a contract under which a lessor buys or leases goods to be leased.

(26) "Termination" occurs when either party pursuant to a power created by agreement or law puts an end to the lease contract otherwise than for default.

(b) Other definitions applying to this division and the sections in which they appear are:

"Accessions." Subdivision (a) of Section 10310.

"Construction mortgage." Paragraph (4) of subdivision (a) of Section 10309.

"Encumbrance." Paragraph (5) of subdivision (a) of Section 10309.

"Fixtures." Paragraph (1) of subdivision (a) of Section 10309.

"Fixture filing." Paragraph (2) of subdivision (a) of Section 10309.

"Purchase money lease." Paragraph (3) of subdivision (a) of Section 10309.

(c) The following definitions in other divisions apply to this division:

"Account." Section 9106.

"Between merchants." Subdivision (3) of Section 2104.

"Buyer." Paragraph (a) of subdivision (1) of Section 2103.

"Chattel paper." Paragraph (b) of subdivision (1) of Section 9105.

"Consumer goods." Subdivision (1) of Section 9109.

"Document." Paragraph (f) of subdivision (1) of Section 9105.

"Entrusting." Subdivision (3) of Section 2403.

"General intangibles." Section 9106.

"Good faith." Paragraph (b) of subdivision (1) of Section 2103.

"Instrument." Paragraph (i) of subdivision (1) of Section 9105.

"Merchant." Subdivision (1) of Section 2104.

"Mortgage." Paragraph (j) of subdivision (1) of Section 9105.

"Pursuant to commitment." Paragraph (k) of subdivision (1) of Section 9105.

"Receipt." Paragraph (c) of subdivision (1) of Section 2103.

"Sale." Subdivision (1) of Section 2106.

"Sale on approval." Section 2326.

"Sale or return." Section 2326.

"Seller." Paragraph (d) of subdivision (1) of Section 2103.

(d) In addition, Division 1 * * * contains general definitions and principles of construction and interpretation applicable throughout this division. (Added by Stats.1988, c. 1359, § 5, operative Jan. 1, 1990. Amended by Stats.1988, c. 1368, § 12.2, operative Jan. 1, 1990; Stats.1991, c. 111 (S.B.972), § 3, eff. July 15, 1991.)

California Comment
Report of the Assembly Committee on Judiciary
August 15, 1989

(a) "Buyer in ordinary course of business". Subdivision (9), Section 1201.

(b) "Cancellation". Subdivision (4), Section 2106.

(c) "Commercial unit". Subdivision (6), Section 2105.

(d) "Conforming". Subdivision (2), Section 2106.

(e) "Consumer lease". New. This Division includes a subset of rules that applies only to consumer leases. Section 10106; subdivision (2), Section 10108; subdivision (4), Section 10108; subdivision (2), Section 10109; Section 10221; Section 10309; Section 10406; Section 10407; paragraph (b), subdivision (3), Section 10504; and paragraph (b), subdivision (3), Section 10516.

For a transaction to qualify as a consumer lease it must first qualify as a lease. Paragraph (j), subdivision (1), Section 10103. Note that this Division regulates the transactional elements of a lease, including a consumer lease; consumer protection statutes — present and future — are unaffected by this Division. Paragraphs (a) and (d), subdivision (1), Section 10104.

This definition is modeled after the definition of consumer lease in the Vehicle Leasing Act, Chapter 2d (commencing with Section 2985.7) of Title 14 of Part 4 of Division 3 of the Civil Code. The lessor can be a person regularly engaged either in the business of leasing or of selling goods, the lease need not be for a term exceeding four months, and a lease primarily for an agricultural purpose is not covered.

This definition focuses on the parties as well as the transaction. If a lease is within this definition, the lessor must be regularly engaged in the business of leasing or selling, and the lessee must be an individual not an organization; note that a lease to two or more individuals having a common interest through marriage or the like should not be considered excluded as a lease to an organization under subdivision (28) of Section 1201. The lessee must take the interest primarily for a personal, family or household purpose.

(f) "Fault". Subdivision (16), Section 1201.

(g) "Finance Lease". New. This Division includes a subset of rules that applies only to finance leases. Section 10209; subdivision (2), Section 10211; subdivision (1), Section 10212; Section 10213; subdivision (1), Section 10219; paragraph (a), subdivision (1), Section 10220; Section 10221; paragraph (c), Section 10405; Section 10407; subdivision (2), Section 10516; and paragraph (a), subdivision (1), Section 10517.

For a transaction to qualify as a finance lease it must first qualify as a lease. Paragraph (j), subdivision (1), Section 10103. Unless the lessor is comfortable that the transaction will qualify as a finance lease, the lease agreement should include provisions giving the lessor the benefits created by the subset of rules applicable to the transaction that qualifies as a finance lease under this Division.

A finance lease is the product of a three party transaction. The supplier manufactures or supplies the goods pursuant to the lessee's specification, perhaps even pursuant to a purchase order, sales agreement or lease agreement between the supplier and the lessee. After the prospective finance lease is negotiated, a purchase order, sales agreement, or lease agreement is entered into by the lessor (as buyer or prime lessee) or an existing order, agreement or lease is assigned by the lessee to the lessor, and the lessor and the lessee then enter into a lease or sublease of the goods. Due to the limited function usually performed by the lessor, the lessee looks almost entirely to the supplier for representations, covenants and warranties. Yet, this definition does not restrict the lessor's function solely to the supply of funds; if the lessor undertakes or performs other functions, express warranties, covenants and the common law will protect the lessee.

This definition focuses on the transaction, not the status of the parties; to avoid confusion it is important to note that in other contexts, *e.g.*, tax and accounting, the term finance lease has been used to connote different types of lease transactions, including leases that are disguised secured transactions. M. Rice, *Equipment Financing*, 62–71 (1981). A lessor who is a merchant with respect to goods of the kind subject to the lease may be a lessor under a finance lease. Many leases that are leases back to the seller of goods (subdivision (3), Section 10308) will be finance leases. This conclusion is easily demonstrated by a hypothetical. Assume that B has bought goods from C pursuant to a sales contract. After delivery to and acceptance of the goods by B, B negotiates to sell the goods to A and simultaneously to lease the goods back from A, on terms and conditions that, we assume, will qualify the transaction as a lease. Paragraph (j), subdivision (1), Section 10103. In documenting the sale and lease back, B assigns the original sales contract between B, as buyer, and C, as seller, to A. A review of these facts leads to the conclusion that the lease from A to B qualifies as a finance lease, as all three conditions of the definition are satisfied. Subparagraph (i) is satisfied as A, the lessor, had nothing to do with the selection, manufacture, or supply of the equipment. Subparagraph (ii) is satisfied as A, the lessor, bought the equipment at the same time that A leased the equipment to B, which certainly is in connection with the lease. Finally, subparagraph (iii) is satisfied as A entered into the sales contract with B at the same time that A leased the equipment back to B. B, the lessee, will have received a copy of the sales contract in a timely fashion.

Subparagraph (i) requires the lessor to remain outside the selection, manufacture and supply of the goods; that is the rationale for releasing the lessor from most of its traditional liability. The lessor is not prohibited from possession, maintenance or operation of the goods, as policy does not require such prohibition. To insure the lessee's reliance on the supplier, and not on the lessor, subparagraph (ii) requires that the goods (where the lessor is the buyer of the goods) or that the right to possession and use of the goods (where the lessor is the prime lessee and the sublessor of the goods) be acquired in connection with the lease (or sublease) to qualify as a finance lease. The scope of the phrase "in connection with" is to be developed by the courts, case by case. Finally, as the lessee generally relies almost entirely upon the supplier for representations, covenants and warranties with respect to the goods, subparagraph (iii) requires that (A) the lessee receive a copy of the supply contract on or before signing the lease contract, or (B) the lessee approve the supply contract as a condition to the effectiveness of the lease contract, or (C) the lessor identify the supplier, inform the lessee that he may have rights under the supply contract and advise the lessee to contact the supplier for a description of those rights or (D) the lease contract disclose all warranties and other rights provided to the lessee by the lessor and the supplier. Thus, even where oral supply orders or computer placed supply orders are compelled by custom and usage the transaction may still qualify as a finance lease if the lessee approves the supply contract before the lease contract is effective and such approval was a condition to the effectiveness of the lease contract.

With respect to clause (D), if the only warranty provided to the lessee is the manufacturer's standard warranty, a disclosure as required by federal law (Regulation M, 12 C.F.R. § 213.4(g)(7) (1986)) that these warranties shall be available to the lessee would be a sufficient disclosure of such warranties under clause (D).

If a transaction does not qualify as a finance lease, the parties may achieve the same result by agreement; no negative implications are to be drawn if the transaction does not qualify. Further, absent the application of special rules (fraud, duress, and the like), a lease that qualifies as a finance lease and is assigned by the lessor or the lessee to a third party does not lose its status as a finance lease under this Division. Finally, this Division creates no special rule where the lessor is an affiliate of the supplier; whether the transaction qualifies as a finance lease will be determined by the facts of each case.

(h) "Goods". Paragraph (h), subdivision (1), Section 9105. See subdivision (3) of Section 10103 for reference to the definition of "Accounts", "Chattel paper", "Documents", "General intangibles" and "Instruments". See Section 10217 for determination of the time and manner of identification. The definition of "goods" would include a mobilehome which is to be permanently attached to a foundation provided the mobilehome was movable at the time it was identified to the lease contract.

(i) "Installment lease contract". Subdivision (1), Section 2612.

(j) "Lease". New. There are several reasons to codify the law with respect to leases of goods. An analysis of the case law as it applies to leases of goods suggests at least several significant issues to be resolved by codification. First and foremost is the definition of a lease. It is necessary to define lease to determine whether a transaction creates a lease or a security interest disguised as a lease. If the transaction creates a security interest disguised as a lease, the transaction will be governed by the Division on Secured Transactions (Division 9) and the lessor will be required to file a financing statement or take other action to perfect its interest in the goods against third parties. There is no such requirement with respect to leases under the common law and, except with respect to leases of fixtures (Section 10309), this Division imposes no such requirement. Yet the distinction between a lease and a security interest disguised as a lease is not clear from the case law at the time of the promulgation of this Division. DeKoven, *Leases of Equipment: Puritan Leasing Company v. August, A Dangerous Decision*, 12 U.S.F.L.Rev. 257 (1978).

At common law a lease of personal property is a bailment for hire. While there are several definitions of bailment for hire, all require a thing to be let and a price for the letting. Thus, in modern terms and as provided in this definition, a lease is created when the lessee agrees to furnish consideration for the right to the possession and use of goods over a specified period of time. Mooney, *Personal Property Leasing: A Challenge*, 36 Bus.Law. 1605, 1607 (1981). Further, a lease is neither a sale (subdivision (1), Section 2106) nor a retention or creation of a security interest (subdivision (37), Section 1201). Due to extensive litigation to distinguish true leases from security interests, an amendment to subdivision (37) of Section 1201 has been promulgated with this Division to create a sharper distinction.

This section as well as subdivision (37) of Section 1201 must be examined to determine whether the transaction in question creates a lease or a security interest. The following hypotheticals indicate the perimeters of the issue. Assume that A has purchased a number of copying machines, new, for $1,000 each; the machines have an estimated useful economic life of three years. A Advertises that the machines are available to rent for a minimum of one month and that the monthly rental is $100.00. A intends to enter into leases where A provides all maintenance, without charge to the lessee. Further, the lessee will rent the machine, month to month, with no obligation to renew. At the end of the lease term the lessee will be obligated to return the machine to A's place of business. This transaction qualifies as a lease under the first half of the definition, for the transaction includes a transfer by A to a prospective lessee of possession and use of the machine for a stated term, month to month. The machines are goods (paragraph (h), subdivision (1), Section 10103). The lessee is obligated to pay consideration in return, $100.00 for each month of the term.

However, the second half of the definition provides that a sale or a security interest is not a lease. Since there is no passing of title, there is no sale. Subdivision (3), Section 10103 and subdivision (1), Section 2106. Under pre-Code security law this transaction would have created a bailment for hire or a true lease and not a conditional sale. *Da Rocha v. Macomber*, 330 Mass. 611, 614–15, 116 N.E.2d 139, 142 (1953). Under subdivision (37) of Section 1201, as amended with the promulgation of this Division, the same result would follow. While the lessee is obligated to pay rent for the one month term of the lease, one of the other four conditions of paragraph (b) of subdivision (37) of Section 1201 must be met and none is. The term of the lease is one month and the economic life of the machine is 36 months; thus, clause (i) of paragraph (b) of subdivision (37) of Section 1201 is not now satisfied. Considering the amount of the monthly rent, absent economic duress or coercion, the lessee is not bound either to renew the lease for the remaining economic life of the goods or to become the owner. If the lessee did lease the machine for 36 months, the lessee would have paid the lessor $3,600 for a machine that could have been purchased for $1,000; thus, clause (ii) of paragraph (b) of subdivision (37) of Section 1201 is not satisfied. Finally, there are no options; thus, clauses (iii) and (iv) of paragraph (b) of subdivision (37) of Section 1201 are not satisfied. This transaction creates a lease, not a security interest. However, with each renewal of the lease the facts and circumstances at the time of each renewal must be examined to determine if that conclusion remains accurate, as it is possible that a transaction that first creates a lease, later creates a security interest.

Assume that the facts are changed and that A requires each lessee to lease the goods for 36 months, with no right to terminate. Under pre-Code security law this transaction would have created a conditional sale, and not a bailment for hire or true lease. *Hervey v. Rhode Island Locomotive Works*, 93 U.S. 664, 672–73 (1876). Under this paragraph, and subdivision (37) of Section 1201, as amended with the inclusion of this Division in the Code, the same result would follow. The lessee's obligation for the term is not subject to termination by the lessee and the term is equal to the economic life of the machine.

Between these extremes there are many transactions that can be created. Some of the transactions have not been properly categorized by the courts in applying the 1978 and earlier Official Texts of subdivision (37) of Section 1201. This paragraph, together with subdivision (37) of Section 1201, as amended with the promulgation of this Division, draws a brighter line, which should create a clearer signal to the professional lessor and lessee.

(k) "Lease agreement". This definition is derived from the first sentence of subdivision (3) of Section 1201. Because the definition of lease is broad enough to cover future transfers, lease agreement includes an agreement contemplating a current or subsequent transfer. Thus it was not necessary to make an express reference to an agreement for the future lease of goods (subdivision (1), Section 2106). This concept is also incorporated in the definition of lease contract. Note that the definition of lease does not include transactions in ordinary building materials that are incorporated into an improvement on land. Subdivision (2), Section 10309.

The provisions of this Division, if applicable, determine whether a lease agreement has legal consequences; otherwise the law of bailments and other applicable law determine the same. Subdivision (4), Section 10103 and Section 1103.

(*l*) "Lease contract". This definition is derived from the definition of contract in subdivision (11) of Section 1201. Note that a lease contract may be for the future lease of goods, since this notion is included in the definition of lease.

(m) "Leasehold interest". New.

(n) "Lessee". New.

(o) "Lessee in ordinary course of business". Subdivision (9), Section 1201.

(p) "Lessor". New.

(q) "Lessor's residual interest". New.

(r) "Lien". New. This term is used in Section 10307.

(s) "Lot". Subdivision (5), Section 2105.

(t) "Merchant lessee". New. This term is used in Section 10511. A person may satisfy the requirement of dealing in goods of the kind subject to the lease as lessor, lessee, seller, or buyer.

(u) "Present value". New. Authorities agree that present value should be used to determine fairly the damages payable by the lessor or the lessee on default. *E.g., Taylor v. Commercial Credit Equip. Corp.*, 170 Ga.App. 322, 316 S.E.2d 788 (Ct.App.1984). Present value is defined to mean an amount that represents the discounted value as of a date certain of one or more sums payable in the future. This is a function of the economic principle that a dollar today is more valuable to the holder than a dollar payable in two years. While there is no question as to the principle, reasonable people would differ as to the rate of discount to apply in determining the value of that future dollar today. To minimize litigation, this Division allows the parties to specify the discount or interest rate, if the rate was not manifestly unreasonable at the time the transaction was entered into. In all other cases, the interest rate will be a commercially reasonable rate that takes into account the facts and circumstances of each case, as of the time the transaction was entered into.

(v) "Purchase". Subdivision (32), Section 1201. This definition omits the reference to lien contained in the definition of purchase in Division 1 (subdivision (32), Section 1201). This should not be construed to exclude consensual liens from the definition of purchase in this Division; the exclusion was mandated by the scope of the definition of lien in paragraph (r) of subdivision (1) of Section 10103. Further, the definition of purchaser in this Division adds a reference to lease; as purchase is defined in subdivision (32) of Section 1201 to include any other voluntary transaction creating an interest in property, this addition is not substantive.

(w) "Sublease". New.

(x) "Supplier". New.

(y) "Supply contract". New. This definition applies only to finance leases.

(z) "Termination". Subdivision (3), Section 2106.

§ 10104. Leases Subject to Other Statutes

(a) A lease, although subject to this division, is also subject to any applicable:

* * *

(1) Certificate of title statute of this state, including the provisions of the Vehicle Code that require registration of a vehicle or boat and provisions of the Health and Safety Code that require registration of a mobilehome or commercial coach.

(2) Certificate of title statute of another jurisdiction (Section 10105).

(3) Consumer law of this state, both decisional and statutory, including, to the extent that they apply to a consumer lease transaction, Chapter 5 (commencing with Section 17200) of Part 2 of Division 7 of the Business and Professions Code, Chapter 1 (commencing with Section 17500) of Part 3 of Division 7 of the Business and Professions Code, and Part 4 (commencing with Section 1725) of Division 3 of the Civil Code.

(b) In case of conflict between * * * this division, other than Section 10105, subdivision (c) of Section 10304, and subdivision (c) of Section 10305, and a law referred to in subdivision (a), * * * that law controls.

(c) Failure to comply with an applicable law has only the effect specified therein. (Added by Stats.1988, c. 1359, § 5, operative Jan. 1, 1990. Amended by Stats. 1989, c. 464, § 3; Stats.1991, c. 111 (S.B.972), § 4, eff. July 15, 1991.)

California Comment
Report of the Assembly Committee on Judiciary
August 15, 1989

Uniform Statutory Source: Sections 9–203(4) and 9–302(3)(b) and (c).
Changes: Substantially revised.
Purposes: This Division creates a comprehensive scheme for the regulation of transactions that create leases. Section 10102. Thus, the Division supersedes all prior legislation dealing with leases, except to the extent set forth in this Section.

Subdivision (1) states the general rule that a lease, although governed by the scheme of this Division, is also governed by certain other applicable statutes. This may occur in the case of a consumer lease. Paragraph (e), subdivision (1), Section 10103. An illustration of a statute of the United States that governs consumer leases is the Consumer Leasing Act, 15 U.S.C. §§ 1667–1667(e) (1982) and its implementing regulation, Regulation M, 12 C.F.R. § 213 (1986); the statute mandates disclosures of certain lease terms, delimits the liability of a lessee in leasing personal property, and regulates the advertising of lease terms. An illustration of a California statute that governs consumer leases is the Vehicle Leasing Act, Chapter 2d (commencing with Section 2985.7) of Title 14 of Part 4 of Division 3 of the Civil Code. Such statutes may define consumer lease so as to govern transactions within and without the definition of consumer lease under this Division. Paragraph (d) of subdivision (1) makes it clear that consumer protection laws that are preserved include both decisional and statutory laws. Rather than attempt to identify all such laws, this subdivision references in a nonexclusive manner several important statutory sources to the extent they apply to consumer lease transactions.

Under subdivision (2), subject to certain limited exclusions, in case of conflict the provisions of such a statute prevail over the provisions of this Division.

Consumer protection in lease transactions is primarily left to other law. However, several provisions of this division do contain special rules that may not be varied by agreement in the case of a consumer lease. *E.g.*, Section 10106. Were that not so, the ability of the parties to govern their relationship by agreement together with the position of the lessor in a consumer lease too often could result in a one-sided lease agreement.

In construing this provision the reference to statute should be deemed to include applicable regulations.

Cross References:
Paragraph (e), subdivision (1), Section 10103; and Section 10106.
Definitional Cross Reference:
"Lease". Paragraph (j), subdivision (1), Section 10103.

Cross References
Limitation on power of parties to consumer lease to choose applicable law and judicial forum, see Commercial Code § 10106.

§ 10105. Territorial Application of Article to Goods Covered by Certificate of Title

Subject to the provisions of subdivision (c) of Section 10304 and subdivision (c) of Section 10305, with respect to goods covered by a certificate of title issued under a statute of this state or of another jurisdiction, compliance and the effect of compliance or noncompliance with a certificate of title statute are governed by the law (including the conflict of laws rules) of the jurisdiction issuing the certificate until the earlier of (1) surrender of the certificate, or (2) four months after the goods are removed from that jurisdiction and thereafter until a new certificate of title is issued by another jurisdiction. (Added by Stats.1988, c. 1359, § 5, operative Jan. 1, 1990. Amended by Stats.1991, c. 111 (S.B.972), § 5, eff. July 15, 1991.)

California Comment
Report of the Assembly Committee on Judiciary
August 15, 1989

Uniform Statutory Source: Section 9–103(2)(a) and (b).
Changes: Substantially revised. The provisions of the last sentence of paragraph (b) of subdivision (2) of Section 9103 have not been incorporated as it is superfluous in this context. The provisions of paragraph (d) of subdivision (2) of Section 9103 have not been incorporated because the problems dealt with are adequately addressed by this section and subdivision (3) of Section 10304 and subdivision (3) of Section 10305.
Purposes: The new certificate referred to in paragraph (b) must be permanent, not temporary. Generally, the lessor or creditor whose interest is indicated on the most recently issued certificate of title will prevail over interests indicated on certificates issued previously by other jurisdictions. This provision reflects a policy that it is reasonable to require holders of interests in goods covered by a certificate of title to police the goods or risk losing their interests when a new certificate of title is issued by another jurisdiction.

Cross References:
Subdivision (3), Section 10304; subdivision (3), Section 10305; paragraph (b), subdivision (2), Section 9103; and paragraph (d), subdivision (2), Section 9103.
Definitional Cross Reference:
"Goods". Paragraph (h), subdivision (1), Section 10103.

Cross References
Certificate of title, perfection of security interests in multiple state transactions, see Commercial Code § 9103.
Sale or sublease of goods by lessee, see Commercial Code § 10305.
Subsequent lease of goods by lessor, see Commercial Code § 10304.

§ 10106. Limitation on Power of Parties to Consumer Lease to Choose Applicable Law and Judicial Forum

(a) If the law chosen by the parties to a consumer lease is that of a jurisdiction other than a jurisdiction in which the lessee resides at the time the lease agreement becomes enforceable or within 30 days thereafter, in which the goods are to be used, or in which the lease is executed by the lessee, the choice is not enforceable.

(b) If the judicial forum chosen by the parties to a consumer lease is in a county other than the county in which the lessee in fact signed the lease, the county in which the lessee resides at the commencement of the action, the county in which the lessee resided at the time the lease contract became enforceable, or the county in which the goods are permanently stored, the choice is not enforceable. *(Added by Stats.1988, c. 1359, § 5, operative Jan. 1, 1990. Amended by Stats.1988, c. 1368, § 12.4, operative Jan. 1, 1990; Stats.1991, c. 111 (S.B. 972), § 6, eff. July 15, 1991.)*

California Comment
Report of the Assembly Committee on Judiciary
August 15, 1989

Uniform Statutory Source: Unif. Consumer Credit Code § 1.201(8), 7A U.L.A. 36 (1974).

Changes: Substantially revised.

Purposes: There is a real danger that a lessor may induce a consumer lessee to agree that the applicable law will be a jurisdiction that has little effective consumer protection, or to agree that the applicable forum will be a forum that is inconvenient for the lessee in the event of litigation. As a result, this section invalidates these choice of law or forum clauses in certain circumstances.

Subdivision (1) limits potentially abusive choice of law clauses in consumer leases. The 30-day rule in subdivision (1) was suggested by paragraph (c) of subdivision (1) of Section 9103. This section has no effect on choice of law clauses in leases that are not consumer leases. Such clauses would be governed by other law.

Subdivision (2) prevents enforcement of potentially abusive jurisdictional consent clauses in consumer leases. The statutory source for the list of acceptable forums is subdivision (d) of Section 2986.3 of the Civil Code. By using the term judicial forum, this section does not limit selection of a nonjudicial forum, such as arbitration. This section has no effect on choice of forum clauses in leases that are not consumer leases; such clauses are, as a matter of current law, "prima facie valid". *The Bremen v. Zapata Off-Shore Co.*, 407 U.S. 1, 10 (1972). Such clauses would be governed by other law, including the Model Choice of Forum Act (1968).

Cross Reference:
Paragraph (c), subdivision (1), Section 9103.

Definitional Cross References:
"Consumer lease". Paragraph (e), subdivision (1), Section 10103.
"Lease agreement". Paragraph (k), subdivision (1), Section 10103.
"Lessee". Paragraph (n), subdivision (1), Section 10103.
"Goods". Paragraph (h), subdivision (1), Section 10103.
"Party". Subdivision (29), Section 1201.

Cross References
Documents, instruments and ordinary goods, perfection of security interests in multiple state transactions, see Commercial Code § 9103.

§ 10107. Waiver or Renunciation of Claim or Right After Default

Any claim or right arising out of an alleged default or breach of warranty may be discharged in whole or in part without consideration by a written waiver or renunciation signed and delivered by the aggrieved party. *(Added by Stats.1988, c. 1359, § 5, operative Jan. 1, 1990.)*

California Comment
Report of the Assembly Committee on Judiciary
August 15, 1989

Uniform Statutory Source: Section 1–107.

Changes: Revised to reflect leasing practices and terminology. This clause is used throughout the comments to this Division to indicate the scope of change in the provisions of the Uniform Statutory Source included in the section; these changes range from one extreme, *e.g.*, a significant difference in practice (a warranty as to merchantability is not implied in a finance lease (Section 10212)) to the other extreme, *e.g.*, a modest difference in style or terminology (the transaction governed is a lease not a sale (Section 10203)).

Cross References:
Sections 10203 and 10212.

Definitional Cross References:
"Aggrieved party". Subdivision (2), Section 1201.
"Delivery". Subdivision (14), Section 1201.
"Rights". Subdivision (36), Section 1201.
"Signed". Subdivision (30), Section 1201.
"Written". Subdivision (46), Section 1201.

Cross References
Implied warranty of merchantability, see Commercial Code § 10212.

CHAPTER 2. FORMATION AND CONSTRUCTION OF LEASE CONTRACT

Section
10201. Statute of Frauds.
10202. Final Written Expression: Parol or Extrinsic Evidence.
10204. Formation in General.
10205. Firm Offers.
10206. Offer and Acceptance in Formation of Lease Contract.
10207. Course of Performance or Practical Construction.
10208. Modification, Rescission and Waiver.
10209. Lessee's benefit of supplier's promises and warranties; extension to lessee; modification or rescission of supply contract; rights against supplier.
10210. Express Warranties.
10211. Warranties against interference and infringement; specifications furnished by lessee.
10212. Implied Warranty of Merchantability.
10213. Implied Warranty of Fitness for Particular Purpose.
10214. Exclusion or Modification of Warranties.
10215. Cumulation and Conflict of Warranties Express or Implied.
10217. Identification.
10218. Insurance and Proceeds.
10219. Risk of Loss.
10220. Effect of Default on Risk of Loss.
10221. Casualty to Identified Goods.

§ 10201. Statute of Frauds

(a) A lease contract is not enforceable by way of action or defense unless:

(1) In a lease contract that is not a consumer lease, the total payments to be made under the lease contract, excluding payments for options to renew or buy, <u>are</u> less than one thousand dollars ($1,000); or

(2) There is a writing, signed by the party against whom enforcement is sought or by that party's authorized agent, sufficient to indicate that a lease contract

has been made between the parties and to describe the goods leased and the lease term.

(b) Any description of leased goods or of the lease term is sufficient and satisfies paragraph (2) of subdivision (a), whether or not it is specific, if it reasonably identifies what is described.

(c) A writing is not insufficient because it omits or incorrectly states a term agreed upon, but the lease contract is not enforceable under paragraph (2) of subdivision (a) beyond the lease term and the quantity of goods shown in the writing.

(d) A lease contract that does not satisfy the requirements of subdivision (a), but which is valid in other respects, is enforceable:

(1) If the goods are to be specially manufactured or obtained for the lessee and are not suitable for lease or sale to others in the ordinary course of the lessor's business, and the lessor, before notice of repudiation is received and under circumstances that reasonably indicate that the goods are for the lessee, has made either a substantial beginning of their manufacture or commitments for their procurement;

(2) If the party against whom enforcement is sought admits in that party's pleading, testimony, or otherwise in court that a lease contract was made, but the lease contract is not enforceable under this provision beyond the quantity of goods admitted; or

(3) With respect to goods that have been received and accepted by the lessee.

(e) The lease term under a lease contract referred to in subdivision (d) is:

(1) If there is a writing signed by the party against whom enforcement is sought or by that party's authorized agent specifying the lease term, the term so specified;

(2) If the party against whom enforcement is sought admits in that party's pleading, testimony, or otherwise in court a lease term, the term so admitted; or

(3) A reasonable lease term. *(Added by Stats.1988, c. 1359, § 5, operative Jan. 1, 1990. Amended by Stats. 1991, c. 111 (S.B.972), § 7, eff. July 15, 1991.)*

California Comment
Report of the Assembly Committee on Judiciary
August 15, 1989

Uniform Statutory Source: Sections 2–201, 9–203(1) and 9–110.

Changes: This section is modeled on Section 2201, with changes to reflect the differences between a lease contract and a contract for the sale of goods. As is the case with Division 2 (Section 2201), the adoption of this section does not displace estoppel or other non-Code bases for enforcing a contract despite non-compliance with the statute of frauds. In particular, paragraph (b) of subdivision (1) adds a requirement that the writing "describe the goods leased and the lease term", borrowing that concept, with revisions, from the provisions of paragraph (a) of subdivision (1) of Section 9203. One significant departure in paragraph (a) of subdivision (1) from the Section 2201 analogue is that this subdivision requires all consumer leases to be in writing. There is no exemption from the writing requirement for small amount leases. Subdivision (2), relying on the statutory analogue in Section 9110, sets forth the minimum criterion for satisfying that requirement.

Purposes: The changes in this section conform the provisions of Section 2201 to custom and usage in lease transactions. Subdivision (2) of Section 2201, stating a special rule between merchants, was not included in this section as the number of such transactions involving leases, as opposed to sales, was thought to be modest. Subdivision (4) creates no exception for transactions where payment has been made and accepted. This represents a departure from the analogue, paragraph (c) of subdivision (3) of Section 2201. The rationale for the departure is grounded in the distinction between sales and leases. Unlike a buyer in a sales transaction, the lessee does not tender payment in full for goods delivered, but only payment of rent for one or more months. It was decided that, as a matter of policy, this act of payment is not a sufficient substitute for the required memorandum. Subdivision (5) was needed to establish the criteria for supplying the lease term if it is omitted, as the lease contract may still be enforceable under subdivision (4).

Cross References:
Section 2201; Section 9110; and paragraph (a), subdivision (1), Section 9203.

Definitional Cross References:
"Action". Subdivision (1), Section 1201.
"Agreed". Subdivision (3), Section 1201.
"Buying". Paragraph (a), subdivision (1), Section 10103.
"Goods". Paragraph (h), subdivision (1), Section 10103.
"Lease". Paragraph (j), subdivision (1), Section 10103.
"Lease contract". Paragraph (*l*), subdivision (1), Section 10103.
"Lessee". Paragraph (n), subdivision (1), Section 10103.
"Lessor". Paragraph (p), subdivision (1), Section 10103.
"Notice". Subdivision (25), Section 1201.
"Party". Subdivision (29), Section 1201.
"Sale". Subdivision (1), Section 2106.
"Signed". Subdivision (39), Section 1201.
"Term". Subdivision (42), Section 1201.
"Writing". Subdivision (46), Section 1201.

Cross References

Sufficiency of description of personal property, see Commercial Code § 9110.

§ 10202. Final Written Expression: Parol or Extrinsic Evidence

Terms with respect to which the confirmatory memoranda of the parties agree or which are otherwise set forth in a writing intended by the parties as a final expression of their agreement with respect to such terms as are included therein may not be contradicted by evidence of any prior agreement or of a contemporaneous oral agreement but may be explained or supplemented:

(a) By course of dealing or usage of trade or by course of performance; and

(b) By evidence of consistent additional terms unless the court finds the writing to have been intended also as a complete and exclusive statement of the terms of the agreement. *(Added by Stats.1988, c. 1359, § 5, operative Jan. 1, 1990.)*

California Comment
Report of the Assembly Committee on Judiciary
August 15, 1989

Uniform Statutory Source: Section 2–202.

Definitional Cross References:
"Agreement". Subdivision (3), Section 1201.
"Course of dealing". Section 1205.

"Party". Subdivision (29), Section 1201.
"Term". Subdivision (42), Section 1201.
"Usage of trade". Section 1205.
"Writing". Subdivision (46), Section 1201.

§ 10204. Formation in General

(a) A lease contract may be made in any manner sufficient to show agreement, including conduct by both parties which recognizes the existence of a lease contract.

(b) An agreement sufficient to constitute a lease contract may be found although the moment of its making is undetermined.

(c) Although one or more terms are left open, a lease contract does not fail for indefiniteness if the parties have intended to make a lease contract and there is a reasonably certain basis for giving an appropriate remedy. *(Added by Stats.1988, c. 1359, § 5, operative Jan. 1, 1990. Amended by Stats.1991, c. 111 (S.B.972), § 8, eff. July 15, 1991.)*

California Comment
Report of the Assembly Committee on Judiciary
August 15, 1989

Uniform Statutory Source: Section 2–204.
Changes: Revised to reflect leasing practices and terminology.
Definitional Cross References:
"Agreement". Subdivision (3), Section 1201.
"Lease contract". Paragraph (1), subdivision (1), Section 10103.
"Party". Subdivision (29), Section 1201.
"Remedy". Subdivision (34), Section 1201.
"Term". Subdivision (42), Section 1201.

§ 10205. Firm Offers

An offer by a merchant to lease goods to or from another person in a signed writing that by its terms gives assurance it will be held open is not revocable, for lack of consideration, during the time stated or, if no time is stated, for a reasonable time, but in no event may the period of irrevocability exceed three months. Any such term of assurance on a form supplied by the offeree must be separately signed by the offeror. *(Added by Stats.1988, c. 1359, § 5, operative Jan. 1, 1990. Amended by Stats.1991, c. 111 (S.B.972), § 9, eff. July 15, 1991.)*

California Comment
Report of the Assembly Committee on Judiciary
August 15, 1989

Uniform Statutory Source: Section 2–205.
Changes: Revised to reflect leasing practices and terminology. As is the case with Division 2 (Section 2205), the adoption of this Section does not displace estoppel or other non-Code bases for making an offer irrevocable.
Definitional Cross References:
"Goods". Paragraph (h), subdivision (1), Section 10103.
"Lease". Paragraph (j), subdivision (1), Section 10103.
"Merchant". Subdivision (1), Section 2104.
"Person". Subdivision (30), Section 1201.
"Reasonable time". Subdivisions (1) and (2), Section 1204.
"Signed". Subdivision (39), Section 1201.
"Term". Subdivision (42), Section 1201.
"Writing". Subdivision (46), Section 1201.

§ 10206. Offer and Acceptance in Formation of Lease Contract

(a) Unless otherwise unambiguously indicated by the language or circumstances, an offer to make a lease contract must be construed as inviting acceptance in any manner and by any medium reasonable in the circumstances.

(b) If the beginning of a requested performance is a reasonable mode of acceptance, an offeror who is not notified of acceptance within a reasonable time may treat the offer as having lapsed before acceptance. *(Added by Stats.1988, c. 1359, § 5, operative Jan. 1, 1990. Amended by Stats.1991, c. 111 (S.B.972), § 10, eff. July 15, 1991.)*

California Comment
Report of the Assembly Committee on Judiciary
August 15, 1989

Uniform Statutory Source: Section 2–206(1)(a) and (2).
Changes: Revised to reflect leasing practices and terminology.
Definitional Cross References:
"Lease contract". Paragraph (1), subdivision (1), Section 10103.
"Notifies". Subdivision (26), Section 1201.
"Reasonable time". Subdivisions (1) and (2), Section 1204.

§ 10207. Course of Performance or Practical Construction

(a) If a lease contract involves repeated occasions for performance by either party with knowledge of the nature of the performance and opportunity for objection to it by the other, any course of performance accepted or acquiesced in without objection is relevant to determine the meaning of the lease agreement.

(b) The express terms of a lease agreement and any course of performance, as well as any course of dealing and usage of trade, must be construed whenever reasonable as consistent with each other; but if that construction is unreasonable, express terms control course of performance, course of performance controls both course of dealing and usage of trade, and course of dealing controls usage of trade.

(c) Subject to the provisions of Section 10208 on modification and waiver, course of performance is relevant to show a waiver or modification of any term inconsistent with the course of performance. *(Added by Stats.1988, c. 1359, § 5, operative Jan. 1, 1990. Amended by Stats.1991, c. 111 (S.B.972), § 11, eff. July 15, 1991.)*

California Comment
Report of the Assembly Committee on Judiciary
August 15, 1989

Uniform Statutory Source: Sections 2–208 and 1–205(4).
Changes: Revised to reflect leasing practices and terminology, except that subdivision (2) was further revised to make the subdivision parallel the provisions of subdivision (4) of Section 1205 by adding that course of dealing controls usage of trade.
Purposes: The section should be read in conjunction with Section 10208. In particular, although a specific term may control over course of performance as a matter of lease construction under subdivision (2),

subdivision (3) allows the same course of dealing to show a waiver or modification, if Section 10208 is satisfied.

Cross References:
Subdivision (4), Section 1205; Section 2208; and Section 10208.

Definitional Cross References:
"Course of dealing". Section 1205.
"Knowledge". Subdivision (25), Section 1201.
"Lease agreement". Paragraph (k), subdivision (1), Section 10103.
"Lease contract". Paragraph (1), subdivision (1), Section 10103.
"Party". Subdivision (29), Section 1201.
"Term". Subdivision (42), Section 1201.
"Usage of trade". Section 1205.

Cross References

Course of dealing and usage of trade, see Commercial Code § 1205.
Course of performance or practical construction, see Commercial Code § 2208.

§ 10208. Modification, Rescission and Waiver

(a) An agreement modifying a lease contract needs no consideration to be binding.

(b) A signed lease agreement that excludes modification or rescission except by a signed writing may not be otherwise modified or rescinded, but, except as between merchants, such a requirement on a form supplied by a merchant must be separately signed by the other party.

(c) Although an attempt at modification or rescission does not satisfy the requirements of subdivision (b), it may operate as a waiver.

(d) A party who has made a waiver affecting an executory portion of a lease contract may retract the waiver by reasonable notification received by the other party that strict performance will be required of any term waived, unless the retraction would be unjust in view of a material change of position in reliance on the waiver. *(Added by Stats.1988, c. 1359, § 5, operative Jan. 1, 1990. Amended by Stats.1991, c. 111 (S.B.972), § 12, eff. July 15, 1991.)*

California Comment
Report of the Assembly Committee on Judiciary
August 15, 1989

Uniform Statutory Source: Section 2–209.

Changes: Revised to reflect leasing practices and terminology, except that the provisions of subdivision (3) of Section 2209 were omitted.

Purposes: Subdivision (3) of Section 2209 provides that "the requirements of the statute of frauds section of this Division (Section 2201) must be satisfied if the contract as modified is within its provisions." This provision was not incorporated as it is unfair to allow an oral modification to make the entire lease contract unenforceable, *e.g.* if the modification takes it a few dollars over the dollar limit. At the same time, the problem could not be solved by providing that the lease contract would still be enforceable in its premodification state (if it then satisfied the statute of frauds) since in some cases that might be worse than no enforcement at all. Resolution of the issue is left to the courts based on the facts of each case.

Cross References:
Sections 2201 and 2209.

Definitional Cross References:
"Agreement". Subdivision (3), Section 1201.
"Between merchants". Subdivision (3), Section 2104.
"Lease agreement". Paragraph (k), subdivision (1), Section 10103.
"Lease contract". Paragraph (1), subdivision (1), Section 10103.
"Merchant". Subdivision (1), Section 2104.
"Notification". Subdivision (26), Section 1201.
"Party". Subdivision (29), Section 1201.
"Signed". Subdivision (39), Section 1201.
"Term". Subdivision (42), Section 1201.
"Writing". Subdivision (46), Section 1201.

Cross References

Modification, rescission and waiver, see Commercial Code § 2209.

§ 10209. Lessee's benefit of supplier's promises and warranties; extension to lessee; modification or rescission of supply contract; rights against supplier

(a) The benefit of a supplier's promises to the lessor under the supply contract and of all warranties, whether express or implied, * * * including those of any third party provided in connection with or as part of the supply contract, extends to the lessee to the extent of the lessee's leasehold interest under a finance lease related to the supply contract, but is subject to the terms of the warranty and of the supply contract and all * * * defenses or claims arising therefrom.

(b) The extension of the benefit of a supplier's promises and of warranties to the lessee (subdivision (a) of Section 10209) does not: (1) modify the rights and obligations of the parties to the supply contract, whether arising therefrom or otherwise, or (2) impose any duty or liability under the supply contract on the lessee.

(c) Any modification or rescission of the supply contract by the supplier and the lessor is effective * * * between the supplier and the lessee unless, * * * before the modification or rescission, the supplier has received notice that the lessee has entered into a finance lease related to the supply contract. If the * * * modification or rescission is effective between the supplier and the lessee, the lessor is deemed to have assumed, in addition to the obligations of the lessor to the lessee under the lease contract, promises of the supplier to the lessor and warranties that were so modified or rescinded as they existed and were available to the lessee before modification or rescission * * *.

(d) In addition to the extension of the benefit of the supplier's promises and of warranties to the lessee under subdivision (a), the lessee retains all rights * * * that the lessee may have against the supplier which arise from an agreement between the lessee and the supplier or * * * under other law. *(Added by Stats.1988, c. 1359, § 5, operative Jan. 1, 1990. Amended by Stats. 1988, c. 1368, § 12.6, operative Jan. 1, 1990; Stats.1991, c. 111 (S.B.972), § 13, eff. July 15, 1991.)*

California Comment
Report of the Assembly Committee on Judiciary
August 15, 1989

Uniform Statutory Source: None.

Changes: This section is modeled on Section 9318, the Restatement (Second) of Contracts §§ 302–315 (1981), and leasing practices. See *Earman Oil Co. v. Burroughs Corp.*, 625 F.2d 1291, 1296–97 (5th Cir.1980).

Purposes: The function performed by the lessor in a finance lease is extremely limited. Paragraph (g), subdivision (1), Section 10103. The

§ 10209

lessee looks to the supplier of the goods for warranties and the like. That expectation is reflected in subdivision (1), which is self-executing. As a matter of policy, the operation of this provision may not be excluded, modified or limited; however, an exclusion, modification, or limitation of any term of the supply contract, including any with respect to rights and remedies, effective against the lessor as buyer under the supply contract, is also effective against the lessee as the beneficiary designated under this provision. The supplier is not precluded from excluding or modifying an express or implied warranty under a supply contract. Subdivision (2), Section 2312 and Section 2316. Further, the supplier is not precluded from limiting the rights and remedies of the lessor, as buyer, and from liquidating damages. Sections 2718 and 2719. If the supply contract excludes or modifies warranties, limits remedies for breach, or liquidates damages with respect to the lessor, such provisions are enforceable against the lessee as beneficiary. Thus, only selective discrimination against the beneficiaries designated under this section is precluded, *i.e.*, exclusion of the supplier's liability to the lessee with respect to warranties made to the lessor.

Enforcement of this benefit is by action. Subdivision (4), Section 10103 and subdivision (2), Section 1106.

The benefit extended by these provisions is not without a price, as this Division also provides in the case of a finance lease that is not a consumer lease that the lessee's promises to the lessor under the lease contract become irrevocable and independent upon the lessee's acceptance of the goods. Section 10407. In the case of a finance lease that is a consumer lease, the lessee's promises to the lessor under the lease contract do not become irrevocable and independent upon the lessee's acceptance of the goods unless the lease agreement so provides. The enforceability of such a provision in the lease is determined by the facts of each case and other applicable law; and this Division carries no negative or positive implication on this issue of enforceability. Subdivision (3), Section 10407.

Subdivision (2) limits the effect of subdivision (1) on the supplier and the lessor by preserving, notwithstanding the transfer of the benefits of the supply contract to the lessee, all of the supplier's and the lessor's rights and obligations with respect to each other and others; it further absolves the lessee of any duties with respect to the supply contract that might have been inferred from the extension of the benefits thereof. Subdivisions (2) and (3) also deal with difficult issues related to modification or rescission of the supply contract. Subdivision (2) states a rule that determines the impact of the statutory extension of benefit contained in subdivision (1) upon the relationship of the parties to the supply contract and, in a limited respect, upon the lessee. This statutory extension of benefit, like that contained in Sections 10216 and 2318, is not a modification of the supply contract by the parties. Thus, subdivision (3) states the rules that apply to a modification or rescission of the supply contract by the parties. Subdivision (3) recognizes the lessee's potential causes of action against the lessor arising from modification or rescission of the supply contract. The existence and extent of a cause of action by the supplier against the lessor is left to resolution by the courts based on the facts of each case.

Subdivision (4) confirms that the lessee retains all rights and remedies against the supplier that arise from applicable law or from any agreement between the lessee and the supplier. This subdivision merely preserves rights the lessee may have against the supplier. Nothing in this subdivision implies that any such rights against the supplier exist against the lessor.

Cross References:

Subdivision (g), Section 10103; Section 10407; and Section 9318.

Definitional Cross References:

"Action". Subdivision (1), Section 1201.
"Finance lease". Paragraph (g), subdivision (1), Section 10103.
"Leasehold interest". Paragraph (m), subdivision (1), Section 10103.
"Lessee". Paragraph (n), subdivision (1), Section 10103.
"Lessor". Paragraph (p), subdivision (1), Section 10103.
"Notice". Subdivision (25), Section 1201.
"Party". Subdivision (29), Section 1201.
"Rights". Subdivision (36), Section 1201.
"Supplier". Paragraph (x), subdivision (1), Section 10103.
"Supply contract". Paragraph (y), subdivision (1), Section 10103.
"Term". Subdivision (42), Section 1201.

Cross References

Defenses against assignees, modification of contracts after notification of assignment, etc., see Commercial Code § 9318.
Finance lease, defined, see Commercial Code § 10103.
Irrevocable promises, finance leases, see Commercial Code § 10407.

§ 10210. Express Warranties

(a) Express warranties by the lessor are created as follows:

(1) Any affirmation of fact or promise made by the lessor to the lessee which relates to the goods and becomes part of the basis of the bargain creates an express warranty that the goods will conform to the affirmation or promise.

(2) Any description of the goods which is made part of the basis of the bargain creates an express warranty that the goods will conform to the description.

(3) Any sample or model that is made part of the basis of the bargain creates an express warranty that the whole of the goods will conform to the sample or model.

(b) It is not necessary to the creation of an express warranty that the lessor use formal words, such as "warrant" or "guarantee," or that the lessor have a specific intention to make a warranty, but an affirmation merely of the value of the goods or a statement purporting to be merely the lessor's opinion or commendation of the goods does not create a warranty. *(Added by Stats.1988, c. 1359, § 5, operative Jan. 1, 1990. Amended by Stats.1991, c. 111 (S.B.972), § 14, eff. July 15, 1991.)*

California Comment
Report of the Assembly Committee on Judiciary
August 15, 1989

Uniform Statutory Source: Section 2–313.
Changes: Revised to reflect leasing practices and terminology.
Purposes: All of the express and implied warranties of the Division on Sales (Division 2) are included in this Division, revised to reflect the differences between a sale of goods and a lease of goods. Sections 10210 through 10216. The lease of goods is sufficiently similar to the sale of goods to justify this decision. Hawkland, *The Impact of the Uniform Commercial Code on Equipment Leasing*, 1972 Ill.L.F. 446, 459–60. Many state and federal courts have reached the same conclusion.

Value of the goods, as used in subdivision (2), includes rental value.

Cross References:
Division 2, esp. Section 2313, and Sections 10210 through 10216.

Definitional Cross References:
"Conforming". Paragraph (d), subdivision (1), Section 10103.
"Goods". Paragraph (h), subdivision (1), Section 10103.
"Lessee". Paragraph (n), subdivision (1), Section 10103.
"Lessor". Paragraph (p), subdivision (1), Section 10103.
"Value". Subdivision (44), Section 1201.

Cross References

Express warranties by affirmation, promise, description, etc., see Commercial Code § 2313.

§ 10211. Warranties against interference and infringement; specifications furnished by lessee

(a) There is in a lease contract a warranty that for the lease term no person holds a claim to or interest in the goods that arose from an act or omission of the lessor, other than a claim by way of infringement or the like, which will interfere with the lessee's enjoyment of its leasehold interest.

(b) Except in a finance lease * * * there is in a lease contract by a lessor who is a merchant regularly dealing in goods of the kind a warranty that the goods are delivered free of the rightful claim of any person by way of infringement or the like.

(c) A lessee who furnishes specifications to a lessor or a supplier shall hold the lessor and the supplier harmless against any claim by * * * way of infringement or the like that arises out of compliance with the specifications. *(Added by Stats.1988, c. 1359, § 5, operative Jan. 1, 1990. Amended by Stats.1991, c. 111 (S.B.972), § 15, eff. July 15, 1991.)*

California Comment
Report of the Assembly Committee on Judiciary
August 15, 1989

Uniform Statutory Source: Section 2–312.

Changes: This section is modeled on the provisions of Section 2312, with modifications to reflect the limited interest transferred by a lease contract and the total interest transferred by a sale. Subdivision (2) of Section 2312, which is omitted here, is incorporated in Section 10214. The warranty of quiet possession was abolished with respect to sales of goods. Section 2312 Comment 1. Subdivision (1) of Section 10211 reinstates the warranty of quiet possession with respect to leases. Inherent in the nature of the limited interest transferred by the lease—the right to possession and use of the goods—is the need of the lessee for protection greater than that afforded to the buyer. Since the scope of the protection is limited to claims or interests that arose from acts or omissions of the lessor, the lessor will be in position to evaluate the potential cost, certainly a far better position than that enjoyed by the lessee. Further, to the extent the market will allow, the lessor can attempt to pass on the anticipated additional cost to the lessee in the guise of higher rent.

Purposes: General language was chosen for subdivision (1) that expresses the essence of the lessee's expectation: with an exception for infringement and the like, no person holding a claim or interest that arose from an act or omission of the lessor will be able to interfere with the lessee's use and enjoyment of the goods for the lease term. Subdivision (2), like other similar provisions in later sections, excludes the finance lessor from extending this warranty; with few exceptions (Section 10210 and subdivision (1), Section 10211), the lessee under a finance lease is to look to the supplier for warranties and the like. Subdivisions (2) and (3) are derived from subdivision (3) of Section 2312. These subdivisions, as well as the analogue, should be construed so that applicable principles of law and equity supplement their provisions. Subdivision (4), Section 10103 and Section 1103.

Cross References:
Section 2312; subdivision (1), Section 2312; subdivision (2), Section 2312; Section 2312 Comment 1; Section 10210; subdivision (1), Section 10211; and Section 10214.

Definitional Cross References:
"Delivery". Subdivision (14), Section 1201.
"Finance lease". Paragraph (g), subdivision (1), Section 10103.
"Goods". Paragraph (h), subdivision (1), Section 10103.
"Lease". Paragraph (j), subdivision (1), Section 10103.
"Lease contract". Paragraph (l), subdivision (1), Section 10103.
"Leasehold interest". Paragraph (m), subdivision (1), Section 10103.
"Lessee". Paragraph (n), subdivision (1), Section 10103.
"Lessor". Paragraph (p), subdivision (1), Section 10103.
"Merchant". Subdivision (1), Section 2104.
"Person". Subdivision (30), Section 1201.
"Supplier". Paragraph (x), subdivision (1), Section 10103.

Cross References
Exclusion or modification of warranty, see Commercial Code § 10214
Warranty of title and against infringement, buyer's obligation against infringement, see Commercial Code § 2312

§ 10212. Implied Warranty of Merchantability

(a) Except in a finance lease, a warranty that the goods will be merchantable is implied in a lease contract if the lessor is a merchant with respect to goods of that kind.

(b) Goods to be merchantable must be at least such as:

(1) Pass without objection in the trade under the description in the lease agreement;

(2) In the case of fungible goods, are of fair average quality within the description;

(3) Are fit for the ordinary purposes for which goods of that type are used;

(4) Run, within the variation permitted by the lease agreement, of even kind, quality, and quantity within each unit and among all units involved;

(5) Are adequately contained, packaged, and labeled as the lease agreement may require; and

(6) Conform to any promises or affirmations of fact made on the container or label.

(c) Other implied warranties may arise from course of dealing or usage of trade. *(Added by Stats.1988, c. 1359, § 5, operative Jan. 1, 1990. Amended by Stats. 1991, c. 111 (S.B.972), § 16, eff. July 15, 1991.)*

California Comment
Report of the Assembly Committee on Judiciary
August 15, 1989

Uniform Statutory Source: Section 2–314.

Changes: Revised to reflect leasing practices and terminology. *E.g., Glenn Dick Equip. Co. v. Galey Constr., Inc.*, 97 Idaho 216, 225, 541 P.2d 1184, 1193 (1975) (implied warranty of merchantability (Division 2) extends to lease transactions).

Definitional Cross References:
"Conforming". Paragraph (d), subdivision (1), Section 10103.
"Course of dealing". Section 1205.
"Finance lease". Paragraph (g), subdivision (1), Section 10103.
"Fungible". Subdivision (17), Section 1201.
"Goods". Paragraph (h), subdivision (1), Section 10103.
"Lease agreement". Paragraph (k), subdivision (1), Section 10103.
"Lease contract". Paragraph (l), subdivision (1), Section 10103.
"Lessor". Paragraph (p), subdivision (1), Section 10103.
"Merchant". Subdivision (1), Section 2104.
"Usage of trade". Section 1205.

§ 10213. Implied Warranty of Fitness for Particular Purpose

Except in a finance lease, if the lessor at the time the lease contract is made has reason to know of any particular purpose for which the goods are required and that the lessee is relying on the lessor's skill or judgment to select or furnish suitable goods, there is in the lease contract an implied warranty that the goods will be fit for that purpose. *(Added by Stats.1988, c. 1359, § 5, operative Jan. 1, 1990.)*

California Comment
Report of the Assembly Committee on Judiciary
August 15, 1989

Uniform Statutory Source: Section 2–315.

Changes: Revised to reflect leasing practices and terminology. *E.g., All-States Leasing Co. v. Bass*, 96 Idaho 873, 879, 538 P.2d 1177, 1183 (1975) (implied warranty of fitness for a particular purpose (Division 2) extends to lease transactions).

Definitional Cross References:

"Finance lease". Paragraph (g), subdivision (1), Section 10103.
"Goods". Paragraph (h), subdivision (1), Section 10103.
"Knows". Subdivision (25), Section 1201.
"Lease contract". Paragraph (1), subdivision (1), Section 10103.
"Lessee". Paragraph (n), subdivision (1), Section 10103.
"Lessor". Paragraph (p), subdivision (1), Section 10103.

§ 10214. Exclusion or Modification of Warranties

(a) Words or conduct relevant to the creation of an express warranty and words or conduct tending to negate or limit a warranty must be construed wherever reasonable as consistent with each other; but, subject to the provisions of Section 10202 on parol or extrinsic evidence, negation or limitation is inoperative to the extent that the construction is unreasonable.

(b) Subject to subdivision (c), to exclude or modify the implied warranty of merchantability or any part of it the language must mention "merchantability," be by a writing, and be conspicuous. Subject to subdivision (c), to exclude or modify any implied warranty of fitness the exclusion must be by a writing and be conspicuous. Language to exclude all implied warranties of fitness is sufficient if it is in writing, is conspicuous and states, for example, "There is no warranty that the goods will be fit for a particular purpose."

(c) Notwithstanding subdivision (b), but subject to subdivision (d),

(1) Unless the circumstances indicate otherwise, all implied warranties are excluded by expressions like "as is," or "with all faults," or by other language that in common understanding calls the lessee's attention to the exclusion of warranties and makes plain that there is no implied warranty, if in writing and conspicuous;

(2) If the lessee before entering into the lease contract has examined the goods or the sample or model as fully as desired or has refused to examine the goods, there is no implied warranty with regard to defects that an examination ought in the circumstances to have revealed; and

(3) An implied warranty may also be excluded or modified by course of dealing, course of performance, or usage of trade.

(d) To exclude or modify a warranty against interference or against infringement (Section 10211) or any part of it, the language must be specific, be by a writing, and be conspicuous, unless the circumstances, including course of performance, course of dealing, or usage of trade, give the lessee reason to know that the goods are being leased subject to a claim or interest of any person. *(Added by Stats.1988, c. 1359, § 5, operative Jan. 1, 1990.*

Amended by Stats.1991, c. 111 (S.B.972), § 17, eff. July 15, 1991.)

California Comment
Report of the Assembly Committee on Judiciary
August 15, 1989

Uniform Statutory Source: Sections 2–316 and 2–312(2).

Changes: Subdivision (2) requires that a disclaimer of the warranty of merchantability be conspicuous and in writing as is the case for a disclaimer of the warranty of fitness; this is contrary to the rule stated in subdivision (2) of Section 2316 with respect to the disclaimer of the warranty of merchantability. This section also provides that to exclude or modify the implied warranty of merchantability, fitness or against interference or infringement the language must be in writing and conspicuous. There are, however, exceptions to the rule. *E.g.,* course of dealing, course of performance, or usage of trade may exclude or modify an implied warranty. Paragraph (c), subdivision (3), Section 10214. The analogue of subdivision (2) of Section 2312 has been moved to subdivision (4) of this section for a more unified treatment of disclaimers; there is no policy with respect to leases of goods that would justify continuing certain distinctions found in the Division on Sales (Division 2) regarding the treatment of the disclaimer of various warranties. *Compare* subdivision (2) of Section 2312 and subdivision (2) of Section 2316. Finally, the example of a disclaimer of the implied warranty of fitness stated in subdivision (2) differs from the analogue stated in subdivision (2) of Section 2316; this example should promote a better understanding of the effect of the disclaimer.

Purposes: These changes were made to reflect leasing practices. *E.g., FMC Finance Corp. v. Murphree*, 632 F.2d 413, 418 (5th Cir.1980) (disclaimer of implied warranty under lease transactions must be conspicuous and in writing). The omission of the provisions of subdivision (4) of Section 2316 was not substantive. Sections 10503 and 10504.

Cross References:

Division 2, esp. subdivision (2), Section 2312; Section 2316; Section 10503; and Section 10504.

Definitional Cross References:

"Conspicuous". Subdivision (10), Section 1201.
"Course of dealing". Section 1205.
"Fault". Paragraph (f), subdivision (1), Section 10103.
"Goods". Paragraph (h), subdivision (1), Section 10103.
"Knows". Subdivision (25), Section 1201.
"Lease". Paragraph (j), subdivision (1), Section 10103.
"Lease contract". Paragraph (1), subdivision (1), Section 10103.
"Lessee". Paragraph (n), subdivision (1), Section 10103.
"Person". Subdivision (30), Section 1201.
"Usage of trade". Section 1205.
"Writing". Subdivision (46), Section 1201.

Cross References

Exclusion or modification of warranties, see Commercial Code § 2316.
Liquidation of damages payable by either party for default, or any other act or omission, see Commercial Code § 10504.
Modification or impairment of rights and remedies, see Commercial Code § 10503.
Warranty of title and against infringement, buyer's obligation against infringement, see Commercial Code § 2312.

§ 10215. Cumulation and Conflict of Warranties Express or Implied

Warranties, whether express or implied, must be construed as consistent with each other and as cumulative, but if that construction is unreasonable, the intention of the parties determines which warranty is dominant. In ascertaining that intention the following rules apply:

(1) Exact or technical specifications displace an inconsistent sample or model or general language of description.

(2) A sample from an existing bulk displaces inconsistent general language of description.

(3) Express warranties displace inconsistent implied warranties other than an implied warranty of fitness for a particular purpose. (Added by Stats.1988, c. 1359, § 5, operative Jan. 1, 1990. Amended by Stats.1991, c. 111 (S.B.972), § 18, eff. July 15, 1991.)

California Comment

Report of the Assembly Committee on Judiciary

August 15, 1989

Uniform Statutory Source: Section 2–317.
Definitional Cross Reference:
 "Party". Subdivision (29), Section 1201.

§ 10217. Identification

Identification of goods as goods to which a lease contract refers may be made at any time and in any manner explicitly agreed to by the parties. In the absence of explicit agreement, identification occurs:

(1) When the lease contract is made, if the lease contract is for a lease of goods that are existing and identified;

(2) When the goods are shipped, marked, or otherwise designated by the lessor as goods to which the lease contract refers, if the lease contract is for a lease of goods that are not existing and identified; or

(3) When the young are conceived, if the lease contract is for a lease of unborn young of animals. (Added by Stats.1988, c. 1359, § 5, operative Jan. 1, 1990. Amended by Stats.1991, c. 111 (S.B.972), § 19, eff. July 15, 1991.)

California Comment

Report of the Assembly Committee on Judiciary

August 15, 1989

Uniform Statutory Source: Section 2–501.
Changes: This section, together with Section 10218, is derived from the provisions of Section 2501, with changes to reflect lease terminology; however, this section omits as irrelevant to leasing practice the treatment of special property.
Purposes: With respect to paragraph (b) there is a certain amount of ambiguity in the reference to when goods are designated, *e.g.*, when the lessor is both selling and leasing goods to the same lessee/buyer and has marked goods for delivery but has not distinguished between those related to the lease contract and those related to the sales contract. As in paragraph (b) of subdivision (1) of Section 2501, this issue has been left to be resolved by the courts, case by case.
Cross References:
 Sections 2501 and 10218.
Definitional Cross References:
 "Agreement". Subdivision (3), Section 1201.
 "Goods". Paragraph (h), subdivision (1), Section 10103.
 "Lease". Paragraph (j), subdivision (1), Section 10103.
 "Lease contract". Paragraph (1), subdivision (1), Section 10103.
 "Lessor". Paragraph (p), subdivision (1), Section 10103.
 "Party". Subdivision (29), Section 1201.

Cross References
Insurable interest in goods, manner of identification of goods, see Commercial Code § 2501.

§ 10218. Insurance and Proceeds

(a) A lessee obtains an insurable interest when existing goods are identified to the lease contract even though the goods identified are nonconforming and the lessee has an option to reject them.

(b) If a lessee has an insurable interest only by reason of the lessor's identification of the goods, the lessor, until default or insolvency or notification to the lessee that identification is final, may substitute other goods for those identified.

(c) Notwithstanding a lessee's insurable interest under subdivisions (a) and (b), the lessor retains an insurable interest until an option to buy has been exercised by the lessee and risk of loss has passed to the lessee.

(d) Nothing in this section impairs any insurable interest recognized under any other statute or rule of law.

(e) The parties by agreement may determine that one or more parties have an obligation to obtain and pay for insurance covering the goods and by agreement may determine the beneficiary of the proceeds of the insurance. (Added by Stats.1988, c. 1359, § 5, operative Jan. 1, 1990. Amended by Stats.1991, c. 111 (S.B.972), § 20, eff. July 15, 1991.)

California Comment

Report of the Assembly Committee on Judiciary

August 15, 1989

Uniform Statutory Source: Section 2–501.
Changes: This section, together with Section 10217, is derived from the provisions of Section 2501, with changes and additions to reflect leasing practices and terminology.
Purposes: Subdivision (2) states a rule allowing substitution of goods by the lessor under certain circumstances, until default or insolvency of the lessor, or until notification to the lessee that identification is final. Subdivision (3) states a rule regarding the lessor's insurable interest that, by virtue of the difference between a sale and a lease, necessarily is different from the rule stated in subdivision (2) of Section 2501 regarding the seller's insurable interest. For this purpose the option to buy shall be deemed to have been exercised by the lessee when the resulting sale is closed, not when the lessee gives notice to the lessor. Further, subdivision (5) is new and reflects the common practice of shifting the responsibility and cost of insuring the goods between the parties to the lease transaction.
Cross References:
 Section 2501; subdivision (2), Section 2501; and Section 10217.
Definitional Cross References:
 "Agreement". Subdivision (3), Section 1201.
 "Buying". Paragraph (a), subdivision (1), Section 10103.
 "Conforming". Paragraph (d), subdivision (1), Section 10103.
 "Goods". Paragraph (h), subdivision (1), Section 10103.
 "Insolvent". Subdivision (23), Section 1201.
 "Lease contract". Paragraph (1), subdivision (1), Section 10103.
 "Lessee". Paragraph (n), subdivision (1), Section 10103.
 "Lessor". Paragraph (p), subdivision (1), Section 10103.
 "Notification". Subdivision (26), Section 1201.
 "Party". Subdivision (29), Section 1201.

§ 10218

Cross References

Insurable interest in goods, manner of identification of goods, see Commercial Code § 2501.

§ 10219. Risk of Loss

(a) Except in the case of a finance lease, risk of loss is retained by the lessor and does not pass to the lessee. In the case of a finance lease, risk of loss passes to the lessee.

(b) Subject to the provisions of this division on the effect of default on risk of loss (Section 10220), if risk of loss is to pass to the lessee and the time of passage is not stated, the following rules apply:

(1) If the lease contract requires or authorizes the goods to be shipped by carrier

(A) And it does not require delivery at a particular destination, the risk of loss passes to the lessee when the goods are duly delivered to the carrier; but

(B) If it does require delivery at a particular destination and the goods are there duly tendered while in the possession of the carrier, the risk of loss passes to the lessee when the goods are there duly so tendered as to enable the lessee to take delivery.

(2) If the goods are held by a bailee to be delivered without being moved, the risk of loss passes to the lessee on acknowledgment by the bailee of the lessee's right to possession of the goods.

(3) In any case not within * * * paragraph (1) or (2), the risk of loss passes to the lessee on the lessee's receipt of the goods if the lessor, or, in the case of a finance lease, the supplier, is a merchant; otherwise the risk passes to the lessee on tender of delivery. *(Added by Stats.1988, c. 1359, § 5, operative Jan. 1, 1990. Amended by Stats.1991, c. 111 (S.B.972), § 21, eff. July 15, 1991.)*

California Comment

Report of the Assembly Committee on Judiciary

August 15, 1989

Uniform Statutory Source: Section 2-509(1) through (3).

Changes: Subdivision (1) is new. The introduction to subdivision (2) is new, but paragraph (a) incorporates the provisions of subdivision (1) of Section 2509; paragraph (b) incorporates the provisions of subdivision (2) of Section 2509 only in part, reflecting current practice in lease transactions.

Purposes: Subdivision (1) states rules related to retention or passage of risk of loss consistent with current practice in lease transactions. The provisions of subdivision (4) of Section 2509 are not incorporated as they are not necessary. This section does not deal with responsibility for loss caused by the wrongful act of either the lessor or the lessee.

Cross References:

Subdivision (1), Section 2509; subdivision (2), Section 2509; and subdivision (4), Section 2509.

Definitional Cross References:

"Delivery". Subdivision (14), Section 1201.
"Finance lease". Paragraph (g), subdivision (1), Section 10103.
"Goods". Paragraph (h), subdivision (1), Section 10103.
"Lease contract". Paragraph (1), subdivision (1), Section 10103.
"Lessee". Paragraph (n), subdivision (1), Section 10103.
"Lessor". Paragraph (p), subdivision (1), Section 10103.
"Merchant". Subdivision (1), Section 2104.
"Receipt". Paragraph (c), subdivision (1), Section 2103.
"Rights". Subdivision (36), Section 1201.
"Supplier". Paragraph (x), subdivision (1), Section 10103.

§ 10220. Effect of Default on Risk of Loss

(a) Where risk of loss is to pass to the lessee and the time of passage is not stated:

(1) If a tender or delivery of goods so fails to conform to the lease contract as to give a right of rejection, the risk of their loss remains with the lessor, or, in the case of a finance lease, the supplier, until cure or acceptance.

(2) If the lessee rightfully revokes acceptance, he or she, to the extent of any deficiency in his or her effective insurance coverage, may treat the risk of loss as having remained with the lessor from the beginning.

(b) Whether or not risk of loss is to pass to the lessee, if the lessee as to conforming goods already identified to a lease contract repudiates or is otherwise in default under the lease contract, the lessor, or, in the case of a finance lease, the supplier, to the extent of any deficiency in his or her effective insurance coverage may treat the risk of loss as resting on the lessee for a commercially reasonable time. *(Added by Stats.1988, c. 1359, § 5, operative Jan. 1, 1990. Amended by Stats.1991, c. 111 (S.B.972), § 22, eff. July 15, 1991.)*

California Comment

Report of the Assembly Committee on Judiciary

August 15, 1989

Uniform Statutory Source: Section 2-510.

Changes: Revised to reflect leasing practices and terminology. The rule in paragraph (b) of subdivision (1) does not allow the lessee under a finance lease to treat the risk of loss as having remained with the supplier from the beginning. This is appropriate given the limited circumstances under which the lessee under a finance lease is allowed to revoke acceptance. Section 10517 and Section 10516 Comment.

Definitional Cross References:

"Conforming". Paragraph (d), subdivision (1), Section 10103.
"Delivery". Subdivision (14), Section 1201.
"Finance lease". Paragraph (g), subdivision (1), Section 10103.
"Goods". Paragraph (h), subdivision (1), Section 10103.
"Lease contract". Paragraph (1), subdivision (1), Section 10103.
"Lessee". Paragraph (n), subdivision (1), Section 10103.
"Lessor". Paragraph (p), subdivision (1), Section 10103.
"Reasonable time". Subdivisions (1) and (2), Section 1204.
"Rights". Subdivision (36), Section 1201.
"Supplier". Paragraph (x), subdivision (1), Section 10103.

§ 10221. Casualty to Identified Goods

If a lease contract requires goods identified when the lease contract is made, and the goods suffer casualty without fault of the lessee, the lessor, or the supplier before delivery, or the goods suffer casualty before risk of loss passes to the lessee pursuant to the lease agreement or Section 10219, then:

(1) If the loss is total, the lease contract is avoided; and

(2) If the loss is partial or the goods have so deteriorated as to no longer conform to the lease contract, the lessee may nevertheless demand inspection and at his or her option either treat the lease contract as

avoided or, except in a finance lease, accept the goods with due allowance from the rent payable for the balance of the lease term for the deterioration or the deficiency in quantity but without further right against the lessor. *(Added by Stats.1988, c. 1359, § 5, operative Jan. 1, 1990. Amended by Stats.1991, c. 111 (S.B.972), § 23, eff. July 15, 1991.)*

California Comment
Report of the Assembly Committee on Judiciary
August 15, 1989

Uniform Statutory Source: Section 2–613.

Changes: Revised to reflect leasing practices and terminology.

Purposes: Due to the vagaries of determining the amount of due allowance (paragraph (b), Section 2613), no attempt was made in paragraph (b) to treat a problem unique to lease contracts and installment sales contracts: determining how to recapture the allowance, *e.g.,* application to the first or last rent payments or allocation, *pro rata,* to all rent payments.

Cross Reference:
Section 2613.

Definitional Cross References:
"Conforming". Paragraph (d), subdivision (1), Section 10103.
"Consumer lease". Paragraph (e), subdivision (1), Section 10103.
"Delivery". Subdivision (14), Section 1201.
"Fault". Paragraph (f), subdivision (1), Section 10103.
"Finance lease". Paragraph (g), subdivision (1), Section 10103.
"Goods". Paragraph (h), subdivision (1), Section 10103.
"Lease". Paragraph (j), subdivision (1), Section 10103.
"Lease agreement". Paragraph (k), subdivision (1), Section 10103.
"Lease contract". Paragraph (*l*), subdivision (1), Section 10103.
"Lessee". Paragraph (n), subdivision (1), Section 10103.
"Lessor". Paragraph (p), subdivision (1), Section 10103.
"Rights". Subdivision (36), Section 1201.
"Supplier". Paragraph (x), subdivision (1), Section 10103.

Cross References
Casualty to identified goods, see Commercial Code § 2613.

CHAPTER 3. EFFECT OF LEASE CONTRACT

Section
10301. Enforceability of Lease Contract.
10302. Title To and Possession of Goods.
10303. Creation of security interests; provisions prohibiting transfers of interests or rights; provisions prohibiting creation or enforcement of security interests.
10304. Subsequent Lease of Goods by Lessor.
10305. Sale or Sublease of Goods by Lessee.
10306. Priority of Certain Liens Arising by Operation of Law.
10307. Priority of Liens Arising by Attachment or Levy on, Security Interests in, and Other Claims to Goods.
10308. Special Rights of Creditors.
10309. Lessor's and Lessee's Rights When Goods Become Fixtures.
10310. Lessor's and Lessee's Rights When Goods Become Accessions.
10311. Priority; subordination agreements.

§ 10301. Enforceability of Lease Contract

Except as otherwise provided in this division, a lease contract is effective and enforceable according to its terms between the parties, against purchasers of the goods, and against creditors of the parties. *(Added by Stats.1988, c. 1359, § 5, operative Jan. 1, 1990. Amended by Stats.1991, c. 111 (S.B.972), § 24, eff. July 15, 1991.)*

California Comment
Report of the Assembly Committee on Judiciary
August 15, 1989

Uniform Statutory Source: Section 9–201.

Changes: The first sentence of Section 9201 was incorporated, modified to reflect leasing terminology. The second sentence of Section 9201 was eliminated as not relevant to leasing practices.

Purposes: This section establishes a general rule regarding the validity and enforceability of a lease contract. The lease contract is effective and enforceable between the parties and against third parties. Exceptions to this general rule arise where there is a specific rule to the contrary in this Division. Enforceability is, thus, dependent upon the lease contract meeting the requirements of the Statute of Frauds provisions of Section 10201. Enforceability is also a function of the lease contract conforming to the principles of construction and interpretation contained in the Division on General Provisions (Division 1). Subdivision (4), Section 10103.

The effectiveness or enforceability of the lease contract is not dependent upon the lease contract or any financing statement or the like being filed or recorded; however, the priority of the interest of a lessor of fixtures with respect to the interests of certain third parties in such fixtures is subject to the provisions of the Division on Secured Transactions (Division 9). Section 10309. Prior to the adoption of this Division filing or recording was not required with respect to leases, only leases intended as security. The definition of security interest, as amended concurrently with the adoption of this Division, more clearly delineates leases and leases intended as security and thus signals the need to file. Subdivision (37), Section 1201. Those lessors who are concerned about whether the transaction creates a lease or a security interest will continue to file a protective financing statement. Section 9408. Coogan, Leasing and the Uniform Commercial Code, in *Equipment Leasing-Leveraged Leasing* 681, 744–46 (2d ed. 1980).

Hypothetical: 1. In construing this section it is important to recognize its relationship to other sections in this Division. This is best demonstrated by reference to a hypothetical. Assume that, on February 1, A, a manufacturer of combines and other farm equipment, leased a fleet of six combines to B, a corporation engaged in the business of farming, for a 12 month term. Under the lease agreement between A and B, A agreed to defer B's payment of the first two months' rent to April 1. On March 1, B recognized that it would need only four combines and thus subleased two combines to C for an 11 month term.

2. This hypothetical raises a number of issues that are answered by the sections contained in this part. Since lease is defined to include sublease (paragraphs (j) and (w), subdivision (1), Section 10103), this section provides that the prime lease between A and B and the sublease between B and C are enforceable in accordance with their terms, except as otherwise provided in this Division; that exception, in this case, is one of considerable scope.

3. The separation of ownership, which is in A, and possession, which is in B with respect to four combines and which is in C with respect to two combines, is not relevant. Section 10302. A's interest in the six combines cannot be challenged simply because A parted with possession to B, who in turn parted with possession of some of the combines to C. Yet it is important to note that by the terms of Section 10302 this conclusion is subject to change if otherwise provided in this Division.

4. B's entering the sublease with C raises an issue that is treated by this part. In a dispute over the leased combines A may challenge B's right to sublease. The general rule is permissive as to transfers of interest under a lease contract, including subleases. Subdivision (1), Section 10103. However, the rule creates two significant exceptions. If the prime lease contract between A and B prohibits B from subleasing the combines, paragraph (a) of subdivision (1) of Section 10303 applies, as the transfer is voluntary and prohibited; thus, B's interest under the prime lease may not be transferred under the sublease to C. Absent a prohibition in the prime lease contract A might be able to argue that the sublease to C materially increases A's risk; thus B's interest under the prime lease may not be transferred under the sublease to C, if after demand by A, C fails to provide the assurances required by subdivision (2) of Section 10303. Paragraph (b), subdivision (1), Section 10303.

§ 10301   PERSONAL PROPERTY LEASES   548

5. Resolution of this issue is also a function of the section dealing with the sublease of goods by a prime lessee (Section 10305). Subdivision (1) of Section 10305, which is subject to the rule of Section 10303 stated above, provides that C takes subject to the interest of A under the prime lease between A and B. However, there are two exceptions. First, if B is a merchant (subdivision (3), Section 10103 and subdivision (1), Section 2104) dealing in goods of that kind and C is a sublessee in the ordinary course of business (paragraphs (n) and (o), subdivision (1), Section 10103), C takes free of the prime lease between A and B. Second, if B has rejected the six combines under the prime lease with A, and B disposes of the goods by sublease to C, C takes free of the prime lease if C can establish good faith. Subdivision (4), Section 10511.

6. If the facts of this hypothetical are expanded and we assume that the prime lease obligated B to maintain the combines, an additional issue may be presented. Prior to entering the sublease, B, in satisfaction of its maintenance covenant, brought the two combines that it desired to sublease to a local independent dealer of A's. The dealer did the requested work for B. C inspected the combines on the dealer's lot after the work was completed. C signed the sublease with B two days later. C, however, was prevented from taking delivery of the two combines as B refused to pay the dealer's invoice for the repairs. The dealer furnished the repair service to B in the ordinary course of the dealer's business. If under applicable law the dealer has a lien on repaired goods in the dealer's possession, the dealer's lien will take priority over A's, B's and C's interests. Section 10306.

7. Now assume that C is in financial straits and one of C's creditors obtains a judgment against C. If the creditor levies on C's subleasehold interest in the two combines, who will prevail? Unless the levying creditor also holds a lien covered by Section 10306, discussed above, the judgment creditor will take its interest subject to B's rights under the sublease and A's rights under the prime lease. Subdivision (1), Section 10307. The hypothetical becomes more complicated if we assume that B is in financial straits and B's creditor holds the judgment. Here the judgment creditor takes subject to the sublease unless the lien attached to the two combines before the sublease contract became enforceable. Paragraph (a), subdivision (2), Section 10307. However, B's judgment creditor cannot prime A's interest in the goods because, with respect to A, the judgment creditor is a creditor of B in its capacity as lessee under the prime lease between A and B. Thus, here the judgment creditor's interest is subject to the lease between A and B. Subdivision (1), Section 10307.

8. Finally, assume that, on April 1, B is unable to pay A the deferred rent then due under the prime lease, but that C is current in its payments under the sublease from B. What effect will B's default under the prime lease between A and B have on C's rights under the sublease between B and C? Section 10301 provides that a lease contract is effective against the creditors of either party. Since a lease contract includes a sublease contract (paragraph (l), subdivision (1), Section 10103), the sublease contract between B and C arguably could be enforceable against A, a prime lessor who has extended unsecured credit to B, the prime lessee/sublessor, if the sublease contract meets the requirements of Section 10201. However, the rule stated in Section 10301 is subject to other provisions in this Division. Under Section 10305, C, as sublessee, would take subject to the prime lease contract in most cases. Thus, B's default under the prime lease will in most cases lead to A's recovery of the goods from C. Section 10523. C's recourse will be to assert a claim for damages against B. Section 10508.

Relationship Between Sections: 1. As the analysis of the hypothetical demonstrates, Chapter 3 of the Division focuses on issues that relate to the enforceability of the lease contract (Sections 10301, 10302, and 10303) and to the priority of various claims to the goods subject to the lease contract (Sections 10304, 10305, 10306, 10307, 10308, 10309, and 10310).

2. This section states a general rule of enforceability, which is subject to specific rules to the contrary stated elsewhere in the Division. Section 10302 negates any notion that the separation of title and possession is fraudulent as a rule of law. Finally, Section 10303 states a permissive rule with respect to the transfer of the lessor's interest (as well as the residual interest in the goods) or the lessee's interest under the lease contract. Conditions are imposed as a function of various issues including whether the transfer is voluntary or involuntary. In addition, a system of rules is created to deal with the rights and duties among assignor, assignee and the other party to the lease contract.

3. Sections 10304 and 10305 are twins that deal with good faith transferees of goods subject to the lease contract. Section 10304 creates a set of rules with respect to transfers by the lessor of goods subject to a lease contract; the transferee considered is a subsequent lessee of the goods. The priority dispute covered here is between the subsequent lessee and the original lessee of the goods (or persons claiming through the original lessee). Section 10305 creates a set of rules with respect to transfers by the lessee of goods subject to a lease contract; the transferees considered are buyers of the goods or sublessees of the goods. The priority dispute covered here is between the transferee and the lessor of the goods (or persons claiming through the lessor).

4. Section 10306 creates a rule with respect to priority disputes between holders of liens for services or materials furnished with respect to goods subject to a lease contract and the lessor or the lessee under that contract. Section 10307 creates a rule with respect to priority disputes between the lessee and creditors of the lessor and priority disputes between the lessor and creditors of the lessee.

5. Section 10308 creates a series of rules relating to allegedly fraudulent transfers and preferences. The most significant rule is that set forth in subdivision (3) which validates sale-leaseback transactions if the buyer-lessor can establish that he or she bought for value and in good faith.

6. Finally, Sections 10309 and 10310 create a series of rules with respect to priority disputes between various third parties and a lessor of fixtures or accessions, respectively, with respect thereto.

Cross References:

Division 1, esp. subdivision (37), Section 1201; subdivision (1), Section 2104; paragraph (j), subdivision (1), Section 10103; paragraph (l), subdivision (1), Section 10103; paragraph (n), subdivision (1), Section 10103; paragraph (o), subdivision (1), Section 10103; paragraph (w), subdivision (1), Section 10103; subdivision (3), Section 10103; subdivision (4), Section 10103; Section 10201; Sections 10301 through 10303; subdivision (1), Section 10303; paragraph (a), subdivision (1), Section 10303; paragraph (b), subdivision (1), Section 10303; Sections 10304 through 10307; subdivision (1), Section 10307; paragraph (a), subdivision (2), Section 10307; Sections 10308 through 10310; Section 10508; subdivision (4), Section 10511; Section 10523; Division 9, esp. Sections 9201 and 9408.

Definitional Cross References:

"Creditor". Subdivision (12), Section 1201.
"Goods". Paragraph (h), subdivision (1), Section 10103.
"Lease contract". Paragraph (l), subdivision (1), Section 10103.
"Party". Subdivision (29), Section 1201.
"Purchaser". Subdivision (33), Section 1201.
"Term". Subdivision (42), Section 1201.

Cross References

Definitions, merchant, between merchants, financing agency, see Commercial Code § 2104.
Installment lease contracts, rejection and default, see Commercial Code § 10510.
Lessee's remedies, see Commercial Code § 10508.
Priority of liens arising by attachment or levy on, security interests in, and other claims to goods, see Commercial Code § 10307.
Statute of Frauds, see Commercial Code § 10201.
Subsequent lease of goods by lessor, see Commercial Code § 10304.
Transfer party's interest under lease contract or of lessor's residual interest in goods, see Commercial Code § 10303.

§ 10302. Title To and Possession of Goods

Except as otherwise provided in this division, each provision of this division applies whether the lessor or a third party has title to the goods, and whether the lessor, the lessee, or a third party has possession of the goods, notwithstanding any statute or rule of law that possession or the absence of possession is fraudulent. *(Added by Stats.1988, c. 1359, § 5, operative Jan. 1, 1990.)*

California Comment
Report of the Assembly Committee on Judiciary
August 15, 1989

Uniform Statutory Source: Section 9–202.

Changes: Section 9202 was modified to reflect leasing terminology and to clarify the law of leases with respect to fraudulent conveyances or transfers.

Purposes: The separation of ownership and possession of goods between the lessor and the lessee (or a third party) has created problems under certain fraudulent conveyance statutes. See, *e.g.*, *In re Ludlum Enters.*, 510 F.2d 996 (5th Cir. 1975); *Suburbia Fed. Sav. & Loan Ass'n v. Bel-Air Conditioning Co.*, 385 So.2d 1151 (Fla.Dist.Ct.App.1980). This section provides, among other things, that separation of ownership and possession *per se* does not affect the enforceability of the lease contract. Sections 10301 and 10308.

Cross References:
Sections 10301, 10308 and 9202.

Definitional Cross References:
"Goods". Paragraph (h), subdivision (1), Section 10103.
"Lessee". Paragraph (n), subdivision (1), Section 10103.
"Lessor". Paragraph (p), subdivision (1), Section 10103.

Cross References

Special rights of creditors, see Commercial Code § 10308.
Title to collateral immaterial, see Commercial Code § 9202.

§ 10303. Creation of security interests; provisions prohibiting transfers of interests or rights; provisions prohibiting creation or enforcement of security interests

* * * (a) As used in the section, "creation of a security interest" includes the sale of a lease contract that is subject to Division 9 (commencing with Section 9101), Secured Transactions, by reason of paragraph (b) of subdivision (1) of Section 9102.

(b) Except as provided in subdivisions (c) and (d), a provision in a lease agreement which (1) prohibits the voluntary or involuntary transfer, including a transfer by sale, sublease, creation or enforcement of a security interest, or attachment, levy, or other judicial process, of an interest of a party under the lease contract * * * or of the lessor's residual interest in the goods * * *, or (2) makes such a transfer an event of default, gives rise to the rights and remedies provided in subdivision (e), but a transfer that is prohibited or is an event of default under the lease agreement is otherwise effective.

* * *

(c) A provision in a lease agreement which (1) prohibits the creation or enforcement of a security interest in an interest of a party under the lease contract or in the lessor's residual interest in the goods, or (2) makes such a transfer an event of default, is not enforceable unless, and then only to the extent that, there is an actual transfer by the lessee of the lessee's right of possession or use of the goods in violation of the provision or an actual delegation of a material performance of either party to the lease contract in violation of the provision. Neither the granting nor the enforcement of a security interest in (1) the lessor's interest under the lease contract or (2) the lessor's residual interest in the goods is a transfer that materially impairs the prospect of obtaining return performance by, materially changes the duty of, or materially increases the burden or risk imposed on, the lessee within the purview of subdivision (e) unless, and then only to the extent that, there is an actual delegation of a material performance of the lessor.

(d) A provision in a lease agreement which (1) prohibits a transfer of a right to damages for default with respect to the whole lease contract or of a right to payment arising out of the transferor's due performance of the transferor's entire obligation, or (2) makes such a transfer an event of default, is not enforceable, and such a transfer is not a transfer that materially impairs the prospect of obtaining return performance by, materially changes the duty of, or materially increases the burden or risk imposed on, the other party to the lease contract within the purview of subdivision (e).

(e) Subject to subdivisions (c) and (d):

(1) If a transfer is made which is made an event of default under a lease agreement, the party to the lease contract not making the transfer, unless that party waives the default or otherwise agrees, has the rights and remedies described in subdivision (b) of Section 10501.

(2) If paragraph (1) is not applicable and if a transfer is made that (A) is prohibited under a lease agreement or (B) materially impairs the prospect of obtaining return performance by, materially changes the duty of, or materially increases the burden or risk imposed on, the other party to the lease contract, unless the party not making the transfer agrees at any time to the transfer in the lease contract or otherwise, then, except as limited by contract, (C) the transferor is liable to the party not making the transfer for damages caused by the transfer to the extent that the damages could not reasonably be prevented by the party not making the transfer and (D) a court having jurisdiction may grant other appropriate relief, including cancellation of the lease contract or an injunction against the transfer.

* * * (f) A transfer of "the lease" or of "all my rights under the lease," or * * * a transfer in similar general terms, is a transfer of rights * * * and, unless the language or the circumstances, as in * * * a transfer for security, indicate the contrary, the transfer is a delegation of duties by the transferor to the * * * transferee. Acceptance by the transferee constitutes a promise by * * * the transferee to perform those duties. The promise is enforceable by either the transferor or the other party to the lease contract.

(g) Unless otherwise agreed by the lessor and the lessee, a delegation of performance does * * * not relieve the transferor as against the other party of any duty to perform or of any liability for default.

* * *

* * * (h) In a consumer lease, to prohibit the transfer of an interest of a party under the lease contract or to make a transfer an event of default, the language * * * must be specific, by a writing, and conspicuous. (Added by Stats.1988, c. 1359, § 5, operative Jan. 1, 1990. Amended by Stats.1991, c. 111 (S.B.972), § 25, eff. July 15, 1991.)

California Comment
Report of the Assembly Committee on Judiciary
August 15, 1989

Uniform Statutory Source: Section 2210.

Changes: The provisions of Section 2210 were incorporated in this Division, with substantial modifications to reflect leasing terminology and practice, as well as certain developments of the law with respect to creditors' rights.

Purposes: Unlike Section 2210, which deals with voluntary transfers of rights and duties under a sales contract, this section deals with involuntary as well as voluntary transfers of rights and duties under a lease contract. Voluntary transfers are permitted unless prohibited by the lease contract or, as is also the case for involuntary transfers, there is a material change in the duty of, or a material increase in the burden or risk to, the other party to the lease contract and the transferee fails to comply with the conditions in subdivision (2) within a reasonable time after a demand, which need not be in writing, has been made for such compliance.

Although paragraph (a) of subdivision (1) generally validates lease contract prohibitions upon voluntary transfers, there is an important exception in the case of transfers consisting of the grant of a security interest by the lessor. Paragraph (a) of subdivision (1), in combination with paragraph (a) of subdivision (3), invalidates any prohibition upon the creation or enforcement of a security interest in the interest of the lessor under the lease contract or the lessor's residual interest in the goods. This is in furtherance of the policy of the law to permit the free alienability for security purposes of intangible assets such as accounts and general intangibles. Subdivision (4), Section 9318.

Paragraph (b) of subdivision (1) does not apply to the creation of a security interest in the interest of the lessor under the lease contract or the lessor's residual interest in the goods; and it also does not apply to collections by the secured party of lease rentals or to any other exercise of rights by the secured party pursuant to the security interest; provided that a transfer of the interest of the lessor under the lease contract or the lessor's residual interest in the goods pursuant to a Division 9 foreclosure by the secured party (Sections 9504 and 9505) will permit the lessee to invoke its rights under paragraph (b) of subdivision (1). Whether a lessee can satisfy the criteria set forth in paragraph (b) of subdivision (1) in a case in which the secured party has exercised foreclosure rights with respect to the lessor's interest in the lease contract or the lessor's residual interest in the goods will depend upon the facts of each case. As a threshold matter, the lessee must first be able to establish that the transfer resulting from the foreclosure has materially increased the burden or risk imposed on the lessee. The lessee would not satisfy this requirement by merely showing that the lessor's interest in the lease contract or the goods has been terminated and is now owned by the transferee upon foreclosure. However, the lessee would satisfy this requirement by showing a reasonable probability that the transferee upon foreclosure cannot or will not perform any material continuing obligation owed by the lessor to the lessee under the lease contract.

The term "security interest" as used in paragraph (a) of subdivision (3) and paragraph (c) of subdivision (3) includes the sale of a lease contract since the lease contract constitutes chattel paper. Paragraph (b), subdivision (1), Section 9102.

Subdivision (2) establishes four criteria that must be satisfied by the transferee after a demand has been made. These criteria are modeled on the requirements contained in the Bankruptcy Reform Act of 1978, as amended, 11 U.S.C. § 365 (1982 & Supp. II 1984), governing the assumption and assignment of an unexpired lease or executory contract by a trustee in bankruptcy. Subdivision (5) of Section 2210 resolves this issue for sales by allowing the other party to demand assurances from the transferee (Section 2609). Section 365 of the Bankruptcy Code, a modern version of the provisions of Section 2609, provided a better model for resolving this issue for leases. If the lease contract requires the lessee to keep the goods free from liens and encumbrances, paragraph (d) of subdivision (3) makes it clear that the lessor may enforce this obligation under the lease contract. Paragraph (b) of subdivision (1) would not permit a lien creditor to override this lease provision by satisfying or agreeing to satisfy the requirements of subdivision (2).

Sections 9206 and 9318 are also relevant in this context. Section 9206 sanctions an agreement by a lessee not to assert certain types of claims or defenses against the lessor's assignee. Section 9318 deals with, among other things, the other party's rights against the assignee where subdivision (1) of Section 9206 does not apply. Since the definition of contract under subdivision (11) of Section 1201 includes a lease agreement, the definition of account debtor under paragraph (a) of subdivision (1) of Section 9105 includes a lessee of goods and Section 9202 applies to lease agreements; thus, there is no need to restate those sections in this Division. However, the reference to "defenses or claims arising out of a sale" in subdivision (1) of Section 9318 should be interpreted broadly to include defenses or claims arising out of a lease. This should follow as subdivision (1) of Section 9318 codifies the common law rule with respect to contracts, including contracts of sale and contracts of lease.

Subdivision (4) is taken almost verbatim from the provisions of subdivision (4) of Section 2210. The subdivision states a rule of construction that distinguishes a commercial assignment, which substitutes the assignee for the assignor as to rights and duties, and an assignment for security or financing assignment, which substitutes the assignee for the assignor only as to rights. Note that the assignment for security or financing assignment is a subset of all security interests. Security interest is defined to include "any interest of a buyer of ... chattel paper". Subdivision (37), Section 1201. Chattel paper is defined to include a lease. Paragraph (b), subdivision (1), Section 9105. Thus, a buyer of leases is the holder of a security interest in the leases. That conclusion should not influence this issue, as the policy is quite different. Whether a buyer of leases is the holder of a commercial assignment, or an assignment for security or financing assignment should be determined by the language of the assignment or the circumstances of the assignment.

While it is recognized that a lease contract may impose restrictions on the transfer of an interest of a party under a lease, such restrictions are not generally favored in law. Subdivision (7) balances these competing interests and ensures that both parties knowingly impose prohibitions on transfer, by providing that the language of prohibition be specific, by a writing, and conspicuous.

Cross References:

Subdivision (11), Section 1201; subdivision (37), Section 1201; Section 2210; Section 2609; paragraph (a), subdivision (1), Section 9105; Section 9206; and Section 9318.

Definitional Cross References:

"Agreed" and "Agreement". Subdivision (3), Section 1201.
"Conspicuous". Subdivision (10), Section 1201.
"Goods". Paragraph (h), subdivision (1), Section 10103.
"Lease". Paragraph (j), subdivision (1), Section 10103.
"Lease contract". Paragraph (*l*), subdivision (1), Section 10103.
"Lessee". Paragraph (n), subdivision (1), Section 10103.
"Lessor". Paragraph (p), subdivision (1), Section 10103.
"Lessor's residual interest". Paragraph (q), subdivision (1), Section 10103.
"Notice". Subdivision (25), Section 1201.
"Party". Subdivision (29), Section 1201.
"Person". Subdivision (30), Section 1201.
"Reasonable time". Subdivisions (1) and (2), Section 1204.
"Rights". Subdivision (36), Section 1201.
"Term". Subdivision (42), Section 1201.
"Writing". Subdivision (46), Section 1201.

Cross References

Agreement not to assert defenses against assignee, modification of sales warranties where security agreement exists, see Commercial Code § 9206.

Defenses against assignee, modification of contract after notification of assignment, terms prohibiting assignment, etc., see Commercial Code § 9318.

Delegation of performance, assignment of rights, see Commercial Code § 2210.

General definitions, see Commercial Code § 1201.

§ 10304. Subsequent Lease of Goods by Lessor

(a) Subject to * * * Section 10303, a subsequent lessee from a lessor of goods under an existing lease contract obtains, to the extent of the leasehold interest transferred, the leasehold interest in the goods that the lessor had or had power to transfer, and, except as provided in subdivision (b) of this section and subdivision (d) of Section 10527, takes subject to the existing lease contract. A lessor with voidable title has power to transfer a good leasehold interest to a good faith subsequent lessee for value, but only to the extent set forth in the preceding sentence. If goods have been delivered under a transaction of purchase, the lessor has that power even though:

(1) The lessor's transferor was deceived as to the identity of the lessor;

(2) The delivery was in exchange for a check which is later dishonored;

(3) It was agreed that the transaction was to be a "cash sale * * *"; or

(4) The delivery was procured through fraud punishable as larcenous under the criminal law.

(b) A subsequent lessee in the ordinary course of business from a lessor who is a merchant dealing in goods of that kind to whom the goods were entrusted by the existing lessee of that lessor before the interest of the subsequent lessee became enforceable against that lessor obtains, to the extent of the leasehold interest transferred, all of that lessor's and the existing lessee's rights to the goods, and takes free of the existing lease contract.

(c) A subsequent lessee from the lessor of goods that are subject to an existing lease contract and are covered by a certificate of title issued under a statute of this state or of another jurisdiction takes no greater rights than those provided by this section and by the certificate of title statute. *(Added by Stats.1988, c. 1359, § 5, operative Jan. 1, 1990. Amended by Stats.1991, c. 111 (S.B.972), § 26, eff. July 15, 1991.)*

California Comment
Report of the Assembly Committee on Judiciary
August 15, 1989

Uniform Statutory Source: Section 2–403.

Changes: While Section 2403 was used as a model for this section, the provisions of Section 2403 were significantly revised to reflect leasing practices and to integrate this Division with certificate of title statutes.

Purposes: This section must be read in conjunction with, as it is subject to, the provisions of Section 10303, which govern voluntary and involuntary transfers of rights and duties under a lease contract, including the lessor's residual interest in the goods.

This section must also be read in conjunction with Section 2403. This section and Section 10305 are derived from Section 2403, which states a unified policy on good faith purchases of goods. Given the scope of the definition of purchaser (subdivision (33), Section 1201), a person who bought goods to lease as well as a person who bought goods subject to an existing lease from a lessor will take pursuant to Section 2403. Further, a person who leases such goods from the person who bought them should also be protected under Section 2403, first because the lessee's rights are derivative and second because the definition of purchaser should be interpreted to include one who takes by lease; no negative implication should be drawn from the inclusion of lease in the definition of purchase in this Division. Paragraph (v), subdivision (1), Section 10103.

There are hypotheticals that relate to an entrustee's unauthorized lease of entrusted goods to a third party that are outside the provisions of Sections 2403, 10304 and 10305. Consider a sale of goods by M, a merchant, to B, a buyer. After paying for the goods B allows M to retain possession of the goods as B is short of storage. Before B calls for the goods M leases the goods to L, a lessee. This transaction is not governed by subdivision (2) of Section 2403 as L is not a buyer in the ordinary course of business. Subdivision (9), Section 1201. Further, this transaction is not governed by subdivision (2) of Section 10304 as B is not an existing lessee. Finally, this transaction is not governed by subdivision (2) of Section 10305 as B is not M's lessor. Subdivision (2) of Section 10307 resolves the potential dispute between B, M and L. By virtue of B's entrustment of the goods to M and M's lease of the goods to L, B has a cause of action against M under the common law. Subdivision (4), Section 10103 and Section 1103. See, *e.g.*, Restatement (Second) of Torts §§ 222A–243. Thus, B is a creditor of M. Subdivision (4), Section 10103 and subdivision (12), Section 1201. Subdivision (2) of Section 10307 provides that B, as M's creditor, takes subject to M's lease to L. Thus, if L does not default under the lease, L's enjoyment and possession of the goods should be undisturbed. However, B is not without recourse. B's action should result in a judgment against M providing, among other things, a turnover of all proceeds arising from M's lease to L, as well as a transfer of all of M's right, title and interest as lessor under M's lease to L, including M's residual interest in the goods. Paragraph (q), subdivision (1), Section 10103.

Subdivision (1) states a rule with respect to the leasehold interest obtained by a subsequent lessee from a lessor of goods under an existing lease contract. The interest will include such leasehold interest as the lessor has in the goods as well as the leasehold interest that the lessor had the power to transfer. Thus, the subsequent lessee obtains unimpaired all rights acquired under the law of agency, apparent agency, ownership or other estoppel, whether based upon statutory provisions or upon case law principles. Subdivision (4), Section 10103 and Section 1103. In general, the subsequent lessee takes subject to the existing lease contract, including the existing lessee's rights thereunder. Furthermore, the subsequent lease contract is, of course, limited by its own terms, and the subsequent lessee takes only to the extent of the leasehold interest transferred thereunder.

Subdivision (1) further provides that a lessor with voidable title has power to transfer a good leasehold interest to a good faith subsequent lessee for value. In addition, paragraphs (a) through (d) of subdivision (1) provide specifically for the protection of the good faith subsequent lessee for value in a number of specific situations which have been troublesome under prior law.

The position of an existing lessee who entrusts leased goods to its lessor is not distinguishable from the position of other entrusters. Thus, subdivision (2) provides that the subsequent lessee in the ordinary course of business takes free of the existing lease contract between the lessor entrustee and the lessee entruster, if the lessor is a merchant dealing in goods of that kind. Further, the subsequent lessee obtains all of the lessor entrustee's and the lessee entruster's rights to the goods, but only to the extent of the leasehold interest transferred by the lessor entrustee. Thus, the lessor entrustee retains the residual interest in the goods. Paragraph (q), subdivision (1), Section 10103. However, entrustment by the existing lessee must have occurred before the interest of the subsequent lessee became enforceable against the lessor. Entrusting is defined in subdivision (3) of Section 2403 and that definition applies here. Subdivision (3), Section 10103.

Subdivision (3) states a rule with respect to a transfer of goods from a lessor to a subsequent lessee where the goods are subject to an existing lease and covered by a certificate of title. The subsequent lessee's rights are no greater than those provided by this section and the applicable certificate of title statute, including any applicable case law construing such statute. Where the relationship between the certificate of title statute and Section 2403, the statutory analogue to this section, has been construed by a court, that construction is incorporated here. Subdivision (4), Section 10103 and subdivisions (1) and (2), Section 1102. The better rule is that the certificate of title statutes are in harmony with Section 2403 and thus would be in harmony with this section. *E.g., Atwood Chevrolet-Olds v. Aberdeen Mun. School Dist.*, 431 So.2d 926, 928 (Miss. 1983); *Godfrey v. Gilsdorf*, 476 P.2d 3, 6, 86 Nev. 714, 718 (1970); *Martin v. Nager*, 192 N.J. Super. 189, 197–98, 469 A.2d 519, 523 (Super.Ct.Ch.Div.1983). Where the certificate of title statute is silent on this issue of transfer, this section will control.

Cross References:

Section 1102; Section 1103; subdivision (33), Section 1201; Section 2403; paragraph (v), subdivision (1), Section 10103; subdivision (3),

§ 10304

Section 10103; subdivision (4), Section 10103; Section 10303; and Section 10305.

Definitional Cross References:
"Agreed". Subdivision (3), Section 1201.
"Delivery". Subdivision (14), Section 1201.
"Entrusting". Subdivision (3), Section 2403.
"Good faith". Subdivision (19), Section 1201 and paragraph (b), subdivision (1), Section 2103.
"Goods". Paragraph (h), subdivision (1), Section 10103.
"Lease". Paragraph (j), subdivision (1), Section 10103.
"Lease contract". Paragraph (*l*), subdivision (1), Section 10103.
"Leasehold interest". Paragraph (m), subdivision (1), Section 10103.
"Lessee". Paragraph (n), subdivision (1), Section 10103.
"Lessee in the ordinary course of business". Paragraph (*o*), subdivision (1), Section 10103.
"Lessor". Paragraph (p), subdivision (1), Section 10103.
"Merchant". Subdivision (1), Section 2104.
"Purchase". Paragraph (v), subdivision (1), Section 10103.
"Rights". Subdivision (36), Section 1201.
"Value". Subdivision (44), Section 1201.

Cross References

General definitions, see Commercial Code § 1201.
Power to transfer title, good faith purchase of goods, entrusting, see Commercial Code § 2403.
Rules of construction of code, variation by agreement, see Commercial Code § 1102.
Supplementary general principles of law applicable, see Commercial Code § 1103.

§ 10305. Sale or Sublease of Goods by Lessee

(a) Subject to the provisions of Section 10303, a buyer or sublessee from the lessee of goods under an existing lease contract obtains, to the extent of the interest transferred, the leasehold interest in the goods that the lessee had or had power to transfer, and, except as provided in subdivision (b) of this section and subdivision (d) of Section 10511, takes subject to the existing lease contract. A lessee with a voidable leasehold interest has power to transfer a good leasehold interest to a good faith buyer for value or a good faith sublessee for value, but only to the extent set forth in the preceding sentence. When goods have been delivered under a transaction of lease the lessee has that power even though:

(1) The lessor was deceived as to the identity of the lessee;

(2) The delivery was in exchange for a check which is later dishonored; or

(3) The delivery was procured through fraud punishable as larcenous under the criminal law.

(b) A buyer in the ordinary course of business or a sublessee in the ordinary course of business from a lessee who is a merchant dealing in goods of that kind to whom the goods were entrusted by the lessor obtains, to the extent of the interest transferred, all of the lessor's and lessee's rights to the goods, and takes free of the existing lease contract.

(c) A buyer or sublessee from the lessee of goods that are subject to an existing lease contract and are covered by a certificate of title issued under a statute of this state or of another jurisdiction takes no greater rights than those provided both by this section and by the certificate of title statute. *(Added by Stats.1988, c. 1359, § 5, operative Jan. 1, 1990. Amended by Stats. 1991, c. 111 (S.B.972), § 27, eff. July 15, 1991.)*

California Comment

Report of the Assembly Committee on Judiciary

August 15, 1989

Uniform Statutory Source: Section 2–403.

Changes: While Section 2403 was used as a model for this section, the provisions of Section 2403 were significantly revised to reflect leasing practice and to integrate this Division with certificate of title statutes.

Purposes: This section, a companion to Section 10304, states the rule with respect to the leasehold interest obtained by a buyer or sublessee from a lessee of goods under an existing lease contract. *Compare* Section 10304 Comment. Note that this provision is consistent with existing case law, which prohibits the bailee's transfer of title to a good faith purchaser for value under subdivision (1) of Section 2403. *Rohweder v. Aberdeen Product. Credit Ass'n*, 765 F.2d 109 (8th Cir. 1985).

Subdivision (2) is also consistent with existing case law. *American Standard Credit, Inc. v. National Cement Co.*, 643 F.2d 248, 269–70 (5th Cir. 1981); *but compare Exxon Co., U.S.A. v. TLW Computer Indus.*, 37 U.C.C. Rep.Serv. (Callaghan) 1052, 1057–58 (D.Mass.1983). Unlike subdivision (2) of Section 10304, this subdivision does not contain any requirement with respect to the time that the goods were entrusted to the merchant. In subdivision (2) of Section 10304 the competition is between two customers of the merchant lessor; the time of entrusting was added as a criterion to create additional protection to the customer who was first in time: the existing lessee. In subdivision (2) the equities between the competing interests were viewed as balanced.

There appears to be some overlap between subdivision (2) of Section 2403 and subdivision (2) of Section 10305 with respect to a buyer in the ordinary course of business. However, an examination of this Division's definition of buyer in the ordinary course of business (paragraph (a), subdivision (1), Section 10103) makes clear that this reference was necessary to treat entrusting in the context of a lease.

Subdivision (3) states a rule of construction with respect to a transfer of goods from a lessee to a buyer or sublessee, where the goods are subject to an existing lease and covered by a certificate of title. *Compare* Section 10304 Comment.

Cross References:
Section 2403; paragraph (a), subdivision (1), Section 10103; Section 10304; and subdivision (2), Section 10305.

Definitional Cross References:
"Buyer". Paragraph (a), subdivision (1), Section 2103.
"Buyer in the ordinary course of business". Paragraph (a), subdivision (1), Section 10103.
"Delivery". Subdivision (14), Section 1201.
"Entrusting". Subdivision (3), Section 2403.
"Good faith". Subdivision (19), Section 1201 and paragraph (b), subdivision (1), Section 2103.
"Goods". Paragraph (h), subdivision (1), Section 10103.
"Lease". Paragraph (j), subdivision (1), Section 10103.
"Lease contract". Paragraph (*l*), subdivision (1), Section 10103.
"Leasehold interest." Paragraph (m), subdivision (1), Section 10103.
"Lessee". Paragraph (n), subdivision (1), Section 10103.
"Lessee in the ordinary course of business". Paragraph (*o*), subdivision (1), Section 10103.
"Lessor". Paragraph (p), subdivision (1), Section 10103.
"Merchant". Subdivision (1), Section 2104.
"Rights". Subdivision (36), Section 1201.
"Sale". Subdivision (1), Section 2106.
"Sublease". Paragraph (w), subdivision (1), Section 10103.
"Value". Subdivision (44), Section 1201.

Cross References

Power to transfer title, good faith purchase of goods, entrusting, see Commercial Code § 2403.

Subsequent lease of goods by lessor, see Commercial Code § 10304.

§ 10306. Priority of Certain Liens Arising by Operation of Law

If a person in the ordinary course of his or her business furnishes services or materials with respect to goods subject to a lease contract, a lien upon those goods in the possession of that person given by statute or rule of law for those materials or services takes priority over any interest of the lessor or lessee under the lease contract or this division unless the lien is created by statute and the statute provides otherwise or unless the lien is created by rule of law and the rule of law provides otherwise. *(Added by Stats.1988, c. 1359, § 5, operative Jan. 1, 1990.)*

California Comment
Report of the Assembly Committee on Judiciary
August 15, 1989

Uniform Statutory Source: Section 9–310.
Changes: The approach reflected in the provisions of Section 9310 was included, but revised to conform to leasing terminology and to expand the exception to the special priority granted to protected liens to cover liens created by rule of law as well as those created by statute. The reference to "priority" in this section means that, in the circumstances prescribed by this section, the statutory lien attaches to the prescribed goods and becomes a charge upon the goods that is superior to the interests of both the lessee and the lessor in the goods.
Purposes: This section should be interpreted to allow a qualified lessor or a qualified lessee to be the competing lienholder if the statute or rule of law so provides. The reference to statute includes applicable regulations and cases; these sources must be reviewed in resolving a priority dispute under this section.
Cross Reference:
Section 9310.
Definitional Cross References:
"Goods". Paragraph (h), subdivision (1), Section 10103.
"Lease Contract". Paragraph (*l*), subdivision (1), Section 10103.
"Lessee". Paragraph (n), subdivision (1), Section 10103.
"Lessor". Paragraph (p), subdivision (1), Section 10103.
"Lien". Paragraph (r), subdivision (1), Section 10103.
"Person". Subdivision (30), Section 1201.

Cross References

Priority of certain liens arising by operation of law, see Commercial Code § 9310.

§ 10307. Priority of Liens Arising by Attachment or Levy on, Security Interests in, and Other Claims to Goods

(a) Except as otherwise provided in Section 10306, a creditor of a lessee takes subject to the lease contract.

(b) Except as otherwise provided in subdivisions (c) and * * * (d) and in Sections 10306 and 10308, a creditor of a lessor takes subject to the lease contract unless:

* * * (1) The creditor holds a lien that attached to the goods before the lease contract became enforceable,

* * * (2) The creditor holds a security interest in the goods and the lessee did not give value and receive delivery of the goods without knowledge of the security interest, or

* * * (3) The creditor holds a security interest in the goods * * * which was perfected (Section 9303) before * * * the lease contract became enforceable * * *.

(c) A lessee in the ordinary course of business takes the leasehold interest free of a security interest in the goods created by the lessor even though the security interest is perfected (Section 9303) and the lessee knows of its existence.

(d) A lessee other than a lessee in the ordinary course of business takes the leasehold interest free of a security interest to the extent that it secures future advances made after the secured party acquires knowledge of the lease unless the future advances are made pursuant to a commitment entered into without knowledge of the lease. *(Added by Stats.1988, c. 1359, § 5, operative Jan. 1, 1990. Amended by Stats.1988, c. 1368, § 13, operative Jan. 1, 1990; Stats.1991, c. 111 (S.B.972), § 28, eff. July 15, 1991.)*

California Comment
Report of the Assembly Committee on Judiciary
August 15, 1989

Uniform Statutory Source: None for subdivisions (1) and (2). Subdivisions (3) and (4) are derived from the provisions of subdivisions (1) and (3) of Section 9307, respectively.
Changes: The provisions of subdivisions (1) and (3) of Section 9307 were incorporated, and modified to reflect leasing terminology and the basic concepts reflected in this Division.
Purposes: Subdivision (1) states a general rule of priority that a creditor of the lessee takes subject to the lease contract. The term lessee (paragraph (n), subdivision (1), Section 10103) includes sublessee. Therefore, this subdivision not only covers disputes between the prime lessor and a creditor of the prime lessee but also disputes between the prime lessor, or the sublessor, and a creditor of the sublessee. Section 10301 Comment. Further, by using the term creditor (subdivision (12), Section 1201), this subdivision will cover disputes with a general creditor, a secured creditor, a lien creditor and any representative of creditors. Subdivision (4), Section 10103. The words "takes subject to the lease contract" mean that a creditor's lien or security interest can attach only to what the debtor (lessee) has. This is consistent with California law. For example, Section 701.640 of the Code of Civil Procedure states what a purchaser at an execution sale acquires at the sale. Section 701.640 provides:

"The purchaser of property at an execution sale acquires any interest of the judgment debtor in the property sold (1) that is held on the effective date of the lien under which the property was sold or (2) that is acquired between such effective date and the date of sale."

Whether a lien or security interest will ever attach to such property is a question that must be answered by other law. Are the goods property subject to attachment or enforcement of a money judgment? Are the debtor's contractual rights embodied in the lease contract itself property that is subject to statutory, consensual or judicial liens? These are issues that are not covered by this Division.

Subdivision (2) states a general rule of priority that a creditor of a lessor takes subject to the lease contract. Note the discussion above with regard to the scope of these rules. Section 10301 Comment. Thus, the section will not only cover disputes between the prime lessee and a creditor of the prime lessor but also disputes between a sublessee and a creditor of the sublessor. Subdivision (2) necessarily addresses two very different questions where the debtor is the lessor: (1) what interests of the lessor under a lease contract can be subjected to the claims of the lessor's creditors; and (2) whether, and under what circumstances, the interest of the lessee under a lease contract can be subjected to the claims of the lessor's creditors.

As to the first of these questions, the analysis is much the same as that in the discussion of subdivision (1). The lessor under a lease contract has a reversionary interest in the goods that are the subject of the lease contract and also has an interest in the lease contract itself. In general,

§ 10307

but subject to the exceptions stated in subdivision (2), a lien or security interest obtained by a creditor of the lessor in the goods that are the subject of a lease contract or in the lease contract itself can attach only to the lessor's interest in the lease contract (chattel paper) or to the lessor's residual interest in the goods that are the subject of the lease contract.

The second question focuses on the ability of a lessor's creditor to subject the interests of a lessee to the creditor's claim. The stated rule is subject to several important exceptions. If none of the exceptions is applicable, the subdivision provides that any lien or security interest obtained by a creditor of the lessor attaches to neither the lessee's interest in the lease contract nor the lessee's interest in the goods which are the subject of the lease contract. Thus, it is enforceable only against the lessor's interest, and then only to the extent permitted by the law creating the lien or security interest. Suppose, for example, that a judgment creditor of the lessor were to levy upon goods in the possession of the lessee. The lessee would be entitled to file a third-party claim pursuant to Section 720.110 of the Code of Civil Procedure and should be awarded judgment that the lessee is entitled to retain possession in accordance with the lease contract. If the levying officer does not have possession, the goods cannot be sold. Subdivision (a), Section 701.510, Code of Civil Procedure. Thus, the principle set forth in subdivision (2) would be carried into effect by the Enforcement of Judgments Law (Title 9 (commencing with Section 680.010) of Part 2 of the Code of Civil Procedure). However, the interest of the lessor in the lease contract is chattel paper. As such, a creditor may enforce a claim against it by way of attachment, execution, or other post-judgment remedy. A lessor's creditor may, be agreement, obtain a security interest in this chattel paper. None of these approaches will interfere with the lessee's rights under the lease contract.

As noted above, there are various exceptions to the general rule of subdivision (2), as follows:

1. One exception is that the rule is applicable except as otherwise provided in Section 10306. Section 10306 states a rule with respect to the enforceability and priority of an improver's possessory statutory or common law lien. Since subdivision (2) is concerned with the rights of creditors of the lessor, it appears that the rights of the lienor under Section 10306 do not depend on whether it is the lessee or the lessor who incurred the debt which gave rise to the statutory or common law lien. Thus, the lessee's leasehold interest may be subject to the improver's lien even though the lessee may not be liable for the debt.

2. A second exception is that the rule of subdivision (2) is applicable except as otherwise provided in Section 10308. That section, which is discussed below, deals with rights that a creditor of the lessor may have under fraudulent transfer law to avoid a lease contract as fraudulent.

3. Paragraph (a) of subdivision (2) provides an important exception to the basic rule that a creditor of the lessor takes subject to the lease contract. That exception is that the interest of a lessee is subject to the lien (paragraph (r), subdivision (1), Section 10103) of a creditor of the lessor if the lien attached to the goods before the lease contract became enforceable. Section 10301. This could result in a lessee's interest being subject to non-possessory statutory liens and non-possessory judicial liens of which there is no public record. Suppose, for example, that prior to the time when a lease contract became enforceable, the lessor, as a judgment debtor, was served with an order to appear for examination proceedings. Under subdivision (d) of Section 708.110 of the Code of Civil Procedure, the service of the order would create a secret lien in favor of the lessor's judgment creditor. However, under the Enforcement of Judgments Law, the lessee probably would take free of the lien as a person who had acquired an interest in property under the law of this state for fair consideration without knowledge of the lien. See subdivision (a), Section 697.910, Section 697.020, and subdivision (a), Section 697.740, Code of Civil Procedure.

4. Paragraph (b) of subdivision (2) provides that the holder of a security interest in the leased goods will not take subject to the lease contract if the lessee did not both give value and receive delivery of the goods without knowledge of the security interest. Under this paragraph, the holder of the security interest need not have perfected the security interest under Division 9. This paragraph places the rights of the lessee on a par with those of a buyer not in the ordinary course of business under Division 9 who must give value and receive delivery of the goods without knowledge of the security interest in order to take free of that security interest. Paragraph (c), subdivision (1), Section 9301.

5. Paragraph (c) of subdivision (2) offers protection to the holder of a perfected Division 9 security interest in the goods in the three enumerated circumstances. The 20-day grace period provided in this paragraph for the holder of a purchase money security interest is derived from the super priority rules of Division 9. See subdivision (4), Section 9312. This 20-day grace period is applicable whether the leased goods constitute "equipment" or "inventory" while owned by the debtor/lessor.

6. Subdivisions (3) and (4), which are modeled on the provisions of subdivisions (1) and (3) of Section 9307, respectively, state two exceptions to the priority rule stated in subdivision (2) with respect to a creditor who holds a security interest. The lessee in the ordinary course of business will be treated in the same fashion as the buyer in the ordinary course of business, given a priority dispute with a secured creditor over goods subject to a lease contract. Subdivision (4) protects a lessee, other than a lessee in the ordinary course of business, against certain future advances made by a secured party after the secured party acquires knowledge of the lease.

7. The rules stated in paragraph (b) of subdivision (2), paragraph (c) of subdivision (2), and subdivisions (3) and (4) can be illustrated by reviewing several hypotheticals. Assume that a corporation which is not a merchant acquires an item of equipment on credit from a supplier. To secure payment of the purchase price, the corporation grants to the supplier a purchase money security interest in the equipment. The supplier does not perfect the security interest under Division 9. Thereafter, the corporation, as lessor, enters into a lease of the equipment to an individual who was aware of the supplier's unperfected security interest before taking delivery of the equipment. In this circumstance, under paragraph (b) of subdivision (2) the supplier would not take subject to the lease contract since, even though its security interest was unperfected, the lessee was aware of the security interest before it took possession of the equipment. Assume the same facts except that the lessee was not aware of the security interest and gave value and took delivery of the equipment before the supplier perfected its security interest. In this circumstance, under paragraph (c) of subdivision (2) the supplier would take subject to the lease contract unless the supplier perfected its security interest in the equipment within 20 days after the earlier of the date that either the corporation or the lessee received possession of the equipment. If the secured party in the hypothetical was not a supplier but was the holder of a nonpurchase money security interest in the equipment, this 20-day grace period would not apply. In this instance, the secured party would therefore take subject to the lease contract since the lessee would have given value and taken possession of the equipment without knowledge of the security interest and before the secured party perfected its security interest. If the secured party in our hypothetical was a lender to the corporation and had perfected its security interest in the equipment before the lessee received possession of the equipment, the secured party would prevail under paragraph (c) of subdivision (2). However, if the lessee gave notice of the lease to the lender, under subdivision (4), the lessee would not take subject to the lender's security interest to the extent that it secured optional advances made after the lender received the notice. If the corporation was a merchant engaged in the business of selling or leasing equipment of the type purchased from the supplier, a different result would follow because the rules of subdivision (2) are subject to the rules of subdivisions (3) and (4). Under the revised hypothetical, the lessee should qualify as a "lessee in the ordinary course of business" (paragraph (o), subdivision (1), Section 10103); and subdivision (3) states that a lessee in the ordinary course of business will prevail over a prior perfected security interest even if the lessee knows of the existence of the security interest.

Cross References:

Subdivision (12), Section 1201; subdivision (37), Section 1201; paragraph (n), subdivision (1), Section 10103; paragraph (o), subdivision (1), Section 10103; paragraph (r), subdivision (1), Section 10103; subdivision (4), Section 10103; Section 10301 Comment; Division 9, esp. subdivision (1), Section 9307; subdivision (3), Section 9307; and paragraph (a), subdivision (5), Section 9312.

Definitional Cross References:

"Creditor". Subdivision (12), Section 1201.
"Goods". Paragraph (h), subdivision (1), Section 10103.
"Knowledge" and "Knows". Subdivision (25), Section 1201.
"Lease". Paragraph (j), subdivision (1), Section 10103.
"Lease contract". Paragraph (l), subdivision (1), Section 10103.

"Leasehold interest". Paragraph (m), subdivision (1), Section 10103.
"Lessee". Paragraph (n), subdivision (1), Section 10103.
"Lessee in the ordinary course of business". Paragraph (o), subdivision (1), Section 10103.
"Lessor". Paragraph (p), subdivision (1), Section 10103.
"Lien". Paragraph (r), subdivision (1), Section 10103.
"Party". Subdivision (29), Section 1201.
"Pursuant to commitment". Subdivision (3), Section 10103.
"Security interest". Subdivision (37), Section 1201.

Cross References

Priorities among conflicting security interest in the same collateral, see Commercial Code § 9312.
Protection of buyers of goods, see Commercial Code § 9307.

§ 10308. Special Rights of Creditors

(a) A creditor of a lessor in possession of goods subject to a lease contract may treat the lease contract as void if as against the creditor retention of possession by the lessor is fraudulent or void under any statute or rule of law, but retention of possession in good faith and current course of trade by the lessor for a commercially reasonable time after the lease contract becomes enforceable is not fraudulent or void.

(b) Nothing in this division impairs the rights of creditors of a lessor if the lease contract is made under circumstances which under any statute or rule of law apart from this division would constitute the transaction a fraudulent transfer or voidable preference.

(c) A creditor of a seller may treat a sale or an identification of goods to a contract for sale as void if as against the creditor retention of possession by the seller is fraudulent under any statute or rule of law, but retention of possession of the goods pursuant to a lease contract entered into by the seller as lessee and the buyer as lessor in connection with the sale or identification of the goods is not fraudulent if the buyer bought for value and in good faith. *(Added by Stats.1988, c. 1359, § 5, operative Jan. 1, 1990. Amended by Stats. 1991, c. 111 (S.B.972), § 29, eff. July 15, 1991.)*

California Comment
Report of the Assembly Committee on Judiciary
August 15, 1989

Uniform Statutory Source: Section 2–402(2) and (3)(b).
Changes: Rephrased and new material added to conform to leasing terminology and practice.
Purposes: Subdivision (1) states a general rule of avoidance where the lessor has retained possession of goods if such retention is fraudulent under any statute or rule of law. However, the subdivision creates an exception under certain circumstances for retention of possession of goods for a commercially reasonable time after the lease contract becomes enforceable.

Subdivision (2) also preserves the possibility of an attack on the lease by creditors of the lessor if the lease would constitute a fraudulent transfer or voidable preference under other law.

Finally, subdivision (3) states a new rule with respect to sale-leaseback transactions, *i.e.*, transactions where the seller sells goods to a buyer but possession of the goods is retained by the seller pursuant to a lease contract between the buyer as lessor and the seller as lessee. Notwithstanding any statute or rule of law that would treat such retention as fraud, whether *per se, prima facie,* or otherwise, such as Section 3440 of the Civil Code, the retention is not fraudulent if the buyer bought for value (subdivision (44), Section 1201) and in good faith (subdivision (19), Section 1201 and paragraph (b), subdivision (1), Section 2103).

Subdivisions (3) and (4), Section 10103. This provision overrides subdivision (2) of Section 2402 to the extent it would otherwise apply to a sale-leaseback transaction.

Cross References:
Subdivision (19), Section 1201; subdivision (44), Section 1201; subdivision (2), Section 2402; and subdivision (4), Section 10103.

Definitional Cross References:
"Buyer". Paragraph (a), subdivision (1), Section 2103.
"Contract". Subdivision (11), Section 1201.
"Creditor". Subdivision (12), Section 1201.
"Good faith". Subdivision (19), Section 1201 and paragraph (b), subdivision (1), Section 2103.
"Goods". Paragraph (h), subdivision (1), Section 10103.
"Lease contract". Paragraph (*l*), subdivision (1), Section 10103.
"Lessee". Paragraph (n), subdivision (1), Section 10103.
"Lessor". Paragraph (p), subdivision (1), Section 10103.
"Money". Subdivision (24), Section 1201.
"Reasonable time". Subdivisions (1) and (2), Section 1204.
"Rights". Subdivision (36), Section 1201.
"Sale". Subdivision (1), Section 2106.
"Seller". Paragraph (d), subdivision (1), Section 2103.
"Value". Subdivision (44), Section 1201.

Cross References

Inapplicability of provisions on conveyances of personal property without delivery, see Civil Code § 3440.9.
Rights of seller's creditors against sold goods, see Commercial Code § 2402.

§ 10309. Lessor's and Lessee's Rights When Goods Become Fixtures

(a) In this section:

(1) Goods are "fixtures" when they become so related to particular real estate that an interest in them arises under real estate law;

(2) A "fixture filing" is the filing, in the office where a mortgage on the real estate would be recorded, of a financing statement covering goods that are or are to become fixtures and conforming to the requirements of subdivision (5) of Section 9402;

(3) A lease is a "purchase money lease" unless the lessee has possession or use of the goods or the right to possession or use of the goods before the lease agreement is enforceable;

(4) A mortgage is a "construction mortgage" to the extent it secures an obligation incurred for the construction of an improvement on land including the acquisition cost of the land, if the recorded writing so indicates * * *; and

(5) "Encumbrance" includes real estate mortgages and other liens on real estate and all other rights in real estate that are not ownership interests.

(b) Under this division a lease may be of goods that are fixtures or may continue in goods that become fixtures, but no lease exists under this division of ordinary building materials incorporated into an improvement on land.

(c) This division does not prevent creation of a lease of fixtures pursuant to real estate law.

(d) The interest of a lessor of fixtures has priority over a conflicting interest of an encumbrancer or owner of the real estate if:

§ 10309

(1) The lease is a purchase money lease, the conflicting interest of the encumbrancer or owner arises before the goods become fixtures, a fixture filing covering the fixtures is filed before the goods become fixtures or within 20 days thereafter, and the lessee has an interest of record in the real estate or is in possession of the real estate;

(2) A fixture filing covering the fixtures is filed before the interest of the encumbrancer or owner is of record, the lessor's interest has priority over any conflicting interest of a predecessor in title of the encumbrancer or owner, and the lessee has an interest of record in the real estate or is in possession of the real estate;

(3) The fixtures are readily removable factory or office machines, readily removable equipment that is not primarily used or leased for use in the operation of the real estate, or readily removable replacements of domestic appliances that are goods subject to a consumer lease;

(4) The conflicting interest is a lien on the real estate obtained by legal or equitable proceedings after the lease contract is enforceable;

(5) The encumbrancer or owner has consented in writing to the lease or has disclaimed an interest in the goods as fixtures; or

(6) The lessee has a right to remove the goods as against the encumbrancer or owner. If the lessee's right to remove terminates, the priority of the interest of the lessor continues for a reasonable time.

(e) Notwithstanding paragraph (1) of subdivision (d) but otherwise subject to subdivision (d), the interest of a lessor of fixtures, including the lessor's residual interest, is subordinate to the conflicting interest of an encumbrancer of the real estate under a construction mortgage recorded before the goods become fixtures if the goods become fixtures before the completion of the construction. To the extent given to refinance a construction mortgage, the conflicting interest of an encumbrancer of the real estate under a mortgage has this priority to the same extent as the encumbrancer of the real estate under the construction mortgage.

(f) In cases not within the preceding subdivisions, priority between the interest of a lessor of fixtures, including the lessor's residual interest, and the conflicting interest of an encumbrancer or owner of the real estate who is not the lessee is determined by the priority rules governing conflicting interests in real estate.

(g) If the interest of a lessor of fixtures, including the lessor's residual interest, has priority over all conflicting interests of all owners and encumbrancers of the real estate, the lessor or the lessee may (1) on default, expiration, termination, or cancellation of the lease agreement * * * but subject to the * * * lease agreement and this division, or (2) if necessary to enforce * * * other rights and remedies of the lessor or lessee under this division, remove the goods from the real estate, free and clear of all conflicting interests of all owners and encumbrancers of the real estate, but * * * the lessor or lessee must reimburse any encumbrancer or owner of the real estate who is not the lessee and who has not otherwise agreed for the cost of repair of any physical injury, but not for any diminution in value of the real estate caused by the absence of the goods removed or by any necessity of replacing them. A person entitled to reimbursement may refuse permission to remove until the party seeking removal gives adequate security for the performance of this obligation. *(Added by Stats.1988, c. 1359, § 5, operative Jan. 1, 1990. Amended by Stats.1991, c. 111 (S.B.972), § 30, eff. July 15, 1991.)*

California Comment
Report of the Assembly Committee on Judiciary
August 15, 1989

Uniform Statutory Source: Section 9–313.

Changes: Revised to reflect leasing terminology and to add new material.

Purposes: While Section 9313 provided a model for this section, certain provisions were revised.

Paragraph (c) of subdivision (1) of Section 10309, which is new, defines purchase money lease to exclude leases where the lessee had possession or use of the goods or the right thereof before the lease agreement became enforceable. This term is used in paragraph (a) of subdivision (4) as one of the conditions that must be satisfied to obtain priority over the conflicting interest of an encumbrancer or owner of the real estate.

Subdivision (4) of Section 10309 states several priority rules found in this section. Paragraph (a) of subdivision (5) expands the scope of the provisions of paragraph (c) of subdivision (4) of Section 9313 to include readily removable equipment not primarily used or leased for use in the operation of real estate; the qualifier is intended to exclude from the expanded rule equipment integral to the operation of real estate, *e.g.*, heating and air conditioning equipment.

The rule stated in subdivision (6) is more liberal than the rule stated in subdivision (7) of Section 9313 in that issues of priority not otherwise resolved in this subdivision are left for resolution by the priority rules governing conflicting interests in real estate, as opposed to the subdivision (7) of Section 9313 automatic subordination of the security interest in fixtures.

The rule stated in subdivision (7) is more liberal than the rule stated in subdivision (8) of Section 9313 in that the right of removal is extended to both the lessor and the lessee and the occasion for removal includes expiration, termination or cancellation of the lease agreement, and enforcement of rights and remedies under this Division, as well as default. The new language also provides that upon removal the goods are free and clear of conflicting interests of owners and encumbrancers of the real estate.

Cross References:

Subdivision (37), Section 1201; paragraph (c), subdivision (1), Section 10309; subdivision (4), Section 10309; Division 9, esp. Section 9313; paragraph (c), subdivision (4), Section 9313; paragraph (d), subdivision (4), Section 9313; subdivision (7), Section 9313; subdivision (8), Section 9313; and Section 9408.

Definitional Cross References:

"Agreed". Subdivision (3), Section 1201.
"Cancellation". Paragraph (b), subdivision (1), Section 10103.
"Conforming". Paragraph (d), subdivision (1), Section 10103.
"Consumer lease". Paragraph (e), subdivision (1), Section 10103.
"Goods". Paragraph (h), subdivision (1), Section 10103.
"Lease". Paragraph (j), subdivision (1), Section 10103.
"Lease agreement". Paragraph (k), subdivision (1), Section 10103.
"Lease contract". Paragraph (l), subdivision (1), Section 10103.
"Lessee". Paragraph (n), subdivision (1), Section 10103.
"Lessor". Paragraph (p), subdivision (1), Section 10103.
"Lien". Paragraph (r), subdivision (1), Section 10103.

"Mortgage". Paragraph (j), subdivision (1), Section 9105.
"Party". Subdivision (29), Section 1201.
"Person". Subdivision (30), Section 1201.
"Reasonable time". Subdivisions (1) and (2), Section 1204.
"Remedy". Subdivision (34), Section 1201.
"Rights". Subdivision (36), Section 1201.
"Security interest". Subdivision (37), Section 1201.
"Termination". Paragraph (z), subdivision (1), Section 10103.
"Value". Subdivision (44), Section 1201.
"Writing". Subdivision (46), Section 1201.

Cross References

Fixtures, fixture filing, construction mortgages, see Commercial Code § 9313.

§ 10310. Lessor's and Lessee's Rights When Goods Become Accessions

(a) Goods are "accessions" when they are installed in or affixed to other goods.

(b) The interest of a lessor or a lessee under a lease contract entered into before the goods became accessions is superior to all interests in the whole except as stated in subdivision (d).

(c) The interest of a lessor or a lessee under a lease contract entered into at the time or after the goods became accessions is superior to all subsequently acquired interests in the whole except as stated in subdivision (d) but is subordinate to interests in the whole existing at the time the lease contract was made unless the holders of such interests in the whole have in writing consented to the lease or disclaimed an interest in the goods as part of the whole.

(d) The interest of a lessor or a lessee under a lease contract described in subdivision (b) or (c) is subordinate to the interest of:

(1) A buyer in the ordinary course of business or a lessee in the ordinary course of business of any interest in the whole acquired after the goods became accessions; or

(2) A creditor with a security interest in the whole perfected before the lease contract was made to the extent that the creditor makes subsequent advances without knowledge of the lease contract.

(e) When under subdivision (b) or * * * subdivisions (c) and (d) a lessor or a lessee of accessions holds an interest that is superior to all interests in the whole, the lessor or the lessee may (1) on default, expiration, termination, or cancellation of the lease contract by the other party but subject to the provisions of the lease contract and this division, or (2) if necessary to enforce his or her other rights and remedies under this division, remove the goods from the whole, free and clear of all interests in the whole, but he or she must reimburse any holder of an interest in the whole who is not the lessee and who has not otherwise agreed for the cost of repair of any physical injury but not for any diminution in value of the whole caused by the absence of the goods removed or by any necessity for replacing them. A person entitled to reimbursement may refuse permission to remove until the party seeking removal gives adequate security for the performance of this obligation. *(Added by Stats.1988, c. 1359, § 5, operative Jan. 1, 1990. Amended by Stats.1991, c. 111 (S.B.972), § 31, eff. July 15, 1991.)*

California Comment
Report of the Assembly Committee on Judiciary
August 15, 1989

Uniform Statutory Source: Section 9–314.

Changes: Revised to reflect leasing terminology and to add new material.

Purposes: Subdivisions (1) and (2) restate the provisions of subdivision (1) of Section 9314 to clarify the definition of accession and to add leasing terminology to the priority rule that applies when the lease is entered into before the goods become accessions. Subdivision (3) restates the provisions of subdivision (2) of Section 9314 to add leasing terminology to the priority rule that applies when the lease is entered into on or after the goods become accessions. Unlike the rule with respect to security interests, the lease is merely subordinate, not invalid.

Subdivision (4) creates two exceptions to the priority rules stated in subdivisions (2) and (3). Subdivision (4) deletes the special priority rule found in the provisions of paragraph (b) of subdivision (4) of Section 9314 as the interests of the lessor and lessee are entitled to greater protection.

Finally, subdivision (5) is modeled on the provisions of subdivision (4) of Section 9314 with respect to removal of accessions, restated to reflect the parallel changes in subdivision (8) of Section 10309.

Neither this section nor Section 9314 governs where the accession to the goods is not subject to the interest of a lessor or a lessee under a lease contract and is not subject to the interest of a secured party under a security agreement. This issue is to be resolved by the courts, case by case.

Cross References:

Subdivision (8), Section 10309; subdivision (1), Section 9314; subdivision (2), Section 9314; paragraph (b), subdivision (3), Section 9314; and subdivision (4), Section 9314.

Definitional Cross References:

"Agreed". Subdivision (3), Section 1201.
"Buyer in the ordinary course of business". Paragraph (a), subdivision (1), Section 10103.
"Cancellation". Paragraph (b), subdivision (1), Section 10103.
"Creditor". Subdivision (12), Section 1201.
"Goods". Paragraph (h), subdivision (1), Section 10103.
"Holder". Subdivision (20), Section 1201.
"Knowledge". Subdivision (25), Section 1201.
"Lease". Paragraph (j), subdivision (1), Section 10103.
"Lease contract". Paragraph (*l*), subdivision (1), Section 10103.
"Lessee". Paragraph (n), subdivision (1), Section 10103.
"Lessee in the ordinary course of business". Paragraph (o), subdivision (1), Section 10103.
"Lessor". Paragraph (p), subdivision (1), Section 10103.
"Party". Subdivision (29), Section 1201.
"Person". Subdivision (30), Section 1201.
"Remedy". Subdivision (34), Section 1201.
"Rights". Subdivision (36), Section 1201.
"Security interest". Subdivision (37), Section 1201.
"Termination". Paragraph (z), subdivision (1), Section 10103.
"Value". Subdivision (44), Section 1201.
"Writing". Subdivision (46), Section 1201.

Cross References

Accessions, generally, see Commercial Code § 9314.

§ 10311. Priority; subordination agreements

Nothing in this division prevents subordination by agreement by any person entitled to priority. *(Added by Stats.1991, c. 111 (S.B.972), § 32, eff. July 15, 1991.)*

CHAPTER 4. PERFORMANCE OF LEASED CONTRACT: REPUDIATED, SUBSTITUTED, AND EXCUSED

Section
10401. Insecurity: Adequate Assurance of Performance.
10402. Anticipatory Repudiation.
10403. Retraction of Anticipatory Repudiation.
10404. Substituted Performance.
10405. Excused Performance.
10406. Procedure on Excused Performance.
10407. Irrevocable Promises: Finance Leases.

§ 10401. Insecurity: Adequate Assurance of Performance

(a) A lease contract imposes an obligation on each party that the other's expectation of receiving due performance will not be impaired.

(b) If reasonable grounds for insecurity arise with respect to the performance of either party, the insecure party may demand in writing adequate assurance of due performance. Until the insecure party receives that assurance, if commercially reasonable the insecure party may suspend any performance for which he or she has not already received the agreed return.

(c) A repudiation of the lease contract occurs if assurance of due performance adequate under the circumstances of the particular case is not provided to the insecure party within a reasonable time, not to exceed 30 days after receipt of a demand by the other party.

(d) Between merchants, the reasonableness of grounds for insecurity and the adequacy of any assurance offered must be determined according to commercial standards.

(e) Acceptance of any nonconforming delivery or payment does not prejudice the aggrieved party's right to demand adequate assurance of future performance. (Added by Stats.1988, c. 1359, § 5, operative Jan. 1, 1990. Amended by Stats.1991, c. 111 (S.B.972), § 33, eff. July 15, 1991.)

California Comment
Report of the Assembly Committee on Judiciary
August 15, 1989

Uniform Statutory Source: Section 2–609.
Changes: Revised to reflect leasing practices and terminology. Note that in the analogue to subdivision (3) (subdivision (4), Section 2609), the adjective "justified" modifies demand. The adjective was deleted here as unnecessary, implying no substantive change.
Definitional Cross References:
 "Aggrieved party". Subdivision (2), Section 1201.
 "Agreed". Subdivision (3), Section 1201.
 "Between merchants". Subdivision (3), Section 2104.
 "Conforming". Paragraph (d), subdivision (1), Section 10103.
 "Delivery". Subdivision (14), Section 1201.
 "Lease contract". Paragraph (*l*), subdivision (1), Section 10103.
 "Party". Subdivision (29), Section 1201.
 "Reasonable time". Subdivisions (1) and (2), Section 1204.
 "Receipt". Paragraph (c), subdivision (1), Section 2103.
 "Rights". Subdivision (36), Section 1201.
 "Writing". Subdivision (46), Section 1201.

§ 10402. Anticipatory Repudiation

(a) If either party repudiates a lease contract, other than a consumer lease, with respect to a performance not yet due under the lease contract, the loss of which performance will substantially impair the value of the lease contract to the other, the aggrieved party may:

(1) For a commercially reasonable time, await retraction of repudiation and performance by the repudiating party;

(2) Make demand pursuant to Section 10401 and await assurance of future performance adequate under the circumstances of the particular case; or

(3) Resort to any right or remedy upon default under the lease contract or this division, even though the aggrieved party has notified the repudiating party that the aggrieved party would await the repudiating party's performance and assurance and has urged retraction. In addition, whether or not the aggrieved party is pursuing one of the foregoing remedies, the aggrieved party may suspend performance or, if the aggrieved party is the lessor, proceed in accordance with the provisions of this division on the lessor's right to identify goods to the lease contract notwithstanding default or to salvage unfinished goods (Section 10524).

(b) The rights and remedies of the parties to a consumer lease in connection with a repudiation of that lease shall be determined under other laws, and this section shall not affect the applicability or interpretation of those laws. (Added by Stats.1988, c. 1359, § 5, operative Jan. 1, 1990. Amended by Stats.1988, c. 1368, § 13.2, operative Jan. 1, 1990; Stats.1991, c. 111 (S.B. 972), § 34, eff. July 15, 1991.)

California Comment
Report of the Assembly Committee on Judiciary
August 15, 1989

Uniform Statutory Source: Section 2–610.
Changes: Revised to reflect leasing practices and terminology. Subdivision (2) leaves to other laws the rules governing repudiation in the case of consumer leases. The failure to include consumer leases in this section carries no negative or positive implications as to the applicability of such laws; nor does such failure in any way affect the interpretation of any such laws that are deemed applicable to consumer leases.
Definitional Cross References:
 "Aggrieved party". Subdivision (2), Section 1201.
 "Goods". Paragraph (h), subdivision (1), Section 10103.
 "Lease contract". Paragraph (*l*), subdivision (1), Section 10103.
 "Lessor". Paragraph (p), subdivision (1), Section 10103.
 "Notifies". Subdivision (26), Section 1201.
 "Party". Subdivision (29), Section 1201.
 "Reasonable time". Subdivisions (1) and (2), Section 1204.
 "Remedy". Subdivision (34), Section 1201.
 "Rights". Subdivision (36), Section 1201.
 "Value". Subdivision (44), Section 1201.

§ 10403. Retraction of Anticipatory Repudiation

(a) Until the repudiating party's next performance is due, the repudiating party can retract the repudiation unless, since the repudiation, the aggrieved party has canceled the lease contract or materially changed the aggrieved party's position or otherwise indicated that the aggrieved party considers the repudiation final.

(b) Retraction may be by any method that clearly indicates to the aggrieved party that the repudiating party intends to perform under the lease contract and includes any assurance demanded under Section 10401.

(c) Retraction reinstates a repudiating party's rights under a lease contract with due excuse and allowance to the aggrieved party for any delay occasioned by the repudiation. *(Added by Stats.1988, c. 1359, § 5, operative Jan. 1, 1990. Amended by Stats.1991, c. 111 (S.B.972), § 35, eff. July 15, 1991.)*

California Comment
Report of the Assembly Committee on Judiciary
August 15, 1989

Uniform Statutory Source: Section 2–611.

Changes: Revised to reflect leasing practices and terminology. Note that in the analogue to subdivision (2) (subdivision (2), Section 2611) the adjective "justifiably" modifies demanded. The adjective was deleted here (as it was in Section 10401) as unnecessary, implying no substantive change.

Definitional Cross References:
"Aggrieved party". Subdivision (2), Section 1201.
"Cancellation". Paragraph (b), subdivision (1), Section 10103.
"Lease contract". Paragraph (*l*), subdivision (1), Section 10103.
"Party". Subdivision (29), Section 1201.
"Rights". Subdivision (36), Section 1201.

§ 10404. Substituted Performance

(a) If without fault of the lessee, the lessor, and the supplier, the agreed berthing, loading, or unloading facilities fail or the agreed type of carrier becomes unavailable or the agreed manner of delivery otherwise becomes commercially impracticable, but a commercially reasonable substitute is available, the substitute performance must be tendered and accepted.

(b) If the agreed means or manner of payment fails because of domestic or foreign governmental regulation:

(1) The lessor may withhold or stop delivery or cause the supplier to withhold or stop delivery unless the lessee provides a means or manner of payment that is commercially a substantial equivalent; and

(2) If delivery has already been taken, payment by the means or in the manner provided by the regulation discharges the lessee's obligation unless the regulation is discriminatory, oppressive, or predatory. *(Added by Stats.1988, c. 1359, § 5, operative Jan. 1, 1990. Amended by Stats.1991, c. 111 (S.B.972), § 36, eff. July 15, 1991.)*

California Comment
Report of the Assembly Committee on Judiciary
August 15, 1989

Uniform Statutory Source: Section 2–614.

Changes: Revised to reflect leasing practices and terminology.

Definitional Cross References:
"Agreed". Subdivision (3), Section 1201.
"Delivery". Subdivision (14), Section 1201.
"Fault". Paragraph (f), subdivision (1), Section 10103.
"Lessee". Paragraph (n), subdivision (1), Section 10103.
"Lessor". Paragraph (p), subdivision (1), Section 10103.
"Supplier". Paragraph (x), subdivision (1), Section 10103.

§ 10405. Excused Performance

Subject to Section 10404 on substituted performance, the following rules apply:

(1) Delay in delivery or nondelivery in whole or in part by a lessor or a supplier who complies with paragraphs (2) and (3) is not a default under the lease contract if performance as agreed has been made impracticable by the occurrence of a contingency the nonoccurrence of which was a basic assumption on which the lease contract was made or by compliance in good faith with any applicable foreign or domestic governmental regulation or order, whether or not the regulation or order later proves to be invalid.

(2) If the causes mentioned in paragraph (1) affect only part of the lessor's or the supplier's capacity to perform, he or she shall allocate production and deliveries among his or her customers but at his or her option may include regular customers not then under contract for sale or lease as well as his or her own requirements for further manufacture. He or she may so allocate in any manner that is fair and reasonable.

(3) The lessor seasonably shall notify the lessee and in the case of a finance lease the supplier seasonably shall notify the lessor and the lessee, if known, that there will be delay or nondelivery and, if allocation is required under paragraph (2), of the estimated quota thus made available for the lessee. *(Added by Stats. 1988, c. 1359, § 5, operative Jan. 1, 1990. Amended by Stats.1991, c. 111 (S.B.972), § 37, eff. July 15, 1991.)*

California Comment
Report of the Assembly Committee on Judiciary
August 15, 1989

Uniform Statutory Source: Section 2–615.

Changes: Revised to reflect leasing practices and terminology.

Definitional Cross References:
"Agreed". Subdivision (3), Section 1201.
"Contract". Subdivision (11), Section 1201.
"Delivery". Subdivision (14), Section 1201.
"Finance lease". Paragraph (g), subdivision (1), Section 10103.
"Good faith". Subdivision (19), Section 1201 and Paragraph (b), subdivision (1), Section 2103.
"Knows". Subdivision (25), Section 1201.
"Lease". Paragraph (j), subdivision (1), Section 10103.
"Lease contract". Paragraph (*l*), subdivision (1), Section 10103.
"Lessee". Paragraph (n), subdivision (1), Section 10103.
"Lessor". Paragraph (p), subdivision (1), Section 10103.
"Notifies". Subdivision (26), Section 1201.
"Sale". Subdivision (1), Section 2106.
"Seasonably". Subdivision (3), Section 1204.
"Supplier". Paragraph (x), subdivision (1), Section 10103.

§ 10406. Procedure on Excused Performance

(a) If the lessee receives notification of a material or indefinite delay or an allocation justified under Section

10405, the lessee may by written notification to the lessor as to any goods involved, and with respect to all of the goods if under an installment lease contract the value of the whole lease contract is substantially impaired (Section 10510):

(1) Terminate the lease contract (subdivision (b) of Section 10505); or

(2) Except in a finance lease, modify the lease contract by accepting the available quota in substitution, with due allowance from the rent payable for the balance of the lease term for the deficiency but without further right against the lessor.

(b) If, after receipt of a notification from the lessor under Section 10405, the lessee fails so to modify the lease agreement within a reasonable time not exceeding 30 days, the lease contract lapses with respect to any deliveries affected. *(Added by Stats.1988, c. 1359, § 5, operative Jan. 1, 1990. Amended by Stats.1991, c. 111 (S.B.972), § 38, eff. July 15, 1991.)*

California Comment

Report of the Assembly Committee on Judiciary

August 15, 1989

Uniform Statutory Source: Section 2–616(1) and (2).

Changes: Revised to reflect leasing practices and terminology. Note that paragraph (a) of subdivision (1) allows the lessee under a lease, including a finance lease, the right to terminate the lease for excused performance (Sections 10404 and 10405). However, paragraph (b) of subdivision (1), which allows the lessee the right to modify the lease for excused performance, excludes a finance lease. This exclusion is compelled by the same policy that led to codification of provisions with respect to irrevocable promises. Section 10407.

Definitional Cross References:

"Consumer lease". Paragraph (e), subdivision (1), Section 10103.
"Delivery". Subdivision (14), Section 1201.
"Finance lease". Paragraph (g), subdivision (1), Section 10103.
"Goods". Paragraph (h), subdivision (1), Section 10103.
"Installment lease contract". Paragraph (i), subdivision (1), Section 10103.
"Lease agreement". Paragraph (k), subdivision (1), Section 10103.
"Lease contract". Paragraph (*l*), subdivision (1), Section 10103.
"Lessee". Paragraph (n), subdivision (1), Section 10103.
"Lessor". Paragraph (p), subdivision (1), Section 10103.
"Notice". Subdivision (25), Section 1201.
"Reasonable time". Subdivisions (1) and (2), Section 1204.
"Receipt". Paragraph (c), subdivision (1), Section 2103.
"Rights". Subdivision (36), Section 1201.
"Termination". Paragraph (z), subdivision (1), Section 10103.
"Value". Subdivision (44), Section 1201.
"Written". Subdivision (46), Section 1201.

§ 10407. Irrevocable Promises: Finance Leases

(a) In the case of a finance lease that is not a consumer lease * * * the lessee's promises under the lease contract become irrevocable and independent upon the lessee's acceptance of the goods.

(b) A promise that has become irrevocable and independent under subdivision (a):

(1) Is effective and enforceable between the parties, and by or against third parties including assignees of the parties; and

(2) Is not subject to cancellation, termination, modification, repudiation, excuse, or substitution without the consent of the party to whom the promise runs.

(c) This section does not affect the validity under any other law of a covenant in any lease contract making the lessee's promises irrevocable and independent upon the lessee's acceptance of the goods. *(Added by Stats.1988, c. 1359, § 5, operative Jan. 1, 1990. Amended by Stats.1991, c. 111 (S.B.972), § 39, eff. July 15, 1991.)*

California Comment

Report of the Assembly Committee on Judiciary

August 15, 1989

Uniform Statutory Source: None.

Purposes: This section extends the benefits of the classic "hell or high water" clause to a finance lease that is not a consumer lease. This section is self-executing; no special provision need be added to the contract. This section makes covenants in a finance lease irrevocable and independent due to the function of the finance lessor in a three party relationship: the lessee is looking to the supplier to perform the essential covenants and warranties. Section 10209. Thus, upon the lessee's acceptance of the goods the lessee's promises to the lessor under the lease contract become irrevocable and independent. The provisions of this section remain subject to the obligation of good faith (subdivision (4), Section 10103 and Section 1203), and the lessee's revocation of acceptance (Section 10517).

The section requires the lessee to perform even if the lessor's performance after the lessee's acceptance is not in accordance with the lease contract; the lessee may, however, have and pursue a cause of action against the lessor, *e.g.,* breach of certain limited warranties (Section 10210 and subdivision (1), Section 10211). This is appropriate because the benefit of the supplier's promises and warranties to the lessor under the supply contract is extended to the lessee under the finance lease. Section 10209. Despite this balance, this section excludes a finance release that is a consumer lease.

The relationship of the three parties to a transaction that qualifies as a finance lease is best demonstrated by a hypothetical. A, the potential lessor, has been contacted by B, the potential lessee, to discuss the lease of an expensive line of equipment that B has recently placed an order for with C, the manufacturer of such goods. The negotiation is completed and A, as lessor, and B, as lessee, sign a lease of the line of equipment for a 60-month term. B, as buyer, assigns the purchase order with C to A. If this transaction creates a lease (paragraph (j), subdivision (1), Section 10103), this transaction should qualify as a finance lease. Paragraph (g), Subdivision (1), Section 10103.

The line of equipment is delivered by C to B's place of business. After installation by C and testing by B, B accepts the goods by signing a certificate of delivery and acceptance, a copy of which is sent by B to A and C. One year later the line of equipment malfunctions and B falls behind in its manufacturing schedule.

Under this Division, because the lease is a finance lease, no warranty of fitness or merchantability is extended by A to B. Subdivision (1), Section 10212 and Section 10213. Absent an express provision in the lease agreement, application of Section 10210 or subdivision (1) of Section 10211, or application of the principles of law and equity, including the law with respect to fraud, duress, or the like (subdivision (4), Section 10103 and Section 1103), B has no claim against A. B's obligation to pay rent to A continues as the obligation became irrevocable and independent when B accepted the line of equipment (subdivision (1), Section 10407). B has no right of set-off with respect to any part of the rent still due under the lease. Subdivision (6), Section 10508. However, B may have another remedy. Despite the lack of privity between B and C (the purchase order with C having been assigned by B to A), B may have a claim against C. Subdivision (1), Section 10209.

This section is silent as to whether a "hell or high water" clause, *i.e.,* a clause that is to the effect of this section, is enforceable if included in a finance lease that is a consumer lease or a lease that is not a finance lease. That issue will continue to be determined by the facts of each case under other applicable law. Section 10104; subdivision (4),

Section 10103; Section 9206; and Section 9318. However, with respect to finance leases that are not consumer leases courts have enforced "hell or high water" clauses. *In re O.P.M. Leasing Servs.*, 21 Bankr. 993, 1006 (Bankr.S.D.N.Y.1982). Subdivision (3) makes it clear that this section carries no positive or negative implication as to the validity of such clauses in contexts where the section does not apply.

Subdivision (2) further provides that a promise that has become irrevocable and independent under subdivision (1) is enforceable not only between the parties but also against third parties. Thus, the finance lease can be transferred or assigned without disturbing enforceability. Further, subdivision (2) also provides that the promise cannot, among other things, be cancelled or terminated without the consent of the lessor.

Cross References:

Section 1103; Section 1203; paragraph (g), subdivision (1), Section 10103; paragraph (j), subdivision (1), Section 10103; subdivision (4), Section 10103; Section 10104; Section 10209; subdivision (1), Section 10209; Section 10210; subdivision (1), Section 10211; subdivision (1), Section 10212; Section 10213; paragraph (b), subdivision (1), Section 10517; Section 9206; and Section 9318.

Definitional Cross References:

"Cancellation". Paragraph (b), subdivision (1), Section 10103.
"Consumer lease". Paragraph (e), subdivision (1), Section 10103.
"Finance lease". Paragraph (g), subdivision (1), Section 10103.
"Goods". Paragraph (h), subdivision (1), Section 10103.
"Lease contract". Paragraph (*l*), subdivision (1), Section 10103.
"Lessee". Paragraph (n), subdivision (1), Section 10103.
"Party". Subdivision (29), Section 1201.
"Termination". Paragraph (z), subdivision (1), Section 10103.

Cross References

Agreement not to assert defenses against assignee, see Commercial Code § 9206.
Defenses against assignee, terms prohibiting assignment ineffective, see Commercial Code § 9318.
Exclusion or modification of warranties, see Commercial Code § 10214.
Implied warranty of fitness for particular purpose, see Commercial Code § 10213.
Implied warranty of merchantability, see Commercial Code § 10212.
Leases subject to other statutes, see Commercial Code § 10104.
Lessee under finance lease as beneficiary of supply contract, see Commercial Code § 10209.
Revocation of acceptance of goods, see Commercial Code § 10517.
Supplementary general principles of law applicable, see Commercial Code § 1103.
Warranties against interference and against infringement, lessee's obligation against infringement, see Commercial Code § 10211.

CHAPTER 5. DEFAULT

Article	Section
1. In General	10501
2. Default by Lessor	10508
3. Default by Lessee	10523

ARTICLE 1. IN GENERAL

Section
10501. Default: Procedure.
10502. Notice after Default.
10503. Rights and remedies included in lease agreement; exclusive remedies; consequential damages; rights and remedies on default of obligation or promise collateral or ancillary to lease contract.
10504. Liquidation of damages; lessee's right to restitution.
10505. Cancellation, termination, or rescission; effect on obligations, rights, and remedies; rights and remedies for material misrepresentation or fraud.
10506. Statute of Limitations.
10507. Proof of Market Rent; Time and Place.

§ 10501. Default: Procedure

(a) Whether the lessor or the lessee is in default under a lease contract is determined by the lease agreement and this division.

(b) If the lessor or the lessee is in default under the lease contract, the party seeking enforcement has rights and remedies as provided in this division and, except as limited by this division, as provided in the lease agreement.

(c) If the lessor or the lessee is in default under the lease contract, the party seeking enforcement may reduce the party's claim to judgment, or otherwise enforce the lease contract by self-help or any available judicial procedure or nonjudicial procedure, including administrative proceeding, arbitration, or the like, in accordance with this division.

(d) Except as otherwise provided in subdivision (1) of Section 1106 or this division or the lease agreement, the rights and remedies referred to in subdivisions (b) and (c) are cumulative.

(e) If the lease agreement covers both real property and goods, the party seeking enforcement may proceed under this chapter as to the goods, or under other applicable law as to both the real property and the goods in accordance with * * * that party's rights and remedies in respect of the real property, in which case this chapter does not apply. (Added by Stats.1988, c. 1359, § 5, operative Jan. 1, 1990. Amended by Stats. 1991, c. 111 (S.B.972), § 40, eff. July 15, 1991.)

California Comment
Report of the Assembly Committee on Judiciary
August 15, 1989

Uniform Statutory Source: Section 9–501.

Changes: Substantially revised.

Purposes: Subdivision (1) is new and represents a departure from the Division on Secured Transactions (Division 9) as the subdivision makes clear that whether a party to the lease agreement is in default is determined by the agreement as well as this Division. Sections 10508 and 10523. It further departs from Division 9 in recognizing the potential default of either party, a function of the bilateral nature of the obligations between the parties to the lease contract. In determining whether a default exists, reference should also be made to all applicable laws and statutes. See Section 10104.

Subdivision (2) is a version of the first sentence of subdivision (1) of Section 9501, revised to reflect leasing terminology.

Subdivision (3), an expansive version of the second sentence of subdivision (1) of Section 9501, lists the procedures that may be followed by the party seeking enforcement; in effect, the scope of the procedures listed in subdivision (3) is consistent with the scope of the procedures available to the foreclosing secured party.

Subdivision (4) establishes that the parties' rights and remedies are cumulative. DeKoven, *Leases of Equipment: Puritan Leasing Company v. August, A Dangerous Decision,* 12 U.S.F.L. Rev. 257, 276–80 (1978).

Subdivision (3) of Section 9501, which, among other things, states that certain rules, to the extent they give rights to the debtor and impose duties on the secured party, may not be waived or varied, was not incorporated in this Division. Given the significance of freedom of contract in the development of the common law as it applies to bailments for hire and the lessee's lack of an equity of redemption, there was no reason to impose that restraint.

Cross References:

Section 10508; Section 10523; Division 9, esp. subdivision (1), Section 9501 and subdivision (3), Section 9501.

§ 10501

Definitional Cross References:
"Goods". Paragraph (h), subdivision (1), Section 10103.
"Lease agreement". Paragraph (k), subdivision (1), Section 10103.
"Lease contract". Paragraph (*l*), subdivision (1), Section 10103.
"Lessee". Paragraph (n), subdivision (1), Section 10103.
"Lessor". Paragraph (p), subdivision (1), Section 10103.
"Party". Subdivision (29), Section 1201.
"Remedy". Subdivision (34), Section 1201.
"Rights". Subdivision (36), Section 1201.

Cross References

Default, procedure when security agreement covers both real and personal property, see Commercial Code § 9501.
Lessee's remedies, see Commercial Code § 10508.

§ 10502. Notice after Default

Except as otherwise provided in this division or the lease agreement, the lessor or lessee in default under the lease contract is not entitled to notice of default or notice of enforcement from the other party to the lease agreement. *(Added by Stats.1988, c. 1359, § 5, operative Jan. 1, 1990.)*

California Comment
Report of the Assembly Committee on Judiciary
August 15, 1989

Uniform Statutory Source: None.

Purposes: This section makes clear that absent agreement to the contrary or provision in this Division to the contrary, *e.g.*, paragraph (a) of subdivision (3) of Section 10516, the party in default is not entitled to notice of default or enforcement. While a review of Chapter 5 of Division 9 leads to the same conclusion with respect to giving notice of default to the debtor, it is never stated. Although Division 9 requires notice of disposition and strict foreclosure, the different scheme of lessors' and lessees' rights and remedies developed under the common law, and codified by this Division, generally does not require notice of enforcement; furthermore, such notice is not mandated by due process requirements. However, certain sections of this Division do require notice. *E.g.*, subdivision (2), Section 10517.

Cross References:

Paragraph (a), subdivision (3), Section 10516; subdivision (2), Section 10517; and Division 9, esp. Chapter 5.

Definitional Cross References:
"Lease agreement". Paragraph (k), subdivision (1), Section 10103.
"Lease contract". Paragraph (*l*), subdivision (1), Section 10103.
"Lessee". Paragraph (n), subdivision (1), Section 10103.
"Lessor". Paragraph (p), subdivision (1), Section 10103.
"Notice". Subdivision (25), Section 1201.
"Party". Subdivision (29), Section 1201.

Cross References

Effect of acceptance of goods, notice of default, burden of establishing default after acceptance, see Commercial Code § 10516.
Revocation of acceptance of goods, see Commercial Code § 10517.

§ 10503. Rights and remedies included in lease agreement; exclusive remedies; consequential damages; rights and remedies on default of obligation or promise collateral or ancillary to lease contract

(a) Except as otherwise provided in this division, the lease agreement may include rights and remedies for default in addition to or in substitution for those provided in this division and may limit or alter the measure of damages recoverable under this division.

(b) Resort to a remedy provided under this division or in the lease agreement is optional unless the remedy is expressly agreed to be exclusive. If circumstances cause an exclusive or limited remedy to fail of its essential purpose, or provision for an exclusive remedy is unconscionable, remedy may be had as provided in this division.

(c) Consequential damages may be liquidated under Section 10504, or may otherwise be limited, altered, or excluded unless the limitation, alteration, or exclusion is unconscionable. Limitation, alteration, or exclusion of consequential damages for injury to the person in the case of consumer goods is * * * prima facie unconscionable * * * but limitation * * *, alteration, or exclusion of damages where the loss is commercial is * * * not prima facie unconscionable.

(d) Rights and remedies on default by the lessor or the lessee with respect to any obligation or promise collateral or ancillary to the lease contract are not impaired by this division. *(Added by Stats.1988, c. 1359, § 5, operative Jan. 1, 1990. Amended by Stats.1991, c. 111 (S.B.972), § 41, eff. July 15, 1991.)*

California Comment
Report of the Assembly Committee on Judiciary
August 15, 1989

Uniform Statutory Source: Sections 2–719 and 2–701.

Changes: Rewritten to reflect lease terminology and to clarify the relationship between this section and Section 10504.

Purposes: A significant purpose of this Chapter is to provide rights and remedies for those parties to a lease who fail to provide them by agreement or whose rights and remedies fail of their essential purpose or are unenforceable. However, it is important to note that this implies no restriction on freedom to contract. Subdivision (4), Section 10103 and subdivision (3), Section 1102. Thus, subdivision (1), a revised version of the provisions of subdivision (1) of Section 2719, allows the parties to the lease agreement freedom to provide for rights and remedies in addition to or in substitution for those provided in this Division and to alter or limit the measure of damages recoverable under this Division. Except to the extent otherwise provided in this Division (*e.g.*, Section 10105; Section 10106; and subdivisions (1) and (2), Section 10108), this Chapter shall be construed neither to restrict the parties' ability to provide for rights and remedies or to limit or alter the measure of damages by agreement, nor to imply disapproval of rights and remedy schemes other than those set forth in this Chapter.

Subdivision (2) makes explicit with respect to this Division what is implicit in Section 2719 with respect to the Division on Sales (Division 2): if an exclusive remedy is held to be unconscionable, remedies under this Division are available. Section 2719 Comment 1. Subdivision (2) should be interpreted to provide that the effect of a holding that an exclusive or limited remedy has failed of its essential purpose or is unconscionable is merely to delete that particular limitation or exclusivity provision, leaving the rest of the lease agreement intact as if that provision had never been part of the lease agreement. For example, an otherwise effective exclusion or limitation of consequential damages would continue to be effective.

Subdivision (3), a revision of subdivision (3) of Section 2719, makes clear that consequential damages may also be liquidated. Subdivision (1), Section 10504.

Subdivision (4) is a revision of the provisions of Section 2701. This subdivision leaves the treatment of default with respect to obligations or promises collateral or ancillary to the release contract to other law. Subdivision (4), Section 10103 and Section 1103. An example of such an obligation would be that of the lessor to the secured creditor which has provided the funds to leverage the lessor's lease transaction; an example of such a promise would be that of the lessee, as seller, to the lessor, as buyer, in a sale-leaseback transaction.

Cross References:

Subdivision (3), Section 1102; Section 1103; Division 2, esp. Section 2701; Section 2719; subdivision (1), Section 2719; subdivision (3), Section 2719; Section 2719 Comment 1; subdivision (4), Section 10103; Section 10105; Section 10106; subdivision (1), Section 10108; subdivision (2), Section 10108; Section 10504; and subdivision (1), Section 10504.

Definitional Cross References:
"Agreed". Subdivision (3), Section 1201.
"Consumer goods". Subdivision (1), Section 9109.
"Lease agreement". Paragraph (k), subdivision (1), Section 10103.
"Lease contract". Paragraph (*l*), subdivision (1), Section 10103.
"Lessee". Paragraph (n), subdivision (1), Section 10103.
"Lessor". Paragraph (p), subdivision (1), Section 10103.
"Person". Subdivision (30), Section 1201.
"Remedy". Subdivision (34), Section 1201.
"Rights". Subdivision (36), Section 1201.

Cross References

Contractual modification or limitation of remedy, see Commercial Code § 2719.
Limitation on power of parties to consumer lease to choose applicable law and judicial forum, see Commercial Code § 10106.
Purposes of code, rules of construction, variation by agreement, see Commercial Code § 1102.
Remedies for breach of collateral contracts not impaired, see Commercial Code § 2701.
Supplementary general principles of law applicable, see Commercial Code § 1103.
Territorial application of article to goods covered by certificate of title, see Commercial Code § 10105.

§ 10504. Liquidation of damages; lessee's right to restitution

(a) Damages payable by either party for default, or any other act or omission, including indemnity for loss or diminution of anticipated tax benefits or loss or damage to the lessor's residual interest, may be liquidated in the lease agreement subject to and in compliance with Section 1671 of the Civil Code.

(b) If the lease agreement provides for liquidation of damages, and such provision does not comply with * * * subdivision (a), remedy may be had as provided in this division.

(c) If the lessor justifiably withholds or stops delivery of goods because of the lessee's default or insolvency (Section 10525 or 10526), the lessee is entitled to restitution of any amount by which the sum of his or her payments exceeds:

(1) The amount to which the lessor is entitled by virtue of terms liquidating the lessor's damages in accordance with subdivision (a); or

(2) In the absence of those terms, 20 percent of the then present value of the total rent the lessee was obligated to pay for the balance of the lease term, or, in the case of a consumer lease, the lesser of such amount or five hundred dollars ($500).

(d) A lessee's right to restitution under subdivision (c) is subject to offset to the extent the lessor establishes:

(1) A right to recover damages under the provisions of this division other than subdivision (a); and

(2) The amount or value of any benefits received by the lessee directly or indirectly by reason of the lease contract. *(Added by Stats.1988, c. 1359, § 5, operative Jan. 1, 1990. Amended by Stats.1991, c. 111 (S.B.972), § 42, eff. July 15, 1991.)*

California Comment
Report of the Assembly Committee on Judiciary
August 15, 1989

Uniform Statutory Source: Sections 2–718(1), (2), (3) and 2–719(2).
Changes: Substantially rewritten.
Purposes: Many leasing transactions are predicated on the parties' ability to agree to an appropriate amount of damages or formula for damages in the event of default or other act or omission. The rule with respect to sales of goods (Section 2718) may not be sufficiently flexible to accommodate this practice. Thus, consistent with the common law emphasis upon freedom to contract with respect to bailments for hire, this section has created a revised rule that allows greater flexibility with respect to leases of goods.

Subdivision (1) provides for liquidation of damages in the lease agreement subject to and in compliance with Section 1671 of the Civil Code. Subdivision (1), in an expansion of its Division 2 analogue (subdivision (1), Section 2718), provides for liquidation of damages for default as well as any other act or omission.

A liquidated damages formula that is common in leasing practice provides that the sum of lease payments past due, accelerated future lease payments, and the lessor's estimated residual interest, less the net proceeds of disposition (whether by sale or release) of the leased goods is the lessor's damages. Tax indemnities, costs, interest and attorney's fees are also added to determine the lessor's damages. Another common liquidated damages formula utilizes a periodic depreciation allocation as a credit to the aforesaid amount in mitigation of a lessor's damages. A third formula provides for a fixed number of periodic payments as a means of liquidating damages. Stipulated loss or stipulated damage schedules are also common. Whether these formulae are enforceable will be determined in the context of each case by applying the standards set forth in Section 1671 of the Civil Code.

This section does not incorporate two other tests that under sales law determine enforceability of liquidated damages, *i.e.,* difficulties of proof of loss and inconvenience or nonfeasibility of otherwise obtaining an adequate remedy. The ability to liquidate damages is critical to modern leasing practice; given the parties' freedom to contract at common law, the policy behind retaining these two additional requirements here was thought to be outweighed. Further, given the expansion of subdivision (1) to enable the parties to liquidate the amount payable with respect to an indemnity for loss or diminution of anticipated tax benefits resulted in another change: the last sentence of subdivision (1) of Section 2718, providing that a term fixing unreasonably large liquidated damages is void as a penalty, was also not incorporated. The impact of local, state and federal tax laws on a leasing transaction can result in an amount payable with respect to the tax indemnity many times greater than the original purchase price of the goods. By deleting the reference to unreasonably large liquidated damages the parties are free to negotiate a formula, restrained only by the rules in Section 1671 of the Civil Code. These changes should invite the parties to liquidate damages. Peters, *Remedies for Breach of Contracts Relating to the Sale of Goods Under the Uniform Commercial Code: A Roadmap for Article Two,* 73 Yale L.J. 199, 278 (1963).

Subdivision (2), a revised version of subdivision (2) of Section 2719, provides that if the liquidated damages provision is not enforceable, remedy may be had as provided in this Division. The effect of a finding that a liquidated damages provision is unenforceable should be that the lease contract may be enforced under the remedial provisions of Chapter 5 of Division 10 without reference to the unenforceable liquidated damages provision, as if such liquidated damages provision had never existed, but with the balance of the lease contract otherwise remaining intact.

Paragraph (b) of subdivision (3) of this section differs from paragraph (b) of subdivision (2) of Section 2718; in the absence of a valid liquidated damages amount or formula the lessor is permitted to retain 20 percent of the present value of the total rent payable under the lease. The alternative limitation of $500 contained in Section 2718 is deleted as unrealistically low with respect to a lease other than a consumer lease.

§ 10504

Cross References:
Subdivision (37), Section 1201; Section 2718; subdivision (1), Section 2718; paragraph (b), subdivision (2), Section 2718; and subdivision (2), Section 2719.

Definitional Cross References:
"Consumer lease". Paragraph (e), subdivision (1), Section 10103.
"Delivery". Subdivision (14), Section 1201.
"Goods". Paragraph (h), subdivision (1), Section 10103.
"Insolvent". Subdivision (23), Section 1201.
"Lease agreement". Paragraph (k), subdivision (1), Section 10103.
"Lease contract". Paragraph (l), subdivision (1), Section 10103.
"Lessee". Paragraph (n), subdivision (1), Section 10103.
"Lessor". Paragraph (p), subdivision (1), Section 10103.
"Lessor's residual interest". Paragraph (q), subdivision (1), Section 10103.
"Party". Subdivision (29), Section 1201.
"Present value". Paragraph (u), subdivision (1), Section 10103.
"Remedy". Subdivision (34), Section 1201.
"Rights". Subdivision (36), Section 1201.
"Term". Subdivision (42), Section 1201.
"Value". Subdivision (44), Section 1201.

Cross References

Contractual modification or limitation of remedy, see Commercial Code § 2719.
Liquidation or limitation of damages, deposits, see Commercial Code § 2718.

§ 10505. Cancellation, termination, or rescission; effect on obligations, rights, and remedies; rights and remedies for material misrepresentation or fraud

(a) On cancellation of the lease contract, all obligations that are still executory on both sides are discharged, but any right based on prior default or performance survives, and the canceling party also retains any remedy for default of the whole lease contract or any unperformed balance.

(b) On termination of the lease contract, all obligations that are still executory on both sides are discharged but any right based on prior default or performance survives.

(c) Unless the contrary intention clearly appears, expressions of "cancellation," "rescission," or the like of the lease contract may not be construed as a renunciation or discharge of any claim in damages for an antecedent default.

(d) Rights and remedies for material misrepresentation or fraud include all rights and remedies available under this division for default.

(e) Neither rescission nor a claim for rescission of the lease contract nor rejection or return of the goods may bar or be deemed inconsistent with a claim for damages or other right or remedy. *(Added by Stats.1988, c. 1359, § 5, operative Jan. 1, 1990. Amended by Stats.1991, c. 111 (S.B.972), § 43, eff. July 15, 1991.)*

California Comment
Report of the Assembly Committee on Judiciary
August 15, 1989

Uniform Statutory Source: Sections 2–106(3) and (4), 2–720 and 2–721.
Changes: Revised to reflect leasing practices and terminology.

Definitional Cross References:
"Cancellation". Paragraph (b), subdivision (1), Section 10103.
"Goods". Paragraph (h), subdivision (1), Section 10103.
"Lease contract". Paragraph (l), subdivision (1), Section 10103.
"Party". Subdivision (29), Section 1201.
"Remedy". Subdivision (34), Section 1201.
"Rights". Subdivision (36), Section 1201.
"Termination". Paragraph (z), subdivision (1), Section 10103.

§ 10506. Statute of Limitations

(a) An action for default under a lease contract, including breach of warranty or indemnity, must be commenced within four years after the cause of action accrued. In a lease contract that is not a consumer lease, by the original lease contract the parties may reduce the period of limitation to not less than one year.

(b) A cause of action for default accrues when the act or omission on which the default or breach of warranty is based is or should have been discovered by the aggrieved party, or when the default occurs, whichever is later. A cause of action for indemnity accrues * * * when the act or omission on which the claim for indemnity is based is or should have been discovered by the indemnified party, whichever is later * * *.

(c) If an action commenced within the time limited by subdivision (a) is so terminated as to leave available a remedy by another action for the same default or breach of warranty or indemnity, the other action may be commenced after the expiration of the time limited and within six months after the termination of the first action unless the termination resulted from voluntary discontinuance or from dismissal for failure or neglect to prosecute.

(d) This section does not alter the law on tolling of the statute of limitations nor does it apply to causes of action that have accrued before the operative date of this division. *(Added by Stats.1988, c. 1359, § 5, operative Jan. 1, 1990. Amended by Stats.1989, c. 464, § 4; Stats.1991, c. 111 (S.B.972), § 44, eff. July 15, 1991.)*

California Comment
Report of the Assembly Committee on Judiciary
August 15, 1989

Uniform Statutory Source: Section 2–725.
Changes: Substantially rewritten.
Purposes: Subdivision (1) does not incorporate the limitation found in subdivision (1) of Section 2725 prohibiting the parties from extending the period of limitation. Breach of warranty and indemnity claims often arise in a lease transaction; with the passage of time such claims often diminish or are eliminated. To encourage the parties to commence litigation under these circumstances makes little sense.

Subdivision (2) states two rules for determining when a cause of action accrues. With respect to default, the rule of subdivision (2) of Section 2725 is not incorporated in favor of a more liberal rule of the later of the date when the default occurs or when the act or omission on which it is based is or should have been discovered. With respect to indemnity, the subdivision recognizes the difference under California law between an indemnity against liability and an indemnity against loss or damage. In the case of an indemnity against liability, the cause of action accrues when the act or omission on which the claim for indemnity is based is or should have been discovered by the indemnified party. In the case of an indemnity against loss or damage, the cause of action does not accrue until the indemnified person makes payment of the loss or damage. See *E.L. White, Inc. v. City of Huntington Beach,* 21 Cal.3d 497 (1978).

Cross References:
Subdivision (1), Section 2725 and subdivision (2), Section 2725.

Definitional Cross References:
"Action". Subdivision (1), Section 1201.
"Aggrieved party". Subdivision (2), Section 1201.
"Lease contract". Paragraph (*l*), subdivision (1), Section 10103.
"Party". Subdivision (29), Section 1201.
"Remedy". Subdivision (34), Section 1201.
"Termination". Paragraph (z), subdivision (1), Section 10103.

Cross References

Statute of limitations in contracts for sale, see Commercial Code § 2725.

§ 10507. Proof of Market Rent; Time and Place

(a) Damages based on market rent (Section 10519 or 10528) are determined according to the rent for the use of the goods concerned for a lease term identical to the remaining lease term of the original lease agreement and prevailing at the * * * <u>times specified in Sections 10519 and 10528</u>.

(b) If evidence of rent for the use of the goods concerned for a lease term identical to the remaining lease term of the original lease agreement and prevailing at the times or places described in this division is not readily available, the rent prevailing within any reasonable time before or after the time described or at any other place or for a different lease term which in commercial judgment or under usage of trade would serve as a reasonable substitute for the one described may be used, making any proper allowance for the difference, including the cost of transporting the goods to or from the other place.

(c) Evidence of a relevant rent prevailing at a time or place or for a lease term other than the one described in this division offered by one party is not admissible unless and until he or she has given the other party notice the court finds sufficient to prevent unfair surprise.

(d) If the prevailing rent or value of any goods regularly leased in any established market is in issue, reports in official publications or trade journals or in newspapers or periodicals of general circulation published as the reports of that market are admissible in evidence. The circumstances of the preparation of the report may be shown to affect its weight but not its admissibility. *(Added by Stats.1988, c. 1359, § 5, operative Jan. 1, 1990. Amended by Stats.1991, c. 111 (S.B.972), § 45, eff. July 15, 1991.)*

California Comment
Report of the Assembly Committee on Judiciary
August 15, 1989

Uniform Statutory Source: Sections 2–723 and 2–724.
Changes: Revised to reflect leasing practices and terminology. Subdivision (2) of Section 10519 provides an example of one of the several times this Division refers to a determination of market rent prevailing at a given time or place. Subdivision (2), Section 10507.
Definitional Cross References:

"Goods". Paragraph (h), subdivision (1), Section 10103.
"Lease". Paragraph (j), subdivision (1), Section 10103.
"Lease agreement". Paragraph (k), subdivision (1), Section 10103.
"Notice". Subdivision (25), Section 1201.
"Party". Subdivision (29), Section 1201.
"Reasonable time". Subdivisions (1) and (2), Section 1204.
"Usage of trade". Section 1205.
"Value". Subdivision (44), Section 1201.

ARTICLE 2. DEFAULT BY LESSOR

Section
10508. Lessee's Remedies.
10509. Lessee's Rights on Improper Delivery; Rightful Rejection.
10510. Installment Lease Contracts: Rejection and Default.
10511. Merchant Lessee's Duties as to Rightfully Rejected Goods.
10512. Lessee's Duties as to Rightfully Rejected Goods.
10513. Cure by Lessor of Improper Tender or Delivery; Replacement.
10514. Waiver of Lessee's Objections.
10515. Acceptance of Goods.
10516. Effect of Acceptance of Goods; Notice of Default; Burden of Establishing Default After Acceptance; Notice of Claim or Litigation to Person Answerable Over.
10517. Revocation of Acceptance of Goods.
10518. Cover; Substitute Goods.
10519. Damages; nondelivery or repudiation by lessor; revocation of acceptance by lessee; nonconforming tender or delivery or other default by lessor; breach of warranty; measure.
10520. Lessee's Incidental and Consequential Damages.
10521. Lessee's Right to Specific Performance or Replevin.
10522. Lessee's Right to Goods on Lessor's Insolvency.

§ 10508. Lessee's Remedies

(a) If a lessor fails to deliver the goods in conformity to the lease contract (Section 10509) or repudiates the lease contract (Section 10402), or a lessee rightfully rejects the goods (Section 10509) or justifiably revokes acceptance of the goods (Section 10517), then with respect to any goods involved, and with respect to all of the goods if under an installment lease contract the value of the whole lease contract is substantially impaired (Section 10510), the lessor is in default under the lease contract and the lessee may:

(1) Cancel the lease contract (subdivision <u>(a)</u> of Section 10505);

(2) Recover so much of the rent and security as has been paid * * * <u>and</u> is just under the circumstances;

(3) Cover and recover damages as to all goods affected whether or not they have been identified to the lease contract (Sections 10518 and 10520), or recover damages for nondelivery (Sections 10519 and 10520)<u>;</u>

<u>(4) Exercise any other rights or pursue any other remedies provided in the lease contract.</u>

(b) If a lessor fails to deliver the goods in conformity to the lease contract or repudiates the lease contract, the lessee may also:

§ 10508   PERSONAL PROPERTY LEASES

(1) If the goods have been identified, recover them (Section 10522); or

(2) In a proper case, obtain specific performance or replevy the goods (Section 10521).

(c) If a lessor is otherwise in default under a lease contract, the lessee may exercise * * * the rights and pursue the remedies provided in * * * the lease contract, which may include a right to cancel the lease, and in subdivision * * * (c) of Section 10519.

(d) If a lessor has breached a warranty, whether express or implied, the lessee may recover damages (subdivision (d) of Section 10519).

(e) On rightful rejection or justifiable revocation of acceptance, a lessee has a security interest in goods in the lessee's possession or control for any rent and security that has been paid and any expenses reasonably incurred in their inspection, receipt, transportation, and care and custody, and may hold those goods and dispose of them in good faith and in a commercially reasonable manner, subject to * * * subdivision (e) of Section 10527.

(f) Subject to the provisions of Section 10407, a lessee, on notifying the lessor of the lessee's intention to do so, may deduct all or any part of the damages resulting from any default under the lease contract from any part of the rent still due under the same lease contract. *(Added by Stats.1988, c. 1359, § 5, operative Jan. 1, 1990. Amended by Stats.1991, c. 111 (S.B.972), § 46, eff. July 15, 1991.)*

California Comment

Report of the Assembly Committee on Judiciary

August 15, 1989

Uniform Statutory Source: Sections 2–711 and 2–717.

Changes: Substantially rewritten.

Purposes: This section is an index to Sections 10509 through 10522 and their effect on the lessee's rights and remedies after the lessor's default. The lessor and the lessee can otherwise agree; thus, the parties can, among other things, raise or lower the threshold of events that give rise to a lessor's default or create a new scheme of rights and remedies triggered by the occurrence of the default. Section 10503; subdivision (4), Section 10103 and subdivision (3), Section 1102.

Subdivision (1), a substantially rewritten version of the provisions of subdivision (1) of Section 2711, lists three cumulative remedies of the lessee where the lessor has failed to deliver conforming goods or has repudiated the contract, or the lessee has rightfully rejected or justifiably revoked. Subdivisions (2) and (4), Section 10501. This Division rejects any doctrine of election of remedy. To determine if one remedy bars another in a particular case is a function of whether the lessee has been put in as good a position as if the lessor had fully performed the lease agreement. Subdivision (4), Section 10103 and subdivision (1), Section 1106. Note that a special rule has been created regarding the lessee's recovery of rent and security that have been paid in the case of an installment lease—recovery is limited to that which is just under the circumstances. With the various different types of installment leases, no bright line can be created that would operate fairly in all cases; in addition, this provision should further encourage the parties to establish their own rules by agreement.

Subdivision (2), a version of the provisions of subdivision (2) of Section 2711 revised to reflect leasing terminology, lists two alternative remedies for the recovery of the goods by the lessee; however, each of these remedies is cumulative with respect to those listed in subdivision (1).

Subdivision (3) is new. If the lessor is in default for reasons other than those stated in subdivision (1), the lessee has all of the rights and remedies provided for in the lease contract (subdivision (2), Section 10501 and subdivision (1), Section 10503); and, in addition, subdivision (3) allows the lessee access to the remedy scheme of this Division except to the extent that this Division makes the right or remedy available only upon the occurrence of a default described in subdivision (1). Note that the reference to this Division includes supplemental principles of law and equity. Subdivision (4), Section 10103 and Section 1103.

Subdivision (4) is new and merely adds to the completeness of the index by including a reference to the lessee's recovery of damages upon the lessor's breach of warranty; such breach may not rise to the level of a default by the lessor (*e.g.,* breach of an express warranty that the goods subject to the lease conform to description where the non-conformity is such that when measured by objective criteria it reflects a minimal deviation from description) unless the breach is material or unless so provided by the lease agreement.

Subdivision (5), a revised version of the provisions of subdivision (3) of Section 2711, recognizes, on rightful rejection or justifiable revocation, the lessee's security interest in goods in its possession and control. Section 9113, which recognized security interests arising under the Division on Sales (Division 2), was amended with the adoption of this Division to reflect the security interests arising under this Division. Pursuant to subdivision (4) of Section 10511, a purchaser who purchases goods from the lessee in good faith takes free of any rights of the lessor, or in the case of a finance lease the supplier. Such goods, however, must have been rightfully rejected and disposed of pursuant to Section 10511 or 10512. However, subdivision (3) of Section 10517 provides that the lessee will have the same rights and duties with respect to goods where acceptance has been revoked as with respect to goods rejected. Thus, subdivision (4) of Section 10511 will apply to the lessee's disposition of such goods.

Pursuant to subdivision (5) of Section 10527, the lessee must account to the lessor for the excess proceeds of such disposition, after satisfaction of the claim secured by the lessee's security interest.

Subdivision (6), a slightly revised version of the provisions of Section 2717, sanctions a right of set-off by the lessee, subject to the rule of Section 10407 with respect to irrevocable promises in a finance lease that is not a consumer lease, and further subject to an enforceable "hell or high water" clause in the lease agreement. Section 10407 Comment. No attempt is made to state how the set-off should occur; this is to be determined by the facts of each case.

There is no special treatment of the finance lease in this section. Absent supplemental principles of law and equity to the contrary, in the case of most finance leases, following the lessee's acceptance of the goods the lessee will have no rights or remedies against the lessor, because the lessor's obligations to the lessee are minimal. Section 10210 and subdivision (1), Section 10211. Since the lessee will look to the supplier for performance, this is appropriate. Section 10209.

Cross References:

Subdivision (3), Section 1102; Section 1103; subdivision (1), Section 1106; Division 2, esp. Sections 2711 and 2717; subdivision (4), Section 10103; Section 10209; Section 10210; subdivision (1), Section 10211; Section 10407; subdivision (2), Section 10501; subdivision (4), Section 10501; Sections 10509 through 10522; subdivision (3), Section 10511; subdivision (3), Section 10517; subdivision (5), Section 10527; and Section 9113.

Definitional Cross References:

"Conforming". Paragraph (d), subdivision (1), Section 10103.

"Delivery". Subdivision (14), Section 1201.

"Good faith". Subdivision (19), Section 1201 and paragraph (b), subdivision (1), Section 2103.

"Goods". Paragraph (h), subdivision (1), Section 10103.

"Installment lease contract". Paragraph (i), subdivision (1), Section 10103.

"Lease contract". Paragraph (*l*), subdivision (1), Section 10103.

"Lessee". Paragraph (n), subdivision (1), Section 10103.

"Lessor". Paragraph (p), subdivision (1), Section 10103.

"Notifies". Subdivision (26), Section 1201.

"Receipt". Paragraph (c), subdivision (1), Section 2103.

"Remedy". Subdivision (34), Section 1201.

"Rights". Subdivision (36), Section 1201.

"Security interest". Subdivision (37), Section 1201.
"Value". Subdivision (44), Section 1201.

Cross References

Buyer's remedies in general, buyer's security interest in rejected goods, see Commercial Code § 2711.
Default, procedure, see Commercial Code § 10501.
Express warranties, see Commercial Code § 10210.
Irrevocable promises, finance leases, see Commercial Code § 10407.
Lessee under finance lease as beneficiary of supply contract, see Commercial Code § 10209.
Lessor's rights to dispose of goods, see Commercial Code § 10527.
Merchant lessee's duties as to rightfully rejected goods, see Commercial Code § 10511.
Purposes of code, rules of construction, variation by agreement, see Commercial Code § 1102.
Remedies to be liberally administered, see Commercial Code § 1106.
Revocation of acceptance of goods, see Commercial Code § 10517.
Security interest arising under divisions on sales or leases, see Commercial Code § 9113.
Supplementary general principles of law applicable, see Commercial Code § 1103.
Warranties against interference and against infringement, see Commercial Code § 10211.

§ 10509. Lessee's Rights on Improper Delivery; Rightful Rejection

(a) Subject to the provisions of Section 10510 on default in installment lease contracts, if the goods or the tender or delivery fail in any respect to conform to the lease contract, the lessee may reject or accept the goods or accept any commercial unit or units and reject the rest of the goods.

(b) Rejection of goods is ineffective unless it is within a reasonable time after tender or delivery of the goods and the lessee seasonably notifies the lessor. *(Added by Stats.1988, c. 1359, § 5, operative Jan. 1, 1990. Amended by Stats.1991, c. 111 (S.B.972), § 47, eff. July 15, 1991.)*

California Comment
Report of the Assembly Committee on Judiciary
August 15, 1989

Uniform Statutory Source: Sections 2–601 and 2–602(1).
Changes: Revised to reflect leasing practices and terminology.
Definitional Cross References:
"Commercial unit". Paragraph (c), subdivision (1), Section 10103.
"Conforming". Paragraph (d), subdivision (1), Section 10103.
"Delivery". Subdivision (14), Section 1201.
"Goods". Paragraph (h), subdivision (1), Section 10103.
"Installment lease contract". Paragraph (i), subdivision (1), Section 10103.
"Lease contract". Paragraph (*l*), subdivision (1), Section 10103.
"Lessee". Paragraph (n), subdivision (1), Section 10103.
"Lessor". Paragraph (p), subdivision (1), Section 10103.
"Notifies". Subdivision (26), Section 1201.
"Reasonable time". Subdivisions (1) and (2), Section 1204.
"Rights". Subdivision (36), Section 1201.
"Seasonably". Subdivision (3), Section 1204.

§ 10510. Installment Lease Contracts: Rejection and Default

(a) Under an installment lease contract, a lessee may reject any delivery that is nonconforming if the nonconformity substantially impairs the value of that delivery and cannot be cured or the nonconformity is a defect in the required documents; but if the nonconformity does not fall within subdivision (b) and the lessor or the supplier gives adequate assurance of its cure, the lessee must accept that delivery.

(b) Whenever nonconformity or default with respect to one or more deliveries substantially impairs the value of the installment lease contract as a whole there is a default with respect to the whole. But, the aggrieved party reinstates the installment lease contract as a whole if the aggrieved party accepts a nonconforming delivery without seasonably notifying of cancellation or brings an action with respect only to past deliveries or demands performance as to future deliveries. *(Added by Stats. 1988, c. 1359, § 5, operative Jan. 1, 1990. Amended by Stats.1991, c. 111 (S.B.972), § 48, eff. July 15, 1991.)*

California Comment
Report of the Assembly Committee on Judiciary
August 15, 1989

Uniform Statutory Source: Section 2–612.
Changes: Revised to reflect leasing practices and terminology.
Definitional Cross References:
"Action". Subdivision (1), Section 1201.
"Aggrieved party". Subdivision (2), Section 1201.
"Cancellation". Paragraph (b), subdivision (1), Section 10103.
"Conforming". Paragraph (d), subdivision (1), Section 10103.
"Delivery". Subdivision (14), Section 1201.
"Installment lease contract". Paragraph (i), subdivision (1), Section 10103.
"Lessee". Paragraph (n), subdivision (1), Section 10103.
"Lessor". Paragraph (p), subdivision (1), Section 10103.
"Notifies". Subdivision (26), Section 1201.
"Seasonably". Subdivision (3), Section 1204.
"Supplier". Paragraph (x), subdivision (1), Section 10103.
"Value". Subdivision (44), Section 1201.

§ 10511. Merchant Lessee's Duties as to Rightfully Rejected Goods

(a) Subject to any security interest of a lessee (subdivision (e) of Section 10508), if a lessor or a supplier has no agent or place of business at the market of rejection, a merchant lessee, after rejection of goods in his or her possession or control, shall follow any reasonable instructions received from the lessor or the supplier with respect to the goods. In the absence of those instructions, a merchant lessee shall make reasonable efforts to sell, lease, or otherwise dispose of the goods for the lessor's account if they threaten to decline in value speedily. Instructions are not reasonable if on demand indemnity for expenses is not forthcoming.

(b) If a merchant lessee (subdivision (a)) or any other lessee (Section 10512) disposes of goods, he or she is entitled to reimbursement either from the lessor or the supplier or out of the proceeds for reasonable expenses of caring for and disposing of the goods and, if the expenses include no disposition commission, to such commission as is usual in the trade, or * * * if there is none, to a reasonable sum not exceeding 10 percent of the gross proceeds.

(c) In complying with this section or Section 10512, the lessee is held only to good faith. Good faith

§ 10511

conduct hereunder is neither acceptance or conversion nor the basis of an action for damages.

(d) A purchaser who purchases in good faith from a lessee pursuant to this section or Section 10512 takes the goods free of any rights of the lessor and the supplier even though the lessee fails to comply with one or more of the requirements of this division. *(Added by Stats.1988, c. 1359, § 5, operative Jan. 1, 1990. Amended by Stats.1991, c. 111 (S.B.972), § 49, eff. July 15, 1991.)*

California Comment
Report of the Assembly Committee on Judiciary
August 15, 1989

Uniform Statutory Source: Sections 2–603 and 2–706(5).
Changes: Revised to reflect leasing practices and terminology. This section, by its terms, applies to merchants as well as others. Thus, in construing the section it is important to note that under this Code the term good faith is defined differently for merchants (paragraph (b), subdivision (1), Section 2103) than for others (subdivision (19), Section 1201). Subdivisions (3) and (4), Section 10103.
Definitional Cross References:
"Action". Subdivision (1), Section 1201.
"Good faith". Subdivision (19), Section 1201 and paragraph (b), subdivision (1), Section 2103.
"Goods". Paragraph (h), subdivision (1), Section 10103.
"Lease". Paragraph (j), subdivision (1), Section 10103.
"Lessee". Paragraph (n), subdivision (1), Section 10103.
"Lessor". Paragraph (p), subdivision (1), Section 10103.
"Merchant lessee". Paragraph (t), subdivision (1), Section 10103.
"Purchaser". Subdivision (33), Section 1201.
"Rights". Subdivision (36), Section 1201.
"Security interest". Subdivision (37), Section 1201.
"Supplier". Paragraph (x), subdivision (1), Section 10103.
"Value". Subdivision (44), Section 1201.

§ 10512. Lessee's Duties as to Rightfully Rejected Goods

(a) Except as otherwise provided with respect to goods that threaten to decline in value speedily (Section 10511) and subject to any security interest of a lessee (subdivision (e) of Section 10508):

(1) The lessee, after rejection of goods in the lessee's possession, shall hold them with reasonable care at the lessor's or the supplier's disposition for a reasonable time after the lessee's seasonable notification of rejection;

(2) If the lessor or the supplier gives no instructions within a reasonable time after notification of rejection, the lessee may store the rejected goods for the lessor's or the supplier's account or ship them to the lessor or the supplier or dispose of them for the lessor's or the supplier's account with reimbursement in the manner provided in Section 10511; but

(3) The lessee has no further obligations with regard to goods rightfully rejected.

(b) Action by the lessee pursuant to subdivision (a) is not acceptance or conversion. *(Added by Stats.1988, c. 1359, § 5, operative Jan. 1, 1990. Amended by Stats. 1991, c. 111 (S.B.972), § 50, eff. July 15, 1991.)*

California Comment
Report of the Assembly Committee on Judiciary
August 15, 1989

Uniform Statutory Source: Sections 2–602(2)(b) and (c) and 2–604.
Changes: Substantially rewritten.
Purposes: The introduction to subdivision (1) references goods that threaten to decline in value speedily and not perishables, the reference in Section 2604, the statutory analogue. This is a change in style, not substance, as the first phrase includes the second. Paragraphs (a) and (c) are revised versions of the provisions of paragraphs (b) and (c) of subdivision (2) of Section 2602. Paragraph (a) states the rule with respect to the lessee's treatment of goods in its possession following rejection; paragraph (b) states the rule regarding such goods if the lessor or supplier then fails to give instructions to the lessee. If the lessee performs in a fashion consistent with paragraphs (a) and (b), paragraph (c) exonerates the lessee.
Cross References:
Paragraph (b), subdivision (2), Section 2602; paragraph (c), subdivision (2), Section 2602; and Section 2604.
Definitional Cross References:
"Action". Subdivision (1), Section 1201.
"Goods". Paragraph (h), subdivision (1), Section 10103.
"Lessee". Paragraph (n), subdivision (1), Section 10103.
"Lessor". Paragraph (p), subdivision (1), Section 10103.
"Notification". Subdivision (26), Section 1201.
"Reasonable time". Subdivisions (1) and (2), Section 1204.
"Seasonably". Subdivision (3), Section 1204.
"Security interest". Subdivision (37), Section 1201.
"Supplier". Paragraph (x), subdivision (1), Section 10103.
"Value". Subdivision (44), Section 1201.

Cross References
Buyer's options as to salvage of rightfully rejected goods, see Commercial Code § 2604.
Manner and effect of rightful rejection, see Commercial Code § 2602.

§ 10513. Cure by Lessor of Improper Tender or Delivery; Replacement

(a) If any tender or delivery by the lessor or the supplier is rejected because it is nonconforming and the time for performance has not yet expired, the lessor or the supplier may seasonably notify the lessee of the lessor's or the supplier's intention to cure and may then make a conforming delivery within the time provided in the lease contract.

(b) If the lessee rejects a nonconforming tender that the lessor or the supplier had reasonable grounds to believe would be acceptable with or without money allowance, the lessor or the supplier may have a further reasonable time to substitute a conforming tender if he or she seasonably notifies the lessee. *(Added by Stats. 1988, c. 1359, § 5, operative Jan. 1, 1990. Amended by Stats.1991, c. 111 (S.B.972), § 51, eff. July 15, 1991.)*

California Comment
Report of the Assembly Committee on Judiciary
August 15, 1989

Uniform Statutory Source: Section 2–508.
Changes: Revised to reflect leasing practices and terminology.
Definitional Cross References:
"Conforming". Paragraph (d), subdivision (1), Section 10103.
"Delivery". Subdivision (14), Section 1201.
"Lease contract". Paragraph (l), subdivision (1), Section 10103.
"Lessee". Paragraph (n), subdivision (1), Section 10103.

"Lessor". Paragraph (p), subdivision (1), Section 10103.
"Money". Subdivision (24), Section 1201.
"Notifies". Subdivision (26), Section 1201.
"Reasonable time". Subdivisions (1) and (2), Section 1204.
"Seasonably". Subdivision (3), Section 1204.
"Supplier". Paragraph (x), subdivision (1), Section 10103.

§ 10514. Waiver of Lessee's Objections

(a) In rejecting goods, a lessee's failure to state a particular defect that is ascertainable by reasonable inspection precludes the lessee from relying on the defect to justify rejection or to establish default:

(1) If, stated seasonably, the lessor or the supplier could have cured it (Section 10513); or

(2) Between merchants if the lessor or the supplier after rejection has made a request in writing for a full and final written statement of all defects on which the lessee proposes to rely.

(b) A lessee's failure to reserve rights when paying rent or other consideration against documents precludes recovery of the payment for defects apparent on the face of the documents. *(Added by Stats.1988, c. 1359, § 5, operative Jan. 1, 1990. Amended by Stats. 1991, c. 111 (S.B.972), § 52, eff. July 15, 1991.)*

California Comment
Report of the Assembly Committee on Judiciary
August 15, 1989

Uniform Statutory Source: Section 2–605.

Changes: Revised to reflect leasing practices and terminology.

Purposes: The principles applicable to the commercial practice of payment against documents (subdivision 2) are explained in Comment 4 to Section 2605, the statutory analogue to this section.

Cross Reference:
Section 2605 Comment 4.

Definitional Cross References:
"Between merchants". Subdivision (3), Section 2104.
"Goods". Paragraph (h), subdivision (1), Section 10103.
"Lessee". Paragraph (n), subdivision (1), Section 10103.
"Lessor". Paragraph (p), subdivision (1), Section 10103.
"Rights". Subdivision (36), Section 1201.
"Seasonably". Subdivision (3), Section 1204.
"Supplier". Paragraph (x), subdivision (1), Section 10103.
"Writing". Subdivision (46), Section 1201.

Cross References

Waiver of buyer's objections by failure to particularize, see Commercial Code § 2605.

§ 10515. Acceptance of Goods

(a) Acceptance of goods occurs after the lessee has had a reasonable opportunity to inspect the goods and

(1) The lessee signifies or acts with respect to the goods in a manner that signifies to the lessor or the supplier that the goods are conforming or that the lessee will take or retain them in spite of their nonconformity; or

(2) The lessee fails to make an effective rejection of the goods (subdivision (b) of Section 10509).

(b) Acceptance of a part of any commercial unit is acceptance of that entire unit. *(Added by Stats.1988, c. 1359, § 5, operative Jan. 1, 1990. Amended by Stats. 1991, c. 111 (S.B.972), § 53, eff. July 15, 1991.)*

California Comment
Report of the Assembly Committee on Judiciary
August 15, 1989

Uniform Statutory Source: Section 2–606.

Changes: The provisions of paragraph (a) of subdivision (1) of Section 2606 were substantially rewritten to provide that the lessee's conduct may signify acceptance. Further, the provisions of paragraph (c) of subdivision (1) of Section 2606 were not incorporated as irrelevant given the lessee's possession and use of the leased goods.

Cross References:
Paragraph (a), subdivision (1), Section 2606 and paragraph (c), subdivision (1), Section 2606.

Definitional Cross References:
"Commercial unit". Paragraph (c), subdivision (1), Section 10103.
"Conforming". Paragraph (d), subdivision (1), Section 10103.
"Goods". Paragraph (h), subdivision (1), Section 10103.
"Lessee". Paragraph (n), subdivision (1), Section 10103.
"Lessor". Paragraph (p), subdivision (1), Section 10103.
"Supplier". Paragraph (x), subdivision (1), Section 10103.

Cross References

What constitutes acceptance of goods, see Commercial Code § 2606.

§ 10516. Effect of Acceptance of Goods; Notice of Default; Burden of Establishing Default After Acceptance; Notice of Claim or Litigation to Person Answerable Over

(a) A lessee must pay rent for any goods accepted in accordance with the lease contract, with due allowance for goods rightfully rejected or not delivered.

(b) A lessee's acceptance of goods precludes rejection of the goods accepted. In the case of a finance lease, other than a consumer lease in which the supplier assisted in the preparation of the lease contract or participated in negotiating the terms of the lease contract with the lessor, if made with knowledge of a nonconformity, acceptance cannot be revoked because of it. In any other case, if made with knowledge of a nonconformity, acceptance cannot be revoked because of it unless the acceptance was on the reasonable assumption that the nonconformity would be seasonably cured. Acceptance does not of itself impair any other remedy provided by this division or the lease agreement for nonconformity.

(c) If a tender has been accepted:

(1) Within a reasonable time after the lessee discovers or should have discovered any default, * * * the lessee shall notify the lessor <u>and the supplier, if any</u>, or be barred from any remedy against the * * * <u>party not notified</u>;

(2) Within a reasonable time after the lessee receives notice of litigation for infringement or the like (Section 10211) the lessee shall notify the lessor or be barred from any remedy over for liability established by the litigation; and

(3) The burden is on the lessee to establish any default.

(d) If a lessee is sued for breach of a warranty or other obligation for which a lessor or a supplier is answerable over the following apply:

(1) The lessee may give the lessor or the supplier, or both, written notice of the litigation. If the notice states that the * * * person notified may come in and defend and that if the * * * person notified does not do so * * * that person will be bound in any action against * * * that person by the lessee by any determination of fact common to the two litigations, then unless the * * * person notified after seasonable receipt of the notice does come in and defend * * * that person is so bound.

(2) The lessor or the supplier may demand in writing that the lessee turn over control of the litigation including settlement if the claim is one for infringement or the like (Section 10211) or else be barred from any remedy over. If the demand states that the lessor or the supplier agrees to bear all expense and to satisfy any adverse judgment, then unless the lessee after seasonable receipt of the demand does turn over * * * control the lessee is so barred.

* * * (e) Subdivisions (c) and (d) apply to any obligation of a lessee to hold the lessor or the supplier harmless against infringement or the like (Section 10211).

(f) Subdivision (c) shall not apply to a consumer lease. (Added by Stats.1988, c. 1359, § 5, operative Jan. 1, 1990. Amended by Stats.1988, c. 1368, § 13.4, operative Jan. 1, 1990; Stats.1991, c. 111 (S.B.972), § 54, eff. July 15, 1991.)

California Comment
Report of the Assembly Committee on Judiciary
August 15, 1989

Uniform Statutory Source: Section 2–607.
Changes: Substantially revised.
Purposes: Subdivision (2) creates a special rule for finance leases, other than a finance lease that is a consumer lease in which the supplier assisted in the preparation of the lease contract or participated in negotiating the terms of the lease contract with the lessor. Subdivision (2) precludes revocation if acceptance is made with knowledge of nonconformity with respect to the lease agreement, as opposed to the supply agreement; this is not inequitable as the lessee has a direct claim against the supplier. Subdivision (1), Section 10209. The exception to this rule, applicable to a finance lease that is a supplier-assisted consumer lease is derived from California law regarding "seller-assisted" financing. See *Hernandez v. Atlantic Finance Company*, 105 Cal.App.3d 65, (1980); subdivision (b), Section 2982.5, Civil Code. Revocation of acceptance of a finance lease is permitted if the lessee's acceptance was without discovery of the nonconformity (with respect to the lease agreement, not the supply agreement) and was reasonably induced by the lessor's assurances. Paragraph (b), subdivision (1), Section 10517. Absent exclusion or modification, the lessor under a finance lease makes certain warranties to the lessee. Section 10210 and subdivision (1), Section 10211. Revocation of acceptance is not prohibited even after the lessee's promise has become irrevocable and independent. Section 10407 Comment. Where the finance lease creates a security interest, the rule may be to the contrary. *General Elec. Credit Corp. of Tennessee v. Ger-Beck Mach. Co.*, 806 F.2d 1207 (3rd Cir. 1986).

Paragraph (a) of subdivision (3) requires the lessee to give notice of default, within a reasonable time after the lessee discovered or should have discovered the default. In the case of a finance lease, notice of default must be given to the supplier in order to preserve claims against the supplier. The definition of supplier is a person from whom a lessor buys or leases goods to be leased under a finance lease. Paragraph (x), subdivision (1), Section 10103. Thus, not all sellers or lessors of goods to be leased are included within the set of persons to be given notice of default, as suppliers. The time of notification is to be determined by applying commercial standards to a merchant lessee. The content of the notification need merely be sufficient to let the lessor or supplier know that the transaction is still troublesome and must be watched. There is no reason to require that the notification which saves the lessee's rights under this section must include a clear statement of all the objections that will be relied on by the lessee, as under the section covering statements of defects upon rejection (Section 10514). Nor is there reason for requiring the notification to be a claim for damages or any threat in litigation or other resort to a remedy. This notification which saves the lessee's rights under this Division need only be such as informs the lessor or supplier that the transaction is claimed to involve a breach and thus opens the way for normal settlement through negotiation.

Pursuant to subdivision (6), subdivision (3) does not apply to consumer leases. The rules governing the lessee's duty to give notice of default to the lessor or supplier in the case of a consumer lease shall be determined by other laws. The failure to include consumer leases in subdivision (3) shall carry no negative or positive implications as to the applicability of such laws; nor shall such failure in any way affect the interpretation of any such laws that are deemed applicable to consumer leases.

Paragraph (b) of subdivision (3) requires the lessee to give the lessor notice of litigation for infringement or the like. An exception was considered for a finance lease, but was not created because it was not necessary—the lessor in a finance lease does not give a warranty against infringement. Subdivision (2), Section 10211. Even though not required under paragraph (b) of subdivision (3), the lessee who takes under a finance lease should consider giving notice of litigation for infringement or the like to the supplier, because the lessee obtains the benefit of the suppliers' promises subject to the suppliers' defenses or claims. Subdivision (1), Section 10209 and paragraph (b), subdivision (3), Section 2607.

Cross References:
Paragraph (b), subdivision (3), Section 2607; subdivision (1), Section 10209; Section 10210; subdivision (1), Section 10211; subdivision (2), Section 10211; Section 10407 Comment; and paragraph (b), subdivision (1), Section 10517.

Definitional Cross References:
"Action". Subdivision (1), Section 1201.
"Agreement." Subdivision (3), Section 1201.
"Burden of establishing". Subdivision (8), Section 1201.
"Conforming". Paragraph (d), subdivision (1), Section 10103.
"Consumer lease". Paragraph (e), subdivision (1), Section 10103.
"Delivery". Subdivision (14), Section 1201.
"Discover". Subdivision (25), Section 1201.
"Finance lease". Paragraph (g), subdivision (1), Section 10103.
"Goods". Paragraph (h), subdivision (1), Section 10103.
"Knowledge". Subdivision (25), Section 1201.
"Lease agreement". Paragraph (k), subdivision (1), Section 10103.
"Lease contract". Paragraph (*l*), subdivision (1), Section 10103.
"Lessee". Paragraph (n), subdivision (1), Section 10103.
"Lessor". Paragraph (p), subdivision (1), Section 10103.
"Notice". Subdivision (25), Section 1201.
"Notifies". Subdivision (26), Section 1201.
"Person". Subdivision (30), Section 1201.
"Reasonable time". Subdivisions (1) and (2), Section 1204.
"Receipt". Paragraph (c), subdivision (1), Section 2103.
"Remedy". Subdivision (34), Section 1201.
"Seasonably". Subdivision (3), Section 1204.
"Supplier". Paragraph (x), subdivision (1), Section 10103.
"Written". Subdivision (46), Section 1201.

Cross References
Effect of acceptance, notice of breach, burden of establishing breach after acceptance, see Commercial Code § 2607.
Express warranties, see Commercial Code § 10210.

Irrevocable promises, finance leases, see Commercial Code § 10407.
Lessee under finance lease as beneficiary of supply contract, see Commercial Code § 10209.
Warranties against interference and against infringement, lessee's obligation against infringement, see Commercial Code § 10211.

§ 10517. Revocation of Acceptance of Goods

(a) A lessee may revoke acceptance of a lot or commercial unit whose nonconformity substantially impairs its value to the lessee if * * * the lessee has accepted it:

(1) Except in the case of a finance lease, on the reasonable assumption that its nonconformity would be cured and it has not been seasonably cured; or

(2) Without discovery of the nonconformity if the lessee's acceptance was reasonably induced either by the lessor's assurances or, except in the case of a finance lease, by the difficulty of discovery before acceptance.

(b) A lessee may revoke acceptance of a lot or commercial unit if the lessor defaults under the lease contract and the default substantially impairs the value of that lot or commercial unit to the lessee.

(c) If the lease agreement so provides, the lessee may revoke acceptance of a lot or commercial unit because of other defaults by the lessor.

(d) Revocation of acceptance must occur within a reasonable time after the lessee discovers or should have discovered the ground for it and before any substantial change in condition of the goods which is not caused by the nonconformity. Revocation is not effective until the lessee notifies the lessor.

(e) A lessee who so revokes has the same rights and duties with regard to the goods involved as if the lessee had rejected them. *(Added by Stats.1988, c. 1359, § 5, operative Jan. 1, 1990. Amended by Stats.1991, c. 111 (S.B.972), § 55, eff. July 15, 1991.)*

California Comment
Report of the Assembly Committee on Judiciary
August 15, 1989

Uniform Statutory Source: Section 2–608.

Changes: Revised to reflect leasing practices and terminology. Note that in the case of a finance lease the lessee retains a limited right to revoke acceptance. Paragraph (b), subdivision (1), Section 10517 and Section 10516 Comment.

Cross References:
Section 10516 Comment and paragraph (b), subdivision (1), Section 10517.

Definitional Cross References:
"Commercial unit". Paragraph (c), subdivision (1), Section 10103.
"Conforming". Paragraph (d), subdivision (1), Section 10103.
"Discover". Subdivision (25), Section 1201.
"Finance lease". Paragraph (g), subdivision (1), Section 10103.
"Goods". Paragraph (h), subdivision (1), Section 10103.
"Lessee". Paragraph (n), subdivision (1), Section 10103.
"Lessor". Paragraph (p), subdivision (1), Section 10103.
"Lot". Paragraph (s), subdivision (1), Section 10103.
"Notifies." Subdivision (26), Section 1201.
"Reasonable time". Subdivisions (1) and (2), Section 1204.
"Rights". Subdivision (36), Section 1201.
"Seasonably". Subdivision (3), Section 1204.
"Value". Subdivision (44), Section 1201.

§ 10518. Cover; Substitute Goods

(a) After a default by a lessor under the lease contract * * of the type described in subdivision (a) of Section 10508 * * *, or, if agreed, after other default by the lessor, the lessee may cover by making any purchase or lease of or contract to purchase or lease goods in substitution for those due from the lessor.

(b) Except as otherwise provided with respect to damages liquidated in the lease agreement (Section 10504) or otherwise determined pursuant to agreement of the parties (Section 10503 and subdivision (3) of Section 1102), if a lessee's cover is by a lease agreement substantially similar to the original lease agreement and the new lease agreement is made in good faith and in a commercially reasonable manner, the lessee may recover from the lessor as damages (1) the present value, as of the date of the commencement of the term of the new lease agreement, of the * * * rent under the new lease agreement applicable to that period of the new lease term * * * which is comparable to the then remaining term of the original lease agreement * * * minus the present value as of the same date of the total rent for the then remaining lease term of the original lease agreement, and (2) any incidental or consequential damages, less expenses saved in consequence of the lessor's default.

* * * (c) If a lessee's cover is by lease agreement that for any reason does not qualify for treatment under subdivision (b), or is by purchase or otherwise, the lessee may recover from the lessor * * * as if the lessee had elected not to cover and Section 10519 governs. *(Added by Stats.1988, c. 1359, § 5, operative Jan. 1, 1990. Amended by Stats.1988, c. 1368, § 14, operative Jan. 1, 1990; Stats.1991, c. 111 (S.B.972), § 56, eff. July 15, 1991.)*

California Comment
Report of the Assembly Committee on Judiciary
August 15, 1989

Uniform Statutory Source: Section 2–712.

Changes: Substantially revised.

Purposes: Subdivision (1) allows the lessee to take action to fix its damages after default by the lessor. Such action may consist of the purchase or lease of goods. The decision to cover is a function of commercial judgment, not a statutory mandate replete with sanctions for failure to comply. *Compare* Section 9507.

Subdivision (2) states a rule for determining the amount of lessee's damages provided that there is no agreement to the contrary. The lessee's damages will be established using the new lease agreement as a measure if the following three criteria are met: (i) the lessee's cover is by lease agreement, (ii) the lease agreement is substantially similar to the original lease agreement, and (iii) such cover was effected in good faith, and in a commercially reasonable manner. Thus, the lessee will be entitled to recover from the lessor the present value, as of the date of the commencement of the term of the new lease agreement, of the difference between the rent reserved under the new lease and the original lease, together with incidental or consequential damages less expenses saved in consequence of the lessor's default.

Two of the three criteria to be met by the lessee are familiar, but the concept of the new lease agreement being substantially similar to the original lease agreement is not. Given the many variables facing a party who intends to lease goods and the rapidity of changes in the market place, the policy decision was made not to draft with specificity. It was thought unwise to seek to establish certainty at the cost of fairness. Thus, the decision of whether the new lease agreement is substantially similar to the original will be determined case by case.

While the section does not draw a bright line, it is possible to describe some of the factors that should be considered in finding that a new lease agreement is substantially similar to the original. First, the goods subject to the new lease agreement should be examined. For example, in a lease of computer equipment the new lease might be for more modern equipment. However, it may be that at the time of the lessor's breach it was not possible to obtain the same type of goods in the market place. Because the lessee's remedy under Section 10519 is intended to place the lessee in essentially the same position as if he had covered, if goods similar to those to have been delivered under the original lease are not available, then the computer equipment in this hypothetical should qualify as a commercially reasonable substitute. See subdivision (1), Section 2712.

Second, the various elements of the new lease agreement should also be examined. Those elements include the term of the new lease (because the damages are calculated under subdivision (2) as the difference between the total rent payable for the entire term of the new lease agreement and the remaining term of the original lease); the presence or absence of options to purchase or release; the lessor's representations, warranties and covenants to the lessee, as well as those to be provided by the lessee to the lessor; and the services, if any, to be provided by the lessor or by the lessee. All of these factors allocate cost and risk between the lessor and the lessee and thus affect the amount of rent to be paid.

Having examined the goods and the agreement, the test to be applied is whether, in light of these comparisons, the new lease agreement is substantially similar to the original lease agreement. These findings should not be made with scientific precision, as they are a function of economics, nor should they be made independently with respect to the goods and each element of the agreement, as it is important that a sense of commercial judgment pervade the finding. To establish the new lease as a proper measure of damage under subdivision (2), these factors, taken as a whole, must result in a finding that the new lease agreement is substantially similar to the original.

Subdivision (3), which is new, provides that if a lessee's cover is by lease substantially similar to the original lease and the lease is made in good faith and in a commercially reasonable manner, the lessee may elect to proceed under subdivision (2) or Section 10519. If the lessee's cover is by lease that does not qualify under subdivision (2), or is by purchase or otherwise, Section 10519 governs.

Cross References:
Subdivision (1), Section 2712; Section 10519; and Section 9507.

Definitional Cross References:
"Agreement". Subdivision (3), Section 1201.
"Contract". Subdivision (11), Section 1201.
"Good faith". Subdivision (19), Section 1201 and paragraph (b), subdivision (1), Section 2103.
"Goods". Paragraph (h), subdivision (1), Section 10103.
"Lease". Paragraph (j), subdivision (1), Section 10103.
"Lease agreement". Paragraph (k), subdivision (1), Section 10103.
"Lease contract". Paragraph (*l*), subdivision (1), Section 10103.
"Lessee". Paragraph (n), subdivision (1), Section 10103.
"Lessor". Paragraph (p), subdivision (1), Section 10103.
"Party". Subdivision (29), Section 1201.
"Present value". Paragraph (u), subdivision (1), Section 10103.
"Purchase". Paragraph (v), subdivision (1), Section 10103.

Cross References

Cover, buyer's procurement of substitute goods, see Commercial Code § 2712.
Secured party's liability for failure to comply with provisions relating to default, see Commercial Code § 9507.

§ 10519. Damages; nondelivery or repudiation by lessor; revocation of acceptance by lessee; nonconforming tender or delivery or other default by lessor; breach of warranty; measure

(a) Except as otherwise provided with respect to damages liquidated in the lease agreement (Section 10504) or <u>otherwise</u> determined * * * <u>pursuant to</u> agreement of the parties (Section 10503 and subdivision (3) of Section 1102), if a lessee elects not to cover or a lessee elects to cover and the cover is by lease agreement * * * <u>that for any reason does not qualify</u> for treatment under subdivision <u>(b)</u> of Section 10518, or is by purchase or otherwise, the measure of damages for * * * <u>nondelivery or repudiation</u> by the lessor * * * <u>or for rejection or revocation of acceptance by the lessee</u> is the present value, as of the date of the default * * *, of the * * * then market rent * * * <u>minus the present value as of the same date of</u> the original rent, computed for the remaining lease term of the original lease agreement, together with incidental and consequential damages, less expenses saved in consequence of the lessor's default.

(b) Market rent is to be determined as of the place for tender or, in cases of rejection after arrival or revocation of acceptance, as of the place of arrival.

* * * (c) Except as otherwise agreed, if the lessee has accepted goods and given notification (subdivision (c) of Section 10516), the measure of damages for nonconforming tender or delivery <u>or other default</u> by a lessor is the loss resulting in the ordinary course of events from the lessor's default as determined in any manner that is reasonable together with incidental and consequential damages, less expenses saved in consequence of the lessor's default.

* * * (d) Except as otherwise agreed, the measure of damages for breach of warranty is the present value at the time and place of acceptance of the difference between the value of the use of the goods accepted and the value if they had been as warranted for the lease term, unless special circumstances show proximate damages of a different amount, together with incidental and consequential damages, less expenses saved in consequence of the lessor's default or breach of warranty. (Added by Stats.1988, c. 1359, § 5, operative Jan. 1, 1990. Amended by Stats.1988, c. 1368, § 15, operative Jan. 1, 1990; Stats.1991, c. 111 (S.B.972), § 57, eff. July 15, 1991.)

California Comment
Report of the Assembly Committee on Judiciary
August 15, 1989

Uniform Statutory Source: Sections 2–713 and 2–714.
Changes: Substantially revised.
Purposes: Subdivision (1), a revised version of the provisions of subdivision (1) of Section 2713, states the basic rule governing the measure of lessee's damages for default by the lessor. Subdivision (1), Section 10508. This measure will apply, absent agreement to the contrary, if the lessee does not cover or the lessee elects to cover whether or not the cover qualifies under Section 10518. There is no sanction for cover that does not qualify.

The measure of damage is the present value, as of the date of default, of the difference between market rent and original rent for the remaining term of the lease, less expenses saved in consequence of the default. Note that the reference in subdivision (1) of Section 10519 is to the date of default not to the date of an event of default. An event of default under a lease agreement becomes a default under a lease agreement only after the expiration of any relevant period of grace and compliance with any notice requirements under this Article and the lease agreement. American Bar Foundation, *Commentaries on Indentures,* § 5-1, at 216-217 (1971). Subdivision (1), Section 10501. This conclusion is also a function of whether, as a matter of fact or law, the event of default has been waived, suspended or cured. Subdivision (4), Section 10103 and Section 1103.

Subdivision (2), a revised version of the provisions of subdivision (2) of Section 2713, states the rule with respect to determining market rent.

Subdivision (3), a revised version of the provisions of subdivisions (1) and (3) of Section 2714, states the measure of damages where goods have been accepted and acceptance is not revoked. The measure in essence is the loss, in the ordinary course of events, flowing from the default.

Subdivision (4), a revised version of the provisions of subdivision (2) of Section 2714, states the measure of damages for breach of warranty. The measure in essence is the present value of the difference between the value of the goods accepted and of the goods if they had been as warranted.

Cross References:

Subdivision (1), Section 2713; subdivision (2), Section 2713; Section 2714; and Section 10518.

Definitional Cross References:

"Conforming". Paragraph (d), subdivision (1), Section 10103.
"Delivery". Subdivision (14), Section 1201.
"Goods". Paragraph (h), subdivision (1), Section 10103.
"Lease". Paragraph (j), subdivision (1), Section 10103.
"Lease agreement". Paragraph (k), subdivision (1), Section 10103.
"Lessee". Paragraph (n), subdivision (1), Section 10103.
"Lessor". Paragraph (p), subdivision (1), Section 10103.
"Notification". Subdivision (26), Section 1201.
"Present value". Paragraph (u), subdivision (1), Section 10103.
"Value". Subdivision (44), Section 1201.

Cross References

Buyer's damages for breach in regard to accepted goods, see Commercial Code § 2714.
Buyer's damages for non-delivery or repudiation, see Commercial Code § 2713.
Determination of damages based on market rent, see Commercial Code § 10507.

§ 10520. Lessee's Incidental and Consequential Damages

(a) Incidental damages resulting from a lessor's default include expenses reasonably incurred in inspection, receipt, transportation, and care and custody of goods rightfully rejected or goods the acceptance of which is justifiably revoked, any commercially reasonable charges, expenses, or commissions in connection with effecting cover, and any other reasonable expense incident to the default.

(b) Consequential damages resulting from a lessor's default include:

(1) Any loss resulting from general or particular requirements and needs of which the lessor at the time of contracting had reason to know and which could not reasonably be prevented by cover or otherwise; and

(2) Injury to person or property proximately resulting from any breach of warranty. *(Added by Stats.1988, c. 1359, § 5, operative Jan. 1, 1990. Amended by Stats. 1991, c. 111 (S.B.972), § 58, eff. July 15, 1991.)*

California Comment
Report of the Assembly Committee on Judiciary
August 15, 1989

Uniform Statutory Source: Section 2-715.

Changes: Revised to reflect leasing terminology and practices.

Purposes: Subdivision (1), a revised version of the provisions of subdivision (1) of Section 2715, lists some examples of incidental damages resulting from a lessor's default; the list is not exhaustive. Subdivision (1) makes clear that it applies not only to rightful rejection, but also to justifiable revocation.

Subdivision (2), a revised version of the provisions of subdivision (2) of Section 2715, lists some examples of consequential damages resulting from a lessor's default; the list is not exhaustive.

Cross Reference:

Section 2715.

Definitional Cross References:

"Goods". Paragraph (h), subdivision (1), Section 10103.
"Knows". Subdivision (25), Section 1201.
"Lessee". Paragraph (n), subdivision (1), Section 10103.
"Lessor". Paragraph (p), subdivision (1), Section 10103.
"Person". Subdivision (30), Section 1201.
"Receipt". Paragraph (c), subdivision (1), Section 2103.

Cross References

Buyer's incidental and consequential damages, see Commercial Code § 2715.

§ 10521. Lessee's Right to Specific Performance or Replevin

(a) Specific performance may be decreed if the goods are unique or in other proper circumstances.

(b) A decree for specific performance may include any terms and conditions as to payment of the rent, damages, or other relief that the court deems just.

(c) A lessee has a right of replevin, detinue, sequestration, claim and delivery, or the like for goods identified to the lease contract if after reasonable effort the lessee is unable to effect cover for those goods or the circumstances reasonably indicate that the effort will be unavailing. *(Added by Stats.1988, c. 1359, § 5, operative Jan. 1, 1990. Amended by Stats.1991, c. 111 (S.B.972), § 59, eff. July 15, 1991.)*

California Comment
Report of the Assembly Committee on Judiciary
August 15, 1989

Uniform Statutory Source: Section 2-716.

Changes: Revised to reflect leasing practices and terminology, and to expand the reference to the right of replevin in subdivision (3) to include other similar rights of the lessee.

Definitional Cross References:

"Delivery". Subdivision (14), Section 1201.
"Goods". Paragraph (h), subdivision (1), Section 10103.
"Lease contract". Paragraph (*l*), subdivision (1), Section 10103.
"Lessee." Paragraph (n), subdivision (1), Section 10103.
"Rights". Subdivision (36), Section 1201.
"Term". Subdivision (42), Section 1201.

§ 10522. Lessee's Right to Goods on Lessor's Insolvency

(a) Subject to subdivision (b) and even though the goods have not been shipped, a lessee who has paid a part or all of the rent and security for goods identified to a lease contract (Section 10217) on making and keeping good a tender of any unpaid portion of the rent and security due under the lease contract may recover the goods identified from the lessor if the lessor becomes insolvent within 10 days after receipt of the first installment of rent and security.

(b) A lessee acquires the right to recover goods identified to a lease contract only if they conform to the lease contract. *(Added by Stats.1988, c. 1359, § 5, operative Jan. 1, 1990. Amended by Stats.1991, c. 111 (S.B.972), § 60, eff. July 15, 1991.)*

California Comment
Report of the Assembly Committee on Judiciary
August 15, 1989

Uniform Statutory Source: Section 2–502.
Changes: Revised to reflect leasing practices and terminology.
Definitional Cross References:
"Conforming". Paragraph (d), subdivision (1), Section 10103.
"Goods". Paragraph (h), subdivision (1), Section 10103.
"Insolvent". Subdivision (23), Section 1201.
"Lease contract". Paragraph (*l*), subdivision (1), Section 10103.
"Lessee". Paragraph (n), subdivision (1), Section 10103.
"Lessor". Paragraph (p), subdivision (1), Section 10103.
"Receipt". Paragraph (c), subdivision (1), Section 2103.
"Rights". Subdivision (36), Section 1201.

ARTICLE 3. DEFAULT BY LESSEE

Section
10523. Lessor's Remedies.
10524. Goods wrongfully rejected or acceptance wrongfully revoked; failure to make payment; lessor's rights.
10525. Lessor's Right to Possession of Goods.
10526. Lessor's Stoppage of Delivery in Transit or Otherwise.
10527. Lessor's Rights to Dispose of Goods.
10528. Lessor's Damages for Default.
10529. Lessor's Action for the Rent.
10530. Lessor's Incidental Damages.
10531. Standing to Sue Third Parties for Injury to Goods.
10532. Recovery by Lessor for Loss of or Damage to Residual Interest.

§ 10523. Lessor's Remedies

(a) If a lessee wrongfully rejects or revokes acceptance of goods or fails to make a payment when due or repudiates with respect to a part or the whole, then, with respect to any goods involved, and with respect to all of the goods if under an installment lease contract the value of the whole lease contract is substantially impaired (Section 10510), the lessee is in default under the lease contract and the lessor may:

(1) Cancel the lease contract (subdivision (a) of Section 10505);

(2) Proceed respecting goods not identified to the lease contract (Section 10524);

(3) Withhold delivery of the goods and take possession of goods previously delivered (Section 10525);

(4) Stop delivery of the goods by any bailee (Section 10526);

(5) Dispose of the goods and recover damages (Section 10527), or retain the goods and recover damages (Section 10528), or in a proper case recover rent (Section 10529);

(6) Exercise any other rights or pursue any other remedies provided in the lease contract.

(b) If a lessor does not fully exercise a right or obtain a remedy to which the lessor is entitled under subdivision (a), the lessor may recover the loss resulting in the ordinary course of events from the lessee's default as determined in any reasonable manner, together with incidental damages, less expenses saved in consequence of the lessee's default.

(c) If a lessee is otherwise in default under a lease contract, the lessor may exercise * * * the rights and pursue the remedies provided in * * * the lease contract, which may include a right to cancel the lease. In addition, unless otherwise provided in the lease contract:

(1) If the default substantially impairs the value of the lease contract to the lessor, the lessor may exercise the rights and pursue the remedies provided in subdivisions (a) and (b); or

(2) If the default does not substantially impair the value of the lease contract to the lessor, the lessor may recover as provided in subdivision (b). *(Added by Stats.1988, c. 1359, § 5, operative Jan. 1, 1990. Amended by Stats.1991, c. 111 (S.B.972), § 61, eff. July 15, 1991.)*

California Comment
Report of the Assembly Committee on Judiciary
August 15, 1989

Uniform Statutory Source: Section 2–703.
Changes: Substantially revised.
Purposes: This section is an index to Sections 10524 through 10531 and their effect on the lessor's rights and remedies upon the lessee's default. The lessor and the lessee can agree otherwise; thus, the parties can, among other things, raise or lower the threshold that gives rise to lessee's default or create a new scheme of rights and remedies triggered by the occurrence of the default. Subdivision (4), Section 10503; subdivision (4), Section 10103; and subdivision (3), Section 1102.

Subdivision (1), a substantially rewritten version of Section 2703, lists various cumulative remedies of the lessor where the lessee wrongfully rejects or revokes acceptance, fails to make a payment when due, or repudiates. Subdivision (4), Section 10501. This Division rejects the doctrine of election of remedy. Whether, in a particular case, one remedy bars another, is a function of whether lessor has been put in as good a position as if the lessee had fully performed the lease contract. Subdivision (4), Section 10103 and subdivision (1), Section 1106.

Hypothetical: 1. To better understand the application of paragraphs (a) through (e), it is useful to review a hypothetical. Assume that A is a merchant in the business of selling and leasing new bicycles of various types. B is about to engage in the business of subleasing bicycles to summer residents of and visitors to an island resort. A, as lessor, has agreed to lease 60 bicycles to B. While there is one master lease, deliveries and terms are staggered. 20 bicycles are to be delivered by A to B's island location on June 1; the term of the lease of these bicycles is four months. 20 bicycles are to be delivered by A to B's island location on July 1; the term of the lease of these bicycles is three months. Finally, 20 bicycles are to be delivered by A to B's island location on August 1; the term of the lease of these bicycles is two months. B is obligated to pay rent to A on the 15th day of each month during the term for the lease. Rent is $50 per month, per bicycle. B has no option to purchase or release and must return the bicycles to A at the end of the term, in good condition, reasonable wear and tear excepted. Since the retail price of each bicycle is $400 and bicycles used in the retail rental business have a useful economic life of 36 months, this transaction creates a lease. Paragraph (j), subdivision (1), Section 10103 and subdivision (37), Section 1201.

2. A's current inventory of bicycles is not large. Thus, upon signing the lease with B in February, A agreed to purchase 60 new bicycles from A's principal manufacturer, with special instructions to drop ship the bicycles to B's island location in accordance with the delivery schedule set forth in the lease.

3. The first shipment of 20 bicycles was received by B on May 21. B inspected the bicycles, accepted the same as conforming to the lease and signed a receipt of delivery and acceptance. However, due to poor weather that summer, business was terrible and B was unable to pay the rent due on June 15. Pursuant to the lease A sent B notice of default and proceeded to enforce A's rights and remedies against B.

4. A's counsel first advised A that under subdivision (2) of Section 10510 and the terms of the lease B's failure to pay was a default with respect to the whole. Thus, to minimize A's continued exposure, A was advised to take possession of the bicycles. If A had possession of the goods A could refuse to deliver. Subdivision (1), Section 10525. However, the facts here are different. With respect to the bicycles, in B's possession, A has the right to take possession of the bicycles, without breach of the peace. Subdivision (2), Section 10525. If B refuses to allow A access to the bicycles, A can proceed by action, including replevin or injunctive relief.

5. With respect to the 40 bicycles that have not been delivered, this Division provides various alternatives. First, assume that 20 of the remaining 40 bicycles have been manufactured and delivered by the manufacturer to a carrier for shipment to B. Given the size of the shipment, the carrier was using a small truck for the delivery and the truck had not yet reached the island ferry when the manufacturer (at the request of A) instructed the carrier to divert the shipment to A's place of business. A's right to stop delivery is recognized under these circumstances. Subdivision (1), Section 10526. Second, assume that the 20 remaining bicycles were in the process of manufacture when B defaulted. A retains the right (as between A as lessor and B as lessee) to exercise reasonable commercial judgment whether to complete manufacture or to dispose of the unfinished goods for scrap. Since A is not the manufacturer and A has a binding contract to buy the bicycles, A elected to allow the manufacturer to complete the manufacture of the bicycles, but instructed the manufacturer to deliver the completed bicycles to A's place of business. Subdivision (2), Section 10524.

6. Thus, so far A has elected to exercise the remedies referred to in paragraphs (b) through (d) in subdivision (1). None of these remedies bars any of the others because A's election and enforcement merely resulted in A's possession of the bicycles. Had B performed A would have recovered possession of the bicycles. Thus A is in the process of obtaining the benefit of A's bargain.

7. A's counsel next would determine what action, if any, should be taken with respect to the goods. As stated in paragraph (e) and as discussed fully in subdivision (1) of Section 10527 the lessor may, but has no obligation to, dispose of the goods by lease, sale or otherwise. In this case, since A is in the business of leasing and selling bicycles, A will probably inventory the 60 bicycles for its retail trade.

8. A's counsel then will determine which of the various, alternate means of ascertaining A's claim for damages against B will be computed. Paragraph (e) catalogues each relevant section. First, under subdivision (2) of Section 10527 the amount of A's claim will be computed by comparing the original lease between A and B with any subsequent lease of the bicycles but only if the subsequent lease is substantially similar to the lease contract. While the section does not define this term, the comment does establish some parameters. If, however, A elects to lease the bicycles to his retail trade, it is unlikely that the resulting lease will be substantially similar to the original, as leases to retail customers are considerably different from leases to wholesale customers like B. If, however, the leases were substantially similar, the damage claim is for accrued and unpaid rent, the present value of the difference between the rent reserved under both leases for the balance of their terms, together with incidental damages less expenses saved in consequence of the lessee's default.

9. If the new lease is not substantially similar or if A elects to sell the bicycles or to hold the bicycles, damages are computed under Section 10528 or 10529. In addition, the lessor may elect to proceed under Section 10528 whether or not any new lease of the goods is a substantially similar lease within the meaning of Section 10527.

10. If A elects to pursue A's claim under subdivision (1) of Section 10528 the damage rule is the same as that stated in subdivision (2) of Section 10527 except that the standard of comparison is not the rent reserved under a substantially similar lease entered into by the lessor but a market rent, as defined in Section 10507. Further, if the facts of this hypothetical were more elaborate A may be able to establish that the measure of damage under subdivision (1) is inadequate to put A in the same position that B's performance would have, in which case A can claim lost profits.

11. Yet another alternative for computing A's damage claim against B is prescribed by Section 10529. That section permits the lessor under certain circumstances to recover from the lessee accrued and unpaid rent plus the present value of the rent reserved for the then remaining lease term of the lease agreement. However, to use the formula under paragraph (b) of subdivision (1), A must have made reasonable efforts to dispose of the bicycles at a reasonable price or establish that such efforts would have been unavailing. In addition, A must, among other things, hold the bicycles identified in the lease contract for B. Since this would include all 60 bicycles and A is a merchant, it is unlikely to occur. Further, paragraph (a) of subdivision (1), which in essence allows A to receive the present value of the rent reserved under the lease without making reasonable efforts to dispose of the bicycles, would in this case apply only to the 20 bicycles accepted by B in May and only if A did not take possession of the bicycles from B. If A took possession of the 20 bicycles from B or if possession was tendered to A by B, then A would be required to proceed under paragraph (b) of subdivision (1) and make reasonable efforts to dispose of the bicycles or establish that such efforts would be unavailing. With respect to the remaining 40 bicycles, paragraph (b) of subdivision (1) will apply only if A is unable to dispose of them, or circumstances indicate the effort will be unavailing, in which case the damage formula identical to the one set forth in paragraph (a) of subdivision (1) will apply. At any time up to collection of a judgment by A against B, A may dispose of the bicycles. In such case A's claim for damages against B is governed by Section 10527 or 10528. Subdivision (3), Section 10529. The resulting recalculation of claim should reduce the amount recoverable by A against B. However, the nature of the post-judgment proceedings to resolve this issue, and the sanctions for abuse, if any, will be determined by other law.

12. Finally, if the lease agreement had provided, A's claim against B would not be determined under any of these statutory formulae, but pursuant to a liquidated damages clause. Subdivision (1), Section 10504.

13. These various methods of computing A's damage claim against B are alternatives. However, the pursuit of any one of these alternatives is not a bar to, nor has it been barred by, A's earlier action to obtain possession of the 60 bicycles. These formulae, which vary as a function of an overt or implied mitigation of damage theory, focus on allowing a recovery of the benefit of A's bargain with B. Had B performed, A would have received the rent as well as the return of the 60 bicycles at the end of the term.

14. Finally, A's counsel should also advise A of the right to cancel the lease contract under paragraph (a). Subdivision (1), Section 10505. Cancellation will discharge all existing obligations but preserve A's rights and remedies.

Subdivision (2) is new. If the lessee is in default for reasons other than those stated in subdivision (1), the lessor has all of the rights and remedies provided for in the lease contract (subdivision (2), Section 10501 and subdivision (1), Section 10503); and, in addition, subdivision (2) allows the lessor access to the remedy scheme of this Division except to the extent that this Division makes the right or remedy available only upon the occurrence of a default described in subdivision (1). However, if a default occurs which is other than a default described in subdivision (1) and such default results in the occurrence of a default described in subdivision (1), then the lessor may have access to the entire remedy scheme of this Division including the remedies described in subdivision (1). Thus, the lessor's invocation of a clause in the lease permitting the lessor to accelerate all rentals provided for under the lease upon the lessee's default would, in the absence of a payment of the accelerated rentals, enable the lessor to invoke the remedies listed in subdivision (1). For example, assume that the lease contract requires the lessee to maintain insurance on the goods and provides that a failure to maintain such insurance shall permit the lessor to accelerate all rental payments under the lease. The lessee's failure to perform this insurance covenant would not be a default of the type described in subdivision (1) so that the lessee's failure to maintain such insurance would not alone permit the lessor to invoke the remedies provided in subdivision (1). However, if the lessor accelerates all rental payments as a result of the lessee's failure to maintain such insurance and the lessee fails to pay such accelerated rentals, the failure to pay such rental would constitute a default described in subdivision (1) entitling the lessor to invoke the remedies listed in subdivision (1). Note that the reference to this Division includes supplementary principles of law and equity, *e.g.*, fraud, misrepresentation and duress. Subdivision (4), Section 10103 and Section 1103.

There is no special treatment of the finance lease in this section. Absent supplementary principles of law to the contrary, in most cases the supplier will have no rights or remedies against the defaulting lessee. Paragraph (b), subdivision (2), Section 10209. Given that the supplier will look to the lessor for payment, this is appropriate. However, there is a specific exception to this rule with respect to the right to identify goods to the lease contract. Subdivision (2), Section 10524. The parties are free to create a different result in a particular case. Subdivision (4), Section 10103 and subdivision (3), Section 10102.

Cross References:

Subdivision (3), Section 1102; Section 1103; subdivision (1), Section 1106; subdivision (37), Section 1201; Section 2703; paragraph (j), subdivision (1), Section 10103; subdivision (4), Section 10103; paragraph (b), subdivision (2), Section 10209; subdivision (4), Section 10501; subdivision (1), Section 10504; subdivision (1), Section 10505; Section 10507; subdivision (2), Section 10510; Sections 10524 through 10531; subdivision (2), Section 10524; subdivision (1), Section 10525; subdivision (2), Section 10525; subdivision (1), Section 10526; subdivision (1), Section 10527; subdivision (2), Section 10527; subdivision (1), Section 10528; and subdivision (3), Section 10529.

Definitional Cross References:

"Delivery". Subdivision (14), Section 1201.
"Goods". Paragraph (h), subdivision (1), Section 10103.
"Installment lease contract". Paragraph (i), subdivision (1), Section 10103.
"Lease contract". Paragraph (*l*), subdivision (1), Section 10103.
"Lessee". Paragraph (n), subdivision (1), Section 10103.
"Lessor". Paragraph (p), subdivision (1), Section 10103.
"Remedy". Subdivision (34), Section 1201.
"Rights". Subdivision (36), Section 1201.
"Value". Subdivision (44), Section 1201.

Cross References

Cancellation and termination and effect of cancellation, termination, etc., see Commercial Code § 10505.
Default, procedure on, see Commercial Code § 10501.
Installment lease contracts, rejection and default, see Commercial Code § 10510.
Lessee under finance lease as beneficiary of supply contract, see Commercial Code § 10209.
Liquidation of damages, see Commercial Code § 10504.
Proof of market and rent, time and place, see Commercial Code § 10507.
Purpose of code, rules of construction, variations by agreement, see Commercial Code § 1102.
Supplementary general principles of law applicable, see Commercial Code § 1103.

§ 10524. Goods wrongfully rejected or acceptance wrongfully revoked; failure to make payment; lessor's rights

* * * (a) After a default by the lessee under the lease contract of the type described in subdivision (a) of, or paragraph (1) of subdivision (c) of, Section 10523 or, if agreed, after other default by the lessee, the lessor * * * may:

(1) Identify to the lease contract conforming goods not already identified if at the time the lessor learned of the default they were in the lessor's or the supplier's possession or control; and

(2) Dispose of goods (subdivision (a) of Section 10527) that demonstrably have been intended for the particular lease contract even though those goods are unfinished.

(b) If the goods are unfinished, in the exercise of reasonable commercial judgment for the purposes of avoiding loss and of effective realization, an aggrieved lessor or the supplier may either complete manufacture and wholly identify the goods to the lease contract or cease manufacture and lease, sell, or otherwise dispose of the goods for scrap or salvage value or proceed in any other reasonable manner. *(Added by Stats.1988, c. 1359, § 5, operative Jan. 1, 1990. Amended by Stats. 1991, c. 111 (S.B.972), § 62, eff. July 15, 1991.)*

California Comment
Report of the Assembly Committee on Judiciary
August 15, 1989

Uniform Statutory Source: Section 2–704.
Changes: Revised to reflect leasing practices and terminology.
Definitional Cross References:
"Aggrieved party". Subdivision (2), Section 1201.
"Conforming". Paragraph (d), subdivision (1), Section 10103.
"Goods". Paragraph (h), subdivision (1), Section 10103.
"Learn". Subdivision (25), Section 1201.
"Lease". Paragraph (j), subdivision (1), Section 10103.
"Lease contract". Paragraph (*l*), subdivision (1), Section 10103.
"Lessor". Paragraph (p), subdivision (1), Section 10103.
"Rights". Subdivision (36), Section 1201.
"Supplier". Paragraph (x), subdivision (1), Section 10103.
"Value". Subdivision (44), Section 1201.

§ 10525. Lessor's Right to Possession of Goods

(a) If a lessor discovers the lessee to be insolvent, the lessor may refuse to deliver the goods.

* * * (b) After a default by the lessee under the lease contract of the type described in subdivision (a) of, or paragraph (1) of subdivision (c) of, Section 10523 or, if agreed, after other default by the lessee, the lessor has the right to take possession of the goods. If the lease contract so provides, the lessor may require the lessee to assemble the goods and make them available to the lessor at a place to be designated by the lessor which is reasonably convenient to both parties. Without removal, the lessor may render unusable any goods employed in trade or business, and may dispose of goods on the lessee's premises (Section 10527).

(c) The lessor may proceed under subdivision (b) without judicial process if it can be done without breach of the peace or the lessor may proceed by action. *(Added by Stats.1988, c. 1359, § 5, operative Jan. 1, 1990. Amended by Stats.1991, c. 111 (S.B.972), § 63, eff. July 15, 1991.)*

California Comment
Report of the Assembly Committee on Judiciary
August 15, 1989

Uniform Statutory Source: Sections 2–702(1) and 9–503.
Changes: Substantially revised.
Purposes: Subdivision (1), a revised version of the provisions of subdivision (1) of Section 2702, allows the lessor to refuse to deliver goods if the lessee is insolvent. Note that the provisions of subdivision (2) of Section 2702, granting the unpaid seller certain rights of reclamation, were not incorporated in this section. Subdivision (2) made this unnecessary.

Subdivision (2), a revised version of the provisions of Section 9503, allows the lessor, on default by the lessee, the right to take possession of or reclaim the goods; since the lessee's insolvency is an event of default in a standard lease agreement, subdivision (2) is the functional equivalent of subdivision (2) of Section 2702. Further, subdivision (2) sanctions the classic crate and delivery clause obligating the lessee to assemble the goods and to make them available to the lessor. Finally, the lessor may leave the goods in place, render them unusable (if they are goods employed in trade or business), and dispose of them on the lessee's premises.

Subdivision (3), a revised version of the provisions of Section 9503, allows the lessor to proceed under subdivision (2) without judicial process, absent breach of the peace, or by action. Subdivision (3), Section 10501; subdivision (4), Section 10103; and subdivision (1), Section 1201. In the appropriate case action includes injunctive relief. *Clark Equip. Co. v. Armstrong Equip. Co.*, 431 F.2d 54 (5th Cir.1970), cert. denied, 402 U.S. 909 (1971).

Cross References:
Subdivision (2), Section 1106; subdivision (1), Section 2702; subdivision (2), Section 2702; subdivision (4), Section 10103; subdivision (3), Section 10501; and Section 9503.

Definitional Cross References:
"Action". Subdivision (1), Section 1201.
"Delivery". Subdivision (14), Section 1201.
"Discover". Subdivision (25), Section 1201.
"Goods". Paragraph (h), subdivision (1), Section 10103.
"Insolvent". Subdivision (23), Section 1201.
"Lease contract". Paragraph (*l*), subdivision (1), Section 10103.
"Lessee". Paragraph (n), subdivision (1), Section 10103.
"Lessor". Paragraph (p), subdivision (1), Section 10103.
"Party". Subdivision (29), Section 1201.
"Rights". Subdivision (36), Section 1201.

Cross References

Default procedure, see Commercial Code § 10510.
Remedies to be liberally administered, see Commercial Code § 1106.
Secured party's rights to take possession after default, see Commercial Code § 9503.
Seller's remedies on discovery of buyer's insolvency, see Commercial Code § 2702.

§ 10526. Lessor's Stoppage of Delivery in Transit or Otherwise

(a) A lessor may stop delivery of goods in the possession of a carrier or other bailee if the lessor discovers the lessee to be insolvent and may stop delivery of carload, truckload, planeload, or larger shipments of express or freight if the lessee repudiates or fails to make a payment due before delivery, whether for rent, security, or otherwise under the lease contract, or for any other reason the lessor has a right to withhold or take possession of the goods.

(b) In pursuing its remedies under subdivision (a), the lessor may stop delivery until:

(1) Receipt of the goods by the lessee;

(2) Acknowledgment to the lessee by any bailee of the goods, except a carrier, that the bailee holds the goods for the lessee; or

(3) Such an acknowledgment to the lessee by a carrier via reshipment or as warehouseman.

* * * (c) (1) To stop delivery, a lessor shall so notify as to enable the bailee by reasonable diligence to prevent delivery of the goods.

(2) After notification, the bailee shall hold and deliver the goods according to the directions of the lessor, but the lessor is liable to the bailee for any ensuing charges or damages.

(3) A carrier who has issued a nonnegotiable bill of lading is not obliged to obey a notification to stop received from a person other than the consignor. (Added by Stats.1988, c. 1359, § 5, operative Jan. 1, 1990. Amended by Stats.1991, c. 111 (S.B.972), § 64, eff. July 15, 1991.)

California Comment
Report of the Assembly Committee on Judiciary
August 15, 1989

Uniform Statutory Source: Section 2–705.
Changes: Revised to reflect leasing practices and terminology.
Definitional Cross References:
"Bill of lading". Subdivision (6), Section 1201.
"Delivery". Subdivision (14), Section 1201.
"Discover". Subdivision (25), Section 1201.
"Goods". Paragraph (h), subdivision (1), Section 10103.
"Insolvent". Subdivision (23), Section 1201.
"Lease contract". Paragraph (*l*), subdivision (1), Section 10103.
"Lessee". Paragraph (n), subdivision (1), Section 10103.
"Lessor". Paragraph (p), subdivision (1), Section 10103.
"Notifies" and "Notification". Subdivision (26), Section 1201.
"Person". Subdivision (30), Section 1201.
"Receipt". Paragraph (c), subdivision (1), Section 2103.
"Remedy". Subdivision (34), Section 1201.
"Rights". Subdivision (36), Section 1201.

§ 10527. Lessor's Rights to Dispose of Goods

(a) After a default by a lessee under the lease contract * * * of the type described in subdivision (a) of, or paragraph (1) of subdivision (c) of, Section 10523 * * * or after the lessor refuses to deliver or takes possession of goods (Section 10525 or 10526), or, if agreed, after other default by a lessee, the lessor may dispose of the goods concerned or the undelivered balance thereof by lease, sale, or otherwise.

(b) Except as otherwise provided with respect to damages liquidated in the lease agreement (Section 10504) or otherwise determined * * * pursuant to agreement of the parties (Section 10503 and subdivision (3) of Section 1102), if the disposition is by lease agreement substantially similar to the original lease agreement and the new lease agreement is made in good faith and in a commercially reasonable manner, the lessor may recover from the lessee as damages (1) accrued and unpaid rent as of the date of the commencement of the term of the new lease agreement, (2) the present value, as of the same date, of the * * * total rent for the then remaining lease term of the original lease agreement * * * minus the present value, as of the same date, of the rent * * * under the new lease agreement applicable to that period of the new lease term which is comparable to the then remaining term of the original lease agreement, and (3) any incidental damages allowed under Section 10530, less expenses saved in consequence of the lessee's default.

* * * (c) If the lessor's disposition is by lease agreement that for any reason does not qualify for treatment under subdivision (b), or is by sale or

otherwise, the lessor may recover from the lessee * * * as if the lessor had elected not to dispose of the goods and Section 10528 governs.

(d) A subsequent buyer or lessee who buys or leases from the lessor in good faith for value as a result of a disposition under this section takes the goods free of the original lease contract and any rights of the original lessee even though the lessor fails to comply with one or more of the requirements of this division.

(e) The lessor is not accountable to the lessee for any profit made on any disposition. A lessee who has rightfully rejected or justifiably revoked acceptance shall account to the lessor for any excess over the amount of the lessee's security interest (subdivision (e) of Section 10508). *(Added by Stats.1988, c. 1359, § 5, operative Jan. 1, 1990. Amended by Stats.1991, c. 111 (S.B.972), § 65, eff. July 15, 1991.)*

California Comment
Report of the Assembly Committee on Judiciary
August 15, 1989

Uniform Statutory Source: Section 2–706(1), (5) and (6).
Changes: Substantially revised.
Purposes: Subdivision (1), a revised version of the first sentence of subdivision (1) of Section 2706, allows the lessor the right to dispose of goods after default by the lessee (even if the goods remain in the lessee's possession—subdivision (2) of Section 10525) or after the lessor refuses to deliver or takes possession of the goods. The lessor's decision to exercise this right is a function of commercial judgment, not a statutory mandate replete with sanctions for failure to comply. *Compare* Section 9507. As the owner of the goods, in the case of a lessor, or as the prime lessee of the goods, in the case of a sublessor, compulsory disposition of the goods is inconsistent with the nature of the interest held by the lessor or the sublessor and is not necessary because the interest held by the lessee or the sublessee is not protected by a right of redemption under the common law or this Division. Subdivision (5), Section 10527.

The rule for determining the measure of damages recoverable by the lessor against the lessee is a function of several variables. If the lessor has elected to effect disposition under subdivision (1) and such disposition is by lease that qualifies under subdivision (2), the measure of damages set forth in subdivision (2) will apply, absent agreement to the contrary. Section 10504; subdivision (4), Section 10103; and subdivision (3), Section 1102.

The lessor's damages will be established using the new lease agreement as a measure if the following three criteria are satisfied: (i) the lessor disposed of the goods by lease, (ii) the lease agreement is substantially similar to the original lease agreement, and (iii) such disposition was in good faith, and in a commercially reasonable manner. Thus, the lessor will be entitled to recover from the lessee the accrued and unpaid rent as of the date of the commencement of the term of the new lease agreement, and the present value, as of such date, of the difference between the rent reserved under the new lease and the original lease, together with incidental damages less expenses saved in consequence of the lessee's default. Whether or not the lessor's disposition satisfies the criteria of subdivision (2), the lessor may elect to calculate its claim against the lessee pursuant to Section 10528. Subdivision (3), Section 10527.

Two of the three criteria to be met by the lessor are familiar, but the concept of the new lease agreement that is substantially similar to the original lease agreement is not. Given the many variables facing a party who intends to lease goods and the rapidity of change in the market place, the policy decision was made not to draft with specificity. It was thought unwise to seek to establish certainty at the cost of fairness. The decision of whether the new lease agreement is substantially similar to the original will be determined case by case.

While the section does not draw a bright line, it is possible to describe some of the factors that should be considered in a finding that a new lease agreement is substantially similar to the original. The various elements of the new lease agreement should be examined. Those elements include the term of the new lease (because the damages are calculated under subdivision (2) as the difference between the total rent payable for the entire term of the new lease agreement and the remaining lease term of the original lease); the options to purchase or release; the lessor's representations, warranties and covenants to the lessee as well as those to be provided by the lessee to the lessor; and the services, if any, to be provided by the lessor or by the lessee. All of these factors allocate cost and risk between the lessor and the lessee and thus affect the amount of rent to be paid. These findings should not be made with scientific precision, as they are a function of economics, nor should they be made independently, as it is important that a sense of commercial judgment pervade the finding. See subdivision (2), Section 10507. To establish the new lease as a proper measure of damage under subdivision (2), these various factors, taken as a whole, must result in a finding that the new lease agreement is substantially similar to the original.

The following hypothetical illustrates the difficulty of providing a bright line. Assume that A buys a jumbo tractor for $1 million and then leases the tractor to B for a term of 36 months. The tractor is delivered to and is accepted by B on May 1. On June 1 B fails to pay the monthly rent to A. B returns the tractor to A, who immediately releases the tractor to C for a term identical to the term remaining under the lease between A and B. All terms and conditions under the lease between A and C are identical to those under the original lease between A and B, except that C does not provide any property damage or other insurance coverage, and B agreed to provide complete coverage. Coverage is expensive and difficult to obtain. The new lease should be viewed as not substantially similar to the original. However, if the lessor seeks a recovery under Section 10528 the new lease can be introduced into evidence to establish market rent (Section 10507), with a proper allowance for the lessor's cost of replacing the lost insurance coverage.

Subdivision (3), which is new, provides that if the lessor's disposition is by lease that qualifies for treatment under subdivision (2), the lessor may elect to proceed under subdivision (2) or Section 10528. If the lessor's disposition is by lease that does not qualify under subdivision (2), or is by sale or otherwise, Section 10528 governs.

Subdivision (4), a revised version of subdivision (5) of Section 2706, applies to protect a subsequent buyer or lessee who buys or leases from the lessor in good faith and for value, pursuant to a disposition under this section. Note that by its terms, the rule in subdivision (1) of Section 10304, which provides that the subsequent lessee takes subject to the original lease contract, is controlled by the rule stated in this subdivision.

Subdivision (5), a revised version of subdivision (6) of Section 2706, provides that the lessor is not accountable to the lessee for any profit made by the lessor on a disposition. This rule follows from the fundamental premise of the bailment for hire that the lessee under a lease of goods has no equity of redemption to protect. Nothing in subdivision (5) relieves the lessor of any contractual duty to account to the lessee for the amount of proceeds obtained after any disposition of the goods to the extent that the lessee's liability to the lessor is determined, pursuant to the lease, by reference to the amount of such proceeds.

Cross References:

Subdivision (3), Section 1102; subdivision (1), Section 2706; subdivision (5), Section 2706; subdivision (6), Section 2706; subdivision (4), Section 10103; subdivision (1), Section 10304; Section 10504; subdivision (2), Section 10507; paragraph (e), subdivision (1), Section 10523; subdivision (2), Section 10525; subdivision (5), Section 10527; Section 10528; and Section 9507.

Definitional Cross References:

"Buyer" and "Buying". Paragraph (a), subdivision (1), Section 2103.
"Delivery". Subdivision (14), Section 1201.
"Good faith". Subdivision (19), Section 1201 and paragraph (b), subdivision (1), Section 2103.
"Goods". Paragraph (h), subdivision (1), Section 10103.
"Lease". Paragraph (j), subdivision (1), Section 10103.
"Lease contract". Paragraph (l), subdivision (1), Section 10103.
"Lessee". Paragraph (n), subdivision (1), Section 10103.
"Lessor". Paragraph (p), subdivision (1), Section 10103.
"Present value". Paragraph (u), subdivision (1), Section 10103.
"Rights". Subdivision (36), Section 1201.

"Sale". Subdivision (1), Section 2106.
"Security interest". Subdivision (37), Section 1201.
"Value". Subdivision (44), Section 1201.

Cross References

Lessor's remedies, see Commercial Code § 10523.
Lessor's right to possession of goods, see Commercial Code § 10525.
Liquidation of damages, see Commercial Code § 10504.
Proof of market rent, time and place, see Commercial Code § 10507.
Purposes of code, rules of construction, variation by agreement, see Commercial Code § 1102.
Secured party's liability for failure to comply with default provisions, see Commercial Code § 9507.
Seller's resale including contract for resale, see Commercial Code § 2706.
Subsequent lease of goods by lessor, see Commercial Code § 10304.

§ 10528. Lessor's Damages for Default

(a) Except as otherwise provided with respect to damages liquidated in the lease agreement (Section 10504) or <u>otherwise</u> determined * * * <u>pursuant to agreement of the parties (Section 10503 and subdivision (3) of Section 1102)</u>, if a lessor elects to retain the goods or a lessor elects to dispose of the goods and <u>the disposition is by lease agreement</u> * * * <u>that for any reason does not qualify</u> for treatment under subdivision <u>(b)</u> of Section 10527, or is by sale or otherwise, the lessor may recover from the lessee as damages for a default * * * <u>of the type described in subdivision (a) of, or paragraph (1) of subdivision (c) of, Section 10523</u> * * *, or, if agreed, for other default of the lessee, (1) accrued and unpaid rent as of the date * * * <u>of default if the lessee has never taken</u> possession of the goods, or * * *, <u>if the lessee has taken possession of the goods, as of the date the lessor repossesses the goods or an earlier date</u> * * * <u>on which the lessee</u> * * * <u>makes a tender of</u> * * * the <u>goods</u> * * * to the lessor, (2) the present value as of the date determined under paragraph (1) of the * * * total rent for the then remaining lease term of the original lease agreement * * * <u>minus the present value as of the same date of</u> the market rent at the * * * place where the goods <u>are</u> located * * * computed for the same lease term, and (3) any incidental damages allowed under Section 10530, less expenses saved in consequence of the lessee's default.

(b) If the measure of damages provided in subdivision (a) is inadequate to put a lessor in as good a position as performance would have, the measure of damages is the present value of the profit, including reasonable overhead, the lessor would have made from full performance by the lessee, together with any incidental damages allowed under Section 10530, due allowance for costs reasonably incurred and due credit for payments or proceeds of disposition. *(Added by Stats.1988, c. 1359, § 5, operative Jan. 1, 1990. Amended by Stats.1991, c. 111 (S.B.972), § 66, eff. July 15, 1991.)*

California Comment
Report of the Assembly Committee on Judiciary
August 15, 1989

Uniform Statutory Source: Section 2–708.

Changes: Substantially revised.

Purposes: Subdivision (1), a substantially revised version of subdivision (1) of Section 2708, states the basic rule governing the measure of lessor's damages for default by the lessee. Subdivision (1), Section 10523. This measure will apply if the lessor elects to retain the goods (whether undelivered, returned by the lessee, or repossessed by the lessor after acceptance and default by the lessee) and whether or not the lessor's disposition qualifies under subdivision (2) of Section 10527. Subdivision (3), Section 10527. There is no sanction for disposition that does not qualify under subdivision (2) of Section 10527. Application of the rule set forth in this section is subject to agreement to the contrary. Section 10504; subdivision (4), Section 10103; and subdivision (3), Section 1102.

The measure of damage is the accrued and unpaid rent as of the date the lessor obtained possession of the goods or such earlier date as possession was tendered to the lessor together with the present value, as of such date, of the difference between market rent and the original rent for the then remaining term of the lease, and incidental damages, less expenses saved in consequence of the default. Market rent will be computed pursuant to Section 10507. If, as of the date of default, the lessor has attempted and failed to obtain possession of the goods, the lessor has, among various additional rights and remedies, a cause of action against the lessee for damages due to loss of use of possession of the goods between the date of default and the date the lessor obtains possession of the goods. Subdivision (3), Section 10525; subdivision (4), Section 10103; and subdivision (1), Section 1201. See also Section 10530. This conclusion is critical to an important policy decision to protect the lessor's residual interest in the goods. Paragraph (q), subdivision (1), Section 10103.

Subdivision (2), a somewhat revised version of the provisions of subdivision (2) of Section 2708, states a measure of damages which applies in each case that subdivision (1) applies but the measure of damages in subdivision (1) is inadequate to put the lessor in as good a position as performance would have. The measure of damage is the present value of the lessor's profit, including overhead, together with incidental damages, with allowance for costs reasonably incurred and credit for payments or proceeds of disposition. In determining the amount of due credit with respect to proceeds of disposition a proper value should be attributed to the lessor's residual interest in the goods. Paragraph (q), subdivision (1), Section 10103 and subdivision (4), Section 10507.

In calculating profit, a court should include any expected appreciation of the goods, *e.g.* the foal of a leased brood mare. Because this subdivision is intended to give the lessor the benefit of the bargain, a court should consider any reasonable benefit or profit expected by the lessor from the performance of the lease agreement. See *Honeywell, Inc. v. Lithonia Lighting, Inc.*, 317 F.Supp. 406, 413 (N.D. Ga. 1970); *Locks v. Wade*, 36 N.J.Super. 128, 131, 114 A.2d 875, 877 (Super.Ct.App.Div.1955).

Cross References:
Subdivision (3), Section 1102; Section 2708; paragraph (u), subdivision (1), Section 10103; Section 10402; Section 10504; Section 10507; subdivision (2), Section 10527; and Section 10529.

Definitional Cross References:
"Agreement". Subdivision (3), Section 1201.
"Goods". Paragraph (h), subdivision (1), Section 10103.
"Lease". Paragraph (j), subdivision (1), Section 10103.
"Lease agreement". Paragraph (k), subdivision (1), Section 10103.
"Lessee". Paragraph (n), subdivision (1), Section 10103.
"Lessor". Paragraph (p), subdivision (1), Section 10103.
"Party". Subdivision (29), Section 1201.
"Present value". Paragraph (u), subdivision (1), Section 10103.
"Sale". Subdivision (1), Section 2106.

Cross References

Anticipatory repudiation of lease contract, see Commercial Code § 10402.
Determination of damages based on market rent, see Commercial Code § 10507.
Liquidation of damages payable by either party for default, see Commercial Code § 10504.
Proof of market rent, time and place, see Commercial Code § 10507.

Purposes of code, rules of construction, variation by agreement, see Commercial Code § 1102.

Seller's damages for non-acceptance or repudiation, see Commercial Code § 2708.

§ 10529. Lessor's Action for the Rent

(a) After default by the lessee under the lease contract * * * of the type described in subdivision (a) of, or paragraph (1) of subdivision (c) of, Section 10523 * * * or, if agreed, after other default by the lessee, if the lessor complies with subdivision (b), the lessor may recover from the lessee as damages:

(1) For goods accepted by the lessee and not repossessed by or * * * tendered * * * to the lessor, and for conforming goods lost or damaged after risk of loss passes to the lessee (Section 10219), (A) accrued and unpaid rent as of the date of entry of judgment in favor of the lessor, (B) the present value as of the same date * * * of the rent for the then remaining lease term of the lease agreement, and (C) any incidental damages allowed under Section 10530, less expenses saved in consequence of the lessee's default; and

(2) For goods identified to the lease contract where the lessor has never delivered the goods or has taken possession of them or the lessee has * * * tendered them * * * to the lessor, if the lessor is unable after reasonable effort to dispose of them at a reasonable price or the circumstances reasonably indicate that * * * effort will be unavailing, (A) accrued and unpaid rent as of the date of entry of judgment in favor of the lessor, (B) the present value as of the same date * * * of the rent for the then remaining lease term of the lease agreement, and (C) any incidental damages allowed under Section 10530, less expenses saved in consequence of the lessee's default.

(b) Except as provided in subdivision (c), the lessor shall hold for the lessee for the remaining lease term of the lease agreement any goods that have been identified to the lease contract and are in the lessor's control.

(c) The lessor may dispose of the goods at any time before collection of the judgment for damages obtained pursuant to subdivision (a). If the disposition is before the end of the remaining lease term of the lease agreement, the lessor's recovery against the lessee for damages * * * is governed by Section 10527 or 10528, and the lessor will cause an appropriate credit to be provided against a judgment for damages to the extent that the amount of the judgment exceeds the recovery available pursuant to Section 10527 or 10528.

(d) Payment of the judgment for damages obtained pursuant to subdivision (a) entitles the lessee to the use and possession of the goods not then disposed of for the remaining lease term of * * * and in accordance with the lease agreement.

(e) After * * * default by the lessee under the lease contract of the type described in subdivision (a) of, or paragraph (1) of subdivision (c) of, Section 10523 or, if agreed, after other default by the lessee, a lessor who is held not entitled to rent under this section must nevertheless be awarded damages for nonacceptance under Section 10527 or 10528. *(Added by Stats.1988, c. 1359, § 5, operative Jan. 1, 1990. Amended by Stats. 1991, c. 111 (S.B.972), § 67, eff. July 15, 1991.)*

California Comment

Report of the Assembly Committee on Judiciary

August 15, 1989

Uniform Statutory Source: Section 2–709.

Changes: Substantially revised.

Purposes: Subdivision (1) provides another method of determining the measure of lessor's damages after default by the lessee. Absent agreement to the contrary (Section 10504), this Division provides the lessor, in this section and the two preceding sections, three alternate methods of computing damages recoverable from the defaulting lessee (paragraph (e), subdivision (1), Section 10523). This section, as well as the two preceding sections, applies to goods subject to the lease, even if such goods have been repossessed from the lessee or otherwise (subdivision (2), Section 10525). This is a departure from Section 2709, the statutory analogue. The departure is not surprising given the essential difference between a sale and a lease.

Absent the right to repossess the goods, the recovery stated in paragraph (a) of subdivision (1) would not compensate the lessor for his or her loss. Consider a lease of a carpet cleaner by A to B, for a term of two days. A purchased the carpet cleaner for $500.00. The rent for the two day term is $75.00. If B defaulted by not paying the rent and refusing to return the carpet cleaner and A was not allowed to repossess the carpet cleaner, the measure of damage stated in this section would allow a recovery of not more than $75.00, together with incidental damages. The rule stated in this Division, which allows the lessor the right to repossess the goods from the lessee and to recover damages, is consistent with the lessor's ownership of the goods. DeKoven, Proceedings After Default by the Lessee Under a True Lease of Equipment, in 1C P. Coogan, W. Hogan, D. Vagts, *Secured Transactions Under the Uniform Commercial Code*, § 29B.06[4] (1986). The statutory analogue, Section 2709, only provides an action for the price of the goods sold, which is consistent with the seller's agreement to dispose of all of the seller's right, title and interest in the goods to the buyer. That measure of damage would not have been appropriate here as the lessor's agreement is to dispose of possession and use of the goods for a term; the bargain includes the return of the goods at the end of the term. It would be anomalous to allow the lessee to improve on the bargain, i.e. retain the goods, solely by virtue of the lessee's default, even if that had been balanced by allowing the lessor to sue to recover the price or value of the goods.

The measure of the lessor's damages under this section is a function of a two-part rule. Paragraph (a) of subdivision (1) establishes a rule of recovery with respect to goods (i) accepted by the lessee and not repossessed by or tendered back to the lessor and (ii) conforming goods lost or damaged after risk of loss passed to the lessee. This rule of recovery permits the lessor to recover accrued and unpaid rent as of the date of entry of judgment in favor of the lessor plus the present value of rentals for the remaining lease term and any incidental damages permitted under Section 10530. Paragraph (b) of subdivision (1) establishes a rule of recovery with respect to goods that have been identified to the lease contract where the lessor has never delivered the goods or after delivery has taken possession of the goods or the lessee has effectively tendered possession of the goods to the lessor. In this instance, the lessor may recover the same measure of damages as under paragraph (a) of subdivision (1) but only if the lessor is unable after reasonable efforts to dispose of the goods at a reasonable price or the circumstances indicate that such an effort would not be successful. If the lessor proceeds under paragraph (b) of subdivision (1), except as provided in subdivision (3), the lessor must hold the goods for the lessee for the remaining lease term if the goods are in the lessor's control. Subdivision (2). This eliminates the possibility of a double recovery by the lessor and preserves the value of the leasehold estate to the lessee. Under subdivision (3) the lessor may dispose of the goods at any time before collection of the judgment for damages; and if such disposition is before the end of the lease term, the lessor's recovery against the lessee will be determined in accordance with Section 10527 or 10528. Upon such disposition, the lessor must provide the lessee with an appropriate credit against any judgment for damages to the extent that the judgment exceeds the recovery that would be available under Section 10527 or 10528.

As a condition to the lessor's election to employ the method to measure the lessor's claim against the lessee set forth in subdivision (1), the lessor must comply with subdivision (2), which provides that, with one exception, goods identified to the lease contract and in the lessor's control (whether as a result of repossession or otherwise) must be held for the lessee for the balance of the lease term. This eliminates the possibility of a double recovery by the lessor and preserves the value of the leasehold estate to the lessee.

Subdivision (3) creates an exception to the requirement set forth as a condition to subdivision (1), that goods identified to the contract and in the lessor's control be held by the lessor. (subdivision (2), Section 10529). If the lessor disposes of those goods prior to collection of the judgment (whether as a matter of law or agreement), the lessor's recovery is governed by the measure of damages in Section 10527 or 10528. See Section 10523 Comment 11.

The relationship between subdivisions (2) and (3) is best stated by examining a hypothetical. Assume the lease is for a term of two years and after default by the lessee the lessor recovers the goods from the lessee and obtains judgment against the lessee for damages pursuant to subdivision (1). If the lessor holds the goods so recovered until the end of the two year term, any subsequent disposition will have no effect on the lessor's judgment. If, however, the lessor determines that the lessee is judgment proof, the lessor might be wise to dispose of the goods before the end of the remaining lease term, even though the amount that the lessor then will be allowed to recover from the lessee, as determined by the provisions of Section 10527 or 10528, is less than the judgment. Subdivision (3) allows the lessor to make this election at any time before collection of the judgment.

Subdivision (4), which is new, further reinforces the requisites of subdivision (2). In the event the judgment for damages obtained by the lessor against the lessee pursuant to subdivision (1) is satisfied, the lessee regains the right to use and possession of the remaining goods for the balance of the original lease term provided that the lessee complies with all of the other terms and conditions of the lease agreement; a partial satisfaction of the judgment creates no right in the lessee to use and possession of the goods.

The relationship between subdivisions (2) and (4) is important to understand. Subdivision (2) requires the lessor to hold for the lessee identified goods in the lessor's possession. Absent agreement to the contrary, whether in the lease or otherwise, under most circumstances the requirement that the lessor hold the goods for the lessee for the term will mean that the lessor is not allowed to use them. Subdivision (4), Section 10103 and Section 1203. Further, the lessor's use of the goods could be viewed as a disposition of the goods that would bar the lessor from recovery under this section, remitting the lessor to the two preceding sections for a determination of the lessor's claim for damages against the lessee.

Subdivision (5), the analogue of subdivision (3) of Section 2709, further reinforces the thrust of subdivision (3) by stating that a lessor who is held not entitled to rent under this section has not elected a remedy; the lessor must be awarded damages under Sections 10527 and 10528. This is a function of two significant policies of this Division—that resort to a remedy is optional, unless expressly agreed to be exclusive (subdivision (2), Section 10503) and that rights and remedies provided in this Division are cumulative. (subdivisions (2) and (4), Section 10501).

Cross References:
Section 1203; Section 2709; subdivision (3), section 2709; subdivision (4), Section 10103; subdivision (2), Section 10501; subdivision (4), Section 10501; subdivision (2), Section 10503; Section 10504; paragraph (e), subdivision (1), Section 10523; subdivision (2), Section 10525; Section 10527; Section 10528; and subdivision (2), Section 10529.

Definitional Cross References:
"Action". Subdivision (1), Section 1201.
"Conforming". Paragraph (d), subdivision (1), Section 10103.
"Goods". Paragraph (h), subdivision (1), Section 10103.
"Lease". Paragraph (j), subdivision (1), Section 10103.
"Lease agreement". Paragraph (k), subdivision (1), Section 10103.
"Lease contract". Paragraph (*l*), subdivision (1), Section 10103.
"Lessee". Paragraph (n), subdivision (1), Section 10103.
"Lessor". Paragraph (p), subdivision (1), Section 10103.
"Present value". Paragraph (u), subdivision (1), Section 10103.
"Reasonable time". Subdivisions (1) and (2), Section 1204.

Cross References
Action for price, see Commercial Code § 2709.
Default procedure, see Commercial Code § 10501.
Lessor's remedies, see Commercial Code § 10523.
Lessor's right to possession of goods, see Commercial Code § 10525.
Liquidation of damages, see Commercial Code § 10504.
Modification or impairment of rights and remedies, see Commercial Code § 10503.
Obligation of good faith, see Commercial Code § 1203.

§ 10530. Lessor's Incidental Damages

Incidental damages to an aggrieved lessor include any commercially reasonable charges, expenses, or commissions incurred in stopping delivery, in the transportation, care and custody of goods after the lessee's default, in connection with return or disposition of the goods, or otherwise resulting from the default. *(Added by Stats. 1988, c. 1359, § 5, operative Jan. 1, 1990.)*

California Comment
Report of the Assembly Committee on Judiciary
August 15, 1989

Uniform Statutory Source: Section 2–710.
Changes: Revised to reflect leasing practices and terminology.
Definitional Cross References:
"Aggrieved party". Subdivision (2), Section 1201.
"Delivery". Subdivision (14), Section 1201.
"Goods". Paragraph (h), subdivision (1), Section 10103.
"Lessee". Paragraph (n), subdivision (1), Section 10103.
"Lessor". Paragraph (p), subdivision (1), Section 10103.

§ 10531. Standing to Sue Third Parties for Injury to Goods

(a) If a third party so deals with goods that have been identified to a lease contract as to cause actionable injury to a party to the lease contract (1) the lessor has a right of action against the third party, and (2) the lessee also has a right of action against the third party if the lessee:

(A) Has a security interest in the goods;

(B) Has an insurable interest in the goods; or

(C) Bears the risk of loss under the lease contract or has since the injury assumed that risk as against the lessor and the goods have been converted or destroyed.

(b) If at the time of the injury the party plaintiff did not bear the risk of loss as against the other party to the lease contract and there is no arrangement between them for disposition of the recovery, his or her suit or settlement, subject to his or her own interest, is as a fiduciary for the other party to the lease contract.

(c) Either party with the consent of the other may sue for the benefit of whom it may concern. *(Added by Stats.1988, c. 1359, § 5, operative Jan. 1, 1990. Amended by Stats.1991, c. 111 (S.B.972), § 68, eff. July 15, 1991.)*

§ 10531

California Comment
Report of the Assembly Committee on Judiciary
August 15, 1989

Uniform Statutory Source: Section 2–722.
Changes: Revised to reflect leasing practices and terminology.
Definitional Cross References:
  "Action". Subdivision (1), Section 1201.
  "Goods". Paragraph (h), subdivision (1), Section 10103.
  "Lease contract". Paragraph (l), subdivision (1), Section 10103.
  "Lessee". Paragraph (n), subdivision (1), Section 10103.
  "Lessor". Paragraph (p), subdivision (1), Section 10103.
  "Party". Subdivision (29), Section 1201.
  "Rights". Subdivision (36), Section 1201.
  "Security interest". Subdivision (37), Section 1201.

§ 10532. Recovery by Lessor for Loss of or Damage to Residual Interest

In addition to any other recovery permitted by this division <u>or other law</u>, the lessor * * * <u>may</u> recover from the lessee an amount that will fully compensate the lessor for any loss of or damage to the lessor's residual interest in the goods caused by the default of the lessee. *(Added by Stats.1988, c. 1359, § 5, operative Jan. 1, 1990. Amended by Stats.1991, c. 111 (S.B.972), § 69, eff. July 15, 1991.)*

California Comment
Report of the Assembly Committee on Judiciary
August 15, 1989

Uniform Statutory Source: None.

Purposes: This section, as well as a number of other sections in Division 10, codify the lessor's common-law right to protect the lessor's reversionary interest in the goods. Paragraph (q), subdivision (1), Section 10103. The rights provided by this section are in addition to any other rights and remedies provided by Division 10. This section is intended to supplement and not displace principles of law and equity with respect to the protection of this reversionary interest. Section 1103 and subdivision (4), Section 10103. Such principles apply in many instances, e.g., loss or damages to the goods if the risk of loss passes to the lessee, failure of the lessee to return the goods to the lessor in the condition stipulated in the lease, and refusal of the lessee to return the goods to the lessor after termination or cancellation of the lease.

CHAPTER 6. TRANSITION PROVISIONS

Section
10600. Date of Application; Written Agreement to Modify.

§ 10600. Date of Application; Written Agreement to Modify

This division shall apply to all lease contracts that are first made or that first become effective between the parties on or after January 1, 1990. This division shall not apply to any lease contract first made or that first became effective between the parties prior to January 1, 1990, or to any extension, amendment, modification, renewal, or supplement of or to the lease contract, unless the parties thereto specifically agree in writing that the lease contract, as extended, amended, modified, renewed, or supplemented, shall be governed by this division. *(Added by Stats.1988, c. 1359, § 5, operative Jan. 1, 1990.)*

Division 11

FUNDS TRANSFERS

Chapter	Section
1. Subject Matter and Definitions	11101
2. Issue and Acceptance of Payment Order	11201
3. Execution of Sender's Payment Order by Receiving Bank	11301
4. Payment	11401
5. Miscellaneous Provisions	11501

CHAPTER 1. SUBJECT MATTER AND DEFINITIONS

Section
11101. Short Title.
11102. Subject Matter.
11103. Payment Order—Definitions.
11104. Funds Transfer—Definitions.
11105. Other Definitions.
11106. Time Payment Order is Received.
11107. Federal Reserve Regulations and Operating Circulars.
11108. Exclusion of Consumer Transactions.
11109. Repealed.

Cross References

Payment order governed by this division not included in definition of item, see Commercial Code § 4104.

§ 11101. Short Title

This division may be cited as Uniform Commercial Code—Funds Transfers. *(Added by Stats.1990, c. 125 (S.B.1759), § 2.)*

§ 11102. Subject Matter

Except as otherwise provided in Section 11108, this division applies to funds transfers defined in Section 11104. *(Added by Stats.1990, c. 125 (S.B.1759), § 2.)*

Uniform Commercial Code Comment

Article 4A governs a specialized method of payment referred to in the Article as a funds transfer but also commonly referred to in the commercial community as a wholesale wire transfer. A funds transfer is made by means of one or more payment orders. The scope of Article 4A is determined by the definitions of "payment order" and "funds transfer" found in Section 4A–103 and Section 4A–104.

The funds transfer governed by Article 4A is in large part a product of recent and developing technological changes. Before this Article was drafted there was no comprehensive body of law—statutory or judicial—that defined the juridical nature of a funds transfer or the rights and obligations flowing from payment orders. Judicial authority with respect to funds transfers is sparse, undeveloped and not uniform. Judges have had to resolve disputes by referring to general principles of common law or equity, or they have sought guidance in statutes such as Article 4 which are applicable to other payment methods. But attempts to define rights and obligations in funds transfers by general principles or by analogy to rights and obligations in negotiable instrument law or the law of check collection have not been satisfactory.

In the drafting of Article 4A, a deliberate decision was made to write on a clean slate and to treat a funds transfer as a unique method of payment to be governed by unique rules that address the particular issues raised by this method of payment. A deliberate decision was also made to use precise and detailed rules to assign responsibility, define behavioral norms, allocate risks and establish limits on liability, rather than to rely on broadly stated, flexible principles. In the drafting of these rules, a critical consideration was that the various parties to funds transfers need to be able to predict risk with certainty, to insure against risk, to adjust operational and security procedures, and to price funds transfer services appropriately. This consideration is particularly important given the very large amounts of money that are involved in funds transfers.

Funds transfers involve competing interests—those of the banks that provide funds transfer services and the commercial and financial organizations that use the services, as well as the public interest. These competing interests were represented in the drafting process and they were thoroughly considered. The rules that emerged represent a careful and delicate balancing of those interests and are intended to be the exclusive means of determining the rights, duties and liabilities of the affected parties in any situation covered by particular provisions of the Article. Consequently, resort to principles of law or equity outside of Article 4A is not appropriate to create rights, duties and liabilities inconsistent with those stated in this Article.

§ 11103. Payment Order—Definitions

(a) In this division:

(1) "Payment order" means an instruction of a sender to a receiving bank, transmitted orally, electronically, or in writing, to pay, or to cause another bank to pay, a fixed or determinable amount of money to a beneficiary if all of the following apply:

(i) The instruction does not state a condition to payment to the beneficiary other than time of payment.

(ii) The receiving bank is to be reimbursed by debiting an account of, or otherwise receiving payment from, the sender.

(iii) The instruction is transmitted by the sender directly to the receiving bank or to an agent, funds-transfer system, or communication system for transmittal to the receiving bank.

(2) "Beneficiary" means the person to be paid by the beneficiary's bank.

(3) "Beneficiary's bank" means the bank identified in a payment order in which an account of the beneficiary is to be credited pursuant to the order or which otherwise is to make payment to the beneficiary if the order does not provide for payment to an account.

(4) "Receiving bank" means the bank to which the sender's instruction is addressed.

(5) "Sender" means the person giving the instruction to the receiving bank.

(b) If an instruction complying with paragraph (1) of subdivision (a) is to make more than one payment to a beneficiary, the instruction is a separate payment order with respect to each payment.

(c) A payment order is issued when it is sent to the receiving bank. *(Added by Stats.1990, c. 125 (S.B.1759), § 2.)*

§ 11103

Uniform Commercial Code Comment

This section is discussed in the Comment following Section 4A–104.

§ 11104. Funds Transfer—Definitions

In this division:

(a) "Funds transfer" means the series of transactions, beginning with the originator's payment order, made for the purpose of making payment to the beneficiary of the order. The term includes any payment order issued by the originator's bank or an intermediary bank intended to carry out the originator's payment order. A funds transfer is completed by acceptance by the beneficiary's bank of a payment order for the benefit of the beneficiary of the originator's payment order.

(b) "Intermediary bank" means a receiving bank other than the originator's bank or the beneficiary's bank.

(c) "Originator" means the sender of the first payment order in a funds transfer.

(d) "Originator's bank" means (i) the receiving bank to which the payment order of the originator is issued if the originator is not a bank, or (ii) the originator if the originator is a bank. *(Added by Stats.1990, c. 125 (S.B.1759), § 2.)*

Uniform Commercial Code Comment

1. Article 4A governs a method of payment in which the person making payment (the "originator") directly transmits an instruction to a bank either to make payment to the person receiving payment (the "beneficiary") or to instruct some other bank to make payment to the beneficiary. The payment from the originator to the beneficiary occurs when the bank that is to pay the beneficiary becomes obligated to pay the beneficiary. There are two basic definitions: "Payment order" stated in Section 4A–103 and "Funds transfer" stated in Section 4A–104. These definitions, other related definitions, and the scope of Article 4A can best be understood in the context of specific fact situations. Consider the following cases:

Case #1. X, which has an account in Bank A, instructs that bank to pay $1,000,000 to Y's account in Bank A. Bank A carries out X's instruction by making a credit of $1,000,000 to Y's account and notifying Y that the credit is available for immediate withdrawal. The instruction by X to Bank A is a "payment order" which was issued when it was sent to Bank A. Section 4A–103(a)(1) and (c). X is the "sender" of the payment order and Bank A is the "receiving bank." Section 4A–103(a)(5) and (a)(4). Y is the "beneficiary" of the payment order and Bank A is the "beneficiary's bank." Section 4A–103(a)(2) and (a)(3). When Bank A notified Y of receipt of the payment order, Bank A "accepted" the payment order. Section 4A–209(b)(1). When Bank A accepted the order it incurred an obligation to Y to pay the amount of the order. Section 4A–404(a). When Bank A accepted X's order, X incurred an obligation to pay Bank A the amount of the order. Section 4A–402(b). Payment from X to Bank A would normally be made by a debit to X's account in Bank A. Section 4A–403(a)(3). At the time Bank A incurred the obligation to pay Y, payment of $1,000,000 by X to Y was also made. Section 4A–406(a). Bank A paid Y when it gave notice to Y of a withdrawable credit of $1,000,000 to Y's account. Section 4A–405(a). The overall transaction, which comprises the acts of X and Bank A, in which the payment by X to Y is accomplished is referred to as the "funds transfer." Section 4A–104(a). In this case only one payment order was involved in the funds transfer. A one-payment-order funds transfer is usually referred to as a "book transfer" because the payment is accomplished by the receiving bank's debiting the account of the sender and crediting the account of the beneficiary in the same bank. X, in addition to being the sender of the payment order to Bank A, is the "originator" of the funds transfer. Section 4A–104(c). Bank A is the "originator's bank" in the funds transfer as well as the beneficiary's bank. Section 4A–104(d).

Case #2. Assume the same facts as in Case #1 except that X instructs Bank A to pay $1,000,000 to Y's account in Bank B. With respect to this payment order, X is the sender, Y is the beneficiary, and Bank A is the receiving bank. Bank A carries out X's order by instructing Bank B to pay $1,000,000 to Y's account. This instruction is a payment order in which Bank A is the sender, Bank B is the receiving bank, and Y is the beneficiary. When Bank A issued its payment order to Bank B, Bank A "executed" X's order. Section 4A–301(a). In the funds transfer, X is the originator, Bank A is the originator's bank, and Bank B is the beneficiary's bank. When Bank A executed X's order, X incurred an obligation to pay Bank A the amount of the order. Section 4A–402(c). When Bank B accepts the payment order issued to it by Bank A, Bank B incurs an obligation to Y to pay the amount of the order (Section 4A–404(a)) and Bank A incurs an obligation to pay Bank B. Section 4A–402(b). Acceptance by Bank B also results in payment of $1,000,000 by X to Y. Section 4A–406(a). In this case two payment orders are involved in the funds transfer.

Case #3. Assume the same facts as in Case #2 except that Bank A does not execute X's payment order by issuing a payment order to Bank B. One bank will not normally act to carry out a funds transfer for another bank unless there is a preexisting arrangement between the banks for transmittal of payment orders and settlement of accounts. For example, if Bank B is a foreign bank with which Bank A has no relationship, Bank A can utilize a bank that is a correspondent of both Bank A and Bank B. Assume Bank A issues a payment order to Bank C to pay $1,000,000 to Y's account in Bank B. With respect to this order, Bank A is the sender, Bank C is the receiving bank, and Y is the beneficiary. Bank C will execute the payment order of Bank A by issuing a payment order to Bank B to pay $1,000,000 to Y's account in Bank B. With respect to Bank C's payment order, Bank C is the sender, Bank B is the receiving bank, and Y is the beneficiary. Payment of $1,000,000 by X to Y occurs when Bank B accepts the payment order issued to it by Bank C. In this case the funds transfer involves three payment orders. In the funds transfer, X is the originator, Bank A is the originator's bank, Bank B is the beneficiary's bank, and Bank C is an "intermediary bank." Section 4A–104(b). In some cases there may be more than one intermediary bank, and in those cases each intermediary bank is treated like Bank C in Case #3.

As the three cases demonstrate, a payment under Article 4A involves an overall transaction, the funds transfer, in which the originator, X, is making payment to the beneficiary, Y, but the funds transfer may encompass a series of payment orders that are issued in order to effect the payment initiated by the originator's payment order.

In some cases the originator and the beneficiary may be the same person. This will occur, for example, when a corporation orders a bank to transfer funds from an account of the corporation in that bank to another account of the corporation in that bank or in some other bank. In some funds transfers the first bank to issue a payment order is a bank that is executing a payment order of a customer that is not a bank. In this case the customer is the originator. In other cases, the first bank to issue a payment order is not acting for a customer, but is making a payment for its own account. In that event the first bank to issue a payment order is the originator as well as the originator's bank.

2. "Payment order" is defined in Section 4A–103(a)(1) as an instruction to a bank to pay, or to cause another bank to pay, a fixed or determinable amount of money. The bank to which the instruction is addressed is known as the "receiving bank." Section 4A–103(a)(4). "Bank" is defined in Section 4A–105(a)(2). The effect of this definition is to limit Article 4A to payments made through the banking system. A transfer of funds made by an entity outside the banking system is excluded. A transfer of funds through an entity other than a bank is usually a consumer transaction involving relatively small amounts of money and a single contract carried out by transfers of cash or a cash equivalent such as a check. Typically, the transferor delivers cash or a check to the company making the transfer, which agrees to pay a like amount to a person designated by the transferor. Transactions covered by Article 4A typically involve very large amounts of money in which several transactions involving several banks may be necessary to carry out the payment. Payments are normally made by debits or credits to bank accounts. Originators and beneficiaries are almost always business organizations and the transfers are usually made to pay obligations. Moreover, these transactions are frequently done on the basis of very short-term credit granted by the receiving bank to the sender of the payment order. Wholesale wire transfers involve policy questions that

are distinct from those involved in consumer-based transactions by nonbanks.

3. Further limitations on the scope of Article 4A are found in the three requirements found in subparagraphs (i), (ii), and (iii) of Section 4A-103(a)(1). Subparagraph (i) states that the instruction to pay is a payment order only if it "does not state a condition to payment to the beneficiary other than time of payment." An instruction to pay a beneficiary sometimes is subject to a requirement that the beneficiary perform some act such as delivery of documents. For example, a New York bank may have issued a letter of credit in favor of X, a California seller of goods, to be shipped to the New York bank's customer in New York. The terms of the letter of credit provide for payment to X if documents are presented to prove shipment of the goods. Instead of providing for presentment of the documents to the New York bank, the letter of credit states that they may be presented to a California bank that acts as an agent for payment. The New York bank sends an instruction to the California bank to pay X upon presentation of the required documents. The instruction is not covered by Article 4A because payment to the beneficiary is conditional upon receipt of shipping documents. The function of banks in a funds transfer under Article 4A is comparable to the role of banks in the collection and payment of checks in that it is essentially mechanical in nature. The low price and high speed that characterize funds transfers reflect this fact. Conditions to payment by the California bank other than time of payment impose responsibilities on that bank that go beyond those in Article 4A funds transfers. Although the payment by the New York bank to X under the letter of credit is not covered by Article 4A, if X is paid by the California bank, payment of the obligation of the New York bank to reimburse the California bank could be made by an Article 4A funds transfer. In such a case there is a distinction between the payment by the New York bank to X under the letter of credit and the payment by the New York bank to the California bank. For example, if the New York bank pays its reimbursement obligation to the California bank by a Fedwire naming the California bank as beneficiary (see Comment 1 to Section 4A-107), payment is made to the California bank rather than to X. That payment is governed by Article 4A and it could be made either before or after payment by the California bank to X. The payment by the New York bank to X under the letter of credit is not governed by Article 4A and it occurs when the California bank, as agent of the New York bank, pays X. No payment order was involved in that transaction. In this example, if the New York bank had erroneously sent an instruction to the California bank unconditionally instructing payment to X, the instruction would have been an Article 4A payment order. If the payment order was accepted (Section 4A-209(b)) by the California bank, a payment by the New York bank to X would have resulted (Section 4A-406(a)). But Article 4A would not prevent recovery of funds from X on the basis that X was not entitled to retain the funds under the law of mistake and restitution, letter of credit law or other applicable law.

4. Transfers of funds made through the banking system are commonly referred to as either "credit" transfers or "debit" transfers. In a credit transfer the instruction to pay is given by the person making payment. In a debit transfer the instruction to pay is given by the person receiving payment. The purpose of subparagraph (ii) of subsection (a)(1) of Section 4A-103 is to include credit transfers in Article 4A and to exclude debit transfers. All of the instructions to pay in the three cases described in Comment 1 fall within subparagraph (ii). Take Case #2 as an example. With respect to X's instruction given to Bank A, Bank A will be reimbursed by debiting X's account or otherwise receiving payment from X. With respect to Bank A's instruction to Bank B, Bank B will be reimbursed by receiving payment from Bank A. In a debit transfer, a creditor, pursuant to authority from the debtor, is enabled to draw on the debtor's bank account by issuing an instruction to pay to the debtor's bank. If the debtor's bank pays, it will be reimbursed by the debtor rather than by the person giving the instruction. For example, the holder of an insurance policy may pay premiums by authorizing the insurance company to order the policyholder's bank to pay the insurance company. The order to pay may be in the form of a draft covered by Article 3, or it might be an instruction to pay that is not an instrument under that Article. The bank receives reimbursement by debiting the policyholder's account. Or, a subsidiary corporation may make payments to its parent by authorizing the parent to order the subsidiary's bank to pay the parent from the subsidiary's account. These transactions are not covered by Article 4A because subparagraph (2) is not satisfied. Article 4A is limited to transactions in which the account to be debited by the receiving bank is that of the person in whose name the instruction is given.

If the beneficiary of a funds transfer is the originator of the transfer, the transfer is governed by Article 4A if it is a credit transfer in form. If it is in the form of a debit transfer it is not governed by Article 4A. For example, Corporation has accounts in Bank A and Bank B. Corporation instructs Bank A to pay to Corporation's account in Bank B. The funds transfer is governed by Article 4A. Sometimes, Corporation will authorize Bank B to draw on Corporation's account in Bank A for the purpose of transferring funds into Corporation's account in Bank B. If Corporation also makes an agreement with Bank A under which Bank A is authorized to follow instructions of Bank B, as agent of Corporation, to transfer funds from Customer's account in Bank A, the instruction of Bank B is a payment order of Customer and is governed by Article 4A. This kind of transaction is known in the wire-transfer business as a "drawdown transfer." If Corporation does not make such an agreement with Bank A and Bank B instructs Bank A to make the transfer, the order is in form a debit transfer and is not governed by Article 4A. These debit transfers are normally ACH transactions in which Bank A relies on Bank B's warranties pursuant to ACH rules, including the warranty that the transfer is authorized.

5. The principal effect of subparagraph (iii) of subsection (a) of Section 4A-103 is to exclude from Article 4A payments made by check or credit card. In those cases the instruction of the debtor to the bank on which the check is drawn or to which the credit card slip is to be presented is contained in the check or credit card slip signed by the debtor. The instruction is not transmitted by the debtor directly to the debtor's bank. Rather, the instruction is delivered or otherwise transmitted by the debtor to the creditor who then presents it to the bank either directly or through bank collection channels. These payments are governed by Articles 3 and 4 and federal law. There are, however, limited instances in which the paper on which a check is printed can be used as the means of transmitting a payment order that is covered by Article 4A. Assume that Originator instructs Originator's Bank to pay $10,000 to the account of Beneficiary in Beneficiary's Bank. Since the amount of Originator's payment order is small, if Originator's Bank and Beneficiary's Bank do not have an account relationship, Originator's Bank may execute Originator's order by issuing a teller's check payable to Beneficiary's Bank for $10,000 along with instructions to credit Beneficiary's account in that amount. The instruction to Beneficiary's Bank to credit Beneficiary's account is a payment order. The check is the means by which Originator's Bank pays its obligation as sender of the payment order. The instruction of Originator's Bank to Beneficiary's Bank might be given in a letter accompanying the check or it may be written on the check itself. In either case the instruction to Beneficiary's Bank is a payment order but the check itself (which is an order to pay addressed to the drawee rather than to Beneficiary's Bank) is an instrument under Article 3 and is not a payment order. The check can be both the means by which Originator's Bank pays its obligation under § 4A-402(b) to Beneficiary's Bank and the means by which the instruction to Beneficiary's Bank is transmitted.

6. Most payments covered by Article 4A are commonly referred to as wire transfers and usually involve some kind of electronic transmission, but the applicability of Article 4A does not depend upon the means used to transmit the instruction of the sender. Transmission may be by letter or other written communication, oral communication or electronic communication. An oral communication is normally given by telephone. Frequently the message is recorded by the receiving bank to provide evidence of the transaction, but apart from problems of proof there is no need to record the oral instruction. Transmission of an instruction may be a direct communication between the sender and the receiving bank or through an intermediary such as an agent of the sender, a communication system such as international cable, or a funds transfer system such as CHIPS, SWIFT or an automated clearing house.

§ 11105. Other Definitions

(a) In this division:

(1) "Authorized account" means a deposit account of a customer in a bank designated by the customer as a source of payment of payment orders issued by the customer to the bank. If a customer does not so designate an account, any account of the customer is an authorized account if payment of a payment order from

§ 11105

that account is not inconsistent with a restriction on the use of that account.

(2) "Bank" means a person engaged in the business of banking and includes a savings bank, savings and loan association, credit union, and trust company. A branch or separate office of a bank is a separate bank for purposes of this division.

(3) "Customer" means a person, including a bank, having an account with a bank or from whom a bank has agreed to receive payment orders.

(4) "Funds-transfer business day" of a receiving bank means the part of a day during which the receiving bank is open for the receipt, processing, and transmittal of payment orders and cancellations and amendments of payment orders.

(5) "Funds-transfer system" means a wire transfer network, automated clearinghouse, or other communication system of a clearinghouse or other association of banks through which a payment order by a bank may be transmitted to the bank to which the order is addressed.

(6) "Good faith" means honesty in fact and the observance of reasonable commercial standards of fair dealing.

(7) "Prove" with respect to a fact means to meet the burden of establishing the fact under subdivision (8) of Section 1201.

(b) Other definitions applying to this division and the sections in which they appear are:

Acceptance: Section 11209.

Beneficiary: Section 11103.

Beneficiary's bank: Section 11103.

Executed: Section 11301.

Execution date: Section 11301.

Funds transfer: Section 11104.

Funds-transfer system rule: Section 11501.

Intermediary bank: Section 11104.

Originator: Section 11104.

Originator's bank: Section 11104.

Payment by beneficiary's bank to beneficiary: Section 11405.

Payment by originator to beneficiary: Section 11406.

Payment by sender to receiving bank: Section 11403.

Payment date: Section 11401.

Payment order: Section 11103.

Receiving bank: Section 11103.

Security procedure: Section 11201.

Sender: Section 11103.

(c) The following definitions in Division 4 (commencing with Section 4101) apply to this division:

Clearinghouse: Section 4104.

Item: Section 4104.

Suspends payments: Section 4104.

(d) In addition Division 1 (commencing with Section 1101) contains general definitions and principles of construction and interpretation applicable throughout this division. *(Added by Stats.1990, c. 125 (S.B.1759), § 2.)*

Uniform Commercial Code Comment

1. The definition of "bank" in subsection (a)(2) includes some institutions that are not commercial banks. The definition reflects the fact that many financial institutions now perform functions previously restricted to commercial banks, including acting on behalf of customers in funds transfers. Since many funds transfers involve payment orders to or from foreign countries the definition also covers foreign banks. The definition also includes Federal Reserve Banks. Funds transfers carried out by Federal Reserve Banks are described in Comments 1 and 2 to Section 4A–107.

2. Funds transfer business is frequently transacted by banks outside of general banking hours. Thus, the definition of banking day in Section 4–104(1)(c) cannot be used to describe when a bank is open for funds transfer business. Subsection (a)(4) defines a new term, "funds transfer business day," which is applicable to Article 4A. The definition states, "is open for the receipt, processing, and transmittal of payment orders and cancellations and amendments of payment orders." In some cases it is possible to electronically transmit payment orders and other communications to a receiving bank at any time. If the receiving bank is not open for the processing of an order when it is received, the communication is stored in the receiving bank's computer for retrieval when the receiving bank is open for processing. The use of the conjunctive makes clear that the defined term is limited to the period during which all functions of the receiving bank can be performed, i.e., receipt, processing, and transmittal of payment orders, cancellations and amendments.

3. Subsection (a)(5) defines "funds transfer system." The term includes a system such as CHIPS which provides for transmission of a payment order as well as settlement of the obligation of the sender to pay the order. It also includes automated clearing houses, operated by a clearing house or other association of banks, which process and transmit payment orders of banks to other banks. In addition the term includes organizations that provide only transmission services such as SWIFT. The definition also includes the wire transfer network and automated clearing houses of Federal Reserve Banks. Systems of the Federal Reserve Banks, however, are treated differently from systems of other associations of banks. Funds transfer systems other than systems of the Federal Reserve Banks are treated in Article 4A as a means of communication of payment orders between participating banks. Section 4A–206. The Comment to that section and the Comment to Section 4A–107 explain how Federal Reserve Banks function under Article 4A. Funds transfer systems are also able to promulgate rules binding on participating banks that, under Section 4A–501, may supplement or in some cases may even override provisions of Article 4A.

4. Subsection (d) incorporates definitions stated in Article 1 as well as principles of construction and interpretation stated in that Article. Included is Section 1–103. The last paragraph of the Comment to Section 4A–102 is addressed to the issue of the extent to which general principles of law and equity should apply to situations covered by provisions of Article 4A.

§ 11106. Time Payment Order is Received

(a) The time of receipt of a payment order or communication canceling or amending a payment order is determined by the rules applicable to receipt of a notice stated in subdivision (27) of Section 1201. A receiving bank may fix a cutoff time or times on a funds-transfer business day for the receipt and processing of payment orders and communications canceling or amending payment orders. Different cutoff times may apply to payment orders, cancellations, or amendments, or to different categories of payment orders, cancellations, or amendments. A cutoff time may apply to senders generally or different cutoff times may apply to different senders or categories of payment orders. If a payment order or communication canceling or amending a payment order is received after the close of a funds-transfer business day or after the appropriate cutoff time on a funds-transfer business day, the receiving bank may treat the payment order or communication as received at the opening of the next funds-transfer business day.

(b) If this division refers to an execution date or payment date or states a day on which a receiving bank is required to take action, and the date or day does not fall on a funds-transfer business day, the next day that is a funds-transfer business day is treated as the date or day stated, unless the contrary is stated in this division. *(Added by Stats.1990, c. 125 (S.B.1759), § 2.)*

Uniform Commercial Code Comment

The time that a payment order is received by a receiving bank usually defines the payment date or the execution date of a payment order. Section 4A–401 and Section 4A–301. The time of receipt of a payment order, or communication cancelling or amending a payment order is defined in subsection (a) by reference to the rules stated in Section 1–201(27). Thus, time of receipt is determined by the same rules that determine when a notice is received. Time of receipt, however, may be altered by a cut-off time.

§ 11107. Federal Reserve Regulations and Operating Circulars

Regulations of the Board of Governors of the Federal Reserve System and operating circulars of the Federal Reserve Banks supersede any inconsistent provision of this division to the extent of the inconsistency. *(Added by Stats.1990, c. 125 (S.B.1759), § 2.)*

Uniform Commercial Code Comment

1. Funds transfers under Article 4A may be made, in whole or in part, by payment orders through a Federal Reserve Bank in what is usually referred to as a transfer by Fedwire. If Bank A, which has an account in Federal Reserve Bank X, wants to pay $1,000,000 to Bank B, which has an account in Federal Reserve Bank Y, Bank A can issue an instruction to Reserve Bank X requesting a debit of $1,000,000 to Bank A's Reserve account and an equal credit to Bank B's Reserve account. Reserve Bank X will debit Bank A's account and will credit the account of Reserve Bank Y. Reserve Bank X will issue an instruction to Reserve Bank Y requesting a debit of $1,000,000 to the account of Reserve Bank X and an equal credit to Bank B's account in Reserve Bank Y. Reserve Bank Y will make the requested debit and credit and will give Bank B an advice of credit. The definition of "bank" in Section 4A–105(a)(2) includes both Reserve Bank X and Reserve Bank Y. Bank A's instruction to Reserve Bank X to pay money to Bank B is a payment order under Section 4A–103(a)(1). Bank A is the sender and Reserve Bank X is the receiving bank. Bank B is the beneficiary of Bank A's order and of the funds transfer. Bank A is the originator of the funds transfer and is also the originator's bank. Section 4A–104(c) and (d). Reserve Bank X, an intermediary bank under Section 4A–104(b), executes Bank A's order by sending a payment order to Reserve Bank Y instructing that bank to credit the Federal Reserve account of Bank B. Reserve Bank Y is the beneficiary's bank.

Suppose the transfer of funds from Bank A to Bank B is part of a larger transaction in which Originator, a customer of Bank A, wants to pay Beneficiary, a customer of Bank B. Originator issues a payment order to Bank A to pay $1,000,000 to the account of Beneficiary in Bank B. Bank A may execute Originator's order by means of Fedwire which simultaneously transfers $1,000,000 from Bank A to Bank B and carries a message instructing Bank B to pay $1,000,000 to the account of Y. The Fedwire transfer is carried out as described in the previous paragraph, except that the beneficiary of the funds transfer is Beneficiary rather than Bank B. Reserve Bank X and Reserve Bank Y are intermediary banks. When Reserve Bank Y advises Bank B of the credit to its Federal Reserve account it will also instruct Bank B to pay to the account of Beneficiary. The instruction is a payment order to Bank B which is the beneficiary's bank. When Reserve Bank Y advises Bank B of the credit to its Federal Reserve account Bank B receives payment of the payment order issued to it by Reserve Bank Y. Section 4A–403(a)(1). The payment order is automatically accepted by Bank B at the time it receives the payment order of Reserve Bank Y. Section 4A–209(b)(2). At the time of acceptance by Bank B payment by Originator to Beneficiary also occurs. Thus, in a Fedwire transfer, payment to the beneficiary's bank, acceptance by the beneficiary's bank and payment by the originator to the beneficiary all occur simultaneously by operation of law at the time the payment order to the beneficiary's bank is received.

If Originator orders payment to the account of Beneficiary in Bank C rather than Bank B, the analysis is somewhat modified. Bank A may not have any relationship with Bank C and may not be able to make payment directly to Bank C. In that case, Bank A could send a Fedwire instructing Bank B to instruct Bank C to pay Beneficiary. The analysis is the same as the previous case except that Bank B is an intermediary bank and Bank C is the beneficiary's bank.

2. A funds transfer can also be made through a Federal Reserve Bank in an automated clearing house transaction. In a typical case, Originator instructs Originator's Bank to pay to the account of Beneficiary in Beneficiary's Bank. Originator's instruction to pay a particular beneficiary is transmitted to Originator's Bank along with many other instructions for payment to other beneficiaries by many different beneficiary's banks. All of these instructions are contained in a magnetic tape or other electronic device. Transmission of instructions to the various beneficiary's banks requires that Originator's instructions be processed and repackaged with instructions of other originators so that all instructions to a particular beneficiary's bank are transmitted together to that bank. The repackaging is done in processing centers usually referred to as automated clearing houses. Automated clearing houses are operated either by Federal Reserve Banks or by other associations of banks. If Originator's Bank chooses to execute Originator's instructions by transmitting them to a Federal Reserve Bank for processing by the Federal Reserve Bank, the transmission to the Federal Reserve Bank results in the issuance of payment orders by Originator's Bank to the Federal Reserve Bank, which is an intermediary bank. Processing by the Federal Reserve Bank will result in the issuance of payment orders by the Federal Reserve Bank to Beneficiary's Bank as well as payment orders to other beneficiary's banks making payments to carry out Originator's instructions.

3. Although the terms of Article 4A apply to funds transfers involving Federal Reserve Banks, federal preemption would make ineffective any Article 4A provision that conflicts with federal law. The payments activities of the Federal Reserve Banks are governed by regulations of the Federal Reserve Board and by operating circulars issued by the Reserve Banks themselves. In some instances, the operating circulars are issued pursuant to a Federal Reserve Board regulation. In other cases, the Reserve Bank issues the operating circular under its own authority under the Federal Reserve Act, subject to review by the Federal Reserve Board. Section 4A–107 states that Federal Reserve Board regulations and operating circulars of the Federal Reserve Banks supersede any inconsistent provision of Article 4A to the extent of the inconsistency. Federal Reserve Board regulations, being valid exercises of regulatory authority pursuant to a federal statute, take precedence over state law if there is an inconsistency. Childs v. Federal Reserve Bank of Dallas, 719 F.2d 812 (5th Cir.1983), reh. den. 724 F.2d 127 (5th Cir.1984). Section 4A–107 treats operating circulars as having the same effect whether issued under the Reserve Bank's own authority or under a Federal Reserve Board regulation.

§ 11108. Exclusion of Consumer Transactions

This division does not apply to a funds transfer any part of which is governed by the Electronic Fund Transfer Act of 1978 (Title XX, Public Law 95-630, 92 Stat. 3728, 15 U.S.C. Sec. 1693 et seq.) as amended from time to time. *(Added by Stats.1990, c. 125 (S.B.1759), § 2.)*

Uniform Commercial Code Comment

The Electronic Fund Transfer Act of 1978 is a federal statute that covers a wide variety of electronic funds transfers involving consumers. The types of transfers covered by the federal statute are essentially different from the wholesale wire transfers that are the primary focus of Article 4A. Section 4A–108 excludes a funds transfer from Article 4A if any part of the transfer is covered by the federal law. Existing procedures designed to comply with federal law will not be affected by Article 4A. The effect of Section 4A–108 is to make Article 4A and EFTA mutually exclusive. For example, if a funds transfer is to a consumer account in the beneficiary's bank and the funds transfer is made in part by use of Fedwire and in part by means of an automated clearing house, EFTA applies to the ACH part of the transfer but not to the Fedwire part. Under Section 4A–108, Article 4A does not apply to any part of the transfer. However, in the absence of any law to govern the part of the funds transfer that is not subject to EFTA, a court might apply appropriate principles from Article 4A by analogy.

§ 11109. Repealed by Stats.1988, c. 1359, § 6, operative Jan. 1, 1990

CHAPTER 2. ISSUE AND ACCEPTANCE OF PAYMENT ORDER

Section
11201. Security Procedure.
11202. Authorized and Verified Payment Orders.
11203. Unenforceability of Certain Verified Payment Orders.
11204. Refund of Payment and Duty of Customer to Report With Respect to Unauthorized Payment Order.
11205. Erroneous Payment Orders.
11206. Transmission of Payment Order Through Funds–Transfer or Other Communication System.
11207. Misdescription of Beneficiary.
11208. Misdescription of Intermediary Bank or Beneficiary's Bank.
11209. Acceptance of Payment Order.
11210. Rejection of Payment Order.
11211. Cancellation and Amendment of Payment Order.
11212. Liability and Duty of Receiving Bank Regarding Unaccepted Payment Order.

§ 11201. Security Procedure

"Security procedure" means a procedure established by agreement of a customer and a receiving bank for the purpose of (i) verifying that a payment order or communication amending or canceling a payment order is that of the customer, or (ii) detecting error in the transmission or the content of the payment order or communication. A security procedure may require the use of algorithms or other codes, identifying words or numbers, encryption, callback procedures, or similar security devices. Comparison of a signature on a payment order or communication with an authorized specimen signature of the customer is not by itself a security procedure. *(Added by Stats.1990, c. 125 (S.B. 1759), § 2.)*

§ 11202. Authorized and Verified Payment Orders

(a) A payment order received by the receiving bank is the authorized order of the person identified as sender if that person authorized the order or is otherwise bound by it under the law of agency.

(b) If a bank and its customer have agreed that the authenticity of payment orders issued to the bank in the name of the customer as sender will be verified pursuant to a security procedure, a payment order received by the receiving bank is effective as the order of the customer, whether or not authorized, if (i) the security procedure is a commercially reasonable method of providing security against unauthorized payment orders, and (ii) the bank proves that it accepted the payment order in good faith and in compliance with the security procedure and any written agreement or instruction of the customer restricting acceptance of payment orders issued in the name of the customer. The bank is not required to follow an instruction that violates a written agreement with the customer or notice of which is not received at a time and in a manner affording the bank a reasonable opportunity to act on it before the payment order is accepted.

(c) Commercial reasonableness of a security procedure is a question of law to be determined by considering the wishes of the customer expressed to the bank, the circumstances of the customer known to the bank, including the size, type, and frequency of payment orders normally issued by the customer to the bank, alternative security procedures offered to the customer, and security procedures in general use by customers and receiving banks similarly situated. A security procedure is deemed to be commercially reasonable if (i) the security procedure was chosen by the customer after the bank offered, and the customer refused, a security procedure that was commercially reasonable for that customer, and (ii) the customer expressly agreed in writing to be bound by any payment order, whether or not authorized, issued in its name and accepted by the bank in compliance with the security procedure chosen by the customer.

(d) The term "sender" in this division includes the customer in whose name a payment order is issued if the order is the authorized order of the customer under subdivision (a), or it is effective as the order of the customer under subdivision (b).

(e) This section applies to amendments and cancellations of payment orders to the same extent it applies to payment orders.

(f) Except as provided in this section and in paragraph (1) of subdivision (a) of Section 11203, rights and obligations arising under this section or Section 11203 may not be varied by agreement. *(Added by Stats.1990, c. 125 (S.B.1759), § 2.)*

Uniform Commercial Code Comment

This section is discussed in the Comment following Section 4A–203 [11203].

§ 11203. Unenforceability of Certain Verified Payment Orders

(a) If an accepted payment order is not, under subdivision (a) of Section 11202, an authorized order of a customer identified as sender, but is effective as an order of the customer pursuant to subdivision (b) of Section 11202, the following rules apply:

(1) By express written agreement, the receiving bank may limit the extent to which it is entitled to enforce or retain payment of the payment order.

(2) The receiving bank is not entitled to enforce or retain payment of the payment order if the customer proves that the order was not caused, directly or indirectly, by a person (i) entrusted at any time with duties to act for the customer with respect to payment orders or the security procedure, or (ii) who obtained access to transmitting facilities of the customer or who obtained, from a source controlled by the customer and without authority of the receiving bank, information facilitating breach of the security procedure, regardless of how the information was obtained or whether the customer was at fault. Information includes any access device, computer software, or the like.

(b) This section applies to amendments of payment orders to the same extent it applies to payment orders. *(Added by Stats.1990, c. 125 (S.B.1759), § 2.)*

Uniform Commercial Code Comment

1. Some person will always be identified as the sender of a payment order. Acceptance of the order by the receiving bank is based on a belief by the bank that the order was authorized by the person identified as the sender. If the receiving bank is the beneficiary's bank, acceptance means that the receiving bank is obliged to pay the beneficiary. If the receiving bank is not the beneficiary's bank, acceptance means that the receiving bank has executed the sender's order and is obliged to pay the bank that accepted the order issued in execution of the sender's order. In either case the receiving bank may suffer a loss unless it is entitled to enforce payment of the payment order that it accepted. If the person identified as the sender of the order refuses to pay on the ground that the order was not authorized by that person, what are the rights of the receiving bank? In the absence of a statute or agreement that specifically addresses the issue, the question usually will be resolved by the law of agency. In some cases, the law of agency works well. For example, suppose the receiving bank executes a payment order given by means of a letter apparently written by a corporation that is a customer of the bank and apparently signed by an officer of the corporation. If the receiving bank acts solely on the basis of the letter, the corporation is not bound as the sender of the payment order unless the signature was that of the officer and the officer was authorized to act for the corporation in the issuance of payment orders, or some other agency doctrine such as apparent authority or estoppel causes the corporation to be bound. Estoppel can be illustrated by the following example. Suppose P is aware that A, who is unauthorized to act for P, has fraudulently misrepresented to T that A is authorized to act for P. T believes A and is about to rely on the misrepresentation. If P does not notify T of the true facts although P could easily do so, P may be estopped from denying A's lack of authority. A similar result could follow if the failure to notify T is the result of negligence rather than a deliberate decision. Restatement, Second, Agency § 8B. Other equitable principles such as subrogation or restitution might also allow a receiving bank to recover with respect to an unauthorized payment order that it accepted. In Gatoil (U.S.A.), Inc. v. Forest Hill State Bank, 1 U.C.C.Rep.Serv.2d 171 (D.Md.1986), a joint venturer not authorized to order payments from the account of the joint venture, ordered a funds transfer from the account. The transfer paid a bona fide debt of the joint venture. Although the transfer was unauthorized the court refused to require recredit of the account because the joint venture suffered no loss. The result can be rationalized on the basis of subrogation of the receiving bank to the right of the beneficiary of the funds transfer to receive the payment from the joint venture.

But in most cases these legal principles give the receiving bank very little protection in the case of an authorized payment order. Cases like those just discussed are not typical of the way that most payment orders are transmitted and accepted, and such cases are likely to become even less common. Given the large amount of the typical payment order, a prudent receiving bank will be unwilling to accept a payment order unless it has assurance that the order is what it purports to be. This assurance is normally provided by security procedures described in Section 4A–201.

In a very large percentage of cases covered by Article 4A, transmission of the payment order is made electronically. The receiving bank may be required to act on the basis of a message that appears on a computer screen. Common law concepts of authority of agent to bind principal are not helpful. There is no way of determining the identity or the authority of the person who caused the message to be sent. The receiving bank is not relying on the authority of any particular person to act for the purported sender. The case is not comparable to payment of a check by the drawee bank on the basis of a signature that is forged. Rather, the receiving bank relies on a security procedure pursuant to which the authenticity of the message can be "tested" by various devices which are designed to provide certainty that the message is that of the sender identified in the payment order. In the wire transfer business the concept of "authorized" is different from that found in agency law. In that business a payment order is treated as the order of the person in whose name it is issued if it is properly tested pursuant to a security procedure and the order passes the test.

Section 4A–202 reflects the reality of the wire transfer business. A person in whose name a payment order is issued is considered to be the sender of the order if the order is "authorized" as stated in subsection (a) or if the order is "verified" pursuant to a security procedure in compliance with subsection (b). If subsection (b) does not apply, the question of whether the customer is responsible for the order is determined by the law of agency. The issue is one of actual or apparent authority of the person who caused the order to be issued in the name of the customer. In some cases the law of agency might allow the customer to be bound by an unauthorized order if conduct of the customer can be used to find an estoppel against the customer to deny that the order was unauthorized. If the customer is bound by the order under any of these agency doctrines, subsection (a) treats the order as authorized and thus the customer is deemed to be the sender of the order. In most cases, however, subsection (b) will apply. In that event there is no need to make an agency law analysis to determine authority. Under Section 4A–202, the issue of liability of the purported sender of the payment order will be determined by agency law only if the receiving bank did not comply with subsection (b).

2. The scope of Section 4A–202 can be illustrated by the following cases. *Case #1.* A payment order purporting to be that of Customer is received by Receiving Bank but the order was fraudulently transmitted by a person who had no authority to act for Customer. *Case #2.* An authentic payment order was sent by Customer, but before the order was received by Receiving Bank the order was fraudulently altered by an unauthorized person to change the beneficiary. *Case #3.* An authentic payment order was received by Receiving Bank, but before the order was executed by Receiving Bank a person who had no authority to act for Customer fraudulently sent a communication purporting to amend the order by changing the beneficiary. In each case Receiving Bank acted on the fraudulent communication by accepting the payment order. These cases are all essentially similar and they are treated identically by Section 4A–202. In each case Receiving Bank acted on a communication that it thought was authorized by Customer when in fact the communication was fraudulent. No distinction is made between Case #1 in which Customer took no part at all in the transaction and Case #2 and Case #3 in which an authentic order was fraudulently altered or amended by an unauthorized person. If subsection (b) does not apply, each case is governed by subsection (a). If there are no additional facts on which an estoppel might be found, Customer is not responsible in Case #1 for the fraudulently issued payment order, in Case #2 for the fraudulent alteration or in Case #3 for the fraudulent amendment. Thus, in each case Customer is not liable to pay the order and Receiving Bank takes the loss. The only remedy of Receiving Bank is to seek recovery from the person who received payment as beneficiary of the fraudulent order. If there was verification in compliance with subsection (b), Customer will take the loss unless Section 4A–203 applies.

3. Subsection (b) of Section 4A–202 is based on the assumption that losses due to fraudulent payment orders can best be avoided by the use of commercially reasonable security procedures, and that the use of such procedures should be encouraged. The subsection is designed to protect both the customer and the receiving bank. A receiving bank

needs to be able to rely on objective criteria to determine whether it can safely act on a payment order. Employees of the bank can be trained to "test" a payment order according to the various steps specified in the security procedure. The bank is responsible for the acts of these employees. Subsection (b)(ii) requires the bank to prove that it accepted the payment order in good faith and "in compliance with the security procedure." If the fraud was not detected because the bank's employee did not perform the acts required by the security procedure, the bank has not complied. Subsection (b)(ii) also requires the bank to prove that it complied with any agreement or instruction that restricts acceptance of payment orders issued in the name of the customer. A customer may want to protect itself by imposing limitations on acceptance of payment orders by the bank. For example, the customer may prohibit the bank from accepting a payment order that is not payable from an authorized account, that exceeds the credit balance in specified accounts of the customer, or that exceeds some other amount. Another limitation may relate to the beneficiary. The customer may provide the bank with a list of authorized beneficiaries and prohibit acceptance of any payment order to a beneficiary not appearing on the list. Such limitations may be incorporated into the security procedure itself or they may be covered by a separate agreement or instruction. In either case, the bank must comply with the limitations if the conditions stated in subsection (b) are met. Normally limitations on acceptance would be incorporated into an agreement between the customer and the receiving bank, but in some cases the instruction might be unilaterally given by the customer. If standing instructions or an agreement state limitations on the ability of the receiving bank to act, provision must be made for later modification of the limitations. Normally this would be done by an agreement that specifies particular procedures to be followed. Thus, subsection (b) states that the receiving bank is not required to follow an instruction that violates a written agreement. The receiving bank is not bound by an instruction unless it has adequate notice of it. Subsections (25), (26) and (27) of Section 1–201 apply.

Subsection (b)(i) assures that the interests of the customer will be protected by providing an incentive to a bank to make available to the customer a security procedure that is commercially reasonable. If a commercially reasonable security procedure is not made available to the customer, subsection (b) does not apply. The result is that subsection (a) applies and the bank acts at its peril in accepting a payment order that may be unauthorized. Prudent banking practice may require that security procedures be utilized in virtually all cases except for those in which personal contact between the customer and the bank eliminates the possibility of an unauthorized order. The burden of making available commercially reasonable security procedures is imposed on receiving banks because they generally determine what security procedures can be used and are in the best position to evaluate the efficacy of procedures offered to customers to combat fraud. The burden on the customer is to supervise its employees to assure compliance with the security procedure and to safeguard confidential security information and access to transmitting facilities so that the security procedure cannot be breached.

4. The principal issue that is likely to arise in litigation involving subsection (b) is whether the security procedure in effect when a fraudulent payment order was accepted was commercially reasonable. The concept of what is commercially reasonable in a given case is flexible. Verification entails labor and equipment costs that can vary greatly depending upon the degree of security that is sought. A customer that transmits very large numbers of payment orders in very large amounts may desire and may reasonably expect to be provided with state-of-the-art procedures that provide maximum security. But the expense involved may make use of a state-of-the-art procedure infeasible for a customer that normally transmits payment orders infrequently or in relatively low amounts. Another variable is the type of receiving bank. It is reasonable to require large money center banks to make available state-of-the-art security procedures. On the other hand, the same requirement may not be reasonable for a small country bank. A receiving bank might have several security procedures that are designed to meet the varying needs of different customers. The type of payment order is another variable. For example, in a wholesale wire transfer, each payment order is normally transmitted electronically and individually. A testing procedure will be individually applied to each payment order. In funds transfers to be made by means of an automated clearing house many payment orders are incorporated into an electronic device such as a magnetic tape that is physically delivered. Testing of the individual payment orders is not feasible. Thus, a different kind of security procedure must be adopted to take into account the different mode of transmission.

The issue of whether a particular security procedure is commercially reasonable is a question of law. Whether the receiving bank complied with the procedure is a question of fact. It is appropriate to make the finding concerning commercial reasonability a matter of law because security procedures are likely to be standardized in the banking industry and a question of law standard leads to more predictability concerning the level of security that a bank must offer to its customers. The purpose of subsection (b) is to encourage banks to institute reasonable safeguards against fraud but not to make them insurers against fraud. A security procedure is not commercially unreasonable simply because another procedure might have been better or because the judge deciding the question would have opted for a more stringent procedure. The standard is not whether the security procedure is the best available. Rather it is whether the procedure is reasonable for the particular customer and the particular bank, which is a lower standard. On the other hand, a security procedure that fails to meet prevailing standards of good banking practice applicable to the particular bank should not be held to be commercially reasonable. Subsection (c) states factors to be considered by the judge in making the determination of commercial reasonableness. Sometimes an informed customer refuses a security procedure that is commercially reasonable and suitable for that customer and insists on using a higher-risk procedure because it is more convenient or cheaper. In that case, under the last sentence of subsection (c), the customer has voluntarily assumed the risk of failure of the procedure and cannot shift the loss to the bank. But this result follows only if the customer expressly agrees in writing to assume that risk. It is implicit in the last sentence of subsection (c) that a bank that accedes to the wishes of its customer in this regard is not acting in bad faith by so doing so long as the customer is made aware of the risk. In all cases, however, a receiving bank cannot get the benefit of subsection (b) unless it has made available to the customer a security procedure that is commercially reasonable and suitable for use by that customer. In most cases, the mutual interest of bank and customer to protect against fraud should lead to agreement to a security procedure which is commercially reasonable.

5. The effect of Section 4A–202(b) is to place the risk of loss on the customer if an unauthorized payment order is accepted by the receiving bank after verification by the bank in compliance with a commercially reasonable security procedure. An exception to this result is provided by Section 4A–203(a)(2). The customer may avoid the loss resulting from such a payment order if the customer can prove that the fraud was not committed by a person described in that subsection. Breach of a commercially reasonable security procedure requires that the person committing the fraud have knowledge of how the procedure works and knowledge of codes, identifying devices, and the like. That person may also need access to transmitting facilities through an access device or other software in order to breach the security procedure. This confidential information must be obtained either from a source controlled by the customer or from a source controlled by the receiving bank. If the customer can prove that the person committing the fraud did not obtain the confidential information from an agent or former agent of the customer or from a source controlled by the customer, the loss is shifted to the bank. "Prove" is defined in Section 4A–105(a)(7). Because of bank regulation requirements, in this kind of case there will always be a criminal investigation as well as an internal investigation of the bank to determine the probable explanation for the breach of security. Because a funds transfer fraud usually will involve a very large amount of money, both the criminal investigation and the internal investigation are likely to be thorough. In some cases there may be an investigation by bank examiners as well. Frequently, these investigations will develop evidence of who is at fault and the cause of the loss. The customer will have access to evidence developed in these investigations and that evidence can be used by the customer in meeting its burden of proof.

6. The effect of Section 4A–202(b) may also be changed by an agreement meeting the requirements of Section 4A–203(a)(1). Some customers may be unwilling to take all or part of the risk of loss with respect to unauthorized payment orders even if all of the requirements of Section 4A–202(b) are met. By virtue of Section 4A–203(a)(1), a receiving bank may assume all of the risk of loss with respect to unauthorized payment orders or the customer and bank may agree that losses from unauthorized payment orders are to be divided as provided in the agreement.

7. In a large majority of cases the sender of a payment order is a bank. In many cases in which there is a bank sender, both the sender and the receiving bank will be members of a funds transfer system over which the payment order is transmitted. Since Section 4A–202(f) does not prohibit a funds transfer system rule from varying rights and obligations under Section 4A–202, a rule of the funds transfer system can determine how loss due to an unauthorized payment order from a participating bank to another participating bank is to be allocated. A funds transfer system rule, however, cannot change the rights of a customer that is not a participating bank. § 4A–501(b). Section 4A–202(f) also prevents variation by agreement except to the extent stated.

§ 11204. Refund of Payment and Duty of Customer to Report With Respect to Unauthorized Payment Order

(a) If a receiving bank accepts a payment order issued in the name of its customer as sender which is (i) not authorized and not effective as the order of the customer under Section 11202, or (ii) not enforceable, in whole or in part, against the customer under Section 11203, the bank shall refund any payment of the payment order received from the customer to the extent the bank is not entitled to enforce payment and shall pay interest on the refundable amount calculated from the date the bank received payment to the date of the refund. However, the customer is not entitled to interest from the bank on the amount to be refunded if the customer fails to exercise ordinary care to determine that the order was not authorized by the customer and to notify the bank of the relevant facts within a reasonable time not exceeding 90 days after the date the customer received notification from the bank that the order was accepted or that the customer's account was debited with respect to the order. The bank is not entitled to any recovery from the customer on account of a failure by the customer to give notification as stated in this section.

(b) Reasonable time under subdivision (a) may be fixed by agreement as stated in subdivision (1) of Section 1204, but the obligation of a receiving bank to refund payment as stated in subdivision (a) may not otherwise be varied by agreement. *(Added by Stats. 1990, c. 125 (S.B.1759), § 2.)*

Uniform Commercial Code Comment

1. With respect to unauthorized payment orders, in a very large percentage of cases a commercially reasonable security procedure will be in effect. Section 4A–204 applies only to cases in which (i) no commercially reasonable security procedure is in effect, (ii) the bank did not comply with a commercially reasonable security procedure that was in effect, (iii) the sender can prove, pursuant to Section 4A–203(a)(2), that the culprit did not obtain confidential security information controlled by the customer, or (iv) the bank, pursuant to Section 4A–203(a)(1) agreed to take all or part of the loss resulting from an unauthorized payment order. In each of these cases the bank takes the risk of loss with respect to an unauthorized payment order because the bank is not entitled to payment from the customer with respect to the order. The bank normally debits the customer's account or otherwise receives payment from the customer shortly after acceptance of the payment order. Subsection (a) of Section 4A–204 states that the bank must recredit the account or refund payment to the extent the bank is not entitled to enforce payment.

2. Section 4A–204 is designed to encourage a customer to promptly notify the receiving bank that it has accepted an unauthorized payment order. Since cases of unauthorized payment orders will almost always involve fraud, the bank's remedy is normally to recover from the beneficiary of the unauthorized order if the beneficiary was party to the fraud. This remedy may not be worth very much and it may not make any difference whether or not the bank promptly learns about the fraud. But in some cases prompt notification may make it easier for the bank to recover some part of its loss from the culprit. The customer will routinely be notified of the debit to its account with respect to an unauthorized order or will otherwise be notified of acceptance of the order. The customer has a duty to exercise ordinary care to determine that the order was unauthorized after it has received notification from the bank, and to advise the bank of the relevant facts within a reasonable time not exceeding 90 days after receipt of notification. Reasonable time is not defined and it may depend on the facts of the particular case. If a payment order for $1,000,000 is wholly unauthorized, the customer should normally discover it in far less than 90 days. If a $1,000,000 payment order was authorized but the name of the beneficiary was fraudulently changed, a much longer period may be necessary to discover the fraud. But in any event, if the customer delays more than 90 days the customer's duty has not been met. The only consequence of a failure of the customer to perform this duty is a loss of interest on the refund payable by the bank. A customer that acts promptly is entitled to interest from the time the customer's account was debited or the customer otherwise made payment. The rate of interest is stated in Section 4A–506. If the customer fails to perform the duty, no interest is recoverable for any part of the period before the bank learns that it accepted an unauthorized order. But the bank is not entitled to any recovery from the customer based on negligence for failure to inform the bank. Loss of interest is in the nature of a penalty on the customer designed to provide an incentive for the customer to police its account. There is no intention to impose a duty on the customer that might result in shifting loss from the unauthorized order to the customer.

§ 11205. Erroneous Payment Orders

(a) If an accepted payment order was transmitted pursuant to a security procedure for the detection of error and the payment order (i) erroneously instructed payment to a beneficiary not intended by the sender, (ii) erroneously instructed payment in an amount greater than the amount intended by the sender, or (iii) was an erroneously transmitted duplicate of a payment order previously sent by the sender, the following rules apply:

(1) If the sender proves that the sender or a person acting on behalf of the sender pursuant to Section 11206 complied with the security procedure and that the error would have been detected if the receiving bank had also complied, the sender is not obliged to pay the order to the extent stated in paragraphs (2) and (3).

(2) If the funds transfer is completed on the basis of an erroneous payment order described in clause (i) or (iii) of this subdivision, the sender is not obliged to pay the order and the receiving bank is entitled to recover from the beneficiary any amount paid to the beneficiary to the extent allowed by the law governing mistake and restitution.

(3) If the funds transfer is completed on the basis of a payment order described in clause (ii) of this subdivision, the sender is not obliged to pay the order to the extent the amount received by the beneficiary is greater than the amount intended by the sender. In that case, the receiving bank is entitled to recover from the beneficiary the excess amount received to the extent allowed by the law governing mistake and restitution.

(b) If (i) the sender of an erroneous payment order described in subdivision (a) is not obliged to pay all or part of the order, and (ii) the sender receives notification from the receiving bank that the order was

§ 11205

accepted by the bank or that the sender's account was debited with respect to the order, the sender has a duty to exercise ordinary care, on the basis of information available to the sender, to discover the error with respect to the order and to advise the bank of the relevant facts within a reasonable time, not exceeding 90 days, after the bank's notification was received by the sender. If the bank proves that the sender failed to perform that duty, the sender is liable to the bank for the loss the bank proves it incurred as a result of the failure, but the liability of the sender may not exceed the amount of the sender's order.

(c) This section applies to amendments to payment orders to the same extent it applies to payment orders. *(Added by Stats.1990, c. 125 (S.B.1759), § 2.)*

Uniform Commercial Code Comment

1. This section concerns error in the content or in the transmission of payment orders. It deals with three kinds of error. *Case #1.* The order identifies a beneficiary not intended by the sender. For example, Sender intends to wire funds to a beneficiary identified only by an account number. The wrong account number is stated in the order. *Case #2.* The error is in the amount of the order. For example, Sender intends to wire $1,000 to Beneficiary. Through error, the payment order instructs payment of $1,000,000. *Case #3.* A payment order is sent to the receiving bank and then, by mistake, the same payment order is sent to the receiving bank again. In Case #3, the receiving bank may have no way of knowing whether the second order is a duplicate of the first or is another order. Similarly, in Case #1 and Case #2, the receiving bank may have no way of knowing that the error exists. In each case, if this section does not apply and the funds transfer is completed, Sender is obliged to pay the order. Section 4A–402. Sender's remedy, based on payment by mistake, is to recover from the beneficiary that received payment.

Sometimes, however, transmission of payment orders of the sender to the receiving bank is made pursuant to a security procedure designed to detect one or more of the errors described above. Since "security procedure" is defined by Section 4A–201 as "a procedure established by agreement of a customer and a receiving bank for the purpose of * * * detecting error * * *," Section 4A–205 does not apply if the receiving bank and the customer did not agree to the establishment of a procedure for detecting error. A security procedure may be designed to detect an account number that is not one to which Sender normally makes payment. In that case, the security procedure may require a special verification that payment to the stated account number was intended. In the case of dollar amounts, the security procedure may require different codes for different dollar amounts. If a $1,000,000 payment order contains a code that is inappropriate for that amount, the error in amount should be detected. In the case of duplicate orders, the security procedure may require that each payment order be identified by a number or code that applies to no other order. If the number or code of each payment order received is registered in a computer base, the receiving bank can quickly identify a duplicate order. The three cases covered by this section are essentially similar. In each, if the error is not detected, some beneficiary will receive funds that the beneficiary was not intended to receive. If this section applies, the risk of loss with respect to the error of the sender is shifted to the bank which has the burden of recovering the funds from the beneficiary. The risk of loss is shifted to the bank only if the sender proves that the error would have been detected if there had been compliance with the procedure and that the sender (or an agent under Section 4A–206) complied. In the case of a duplicate order or a wrong beneficiary, the sender doesn't have to pay the order. In the case of an overpayment, the sender does not have to pay the order to the extent of the overpayment. If subsection (a)(1) applies, the position of the receiving bank is comparable to that of a receiving bank that erroneously executes a payment order as stated in Section 4A–303. However, failure of the sender to timely report the error is covered by Section 4A–205(b) rather than by Section 4A–304 which applies only to erroneous execution under Section 4A–303. A receiving bank to which the risk of loss is shifted by subsection (a)(1) or (2) is entitled to recover the amount erroneously paid to the beneficiary to the extent allowed by the law of mistake and restitution. Rights of the receiving bank against the beneficiary are similar to those of a receiving bank that erroneously executes a payment order as stated in Section 4A–303. Those rights are discussed in Comment 2 to Section 4A–303.

2. A security procedure established for the purpose of detecting error is not effective unless both sender and receiving bank comply with the procedure. Thus, the bank undertakes a duty of complying with the procedure for the benefit of the sender. This duty is recognized in subsection (a)(1). The loss with respect to the sender's error is shifted to the bank if the bank fails to comply with the procedure and the sender (or an agent under Section 4A–206) does comply. Although the customer may have been negligent in transmitting the erroneous payment order, the loss is put on the bank on a last-clear-chance theory. A similar analysis applies to subsection (b). If the loss with respect to an error is shifted to the receiving bank and the sender is notified by the bank that the erroneous payment order was accepted, the sender has a duty to exercise ordinary care to discover the error and notify the bank of the relevant facts within a reasonable time not exceeding 90 days. If the bank can prove that the sender failed in this duty it is entitled to compensation for the loss incurred as a result of the failure. Whether the bank is entitled to recover from the sender depends upon whether the failure to give timely notice would have made any difference. If the bank could not have recovered from the beneficiary that received payment under the erroneous payment order even if timely notice had been given, the sender's failure to notify did not cause any loss of the bank.

3. Section 4A–205 is subject to variation by agreement under Section 4A–501. Thus, if a receiving bank and its customer have agreed to a security procedure for detection of error, the liability of the receiving bank for failing to detect an error of the customer as provided in Section 4A–205 may be varied as provided in an agreement of the bank and the customer.

§ 11206. Transmission of Payment Order Through Funds–Transfer or Other Communication System

(a) If a payment order addressed to a receiving bank is transmitted to a funds-transfer system or other third-party communication system for transmittal to the bank, the system is deemed to be an agent of the sender for the purpose of transmitting the payment order to the bank. If there is a discrepancy between the terms of the payment order transmitted to the system and the terms of the payment order transmitted by the system to the bank, the terms of the payment order of the sender are those transmitted by the system. This section does not apply to a funds-transfer system of the Federal Reserve Banks.

(b) This section applies to cancellations and amendments of payment orders to the same extent it applies to payment orders. *(Added by Stats.1990, c. 125 (S.B. 1759), § 2.)*

Uniform Commercial Code Comment

1. A payment order may be issued to a receiving bank directly by delivery of a writing or electronic device or by an oral or electronic communication. If an agent of the sender is employed to transmit orders on behalf of the sender, the sender is bound by the order transmitted by the agent on the basis of agency law. Section 4A–206 is an application of that principle to cases in which a funds transfer or communication system acts as an intermediary in transmitting the sender's order to the receiving bank. The intermediary is deemed to be an agent of the sender for the purpose of transmitting payment orders and related messages for the sender. Section 4A–206 deals with error by the intermediary.

2. Transmission by an automated clearing house of an association of banks other than the Federal Reserve Banks is an example of a transaction covered by Section 4A–206. Suppose Originator orders Originator's Bank to cause a large number of payments to be made to many accounts in banks in various parts of the country. These payment

orders are electronically transmitted to Originator's Bank and stored in an electronic device that is held by Originator's Bank. Or, transmission of the various payment orders is made by delivery to Originator's Bank of an electronic device containing the instruction to the bank. In either case the terms of the various payment orders by Originator are determined by the information contained in the electronic device. In order to execute the various orders, the information in the electronic device must be processed. For example, if some of the orders are for payments to accounts in Bank X and some to accounts in Bank Y, Originator's Bank will execute these orders of Originator by issuing a series of payment orders to Bank X covering all payments to accounts in that bank, and by issuing a series of payment orders to Bank Y covering all payments to accounts in that bank. The orders to Bank X may be transmitted together by means of an electronic device, and those to Bank Y may be included in another electronic device. Typically, this processing is done by an automated clearing house acting for a group of banks including Originator's Bank. The automated clearing house is a funds transfer system. Section 4A–105(a)(5). Originator's Bank delivers Originator's electronic device or transmits the information contained in the device to the funds transfer system for processing into payment orders of Originator's Bank to the appropriate beneficiary's banks. The processing may result in an erroneous payment order. Originator's Bank, by use of Originator's electronic device, may have given information to the funds transfer system instructing payment of $100,000 to an account in Bank X, but because of human error or an equipment malfunction the processing may have converted that instruction into an instruction to Bank X to make a payment of $1,000,000. Under Section 4A–206, Originator's Bank issued a payment order for $1,000,000 to Bank X when the erroneous information was sent to Bank X. Originator's Bank is responsible for the error of the automated clearing house. The liability of the funds transfer system that made the error is not governed by Article 4A. It is left to the law of contract, a funds transfer system rule, or other applicable law.

In the hypothetical case just discussed, if the automated clearing house is operated by a Federal Reserve Bank, the analysis is different. Section 4A–206 does not apply. Originator's Bank will execute Originator's payment orders by delivery or transmission of the electronic information to the Federal Reserve Bank for processing. The result is that Originator's Bank has issued payment orders to the Federal Reserve Bank which, in this case, is acting as an intermediary bank. When the Federal Reserve Bank has processed the information given to it by Originator's Bank it will issue payment orders to the various beneficiary's banks. If the processing results in an erroneous payment order, the Federal Reserve Bank has erroneously executed the payment order of Originator's Bank and the case is governed by Section 4A–303.

§ 11207. Misdescription of Beneficiary

(a) Subject to subdivision (b), if, in a payment order received by the beneficiary's bank, the name, bank account number, or other identification of the beneficiary refers to a nonexistent or unidentifiable person or account, no person has rights as a beneficiary of the order and acceptance of the order cannot occur.

(b) If a payment order received by the beneficiary's bank identifies the beneficiary both by name and by an identifying or bank account number and the name and number identify different persons, the following rules apply:

(1) Except as otherwise provided in subdivision (c), if the beneficiary's bank does not know that the name and number refer to different persons, it may rely on the number as the proper identification of the beneficiary of the order. The beneficiary's bank need not determine whether the name and number refer to the same person.

(2) If the beneficiary's bank pays the person identified by name or knows that the name and number identify different persons, no person has rights as beneficiary except the person paid by the beneficiary's bank if that person was entitled to receive payment from the originator of the funds transfer. If no person has rights as beneficiary, acceptance of the order cannot occur.

(c) If (i) a payment order described in subdivision (b) is accepted, (ii) the originator's payment order described the beneficiary inconsistently by name and number, and (iii) the beneficiary's bank pays the person identified by number as permitted by paragraph (1) of subdivision (b), the following rules apply:

(1) If the originator is a bank, the originator is obliged to pay its order.

(2) If the originator is not a bank and proves that the person identified by number was not entitled to receive payment from the originator, the originator is not obliged to pay its order unless the originator's bank proves that the originator, before acceptance of the originator's order, had notice that payment of a payment order issued by the originator might be made by the beneficiary's bank on the basis of an identifying or bank account number even if it identifies a person different from the named beneficiary. Proof of notice may be made by any admissible evidence. The originator's bank satisfies the burden of proof if it proves that the originator, before the payment order was accepted, signed a writing stating the information to which the notice relates.

(d) In a case governed by paragraph (1) of subdivision (b), if the beneficiary's bank rightfully pays the person identified by number and that person was not entitled to receive payment from the originator, the amount paid may be recovered from that person to the extent allowed by the law governing mistake and restitution as follows:

(1) If the originator is obliged to pay its payment order as stated in subdivision (c), the originator has the right to recover.

(2) If the originator is not a bank and is not obliged to pay its payment order, the originator's bank has the right to recover. *(Added by Stats.1990, c. 125 (S.B. 1759), § 2.)*

Uniform Commercial Code Comment

1. Subsection (a) deals with the problem of payment orders issued to the beneficiary's bank for payment to nonexistent or unidentifiable persons or accounts. Since it is not possible in that case for the funds transfer to be completed, subsection (a) states that the order cannot be accepted. Under Section 4A–402(c), a sender of a payment order is not obliged to pay its order unless the beneficiary's bank accepts a payment order instructing payment to the beneficiary of that sender's order. Thus, if the beneficiary of a funds transfer is nonexistent or unidentifiable, each sender in the funds transfer that has paid its payment order is entitled to get its money back.

2. Subsection (b), which takes precedence over subsection (a), deals with the problem of payment orders in which the description of the beneficiary does not allow identification of the beneficiary because the beneficiary is described by name and by an identifying number or an account number and the name and number refer to different persons. A very large percentage of payment orders issued to the beneficiary's bank by another bank are processed by automated means using machines capable of reading orders on standard formats that identify the beneficiary by an identifying number or the number of a bank account. The processing of the order by the beneficiary's bank and the crediting of the beneficiary's account are done by use of the identifying

or bank account number without human reading of the payment order itself. The process is comparable to that used in automated payment of checks. The standard format, however may also allow the inclusion of the name of the beneficiary and other information which can be useful to the beneficiary's bank and the beneficiary but which plays no part in the process of payment. If the beneficiary's bank has both the account number and name of the beneficiary supplied by the originator of the funds transfer, it is possible for the beneficiary's bank to determine whether the name and number refer to the same person, but if a duty to make that determination is imposed on the beneficiary's bank the benefits of automated payment are lost. Manual handling of payment orders is both expensive and subject to human error. If payment orders can be handled on an automated basis there are substantial economies of operation and the possibility of clerical error is reduced. Subsection (b) allows banks to utilize automated processing by allowing banks to act on the basis of the number without regard to the name if the bank does not know that the name and number refer to different persons. "Know" is defined in Section 1–201(25) to mean actual knowledge, and Section 1–201(27) states rules for determining when an organization has knowledge of information received by the organization. The time of payment is the pertinent time at which knowledge or lack of knowledge must be determined.

Although the clear trend is for beneficiary's banks to process payment orders by automated means, Section 4A–207 is not limited to cases in which processing is done by automated means. A bank that processes by semi-automated means or even manually may rely on number as stated in Section 4A–207.

In cases covered by subsection (b) the erroneous identification would in virtually all cases be the identifying or bank account number. In the typical case the error is made by the originator of the funds transfer. The originator should know the name of the person who is to receive payment and can further identify that person by an address that would normally be known to the originator. It is not unlikely, however, that the originator may not be sure whether the identifying or account number refers to the person the originator intends to pay. Subsection (b)(1) deals with the typical case in which the beneficiary's bank pays on the basis of the account number and is not aware at the time of payment that the named beneficiary is not the holder of the account which was paid. In some cases the false number will be the result of error by the originator. In other cases fraud is involved. For example, Doe is the holder of shares in Mutual Fund. Thief, impersonating Doe, requests redemption of the shares and directs Mutual Fund to wire the redemption proceeds to Doe's account #12345 in Beneficiary's Bank. Mutual Fund originates a funds transfer by issuing a payment order to Originator's Bank to make the payment to Doe's account #12345 in Beneficiary's Bank. Originator's Bank executes the order by issuing a conforming payment order to Beneficiary's Bank which makes payment to account #12345. That account is the account of Roe rather than Doe. Roe might be a person acting in concert with Thief or Roe might be an innocent third party. Assume that Roe is a gem merchant that agreed to sell gems to Thief who agreed to wire the purchase price to Roe's account in Beneficiary's Bank. Roe believed that the credit to Roe's account was a transfer of funds from Thief and released the gems to Thief in good faith in reliance on the payment. The case law is unclear on the responsibility of a beneficiary's bank in carrying out a payment order in which the identification of the beneficiary by name and number is conflicting. See Securities Fund Services, Inc. v. American National Bank, 542 F.Supp. 323 (N.D.Ill.1982) and Bradford Trust Co. v. Texas American Bank, 790 F.2d 407 (5th Cir.1986). Section 4A–207 resolves the issue.

If Beneficiary's Bank did not know about the conflict between the name and number, subsection (b)(1) applies. Beneficiary's Bank has no duty to determine whether there is a conflict and it may rely on the number as the proper identification of the beneficiary of the order. When it accepts the order, it is entitled to payment from Originator's Bank. Section 4A–402(b). On the other hand, if Beneficiary's Bank knew about the conflict between the name and number and nevertheless paid Roe, subsection (b)(2) applies. Under that provision, acceptance of the payment order of Originator's Bank did not occur because there is no beneficiary of that order. Since acceptance did not occur Originator's Bank is not obliged to pay Beneficiary's Bank. Section 4A–402(b). Similarly, Mutual Fund is excused from its obligation to pay Originator's Bank. Section 4A–402(c). Thus, Beneficiary's Bank takes the loss. Its only cause of action is against Thief. Roe is not obliged to return the payment to the beneficiary's bank because Roe received the payment in good faith and for value. Article 4A makes irrelevant the issue of whether Mutual Fund was or was not negligent in issuing its payment order.

3. Normally, subsection (b)(1) will apply to the hypothetical case discussed in Comment 2. Beneficiary's Bank will pay on the basis of the number without knowledge of the conflict. In that case subsection (c) places the loss on either Mutual Fund or Originator's Bank. It is not unfair to assign the loss to Mutual Fund because it is the person who dealt with the imposter and it supplied the wrong account number. It could have avoided the loss if it had not used an account number that it was not sure was that of Doe. Mutual Fund, however, may not have been aware of the risk involved in giving both name and number. Subsection (c) is designed to protect the originator, Mutual Fund, in this case. Under that subsection, the originator is responsible for the inconsistent description of the beneficiary if it had notice that the order might be paid by the beneficiary's bank on the basis of the number. If the originator is a bank, the originator always has that responsibility. The rationale is that any bank should know how payment orders are processed and paid. If the originator is not a bank, the originator's bank must prove that its customer, the originator, had notice. Notice can be proved by any admissible evidence, but the bank can always prove notice by providing the customer with a written statement of the required information and obtaining the customer's signature to the statement. That statement will then apply to any payment order accepted by the bank thereafter. The information need not be supplied more than once.

In the hypothetical case if Originator's Bank made the disclosure stated in the last sentence of subsection (c)(2), Mutual Fund must pay Originator's Bank. Under subsection (d)(1), Mutual Fund has an action to recover from Roe if recovery from Roe is permitted by the law governing mistake and restitution. Under the assumed facts Roe should be entitled to keep the money as a person who took it in good faith and for value since it was taken as payment for the gems. In that case, Mutual Fund's only remedy is against Thief. If Roe was not acting in good faith, Roe has to return the money to Mutual Fund. If Originator's Bank does not prove that Mutual Fund had notice as stated in subsection (c)(2), Mutual Fund is not required to pay Originator's Bank. Thus, the risk of loss falls on Originator's Bank whose remedy is against Roe or Thief as stated above. Subsection (d)(2).

§ 11208. Misdescription of Intermediary Bank or Beneficiary's Bank

(a) This subdivision applies to a payment order identifying an intermediary bank or the beneficiary's bank only by an identifying number.

(1) The receiving bank may rely on the number as the proper identification of the intermediary or beneficiary's bank and need not determine whether the number identifies a bank.

(2) The sender is obliged to compensate the receiving bank for any loss and expenses incurred by the receiving bank as a result of its reliance on the number in executing or attempting to execute the order.

(b) This subdivision applies to a payment order identifying an intermediary bank or the beneficiary's bank both by name and an identifying number if the name and number identify different persons.

(1) If the sender is a bank, the receiving bank may rely on the number as the proper identification of the intermediary or beneficiary's bank if the receiving bank, when it executes the sender's order, does not know that the name and number identify different persons. The receiving bank need not determine whether the name and number refer to the same person or whether the number refers to a bank. The sender is obliged to compensate the receiving bank for any loss and expenses incurred by the receiving bank as a result of its

reliance on the number in executing or attempting to execute the order.

(2) If the sender is not a bank and the receiving bank proves that the sender, before the payment order was accepted, had notice that the receiving bank might rely on the number as the proper identification of the intermediary or beneficiary's bank even if it identifies a person different from the bank identified by name, the rights and obligations of the sender and the receiving bank are governed by paragraph (1) of subdivision (b), as though the sender were a bank. Proof of notice may be made by any admissible evidence. The receiving bank satisfies the burden of proof if it proves that the sender, before the payment order was accepted, signed a writing stating the information to which the notice relates.

(3) Regardless of whether the sender is a bank, the receiving bank may rely on the name as the proper identification of the intermediary or beneficiary's bank if the receiving bank, at the time it executes the sender's order, does not know that the name and number identify different persons. The receiving bank need not determine whether the name and number refer to the same person.

(4) If the receiving bank knows that the name and number identify different persons, reliance on either the name or the number in executing the sender's payment order is a breach of the obligation stated in paragraph (1) of subdivision (a) of Section 11302. (Added by Stats.1990, c. 125 (S.B.1759), § 2.)

Uniform Commercial Code Comment

1. This section addresses an issue similar to that addressed by Section 4A–207. Because of automation in the processing of payment orders, a payment order may identify the beneficiary's bank or an intermediary bank by an identifying number. The bank identified by number might or might not also be identified by name. The following two cases illustrate Section 4A–208(a) and (b):

Case #1. Originator's payment order to Originator's Bank identifies the beneficiary's bank as Bank A and instructs payment to Account #12345 in that bank. Originator's Bank executes Originator's order by issuing a payment order to Intermediary Bank. In the payment order of Originator's Bank the beneficiary's bank is identified as Bank A but is also identified by number, #67890. The identifying number refers to Bank B rather than Bank A. If processing by Intermediary Bank of the payment order of Originator's Bank is done by automated means, Intermediary Bank, in executing the order, will rely on the identifying number and will issue a payment order to Bank B rather than Bank A. If there is an Account #12345 in Bank B, the payment order of Intermediary Bank would normally be accepted and payment would be made to a person not intended by Originator. In this case, Section 4A–208(b)(1) puts the risk of loss on Originator's Bank. Intermediary Bank may rely on the number #67890 as the proper identification of the beneficiary's bank. Intermediary Bank has properly executed the payment order of Originator's Bank. By using the wrong number to describe the beneficiary's bank, Originator's Bank has improperly executed Originator's payment order because the payment order of Originator's Bank provides for payment to the wrong beneficiary, the holder of Account #12345 in Bank B rather than the holder of Account #12345 in Bank A. Section 4A–302(a)(1) and Section 4A–303(c). Originator's Bank is not entitled to payment from Originator but is required to pay Intermediary Bank. Section 4A–303(c) and Section 4A–402(c). Intermediary Bank is also entitled to compensation for any loss and expenses resulting from the error by Originator's Bank.

If there is no Account #12345 in Bank B, the result is that there is no beneficiary of the payment order issued by Originator's Bank and the funds transfer will not be completed. Originator's Bank is not entitled to payment from Originator and Intermediary Bank is not entitled to payment from Originator's Bank. Section 4A–402(c). Since Originator's Bank improperly executed Originator's payment order it may be liable for damages under Section 4A–305. As stated above, Intermediary Bank is entitled to compensation for loss and expenses resulting from the error by Originator's Bank.

Case #2. Suppose the same payment order by Originator to Originator's Bank as in Case #1. In executing the payment order Originator's Bank issues a payment order to Intermediary Bank in which the beneficiary's bank is identified only by number, #67890. That number does not refer to Bank A. Rather, it identifies a person that is not a bank. If processing by Intermediary Bank of the payment order of Originator's Bank is done by automated means, Intermediary Bank will rely on the number #67890 to identify the beneficiary's bank. Intermediary Bank has no duty to determine whether the number identifies a bank. The funds transfer cannot be completed in this case because no bank is identified as the beneficiary's bank. Subsection (a) puts the risk of loss on Originator's Bank. Originator's Bank is not entitled to payment from Originator. Section 4A–402(c). Originator's Bank has improperly executed Originator's payment order and may be liable for damages under Section 4A–305. Originator's Bank is obliged to compensate Intermediary Bank for loss and expenses resulting from the error by Originator's Bank.

Subsection (a) also applies if #67890 identifies a bank, but the bank is not Bank A. Intermediary Bank may rely on the number as the proper identification of the beneficiary's bank. If the bank to which Intermediary Bank sends its payment order accepts the order, Intermediary Bank is entitled to payment from Originator's Bank, but Originator's Bank is not entitled to payment from Originator. The analysis is similar to that in Case #1.

2. Subsection (b)(2) of Section 4A–208 addresses cases in which an erroneous identification of a beneficiary's bank or intermediary bank by name and number is made in a payment order of a sender that is not a bank. Suppose Originator issues a payment order to Originator's Bank that instructs that bank to use an intermediary bank identified as Bank A and by an identifying number, #67890. The identifying number refers to Bank B. Originator intended to identify Bank A as intermediary bank. If Originator's Bank relied on the number and issued a payment order to Bank B the rights of Originator's Bank depend upon whether the proof of notice stated in subsection (b)(2) is made by Originator's Bank. If proof is made, Originator's Bank's rights are governed by subsection (b)(1) of Section 4A–208. Originator's Bank is not liable for breach of Section 4A–302(a)(1) and is entitled to compensation from Originator for any loss and expenses resulting from Originator's error. If notice is not proved, Originator's Bank may not rely on the number in executing Originator's payment order. Since Originator's Bank does not get the benefit of subsection (b)(1) in that case, Originator's Bank improperly executed Originator's payment order and is in breach of the obligation stated in Section 4A–302(a)(1). If notice is not given, Originator's Bank can rely on the name if it is not aware of the conflict in name and number. Subsection (b)(3).

3. Although the principal purpose of Section 4A–208 is to accommodate automated processing of payment orders, Section 4A–208 applies regardless of whether processing is done by automation, semi-automated means or manually.

§ 11209. Acceptance of Payment Order

(a) Subject to subdivision (d), a receiving bank other than the beneficiary's bank accepts a payment order when it executes the order.

(b) Subject to subdivisions (c) and (d), a beneficiary's bank accepts a payment order at the earliest of the following times:

(1) When the bank (i) pays the beneficiary as stated in subdivision (a) or (b) of Section 11405, or (ii) notifies the beneficiary of receipt of the order or that the account of the beneficiary has been credited with respect to the order unless the notice indicates that the bank is rejecting the order or that funds with respect to

§ 11209

the order may not be withdrawn or used until receipt of payment from the sender of the order.

(2) When the bank receives payment of the entire amount of the sender's order pursuant to paragraph (1) or (2) of subdivision (a) of Section 11403.

(3) The opening of the next funds-transfer business day of the bank following the payment date of the order if, at that time, the amount of the sender's order is fully covered by a withdrawable credit balance in an authorized account of the sender or the bank has otherwise received full payment from the sender, unless the order was rejected before that time or is rejected within (i) one hour after that time, or (ii) one hour after the opening of the next business day of the sender following the payment date if that time is later. If notice of rejection is received by the sender after the payment date and the authorized account of the sender does not bear interest, the bank is obliged to pay interest to the sender on the amount of the order for the number of days elapsing after the payment date to the day the sender receives notice or learns that the order was not accepted, counting that day as an elapsed day. If the withdrawable credit balance during that period falls below the amount of the order, the amount of interest payable is reduced accordingly.

(c) Acceptance of a payment order cannot occur before the order is received by the receiving bank. Acceptance does not occur under paragraph (2) or (3) of subdivision (b) if the beneficiary of the payment order does not have an account with the receiving bank, the account has been closed, or the receiving bank is not permitted by law to receive credits for the beneficiary's account.

(d) A payment order issued to the originator's bank cannot be accepted until the payment date if the bank is the beneficiary's bank, or the execution date if the bank is not the beneficiary's bank. If the originator's bank executes the originator's payment order before the execution date or pays the beneficiary of the originator's payment order before the payment date and the payment order is subsequently canceled pursuant to subdivision (b) of Section 11211, the bank may recover from the beneficiary any payment received to the extent allowed by the law governing mistake and restitution. *(Added by Stats.1990, c. 125 (S.B.1759), § 2.)*

Uniform Commercial Code Comment

1. This section treats the sender's payment order as a request by the sender to the receiving bank to execute or pay the order and that request can be accepted or rejected by the receiving bank. Section 4A–209 defines when acceptance occurs. Section 4A–210 covers rejection. Acceptance of the payment order imposes an obligation on the receiving bank to the sender if the receiving bank is not the beneficiary's bank, or to the beneficiary if the receiving bank is the beneficiary's bank. These obligations are stated in Section 4A–302 and Section 4A–404.

2. Acceptance by a receiving bank other than the beneficiary's bank is defined in Section 4A–209(a). That subsection states the only way that a bank other than the beneficiary's bank can accept a payment order. A payment order to a bank other than the beneficiary's bank is, in effect, a request that the receiving bank execute the sender's order by issuing a payment order to the beneficiary's bank or to an intermediary bank. Normally, acceptance occurs at the time of execution, but there is an exception stated in subsection (d) and discussed in Comment 9. Execution occurs when the receiving bank "issues a payment order intended to carry out" the sender's order. Section 4A–301(a). In some cases the payment order issued by the receiving bank may not conform to the sender's order. For example, the receiving bank might make a mistake in the amount of its order, or the order might be issued to the wrong beneficiary's bank or for the benefit of the wrong beneficiary. In all of these cases there is acceptance of the sender's order by the bank when the receiving bank issues its order intended to carry out the sender's order, even though the bank's payment order does not in fact carry out the instruction of the sender. Improper execution of the sender's order may lead to liability to the sender for damages or it may mean that the sender is not obliged to pay its payment order. These matters are covered in Section 4A–303, Section 4A–305, and Section 4A–402.

3. A receiving bank has no duty to accept a payment order unless the bank makes an agreement, either before or after issuance of the payment order, to accept it, or acceptance is required by a funds transfer system rule. If the bank makes such an agreement it incurs a contractual obligation based on the agreement and may be held liable for breach of contract if a failure to execute violates the agreement. In many cases a bank will enter into an agreement with its customer to govern the rights and obligations of the parties with respect to payment orders issued to the bank by the customer or, in cases in which the sender is also a bank, there may be a funds transfer system rule that governs the obligations of a receiving bank with respect to payment orders transmitted over the system. Such agreements or rules can specify the circumstances under which a receiving bank is obliged to execute a payment order and can define the extent of liability of the receiving bank for breach of the agreement or rule. Section 4A–305(d) states the liability for breach of an agreement to execute a payment order.

4. In the case of a payment order issued to the beneficiary's bank, acceptance is defined in Section 4A–209(b). The function of a beneficiary's bank that receives a payment order is different from that of a receiving bank that receives a payment order for execution. In the typical case, the beneficiary's bank simply receives payment from the sender of the order, credits the account of the beneficiary and notifies the beneficiary of the credit. Acceptance by the beneficiary's bank does not create any obligation to the sender. Acceptance by the beneficiary's bank means that the bank is liable to the beneficiary for the amount of the order. Section 4A–404(a). There are three ways in which the beneficiary's bank can accept a payment order which are described in the following comments.

5. Under Section 4A–209(b)(1), the beneficiary's bank can accept a payment order by paying the beneficiary. In the normal case of crediting an account of the beneficiary, payment occurs when the beneficiary is given notice of the right to withdraw the credit, the credit is applied to a debt of the beneficiary, or "funds with respect to the order" are otherwise made available to the beneficiary. Section 4A–405(a). The quoted phrase covers cases in which funds are made available to the beneficiary as a result of receipt of a payment order for the benefit of the beneficiary but the release of funds is not expressed as payment of the order. For example, the beneficiary's bank might express a release of funds equal to the amount of the order as a "loan" that will be automatically repaid when the beneficiary's bank receives payment by the sender of the order. If the release of funds is designated as a loan pursuant to a routine practice of the bank, the release is conditional payment of the order rather than a loan, particularly if normal incidents of a loan such as the signing of a loan agreement or note and the payment of interest are not present. Such a release of funds is payment to the beneficiary under Section 4A–405(a). Under Section 4A–405(c) the bank cannot recover the money from the beneficiary if the bank does not receive payment from the sender of the payment order that it accepted. Exceptions to this rule are stated in § 4A–405(d) and (e). The beneficiary's bank may also accept by notifying the beneficiary that the order has been received. "Notifies" is defined in Section 1–201(26). In some cases a beneficiary's bank will receive a payment order during the day but settlement of the sender's obligation to pay the order will not occur until the end of the day. If the beneficiary's bank wants to defer incurring liability to the beneficiary until the beneficiary's bank receives payment, it can do so. The beneficiary's bank incurs no liability to the beneficiary with respect to a payment order that it receives until it accepts the order. If the bank does not accept pursuant to subsection (b)(1), acceptance does not

occur until the end of the day when the beneficiary's bank receives settlement. If the sender settles, the payment order will be accepted under subsection (b)(2) and the funds will be released to the beneficiary the next morning. If the sender doesn't settle, no acceptance occurs. In either case the beneficiary's bank suffers no loss.

6. In most cases the beneficiary's bank will receive a payment order from another bank. If the sender is a bank and the beneficiary's bank receives payment from the sender by final settlement through the Federal Reserve System or a funds transfer system (Section 4A–403(a)(1)) or, less commonly, through credit to an account of the beneficiary's bank with the sender or another bank (Section 4A–403(a)(2)), acceptance by the beneficiary's bank occurs at the time payment is made. Section 4A–209(b)(2). A minor exception to this rule is stated in Section 4A–209(c). Section 4A–209(b)(2) results in automatic acceptance of payment orders issued to a beneficiary's bank by means of Fedwire because the Federal Reserve account of the beneficiary's bank is credited and final payment is made to that bank when the payment order is received.

Subsection (b)(2) would also apply to cases in which the beneficiary's bank mistakenly pays a person who is not the beneficiary of the payment order issued to the beneficiary's bank. For example, suppose the payment order provides for immediate payment to Account #12345. The beneficiary's bank erroneously credits Account #12346 and notifies the holder of that account of the credit. No acceptance occurs in this case under subsection (b)(1) because the beneficiary of the order has not been paid or notified. The holder of Account #12345 is the beneficiary of the order issued to the beneficiary's bank. But acceptance will normally occur if the beneficiary's bank takes no other action, because the bank will normally receive settlement with respect to the payment order. At that time the bank has accepted because the sender paid its payment order. The bank is liable to pay the holder of Account #12345. The bank has paid the holder of Account #12346 by mistake, and has a right to recover the payment if the credit is withdrawn, to the extent provided in the law governing mistake and restitution.

7. Subsection (b)(3) covers cases of inaction by the beneficiary's bank. It applies whether or not the sender is a bank and covers a case in which the sender and the beneficiary both have accounts with the receiving bank and payment will be made by debiting the account of the sender and crediting the account of the beneficiary. Subsection (b)(3) is similar to subsection (b)(2) in that it bases acceptance by the beneficiary's bank on payment by the sender. Payment by the sender is effected by a debit to the sender's account if the account balance is sufficient to cover the amount of the order. On the payment date (Section 4A–401) of the order the beneficiary's bank will normally credit the beneficiary's account and notify the beneficiary of receipt of the order if it is satisfied that the sender's account balance covers the order or is willing to give credit to the sender. In some cases, however, the bank may not be willing to give credit to the sender and it may not be possible for the bank to determine until the end of the day on the payment date whether there are sufficient good funds in the sender's account. There may be various transactions during the day involving funds going into and out of the account. Some of these transactions may occur late in the day or after the close of the banking day. To accommodate this situation, subsection (b)(3) provides that the status of the account is determined at the opening of the next funds transfer business day of the beneficiary's bank after the payment date of the order. If the sender's account balance is sufficient to cover the order, the beneficiary's bank has a source of payment and the result in almost all cases is that the bank accepts the order at that time if it did not previously accept under subsection (b)(1). In rare cases, a bank may want to avoid acceptance under subsection (b)(3) by rejecting the order as discussed in Comment 8.

8. Section 4A–209 is based on a general principle that a receiving bank is not obliged to accept a payment order unless it has agreed or is bound by a funds transfer system rule to do so. Thus, provision is made to allow the receiving bank to prevent acceptance of the order. This principle is consistently followed if the receiving bank is not the beneficiary's bank. If the receiving bank is not the beneficiary's bank, acceptance is in the control of the receiving bank because it occurs only if the order is executed. But in the case of the beneficiary's bank acceptance can occur by passive receipt of payment under subsection (b)(2) or (3). In the case of a payment made by Fedwire acceptance cannot be prevented. In other cases the beneficiary's bank can prevent acceptance by giving notice of rejection to the sender before payment occurs under Section 4A–403(a)(1) or (2). A minor exception to the ability of the beneficiary's bank to reject is stated in Section 4A–502(c)(3).

Under subsection (b)(3) acceptance occurs at the opening of the next funds transfer business day of the beneficiary's bank following the payment date unless the bank rejected the order before that time or it rejects within one hour after that time. In some cases the sender and the beneficiary's bank may not be in the same time zone or the beginning of the business day of the sender and the funds transfer business day of the beneficiary's bank may not coincide. For example, the sender may be located in California and the beneficiary's bank in New York. Since in most cases notice of rejection would be communicated electronically or by telephone, it might not be feasible for the bank to give notice before one hour after the opening of the funds transfer business day in New York because at that hour, the sender's business day may not have started in California. For that reason, there are alternative deadlines stated in subsection (b)(3). In the case stated, the bank acts in time if it gives notice within one hour after the opening of the business day of the sender. But if the notice of rejection is received by the sender after the payment date, the bank is obliged to pay interest to the sender if the sender's account does not bear interest. In that case the bank had the use of funds of the sender that the sender could reasonably assume would be used to pay the beneficiary. The rate of interest is stated in Section 4A–506. If the sender receives notice on the day after the payment date the sender is entitled to one day's interest. If receipt of notice is delayed for more than one day, the sender is entitled to interest for each additional day of delay.

9. Subsection (d) applies only to a payment order by the originator of a funds transfer to the originator's bank and it refers to the following situation. On April 1, Originator instructs Bank A to make a payment on April 15 to the account of Beneficiary in Bank B. By mistake, on April 1, Bank A executes Originator's payment order by issuing a payment order to Bank B instructing immediate payment to Beneficiary. Bank B credited Beneficiary's account and immediately released the funds to Beneficiary. Under subsection (d) no acceptance by Bank A occurred on April 1 when Originator's payment order was executed because acceptance cannot occur before the execution date which in this case would be April 15 or shortly before that date. Section 4A–301(b). Under Section 4A–402(c), Originator is not obliged to pay Bank A until the order is accepted and that can't occur until the execution date. But Bank A is required to pay Bank B when Bank B accepted Bank A's order on April 1. Unless Originator and Beneficiary are the same person, in almost all cases Originator is paying a debt owed to Beneficiary and early payment does not injure Originator because Originator does not have to pay Bank A until the execution date. Section 4A–402(c). Bank A takes the interest loss. But suppose that on April 3, Originator concludes that no debt was owed to Beneficiary or that the debt was less than the amount of the payment order. Under Section 4A–211(b) Originator can cancel its payment order if Bank A has not accepted. If early execution of Originator's payment order is acceptance, Originator can suffer a loss because cancellation after acceptance is not possible without the consent of Bank A and Bank B. Section 4A–211(c). If Originator has to pay Bank A, Originator would be required to seek recovery of the money from Beneficiary. Subsection (d) prevents this result and puts the risk of loss on Bank A by providing that the early execution does not result in acceptance until the execution date. Since on April 3 Originator's order was not yet accepted, Originator can cancel it under Section 4A–211(b). The result is that Bank A is not entitled to payment from Originator but is obliged to pay Bank B. Bank A has paid Beneficiary by mistake. If Originator's payment order is cancelled, Bank A becomes the originator of an erroneous funds transfer to Beneficiary. Bank A has the burden of recovering payment from Beneficiary on the basis of a payment by mistake. If Beneficiary received the money in good faith in payment of a debt owed to Beneficiary by Originator, the law of mistake and restitution may allow Beneficiary to keep all or part of the money received. If Originator owed money to Beneficiary, Bank A has paid Originator's debt and, under the law of restitution, which applies pursuant to Section 1–103, Bank A is subrogated to Beneficiary's rights against Originator on the debt.

If Bank A is the Beneficiary's bank and Bank A credited Beneficiary's account and released the funds to Beneficiary on April 1, the analysis is similar. If Originator's order is cancelled, Bank A has paid Beneficiary by mistake. The right of Bank A to recover the payment from Beneficiary is similar to Bank A's rights in the preceding paragraph.

§ 11210. Rejection of Payment Order

(a) A payment order is rejected by the receiving bank by a notice of rejection transmitted to the sender orally, electronically, or in writing. A notice of rejection need not use any particular words and is sufficient if it indicates that the receiving bank is rejecting the order or will not execute or pay the order. Rejection is effective when the notice is given if transmission is by a means that is reasonable in the circumstances. If notice of rejection is given by a means that is not reasonable, rejection is effective when the notice is received. If an agreement of the sender and receiving bank establishes the means to be used to reject a payment order, (i) any means complying with the agreement is reasonable and (ii) any means not complying is not reasonable unless no significant delay in receipt of the notice resulted from the use of the noncomplying means.

(b) This subdivision applies if a receiving bank other than the beneficiary's bank fails to execute a payment order despite the existence on the execution date of a withdrawable credit balance in an authorized account of the sender sufficient to cover the order. If the sender does not receive notice of rejection of the order on the execution date and the authorized account of the sender does not bear interest, the bank is obliged to pay interest to the sender on the amount of the order for the number of days elapsing after the execution date to the earlier of the day the order is canceled pursuant to subdivision (d) of Section 11211 or the day the sender receives notice or learns that the order was not executed, counting the final day of the period as an elapsed day. If the withdrawable credit balance during that period falls below the amount of the order, the amount of interest is reduced accordingly.

(c) If a receiving bank suspends payments, all unaccepted payment orders issued to it are deemed rejected at the time the bank suspends payments.

(d) Acceptance of a payment order precludes a later rejection of the order. Rejection of a payment order precludes a later acceptance of the order. *(Added by Stats.1990, c. 125 (S.B.1759), § 2.)*

Uniform Commercial Code Comment

1. With respect to payment orders issued to a receiving bank other than the beneficiary's bank, notice of rejection is not necessary to prevent acceptance of the order. Acceptance can occur only if the receiving bank executes the order. Section 4A–209(a). But notice of rejection will routinely be given by such a bank in cases in which the bank cannot or is not willing to execute the order for some reason. There are many reasons why a bank doesn't execute an order. The payment order may not clearly instruct the receiving bank because of some ambiguity in the order or an internal inconsistency. In some cases, the receiving bank may not be able to carry out the instruction because of equipment failure, credit limitations on the receiving bank, or some other factor which makes proper execution of the order infeasible. In those cases notice of the rejection is a means of informing the sender of the facts so that a corrected payment order can be transmitted or the sender can seek alternate means of completing the funds transfer. The other major reason for not executing an order is that the sender's account is insufficient to cover the order and the receiving bank is not willing to give credit to the sender. If the sender's account is sufficient to cover the order and the receiving bank chooses not to execute the order, notice of rejection is necessary to prevent liability to pay interest to the sender if the case falls within Section 4A–210(b) which is discussed in Comment 3.

2. A payment order to the beneficiary's bank can be accepted by inaction of the bank. Section 4A–209(b)(2) and (3). To prevent acceptance under those provisions it is necessary for the receiving bank to send notice of rejection before acceptance occurs. Subsection (a) of Section 4A–210 states the rule that rejection is accomplished by giving notice of rejection. This incorporates the definitions in Section 1–201(26). Rejection is effective when notice is given if it is given by a means that is reasonable in the circumstances. Otherwise it is effective when the notice is received. The question of when rejection is effective is important only in the relatively few cases under subsection (b)(2) and (3) in which a notice of rejection is necessary to prevent acceptance. The question of whether a particular means is reasonable depends on the facts in a particular case. In a very large percentage of cases the sender and the receiving bank will be in direct electronic contact with each other and in those cases a notice of rejection can be transmitted instantaneously. Since time is of the essence in a large proportion of funds transfers, some quick means of transmission would usually be required, but this is not always the case. The parties may specify by agreement the means by which communication between the parties is to be made.

3. Subsection (b) deals with cases in which a sender does not learn until after the execution date that the sender's order has not been executed. It applies only to cases in which the receiving bank was assured of payment because the sender's account was sufficient to cover the order. Normally, the receiving bank will accept the sender's order if it is assured of payment, but there may be some cases in which the bank chooses to reject. Unless the receiving bank had obligated itself by agreement to accept, the failure to accept is not wrongful. There is no duty of the receiving bank to accept the payment order unless it is obliged to accept by express agreement. Section 4A–212. But even if the bank has not acted wrongfully, the receiving bank had the use of the sender's money that the sender could reasonably assume was to be the source of payment of the funds transfer. Until the sender learns that the order was not accepted the sender is denied the use of that money. Subsection (b) obliges the receiving bank to pay interest to the sender as restitution unless the sender receives notice of rejection on the execution date. The time of receipt of notice is determined pursuant to § 1–201(27). The rate of interest is stated in Section 4A–506. If the sender receives notice on the day after the execution date, the sender is entitled to one day's interest. If receipt of notice is delayed for more than one day, the sender is entitled to interest for each additional day of delay.

4. Subsection (d) treats acceptance and rejection as mutually exclusive. If a payment order has been accepted, rejection of that order becomes impossible. If a payment order has been rejected it cannot be accepted later by the receiving bank. Once notice of rejection has been given, the sender may have acted on the notice by making the payment through other channels. If the receiving bank wants to act on a payment order that it has rejected it has to obtain the consent of the sender. In that case the consent of the sender would amount to the giving of a second payment order that substitutes for the rejected first order. If the receiving bank suspends payments (Section 4–104(1)(k)), subsection (c) provides that unaccepted payment orders are deemed rejected at the time suspension of payments occurs. This prevents acceptance by passage of time under Section 4A–209(b)(3).

§ 11211. Cancellation and Amendment of Payment Order

(a) A communication of the sender of a payment order canceling or amending the order may be transmitted to the receiving bank orally, electronically, or in writing. If a security procedure is in effect between the sender and the receiving bank, the communication is not effective to cancel or amend the order unless the communication is verified pursuant to the security procedure or the bank agrees to the cancellation or amendment.

(b) Subject to subdivision (a), a communication by the sender canceling or amending a payment order is effective to cancel or amend the order if notice of the communication is received at a time and in a manner affording the receiving bank a reasonable opportunity to act on the communication before the bank accepts the payment order.

(c) After a payment order has been accepted, cancellation or amendment of the order is not effective unless the receiving bank agrees or a funds-transfer system rule allows cancellation or amendment without agreement of the bank.

(1) With respect to a payment order accepted by a receiving bank other than the beneficiary's bank, cancellation or amendment is not effective unless a conforming cancellation or amendment of the payment order issued by the receiving bank is also made.

(2) With respect to a payment order accepted by the beneficiary's bank, cancellation or amendment is not effective unless the order was issued in execution of an unauthorized payment order, or because of a mistake by a sender in the funds transfer which resulted in the issuance of a payment order (i) that is a duplicate of a payment order previously issued by the sender, (ii) that orders payment to a beneficiary not entitled to receive payment from the originator, or (iii) that orders payment in an amount greater than the amount the beneficiary was entitled to receive from the originator. If the payment order is canceled or amended, the beneficiary's bank is entitled to recover from the beneficiary any amount paid to the beneficiary to the extent allowed by the law governing mistake and restitution.

(d) An unaccepted payment order is canceled by operation of law at the close of the fifth funds-transfer business day of the receiving bank after the execution date or payment date of the order.

(e) A canceled payment order cannot be accepted. If an accepted payment order is canceled, the acceptance is nullified and no person has any right or obligation based on the acceptance. Amendment of a payment order is deemed to be cancellation of the original order at the time of amendment and issue of a new payment order in the amended form at the same time.

(f) Unless otherwise provided in an agreement of the parties or in a funds-transfer system rule, if the receiving bank, after accepting a payment order, agrees to cancellation or amendment of the order by the sender or is bound by a funds-transfer system rule allowing cancellation or amendment without the bank's agreement, the sender, whether or not cancellation or amendment is effective, is liable to the bank for any loss and expenses, including reasonable attorney's fees, incurred by the bank as a result of the cancellation or amendment or attempted cancellation or amendment.

(g) A payment order is not revoked by the death or legal incapacity of the sender unless the receiving bank knows of the death or of an adjudication of incapacity by a court of competent jurisdiction and has reasonable opportunity to act before acceptance of the order.

(h) A funds-transfer system rule is not effective to the extent it conflicts with paragraph (2) of subdivision (c). *(Added by Stats.1990, c. 125 (S.B.1759), § 2.)*

Uniform Commercial Code Comment

1. This section deals with cancellation and amendment of payment orders. It states the conditions under which cancellation or amendment is both effective and rightful. There is no concept of wrongful cancellation or amendment of a payment order. If the conditions stated in this section are not met the attempted cancellation or amendment is not effective. If the stated conditions are met the cancellation or amendment is effective and rightful. The sender of a payment order may want to withdraw or change the order because the sender has had a change of mind about the transaction or because the payment order was erroneously issued or for any other reason. One common situation is that of multiple transmission of the same order. The sender that mistakenly transmits the same order twice wants to correct the mistake by cancelling the duplicate order. Or, a sender may have intended to order a payment of $1,000,000 but mistakenly issued an order to pay $10,000,000. In this case the sender might try to correct the mistake by cancelling the order and issuing another order in the proper amount. Or, the mistake could be corrected by amending the order to change it to the proper amount. Whether the error is corrected by amendment or cancellation and reissue the net result is the same. This result is stated in the last sentence of subsection (e).

2. Subsection (a) allows a cancellation or amendment of a payment order to be communicated to the receiving bank "orally, electronically, or in writing." The quoted phrase is consistent with the language of Section 4A–103(a) applicable to payment orders. Cancellations and amendments are normally subject to verification pursuant to security procedures to the same extent as payment orders. Subsection (a) recognizes this fact by providing that in cases in which there is a security procedure in effect between the sender and the receiving bank the bank is not bound by a communication cancelling or amending an order unless verification has been made. This is necessary to protect the bank because under subsection (b) a cancellation or amendment can be effective by unilateral action of the sender. Without verification the bank cannot be sure whether the communication was or was not effective to cancel or amend a previously verified payment order.

3. If the receiving bank has not yet accepted the order, there is no reason why the sender should not be able to cancel or amend the order unilaterally so long as the requirements of subsection (a) and (b) are met. If the receiving bank has accepted the order, it is possible to cancel or amend but only if the requirements of subsection (c) are met.

First consider the case of a receiving bank other than the beneficiary's bank. If the bank has not yet accepted the order, the sender can unilaterally cancel or amend. The communication amending or cancelling the payment order must be received in time to allow the bank to act on it before the bank issues its payment order in execution of the sender's order. The time that the sender's communication is received is governed by Section 4A–106. If a payment order does not specify a delayed payment date or execution date, the order will normally be executed shortly after receipt. Thus, as a practical matter, the sender will have very little time in which to instruct cancellation or amendment before acceptance. In addition, a receiving bank will normally have cut-off times for receipt of such communications, and the receiving bank is not obliged to act on communications received after the cut-off hour. Cancellation by the sender after execution of the order by the receiving bank requires the agreement of the bank unless a funds transfer rule otherwise provides. Subsection (c). Although execution of the sender's order by the receiving bank does not itself impose liability on the receiving bank (under Section 4A–402 no liability is incurred by the receiving bank to pay its order until it is accepted), it would commonly be the case that acceptance follows shortly after issuance. Thus, as a practical matter, a receiving bank that has executed a payment order will incur a liability to the next bank in the chain before it would be able to act on the cancellation request of its customer. It is unreasonable to impose on the receiving bank a risk of loss with respect to a cancellation request without the consent of the receiving bank.

The statute does not state how or when the agreement of the receiving bank must be obtained for cancellation after execution. The receiving bank's consent could be obtained at the time cancellation occurs or it could be based on a preexisting agreement. Or, a funds transfer system rule could provide that cancellation can be made unilaterally by the sender. By virtue of that rule any receiving bank covered by the rule is bound. Section 4A–501. If the receiving bank has already executed the sender's order, the bank would not consent to cancellation unless the bank to which the receiving bank has issued its payment order consents to cancellation of that order. It makes no sense to allow cancellation of a payment order unless all subsequent payment orders in the funds transfer that were issued because of the cancelled payment order are also cancelled. Under subsection (c)(1), if a receiving bank consents to cancellation of the payment order after it is executed, the cancellation is not effective unless the receiving bank also cancels the payment order issued by the bank.

4. With respect to a payment order issued to the beneficiary's bank, acceptance is particularly important because it creates liability to pay the beneficiary, it defines when the originator pays its obligation to the beneficiary, and it defines when any obligation for which the payment is made is discharged. Since acceptance affects the rights of the originator and the beneficiary it is not appropriate to allow the beneficiary's bank to agree to cancellation or amendment except in unusual cases. Except as provided in subsection (c)(2), cancellation or amendment after acceptance by the beneficiary's bank is not possible unless all parties affected by the order agree. Under subsection (c)(2), cancellation or amendment is possible only in the four cases stated. The following examples illustrate subsection (c)(2):

Case #1. Originator's Bank executed a payment order issued in the name of its customer as sender. The order was not authorized by the customer and was fraudulently issued. Beneficiary's Bank accepted the payment order issued by Originator's Bank. Under subsection (c)(2) Originator's Bank can cancel the order if Beneficiary's Bank consents. It doesn't make any difference whether the payment order that Originator's Bank accepted was or was not enforceable against the customer under Section 4A–202(b). Verification under that provision is important in determining whether Originator's Bank or the customer has the risk of loss, but it has no relevance under Section 4A–211(c)(2). Whether or not verified, the payment order was not authorized by the customer. Cancellation of the payment order to Beneficiary's Bank causes the acceptance of Beneficiary's Bank to be nullified. Subsection (e). Beneficiary's Bank is entitled to recover payment from the beneficiary to the extent allowed by the law of mistake and restitution. In this kind of case the beneficiary is usually a party to the fraud who has no right to receive or retain payment of the order.

Case #2. Originator owed Beneficiary $1,000,000 and ordered Bank A to pay that amount to the account of Beneficiary in Bank B. Bank A issued a complying order to Bank B, but by mistake issued a duplicate order as well. Bank B accepted both orders. Under subsection (c)(2)(i) cancellation of the duplicate order could be made by Bank A with the consent of Bank B. Beneficiary has no right to receive or retain payment of the duplicate payment order if only $1,000,000 was owed by Originator to Beneficiary. If Originator owed $2,000,000 to Beneficiary, the law of restitution might allow Beneficiary to retain the $1,000,000 paid by Bank B on the duplicate order. In that case Bank B is entitled to reimbursement from Bank A under subsection (f).

Case #3. Originator owed $1,000,000 to X. Intending to pay X, Originator ordered Bank A to pay $1,000,000 to Y's account in Bank B. Bank A issued a complying payment order to Bank B which Bank B accepted by releasing the $1,000,000 to Y. Under subsection (c)(2)(ii) Bank A can cancel its payment order to Bank B with the consent of Bank B if Y was not entitled to receive payment from Originator. Originator can also cancel its order to Bank A with Bank A's consent. Subsection (c)(1). Bank B may recover the $1,000,000 from Y unless the law of mistake and restitution allows Y to retain some or all of the amount paid. If no debt was owed to Y, Bank B should have a right of recovery.

Case #4. Originator owed Beneficiary $10,000. By mistake Originator ordered Bank A to pay $1,000,000 to the account of Beneficiary in Bank B. Bank A issued a complying order to Bank B which accepted by notifying Beneficiary of its right to withdraw $1,000,000. Cancellation is permitted in this case under subsection (c)(2)(iii). If Bank B paid Beneficiary it is entitled to recover the payment except to the extent the law of mistake and restitution allows Beneficiary to retain payment. In this case Beneficiary might be entitled to retain $10,000, the amount of the debt owed to Beneficiary. If Beneficiary may retain $10,000, Bank B would be entitled to $10,000 from Bank A pursuant to subsection (f).

In this case Originator also cancelled its order. Thus Bank A would be entitled to $10,000 from Originator pursuant to subsection (f).

5. Unless constrained by a funds transfer system rule, a receiving bank may agree to cancellation or amendment of the payment order under subsection (c) but is not required to do so regardless of the circumstances. If the receiving bank has incurred liability as a result of its acceptance of the sender's order, there are substantial risks in agreeing to cancellation or amendment. This is particularly true for a beneficiary's bank. Cancellation or amendment after acceptance by the beneficiary's bank can be made only in the four cases stated and the beneficiary's bank may not have any way of knowing whether the requirements of subsection (c) have been met or whether it will be able to recover payment from the beneficiary that received payment. Even with indemnity the beneficiary's bank may be reluctant to alienate its customer, the beneficiary, by denying the customer the funds. Subsection (c) leaves the decision to the beneficiary's bank unless the consent of the beneficiary's bank is not required under a funds transfer system rule or other interbank agreement. If a receiving bank agrees to cancellation or amendment under subsection (c)(1) or (2), it is automatically entitled to indemnification from the sender under subsection (f). The indemnification provision recognizes that a sender has no right to cancel a payment order after it is accepted by the receiving bank. If the receiving bank agrees to cancellation, it is doing so as an accommodation to the sender and it should not incur a risk of loss in doing so.

6. Acceptance by the receiving bank of a payment order issued by the sender is comparable to acceptance of an offer under the law of contracts. Under that law the death or legal incapacity of an offeror terminates the offer even though the offeree has no notice of the death or incapacity. Restatement Second, Contracts § 48. Comment a. to that section state that the "rule seems to be a relic of the obsolete view that a contract requires a 'meeting of minds,' and it is out of harmony with the modern doctrine that a manifestation of assent is effective without regard to actual mental assent." Subsection (g), which reverses the Restatement rule in the case of a payment order, is similar to Section 4–405(1) which applies to checks. Subsection (g) does not address the effect of the bankruptcy of the sender of a payment order before the order is accepted, but the principle of subsection (g) has been recognized in Bank of Marin v. England, 385 U.S. 99 (1966). Although Bankruptcy Code Section 542(c) may not have been drafted with wire transfers in mind, its language can be read to allow the receiving bank to charge the sender's account for the amount of the payment order if the receiving bank executed it in ignorance of the bankruptcy.

7. Subsection (d) deals with stale payment orders. Payment orders normally are executed on the execution date or the day after. An order issued to the beneficiary's bank is normally accepted on the payment date or the day after. If a payment order is not accepted on its execution or payment date or shortly thereafter, it is probable that there was some problem with the terms of the order or the sender did not have sufficient funds or credit to cover the amount of the order. Delayed acceptance of such an order is normally not contemplated, but the order may not have been cancelled by the sender. Subsection (d) provides for cancellation by operation of law to prevent an unexpected delayed acceptance.

8. A funds transfer system rule can govern rights and obligations between banks that are parties to payment orders transmitted over the system even if the rule conflicts with Article 4A. In some cases, however, a rule governing a transaction between two banks can affect a third party in an unacceptable way. Subsection (h) deals with such a case. A funds transfer system rule cannot allow cancellation of a payment order accepted by the beneficiary's bank if the rule conflicts with subsection (c)(2). Because rights of the beneficiary and the originator are directly affected by acceptance, subsection (c)(2) severely limits cancellation. These limitations cannot be altered by funds transfer system rule.

§ 11212. Liability and Duty of Receiving Bank Regarding Unaccepted Payment Order

If a receiving bank fails to accept a payment order that it is obliged by express agreement to accept, the bank is liable for breach of the agreement to the extent provided in the agreement or in this division, but does not otherwise have any duty to accept a payment order or, before acceptance, to take any action, or refrain from taking action, with respect to the order except as provided in this division or by express agreement. Liability based on acceptance arises only when acceptance occurs as stated in Section 11209, and liability is limited to that provided in this division. A receiving bank is not the agent of the sender or beneficiary of the payment order it accepts, or of any other party to the funds transfer, and the bank owes no duty to any party to the funds transfer except as provided in this division or by express agreement. *(Added by Stats.1990, c. 125 (S.B.1759), § 2.)*

Uniform Commercial Code Comment

With limited exceptions stated in this Article, the duties and obligations of receiving banks that carry out a funds transfer arise only as a result of acceptance of payment orders or of agreements made by receiving banks. Exceptions are stated in Section 4A–209(b)(3) and Section 4A–210(b). A receiving bank is not like a collecting bank under Article 4. No receiving bank, whether it be an originator's bank, an intermediary bank or a beneficiary's bank, is an agent for any other party in the funds transfer.

CHAPTER 3. EXECUTION OF SENDER'S PAYMENT ORDER BY RECEIVING BANK

Section
11301. Execution and Execution Date.
11302. Obligations of Receiving Bank in Execution of Payment Order.
11303. Erroneous Execution of Payment Order.
11304. Duty of Sender to Report Erroneously Executed Payment Order.
11305. Liability for Late or Improper Execution or Failure to Execute Payment Order.

§ 11301. Execution and Execution Date

(a) A payment order is "executed" by the receiving bank when it issues a payment order intended to carry out the payment order received by the bank. A payment order received by the beneficiary's bank can be accepted but cannot be executed.

(b) "Execution date" of a payment order means the day on which the receiving bank may properly issue a payment order in execution of the sender's order. The execution date may be determined by instruction of the sender but cannot be earlier than the day the order is received and, unless otherwise determined, is the day the order is received. If the sender's instruction states a payment date, the execution date is the payment date or an earlier date on which execution is reasonably necessary to allow payment to the beneficiary on the payment date. *(Added by Stats.1990, c. 125 (S.B.1759), § 2.)*

Uniform Commercial Code Comment

1. The terms "executed," "execution" and "execution date" are used only with respect to a payment order to a receiving bank other than the beneficiary's bank. The beneficiary's bank can accept the payment order that it receives, but it does not execute the order. Execution refers to the act of the receiving bank in issuing a payment order "intended to carry out" the payment order that the bank received. A receiving bank has executed an order even if the order issued by the bank does not carry out the order received by the bank. For example, the bank may have erroneously issued an order to the wrong beneficiary, or in the wrong amount or to the wrong beneficiary's bank. In each of these cases execution has occurred but the execution is erroneous. Erroneous execution is covered in Section 4A–303.

2. "Execution date" refers to the time a payment order should be executed rather than the day it is actually executed. Normally the sender will not specify an execution date, but most payment orders are meant to be executed immediately. Thus, the execution date is normally the day the order is received by the receiving bank. It is common for the sender to specify a "payment date" which is defined in Section 4A–401 as "the day on which the amount of the order is payable to the beneficiary by the beneficiary's bank." Except for automated clearing house transfers, if a funds transfer is entirely within the United States and the payment is to be carried out electronically, the execution date is the payment date unless the order is received after the payment date. If the payment is to be carried out through an automated clearing house, execution may occur before the payment date. In an ACH transfer the beneficiary is usually paid one or two days after issue of the originator's payment order. The execution date is determined by the stated payment date and is a date before the payment date on which execution is reasonably necessary to allow payment on the payment date. A funds transfer system rule could also determine the execution date of orders received by the receiving bank if both the sender and the receiving bank are participants in the funds transfer system. The execution date can be determined by the payment order itself or by separate instructions of the sender or an agreement of the sender and the receiving bank. The second sentence of subsection (b) must be read in the light of Section 4A–106 which states that if a payment order is received after the cut-off time of the receiving bank it may be treated by the bank as received at the opening of the next funds transfer business day.

3. Execution on the execution date is timely, but the order can be executed before or after the execution date. Section 4A–209(d) and Section 4A–402(c) state the consequences of early execution and Section 4A–305(a) states the consequences of late execution.

§ 11302. Obligations of Receiving Bank in Execution of Payment Order

(a) Except as provided in subdivisions (b) to (d), inclusive, if the receiving bank accepts a payment order pursuant to subdivision (a) of Section 11209, the bank has the following obligations in executing the order:

(1) The receiving bank is obliged to issue, on the execution date, a payment order complying with the sender's order and to follow the sender's instructions concerning (i) any intermediary bank or funds-transfer system to be used in carrying out the funds transfer, or (ii) the means by which payment orders are to be transmitted in the funds transfer. If the originator's bank issues a payment order to an intermediary bank, the originator's bank is obliged to instruct the intermediary bank according to the instruction of the originator. An intermediary bank in the funds transfer is similarly bound by an instruction given to it by the sender of the payment order it accepts.

(2) If the sender's instruction states that the funds transfer is to be carried out telephonically or by wire transfer or otherwise indicates that the funds transfer is to be carried out by the most expeditious means, the receiving bank is obliged to transmit its payment order by the most expeditious available means, and to instruct any intermediary bank accordingly. If a sender's instruction states a payment date, the receiving bank is obliged to transmit its payment order at a time and by means reasonably necessary to allow payment to the beneficiary on the payment date or as soon thereafter as is feasible.

§ 11302

(b) Unless otherwise instructed, a receiving bank executing a payment order may (i) use any funds-transfer system if use of that system is reasonable in the circumstances, and (ii) issue a payment order to the beneficiary's bank or to an intermediary bank through which a payment order conforming to the sender's order can expeditiously be issued to the beneficiary's bank if the receiving bank exercises ordinary care in the selection of the intermediary bank. A receiving bank is not required to follow an instruction of the sender designating a funds-transfer system to be used in carrying out the funds transfer if the receiving bank, in good faith, determines that it is not feasible to follow the instruction or that following the instruction would unduly delay completion of the funds transfer.

(c) Unless paragraph (2) of subdivision (a) applies or the receiving bank is otherwise instructed, the bank may execute a payment order by transmitting its payment order by first-class mail or by any means reasonable in the circumstances. If the receiving bank is instructed to execute the sender's order by transmitting its payment order by a particular means, the receiving bank may issue its payment order by the means stated or by any means as expeditious as the means stated.

(d) Unless instructed by the sender, (i) the receiving bank may not obtain payment of its charges for services and expenses in connection with the execution of the sender's order by issuing a payment order in an amount equal to the amount of the sender's order less the amount of the charges, and (ii) may not instruct a subsequent receiving bank to obtain payment of its charges in the same manner. *(Added by Stats.1990, c. 125 (S.B.1759), § 2.)*

Uniform Commercial Code Comment

1. In the absence of agreement, the receiving bank is not obliged to execute an order of the sender. Section 4A–212. Section 4A–302 states the manner in which the receiving bank may execute the sender's order if execution occurs. Subsection (a)(1) states the residual rule. The payment order issued by the receiving bank must comply with the sender's order and, unless some other rule is stated in the section, the receiving bank is obliged to follow any instruction of the sender concerning which funds transfer system is to be used, which intermediary banks are to be used, and what means of transmission is to be used. The instruction of the sender may be incorporated in the payment order itself or may be given separately. For example, there may be a master agreement between the sender and receiving bank containing instructions governing payment orders to be issued from time to time by the sender to the receiving bank. In most funds transfers, speed is a paramount consideration. A sender that wants assurance that the funds transfer will be expeditiously completed can specify the means to be used. The receiving bank can follow the instructions literally or it can use an equivalent means. For example, if the sender instructs the receiving bank to transmit by telex, the receiving bank could use telephone instead. Subsection (c). In most cases, the sender will not specify a particular means but will use a general term such as "by wire" or "wire transfer" or "as soon as possible." These words signify that the sender wants a same-day transfer. In these cases the receiving bank is required to use a telephonic or electronic communication to transmit its order and is also required to instruct any intermediary bank to which it issues its order to transmit by similar means. Subsection (a)(2). In other cases, such as an automated clearing house transfer, a same-day transfer is not contemplated. Normally the sender's instruction or the context in which the payment order is received makes clear the type of funds transfer that is appropriate. If the sender states a payment date with respect to the payment order, the receiving bank is obliged to execute the order at a time and in a manner to meet the payment date if that is feasible. Subsection (a)(2). This provision would apply to many ACH transfers made to pay recurring debts of the sender. In other cases, involving relatively small amounts, time may not be an important factor and cost may be a more important element. Fast means, such as telephone or electronic transmission, are more expensive than slow means such as mailing. Subsection (c) states that in the absence of instructions the receiving bank is given discretion to decide. It may issue its payment order by first class mail or by any means reasonable in the circumstances. Section 4A–305 states the liability of a receiving bank for breach of the obligations stated in Section 4A–302.

2. Subsection (b) concerns the choice of intermediary banks to be used in completing the funds transfer, and the funds transfer system to be used. If the receiving bank is not instructed about the matter, it can issue an order directly to the beneficiary's bank or can issue an order to an intermediary bank. The receiving bank also has discretion concerning use of a funds transfer system. In some cases it may be reasonable to use either an automated clearing house system or a wire transfer system such as Fedwire or CHIPS. Normally, the receiving bank will follow the instruction of the sender in these matters, but in some cases it may be prudent for the bank not to follow instructions. The sender may have designated a funds transfer system to be used in carrying out the funds transfer, but it may not be feasible to use the designated system because of some impediment such as a computer breakdown which prevents prompt execution of the order. The receiving bank is permitted to use an alternate means of transmittal in a good faith effort to execute the order expeditiously. The same leeway is not given to the receiving bank if the sender designates an intermediary bank through which the funds transfer is to be routed. The sender's designation of that intermediary bank may mean that the beneficiary's bank is expecting to obtain a credit from that intermediary bank and may have relied on that anticipated credit. If the receiving bank uses another intermediary bank the expectations of the beneficiary's bank may not be realized. The receiving bank could choose to route the transfer to another intermediary bank and then to the designated intermediary bank if there was some reason such as a lack of a correspondent-bank relationship or a bilateral credit limitation, but the designated intermediary bank cannot be circumvented. To do so violates the sender's instructions.

3. The normal rule, under subsection (a)(1), is that the receiving bank, in executing a payment order, is required to issue a payment order that complies as to amount with that of the sender's order. In most cases the receiving bank issues an order equal to the amount of the sender's order and makes a separate charge for services and expenses in executing the sender's order. In some cases, particularly if it is an intermediary bank that is executing an order, charges are collected by deducting them from the amount of the payment order issued by the executing bank. If that is done, the amount of the payment order accepted by the beneficiary's bank will be slightly less than the amount of the originator's payment order. For example, Originator, in order to pay an obligation of $1,000,000 owed to Beneficiary, issues a payment order to Originator's Bank to pay $1,000,000 to the account of Beneficiary in Beneficiary's Bank. Originator's Bank issues a payment order to Intermediary Bank for $1,000,000 and debits Originator's account for $1,000,010. The extra $10 is the fee of Originator's Bank. Intermediary Bank executes the payment order of Originator's Bank by issuing a payment order to Beneficiary's Bank for $999,990, but under § 4A–402(c) is entitled to receive $1,000,000 from Originator's Bank. The $10 difference is the fee of Intermediary Bank. Beneficiary's Bank credits Beneficiary's account for $999,990. When Beneficiary's Bank accepts the payment order of Intermediary Bank the result is a payment of $999,990 from Originator to Beneficiary. Section 4A–406(a). If that payment discharges the $1,000,000 debt, the effect is that Beneficiary has paid the charges of Intermediary Bank and Originator has paid the charges of Originator's Bank. Subsection (d) of Section 4A–302 allows Intermediary Bank to collect its charges by deducting them from the amount of the payment order, but only if instructed to do so by Originator's Bank. Originator's Bank is not authorized to give that instruction to Intermediary Bank unless Originator authorized the instruction. Thus, Originator can control how the charges of Originator's Bank and Intermediary Bank are to be paid. Subsection (d) does not apply to charges of Beneficiary's Bank to Beneficiary.

In the case discussed in the preceding paragraph the $10 charge is trivial in relation to the amount of the payment and it may not be important to Beneficiary how the charge is paid. But it may be very important if the $1,000,000 obligation represented the price of exercising a right such as an option favorable to Originator and unfavorable to Beneficiary. Beneficiary might well argue that it was entitled to receive $1,000,000. If the option was exercised shortly before its expiration date, the result could be loss of the option benefit because the required payment of $1,000,000 was not made before the option expired. Section 4A–406(c) allows Originator to preserve the option benefit. The amount received by Beneficiary is deemed to be $1,000,000 unless Beneficiary demands the $10 and Originator does not pay it.

§ 11303. Erroneous Execution of Payment Order

(a) A receiving bank that (i) executes the payment order of the sender by issuing a payment order in an amount greater than the amount of the sender's order, or (ii) issues a payment order in execution of the sender's order and then issues a duplicate order, is entitled to payment of the amount of the sender's order under subdivision (c) of Section 11402 if that subdivision is otherwise satisfied. The bank is entitled to recover from the beneficiary of the erroneous order the excess payment received to the extent allowed by the law governing mistake and restitution.

(b) A receiving bank that executes the payment order of the sender by issuing a payment order in an amount less than the amount of the sender's order is entitled to payment of the amount of the sender's order under subdivision (c) of Section 11402 if (i) that subdivision is otherwise satisfied and (ii) the bank corrects its mistake by issuing an additional payment order for the benefit of the beneficiary of the sender's order. If the error is not corrected, the issuer of the erroneous order is entitled to receive or retain payment from the sender of the order it accepted only to the extent of the amount of the erroneous order. This subdivision does not apply if the receiving bank executes the sender's payment order by issuing a payment order in an amount less than the amount of the sender's order for the purpose of obtaining payment of its charges for services and expenses pursuant to instruction of the sender.

(c) If a receiving bank executes the payment order of the sender by issuing a payment order to a beneficiary different from the beneficiary of the sender's order and the funds transfer is completed on the basis of that error, the sender of the payment order that was erroneously executed and all previous senders in the funds transfer are not obliged to pay the payment orders they issued. The issuer of the erroneous order is entitled to recover from the beneficiary of the order the payment received to the extent allowed by the law governing mistake and restitution. *(Added by Stats. 1990, c. 125 (S.B.1759), § 2.)*

Uniform Commercial Code Comment

1. Section 4A–303 states the effect of erroneous execution of a payment order by the receiving bank. Under Section 4A–402(c) the sender of a payment order is obliged to pay the amount of the order to the receiving bank if the bank executes the order, but the obligation to pay is excused if the beneficiary's bank does not accept a payment order instructing payment to the beneficiary of the sender's order. If erroneous execution of the sender's order causes the wrong beneficiary to be paid, the sender is not required to pay. If erroneous execution causes the wrong amount to be paid the sender is not obliged to pay the receiving bank an amount in excess of the amount of the sender's order. Section 4A–303 takes precedence over Section 4A–402(c) and states the liability of the sender and the rights of the receiving bank in various cases of erroneous execution.

2. Subsections (a) and (b) deal with cases in which the receiving bank executes by issuing a payment order in the wrong amount. If Originator ordered Originator's Bank to pay $1,000,000 to the account of Beneficiary in Beneficiary's Bank, but Originator's Bank erroneously instructed Beneficiary's Bank to pay $2,000,000 to Beneficiary's account, subsection (a) applies. If Beneficiary's Bank accepts the order of Originator's Bank, Beneficiary's Bank is entitled to receive $2,000,000 from Originator's Bank, but Originator's Bank is entitled to receive only $1,000,000 from Originator. Originator's Bank is entitled to recover the overpayment from Beneficiary to the extent allowed by the law governing mistake and restitution. Originator's Bank would normally have a right to recover the overpayment from Beneficiary, but in unusual cases the law of restitution might allow Beneficiary to keep all or part of the overpayment. For example, if Originator owed $2,000,000 to Beneficiary and Beneficiary received the extra $1,000,000 in good faith in discharge of the debt, Beneficiary may be allowed to keep it. In this case Originator's Bank has paid an obligation of Originator and under the law of restitution, which applies through Section 1–103, Originator's Bank would be subrogated to Beneficiary's rights against Originator on the obligation paid by Originator's Bank.

If Originator's Bank erroneously executed Originator's order by instructing Beneficiary's Bank to pay less than $1,000,000, subsection (b) applies. If Originator's Bank corrects its error by issuing another payment order to Beneficiary's Bank that results in payment of $1,000,000 to Beneficiary, Originator's Bank is entitled to payment of $1,000,000 from Originator. If the mistake is not corrected, Originator's Bank is entitled to payment from Originator only in the amount of the order issued by Originator's Bank.

3. Subsection (a) also applies to duplicate payment orders. Assume Originator's Bank properly executes Originator's $1,000,000 payment order and then by mistake issues a second $1,000,000 payment order in execution of Originator's order. If Beneficiary's Bank accepts both orders issued by Originator's Bank, Beneficiary's Bank is entitled to receive $2,000,000 from Originator's Bank, but Originator's Bank is entitled to receive only $1,000,000 from Originator. The remedy of Originator's Bank is the same as that of a receiving bank that executes by issuing an order in an amount greater than the sender's order. It may recover the overpayment from Beneficiary to the extent allowed by the law governing mistake and restitution and in a proper case as stated in Comment 2 may have subrogation rights if it is not entitled to recover from Beneficiary.

4. Suppose Originator instructs Originator's Bank to pay $1,000,000 to Account #12345 in Beneficiary's Bank. Originator's Bank erroneously instructs Beneficiary's Bank to pay $1,000,000 to Account #12346 and Beneficiary's Bank accepted. Subsection (c) covers this case. Originator is not obliged to pay its payment order, but Originator's Bank is required to pay $1,000,000 to Beneficiary's Bank. The remedy of Originator's Bank is to recover $1,000,000 from the holder of Account #12346 that received payment by mistake. Recovery based on the law of mistake and restitution is described in Comment 2.

§ 11304. Duty of Sender to Report Erroneously Executed Payment Order

If the sender of a payment order that is erroneously executed as stated in Section 11303 receives notification from the receiving bank that the order was executed or that the sender's account was debited with respect to the order, the sender has a duty to exercise ordinary care to determine, on the basis of information available to the sender, that the order was erroneously executed and to notify the bank of the relevant facts within a reasonable time not exceeding 90 days after the notification from the bank was received by the sender. If the sender fails to perform that duty, the bank is not obliged to pay interest on any amount refundable to the sender under subdivision (d) of Section 11402 for the period before the bank learns of the execution error. The bank is not entitled to any recovery from the sender on account of a

§ 11304

failure by the sender to perform the duty stated in this section. *(Added by Stats.1990, c. 125 (S.B.1759), § 2.)*

Uniform Commercial Code Comment

This section is identical in effect to Section 4A–204 which applies to unauthorized orders issued in the name of a customer of the receiving bank. The rationale is stated in Comment 2 to Section 4A–204.

§ 11305. Liability for Late or Improper Execution or Failure to Execute Payment Order

(a) If a funds transfer is completed but execution of a payment order by the receiving bank in breach of Section 11302 results in delay in payment to the beneficiary, the bank is obliged to pay interest to either the originator or the beneficiary of the funds transfer for the period of delay caused by the improper execution. Except as provided in subdivision (c), additional damages are not recoverable.

(b) If execution of a payment order by a receiving bank in breach of Section 11302 results in (i) noncompletion of the funds transfer, (ii) failure to use an intermediary bank designated by the originator, or (iii) issuance of a payment order that does not comply with the terms of the payment order of the originator, the bank is liable to the originator for its expenses in the funds transfer and for incidental expenses and interest losses, to the extent not covered by subdivision (a), resulting from the improper execution. Except as provided in subdivision (c), additional damages are not recoverable.

(c) In addition to the amounts payable under subdivisions (a) and (b), damages, including consequential damages, are recoverable to the extent provided in an express written agreement of the receiving bank.

(d) If a receiving bank fails to execute a payment order it was obliged by express agreement to execute, the receiving bank is liable to the sender for its expenses in the transaction and for incidental expenses and interest losses resulting from the failure to execute. Additional damages, including consequential damages, are recoverable to the extent provided in an express written agreement of the receiving bank, but are not otherwise recoverable.

(e) Reasonable attorney's fees are recoverable if demand for compensation under subdivision (a) or (b) is made and refused before an action is brought on the claim. If a claim is made for breach of an agreement under subdivision (d) and the agreement does not provide for damages, reasonable attorney's fees are recoverable if demand for compensation under subdivision (d) is made and refused before an action is brought on the claim.

(f) Except as stated in this section, the liability of a receiving bank under subdivisions (a) and (b) may not be varied by agreement. *(Added by Stats.1990, c. 125 (S.B.1759), § 2.)*

Uniform Commercial Code Comment

1. Subsection (a) covers cases of delay in completion of a funds transfer resulting from an execution by a receiving bank in breach of Section 4A–302(a). The receiving bank is obliged to pay interest on the amount of the order for the period of the delay. The rate of interest is stated in Section 4A–506. With respect to wire transfers (other than ACH transactions) within the United States, the expectation is that the funds transfer will be completed the same day. In those cases, the originator can reasonably expect that the originator's account will be debited on the same day as the beneficiary's account is credited. If the funds transfer is delayed, compensation can be paid either to the originator or to the beneficiary. The normal practice is to compensate the beneficiary's bank to allow that bank to compensate the beneficiary by back-valuing the payment by the number of days of delay. Thus, the beneficiary is in the same position that it would have been in if the funds transfer had been completed on the same day. Assume on Day 1, Originator's Bank issues its payment order to Intermediary Bank which is received on that day. Intermediary Bank does not execute that order until Day 2 when it issues an order to Beneficiary's Bank which is accepted on that day. Intermediary Bank complies with subsection (a) by paying one day's interest to Beneficiary's Bank for the account of Beneficiary.

2. Subsection (b) applies to cases of breach of Section 4A–302 involving more than mere delay. In those cases the bank is liable for damages for improper execution but they are limited to compensation for interest losses and incidental expenses of the sender resulting from the breach, the expenses of the sender in the funds transfer and attorney's fees. This subsection reflects the judgment that imposition of consequential damages on a bank for commission of an error is not justified.

The leading common law case on the subject of consequential damages is Evra Corp. v. Swiss Bank Corp., 673 F.2d 951 (7th Cir.1982), in which Swiss Bank, an intermediary bank, failed to execute a payment order. Because the beneficiary did not receive timely payment the originator lost a valuable ship charter. The lower court awarded the originator $2.1 million for lost profits even though the amount of the payment order was only $27,000. The Seventh Circuit reversed, in part on the basis of the common law rule of Hadley v. Baxendale that consequential damages may not be awarded unless the defendant is put on notice of the special circumstances giving rise to them. Swiss Bank may have known that the originator was paying the shipowner for the hire of a vessel but did not know that a favorable charter would be lost if the payment was delayed. "Electronic payments are not so unusual as to automatically place a bank on notice of extraordinary consequences if such a transfer goes awry. Swiss Bank did not have enough information to infer that if it lost a $27,000 payment order it would face liability in excess of $2 million." 673 F.2d at 956.

If *Evra* means that consequential damages can be imposed if the culpable bank has notice of particular circumstances giving rise to the damages, it does not provide an acceptable solution to the problem of bank liability for consequential damages. In the typical case transmission of the payment order is made electronically. Personnel of the receiving bank that process payment orders are not the appropriate people to evaluate the risk of liability for consequential damages in relation to the price charged for the wire transfer service. Even if notice is received by higher level management personnel who could make an appropriate decision whether the risk is justified by the price, liability based on notice would require evaluation of payment orders on an individual basis. This kind of evaluation is inconsistent with the high-speed, low-price, mechanical nature of the processing system that characterizes wire transfers. Moreover, in *Evra* the culpable bank was an intermediary bank with which the originator did not deal. Notice to the originator's bank would not bind the intermediary bank, and it seems impractical for the originator's bank to convey notice of this kind to intermediary banks in the funds transfer. The success of the wholesale wire transfer industry has largely been based on its ability to effect payment at low cost and great speed. Both of the these essential aspects of the modern wire transfer system would be adversely affected by a rule that imposed on banks liability for consequential damages. A banking industry amicus brief in *Evra* stated: "Whether banks can continue to make EFT services available on a widespread basis, by charging reasonable rates, depends on whether they can do so without incurring unlimited consequential risks. Certainly, no bank would handle for $3.25 a transaction entailing potential liability in the millions of dollars."

As the court in *Evra* also noted, the originator of the funds transfer is in the best position to evaluate the risk that a funds transfer will not be made on time and to manage that risk by issuing a payment order in time to allow monitoring of the transaction. The originator, by asking the beneficiary, can quickly determine if the funds transfer has been completed. If the originator has sent the payment order at a time that allows a reasonable margin for correcting error, no loss is likely to result if the transaction is monitored. The other published cases on this issue reach the *Evra* result. Central Coordinates, Inc. v. Morgan Guaranty Trust Co., 40 U.C.C. Rep.Serv. 1340 (N.Y.Sup.Ct.1985), and Gatoil (U.S.A.), Inc. v. Forest Hill State Bank, 1 U.C.C. Rep.Serv.2d 171 (D.Md.1986).

Subsection (c) allows the measure of damages in subsection (b) to be increased by an express written agreement of the receiving bank. An originator's bank might be willing to assume additional responsibilities and incur additional liability in exchange for a higher fee.

3. Subsection (d) governs cases in which a receiving bank has obligated itself by express agreement to accept payment orders of a sender. In the absence of such an agreement there is no obligation by a receiving bank to accept a payment order. Section 4A–212. The measure of damages for breach of an agreement to accept a payment order is the same as that stated in subsection (b). As in the case of subsection (b), additional damages, including consequential damages, may be recovered to the extent stated in an express written agreement of the receiving bank.

4. Reasonable attorney's fees are recoverable only in cases in which damages are limited to statutory damages stated in subsection (a), (b) and (d). If additional damages are recoverable because provided for by an express written agreement, attorney's fees are not recoverable. The rationale is that there is no need for statutory attorney's fees in the latter case, because the parties have agreed to a measure of damages which may or may not provide for attorney's fees.

5. The effect of subsection (f) is to prevent reduction of a receiving bank's liability under Section 4A–305.

CHAPTER 4. PAYMENT

Section
11401. Payment Date.
11402. Obligation of Sender to Pay Receiving Bank.
11403. Payment by Sender to Receiving Bank.
11404. Obligation of Beneficiary's Bank to Pay and Give Notice to Beneficiary.
11405. Payment by Beneficiary's Bank to Beneficiary.
11406. Payment by Originator to Beneficiary; Discharge of Underlying Obligation.

§ 11401. Payment Date

"Payment date" of a payment order means the day on which the amount of the order is payable to the beneficiary by the beneficiary's bank. The payment date may be determined by instruction of the sender but cannot be earlier than the day the order is received by the beneficiary's bank and, unless otherwise determined, is the day the order is received by the beneficiary's bank. *(Added by Stats.1990, c. 125 (S.B.1759), § 2.)*

Uniform Commercial Code Comment

"Payment date" refers to the day the beneficiary's bank is to pay the beneficiary. The payment date may be expressed in various ways so long as it indicates the day the beneficiary is to receive payment. For example, in ACH transfers the payment date is the equivalent of "settlement date" or "effective date." Payment date applies to the payment order issued to the beneficiary's bank, but a payment order issued to a receiving bank other than the beneficiary's bank may also state a date for payment to the beneficiary. In the latter case, the statement of a payment date is to instruct the receiving bank concerning time of execution of the sender's order. Section 4A–301(b).

§ 11402. Obligation of Sender to Pay Receiving Bank

(a) This section is subject to Sections 11205 and 11207.

(b) With respect to a payment order issued to the beneficiary's bank, acceptance of the order by the bank obliges the sender to pay the bank the amount of the order, but payment is not due until the payment date of the order.

(c) This subdivision is subject to subdivision (e) and to Section 11303. With respect to a payment order issued to a receiving bank other than the beneficiary's bank, acceptance of the order by the receiving bank obliges the sender to pay the bank the amount of the sender's order. Payment by the sender is not due until the execution date of the sender's order. The obligation of that sender to pay its payment order is excused if the funds transfer is not completed by acceptance by the beneficiary's bank of a payment order instructing payment to the beneficiary of that sender's payment order.

(d) If the sender of a payment order pays the order and was not obliged to pay all or part of the amount paid, the bank receiving payment is obliged to refund payment to the extent the sender was not obliged to pay. Except as provided in Sections 11204 and 11304, interest is payable on the refundable amount from the date of payment.

(e) If a funds transfer is not completed as stated in subdivision (c) and an intermediary bank is obliged to refund payment as stated in subdivision (d) but is unable to do so because it is not permitted by applicable law or because the bank suspends payments, a sender in the funds transfer that executed a payment order in compliance with an instruction, as stated in paragraph (1) of subdivision (a) of Section 11302, to route the funds transfer through that intermediary bank is entitled to receive or retain payment from the sender of the payment order that it accepted. The first sender in the funds transfer that issued an instruction requiring routing through that intermediary bank is subrogated to the right of the bank that paid the intermediary bank to refund as stated in subdivision (d).

(f) The right of the sender of a payment order to be excused from the obligation to pay the order as stated in subdivision (c) or to receive refund under subdivision (d) may not be varied by agreement. *(Added by Stats.1990, c. 125 (S.B.1759), § 2.)*

Uniform Commercial Code Comment

1. Subsection (b) states that the sender of a payment order to the beneficiary's bank must pay the order when the beneficiary's bank accepts the order. At that point the beneficiary's bank is obliged to pay the beneficiary. Section 4A–404(a). The last clause of subsection (b) covers a case of premature acceptance by the beneficiary's bank. In some funds transfers, notably automated clearing house transfers, a beneficiary's bank may receive a payment order with a payment date after the day the order is received. The beneficiary's bank might accept the order before the payment date by notifying the beneficiary of receipt of the order. Although the acceptance obliges the beneficiary's bank to pay the beneficiary, payment is not due until the payment date. The last clause of subsection (b) is consistent with that result. The beneficiary's bank is also not entitled to payment from the sender until the payment date.

2. Assume that Originator instructs Bank A to order immediate payment to the account of Beneficiary in Bank B. Execution of

§ 11402

Originator's payment order by Bank A is acceptance under Section 4A–209(a). Under the second sentence of Section 4A–402(c) the acceptance creates an obligation of Originator to pay Bank A the amount of the order. The last clause of that sentence deals with attempted funds transfers that are not completed. In that event the obligation of the sender to pay its payment order is excused. Originator makes payment to Beneficiary when Bank B, the beneficiary's bank, accepts a payment order for the benefit of Beneficiary. Section 4A–406(a). If that acceptance by Bank B does not occur, the funds transfer has miscarried because Originator has not paid Beneficiary. Originator doesn't have to pay its payment order, and if it has already paid it is entitled to refund of the payment with interest. The rate of interest is stated in Section 4A–506. This "money-back guarantee" is an important protection of Originator. Originator is assured that it will not lose its money if something goes wrong in the transfer. For example, risk of loss resulting from payment to the wrong beneficiary is borne by some bank, not by Originator. The most likely reason for noncompletion is a failure to execute or an erroneous execution of a payment order by Bank A or an intermediary bank. Bank A may have issued its payment order to the wrong bank or it may have identified the wrong beneficiary in its order. The money-back guarantee is particularly important to Originator if noncompletion of the funds transfer is due to the fault of an intermediary bank rather than Bank A. In that case Bank A must refund payment to Originator, and Bank A has the burden of obtaining refund from the intermediary bank that it paid.

Subsection (c) can result in loss if an intermediary bank suspends payments. Suppose Originator instructs Bank A to pay to Beneficiary's account in Bank B and to use Bank C as an intermediary bank. Bank A executes Originator's order by issuing a payment order to Bank C. Bank A pays Bank C. Bank C fails to execute the order of Bank A and suspends payments. Under subsections (c) and (d), Originator is not obliged to pay Bank A and is entitled to refund from Bank A of any payment that it may have made. Bank A is entitled to a refund from Bank C, but Bank C is insolvent. Subsection (e) deals with this case. Bank A was required to issue its payment order to Bank C because Bank C was designated as an intermediary bank by Originator. Section 4A–302(a)(1). In this case Originator takes the risk of insolvency of Bank C. Under subsection (e), Bank A is entitled to payment from Originator and Originator is subrogated to the right of Bank A under subsection (d) to refund of payment from Bank C.

3. A payment order is not like a negotiable instrument on which the drawer or maker has liability. Acceptance of the order by the receiving bank creates an obligation of the sender to pay the receiving bank the amount of the order. That is the extent of the sender's liability to the receiving bank and no other person has any rights against the sender with respect to the sender's order.

§ 11403. Payment by Sender to Receiving Bank

(a) Payment of the sender's obligation under Section 11402 to pay the receiving bank occurs as follows:

(1) If the sender is a bank, payment occurs when the receiving bank receives final settlement of the obligation through a Federal Reserve Bank or through a funds-transfer system.

(2) If the sender is a bank and the sender (i) credited an account of the receiving bank with the sender, or (ii) caused an account of the receiving bank in another bank to be credited, payment occurs when the credit is withdrawn or, if not withdrawn, at midnight of the day on which the credit is withdrawable and the receiving bank learns of that fact.

(3) If the receiving bank debits an account of the sender with the receiving bank, payment occurs when the debit is made to the extent the debit is covered by a withdrawable credit balance in the account.

(b) If the sender and receiving bank are members of a funds-transfer system that nets obligations multilaterally among participants, the receiving bank receives final settlement when settlement is complete in accordance with the rules of the system. The obligation of the sender to pay the amount of a payment order transmitted through the funds-transfer system may be satisfied, to the extent permitted by the rules of the system, by setting off and applying against the sender's obligation the right of the sender to receive payment from the receiving bank of the amount of any other payment order transmitted to the sender by the receiving bank through the funds-transfer system. The aggregate balance of obligations owed by each sender to each receiving bank in the funds-transfer system may be satisfied, to the extent permitted by the rules of the system, by setting off and applying against that balance the aggregate balance of obligations owed to the sender by other members of the system. The aggregate balance is determined after the right of setoff stated in the second sentence of this subdivision has been exercised.

(c) If two banks transmit payment orders to each other under an agreement that settlement of the obligations of each bank to the other under Section 11402 will be made at the end of the day or other period, the total amount owed with respect to all orders transmitted by one bank shall be set off against the total amount owed with respect to all orders transmitted by the other bank. To the extent of the setoff, each bank has made payment to the other.

(d) In a case not covered by subdivision (a), the time when payment of the sender's obligation under subdivision (b) or (c) of Section 11402 occurs is governed by applicable principles of law that determine when an obligation is satisfied. *(Added by Stats.1990, c. 125 (S.B.1759), § 2.)*

Uniform Commercial Code Comment

1. This section defines when a sender pays the obligation stated in Section 4A–402. If a group of two or more banks engage in funds transfers with each other, the participating banks will sometimes be senders and sometimes receiving banks. With respect to payment orders other than Fedwires, the amounts of the various payment orders may be credited and debited to accounts of one bank with another or to a clearing house account of each bank and amounts owed and amounts due are netted. Settlement is made through a Federal Reserve Bank by charges to the Federal Reserve accounts of the net debtor banks and credits to the Federal Reserve accounts of the net creditor banks. In the case of Fedwires the sender's obligation is settled by a debit to the Federal Reserve account of the sender and a credit to the Federal Reserve account of the receiving bank at the time the receiving bank receives the payment order. Both of these cases are covered by subsection (a)(1). When the Federal Reserve settlement becomes final the obligation of the sender under Section 4A–402 is paid.

2. In some cases a bank does not settle an obligation owed to another bank through a Federal Reserve Bank. This is the case if one of the banks is a foreign bank without access to the Federal Reserve payment system. In this kind of case, payment is usually made by credits or debits to accounts of the two banks with each other or to accounts of the two banks in a third bank. Suppose Bank B has an account in Bank A. Bank A advises Bank B that its account in Bank A has been credited $1,000,000 and that the credit is immediately withdrawable. Bank A also instructs Bank B to pay $1,000,000 to the account of Beneficiary in Bank B. This case is covered by subsection (a)(2). Bank B may want to immediately withdraw this credit. For example, it might do so by instructing Bank A to debit the account and pay some third party. Payment by Bank A to Bank B of Bank A's payment order occurs when the withdrawal is made. Suppose Bank B

does not withdraw the credit. Since Bank B is the beneficiary's bank, one of the effects of receipt of payment by Bank B is that acceptance of Bank A's payment order automatically occurs at the time of payment. Section 4A–209(b)(2). Acceptance means that Bank B is obliged to pay $1,000,000 to Beneficiary. Section 4A–404(a). Subsection (a)(2) of Section 4A–403 states that payment does not occur until midnight if the credit is not withdrawn. This allows Bank B an opportunity to reject the order if it does not have time to withdraw the credit to its account and it is not willing to incur the liability to Beneficiary before it has use of the funds represented by the credit.

3. Subsection (a)(3) applies to a case in which the sender (bank or nonbank) has a funded account in the receiving bank. If Sender has an account in Bank and issues a payment order to Bank, Bank can obtain payment from Sender by debiting the account of Sender, which pays its Section 4A–402 obligation to Bank when the debit is made.

4. Subsection (b) deals with multilateral settlements made through a funds transfer system and is based on the CHIPS settlement system. In a funds transfer system such as CHIPS, which allows the various banks that transmit payment orders over the system to settle obligations at the end of each day, settlement is not based on individual payment orders. Each bank using the system engages in funds transfers with many other banks using the system. Settlement for any participant is based on the net credit or debit position of that participant with all other banks using the system. Subsection (b) is designed to make clear that the obligations of any sender are paid when the net position of that sender is settled in accordance with the rules of the funds transfer system. This provision is intended to invalidate any argument, based on common-law principles, that multilateral netting is not valid because mutuality of obligation is not present. Subsection (b) dispenses with any mutuality of obligation requirements. Subsection (c) applies to cases in which two banks send payment orders to each other during the day and settle with each other at the end of the day or at the end of some other period. It is similar to subsection (b) in that it recognizes that a sender's obligation to pay a payment order is satisfied by a setoff. The obligations of each bank as sender to the other as receiving bank are obligations of the bank itself and not as representative of customers. These two sections are important in the case of insolvency of a bank. They make clear that liability under Section 4A–402 is based on the net position of the insolvent bank after setoff.

5. Subsection (d) relates to the uncommon case in which the sender doesn't have an account relationship with the receiving bank and doesn't settle through a Federal Reserve Bank. An example would be a customer that pays over the counter for a payment order that the customer issues to the receiving bank. Payment would normally be by cash, check or bank obligation. When payment occurs is determined by law outside Article 4A.

§ 11404. Obligation of Beneficiary's Bank to Pay and Give Notice to Beneficiary

(a) Subject to subdivision (e) of Section 11211, and subdivisions (d) and (e) of Section 11405, if a beneficiary's bank accepts a payment order, the bank is obliged to pay the amount of the order to the beneficiary of the order. Payment is due on the payment date of the order, but if acceptance occurs on the payment date after the close of the funds-transfer business day of the bank, payment is due on the next funds-transfer business day. If the bank refuses to pay after demand by the beneficiary and receipt of notice of particular circumstances that will give rise to consequential damages as a result of nonpayment, the beneficiary may recover damages resulting from the refusal to pay to the extent the bank had notice of the damages, unless the bank proves that it did not pay because of a reasonable doubt concerning the right of the beneficiary to payment.

(b) If a payment order accepted by the beneficiary's bank instructs payment to an account of the beneficiary, the bank is obliged to notify the beneficiary of receipt of the order before midnight of the next funds-transfer business day following the payment date. If the payment order does not instruct payment to an account of the beneficiary, the bank is required to notify the beneficiary only if notice is required by the order. Notice may be given by first-class mail or any other means reasonable in the circumstances. If the bank fails to give the required notice, the bank is obliged to pay interest to the beneficiary on the amount of the payment order from the day notice should have been given until the day the beneficiary learned of receipt of the payment order by the bank. No other damages are recoverable. Reasonable attorney's fees are also recoverable if demand for interest is made and refused before an action is brought on the claim.

(c) The right of a beneficiary to receive payment and damages as stated in subdivision (a) may not be varied by agreement or a funds-transfer system rule. The right of a beneficiary to be notified as stated in subdivision (b) may be varied by agreement of the beneficiary or by a funds-transfer system rule if the beneficiary is notified of the rule before initiation of the funds transfer. *(Added by Stats.1990, c. 125 (S.B.1759), § 2.)*

Uniform Commercial Code Comment

1. The first sentence of subsection (a) states the time when the obligation of the beneficiary's bank arises. The second and third sentences state when the beneficiary's bank must make funds available to the beneficiary. They also state the measure of damages for failure, after demand, to comply. Since the Expedited Funds Availability Act, 12 U.S.C. 4001 et seq., also governs funds availability in a funds transfer, the second and third sentences of subsection (a) may be subject to preemption by that Act.

2. Subsection (a) provides that the beneficiary of an accepted payment order may recover consequential damages if the beneficiary's bank refuses to pay the order after demand by the beneficiary if the bank at that time had notice of the particular circumstances giving rise to the damages. Such damages are recoverable only to the extent the bank had "notice of the damages." The quoted phrase requires that the bank have notice of the general type or nature of the damages that will be suffered as a result of the refusal to pay and their general magnitude. There is no requirement that the bank have notice of the exact or even the approximate amount of the damages, but if the amount of damages is extraordinary the bank is entitled to notice of that fact. For example, in Evra Corp. v. Swiss Bank Corp., 673 F.2d 951 (7th Cir.1982), failure to complete a funds transfer of only $27,000 required to retain rights to a very favorable ship charter resulted in a claim for more than $2,000,000 of consequential damages. Since it is not reasonably foreseeable that a failure to make a relatively small payment will result in damages of this magnitude, notice is not sufficient if the beneficiary's bank has notice only that the $27,000 is necessary to retain rights on a ship charter. The bank is entitled to notice that an exceptional amount of damages will result as well. For example, there would be adequate notice if the bank had been made aware that damages of $1,000,000 or more might result.

3. Under the last clause of subsection (a) the beneficiary's bank is not liable for damages if its refusal to pay was "because of a reasonable doubt concerning the right of the beneficiary to payment." Normally there will not be any question about the right of the beneficiary to receive payment. Normally, the bank should be able to determine whether it has accepted the payment order and, if it has been accepted, the first sentence of subsection (a) states that the bank is obliged to pay. There may be uncommon cases, however, in which there is doubt whether acceptance occurred. For example, if acceptance is based on receipt of payment by the beneficiary's bank under Section 4A–403(a)(1) or (2), there may be cases in which the bank is not certain that payment has been received. There may also be cases in which there is doubt about whether the person demanding payment is the person identified in the payment order as beneficiary of the order.

§ 11404

The last clause of subsection (a) does not apply to cases in which a funds transfer is being used to pay an obligation and a dispute arises between the originator and the beneficiary concerning whether the obligation is in fact owed. For example, the originator may try to prevent payment to the beneficiary by the beneficiary's bank by alleging that the beneficiary is not entitled to payment because of fraud against the originator or a breach of contract relating to the obligation. The fraud or breach of contract claim of the originator may be grounds for recovery by the originator from the beneficiary after the beneficiary is paid, but it does not affect the obligation of the beneficiary's bank to pay the beneficiary. Unless the payment order has been cancelled pursuant to Section 4A–211(c), there is no excuse for refusing to pay the beneficiary and, in a proper case, the refusal may result in consequential damages. Except in the case of a book transfer, in which the beneficiary's bank is also the originator's bank, the originator of a funds transfer cannot cancel a payment order to the beneficiary's bank, with or without the consent of that bank, because the originator is not the sender of that order. Thus, the beneficiary's bank may safely ignore any instruction by the originator to withhold payment to the beneficiary.

4. Subsection (b) states the duty of the beneficiary's bank to notify the beneficiary of receipt of the order. If acceptance occurs under Section 4A–209(b)(1) the beneficiary is normally notified. Thus, subsection (b) applies primarily to cases in which acceptance occurs under Section 4A–209(b)(2) or (3). Notice under subsection (b) is not required if the person entitled to the notice agrees or a funds transfer system rule provides that notice is not required and the beneficiary is given notice of the rule. In ACH transactions the normal practice is not to give notice to the beneficiary unless notice is requested by the beneficiary. This practice can be continued by adoption of a funds transfer system rule. Subsection (a) is not subject to variation by agreement or by a funds transfer system rule.

§ 11405. Payment by Beneficiary's Bank to Beneficiary

(a) If the beneficiary's bank credits an account of the beneficiary of a payment order, payment of the bank's obligation under subdivision (a) of Section 11404 occurs when and to the extent (i) the beneficiary is notified of the right to withdraw the credit, (ii) the bank lawfully applies the credit to a debt of the beneficiary, or (iii) funds with respect to the order are otherwise made available to the beneficiary by the bank.

(b) If the beneficiary's bank does not credit an account of the beneficiary of a payment order, the time when payment of the bank's obligation under subdivision (a) of Section 11404 occurs is governed by principles of law that determine when an obligation is satisfied.

(c) Except as stated in subdivisions (d) and (e), if the beneficiary's bank pays the beneficiary of a payment order under a condition to payment or agreement of the beneficiary giving the bank the right to recover payment from the beneficiary if the bank does not receive payment of the order, the condition to payment or agreement is not enforceable.

(d) A funds-transfer system rule may provide that payments made to beneficiaries of funds transfers made through the system are provisional until receipt of payment by the beneficiary's bank of the payment order it accepted. A beneficiary's bank that makes a payment that is provisional under the rule is entitled to refund from the beneficiary if (i) the rule requires that both the beneficiary and the originator be given notice of the provisional nature of the payment before the funds transfer is initiated, (ii) the beneficiary, the beneficiary's bank and the originator's bank agreed to be bound by the rule, and (iii) the beneficiary's bank did not receive payment of the payment order that it accepted. If the beneficiary is obliged to refund payment to the beneficiary's bank, acceptance of the payment order by the beneficiary's bank is nullified and no payment by the originator of the funds transfer to the beneficiary occurs under Section 11406.

(e) This subdivision applies to a funds transfer that includes a payment order transmitted over a funds-transfer system that (i) nets obligations multilaterally among participants, and (ii) has in effect a loss-sharing agreement among participants for the purpose of providing funds necessary to complete settlement of the obligations of one or more participants that do not meet their settlement obligations. If the beneficiary's bank in the funds transfer accepts a payment order and the system fails to complete settlement pursuant to its rules with respect to any payment order in the funds transfer, (i) the acceptance by the beneficiary's bank is nullified and no person has any right or obligation based on the acceptance, (ii) the beneficiary's bank is entitled to recover payment from the beneficiary, (iii) no payment by the originator to the beneficiary occurs under Section 11406, and (iv) subject to subdivision (e) of Section 11402, each sender in the funds transfer is excused from its obligation to pay its payment order under subdivision (c) of Section 11402 because the funds transfer has not been completed. *(Added by Stats.1990, c. 125 (S.B. 1759), § 2.)*

Uniform Commercial Code Comment

1. This section defines when the beneficiary's bank pays the beneficiary and when the obligation of the beneficiary's bank under Section 4A–404 to pay the beneficiary is satisfied. In almost all cases the bank will credit an account of the beneficiary when it receives a payment order. In the typical case the beneficiary is paid when the beneficiary is given notice of the right to withdraw the credit. Subsection (a)(i). In some cases payment might be made to the beneficiary not by releasing funds to the beneficiary, but by applying the credit to a debt of the beneficiary. Subsection (a)(ii). In this case the beneficiary gets the benefit of the payment order because a debt of the beneficiary has been satisfied. The two principal cases in which payment will occur in this manner are setoff by the beneficiary's bank and payment of the proceeds of the payment order to a garnishing creditor of the beneficiary. These cases are discussed in Comment 2 to Section 4A–502.

2. If a beneficiary's bank releases funds to the beneficiary before it receives payment from the sender of the payment order, it assumes the risk that the sender may not pay the sender's order because of suspension of payments or other reason. Subsection (c). As stated in Comment 5 to Section 4A–209, the beneficiary's bank can protect itself against this risk by delaying acceptance. But if the bank accepts the order it is obliged to pay the beneficiary. If the beneficiary's bank has given the beneficiary notice of the right to withdraw a credit made to the beneficiary's account, the beneficiary has received payment from the bank. Once payment has been made to the beneficiary with respect to an obligation incurred by the bank under Section 4A–404(a), the payment cannot be recovered by the beneficiary's bank unless subsection (d) or (e) applies. Thus, a right to withdraw a credit cannot be revoked if the right to withdraw constituted payment of the bank's obligation. This principle applies even if funds were released as a "loan" (see Comment 5 to Section 4A–209), or were released subject to a condition that they would be repaid in the event the bank does not receive payment from the sender of the payment order, or the beneficiary agreed to return the payment if the bank did not receive payment from the sender.

3. Subsection (c) is subject to an exception stated in subsection (d) which is intended to apply to automated clearing house transfers. ACH transfers are made in batches. A beneficiary's bank will normally accept, at the same time and as part of a single batch, payment orders with respect to many different originator's banks. Comment 2 to Section 4A–206. The custom in ACH transactions is to release funds to the beneficiary early on the payment date even though settlement to the beneficiary's bank does not occur until later in the day. The understanding is that payments to beneficiaries are provisional until the beneficiary's bank receives settlement. This practice is similar to what happens when a depositary bank releases funds with respect to a check forwarded for collection. If the check is dishonored the bank is entitled to recover the funds from the customer. ACH transfers are widely perceived as check substitutes. Section 4A–405(d) allows the funds transfer system to adopt a rule making payments to beneficiaries provisional. If such a rule is adopted, a beneficiary's bank that releases funds to the beneficiary will be able to recover the payment if it doesn't receive payment of the payment order that it accepted. There are two requirements with respect to the funds transfer system rule. The beneficiary, the beneficiary's bank and the originator's bank must all agree to be bound by the rule and the rule must require that both the beneficiary and the originator be given notice of the provisional nature of the payment before the funds transfer is initiated. There is no requirement that the notice be given with respect to a particular funds transfer. Once notice of the provisional nature of the payment has been given, the notice is effective for all subsequent payments to or from the person to whom the notice was given. Subsection (d) provides only that the funds transfer system rule must require notice to the beneficiary and the originator. The beneficiary's bank will know what the rule requires, but it has no way of knowing whether the originator's bank complied with the rule. Subsection (d) does not require proof that the originator received notice. If the originator's bank failed to give the required notice and the originator suffered as a result, the appropriate remedy is an action by the originator against the originator's bank based on that failure. But the beneficiary's bank will not be able to get the benefit of subsection (d) unless the beneficiary had notice of the provisional nature of the payment because subsection (d) requires an agreement by the beneficiary to be bound by the rule. Implicit in an agreement to be bound by a rule that makes a payment provisional is a requirement that notice be given of what the rule provides. The notice can be part of the agreement or separately given. For example, notice can be given by providing a copy of the system's operating rules.

With respect to ACH transfers made through a Federal Reserve Bank acting as an intermediary bank, the Federal Reserve Bank is obliged under Section 4A–402(b) to pay a beneficiary's bank that accepts the payment order. Unlike Fedwire transfers, under current ACH practice a Federal Reserve Bank that processes a payment order does not obligate itself to pay if the originator's bank fails to pay the Federal Reserve Bank. It is assumed that the Federal Reserve will use its right of preemption which is recognized in Section 4A–107 to disclaim the Section 4A–402(b) obligation in ACH transactions if it decides to retain the provisional payment rule.

4. Subsection (e) is another exception to subsection (c). It refers to funds transfer systems having loss-sharing rules described in the subsection. CHIPS has proposed a rule that fits the description. Under the CHIPS loss-sharing rule the CHIPS banks will have agreed to contribute funds to allow the system to settle for payment orders sent over the system during the day in the event that one or more banks are unable to meet their settlement obligations. Subsection (e) applies only if CHIPS fails to settle despite the loss-sharing rule. Since funds under the loss-sharing rule will be instantly available to CHIPS and will be in an amount sufficient to cover any failure that can be reasonably anticipated, it is extremely unlikely that CHIPS would ever fail to settle. Thus, subsection (e) addresses an event that should never occur. If that event were to occur, all payment orders made over the system would be cancelled under the CHIPS rule. Thus, no bank would receive settlement, whether or not a failed bank was involved in a particular funds transfer. Subsection (e) provides that each funds transfer in which there is a payment order with respect to which there is a settlement failure is unwound. Acceptance by the beneficiary's bank in each funds transfer is nullified. The consequences of nullification are that the beneficiary has no right to receive or retain payment by the beneficiary's bank, no payment is made by the originator to the beneficiary and each sender in the funds transfer is, subject to Section 4A–402(e), not obliged to pay its payment order and is entitled to refund under Section 4A–402(d) if it has already paid.

§ 11406. Payment by Originator to Beneficiary; Discharge of Underlying Obligation

(a) Subject to subdivision (e) of Section 11211 and subdivisions (d) and (e) of Section 11405, the originator of a funds transfer pays the beneficiary of the originator's payment order (i) at the time a payment order for the benefit of the beneficiary is accepted by the beneficiary's bank in the funds transfer and (ii) in an amount equal to the amount of the order accepted by the beneficiary's bank, but not more than the amount of the originator's order.

(b) If payment under subdivision (a) is made to satisfy an obligation, the obligation is discharged to the same extent discharge would result from payment to the beneficiary of the same amount in money, unless (i) the payment under subdivision (a) was made by a means prohibited by the contract of the beneficiary with respect to the obligation, (ii) the beneficiary, within a reasonable time after receiving notice of receipt of the order by the beneficiary's bank, notified the originator of the beneficiary's refusal of the payment, (iii) funds with respect to the order were not withdrawn by the beneficiary or applied to a debt of the beneficiary, and (iv) the beneficiary would suffer a loss that could reasonably have been avoided if payment had been made by a means complying with the contract. If payment by the originator does not result in discharge under this section, the originator is subrogated to the rights of the beneficiary to receive payment from the beneficiary's bank under subdivision (a) of Section 11404.

(c) For the purpose of determining whether discharge of an obligation occurs under subdivision (b), if the beneficiary's bank accepts a payment order in an amount equal to the amount of the originator's payment order less charges of one or more receiving banks in the funds transfer, payment to the beneficiary is deemed to be in the amount of the originator's order unless upon demand by the beneficiary the originator does not pay the beneficiary the amount of the deducted charges.

(d) Rights of the originator or of the beneficiary of a funds transfer under this section may be varied only by agreement of the originator and the beneficiary. *(Added by Stats.1990, c. 125 (S.B.1759), § 2.)*

Uniform Commercial Code Comment

1. Subsection (a) states the fundamental rule of Article 4A that payment by the originator to the beneficiary is accomplished by providing to the beneficiary the obligation of the beneficiary's bank to pay. Since this obligation arises when the beneficiary's bank accepts a payment order, the originator pays the beneficiary at the time of acceptance and in the amount of the payment order accepted.

2. In a large percentage of funds transfers, the transfer is made to pay an obligation of the originator. Subsection (a) states that the beneficiary is paid by the originator when the beneficiary's bank accepts a payment order for the benefit of the beneficiary. When that happens the effect under subsection (b) is to substitute the obligation of the beneficiary's bank for the obligation of the originator. The effect is similar to that under Article 3 if a cashier's check payable to the beneficiary has been taken by the beneficiary. Normally, payment by funds transfer is sought by the beneficiary because it puts money into

the hands of the beneficiary more quickly. As a practical matter the beneficiary and the originator will nearly always agree to the funds transfer in advance. Under subsection (b) acceptance by the beneficiary's bank will result in discharge of the obligation for which payment was made unless the beneficiary had made a contract with respect to the obligation which did not permit payment by the means used. Thus, if there is no contract of the beneficiary with respect to the means of payment of the obligation, acceptance by the beneficiary's bank of a payment order to the account of the beneficiary can result in discharge.

3. Suppose Beneficiary's contract stated that payment of an obligation owed by Originator was to be made by a cashier's check of Bank A. Instead Originator paid by a funds transfer to Beneficiary's account in Bank B. Bank B accepted a payment order for the benefit of Beneficiary by immediately notifying Beneficiary that the funds were available for withdrawal. Before Beneficiary had a reasonable opportunity to withdraw the funds Bank B suspended payments. Under the unless clause of subsection (b) Beneficiary is not required to accept the payment as discharging the obligation owed by Originator to Beneficiary if Beneficiary's contract means that Beneficiary was not required to accept payment by wire transfer. Beneficiary could refuse the funds transfer as payment of the obligation and could resort to rights under the underlying contract to enforce the obligation. The rationale is that Originator cannot impose the risk of Bank B's insolvency on Beneficiary if Beneficiary had specified another means of payment that did not entail that risk. If Beneficiary is required to accept Originator's payment, Beneficiary would suffer a loss that would not have occurred if payment had been made by a cashier's check on Bank A, and Bank A has not suspended payments. In this case Originator will have to pay twice. It is obliged to pay the amount of its payment order to the bank that accepted it and has to pay the obligation it owes to Beneficiary which has not been discharged. Under the last sentence of subsection (b) Originator is subrogated to Beneficiary's right to receive payment from Bank B under Section 4A-404(a).

4. Suppose Beneficiary's contract called for payment by a Fedwire transfer to Bank B, but the payment order accepted by Bank B was not a Fedwire transfer. Before the funds were withdrawn by Beneficiary, Bank B suspended payments. The sender of the payment order to Bank B paid the amount of the order to Bank B. In this case the payment by Originator did not comply with Beneficiary's contract, but the noncompliance did not result in a loss to Beneficiary as required by subsection (b)(iv). Fedwire transfer avoids the risk of insolvency of the sender of the payment order to Bank B, but it does not affect the risk that Bank B will suspend payments before withdrawal of the funds by Beneficiary. Thus, the unless clause of subsection (b) is not applicable and the obligation owed to Beneficiary is discharged.

5. Charges of receiving banks in a funds transfer normally are nominal in relationship to the amount being paid by the originator to the beneficiary. Wire transfers are normally agreed to in advance and the parties may agree concerning how these charges are to be divided between the parties. Subsection (c) states a rule that applies in the absence of agreement. In some funds transfers charges of banks that execute payment orders are collected by deducting the charges from the amount of the payment order issued by the bank, i.e. the bank issues a payment order that is slightly less than the amount of the payment order that is being executed. The process is described in Comment 3 to Section 4A-302. The result in such a case is that the payment order accepted by the beneficiary's bank will be slightly less than the amount of the originator's order. Subsection (c) recognizes the principle that a beneficiary is entitled to full payment of a debt paid by wire transfer as a condition to discharge. On the other hand, Subsection (c) prevents a beneficiary from denying the originator the benefit of the payment by asserting that discharge did not occur because deduction of bank charges resulted in less than full payment. The typical case is one in which the payment is made to exercise a valuable right such as an option which is unfavorable to the beneficiary. Subsection (c) allows discharge notwithstanding the deduction unless the originator fails to reimburse the beneficiary for the deducted charges after demand by the beneficiary.

Cross References

Settlement by bank by payment through funds transfer under this section, see Commercial Code § 4213.

CHAPTER 5. MISCELLANEOUS PROVISIONS

Section
11501. Variation by Agreement and Effect of Funds—Transfer System Rule.

Section
11502. Creditor Process Served on Receiving Bank; Set-off by Beneficiary's Bank.
11503. Injunction or Restraining Order With Respect to Funds Transfer.
11504. Order in Which Items and Payment Orders May be Charged to Account; Order of Withdrawals From Account.
11505. Preclusion of Objection to Debit of Customer's Account.
11506. Rate of Interest.
11507. Choice of Law.

§ 11501. Variation by Agreement and Effect of Funds—Transfer System Rule

(a) Except as otherwise provided in this division, the rights and obligations of a party to a funds transfer may be varied by agreement of the affected party.

(b) "Funds-transfer system rule" means a rule of an association of banks (i) governing transmission of payment orders by means of a funds-transfer system of the association or rights and obligations with respect to those orders, or (ii) to the extent the rule governs rights and obligations between banks that are parties to a funds transfer in which a Federal Reserve Bank, acting as an intermediary bank, sends a payment order to the beneficiary's bank. Except as otherwise provided in this division, a funds-transfer system rule governing rights and obligations between participating banks using the system may be effective even if the rule conflicts with this division and indirectly affects another party to the funds transfer who does not consent to the rule. A funds-transfer system rule may also govern rights and obligations of parties other than participating banks using the system to the extent stated in subdivision (c) of Section 11404, subdivision (d) of Section 11405, and subdivision (c) of Section 11507. *(Added by Stats.1990, c. 125 (S.B.1759), § 2.)*

Uniform Commercial Code Comment

1. This section is designed to give some flexibility to Article 4A. Funds transfer system rules govern rights and obligations between banks that use the system. They may cover a wide variety of matters such as form and content of payment orders, security procedures, cancellation rights and procedures, indemnity rights, compensation rules for delays in completion of a funds transfer, time and method of settlement, credit restrictions with respect to senders of payment orders and risk allocation with respect to suspension of payments by a participating bank. Funds transfer system rules can be very effective in supplementing the provisions of Article 4A and in filling gaps that may be present in Article 4A. To the extent they do not conflict with Article 4A there is no problem with respect to their effectiveness. In that case they merely supplement Article 4A. Section 4A–501 goes further. It states that unless the contrary is stated, funds transfer system rules can override provisions of Article 4A. Thus, rights and obligations of a sender bank and a receiving bank with respect to each other can be different from that stated in Article 4A to the extent a funds transfer system rule applies. Since funds transfer system rules are defined as those governing the relationship between participating banks, a rule can have a direct effect only on participating banks. But a rule that affects the conduct of a participating bank may indirectly affect the rights of nonparticipants such as the originator or beneficiary of a funds transfer, and such a rule can be effective even though it may affect nonparticipants without their consent. For example, a rule might prevent execution of a payment order or might allow cancellation of a payment order with the result that a funds transfer is not completed or is delayed. But a rule purporting to define rights and obligations of nonparticipants

in the system would not be effective to alter Article 4A rights because the rule is not within the definition of funds transfer system rule. Rights and obligations arising under Article 4A may also be varied by agreement of the affected parties, except to the extent Article 4A otherwise provides. Rights and obligations arising under Article 4A can also be changed by Federal Reserve regulations and operating circulars of Federal Reserve Banks. Section 4A–107.

2. Subsection (b)(ii) refers to ACH transfers. Whether an ACH transfer is made through an automated clearing house of a Federal Reserve Bank or through an automated clearing house of another association of banks, the rights and obligations of the originator's bank and the beneficiary's bank are governed by uniform rules adopted by various associations of banks in various parts of the nation. With respect to transfers in which a Federal Reserve Bank acts as intermediary bank these rules may be incorporated, in whole or in part, in operating circulars of the Federal Reserve Bank. Even if not so incorporated these rules can still be binding on the association banks. If a transfer is made through a Federal Reserve Bank, the rules are effective under subsection (b)(ii). If the transfer is not made through a Federal Reserve Bank, the association rules are effective under subsection (b)(i).

§ 11502. Creditor Process Served on Receiving Bank; Set-off by Beneficiary's Bank

(a) As used in this section, "creditor process" means levy, attachment, garnishment, notice of lien, sequestration, or similar process issued by or on behalf of a creditor or other claimant with respect to an account.

(b) This subdivision applies to creditor process with respect to an authorized account of the sender of a payment order if the creditor process is served on the receiving bank. For the purpose of determining rights with respect to the creditor process, if the receiving bank accepts the payment order the balance in the authorized account is deemed to be reduced by the amount of the payment order to the extent the bank did not otherwise receive payment of the order, unless the creditor process is served at a time and in a manner affording the bank a reasonable opportunity to act on it before the bank accepts the payment order.

(c) If a beneficiary's bank has received a payment order for payment to the beneficiary's account in the bank, the following rules apply:

(1) The bank may credit the beneficiary's account. The amount credited may be set off against an obligation owed by the beneficiary to the bank or may be applied to satisfy creditor process served on the bank with respect to the account.

(2) The bank may credit the beneficiary's account and allow withdrawal of the amount credited unless creditor process with respect to the account is served at a time and in a manner affording the bank a reasonable opportunity to act to prevent withdrawal.

(3) If creditor process with respect to the beneficiary's account has been served and the bank has had a reasonable opportunity to act on it, the bank may not reject the payment order except for a reason unrelated to the service of process.

(d) Creditor process with respect to a payment by the originator to the beneficiary pursuant to a funds transfer may be served only on the beneficiary's bank with respect to the debt owed by that bank to the beneficiary. Any other bank served with the creditor process is not obliged to act with respect to the process. *(Added by Stats.1990, c. 125 (S.B.1759), § 2.)*

Uniform Commercial Code Comment

1. When a receiving bank accepts a payment order, the bank normally receives payment from the sender by debiting an authorized account of the sender. In accepting the sender's order the bank may be relying on a credit balance in the account. If creditor process is served on the bank with respect to the account before the bank accepts the order but the bank employee responsible for the acceptance was not aware of the creditor process at the time the acceptance occurred, it is unjust to the bank to allow the creditor process to take the credit balance on which the bank may have relied. Subsection (b) allows the bank to obtain payment from the sender's account in this case. Under that provision, the balance in the sender's account to which the creditor process applies is deemed to be reduced by the amount of the payment order unless there was sufficient time for notice of the service of creditor process to be received by personnel of the bank responsible for the acceptance.

2. Subsection (c) deals with payment orders issued to the beneficiary's bank. The bank may credit the beneficiary's account when the order is received, but under Section 4A–404(a) the bank incurs no obligation to pay the beneficiary until the order is accepted pursuant to Section 4A–209(b). Thus, before acceptance, the credit to the beneficiary's account is provisional. But under Section 4A–209(b) acceptance occurs if the beneficiary's bank pays the beneficiary pursuant to Section 4A–405(a). Under that provision, payment occurs if the credit to the beneficiary's account is applied to a debt of the beneficiary. Subsection (c)(1) allows the bank to credit the beneficiary's account with respect to a payment order and to accept the order by setting off the credit against an obligation owed to the bank or applying the credit to creditor process with respect to the account.

Suppose a beneficiary's bank receives a payment order for the benefit of a customer. Before the bank accepts the order, the bank learns that creditor process has been served on the bank with respect to the customer's account. Normally there is no reason for a beneficiary's bank to reject a payment order, but if the beneficiary's account is garnished, the bank may be faced with a difficult choice. If it rejects the order, the garnishing creditor's potential recovery of funds of the beneficiary is frustrated. It may be faced with a claim by the creditor that the rejection was a wrong to the creditor. If the bank accepts the order, the effect is to allow the creditor to seize funds of its customer, the beneficiary. Subsection (c)(3) gives the bank no choice in this case. It provides that it may not favor its customer over the creditor by rejecting the order. The beneficiary's bank may rightfully reject only if there is an independent basis for rejection.

3. Subsection (c)(2) is similar to subsection (b). Normally the beneficiary's bank will release funds to the beneficiary shortly after acceptance or it will accept by releasing funds. Since the bank is bound by a garnishment order served before funds are released to the beneficiary, the bank might suffer a loss if funds were released without knowledge that a garnishment order had been served. Subsection (c)(2) protects the bank if it did not have adequate notice of the garnishment when the funds were released.

4. A creditor may want to reach funds involved in a funds transfer. The creditor may try to do so by serving process on the originator's bank, an intermediary bank or the beneficiary's bank. The purpose of subsection (d) is to guide the creditor and the court as to the proper method of reaching the funds involved in a funds transfer. A creditor of the originator can levy on the account of the originator in the originator's bank before the funds transfer is initiated, but that levy is subject to the limitations stated in subsection (b). The creditor of the originator cannot reach any other funds because no property of the originator is being transferred. A creditor of the beneficiary cannot levy on property of the originator and until the funds transfer is completed by acceptance by the beneficiary's bank of a payment order for the benefit of the beneficiary, the beneficiary has no property interest in the funds transfer which the beneficiary's creditor can reach. A creditor of the beneficiary that wants to reach the funds to be received by the beneficiary must serve creditor process on the beneficiary's bank to reach the obligation of the beneficiary's bank to pay the beneficiary which arises upon acceptance by the beneficiary's bank under Section 4A–404(a).

5. "Creditor process" is defined in subsection (a) to cover a variety of devices by which a creditor of the holder of a bank account or a claimant to a bank account can seize the account. Procedure and nomenclature varies widely from state to state. The term used in Section 4A–502 is a generic term.

§ 11503. Injunction or Restraining Order With Respect to Funds Transfer

For proper cause and in compliance with applicable law, a court may restrain (i) a person from issuing a payment order to initiate a funds transfer, (ii) an originator's bank from executing the payment order of the originator, or (iii) the beneficiary's bank from releasing funds to the beneficiary or the beneficiary from withdrawing the funds. A court may not otherwise restrain a person from issuing a payment order, paying or receiving payment of a payment order, or otherwise acting with respect to a funds transfer. *(Added by Stats.1990, c. 125 (S.B.1759), § 2.)*

Uniform Commercial Code Comment

This section is related to Section 4A–502(d) and to Comment 4 to Section 4A–502. It is designed to prevent interruption of a funds transfer after it has been set in motion. The initiation of a funds transfer can be prevented by enjoining the originator or the originator's bank from issuing a payment order. After the funds transfer is completed by acceptance of a payment order by the beneficiary's bank, that bank can be enjoined from releasing funds to the beneficiary or the beneficiary can be enjoined from withdrawing the funds. No other injunction is permitted. In particular, intermediary banks are protected, and injunctions against the originator and the originator's bank are limited to issuance of a payment order. Except for the beneficiary's bank, nobody can be enjoined from paying a payment order, and no receiving bank can be enjoined from receiving payment from the sender of the order that it accepted.

§ 11504. Order in Which Items and Payment Orders May be Charged to Account; Order of Withdrawals From Account

(a) If a receiving bank has received more than one payment order of the sender or one or more payment orders and other items that are payable from the sender's account, the bank may charge the sender's account with respect to the various orders and items in any sequence.

(b) In determining whether a credit to an account has been withdrawn by the holder of the account or applied to a debt of the holder of the account, credits first made to the account are first withdrawn or applied. *(Added by Stats.1990, c. 125 (S.B.1759), § 2.)*

Uniform Commercial Code Comment

1. Subsection (a) concerns priority among various obligations that are to be paid from the same account. A customer may have written checks on its account with the receiving bank and may have issued one or more payment orders payable from the same account. If the account balance is not sufficient to cover all of the checks and payment orders, some checks may be dishonored and some payment orders may not be accepted. Although there is no concept of wrongful dishonor of a payment order in Article 4A in the absence of an agreement to honor by the receiving bank, some rights and obligations may depend on the amount in the customer's account. Section 4A–209(b)(3) and Section 4A–210(b). Whether dishonor of a check is wrongful also may depend upon the balance in the customer's account. Under subsection (a), the bank is not required to consider the competing items and payment orders in any particular order. Rather it may charge the customer's account for the various items and orders in any order. Suppose there is $12,000 in the customer's account. If a check for $5,000 is presented for payment and the bank receives a $10,000 payment order from the customer, the bank could dishonor the check and accept the payment order. Dishonor of the check is not wrongful because the account balance was less than the amount of the check after the bank charged the account $10,000 on account of the payment order. Or, the bank could pay the check and not execute the payment order because the amount of the order is not covered by the balance in the account.

2. Subsection (b) follows Section 4–208(b) in using the first-in-first-out rule for determining the order in which credits to an account are withdrawn.

§ 11505. Preclusion of Objection to Debit of Customer's Account

If a receiving bank has received payment from its customer with respect to a payment order issued in the name of the customer as sender and accepted by the bank, and the customer received notification reasonably identifying the order, the customer is precluded from asserting that the bank is not entitled to retain the payment unless the customer notifies the bank of the customer's objection to the payment within one year after the notification was received by the customer. *(Added by Stats.1990, c. 125 (S.B.1759), § 2.)*

Uniform Commercial Code Comment

This section is in the nature of a statute of repose for objecting to debits made to the customer's account. A receiving bank that executes payment orders of a customer may have received payment from the customer by debiting the customer's account with respect to a payment order that the customer was not required to pay. For example, the payment order may not have been authorized or verified pursuant to Section 4A–202 or the funds transfer may not have been completed. In either case the receiving bank is obliged to refund the payment to the customer and this obligation to refund payment cannot be varied by agreement. Section 4A–204 and Section 4A–402. Refund may also be required if the receiving bank is not entitled to payment from the customer because the bank erroneously executed a payment order. Section 4A–303. A similar analysis applies to that case. Section 4A–402(d) and (f) require refund and the obligation to refund may not be varied by agreement. Under 4A–505, however, the obligation to refund may not be asserted by the customer if the customer has not objected to the debiting of the account within one year after the customer received notification of the debit.

§ 11506. Rate of Interest

(a) If, under this division, a receiving bank is obliged to pay interest with respect to a payment order issued to the bank, the amount payable may be determined (i) by agreement of the sender and receiving bank, or (ii) by a funds-transfer system rule if the payment order is transmitted through a funds-transfer system.

(b) If the amount of interest is not determined by an agreement or rule as stated in subdivision (a), the amount is calculated by multiplying the applicable federal funds rate by the amount on which interest is payable, and then multiplying the product by the number of days for which interest is payable. The applicable federal funds rate is the average of the federal funds rates published by the Federal Reserve Bank of New York for each of the days for which interest is payable divided by 360. The federal funds rate for any day on which a published rate is not available is the same as the published rate for the next preceding day for which there is a published rate. If a receiving bank that accepted a payment order is required to refund payment to the sender of the order because the funds transfer was not completed, but the failure to complete was not due to any fault by the bank, the interest payable is reduced by a percentage equal to the reserve requirement on deposits of the receiving bank. *(Added by Stats.1990, c. 125 (S.B.1759), § 2.)*

Uniform Commercial Code Comment

1. A receiving bank is required to pay interest on the amount of a payment order received by the bank in a number of situations. Sometimes the interest is payable to the sender and in other cases it is payable to either the originator or the beneficiary of the funds transfer. The relevant provisions are Section 4A–204(a), Section 4A–209(b)(3), Section 4A–210(b), Section 4A–305(a), Section 4A–402(d) and Section 4A–404(b). The rate of interest may be governed by a funds transfer system rule or by agreement as stated in subsection (a). If subsection (a) doesn't apply, the rate is determined under subsection (b). Subsection (b) is illustrated by the following example. A bank is obliged to pay interest on $1,000,000 for three days, July 3, July 4, and July 5. The published Fed Funds rate is .082 for July 3 and .081 for July 5. There is no published rate for July 4 because that day is not a banking day. The rate for July 3 applies to July 4. The applicable Fed Funds rate is .08167 (the average of .082, .082, and .081) divided by 360 which equals .0002268. The amount of interest payable is $1,000,000 × .0002268 × 3 = $680.40.

2. In some cases, interest is payable in spite of the fact that there is no fault by the receiving bank. The last sentence of subsection (b) applies to those cases. For example, a funds transfer might not be completed because the beneficiary's bank rejected the payment order issued to it by the originator's bank or an intermediary bank. Section 4A–402(c) provides that the originator is not obliged to pay its payment order and Section 4A–402(d) provides that the originator's bank must refund any payment received plus interest. The requirement to pay interest in this case is not based on fault by the originator's bank. Rather, it is based on restitution. Since the originator's bank had the use of the originator's money, it is required to pay the originator for the value of that use. The value of that use is not determined by multiplying the interest rate by the refundable amount because the originator's bank is required to deposit with the Federal Reserve a percentage of the bank's deposits as a reserve requirement. Since that deposit does not bear interest, the bank had use of the refundable amount reduced by a percentage equal to the reserve requirement. If the reserve requirement is 12%, the amount of interest payable by the bank under the formula stated in subsection (b) is reduced by 12%.

§ 11507. Choice of Law

(a) The following rules apply unless the affected parties otherwise agree or subdivision (c) applies:

(1) The rights and obligations between the sender of a payment order and the receiving bank are governed by the law of the jurisdiction in which the receiving bank is located.

(2) The rights and obligations between the beneficiary's bank and the beneficiary are governed by the law of the jurisdiction in which the beneficiary's bank is located.

(3) The issue of when payment is made pursuant to a funds transfer by the originator to the beneficiary is governed by the law of the jurisdiction in which the beneficiary's bank is located.

(b) If the parties described in each paragraph of subdivision (a) have made an agreement selecting the law of a particular jurisdiction to govern rights and obligations between each other, the law of that jurisdiction governs those rights and obligations, whether or not the payment order or the funds transfer bears a reasonable relation to that jurisdiction.

(c) A funds-transfer system rule may select the law of a particular jurisdiction to govern (i) rights and obligations between participating banks with respect to payment orders transmitted or processed through the system, or (ii) the rights and obligations of some or all parties to a funds transfer any part of which is carried out by means of the system. A choice of law made pursuant to clause (i) is binding on participating banks. A choice of law made pursuant to clause (ii) is binding on the originator, other sender, or a receiving bank having notice that the funds-transfer system might be used in the funds transfer and of the choice of law by the system when the originator, other sender, or receiving bank issued or accepted a payment order. The beneficiary of a funds transfer is bound by the choice of law if, when the funds transfer is initiated, the beneficiary has notice that the funds-transfer system might be used in the funds transfer and of the choice of law by the system. The law of a jurisdiction selected pursuant to this subdivision may govern, whether or not that law bears a reasonable relation to the matter in issue.

(d) In the event of inconsistency between an agreement under subdivision (b) and a choice-of-law rule under subdivision (c), the agreement under subdivision (b) prevails.

(e) If a funds transfer is made by use of more than one funds-transfer system and there is inconsistency between choice-of-law rules of the systems, the matter in issue is governed by the law of the selected jurisdiction that has the most significant relationship to the matter in issue. *(Added by Stats.1990, c. 125 (S.B.1759), § 2.)*

Uniform Commercial Code Comment

1. Funds transfers are typically interstate or international in character. If part of a funds transfer is governed by Article 4A and another part is governed by other law, the rights and obligations of parties to the funds transfer may be unclear because there is no clear consensus in various jurisdictions concerning the juridical nature of the transaction. Unless all of a funds transfer is governed by a single law it may be very difficult to predict the result if something goes wrong in the transfer. Section 4A–507 deals with this problem. Subsection (b) allows parties to a funds transfer to make a choice-of-law agreement. Subsection (c) allows a funds transfer system to select the law of a particular jurisdiction to govern funds transfers carried out by means of the system. Subsection (a) states residual rules if no choice of law has occurred under subsection (b) or subsection (c).

2. Subsection (a) deals with three sets of relationships. Rights and obligations between the sender of a payment order and the receiving bank are governed by the law of the jurisdiction in which the receiving bank is located. If the receiving bank is the beneficiary's bank the rights and obligations of the beneficiary are also governed by the law of the jurisdiction in which the receiving bank is located. Suppose Originator, located in Canada, sends a payment order to Originator's Bank located in a state in which Article 4A has been enacted. The order is for payment to an account of Beneficiary in a bank in England. Under subsection (a)(1), the rights and obligations of Originator and Originator's Bank toward each other are governed by Article 4A if an action is brought in a court in the Article 4A state. If an action is brought in a Canadian court, the conflict of laws issue will be determined by Canadian law which might or might not apply the law of the state in which Originator's Bank is located. If that law is applied, the execution of Originator's order will be governed by Article 4A, but with respect to

the payment order of Originator's Bank to the English bank, Article 4A may or may not be applied with respect to the rights and obligations between the two banks. The result may depend upon whether action is brought in a court in the state in which Originator's Bank is located or in an English court. Article 4A is binding only on a court in a state that enacts it. It can have extraterritorial effect only to the extent courts of another jurisdiction are willing to apply it. Subsection (c) also bears on the issues discussed in this Comment.

Under Section 4A–406 payment by the originator to the beneficiary of the funds transfer occurs when the beneficiary's bank accepts a payment order for the benefit of the beneficiary. A jurisdiction in which Article 4A is not in effect may follow a different rule or it may not have a clear rule. Under Section 4A–507(a)(3) the issue is governed by the law of the jurisdiction in which the beneficiary's bank is located. Since the payment to the beneficiary is made through the beneficiary's bank it is reasonable that the issue of when payment occurs be governed by the law of the jurisdiction in which the bank is located. Since it is difficult in many cases to determine where a beneficiary is located, the location of the beneficiary's bank provides a more certain rule.

3. Subsection (b) deals with choice-of-law agreements and it gives maximum freedom of choice. Since the law of funds transfers is not highly developed in the case law there may be a strong incentive to choose the law of a jurisdiction in which Article 4A is in effect because it provides a greater degree of certainty with respect to the rights of various parties. With respect to commercial transactions, it is often said that "[u]niformity and predictability based upon commercial convenience are the prime considerations in making the choice of governing law . . . ." R. Leflar, American Conflicts Law, § 185 (1977). Subsection (b) is derived in part from recently enacted choice-of-law rules in the States of New York and California. N.Y. Gen. Obligations Law 5–1401 (McKinney's 1989 Supp.) and California Civil Code § 1646.5. This broad endorsement of freedom of contract is an enhancement of the approach taken by Restatement (Second) of Conflict of Laws § 187(b) (1971). The Restatement recognizes the basic right of freedom of contract, but the freedom granted the parties may be more limited than the freedom granted here. Under the formulation of the Restatement, if there is no substantial relationship to the jurisdiction whose law is selected and there is no "other" reasonable basis for the parties' choice, then the selection of the parties need not be honored by a court. Further, if the choice is violative of a fundamental policy of a state which has a materially greater interest than the chosen state, the selection could be disregarded by a court. Those limitations are not found in subsection (b).

4. Subsection (c) may be the most important provision in regard to creating uniformity of law in funds transfers. Most rights stated in Article 4A regard parties who are in privity of contract such as originator and beneficiary, sender and receiving bank, and beneficiary's bank and beneficiary. Since they are in privity they can make a choice of law by agreement. But that is not always the case. For example, an intermediary bank that improperly executes a payment order is not in privity with either the originator or the beneficiary. The ability of a funds transfer system to make a choice of law by rule is a convenient way of dispensing with individual agreements and to cover cases in which agreements are not feasible. It is probable that funds transfer systems will adopt a governing law to increase the certainty of commercial transactions that are effected over such systems. A system rule might adopt the law of an Article 4A state to govern transfers on the system in order to provide a consistent, unitary, law governing all transfers made on the system. To the extent such system rules develop, individual choice-of-law agreements become unnecessary.

Subsection (c) has broad application. A system choice of law applies not only to rights and obligations between banks that use the system, but may also apply to other parties to the funds transfer so long as some part of the transfer was carried out over the system. The originator and any other sender or receiving bank in the funds transfer is bound if at the time it issues or accepts a payment order it had notice that the funds transfer involved use of the system and that the system chose the law of a particular jurisdiction. Under Section 4A–107, the Federal Reserve by regulation could make a similar choice of law to govern funds transfers carried out by use of Federal Reserve Banks. Subsection (d) is a limitation on subsection (c). If parties have made a choice-of-law agreement that conflicts with a choice of law made under subsection (c), the agreement prevails.

5. Subsection (e) addresses the case in which a funds transfer involves more than one funds transfer system and the systems adopt conflicting choice-of-law rules. The rule that has the most significant relationship to the matter at issue prevails. For example, each system should be able to make a choice of law governing payment orders transmitted over that system without regard to a choice of law made by another system.

Division 12

EFFECTIVE DATE AND TRANSITION PROVISIONS [REPEALED]

§§ 12101 to 12104. Repealed by Stats.1988, c. 1359, § 7, operative Jan. 1, 1990

Division 13

EFFECTIVE DATE AND REPEALER

Section
13101. Effective Date.
13102. Provision for Transition; Continuation Statement.
13103. General Repealer.
13104. Laws Not Repealed.
13105. Validation of Prior Filings; Requirements After Jan. 1, 1971.

WESTLAW Computer Assisted Legal Research

WESTLAW supplements your legal research in many ways. WESTLAW allows you to
- update your research with the most current information
- expand your library with additional resources
- retrieve direct history, precedential history and parallel citations with the Insta-Cite service

For more information on using WESTLAW to supplement your research, see the WESTLAW Electronic Research Guide, which follows the Preface.

Continuation of Division

Continuing application of this division to the Commercial Code as it existed on Jan. 1, 1993, see Commercial Code § 16102.

Cross References

Continued application of this division to this code, see Commercial Code §§ 14102, 15102.

§ 13101. Effective Date

This code shall become effective on January 1, 1965. It applies to transactions entered into and events occurring after that date. *(Added by Stats.1988, c. 1359, § 8, operative Jan. 1, 1990.)*

Uniform Commercial Code Comment

This effective date is suggested so that there may be ample time for all those who will be affected by the provisions of the Code to become familiar with them.

Cross References

Effective date of statutes, see Const. Art. 2, § 10, Art. 4, § 8; Government Code § 9600.

§ 13102. Provision for Transition; Continuation Statement

Transactions validly entered into before January 1, 1965, and the rights, duties, and interests flowing from them remain valid thereafter and may be terminated, completed, consummated, or enforced as required or permitted by any statute or other law amended or repealed by this act as though such repeal or amendment had not occurred; provided, however, that the perfection of a security interest (other than a security interest (i) in a motor vehicle or vessel required to be registered under the Vehicle Code unless such vehicle or vessel is inventory or (ii) in personal property, including fixtures, which constitutes a portion of the properties included in an agreement which is a mortgage or deed of trust of both real and personal property made to secure the payment of bonds or other evidences of indebtedness authorized or permitted to be issued by the Commissioner of Corporations, or made by a public utility as defined in the Public Utilities Code), as defined in this code (Section 1201), and however denominated in any law repealed by this act,

(a) Which was perfected on or before January 1, 1965, by a filing or recording under a law repealed by this act and requiring a further filing or recording to continue its perfection, continues until and will lapse on the date provided by the law so repealed for such further filing or recording.

(b) Which was perfected on or before January 1, 1965, by a filing or recording under a law repealed by this act and requiring no further filing or recording to continue its perfection, continues until and will lapse 12 months after January 1, 1965.

(c) Which was perfected on or before January 1, 1965, without any filing or recording, but with respect to which a financing statement is required to be filed in order for it to be perfected under this code, continues until and will lapse 12 months after January 1, 1965;

unless, in each case, a continuation statement is filed by the secured party within 12 months before the perfection of the security interest would otherwise lapse. Any such continuation statement must be signed by the secured party, identify the original security agreement, however denominated, state the office where and the date when last filed or refiled, or recorded or rerecorded, and the filing number or recordation data and further state that the original security agreement is still effective. Subdivision (1) of Section 9401 determines the proper place to file such a continuation statement. Except as herein specified the provisions of subdivision (3) of Section 9403 apply to such a continuation statement. *(Added by Stats.1988, c. 1359, § 8, operative Jan. 1, 1990.)*

Cross References

Filing to perfect security interest, see Commercial Code § 9401.
Motor vehicles, filing instruments evidencing liens or encumbrances, see Vehicle Code § 6300 et seq.
Repeal of repealing statute, see Government Code § 9607.
Repeal of statutes, see Government Code § 9606.

Transfer of title to, or interest in, undocumented vessels, see Vehicle Code § 9900 et seq.

§ 13103. General Repealer

Except as provided in the following section, all acts and parts of acts inconsistent with this act are hereby repealed. *(Added by Stats.1988, c. 1359, § 8, operative Jan. 1, 1990.)*

Uniform Commercial Code Comment

This section provides for the repeal of all other legislation inconsistent with this Act.

Uniform Law:

Cross References

Construction against implicit repeal, see Commercial Code § 1104.
Repeal of repealing statute, see Government Code § 9607.
Repeal of statutes, see Government Code § 9606.

§ 13104. Laws Not Repealed

The division on documents of title (Division 7) does not repeal or modify any laws prescribing the form or contents of documents of title or the services or facilities to be afforded by bailees, or otherwise regulating bailees' businesses in respects not specifically dealt with herein; but the fact that such laws are violated does not affect the status of a document of title which otherwise complies with the definition of a document of title (Section 1201). *(Added by Stats.1983, c. 1359, § 8, operative Jan. 1, 1990.)*

Uniform Commercial Code Comment

This section subordinates the Article of this Act on Documents of Title (Article 7) to the more specialized regulations of particular classes of bailees under other legislation and international treaties. Particularly, the provisions of that Article are superseded by applicable inconsistent provisions regarding the obligation of carriers and the limitation of their liability found in federal legislation dealing with transportation by water (including the Harter Act, Act of February 13, 1893, 27 Stat. 445, and the Carriage of Goods by Sea Act, Act of April 16, 1936, 49 Stat. 1207); the Warsaw Convention on International Air Transportation, 49 Stat. 3000, and Section 20(11) of the Interstate Commerce Act, Act of February 20, 1887, 24 Stat. 386, as amended. The Documents of Title provisions of this Act supplement such legislation largely in matters other than obligation of the bailee, e.g., form and effects of negotiation, procedure in the case of lost documents, effect of over-issue, possibility of rapid transmission.

Cross Reference:

Section 7–103.

Cross References

Construction against implicit repeal, see Commercial Code § 1104.
Documents of title,
  Generally, see Commercial Code § 7101 et seq.
  Effect of provisions outside code, see Commercial Code § 7103.
General repealer, see Commercial Code § 13103.
Obligations of carriers of property, see Civil Code §§ 2114, 2115, 2118 et seq., 2194 et seq.
Obligations of depositary, see Civil Code § 1822 et seq.
Repeal of repealing statute, see Government Code § 9607.
Repeal of statutes, see Government Code § 9606.

§ 13105. Validation of Prior Filings; Requirements After Jan. 1, 1971

(1) A financing statement or a continuation thereof, properly filed and effective pursuant to Section 9401 as it existed prior to January 1, 1971, remains valid and effective after January 1, 1971, until expiration of the usual five-year period from date of filing. Any termination, release, assignment, or amendment of the financing statement prior to expiration of the five-year period of effectiveness shall be filed, as previously required, with the county recorder who has filed the financing statement.

(2) After January 1, 1971, any continuation of a financing statement which had been properly filed with a county recorder prior to January 1, 1971, and which now would be required to be filed with the Secretary of State, shall be filed with the Secretary of State in accordance with Section 9403. The continuation statement shall be accompanied by a certified copy of the entire record of the county recorder related to the financing statement. After filing of the continuation statement with the Secretary of State, any termination, release, assignment, amendment, or continuation of the financing statement shall also be filed with the Secretary of State and any documents affecting the financing statement that are not filed with the Secretary of State shall not be effective. *(Added by Stats.1988, c. 1359, § 8, operative Jan. 1, 1990.)*

Division 14

EFFECTIVE DATE AND TRANSITION PROVISIONS

Section
14101. Effective Date.
14102. Preservation of Old Transition Provision.
14103. Transition to 1973–74 Amendments—General Rule.
14104. Transition Provision on Change of Requirement of Filing.
14105. Transition Provision on Change of Place of Filing.
14106. Required Refilings.
14107. Transition Provisions as to Priorities.
14108. Presumption that Rule of Law Continues Unchanged.
14109. Application of 1979–80 Amendments Related to Fixtures.

WESTLAW Computer Assisted Legal Research

WESTLAW supplements your legal research in many ways. WESTLAW allows you to
- update your research with the most current information
- expand your library with additional resources
- retrieve direct history, precedential history and parallel citations with the Insta-Cite service

For more information on using WESTLAW to supplement your research, see the WESTLAW Electronic Research Guide, which follows the Preface.

Continuation of Division

Continuing application of this division to the Commercial Code as it existed on Jan. 1, 1993, see Commercial Code § 16102.

Cross References

Continued application of this division to this code, see Commercial Code § 15102.

§ 14101. Effective Date

The amendments to this code, as adopted by the Legislature at the 1973–74 Regular Session, shall become effective at 12:01 a.m. on January 1, 1976. *(Added by Stats.1988, c. 1359, § 9, operative Jan. 1, 1990.)*

§ 14102. Preservation of Old Transition Provision

The provisions of Division 13 shall continue to apply to this code, as amended by the Legislature at the 1973–74 Regular Session, and for this purpose this code as it existed prior to January 1, 1976, and this code, as amended by the Legislature at the 1973–74 Regular Session, shall be considered one continuous statute. *(Added by Stats.1988, c. 1359, § 9, operative Jan. 1, 1990.)*

§ 14103. Transition to 1973–74 Amendments—General Rule

Transactions validly entered into after January 1, 1965, and before January 1, 1976, and which were subject to the provisions of this code and which would be subject to this code as amended by the Legislature at the 1973–74 Regular Session if they had been entered into after January 1, 1976, and the rights, duties, and interests flowing from the transactions remain valid after January 1, 1976, and may be terminated, completed, consummated, or enforced as required or permitted by this code as amended by the Legislature at the 1972 Regular Session. Security interests arising out of these transactions which are perfected on January 1, 1976, shall remain perfected until they lapse as provided in this code as amended by the Legislature at the 1973–74 Regular Session, and may be continued as permitted by this code as amended by the Legislature at the 1973–74 Regular Session, except as stated in Section 14105. *(Added by Stats.1988, c. 1359, § 9, operative Jan. 1, 1990.)*

§ 14104. Transition Provision on Change of Requirement of Filing

A security interest for the perfection of which filing or the taking of possession was required under this code and which attached prior to January 1, 1976, but was not perfected shall be deemed perfected on January 1, 1975, if this code as amended by the Legislature at the 1973–74 Regular Session permits perfection without filing or authorizes filing in the office or offices where a prior ineffective filing was made. *(Added by Stats.1988, c. 1359, § 9, operative Jan. 1, 1990.)*

§ 14105. Transition Provision on Change of Place of Filing

(1) A financing statement or continuation statement filed prior to January 1, 1976, which shall not have lapsed prior to January 1, 1976, shall remain effective for the period provided in this code as it existed prior to January 1, 1976, but not less than five years after the filing.

(2) With respect to any collateral acquired by the debtor subsequent to January 1, 1976, any effective financing statement or continuation statement described in this section shall apply only if the filing or filings are in the office or offices that would be appropriate to perfect the security interests in the new collateral under this code as amended by the Legislature at the 1973–74 Regular Session.

(3) The effectiveness of any financing statement or continuation statement filed prior to January 1, 1976,

may be continued by a continuation statement as permitted by this code as amended by the Legislature at the 1973–74 Regular Session, except that if this code, as amended by the Legislature at the 1973–74 Regular Session, requires a filing in an office where there was no previous financing statement, a new financing statement conforming to Section 14106 shall be filed in that office. *(Added by Stats.1988, c. 1359, § 9, operative Jan. 1, 1990.)*

§ 14106. Required Refilings

(1) If a security interest is perfected or has priority on January 1, 1976, as to all persons or as to certain persons without any filing or recording, and if the filing of a financing statement would be required for the perfection or priority of the security interest against those persons under this code, as amended by the Legislature at the 1973–74 Regular Session, the perfection and priority rights of the security interest continue until January 1, 1979. The perfection will then lapse unless a financing statement is filed as provided in subdivision (4) or unless the security interest is perfected otherwise than by filing.

(2) If a security interest is perfected on January 1, 1976, under a law other than this code which requires no further filing, refiling or recording to continue its perfection, perfection continues until and will lapse January 1, 1979, unless a financing statement is filed as provided in subdivision (4) or unless the security interest is perfected otherwise than by filing, or unless under subdivision (3) of Section 9302 the other law continues to govern filing.

(3) If a security interest is perfected by a filing, refiling or recording under a law repealed by this code as amended by the Legislature at the 1973–74 Regular Session which required further filing, refiling or recording to continue its perfection, perfection continues and will lapse on the date provided by the law so repealed for a further filing, refiling, or recording unless a financing statement is filed as provided in subdivision (4) or unless the security interest is perfected otherwise than by filing.

(4) A financing statement may be filed within six months before the perfection of a security interest would otherwise lapse. Any such financing statement may be signed by either the debtor or the secured party. It must identify the security agreement, statement, or notice (however denominated in any statute or other law repealed or modified by this code as amended by the Legislature at the 1973–74 Regular Session), state the office where and the date when the last filing, refiling, or recording, if any, was made with respect thereto, and the filing number, if any, was made with respect thereto, and the filing number, if any, or book and page, if any, of recording and further state that the security agreement, statement, or notice, however denominated, in another filing office under this code or under any statute or other law repealed or modified by this code as amended by the Legislature at the 1973–74 Regular Session is still effective. Section 9401 and Section 9103 determine the proper place to file such a financing statement. Except as specified in this subdivision, the provisions of Section 9403(3) for continuation statements apply to such a financing statement. *(Added by Stats.1988, c. 1359, § 9, operative Jan. 1, 1990.)*

§ 14107. Transition Provisions as to Priorities

Except as otherwise provided in this division, this code as it existed prior to January 1, 1976, shall apply to any questions of priority if the positions of the parties were fixed prior to January 1, 1976. In other cases questions of priority shall be determined by this code as amended by the Legislature at the 1973–74 Regular Session. *(Added by Stats.1988, c. 1359, § 9, operative Jan. 1, 1990.)*

§ 14108. Presumption that Rule of Law Continues Unchanged

Unless a change in law has clearly been made, the provisions of this code as amended by the Legislature at the 1973–74 Regular Session shall be deemed declaratory of the meaning of this code as it existed prior to January 1, 1976. The amendments to subdivision (38) of Section 1201 and to subdivision (j) of Section 9104 of this code as amended by the Legislature at the 1973–74 Regular Session shall be deemed declaratory of the meaning of this code as it existed prior to January 1, 1976. *(Added by Stats.1988, c. 1359, § 9, operative Jan. 1, 1990.)*

§ 14109. Application of 1979–80 Amendments Related to Fixtures

(1) The amendments to this code relating to fixtures adopted by the Legislature at the 1979–1980 Regular Session shall apply to security interests which attach on or after January 1, 1981, in goods which become fixtures on or after January 1, 1981.

(2) If the record of a mortgage of real estate would have been effective as a fixture filing of goods described therein if the amendments to this code relating to fixtures adopted by the Legislature at the 1979–1980 Regular Session had been in effect on the date of recording the mortgage, the mortgage shall be deemed effective as a fixture filing as to such goods under subdivision (6) of Section 9402 as of January 1, 1981. *(Added by Stats.1988, c. 1359, § 9, operative Jan. 1, 1990.)*

Division 15

EFFECTIVE DATE AND TRANSITION PROVISIONS

Section
15101. Repeal and Addition of Division 8.
15102. Continuous Application of Division 13 and Division 14.
15103. Interests in Uncertificated Securities; Governing Law.
15104. Security Interests in Uncertificated Securities; Governing Law; Continuation of Perfection of Security interest.

WESTLAW Computer Assisted Legal Research

WESTLAW supplements your legal research in many ways. WESTLAW allows you to
• update your research with the most current information
• expand your library with additional resources
• retrieve direct history, precedential history and parallel citations with the Insta-Cite service
For more information on using WESTLAW to supplement your research, see the WESTLAW Electronic Research Guide, which follows the Preface.

Continuation of Division

Continuing application of this division to the Commercial Code as it existed on Jan. 1, 1993, see Commercial Code § 16102.

§ 15101. Repeal and Addition of Division 8

The repeal and addition of Division 8 (commencing with Section 8101) made at the 1984 portion of the 1983–84 Regular Session shall become effective on January 1, 1985. *(Added by Stats.1988, c. 1359, § 10, operative Jan. 1, 1990.)*

§ 15102. Continuous Application of Division 13 and Division 14

The provisions of Division 13 (commencing with Section 13101) and Division 14 (commencing with Section 14101) shall continue to apply to this code, as revised by the Legislature at the 1983–84 Regular Session, and for this purpose, this code as it existed prior to January 1, 1985, and this code, as revised by the Legislature at the 1984 portion of the 1983–84 Regular Session, shall be considered one continuous statute. *(Added by Stats.1988, c. 1359, § 10, operative Jan. 1, 1990.)*

§ 15103. Interests in Uncertificated Securities; Governing Law

The owner of an interest (other than a security interest) in an uncertificated security (paragraph (b) of subdivision (1) of Section 8102) whose interest was acquired prior to January 1, 1985, or was acquired after January 1, 1985, in an uncertificated security issued in respect of a security in which the owner had such an interest, shall not be required to take any action under Section 8313 or otherwise to preserve or protect that ownership interest, which shall remain effective and enforceable to the same extent it was prior to January 1, 1985, in the absence of that action. However, if a security interest first attaches to the security or any other interest in the security first becomes effective after that date, the provisions of Division 8 (commencing with Section 8101) as revised shall govern the rights and obligations of all persons with respect to those interests. Except as otherwise provided in this division, the rights and obligations of all persons with respect to uncertificated securities issued prior to January 1, 1985, shall be governed by Division 8 (commencing with Section 8101) as revised by * * * Chapter 927 of the Statutes of 1984. All references in this section to Division 8 (commencing with Section 8101) or a section thereof are references to Division 8 (commencing with Section 8101) as revised by Chapter 927 of the Statutes of 1984. *(Added by Stats.1988, c. 1359, § 10, operative Jan. 1, 1990. Amended by Stats.1996, c. 497 (S.B.1591), § 23, operative Jan. 1, 1997.)*

Legislative Committee Comment—Assembly
1984 Addition

This provision "grandfathers" ownership of uncertificated securities acquired prior to the effective date of new Division 8, without the requirement of any further action on the part of the owner. It also "grandfathers" ownership of uncertificated securities acquired after the effective date, but only if the securities were issued "in respect of" (i.e., by way of a stock split or stock dividend) securities acquired prior to the effective date.

In the event that the owner grants a security interest in or otherwise transfers the security, the new requirements of Division 8 applicable to uncertificated securities must be complied with. Thus, no shelter principle is applicable.

It should be noted that the reference to the definition of uncertificated securities in Section 8102(1)(b) leaves open the question whether a particular item of property is or is not an uncertificated security, making the application of this provision conditional on an independent determination that the property in question is an uncertificated security. [84 A.J. 18471].

§ 15104. Security Interests in Uncertificated Securities; Governing Law; Continuation of Perfection of Security interest

A secured party who has a security interest in an uncertificated security (paragraph (b) of subdivision (1) of Section 8102), which security interest attached to that uncertificated security (a) prior to January 1, 1985, or (b) after that date in an uncertificated security issued in respect of a security in which the secured party had the pre-January 1, 1985, security interest, shall not be required to take any action under Division 8 (commencing with Section 8101) to protect, preserve, or perfect that security interest, which shall remain attached and perfected to the same extent it was prior to that date in the absence of any such action. The priority and perfection of those security interests shall continue to be governed by Division 9 (commencing with Section 9101) as it existed prior to that date. However, on or before the last date on which any action is required under Division 9 (commencing with Section 9101) (as it existed prior to that date) to continue the perfection of the security interest, in order to continue the perfection of the security interest the secured party, rather than complying with Division 9 (commencing with Section 9101), shall furnish to a party described in subparagraph (i), (iii), or (iv) of paragraph (h) of subdivision (1) of Section 8313, or if none of those is applicable, then to the issuer of the uncertificated security, either (x) a copy of either the financing statement previously filed to perfect the security interest or the security agreement that created the security interest, in either case bearing a copy or an original of the debtor's signature, or (y) a written notification from the registered owner under paragraph (b) of subdivision (7) of Section 8403. Any such notice to an issuer shall be deemed a written notification under paragraph (b) of subdivision (7) of Section 8403, subject to the limitation that there can be no more than one registered pledge of an uncertificated security at any time (Section 8108). Except as otherwise provided in this division, the provisions of Division 8 (commencing with Section 8101) as revised shall govern the rights and obligations of all persons with respect to a security interest in an uncertificated security that first attaches after January 1, 1985. All references in this section to Division 8 (commencing with Section 8101) or a section thereof are references to Division 8 (commencing with Section 8101) as revised by Chapter 927 of the Statutes of 1984. *(Added by Stats.1988, c. 1359, § 10, operative Jan. 1, 1990. Amended by Stats. 1996, c. 497 (S.B.1591), § 24, operative Jan. 1, 1997.)*

Legislative Committee Comment—Assembly
1984 Addition

This provision "grandfathers" security interests in uncertificated securities created prior to the effective date of new Division 8, or after the effective date in uncertificated securities issued "in respect of" (i.e., by way of a stock split or stock dividend) securities in which the secured party had a pre-effective date security interest. However, a secured party must eventually comply with the requirements of Division 8. If perfected by filing (as required by Section 9302 prior to the effective date of new Division 8), the secured party would have to take periodic action under Section 9403 in any event. If the secured party is concerned that its collateral might be uncertificated securities (as, for instance, if it has taken a security interest in mutual fund shares or dividend reinvestment plan interests), then it can protect itself by complying with the requirements of this section.

As in Section 9403, this section provides a method for continuation of perfection that does not require the cooperation of the debtor. The secured party already should have a security agreement signed by the debtor, since the only alternative under Section 9203(1) (possession of the collateral by the secured party) is not possible as to uncertificated securities, and should have a copy of the financing statement signed by the debtor (Sections 9302, 9402(1)). The secured party need only put the appropriate party (as described in this section) on notice of its security interest, and thus continue perfection, by furnishing it with a copy of the financing statement or the security agreement.

Notice to an issuer under this section will give rise to an adverse claim as to which the issuer has a duty under Section 8403. However, this does not expand the issuer's duty to register no more than one pledge at any time (Section 8108). If the issuer receives more than one notice under this section, it should register the first one received. Upon such registration Section 8313(1)(h) becomes applicable, and the issuer is no longer the proper party to receive notice under this section. [84 A.J. 18471].

Division 16

EFFECTIVE DATE AND TRANSITION PROVISIONS

Section
16101. Division 3 and Division 4; construction of changes made by Stats.1992, c. 914.
16102. Application of Divisions 13 to 15 to Code in existence on Jan. 1, 1993.
16103. Limitation of actions.
16104. Code in existence on Jan. 1, 1993; construction.

§ 16101. Division 3 and Division 4; construction of changes made by Stats.1992, c. 914

The repeal and addition of Division 3 (commencing with Section 3101) and the repeal and addition, the amendment, and the addition of provisions of Division 4 (commencing with Section 4101), and the amendment of related sections, adopted by the Legislature in Chapter 914 of the Statutes of 1992, shall become effective on January 1, 1993. The Legislature intends that the that [1] action be construed as an amendment of Division 3 (commencing with Section 3101) and Division 4 (commencing with Section 4101), notwithstanding that the action took the form of a repeal and addition of Division 3 (commencing with Section 3101), and a repeal and addition to, and amendment of, or an addition to the provisions of Division 4 (commencing with Section 4101). *(Added by Stats.1994, c. 668 (S.B.1405), § 15.)*

[1] So in chaptered copy.

§ 16102. Application of Divisions 13 to 15 to Code in existence on Jan. 1, 1993

The provisions of Division 13 (commencing with Section 13101), Division 14 (commencing with Section 14101), and Division 15 (commencing with Section 15101) shall continue to apply to this code, as this code existed on January 1, 1993, and for this purpose, this code, as it existed prior to January 1, 1993, and this code, as it existed on January 1, 1993, shall be considered one continuous statute. *(Added by Stats.1994, c. 668 (S.B.1405), § 15.)*

§ 16103. Limitation of actions

Nothing in this division shall have the effect of (a) reviving a cause of action barred by limitation before January 1, 1993, or (b) applying Section 3118 or 4111 on limitation of actions to an action commenced before January 1, 1993. *(Added by Stats.1994, c. 668 (S.B. 1405), § 15.)*

§ 16104. Code in existence on Jan. 1, 1993; construction

Unless a change in law, as contrasted with a clarification, has clearly been made, this code, as it existed on January 1, 1993, shall be deemed declaratory of the meaning of this code as it existed prior to January 1, 1993. *(Added by Stats.1994, c. 668 (S.B.1405), § 15.)*

INDEX TO COMMERCIAL CODE

ABSENCE AND ABSENTEES
Sales contracts,
   Specific time provisions, **Com 2309**
   Specified place for delivery, **Com 2308**

ACCELERATION
Commercial Paper, this index

ACCEPTOR
Defined, negotiable instruments, **Com 3103**

ACCESSION, ACCRETION AND AVULSION
Defined, leases, **Com 10310**
Secured transactions, **Com 9314**

ACCESSIONS
Defined, leases, **Com 10310**

ACCIDENTS
Documents of title, **Com 7502**
Insurance, generally, this index

ACCOMMODATIONS
Non-conforming goods offered buyer, **Com 2206**

ACCORD AND SATISFACTION
Delivery of goods excused, **Com 7403**
Negotiable instruments, use of instrument, **Com 3311**

ACCOUNT DEBTOR
Defined,
   Secured transactions, **Com 9105**

ACCOUNTS AND ACCOUNTING
Bank Deposits and Collections, this index
Commercial Paper, this index
Defined,
   Bank deposits and collections, **Com 4104**
   Commercial code, **Com 10103**
   Secured transactions, **Com 9106**
Deposit accounts,
   Secured transactions, filing exclusion, **Com 9302**
Investment securities,
   Delivery to, warranties, **Com 8109**
   Entitlements, **Com 8501**
Sales, resale of goods, **Com 2706**
Secured Transactions, this index
Security interest, defined, **Com 1201**

ACCOUNTS RECEIVABLE
Secured transactions, assignments, exemptions, **Com 9104**

ACTIONS AND PROCEEDINGS
Aggrieved party, defined, Commercial Code, **Com 1201**
Arbitration and Award, generally, this index
Attachment, generally, this index
Bills of Lading, this index
Claim and Delivery, generally, this index
Commercial code, enforcement of remedies, **Com 1106**
Counterclaim. Set-Off and Counterclaim, generally, this index
Damages, generally, this index
Definitions, **Com 1201**
Enforcement of remedies, commercial code, **Com 1106**
Equity, generally, this index
Evidence, generally, this index
Executions, generally, this index
Foreclosure, generally. Mortgages, this index
Injunction, generally, this index
Investment Securities, this index
Judgments and Decrees, generally, this index
Leases, this index
Limitation of Actions, generally, this index
Mechanics Liens, generally, this index
Negligence, generally, this index
Parties, generally, this index
Probate Proceedings, generally, this index
Process, generally, this index
Receivers and Receivership, generally, this index
Sales, this index
Security interest, levy, limitation of actions, **Com 6111**
Set-Off and Counterclaim, generally, this index
Third Parties, generally, this index
Warehouse receipts, provisions, **Com 7204**

ACTS OF LEGISLATURE
Statutes, generally, this index

AD VALOREM TAXES
Taxation, generally, this index

ADDITIONAL TERMS
Acceptance of offer, **Com 2207**

ADDRESS
Secured transactions, financing statement, **Com 9402**

ADDRESS—Cont'd
Send, defined, commercial code, **Com 1201**

ADJOINING STATES
Foreign States, generally, this index

ADMINISTRATION OF ESTATES
Probate Proceedings, generally, this index

ADMINISTRATIVE LAW AND PROCEDURE
Leases,
   Default, **Com 10501**

ADMISSIBILITY OF EVIDENCE
Evidence, generally, this index

ADMISSIONS
Investment securities, signatures, **Com 8114**

ADULTERATION
Food, generally, this index

ADVANCES AND ADVANCEMENTS
Financing agency, defined, Sales Act, **Com 2104**
Secured Transactions, this index
Warehouse receipts, forms, **Com 7202**

ADVISORS
Defined,
   Letters of credit, **Com 5102**

AERONAUTICS
Aircraft, generally, this index

AFTER–ACQUIRED PROPERTY
Secured transactions, application of law, **Com 9102**

AFTERNOON
Bank deposits and collections, cut-off time, **Com 4108**
Defined, bank deposits and collections, **Com 4104**

AGE
Checks, bank deposits and collections, **Com 4404**

AGENTS
Bank deposits and collections, **Com 4201**
Commercial code, application of law, **Com 1103**
Funds transfers, transfer system, **Com 11206**
Investment Securities, this index

623

AGENTS

AGENTS—Cont'd
Issuer, defined, documents of title, **Com 7102**
Sales, this index
Seller under Sales Act, **Com 2707**
Signatures,
    Negotiable instruments, **Com 3403**
    Warehouse receipts, **Com 7202**
Transfer agent, generally. Investment Securities, this index

AGGRIEVED PARTIES
Parties, this index

AGREEMENTS
Contracts, generally, this index
Defined,
    Commercial Code, **Com 1201**
    Sales Act, **Com 2106**

AGRICULTURAL COOPERATIVE ASSOCIATIONS
Merchants, secured transactions, **Com 9102**
Secured transactions, security interest in inventory, retail merchant, **Com 9102**

AGRICULTURAL MACHINERY AND EQUIPMENT
Secured transactions, **Com 9103**
    Application of law, **Com 9102**
Security interest,
    Filing, **Com 9401**
    Perfection, **Com 9302**

AGRICULTURAL PRODUCTS
Contracts,
    Sale, growing crops, **Com 2107**
Definitions,
    Secured transactions, **Com 9109**
Future crops, sales, insurable interest, **Com 2501**
Insurable interest of buyer, growing crop, **Com 2501**
Protection of buyer, **Com 9307**
Sales, **Com 2102**
    Goods, defined, **Com 2105**
Sales Act,
    Application, **Com 2102**
    Goods, defined, **Com 2105**
Secured Transactions, this index
Third-party rights, **Com 2107**
Warehouse receipts, **Com 7201**
Warehouses and Warehousemen, generally, this index

AIRBILL
Defined, commercial code, **Com 1201**

AIRCRAFT
Foreign,
    Secured transactions, location of debtor, **Com 9103**

ALCOHOLIC BEVERAGES
Bank deposits and collections, incompetency of customer, **Com 4405**
Secured transactions, application of law, **Com 9102**

ALCOHOLIC BEVERAGES—Cont'd
Warehouse receipts, **Com 7201 et seq.**

ALIENATION
Deeds and Conveyances, generally, this index

ALTERATION OF INSTRUMENTS
Banks and banking,
    Duty of customer, **Com 4406**
Bills of lading, **Com 7306**
Forgery, generally, this index
Investment securities, **Com 8206**
Warehouse receipts, **Com 7208**

ALTERNATIVE PAYEES
Negotiable instruments, payable to order, **Com 3110**

AMBASSADORS AND CONSULS
Invoices, presumptions, **Com 1202**
Negotiable instruments, certificate of dishonor, **Com 3505**
Third party documents, presumptions, **Com 1202**

AMOUNT IN CONTROVERSY
Statute of frauds, personal property not otherwise covered, **Com 1206**

ANIMALS
Farm products, defined, **Com 9109**
Fish and Game, generally, this index
Issue, security interest, attachment, **Com 9204**
Sales,
    Goods, defined, **Com 2105**
    Insurable interest, **Com 2501**
Secured transactions,
    Farm products defined, **Com 9109**
    Security interest, attaching, **Com 9204**
Unborn young of animals, sales, insurable interest, **Com 2501**
Wild animals and birds. Fish and Game, generally, this index

ANOMALOUS INDORSEMENTS
Defined, negotiable instruments, **Com 3205**

ANTECEDENT DEBT
Secured transactions, after-acquired collateral, **Com 9108**

ANTEDATED INSTRUMENTS
Negotiable instruments, **Com 3113**

ANTICIPATORY REPUDIATION
Sales, this index

APPLIANCES
Retail sales, warranty cards, **Com 2800, 2801**

APPLICANT
Defined,
    Letters of credit, **Com 5102**

APPORTIONMENT
Sales, delivery of goods, **Com 2307**

APPROPRIATE PERSON
Defined, investment securities, **Com 8107**

AQUATIC ORGANISMS
Fish and Game, generally, this index

ARBITRATION AND AWARD
Attorneys, generally, this index
Leases,
    Default, **Com 10501**

ASSESSMENTS
Investment securities, registered owner, **Com 8207**

ASSIGNMENT FOR BENEFIT OF CREDITORS
Bulk sales, **Com 6103**
Definitions,
    Commercial code, **Com 1201**
Financing statements, filing, **Com 9302**

ASSIGNMENTS
Damages,
    Breach of sales contract, **Com 2210**
Letters of credit, proceeds, **Com 5114**
Recorders, index, destruction, **Com 9403.1**
Sales contract, **Com 2210**
Secured Transactions, this index

ASSOCIATIONS AND SOCIETIES
Business Trusts, generally, this index
Definitions,
    Organization, **Com 1201**
Organization, defined,
    Commercial code, **Com 1201**
Partnership, generally, this index
Savings and Loan Associations, generally, this index

ASSUMED OR FICTITIOUS NAMES
Negotiable instruments, signatures, **Com 3401**

ATTACHMENT
Bulk sales, sellers payments, disputed claims by sellers creditors, **Com 6106.2**
Certificates and certification,
    Attachment liens, combined certificates, **Com 9409**
Funds transfers, **Com 11502**
Goods under document of title, **Com 7602**
Secured Transactions, this index

ATTORNEY FEES
Documents of title, lost, stolen or destroyed, bailee, **Com 7601**
Funds transfers,
    Execution of payment orders, receiving banks, liability, **Com 11305**
    Payment orders, cancellation or amendment, losses and expenses, **Com 11211**
Letters of credit, **Com 5111**

ATTORNEYS
Documents of title, fees, lost, stolen or destroyed documents, bailee, **Com 7601**
Secured transactions, fees, collateral,
Disposition after default, **Com 9504**
Redeemed after default, **Com 9506**

AUCTIONS AND AUCTIONEERS
Bids,
Retraction, **Com 2328**
Bulk sales, **Com 6108**
Limitation of actions, **Com 6110**
Buyer, **Com 2328**
Completion of sale, **Com 2328**
Defined,
Bulk sales, **Com 6102**
Elections of bids, **Com 2328**
Forced sales, **Com 2328**
Fraud, **Com 2328**
Good faith, bidding, **Com 2328**
Lots, Sales Act, **Com 2328**
Motor carriers, enforcement of liens, **Com 7308**
Reopen bidding, **Com 2328**
Resale by seller, **Com 2706**
Reserve, **Com 2328**
Sales Act, **Com 2328**
Secured transactions, collateral, default, **Com 9504**
Warehousemen,
Lien, enforcement, **Com 7210**
Termination of storage, **Com 7206**
Without reserve, **Com 2328**

AUTHENTICATING TRUSTEES
Investment Securities, this index

AUTOMOBILES
Motor Vehicles, generally, this index

AVIATION
Aircraft, generally, this index

BABIES
Children and Minors, generally, this index

BAD FAITH
Good Faith, generally, this index

BAGS
Containers, generally, this index

BAILMENT
Acknowledgment goods held for buyer, **Com 2705**
Bills of Lading, generally, this index
Defined, documents of title, **Com 7102**
Delay, delivery of goods, **Com 7403**
Delivery of property, **Com 7403**
Documents of Title, generally, this index
Good faith delivery of goods, documents of title, **Com 7404**
Investment securities,
Financial assets, transfer, **Com 8115**
Sales, this index
Stoppage of delivery, **Com 2703, 2705**
Leases of personal property, default by lessee, **Com 10526**

BAILMENT—Cont'd
Warehouse Receipts, generally, this index
Warehouses and Warehousemen, generally, this index

BANK DEPOSITS AND COLLECTIONS
Generally, **Com 4101 et seq.**
Acceptance,
Death of customer, **Com 4405**
Defined, commercial paper,
Application, **Com 4104**
Incompetency of customer, **Com 4405**
Notice of holding, **Com 4212**
Presentment warranties, **Com 4208**
Settlement, **Com 4213**
Warranties, **Com 4207**
Accounts and accounting,
Defined, **Com 4104**
Late return of items, **Com 4302**
Actions and proceedings,
Conflict of laws, **Com 4102**
Afternoon, defined, **Com 4104**
Afternoon hour, cut-off time, **Com 4108**
Age of check, **Com 4404**
Agency relationship, **Com 4201**
Agreements,
Electronic presentment, **Com 4110**
Settlement, **Com 4213**
Variation, **Com 4103**
Alteration of instruments,
Duty of customer, **Com 4406**
Presentment warranties, **Com 4208**
Transfer warranties, **Com 4207**
Alterations, duty of customer, **Com 4406**
Application of law, **Com 4102, 4201**
Negotiable instruments, **Com 3102**
Bank offered spot rates, charge-back or refund, **Com 4214**
Banking day, defined, **Com 4104**
Branch banks,
Defined, **Com 1201**
Payment, time and place, **Com 4107**
Separate bank, **Com 4105**
Breach of warranties,
Damages, **Com 4207**
Encoding, retention, **Com 4209**
Presentment, **Com 4208**
Warranties, **Com 4208**
Statute of limitations, **Com 4111**
Transfer warranties, **Com 4207**
Burden of proof,
Damages, payment after stop payment order, **Com 4403**
Reasonable time, **Com 4202**
Cashiers check, settlement, **Com 4213**
Certificates of deposit,
Defined, commercial paper,
Application, **Com 4104**
Certification,
Defined, **Com 3411**
Commercial paper,
Application, **Com 4104**
Certified checks,
Time for presenting, **Com 4404**
Charge-back, **Com 4214**
Charging items against accounts, **Com 4401**

BANK DEPOSITS AND COLLECTIONS —Cont'd
Checks,
Defined,
Commercial paper,
Application, **Com 4104**
Electronic presentment, **Com 4110**
More than six months old, payment, **Com 4404**
Postdating, charging against account, **Com 4401**
Presentment warranties, **Com 4208**
Transfer warranties, **Com 4207**
Clearinghouse, **Com 4215**
Defined, **Com 4104**
Electronic presentment, **Com 4110**
Provisional settlements, **Com 4215**
Return, item received through, **Com 4301**
Rules varied by agreement, **Com 4103**
Settlement, **Com 4213**
Collecting bank,
Care required, **Com 4202**
Charge-back, **Com 4214**
Death of customer, **Com 4405**
Defined, **Com 4105**
Application, **Com 4104**
Sales Act, **Com 2104**
Delay beyond time limit, **Com 4109**
Documents of title, warranties, **Com 7508**
Final payment, **Com 4215**
Incompetence of customer, **Com 4405**
Instructions, **Com 4203, 4204**
Methods of sending and presenting, **Com 4204**
Modification of time limit, **Com 4109**
Nonbank payor, sending items to, **Com 4204**
Nonpayment, **Com 4202**
Notice of dishonor, **Com 4202**
Ordinary care required, **Com 4202**
Payable at or through, **Com 4106**
Payment suspended, **Com 4216**
Presentment, **Com 4202**
Item not payable by, through, or at bank, **Com 4212**
Presumption and duration of agency status, **Com 4201**
Refund, **Com 4214**
Restrictive indorsement, **Com 3206**
Seasonable action, **Com 4202**
Secured transactions, **Com 9203**
Priorities, **Com 9312**
Sending direct to payor bank, **Com 4204**
Transfer warranties, **Com 4207**
Warranties, **Com 4207**
Transfer, **Com 4207**
Unindorsed items, **Com 4205**
Collection non-action, **Com 4102**
Compromise and settlement,
Agency, **Com 4201**
Final payment, **Com 4215**
Revocation, **Com 4214, 4301**
Warranties, **Com 4207**
Conflict of laws, **Com 1105, 4102**

BANK

BANK DEPOSITS AND COLLECTIONS
—Cont'd
Consideration, damages for breach of warranty, **Com 4207**
Conversion, **Com 4203**
Copies,
  Payment of items, **Com 4406**
Customers,
  Alterations, duty, **Com 4406**
  Charging against account, **Com 4401**
  Damages for wrongful dishonor, **Com 4402**
  Death, **Com 4405**
  Defined, **Com 4104**
  Depository banks, encoding, warranties, **Com 4209**
  Incompetence, **Com 4405**
  Stop payment orders, **Com 4403**
  Transfer warranties, **Com 4207**
  Unauthorized signature, duty, **Com 4406**
  Warranties, **Com 4207**
    Encoding, depository banks, **Com 4209**
    Transfer warranties, **Com 4207**
Cutoff hour,
  Items subject to notice, stop-order, legal process or setoff, **Com 4303**
Damages, **Com 4103**
  Breach of warranties, **Com 4207**
  Encoding retention, **Com 4209**
  Presentment, **Com 4208**
  Transfer warranties, **Com 4207**
  Payment after stop payment order, **Com 4403**
  Presentment, **Com 4208**
  Transfer warranties, **Com 4207**
  Wrongful dishonor, **Com 4402**
Death of customer, **Com 4405**
Default, **Com 4202**
Definitions, **Com 4104, 4105**
  Electronic presentment, **Com 4110**
Delay,
  Beyond time limit, **Com 4109**
  Notice, **Com 4202**
Demand deposits,
  Restrictive endorsement, effect, **Com 4204**
Demand drafts,
  Presentment warranties, **Com 4208**
  Transfer warranties, **Com 4207**
Depositary bank, **Com 4209**
  Charge-back, **Com 4214**
  Defined, **Com 4105**
    Application, **Com 4104**
  Final payment, **Com 4215**
  Holder, unindorsed items, **Com 4205**
  Refund, **Com 4214**
  Restrictive indorsement, **Com 3206, 4204**
  Unindorsed items, **Com 4205**
Discharge. Release and discharge, generally, post
Disclaimers,
  Presentment warranties, **Com 4208**
  Transfer warranties, **Com 4207**
Dishonor,
  Documentary drafts, **Com 4501 et seq.**

BANK DEPOSITS AND COLLECTIONS
—Cont'd
Dishonor—Cont'd
  Documentary drafts—Cont'd
    Defined, **Com 4104**
    Security interest, **Com 4504**
  Electronic presentment, **Com 4110**
  Notice of dishonor, generally, post
  Presenting bank, collections, **Com 4503**
  Presentment warranties, **Com 4208**
  Time, **Com 4301**
  Transfer warranties, **Com 4207**
  Warranties, **Com 4207**
    Presentment warranties, **Com 4208**
    Transfer, **Com 4207**
  Wrongful, damages, **Com 4402**
Documentary drafts,
  Handling, **Com 4501**
  Notice of dishonor, **Com 4501**
  Presentment, **Com 4501**
    On-arrival drafts, **Com 4502**
  Privilege of presenting bank to deal with goods, **Com 4504**
  Referees, **Com 4503**
  Report of reasons for dishonor, **Com 4503**
  Security interest for expenses, **Com 4504**
Draft,
  Defined, commercial paper,
    Application, **Com 4104**
  Documentary drafts, **Com 4501 et seq.**
  On arrival draft, presentment, **Com 4502**
  Payable at, **Com 4106**
  Unaccepted drafts, presentment warranties, **Com 4208**
Drugs, incompetency caused by, **Com 4405**
Effective date, **Com 16101**
Electronic funds transfers. Funds Transfers, generally, this index
Electronic presentment,
  Agreements, **Com 4209**
  Defined, **Com 4110**
Encoding, **Com 4209**
  Warranties, **Com 4209**
Endorsements. Indorsements, generally, post
Expenses,
  Lien on goods for expenses following dishonor, **Com 4504**
  Reimbursement for expenses incurred following instructions after dishonor, **Com 4503**
Extension, time limits, **Com 4109**
Federal reserve banks,
  Methods of sending and presenting, **Com 4204**
Federal reserve regulations, **Com 4103**
  Electronic presentment agreement, **Com 4110**
  Settlement, **Com 4213**
Final payment, **Com 4215**
Finality, settlement, **Com 4213**
  Charge-back or refund, **Com 4214**
Finance charges, damages for breach of warranty, **Com 4207**

BANK DEPOSITS AND COLLECTIONS
—Cont'd
Foreclosure of liens, dishonor of documentary draft, **Com 4504**
Foreign currency, charge-back or refund, **Com 4214**
Forgeries, customers duty to report, **Com 4406**
Funds Transfers, generally, this index
Guaranty, warranties, **Com 4207**
Holder,
  Acquisition of rights, **Com 4201**
  Unindorsed items, depositary banks, **Com 4205**
Holder in due course, **Com 4201, 4211**
  Defined, commercial paper,
    Application, **Com 4104**
  Subrogation of bank, **Com 4108, 4407**
  Unindorsed items, depositary banks, **Com 4205**
  Warranties, **Com 4207**
Identity, transferor bank, **Com 4206**
Incompetents, customers, rights of bank, **Com 4405**
Incomplete items, transfer warranties, **Com 4207**
Index of definitions, **Com 4104**
Indorsements,
  Presentment warranties, **Com 4208**
  Restrictive indorsements, **Com 3206, 4203**
  Settlement, **Com 4201**
  Transfer warranties, **Com 4207**
Insolvency, **Com 4202**
  Transfer warranties, **Com 4207**
  Warranties, **Com 4207**
  Transferor, **Com 4207**
Instructions,
  Collecting bank, **Com 4203**
  Method of sending and presenting instruments, **Com 4204**
  Documentary drafts, presentment, **Com 4503**
  Remitting bank, **Com 4105**
Intermediary banks,
  Defined, **Com 4105**
Intoxicated persons, payment of items, **Com 4405**
Investments securities, application, **Com 4102**
Item, defined, **Com 4104, 4110**
Knowledge,
  Presentment warranties, **Com 4208**
  Transfer warranties, **Com 4207**
Late return of item, **Com 4302**
Liability,
  Adverse claimants,
    Handling goods, expenses, **Com 4504**
  Charge-back, **Com 4214**
  Customers, overdrafts, **Com 4401**
  Refund, **Com 4214**
Limitation of actions, **Com 4111**
  Damages, agreement, **Com 4103**
Liquor, incompetency caused by, **Com 4405**
Losses, negligence, **Com 4403**
Lost or destroyed property, notice to transferor, **Com 4202**

BANK

BANK DEPOSITS AND COLLECTIONS
—Cont'd
Medium of settlement, **Com 4213**
Mentally deficient and mentally ill persons, patients,
    Payment of items, **Com 4405**
Methods, sending and presenting, **Com 4204**
Midnight deadline,
    Defined, **Com 4104**
    Late return of item, **Com 4302**
    Return of items, **Com 4301**
    Seasonable action, **Com 4202**
Misconduct, **Com 4202**
Mistake, **Com 4202**
    Wrongful dishonor, **Com 4402**
Modification, time limit, **Com 4109**
Negligence,
    Liability, **Com 4202**
    Other banks, **Com 4202**
    Payment, damages, **Com 4403**
Non-action, liability, **Com 4102**
Nonbank payor, items sent to by collecting bank, **Com 4204**
Nonpayment, collecting bank, **Com 4202**
Notice,
    Duty of customer, unauthorized payment, **Com 4406**
    Negotiable instruments, dishonor, **Com 3503**
    Presentment, **Com 4110**
    Item not payable by, through, or at bank, **Com 4212**
    Warranties, **Com 4208**
    Transfer warranties, **Com 4207**
Notice of dishonor, **Com 4202, 4301**
    Collecting bank, **Com 4202**
    Defined, commercial paper,
    Application, **Com 4104**
    Documentary draft, **Com 4501**
    Sending notice, **Com 4202**
    Warranties, **Com 4207**
Operating circular, electronic presentment, **Com 4110**
Orders,
    Branch banks, **Com 4107**
    Stop payment, **Com 4303, 4403**
Overdrafts,
    Charging against account, **Com 4401**
Payable at, **Com 4106**
Payable through, **Com 4106**
Payment, **Com 4215**
    Branch banks, **Com 4107**
    Charging against accounts, **Com 4401**
    Check, time limit for presenting, **Com 4404**
    Death of customer, **Com 4405**
    Electronic presentment, **Com 4110**
    Incompetence of customer, **Com 4405**
    Non-action, **Com 4102**
    Nonpayment, collecting bank, **Com 4202**
    Payable at or through, **Com 4106**
    Presentment warranties, **Com 4208**
    Revocation, **Com 4301**
    Subrogation, **Com 4407**
    Suspended, **Com 4216**
    Transfer warranties, **Com 4207**

BANK DEPOSITS AND COLLECTIONS
—Cont'd
Payment—Cont'd
    Warranties, **Com 4207**
    Presentment warranties, **Com 4208**
    Transfer, **Com 4207**
Payor bank,
    Death of customer, **Com 4405**
    Defined, **Com 4105**
    Application, **Com 4104**
    Delayed beyond time limits, **Com 4109**
    Final payment, **Com 4215**
    Incompetence of customer, **Com 4405**
    Late return of item, **Com 4302**
    Notice of dishonor, **Com 4201**
    Payment suspended, **Com 4216**
    Remitting bank, **Com 4105**
    Revocation of payment, **Com 4301**
    Stop orders, **Com 4303**
    Subrogation, **Com 4407**
    Waiver of defense against unauthorized signature or alteration, **Com 4406**
    Warranties, unindorsed items, **Com 4205**
Place of payment,
    Branch banks, **Com 4107**
Place of presentment, **Com 4204**
Postdated checks, charging against account, **Com 4401**
Preferences. Priorities and preferences, generally, post
Preferred claims, **Com 4216**
Presenting bank,
    Defined, **Com 4105**
    Application, **Com 4104**
    Place of presentment, **Com 4204**
Presentment,
    Agreement, **Com 4110**
    Collecting bank, **Com 4202**
    Payable through, **Com 4106**
    Defined, commercial paper,
    Application, **Com 4104**
    Documentary drafts, **Com 4501 to 4504**
    Electronic presentment agreements, retention, warranties, **Com 4209**
    Methods, **Com 4204**
    Non-action, **Com 4102**
    Notice, item not payable by, through, or at bank, **Com 4212**
    Place, **Com 4204**
    Time limit, check, **Com 4404**
    Warranties, **Com 4207, 4208**
Presentment warranties, **Com 4208**
Presumptions,
    Agency status of collecting bank, **Com 4201**
Priorities and preferences, **Com 4216**
    Charging or certifying items, **Com 4303**
Process, items subject to, time, **Com 4303**
Properly payable, defined, **Com 4104**
Protests,
    Collecting bank, **Com 4202**
Provisional settlement, **Com 4215**
    Charge back or refund, **Com 4214**
    Final payment, **Com 4215**
    Payment suspended, **Com 4216**

BANK DEPOSITS AND COLLECTIONS
—Cont'd
Proximate cause, damages, wrongful dishonor, **Com 4402**
Rates and charges,
    Bank offered spot rate, charge-backs and refunds, **Com 4214**
Receipts,
    Time, **Com 4108**
Recoupment,
    Transfer warranties, **Com 4207**
Refunds, **Com 4214**
    Overdrafts, charging against account, **Com 4401**
Release and discharge,
    Damages for breach of warranty, **Com 4207**
    Transfer warranties, breach of warranty, **Com 4207**
Remitting bank,
    Defined, **Com 4105**
    Application, **Com 4104**
Repayment. Payment, generally, ante
Repossession, liability for inability to obtain repossession, **Com 4202**
Restrictive indorsement. Indorsements, ante
Retention,
    Electronic presentment agreement, **Com 4110**
    Items not returned, **Com 4406**
    Warranties, **Com 4209**
Returns, **Com 4214**
    Items, **Com 4301**
    Suspension of payment, **Com 4216**
Revocation of payment, **Com 4301**
Sales,
    Security interest, dishonor of documentary draft, **Com 4504**
Savings deposits,
    Incompetent depositors, **Com 4405**
Secondary party, defined, commercial paper,
    Application, **Com 4104**
Secured transactions, **Com 9104**
    Proceeds on disposition of collateral, **Com 9306**
Security interest,
    Dishonor of documentary draft, **Com 4504**
    Holder in due course, **Com 4211**
Sending item, method, **Com 4204**
Set-Off and Counterclaim, this index
Settle, defined, **Com 4104**
Settlement. Compromise and settlement, generally, ante
Signatures,
    Presentment warranties, **Com 4208**
    Transfer warranties, **Com 4207**
    Unauthorized signature, duty of customer, **Com 4406**
    Warranties, **Com 4207**
Six months after writing check, payment, **Com 4404**
Special endorsements, status of collecting banks, **Com 4201**
Statement of account, **Com 4406**
Statute of limitations, **Com 4111**

BANK

BANK DEPOSITS AND COLLECTIONS
—Cont'd
Stop payment orders, **Com 4303, 4403**
   Subrogation, **Com 4407**
Subrogation, payor bank, **Com 4407**
Suspends payments, defined, **Com 4104**
Suspension of payment, **Com 4216**
Tellers check,
   Settlement, **Com 4213**
Tender,
   Settlement, **Com 4213**
Time, **Com 4108**
   Branch banks, **Com 4107**
   Charge-back or refund, **Com 4214**
   Damages for breach of warranty, **Com 4207**
   Electronic presentment, **Com 4110**
   Limit for presenting check, **Com 4404**
   Limitation of actions, **Com 4111**
   Modification, **Com 4109**
   Notice of holding, **Com 4212**
   Receipt of items,
      Obligation of bank to determine, **Com 4303**
      Retention of items not returned, **Com 4406**
   Settlement, **Com 4213**
   Stop payment orders, **Com 4403**
   Withdrawal of deposits, **Com 4215**
Transfers. Funds Transfers, generally, this index
Unauthorized signatures, duty of customer, **Com 4406**
Unindorsed items, depositary bankholders, **Com 4205**
Value, holder in due course, **Com 4211**
Variation, agreement, **Com 4103**
Waiver,
   Defense against unauthorized signature or alteration, **Com 4406**
   Time limits, **Com 4109**
Warranties,
   Breach, late return of items, **Com 4302**
   Collecting bank, **Com 4207**
      Documents of title, **Com 7508**
      Transfer warranties, **Com 4207**
   Customers, **Com 4207**
   Damages for breach, **Com 4207**
      Transfer warranties, **Com 4207**
   Depositary bankholders, unindorsed items, **Com 4205**
   Dishonor and protest, **Com 4207**
      Transfer warranties, **Com 4207**
   Encoding, **Com 4209**
   Retention warranties, **Com 4209**
   Transfer warranties, **Com 4207**
   Transferor, **Com 4207**
   Unindorsed items, depositary bankholders, **Com 4205**
Wrongful dishonor, damages, **Com 4402**

BANKERS CREDIT
Defined, Sales Act, **Com 2325**
Application, **Com 2103**

BANKING DAY
Defined, bank deposits and collections, **Com 4104**

BANKRUPTCY
Bulk sales, application of law, **Com 6103**
Commercial code, application of law, **Com 1103**
Insolvency, generally, this index
Trusts and trustees,
   Bulk sales, application of law, **Com 6103**
   Creditor, defined, Commercial Code, **Com 1201**

BANKS AND BANKING
Accounts and accounting,
   Funds Transfers, generally, this index
Bills and notes. Commercial Paper, generally, this index
Branch offices,
   Deposits and collections, **Com 4102**
Business Trusts, generally, this index
Certificates of deposit, generally. Bank Deposits and Collections, this index
Collections. Bank Deposits and Collections, generally, this index
Commercial Paper, generally, this index
Credit Unions, generally, this index
Definitions, **Com 1201**
   Funds transfers, **Com 11105**
   Obligated bank, negotiable instruments, **Com 3312**
Deposits,
   Bank Deposits and Collections, generally, this index
Documents,
   Title, delivery, **Com 2308**
Electronic funds transfers,
   Funds Transfers, generally, this index
Federal Reserve Banks, generally, this index
Financing agency, Sales Act, **Com 2104**
Funds Transfers, generally, this index
Letters of Credit, generally, this index
Obligated bank,
   Defined, negotiable instruments, **Com 3411**

BAR
Attorneys, generally, this index

BEARER
Defined, **Com 1201**

BEARER FORM
Defined, investment securities, certificated securities, **Com 8102**

BENEFICIARIES
Definitions,
   Funds transfer, **Com 11103**
   Letters of credit, **Com 5102**
Funds Transfers, this index
Letters of Credit, this index

BEQUESTS
Gifts, Devises and Bequests, generally, this index

BETWEEN MERCHANTS
Defined, Sales Act, **Com 2104**
Application, **Com 2103**

BEVERAGES
Alcoholic Beverages, generally, this index
Merchantable warranty, **Com 2314**
Sales,
   Merchantable warranty, **Com 2314**

BIDS AND BIDDING
Auctions and Auctioneers, generally, this index

BILLS AND NOTES
Commercial Paper, generally, this index

BILLS OF EXCHANGE
Commercial Paper, generally, this index

BILLS OF LADING
See, also, Documents of Title, generally, this index
Generally, **Com 7301 et seq.**
Actions and proceedings,
   Damages, generally, post
   Provisions, **Com 7309**
   Through bills, **Com 7302**
Airbill, defined, commercial code, **Com 1201**
Alterations, **Com 7306**
Attachment,
   Goods covered by document, **Com 7602**
Authenticity, presumptions, **Com 1202**
Blanks, filling, **Com 7306**
   Unauthorized alteration or filling, **Com 7306**
Bona fide purchaser, **Com 7501**
   Defenses, **Com 7504**
   Judicial process lien, **Com 7602**
Bonds (officers and fiduciaries), lost, stolen or destroyed documents, **Com 7601**
Breach of obligation, through bills, **Com 7302**
Bulk freight, shipper's weight, **Com 7301**
Care required, **Com 7309**
Change of instructions, **Com 7303**
Charges, lien of carrier, **Com 7307**
C.I.F., Sales Act, **Com 2320**
Claims, provisions, **Com 7309**
Connecting carriers, damages, **Com 7302**
Consignee, delivery of goods, **Com 7303**
Consignor,
   Carriers lien effective against, **Com 7307**
   Diversion instructions, **Com 7303**
Containers, description of goods, **Com 7301**
Contracts for sale, application of law, **Com 7509**
Conversion, **Com 7308**
   Bailee, **Com 7601**
   Carrier's liability, **Com 7309**
   Carrier's sale to enforce lien, **Com 7308**
   Limitation of liability, **Com 7309**
   Title and rights acquired by negotiation, **Com 7502**
Damages,
   Description of goods, **Com 7301**
   Reliance, **Com 7203**

BILLS OF LADING—Cont'd
Damages—Cont'd
  Limitation, **Com 7309**
  Non-receipt or misdescription, **Com 7203**
  Overissue, **Com 7402**
  Sale by carrier, **Com 7308**
  Sets, **Com 7304**
  Through bills, **Com 7302**
Deceit. Fraud, generally, post
Defined, commercial code, **Com 1201**
Degree of care required, **Com 7309**
Delivery of goods, **Com 7403**
  Good faith delivery, **Com 7404**
  Negotiation, **Com 7501**
Demurrage charges, lien of carrier, **Com 7307**
Description of goods,
  Damages, **Com 7301**
  Reliance, **Com 7203**
Destination bills, **Com 7305**
Discharge of obligation, through bills, delivery, **Com 7302**
Diversion of goods, **Com 7303**
Duplicates, lost instruments, **Com 7601**
Endorsement,
  Delivery without endorsement, **Com 7506**
  Guarantor for other parties, **Com 7505**
Enforcement of carrier's lien, **Com 7308**
Evidence, **Com 1201**
Expenses, lien of carrier, **Com 7307**
F.A.S., Sales Act, **Com 2319**
Foreign countries,
  Agreement as to liabilities, **Com 7302**
  Sales, **Com 2323**
Fraud,
  Negotiation, **Com 7502**
Genuineness, presumptions, **Com 1202**
Good faith,
  Sale of goods by carrier, **Com 7308**
Guaranty, accuracy of descriptions, marks, etc., **Com 7301**
Holder, diversion instructions, **Com 7303**
Indemnification,
  Rights of issuer, **Com 7301**
  Sellers stoppage of delivery, expenses of bailee, **Com 7504**
Indorsement, **Com 7501**
Injunction, surrender of documents, **Com 7602**
Instructions,
  Change of shipping instructions, effect, **Com 7504**
  Delivery of goods, **Com 7303**
Intent, **Com 1201**
Interpleader, conflicting claims, **Com 7603**
Labels, description of goods, **Com 7301**
Liens and incumbrances,
  Carriers, **Com 7307, 7308**
  Goods covered by negotiable document, **Com 7602**
Limitation of damages, **Com 7309**
Loss, lien of carrier, **Com 7307**
Lost or destroyed documents, duplicates, **Com 7601**

BILLS OF LADING—Cont'd
Marks,
  Description of goods, **Com 7301**
  Non-negotiable bill, **Com 7104**
Misdating, **Com 7301**
Misdescription of goods, damages, **Com 7203, 7301**
Misrepresentation. Fraud, generally, ante
Mistakes, obligations of issuer, **Com 7401**
Negligence, carrier, **Com 7309**
Negotiability, **Com 7104**
Negotiation, **Com 7501 et seq.**
Non-negotiable, **Com 7104**
Non-receipt of goods, damages, **Com 7203, 7301**
Notice, lien of carrier, enforcement, **Com 7308**
Numbering, sets, **Com 7304**
Omissions, implication, **Com 7105**
Overseas shipment, **Com 2323**
  Sets, **Com 7304**
Packages of goods, issuer to count, **Com 7301**
Preservation of goods, expenses, lien of carrier, **Com 7307**
Presumptions, **Com 1202**
Proceedings. Actions and proceedings, generally, ante
Reconsignment, **Com 7303**
Reservation of interest,
  Security interest, **Com 2401**
  Seller, **Com 2505**
Satisfaction, lien of carrier, **Com 7308**
Secured transactions, protection of security interest, **Com 9304**
Security interest, negotiation, **Com 7503**
Sets, **Com 7304**
  Overseas shipment, **Com 2323**
Shipper's weight, bulk freight, **Com 7301**
Stoppage in transit, sellers remedies, **Com 2705**
Stopping delivery, defenses, **Com 7504**
Substitute bills, **Com 7305**
Suits. Actions and proceedings, generally, ante
Surrender of documents, **Com 7601**
Tender, overseas shipment, set of parts, **Com 2323**
Terminal charges, lien of carrier, **Com 7307**
Third party documents, presumptions, **Com 1202**
Through bills, **Com 7302**
Warranties, **Com 7507**
  Collecting bank, **Com 7508**

BLANK FORMS
Forms, generally, this index

BLANK INDORSEMENT
Negotiable instruments, **Com 3205**

BLANKS
Bills of lading, filling in, **Com 7306**
Investment securities, filling, **Com 8206**
Warehouse receipts, filling, authority, **Com 7208**

BLUE SKY LAW
Securities, generally, this index

BOATS AND BOATING
Secured transactions, perfecting security interest, **Com 9302**
Ships and Shipping, generally, this index

BONA FIDE PURCHASERS
Innocent Purchasers, generally, this index

BONDS
  See, also, Securities, generally, this index
Fiduciaries. Bonds (Officers and Fiduciaries), generally, this index
Investments, generally, this index

BONDS (OFFICERS AND FIDUCIARIES)
Bills of lading, lost, stolen or destroyed documents, **Com 7601**
Documents of title, lost, stolen or destroyed documents, **Com 7601**
Investment securities,
  Lost or stolen securities, **Com 8405**
  Registration, **Com 8403**
Receipt issued for goods stored under statute requiring, **Com 7201**
Warehouse receipts, lost or destroyed documents, **Com 7601**

BOOKS AND PAPERS
Negotiable instruments, evidence of dishonor, **Com 3505**

BORROWING MONEY
Loans, generally, this index

BOXES
Containers, generally, this index

BRANCH BANKS
Bank Deposits and Collections, this index

BRANCH OFFICES
Banks and Banking, this index
Secured transactions, statement of account or approval of list of collateral, **Com 9208**

BRANDS, MARKS AND LABELS
Bills of lading, guaranty, **Com 7301**
Merchantability requirements, **Com 2314**
Negotiable instruments, signatures, **Com 3401**
Trade Names, generally, this index

BREACH OF WARRANTY
Sales, this index

BROKERS
Definitions,
  Investment securities, **Com 8102**
Investment Securities, this index
Secured transactions, application of law, **Com 9203**

BUILDINGS
Contractors, generally, this index
Fixtures, generally, this index
Mechanics Liens, generally, this index

BULK

BULK SALES
Generally, **Com 6101 et seq.**
Actions and proceedings,
  Limitation of actions, **Com 6110**
Amount, application of law, **Com 6103**
Application of law, **Com 6103, 6111**
Assignment for benefit of creditors, application of law, **Com 6103**
Attachment, sellers payments, disputed claims by sellers creditors, **Com 6106.2**
Auctions and auctioneers, **Com 6108**
  Limitation of actions, **Com 6110**
Bankruptcy, application of law, **Com 6103**
Burden of proof,
  Buyer, action against, **Com 6107**
Business names, addresses, notice to creditors, **Com 6105**
Business property statements, notice to creditors, **Com 6105**
Buyers obligations, **Com 6104**
  Auctions, liquidations, **Com 6108**
Claims, sellers creditors, claims against sale proceeds, **Com 6106.2, 6106.4**
Collateral, sale, retention, application of law, **Com 6103**
Concealed sales, limitation of actions, **Com 6110**
Conflict of laws, **Com 1105**
Consideration, application to sellers debts by buyer or escrow agent, **Com 6106.2, 6106.4**
Corporate reorganization, application of law, **Com 6103**
Damage,
  Notice, buyers failure, **Com 6107**
Definitions, **Com 6102**
Delivery, notice to creditors, **Com 6105**
Deposits in court, consideration, distribution, **Com 6106.2, 6106.4**
Discovery, concealed sales, limitation of actions, **Com 6110**
Encumbrances. Liens and incumbrances, generally, post
Escrows, **Com 6106.2**
Execution sales, **Com 6103**
Executors and administrators, application of law, **Com 6103**
Exemptions from law, **Com 6103**
Interpleader, consideration, distribution, **Com 6106.2**
Inventory, sale from stock, principal business, application of law, **Com 6103**
Judicial sales, exemptions, **Com 6103**
Liens and incumbrances,
  Claims, priorities, **Com 6106.4**
  Exemptions, **Com 6103**
  Release, **Com 6106.2**
Limitation,
  Buyers liability,
    Auctions, liquidations, **Com 6108**
  Damages, **Com 6107**
Limitation of actions, **Com 6110**
Liquidation,
  Limitation of actions, **Com 6110**
Liquidators, **Com 6108**

BULK SALES—Cont'd
List,
  Sellers business names, addresses, **Com 6104**
  Location, property, notice to creditors, **Com 6105**
  Location of seller, agreement, application of law, **Com 6103**
Mail and mailing, notice to creditors, **Com 6105**
Names, notice to creditors, **Com 6105**
Negotiable instruments, holder in due course, **Com 3302**
Newspapers, notice to creditors, publication, **Com 6105**
Notice,
  Auction, liquidation, sale by, statement, **Com 6108**
  Business property statements, notices to creditors, **Com 6105**
  Buyers obligation, **Com 6104, 6105**
  Damages, **Com 6107**
Payment of claims, priorities, **Com 6106.4**
Personal property immediately leased back to transferor, application of law, **Com 6103**
Priorities, creditors claims, proceeds, distribution, **Com 6106.4**
Proceeds, attachment by creditors, **Com 6106.2**
Property in more than one judicial district, notice to creditors, publication, **Com 6105**
Public officers, sales, application of law, **Com 6103**
Publication, notice to creditors, **Com 6105**
Receivers, exemptions, **Com 6103**
Records and recordation,
  Notice to creditors, **Com 6105**
Reimbursement, buyer, damages paid, **Com 6107**
Restaurants, application of law, **Com 6103**
Sale leaseback transactions, application of law, **Com 6103**
Securing payment, performance of obligation, transfers made, application of law, **Com 6103**
Security interest,
  Application of law, **Com 6103**
  Priority, **Com 6106.4**
  Release, **Com 6106.2**
Statutory sales, application of law, **Com 6103**
Title to property, buyer, impairment, **Com 6107**
Trustees, bankruptcy, application of law, **Com 6103**
Warehouses, property under warehouse receipt, **Com 6103**
Withholding,
  Sellers consideration, disputed claim, sellers creditors, **Com 6106.2**

BULK TRANSFERS
Bulk Sales, generally, this index

BURDEN OF ESTABLISHING A FACT
Defined, commercial code, **Com 1201**

BURDEN OF PROOF
Evidence, this index

BURNED OR DESTROYED RECORDS AND DOCUMENTS
Lost or Destroyed Documents, generally, this index

BUSINESS ADDRESS
Bulk sales, notice, **Com 6105**

BUSINESS AND COMMERCE
Corporations, generally, this index
Customs and usages, commercial code, **Com 1205**
Inventories, generally, this index
Journals,
  Market quotations, evidence, **Com 2724**
Partnership, generally, this index
Trade Names, generally, this index

BUSINESS CORPORATIONS
Corporations, generally, this index

BUSINESS DAY
Defined,
  Bulk sales, notice to creditors, **Com 6107**

BUSINESS NAME
Bulk sales, notice, **Com 6105**

BUSINESS PROPERTY STATEMENTS
Bulk sales, notice to creditors, **Com 6105**

BUSINESS RECORDS
Negotiable instruments, dishonor, **Com 3505**

BUSINESS TRUSTS
Organization, defined, commercial code, **Com 1201**

BUYER
Defined,
  Bulk sales, **Com 6102, 6108**
Sales, this index

BUYER IN ORDINARY COURSE OF BUSINESS
Defined,
  Commercial code, **Com 1201**

BUYING
Defined, commercial code, **Com 1201**

C. & F.
Defined, Sales Act, **Com 2320**
Sales, this index

CALLS
Investment securities,
  Registered owner, liability, **Com 8207**
  Revoked, **Com 8203**

CARLOAD
Commercial unit, defined, Sales Act, **Com 2105**

CARRIERS
See, also, Public Utilities, generally, this index
Bills of Lading, generally, this index
Highway carriers. Motor Carriers, generally, this index
Leases,
   Stoppage of delivery, default by lessee, **Com 10526**
Liens and incumbrances,
   Enforcement, **Com 7308**
Motor Carriers, generally, this index
Railroads, generally, this index
Sales,
   Liens and incumbrances, **Com 7308**
Ships and Shipping, generally, this index

CARS
Motor Vehicles, generally, this index
Railroads, generally, this index

CARTONS
Containers, generally, this index

CASH
Money, generally, this index

CASH SALES
Sales, this index

CASUALTY INSURANCE
Insurance, generally, this index

CATTLE
Animals, generally, this index

CAUSES OF ACTION
Actions and Proceedings, generally, this index

CERTAINTY
Sale contract, **Com 2204**

CERTIFICATED SECURITIES
Defined,
   Investment securities, **Com 8102**

CERTIFICATES AND CERTIFICATION
Application of law, **Com 10105**
Definitions,
   Commercial paper,
     Application,
       Bank deposits and collections, **Com 4104**
Presumptions, third party documents, **Com 1202**
Secured transactions,
   Condition of perfection, **Com 9103**
   Filing officer, **Com 9407**
   Perfection, international treaty, **Com 9302**
Third party documents, presumptions, **Com 1202**
Weights and Measures, this index

CERTIFICATES OF DEPOSIT
Bank Deposits and Collections, this index
Defined,
   Negotiable instruments, **Com 3104**

CERTIFIED CHECKS
Commercial Paper, this index

CERTIFIED OR REGISTERED MAIL
Mail and Mailing, this index

CHANCERY
Equity, generally, this index

CHANGE
Modification or Change, generally, this index

CHANGE OF POSITION
Sales,
   Anticipatory repudiation, **Com 2610, 2611**
   Reliance on term waiver, **Com 2209**

CHARGE-BACK
Bank deposits and collections, **Com 4214**

CHARGES
Rates and Charges, generally, this index

CHATTEL PAPER
Defined,
   Secured transactions, **Com 9105**
Secured Transactions, this index
Security interest, defined, commercial code, **Com 1201**

CHATTEL TRUST
Secured transactions, applicability of law, **Com 9102**

CHATTELS
Personal Property, generally, this index

CHECKS
Commercial Paper, this index
Defined,
   Application,
     Bank deposits and collections, **Com 4104**
     Sales Act, **Com 2103**

CHILDREN AND MINORS
Defenses,
   Accommodation parties, negotiable instruments, **Com 3305**
   Negotiable instruments, recoupment, **Com 3305**
Duress,
   Recoupment, negotiable instruments, **Com 3305**
Holders in due course, defenses, **Com 3305**
Negotiable instruments,
   Accommodation parties, defenses, **Com 3305**
   Recoupment, defenses, claims, **Com 3305**
   Rescission of negotiation, **Com 3202**
Negotiation of commercial paper, rescission, **Com 3207**
Rescission,
   Negotiation of commercial paper, **Com 3202, 3207**

C.I.F.
Bills of lading, provision, **Com 2323**
Defined, sales act, **Com 2320**
Price settlement, **Com 2321**

C.I.F.—Cont'd
Sales, this index

CITIES AND TOWNS
Municipalities, generally, this index

CIVIL ACTIONS
Actions and Proceedings, generally, this index

CIVIL PROCESS
Process, generally, this index

CLAIM AND DELIVERY
Definitions,
   Bulk sales, **Com 6102**
Leases, personal property, **Com 10521**
Sales Act, **Com 2711**
   Buyer, **Com 2716**

CLAIMANT
Defined,
   Bulk sales, **Com 6102**
   Negotiable instruments, lost, destroyed or stolen checks, **Com 3312**

CLEARING CORPORATION
Defined, investment securities, **Com 8102**

CLEARINGHOUSE
Bank Deposits and Collections, this index
Defined,
   Bank deposits and collections, **Com 4104**
Negotiable instruments, presentment, **Com 3501**
Return, item received, **Com 4301**
Rules, varying by agreement, **Com 4103**

C.O.D.
Inspection of goods, **Com 2513**

COERCION
Duress or Coercion, generally, this index

COLLATERAL
Additional collateral required at will, **Com 1208**
Defined,
   Secured transactions, **Com 9105**
Investment securities,
   Perfection of security interest, **Com 9115**
Secured Transactions, this index

COLLECTING BANK
Bank Deposits and Collections, this index

COLLISIONS
Accidents, generally, this index

COLLUSION
Fraud, generally, this index

COMMERCE
Business and Commerce, generally, this index

COMMERCIAL BANKS
Banks and Banking, generally, this index

COMMERCIAL CODE
Generally, **Com 1101 et seq.**

COMMERCIAL

COMMERCIAL CODE—Cont'd
Acceptance under reservation of right, **Com 1207**
Actions and proceedings, enforcement of remedies, **Com 1106**
Bank deposits and collections, **Com 4101 et seq.**
Bankruptcy, **Com 1103**
Bills of lading, **Com 7101 et seq.**
Breach of contract, waiver, **Com 1107**
Bulk sales, **Com 6101 et seq.**
Burden of proof, **Com 1202, 1210**
Coercion, **Com 1103**
Conflict of laws, **Com 1105**
Consideration, waiver of breach of contract, **Com 1107**
Construction against implicit repeal, **Com 1104**
Construction of law, **Com 1102, 16104**
Contract Law, **Com 1103**
Course of dealing, **Com 1205**
Damages, **Com 1106**
Definitions, **Com 1201**
Documents of title, **Com 7101 et seq.**
Duress, **Com 1103**
Effective date, **Com 13101 et seq., 14101 et seq., 15101 et seq., 16101 et seq.**
Electronic funds transfers. Funds Transfers, generally, this index
Enforcement of act, **Com 1106**
Estoppel, **Com 1103**
Evidence, **Com 1202, 1210**
　Presumptions, **Com 1202, 1210**
Fraud, **Com 1103**
Funds Transfers, generally, this index
Implicit repeal, **Com 1104**
Investment securities, **Com 8101 et seq.**
Law merchant, **Com 1103**
Leases, **Com 10101 et seq.**
Limitation of actions, **Com 16103**
Misrepresentation, **Com 1103**
Mistake, **Com 1103**
Negotiable instruments, **Com 3101 et seq.**
Notice, proper sending, registered or certified mail, **Com 1201**
Obligations,
　Good faith, **Com 1203**
　Subordination of right to payment, **Com 1209**
Partial invalidity, **Com 1108**
Performance under reservation of rights, **Com 1207**
Power to choose applicable law, **Com 1105**
Presumptions, **Com 1202, 1210**
Principal and agent, **Com 1103**
Principles of law and equity, **Com 1103**
Purpose of code, **Com 1102**
Reasonable time, **Com 1104, 1204**
Remedies liberally administered, **Com 1106**
Renunciation, claim or right after breach, **Com 1107**
Repeals, **Com 13101 et seq.**
Rules of construction, **Com 1102**
Sales, **Com 2101 et seq.**
Seasonably, **Com 1204**
Secured transactions, **Com 9109 et seq.**

COMMERCIAL CODE—Cont'd
Severability of actions, **Com 1108**
Statute of frauds, **Com 1206**
Subordination of right to payment of obligations, **Com 1209**
Territorial application of law, **Com 1105**
Third party documents, evidence, **Com 1202**
Time, **Com 1204**
Transition provisions, **Com 10600, 14101 et seq., 15101 et seq., 16101 et seq.**
Usage of trade, **Com 1205**
Variation by agreement, **Com 1102**
Waiver, claim or right after breach, **Com 1107**
Warehouse receipts, **Com 7101 et seq.**

COMMERCIAL FINANCE LENDERS
Secured transactions, application of law, **Com 9203**

COMMERCIAL PAPER
Acceleration, **Com 1208**
　Payment, **Com 1208**
Accounts and accounting,
　Defined,
　　Bank deposits and collections, **Com 4104**
Bank deposits and collection, application, **Com 4102**
Banking day, defined,
　Bank deposits and collections, **Com 4104**
Bills of Lading, generally, this index
Certified checks,
　Time for presenting, **Com 4404**
Checks,
　Certified checks, generally, ante
　Defined,
　　Application,
　　　Bank deposits and collections, **Com 4104**
　　　Sales Act, **Com 2103**
　Drugs, incompetency caused by, **Com 4405**
　Liquor, incompetency caused by, **Com 4405**
　Payment by financing agency, **Com 2506**
　Presentment, six months after date, **Com 4404**
　Refusal of bank to pay, incompetency caused by liquor or drugs, **Com 4405**
　Sales, this index
　Secured transactions, cash proceeds, **Com 9306**
　Six months old, payment, **Com 4404**
　Tender under sales act, **Com 2511**
　Title to goods, delivery in exchange for check later dishonored, **Com 2403**
Clearinghouse,
　Defined,
　　Bank deposits in collections, **Com 4104**

COMMERCIAL PAPER—Cont'd
Collecting bank,
　Defined,
　　Bank deposits and collections, **Com 4105**
Continuation statements, effectiveness, period, **Com 9403.5**
Custom and usage, **Com 1205**
Customer, defined,
　Bank deposits and collections, **Com 4104**
Definitions,
　Commercial code, **Com 10103**
Depository bank, defined,
　Bank deposits and collections, **Com 4105**
Dishonor,
　Letter of credit, sales act, **Com 2325**
　Notice of dishonor, generally, post
Documentary drafts,
　Bank deposits and collections, **Com 4104**
Documents of Title, generally, this index
Drafts,
　Checks, generally, ante
　Defined,
　　Application,
　　　Sales Act, **Com 2103**
　Incompetency caused by liquor or drugs, **Com 4405**
Electronic funds transfers. Funds Transfers, generally, this index
Equity, action, definition, **Com 1201**
Evidence,
　Third party documents, **Com 1202**
Expenses, presenting bank,
　Lien on goods following dishonor, **Com 4504**
　Right to reimbursement for following instructions after dishonor, **Com 4503**
Financing statements,
　Effective, period, **Com 9403.5**
　Originals, return to parties, **Com 9407.3**
Frauds, statute of, **Com 1206**
Funds Transfers, generally, this index
Good faith, **Com 1203**
　Acceleration, **Com 1208**
Holder in due course,
　Secured transactions,
　　Priorities, **Com 9309**
Intermediary bank,
　Defined,
　　Bank deposits and collections, **Com 4105**
Investment Securities, generally, this index
Item,
　Bank deposits and collections, **Com 4104**
Letters of Credit, generally, this index
Midnight deadline, defined,
　Bank deposits and collections, **Com 4104**
Notice of dishonor,
　Protests, generally, post

COMMERCIAL PAPER—Cont'd
Options,
    Acceleration, **Com 1208**
Order,
    Withdrawal of funds, incompetency due to liquor or drugs, **Com 4405**
Payment,
    Subordination of rights, **Com 1209**
Payor bank, defined,
    Bank deposits and collections, **Com 4105**
Presentment,
    Six months after date, **Com 4404**
Presumptions,
    Defined, **Com 1210**
    Third party documents, **Com 1202**
Protests,
    Reservation of rights, **Com 1207**
Reservation of rights, **Com 1207**
Secured Transactions, generally, this index
Security interest,
    Subordination of rights, **Com 1209**
Six months after date, presentment, **Com 4404**
Subordinated obligations, **Com 1209**
Third party,
    Documents, authenticity, presumptions, **Com 1202**
Time,
    Continuation statement effectiveness, **Com 9403.5**
    Financing statement effectiveness, **Com 9403.5**
Transfer,
    Funds Transfers, generally, this index
Warehouse Receipts, generally, this index
Warranties, express, creation by seller, **Com 2313**

COMMERCIAL UNIT
Defined,
    Commercial code, **Com 10103**
    Sales act, **Com 2105**
        Application, **Com 2103**
Sales, this index

COMMINGLING GOODS
Secured Transactions, this index
Warehousemen, fungible goods, **Com 7207**

COMMODITIES
Law governing, secured transactions, **Com 9103**
Securities,
    Secured transactions, law governing, **Com 9103**

COMMODITY ACCOUNT
Defined, secured transactions, **Com 9115**

COMMODITY CONTRACT
Defined, secured transactions, **Com 9115**

COMMODITY CUSTOMER
Defined, secured transactions, **Com 9115**

COMMODITY INTERMEDIARIES JURISDICTION
Defined, secured transactions, **Com 9103**

COMMODITY INTERMEDIARY
Defined, secured transactions, **Com 9115**

COMMODITY MARKETS
Sales, use in determining market price, **Com 2724**

COMMON CARRIERS
Carriers, generally, this index
Marine carriers. Ships and Shipping, generally, this index
Motor Carriers, generally, this index
Railroads, generally, this index

COMMUNICATE
Defined, investment securities, **Com 8102**

COMMUNICATIONS
Telegraphs and Telephones, generally, this index

COMPENSATION AND SALARIES
Assignments,
    Secured transactions, **Com 9104**
Attachment, generally, this index
Attorney Fees, generally, this index

COMPETENCY
Evidence, negotiable instruments, signature, burden of proof, **Com 3308**

COMPRESS RECEIPT
Document of title, defined, **Com 1201**

COMPROMISE AND SETTLEMENT
Arbitration and Award, generally, this index
Bank Deposits and Collections, this index

COMPUTERS
Electronic funds transfers. Funds Transfers, generally, this index

CONCEALMENT
Bulk sales, **Com 6110**

CONDUCT OF PARTIES
Contract for sale of goods, existence recognized, **Com 2204, 2207**

CONFIRMED CREDIT
Defined, Sales Act, **Com 2325**
    Application, **Com 2103**

CONFLICT OF LAWS
Bank deposits and collections, **Com 1105, 4102**
    Bank liability, **Com 4102**
Bulk sales, **Com 1105**
Commercial code, **Com 1102, 1105**
Funds transfers, **Com 1105, 11507**
Investment securities, **Com 1105**
Sales, **Com 1105**
    Rights of seller's creditors, **Com 2402**
Secured transactions, **Com 1105, 9103, 9203**

CONFORMING
Defined, Sales Act, **Com 2106**
    Application, **Com 2103**

CONSIDERATION
Commercial code, waiver of breach of contract, **Com 1107**
Firm offers, **Com 2205**
Sales contract, agreement modifying, **Com 2209**
Value, defined, **Com 1201**
Waiver or relinquishment of claim or right, Commercial Code, **Com 1107**

CONSIGNEE
Defined, documents of title, **Com 7102**
    Application, Sales Act, **Com 2103**

CONSIGNMENT
Creditors claims, **Com 2326**
Debtors and creditors, rights of creditors against consignee, **Com 2403**
Priorities, secured transactions, **Com 9114**
Secured transactions, perfecting security interest, filing financing statement, **Com 9408**
Security interest, defined, **Com 1201**

CONSIGNOR
Bills of lading,
    Carriers lien, **Com 7307**
    Delivery of goods, **Com 7303**
Defined,
    Documents of title, **Com 7102**
        Application, Sales Act, **Com 2103**

CONSPICUOUS
Defined, Commercial Code, **Com 1201**

CONSTRUCTION MORTGAGES
Defined,
    Leases, **Com 10309**

CONSTRUCTION OF STATUTES
Statutes, this index

CONSULAR INVOICE
Evidence, **Com 1202**

CONSULS
Ambassadors and Consuls, generally, this index

CONSUMER GOODS
Defined,
    Secured transactions, **Com 9109**
    Application,
        Sales Act, **Com 2103**
Sales, this index
Secured Transactions, this index

CONSUMER LEASES
Defined,
    Commercial code, **Com 10103**

CONTAINERS
Bills of lading, description of goods, **Com 7301**
Brands, Marks and Labels, generally, this index

CONTAINERS

CONTAINERS—Cont'd
Labels. Brands, Marks and Labels, generally, this index
Sale warranty, **Com 2314**
Shipping, security interest perfection, applicable law, **Com 9103**

CONTEMPORANEOUS ORAL AGREEMENT
Contract for sale, **Com 2202**

CONTINUITY
Secured transactions, perfection of security interest, **Com 9303**

CONTRACTORS
Goods, offers to supply, irrevocability, **Com 2205**
Mechanics Liens, generally, this index
Offers to supply goods, irrevocability, **Com 2205**
Sales,
 Bids, offers to supply, irrevocability, **Com 2205**
 Secured transactions, **Com 9102**
Supplying goods, irrevocable offers, **Com 2205**

CONTRACTS
Accord and Satisfaction, generally, this index
Agricultural Products, this index
Arbitration and Award, generally, this index
C.I.F. or C. & F., **Com 2320**
 Foreign shipment, **Com 2323**
 Inspection of goods, **Com 2513**
 Price basis, **Com 2321**
Commercial code,
 Application of law, **Com 1103**
 Construction and operation, **Com 1102**
Course of dealing, Commercial Code, **Com 1205**
Definitions, **Com 1201**
 Sales Act, **Com 2106**
Deterioration of goods, "no arrival, no sale" term, **Com 2324**
Foreign States, this index
Fraud, generally, this index
Frauds, Statute of, generally, this index
Funds transfers, variation of law, **Com 11501**
General intangibles, terms prohibiting creation of security interest, **Com 9318**
Installment Sales, generally, this index
Insurance, generally, this index
Mortgages, generally, this index
Obligation of good faith, **Com 1203**
Principles of law applicable, Commercial Code, **Com 1103**
Sales, this index
Satisfaction. Accord and Satisfaction, generally, this index
Secured transactions, terms prohibiting creation of security interest, general intangibles, **Com 9318**
Security agreements, generally. Secured Transactions, this index

CONTRACTS—Cont'd
Statute of frauds. Frauds, Statute of, generally, this index
Subordination of rights to payment of obligations, **Com 1209**
Supplementary, commercial code, **Com 1103**

CONTRAST
Conspicuous, defined, commercial code, **Com 1201**

CONTRIBUTIONS
Gifts, Devises and Bequests, generally, this index

CONVERSION
Bank deposits and collections, **Com 4203**
Bills of Lading, this index
Documents of title, title and rights, **Com 7502**
Indorsements,
 Restrictive, **Com 3206**
Negotiation,
 Anomalous indorsement, **Com 3205**
Restrictive indorsements, **Com 3206**
Sales, merchant buyer, rejected goods, **Com 2603, 2604**
Secured transactions, possession after default, **Com 9505**
Warehouse Receipts, this index
Warehousemans lien, enforcement, **Com 7210**

CONVEYANCES
Deeds and Conveyances, generally, this index

COOPERATION
Sales agreement, particulars of performance, **Com 2311**
Secured transactions, debtor, residence, **Com 9401**

COOPERATIVE ASSOCIATIONS
Fish marketing cooperative associations, secured transactions, inventory, merchants, **Com 9102**

COOPERATIVE CORPORATIONS
Credit Unions, generally, this index

COPARTNERSHIP
Partnership, generally, this index

CORPORATE SECURITIES LAW OF 1968
Securities, generally, this index

CORPORATIONS
Banks and Banking, generally, this index
Business Trusts, generally, this index
Credit Unions, generally, this index
Directors,
 Breach of duty,
  Fiduciary duties, notice, **Com 3307**
 Fiduciary duties, breach, notice, **Com 3307**
Foreign Corporations, generally, this index
Insurance companies. Insurance, generally, this index

CORPORATIONS—Cont'd
Negotiable instruments,
 Breach of fiduciary duty, notice, **Com 3307**
 Ultra vires, rescission, **Com 3202**
Notice,
 Negotiable instruments, breach of fiduciary duty, **Com 3307**
Officers and employees,
 Negotiable instruments, breach of fiduciary duty, notice, **Com 3307**
Public Utilities, generally, this index
Railroads, generally, this index
Receivers and Receivership, generally, this index
Reorganization,
 Bulk sales, application of law, **Com 6103**
 Claims after breach, commercial code, **Com 1107**
 Negotiable instruments, discharge, **Com 3604**
 Rights after breach, commercial code, **Com 1107**
Representative, defined, **Com 1201**
Secured transactions,
 Debtor, residence, **Com 9401**
 Financing statement, names, **Com 9402**
 Structure change, financing statement, **Com 9402**
Ultra vires acts,
 Negotiable instruments, rescission, **Com 3202**

COUNSEL
Attorneys, generally, this index

COUNSELORS AND COUNSELING
Invoices, presumptions, **Com 1202**

COUNTERCLAIM
Set-Off and Counterclaim, generally, this index

COUNTERFEITING
See, also, Forgery, generally, this index
Definitions,
 Genuine, commercial paper, **Com 1201**
Genuine, defined, commercial paper, **Com 1201**

COUNTERSIGNATURE
Signatures, this index

COUNTIES
Secured transactions, security interest, **Com 9104**
Taxation, generally, this index

COUNTY RECORDERS
Recorders, generally, this index

COURSE OF DEALING
Sales, this index

COURSE OF PERFORMANCE
Sales, this index

COVER
Defined, Sales Act, **Com 2712**
 Application, **Com 2103**

DEEDS

COWS
Animals, generally, this index

CRATES
Containers, generally, this index

CREATION OF A SECURITY INTEREST
Defined,
    Leases, Com 10303

CREDIT
Banker's credit, defined, Sales Act, Com 2103
Buyer in ordinary course of business, defined, Commercial Code, Com 1201
Confirmed credit, defined, Sales Act, Com 2103
Letters of Credit, generally, this index
Sales, beginning of period, Com 2310
Value, defined, Com 1201

CREDIT UNIONS
Electronic funds transfers. Funds Transfers, generally, this index
Funds Transfers, generally, this index
Secured transactions, application of law, Com 9104

CREDITORS
Debtors and Creditors, generally, this index

CRIMES AND OFFENSES
Alteration of Instruments, generally, this index
Counterfeiting, generally, this index
Duress or Coercion, generally, this index
Forgery, generally, this index
Fraud, generally, this index
Indorsements, commercial paper, Com 3405
Leases, this index
Theft, generally, this index

CROPS
Agricultural Products, generally, this index
Defined, secured transactions, Com 9109

CROSS–ACTION
Defendant, defined, Commercial Code, Com 1201

CURATIVE AND VALIDATING ACTS
Commercial code,
    Application of law, Com 1103

CURRENCY
Money, defined, Commercial Code, Com 1201

CUSTOM AND USAGE
Agreement, defined, Commercial Code, Com 1201
Bank deposits and collections, variation by agreement, Com 4103
Commercial paper, Com 1205
Commercial practices, continued expansion, Com 1102
Definitions, Commercial Code, Com 1205

CUSTOM AND USAGE—Cont'd
Fungible, defined, Commercial Code, Com 1201
Sales, this index

CUSTOMERS
Bank Deposits and Collections, this index
Defined,
    Bank deposits and collections, Com 4104

CUSTOMS DUTIES
Documents of title, application of law, Com 7103

CUTOFF HOUR
Bank deposits and collections,
    Items subject to notice, stop-order, legal process or setoff, Com 4303

DAMAGES
Assignment, breach of sales contract, Com 2210
Bank Deposits and Collections, this index
Bills of Lading, this index
Breach of warranty, Com 2316
Commercial code, Com 1106
Consequential damages, commercial code, Com 1106
Documents of Title, this index
Funds Transfers, this index
Incidental damages, Sales Act, Com 2710
Leases, this index
Letters of credit, Com 5111
Limitations,
    Bank deposits and collections, Com 4103
    Bills of lading, Com 7309
    Sales Act, Com 2718, 2719
Liquidated damages,
    Letters of credit, Com 5111
Measure of damages,
    Bank deposits and collections, agreements, Com 4103
Misdescription of goods, consignee, Com 7301
Non-receipt of goods, consignee, Com 7301
Penal damages, Commercial Code, Com 1106
Proximate cause, wrongful dishonor, Com 4402
Sales, this index
Secured transactions, secured party, Com 9507
    Failure to furnish termination statement, Com 9404
Special damages,
    Commercial Code, Com 1106
Warehouse Receipts, this index
Warehousemen, sale to enforce lien, Com 7210
Wrongful dishonor of bank item, Com 4402

DATE OF THE BULK SALE
Defined,
    Bulk sales, Com 6102

DATE OF THE BULK SALE AGREEMENT
Defined,
    Bulk sales, Com 6102

DEATH
Bank customer, authority of bank, Com 4405
Funds transfers, payment orders, cancellation, Com 11211

DEBENTURES
Bonds, generally, this index

DEBTORS AND CREDITORS
Accord and Satisfaction, generally, this index
Assignment for Benefit of Creditors, generally, this index
Attachment, generally, this index
Bankruptcy, generally, this index
Bulk Sales, generally, this index
Creditor, defined, Com 1201
Debtor, defined, secured transactions, Com 9105
Definitions,
    Bulk sales, Com 6102
Funds transfers, process, Com 11502
Insolvency,
    Sellers remedies, Com 2702
Investment securities, Com 8112
    Entitlements, intermediaries, Com 8503
Leases, Com 10308
Notice,
    Bulk sales, Com 6104, 6105
Sale on approval, Com 2326
Sale or return, Com 2326
Satisfaction. Accord and Satisfaction, generally, this index
Secured Transactions, generally, this index
Seller of goods, rights, Com 2402
Unsecured creditors,
    Rights against buyer, Com 2402

DEBTS
Defined,
    Bulk transfer, Com 6102
Indebtedness, generally, this index

DECEDENTS ESTATES
Probate Proceedings, generally, this index

DECEPTION
Fraud, generally, this index

DECLARATION OF LOSS
Defined, negotiable instruments, lost, destroyed or stolen checks, Com 3312

DECREES
Judgments and Decrees, generally, this index

DEEDS AND CONVEYANCES
Contracts for sale of land,
    Structures, Com 2107
Trust Deeds, generally, this index

DEFAULT

DEFAULT
Bank,
  Deposits and collections, **Com 4202**
Leases, **Com 10501 et seq.**
Secured Transactions, this index

DEFENDANTS
Defined,
  Commercial code, **Com 1201**
Parties, generally, this index

DEFINITIONS
Words and Phrases, generally, this index

DELIVERED WEIGHTS
C.I.F. or C. & F. contracts, basis of price, **Com 2321**

DELIVERY
Bailee, duty to deliver goods, **Com 7403**
Bulk sales, notice, **Com 6105**
Defined,
  Commercial Code, **Com 1201**
Delay, bailee, **Com 7403**
Documents of title, delivery of goods, **Com 7403**
Investment Securities, this index
Sales, this index

DEPOSITARY BANK
Bank Deposits and Collections, this index

DEPOSITS IN BANKS
Bank Deposits and Collections, generally, this index

DESCENT AND DISTRIBUTION
Probate Proceedings, generally, this index

DESCRIPTION OF PROPERTY
Warehouse receipts, **Com 7202**

DESTINATION BILL OF LADING
Request of consignor, **Com 7305**

DESTROYED DOCUMENTS
Lost or Destroyed Documents, generally, this index

DESTROYED PROPERTY
Lost or Destroyed Property, generally, this index

DETERIORATION OF GOODS
Buyer's option, **Com 2613**
C.I.F. or C. & F. contracts, risk on seller, **Com 2321**
No arrival, no sale, term, goods no longer conforming to contract, **Com 2324**
Sales, this index
Warehousemen, right to sell, **Com 7206**

DETINUE
Leases, personal property, **Com 10521**

DEVISES AND DEVISEES
Gifts, Devises and Bequests, generally, this index

DILIGENCE
Agreement, disclaiming, commercial code, **Com 1102**
Exercising, commercial code, **Com 1201**

DIPLOMATIC AND CONSULAR OFFICERS
Ambassadors and Consuls, generally, this index

DISCHARGE
Bank deposits and collections,
  Breach of warranty, transfer, **Com 4207**
  Damages, breach of warranty, **Com 4207**

DISCLAIMER
Commercial code, **Com 1102**

DISCOUNTS
Purchase of instruments, Commercial Code, **Com 1201**

DISCOVER
Defined, Commercial Code, **Com 1201**

DISCRIMINATION
Sales, substituted performance, **Com 2614**

DISHONOR
Bank Deposits and Collections, this index
Checks, payment of instrument, **Com 2511**
Collecting banks,
  Notice, **Com 4202**
Commercial Paper, this index
Defined,
  Commercial paper, application, sales act, **Com 2103**
  Letters of credit, **Com 5102**
Letters of Credit, this index
Presenting bank, collections, **Com 4503**
Sales, this index

DISPUTES
Evidence of goods, preservation, **Com 2515**

DOCK RECEIPTS
Documents of Title, generally, this index

DOCUMENTARY DRAFTS
Bank deposits and collections, **Com 4501 et seq.**
Defined, **Com 4104**
Commercial Paper, this index
Defined,
  Bank deposits and collections, **Com 4104**

DOCUMENTARY EVIDENCE
Evidence, generally, this index

DOCUMENTS OF TITLE
Generally, **Com 7101 et seq.**
Accident, title and rights, **Com 7502**
Adequacy, **Com 7509**
Adverse claims, **Com 7603**
Attachment,
  Goods, **Com 7602**
Attorney fees, lost, stolen or destroyed documents, bailee, **Com 7601**
Bailee,
  Attorney fees, lost, stolen or destroyed documents, **Com 7601**

DOCUMENTS OF TITLE—Cont'd
Bailee—Cont'd
  Defined, **Com 7102**
  Possession, tender of delivery, **Com 2503**
Banking channels, delivery, **Com 2308**
Bills of Lading, generally, this index
Bona fide purchasers, defenses, **Com 7504**
Bonds (officers and fiduciaries), stolen or destroyed documents, **Com 7601**
Citation, **Com 7101**
Collecting bank, warranties, **Com 7508**
Conflicting claims, **Com 7603**
Consignee, defined, **Com 7102**
Consignor, defined, **Com 7102**
Contract for sale,
  Adequacy, **Com 7509**
  Defined, **Com 2106**
  Application, **Com 7102**
Conversion, **Com 7601**
Title and rights, **Com 7502**
Creditors, title to goods, **Com 7504**
Customs duties, application of law, **Com 7103**
Damage to goods, delivery, **Com 7403**
Damages,
  Description of goods, reliance, **Com 7203**
  Duplicate documents, **Com 7402**
  Good faith delivery, **Com 7404**
Definitions, **Com 1201, 7102**
Delay, delivery, **Com 7403**
Delivery, **Com 2308, 2310**
  Document, title and rights, **Com 7504**
  Goods,
    Good faith, damages, **Com 7404**
    Stoppage, **Com 7504**
  Negotiation, **Com 7501**
  Obligation, **Com 7403**
  Payment due and demanded, **Com 2507**
  Without indorsement, **Com 7506**
Description of goods, reliance, **Com 7203**
Destruction, **Com 7601**
Goods, delivery, **Com 7403**
Diversion of goods,
  Delivery, **Com 7403**
  Title, **Com 7504**
Documents, definition, **Com 7102**
Duly negotiate, defined, **Com 7501**
  Application, **Com 7102**
  Warehouse receipts and bills of lading, **Com 7501**
Duplicates, **Com 7402**
  Lost instruments, **Com 7601**
Duress or coercion, title and rights, **Com 7502**
Endorsement,
  Delivery without endorsement, **Com 7506**
  Liability, **Com 7505**
  Negotiations, **Com 7501**
  Right to compel indorsement, **Com 7506**
Exception, **Com 3102**
Excuses for delivery of goods, **Com 7403**

ENDORSEMENT

DOCUMENTS OF TITLE—Cont'd
Financing agency, rights secured, **Com 2506**
Fraud, title and rights, **Com 7502**
Fungible goods, rights of holder, **Com 7502**
Genuine, warranties, on transfer, **Com 7507**
Good faith delivery, damages, **Com 7404**
Goods, defined, **Com 7102**
Holder,
  Rights, **Com 7502**
  Secured transactions, priorities, **Com 9309**
Indemnity,
  Lost or missing document, security of claimant, **Com 7601**
  Overissue, **Com 7402**
Index of definitions, **Com 7102**
Injunction, rights of purchaser, **Com 7602**
Insurance, warehousemen, lien for cost, **Com 7209**
Interpleader, **Com 7603**
Irregular document, **Com 7401**
Issuer,
  Defined, **Com 7102**
  Obligations, **Com 7401**
Larceny, **Com 7601**
  Title and rights, **Com 7502**
Legal interest before issuance of document, **Com 7503**
Letters of credit, adequacy, **Com 7509**
Liens and incumbrances,
  Bailees lien, satisfaction, **Com 7403**
  Judicial process, **Com 7602**
  Warehousemen, satisfaction, **Com 7403**
Loss of goods, delivery, **Com 7403**
Lost or destroyed documents, **Com 7601**
  Duplicates, **Com 7402**
  Title and rights, **Com 7502**
Mail, warehouseman's lien, enforcement, **Com 7210**
Misdescription, damages, **Com 7203**
Mistakes,
  Obligations of issuer, **Com 7401**
  Title and rights, **Com 7502**
Negotiability, **Com 7104**
Negotiation, **Com 7501**
  Rights acquired, **Com 7502**
Nonnegotiable, title and rights, **Com 7104, 7504**
Nonreceipt of goods, damages, **Com 7203**
Obligation,
  Delivery, **Com 7403**
  Issuer, **Com 7401**
Omissions, implication, **Com 7105**
Overissue,
  Damages, **Com 7402**
  Liabilities of issuer, **Com 7402**
Overseas, defined, **Com 2323**
  Application, **Com 7102**
Partial delivery, **Com 7403**
Passing title to goods, **Com 2401**
Person entitled under the document, defined, **Com 7403**
  Application, **Com 7102**
Place of delivery, **Com 2308**
Presumptions, **Com 1202**

DOCUMENTS OF TITLE—Cont'd
Receipt of goods, defined, **Com 2103**
  Application, **Com 7102**
Reconsignment, delivery, **Com 7403**
Registered mail, warehouseman's lien, enforcement, **Com 7210**
Release, warehousemen, delivery excused, **Com 7403**
Right in goods defeated, **Com 7503**
Rights of holder, **Com 7502**
Risk of loss, passage on receipt, **Com 2509**
Sales, delivery, **Com 2310**
Secured Transactions, generally, this index
Security interest, title to goods, **Com 7503**
Shipment of seller, **Com 2504**
Statutes, application of law, **Com 7103**
Stoppage in transit, **Com 7502**
Stopping delivery,
  Defenses, **Com 7504**
  Exercise of right, **Com 7403**
Surrender of documents, **Com 7601**
Tender of delivery, bailee in possession, **Com 2503**
Transfer, warranties, **Com 7507**
Treaties, application, **Com 7103**
United States statutes, application, **Com 7103**
Warehouse Receipts, generally, this index
Warehouseman, defined, **Com 7102**
Warranties, **Com 7507**
  Collecting bank, **Com 7508**

DOMESTIC CORPORATIONS
Corporations, generally, this index

DONATIONS
Gifts, Devises and Bequests, generally, this index

DRAFTS
Commercial Paper, this index
Defined, commercial paper,
  Application,
    Bank deposits and collections, **Com 4104**
    Documentary drafts, **Com 4104**
    Sales Act, **Com 2103**
Delivery of documents, **Com 2514**
Documentary drafts, **Com 4501 et seq.**
  Bank Deposits and Collections, this index
  Defined, **Com 4104**
Purchases, rights of financing agency, **Com 2506**
Sales, this index

DRAWEE
Defined,
  Negotiable instruments, **Com 3103**

DRAWER
Defined, negotiable instruments, **Com 3103**

DRUGS AND MEDICINE
Bank deposits and collections, incompetency of customer caused by, **Com 4405**

DULY NEGOTIATED
Defined, documents of title, **Com 7501**
  Application, **Com 7102**
    Warehouse receipts and bills of lading, **Com 7501**

DURESS OR COERCION
Commercial code, supplementary, **Com 1103**
Documents of title, title and rights, **Com 7502**
Holder in due course, defense, **Com 3305**

EARNINGS
Compensation and Salaries, generally, this index

ELECTION OF RIGHTS AND REMEDIES
Sale on approval, sales act, **Com 2327**

ELECTRICITY
Secured transactions, exemptions, transition property, **Com 9104**
Transition property,
  Secured transactions, exemptions, **Com 9104**

ELECTRONIC FUNDS TRANSFERS
Funds Transfers, generally, this index

ELECTRONIC PRESENTMENT AGREEMENT
Defined, bank deposits and collections, **Com 4110**

EMPLOYEES
Defined,
  Negotiable instruments, **Com 3405**

EMPLOYEES EARNING PROTECTION LAW
Secured transactions, **Com 9311**

EMPLOYMENT
Labor and Employment, generally, this index

ENCUMBRANCES
Liens and Incumbrances, generally, this index
Mortgages, generally, this index

ENDORSEMENT
Bills of lading, **Com 7501**
Defined,
  Investment securities, **Com 8102**
  Negotiable instruments, **Com 3204**
Documents of Title, this index
Investment Securities, this index
Unauthorized indorsement, defined, commercial code, **Com 1201**
Unindorsed items, depository banks, **Com 4205**
Warehouse receipts, transfer by indorsement, **Com 7501**

ENTITLEMENT

ENTITLEMENT HOLDER
Defined,
    Investment securities, **Com 8102**

ENTITLEMENT ORDER
Defined,
    Investment securities, **Com 8102**

ENTRUSTING
Defined, Sales Act, **Com 2403**
    Application, **Com 2103**

EQUIPMENT TRUSTS
Application of article, commercial code, **Com 9104**
Policy and scope of article, commercial code, **Com 9102**

EQUITY
Definitions,
    Commercial Code, **Com 1201**
Law applicable, commercial code, **Com 1103**

ESTATES
Organization includes an estate, commercial code, **Com 1201**
Probate Proceedings, generally, this index

ESTATES OF DECEDENTS
Probate Proceedings, generally, this index

ESTOPPEL
Supplementary, Commercial Code, **Com 1103**

EVIDENCE
Bill of lading, **Com 1201, 1202**
Burden of proof, **Com 1202, 1210**
    Bank deposits and collections,
        Damages, stop payment order, **Com 4403**
        Reasonable time, **Com 4202**
Commercial Code, **Com 1202, 1210**
Defined,
    Commercial Code, **Com 1201**
Investment securities,
    Signatures, **Com 8114**
Lack of good faith, **Com 1208**
Nonconformance of goods, **Com 2607**
Reasonable time, bank collections, **Com 4202**
Certificates and certification,
    Presumptions,
        Third party documents, **Com 1202**
Commercial Paper, this index
Consular invoice, **Com 1202**
Dishonor, negotiable instruments, **Com 3505**
Inspection and inspectors,
    Certificates and certification, **Com 1202**
Insurance, this index
Leases, this index
Market price, sales act, **Com 2723**
Notice,
    Dishonor, negotiable instrument, **Com 3505**
Parol evidence,
    Contract for sale, **Com 2202**

EVIDENCE—Cont'd
Parol evidence—Cont'd
    Sale or return, **Com 2326**
    Warranties, sales, **Com 2316**
Presumptions, **Com 1210**
    Collecting banks, agencies status, **Com 4201**
    Commercial code, **Com 1202, 1210**
    Investment securities, signatures, **Com 8114**
Records and Recordation, generally, this index
Sales, this index
Secured transactions,
    Assignment, **Com 9318**
    Subordinate security interest, **Com 9504**
Signatures,
    Representatives, negotiable instruments, **Com 3403**
Third party documents, **Com 1202**
Usage of trade, Commercial Code, **Com 1205**
Weighers certificate, **Com 1202**

EXCHANGE
Negotiable instruments, value, **Com 3303**

EXCHANGE, BILLS OF
Commercial Paper, generally, this index

EXCHANGE OF PROPERTY
Buyer in ordinary course of business, defined, Commercial Code, **Com 1201**

EXECUTIONS
Bulk sales, application of law, **Com 6103**
Bulk Transfer Law, exemption, **Com 6103**
Funds transfers, **Com 11502**
Secured transactions, **Com 9311**
    Default, **Com 9501**

EXEMPTIONS
Bulk sales, application of law, **Com 6103**
Secured transactions, **Com 9104**
    Filing provisions, **Com 9302**
Warranty of merchantability, **Com 2316**

EXPRESS WARRANTIES
Sales, this index

EX-SHIP
Goods, delivery, **Com 2322**

FAIR DEALING
Good faith, defined, Sales Act, **Com 2103**

FALSE PERSONATION
Negotiable instruments, issuance induced by, **Com 3404**

FALSE REPRESENTATIONS
Fraud, generally, this index

FARM MACHINERY AND EQUIPMENT
Agricultural Machinery and Equipment, generally, this index

FARM PRODUCTS
Agricultural Products, generally, this index

F.A.S.
Defined, Sales Act, **Com 2319**

FAULT
Defined,
    Commercial code, **Com 1201, 10103**

FEDERAL GOVERNMENT
United States, generally, this index

FEDERAL RESERVE BANKS
Bank deposits and collections, **Com 4103**
    Methods of sending and presenting, **Com 4204**
Regulations, negotiable instruments, **Com 3102**

FIDELITY BONDS
Bonds (Officers and Fiduciaries), generally, this index

FIDELITY INSURANCE
Suretyship and Guaranty, generally, this index

FIDUCIARIES
Bonds (Officers and Fiduciaries), generally, this index
Defined,
    Negotiable instruments, **Com 3307**
Investment securities, registration, endorsements, evidence, **Com 8402**
Receivers and Receivership, generally, this index
Trusts and Trustees, generally, this index

FILING OFFICER
Defined,
    Secured transactions, **Com 9401**
Secured transactions, **Com 9401**
    Financing statement, acceptance for filing **Com 9402**

FINAL PAYMENT
Bank deposits and collections, **Com 4215**

FINANCE LEASES
Defined,
    Commercial code, **Com 10103**

FINANCIAL ASSET
Defined,
    Investment securities, **Com 8102**

FINANCIAL INSTITUTIONS
Banks and Banking, generally, this index

FINANCING AGENCY
Defined,
    Sales act, **Com 2104**
        Application, **Com 2103**
Sales, this index

FINANCING STATEMENT
Certificates and certification, combined certificates, **Com 9409**
Commingled goods, **Com 9315**
Continuation statement, effectiveness, **Com 9403.5**
Defined, secured transactions, **Com 9402**
Filing fee, **Com 9407**
Processed goods, **Com 9315**

FINANCING STATEMENT—Cont'd
Secured Transactions, this index
Security interest, perfection, **Com 9302**

FISH AND GAME
Fish marketing associations,
Secured transactions, security, interests in inventory, retail merchants, **Com 9102**
Livestock. Animals, generally, this index
Secured transactions,
Attachment of interest, **Com 9204**
Fish marketing associations, **Com 9102**

FITNESS
Warranties, **Com 2314 et seq.**

FIXTURE FILING
Defined,
Leases, **Com 10309**

FIXTURES
Defined,
Leases, **Com 10309**
Secured Transactions, this index

F.O.B.
Defined, sales act, **Com 2319**
Overseas shipments, bill of lading required, **Com 2323**

FOOD
Agricultural Products, generally, this index
Beverages, generally, this index
Sales,
Warranty, **Com 2314**
Warranty sales, **Com 2314**

FORCED SALES
Auctions, **Com 2328**

FORECLOSURE
Mortgages, this index
Secured transactions, **Com 9501**

FOREIGN AIR CARRIERS
Secured transactions, location of debtor, **Com 9103**

FOREIGN CORPORATIONS
Secured transactions, debtor, residence, **Com 9401**

FOREIGN COUNTRIES
Ambassadors and Consuls, generally, this index
Bills of lading, agreements as to liabilities, **Com 7302**
Commercial code, application of law, **Com 1105**
Conflict of Laws, generally, this index
Contract for sale,
Excuse by failure of presupposed conditions, **Com 2615**
Payment regulations, substituted performance, **Com 2614**
Money,
Defined, commercial code, **Com 1201**
Sales, bills of lading, **Com 2323**

FOREIGN COUNTRIES—Cont'd
Secured transactions, perfection of security interest, **Com 9103**

FOREIGN CURRENCY
Collecting bank, charge back or refund, **Com 4214**
Negotiable instruments, form of payment, **Com 3107**

FOREIGN STATES
Commercial code, application of law, **Com 1105**
Conflict of Laws, generally, this index
Contracts,
Excuse by failure of presupposed conditions, **Com 2615**
Payment regulations, substituted performance, **Com 2614**
Secured Transactions, this index

FOREST PRODUCTS
Timber and Lumber, generally, this index

FORGERY
Genuine, defined, Commercial Code, **Com 1201**
Investment securities, alteration, **Com 8206**
Letters of credit, **Com 5109**
Negotiable instruments, fraudulent indorsement by employee, **Com 3405**
Unauthorized signature, definition, Commercial Code, **Com 1201**
Warehouse receipts, **Com 7208**

FORMS
Conspicuous language, defined, Commercial Code, **Com 1201**
Contracts, **Com 2204**
Financing statements, secured transactions, **Com 9402**
Warehouse receipts, **Com 7202**

FRAUD
Alterations,
Investment securities, **Com 8206**
Bills of Lading, this index
Buyers misrepresentation of solvency, **Com 2702**
Commercial code, supplementary, **Com 1103**
Commercial Paper, this index
Documents of title,
Title and rights, **Com 7502**
Holder in due course, defense, **Com 3305**
Investment Securities, this index
Leases, this index
Letters of credit, **Com 5109**
Remedies, **Com 2721**
Rights of creditor, **Com 2402**
Sales, this index
Statute of frauds. Frauds, Statute of, generally, this index

FRAUDS, STATUTE OF
Commercial paper, **Com 1206**
Formal requirements of contract, **Com 2201**
Investment securities, **Com 1206**

FRAUDS, STATUTE OF—Cont'd
Modification of contract, **Com 2209**
Negotiable instruments, accommodation parties, **Com 3419**
Personal property not otherwise covered, **Com 1206**
Sales, **Com 2201, 2326**
Commercial code, **Com 1206**
Contract modification, **Com 2209**
Personal property not otherwise covered, **Com 1206**
Secured transaction, **Com 1206**

FRAUDULENT TRANSFERS
Sale of goods, retention of possession in fraud of creditors, **Com 2402**

FRAUDULENT INDORSEMENT
Defined, negotiable instruments, **Com 3405**

FUNDS
Investments, generally, this index
Trust funds. Trusts and Trustees, generally, this index

FUNDS TRANSFERS
Generally, **Com 11101 et seq.**
Acceptance, payment orders, **Com 11209**
Agents, transfer system, **Com 11206**
Amendments, payment orders, **Com 11211**
Application of law, **Com 11102**
Choice of law and jurisdiction, **Com 11507**
Consumer transactions, federal law, **Com 11108**
Definitions, **Com 11105**
Attachment, **Com 11502**
Attorney fees,
Execution of payment orders, receiving banks, liability, **Com 11305**
Payment orders, cancellation or amendment, losses and expenses, **Com 11211**
Beneficiaries,
Acceptance of payment orders, **Com 11209**
Creditor process, **Com 11502**
Defined, **Com 11103**
Identification of banks, payment orders, **Com 11208**
Interest, payment by beneficiary banks, **Com 11404**
Liability, beneficiary banks, payment, **Com 11404**
Misdescription, payment orders, **Com 11207**
Notice,
Payment by beneficiary banks, **Com 11404**
Refusal of payment, **Com 11406**
Payment, **Com 11406**
By beneficiary banks, **Com 11404, 11405**
Refunds, payment by beneficiary banks, **Com 11405**

FUNDS

FUNDS TRANSFERS—Cont'd
Beneficiaries—Cont'd
  Time,
    Payment by beneficiary banks, **Com 11404, 11405**
    Payment of obligation, **Com 11406**
Between banks, **Com 4206**
Cancellation, payment orders, **Com 11211**
Completions of transfers, acceptance of payment, **Com 11104**
Conflict of laws, **Com 1105, 11507**
Consumer transactions, federal law, application of law, **Com 11108**
Contracts,
  Variation of law, **Com 11501**
Damages. Liability, generally, post
Death, payment orders, cancellation, **Com 11211**
Debtors and creditors, process, **Com 11502**
Definitions, **Com 11103 et seq.**
  Creditor process, **Com 11502**
  Execution, **Com 11301**
  Payment, **Com 11401**
  Security procedure, **Com 11201 et seq.**
Errors. Mistake, generally, post
Executions, **Com 11502**
  Payment orders, **Com 11301 et seq.**
Federal reserve system, rules and regulations, **Com 11107**
Fees, receiving banks, execution of payment orders, **Com 11302**
Garnishment, **Com 11502**
Incompetency, payment orders, cancellation, **Com 11211**
Injunction, **Com 11503**
Instructions. Payment orders, generally, post
Interest,
  Beneficiaries, payment by beneficiary banks, **Com 11404**
  Payment orders,
    Execution, delay, **Com 11305**
    Pending disposition by receiving banks, **Com 11210**
  Receiving banks, rate, **Com 11506**
  Unauthorized payment orders, refunds, **Com 11204**
Intermediary banks,
  Defined, **Com 11104**
  Execution of payment orders, **Com 11302**
  Identification, payment orders, **Com 11208**
  Refunds, **Com 11402**
Jurisdiction, application of law, **Com 11507**
Liability,
  Beneficiaries, payment by beneficiary banks, **Com 11404**
  Payment orders, post
Liens and incumbrances, process, **Com 11502**
Mistake. Payment orders, post
Negotiable instruments, exception, **Com 3102**

FUNDS TRANSFERS—Cont'd
Notice,
  Beneficiaries,
    Payment by beneficiary banks, **Com 11404**
    Refusal of payment, **Com 11406**
  Objections, payment, **Com 11505**
  Payment orders, post
Orders. Payment orders, generally, post
Payment, **Com 11401 et seq.**
  Beneficiaries, **Com 11404, 11406**
  Discharge of obligations, **Com 11406**
  Obligation of sender of payment orders, **Com 11402**
  Receiving banks, by senders, **Com 11403**
  Time, **Com 11401**
Payment orders, **Com 11201 et seq.**
  Acceptance, **Com 11209**
    Completion of transfers, **Com 11104**
  Amendments, **Com 11211**
  Authorization, **Com 11202**
  Cancellation, **Com 11211**
  Defined, **Com 11103**
  Enforceability, **Com 11203**
  Execution, **Com 11301 et seq.**
  Injunction, **Com 11503**
  Instructions, execution of orders, **Com 11302**
  Interest,
    Execution, delay, **Com 11305**
    Pending disposition by receiving banks, **Com 11210**
    Refunds, **Com 11204**
  Liability,
    Cancellation and amendments, **Com 11211**
    Execution,
      Failures, **Com 11305**
      Mistake, **Com 11303**
    Misdescription of beneficiaries, **Com 11207**
    Misdescription of intermediary or beneficiary banks, **Com 11208**
    Mistake, **Com 11205**
    Payment before time, **Com 11209**
    Receiving banks, **Com 11212**
    Transfer system, **Com 11206**
    Unauthorized orders, **Com 11203, 11204**
  Mistake, **Com 11205**
    Beneficiaries, misdescription, **Com 11207**
    Execution, **Com 11303**
    Intermediary or beneficiary banks, identification, **Com 11208**
    Reports, execution, **Com 11304**
  Notice,
    Cancellation or amendment, **Com 11211**
    Errors and mistakes, **Com 11205**
    Execution, mistake, **Com 11304**
    Misdescription of beneficiaries, **Com 11207**
    Misdescription of intermediary or beneficiary banks, **Com 11208**
    Rejection, **Com 11210**
    Unauthorized orders, **Com 11204**

FUNDS TRANSFERS—Cont'd
Payment orders—Cont'd
  Objections, customers, **Com 11505**
  Obligations of senders, **Com 11402**
  Priorities and preferences, **Com 11504**
    Acceptance and rejection, **Com 11210**
  Refunds, unauthorized orders, **Com 11204**
  Rejection, **Com 11210**
  Security procedure, **Com 11201, 11202**
  Separate payments, **Com 11103**
  System transmittal, **Com 11105**
  Time,
    Acceptance, **Com 11209**
    Cancellation, **Com 11211**
    Execution, **Com 11301**
    Issuance, **Com 11103**
    Objections, customers, **Com 11505**
    Receipt, **Com 11106**
    Rejection, **Com 11210**
  Transfer system, liability, **Com 11206**
  Unenforceability, **Com 11203**
  Verification, **Com 11202**
Presentment warranties, **Com 4208**
Priorities and preferences,
  Payment and withdrawals, **Com 11504**
  Payment orders,
    Acceptance and rejection, **Com 11210**
Receiving banks,
  Creditor process, **Com 11502**
  Damages, execution of payment orders, **Com 11305**
  Defined, **Com 11104**
  Erroneous execution of payment orders, **Com 11303**
  Execution of payment orders, **Com 11302**
  Interest, rates, **Com 11506**
  Liability, payment orders, **Com 11212**
  Payment by senders, **Com 11403**
  Time, payment by senders, **Com 11403**
Recovery, execution of payment orders, mistake, **Com 11303**
Refunds,
  Beneficiaries, payment by beneficiary banks, **Com 11405**
  Payment, **Com 11402**
  Unauthorized payment orders, **Com 11204**
Rejection, payment orders, **Com 11210**
Reports, execution of payment orders, mistake, **Com 11304**
Restraining orders, **Com 11503**
Rules and regulations,
  Choice of law, **Com 11507**
  Federal reserve system, **Com 11107**
  Transfer system, **Com 11501**
Security procedure, payment orders, **Com 11201, 11202**
Settlement, bank deposits and collections, **Com 4213**
Time,
  Beneficiaries,
    Payment by beneficiary banks, **Com 11404, 11405**
    Payment of obligation, **Com 11406**

FUNDS TRANSFERS—Cont'd
Time—Cont'd
  Business days, **Com 11105**
  Payment, **Com 11401**
  Payment orders, ante
  Receiving banks, payment by senders, **Com 11403**
Transfer system,
  Agents, liability, **Com 11206**
  Application of law, jurisdiction, **Com 11507**
  Beneficiaries, payment by beneficiary banks. **Com 11405**
  Defined, **Com 11105**
  Payment to receiving banks by senders, **Com 11403**
  Receiving banks, **Com 11302**
  Rules and regulations, **Com 11501**
Warranties, **Com 4207**

FUNGIBLE
Defined, commercial code, **Com 1201**

FUNGIBLE GOODS
Commingling, effect, **Com 7207**
Defined, commercial code, **Com 1201**
Implied warranties, **Com 2314**
Merchantability, **Com 2314**
Sales, this index
Undivided shares, identification, **Com 2105**
Warehouse Receipts, this index

FUNGIBLE SECURITIES
Defined, Commercial Code, **Com 1201**

FURNITURE
Commercial unit, defined, Sales Act, **Com 2105**
Defined,
  Household goods, warehouse receipts, **Com 7209**
Warehousemen, liens, **Com 7209**

FUTURE GOODS
Defined, Sales Act, **Com 2105**
  Application, **Com 2103**
Insurable interest, time of acquisition, **Com 2501**
Sales, this index

GAME
Fish and Game, generally, this index

GARNISHMENT
Funds transfers, **Com 11502**

GAS
Oil and Gas, generally, this index

GENERAL CREDITOR
Creditor, defined, commercial code, **Com 1201**

GENERAL INTANGIBLES
Defined,
  Secured transactions, **Com 9106**

GENUINE
Defined, commercial code, **Com 1201**

GENUINE—Cont'd
Documents of title, warranties on transfer, **Com 7507**
Investment Securities, this index
Third party document, presumptions, **Com 1202**

GIFTS, DEVISES AND BEQUESTS
Definitions,
  Purchase, commercial code, **Com 1201**
Goods, place of delivery, **Com 2308**

GIN TICKET
Document of title, defined, commercial code, **Com 1201**

GIVES NOTICE
Defined, commercial code, **Com 1201**

GOOD FAITH
Accelerate payments or performance, commercial code, **Com 1208**
Agreement disclaiming, commercial code, **Com 1102**
Auction bidding, **Com 2328**
Bailee's liability, **Com 7404**
Buyer in ordinary course of business, defined, commercial code, **Com 1201**
Commercial code, construction of act, commercial code, **Com 1102**
Defined,
  Commercial code, **Com 1201**
  Sales Act, **Com 2103**
  Investment securities, **Com 8102**
  Letters of credit, **Com 5102**
  Negotiable instruments, **Com 3103**
Duties, obligation of, commercial code, **Com 1203**
Holder in due course,
  Negotiable instruments, **Com 3302**
Obligation, commercial code, **Com 1203**
Purchasers, voidable title, **Com 2403**
Rejected goods, duties of buyer, **Com 2603**
Sales, this index

GOODS, WARES AND MERCHANDISE
Bailment, generally, this index
Consumer Goods, generally, this index
Contract for sale, payment of price, **Com 2304**
Defined,
  Documents of title, **Com 7102**
  Sales Act, **Com 2105**
    Application, **Com 2103**
    Personal or household, return of warranty forms, **Com 2800**
  Secured transactions, **Com 9105**
Deterioration of Goods, generally, this index
Expenses and expenditures,
  Inspection of goods, liabilities, **Com 2513**
  Rejected goods,
    Buyers security interest, **Com 2711**
    Care and sale, **Com 2603**
Installment Sales, generally, this index
Misdescription, bills of lading, **Com 7301**

GRAIN
Agricultural Products, generally, this index

GROSS
Commercial unit, defined, Sales Act, **Com 2105**

GUARANTOR
Surety, defined, commercial code, **Com 1201**

GUARANTY
Suretyship and Guaranty, generally, this index

HAMMERS
Auction sales, completed sale by fall, **Com 2328**

HANDWRITING
Negotiable instruments, contradictory terms, **Com 3114**

HEIRS
Probate Proceedings, generally, this index

HIGHWAYS AND ROADS
Construction or maintenance equipment,
  Security interest, perfection, place, **Com 9103**

HOLDER
Banks, acquisition of right, **Com 4201**
Commercial Paper, this index
Defined,
  Commercial Code, **Com 1201**

HOLDER IN DUE COURSE
Bank Deposits and Collections, this index
Commercial Paper, this index
Defined, commercial paper,
  Application,
    Bank deposits and collections, **Com 4104**
Secured Transactions, this index
Transfer, rights, **Com 3203**

HONESTY
Good faith, defined, Sales Act, **Com 2103**

HONOR
Defined, Commercial Code, **Com 1201**
Letters of Credit, this index

HOUSEHOLD APPLIANCES
Retail sales, warranty cards, **Com 2800, 2801**

HOUSEHOLD GOODS
Furniture, generally, this index

HOUSING
Factory-built housing,
  Secured transactions, application of law, **Com 9203**

IDENTIFIED GOODS TO CONTRACTS
Sales, this index

IDENTITY AND IDENTIFICATION
Definitions, Sales Act, **Com 2501**
  Application, **Com 2103**

IDENTITY

IDENTITY AND IDENTIFICATION—Cont'd
Purchaser rights of transferor, **Com 2403**
Sales, this index
Secured transactions,
    Collateral in secured party's possession, **Com 9207**
    Identifying property, description, **Com 9110**

ILLEGALITY
Negotiable instruments, rescission, **Com 3202**

IMPLIED REPEAL
Construction, Commercial Code, **Com 1104**

IMPLIED WARRANTIES
Sales, this index
Warranties, generally, this index

IMPROVEMENT ACT OF 1911
Assignments,
    Public construction contracts, security interest, **Com 9104**
Contracts,
    Secured transactions, assignment of benefits, security interests created by, **Com 9104**
Secured transactions, public construction contracts, assignment of benefits, **Com 9104**

IMPROVEMENTS
Secured transactions, real property, accounts or contract rights, financing statement, filing, **Com 9302**

IN THE ORDINARY COURSE OF THE SELLERS BUSINESS
Defined,
    Bulk sales, **Com 6102**

INCUMBRANCES
Liens and Incumbrances, generally, this index

INDEBTEDNESS
Assignment for Benefit of Creditors, generally, this index
Bankruptcy, generally, this index
Bonds, generally, this index
Insolvency, generally, this index

INDEMNITY
Bills of lading, rights of issuer, **Com 7301**
Lost or destroyed instruments,
    Security of claimant, **Com 7601**
Negotiable instruments, payment, **Com 3602**
Security transactions, filing bond with secured party, holder of subordinate security interest, **Com 9504**
Sellers stoppage of delivery, expenses of bailee, **Com 7504**
Subrogation, generally, this index

INDEPENDENT CONTRACTORS
Negotiable instruments, fraudulent indorsement by employee, **Com 3405**

INDORSEMENTS
Endorsement, generally, this index

INDORSER
Defined, negotiable instruments, discharge, **Com 3605**

INDUSTRIAL LOANS
Secured transaction, application of law, **Com 9203**

INJUNCTION
Documents of title, rights of purchaser, **Com 7602**
Funds transfers, **Com 11503**
Investment Securities, this index
Letters of credit, forgery or fraud, **Com 5109**
Negotiable instruments, knowledge, payment, **Com 3602**
Secured transactions,
    Noncompliance of law by secured party, **Com 9507**
    Owner of collateral, **Com 9112**

INJURIES
Damages, breach of warranty, **Com 2715**

INNOCENT PURCHASERS
Bills of lading, **Com 7501**
    Judicial process, lien, **Com 7602**
Purchasers for value, generally. Investment Securities, this index
Resale by seller, **Com 2706**
Seller, right to reclaim goods, **Com 2702**
Title to goods, **Com 2403**
Warehouse receipts, alteration, **Com 7208**
Warehousemens lien, sale to enforce, **Com 7210**

INSOLVENCY
    See, also, Bankruptcy, generally, this index
Bank deposits and collections, **Com 4202**
    Warranties of transferor, **Com 4207**
Defined,
    Commercial Code, **Com 1201**
Holder in due course, defenses, **Com 3305**
Leases,
    Recovery of goods by lessee, **Com 10522**
    Refusal of delivery of goods, **Com 10525**
Sales, this index
Secured parties, rights on disposition of collateral, **Com 9306**
Secured transactions,
    Financing statement, filing, **Com 9403**
    Proceeds, **Com 9306**

INSOLVENCY PROCEEDINGS
Defined, Commercial Code, **Com 1201**

INSPECTION AND INSPECTORS
Certificates, presumptions, **Com 1202**
Presumptions, certificates, **Com 1202**
Resale of goods, right of inspection, **Com 2706**

INSPECTION AND INSPECTORS—Cont'd
Sales, this index

INSTALLMENT CONTRACT
Defined, Sales Act, **Com 2612**
    Application, **Com 2103**

INSTALLMENT LEASE CONTRACTS
Defined,
    Commercial code, **Com 10103**

INSTALLMENT SALES
Breach, **Com 2612**
Definitions,
    Installment contract, **Com 2612**
        Application, **Com 2103**
Delay in performance, **Com 2616**

INSTALLMENTS
Secured Transactions Law, effect, **Com 9201**

INSTRUCTIONS
Bank Deposits and Collections, this index
Banks, documentary draft, presentation, **Com 4503**
Bill of lading,
    Change of shipping instructions, effect, **Com 7504**
    Delivery of goods, **Com 7303**
Collecting banks, method of sending and presenting instruments, **Com 4204**
Defined,
    Investment securities, **Com 8102**
Investment Securities, this index
Rejected goods, **Com 2603**
Sales, delivery instructions, **Com 2319**

INSTRUMENTS
Defined,
    Negotiable instruments, **Com 3104**

INSURANCE
Bonds,
    Fidelity bonds. Bonds (Officers and Fiduciaries), generally, this index
Buyer under Sales, Act, **Com 2501**
C.I.F., Sales Act, **Com 2320**
Collateral in secured party's possession, **Com 9207**
Evidence,
    Policy or certificate, **Com 1202**
    Presumptions, generally, post
Fidelity insurance,
    Bonds (Officers and Fiduciaries), generally, this index
    Suretyship and Guaranty, generally, this index
Guaranty insurance,
    Suretyship and Guaranty, generally, this index
Policies,
    Presumptions, **Com 1202**
Presumptions,
    Policy or certificate, **Com 1202**
Records and recordation,
    Negotiable instruments, notice of dishonor, **Com 3505**
Sales,
    Buyer, **Com 2501**

INVESTMENT

INSURANCE—Cont'd
Sales—Cont'd
  Price, **Com 2320**
  Risk of loss, **Com 2510**
Secured Transactions, this index
Seller under Sales Act, **Com 2501**
Subrogation, generally, this index
Suretyship and Guaranty, generally, this index
Third party documents, presumptions, **Com 1202**
Warehousemen, lien for costs, **Com 7209**

INTANGIBLES
Secured Transactions, this index
Security Interest, this index

INTER VIVOS TRUSTS
Trusts and Trustees, generally, this index

INTEREST
Funds Transfers, this index
Letters of credit, **Com 5111**
Priorities, secured transactions, **Com 9312**
Usury,
  Secured transactions, **Com 9201**

INTERMEDIARY BANKS
Bank Deposits and Collections, this index
Funds Transfers, this index

INTERPLEADER
Documents of title, **Com 7603**

INTIMIDATION
Duress or Coercion, generally, this index

INVENTORIES
Defined,
  Bulk sales, **Com 6102**
  Secured transactions, **Com 9109**
Purchase money security interest, priority, **Com 9312**
  Application of law, **Com 9102**
  Priorities, **Com 9308**
Secured Transactions, this index

INVESTMENT COMPANY SECURITY
Defined, investment securities, **Com 8103**

INVESTMENT SECURITIES
Generally, **Com 8101 et seq.**
Accounts and accounting,
  Delivery to, warranties, **Com 8109**
  Entitlements, **Com 8501**
Acquisition, **Com 8104**
  Entitlement, intermediaries, **Com 8116**
Actions and proceedings, **Com 8114**
  Financial assets, adverse claims, **Com 8502**
Admissions, signatures, **Com 8114**
Adverse claims,
  Conflict of laws, **Com 8110**
  Entitlements, **Com 8510, 8511**
  Notice, **Com 8105**
    Endorsements, bearer form, **Com 8304**
    Purchaser, **Com 8302**
Agents,
  Delivery, warranties, **Com 8108**

INVESTMENT SECURITIES—Cont'd
Agents—Cont'd
  Endorsements, signature, warranties, **Com 8306**
  Financial assets, transfer, **Com 8115**
  Registration of transfer, **Com 8407**
    Signatures, assurance, **Com 8402**
  Signatures,
    Instructions, warranties, **Com 8306**
  Transfer agents, generally, post
Alteration, **Com 8206**
Application of law,
  Transition provisions, **Com 8601, 8603**
Assessments, registered owner, liability, **Com 8207**
Assurances, registration, **Com 8402**
Attachment, security interest, **Com 9115**
Authenticating trustees,
  Registration of transfer, **Com 8407**
  Signature, **Com 8205**
  Warranties, **Com 8208**
Authentication, warranty, **Com 8208**
Bailee,
  Financial assets, transfer, **Com 8115**
Bank deposits and collections, application, **Com 4102**
Bearer form,
  Adverse claims, notice, **Com 8105**
  Control, **Com 8106**
  Endorsements, **Com 8304**
Blanks,
  Completion of instrument, **Com 8206**
  Endorsements, **Com 8304**
Bona fide purchaser. Purchasers for value, generally, post
Bonds (officers and fiduciaries),
  Lost or stolen securities, **Com 8405**
  Registration, **Com 8403**
Brokers,
  Financial assets, transfer, **Com 8115**
Burden of proof, signatures, **Com 8114**
Calls,
  Registered owner, liability, **Com 8207**
  Revoked, **Com 8203**
Capacity,
  Signatures,
    Endorsements, **Com 8306**
    Instructions, **Com 8306**
Certificated securities,
  Security interest, **Com 9116**
  Warranties, **Com 8108**
Citation, **Com 8101**
Clearing corporation,
  Entitlements, priorities and preferences, **Com 8511**
  Rules, **Com 8111**
Collateral,
  Perfection of security interest, **Com 9115**
Collusion, wrongful registration of transfer, liability, **Com 8404**
Commodities, secured transactions, law governing, **Com 9103**
Completion of instrument, **Com 8206**
Conditional delivery, defenses of issuer, **Com 8202**

INVESTMENT SECURITIES—Cont'd
Conflict of laws, **Com 1105, 8110**
  Intermediaries, entitlements, **Com 8509**
  Secured transactions, **Com 9103**
Constructive trust, financial assets, adverse claims, **Com 8502**
Contract of purchase,
  Statute of frauds, **Com 8113**
Control, **Com 8106**
  Perfection of security interest, **Com 9115**
Conversion,
  Endorsements, **Com 8304**
  Financial assets, adverse claims, **Com 8502**
Countersignature, warranty, **Com 8208**
Damages,
  Entitlements, wrongful transfer, **Com 8507**
Dates, presentment or surrender, notice of adverse claim, **Com 8105**
Debtors and creditors, **Com 8112**
  Entitlements, intermediaries, **Com 8503**
Defect,
  Burden of proof, **Com 8114**
  Laches, **Com 8203**
  Notice to purchaser, **Com 8202, 8203**
Defenses,
  Burden of proof, **Com 8114**
  Genuineness, **Com 8202**
  Staleness of security as notice, **Com 8203**
Definitions, **Com 8102, 8103**
  Appropriate evidence of appointment or incumbency, registration, **Com 8402**
  Appropriate person, **Com 8107**
  Guaranty of the signature, registration, **Com 8402**
  Issuer, **Com 8201**
  Issuers jurisdiction, conflict of laws, **Com 8110**
  Overissue, **Com 8210**
  Protected purchaser, **Com 8303**
  Securities account, entitlements, **Com 8501**
Delay, registration, liability, **Com 8401**
Delivery, **Com 8301 et seq.**
  Agents, warranties, **Com 8108**
  Conditional delivery, **Com 8202**
  Control, purchaser, **Com 8106**
  Endorsements, transfer, **Com 8304**
  Purchaser, rights acquired, **Com 8302**
Demand,
  Not to register transfer, **Com 8403**
  Proof of authority to transfer, **Com 8307**
  Registration of transfer, **Com 8401**
    Wrongful registration, liability, **Com 8404**
Destroyed instruments, registration of transfer, **Com 8405**
  Notice, time, **Com 8406**
Distribution, entitlements, **Com 8505**

INVESTMENT

INVESTMENT SECURITIES—Cont'd
Due care,
  Intermediaries, financial assets, **Com 8504**
  Payment or distribution, **Com 8505**
Effectiveness, endorsements, instructions, entitlement orders, **Com 8107**
Employees, unauthorized signature, **Com 8205**
Endorsements, **Com 8304**
  Adverse claims, notice, **Com 8105**
  Assurance, **Com 8402**
  Control, **Com 8106**
  Effective, **Com 8107**
  Liability for registration, **Com 8404**
  Registration, **Com 8401**
    Assurances, **Com 8402**
  Registration of transfer, liability, **Com 8404**
  Signatures, warranties, **Com 8306**
  Warranties, **Com 8306**
Entitlements, **Com 8501 et seq.**
  Account, **Com 8501**
  Acquisition, **Com 8104**
  Adverse claims, **Com 8502**
  Change in form of holding, **Com 8508**
  Conflict of laws, **Com 8110**
  Control, **Com 8106**
  Debtors and creditors, process, **Com 8112**
  Financial assets, **Com 8504**
    Payments or distributions, **Com 8505**
  Form,
    Change in form of holding, **Com 8508**
  Intermediaries,
    Acquisition for value, **Com 8116**
    Duties, **Com 8506**
  Legal duties, fulfillment, **Com 8509**
  Orders,
    Compliance, **Com 8507**
    Effective, **Com 8107**
    Warranties, **Com 8109**
  Priorities and preferences,
    Intermediaries, claims against, **Com 8510**
    Purchasers for value, **Com 8510**
  Property interest, **Com 8503**
  Purchaser for value, **Com 8510**
  Wrongful transfer, **Com 8507**
Equity,
  Liens, financial assets, adverse claims, **Com 8502**
Evidence,
  Signatures, **Com 8114**
Exception, **Com 3102**
Exemptions, **Com 8103**
Fiduciaries, registration, endorsements, evidence, **Com 8402**
Filing, security interest, perfection, **Com 9115**
Financial assets,
  Acquisition, **Com 8104**
  Entitlements, **Com 8501 et seq.**
  Perfection of security interest, **Com 9116**
  Purchaser for value, **Com 8116**
  Security interest, **Com 9116**

INVESTMENT SECURITIES—Cont'd
Financial assets—Cont'd
  Transfer, **Com 8115**
Financing statements, security interests, transition provisions, **Com 8603**
Forgery, alteration, **Com 8206**
Forms,
  Entitlements, change in form of holding, **Com 8508**
Fraud,
  Alteration, **Com 8206**
Frauds, statute of,
  Commercial code, **Com 1206**
Genuine,
  Defenses, **Com 8202**
  Signatures,
    Authenticating trustee, registrar or transfer agent, **Com 8208**
    Endorsements, warranties, **Com 8306**
Government, issuance, responsibilities, **Com 8202**
Guarantees,
  Endorsements, signature, **Com 8306**
  Signatures, registration, **Com 8402**
Guaranty,
  Liabilities of guarantor, **Com 8201**
Incomplete instruments, **Com 8206**
Incorporation by reference, terms, **Com 8202**
Indorsement. Endorsements, generally, ante
Initial transaction statements,
  Unauthorized signature, **Com 8205**
Injunction,
  Debtors and creditors, **Com 8112**
  Demand, issuer not to register transfer, **Com 8403**
  Registration of transfer,
    Wrongful registration, liability, **Com 8404**
Innocent purchasers. Purchasers for value, generally, post
Instructions,
  Assurances, registration, **Com 8402**
  Completion, **Com 8305**
  Effective, **Com 8107**
  Registration, **Com 8401**
    Assurances, **Com 8402**
  Signatures,
    Warranties, **Com 8306**
  Warranties, registration of transfer, **Com 8108**
  Wrongful registration, liability, **Com 8404**
Intermediaries,
  Conflict of laws, **Com 8110**
  Control, **Com 8106**
  Entitlements, **Com 8501 et seq.**
  Exercise of rights, entitlements, **Com 8506**
  Financial assets,
    Purchaser for value, **Com 8116**
    Transfer, **Com 8115**
Intermediary bank, defined,
  Bank deposits and collections, **Com 4105**
Issue. Overissue, generally, post

INVESTMENT SECURITIES—Cont'd
Issuer, **Com 8201 et seq.**
  Actions and proceedings, **Com 8114**
  Assurances, registration, **Com 8402**
  Defenses, **Com 8202**
  Demand, not to register transfer, **Com 8403**
  Government or governmental agency or unit, validity, **Com 8202**
  Liens and incumbrances, **Com 8209**
  Overissue, **Com 8210**
  Registration,
    Duties, **Com 8401**
    Liabilities, **Com 8404**
  Registration of transfer,
    Assurances, **Com 8402**
    Demand not to register, **Com 8403**
    Responsibility, **Com 8202**
    Restrictions on transfer, **Com 8204**
    Rights with respect to registered owners, **Com 8207**
Jurisdiction, conflict of laws, **Com 8110**
Laches, **Com 8203**
Lack of genuineness, defense, **Com 8202**
Larceny,
  Notice to issuer, time, **Com 8406**
  Reissuance, **Com 8405**
Liens and incumbrances,
  Financial assets, adverse claims, **Com 8502**
  Issuer, **Com 8209**
Limited interest, purchaser, **Com 8302**
Lost instruments, registration of transfer, **Com 8405**
  Notice, time, **Com 8406**
Modification, contract for purchase, statute of frauds, **Com 8113**
Negotiable instruments, exception, **Com 3102**
Nondelivery, defenses of issuer, **Com 8202**
Notice,
  Adverse claims, ante
  Defect or defense, **Com 8202**
    Staleness, **Com 8203**
  Lost, destroyed or stolen securities, failure to notify issuer within reasonable time, **Com 8406**
  Registered owners, rights, **Com 8207**
  Registration of transfer, **Com 8403**
Overissue, **Com 8210**
  Delivery, registration, **Com 8404**
  Establishment of entitlement, **Com 8501**
Owners and ownership,
  Registered owner, rights, **Com 8207**
Payment,
  Entitlements, **Com 8505**
Perfection of security interests, **Com 9115**
  Law governing, **Com 9103**
  Transition provisions, **Com 8603**
Pledges,
  Uncertificated securities, **Com 8106**
Possession,
  Delivery, **Com 8301**
Powers and duties,
  Intermediaries, entitlements, **Com 8501 et seq.**

INVESTMENT SECURITIES—Cont'd
Presumptions, signatures, **Com 8114**
Priorities and preferences,
  Entitlements,
    Intermediaries, claims of creditors, **Com 8511**
    Purchaser for value, **Com 8510**
  Secured transactions, **Com 9312**
  Law governing, **Com 9103**
Process,
  Debtors and creditors, **Com 8112**
Proof of authority to transfer, demand, **Com 8307**
Property interest, entitlements, **Com 8503**
Protected purchasers,
  Endorsements, **Com 8304**
  Lost, destroyed or wrongfully taken securities, **Com 8405**
  Secured transactions, **Com 9309**
Purchaser,
  Delivery, rights acquired, **Com 8302**
  Limited interest, **Com 8302**
  Notice,
    Adverse claims, **Com 8105, 8302**
    Defect in issue or defense of issuer, **Com 8203**
Purchasers for value,
  Blanks, completion of instrument, **Com 8206**
  Defects, **Com 8202**
  Entitlements, **Com 8503, 8510**
    Priorities and preferences, **Com 8510**
  Financial assets, intermediary, **Com 8116**
  Registration of transfer, warranties, **Com 8108**
  Secured transactions, priorities, **Com 9309**
  Unauthorized signatures, **Com 8205**
  Warranties, **Com 8108**
Reference, incorporation of terms, **Com 8202**
Registered form,
  Adverse claims, notice, **Com 8105**
  Control, **Com 8106**
Registered owner, rights, **Com 8207**
Registrar,
  Registration of transfer, **Com 8407**
  Unauthorized signature, **Com 8205**
  Warranties, **Com 8208**
Registration of transfer, **Com 8401 et seq.**
  Agents, **Com 8407**
  Assurances, endorsements, instructions, **Com 8402**
  Control, purchaser, **Com 8106**
  Delivery, **Com 8301**
  Demand not to register, **Com 8403**
  Destroyed instruments, **Com 8405**
  Issuer, conflict of laws, **Com 8110**
    Liability, **Com 8404**
  Liability of issuer, **Com 8404**
  Lost instruments, **Com 8405**
  Notice, **Com 8403**
    Lost, destroyed or wrongfully taken instruments, **Com 8406**
  Registered owner, rights, **Com 8207**
  Registrar, **Com 8407**

INVESTMENT SECURITIES—Cont'd
Registration of transfer—Cont'd
  Stolen instruments, **Com 8405**
  Transfer agent, **Com 8407**
  Trustee, **Com 8407**
Reissue,
  Overissue, **Com 8210**
Rejectment or rescission of transfer, **Com 8307**
Replevin,
  Financial assets, adverse claims, **Com 8502**
Representatives, effectiveness of endorsements, instructions or entitlement orders, **Com 8107**
Rescission or rejectment of transfer, **Com 8307**
Restriction on transfer, **Com 8204**
Rules and regulations,
  Clearing corporation, **Com 8111**
Sales, this index
Secured transactions, priorities, **Com 9309**
Securities, generally, this index
Security interests,
  Application of law, **Com 9203**
  Certificated securities, **Com 9116**
  Entitlements, **Com 8504**
    Priorities and preferences, **Com 8511**
  Financial assets, **Com 9116**
  Law governing, **Com 9103**
  Perfecting, filing, **Com 9302**
  Priorities, **Com 9312**
  Proceeds on disposition of collateral, **Com 9306**
  Protected purchasers, **Com 9309**
  Transition provisions, **Com 8603**
Seizures, **Com 8112**
Signatures,
  Admissions, proceedings, **Com 8114**
  Endorsements, generally, ante
  Evidence, **Com 8114**
  Guarantee, registration, **Com 8402**
  Registrar,
    Unauthorized signature, **Com 8205**
    Warranties, **Com 8208**
  Transfer agent,
    Unauthorized signature, **Com 8205**
    Warranties, **Com 8208**
  Trustees,
    Unauthorized signature, **Com 8205**
    Warranties, **Com 8208**
  Unauthorized signature, **Com 8205**
  Warranties, **Com 8208**
Special endorsements, **Com 8304**
Specific performance,
  Notice, adverse claim, **Com 8105**
Staleness,
  Notice of defects, **Com 8203**
Statute of frauds, **Com 1206, 8113**
Stolen instruments, registration of transfer, **Com 8405**
Taxes, compliance with law, **Com 8401**
Terms, **Com 8202**
Theft, reissuance, **Com 8405**

INVESTMENT SECURITIES—Cont'd
Time,
  Effectiveness of endorsements, instructions or entitlement orders, **Com 8107**
Trailers, security interest, **Com 9102**
Transfer, **Com 8301 et seq.**
  Adverse claims, knowledge of transfer, notice, **Com 8105**
  Demand, proof of authority, **Com 8307**
  Endorsements, **Com 8304**
  Entitlements, wrongful transfer, **Com 8507**
  Financial assets, **Com 8115**
  Lost, destroyed or stolen securities, failure to notify issuer within reasonable time, **Com 8405, 8406**
  Notice, adverse claims, **Com 8105**
  Proof of authority, demand, **Com 8307**
  Registration of transfer, generally, ante
  Rejection or rescission, **Com 8307**
  Rescission or rejectment, **Com 8307**
  Restriction, **Com 8204**
  Units, endorsements, **Com 8304**
  Warranties, **Com 8108**
Transfer agents,
  Registration of transfer, **Com 8407**
  Unauthorized signature, **Com 8205**
  Warranties, **Com 8208**
Trusts and trustees,
  Constructive trusts, financial assets, adverse claims, **Com 8502**
  Registration of transfer, **Com 8407**
  Unauthorized signature, **Com 8205**
  Warranties, **Com 8208**
Unauthorized signature, **Com 8205**
Uncertificated securities,
  Control, **Com 8106**
Unit transfers, endorsements, **Com 8304**
Validation, overissue, **Com 8210**
Validity, conflict of laws, **Com 8110**
Warranties,
  Accounts, delivery to, **Com 8109**
  Agents, delivery, **Com 8108**
  Endorsements, **Com 8306**
  Entitlement orders, **Com 8109**
  Purchaser for value, **Com 8108**
  Registrar, **Com 8208**
  Transfer agent, **Com 8208**
  Trustees, **Com 8208**
Wrongful transfer,
  Entitlements, **Com 8507**

INVESTMENTS
Defined,
  Secured transactions, **Com 9115**
Secured transactions, application of law, **Com 9103**

INVOICES
C.I.F. and C. & F. terms, preparation by seller, **Com 2320**
Consular invoices, presumptions, **Com 1202**

ISSUER
Defined,
  Documents of title, **Com 7102**
  Investment securities, **Com 8201**

ISSUER

ISSUER—Cont'd
Defined—Cont'd
  Letters of credit, **Com 5102**
Investment Securities, this index
Letters of Credit, this index

ITEM
Defined,
  Bank deposits and collections, **Com 4104**

JOINT INTEREST
Organization, defined, commercial code, **Com 1201**

JOINT TENANTS
Warehouse receipts, **Com 7202**

JUDGMENT LIENS
Priorities and preferences,
  Secured transactions, **Com 9301**
Secured transactions, priorities, **Com 9301**

JUDGMENTS AND DECREES
Attachment, generally, this index
Mortgages, generally, this index
Secured transactions, **Com 9104**

JUDICIAL SALES
Bulk sales, application of law, **Com 6103**
Executions, generally, this index
Instruments purchased, holder in due course, **Com 3302**
Negotiable instruments, holder in due course, **Com 3302**
Secured transactions, **Com 9311, 9501**

JURISDICTION
Investment securities, conflict of laws, **Com 8110**
Letters of credit, **Com 5116**

KNOWLEDGE
Notice, generally, this index

LABOR AND EMPLOYMENT
Compensation and Salaries, generally, this index
Investment securities, unauthorized signatures, effect, **Com 8205**
Liens and incumbrances,
  Mechanics Liens, generally, this index
  Warehousemen, **Com 7209**
Mechanics Liens, generally, this index

LACHES
Investment securities, **Com 8203**

LAKES AND PONDS
Fish and Game, generally, this index

LAND
Real Estate, generally, this index

LANDLORD AND TENANT
Liens and incumbrances,
  Application of law, commercial code, **Com 9104**

LANGUAGE
Conspicuous, defined, Commercial Code, **Com 1201**

LAPSE
Offer before acceptance, **Com 2206**

LARCENY
Theft, generally, this index

LAW GOVERNING
Conflict of Laws, generally, this index

LAW MERCHANT
Supplementary, Commercial Code, **Com 1103**

LAWYERS
Attorneys, generally, this index

LEARN
Defined, commercial code, **Com 1201**

LEASES
Acceptance of goods,
  Default by lessor, **Com 10515**
  Rejection, **Com 10516**
  Revocation,
    Defaults, **Com 10517**
    Incidental damages, **Com 10520**
Accessions, **Com 10310**
Actions and proceedings,
  Breach of warranty, **Com 10516**
  Damages, generally, post
  Default, **Com 10506**
  Enforceability, **Com 10201**
  Evidence, generally, ante
  Limitation of actions, generally, post
  Warranties, **Com 10107**
Administrative law and procedure,
  Default, **Com 10501**
Application of law, **Com 10102, 10104**
Arbitration of disputes,
  Default, **Com 10501**
Bailment, generally, this index
Breach of lease. Damages, generally, post
Cancellation,
  Contract, default by lessee, **Com 10523**
  Default,
    Lessor, **Com 10508**
  Executory obligations, **Com 10505**
Carriers, this index
Claim and delivery, **Com 10521**
Consent,
  Modification, repudiation, excuse, substitution, cancellation, termination, **Com 10406**
Consequential damages, **Com 10503**
  Default by lessor, **Com 10519**
Construction of contracts, **Com 10201 et seq.**
Consumer leases,
  Repudiation, **Com 10402**
Course of dealing,
  Construction, **Com 10207**
  Oral agreements, **Com 10202**
Course of performance,
  Construction, **Com 10207**
Cover, incidental damages, **Com 10520**

LEASES—Cont'd
Crimes and offenses,
  Fraud, generally, post
Damages,
  Breach of warranty,
    Default by lessor, **Com 10519**
  Consequential damages, **Com 10503, 10520**
    Default by lessor, **Com 10519**
  Default, **Com 10508**
    Lessee, **Com 10529 et seq.**
    Lessor, **Com 10508**
  Incidental damages, **Com 10520**
    Default by lessee, **Com 10530**
  Liquidation,
    Default by lessor, **Com 10518, 10519**
  Market rent, **Com 10507**
  Residual interest of lessor, recovery for, **Com 10532**
Debtor and creditor, **Com 10308**
Default, **Com 10501 et seq., 10523 et seq.**
  Actions and proceedings, discharges, **Com 10107**
  Burden of proof, **Com 10516**
  Lessor, **Com 10508 et seq.**
  Notice, post
  Repudiation, **Com 10402**
  Revoking acceptance of lot or commercial unit, **Com 10517**
  Security interest, creation, **Com 10303**
Defined,
  Commercial code, **Com 10103**
Delay in delivery or nondelivery, **Com 10405**
Delivery,
  Commercially impractical, **Com 10404**
  Refusal, insolvency of lessee, **Com 10525**
  Stopping, carriers or bailees, **Com 10526**
  Withholding or stopping, default by lessee, **Com 10523**
Detinue, **Com 10521**
Discharges, actions and proceedings, default or breach of warranty, **Com 10107**
Disposal of goods,
  Default by lessee, **Com 10529**
Effect of lease contract, **Com 10301 et seq.**
Evidence,
  Damages, rent, **Com 10507**
Excuse, **Com 10401 et seq.**
Executory obligations,
  Cancellation, termination or recision, **Com 10505**
Express warranties, **Com 10210**
Filing, secured transactions, **Com 9113**
Fixtures,
  Liens and incumbrances, **Com 10309**
Fraud, **Com 10304**
  Default, **Com 10505**
Fraudulent transfers, **Com 10308**
Identification of goods, **Com 10217**
  Casualty, **Com 10221**
  Insurable interest, **Com 10218**
  Repudiation, **Com 10402**

LEASES—Cont'd
Incidental damages, default, **Com 10520**
Lessee, **Com 10530**
Indefiniteness, enforceability, **Com 10204**
Infringement,
  Actions and proceedings,
    Breech of warranty, **Com 10517**
Insolvency,
  Lessee, refusal of delivery, **Com 10525**
  Lessor, recovery of goods by lessee, **Com 10522**
Installment leases,
  Default, **Com 10509**
    Deliveries, **Com 10510**
    Rejection of goods, **Com 10509, 10510**
Irrevocability, **Com 10406**
Jurisdiction, **Com 10106**
Liens and incumbrances, **Com 10306, 10307**
  Fixtures, **Com 10309**
Limitation of actions,
  Default, **Com 10506**
Liquidation,
  Damages, **Com 10504**
    Consequential damages, **Com 10503**
    Default by lessor, **Com 10518, 10519**
Material misrepresentation, default, **Com 10505**
Modification,
  Consideration, **Com 10208**
  Course of performance, **Com 10207**
  Supply contracts, **Com 10209**
Nonconformities, revocation of acceptance, **Com 10517**
Notice,
  Actions and proceedings,
    Breech of warranty, **Com 10516**
  Cancellation,
    Nonconformities, **Com 10510**
  Default, **Com 10501**
    Acceptance of goods, **Com 10519**
    Installment contracts, **Com 10509**
    Lessor, **Com 10508**
    Rent, **Com 10507**
  Delay or nondelivery, **Com 10405**
  Material or incident delay, **Com 10406**
  Modification or rescission, supply contracts, finance leases, **Com 10209**
  Rejection of goods, **Com 10512**
  Repudiation, default, **Com 10402**
  Retraction of waivers, **Com 10208**
Offers,
  Construction, **Com 10206**
Oral agreements, **Com 10202**
Performance of lease contracts, **Com 10401 et seq.**
Personal property, **Com 10101 et seq.**
Possession,
  Application of law, **Com 10302**
Prevailing rent,
  Damages, default, **Com 10507**
Priorities and preferences,
  Fixtures, liens and incumbrances, **Com 10309**
  Subordination agreements, personal property, **Com 10311**

LEASES—Cont'd
Proceedings. Actions and proceedings, generally, ante
Prohibition,
  Security interest creation, **Com 10303**
Proof. Evidence, generally, ante
Recision, default, **Com 10505**
Reinstatement,
  Retraction, repudiation, **Com 10403**
Rejection,
  Default by lessor, **Com 10508, 10514**
  Incidental damages, **Com 10520**
  Justification, **Com 10514**
  Security interest, **Com 10511**
Remedies,
  Default of lessee, **Com 10523 et seq.**
Rent, generally, this index
Renunciation,
  Actions and proceedings,
    Default or breech of warranty, **Com 10107**
Replevin,
  Default by lessor, **Com 10508**
Repudiation, **Com 10401 et seq.**
Residual interest of lessor, recovery of damages for, **Com 10532**
Restitution,
  Lessees rights, **Com 10504**
Retraction,
  Repudiation, **Com 10402**
Revocation,
  Default by lessor, **Com 10508**
  Incidental damages, **Com 10520**
  Merchants, **Com 10205**
Risks of loss, **Com 10219, 10220**
Secured Transactions, generally, this index
Security,
  Default, lessor, **Com 10508**
Security interest,
  Defined, commercial code, **Com 1201**
  Prohibiting, making default, enforcement, **Com 10303**
  Rejection of goods, **Com 10511**
Sequestration, **Com 10521**
Special manufactured goods, **Com 10201**
Specific performance, **Com 10521**
  Default by lessor, **Com 10508**
Statutes of limitation. Limitation of actions, generally, ante
Subleases,
  Defined, Commercial Code, **Com 10103**
  Transfer of interest, **Com 10305**
Subordination agreements, **Com 10311**
Substitute performance, **Com 10404, 10405**
Substitution, **Com 10401 et seq.**
  Default by lessor, **Com 10518**
Suits. Actions and proceedings, generally, ante
Supply **Com 10208, 10209**
Termination,
  Delay, **Com 10406**
Third parties,
  Actions against, **Com 10530**
  Application of law, **Com 10302**

LEASES—Cont'd
Time,
  Agreement, **Com 10204**
  Limitation of actions, generally, ante
  Substitution of conforming tender, **Com 10513**
Title to property,
  Application of law, **Com 10302**
  Transfer of interest, **Com 10303**
  Subleases, **Com 10305**
Uniform Commercial Code, **Com 10101 et seq.**
Unpaid rent, recovery by lessor, default by lessee, **Com 10529**
Usage of trade,
  Construction, **Com 10207**
  Oral agreements, **Com 10202**
Waiver,
  Actions and proceedings,
    Default or breech of warranty, **Com 10107**
  Course of performance, **Com 10207**
  Executory portions, **Com 10208**
Warranties,
  Actions and proceedings, **Com 10107**
  Discharges, **Com 10107**
  Adverse claims, **Com 10211**
  Breaches,
    Damages,
      Default by lessor, **Com 10508**
  Construction, **Com 10215**
  Express warranties, **Com 10210, 10214**
  Fitness, implied warranty, **Com 10213**
  Implied warranties, fitness, **Com 10213**
  Merchantability, **Com 10212**

LEGAL TENDER
Sales, demand for payment, **Com 2511**

LETTERS OF CREDIT
Generally, **Com 2325, 5101 et seq.**
Acceptance,
  Definitions, **Com 5102**
Advisors, **Com 5107**
  Definitions, **Com 5102**
Amendment, **Com 5106**
Applicants,
  Definitions, **Com 5102**
Application of law, **Com 5103**
  Commercial code, **Com 1105**
Assignments, proceeds, **Com 5114**
Attorney fees, **Com 5111**
Authentication, **Com 5104**
Beneficiaries,
  Assignments, proceeds, **Com 5114**
  Definitions, **Com 5102**
  Name change, **Com 5113**
  Successors, **Com 5113**
  Transferee beneficiaries, notice, **Com 5107**
  Warranties, **Com 5110**
Cancellation, **Com 5106**
Change of name, beneficiaries, **Com 5113**
Choice of law, **Com 5116**
Commercial code, application of law, **Com 1105**
Confirmers, **Com 5107**
  Definitions, **Com 5102**

LETTERS

LETTERS OF CREDIT—Cont'd
Conflict of laws, **Com 1105**
Consent,
    Amendment or cancellation, **Com 5106**
    Assignments, proceeds, **Com 5114**
Consideration, **Com 5105**
Contract for sale, defined, **Com 2106**
Damages, **Com 5111**
Definitions, **Com 5102**
    Sales Act, **Com 2325**
        Application, **Com 2103**
Discharge, issuer, **Com 5108**
Dishonor, **Com 5108**
    Definitions, **Com 5102**
    Notice, **Com 5108**
    Rights of seller, **Com 2325**
    Wrongful dishonor, **Com 5111**
Documents,
    Definitions, **Com 5102**
Duration, **Com 5106**
Enforceability, **Com 5106**
Expiration, **Com 5106**
Forgery, **Com 5109**
Fraud, **Com 5109**
Good faith,
    Definitions, **Com 5102**
Honor, **Com 5108**
    Definitions, **Com 5102**
    Injunction, forgery or fraud, **Com 5109**
Injunction, forgery or fraud, **Com 5109**
Interest, **Com 5111**
Issuance, **Com 5104, 5106**
Issuers, **Com 5108**
    Definitions, **Com 5102**
Jurisdiction, **Com 5116**
Limitation of actions, **Com 5115**
Liquidated damages, **Com 5111**
Midnight deadline, defined, bank deposits and collections, **Com 4104**
Nominated persons, **Com 5107**
    Definitions, **Com 5102**
Nondocumentary conditions, **Com 5108**
Notice,
    Advisors, **Com 5107**
    Dishonor, **Com 5108**
    Transferee beneficiaries, **Com 5107**
Perfecting interest, secured transactions, **Com 9305**
Perpetual letters of credit, **Com 5106**
Presentation, **Com 5108**
    Definitions, **Com 5102**
    Forgery, **Com 5109**
    Fraud, **Com 5109**
Presenter,
    Definitions, **Com 5102**
Proceeds, assignments, **Com 5114**
Records and recordation, **Com 5104**
    Definitions, **Com 5102**
Reimbursement, issuer, **Com 5108**
Repudiation, **Com 5111**
Restitution, issuer, **Com 5108**
Revocability, **Com 5106**
Secured transactions,
    Application of law, **Com 9103**
    Perfecting interest, **Com 9304, 9305**
    Security interests, **Com 9103, 9104, 9304, 9305**
        Application of law, **Com 9103**

LETTERS OF CREDIT—Cont'd
Signatures, authentication, **Com 5104**
Specific performance, wrongful dishonor or repudiation, **Com 5111**
Standard practice, issuers, **Com 5108**
Subrogation, **Com 5117**
Successors of beneficiaries, **Com 5113**
    Definitions, **Com 5102**
Time, **Com 5106**
Transferee beneficiaries, notice, **Com 5107**
Transfers, **Com 5112**
Transmission, **Com 5106**
Value,
    Definitions, **Com 5102**
Warranties, **Com 5110**
Wrongful dishonor, **Com 5111**

LICENSES AND PERMITS
Warehouse receipts, issuance, **Com 7201**

LIEN CREDITOR
Creditor, defined, Commercial Code, **Com 1201**
Defined, secured transactions, **Com 9301**

LIENS AND INCUMBRANCES
Bailees lien, satisfaction, **Com 7403**
Bills of lading, **Com 7307**
    Enforcement, **Com 7308**
Bulk Sales, this index
Carriers, this index
Certificates and certification,
    Combined certificates, **Com 9409**
Defined,
    Commercial code, **Com 10103**
    Leases, **Com 10309**
    Secured transactions, **Com 9105**
Delivery of goods ex-ship, satisfaction, **Com 2322**
Documents of Title, this index
Employment. Mechanics Liens, generally, this index
Funds transfers, process, **Com 11502**
Investment securities, issuer, **Com 8209**
Judgment Liens, generally, this index
Labor and Employment, this index
Leases, **Com 10306, 10307**
Mechanics Liens, generally, this index
Mortgages, generally, this index
Policy and scope of law, **Com 9102**
Presenting banks, expenses, **Com 4504**
Sale of property,
    Fraudulent transfers, **Com 2403**
Sales contracts, warranties, **Com 2312**
Secured Transactions, this index
Settlement, bulk sales, application of law, **Com 6103**
Warehouse Receipts, this index
Warehouses and Warehousemen, this index
Warranty of freedom, **Com 2312**

LIMITATION OF ACTIONS
Bank Deposits and Collections, this index
Bulk sales, **Com 6110**
Commercial code, **Com 16103**
Laches, generally, this index
Leases, this index

LIMITATION OF ACTIONS—Cont'd
Letters of credit, **Com 5115**
Sales, this index

LIMITED LIABILITY COMPANIES
Fiduciaries,
    Negotiable instruments, breach of duty, notice, **Com 3307**
Negotiable instruments,
    Breach of fiduciary duty, notice, **Com 3307**
Officers and employees,
    Negotiable instruments, breach of fiduciary duty, notice, **Com 3307**

LIQUIDATION
Bulk sales,
    Limitation of actions, **Com 6110**

LIQUIDATORS
Bulk sales, **Com 6108**
Defined,
    Bulk sales, **Com 6102**

LISTS
Secured transactions, collateral request, **Com 9208**

LIVESTOCK
Animals, generally, this index

LOANS
Commercial Finance Lenders, generally, this index
Consumer goods, default, disposal of property and recovery, **Com 9505**

LOST OR DESTROYED DOCUMENTS
Documents of Title, this index
Investment securities, registration of transfer, **Com 8405**

LOST OR DESTROYED PROPERTY
Bank deposits and collections, notice to transferor, **Com 4202**
Documents. Lost or Destroyed Documents, generally, this index
Investment securities, registration of transfer, **Com 8405**
Sales,
    Payment, time, **Com 2321**
Warehouse receipts, damages, **Com 7204**
Warehousemen, liabilities, **Com 7403**

LOTS
Auctions, **Com 2328**
Defined,
    Sales Act, **Com 2105**
        Application, **Com 2103**
Sales, this index

MACHINERY AND EQUIPMENT
Agricultural Machinery and Equipment, generally, this index
Commercial unit, defined, Sales Act, **Com 2105**
Construction equipment,
    Secured transactions,
        Application of law, **Com 9102**
        Security interest, validity and perfection, **Com 9103**

MACHINERY AND EQUIPMENT—Cont'd
Defined,
  Bulk sales, **Com 6102**
  Secured transactions, **Com 9109**
Negotiable instruments,
  Signatures, **Com 3401**
Roadbuilding equipment, secured transactions, security interest, perfection, applicable law, **Com 9103**
Secured transactions,
  Defined, **Com 9109**
  Security interest, perfection, **Com 9103**

MAIL AND MAILING
Bulk sales, notice, **Com 6105**
Certified or registered mail,
  Bulk sales,
    Notice to creditors, **Com 6105**
  Commercial code, notices and writings, **Com 1201**
  Notice, **Com 1201**
    Commercial code, **Com 1201**
    Warehousemen's lien, **Com 7210**
Notice,
  Certified or registered mail, ante
Registered mail. Certified or registered mail, generally, ante
Send, defined, Commercial Code, **Com 1201**
Warehousemen lien, enforcement, **Com 7210**

MAKER
Defined, negotiable instruments, **Com 3103**

MARKET PRICES
Sale, nondelivery, measure of damages, **Com 2713**

MATERIALMAN
Mechanics Liens, generally, this index

MEASUREMENTS
Weights and Measures, generally, this index

MECHANICS LIENS
Secured transactions, **Com 9104**
  Priority, **Com 9310**

MEDIATION
Arbitration and Award, generally, this index

MEDICINE
Drugs and Medicine, generally, this index

MEDIUM OF EXCHANGE
Money, defined, Commercial Code, **Com 1201**

MEMORANDUM
Contract for sale, **Com 2201**

MENACE
Duress or Coercion, generally, this index

MENTALLY ILL PERSONS
Bank customers, authority, **Com 4405**

MENTALLY RETARDED AND DEVELOPMENTALLY DISABLED PERSONS
Bank customer, authority of bank, **Com 4405**

MERCHANTABILITY
Sales, implied warranty, **Com 2314**

MERCHANTS
Defined,
  Sales Act, **Com 2104**
    Application, **Com 2103**

MESSAGES
Telegram, defined, commercial code, **Com 1201**

MICROFILMS
Secured transactions, recording instruments in lieu of filing, **Com 9407.1 et seq.**

MIDNIGHT DEADLINE
Bank Deposits and Collections, this index
Defined, bank deposits and collections, **Com 4104**

MINERAL, OIL AND GAS BROKERS
Buyer in ordinary course of business, Commercial Code, **Com 1201**
Mineralhead, sales, buyer in ordinary course of business, Commercial Code, **Com 1201**
Sales,
  Buyer in ordinary course of business, Commercial Code, **Com 1201**
  Wellhead, sales, buyer in ordinary course of business, Commercial Code, **Com 1201**

MINES AND MINERALS
Buyer in ordinary course of business, commercial code, **Com 1201**
Contract for sale, **Com 2107**
Mineralhead, sales, buyer in ordinary course of business, Commercial Code, **Com 1201**
Oil and Gas, generally, this index
Sales,
  Buyer in ordinary course of business, Commercial Code, **Com 1201**
  Contract for sale, **Com 2107**
  Minehead, security, interest perfection, applicable law, **Com 9103**
Secured transactions,
  Attachment of interest, **Com 9204**
  Enforcement, **Com 9203**
  Financing statement,
    Recordation and indexing, **Com 9403**
    Requirements, **Com 9402**
  Perfection, applicable law, **Com 9103**
  Place of filing, **Com 9401**
Security interest, profession, applicable law, **Com 9103**

MINORS
Children and Minors, generally, this index

MISBRANDED
Brands, Marks and Labels, generally, this index

MISREPRESENTATION
Fraud, generally, this index

MISSING RECORDS
Lost or Destroyed Documents, generally, this index

MISSPELLED NAMES
Commercial paper, **Com 3203**

MOBILEHOMES AND MOBILEHOME PARKS
Financing statements,
  Filing, perfecting security interest, **Com 9302**
Secured transactions,
  Application of law, **Com 9102, 9203**
  Perfecting security interests, **Com 9302**

MODIFICATION OR CHANGE
Bank deposits and collections, time limit, **Com 4109**
Sale agreement, **Com 2208, 2209**
  Warranties, **Com 2312**
Secured transaction,
  Right of assignee, **Com 9318**
  Seller's warranties, application of law, **Com 9206**
Warranty of merchantability, **Com 2316**

MONEY
Cash proceeds, definitions, **Com 9306**
Defined,
  Commercial code, **Com 1201**
  Foreign Countries, this index
Sales,
  Legal tender, payment demands, **Com 2511**
  Payment of price, **Com 2304**
Secured transactions, perfecting security interest, **Com 9305**

MORTGAGES
See, also, Trust Deeds, generally, this index
Definitions,
  Commercial code, **Com 10103**
  Secured transactions, **Com 9105**
Foreclosure,
  Secured transactions, **Com 9501**
Purchasers and purchasing,
  Definition, commercial code, **Com 1201**
Secured transactions, corporation, financing statement, filing to perfect security interest, **Com 9302**

MOTOR CARRIERS
See, also, Public Utilities, generally, this index
Bills of Lading, generally, this index
Connecting carriers, bills of lading, damages, **Com 7302**
Investment securities, security interest, semitrailers, **Com 9102**

MOTOR

MOTOR CARRIERS—Cont'd
Liens and incumbrances,
  Bills of lading, **Com 7307**
Possessory liens, bills of lading, **Com 7307**
Sales,
  Market price, computation, **Com 2723**
  Risk of loss, **Com 2509**
  Shipment by seller, **Com 2504**
  Stoppage in transit, sellers remedies, **Com 2705**
  Substituted performance, **Com 2614**
  Terms of delivery, **Com 2319**
Secured transactions,
  Application of law, **Com 9102**

MOTOR VEHICLES
Agricultural Machinery and Equipment, generally, this index
Carriers. Motor Carriers, generally, this index
Equipment,
  Secured transactions, applicability of law, **Com 9103**
F.O.B., Sales Act, **Com 2319**
Security deposits,
  Perfection, applicable law, **Com 9103**
Security interest,
  Application of law, **Com 9102, 9203**
  Equipment, applicability of law, **Com 9103**
  Perfecting security interest, **Com 9103, 9302**
Transactions,
  Equipment, **Com 9103**
  Perfecting security interest, **Com 9302**
  Applicable law, **Com 9103**

MUNICIPAL BONDS
Security, **Com 9104**

MUNICIPALITIES
Security interest, secured transactions, **Com 9104**
Taxation, generally, this index

NAMES
Bulk sales, business, notice to credits, **Com 6105**
Change of name,
  Letters of credit, beneficiaries, **Com 5113**
Secured transactions, financing statements, **Com 9402**
Signatures, generally, this index
Trade Names, generally, this index

NATURAL GAS
Oil and Gas, generally, this index

NEGLIGENCE
Bank deposits and collections, other banks, **Com 4202**
Secured transactions, loss to collateral in secured party's possession, **Com 9207**

NEGOTIABLE INSTRUMENTS
  See, also, Commercial Paper, generally, this index

NEGOTIABLE INSTRUMENTS—Cont'd
  Generally, **Com 3101 et seq.**
Acceleration,
  Overdue instrument, **Com 3304**
  Payable at a definite time, **Com 3108**
Acceptance,
  Cancellation, **Com 3410**
  Defined, **Com 3409**
  Dishonor, **Com 3502**
  Draft, obligation of indorser, **Com 3415**
  Excuse, presentment, **Com 3504**
  Mistake, **Com 3418**
  Obligation,
    Acceptor, **Com 3413**
    Drawer, **Com 3413**
  Revocation, payment by acceptance or mistake, **Com 3418**
  Transfer warranties, **Com 3416**
  Variance, **Com 3410**
Accepted drafts,
  Dishonor, **Com 3502**
Acceptor,
  Conversion, **Com 3420**
  Defined, **Com 3103**
  Drafts, obligations, **Com 3413**
  Excuse, presentment, **Com 3504**
  Liability, **Com 3116**
  Transfer warranties, **Com 3416**
Accommodation parties, **Com 3419**
  Defenses, **Com 3305**
  Discharge, **Com 3605**
  Insolvency, **Com 3305**
Accord and satisfaction, use of instrument, **Com 3311**
Accounts and accounting,
  Breach of fiduciary duty, notice, **Com 3307**
  Identification of payee, **Com 3110**
Actions and proceedings,
  Conversion, **Com 3420**
  Enforcements, **Com 3301 et seq.**
  Limitation of actions, **Com 3118**
  Lost, destroyed or stolen instruments, **Com 3309**
  Notice, third party, **Com 3119**
  Transfer, **Com 3203**
Address of drawee, place of payment, **Com 3111**
Admissibility of evidence, dishonor, **Com 3505**
Admissions,
  Signatures, **Com 3308**
Adoption,
  Signatures, **Com 3401**
Agents,
  Breach of fiduciary duty, notice, **Com 3307**
  Conversion, **Com 3420**
  Identification of payee, **Com 3110**
  Restrictive indorsement, **Com 3206**
  Signatures, **Com 3401, 3403**
Agreements,
  Liability, **Com 3116**
  Other agreements affecting instrument, **Com 3117**
  Separate written agreement, **Com 3117**

NEGOTIABLE INSTRUMENTS—Cont'd
Alteration of instruments,
  Defined, **Com 3407**
  Incomplete instrument, **Com 3115**
  Negligence, **Com 3406**
  Presentment warranties, **Com 3417**
  Transfer warranties, **Com 3416**
Alternative payees, identification, **Com 3110**
Antedating, **Com 3113**
Application of law,
  Bank deposits and collections, **Com 3102**
As originally drawn, obligation of acceptor, **Com 3413**
Assignments,
  Unaccepted drafts, drawee liabilities, **Com 3408**
Associations and societies,
  Discharge, **Com 3311**
  Identification of payee, **Com 3110**
  Signature, unauthorized, **Com 3403**
Assumed name, signature, **Com 3401**
Authenticity,
  Burden of proof, **Com 3308**
  Holder in due course, **Com 3302**
  Signatures, **Com 3401**
Bearer instruments, **Com 3109**
  Blank indorsement, **Com 3205**
  Interest, **Com 3112**
  Payable to order, **Com 3109**
  Special indorsement, **Com 3205**
Beneficiaries,
  Breach of fiduciary duty, notice, **Com 3307**
Blank indorsement, **Com 3205**
Books and papers, evidence of dishonor, **Com 3505**
Branch bank, action taken, notices or orders given, **Com 4107**
Breach,
  Fiduciaries, **Com 3307**
  Notice to third party, **Com 3119**
  Rescission, **Com 3202**
Breach of warranties, **Com 3416**
  Limitation of actions, **Com 3118**
  Presentment warranties, **Com 3417**
Bulk transactions, holder in due course, **Com 3302**
Business records, dishonor, **Com 3505**
Businesses, place of payment, **Com 3111**
Cancellation,
  Acceptance, **Com 3410**
  Discharge, **Com 3604**
  Indorsement, reacquisition, **Com 3207**
Capacity,
  Accommodation parties, defenses, **Com 3305**
  Recoupment, **Com 3305**
  Rescission, **Com 3202**
Cash, payable to bearer, **Com 3109**
Cashiers checks,
  Defined, **Com 3104**
  Discharge of obligation, **Com 3310**
  Limitation of actions, **Com 3118**
  Lost, destroyed or stolen, **Com 3312**
  Obligations of issuer, **Com 3412**
  Refusal to pay, **Com 3411**

NEGOTIABLE INSTRUMENTS—Cont'd
Cashiers checks—Cont'd
  Settlement, **Com 4213**
Certificate of deposit,
  Defined, **Com 3104**
  Limitation of actions, **Com 3118**
Certificates and certification,
  Acceptance, **Com 3409**
  Protest, **Com 3505**
Certified checks,
  Acceptance, **Com 3409**
  Defined, **Com 3409**
  Discharge of obligation, **Com 3310**
  Limitation of actions, **Com 3118**
  Lost, destroyed or stolen checks, **Com 3312**
  Obligation of acceptor, **Com 3413**
  Refusal to pay, **Com 3411**
Checks, **Com 4213**
  Acceptance, **Com 3409**
    Variation, **Com 3410**
  Accepted drafts, dishonor, **Com 3502**
  Damages, refusal to pay, **Com 3411**
  Defined, **Com 3104**
    Lost, destroyed or stolen checks, **Com 3312**
  Demand instrument, overdue, **Com 3304**
  Destroyed **Com 3312**
  Disclaimer, warranties, **Com 3416**
  Dishonor, **Com 3502**
  Liability of drawee, **Com 3408**
  Limitation of actions, **Com 3118**
  Lost, destroyed or stolen, **Com 3312**
  Money orders, **Com 3104**
  Obligations,
    Acceptor, **Com 3413**
    Drawer, **Com 3414**
    Indorser, **Com 3415**
    Issuer, cashiers check, **Com 3412**
  Payment,
    Mistake, **Com 3418**
    Refusal, **Com 3411**
  Presentment,
    Warranties, **Com 3417**
  Refusal to pay, **Com 3411**
  Stolen, **Com 3312**
  Transfer warranties, **Com 3416**
  Unaccepted drafts,
    Dishonor, obligation of drawer, **Com 3413**
    Liability of drawee, **Com 3408**
    Transfer warranties, **Com 3416**
  Variance of draft, **Com 3410**
  Without recourse, obligation of drawer, **Com 3414**
Citation, **Com 3101**
Claimant, defined, lost, destroyed or stolen checks, **Com 3312**
Claims,
  Accommodation parties, **Com 3305**
  Accord and satisfaction, **Com 3311**
  Checks,
    Lost, destroyed or stolen, **Com 3312**
    Holder in due course, **Com 3302, 3305**
    Knowledge, discharge, **Com 3602**
  Lost, destroyed or stolen instruments, **Com 3309**

NEGOTIABLE INSTRUMENTS—Cont'd
Claims—Cont'd
  Notice, breach of fiduciary duty, **Com 3307**
  Presentment warranties, **Com 3417**
  Recoupment, **Com 3305**
  Signatures, burden of proof, **Com 3308**
  Taking subject to, **Com 3306**
  Transfer warranties, **Com 3416**
Collateral,
  Discharge, **Com 3605**
  Impairment, discharge, **Com 3605**
  Securing payment, negotiability, **Com 3104**
Collecting banks,
  Notice of dishonor, **Com 3503**
Competency,
  Burden of proof, signatures, **Com 3308**
Completion, **Com 3115**
Conditions,
  Issue, **Com 3105**
  Promise or order, unconditional, **Com 3106**
  Restrictive indorsement, **Com 3206**
Confession of judgment,
  Negotiability, **Com 3104**
Consent,
  Discharge, **Com 3605**
Consequential damages, refusal to pay checks, **Com 3411**
Consideration,
  Accommodation parties, **Com 3419**
  Defined, **Com 3303**
Consuls, certificate of dishonor, **Com 3505**
Contracts, fraudulent indorsement by employee, **Com 3405**
Contradictory terms, **Com 3114**
Contributions, **Com 3116**
  Accommodation party, **Com 3419**
  Discharge, **Com 3605**
Conversion, **Com 3420**
  Blank indorsements, **Com 3205**
  Limitation of actions, **Com 3118**
  Restrictive indorsement, **Com 3206**
Countersignatures,
  Unconditional promise or order, **Com 3106**
Creditor sale, holder in due course, **Com 3302**
Cut-off hour, presentment, **Com 3501**
Damages,
  Breach of warranty, **Com 3416**
  Presentment, **Com 3417**
  Consequential damages, refusal to pay checks, **Com 3411**
  Presentment warranties, **Com 3417**
Death,
  Excuse, presentment, **Com 3504**
  Signature, burden of proof, **Com 3308**
Declaration of loss, defined, lost, destroyed or stolen checks, **Com 3312**
Default,
  Overdue instrument, **Com 3304**
Defenses,
  Accommodation parties, **Com 3305**
  Breach of warranty, presentment warranties, **Com 3417**

NEGOTIABLE INSTRUMENTS—Cont'd
Defenses—Cont'd
  Consideration, **Com 3303**
  Countersignatures, unconditional promise or order, **Com 3106**
  Holder in due course, **Com 3305**
  Negligence contributing to forged signature or alternation, **Com 3406**
  Nonissuance, **Com 3105**
  Notice, holder in due course, **Com 3302**
  Recoupment, **Com 3305**
  Restrictive indorsement, **Com 3206**
  Separate agreements, **Com 3117**
  Signatures, burden of proof, **Com 3308**
  Waiver, discharge, **Com 3605**
  Warranties on transfer, **Com 3416**
Definitions, **Com 3103, 3104**
  Acceptance, **Com 3409**
  Alternation, **Com 3407**
  Certified check, **Com 3409**
  Checks,
    Lost, destroyed or stolen, **Com 3312**
  Consideration, **Com 3303**
  Fiduciary, **Com 3307**
  Fraudulent indorsements by employee, **Com 3405**
  Holder in due course, **Com 3302**
  Incomplete instrument, **Com 3115**
  Indorsements, **Com 3204**
  Indorser, discharge, **Com 3605**
  Issue, **Com 3105**
  Negotiation, **Com 3201**
  Obligated bank, **Com 3411**
  Person entitled to enforce, **Com 3301**
  Presentment, **Com 3501**
  Protest, **Com 3505**
  Represented person, **Com 3307**
Delay,
  Notice of dishonor, excuse, **Com 3504**
Delivery, **Com 3105**
  Transfer, **Com 3203**
Demand,
  Presentment, **Com 3501**
Demand drafts,
  Defined, **Com 3104**
  Presentment warranties, **Com 3417**
  Transfer warranties, **Com 3416**
Demand instrument,
  Dishonor, **Com 3502**
  Limitation of actions, **Com 3118**
  Overdue, **Com 3304**
  Payable on demand, **Com 3108**
Description, payable to named persons, **Com 3110**
Destroyed checks, **Com 3312**
Destroyed instruments, **Com 3309**
Destruction,
  Discharge, **Com 3604**
Discharge, **Com 3601 et seq.**
  Acceptance of draft, **Com 3413**
  Accord and satisfaction, **Com 3311**
  Alteration, **Com 3407**
  Cancellation, **Com 3604**
  Cashier checks, **Com 3310**
  Certified checks, **Com 3310**
  Defenses, recoupment, **Com 3305**

NEGOTIABLE

NEGOTIABLE INSTRUMENTS—Cont'd
Discharge—Cont'd
  Insolvency, defense, recoupment, **Com 3305**
  Liability, **Com 3116**
  Notice,
    Holder in due course, **Com 3302, 3601**
    Organizations, **Com 3311**
  Obligation of indorser, **Com 3415**
  Organizations, **Com 3311**
  Payment, **Com 3310, 3602**
    Effect, **Com 3601 et seq.**
  Presentment warranties, **Com 3417**
  Renunciation, **Com 3604**
  Secured transactions, **Com 3605**
  Tellers checks, **Com 3310**
  Tender of payment, **Com 3603**
  Transfer warranties, **Com 3416**
  Variance of draft, **Com 3410**
Disclaimers,
  Liability, obligation of drawer, **Com 3414**
  Presentment warranties, **Com 3417**
  Transfer warranties, **Com 3416**
Dishonor,
  Acceptance, **Com 3409**
  Drafts, acceptance varying, **Com 3410**
  Evidence, **Com 3505**
  Notes, suspension of obligations, **Com 3310**
  Obligation of indorser, **Com 3415**
  Payment by acceptance or mistake, **Com 3418**
  Presentment, **Com 3501**
    Warranties, **Com 3417**
  Rules and regulations, **Com 3502**
  Unaccepted drafts, obligation of drawer, **Com 3413**
  Variance of draft, **Com 3410**
Disputes, accord and satisfaction, **Com 3311**
Dollars, foreign money, payable in, **Com 3107**
Domicile and residence, place of payment, **Com 3111**
Drafts,
  Defined, **Com 3104**
Drawee,
  Defined, **Com 3103**
  Payment by acceptance or mistake, **Com 3418**
  Presentment warranties, **Com 3417**
Drawer,
  Declaration of loss, **Com 3312**
  Defined, **Com 3103**
  Issuer, **Com 3105**
  Liability, **Com 3116**
  Notice of dishonor, **Com 3503**
  Obligations, **Com 3413**
  Signature, representative, **Com 3402**
Duress or coercion,
  Recoupment, **Com 3305**
  Rescission, **Com 3202**
Effective date, **Com 16101**
Electronic communications,
  Notice of dishonor, **Com 3503**
  Presentment, **Com 3501**

NEGOTIABLE INSTRUMENTS—Cont'd
Employee, defined, **Com 3405**
Enforcement, **Com 3301 et seq.**
Estates,
  Holder in due course, **Com 3302**
  Identification of payee, **Com 3110**
Evidence,
  Burden of proof,
    Accord and satisfaction, **Com 3311**
    Holder in due course, **Com 3308**
    Impairment, discharge, **Com 3605**
    Incomplete instrument, **Com 3115**
    Lost, destroyed or stolen instruments, **Com 3309**
    Negligence contributing to forged signature or alternation, **Com 3406**
  Dishonor, **Com 3505**
  Presentment, **Com 3501**
  Presumptions,
    Accommodation parties, **Com 3419**
    Conversion, **Com 3420**
    Dishonor, **Com 3505**
  Signatures, intent, **Com 3308, 3403**
Exceptions, **Com 3102**
Exchange, value, **Com 3303**
Excuse,
  Notice of dishonor, **Com 3504**
  Presentment, **Com 3504**
Executions,
  Accommodation parties, **Com 3419**
  Holder in due course, **Com 3302**
  Signature, **Com 3401**
Exhibition of instruments, presentment, **Com 3501**
Expenses,
  Presentment warranties, **Com 3417**
  Refusal to pay checks, **Com 3411**
  Transfer warranties, **Com 3416**
Extensions,
  Discharge, indorsers, accommodation parties, **Com 3605**
  Payable at definite time, **Com 3108**
Federal reserve banks, regulations, **Com 3102**
Fictitious payees, **Com 3404**
Fiduciaries,
  Definitions, **Com 3307**
  Identification of payee, **Com 3110**
  Notice, breach of duty, **Com 3307**
  Restrictive indorsement, **Com 3206**
First delivery, **Com 3105**
Fixed dates, payable at definite time, **Com 3108**
Foreign money, **Com 3107**
Forged indorsements, employer responsibility, **Com 3405**
Forged signatures,
  Negligence, **Com 3406**
Fraud,
  Alternation, **Com 3407**
  Defense, recoupment, **Com 3305**
  Indorsement by employee, **Com 3405**
  Rescission, **Com 3202**
Frauds, statute of, accommodation parties, **Com 3419**
Fraudulent indorsement, defined, **Com 3405**

NEGOTIABLE INSTRUMENTS—Cont'd
Funds,
  Discharge of drawer, **Com 3414**
  Identification of payee, **Com 3110**
Funds transfers,
  Exception, **Com 3102**
Good faith,
  Defined, **Com 3103**
  Holder in due course, **Com 3302**
  Tender, accord and satisfaction, **Com 3311**
Guarantors, accommodation parties, **Com 3419**
Holder,
  Claims, **Com 3306**
  Countersignatures, **Com 3106**
  Determination, **Com 3110**
  Enforcement of instruments, **Com 3301 et seq.**
  Indorsements, **Com 3204**
  Negotiation, **Com 3201**
  Payable at will, demand instrument, **Com 3108**
  Reacquisition, **Com 3207**
Holder in due course, **Com 3302**
  Alternation, defense, **Com 3406, 3407**
  Burden of proof, signature, **Com 3308**
  Claims, **Com 3306**
  Discharge, **Com 3601 et seq.**
  Lost, destroyed or stolen checks, payment, **Com 3312**
  Obligation of acceptor, **Com 3413**
  Payment by acceptance or mistake, **Com 3418**
  Recoupment, **Com 3305**
  Remedies, **Com 3202**
  Restrictive indorsement, **Com 3206**
  Secured transactions, **Com 9206**
  Signature by representative, liability, **Com 3402**
  Unauthorized signatures,
    Defense, **Com 3406**
    Liability, **Com 3403**
  Unconditional promise or order, **Com 3106**
Identity and identification,
  Notice of dishonor, **Com 3503**
  Payees, **Com 3110**
  Presentment, **Com 3501**
Illegal transactions,
  Recoupment, **Com 3305**
  Rescission, **Com 3202**
Impairment, recourse or collateral, discharge, **Com 3605**
Imposters, issuance, **Com 3404**
Incomplete instruments,
  Acceptance, **Com 3409**
  Alteration, **Com 3407**
  Defined, **Com 3115**
  Obligations,
    Drawer, **Com 3413**
    Indorser, **Com 3415**
    Issuer, **Com 3412**
Indemnification, payment, **Com 3602**
Independent contractors, fraudulent indorsement by employee, **Com 3405**
Indorsements,
  Anomalous, **Com 3205**

NEGOTIABLE

NEGOTIABLE INSTRUMENTS—Cont'd
Indorsements—Cont'd
  Anomalous—Cont'd
    Accommodation parties, **Com 3419**
    Liability, **Com 3116**
  Blank, **Com 3205**
  Cancellation, reacquisition, **Com 3207**
  Conversion, **Com 3420**
  Defined, **Com 3204**
  Discharge, **Com 3207, 3605**
    Cancellation or striking out, **Com 3207, 3604**
    Liability, **Com 3310**
  Dishonor, presentment, **Com 3501**
  Effect, **Com 3201**
  Fraud, employer responsibility, **Com 3405**
  Imposter, **Com 3404**
  Names, **Com 3204**
    Imposters, **Com 3404**
  Negotiation, **Com 3201**
    Transfer, **Com 3203**
  Notice of dishonor, **Com 3503**
  Obligations,
    Drawer, **Com 3413**
    Indorser, **Com 3415**
  Presentment, **Com 3501**
    Warranties, **Com 3417**
  Right of transferee, **Com 3203**
  Transfer warranties, **Com 3416**
  Without recourse, obligation of indorser, **Com 3415**
Indorser,
  Defined, **Com 3204, 3605**
  Liability, **Com 3116**
Injunctions, knowledge, payment, **Com 3602**
Insolvency,
  Accommodation parties, **Com 3419**
    Defenses, **Com 3305**
  Defense, recoupment, **Com 3305**
  Excuse, presentment, **Com 3504**
  Holder in due course, **Com 3302**
  Transfer warranties, **Com 3416**
Installments,
  Overdue, **Com 3304**
Instruments,
  Defined, **Com 3104**
  Unconditional **Com 3106**
Intent,
  Identification of payee, **Com 3110**
  Imposters, indorsement, **Com 3404**
  Incomplete instruments, **Com 3115**
  Indorsements, **Com 3204**
  Signatures, **Com 3403**
Interest, **Com 3112**
  Presentment warranties, **Com 3417**
  Refusal to pay checks, **Com 3411**
  Tender of payment, discharge, **Com 3603**
  Transfer warranties, **Com 3416**
Issue,
  Cashiers checks, obligation, **Com 3412**
  Conversion, **Com 3420**
  Date of payment, **Com 3113**
  Defined, **Com 3105**
  Fiduciaries, breach of duty, notice, **Com 3307**

NEGOTIABLE INSTRUMENTS—Cont'd
Issue—Cont'd
  Imposters, **Com 3404**
  Notes, obligation, **Com 3412**
  Obligations, notes, cashiers check, **Com 3412**
  Value, **Com 3303**
Issuer, defined, **Com 3105**
Joint and several liability, **Com 3116**
  Discharge, **Com 3605**
Judgments,
  Rate of interest, **Com 3112**
Judicial sales, holder in due course, **Com 3302**
Knowledge,
  Discharge, **Com 3602**
  Transfer warranties, **Com 3416**
Liability, **Com 3116**
  Conversion, **Com 3420**
  Discharge of obligations, **Com 3310**
  Drawee, unaccepted drafts, **Com 3408**
  Fraudulent indorsement by employee, **Com 3405**
  Obligations,
    Drawer, **Com 3414**
    Indorser, **Com 3415**
  Presentment warranties, **Com 3417**
  Restrictive indorsement, **Com 3206**
  Transfer warranties, **Com 3416**
  Unauthorized signatures, **Com 3403**
Limitation of actions, **Com 3118**
Limited liability companies,
  Fiduciaries, breach of duty, notice, **Com 3307**
Loss,
  Discharge,
    Modification, **Com 3605**
  Fraudulent indorsement by employee, liability, **Com 3405**
  Imposters, fictitious payees, **Com 3404**
  Negligence contributing to forged signature or alteration, **Com 3406**
  Presentment warranties, **Com 3417**
  Transfer warranties, **Com 3416**
Lost checks, **Com 3312**
Lost instruments, **Com 3309**
Machines, signatures, **Com 3401**
Maker,
  Defined, **Com 3103**
  Excuse, presentment, **Com 3504**
  Issuer, **Com 3105**
  Liability, **Com 3116**
  Transfer warranties, **Com 3416**
Manual signatures, **Com 3401**
Mark, signatures, **Com 3401**
Mistake,
  Payment or acceptance, **Com 3418**
  Rescission, **Com 3202**
Modification, **Com 3117, 3407**
  Discharge, **Com 3605**
Money,
  Exceptions, **Com 3102**
  Foreign money, payable in, **Com 3107**
  Interest, **Com 3112**
  Limitation of actions, **Com 3118**
Money orders,
  Checks, **Com 3104**

NEGOTIABLE INSTRUMENTS—Cont'd
Mutilation,
  Discharge, **Com 3604**
Names,
  Fraudulent indorsement by employee, **Com 3405**
  Identification of payee, **Com 3110**
  Signatures, **Com 3401**
  Trade names, **Com 3401**
Negligence,
  Alteration, **Com 3406**
  Forged signatures, **Com 3406**
Negotiation,
  Defined, **Com 3201**
  Partial transfer, **Com 3203**
  Reacquisition, **Com 3207**
  Rescission, **Com 3202**
  Restrictive indorsement, **Com 3206**
  Special indorsement, **Com 3205**
Nonnegotiability, **Com 3104**
Notaries public, certificate of dishonor, **Com 3505**
Notes,
  Certificates of deposit, **Com 3104**
  Defined, **Com 3104**
  Obligation of issuer, **Com 3412**
  Suspension of obligation, **Com 3310**
Notice,
  Acceptance of draft, **Com 3409**
  Breach of warranty, **Com 3416**
    Presentment warranties, **Com 3417**
  Fiduciaries, breach of duty, **Com 3307**
  Holder in due course, **Com 3302**
  Indorsements, obligation of indorser, **Com 3415**
  Restrictive indorsement, **Com 3206**
  Separate office or branch bank, **Com 4107**
  Signature for accommodation, **Com 3419**
  Third party, obligation, **Com 3119**
Nullified by separate agreement, **Com 3117**
Numbers and numbering,
  Contradictory terms, **Com 3114**
  Identification of payee, **Com 3110**
  Incomplete instrument, **Com 3115**
Obligated bank, defined, **Com 3312, 3411**
Obligations,
  Acceptance, **Com 3409**
  Acceptor, **Com 3413**
  Discharge, **Com 3310, 3601 et seq.**
  Drawer, **Com 3413**
  Indorser, **Com 3415**
  Issuer of note or cashiers checks, **Com 3412**
  Notice to third party, **Com 3119**
  Presentment, excuse, **Com 3504**
  Suspension, **Com 3310**
  Tender of payment, **Com 3603**
Office, instruments payable to, **Com 3110**
Officers and employees,
  Fraudulent indorsement by employee, **Com 3405**
Oral communication,
  Notice of dishonor, **Com 3503**
  Presentment, **Com 3501**

NEGOTIABLE

NEGOTIABLE INSTRUMENTS—Cont'd
Orders,
  Defined, **Com 3103**
  Negotiability, **Com 3104**
  Payment, payable to order, **Com 3109**
  Separate office or branch bank, **Com 4107**
  Unconditional, **Com 3106**
    Negotiability, **Com 3104**
Ordinary care, defined, **Com 3103**
Overdue,
  Acceptance, **Com 3409**
  Demand instruments, **Com 3304**
Partial assignment, transfer, **Com 3203**
Partial transfer, **Com 3203**
Parties,
  Defined, **Com 3103**
  Liability, **Com 3116**
Partnership,
  Breach of fiduciary duty, notice, **Com 3307**
Payable at a definite time, **Com 3108**
  Limitation of actions, **Com 3118**
  Negotiability, **Com 3104**
Payable at place of payment, **Com 3111**
Payable on demand, **Com 3108**
  Date of instrument, **Com 3113**
  Negotiability, **Com 3104**
Payable to bearer, **Com 3109**
  Negotiability, **Com 3104**
Payable to named person, description, **Com 3110**
Payable to order, **Com 3109**
  Negotiability, **Com 3104**
Payee,
  Conversion, **Com 3420**
  Declaration of loss, **Com 3312**
  Fictitious payees, **Com 3404**
  Identification, **Com 3110**
  Unstated, payable to bearer, **Com 3109**
Payment, **Com 3602**
  Accommodation parties, **Com 3419**
  Accord and satisfaction, **Com 3311**
  Definite time,
    Overdue, **Com 3304**
    Prepayment, **Com 3108**
  Dishonor, **Com 3502**
  Excuse, presentment, **Com 3504**
  Foreign money, **Com 3107**
  Mistake, **Com 3418**
  Notice,
    Breach of fiduciary duty, **Com 3307**
  Obligation of indorser, **Com 3415**
  Orders, exception, **Com 3102**
  Presentment, **Com 3501**
    Warranties, **Com 3417**
  Refusal, checks, **Com 3411**
  Signatures, burden of proof, **Com 3308**
  Suspension, obligation of drawer, **Com 3414**
  Tender, discharge, **Com 3603**
  Unaccepted drafts, obligation of drawer, **Com 3413**
  Value, **Com 3303**
Payment at definite time,
  Overdue, **Com 3304**
Person entitled to enforce, defined, **Com 3301**

NEGOTIABLE INSTRUMENTS—Cont'd
Place of payment, **Com 3111**
  Presentment, **Com 3501**
  Separate office or branch bank, **Com 4107**
  Terms of draft, variance, **Com 3410**
Prepayment,
  Payable at a definite time, **Com 3108**
Presentment,
  Acceptance, **Com 3501**
    Warranties, **Com 3417**
  Dishonor, **Com 3502**
  Excuse, **Com 3504**
  Tender of payment, **Com 3603**
  Waiver, **Com 3504**
  Warranties, **Com 3417**
Principals,
  Breach of fiduciary duty, notice, **Com 3307**
Printed terms,
  Handwritten terms, **Com 3114**
Process,
  Services of process,
    Accommodation parties, **Com 3419**
    Taking under, status of holder, **Com 3302**
Production of documents, lost, destroyed or stolen instruments, **Com 3309**
Promises,
  Defined, **Com 3103**
  Unconditional, **Com 3106**
    Negotiability, **Com 3104**
  Value, **Com 3303**
Protection against loss, **Com 3309**
Protests, **Com 3501**
  Defined, **Com 3505**
Prove, defined, **Com 3103**
Rates and charges,
  Interest, **Com 3112**
  Spot rates, foreign money, **Com 3107**
Ratification, unauthorized signatures, **Com 3403**
Reacquisition, **Com 3207**
Receipts,
  Presentment, **Com 3501**
Records, evidence of dishonor, **Com 3505**
Recoupment,
  Defenses, **Com 3305**
  Notice, **Com 3302**
  Signatures, burden of proof, **Com 3308**
Recourse, discharge, **Com 3605**
Reference to other writings,
  Unconditional promise, **Com 3106**
Reimbursement,
  Accommodation parties, **Com 3419**
Remedies, rescission, **Com 3202**
Remitter,
  Declaration of loss, **Com 3312**
  Defined, **Com 3103**
Renunciation,
  Discharge, **Com 3604**
Representatives,
  Conversion, **Com 3420**
  Identification of payee, **Com 3110**
  Signatures, **Com 3401, 3402**
Represented person, defined, **Com 3307**
Repudiation,
  Excuse, presentment, **Com 3504**

NEGOTIABLE INSTRUMENTS—Cont'd
Requirements, **Com 3104**
Rescission,
  Negotiation, **Com 3202**
Residence, place of payment, **Com 3111**
Responsibility, defined, **Com 3405**
Restitution,
  Payment by acceptance or mistake, **Com 3418**
Return,
  Notice of dishonor, **Com 3503**
Rules and regulations,
  Restrictive indorsement, **Com 3206**
Satisfaction, use of instruments, **Com 3311**
Security,
  Breach of fiduciary duty, notice, **Com 3307**
  Value, **Com 3303**
Seizure,
  Lost, destroyed or stolen checks, **Com 3312**
Separate office of bank, action taken, notices or orders given, **Com 4107**
Separate written agreements, **Com 3117**
  Unconditional promise, **Com 3106**
Settlement, **Com 4213**
Signatures,
  Acceptance of draft, **Com 3409**
  Accommodation parties, **Com 3419**
    Discharge, **Com 3605**
  Assumed names, **Com 3401**
  Automated means, identification of payee, **Com 3110**
  Burden of proof, **Com 3308**
  Countersignatures, unconditional promise or order, **Com 3106**
  Discharge, **Com 3604**
  Forgery,
    Negligence, **Com 3406**
  Incomplete instruments, **Com 3115**
  Issuers, identification of payee, **Com 3110**
  Liability, **Com 3116, 3401**
    Burden of proof, **Com 3308**
    Representatives, **Com 3402**
  Mark, **Com 3401**
  Presentment warranties, **Com 3417**
  Presumptions, **Com 3308**
  Representatives, **Com 3402**
  Specimen signatures, unconditional promise or order, **Com 3106**
  Striking out, discharge, **Com 3604**
  Symbols, **Com 3401**
  Transfer warranties, **Com 3416**
  Travelers checks, **Com 3104**
  Unauthorized, **Com 3403**
Site, payable on demand, **Com 3108**
Special indorsements, **Com 3205**
  Imposters, **Com 3404**
  Payable to bearer, **Com 3109**
Specimen signatures, unconditional promise or order, **Com 3106**
Spot rates, foreign money, **Com 3107**
Statute of frauds, accommodation parties, **Com 3419**
Stolen checks, **Com 3312**
Stolen instruments, **Com 3309**

NOTICE

NEGOTIABLE INSTRUMENTS—Cont'd
Successor,
   Holder in due course, **Com 3302**
   Identification of payees, **Com 3110**
Sufficiency,
   Notice of dishonor, **Com 3503**
Supplementation, **Com 3117**
Suretyship and guaranty,
   Accommodation parties, **Com 3419**
Surrender,
   Discharge, **Com 3604**
   Presentment, **Com 3501**
Suspension,
   Obligations, **Com 3310**
   Payments, damages, **Com 3411**
Symbols, signatures, **Com 3401**
Tellers checks,
   Defined, **Com 3104**
   Discharge of obligations, **Com 3310**
   Limitation of actions, **Com 3118**
   Lost, destroyed or stolen, **Com 3312**
   Refusal to pay, **Com 3411**
   Settlement, **Com 4213**
Tender,
   Accord and satisfaction, **Com 3311**
   Discharge, **Com 3603**
Theft, payment, **Com 3602**
Third parties,
   Discharge, **Com 3310**
   Notice of right to defend, **Com 3119**
Time,
   Acceptance of draft, **Com 3409**
   Checks, lost, destroyed or stolen checks, enforceable claims, **Com 3312**
   Date of instrument, **Com 3113**
   Definite time,
     Overdue instrument, **Com 3304**
     Payment, **Com 3108**
   Dishonor, **Com 3502**
   Extension, discharge, **Com 3605**
   Interest, **Com 3112**
   Limitation of actions, **Com 3118**
   Notice of dishonor, **Com 3503**
     Delay, excuse, **Com 3504**
   Overdue instrument, **Com 3304**
   Payable at a definite time, **Com 3108**
   Presentment, **Com 3501**
   Separate office or branch bank, action taken, notices or orders given, **Com 4107**
   Tender of payment, discharge, **Com 3603**
Trade names, signatures, **Com 3401**
Transfer, **Com 3203**
   Checks, lost, destroyed or stolen, **Com 3312**
   Declaration of loss, **Com 3312**
   Indorsements, **Com 3204**
   Lost or stolen instruments, **Com 3309**
   Negotiation, **Com 3201**
   Presentment warranties, **Com 3417**
   Reacquisition, **Com 3207**
   Recoupment, **Com 3305**
   Restrictive indorsement, **Com 3206**
   Value, **Com 3303**
   Warranties, **Com 3416**
Transfer warranties, **Com 3416**

NEGOTIABLE INSTRUMENTS—Cont'd
Travelers checks,
   Defined, **Com 3104**
   Limitation of actions, **Com 3118**
Trusts and trustees,
   Breach of fiduciary duty, notice, **Com 3307**
   Identification of payee, **Com 3110**
   Restrictive indorsement, **Com 3206**
Typewritten terms, **Com 3114**
Unaccepted drafts,
   Dishonor, **Com 3502**
Unauthorized signatures, **Com 3403**
Uncertified checks, suspension of obligations, **Com 3310**
Unconditional promise or order, **Com 3106**
   Negotiability, **Com 3104**
Undated instruments, **Com 3113**
Unissued instrument,
   Date of payment, **Com 3113**
United States consul, certificate of dishonor, **Com 3505**
Unliquidated amounts, accord and satisfaction, **Com 3311**
Unqualified indorsement, **Com 3204**
Value,
   Holder in due course, **Com 3302**
   Issue or transfer, **Com 3303**
Variance, acceptance, **Com 3410**
Vested rights, transfer, **Com 3203**
Vice consul, certificate of dishonor, **Com 3505**
Waiver,
   Benefits of law, negotiability, **Com 3104**
   Discharge, **Com 3605**
   Excuse, presentment, notice of dishonor, **Com 3504**
Warranties,
   Declaration of loss, lost, destroyed or stolen checks, **Com 3312**
   Presentment warranties, **Com 3417**
   Transfer warranties, **Com 3416**
Without recourse,
   Drafts, obligation of drawer, **Com 3414**
   Obligation of indorser, **Com 3415**
Words,
   Contradictory terms, **Com 3114**
   Incomplete instruments, **Com 3115**
Written communications,
   Notice of dishonor, **Com 3503**
   Presentment, **Com 3501**

NEGOTIATION
Warehouse receipts, delivery, **Com 7501**

NET CONTRACT PRICE
Defined, **Com 6108**
   Bulk sales, **Com 6102**

NET LANDED WEIGHT
Sales, C.I.F. or C. & F. contracts, payment, **Com 2321**

NET PROCEEDS
Defined,
   Bulk sales, **Com 6102**

NEW VALUE
After-acquired collateral, secured transactions, **Com 9108**
Defined,
   Secured transactions, **Com 9105**

NEWSPAPERS
Market quotations, evidence, **Com 2724**

NO ARRIVAL, NO SALE
Sales,
   Casualty, identified goods, **Com 2613**
   Conforming goods, **Com 2324**

NONCONFORMING GOODS
Sales, this index

NONCONFORMING TENDER
Sales,
   Cure, **Com 2508**
   Risk of loss, **Com 2510**

NONPAYMENT
Collecting bank, **Com 4202**

NONPROFIT CORPORATIONS
Credit Unions, generally, this index
Insurance, generally, this index

NONRESIDENTS
Security interest, filing, **Com 9401**

NOTARIES PUBLIC
Negotiable instruments,
   Certificate of dishonor, **Com 3505**

NOTES
Commercial Paper, generally, this index

NOTICE
Adverse claims. Investment Securities, this index
Bank Deposits and Collections, this index
Bulk Sales, this index
Certified or registered mail. Mail and Mailing, this index
Commercial code, sending notices, certified or registered mail, **Com 1201**
Commercial paper, this index
Conspicuous, defined, Commercial Code, **Com 1201**
Constructive notice,
   Real estate, purchaser or encumbrancer, financing or continuation statement, crops or timber, **Com 9403**
Debtors and Creditors, this index
Definitions,
   Commercial Code, **Com 1201**
Investment Securities, this index
Leases, this index
Sales, this index
Secured Transactions, this index
Send, defined, Commercial Code, **Com 1201**
Usage of trade, offer of evidence, **Com 1205**

NOTICE OF DISHONOR
Bank Deposits and Collections, this index
Commercial Paper, this index

NOTICE

NOTICE OF DISHONOR—Cont'd
Defined, commercial paper,
  Application,
    Bank deposits and collections, **Com 4104**

NOTIFIES
Defined, commercial code, **Com 1201**

OATHS AND AFFIRMATIONS
Warranties, express warranty by seller, **Com 2313**

OBLIGATED BANK
Defined,
  Negotiable instruments, **Com 3411**

OFFENSES
Crimes and Offenses, generally, this index

OFFERS
Sales, this index

OFFICERS AND EMPLOYEES
Public Officers and Employees, generally, this index

OFFICIAL BONDS
Bonds (Officers and Fiduciaries), generally, this index

OFFSET
Set-off and Counterclaim, generally, this index

OIL AND GAS
Buyer in ordinary course of business, Commercial Code, **Com 1201**
Contracts,
  Sale, goods, severed from realty, **Com 2107**
Goods, severed from realty, **Com 2107**
Sales,
  Goods, severed from realty, **Com 2107**
  Wellhead,
    Buyer in ordinary course of business, Commercial Code, **Com 1201**
    Security interest perfection, applicable law, **Com 9103**
Secured transactions,
  Attachment of interest, **Com 9204**
  Financing statement requirements, **Com 9402, 9403**
  Perfection, applicable law, **Com 9103**
  Place of filing, **Com 9401**
  Recording, **Com 9403**
  Security interest,
    Enforcement, **Com 9203**
    Perfection, applicable law, **Com 9103**
  Wellhead, sales, buyer in ordinary course of business, Commercial Code, **Com 1201**

OPEN PRICE TERM
Sales contracts, cure, **Com 2305**

OPINIONS
Express warranties, creation, **Com 2313**

OPTICAL DISKS
Secured transactions, recording instruments in lieu of filing, **Com 9407.1 et seq.**

OPTIONS
Commercial paper, acceleration, **Com 1208**
Leases,
  Security interest, defined, commercial code, **Com 1201**
Payment, acceleration at will, commercial code, **Com 1208**
Performance, acceleration at will, commercial code, **Com 1208**
Sales, this index
Warehousemen, termination of storage, **Com 7206**

ORAL EVIDENCE
Parol evidence, generally. Evidence, this index

ORDERS
Branch banks, bank deposits and collections, **Com 4107**
Definitions,
  Negotiable instruments, **Com 3103**
Funds Transfers, this index
Stop payment, bank deposits and collections, **Com 4303, 4403**

ORDINARY CARE
Defined, negotiable instruments, **Com 3103**

ORDINARY COURSE OF BUSINESS
Insolvent, defined, Commercial Code, **Com 1201**

ORGANIZATIONS
Associations and Societies, generally, this index
Defined,
  Commercial Code, **Com 1201**

OTHER STATES
Foreign States, generally, this index

OVERDRAFTS
Bank Deposits and Collections, this index

OVERISSUE
Documents and title, liabilities of issuer, **Com 7402**
Investment securities, delivery, registration, **Com 8404**
Warehouse receipts,
  Fungible goods, liability of warehousemen, **Com 7207**
  Liabilities, **Com 7402**

OVERSEAS
Defined,
  Bills of lading, overseas shipment, **Com 2103, 2323**
  Documents of title, **Com 2323, 7102**

OVERSEAS SHIPMENT
Bill of lading, form, **Com 2323**
Defined, Sales Act, **Com 2323**

PACKAGES
Containers, generally, this index

PAPERS
Commercial Paper, generally, this index
Newspapers, generally, this index

PAROL EVIDENCE
Evidence, this index

PARTIES
Aggrieved parties,
  Definition, commercial code, **Com 1201**
  Liberally administered remedies, commercial code, **Com 1106**
  Remedy, defined, commercial code, **Com 1201**
Definitions,
  Negotiable instruments, **Com 3103**
Third Parties, generally, this index

PARTNERSHIP
Organization, defined, Commercial Code, **Com 1201**
Secured transactions,
  Debtor, residence, **Com 9401**
  Financing statement, names, **Com 9402**

PASSBOOKS
Financial institutions, secured transactions, application of law, **Com 9104**

PAWNBROKERS
Buyer in the ordinary course of business, definition, Commercial Code, **Com 1201**
Secured transaction, application of law, **Com 9203**

PAY
Compensation and Salaries, generally, this index

PAYMENT
Bank Deposits and Collections, this index
Commercial Paper, this index
Funds Transfers, this index
Option to accelerate at will, Commercial Code, **Com 1208**
Receipts, generally, this index
Sales, this index
Secured transactions,
  Assignments, **Com 9318**
  Default, **Com 9502**
  Subordination of right to payment of obligations, Commercial Code, **Com 1209**

PAYMENT ORDERS
Funds Transfers, this index

PAYOR BANK
Bank Deposits and Collections, this index

PERFECTING INTEREST
Secured Transactions, this index

PERFORMANCE BONDS
Bonds (Officers and Fiduciaries), generally, this index

PERISHABLE PROPERTY
Sales, rejected goods, options of buyer, **Com 2604**

PERSONAL PROPERTY
Attachment, generally, this index
Auctions and Auctioneers, generally, this index
Bailment, generally, this index
Goods, Wares and Merchandise, generally, this index
Liens and Incumbrances, generally, this index
Sales, generally, this index
Secured Transactions, generally, this index
Statute of frauds, **Com 1206**
Theft, generally, this index
Title to property, generally, this index

PERSONAL PROPERTY BROKERS
Secured transactions, application of law, **Com 9203**

PETROLEUM
Oil and Gas, generally, this index

PLANES
Aircraft, generally, this index

PLEDGES
Defined,
    Purchase, **Com 1201**
Investment Securities, this index
Purchase, definition, commercial code, **Com 1201**
Secured Transactions, generally, this index

POLITICAL SUBDIVISIONS
Counties, generally, this index
Municipalities, generally, this index
Organization,
    Defined, Commercial Code, **Com 1201**
Secured transactions, exemptions, **Com 9104**
Taxation, generally, this index

POST DATING
Invoices, credit period, beginning, **Com 2310**

PRACTICE OF LAW
Attorneys, generally, this index

PREEXISTING CLAIM
Value, defined, Commercial Code, **Com 1201**

PREFERENCES
Priorities and Preferences, generally, this index

PRESENT SALE
Defined, Sales Act, **Com 2106**
    Application, **Com 2103**

PRESENTING BANK
Defined, bank deposits and collections, **Com 4105**
    Application, **Com 4104**

PRESENTMENT
Bank Deposits and Collections, this index
Commercial Paper, this index
Defined, commercial paper,
    Application,
        Bank deposits and collections, **Com 4104**
Negotiable instruments, **Com 3501**

PRESENTMENT WARRANTIES
Bank deposits and collections, **Com 4208**
Negotiable instruments, **Com 3417**

PRESUMPTIONS
Evidence, this index

PRICES
Sales, this index

PRINCIPAL AND AGENT
Agents, generally, this index

PRINCIPAL AND SURETY
Suretyship and Guaranty, generally, this index

PRINTING
Written or writing, defined, commercial code, **Com 1201**

PRIORITIES AND PREFERENCES
Bank Deposits and Collections, this index
Funds transfers,
    Payment orders, acceptance and rejection, **Com 11210**
    Payments and withdrawals, **Com 11504**
Leases,
    Fixtures,
        Liens and incumbrances, **Com 10309**
Sales, rights of sellers creditors, **Com 2402**
Secured Transactions, this index

PROBATE PROCEEDINGS
Assignment of beneficial interests, secured transactions, filing exclusion, **Com 9302**
Bulk sales, application of law, **Com 6103**
Creditors,
    Defined, **Com 1201**
Executors and administrators,
    Bulk sales, exemptions, **Com 6103**
Sales,
    Bulk sales, **Com 6103**

PROCEEDINGS
Actions and Proceedings, generally, this index

PROCESS
Attachment, generally, this index
Bank deposit and collections, items subject to, time, **Com 4303**
Injunction, generally, this index
Investment securities,
    Debtors and creditors, **Com 8112**

PROCESSED GOODS
Secured transactions, priorities, **Com 9315**

PRODUCE
Agricultural Products, generally, this index

PROFESSIONS AND OCCUPATIONS
Attorneys, generally, this index
Contractors, generally, this index
Customs and usages, commercial code, **Com 1205**

PROFITS
Secured transactions, sale of collateral, disposition, **Com 9207**

PROMISSORY NOTES
Commercial Paper, generally, this index
Defined,
    Negotiable instruments, **Com 3103**

PROPERLY PAYABLE
Defined, bank deposits and collections, **Com 4104**

PROPERTY
Deeds and Conveyances, generally, this index
Investment securities, entitlements, holders interest, **Com 8503**
Personal Property, generally, this index
Real Estate, generally, this index
Title to Property, generally, this index

PROPERTY TAXES
Taxation, generally, this index

PROTECTED PURCHASER
Defined, investment securities, **Com 8303**

PROTESTS
Bank Deposits and Collections, this index
Commercial Paper, this index
Defined,
    Commercial paper,
        Application,
            Bank deposits and collections, **Com 4104**

PROVE
Defined, negotiable instruments, **Com 3103**

PROXIMATE CAUSE
Damages, wrongful dishonor, **Com 4402**

PUBLIC FUNDS
Funds, generally, this index

PUBLIC OFFICERS AND EMPLOYEES
Bonds (Officers and Fiduciaries), generally, this index

PUBLIC POLICY
Retail sales, warranties, return of card to manufacturer, **Com 2801**
Secured transactions, **Com 9102**

PUBLIC RECORDS
Records and Recordation, generally, this index

PUBLIC SERVICE CORPORATIONS
Public Utilities, generally, this index

PUBLIC

PUBLIC UTILITIES
Carriers, generally, this index
Motor Carriers, generally, this index
Railroads, generally, this index
Warehouse receipts, rates and charges, **Com 7202**

PUBLICATION
Bulk sales, notice, **Com 6105**
Market quotations, evidence, **Com 2724**

PURCHASE MONEY LEASES
Defined,
　Commercial code, **Com 10103**
Leases, **Com 10309**

PURCHASE MONEY SECURITY INTEREST
Defined, secured transactions, **Com 9107**
Secured transactions,
　Consumer goods, default, disposal of property and recovery, **Com 9505**
　Inventory, after-acquired property, **Com 9102**
　Priorities, **Com 9301, 9312**

PURCHASER
Defined,
　Commercial code, **Com 1201**
Investment Securities, this index

PURCHASES
Defined,
　Commercial code, **Com 1201**
Sales, generally, this index

QUOTA
Sales,
　Acceptance by buyer due to delay, **Com 2616**
　Necessity by failure of presupposed conditions, **Com 2615**

RAILROADS
Carload, commercial unit, **Com 2105**
Secured Transactions, this index

RATES AND CHARGES
Handling, warehouse receipts, **Com 7202**
Interest, generally, this index
Liens and incumbrances, warehousemen, **Com 7209**
Storage, warehouse receipts, **Com 7202**
Warehouse receipts, storage, **Com 7202**
Warehousemen,
　Lien, **Com 7209**

RATIFICATION
Sales, acceptance of goods, **Com 2606**

REAL ESTATE
Deeds and Conveyances, generally, this index
Fixtures, generally, this index
Interest,
　Transfer, Los Angeles county, to water agencies without consideration,
　　Application of law, **Com 9104**
Leases, generally, this index
Liens and Incumbrances, generally, this index
Mortgages, generally, this index

REAL ESTATE—Cont'd
Sales,
　Goods to be severed from realty, **Com 2107**
　Price payable in, **Com 2304**
Secured Transactions, this index
Security interest,
　Default, procedure, **Com 9501**
　Structures to be moved, contract for sale, **Com 2107**
Taxation, generally, this index
Title to Property, generally, this index

REASONABLE TIME
Acceptance of offer, **Com 2206, 2207**
Definitions,
　Commercial code, **Com 1204**
Firm offers, revocability, **Com 2205**

REASONABLENESS
Commercial transactions, disclaimer, **Com 1102**

RECEIPT OF GOODS
Defined, Sales Act, **Com 2103**
　Application, documents of title, **Com 7102**
　Delivery under C.I.F. and C & F terms, **Com 2320**
　Delivery under F.A.S. terms, **Com 2319**

RECEIPTS
Bank Deposits and Collections, this index
Negotiable instruments, presentment, **Com 3501**
Warehouse Receipts, generally, this index

RECEIVERS AND RECEIVERSHIP
Bulk sales, **Com 6103**
Creditors,
　Definition, commercial code, **Com 1201**
Sales,
　Bulk sales, application of law, **Com 6103**

RECEIVES NOTICE
Defined, Commercial Code, **Com 1201**

RECENTLY PREDICTABLE
Defined, commercial code, **Com 1201**

RECLAMATION
Goods, sellers remedy on discovery by buyer's insolvency, **Com 2702**

RECONSIGNMENT
Bills of lading, **Com 7303**

RECORDERS
Assignments,
　Index, destruction, **Com 9403.1**
Deeds and Conveyances, generally, this index
Destruction by recorder,
　Financing statements, index, **Com 9403.1**
Financing statements, index, destruction, **Com 9403.1**

RECORDERS—Cont'd
Indexes,
　Financing statements, destruction, **Com 9403.1**
Releases,
　Index, destruction, **Com 9403.1**

RECORDS AND RECORDATION
Bulk Sales, this index
Defined,
　Letters of credit, **Com 5102**
Lost records,
　Lost or Destroyed Documents, generally, this index
Sales,
　Contracts, goods to be severed from realty, **Com 2107**
Secured Transactions, this index

RECOUPMENT
Definition, commercial code, **Com 1201**

RECOURSE
Negotiable instruments, discharge, **Com 3605**

REDEMPTION
Secured transactions, collateral, **Com 9501, 9506**

REFERENCE AND REFEREES
Bank deposits and collections, dishonor, **Com 4503**

REFUNDS
Bank deposits and collections, **Com 4214**
　Overdrafts, charging against account, **Com 4401**
Funds Transfers, this index

REGISTERED FORM
Defined, investment securities, certificated security, **Com 8102**

REGISTRAR
Investment Securities, this index

REIMBURSEMENT
Negotiable instruments,
　Accommodation party, **Com 3419**

REJECTION
Investment securities, transfer, **Com 8307**
Sales, this index

RELEASE
Bank Deposits and Collections, this index
Secured transactions, collateral, **Com 9405**
Warehousemen, delivery, **Com 7403**

REMAINING ECONOMIC LIFE OF THE GOODS
Defined,
　Commercial code, **Com 1201**

REMITTER
Defined, negotiable instruments, **Com 3103**

REMITTING BANK
Defined, bank deposits and collections, **Com 4105**
Application, **Com 4104**

REMUNERATION
Compensation and Salaries, generally, this index

RENT
Acceptance of goods, **Com 10515**
Recovery,
  Default,
    Leasee, **Com 10529**
    Lessor, **Com 10508**
Secured transactions, **Com 9104**

REORGANIZATION
Corporations, this index

REPLEVIN
Investment securities, financial assets, adverse claims, **Com 8502**

REPORTS
Funds transfers, execution of payment orders, mistake, **Com 11304**

REPRESENTATIVES
Defined,
  Commercial code, **Com 1201**

REPRESENTED PERSONS
Defined,
  Negotiable instruments, **Com 3307**

REPUDIATION
Sales, this index

RESALE
Defined,
  Secured transactions, **Com 9102**
Sales, this index

RESCISSION
Investment securities, transfer, **Com 8307**

RESERVATION OF INTEREST
Bills of lading,
  Security interest, **Com 2401**
  Seller, **Com 2505**
Security interest, defined, commercial code, **Com 1201**

RESERVATION OF RIGHTS
Commercial transactions,
  Acceptance under, **Com 1207**
  Performance under, **Com 1207**

RESERVATIONS
Sales, shipments under, rights of seller, **Com 2310**
Title, security interest, defined, Commercial Code, **Com 1201**

RESTAURANTS
Bulk sales, application of law, **Com 6103**

RESTITUTION
Buyers right, **Com 2718**

RESTRAINING ORDER
Injunction, generally, this index

RETAIL SALES
Defined, **Com 2800**
Sales, generally, this index

RETENTION WARRANTIES
Bank deposits and collections, **Com 4209**

RETURNS
Bank deposits and collections, **Com 4214**

REVENUE
Taxation, generally, this index

RIGHTS
Defined, Commercial Code, **Com 1201**

RISK
Sales, this index
Secured transactions, collateral in secured party's possession, **Com 9207**

ROLLING STOCK
Security interest, perfection, **Com 9103**

SALARIES
Compensation and Salaries, generally, this index

SALE ON APPROVAL
Acceptance, **Com 2327**
Defined, sales act, **Com 2326**
  Application, **Com 2103**
Risk of loss, **Com 2509**

SALE OR RETURN
Defined, sales act, **Com 2326**
  Application, **Com 2103**

SALE–LEASEBACK TRANSACTIONS
Bulk sales, application of law, **Com 6103**

SALES
Generally, **Com 2101 et seq.**
Absence,
  Specific time provisions, **Com 2309**
  Specified place for delivery, **Com 2308**
Acceptance, **Com 2206, 2606**
  Assurance of future performance, **Com 2609**
  Condition, tender of delivery, **Com 2507**
  Conditional, **Com 2207**
  Damages,
    Nonacceptance, **Com 2708**
    Nonconformity of tender, **Com 2714**
  Defined, **Com 2606**
    Application, **Com 2103**
  Draft, documents delivered, **Com 2514**
  Improper delivery, **Com 2601**
  Inspection of goods, **Com 2513**
  Measure of damages, non-acceptance, **Com 2708**
  Nonacceptance, measure of damages, **Com 2708**
  Nonconforming goods, **Com 2206**
  Nonconformity of tender, **Com 2714**
  Obligation of buyer, **Com 2301**
  Part of unit, **Com 2606**
  Payment, **Com 2607**
    Before inspection, **Com 2512**
  Reasonable time, **Com 2206**

SALES—Cont'd
Acceptance—Cont'd
  Rejection precluded, **Com 2607**
  Revocation of acceptance, generally, post
  Risk of loss, **Com 2510**
  Sale on approval, **Com 2327**
  Substituted performance, **Com 2614**
  Written confirmation, **Com 2207**
Accounts and accounting, resale of goods, **Com 2706**
Actions and proceedings, **Com 2201**
  Breach of installment contracts, **Com 2612**
  Enforcement, **Com 2201**
  Good faith conduct, buyer, **Com 2603**
  Injury to goods, third parties, **Com 2722**
  Installment contracts, **Com 2612**
  Limitation of actions, generally, post
  Price, **Com 2709**
  Replevin, **Com 2711, 2716**
  Specific performance, **Com 2711, 2716**
  Third party actions, **Com 2722**
Affirmation of fact, express warranty, **Com 2313**
Agents,
  Position of seller, **Com 2707**
Agreement, defined, **Com 2106**
Agricultural Products, this index
Allocation,
  Delay in performance, **Com 2616**
  Performance, **Com 2615**
  Risk under sales contract, **Com 2303**
Alteration of terms, **Com 2207**
Ancillary obligation or promise,
Contract, remedies for breach, **Com 2701**
Animals, this index
Anticipatory repudiation,
  Market price, **Com 2723**
  Performance not due, **Com 2610**
  Retraction, **Com 2610, 2611**
Application of law, **Com 2102**
Apportionment of price, lots, **Com 2307**
Approval, sale on approval, **Com 2326**
  Acceptance, **Com 2327**
  Defined, application, **Com 2103**
  Delivered goods, return, **Com 2326**
  Risk of loss, **Com 2509**
  Special incidents, **Com 2327**
Assignment of rights, **Com 2210**
Assortment of goods, option, **Com 2311**
Assurance of due performance, **Com 2609**
Auctions and Auctioneers, generally, this index
Bailment,
  Acknowledgment goods held for buyer, **Com 2705**
  Risk of loss, **Com 2509**
  Tender of delivery, **Com 2503**
Banker's credit, defined, **Com 2325**
  Application, **Com 2103**
Between merchants,
  Assurance of performance, **Com 2609**
  Contract for sale, **Com 2201**
  Defined, **Com 2104**

SALES

SALES—Cont'd
Between merchants—Cont'd
  Defined—Cont'd
    Application, **Com 2103**
  Modification of contract, **Com 2209**
  Rescission of contract, **Com 2209**
Bills of Lading, generally, this index
Bona fide purchasers. Innocent Purchasers, generally, this index
Brands and labels, merchantability requirements, **Com 2314**
Breach of contract,
  Anticipatory repudiation, **Com 2610**
  Collateral contract, **Com 2701**
  Damages, assignment, **Com 2210**
  Deduction of damages from price, **Com 2717**
  Delegation of duty, **Com 2210**
  Installment contracts, **Com 2612**
  Letter of credit, **Com 2325**
  Limitation of actions, **Com 2725**
  Risk of loss, **Com 2509, 2510**
  Waiver or renunciation of claim or right after breach, commercial code, **Com 1107**
Breach of warranty,
  Cause of action, accrual basis, **Com 2725**
  Consequential damages, **Com 2715**
  Damages, **Com 2316, 2714**
  Incidental damages, **Com 2715**
  Notice to seller, **Com 2607**
Bulk Sales, generally, this index
Burden of proof, conformance, **Com 2607**
Buyer,
  Acceptance of goods, **Com 2301, 2606**
  Assignment of rights, **Com 2210**
  Cover, **Com 2711**
  Defined, **Com 2103**
  Deterioration of goods, option, **Com 2613**
  Insolvency, **Com 2702**
    Remedy of seller, **Com 2702**
  Insolvency of seller, **Com 2502**
  Inspection, **Com 2513**
  Insurable interest, **Com 2501**
  Limited interest, **Com 2403**
  Merchant buyer, rejection, duties, **Com 2603**
  Objections, waiver, **Com 2605**
  Obligations, **Com 2301**
    Exclusive dealing, **Com 2306**
  Perishable goods rejected, **Com 2604**
  Rejection of goods, **Com 2401, 2602**
  Replevin, **Com 2716**
  Resale, **Com 2711**
  Rights on improper delivery, **Com 2601**
  Risk of loss, **Com 2509**
  Special property, identification of goods, **Com 2401**
  Specific performance, **Com 2716**
  Third party actions, **Com 2722**
  Title acquired, **Com 2403**
C. & F., **Com 2320**
  Foreign shipment, **Com 2323**
  Price, **Com 2321**

SALES—Cont'd
Cancellation, **Com 2703, 2711**
  Construed, **Com 2720**
  Defined, **Com 2106**
    Application, **Com 2103**
  Open price term, **Com 2305**
Cards, warranty cards, return to manufacturer, **Com 2801**
Cash sales, **Com 2403**
  Buyer in ordinary course of business, defined, commercial code, **Com 1201**
  Title to goods, **Com 2403**
Casualty, identified goods, **Com 2613**
Cats, **Com 2613**
Certainty of contract, **Com 2204**
Change of position,
  Anticipatory repudiation, **Com 2610, 2611**
  Reliance on waiver, **Com 2209**
Checks, **Com 2403, 2514**
  Conditional payment, **Com 2511**
  Defined,
    Application, **Com 2103**
  Dishonored, **Com 2403**
    Nonacceptance or rejection of tender of delivery, **Com 2503**
  Financing agency, rights, **Com 2506**
  Tender of payment, **Com 2511**
C.I.F., **Com 2320**
  Inspection of goods, **Com 2513**
  Overseas shipment, **Com 2323**
  Price, **Com 2321**
Citation, **Com 2101**
Claims, adjustment, **Com 2515**
C.O.D., inspection of goods, **Com 2513**
Collateral promises, breach, **Com 2701**
Commercial unit,
  Acceptance of part, **Com 2606**
  Defined, **Com 2105**
    Application, **Com 2103**
Commission,
  Incidental damages,
    Aggrieved seller, **Com 2710**
    Sellers breach, **Com 2715**
  Merchant buyer on sale after rejection of goods, **Com 2603**
  Perishable goods rejected, **Com 2603**
Conditional acceptance, **Com 2207**
Conditional delivery, transfer of title, **Com 2505**
Conditional payment, checks, **Com 2511**
Conditional sales,
  Secured Transactions, generally, this index
Conditions,
  Acceptance, **Com 2207**
  Tender of delivery, acceptance of goods, **Com 2507**
Confirmed credit, defined, **Com 2325**
  Application, **Com 2103**
Conflict of laws, **Com 1105**
  Rights of seller's creditors, **Com 2402**
Conformance to description, warranty, **Com 2313**
Conforming,
  Defined, **Com 2106**
    Application, **Com 2103**

SALES—Cont'd
Conforming—Cont'd
  Nonconforming goods, generally, post
Conforming goods,
  Identity to contract, **Com 2704**
  No arrival, no sale, **Com 2324**
Consequential damages,
  Breach of warranty, **Com 2715**
  Limitation, **Com 2719**
Consideration,
  Modification of contract, **Com 2209**
  Revocation of offer, lack of consideration, **Com 2205**
Consignee, defined, documents of title, **Com 7102**
  Application, **Com 2103**
Consignment, generally, this index
Consumer goods,
  Application, **Com 2102**
  Consequential damages, limitation, **Com 2719**
  Defined, secured transactions, **Com 9109**
    Application, **Com 2103**
Containers,
  Warranty, **Com 2314**
Contemporaneous oral agreement, **Com 2202**
Contracts for sale,
  Breach of contract, generally, ante
  Conduct of parties, **Com 2207**
  Course of dealing, **Com 2202, 2208**
    Implied warranty, exclusion or modification, **Com 2316**
  Defined, **Com 2106**
    Application,
      Documents of title, **Com 7102**
  Explained or supplemented, **Com 2202**
  Foreign nations,
    Excuse by failure of principal's conditions, **Com 2615**
    Payment regulations, substituted performance, **Com 2614**
  Foreign states,
    Excuse by failure of principal's conditions, **Com 2615**
    Payment regulations, substituted performance, **Com 2614**
  Form, **Com 2204**
  Growing corps, **Com 2107**
  Indefiniteness, **Com 2204**
  Limitation of actions, **Com 2725**
Conversion, merchant buyer,
  After rejection of goods, **Com 2603**
  Rejected goods, **Com 2604**
Cooperation between parties, **Com 2311**
  Contract of performance, particulars, **Com 2311**
Costs, damages for repudiation, **Com 2708**
Course of dealing, commercial code, **Com 1205**
  Agreement, defined, commercial code, **Com 1201**
  Controlling construction, **Com 2208**
  Implied warranty, exclusion or modification, **Com 2316**

SALES—Cont'd
Course of performance,
  Agreement, defined, commercial code, **Com 1201**
  Controlling construction, **Com 2208**
  Implied warranty, exclusion or modification, **Com 2316**
Cover by buyer, **Com 2711, 2712**
  Application, **Com 2103**
Credit period, duration, **Com 2310**
Credit sales. Installment Sales, generally, this index
Creditors, sale or return, **Com 2326**
  Sellers, creditors rights, **Com 2402**
Crops, insurable interest, **Com 2501**
Cure of defects, **Com 2605**
Custom and usage,
  Alteration of agreement, **Com 2202**
  Contract for sale, **Com 2202, 2208**
  Final expression of agreement, **Com 2202**
  Foreign countries, bills of lading, **Com 2323**
  Implied warranty, **Com 2314**
    Exclusion, **Com 2316**
  Market price, **Com 2723**
  Shipment by seller, **Com 2504**
Damages,
  Action for price, **Com 2709**
  Assignment, breach of contract, **Com 2210**
  Breach of contract, mitigation of damages, **Com 2715**
  Breach of warranty, **Com 2316, 2714**
    Consequential damages, **Com 2715**
  Cancellation construed, **Com 2720**
  Consequential damages, **Com 2715**
    Limitation, **Com 2719**
  Cover, **Com 2711, 2712**
  Deduction from price, **Com 2717**
  Fraud, **Com 2721**
  Incidental damages, **Com 2710**
    Accepted goods, **Com 2714**
    Breach of warranty, **Com 2715**
    Cover by buyer, **Com 2712**
    Nondelivery or repudiation, **Com 2713**
  Limitation, **Com 2718**
  Liquidated, **Com 2718**
  Market price, determination, **Com 2713, 2723**
  Modification, **Com 2719**
  Nonacceptance, **Com 2703, 2708**
  Nonconforming goods, **Com 2714**
  Nondelivery, **Com 2713**
  Person in position of seller, **Com 2707**
  Prevailing price, evidence, **Com 2724**
  Rejection of goods, **Com 2603**
  Replevin, **Com 2716**
  Repudiation, **Com 2708**
  Repudiation by seller, **Com 2713**
  Rescission construed, **Com 2720**
  Resale, **Com 2706**
  Sales contract, breach, assignment, **Com 2210**
  Specific performance, **Com 2716**
  Third party actions, **Com 2722**
Default, installment contracts, **Com 2612**

SALES—Cont'd
Defects,
  Documents, reimbursement of financing agency, **Com 2506**
  Waiver by buyer, **Com 2605**
Deficiency,
  Casualty to identified goods, **Com 2613**
  Secured transactions, after resale, **Com 9112**
Definitions, **Com 2103, 2104, 2105, 2106**
  Commercial code, **Com 10103**
  Resale, secured transactions, **Com 9102**
  Secured transactions, **Com 9105**
Delay,
  Delivery, post
  Repudiation of contract, **Com 2611**
Delegation of performance, **Com 2210**
Delivery,
  Apportionment, **Com 2307**
  Bailee, previous sale enforcing lien or termination of storage, **Com 7403**
  Conditions, delivery on condition, **Com 2507**
  Delay, **Com 2615, 2616**
    Breach of duty, **Com 2615**
    Excuse, **Com 2311**
    Notice of excuse, **Com 2616**
  Entrusting as including delivery, **Com 2403**
  Ex-ship, **Com 2322**
  Failure, buyer's right to cancel, **Com 2711**
  F.A.S., **Com 2319**
  Financing agency, right to stoppage, **Com 2506**
  F.O.B., **Com 2319**
  Improper,
    Acceptance, **Com 2609**
    Buyer's rights, **Com 2601**
  Insolvent buyer, **Com 2702**
  Installment contract, **Com 2612**
  Letter of credit, **Com 2325**
  Nonconformance, risk of loss, **Com 2510**
  Nondelivery, remedy of buyer, **Com 2711**
  Obligation of seller, **Com 2301**
  Open price term, **Com 2305**
  Option, **Com 2311**
  Passage of title, **Com 2401**
  Place, **Com 2308**
  Procured through fraud, **Com 2403**
  Rejection, **Com 2508**
    Seller's remedy, **Com 2703**
  Risk of loss, shipment by seller, **Com 2509**
  Shipment by seller, **Com 2504**
  Single delivery, **Com 2307**
  Stoppage, **Com 2705**
    Financing agency's rights, **Com 2506**
  Substitute, **Com 2614**
  Tender, post
  Time, **Com 2309**
Description,
  Inconsistent specifications, **Com 2317**
  Warranty of conformance, **Com 2313**

SALES—Cont'd
Deterioration of goods,
  Casualty to identified goods, **Com 2613**
  No arrival, no sale, **Com 2324**
  Risk, **Com 2321**
Dishonor,
  Checks,
    Nonacceptance or rejection of tender of delivery, **Com 2503**
    Payment of instruments, **Com 2511**
  Defined, commercial paper,
    Application, **Com 2103**
  Letter of credit, **Com 2325**
  Sale of goods for dishonored check, **Com 2403**
Disputes, evidence of goods, preservation, **Com 2515**
Division of risk, **Com 2303**
Document, draft drawn, **Com 2514**
Documents of Title, generally, this index
Domicile and residence, place of delivery, **Com 2308**
Drafts,
  Defined, commercial paper,
    Application, **Com 2103**
  Delivery of document, **Com 2514**
  Payment by financing agency, **Com 2506**
  Purchases, rights of financing agency, **Com 2506**
Drinks, merchantable warranty, **Com 2314**
Duration, contract calling for successive performances, **Com 2309**
Election to return, sale on approval, **Com 2327**
Encumbrances, warranties, **Com 2312**
Enforcement, contract for sale, **Com 2201**
Entrusting, defined, **Com 2403**
  Application, **Com 2103**
Evidence,
  Conformance of goods, **Com 2515**
  Exclusion or modification of warranties, **Com 2316**
  Intent, **Com 2202**
  Market price, **Com 2723**
  Prevailing price, **Com 2724**
  Warranties, purchase and date, returnable forms, **Com 2800, 2801**
Examination of goods, implied warranties, **Com 2316**
Exclusion, warranty of merchantability, **Com 2316**
Exclusive dealing, **Com 2306**
Excuse,
  Delayed performance, **Com 2311, 2615, 2616**
  Failure of presupposed conditions, **Com 2615**
  Performance of agreements, **Com 2311**
Exemptions, **Com 2102**
Expenses and expenditures,
  Incidental damages from seller's breach, **Com 2715**
  Inspection of goods, liabilities, **Com 2513**

SALES

SALES—Cont'd
Expenses and expenditures—Cont'd
  Rejected goods,
    Buyer's security interest, **Com 2711**
    Rights of buyer, **Com 2603**
  Sellers incidental damages after
    breach, definition, **Com 2710**
Express warranties, **Com 2313**
  Cumulative, **Com 2317**
  Intention of parties, **Com 2317**
Ex-ship, delivery, **Com 2322**
Farmers, application, **Com 2102**
F.A.S., **Com 2319**
Filing, secured transactions, **Com 9113**
Financing agency,
  Defined, **Com 2104**
    Application, **Com 2103**
  Letter of credit, **Com 2325**
  Reservation of security interest, **Com 2505**
  Rights, **Com 2506**
Firm offers, **Com 2205**
Fitness for particular purpose. Implied warranties, post
F.O.B., **Com 2319**
  Foreign shipment, **Com 2323**
Food, this index
Forces sales, auctions, **Com 2328**
Foreign countries, bills of lading, **Com 2323**
Foreign shipment, letter of credit, **Com 2325**
Form, contract for sale, **Com 2204**
Fraud,
  Insolvency of buyer, **Com 2702**
  Remedies, **Com 2721**
  Retention of possession in fraud of creditors, **Com 2402**
Frauds, Statute of, this index
Freight, C.I.F. and C. & F., definitions, **Com 2320**
Fungible goods,
  Implied warranties, **Com 2314**
  Merchantability, **Com 2314**
  Undivided share, **Com 2105**
Future goods,
  Defined, **Com 2105**
    Application, **Com 2103**
  Insurable interest, time of acquisition, **Com 2501**
Future installments, performance demanded, **Com 2612**
Future performance, assurance, **Com 2609**
Future sales, identification of goods, **Com 2501**
Good faith,
  Cover by buyer, **Com 2712**
  Defined, **Com 2103**
  Open price term, **Com 2305**
  Purchaser, voidable title, **Com 2403**
  Rejected goods, duties of buyer, **Com 2603**
  Seller's resale, **Com 2706**
  Specification for performance, **Com 2311**
Goods,
  Defined, **Com 2105**

SALES—Cont'd
Goods—Cont'd
  Defined—Cont'd
    Application, **Com 2103**
    Personal or household, returnable warranty form, **Com 2800**
    Nonconforming goods, generally, post
    Payment of price, **Com 2304**
Governmental regulations,
  Delay in delivery, **Com 2615**
  Substituted performance, **Com 2614**
Growing crops, **Com 2107**
Guaranty. Warranties, generally, post
Identification, defined, **Com 2501**
  Application, **Com 2103**
Identification of goods, **Com 2501**
  Action for price, **Com 2709**
  Purchaser, rights of transferor, **Com 2403**
  Resale of goods by seller, **Com 2706**
Identified goods to contracts, **Com 2704**
  Casualty, **Com 2613**
  Place of delivery, **Com 2308**
Identity of goods, passing title, **Com 2401**
Implied warranties, **Com 2314, 2315**
  Cumulative, **Com 2317**
  Examination of goods, **Com 2316**
  Fitness for particular purpose, **Com 2315**
    Exclusion or modification, **Com 2316**
    Inconsistent express warranty, **Com 2317**
  Intention of parties, **Com 2317**
  Merchantability, exclusion or modification, **Com 2316**
Improper delivery, buyer's rights, **Com 2601**
Incidental damages. Damages, ante
Inconsistent claims, **Com 2721**
Indefiniteness, contracts, validity, **Com 2204**
Index of definitions, **Com 2103**
Infringement,
  Burden of proof, **Com 2607**
  Buyer's warranties, **Com 2312**
  Claims, duties of buyer, **Com 2607**
  Warranty, **Com 2312**
Injuries,
  Breach of warranty, **Com 2715**
  Consequential damages, limitation, **Com 2719**
Innocent Purchasers, generally, this index
Insolvency,
  Buyer, **Com 2702**
  Remedy, **Com 2702**
  Rights of buyer, **Com 2502**
  Seller, **Com 2502**
  Stoppage of delivery, **Com 2705**
Inspection and inspectors, **Com 2310**
  Buyer, **Com 2513**
  Conformance of goods, **Com 2515**
  Incidental damages from seller's breach, **Com 2715**
  Payment, **Com 2321, 2512**
  Resale of goods, right of inspection, **Com 2706**
Installment Sales, generally, this index

SALES—Cont'd
Instructions,
  Delivery instructions, **Com 2319**
  Rejected goods, **Com 2603**
Insurance, this index
Intention of parties, warranties, **Com 2317**
  Express warranty, creation, **Com 2313**
Interest in land, contract for sale, **Com 2107**
Investment securities,
  Limitation of actions, **Com 2725**
  Minerals, **Com 2107**
  Parol agreement, modification, **Com 2209**
  Performance, **Com 2208**
  Practical construction, **Com 2208**
  Price, **Com 2305**
  Requirements, **Com 2201**
  Single delivery, **Com 2307**
  Specially manufactured, **Com 2201**
  Statute of frauds, **Com 1206**
    Modification of contracts, **Com 2107**
  Structures on realty, **Com 2107**
  Timber, **Com 2107**
  Usage of trade, **Com 2202, 2208**
  Waiver, of terms, **Com 2208**
  Written agreement, **Com 2201**
Invoices,
  C.I.F., **Com 2320**
Irrevocable offers, period of irrevocability, **Com 2205**
Judicial Sales, generally, this index
Lack of consideration, revocation of offer, **Com 2205**
Lapse, offer before acceptance, **Com 2206**
Larceny, transfer of title, **Com 2403**
Legal tender, demand of payment, **Com 2511**
Letters of Credit, generally, this index
Liens and encumbrances, fraudulent transfers, **Com 2403**
Limitation of actions,
  Contract breaches, **Com 2725**
Limitation of damages, **Com 2718, 2719**
Limitation of warranty, **Com 2316**
  Returnable forms, proof of purchase, **Com 2800, 2801**
Limited interest, **Com 2403**
Liquidated damages, **Com 2718**
Lots,
  Auctions, **Com 2328**
  Defined, **Com 2105**
    Application, **Com 2103**
  Price, apportionment, **Com 2307**
Market price,
  Anticipatory repudiation, **Com 2723**
  Determination, **Com 2713**
Market quotations, evidence, admissibility, **Com 2724**
Memoranda, contract for sale, **Com 2201**
Merchant buyer, rejection, duties, **Com 2603**
Merchantability, warranty, **Com 2314**
Merchants,
  Between merchants, generally, ante
Mines and Minerals, this index

SALES

SALES—Cont'd
Models,
  Examination, implied warranty, **Com 2316**
  Inconsistent specifications, **Com 2317**
  Warranty of conformance, **Com 2313**
Modification,
  Contract, **Com 2208, 2209**
  Damages, **Com 2719**
  Warranty of merchantability, **Com 2316**
  Warranty of title, **Com 2312**
Money,
  Legal tender, payment demand, **Com 2511**
  Payment of price, **Com 2304**
Motor Carriers, this index
Negation of warranty, **Com 2316**
Net landed weights, C.I.F. or C. & F. contracts, payment, **Com 2321**
Newspapers, market quotations, **Com 2724**
No arrival, no sale,
  Casualty, identified goods, **Com 2613**
  Conforming goods, **Com 2324**
Nonacceptance, damages, **Com 2708, 2709**
Nonconforming goods,
  Acceptance, **Com 2206**
    Effect, **Com 2607**
  Damages, **Com 2714**
  Identification, rights of buyer, **Com 2501**
  Installment contracts, **Com 2612**
  Partial acceptance, **Com 2608**
  Payment before inspection, **Com 2512**
  Preserving evidence, **Com 2515**
  Rejection, **Com 2508**
  Revocation of acceptance, **Com 2608**
  Risk of loss, **Com 2510**
Nonconforming tender,
  Cure, **Com 2508**
  Risk of loss, **Com 2510**
Nondelivery, damages, **Com 2713**
Notice,
  Allocation of performance, **Com 2616**
  Buyer's rights in realty, **Com 2107**
  Deduction of damages from price, **Com 2717**
  Delay, **Com 2615**
  Delay in performance, **Com 2616**
  Inspection of goods, **Com 2515**
  Litigation notice given seller, **Com 2607**
  Nonconforming tender or delivery, intention to cure, **Com 2508**
  Nondelivery, **Com 2615**
  Rejection, **Com 2602, 2604**
  Repudiating party, performance awaited, **Com 2610**
  Revocation of acceptance, **Com 2608**
  Sampling goods, **Com 2515**
  Seller's resale, **Com 2706**
  Shipment by seller, **Com 2504**
  Stopped delivery, **Com 2705**
  Tender of delivery, **Com 2503**
  Termination, **Com 2309**
  Test of goods, **Com 2515**

SALES—Cont'd
Notice—Cont'd
  Waiver, retraction, **Com 2209**
Obligations, **Com 2301**
  Exclusive dealing, **Com 2306**
Offers, **Com 2206**
  Additional terms, acceptance, **Com 2207**
  Revocation, **Com 2205**
Official publications, market quotations, evidence, **Com 2724**
Offset, buyer's right to restitution, **Com 2718**
Oil and Gas, this index
Open price term, **Com 2305**
  Contracts, cure, **Com 2305**
Operation of law, rejection, revesting of title in seller, **Com 2401**
Opinions warranty, **Com 2313**
Options,
  Allocation of production and deliveries, **Com 2615**
  Assortment of goods, **Com 2311**
  Casualty to identified goods, **Com 2613**
  Open price term, **Com 2305**
  Performance, **Com 2311**
  Remedy, **Com 2719**
  Return, insurable interest, **Com 2501**
    Time of exercising option, **Com 2327**
  Sale or return, **Com 2327**
Oral agreements, contract for sale, **Com 2202**
Output of seller, quantity, **Com 2306**
Overseas,
  Application, **Com 2103**
  Defined, **Com 2323**
  Shipment, bill of lading, form, **Com 2323**
Parol agreement, modification of written contract, **Com 2209**
Parol evidence,
  Contract for sale, **Com 2202**
  Sale or return, **Com 2326**
  Warranties, **Com 2316**
Part interest, **Com 2105**
Partial acceptance of goods, **Com 2608**
Passing of title, **Com 2401**
Payment,
  Acceptance of goods, **Com 2607**
  Before inspection, **Com 2512**
  C.I.F., **Com 2320**
  F.A.S., **Com 2319**
  F.O.B., **Com 2319**
  Insolvent buyer, **Com 2702**
  Inspection of goods, **Com 2321, 2513**
  Obligation of buyer, **Com 2301**
  Open time, **Com 2310**
  Price, **Com 2304**
  Substituted performance, **Com 2614**
  Tender, **Com 2511**
    Delivery, **Com 2507**
  Time and place, **Com 2310**
Performance, **Com 2501 et seq.**
  Anticipatory repudiation, **Com 2610**
    Retraction, **Com 2611**
  Assurance, **Com 2609**
  Contract for sale, **Com 2208**
  Delegation of duty, **Com 2210**

SALES—Cont'd
Performance—Cont'd
  Specific performance, **Com 2711, 2716**
  Specified by parties, **Com 2311**
  Substitute, **Com 2614**
Perishable goods rejected, **Com 2603, 2604**
Person in position of seller, defined, **Com 2707**
  Application, **Com 2103**
Personal injuries,
  Breach of warranty, **Com 2715**
  Consequential damages, limitation, **Com 2719**
Place,
  Delivery, **Com 2308**
  Payment, **Com 2310**
Possession,
  Merchant buyer, rejection, **Com 2603**
  Rejection by buyer, **Com 2602**
Postdating invoice, credit period, **Com 2310**
  Beginning, **Com 2310**
Practical construction of contract, **Com 2208**
Preexisting claims, satisfaction, rights of creditors, **Com 2402**
Preference, right of seller's creditors, **Com 2402**
Present sale, defined, **Com 2106**
  Application, **Com 2103**
Prevailing price, evidence, **Com 2724**
Prices,
  Action to recover, **Com 2709**
  C. & F., **Com 2321**
  C.I.F., **Com 2321**
  Contract for sale, **Com 2305**
  Deduction of damages, **Com 2717**
  F.O.B., **Com 2319**
  Lots, **Com 2307**
  Market price, evidence, **Com 2723**
  Payment, **Com 2304**
Prior agreement, **Com 2202**
Proceedings. Actions and proceedings, generally, ante
Profits, resale of goods, accounting, **Com 2706**
Promises,
  Creation by seller, **Com 2313**
  Express warranties, **Com 2313**
Quantity,
  Output of seller, **Com 2306**
  Requirements of buyer, **Com 2306**
Quota,
  Acceptance by buyer due to delay, **Com 2616**
  Necessity by failure of presupposed conditions, **Com 2615**
Ratification, acceptance of goods, **Com 2606**
Real Estate, this index
Reasonable price, open price term, **Com 2305**
Reasonable time,
  Acceptance, **Com 2206, 2207**
  Anticipatory repudiation, **Com 2610**
  Firm offers, revocability, **Com 2205**
  Inspection of goods, **Com 2513**

SALES

SALES—Cont'd
Reasonable time—Cont'd
  Notice of breach, **Com 2607**
  Rejection of goods, **Com 2602**
  Revocation of acceptance, **Com 2608**
  Specific time provision absent, **Com 2309**
Receipt of goods,
  Defined, **Com 2103**
  Delivery under C.I.F. and C. & F. terms, **Com 2320**
  Delivery under F.A.S. terms, **Com 2319**
  Incidental damages from seller's breach, **Com 2715**
Reclamation, seller's remedies on discovery of buyer's insolvency, **Com 2702**
Rejection,
  Buyer, **Com 2401**
  Improper delivery, **Com 2601**
  Inconsistent claims, **Com 2721**
  Installment, **Com 2612**
  Merchant buyer, duties, **Com 2603**
  Nonconformance, **Com 2508**
  Perishable goods, **Com 2604**
  Precluded by acceptance, **Com 2607**
  Remedies,
    Buyer, **Com 2711**
    Seller, **Com 2703**
  Revesting of title in seller, **Com 2401**
  Salvage of rejected goods, **Com 2604**
  Time, **Com 2602**
  Waiver, **Com 2605**
Remedies, **Com 2701 et seq.**
  Action for price, **Com 2709**
  Breach of collateral contract, **Com 2701**
  Breach of warranty, **Com 2714**
    Consequential damages, **Com 2715, 2719**
  Cover, **Com 2711, 2712**
  Defined, commercial code, **Com 1201**
  Delivery not made, **Com 2711**
  Fraud, **Com 2721**
  Identified goods to contract, **Com 2704**
  Incidental damages, **Com 2710**
    Breach of warranty, **Com 2715**
  Insolvency of buyer, **Com 2702**
  Misrepresentation, **Com 2721**
  Nonacceptance, **Com 2708, 2709**
  Nonconforming goods, **Com 2714**
  Nondelivery, **Com 2713**
  Rejection of goods, **Com 2703**
  Replevin, buyer, **Com 2716**
  Repudiation, **Com 2708**
    Seller, **Com 2713**
  Resales, generally, post
  Revocation of acceptance, **Com 2703**
  Seller, **Com 2703**
  Specific performance, **Com 2716**
  Stoppage in transit, **Com 2705**
  Substitution, **Com 2719**
  Unfinished goods, **Com 2704**
Replevin, **Com 2711**
  Unique goods, **Com 2716**
Repudiation,
  Anticipatory repudiation, generally, ante
  Damages, **Com 2708**

SALES—Cont'd
Repudiation—Cont'd
  Evidence of market price, **Com 2723**
  Performance not due, **Com 2610**
  Remedy of buyer, **Com 2711**
  Risk of loss, **Com 2510**
  Seller, **Com 2713**
  Specially manufactured goods, **Com 2201**
Requirements, **Com 2306**
Resales, **Com 2706**
  Action for price, **Com 2709**
  Buyer, **Com 2711**
  Damages, **Com 2703**
  Defined, secured transactions, **Com 9102**
  Incidental damages, **Com 2710**
  Liquidated damages, **Com 2718**
  Unfinished goods, **Com 2704**
Rescission, **Com 2209**
  Construed, **Com 2720**
  Effect,
    Claims for antecedent breach, **Com 2720**
    Remedies for fraud, **Com 2721**
  Written instrument, **Com 2209**
Reservation, shipments under, rights of seller, **Com 2310**
Reservation of security interest, **Com 2505**
Reservation of title, security interest, **Com 2401**
Reshipment of rejected goods, **Com 2604**
Residence, place of delivery, **Com 2308**
Restitution, delivery of goods withheld, **Com 2718**
Retail installment sales. Installment Sales, generally, this index
Retention of possession by seller, fraud, **Com 2402**
Retraction, anticipatory repudiation, **Com 2610, 2611**
Returnable proof of purchase forms, warranties, **Com 2800, 2801**
Returns,
  Inconsistent claims, **Com 2721**
  Open price term, price not fixed, **Com 2305**
  Rights of buyer, **Com 2326**
  Risk,
    Sale on approval, **Com 2327**
    Sale or return, **Com 2326**
  Defined, **Com 2326**
    Application, **Com 2103**
  Special incidents, **Com 2327**
Revesting title in seller, rejection of goods, **Com 2401**
Revocation of acceptance, **Com 2608, 2703**
Firm offers, **Com 2205**
Offer to buy or sell, **Com 2205**
Remedies,
  Buyer, **Com 2711**
  Seller, **Com 2401, 2703, 2704**
Risk of loss, **Com 2510**
Risk of loss, **Com 2509**
  Assignment of rights, **Com 2210**
  Casualty, identified goods, **Com 2613**

SALES—Cont'd
Risk of loss—Cont'd
  C.I.F., **Com 2320**
  Deterioration, **Com 2321**
  Division, **Com 2303**
  Ex-ship, delivery, **Com 2322**
  F.O.B., **Com 2319**
  No arrival, no sale terms, **Com 2324**
  Nonconforming tender, **Com 2510**
  Return, sale on approval, **Com 2327**
  Sale on approval, **Com 2327**
  Sale or return, **Com 2327**
  Shifting allocation, **Com 2303**
  Shrinkage, **Com 2321**
Running of credit, open time, **Com 2310**
Sale on approval, **Com 2326**
  Risk, **Com 2327, 2509**
Salvage,
  Anticipatory repudiation, **Com 2610**
  Rejected goods, **Com 2604**
Salvageable personal property,
  Unfinished goods, **Com 2704**
Samples,
  Examination, implied warranties, **Com 2316**
  Inconsistent specifications, **Com 2317**
  Preserving evidence of goods in dispute, **Com 2515**
  Warranty of conformance, **Com 2313**
Scope of law, **Com 2102**
Secured Transactions, this index
Securities, generally, this index
Security interest,
  Preferences, creditors, **Com 2402**
  Rejected goods, **Com 2711**
  Reservation, **Com 2505**
  Reservation of title, **Com 2401**
  Warranty of freedom from, **Com 2312**
Seller,
  Action for price, **Com 2709**
  Assignment of rights, **Com 2210**
  Cancellation of contract, **Com 2703**
  Creditors, rights, **Com 2402**
  Cure of nonconformance, **Com 2508**
  Defined, **Com 2103**
  Identified goods to contract, **Com 2704**
  Incidental damages, **Com 2710**
  Insolvency, rights of buyer, **Com 2502**
  Insurable interest, **Com 2501**
  Nondelivery, **Com 2713**
  Obligations, **Com 2301**
    Exclusive dealing, **Com 2306**
  Persons included, **Com 2707**
  Repudiation, damages, **Com 2713**
  Resale, **Com 2706**
  Reservation of security interest, **Com 2505**
  Risk of loss, **Com 2509**
    Nonconforming goods, **Com 2510**
  Security interest, **Com 2401**
  Shipment, **Com 2504**
  Stop delivery, **Com 2703**
  Stoppage in transit, **Com 2705**
  Tender of delivery, **Com 2503, 2507**
  Third party actions, **Com 2722**
Shipment by seller, **Com 2504**
Shrinkage, risk, **Com 2321**
Specially manufactured, **Com 2201**

SALES—Cont'd
Specific performance, **Com 2711, 2716**
Specification of performance, **Com 2311**
Specifications,
 Inconsistent sample or model, **Com 2317**
 Warranties, **Com 2312**
Statute of limitations. Limitation of actions, generally, ante
Stop delivery, insolvent buyer, **Com 2702**
Stoppage in transit, **Com 2705**
 Bailee excused from delivery, **Com 7403**
 Damages, expenses, **Com 2710**
 Person in position of seller, **Com 2707**
 Structure to be moved from realty, **Com 2107**
Substituted goods, buyer's procurement, **Com 2712**
Substituted performance, **Com 2614**
 Delay in delivery, **Com 2615**
Substitution, conforming tender for nonconforming tender, **Com 2508**
Successive performances, termination, **Com 2309**
Tender, **Com 2503**
 Bill of lading, overseas shipment, **Com 2323**
 Delivery, **Com 2507**
  Manner, **Com 2503**
  Rejection, **Com 2508**
  Risk of loss, **Com 2509, 2510**
 No arrival, no sale terms, conforming goods on arrival, **Com 2324**
 Nonconformance, risk of loss, **Com 2510**
 Payment, **Com 2511**
 Risk of loss passing, **Com 2509**
 Substituted performance, **Com 2614**
Termination,
 Defined, **Com 2106**
  Application, **Com 2103**
 Notice, **Com 2309**
Third parties,
 Actions, **Com 2722**
 Inspection of goods, **Com 2515**
 Notice of buyer's right, **Com 2107**
Time,
 Anticipatory repudiation, **Com 2610**
 Assurance of due performance, **Com 2609**
 Delivery, **Com 2309**
 Offer and acceptance, **Com 2205**
 Open time, **Com 2310**
 Passing of title, **Com 2401**
 Payment, **Com 2310**
 Reasonable time, generally, ante
 Rejection, **Com 2602**
 Revocation of acceptance, **Com 2608**
 Sales contract breaches, limitation of actions, **Com 2725**
 Tender of delivery, **Com 2503**
Title to property, **Com 2403**
 Passing, **Com 2401**
 Sale on approval, **Com 2327**
 Warranty, **Com 2312**
Trade journals, market quotations, evidence, **Com 2724**

SALES—Cont'd
Transfer,
 Interest in realty, price, **Com 2304**
 Obligation of seller, **Com 2301**
Unborn young, insurable interest, **Com 2501**
Unconscionable contracts, damages, **Com 2719**
Undivided share in identified bulk, **Com 2105**
Unfinished goods, **Com 2704**
Uniform Commercial Code, **Com 2101 et seq.**
Unique goods, specific performance, **Com 2716**
Unsecured creditors, rights against buyer, **Com 2402**
Usage of trade. Custom and usage, generally, ante
Voidable title, good faith purchaser, **Com 2403**
Waiver, **Com 2209**
 Contract for sale terms, **Com 2208**
 Rejection, **Com 2605**
 Retraction, **Com 2209**
 Warranty cards, return to manufacturer, **Com 2801**
War risk insurance, C.I.F., **Com 2320**
Warehouses and warehousemen,
 Deterioration of goods, **Com 7206**
 Enforcement of lien, **Com 7210**
Warranties, **Com 2312**
 Affirmation of fact, **Com 2313**
 Breach of warranty, generally, ante
 Course of dealing, **Com 2314**
 Cumulative, **Com 2317**
 Damages for breach, incidental damages, **Com 2715**
 Description, conformance, **Com 2313**
 Encumbrances, **Com 2312**
 Exclusions or modifications, **Com 2316**
 Express warranties, generally, ante
 Food, **Com 2314**
 Implied warranties, generally, ante
 Infringement, **Com 2312**
 Intention of parties, **Com 2317**
  Express warranty, **Com 2313**
 Liens, freedom from, **Com 2312**
 Limitation, **Com 2316**
 Limitation of actions, **Com 2725**
 Merchantability, **Com 2314**
  Exclusion or modification, **Com 2316**
 Models, conformance, **Com 2313**
 Modification, **Com 2316**
 Negation, **Com 2316**
 Opinion, **Com 2313**
 Promise, **Com 2313**
 Return, forms, personal or household goods, **Com 2800, 2801**
 Sample, conformance, **Com 2313**
 Security interest, free from, **Com 2312**
 Title, **Com 2312**
 Usage of trade, **Com 2314**
Written instruments,
 Confirmation of acceptance, **Com 2207**
 Contract for sale, **Com 2201**
 Modification, **Com 2209**
 Offers, **Com 2205**

SALES—Cont'd
Written instruments—Cont'd
 Rescission, **Com 2209**

SALVAGE
Sales, anticipatory repudiation, **Com 2610**
Unfinished goods, sales, **Com 2704**

SATISFACTION
Accord and Satisfaction, generally, this index

SAVINGS AND LOAN ASSOCIATIONS
Funds Transfers, generally, this index
Secured transaction, application of law, **Com 9104**

SAVINGS ASSOCIATIONS
Funds Transfers, generally, this index

SAVINGS BANKS
Funds Transfers, generally, this index

SCALES
Weights and Measures, generally, this index

SEARCHES AND SEIZURES
Investment securities, **Com 8112**

SEASONABLY
Defined, commercial code, **Com 1204**

SECONDARY PARTY
Defined, bank deposits and collections, **Com 4104**

SECRETARY OF STATE
Filing fees,
 Summaries, **Com 9407**

SECURED CREDITOR
Creditor, defined, commercial code, **Com 1201**

SECURED PARTIES
Defined,
 Secured transactions, **Com 9105**

SECURED TRANSACTIONS
Generally, **Com 9101 et seq.**
Accessions, priorities, **Com 9314**
Accounts and accounting,
 Application of law, **Com 9102**
 Assignment, financing, statement, filing, **Com 9302**
 Attachment of interest, **Com 9204**
 Collect or compromise, debtor's liberty, **Com 9205**
 Default, **Com 9502**
  Surplus funds, **Com 9504**
 Deposit account, generally, post
 Financing statement,
  Financing to perfect security interest, **Com 9302**
  Requirements, **Com 9402**
 Jurisdiction, **Com 9103**
 Minerals, perfection, applicable law, **Com 9103**
 Oil and gas, perfection, applicable law, **Com 9103**

SECURED

SECURED TRANSACTIONS—Cont'd
Accounts and accounting—Cont'd
  Perfection of security interest, applicable law, **Com 9103**
  Sale, **Com 9102, 9104**
  Security interest, place of filing, **Com 9401**
  Statement of account, verification by secured party, **Com 9208**
Accounts receivable, subordination of rights, **Com 9301**
Acts or omissions of debtor, liability of secured party, **Com 9317**
Advances and advancements,
  After-acquired property, **Com 9108**
  Future advances, **Com 9204**
  Lien creditors, priorities, **Com 9301**
  Priorities, **Com 9312**
  Termination statement, **Com 9404**
  Warehouse receipts, statement, **Com 7202**
After-acquired collateral,
  Antecedent debt, **Com 9108**
  Attachment of interest, **Com 9204**
  Purchase money security interests, inventory, **Com 9102**
Agreements,
  Security agreements, generally, post
  Subordination of priorities, **Com 9316**
Agricultural Machinery and Equipment, this index
Agricultural products,
  Attachment of interest, **Com 9203, 9204**
  Definition, farm products, **Com 9109**
  Filing of security interest, **Com 9401**
  Financing or continuation statements, index, **Com 9403**
  Financing statement, description, **Com 9402**
  Place of filing, **Com 9401**
    Protection of buyer, **Com 9307**
  Security interest, enforcement, **Com 9203**
Air carriers, foreign, debtor, location, **Com 9103**
Aircraft, **Com 9103**
  Application of law, **Com 9102**
  Security interest, perfection, applicable law, **Com 9103**
Alcoholic beverages, application of law, **Com 9102**
Amendment of financing statement, **Com 9402**
Animals, this index
Antecedent debt, after-acquired collateral, **Com 9108**
Application of law, **Com 9102**
  Conditional sales, **Com 9203**
  Negotiable instruments, **Com 3102**
Assignee, defenses, **Com 9318**
Assignments, **Com 9318**
  Accounts or contract rights, **Com 9302**
  Accounts receivable, exemptions, **Com 9104**
  Application of law, **Com 9102**
  Claim or defense, asserting, **Com 9206**
  Debtor's rights in collateral, **Com 9311**

SECURED TRANSACTIONS—Cont'd
Assignments—Cont'd
  Filing, **Com 9406**
  Improvement Act of 1911, public construction contracts, **Com 9104**
  Recording in lieu of filing, **Com 9407.1 et seq.**
  Wages, **Com 9104**
Attachment of interest, **Com 9203, 9204, 9311**
  Agricultural products, **Com 9204**
  Liens, combined certificates, **Com 9409**
  Perfecting, **Com 9303**
Attorney fees,
  Collateral,
    Disposition after default, **Com 9504**
    Redeemed after default, **Com 9506**
Auctions and auctioneers, default, disposition of collateral, **Com 9504**
Bank deposits, **Com 9104**
  Proceeds on disposition of collateral, **Com 9306**
Bills of lading, protection of security interest, **Com 9304**
Boats,
  Perfecting security interest, **Com 9302**
Bona fide purchasers,
  Priorities, **Com 9314**
  Protection, **Com 9307**
  Rights, **Com 9309**
Branch office of secured party, statement of account or approval of list of collateral, **Com 9208**
Brokers, application of law, **Com 9203**
Bulk sales, transfer of collateral, application of law, **Com 6103**
Bulk Transfer Law,
  Transferee, subordination of rights, **Com 9301**
Buyer, protection, **Com 9307**
Certificates and certification,
  Combined certificate, financing statements, **Com 9409**
  Filing officer, **Com 9407**
Certificates of title,
  Condition of perfection, **Com 9302**
  International, perfection, **Com 9302**
  Out of state, perfection of security interest, **Com 9103**
Chattel paper,
  Application of law, **Com 9102, 9203**
  Defined, **Com 1201**
  Nonpossessory security interest, perfection, **Com 9103**
  Possessory security interest, perfection, **Com 9103**
  Priorities, **Com 9308**
  Promissory, perfection, **Com 9103**
Chattel trust, application of law, **Com 9102**
Citation, **Com 9101**
Cities, security interest, **Com 9104**
City and county, security interest, **Com 9104**
Claims, agreement, **Com 9206**
Classification of goods, **Com 9109**

SECURED TRANSACTIONS—Cont'd
Collateral,
  After-acquired, antecedent, debt, **Com 9108**
  After-acquired property, **Com 9204**
  Attachment, **Com 9203, 9311**
  Commingled, **Com 9205**
  Compulsory disposition, **Com 9505**
  Debtor, collateral not owned, **Com 9112**
  Debtors and creditors, right to redeem, **Com 9506**
  Default, possession, **Com 9503**
  Description, **Com 9203**
  Disposition,
    After default, **Com 9504**
    Secured party's rights to proceeds, **Com 9306**
  Financing statement, filing to perfect security interest, **Com 9402**
  Garnishment, **Com 9311**
  Investment securities, perfecting security interest, **Com 9115**
  Judicial process, **Com 9311**
  Lapsed filing, financing statement, **Com 9402**
  Levy, **Com 9311**
  List, approval, **Com 9208**
  Out-of-state, security interest perfection, applicable law, **Com 9103**
  Owned by other than debtor, **Com 9112**
  Possession, perfecting interest, **Com 9305**
  Possession by secured party, **Com 9207**
    Financing statement, filing, **Com 9302**
  Priorities among conflicting security interest, **Com 9312**
    Financing statement, **Com 9402**
  Proceeds, **Com 9203**
  Redemption, **Com 9506**
  Owner, **Com 9112**
  Release, **Com 9405**
  Sale, **Com 9311**
  Security interest, perfection, applicable law, **Com 9103**
  Title, **Com 9202**
  Use or disposal, **Com 9205**
  Vehicles or boats, inventory, perfection, **Com 9302**
Collecting bank,
  Enforcement of interest, **Com 9203**
  Priority, **Com 9312**
Collection purposes, **Com 9104**
Collection rights of secured party on default, **Com 9502**
Commercial coach, perfecting security interests, **Com 9302**
Commercial finance lenders, application of law, **Com 9203**
Commingling goods, **Com 9315**
  Fraud, **Com 9205**
  Fungible collateral, **Com 9207**
  Priorities, **Com 9315**
Conflict of laws, **Com 1105, 9103, 9203**
Conflicting interest, same collateral, priorities, **Com 9312**

SECURED

SECURED TRANSACTIONS—Cont'd
Conflicting security interests, priorities and preferences, **Com 9304**
Consecutive filing members, financing statements, **Com 9403**
Consigned goods, priority, **Com 9114**
Consignment,
   Financing statements, filing, terms, **Com 9408**
   Perfection of security interest, filing financing statement, **Com 9408**
   Priority, **Com 9114**
Construction machinery,
   Application of law, **Com 9102**
   Security interest, validity and perfection, **Com 9103**
Consumer goods,
   Attachment of interest, **Com 9204**
   Default,
     Disposal of property, **Com 9505**
     Renunciation or modification of debtors rights, **Com 9508**
     Right to deficiency, waiver by secured party, **Com 9508**
   Purchase money security interest, **Com 9302**
   Security interest, place of filing to perfect, **Com 9401**
Containers, shipping, security interest, perfection, applicable law, **Com 9103**
Continuation statement,
   Application of law, **Com 9102**
   Effectiveness, period, **Com 9403.5**
   Fixture filing, **Com 9403**
   Perfection of security interest, Filing, **Com 9403**
Continuing interest, **Com 9306**
Continuous perfection, **Com 9303**
Contract liability of secured party, **Com 9317**
Contract right,
   Application of law, **Com 9102**
   Jurisdiction, rights relating to another jurisdiction, **Com 9103**
Contract terms, prohibiting creation of security interest, general intangibles, **Com 9318**
Control of proceeds, default, **Com 9502**
Conversion, possession after default, **Com 9505**
Cooperative associations, fish marketing and agricultural inventory, merchants, **Com 9102**
Copies,
   Assignments, **Com 9406**
   Filed statements, **Com 9407**
   Security interest, financing statement, **Com 9402**
Corporations, this index
Counties, security interest, **Com 9104**
Credit union, application of law, **Com 9104**
Creditor of seller, rights, **Com 2402**
Creditors, validity of agreement, **Com 9201**
Crops,
   Agricultural products, generally, ante
   Defined, **Com 9109**

SECURED TRANSACTIONS—Cont'd
Damages,
   Against secured party, **Com 9507**
   Failure to furnish termination statement, **Com 9404**
Debtor,
   Corporate structure, change, financing statement, **Com 9402**
   Identity change, financing statement, **Com 9402**
   Location, perfection,
     Accounts, **Com 9103**
     General intangibles, **Com 9103**
     Mobile goods, **Com 9103**
   Location change, financing statement, **Com 9402**
   Name change, financing statement, **Com 9402**
   Names, financing statements, **Com 9402**
Decedents estate, assignment of beneficial interest, filing exclusion, **Com 9302**
Default, **Com 9501 et seq.**
   Consumer goods, ante
   Control of proceeds, **Com 9502**
   Damages against secured party, **Com 9507**
   Debtors rights, renunciation or modification, **Com 9508**
   Deeds of trust, **Com 9501**
   Deficiency, waiver by secured party, **Com 9508**
   Disposal of property, **Com 9504, 9505, 9507**
   Foreclosure, **Com 9501**
   Judgment, **Com 9501**
   Judicial sale, **Com 9501**
   Modification, debtors rights, **Com 9508**
   Mortgage foreclosure, **Com 9501**
   Payment, **Com 9502**
   Possession, **Com 9503**
   Recovery, **Com 9505**
   Redemption, **Com 9506**
   Renunciation, debtors rights, **Com 9508**
   Sales, **Com 9113**
   Transfer of debtor's rights in collateral, **Com 9311**
Defenses,
   Against assignee, **Com 9318**
   Agreements, **Com 9206**
Deficiency,
   Default, **Com 9502**
   Owner of collateral, **Com 9112**
   Waiver by secured party, **Com 9508**
Definitions, **Com 9105**
   Account, **Com 9106**
   Commodity account, **Com 9115**
   Commodity contract, **Com 9115**
   Commodity customer, **Com 9115**
   Commodity intermediaries jurisdiction, **Com 9103**
   Commodity intermediary, **Com 9115**
   Consumer goods, **Com 9109**
   Contract for sale, **Com 2106**
   Crops, **Com 9109**
   Equipment, **Com 9109**

SECURED TRANSACTIONS—Cont'd
Definitions—Cont'd
   Farm products, **Com 9109**
   Filing officer, **Com 9401**
   Financing statement, **Com 9402**
   General intangibles, **Com 9106**
   Holder in due course, **Com 9206**
   Inventory, **Com 9109**
   Investment property, **Com 9115**
   Lien creditor, **Com 9301**
   Proceeds, **Com 9306**
   Purchase money security interest, **Com 9107**
   Resale, **Com 9102**
   Sales, **Com 2106**
   Secured party of record, **Com 9406**
   Security interest, **Com 9107**
Deposit account,
   Cash proceeds, **Com 9306**
   Filing exclusion, **Com 9302**
   Proceeds, insolvency proceedings, perfected security interest, **Com 9306**
Deposits in banks, **Com 9104**
Descriptions,
   Collateral, **Com 9203**
   Financing statement, **Com 9402**
   Sufficiency, **Com 9110**
Discharge, negotiable instruments, **Com 3605**
Disposal of,
   Goods, **Com 9205**
   Property after default, **Com 9504, 9505**
Disposition of collateral, default, **Com 9503**
Dual security interests, personal property and real estate, secured party rights, **Com 9501**
Duration of filing, **Com 9403**
Electric utilities, transition property, exemptions, **Com 9104**
Enforcement of security interest, **Com 9203**
Equipment, security interests, perfection, application of law, **Com 9103**
Equipment trust,
   Policy and scope of law, **Com 9102**
   Railway rolling stock, **Com 9104**
Evidence,
   Assignment, **Com 9318**
   Subordinate security interest, **Com 9504**
Exclusions, **Com 9104**
   Filing provisions, **Com 9302**
Execution,
   Default, **Com 9501**
   Transfer of debtors rights, **Com 9311**
Exemptions, **Com 9104**
Expenses, secured party, statement of account or approval of list of collateral, **Com 9208**
Farm products,
   Agricultural products, generally, ante
   Defined, **Com 9109**
Fees,
   Certificate of filing officer, **Com 9407**
   Combined certificate concerning financing statements, **Com 9409**
   Continuation statement, **Com 9403**

SECURED

SECURED TRANSACTIONS—Cont'd
Fees—Cont'd
  Filed statements, copies, **Com 9407**
  Filing financing statement, **Com 9403**
  Filing statement of assignment, **Com 9406**
  Statement of release, **Com 9405**
  Termination statement, **Com 9404**
Filing, **Com 9401 et seq., 9403**
  Exclusions, **Com 9302**
  Fees, **Com 9404**
  Financing statement, **Com 9302, 9401, 9402**
    Lapse, **Com 9402, 9403**
  Governing law, **Com 9103**
  Insolvency proceedings, **Com 9403**
  Investment securities, perfection of security interest, **Com 9115**
  Lapse, financing statement, **Com 9402, 9403**
  Perfecting interest, **Com 9304**
    Treaties or statutes, **Com 9302**
  Presentation, **Com 9403**
  Recording in lieu of, **Com 9407.1 et seq.**
  Release,
    Collateral, **Com 9405**
  Sales act, **Com 9113**
  Termination statement, **Com 9404**
Filing officer, **Com 9407**
  Defined, **Com 9401**
  Duties, **Com 9403**
  Financing statement, acceptance for filing, **Com 9402**
  Insolvency proceeding, information, **Com 9407**
  Recording of instruments in lieu of filing, **Com 9407.1 et seq.**
Financial statements and reports, fixtures, **Com 9401, 9402**
Financing statement,
  Amendment, **Com 9402**
  Application of law, **Com 9102**
  Assignment, filing, **Com 10105**
  Assignments for benefit of creditors, **Com 9302**
  Certified copy, **Com 9402**
  Combined certificates, **Com 9409**
  Commingled goods, **Com 9315**
  Defined, **Com 9402**
  Destruction, **Com 9404**
  Effectiveness period, **Com 9403.5**
  Filing, **Com 9302, 9401, 9402, 9403**
    Recording in lieu of filing, **Com 9407.1 et seq.**
  Fixtures, **Com 9401, 9402**
  Formal requisites, **Com 9402**
  Forms, **Com 9402**
  Indexing, **Com 9407.2**
  Investment securities, transition provisions, **Com 8603**
  Lapse,
    Lien creditors and purchasers, **Com 9403**
    Statement, **Com 9402**
  Perfection of security interest, **Com 9302**
  Process goods, **Com 9315**

SECURED TRANSACTIONS—Cont'd
Financing statement—Cont'd
  Recording, **Com 9407.1 et seq.**
  Termination statement, **Com 9404**
    Transmitting utilities, **Com 9403**
  Terms, consignors and lessors of goods, **Com 9408**
  Transmitting utilities, period of effectiveness, **Com 9403**
Fish, attachment of interest, **Com 9204**
Fixtures, **Com 9102 et seq.**
  Application of law, **Com 9102**
  Financial statements, **Com 9401, 9402**
  Goods which are fixtures or could become fixtures, security interest, **Com 9313**
  Insolvency, **Com 9403**
  Priorities and preferences, **Com 9302**
Foreclosure, **Com 9501**
Foreign corporation,
  Debtor, residence, **Com 9401**
Foreign countries, perfection of security interest, **Com 9103**
Foreign states,
  Auction sale of collateral, default, **Com 9504**
  Financing statement, description, **Com 9402**
  Perfection of security interest, **Com 9103**
Forms, financing statements, **Com 9402**
Frauds, statute of, commercial code, **Com 1206**
Future advances,
  Priorities, **Com 9312**
  Third persons, protection of buyers, **Com 9307**
Garnishment, **Com 9311**
Gas. Oil and Gas, this index
General intangibles,
  Security interest, contracts terms prohibiting creation, **Com 9318**
Goods,
  Classified, **Com 9109**
Harvesting equipment, **Com 9103**
Holder, documents of title, rights, **Com 9309**
Holder in due course, **Com 3302, 9309**
  Negotiable instruments, **Com 9206**
  Rights, **Com 9309**
House trailers, application of law, **Com 9102**
Identification,
  Collateral in secured party's possession, **Com 9207**
  Property, sufficiency of description, **Com 9110**
Improvement, real property, accounts or contract rights, financing statement, filing, **Com 9302**
Improvement Act of 1911, public construction contracts, assignment of benefits, **Com 9104**
Indemnity bond, filing with secured party by holder of subordinate security interest, **Com 9504**
Indexes,
  Continuation statement, **Com 9403**

SECURED TRANSACTIONS—Cont'd
Indexes—Cont'd
  Financing statements, **Com 9403**
  Release of collateral, **Com 9405**
  Termination statement, **Com 9404**
Industrial loans, application of law, **Com 9203**
Injunction,
  Noncompliance with law by secured party, **Com 9507**
  Owner of collateral, **Com 9112**
Insolvency, fixtures, **Com 9403**
Insolvency proceedings,
  Financing statements, filing, perfection of security interest, **Com 9403**
  Fixtures, **Com 9403**
  Information, filing officer, **Com 9407**
  Secured parties, rights on disposition of collateral, **Com 9306**
Installment sales, effect of law, **Com 9201**
Instrument,
  Filing, **Com 9304**
  Policy of law, **Com 9102**
  Scope of law, **Com 9102**
  Security interest, perfection, **Com 9305**
Insurance,
  Claims, security interest, perfection, filing exclusion, **Com 9302**
  Collateral in secured party's possession, **Com 9207**
  Loans, application of law, **Com 9104**
  Proceeds, **Com 9306**
Intangibles,
  Perfection, law governing, **Com 9103**
  Policy of law, **Com 9102**
  Scope of law, **Com 9102**
  Security interest, place of filing, **Com 9401**
  Unperfected security interest, priorities, **Com 9301**
Interest,
  Priorities, **Com 9312**
Inventories,
  Application of law, **Com 9102**
  Defined, **Com 9109**
  Priorities, **Com 9308**
  Purchase money security interest, priorities, **Com 9312**
  Security interest, perfection, applicable law, **Com 9103**
  Vehicles or boats, perfection, **Com 9302**
Investments, application of law, **Com 9103**
Judgment,
  Default, **Com 9501**
  Rights, **Com 9104**
Judgment liens, combined certificates, **Com 9409**
Judicial process, **Com 9311**
Judicial sales, **Com 9501**
Jurisdiction, **Com 9103**
Landlord lien, **Com 9104**
Lapsed filing, financing statement, **Com 9402, 9403**
Leases, goods,
  Application of law, **Com 9203**
  Default, **Com 9504**

SECURED TRANSACTIONS—Cont'd
Leases, goods—Cont'd
  Exemption, **Com 9104**
  Financing statements, **Com 9408**
  Perfection of security interest, filing financing statement, **Com 9408**
  Sales act, **Com 9113**
Letters of credit, **Com 9103, 9104, 9304, 9305**
  Application of law, **Com 9103**
  Perfecting interest, **Com 9304**
Levy, **Com 9311**
Lien creditor,
  Defined, **Com 9301**
  Financing statement, lapse, **Com 9403**
  Notice, secured party, **Com 9301**
  Priorities, **Com 9301**
  Purchase money security interest, priorities, **Com 9301**
Liens and incumbrances,
  Collateral, default, **Com 9504**
  Combined certificates, **Com 9409**
  Landlord, **Com 9104**
  Mechanics' liens, **Com 9104**
    Priority, **Com 9310**
  Policy and scope of article, **Com 9102**
  Priority, arising by operation of law, **Com 9310**
List of collateral, approval, **Com 9208**
Loans,
  Default, consumer goods, disposal of property, **Com 9505**
  Small loans, application of law, **Com 9201**
Location, change, financing statement, **Com 9402**
Losses, owner of collateral, **Com 9112**
Machinery and Equipment, this index
Mechanic's liens, **Com 9104**
  Priority, **Com 9310**
Merchant, fish marketing and agricultural cooperative associations, security interest in inventory, **Com 9102**
Microphotography, recording instruments in lieu of filing, **Com 9407.1 et seq.**
Mines and Minerals, this index
Mistake,
  Financing statements, **Com 9402**
  Place of filing, **Com 9401**
Mobilehomes and Mobilehome Parks, this index
Modification of contract, **Com 9318**
  Seller's warranties, application of law, **Com 9206**
Modification of rights by debtor, default, **Com 9508**
Money,
  Cash proceeds, definition, **Com 9306**
  Perfecting security interest, **Com 9304**
  Possession, **Com 9305**
Mortgages,
  Corporation, financing statement, filing to perfect security interest, **Com 9302**
  Foreclosure, **Com 9501**
Municipal corporations, security interest, **Com 9104**

SECURED TRANSACTIONS—Cont'd
Names, financing statement, change of name, **Com 9402**
Negligence, loss to collateral in secured party's possession, **Com 9207**
New value,
  After-acquired collateral, **Com 9108**
Noncompliance by secured party, **Com 9507**
Non-negotiable instruments, priorities, **Com 9308**
Nonpossessory security interest in inventory, purchase money security interest, **Com 9102**
Nonresidents, filing security interest, **Com 9401**
Notice,
  Assignment, **Com 9318**
  Consigned goods, priorities, **Com 9114**
  Default sales, **Com 9504**
  Owner of collateral, **Com 9112**
Numbers, financing statement, filing, **Com 9403**
Obligation payable on demand, statement in filed financing statement, period effective, **Com 9403**
Oil and Gas, this index
Optical disks, recording instruments in lieu of filing, **Com 9407.1 et seq.**
Owner of collateral, rights, **Com 9112**
Partnership,
  Debtor, residence, **Com 9401**
  Financing statement, names, **Com 9402**
Passbooks, financial institutions, application of law, **Com 9104**
Pawnbrokers, application of law, **Com 9203**
Payment,
  Assignments, **Com 9318**
  Default, **Com 9502**
Penalty, failure to furnish termination statement, **Com 9404**
Perfecting interest, **Com 9103, 9113, 9303**
  Collateral, applicable law, **Com 9103**
  Consignment, filing financing statement, **Com 9408**
  Filing, **Com 9304**
    Treaties or statutes, **Com 9302**
  Insurance claim, **Com 9302**
  Investment securities, law governing, **Com 9103**
  Leased goods, filing financing statement, **Com 9408**
  Possession,
    Collateral, **Com 9305**
    Proceeds, **Com 9304**
  Property subject to treaty, filing, **Com 9302**
  Purchase money security interest, goods, applicable law, **Com 9103**
  Specification of applicable law, **Com 1105**
  Temporary perfection without filing or transfer of possession, **Com 9304**
Perishable goods, disposition on default, **Com 9504**

SECURED TRANSACTIONS—Cont'd
Personal property, application of law, **Com 10102**
  Foreclosure, default, **Com 9501**
Place, filing security interest, **Com 9401**
Possession,
  Default, **Com 9503**
  Perfecting interest, **Com 9305**
  Secured party, **Com 9207**
Presentation for filing, **Com 9403**
Preservation, collateral in secured party's possession, **Com 9207**
Priorities and preferences, **Com 9308, 9309, 9312**
  Accessions, **Com 9314**
  Buyers, future advances, **Com 9307**
  Chattel paper or non-negotiable instruments, **Com 9308**
  Commingled goods, **Com 9315**
  Consigned goods, **Com 9114**
  Fixtures, **Com 9302, 9313**
  Liens, **Com 9104**
    Arising by operation of law, **Com 9310**
  Mechanic's liens, **Com 9310**
  Processed goods, **Com 9315**
  Purchase money security, **Com 9301, 9312**
  Subordination, **Com 9316**
  Unperfected security interests, **Com 9301**
Proceeds,
  Cash proceeds, inventory, purchase money security interest, priority, **Com 9312**
  Control on default, **Com 9502**
  Definitions, **Com 9203, 9306**
  Deposit accounts, **Com 9306**
  Insurance, **Com 9306**
  Perfecting security interest, **Com 9304**
  Purchase money security interest, priority, **Com 9312**
  Security agreement, **Com 9203**
  Sufficiency of description, **Com 9110**
Processed goods, priorities, **Com 9315**
Profits, sale of collateral, disposition, **Com 9207**
Property, subject to treaty, perfection, filing, **Com 9302**
Protection of buyer, **Com 9307**
Public authority, security interest, **Com 9104**
Public districts, security interest, **Com 9104**
Public improvements, financing statement, filing to perfect security interest, **Com 9302**
Public sales, collateral default, **Com 9504**
Purchase money security interest,
  Consumer goods, default, disposal of property, **Com 9505**
  Defined, **Com 9107**
  Goods, perfection, applicable law, **Com 9103**
  Inventory, after-acquired property, **Com 9102**
  Perfection, applicable law, **Com 9103**
  Priorities, **Com 9301, 9312**

SECURED

SECURED TRANSACTIONS—Cont'd
Purchase money security interest
—Cont'd
Sales, **Com 9206**
Purchasers,
Financing statement, lapse, **Com 9403**
Validity of agreement, **Com 9201**
Railroads,
Equipment trusts covering rolling stock, application of law, **Com 9104**
Rolling stock, security interest, perfection, place, **Com 9103**
Real estate,
Constructive notice, crops or timber, financing statement, **Com 9403**
Description,
Financing statement, **Com 9402**
Sufficiency, **Com 9110**
Interest, transfer, application of law, **Com 9104**
Record owner, financing statement, **Com 9402**
Records, financing statement, **Com 9402**
Security interest,
Default, procedure, **Com 9501**
Recording,
In lieu of filing, **Com 9407.1 et seq.**
Recording officer, defined, **Com 9401**
Records and recordation,
Filing, perfecting security interest, **Com 9401**
Real estate, financing statement, **Com 9402**
Redemption,
After default, **Com 9506**
Collateral,
Default, **Com 9501**
Rights of debtor, **Com 9506**
Owner, **Com 9112**
Release of collateral, **Com 9405**
Rents, application of law, **Com 9104**
Renunciation of rights, default, **Com 9508**
Repair parts, application of law, **Com 9102**
Repledging collateral in secured party's possession, **Com 9207**
Repossession, **Com 9205**
Resale, defined, **Com 9102**
Residence of debtor, **Com 9401**
Retail installment sales, **Com 9201**
Application of law, **Com 9203**
Risk of loss, collateral in secured party's possession, **Com 9207**
Road building equipment, security interest, perfection, place, **Com 9103**
Rolling stock, security interest, perfection, place, **Com 9103**
Sales, **Com 9113**
Application of law, **Com 2102**
Collateral, **Com 9311**
Owned by other than debtor, **Com 9112**
Conditional sales, **Com 9203**
Default, **Com 9504**
Defined, sales act, **Com 2106**

SECURED TRANSACTIONS—Cont'd
Sales—Cont'd
Enforcement of interest, **Com 9203**
Purchase money security, **Com 9206**
Rights of creditor, **Com 2402**
Savings and loan association deposits, excluded, **Com 9104**
Scope of article, **Com 9102**
Secretary of state,
Filing, generally, ante
Form, financing statement, standards prescribed by, **Com 9403 et seq.**
Secured party,
Possession of collateral, **Com 9207**
Title to collateral, **Com 9202**
Secured party of record, defined, **Com 9406**
Security agreements,
Financing statement, **Com 9402**
Proceeds, **Com 9203**
Security interest,
Defined, **Com 9107**
Fixtures, **Com 9313**
Release, **Com 9405**
Semitrailers, application of law, **Com 9102**
Set-off, **Com 9104**
Security interest, **Com 9306**
Ship Mortgage Act, **Com 9104**
Shipping containers, security interest, perfection, applicable law, **Com 9103**
Signatures,
Financing statement, **Com 9402**
Termination statement, **Com 9404**
Small loans act, **Com 9201, 9203**
State, security interest, **Com 9104**
Statement of account, **Com 9208**
Statement of release, fees, **Com 9405**
Statements,
Owner of collateral, **Com 9112**
Unpaid indebtedness, **Com 9208**
Statute of frauds, **Com 1206**
Statutes,
Liens arising by operation of law, priorities, **Com 9310**
Perfecting security interest, filing, **Com 9302**
Subdivisions, security interest, **Com 9104**
Subordination of rights, **Com 9301**
Obligations, **Com 1209**
Priorities, **Com 9316**
Subrogation, default, **Com 9504**
Substitution of contract, **Com 9318**
Sufficiency of description, **Com 9110**
Surplus,
Accounting by secured party, **Com 9502, 9504**
Default, **Com 9502**
Owner of collateral, **Com 9112**
Tax liens, combined certificates, **Com 9409**
Taxes, expenses incurred, **Com 9207**
Temporary perfection,
Purchase money security interest, priority, **Com 9312**
Temporary perfection of security interest, **Com 9304**

SECURED TRANSACTIONS—Cont'd
Termination statement, **Com 9404**
Filing,
Recording in lieu of filing, **Com 9407.1 et seq.**
Third persons, priorities and preferences, **Com 9301**
Timber and Lumber, this index
Time,
Attachment of security interest, **Com 9204**
Continuation statements, period of effectiveness, **Com 9403.5**
Financing statement,
Duration of filing, **Com 9403**
Period of effectiveness, **Com 9403.5**
Perfection of security interest, **Com 9303**
Title to collateral, **Com 9202**
Tort claims, application of law, **Com 9104**
Tort liability of secured party, **Com 9317**
Trademarks and trade names, financing statement, **Com 9402**
Trailers,
Application of law, **Com 9102**
Perfection of security interest, applicable law, **Com 9103**
Transfer of right, **Com 9311**
Transition property, electric utilities, application of law, **Com 9104**
Treaties, perfecting security interest, filing, **Com 9302**
Trust deeds, **Com 9102**
Trusts, assignment of beneficial interest, filing exclusion, **Com 9302**
Unified sales, application of law, **Com 9501**
United States,
Defined, **Com 9103**
Liens, combined certificate with financing statement, **Com 9409**
United States statutes, application, **Com 9104**
Filing provisions, **Com 9302**
Unperfected security interest, **Com 9301**
Use of goods, **Com 9205**
Collateral in secured party's possession, **Com 9207**
Usury laws, **Com 9201**
Utilities, transmitting,
Financing statement, period of effectiveness, **Com 9403**
Place of filing, **Com 9401**
Validity,
Interest, **Com 9103**
Security agreement, **Com 9201**
Value, negotiable instruments, **Com 3303**
Verification by secured party, statement of account or list of collateral, **Com 9208**
Vessels, vehicle code registration, security interest, filing, **Com 9302**
Waiver, default, modification of terms, **Com 9508**
Warranties, application of law, **Com 9206**
Zones, security interest, **Com 9104**

SECURITIES
Application of law,
  Negotiable instruments, **Com 3102**
Negotiable instruments,
  Application of law, **Com 3102**
  Discharge, **Com 3605**
  Exemptions, **Com 3102**

SECURITIES ACCOUNT
Defined,
  Investment securities, entitlements, **Com 8501**

SECURITIES INTERMEDIARY
Defined, investment securities, **Com 8102**

SECURITY
See, also, Bonds (Officers and Fiduciaries), generally, this index
Defined,
  Investment securities, **Com 8102**
Lost or destroyed documents of title, **Com 7601**

SECURITY AGREEMENT
Defined,
  Secured transactions, **Com 9105**

SECURITY CERTIFICATE
Defined, investment securities, **Com 8102**

SECURITY ENTITLEMENT
Defined,
  Investment securities, **Com 8102**

SECURITY INTEREST
Bills of lading, reservation of interest, **Com 2401**
Bulk Sales, this index
Collecting banks, **Com 4208**
Commercial Paper, this index
Defined,
  Commercial code, **Com 1201**
  Secured transactions, **Com 9107**
Intangibles,
  Perfection, law governing, **Com 9103**
  Place of filing, **Com 9401**
  Policy of law, **Com 9102**
  Unperfected security interest, priorities, **Com 9301**
Inventories, perfected purchase money security interest, priority over judgment lien on after-acquired inventory, **Com 9102**
Investment Securities, this index
Leases, this index
Motor Vehicles, this index
Sales, this index
Secured Transactions, generally, this index
Seller of goods, insurable interest, **Com 2501**
Subordination of right to payment of obligations, commercial code, **Com 1209**

SELLER
Defined,
  Bulk sales, **Com 6102**
  Sales Act, **Com 2103**

SELLER—Cont'd
Deterioration, risk, C.I.F. or C. & F. contract, **Com 2321**
Reservation of interest, bill of lading, **Com 2505**
Sales, this index

SEND
Defined, commercial code, **Com 1201**

SEQUESTRATION
Leases, personal property, **Com 10521**

SET-OFF AND COUNTERCLAIM
Action, included in term, commercial code, **Com 1201**
Bank deposits and collections, **Com 4201**
  Payor bank, **Com 4303**
Buyer's right to restitution, **Com 2718**
Defendant, defined, Commercial Code, **Com 1201**
Definitions, Commercial Code, **Com 1201**
Secured transactions, **Com 9104**
  Security interest, **Com 9306**

SETTLE
Defined, bank deposits and collections, **Com 4104**

SEVERANCE
Contract for sale of goods, **Com 2107**

SHIP MORTGAGE ACT
Secured transactions, exclusion, **Com 9104**

SHIPS AND SHIPPING
Containers,
  Security interest, perfection, applicable law, **Com 9103**
F.A.S., **Com 2319**
F.O.B., Sales Act, **Com 2319**
Secured transactions,
  Perfecting security interest, **Com 9302**
Security interest,
  Perfecting, **Com 9302**

SIGNATURES
Agents,
  Negotiable instruments, **Com 3403**
  Warehouse receipts, **Com 7202**
Bank Deposits and Collections, this index
Burden of proof,
  Negotiable instruments, **Com 3308**
Countersignature,
  Investment securities, warranty, **Com 8208**
Forgery, generally, this index
Investment Securities, this index
Letters of credit, authentication, **Com 5104**
Renunciation, claim or right after breach, Commercial Code, **Com 1107**
Representatives,
  Negotiable instruments, **Com 3403**
Secured Transactions, this index
Waiver, claim or right after breach, Commercial Code, **Com 1107**
Warehouse receipts, **Com 7202**

SIGNED
Defined,
  Commercial Code, **Com 1201**

SIMPLIFICATION
Commercial transactions, law governing, **Com 1102**

SMALL LOANS
Application of law, **Com 9201**

SPECIAL DAMAGES
Restriction, commercial code, **Com 1106**

SPECIALLY MANUFACTURED GOODS
Sales Act, exception, **Com 2201**

STANDARDS
Buyer, Sales Act, **Com 2716**
Investment securities,
  Delivery without endorsement, right to compel, **Com 8307**
Leases, personal property, **Com 10521**
Letters of credit, wrongful dishonor or repudiation, **Com 5111**
Sales Act, **Com 2711, 2716**
Weights and Measures, generally, this index

STATE
Foreign States, generally, this index
Security interest,
  Secured transactions, **Com 9104**
Taxation, generally, this index

STATEMENTS
Advances, warehouse receipts, **Com 7202**
Owner of collateral, **Com 9112**
Secured transactions, amount of unpaid indebtedness, **Com 9208**

STATES
Foreign States, generally, this index

STATUTE OF FRAUDS
Frauds, Statute of, generally, this index
Investment securities, **Com 8113**

STATUTE OF LIMITATIONS
Limitation of Actions, generally, this index

STATUTES
Conflict of Laws, generally, this index
Construction of statutes,
  Against implicit repeal, commercial code, **Com 1104**
  Liberal, commercial code, **Com 1102**
  Negative implications, **Com 7105**
  Severability of provisions, commercial code, **Com 1108**
Documents of title, application of law, **Com 7103**
Frauds, Statute of, generally, this index
Limitation of Actions, generally, this index
Uniform Laws, generally, this index
United States, this index

STEALING
Theft, generally, this index

STOLEN

STOLEN DOCUMENTS
Investment securities, claims, **Com 8405**
Warehouse receipts and bills of lading, delivery of goods, **Com 7601**

STOLEN PROPERTY
Theft, generally, this index

STOP DELIVERY
Insolvent buyer, **Com 2702**
Person in position of seller, **Com 2707**
Sellers incidental damages, **Com 2710**
Sellers remedies, **Com 2703**

STOP PAYMENT
Bank Deposits and Collections, this index

STORAGE
Liens and encumbrances,
    Warehousemen, **Com 7202, 7209**
Warehouse Receipts, generally, this index

SUBCONTRACTORS
Contractors, generally, this index

SUBLEASES
Leases, this index

SUBORDINATION
Personal property, leases, priority, agreements, **Com 10311**
Right to payment of obligations, **Com 1209**

SUBROGATION
Letters of credit, **Com 5117**
Payor bank, **Com 4407**
Secured transactions, **Com 9504**

SUCCESSION
Assignment by beneficiary,
    Secured transactions, exclusion, **Com 9302**

SUITS
Actions and Proceedings, generally, this index

SURETY BONDS
Bonds (Officers and Fiduciaries), generally, this index

SURETYSHIP AND GUARANTY
Bills of lading, brands, marks and labels, **Com 7301**
Bonds (Officers and Fiduciaries), generally, this index
Definitions,
    Commercial code, **Com 1201**
Documents of title, endorser, **Com 7505**
Investment securities,
    Liabilities of guarantor, **Com 8201**
    Signature of endorser, **Com 8402**

SURPLUS
Secured Transactions, this index

SURPRISE
Usage of trade, offer of evidence, commercial code, **Com 1205**

SUSPENDS PAYMENTS
Defined, bank deposits and collections, **Com 4104**

SYMBOLS
Signed, defined, Commercial Code, **Com 1201**

TAX COLLECTION
Investment securities, compliance with law, registration, **Com 8401**

TAX LIENS
Certificates and certification,
    Combined certificate, **Com 9409**

TAXATION
Investment securities, compliance with law, **Com 8401**
Secured transactions, expenses incurred, **Com 9207**
Senior citizens tax postponement, **Com 9207**

TELECOMMUNICATIONS
Definitions,
    Commercial code, **Com 1201**
    Telegram, commercial code, **Com 1201**

TELEGRAPHS AND TELEPHONES
Funds Transfers, generally, this index

TELETYPE
Telegram, defined, **Com 1201**

TELLERS CHECK
Bank deposits and collections, settlement, **Com 4213**
Defined,
    Negotiable instruments, **Com 3104**

TENANCY IN COMMON
Warehouse receipts, form, **Com 7202**

TENDER
Sales, this index

TERMS
Defined,
    Commercial code, **Com 1201**

THEFT
Documents of title, **Com 7601**
    Title and rights, **Com 7502**
Investment securities,
    Notice to issuer, **Com 8405**
    Reissuance, **Com 8405**
Negotiable instruments,
    Payment, **Com 3602**
Sales,
    Transfer of title, **Com 2403**

THIRD PARTIES
Documents, presumptions, **Com 1202**
Inspection of goods, **Com 2515**
Leases,
    Application of law, **Com 10302**
Party distinct, Commercial Code, **Com 1201**
Sales, this index
Secured transactions, priorities and preferences, **Com 9301**

THREATS
Duress or Coercion, generally, this index

THROUGH BILLS OF LADING
Generally, **Com 7302**

TIMBER AND LUMBER
Contracts, **Com 2107**
Secured transactions,
    Attachment of interest, **Com 9203**
    Financing or continuation statement, indexing, **Com 9403**
    Financing statement, **Com 9402**
    Place of filing, **Com 9401**
    Security interest, timber to cut, **Com 9203**

TIME
Bank Deposits and Collections, this index
Commercial Paper, this index
Extension of time,
    Collecting bank, negotiable instruments, **Com 4109**
Funds Transfers, this index
Leases, this index
Limitation of Actions, generally, this index
Reasonable Time, generally, this index
Sales, this index
Secured Transactions, this index

TITLE TO PROPERTY
Documents of Title, generally, this index
Sales, this index
Secured transactions, title to collateral, **Com 9202**
Warehousemens lien, enforcement, **Com 7210**

TORTS
Negligence, generally, this index
Secured party, liability, **Com 9317**
Secured transactions, application of law, **Com 9104**

TRADE NAMES
Negotiable instruments, signatures, **Com 3401**
Secured transactions, financing statement, description, **Com 9402**

TRAILERS
Motor Carriers, generally, this index
Secured transactions,
    Application of law, **Com 9102**
    Security interest, perfection, applicable law, **Com 9103**

TRAINS
Railroads, generally, this index

TRANSFER AGENTS
Investment Securities, this index

TRANSFER WARRANTIES
Bank deposits and collections, **Com 4207**
Negotiable instruments, **Com 3416**

TRAVELERS CHECKS
Definitions,
    Negotiable instruments, **Com 3104**

WAREHOUSE

TREATIES
Documents of title, application, **Com 7103**
Property, security interests, perfection, **Com 9302**
Secured transactions, property, filing, **Com 9302**

TRUST COMPANIES
Funds Transfers, generally, this index

TRUST DEEDS
Foreclosure, **Com 9501**
Secured Transactions, generally, this index

TRUSTS AND TRUSTEES
Investment Securities, this index
Organization, defined, Commercial Code, **Com 1201**
Representative, defined, commercial code, **Com 1201**
Secured Transactions, generally, this index
Unauthorized signature, investment securities, **Com 8205**

TYPEWRITING
Negotiable instruments, contradictory terms, **Com 3114**

TYPEWRITTEN TERMS
Defined, **Com 1201**

UNAUTHORIZED
Defined, commercial code, **Com 1201**

UNBORN ANIMALS
Defined, Sales Act, **Com 2105**

UNCERTIFICATED SECURITIES
Defined,
  Investment securities, **Com 8102**

UNDIVIDED SHARES
Fungible goods, sale, **Com 2105**

UNIFORM COMMERCIAL CODE
Commercial Code, generally, this index
Negotiable instruments, **Com 3101 et seq.**

UNIFORM COMMERCIAL CODE–LEASES
Generally, **Com 10101 et seq.**

UNIFORM LAWS
Bank deposits and collections, **Com 4101 et seq.**
Bills of Lading Act, see now, documents of title, **Com 7101 et seq.**
Bulk sales, **Com 6101 et seq.**
Commercial code, **Com 1101 et seq.**
  Bank deposits and collections, **Com 4101 et seq.**
  Bulk sales, **Com 6101 et seq.**
  Documents of title, **Com 7101 et seq.**
  Funds transfers, **Com 11101 et seq.**
  Investment securities, **Com 8101 et seq.**
  Leases, **Com 10101 et seq.**
  Negotiable instruments, **Com 3101 et seq.**
  Personal property leases, **Com 10101 et seq.**

UNIFORM LAWS—Cont'd
Commercial code—Cont'd
  Sales, **Com 2101 et seq.**
  Secured transactions, **Com 9101 et seq.**
Documents of title, **Com 7101 et seq.**
Investment securities, **Com 8101 et seq.**
Leases, commercial code, **Com 10101 et seq.**
Letters of credit, **Com 5101 et seq.**
Negotiable instruments, **Com 3101 et seq.**
Sales, **Com 2101 et seq.**
Secured transactions, **Com 9101 et seq.**
Trust Receipts Act, see now, secured transactions, **Com 9101 et seq.**
Warehouse Receipts Act, documents of title, **Com 7101 et seq.**

UNITED STATES
Defined,
  Bulk sales, **Com 6102**
  Secured transactions, **Com 9103**
Federal Reserve Banks, generally, this index
Ships and shipping,
  Ship Mortgage Act, secured transactions, **Com 9104**
Statutes,
  Documents of title, **Com 7103**
  Secured transactions, **Com 9104**
  Filing provision, **Com 9302**

USAGE
Custom and Usage, generally, this index

USAGE OF TRADE
Defined, Commercial Code, **Com 1205**

UTILITIES
Public Utilities, generally, this index

VALUATION
Defined,
  Commercial code, **Com 1201**
  Letters of credit, **Com 5102**

VALUE
Defined,
  Bulk sales, **Com 6102**

VEHICLES
Motor Vehicles, generally, this index

VERIFIED
Defined,
  Bulk sales, **Com 6102**

VESSELS
Boats and Boating, generally, this index
Ships and Shipping, generally, this index

VESTED RIGHTS
Negotiable instruments, **Com 3203**

VOIDABLE TITLE
Transfer, **Com 2403**

WAGES
Compensation and Salaries, generally, this index

WAR RISK INSURANCE
C.I.F., Sales Act, **Com 2320**

WAREHOUSE RECEIPTS
See, also, Documents of Title, generally, this index
Generally, **Com 7201 et seq.**
Advances, made, statement, **Com 7202**
Agents, signatures, **Com 7202**
Agricultural commodities, **Com 7201**
Alcoholic Beverages, this index
Alteration, **Com 7208**
Attachment,
  Goods covered by document, **Com 7602**
Blanks, filling, **Com 7208**
Bonded warehouse, **Com 7201 et seq.**
Bonds (officers and fiduciaries), lost or destroyed documents, **Com 7601**
Bulk sales, exemptions, **Com 6103**
Claims, provisions, **Com 7204**
Commingling goods, **Com 7207**
Common ownership, **Com 7202**
Contracts for sale, application of law, **Com 7509**
Conversion,
  Bailee, **Com 7601**
  Damages, **Com 7204**
  Delivery of goods under missing document, **Com 7601**
  Description of goods, reliance, **Com 7203**
  Overissue, **Com 7402**
  Title and rights acquired by negotiation, **Com 7502**
Damages, **Com 7204**
  Forms, **Com 7202**
  Fungible goods, shortage, **Com 7207**
  Limitations, **Com 7204**
  Loss of goods, **Com 7204**
  Nonreceipt or misdescription, **Com 7203**
  Overissue, **Com 7402**
Defined, commercial code, **Com 1201**
Delivery of goods,
  Adverse claim, **Com 7603**
  Bailee duty, **Com 7403**
  Conversion, **Com 7601**
  Demand, **Com 7206**
  Good faith, liability of bailee, **Com 7404**
  Indorsements, documents of title, **Com 7506**
  Liens and incumbrances, loss, **Com 7209**
  Negotiation, **Com 7501**
  Statement as to delivery, **Com 7202**
  Stoppage by seller, **Com 7504**
Demand, delivery of goods, **Com 7206**
Description of goods, **Com 7202**
  Enforcement of warehouseman's lien, **Com 7210**
  Reliance, **Com 7203**
Deterioration of goods, sale, **Com 7206**
Distilled spirits, issuance, **Com 7201**
Duplicates, lost instruments, **Com 7601**
Endorsement,
  Delivery without endorsement, **Com 7506**
  Guarantor for other parties, **Com 7505**
Enforcement of lien, **Com 7210**

WAREHOUSE

WAREHOUSE RECEIPTS—Cont'd
Field warehousing arrangement, **Com 7202**
Forgery, **Com 7208**
Form, **Com 7202**
Fraud, negotiation, **Com 7502**
Fungible goods, **Com 7207**
  Bona fide purchasers, **Com 7205**
  Commingling, effect, **Com 7207**
  Overissue of receipts, **Com 7402**
  Title, **Com 7205**
Good faith delivery of goods, liability of bailee, **Com 7404**
Handling charges, **Com 7202**
Indorsement, transfer by indorsement, **Com 7501**
Injunction, surrender of documents, **Com 7602**
Innocent purchasers, **Com 7501**
  Blanks filled in without authority, **Com 7208**
  Defenses, **Com 7504**
  Judicial process, lien, **Com 7602**
  Sale to enforce warehousemans lien, **Com 7210**
  Title to property, **Com 7205**
Insertions without authority, **Com 7208**
Interpleader, conflicting claims, **Com 7603**
Irregularity in issue, **Com 7401**
Issuance, **Com 7201**
Joint owner, **Com 7202**
Labor and employment, lien of warehousemen, **Com 7209**
Licenses and permits,
  Issuance, **Com 7201**
Liens and incumbrances, **Com 7209**
  Enforcement, **Com 7210**
  Form, **Com 7202**
  Goods covered by negotiable document, **Com 7602**
  Limitations, damages, **Com 7204**
  Proceeds of sale, **Com 7206**
Location, warehouse, form, **Com 7202**
Lost or destroyed documents, duplicates, **Com 7601**
Lost or destroyed property, warehousemen, liabilities, **Com 7403**
Marking nonnegotiable receipt, **Com 7104**
Misdescription, damages, **Com 7203**
Mistakes, obligations of issuer, **Com 7401**
Negotiability, **Com 7104**
Negotiation,
  Delivery, **Com 7501**
  Rights acquired, **Com 7502**
Nonnegotiable, marking, **Com 7104**
Nonreceipt of goods, damages, **Com 7203**
Notice, termination of storage, **Com 7206**
Numbering, **Com 7202**
Omissions, implication, **Com 7105**
Option, termination of storage, **Com 7206**
Over-issue,
  Fungible goods, liability of warehousemen, **Com 7207**
  Liabilities, **Com 7402**
Owners, sole owner, **Com 7202**

WAREHOUSE RECEIPTS—Cont'd
Public utility warehouse, storage and handling charges, **Com 7202**
Rate of storage, **Com 7202**
  Liens and incumbrances, **Com 7209**
Sales,
  Deterioration of goods, **Com 7206**
  Enforcement of lien, **Com 7210**
Security interest, **Com 7209**
  Forms, **Com 7202**
  Negotiation, **Com 7503**
Separation of goods, **Com 7207**
Signature, **Com 7202**
Statements, advances made, **Com 7202**
Stopping delivery, defenses, **Com 7504**
Storage and handling charges, terms, **Com 7202**
Surrender of documents, **Com 7601**
Tenancy in common, fungible goods, **Com 7207**
Termination of storage, **Com 7206**
Title,
  Acquired by negotiation, **Com 7502**
  Fungible goods, **Com 7205**
Value of property, **Com 7204**
Warranties, **Com 7507**
  Collecting bank, **Com 7508**

WAREHOUSES AND WAREHOUSEMEN
Auction sales,
  Enforcement of lien, **Com 7210**
  Termination of storage, **Com 7206**
Bulk sales, property subject to warehouse receipt, exemptions, **Com 6103**
Commingling goods, fungible goods, **Com 7207**
Conversion, sale to enforce lien, **Com 7210**
Damages,
  Fungible goods, shortages, **Com 7207**
  Sale to enforce lien, **Com 7210**
Definition,
  Documents of title, **Com 7102**
Deteriorating goods, right to sell, **Com 7206**
Furniture, liens, **Com 7209**
Household goods, defined, **Com 7209**
Liens and incumbrances, **Com 7206, 7209, 7210**
  Enforcement, **Com 7210**
  Household goods, **Com 7209**
  Satisfaction, **Com 7403**
Notice, termination of storage, **Com 7206**
Security interest, rates and charges, **Com 7209**
Storage charges, lien, **Com 7209**
Statement, **Com 7202**
Tenancy in common, fungible goods, **Com 7207**
Termination of storage, options, **Com 7206**
Title of property, enforcement of lien, **Com 7210**
Warehouse Receipts, generally, this index

WARRANTIES
Bank Deposits and Collections, this index

WARRANTIES—Cont'd
Documents of title,
  Collecting bank, **Com 7508**
  Negotiation or transfer, **Com 7507**
Investment Securities, this index
Leases, this index
Letters of credit, **Com 5110**
Presentment warranties,
  Bank deposits and collections, **Com 4207**
  Negotiable instruments, **Com 3417**
Sales, this index
Secured transactions, application of law, **Com 9206**
Transfer warranties,
  Bank deposits and collections, **Com 4208**
  Negotiable instruments, **Com 3416**

WATERS AND WATER COURSES
Boats and Boating, generally, this index
Fish and Game, generally, this index

WEIGHTS AND MEASURES
Certificates and certification,
  Presumptions, **Com 1202**
Fungible goods, identified bulk, sale of undivided share, **Com 2105**

WILDLIFE
Fish and Game, generally, this index

WITHHOLDING
Bulk Sales, this index

WOOD
Timber and Lumber, generally, this index

WORDS AND PHRASES
Accept,
  Letters of credit, **Com 5102**
Acceptance,
  Commercial paper,
    Application,
      Bank deposits and collections, **Com 4104**
  Letters of credit, **Com 5102**
  Negotiable instruments, **Com 3409**
  Sales act, **Com 2606**
    Application, **Com 2103**
Acceptor, negotiable instruments, **Com 3103**
Accessions,
  Commercial code, **Com 10103**
  Leases, **Com 10310**
Account,
  Bank deposits and collections, **Com 4104**
  Commercial code, **Com 10103**
  Secured transactions, **Com 9106**
Account debtor,
  Secured transactions, **Com 9105**
Action,
  Commercial code, **Com 1201**
Adverse claims, investment securities, **Com 8102**
Advisor,
  Letters of credit, **Com 5102**
Afternoon, bank deposits and collections, **Com 4104**

WORDS

WORDS AND PHRASES—Cont'd
Agreements,
  Commercial code, **Com 1201**
  Sales Act, **Com 2106**
Air bill, commercial code, **Com 1201**
Alteration,
  Negotiable instruments, **Com 3407**
Applicant,
  Letters of credit, **Com 5102**
Appropriate evidence of appointment or incumbency, investment securities, **Com 8402**
Appropriate person, investment securities, **Com 8107**
Assets,
  Bulk sales, **Com 6102**
Auctioneer,
  Bulk sales, **Com 6102**
Authorized account, funds transfers, **Com 11105**
Bailee,
  Documents of title, **Com 7102**
Bank,
  Funds transfers, **Com 11105**
Banker, Commercial Code, **Com 1201**
Bankers credit, Sales Act, **Com 2325**
  Application, **Com 2103**
Banking day,
  Bank deposits and collections, **Com 4104**
Bearer, commercial code, **Com 1201**
Bearer form, investment securities, certificated securities, **Com 8102**
Beneficiaries bank,
  Funds transfers, **Com 11103**
Beneficiary,
  Funds transfers, **Com 11103**
  Letters of credit, **Com 5102**
Between merchants,
  Commercial code, **Com 10103**
  Sales act, **Com 2104**
  Application, **Com 2103**
Bill of lading, commercial code, **Com 1201**
Branch,
  Commercial code, **Com 1201**
Brokers,
  Investment securities, **Com 8102**
Bulk sale, **Com 6102**
Burden of establishing a fact, commercial code, **Com 1201**
Business day,
  Bulk sales, notice to creditors, **Com 6105**
Buyer in ordinary course of business,
  Commercial code, **Com 1201, 10103**
Buyers,
  Bulk sales, **Com 6102, 6108**
  Commercial code, **Com 10103**
Buying, commercial code, **Com 1201**
C. & F., Sales Act, **Com 2320**
Cancellation,
  Commercial code, **Com 10103**
  Sales Act, **Com 2106**
    Application, **Com 2103**
Cashiers check,
  Negotiable instruments, **Com 3104**

WORDS AND PHRASES—Cont'd
Certificate of deposit,
  Commercial paper,
    Application,
      Bank deposits and collections, **Com 4104**
  Negotiable instruments, **Com 3104**
Certificated securities,
  Investment securities, **Com 8102**
Certification,
  Commercial paper,
    Application,
      Bank deposits and collections, **Com 4104**
Certified check,
  Negotiable instruments, **Com 3409**
Chattel papers,
  Commercial code, **Com 10103**
  Secured transactions, **Com 9105**
Checks,
  Bank deposits and collections,
    Electronic presentment, **Com 4110**
  Commercial paper,
    Application,
      Bank deposits and collections, **Com 4104**
  Lost, destroyed or stolen, negotiable instruments, **Com 3312**
  Negotiable instruments, **Com 3104**
C.I.F., Sales Act, **Com 2320**
Claim,
  Bulk sales, **Com 6102**
Claimants,
  Bulk sales, **Com 6102**
  Negotiable instruments, lost, destroyed or stolen checks, **Com 3312**
Clearing corporation, investment securities, **Com 8102**
Clearinghouse,
  Bank deposits and collections, **Com 4104**
Collaterals, secured transactions, **Com 9105**
Collecting bank, bank deposits and collections, **Com 4105**
  Application, **Com 4104**
Commercial unit,
  Commercial code, **Com 10103**
  Sales Act, **Com 2105**
    Application, **Com 2103**
Commodity account, secured transactions, **Com 9115**
Commodity contract, secured transactions, **Com 9115**
Commodity customer, secured transactions, **Com 9115**
Commodity intermediaries jurisdiction, secured transactions, **Com 9103**
Commodity intermediary, secured transactions, **Com 9115**
Communicate,
  Investment securities, **Com 8102**
Confirmed credit, Sales Act, **Com 2325**
  Application, **Com 2103**
Confirmer,
  Letters of credit, **Com 5102**
Conforming,
  Commercial code, **Com 10103**

WORDS AND PHRASES—Cont'd
Conforming—Cont'd
  Sales Act, **Com 2106**
Conforming to contract, Sales Act, **Com 2106**
  Application, **Com 2103**
Consideration,
  Negotiable instruments, **Com 3303**
Consignee,
  Documents of title, **Com 7102**
    Application, Sales Act, **Com 2103**
Consignor,
  Documents of title, **Com 7102**
    Application, Sales Act, **Com 2103**
Conspicuous, commercial code, **Com 1201**
Construction and operation, **Com 1102**
Construction mortgages,
  Commercial code, **Com 10103**
  Leases, **Com 10309**
  Secured transactions, **Com 9313**
Consumer goods,
  Commercial code, **Com 10103**
  Secured transactions, **Com 9109**
    Application,
      Sales Act, **Com 2103**
Consumer lease,
  Commercial code, **Com 10103**
Contract for sale, Sales Act, **Com 2106**
  Application,
    Documents of title, **Com 7102**
Contracts,
  Commercial code, **Com 1201**
Control,
  Secured transactions, **Com 9115**
Course of dealing, commercial code, **Com 1205**
Cover, Sales Act, **Com 2712**
  Application, **Com 2103**
Creation of a security interest,
  Leases, **Com 10303**
Creditor,
  Bulk sales, **Com 6102**
  Commercial code, **Com 1201**
Creditor process, funds transfers, **Com 11502**
Crops, secured transactions, **Com 9109**
Customer,
  Bank deposits and collections, **Com 4104**
  Funds transfers, **Com 11105**
Date of the bulk sale,
  Bulk sales, **Com 6102**
Date of the bulk sale agreement,
  Bulk sales, **Com 6102**
Debt,
  Bulk sales, **Com 6102**
Debtor,
  Secured transactions, **Com 9105**
Declaration of loss,
  Negotiable instruments, **Com 3312**
Defendant,
  Commercial code, **Com 1201**
Delivery,
  Commercial code, **Com 1201**
Deposit account,
  Secured transactions, **Com 9105**

WORDS

WORDS AND PHRASES—Cont'd
Depository bank, bank deposits and collections, **Com 4105**
    Application, **Com 4104**
Discover, commercial code, **Com 1201**
Dishonor,
    Commercial paper, application, sales act, **Com 2103**
    Letters of credit, **Com 5102**
Documentary draft,
    Bank deposits and collections, **Com 4104**
Documents,
    Commercial code, **Com 10103**
    Documents of title, **Com 7102**
    Letters of credit, **Com 5102**
    Secured transactions, **Com 9105**
Documents of title, **Com 7102**
    Commercial code, **Com 1201**
Drafts,
    Commercial paper,
        Application,
            Bank deposits and collections, **Com 4104**
            Sales Act, **Com 2103**
    Negotiable instruments, **Com 3104**
Drawee,
    Negotiable instruments, **Com 3103**
Drawer, negotiable instruments, **Com 3103**
Duly negotiate, documents of title, **Com 7501**
    Application, **Com 7102**
        Warehouse receipts and bills of lading, **Com 7501, 7502**
Electronic presentment agreement, bank deposits and collections, **Com 4110**
Employees,
    Negotiable instruments, **Com 3405**
Encumbrance,
    Leases, **Com 10309**
    Secured transactions, **Com 9105**
Endorsement,
    Investment securities, **Com 8102**
Entitlement holder,
    Investment securities, **Com 8102**
Entitlement order, investment securities, **Com 8102**
Entrusting,
    Commercial code, **Com 10103**
    Sales Act, **Com 2403**
        Application, **Com 2103**
Equipment,
    Bulk sales, **Com 6102**
    Secured transactions, **Com 9109**
Execution date, funds transfers, payment orders, **Com 11301**
Express,
    Sales Act, **Com 2106**
Farm products,
    Secured transactions, **Com 9109**
F.A.S., Sales Act, **Com 2319**
Fault,
    Commercial code, **Com 1201, 10103**
Fiduciary,
    Negotiable instruments, **Com 3307**
Filing officer,
    Secured transactions, **Com 9401**

WORDS AND PHRASES—Cont'd
Finance lease,
    Commercial code, **Com 10103**
Financial asset,
    Investment securities, **Com 8102**
Financing agency,
    Sales Act, **Com 2104**
        Application, **Com 2103**
Financing statement, secured transactions, **Com 9402**
Fixture filing,
    Commercial code, **Com 10103**
    Leases, **Com 10309**
    Secured transactions, **Com 9313**
Fixtures,
    Commercial code, **Com 10103**
    Leases, **Com 10309**
    Secured transactions, **Com 9313**
F.O.B., Sales Act, **Com 2319**
Fraudulent indorsements,
    Negotiable instruments, **Com 3405**
Funds transfer, **Com 11104**
Funds-transfer business day, **Com 11105**
Funds-transfer system, **Com 11105**
Funds-transfer system rule, **Com 11501**
Fungible, commercial code, **Com 1201**
Future goods, Sales Act, **Com 2105**
    Application, **Com 2103**
General intangibles,
    Commercial code, **Com 10103**
    Secured transactions, **Com 9106**
Genuine, commercial code, **Com 1201**
Gives notice, commercial code, **Com 1201**
Good faith,
    Commercial code, **Com 1201, 10103**
    Sales, **Com 2103**
    Funds transfers, **Com 11105**
    Investment securities, **Com 8102**
    Letters of credit, **Com 5102**
    Negotiable instruments, **Com 3103**
Goods,
    Commercial code, **Com 10103**
    Documents of title, **Com 7102**
    Sales Act, **Com 2105**
        Application, **Com 2103**
    Secured transactions, **Com 9105**
Guaranty of the signature, investment securities, **Com 8402**
Holder,
    Commercial code, **Com 1201**
Holder in due course,
    Commercial paper,
        Application,
            Bank deposits and collections, **Com 4104**
    Negotiable instruments, **Com 3302**
Honor,
    Commercial code, **Com 1201**
    Letters of credit, **Com 5102**
Household goods,
    Warehouse receipts, **Com 7209**
Identification,
    Sales Act, **Com 2501**
        Application, **Com 2103**
In the ordinary course of the sellers business,
    Bulk sales, **Com 6102**

WORDS AND PHRASES—Cont'd
Incomplete instrument,
    Negotiable instruments, **Com 3115**
Incumbrances,
    Commercial code, **Com 10103**
Indorsement,
    Negotiable instruments, **Com 3204**
Indorser,
    Negotiable instruments, **Com 3204, 3605**
Insolvency,
    Proceedings, **Com 1201**
Insolvent,
    Commercial code, **Com 1201**
Installment contract, Sales Act, **Com 2612**
    Application, **Com 2103**
Installment lease contract,
    Commercial code, **Com 10103**
Instruction,
    Investment securities, **Com 8102**
Instruments,
    Commercial code, **Com 10103**
    Negotiable instruments, **Com 3104**
    Secured transactions, **Com 9105**
Intermediary bank,
    Bank deposits and collections, **Com 4105**
        Application, **Com 4104**
    Funds transfers, **Com 11104**
Inventory,
    Bulk sales, **Com 6102**
    Secured transactions, **Com 9109**
Investment company security, investment securities, **Com 8103**
Investment property,
    Secured transactions, **Com 9115**
Issue,
    Negotiable instruments, **Com 3105**
Issuer,
    Documents of title, **Com 7102**
    Investment securities, **Com 8201**
    Letters of credit, **Com 5102**
    Negotiable instruments, **Com 3105**
Issuers jurisdiction, investment securities, conflict of laws, **Com 8110**
Item,
    Bank deposits and collections, **Com 4104**
        Electronic presentment, **Com 4110**
Learn, Commercial code, **Com 1201**
Lease agreement,
    Commercial code, **Com 10103**
Lease contract,
    Commercial code, **Com 10103**
Leasehold interest,
    Commercial code, **Com 10103**
Leases,
    Commercial code, **Com 10103**
Lessee,
    Commercial code, **Com 10103**
Lessee in ordinary course of business,
    Commercial code, **Com 10103**
Lessor,
    Commercial code, **Com 10103**
Lessor residual interest,
    Commercial code, **Com 10103**

WORDS AND PHRASES—Cont'd

Letter of credit, **Com 5102**
  Sales act, **Com 2325**
    Application, **Com 2103**
Lien creditor,
  Secured transactions, **Com 9301**
Liens,
  Commercial code, **Com 10103**
Liquidator,
  Bulk sales, **Com 6102**
Lots,
  Commercial code, **Com 10103**
  Sales act, **Com 2105**
    Application, **Com 2103**
Marker, negotiable instruments, **Com 3103**
Merchant,
  Commercial code, **Com 10103**
  Sales act, **Com 2104**
    Application, **Com 2103**
Merchant lessee,
  Commercial code, **Com 10103**
Midnight deadline, bank deposits and collections, **Com 4104**
Monetary judgment on the debt, secured transactions, **Com 9501**
Money,
  Commercial Code, **Com 1201**
Mortgages,
  Commercial code, **Com 10103**
  Secured transactions, **Com 9105**
Negotiability, documents of title, **Com 7104**
Negotiable instrument, **Com 3104, 7104**
Negotiation,
  Negotiable instruments, **Com 3201**
Net contract price,
  Bulk sales, **Com 6102, 6108**
Net proceeds,
  Bulk sales, **Com 6102**
Net value,
  Bulk sales, **Com 6107**
New value,
  Secured transactions, **Com 9105**
Nominated person,
  Letters of credit, **Com 5102**
Notes,
  Negotiable instruments, **Com 3104**
  Secured transactions, **Com 9105**
Notice,
  Commercial Code, **Com 1201**
Notice of dishonor, commercial paper,
  Application,
    Bank deposits and collections, **Com 4104**
Notifies, **Com 1201**
Obligated bank,
  Negotiable instruments, **Com 3311, 3412**
Ordinary care, negotiable instruments, **Com 3103**
Organization,
  Commercial Code, **Com 1201**
Originator, funds transfers, **Com 11104**
Originators bank, funds transfers, **Com 11104**
Overseas, Sales Act, **Com 2323**
  Application, **Com 2103**

WORDS AND PHRASES—Cont'd

Overseas, Sales Act—Cont'd
  Application—Cont'd
    Documents of title, **Com 7102**
Party,
  Commercial code, **Com 1201**
  Negotiable instruments, **Com 3103**
Payment date,
  Funds transfers, **Com 11401**
Payment order,
  Funds transfers, **Com 11103**
Payor bank,
  Bank deposits and collections, **Com 4105**
    Application, **Com 4104**
Person entitled to enforce,
  Negotiable instruments, **Com 3301**
Person entitled under the document,
  Documents of title, **Com 7403**
    Application, **Com 7102**
Person in the position of a seller,
  Sales act, **Com 2707**
    Application, **Com 2103**
Persons,
  Commercial Code, **Com 1201**
Present sale, Sales Act, **Com 2106**
  Application, **Com 2103**
Present value,
  Commercial code, **Com 10103**
  Defined,
    Commercial code, **Com 1201**
Presentation,
  Letters of credit, **Com 5102**
Presenter,
  Letters of credit, **Com 5102**
Presenting bank, bank deposits and collections, **Com 4105**
  Application, **Com 4104**
Presentment,
  Commercial paper,
    Application,
      Bank deposits and collections, **Com 4104**
  Negotiable instruments, **Com 3501**
Presumptions,
  Commercial paper, **Com 1210**
Proceeds,
  Secured transactions, **Com 9306**
Proceeds of a letter of credit, **Com 5114**
Promise,
  Negotiable instruments, **Com 3103**
Properly payable bank deposits and collections, **Com 4104**
Protected purchaser, investment securities, **Com 8303**
Protest,
  Application,
    Bank deposits and collections, **Com 4104**
  Negotiable instruments, **Com 3505**
Prove,
  Funds transfers, **Com 11105**
  Negotiable instruments, **Com 3103**
Purchase,
  Commercial code, **Com 1201, 10103**
Purchase money lease,
  Commercial code, **Com 10103**
  Leases, **Com 10309**

WORDS AND PHRASES—Cont'd

Purchase money security interest,
  Secured transactions, **Com 9102, 9107**
Purchaser,
  Commercial Code, **Com 1201**
Pursuant to commitment,
  Commercial code, **Com 10103**
Reasonable time, Commercial Code, **Com 1204**
Reasonably predictable,
  Commercial code, **Com 1201**
Receipts,
  Commercial code, **Com 10103**
Receipts of goods, Sales Act, **Com 2103**
  Documents of title, application, **Com 7102**
Receives notice, Commercial Code, **Com 1201**
Receiving bank, funds transfers, **Com 11103**
Record,
  Letters of credit, **Com 5102**
Recording officer,
  Secured transactions, **Com 9401**
Registered form, investment securities,
  certificated securities, **Com 8102**
Remedy,
  Commercial Code, **Com 1201**
Remitter, negotiable instruments, **Com 3103**
Remitting bank, bank deposits and collections, **Com 4105**
  Application, **Com 4104**
Representatives,
  Commercial Code, **Com 1201**
Represented person,
  Negotiable instruments, **Com 3307**
Resale,
  Secured transactions, **Com 9102**
Responsibility,
  Negotiable instruments, **Com 3405**
Retail merchant,
  Secured transactions, **Com 9102**
Retail sales, **Com 2800**
Rights, Commercial Code, **Com 1201**
Sale on approval, Sales Act, **Com 2326**
  Application, **Com 2103**
Sale or return,
  Commercial code, **Com 10103**
  Sales Act, **Com 2326**
    Application, **Com 2103**
Sales, **Com 2106**
  Bulk sales, **Com 6102**
  Commercial code, **Com 10103**
  Sales Act, **Com 2106**
Sales Act, **Com 2103**
Sales on approval,
  Commercial code, **Com 10103**
Seasonably taking action, Commercial Code, **Com 1204**
Secured party,
  Secured transactions, **Com 9105**
Secured party of record,
  Secured transactions, **Com 9406**
Secured transaction, **Com 9105**
Securities,
  Investment securities, **Com 8102**

WORDS

WORDS AND PHRASES—Cont'd
Securities account, investment securities, entitlements, **Com 8501**
Securities intermediary, investment securities, **Com 8102**
Security agreements,
  Secured transactions, **Com 9105**
Security certificate,
  Investment securities, **Com 8102**
Security entitlement,
  Investment securities, **Com 8102**
Security interest,
  Commercial Code, **Com 1201**
    Secured transactions, **Com 9107**
Security procedure, funds transfers, **Com 11201 et seq.**
Seller,
  Bulk sales, **Com 6102**
  Commercial code, **Com 10103**
  Sales Act, **Com 2103**
Send, Commercial Code, **Com 1201**
Sender, funds transfers, **Com 11103**
Settle, bank deposits and collections, **Com 4104**
Signed,
  Commercial code, **Com 1201**
Sublease, commercial code, **Com 10103**

WORDS AND PHRASES—Cont'd
Successor of beneficiary,
  Letters of credit, **Com 5102**
Supplier,
  Commercial code, **Com 10103**
Supply contract, commercial code, **Com 10103**
Surety,
  Commercial code, **Com 1201**
Suspends payments, bank deposits and collections, **Com 4104**
Telegram, Commercial Code, **Com 1201**
Tellers check,
  Negotiable instruments, **Com 3104**
Term,
  Commercial Code, **Com 1201**
Termination,
  Commercial code, **Com 10103**
  Sales Act, **Com 2106**
    Application, **Com 2103**
Transmitting utility, secured transactions, **Com 9105**
Travelers checks,
  Negotiable instruments, **Com 3104**
Unauthorized, Commercial Code, **Com 1201**
Uncertificated security,
  Investment securities, **Com 8102**

WORDS AND PHRASES—Cont'd
United States,
  Bulk sales, **Com 6102**
  Secured transactions, **Com 9103**
Usage of trade, Commercial Code, **Com 1205**
Value,
  Bulk sales, **Com 6102**
  Commercial Code, **Com 1201**
  Letters of credit, **Com 5102**
Verified,
  Bulk sales, **Com 6102**
Warehouse receipt, Commercial Code, **Com 1201**
Warehouseman,
  Documents of title, **Com 7102**
Writings,
  Commercial code, **Com 1201**
Written,
  Commercial code, **Com 1201**

WRITING
Defined,
  Commercial Code, **Com 1201**

WRITS
Attachment, generally, this index

WRITTEN INSTRUMENTS
Sales, this index

Warranties:

① **Express warranty: 2-313(1)** — an affirmation of fact or promise which relates to the goods and becomes part of the basis of the bargain. (description of goods, sample, model, brochure, box)

② **Implied warranty's:**
  A) Implied warranty of merchantability: **2-314**
    1) Seller must be a <u>merchant</u> w/ respect to <u>goods of that kind</u>
    2) Goods must be merchantable
      a) Fair ave quality
      b) fit for ordinary purpose for which goods are used.
      c) Goods pass w/o objection in the Trade (course of dealing, usage of Trade)
      d) Goods conform to description on label or container

(defense: puffing or opinion)

  B) Implied warranty of fitness for a particular purpose: **2-315**
    1) arises whenever any seller (merchant or not) has reason to know the particular purpose for which the goods are to be used.
    2) That the buyer is relying upon the sellers skill & judgment to select suitable goods. (High degree of reliance is required)
    3) Actual reliance by the buyer is required. Seller must know buyer is relying.

Exclusion or modification of warranties: 2-316(1)
1) Expressed warranty — Code language makes it impossible to negate an express warranty. (Language limiting x-press warranty must be read together & consistent w/ the warranty.
2) Implied warranty of merchantability: In writing limitation. Must be conspicuous and mention word "merchantability" **2-316 (3)(b)(c)** "as is" w/ all faults
3) Implied warranty of fitness for a particular purpose: — Exclusion must be by a writing and conspicuous, 10 PT type or larger. [all implied war. may be excluded by **2-316 (a)(b)** ① "as is" with all faults → ② Buyer examines goods. ③ course of dealing 316

Breach of Warranty — 2-607

1) Buyer must pay the (K) price for any goods accepted.
2) Acceptance of goods precludes rejection of these goods accepted, if:
   a) Acceptance is made w/ knowledge of non-conformity. (cannot be revoked)
      1) unless: acceptance was on the reasonable assumption that non-conf.
         would be reasonably cured.
      2) Acceptance does not impair other remedies available for non-conf. goods.
3) If a Tender has been accepted: (notice)
   Buyer w/i a reasonable time after he discovers or should have discovered
   breach, must notify seller of breach or he is barred from remedy. 2-607(3)
   give opportunity to cure.
4) Burden of Proof to establish breach is on buyer: can be shown by circum. evidence.

Statute of Limitations — 2-725
4 years after the action accrued.
1) may be reduced by agreement to no less than 1 year.
2) accrues when breach occurs.
Breach of warranty: 1) occurs when Tender of delivery is made.
                    2) if warranty extends to future performance.
                       a) discovery must await future perf.
                       b) cause of action arises when breach should have been discovered.

Buyers Remedies for Breach of Warranty:
1) 2-714(2) difference @ the time & place of acceptance, between the value
   of the goods accepted and the value they would have had if
   they had been warranted.
   (Diff. between (K) price + value of what you got) can limit c/Dmg's if not unreasonable.
2) Incidental damages: 2-715(1) / consequential damages 2-715(2)
3) 2-316(4) Remedies can be modified or limited.
4) Buyer can reject + seller must cure. When limiting dmg's must state "exclusive" remedy.
5) Buyer can cover.

Article 9: Secured Creditors
Creditors rt's in Collateral.

Security interest: 1-201(37) an interest in personal property or fixtures which secures
payment or performance of an obligation.

Secured creditor: Has an interest in the collateral such that he has the rt.
to take title + possession if he is not paid.

Attachment: a lien attaches to a specific piece of property, and remains on the
property even if the property is sold or destroyed. If sold, lien
attaches to the proceeds.

3 Requirements to create a lien:
① Written document
   a) must specifically describe the collateral w/ particularity.
   b) must grant a security interest in the collateral.
   c) signed by the debtor.
   Exception: can be oral if creditor takes possession of the collateral.
              9-204 (after acquired collateral ok)
② Debtor must own the collateral.
③ Must be perfected.

Perfection: 9-302
UCC-1 must be filed w/ Sec of State 9-401(a) county.
  Exceptions: 1) when collateral is in possession of Secured Party (Pawn Shop)
  9-302(1)   2) Purchase money security interest in consumer goods
             (automatically recorded) 9-109

UCC-1 must have: 9-402(1)
  ① Names of debtor + secured party
  ② address of secured party
  ③ address of debtor
  ④ Statement indicating the type or describing the items of collateral (must
                                                                         exa
                                                                         or not
  ⑤ signature of debtor.

Duration: ① 5 years from date of filing   UCC-4
            ② can be extended by filing a Continuation stmt, w/i 6 mo's
               before expiration of UCC-1.

9-109 Goods: 1) Consumer goods – Cty recorder
             2) Inventory –
             3) Farm Products –   Filing
             4) Equipment –   9-401

  Test: principle use of property

Fixtures: 9-313 a fixture is a good that has become so
                    related to a particular real estate that a
                    interest in them arises under law.
                    (goods permanently attached to real property)

  Test: what a(n) Ave. reasonable person would believe the owner wa
        doing when he affixed the good to the property.
        Did he intend to make it permanent?

  Perfection: must be filed at Cty recorder where property i
              filed ~~9-310(6)~~ 9-313(1)(b)

  A purchase money security interest in goods that will be attac
  to real property must be perfected by filing in Cty recor
  office where property is located prior to affixation or w/i 10 da
  thereafter.

  Priority: 1st to file or perfect 9-312(5)

              Priorities:
  If more than 1 person claims the rt to certain property, w
  of them prevails over the others?

  A) To Establish priorities ask:
     1) Is the Secured Party's interest unperfected? If so, that
        has very little priority   1st to attach 9-312(5)(b)

2.) Is the secured party's interest Perfected? If so, then that party is entitled to priority over unperfected creditors & Perfected creditors under 1st to file 9-312(5).

Priority among Perfected creditors:
1) General Rule: 1st to file or Perfect has priority 9-312(5).
2) Special rule for Purchase money Security interest 9-312(4)
  A) Non-Inventory PMSI: a creditor who advances value to a debtor that enables the debtor to acquire an interest in collateral has a PMSI.
    1) Takes priority over conflicting security interests in the same collateral if the Interest is
      a) Perfected when debtor takes possession of the collateral
      b) or within 20 days thereafter.

Purchase money security agreement which is for non-consumer goods & UCC-1 filed w/I 20 days have priority.

  B) PMSI in Inventory: a lender who advances money to a retailer & takes a security interest in inventory.
    1) has priority if:
      A) PMSI is perfected at the time debtor receives possession of the collateral
      B) written notice to any other security interest holder who has previously filed a UCC-1 covering inventory of the same type of goods.